USA

Sara Benson

Amy C Balfour, Andrew Bender, Glenda Bendure, Alison Bing, Becca Blond, Jeff Campbell, Nate Cavalieri, Jim DuFresne, Lisa Dunford, Ned Friary, Michael Grosberg, Adam Karlin, Mariella Krause, Josh Krist, Emily Matchar, Brendan Sainsbury, César Soriano, Ellee Thalheimer, Ryan Ver Berkmoes, John A Vlahides, Karla Zimmerman

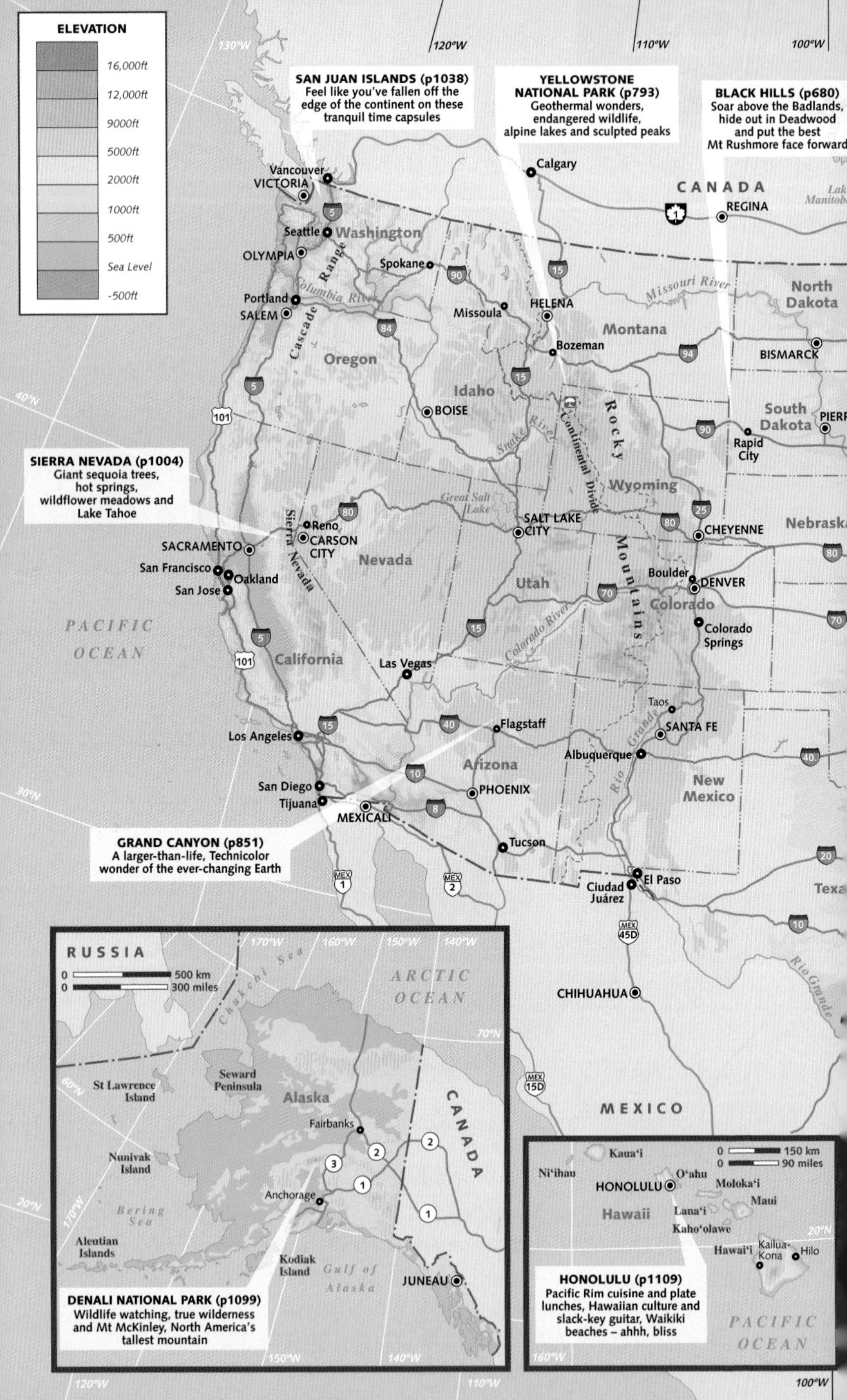

ELEVATION
16,000ft
12,000ft
9000ft
5000ft
2000ft
1000ft
500ft
Sea Level
-500ft
SAN JUAN ISLANDS (p1038)
Feel like you've fallen off the edge of the continent on these tranquil time capsules
YELLOWSTONE NATIONAL PARK (p793)
Geothermal wonders, endangered wildlife, alpine lakes and sculpted peaks
BLACK HILLS (p680)
Soar above the Badlands, hide out in Deadwood and put the best Mt Rushmore face forward
SIERRA NEVADA (p1004)
Giant sequoia trees, hot springs, wildflower meadows and Lake Tahoe
GRAND CANYON (p851)
A larger-than-life, Technicolor wonder of the ever-changing Earth
DENALI NATIONAL PARK (p1099)
Wildlife watching, true wilderness and Mt McKinley, North America's tallest mountain
HONOLULU (p1109)
Pacific Rim cuisine and plate lunches, Hawaiian culture and slack-key guitar, Waikiki beaches – ahhh, bliss
CANADA
PACIFIC OCEAN
MEXICO
Washington
Oregon
Idaho
Montana
Wyoming
North Dakota
South Dakota
Nebraska
Nevada
Utah
Colorado
California
Arizona
New Mexico
Texas
Vancouver
VICTORIA
Seattle
OLYMPIA
Spokane
Portland
SALEM
Calgary
REGINA
HELENA
Missoula
Bozeman
BISMARCK
BOISE
Rapid City
PIERRE
Reno
CARSON CITY
SACRAMENTO
San Francisco
Oakland
San Jose
SALT LAKE CITY
CHEYENNE
Boulder
DENVER
Colorado Springs
Las Vegas
Taos
SANTA FE
Flagstaff
Albuquerque
Los Angeles
San Diego
Tijuana
MEXICALI
PHOENIX
Tucson
El Paso
Ciudad Juárez
CHIHUAHUA
Cascade Range
Sierra Nevada
Rocky Mountains
Continental Divide
Columbia River
Snake River
Missouri River
Colorado River
Rio Grande
Great Salt Lake
Lake Manitoba
130°W
120°W
110°W
100°W
40°N
30°N
20°N
RUSSIA
500 km
300 miles
Chukchi Sea
ARCTIC OCEAN
St Lawrence Island
Seward Peninsula
Alaska
Fairbanks
Nunivak Island
Anchorage
Bering Sea
Aleutian Islands
Kodiak Island
Gulf of Alaska
JUNEAU
170°W
160°W
150°W
140°W
70°N
60°N
150 km
90 miles
Kaua'i
Ni'ihau
O'ahu
HONOLULU
Moloka'i
Maui
Hawaii
Lana'i
Kaho'olawe
Hawai'i
Kailua-Kona
Hilo
160°W

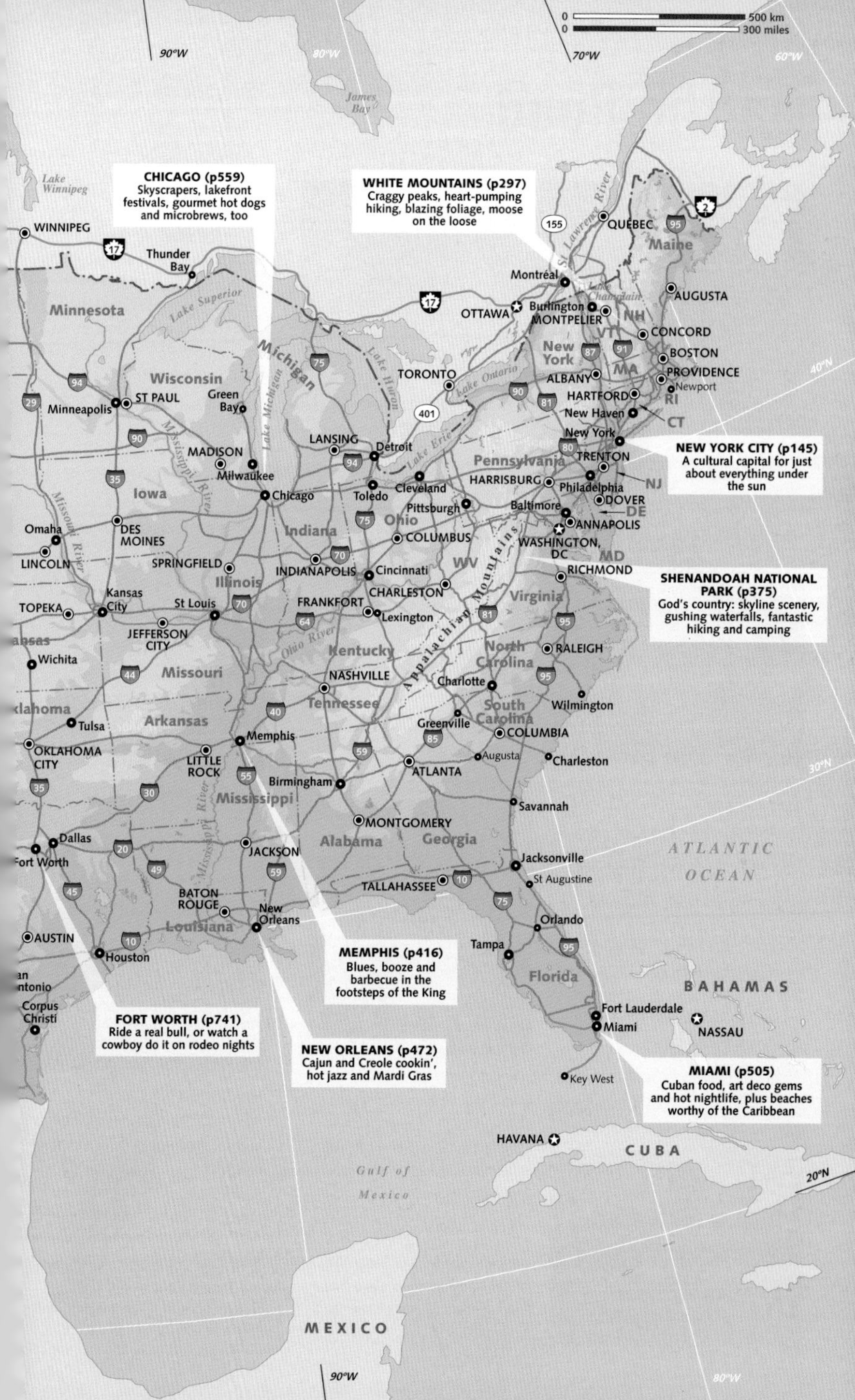
0 500 km
0 300 miles
90°W
80°W
70°W
60°W
40°N
30°N
20°N
James Bay
Lake Winnipeg
CHICAGO (p559)
Skyscrapers, lakefront festivals, gourmet hot dogs and microbrews, too
WHITE MOUNTAINS (p297)
Craggy peaks, heart-pumping hiking, blazing foliage, moose on the loose
NEW YORK CITY (p145)
A cultural capital for just about everything under the sun
SHENANDOAH NATIONAL PARK (p375)
God's country: skyline scenery, gushing waterfalls, fantastic hiking and camping
MEMPHIS (p416)
Blues, booze and barbecue in the footsteps of the King
FORT WORTH (p741)
Ride a real bull, or watch a cowboy do it on rodeo nights
NEW ORLEANS (p472)
Cajun and Creole cookin', hot jazz and Mardi Gras
MIAMI (p505)
Cuban food, art deco gems and hot nightlife, plus beaches worthy of the Caribbean
WINNIPEG
Thunder Bay
Lake Superior
Minnesota
Wisconsin
Michigan
Lake Michigan
Lake Huron
Lake Ontario
Lake Erie
St Lawrence River
Lake Champlain
QUEBEC
Maine
Montréal
OTTAWA
Burlington
MONTPELIER
AUGUSTA
NH
VT
CONCORD
New York
BOSTON
MA
ALBANY
PROVIDENCE
Newport
HARTFORD
RI
New Haven
CT
TORONTO
Minneapolis
ST PAUL
Green Bay
MADISON
Milwaukee
Mississippi River
Missouri River
LANSING
Detroit
Pennsylvania
TRENTON
NJ
HARRISBURG
Philadelphia
DOVER
DE
Baltimore
ANNAPOLIS
WASHINGTON, DC
MD
Iowa
Chicago
Toledo
Cleveland
Pittsburgh
Ohio
Indiana
COLUMBUS
Omaha
DES MOINES
LINCOLN
SPRINGFIELD
Illinois
INDIANAPOLIS
Cincinnati
WV
Appalachian Mountains
RICHMOND
CHARLESTON
Virginia
TOPEKA
Kansas City
St Louis
FRANKFORT
Lexington
JEFFERSON CITY
Ohio River
Kentucky
North Carolina
RALEIGH
Wichita
Missouri
NASHVILLE
Charlotte
Tennessee
South Carolina
Wilmington
Tulsa
Arkansas
Greenville
COLUMBIA
Memphis
OKLAHOMA CITY
LITTLE ROCK
Augusta
Charleston
Birmingham
ATLANTA
Mississippi
Savannah
MONTGOMERY
Dallas
Fort Worth
JACKSON
Alabama
Georgia
ATLANTIC OCEAN
Jacksonville
St Augustine
TALLAHASSEE
BATON ROUGE
New Orleans
Louisiana
Orlando
AUSTIN
Tampa
Houston
Florida
BAHAMAS
Corpus Christi
Fort Lauderdale
Miami
NASSAU
Key West
HAVANA
CUBA
Gulf of Mexico
MEXICO
155
401
17
2
29
94
90
35
75
80
81
87
91
95
70
64
44
40
59
85
55
30
20
49
45
10

On the Road

SARA BENSON
Coordinating Author
Having visited the Sierra Nevada before in every season except winter, I hadn't expected to see such thundering waterfalls pouring down into Yosemite Valley (p1006) in March, along with a winter wonderland of snow, perfect for skiing. Even better, trails with almost no people on them! That rarely happens here.

AMY C BALFOUR I'm standing on the patio of the View Hotel at Monument Valley Navajo Tribal Park (p858), soaking in the awesomeness of the landscape. Behind me there's a fun 17-mile driving loop around the colossal formations.

BECCA BLOND I'm on the road for Lonely Planet a lot, which doesn't make my oversized bulldog Duke happy. So when I get to write about my Colorado backyard, he follows me everywhere – including onto this bench. My husband snapped this picture on a cloudless April morning at our Boulder home as I soaked up the rays and wrote up my notes.

LISA DUNFORD A family was sticking their feet in the hot-spring 'hot tub' in an old foundation ruin when we arrived on a surprisingly cool May morning (77°F) in Big Bend (p746). After they'd gone, we had a perfect moment of steaming water, refreshing breeze and the rushing sound of the Rio Grande below.

NED FRIARY & GLENDA BENDURE Walking into Burlington's Magic Hat Brewery (p293) reminds us of an amusement-park fun house, but they do take their beer seriously here. After all, Vermont has more microbreweries per capita than any other state in the USA. Don't think we'll manage to get to them all…

MICHAEL GROSBERG Even on a soggy day, work calls. I braved the approaching storm to take a canoe out on the dark waters of Lake Mohonk (p196). You can't see them but I also had to brave three other canoes with water-fighting teenagers on board.

ADAM KARLIN I figured I'd combine the disparate elements of my research for this picture: me in a Coop's T-shirt from New Orleans (p472), sitting on my buddy's pickup truck in Washington, DC (p318). I love both cities, and I'm thrilled I got to cover each of them for this book.

MARIELLA KRAUSE I happened to be in Key West during the three weeks the USS *Vandenberg* (p528) was docked there, right before it was sunk 7 miles off the coast to create an artificial reef. It was humongous! My new goal? Learn to scuba dive so I can go back and see it underwater.

JOSH KRIST This self-portrait is at the edge of the Grand Canyon (p851). One of the highlights of my life was watching a black cloud full of lightning sparking over the middle of the canyon, slowly approaching as I stood on the South Rim. I could smell the scent of imminent rain and felt a charge in the air.

EMILY MATCHAR Here's Emily at Lake Mattamuskeet, in eastern North Carolina, not too far from the Outer Banks (p391). Eighteen inches deep! And no, she still can't spell 'Mattamuskeet.'

CÉSAR SORIANO I've been picking Maryland blue crabs (p351) as long as I can remember. It's messy, time-consuming, dangerous work, but it's all worth it once you taste that delicate, sweet, buttery flesh, seasoned with lots of Old Bay spice and accompanied by corn on the cob and cold beer. It tastes like – home.

BRENDAN SAINSBURY I thought I'd seen it all but I hadn't. Even in a region as jaw-droppingly spectacular as the Pacific Northwest, Crater Lake (p1064) appears like a jolting epiphany, defying every cliché you've ever heard about it.

ELLEE THALHEIMER One rainy afternoon in Hot Springs (p495), AR, I decided it was time to dig into some crawfish boil. Our waiter obligingly taught us how to traditionally gut the little guys and heartily suck their delicious juices from every nook and crack. This is not a first-date activity.

KARLA ZIMMERMAN Me and Abe share a moment at the Henry Ford Museum (p617) in Dearborn, MI. Lincoln is the Midwest's main man, and shrines pop up throughout the Midwest. The Ford contains the chair he was sitting in when assassinated. Oddly, that's not the image they use for marketing in the gift shop.

RYAN VER BERKMOES The joy of driving the myriad two-laners across the Great Plains is that you never know what surprise you'll find. Here on a lonely stretch of US 30 somewhere east of Kearney (p688) in Nebraska I found my future selling used cars.

For full author biographies see p1176.

USA ITINERARIES

Forget all of your preconceptions. Take a look at America the way it really, truly is today: a land of limitless road trips, astonishing natural beauty and diverse multiethnic cities from coast to coast. Pay your respects to the heritage of Native American tribes, then explore the kitschy side of stateside life at oddball roadside attractions. Taste the American dream – sweet as apple pie, strong as homemade moonshine – for yourself.

Legendary Drives

With more than 4 million miles of highway, the USA offers more road trips than anyone could tackle in one lifetime. Whether you're into Wild West history or nature's vistas, you'll find them along America's back roads and byways.

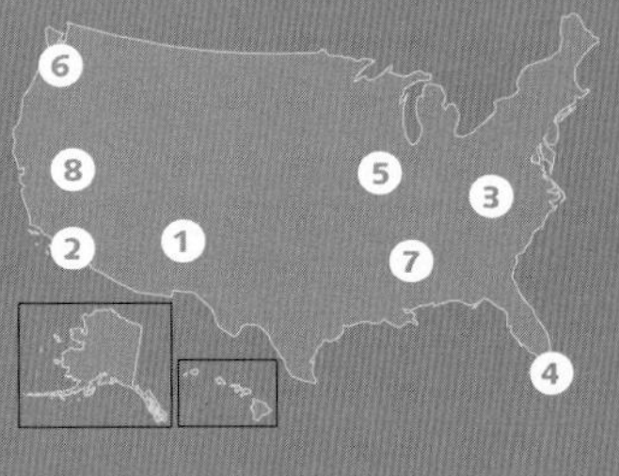

❶ Route 66
Get your kicks on the USA's Mother Road (p44), a ribbon of concrete stretching from Chicago to LA. Take snapshots of retro roadside relics, stuff yourself silly at mom-and-pop diners and snooze in 1950s motor courts.

❷ Pacific Coast Highway
Curve alongside the ocean on California's Hwys 1 and 101 (p45) past SoCal's celebrity enclaves and golden beaches, over San Francisco's Golden Gate Bridge and north into misty coast redwood forests.

❸ Blue Ridge Parkway
Cruise the Appalachian Mountains on this historic route (p46), with its rustic wooden-cabin hideaways and bluegrass-music joints, while soaking up glorious sunsets.

❹ Florida's Highway 1
Fly along breathtaking bridges and causeways across the Florida Keys (p523), an archipelago that feels as close to Cuba as it does to Miami. Your final destination? Kooky, anything-goes Key West.

❺ Great River Road
Wind alongside the mighty Mississippi (p48), stopping off at 19th-century-author Mark Twain's hometown of Hannibal, St Louis' Gateway Arch and Missouri's pastoral French-colonial countryside.

❻ Columbia River Highway
Oregon's most scenic byway (p1061) was the first route in the USA to become a National Historic Landmark. Travel in spring, when waterfalls and wildflowers spread along the dramatic Columbia River Gorge.

❼ Natchez Trace Parkway
After kicking up your heels in country-and-western Nashville, drive into the Deep South and enter Alabama and Mississippi (p432), with their swampy marshes and old-fashioned roadhouses dishing up good ol' barbecue, biscuits and beer.

❽ US Highway 50
Running through Nevada, 'the Loneliest Road in America' (p837) is a winner if you're seeking solitude amid arid deserts, skyscraping peaks, Basque-flavored cowboy country and Old West mining ghost towns.

3
Urban Scenes
7
1
2
8
3
5
6
4
1

❶ New York City
It all starts here, the USA's original mecca for immigrants, where the mosaic of human life still throbs with the lifeblood of hundreds of nations. Everything about NYC (p145) is an electrifying experience.

❷ Chicago
With skyscrapers perched on the shores of Lake Michigan, this big-shouldered capital (p559) of the Midwestern prairies may have the nickname 'Second City,' but we say it's second to none. Show up for live blues music, Cubs baseball and more.

❸ San Francisco
Birthed by the 19th-century gold rush, the hurly-burly 'City by the Bay' (p966) may call to mind hippies, cable cars and the Golden Gate. Modern reality is more edgy: bohemian artists, high-tech entrepreneurs, ecoactivists and foodies.

❹ Nashville
A big-lights destination for many aspiring stars, Nashville (p423) is the self-proclaimed country-music capital of the world. Dig into Southern soul food and keep your toes tapping all night long at honky-tonks.

❺ Las Vegas
Everyone needs a place where they can let loose and misbehave, and no one cares. For Americans, that's Las Vegas (p822), a world-famous gambling destination with a surprisingly posh urban vibe and an artistic side, too.

❻ Los Angeles
The dark side of LA (p914) is often portrayed in noir fiction and films, but the home of Hollywood still has celebrity cachet. Dozens of independent 'hoods await, from hipster haunts to ethnic enclaves.

❼ Seattle
Tucked into a corner of the Pacific Northwest, this dynamic city (p1021) harbors artists and musicians, with waterfront markets, Old West history and the great outdoors just outside the city limits.

❽ Washington, DC
Forget about boring bureaucracy and policy wonks: DC isn't just the nation's capital (p318), it's a multiethnic metropolis with buzzing nightlife and arts and cultural scenes. Oh, yes, and plenty of history, too.

American Beauty

'O beautiful for spacious skies' is not just a song, it's practically the national motto. Wilderness lies at the heart of the American identity. It's where the USA's bittersweet history was forged and where its soul finds sweet relief today, whether in mountain highs or the dizzying depths of desert canyons.

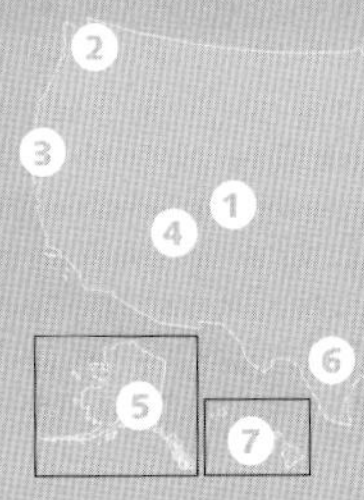

1 Rocky Mountains

Peaks above 14,000ft are just the tip of this range (p754), full of glaciers, alpine lakes, hot springs, geysers, and megafauna – bears, bison, moose and wolves – all protected by a web of preserves.

2 Olympic Peninsula & San Juan Islands

Head to this peninsula (p1034), where glacial lakes, rainforests and Pacific beaches await, then hop on a ferry to the West Coast's most pastoral island idylls (p1038), where forests, farmlands and smugglers' coves mix.

3 Coast Redwoods

Amble through peaceful virgin groves of the world's tallest trees along California's foggy, mysterious-looking north coast (p995), then retire to a cozy brewpub for a pint with the bohemian locals.

4 Canyon Country

Starting from Arizona's Grand Canyon (p851), wander the Southwest's deserts, from the saguaro cacti of Arizona to the geological wonderlands of southern Utah and the homelands of Native American nations, with cliff dwellings and sacred rock art.

5 Alaska's Marine Highway

Ride the ferries through the Inside Passage and along Alaska's remote southeastern coast (p1078). Expect jaw-droppingly spectacular wildlife-watching, and jagged, snowy cliffs rising up out of the sea.

6 Texas Hill Country

All-natural swimming holes and highland lakes with cool, crystal-clear waters; vast swaths of wildflower fields; and horizons as huge as the Lone Star State are what you'll find along these rolling rural byways (p717).

7 Hawaiian Islands

About 2500 miles away from the US mainland, these Polynesian islands (p1104) feel like another country: icy volcano summits, fiery lava flows, cloud forests flush with rare birds, jungly waterfalls and pristine sands compose a dreamy tropical landscape.

8 Great Lakes

Be awed by the planet's largest supply of freshwater, harbored by a chain of lakes (p555) strung with beaches, sand dunes, offshore islands and forests that are home to black bears, beavers and bald eagles.

Weird & Wonderful

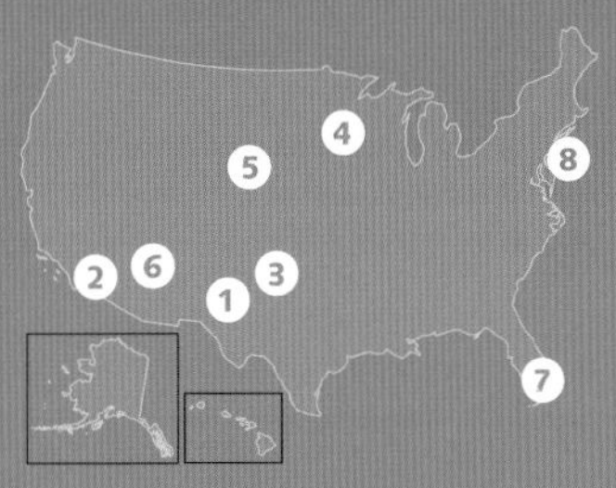

Don't worry: Americans may sometimes take themselves too seriously, but they also have a sense of humor. How else to explain those wacky, way-out-in-left-field roadside attractions you stumble upon while driving cross-country? Muffler men, mystery spots and antigravity hills are just the start.

❶ Roswell

Scan the skies for UFOs in the New Mexico desert (p907), near where conspiracy theorists believe a top-secret US military operation recovered alien technology that crash-landed on earth.

❷ Salton Sea

An early-20th-century accident spawned this lake (p953) in California's Mojave Desert. Examine the ruined skeletons of yesteryear vacation resorts, soak in hot springs and meet eccentrics, including at the folk-art monument Salvation Mountain.

❸ Cadillac Ranch

Immortalized in American rock songs, this eye-catching art installation (p746) along Route 66 in Amarillo, Texas lines up classic Caddies with their beautiful fins pointing skyward out of the dirt.

❹ World's Largest Ball of Twine

There's much ado about which ball of twine actually holds the record these days. But why not pay your respects to the original (p646) that started all the fuss? It's near Minnesota's Twin Cities.

❺ Wall Drug

This tourist-trap drugstore (p679) in South Dakota is famous for its billboards advertising 'free ice water' from several states away. Join generations of Americans who've been suckered into stopping here. Don't miss the animatronic dinosaurs.

❻ Meteor Crater

Half pop-culture kitsch and half pseudo-scientific attraction, Arizona's giant meteor-impact crater (p848) is the place where NASA astronauts once trained. Be amazed by a 1400lb meteorite, then take a guided hike around the crater rim.

❼ Coral Castle

Just one lovelorn man, all by himself, excavated over 2 million lb of coral rock to build this odd monument (p522), which some even claim has unusual electromagnetic properties.

❽ Lucy the Margate Elephant

Not that the New Jersey gambling mecca of Atlantic City needs anything more eccentric, but this 65ft-high wooden replica of a pachyderm (p211) will still stop you in your tracks.

Native America

Dig deep down into the soil of America to discover the sacred ancestral roots of the continent's indigenous peoples. Today, tribal traditions are most visible to travelers across the Great Plains and the Southwest, where you'll encounter ancient cliff dwellings, historic battlefields, contemporary pueblos and ceremonial powwows.

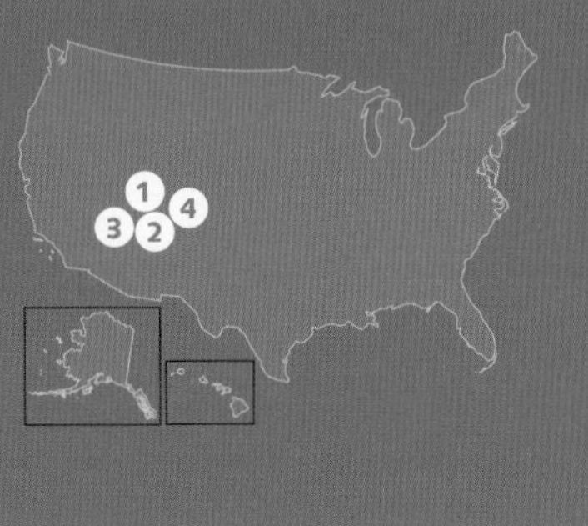

1 Monument Valley Navajo Tribal Park

Be captivated by classic Southwestern scenery of flat-topped sandstone mesas and buttes, where Western movies were filmed and Navajo tribespeople lead guided tours (p858).

2 Navajo Nation

Take an overland journey through the largest Native American reservation (p857) in the USA, encompassing Southwestern cliff dwellings, natural and national monuments, museums and a kinetic calendar of annual festivals and celebrations.

3 Hopi Mesas

Among the oldest continuously inhabited settlements in North America, some of these Southwestern villages (p858) date from 1400 AD. The cultural museum is a must-stop, as are artisan jewelry workshops.

4 Mesa Verde National Park

Drive up onto the cool, thickly forested mesas of southwestern Colorado to clamber inside Ancestral Puebloan cliff dwellings at this archaeological national park (p789).

Contents

Regional Map Contents

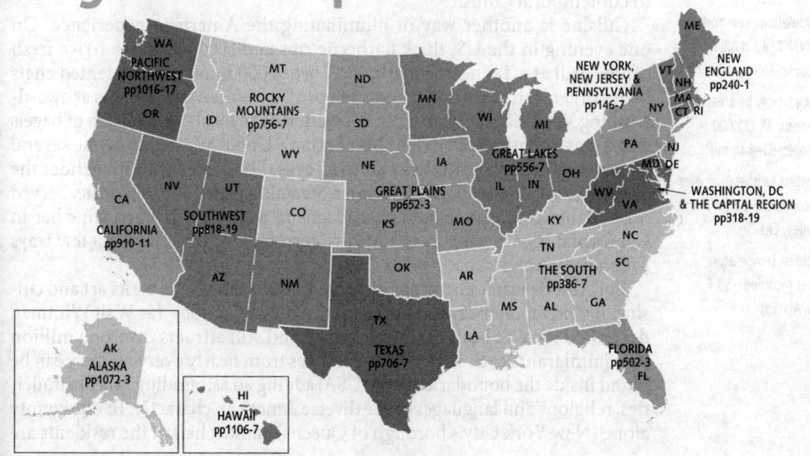

Destination USA

Regis St. Louis

The playwright Arthur Miller once said that the essence of America was its promise. For newly arrived immigrants and jet-lagged travelers alike, that promise of America can take on near mythic proportions. America is a land of dazzling cities, towering coast redwoods, alpine lakes, rolling vineyards, chiseled peaks, barren deserts and a dramatic coastline of unrivaled beauty. And that's just one state (California).

In the other 49 lie an astounding collection of natural and cultural wonders, from the wildly multihued tapestry of urban streets to the mountains, plains and forests that cover vast swaths of the continent. America is the birthplace of LA, Las Vegas, Chicago, Miami, Boston and New York City – each a brimming metropolis whose name alone conjures a million different notions of culture, cuisine and entertainment.

Look more closely, and the American quilt unfurls in all its surprising variety: the eclectic music scene of Austin, the easygoing charms of antebellum Savannah, the ecoconsciousness of free-spirited Portland, the magnificent waterfront of San Francisco, and the captivating old quarters of New Orleans, still rising up from its waterlogged ashes.

This is a country of road trips and great open skies, where four million miles of highways lead past red-rock deserts, below towering mountain peaks, and across fertile wheat fields that roll off toward the horizon. The sun-bleached hillsides of the Great Plains, the lush forests of the Pacific Northwest and the scenic country lanes of New England are a few fine starting points for the great American road trip.

The world's third-largest nation has made substantial contributions to the arts. Georgia O'Keeffe's wild landscapes, Robert Rauschenberg's surreal collages, Alexander Calder's elegant mobiles and Jackson Pollock's drip paintings have entered the vernacular of modern 20th-century art. Cities such as Chicago and New York have become veritable drawing boards for the great architects of the modern era. Musically speaking, America has few peers on the world stage. From the big-band jazz that was born in New Orleans, to the Memphis blues, Detroit's Motown sound, plus funk, hip-hop, country, and rock and roll – America has invented sounds that are integral to contemporary music.

Cuisine is another way of illuminating the American experience. On one evening in the US, thick barbecue ribs and sizzling meats arrive fresh off the grill at a Tennessee roadhouse; over 2000 miles away, talented chefs blend organic, fresh-from-the-garden produce with Asian accents at award-winning West Coast restaurants. A smattering of locals get their fix of bagels and lox at a century-old deli in Manhattan's Upper West Side, while several states away, plump pancakes and fried eggs disappear in a hurry under the clatter of cutlery at a 1950s-style diner. Steaming plates of fresh lobster served off a Maine pier, oysters and champagne in a fashion-forward wine bar in California, beer and pizza at a Midwestern pub – these are just a few ways to dine à la Americana.

But America isn't just about its geography, its cities or even its art and cuisine. It's also about people. The 'teeming nation of nations' (as Walt Whitman described it), was built on immigration and still attracts over one million new immigrants each year. Representatives from nearly every country can be found inside the boundaries of the USA, adding an astounding mix of ethnicities, religions and languages to the diverse American character. In one county alone (New York City's borough of Queens), almost half of the residents are

FAST FACTS

Population: 306 million

Gross Domestic Product (GDP): $14.1 trillion

Barrels of oil consumed daily: 21 million

Total hybrid cars sold in 2008: 308,000

TV channels in an average US home: 118.6

States in which gay marriage is legal: 6

Biggest city by population: New York City, NY (8.3 million people; 469 sq mi)

Biggest city by area: Juneau, AK (31,000 people; 3248 sq mi)

Hottest temperature ever recorded: 134°F (in Death Valley, CA)

Coldest temperature ever recorded: -80°F (in Alaska)

foreign born and speak some 138 languages. Although the topic of immigration remains a heated one (historically, the subject has been a source of contention since the country's inception), few Americans contest the enormous contributions made by fresh-faced immigrants over the centuries.

In addition to the wide mix of racial and ethnic groups, America is a mishmash of factory workers and farmers, born-again Christians and Hatha yoga practitioners, literary-minded college students, tradition-conscious Native Americans, beer-swilling baseball lovers and back-to-nature commune dwellers. This is a country where regional stereotypes help Americans get a handle on their own elusive country, whether the people in question are gracious Southern belles, street-smart New Yorkers, humble Midwesterners, SoCal surfers or straight-talking Texans.

The collective identity, however, goes only so far in defining Americans. This is, after all, a country that celebrates – or rather mythologizes – the feats of 'rugged individualism', a notion well supported by the enormous ranks of the great and dastardly alike that have left their mark on America. This is the land of Eleanor Roosevelt, John Muir, Diane Arbus, Jack Kerouac, Frank Lloyd Wright, Elvis Presley and Amelia Earhart. It is also the birthplace of Billy the Kid, Al Capone, Bonnie and Clyde and hundreds of other real and fictional characters who contribute to that portrait of the American hero or outlaw heading off into the sunset.

'Today's stars...help redefine in some small way what it means to be American'

Today's stars shine no less brightly and each help redefine in some small way what it means to be American. From the inspiring social activism of singer-songwriter Willie Nelson and feminist Gloria Steinem to revolutionary chef Alice Waters; Al Gore's laudatory dedication to fighting climate change and the powerful lyricism of Nobel Prize–winner Toni Morrison; or the record-breaking run by Olympic-swimmer Michael Phelps: each have followed a dream that led them to undoubtedly surprising places.

America is still a place where big dreamers can triumph over adversity. Although 40 years have passed since Martin Luther King was assassinated, his message of hope lives on. No one in recent history has demonstrated that more clearly than Barack Obama, America's first African American president.

'If there is anyone out there who still doubts that America is a place where all things are possible; who still wonders if the dream of our founders is alive in our time; who still questions the power of our democracy, tonight is your answer.' So began Barack Obama's election-night victory speech in November 2008, following one of the most surprising presidential victories in history.

The next day, newspapers across the country sold out quickly, despite enormously increased press runs, as Americans hurried out to snatch up a piece of history, for which they themselves were responsible. Indeed, it was a historic moment for America. This once bitterly divided nation – with a dark legacy of slavery – looked past its differences and elected an African American man to the highest office in the land. And voters did so by an overwhelming margin.

As Obama went on to say in his victory speech, 'It's been a long time coming, but tonight, because of what we did on this day, in this election, at this defining moment, change has come to America.' Change – that magic word so bandied about by both parties in the run-up to the election – played a pivotal role in Obama's success. Yet, despite the unprecedented moment in US history, change is no stranger to the American scene. Even America's creation was a daring paradigm shift in a world of monarchies and autocracies. A country founded as a refuge for religious tolerance by early colonists later became the world's first – and perhaps its most brilliantly envisaged – democratic republic. Over the centuries, visionary statesman such as Jefferson, Lincoln and Roosevelt have helped move the country in bold new directions, but it was courageous citizens, fighting (and sometimes sacrificing their lives) in the battle against injustice, who've brought about some of America's most profound changes – in abolishing slavery, earning equal rights for women, protecting the environment and enshrining fair wages and working conditions for laborers.

Citizens from all walks of life have participated in 'the great American experiment', a concept that rewards bold ideas and hard work, no matter one's place in society. The results of nurturing this entrepreneurial spirit have been far-reaching. From the historic flight by the Wright Brothers to the Apollo moon landing, Americans have achieved ambitious goals. Technological revolutions beginning with Thomas Edison's light bulb and Henry Ford's automobile continue today in the pioneering work by Bill Gates, Steve Jobs and Larry Page. Microsoft, Apple and Google have changed the way people work, learn and interact across the industrialized world. American advances in science, medicine and countless other fields have brought meaningful changes to many lives.

'Citizens from all walks of life have participated in 'the great American experiment'

The spirit of innovation remains alive and well, but on other fronts, Americans seem less optimistic. As this book went to press, the US was just starting to show signs of recovery from a deep recession stemming in part from the mortgage meltdown that erupted late in the Bush presidency. In 2008, over three million Americans lost their homes to foreclosure as unemployment soared – with some 15 million out of work in late 2009 (the highest figure since WWII).

Health care is another dispiriting topic for many Americans. Despite playing a leading role in medical technology, the USA remains the world's only wealthy industrialized country that does not provide universal health care for its citizens. More than 46 million Americans currently live without health insurance, and analysts predict that the economic downturn and rising unemployment will add another two million to their ranks.

Addressing these grievous issues – plus the ongoing conflicts in Iraq and Afghanistan – remain the biggest challenges of the day. Americans, however, aren't a nation easily put down. As John F Kennedy once said in an inaugural address, 'The American, by nature, is optimistic. He is experimental, an inventor and a builder who builds best when called upon to build greatly.'

Getting Started

Got your map? Ready to plot out your road trip? Just remember: the USA covers a continent and more. Texas alone is twice the size of Germany, so you may need to adjust your sense of scale. It's easy to get overambitious, blow your budget and spend more time getting to sights than actually seeing them. Our best advice? Plan what you want to see in the time that you think you will have, then take out half the stops.

Reservations are essential during peak travel seasons, especially during the summer months and around major holidays (p1141). But don't let a lack of advance planning stop you from traveling any time, because spontaneity and the adventure of the open road are what America is really all about.

You'll need to consider your transportation options carefully, balancing cost, time and flexibility – as well as your carbon footprint. The 'best' way to get around can vary by region and route. For more ecotravel advice, see p26.

WHEN TO GO

America's size plays to the traveler's advantage when it comes to weather: it's always perfect somewhere in the USA and just shy of hell somewhere else. In other words, either your destination or your trip's timing may need tweaking depending on the season. For specific regional info, see each chapter's Land & Climate section. For current weather forecasts, check the **Weather Channel** (www.weather.com).

The busiest travel season is summer, which typically begins on Memorial Day (the last Monday in May) and ends on Labor Day (the first Monday in September). Americans take their vacations mainly in summer because schools are closed, not because the weather's uniformly ideal. But yes, you should hit the beaches in August, when Manhattan is a shimmering sweat bath and the deserts are frying pans.

See Climate Charts (p1137) for more information.

The seasons don't arrive uniformly either. Spring (typically March to May) and fall (usually September to November) are often the best travel times, but 'spring' in parts of the Rockies and Sierras may not come till June. By then it's only a sweet memory in Austin, while in Seattle, spring often means rain, rain, rain.

And winter? It's expensive during thehigh season at ski resorts and in parts of the southern US (RV-driving retirees, aka 'snowbirds,' head down to Florida, Texas and other sunny climes by Thanksgiving on the fourth Thursday of November). But planned well, winter can mean you have the riches of some American landscapes virtually all to yourself.

Whether you're planning to join the crowds or avoid them, holidays (p1141) and festivals (p1140) are factors to think about.

COSTS & MONEY

An economical US trip is possible, but it is easy to spend much more than you bargained for, no matter what your travel style. Mode of transportation is a big factor, as is destination: cities don't chip away at budgets, they jackhammer them into pieces.

Only the creatively thrifty backpacker or road-tripper will spend less than $100 a day. A comfortable midrange budget ranges from $150 to $250 a day; this usually gets you a car, gas, two meals, a decent hotel and a museum admission or two. Spending over $300 a day isn't hard: just

DON'T LEAVE HOME WITHOUT...

- Checking current US visa (p1148) and passport (p1152) requirements
- Adequate travel and medical insurance (p1141)
- Up-to-date medical vaccinations (p1168)
- Hotel reservations, particularly for your first night and near national parks (p1131)
- Your driver's license (p1163). Not driving? Take it anyway – you might change your mind once you see exactly how big the USA is
- Nerves of steel for driving on urban freeways (p1165)
- A handful of credit cards – they're often easier and safer than cash, and are sometimes required (eg for hotel reservations, car rentals, show tickets)
- An open mind: you'll find foodies in the Ozarks and hicks in Manhattan, and everything in between in the USA

splash out a few times, drive a lot, and stay, eat and whoop it up in the likes of New York, Chicago, San Francisco.

In this guide, we define a 'midrange' hotel, broadly, as costing from $80 to $200 per night per double occupancy. In rural areas, $100 buys a princely night's sleep, but in some cities, clean budget places *start* at $200. The same holds true for meals.

To travel on the cheap, plan on camping (sometimes free but up to $35 per night) or hostelling ($20 to $35 a night), cooking some of your own meals, and touring by bus and train, both of which limit your flexibility and are slower than driving or flying (that's not necessarily a bad thing). Be wary of budget motel come-ons; the sign might flash $39, but that's probably for a single room and doesn't include taxes. For money-saving advice on accommodations, see p1131.

HOW MUCH?

Broadway show $100-300

Major-league baseball game $27

Internet access per hour $3-12

Gallon of milk $3.35

Local payphone call 35-50¢

Traveling by car is often a necessity. A rental is a bare minimum of $30 a day (type of car, taxes, fees and insurance can push it higher), plus gas. Planning the great American road trip? Gas could actually cost more than the car itself (say, another $20 to $40 per day, depending on how far you're driving and on what kind of roads).

Families can save money by booking accommodations that don't charge extra for children staying in the same room, by asking for kids' menus at restaurants and by taking advantage of family discounts at museums, theme parks and other sights. For more on traveling with children, see p1136. For discounts that everyone can use, see p1139.

Don't forget that old travel chestnut: after you halve the clothes you've packed in your suitcase, double your estimated budget, and it'll all work out fine.

TRAVELING RESPONSIBLY

Since 1973, Lonely Planet has inspired readers to tread lightly, travel responsibly and enjoy the serendipitous magic of independent travel. Globally, travel is growing at a jaw-dropping rate, and we still firmly believe in the benefits it can bring. As always, we encourage you to consider the impact your visit will have on local economies, indigenous cultures and the environment, especially native ecosystems and wildlife.

In the USA, 'going green' has become trendy, and businesses of all stripes now slap 'eco' stickers on their products and services. For the traveler, determining how ecofriendly they actually are can be difficult. Throughout this guide, our authors have carefully researched and recommended ecofriendly, sustainable tourism practices (see also the GreenDex, p1212) that support environmental and conservation efforts; help preserve local, regional and ethnic identity; and/or support indigenous arts and culture, particularly that of Native Americans.

Many other resources are springing up to certify ecofriendly businesses, hotels, services, tours and outfitters, including state and local tourism bureaus. Be sure to review the listings' criteria for reliability and independence carefully. Here are a few:

Alaska Wilderness Recreation & Tourism Association (www.awrta.org) Resources for Native Alaska culture and arts, special events and discounts on outdoor activities.

Alternative Hawaii (www.alternative-hawaii.com) Ecotourism website promoting Hawaiian culture and independent ecotravel.

Chicago Sustainable Business Alliance (http://csba.foresightdesign.org) For ecotourism news, events and a 'green' business directory.

Green Hotel Association (www.greenhotels.com) Self-selecting pay-to-play membership, but a useful online directory nonetheless.

Greenopia (www.greenopia.com/USA) City guides for ecoliving in San Francisco, Los Angeles, New York City and more.

Handmade in America (www.handmadeinamerica.org) Art roads and farm trails in North Carolina.

Hawaii Ecotourism Association (www.hawaiiecotourism.org) Travel tips, cultural events and 'green' business listings.

Historic Hotels of America (www.historichotels.org) Online directory and accommodations booking from the National Trust for Historic Preservation.

offManhattan (www.offmanhattan.com) Green travel around New York City, always accessible by public transportation.

Travel Green Wisconsin (www.travelgreenwisconsin.com) Comprehensive, engaging website for trip planning, from agritourism, outdoor adventures and festivals to hotels, restaurants and shops.

Vital Communities (www.vitalcommunities.org) Green restaurants and local farmers markets in New England's Vermont and New Hampshire.

'Sustainable tourism is about more than making 'green' choices; it's a way of interacting with people and the environment as you travel'

Choosing public transportation instead of renting a car will decrease your carbon footprint. But realistically, a car is often a necessity in the USA – so, consider renting ecofriendly cars when available from national agencies such as Avis, Budget or Hertz (see p1164). Also look for independent rental agencies specializing in hybrid and electric rental cars (p1164). Zipcar (p1164) is a car-sharing service now available in cities and towns in 25 states. The automobile association Better World Club (p1161) supports environmental legislation and offers ecofriendly services for members, including roadside assistance for both cars and bicycles.

While hitchhiking (p1165) is always risky, ride-sharing using online bulletin boards like **Craigslist** (CL; www.craigslist.org) is not uncommon. CL also has listings for vacation rentals and housing sublets, short-term jobs and community activities, and free classified ads for anything you might want to buy, sell or barter during your trip, whether a surfboard, bicycle or used car.

Of course, sustainable tourism is about more than making 'green' choices; it's a way of interacting with people and the environment as you travel. It's practicing low-impact hiking and camping (see p126). It's volunteering during your vacation (see p1150). It's also learning about indigenous cultures and understanding the challenges they face today. For more on US environmental issues, see p128 and check out the following:

Climatecrisis.net (www.climatecrisis.net) Official website for the documentary *An Inconvenient Truth;* offers carbon-offset programs, advice and information.

National Geographic Center for Sustainable Destinations (www.nationalgeographic.com/travel/sustainable) Promotes 'geotourism' with webcams, digital images, maps, blogs and online traveler resources.

Sierra Club (www.sierraclub.org) Environmental and conservation news, political activism, group hikes and volunteer vacations.

TOP 10

SCENIC DRIVES

A road trip can't exist without roads. Here are 10 doozies. Frankly, we had to arm wrestle over our favorites, so consider this list *very* incomplete. Turn to the USA Road Trips (p44) and Itineraries (p33) chapters for more. For America's 'official' scenic drives, visit www.byways.org.

1 Pacific Coast Hwy (Hwy 1), California: officially, just 42 miles through Orange County (p938); for the full Mexico–Canada trip, see p45
2 Route 66: 2400 miles from Chicago, Illinois, to Los Angeles, California (p44)
3 Blue Ridge Parkway: 469 miles from Shenandoah National Park (VA; p375), to Great Smoky Mountains National Park (NC; (p46)
4 Great River Road: 2000 miles from Lake Itasca, Minnesota, to New Orleans, Louisiana (p48)
5 Overseas Hwy (Hwy 1), Florida: 160 miles from Miami to Key West (p523)
6 Hana Hwy (Hwy 360), Maui, Hawaii: 38 miles from Pauwela to Hana (p1126)
7 Natchez Trace Parkway: 444 miles from Nashville, Tennessee, to Natchez, Mississippi (p432)
8 Hwy 12, Utah: 110 miles from Torrey to Bryce Canyon National Park (p881)
9 Columbia River Hwy (Hwy 30), Oregon: 74 miles from Troutdale to the Dalles (p1061)
10 Turquoise Trail (Hwy 14), New Mexico: 45 miles from Tijeras to Santa Fe (p894)

PARTIES & PARADES

Americans will use any excuse to party. Seriously. Here are 10 festivals worth planning a trip around. For more, browse the destination chapters, see p1140 and p98, and visit www.festivals.com.

1 Mardi Gras, New Orleans, Louisiana, February/early March (p481)
2 Mummers Parade, Philadelphia, Pennsylvania, New Year's Day (p221)
3 National Cherry Blossom Festival, Washington, DC, late March/April (p331)
4 Conch Republic Independence Celebration, Key West, Florida, April (p530)
5 Fiesta San Antonio, San Antonio, Texas, mid-April (p723)
6 Gullah Festival, Beaufort, South Carolina, late May (p413)
7 Red Earth Native American Cultural Festival, Oklahoma City, Oklahoma, early June (p697)
8 SF Gay Pride Month, San Francisco, California, June (p980)
9 St Paul Winter Carnival, St Paul, Minnesota, late January (p644)
10 Burning Man Festival, Black Rock Desert, Nevada, late August/early September (p835)

BIZARRE LODGINGS

From haunted mansions to wacky themed rooms, and futuristic ecobubbles to retro concrete tipis, Americans seem to like a little variety when they hit the pillow. To break up the motel monotony, try these 10 places. For more accommodations tips, see p1131.

1 Madonna Inn, San Luis Obispo, California (p959)
2 Earthship Rentals, Taos, New Mexico (p900)
3 Queen Mary Hotel, Long Beach, California (p928)
4 Wigwam Village Inn, Cave City, Kentucky (p441)
5 Stanley Hotel, Estes Park, Colorado (p776)
6 Pelican Hotel, Miami Beach, Florida (p514)
7 Arcosanti, Phoenix, Arizona (p845)
8 Myrtles Planatation, St Francisville, Louisiana (p489)
9 Belfry Inne, Sandwich, Massachusetts (p262)
10 Covington Inn, St Paul, Minnesota (p644)

TOP 10

OUTDOOR ADVENTURES

You can satisfy your jonesing for an adrenaline rush from coast to coast, whether on foot, bicycle or boat, while high in the sky or under the sea. For more about the USA's great outdoors, turn to p131. For national park adventures, see p106.

1. Trekking the epic Appalachian Trail through 14 states (p134)
2. Kayaking the icy waters of Glacier Bay National Park & Preserve, Alaska (p1083)
3. Climbing Mt Rainier, Washington (p1043)
4. Scuba diving and snorkeling at Dry Tortugas National Park, Florida(p531)
5. Hiking the Narrows of the Virgin River in Zion National Park, Utah (p884)
6. Canoeing the Boundary Waters, Minnesota (p648)
7. Watching lava flow around Hawai'i Volcanoes National Park, Hawaii (p1122)
8. White-water rafting the Middle Fork of the Salmon River, Idaho (p815)
9. Cycling through Northern California's wine country (p995)
10. Surfing the waves off Southern California's Huntington Beach (p939)

SMALL TOWNS

Forget NYC, DC, LA and just about anywhere else with an initialism, because it's small towns that will give you the real scoop on American life. So, go on. Get to know the locals and find out why they are proud to call these blink-and-you'll-miss-them blips on the map home.

1. Key West, Florida (p527)
2. Montpelier, Vermont (p290)
3. Luckenbach, Texas (p719)
4. Seward, Alaska (p1093)
5. Telluride, Colorado (p788)
6. Hilo, Hawai'i the Big Island (p1121)
7. Bisbee, Arizona (p865)
8. Bozeman, Montana (p801)
9. Ocean Springs, Mississippi (p470)
10. Grand Marais, Minnesota (p648)

MICROBREWERIES

Here's proof that the liquid lunch exists in America, especially out West. You'll also find good suds up and down the East Coast, deep into the South, across the Midwest and the Great Plains, and even in far-flung Alaska. Once you've gulped down these 10, peruse www.beerinfo.com for more microbreweries and brewpubs in all 50 states.

1. Ska Brewing Company, Durango, Colorado (p785)
2. Abita Brewery, Abita Springs, Louisiana (p486)
3. Lost Coast Brewery, Eureka, California (p998)
4. Magic Hat Brewery, Burlington, Vermont (p293)
5. Mountain Sun Pub & Brewery, Boulder, Colorado (p773)
6. Lakefront Brewery, Milwaukee, Wisconsin (p628)
7. Hopworks Urban Brewery, Portland, Oregon (p1056)
8. Haines Brewing Company, Haines, Alaska (p1085)
9. Free State Brewing, Lawrence, Kansas (p692)
10. Spoetzl Brewery, Texas (p714)

TOP 10

FOODIE PILGRIMAGES

McDonald who?! In contemporary, food-obsessed America, Iron Chefs do battle on TV's Food Network and gastronomic wunderkinds attain the celebrity status of Hollywood stars. It's worth detouring to these 10 culinary temples. For tastebud-tempting regional specialties, see p93. For cooking schools, see p102.

1 French Laundry, Yountville, California (p992)
2 Chez Panisse, Berkeley, California (p990)
3 Mat and Naddie's, New Orleans, Louisiana (p485)
4 Alinea, Chicago, Illinois (p581)
5 Daniel, New York City, New York (p184)
6 Alan Wong's, Honolulu, Hawaii (p1115)
7 FIG, Charleston, South Carolina (p410)
8 Arthur Bryant's, Kansas City, Missouri (p668)
9 Azul, Miami, Florida (p515)
10 Hugo's, Portland, Maine (p307)

SPOTS FOR SOLITUDE

When the USA's more than 306 million residents and 50 million other tourists cause claustrophobia and just make you want to scream, escape to these places. For the USA's most uncrowded national parks, see p115.

1 Death Valley National Park, California (p954)
2 Ka'ena Point, O'ahu, Hawaii (p1118)
3 North Cascades National Park, Washington (p1041)
4 Race Point Beach, Provincetown, Massachusetts (p265)
5 Absaroka Beartooth Wilderness, Montana (p803)
6 Hwy 2 through the Sandhills, Nebraska (p689)
7 South Manitou Island, Michigan (p621)
8 Guadalupe Mountains National Park, Texas (p753)
9 Little Palm Island, Florida Keys (p527)
10 Portsmouth Island, North Carolina (p394)

LANDMARK BUILDINGS

From skyscraping towers and sprawling private estates to postmodern urban icons, the building blocks of this nation are diverse. Many of these 10 are instantly recognizable worldwide, too, thanks to Hollywood. For more about the USA's groundbreaking architecture, see p90.

1 Empire State Building, New York City, New York (p161)
2 White House, Washington, DC (p328)
3 Willis Tower, Chicago, Illinois (p566)
4 Monticello, Virginia (p373)
5 Fallingwater, Pennsylvania (p236) – or anything else by Frank Lloyd Wright (see the boxed text, p92)
6 Walt Disney Concert Hall, Los Angeles, California (p920)
7 Biltmore Estate, Asheville, North Carolina (p401)
8 Space Needle, Seattle, Washington (p1026)
9 'Iolani Palace, Honolulu, Hawaii (p1111)
10 Las Vegas Strip, Las Vegas, Nevada (p823)

TOP 10

MOVIE & TV LOCATIONS

Even if it's your first time traveling in the USA, you might feel some déjà vu when you see these 10 locations, made famous by Hollywood on the silver screen. For more recommended made-in-America films, see p84. For TV, see p83.

1. Los Angeles, California (p914) – just about everywhere in the city!
2. O'ahu's North Shore, Hawaii (p1118) – as seen on TV's *Lost* and *Baywatch*
3. National Mall, Washington, DC (p321) – as seen in thrillers, spy movies and disaster flicks
4. Monument Valley Navajo Tribal Park, Navajo Nation (p858) – as seen in classic Westerns such as *Stagecoach* and *The Searchers*
5. Alabama Hills, California (p1013) – as seen in even more Westerns such as *High Sierra*
6. Mt Rushmore, South Dakota (p683) – as seen in Alfred Hitchcock's North by Northwest
7. Missoula, Montana (p805) – as seen in A River Runs Through It
8. Dead Horse Point State Park, Utah (p879) – as seen in the Mission Impossible II opening and Thelma & Louise finale
9. Union Station, Chicago, Illinois (p586) – as seen in The Untouchables
10. Timberline Lodge, Mt Hood, Oregon (p1062) – as seen in Stanley Kubrick's *The Shining*

BEACHES

So, you already know that California, Hawaii and Florida have drop-dead gorgeous beaches? Fine. But what about Texas, Alaska and Chicago? See, we knew we could still surprise you. Here are 10 gems you might not know about, and there are hundreds more waiting to be discovered: just go find 'em.

1. DT Fleming Beach Park, Maui, Hawaii (p1123)
2. Coast Guard Beach, Cape Cod, Massachusetts (p264)
3. Padre Island National Seashore, Corpus Christi, Texas (p733)
4. Siesta Key Beach, Sarasota, Florida (p543)
5. Assateague Island National Seashore, Berlin, Maryland (p353)
6. Point Lobos State Reserve, Carmel-by-the-Sea, California (p962)
7. Cumberland Island National Seashore, St Marys, Georgia (p458)
8. Fire Island National Seashore, Long Island, New York (p193)
9. North Avenue Beach, Chicago, Illinois (p569)
10. Golden Sands Beach, Nome, Alaska (p1103)

HISTORICAL SITES

Tangled, embattled, bittersweet and triumphant – that's the USA's history in a nutshell (see p51). At these 10 sites you can walk in the footsteps of giants, including Native Americans, Western explorers and modern civil-rights activists. For more destination-worthy historic sites and itineraries, see p120.

1. Historic Triangle, Virginia (p367)
2. Freedom Trail, Boston, Massachussetts (p252)
3. Klondike Gold Rush National Historical Park, Skagway, Alaska (p1085)
4. Gettysburg National Military Park, Gettysburg, Pennsylvania (p229)
5. Lewis & Clark National Historical Park, Oregon (p1068)
6. Mission San Juan Capistrano, Orange County, California (p939)
7. The Alamo, San Antonio, Texas (p720)
8. Brown vs Board of Education National Historic Site, Kansas (p693)
9. Mesa Verde National Park, Colorado (p789)
10. Pu'uhonua O Honaunau National Historical Park, Hawaii (p1119)

TRAVEL LITERATURE

The American travelogue is its own literary genre. One could argue that the first (and still the best) is *Democracy in America* (1835), by Alexis de Tocqueville, who wandered around talking to folks, then in pithy fashion distilled the philosophical underpinnings of the then-new American experiment.

America is often most vividly described by non-Americans: two Russian satirists road-tripped during the Great Depression searching for the 'real America' (doesn't everyone?), and their *Ilf and Petrov's American Road Trip* (1935) is a comic masterpiece laced with pungent critiques.

'Perhaps the most famous American travelogue is Jack Kerouac's headlong *On the Road*'

Those who prefer their commentary and humor, like their coffee, bitter and black should stuff *The Air-Conditioned Nightmare* (1945) by Henry Miller in their backpack, written while the irascible and notoriously obscene writer canvassed America during WWII.

Celebrated travel writer and historian Jan Morris was clearly smitten with the country in *Coast to Coast* (1956), originally titled *As I Saw the USA;* it's crisp, elegant and poignant, particularly her experience in the pre-Civil Rights–era South.

Perhaps the most famous American travelogue is Jack Kerouac's headlong *On the Road* (1957), a Beat Generation classic that's full of hot jazz, poetry and drugs in post-WWII America.

John Steinbeck's *Travels with Charley* (1962), about the novelist's trek across America with his poodle for company, takes a critical look at how technology, tradition and prejudice have shaped the regional character of this country.

Written during a crossroads in midlife, William Least Heat-Moon's *Blue Highways* (1982) is a moving pastiche of 'average Americans' as it follows one man's attempt to find himself by losing himself on the road.

Not strictly a travelogue, *On the Rez* (2000), by Ian Frazier, provides a good taste of contemporary life on Native American reservations. It's a journey of history and heart that goes into America, rather than across it.

See p79 for more on American literature.

INTERNET RESOURCES

Away.com (www.away.com) Boundless ideas for outdoor and urban adventure travel across the 50 states, from Hawaii's beaches to Boston's Freedom Trail.

Festivals.com (www.festivals.com) From coast to coast, find where the best parties are – live-music shows, food fiestas and even more unlikely celebrations, such as of pirates and covered bridges.

Lonely Planet (www.lonelyplanet.com) Travel news and summaries, savvy hotel and hostel reviews, the Thorn Tree community forum, and links to more web resources.

New York Times Travel (http://travel.nytimes.com) Travel news, practical advice and features including 36-hour city breaks and authentic 'American Journeys.'

Roadside America (www.roadsideamerica.com) For all things weird and wacky: who needs the Statue of Liberty when you've got 'Muffler Men' and 'Mega-Messiahs'?!

USA.gov (www.usa.gov/Citizen/Topics/Travel.shtml) The closest thing to a national tourism information resource, on the US federal government's official website.

Itineraries
CLASSIC ROUTES

CITIES BY THE SEA
Two to Three Weeks / Boston to Maryland

The nice thing about East Coast metropolises? They're near the beach! Here you can balance culture, history and cuisine with coastal idylls and long naps in the sun.

Arrive in revolutionary **Boston** (p243), then go to sandy **Cape Cod** (p260), and keep going till you reach **Provincetown** (p265), where the Pilgrims landed. Pretty, ain't it? Then scoot down I-195 to Rhode Island's quaint **Newport** (p276); time your visit for a music festival.

Now, tackle **New York City** (p145). Once you've had your fill of the bustling Big Apple, escape to the **Hamptons** (p194) on Long Island; what was the hurry, again?

In New Jersey, go 'down the shore' to **Long Beach Island** (p210), and if you're a casino gambler, **Atlantic City** (p210) and its boardwalk.

Then, make time for **Philadelphia** (p213), **Baltimore** (p339), and **Washington, DC** (p318).

Finally, cross Chesapeake Bay and relax on Maryland's **Eastern Shore** (p350).

Why are East Coasters so stressed out? Because eastern seaboard highways couldn't be more congested. So why on earth do this road trip? Slow down, avoid rush hour, hit the beaches often, and for 1100 detour-laden miles, it's one first-class metropolis after another.

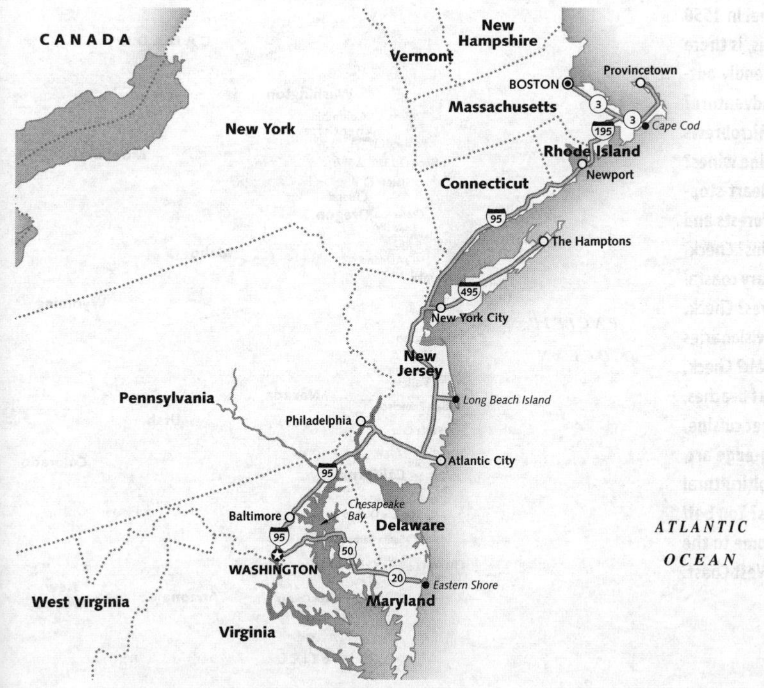

THE LEFT COAST

Two to Three Weeks / Portland to San Diego

Geographically and politically, the West Coast couldn't be further from Washington, DC. This is a trip for those who lean left, and who like their nature ancient and wild, and their horizons and beaches wide-open.

Affable **Portland** (p1046) is a pretty place to start. Then jump into nature's bounty by driving east along the **Columbia River Gorge** (p1061). At The Dalles, turn south and make for **Mt Hood** (p1061) for winter skiing and summer hiking. From **Bend** (p1063), enjoy Cascades adventures around **Sisters** (p1062) and **Crater Lake** (p1064). Catch a Shakespearian play in sunny **Ashland** (p1064), then trade the mountains for the foggy coast. Enter California via Hwy 199 and magnificent **Redwood National & State Parks** (p998).

Hug the coast as it meanders south through funky **Arcata** and seaside **Eureka** (p997), get lost on the **Lost Coast** (p997), then catch Hwy 1 through quaint **Mendocino** (p996).

Make your way inland to the **Napa & Sonoma Valleys** (p991) for a wash-up and wine tasting, and thence to the romantically hilly, bohemian burg of **San Francisco** (p966).

Return to scenic **Hwy 1** (p966) through weird **Santa Cruz** (p964), bayfront **Monterey** (p962) and beatnik-flavored **Big Sur** (p960), where you can get scruffy again. In no time you'll reach **Hearst Castle** (p960) and laid-back, collegiate **San Luis Obispo** (p959).

Roll into Mediterranean-esque **Santa Barbara** (p956), then hop aboard a ferry in Ventura to the wildlife-rich **Channel Islands** (p956) At last, **Los Angeles** (p914) – aka LA, La-la Land, City of Angels. Go ahead, indulge your fantasies of **Hollywood** (p921) and gawk at the beautiful people of the **OC** (p938) before kicking back in **San Diego** (p939).

Let's see. In 1550 miles, is there eco-friendly outdoor adventure? Check. Microbrews and fine wines? Check. Heart-stopping forests and mountains? Check. Legendary coastal drives? Check. Freaks, visionaries and radicals? Check. Surf beaches, gourmet cuisine, cutting-edge art, multicultural cities? You bet! Welcome to the West Coast.

WESTERN MIGRATIONS **Three to Four Weeks / Chicago to Seattle**

'The West' is not one thing. It's a panoply of landscapes and personalities that unfold as you journey west from the past into the future. No single route could capture it all, but this stretch of I-90 is book-ended by world-class cities and packed with heartbreakingly beautiful country.

Chicago (p559) – aka Second City, the Windy City – is the Midwest's greatest city. Follow I-90 to youthful **Madison** (p630) and quirky **US 12** (p632) to dispel any myths about Midwestern sobriety.

Detour north to friendly, arty **Minneapolis** (p636) for more Midwest liberalism. Return to I-90 and activate cruise control, admiring the corn (and the **Corn Palace**, p678) and the flat, flat South Dakota plains. See why lonely Westerners go stir crazy?

Hit the brakes for the **Badlands National Park** (p679) and plunge into the Wild West. In the **Black Hills** (p680), contemplate competing monuments at **Mt Rushmore** (p683) and **Crazy Horse** (p684). Watch mythic gunfights in **Deadwood** (p682) and visit **Pine Ridge Indian Reservation** (p679).

Halfway across Wyoming, cruise Hwy 14 into **Cody** (p792) to catch a summer rodeo. Save time for the wild majesty and wildlife of **Yellowstone National Park** (p793) and **Grand Teton National Park** (p798).

Through rural Montana, the outdoorsy towns of **Bozeman** (p801) and **Missoula** (p805) make fun stops. For serious adventure, detour to **Glacier National Park** (p808) and the **Bob Marshall Wilderness Complex** (p806).

Back on I-90 in Washington, stop in unassuming **Spokane** (p1042) and end in **Seattle** (p1021), which embodies the high-tech, ecoconscious New West. Still got time? Take in **Mt Rainier** (p1043), **Olympic National Park** (p1034), and the **San Juan Islands** (p1038). Ah, bliss.

From Midwest to Wild West to New West: this route is a 3400-mile meditation on America's evolving final frontier. Only by seeing the West's endless plains, towering mountains and rugged coastline for yourself can you begin to understand its inhabitants' singular multiple personalities.

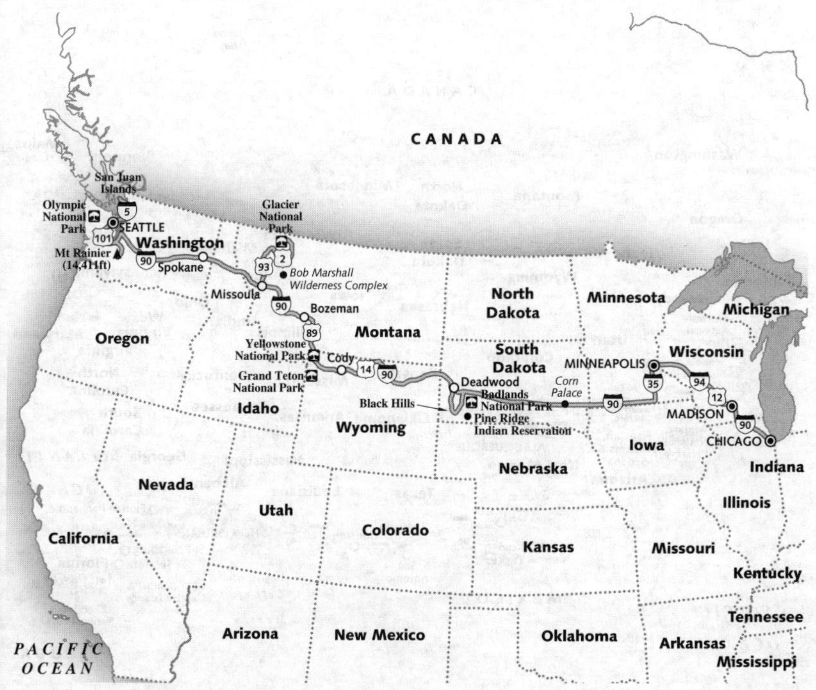

GO EAST, YOUNG MAN

One Month to Six Weeks / San Francisco to Miami

For those contemplating an epic coast-to-coast road trip, here's a suggestion: start in San Francisco and head toward the rising sun. This route snags some seriously cool cities and classic American scenery, but be warned: it'll be *hot* come July and August.

From anything-goes **San Francisco** (p966), head for **Yosemite National Park** (p1006) and **Sequoia & Kings Canyon National Parks** (p1010) in the Sierra Nevada – now that's scenery! Skirt the **Mojave National Preserve** (p953) on I-15 and head for **Las Vegas** (p822), baby. Stop at **Grand Canyon National Park** (p851) for a photo-op, rattle along Route 66 through **Williams** (p849) and **Flagstaff** (p847), detour to red-rock **Sedona** (p849), then roll east on I-40.

In New Mexico, unlike Bugs Bunny, take that left at **Albuquerque** (p886) along the **Turquoise Trail** (p894) up to artsy **Santa Fe** (p892) and far-out **Taos** (p899). Drop south on I-25 through scenic **Southwestern New Mexico** (p903).

Pick up I-10 into Texas, dip through **Marfa** (p749) and jaw-dropping **Big Bend National Park** (p746). Saunter through Texas' bucolic **Hill Country** (p717) to **Austin** (p709) for live music and drinkin'. Follow the Mission Trail in **San Antonio** (p720), hit the beach at **Galveston Island** (p731) outside **Houston** (p725). Giddy-up for party-central, **New Orleans** (p472), then keep dancing and eatin' in **Cajun Country** (p489).

Explore the **Florida Panhandle** (p550) beaches. Inland, **Walt Disney World** (p548) must be seen to be believed. Along the Gulf Coast, enjoy **St Petersburg** (p541), clown around in **Sarasota** (p543) and see seashells at **Sanibel & Captiva Islands** (p544). Bisect the alligator-filled swamps of the **Everglades** (p519) and arrive in **Miami** (p505). With a beach, a mojito and some Cuban fare, party till sunrise!

Cruising from coast to coast, ocean to ocean, sunrise to sunset (or in this case, vice versa) – it's 4500 miles, give or take. Some do it in weeks, others take months. There's no right or wrong, no rules, no 'best' route, really. Just go!

ROADS LESS TRAVELED

BLUES & BBQ

Two to Three Weeks / Chicago to New Orleans

The Mississippi River marks a physical and psychological divide, and along this spine runs America's greatest music: blues, jazz, and rock and roll. Hwy 61 is the heart of the route, which starts in soulful **Chicago** (p559), legendary home of Chess Records, home of true-blue Mississippi Delta musicians who migrated northward, along with rhythm and blues (R & B) and early rock and roll. Scarf down a plate of juicy barbecued ribs before speeding downstate on I-55.

You'll meet the mighty Mississippi River in **St Louis** (p656), which bills itself as the 'Home of the Blues,' though original rock-and-roller Chuck Berry still plays here, too. Order up pork steaks slow-cooked in St Louis' signature barbecue sauce. Motor south to **Memphis** (p416). Pay homage to Elvis Presley at Graceland and rock and roll at Sun Studio. Smoked, dry-rubbed racks of ribs are a must. For even more of a musical pilgrimage, detour on I-40 to **Nashville** (p423), the home of country music – and yes, lip-smackin' spicy fried chicken. South of Memphis, Hwy 61 runs through the **Mississippi Delta** (p465), where the blues was born: **Clarksdale** (p466) is where Robert Johnson bargained with the devil. The town's still jumpin' with blues joints and roadside shacks dishing up wood-smoked pit barbecue with vinegary slaw.

Finally, you'll arrive at **New Orleans** (p472), birthplace of jazz. The 'Big Easy,' despite recent hard times (p472), is a place where lazy mornings blend into late nights with a soundtrack of smokin' hot funk brass bands, and succulent Cajun and Creole food always at hand.

Much of the epic, legendary, even revolutionary history of home-grown American music can be experienced along this 1100-mile stretch running (mostly) alongside the Mississippi River. Throw in a 425-mile side trip to Nashville, and you've got the musical – and gastronomic – journey of a lifetime.

THE FOUR CORNERS

Ten Days to Two Weeks / Flagstaff to Moab

A stronghold of Native American lands and traditions, the center of the Southwest is actually not a circle, but a square. The Four Corners – where Utah, Colorado, New Mexico and Arizona meet – is a gorgeously remote, wild region that you could lose yourself in for weeks, or even months.

Kick up your heels in Old West frontier-flavored **Flagstaff** (p847), then take Hwy 180 north to tackle the vast **Grand Canyon** (p851), or detour west along Route 66 to visit the **Hualapai** (p856) and **Havasupai** (p856) tribal nations first.

Traveling east of the Grand Canyon's South Rim (p853) on Hwy 264, you'll enter the sacred **Hopi Mesas** (p858), bordering the vast **Navajo Nation** (p857), which is networked by rugged roads and tribal parks protecting pockets of wilderness. Head east of **Hubbell Trading Post National Historic Site** (p858) on Hwy 264, then north on Hwy 191 to **Canyon de Chelly National Monument** (p858).

Drive west on lonely Hwy 160, then take your natural wonder north on Hwy 163 through the classic Hollywood Western scenery of **Monument Valley Navajo Tribal Park** (p858). Rest and refuel in **Bluff** (p880), then take Hwy 191 south and Hwy 160 east for an irresistibly kitschy photo-op – yes, you can put your hands and feet in four states at once! – at the **Four Corners Monument** (p858).

Keep going east on Hwy 160 to hilltop **Mesa Verde National Park** (p789), with its famous cliff dwellings, then zoom north on Hwy 491 then 191 to **Moab** (p878), a sporty outdoor-adventure mecca and the gateway to the ancient earth of **Arches National Park** (p879) and wilder **Canyonlands National Park** (p880).

Deep canyons, deserts painted a rainbow, crumbling buttes, delicate sandstone arches, pueblo-topped mesas, ancient civilizations hidden in the cliffs – you really can't make this stuff up. To see it all requires almost 1000 brutal miles of slow, sun-baked roads, and it's worth every saddle sore.

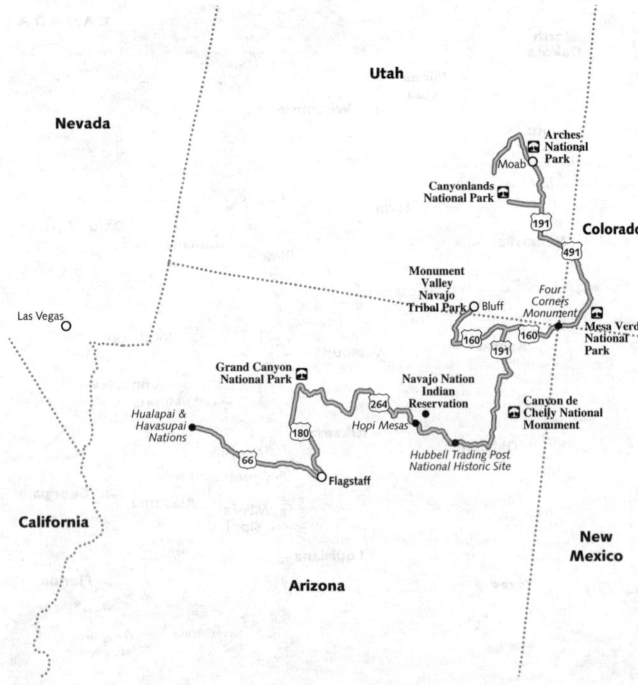

SAILORS, FARMERS & DAMN YANKEES

Ten Days to Two Weeks / New York City to Acadia National Park

This is a good spring or summer trip, but in early fall – wow! Autumn dresses New England in auburn and scarlet, and the air is so crisp you can bite it. Stalwart, fiercely independent personalities settled this region, a mix of rugged wilderness, tidy towns and fruitful farms.

Launch in **New York City** (p145); soak up the excitement, the cacophony, the crowds. When you're ready, rent a car and head north on I-87. Dip into the **Catskills** (p197) along Hwy 28 for a first taste of forests, then continue north for the real deal: the **Adirondacks** (p201). Settle in for a few days at **Lake Placid** (p201) and explore the wilderness.

Take the ferry across Vermont's Lake Champlain to youthful, outdoorsy **Burlington** (p292), a vibrant introduction to New England. The **Lake Champlain Islands** (p293) are splendid. Take I-89 southeast, stopping at the four-seasons resorts of **Stowe** (p291). From **Montpelier** (p290), America's smallest capital city, take Hwy 302 east into New Hampshire. Hwy 302 runs into Hwy 112, the **Kancamagus Hwy** (p299), perhaps the prettiest drive in New England, through the magnificent **White Mountains** (p297): waterfalls, hikes and quaint villages abound. At Hwy 16, go south to historic, maritime **Portsmouth** (p295).

Now follow I-95 into Maine. Lively **Portland** (p305) has foodie-worthy eats. From Hwy 1, meander the **Central Maine Coast** (p307): you're hunting clam chowder, fresh lobster and nautical ports to let loose your inner sailor. Visit **Boothbay Harbor** (p308) for fresh-off-the-boat lobster, and **Camden** (p308) for memorable **windjammer cruises** (p310).

Finally, book yourself a historic inn at **Bar Harbor** (p311) and dive into the unspoiled splendor of **Acadia National Park** (p310).

Never experienced fall in New England? Tired of hearing everyone blather on about it? Time this 1000-mile trip right, and you'll join the proselytizers. Heck, it's gorgeous any season: the chowder fills your belly, the maritime air stirs your blood, and that damn Yankee ingenuity is a marvel.

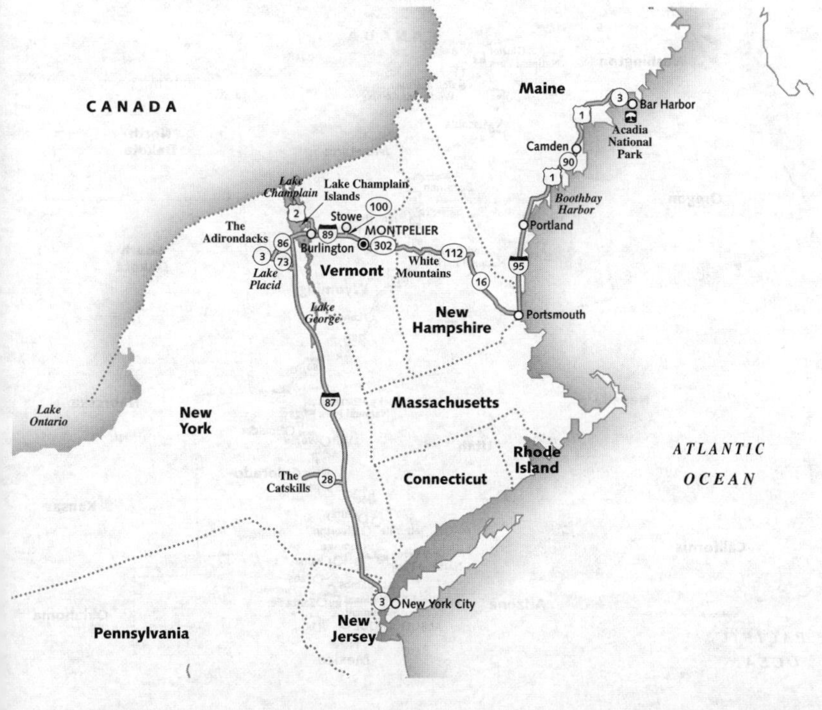

THE CONTINENTAL DIVIDE

Three to Four Weeks / Albuquerque to Glacier National Park

On one side rivers run east, on the other, west. You'll trace the mountains in between, finding constant excuses to ditch the car and hike, climb, raft, bike, ski and get dirty.

Start in **Albuquerque** (p886) and take the **Turquoise Trail** (Hwy 14; p894) to genteel **Santa Fe** (p892). Between here and trippy **Taos** (p899), check out Native American **pueblos** (p898), atomic **Los Alamos** (p898) and the spectacular scenery of **Bandelier National Monument** (p898).

Follow Hwy 84 through **Chama** (p902) into Colorado. Enjoy bikes and brews in **Durango** (p784). Take the 'Million Dollar Hwy' (Hwy 550) north, stopping in **Silverton** (p786); for hot springs in **Ouray** (p786); and a quick detour to gorgeous **Telluride** (p788). Then go east on Hwy 50, through the Black Canyon of the Gunnison and north on Hwy 24 to ritzy **Vail** (p780).

Relax a spell in laid-back **Boulder** (p770) and **Rocky Mountain National Park** (p774). For time's sake, stay north on I-25, and in Wyoming, take I-80 west to Hwy 287: follow this to **Lander** (p793) for rock climbing. Now get thee to **Grand Teton National Park** (p798) and **Yellowstone National Park** (p793).

In Montana, take Hwy 89 north and I-90 west to **Bozeman** (p801) and **Missoula** (p805), both fun places to stock up before the final push. Serious nature awaits in the **Bob Marshall Wilderness Complex** (p806) and **Glacier National Park** (p808).

And really, there's no reason not to keep following the Rocky Mountains right into Canada – but that's a story for another book.

Work hard, play hard – or at least, play hard. Name it, and you can probably do it in the Rocky Mountains. This 2150-mile route is built for those who don't want to just admire nature, but roll around in it, then swap stories over beer.

ALASKA'S INSIDE PASSAGE One to Three Weeks / Bellingham to Skagway

You can take a car along, but if you are looking for an unforgettable journey that doesn't involve an automobile, cruise Alaska's Inside Passage. In summer, the Alaska Marine Highway ferries stop at towns nearly every day, and with advance notice you can get on and off at every one, just as long as you keep traveling in the same direction. See p1077 for ferry information.

Fly into **Seattle** (p1021), Washington, and linger awhile or take a shuttle directly to **Bellingham** (p1038), where you catch the Alaska Marine Highway ferry. The first stop is characterful **Ketchikan** (p1078), where you can zip-line down to watch wild bears feeding on salmon midstream. It might be worth renting a car once you land on **Prince of Wales Island** (p1079), the third-largest island in the USA and a haven for mountain biking, kayaking, caving and seeking out Alaska Native petroglyphs.

Wrangell (p1079) has an impressive collection of totems on Chief Shakes Island, while pretty **Petersburg** (p1080) has Norwegian pride and great seafood. Rich with Russian heritage and beautifully situated, **Sitka** (p1080) shouldn't be missed. Busy **Juneau** (p1081) is Alaska's capital, and from there it's easy to get close to magnificent **Mendenhall Glacier** (p1082) or take a tram from the dock to the timberline.

Haines (p1084) is another sizable town, full of gold mining, missionary and trading post history, with a Native arts center. Historic **Skagway** (p1085) is the end of the line: it's a well-preserved, atmospheric version of its once-lawless gold-rush self.

You can also fly into or out of Juneau, or make it a round-trip and take the ferry back to Bellingham.

A trip through Alaska's Inside Passage is proof that Mother Nature is one wild woman. Awesome doesn't begin to describe it. Calving glaciers, forests thick as night, pods of whales, trees full of eagles: it's one of the most memorable trips ever.

TAILORED TRIPS

DUDE, THAT'S WEIRD

Combine fierce independence with a vast landscape and what you get are lotsa crazies giving free rein to their obsessions. Call it kitschy 'Americana.' You've probably heard of the biggies (ahem, Las Vegas); here are some others.

First, what's up with Stonehenge? Modern, personal iterations include Nebraska's **Carhenge** (p689). Even Florida's megalomaniacal **Coral Castle** (p522) has been nicknamed 'America's Stonehenge.' Or maybe you're looking for the world's largest…**ball of twine** (p646)? Or **chair** (p330)? Perhaps the **world's tallest filing cabinet** (p292) or **world's biggest dinosaurs** (p950)?

For sublime examples of 'outsider' folk art, aim for **Lucas** (p693) in Kansas; California's **Salvation Mountain** (p950); **Dr Evermor's Sculpture Park** (p632) in Wisconsin; and Texas' **Beer Can House** (p728) and **Cadillac Ranch** (p746).

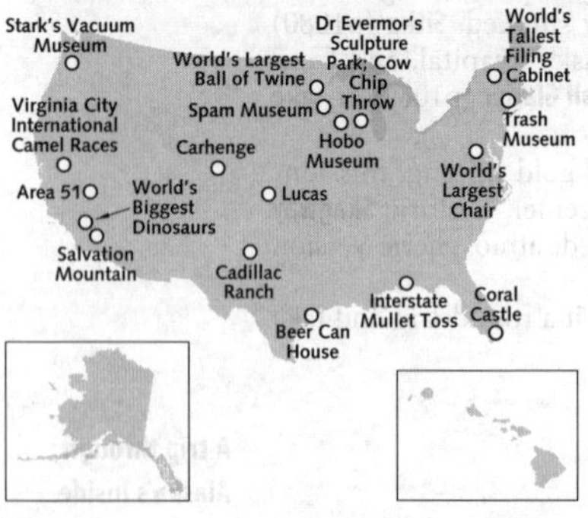

Sometimes Americans dress up madness and call it a 'museum.' What do *you* make of the **Spam Museum** (p646), the **Hobo Museum** (p673), **Stark's Vacuum Museum** (p1052) or the **Trash Museum** (p284)?

Americans celebrate strangely too. Show up for the **Interstate Mullet Toss** (p554) and **Cow Chip Throw** (p632), then cheer on the galumphing dromedaries at Nevada's **Virginia City International Camel Races** (p836).

Finally, if the folks on the ground aren't alien enough for you, look for the outer-space kind along Nevada's Extraterrestrial Hwy outside **Area 51** (p838).

BOOZIN' ACROSS THE USA

Americans like to drink. The US Constitution's 21st Amendment – which ended a 14-year dry spell called Prohibition – establishes the right of every adult over the age of 21 to drink legally, even emphatically. Americans are quite good at making the stuff, too.

Most states tout their 'wine countries' these days, and it ain't all bunkum. California's **Napa** and **Sonoma Valleys** (p991) are justifiably famous, but don't neglect **Santa Barbara** (p956) or rural **Anderson Valley** (p994). Other regions for tippling include **Willamette Valley** (OR; p1058), **Walla Walla** (WA; p1045), **Finger Lakes** (NY; p198), Long Island's **North Fork** (NY; p195), **Charlottesville** (VA; p375) and the **Hill Country** (TX; p718). Cowboys knocking back syrah? Hell yeah.

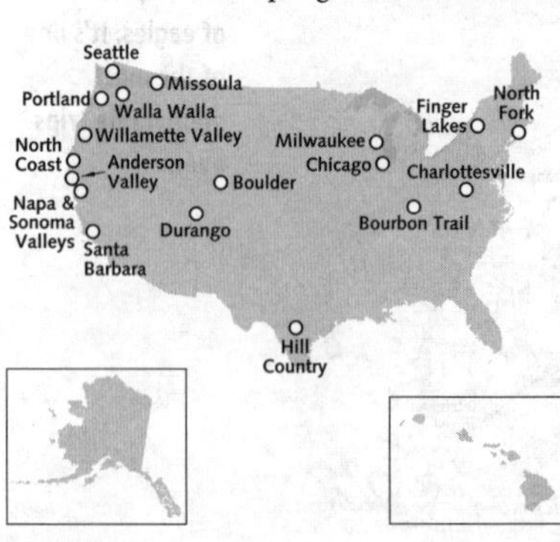

Americans have been brewing beer since before the Revolutionary War. Despite being the home of lightweight major-label beers, **Milwaukee** (p627) remains a beer-lover's destination, and so is **Chicago** (p559). But the microbrewery renaissance began way out West: notable brewmeister cities include **Portland** (p1046), **Seattle** (p1021), **Boulder** (p770), **Durango** (p784) and **Missoula** (p805). In California, the **North Coast** (p995) is doused in good homemade suds.Those who prefer the hard stuff should make time for Kentucky's **Bourbon Trail** (p440), a genteel Southern experience.

ISLAND HOPPING

Everybody wants to go straight across the USA, but traveling around it might make an even better trip. Start at Maine's **Acadia National Park** (p310) for a sunrise hike. Then go to historic **Martha's Vineyard** (p268), from where it's a quick tack to the USA's most famous island, **Manhattan** (p145). Off the Virginia coast is **Chincoteague Island** (p373), famous for its wild horses, and off North Carolina are the **Outer Banks** (p391) and **Cape Hatteras National Seashore** (p392). Farther south off the coast of Georgia lie the Golden Isles (p457), where **Cumberland Island** (p458) is an unspoiled paradise.

Florida boasts **Amelia Island** (p538), the string-of-pearls **Florida Keys** (p523), the islands of **Dry Tortugas National Park** (p531) and lush, tropical **Sanibel and Captiva Islands** (p544).

Along the Gulf of Mexico is the Texas resort town of **Galveston** (p731 and gorgeously wild **Padre Island National Seashore** (p733) – not to be confused with **South Padre Island** (p734), where 'gorgeous and wild' describes the spring-break party scene.

Sail through the Panama Canal or go overland to California, where **Catalina Island** (p937) has Mediterranean flavor, and **Channel Islands National Park** (p956) is 'California's Galápagos.' Keep going to Washington's **San Juan Islands** (p1038) and from there to the islands of Alaska's **Inside Passage** (p1078). Finally, don't forget **Hawaii** (p1104)!

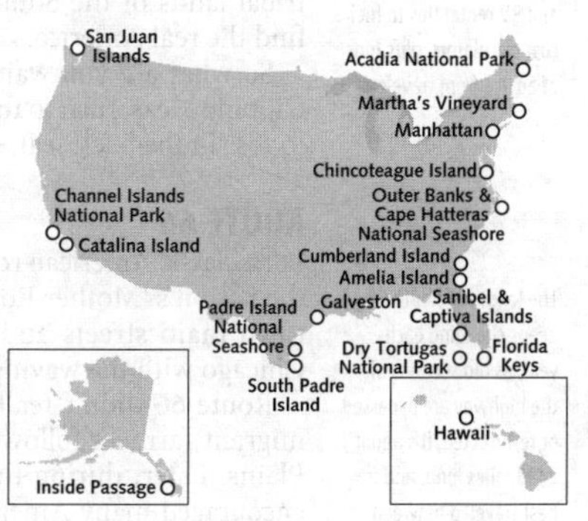

WE'RE HERE, WE'RE QUEER

It's never been a better time to be gay in the USA. GLBT travelers will find lots of places where they can be themselves without thinking twice. Naturally, beaches and big cities typically are the gayest destinations.

Manhattan (p145) is too crowded and cosmopolitan to worry about who's holding hands, while **Fire Island** (p193) is the sandy gay mecca on Long Island. Other East Coast cities that flaunt it are **Boston** (p257), **Philadelphia** (p213), **Washington, DC** (p318), Massachusetts' **Provincetown** (p265) and Delaware's **Rehoboth Beach** (p355). Why even Maine brags a gay beach destination: **Ogunquit** (p302).

In the South, there's always steamy **'Hotlanta'** (p448) and Texas gets darn-right gay-friendly in **Austin** (p716) and parts of **Houston** (p730). In Florida, **Miami** (p505) and the 'Conch Republic' of **Key West** (p527) support thriving gay communities, though **Fort Lauderdale** (p517) attracts bronzed boys and girls too. Of course, everyone gets their freak on in **New Orleans** (p472).

In the Midwest, seek out **Chicago** (p578) and **Minneapolis** (p641). You will have heard of **San Francisco** (p986), the happiest gay city in America, and what can gays and lesbians do in **Los Angeles** (p934) and **Las Vegas** (p832)? Hmmm, just about anything. In fact, when LA or Vegas gets to be too much, flee to the desert resorts of **Palm Springs** (p949).

Lastly, for an island idyll, **Hawaii** (p1104) is generally gay-friendly, especially in **Waikiki** (p1104).

USA Road Trips

Fill up the gas tank and buckle up. Everyone knows road-tripping is the ultimate way to experience America. You can drive up, down, across, around or straight through every state on the map. (OK, maybe not Hawaii, but even that remote Polynesian archipelago has some stunning drives – as does far-flung Alaska.) Revel in yesteryear Route 66 or the dramatic Pacific Coast Highway, or carve your own path through the Appalachian Mountains, cruising alongside the Mississippi River and around the Native American tribal lands of the Southwest. Those 'in-between' are places where you'll find the real America.

RoadTrip America (www.roadtripamerica.com) helps with the nitty-gritty of trip planning, from audiobook reviews and RV rental tips to fuel cost calculators, plus tons of advice from travelers.

So what are you waiting for? It's time to hit the road. For more road-tripping ideas, turn to the Itineraries chapter (p33). For some riveting reads to toss in the back seat, see p32.

ROUTE 66

For a classic American road trip, nothing beats good ol' Route 66. Nicknamed the nation's 'Mother Road' by novelist John Steinbeck, this string of small-town main streets and country byways first connected big-shouldered Chicago with the waving palm trees of Los Angeles in 1926.

The length of Route 66 keeps changing each year, as old sections of the highway are bypassed or resurrected. It's about 2400 miles long, and is best traveled between May and September to avoid winter snow.

Route 66 didn't really hit its stride until the Great Depression, when migrant farmers followed it as they fled the Dust Bowl across the Great Plains. Later, during the post-WWII baby boom, new-found prosperity encouraged many Americans to hit the road and 'get their kicks' on Route 66, which ran through Illinois (p590), Missouri (p666), Kansas (p694), Oklahoma (p696), Texas (p745), New Mexico (p885), Arizona (p860) and California (p954).

Almost as soon as it came of age, however, Route 66 began to lose steam. The shiny blacktop of an ambitious new interstate system started systematically paving over Route 66, bypassing its mom-and-pop diners, drugstore soda fountains and once-stylish motor courts. Railway towns

BEFORE YOU HIT THE ROAD

A few things to remember to ensure your road trip is as happy-go-lucky as possible:

- Join an automobile club (p1161) that provides members with 24-hour emergency roadside assistance and discounts on lodging and attractions; some international clubs have reciprocal agreements with US automobile associations, so check first and bring your member card from home.
- Check the spare tire, tool kit (eg jack, jumper cables, ice scraper, tire pressure gauge) and emergency equipment (eg flashers) in your car; if you're renting a vehicle and these essential safety items are not provided, consider buying them.
- Bring good maps (p1143), especially if you're touring off-road or away from highways; don't rely on a GPS unit – they can malfunction, and in remote areas such as deep canyons or thick forests they may not even work.
- Always carry your driver's license (p1163) and proof of insurance (p1163).
- If you're an international traveler, review the USA's road rules (p1165) and common road hazards (p1164).
- Fill up the tank often, because gas stations can be few and far between on the USA's scenic byways.

were forgotten and way stations for travelers became dusty. Even entire towns began to disappear.

By the time Route 66 was officially decommissioned in 1984, preservation associations of Mother Road fans had sprung up. Today you can still get your kicks on Route 66, following gravel frontage roads and blue-line highways across the belly of America. It's like a time warp – connecting places where the 1950s seem to have stopped just yesterday.

Even if you're not a fan of retro Americana, it's still a great road trip. Or maybe you're after big horizons and natural beauty? Route 66 runs by some of the USA's greatest outdoor attractions – not just the Grand Canyon, but also the Mississippi River, Arizona's Painted Desert and Petrified Forest National Park, and, at road's end, the Pacific beaches of sun-kissed Santa Monica.

The National Historic Route 66 Federation website (www.national66.com) has links to local preservation associations, as well as fan clubs overseas, ranging from the Czech Republic to Norway.

Culturally speaking, Route 66 can be an eye-opener. Discard your preconceptions of small-town American life and unearth the joys of what bicoastal types dismissively term 'flyover' states. Mingle with farmers in Illinois and country-and-western stars in Missouri. Hear the legends of cowboys and Indians in Oklahoma. Visit Native American tribal nations and contemporary pueblos across the Southwest, all the while discovering the traditions of the USA's indigenous peoples. Then follow the trails of miners and desperados deep into the Old West.

You need to be an amateur sleuth to follow Route 66 these days. Historical realignments of the route, dead-ends in farm fields and tumbleweed-filled desert patches, and rough, rutted driving conditions are par for the course. For free turn-by-turn directions, check out www.historic66.com, or purchase the illustrated 'Here It Is!' map series (Ghost Town Press). Remember that getting lost every now and then is inevitable. But never mind, since what the road offers is so valuable: a leap back through time to see what America once was, and still sometimes is. Nostalgia never tasted so sweet.

If you need a break from behind the wheel, why not ride the rails? Amtrak (p1166) runs *Coast Starlight* and commuter trains along the California coast from San Diego to San Francisco.

PACIFIC COAST HIGHWAY

Stretching almost 2000 miles from border to border – that is, from Tijuana, Mexico to British Columbia, Canada – the Pacific Coast Highway (PCH) is an epic adventure for water babies, surfers, kayakers, scuba divers and every other kind of outdoor enthusiast, including landlubbers. Or if you're a more laid-back road-tripper, who just dreams of cruising alongside the ocean in a cherry-red convertible, drifting from sunrise to sunset, the insanely scenic PCH can deliver that, too.

The PCH is a road trip for lovers, nomadic ramblers, bohemians, beatniks and curiosity seekers keen to search out every nook and cranny of forgotten beachside hamlets and pastoral farm towns along the way. It connects the

ROADSIDE ODDITIES: ROUTE 66

Kitschy, time-warped and just plain weird roadside attractions? Route 66 has got 'em in spades. Here are a few beloved Mother Road landmarks to make your own scavenger hunt:

- Gemini Giant (p590) in Illinois
- Pacific's Black Madonna Shrine and Red Oak II outside Carthage in Missouri
- Blue Whale (p696) in Oklahoma
- Devil's Rope Museum (p745), Cadillac Ranch and Bug Ranch (p746) in Texas
- Seligman's Snow Cap Drive-In and Holbrook's WigWam Motel and Meteor Crater (p848) in Arizona (p860)
- Roy's Motel & Cafe in Amboy, in the middle of California's Mojave Desert

dots between some of the West Coast's most striking cities, starting from surf-style San Diego, glamorous Los Angeles and offbeat San Francisco in California, then moving north to equally alternative-minded and arty Seattle, Washington. When pounding the pavement starts to make you feel claustrophobic, just head out back on the open road and hit the coast again, heading north or south – the direction doesn't really matter.

You could bypass metro areas and just stick to the places in between, like the almost too-perfect beaches of California's Orange County ('the OC') and Santa Barbara (the 'American Riviera'); wacky Santa Cruz, a university town and surfers' paradise; redwood forests along the Big Sur coast and north of Mendocino; the sand dunes, seaside resorts and fishing villages of coastal Oregon; and finally, the wild lands of Washington's Olympic Peninsula, with its primeval rain forest, and bucolic San Juan Islands, served by coastal ferries.

For traveling every back road in the western US, it's hard to beat the comprehensive Benchmark Maps (www.benchmarkmaps.com) series of topographical road and recreational atlases.

There's no very bad time of year to drive the PCH, although northern climes will be rainier and snowier during winter. Peak travel season is June through August, despite that being when many stretches of the coast are socked in by fog during early summer (locals call it 'June Gloom'). The shoulder seasons before Memorial Day (ie April and May) and after Labor Day (ie September and October) can be ideal, with sunny days, crisply cool nights and fewer crowds.

BLUE RIDGE PARKWAY

What's the USA's most visited national parkland? If you said the Grand Canyon or Yosemite, you're wrong. Surprisingly, it's the Blue Ridge Parkway (p401), which snakes for nearly 500 miles through the southern Appalachian Mountains. Finished in 1940, the parkway was officially commissioned by President Franklin D Roosevelt during the Great Depression as a public-works project. Today, this rolling, rural scenic byway still connects Virginia's Shenandoah National Park with Great Smoky Mountains National Park, straddling the North Carolina–Tennessee border.

The Blue Ridge Parkway celebrates its 75th anniversary in 2010 – get the lowdown on heritage festivities in historical communities all along the route at www.blueridgeparkway75.org.

Although it skirts dozens of small towns and a few metropolitan areas, this backwoods byway really feels decades removed from the 'New South'. Here, rustic log cabins with creaky rocking chairs on the front porch still dot the rolling hillsides. Folk-art shops and live bluegrass music joints are strung along the route. The parkway is also steeped in history, from Cherokee tribal lands to early European homesteads and later Civil War battlefields. Early-20th-century mountain and lakeside resorts still welcome families like old friends, while log-cabin diners dish up heaping piles of buckwheat pancakes with blackberry preserves and a side of country ham.

When you need to work off all that good Southern cooking, over 100 hiking trails can be accessed along the Blue Ridge Parkway, from gentle nature walks and easily summited peaks to rough-and-ready tramps along the legendary Appalachian Trail (p134). Or clamber on a horse and ride off into

DETOURS: OFF THE PACIFIC COAST HIGHWAY

Let yourself be lured inland by:

- Mission San Juan Capistrano (p939)
- Northern California's wine country (p991)
- Portland (p1046)
- Columbia River Gorge (p1060)
- Mt Rainier National Park (p1043)

the refreshingly shady forests. Then go canoeing, kayaking or inner tubing along rushing rivers, or dangle a fishing line over the side of a rowboat on petite lakes. And who says you even have to drive? The parkway makes an epic trip for long-distance cyclists, too.

Keep in mind that the weather can vary greatly, depending on your elevation. While mountain peaks are snowed in during winter, the valleys can still be invitingly warm. Most visitor services along the parkway are only open from April through October. May is best for wildflowers, although most people come for leaf-peeping during fall. Spring and fall are good times for bird-watching, with nearly 160 species having been spotted in the skies over the parkway.

Discover Navajo (http://discovernavajo.com) offers free downloads of the Navajo Nation's official travel guide, written by tribal members. For the uninitiated, it even explains exactly what a 'Navajo taco' is.

THE GRAND CIRCLE

In the early-20th-century era of tourism, the Grand Circle was a leisure-class railway and overland journey to see all the rugged, raw natural splendors of the American Southwest. It took several months, but today you need only a few weeks to witness some of the most amazing spectacles that Mother Nature has yet devised – and to get acquainted with the Southwest's rich Native American heritage.

This road trip, which covers 1800 miles or more depending on where you choose to roam, is the antithesis of a straight line. It slowly winds around and roughly encircles the Four Corners region (p38). Some backtracking is unavoidable. You can start in any of the main air-travel hubs – Las Vegas, Albuquerque, Flagstaff, Salt Lake City or Denver – and be just a half-day's drive from the heart of this remote region. Travel during spring and fall to avoid the most extreme temperatures.

The National Scenic Byways Program website (www.byways.org) has a clickable map of drives across the country, from Vermont's Mad River Byway to Alaska's Top-of-the-World Highway.

In Arizona, the Grand Canyon awaits, just north of the vintage Route 66 towns of Williams and Flagstaff. Explore the Hopi mesas, with their hilltop pueblos, and the Navajo Nation, home to the majestic buttes of Monument Valley (as seen in heaps of Hollywood Western movies), and the Ancestral Puebloan of in Canyon de Chelly.

Zuni Pueblo is just outside Gallup, a Route 66 town and the unofficial 'Capital of Indian Country.' New Mexico is also where you'll find quirky

DOWNLOADS: BLUEGRASS SOUNDS

If you can't catch a live show at Virginia's **Blue Ridge Music Center** (www.blueridgemusiccenter.org), open from May through October, then load up your Mp3 player with beloved 'hillbilly' classics like:

- 'Blue Moon of Kentucky,' Bill Monroe and the Blue Grass Boys
- 'Foggy Mountain Breakdown,' Earl Scruggs
- 'Orange Blossom Special,' Rouse Brothers
- 'Rocky Top,' Osborne Brothers
- 'Windy Mountain,' Lonesome Pine Fiddlers
- 'Flame of Love,' Jim and Jesse
- 'I'm a Man of Constant Sorrow,' Stanley Brothers
- 'Every Time You Say Goodbye,' Alison Krauss and Union Station
- 'Like a Hurricane,' The Dillards
- 'Angel Band,' Emmylou Harris

For a short history of bluegrass music, see p77.

Albuquerque, followed by a scenic drive up to arty Santa Fe and Taos. To stand on the Four Corners itself, trek west of Chaco Canyon, a ceremonial center for Ancestral Puebloans. Afterward, backtrack across the Colorado border to the equally ancient cliff dwellings of Mesa Verde National Park.

Red-rock Moab is the adventure-hound capital of Utah, just outside Arches and Canyonlands National Parks. Sublimely scenic Hwy 12 winds west through Utah's wild 'color country,' ending in the river oasis of Zion National Park. To bring your road trip full circle, detour to the Grand Canyon's North Rim before zipping down to the neon lights of Las Vegas.

The Indian Pueblo Cultural Center website (www.indianpueblo.org) has information about New Mexico's indigenous peoples, from Acoma to Zuni, with an online calendar of ceremonial feast days.

GREAT RIVER ROAD

The Mississippi River splits the USA in two, not just geographically and historically but also psychologically speaking, defining every citizen as either an Easterner or a Westerner. After the Louisiana Purchase of 1803, when Napoleon Bonaparte sold off vast French colonial lands in the New World to President Thomas Jefferson, the Mississippi became the new American frontier.

Explorers Lewis and Clark soon crossed the Mississippi while making their way overland to the Pacific Coast. Earlier French voyageurs and Native American peoples used the river for trade and travel, as did African slaves seeking freedom along the Underground Railroad before the Civil War. Later novelist Mark Twain set his great American novel, *The Adventures of Huckleberry Finn,* along this iconic waterway.

Can anyone capture the whole history of the blues? Martin Scorsese's concert film, *Lightning in a Bottle* (2004), and the CD boxed set *Martin Scorsese Presents the Blues: A Musical Journey* (2003), come mighty close.

Established in the late 1930s, the Great River Road is a 2000-mile journey from the Mississippi's headwaters in the northern lakes of Minnesota, floating downstream all the way to where the river empties into the Gulf of Mexico near New Orleans, Louisiana. You'll be awed by the sweeping scenery as you meander alongside North America's second-longest river, from the rolling plains of Iowa down past the cotton fields of the Mississippi Delta. And you'll never be more than 100 miles from a riverboat casino anywhere along the route.

But seriously, this trip is worth taking for other reasons. The Great River Road diverts you off the interstate to small towns you'd otherwise miss, including Hibbing, MN, where folk rocker Bob Dylan grew up; Brainerd, MN, as seen in the Coen Brothers' indie flick *Fargo;* Spring Green, WI, where

DOWNLOADS: ROAD-TRIPPIN' BLUES, JAZZ & ZYDECO

If you're out of range of New Orleans' community-run WWOZ radio station (90.7FM), try grooving to these rhythms out on the road:

- 'Walkin' Blues,' Robert Johnson
- 'Mississippi River Blues,' Ida Cox
- 'I've Got My Mojo Working.' Muddy Waters
- 'Johnny B Goode,' Chuck Berry
- 'Zydeco La Louisianne,' Buckwheat Zydeco
- 'Bourbon Street Parade,' Preservation Hall Jazz Band
- 'Do You Know What It Means to Miss New Orleans,' Louis Armstrong
- 'St Louis Blues,' Louis Armstrong and Bessie Smith
- 'Me & My Chauffeur,' Memphis Minnie
- 'Let the Good Times Roll,' BB King

For more about American blues see p76; and for more on jazz, see p76.

DETOURS: BETWEEN DC & MIAMI

Going out of your way is always a pleasure, never an annoyance, whether you're heading toward the sea or inland to explore the South's spooky swamps.

- Virginia's Eastern Shore (p373)
- North Carolina's Outer Banks (p391) and Crystal Coast (p394)
- South Carolina's most genteel city, Charleston (p404), and wild swamps (p487)
- Georgia's 'Golden Isles' (p457) and Okefenokee National Wildlife Refuge (p459)
- Florida's Space Coast (p532) and Everglades National Park (p520)

architect Frank Lloyd Wright once worked (see p92); pastoral Hannibal, MO, boyhood home of Mark Twain; and Metropolis, IL, where you'll find Superman's quick-change phone booth.

The southern section of this route (see p37) traces American musical history, from rock and roll in St Louis to Memphis blues and N'awlins jazz. And you won't go hungry either, with retro Midwestern diners serving homemade pies, Southern barbecue joints and smokehouses, and lip-smackin' Cajun taverns and dance halls in Louisiana. By the time you reach N'awlins, you'll be ready to party.

'Ten states, one river' is the slogan for the Official Site for Mississippi River Travel (www.experiencemississippiriver.com), a comprehensive resource for history, outdoor recreation, live music and much more.

SOUTH FROM DC TO THE SUNSHINE STATE

You could never pin down exactly how many millions of Americans have made the trip from Washington, DC, to Florida during some family summer vacation long, long ago. But there's no denying just how popular a road trip this is – I-95 isn't nicknamed the 'Disney World Expressway' for nothing, you know.

Don't start panicking: no Mickey Mouse ears are required for our sybaritic, all-ages southern road trip. We encourage you to leave behind the interstate highway as often as you can and meander over to the coast (see the Detours boxed text, above) the instant you start missing those Atlantic sea breezes, letting you soak up as much fresh air and Dixie sunshine as possible.

Start in the nation's capital, Washington, DC, wandering the National Mall's monuments and museums. Then dive right into the South, starting with the rolling hills of Virginia, dipping into colonial-era history outside of Richmond. Back on the road in North Carolina's Piedmont region, stop over in the college towns of Chapel Hill and Raleigh-Durham. In South Carolina, don't miss a side trip to Charleston, with its gracious antebellum architecture and old-fashioned romance. Savannah is another charming southern belle, just further down the coast of Georgia.

The Roadside America website (www.roadsideamerica.com) is a handy go-to source for finding obscure, infamous and kitschy roadside attractions and oddities from coast to coast.

Expect a sea change of personality when you motor into Florida, with its bronzed bods, beaches, surfers and retro seaside resorts galore. Walt Disney World exerts an irresistible pull inland on I-95, but south of plasticky Orlando, the interstate quickly swings back to the coast. Get ready to cruise into spicy-hot Miami, beyond which lies the lotusland of the Florida Keys, an archipelago of island idylls in the Gulf of Mexico reached via the gorgeous Overseas Hwy (Hwy 1). At road's end, Key West is less than 100 nautical miles from Cuba – so go on, reward yourself with a mojito.

ALSO WORTH A SPIN

So far we've only described a half-dozen of the best road trips that the USA has to offer. But there are scores of other scenic byways, country roads and blue-line highways webbing across the nation. For more faves,

WORTHWHILE DETOURS

Route	State(s)	Start/End	Sights & Activities	Best Time to Drive	More Info
Seward Hwy	AK	Anchorage/Seward	glaciers, fjords, waterfalls, wildflower meadows; watching wildlife	May-Oct	p1093
Natchez Trace Hwy	AL/MS/TN	Nashville/Natchez	'Old South' history, archaeological sites, scenic waterways; biking, camping, hiking	Mar-Nov	p432
Eastern Sierra Scenic Byway	CA	Topaz Lake/ Little Lake	snowy peaks, alpine lakes, desert basins, hot springs; camping, hiking, mountain & rock climbing	May-Sep	p1012
Hwy 49	CA	Oakhurst/Sierraville	Gold Rush–era towns & historic sites; wine tasting	Apr-Oct	p1000
San Juan Skyway	CO	Durango/Durango	Old West mining & railway towns, archaeological sites; hiking, skiing	Jun-Sep	p784
Maui's Road to Hana	HI	Paia/Hana	Jungle waterfalls, beaches; hiking, surfing, swimming	year-round	p1126
Sawtooth Scenic Byway	ID	Ketchum/Stanley	jagged mountains, verdant forests; backpacking, hiking	May-Sep	p813
Going-to-the-Sun Road	MT	Glacier National Park	dizzying mountain passes, glacier views; camping, wildlife watching	Jul & Aug	p808
Turquoise Trail	NM	Albuquerque/Santa Fe	mining towns, quirky museums & folk art; cycling, hiking	Mar-May & Sep-Nov	p894
US 50	NV	Fernley/Baker	'Loneliest Road in America', epic wilderness; biking, hiking, spelunking	May-Sep	p837
Rte 28	NY	Stony Hollow/Arkville	Catskills mountains, lakes, rivers; hiking, leaf-peeping, tubing	May-Sep	p198
Historic Columbia River Hwy	OR	Portland/Portland	'gorge-ous' scenery, waterfalls, wildflowers; cycling, hiking	Apr-Sep	p1061
Rte 170	TX	Lajitas/Presidio	vast desert & mountain landscapes, hot springs; hiking, horseback riding	Feb-Apr & Oct-Nov	p749
Monument Valley	UT	Monument Valley	iconic buttes, movie-set locations; 4WD tours, horseback riding	year-round	p858
VT 100	VT	Stamford/Newport	rolling pastures, green mountains; hiking, skiing	Jun-Sep	p291
Hwy 13	WI	Bayfield/Superior	lakeside beaches, forests, farmlands; nature walks	May-Sep	p636
Kancamagus Hwy	VT	Conway/Lincoln	craggy mountains, streams & waterfalls; camping, hiking, swimming	May-Sep	p299

see the table below. Also look for the Scenic Drive boxed texts scattered throughout the destination chapters. Lonely Planet's Trips series of guidebooks covers more micro-regional to sprawling, epic road trips throughout the US, including top picks by local experts – click to www.lonelyplanet.com/campaigns/usatrips for free itinerary downloads and more.

History

TURTLE ISLAND

According to oral traditions and sacred myths, indigenous peoples have always lived on the North American continent, which some called 'Turtle Island.' At the time of first European contact, approximately two to 18 million Native American people occupied every corner of the turtle's back north of present-day Mexico and spoke over 300 languages.

The Western scientific explanation of the continent's peopling – that Asians migrated over a land bridge between Siberia and Alaska at least 20,000 years ago – likely occurred but is considered insufficient to explain all the evidence of prehistoric civilization on the North American continent. Also, because it turns Native Americans into 'immigrants,' this theory has been criticized as it provides an occasional justification for the US taking Native American lands.

The earliest identifiable Paleo-Indian cultures were the Clovis and Folsom, who lived throughout North America from about 10,000 to 8000 BC, at the end of the last ice age. From then, a vibrant mix of complex societies developed across the continent: first nomadic hunters and gatherers (often called 'Archaic' peoples) and later incorporating some settled farming communities.

Among North America's most significant prehistoric cultures were the Mound Builders, who inhabited the Ohio and Mississippi River valleys from around 3000 BC to AD 1300. In Illinois, Cahokia Mounds State Historic Site (p590) was once a metropolis of 20,000 people, the largest in pre-Columbian North America. In Ohio, Hopewell Culture National Historic Park (p606) protects a more mysterious, sacred ceremonial center nicknamed 'Mound City.'

The People: Indians of the American Southwest (1993), by Stephen Trimble, is a diverse account of indigenous history and contemporary culture as related by Native Americans themselves.

In the Southwest, Ancestral Puebloans occupied the Colorado Plateau from around AD 100 to AD 1300, until warfare, drought and scarcity of resources likely drove them out. You can still see their cliff dwellings at Colorado's Mesa Verde National Park (p789) and desert adobe pueblos at New Mexico's Chaco Culture National Historic Park (p902). These people's descendents include the Hopi, whose 13th-century mesa-top pueblos (p858) are among North America's oldest continuously inhabited settlements.

Meanwhile, in Hawaii Polynesian voyagers started arriving between AD 500 and AD 1000 (see p1105). In the Pacific Northwest and Alaska, hallmarks of indigenous cultures also included seafaring canoes, as well as carved wooden totem poles. On Washington state's Olympic Peninsula, the Makah Nation (p1037) encompasses an excavated 15th-century Native American

TIMELINE

8000 BC

Widespread extinction of ice age mammals including the woolly mammoth, due partly to cooperative hunting by humans and partly to a warming climate. Indigenous peoples begin hunting smaller game and gathering native plants.

7000 BC–AD 100

'Archaic period' marked by nomadic hunter-gatherer lifestyle. By the end of this period, corn, beans and squash (the agricultural 'three sisters') and permanent settlements are well established.

1492

Italian explorer Christopher Columbus 'discovers' America, eventually making three voyages throughout the Caribbean. He names the indigenous inhabitants 'Indians,' mistakenly thinking he had reached the Indies.

village that was buried by a mudslide, thus preserving its pre-Columbian artifacts, including a traditional longhouse. In Anchorage, the Alaska Native Heritage Center (p1087) is the best place to learn about indigenous peoples of the far north.

THE LAST AMERICANS

One of America's formative paradoxes is that the continent's 'first peoples' were among the last to become citizens. When this finally happened in 1924 (in part to honor Native American service in WWI), it cemented an unresolved end to the 19th-century's brutal Indian Wars: Native American reservations would remain separate nations within the USA, with their own laws and sometimes unclear obligations on both sides.

This isn't what anyone wanted, and opinions always differed on who should get to live exactly where. Intending to end these conflicts forever almost a century earlier, President Andrew Jackson enacted the Indian Removal Act of 1830. This designated land west of the Mississippi River as 'Indian territory.' Indians were meant to remove themselves there, thus clearing the fertile valleys west of the Appalachians for US settlement and capitalism.

Many tribes resisted forced removal, including the Seminole in Florida, but the US cajoled, threatened and bribed Indians to sign treaties and cooperate; when that failed, the government used guns. Among the most infamous incidents was the 1838 Trail of Tears, a forced march that alone killed over 4000 Cherokee. By 1844, three-quarters of the 120,000 Indians who lived east of the Mississippi had been successfully 'removed.'

By 1853, after annexing Texas and winning the Mexican-American War, the US found itself holding nearly the entire continent, with Indian territory smack in the middle. Particularly after the Civil War, pioneers and miners flooded west, settling everywhere, regardless of treaty boundaries. By 1871, the US was making and breaking new treaties so fast that they simply quit writing them. Ultimately, the US broke over 470 treaties, every one understood by Native Americans to have lasted 'as long as grass grows or water runs.'

The new nation kept finding gold, or it wanted the real estate, and it tired of asking permission to take it. Disregarding fairness, the US abandoned any pretense at peaceful coexistence. In the late 19th century, buffalo were exterminated as an explicit (and successful) military strategy to starve the 'wild' nomadic Great Plains tribes who resisted forced relocation to reservations. In 1876, when the Sioux won the Battle of Little Bighorn, US restraint vanished. The military relentlessly hounded tribes until, with the end of the Apache Wars in 1886, no armed Native American resistance remained.

Sequestered on impoverished reservations, Native American tribes needed US help to survive. What they got was the 1887 Dawes Act, aimed to 'assimilate' Indians into white society by forcing them to abandon their language and cultural heritage. With insult heaped upon misery, many Native Americans staunchly refused to be assimilated. This policy extended to the 1924 Indian Citizenship Act, which some tribes welcomed but others regarded as a violation of their inherent sovereignty.

For more about contemporary Native American culture, see p70.

1607

Within the first year of the Jamestown settlement, 80 out of 108 people die. The next year, called the 'starving time,' 440 of 500 settlers are buried. From 1619–22, 3000 of 3600 Jamestown settlers perish.

1620

The *Mayflower* lands at Plymouth with 102 English Pilgrims. Sick and starving, they are saved by gifts of food from the Wampanoag tribe. Grateful Pilgrims throw a harvest festival, which today is celebrated annually as Thanksgiving.

1756–63

In the Seven Years' War (or the 'French and Indian War'), France loses to England and gets kicked out of Canada. Britain now controls most of the territory east of the Mississippi River.

It was the Great Plains cultures that came to epitomize 'Indians' in the popular American imagination, in part because these tribal peoples put up the longest fight against the USA's westward expansion. Oklahoma is rich in sites that interpret Native American life before Europeans arrived, including at Anadarko (p700) and along the Trail of Tears (p702).

A NEW WORLD FOR EUROPEANS

When Europeans first sailed into the western hemisphere, they called its continents a 'New World.' The unexpected land was certainly startling, but the real new world was seafaring across oceans: as it turned out, the sea wasn't earth's edge, but instead a superhighway. This discovery radically altered the political landscape of Europe and Asia and spurred modern capitalism, affecting the way Europeans reacted to the Americas.

Authoritative and sobering, *Bury My Heart at Wounded Knee* (1970), by Dee Brown, tells the story of the late-19th-century Indian Wars from the perspective of Native Americans.

In 1492, Italian explorer Christopher Columbus, backed by Spain, voyaged west – looking for the East Indies. He found the Bahamas. With visions of gold, more Spanish explorers quickly followed: Hernán Cortés conquered much of today's Mexico; Francisco Pizarro conquered Peru; Juan Ponce de León wandered through Florida looking for the fountain of youth. Not to be left out, the French explored Canada and the Midwest, while the Dutch and English cruised North America's eastern seaboard.

European explorers left in their wake diseases to which indigenous peoples had no immunity. More than any other factor – war, slavery or famine – disease epidemics decimated Native populations by anywhere from 50% to 90%. By the 17th century, indigenous North Americans numbered only about a million, and many of the continent's once-thriving societies were in turmoil and transition.

In addition to seeking riches, European colonizers were driven by religious fervor: it seemed to many of them that this underpopulated New World must have been reserved by divine providence for Christians. Spanish Catholic missionaries sought intensely to convert the continent's indigenous cultures, eventually establishing strings of missions across the Southwest and in Texas and California.

In 1502, Italian explorer Amerigo Vespucci used the term 'Mundus Novus,' or New World, to describe his discoveries. His reward? In 1507, new maps labeled the western hemisphere 'America.'

In 1607, English noblemen established North America's first permanent European settlement in Jamestown (p369). Earlier settlements had ended badly, and Jamestown almost did too: the English chose a swamp, planted their crops late and died from disease and starvation. Some despairing colonists ran off to live with the local tribes, who provided the settlement with enough aid to survive.

For Jamestown and America, 1619 proved a pivotal year: the colony established the House of Burgesses, a representative assembly of citizens to decide local laws, and it received its first boatload of 20 African slaves. Having finally grown a successful export crop – tobacco – colonists needed workers: they didn't have enough English servants (who disdained field

1773

To protest a British tax on tea, Bostonians crudely 'disguise' themselves as Mohawks, board East India Company ships and toss their tea overboard during what would be named the Boston Tea Party.

1775

On April 18, Paul Revere rides from Boston to warn colonial 'Minutemen' that the British are coming. The next day, 'the shot heard round the world' is fired at Lexington, starting the Revolutionary War.

1776

On July 4, American colonies sign the Declaration of Independence. Famous figures who helped create this document include John Hancock, Samuel Adams, John Adams, Benjamin Franklin and Thomas Jefferson.

labor) and Native Americans were difficult to convince or subdue. African slaves, already established on Caribbean sugar plantations, fit the bill.

The next year, 1620, was equally momentous, as a boatload of radically religious Puritans pulled ashore at what would become Plymouth, Massachusetts (p260). The Pilgrims were escaping religious persecution under the 'corrupt' Church of England, and in the New World they saw a divine opportunity to create a new society that would be a religious and moral beacon. The Pilgrims signed a 'Mayflower Compact,' one of the seminal texts of American democracy, to govern themselves by consensus.

The New World (2005), directed by Terrence Malick, is a brutal but passionate film that retells the tragic story of the Jamestown colony and the pivotal peacemaking role of Pocahontas, a Powhatan chief's daughter.

For decades, the Pilgrims and local Native American tribes lived fairly cooperatively, but deadly conflict erupted in 1675. King Philip's War lasted 14 months and killed over 5000 people (mostly Native Americans), with most remaining tribal members being put on Caribbean-bound slave ships. And so, the 'American paradox' was born: white political and religious freedom would come to be founded through the enslavement of blacks and the disappearance of Native Americans.

CAPITALISM & COLONIALISM

For the next two centuries, European powers – particularly England, France, Portugal and Spain – competed for position and territory in the New World, extending European politics into the Americas. As Britain's Royal Navy came to rule Atlantic seas, England increasingly profited from its colonies and eagerly consumed the fruits of their labors – sweet tobacco from Virginia, sugar and coffee from the Caribbean.

Anticipating the industrial revolution, these luxuries were profitable only when mass-produced as export goods using cheap labor in rigidly organized plantations. Over the 17th and 18th centuries, slavery in America was slowly legalized into a formal institution to support this plantation economy. North America received only about 5% of all slaves transported from Africa to the Americas, but slaves made up a large proportion of the American colonies' population: by 1800, one out of every five persons was a slave.

If history is a partisan affair, Howard Zinn makes his allegiance clear in *A People's History of the United States* (1980 & 2005), which tells the often-overlooked stories about laborers, minorities, immigrants, women and radicals.

Meanwhile, Britain mostly left the American colonists to govern themselves. Town meetings and representative assemblies, in which local citizens (that is, white men with property) debated community problems and voted on laws and taxes, became common.

However, by the end of the Seven Years' War in 1763, Britain was feeling the strains of running an empire: it had been fighting France for a century and had colonies scattered all over the world. It was time to clean up bureaucracies and share financial burdens. Britain stationed a permanent army in America. It passed laws forbidding settlement west of the Appalachian Mountains and north of the Ohio River (to avoid more wars) and a series of taxes to raise funds for the Crown and its defense.

1787

Constitutional Convention in Philadelphia draws up the US Constitution; Alexander Hamilton and particularly James Madison play important roles. Federal power is balanced between the presidency, Congress and the judiciary.

1791

Bill of Rights adopted as constitutional amendments articulating citizens' rights, including those of freedom of speech, assembly, religion and the press; the right to bear arms; and the prohibition of 'cruel and unusual punishments.'

1803

France's Napoleon (preparing for war with England) sells the Louisiana Territory to the US for just $15 million, thereby extending the boundaries of the new nation from the Mississippi River to the Rocky Mountains.

From 1763 onward, the colonies protested and boycotted English policies and engaged in a running public discussion of political theory that would culminate in the 1776 Declaration of Independence and the Federalist Papers. With these documents, the American colonists took many of the Enlightenment ideas then circulating worldwide – of individualism, equality and freedom; of John Locke's 'natural rights' of life, liberty and property – and fashioned a new type of government to put them into practice.

Frustrations came to a head with the Boston Tea Party in 1773, after which Britain clamped down hard, shutting Boston's harbor, increasing its military presence and enforcing imperial authority. In 1774 representatives from 12 colonies convened the First Continental Congress in Philadelphia's Independence Hall to air complaints and debate how to respond. Colonists, still identifying as aggrieved Englishmen, worked themselves up, and both sides readied for a fight.

Want to read the Constitution, Emancipation Proclamation, Federalist Papers and much, much more? Peruse the National Archives at www.archives.gov or '100 Milestone Documents' at www.ourdocuments.gov.

REVOLUTION & THE REPUBLIC

In April 1775, British troops skirmished with armed colonists in Massachusetts, and the Revolutionary War began. Soon after shooting started, the Second Continental Congress met in Philadelphia and chose George Washington, a wealthy Virginia farmer, to lead the American army. Trouble was, Washington lacked gunpowder and money (the colonists resisted taxes even for their own military), and his troops were a motley collection of poorly armed farmers, hunters and merchants, who regularly quit and returned to their farms due to lack of pay. On the other side, the British 'Redcoats,' represented the world's most powerful military. The inexperienced General Washington had to improvise constantly, sometimes wisely retreating, sometimes engaging in 'ungentlemanly' sneak attacks. During the winter of 1777–78, the American army nearly starved at Valley Forge (p227).

The HBO miniseries *John Adams* (2008) is a riveting story, told from all sides, of the years when the American Revolution hung in the balance and fate could have swung either way.

Meanwhile, the Second Continental Congress tried to articulate what exactly they were fighting for. In January 1776, Thomas Paine published the wildly popular *Common Sense,* which passionately argued for independence from England. Soon, independence seemed not just logical, but noble and necessary, and on July 4, 1776, the Declaration of Independence was finalized and signed. Largely written by Thomas Jefferson, it elevated the 13 colonies' particular gripes against the monarchy into a universal declaration of individual rights and republican government. It was so moving it helped inspire revolutions elsewhere, and famously states:

> We hold these truths to be self-evident: That all men are created equal; that they are endowed by their Creator with certain unalienable Rights; that among these are Life, Liberty, and the Pursuit of Happiness. That to secure these rights, Governments are instituted among Men, deriving their just powers from the consent of the governed.

1803–6

President Thomas Jefferson sends Meriwether Lewis and William Clark west through the Louisiana Purchase. Guided by the Shoshone tribeswoman Sacajawea, they trailblaze from St Louis, Missouri, to the Pacific Ocean and back.

1812

The War of 1812 begins with battles against the British and Native Americans in the Great Lakes region. Even after the 1815 Treaty of Ghent, fighting continues along the Gulf Coast, notably at New Orleans.

1823

President Monroe articulates the Monroe Doctrine, which seeks to end European military interventions in the Americas. President Teddy Roosevelt later extends it to justify US interventions in Latin America and the western hemisphere.

However, to succeed on the battlefield, General Washington needed help, not just patriotic sentiment. In 1778, Benjamin Franklin persuaded France (always eager to trouble England) to ally with the revolutionaries, and they provided the troops, material and sea power that won the war. The British surrendered at Yorktown, Virginia, in 1781, and two years later the Treaty of Paris formally recognized the 'United States of America.'

At first, the nation's loose confederation of fractious states, squabbling and competing like hens at a grain bucket, were hardly 'united.' So the founders gathered again in Philadelphia, tinkered like mechanics, and in 1787 drafted a new-and-improved Constitution: the US government was given a stronger federal center, with checks and balances between its three major branches; and to guard against the abuse of centralized power, a citizen's Bill of Rights was approved in 1791.

According to apocryphal legend, George Washington was so honest that after chopping down his father's cherry tree when he was just a child, he admitted, 'I cannot tell a lie. I did it with my little hatchet.'

With the Constitution, the scope of the American Revolution solidified: a radical change in government; and preservation of the economic and social status quos. Rich landholders kept their property, which included their slaves; Native Americans were excluded from the nation; and women were excluded from politics. These blatant discrepancies and injustices, which were widely noted, were the results of both pragmatic compromise (eg to get slave-dependent Southern states to agree) and also widespread beliefs in the essential rightness of things as they were.

As a result, from that moment till now, US history has pulsed with the ongoing struggle to define 'all' and 'equal' and 'liberty' – to take the universal language of America's founding and either rectify or justify the inevitable disparities that have bedeviled this democratic society.

You can follow the Lewis and Clark expedition on its extraordinary journey west to the Pacific and back again online at www.pbs.org/lewisandclark, which features historical maps, photo albums and journal excerpts.

WESTWARD, HO!

As the 19th century dawned on the young nation, the 'rightness' of the American experiment appeared to have been proven, and self-satisfied optimism was the mood of the day. With the invention of the cotton gin in 1793 – followed by threshers, reapers, mowers and later combines – agriculture was industrialized, and US commerce surged. The 1803 Louisiana Purchase doubled US territory, and expansion west of the Appalachian Mountains began in earnest.

Relations between the US and Britain – despite lively trade – remained tense. The British maintained forts in the Ohio Valley, and were known to incite Native Americans to attack American settlers, while Britain's navy harassed US ships. In 1812, the US declared war on England again, but the two-year conflict ended without much gained by either side. The British abandoned their forts, and the US renewed its vow to avoid Europe's 'entangling alliances.' One result was the 1823 Monroe Doctrine, which declared the Americas closed to European colonialism.

In the 1830s and 1840s, with growing nationalist fervor and dreams of continental expansion, many Americans came to believe it was 'Manifest Destiny'

1841

First wagon trains follow the Oregon Trail, which extends the route followed by the Lewis and Clark Expedition. By 1847, over 6500 emigrants a year are heading West, to states such as Oregon, California and Mormon-dominated Utah.

1844

First telegraph line is inaugurated in 1844 with the phrase 'What hath God wrought?'. In 1845, Congress considers building a transcontinental railroad, finally completed in 1869. Together, telegraph and train open the frontier.

1849

After the 1848 discovery of gold near Sacramento, an epic cross-country gold rush sees 60,000 'forty-niners' flock to California's Mother Lode. The population of San Francisco explodes from 850 to 25,000 hardy souls.

that all the land should be theirs. The 1830 Indian Removal Act aimed to clear one obstacle (see p52), while the building of the railroads cleared another hurdle, linking Midwestern farmers with East Coast markets.

In 1836 a group of Texans fomented a revolution against Mexico. (Remember the Alamo? See p722.) Ten years later, the US annexed the Texas Republic, and when Mexico complained, the US simply waged war for it – and while they were at it, took California too. In 1848, Mexico was soundly defeated and ceded this territory to the US, adding more land with the 1853 Gadsden Purchase. This completed the USA's continental expansion. Except for Native American tribal lands, Americans had nabbed it all, from sea to shining sea.

By a remarkable coincidence, only days after the 1848 treaty with Mexico was signed, gold was discovered in California (p1000). By 1849, surging rivers of wagon trains were creaking west filled with miners, pioneers, entrepreneurs, immigrants, outlaws and prostitutes, all seeking their fortunes. This made for exciting, legendary times, but throughout loomed a troubling question: as new states joined the USA, would they be slave states or free states? The nation's future depended on the answer.

By turns gritty and heroic, the Western TV series *Deadwood* (2004–06) dramatically brings to life the chaos and twisted up-and-down fortunes of a 19th-century mining town, with characters as dramatic as any Shakespearean tragedy.

A HOUSE DIVIDED

The US Constitution hadn't ended slavery, but it had given Congress the power to approve (or not) slavery in new states. Public debates raged constantly over the expansion of slavery, particularly since this shaped the unfolding balance of political power between the industrial North and the agrarian South.

Since the founding, Southern politicians had dominated government and defended slavery as 'natural and normal,' which an 1856 *New York Times* editorial called 'insanity.' The Southern proslavery lobby enraged northern abolitionists (who aided the 'Underground Railroad,' a series of safe havens for runaway slaves heading North). But even many Northern politicians feared that ending slavery with a penstroke would be ruinous. Limit slavery, they reasoned, and in the competition with industry and free labor, slavery would wither without inciting a violent slave revolt – a constantly feared possibility. Indeed, in 1859, radical abolitionist John Brown tried unsuccessfully to spark just that at Harpers Ferry (p381).

The UN estimates there are 12 million humans in slavery worldwide today, mostly woman and children. According to the CIA, an estimated 14,500 human-trafficking victims are brought into the US each year.

The economics of slavery were undeniable. In 1860, there were over four million slaves in the US, most held by Southern planters. Were those plantation owners going to let their labor force just walk free? Also, the South grew 75% of the world's cotton, which accounted for over half of US exports. Thus, the Southern economy supported the nation's economy, and it required slaves. The 1860 presidential election became a referendum on this issue, and the election was won by a young politician who favored limiting slavery: Abraham Lincoln.

1861–65

American Civil War between the North and the South (delineated by the Mason–Dixon line). The war's end on April 9, 1865, is marred by President Lincoln's assassination five days later.

1882

Racist, anti-Chinese sentiment, particularly in California (where over 50,000 Chinese immigrants have arrived since 1848) leads to the Chinese Exclusion Act, the only US immigration law to exclude a specific race.

1896

In *Plessy v. Ferguson,* the US Supreme Court rules that 'separate but equal' public facilities for blacks and whites are legal, arguing that the Constitution addresses only political, not social, equality.

In the South, even the threat of federal limits was too onerous to abide, and as President Lincoln took office, 11 states eventually seceded from the union and formed the Confederate States of America (called the Confederacy). Now, could Lincoln allow these states to walk free? If any unhappy state could leave the nation 'at pleasure,' wouldn't that destroy republican government itself? In 1865, in his second inaugural address, Lincoln eloquently expressed this dilemma: 'Both parties deprecated war; but one of them would make war rather than let the nation survive; and the other would accept war rather than let it perish. And the war came.'

James McPherson is a preeminent Civil War historian, and his Pulitzer Prize–winning *Battle Cry of Freedom* (1988) somehow gets the whole heartbreaking saga between two covers.

In April 1861, the Confederacy attacked Fort Sumter in Charleston, South Carolina, and the Civil War came. Over the next four years the carnage was as gruesome as any war up to that point in history. By the end, over 600,000 soldiers, nearly an entire generation of young men, were dead; Southern plantations and cities (most notably Atlanta) lay sacked and burned. The course of the war, and all the ways it could have unfolded, remain the subject of impassioned debate. Both sides had their share of ineffectual and cunning leaders and used troops recklessly; both had moments of demoralization and determination. The North's industrial might provided an advantage, but its victory was not preordained; it unfolded battle by bloody battle.

As fighting progressed, Lincoln recognized that if the war didn't end slavery outright, victory would be pointless. In 1863, his Emancipation Proclamation expanded the war's aims and freed all slaves (an act legally accomplished two years later by the Constitution's 13th Amendment). In April 1865, Confederate General Robert E Lee surrendered to Union General Ulysses S Grant in Appomattox, Virginia. The Union had been preserved.

This Republic of Suffering (2008), by historian Drew Gilpin Faust, is a poignant look at the Civil War through the eyes of loved ones left behind by fallen soldiers on both sides of the Mason–Dixon line.

STIRRING THE MELTING POT: SEGREGATION & IMMIGRATION

The Civil War ended an economic system of forced labor, but the society that newly free African Americans entered remained largely, and often deeply, racist. During Reconstruction (1865–77), the civil rights of ex-slaves were protected by the federal government, which also extracted reparations from Southern states. Ill-will and bad feelings ran so deep that Civil War grudges were nursed for many decades afterward.

After Reconstruction, Southern states developed a system of 'sharecropping' that kept blacks indentured to the land for a measly share of crops, and they enacted endless laws aimed at keeping whites and blacks 'separate but equal.' Freed black men were given the vote in 1870, but the South's segregationist 'Jim Crow' laws (which remained in place until the 1960s Civil Rights movement) effectively disenfranchised and impoverished blacks in every meaningful sphere of daily life.

Meanwhile, the US turned its full attention to the West: the telegraph and the transcontinental railroad shrank time and space; the interior West was systematically explored and mapped for the first time; and the continent's

1898

US annexes Hawaii, and victory in the Spanish-American War gives US control of the Philippines, Puerto Rico and Guam, and indirect control of Cuba. The ensuing, bloody Philippine war for independence deters future US colonialism.

1908

The first Model T (aka 'Tin Lizzie') car is built in Detroit, MI; assembly-line innovator Henry Ford is soon selling one million automobiles annually.

1914

Panama Canal opens, linking Atlantic and Pacific Oceans. US won the right to build and run the canal by inciting a Panamanian revolt over independence from Colombia, and then sending forces to 'protect' Panama's freedom.

overflowing natural resources (its gold and silver, its coal and forests) fueled a galloping industrialization. Despite its lingering 'Indian problem' (p52), the West appeared like a 'land of opportunity.' Immigrants flooded in from Europe and Asia (in total, about 25 million people arrived from 1880 to 1920). Poles, Germans, Irish, Italians, Russians, Eastern Europeans, Chinese and more came to build the nation's railroads, smelt its steel, harvest its grain, mine its minerals and slaughter its cattle.

This also fed the urban migration that made the late 19th century the age of cities. In particular, New York, Chicago and Philadelphia swelled to rival London and Paris as global centers of industry and commerce. These crowded, buzzing multiethnic hives both spurred the xenophobic fears of whites and gave rise to the dream that America could become a unique 'melting pot' of the world's cultures.

Beyond the Hundredth Meridian (1954), Wallace Stegner's biography of Western explorer and scientist John Wesley Powell, is a wise, sharply written account of when America's Edenic continental visions first met the West's dry reality.

ROBBER BARONS & PROGRESSIVE REFORMERS

For American business, laissez-faire economic policy, the industrial revolution and hordes of cheap labor equaled towering piles of cash. Industrialists such as JP Morgan, Andrew Carnegie and John D Rockefeller became politically powerful 'robber barons' controlling vast monopolies (or trusts) in oil, banking, railroads and steel. These paragons of capitalism were America's version of royalty, crowned by Wall Street.

As industrialism created wealth for the few, it consigned many to poverty and dangerous, even deadly, work in choking factories and sweatshops, as vividly depicted in *The Jungle* (1906), Upton Sinclair's muckraking exposé of Chicago's unsavory meatpacking industry. Mechanization and piecework might be godsends to farming, textiles and automobile manufacturing, but unchecked they sowed pain and injustice.

Increasing political protests sparked new, heated arguments pitting the rights of private property against the rights of everyday people. Wasn't it the federal government's duty to intervene when an unregulated free market was, in effect, abusing, impoverishing and killing its own citizens? Whose liberty, whose welfare, deserved society's protection: business or labor?

In *The Souls of Black Folk* (1903), WEB Du Bois, who helped found the National Association for the Advancement of Colored People (NAACP), eloquently describes the racial dilemmas of politics and culture facing early-20th-century America.

In the 1880s, the Populist movement, which sought to help farmers, was an early effort to transform America's emerging class anger into a political force. Populism eventually petered out, replaced by the urban and more radical socialist movement, whose militant fringe was occupied by the International Workers of the World (IWW, aka Wobblies). Labor unions blossomed and strikes were frequent and often violent.

In the first decades of the 20th century, socialist movements developed worldwide; in the US, most citizens rejected actual socialism, but many embraced its ideas and ways of thinking. Still, the Socialist party was a real force, so much so that socialist candidate Eugene Debs won 6% of the vote in the 1912 presidential election. In order to calm labor unrest and thwart

1917

President Woodrow Wilson enters US into WWI, pledging 'the world must be made safe for democracy.' The US mobilizes over 4.7 million troops, and suffers around 110,000 of the war's more than 9 million military deaths.

1919

The temperance movement champions the 18th amendment, which bans alcohol. Prohibition is wildly unsuccessful, leading to increased drinking, large-scale bootlegging and a heyday for organized crime. The amendment is repealed in 1933.

1920s

Spurred by massive African American migration to northern cities, the Harlem Renaissance inspires an intellectual flowering of literature, art, music and cultural pride. Important figures include WEB Du Bois, Langston Hughes and Zora Neale Hurston.

socialism, Progressives pursued a slew of reforms: trusts were busted up, and eventually regulations were established, including a 40-hour work week, improved worker and food safety, and outlawed child labor.

Meanwhile, the US was developing a novel approach to imperialism, which President William Howard Taft dubbed 'dollar diplomacy.' To feed its overproductive economic engine, the US was desperate to gain access to new international markets. The 1898 Spanish-American War showed the way: rather than wage war for territory, the US would henceforth pursue an 'informal empire' using private commerce and banking. America would intervene militarily only as a paternalistic global 'policeman': not to impose its own colonial rule, but instead to protect regional security, financial stability, private property and open markets.

Industrialization really did speed up American life. On farms, a bushel of wheat took three hours to produce in 1830, but only 10 minutes by 1900.

President Woodrow Wilson also helped develop this approach, which still informs US foreign policy. By the start of WWI, the US had transitioned from a debtor to a creditor nation, and Wilson understood that, despite widespread parochial isolationism, the US needed to be engaged in the international community. Though Wilson's League of Nations failed, his idea of a cooperative 'concert of nations' would be realized after WWII with the founding of the UN.

As the Great War erupted in Europe in 1914, the US officially maintained neutrality, though it profitably sold armaments to the Allies. Germany responded by attacking US freighters, and in 1917 the US reluctantly entered the fight against the Central Powers. Wilson was hard pressed to sell the war at home, and suppression of antiwar dissent became standing policy. After the war, moralistic calls for social reform resumed: prohibition outlawing alcohol was inaugurated in 1920, the same year that the 19th amendment gave women the right to vote.

Iron Jawed Angels (2005), starring Hillary Swank, is a moving docudrama about the struggles of early-20th-century suffragettes, including hunger strikes while being unjustly jailed for political activism in pursuit of women's equality.

A tide of good feeling drowned out further reformist voices. America had won the war, the economy was humming, capitalism's worst abuses were softened, wages were rising, unemployment was falling, and the Jazz Age was in full swing. Middle-class Americans became modern-day consumers, oohing and aahing over their new electric appliances. For a while, despite poverty, crime and corruption, optimism ruled. Flappers danced the Charleston, radio and movies captivated millions, and stock prices kept going up, and up.

GREAT DEPRESSION, THE NEW DEAL & WORLD WAR II

Everything looked rosy, but the good times couldn't last. In October 1929, investors, worried over a gloomy global economy, started selling stocks, and seeing the selling, everyone panicked until they'd sold everything. The stock market crashed, and the US economy collapsed like a house of cards – revealing just how jerryrigged it actually was.

Thus began the Great Depression. Frightened banks called in their dodgy loans, people couldn't pay, and the banks folded. Millions lost their homes,

1933–38

Franklin D Roosevelt's New Deal establishes federal programs and legislation including Social Security, the Fair Labor Standards Act, and the Works Progress Administration (WPA) and Civilian Conservation Corps (CCC) to provide unemployment relief.

1941–45

US engages in WWII. America deploys over 16 million troops and suffers around 400,000 deaths. Overall, WWII civilian deaths outpace military deaths two to one, and total 50 to 70 million people from over 50 countries.

1948–51

The US-led Marshall Plan funnels $12 billion in material and financial aid to help Europe recover from WWII, and not, coincidentally, to also help contain Soviet communist influence and reignite the US economy.

farms, businesses and savings, and as much as 50% of the American workforce became unemployed. Scores hit the roads in search of work. With despairing immediacy, Americans decided they didn't just need protection from industrialism's workplace sins, but society-wide insurance from market forces beyond their control. The US belatedly moved to establish social programs that had already been created decades earlier by other industrialized nations.

In 1932, Democrat Franklin D Roosevelt was elected president on the promise of a 'New Deal' to rescue the US from its crisis, and he would become a pivotal figure in US history. He significantly expanded the role of the federal government to protect citizens, such as with Social Security (insuring retirement savings), and he instituted government-funded employment programs and enormous public-works projects (such as Hoover Dam, p833). Roosevelt did much to ameliorate the pain of the Great Depression, and New Deal programs remain the foundation of US social policy.

John Steinbeck's *The Grapes of Wrath* (1940) tells the saga of Depression-era farmers from the Great Plains desperately trying to escape the Dust Bowl by heading for the promised land of California.

When war once again broke out in Europe in 1939, the isolationist mood in America was as strong as ever. However, the extremely popular President Roosevelt, elected to an unprecedented third term in 1940, understood that the US couldn't sit by and allow victory for the fascist, totalitarian regimes of Germany, Italy, Spain and Japan. Roosevelt sent aid to Britain and used his considerable persuasive powers to get a skittish Congress to go along with it.

Then, on December 7, 1941, Japan launched a surprise attack on Hawaii's Pearl Harbor (p1117), killing over 2000 Americans and sinking several battleships. As US isolationism transformed overnight into outrage, Roosevelt suddenly had the support he needed. Germany also declared war on the US, and America joined the Allied fight against Hitler and the Axis powers. From that moment, the US put almost its entire will and industrial prowess into the war effort.

The Perilous Fight: America's World War II in Color (2003) is a groundbreaking documentary featuring previously lost footage of US military battles abroad, focusing on the Pacific theater and war efforts on the home front.

Initially, neither the Pacific nor European theaters went well for the US. In the Pacific, fighting didn't turn around until the US unexpectedly routed the Japanese navy at Midway Island in June 1942. Afterward, the US drove Japan back with a series of brutal battles recapturing Pacific islands.

In Europe, the US dealt the fatal blow to Germany with its massive D-Day invasion of France on June 6, 1944: unable to sustain a two-front war (the Soviet Union was savagely fighting on the eastern front), Germany surrendered in May 1945.

Nevertheless, Japan continued fighting. Newly elected President Harry Truman – ostensibly worried that a US invasion of Japan would lead to unprecedented carnage – chose to drop experimental atomic bombs on Hiroshima and Nagasaki in August 1945. Created by the government's top-secret Manhattan Project, the bombs devastated both cities, killing over 200,000 people. Japan surrendered days later. The nuclear age was born.

1954

In *Brown v. Board of Education,* the Supreme Court rules that segregation in public schools is 'inherently unequal' and orders desegregation 'with all deliberate speed.' The fight to integrate schools spurs the civil rights movement.

1963

On November 22, President John F Kennedy is publically assassinated by Lee Harvey Oswald while riding in a motorcade through Dealey Plaza in Dallas, Texas.

1965–75

US involvement in the Vietnam War, in which it supports South Vietnam against communist North Vietnam. The war results in 58,000 American troop fatalities, compared to four million Vietnamese and 1.5 million Laotians and Cambodians.

SUBURBIA & THE SECOND AMERICAN REVOLUTION

The US enjoyed unprecedented prosperity in the decades after WWII but little peace.

Formerly wartime allies, the communist Soviet Union and the capitalist USA soon engaged in a running competition to dominate the globe. The superpowers engaged in proxy wars – notably the Korean War (1950–53) and Vietnam War (1959–75) – with only the mutual threat of nuclear annihilation preventing direct war. Founded in 1945, the UN couldn't overcome this worldwide ideological split and was largely ineffectual in preventing Cold War conflicts.

The Fifties (1993), by David Halberstam, explores an almost schizophrenic era: TV, civil rights, McCarthyism, Elvis Presley, suburbia and more coalesced into the decade that spawned modern America.

Meanwhile, with its continent unscarred and its industry bulked up by WWII, the American homeland entered an era of surreal affluence. In the 1950s, a mass migration left the inner cities for the suburbs, where affordable single-family homes sprang up. Americans drove cheap cars using cheap gas over brand-new interstate highways. They relaxed with the comforts of modern technology, swooned over TV, and got busy, giving birth to a 'baby boom.'

Middle-class whites did, anyway. African Americans remained segregated, poor and unwelcome at the party. Echoing 19th-century abolitionist Frederick Douglass, the Southern Christian Leadership Coalition (SCLC), led by African American preacher Martin Luther King Jr (p447), aimed to end segregation and 'save America's soul': to realize color-blind justice, racial equality and fairness of economic opportunity for all.

Beginning in the 1950s, King preached and organized nonviolent resistance in the form of bus boycotts, marches and sit-ins, mainly in the South. White authorities often met these protests with water hoses and batons, and demonstrations sometimes dissolved into riots, but with the 1964 Civil Rights Act, African Americans spurred a wave of legislation that swept away racist laws in what some called America's 'second revolution.' However, African Americans and other minorities still struggle to overcome persistent inequalities in education and employment today.

In biopic *Malcolm X* (1992), directed by Spike Lee, Denzel Washington plays the role of one of America's most militant black liberation-movement leaders, who was assassinated in 1965.

Meanwhile, the 1960s saw further social upheavals: rock 'n' roll spawned a youth rebellion, and drugs sent Technicolor visions spinning in their heads. President John F Kennedy was assassinated in Dallas in 1963, followed by the assassinations in 1968 of his brother, Senator Robert Kennedy, and of Martin Luther King. Americans' faith in their leaders and government were further shocked by the bombings and brutalities of the Vietnam War, as seen on TV, which led to widespread student protests.

Yet President Richard Nixon, elected in 1968 partly for promising an 'honorable end to the war,' instead escalated US involvement and secretly bombed Laos and Cambodia. Then, in 1972, the Watergate scandal broke: a burglary at Democratic Party offices was, through dogged journalism, tied to 'Tricky Dick,' who, in 1974, became the first US president to resign from office.

1969

American astronauts land on the moon, fulfilling President Kennedy's unlikely 1961 promise to accomplish this feat within a decade and culminating the 'space race' between the US and USSR.

1973

In *Roe v. Wade*, the Supreme Court legalizes abortion. Still today, this decision remains controversial and socially divisive, pitting the 'right to choose' advocates against the 'right to life' anti-abortion lobby.

1980s

Hundreds of New Deal–era financial institutions, deregulated under President Reagan, play fast and loose with their customers' savings and loans, and ultimately fail, leaving the government on the hook for a $125 billion bailout.

The tumultuous 1960s and '70s also witnessed the sexual revolution, women's liberation, struggles for gay rights, energy crises over the supply of crude oil from the Middle East, and, with the 1962 publication of Rachel Carson's *Silent Spring*, the realization that the USA's industries had created a polluted, diseased environmental mess (p126).

Having failed to stop communism, the US finally left Vietnam in 1975, just as the economy really hit the skids. Cynical Americans, perhaps tired of fighting each other and being lied to by politicians, turned up the disco, popped birth-control pills and got their freak on right through into the narcissistic, name-brand consumerist 'Me' decade of the 1980s.

Starring Kevin Spacey, Laura Dern and Denis Leary, *Recount* (2008) dramatizes the events of the hotly contested 2000 US presidential election, including the issues surrounding voter fraud and disenfranchisement in Florida.

PAX AMERICANA & THE WAR ON TERROR

In 1980, Republican California governor and former actor Ronald Reagan, correctly sensing the country's mood, campaigned for president by promising to make Americans feel good about America again. The affable Reagan won easily, and his election marked the start of a nearly three-decade conservative shift in US politics.

Reagan wanted to defeat communism, restore the economy, deregulate business and cut taxes. To tackle the first two, he launched the biggest peacetime military build-up in history, and dared the Soviets to keep up. They went broke trying, and the USSR collapsed. Thus, the Cold War ended without direct conflict between the two superpowers.

Military spending and tax cuts created enormous federal deficits, which hampered the presidency of Reagan's successor, George HW Bush. Despite winning the Gulf War – liberating Kuwait in 1991 after an Iraqi invasion – Bush was soundly defeated in the 1992 presidential election by Southern Democrat Bill Clinton. Clinton had the good fortune to catch the 1990s high-tech internet boom, which seemed to augur a 'new economy' based on white-collar telecommunications. The US economy erased its deficits and ran a surplus, and Clinton tried to pass universal health coverage, but conservatives blocked this expansion of the 'welfare state.'

Director Spike Lee's monumental documentary *When the Levees Broke* (2006) is an intimate, moving account of Hurricane Katrina's devastation of New Orleans and a shameful indictment of the government's response.

In 2000 and 2004, George W Bush, the eldest son of George HW Bush, won the presidential elections so narrowly that the divided results seemed to epitomize an increasingly divided nation. 'Dubya' had the misfortune of being president when the high-tech stock bubble burst in 2000, but he nevertheless enacted tax cuts (mostly for the wealthy) that returned federal deficits even greater than before. He also championed the right-wing conservative 'backlash' that had been building since Reagan, which involved undoing environmental regulations, labor reforms and civil rights legislation; continuing Reagan's laissez-faire deregulation of industry; and fostering a moral, religious and cultural crusade of 'family values.'

On September 11, 2001, Islamic terrorists flew hijacked planes into New York's World Trade Center and the Pentagon in Washington, DC.

1989

The 1960s-era Berlin Wall is torn down, marking the official end of the Cold War between the US and the USSR (now Russia). The USA becomes the world's last remaining superpower.

1990s

The World Wide Web debuts in 1991. Silicon Valley, CA, leads a high-tech internet revolution, remaking communications and media, and overvalued tech stocks drive the biggest boom and bust since the Great Depression.

2001

On September 11, Al-Qaeda terrorists hijack four commercial airplanes, flying two into NYC's World Trade Center towers, which collapse, and one into the Pentagon (the fourth plane crashes in rural Pennsylvania); nearly 3000 people are killed.

This catastrophic attack united Americans behind their president as he vowed revenge and declared a 'war on terror.' But the Al-Qaeda terrorists belonged to no nation, and it was quickly apparent this would mean a new kind of war.

Congress quickly passed the Patriot Act, which abridged citizen's civil rights in an effort to catch potential terrorists, and President Bush revised long-standing US military policy to allow for 'preemptive attacks.' Bush soon attacked Afghanistan in an unsuccessful hunt for Al-Qaeda terrorist cells, then he attacked Iraq in 2003 and toppled its anti-US dictator, Saddam Hussein. Later one of the president's main justifications for starting the Iraq War – that Iraq possessed weapons of mass destruction – was proven false. Meanwhile, Iraq descended into civil war.

Suspicious of political factoids? So are we – particularly during political elections. That's why we turn to www.factcheck.org to help discern truth from 'truthiness.'

The USA's most expensive natural disaster to date occurred in 2005 when Hurricane Katrina devastated the Gulf Coast, including New Orleans (p476). When federal relief efforts were slow to arrive and then proved inadequate, a sour mood settled over the nation: government was untrustworthy, the economy was debt-ridden, and the country was mired in a seemingly unwinnable war.

Hungry for change, Americans responded to a message of hope from political newcomer, Barack Obama. In 2008, after winning the Democratic primary (see p755) against Senator Hillary Clinton, Obama went on to defeat his Republican rival Senator John McCain. In 2009 Obama became the first African American to assume the country's highest office, a significant step forward in bridging racial divides that have plagued the nation since its founding.

During his first 100 days in office, President Obama passed a massive economic stimulus bill; shored up the failing banking, insurance and auto industries with taxpayer bailouts; set a timetable for US troop withdrawal from Iraq; overturned Bush-era restrictions on stem-cell research and nonsectarian family-planning services; moved to overhaul the broken US health-care system; and engaged in foreign diplomacy to help restore faith in America's leadership abroad, including with Islamic nations.

2003

On March 20, after citing evidence that Iraq possesses 'weapons of mass destruction,' President George W Bush launches a preemptive war. Bush declares 'mission accomplished' on May 1, but guerrilla fighting and war continue.

2005

On August 29, Hurricane Katrina hits the Mississippi and Louisiana coasts, rupturing levees and flooding below-sea-level New Orleans. Over 1800 people die, and cost estimates exceed $80 billion.

2008–9

The US stock market crashes due to the failure of several banking and financial institutions, causing the subprime mortgage lending bubble to burst. In 2009, the US struggles with the worst economic recession since the Great Depression.

The Culture

THE NATIONAL PSYCHE

For all their differences – Americans don't all look alike or eat the same foods, they don't worship alike or have equal bank accounts – they do share a common thread. It unspools to this: the belief that America is a land of possibility, and if you apply yourself, you can achieve your dreams. Really – as cheesy as its sounds, it's the core of the national psyche.

When the founding fathers rattled on about democracy, government by and for the people, liberty and the pursuit of happiness, they laid the mold for the American character. People expect a large slate of individual rights, and for those rights to prevail if the government tries to curb them. It's also a group effort, where everyone has to trust 'the basic good sense and stability of the great American consensus,' as John F Kennedy once put it.

Americans take their liberty seriously, with 48 places nationwide named after the inalienable right. Iowa takes the prize, with three cities: New Liberty, North Liberty and West Liberty.

It's not always easy. While the country prides itself on freedom and democracy, some citizens see these cornerstones slipping away. They are incensed about the government's expanded powers to wiretap, web-tap, and detain and seize property, all of which have been implemented in the name of fighting terrorism. Other citizens say such powers are necessary to keep the country safe, and if they have to forgo a civil liberty here or there, so be it.

One thing's for sure: freedom gets its due each Fourth of July, during the nation's whopping Independence Day celebration. Almost every city holds a fireworks-laden parade or festival to rock the nation's birthday. In Chicago, for instance, more than a million people fill downtown to watch red, white and blue pyrotechnics explode over a score of patriotic music. The scene plays out across the country, complemented by barbecues, picnics and cold beer.

NPR radio host Terry Gross interviews Americans from all walks of life, from rock stars to environmental activists to nuclear scientists. Listen online at www.npr.org/freshair.

But we don't mean to get overly sentimental here. An unpopular war, an unpopular former president (Bush had his lowest approval rating ever – about 22% – by his term's end) and a jittery economy have taken their toll on the American mindset. A 2008 Pew/Gallup poll showed that most Americans do not believe they're moving forward in life (25%) or they believe they are falling backward (31%) – the worst numbers in a half-century. But most are confident their quality of life in five years will be better than it is now. Is that optimistic or what?

Perhaps Barack Obama sums up the American spirit best. 'America is a place where all things are possible,' he said on election night in 2008, and him standing there on the great stage seemed to prove it. He was young, a relative newcomer to politics, and the first African American to become president – an American dream story, indeed.

In *Roads to Quoz: An American Mosey* (2008), William Least Heat-Moon writes about the strange, mysterious people and places he encounters while driving through the USA's small towns and along rural backroads and byways.

LIFESTYLE

The USA has one of the world's highest standards of living. The median household income is just over $50,000, though it varies by ethnicity, with African Americans and Hispanics earning less than whites and Asians ($34,000 and $41,000 respectively, versus $54,000 and $67,000, according to census data).

Eighty percent of Americans are high-school graduates, while 24% go on to graduate from college with a four-year bachelor's degree.

More often than not there are two married parents in an American household, and both of them work. Single parents head 9% of households. Twenty-eight percent of Americans work over 40 hours per week. Divorce is common – more than 40% of first marriages go kaput – but both divorce and marriage rates have declined over the last three decades. Despite the high divorce rate, Americans spend more than $160 billion annually on weddings. The average number of children in an American family is two.

Despite the current economic crisis, two-thirds of Americans still own their house. Nearly all households (87%) have a TV, and 66% plug in three or more TVs; today, an average household has more TVs than people. Adding to the screen-time: 80% of homes have a DVD player, and 25% pay for satellite channels. Tallied up, the average American watches 140-plus hours of TV each month, according to Nielsen Media Research.

One in three American households owns a gun, according to the CDC. The National Rifle Association says it's more – that 40% to 45% pack heat.

While many Americans hit the gym or walk, bike or jog regularly, 40% don't exercise at all during their free time, according to the Centers for Disease Control (CDC). Health researchers speculate this lack of exercise and Americans' fondness for sugary and fatty foods have led to rising obesity and diabetes rates. More than two-thirds of Americans are overweight, with one-third considered obese, the CDC says.

About 26% of Americans volunteer their time to help others or help a cause. This is truer in the Midwest, followed by the West, South and Northeast, according to the Corporation for National and Community Service. Ecoconsciousness has entered the mainstream: 77% of Americans recycle at home, as per a recent Harris poll, and most big chain grocery stores – including Wal-Mart – now sell organic foods.

Americans tend to travel close to home. Just over one-third of Americans have passports so most people take vacations within the 50 states. According to the US Department of Commerce's Office of Travel and Tourism Industries, Mexico and Canada are the top countries for international getaways, followed by the UK, Italy, France, Germany and Japan. America's reputation as the 'no-vacation nation,' with many workers having only five to 10 paid annual vacation days, contributes to this stay-at-home scenario.

Sicko (2007), a documentary by 'love him or hate him' filmmaker Michael Moore, examines the US health-care system and its impact on citizens.

Finally, there's health care, which has become a unique issue for Americans. No national service exists, so citizens must pay for care on their own – and it's incredibly expensive. Health insurance is cost-prohibitive for many families, and as a result, more than 15% of Americans are uninsured. Thus, they often forgo routine care and medications until their health conditions become a problem. A study by Harvard researchers found that medical bills trigger half of all bankruptcies.

KNOW YOUR GENERATIONS

American culture is often stratified by age groups. Here's a quick rundown to help you tell Generation X from Y, and then some.

- **Baby Boomers** – those born from 1946 to 1964. After American soldiers came home from WWII, they got busy with the ladies, and the birthrate exploded (hence the term 'baby boom'). Youthful experimentation, self-expression and social activism was often followed by midlife affluence.
- **Generation X** – those born between 1961 and 1981. Characterized by their rejection of Baby Boomer values, skepticism and alienation are X's pop-culture hallmarks.
- **Generation Y** – those born from roughly the early 1980s to early 1990s (aka Millennials). Known for being brash and self-confident, they were the first to grow up with the internet.
- **Generation Next** – overlaps with Gen Y, but basically applies to those born in the 1990s. Weaned on iPods, text messaging, instant messaging and social-networking websites, they are a work in progress. Stay tuned (and check their Facebook page for updates).

DOS & DON'TS

By and large, the American motto is to live and let live. But there are certain norms of behavior foreign visitors should be aware of.

- Do return friendly greetings. 'Hi. How are you?' is expected to receive a cheerful, 'Thanks, I'm fine,' not 'My boyfriend dumped me, my irritable bowel is acting up and my car got towed.' Actual complaints are frowned upon.
- Don't be overly physical when you greet someone. Some Americans will hug, but many more, especially men, will just shake hands. Big juicy lip kisses will likely get you slapped. Or arrested.
- Don't take your clothes off in public. Especially on beaches, don't disrobe or, for women, go topless, unless many other people are already showing skin.
- Some Americans you encounter may not know much about your country. Americans are usually excited to meet foreigners, but their geo-cultural knowledge is often low. Don't take it personally – only half of 18 to 24 year olds in the USA can even find New York on a map, according to a 2006 National Geographic Society survey.
- Do be on time. Many Americans consider it rude to be kept waiting.
- Don't smoke inside a building without asking first. Nonsmoking laws are increasingly common, and many people are strongly against second-hand smoke in their homes.
- Do be respectful of police officers. Americans may be casual, but the police expect to be called 'Sir,' 'Ma'am' or simply 'Officer.' Slang terms such as 'Pig' are *not* terms of endearment.

ECONOMY

America's economy forged ahead throughout most of the last 25 years. Yes, there were ups and downs, but overall the stock market was reaching historic highs, alongside home-ownership rates and housing prices. Productivity was up, and unemployment was down.

But a problem lurked beneath the surface. The economy and productivity were growing without wage gains for the average worker. So Americans began borrowing money to make up the difference. As the economy zipped along, credit and home loans were easy to obtain. Soon the median debt-to-income ratio for middle-class adults had jumped from 0.45 in 1983 to 1.19 two decades later, according to Pew Research Center statistics. You'll often hear people say America's middle class is disappearing. Many economists agree, and peg it to this rising debt. There's certainly more to the story, but we'll get to that later…

Four million Americans tune in every week to Midwestern raconteur Garrison Keillor's old-timey radio show, *A Prairie Home Companion;* listen to the live music, sketches and storytelling online at http://prairie home.publicradio.org.

Americans' real median household income was $50,233 in 2007. It's one of the world's highest incomes (in terms of purchasing power), according to the Organization for Economic Co-operation and Development. However, it also represents the world's second-greatest income inequality – the gap between what America's richest 10% of workers earn and what the poorest 10% earn is wider than in every other developed country except Hungary. Perhaps the fact isn't a surprise, since median income combines citizens such as Bill Gates, the nation's richest person (with a net worth of $58 billion), and citizens earning minimum wage ($7.25 per hour, or $15,080 per year). Note the federal poverty level for a family of three is $18,310 per year – more than what a minimum-wage job alone provides.

The documentary *Maxed Out: Hard Times, Easy Credit and the Era of Predatory Lenders* (2006) tries to figure out why Americans keep spending money they don't have.

What drives this wild economy, the world's largest for a single country? The service sector and industries such as banking, retail and health care account for about 68% of GDP. Manufacturing (autos, aircraft and machinery) comprises 12%, construction 4%, oil drilling and mining 2%, and agriculture 1%. The government sector makes up the remaining 13%.

Industries on the rise include scientific, technical and health-care services. Those on the wane include agriculture, mining and some kinds of manufacturing, such as textiles and autos. Even for a 'waning' segment of the economy we're still talking huge numbers. Agriculture, for instance, is a $300 billion-plus industry, according to US Department of Commerce data.

An old economists' proverb says, 'When the United States sneezes, the rest of the world catches a cold.' A big *achoo* happened in mid-2008. Remember those easy-to-get home loans mentioned earlier? They set off a domino effect that plunged the economy into crisis. In short, financial institutions had been giving risky mortgages, financed through maneuverings in the booming stock market, to people with not-so-great credit. The economy tightened, and suddenly there was a record surge in mortgage defaults. Financial firms were caught holding the bag, and they began losing billions of dollars. This, in turn, set off a severe credit crisis and general all-round panic in the stock market, both here and abroad, making it difficult for businesses to pick up again. The US economy ground to a halt amid headlines of the 'Worst Economic Downturn since the Great Depression.'

The US spends 4.1% of its GDP on the military. By comparison, Canada spends 1.1%, China 4.3% and Israel 7.3% (stats from the CIA's World Factbook at www.cia.gov).

The federal government took unprecedented steps to spark the economy. Usually known for letting the market work out its own kinks, the feds loaned billions of dollars to failed banks and other big companies. It cut interest rates. But the stock market kept on quivering. Over three-fourths of America believe the country is now in a recession, of which the upward-ticking unemployment rate (9.4% in July 2009, a 25-year high) is just one indicator.

POPULATION

Of the 12 companies that Dow Jones listed in 1896 when it created its famous stock index, only one, General Electric, remains today.

'The times they are a-changin',' Bob Dylan once famously crooned, and it could be the theme song for America's population make-up. During the next four decades the country's population will undergo two major shifts: it will become significantly older, and it will become far more Hispanic/Latino.

Let's start with the here and now. The total US population is around 305 million, making it the world's third-most populous country, but still well behind India and China, each of which pack in over a billion people. Broken down by ethnicity, the USA is 66% white, 15% Hispanic, 13% African American, 5% Asian and 1% Native American, according to 2007–08 census data.

Since the 2000 census, the US population has grown by roughly 8%, with Hispanics leading the charge. Their numbers ballooned by 24% in the new millennium, fueled by both immigration and the fact that Hispanic families tend to be younger and have more children than other population segments (the median age for Hispanics is 27.6 compared with 36.6 for the overall population).

A 2009 Gallup poll showed that for the first time in 25 years, a majority of Americans are willing to sacrifice environmental protections to boost economic growth.

By 2050, America is going to look a whole lot different. Census demographers project the country will be 46% white, 30% Hispanic, 15% African American and 9% Asian; Native Americans will rise to about 2% (rounding errors mean that the total does not equal 100). The upshot? Minorities will become the majority (for all the statistics wonks out there, 2042 is the momentous year when this transformation is set to occur).

The other big change will be the nation's elderly population. It will more than double in size by 2050, as baby boomers roll into their retirement years. One in five Americans will be aged over 65 by then (pay attention, prune marketers). The skew can best be seen in the 'dependency ratio,' which is the number of children and elderly compared to the number of working-age Americans. It will shoot up from 59 to 72 per 100 workers, according to the Pew Research Center, and create a new challenge: how will the country take care of all these older citizens?

WHO'S NAUGHTY OR NICE?

Regional US stereotypes now have solid data behind them, thanks to a 2008 study titled 'The Geography of Personality.' Researchers processed more than a half-million personality assessments collected from individual US citizens, then looked at where certain traits stacked up on the map. Turns out 'Minnesota nice' is for real – the most 'agreeable' states cluster in the Midwest, Great Plains and South. These places rank highest for friendliness and cooperation. The most neurotic states? They line up in the Northeast. But New York didn't place number one, as you might expect; that honor goes to West Virginia. Many of the most 'open' states lie out West. California, Nevada, Oregon and Washington all rate high for being receptive to new ideas, although they lag behind Washington DC and New York. The most dutiful and self-disciplined states sit in the Great Plains and Southwest, led by New Mexico. Go figure.

The changes will play out across America, and in particular in states such as California, Texas, New York, Florida and Illinois. These are not only the five most populous states, but also the ones with major metropolitan gateways where immigrants tend to put down stakes. Florida has the highest share of elderly residents, to boot.

Most Americans are city folk, with almost 80% living in an urban environment. They favor the coasts, leaving the middle of the country sparsely populated. So there's lots of room to roam out on the range. States such as Wyoming, Montana and North Dakota each have fewer than 10 persons per sq mile (psm). Alaska is the loneliest place of all, with a mere 1.1 psm (a number that pleases the local moose population greatly). Compare that to New Jersey, the most densely populated state, where people are practically living on top of each other at 1135 psm. The USA as a whole has an average density of 80 psm – roomy, when stacked up next to Europe (134 psm) and Asia (203 psm).

MULTICULTURALISM

From the get-go, America was called a 'melting pot,' which presumed that newcomers came and blended into the existing American fabric. The country hasn't let go of that sentiment completely. On one hand, diversity is celebrated (Cinco de Mayo, Martin Luther King Day and Chinese New Year all get their due), but on the other hand, many Americans are comfortable with the status quo.

State by State: A Panoramic Portrait of America (2008) collects 50 essays about the 50 states, many by well-known literary personalities including Dave Eggers (Illinois), SE Hinton (Oklahoma) and Jhumpa Lahiri (Rhode Island).

Immigration is at the crux of the matter. Immigrants currently make up over 12% of the population, and their numbers are growing fast. About 1.1 million newcomers enter the US legally each year, with the majority from Mexico, followed by Asia and Europe. Another 11.5 million or so are in the country illegally. This is the issue that makes Americans edgy, especially as it gets politicized.

'Immigration reform' has become a Washington buzzword. Some people believe the nation's current system deals with illegal immigrants too leniently – that we should build more walls on the border, deport immigrants who are here unlawfully and fine employers who hire them. Other Americans think those rules are too harsh – that immigrants who have been here for years working, contributing to society and abiding by the law deserve amnesty. Perhaps they could pay a fine and fill out the paperwork to become citizens while continuing to live here with their families. It's an ongoing conflict. Despite several attempts, Congress has not been able to pass a comprehensive package addressing illegal immigration, though it has put through various measures to beef up enforcement. Stay tuned, because the issue isn't going away anytime soon.

Age has a lot to do with Americans' multicultural tolerance. When asked in a recent survey if immigration strengthens the nation, only about one-third of older Americans said yes, whereas more than half of 18 to 26 year olds said yes, according to the Pew Research Center. In a similar survey, those aged 60 and older were asked if it's acceptable for whites and African Americans to date each other: 35% said no, but that dropped to 6% when asked of Americans aged 30 and younger.

Many people point to the election of President Barack Obama as proof of America's multicultural achievements. It's not just his personal story (white mother, black father, Muslim name, has lived among the diverse cultures

NATIVE AMERICANS TODAY

Not that long ago they had the whole wide country to themselves. Today, single-race Native Americans represent only 1.5% of the USA's total population, according to 2007 census data.

About 4.5 million people of Native American descent are spread out across the country, though most live west of the Mississippi River (see the boxed text, p52, for the historical explanation of why this is). Over half reside in 10 states: California and Oklahoma, which together contain 25% of the USA's Native American population, followed by Arizona, Texas, New Mexico, New York, Washington, North Carolina, Michigan and Alaska. One-third of all Native Americans live on reservations. Many others have packed up to look for better opportunities in urban areas. Los Angeles is the city with the largest number of Native Americans, while the nation's capital, Washington DC, has the lowest.

The Cherokee, Navajo, Chippewa, Sioux and Choctaw are the largest tribal groupings in the lower 48 (ie barring Alaska and Hawaii), with Cherokee leading the pack. The majority of groups speak English as their everyday language; the Navajo are the exception; about two-thirds of Navajo people speak their own language at home. The state with the largest percentage of indigenous people is Alaska, where over 15% of people identify as either Alaska Native or Native American. In Hawaii, almost 10% of residents are Native Hawaiian – though the federal government has yet to recognize them as an indigenous people with rights to self-determination and self-governance.

Today Native Americans face many social challenges. One in four lives in poverty, a rate that's twice that of the rest of the US population. Rates of alcoholism (550% higher), diabetes (190% higher), homicide (100% higher) and suicide (70% higher) are also disproportionate compared to other Americans, according to the Indian Health Service.

Are better times ahead? Tax-free gambling on reservations (in the form of casinos) has provided an influx of money for some tribal groups. In recent decades, a cultural renaissance has revived traditional chanting, music and dance, ritual ceremonies and native languages. Political activism has been on the rise ever since the American Indian Movement (AIM) was founded back in 1968 during the peak of civil-rights protests nationwide.

Many authors offer insight into contemporary Native American life. Sherman Alexie Jr, a Spokane/Coeur d'Alene Indian, uses humor and wit to reshape Native American stereotypes. His book of short stories *The Lone Ranger and Tonto Fistfight in Heaven* (1994) talks about life on the rez. Alexie's *The Absolutely True Diary of a Part-Time Indian* (2007), a young-adult novel about teen cartoonist Junior, who breaks away from the reservation to attend an all-white high school, won the National Book Award. Louise Erdrich is a novelist and poet who draws on her Chippewa heritage to examine relationships among full- and mixed-blood Native Americans and their questions of identity. Her novel *Love Medicine* (1984) weaves the complex story of multigenerational families living on a North Dakota reservation; it won the National Book Critics Circle Award.

To dig deeper, the **Native American Virtual Library** (www.hanksville.org/naresources) has links to activist, media and tribal sites. The **Native Radio Network** (www.airos.org) has downloadable podcasts on Native American issues. In Washington, DC, the Smithsonian's **National Museum of the American Indian** (p326) provides a high-level introduction to myriad Native American cultures, covering languages, literature, arts, history and even foods through its café. Powwows, ceremonies and cultural festivals take place year-round nationwide; New Mexico's **Gathering of Nations** (www.gatheringofnations.com) and Oklahoma's **Red Earth Native American Cultural Festival** (p697) are among the country's largest annual intertribal gatherings.

of Hawaii, Indonesia and the Midwest, among others). Or that he's the first African American to hold the nation's highest office (in a country where as recently as the 1960s blacks couldn't even vote in certain regions). It's that Americans of all races and creeds voted overwhelmingly to elect the self-described 'mutt' and embrace his message of diversity and change.

RELIGION

When the Pilgrims (early settlers to the United States who fled their European homeland to escape religious persecution) came ashore, they were adamant that their new country would be one of religious tolerance. They valued the freedom to practice religion so highly they refused to make their Protestant faith official state policy. What's more, they forbade the government from doing anything that might sanction one religion or belief over another. Separation of church and state became the law of the land.

The US holds the world's second-largest Hispanic population, behind Mexico and just ahead of Spain.

Today, Protestants are on the verge of becoming a minority in the country they founded. According to the Pew Research Center, Protestant numbers have declined steadily to just over 50%. Meanwhile, other faiths have held their own or seen their numbers rise. Catholics represent about 25% of the country, with the denomination receiving a boost from the many Hispanics who have immigrated here. Those practicing non-Christian 'world religions' – Islam, Buddhism, Hindu, Judaism – have grown collectively to represent 5% of the country. Mormons comprise about 2%.

Interestingly, one of the fastest-growing categories is 'unaffiliated.' The proportion of those who say they have 'no religion' is now around 16%. Some in this catch-all category disavow religion altogether (around 4%), but the majority sustain spiritual beliefs that simply fall outside the box.

What's more, the country is in a period of exceptional religious fluidity. Forty-four percent of American adults have left the denomination of their childhood for another denomination, another faith or no faith at all, according to Pew. A unique era of 'religion shopping' has been ushered in. As for the geographic breakdown: the USA's most Catholic region is shifting from the Northeast to the Southwest; the South is the most evangelical; and the West is the most unaffiliated.

Hindus, Mormons and Catholics are least likely to marry outside their faith, while Buddhists and mainline Protestants more often partner with a person of a different faith (from the 2008 Pew Center 'US Religious Landscape' survey).

All that said, America's biggest schism isn't between religions or even between faith and skepticism. It's between fundamentalist and progressive interpretations within each faith. Most Americans don't care much if you're Catholic, Episcopalian, Buddhist or atheist. What they do care about are your views on abortion, contraception, gay rights, stem-cell research, teaching of evolution, school prayer and government displays of religious icons. The country's Religious Right (the oft-used term for evangelical Christians) has pushed these issues onto center stage, and the group has been effective at using politics to codify its conservative beliefs into law. This effort has prompted a slew of court cases, testing the nation's principles on separation of church and state. The split remains one of America's biggest culture wars, and it almost always plays a role in politics, especially elections.

MEDIA

Once the domain of the daily newspaper and a handful of TV networks, American media has become so much more over the past 20 years. And less too – while the internet provides a dynamic free-for-all of expression, traditional media ownership continues to consolidate. Rupert Murdoch's News Corporation, Walt Disney Company, General Electric, Time Warner, Viacom and Vivendi control much of the US market. Such concentration is a newish state of affairs. It harkens back to 1996, when the Federal Communications Commission (FCC) started to deregulate media ownership.

The main TV networks are ABC (Disney owned), CBS (formerly Viacom-affiliated), NBC (General Electric/Vivendi owned) and Fox (Murdoch owned). Univision (independently owned) and Telemundo (General Electric owned) are the main Spanish-language networks. PBS is the nonprofit, public TV network; its radio equivalent is National Public Radio (NPR). While many Americans complain that both PBS and NPR are becoming too commercialized and beholden to corporate sponsors, both networks remain the country's main independent sources of news. Over half of Americans get their local news from TV, according to a 2008 Gallup poll. Yet younger, college-educated audiences prefer national news-satire programs such as *The Daily Show* and *Colbert Report* (for clips of both, visit www.comedycentral.com).

The Independent Media Institute runs www.alternet.org, a haven for independent, progressive journalism that includes news, national columnists and individual blogs.

Newspapers have their own set of title holders. Large chains such as Gannett, Hearst and Cox own many US newspapers, and they're shrinking like mad. Average daily circulation across the country fell from 53.3 million to 34.4 million between 2006 and 2009, and over 100 papers folded during 2008. Even venerable, Pulitzer Prize–winning papers such as the *Christian Science Monitor* can no longer make it. In 2009, the *Monitor* became the first national daily to replace its daily print edition with a web-only version. Of those papers that remain on the newsstand, *USA Today*, the *Wall Street Journal*, the *New York Times*, the *Washington Post* and the *Los Angeles Times* are the most popular.

Where are all the lost readers going? To the internet, of course. Over 80% of Americans log onto the internet regularly, according to University of Southern California Annenberg data, and on average they spend almost an hour a week reading news online. Blogs, websites and podcasts are so mainstream now that more than 44% of internet users – 100 million-plus Americans – have posted content to the web.

Blogs, in particular, have captured American eyeballs. Almost half of US internet users read blogs, and over 25% are blogging themselves, eMarketer reported in 2009. As the Blogosphere grows in size and influence, the lines between what constitutes a blog and what constitutes mainstream media are becoming blurred. For instance, 95% of the top 100 US newspapers now have reporter blogs that provide news content. If you want to see what the blogging scene is all about, check out popular US sites such as the **Huffington Post** (www.huffingtonpost.com), **Daily Kos** (www.dailykos.com) and green-oriented **TreeHugger** (www.treehugger.com).

'Recession-Plagued Nation Demands New Bubble To Invest In' is but one of *The Onion*'s (www.theonion.com) outrageous, cheeky news story headlines.

SPORTS

You want to see American culture in all its glory? Head to the ballpark, football field or basketball court, and prepare for mania.

What really draws Americans together, sometimes slathered in blue body paint or with foam-rubber cheese wedges on their heads, is sports. It provides a social glue, so whether a person is conservative or liberal, married or single, Mormon or pagan, chances are come Monday at the office they'll be chatting about the weekend performance of their favorite team.

And Americans aren't just watching sports. They're also wagering on them. Football, in particular, brings out wallets for a friendly bet. Fantasy Leagues do, too. It's estimated that 17 million adults, age 18 to 55, play fantasy sports in the USA, which entails not only minute statistical analysis of favorite players but also shelling out the cash to back up one's picks.

The fun and games go on all year long. In spring and summer there's baseball nearly every day. In fall and winter, a weekend or Monday night doesn't feel right without a football game on, and through the long days and nights of winter there's plenty of basketball to keep the adrenaline going. Those are the big three sports. Car racing (see boxed text, p74) has revved up interest in recent years. Major League Soccer (MLS) is attracting an ever-increasing following, especially after international superstar David Beckham's brief stint with the LA Galaxy team. And ice hockey, once favored only in northern climes (eg anywhere close to Canada like Detroit, MI), is popular nationwide, with three Stanley Cup winners since 2000 hailing from either California or the South.

Baseball

C'mon, despite obnoxiously high salaries and its biggest stars being dogged by steroid rumors, baseball remains America's pastime. It may not command the same TV viewership (and subsequent advertising dollars) as football, but hey, baseball has 162 games over a season versus 16 for football.

Besides, baseball isn't about seeing it on TV – it's all about the live version. There's nothing better than being at the ballpark on a sunny day, sitting in the bleachers with a beer and hot dog, and indulging in the seventh-inning stretch, when the entire park erupts in a communal sing-along of 'Take Me Out to the Ballgame.' The play-offs, held every October, still deliver excitement and unexpected champions. The New York Yankees, Boston Red Sox and Chicago Cubs continue to be America's favorite teams, even when they suck (the Cubs haven't won a World Series in over 100 years).

Arguably the most hallowed grounds are Chicago's Wrigley Field and Boston's Fenway Park, both beautiful in a historic kind of way and smack-dab in the middle of urban neighborhoods with bars on every corner. Newer stadiums attract crowds with gimmicks such as an on-site swimming pool (Arizona's Chase Field), carousel and Ferris wheel rides (Detroit's Comerica Park) and sushi sold at the concession stands (LA's Dodger Stadium, San Diego's Qualcomm Stadium and San Francisco's AT&T Park).

The website www.mlb.com is baseball's official home. Tickets are relatively inexpensive – seats average about $14 at most stadiums – and are easy to get for most games. Minor-league baseball games cost half as much, and can be even more fun, with lots of audience participation, stray chickens and dogs running across the field and wild throws from the pitcher's mound. For info, click to www.minorleaguebaseball.com.

The Super Bowl costs America $800 million dollars in lost workplace productivity as employees gossip about the game, make bets and shop for new TVs online.

Live out your sports-nerd fantasies at www.fantasysports.yahoo.com, Yahoo's website for football, basketball, baseball and other fantasy-league teams.

Basketball

Despite its prominence, professional basketball is starting to show signs of strain – mounting ticket prices prevent much of its traditional fan base from attending. At the same time, disadvantaged urban youth still play on street courts from coast to coast and hope that a college sports scholarship and professional basketball career will be a way out. Increasing numbers of players are being recruited from Europe, South America and even China, giving the game an unexpectedly cosmopolitan flavor.

The teams bringing in the most fans these days include the Chicago Bulls (thanks to the lingering Michael Jordan effect), Detroit Pistons (a rowdy crowd where riots have broken out), Cleveland Cavaliers (home of Lebron James, aka the new Michael Jordan), the San Antonio Spurs and last but not least, the Los Angeles Lakers (led by ex-Chicago Bulls head coach Phil Jackson), which has won four championships since 2000. Small-market teams like Sacramento and Portland have true-blue fans, and such cities can be great places to take in a game. Check the National Basketball Association website (www.nba.com) for info.

College level basketball also draws millions of fans, especially every spring when March Madness rolls around. This series of college play-off games

Don't know your on-base percentage (OBP) from gross production average (GPA)? The Hardball Times (www.hardballtimes.com) can unleash your inner baseball stats-geek.

START YOUR ENGINES

NASCAR – officially, the National Association for Stock Car Auto Racing – has played an unusual role in American culture. It flew under the radar for years, mostly thrilling fans in the Southeast, where it originated. Money started to flow in during the 1990s, and then it burst onto the national scene in a big way in 2002.

That's when the term 'NASCAR dad' entered the national lexicon as part of political campaigning, and came to typify white, working-class, typically conservative men who also happened to be fans of fast cars that drive around in circles. Soon NASCAR races became the second most-watched sport on TV, trailing only pro football games. And more than a hundred Fortune 500 companies became involved via sponsorship. Dollar signs flashed.

Lately though, NASCAR is having an identity crisis. Its traditional fan base is irked that the sport tried to go upscale – merlot versus moonshine, as they say – and now NASCAR must woo them back. Big names on the circuit today include Jeff Gordon and Dale Earnhardt Jr. The Nextel Cup is the top-tier tour, with the Daytona 500 (p535) being the year's biggest race, attracting nearly 250,000 spectators – more than an NFL Superbowl, MLB World Series game and NBA finals match-up combined.

culminates in the Final Four, when the four remaining teams compete for a spot in the championship game. The Cinderella stories and unexpected outcomes rival the pro league for excitement. The games are widely televised – and bet upon. This is when Las Vegas bookies earn their keep.

Women play too, at both college and pro levels. It's not uncommon for certain college women's teams to outdraw the men's.

Football

Football has tackled the rest of American sports. It's big, it's physical, and it's rolling in dough. With the shortest season and least number of games of any of the major sports, every match takes on the emotion of an epic battle, where the results matter and an unfortunate injury can be devastatingly lethal to the chances of an entire team.

In *Talladega Nights* (2006), comedian Will Ferrell spoofs NASCAR. He plays dim-witted driver Ricky Bobby, racing's top star until pride brings him down. Can he regain his integrity (and wife, kids, money and car)?

Football's also the toughest because it's played in fall and winter in all manner of rain, sleet and snow. Some of history's most memorable matches have occurred at below-freezing temperatures. Green Bay Packers fans are in a class by themselves when it comes to severe weather. Their stadium in Wisconsin, known as Lambeau Field, was the site of the infamous Ice Bowl, a 1967 championship game against the Dallas Cowboys where the temperature plummeted to 13°F below zero – mind you, that was with a wind-chill factor of -48°F.

Different teams have dominated different decades: the Pittsburgh Steelers in the 1970s, the San Francisco 49ers in the 1980s, the Cowboys in the 1990s and the New England Patriots in the 2000s. The pro league's official website, www.nfl.com, is packed with information. Tickets are expensive and hard to get (that's why many fans congregate in bars to watch instead).

Even college and high-school football games enjoy an intense amount of pomp and circumstance, with cheerleaders, marching bands, mascots, songs and mandatory pre- and postgame rituals, especially the tailgate – a full-blown beer-and-barbecue feast that takes place over portable grills in parking lots where games are played.

The rabidly popular Super Bowl is pro football's championship match, held in late January or early February. The bowl games (such as Rose Bowl and Orange Bowl) are college football's title matches, held on and around New Year's Day.

Arts

When searching for a metaphor that encapsulates America's arts, one is sorely tempted to use the web (or, to be current, Web 2.0). Many of the characteristics of the internet revolution so perfectly match and amplify America's artistic persona that, if set free in a metaverse, the web could be America's digital avatar.

Both are chaotic, democratic jumbles of high and low culture, in which the individual takes the reins of criticism and self-defined communities perform for themselves. Both are rebellious, obsessively personal, ahistorical (even antihistorical), deconstructive, collaborative and given to appropriation, if not outright theft. Both enjoy upsetting apple carts and revel in the transformative nature of technology.

Historically, America's arts have shined brightest during modernism and postmodernism – and what's more postmodern than the internet? However, what the web lacks is ethnicity and place, and no analogy for America will ever work without those. Geography and race together create the varied regionalism that is key to understanding America's arts. And despite a popular affinity for technology, nature and wilderness still inspire the nation's soul and, consequently, much of its art.

Discarding the web as analogy and simply considering the fact of it, there is no question that digital technology is currently unmaking and remaking every medium and influencing every aesthetic in the US. It's impossible to say exactly where this is going or how much, once the binary dusts settle, will be different. America is in the middle of a global revolution, in which economics, production, distribution, tools, community, performance, expression and audience experience are all changing.

Yet to understand the art of tomorrow, you've got to first look at the history of the arts in America – including music, literature, architecture, painting, photography, theater, dance, cinema and TV – today.

MUSIC

American popular music is the nation's heartbeat. It's John Lee Hooker's deep growls and John Coltrane's soulful cascades. It's Hank Williams' yodel and Elvis' pout. It's Beyoncé and Bob Dylan, Duke Ellington and Patti Smith. It's a feeling as much as a form – always a foot-stomping, defiant good time, whether folks are boot scootin' to bluegrass, sweating to zydeco or jumpin' to hip-hop.

No other American art has been as influential. Blues, jazz, country, rock and roll, hip-hop: download them to your iPod and you've got the soundtrack for the story of American music as it evolved in the 20th century. The rest of the world has long returned the love, and American music today is a joyful, freewheeling multicultural feast, in which genres and styles are mixed, matched, blended and blurred.

Only the industry does not have happy feet. The digital revolution hit music first, and the 'problems' new technology poses to business hit music hardest: the obsolescence of physical media, uncontrolled public access and lack of copyright protections. CD sales (still over 80% of all music sales) have been falling for eight years; digital sales are rising fast, but not enough to stop an overall decline. Music, a $14.5 billion industry in 1999, dropped to a $10.4 billion industry in 2007, with music retailers closing faster than independent bookstores. In 2008, the US accounted for half of the global digital music market, with annual downloads surpassing the one billion mark.

Reading *Hip: The History* (2004), by John Leland, is like watching an expert mechanic disassemble the racially charged, high-octane engine of American pop culture. It's so good, it's badass.

Despite waves of lawsuits, the industry seems powerless to stop illegal downloading. Estimates are that a billion songs are traded illegally every month – a testament to both the power of music and the consequences of new media.

Blues

The South is the mother of American music, most of which has roots in the frisson and interplay of black-white racial relations, whose troubled course was first set by the 'peculiar institution' of slavery. The blues developed out of the work songs, or 'shouts,' of black slaves and out of black spiritual songs and their 'call-and-response' pattern, both of which were adaptations of African music.

Cadillac Records (2008) may not tell the strict historical truth about the influential Chicago-based music label, but it's still a ripping good story about legendary blues musicians including Muddy Waters, Howlin' Wolf and Etta James.

After the Civil War, transformed by the crucible of African American life in white US society, slave work songs became the blues. Improvisational and intensely personal, the blues remain at heart an immediate expression of individual pain, suffering, hope, desire and pride. Nearly all subsequent American music has tapped this deep well.

At the turn of the 20th century, traveling blues musicians, and particularly female blues singers, gained fame and employment across the South. Early pioneers included Robert Johnson, WC Handy, Ma Rainey, Huddie Ledbetter (aka Lead Belly) and Bessie Smith, who some consider the best blues singer who ever lived. At the same time, African American Christian choral music evolved into gospel, whose greatest singer, Mahalia Jackson, came to prominence in the 1920s.

After WWII, blues from Memphis and the Mississippi Delta dispersed northward, particularly to Chicago, in the hands of a new generation of musicians like Muddy Waters, Buddy Guy, BB King, John Lee Hooker and Etta James. Today, the blues flame is tended, and updated, by musicians like Robert Cray, Bettye LaVette and Keb' Mo'.

An African American euphemism for sex, the term 'rock and roll' first appeared in blues singer Trixie Smith's 1922 song 'My Man Rocks Me (With One Steady Roll).'

Jazz

Down in New Orleans, Congo Sq, where slaves gathered to sing and dance from the late 18th century onward, is considered the 'birthplace' of jazz. There ex-slaves adapted the reed, horn and string instruments used by the city's often French-speaking, multiracial Creoles – who themselves preferred formal European music – to play their own 'primitive,' African-influenced music. This fertile cross-pollination produced a steady stream of innovative sounds.

The first variation was ragtime, so-called because of its 'ragged,' syncopated African rhythms. Beginning in the 1890s, ragtime was popularized by musicians like Scott Joplin, and was made widely accessible through sheet music and player-piano rolls.

Ken Burns' documentary miniseries *Jazz* (2001) celebrates the multiracial mosaic of this American musical invention, from the early days of slavery through to the contributions of 20th-century innovators. For audio clips and more, visit www.pbs.org/jazz.

Dixieland jazz, centered on New Orleans' infamous Storyville red-light district, soon followed. Coronet player Buddy Bolden is credited with being the first true jazz musician, although pianist Jelly Roll Morton liked to boast that he was the one who created jazz. In 1917 Storyville shut down and New Orleans' jazz musicians dispersed. In 1919, bandleader King Oliver moved to Chicago, and his star trumpet player, Louis Armstrong, soon followed. Armstrong's distinctive vocals and talented improvisations led to the solo becoming an integral part of jazz throughout much of the 20th century.

The 1920s and '30s are known as the Jazz Age, but music was just part of the greater flowering of African American culture during New York's Harlem Renaissance. Swing – an urbane, big-band jazz style – swept the country, led by innovative bandleaders Duke Ellington and Count Basie.

Jazz singers Ella Fitzgerald and Billie Holiday combined jazz with its Southern sibling, the blues.

After WWII, bebop (aka bop) arose, reacting against the smooth melodies and confining rhythms of big-band swing. Saxophonist Lester Young influenced a new crop of musicians, including Charlie Parker, Dizzy Gillespie and Thelonious Monk. Critics at first derided such 1950s and '60s permutations as cool jazz, hard-bop, free or avant-garde jazz, and fusion (which combined jazz and Latin or rock music) – but there was no stopping the postmodernist tide deconstructing jazz. Pioneers of this era include Miles Davis, Dave Brubeck, Chet Baker, Charles Mingus, John Coltrane, Melba Liston and Ornette Coleman.

Excellent jazz magazines include *Down Beat* (www.downbeat.com), with an online 'Jazz 101' history section, and *Jazz Times* (www.jazztimes.com) for an online concert and events guide.

Today, no particular jazz style predominates. Ragtime, Dixieland and swing all enjoy revivals, especially under the leadership of trumpeter Wynton Marsalis, while musicians such as pianist Herbie Hancock, saxophonists Wayne Shorter and Joshua Redman, and 'vocalese' singer Kurt Elling keep expanding this ever malleable, brilliantly resilient form.

Folk & Country

Early Scottish, Irish and English immigrants brought their own instruments and folk music to America, and what emerged over time in the secluded Appalachian Mountains was fiddle-and-banjo hillbilly, or 'country,' music. In the Southwest, 'western' music was distinguished by steel guitars and larger bands. In the 1920s, these styles merged into 'country-and-western' music and became centered on Nashville, Tennessee, especially once the *Grand Ole Opry* began its radio broadcasts in 1925 (see p424).

Jimmie Rodgers and the Carter Family were some of the first country musicians to become widely popular. In Kentucky, Bill Monroe and his Blue Grass Boys mixed country with jazz and blues to create 'bluegrass.' Other notable country musicians include Hank Williams, Johnny Cash, Willie Nelson, Patsy Cline and Loretta Lynn.

The tradition of American folk music was crystallized in Woody Guthrie, who traveled the country during the Depression singing politically conscious songs. In the 1940s, Pete Seeger emerged as a tireless preserver of America's folk heritage. Folk music experienced a revival during 1960s protest movements, but then-folkie Bob Dylan ended it almost single-handedly when he plugged in an electric guitar to shouts of 'traitor!'

Part of the 'outlaw country' movement of the late 1960s and '70s, Willie Nelson's pioneering brand of country music appealed to cowboys and hippies alike, as heard on the concept album *Red Headed Stranger* (1975).

Country music influenced rock and roll in the 1950s, while rock-flavored country was dubbed 'rockabilly.' In the 1980s, country and western achieved new levels of popularity with stars like Garth Brooks. Today, famous country musicians include Shania Twain, the Dixie Chicks, Dwight Yoakam and Tim McGraw. Occupying the eclectic 'alt country' category are Lucinda Williams and Lyle Lovett. For the Austin music scene, see p715.

Rock & Roll

Most say rock and roll was born in 1954 the day Elvis Presley walked into Sam Philips' Sun Studio and recorded 'That's All Right.' Initially, radio stations weren't sure why a white country boy was singing black music, or whether they should play it. Two years later Presley scored his first big breakthrough with 'Heartbreak Hotel.'

Musically, rock and roll was a hybrid of guitar-driven blues, black rhythm and blues (R & B), and white country-and-western music. R & B evolved in the 1940s out of swing and the blues and was then known as 'race music.' With rock and roll, white performers and some African American musicians transformed 'race music' into something that white youths could embrace freely – and oh, did they.

Rock and roll instantly abetted a social revolution even more significant than its musical one: openly sexual, celebrating youth and dancing freely across color lines, rock scared the nation. Authorities worked diligently to control 'juvenile delinquents' and to sanitize and suppress rock and roll, which might have withered if not for the early 1960s 'British invasion,' in which the Beatles and the Rolling Stones, emulating Buddy Holly, Little Richard and others, shocked rock and roll back to life.

The 1960s witnessed a full-blown youth rebellion, epitomized by the drug-inspired psychedelic sounds of the Grateful Dead and Jefferson Airplane, and the electric wails of Janis Joplin, Jimi Hendrix, Bob Dylan and Patti Smith. Ever since, rock has been about music *and* lifestyle, alternately torn between hedonism and seriousness, commercialism and authenticity.

Punk arrived in the late 1970s, led by the Ramones and the Dead Kennedys, as did the working-class rock of Bruce Springsteen and Tom Petty. As the counterculture became the culture in the 1980s, critics prematurely pronounced 'rock is dead.' Rock was saved (including by the Talking Heads, REM, Nirvana and Pearl Jam) as it always has been: by splintering and evolving, whether it's called new wave, heavy metal, grunge, alt rock, world beat, skate punk, goth, electronica, and on and on.

The album is dead! Long live the album! My Chemical Romance's *The Black Parade* (2006) is old-school, bombastic, self-conscious and rock-laden with sly winks, infectious hooks and emo-punk wails.

Even though hip-hop has become today's outlaw sound, rock remains relevant, and it's not going anywhere. Cue up the White Stripes, the Killers, Yeah Yeah Yeahs, Kings of Leon or Beck to hear why.

Hip-Hop TophOne

From the ocean of sounds coming out of the early 1970s – funk, soul, Latin, reggae and rock and roll – young DJs from the Bronx in New York City began to spin a groundbreaking mixture of records together in an effort to drive dance floors wild. An emcee would take over the microphone, calling out rhymes and urging the dancers, or b-boys and b-girls, into a frenzy.

And so hip-hop was born. Groups like Grandmaster Flash and the Furious Five and Afrika Bambaataa and the SoulSonic Force were soon taking the party from the streets to the trendy clubs of Manhattan and mingling with punk and new wave bands like the Clash and Blondie. Break-out artists Futura 2000, Keith Haring and Jean-Michel Basquiat moved from the subways and the streets to the galleries, and soon to the worlds of fashion and advertising. By the mid-1980s, hip-hop touched everyone, young and old, black and white, and everybody in between.

For all the alt rock and garage bands (still playing garages!) that fly below the music industry's promotional juggernaut, plug into *Magnet* (www.magnetmagazine.com).

As groups like RunDMC and the Beastie Boys sold millions, the sounds and styles of the growing hip-hop culture rapidly diversified. The 'gangsta rap' sound of NWA came out of Los Angeles, as Japan's DJ Krush composed monumental soundscapes and MC Solaar rapped about Parisian housing projects. Throughout the 1990s kids from all corners of the globe were rapping, break dancing, and painting their names on urban walls in emulation of the artists they adored.

Come the turn of the millennium, what started as some raggedy gang kids playing their parents' funk records at illegal block parties had evolved into a multibillion-dollar business. Russell Simmons and P Diddy stood atop media empires, and stars Queen Latifah and Will Smith were Hollywood royalty. A white rapper from Detroit, Eminem, sold millions of records and hip-hop overtook country as America's second-most-popular music behind pop rock.

At the same time, the underground essence of hip-hop kept thriving. Pictures of fresh graffiti spread instantly over websites, and the development of cheaper and simpler music programs gave rise to thousands of bedroom producers. Regional styles such as the American South's 'krunk'

MUSIC IN THE HOT, HOT SUN

Americans love a grassy lawn and an outdoor stage, and recent decades have seen a renaissance in music festival extravaganzas. More than bandstands, these are some of the nation's top 'musical, cultural, community experiences,' to quote grandpappy Lollapalooza.

In general, single-day tickets run from $40 to $85 and multiday passes from $150 to over $300. Book early on festival websites, which often link to hotel and transportation options (and sometimes offer special package deals, too).

For more music festivals, check the listings throughout this book or browse online at www.bluesfestivalguide.com, www.jazzonjazz.com, www.dirtylinen.com and www.festivalfinder.com.

Bill Monroe Memorial Bluegrass Festival (Bean Blossom, IN; www.beanblossom.com) USA's oldest bluegrass festival; eight days in mid-June.

Bonnaroo Music & Arts Festival (Manchester, TN; www.bonnaroo.com) Big-name rock, soul, country and more, plus a comedy tent; four days in mid-June.

Bumbershoot (Seattle, WA; www.bumbershoot.org) Not just rock but dance, theater and comedy too; three days in early September.

Coachella (Indio, CA; www.coachella.com) Hard rock, DJs, musical icons and alternative bands in the desert; three days in mid-April.

Folk Festival 50 (Newport, RI; www.folkfestival50.com) Dylan went electric in Newport at the nation's preeminent folk gathering; three days in early August.

Lollapalooza (Chicago, IL; www.lollapalooza.com) Major-player rock and DJ lineup; three dazed days in early August.

Monterey Jazz Festival (Monterey, CA; www.montereyjazzfestival.org) A don't-miss jazz celebration with legendary showstoppers; three days in mid-September.

New Orleans Jazz Fest (New Orleans, LA; www.nojazzfest.com) Premier jazz fest, from Cajun and funk to blues and zydeco; two weekends in late April/early May. See also p481.

Sasquatch! Music Festival (Quincy, WA; www.sasquatchfestival.com) Rock and roll in the gorgeous Columbia River Gorge; three days in late May.

South by Southwest (Austin, TX; http://sxsw.com); Gargantuan event with nearly 2000 bands, 110 films and an interactive digital expo; 10 days in mid-March. See also p715.

and the Bay Area's 'hyphy movement' rose from the grassroots to gain major airplay.

Today, many view hip-hop as a vapid wasteland of commercial excess – glorifying consumerism, misogyny, homophobia, drug use and a host of other social ills. But just as the hedonistic days of arena rock and roll gave birth to the rebel child of punk, the evolving offspring of hip-hop and DJ culture are constantly breaking the rules to create something new and even more energizing.

Layered with pop, rap, soul, retro and hip-hop, *St Elsewhere* (2006), by Gnarls Barkley, is wickedly good. So is DJ Danger Mouse's *Grey Album* (2004), a mashup of rapper Jay-Z's *The Black Album* and the Beatles' 'White Album.'

LITERATURE

Not so long ago, the nation's imagination stirred when critics heralded the next Great American Novel. Not everyone cared, but for over a century the novel was still the vital engine of US culture and art. In today's glutted multimedia environment, American writers have to fight for wallets – and ever-decreasing attention spans – so much so that the Great American Novel has practically become niche publishing.

Yet reading survives. Americans spend over $37 billion a year on books, which is more than they spend on music and movie tickets combined. Overall book sales are steady, but physical bookstores are suffering due to web-retailers and digital reading devices for ebooks like Kindle from online mega-bookseller Amazon.com.

Americans are in no danger of losing their love of a well-told tale, even though the distinction between literature and genre fiction is often playfully blurred. Each year reveals a pluralistic wealth of new and talented voices, all feverishly digesting what life in these United States is all about. In whatever form, great American writers still stir the melting pot.

The Great American Novel

America first articulated a vision of itself through its literature. Until the American Revolution, the continent's citizens identified largely with England, but after independence, an immediate call went out to develop an American national voice. Despite much parochial hand-wringing, little progress was made until the 1820s, when writers took up the two aspects of American life that had no counterpart in Europe: the untamed wilderness and the frontier experience.

Since the 1970s, the nonprofit Gutenberg Project (www.gutenberg.org) has been expanding its free digital library of ebooks, with over 28,000 titles currently available for download.

James Fenimore Cooper is credited with creating the first truly American literature with *The Pioneers* (1823), the first of his famous Leatherstocking adventure stories. Cooper portrayed the humble pioneer, gathering ethical and spiritual lessons through his contact with wilderness, as a more authentic, admirable figure than the refined European. In Cooper's 'everyman' humor and individualism, Americans first recognized themselves.

In his essay *Nature* (1836), Ralph Waldo Emerson articulated similar ideas, but in more philosophical and spiritual terms. Emerson claimed that nature reflected God's instructions for humankind as plainly as the Bible did, and that individuals could understand these through rational thought and self-reliance. Emerson's writings became the core of the transcendentalist movement, which Henry David Thoreau championed in *Walden; or, Life in the Woods* (1854).

Unknown authors languishing in dusty garrets pining for publication? That's no longer necessary, now that writers are telling stories in serial podcasts at Podiobooks (http://podiobooks.com).

Herman Melville's ambitious *Moby Dick* (1851) was, in part, a cautionary tale of what happens when the individual accepts transcendentalist beliefs, and thus thinks that he can distinguish good from evil with God-like clarity. Nathaniel Hawthorne examined the dark side of conservative New England in *The Scarlet Letter* (1850), as did recluse Emily Dickinson in her haunting, tightly structured poems, which were first published in 1890, four years after her death.

Standing somewhat outside this dialogue, Edgar Allan Poe was the first American writer to achieve international acclaim. His gruesome stories (such as 'The Tell-Tale Heart,' 1843) helped popularize the short-story form, and he is credited with inventing the mystery story, the horror story and science fiction, all extremely popular and enduring genres in America.

The celebration of common humanity and nature reached its apotheosis in Walt Whitman, whose poetry collection *Leaves of Grass* (1855) signaled the arrival of an American literary visionary. In Whitman's informal, intimate, rebellious free verse were songs of individualism, democracy, earthy spirituality, taboo-breaking sexuality and joyous optimism that encapsulated the heart of a throbbing new nation.

American poets still struggle for notice, but the US has an active scene: *Poetry* magazine (www.poetryfoundation.org) publishes news, interviews with authors, contemporary verse and podcasts.

But not everything was coming up roses. Abolitionist Harriet Beecher Stowe's controversial novel *Uncle Tom's Cabin* (1852) depicted African American life under slavery with Christian romanticism but also enough realism to inflame passions on both sides of the 'great debate' over slavery, which would shortly plunge the nation into civil war.

After the Civil War (1861–65), two enduring literary trends emerged: realism and regionalism. Stephen Crane's *The Red Badge of Courage* (1895) depicted the horrors of war, while Upton Sinclair's *The Jungle* (1906) was a shocking exposé of Chicago's meatpacking industry. Regionalism was especially spurred by the rapid late-19th-century settlement of the West. Novelist Jack London (*Call of the Wild*, 1903) serialized his adventures throughout the West, as well as in Alaska and Hawaii, for popular magazines such as the *Saturday Evening Post.*

However, it was Samuel Clemens (aka Mark Twain) who came to define American letters. Twain wrote in the vernacular, loved 'tall tales' and reveled in satirical humor and absurdity, while his folksy, 'anti-intellectual' stance endeared him to everyday readers. In *Huckleberry Finn* (1884), Twain made explicit the quintessential American narrative of an individual journey of self-discovery. The image of Huck and Jim – a poor white teenager and a runaway black slave – standing outside society's norms and floating together toward an uncertain future down the Mississippi River challenges American society still.

Orion Horncrackle, Fiesta Punch and Plato Bucklew are just a few of the Wyoming denizens populating Annie Proulx's *Bad Dirt* (2004), a Twain-esque collection of tall tales, hard luck and barbed-wire wit.

Disillusionment & Diversity

With the dramas of world wars and a newly industrialized society for artistic fodder, American literature came into its own in the 20th century.

Dubbed the 'Lost Generation,' many US writers became expatriates in Europe, most famously Ernest Hemingway. His novel *The Sun Also Rises* (1926) exemplified the era, and his spare, stylized realism has often been imitated, never bettered. Other notable American figures at Parisian literary salons included modernist writers Gertrude Stein and Ezra Pound, and iconoclast Henry Miller, whose semiautobiographical novels, including *Tropic of Cancer* (1934), were published in Paris, only to be banned for obscenity and pornography in the USA until the 1960s.

F Scott Fitzgerald (*The Great Gatsby,* 1925) eviscerated East Coast society life, while John Steinbeck (*The Grapes of Wrath,* 1939) became the great voice of rural working poor in the West, especially during the Great Depression. William Faulkner (*The Sound and the Fury,* 1929) examined the South's social rifts in dense prose riddled by bullets of black humor.

Spanning more than four decades, the Rabbit series by novelist John Updike's used dark angst and humor to capture the ironic disaffections of modern life in suburban America; *Rabbit is Rich* (1981) won the Pulitzer Prize.

In the 1930s, the classic detective story got hammered by writers like Dashiell Hammett (*The Maltese Falcon,* 1930) and Raymond Chandler (*The Big Sleep,* 1939), whose hard-boiled urban realism was so morally dark it was dubbed 'noir' fiction. This tradition is carried on today by crime writers such as James Ellroy (*The Black Dahlia,* 1987), Walter Mosley (*Devil in a Blue Dress,* 1990) and Elmore Leonard (*Out of Sight,* 1996).

Between the world wars, the Harlem Renaissance also flourished, as African American intellectuals and artists took pride in their culture and undermined racist stereotypes. Among the most well-known writers were poet Langston Hughes and novelist Zora Neale Hurston (*Their Eyes Were Watching God,* 1937).

After WWII, American writers delineated ever-sharper regional and ethnic divides, pursued stylistic experimentation and often caustically repudiated conservative middle-class American values. Writers of the 1950s Beat Generation threw themselves like Molotov cocktails onto the profusion of smug suburban lawns: Jack Kerouac (*On the Road,* 1957), Allen Ginsberg (*Howl,* 1956) and William S Burroughs (*Naked Lunch,* 1959) celebrated nonconformity and transgressive, stream-of-consciousness writing. Meanwhile, JD Salinger (*The Catcher in the Rye,* 1951), Russian immigrant Vladimir Nabokov (*Lolita,* 1958), Ken Kesey (*One Flew Over the Cuckoo's Nest,* 1962) and Sylvia Plath (*The Bell Jar,* 1963) darkly chronicled descents into madness by characters who struggled against stifling social norms.

And now for something really different: Kurt Vonnegut's *Cat's Cradle* (1963) and *Slaughterhouse-Five* (1969) are genre-bending novels that mix science fiction with postmodern Cold War–era political satire and a hefty dose of dark humor.

The South, always ripe with paradox, inspired masterful short-story writers Flannery O'Connor (*Wise Blood,* 1952) and Eudora Welty (*The Optimist's Daughter,* 1972) and novelist Dorothy Allison (*Bastard Out of Carolina,* 1992). The mythical romance and modern tragedies of the West have found their champions in Chicano writer Rudolfo Anaya (*Bless Me Ultima,* 1972),

Larry McMurtry (*Lonesome Dove,* 1985) and Cormac McCarthy (*All the Pretty Horses,* 1982), whose characters poignantly tackle the rugged realities of Western life.

African American writers also rose to prominence as the 20th century progressed. Richard Wright (*Black Boy,* 1945) and Ralph Ellison (*Invisible Man,* 1952) wrote passionately about racism, while James Baldwin became both an acclaimed African American writer (*Go Tell It on the Mountain,* 1953) and a groundbreaking openly gay writer (*Giovanni's Room,* 1956). African American women writers were led by Toni Morrison (*The Bluest Eye,* 1970), Maya Angelou (*I Know Why the Caged Bird Sings,* 1971) and Alice Walker (*The Color Purple,* 1982).

Pick up *The Namesake* (2003) for Jhumpa Lahiri's exquisite prose, which describes a moving intergenerational tale of a Bengali Indian family settling and assimilating in America.

As the 20th century ended, American literature became ever more personalized, starting in the 'me' decade of the 1980s. Narcissistic, often nihilistic narratives catapulted the 'Brat Pack' into pop culture: Jay McInerney (*Bright Lights, Big City,* 1984), Brett Easton Ellis (*Less Than Zero,* 1985) and Tama Janowitz (*Slaves of New York,* 1986). The spare prose of short-story master Raymond Carver (*What We Talk about When We Talk about Love,* 1981) stood in stark contrast to these youngsters, as well as to the ever-expanding ego of sprawling novels by David Foster Wallace (*Infinite Jest,* 1996) and Don DeLillo (*Underworld,* 1997) that came later.

Today, an increasingly diverse, multiethnic panoply of voices reflects the kaleidoscopic society Americans live in. Ethnic identity (especially that of immigrant cultures), regionalism and narratives of self-discovery remain at the forefront of American literature, no matter how experimental. The quarterly journal *McSweeney's,* founded by Dave Eggers (*A Heartbreaking Work of Staggering Genius,* 2000), publishes titans of contemporary literature such as Joyce Carol Oates (*We Were the Mulvaneys,* 1996) and Michael Chabon (*The Amazing Adventures of Kavalier & Clay,* 2000) alongside emerging writers.

Get the insiders' low-down on the bounty of US film festivals, both large and small, from coast to coast and everywhere in between at www.filmfestivals.com.

FILM

No less an American icon, Hollywood is increasingly the product of an internationalized cinema and film culture. This evolution is partly pure business: Hollywood studios are the showpieces of multinational corporations, and funding flows to talent that brings the biggest grosses, regardless of nationality.

But this shift is also creative. It's Hollywood's recognition that if the studios don't incorporate the immense filmmaking talent emerging worldwide, they will be made irrelevant by it. Cooption is an old Hollywood strategy, used most recently to subvert the challenge posed by the independent film movement of the 1990s. That said, mainstream American audiences remain steadfastly indifferent to foreign films.

For downloading or screening independent movies at home and partaking in 'social cinema,' join up with GreenCine (www.greencine.com), Jaman (www.jaman.com) or IndieFlix (http://indieflix.com).

Perhaps most significantly, computers are killing celluloid; movies can now be made and shown without using film. With celluloid increasingly out of the picture, production and distribution, once so prohibitively expensive and complex they were easily controlled by a few privileged gatekeepers (ie studios, have never been more accessible.

The Magic of Moving Pictures

In the late 19th century, motion-picture cameras and projectors were developed simultaneously in France and the USA (though Thomas Edison was the first to use sprocketed celluloid film). The first movie house – called the Nickelodeon because shows cost just a nickel (5¢) – opened in Pittsburgh in 1905.

The Great Train Robbery (1903) is famous because it was the first to be edited for dramatic effect: it cut to the chase. Emulating the stage, moviemakers enticed audiences by developing appealing stars and dependable genres. In the 1910s, Charlie Chaplin became the first movie star, and producer Mack Sennett's slapstick comedies – and his ever-bumbling Keystone cops – became cultural institutions.

DW Griffith was a pioneer of cinematic techniques. His landmark films *Birth of a Nation* (1915) and *Intolerance* (1916) introduced much of cinema's now-familiar language, such as the fade, the close-up and the flashback.

indieWIRE (http://indiewire.com) is a rich source of reviews, news and box office and festival information about independent films that are actually independent of the studios.

Meanwhile, competition fostered the studio system, which began in Manhattan, where Edison tried to create a monopoly with his patents. This drove many independents to move to a suburb of Los Angeles, where they could easily flee to Mexico in case of legal trouble – and ta-da, Hollywood was born.

In 1927, sound was introduced in *The Jazz Singer*, and the 'talkies' ushered in the golden age of the movies, lasting from the 1930s to the '50s. Movie palaces and drive-in theaters sprung up across the country, and glamorous stars such as Humphrey Bogart, Katherine Hepburn, Bette Davis and Cary Grant enthralled the nation. Hollywood studios had the perfect racket: they locked actors into exclusive contracts, ran production departments that handled every aspect of filmmaking and controlled distribution in theaters.

Then, in the 1950s, TV arrived, and Americans discovered that laughing at Ralph Kramden in their living rooms was easier than driving to the movies. Plus, the feds broke up Hollywood's monopoly. In the 1960s, struggling studios cut costs, ended actors' contracts, sold production departments and sometimes went bankrupt.

The pinnacle of pop-culture irony, sublime vacuousness and cartoonish American optimism, *The Simpsons Movie* (2007) may be the only cultural handbook foreign visitors will need.

In the 1970s, desperate studios took a risk on a generation of young, anti-establishment filmmakers who, reflecting the times, were interested in social realism, not musicals, romantic comedies or Westerns. Break-out directors included Martin Scorsese, Robert Altman and Francis Ford Coppola, whose provocative films remain high-water marks of excellence.

The '70s also spawned the blockbuster, courtesy of two innovators now synonymous with pop culture: Steven Spielberg and George Lucas. Spielberg's *Jaws* (1975) and Lucas' *Star Wars* (1977) were such cultural phenomena, and their pleasures so visceral, that they provided a blueprint for the future: keep the action fast, characters simple, pile on special effects and open big. Lessons learned, the studios recovered and have drawn record audiences ever since.

In the 1990s, small, edgy, independently produced films (led by maverick Miramax, now owned by media conglomerate Disney) became the rage; they experimented with new tools of digital filmmaking and rode the buzz generated in a burgeoning US film-festival circuit. Today, Utah's Sundance Film Festival (p874), chaired by Robert Redford; New York City's Tribeca Film Festival (p176); Colorado's Telluride Film Festival (p788); and Nevada's **CineVegas** (www.cinevegas.com) rank highly among America's almost 500 independent film festivals.

Admit it: you *want* Hollywood gossip with your film criticism. In the deliciously dishy *Easy Riders, Raging Bulls: How the Sex-Drugs-and-Rock-'N'-Roll Generation Saved Hollywood* (1997), Peter Biskind rips the lid off the 1970s 'auteur era.'

TELEVISION

In the 20th century, it could be argued that TV was the defining medium of the modern age. An average American still watches 35 hours of TV a week, an all-time high. Americans *love* TV, but they are watching differently: recording or downloading online, viewing according to their schedules (not the networks') and skipping the commercials. As the internet messes with the economics of this corporate-owned, ad-driven entertainment, TV executives shudder.

TV was developed in the USA and Europe in the 1920s and '30s, and the first commercial TV set was introduced at the 1939 New York World's Fair. After WWII, owning a set became a status symbol for America's blossoming middle class, and radio and movies wilted under TV's cathode-tube glow. Cable arrived in the 1980s and satellite services rapidly grew in the 1990s, expanding TV's handful of channels into dozens, and then hundreds.

For many decades, critics sneered that TV was low-brow, and movie stars wouldn't be caught dead on it. But well-written, thought-provoking shows have existed almost since the beginning. In the 1950s, the original *I Love Lucy* show was groundbreaking: shot on film before a live audience and edited before airing, it pioneered syndication. It established the sitcom

ALL-AMERICAN FLICKS

Genres have defined cinema since its birth. Here are some distinctly American ones.

The Western

In pop cinema terms, the mythic West *is* America: good guys versus bad guys (and girls), law versus lawlessness, and duking it out on the rugged frontier. The 1940s and '50s were the Western's heyday. For an unironic paragon of manhood, check out Gary Cooper in *High Noon* (1952). John Ford's influential *The Searchers* (1956) is pure Western poetry: John Wayne, Monument Valley and a deadly score to settle. Sam Peckinpah's ode to nihilistic violence, *The Wild Bunch* (1969), dragged the Western into the antiheroic modern day, as did Clint Eastwood's *Unforgiven* (1992) and *3:10 to Yuma* (2007) starring Russell Crowe and Christian Bale.

The Musical

The golden age of Hollywood was defined by the musical, and *42nd Street* (1933) encapsulates the genre. Fred Astaire and Ginger Rogers were a match made in heaven; *Top Hat* (1935) adds a classic Irving Berlin score. The exuberant, impish Gene Kelly is showcased in *Singin' in the Rain* (1952) and the jazz-scored *An American in Paris* (1951). No musical-fantasy is more parodied and exalted than *The Wizard of Oz* (1939). These days, musicals are occasionally updated for modern tastes, as with *Moulin Rouge!* (2001), *Chicago* (2002), and *Dreamgirls* (2006).

Gangsters & Crime

The outsider status of the urban gangster is an often explicit metaphor for the American immigrant experience, and the crime genre includes many of America's greatest films.

Francis Ford Coppola's *Godfather* trilogy (1972–90), which examines immigrants and American society through the prism of organized crime, is an unrivaled cinematic achievement. Martin Scorsese is the auteur of American mobsters: don't miss *Mean Streets* (1973), *GoodFellas* (1990), *Casino* (1995) and *The Departed* (2006).

The influential subgenre 'film noir' got the star treatment in John Huston's *The Maltese Falcon* (1941), Orson Welles' *Touch of Evil* (1958), Roman Polanski's *Chinatown* (1974) and the star-studded *LA Confidential* (1997). For kinetic jolts of pop irony, see *Pulp Fiction* (1994), by Quentin Tarantino and *Fargo* (1996), by the Coen brothers.

Science Fiction

Inherently cinematic and ever popular, sci-fi is often just the wild West tricked out with lasers and spaceships, but it can also be rivetingly shot through with existential dread and postmodern fears of otherness and technology, starting with the silent film *Metropolis* (1927).

For existentialism, watch Stanley Kubrick's *2001: A Space Odyssey* (1968). Equally jittery with techno-fears are *The Terminator* (1984–2009) quartet and *The Matrix* (1999–2003) trilogy. Steven Spielberg is virtually a one-man sci-fi factory, from *Close Encounters of the Third Kind* (1977) and *E.T: The Extra-Terrestrial* (1982) to *War of the Worlds* (2005). Other sci-fi classics include James Cameron's *Alien* (1979) and *Aliens* (1986), and Ridley Scott's moody *Blade Runner* (1982). For pure pulp, see George Lucas' *Star Wars* (1977–2000) series and JJ Abrams' *Star Trek* (2009). Terry Gilliam's *Brazil* (1985) is hilarious future shock.

('situation comedy') formula, and showcased a dynamic female comedian, Lucille Ball, in an interethnic marriage.

The 1970s comedy *All in the Family* aired an unflinching examination of prejudice, as embodied by bigoted patriarch Archie Bunker, played by Carol O'Connor. Similarly, the sketch-comedy show *Saturday Night Live,* which debuted in 1975, pushed social hot buttons with its subversive, politically charged humor.

In the 1980s, videotapes brought movies into American homes, blurring the distinction between big and small screens, and the stigma Hollywood attached to TV slowly faded. Another turning point in this decade was *The Cosby Show,* starring comedian Bill Cosby. While not the first successful African American show, it became the nation's highest-rated program and spurred more multicultural TV shows.

In the 1990s, TV audiences embraced the unformulaic, no-holds-barred weird cult show *Twin Peaks,* leading to a slew of provocative idiosyncrasies like *The X-Files.* By the 21st century, pay cable was targeting all manner of niche audiences and producing sophisticated, complex dramas that surpassed most risk-averse Hollywood fare: *The Sopranos, Deadwood, The Wire, Weeds, Dexter* and more.

Now, YouTube, Blip.tv and its ilk are changing the rules again. The networks have responded by creating more edgy, long-narrative serial dramas, like *Lost* and *24,* as well as cheap-to-produce, 'unscripted' reality TV: what *Survivor* started in 2000, the contestants of *American Idol* and *Dancing with the Stars* keep alive today, for better or for worse.

If Shakespeare lived today, he couldn't write a better drama than *The Wire,* an epic, morally ambiguous TV show about Baltimore's drug trade. In 2008 Barack Obama said it was his favorite TV show.

Still don't believe the future of TV is on the internet? Start surfing at www.youtube.com, www.blip.tv, www.atom.com, www.joost.com or www.hulu.com.

PAINTING & SCULPTURE Karen Levine

An ocean away from Europe's aristocratic patrons, religious commissions and historic art academies, colonial America was not exactly fertile ground for the visual arts. Few settlers had the time or money to devote to fine art, and the modest portraits and prints of the time reflect their makers' old-world tastes.

It is telling that the best-known American-born painter of the 18th century, Benjamin West, only made his name after going to Rome. When West first visited the Vatican and saw the Apollo Belvedere, he is said to have betrayed his Yankee roots by exclaiming, 'My God! How like it is to a young Mohawk warrior!'

Shaping a National Identity

Artists played a pivotal role in the USA's 19th-century expansion, disseminating images of far-flung territories and reinforcing the call to Manifest Destiny. Thomas Cole and his colleagues in the Hudson River School translated European romanticism to the luminous wild landscapes of upstate New York, while Frederic Remington offered idealized, often stereotypical portraits of the Western frontier. Other artists such as George Caleb Bingham focused on genre paintings or scenes of everyday life and exalted the American virtues of hard work and democracy.

After the Civil War and the advent of industrialization, realism increasingly became prominent. Augustus Saint-Gaudens, a student of Paris' École des Beaux-Arts, and John Quincy Adams Ward produced masterful marbles and bronzes for national monuments. Eastman Johnson painted nostalgic scenes of rural life, as did Winslow Homer, who later became renowned for watercolor seascapes. Perhaps the most daring example of realism was Thomas Eakins' *The Gross Clinic* (1875), which scandalized Philadelphia with its graphic depiction of a surgical procedure.

Keep up with art-world happenings and exhibitions around the country with monthly magazines *ARTnews* (www.artnewsonline.com), *Artforum* (http://artforum.com) and *Art in America* (www.artinamericamagazine.com).

NATIVE AMERICAN ART & CRAFTS

It would take an encyclopedia to cover the myriad artistic traditions of America's tribal peoples, from pre-Columbian rock art to the contemporary multimedia scene.

What ties such diverse traditions together is that Native American art and crafts are not just functional for everyday life, but can also serve ceremonial purposes and have social and religious significance. The patterns and symbols are not merely pretty, but are woven with meanings that provide an intimate window into the heart of Native American peoples. This is as true of Zuni fetish carvings as it is of patterned Navajo rugs, Southwestern pueblo pottery, Sioux beadwork, Inuit sculptures and Cherokee and Hawaiian wood carvings, to name just a few examples.

In addition to preserving their culture, contemporary Native American artists have used sculpture, painting, textiles, film, literature, live performance and more to reflect and critique modernity since the mid-20th century, especially after the civil rights activism of the 1960s and cultural renaissance of the '70s. Contemporary Native American artists' messages are concerned with not just political, environmental and community activism, but also experimenting and engaging with artistic genres, from abstraction to documentary realism. *North American Indian Art* (2004) by David W Penney offers an accessible introduction to the varied artistic traditions of America's diverse indigenous cultures.

By purchasing arts from Native Americans themselves, travelers can have a direct, positive impact on tribal economies, which in part depend on tourist dollars. Many tribes run craft outlets and galleries, usually in the main towns of reservations. The **Indian Arts & Crafts Board** (☎ 202-208-3773, 888-278-3253; www.doi.gov/iacb) publishes a directory of Native American–owned galleries and shops.

An American Avant-Garde

Polite society's objections to Eakins' painting had nothing on the near-riots inspired by New York's Armory Show of 1913. This exhibition introduced the nation to European modernism and changed the face of American art. It showcased impressionism, fauvism and cubism, including the notorious 1912 *Nude Descending a Staircase (No. 2)* by Marcel Duchamp, a French artist who later became an American citizen. In 1917 Duchamp shocked audiences again with *Fountain*. The sculpture – an upended porcelain urinal signed 'R. Mutt' that was Duchamp's first publicly exhibited 'readymade' – was rejected by exhibition organizers on the grounds it wasn't art, but Duchamp's gesture has inspired generations of American artist-provocateurs, from Robert Rauschenberg and Andy Warhol to Sherrie Levine and Bruce Nauman.

Many museums offer free podcasts about current artworks. The best include SFMOMA (www.sfmoma.org), MoMA (http://moma.org), the Walker (www.walkerart.org) and the Met (www.metmuseum.org). Before you visit, load up your iPod!

New York's 1913 Armory Show was merely the first in a series of exhibitions evangelizing the radical aesthetic shifts of European modernism, and it was inevitable that American artists would begin to grapple with what they had seen. Alexander Calder, Joseph Cornell and Isamu Noguchi produced sculptures inspired by surrealism and constructivism; the precisionist paintings of Charles Demuth, Georgia O'Keeffe and Charles Sheeler combined realism with a touch of cubist geometry.

In the 1930s, the Works Progress Administration's (WPA) Federal Art Project, part of FDR's New Deal (p60), commissioned murals, paintings and sculptures for public buildings nationwide. Thomas Hart Benton, Ben Shahn and Grant Wood, among other WPA artists, borrowed from Soviet social realism and Mexican muralists to forge a socially engaged figurative style with regional flavor. African American and female artists also benefited from the nondiscriminatory policies of the WPA, which employed Romare Bearden, Aaron Douglas and other figures associated with the Harlem Renaissance, as well as Lee Krasner and Alice Neel.

A History of African-American Artists: From 1792 to the Present (1993) by Romare Bearden and Harry Henderson: this delightfully anecdotal survey was a labor of love for artist Bearden, a central figure of the Harlem Renaissance.

Abstract Expressionism

In the wake of WWII, American art underwent a sea change at the hands of New York school painters such as Franz Kline, Jackson Pollock and

Mark Rothko. Moved by surrealism's celebration of spontaneity and the unconscious, these artists explored abstraction and its psychological potency through imposing scale and the gestural handling of paint. The movement's 'action painter' camp went extreme; Pollock, for example, made his drip paintings by pouring and splattering pigments over large canvases. Barnett Newman and Rothko exercised more subdued brushwork, creating epic yet ethereal paintings dominated by carefully composed fields of color.

Abstract expressionism is widely considered to be the first truly original school of American art. Intriguingly, art historians have argued that the US used it as a tool for Cold War propaganda. Evidence suggests that the CIA funded traveling exhibitions of abstract expressionist works to promote American individualism and democracy overseas, in the hope that abstraction would serve as an instructive antidote to the realist styles favored by Soviet regimes.

Picasso and American Art (2006), by Michael Fitzgerald and Julia May Boddewyn, describes how American artists reacted when Picasso's provocations landed on these shores, narrating from modernism through pop art and postmodernism.

Art + Commodity = Pop

Once established in America, abstract expressionism reigned supreme; indeed, one of its best-known practitioners, Philip Guston, was attacked by critics when he unveiled his first figurative paintings in 1970.

However, stylistic revolts had begun much earlier, in the 1950s. Most notably, Jasper Johns came to prominence with thickly painted renditions of ubiquitous symbols, including targets and the American flag, while Robert Rauschenberg assembled artworks from comics, ads and even – à la Duchamp – found objects (a mattress, a tire, a stuffed goat). Both artists helped break down traditional boundaries between painting and sculpture, opening the field for pop art in the 1960s.

America's postwar economic boom also influenced pop. Not only did artists embrace representation, they drew inspiration from consumer images such as billboards, product packaging and media icons. Employing mundane mass-production techniques to silkscreen paintings of movie

AMERICAN PHOTOGRAPHY *Karen Levine*

Americans took up photography as soon as news of its invention crossed the Atlantic in 1839, and portrait studios – some on four wheels – began to crop up as entrepreneurs of all stripes (some former painters or miniaturists) exploited the commercial possibilities.

Translated into engravings and published in journals such as *Harper's Weekly*, photographs brought the visages of politicians and celebrities to a fast-growing American public. More accessible than painted portraits, photography also allowed people from all walks of life, in rural settlements and big cities alike, to commission keepsake images of relatives, friends and even recently deceased loved ones.

It was not long before intrepid photographers were lugging their heavy equipment into the American wilderness. Figures such as Carleton Watkins and Timothy O'Sullivan produced awe-inspiring views of the Rocky Mountains and the Sierra Nevada that helped to encourage westward expansion, while Mathew Brady famously documented devastated Civil War battlefields.

Unlike paintings and sculptures, which could rarely be seen by large audiences, photographs were easily and inexpensively reproduced in books, magazines and as picture postcards. As it became a ubiquitous part of popular culture, photography contributed greatly to Americans' understanding of their shifting social and political landscape.

Modern American photographers have influenced historic events while advancing the medium as an art form. Lewis Hine's and Jacob Riis' early-20th-century scenes of poverty are crucial to our understanding of social injustices of the time, as are Walker Evans and Dorothea Lange's portraits of Depression-era poverty and Joe Rosenthal and Thérèse Bonney's images of WWII battles.

Other celebrated modern American photographers worth seeking out images by include Edward Weston, Ansel Adams, Diane Arbus, William Eggleston and Robert Frank.

stars and Coke bottles, Andy Warhol helped topple the myth of the solitary artist laboring heroically in the studio. Roy Lichtenstein combined news print's humble Benday dots with the representational conventions of comics. Other prominent pop artists include James Rosenquist, Ed Ruscha and Wayne Thiebaud.

Minimalism & Beyond

What became known as minimalism shared pop's interest in mass production, but all similarities ended there. Like the abstract expressionists, artists such as Donald Judd, Agnes Martin and Robert Ryman eschewed representational subject matter; their cool, reductive works of the 1960s and '70s were often arranged in gridded compositions and fabricated from industrial materials.

Outrageous and thought-provoking, *The Guerrilla Girls' Bedside Companion to the History of Western Art* (1998) aims to throttle 'the white male stronghold over the art world' with 'a colorful reinterpretation of classic and modern art.'

Meanwhile, Sol LeWitt was busy theorizing the related strand of conceptualism, arguing that the idea behind an artwork was more important than the object itself. Robert Irwin and James Turrell explored the realm of perception through spare, dematerialized installations of light, while Eva Hesse, Robert Morris, Richard Serra and Richard Tuttle lent their sculptures a sense of impermanence through malleable materials such as latex, fabric, sheet metal and wire.

In many ways, minimalism aimed to critique the gallery context and undermine the status of art as commodity. This was perhaps most dramatically demonstrated by land artists Walter De Maria, Betty Beaumont and Robert Smithson, who created immense environmental earthworks across America that no one could buy or sell.

The Contemporary Scene

By the 1980s, civil rights, feminism and AIDS activism had made inroads in visual culture; artists not only voiced political dissent through their work but embraced a range of once-marginalized media, from textiles and graffiti to video, sound and performance. The decade also ushered in the so-called Culture Wars, which commenced with tumult over photographs by Robert Mapplethorpe and Andres Serrano. In 1998, the Supreme Court ruled that the National Endowment for the Arts could withhold funding from artists violating 'general standards of decency and respect for the beliefs and values of the American public.'

Looking for a carrot museum, a gallery of monster toys or a survey of restroom hand dryers? Find these and more at the Museum of Online Museums (www.coudal.com/moom).

Throughout this firestorm and beyond, American artists have continued to innovate – and not just domestically. In 2008 the Whitney Biennial – originally conceived as a show of Americans, for Americans – advertised that it would show 'where American art stands today,' to which a *New York Times* critic responded: '[W]e basically already know. A lot of new art stands today in the booths of international art fairs.'

Many of the best American artists working today are as well known abroad as they are on home soil. Several worthy of attention: painters Jeff Koons, Barry McGee and Nancy Spero; sculptors Robert Gober and Kiki Smith; sculptor and filmmaker Matthew Barney; video and multimedia artists Doug Aitken, Barbara Kruger, Tony Oursler and Bill Viola; photographers Tina Barney and Cindy Sherman; and installation artists Ann Hamilton, Jenny Holzer, Mike Kelley and Kara Walker.

THEATER

American theater is a three-act play of sentimental entertainment, classic revivals and urgent social commentary. From the beginning, Broadway musicals (www.livebroadway.com) have aspired to be 'don't-miss-this-show!' tourist attractions. Considering that Broadway sells 12 million tickets a year, they've apparently succeeded. Independent theater arrived in the

1920s and '30s, with the Little Theatre Movement, which emulated progressive European theater and developed into today's 'off-Broadway' scene. Always struggling and scraping, and mostly surviving, the country's 1500 nonprofit regional theaters are breeding grounds for new plays and foster new playwrights. Some also develop Broadway-bound productions, while others sponsor festivals dedicated to the Bard himself, William Shakespeare (see the boxed text, p1065).

Eugene O'Neill – the first major US playwright, and still widely considered the best – put American drama on the map with his magnificent trilogy *Mourning Becomes Electra* (1931), which sets a tragic Greek myth in post–Civil War New England. Other frequently revived works of his are *The Iceman Cometh* (1946) and the autobiographical *Long Day's Journey into Night* (1956).

Critic Tyler Green's blog Modern Art Notes (www.artsjournal.com/man) offers a smart, opinionated roundup of all the latest art-world news, from the joyful to the scandalous.

After WWII, American playwrights joined the nationwide artistic renaissance. Two of the most famous were Arthur Miller, who wrote *Death of a Salesmen* (1949) and *The Crucible* (1953), and the prolific Southerner Tennessee Williams, who wrote *The Glass Menagerie* (1945), *A Streetcar Named Desire* (1947) and *Cat on a Hot Tin Roof* (1955). Meanwhile, another Southerner, Lillian Hellman (*Toys in the Attic,* 1963), tackled the provocative social issues of feminism, class privilege, racism and homosexuality. All of these plays, and more, have been adapted into films.

As in Europe, American theater in the 1960s was marked by absurdism and the avant-garde. Few were more scathing than Edward Albee, who started provoking bourgeois sensibilities with *Who's Afraid of Virginia Woolf?* (1962). Neil Simon arrived at around the same time; his ever-popular comedies kept Broadway humming for 40 years, but it was his Jewish American drama *Lost in Yonkers* (1991) that won the Pulitzer Prize.

In the amusing documentary *OT: Our Town* (2002), inner-city students in Los Angeles turn Thornton Wilder's hoary chestnut inside-out and learn that, sometimes, theater really can make a difference.

Emerging in the 1970s, other prominent, active American dramatists include David Mamet (*Glengarry Glen Ross,* 1984), Sam Shepard (*Buried Child,* 1978) and innovative 'concept musical' composer Stephen Sondheim (*Sweeney Todd,* 1979). August Wilson (*Fences,* 1985) created a monumental 10-play 'Pittsburgh Cycle' dissecting 20th-century African American life. Christopher Durang (*Sister Mary Ignatius Explains It All for You,* 1979) is an absurdist playwright of pop-culture parodies.

Today, American theater is evolving in its effort to remain a relevant communal experience in an age of ever-isolating media. One-person shows, such as *Bridge & Tunnel* (2004) by Sarah Jones, are increasingly popular. Hip-hop theater is a growing, if eclectic, phenomena, merging diverse aesthetics. Meanwhile, young playwrights like Suzan-Lori Parks (*Topdog/Underdog,* 2001), whose *365 Plays/365 Days* (2006) became a year-long play cycle unfolding across the country, keep experimenting.

For updates on the US regional theater scene, check out *American Theatre* (www.tcg.org) magazine; its website provides links to theater events and festivals nationwide.

DANCE

America fully embraced dance in the 20th century. New York City has always been the epicenter for dance innovation and the home of many premier dance companies, but every major city supports resident and touring troupes, both ballet and modern.

Ballet

Modern ballet is said to have begun with Russian-born choreographer George Balanchine's *Apollo* (1928) and *Prodigal Son* (1929). With these, Balanchine invented the 'plotless ballet' – in which he choreographed the inner structure of music, not a pantomimed story – and thereby created a new, modern vocabulary of ballet movement. In 1934, Balanchine founded the School of American Ballet; in 1948 he founded the New York City Ballet, turning it into one of the world's foremost ballet companies. Jerome Robbins took over that company in 1983, after achieving fame choreographing huge Broadway musicals, such as *West Side Story* (1957). Broadway remains an important venue for dance today. National companies elsewhere, like San Francisco's Lines Ballet, keep evolving contemporary ballet. **Dance** (www.dancemagazine.com) is an excellent resource for contemporary ballet.

Modern Dance

The pioneer of modern dance, Isadora Duncan, didn't find success until she began performing in Europe at the turn of the 20th century. Basing her ideas on ancient Greek myths and concepts of beauty, she challenged the strictures of classical ballet and sought to make dance an intense form of self-expression.

Founded in 1915, Los Angeles–based Denishawn was the nation's leading modern-dance school, and its most famous and influential student was Martha Graham. She founded the Martha Graham School for Contemporary Dance in 1926 after moving to New York, and many of today's major American choreographers developed under her tutelage. In her long career she choreographed more than 140 works and developed a new dance technique, now taught worldwide, aimed at expressing inner emotion and dramatic narrative. Her most famous work was *Appalachian Spring* (1944).

Merce Cunningham, Paul Taylor and Twyla Tharp succeeded Graham as leading exponents of modern dance; they all have companies that are active today. In the 1960s and '70s, Cunningham explored abstract expressionism in movement, collaborating famously with musician John Cage. Taylor experimented with everyday movements and expressions, while Tharp is known for incorporating pop music, jazz and ballet.

Another student of Martha Graham, Alvin Ailey, was part of the post-WWII flowering of African American culture. He made his name with *Revelations* (1960), two years after he founded the still-lauded Alvin Ailey American Dance Theater in New York City.

Other celebrated postmodern choreographers include Mark Morris and Bill T Jones. Beyond New York, San Francisco, Los Angeles, Chicago, Minneapolis and Philadelphia are noteworthy for modern dance.

The film *Ballet Russes* (2005) is a warm remembrance, told by the dancers, of this revolutionary troupe and how they changed ballet and then introduced it – and Balanchine – to America.

Carolyn Brown describes dancing with Merce Cunningham and rubbing elbows with John Cage and other artistic lions of the 1950s and '60s avant-garde in *Chance and Circumstance: Twenty Years with Cage and Cunningham* (2007).

ARCHITECTURE

In the 21st century, computer technology and innovations in materials and manufacturing allow for curving, asymmetrical buildings once considered impossible, if not inconceivable. Architects are being challenged to 'go green,' and the creativity unleashed is riveting, transforming skylines and changing the way Americans think about their built environments. The public's architectural taste remains conservative, but never mind: avant-garde 'starchitects' are revising urban landscapes with radical visions that the nation will catch up with – one day.

The Colonial Period

Perhaps the only lasting indigenous influence on American architecture has been the adobe dwellings of the Southwest. In the 17th and 18th centuries, Spanish colonists incorporated elements of what they called the Native American *pueblo* (village). It reappeared in late-19th and early-20th-century architecture in both the Southwest's pueblo revival style and Southern California's mission revival style.

Elsewhere until the 20th century, immigrant Americans mainly adopted English and continental European styles and followed their trends. For most early colonists in the eastern US, architecture served necessity rather than taste, while the would-be gentry aped grander English homes, a period well preserved in Williamsburg, Virginia (p367).

In 2007, the American Institute of Architects (AIA) asked average US citizens to name their 150 favorite buildings. To their dismay, the list (www.aia150.org) is packed with nostalgic kitsch and tourist attractions.

After the Revolutionary War, the nation's leaders wanted a style befitting the new republic and adopted neoclassicism. Virginia's capitol (p363), designed by Thomas Jefferson, was modeled on an ancient Roman temple, and Jefferson's own private estate, Monticello (p373), sports a Romanesque rotunda.

Professional architect Charles Bulfinch helped develop the more monumental federal style, which paralleled the English Georgian style. The grandest example is the US Capitol in Washington, DC (p326), which became a model for state legislatures nationwide. As they moved into the 19th century, Americans, mirroring English fashions, gravitated toward the Greek and Gothic revival styles, still seen today in many churches and college campuses.

Building the Nation

Meanwhile, small-scale architecture was revolutionized by 'balloon-frame' construction: a light frame of standard-milled timber joined with cheap nails. Easy and economical, balloon-frame stores and houses made possible swift settlement of the expanding West and, later, the surreal proliferation of the suburbs. Though disposable and mass-produced, balloon-frame houses brought home-ownership within reach of average middle-class families, making real the enduring American Dream.

After the Civil War, influential American architects studied at Paris' École des Beaux-Arts, and American buildings began to show increasing refinement and confidence. Major examples of the beaux-arts style include Richard Morris Hunt's Biltmore Estate in North Carolina (p401) and New York's Public Library (p164).

In San Francisco and other cities across America, Victorian architecture appeared as the 19th century progressed. Among well-to-do classes, larger and fancier private houses added ever more adornments: balconies, turret, towers, ornately painted trim and intricate 'gingerbread' wooden millwork.

In reaction against Victorian opulence, the Arts and Crafts movement arose after 1900 and remained popular until the 1930s. Its modest bungalows, such as the Gamble House in Pasadena, California (p928), featured locally handcrafted wood- and glasswork, ceramic tiles and other artisan details.

As the nation relentlessly expanded westward during the late 19th and early 20th centuries, two prominent female architects emerged. Mary Elizabeth Jane Colter built Harvey Houses for the railroad and also designed some of the iconic tourist lodgings and landmarks at the Grand Canyon, incorporating Native American motifs. Julia Morgan, the first woman architect to receive a diploma from the École des Beaux-Arts, designed over 700 buildings in myriad styles, from California bungalows to grandiose Hearst Castle (p960).

In the 1950s, sprawling middle-class suburbs appeared almost literally overnight. One major housing developer, Levitt and Sons, produced a new four-bedroom house every 16 minutes.

Reaching for the Sky

By the 1850s, internal iron-framed buildings had appeared in Manhattan, and this freed up urban architectural designs, especially after the advent of Otis hydraulic elevators in the 1880s. The Chicago School of architecture transitioned beyond beaux-arts style to produce the skyscraper – considered the first truly 'modern' architecture, and America's most prominent architectural contribution to the world at that time.

In the 1930s, the influence of art deco – which became instantly popular in the US after the Paris Exposition of 1925 – meant that urban high-rises soared, becoming fitting symbols of America's technical achievements, grand aspirations, commerce and an affinity for modernism. Design emphasized the structural grid and surfaces of concrete, glass and steel. Remarkable examples of art deco skyscrapers include New York City's Chrysler Building (p161) and Empire State Building (p161). Art deco simultaneously appeared nationwide

MASTER OF THE PRAIRIES

Initially an apprentice to modernist architect Louis Sullivan's firm in Chicago, Frank Lloyd Wright (1867–1959) was one of the 20th century's great visionaries.

Working mainly on private houses, Wright abandoned traditional architectural elements and historical references, making each building a unique form characterized by strong horizontal lines and overhanging eaves. Wright called them 'prairie houses,' though invariably they were built in the suburbs, especially in Oak Park, IL (p587). Wright also pioneered radiant panel heating, indirect lighting, double glazing and air-conditioning.

Wright later evolved the concept of 'organic architecture,' in which building designs harmonize with the natural environment, as at Fallingwater outside Pittsburgh, PA (p236). Interior spaces flowed openly rather than being divided into rooms, and the inside was connected to the outside rather than being separated by solid walls. Wright was innovative in his use of steel, glass and concrete – structural materials, not applied decoration, provided texture and color.

Today, you can also visit Frank Lloyd Wright's summer home, Taleisin, in southern Wisconsin (p633), and Wright's winter home and architectural school, Taleisin West, in southern Arizona (p842).

in the design of movie houses, train stations, office buildings like in downtown Tulsa, OK, and hotels such as those in Miami's South Beach neighborhood.

Modernism & Beyond

When the Bauhaus school fled the rise of Nazism in Germany, architects such as Walter Gropius and Ludwig Mies van der Rohe brought their pioneering modern designs to American shores. Van der Rohe landed in Chicago, where Louis Sullivan, considered to be the inventor of the modern skyscraper, was already working on a simplified style of architecture in which 'form ever follows function.' This evolved into the International style, which favored glass 'curtain walls' over a steel frame. IM Pei, who designed Cleveland's Rock and Roll Hall of Fame and the Louvre Pyramid in Paris, is considered the last living high-modernist architect in America.

In the mid-20th century, modernism transitioned into America's suburbs, especially in Southern California. Midcentury modern architecture was influenced not only by the organic nature of Frank Lloyd Wright homes (see the boxed text, above) but also the spare, geometric, clean-lined designs of Scandinavia. Post-and-beam construction allowed for walls of sheer glass that gave the illusion of merging indoor and outdoor living spaces. Today, a striking collection of midcentury modern homes and public buildings by Albert Frey, Richard Neutra and other luminaries is found in Palm Springs, CA.

The first true skyscraper is in neither Chicago nor Manhattan but Buffalo, NY: the 13-story Guaranty Building, designed by Louis Sullivan and completed in 1895.

Rejecting modernism's 'ugly boxes' later in the 20th century, postmodernism reintroduced decoration, color, historical references and whimsy. In this, architects like Michael Graves and Philip Johnson took the lead. Another expression of postmodernism is the brash, mimetic architecture of the Las Vegas Strip, which Pritzker Prize–winning architect Robert Venturi held up as the triumphant antithesis of modernism (he sardonically described the latter as 'less is a bore').

Today, aided and abetted by digital tools, architectural design favors the bold and the unique. Leading this plunge into futurama has been Frank Gehry; his Walt Disney Concert Hall in Los Angeles (p920) is but one example. Other notable contemporary architects include Richard Meier (Los Angeles' Getty Center), Thom Mayne (San Francisco's Federal Building) and Daniel Libeskind (San Francisco's Contemporary Jewish Museum and the Denver Art Museum's Hamilton Building). Newly built and expanded museums and public buildings in cities across America also bear witness to this innovative surge in architecture.

Food & Drink

Sara Benson & John Mariani

Ever since Wampanoag tribespeople helped the Pilgrims stave off starvation over the winter of 1620 and brought food to the first Thanksgiving, Americans have mixed myriad food cultures to create their own, based on the rich bounty of the continent. Americans took pride in that bounty, drawing on the seafood of the North Atlantic, Gulf of Mexico and Pacific Ocean; the fertility of Midwest farmlands; and vast Western ranchlands that made beef, pork and chicken everyday staples.

Massive waves of immigrants enriched American gastronomy by adapting foreign ideas to home kitchens, from Italian pizza and German hamburgers to Eastern European borscht, Mexican huevos rancheros and Japanese sushi. Later, a vast market and transportation system made fresh, canned, boxed and frozen foods available to everyone – so much so, it can be argued, that many Americans grew fat (and even obese) on the abundance of fast food and junk food. It is not by accident that phrases such as 'grab a bite,' and 'pick up some takeout' are quintessential American colloquialisms, along with 'road food' and 'the munchies.' Such ideas had the effect of American cooking not being taken seriously by the rest of the world.

Not until the 1960s did food and wine become serious topics for newspapers, magazines and TV, led by a Californian named Julia Child who taught Americans how to cook French food through black-and-white programs broadcast from Boston's public TV station. By the 1970s, everyday folks (and not just hippies) had started turning their attention to issues of organic, natural foods and sustainable agriculture. In the 1980s and '90s, the 'foodie revolution' – choosing 'arugula over iceberg' lettuce, as *Time* magazine put it in 2007 – encouraged entrepreneurs to open restaurants featuring regional American cuisine, from the South to the Pacific Northwest, that would rank with Europe's best.

Roadfood (revised 2005), by intrepid noshers Jane and Michael Stern, ferrets out top-notch local and regional eateries from Maine to Oregon. The authors also maintain a website (www.roadfood.com) with heaps of free listings.

More recently, the 'Slow Food' movement and renewed enthusiasm for eating local, often organically grown fare is a leading trend in American restaurants. The movement, which was arguably started in 1971 by chef Alice Waters at Berkeley's Chez Panisse (p990), continues with First Lady Michelle Obama and her daughters, who have planted an organic garden on the White House lawn. Recently, farmers markets have been popping up all across the country and they're a great place to meet locals and take a big bite out of America's cornucopia of foods, from heritage fruit and vegetables to fresh, savory and sweet regional delicacies.

STAPLES & SPECIALTIES

Americans have such easy access to regional foods that once-unique specialties are now often readily available everywhere: a Bostonian might just as easily have a taco or barbecue ribs for lunch as a Houstonian would eat Maine lobster for dinner.

Usually after a midmorning coffee break, an American worker's lunch hour affords only a sandwich, quick burger or hearty salad. The formal 'business lunch' is more common in big cities like New York, where food is not necessarily as important as the conversation. Many business dinners take place at steakhouses or other splashy restaurants. Most workers have a midafternoon snack – maybe a candy bar, bag of chips or piece of fruit.

Usually early in the evening, Americans settle in to a more substantial weeknight dinner, which, given the workload of so many two-career families, might be takeout (eg pizza or Chinese food) or prepackaged meals cooked in a microwave. Desserts tend toward ice cream, pies and cakes. Some families still cook a traditional Sunday night dinner, when relatives and friends gather for a big feast, or grill outside and go picnicking on weekends.

New York City

Owing to its huge immigrant population and an influx of 47 million tourists annually, New York captures the title of America's greatest restaurant city, hands down. Its diverse neighborhoods serve up authentic Italian food and thin crust–style pizza, all manner of Asian food, French *haute cuisine* and classic Jewish deli food, from bagels to piled-high pastrami on rye with crunchy pickles. More exotic cuisines are found here as well, from Ethiopian to Slavic. Breakfasts are casual and often on the go; lunch may be from a takeout deli or street vendor; and dinner is often eaten out either at little bistros or among the torrent of new, exciting restaurants that open (and close) weekly in the city. Arthur Schwartz's *New York City Food* (2008), by famous foodie Arthur Schwartz, reveals where to find every NYC specialty, from bagels and pizza to Gray's Papaya juice and cheesecake, and includes more than 100 recipes.

In the 2008 Nathan's Famous Fourth of July International Hot Dog Eating Contest, two-time champion Joey Chestnut stuffed down 64 wieners in less than 11 minutes.

New England

New England's claim to have the nation's best seafood is hard to beat, because the North Atlantic offers up clams, mussels, oysters and huge lobsters, along with shad, bluefish and cod. New Englanders love a good chowder (seafood stew) and a good clambake, an almost ritual meal where the shellfish are buried in a pit fire with corn, chicken, potatoes and sausages. Fried clam fritters and lobster rolls (lobster meat with mayonnaise served in a bread bun) are served throughout the region. There are excellent cheeses made in Vermont, cranberries (a Thanksgiving staple) harvested in Massachusetts and maple syrup from New England's forests. Maine's coast is lined with lobster shacks; baked beans and brown bread are Boston specialties; and Rhode Islanders pour coffee syrup into milk and embrace traditional cornmeal johnnycakes.

Mid-Atlantic

From New York down through Maryland and Virginia, the Middle Atlantic states share a long coastline and a cornucopia of apple, pear and berry farms. New Jersey and New York's Long Island are famous for their spuds (potatoes). Chesapeake Bay's blue crabs are the finest anywhere and Virginia salt-cured 'country-style' hams are served with biscuits. In Philadelphia, you can gorge on 'Philly' cheesesteaks, made with thin, sautéed beef and onions and melted cheese on a bun. In Pennsylvania Dutch country, stop by a farm restaurant for chicken pot pie, noodles and meatloaf-like scrapple. The wines of New York's Finger Lakes, Hudson Valley and Long Island are well worth sampling.

Big Night (1996) is an amusing film about Italian brothers who struggle to run an authentic, refined restaurant on the New Jersey shore in the 1950s, but whose clients want old Italian American favorites.

The South

No region is prouder of its food culture than the South, which has a long history of mingling Anglo, French, African, Spanish and Native American foods in dishes such as slow-cooked barbecue, which has as many meaty and saucy variations as there are towns in the South. Southern fried chicken is crisp outside and moist inside. In Florida, dishes made with alligator, shrimp and conch incorporate hot chili peppers and tropical spices. Breakfasts are as big as can be, and treasured dessert recipes tend to produce big layer cakes or pies made with pecans, bananas and citrus. Light, fluffy hot biscuits are served well buttered, and grits (ground corn cooked to a porridge-like consistency) are a passion among Southerners, as are cool mint julep cocktails.

Louisiana's legendary cuisine is influenced by colonial French and Spanish cultures, Afro-Caribbean cooking and Choctaw Indians' traditions. Cajun food is found in the bayou country and marries native spices such as sassafras and chili peppers with provincial French cooking. Creole food is more urban, and centered in New Orleans, where dishes such as shrimp remoulade, crabmeat ravigote, crawfish étouffée and beignets are ubiquitous. Louisiana's most famous dishes include gumbo, a roux-based stew of chicken and shellfish, or sausage and often okra; jambalaya, a rice-based dish with tomatoes, sausage and shrimp; and blackened catfish. Classic po'boy sandwiches are stuffed with everything from oysters to fried shrimp. Try coffee made with chicory, or join the locals swilling famous cocktails like the Sazerac or Ramos gin fizz.

New Mexico is the only US state with an official state question: 'Red or green?' It refers to chili sauces; if you want both, ask for your enchiladas 'Christmas style.'

Midwest

In the Midwest you eat big and with gusto. Portions are huge – this is farm country, where people need sustenance to get their work done. So you might start off the day with eggs, bacon and toast; have a double cheeseburger and potato salad for lunch; and fork into steak and baked potatoes for dinner – all washed down with a cold brew, often one of the growing numbers of microbrews. Barbecue is very popular here, especially in Kansas City, St Louis and Chicago. Chicago is also an ethnically diverse culinary center, with some of the country's top restaurants. One of the best places to sample Midwestern foods is at a county fair, which offers everything from bratwurst to fried dough to grilled corn on the cob. Elsewhere at diners and family restaurants, you'll taste the varied influences of Eastern European, Scandinavian, Latino and Asian immigrants, especially in the cities.

Southwest

Southwestern food culture is defined by two ethnic groups: the Spanish and Mexicans, who controlled territories from Texas to California until well into the 19th century. While there is little actual Spanish food today, the Spanish brought cattle to Mexico, which the Mexicans adapted to their own corn-and-chili-based gastronomy to make tacos, tortillas, enchiladas, burritos, chimichangas and other dishes made of corn or flour pancakes filled with everything from chopped meat and poultry to beans. Steaks and barbecue are always favorites on Southwestern menus, and beer is the drink of choice for dinner and a night out. For a cosmopolitan foodie scene, visit Las Vegas, where top chefs from NYC, LA and even Paris are sprouting satellite restaurants.

Bottle Shock (2008) is a nostalgic romp through the early days of winemaking in California's Sonoma and Napa Valleys, ending with the triumph of California wines over the French at the Judgment of Paris in 1976.

California

Owing to its vastness and variety of microclimates, California is truly America's cornucopia for fruits and vegetables, and a gateway to myriad Asian markets. The state's natural resources are overwhelming, with wild salmon, Dungeness crab and oysters from the ocean; robust produce year-round; and artisanal products such as cheese, bread, olive oil, wine and chocolate. Starting in the 1970s and '80s, star chefs such as Alice Waters and Wolfgang Puck pioneered 'California cuisine' by incorporating the best local ingredients into simple yet delectable preparations. The influx of Asian immigrants, especially after the Vietnam War, enriched the state's urban food cultures with Chinatowns, Koreatowns and Japantowns, along

'ORGANIC' VERSUS 'NATURAL' FOODS

The US Department of Agriculture defines 'organic' and 'natural' according to distinct standards. For crops, 'organic' means they were grown without the use of conventional pesticides, artificial fertilizers, human waste or sewage sludge. It also specifies that the crops must have been processed without being irradiated or having food additives. For animals, they must have been reared without routine use of antibiotics or growth hormones, and have not been genetically modified. 'Natural' products are those that have been minimally processed and contain no artificial colorings or preservatives.

with huge enclaves of Mexican Americans who maintain their own culinary traditions across the state. Global fusion restaurants are another hallmark of California's cuisine scene.

Pacific Northwest

The cuisine of the Pacific Northwest region draws on the traditions of the local tribes of Native Americans, whose diets traditionally centered on game, seafood – especially salmon – and foraged mushrooms, fruits and berries. Seattle spawned the modern international coffeehouse craze with Starbucks; and the beers and wines from both Washington and Oregon have come up to international standards, especially Pinot Noirs and Rieslings.

Hawaii

In the middle of the Pacific Ocean, Hawaii is rooted in a Polynesian food culture that takes full advantage of locally caught fish such as mahimahi, 'opakapaka, 'ono and 'ahi. Traditional luau celebrations include cooking kalua pig in an underground pit layered with hot stones and ti leaves. Hawaii's contemporary cuisine incorporates fresh, island-grown produce and borrows liberally from the islands' many Asian and European immigrant groups. This also happens to be the only state to grow coffee commercially; 100% Kona beans from the Big Island have the most gourmet cachet.

DRINKS

Americans are far from teetotalers. While alcohol sales in the USA have soared to record highs in recent years, only about 20% of Americans drink wine on a regular basis; the majority of drinkers still prefer beer. Beer is more than a thirst-quencher; it is a social beverage that's almost essential for a good picnic, a day at the beach or a 'tailgate party' held outside a sports stadium before the game.

Jack Daniels whiskey is distilled in the town of Lynchburg in Moore County, Tennessee, which has been a dry county since Prohibition days.

After all, it's understandable: 19th-century German immigrants developed ways to make beer in vast quantities and to deliver it all over America. Today 80% of domestic beer comes from the Midwest. Craft beer production is rising meteorically, accounting for 6% of the domestic market in 2008. Over 1500 craft breweries across the USA now churn out over 8.5 million barrels each year, with Vermont boasting the most microbreweries per capita: one for every 33,000 residents.

That said, Americans are still drinking more wine than ever and the nation is the world's 4th largest producer of wine, behind Italy, France and Spain. Today almost 90% of US wine comes from California; and Oregon, Washington and New York wines have achieved international status. Scores of varietal grapes are used to make wines, all based on imported root stocks.

Rye, whiskey, gin and vodka are also crafted in the USA. Bourbon, made from corn, is the only native spirit and traditionally is made in Kentucky. American cocktails created at bars in the late 19th and early 20th centuries include such long-standing classics as the martini and the Manhattan. The tequila-based margarita came from Tijuana, Mexico. The current fashion is for mojitos (rum cocktails with muddled mint leaves), born in Cuba. For a comforting nightcap, Irish coffee is a mix of hot coffee with Irish whiskey and whipped cream.

Tap water in the USA is safe to drink. Most nonalcoholic drinks are quite sugary and served over ice, from Southern-style iced 'sweet tea' and

WINE'S BRAVE NEW WORLD

From the moment Europeans arrived in the New World they made wine, first from wild native grapes with names like Scuppernong, Catawba, Concord and Niagara, then from imported European varietals. Spanish missionaries brought vines to California in the 16th century.

By the 19th century there were flourishing vineyards in California, as well as in New York, Missouri and Ohio. In fact, when the phylloxera bug devastated vineyards throughout Europe in the late 19th century, phylloxera-resistant American vines were grafted onto European stocks to replenish the wine industries in France, Spain, Italy and Germany.

The 1920s Prohibition era outlawed alcohol in the USA, effectively putting the American wine industry out of business until Prohibition was repealed in 1933. Afterward, vineyards devoted themselves to producing mediocre wine in bulk, especially 'jug wines' in big bottles that held a liter or more.

Not until the 1960s did California wineries begin to make wines that could compete with Europe's best. Based on varietals like Cabernet Sauvignon, Chardonnay, Pinot Noir and Riesling, American wines were often more intense in taste and higher in alcohol than their Old World counterparts. In 1976 at the Judgment of Paris, after blind tastings by wine critics, California vintages beat the French, much to the world's shock.

The success of California winemaking, especially in the Napa and Sonoma Valleys, brought improvements in technology and viticulture that marked the production of wines elsewhere. Today wine is made in all 50 states. Of course, not all *terroir* (soil) is created equal. The West Coast is the pinnacle of US winemaking, with wineries found throughout California, Washington and Oregon. Some surprisingly excellent wines are being made in the Great Lakes region (especially New York and Michigan) and in the Hill Country of Texas, too.

If you long to visit unpretentious, off-the-beaten-path wine countries in California, try these:

- **Amador County** (www.amadorwine.com) – rural Sierra Foothills wineries identify with Zinfandel, but also a dizzying array of sun-loving Italian and southern French varietals
- **Lodi** (www.lodiwine.com) – meet multigeneration family vintners specializing in old-growth Zinfandel vines
- **Mendocino County** (www.truemendocinowine.com) – just outside Napa and Sonoma, follow back roads through the Anderson Valley to find stellar Syrah and Reisling
- **Paso Robles** (www.pasowine.com) – California's fastest-growing wine region makes outstanding Cabernet Sauvignon, Syrah and Zinfandel; look for Chardonnay in the nearby Edna Valley
- **Santa Barbara County** (www.sbcountywines.com) – made famous by the movie *Sideways* (2004), the Santa Maria and Santa Ynez Valleys produce top-rated Pinot Noir
- **Santa Cruz Mountains** (www.scmwa.com) – some of California's oldest and most revered winemakers are open to the public only on quarterly 'passport' days

Wine Spectator (www.winespectator.com) offers a comprehensive online database of wine reviews for subscribers, and free blogs, archived articles, tasting reports and critics' top picks lists.

lemonade to quintessential American soft drinks (called 'soda' or 'pop') such as Coca-Cola, Pepsi and Dr Pepper. Retro and nouveau soft-drink labels found on restaurant menus and in grocery stores include Jones Soda, made with cane sugar instead of corn syrup, and Dr Brown's, which originated at NYC's delicatessens.

CELEBRATIONS

The late historian Arthur Schlesinger Jr noted that after just a single generation, the children of American immigrants lost nearly all ties to their ethnicities – except with regard to food culture.

Thanksgiving may be the only holiday (held the last Thursday in November) where most Americans would agree on the menu – roast turkey, stuffing, mashed potatoes, cranberry sauce, perhaps pumpkin pie – but even then appetizers, side dishes and desserts might be Latino, African or Hawaiian.

Americans celebrate their ethnic heritage on other holidays in many ways. At Christmas, Italian Americans may, by tradition, serve fish the night before and a pasta dish on Christmas Day. At Easter many Americans will serve roast ham, while Greek Americans will serve lamb. Oddly, on St Patrick's Day Americans traditionally serve corned beef and cabbage, which is practically unknown in Ireland. Traditional good-luck New Year's Day dishes in America include lentils for Italians, cabbage for Irish, black-eyed peas and rice for Southerners, and sauerkraut for the Pennsylvania Dutch.

Other holidays may be observed only by certain groups. Jews celebrate Passover seder meals with matzoh ball soup and Hanukkah with fried foods such as potato latkes. African Americans celebrate a heritage festival in December called Kwanzaa with the foods of Africa, the Caribbean and the US South. The lunar New Year (held in late January or early February) is a gourmet feast day for Chinese Americans, while Italians hold street festivals serving fried seafood, sausage sandwiches and pastries in honor of their favorite saints.

Far less formal are national holidays such as Memorial Day, the Fourth of July and Labor Day, which denote the beginning, middle and end of summer. Barbecues and beer predominate the festivities, with large gatherings of family and friends in backyards or parks for hamburgers, hot dogs, and ribs with corn on the cob, potato salad and fruit pies.

TOP PICKS: US FOOD & DRINK FESTIVALS

Every year, you can catch Americans chowing down at hundreds of regional food (and beer and wine) festivals across the USA. Here are just a few of our faves:

- **American Royal Barbecue** (Kansas City, MO; p667)
- **Breaux Bridge Crawfish Festival** (Breaux Bridge, LA; p491)
- **Kentucky Bourbon Festival** (Bardstown, KY; p439)
- **Maine Lobster Festival** (Rockland, ME; p309)
- **National Buffalo Wing Festival** (Buffalo, NY; p205)
- **Newport Seafood & Wine Festival (**Newport, OR; p1069)
- **Spam Jam** (Waikiki, HI; p1112)
- **Taste of Chicago** (Chicago, IL; p577)
- **Terlingua International Chili Cook-off** (Terlingua, TX; p748)
- **Castroville Artichoke Festival** (Castroville, CA; p963)

TIPPING

Service is almost never included on restaurant bills in the USA. A standard tip on the bill (to which taxes have already been added) is 15% for good service or 20% for excellent service. A restaurant *may* add a service charge for parties of six or more. If you do receive poor service, by all means bring it to the manager's attention and tip below 15%. But only withhold a tip for outrageously bad service.

The biggest, most expensive parties by far are wedding receptions, which in recent decades have become incredibly sumptuous, often held at a restaurant or banquet hall, with copious amounts of food and drink – and of course, the multitiered wedding cake. Traditionally, the bride and groom feed the first bite of cake to each other by hand. In Latino communities, *quinceañera* (coming-of-age parties) in honor of girls' fifteenth birthdays can also be incredibly lavish affairs.

WHERE TO EAT & DRINK

Much of the USA is blanketed with lookalike chain restaurants. Most Americans outside of major cities do not often eat out at expensive restaurants, and consider one of the scores of family-style chain restaurants– TGI Friday's, Denny's or Applebee's, for example – a more reasonable alternative. Such places are dependable and consistent, the prices moderate and the setting casual, but the food rarely rises above mediocre.

A much better idea: ask locals for their recommendations to find the best independent neighborhood restaurants around, maybe one that specializes in barbecue, fresh seafood or pancakes. These spots often have an authentic atmosphere, warmer hospitality and higher-quality food, which all give a truer sense of local color and American culture than chain eateries ever could. On the other hand, the few remaining cafeteria-style buffet chains like Piccadilly in the South can also provide decent regional food at a very fair price and allow you to mix with the locals.

It's easy and fast to make restaurant reservations for free online at www.opentable.com, which serves over 10,000 restaurants in all 50 states, including 18 US metro areas.

The best breakfasts in America – often amazingly good value – are found at diners, coffee shops, cafés and some family restaurants. These all tend to open early and close late, which makes them a good stop for a light meal or snack throughout the day. The most expensive breakfasts are from hotel room service, and they're rarely very tasty; avoid them.

A bar-and-grill may be little more than a tavern that serves modest food or, in an upscale version, a trendy brewpub or restaurant that serves excellent American fare and has a good beer and wine list. Very often these have bars where solo diners can eat well and feel quite comfortable doing so. For those with heartier appetites, the all-you-can-eat buffet is a cultural phenomenon: for a set price you can revisit the buffet as many times as you like – until you're either completely stuffed or just too plain embarrassed to eat any more.

Chowhound (www.chowhound.com) is 'for those who live to eat.' Come here to ask locals about VIP issues – like finding the tastiest taco trucks in San Francisco.

In bigger cities you'll find high-end restaurants with prix-fixe menus and European-style service that lets you linger romantically over your espresso and crème brûlée. But be prepared to pay for it. That said, these days the weak US dollar makes the occasional foray into a posh restaurant far less expensive than in cities like London, Paris and Tokyo. If you go for it, always call to make a reservation (or ask your hotel concierge to do so), ask if there is a dress code, and be prepared to accept a very early or quite late table at popular star-chefs' restaurants.

For typical restaurant opening hours, see p1136, and for average meal costs, see p1141.

Quick Eats

Eating hot dogs or pretzels from city street carts or tacos and barbecue from roadside trucks carries a small risk that you might pick up some nasty bacteria, but generally fast food tends to be safe and vendors are usually supervised by the local health department. At festivals and county fairs, you can take your pick from cotton candy, corn dogs, candy apples, funnel cakes, chocolate-covered frozen bananas and plenty of tasty regional specialties. Farmers markets often have more wholesome, affordable prepared foods.

Approximately two-thirds of adult Americans (and 32% of children) are overweight. That's up from 47% in the late 1970s.

VEGETARIANS & VEGANS

Vegetarianism and veganism once carried something of a cult-like onus in the USA, but those days are long gone. Indeed, some of the most highly regarded American restaurants cater exclusively to vegetarians and vegans, for example, Greens (p983), run by the San Francisco Zen Center. In a 2006 nationwide poll, the Vegetarian Resource Group found that fewer than 3% of Americans are completely vegetarian, but almost 10% of the population never eats red meat.

Even many fast-food eateries now offer vegetarian options, perhaps a fruit-yogurt parfait or vegetable salad, and nonmeat-eaters can do very well in Asian restaurants. At upscale restaurants, daytime menus offer lighter soups, salads and pastas, and most will make a vegetarian dinner plate upon request.

If you dine at a nonvegetarian restaurant that claims to have vegetarian or vegan options, check that the food has been made without animal-based fats or broths. Do not assume that the waiter or even the cook knows all of the variations.

Vegetarian and vegan restaurants abound in major US cities, though not always in small towns and rural areas away from the coasts. Eateries that are exclusively vegetarian or vegan are noted throughout this book using the Ⓥ icon. To find more vegetarian and vegan restaurants, browse the online directory at www.happycow.net.

DOS & DON'TS

Americans are pretty casual even about fine dining, but they still have their customs and rules:

- If invited to dinner, take flowers or a bottle of wine as a gift, though your host may not serve the wine you have brought that evening.
- Cell phones are a big annoyance in restaurants, so excuse yourself and step outside to make or take a call.
- Many cities and states outlaw smoking in restaurants and bars, so don't smoke inside unless there's an ashtray on your table.
- If you have your heart set on going to a trendy restaurant, try to reserve a table for before 6pm or after 8:30pm, and you'll have a much better chance of getting in. Also, hotel concierges can work wonders in getting reservations on short notice for you.
- Most restaurants will not hold reservations more than 15 minutes. If you're running late, call to let them know.
- Expect restaurant wine lists to be marked up 100% to 300% above retail shop prices.
- Always check your bill for questionable charges. Mistakes, intentional and otherwise, do occur.
- Ask for a 'doggie bag' to take leftovers home with you, even at haute restaurants. Americans hate to waste food and portions tend to be large.

BAGELS: THE REAL THING

Bagels are a big deal in the USA, but if you buy a stale one in a random Midwestern supermarket you may find yourself wondering what all the fuss about. It's just a bread roll with a hole in the middle, right? But if you get your hands on a genuine NYC bagel, like those made by **H & H Bagels** (☎ 212-595-8003; 2239 Broadway; www.hhbagels.com), you might just find bakery heaven.

A true bagel, brought to this country by Jewish immigrants from Eastern Europe, is made of just flour, water, salt – and sometimes barley malt for a little sweetness – and often is still rolled by hand. It is boiled, then baked, making it slightly crisp on the outside and deliciously dense and chewy inside.

Traditional bagel flavors include plain, poppy seed, sesame seed, onion, pumpernickel and egg, but modern-day bakeries often add more unusual ingredients such as blueberries or sundried tomatoes. Bagels are sliced in half, sometimes toasted and then spread with cream cheese or butter, or occasionally topped with lox (brine-cured salmon).

How good are real bagels? They've even been shipped to the international space station (poppy seed was the astronauts' chosen flavor).

EATING WITH KIDS

The US restaurant industry seems built on family-style service: children are not just accepted almost everywhere, but usually are encouraged by special children's menus with smaller portions and lower prices. In some restaurants children under a certain age even eat for free. Restaurants usually provide high chairs and booster seats. Some restaurants may also offer children crayons and puzzles, and occasionally live performances by cartoon-like characters.

Restaurants without children's menus don't necessarily discourage kids, though higher-end restaurants might; always call ahead. You can ask if the kitchen will make a smaller order of a dish (also ask how much it will cost), or if they will split a normal-size main dish among two plates for the kids. Chinese, Mexican and Italian restaurants seem to be the best bet for finicky young eaters.

For more advice on traveling with kids, see p1136.

HABITS & CUSTOMS

Americans tend to eat early at restaurants and at home, so don't be surprised to find a restaurant half full at noon or 5:30pm. In smaller towns, it may be hard to find anywhere to eat after 8:30pm or 9pm. Dinner parties for adults usually begin around 6:30pm or 7pm with cocktails followed by a buffet or sit-down meal. If invited to dinner, it's polite to be prompt: ideally, you should plan to arrive within 15 minutes of the designated time.

Americans are notoriously informal in their dining manners, although they will usually wait until everyone is served before eating. They also eat with their fork in their right hand, after picking it up with, then switching it from, their left. Many foods are eaten with the fingers, and an entire piece of bread may be buttered and eaten all at once. Beer bottles are not uncommon on a dinner table and iced tea is more typical at lunch than beer or wine.

DUI (driving under the influence) is taken very seriously in the USA (see p1165). Designating a sober driver who doesn't drink has become widespread practice among groups of friends consuming alcohol at restaurants, bars, nightclubs and parties.

COOKING COURSES

Even more Americans are realizing that they want to be able to cook better (or just plain cook). Cooking shows have become popular on TV, and cooking classes taught by culinary professionals are now offered at some high-end cookware shops such as **Williams-Sonoma** (www.williams-sonoma.com) and **Sur la Table** (www.surlatable.com).

Cooking schools that offer courses for enthusiastic amateur chefs on vacation include the following (though this list is by no means exhaustive):

California Sushi Academy (www.sushi-academy.com) Apprentice in the art of finessing raw fish in Los Angeles.

Central Market Cooking School (www.centralmarket.com) Heat things up in the kitchen in major Texas cities.

Chopping Block Cooking School (www.thechoppingblock.net) Master knife skills and meet the 'Wine Goddess' in Chicago.

Cookin' Cajun Cooking School (www.cookincajun.com) Feast on Cajun and Creole delicacies in New Orleans.

Cook's World (www.cooksworld.net) Try rustic breadbaking or street-food recipes from around the world in Seattle.

Heat and Spice Cooking School (http://heatandspice.com) Vegetarian, grilling, New Orleans–style, Floribbean and world cuisine classes in Chicago.

International Culinary Center (www.internationalculinarycenter.com) Hosts the French Culinary Institute and Italian Culinary Academy in New York City.

Natural Gourmet Cookery School (www.naturalgourmetschool.com) Focuses on vegetarian and healthy 'flexitarian' cooking in NYC.

New School of Cooking (www.newschoolofcooking.com) Learn ethnic cooking from around the world in Los Angeles County.

Santa Fe School of Cooking (www.santafeschoolofcooking.com) Unlock the chili-spiced secrets of Southwestern cuisine in New Mexico.

Tante Marie's Cooking School (www.tantemarie.com) Sharing farmers market recipes and passing on world culinary traditions in San Francisco.

Epicurious (www.epicurious.com) and the Food Network (www.foodnetwork.com) have vast databases of recipes from popular cooking magazines, TV shows and some of the USA's star chefs.

EAT YOUR WORDS

angel food cake – light, tall puffy cake made with beaten egg whites

bagel – circular New York bread roll that is boiled, then baked

Bananas Foster – New Orleans dessert of sliced bananas sautéed in butter, brown sugar and rum, then set aflame and served with vanilla ice cream

barbecue – a technique of slow-smoking spice-rubbed and basted meat over a grill

beignet – New Orleans doughnut-like fritter dusted with powdered sugar

biscuit – flaky yeast-free roll served in the South

blintz – Jewish pancake stuffed with various fillings such as jam, cheese or potatoes

Bloody Mary – cocktail made with vodka, tomato juice, hot sauce and seasonings

BLT – bacon, lettuce and tomato sandwich

blue plate – special of the day in a diner or luncheonette

Boston baked beans – beans cooked with molasses and bacon in a casserole

brownie – fudgy, cake-like bar rich in chocolate, sometimes with nuts

Buffalo wings – deep-fried chicken wings glazed with a buttery hot sauce and served with blue cheese dressing; originated in Buffalo, NY

burrito – Mexican American flour tortilla wrapped around beans, meat, salsa and rice

Caesar salad – romaine lettuce tossed with croutons and shaved Parmesan cheese in a dressing made from raw eggs

California roll – fusion sushi made with avocado, crabmeat and cucumbers wrapped in vinegared rice and *nori* (dried seaweed)

chicken-fried steak – thin beef steak battered, floured and fried like chicken; aka country-fried steak

chili – hearty meat stew spiced with ground chilies, vegetables and beans; also called chili con carne
chimichanga – deep-fried wheat tortilla stuffed with minced beef, potatoes and seasonings
chips – thin, deep-fried potato slices; also crisp tortilla wedges
chop suey – Chinese American dish of noodles, water chestnuts, bean sprouts, cabbage and meat
clam chowder – potato-based soup full of clams, vegetables and sometimes bacon, thickened with milk
club sandwich – three-layered sandwich with chicken or turkey, bacon, lettuce and tomato
Cobb salad – a California chopped salad of avocado, lettuce, tomato, bacon, chicken, hard-boiled egg and blue cheese
cobbler – baked fruit dessert with a biscuit or pie-crust topping
cold cuts – thinly sliced deli meats and cheese served cold
continental breakfast – usually coffee or tea, pastry and juice or fruit
corned beef – salt-cured or brined beef, traditionally served with cabbage on St Patrick's Day (March 17)
crab cake – crabmeat bound with breadcrumbs and eggs then fried
cream cheese – soft cow's milk cheese that can be spread on a bagel
devil's food cake – dark chocolate layer cake with chocolate icing
eggs Benedict – poached eggs, ham and hollandaise sauce on top of English muffins
enchilada – baked tortilla stuffed with shredded meats and cheese and topped with chili sauce
English muffin – round flat yeast muffin dusted with cornmeal
fajita – marinated grilled meat and vegetables served with tortillas and various toppings (eg guacamole, sour cream, shredded cheese)
French fries – deep-fried sliced potatoes
French toast – egg-dipped fried bread served with maple syrup
fudge – semisoft, buttery candy, usually chocolate-flavored, sometimes with walnuts
granola – breakfast cereal of oats, honey and nuts
grits – white cornmeal porridge; a Southern breakfast or side dish
guacamole – mashed avocado dip with lime juice, onions, chilies and cilantro, served with tortilla chips
hash browns – shredded pan-fried potatoes
huevos rancheros – Mexican breakfast of corn tortillas topped with fried eggs and salsa
jambalaya – Louisiana stew of rice, ham, sausage, shrimp and seasonings
jelly – fruit preserve; thinner than jam
knish – baked, grilled or fried Jewish American pastry stuffed with potato, onions, cheese or buckwheat groats
lobster roll – lobster meat mixed with mayonnaise and seasonings, and served in a toasted frankfurter bun.
lox – Jewish version of brine-cured salmon
muffuletta – New Orleans sandwich made with a round bread loaf, ham, salami, cheese and pickled olives
nacho – Mexican American fried tortilla chips often topped with cheese, ground beef, jalapeño peppers, salsa and sour cream
pastrami – Jewish American brined brisket beef that is smoked and steamed
pickle – cucumber brined in vinegar
ranch dressing – salad dressing of mayonnaise, onion, garlic, buttermilk and seasonings
refried beans – Mexican American side dish of fried, mashed pinto beans
Reuben sandwich – sandwich of corned beef, Swiss cheese and sauerkraut on rye bread
sloppy Joe – ground beef, onions, green peppers and ketchup cooked in a skillet
smoothie – cold, thick drink made with pureed fruit, ice and sometimes yogurt
stone crab – Floribbean crab whose claws are eaten with melted butter or mustard-mayonnaise sauce

'Even more Americans are realizing that they want to be able to cook better (or just plain cook)'

strawberry shortcake – biscuit pastry topped with strawberries and whipped cream
submarine sandwich – sandwich served on a thick roll filled with cold cuts, as well as lettuce, onions, pickles and tomato; also called a hoagie, po'boy, hero or grinder
surf 'n' turf – combination plate of seafood (often lobster) and steak
veal (or chicken) parmesan – Italian American dish of pounded cutlet baked with a topping of mozzarella cheese and tomato sauce
wrap – tortilla or pita bread stuffed with a variety of fillings

USA's National Parks

Explore the highs and lows of Grand Canyon National Park (p851), Arizona

JOHN ELK III

National parks are the USA's big backyards. Many cross-country road trips connect the dots between the USA's big-shouldered cities, but not everyone takes time to drive off interstate highways onto the rustic doorsteps of the USA's national parks. If you do take that kind of detour – and we really think you should – you'll encounter truly remarkable places, rich in unspoiled wilderness and native wildlife. Some parklands look much the same as they did centuries ago, when this nation was just starting out. From craggy islands off the Atlantic Coast to prairie grasslands and buffalo herds roaming across the Great Plains to the Rocky Mountains raising their jagged teeth along the Continental Divide, and onward to the tallest trees on earth – coast redwoods – standing sentinel on Pacific shores, you'll be amazed by the USA's natural bounty. (See also the Environment chapter, p121).

Historically speaking, the USA's voracious appetite for land and the material riches it promised drove not only the false doctrine of Manifest Destiny, but also a bonanza of building pioneer homesteads, farms, barrier fences, great dams, concrete roadways and train tracks from sea to shining sea. This artificial infrastructure, which was entirely foreign to Native Americans, quickly swallowed up and devastated vast tracts of wilderness from the Appalachian Mountains across the mighty Mississippi River and far into the West.

Yosemite National Park (p1006), California
CAROL POLICH

That is, until the creation of a well-defended web of federally protected public lands, starting with the national parks; the express mission of the National Park Service (NPS) is to 'preserve unimpaired the natural and cultural resources and values of the national park system for the enjoyment, education, and inspiration of this and future generations.' That means you, too.

ADVENTURES

The USA's national parks are like open-air museums of living natural and cultural history, a gigantic outdoor playground designed for everyone to enjoy, from grandparents and tots toddling down nature trails to rock climbers scaling high-flying canyon walls.

Hiking & Mountaineering

Nothing is easier than just getting out of your vehicle and walking around. National parks enfold thousands of miles of hiking and backpacking trails. Stroll through an alpine wildflower meadow or along a wild, natural beach. Long-distance hiking trails include the 2175-mile Appalachian National

Scenic Trail (NST), which clambers along the mountains from Georgia up to Maine. Not feeling that hard-core? You only need a few days to trek the Grand Canyon (p851) from rim to rim, or just one night to sleep inside a technically-still-active volcano at Haleakalā National Park (NP; p1127). For the most popular backpacking routes, reserve wilderness permits in advance (see p115).

Mountaineering is a way to get even higher. Some backpackers tackle the entire 211-mile John Muir Trail, connecting Yosemite NP (p1006) through Sequoia and Kings Canyon NPs (p1010), just to climb Mt Whitney (14,505ft), the continental USA's highest mountain. Peak bagging is a coast-to-coast pursuit, although die-hard alpinists should look west of the Mississippi River to Rocky Mountain NP (p774), Grand Teton NP (p798), Mt Rainier NP (p1043), North Cascades NP (p1041) and Olympic NP (p1034), or almost anywhere in Alaska (p1071).

top five NATIONAL PARKS FOR JAW-DROPPING SCENERY

Acadia NP (p310), ME
Rocky coastlines and end-of-the-world Atlantic islands.

Blue Ridge Pkwy (p46), NC & VA
Appalachian horizons stretch beside a rolling highway from **Shenandoah NP** (p375) to **Great Smoky Mountains NP**(p402).

Glacier NP (p808), MT
Wildflower-strewn meadows and lakes along the spine of the Continental Divide.

Grand Canyon NP (p851), AZ
An ancient, colorful chasm carved by the mighty Colorado River.

Yosemite NP (p1006), CA
Verdant valleys with thunderous waterfalls and the sirens' call of Sierra Nevada peaks.

Rock Climbing & Canyoneering

For rock climbers, Glen Denny's photographic history *Yosemite: In the Sixties* may challenge you to tackle big walls in Yosemite NP (p1006), arrayed with granite domes. You can scramble

Watch lava flow into the ocean at Hawai'i Volcanoes National Park (p1122), Hawaii MARK NEWMAN

around boulders in the wonderland of Joshua Tree NP (p951), which beckons with over 8000 climbing routes. Meanwhile, experts belay the sea cliffs of Acadia NP (p310). Sounds like too much work? Go canyoneering in Zion NP (p884) instead, where instead of painstakingly inching upward you can rapidly rappel down sheer walls and through twisting slot canyons.

Horseback Riding

Horseback riding is a mighty pleasurable way to survey the landscape. Trot along Point Reyes National Seashore (NS; p989), or gallop along dizzying canyon rim trails all over the Southwest, including into the Grand Canyon (p851) itself. You can cross mountain passes from the Appalachians to the Rockies on the back of a trusty steed or a humble mule, too. Pack stations in dozens of national parks across the country can arrange stock rental and outfit guided rides, lasting from an hour to a couple of days or a week; overnight trips usually require advance reservations.

Caving

Whether you're a novice or an expert spelunker, you can get your knees dirty inside lava tubes at Lava Beds National Monument (NM; p1003) and Hawai'i Volcanoes NP (p1122). Or get down underground at Carlsbad Caverns NP (p908), where subterranean adventures await in some of

top five
NATIONAL PARKS FOR WATCHING WILDLIFE

The USA's national parks are unmatched havens for glimpsing wildlife, from brightly colored tropical birds in Hawaii and Florida to majestic megafauna out West. For more wildlife-watching hot spots, see p140 and p123.

Channel Islands NP (p956), CA
The USA's answer to the Galapagos Islands.

Denali NP (p1099), AK
Domain of grizzlies, caribou, moose and other majestic giants.

Everglades NP (p520), FL
Home to crocs, panthers, manatees and more.

Theodore Roosevelt NP (p675), ND
Where the buffalo still roam (bighorn sheep and wild horses, too).

Yellowstone NP (p793), ID, MT & WY
North America's largest intact ecosystem.

Elk fighting in Wyoming's Yellowstone National Park (p793), a prime spot for watching wildlife
MARK NEWMAN

North America's largest limestone caves. Guided tours at Wind Cave NP (p685), Jewel Cave NM (p685), Mammoth Cave NP (p441), Sequoia NP and Great Basin NP (p837) will show you sci-fi–looking stalactites and stalagmites, and more.

See Denali National Park (p1099), Alaska, from the seat of a 'cycle ALASKA STOCK LLC / ALAMY

Cycling & Mountain Biking

Almost all national parks prohibit mountain biking on trails, but cyclists are often allowed on designated, dirt 4WD roads like those in the wilderness of Utah's Capitol Reef NP (p881) and Joshua Tree NP. Road cyclists should look for multi-use recreational paths and scenic loop drives inside the parks, for example along a historic rail route in Cuyahoga Valley NP. Bicycles are also ideal for getting around congested park hubs like Grand Canyon Village and Yosemite Valley, and in blissfully car-free zones such as at Grand Canyon's South Rim, Zion NP, Bryce Canyon NP (p883) and Acadia NP. The rolling Blue Ridge Pkwy (p401) and the vertiginous Going-to-the-Sun Rd in Glacier NP (p808) will challenge experienced long-distance cyclists.

Water Sports

In summer, national parks are great places for getting your feet wet and cooling off. Discover your own perfect swimming hole in Yosemite NP or Yellowstone NP, sea kayak in Alaska's Kenai Fjords NP (p1094) or California's Channel Islands NP (p956), paddle a river-running raft through white-water rapids in Grand Canyon NP, go snorkeling and scuba diving at Michigan's Isle Royale NP (p625) or Florida's Dry Tortugas NP (p531), canoe beside the borderlands of Minnesota's Voyageurs NP (p649), or go boating in Florida's sweaty Everglades NP (p520) or Alaska's icy Glacier Bay NP & Preserve (p1083). Subject to local regulations and restrictions, fishing (p141) is also permitted in many national parks.

Winter Sports

Summer is high season at most national parks, but winter sports including snowshoeing, skiing, ice skating and snowmobiling attract crowds, too. Expert downhill skiers won't find groomed black-diamond trails in national parks, but beginners can hit the slopes on skis or a snowboard in Yosemite NP (p1006), where magical cross-country routes lead to backcountry huts. Hardier types can go mountain skiing in Mount Rainier NP (p1043), sometimes even on the Fourth of July holiday. For guided snowmobile adventures, Yellowstone NP (p793) is unbeatable. Other fave spots for myriad winter sports include Glacier NP (p808), Grand Teton NP (p798), Rocky Mountain NP (p774) and California's little-known Lassen Volcanic NP (p1004). Anyone with a nuclear-powered body core can go snow camping in many national parks, perhaps most spectacularly inside Yosemite's groves of giant sequoias. Brrr!

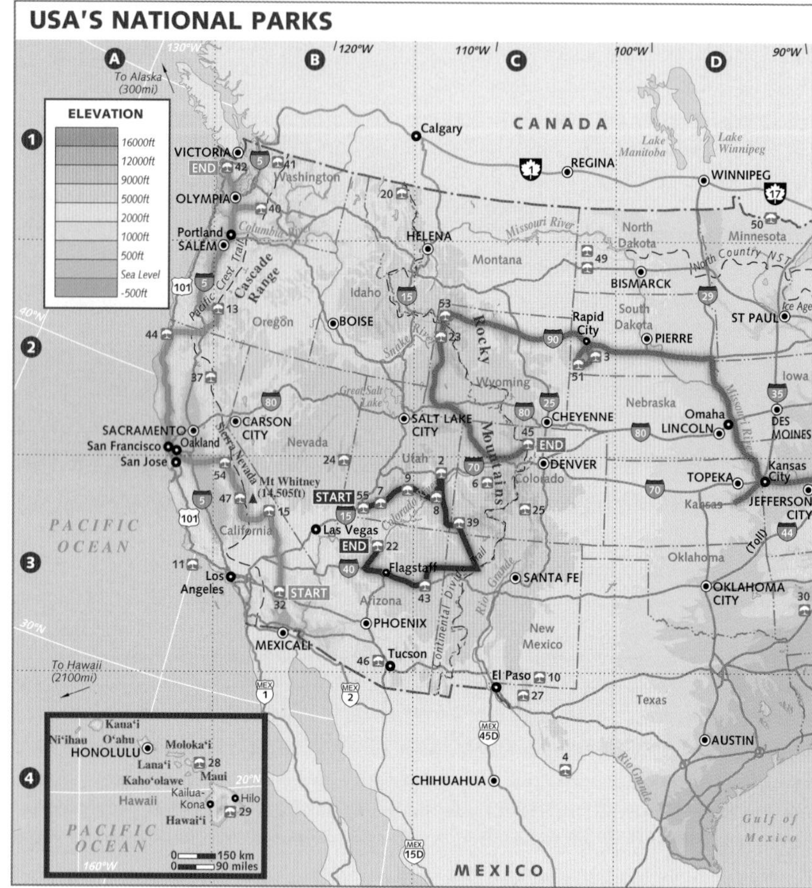

Ranger-Led Activities

For many Americans, a visit to a national park just isn't complete without attending a ranger-led program. Those classic, heart-warming evening campfire sing-alongs and slide-show programs still happen at most parks. So do guided nature walks and hikes for exploring miles of trails while learning about human history, wildlife, ecology, geology and much more.

Some national parks offer extraordinary opportunities for outdoor adventures with the same friendly rangers as your guide. Such special activities may happen only at certain times of year, might cost a bit extra and sometimes require advance reservations, so plan ahead. Rangers can often accompany you on outdoor activities, including snorkeling in Biscayne NP (p522), river rafting at Glen Canyon National Recreation Area (NRA; p857) and boating in Everglades NP (p520). At Carlsbad Caverns NP (p908), you can follow a ranger on caving tours that involve free climbing, twisting through tight spaces and navigating slippery flowstone. At Yosemite NP (p1006) and Mount Rainier NP (p1043), rangers will take you

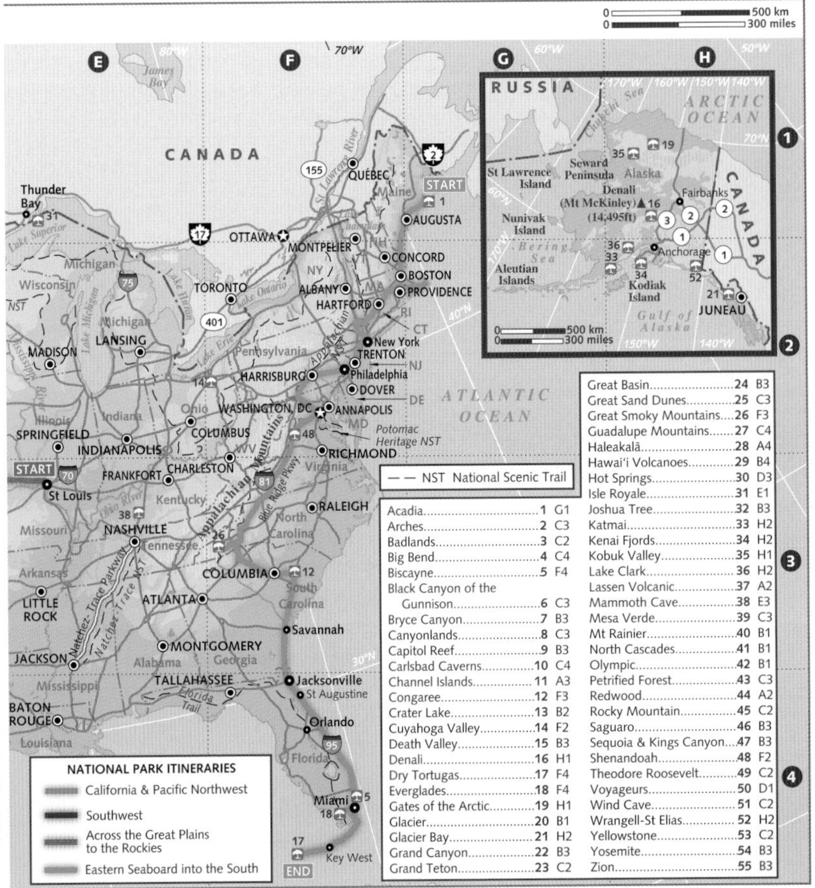

snowshoeing, and accompany you while cycling around the National Mall and Memorial Parks in Washington, DC (p321).

After dark is an amazing time to explore the parks with a ranger. Guided moonlight hikes are popular all over the map, especially in the Southwest's canyon country. Many parks now offer astronomy programs, from telescopes set up atop the north rim of the Grand Canyon (p855) and Yosemite's Glacier Point (p1006) to the small observatory at Chaco Culture National Historic Park (NHP; p902), which also offers daytime solar viewing.

National parks can also allow you to access indigenous culture and regional history in authentic ways that travelers do not often get to experience. At Canyon de Chelly NM (p858), Navajo guides lead horseback and 4WD tours of ancient cliff dwellings. Native Americans also demonstrate traditional artisan crafts, especially in western parks, such as Lassen Volcanic NP (p1004). NPS rangers and an army of volunteers also engage in living-history programs and historical reenactments, especially in the eastern USA, for example at Colonial NHP in Virginia's Historic Triangle (p367). At New Orleans Jazz NHP (p473) live concerts go on stage twice weekly, occasionally with musical instruments played by the rangers themselves.

Wired, tech-savvy national parks now offer video podcasts and audio tours that you can download from home before your visit. That way, you'll always have a ranger in your pocket.

ITINERARIES

Enthusiasts spend a lifetime checking off every NPS site on the master list, collecting special stamps along the way in their official gold-embossed, blue-covered national-parks passports, which are sold at visitor centers and online at www.eparks.com/store.

But assuming you don't have quite that much time on your hands, the following itineraries highlight some of the stars of the NPS system. These trips are meant to be inspirational, not prescriptive: take a look at our recommended routes, then design your own connect-the-dots national-parks tour. See p33 for more ideas.

Eastern Seaboard into the South

Two to Three Weeks / 2325 Miles

Skip down the Atlantic coast, from **Acadia NP** (p310) to **Cape Cod NS** (p264) before braving NYC to visit the **Statue of Liberty NM** (p151) and **Ellis Island NM** (p151), a gateway for early-20th-century immigrants. Learn of Civil War heartbreak at **Gettysburg National Military Park** (p229). Walk the USA's corridors of political power and its national monuments, memorials and historic sites in **Washington, DC** (p321). Slow down for the Appalachians and cruise the **Blue Ridge Pkwy** (p46) from pastoral **Shenandoah NP** (p375) to **Great Smoky Mountains NP** (p402). Continuing south, paddle around **Congaree NP** (p415) before diving into **Biscayne NP** (p522) and lush **Everglades NP** (p520). Finally, board a catamaran for snorkeling and diving in one of the USA's most remote national parks, **Dry Tortugas NP** (p531).

Dry Tortugas National Park (p531), Florida, is home to the endangered hawksbill sea turtle
MICHAEL PATRICK O'NEILL / ALAMY

Across the Great Plains to the Rockies

Two to Three Weeks / 2550 Miles

Start your epic journey west inside St Louis' Gateway Arch at **Jefferson National Expansion Memorial** (p658). Head straight into the USA's heartland to **Tallgrass Prairie National Preserve** (NPreserve; p694), the last vestige of a native ecosystem. Make the long haul north into the Dakotas, formerly frontier territory. Stop by the fossil-laden landscapes of **Badlands NP** (p679) and tour a Cold War–era nuclear-weapons silo at **Minuteman Missile National Historic Site** (p678). Gawk at **Mount Rushmore National Memorial** (p683), then clamber through honeycombed **Wind Cave NP** (p685) or **Jewel Cave NM** (p685), home of the world's second-longest cave. Tip your hat to **Devil's Tower NM** (p801),

The granite peaks of the Teton Range dominate Wyoming's Grand Teton National Park (p798) DAVID TOMLINSON

a sacred site for Native Americans, en route to **Yellowstone NP** (p793), the country's most venerated national park, stuffed full of wildlife, geysers and hot springs. Next door are the peaks of **Grand Teton NP** (p798). Delve into geology and paleontology at **Dinosaur National Monument** (p877) before finishing at top-of-the-world **Rocky Mountain NP** (p774).

Southwest

Two Weeks / 1250 Miles

Find the biblical promised land at **Zion NP** (p884), with its waterfalls and natural springs hidden in the desert. Nearby **Bryce Canyon NP** (p883) exhibits quirky hoodoo formations and horseshoe-shaped natural amphitheaters. Follow back roads and byways through **Grand Staircase-Escalante NM** (p882) and over to **Capitol Reef NP** (p881), which sits atop a wrinkle in the earth's crust. Plumb the mazelike topography of **Canyonlands NP** (p880) and trek to eroded sandstone formations in **Arches NP** (p879). Wander through Native American lands, paying your respects to Ancestral Puebloan ruins in **Mesa Verde NP** (p789), **Chaco Culture NHP** (p902), **Bandelier NM** (p898) and **Canyon de Chelly NM** (p858). Don't miss the Navajo rug room at **Hubbell Trading Post NHS** (p858). Cruise ol' Route 66 through the painted desert of **Petrified Forest NP** (p859) to **Williams** (p849), where vintage trains depart for the south rim of **Grand Canyon NP** (p851).

California & the Pacific Northwest

Two to Three Weeks / 2200 Miles

Starting in Southern California's deserts, hop between boulders and palm oases in **Joshua Tree NP** (p951) and slide down sand dunes and stroll across salt flats at Badwater, the USA's lowest elevation, in **Death Valley NP** (p954). Climb into the Sierra Nevada to wander giant sequoia forests and marble caves in **Sequoia and Kings Canyon NPs**, (p1010), then explore the glaciated valleys, alpine wildflower meadows and majestic waterfalls of **Yosemite NP** (p1006). Head to San Francisco for a ferry ride over to **Alcatraz Island** (p978), once an infamous prison, inside Golden Gate NRA. Drive over the **Golden Gate Bridge** (p978) out to the rocky headlands of **Point Reyes NS** (p989), a wildlife haven. Keep heading north to the towering trees of **Redwood NP** (p998). See the sky reflected in volcanic **Crater Lake NP** (p1064), meet a glacier-covered, rumbling giant in **Mount Rainier NP** (p1043) and lose yourself in the rainforest, mountains and Pacific Coast beaches of **Olympic NP** (p1034).

NATIONAL PARKS: A USER'S GUIDE

Before you visit any national park, check out its website, using the navigational search tool on the **NPS home page** (www.nps.gov). You can find a lot of information online, from driving directions and printable maps to operating hours and updates on road closures and trail conditions to campground maps and lodging links. You can also take a closer look at outdoor activities, wilderness areas and ranger-led programs happening in the parks. Some individual park websites also have downloadable podcasts, PDF brochures, virtual hiking guides, webcams and interactive activities for junior rangers (ie kids).

At the park's entrance, be ready to hand over some cash (credit cards may not be accepted). Entrance fees vary, from nothing at all to $25 per vehicle for a seven-day pass. Due to federal budget shortfalls and chronic underfunding, parks fees regularly rise. That makes the **'America the Beautiful' annual pass** (http://store.usgs.gov/pass; pass $80) quite a deal. It admits four adults and their children under 16 years old for free to all national parks and federal recreational lands for one year. For US citizens and permanent residents only, those aged 62 years and older are eligible for a lifetime pass ($10), which is free for those with eligible disabilities.

Joshua Tree National Park (p951), California, offers more than 8000 climbing routes

MAX PAOLI & RUTH EA

Wheeler Peak in Great Basin National Park (p837), Nevada

ANDREW BAIN

top five NATIONAL PARKS FOR ESCAPING THE CROWDS

Big Bend NP (p746), TX
Find solitude in the desert and along the banks of the Rio Grande.

Great Basin NP (p837), NV
Meditate among ancient bristlecone pines or in underground caverns.

Dry Tortugas NP (p531), FL
Hop aboard a catamaran for spectacular diving, snorkeling and birding.

Lassen Volcanic NP (p1004), CA
Daringly circumnavigate boiling mud pots, hissing fumaroles and more.

North Cascades NP (p1041), WA
Climb icy glaciers and discover wild, lonely waterfalls.

Bring extra cash to pay for campsites, wilderness permits, guided tours and other recreation. There often aren't many ATMs inside the parks, and all apply a transactional surcharge. Credit cards are accepted at some park visitor centers – great news for all of those books, maps, posters and souvenirs you'll soon be buying – and private concessionaire businesses inside the parks (eg restaurants, lodges).

If you don't have accommodations booked, that should be your first priority when you arrive in the park. National park lodges are incredibly popular family vacation destinations; during peak seasons, reserve a room far in advance (six months to a year ahead). To check on last-minute availability, call the lodges directly. Campsite reservations (see p1132) are also necessary during busy times, especially weekends and holidays from Memorial Day through Labor Day. Some parks have first-come, first-served campgrounds, in which case you should try to arrive between 10am and noon to nab a spot while some of last night's campers are vacating their sites.

For overnight camping in the backcountry and occasionally for longer day hikes, you'll need a wilderness permit. Permit fees and reservation procedures vary from park to park, so before your trip check out the park's website, or call its general information number and ask for the wilderness office. Walk-up permits may be available in person the day before or the morning of departure for less-popular backpacking routes, but even then you should plan to get in

The future of Montana's Glacier National Park (p808) is threatened due to climate change
ROB BLAKERS

line an hour before the permit station opens. The number of permits available is often subject to quotas aimed at protecting natural resources from being trampled to death.

Once you're ready to explore the park, stop by a visitor center first. If the rangers on duty are busy, take time to browse the signposted information while you wait. Want to know the weather forecast? The best trails for day hikes? If it's OK to build campfires? All of the answers are available to help you make the most of your visit. You'll also find schedules and information about park shuttles, so you can leave your car behind. Families should ask about junior ranger programs: kids get an activity book to work on during their visit, after which they're awarded an official badge and sworn in as junior rangers. Some parks have fully loaded activity backpacks for families to borrow.

If you're camping or doing any specialized activities (basically, anything more than just rambling around), bring your own equipment. Park stores may sell basic camping and outdoor supplies, but prices are inflated and some items may be out of stock (eg your particular type of camp-stove fuel). Outdoor gear is usually only rentable in the biggest parks (eg Yosemite, the Grand Canyon); bearproof canisters are generally available when required for backcountry travel.

During your visit, do your utmost to preserve the park's wild and beautiful natural environment. Review the principles of the **Leave No Trace** (www.lnt.org) outdoor ethics (see the boxed text, p126). National-park policies and regulations may seem restrictive, but they're intended to keep you safe and to protect the park's natural and cultural resources. Pets are not allowed outside of the parks' developed areas, where they must be kept on a leash and attended by their owner at all times – not much fun for you or your canine companion.

EXPLORING BEYOND THE NATIONAL PARKS

Thanks to more than 20,000 employees and 150,000 volunteers, the National Park Service (NPS) protects 319 different sites – so much more than just 58 national parks, although that's what people usually think of first. The eastern USA's 'cannonball' historic parks can never compete with lodestars like Yellowstone or Yosemite, but that doesn't mean you shouldn't check out NPS sites that aren't, in fact, national parks. You can often avoid big crowds, engage in more recreational activities and see just as many amazing landscapes and wildlife species.

Besides national parks, the most popular places to visit in the NPS system are National Preserves (NPreserve) and National Monuments (NM). The former are like national parks but with hunting and mining permitted, while the latter protect places of historical and scientific interest. The NPS offers a lot more for history buffs, too, from National Historic Sites (NHS) and Parks (NHP) to National Memorials (NMem) and National Battlefields (NB). If it's wild scenery and adventure you're after, head for a National Recreation Area (NRA) or National Seashore (NS). Motorists can cruise National Parkways (Pkwy) and National Historic Trails (NHT), while hikers amble along National Scenic Trails (NST). Finally, there are a dozen or so miscellaneous NPS lands, like the National Mall in Washington, DC (p321).

Not only does it grant you access to *every* NPS site, but an 'America the Beautiful' pass (see p114) also throws open the doors to thousands of natural areas overseen by other federal land management agencies, including the **US Forest Service** (USFS; www.fs.fed.us), **US Fish & Wildlife Service** (USFWS; www.fws.gov) and **Bureau of Land Management** (BLM; www.blm.gov). Much like NPS sites, all of these public lands have uniquely valuable properties that justify putting them into the country's wilderness treasure chest.

National forests provide plenty of solitude easily accessed via scenic byways and 4WD roads, along with mountain-biking trails and sport fishing and hunting. For epic journeys, the USA's largest land manager, the BLM, has hidden nooks and crannies of wilderness still waiting to be discovered. The USFWS, which works to preserve threatened and endangered species, offers unparalleled opportunities for wildlife watching, especially birding in protected wetlands. Some of the USFWS' 540-plus National Wildlife Refuges (NWRs) are situated close to urban areas, if you want a quick adventure in the great outdoors.

If your time is limited, know that visiting any of these places is usually more of a do-it-yourself experience than national parks. Visitor centers and other facilities may be few and far between. The biggest payoff is solitude. Free dispersed camping is allowed on many of these public lands (free campfire permits may be required), while developed campgrounds, which may be booked and paid for in advance (see p1132), tend to be less busy than in nearby national parks.

EVOLUTION OF THE PARKS

Although the NPS didn't exist until 1916, the idea of national parks began during the era of helter-skelter nation building. During a trip to the Dakotas in 1831, artist George Catlin had a dream. As he watched the USA's rapid westward expansion damage both the wilderness and Native American peoples, Catlin penned a call to action, to create 'a nation's park, containing man and beast, in all the wild and freshness of their nature's beauty!' Four decades later, in 1872, Congress designated Yellowstone NP 'for the benefit and enjoyment of the people.'

The 1890s saw a rush of new parks – Yosemite NP, Sequoia NP, Mount Rainier NP, Crater Lake NP and Glacier NP – as well as a nascent environmental movement (see p126) as the idea of a national-park system fired up the public's imagination. The Antiquities Act of 1906, signed by President Theodore Roosevelt, preserved a trove of archaeological sites from Native American cultures, including Mesa Verde NP and Chaco Culture NHP. In the 1930s, President Franklin Delano Roosevelt added 50 more historic sites and monuments to the NPS portfolio while hiring Depression-era Civilian Conservation Corps

Glimpse a gator in Everglades National Park (p520), Florida

MARK NEWMAN

(CCC) workers to build scenic byways and create new recreational opportunities in the parks.

Throughout the 20th century, the NPS kept expanding. The biggest growth spurt to date happened in 1980, when the Alaska National Interest Lands Conservation Act turned over 47 million acres of wilderness to the NPS, more than doubling the federal agency's holdings. However, some NPS growth has been controversial, for example when local residents protested new restrictions on land use in the Mojave NPreserve or when NPS goals have come into conflict with the aims of Native American communities (for background reading on the latter, pick up *American Indians and National Parks* by Robert Keller and Michael Turek).

Today the NPS protects more than 300 parklands and more than 84 million acres of wilderness from coast to coast. Its newest sites are NYC's **African Burial Ground NM** (www.nps.gov/afbg) and Colorado's **Sand Creek Massacre NHS** (www.nps.gov/sand), both established since 2000. But today, the NPS is in crisis. Federal budget cuts and the enormous pressures of 275 million visitors every year together have taken huge tolls on parks' infrastructure. An ambitious **National Parks Centennial Initiative** (www.nps.gov/2016) aims to restore the luster of the parks by funding major

NATURAL BORN HEROES

In a country founded on the philosophy that individuals matter, the solo voices of artists, explorers, environmentalists and presidents have given shape to the USA's national parks as much as, if not more than, governmental bureaucrats.

In the late 19th century, the poetic herald of the Sierra Nevada, John Muir (1838–1914), galvanized the public while campaigning for a national park system, delivering open-air lectures and writing about the spiritual value of wilderness beyond just its economic advantages. He inspired Teddy Roosevelt (1858–1919), a big-game hunter and US president, to establish wildlife preserves, national forests and new national parks and monuments.

Women have also been influential in protecting national parks, as narrated in Polly Kaufman's *National Parks and the Woman's Voice: A History*. Western architect Mary Elizabeth Jane Colter (1869–1958), who built grand railway hotels for the Fred Harvey Company, helped devise the classic national-park architectural style, seen in her masterworks at Grand Canyon Village.

First lady during the 1960s, 'Lady Bird' Johnson (1912–2007) started out small by beautifying the nation's capital and its highways by planting wildflowers. Then she contributed to the groundbreaking report *With Heritage So Rich*, which led to the National Historic Preservation Act of 1966 that expanded the NPS system. Her advocacy for national parks influenced her husband, President Lyndon B Johnson, who enacted more environmental-protection legislation than any administration since Franklin D Roosevelt. Lady Bird and her legacy of conservation are fittingly honored by a majestic memorial grove of trees in Redwood NP (p998).

TALK WITH A NATIONAL PARK RANGER: KEN HIRES

Why did you become a park ranger? When I was a child, I read a comic book with characters that traveled all over the American West. That's when I knew I wanted to work in the mountains someday. Since then, I've worked at Yellowstone NP, Mt St Helens National Volcanic Monument and Kings Canyon NP.

What kind of work do you do? I'm an interpretive ranger, which means I turn nature into English. I conduct evening programs, take visitors on guided walks, explain the various intricate workings of nature, give lots of directions and when anyone needs assistance, I help out.

What makes your job fun? I like working with kids and folks who really want to know things, the ones who ask me lots of questions about the natural environment.

How many visitors do you talk to a day? At least a hundred, sometimes many more.

What do visitors often forget to do in national parks? They go for hikes without taking any water.

What other parks do you like to visit? Point Reyes NS, the Mojave Desert, Grand Canyon NP, Zion NP and Bryce Canyon NP – the Western parks.

What's the oddest job you've done as a ranger? At Yellowstone, I went out and checked the temperatures of hot pools and geysers once a month with a thermometer and a fishing pole.

What do national parks need most right now? Maintenance funds to take care of the backlog of infrastructure repairs.

Do you think increased visitation has helped or hurt the parks? While more people have been coming to national parks, it represents a smaller percentage of the USA's total population. At the same time, more people are learning to appreciate parks, which is a good thing. In fact, 99.9% of the people I meet are very happy to be here.

Why is it important for visitors to follow the rules? The rules are in place to protect natural resources, like vegetation from being trampled by too many feet and wildlife from being pushed out of its habitat. Without rules, eventually the wilderness would not be itself. The very things that people come here to love would be destroyed.

Any last words? When you visit a park, remember rangers are not there to hassle you; they're there to protect the park and help you enjoy it. And no, we don't feed the bears!

Hike your way around Mt Rainier National Park (p1043), Washington, on one of its many trails RICHARD CUMMINS

Hike through the Narrows in Zion National Park (p884), Utah

RICHARD CUMMINS

top five
NATIONAL HISTORIC PLACES

For travel itineraries that visit nationally registered historic sites, from shipwrecks in Florida to stops on the Underground Railroad, click to www.nps.gov/history/nr/travel.

Antietam National Battlefield (p353), MD
Learn how the USA's bloodiest day-long battle became a Civil War turning point.

Martin Luther King Jr NHS (p447), GA
Follow in the footsteps of the influential 1960s civil-rights activist.

Manzanar NHS (p1013), CA
Examine the heartbreaking history of WWII-era Japanese American internment camps.

National Mall & Memorial Parks (p321), Washington, DC
Walk the paths of history in the nation's capitol district.

San Antonio Missions NHP (p722), TX
Trace the influences of Spanish colonization on Native Americans in the 'New World.'

park improvements and repairs in time for the NPS's 100th anniversary in 2016. Centennial projects include restoring historic buildings, controlling invasive plant and animal species, and inventorying archaeological sites before they are lost.

Nonprofit partners such as the **National Parks Conservation Association** (www.npca.org) and **Western National Parks Association** (www.wnpa.org) are critical to the parks' survival. These organizations raise money, staff visitor centers and educational programs, publish books and maps, and promote conservation in the parks. Recent media spotlights on national parks have also increased public awareness of their importance, as has Ken Burns' inspiring documentary, *The National Parks: America's Best Idea* (www.pbs.org/nationalparks).

Environment

Through luck, wars and purchase, the USA gathered to itself the entire lower half of the North American continent. Without this land, would the 'American experiment' in republican democracy have grown into the powerful nation it is today?

Decidedly not. The continent's immense riches fueled the USA's industrial might and inspired self-congratulatory dreams of Manifest Destiny, even as the continent's raw beauty wove itself into the nation's collective soul. Despite over 400 years of settlement and cities, of farming and mining, and sometimes raging conflicts over resources and environmental impacts, Americans regard the continent's unsurpassed natural wonders as a national treasure.

In the last century and a half, Americans have tried to make all that good feeling concrete by establishing an array of parks, preserves and wildlife refuges. Exploring these can be the highlight of your trip: for a taste of the USA's national parks, see p105. But also, nature writing is one of the richest genres of American nonfiction, bringing to life America's distinctive spirit and its inextricable relationship to the land.

THE LAND

The USA is big, no question. Covering some 3,537,000 sq miles, it's the world's third-largest country by size, trailing only Russia and Canada, its friendly neighbor to the north. The continental USA is made up of 48 contiguous states ('the lower 48'), while Alaska, its largest state, is northwest of Canada, and the volcanic islands of Hawaii, the 50th state, are 2600 miles southwest of the mainland in the Pacific Ocean.

Where the Bluebird Sings to the Lemonade Springs (1993) is an essential primer in Wallace Stegner and his writing about the misunderstood and mostly abused West. These essays are classics.

It's more than just size, though. America feels big because of its incredibly diverse topography, which began to take shape around 50 to 60 million years ago.

In the contiguous USA, the east is a land of temperate, deciduous forests and contains the ancient Appalachian Mountains, a low range that parallels the coast along the Atlantic Ocean. This coast is the country's most populated, urbanized region, particularly in the corridor between Washington, DC, and Boston, MA.

To the north are the Great Lakes, which the USA shares with Canada. These five lakes, part of the Canadian Shield, are the greatest expanse of fresh water on the planet, constituting nearly 20% of the world's supply.

Going south along the East Coast, things get wetter and warmer till you reach the swamps of southern Florida and make the turn into the Gulf of Mexico, which provides the USA with a southern coastline.

Geology is rarely a page-turner, but in *Annals of the Former World* (1998) John McPhee turns the history of North American plate tectonics into a thrilling, human spectacle of discovery.

West of the Appalachians are the vast interior plains, which lie flat all the way to the Rocky Mountains. The eastern plains are the nation's breadbasket, roughly divided into the northern 'corn belt' and the southern 'cotton belt.' The plains, an ancient sea bottom, are drained by the mighty Mississippi River, which together with the Missouri River forms the world's fourth-longest river system, beat out only by the Nile, Amazon and Yangtze Rivers. Going west, farmland slowly gives way to cowboys and ranches in the semi-arid, big-sky Great Plains.

The young, jagged Rocky Mountains are a complex set of tall ranges that runs all the way from Mexico to Canada, providing excellent skiing. West of these mountains are the Southwestern deserts, an arid region of extremes that has been cut to dramatic effect by the Colorado River system. This land of eroded canyons leads to the unforgiving Great Basin as you go across

Nevada. Also an ancient sea bottom, the Great Basin is where the military practices and the where the USA plans to bury its nuclear waste.

Then you reach America's third major mountain system: the southern, granite Sierra Nevada and the northern, volcanic Cascades, which both parallel the Pacific Coast. California's Central Valley is one of the most fertile places on earth, while the coastline from San Diego to Seattle is celebrated in folk songs and Native American legends – a stretch of sandy beaches and old-growth forests, including coast redwoods.

But wait, there's more. Northwest of Canada, Alaska reaches the Arctic Ocean and contains tundra, glaciers, an interior rainforest and the lion's share of federally protected wilderness. Hawaii, in the Pacific Ocean, is a string of tropical island idylls.

WILDLIFE

Standing in one of the carefully tended, surviving patches of original American wilderness, it's possible to imagine the continent as it appeared long ago: the great plains a rustling ocean of grass; the eastern seaboard a chattering blanket of forest; buffalo by the millions; howling wolves in every corner.

The Wilderness Society (www.wilderness.org) is the USA's main advocacy organization for wilderness. Aldo Leopold (1887–1948), author of *A Sand County Almanac*, was the organization's founder.

Occupying the same vast horizon, you can see why the new nation believed its natural resources to be limitless. They weren't, though, and the USA quickly proved it during its 19th-century westward expansion. By century's end, alarmed citizens and politicians suddenly realized they could actually use everything up.

In 1903, America began preserving its wildlife when President Teddy Roosevelt set aside Florida's Pelican Island as the nation's first bird sanctuary, thereby creating a National Wildlife Refuge System (NWRS). Today, managed by the **US Fish & Wildlife Service** (www.fws.gov), NWRS comprises over 150 million acres, making it the world's largest system of preserves dedicated to protecting wildlife and habitat. In 1964 Congress passed the Wilderness Act, which preserves entire, self-regulating ecosystems. The USA now has over 750 official wilderness areas totaling almost 110 million acres, over half of which are in Alaska.

The most powerful and controversial environmental tool remains the 1973 Endangered Species Act (ESA). Since its inception, the ESA has been criticized for obstructing industry and commerce, but never more so than by George W Bush's administration, which threw up 'pervasive bureaucratic obstacles,' according to a 2008 *Washington Post* article. In 2009, Secretary of the Interior Ken Salazar announced that the Obama administration was overturning the Bush-era rule that had weakened the ESA by allowing federal agencies to essentially ignore the input of conservation scientists.

Given all the stresses that nature is enduring here, what is most remarkable is how wild it still seems. Hiking in a national park or wilderness area – spotting bears and wolves, elephant seals and condors, herds of bison and elk, old-growth redwoods and primordial swamps – is pure joy. Here are just some tantalizing highlights.

Animals

LAND MAMMALS

Nineteenth-century Americans did not willingly suffer competing predators, and federal eradication programs nearly wiped out every single wolf and big cat and many of the bears in the continental US. Almost all share the same story of abundance, precipitous loss and, today, partial recovery.

The grizzly bear, a subspecies of brown bear, is one of North America's largest land mammals. Male grizzlies can stand 7ft tall, weigh up to 850lb and

USA'S ENDANGERED SPECIES: THERE'S STILL TIME

Currently, over 1300 plants and animals are listed in the USA as either endangered or threatened. Some are mighty creatures like grizzly and polar bears, but most are just not that big (eg freshwater mussels, chubs, grasses).

Although all endangered species are vital to the ecosystem, if it's brag-worthy animals that you're keen to see (and photograph), here are places to spot them before it's too late:

- **Bighorn sheep** – Anza-Borrego Desert State Park, CA (p952) & Zion National Park (p884), UT
- **California condor** – Big Sur, CA (p960) & Grand Canyon National Park, AZ (p851)
- **Desert tortoise** – Mojave National Preserve, CA (p953)
- **Florida panther** – Everglades National Park, FL (p520)
- **Gray wolf** – Yellowstone National Park, WY (p793)
- **Hawaiian goose** – Haleakalā National Park (p1127)
- **Hawaiian monk seal** – Papahanaumokuakea Marine National Monument (p1130) & Waikiki Aquarium, HI (p1111)
- **Manatee** – Everglades National Park, FL (p520)
- **Mexican long-nosed bat** – Big Bend National Park, TX (p746)
- **Whooping cranes** – Aransas National Wildlife Refuge, TX (p733) & Bosque del Apache National Wildlife Refuge, NM (p903)

consider 500 sq miles home. At one time, perhaps 50,000 grizzlies roamed the West, but by 1975 fewer than 300 remained. Conservation efforts, particularly in the Greater Yellowstone Region, have increased the population in the lower 48 states to around 1300. By contrast, Alaska remains chock-full of grizzlies, with upwards of 30,000. Despite a decline in numbers, black bears survive nearly everywhere. Smaller than grizzlies, these opportunistic, adaptable and curious animals can survive on very small home ranges.

Another extremely adaptable creature is the coyote, which looks similar to a wolf but is about half the size, ranging from 15lb to 45lb. An icon of the Southwest, coyotes are found all over, even in cities. The USA has one primary big-cat species, which goes by several names: mountain lion, cougar, puma and panther. In the east, a remnant population of panthers is defended within Everglades National Park. In the west, mountain lions are common enough that human encounters have increasingly occurred. These powerful cats are about 150lb of pure muscle, with short tawny fur, long tails and a secretive nature.

When it comes to wildlife slaughter, nothing can match what happened to the buffalo, or bison. No accurate count can ever be made, but they may have originally numbered as many as 65 million, in herds so thick they 'darkened the whole plains,' as explorers Lewis and Clark wrote. They were killed for food, hides, sport, cash and to impoverish Native Americans, who depended on them to live. By the 20th century, a couple of hundred bison remained. From these, new herds have been built up, so that one of America's quintessential animals can again be admired in its gruff majesty – among other places, in Yellowstone, Grand Teton and Badlands National Parks.

Defenders of Wildlife (www.defenders.org) is a major champion of endangered plants and animals, particularly wolves. Its website has species fact sheets and status updates.

Due to melting glaciers, the polar bear is becoming an endangered species. After years of debate, the USFWS has finally listed it as threatened due to climate change.

MARINE MAMMALS & FISH

Perhaps no native fish gets more attention than salmon, whose spawning runs up Pacific Coast rivers are famous spectacles. However, both Pacific and Atlantic salmon are considered endangered; hatcheries release

RETURN OF THE WOLF

The wolf is a potent icon of America's wilderness. This smart, social predator is the largest species of canine – averaging over 100lbs and reaching nearly 3ft at the shoulder – and an estimated 400,000 once roamed the continent from coast to coast, from Alaska to Mexico.

Unlike domestic dogs, wolves were not regarded warmly by European settlers. The first wildlife legislation in the British colonies was a wolf bounty. As 19th-century Americans tamed the West, they slaughtered the once-uncountable herds of bison, elk, deer and moose, replacing them with domestic cattle and sheep, which wolves found equally tasty.

To stop their inevitable poaching of livestock, the wolf's extermination soon became official government policy. For $20 to $50 an animal, wolves were shot, poisoned, trapped and dragged from dens until in the lower 48 states only a few hundred gray wolves remained in northern Minnesota and Michigan. Lacking wolves, bounty programs ended in 1965.

In 1944, naturalist Aldo Leopold called for the return of the wolf. His argument was ecology, not nostalgia. His studies showed that wild ecosystems need their top predators to maintain a healthy biodiversity; in complex interdependence, all animals and plants suffered with the wolf gone.

When the Endangered Species Act was enacted in 1973, gray and red wolves were among the first species listed. Despite dire predictions from ranchers and hunters, gray wolves were reintroduced to the Greater Yellowstone Region in 1995–96 and red wolves were reintroduced to Arizona in 1998.

Protected and encouraged, wolf populations have recovered rapidly, with over 5500 now counted in the wild. In 2009, the western Great Lakes population of gray wolves was considered self-sustaining and 'delisted,' although the species remains protected elsewhere in the USA. Red wolves and Mexican gray wolves are still endangered nationwide.

millions of young every year, but there is debate whether this practice hurts or helps wild populations.

As for marine life, gray, humpback and blue whales migrate annually along the Pacific Coast, making whale-watching very popular. Alaska and Hawaii are important breeding grounds for whales and marine mammals, and Washington's San Juan Islands are visited by orcas. The Pacific Coast is also home to ponderous elephant seals, playful sea lions and endangered sea otters.

Peak mating season for elephants seals along the Pacific coast just happens to coincide with Valentine's Day (February 14), when love is in the air – and on the beach!

In California, Channel Islands National Park and Monterey Bay preserve unique, highly diverse marine worlds. For coral reefs and tropical fish, Hawaii and the Florida Keys are the prime destinations. The coast of Florida is also home to the unusual, gentle manatee, which moves between freshwater rivers and the ocean. Around 10ft long and weighing on average 1000lb, these agile, expressive creatures number over 3800 today, and may once have been mistaken for mermaids.

The Gulf of Mexico is another vital marine habitat, perhaps most famously for endangered sea turtles, which nest on coastal beaches.

At eBird (http://ebird.org), which offers a trove of birding knowledge, avid birders can put their efforts to good use by logging their counts and helping science.

BIRDS

Birding is the most popular wildlife-watching activity in the US, and little wonder – all the hemisphere's migratory songbirds and shorebirds rest here at some point, and the USA consequently claims some 800 native avian species. For help finding and identifying them, Sibley Field Guides are an indispensable resource, as is the **National Audubon Society** (www.audubon.org).

The bald eagle was adopted as the nation's symbol in 1782. It's the only eagle unique to North America, and perhaps half a million once ruled the continent's skies. By 1963, habitat destruction and, in particular, poisoning from DDT had caused the population to plummet to 487 breeding pairs in the lower 48. However, by 2006, bald eagles had recovered so well, increasing to almost 9800 breeding pairs across the continent (plus 50,000 in Alaska), that they've been delisted as an endangered species.

Another impressive bird is the endangered California condor, a prehistoric, carrion-eating bird that weighs about 20lb and has a wingspan over 9ft. Condors were virtually extinct by the 1980s (reduced to just 22 birds), but they have been successfully bred and reintroduced in California and northern Arizona, where they can sometimes be spotted soaring above the Grand Canyon.

Plants

The eastern United States was originally one endless, complex deciduous forest that mixed with evergreens depending on altitude and latitude. Great Smoky Mountains National Park contains all five eastern forest types – spruce fir, hemlock, pine-oak, and northern and cove hardwood – which support over 100 native species of trees. Spring wildflower and colorful autumn foliage displays are a New England specialty.

In Florida, the Everglades is the last subtropical wilderness in the US. This vital, endangered habitat is a fresh- and salt-water world of marshes, sloughs and coastal prairies that support mangroves, cypresses, sea grasses, tropical plants, pines and hardwoods.

The grasslands of the interior plains are perhaps America's most abused ecosystem. The 19th-century 'sodbusters' converted them largely to agriculture, particularly the eastern tallgrass prairies, of which less than 4% remains. The semiarid shortgrass prairies have survived somewhat better, but farmers have still cultivated them for monoculture row crops by tapping the underground aquifer. Theodore Roosevelt National Park in North Dakota is a good destination to see America's remaining grasslands.

The fastest bird in North America is believed to be the peregrine falcon, which has been clocked diving for prey at speeds of up to 175mph.

The Southwest deserts are horizon-stretching expanses of sage, scrub and cacti that abut western mountain ranges, where abundant wildflowers in spring and yellow quaking aspens in fall inspire pilgrimages.

West of the Cascades in wet, milder Washington and Oregon are the last primeval forests in America. These diverse, ancient evergreen stands, of which only 10% remain, contain hemlocks, cedars, spruces and towering Douglas firs.

California, meanwhile, is famous for its two species of sequoias, or redwoods. The coast redwood is the world's tallest tree, with the tallest specimens in Redwood National Park. Its relative, the giant sequoia, is the world's biggest tree by volume; Sequoia National Park has the granddaddy of 'em all.

NATIONAL PARKS & FEDERAL LANDS

Over a quarter of the USA (over 640 million acres) falls under some kind of federal protection or stewardship. That's a lot of public land, and nearly all of it can be visited. These diverse areas span the country, but are most extensive in the West and Alaska. Some have entrance fees and require permits (for instance, to camp or go backpacking). Visitor facilities range from nothing at all to full-service lodges serving meals.

These public lands have a bewildering array of designations, but they are managed mainly by four agencies: the **Bureau of Land Management** (BLM; www.blm.gov), **US Forest Service** (USFS; www.fs.fed.us), **US Fish and Wildlife Service** (USFWS; www.fws.gov) and **National Park Service** (NPS; www.nps.gov).

If you're looking for iconographic America – the Grand Canyon, perhaps? – chances are it's within the National Park Service (NPS). The NPS manages 391 units, totaling 79 million acres. The jewels of the system are its 58 national parks, which generally contain the best facilities and the most visitor services. For a complete introduction to the USA's national parks, see p105.

ARRIVE PREPARED, LEAVE NO TRACE

Many of America's most beloved landscapes are being loved to death. As you're out having an adventure in the wilderness, remember: one thoughtless gesture – hiking off-trail through fragile soil or building an illegal fire – can take years for nature to repair. Each person makes a difference.

Most hiking and camping advice is common sense. First, know what you are getting into. Find out what weather to expect and pack accordingly, even for just a few hours. Get trail maps and take five minutes to talk to a ranger before plunging ahead. Rangers can alert you to crowds, weather reports, trail conditions and the possibilities of flash floods or wildfires.

In the wild, do everything possible to minimize your impact. As they say, take only pictures, leave only footprints. Stick to established trails and campsites. Be particularly sensitive to riparian areas: don't wash yourself or dishes in streams or rivers, and camp at least 200ft away from them. Use a stove for cooking and make fires only in established fire rings (using dead, downed wood). When you leave, take out everything you brought in (trash, recycling and toilet paper, too).

Basically, conduct yourself as if you were a guest in someone's home – which you are. Observe wildlife, but don't approach or feed it. Leave cultural or historic artifacts where you find them. And finally, be respectful of other hikers, both those around you and those to follow. Far-reaching human noise is the fastest way to spoil a whole valley's worth of solitude.

For more advice, consult **Tread Lightly** (www.treadlightly.org) or the **Leave No Trace Center** (www.lnt.org).

Most other federal lands, such as the BLM's 264 million acres and the USFS' 193 million acres, are managed under the concept of 'mixed use,' which means they must balance recreation, resource extraction, grazing and preservation. Visitor facilities tend to be minimal, when they exist at all, but the scenery is often wonderful and less crowded than at higher-profile national parks.

A great place to start is by visiting www.recreation.gov, the government's main public-lands web portal. For details of annual passes, see National Parks: A User's Guide (p114). For camping facilities, fees and reservations, see p1132.

THE ENVIRONMENTAL MOVEMENT

The USA is well known for its political and social revolutions, but it also birthed environmentalism. The USA was the first nation to make significant efforts to preserve its wilderness, and US environmentalists often spearhead preservation efforts worldwide.

Nature Noir (2005), by Jordan Fisher Smith, is utterly unique and actually pulse-pounding: Smith's tales of being a state park ranger in the rural Sierra Nevada would make Raymond Chandler blanch.

The nation did not start out this way. Indeed, America's Protestant settlers believed that civilization's Christian mandate was to bend nature to its will. Not only was wilderness deadly and difficult, but it was a potent symbol of humanity's godless impulses, and the Pilgrims set about subduing both with gusto.

Then, in the mid-19th-century, taking their cue from European Romantics, the USA's transcendentalists claimed that nature was not fallen, but holy. In *Walden; or, Life in the Woods* (1854), iconoclast Henry David Thoreau described living for two years in the woods, blissfully free of civilization's comforts. He persuasively argued that human society was harmfully distant from nature's essential truths. While largely anthropomorphic, this view marked a profound shift to believing that nature, the soul and God were one.

The continent's natural wonders – vividly captured by America's 19th-century landscape painters – had a way of selling themselves, and rampant nationalism led to a desire to promote them. In 1864, President Abraham Lincoln set aside a part of Yosemite Valley as a state park. In 1872, President Ulysses S Grant designated over two million acres as Yellowstone

National Park, the world's first such large-scale preserve, established expressly to preserve its unique features for human enjoyment.

Scottish naturalist John Muir soon emerged to champion wilderness for its own sake. Muir considered nature superior to civilization, and he spent much of his life wandering the Sierra Nevada mountain range and passionately advocating on its behalf. Muir was the driving force behind the USA's emerging conservation movement, which had its first big victory in 1890 when Yosemite National Park was established. Muir founded the Sierra Club two years later.

To learn more about wilderness in America – its history, advocates, laws, current status and helpful trip-planning tools such as descriptions, maps and photos – visit www.wilderness.net.

By the end of the 19th century, the nation was realizing the limits of its once boundless resources. In 1891 the Forest Reserve Act was passed to maintain and manage forests to ensure they'd keep fueling America's growth. This epitomized the conservation movement's central conflict: whether to preserve nature for human use or for its own sake. These mutually exclusive aims underlie many conflicts today.

In the early 20th century, industrial progress raised urgent new concerns. The 1916 National Park Service Act established a permanent federal mechanism for wilderness preservation (for more national parks history, see p117). But more importantly, the science of ecology emerged. Ecology proved yet another humbling of humankind – already knocked from the center of the universe, and swinging arm in arm with monkeys, thanks to Charles Darwin – with its assertion that people were in fact interdependent with nature, not in charge of it.

US WORLD HERITAGE SITES

For more info on World Heritage sites, visit Unesco's website (http://whc.unesco.org/en/list).

- Cahokia Mounds State Historic Site (p590)
- Carlsbad Caverns National Park (p908)
- Chaco Culture National Historic Park (p902)
- Everglades National Park (p520)
- Glacier Bay National Park & Preserve (p1083)
- Grand Canyon National Park (p851)
- Great Smoky Mountains National Park (p402)
- Hawai'i Volcanoes National Park (p1122)
- Independence Hall (p214)
- Mammoth Cave National Park (p441)
- Mesa Verde National Park (p789)
- Monticello (p373) and the University of Virginia (p374) in Charlottesville
- Olympic National Park (p1034)
- Redwood National & State Parks (p998)
- Statue of Liberty (p151)
- Taos Pueblo (p901)
- Waterton-Glacier International Peace Park (p808)
- Wrangell-St Elias National Park & Preserve (p1097)
- Yellowstone National Park (p793)
- Yosemite National Park (p1006)

With ecology, America's 19th-century conservation movement became the modern environmental movement. Aldo Leopold was the first writer to popularize an ecological world view with his idea of a 'land ethic,' which proposed that humans must act with respectful stewardship toward all of nature, rather than celebrating the parts they like and abusing the rest. The 1962 publication of *Silent Spring*, by Rachel Carson, provided the shocking proof: this exposé of how chemicals such as DDT were killing animals and poisoning the land horrified the nation and inspired activists.

Aldo Leopold's *A Sand County Almanac* (1949) became a touchstone for American naturalists, and it remains a humble, unpretentious and powerfully moving testimony to the power of leaving wilderness undisturbed.

Over the next decades, the USA passed a series of landmark environmental and wildlife laws that have since resulted in significant improvements in the nation's water and air quality, and the partial recovery of many near-extinct plants and animals. The movement's focus steadily broadened – to preserving entire ecosystems, not just establishing parks – as it confronted the 'five horsemen of the environmental apocalypse': disease, pollution, overkill of species, habitat destruction through human impact, and the introduction of alien (that is, nonnative) species.

Today, environmentalism is a worldwide movement, one that understands that each nation's local problems also contribute to a global threat: climate change. In the USA, the dangers of global warming are inspiring an environmental awareness as widespread as at any time in US history. Whether or not average Americans believe God speaks through nature, they're increasingly disturbed by the messages they are hearing.

The Sierra Club (www.sierraclub.org) was the USA's first conservation group and it remains the nation's most active, with educational programs, organized trips and tons of information.

ENVIRONMENTAL ISSUES

The USA seems to have reached a tipping point: most Americans now accept the reality of global warming, regardless of their political affiliation. National discussions have steadily shifted from whether climate change exists to what the country should do about it. Even the Bush administration, which once shut its eyes tight against the possibility (and when that failed, censored climate-change scientists to discredit it, as concluded by the Congressional Committee on Oversight and Government Reform in late 2007), finally conceded that, yes, perhaps the weather is changing after all.

In 2009 at the Major Economies Forum on Energy and Climate, Secretary of State Hillary Clinton said that 'the science is unambiguous, and the logic that flows from it is inescapable: climate change is a clear and present danger to our world that demands immediate attention.' President Obama has promised to limit greenhouse gas emissions by 80% before 2050 using an economy-wide cap-and-trade program, and has stated his support for finding alternative 'clean energy' sources to power America. After his first 100 days in office, however, no meaningful legislation to combat climate change had been passed.

Why not? To be sure, some sectors of the government and industry are dragging their feet, hard. They argue that global warming is a natural (not human-caused) cycle; that it won't be that bad; that there's nothing we can do about it; or that, most especially, in a country already mired in a deep recession, making drastic changes to quickly combat global warming is too costly to the nation's economic health to consider.

Famously cranky environmentalist Edward Abbey turned his job as an Arches National Park seasonal ranger into *Desert Solitaire* (1967), which swings from desert rhapsodies to prescient warnings about the onslaught of mass tourism on wild places.

Battles over the environment have been a fixture of the American political landscape for over a century, and for business, this last argument has been a winner, whether the issue is pollution, dwindling resources or endangered species. This effectiveness rests, in part, on the reluctance of some US residents to make sacrifices in their consumptive lifestyles (annually, each US citizen is responsible for emitting 20 tons of carbon dioxide; the global average is 4.5 tons per person). Over the past centuries, Americans have often altered their habits only when environmental problems become undeniable, quantifiable and urgent. With global warming, that moment seems to have arrived.

TERRY TEMPEST WILLIAMS: LOVE AND HUMILITY IN THE DESERT *Jeff Campbell*

A naturalist, teacher and writer, Terry Tempest Williams forms part of the West's long, distinguished heritage of conservationists and ecologists. Her latest book is *Finding Beauty in a Broken World*. We asked her to talk about the environmental state of the nation and what she loves about her home, the canyon country of southern Utah.

'One of the beautiful aspects of American democracy,' Williams said, 'is that we have given value to national parks and refuges. We have a Wilderness Act and an Endangered Species Act. To me this is a transformative, restorative justice. It's a movement born out of love and idealism. It's an expansive movement born out of expansive country. I love that.'

When asked about today's seemingly endless list of environmental threats, Williams didn't hesitate: 'I refuse to engage in doomsday approaches. I don't think we can know what's ahead. The problem before us now is that we've failed to see the interconnectedness of things. To me the very heart of an environmental ethic is the notion of empathy based in community in the broadest sense.

'I love thinking of those two words "climate change" literally – you know, a change of attitudes. And I do see a climate change in the American Southwest. The world is so beautiful, so fragile, particularly in desert landscapes, how can we not respond? It's important to look at global warming as local warming, which brings an immediacy to our own communities that we can no longer ignore.'

She added, 'It's going to take us decades to undo what George Bush has set in motion environmentally. All one has to do is fly over southwest Colorado, the Colorado Plateau in Utah, western Wyoming, and your heart breaks. The Clean Air Act, the Clean Water Act, wetlands legislation – all these have been gravely undermined for short-term gain, and who's paying the price? Ecological communities from pronghorns and sage to red rock and ravens.'

Williams also noted, 'It's so important that we venture out into these vast wildlands because I think it reminds us what endures. There's something so profoundly wonderful about the humility that one faces walking in a wild place. These rocks tell time differently, and they ask us to do the same. Perhaps therein lies our humility as a species.'

'What I love is, you know, talk to me about politics and greed in the middle of a flash flood. Just the other day I was out walking and I heard this dry rattle. I stopped and thought, *Where are you?* All of sudden just square in the wash was this rattlesnake. It's that kind of pause that makes me smile. There's no word for that kind of encounter.'

How to tell? State and local governments have started passing environmental legislation of their own, and businesses are going green by investing in alternative energy. Fourteen states have adopted stricter auto-emissions standards than the federal government's. When the **Environmental Protection Agency** (EPA; www.epa.gov) withheld permission to implement them, these states (led by California) sued, and in 2007 the Supreme Court ruled that the EPA has both the authority and a 'duty' to regulate greenhouse gases under the Clean Air Act. Not coincidentally, in 2007 Congress introduced a bill to tighten federal auto-emissions standards for the first time in 20 years. In June 2009, the EPA began to comply with the Supreme Court ruling by granting California's petition to be allowed to regulate its own more-stringent greenhouse gas emissions.

By turns self-effacing and earnest, Bill McKibben talks with Vermont farmers and friends about how to turn an ecological mind-set into a practical everyday reality in *Wandering Home* (2005).

Energy

Although China doesn't lag far behind, the USA is the world's greatest consumer of energy (using more oil, electricity and natural gas per day than any other country) and hence its greatest polluter, accounting for a quarter of the world's greenhouse gases. Greenhouse gas emissions in the USA have increased 6% over the last decade alone. Coal provides just under half of the nation's electricity, natural gas and nuclear power about 20% each, and renewable sources (mainly hydroelectric) and petroleum account for the rest. Coal accounts for roughly 90% of the country's energy reserves, though it's among the dirtiest methods of generating electricity.

Credit former vice president Al Gore. His documentary *An Inconvenient Truth* (2006) finally convinced Americans that global warming exists and that the US is throwing fuel on the fire.

Nuclear energy emits no greenhouse gases, but its waste poses other problems. In 2007 the **US Nuclear Regulatory Commission** (NRC; www.nrc.gov) approved the first new nuclear plant site in 30 years. As of 2009, the NRC was reviewing applications for opening a few dozen more light-water reactor facilities across the country. Nevada's Yucca Mountain was chosen as the nation's sole permanent nuclear-waste repository in 2001. However, the project was plagued with controversy over the potential for leaks, and President Obama has vowed to stop it. But what happens then to high-level radioactive waste being produced at 104 sites nationwide?

The Union of Concerned Scientists (www.ucsusa.org) is a reliable source for independent updates on global warming, vehicle emissions, energy, nuclear technology and invasive species.

Meanwhile, interest in renewable-energy technologies and fuels is increasing markedly. One indication is that venture-capital investments in alternative fuels hit a record high of $2.7 billion in 2008, more than 10 times what it was less than a decade ago. The USA currently leads the world in installing wind turbines and wind-power generation capacity, though so far it only provides 2.5% of the nation's electricity. The USA has leaped ahead globally in the production of ethanol and biodiesel fuels, with the latter predicted to account for as much as 20% of the nation's total domestic fuel consumption by 2012. Even chain retailers such as Wal-Mart and Target have been putting solar panels on their buildings. Hydrogen technology may hold the most promise for zero-emission production, but developing hydrogen into an affordable energy fuel option could take decades.

Why is the need to increase domestic oil production such a big issue? The US imports over 60% of its supply (a percentage that rose during George W Bush's presidency), which makes the US reliant on external resources and circumstances for its oil supply.

Air

Concern for air pollution has lead to a society-wide discussion about greenhouse gases touching every aspect of modern life: from building design and light bulbs to auto emissions and planting trees. While states wrestle with the federal government over how much and how quickly to raise auto fuel-economy standards (currently averaging just 21mpg), some US automakers who accepted a multibillion dollar federal bailout have promised to expand their line of hybrid and electric models. Even import companies such as Toyota and Honda have dropped their hybrid car prices, making it more affordable. In 2009, the EPA gave away over $85 million dollars to help 49 states meet new 'clean' diesel emissions standards, while Congress spent 3 billion dollars on the Car Allowance Rebate System (CARS). Also known as the 'cash for clunkers' program, it allowed consumers to trade in their old cars and get cash back when buying new, more fuel-efficient models. The CARS program was so successful that it ran out of funding in less than two months. Recently, the EPA has also begun developing emissions standards for coal-burning power plants, which currently account for about 30% of the nation's greenhouse gas emissions.

Water

The EPA estimates that over 60% of US waters remain 'impaired,' despite significant improvements in water quality since the Clean Water Act was enacted in 1972. One of the most widespread pollution problems is the discovery of perchlorate, a chemical used in missile and rocket fuel, in the drinking water in 26 states. As of 2009, the EPA was working to finalize contamination standards that may require nationwide cleanup.

When Smoke Ran Like Water (2002), by Devra Davis, chillingly traces how scientists painstakingly link pollution to disease and how easily politics and industry undermine their conclusions.

Water issues are particularly acute in the West: the region's underground aquifer is being drained at a phenomenal rate – not just for suburban homes with their grassy lawns, but also for golf courses and swimming pools – and increasing water salinity is playing havoc with farming. The West has also witnessed a surge in new oil and gas drilling, especially since the federal government approved industry exemptions to the Clean Water Act in 2005. An unlikely coalition of ranchers, hunters and conservationists is fighting this sacrifice of water for cheap energy.

USA Outdoors

Amy Marr

No matter what type of outdoor enthusiast you might be – curious first-timer, recent convert or seasoned pro – you've definitely come to the right place. And while you may be familiar with the country's more illustrious standouts – exploring magnificent national parks like Yosemite and Yellowstone, rafting in the Grand Canyon, skiing in the legendary powder snow of the Rocky Mountains – it's the lesser-known treasures, such as kayaking in Washington's San Juan Islands, canoeing in Minnesota's Boundary Waters, skiing in the maple woods of Vermont, that beg discovery, and unveil the country's true, untamed essence.

Consider the USA your enormous playpen for outdoor activities, and yours to customize as you wish. The country is so full of accessible and diverse terrain that choosing where to go and what to do is the biggest challenge. You simply need to pick your desired activity and terrain, whether it's hiking to glacial lakes, fly-fishing in streams, backpacking over mountain passes, riding horseback through Aspen thickets, walking in the desert or surfing ocean – or lake – waves.

Check out www.randmcnally.com for useful tools highlighting interesting sites and activities, as well as maps with overnight suggestions.

So after reveling in the music, museums and mayhem of urban USA, take it outside. Steer in any direction into the country's wild soul, stretching your legs and your horizons. Hike along a ridgeline, learn to surf, mountain bike past redwoods, spot an eagle, go spelunking. Just get out there and dunk yourself, or at least your toes, in the invigorating, eye-popping natural splendors on offer in every state. The outdoor pleasures will likely become a memorable highlight.

For a wealth of resources on all of the activities described in this chapter, see p1134, and for more suggestions of places to go and things to do, see p106.

Website www.americaoutdoors.org is an international association representing travel outfitters, tour companies and outdoor educators; you can search by state or activity.

SKIING & SNOWBOARDING

You can hit the slopes in 40 states, making for tremendous variety in terrain and ski-town vibe. Vermont's top-notch Stowe (p291) draws seasoned souls – freeze your tail off on the lifts, but thaw out nicely après ski in timbered bars with local brews. Find more snow, altitude and attitude out west at Vail, CO (p780), Squaw Valley, CA (p1005) and high-glitz Aspen, CO (p781). For an unfussy scene and steep vertical chutes, try Alta, UT (p874), Telluride, CO (p788), Jackson, WY (p799) and Taos, NM (p900). In Alaska, slopes slice through spectacular terrain outside Juneau, Anchorage and Fairbanks. Mt Aurora SkiLand has the most northerly chairlift in North America and, from spring to summer, the shimmering green-blue aurora borealis.

Here's a snow-stash secret: Hawai'i. Mauna Kea (p1120), the Big Island's 'white mountain' (actually a cone-shaped volcano) soars nearly 14,000ft and is often covered with snow, as is neighboring Mauna Loa. Don't expect lifts, grooming or resorts; your rented 4WD does the hard work. Granted, it takes planning, but what a day! Skiing in the morning and snorkeling in the afternoon, powered by Kona coffee.

Thrill-seekers take note: Colorado's Steamboat Springs has five ski jumps and the largest natural ski-jump area in North America.

Wherever you ski, it won't come cheap. Find the best deals by purchasing multiday tickets, heading to lesser-known 'sibling' resorts (like Alpine Meadows near Lake Tahoe) or checking out mountains that cater to locals including Vermont's Mad River Glen (p290), Santa Fe Ski Area (p893) and Colorado's Wolf Grade.

On powdered slopes across the USA, snowboarding has become as popular as downhill skiing – all thanks to snow-surfing pioneer Jake Burton

THE USA'S BEST CLASSROOM: OUTDOORS

Whether you're jonesing to catch a wave or dangle from a cliff, learn some new outdoor tricks in these high-thrill programs.

Club Ed Surf Camp (www.club-ed.com) Learn to ride the waves from Manresa Beach to Santa Cruz, CA, with field trips to the surfing museum and surfboard companies included.

Craftsbury Outdoor Center (www.craftsbury.com) Come here for sculling, cross-country skiing, biking and running, Vermontstyle (crisp air and maple woods).

Joshua Tree Rock Climbing School (www.joshuatreerockclimbing.com) Local guides lead beginners to experts on 7000 different climbs in Joshua Tree National Park, CA.

Nantahala Outdoor Center (www.noc.com) Learn to paddle like a pro at this North Carolina–based school, which offers world-class instruction in canoeing and kayaking in the Great Smoky Mountains.

Otterbar Lodge Kayak School (www.otterbar.com) Top-notch whitewater kayaking instruction is complemented by saunas, hot tubs, salmon dinners and a woodsy lodge tucked away on California's north coast.

Steep and Deep Ski Camp (http://www.jacksonhole.com/info/ski.ac.steepski.asp) Finesse skiing extreme terrain (and snagging first tracks) then wind down over dinner parties. You can also ski with Olympian Tommy Moe.

Carpenter, who set up a workshop in his Vermont garage and began to build snowboards in the mid-1970s. Vermont is still home central for snowboarders but airdogs also flock almost everywhere out west, including Sun Valley and Tahoe. After years of holding out, Taos finally opened its coveted slopes – marked by great snow and killer chutes – to snowboarders. For a fix during the summer months, head to Oregon's Mt Hood area (p1061), where several resorts offer snowboard camps.

Washington's Mt Baker, aka King of Snow, has the highest average accumulation (647in) of any lift-served ski resort in the world.

For a mellower schuss, find superb trail networks for Nordic skiers and snowshoers in New York's Lake Placid (p201); quaint Jackson, NH; California's Royal Gorge (North America's largest Nordic ski area); and Washington's sublime and crowd-free Methow Valley (p1041). Backcountry passionistas will be happily rewarded throughout the Sierra Nevada, with its many ski-in huts, and West Virginia's storm-pounded Dolly Sods Wilderness.

Novice dogsledders may not be ready for the Iditarod – Alaska's legendary, 1049-mile race from Anchorage to Nome, first forged by gold diggers – but how about a weekend on the trails of the gorgeous White Mountains National Recreation Area, 30 miles north of Fairbanks? Or combine mushing and memorable dining with a twilight ride at Colorado's Krabloonik, North America's largest touring dogsled kennel.

For information on resources, see p1135.

CYCLING & MOUNTAIN BIKING

Thanks to media-favorite Lance Armstrong, coupled with an ever-expanding concern for the environment, cycling's popularity grows by the day in the USA.

You can rent a road bike in any city, with bike-friendly all-stars including Madison, WI, Boulder, CO, Austin, TX, Burlington, VT, and Portland, OR. Some of the country's best cycling is around San Francisco, where a pedal over the Golden Gate Bridge lands you in the stunningly beautiful, and stunningly hilly, Marin Headlands, where you might spot comedian Robin Williams out on his bike. For a memorably tough urban biking challenge, try keeping upright when riding around the bridge's famous art-deco towers while battling gusty crosswinds off the Pacific.

The fact is, every state in the USA is proud of its cycling trails, and you'll find die-hard enthusiasts in every town. Numerous outfitters offer guided trips for all levels and durations. For the best advice on rides and rentals, stop by a local bike shop or Google the area you plan to visit.

Many states offer social multiday rides, such as Ride the Rockies in Colorado. For a modest fee, you can join the peloton on a scenic, well-supported route; your gear is ferried ahead to that night's camping spot (usually the football field in a scenic town). Other standout rides include Arizona's Mt Lemmon, a thigh-zinging 28-mile climb from the Sonoran Desert floor to the 9157ft summit; Tennessee's Cherohala Skyway, 51 glorious miles of undulating road and Great Smoky Mountain views; and Missouri's Katy Trail (p664), a 200-mile crushed-limestone bike path through the heartland.

Fat-tire fans will love *Klunkerz*, a movie about the history of mountain bikes and the bunch of Californian hippies who took the sport forward from fringe to mainstream.

Mountain-biking enthusiasts will find trail nirvana in Boulder, CO, Moab, UT, Bend, OR, Ketchum, ID and Marin, CA, where Gary Fisher and Co. bunny-hopped the sport forward by careening down the rocky flanks of Mt Tamalpais on home-rigged bikes. Premier long-distance trails abound, from North Dakota's Maah Daah Hey Trail, a 96-mile jaunt over rolling buttes along the Little Missouri River, to the Sun Top Loop, bouncing across the western slopes of Washington's Cascade Mountains. The 206-mile, hut-to-hut ride between Telluride, CO, and Moab, UT, is a sure thing. Both towns are dazzling, and the scenery between them will make you feel like you've pedaled onto the set of a classic Western flick. For a shorter high-altitude experience, ride from Aspen to Crested Butte and back, an equally stunning ride.

In pristine Alaska, even a ride on the highway feels like a wilderness encounter. Bike outfits with tours originating in Anchorage, Homer or Fairbanks will take you on your ideal ride – from an easy day trip to a nine-day expedition along mountain ranges and salmon-filled rivers. Then of course, there's the Iditarod Trail, which, come summer, morphs into the state's best mountain-biking adventure.

The nonprofit Rails-to-Trails (www.railtrails.org) has created more than 13,900 miles of scenic trails nationwide from America's unused rail corridors.

For more information on cycling and mountain biking, see p1134.

HIKING & BACKPACKING

Fitness-focused Americans take great pride in their formidable network of trails – literally tens of thousands of miles – and there's no better way (besides cycling!) to experience the countryside up close and at your own pace.

The wilderness is amazingly accessible, making for easy exploration. Within a few hours' drive from virtually any city, you'll find yourself engulfed by glorious scenery: jagged peaks, wildflower-dappled meadows, towering redwood forests, streaming waterfalls, pristine seashore. For instance, a mere 30-mile drive north of San Francisco will land you in Point Reyes National Seashore (p989), where the eucalyptus-fringed trails reward with Pacific views and sand-soft camping spots – and, if you're lucky, a glimpse of the resident tule elk.

The real issue is deciding what kind of hike you're after. The national parks, for example, can be approached from three different perspectives. For the visitor on the go, there are short hikes – many less than a mile long – that showcase the natural highlights. In just a few hours, you can absorb the beauty of national parks like King's Canyon (p1010), Glacier (p808) and Acadia (p310), to name a few. If you have more time to spare, ask a ranger (stop in at the visitor centers) to recommend a longer hike, from gentle ambles to sweaty slogs (the most popular of the these may well be Yosemite's Half Dome, a 12-hour trek tackled by dozens every day). If you're hankering for nights in the wilderness in the company of Orion and Cassiopeia, plan on securing a backcountry permit in advance, especially in places like the Grand Canyon – spaces are limited, particularly during summer.

New Hampshire's 3165ft Mt Monadnock, America's most-climbed peak, has 40 miles of trails and a summit view of all six New England states.

Beyond the parks, you'll find troves of trails in every state. There's no limit to the places you can explore, from the sun-blasted hoodoos and red spires

TOP TRAILS IN THE USA

Ask 10 people for their top trail recommendations and no two answers will be alike. The country is so varied and distances so enormous, there's little consensus. That said, you can't go wrong with the following all-star sampler. For more ideas, check out award-winning **Trails.com** (www.trails.com), with a database of 45,000 trails (and lots of topo maps so you won't get lost).

Hiking

Appalachian Trail (www.appalachiantrail.org) Completed in 1937, the country's longest footpath is 2178 miles long, crosses six national parks, traverses eight national forests and hits 14 states. Pick a leg, any leg, and wallow in the splendor.

Enchanted Valley, Olympic National Park, WA (p1036) Magnificent mountain views, roaming wildlife and lush rainforests – all on a 13-mile out-and-back trail.

Great Northern Traverse, Glacier National Park, MT (p808) A 58-mile haul that cuts through the heart of grizzly country and crosses the Continental Divide.

Kalalau Trail, Na Pali Coast, Kaua'i, HI (p1128) Wild Hawaii at its finest – 11 miles of lush waterfalls, hidden beaches, verdant valleys and crashing surf.

Mount Katahdin, Baxter State Park, ME (p314) A 9.5-mile hike over the 5268ft summit, with panoramic views of the park's 46 peaks.

South Kaibab/North Kaibab Trail, Grand Canyon, AZ (p853) A multiday cross-canyon tramp down to the Colorado River and back up to the rim.

South Rim, Big Bend National Park, TX (p746) A 13-mile loop through the ruddy, 7000ft Chisos Mountains, with views into Mexico.

Tahoe Rim Trail, Lake Tahoe, CA (p1004) This 165-mile all-purpose trail circumnavigates the lake from high above, affording glistening Sierra views.

Mountain Biking

Downieville Downhill, Downieville, CA Not for the faint of heart, this piney trail, located near its namesake Sierra foothill town in Tahoe's National Forest, skirts river-hugging cliffs, passes through old-growth forest and drops 4200ft in under 14 miles.

Finger Lakes Trail, Letchworth State Park, NY A little-known treasure, 35 miles south of Rochester in upstate New York, featuring over 20 miles of singletrack along the rim of the 'Grand Canyon of the East'.

McKenzie River Trail, Wilamette National Forest, OR (www.mckenzierivertrail.com) Twenty-two miles of blissful single-track winding through deep forests and volcanic formations. The town of McKenzie is located about 50 miles east of Eugene (p1059).

Porcupine Rim, Moab, UT (p878) A 30-mile loop from town, this venerable high-desert romp features stunning views and hairy downhills.

in Arizona's Chiricahua Mountains to the dripping trees and mossy nooks in Washington's Hoh River Rainforest (p1035); from the dogwood-choked Wild Azalea Trail in Louisiana to the tropical paradise of Kaua'i's Na Pali Coast (p1128). Almost anywhere you go, there's great hiking and backpacking within easy striking distance. All you need is a sturdy pair of shoes (sneakers or hiking boots) and a water bottle.

Check out the world's best-preserved Permian-aged fossil reef at Carlsbad Caverns National Park in New Mexico.

Commitment-phobes should steer clear of the John Muir Trail in Yosemite (p1008): 222 miles of scenic bliss, from Yosemite Valley up to Mt Whitney. The Appalachian Trail (AT) stretches north–south from Maine to Georgia, while the Colorado Trail spans almost 500 miles from Denver to Durango. The Pacific Coast Trail (PCT) follows the spines of the Cascades and Sierra Nevada, traipsing the continent's edge from Canada to Mexico: that's 2650 miles, passing through six of North America's seven ecozones. About 300 hikers go for it every year; why not be number 301?

For information on these regional trails and other hiking resources, see p1135.

ROCK CLIMBING

Scads of climbers flock to Joshua Tree National Park, an otherworldly shrine in southern California's sun-scorched desert. There, amid craggy monoliths and the country's oldest trees, they pay pilgrimage on more than 8000 routes, tackling sheer vertical, sharp edges and bountiful cracks with aplomb. Or not. Fortunately, a top-notch climbing school offers classes for all levels (see p132).

Cool and piney by comparison, Yosemite National Park (p1006), with its signature glacially polished domes, is climbing's most hallowed shrine – this is where American climbing first took hold in the 1930s. Surely anyone with a passion for rocks has seen gravity-defying pictures of climbers bivouacking on Half Dome, or Lynn Hill's legendary free ascent of the Nose. This venerable national park, protected by president Abraham Lincoln in 1890, offers superb climbing courses for first timers as well as for those craving a night in a hammock 1000ft above terra firma. South of the park and favored by many top climbers is Bishop (p1012), a sleepy town in the Eastern Sierra, with fantastic boulders in the nearby Owens River Gorge and Buttermilk Hills.

A Walk in the Woods: Rediscovering America on the Appalachian Trail is Bill Bryson's hilarious travelogue about tackling the venerable AT with a college buddy, both of them middle-aged and out of shape.

Fortunately, California didn't reap all the climbing spoils. Ten miles west of Las Vegas is Red Rock Canyon (p833) and some of the world's finest sandstone climbing. In Wyoming's Grand Teton National Park, Exum Mountain Guides (p798) offers programs from basic climbing courses to two-day expeditions up to the top of Grand Teton itself: a 13,770ft peak with majestic views. Idaho's City of Rocks National Reserve has more than 500 routes up wind-scoured granite and pinnacles 60 stories tall. Located 70 miles west from Austin, TX, the Enchanted Rock State Natural Area, with its huge pink granite dome, has hundreds of routes and stellar views of the Texas Hill Country. And in Colorado, versatility's the word, from multipitch ascents in the Flatirons to alpine climbing in Rocky Mountain National Park, both close to Boulder.

John Muir's spectacular *The Yosemite* features gorgeous photographs by Galen Rowell, who died in 2002 when his plane crashed near his home in Bishop, CA.

Near Zion National Park, UT, multiday canyoneering classes teach the fine art of going *down:* rappelling off sheer sandstone cliffs into glorious, red-rock canyons filled with trees. Some of the sportier pitches are made in dry suits, down the flanks of roaring waterfalls into ice-cold pools.

East of the Mississippi, upstate New York's Shawangunk Ridge (p196) is located within a two-hour drive north of New York City. The ridge stretches some 50 miles, and the 'Gunks' are where many East Coast climbers tied their first billets.

For information on climbing and canyoneering resources, see p1135.

CANOEING, KAYAKING, RAFTING & SAILING

East of the Mississippi, West Virginia has an arsenal of legendary white water. First, there's the New River Gorge National River (p383), which, despite its name, is one of the oldest rivers in the world. Slicing from North Carolina into West Virginia, it cuts a deep gorge, known as the 'Grand Canyon of the East,' producing frothy rapids in its wake. Then there's the Gauley, arguably among the world's finest white water. Revered for its ultrasteep and turbulent chutes, this venerable Appalachian river is a watery roller-coaster, dropping more than 668ft and churning up 100-plus rapids in a mere 28 miles. Too gnarly? Six more rivers, all in the same neighborhood, offer training grounds for less-experienced river rats.

Vermont's 270-mile Long Trail – America's oldest long-distance hiking path – follows the spine of the Green Mountains. It spans the entire state, and inspired the Appalachian Trail.

Out west there's no shortage of scenic and spectacular rafting, from Utah's Cataract Canyon, a thrilling romp through the red rocks of Canyonlands National Park, to the Rio Grande in Texas, a lazy run

TOP SPECTATOR ACTIVITIES

Insane or inspiring? Decide for yourself. These outdoor events – some quirky, others legendary – are fun to watch and grueling to do.

24 Hours of Moab (www.grannygear.com) Relay teams gather in the red-rock desert to ride a gnarly 15-mile loop under sun and stars.

American Birkebeiner Ski Race (www.birkie.com) Come February, 8000 cross-country skiers snow-sprint 30 tree-lined miles in Wisconsin's wilderness (in summer, swap skis for a mountain bike).

Boston Marathon (www.bostonmarathon.org) Held annually on the third Monday of April, the world's oldest marathon follows a historic, heart-pounding route.

Dipsea (www.dipsea.org) For over 100 years, sure-footed souls have been tackling this hilly 7.1-mile trail to Stinson Beach, CA, in America's oldest cross-country race. For sick kicks, there's a double and a quad, too.

Ironman (www.ironman.com) The big daddy of triathlons, held on Hawai'i's Kona coast every October, is known for killer head winds, ocean waves and black lava–covered terrain.

Mavericks (www.maverickssurf.com) Violent tides, sharky waters, hidden rocks, supersonic swells and the world's top big-wave riders guarantee a dazzling show just south of San Francisco. Mavericks goes off in winter, but the exact date is determined by Mother Nature and announced only a few days before the event.

Mt Washington Auto Rd Bicycle Hillclimb (www.mtwashingtonbicyclehillclimb.org) A 7.6-mile uphill race along grades of between 12% and 22% to the summit of New England's highest peak. It's held in August.

through limestone canyons. The North Fork of the Owyhee – which snakes from the high plateau of southwest Oregon to the rangelands of Idaho – is rightfully popular and features towering hoodoos. In California, both the Tuolumne and American Rivers surge with moderate-to-extreme rapids while in Idaho, the Middle Fork of the Salmon River has it all: abundant wildlife, thrilling rapids, a rich homesteader history, waterfalls and hot springs. If you're organized enough to plan a few years in advance, snag a spot on the Colorado River, the quintessential river trip. And if you're not after white-knuckle rapids, fret not – many rivers have sections suitable for peaceful float trips or inner-tube drifts you can traverse with a cold beer in hand.

For exploring flatwater (no rapids or surf), opt for a kayak or canoe. While kayaks are seaworthy, they are not always suited for carrying bulky gear. For big lakes and the seacoast (including the San Juan Islands), use a sea kayak. For month-long wilderness trips – including the 12,000 miles of watery routes in Minnesota's Boundary Waters or Alabama's Bartram Canoe Trail, with 300,000 acres of marshy delta bayous, lakes and rivers – use a canoe.

You can kayak or canoe almost anywhere in the USA. Rentals and instruction are yours for the asking, from Wisconsin's Apostle Islands National Seashore and Utah's celebrated Green River (p877) to Hawaii's Na Pali Coast (p1128). Hire kayaks in Maine's Penobscot Bay to poke around the briny waters and spruce-fringed islets, or join a full-moon paddle in Sausalito's Richardson Bay, CA.

If you prefer your water vessel to be wind-propelled, sign up for a sailing charter. With the snow-capped Sierra as a backdrop, Lake Tahoe is ideal for an afternoon sail; on the East Coast, Chesapeake Bay is chock-full of schooners and racing catamarans, while Cape Cod and the islands harbor quiet coves and salty New Englanders.

For information on rafting resources, see p1134.

SURFING, WINDSURFING & KITESURFING

Some of the best surf in continental USA breaks off the beaches of funky and low-key Santa Cruz, CA (p964). Bribe a local (a cold beer or two should do the trick) to share sweet spots, or plan to wait your turn at legendary sites such as Pleasure Point, Sharks and Steamer Lane, the fabled Westside surf break.

An hour north is Mavericks, where the 30ft waves have been commanding surfers' respect since the 1970s. Supremely harsh and unpredictable, this offshore break draws the kings of big-wave riding to an (almost) annual winter competition: when Mavericks starts to go, the world's top 24 surfers get the call and have 24 hours to get there.

There are good breaks up north in California as well, just be prepared for chillier water (and the occasional shark). In San Francisco, urban swellers get their daily fix at Ocean Beach (a tough spot to learn!) or in Bolinas, 30 miles north, where locals routinely take down the town's sign to dissuade visitors. South, you'll find strong swells and Santa Ana winds in San Diego, La Jolla, Malibu and Santa Barbara, all sporting warmer waters, fewer sharks of the great white variety, and a saucy SoCal beach scene; the best conditions are from September to November. Along the coast of Oregon and Washington, you'll find miles and miles of crowd-free beaches and pockets of surfing communities.

Surf buffs shouldn't miss Stacy Peralta's ultra-engaging documentary, *Riding Giants*, about the history of surfing, with its stellar clips from Hawaii and California in the 1950s and '60s.

Other good surf spots include Seaside Beach on Oregon's Pacific Coast (about 75 miles northwest of Portland), and North Carolina's Cape Hatteras (p392). During summer and fall, East Coasters rip it up at Ditch Plains on Long Island, New Hampshire's Hampton Beach and Cape Cod's Nauset Beach.

The true surfer adventurer might even consider Alaska, with more coastline than the rest of the states combined and loads of potential for uncharted breaks.

But for the serious surfer looking for wave action between October and March, there's only one destination worth mentioning: Hawaii, the birthplace of surfing and the winter home of big waves (they regularly tower over 20ft), where the famed annual Pipeline Masters competition draws the world's best surfers to Oahu's North Shore (p1118). Other excellent areas include Honolua Bay on the North Shore of Maui, Ehukai Beach and Waimea Beach. Beginners beware: these waves have pro written all over them.

If you think you need an ocean for stupendous sets, just watch *Unsalted*, an engaging documentary by Grand Rapids–based Vince Deur, about surfing the Great Lakes.

Hawaii is also a great place for kitesurfing (also known as kiteboarding), yet another exhilarating water sport. The concept is simple: use an inflatable kite (from 15ft to nearly 50ft across) and a board like a surfboard, harness the power of the wind and ride the water surface at amazing speeds with acrobatic agility. Experienced kitesurfers take to the air, zipping off wave crests and flying above the whitecaps.

Kitesurfers can find the prerequisite warm water and consistent winds at Kanaha Beach in Maui (p1125) and scattered locations around O'ahu. Popular California haunts include Long Beach and, further north, San Francisco Bay, where the summer gusts provide thrilling rides off the Emeryville breakwater, and novices can take lessons.

As kitesurfing and its cousin, windsurfing (which uses a sailboard, and was first developed by a 20-year-old sailor named Newman Darby in 1948), rely on similar conditions, you'll find that both sports sometimes share locales: places with good wind, ready access to the waves and reasonable proximity to a watering hole serving local microbrews. Texas' South Padre Island and Oregon's Columbia River Gorge, with wicked west gales and a frisky chop, both qualify.

For more information on surfing resources, see p1136.

SCUBA DIVING & SNORKELING

If you're hankering for a thrilling and colorful underwater experience, it's hard to beat scuba diving. Novice and expert divers alike can take

TOP SURFING SPOTS FROM COAST-TO-COAST

Wherever the surf's up, you're bound to find colorful characters, a laid-back beach town and, of course, a break that warrants bragging rights. Herewith, a sampling of top-rate spots selected for both quality of waves and local/legendary lore. Don a wet suit (or not) and ingratiate yourself with the locals.

Hawaii

Blessed is the state that started it all, where the best swells generally arrive between November and March.

Waikiki (South Shore of Oahu) Hawaii's ancient kings rode waves on wooden boards well before 19th-century missionaries deemed the sport a godless activity. With warm water and gentle rolling waves, Waikiki is perfect for novices, offering long and sudsy rides. Rent boards by the hour from the beachside shacks or take a lesson from one of the many local surf schools.

Pipeline & Sunset Beach (North Shore of Oahu) Home to the classic tubing wave, which form as deep-water swells break over reefs into shallows, these are expert-only spots but well worth an ogle; the Pipeline Masters pro contest is held here annually.

West Coast/California

If big waves reign in Hawaii, California rules surf culture as much of the world knows it. Huntington Beach (aka Surf City, USA) is the quintessential capital, with perpetual sun and a 'perfect' break, particularly during winter when the winds are calm.

Black's Beach, San Diego This 2-mile sandy strip at the base of 300ft cliffs in La Jolla is known as one of the most powerful beach breaks in SoCal, thanks to an underwater canyon just offshore.

Huntington Beach Pier, Huntington Beach, CA Surfer central is a great place to take in the scene – and some lessons (try Corky Carroll's Surf School at www.surfschool.net/).

Ocean Beach, San Francisco, CA Strong currents, cold water and fierce waves add to this break's allure and popularity among serious aficionados.

Oceanside Beach, Oceanside, CA One of SoCal's prettiest beaches boasts one of the world's most consistent surf breaks come summer. It's a family-friendly spot.

Rincon, Santa Barbara, CA Arguably one of the planet's top surfing spots; nearly every major surf champion on the globe has taken Rincon for a ride.

Steamer Lane & Pleasure Point, Santa Cruz, CA The home of O'Neill Wetsuits is a pantheon to surfers – and rumored to be the site of California's first surfing, c 1885. There are 11 world-class breaks, including the point breaks over rock bottoms at these two sweet spots.

their pick of dive sites (some colder and darker than others), spanning the country.

Let's be frank: the most exotic underwater destination in the USA is Hawaii. There, in shimmering aquamarine waters that stay warm year-round, you'll be treated to a psychedelic display of surreal colors and shapes. Swim alongside sea turtles, octopuses and fiesta-colored parrot-fish – not to mention lava tubes and black coral. Back on shore, cap off the reverie with a Kona brew and *poke* made from just-caught 'ahi.

Despite the crowds, Oahu's Hanauma Bay Nature Preserve (p1117) is still one of the world's great spots for snorkeling, with over 450 resident species of reef fish, some of which will swim right up to your mask. There's also fine snorkeling near Maui, with wild spinner dolphins, and on the Big Island in Kealakekua Bay (p1119), Captain Cook's old haunt. The best diving is off the coast or between the islands, so liveaboards are the way to go for scuba buffs. From the green turtles and WWII wrecks off the shores of Oahu to the undersea lava sculptures near little Lana'i, the Aloha State offers endless underwater bliss – but plan ahead, as the dive sites change with the seasons.

Swami's, Encinitas, CA Located below Seacliff Roadside Park, this popular surfing beach has multiple breaks guaranteeing you some fantastic waves; the surrounding kelp beds make it a good spot for some diving action as well.

Midwest

'Third Coast' surfers get their year-round fix on the Great Lake breakers, thanks to over 10,500 miles of shoreline.

Lake Michigan, Michigan, IL Bowing to the popularity of the sport on this vast lake, Chicago is poised to allow surfing at five Windy City beaches.

East Coast

The Atlantic seaboard states harbor some terrific and unexpected surfing spots – especially if you're after more moderate swells. Still, these waters can be fickle, cold and crowded. You'll find the warmest waters off Florida's Gulf Coast, where jetties, piers, and sandbars offer many fine surfing opportunities.

Cocoa Beach, Melbourne Beach, FL World Champion Kelly Slater has called this beach home. Small crowds and mellow waves make it a paradise for beginners and longboarders. Just south is the Inlet, known for consistent surf and crowds to match; beginners will be happy riding 'Second Peak' and 'Third Peak' north of the jetty.

Reef Rd, Palm Beach, FL This stellar spot features exposed beach and reef breaks with consistent surf, especially at low tide; winter is best. Beware of sharks, rocks and crowds at all times.

Cape Hatteras Lighthouse, NC This very popular area has several quality spots and infinitely ridable breaks that gracefully handle swells of all sizes and winds from any direction. Scuba divers take note: if you love wrecks, check out the nearby 'Graveyard of the Atlantic.'

Long Island, Montauk, NY More than a dozen surfing areas dot the length of Long Island from Montack's oft-packed Ditch Plains to Nassau County's Long Beach, with its 3-mile stretch of curling waves.

Casino Pier, Seaside Heights, NJ Both sides of the pier offer arguably the longest tube rides in NJ – just be prepared to compete with the crowds and entitled locals.

Point Judith, Narragansett, RI Rhode Island has some of the most premier surfing in the Northeast, with 40 miles of coastline and more than 30 surf spots, including this rocky point break offering an array of wave types, from long rollers to hollow barrels. Not for beginners.

Coast Guard Beach, Eastham, MA Part of the Cape Cod National Seashore, this family-friendly beach is known for its consistent shortboard/longboard swell all summer long.

Throughout the year, California's coastal waters host an impressive variety of life: colorful nudibranchs (fancy for sea slugs), wild dolphins, and gray whales on their annual migration between Mexico and Alaska. Diving beneath Monterey Bay (p962), you'll feel like you've landed in a dark forest, with shafts of sunlight casting eerie shadows as sea lions dart by. In all directions, 100ft-high kelp stalks sway toward the glittering surface while jumbo starfish float along the ocean's bottom. The aptly named Jade Cove (about 10 miles south of Lucia on Hwy 1) has the world's only underwater concentration of jade, making for an unforgettable dive. In Limekiln State Park, Soberanes Point and Lopez Point, look out for orcas, dolphins and seals. The **Monterey Bay Dive Company** (www.montereyscubadiving.com) is a handy resource for sites and guides.

One of the most popular dive areas is the Point Lobos State Reserve (p961), part of the spectacular Monterey Bay (also home of perhaps the world's finest aquarium, complete with resident great white sharks; see p962). The Channel Islands (p956), lying between Santa Barbara and Los Angeles, harbor spiny lobsters, angel sharks and numerous dive sites best accessed by liveaboard charter. In the chillier waters north of San

Francisco, thick-skinned divers await April 1, the start of the season for north-coast red abalone, a local delicacy.

With more than 1000 miles of coastline boasting over 20 different areas offering undersea adventures from Pensacola (p553) to Jacksonville (p537), Florida offers some of the finest diving in the States, with hundreds of sites and dive shops offering equipment and guided excursions. The Florida Keys, a curving string of 31 islets, are the crown jewel; expect a brilliant mix of marine habitats, North America's only living coral garden and the occasional shipwreck. Key Largo is home to the John Pennekamp Coral Reef State Park with over 200 miles of underwater bliss. The Atlantic coast, where the waters are brisk, choppy and full of speedy fish, offers the state's most wild and unpredictable diving. South of West Palm Beach, you'll find clearer waters and fantastic year-round diving with ample reefs. In the Panhandle, or northern part of the state, you can scuba in the calm and balmy waters of the Gulf of Mexico; off Pensacola and Destin, there are fabulous wreck dives; and you can dive with manatees near Crystal River.

Over the Edge: Death in Grand Canyon, by a river-guiding biologist and a wilderness doctor (Michael Ghiglieri and Thomas Myers), is a terrifying chronicle of every ill-fated excursion in the Canyon; most adventurers could have avoided their unhappy endings.

Even inland, a vast network of springs, sinkholes, rivers and lakes offer unique opportunities for the scuba set (local dive shops provide specialized cave training). There's terrific diving and snorkeling (and much warmer water) beyond the mangrove swamps of the Florida Keys, FL, boasting the world's third-largest coral system. Look for manatees off Islamorada (p525) or take an expedition to Dry Tortugas (p531), where the expansive reef swarms with barracuda, sea turtles and a couple of hundred sunken ships.

Along the northern coast of North Carolina, in the Cape Hatteras National Seashore, divers can explore historical wrecks from the Civil War (and encounter tiger sand sharks), and there are numerous options for dive charters within the Outer Banks and the Cape Lookout areas; the peak diving season is May to October. If you find yourself in Arkansas, hit Lake Ouachita, the state's largest lake, ringed by forested mountains and known for its pristine waters and some 30 distinct dive spots. Camp along the lakeshore and, quite literally, dive in. It's also the site of a 16-mile water-based trail, the first of its kind in the country. Get information at local marinas, which also cater to divers.

The USA's most unexpected dive spot? Michigan's Lakes Superior and Huron, with thousands of shipwrecks lying strewn on the sandy bottoms – just don't expect to see any angelfish!

For responsible snorkeling tips, see p525.

WATCHING WILDLIFE

If your must-see list includes a bear, a moose or even a roseate spoonbill, you've come to the right country: there are loads of accessible spots for watching wildlife in its natural habitat. Of course, sightings are never guaranteed. Pick your season and time of day (hint: dawn and dusk), get yourself into the heart of the habitat (preferably by foot, bike or boat) and chances are you'll be rewarded.

Start with the national parks, which represent a cross-section of natural habitats. (For the top national parks for wildlife, see p108). Glacier (p808) is bear-country central, so be prepared for a personal encounter. Yellowstone (p793) is terrific for seeing elk (more than 30,000 are in residence during the summer months), gray wolves (reintroduced not long ago), bison (North America's largest mammal) and deer, while the classic North Woods of Isle Royale (p625) showcases wolves and moose. Big Bend (p746) is tops for spotting birds and whitetail deer, while beavers and turtles haul out along the Rio Grande's big bend, for which the park is named. Spot cartoonish, colorful puffins and playful harbor seals in the waters surrounding Acadia (p310).

TOP WHALE-WATCHING SPOTS

For a spectacular – if not terrifying – wildlife encounter, it's hard to beat seeing orcas breaching. Ten feet in front of you. From a kayak.

- Alaska: Glacier Bay (p1083)
- California: Monterey Bay (p962), SoCal's Channel Islands (p956) and Point Reyes National Seashore (p989).
- Hawaii: Maui's southern and western shores (p1123).
- Massachusetts: Cape Cod (p260)
- Washington: Orcas Island (p1039), Lime Kiln Point State Park on San Juan Island (p1039)

For alligators, manatees, crocodiles and sea turtles, paddle the Everglades (p519), or hike Ding Darling National Preserve on Sanibel Island, FL, where the warm gulf waters draw frolicking dolphins. In Alaska, Denali's wide-open tundra (p1099) makes for unobstructed viewing of Dall sheep, caribou, moose, grizzlies and wolves. Rocky Mountain National Park (p774) is home to mountain goats, elk, marmots and sure-footed bighorn sheep. And for that iconic image of buffalo roaming the Great Plains? Head to Theodore Roosevelt National Park (p675), Lewis and Clark territory, where wild horses and bison meander freely.

Boston's North Shore, particularly Plum Island, is one of the best places in the East to spot migrating birds (and sample outstanding lobster rolls). California's Monterey Bay teems with five species of seals and sea lions, cavorting in the kelp ribbons with otters, dolphins and porpoises. Ano Nuevo State Reserve, 55 miles south of San Francisco, hosts the world's largest mainland breeding colony for elephant seals; plan ahead to view the riveting (and loud!) spectacle of battling males and birthing females from December through March.

FISHING

No sport – except maybe baseball – is as central to the American mythos as fishing. From cruises in pursuit of deep-sea marlin off the Florida Keys and remote coastal fishing camps in salmon-rich Alaska, to the many fly-fishing outfits in the Rockies, the entire USA is, in the eyes of many anglers, one big, glorious fishery.

Scores of websites and books provide advice and instruction on how to indulge in this ancient (but highly evolved) enterprise. Your best clues, however, will come from plying locals for secret spots. Five species of salmon spawn in Alaska, while Georgia produces the buttery Mississippi catfish (delicious pan-fried). Big-game fish, such as tarpon and sailfish, leap above Florida's waters, and Minnesota offers the opportunity to reel in great northern pike. Deep-sea fishing is divine in Hawaii's Kona area, where you can tackle yellowfin and mahimahi for boat-side sushi. Beautiful Maine is where you'll go to tangle – from shore – with striped bass, the quintessential sporting fish. And on Cape Cod and the islands of Nantucket and Martha's Vineyard, summer means surfcasting for bluefish and striped bass at sunrise – or with a cooler of beer at sunset.

For sheer fishing delight, not to mention culinary enjoyment, think trout. Most anglers agree that fly-fishing is at its Zen best in the Colorado Rockies, Idaho, Washington's Methow Valley, and especially in Montana, 'Big Sky' country. This is the state that spawned the filming of *A River Runs Through It,* and where one river alone – the Bighorn, beginning in

Wyoming – is said to host over 6000 trout per mile. A guaranteed catch spot? Missouri's Bennett Spring, where the cool, clear waters are stocked with farm-fed trout every night.

HORSEBACK RIDING

Chances are you've seen a classic Western and could recognize a cowboy anywhere: a burly guy in chaps who boldly expunges evil from frontier towns, thunders across the sage-studded plains on horseback and always gets the beautiful girl in the end.

Cowboy wannabes will be happy to learn that horseback riding of every style, from Western to bareback, is available across the USA. The best opportunities, through country that's still rugged and wild and, yes, resembles those old Westerns, are (of course!) in the West. We're talking everything from week-long expeditions through the canyons of southern Utah and cattle wrangling in Wyoming, to pony rides along the Oregon coast. Finding horses is easy; rental stables and riding schools are located around and in many of the national parks. Experienced equestrians can explore alone or in the company of guides familiar with local flora, fauna and history (much of which was made on horseback). Half- and full-day group trail rides, which usually include lunch in a wildflower-speckled meadow, are popular and plentiful.

To be the first in the continental USA to see the sun pop over the horizon, park yourself atop Cadillac Mountain in Acadia National Park.

California is terrific for riding, with fog-swept trails leading along the cliffs of Point Reyes National Seashore, longer excursions through the high-altitude lakes of the Ansel Adams Wilderness, and multiday pack trips in Yosemite. Utah's Capitol Reef (p881) and Canyonlands (p880) also provide spectacular four-hoofed outings, as can the mountains, arroyos and plains of Colorado, Arizona, New Mexico, Montana and Texas.

Dude ranches come in all varieties, from down-duvet luxurious to barn-duty authentic on working cattle ranches. Decide what kind of experience you want and do diligent research. They're found in most of the western states, and even some eastern ones (such as Tennessee and North Carolina). Real-life cowboys are included.

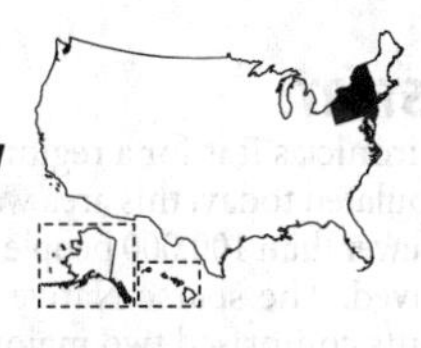

New York, New Jersey & Pennsylvania

Full of places where jaded city dwellers escape to seek simple lives, where artists retreat for inspiration, and where pretty houses line main streets, this is a region of defining American locales. It's provincial in many ways, with rough-around-the edges towns in the midst of reinventing themselves as tourist destinations. Even though it's the most populated and industrialized part of the US, it's also proof that America is really a nation of small places, many here set amid stunning scenery but often overlooked in a country so large.

New York City, one of the world's great cities, looms like an alien mothership and serves as a sort of Rorschach test; even the most jaded upstater will have a say on it. Overall, there is a conflicted relationship between urban and rural ways of life. For every teenage suburbanite itching to make it to Broadway, there is a downtown family ready to leave and start a B&B in the peaceful Catskills. Miles and miles of glorious beaches are within reach, from glamorous Long Island to the Jersey Shore – the latter ranges from stately to kitschy.

River-rich Pittsburgh and bohemian Buffalo, not to mention the lively historic gem that is Philadelphia, are all worthy destinations in their own right. A trip to Amish country in southern Pennsylvania serves as a reminder that it's possible, though challenging, to resist modernity's rushing pull. The mountain wilderness of the Adirondacks reaches skyward just a day's drive north of New York City, a journey that perfectly encapsulates this region's heady character.

HIGHLIGHTS

- Traveling round the world without ever leaving the kaleidoscope of neighborhoods and cultures that is **New York City** (p145)
- Enjoying the kitsch and calm of the **Jersey Shore** (p208)
- Absorbing the story of the birth of the nation in Philadelphia's **Independence National Historic Park** (p214)
- Walking the densely forested paths of the unspoiled **Catskills** (p197)
- Exploring the impressive wilderness beauty of the **Adirondacks** (p201)
- Camping along the shores of the St Lawrence River in the **Thousand Islands** (p202)
- Bar-hopping on the Strip in **Pittsburgh** (p230)
- Wine tasting on Long Island's **North Fork** (p195)
- Cycling the back roads of **Pennsylvania Dutch Country** (p228)
- Floating past bucolic scenery in the **Delaware Water Gap** (p208)

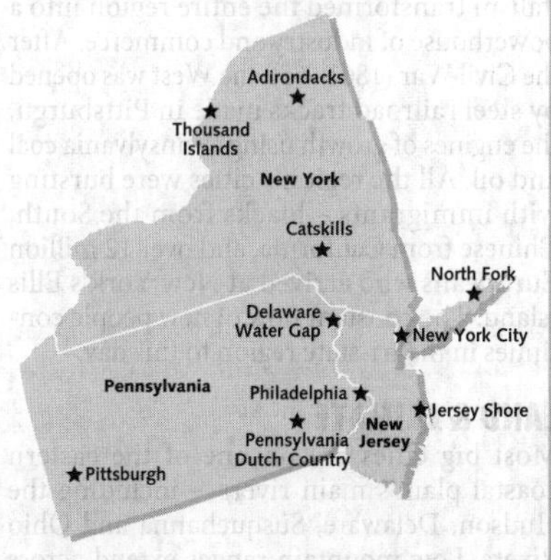

HISTORY

As ironic as it is for a region that is so thickly populated today, this area was probably home to fewer than 100,000 people before Europeans arrived. The sparse Native American settlements comprised two major cultural groups: the Algonquians and the Iroquois.

But by the mid-16th century, French fur trappers and traders had found their way from Canada to the region via the St Lawrence River. In 1609 explorer Henry Hudson found, sailed and named the Hudson River, claiming the land for the Dutch, who started several settlements in 'New Netherlands,' where the Iroquois took over control of the booming fur trade.

The tiny Dutch settlement on Manhattan Island soon surrendered to a Royal Navy warship and the new colonial power created two territories, 'New York' and 'New Jersey,' which soon attracted a great number of settlers from nearby New England. New Jersey's population grew rapidly, due in no small part to the great neighboring colonies of New York and Pennsylvania – the latter of which played a leading role in the Revolutionary War (1775–83), though important battles occurred in all three states. Many Iroquois allied themselves with the British and suffered badly from military defeats, disease, European encroachment and reprisals. Farmers, meanwhile, displaced the Algonquians from coastal areas and river valleys.

As early as the 1840s the region's major cities were linked by railways; the population also grew with waves of immigration, starting with the Irish in the 1840s and 1850s. Natural resources, abundant labor and unfettered capitalism transformed the entire region into a powerhouse of industry and commerce. After the Civil War (1861–65), the West was opened by steel railroad tracks made in Pittsburgh, the engines of growth using Pennsylvania coal and oil. All the region's cities were bursting with immigrants – blacks from the South, Chinese from California, and over 12 million Europeans who arrived at New York's Ellis Island. The constant flow of new people continues in the tri-state region to this day.

LAND & CLIMATE

Most big cities are on one of the eastern coastal plain's main rivers – including the Hudson, Delaware, Susquehanna and Ohio Rivers. Low mountain ranges extend across the region's interior and are heavily forested with pine, red spruce, maple, oak, ash and birch trees.

All three states experience the full range of the four seasons. Temperatures are always a bit cooler to the north and warmer in the south, but generally, fall temperatures hover around the 40°F to 50°F (4.4°C to 10°C) mark, while winter can range from the teens to the high 30s (-10°C to 3°C). Expect spring temperatures to be between 50°F to 70°F (10°C to 22°C) – plus some extra doses of rain – and in summer from the high 60°F mark to the mid-80s (15.5°C to 31°C).

PARKS & WILDLIFE

Parklands and recreation areas are in big supply here, as is wildlife, at first surprising to many who associate these states only with large urban areas. Black bears, bobcats and even elk can be found in forested parts of the states; more common are various species of deer. Falcons, eagles, hawks and migrating species of birds stop over in the region, some even within only a few miles of New York City. In New York alone, you'll find a few dozen spots managed by the **National Parks Service** (NPS; www.nps.gov), many of them more of the historic-site than pure-green-space variety, and hundreds of **state parks** (☎ 518-474-0456; www.nysparks.state.ny.us), ranging from waterfalls and forests to beaches.

New Jersey is home to many federally managed areas, including its southeastern **Pinelands National Reserve** (p210) and the **Delaware Water Gap National Recreation Area** (p208). Its many **state parks** (☎ 609-984-0370; www.state.nj.us/dep/parksandforests) range from the beachy **Cape May Point State Park** (p212) to the mountainous, forested **Kittatinny Valley State Park** (p208) in the north.

Pennsylvania is home to dozens of NPS areas that range from historic sites to a significant portion of the Appalachian National Scenic Trail, a 2175-mile footpath that snakes its way from Maine to Georgia. The **state parks** (☎ 888-727-2757; www.dcnr.state.pa.us/stateparks) include a huge array of thick forests, rolling parklands and trails, as well as **Presque Isle State Park** (p237), a beach that juts out into Lake Erie.

INFORMATION

For this vast and varied region, see individual states – New York p193, New Jersey p206 and Pennsylvania p213.

GETTING THERE & AROUND

The big cities all have airports, but New York's John F Kennedy (JFK; p190) is the region's major international gateway. Alternatives include Newark International Airport (EWR; p190); La Guardia (LGA; p190), in Queens, with mostly domestic flights; and the Long Island MacArthur Airport (ISP) in Islip, also offering domestic travel (see p191). Philadelphia and Pittsburgh also have small international airports.

Greyhound (p1160) buses serve main cities and towns, while **Peter Pan Bus Lines** (☎ 800-343-9999; www.peterpanbus.com) and **Adirondack Trailways** (☎ 800-776-7548; www.trailwaysny.com) are two regional bus lines. Amtrak (p1166) provides rail services throughout the New York metropolitan area, linking New York with much of New Jersey, as well as Philadelphia and Pittsburgh. Most popular day trips, at least when leaving from New York City, are easily accessible by one of the three commuter-rail lines (see p191). If you're driving, the main north–south highway is the I-95.

NEW YORK CITY

The fin de siècle Gilded Age may be over, what with Wall Street's implosion in 2008, but the city lives on. Loud and fast and pulsing with energy, New York City (population 8.3 million), is symphonic, exhausting and always evolving. Storefronts are being shuttered more than usual and if there is a malaise in the air, there's also a palpable feeling that maybe the city is shifting, reorganizing, once again in the process of reinventing itself. The darker aspects of the city perhaps aren't as immediately visible as they once were – after all, neighborhoods such as Times Square and the Meatpacking District have been scrubbed clean for years now. However, *Law & Order*–type scenarios are still splashed across the headlines daily and surely the bottom of the East River continues to harbor secrets.

Maybe only a Walt Whitman poem cataloguing typical city scenes, from the humblest hole-in-the-wall to grand buildings, could begin to do the city justice. It remains one of the world centers of fashion, theater, food, music, publishing, advertising and, of course, finance. And as Groucho Marx once said, 'When it's 9:30 in New York, it's 1937 in Los Angeles.' Coming here for the first time from anywhere else is like stepping into a movie, one you've probably been unknowingly writing, one that contains all imagined possibilities. From the middle of Times Square to the most obscure corner of the Bronx, you'll find extremes. From Brooklyn's Russian enclave in Brighton Beach to the mini South America in Queens, virtually every country in the world has a bustling proxy community in the city. You can experience a little bit of everything on a visit here, as long as you take care to travel with a loose itinerary and an open mind.

HISTORY

After Henry Hudson first claimed this land in 1609 for his Dutch East India Company sponsors, he reported it to be 'as beautiful a land as one can hope to tread upon.' Soon after it was named 'Manhattan,' derived from local Munsee Indian words and meaning 'Island of Hills.'

By 1625 a colony, soon called New Amsterdam, was established, and the island was bought from the Munsee Indians by Peter Minuit. George Washington was sworn in here as the republic's first president in 1789, and when the Civil War broke out, New York City, which supplied a significant contingent of volunteers to defend the Union, became an organizing center for the movement to emancipate slaves.

Throughout the 19th century successive waves of immigrants – Irish, German, English, Scandinavian, Slavic, Italian, Greek and central European Jewish – led to a swift population increase, followed by the building of empires in industry and finance, and a golden age of skyscrapers.

After WWII New York City was the premier city in the world, but it suffered from a new phenomenon: 'white flight' to the suburbs. By the 1970s the graffiti-ridden subway system had become a symbol of New York's civic and economic decline. But NYC regained much of its swagger in the 1980s, led by colorful three-term mayor Ed Koch. The city elected its first African American mayor, David Dinkins, in 1989, but ousted him after a single term in favor of Republican Rudolph Giuliani (a 2008 primary candidate for US president). It was during Giuliani's reign that catastrophe struck on September 11, 2001, when the

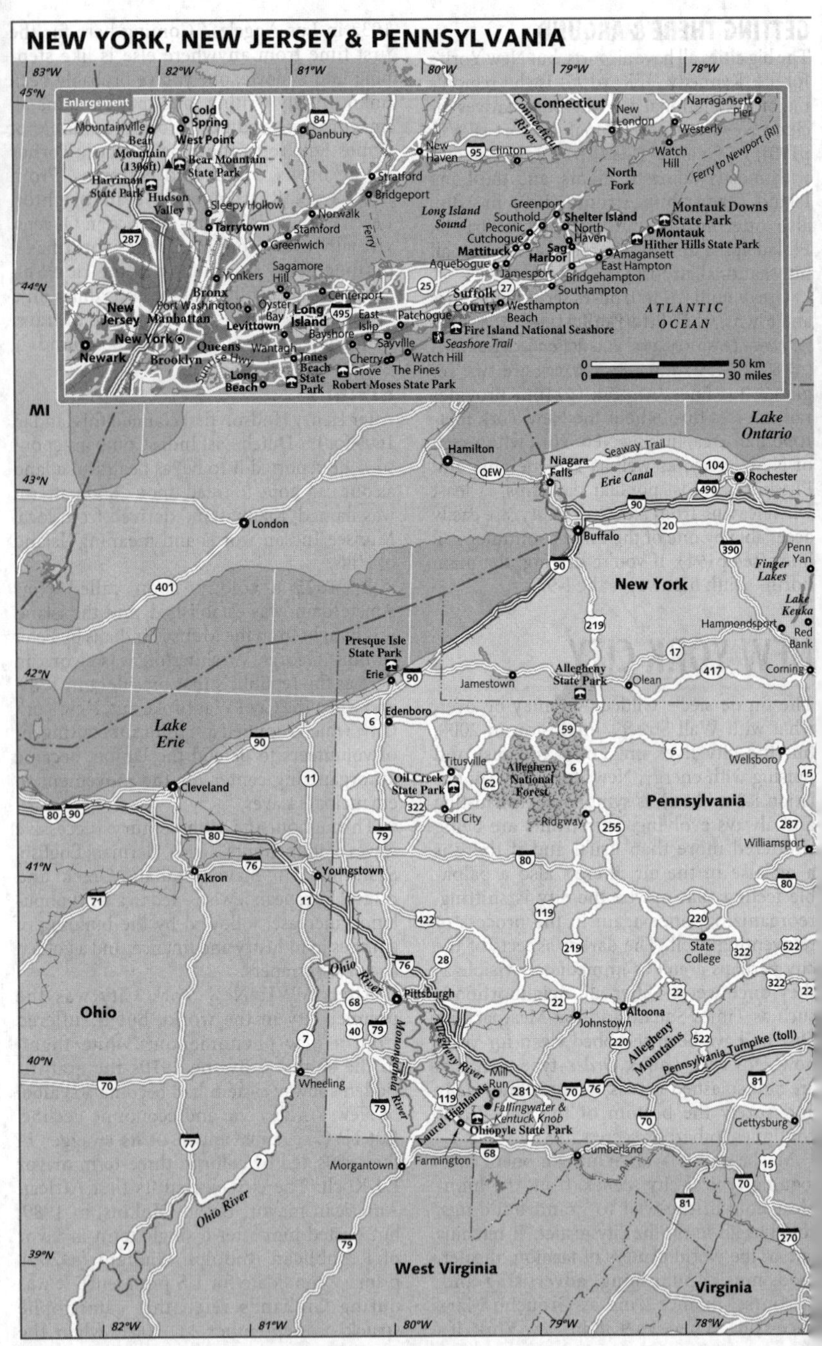
NEW YORK, NEW JERSEY & PENNSYLVANIA
Enlargement
Cold Spring
West Point
Bear Mountain (1306ft)
Bear Mountain State Park
Harriman State Park
Hudson Valley
Mountainville
Danbury
New Haven
Clinton
Connecticut
Connecticut River
New London
Westerly
Narragansett Pier
Watch Hill
Ferry to Newport (RI)
Stratford
Bridgeport
North Fork
Sleepy Hollow
Tarrytown
Norwalk
Stamford
Greenwich
Long Island Sound
Ferry
Greenport
Southold
Shelter Island
Peconic
North Haven
Cutchogue
Mattituck
Sag Harbor
Montauk Downs State Park
Montauk
Hither Hills State Park
Amagansett
East Hampton
Bridgehampton
Southampton
Aquebogue
Jamesport
Yonkers
Sagamore Hill
Centerport
Bronx
Port Washington
Oyster Bay
Long Island
New Jersey
Manhattan
Levittown
East Islip
Patchogue
Suffolk County
Westhampton Beach
ATLANTIC OCEAN
New York
Queens
Wantagh
Bayshore
Sayville
Fire Island National Seashore
Seashore Trail
Newark
Brooklyn
Sunrise Hwy
Jones Beach State Park
Cherry Grove
Watch Hill
The Pines
Long Beach
Robert Moses State Park
50 km
30 miles
MI
Lake Ontario
Hamilton
QEW
Niagara Falls
Seaway Trail
Erie Canal
Rochester
London
Buffalo
Penn Yan
Finger Lakes
New York
Lake Keuka
Hammondsport
Red Bank
Presque Isle State Park
Erie
Jamestown
Allegheny State Park
Olean
Corning
Edenboro
Lake Erie
Titusville
Oil Creek State Park
Allegheny National Forest
Oil City
Ridgway
Pennsylvania
Wellsboro
Williamsport
Cleveland
Akron
Youngstown
State College
Ohio River
Pittsburgh
Altoona
Johnstown
Allegheny Mountains
Pennsylvania Turnpike (toll)
Ohio
Monongahela River
Allegheny River
Mill Run
Wheeling
Laurel Highlands
Fallingwater & Kentuck Knob
Ohiopyle State Park
Gettysburg
Cumberland
Morgantown
Farmington
Ohio River
West Virginia
Virginia

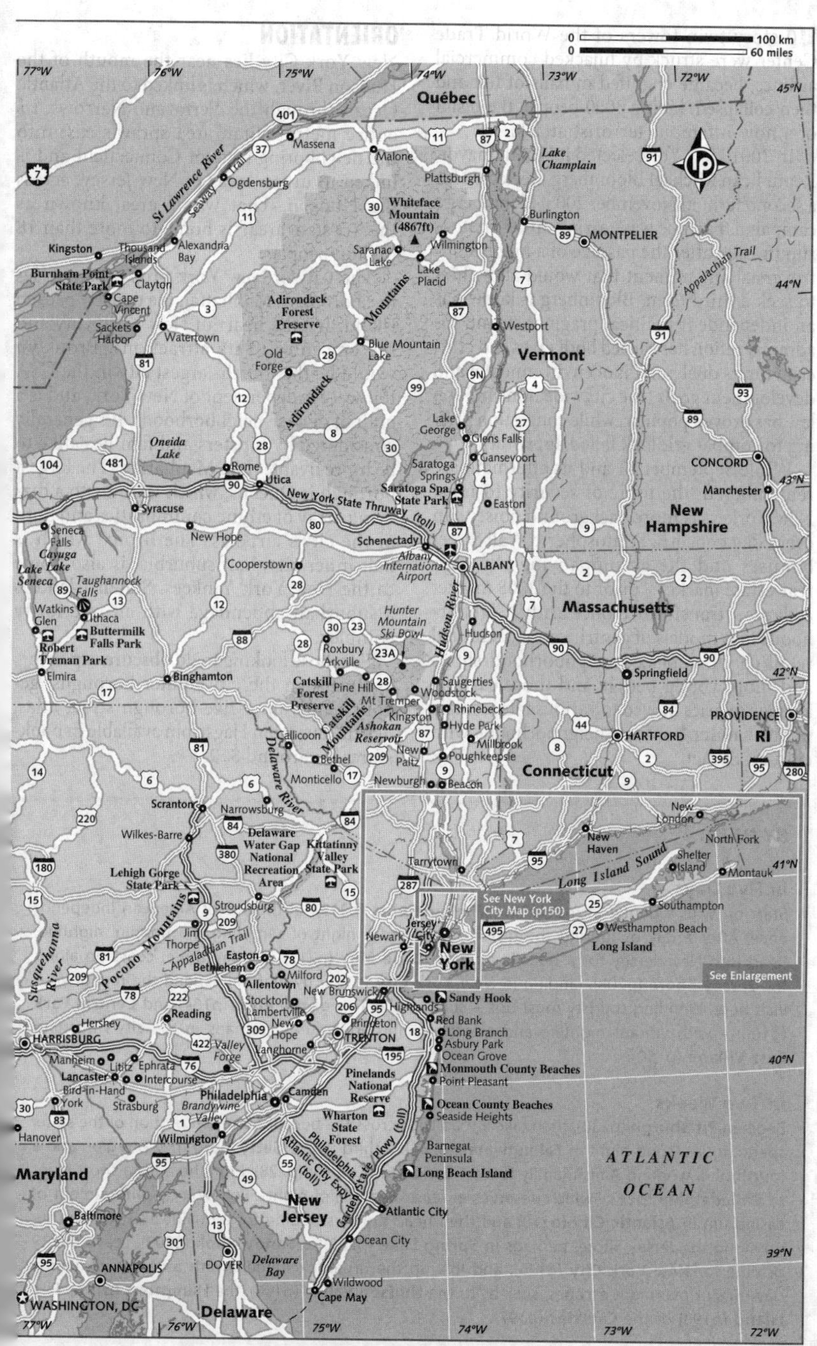
0 100 km
0 60 miles
77°W
76°W
75°W
74°W
73°W
72°W
45°N
44°N
43°N
42°N
41°N
40°N
39°N
Québec
Massena
Malone
Plattsburgh
Lake Champlain
St Lawrence River
Seaway Trail
Ogdensburg
Whiteface Mountain (4867ft)
Burlington
MONTPELIER
Kingston
Thousand Islands
Alexandria Bay
Saranac Lake
Wilmington
Lake Placid
Burnham Point State Park
Clayton
Cape Vincent
Appalachian Trail
Sackets Harbor
Watertown
Adirondack Forest Preserve
Mountains
Westport
Blue Mountain Lake
Old Forge
Vermont
Adirondack
Lake George
Glens Falls
Gansevoort
Oneida Lake
Rome
Utica
Saratoga Springs
Saratoga Spa State Park
Easton
CONCORD
Manchester
New Hampshire
Syracuse
New York State Thruway (toll)
Seneca Falls
New Hope
Schenectady
Cayuga Lake
Lake Seneca
Albany International Airport
ALBANY
Cooperstown
Taughannock Falls
Watkins Glen
Ithaca
Buttermilk Falls Park
Robert Treman Park
Elmira
Hunter Mountain Ski Bowl
Hudson River
Hudson
Massachusetts
Roxbury
Arkville
Springfield
Binghamton
Catskill Forest Preserve
Pine Hill
Saugerties
Woodstock
Mt Tremper
Catskill Mountains
Kingston
Rhinebeck
Hyde Park
Ashokan Reservoir
Callicoon
Delaware River
Millbrook
Poughkeepsie
Bethel
New Paltz
HARTFORD
PROVIDENCE
RI
Monticello
Newburgh
Beacon
Connecticut
Scranton
Narrowsburg
New London
New Haven
North Fork
Wilkes-Barre
Delaware Water Gap National Recreation Area
Kittatinny Valley State Park
Tarrytown
Shelter Island
Montauk
Long Island Sound
Lehigh Gorge State Park
Stroudsburg
See New York City Map (p150)
Southampton
Westhampton Beach
Long Island
Pocono Mountains
Jim Thorpe
Jersey City
Newark
New York
Easton
Bethlehem
Allentown
Milford
See Enlargement
Susquehanna River
New Brunswick
Sandy Hook
Reading
Stockton
Lambertville
Highlands
Hershey
New Hope
Princeton
Red Bank
HARRISBURG
TRENTON
Long Branch
Asbury Park
Valley Forge
Langhorne
Ocean Grove
Manheim
Lititz
Ephrata
Monmouth County Beaches
Lancaster
Intercourse
Pinelands National Reserve
Point Pleasant
Bird-in-Hand
Philadelphia
Camden
York
Strasburg
Brandywine Valley
Ocean County Beaches
Seaside Heights
Wharton State Forest
Hanover
Wilmington
Barnegat Peninsula
Atlantic City Expy (toll)
Philadelphia
Garden State Pkwy (toll)
Long Beach Island
ATLANTIC OCEAN
Maryland
New Jersey
Atlantic City
Baltimore
Ocean City
ANNAPOLIS
DOVER
Delaware Bay
Wildwood
Cape May
WASHINGTON, DC
Delaware

110-story twin towers of the World Trade Center were struck by hijacked commercial airlines, became engulfed in balls of fire and then collapsed, killing 3000 people, the result of a now-infamous terrorist attack.

In 2001 New York elected its 108th mayor, Republican Michael Bloomberg. Reelected for a second term in November 2005, Bloomberg's campaign machine was gearing up for another run in 2009 after the passage of a highly controversial amendment that would allow him to seek a third term. Bloomberg is known as an independent political pragmatist, and his administration has earned both raves and criticism for its dual pursuit of environmental and development goals (the citywide nonsmoking law has proved popular, while congestion pricing to combat gridlock failed approval).

While September 11 and its aftermath are remembered, the topic of security to most New Yorkers is more background noise than every day concern. Stratospheric Wall Street bonuses and the accompanying sky-high real-estate market – prior to the 2008 market collapse – transformed once gritty neighborhoods into models of gentrification. National retail chains replaced neighborhood shops and more young people and those earning average salaries moved to various increasingly popular outer-borough neighborhoods with cultural cachet.

ORIENTATION

New York City lies near the mouth of the Hudson River, which is linked to the Atlantic Ocean through the Verrazano Narrows. Its entire metropolitan area sprawls east into the neighboring state of Connecticut and is linked to urban areas of New Jersey, across the Hudson. That whole area, known as the 'tri-state area,' is home to more than 18 million people.

The City of New York proper comprises five boroughs. Manhattan is a densely packed island. It's the heart of New York City and the epicenter of its attractions. Brooklyn would be the fourth-largest city in the USA if it were independent of New York, and is a quilt of diverse neighborhoods. It's generally considered by hipsters and families alike to be more livable than Manhattan. The largest borough is Queens, which is home to a dizzying array of ethnic communities and both of the city's airports. The Bronx, which is half inner city, half suburbia, is also home to the New York Yankees. Staten Island is a suburban appendage with an inferiority complex.

For those looking to do obscure exploring, especially in the city's outer boroughs, get your hands on a five-borough street atlas, like the one from Hagstrom available in bookstores for around $19.

NY-NJ-PA...

In Five Days

Start off with a gentle introduction in **Philadelphia** (p213), birthplace of American independence. After a day of touring the historic sites and a night of sampling the hoppin' nightlife, head into New Jersey for a bucolic night in **Cape May** (p212). On day three, coast up along the **Jersey Shore** (p208), landing in **New York City** (p145) by nightfall. Spend the rest of your visit here, blending touristy must-dos – such as the **Top of the Rock** (p164) and **Central Park** (p166) – with vibrant nightlife and eclectic dining adventures, perhaps in the city's bustling **East Village** (p158).

In Two Weeks

Begin in **Pittsburgh** (p230), then take a road trip across the bucolic southern portion of the state, spending a second night in **Fallingwater** (p236), a third in the **Gettysburg** (p229) region and a fourth on a working Amish family farm in **Lancaster County** (p228). From here it's a short jaunt to **Philadelphia** (p213), which deserves at least a couple of nights. Follow it up with a night of casino fun in **Atlantic City** (p210) and then head north, stopping for a quaint B&B stay further up along the Jersey Shore, perhaps in **Spring Lake** (p209) or **Sandy Hook** (p208). Leave plenty of time for **New York City** (p145), and mix up the urban excitement with a couple of nearby day trips or overnight escapes, such as to the **Hudson Valley** (p196), the **Hamptons** (p194), **Fire Island** (p193) or the **Catskills** (p197).

INFORMATION

Bookstores

There is a handful of **Barnes & Noble** (www.barnesandnoble.com) and **Borders** (www.borders.com) superstores, but also some great independent shops:

Bluestockings Bookstore (Map pp152-3; ☎ 212-777-6028; 172 Allen St; 🕑 11am-11pm) A homegrown women's bookstore-café with frequent readings and other events.

Book Culture (Map pp168-9; ☎ 212-865-1588; 536 W 112th St; 🕑 9am-10pm Mon-Fri, to 8pm Sat, 11am-7pm Sun) Formerly Labyrinth Books, and still going strong in the Columbia University neighborhood.

Idlewild Books (Map pp162-3; ☎ 212-414-8888; 12 W 19th St; 🕑 11:30am-8pm Mon-Fri, noon-7pm Sat & Sun) Near Union S. Fiction and nonfiction are uniquely organized by country and regions of the world.

McNally Jackson Books (Map pp152-3; ☎ 212-274-1160; 52 Prince St; 🕑 10am-10pm Mon-Sat, to 9pm Sun) A NoLita refuge with a nice café and regular author readings.

Shakespeare & Co Booksellers (Map pp152-3; ☎ 212-979-5711; 716 Broadway, at Washington Pl; 🕑 10am-11pm Mon-Fri, noon-9pm Sat & Sun) A general bookseller with especially good sections on NY history; more academic subjects downstairs.

St Mark's Bookshop (Map pp152-3; ☎ 212-260-7853; 31 Third Ave; 🕑 10am-midnight Mon-Sat, from 11am Sun) Especially good for academics and those who want to read like one.

Strand Bookstore (Map pp152-3; ☎ 212-473-1452; 828 Broadway, at E 12th St; 🕑 9:30am-10:30pm Mon-Sat, from 11am Sun) The city's preeminent bibliophile warehouse, selling new and used books.

Internet Access

There are many wi-fi access hot spots around the city, including the Lincoln Center (see p167) uptown, Bryant Park (see p164) in midtown and Union Square (see p160) downtown. The hourly fee for surfing the web at internet cafés ranges from $3 to $12. Full-service **FedEx Office** (www.fedex.com) stores scattered around the city offer web access.

Cybercafe Times Square (Map pp162–3; ☎ 212-333-4109; 250 W 49th St, btwn Broadway & 8th Ave; per 30min $7; 🕑 8am-11pm Mon-Fri, from 11am Sat & Sun)

Netzone Internet Cafe (Map pp162-3; ☎ 212-239-770; 28 W 32nd St, 5th fl; per hr $4; 🕑 9am-5am)

New York Public Library (Map pp162-3; ☎ 212-930-800; www.nypl.org/branch/local; E 42nd St, at Fifth Ave) Offers free half-hour internet access, though there may be a wait in the afternoons; more than 80 other local branches also have free access.

Web2Zone (Map pp152-3; ☎ 212-614-7300; 54 Cooper Sq, btwn Astor Pl & Fourth Ave; per hr $6; 🕑 9am-11pm Mon-Fri, 10am-11pm Sat, noon-10pm Sun)

If you have a laptop, there are a few more friendly and comfortable places with wi-fi access:

Aroma Café (Map pp152-3; ☎ 212-533-1094; 145 Greene St; 🕑 7am-11pm; 📶) Trendy café in SoHo.

Think Coffee (Map pp152-3; ☎ 212-228-6226; 248 Mercer St; 🕑 7am-11:30pm Mon-Fri, from 8am Sat & Sun; 📶) Swamped with NYU students.

Pe'Can Café (Map pp152-3; ☎ 646-613-8293; 130 Franklin St; 🕑 7:30am-6pm Mon-Fri, 8am-5pm Sat & Sun; 📶) In Tribeca, across the street from the Franklin St subway stop (1 line). Also serves good sandwiches and salads.

Media

Daily News (www.nydailynews.com) A daily tabloid, leans toward the sensational – archrivals of the *New York Post*.

New York (www.newyorkmagazine.com) Weekly featuring listings and NYC-oriented news and gossip for the hip but established urbanite.

New York Post (www.nypost.com) Media mogul Rupert Murdoch publishes this daily tabloid, famous for spicy headlines, celebrity scandal–laden Page Six and good sports coverage.

New York Times (www.nytimes.com) The 'Gray Lady' is struggling in these lean economic times but is still the newspaper of record for readers throughout the US and much of the English-speaking world.

NY1 An excellent source of local news, this is the city's all-day news station on Time Warner cable's Channel 1.

Onion (www.onion.com) Weekly fake news and satire website; the print edition has real and extensive listings for goings-on about town, especially comedy.

Village Voice (www.villagevoice.com) The weekly tabloid's rep is on the wane as far as investigative news goes, but it's still a place to go for events, clubs and music listings.

WNYC 820am or 93.9FM National Public Radio's local affiliate.

WFUV-90.7FM The area's best alternative-music radio station is run by the Bronx's Fordham University.

Medical Services

Big retail pharmacies are everywhere and some stay open late.

Interchurch Center Medical Office (Map pp168-9; ☎ 212-870-3053; www.interchurch-center.org; 475 Riverside Dr) Upper West Side office open to general public. Recommended for reasonably priced travel immunizations; expert consultation as well.

New York University Langone Medical Center (Map pp162-3; ☎ 212-263-7300; 550 First Ave; 🕑 24hr)

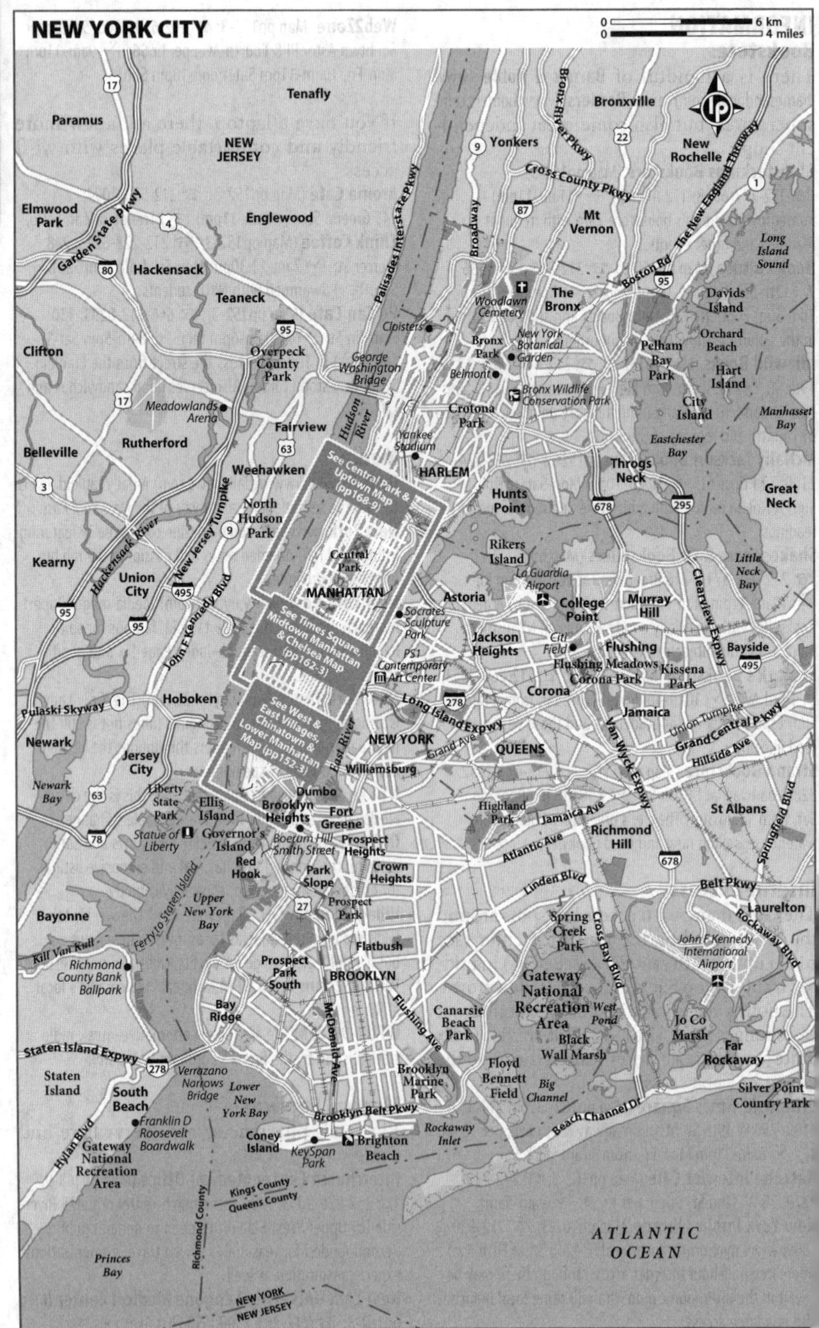
NEW YORK CITY
0 6 km
0 4 miles
Paramus
Tenafly
NEW JERSEY
Yonkers
Bronxville
New Rochelle
Elmwood Park
Englewood
Mt Vernon
Hackensack
Teaneck
The Bronx
Clifton
Overpeck County Park
George Washington Bridge
Meadowlands Arena
Fairview
Belleville
Rutherford
Weehawken
HARLEM
North Hudson Park
Kearny
Union City
Central Park
MANHATTAN
Hoboken
Newark
Jersey City
Newark Bay
Liberty State Park
Ellis Island
Statue of Liberty
Governor's Island
Red Hook
Upper New York Bay
Bayonne
Richmond County Bank Ballpark
Bay Ridge
Staten Island
South Beach
Gateway National Recreation Area
Princes Bay
See Central Park & Uptown Map (pp168-9)
See Times Square, Midtown Manhattan & Chelsea Map (pp162-3)
See West & East Villages, Chinatown & Lower Manhattan Map (pp152-3)
Astoria
Jackson Heights
Corona
NEW YORK
QUEENS
Williamsburg
Dumbo
Brooklyn Heights
Fort Greene
Prospect Heights
Park Slope
Crown Heights
Prospect Park
Flatbush
Prospect Park South
BROOKLYN
Brooklyn Marine Park
Coney Island
KeySpan Park
Brighton Beach
Canarsie Beach Park
Floyd Bennett Field
Gateway National Recreation Area
Black Wall Marsh
Jamaica
Richmond Hill
St Albans
Laurelton
John F Kennedy International Airport
Jo Co Marsh
Far Rockaway
Silver Point Country Park
Hunts Point
Rikers Island
La Guardia Airport
College Point
Murray Hill
Flushing
Bayside
Flushing Meadows Corona Park
Kissena Park
Throgs Neck
Great Neck
Little Neck Bay
Pelham Bay Park
City Island
Hart Island
Orchard Beach
Davids Island
Long Island Sound
Manhasset Bay
Eastchester Bay
Woodlawn Cemetery
Cloisters
Bronx Park
New York Botanical Garden
Belmont
Bronx Wildlife Conservation Park
Crotona Park
Yankee Stadium
Socrates Sculpture Park
PS1 Contemporary Art Center
Citi Field
Highland Park
Spring Creek Park
West Pond
Big Channel
Rockaway Inlet
Lower New York Bay
Verrazano Narrows Bridge
Franklin D Roosevelt Boardwalk
Boerum Hill
Smith Street
ATLANTIC OCEAN
Kings County
Queens County
Richmond County
NEW YORK
NEW JERSEY
Hudson River
East River
Hackensack River
Kill Van Kull
Ferry to Staten Island
Garden State Pkwy
Palisades Interstate Pkwy
Broadway
Bronx River Pkwy
Cross County Pkwy
The New England Thruway
Boston Rd
New Jersey Turnpike
John F Kennedy Blvd
Pulaski Skyway
Long Island Expwy
Grand Ave
Van Wyck Expwy
Clearview Expwy
Union Turnpike
Grand Central Pkwy
Hillside Ave
Jamaica Ave
Atlantic Ave
Linden Blvd
Belt Pkwy
Springfield Blvd
Rockaway Blvd
Cross Bay Blvd
Flushing Ave
McDonald Ave
Brooklyn Belt Pkwy
Beach Channel Dr
Staten Island Expwy
Hylan Blvd
17
4
80
95
9
22
87
1
63
3
495
678
295
278
78
27

St Vincent's Medical Center (Map pp152-3; ☎ 212-604-7070; 170 W 12th St, at Sixth Ave; 24hr) In the Village.

Travel MD (☎ 212-737-1212; www.travelmd.com) A 24-hour house-call service for travelers and residents.

Money

Withdrawal fees average $2.75 at ATMs found in some of the most convenient places – nightclubs, supermarkets, delis, restaurants, you name it.

Post

Find a local branch with regular daytime hours by checking www.usps.com. The city's main post office, the James A Farley building occupying two full city blocks (p165), is an architectural sight worth seeing.

Telephone

There are thousands of pay telephones lining the streets, but many are out of order. Manhattan's telephone area codes are ☎ 212, ☎ 646 and ☎ 917; in the four other boroughs they're ☎ 718 and ☎ 347. You must dial 1 + the area code, even if you're calling from a borough that uses the same one you're calling to.

The city's wonderful ☎ 311 service allows you to dial from anywhere within the city for info or help with any city agency, from the parking-ticket bureau to the noise complaint department.

Tourist Information

New York City & Company (Map pp162-3; ☎ 212-484-1222/1200, toll-free 800-692-8474; www.nycgo.com; 810 Seventh Ave, at 53rd St; 8:30am-6pm Mon-Fri, 9am-5pm Sat & Sun) The official information service of the Convention & Visitors Bureau, it has helpful multilingual staff. The toll-free line provides information on special events and reservations. Other branches include Chinatown (Map pp152-3; cnr Canal, Walker & Baxter Sts; 10am-6pm Mon-Fri, to 7pm Sat); Harlem (Map pp168-9; 144 W 125th St btwn Adam Clayton Powell & Malcolm X Blvds; noon-6pm Mon-Fri, 10am-6pm Sat & Sun); Lower Manhattan (Map pp152-3; City Hall Park at Broadway; 9am-6pm Mon-Fri, 10am-5pm Sat & Sun); Times Square (Map pp162-3; 1560 Broadway, btwn 46th & 47th Sts; 8am-8pm Mon-Sun) .

SIGHTS

While there's something to see on every block of every neighborhood, the most popular stops on the tourist circuit are clustered in or near Midtown. Others are way downtown, such as the Statue of Liberty and the New York Stock Exchange, or way uptown, like the Apollo Theater in Harlem.

Lower Manhattan & the Financial District

STATUE OF LIBERTY

In a city full of American icons, the Statue of Liberty is perhaps the most famous. Conceived as early as 1865 by French intellectual Edouard Laboulaye as a monument to the republican principals shared by France and the USA, it's still generally recognized as a symbol for at least the ideals of opportunity and freedom to many. French sculptor Frédéric-Auguste Bartholdi traveled to New York in 1871 to select the site, then spent more than 10 years in Paris designing and making the 151ft-tall figure *Liberty Enlightening the World*. It was then shipped to New York, erected on a small island in the harbor and unveiled in 1886. Structurally, it consists of an iron skeleton (designed by Gustave Eiffel) with a copper skin attached to it by stiff but flexible metal bars.

Beginning July 4, 2009, for the first time since it was closed for security concerns after September 11, the crown is once again open to the public – numbers are quite limited, however, so reservations are required, probably months in advance. For those without crown reservations, a visit to **Statue of Liberty National Monument** (Map p150; ☎ 212-363-3200; www.nps.gov/stli; New York Harbor, Liberty Island; 9:30am-5pm) means you can wander the grounds and enjoy the view from the 16-story observation deck; a specially designed glass ceiling lets you look up into the statue's striking interior. The trip to its island, via ferry, is usually visited in conjunction with nearby Ellis Island. **Ferries** (Map pp152-3; ☎ 212-269-5755, 877-523-9849; www.statuecruises.com; adult/child $12/5; every 30min 9am-5pm, extended summer hours) leave from Battery Park. South Ferry and Bowling Green are the closest subway stations. Ferry tickets (additional $3 for crown admission) include admission to both sights and reservations can be made in advance.

ELLIS ISLAND

The way-station from 1892 to 1954 for more than 12 million immigrants who were hoping to make new lives in the United States, Ellis Island conjures up the humble and sometimes miserable beginnings of the experience of coming to America – as well as

WEST & EAST VILLAGES, CHINATOWN & LOWER MANHATTAN
0 600 m
0 0.3 miles
See Times Square, Midtown Manhattan & Chelsea Map (pp162-3)
To SEA (1.6mi); Spuyten Duyvil (2mi)
Chelsea
Chelsea Market
8th Ave-14th St
14th St
W 14th St
6th Ave-14th St
14th St-Union Sq
Union Square
E 14th St
3rd Ave
Stuyvesant Square
1st Ave
14th St Loop
John Murphy Park
Stuyvesant Town
FDR Dr
High Line
Meatpacking District
West Village
Jefferson Market Library
Abingdon Square
Christopher St-Sheridan Square
W 4th St
Washington Square Park
New York University
8th St-NYU
Astor Pl
East Village
Tompkins Square Park
East River Park
Alphabet City
New York City Marble Cemetery
Greenwich Village
NoHo
Bleecker St
Lower East Side-Second Ave
Hamilton Fish Park
James J Walker Park
W Houston St
E Houston St
Broadway-Lafayette St
Houston St
Sara D Roosevelt Park
NoLita
Prince St
Singer Building
Spring St
Delancey St-Essex St
Williamsburg Bridge
Bernard Downing Playground
SoHo
Bowery
Lower East Side
Antique Market
Little Italy
Grand St
WH Seward Park
Pier 40
Holland Tunnel
Canal St
Hudson Square
Manhattan Bridge Entrance
East Broadway
West Side Hwy
Hudson River Park
Sixth Ave (Avenue of the Americas)
Seventh Ave
Fifth Ave
Fourth Ave
Third Ave
Second Ave
First Ave
Broadway
Eleventh Ave
Tenth Ave
Ninth Ave
Eighth Ave
Ave A
Ave B
Ave C
Ave D

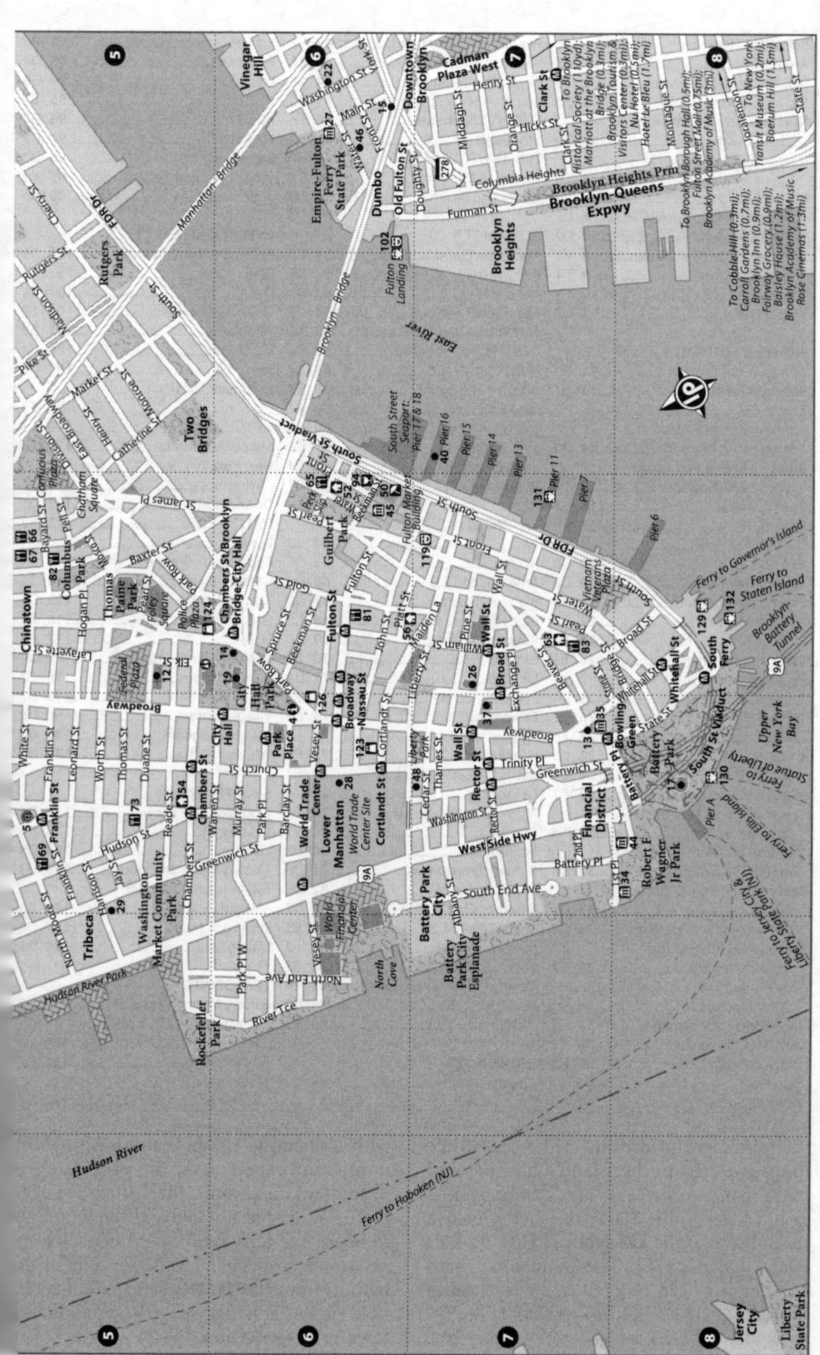
Vinegar Hill
Cadman Plaza West
Downtown Brooklyn
Dumbo
Empire-Fulton Ferry State Park
Old Fulton St
Brooklyn Heights
Brooklyn-Queens Expwy
Brooklyn Heights Prm
Columbia Heights
Fulton Landing
Manhattan Bridge
Brooklyn Bridge
East River
Rutgers Park
Two Bridges
Chinatown
Columbus Park
Thomas Paine Park
Foley Square
Police Plaza
Federal Plaza
City Hall Park
Chambers St/Brooklyn Bridge-City Hall
South St Viaduct
South Street Seaport: Pier 17 & 18
Fulton Market Building
Guilbert Park
FDR Dr
Vietnam Veterans Plaza
Ferry to Governor's Island
Ferry to Staten Island
Brooklyn-Battery Tunnel
South Ferry
Whitehall St
Bowling Green
Battery Park
Upper New York Bay
Ferry to Statue of Liberty
Ferry to Ellis Island
Liberty State Park (NJ) & Ferry to Jersey City
Financial District
Robert F Wagner Jr Park
Battery Park City
Battery Park City Esplanade
North Cove
World Financial Center
World Trade Center Site
Lower Manhattan
West Side Hwy
Washington Market Community Park
Tribeca
Hudson River Park
Rockefeller Park
Hudson River
Ferry to Hoboken (NJ)
Jersey City
Liberty State Park
To Cobble Hill (0.3mi); Carroll Gardens (0.7mi); Brooklyn Inn (0.9mi); Fairway Grocery (0.9mi); Baisley House (1.2mi); Brooklyn Academy of Music Rose Cinemas (1.3mi)
To Brooklyn Borough Hall (0.5mi); Fulton Street Mall (0.75mi); Brooklyn Academy of Music (3mi)
To New York Transit Museum (0.2mi); Boerum Hill (1.5mi)
To Brooklyn Historical Society (110yd); Marriott at the Brooklyn Bridge (0.3mi); Brooklyn Tourism & Visitors Center (0.3mi); Nu Hotel (0.5mi); Hotel Le Bleu (1.7mi)

INFORMATION

Aroma Café........1 C3
Bluestockings Bookstore........2 E3
McNally Jackson Books........3 D3
New York City & Company (Chinatown)........(see 25)
New York City & Company (Lower Manhattan)........4 C6
Pe'Can Café........5 C5
Shakespeare & Co Booksellers........6 D2
St Mark's Bookshop........7 D2
St Vincent's Medical Center........8 B1
Strand Bookstore........9 D1
Think Coffee........10 C3
Web2Zone........11 D2

SIGHTS & ACTIVITIES

African Burial Ground........12 D5
Bowling Green Park........13 C7
Bronze Bull........(see 13)
Brooklyn Bridge Pedestrian & Bicycle Path Entrance........14 D6
Brooklyn Bridge Pedestrian & Bicycle Path Entrance........15 F6
Cage........16 C2
Castle Clinton........17 C8
Christopher Street Pier........18 A3
City Hall........19 D6
Cooper Union........20 D2
Downtown Boathouse........21 A3
Dumbo Arts Center........22 F6
Eldridge Street Synagogue........23 E4
Essex Street Market........24 E3
Explore Chinatown Information Kiosk........25 D4
Federal Hall........26 D7
Galapagos Art Space........27 F6
Ground Zero........28 C6
Harrison Street Townhouses........29 C5
High Line Southern Terminus........30 A1
Lower East Side Tenement Museum........31 E4
Museum of Chinese in the Americas........32 D4
Museum of Comic & Cartoon Art........33 D3
Museum of Jewish Heritage........34 C8
National Museum of the American Indian........35 C7
New Museum of Contemporary Art........36 D3
New York Stock Exchange........37 C7
New York University........38 C2
Old St Patrick's Cathedral........39 D3
Pioneer........40 E7
Ravenite Social Club........41 D3
Russian & Turkish Baths........42 E2
Sheridan Square........43 B2
Skyscraper Museum........44 C8
South Street Seaport Museum........45 D6
St Ann's Warehouse........46 F6
Stonewall Inn........47 B2
Tribute WTC Visitor Center........48 C7
Ukrainian Museum........49 D2
Water Taxi Beach........50 D6

SLEEPING

Abingdon Guest House........51 B1
Best Western Seaport Inn........52 D6
Bowery Hotel........53 D3
Cosmopolitan Hotel........54 C5
East Village Bed & Coffee........55 F2
Gild Hall Wall Street........56 D6
Hotel Gansevoort........57 A1
Hotel on Rivington........58 E3
Jane Hotel........59 A2
Larchmont Hotel........60 C1
Sixty Thompson........61 C3
Soho Grand Hotel........62 C4
Wall Street Inn........63 D7

EATING

7A........64 E2
Acqua........65 D6
Amazing 66........66 D5
Big Wong King........67 D5
Blue Hill........68 C2
Bubby's Pie Company........69 C5
Counter........70 E2
Da Nico........71 D4
Economy Candy........72 E3
Edward's........73 C5
Egg Custard King........74 E4
Hearth........75 E1
Katz's Delicatessen........76 E3
La Esquina........77 D4
Momofuku Noodle Bar........78 E1
Peasant........79 D3
Perilla........80 B2
Ruben's Empanadas........81 D6
Shanghai Cuisine........82 D5
Smorgas Chef Wall St........83 D7
Snack Taverna........84 B3
Spitzer's Corner........85 E3
Taïm........86 B2
Vanessa's Dumpling House........87 E4
Veselka........88 D2
WD-50........89 E3

DRINKING

Cheery Tavern........90 E2
Circa Tabac........91 C4
Fat Cat........92 B2
Freeman's........93 D3
Fresh Salt........94 D6
Henrietta Hudson........95 B3
KGB Bar........96 D2
Mayahuel........97 D2
Sake Bar Decibel........98 D2
Schiller's Liquor Bar........99 E3
Welcome to the Johnsons........100 E3

ENTERTAINMENT

Anthology Film Archives........101 D3
Barge Music........102 F6
Cielo........103 A1
Delancey Lounge........104 E3
Film Forum........105 B3
IFC Center........106 C2
Joe's Pub........107 D2
Landmark Sunshine Cinema........108 E3
Le Poisson Rouge........109 C3
Mercury Lounge........110 E3
New York Theater Workshop........111 D2
Ontological Theater........112 D1
PS 122........113 E2
Public Theater........(see 107)
Regal Union Square Stadium 14........114 D1
Santos Party House........115 D4
Smalls........116 B2
SOBs........117 B3
St Ann's Warehouse........(see 46)
Sullivan Room........118 C2
TKTS Ticket Booth........119 D7
Village Lantern........(see 118)
Village Vanguard........120 B1
Webster Hall........121 D1

SHOPPING

Bloomingdale's SoHo........122 D4
Century 21........123 C6
Citystore........124 D5
Eastern Mountain Sports........125 D3
J&R Music & Computer World........126 C6
Topshop........127 D4
Uniqlo........128 D3

TRANSPORT

Battery Marine Terminal........129 D8
Ferry to Statue of Liberty & Ellis Island........130 C8
Ikea Water Taxi........131 D7
Staten Island Ferry Terminal........132 D8

the fulfillment of dreams. More than three thousand died in the island's hospital and more than two percent were denied admission. Ferries to the Statue of Liberty make a second stop at the **immigration station** on Ellis Island (Map p150). The handsome main building has been restored as the **Immigration Museum** (☎ 212-363-3200; www.ellisisland.org; New York Harbor; adult/child $12/5, audioguide $6; 9:30am-5pm), with fascinating exhibits and a film abou[t] immigrant experiences, the processing o[f] immigrants and how the influx change[d] the USA. Special tip: to avoid the long line[s] to board the ferry, you might consider approaching from the New Jersey side of th[e] harbor, from **Liberty State Park** (p206), accessible via PATH trains (see p191) from downtown or Penn Station (NYC).

GOVERNOR'S ISLAND

Most New Yorkers have gazed out on this mysterious path of green in the harbor, less than half a mile from the southern tip of Manhattan, without a clue as to its purpose. Although it was once reserved only for the Army or Coast Guard personnel who were based here, these days the general public can visit. The 22-acre **Governor's Island National Monument** (Map p150; ☎ 212-825-3045; www.nps.gov/gois; admission free) is accessible by riding the free **ferry** (☎ 212-514-8285; www.nps.gov/gois; 🕑 10am-3pm Wed-Fri, 10am-5pm Sat & Sun, summer only) leaving from the **Battery Marine Terminal** (Map pp152-3; cnr South & Whitehall Sts) next to the Staten Island Ferry Whitehall Terminal in very lower Manhattan. Guided **walking tours** (www.nps.gov/gois; 🕑 10am-1pm Wed & Thu), an hour and a half long, are run by the park service; tickets are free and are available first-come, first-served an hour in advance at the Battery Marine Terminal. Highlights include two 19th-century fortifications – Fort Jay and the three-tiered, sandstone Castle Williams – plus open lawns, massive shade trees and unsurpassed city views. Proposals for the island's future have run the gamut from a big-time casino to a cultural arts center, as well as an enormous cable car to Manhattan. In the near future at least, it is likely that 150 acres will be transformed into parkland and Fort Jay and Castle Williams will be converted into an art exhibition center and interpretative center.

BROOKLYN BRIDGE

Marianne Moore's description of the world's first suspension bridge – which inspired poets from Walt Whitman to Jack Kerouac even before its completion – as a 'climatic ornament, a double rainbow' is perhaps most evocative. Walking across the grand **Brooklyn Bridge** (Map pp152–3) is a rite of passage for New Yorkers and visitors alike. With an unprecedented span of 1596ft, it remains a compelling symbol of US achievement and a superbly graceful structure, despite the fact that its construction was plagued by budget overruns and the deaths of 20 workers. Among the casualties was designer John Roebling, who was knocked off a pier in 1869 while scouting a site for the western bridge tower and later died of tetanus poisoning. The bridge has been renovated several times, and the smooth pedestrian/bicyclist path, beginning just east of City Hall, affords wonderful views of Lower Manhattan and Brooklyn. Observation points under the two stone support towers have illustrations showing panoramas of the waterfront at various points in New York's history.

FINANCIAL DISTRICT

No longer home to Masters of the Universe, these days, in the mind of Main St, **Wall Street** is synonymous with shortsighted greed and decadent irresponsibility. Both an actual street and the metaphorical home of US commerce, named for the wooden barrier built by Dutch settlers in 1653 to protect Nieuw Amsterdam from Native Americans and the British. The area and its industry are considerably diminished following the worldwide economic crash of late 2008/early 2009. Once-venerable banks including Lehman Brothers and Bear Stearns have shuttered and thousands of jobs have been lost. Of course, the future of American business and capitalism and what Wall Street will look like in a year or two is difficult to predict.

To the east is **Federal Hall** (Map pp152-3; ☎ 212-825-6990; www.nps.gov/feha; 26 Wall St; admission free; 🕑 9am-5pm), New York City's 18th-century city hall, distinguished by a huge statue of George Washington on the steps. This is where the first US Congress convened and Washington was sworn in as the first president, though it is not the original building. Across the street, the **New York Stock Exchange** (Map pp152-3; ☎ 212-656-3000; www.nyse.com; 20 Broad St) has a facade like a Roman temple. The visitor center, unfortunately, is closed indefinitely due to security concerns. Outside the exchange, though, you'll see brokers dressed in color-coordinated trading jackets popping out for a cigarette or lunch from a vendor cart.

SOUTH STREET SEAPORT

Known more for the large commercial mall jutting out over the East River on Pier 17, this 11-block enclave of cobblestoned streets and restored historic buildings has been revitalized into an area worthy of a walk. The Fulton Fish Market is long gone but a combination of residents and tourists mix in a handful of bars and restaurants housed in restored mid-19th-century buildings. The **South Street Seaport Museum** (Map pp152-3; ☎ 212-748-8600; www.southstseaport.org; adult/child $10/5; 🕑 10am-6pm Tue-Sun Apr-Dec, 10am-5pm Fri-Sun Jan-Mar) includes three galleries, a children's center and three historic ships to visit just south of the pier. You can also sail on the wonderful 1885 wooden schooner **Pioneer**

(Map pp152-3; ☎ 212-748-8786; www.southstseaport.org; Pier 16; adult $25-30, child $15-20; sail times vary;).

Bringing summer fun to the city is the **Water Taxi Beach** (☎ 877-974-6998; www.watertaxibeach.com; Fulton St, at South St; 11am-11pm), a sandbox for adults, docked on a pier in the East River (another location is in Long Island City, Queens).

When in the area it's worth considering hopping on the **Ikea water taxi** (Map pp152-3; every 40min 2pm-6:40pm Mon-Fri, 11am-7:40pm Sat & Sun) operated by the Swedish furniture store from Pier 11 (six blocks south of South Street Seaport) to its store in Red Hook, Brooklyn. Besides offering the chance to get out on the water and take in breathtaking views of the city, it's free.

BOWLING GREEN PARK & AROUND

At **Bowling Green Park** (Map pp152-3; cnr State & Whitehall Sts), British residents relaxed with quiet games in the late 17th century. The large **bronze bull** (Map pp152–3) here is a tourist photo stop. The **National Museum of the American Indian** (Map pp152-3; ☎ 212-514-3700; www.nmai.si.edu; 1 Bowling Green; admission free; 10am-5pm), housed in the gorgeous and historic Alexander Hamilton US Customs House, has quite an extensive collection of Native American arts, crafts and exhibits, plus a library and a great gift shop. Just up Broadway from here is the **African Burial Ground** (Map pp152-3; ☎ 212-637-2019; www.nps.gov/afbg; 290 Broadway, btwn Duane & Elk Sts; 9am-5pm Mon-Fri), where the skeletal remains of more than 400 free and enslaved African men and women were discovered during preliminary construction of a downtown office building in 1991.

BATTERY PARK & AROUND

'New York, New York, it's a wonderful town. The Bronx is up and the Battery's down.' That's an *On the Town* reference, for all you nonfans of musicals, and it's talking about the southwestern tip of Manhattan Island, which has been extended with landfill over the years to form Battery Park, so-named for the gun batteries that used to be housed at the bulkheads. **Castle Clinton** (Map pp152–3) a fortification built in 1811 to protect Manhattan from the British, was originally 900ft offshore but is now at the edge of Battery Park, with only its walls remaining. Come summertime, it's transformed into a gorgeous outdoor concert arena.

West of the park, the **Museum of Jewish Heritage: A Living Memorial to the Holocaust** (Map pp152-3; ☎ 646-437-4200; www.mjhnyc.org; 36 Battery Pl, Battery Park City; adult/child $12/free; 10am-5:45pm Sun-Tue & Thu, to 8pm Wed, to 5pm Fri) depicts many aspects of New York Jewish history and culture, and includes a holocaust memorial. Also worth a look is the **Skyscraper Museum** (Map pp152-3; ☎ 212-968-1961; www.skyscraper.org; 39 Battery Pl; adult/senior & student $5/2.50; noon-6pm Wed-Sun), occupying the ground-floor space of the Ritz-Carlton Hotel and featuring rotating exhibits plus a permanent study of high-rise history.

Finally, Battery Place is the start of the stunning **Hudson River Park** (☎ 212-627-2020; www.hudsonriverpark.org), which incorporates renovated piers, grassy spaces, gardens, basketball courts, a trapeze school, food concessions and, best of all, a ribbon of a bike/skate/running path that stretches 5 miles up to 59th St.

GROUND ZERO

Tourists snapping photos, local office workers on a lunch break, folks who miss loved ones – all mill about before this high **viewing wall** (Map pp152-3; Church St, at Fulton St; admission free) that wraps around the ever-changing construction site of the former Twin Towers. Photos with accompanying text along the fencelike wall present an eerie and specific timeline of the attacks. Though the city is looking collectively into the future, redevelopment plans have been terribly delayed, fraught with politicking, cost overruns and tightened budgets; the only finished building is a mundane 52-story glass office building. The signature of the site, One World Trade Center, formerly known as the Freedom Tower, along with the National September 11 Memorial and Museum, aren't scheduled for completion until 2013.

Nearby is the **Tribute WTC Visitor Center** (Map pp152-3; ☎ 866-737-1184; 120 Liberty St; admission $10; 10am-6pm Mon, Wed-Sat, noon-6pm Tue, to 5pm Sun), which provides exhibits, first-person testimony and walking tours of the site ($10 per person, several from 11am to 3pm Sunday to Friday, and to 4pm Saturday).

City Hall (Map pp152-3; City Hall Park, Broadway), in the Civic Center precinct, has been home to New York City's government since 1812.

Tribeca & SoHo

The 'TRIangle BElow CAnal St,' bordered roughly by Broadway to the east and Chambers St to the south, is the mor

DON'T MISS

Recognizing that any New York City highlights list is inevitably abbreviated, necessary shorthand for a city with so much to do and see, the following offers a few sights not to miss on a short visit:

- **Museums** – The massive and exceptional **Metropolitan Museum of Art** (p170) can occupy your entire visit. Take in the iconic works at the **Museum of Modern Art** (p161) on a weekday morning to avoid the gridlock.
- **Views** – The open-air observation deck of the **Top of the Rock** (p164) offers an unparalleled perspective. On a nighttime stroll, stop midway across the **Brooklyn Bridge** (p155) for one of the more romantic sights the city has to offer.
- **Green Space** – Whatever the season, a walk through **Central Park** (p166) is the quintessential New York experience. To get a sense of how much of the city lives, head out to Brooklyn's **Prospect Park** (p172) for a weekend picnic.

downtown of these two sister 'hoods. It has old warehouses, very expensive loft apartments and chichi restaurants. On the historic side, the **Harrison Street town houses** (Map pp152-3; Harrison St) west of Greenwich St, were built between 1804 and 1828 and are New York's largest remaining collection of Federal architecture.

SoHo has nothing to do with its London counterpart, but instead, like Tribeca, takes its name from its geographical placement: SOuth of HOuston St. SoHo is filled with block upon block of cast-iron industrial buildings that date to the period just after the Civil War, when this was the city's leading commercial district. It had a bohemian/artsy heyday that had ended by the 1980s, and now this super-gentrified area is a major shopping destination, home to many chain stores and boutiques alike and to hordes of consumers, especially on weekends.

The **Museum of Comic & Cartoon Art** (Map pp152-3; ☎ 212-254-3511; www.moccany.org; 594 Broadway; adult/child $5/free; 🕑 noon-5pm Tue-Sun) can help you appreciate comic strips, cartoons, anime, animation, gag cartoons, political illustrations, caricature, graphic novels and more.

SoHo's hip cup overfloweth to the northern side of Houston St and east side of Lafayette St, where two small areas, **NoHo** ('north of Houston') and **NoLita** ('north of Little Italy'), respectively, are known for excellent shopping – lots of small, independent and stylish clothing boutiques for women – and dining. Add them to SoHo and Tribeca for a great experience of strolling, window-shopping and café-hopping, and you'll have quite a lovely afternoon.

Chinatown & Little Italy

More than 150,000 Chinese-speaking residents live in cramped tenements and crowded apartments in Chinatown, the largest Chinese community that exists outside of Asia (though there are two other major Chinatowns in the city – Sunset Park in Brooklyn and Flushing, in Queens). In the 1990s, the neighborhood also attracted a growing number of Vietnamese immigrants, who set up their own shops and opened inexpensive restaurants here; depending on what street you're on, you'll often notice more of a Vietnamese than Chinese presence.

The best reason to visit Chinatown is to experience a feast for the senses – it's the only spot in the city where you can simultaneously see whole roasted pigs hanging in butcher-shop windows, get whiffs of fresh fish and hear the twangs of Cantonese and Vietnamese rise over the calls of knock-off-Prada-bag hawkers on Canal St. Start at the official **Explore Chinatown information kiosk** (Map pp152-3; ☎ 212-346-9288; www.explorechinatown.com; Canal St, btwn Baxter & Walker Sts; 🕑 10am-6pm Mon-Sun, 10am-7pm Sat), where helpful, multilingual folks can guide you to specific spots. The **Museum of Chinese in America** (Map pp152-3; ☎ 212-619-4785; www.mocanyc.org; 215 Centre St; admission $7; 🕑 11am-5pm Mon, to 9pm Thu, 10am-5pm Sat & Sun, closed Tue & Wed) has sophisticated exhibitions and film series as well as walking tours dedicated to the lives and culture of Chinese communities in the US.

Once known as a truly authentic pocket of Italian people, culture and eateries, **Little Italy** (Map pp152–3) is a barely-there remnant that's constantly shrinking (a growing Chinatown keeps moving in). Still, loyal

Italian Americans, mostly from the suburbs, flock here to gather around red-and-white-checked tablecloths at one of a handful of longtime red-sauce restaurants. Join them for a stroll along **Mulberry Street**, and take a peek at the **Old St Patrick's Cathedral** (Map pp152-3; 263 Mulberry St), which became the city's first Roman Catholic cathedral in 1809 and remained so until 1878, when its more famous uptown successor was completed. The former **Ravenite Social Club** (Map pp152-3; 247 Mulberry St), now a fancy shoe shop, is a reminder of the not-so-long-ago days when mobsters ran the neighborhood. Originally known as the Alto Knights Social Club, where big hitters like Lucky Luciano spent time, the Ravenite was a favorite hangout of John Gotti (and the FBI) before his arrest and life sentencing in 1992.

Lower East Side

First came the Jews, then the Latinos, and now, of course, the hipsters. Today the place is either about being cool – by cramming into low-lit lounges and live-music clubs – or about being moneyed, by snagging a table at a pricey restaurant. A bunch of luxury high-rise condominiums and hip boutique hotels coexist with large public housing projects (read Richard Price's novel *Lush Life* for entertaining insight into this class conflict). To keep the humble past in perspective, head to the **Lower East Side Tenement Museum** (Map pp152-3; ☎ 212-982-8420; www.tenement.org; 90 Orchard St, at Broome St; tours $17; 🕑 visitor center 10am-5:30pm, tours 10:15am-5pm), which puts the neighborhood's heartbreaking heritage on full display in several reconstructed tenements. Museum visits are available only as part of scheduled tours (the price of which is included in the admission), which typically operate every 40 or 50 minutes.

The landmark **Eldridge Street Synagogue** (Map pp152-3; ☎ 212-219-0888; www.eldridgestreet.org; 12 Eldridge St, btwn Canal & Division Sts), built in 1887, attracted as many as 1000 worshipers on the High Holidays at the turn of the 20th century. But membership dwindled in the 1920s with restricted immigration laws, and by the 1950s the temple closed altogether. A 20-year restoration project was finally completed in 2007 and now the synagogue holds Friday-evening and Saturday-morning worship services, hosts weddings and offers **tours** (adult/child $10/6; 🕑 10am-3pm Sun-Thu, on the half-hour) of the building. Not far from here is the lively **Essex Street Market** (Map pp152-3; ☎ 212-312-3603; www.essexstreetmarket.com; 120 Essex St, btwn Delancey & Rivington Sts; 🕑 8am-7pm Mon-Sat), a 65-year-old shopping destination with vendors hawking produce, seafood, Latino groceries, kosher wines and freshly baked bread.

East Village

Bordered roughly by 14th St, Lafayette St, E Houston St and the East River, the East Village has gentrified rapidly in the last decade, much to the horror of longtime tenants and punk-kid squatters, who have been floating around for decades. These days the real-estate developers seem to have the upper hand – although the 'hood has not yet shaken its image as an edgy, radical, be-yourself kind of place, which it still is, mostly.

TOMPKINS SQUARE PARK & AROUND

This **park** (Map pp152-3; btwn 7th & 10th Sts & Aves A & B) is an unofficial border between the East Village (to the west) and Alphabet City (to the east). It was once an Eastern European immigrant area; you'll still see old Ukrainians and Poles in the park, but they'll be alongside punks, students, panhandlers and a slew of dog-walking yuppies. The historic **Russian & Turkish Baths** (Map pp152-3; ☎ 212-674-9250; www.russianturkishbaths.com; 268 E 10th St; admission $30; 🕑 noon-10pm Mon, Tue, Thu & Fri, from 9am Sat, 8am-1pm Sun) is a great place to work out your stress in one of the four hot rooms; traditional massages are also offered. It's ladies-only from 10am to 2pm Wednesday, men-only from noon to 5pm Thursday and 8am to 2pm Sunday, and coed the rest of the time. It's authentic and somewhat grungy, and you're as likely to share a sauna with a hipster couple on a date, a well-known actor looking for a time-out or an actual Russian.

Housed in an architecturally ambitious building, a folding silvery column, is the **New Museum of Contemporary Art** (Map pp152-3; ☎ 212-219-1222; www.newmuseum.org; 235 Bowery, at Prince St; adult/senior $12/10, child under 18yr free; 🕑 noon-6pm Wed, Sat & Sun, to 9pm Thu & Fri).

The expanded modern version of the **Ukrainian Museum** (Map pp152-3; ☎ 212-228-0110; www.ukrainianmuseum.org; 222 E 6th St, btwn Second & Third Aves; admission $8; 🕑 11:30am-5pm Wed-Sun) is testament to the fact that Ukrainians have a long history and still-strong presence here. Its collection of folk art includes ceramics and richly woven textiles.

ASTOR PLACE & AROUND

At the west end of St Mark's Pl, **Astor Place** (Map pp152–3) was once an elite neighborhood and some of its impressive original Greek Revival residences remain. These days a large Starbucks anchors one corner and a K-Mart another, while a tall glass condominium dominates the skyline across the street. The landmark rotating sculpture – 'the Cube' – remains, as do the young skateboarders who congregate here.

The large brownstone **Cooper Union** (Map pp152-3; www.cooper.edu; 51 Astor Pl) is a public college founded by glue millionaire Peter Cooper in 1859. Abraham Lincoln gave his 'Right Makes Might' speech condemning slavery before his election to the White House in the college's Great Hall.

West (Greenwich) Village

Once a symbol for all things artistic, outlandish and bohemian, this storied and popular neighborhood – the birthplace of the gay-rights movement as well as former home of Beat poets and important artists – feels worlds away from busy Broadway, in fact almost European. Known by most visitors as 'Greenwich Village,' although that term is not used by locals, it has narrow streets lined with well-groomed and high-priced real estate, as well as cafés and restaurants, making it an ideal place to wander.

NEW YORK UNIVERSITY

Dominating a huge swath of property in the middle of the Village, this university, one of the largest in the country, defines the area architecturally and demographically. Founded in 1831 by Albert Gallatin, the secretary of treasury under President Thomas Jefferson, **New York University** (NYU; Map pp152-3; ☎ 212-998-4550; www.nyu.edu; information center at 50 W 4th St; 🕑 9am-5pm Mon-Fri, 10am-4pm Sat) was an intimate school open to all, regardless of race or class background. The student population has swelled to nearly 47,000, with 14 schools and colleges at six Manhattan locations.

WASHINGTON SQUARE PARK & AROUND

This **park** (Map pp152–3) began as a 'potter's field' – a burial ground for the penniless – and its status as a cemetery protected it from development. It is now an incredibly well-used park, especially on the weekend. Children use the playground, NYU students catch some rays and friends meet 'under the arch,' the recently renovated landmark on the park's northern edge, designed in 1889 by society architect Stanford White. A controversial $16-million renovation plan that some residents feared would reduce the informality and character of the park has meant more symmetry, landscaping and higher fences. The undersized basketball court, the **Cage** (cnr Sixth Ave & W 3rd St), considered one of the more competitive playgrounds in the city, draws onlookers and top ballers – the more people-watching, the more showboating.

CHRISTOPHER STREET PIER (PIER 45)

Formerly the strict domain of young gay hustlers and sassy 'pier queens,' this completely renovated **concrete pier** (Map pp152-3; Christopher St, at the Hudson River; 🕑 closes 1am) is now a magnet for downtowners of all stripe, with a healthy dose of local yuppies and a sprinkling of young gay holdouts, most of whom travel from other boroughs and northern New Jersey to be a part of the scene. Developers of the Hudson River Park Project paid special attention to this prime waterfront spot, adding a lawn and flower bed, wooden deck, tented shade shelters, benches and a grand stone fountain at its entrance.

SHERIDAN SQUARE & AROUND

The western edge of the Village is home to **Sheridan Square** (Stonewall Place; Map pp152–3), a small, triangular park where life-size white statues by George Segal honor the gay community and gay pride movement that began in the nearby renovated **Stonewall Inn** sitting just across the street from the square. A block further east, an appropriately bent street is officially named Gay St (prompting titillated queer folks to periodically swipe the street sign). Although gay social scenes have in many ways moved a bit further uptown to Chelsea, **Christopher Street** is still the center of gay life in the Village.

Meatpacking District

Nestled between the far West Village and the southern border of Chelsea is the gentrified and now inappropriately named **Meatpacking District** (Map pp152–3). Less than 10 years ago, the neighborhood was home to 250 slaughterhouses – today only seven butchers remain – and was best known for its groups of tranny hookers, racy S&M sex clubs and, of course, its sides of beef. These days, only trendy wine bars, eateries, nightclubs, high-end designer clothing stores and chic hotels can afford the rents.

With the completion of the **High Line** (Map pp152-3 www.thehighline.org), a 30ft-high abandoned stretch of elevated railroad track transformed into a long ribbon of parkland (from Gansevoort St to W 34th St), there's finally some greenery amid the asphalt jungle; the project plans also call for a high-end hotel and outpost of the **Whitney Museum of American Art** (Map pp168–9), due to be completed by 2012. Only three stories above the streetscape, this thoughtfully and carefully designed mix of contemporary, industrial and natural elements is nevertheless a refuge and escape from the ordinary.

Chelsea

This 'hood is popular for two main attractions: one, the parade of gorgeous gay men (known affectionately as 'Chelsea boys') who roam Eighth Ave, darting from gyms to trendy happy hours; and two, it's one of the hubs of the city's art-gallery scene – it's currently home to nearly 200 modern-art art spaces, most of which are clustered west of Tenth Ave. Find specific galleries at www.westchelseaarts.com or pick up a copy of the monthly *Gallery Guide* (www.galleryguide.org), hard copies of which are available for free at most venues.

The **Chelsea Market** (Map pp162-3; www.chelseamarket.com; 75 Ninth Ave, btwn W 15th & 16th Sts; ⌚ 7am-10pm Mon-Sat, 8am-8pm Sun) will thrill gourmet food fans with its 800ft-long shopping concourse, while **Chelsea Piers** (Map pp162-3; ☎ 212-336-6666; www.chelseapiers.com; W 23rd St, at Hudson River;) is a waterfront sports center that caters to the athlete in everyone. It's got a four-level driving range, indoor ice rink, jazzy bowling alley, Hoop City for basketball, a sailing school for kids, batting cages, a huge gym, indoor rock-climbing walls – the works.

Flatiron District

At the intersection of Broadway, Fifth Ave and 23rd St, the famous (and absolutely gorgeous) 1902 **Flatiron Building** (Map pp162–3) has a distinctive triangular shape to match its site. It was New York's first iron-frame high-rise, and the world's tallest building until 1909. Its surrounding district is a fashionable area of boutiques and loft apartments, and home to the peaceful **Madison Square Park** (www.madisonsquarepark.org) bordered by 23rd and 26th Sts, and Fifth and Madison Aves, where you'll find an active dog run, rotating outdoor sculptures, shaded park benches and a popular burger joint (see p182). Flatiron is also where you'll find the **Museum of Sex** (Map pp162-3; ☎ 212-689-6337; www.museumofsex.com; 233 Fifth Ave, at W 27th St; admission $14.50; ⌚ 11am-6:30pm Sun-Fri, 11am-8pm Sat), a somewhat intellectualized homage to intercourse.

Union Square

A true town square, albeit one with a grassy interior, **Union Square** (Map pp162-3; 14th St, at Broadway) is a hive of activity with all manner of New Yorkers rubbing elbows, sharing hacky sacks and eyeing each other. A major renovation will include a year-round restaurant, more playgrounds and public toilets. The southern end is the place for antiwar and other liberal-leaning demonstrators and, on most days, its north end hosts the **Greenmarket Farmers Market** (Map pp162-3; ☎ 212-788-7476; www.cenyc.org; 17th St, btwn Broadway & Park Ave S; ⌚ 8am-6pm Mon, Wed, Fri & Sat), the most popular of the nearly 50 greenmarkets throughout the five boroughs, where even celebrity chefs come for just-picked rarities including fiddlehead ferns, heirloom tomatoes and fresh curry leaves.

Gramercy Park

This area, loosely comprising the 20s east of Madison Ave, is named after one of New York's loveliest parks; it's for residents only, though, and you need a key to get in! If you're strolling by, peer through the gates and get a good look at what you're missing. Nearby is **Theodore Roosevelt's Birthplace** (Map pp162-3; ☎ 212-668-2251; www.nps.gov/thrb; 28 E 20th St, btwn Park Ave & Broadway; admission $3; ⌚ 9am-5pm Tue-Sat), a National Historic Site; however, this building is simply a re-creation – the actual house where the 26th president was born was demolished in his lifetime.

Midtown

The classic NYC fantasy – shiny skyscrapers, teeming mobs of worker bees, Fifth Ave store windows, taxi traffic – and some of the city's most popular attractions can be found here. Long ago when print ruled and newspaper and magazines were the cultural currency of the day, Midtown was actually also the literary district – the prime movers and shakers used to meet at the Algonquin Hotel. Major media companies such as the NY Times and Condé Nast, among others, are still based here.

EMPIRE STATE BUILDING

Catapulted to Hollywood stardom both as the planned meeting spot for Cary Grant and Deborah Kerr in *An Affair to Remember,* and the vertical perch that helped to topple King Kong, the classic **Empire State Building** (Map pp162-3; ☎ 212-736-3100; www.esbnyc.org; 350 Fifth Ave, at E 34th St; adult/child $18.50/13; 8am-2am) is one of New York's most famous members of the skyline. It's a limestone classic built in just 410 days, or seven million man-hours, during the depths of the Depression at a cost of $41 million. On the site of the original Waldorf-Astoria Hotel, the 102-story, 1472ft (to the top of the antenna) Empire State Building opened in 1931 after 10 million bricks were laid, 6400 windows installed and 328,000 sq ft of marble laid. Today you can ride the elevator to observatories on the 86th and 102nd floors (for the latter it's an additional $15 and tickets are only sold upon arrival at the building), but be prepared for crowds; try to come very early or very late (and purchase your tickets ahead of time, online) for an optimal experience.

MUSEUM OF MODERN ART

A veritable art universe of more than 100,000 pieces, the 75-year old **Museum of Modern Art** (MoMA; Map pp162-3; ☎ 212-708-9400; www.moma.org; 11 W 53rd St, btwn Fifth & Sixth Aves; adult/child/student/senior $20/free/12/16, free 4-8pm Fri; 10:30am-5:30pm Sat-Mon, Wed-Thu, 10:30am-8pm Fri) houses one of the more significant collections of works in the world. A controversial renovation project designed by the architect Yoshio Taniguchi doubled the museum's capacity to 630,000 sq ft on six floors. Most of the big hitters – Matisse, Picasso, Cézanne, Rothko, Pollock and many others – are housed in the central five-story atrium. Be prepared for long entrance lines and crushing crowds around the artwork.

TIMES SQUARE & THEATER DISTRICT

There are few images more universally iconic than the glittering orb dropping from **Times Square** (Map pp162–3) on New Year's Eve – the first one descended 100 years ago. Smack in the middle of Midtown Manhattan, this area around the intersection of Broadway and Seventh Ave, with its gaudy billboards and glittery marquees, has become so intertwined with New York City in the minds of non-New Yorkers that regardless of how Disneyfied it has become, it's still considered quintessential New York. Once again 'the Crossroads of the World' and unrecognizable from its '70s-era seediness of strip clubs, hookers and pickpockets, the square draws 27 million visitors annually, who spend something over $12 billion in Midtown. Massive chains including Sephora, Skechers and Cold Stone Creamery pull in folks who can find this stuff anywhere, and multiplex theaters draw crowds with large screens and stadium seating. In an effort to make the area more pedestrian-friendly and diminish the perpetual gridlock, Broadway from 47th to 42nd St was turned into a vehicle-free zone in the summer of 2009 – the experiment's fate and design is still uncertain.

Times Square also continues to serve as New York's official **Theater District**, with dozens of Broadway and off-Broadway theaters located in an area that stretches from 41st to 54th Sts, between Sixth and Ninth Aves (see p187). The Times Square branch of **New York City & Company** (☎ 212-763-1560; www.timessquarenyc.org; 1560 Broadway, btwn 46th & 47th Sts; 9am-7pm Mon-Fri, 8am-8pm Sun) sits smack in the middle of this famous crossroads, inside the beautifully restored landmark Embassy Theater. Broadway, the road, once ran all the way to the state capitol in Albany.

GRAND CENTRAL STATION

Built in 1913 as a prestigious terminal by New York Central and Hudson River Railroad, **Grand Central Station** (Map pp162-3; www.grandcentralterminal.com; 42nd St, at Fifth Ave) is no longer a romantic place to begin a cross-country journey, as it's now the terminus for Metro North commuter trains to the northern suburbs and Connecticut. But even if you're not boarding a train to the 'burbs, it's worth exploring the grand, vaulted main concourse and gazing up at the restored ceiling, decorated with a star map that is actually a 'God's-eye' image of the night sky. The bottom floor houses a truly excellent array of eateries, bringing the idea of 'food court' to grand new levels, while the balcony has a cozy '20s-era salon kind of bar called the Campbell Apartment.

CHRYSLER BUILDING

Just east of Grand Central Station, the **Chrysler Building** (Map pp162-3; 405 Lexington Ave), an art-deco masterpiece that's adorned with motorcar

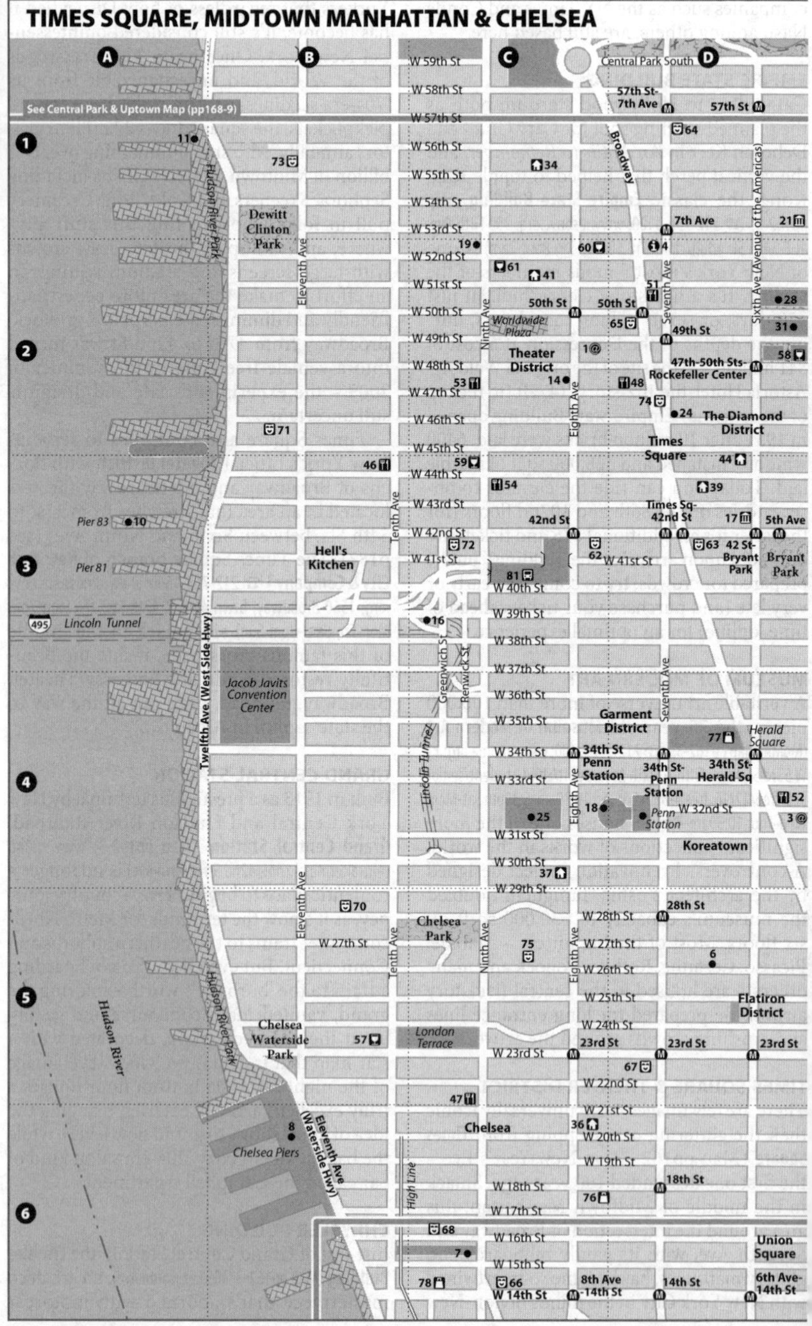
TIMES SQUARE, MIDTOWN MANHATTAN & CHELSEA
See Central Park & Uptown Map (pp168-9)
Central Park South
57th St-7th Ave
57th St
Broadway
7th Ave
50th St
49th St
47th-50th Sts-Rockefeller Center
Theater District
Worldwide Plaza
The Diamond District
Times Square
Times Sq-42nd St
42nd St
5th Ave
42 St-Bryant Park
Bryant Park
Hell's Kitchen
Dewitt Clinton Park
Hudson River Park
Pier 83
Pier 81
Lincoln Tunnel
Twelfth Ave (West Side Hwy)
Jacob Javits Convention Center
Greenwich St
Renwick St
Lincoln Tunnel
Garment District
Herald Square
34th St Penn Station
34th St-Penn Station
34th St-Herald Sq
Penn Station
Koreatown
28th St
Chelsea Park
Flatiron District
Chelsea Waterside Park
London Terrace
23rd St
Chelsea
Chelsea Piers
Eleventh Ave (Waterside Hwy)
High Line
18th St
Hudson River
Union Square
8th Ave-14th St
14th St
6th Ave-14th St
Eleventh Ave
Tenth Ave
Ninth Ave
Eighth Ave
Seventh Ave
Sixth Ave (Avenue of the Americas)
W 59th St
W 58th St
W 57th St
W 56th St
W 55th St
W 54th St
W 53rd St
W 52nd St
W 51st St
W 50th St
W 49th St
W 48th St
W 47th St
W 46th St
W 45th St
W 44th St
W 43rd St
W 42nd St
W 41st St
W 40th St
W 39th St
W 38th St
W 37th St
W 36th St
W 35th St
W 34th St
W 33rd St
W 32nd St
W 31st St
W 30th St
W 29th St
W 28th St
W 27th St
W 26th St
W 25th St
W 24th St
W 23rd St
W 22nd St
W 21st St
W 20th St
W 19th St
W 18th St
W 17th St
W 16th St
W 15th St
W 14th St

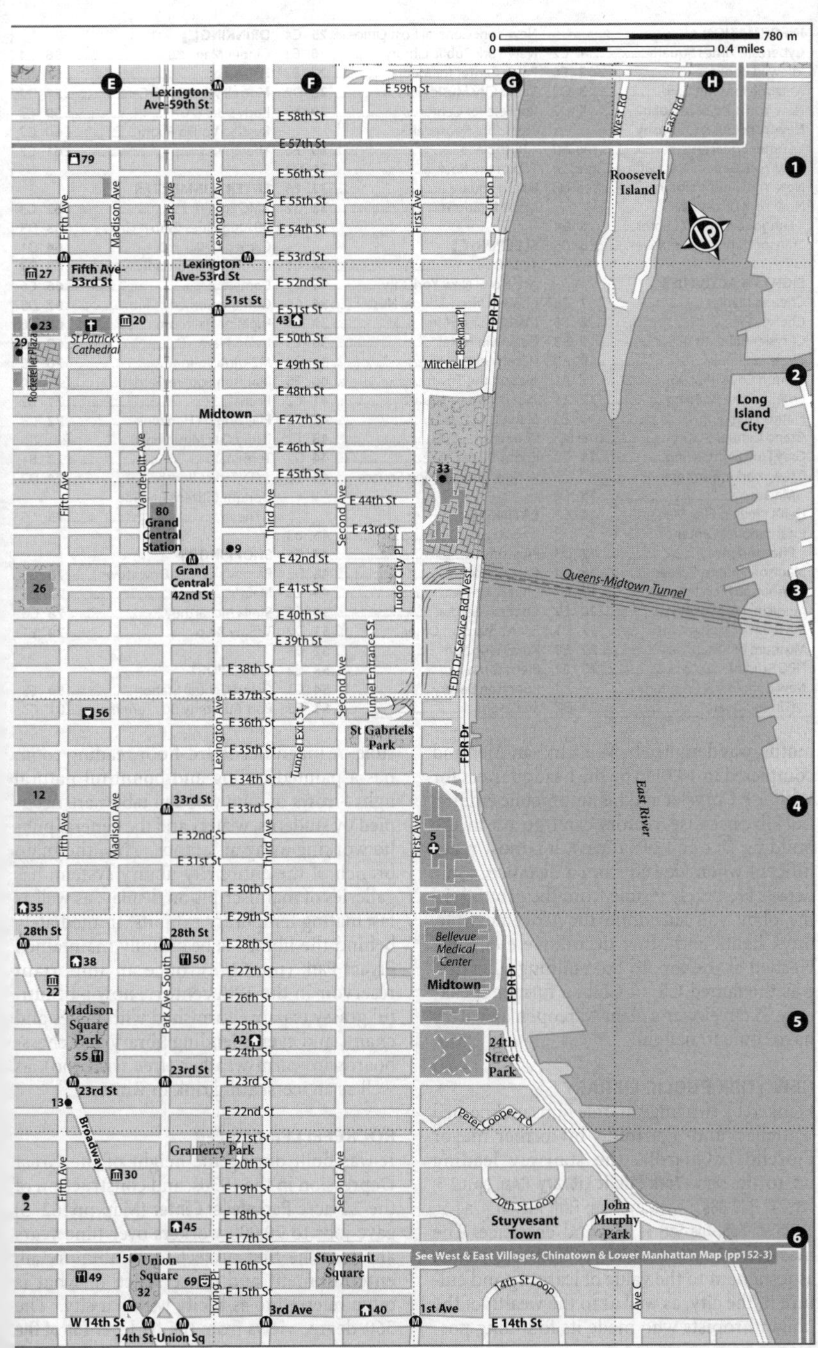
0 780 m
0 0.4 miles
E
F
G
H
1
2
3
4
5
6
Lexington Ave-59th St
E 59th St
E 58th St
E 57th St
E 56th St
E 55th St
E 54th St
E 53rd St
E 52nd St
E 51st St
E 50th St
E 49th St
E 48th St
E 47th St
E 46th St
E 45th St
E 44th St
E 43rd St
E 42nd St
E 41st St
E 40th St
E 39th St
E 38th St
E 37th St
E 36th St
E 35th St
E 34th St
E 33rd St
E 32nd St
E 31st St
E 30th St
E 29th St
E 28th St
E 27th St
E 26th St
E 25th St
E 24th St
E 23rd St
E 22nd St
E 21st St
E 20th St
E 19th St
E 18th St
E 17th St
E 16th St
E 15th St
E 14th St
W 14th St
West Rd
East Rd
Roosevelt Island
Sutton Pl
Fifth Ave
Madison Ave
Park Ave
Lexington Ave
Third Ave
First Ave
Second Ave
Fifth Ave-53rd St
Lexington Ave-53rd St
51st St
St Patrick's Cathedral
Rockefeller Plaza
Beekman Pl
FDR Dr
Mitchell Pl
Long Island City
Midtown
Vanderbilt Ave
Grand Central Station
Grand Central-42nd St
Tudor City Pl
Queens-Midtown Tunnel
FDR Dr Service Rd West
Tunnel Entrance St
Tunnel Exit St
St Gabriels Park
East River
33rd St
28th St
Park Ave South
Bellevue Medical Center
Madison Square Park
23rd St
24th Street Park
Broadway
Peter Cooper Rd
Gramercy Park
20th St Loop
Stuyvesant Town
John Murphy Park
See West & East Villages, Chinatown & Lower Manhattan Map (pp152-3)
Union Square
Stuyvesant Square
Irving Pl
14th St Loop
Ave C
3rd Ave
1st Ave
14th St-Union Sq
79
27
20
23
29
43
33
80
9
26
56
12
5
35
38
50
22
55
42
13
30
2
45
15
49
32
69
40

INFORMATION		
Cybercafe Times Square	1	C2
Idlewild Books	2	E6
Netzone Internet Cafe	3	D4
New York City & Company	4	D2
New York City & Company (Times Square)	(see 24)	
New York General Post Office	(see 25)	
New York Public Library	(see 26)	
New York University Langone Medical Center	5	G4
Transportation Alternatives	6	D5

SIGHTS & ACTIVITIES		
Chelsea Market	7	C6
Chelsea Piers	8	B6
Chrysler Building	9	F3
Circle Line	10	A3
Clinton Cove (Pier 96)	11	A1
Empire State Building	12	E4
Flatiron Building	13	E5
Grand Central Station	(see 80)	
Gray Line Sightseeing	14	C2
Greenmarket Farmers Market	15	E6
Hell's Kitchen Flea Market	16	C3
International Center of Photography	17	D3
Madison Square Garden	18	C4
Manhattan Bicycle	19	C2
Municipal Art Society	20	E2
Museum of Modern Art	21	D1
Museum of Sex	22	E5
NBC Studios	23	E2
New York City & Company (Times Square)	24	D2
New York General Post Office	25	C4
New York Public Library	26	E3
Paley Center for Media	27	E2
Radio City Music Hall	28	D2
Rockefeller Center	29	E2
Theodore Roosevelt's Birthplace	30	E6
Top of the Rock	31	D2
Union Square	32	E6
United Nations	33	G2

SLEEPING		
1291 B&B	34	C1
Ace Hotel New York City	35	E4
Chelsea International Hostel	36	C6
Chelsea Star Hotel	37	C4
Gershwin Hotel	38	E5
Hotel Mela	39	D3
Jazz on the Town	40	F6
Jazz on Times Square	41	C2
Marcel	42	F5
Pod Hotel	43	F2
Room-Mate Grace	44	D3
W New York – Union Square	45	E6

EATING		
44 & X	46	B3
Blossom	47	C5
Café Edison	48	D2
Chat N' Chew	49	E6
Chennai Garden	50	E5
Ellen's Stardust Diner	51	D2
Kum Gang San	52	D4
Pietrasanta	53	C2
Poseidon Bakery	54	C3
Shake Shack	55	E5

DRINKING		
Ginger Man	56	E4
Half King	57	B5
Morrell Wine Bar & Café	58	D2
Rudy's Bar & Grill	59	C3
Russian Vodka Room	60	C2
Therapy	61	C2

ENTERTAINMENT		
AMC Empire 25	62	C3
BB King Blues Club & Grill	63	D3
Carnegie Hall	64	D1
Caroline's on Broadway	65	D2
Comix	66	C6
Gotham Comedy Club	67	D5
Highline Ballroom	68	C6
Irving Plaza	69	E6
M2 Ultra Lounge	70	B5
Madison Square Garden	(see 18)	
Pacha	71	B2
Playwrights Horizons	72	C3
Radio City Music Hall	(see 28)	
Terminal 5	73	B1
TKTS Ticket Booth	74	D2
Upright Citizens Brigade Theatre	75	C5

SHOPPING		
Barney's Co-op (Downtown)	76	C6
Macy's	77	D4
Stella McCartney	78	C6
Tiffany & Co	79	E1

TRANSPORT		
Grand Central Station	80	E3
Port Authority Bus Terminal	81	C3

motifs, was designed by William Van Alen and completed in 1930 to be the headquarters for Walter P Chrysler and his automobile empire. Luckily, because visitors can't go up in the building (it's full of offices), it's most magnificent when viewed from a distance; some details are barely visible from the ground. In the lobby, you can admire the African marble, onyx lights and other decorative elements. Nestled at the top, in the building's heyday, was the famed Cloud Club, a former speakeasy. A developer's plans to reopen an eatery have come to naught.

NEW YORK PUBLIC LIBRARY

Flanked by two huge marble lions nicknamed 'Patience' and 'Fortitude' by former mayor Fiorello LaGuardia, the stairway leading up to the **New York Public Library** (Map pp162-3; ☎ 212-340-0833; www.nypl.org; Fifth Ave, at 42nd St; 10am-6pm Tue-Sat) is a grand entrance. The massive, superb beaux-arts building stands as testament to the value of learning and culture in the city, as well as to the wealth of the philanthropists who made its founding possible. A magnificent 3rd-floor reading room has a painted ceiling and bountiful natural light – rows of long wooden tables are occupied by students, writers and the general public working away at laptops. This, the main branch of the entire city library system, has galleries of manuscripts on display, as well as fascinating temporary exhibits. Immediately behind the library is beautifully maintained **Bryant Park** (pp162–3), once an important reservoir in the 19th century, now a beautiful grassy expanse furnished with tables and chairs, and even a lending library and chessboards in warm weather (free wi-fi too), as well as an ice-skating rink in winter.

ROCKEFELLER CENTER

It was built during the height of the Great Depression in the 1930s, and construction of the 22-acre **Rockefeller Center** (Map pp162–3) gave jobs to 70,000 workers over nine years and was the first project to combine retail, entertainment and office space in what is often referred to as a 'city within a city.' The 360-degree views from the tri-level **Top of the**

Rock (☎ 212-698-2000; main entrance 50th St, btwn Fifth & Sixth Aves; adult/child $18/13; ⌚ 8am-midnight) observation deck are absolutely stunning and should not be missed; on a clear day you can see quite a distance across the river into New Jersey. The 67th and 69th floors have outdoor terraces. Architecture fans should look for the tile work above the Sixth Ave entrance to the GE Building; the entrance to the East River Savings Bank building at 41 Rockefeller Plaza; the triptych above the entrance to 30 Rockefeller Plaza; and the statues of Prometheus and Atlas. In winter the place is abuzz with ice-skaters and Christmas-tree gawkers.

Within the complex is the 1932 **Radio City Music Hall** (Map pp162-3; ☎ 212-247-4777; www.radiocity.com; 1260 Sixth Ave; tours adult/child $18.50/10; ⌚ tours 11am-3pm Mon-Sun), a 6000-seat former movie palace and protected landmark that's been gorgeously restored in all its art-deco grandeur. To get an inside look, join one of the frequent guided tours, which leave the lobby every half-hour.

NBC Studios (Map pp162-3; ☎ 212-664-3700; www.nbcuniversalstore.com; 30 Rockefeller Plaza; tours adult/child $19/16; ⌚ 8:30am-5:30pm Mon-Sat, 9:30am-4:30pm Sun) are here as part of the NBC TV network, which has its headquarters in the 70-story GE Building. *The Today Show* broadcasts live 7am to 11am daily from a glass-enclosed street-level studio near the fountain (fans of Matt Lauer, Meredith Vieira, Al Roker et al take note), and tours of the NBC studios leave from the lobby of the GE Building every 15 minutes; note that children under six are not admitted on tours.

FIFTH AVENUE & AROUND

Immortalized in both film and song, Fifth Ave first developed its high-class reputation in the early 20th century, when it was considered desirable for its 'country' air and open spaces. The series of mansions called **Millionaire's Row** extended right up to 130th St, though most of the heirs to the millionaire mansions on Fifth Ave above 59th St sold them for demolition or converted them to the cultural institutions that now make up Museum Mile.

The avenue's Midtown stretch still boasts upmarket shops and hotels, including Trump Tower (725 Fifth Ave, at 56th St) and the Plaza (cnr Fifth Ave and Central Park South). While a number of the more exclusive boutiques have migrated to Madison Ave – leaving outposts of Gap and H&M in their wake – several superstars still reign over Fifth Ave above 50th St, including the famous Tiffany & Co (p190).

UNITED NATIONS

The **UN headquarters** (Map pp162-3; ☎ 212-963-8687; www.un.org/tours; First Ave, btwn 42nd & 48th Sts; tours adult/child $12.50/6.50; ⌚ tours 9:30am-4:45pm Mon-Fri) is technically on a section of international territory overlooking the East River. Take a guided 45-minute tour of the facility and you'll get to see the General Assembly, where the annual fall convocation of member nations takes place (the Security Council Chamber has been closed to tours because of renovations, due to be completed in 2013); and also the Economic & Social Council Chamber. There is a park to the south of the complex which is home to Henry Moore's *Reclining Figure* as well as several other sculptures with a peace theme. English-language tours of the UN complex depart frequently; limited tours in several other languages are also available.

HERALD SQUARE & AROUND

This crowded convergence of Broadway, Sixth Ave and 34th St is best known as the home of **Macy's** department store (see p190), where you can still ride some of the remaining original wooden elevators to floors ranging from home furnishings to lingerie. But the busy square gets its name from a long-defunct newspaper, the *Herald*, and the small, leafy park here bustles during business hours. (The two indoor malls south of Macy's on Sixth Ave house the standard array of suburban chain stores.) In order to cut down on some of the area gridlock, Broadway, from 33rd to 35th St has been closed to traffic and turned into a pedestrian plaza.

West of Herald Sq, the **Garment District** has most of New York's fashion design offices, and while not much clothing is actually made here anymore, for anyone into pawing through dreamy selections of fabrics, buttons, sequins, lace and zippers it is the place to shop.

Nearby, tens of thousands of train commuters and travelers pass through the sterile confines of **Pennsylvania Station** (Penn Station; Map pp162-3; 33rd St, btwn Seventh & Eighth Aves). **Madison Square Garden** (Map pp162-3; ☎ 212-465-5800; www.thegarden.com; Seventh Ave, btwn W 31st & W 33rd Sts), built over Penn Station, is a major sporting and entertainment venue. A block west, the 1913 **New York General Post Office** (James A Farley Post Office;

Map pp162-3; www.ny.com/general/postoffices.html; 421 Eighth Ave, at 33rd St; 7am-10pm Mon-Fri, 9am-9pm Sat, 11am-7pm Sun) is an imposing beaux-arts building that stands behind a long row of Corinthian columns. A grand project proposed by former senator Daniel Patrick Moynihan in 1999 to move the station into a refurbished Farley post office has fallen by the wayside.

From 31st St to 36th St, between Broadway and Fifth Ave, **Koreatown** pp162–3 is an interesting and lively neighborhood with an ever-expanding number of good restaurants and authentic karaoke spots.

OTHER MIDTOWN MUSEUMS

Among the impressive lineup of cultural institutions in this area is the **Paley Center for Media** (formerly Museum of TV & Radio; Map pp162-3; ☎ 212-621-6800; www.paleycenter.org; 25 W 52nd St; adult/child $10/5, theater $6; noon-6pm Fri-Wed, to 8pm Thu), where more than 100,000 US TV and radio programs and advertisements are available at the click of a mouse. Here you can search the extensive catalogue on computer, and staff will find and play your classic TV or radio selection. A comfy theater shows some great specials on broadcasting history, and there are frequent special programming events.

The stunning **International Center of Photography** (Map pp162-3; ☎ 212-857-0000; www.icp.org; 1133 Sixth Ave, at 43rd St; adult/senior & student $12/8, admission by 'voluntary contribution' 5-8pm Fri; 10am-6pm Tue-Thu, Sat & Sun, 10am-8pm Fri) is the city's most important showcase for major photographers, especially photojournalists. Its past exhibitions have included work by Henri Cartier-Bresson, Matthew Brady and Robert Capa.

HELL'S KITCHEN (CLINTON)

For years, the far west side of Midtown was a working-class district of tenements and food warehouses known as Hell's Kitchen – supposedly its name was muttered by a cop in reaction to a riot in the neighborhood in 1881. A 1990s economic boom seriously altered the character and developers reverted to using the cleaned-up name Clinton, a moniker originating from the 1950s; locals are split on usage. New restaurants exploded along Ninth and Tenth Aves between about 37th and 55th Sts, and now it's a great place to grab a pre- or post-theater meal. Antique-lovers should note that the beloved Annex Antiques Fair & Flea Market (Chelsea Flea Market) has moved here, and that it's now the **Hell's Kitchen Flea Market** (Map pp162-3; ☎ 212-243-5343; www.hellskitchenfleamarket.com; W 39th St, btwn Ninth & Tenth Aves; 7am-5pm Sat & Sun), boasting 170 vendors of vintage clothing, antique jewelry, period furniture and many more treasures.

COLUMBUS CIRCLE/TIME WARNER CENTER

The pair of sleek towers known as the **Time Warner Center** (Map pp168-9; ☎ 212-823-6300; www.shopsatcolumbuscircle.com; 10 Columbus Circle, at 59th St; 9am-9pm), built for $1.8 billion after much angst and anticipation, created a major buzz with their grand entrance. What remains here, in the spot that for years was home to the aging New York Coliseum, is a very tall high-end mall. But the view of Central Park is quite special and there are number of excellent restaurants (p183) on the 3rd floor. On the southern side of the circle is the **Museum of Arts and Design** (Map pp162-3; ☎ 212-299-7777; www.madmuseum.org; 2 Columbus Circle; adult/child $15/12; 11am-6pm Wed-Sun, to 9pm Thu), exhibiting a diverse international collection of modern, folk, craft and fine art pieces.

Central Park

It's hard to imagine what the city would be like without this refuge from the claustrophobia, from the teeming sidewalks and clogged roadways. This enormous wonderland of a **park** (Map pp168-9; ☎ 212-310-6600; www.centralparknyc.org; btwn 57th & 110th Sts & Fifth Ave & Central Park;), sitting right in the middle of Manhattan, provides both metaphorical and spiritual oxygen to its residents. The park's 843 acres were set aside in 1856 on the marshy northern fringe of the city. The landscaping (the first in a US public park), by Frederick Law Olmsted and Calvert Vaux, was innovative in its naturalistic style, with forested groves, meandering paths and informal ponds. Highlights include **Sheep Meadow** (mid-Park from 66th to 69th Sts), where tens of thousands of people lounge and play on warm weather weekends; **Strawberry Fields** at 72nd St, dedicated to John Lennon, who lived at (and was murdered in front of) the **Dakota apartment building** across the street; the sparkling **Jacqueline Kennedy Onassis Reservoir**, encircled by joggers daily; **Central Park zoo** (☎ 212-439-6500; www.wcs.org; 64th St, at Fifth Ave; adult/child $10/5; 10am-5pm Mon-Fri, to 5:30pm Sat & Sun), which opened a naturalistic snow leopard exhibit in spring 2009; and the formal, tree-lined promenade called the **Mall**, which culminates at the elegant **Bethesda Fountain**. A favorite tourist activity is to rent a **horse-drawn carriage** (Map pp168-9; 30min tour $35 plus generous tip) at 59th St (Central Park South). For more information while you're strolling, visit the **Dairy Building visitor centre** (Map pp168-9; ☎ 212-794-6564; Central Park, at 65th St; 10am-5pm Tue-Sat) in the southern section of the park.

Upper West Side

Shorthand for liberal, progressive and intellectual New York – think Woody Allen and Seinfeld – this neighborhood comprising the west side of Manhattan from Central Park to the Hudson River, and from Columbus Circle to 110th St, is no longer as colorful as it once was. Upper Broadway has been taken over by banks, pharmacies and national retail chain stores and many of the mom-and-pop shops and bookstores are long gone. You'll still find massive, ornate apartments and a diverse mix of stable, upwardly mobile folks (with many actors and classical musicians sprinkled throughout); and some lovely green spaces – **Riverside Park** stretches for 4 miles between W 72nd St and W 158th St along the Hudson River, and is a great place for strolling, running, cycling or simply gazing at the sun as it sets over the Hudson River.

NEW YORK HISTORICAL SOCIETY

The **New York Historical Society** (Map pp168-9; ☎ 212-873-3400; www.nyhistory.org; 170 Central Park W, at 77th St; adult/child $10/6; 10am-6pm Tue-Sun), founded in 1804, is the city's oldest museum, featuring original watercolors from John James Audubon's *Birds of America* and a quirky permanent collection: only here can you see 17th-century cowbells and the mounted wooden leg of Gouverneur Morris. The Henry Luce III Center for the Study of American Culture is a 21,000-sq-ft showcase of more than 40,000 objects from the museum's permanent collection.

LINCOLN CENTER

As well as marking the completion of the first phase of a $1.2 billion redevelopment plan for the **Lincoln Center** (Map pp168-9; ☎ 212-875-5456; www.lincolncenter.org; cnr Columbus Ave & Broadway), 2009 was the 50th anniversary the country's largest performing arts center. The dramatically redesigned Alice Tully Hall anchors one end of a courtyard with a massive fountain surrounded by other stunning venues. Plans call for the renovation of Avery Fisher Hall, home to the New York Philharmonic, and upgrading the public spaces. Fascinating one-hour **tours** (☎ 212-875-5350; adult/child $15/8) of the complex leave from the lobby of Avery Fisher Hall from 10:30am to 4:30pm daily. Free wi-fi is available on the property.

AMERICAN MUSEUM OF NATURAL HISTORY

Founded in 1869, this **museum** (Map pp168-9; ☎ 212-769-5100; www.amnh.org; Central Park West, at 79th St; suggested admission adult/child $15/8.50, extra for space shows, IMAX shows & special exhibits; 10am-5:45pm;) includes more than 30 million artifacts, interactive exhibits and loads of taxidermy. It's most famous for its three large dinosaur halls, an enormous (fake) blue whale that hangs from the ceiling above the Hall of Ocean Life and the elaborate **Rose Center for Earth & Space**. Just gazing at its facade – a massive glass box that contains a silver globe, home to space-show theatres and the planetarium – is mesmerizing, especially at night, when all of its otherworldly features are aglow. To get here take the subway to 81st St-Museum of Natural History.

Morningside Heights

The Upper West Side's northern neighbor, comprising the area of Broadway and west up to about 125th St, is anchored by the Ivy League **Columbia University** (Map pp168-9; ☎ 212-854-1754; www.columbia.edu; cnr 116th St & Broadway). The highly rated college, one of the centers of student activism and protest in the late 1960s, features a spacious, grassy central quadrangle that's dominated by the 1895 neoclassical Low Library.

Two churches are big draws, too: the Episcopal **Cathedral of St John the Divine** (Map pp168-9; ☎ 212-316-7540; 1047 Amsterdam Ave, at 112th St; 7am-6pm, to 7pm Sun) is the largest place of worship in the USA, and features High Mass, held at 11am Sunday, often with sermons by well-known intellectuals. It's known by some as 'St John the Unfinished;' scaffolding and restoration crews have been omnipresent since the church was damaged in a large fire in 2001. West of here is the **Riverside Church** (Map pp168-9; ☎ 212-870-6700; www.theriversidechurchny.org; 490 Riverside Dr, at 122nd St; 7am-10pm), a 1930 Gothic-style marvel, famous for its 74 carillon bells that are rung every Sunday at noon and 3pm, as well as for its diverse and activist congregation.

CENTRAL PARK & UPTOWN

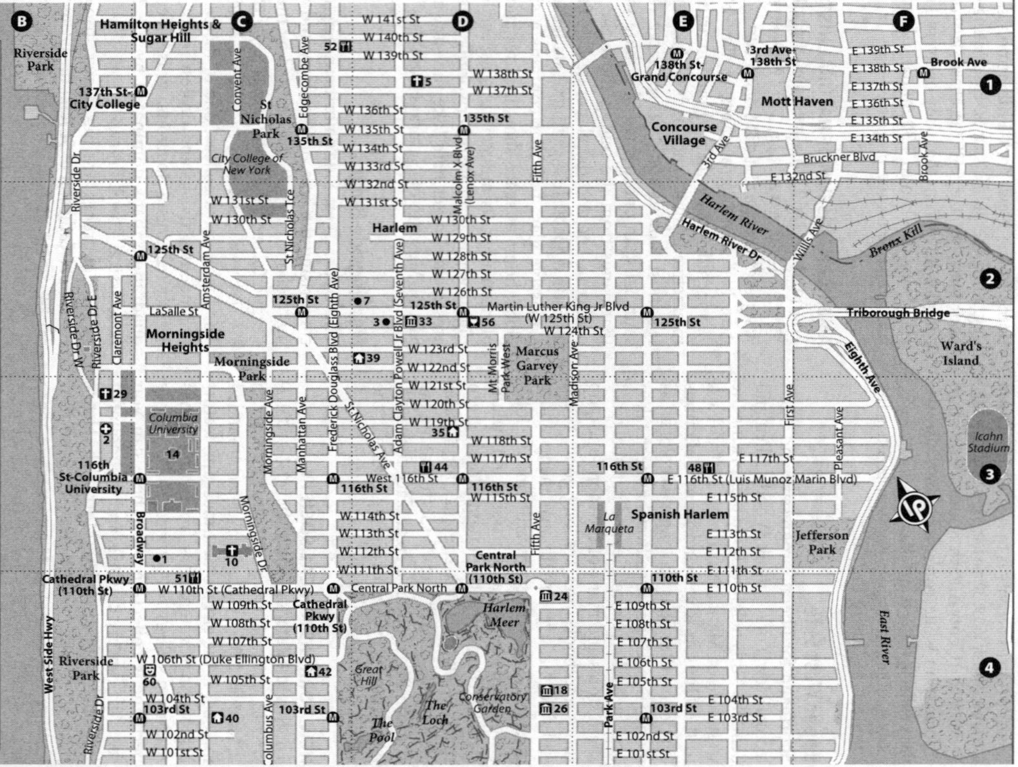

0 — 600 m
0 — 0.3 miles

INFORMATION

Book Culture	1	C3
Interchurch Center Medical Office	2	B3
New York City & Company (Harlem)	3	D2

SIGHTS & ACTIVITIES

92nd St Y	4	E5
Abyssinian Baptist Church	5	D1
American Museum of Natural History	6	C7
Apollo Theater	7	D2
Bethesda Fountain	8	D7
Blades Board & Skate	9	C7
Cathedral of St John the Divine	10	C3
Central Park Zoo	11	D8
Central Park's Safari Playground	12	C5
Children's Museum of Manhattan	13	C6
Columbia University	14	C3
Columbus Circle	15	C8
Dairy Building Visitor Center	16	D8
Dakota Apartment Building	17	C7
El Museo del Barrio	18	D4
Frick Collection	19	D7
Horse-drawn Carriages	20	D8
Jacqueline Kennedy Onassis Reservoir	21	D5
Lincoln Center	(see 59)	
Loeb Boathouse	22	D7
Metropolitan Museum of Art	23	D6
Museum of African Art	24	D4
Museum of Arts & Design	25	C8
Museum of the City of New York	26	D4
Neue Galerie	27	D6
New York Historical Society	28	C7
Riverside Church	29	B3
Sheep Meadow	30	D8
Solomon R Guggenheim Museum	31	D6
Strawberry Fields	32	D7
Studio Museum in Harlem	33	D2
Time Warner Towers	(see 15)	
Whitney Museum of American Art	34	E7

SLEEPING

102 Brownstone	35	D3
Bentley	36	F8
Carlyle	37	E7
Empire Hotel	38	C8

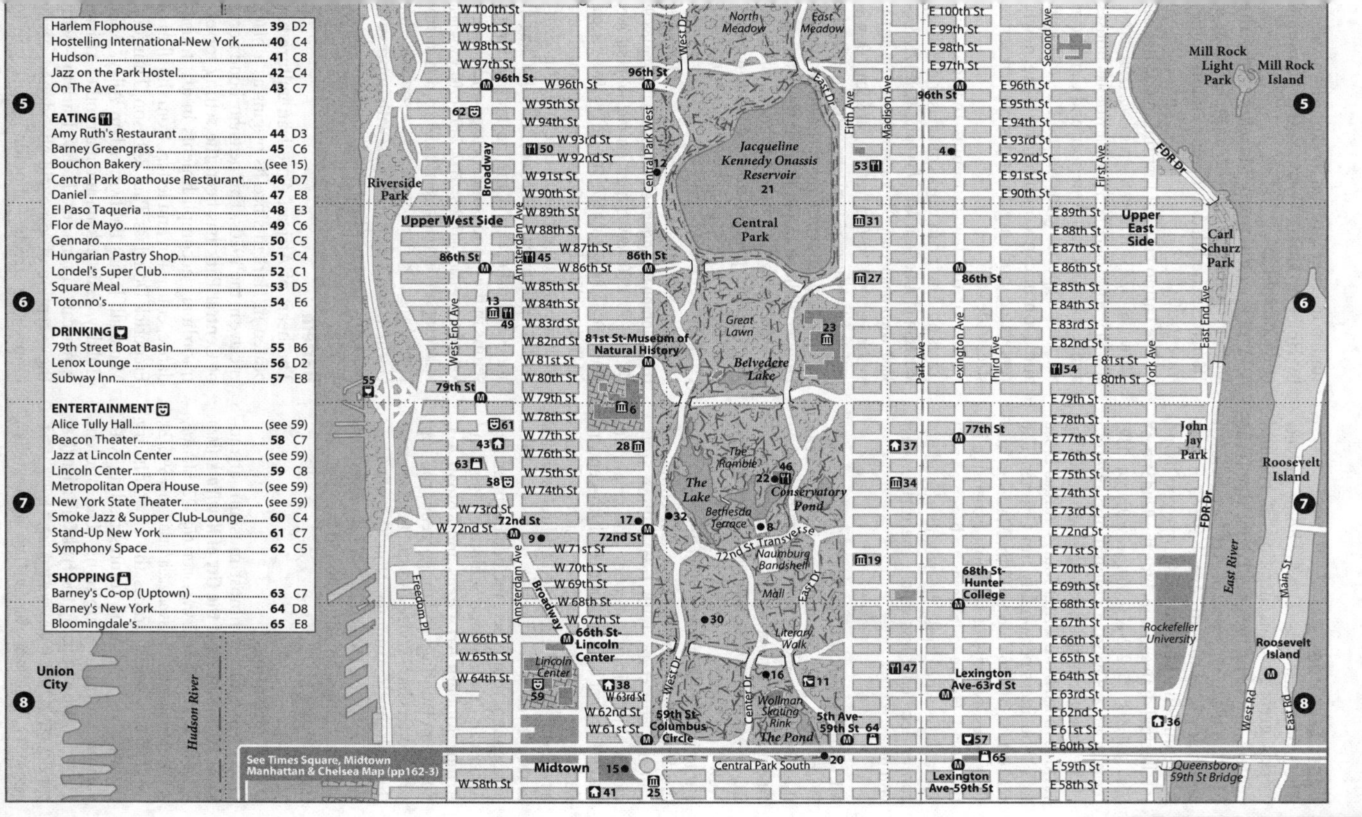
Harlem Flophouse 39 D2
Hostelling International-New York 40 C4
Hudson 41 C8
Jazz on the Park Hostel 42 C4
On The Ave 43 C7
EATING
Amy Ruth's Restaurant 44 D3
Barney Greengrass 45 C6
Bouchon Bakery (see 15)
Central Park Boathouse Restaurant 46 D7
Daniel 47 E8
El Paso Taqueria 48 E3
Flor de Mayo 49 C6
Gennaro 50 C5
Hungarian Pastry Shop 51 C4
Londel's Super Club 52 C1
Square Meal 53 D5
Totonno's 54 E6
DRINKING
79th Street Boat Basin 55 B6
Lenox Lounge 56 D2
Subway Inn 57 E8
ENTERTAINMENT
Alice Tully Hall (see 59)
Beacon Theater 58 C7
Jazz at Lincoln Center (see 59)
Lincoln Center 59 C8
Metropolitan Opera House (see 59)
New York State Theater (see 59)
Smoke Jazz & Supper Club-Lounge 60 C4
Stand-Up New York 61 C7
Symphony Space 62 C5
SHOPPING
Barney's Co-op (Uptown) 63 C7
Barney's New York 64 D8
Bloomingdale's 65 E8
See Times Square, Midtown Manhattan & Chelsea Map (pp162-3)
Hudson River
Union City
Riverside Park
Upper West Side
Midtown
Broadway
Amsterdam Ave
West End Ave
Central Park West
Freedom Pl
81st St-Museum of Natural History
66th St-Lincoln Center
59th St-Columbus Circle
Central Park
Jacqueline Kennedy Onassis Reservoir
North Meadow
East Meadow
Great Lawn
Belvedere Lake
The Ramble
The Lake
Conservatory Pond
Bethesda Terrace
Naumburg Bandshell
Mall
Literary Walk
Wollman Skating Rink
The Pond
Central Park South
5th Ave-59th St
Fifth Ave
Madison Ave
Park Ave
Lexington Ave
Third Ave
Second Ave
First Ave
York Ave
East End Ave
Upper East Side
68th St-Hunter College
Lexington Ave-63rd St
Lexington Ave-59th St
Rockefeller University
John Jay Park
Carl Schurz Park
Mill Rock Light Park
Mill Rock Island
FDR Dr
East River
Roosevelt Island
Main St
West Rd
East Rd
Queensboro 59th St Bridge

Upper East Side

The Upper East Side (UES) is home to New York's greatest concentration of cultural centers, including the grand dame that is the Metropolitan Museum of Art (see below), and many refer to Fifth Ave above 57th St as Museum Mile. Beyond museums, you'll find intellectual draws that include the **92nd Street Y** (Map pp168-9; ☎ 212-415-5500; www.92y.org; 1395 Lexington Ave, at 92nd St), a cultural hub offering classes, performances, readings and talks by various folks, from writer Mario Vargas Llosa to TV business personality Jim Cramer. The real estate, at least along Fifth, Madison and Park Aves, is some of the most expensive in the world. Home to ladies who lunch as well as frat boys who drink, the neighborhood becomes decidedly less chichi the further east you go.

METROPOLITAN MUSEUM OF ART

With more than five million visitors a year, the **Met** (Map pp168-9; ☎ 212-535-7710; www.metmuseum.org; 1000 Fifth Ave, at 82nd St; suggested donation $20; 9:30am-5:30pm Tue-Thu & Sun, to 9pm Fri & Sat) is New York's most popular single-site tourist attraction, with one of the richest coffers in the arts world. The Met is a self-contained cultural city-state, with two million individual objects in its collection and an annual budget of over $120 million; its 19th-century European paintings and sculpture galleries have been greatly expanded and refurbished in recent years.

Highlight rooms here include Egyptian Art, American Paintings and Sculpture, Arms and Armor, Modern Art, Greek and Roman Art, European Paintings and the gorgeous rooftop, which offers bar service and spectacular views throughout the summer. Note that the suggested donation (which is, truly, a *suggestion*) includes same-day admission to the Cloisters (see opposite).

OTHER MUSEUMS

One of the northernmost museum attractions, the **Museum of the City of New York** (Map pp168-9; ☎ 212-534-1672; www.mcny.org; 1220 Fifth Ave, at 123rd St; suggested admission adult/child/family $9/5/20; 10am-5pm Tue-Sun) traces the city's history from beaver trading to futures trading with various cultural exhibitions. The opulent 1914 mansion housing the **Frick Collection** (Map pp168-9; ☎ 212-288-0700; www.frick.org; 1 E 70th St; admission $15; 10am-6pm Tue-Sat, 11am-5pm Sun) tells a similar tale, but through its exquisite artwork by Holbein, Titian, Vermeer, Gainsborough and Constable.

A new addition to Museum Mile, the **Museum of African Art** (www.africanart.org; Fifth Ave, at 110th St) is scheduled to open its doors sometime in 2010.

The Latino cultural institution **El Museo del Barrio** (☎ 212-831-7272; www.elmuseo.org; 1230 Fifth Ave, at 104th St; admission $9; 11am-6pm Wed-Sun) houses a collection of Latin American and Caribbean art with a special focus on the Puerto Rican and Dominican communities. The newly renovated building includes an attractive streetside café.

One of the few museums that concentrates on American works of art is the **Whitney Museum of American Art** (Map pp168-9; ☎ 212-570-3600; www.whitney.org; 945 Madison Ave, at 75th St; admission $15; 11am-6pm Wed, Thu, Sat & Sun, 1-9pm Fri with pay-what-you-wish 6-9pm), specializing in 20th-century and contemporary art, with works by Hopper, Pollock and Rothko, as well as special shows, such as the much-ballyhooed Biennial. The Whitney plans to have a downtown outpost in the Meatpacking District as part of the High Line project.

The inspired work of Frank Lloyd Wright, the **Solomon R Guggenheim Museum** (Map pp168-9; ☎ 212-423-3500; www.guggenheim.org; 1071 Fifth Ave; admission $18, by donation 6-7:45pm Fri; 10am-5:45pm Sat-Wed, to 7:45pm Fri) and its sweeping spiral of a staircase is a superb sculpture, holding 20th-century paintings by Picasso, Pollock, Chagall and Kandinsky. One of the most pleasant museums in the 'hood is the focused and elegant **Neue Galerie** (Map pp168-9; ☎ 212-628-6200; www.neuegalerie.org; 1048 Fifth Ave, at 86th St; adult $15, children under 12 not admitted; 11am-6pm Thu-Mon), a showcase for German and Austrian artists, with impressive works by Gustav Klimt and Egon Schiele.

Harlem

The heart of African American culture has beaten in Harlem since its origins as a black enclave in the 1920s. This neighborhood north of Central Park has been the setting for extraordinary accomplishments in art, music, dance, education and letters from the likes of Frederick Douglass, Paul Robeson, Thurgood Marshall, James Baldwin, Alvin Ailey, Billie Holiday, Jessie Jackson and many other African American luminaries. Today, Harlem – with the exception of some still-abandoned, eerily empty side streets – shouldn't cause you to exercise any more caution than you would anywhere else in New York.

For a traditional view of Harlem, visit on Sunday morning, when well-dressed locals flock to neighborhood churches. Just be respectful of the fact that these people are attending a religious service (rather than being on display for tourists). Unless you're invited by a member of a small congregation, stick to the bigger churches such as the **Abyssinian Baptist Church** (Map pp168-9; ☎ 212-862-7474; www.abyssinian.org; 132 W 138th St). It has a superb choir and a charismatic pastor, Calvin O Butts, who welcomes tourists and prays for them. Sunday services start at 9am and 11am – the later one is *very* well attended.

For straight-up entertainment, head to the historic **Apollo Theater** (Map pp168-9; ☎ 212-663-0499; www.apollotheater.com; 253 W 125th St), which still holds its famous (if very touristed) amateur night ($17 to $27), 'where stars are born and legends are made.'

To glimpse the work of visual artists be sure to visit the **Studio Museum in Harlem** (Map pp168-9; ☎ 212-864-4500; www.studiomuseum.org; 144 W 125th St; suggested donation $7; 🕑 noon-6pm Wed-Fri & Sun, from 10am Sat), one of the premier showcases for black artists; look for excellent rotating exhibits from painters, sculptors, illustrators and other creators.

Washington Heights

Near the northern tip of Manhattan (above 155th St), Washington Heights takes its name from the first US president, who set up a Continental Army fort here during the Revolutionary War. An isolated rural spot until the end of the 19th century, Washington Heights attracted lots of new blood as New Yorkers sniffed out its affordable rents. Still, this neighborhood manages to retain its Latino – mainly Dominican – flavor, and now what you'll find is an interesting mix of blocks that alternate between former downtowners and longtime residents who operate within a tight and warm community.

Most visitors to Washington Heights come to see the **Cloisters** (Map p150; ☎ 212-923-3700; www.metmuseum.org/cloisters; Fort Tryon Park, at 190th St; suggested admission adult/child $20/free; 🕑 9:30am-4:45pm Tue-Sun Nov-Feb, to 5:15pm Mar-Oct), a branch of the Metropolitan Museum of Art in Fort Tryon Park. Constructed in the 1930s using stones and fragments from several French and Spanish medieval monasteries, the romantic, castle-like creation houses medieval frescoes, tapestries, courtyards, gardens and paintings, and has commanding views of the Hudson.

Brooklyn

Brooklyn is a world in and of itself; residents sometimes don't go into Manhattan for days or even weeks at a time. With 2.5 million people and growing, from well-to-do new parents seeking stately brownstones in Carroll Gardens to young band members wanting cheap rents near gigs in Williamsburg, this outer borough has long succeeded Manhattan in the cool and livability factors in many people's minds. From sandy beaches and breezy boardwalks at one end, foodie destinations at the other, with a massive range of ethnic enclaves, world-class entertainment, stately architecture and endless shopping strips in between, Brooklyn is a rival to Manhattan's attractions. The **Brooklyn Tourism & Visitors Center** (off Map pp152-3; ☎ 718-802-3846; www.brooklyntourism.org; 209 Borough Hall, Joralemon St; 🕑 10am-6pm Mon-Fri), in Brooklyn Heights, is an informative place to begin.

BROOKLYN HEIGHTS & DOWNTOWN BROOKLYN

When Robert Fulton's steam ferries started regular services across the East River in the early 19th century, well-to-do Manhattanites began building stellar houses – Victorian Gothic, Romanesque, neo-Greco, Italianate and others – in Brooklyn Heights. Strolling along the tree-lined streets to gaze at them now is a lovely afternoon activity; don't miss the 1881 Queen Anne–style landmark building that houses the **Brooklyn Historical Society** (off Map pp152-3; ☎ 718-222-4111; www.brooklynhistory.org; 128 Pierrepont St; admission $6; 🕑 noon-5pm Wed-Fri & Sun, 10am-5pm Sat), which houses a library (with some 33,000 grainy digitized photos from decades past), auditorium and museum devoted to the borough. The society also leads several walking tours.

Follow **Montague St**, the Heights' main commercial avenue, down to the waterfront until you hit the **Brooklyn Heights Promenade**, which juts out over the Brooklyn–Queens Expwy to offer stunning views of Lower Manhattan. An 85-acre development of green space and condos, **Brooklyn Bridge Park** is being built on piers stretching from the bridge south to Atlantic Ave.

The 1848 beaux-arts **Brooklyn Borough Hall** (209 Joralemon St) straddles both Brooklyn Heights and downtown Brooklyn, characterized by its various courts. Its busy Fulton St feeds into the **Brooklyn Bridge** (see p155). **Fulton Street Mall** is a bustling bazaar of shoe stores, cheap clothing outlets, fast-food and cell-phone shops running from Adams St to Flatbush Ave. Just south of here, the small but fascinating **New York Transit Museum** (off Map pp152-3; ☎ 718-694-1600; www.mta.info/mta/museum; Boerum Pl, at Schermerhorn St; adult/child $5/3; 🕒 10am-4pm Tue-Fri, noon-5pm Sat & Sun) has an amazing collection of original subway cars and transit memorabilia dating back more than a century.

DUMBO

Dumbo's nickname is an acronym for its location: 'Down Under the Manhattan–Brooklyn Bridge Overpass,' and while this north Brooklyn slice of waterfront used to be strictly for industry, it's now the domain of artists and wannabes, who occupy huge loft spaces that are no longer real-estate bargains. A controversial 17-story tower is scheduled to be built next to the Brooklyn Bridge, marring the views in the opinion of those who oppose the project. **St Ann's Warehouse** (Map pp152-3; ☎ 718-254-8779; www.stannswarehouse.org; 45 Main St) is a highly regarded artist-driven performance space; **Dumbo Arts Center** (Map pp152-3; ☎ 718-694-0831; www.dumboartscenter.org; 30 Washington St; 🕒 noon-6pm Wed-Sun) is one of the top galleries here, and host to the annual Dumbo Art Under the Bridge Festival, held each October. Formerly located in Williamsburg, the **Galapagos Art Space** (Map pp152-3; ☎ 718-222-8500; www.galapagosartspace.com; 16 Main St) has a new location in a strikingly renovated century-old horse stable. The mix of theater, cinema, readings and alternative performance is the same.

BOERUM HILL, COBBLE HILL & CARROLL GARDENS (& RED HOOK)

These neighborhoods, home to a mix of families, mostly Italian, who have lived here for generations, and former Manhattanites looking for a real life after the city, are full of tree-lined streets with rows of attractively restored brownstones. There's a distinctively conflicted urge to advertise the area's attractions and to guard them like a secret. **Smith Street** and **Court Street** are the two main arteries connecting to the most southerly area of the three, **Carroll Gardens**. The former is known as 'restaurant row,' while the latter has more of the old-school groceries, bakeries and red-sauce restaurants. A block west of here is **Cobble Hill Park**, a manicured patch of green with benches and picnic tables where locals hang. Even further west (and south) is **Red Hook**, a waterfront area with cobblestoned streets and hulking industrial buildings. Though it's a bit of a hike from the subway line, the formerly gritty area is now home to a handful of bars and eateries, as well as a massive waterfront branch of **Fairway** (☎ 718-694-6868; 480 Van Brunt St), a beloved gourmet grocery with breathtaking views of NY harbor and the Statue of Liberty. Also here is the newest outpost of the Swedish furniture megastore Ikea (see p155 for information on the free water taxi to downtown Manhattan).

PARK SLOPE & PROSPECT HEIGHTS

The **Park Slope** neighborhood is known for its classic brownstones, tons of great eateries and boutiques (especially along Fifth Ave, which is more cutting edge than the other major strip, Seventh Ave), lesbian residents and stroller-pushing couples who resemble those on the Upper West Side (but have a backyard attached to their apartment). Beginning at its eastern border, the 585-acre **Prospect Park** (☎ 718-965-8591; www.prospectpark.org), created in 1866, is considered the greatest achievement of landscape designers Olmsted and Vaux, who also designed Central Park. Next door is the excellent 52-acre **Brooklyn Botanic Garden** (☎ 718-623-7200; www.bbg.org; 1000 Washington Ave; adult/child $8/4, free Tue; 🕒 8am-6pm Tue-Fri, from 10am Sat & Sun), which features impressive cherry-tree blossoms in spring. Beside the garden is the **Brooklyn Museum** (☎ 718-638-5000; www.brooklynmuseum.org; 200 Eastern Pkwy; suggested admission $8, 11am-11pm 1st Sat of each month free; 🕒 10am-5pm Wed-Fri, 11am-6pm Sat & Sun), with comprehensive collections of African, Islamic and Asian art, plus the brand-new Elizabeth A Sackler Center for Feminist Art.

WILLIAMSBURG & GREENPOINT

There is a definite Williamsburg look: skinny jeans, multiple tattoos, a discreet body piercing, shaggy hair for men, maybe some kind of retro head covering for a woman. Denizens of this raggedy and rowdy neighborhood across the East River on the L train seem to have time and money to slouch in cafés and party all night in bars; a fair share of older – early 30s – newcomers and Europeans are changing the makeup slightly. The main artery is **Bedford Ave** between N 10th St and Metropolitan Ave, where there are boutiques, cafés, bars and cheap eateries. But cool spots have also sprouted along N 6th St and Berry St, and even into the next neighborhood, **Greenpoint**, a traditionally Polish neighborhood that's lured those priced out of Billyburg with lower rents. Be sure to visit the excellent **Brooklyn Brewery** (☎ 718-486-7422; www.brooklynbrewery.com; 79 N 11th St; admission free; ⏲ 6-11pm Fri, noon-5pm Sat), which hosts weekend tours (on the hour from noon to 6pm), special events and pub nights.

FORT GREENE

Spike Lee grew up here and Erykah Badu and Rosie Perez live here – and they are not alone. This residential neighborhood of late-19th-century brownstones and gospel churches has been on the real-estate radar for a racially diverse group of young professionals for several years now. Its gem is the **Brooklyn Academy of Music** (Map pp152-3; ☎ 718-636-4100; www.bam.org; 30 Lafayette Ave), the oldest concert center in the country. A well-respected art and architecture school, the **Pratt Institute** (www.pratt.edu) calls the neighborhood home.

CONEY ISLAND & BRIGHTON BEACH

About 50 minutes by subway from Midtown, this popular pair of beach neighborhoods makes for a great day trip. **Coney Island** (Map p150) is all about nostalgic charms, with its wide sandy beach, wood-plank boardwalk and famous 1927 Cyclone roller coaster; Astroland Park used to operate arcade games and a collection of carnival rides, but it was sold to make way for developers (who plan to transform the area into a sleek-residential city complete with high-rise hotels) and closed, to considerable consternation. Still intact, though, is **Sideshows by the Seashore** (☎ 718-372-5159; www.coneyisland.com; adult/child $7.50/5), a burlesque-type show with bearded ladies and tattooed men. The **New York Aquarium** (☎ 718-741-1818; www.nyaquarium.com; Surf Ave, btwn 5th & W 8th Sts; adult/child $13/9; ⏲ 10am-6pm Mon-Fri, to 7pm Sat & Sun) is a big hit with kids, and **KeySpan Park** (Map p150; ☎ 718-449-8497; 1904 Surf Ave) is the waterfront stadium for the minor-league Brooklyn Cyclones baseball team.

A five-minute stroll north along the boardwalk brings you to **Brighton Beach** ('Little Odessa'; Map p150), where old-timers play chess and locals enjoy pierogies (boiled dumplings filled with meat or vegetables) and vodka shots in the sun at several boardwalk eateries. Then head into the heart of the 'hood, busy Brighton Beach Ave, to hit the many Russian shops, bakeries and restaurants.

The Bronx

Brooklyn's fierce northern rival is this 42-sq-mile borough, which has several claims to fame: the Yankees, fondly known as the Bronx Bombers, who can be seen in all their pinstriped glory at the new **Yankee Stadium** (Map p150; ☎ 718-293-6000; www.yankees.com; 161st St, at River Ave) in spring and summer; the 'real' Little Italy, or **Belmont** (Map p150; www.arthuravenuebronx.com), bustling stretches of Arthur and Belmont Aves that burst with Italian gourmet markets and eateries; and a super-sized attitude that's been mythologized in Hollywood movies from *The Godfather* to *Rumble in the Bronx*.

But it's also got some cool surprises up its sleeve: a quarter of the Bronx is parkland, including the city beach of Pelham Bay Park. It's home to the 250-acre **New York Botanical Garden** (Map p150; ☎ 718-817-8700; www.nybg.org; Bronx River Pkwy, at Fordham Rd; adult/child $6/3, free Wed; ⏲ 10am-6pm Tue-Sun; 👶), with nearly 3000 roses. The nearby **Bronx Wildlife Conservation Park** (Map p150; ☎ 718-220-5100; www.bronxzoo.com; Bronx River Pkwy, at Fordham Rd; adult/child $15/11; ⏲ 10am-5pm Apr-Oct; 👶), otherwise known as the Bronx Zoo, is one of the biggest, best and most progressive zoos anywhere; and the famous, historic **Woodlawn Cemetery** (Map p150; ☎ 718-920-0500; www.thewoodlawncemetery.org; Webster Ave, at 233rd St) is the fascinating, 400-acre burial ground of many notable Americans, including Irving Berlin and Herman Melville. Also up in these parts is the magical City Island (see boxed text, p174), a little slice of New England in the Bronx.

The **Bronx Tourism Council** (☎ 718-590-3518; www.ilovethebronx.com) has visitor information, and the **Bronx County Historical Society** (☎ 718-881-8900; www.bronxhistoricalsociety.org) sponsors weekend walking tours.

Queens

There is no longer any typical Queens accent – think Archie and Edith Bunker in *All in the Family*. You're as likely to hear Bengali and Spanish – 170 languages are spoken – in this, the largest (282 sq miles) and most ethnically diverse county in the country. There are few of the tree-lined brownstone streets you find in Brooklyn, and the majority of the neighborhoods, architecturally speaking at least, are unbefitting this borough's grand name. However, because close to half its 2.3 million residents were born abroad, parts of Queens are endlessly reconstituting themselves, creating a vibrant and heady alternative universe to Manhattan. It's also home to two major airports, the Mets, a hip modern-art scene, miles of excellent beaches in the **Rockaways** and walking trails in the **Gateway National Recreation Area** (Map p150; www.nps.gov/gate), a wildlife refuge in Jamaica Bay only minutes from JFK airport. The **Queens Historical Society** (☎ 718-939-0647; www.queenshistoricalsociety.org) offers tours on many areas of the massive borough.

ASTORIA & LONG ISLAND CITY

Home to the largest Greek community outside of Greece, this is obviously the place to find amazing Greek bakeries, restaurants and gourmet shops, mainly along **Broadway**. But it's not as one-note as it used to be, as an influx of Eastern European and Middle Eastern (Steinway Ave is the place for falafel, kebabs and hookah pipes) folks have been pouring in too. Then there are the hipsters, who have made this area Queens' answer to Williamsburg. In the summer, cool off at the **Astoria Pool** (19th St, at 23rd Dr), the city's largest and oldest. Much of the neighborhood, as well as curious Manhattanites, can be found at the **Bohemian Hall & Beer Garden** (☎ 718-274-4925; www.bohemianhall.com; 2919 24th Ave, Astoria) during warm afternoons and evenings.

In recent years neighboring Long Island City has become quite the hub of art museums. **PS 1 Contemporary Art Center** (☎ 718-784-2084; www.ps1.org; 22-25 Jackson Ave, at 46th Ave; suggested donation $5; noon-6pm Thu-Mon), run by MoMA, is dedicated solely to new, cutting-edge works. On Saturdays (2pm to 9pm) from early July through September, the center's outdoor courtyard is transformed into an installation art space and crammed with the highest concentration of hipsters this side of the Mississippi. Several high-rise condominiums line Long Island City's riverfront with fantastic views of Manhattan.

If the weather is pleasant, don't miss the waterside **Socrates Sculpture Park** (☎ 718-956-1819; www.socratessculpturepark.org; Broadway, at Vernon Blvd; admission free; 10am-dusk), an outdoor exhibit of massive, climbable sculptures by greats including Mark DiSuvero, who founded the space. Nearby is the peaceful **Isamu Noguchi Garden Museum** (☎ 718-204-7088; www.noguchi.org; 9-01 33rd Rd, at Vernon Blvd; adult/child $10/free; 10am-5pm Wed-Fri, 11am-6pm Sat & Sun), with the sculptures of this Japanese artist. Also in the area is a reminder that moviemaking started in Astoria in the 1920s: the **American Museum of the Moving Image** (☎ 718-777-6820; www.ammi.org; 35th Ave, at 36th St; admission $7; 10am-5pm Tue-Fri) exposes some of the mysteries of the craft with amazing exhibits and screenings.

> **WORTH THE TRIP: CITY ISLAND**
>
> Only 15 miles from midtown but a complete world away is the surprising neighborhood of **City Island** (Map p150; www.cityislandchamber.org), a 1.5-mile-long fishing community that's filled with boat slips, yacht clubs, waterfront seafood eateries and windswept little spits of sand. Victorian clapboard houses look more New England than the Bronx, and you can even go on a lobster dive with **Captain Mike's Dive Shop** (☎ 718-885-1588; www.captainmikesdiving.com; 530 City Island Ave; dives $55-88).

FLUSHING & CORONA

The intersection of Main St and Roosevelt Ave, downtown Flushing, can feel like the Times Square of a city a world away from NYC. Immigrants from all over Asia, primarily Chinese and Korean, make up this neighborhood bursting at the seams with markets and restaurants filled with delicious and cheap delicacies. The Long Island Rail Road station and terminal for the 7 train see around 100,000 people pass through daily. **Flushing Meadows Corona Park**, meanwhile, is the home of **Citi Field** (Map p150), the **USTA National Tennis Center** and many lakes, ball fields, bike paths and grassy expanses; and was used for the 1939 and 1964 World's Fairs, of which there are quite a few faded leftovers – including Queens' most famous landmark, the stainless steel Unisphere, standing 120ft high and weighing 380 tons. Kids can learn about space and astropohysics while putting through the **Rocket Park Mini Golf Course** (☎ 718-699-0005; $5 per round;). Also within this massive park is the **Queens Museum of Art** (☎ 718-592-9700; www.queensmuseum.org; New York City Bldg, Flushing Meadows Corona Park; suggested donation $5; 10am-5pm Wed-

Fri, from noon Sat & Sun). In nearby Corona, the **Louis Armstrong House** (☎ 718-478-8274; www.louisarmstronghouse.org; 34-56 107th St; 🕑 10am-5pm Tue-Fri, noon-5pm Sat & Sun; admission $8) is the home where the musical great lived during the peak of his career.

JACKSON HEIGHTS

A fascinating mix of Indian (74th St) and South American (Roosevelt Ave) cultures, this is the place to purchase saris and 22-karat gold, dine on South Indian *masala dosas* – huge, paper-thin rice crepes folded around flavorful mixtures of masala potatoes, peas, cilantro and other earthy treats – and continue on with a plate of Colombian arepas (corn pancakes), a bite of Argentine empanadas and a cocktail at one of several Latin gay and lesbian bars, several of which line the main drag of Broadway. It's a crazy convergence that's not to be missed.

Staten Island

While many New Yorkers will say that Staten Island has more in common with its neighbor, New Jersey, because of its suburban house and car cultures, there are some undoubtedly compelling reasons to count this borough in your urban explorations. First and foremost is the free **Staten Island Ferry** (☎ 718-815-2628; www.siferry.com; 🕑 24hr), which shuttles blasé commuters to work while offering breathtaking views of the Statue of Liberty and the Manhattan skyline. Not far from the ferry station on the Staten Island side is the **Richmond County Bank Ballpark** (Map p150; ☎ 718-720-9265; www.siyanks.com; Richmond Terrace), home to the minor-league Staten Island Yankees, as well as the hipper-than-ever neighborhood of St George.

ACTIVITIES

Cycling & Inline Skating

Unless you're a bike messenger or otherwise-experienced urban cyclist, pedaling through the streets can be a high-risk activity in Manhattan, as bike lanes are often blocked by trucks, taxis and double-parked cars. City Hall, however, has committed to improving the situation. **Central Park** has lovely cycling paths, as does **Hudson River Park** (see p156), which has a path shared by cyclists, runners, walkers and skaters. An auto-free road runs round the perimeter of Brooklyn's **Prospect Park** (see p172), and the beautiful **Franklin D Roosevelt Boardwalk** (cnr Father Capadanno Blvd & Sand Ln) along South Beach in Staten Island, hugs 4 miles of unspoiled beaches.

For cycling tips and weekend trips, contact **Five Borough Bicycle Club** (☎ 212-932-2300; www.5bbc.org). **Transportation Alternatives** (Map pp162-3; ☎ 212-629-8080; www.transalt.org; Suite 1002, 127 W 26th St), a nonprofit bicycle-lobbying group, is also a good source of information, as is **Bike Network Development** (www.ci.nyc.ny.us/html/dcp/html/bike/home.html), which offers bicycling map downloads and more information on cycling in the city. Gay cycling enthusiasts should check the website of **Fast & Fabulous** (☎ 212-567-7160; www.fastnfab.org), a gay cycling club that organizes long weekend rides. For bike rentals, try **Loeb Boathouse** (Map pp168-9; ☎ 212-517-2233; Central Park, btwn 74th & 75th Sts; per hr from $9; 🕑 10am-6pm Apr-Nov) or **Manhattan Bicycle** (Map pp162-3; ☎ 212-262-0111; 791 Ninth Ave, btwn 52nd & 53rd Sts; per hr $5; 🕑 9am-7pm Mon-Fri, 10am-6pm Sat & Sun).

In-line skating is also popular in all of the above places, where, especially in Central Park north of Sheep Meadow, funky veterans fueled by loud disco and the music in their heads dance around a circle on summer weekends. For rentals, try **Blades Board & Skate** (Map pp168-9; ☎ 212-787-3911; www.blades.com; 156 W 72nd St; per day $20; 🕑 10am-8pm Mon-Sat, to 7pm Sun), two blocks from Central Park.

Running

The 6-mile roadway in **Central Park** (see p166) is closed to cars from 10am to 3pm weekdays and all weekend, and is perfect for running – as is its gleaming Jacqueline Kennedy Onassis Reservoir, encircled by a soft 1½-mile path. Another good place to sprint is the **Hudson River Park** (see p156), which runs along Manhattan's western edge from Battery Park to 59th St, and north of there through the leafy **Riverside Park** (p167). On the east side of the island, runners compete for space along the narrow **East River Promenade**; despite obstacles like a gap from 34th to 60th Sts where you have to detour to First or Second Ave, the views of the river and bridges are spectacular. Brooklynites run the 3.3-mile loop in **Prospect Park** (see p150), an urban oasis of 500-plus acres. The **New York Road Runners Club** (☎ 212-860-4455; www.nyrr.org) organizes weekend runs and races as well as the early-November **New York City Marathon**, an inspiring spectacle to behold if not to participate in.

Water Sports

This is an island, after all, and as such there are plenty of opportunities for boating and kayaking. The **Downtown Boathouse** (Map pp152-3; www.downtownboathouse.org; Pier 40, near Houston St) offers free 20-minute kayaking (including equipment) in the protected embayment of the Hudson River. You don't need a reservation; just head over on weekends between May 15 and October 15 (9am to 6pm) and occasional weekday evenings. Two other locations include **Clinton Cove** (Map pp162-3; Pier 96, west of 56th St) and **Riverside Park** (Map pp168-9; W 72nd St). It even gives tips to first-timers.

In Central Park, **Loeb Boathouse** (Map pp168-9; ☎ 212-517-2233; Central Park, btwn 74th & 75th Sts; per hr $10; 🕑 10am-dusk Mar-Oct) rents row boats for romantic trysts, and even fills Vienna-style gondolas in summer ($30 for 30 minutes). For a sailing adventure, hop aboard the *Schooner Adirondack* at **Chelsea Piers** (Map pp162–3), or the *Pioneer* at **South Street Seaport** (Map pp152–3).

If you'd rather get all wet, check out the cool new **Floating Pool Lady** (www.floatingpool.org), a 25-meter swimming pool on top of a massive barge that moves around the Hudson and docks in various city locations. Admission is free but limited to 175 people, so expect to wait on hot days.

Surfers may be surprised to find a tight group of wave worshipers within city limits, at Queens' **Rockaway Beach** at 90th St, where you can hang ten after only a 45-minute ride on the A train from midtown.

NEW YORK FOR CHILDREN

Contrary to popular belief, New York can be a pretty child-friendly city – it just takes a bit of guidance to find all the little creature comforts that you're accustomed to having back home. Fun playscape options include **Central Park's Safari Playground** (Map pp168–9), **Battery Park** (p156) and the **Glass Garden** (Map pp162-3; ☎ 212-263-6058; 400 E 34th St, at First Ave; 🕑 8am-5:30pm Mon-Fri, 1-5:30pm Sat-Sun).

The **Children's Museum of Manhattan** (Map pp168-9; ☎ 212-721-1223; www.cmom.org; 212 W 83rd St, btwn Broadway & Amsterdam Ave; admission $10; 🕑 10am-5pm Tue-Sun) and the **Brooklyn Children's Museum** (off Map pp152-3; ☎ 718-735-4400; www.brooklynkids.org; 145 Brooklyn Ave, Prospect Heights; admission $7.50; 🕑 11am-5pm Wed-Fri, from 10am Sat & Sun) are excellent respites, as are children's theaters, movie theaters, book and toy stores, aquariums and kid-friendly restaurants, such as **Bubby's Pie Company** (p181). For more hints and information on traveling with children, pick up Lonely Planet's *Travel with Children*.

TOURS

The following is just a sampling:

Big Onion Walking Tours (☎ 212-439-1090; www.bigonion.com; tours $15) Popular and quirky guided tours specializing in ethnic and neighborhood tours.

Circle Line (Map pp162-3; ☎ 212-563-3200; www.circleline42.com; Pier 83, W 42nd St; tickets $16-34) Ferry boat tours, from semicircle to a full island cruise with guided commentary; definitely recommended at least once.

Famous Fat Dave's Eating Tours (www.famousfatdave.com; tours for 2 people from $200) Customized private eating tours of the five boroughs chauffeured by the eponymous Dave in his retrofitted white checker cab.

Gray Line Sightseeing (☎ 212-445-0848; www.coachusa.com/newyorksights; 49 W 45th St; adult/child from $42/$32) Hop-on, hop-off double-decker multilingual guided bus tours of all the boroughs (except Staten Island).

Municipal Art Society (☎ 212-935-3960; www.mas.org; 457 Madison Ave; tours adult $15) Various scheduled tours focusing on architecture and history.

New York City Audubon (☎ 212-691-7483; www.nycaudubon.org; tours $8-100) Expert instructors and guides lead trips including birding in Central Park and the Bronx and ecology cruises of the Jamaica Bay Wildlife Refuge.

On Location Tours (☎ 212-209-3370; www.screentours.com; tours $15-45) A Gossip Girl tour is the latest addition to the list of tours available for fulfilling your Carrie Bradshaw or Tony Soprano fantasies.

FESTIVALS & EVENTS

Festivities never cease in New York. From cultural street fairs to foodie events and outdoor concerts, you are bound to find something that will excite you, no matter the time of year. There's almost too much to digest in summer, when outdoor celebrations proliferate.

Restaurant Week (☎ 212-484-1222; www.nycgo.com) Dine at top restaurants for $20 and $30 deals – first in February and again in July.

Armory Show (☎ 212-645-6440; www.thearmoryshow.com) New York's biggest contemporary art fair sweeps the city in March, showcasing the new work of thousands of artists from around the world.

Tribeca Film Festival (☎ 212-941-2400; www.tribecafilmfestival.com) Robert DeNiro co-organizes this local downtown film fest, held in late April and early May, that's quickly rising in prestige on the circuit.

Fleet Week (☎ 212-245-0072) Annual convocation of sailors and their naval ships and air rescue teams, who descend upon the city in their formal whites every May.

Lesbian, Gay, Bisexual & Transgender Pride (☎ 212-807-7433; www.nycpride.org) Pride month, in June, with a packed calendar of parties and events, culminates with a major march down Fifth Ave on the last Sunday of the month.

Mermaid Parade (www.coneyisland.com/mermaid) Something of Mardi Gras on the boardwalk, Surf Ave on Coney Island in Brooklyn turns into an artistic, crazy and fun free-expression zone in late June.

New York Film Festival (www.filmlinc.com) Catch major world premieres from prominent directors at this Lincoln Center event, held in late September.

New Yorker Festival (www.newyorker.com) A mid-October lineup of interviews, talks and tours from some of the most prominent literary and cultural figures in the world.

SLEEPING

The average room rate in early 2009 came crashing down to around $200 and the occupancy rate fell precipitously as well. Keep in mind that prices change depending on the value of the euro, yen and other worldwide currencies, as well as the general drift of the global economic climate, not to mention the day of the week and the season, with spring and fall being most expensive. Tax adds an additional 13.25% per night. For longer stays, an apartment rental or sublet can be the best option (there's no tax on rentals), secured with the help of an agency like **City Sonnet** (☎ 212-614-3034; www.westvillagebb.com; apt from $135 per night).

Lower Manhattan

OUR PICK **Gild Hall Wall Street** (Map pp152-3; ☎ 212-232-7700; www.wallstreetdistrict.com; 15 Gold St; r from $225, ste $315;) Part of the Thompson line of fabulous NYC hotels, Gild Hall sports a funky English-hunting-lodge lobby. All the rooms, including the small and simple standards, have oversized leather headboards and notably comfortable beds; the suites have high ceilings and large living areas. Only a few blocks from Wall St and several subway lines, you won't feel stranded.

Wall Street Inn (Map pp152-3; ☎ 212-747-1500; www.thewallstreetinn.com; 9 S William St; r incl breakfast from $275;) Lehman Brothers, the failed bank, once occupied this classic limestone building and, while the mood of the hotel is very early American banker, there's little risk in a stay here. Old-fashioned and warm rather than stuffy, the rooms, with luxurious marble bathrooms, are slightly over-furnished for their size.

Best Western Seaport Inn (Map pp152-3; ☎ 212-766-6600, 800-468-3569; www.seaportinn.com; 33 Peck Slip, btwn Front & Water Sts; d from $215;) Despite its blah chain style, the Best Western offers some striking water views.

Tribeca & SoHo

Cosmopolitan Hotel (Map pp152-3; ☎ 212-566-1900, 888-895-9400; www.cosmohotel.com; 95 W Broadway, at Chambers St; d from $149;) Don't let the name fool you – rather than being urbane and sophisticated, the Cosmopolitan is more akin to the average Main St USA hotel. Clean, carpeted, though decidedly cramped, it's an affordable downtown option with loads of cheap eats a short walk away.

Soho Grand Hotel (Map pp152-3; ☎ 212-965-3000; www.sohogrand.com; 310 W Broadway; d $195-450;) The original boutique hotel of the 'hood still reigns, with its striking glass-and-cast-iron lobby stairway, and 367 rooms with cool, clean lines plus Frette linens, plasma flat-screen TVs and Kiehl's grooming products. The lobby's Grand Lounge buzzes with action.

Sixty Thompson (Map pp152-3; ☎ 212-431-0400; www.60thompson.com; 60 Thompson St, btwn Broome & Spring Sts; s/d/ste $360/425/720;) Another minimalist charmer. Rooms here have down duvets, flat-screen TVs and cozy tweed sofas. The rooftop Thom Bar is a stunning place to see and be seen.

Lower East Side & East Village

East Village Bed & Coffee (Map pp152-3; ☎ 212-533-4175; www.bedandcoffee.com; 110 Ave C, btwn 7th & 8th Sts; r with shared bath from $115;) This hotel, a cheap and stylish place in the heart of a very cool 'hood, is a surprising find. The 10 airy rooms sport different well-executed themes – Mexican (with a bright-yellow wall and pressed-tin doodads), Zen (with a small Buddha and icy tones) and so on – and common areas are lovely, from the high-ceilinged kitchen to the leafy back garden.

Hotel on Rivington (Map pp152-3; ☎ 212-475-2600; www.hotelonrivington.com; 107 Rivington St, btwn Essex & Ludlow Sts; r from $160;) This shimmering 20-floor tower looms large over Lower East Side tenement buildings, its glass-enclosed rooms offering stunning views of the East River and downtown's spread. Rooms vary quite a bit – some have balconies, some have hanging flat-screen TVs – and the ground-floor restaurant is a hipster hot spot.

Bowery Hotel (Map pp152-3; ☎ 212-505-9100; www.theboweryhotel.com; 335 Bowery, btwn E 2nd & 3rd Sts; r from $325;) Perhaps as far as you can get from the Bowery's gritty flophouse history, this stunningly stylish hotel is all 19th-century elegance. Rooms come equipped with lots of light and sleek furnishings mixed with antiques. The baroque-style lobby bar attracts the young and chic, and on-site restaurant Gemma serves upscale Italian with preferred seating saved for hotel guests.

West (Greenwich) Village

Larchmont Hotel (Map pp152-3; ☎ 212-989-9333; www.larchmonthotel.com; 27 W 11th St, btwn Fifth & Sixth Aves; s/d with shared bathroom & breakfast from $90/109;) Housed in a prewar building that blends in with the other fine brownstones on the block, a stay at the Larchmont is about location. The carpeted rooms are basic and in need of updating, as are the communal bathrooms, but it's still a good deal for the price.

Jane Hotel (Map pp152-3; ☎ 212-924-6700; www.thejanenyc.com; 113 Jane St; r with shared bathroom from $100;) If history were the only standard, the Jane would be a fine hotel. Originally built for sailors (which is obvious after one look at the cabin-sized rooms), then a temporary refuge for survivors of the *Titanic*, a YMCA and rock-and-roll venue, the single bunk rooms feature flat-screen TVs and the communal showers are more than adequate.

Abingdon Guest House (Map pp152-3; ☎ 212-243-5384; www.abingdonguesthouse.com; 21 Eighth Ave, at Jane St; s/d from $169/179;) Don't look out the window and you'll swear you've landed in a New England B&B. Elegant, comfortable rooms feature four-poster beds, (nonworking) fireplaces, scads of exposed brick, and billowing curtains. Plus a lovely little garden out back.

Meatpacking District & Chelsea

Chelsea Star Hotel (Map pp162-3; ☎ 877-827-6969; 300 W 30th St, at Eighth Ave; dm/s/d from $30/90/110;) Some of the wall murals are liable to keep you up at night – 'The King & I' room especially is not for insomniacs. Whatever you think of the theme paint jobs on most of the rooms, whether whimsical or cheesy, they're certainly more welcoming than you'd expect from the hotel's exterior. The dorms are cozy brick-walled rooms with wood floors.

Chelsea International Hostel (Map pp162-3; ☎ 212-243-3700; www.chelseahostel.com; 222 W 20th St, btwn Seventh & Eighth Aves; dm with/without bathroom $36/32, r $80;) For those who simply need a place to crash, this well-located hostel draws an international crowd accustomed to partying and bunking down for a few hours. The staff isn't as friendly as one would like, but no doubt you'll make friends in the communal kitchen.

Ace Hotel New York City (Map pp162-3; ☎ 212-679-2222; www.acehotel.com/newyork; 20 W 29th St; r from $99-369;) This outpost of a hip Pacific northwest chain is on the northern edge of Chelsea. Some clever touches such as vintage turntables and handwritten welcome notes elevate the Ace beyond the standard. However, flannel comforters and prison-issued bunk beds in one of the room styles are missteps. Juice, coffee and croissants are available in the morning.

Hotel Gansevoort (Map pp152-3; ☎ 212-206-6700; www.hotelgansevoort.com; 18 Ninth Ave, at 13th St; r/ste from $395/625;) This 187-room luxury hotel in the trendy Meatpacking District has been a hit for its 400-thread-count linens, hypoallergenic down duvets, plasma TVs, chic basement spa and rooftop bar with fabulous views. Down-to-earth types, beware: it's on the nauseatingly trendy side of things.

Union Square, Flatiron District & Gramercy Park

Gershwin Hotel (Map pp162-3; ☎ 212-545-8000; www.gershwinhotel.com; 7 E 27th St, at Fifth Ave; dm/d/ste from $45/109/299;) This popular and funky spot is half youth hostel, half hotel, and buzzes with original pop art, touring bands and a young and artsy European clientele.

Marcel (Map pp162-3; ☎ 212-696-3800; www.nychotels.com; 201 E 24th St, at Third Ave; d from $175;) Minimalist with earth-tone touches, this 97-room inn is a poor-man's chic boutique and that's not a bad thing. Modernist rooms on the avenue have great views, and the sleek lounge is a great place to unwind from a day of touring. Visit its website for other classy affordable inns within the Amsterdam Hospitality group.

W New York – Union Square (Map pp162-3; ☎ 212-253-9119, 877-946-8357; www.whotels.com; 201 Park Ave S, at 17th St; r from $400;) This hipster pad demands a black wardrobe and a platinum credit card. Like all the W hotels, everything is top of the line, comfortable and classy – rooms have somber tones and beds have leather-framed headboards – and its location right near always bustling Union Sq is a big perk for those who like to be near the action.

Also recommended is **Jazz on the Town** (Map pp162-3; ☎ 212.228.2780; www.jazzhostels.com; 307 E 14th St, at Second Ave; dm incl breakfast $27-32, d incl breakfast $95;). See right for other branches in the Jazz chain.

Midtown

1291 B&B (Map pp162-3; ☎ 212-397-9686; www.1291.com; 337 W 55th St, btwn Eighth & Ninth Aves; dm $30, r $70-90;) Depending on your priorities – if you're looking for inexpensive midtown digs – the peeling paint jobs and spotty service can be overlooked. Rough around the edges, 1291's suites, good for groups and families, are more recommended than the cramped doubles. Buffet breakfast – basically coffee, tea, cereal and bread – is available 24-hours in the outdoor garden.

Pod Hotel (Map pp162-3; ☎ 212-355-0300; www.thepodhotel.com; 230 E 51st St, btwn Second & Third Aves; r from $129;) A dream come true for folks who'd like to live inside their iPod – or at least curl up and sleep with it – this affordable hot spot has a range of room types, most barely big enough for the bed. 'Pods' have bright bedding, tight workspaces, flat-screen TVs, iPod docking stations and 'rain' showerheads.

Hotel Mela (Map pp162-3; ☎ 212-730-7900; www.hotelmela.com; 120 W 44th St; r from $155;) Not for the big boned, everything – including the elevator – at this centrally located hotel is diminutive. But good things come in small packages and the Mela does the tried-and-true boutique-trendy style well. Street noise isn't a significant problem and there's a nice gym to work out the kinks from a day of sightseeing.

Hudson (Map pp168-9; ☎ 212-554-6000; www.hudsonhotel.com; 356 W 58th St, btwn Eighth & Ninth Aves; s/d from $135/165;) This delicious marriage between designer Phillipe Starck and hotelier Ian Schrager is an absolute jewel – if you're not aching for quiet, that is. Part hotel and part nightclub, this beauty has several lounge bars that are always jammin', and the teensy rooms are highly stylized, with lots of glass, bright wood and gossamer scrims.

Room-Mate Grace (Map pp162-3; ☎ 212-354-2323; www.room-matehotels.com; 125 W 45th St; r incl breakfast from $165;) Part of a Spanish chain, this ultra-hip hotel is good value when you consider you're steps from the midtown action. Like other hotels of the same genre, space is at a premium and sleekness is prized over warmth. A steam-room, sauna and lively pool-bar are reasons to choose the Mate over others.

Jazz on Times Square (Map pp162-3; ☎ 212.974.6400; www.jazzhostels.com; 341 W 51st St, btwn Eighth & Ninth Aves; dm incl breakfast $27-32, d incl breakfast $95) is also recommended. See left and below for other branches in the Jazz chain.

Upper West Side

Jazz on the Park (Map pp168-9; ☎ 212-932-1600; www.jazzhostels.com; 36 W 106th St, btwn Central Park West & Manhattan Ave; dm incl breakfast $27-32, d incl breakfast $95;) This deservedly popular hostel has small rooms with standard wood-frame bunks, a beautiful roof deck and an exposed-brick lounge that hosts local jazz acts (not to mention the espresso and cheap lasagna). Other branches in midtown (above), Union Sq (left), Harlem and the Upper West Side also have fun atmospheres and great roof decks. All Jazz hostels share the same pricing system.

Hostelling International-New York (Map pp168-9; ☎ 212-932-2300; www.hinewyork.org; 891 Amsterdam Ave, at 103rd St; dm $32-40, d from $135;) It's got clean, safe and air-conditioned dorm rooms in a gorgeous landmark building, with a sprawling and shady patio and a super-friendly vibe.

Empire Hotel (Map pp168-9; ☎ 212-265-7400; www.empirehotelnyc.com; 44 W 63rd St; r from $225;) An uptown version of the W, the Empire is a chic hotel directly across the street from the Lincoln Center. The decor is all classy earth tones and of decent size – for NYC. There's a rooftop pool deck with fabulous views and, when not closed for private functions, it's a nighttime hot spot.

our pick **On the Ave** (Map pp168-9; ☎ 212-362-1100; www.ontheave.com; 2178 Broadway, at W 77th St; r from $225;) A more welcoming feel and larger rooms make On the Ave a cut above the average sleek boutique hotel. And it's a good deal considering the high-concept design, stainless steel and marble baths, featherbeds, flat-screen TVs and original artwork. It's near the Lincoln Center, Central Park and a slew of good eats.

Upper East Side

Bentley (Map pp168-9; ☎ 888-664-6835; www.nychotels.com; 500 E 62nd St, at York Ave; r/ste from $155/265;) Featuring great East River views, the Bentley overlooks FDR Dr, as far east as you can go. Formerly an office building, the hotel has shed its utilitarian past in the form of chic boutique-hotel stylings, a swanky lobby and sleek rooms.

Carlyle (Map pp168-9; ☎ 212-744-1600; www.thecarlyle.com; 35 E 76th St, btwn Madison & Park Aves; r from $450;) This New York classic is the epitome of old-fashioned luxury: a hushed lobby with glossy marble floors, antique boudoir chairs and framed English country scenes or Audubon prints in the rooms; some have terraces and baby grand pianos. If you can't afford to stay here, at least have a cocktail in the legendary art-deco Bemelmans Bar.

Harlem

Harlem Flophouse (Map pp168-9; ☎ 212-662-0678; www.harlemflophouse.com; 242 W 123rd St, btwn Adam Clayton Powell & Frederick Douglass Blvds; s/d with shared bathroom from $100/125;) The four gorgeous bedrooms here conjure up the jazz era with antique light fixtures, glossed-wood floors and big beds, plus classic tin ceilings and wooden shutters. There are radios tuned to local jazz stations (and two cats) on the premises.

102 Brownstone (Map pp168-9; ☎ 212-662-4223; www.102brownstone.com; 102 W 118th St, btwn Lenox Ave & Adam Clayton Powell Blvd; r $125-275;) A wonderfully redone Greek Revival row house on a beautiful residential street; room styles range from Zen to classy boudoir.

Brooklyn

Downtown Brooklyn already boasts a large and full-service Marriott; Sheraton plans to open a hotel nearby in 2010.

Baisley House (☎ 718-935-1959; 294 Hoyt St, btwn Union & Sackett Sts; s/d with shared bathroom & breakfast $125/150;) This three-room inn sits among 18th-century town houses and is overflowing with Victorian touches (wingback chairs, period-piece landscapes) and serves a big, always-different breakfast in the back garden when it's nice out.

Hotel Le Bleu (☎ 718-625-1500; www.hotelbleu.com; 370 4th Ave; d incl breakfast $169-349;) Not exactly everyone's idea of a NYC vacation – belching trucks, autobody shops and gritty streets, but more-welcoming blocks with good shops and restaurants are only a short walk away in Park Slope. Boutique styling – you know the deal: sleek, white, minimalistic – king-sized beds and balconies with good views of Manhattan make Le Bleu worth considering.

Nu Hotel (☎ 718-852-8585; www.nuhotelbrooklyn.com; 85 Smith St; d incl breakfast from $199;) This location, only blocks from Brooklyn Heights, Cobble Hill, Boerum Hill, downtown Brooklyn and Carroll Gardens, is absolutely ideal – except for the fact that it's across the street from the Brooklyn House of Detention. It has a chic minimalist vibe and the clean, all-white rooms are comfortable; street noise can be a nuisance on the Atlantic Ave side.

EATING

In a city with 18,700 restaurants, and new ones opening every single day of the year, where are you supposed to begin? Go with whatever your belly desires, whether it's Italian, French, Israeli, Japanese, South Indian or good ol' American-diner burgers and fries. You'll find whatever it is you're after either a quick walk or subway ride away.

Lower Manhattan

Ruben's Empanadas (Map pp152-3; ☎ 212-962-5330; 64 Fulton St, at Gold St; empanadas $3.75; 8am-8pm) A tiny storefront with no decor, this takeout is Argentine heaven – with greaseless empanadas in endless varieties, from the requisite beef and chicken to broccoli with mozzarella and ricotta, Argentine sausage and gooey guava.

Smorgas Chef Wall St (Map pp152-3; ☎ 212-422-3500; 53 Stone St; mains $9-24; 10:30am-10:30pm) Located on quaint and narrow Stone St, this fine bistro serves Scandinavian fare such as Swedish meatballs as well as lighter fare like fish and salads. During the summer months, Smorgas Chef and neighboring restaurants put tables outside, turning the street into one big block party.

Acqua (Map pp152-3; ☎ 212-349-4433; 21 Peck Slip, at Water St; mains $14-26; noon-11pm Mon-Thu, to 11:30pm Fri & Sat, to 10pm Sun) A sleek wine bar right near South Street Seaport, this charmer offers savory portions of cured meats and cheeses; pizzas and paninis; and fresh pastas including gnocchi with pesto and gorgonzola. Pair any choice with a carafe of wine and you'll be good to stay.

Tribeca, SoHo & NoHo

Edward's (Map pp152-3; ☎ 212-274-8525; 136 W Broadway, btwn Thomas & Duane Sts; mains $7-14; 10am-11pm Mon-Fri, 9am-11pm Sat & Sun) Located on a busy block in Tribeca, Edward's has the feel of a casual European bistro – high ceilings, mirrored walls and dark wood booths. The menu offers everything from pasta to burgers.

La Esquina (Map pp152-3; ☎ 646-613-7100; 114 Kenmare St, at Cleveland Pl; mains $12-20; noon-4pm upstairs, 6pm-midnight upstairs & down) This Mexican hot spot, whose only marking is a huge neon sign that blares 'The Corner' (hence *la esquina*), bustles night and day for good reason. Delectable, authentic treats are served upstairs in a mellow café or downstairs in a dark, loud vault that calls for reservations made way in advance.

Bubby's Pie Company (Map pp152-3; ☎ 212-219-0666; 120 Hudson St, at N Moore St; mains $12-20; 8am-4pm & 6-11pm Mon-Thu, to midnight Fri, 9am-4pm & 6pm-midnight Sat, to 10pm Sun) This kid-friendly Tribeca standby is *the* place for simple, big, delicious food: slow-cooked BBQ, grits, matzo-ball soup, buttermilk potato salad, fried okra and big fat breakfasts, all melt-in-your-mouth good.

Chinatown, Little Italy & NoLita

our pick **Peasant** (Map pp152-3; ☎ 212-965-9511; 194 Elizabeth St, btwn Spring & Prince Sts; mains $15-30; 6-11pm Tue-Sat, to 10pm Sun) A warm dining area of bare oak tables is structured around a brick hearth and open kitchen, which lovingly turns out hearty, pan-Italian, mostly meat-based fare. Solid stunners include gnocchi with wild mushrooms and oven-baked rabbit. After dinner, head downstairs to the dark and cozy cellar wine bar.

Da Nico (Map pp152-3; ☎ 212-343-1212; 164 Mulberry St; mains $18-40; noon-11pm Sun-Thu, to midnight Fri & Sat) If you're hell-bent on having a Little Italy dinner, Da Nico is a classic. It's family-run and traditional in feel and the extensive restaurant highlights both northern and southern Italian cuisine that's red-sauce predictable – shrimp, scampi, chicken cacciatore – but delicious.

Lower East Side

Economy Candy (Map pp152-3; ☎ 212-254-1531; 108 Rivington St; candies from $4; 9am-6pm Sun-Fri, 10am-5pm Sat) Fancy some chocolate-covered matzo? Or maybe a brick of halvah? If not, then surely you can't say no to any of the myriad crazy, nostalgic candies you consumed as a kid. Whatever it is, as long as it contains sugar, it's probably crammed or stacked in this slightly hole-in-the-wallish candy purveyor that smells as sweet as a barrel of jelly beans.

Spitzer's Corner (Map pp152-3; ☎ 212-228-0027; 101 Rivington St; mains $9-19; noon-4am Mon-Sat, 10am-midnight Sun) The corner location of this recent Lower East Side addition offers an open-air gastropub experience with a concise menu designed by a Michelin-starred chef, and more than 40 different beers on tap. Large communal tables and a lengthy counter facing the street encourage socializing.

Katz's Delicatessen (Map pp152-3; ☎ 212-254-2246; 205 E Houston St; sandwiches $13; 8am-9:45pm Mon & Tue, to 10:45pm Wed, Thu & Sun, to 2:45am Fri & Sat) The neighborhood might be changing, but they are still slicing up delicious pastrami by hand at this over 100-year-old New York institution. One of the few remaining Jewish delicatessens in the city, Katz's attracts locals, tourists, and celebrities whose photos line the walls. Massive pastrami, corned beef, brisket, and tongue sandwiches are throwbacks, as is the payment system: hold on to the ticket you're handed when you walk in and pay cash only.

WD-50 (Map pp152-3; ☎ 212-477-2900; 50 Clinton St; mains $30; 6-11pm Wed-Sat, to 10pm Sun) Chef and owner Wylie Dufresne combines food, art, and innovative cooking techniques to produce a cuisine known elsewhere as molecular gastronomy. Expect completely reinvented takes on classic dishes like fried chicken and scrambled eggs. Or interesting combinations like foie gras, passionfruit and chinese celery. Desserts are equally creative.

EATING NYC: CHINATOWN

With hundreds of restaurants, from holes-in-the-wall to banquet-sized dining rooms, Chinatown is wonderful for exploring cheap eats on an empty stomach. One of the best places to lunch for Cantonese cuisine is **Amazing 66** (Map pp152-3; ☎ 212-334-0099; 66 Mott St, at Canal St; mains $5; 11am-pm). The best of the four for $1 dumpling joints is **Vanessa's Dumpling House** (Map pp152-3; ☎ 212-625-8008;118 Eldridge St, at Broome St; mains $5; 7:30am-10:30pm); add a beef pancake to your dumpling order and the bill comes to a whopping $3. Head to **Big Wong King** (☎ 212-964-0540; 67 Mott St, at Canal; mains $5-20; 7am-10pm) for chopped meat over rice and reliable congee (sweet or savory soft rice soup). **Shanghai Cuisine** (Map pp152-3; ☎ 212-732-8988; 89 Bayard St, at Mulberry St; mains $10; 11:30am-10:30pm) is tourist-friendly and does good soup dumplings. And finally, the **Egg Custard King** (Map pp152-3; ☎ 212-226-8882; 271 Grand St; custards $1; 7am-9:30pm) is the place for the eponymous dessert.

East Village

Every cuisine and style is represented in the East Village, though even the very best places are certainly more casual than stuffy. St Marks Place and around, from Third to Second Ave, has turned into a little Tokyo with loads of Japanese sushi and grill restaurants. Cookie-cutter Indian restaurants line Sixth St between First and Second Ave.

OUR PICK **Momofuku Noodle Bar** (Map pp152-3; ☎ 212-777-7773; 171 First Ave, at 11th St; mains $9-16; 🕒 noon-4pm & 5:30-11pm Sun-Thu, to midnight Fri & Sat) Ramen and steamed buns are the name of the game at this infinitely creative Japanese eatery, part of the growing David Chang empire. Seating is on stools at a long bar or at communal tables. Recommended are the smoked chicken wings with garlic and pickled chili ($11), as well as Momofuku's famous steamed chicken and pork buns ($9 for two).

Counter (Map pp152-3; ☎ 212-982-5870; 105 First Ave, btwn E 6th & 7th Sts; mains $15-25; 🕒 5pm-midnight Mon-Thu, to 1am Fri, 11am-1am Sat, to 4pm Sun; V) This unique eatery manages to mix infused-vodka martinis with organic vegetarian cuisine with outlandish success. Credit the futuristic, backlit dining room, fabulous large-scale artwork and innovative dishes, like tournedos of seitan and cauliflower 'risotto.'

Hearth (Map pp152-3; ☎ 646-602-1300; 403 E 12th St, at First Ave; mains $20-40; 🕒 6-10pm Sun-Thu, to 11pm Fri, Sat) A staple for finicky, deep-pocketed diners, Hearth boasts a warm, brick-walled interior. The seasonal menu includes specials such as roasted sturgeon with lentils and bacon, zucchini ravioli and rabbit papardelle with fava beans.

Bustling hot spots, **Veselka** (Map pp152-3; ☎ 212-228-9682; 144 Second Ave, at 9th St; mains $9-14; 🕒 24hr) and **7A** (Map pp152-3; ☎ 212-228-9682; 109 Ave A; mains $9-14; 🕒 24hr) are where to go if you're nursing a hangover or just getting started on one.

West (Greenwich) Village

Taïm (Map pp152-3; ☎ 212-691-1287; 222 Waverly Pl, btwn Perry & W 11th Sts; mains $7-9; 🕒 noon-10pm) Not all Middle Eastern fare is alike, and this tiny little falafel joint proves it with its smoothies, salads and sass – and even its falafel, which ranges from the traditional to those spiced up with roasted red pepper or hot harissa. Excellent smoothies blend exotics from dates to tamarind.

Snack Taverna (Map pp152-3; ☎ 212-929-3499; 63 Bedford St; mains $15-25; 🕒 noon-11pm Mon-Sat, to 10pm Sun) If you can't make it out to the Greek restaurants in Astoria, Queens, try this West Village place. The menu goes beyond the standard gyro and moussaka – the small plates like the smoked trout with barley rusks, tomato, cheese and balsamic vinaigrette are excellent.

Perilla (Map pp152-3; ☎ 212-929-6868; 9 Jones St; mains $22-27; 🕒 5:30-11pm Mon-Thu, to 11:30pm Fri & Sat, 11am-10pm Sun) The inspiration of one of the winners of popular reality-TV show *Top Chef*, Perilla is an extremely creative yet well-grounded American bistro. The spicy duck meatballs and roasted main sardines are both good ways to start off a meal.

Blue Hill (Map pp152-3; ☎ 212-539-1776; 75 Washington Pl, btwn Sixth Ave & MacDougal St; mains $22-50; 🕒 5:30-11pm Mon-Sat, to 10pm Sun) A place for high-rolling Slow Food junkies, Blue Hill is a low-key, high-class dining spot where you can be certain that everything on your plate is fresh and seasonal. Expect barely seasoned veggies as centerpieces for dishes like cod with cauliflower and currants. The below-street-level space is sophisticated and serene.

Chelsea, Union Square, Flatiron District & Gramercy Park

Shake Shack (Map pp162-3; ☎ 212-889-6600; Madison Ave, at E 23rd St; burgers from $4; 🕒 11am-11pm) Tourists line up in droves for the hamburgers at this Madison Square Park counter-window-serving institution. Savvy local lunchgoers know enough to check out their webcam to assess wait times. Grab a shake, a burger, and a seat at one of the park's many outdoor tables.

Chennai Garden (Map pp162-3; ☎ 212-689-1999; 129 E 27th St, btwn Park & Lexington Aves; mains $9-15; 🕒 11:30am-10pm Mon-Fri, noon-10pm Sat & Sun) Come for South Indian faves such as paper-thin dosas (rice-flour pancakes) stuffed with spicy mixtures of potatoes and peas, and a range of more expected curries. The interior is bright and bustling – especially for the popular $7 lunchtime buffet.

Chat N' Chew (Map pp152-3; ☎ 212-243-1616; 10 E 16th St; mains $12-20; 🕒 11am-midnight Mon-Fri, 10am-midnight Sat, 10am-11pm Sun) Nonstatuesque models are welcome – they probably wouldn't be happy here anyway. It's all down-home comfort food, though of a generally high quality, like macaroni and cheese, mashed potatoes, and fried chicken; the onion ring loaf should be divided by a minimum of four people – who don't suffer from heart disease.

Blossom (Map pp152-3; ☎ 212-627-1144; 187 Ninth Ave, btwn 21st & 22nd Sts; mains $25-35; 🕒 noon-2:45pm & 5-10:30pm Fri & Sat, noon-2:45pm & 5-10pm Sun, 5-10pm Mon-Thu; V) A creative and elegant vegan spot, housed in a Chelsea town house, where menu items span the globe and enliven the taste buds. Try the flaky seitan empanada, mojo-marinated tempeh or portobello stuffed with cashew-tahini sauce.

Midtown

Café Edison (Map pp162-3; ☎ 212-840-5000; 228 W 47th St, btwn Broadway & Eighth Ave; mains from $6; 🕒 6am-9:30pm Mon-Sat, to 7:30pm Sun) Where else can you get a bologna sandwich? This landmark New York spot has been in business since the 1930s, serving up American diner classics like grilled cheese, hot corned beef, open-faced turkey sandwiches and cheese blintzes. Cash only.

Kum Gang San (Map pp162-3; ☎ 212-967-0909; 49 W 32nd St, at Broadway; mains $12-26; 🕒 24hr) One of Koreatown's larger and more extravagant restaurants, Kum Gang San serves standout barbecue – you do it at your table. As in most Korean restaurants, the side dishes that accompany the mains are delicious meals in and of themselves. Large, loud and kind of kitschy, it's still a reliable introduction to Koreatown.

Ellen's Stardust Diner (Map pp162-3; ☎ 212-956-5151; 1650 Broadway, at 51st St; mains $15; 🕒 7am-midnight Mon-Thu, to 1am Fri & Sat, to 11pm Sun) No New Yorker would be caught dead here, but this '50s theme diner-cum-dinner theater is a superfun place to head after a show. When the talented waitstaff belt out show tunes and pop songs while picking up your checks, you can't help but applaud.

Pietrasanta (Map pp162-3; ☎ 212-265-9471; 683 9th Ave, at 47th St; mains $16-24; 🕒 noon-10:30pm Mon-Thu & Sun, to midnight Fri & Sat) The best of the many Italian restaurants within several blocks from here, Pietrasanta is as welcoming to neighborhood regulars as to tourists in the city for a night of theater. The pumpkin ravioli is a favorite, as are the hummus and flavored butter spreads.

44 & X (Map pp162-3; ☎ 212-977-1170; 622 Tenth Ave, at W 44th St; mains $16-30; 🕒 5:30pm-midnight Mon-Fri, 11:30am-3pm & 5:30pm-midnight Sat, to 10:30pm Sun) Worth venturing this far west for, 44 & X is one of the pioneers of the Hell's Kitchen stylish foodie trend. This sleek and airy dining room serves a little something for everyone, from macaroni and cheese to grilled braised short ribs.

Poseidon Bakery (Map pp162-3; ☎ 212-757-6173; 629 Ninth Ave, at W 44th St; pastries from $2; 🕒 9am-7pm Tue-Sat). The last family-owned Greek bakery in Manhattan. The handmade baklava (pastry made with walnuts and almonds) and spanakopita (feta cheese and spinach wrapped in phyllo pastry) are delicious.

Bouchon Bakery (Map pp168-9; ☎ 212-823-9366; 3rd fl, 10 Columbus Circle in Time Warner Center; mains $12-20; 🕒 11:30am-9pm Mon-Sat, to 7pm Sun) Of the seven restaurants in the Time Warner Center, most very high-end in terms of price, this bakery from Per Se owner Thomas Keller brings new meaning to 'food court.'

Upper West Side & Morningside Heights

Hungarian Pastry Shop (Map pp168-9; ☎ 212-886-4230; 1030 Amsterdam Ave, btwn W 110th & 111th Sts; pastries $2-4; 🕒 7:30am-11:30pm Mon-Fri, 8:30am-11:30pm Sat, to 10:30pm Sun) Bring a dog-eared copy of Kierkegaard to blend in with the intensely serious Columbia University students working for hours in front of steaming laptops and cooling coffee. Excellent pastries and cakes are also available.

Barney Greengrass (Map pp168-9; ☎ 212-724-4707; 541 Amsterdam Ave, at W 86th St; mains $8-17; 🕒 8:30am-4pm Tue-Fri, to 5pm Sat & Sun) Old-school Upper Westsiders and pilgrims from other neighborhoods crowd this century-old 'sturgeon king' on weekends. It serves a long list of traditional if pricey Jewish delicacies, from bagels and lox to sturgeon scrambled with eggs and onions.

Flor de Mayo (Map pp168-9; ☎ 212-787-3388; 484 Amsterdam Ave, at 83rd St; mains $9-14; 🕒 noon-midnight) One of a handful of unpretentious NYC restaurants combining Peruvian and Chinese cuisine, Flor de Mayo is a favorite of locals from neighborhoods north and south of here. It's somewhat hectic at dinnertime, but it's the place for choosing between egg foo young and ceviche de pescado?

Gennaro (Map pp168-9; ☎ 212-665-5348; 665 Amsterdam Ave, at 92nd St; mains $10-25; 🕒 5-10:30pm Sun-Thu, to 11pm Fri & Sat) Locals line up for the reasonably priced Italian fare at dinnertime – no reservations and cash only. There's a long list of specials and a number of outstanding pastas (the gnocchi is a favorite) fish, chicken and beef dishes, as well as vegetarian options; if you have room be sure to sample the tiramisu.

Upper East Side

Central Park Boathouse Restaurant (Map pp168-9; ☎ 212-517-2233; Central Park Lake, enter Fifth Ave, at 72nd St; mains $15-40; ⌚ noon-4:30pm Mon-Fri, 9:30am-4pm Sat & Sun year-round, 5:30-9:30pm Mon-Fri 6-9:30pm Sat & Sun Apr-Nov) The historic Loeb Boathouse, perched on the shores of the park's lake, is one of the city's more incredible settings for a serene and romantic meal. Food is top-notch, too – reserve early and aim for an outdoor table.

Daniel (Map pp168-9; ☎ 212-288-0033; 60 E 65th St, btwn Madison & Park Aves; 3-course prix fixe dinners $96; ⌚ Mon-Sat 5:30-11pm) This chichi French palace features floral arrangements and wide-eyed foodies who gawk over plates of peekytoe crab and celery-root salad, foie gras terrine with gala apples and black truffle-crusted lobster – and that's just the first course. There's an all-veggie menu, too.

Totonno's (Map pp168-9; ☎ 212-327-2800; 1544 Second Ave; mains $14; ⌚ noon-4pm Mon-Fri) is the Manhattan branch of a Coney Island classic New York pizza joint and **Square Meal** (Map pp168-9; ☎ 212-860-9872; 30 E 92nd St; mains $13-25; ⌚ 11am-10pm Tue-Fri, 9am-10pm Sat, 9am-9pm Sun) is a homey neighborhood bistro with a seasonal menu.

Harlem

Amy Ruth's Restaurant (Map pp168-9; ☎ 212-280-8779; 113 W 116th St, btwn Malcolm X & Adam Clayton Powell Jr Blvds; mains $10-16; ⌚ 11:30am-11pm Mon, from 8:30am Tue-Thu & Sun, to 5:30am Fri & Sat) Though Food Network coverage has amped up the tourist crowds, this place still does a good job with the standards – smoked ham, chicken and dumplings – but it's specialty is waffles; choose from sweet (chocolate, strawberry, blueberry, smothered in sautéed apples) or savory (paired with fried chicken, rib-eye or catfish).

Londel's Supper Club (Map pp168-9; ☎ 212-234-6114; 2620 Frederick Douglass Blvd; mains $12-24; ⌚ 11:30am-11pm Tue-Sat, 11am-5pm Sun) The wall photos of famous patrons are testament to this elegant restaurant's status and popularity. Londel's menu combines Cajun and continental flavors and live jazz Friday and Saturday nights.

For tasty Mexican in East Harlem, try **El Paso Taqueria** (Map pp168-9; ☎ 212-860-9753; 237 E 116th St, btwn Second & Third Aves; mains $5-17; ⌚ 9am-11pm).

Brooklyn

Of course it's impossible to begin to do justice to Brooklyn's eating options – it's as much a foodie's paradise as Manhattan. Virtually every ethnic cuisine has a significant presence somewhere in this area. As far as neighborhoods close to Manhattan go: Williamsburg is chockablock with eateries, as are Fifth and Seventh Aves in Park Slope. Smith St is 'Restaurant Row' in the Carroll Gardens and Cobble Hill neighborhoods. Atlantic Ave, near Court St, has a number of excellent Middle Eastern restaurants and groceries.

our pick Frankies 457 (☎ 718-403-0033; 457 Court St; mains $9-18; ⌚ 11am-11pm Sun-Thu, to midnight Fri & Sat) A Carroll Gardens favorite packing in regulars night after night, Frankies feels both homey and romantic. Dark and candlelit at night, it has an attractive backyard garden for warm weather brunches. Small cheese plates, crostinis and veggie side dishes can be shared by the table; the arugula salad and meatballs with pine nuts and raisins make an excellent meal.

Blue Ribbon Brasserie (☎ 718-840-0404; 280 5th Ave, btwn 1st St & Garfield Pl; mains $15-27; ⌚ 5pm-midnight Mon-Thu & Sun, to 2am Fri & Sat) This restaurant in the heart of Park Slope has something for everyone: an incredible raw bar, pork ribs, matzo-ball soup, paella, fried chicken and chocolate-chip bread pudding. It's open late but doesn't take reservations for parties fewer than six.

Applewood (☎ 718-788-1810; 501 11th St; brunch $12, dinner mains $23; ⌚ 5-11pm Tue-Fri, from 10am Sat, 10am-3pm Sun) Cozy and sweet, like a close friend's dinner party, especially in winter when there's always a roaring fire, this country house in Park Slope is part of the locavore movement. The frequently changing menu is meat-heavy; slim pickings for vegetarians.

Peter Luger Steakhouse (☎ 718-387-7400; 178 Broadway; lunch mains $5-20, dinner mains $30-32; ⌚ 11:30am-9:30pm Mon-Thu, to 10:30pm Fri & Sat, 12:30-9:30pm Sun) The aged porterhouse at this venerable 100-year-old German steakhouse at the foot of the Williamsburg Bridge is often regarded as one of the best steaks in the country. Some Manhattanites even cross the East River for the hamburger, available only at lunchtime. Reservations required and cash only.

Good Fork (☎ 718-643-6636; 391 Van Brunt St; mains $18-22; ⌚ 5:30pm-10:30pm Tue-Sat, to 10pm Sun) Foodies head to this small, warm restaurant in Red Hook for its eclectic and fresh fare.

DRINKING

Watering holes come in many forms in this city: sleek lounges, cozy pubs and booze-soaked dives – no smoke, though, thanks to city law. The majority are open to 4am, though closing (and opening) times do vary. Here's a highly selective sampling.

Downtown

KGB Bar (Map pp152-3; ☎ 212-505-3360; 85 E 4th St, at 2nd Ave) The East Village's own grungy Algonquin roundtable has been drawing literary types to its regular readings since the early 1990s. Even when there's no artist in residence the heavily worn wood bar is good for kicking back.

Sake Bar Decibel (Map pp152-3; ☎ 212-979-2733; 240 E 9th St) Just nod your head and sip. Hearing is a challenge even when you're crammed in a corner touching knees. Nevertheless, this cozy and dark downstairs hideaway feels like an authentic Tokyo dive, from the sake varieties to the delicious snacks.

Mayahuel (Map pp152-3; ☎ 212-253-5888; 304 E 6th St, at Second Ave) About as far from your typical Spring Break tequila bar as you can get – more like the cellar of a monastery. Devotees of the fermented agave can seriously indulge themselves experimenting with dozens of varieties (all cocktails $13); in between drinks, snack on tamales and tortillas.

Cheery Tavern (Map pp152-3; ☎ 212-777-1448; 441 E 6th St, at Ave A) Not for the 40-year-old virgin – hard-drinking 20- and 30-somethings get their flirt on at this small, dimly lit dive. Arrive before 9pm and you have a shot at the bar or a seat at one of the few tables. Otherwise, clunk your quarters down for a game of pool or sidle up to the jukebox filled with indie/alt songs.

Fat Cat (Map pp152-3; ☎ 212-675-6056; 75 Christopher St, at Seventh Ave; cover up to $3; ⌚ 2pm-5am Mon-Thu, from noon Fri-Sun;) For every man who has ever fantasized about the perfect college basement – years and years after graduation – there is Fat Cat. The worn and ratty furniture will remind you of a typical fraternity basement, but all are welcome at this gamers paradise – Ping-Pongers, pool players, chess geeks, even shuffleboarders and cute girls, and, and! there's cheap beer and live music every night.

Fresh Salt (Map pp152-3; ☎ 212-962-0053; 146 Beekman St) Only steps from a beautiful pier on the East River, and close to the financial district, Fresh Salt manages to avoid the boisterous feel of the after-work Wall St crowd. This small and rustic bar has board games (Boggle, chess etc) and a great hummus plate.

Circa Tabac (Map pp152-3; ☎ 212-941-1781; 32 Watts St, btwn Sixth Ave & Thompson St) Healthy-smelthy. By all means puff away. This is one of only five places left in the city where you can and are encouraged to smoke – mainly global cigars – while you drink. The deco-style lounge, with bamboo walls and velvet lounge chairs, is as sumptuous as much of its fine-cut tobacco.

Henrietta Hudson (Map pp152-3; ☎ 212-924-3347; 438 Hudson St, at Morton St) All sorts of cute young girls storm this long-running lesbian spot, a former pool-and-pint joint that's now a sleek lounge with varied DJs.

Welcome to the Johnsons (Map pp152-3; ☎ 212-420-9911; 123 Rivington St) Looking like a set from *The Brady Bunch* or *That '70s Show*, this Lower East Side theme bar can be enjoyed with or without irony. Wash down the free Doritos with a Jack Daniel's and root beer.

The trendy **Schiller's Liquor Bar** (Map pp152-3; ☎ 212-260-4555; 131 Rivington St, at Norfolk St; ⌚ 11am-1am Mon-Wed, to 2am Thu, to 3am Fri, 10am-3am Sat, 10am-1am Sun) and no-signage **Freeman's** (Map pp152-3; ☎ 212-420-0012; Freeman Alley, btwn Bowery & Chrystie Sts) both serve cocktails as delicious as their food (mains $12 to $25); the latter, whose bar seats only around 10 people, is a mix of taxidermy and downtown cool.

Midtown

our pick **Russian Vodka Room** (Map pp162-3; ☎ 212-307-5835; 265 W 52nd St, btwn 8th Ave & Broadway) This swank and welcoming bar keeps things real enough that actual Russians aren't uncommon here. The lighting is dark and the corner booths intimate, but more importantly the dozens of flavored vodkas, from cranberry to horseradish, are fun to experiment with. Eastern European dishes such as latkes, smoked fish and schnitzel can quiet a rumbling stomach.

Rudy's Bar & Grill (Map pp162-3; ☎ 212-974-9169; 627 Ninth Ave) This semi-dive bar – neighborhood newcomers and hipsters rub beer-soaked shoulders with hard-core drinkers – doesn't take itself seriously. It's a good place for cheap beer and even greasy hot dogs, if you don't mind not being able to hear yourself think. A backyard garden with makeshift furniture and artificial turf is open in the summer months.

Therapy (Map pp162-3; ☎ 212-397-1700; 348 W 52nd St, btwn Eighth & Ninth Aves) Multileveled, airy and sleekly contemporary, Therapy is a longstanding gay Hell's Kitchen hot spot. Theme nights abound, from stand-up comedy to musical shows.

Morrell Wine Bar & Café (Map pp162-3; ☎ 212-262-7700; 1 Rockefeller Plaza, W 48th St, btwn Fifth & Sixth Aves; 11:30am-midnight Mon-Sat, noon-6pm Sun) The list of vinos at this pioneering New York City wine bar is over 2000 long, with a whopping 150 available by the glass. And the airy, split-level room, right across from the famous skating rink, is equally intoxicating.

Half King (Map pp162-3; ☎ 212-462-4300; 505 W 23rd St, at Tenth Ave), a cozy pub, and **Ginger Man** (Map pp162-3; ☎ 212-532-3740; 11 E 36th St, btwn Fifth & Madison Aves) are other neighborhood options for those looking for top-flight beer selections.

Uptown

79th Street Boat Basin (Map pp168-9; ☎ 212-496-5592; W 79th St, in Riverside Park) A covered, open-sided party spot under the ancient arches of a park overpass, this is an Upper West Side favorite once spring hits. Order a pitcher, some snacks and enjoy the sunset view over the Hudson River.

Subway Inn (Map pp168-9; ☎ 212-223-8929; 143 E 60th St, btwn Lexington & Third Aves) An old-geezer watering hole with cheap drinks and loads of authenticity, this place should truly be landmarked, as the entire scene – from the vintage neon sign outside to the well-worn red booths and old guys huddled inside – is truly reminiscent of bygone days.

Lenox Lounge (Map pp168-9; ☎ 212-427-0253; www.lenoxlounge.com; 288 Malcolm X Blvd, btwn 124th & 125th Sts) The classic art-deco Lounge, which once hosted the likes of Billie Holiday and Miles Davis and is an old favorite of local jazz cats, is still going strong. The luxe Zebra Room in back is a beautiful and historic setting to hear top-flight musicians.

Brooklyn

our pick **Brooklyn Social** (☎ 718-858-7758; 335 Smith St, at Carroll St, Carroll Gardens) Real old-school social clubs with card-playing men still exist only blocks away from here, but this place is strictly for those who couldn't tell you the roster of the '57 Yankees. Typical of this genre of bar, signage is a no-no and discretion an asset. Young neighborhood types and hipsters from nearby cozy up to the bar or one of the barely lit corner lounges.

Iona Bar (☎ 718-384-5008; 180 Grand St, Williamsburg; 1pm-4am) Hipsters infiltrate this Scottish/Irish bar on weekend nights; other nights it's a less American Apparel crowd enjoying happy hour (beer $4). Meat and veggie pies play second fiddle in summer when the barbecue in the backyard garden turns out hamburgers and hot dogs. Competitive Ping-Pongers enjoy the outdoor table on warm evenings.

Turkey's Nest (☎ 718-384-9774; 94 Bedford Ave, at N 12th St; 8am-4am Mon-Sat, from noon Sun) Local dive bar, sports bar, hipster hangout… The eclectic crowd at the Nest loves the huge Styrofoam containers of cheap beer and cocktails served in plastic cups. Watch the Yankees and watch the Mets or play the hunting video game in the back. Whatever you do, wear a hazmat suit when you use the bathroom.

In Park Slope, head to the creatively idiosyncratic **Union Hall** (☎ 718-638-4400; 702 Union St, at Fifth Ave, Park Slope) – leather chairs à la a snooty London social club, walls lined with bookshelves and two bocce courts, plus live music downstairs and an outdoor patio. **Total Wine Bar** (☎ 718-783-5166; 74 Fifth Ave) is a small sophisticated place for high-quality vino.

ENTERTAINMENT

Those with unlimited fuel and appetites can gorge themselves on a seemingly infinite number of entertainments – from Broadway shows to performance art in someone's Brooklyn living room, and everything in between. *New York* and the weekend editions of the *New York Times* are great guides for what's on once you arrive.

Nightclubs

Santos Party House (Map pp152-3; ☎ 212-584-5492; www.santospartyhouse; 96 Lafayette St; cover $5-15; 10pm-4am) Shaggy rocker Andrew WK created this bilevel 8000-sq-ft cavernous barebones dance club. Devoted to good times and good vibes, this place requires that you check your attitude at the door – funk to electronica, and WK spins some nights.

SOBs (☎ 212-243-4940pp152-3; www.sobs.com; 204 Varick St, at W Houston) Brazilian bossa nova, samba and other Latin vibes draw a mix of those who know how to move smooth and sensually and those who like to watch.

Sullivan Room (Map pp152-3; ☎ 212-505-1703 www.sullivanroom.com; 218 Sullivan St, btwn Bleecker & W 3rd Sts; 10pm-5am Wed-Sun) An eclectic downtown mix and top-flight DJs make Sullivan Room one of the best places to dance the night away. There's nothing pretentious – no need for high heels or cheesy leather jackets,

Cielo (Map pp152-3; ☎ 212-645-5700; www.cieloclub.com; 18 Little W 12th St, btwn Ninth Ave & Washington St; cover $5-20; ⏰ midnight-4am Mon, 10pm-4am Tue-Sat, to midnight Sun) Known for its intimate space and kick-ass sound system, this space age–looking Meatpacking District staple packs in a fashionable, multiculti crowd nightly for its blend of tribal, old-school house and soulful grooves.

Pacha (Map pp162-3; ☎ 212-209-7500; www.pachanyc.com; 618 W 46th St, btwn Eleventh Ave & West Side Hwy) A massive and spectacular place, this is 30,000 sq ft and four levels of glowing, sleek spaces and cozy seating nooks that rise up to surround the main dance-floor atrium. Big-name DJs are always on tap.

M2 Ultra Lounge (Map pp162-3; ☎ 212-629-9000; www.m2ultralounge.com; 530 W 28th St, btwn Tenth & Eleventh Aves; admission $20; ⏰ 10pm-4am Thu-Sat) Formerly Crobar, then Studio Mezmor, this megaclub will blow out your ear drums and your wallet – drinks are expensive ($15). In some ways this is the classic big club – long lines, opulent booths, bottle service and sexy go-go dancers. DJs and live performances depending on the night.

Live Music

Maybe less indie-dominated than music scenes in Austin or Seattle, and certainly diminished with the closing of several important institutions including CBGB and the Knitting Factory, NYC does of course still boast an enormous number of venues varying greatly in size, crowd and genre of music.

Madison Square Garden (Map pp162-3; ☎ 212-465-5800; www.thegarden.com; Seventh Ave, btwn W 31st & W 33rd Sts) For the biggest shows like Green Day and Andrea Bocelli, this place draws stadium-sized crowds.

Radio City Music Hall (Map pp162-3; ☎ 212-247-4777; www.radiocity.com; Sixth Ave, at W 50th St) In the middle of Midtown, the architecturally grand concert hall, built in 1932, hosts the likes of Tori Amos, Aretha Franklin and of course the famous Christmas spectacular; managed by the same team as Madison Square Garden.

Beacon Theatre (Map pp168-9; ☎ 212-465-6500; www.beacontheatre.com; 2124 Broadway, btwn W 74th & 75th Sts) This Upper West Side venue has a pretty cool vibe for such a large, mainstream space. It hosts big (often old-time) acts – Tom Jones, Steely Dan – for folks who want to see shows in an environment that's more intimate than that of a big concert arena.

Joe's Pub (Map pp152-3; ☎ 212-967-7555; www.joespub.com; Public Theater, 425 Lafayette St, btwn Astor Pl & E 4th St) Part cabaret theater, part rock and new-indie venue, this small and lovely supper club has hosted the likes of Booker T and Mandy Moore; a wonderful variety of styles, voices and talent.

BargeMusic (Map pp152-3; ☎ 718-624-2083; www.bargemusic.org; Fulton Ferry Landing) Exceptionally talented classical musicians perform in this intimate space, a decommissioned barge docked under the Brooklyn Bridge.

Le Poisson Rouge (Map pp152-3; ☎ 212-796-0741; 158 Bleecker St, at Sullivan St) Formerly the Village Gate, this Bleecker St basement club reopened in 2008, quickly becoming one of the premier venues for experimental contemporary, from classical to indie rock to electro-acoustic.

Highline Ballroom (Map pp162-3; ☎ 212-414-5994; 431 W 16th St, btwn Ninth & Tenth Aves) A classy Chelsea venue with an eclectic lineup, from Mandy Moore to Moby.

Webster Hall (Map pp152-3; ☎ 212-353-1600; www.websterhall.com; 125 E 11th St, at 3rd Ave), **Irving Plaza** (Map pp162-3; ☎ 212-777-6800; www.irvingplaza.com; 17 Irving Pl) and **Terminal 5** (Map pp162-3; ☎ 212-260-4700; www.terminal5nyc.com; 610 W 56th St, at 11th Ave) all book big and quality acts.

Mercury Lounge (Map pp152-3; ☎ 212-260-4700; www.mercuryloungenyc.com; 217 E Houston St) and **Delancey Lounge** (Map pp152-3; ☎ 212-254-9920; www.thedelancey.com; 168 Delancey St, at Clinton St) have great indie-band bookings. In Park Slope, Brooklyn, head to **Southpaw** (☎ 718-230-0236; www.spsounds.com; 125 5th Ave) for a nightly lineup.

Theater

In general, 'Broadway' productions are staged in the lavish, early-20th-century theaters surrounding Times Square. You'll choose your theater based on its production – *Guys and Dolls, Shrek the Musical, West Side Story* – but all are pretty over-the-top and old-fashioned. Evening performances begin at 8pm.

'Off Broadway' simply refers to shows performed in smaller spaces (between 99 and 500 seats), which is why you'll find many just around the corner from Broadway venues, as well as elsewhere in town. 'Off-off Broadway' events include readings, experimental and cutting-edge performances and improvisations held in spaces with fewer than 100 seats; these venues are primarily downtown.

JAZZ

Second only to New Orleans, Harlem was an early home to a flourishing jazz scene and was one of its principal beating hearts. The neighborhood fostered greats like Duke Ellington, Charlie Parker, John Coltrane and Thelonius Monk. From bebop to free improvisation, in classic art-deco clubs and intimate jam sessions, Harlem and other important venues scattered throughout the city, especially around the Village, continue to foster old-timers and talented newcomers alike. Tune in to **WKCR** (89.9 FM) for jazz and especially from 8:20am to 9:30am Monday through Friday for Phil Schaap's 27-year-old program in which he dazzles listeners with his encyclopedic knowledge and appreciation for the art form. The **National Jazz Museum in Harlem** (212-348-8300; www.jazzmuseuminharlem.org; 104 E 126th St, Suite 2D; admission free; 10am-4pm Mon-Fri) has a collection of books, CDs and photos for passionate fans.

Smalls (Map pp152-3; ☎ 212-252-5091; www.smallsjazzclub.com; 183 W 4th St; cover $20) is a subterranean jazz dungeon that rivals the world-famous **Village Vanguard** (Map pp152-3; ☎ 212-255-4037; www.villagevanguard.com; 178 Seventh Ave, at W 11th St) in terms of sheer talent. Of course, the latter has hosted every major star of the past 50 years; there's a two-drink minimum and a serious no-talking policy. **BB King Blues Club and Grill** (Map pp162-3; ☎ 212-997-4144; www.bbkingblues.com; 237 W 42nd St) in the heart of Times Square offers old-school blues along with rock, folk and reggae acts.

Heading uptown, **Jazz at Lincoln Center** (Map pp168-9; ☎ 212-258-9800; www.jazzatlincolncenter.org; Broadway, at W 60th St) has stunning views overlooking Central Park and nightly shows featuring top lineups in one of three venues. Further north on the Upper West Side, check out the **Smoke Jazz & Supper Club-Lounge** (Map pp168-9; ☎ 212-864-6662; www.smokejazz.com; 2751 Broadway, btwn W 105th & 106th Sts), which gets crowded on weekends.

Some of the world's best theater happens in these more intimate venues before moving to Broadway. Some distinguished theaters include **Playwrights Horizon** (Map pp162-3; ☎ 212-564-1235; www.playwrightshorizon.org; 416 W 42nd St, btwn Ninth & Tenth Aves), **PS 122** (Map pp152-3; ☎ 212-477-5288; www.ps122.org; 150 First Ave, at E 9th St), **New York Theater Workshop** (Map pp152-3; ☎ 212-780-9037; www.nytw.org; 79 E 4th St, btwn Second & Third Aves), **Public Theater** (Map pp152-3; ☎ 212-539-8500; www.publictheater.org; 425 Lafayette St, btwn Astor Pl & E 4th St) and **St Ann's Warehouse** (Map pp152-3; ☎ 718-254-8779; www.stannswarehouse.org; 38 Water St). Richard Foreman, a pioneer of the avant-garde, stages enigmatic and cryptic performances at the **Ontological Theater** (Map pp152-3; ☎ 212-420-1916; www.ontological.com; 131 E 10th St) in the East Village.

Choose from current shows by checking print publications (p149), or at a website such as **Theater Mania** (www.theatermania.com). You can purchase tickets through **Telecharge** (☎ 212-239-6200; www.telecharge.com) & **Ticketmaster** (☎ 212-307-7171; www.ticketmaster.com) for standard ticket sales, or **TKTS ticket booths** (www.tkts.com; Downtown Map pp152-3; Front St, at John St, South St Seaport; 11am-6pm; Midtown Map pp162-3; 47th St, at Broadway; 10am-8pm Mon-Fri, from 11am Sun) for same-day tickets to Broadway and off-Broadway musicals at up to 50% off regular prices.

Comedy

From lowbrow prop comics to experimental conceptual humor, there's a venue for every taste and budget. More-established ones push the alcohol with drink minimums. A good spot for alternative comedy nightly is the **Village Lantern** (Map pp152-3; ☎ 212-260-7993; 167 Bleecker St), underneath a bar of the same name.

Upright Citizens Brigade Theatre (Map pp162-3; ☎ 212-366-9176; www.ucbtheatre.com; 307 W 26th St) features well-known, emerging and probably-won't-emerge comedians as they perform wacky improv, alternative, smart and sometime edgy comedy in this small basement theater nightly. **Caroline's on Broadway** (Map pp162-3; ☎ 212-956-0101; www.carolines.com; 1626 Broadway) is one of the best-known places in the city, and host to the biggest names on the circuit.

Comix (Map pp162-3; ☎ 212-524-2500; 353 W14th St) is the new Caroline's. **Gotham Comedy Club** (Map pp162-3; ☎ 212-367-9000; www.gothamcomedyclub.com; 208 W 23rd St, btwn Seventh & Eighth Aves) is a plush venue featuring mostly mainstream-style comedy and **Stand-Up New York** (Map pp168-9; ☎ 212-595-0850; www.standupny.com; 236 W 78th St; tickets $5-12) gets surprise appearances from star comedians.

Cinemas

Even though movie tickets cost at least $10, long lines on evenings and weekends are the norm. To ensure you'll get in – and not wind up watching with a stiff neck from the front row – it's pretty much imperative that you call and buy your tickets in advance (unless it's midweek, midday or for a film that's been out for months already). Most cinemas are handled either through **Movie Fone** (☎ 212-777-3456; www.moviefone.com) or **Fandango** (www.fandango.com). You'll have to pay an extra $1.50 fee per ticket, but it's worth it.

AMC Empire 25 (Map pp162-3; 234 W 42nd St) in the heart of Times Square, and **Regal Union Square Stadium 14** (Map pp152-3; 859 Broadway, at 13th St), show a mix of mainstream and indie films in theaters with massive screens and stadium seating.

Housed in a former Yiddish theater, **Landmark Sunshine Cinema** (Map pp152-3; ☎ 212-358-7709; 143 E Houston St) shows first-run indies, while film studies majors and East Village hipsters head to **Anthology Film Archives** (Map pp152-3; ☎ 212-505-5181; www.anthologyfilmarchives.org; 32 Second Ave, at E 2nd St), housed in a schoolhouse-like building, for independent and avant-garde cinema.

Brooklyn Academy of Music Rose Cinemas (BAM; Map pp152-3; ☎ 718-636-4100; www.bam.org; 30 Lafayette Ave), in Brooklyn, is comfortable as well as popular for its new-release indies and special festival screenings.

The long and narrow theaters at **Film Forum** (Map pp152-3; ☎ 212-627-2035; www.filmforum.org; 209 W Houston St) can't dent cineastes' love for this institution showing revivals, classics and documentaries. **IFC Center** (Map pp152-3; ☎ 212-924-7771; www.ifccenter.com; 323 Sixth Ave, at 3rd St), formerly the Waverly, is a three-screen art-house cinema showing new indies, cult classics (every Friday and Saturday at midnight) and foreign films – and the popcorn is organic.

Performing Arts

World-class performers and venues mean the city is a year-round Mecca for arts-lovers.

Every top-end genre has a stage at the massive **Lincoln Center** (see p167) complex. Its **Avery Fisher Hall** is the showplace of the New York Philharmonic, while recently redesigned **Alice Tully Hall** houses the Chamber Music Society of Lincoln Center, and the **New York State Theater** is home to both the New York City Ballet and the New York City Opera. Great drama is found at both the **Mitzi E Newhouse** and **Vivian Beaumont** theaters; and frequent concerts at the **Juilliard School**. But the biggest draw is the **Metropolitan Opera House**, home to the Metropolitan Opera and American Ballet Theater.

Since 1891, the historic **Carnegie Hall** (Map pp162-3; ☎ 212-247-7800; www.carnegiehall.org; 154 W 57th St, at Seventh Ave) has hosted performances by the likes of Tchaikovsky, Mahler and Prokofiev. Today it hosts visiting philharmonics, the New York Pops orchestra, piano soloists and various world-music performers.

Symphony Space (Map pp168-9; ☎ 212-864-5400; www.symphonyspace.org; 2537 Broadway, at W 95th St) is a multigenre space with several facilities in one. This Upper West Side gem is home to many performance series as well as theatre, cabaret, comedy, dance and world-music concerts throughout the week.

Sort of a Brooklyn version of the Lincoln Center – in its all-inclusiveness rather than its vibe, which is much edgier – the spectacular **Brooklyn Academy of Music** (BAM; off Map pp152-3; ☎ 718-636-4100; www.bam.org; 30 Lafayette Ave) also hosts everything from modern dance to opera, cutting-edge theater and music concerts.

Sports

In 2009 the city's two major-league baseball teams, the uber-successful **New York Yankees** (www.yankees.com), who play at **Yankee Stadium** (Map p150; ☎ 718-293-4300; cnr 161st St & River Ave, the Bronx), and the more historically beleaguered **New York Mets** (www.mets.com), who play at **Citi Field** (Map p150; ☎ 718-507-8499; Citi Field, 126th St, at Roosevelt Ave, Flushing, Queens), inaugurated long-anticipated brand-new stadiums. For less-grand settings but no-less-pleasant outings, check out the minor-league **Staten Island Yankees** (www.siyanks.com) at **Richmond County Bank Ballpark** (Map p150; ☎ 718-720-9265; 75 Richmond Tce, Staten Island) or the **Brooklyn Cyclones** (www.brooklyncyclones.com) at **KeySpan Park** (Map p150; ☎ 718-449-8497; cnr Surf Ave & W 17th St, Coney Island).

For basketball, you can get courtside with the NBA's **New York Knicks** (www.nba.com/knicks) at **Madison Square Garden** (☎ 212-465-6073; btwn Seventh Ave & 33rd St); called the 'mecca of basketball' by no less than Michael Jordan, the Knicks themselves have been rebuilding for years. The cross-river rivals, **New Jersey Nets** (☎ 800-765-6387; www.nba.com/nets) are scheduled to move to the Atlantic Yards, a large and controversial complex in downtown Brooklyn.

Also playing at Madison Square Garden, the women's WNBA league team **New York Liberty** (☎ 212-564-9622; www.wnba.com/liberty) provides a more laid-back time.

New York City's NFL (pro football) teams, the **Giants** (☎ 201-935-8111; www.giants.com) and **Jets** (☎ 516-560-8200; www.newyorkjets.com), share the **Giants Stadium** in Rutherford's Meadowlands complex; the two teams will begin sharing a brand-new field in the Meadowlands in 2010.

SHOPPING

While the economic downturn has shuttered many shops throughout the city and chain stores have proliferated, turning once-idiosyncratic blocks into versions of generic strip malls, NYC is still the best American city for shopping. From Levis to Prada, iPhones to Buddhist mala beads, you can find it here. It's not unusual for shops – especially downtown boutiques – to stay open until 10pm or 11pm.

Downtown

Lower Manhattan is where you'll find across-the-board bargains, as well as more of the small, stylish boutiques. Downtown's coolest offerings are in NoLita (just east of SoHo), the East Village and the Lower East Side. SoHo has more expensive though no less fashionable stores, while Broadway from Union Sq to Canal St is lined with big retailers like H&M and Urban Outfitters, as well as dozens of jeans and shoe stores – the museum-like Prada NYC flagship is also here. The streets of Chinatown are filled with knock-off designer handbags, jewelry, perfume and watches.

For only-in–New York memorabilia, head to the **Citystore** (Map pp152-3; ☎ 212-669-7452; Municipal Bldg, 1 Centre St, North Plaza; 🕑 9am-4:30pm Mon-Fri). **Century 21** (Map pp152-3; ☎ 212-227-9092; 22 Cortlandt St, at Church St), a four-level department store beloved by New Yorkers of every income, is shorthand for designer bargains. Every electronic need, especially computer, and camera-related, can be satisfied at **J&R Music & Computer World** (Map pp152-3; ☎ 212-238-9000; 15-23 Park Row), which takes up a full city block. **Eastern Mountain Sports** (Map pp152-3; ☎ 212-966-8730; 530 Broadway, at Spring St) is a high-quality outdoor emporium outfitting every imaginable adventure and the staff is extremely knowledgeable and friendly.

Bloomingdale's SoHo (Map pp152-3; ☎ 212-729-5900; 504 Broadway), the smaller, younger outpost of the Upper East Side (right) legend, focuses on designer fashion. The trendy British superstore for women, **Topshop** (Map pp152-3; ☎ 212-966-9555; 478 Broadway, at Broome St), is where to go for shiny spandex and disco tops, while Japanese retailer **Uniqlo** (Map pp152-3; ☎ 917-237-8800; 546 Broadway) has moderately priced men's and women's fashions. For coveted labels like **Stella McCartney** (Map pp152-3; ☎ 212-255-1566; 429 W 14th St), stroll through the Meatpacking District around 14th St and Ninth Ave.

Midtown & Uptown

Midtown's Fifth Ave and the Upper East Side's Madison Ave have the famous high-end fashion and clothing by international designers. Times Square has many supersize stores, though they're all chains. Chelsea has more unique boutiques, though it too has been colonized by banks, drugstores and big box retailers.

Macy's (Map pp162-3; ☎ 212-695-4400; 151 W 34th St), the grande dame of midtown department stores, sells everything from jeans to kitchen appliances. Uptown, the sprawling, overwhelming **Bloomingdale's** (Map pp168-9; ☎ 212-705-2000; 1000 3rd Ave, at E 59th St) is akin to the Metropolitan Museum of Art for shoppers.

Barney's New York (Map pp168-9; ☎ 212-826-8900; 660 Madison Ave) is a classy emporium with spot-on choice collections of the best designer duds (Marc Jacobs, Helmut Lang, Paul Smith, Miu Miu shoes), while **Barney's Co-op** (Downtown (Map pp162-3; 236 W 18th St; Uptown Map pp168-9; 2151 Broadway) offers hipper, less-expensive versions of high-end fashion.

In the cultural imagination, **Tiffany & Co** (Map pp162-3; ☎ 212-755-8000; 727 Fifth Ave) has become synonymous with NYC luxury. This famous jeweler, with the trademark clock-hoisting Atlas over the door, carries fine diamond rings, watches, necklaces etc, as well as crystal and glassware.

GETTING THERE & AWAY

Air

Three major airports serve New York City. The biggest is **John F Kennedy International Airport** (JFK; ☎ 718-244-4444; www.panynj.gov/aviation/jfk frame), in the borough of Queens, which is also home to **La Guardia Airport** (LGA; ☎ 718-533-3400; www.panynj.gov/aviation/lgaframe). **Newark International Airport** (EWR; ☎ 973-961-6000; www.panynj.gov/aviation/ewrframe), across the Hudson River in Newark, NJ, is another option. While using online booking websites, search 'NYC' rather than a specific airport, which will allow most sites to search all three spots at once. **Long Island MacArthur Airport** (ISP; ☎ 631-467-3210; www.macarthurairport.com), in Islip, is a money-saving (though time-consuming) alternative, but may make sense if a visit to the Hamptons or other parts of Long Island are in your plans.

Bus

The massive and confusing **Port Authority Bus Terminal** (Map pp162-3; ☎ 212-564-8484; 625 Eighth Ave, btwn 40th & 42nd St) is the gateway for buses into and out of Manhattan. **Short Line** (☎ 212-736-4700; www.shortlinebus.com) runs numerous buses to towns in northern New Jersey and upstate New York, while **New Jersey Transit** (☎ 973-275-5555; www.njtransit.state.nj.us) buses serve all of New Jersey. For other NYC bus information see p145.

A number of bus companies, including the pioneers based in Chinatown but now expanded to several midtown locations, link NYC to Philadelphia ($10, two hours), Boston ($15, four hours 15 minutes) and Washington, DC ($15, four hours 15 minutes). Cutthroat competition has led to lowered fares and increased amenities; some offer free wi-fi on board. A few of the more reliable ones to check out include **Bolt Bus** (☎ 877-265-8287; www.boltbus.com) and **Megabus** (☎ 877-462-6342; www.megabus.com). Trip durations depend on the time of day you depart, and where in each city you depart from and arrive.

Car & Motorcycle

See p1164 for information about vehicle rentals. Note that renting a car in the city is expensive, starting at about $75 a day for a midsize car – before extra charges like the 13.25% tax and various insurance costs.

Train

Penn Station (Map pp162-3; 33rd St, btwn Seventh & Eighth Aves), not to be confused with the Penn Station in Newark, NJ, is the departure point for all **Amtrak** (☎ 800-872-7245; www.amtrak.com) trains, including the speedy Acela Express service to Boston (three hours 45 minutes) and Washington, DC (two hours 52 minutes). All fares and durations vary based on the day of the week and the time of day you want to travel. Also arriving into Penn Station (NYC), as well as points in Brooklyn and Queens – is the **Long Island Rail Road** (LIRR; ☎ 718-217-5477; www.mta.nyc.ny.us/lirr), which serves several hundred thousand commuters each day. **New Jersey Transit** (☎ 973-275-5555; www.njtransit.com) also operates trains from Penn Station (NYC), with services to the suburbs and the Jersey Shore. Another option for getting into New Jersey, but strictly to points north of the city such as Hoboken and Newark, is the **New Jersey PATH** (☎ 800-234-7284; www.pathrail.com), which runs trains on a separate-fare system ($1.75) along the length of Sixth Ave, with stops at 34th, 23rd, 14th, 9th and Christopher Sts, and the reopened World Trade Center station.

The only train line that still departs from Grand Central Station, Park Ave at 42nd St, is the **Metro-North Railroad** (☎ 212-532-4900; www.mnr.org), which serves the northern city suburbs, Connecticut (eg one way to New Haven $14 to $18.50, one hour 45 minutes) and locations throughout the Hudson Valley.

GETTING AROUND

To/From the Airport

All major airports have on-site car-rental agencies. It's a hassle to drive into NYC, though, and many folks take taxis, shelling out the $45 taxi flat rate (plus toll and tip) from JFK and Newark or a metered fare of about $35 to Midtown from La Guardia.

A cheaper and pretty easy option to/from JFK is the **AirTrain** ($5 one way), which connects to subway lines into the city ($2.25; coming from the city, take the Howard Beach–bound A train) or to the LIRR (about $7 one way) at Jamaica Station in Queens (this is probably the quickest route to Penn Station in the city).

To/from Newark, the **AirTrain** links all terminals to a New Jersey Transit train station, which connects to Penn Station in NYC ($12.50 one way combined NJ Transit/Airtrain ticket).

For La Guardia, a reliable option to consider if you allow plenty of time is the M60 bus ($2.25), which heads to/from Manhattan across 125th St in Harlem and makes stops along Broadway on the Upper West Side.

All three airports are also served by express buses ($12 to $15) and shuttle vans ($20); such companies include the **New York Airport Service Express Bus** (☎ 718-875-8200; www.nyairportservice.com), which leaves every 15 minutes for Port Authority, Penn Station (NYC) and Grand Central Station; and **Super Shuttle Manhattan** (☎ 800-258-3826; www.supershuttle.com), which picks you (and others) up anywhere, on demand, with a reservation.

Car & Motorcycle

Even for the most spiritually centered, road rage is an inevitable byproduct of driving within the city. Traffic is a perpetual problem and topic of conversation. Mayor Bloomberg, a committed proponent of congestion pricing plans, and other transportation advocates will no doubt continue to try to solve the puzzle.

If you are driving out or in, however, know that the worst part is joining the masses as they try to squeeze through tunnels and over bridges to traverse the various waterways that surround Manhattan. Be aware of local laws, such as the fact that you can't make a right on red (like you can in the rest of the state) and also the fact that every other street is one way.

Public Transportation

The **Metropolitan Transport Authority** (MTA; (www.mta.info) runs both the subway and bus sytems. Depending on the train line (the W and G are consistently rated two of the worst), time of day and whether the door slams in your face or not, New York City's 100-year-old round-the-clock subway system (per ride $2.25) is your best friend or worst enemy. The popularized Hollywood version, given life in films like *The Taking of Pelham 1 2 3* (both the original and the 2009 version) are obvious exaggerations, but the system can be frustrating. Mismanagement and budget shortfalls threaten its smooth running. The 656-mile system can be intimidating at first, but regardless of its faults it's an incredible resource and achievement, linking the most disparate neighborhoods in a continually pulsating network. Maps should be available for the taking at every stop. To board, you must purchase a MetroCard, available at windows and self-serve machines, which accept change, dollars or credit/debit cards; purchasing many rides at once works out cheaper per trip.

If you're not in a big hurry, consider taking the bus (per ride $2.25). You get to see the world go by, they run 24/7 and they're easy to navigate – going crosstown at all the major street byways (14th, 23rd, 34th, 42nd, 72nd Sts and all the others that are two-way roads) and uptown or downtown, depending which avenue they serve. You can pay with a MetroCard or exact change but not bills. Transfers from one line to another are free, as are transfers to or from the subway.

Taxi

The classic NYC yellow cab is no longer a boxy gas-guzzling behemoth. More streamlined and outfitted with mini-TVs and credit-card machines, some hybrid models are even being rolled out. No matter the make or year of the car, however, expect a herky-jerky, somewhat out-of-control ride. Current fares are $2.50 for the initial charge (first one-fifth mile), 40¢ each additional one-fifth mile, as well as per 60 seconds of being stopped in traffic, $1 peak surcharge (weekdays 4pm to 8pm), and 50¢ night surcharge (8pm to 6am daily). Tips are expected to be 10% to 15%; minivan cabs can hold five to six passengers. You can only hail a cab that has a lit light on its roof. Also know that it can be difficult to score a taxi in the rain, at rush hour and at around 4pm, when many drivers end their shifts.

Pedicabs – human-powered taxis, basically bicycle rickshaws – roam around Central Park South and other heavily touristy areas. Rides cost around $10 to $20 but fares are negotiable.

NEW YORK STATE

There's upstate and downstate and never the twain shall meet. The two have about as much in common as NYC's Upper East Side and the Bronx. And yet everyone shares the same governor and dysfunctional legislature in the capital, Albany. While this incompatibility produces legislative gridlock and downright operatic drama, it's a blessing for those who cherish quiet and pastoral idylls as much as Lower East Side bars and the subway. Defined largely by its inland waterways – the Hudson River, the 524-mile Erie Canal connecting Albany to Buffalo, and the St Lawrence River – New York stretches to the Canadian border at world-famous Niagara Falls and under-the-radar Thousand Islands. Buffalo is a cheap foodies' paradise and wine aficionados can pick their favorite vintage from around the state, but especially in the Finger Lakes region close to the college town of Ithaca. From wilderness trails with backcountry camping to small-town Americana and miles and miles of sandy beaches, from the historic, grand estates and artists colonies in the Hudson Valley and Catskills to the rugged and remote Adirondacks, it's easy

NEW YORK FACTS

Nicknames Empire State, Excelsior State, Knickerbocker State
Population 19.5 million
Area 47,214 sq miles
Capital city Albany (population 96,000)
Other cities Buffalo (population 276,059)
Sales tax 4%, plus additional county and state taxes (total approximately 8%)
Birthplace of Poet Walt Whitman (1819–92), President Theodore Roosevelt (1858–1919), President Franklin D Roosevelt (1882–1945), first lady Eleanor Roosevelt (1884–1962), painter Edward Hopper (1882–1967), movie star Humphrey Bogart (1899–1957), comic Lucille Ball (1911–89), filmmaker Woody Allen (b 1935), actor Tom Cruise (b 1962), pro athlete Michael Jordan (b 1963), pop star Jennifer Lopez (b 1969)
Home of Six Nations of the Iroquois Confederacy, first US cattle ranch (1747, in Montauk, Long Island), US women's suffrage movement (1872), Erie Canal (1825)
Famous for Niagara Falls (half of it), the Hamptons, Cornell University, Hudson River
Unusual river Genesee River is one of the few rivers in the world that flows south–north, from south central New York into Lake Ontario at Rochester
Driving distances NYC to Albany 160 miles, NYC to Buffalo 375 miles

to understand why so many people leave the city never to return.

Information

New York State Office of Parks, Recreation and Historic Preservation (☎ 518-474-0456, 800-456-2267; www.nysparks.com) Camping, lodging and general info on all state parks. Reservations can be made up to nine months in advance; tent sites cost from $17.
New York State Tourism (☎ 800-225-5697; www.iloveny.com) Info, maps, travel advice available by phone.
New York State Travel Information (www.travelinfony.com) Weather advisories, road information and more.
Uncork New York (☎ 585-394-3620; www.newyorkwines.org) One-stop shop for statewide wine info.

LONG ISLAND

Private-school blazers, nightmare commutes, strip malls colonized by national chains, cookie-cutter suburbia, moneyed resorts, windswept dunes and magnificent beaches – and those accents. Long Island, a long peninsula contiguous with the boroughs of Brooklyn and Queens, has all of these things, which explains its somewhat complicated reputation. The site of small European whaling and fishing ports from as early as 1640, Levittown, just 25 miles east of Manhattan in Nassau County, is where builders first perfected the art of mass-producing homes. But visions of suburban dystopia aside, Long Island has wide ocean and bay beaches, important historic sites, renowned vineyards, rural regions and of course the Hamptons, in all their luxuriously sunbaked glory.

North Shore

In Port Washington, **Sands Point Preserve** (☎ 516-571-7900; www.sandspointpreserve.org; 127 Middleneck Rd; admission per car $5, free Thu; ⏲ 9am-4:30pm) is a wooded bayfront park with nature trails that's also home to the 1923 **Falaise** (admission $6; ⏲ tours hourly noon-3pm Thu-Sun Jun-Oct), one of the few remaining Gold Coast mansions and now a museum. East of there is the bucolic town of Oyster Bay (hometown of Billy Joel), with an even bigger claim to fame: it's home to **Sagamore Hill** (☎ 516-922-4788; www.nps.gov/sahi; admission $5; ⏲ 10am-4pm Wed-Sun), a National Historic Site home where Theodore Roosevelt vacationed during his presidency.

South Shore

Despite the periodic roar of over-flying jets, **Long Beach**, the closest beach to the city and most accessible by train, has a main town strip with ice-cream shops, bars and eateries, a lively surfers' scene and pale city hipsters mixing with suntanned locals.

On summer weekends the mob scene on the 6-mile stretch of pretty **Jones Beach** is a microcosm of the city's diversity, attracting surfers, wild city folk, local teens, nudists, staid families, gay and lesbian people and plenty of old-timers. The Long Island Rail Road (LIRR) service to Wantagh has a bus connection to Jones Beach.

Further east, just off the southern shore, is a separate barrier island. **Fire Island** includes **Fire Island National Seashore** (☎ 631-289-4810; www.nps.gov) and several summer-only villages accessible by ferry from Long Island. The Fire Island Pines and Cherry Grove (both car-free) comprise a historic, gay bacchanalia that attracts men and women in droves from New York City, while villages on the west end cater to straight singles and families. There are limited places to stay, and booking in advance is strongly advised (check www.fireisland.com for accommodations information). Beach camping is allowed in **Watch Hill** (☎ 631-597-3109; www.watchhillfi.com; campsites $20; early May–late Oct), though mosquitoes can be fierce and reservations are a must. At the western end of Fire Island, **Robert Moses State Park** is the only spot accessible by car. **Fire Island Ferries** (☎ 631-665-3600; www.fireislandferries.com) runs services to Fire Island beaches and the national seashore; the terminals are close to LIRR stations at Bayshore, Sayville and Patchogue (round trip $17, May to November).

The Hamptons

Even the Hamptons have been affected by the 2008 market crash – real-estate offices no longer boast two-bedroom inland cottages for $5 million. But no economic downturn can detract from the sheer beauty of the beaches and what's left of the picturesque farms and woodland. Attitudes about the Hamptons are about as varied as the number of Maseratis and Land Rovers cruising the perfectly landscaped streets. If you can bury the envy, a pleasurable day of sightseeing can be had simply driving past the homes of the once and still-by-comparison extravagantly wealthy, ranging from cutting-edge modernist to faux-castle monstrosities. However, many summertime residents are partying the weekends away in much more modest group rentals and at the revolving doors of clubs. While each Hampton is not geographically far from every other, traffic can be a nightmare.

SOUTHAMPTON

Though the village of Southampton appears blemish-free as if it were Botoxed, it gets a face-lift at night when raucous clubgoers let their hair down. Its beaches are sweeping and gorgeous, and the **Parrish Art Museum** (☎ 631-283-2118; www.parrishart.org; 25 Jobs Lane; admission $7; 11am-5pm Mon & Thu-Sat, 1-5pm Sun mid-Sep–May, daily Jun–mid-Sep) is an impressive regional institution. At the edge of the village is a small Native American reservation, home to the Shinnecock Nation, which runs a tiny **museum** (☎ 631-287-4923; 100 Montauk Hwy; adult/child $5/3; 11am-4pm Thu-Sat, from noon Sun). For a quick and reasonable meal try **Golden Pear** (☎ 631-283-8900; 99 Main St; sandwiches $9; 7:30am- 5pm Fri & Sat, 7:30am-5:30pm Sun-Thu), which serves delicious soups, salads and wraps. Well-heeled revelers can down cocktails and Dom Perignon at **La Playa** (formerly Tavern; ☎ 631-251-6292; www.laplayanightclub.com; 125 Tuckahoe Rd), one of the largest spaces around.

BRIDGEHAMPTON & SAG HARBOR

Moving east, Bridgehampton has a more modest-looking drag, but has its fair share of trendy boutiques and fine restaurants. The modest low-slung **Enclave Inn** (☎ 631-537-2900; www.enclaveinnn.com; 2668 Montauk Hwy; r from $99;) is just a few blocks from the heart of the village; there are other branches elsewhere in the Hamptons. For stately classic luxury try the **Bridgehampton Inn** (☎ 631-537-3660; www.bridgehamptoninn.com; 2266 Main St; r $340-390;), a B&B in a traditional country house. Old-fashioned diner **Candy Kitchen** (☎ 646-537-9885; Main St; mains $5-12; 7am-6pm) is as un-Hamptons as you can get; there's a luncheonette counter serving filling breakfasts, burgers and sandwiches.

Seven miles north, on Peconic Bay, is the lovely old whaling town of Sag Harbor; ferries to Shelter Island leave a few miles north of here. Check out its **Whaling & Historical Museum** (☎ 631-725-0770; www.sagharborwhalingmuseum.org; adult/child $5/1; 10am-5pm May-Oct), or simply stroll up and down its narrow, Cape Cod–like streets. Get gourmet sustenance without going broke at **Provisions** (☎ 631-725-3636; cnr Bay & Division Sts; sandwiches $9; 8:30am-8pm), a natural foods market with delicious take-out wraps, burritos and sandwiches.

EAST HAMPTON

Don't be fooled by the oh-so-casual-looking summer attire – the sunglasses alone are probably equal to a month's rent. Steven Spielberg, Martha Stewart and Diddy all have homes here. Long-standing restaurants (by Hamptons standards) such as **Della Femina** (☎ 631-329-6666; 99 N Main St; dishes $20-30; 6-11pm Fri & Sat, 6-10pm Sun-Thu) draw regulars from the celebrity crowd and those trolling for sightings. Housed in the pricey Maidstone Inn is the **Living Room** (☎ 631-324-5440; 207 Main St; mains $30; 8-10:30am, noon-2:30pm & 5:30-10:30pm), featuring both haute design as well as haute cuisine – basically thoughtfully conceived American with a Swedish influence, and sourced from local growers when possible. Catch readings and art exhibits at **Guild Hall** (☎ 631-324-0806; www.guildhall.org; 158 Main St; ⌚ 11am-5pm Mon-Sat, noon-5pm Sun Apr 13–Jan 30, 11am-5pm Thu-Sat, noon-5pm Sun Jan 31–Apr 12), or have a debauched night out at **Lily Pond** (formerly Flirt; ☎ 631-619-1217; 44 Three Mile Rd, at Oak View Hwy; ⌚ 10pm-4am). Nightclubs come and go with the seasons. A word to the wise: strike the phrase 'bottle service' from your vocabulary.

MONTAUK & AROUND

More Jersey Shore, less polo club, Montauk is the humble stepsister of the Hamptons, though its beaches are equally beautiful. There's a slew of relatively reasonable restaurants and a louder bar scene. At the very eastern, wind-whipped tip of the South Fork is **Montauk Point State Park**, with its impressive, 1796 **Montauk Point Lighthouse** (☎ 631-668-2544; www.montauklighthouse.com; adult/child $8/4; ⌚ 10:30am-5:30pm, hours vary), the fourth oldest still-active lighthouse in the US. You can camp about 15 minutes west of here at the dune-swept **Hither Hills State Park** (☎ 631-668-2554; New York residents/nonresidents Mon-Fri $28/56, higher prices Sat & Sun; ⌚ Apr-Nov), right on the beach; just reserve early. Several miles to the north is the Montauk harbor, with dockside restaurants and hundreds of boats in the marinas.

You'll find a string of very basic (but beachfront) motels near the entrance to the town beach, including the **Ocean Resort Inn** (☎ 631-668-2300; www.oceanresortinn.com; 96 S Emerson Ave; r $105-165, ste $175-220; ❄ 📶). A few miles west, just across the street from the beach, is **Sunrise Guesthouse** (☎ 631-668-7286; www.sunrisebnb.com; 681 Old Montauk Hwy; r $115-145; ❄), a modest and comfortable B&B. Nearby is the posh **Gurney's Inn & Spa** (☎ 631-668-2345; www.gurneys-inn.com; 290 Old Montauk Hwy; r $200-750; ❄ 💻 🏊) with fabulous ocean views.

Two great places to wind down the day with drinks and hearty, fresh seafood are the roadside restaurants **Clam Bar** (☎ 631-267-6348; 2025 Montauk Hwy; mains $7-14; ⌚ noon-8pm daily, weather permitting) and **Lobster Roll** (☎ 631-267-3740; 1980 Montauk Hwy; mains $11-22; ⌚ 11:30am-9:30pm Mon-Thu & Sun May-Oct, to 10pm Fri & Sat), now in its fifth decade, both on the highway between Amagansett and Montauk. The bar and restaurant at the new **Surf Lodge** (☎ 631-668-3284; 183 Edgemere St; ⌚ 5pm-late Wed-Mon), set on Fort Pond a half-mile north of the beach, tries to have it both ways: Bob Marley-surfer ethos with a chic vibe.

North Fork & Shelter Island

Mainly, the North Fork is known for its unspoiled farmland and wineries – there are close to 30 vineyards, clustered mainly in the towns of Jamesport, Cutchogue and Southold – and the **Long Island Wine Council** (☎ 631-369-5887; www.liwines.com) provides details of the local wine trail, which runs along Rte 25 north of Peconic Bay. Try **Palmer Vineyards** (☎ 631-722-9463; www.palmervineyards.com; Sound Ave, Aquebogue) and **Macari Vineyards** (☎ 631-298-0100; www.macariwines.com; 150 Bergen Ave, Mattituck) for a tasting.

The main North Fork town and the place for ferries to Shelter Island, **Greenport** (www.greenport.com) is a bit more down-to-earth and affordable than most South Fork villages. Hunker down for some excellent seafood at one of the marina restaurants, and take a free spin on the historic waterfront carousel, the gem of **Harbor Front Park**.

Between the North and South Forks, **Shelter Island** (www.shelter-island.org), accessible by ferry from North Haven to the south and Greenport to the north, is home to a cluster of Victorian buildings and the **Mashomack Nature Preserve**. It's a great spot for hiking or kayaking (no bicycling).

Nestled on a prime piece of property surrounded by woods and fronting a small beach and the bay, **Pridwin Beach Hotel & Cottages** (☎ 631-749-0476; www.pridwin.com; r & cottages from $149-259; P ❄ 📶) on Shelter Island has standard hotel rooms as well as private water-view cottages, some renovated in high-designer style.

Getting There & Around

The most direct driving route is along the I-495, aka the LIE (Long Island Expwy), though be sure to avoid rush hour, when it's commuter hell. Once in the Hamptons, there is one main road to the end, Montauk Hwy. The **Long Island Rail Road** (LIRR; ☎ 718-217-5477; www.mta.nyc.ny.us/lirr) serves all regions of Long Island, including the Hamptons ($20 one way, two hours 45 minutes) and North Fork (two hours 45 minutes), from Penn Station (NYC), Brooklyn and Queens. The **Hampton Jitney** (☎ 631-283-4600; www.hamptonjitney.com; one way Tue-Thu/Fri-Mon $26/30) and **Hampton Luxury Liner** (☎ 631-567-5100; www.hamptonluxuryliner.com; one way $36) bus services connect Manhattan's Upper East Side to various Hamptons villages; the former also has services to/from various spots in Brooklyn.

HUDSON VALLEY

Immediately north of New York City, green becomes the dominant color and the vistas of the Hudson River and the mountains breathe life into your urban-weary body. The region was home to the Hudson River School of painting in the 19th century and its history is preserved in the many grand estates and picturesque villages. The Lower Valley and Middle Valley are more populated and suburban, while the Upper Valley has a rural feel, with hills leading into the Catskills mountain region. For region-wide information, check out the **Hudson Valley Network** (www.hvnet.com).

Lower Hudson Valley

A pristine forested wilderness with miles of hiking trails is available just 40 miles north of New York City: **Harriman State Park** (☎ 845-786-2701) covers 72 sq miles and offers swimming, hiking and camping; adjacent **Bear Mountain State Park** (☎ 845-786-2701; 🕑 8am-dusk) offers great views from its 1306ft peak, with the Manhattan skyline looming beyond the river and surrounding greenery; there's a restaurant and lodging at the inn on Hessian Lake. In both parks there are several scenic roads snaking their way past secluded lakes with gorgeous vistas.

Several magnificent homes and gardens can be found near Tarrytown and Sleepy Hollow, on the east side of the Hudson. **Kykuit**, one of the properties of the Rockefeller family, has an impressive array of Asian and European artwork and immaculately kept gardens with breathtaking views. **Lyndhurst** is the estate of railroad tycoon Jay Gould and **Sunnyside** is the home of author Washington Irving. Go to the **Historic Hudson Valley** (www.hudsonvalley.org) website for info on these and other historic attractions.

West of Rte 9W and 50 miles north of New York City, the **Storm King Art Center** (☎ 845-534-3115; www.stormkingartcenter.org; Old Pleasant Rd, Mountainville; adult/student $10/9; 🕑 10am-5:30pm Wed-Sun Apr-Nov) is a 500-acre outdoor sculpture park with rolling hills that showcases stunning avant-garde sculpture by well-known artists; a free tram gives tours of the grounds. Nearby **West Point** (☎ 845-938-2638; 🕑 9am-5pm), open to visitors on guided tours (☎ 845-446-4724; www.westpointtours.com; tours adult/child $11/8), was a strategic fort before becoming the US Military Academy in 1802. Not far from here, the large, strip mall–filled town of Newburgh is the site of **Washington's Headquarters State Historic Site** (☎ 845-562-1195; Liberty St, at Washington St; donations accepted; 🕑 10am-5pm Wed-Sat, from 1pm Sun, Apr-Oct), General George's longest-lasting base during the Revolutionary War; there's a museum, galleries and maps.

Across the river, near the town of Cold Spring, the **Hudson Valley Shakespeare Festival** (☎ 845-7588; www.hvshakespeare.org) takes place between mid-June and early September, staging impressive open-air productions on a magnificent piece of property.

At Beacon, a fairly nondescript town east of Rte 9W, fashionable regulars of the international art scene stop for **Dia Beacon** (☎ 845-440-0100; www.diaart.org; admission $10; 🕑 11am-6pm Thu-Mon mid-Apr–mid-Oct, 11am-4pm Fri-Mon mid-Oct–mid-Apr), which features a renowned collection from 1960 to the present, and enormous sculptures and installation pieces.

Middle & Upper Hudson Valley

On the western side of the Hudson is **New Paltz**, home of a campus of the State University of New York, natural food stores and a liberal ecofriendly vibe. In the distance behind the town the ridge of the Shawangunk (Shon-gum or just the 'Gunks') mountains rises more than 2000 feet above sea level. **Minnewaska State Park Preserve** has 12,000 acres of wild landscape, the centerpiece of which is a usually ice-cold mountain lake.

The nearby iconic **Mohonk Mountain House** (☎ 845-255-1000; www.mohonk.com; 1000 Mountain Rest Rd; r $320-2500;) looks like it's straight out of a fairy tale: a rustic castle perched magnificently over a dark lake. It's an all-inclusive resort where guests can gorge on elaborate five-course meals, stroll through gardens, hike miles of trails, canoe, swim, etc. A luxury spa center is there to work out the kinks. Nonovernight guests can visit the grounds (adult/child per day $23/18) – well worth the price of admission.

The largest town on the Hudson's east bank, **Poughkeepsie** (puh-*kip*-see) is famous for **Vassar**, a private liberal-arts college that until 1969 only admitted women. Cheap motel chains are clustered along Rte 9, south of the Mid-Hudson Bridge, but try the **Copper Penny Inn** (☎ 845-452-3045; www.copperpennyinn.com; 2406 Hackensack Rd; r incl breakfast $140-230;), a charming and cheerful B&B set on 12 wooded acres. The **Buttermilk Inn & Spa** (☎ 845-795-1310; 220 North Rd; www.buttermilkfallsinn.com; r from $225;) is a luxurious getaway.

Hyde Park is chock-full of history, as it's long been associated with the Roosevelts, a prominent family since the 19th century. The **Franklin D Roosevelt Library & Museum** (☎ 800-337-8474; www.fdrlibrary.marist.edu; 511 Albany Post Rd/Rte 9; admission $14; 9am-6pm May-Oct, to 5pm Nov-Apr) features exhibits on the man who created the New Deal and led the USA into WWII. First Lady Eleanor Roosevelt's peaceful cottage, **Val-Kill** (☎ 877-444-6777; www.nps.gov/elro; admission $8; 9am-5pm), was her retreat from Hyde Park, FDR's mother and FDR himself. The 54-room **Vanderbilt Mansion** (☎ 877-444-6777; www.nps.gov/vama; Rte 9; admission $8; 9am-5pm), a national historic site 2 miles north of Hyde Park on Rte 9, is a spectacle of lavish beaux-arts and eclectic architecture.

Hyde Park's famous **Culinary Institute of America** (☎ 845-471-6608; www.ciachef.edu; 1964 Campus Dr) trains future chefs and can satisfy absolutely anyone's gastronomic cravings; it's home to six student-staffed eateries.

CATSKILLS

The introduction of fine cuisine and cute boutiques has yet to overwhelm the pastoral atmosphere and small-town charm of the Catskills. For some out-of-staters this bucolic region of undulating, forest-covered mountains and picturesque farmland is still synonymous with Borscht-belt family resorts. However, that era is long past, and after some economically tough times the Catskills, though having a lower profile than the Hamptons, have become a popular choice for sophisticated city dwellers seeking second-home getaways.

Woodstock & Around

Shorthand for free love, free expression and the political ferment of the 1960s, world-famous **Woodstock** today still wears its counterculture tie-dye in the form of healing centers, art galleries, cafés and an eclectic mix of aging hippies and young Phish-fan types. The famous 1969 Woodstock music festival, though, actually occurred in Bethel, a town over 40 miles southwest. Overlooking Woodstock's town square, actually in front of the bus stop, is the **Village Green B&B** (☎ 845-679-0313; 12 Tinker St; r incl breakfast $135;), a three-story Victorian with comfortable rooms. Only two miles away and relatively secluded amid tranquil meadows with mountains in the background, try the **Woodstock Country Inn** (☎ 845-679-9380; www.woodstockcountryinn.com; 185 Cooper Lake Rd; r incl breakfast from $150-300;), housed in a 19th-century farmhouse; two rooms have private entrances for those who shy away from socializing. Especially popular for its breakfast omelets and eggs, **Oriole 9** (☎ 845-679-5763; 17 Tinker St; sandwiches $10; 8:30am-4:30pm) also does tasty sandwiches, salads and wraps.

Saugerties, just 7 miles east of Woodstock, is not nearly as quaint and feels comparably like the big city, but there are two highly recommended places to sleep.

our pick **Saugerties Lighthouse** (☎ 845-247-0656; www.saugertieslighthouse.com; r incl breakfast $200; Thu-Sun, closed Feb) offers a truly romantic and unique place to lay your head. The picturesque 1869 landmark sits on a small island in the Esopus Creek, accessible by boat or more commonly by a half-mile-long trail from the parking lot. Rooms are booked far in advance but a walk to the lighthouse is highly recommended regardless. On a verdant piece of property several miles outside town on the way to Woodstock is the five-room **Villa at Saugerties** (☎ 845-246-0682; www.thevillaatsaugerties.com; 159 Fawn Rd; d incl breakfast $145-235;), rustic and country on the outside, hip and cosmopolitan on the inside.

On the eastern side of the river is **Rhinebeck**, with a bustling main street, good antique shops, inns, farms and wineries. There's also an **Aerodrome Museum** (☎ 845-752-3200; www.oldrhinebeck.org) and the destination bistro, worth the trip in itself, **Terrapin** (☎ 845-876-3330; www.terrapinrestaurant.com; 6426 Montgomery St; lunch sandwiches $7, dinner mains from $19; 11:30am-11:30pm Mon-Thu, to 12:30am Fri & Sat, to 11pm Sun). The formal dining room has more-limited hours.

Much further to the north is **Hudson** – a beautiful town with a hip, gay-friendly community of artists, writers and performers who fled the city.

Having a car is near essential in these parts. **Adirondack Trailways** (☎ 800-776-7548; www.trailwaysny.com) operates daily buses from NYC to Kingston (one way $24, two hours), the Catskills' gateway town, as well as to Catskills and Woodstock (one way $26.50, two hours 30 minutes). Buses leave from NYC's Port Authority. The commuter rail line **Metro-North** (☎ 800-638-7646; www.mta.info/mnr) makes stops through the Lower and Middle Hudson Valleys.

FINGER LAKES REGION

A bird's-eye view of this region of rolling hills and 11 long narrow lakes – the eponymous fingers – reveals an outdoor paradise stretching all the way from Albany to far-western New York. Of course there's boating, fishing, bicycling, hiking and cross-country skiing, but this is also the state's premier wine-growing region, with more than 65 vineyards, enough for the most discerning oenophile.

Ithaca & Around

An idyllic home for college students and older generations of hippies who cherish elements of the traditional collegiate lifestyle – laid-back vibe, café poetry readings, art-house cinemas, green quads, good eats – Ithaca is perched above Cayuga Lake. Besides being a destination in and of itself, it is also a convenient halfway point between New York City and Niagara Falls. For tourist information, head to the **Visit Ithaca Information Center** (☎ 607-272-1313; www.visitithaca.com; 904 E Shore Dr; 9am-5pm Mon-Fri, from 10am Sat).

Founded in 1865, **Cornell University** boasts a lovely campus, mixing traditional and contemporary architecture, and sits high on a hill overlooking the picturesque town below. The modern **Herbert F Johnson Museum of Fine Art** (☎ 607-255-6464; www.museum.cornell.edu; University Ave; admission free; 10am-5pm Tue-Sun) – designed by IM Pei – has a major Asian collection, plus pre-Columbian, American and European exhibits.

SCENIC DRIVE: ROUTE 28 & AROUND

One sign you've crossed into the Catskills is that your cell-phone signal dies – another more welcome one is that unending asphalt gives way to dense greenery crowding the snaking roadway when you exit the I-87 and turn onto Rte 28. As you drive through the heart of the region, the vistas open up and the mountains (around 35 peaks are above 3500 ft) take on stunning coloring depending on the season and time of day. Esopus Creek winds its way through the area and **Ashokan Reservoir** is a nice place for a walk or drive.

our pick **Emerson Spa Resort** (☎ 877-688-2828; www.emersonresort.com; 5340 Rte 28, Mt Tremper; r from $129-519;) looks like nothing more than an ordinary country inn from the outside, but is truly worthy of a weekend retreat. From luxurious Asian-inspired retreats to more-ordinary rooms in the rustic-pioneer-style lodge, Emerson aims to please; the Phoenix restaurant (mains $15 to $30) is probably the best in the region. The world's largest kaleidoscope and kaleidoscope boutique, selling sculpture quality pieces, is attached, as well as a coffee/sandwich shop. Only a minute down the road is the **Lazy Meadow Motel** (☎ 845-688-7200; www.lazymeadow.com; 5191 Rte 28, Mt Tremper; r from $150;), where you can choose from retrofitted airstream trailers or more conventional rooms, all decorated with the same '50's-era nostalgia.

Only a few miles further west is the one-lane town of **Phoenicia**. It's a pleasant place to stop for a meal and a tube – **Town Tinker Tube Rental** (☎ 845-688-5553; www.towntinker.com; 10 Bridge St; tubes per day $12) can hook you up for repeated forays down the Esopus rapids. The refreshing water of Pine Hill Lake at nearby **Belleayre Beach** (☎ 845-254-5600; www.belleayre.com;) is the summertime place to cool off. Continuing on Rte 28 takes you past the town of Fleischmann's, where you can stop for the night at the **River Run B&B** (☎ 845-254-4884; www.riverrunbedandbreakfast.com; 882 Main St; r from $85-135;), a professionally run Victorian inn.

In nearby Arkville, you can take a scenic ride on the historic **Delaware & Ulster Rail Line** (☎ 845-586-3877; www.durr.org; Hwy 28; adult/child $12/7; 11am & 2pm, Sat & Sun Jun-Nov, additional trips Thu & Fri Jul-Sep;). In the winter, skiers should head further north, where Rtes 23 and 23A lead you to **Hunter Mountain Ski Bowl** (☎ 518-263-4223; www.huntermtn.com), a year-round resort with challenging runs and a 1600ft vertical drop.

From here you can carry on to the **Roxbury** (☎ 607-326-7200; www.theroxburymotel.com; r $100-330;), in the tiny village of the same name, a wonderfully creative gem of a place with luxuriously designed rooms, each inspired by a particular '60s- or '70s-era TV show; a spa is attached.

West of Roxbury is the 26-mile-long **Catskill Scenic Trail** (a good map is available at www.durr.org), a mostly flat path built on top of a former rail bed, ideal for cycling, hiking and cross-country skiing in the winter. For rougher hikes through dense forest, the **Utsayantha Trail System** intersects at several points around the town of Stamford.

The area around Ithaca is known for its waterfalls, gorges and gorgeous parks. However, downtown has its very own – **Cascadilla Gorge** – starting several blocks from Ithaca Commons and ending, after a steep and stunning vertical climb, at the Performing Arts Center of Cornell. Eight miles north on Rte 89, the spectacular **Taughannock Falls** spills 215ft into the steep gorge below; **Taughannock Falls State Park** (☎ 607-387-6739; www.taughannock.com; Rte 89) has two major hiking trails, craggy gorges, tent-trailer sites and cabins. **Buttermilk Falls Park** (☎ 607-273-5761 summer, 607-273-3440 winter; Rte 13) has a popular swimming hole at the foot of the falls, as does **Robert Treman Park** (☎ 607-273-3440; 105 Enfield Falls Rd), a few miles further out of town.

Dozens of wineries line the shores of Cayuga Lake, Lake Seneca and Lake Keuka. Two recommended Cayuga Lake wineries are **Goose Watch** (☎ 315-549-2599; www.goosewatch.com; 5480 Rte 89), which has stunning lake views, and **Thirsty Owl** (☎ 607-869-5805; www.thirstyowl.com; 6799 Elm Beach Rd).

Around 44 miles to the southwest is the charming town of Corning, home to Corning Glass Works and the hugely popular **Corning Museum of Glass** (☎ 800-732-6845; www.cmog.org; adult/child $12.50/free; 9am-5pm, to 8pm Memorial Day–Labor Day;). The massive complex is home to fascinating exhibits on glassmaking arts, complete with demonstrations and interactive items for kids.

SLEEPING & EATING

The gracious and grand **William Henry Miller Inn** (☎ 607-256-4553; www.millerinn.com; 303 N Aurora St, Ithaca; r incl breakfast $115-215;), only a few steps from the commons, is a completely restored historic home with luxuriously designed rooms – three have Jacuzzis – and a gourmet breakfast. Nearby is the also recommended **Inn on Columbia** (☎ 607-272-0204; www.columbiabb.com; 228 Columbia St, Ithaca; d $150;) which has a more modern, contemporary feel.

Ithaca has a great variety of international, gourmet and vegetarian restaurants. According to locals in the know, **Glenwood Pines** (☎ 607-273-3709; burgers $5; 11am-9:30pm Sun-Thu, 11am-10:30pm Fri & Sat), a modest roadside restaurant overlooking Lake Cayuga on Rte 89 four miles north of Ithaca, serves the best burger. In downtown Ithaca Commons, **Madeline's** (☎ 607-277-2253; 215 East State St; mains $18; 5:30-10pm Sun-Thu, 5:30-11pm Fri & Sat, 10:30am-2:30pm Sat & Sun) does Euro-Asian seasonal dishes like grilled New Zealand rack of lamb marinated with *hoisin*, lime and ginger ($23). Nearby **Moosewood Restaurant** (☎ 607-273-9610; www.moosewoodrestaurant.com; 215 N Cayuga St; mains $8-18; 11:30am-3pm Mon-Sat, 5:30-8:30pm Sun-Thu, 5:30-9pm Fri & Sat; V) is famous for its creative and constantly changing vegetarian menu and recipe books by founder Mollie Katzen.

Seneca Falls

After being excluded from an antislavery meeting, Elizabeth Cady Stanton and her friends drafted an 1848 declaration asserting that 'all men and women are created equal,' transforming this small town into the birthplace of this country's organized women's rights movement. The inspirational **Women's Rights National Historical Park** (☎ 315-568-0024; www.nps.gov/wori; 136 Fall St; 9am-5pm) has a small but impressive museum, as well as a visitor center offering tours of Cady Stanton's house. The surprisingly tiny **National Women's Hall of Fame** (☎ 315-568-8060; www.greatwomen.org; 76 Fall St; admission $3; 10am-5pm Mon-Sat, noon-5pm Sun May-Sep, 11am-5pm Wed-Sat Oct-Apr) honors American women such as first lady Abigail Adams, American Red Cross founder Clara Barton and civil-rights activist Rosa Parks.

ALBANY

Synonymous with legislative dysfunction as much as legislative power, Albany (or 'Smallbany' to jaded locals) remains a tourism backwater. It became New York State's capital in 1797 because of its geographic centrality to local colonies and its strategic importance in the fur trade. The railroad reached town in 1851 and helped solidify the city as an important transportation crossroads and manufacturing center. Albany is an architecturally diverse city, from the ostentatiously modern to the classically Victorian, but several blocks from the city center stately government buildings give way to derelict and neglected streets and a general feeling of malaise. **Lark Street** (www.larkstreet.org), north and uphill of downtown, has several restaurants and bars popular with university students when school is in session. Get information from **Albany Heritage Area Visitor Center** (☎ 518-434-0405; www.albany.org; 25 Quackenbush Sq; 9am-4pm Mon-Fri, 10am-3pm Sat, 11am-3pm Sun).

Sights & Activities

The **Empire State Plaza** comprises 98 acres of land and 10 government buildings, state agencies, a modern-art sculpture display and a performing-arts center that's dubbed 'the Egg' for its oval architecture. The plaza also has the tall Corning Tower, with an **observation deck** (☎ 518-474-2418; Corning Tower; admission free; 10am-4pm Mon-Sat) that overlooks the city and the Hudson River from its 42nd floor; and the **New York State Museum** (☎ 518-474-5877; www.nysm.nysed.gov; admission by donation; 9:30am-5pm), which documents the state's political, cultural and natural history. East of the plaza, **Albany Institute of History & Art** (☎ 518-463-4478; www.albanyinstitute.org; 125 Washington Ave; adult/child $10/6; 10am-5pm Wed-Sat, noon-5pm Sun) houses decorative arts and works by Hudson River School painters. **Albany City Hall** (☎ 518-434-5284; cnr Washington Ave & State St) is also worth a visit for its grand 19th-century architecture; call ahead for tour times.

Sleeping & Eating

There are a handful of chain hotels downtown. For more intimate and elegant accommodations, try the **Morgan State House Inn** (☎ 518-427-6063; www.statehouse.com; 393 State St; r incl breakfast from $135;). **74 State** (☎ 518-434-7410; www.74state.com; 74 State St; r incl breakfast from $180;) is a high-end boutique hotel in the heart of downtown.

To experience Albany in all its elegant and back-room-dealing clubby glory, try **Jack's Oyster House** (☎ 518-465-8854; 42 State St; mains $19-25; 11:30am-10pm), an almost 100-year-old family-owned restaurant serving huge porterhouse steaks and seafood dishes with a French twist. Lunchtime burgers and crab cakes are a more affordable option. A number of restaurants are located along Pearl St and Lark St; **A Taste of Greece** (☎ 518-426-9000; 193 Lark St; dishes $9-15; 11am-10pm Mon-Fri, 4-10pm Sat) does Hellenic standards in a simple setting.

Drinking & Entertainment

A strip of bars and clubs on North Pearl St downtown gets hopping when workers spill out of the nearby government buildings, including the **Bayou Cafe** (☎ 518-426-8550; 79 N Pearl St; mains 11-$19; 11:30-1:30am Mon-Tue, to 3:30am Thu-Sat). North of here on Lark St, one of the city's best spots for a drink is **Wine Bar & Bistro** (formerly Antica, Enoteca Old World Wine Bar; ☎ 518-463-2881; 200 Lark St; 5pm-midnight Mon-Sat), a miniature maze of cozy tables with a selection of several dozen very reasonably priced wines by the glass. **Justin's** (☎ 518-436-7008; www.justinsonlark.com; 301 Lark St; 11am-1am) has live jazz every night of the week, as well as serving dinner and drinks.

Getting There & Around

From the **bus terminal** (34 Hamilton St), **Adirondacks Trailways** (☎ 518-436-9651; www.trailwaysny.com) and **Greyhound** (☎ 518-436-9651; www.greyhound.com) head to/from New York City (one way $25, three hours). Amtrak stops out of New York City ($51 one way, 2½ hours), as do several major airlines flying into **Albany International Airport** (ALB; ☎ 518-242-2200; www.albanyairport.com; 737 Albany Shaker Rd) about 10 miles north from downtown. The **ShuttleFly** service leaves the airport for downtown several times each hour (from 6am to 11pm).

AROUND ALBANY

Cooperstown

For sports fans, **Cooperstown** (Chamber of Commerce; ☎ 607-547-9983; www.cooperstownchamber.org), 50 miles west of Albany, is instantly recognized as the home of the shrine for the national sport (baseball). But the small-town atmosphere and stunning views of the countryside around beautiful Ostego Lake make it worth visiting even for those who don't know the difference between ERA and RBI.

The **National Baseball Hall of Fame & Museum** (☎ 607-547-7200; 25 Main St; www.baseballhalloffame.org; adult/child $16.50/6; 9am-5pm, to 9pm summer;) has exhibits, a theater, library and an interactive statistical database. The old stone **Fenimore Art Museum** (☎ 607-547-1400; www.fenimoreartmuseum.org; 5798 Lake Rd; adult/child $11/5; 10am-4pm Tue-Sun) has an outstanding collection of Americana.

Several affordable low-slung motels line Rte 80 alongside the lake outside of town. The **Inn at Cooperstown** (☎ 607-547-5756; www.innatcooperstown.com; 16 Chestnut St; r incl breakfast from $100;) is a beautifully restored country home located just blocks from Main St. The tiny **Cooperstown Diner** (☎ 607-547-9201; 136½ Main St; mains $8) does burgers and comfort food. For a culinary treat try **Alex & Ika Restaurant** (☎ 607-547-4070; 149 Main St; mains $30; 11am-10pm Mon-Sat, to 3pm Sun); the spicy fried shrimpcake with passionfruit mascaparone can be recommended.

Saratoga Springs

When 'taking the waters' was equivalent to a trip to the hospital, this settlement north of Albany was world famous in its heyday in the early 1800s – Joseph Bonaparte, Napoleon's older brother and King of Spain, took his medicine here once. Despite the continued encroachment of large-scale retail chains, Saratoga Springs' main commercial street retains something of the artsy, laid-back feel of a college town and it's rightly famous for its performing arts, horse racing and the liberal-arts Skidmore College.

The only remaining bathhouse – the first was built in 1784 – is the **Roosevelt Baths and Spa** (☎ 518-226-4790; 40min spa $25; 9am-7pm) in the 2300-acre **Saratoga Spa State Park** (☎ 518-584-2535; www.saratogaspastatepark.org; 19 Roosevelt Dr; per car $4; sunrise-sunset). The mineral- and gas-infused waters are pumped underground from Lincoln Springs over a mile away. These days very hot tap water is added to the mix, though purists insist on going cold. Park grounds include golf courses, an Olympic-sized pool complex, multiuse trails, ice rinks and, world-famous **Saratoga Performing Arts Center** (☎ 518-587-3330; www.spac.org; 108 Ave of the Pines), with orchestra, jazz, pop, rock and dance performances. From late July to September, horse-racing fans flock to **Saratoga Race Course** (☎ 518-584-6200; www.saratogaracetrack.com), the country's oldest thoroughbred track.

In nearby Glens Falls, the remarkable Hyde Collection, housed in the **Hyde Collection Art Museum** (☎ 518-792-1761; www.hydecollection.org; 161 Warren St; admission free; 10am-5pm Tue-Sat, noon-5pm Sun), an impressive 1912 Florentine Renaissance–style villa, includes works by Rembrandt, Degas and Matisse.

There are more campsites around Lake George further north; however, the **Rustic Barn Campground** (☎ 518-654-6588; www.rusticbarncampground.com; 4748 Rte 9; campsites $26-30), on a wooded property with a pond and hiking trails about 9 miles north in Corinth, is an option. There are plenty of inns and B&Bs in town; the **Batcheller Mansion Inn** (☎ 518-584-7012; www.batchellermansion.com; 20 Circular St; r incl breakfast $160-420;) is a Victorian B&B straight out of a fairy tale. Eateries line Broadway and the intimate side streets, including **Ravenous** (☎ 518-581-0560; 21 Phila St; mains $10; 11:30am-8pm Tue-Thu, to 9pm Fri, 10am-9pm Sat, to 3pm Sun) which serves satisfyingly sweet and savory deluxe crepes.

THE ADIRONDACKS

Majestic and wild, the Adirondacks, a mountain range with 42 peaks over 4000ft high, rival any of the nation's wilderness areas for sheer awe-inspiring beauty. The 9375 sq miles of park and forest preserve that climb from central New York State to the Canadian border include towns, mountains, lakes, rivers and more than 2000 miles of hiking trails. There's good trout, salmon and pike fishing, along with excellent camping spots. The Adirondack Forest Preserve covers 40% of the park, preserving the area's pristine integrity. In colonial times settlers exploited the forests for beaver fur, timber and hemlock bark, but by the 19th century 'log cabin' wilderness retreats, both in the form of hotels and grand estates, became fashionable.

Lake George, Lake Placid & Saranac Lake

Maybe it's a blessing that the primary gateway to the Adirondacks, the village of **Lake George** (www.lakegeorgechamber.com), is a kitsch tourist town full of cotton candy, arcades and cheap souvenirs. The real reason for coming is the 32-mile-long lake itself, with its crystalline waters and forested shoreline, and once you leave the town behind the contrast is only more striking. Check out the **visitor center** (☎ 518-668-2846; 1 Beach Rd; 9am-5pm Oct-May, 10am-10pm Jun-Sept) for more information.

The state maintains wonderfully remote **campgrounds** (☎ 800-456-2267) on Lake George's islands, and one of several places for wilderness information is the **Adirondack Mountain Club** (☎ 518-668-4447; www.adk.org; 814 Goggins Rd). Small motels line the main street of Lake George.

It's something of a stretch to imagine this small mountain resort was once at the center of the world's attention – well, twice. In 1932 and 1980, **Lake Placid** hosted the Winter Olympics and the facilities and infrastructure remain; elite athletes still train here. Parts of the **Olympic sports centers** (☎ 518-523-4436; www.orda.org) are open to visitors, including ice arenas, a ski-jumping complex and a chance to **bobsled** ($75, Wed-Sun) with a professional driver. Hotels, restaurants, bookstores and shops line the frontier-like main street in town, which actually fronts Mirror Lake. Skiers should head to nearby **Whiteface Mountain** (www.whiteface.com), with 80 trails and a serious 3400ft vertical drop.

South of Lake Placid town, **Adirondack Loj** (☎ 518-523-3441; www.adk.org; dm/r incl breakfast

$50/155), run by the Adirondack Mountain Club (ADK), is a rustic retreat surrounded by mountains on the shore of peaceful Heart Lake. Wilderness campsites, lean-tos and cabins are also available.

Further north is the **Saranac Lake** region, where you'll find even more secluded wilderness areas – small lakes and ponds, ancient forests and wetlands. The town of Saranac Lake itself, once a center for tuberculosis treatments, feels a little down on its luck. However, the nearby **Porcupine Inn** (☎ 518-891-5160; www.theporcupine.com; 350 Park Ave; r incl breakfast $172-400;), housed in a classic Adirondacks-style lodge house, is run with loving care and perfection. A hike up to nearby Moody Pond and Baker Mountain affords excellent views of the area.

Getting There & Around

Both **Greyhound** (☎ 800-231-2222; www.greyhound.com) and **Adirondack Trailways** (☎ 800-776-7548; www.trailwaysny.com) serve various towns in the region. A car is really essential for exploring the region.

THOUSAND ISLANDS REGION

Virtually unknown to downstate New Yorkers, in part because of its relative inaccessibility, this region of over 1800 islands – from tiny outcroppings just large enough to lie down on to larger islands with roads and towns – is a scenic wonderland separating the US from Canada. From its source in the Atlantic Ocean far to the north, the wide and deceptively fast-moving St Lawrence River East empties into Lake Ontario at Cape Vincent. This portion of the river was once a summer playground for the very rich, who built large, stately homes here. It is still a popular vacation area known for its boating, camping and even shipwreck scuba diving.

Sackets Harbor was the site of a major battle during the War of 1812. While it is on Lake Ontario and not technically part of the Thousand Islands, it is a convenient starting point for touring the region. The centrally located and friendly **Ontario Place Hotel** (☎ 315-646-8000; www.ontarioplacehotel.com; 103 General Smith Dr; d from $90;) has comfortable, well-kept rooms. Several inviting restaurants line the street that runs down to the harbor front with waterside patio seating.

The relaxing, French-heritage village of **Cape Vincent** is at the western end of the river where it meets the lake. Drive out to the **Tibbetts Point Lighthouse** for stunning lake views; an attractive **hostel** (☎ 315-654-3450; www.hihostels.com; dm/r $18/40) shares the property. Nearby **Burnham Point State Park** (☎ 315-654-2522; Rte 12E; campsites $25) has wooded, lakeside campsites.

Clayton, 15 miles to the east along the Seaway Trail (Rte 12), has more than a dozen marinas and a few good eating choices in an area generally bereft of them. **TI Adventures** (☎ 315-686-2500; www.tiadventures.com; 1011 State St; half-day kayak rental $30) rents kayaks and runs white-water rafting trips down the Black River. Such activities are also organized by several companies in Watertown, a sizable city half an hour's drive to the south.

The owner/chef of friendly **Bella's** (☎ 315-686-2341; 602 Riverside Dr, Clayton; mains $6; 7am-6pm Mon-Fri, 8am-5pm Sun Apr-Oct), does excellent breakfast and veggie and meat sandwiches. **Lyric Coffee House** (☎ 315-686-4700; 246 James St, Clayton; 8am-8pm Mon & Sat, to 6pm Tue-Fri, 10am-5pm Sun;), surprisingly modern for this town, serves specialty coffee drinks, gelato, pastries and specials such as lasagna for lunch; there's live music some Fridays and Saturdays.

Further east, **Alexandria Bay** (Alex Bay), an early-20th-century resort town, is still the center of tourism on the American side – its sister city is Gananoque in Canada. While it is run-down and tacky, there's enough around to keep you occupied: go-karts, mini-golf and a **drive-in movie theater** (www.baydrivein.com) are only minutes away. It's also the departure point for ferries to Heart Island, where **Boldt Castle** (☎ 800-847-5263; www.boldtcastle.com; adult/child $6.50/4; 10am-6:30pm mid-May–mid-Oct) marks the love story of a rags-to-riches New York hotelier who built the castle for his beloved wife. Sadly, she died before its completion. The same hotelier once asked his chef to create a new salad dressing, which was popularized as 'Thousand Island' – an unfortunate blend of ketchup, mayonnaise and relish. **Uncle Sam's Boat Tours** (☎ 800-253-9299; www.unclesamboattour.com, 45 James St; 2-nation tour adult/child $17/8.50) has several departures daily for its recommended two-nation cruise (visiting both the US and Canadian sides of the river), which allows you to stop at Boldt Castle and ride back on one of its half-hourly ferries for free.

our pick **Wellesley Island State Park** (☎ 518-482-2722; www.nysparks.com; campsites from $15) offers camping, which is probably the best accommodations option even for the raccoon-averse.

Many sites are almost directly on the riverfront and some have their own 'private' beaches. The island is only accessible by crossing a toll portion ($2.50) of the Thousand Islands Bridge. There is a small convenience store/diner on the way to the campgrounds, but your best bet is to stock up on supplies at one of the large grocery stores in Alex Bay or Clayton.

There are several supposedly upscale resorts around Alex Bay, though none is especially good value. Probably the best midrange choice is **Capt Thomson's Resort** (☎ 315-482-9961; www.captthomsons.com; 45 James St; d from $80;) on the waterfront next to the office for Uncle Sam's Boat Tours.

Ogdensburg, 37 miles north of Alex Bay, is the birthplace of Frederic Remington (1861–1909), an artist who romanticized the American West in paintings and sculpture. The **Frederic Remington Art Museum** (☎ 315-393-2425; www.fredericremington.org; 303 Washington St; admission $8; 11am-5pm Wed-Sat, 1pm -5pm Sun) has some of his sculptures, paintings and personal effects.

Jet Blue (☎ 800-538-2583; www.jetblue.com) has regular daily flights to Hancock International Airport (SYR) in Syracuse, an hour and a half south. Several major car-rental agencies have offices in the airport. Bicyclists will enjoy the mostly flat Scenic Byway Trail.

WESTERN NEW YORK

Still trying to find their feet after hemorrhaging industries and population for over a decade, most of the cities in this region live in the shadow of Niagara Falls, a natural wonder that attracts upward of 12 million visitors from around the world per year. Buffalo was once a booming industrial center and the terminus of the Erie Canal, which used to serve as the transportation lifeline connecting the Great Lakes and the Atlantic Ocean; it now boasts an indigenous culinary scene and bohemian enclaves. Syracuse and Rochester are both home to big universities; the latter is worth a visit for the **George Eastman House and International Museum of Photography & Film** (☎ 585-271-3361; www.eastmanhouse.org; 900 East Ave, Rochester; adult/child/student $10/4/6; 10am-5pm Tue-Sat, to 8pm Thu, 1-5pm Sun).

Niagara Falls

It's a tale of two cities and two falls, though either side of this international border affords views of an undeniably dramatic natural wonder. There are honeymooners and heart-shaped Jacuzzis, arcades, tacky shops and kitsch boardwalk-like sights, but as long as your attention is focused nothing can detract from the majestic sight. The closer to the falls you get the more impressive they seem and the wetter you become. For good reason, the Canadian side is where almost everyone visits, though it's easy to stroll back and forth between the two (see p1157).

ORIENTATION & INFORMATION

The falls are in two separate towns: Niagara Falls, New York (USA) and Niagara Falls, Ontario (Canada). The towns face each other across the Niagara River, spanned by the Rainbow Bridge, which is accessible for cars and pedestrians.

On the US side, the **Niagara Falls Convention & Visitors Bureau** (☎ 800-338-7890; www.nfcvb.com; cnr 4th & Niagara Sts; 8:30am-5pm) has all sorts of guides; its more helpful Canadian counterpart is located near the base of the **Skylon Tower** (☎ 905-356-6061; www.niagarafallstourism.com; 5400 Robinson St; 9am-5pm).

SIGHTS & ACTIVITIES

You can see side views of the **American Falls** and their western portion, the **Bridal Veil Falls**, which drops 180ft, by simply walking across the pedestrian bridge from Canada. Take the **Prospect Point Observation Tower** (☎ 716-278-1796; admission $1, free from 5pm; 9:30am-7pm) elevator up for a vista. Cross the bridge to **Goat Island** for other viewpoints, including Terrapin Point, which has a fine view of Horseshoe Falls and pedestrian bridges to the Three Sisters Islands in the upper rapids. From the north corner of Goat Island, an elevator descends to the **Cave of the Winds** (☎ 716-278-1730; adult/child $11/8), where walkways go within 25ft of the cataracts (raincoats provided). The **Maid of the Mist** (☎ 716-284-8897; www.maidofthemist.com; tours adult/child $13.50/8; 9am-7pm Apr-Sep, to 5pm Oct;) boat trip around the bottom of the falls has been a major attraction since 1846 and is highly recommended. Boats leave every 15 minutes from the base of the Prospect Park Observation Tower on the US side and from the bottom of Clifton Hill on the Canadian side.

For those seeking more of an adrenaline rush, check out **Niagara Helicopters** (☎ 905-357-5672; niagarahelicopters.com; 3731 Victoria Ave; 12min $105) and **Whirlpool Jet Boat Tours** (☎ 888-438-4444; www.whirlpooljet.com; 1 hr adult/child $50/42).

BORDER CROSSING: CANADIAN NIAGARA FALLS

When people say they are visiting the falls they usually mean the Canadian side, which is naturally blessed with a far superior view. Canada's **Horseshoe Falls** are wider and especially photogenic from Queen Victoria Park; at night they're illuminated with a colored light show. The **Journey Behind the Falls** (adult/child US$11/6.50; 9am-8:30pm Mon-Fri, 9am-11pm Sat & Sun Jun-Sep, 9am-8pm daily Sep & Oct, 9am-7pm daily Nov & Dec, 9am-5:30pm Mon-Fri, 9am-7:30pm Sat & Sun Jan-May) gives access to a spray-soaked viewing area beneath the falls.

Casino Niagara (905-374-3598; www.casinoniagara.com; 5705 Falls Ave) pales in comparison to upscale **Fallsview Casino Resort** (888-325-5788; www.fallsviewcasinoresort.com; 6380 Fallsview Blvd), which has a mall of expensive shops and restaurants. Niagara on the Lake, 15km to the north, is a small town full of elegant B&Bs and a famous summertime theater festival.

Virtually every major hotel chain has at least several locations on the Canadian side of the falls. Backpackers can head to the somewhat messy **HI Niagara Falls Hostel** (905-357-0770; www.hostellingniagara.com; 4549 Cataract Ave; dm/r US$18/34;). Newly renovated **Skyline Inn** (800-263-7135; Falls Ave; r from US$60; P) is a good choice if you're seeking a budget place away from the noise. River Rd is lined with B&Bs but **Chestnut Inn** (905-374-7623; www.chestnutinnbb.com; 4983 River Rd; r from US$90;), a tastefully decorated colonial home with a wraparound porch, stands above the rest. Parents looking to keep the kids occupied should head immediately to the **Great Wolf Lodge** (800-605-9653; www.greatwolf.com; 3950 Victoria Ave; ste from US$229; P), whose centerpiece is an enormous indoor water park.

Obvious tourist-trap restaurants are a dime a dozen in and around Clifton Hill. American fare and chains dominate the culinary scene. The Lundy's Lane area has tons of cheap eats.

SLEEPING & EATING

There's virtually no reason to spend the night on the US side of the falls. The purple glass–covered Seneca Niagara Casino & Hotel towers over the surrounding derelict blocks. Some of the hotel chains are represented – Ramada Inn, Howard Johnson, Holiday Inn – but unless you're a fugitive on the run, cross the border to Canada. There are a few restaurants near the bridge area, including several Indian takeaway places. See the boxed text, above for lodging and dining information.

GETTING THERE & AROUND

From the **NFTA Terminal** (Niagara Frontier Transportation Authority; www.nfta.com; Portage Rd, btwn Main & Pine Sts) around one mile east of the Rainbow Bridge (a dodgy area, especially at night), bus 40 goes to Buffalo ($2.65, one hour) for air and bus connections; and there is an extensive local bus service. The **Amtrak train station** (716-285-4224) is about 2 miles northeast of downtown. From Niagara Falls, daily trains go to Buffalo ($11, 35 minutes), Toronto, $30, three hours) and New York City ($80, nine hours). The **Greyhound & Trailways terminal** (905-357-2133; 4555 Erie Ave) is on the Canadian side.

Parking costs $5 to $10 a day on either side of the falls. Most of the midrange hotels offer complimentary parking to guests, while upscale hotels tend to charge $10 to $20 a day for the privilege.

Crossing the Rainbow Bridge to Canada and return costs US$3.25/1 for cars/pedestrians. There are customs and immigration stations at each end – US citizens are now required to have their passport available (see p1152). Driving a rental car from the US over the border should not be a problem (see p1150 and p1157) but check with your rental company before you depart.

Buffalo

This undeservedly maligned working-class city does have long, cold winters and its fair share of abandoned industrial buildings, but Buffalo (population 276,000) also has a vibrant community of college students and 30-somethings living well in cheap real estate and gorging on this city's unique and tasty cuisine. Native local hero Ani DiFranco, who has chosen her hometown as the place to base her indie music label, is at the vanguard of a continuing effort to revitalize this former booming terminus of the Erie Canal. Settled by the French in 1758 – its name is believed to derive from *beau fleuve* (beautiful river) – and just an hour south of Niagara Falls, Buffalo is about an eight-hour trip from New York City.

The helpful **Buffalo Niagara Convention & Visitors Bureau** (☎ 716-852-2356; www.buffalocvb.org; 617 Main St; 10am-4pm Mon-Fri, 10am-2pm Sat) has good walking-tour pamphlets and a great website.

SIGHTS & ACTIVITIES

Architecture buffs will have a field day here, starting at the **Prudential Building** (28 Church St). It was designed by Louis Sullivan in 1895 as the Guaranty Building, and used an innovative steel-frame construction to create the first modern skyscraper. Be sure to glimpse the stunning art-deco **City Hall** (65 Niagara Sq), built in 1931, and the neo-Gothic **Old Post Office** (121 Ellicot St) from 1894. The **M&T Bank** (545 Main St) is topped with a gilded dome of 140,000 paper-thin sheets of 23.75-karat gold leaf. Six **Frank Lloyd Wright houses** are a highlight; the 1904 **Darwin Martin House** (☎ 716-856-3858; 125 Jewett Pkwy; tours $15-40) and neighboring **Barton House** (118 Summit Ave) are accessible by appointment. For details about local architecture check out www.walkbuffalo.com.

North of downtown, sprawling Delaware Park was designed by Frederick Law Olmsted. Its jewel is the **Albright-Knox Art Gallery** (☎ 716-882-8700; www.albrightknox.org; 1285 Elmwood Ave; admission $12, free 3-10pm Fri; 10am-5pm Wed-Thu, Sat & Sun, to 10pm Fri), a sizable museum including some of the best French Impressionists and American masters. Directly across the street is the newest addition to the city's art scene, the **Burchfield Penney** (☎ 716-878-6011; www.yournewburchfieldpenney.com; 1300 Elmwood Ave; admission $7; 10am-5pm Tue, Wed & Fri, to 9pm Thu, 1pm-5pm Sun), exhibiting works, mostly American, from the late 19th century to contemporary. Buffalo also has good science, history and children's museums and a fine zoo. The **Elmwood** neighborhood, stretching along Elmwood Ave between Allen St and Delaware Park, is dotted with hip cafés, restaurants, boutiques and bookstores. Hertle Ave in North Buffalo also has several good restaurants and cafés.

Guided tours of the **Theodore Roosevelt Inaugural National Historic Site** (☎ 716-884-0095; www.nps.gov/thri; 641 Delaware Ave; adult/child $10/5; 9am-5pm Mon-Fri, noon-5pm Sat & Sun) in the Ansley-Wilcox house examine the tale of Teddy's emergency swearing-in here following the assassination of William McKinley in 1901.

This is a hard-core sports town and locals live and die with the **NFL Buffalo Bills** (☎ 716-648-1800; www.buffalobills.com) football team and the **Buffalo Sabres** (☎ 716-855-4100; www.sabres.com), the city's NHL ice-hockey team. A lower-key but no less recommended option to rub elbow's with local sports fanatics is to catch the **Buffalo Bisons** (☎ 716-846-2000; www.bisons.com), the AAA affiliate of the major-league baseball team, the New York Mets, in their trendy-traditional downtown ballpark.

SLEEPING

Standard chains line the highways around the city. Budget travelers can sleep at the **Hostelling International – Buffalo Niagara** (☎ 716-852-5222; www.hostelbuffalo.com; 667 Main St; dm/r $25/60;). The **Beau Fleuve** (☎ 800-278-0245; www.beaufleuve.com; 242 Linwood Ave; r $115-165;) is a historic B&B in the Linwood neighborhood. Downtown has the **Adam's Mark Hotel** (☎ 716-845-5100; www.adamsmark.com; 120 Church St; r from $100;), the Hyatt Regency and Holiday Inn. For truly luxurious accommodations and flawless service, head to the very special and grand **Mansion on Delaware Avenue** (☎ 716-886-3300; www.mansionondelaware.com; 414 Delaware Ave; r incl breakfast from $175;).

EATING

Inspired by the ambitions of a Bill Murray character in an obscure movie, every Labor Day weekend Buffalo celebrates its **National Buffalo Wing Festival** (www.buffalowing.com). Organizers brag that since 2002 nearly two tons of wings have been consumed. One of the largest outdoor markets in the region is the **Elmwood-Bidwell Farmers Market** (Bidwell Ave, at Elmwood Ave; www.elmwoodmarket.org; 8am-1pm Sat mid-May–mid-Dec), open only to local growers of the freshest produce.

Buffalo is curiously blessed with an abundance of eateries serving unique, tasty and cheap dishes. For the famous deep-fried chicken wings covered in a spicy sauce, head to the landmark **Anchor Bar** (☎ 716-886-8920; 1047 Main St; 10 wings $9; 10am-11pm Mon-Thu, 10am-1am Fri & Sat;), which claims credit for inventing the 'delicacy.' Locals in the know say **Duff's** (☎ 716-834-6234; 3651 Sheridan Dr, Amherst; 10 wings $8; 11am-11pm) wings are tastier. **Bob & John's** (☎ 716-836-5411; 1545 Hertel Ave; sandwiches $5, 10 wings $8; 11am-11pm) serves beef-on-weck (sliced roast beef on a crispy German kaiser roll sprinkled with caraway seeds), buffalo wings and, according to some, the best pizza in Buffalo. **Ted's** (☎ 716-834-6287; Sheridan Ave; hot dog $2;

10:30am-11pm Mon-Sun) fast-food specialty is hot dogs, foot-longs, any way you like 'em.

In business for 85 years, **Chef's** (☎ 716-856-9187; 291 Seneca St; mains 7-$17; 11am-9pm Mon-Sat) is a Buffalo landmark doling out classic red-sauce Italian dishes. For slightly more upscale eats try **Betty's** (☎ 716-362-0633; 370 Virginia St; mains $12; 8am-9pm Tue, 8am-10pm Wed-Fri, 9am-10pm Sat, 9am-3pm Sun). In the neighborhood of Allentown, Betty's does interpretations of American comfort food. **Left Bank** (☎ 716-882-3509; 511 Rhode Island St; mains $10-19; 5-11pm Mon-Thu, to midnight Fri & Sat, 11am-10pm Sun), housed in an attractive 100-year-old building, is an atmospheric restaurant serving large portions of homemade ravioli, grilled meat and good wine.

DRINKING & ENTERTAINMENT

Bars along Chippewa St (aka Chip Strip) are open until 4am and cater primarily to the frat-boy crowd. More eclectic neighborhoods such as Elmwood, Linwood and Allentown have more than their fair share of late-night options. From late May through July a **summer concert series** (☎ 716-856-3150; www.buffaloplace.com) draws an eclectic mix of new and established artists to outdoor spaces in downtown.

Nietzches (☎ 716-886-8539; 248 Allen St) is a legendary dive-bar with live music, and a few storefronts down is **Allen Street Hardware Cafe** (☎ 716-882-8843; 245 Allen St), where the best local musicians play to regularly packed houses. Several gay bars are clustered around the south end of Elmwood, including **Fugazi** (☎ 716-881-3588; 503 Franklin St; 5pm-2am Mon-Thu, 8pm-2am Fri & Sat, 8pm-midnight Sun), which specializes in flavored martinis.

GETTING THERE & AROUND

Buffalo Niagara International Airport (BUF; ☎ 716-630-6000; www.buffaloairport.com), about 16 miles east of downtown, is a regional hub. Jet Blue Airways has inexpensive round-trip fares from New York City (one hour, from around $140). Buses arrive and depart from the **Greyhound terminal** (☎ 716-855-7533; 181 Ellicott St). **NFTA** (☎ 716-855-7211; www.nfta.com) local bus 40 goes to the transit center on the American side of Niagara Falls ($2.65, one hour). From the downtown **Amtrak train station** (☎ 716-856-2075; 75 Exchange St), you can catch trains to major cities (to NYC is $55, eight hours; to Albany $43, six hours; to Syracuse $24, 2½ hours). The Exchange Street station can feel dodgy, especially at night; locals recommend the Buffalo-Depew station (55 Dick Rd), 6 miles east.

NEW JERSEY

There are McMansions, à la the *Real Housewives* of New Jersey (NJ), and guys who speak with thick Jersey accents like characters from a TV crime drama. And the areas around the turnpike and harbors near NYC are dystopic landscapes of decaying industry. However, nearby are plenty of high-tech and banking headquarters and sophisticated, progressive people living in charming towns. Unfortunately, political scandals have become at least as synonymous with the state as its beautiful shoreline. Get off the exits, flee the malls and you are privy to a beautiful side of the state: a quarter is farmland and it has 127 miles of beaches, as well, of course, as two of New York City's greatest icons: the statue of Liberty and Ellis Island.

Information

Asbury Park Press (www.app.com)
Jersey Journal (www.nj.com/jjournal)
Newark Star-Ledger (www.nj.com/starledger)
NJ.com (www.nj.com) Statewide news from all the major dailies.
State of New Jersey Division of Travel & Tourism (☎ 609-777-0885; www.visitnj.org) Statewide tips on sights, accommodations and festivals.

Though NJ is made up of folks who love their cars, there are other transportation options:
New Jersey PATH train (see p191) Goes to northern New Jersey.
New Jersey Transit (www.njtransit.com) Operates buses out of NYC's Port Authority and trains out of Penn Station, NYC.
New York Waterway (☎ 800-533-3779; www.nywaterway.com) Ferries to northern New Jersey.

NORTHERN NEW JERSEY

Stay east and you'll experience the Jersey urban jungle. Go west to find its opposite: the peaceful, refreshing landscape of the Delaware Water Gap and rolling Kittatinny Mountains.

Hoboken & Jersey City

A sort of television-land version of a cityscape, Hoboken is a cute little urban pocket just across the Hudson River from New York City – and, because of cheaper rents that lured pioneers over at least a decade

NEW JERSEY FACTS

Nickname Garden State
Population 8.7 million
Area 8722 sq miles
Capital city Trenton (population 83,000)
Other cities Newark (population 281,000)
Sales tax 7%
Birthplace of Musician Count Basie (1904–84), singer Frank Sinatra (1915–98), actor Meryl Streep (b 1949), musician Bruce Springsteen (b 1949), actor John Travolta (b 1954), musician Jon Bon Jovi (b 1962), rapper Queen Latifah (b 1970), pop band Jonas Brothers: Kevin (b 1987), Joseph (b 1989), Nicolas (b 1992)
Home of The first movie (1889), first professional baseball game (1896), first drive-in theater (1933), the Statue of Liberty
Famous for The Jersey Shore, the setting for *The Sopranos,* Bruce Springsteen's musical beginnings
Number of White Castle fast-food restaurants 76
Driving distances Newark to NYC 11 miles, Atlantic City to NYC 135 miles

ago, a sort of sixth city borough, too. It's no longer a cheapo destination – a slick W Hotel opened here in 2008 – but it's still a fun place for a brief jaunt. On weekends the bars and live-music venues come alive – especially the legendary **Maxwell's** (☎ 201-653-1703; www.maxwellsnj.com; 1039 Washington St), which has featured up-and-coming rock bands since 1978. But the town also has some lovely residential streets and a leafy, revitalized waterfront – a far cry from when the gritty *On the Waterfront* was filmed here. The **Hoboken Historical Museum** (☎ 201-656-2240; www.hobokenmuseum.org; 1301 Hudson St; admission free; 🕑 2-7pm Tue-Thu, 1-5pm Fri, noon-5pm Sat & Sun) gives a great overview.

High-rise buildings housing condominiums and the offices of financial firms seeking lower rents have transformed **Jersey City** (www.destinationjerseycity.com) for better or worse from a primarily blue-collar and immigrant neighborhood into a 'restored' area for the upwardly mobile. Its biggest draw is the 1200-acre **Liberty State Park** (☎ 201-915-3440; www.libertystatepark.org; 🕑 6am-10pm), which hosts outdoor concerts with the Manhattan skyline as a backdrop and has a great bike trail, and also operates **ferries** (☎ 877-523-9849; www.statuecruises.com) to Ellis Island and the Statue of Liberty (see p151). Also in the park is the expansive and modern **Liberty Science Center** (☎ 201-200-1000; www.lsc.org; adult/child $11.50, extra for IMAX & special exhibits; 🕑 9am-5pm; 🚸), which is especially great for kids.

Newark & Around

Though many NYC-bound travelers fly into Newark International Airport (see p190), few stick around to see the city they've landed in. Too bad, since **Newark** (population 281,000, www.gonewark.com) – long mired in images of the 1960s race riots that made it off-limits to many for so long – has been in the midst of a renaissance for years now, even more so since its young, high-profile and ambitious mayor, Cory Booker, took office in 2006. Only the city's third mayor since 1970 (Sharpe James, who defeated Booker in 2002 and was convicted of fraud in 2008, was in office for 20 years), Booker has struggled to reduce crime and endemic corruption, all the while dealing with dwindling finances.

Many are drawn here to experience the thriving Portuguese culture of the **Ironbound District**; its restaurant-lined Ferry St lies right outside the city's neoclassic **Penn Station** (accessible from NYC's same-named station via NJ Transit). Also not far from here is the **Newark Museum** (☎ 973-596-6550; www.newarkmuseum.org; 49 Washington St; suggested donation $10; 🕑 noon-5pm Wed-Fri, 10am-5pm Sat & Sun Oct-Jun, noon-5pm Sat & Sun Jul-Sep), which has a renowned Tibetan Collection and hosts the annual Newark Black Film Festival in June. The **New Jersey Performing Arts Center** (🕑 973-642-8989; www.njpac.org; 1 Center St) is the city's crowning jewel, hosting national orchestras, operas, dance, jazz and other performances. The **Prudential Center** (www.prucenter.com) has become the focal point for sports, home to the New Jersey Devils hockey team, plus basketball games and concerts.

Other attractions include the grand **Cathedral Basilica of the Sacred Hearts** (☎ 973-484-4600; www.cathedralbasilica.org; 89 Ridge St) and the

400-acre Frederick Law Olmstead–designed **Branch Brook Park**, with some 2700 cherry trees that blossom in April.

Delaware Water Gap

The Delaware River meanders in a tight S-curve through the ridge of NJ's Kittatinny Mountains, and its beauteous image turned this region into a resort area beginning in the 19th century. The **Delaware Water Gap National Recreation Area** (☎ 570-426-2452; www.nps.gov/dewa), which comprises land in both New Jersey and Pennsylvania, was established as a protected area in 1965, and today it's still an unspoiled place to swim, boat, fish, camp, hike and see wildlife – just 70 miles east of New York City. For more information about rafting the river and on combining a trip here with other nearby regions see p229 and p197.

The 3348-acre **Kittatinny Valley State Park** (☎ 973-786-6445; www.state.nj.us/dep/parksandforests) is home to lakes with boat launches, lime outcroppings and campsites, plus former railroads that have been converted into hiking and cycling trails. **High Point State Park** (☎ 973-875-4800), also great for camping and hiking, has a monument which, at 1803ft above sea level, affords wonderful views of surrounding lakes, hills and farmland.

CENTRAL NEW JERSEY

Otherwise known as the armpit (only for how it looks on a map, of course), this region is home to the state capital, Trenton, and a string of beautiful, wealthy communities including Princeton, at the eastern border of Pennsylvania.

Princeton & Around

Settled by an English Quaker missionary, the tiny town of **Princeton** (www.visitprinceton.org) is filled with lovely architecture and several noteworthy sites, number one of which is its Ivy League **Princeton University** (www.princeton.edu), which was built in the mid-1700s and soon became one of the largest structures in the early colonies. The town's **Palmer Square**, built in 1936, is a lovely place to shop and stroll. The **Historical Society of Princeton** (☎ 609-921-6748; www.princetonhistory.org; 158 Nassau St; tours adult/child $7/4) leads historical walking tours of the town on Sundays at 2pm, and the **Orange Key Guide Service & Campus Information Office** (☎ 609-258-3060; www.princeton.edu/orangekey) offers free university tours.

Accommodations are expensive and hard to find during graduation time in May and June, but beyond that it should be easy to arrange for a stay at one of several atmospheric inns, including the traditionally furnished **Nassau Inn** (☎ 609-921-7500; www.nassauinn.com; 10 Palmer Sq; r incl breakfast from $169;) and the **Inn at Glencairn** (☎ 609-497-1737; www.innatglencairn.com; 3301 Lawrenceville Rd; r incl breakfast from $195;), a renovated Georgian manor with old-world style and modern amenities.

Trenton

It may not be the most beautiful place, but New Jersey's capital, **Trenton** (www.trentonnj.com) has several historic sites worth stopping in on – especially if you can pair it up with a trip to Philly (p213) or Atlantic City (p210).

You can tour the grand **New Jersey Statehouse** (☎ 609-633-2709; 125 West State St; admission free; 10am-3pm Mon-Fri, from noon Sat) and visit the **Old Barracks Museum** (☎ 609-396-1776; www.barracks.org; Barrack St; adult/child $8/6; 10am-5pm), built in 1758 and now the state's last remaining barracks from the French and Indian War. The **New Jersey State Museum** (☎ 609-292-6464; www.state.nj.us/state/museum; 205 W State St; admission free; 9am-5pm Tue-Sat, noon-5pm Sun), with a planetarium, is home to diverse collections from fossils to fine art. The massive **Trenton Farmers Market** (☎ 609-695-2998; www.thetrentonfarmersmarket.com; 960 Spruce St; 9am-6pm Tue-Sat, 10am-4pm Sun May-Oct, 9am-6pm Thu-Sat Nov-Apr) has vendors hawking fresh produce, baked goods and crafts.

JERSEY SHORE

Perhaps the most famous and revered feature of New Jersey is its sparkling shore, stretching from Sandy Hook to Cape May and studded with resort towns from tacky to classy. Though it's mobbed during summer weekends, you could find yourself wonderfully alone on the sand come early fall.

Sandy Hook & Red Bank

At the northernmost tip of the Jersey Shore is the **Sandy Hook Gateway National Recreation Area** (☎ 732-872-5970; www.nps.gov/gate; parking per car $10 7am-4pm Memorial Day–Labor Day; sunrise-sunset), a 6-mile-long sandy barrier beach at the entrance to New York Harbor (and you can see the city skyline from your beach blanket on clear days). The ocean side of the peninsula has wide, sandy beaches (including a nude area at Gunnison Beach) edged by an extensive system of bike trails, while the bay side is great for fishing or wading. The brick buildings of the abandoned coastguard station, **Fort Hancock** (1-5pm Sat & Sun) houses a small museum. The **Sandy Hook Lighthouse**, which offers guided tours, is the oldest in the country.

The town next door, the **Highlands**, has seafood restaurants on the water, offering a great end to your day before hopping on the **Seastreak** (800-262-8743; www.seastreak.com), a fast ferry service that runs between here and NYC (round trip $40, one hour). It's also home to the **Twin Lights Historic Site** (732-872-1814; www.twin-lights.org; admission free; 10am-4:30pm daily late May–early Sep, 10am-4:30pm Wed-Sun early Sep–late May) and a swank hotel, the **Blue Bay Inn** (732-708-7600; www.bluebayinn.com; 51 First Ave; r $159-299;).

About 10 miles inland is the artsy town of **Red Bank**, with a hoppin' main strip of hipster shops, galleries and cafés, plus a sizable Mexican population (and plenty of authentic Mexican-food eateries, New Jersey Transit stops here.

Asbury Park & Ocean Grove

Asbury Park experienced passing prominence in the 1970s when Bruce Springsteen 'arrived' at the **Stone Pony** (732-502-0600; 913 Ocean Ave) nightclub, which is still offering live music. After that, the town went through a major decline, followed by a still-in-progress comeback – led by wealthy gay men from NYC who snapped up blocks of forgotten Victorian homes and storefronts to refurbish. Though the place still has an unfinished quality to it (and rough pockets that should be avoided), there's still plenty to enjoy (especially if you're a gay man). The sprawling **Antique Emporium of Asbury Park** (732-774-8230; 646 Cookman Ave; 11am-5pm Mon-Sat & noon-5pm Sun) has two levels of amazing finds, while trendy **Restaurant Plan B** (732-807-4710; 705 Cookman Ave; mains $10-25; 4:30-9pm Tue-Thu & Sun, to 10pm Fri, to 11pm Sat) serves excellent weekend brunch. **Moonstruck** (732-988-0123; 517 Lake Ave; mains $15-32; 4-9pm Wed, Thu & Sun, to 11pm Fri & Sat), housed in a striking Victorian building, does eclectic Italian fare. The boardwalk is a lovely place for an afternoon stroll.

The town immediately to the south, **Ocean Grove**, is a fascinating place to wander. Founded by Methodists in the 19th century, the place retains what's left of a post–Civil War **Tent City** revival camp – now a historic site with 114 cottage-like canvas tents clustered together that are used for summer homes. The town has well-preserved Victorian architecture and a 6500-seat wooden auditorium, and there are many beautiful, big-porched **Victorian inns** to choose from for a stay; visit www.oceangrovenj.com for guidance.

Monmouth County Beaches

In between Sandy Hook and Asbury Park sits the town of **Long Branch**. Though its elegance is gone, a mall-like food-and-shopping complex by the ocean called **Pier Village** (www.piervillage.com) packs 'em in for everything from Greek dinners to swimwear shopping. Just a bit inland from here is the famed **Monmouth Park Race Track** (732-222-5100; www.monmouthpark.com; grandstand/clubhouse $3/5; 11:30am-6pm May-Aug), where you can see thoroughbred racing in a gracious, historic setting.

Belmar (www.belmar.com) has beautiful beaches, a spirited boardwalk with some arcade games, and beachfront food shacks that can get mobbed when the bars close at 2am. **Bradley Beach** (www.bradleybeachonline.com), next door, is Belmar's quiet, peaceful sister with row after row of adorable summer cottages and a beautiful stretch of shore. **Spring Lake** (www.springlake.org) is a classy community once known as the 'Irish Riviera,' with lush gardens, Victorian houses, gorgeous beaches and elegant accommodations, including the bright and airy **Grand Victorian at Spring Lake** (449-5327; www.grandvictorianspringlake.com; 1505 Ocean Ave; r from $79;) and the more traditionally furnished **Chateau Inn and Suites** (732-974-2000; www.chateauinn.com; 500 Warren Ave; r incl breakfast $119-329;).

Ocean County Beaches

Kids will love nearby **Point Pleasant** (www.pointpleasantbeach.com), home to **Jenkinson's Boardwalk** (732-892-0600; www.jenkinsons.com) with an aquarium, rides, arcade games, funhouse, miniature golf and dining options.

Just below there, the narrow **Barnegat Peninsula** barrier island extends some 22 miles south from Point Pleasant. In its center, **Seaside Heights** (www.seasideheights.net) sucks in the raucous 20-something summer crowds with beaches, boardwalks, bars, nightclubs, arcades, two amusement piers and motel crash pads. Occupying the southern third of Barnegat

Peninsula is **Island Beach State Park** (☎ 732-793-0506; www.islandbeachnj.org; per car weekday/weekend $6/10), a 10-mile barrier island that's pure, untouched dunes and wetlands. **Long Beach Island** (www.longbeachisland.com) is south of here, with beautiful beaches balanced by a string of summer homes, eateries and bars. The latest overnight hot spot is **Daddy O** (☎ 609-361-5100; www.daddyohotel.com; 4401 Long Beach Blvd; r $195-375;), a sleek boutique hotel and restaurant (mains $12 to $35) near the ocean.

SOUTH JERSEY

A mixture of kitsch and country, the state's southern region – closely identified with neighboring Philadelphia in Pennsylvania – represents the best of New Jersey's extremes.

Pine Barrens

Locals call this region the Pinelands – and like to carry on the lore about the one million acres of pine forest being home to a mythical beast known as the 'Jersey Devil.' Containing several state parks and forests, the area is a haven for bird-watchers, hikers, campers, canoeists and all-round nature enthusiasts. A good outfitter is **Pine Barrens Canoe Rental** (☎ 609-726-1515; www.pinebarrenscanoe.com; 3107 Rte 563; per day kayak $37, canoe $48), which has maps and other details about all trips in the area. **Wharton State Forest** (☎ 609-561-0024) is one of the good places to canoe – as well as hike and picnic – and the 40,000-acre **Edwin B Forsythe National Wildlife Refuge** (☎ 609-652-1665; www.forsythe.fws.gov.gov) is paradise for bird-watchers.

Nestled within the Pine Barrens region is the quirky **Historic Village at Allaire** (☎ 732-919-3500; www.allairevillage.org; adult/child $3/2; noon-4pm Wed-Sun late May–early Sep, noon-4pm Sat & Sun Nov-May), the remains of what was a thriving 19th-century village called Howell Works. You can still visit various 'shops,' all run by folks in period costume.

Atlantic City

If you pause and look past the blinging lights and white noise of clanking quarters you'll see busloads of retirees making a beeline for the slots. Inside the casinos that never see the light of day, it's easy to forget there's a wide white-sand beach just outside and boarded-up shop windows a few blocks in the other direction. Since 1977 when the state approved gambling casinos in the hope of revitalizing this fading resort, known throughout the late 19th and early 20th century for its grand boardwalk and oceanside amusement pier, 'AC,' as locals call, it has been on a bumpy ride. New hotel-casinos like the massive Borgata, which has brought glitz and glamour, can seem like harbingers of a real recovery. A slew of nightclubs; the **Pier at Caesars** (www.thepiershopsatcaesars.com), a spiffy shopping mall jutting out into the Atlantic; a trendy boutique hotel; and an express train service from NYC have followed. The developer and TV personality Donald Trump has put his stamp on the city in the form of some of the more ostentatiously designed buildings. If gambling isn't your thing, the boardwalk offers up an all-star roster of summer indulgence, from funnel cakes to go-karts to cheesy gift shops.

ORIENTATION & INFORMATION

The **Atlantic City Convention & Visitors Bureau** (☎ 609-348-7100; www.atlanticcitynj.com; 2314 Pacific Ave; 9am-5pm), under the giant tipi in the middle of the Atlantic City Expwy, with another location right on the boardwalk at Mississippi Ave, can provide you with maps and accommodations deals. **Atlantic City Weekly** (www.acweekly.com) has useful info on events, clubs and eateries. The small **Atlantic City Historical Museum** (☎ 609-347-5839; www.acmuseum.org; cnr Boardwalk & New Jersey Aves; admission free; 10am-4pm) provides a quirky look at AC's past.

SLEEPING & EATING

The noncasino, super-trendy **Chelsea** (☎ 800-548-3030; www.thechelsea-ac.com; 111 S Chelsea Ave; r from $80;) and the 43-story chic boutique-style **Water Club & Spa** (☎ 800-800-8817; www.thewaterclubhotel.com; 1Renaissance Way; r from $119;) are welcome additions to the uninspired standard casino accommodations. The Water Club's next-door sister or rather mother hotel, is the Las Vegas–style **Borgata** (☎ 866-692-6742; www.theborgata.com; r $149-400;), an enormous destination-worthy resort with high-style rooms, a full-service spa, major concert hall, four five-star restaurants and, of course, a grand casino, which draws a relatively classy crowd. After undergoing a thorough renovation, **Harrah's Atlantic City** (☎ 609-441-5000; www.harrahs.com; 777 Harrah's Blvd; r $149-349) features a spa and a massive glass-domed pool that shares space with Jacuzzis, cabanas, a pool bar and deck-lounge

WHAT THE...?

Drive around the beach communities just south of Atlantic City and something massive, gray and kitsch will stop you in your tracks: **Lucy the Margate Elephant** (☎ 609-823-6473; www.lucytheelephant.org; 9200 Atlantic Ave, Margate City, NJ; adult/child $6/3; ⌚ 10am-8pm Mon-Sat, 10am-5pm Sun), a 65ft-high wooden pachyderm constructed in 1881 as a developer's truly weird scheme to attract land buyers to the area. It was variously used as a hotel, beach cottage, private mansion and last, a tavern, but rowdy patrons almost destroyed her. Now recognized on the National Register of Historic Places, Lucy is open for tours during summer, starting every half-hour, weather permitting.

areas – extremely popular with off-duty casino workers late on Saturday nights. A handful of motor inns and cheap motels line Pacific Ave, a block inland from the boardwalk; however, these tend to have questionable hygiene and security standards.

The best in-casino dining is to be had at the Borgata, home to Wolfgang Puck American Grille, Bobby Flay Steak, Fornelletto (Italian) and Tony Luke's in the food court for cheesesteaks and pork sandwiches. Head to **Caesars** (☎ 609-348-4411; www.caesarsac.com; 2100 Pacific Ave) and Harrah's for the best all-you-can-eat buffets ($19 to $24). Good (and more affordable) food can be found in the 'real' part of downtown, too. **Mexico Lindo** (☎ 609-345-1880; 2435 Atlantic Ave; dishes $5-12; ⌚ 8am-10pm) is a no-frills favorite among Mexican locals and serves big, cheap breakfasts – as does **Hannah G's** (☎ 609-823-1466; 7310 Ventnor Ave; dishes $6-10; ⌚ 7am-2pm Mon-Sun), a family-owned spot in nearby Ventnor.

DRINKING & ENTERTAINMENT

It's the **casinos**, as you may have guessed, that are the biggest draw here. As in Las Vegas, they all have themes – Far East, Ancient Rome, Wild West – but they're superficially done. Inside they're all basically the same: nonstop clanging, flashing and miles of blackjack, poker, baccarat and craps tables.

Beyond the casino walls you'll find the wide, oceanfront **boardwalk**, the first in the world. Enjoy a walk or a hand-pushed rolling-chair ride (there's a price chart posted inside each chair) and drop in on one of several casino boardwalk clubs and lounges.

Check out the calendar at the **Borgata** (opposite), which has a comedy club, an intimate concert hall and a massive music venue that hosts big acts. The venerable **House of Blues** (☎ 609-236-2583; www.hob.com; 801 Boardwalk, at the Showboat) is home to various bars, a restaurant and a plush music hall with well-known headliners.

GETTING THERE & AWAY

The small **Atlantic City International Airport** (ACY; ☎ 609-645-7895; www.acairport.com) is a 20-minute drive from the center of Atlantic City, and a great option for reaching any part of South Jersey or Philadelphia. Taxis and a shuttle van service also run from the airport to the city.

There are a busload of bus options to AC, including NJ Transit (round-trip $28.50, 2½ hours) and Greyhound (round-trip $31, 2½ hours), both leaving from New York's Port Authority, and **Capitol Trailways** (☎ 717-564-4900; www.thebusstop.com; round-trip $30-35), from points in Pennsylvania. A casino will often refund much of the fare (in chips, coins or coupons) if you get a bus directly to its door.

New Jersey Transit (☎ 973-762-5100; www.njtransit.com) trains only go to Atlantic City from Philadelphia (one way $13, 1½ hours). A new double-decker train service, **ACES** (Atlantic City Express Train Service; ☎ 877-326-7428; www.aces.com; ⌚ Fri-Sun), connecting AC to Penn Station, (NYC; from $29, two hours 40 minutes) was inaugurated in the summer of 2009.

The Wildwoods & Ocean City

South of Atlantic City, the three towns of **North Wildwood**, **Wildwood** and **Wildwood Crest** are an archaeological find – whitewashed motels with flashing neon signs, turquoise curtains and pink doors, especially in Wildwood Crest, a kitsch slice of 1950s Americana. Wildwood, a party town popular with teens and young overseas visitors, is the main social focus. The **Greater Wildwood Chamber of Commerce** (☎ 609-729-4000; www.gwcoc.com; 3306 Pacific Ave, Wildwood; ⌚ 9am-5pm Mon-Fri, shorter hours in winter) hands out information on self-guided tours around the 'doo-wop' motels. The beach is free, and the 2-mile-long boardwalk has several piers that are host to roller coasters, Ferris wheels and weekly fireworks displays in summer. About 250 motels offer rooms for $50 to

$250, making it a good option if Cape May (below) is booked out.

Ocean City (www.oceancityvacation.com), meanwhile, is a truly kitsch and old-fashioned family holiday spot, home to dune-swept beaches and a dizzying number of child-centric arcades and themed playlands. Motels are plentiful, cheap (average $70 per night) and old-fashioned, as are the myriad crab shacks and seafood joints.

Cape May

Founded in 1620, Cape May – the only place in the state where the sun both rises and sets over the water – is on the state's southern tip and is the country's oldest seashore resort. Its sweeping beaches get crowded in summer, but the stunning Victorian architecture is attractive year-round. Contact the **Cape May County Chamber of Commerce** (☎ 609-465-7181; www.cmccofc.com) for details about the area.

In addition to 600 gingerbread-style houses, the city boasts antique shops and places for whale- and bird-watching, and is just outside **Cape May Point State Park** (☎ 609-884-2159) and its 157ft **Cape May Lighthouse** (☎ 609-884-5404; adult/child $7/3). The sandy **beach** is the main attraction in summer months.

Cape May's B&B options are endless, with the majority leaning toward the overstuffed and chintzy. The classic, sprawling **Congress Hall** (☎ 609-884-8422; www.congresshall.com; 251 Beach Ave; r $100-465; P ⊠ ⁙ ◻) has a range of beautiful quarters for various budgets, plus there's a cool on-site restaurant and bar.

The tiny, eclectic **Louisa's Café** (☎ 609-884-5884; 104 Jackson St; dishes $14-23; ⏲ 5-9pm Tue-Sat June–early Sep) is the town's prize midrange eatery.

PENNSYLVANIA

In a state so large it's unsurprising that geography in part determines identity. The further west you go the closer you are to the rest of America. Philadelphia, once the heart of the British colonial empire and the intellectual and spiritual motor of its demise, is firmly ensconced culturally in the East Coast. Residents of Pittsburgh and western Pennsylvania (PA), on the other hand, are proud to identify themselves as part of the city or immediate region, relishing their distinctiveness from East-Coasters and their blue-collar reputation. Moving east to west, the terrain becomes more rugged and you begin to appreciate the sheer size and diversity of this one state. Philly's Independence Park and historic district offer an ideal opportunity to come to some understanding of this nation's origins. Nearby, the battle sites of Gettysburg and Valley Forge provide another chance to travel back in time. But the city and state offer more than the clichés associated with school field trips. Stunning natural forests and mountain areas including the Poconos and Allegheny National Forest provide endless outdoor adventures. Both Philly and Pittsburgh are vibrant university cities with thriving music, performance and art scenes. Frank Lloyd Wright's architectural masterpiece, Fallingwater, and Amish country, not to mention the region's small, artsy towns, are perfect for weekend getaways.

PENNSYLVANIA FACTS

Nicknames Keystone State, Quaker State
Population 12.4 million
Area 46,058 sq miles
Capital city Harrisburg (population 53,000)
Other cities Philadelphia (population 1.45 million), Pittsburgh (population 313,000), Erie (population 102,000)
Sales tax 6%
Birthplace of Writer Louisa May Alcott (1832–88), dancer Martha Graham (1878–1948), artist Andy Warhol (1928–87), movie star Grace Kelly (1929–82), comic Bill Cosby (b 1937)
Home of US Constitution, the Liberty Bell, first daily newspaper (1784), first auto service station (1913), first computer (1946)
Famous for Soft pretzels, Amish people, Philadelphia cheesesteak, Pittsburgh steel mills
Animal celebrity Punxsutawney Phil (of Groundhog Day)
Driving distances Philadelphia to NYC 100 miles, Philadelphia to Pittsburgh 306 miles

History

William Penn, a Quaker, founded his colony in 1681, making Philadelphia its capital. His 'holy experiment' respected religious freedom (a stance that attracted other minority religious sects, including the well-known Mennonite and Amish communities), liberal government and even indigenous inhabitants. But it didn't take long for European settlers to displace those communities, thus giving rise to Pennsylvania's status as the richest and most populous British colony in North America. It had great influence on the independence movement and, much later, became an economic leader through its major supply of coal, iron and timber, followed by raw materials and labor during WWI and WWII. In the postwar period its industrial importance gradually declined. Urban-renewal programs and the growth of service, high-tech and health-care industries have boosted the economy, most notably in Philadelphia and Pittsburgh.

Information

Pennsylvania Travel and Tourism (☎ 800-847-4872; www.visitpa.com) The official tourism department has a comprehensive website featuring maps, videos and suggested itineraries. It also operates 15 welcome centers scattered around the state's borders, stocked with maps, guides, regional info and well-informed staffers.

PHILADELPHIA

Although it may seem like a little sibling to NYC, which is less than 90 miles away, Philadelphia is more representative of what East Coast city living is like. And in the minds of many, it offers every upside of urban life – burgeoning food, music and art scenes, neighborhoods with distinct personalities, copious parkland and maybe equally importantly, relatively affordable real estate. The older, preserved buildings in historic Philadelphia provide a picture of what colonial American cities once looked like – based on a grid with wide streets and public squares.

For a time the second-largest city in the British Empire (after London), Philadelphia became a center for opposition to British colonial policy. It was the new nation's capital at the start of the Revolutionary War and again after the war until 1790, when Washington, DC, took over. By the 19th century, New York City had superseded Philadelphia as the nation's cultural, commercial and industrial center. Though urban renewal has been going on for decades, some parts of the city formerly populated by industrial workers are blighted and worlds away from the carefully manicured lawns and park-service-glutted historic district around the Liberty Bell and Independence Hall.

Orientation

Philadelphia is easy to navigate. Most sights and accommodations are within walking distance of each other, or a short bus ride away. East–west streets are named; north–south streets are numbered, except for Broad and Front Sts.

Historic Philadelphia includes Independence National Historic Park and Old City, which extends east to the waterfront. West of the historic district is Center City, home to Penn Sq and City Hall. The Delaware and Schuylkill (*skoo*-kill) Rivers border South Philadelphia, which features the colorful Italian Market, restaurants and bars. West of the Schuylkill, University City has two important campuses as well as a major museum. Northwest Philadelphia includes the genteel suburbs of Chestnut Hill and Germantown, plus Manayunk, with plenty of bustling pubs and hip eateries. The South St area, between S 2nd, 10th, Pine and Fitzwater Sts, has bohemian boutiques, bars, eateries and music venues. Northern Liberties is an up-and-coming neighborhood with eclectic cafés and restaurants.

Information

BOOKSTORES

Giovanni's Room (☎ 215-923-2960; 345 S 12th St; 🕑 11:30am-7pm Mon-Sat, from 1pm Sun) Gay and lesbian books and periodicals.

House of Our Own (☎ 215-222-1576; 3920 Spruce St; 🕑 10am-7pm Mon-Sat, noon-5pm Sun) Used books, small-press publications, academic literature and frequent readings.

Joseph Fox Bookshop (☎ 215-563-4184; 1724 Sansom St; 🕑 10-6pm, to 7pm Wed) An independent in Rittenhouse Sq, with good architecture, design, children's and literature sections.

INTERNET ACCESS

The highly touted plan to make Philadelphia the first major American city with free wi-fi has mostly fallen by the wayside.

Central Library (☎ 215-686-5322; 1901 Vine St; 9am-5pm Mon-Wed, to 6pm Thu & Fri, to 5pm Sat, 1-5pm Sun;) Free internet and wi-fi access.

The following nice cafés have free wi-fi:
Green Line (☎ 215-222-0799; 4426 Locust St, at 45th St, West Philadelphia;)
Intermezzo Café & Lounge (☎ 215-222-4300; 3131 Walnut St, West Philadelphia;)
Philadelphia Java Co (☎ 215-928-1811; 518 S 4th St, Society Hill;)

INTERNET RESOURCES & MEDIA

City Paper (www.citypaper.net) Free weekly available at street boxes around town.
HX Philadelphia (www.myspace.com/hxphilly) Free gay weekly with nightlife and culture listings, available at nightspots and Giovanni's Room (p213).
Philadelphia Citysearch (www.philadelphia.citysearch.com) Restaurant, bar, club hotel and shopping listings.
Philadelphia Daily News (www.philly.com/dailynews) A tabloid-style daily.
Philadelphia Inquirer (www.philly.com/mld/inquirer) The region's top daily newspaper.
Philadelphia Magazine (www.phillymag.com) A monthly glossy.
Philadelphia Weekly (www.philadelphiaweekly.com) Free alternative available at street boxes around town.
Philly.com (www.philly.com) News, listings and more, courtesy of the *Philadelphia Inquirer*.
WHYY 91-FM (www.whyy.org) Local National Public Radio affiliate.

MEDICAL SERVICES

Graduate Hospital (☎ 215-893-2000; 1800 Lombard St; 24hr) Close to the business district.
Pennsylvania Hospital (☎ 215-829-3000; www.pennhealth.com/hup; 800 Spruce St; 24hr)

MONEY

There are exchange bureaus in every terminal of the Philadelphia International Airport, though the best rates are at banks in the city. Most banks are open 10am to 5pm or 6pm Monday and to between 1pm and 3pm Saturday.

POST

B Free Franklin Post Office (☎ 215-597-8974; 316 Market St; 9am-5pm Mon-Sat) Postmarks stamps with Franklin's unique signature.
Main Post Office (☎ 215-895-9320; 3000 Chestnut St, at 30th St; 8am-9pm Mon-Sat, 11am-7pm Sun) Call for other branch locations.

TOURIST INFORMATION

Greater Philadelphia Tourism Marketing Corp (www.gophila.com; 6th St, at Market St) The highly developed, nonprofit visitors bureau has comprehensive visitor information. Its welcome center shares space with the NPS center.
Independence Visitor Center (☎ 215-597-8787, 800-537-7676; www.independencevisitorcenter.com; 6th St, at Market St; 8:30am-5:30pm) Run by the NPS, the center distributes useful visitor guides and maps, and sells tickets for the various official tours that depart from nearby locations, including Trolley Works & 76 Carriage Company (p221).

Sights & Activities

INDEPENDENCE NATIONAL HISTORIC PARK

This L-shaped 45-acre **park** (☎ 215-597-8787, 800-537-7676; www.nps.gov/inde), along with Old City, has been dubbed 'America's most historic square mile.' Once the backbone of the United States government, today it is the backbone of Philadelphia's tourist trade. Stroll around and you'll see storied buildings in which the seeds for the Revolutionary War were planted and the US government came into bloom. You'll also find beautiful, shaded urban lawns dotted with large groups of schoolchildren and costumed actors. Most sites are open every day from 9am to 5pm, and some are closed Monday. Note that you must call or stop in to the **Independence Visitor Center** (see above) to make a timed reservation before visiting the high-volume Independence Hall, and beware that lines for the Liberty Bell can be extremely long.

Liberty Bell Center (6th & Market Sts) is Philadelphia's top tourist attraction and was commissioned to commemorate the 50th anniversary of the Charter of Privileges (Pennsylvania's constitution, enacted in 1701 by William Penn). The 2080lb bronze bell was made in London's East End by the Whitechapel Bell Foundry in 1751. The bell's inscription, from Leviticus 25:10, reads: 'Proclaim liberty through all the land, to all the inhabitants thereof.' The bell was secured in the belfry of the Pennsylvania State House (now Independence Hall) and tolled on important occasions, most notably the first public reading of the Declaration of Independence in Independence Sq. The bell became badly cracked during the 19th century; despite initial repairs it became unusable in 1846 after tolling for George Washington's birthday.

Independence Hall (Chestnut St, btwn 5th & 6th Sts) is the 'birthplace of American government,' where delegates from the 13 colonies met to approve the Declaration of Independence on July 4, 1776. An excellent example of Georgian architecture, it sports understated lines that reveal Philadelphia's Quaker heritage. Behind Independence Hall is the spiffy **Independence Square**, where the Declaration of Independence was first read in public.

The highly recommended **National Constitution Center** (☎ 215-409-6700; www.constitutioncenter.org; 525 Arch St; adult/child $12/8; 🕑 9:30am-5pm Mon-Fri, to 6pm Sat, noon-5pm Sun; 👪), right next to the visitor center, makes the United States Constitution sexy and interesting for a general audience through theater-in-the-round reenactments. There are exhibits including interactive voting booths and Signer's Hall, which contains lifelike bronze statues of the signers in action.

Other attractions in this historic park include: **Carpenters' Hall**, owned by the Carpenter Company, the USA's oldest trade guild (1724), which is the site of the First Continental Congress in 1774; **Library Hall**, where you'll find a copy of the Declaration of Independence, handwritten in a letter by Thomas Jefferson, plus first editions of Darwin's *On the Origin of the Species* and Lewis and Clark's field notes; **Congress Hall** (S 6th & Chestnut Sts), the meeting place for US Congress when Philly was the nation's capital; and **Old City Hall**, finished in 1791, which was home to the US Supreme Court until 1800. The **Franklin Court** complex, a row of restored tenements, pays tribute to Benjamin Franklin with a clever underground museum displaying his inventions, as well as details on his many other contributions (as statesman, author and journalist) to society. At the **B Free Franklin Post Office** (see opposite) mail receives a special handwritten Franklin postmark (Ben was also a postmaster) and there's a small **US Postal Service Museum**. **Christ Church** (☎ 215-627-2750; N 2nd St), completed in 1744, is where George Washington and Franklin worshiped.

Philosophical Hall (☎ 215-440-3400; 104 S 5th St; admission $1; 🕑 10am-4pm Thu-Sun Mar–Labor Day & Fri-Sun Labor Day–Feb), south of Old City Hall, is the headquarters of the American Philosophical Society, founded in 1743 by Benjamin Franklin. Past members have included Thomas Jefferson, Marie Curie, Thomas Edison, Charles Darwin and Albert Einstein.

Second Bank of the US (Chestnut St, btwn 4th & 5th Sts), modeled after the Greek Parthenon, is an 1824 marble-faced Greek Revival masterpiece that was home to the world's most powerful financial institution until President Andrew Jackson dissolved its charter in 1836. The building then became the Philadelphia Customs House until 1935, when it became a museum. Today it's home to the **National Portrait Gallery** (Chestnut St; 🕑 11am-4pm Wed-Sun; admission free), housing many paintings by Charles Willson Peale, America's top portrait artist at the time of the American Revolution.

OLD CITY

Old City – the area bounded by Walnut, Vine, Front and 6th Sts – picks up where Independence National Historical Park leaves off. And, along with Society Hill, Old City was early Philadelphia. The 1970s saw revitalization, with many warehouses converted into apartments, galleries and small businesses. Today it's a quaint and fascinating place for a stroll.

The tiny, cobblestoned **Elfreth's Alley** (www.elfrethsalley.org; off 2nd St, btwn Arch & Race Sts) is believed to be the oldest continuously occupied street in the USA. Its 32 well-preserved brick row houses are still inhabited with real live Philadelphians, so be considerate as you stroll along, and be sure to stop into **Elfreth's Alley Museum** (☎ 215-574-0560; No 126; adult/student $5/1; 🕑 10am-5pm Tue-Sat, from noon Sun) which was built in 1755 by blacksmith and alley namesake Jeremiah Elfreth; it's been restored and furnished to its 1790 appearance.

The nearby **Betsy Ross House** (☎ 215-686-1252; www.betsyrosshouse.org; 239 Arch St; suggested donation adult/child $3/2; 🕑 10am-5pm daily Apr-Sep, closed Mon Oct-Mar) is where it is believed that Betsy Griscom Ross (1752–1836), upholsterer and seamstress, may have sewn the first US flag.

The cool **Clay Studio** (☎ 215-925-3453; www.theclaystudio.org; 139 N 2nd St; admission free; 🕑 11am-7pm Tue-Sat, noon-6pm Sun) exhibits staid as well as oddball works in ceramic; it's been in Old City since 1974 and is partially responsible for the development of the area's burgeoning gallery scene. The distinctly translucent facade of the **National Museum of American Jewish History** (☎ 215-923-3811; www.nmajh.org; 55 N 5th St; 🕑 10am-5pm Mon-Thu, to 3pm Fri, noon-5pm Sun)

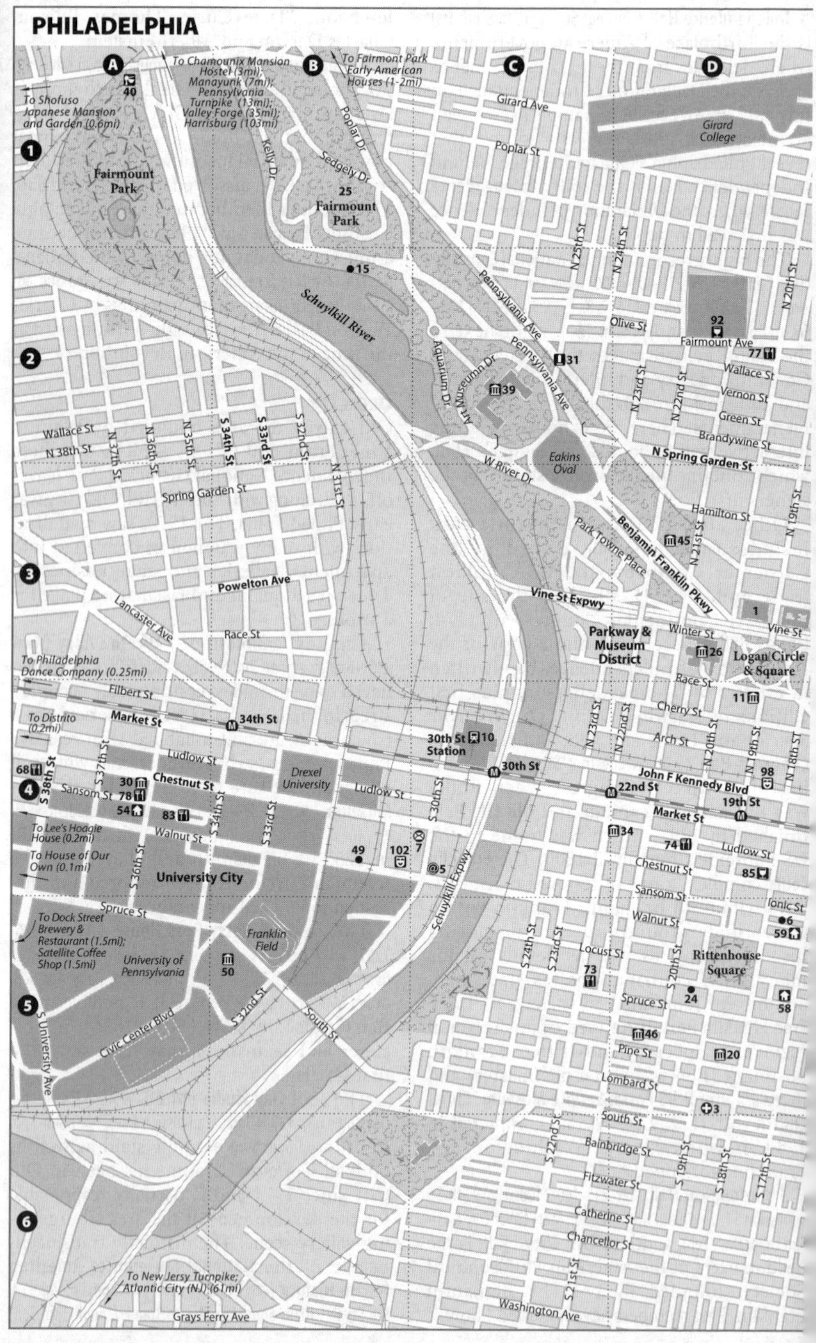
PHILADELPHIA
To Chamounix Mansion Hostel (3mi); Manayunk (7mi); Pennsylvania Turnpike (13mi); Valley Forge (35mi); Harrisburg (103mi)
To Fairmont Park Early American Houses (1-2mi)
To Shofuso Japanese Mansion and Garden (0.6mi)
Fairmount Park
Girard Ave
Girard College
Poplar St
Poplar Dr
Kelly Dr
Sedgely Dr
Schuylkill River
Pennsylvania Ave
Olive St
Fairmount Ave
Wallace St
Vernon St
Green St
Brandywine St
N Spring Garden St
Hamilton St
Aquarium Dr
Art Museum Dr
W River Dr
Eakins Oval
Park Towne Place
Benjamin Franklin Pkwy
Vine St Expwy
Vine St
Winter St
Parkway & Museum District
Logan Circle & Square
Race St
Cherry St
Arch St
John F Kennedy Blvd
Market St
Ludlow St
Chestnut St
Sansom St
Walnut St
Ionic St
Locust St
Rittenhouse Square
Spruce St
Pine St
Lombard St
South St
Bainbridge St
Fitzwater St
Catherine St
Chancellor St
Washington Ave
Wallace St
N 38th St
N 37th St
N 36th St
N 35th St
S 34th St
S 33rd St
S 32nd St
N 31st St
Spring Garden St
Powelton Ave
Lancaster Ave
Race St
Filbert St
Market St
34th St
30th St Station
30th St
22nd St
19th St
Drexel University
University City
Franklin Field
University of Pennsylvania
Civic Center Blvd
South St
S University Ave
Schuylkill Expwy
Grays Ferry Ave
To Philadelphia Dance Company (0.25mi)
To Distrito (0.2mi)
To Lee's Hoagie House (0.2mi)
To House of Our Own (0.1mi)
To Dock Street Brewery & Restaurant (1.5mi); Satellite Coffee Shop (1.5mi)
To New Jersey Turnpike; Atlantic City (NJ) (61mi)
N 25th St
N 24th St
N 23rd St
N 22nd St
N 21st St
N 20th St
N 19th St
N 18th St
S 24th St
S 23rd St
S 22nd St
S 21st St
S 20th St
S 19th St
S 18th St
S 17th St
S 38th St
S 37th St
S 36th St
S 34th St
S 33rd St
S 30th St
S 32nd St

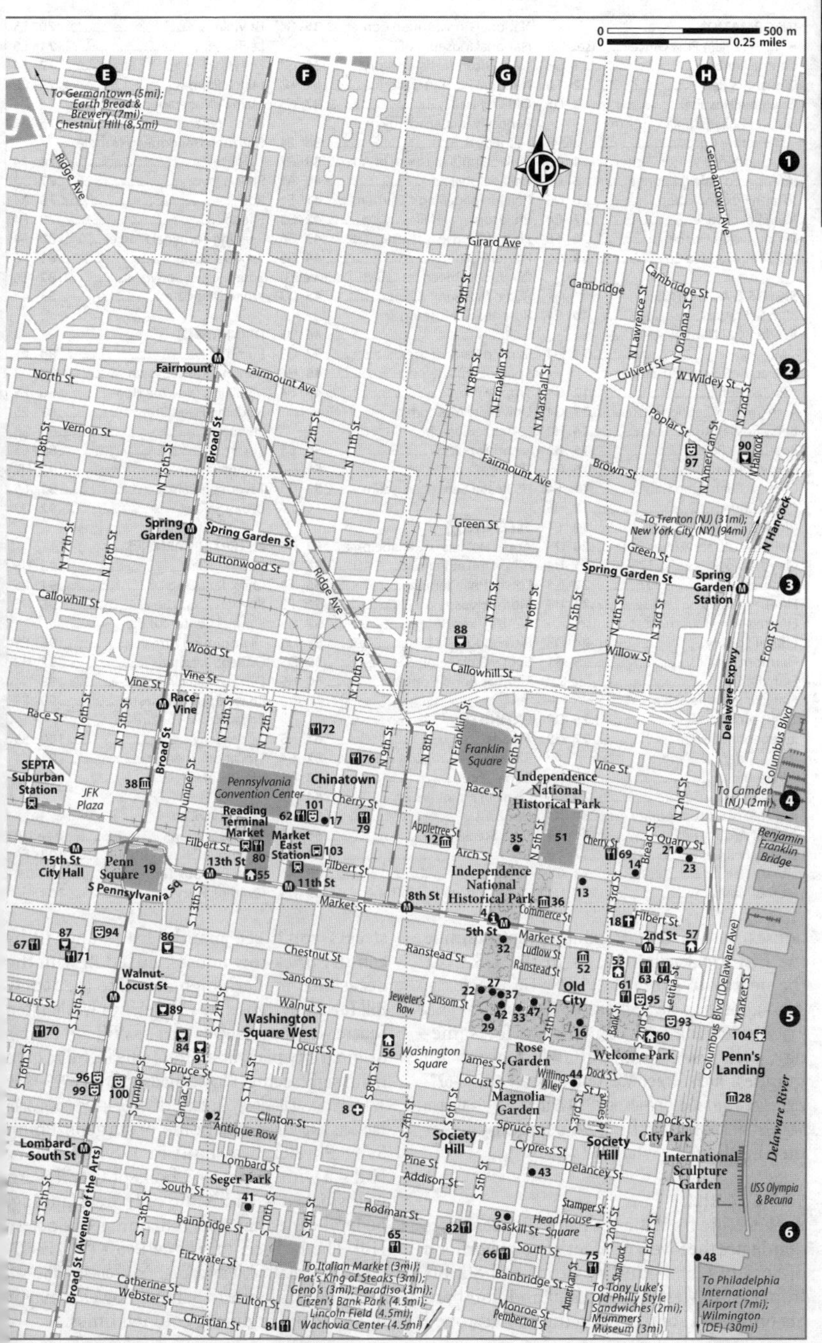
0 500 m
0 0.25 miles
E
F
G
H
1
2
3
4
5
6
To Germantown (5mi); Earth Bread & Brewery (7mi); Chestnut Hill (8.5mi)
Ridge Ave
Germantown Ave
Girard Ave
Cambridge
Cambridge St
N 9th St
N Lawrence St
N Orianna St
Fairmount
North St
Fairmount Ave
N 8th St
N Franklin St
N Marshall St
Culvert St
W Wildey St
N 2nd St
Poplar St
N American St
N Hancock
Vernon St
N 18th St
Broad St
N 15th St
N 12th St
N 11th St
Fairmount Ave
Brown St
90
97
To Trenton (NJ) (31mi); New York City (NY) (94mi)
N Hancock
N 17th St
N 16th St
Spring Garden
Spring Garden St
Green St
Green St
Spring Garden St
Spring Garden Station
Buttonwood St
Ridge Ave
Callowhill St
N 7th St
N 6th St
N 5th St
N 4th St
N 3rd St
Front St
88
Wood St
Willow St
Delaware Expwy
Vine St
Vine St
Callowhill St
Race-Vine
Race St
N 16th St
N 15th St
Broad St
N 13th St
N 12th St
N 10th St
N 9th St
N 8th St
N Franklin St
N 6th St
Columbus Blvd
72
Franklin Square
76
Vine St
SEPTA Suburban Station
38
N Juniper St
Pennsylvania Convention Center
Chinatown
Independence National Historical Park
JFK Plaza
Race St
Cherry St
101
N 2nd St
To Camden (NJ) (2mi)
Reading Terminal Market
62
17
79
Appletree St
12
51
Quarry St
Benjamin Franklin Bridge
Market East Station
103
Filbert St
Arch St
35
Cherry St
69
Bread St
21
23
15th St City Hall
Penn Square
19
13th St
80
55
11th St
Filbert St
Independence National Historical Park
14
S Pennsylvania Sq
13
Market St
8th St
36
N 3rd St
4
Commerce St
18
Filbert St
5th St
Market St
2nd St
57
67
87
94
86
32
Ludlow St
71
Chestnut St
Ranstead St
Ranstead St
52
53
61
63
64
Letitia St
Walnut-Locust St
Sansom St
22
27
37
Old City
Jeweler's Row
Sansom St
47
Locust St
89
S 12th St
Walnut St
42
33
S 4th St
95
93
Washington Square West
29
16
Bank St
S 2nd St
Columbus Blvd (Delaware Ave)
Market St
5
70
S 15th St
84
91
Locust St
56
Rose Garden
60
104
Penn's Landing
S 16th St
S Juniper St
Washington Square
Welcome Park
96
S 11th St
Spruce St
James St
Dock St
99
100
Camac St
S 8th St
Locust St
Willings Alley
44
St James Pl
Magnolia Garden
28
Delaware River
2
8
Clinton St
Antique Row
S 7th St
S 6th St
Spruce St
S 3rd St
Dock St
Lombard-South St
Society Hill
Cypress St
Society Hill
City Park
Lombard St
Pine St
Delancey St
International Sculpture Garden
S 15th St
Seger Park
Addison St
43
S 5th St
USS Olympia & Becuna
South St
41
S 13th St
S 10th St
S 9th St
Rodman St
Stamper St
Bainbridge St
9
Head House Square
Gaskill St
82
Front St
6
65
S 2nd St
Fitzwater St
South St
75
66
Shancock
48
To Italian Market (3mi); Pat's King of Steaks (3mi); Geno's (3mi); Paradiso (3mi); Citzen's Bank Park (4.5mi); Lincoln Field (4.5mi); Wachovia Center (4.5mi)
Catherine St
Webster St
Broad St (Avenue of the Arts)
Bainbridge St
American St
To Tony Luke's Old Philly Style Sandwiches (2mi); Mummers Museum (3mi)
To Philadelphia International Airport (7mi); Wilmington (DE) (30mi)
Fulton St
Monroe St
Pemberton St
Christian St
81

INFORMATION
B Free Franklin Post Office (see 52)
Central Library **1** D3
Giovanni's Room **2** F5
Graduate Hospital **3** D5
Greater Philadelphia Tourism Marketing Corp (see 4)
Independence Visitor Center **4** G5
Intermezzo Café & Lounge **5** C4
Joseph Fox Bookshop **6** D5
Main Post Office **7** C4
Pennsylvania Hospital **8** F5
Philadelphia Java Co **9** G6

SIGHTS & ACTIVITIES
30th St Station **10** C4
Academy of Natural Sciences Museum **11** D4
African American Museum in Philadelphia **12** G4
Arch Street Meeting House **13** G4
Betsy Ross House **14** H4
Boathouse Row **15** B2
Carpenters' Hall **16** G5
Chinese Friendship Gate **17** F4
Christ Church **18** H5
City Hall **19** E4
Civil War Library & Museum **20** D5
Clay Studio **21** H4
Congress Hall **22** G5
Elfreth's Alley **23** H4
Elfreth's Alley Museum (see 23)
Ethical Society **24** D5
Fairmont Park **25** B1
Franklin Court (see 52)
Franklin Institute Science Museum **26** D3
Independence Hall **27** G5
Independence Seaport Museum **28** H5
Independence Square **29** G5
Institute of Contemporary Art **30** A4
Joan of Arc Statue **31** C2
Liberty Bell Center **32** G5
Library Hall **33** G5
Mutter Museum **34** D4
National Constitution Center **35** G4
National Museum of American Jewish History **36** G4
National Portrait Gallery (see 47)
Old City Hall **37** G5
Pennsylvania Academy of the Fine Arts **38** E4
Philadelphia Museum of Art **39** C2
Philadelphia Zoo **40** A1
Philadelpia's Magic Garden **41** F6
Philosopical Hall **42** G5
Physick House **43** G6
Powel House **44** G5
Riverboat Queen (see 23)
Rodin Museum **45** D3
Rosenbach Museum & Library **46** D5
Second Bank of the US **47** G5
Spirit of Philadelphia **48** H6
Trophy Bikes **49** B4
University Museum of Archaeology & Anthropology **50** B5
US Mint **51** G4
US Postal Service Museum **52** G5

SLEEPING
Apple Hostels of Philadelphia **53** H5
Hilton Inn at Penn **54** A4
Lowes Philadelphia **55** F4
Morris House Hotel **56** F5
Penn's View Hotel **57** H5
Rittenhouse 1715 **58** D5
Sofitel Philadelphia **59** D5
Thomas Bond House **60** H5

EATING
Amada **61** H5
Banana Leaf **62** F4
Cuba Libre **63** H5
Franklin Fountain **64** H5
Horizons **65** F6
Jim's Steaks **66** G6
Joe's **67** E5
Koreana **68** A4
La Locanda del Ghiottone **69** H4
La Viola **70** E5
Le Bec-Fin **71** E5
Lee How Fook **72** F4
Mama Palmas **73** C5
Mama's Vegetarian **74** D4
Maoz Vegetarian **75** G6
Nanzhou Handdrawn Noodle House **76** F4
Philly Flavors **77** D2
Pod **78** A4
Rangoon **79** F4
Reading Terminal Market **80** F4
Sabrina's Cafe **81** F6
South Street Souvlaki **82** G6
White Dog Cafe **83** A4

DRINKING
Bump **84** E5
Continental Midtown **85** D4
McGillin's Olde Ale House **86** E5
Nodding Head Brewery **87** E5
Shampoo **88** G3
Sisters **89** E5
Standard Tap **90** H2
Tavern on Camac **91** E5
Urban Saloon **92** D2

ENTERTAINMENT
Brasil's **93** H5
Chris' Jazz Club **94** E5
Khyber **95** H5
Kimmel Center for the Performing Arts **96** E5
Ortlieb's Jazzhaus **97** H2
Pennsylvania Ballet **98** D4
Philadelphia Orchestra **99** E5
Philadelphia Theatre Company **100** E5
Trocadero Theater **101** F4
World Cafe Live **102** B4

TRANSPORT
30th St Station (see 10)
Greyhound Bus Terminal **103** F4
Peter Pan Bus Terminal (see 103)
Riverlink Ferry **104** H5

houses state-of-the-art exhibits that examine the historical role of Jews in the USA. At the nearby **US Mint** (☎ 215-408-0110; www.usmint.gov; Arch St, btwn 4th & 5th Sts; admission free; 🕒 tours 9am-3pm Mon-Fri), you can line up for same-day, self-guided tours that last about 45 minutes. **Arch Street Meeting House** (☎ 215-627-2667; www.archstreetfriends.org; 320 Arch St; 🕒 9am-5pm Mon-Sat, 1-5pm Sun) is the USA's largest Quaker meeting house.

SOCIETY HILL

Architecture from the 18th and 19th centuries dominates the lovely residential neighborhood of Society Hill, bound by Front and 8th Sts from east to west, and Walnut and Lombard Sts north and south. Along the cobblestoned streets you'll see mainly 18th- and 19th-century brick row houses, mixed in with the occasional modern high-rise, like the **Society Hill Towers** designed by IM Pei, but **Washington Square** was conceived as part of William Penn's original city plan, and offers a peaceful respite from sightseeing. **Physick House** (☎ 215-925-7866; 321 S 4th St, at Delancey St; adult/child $5/4; 🕒 noon-4pm Thu-Sat, 1-4pm Sun), the home of surgeon Philip Syng Physick, was built in 1786 by Henry Hill – a wine importer who kept City Tavern well stocked – and is the only freestanding, Federal-style mansion remaining in Society Hill. The 18th-century **Powel House** (☎ 215-627-0364; 244 S 3rd St; adult/child $5/4; 🕒 noon-4pm Thu-Sat, 1-4pm Sun) was home to Samuel Powel, a mayor of Philadelphia during colonial times.

CENTER CITY, RITTENHOUSE SQUARE & AROUND

Philadelphia's center of creativity, commerce, culture and just about everything else, this region is the engine that drives the city. It contains the city's tallest buildings, the financial district, big hotels, museums, concert halls, shops and restaurants.

The leafy **Rittenhouse Square**, with its wading pool and fine statues, is the best known of William Penn's city squares. The majestic **City Hall** (☎ 215-686-2840; www.phila.gov; cnr Broad & Market Sts; admission free; 9:30am-4:30pm Tue-Fri), completed in 1901, stands 548ft tall in Penn Sq. It's the world's tallest masonry construction without a steel frame, and it's topped by a 27-ton bronze statue of William Penn. Just below that is an **observation deck**, where you can get a bird's-eye view of the city.

Highly recommended for Civil War buffs is the comprehensive **Civil War Library & Museum** (☎ 215-735-8196; www.cwurmuseum.org; 1805 Pine St; admission $5; 11am-4:30pm Thu-Sat) boasting artifacts and exhibitions; the museum is moving to a new location and will open, at the earliest, in early 2011. **Rosenbach Museum & Library** (☎ 215-732-1600; www.rosenbach.org; 2010 Delancey Pl; adult/child $10/5; 10am-5pm Tue & Thu-Sun, to 8pm Wed), meanwhile, is for bibliophiles, as it features rare books and manuscripts, including James Joyce's *Ulysses*, and special exhibits.

Skip med school and visit the seriously twisted **Mutter Museum** (☎ 215-563-3737; www.collphyphil.org; 19 S 22nd St; adult/child $14/10; 10am-5pm) to learn all about the history of medicine in the US.

BENJAMIN FRANKLIN PARKWAY & MUSEUM DISTRICT

Modeled after the Champs Elysées in Paris, the parkway is a center of museums and other landmarks. **Philadelphia Museum of Art** (☎ 215-763-8100; www.philamuseum.org; cnr Benjamin Franklin Pkwy & 26th St; adult/senior, student & child $14/10, Sun pay-what-you-wish; 10am-5pm Tue-Thu & Sat & Sun, to 8:45pm Fri) is the highlight. It's one of the nation's largest and most important museums, featuring some excellent collections of Asian art, Renaissance masterpieces, postimpressionist works and modern pieces by Picasso, Duchamp and Matisse. The grand stairway at its entrance was immortalized when star Sylvester Stallone ran up the steps in the 1976 flick *Rocky*.

Pennsylvania Academy of the Fine Arts (☎ 215-972-7600; www.pafa.org; 118 N Broad St; adult/child $10/6; 10am-5pm Tue-Sat, 11am-5pm Sun) is a prestigious academy that has a museum with works by American painters, including Charles Willson Peale and Thomas Eakins. The **Academy of Natural Sciences Museum** (☎ 215-299-1060; www.acnatsci.org; 1900 Benjamin Franklin Pkwy; adult/child $12/10; 10am-4:30pm Mon-Fri, 10am-5pm Sat & Sun) features a terrific dinosaur exhibition where you can dig for fossils on weekends. **Franklin Institute Science Museum** (☎ 215-448-1200; www2.fi.edu; 222 N 20th St; admission $14.75; 9:30am-5pm) is where hands-on science displays were pioneered; a highlight is the Ben Franklin exhibit. At the **Rodin Museum** (☎ 215-568-6026; www.rodinmuseum.org; Benjamin Franklin Pkwy & N 22nd St; suggested donation $5; 10am-5pm Tue-Sun), you'll find Rodin's great works *The Thinker* and *Burghers of Calais*.

SOUTH STREET

Sort of a Greenwich Village of Philly, **South Street** is where one goes to find record shops, art-supply stores, tiny cheapskate eateries and college favorites such as head shops, T-shirt stores and the teenage goth chicks who populate them. A hidden gem worth seeking out is **Philadelphia's Magic Garden** (☎ 215-733-0390; www.philadelphiasmagicgardens.org; 1020 South St), a mystical, art-filled pocket of land that's the passion of mosaic muralist Isaiah Zager.

SOUTH PHILADELPHIA

The **Italian Market** (S 9th St, btwn Wharton & Fitzwater Sts; 9am-5pm Tue-Sat, 9am-2pm Sun) is a highlight of South Philadelphia. The country's largest outdoor market, it's where butchers and artisans hawk produce and cheese, homemade pastas, incredible pastries and freshly slaughtered fish and meats, from lamb to pheasant. A great time to experience it in all its glory is in mid-May, for the annual **Sorrento Cheese Ninth Street Italian Market Festival** (www.9thstreetitalianmarketfestival.com).

In the midst of all the foodie frenzy is the **Mummers Museum** (☎ 215-336-3050; www.mummersmuseum.com; 1100 S 2nd St; adult/child $3.50/2.50; 9:30am-4:30pm Wed-Sat Oct-Apr, to 9:30pm Thu May-Sep), celebrating the tradition of disguise and masquerade. It has an integral role in the famed Mummers Parade, which takes place here every New Year's Day.

CHINATOWN & AROUND

The fourth-largest Chinatown in the USA, Philly's version has existed since the 1860s.

Chinese immigrants who built America's transcontinental railroads started out west and worked their way here. Today's Chinatown remains a center for immigrants, though now many of the neighborhood's residents come from Malaysia, Thailand and Vietnam in addition to every province in China. Though it does hold a few residents, the tone of Chinatown is thoroughly commercial. The **Chinese Friendship Gate** (N 10th St, btwn Cherry & Arch Sts) is a decorative arch built in 1984 as a joint project between Philadelphia and its Chinese sister city, Tianjin. The multicolored, four-story gate is Chinatown's most conspicuous landmark.

Between here and Independence Park is the **African American Museum in Philadelphia** (☎ 215-574-0380; www.aampmuseum.org; 701 Arch St; adult/child $10/8; 🕒 10am-5pm Tue-Sat, noon-5pm Sun). Housed in a foreboding concrete building, it contains excellent collections on African American history and culture.

PENN'S LANDING

Back in its heyday Penn's Landing – the waterfront area along the Delaware River between Market and Lombard Sts – was a very active port area. Eventually those transactions moved farther south down the Delaware, and today most of the excitement is about boarding boats, like the **Riverboat Queen** (☎ 215-923-2628; www.riverboatqueenfleet.com; tours from $15) or **Spirit of Philadelphia** (☎ 866-394-8439; www.spiritcruises.com; from $40), for booze cruises, or simply strolling along the water's edge. The 1.8-mile **Benjamin Franklin Bridge**, the world's largest suspension bridge when completed in 1926, spans the Delaware River and dominates the view here. Nearby is a grassy sculpture garden and the **Independence Seaport Museum** (☎ 215-413-8655; www.phillyseaport.com; 211 S Columbus Blvd; adult/child $12/7, 10am-noon Sun free; 🕒 10am-5pm), which highlights Philadelphia's role as an immigration hub; its shipyard closed in 1995 after 200 years.

Just across the Delaware River in otherwise missable Camden, NJ, is the excellent **Adventure Aquarium** (☎ 856-365-3300; www.adventureaquarium.com; 1 Riverside Dr; adult/child $20/16; 🕒 9:30am-5pm; 👶), featuring an archway where you can pass under schools of fish. To get there, just hop on the **RiverLink Ferry** (☎ 856-365-1166; www.riverlinkferry.org; round trip $6; 🕒 10am-6pm, to 7pm Fri-Sun), which runs hourly from Penn's Landing.

UNIVERSITY CITY

This neighborhood, separated from downtown Philly by the Schuylkill River, feels like one big college town. That's because it's home to both Drexel University and the Ivy League **University of Pennsylvania** (commonly called 'U Penn'), founded in 1740. The leafy, bustling campus makes for a pleasant afternoon stroll, and it's got two museums definitely worth a visit: the **University Museum of Archaeology & Anthropology** (☎ 215-898-4000; www.upenn.edu/museum; 3260 South St; adult/child $10/6; 🕒 10am-4:30pm Tue-Sat, 1-5pm Sun) contains archaeological treasures from ancient Egypt, Mesopotamia, Mesoamerica, Greece, Rome and North America; and the heralded **Institute of Contemporary Art** (☎ 215-898-7108; www.icaphila.org; 118 S 36th St; admission free; 🕒 noon-8pm Wed-Fri, 11am-5pm Sat & Sun) is an excellent place to catch shows by folks making a big splash at the cutting edge of the art world.

Oh, and whether you're catching a train or not, be sure to pop your head into the romantic, neoclassical **30th St Station** (☎ 215-349-2153; 30th St, at Market St) while you're in the 'hood. Flooded with sunlight during the afternoon, it's positively ethereal.

FAIRMOUNT PARK

The snaking Schuylkill River bisects this 9200-acre green space – bigger than New York's Central Park and, in fact, the largest city park in the country. From the earliest days of spring every corner is thrumming with activity – ball games, runners, picnickers, you name it. The enthusiasm is catchy and you'll certainly want to join them. Runners will love the tree-lined, riverside trails, which range from 2 miles to 10 miles in length. **Philly runners** (www.phillyrunners.org) is an all-skills running club that has great maps and information.

Park trails are also great for bicycling. For rentals, **Trophy Bikes** (☎ 215-222-2020; www.trophybikes.com; 3131 Walnut St; bike rental per full/half-day $35/25; 🕒 10am-6pm) stocks the latest hybrids and a couple of tandems, and staff members specialize in touring. For advice and group rides, contact the **Bicycle Club of Philadelphia** (☎ 215-913-3246; www.phillybikeclub.org), which leads rides for all skill levels.

On the east bank, **Boathouse Row** has Victorian-era rowing-club buildings that lend a lovely old-fashioned flavor to this stretch. Across the park are a number of **early American houses** (adult/child $5/2) that are open to the public, including **Laurel Hill** (☎ 215-235-1776; 🕒 10am-4pm

Sat & Sun) and **Woodford** (☎ 215-229-6115; ⌚ 10am-4pm Tue-Sun). Also, check out the **Shofuso Japanese House and Garden** (☎ 215-878-5097; www.shofuso.com; admission $6; ⌚ 10am-4pm Wed-Fri, 11am-5pm Sat & Sun May-Sep), a picturesque home and teahouse constructed in the traditional 16th-century style. Scattered all throughout the park are some notable monuments, including one, at the far east end, for **Joan of Arc**.

Also within park borders is **Philadelphia Zoo** (☎ 215-243-1100; www.philadelphiazoo.org; 3400 Girard Ave; adult/child $18/15 Mar-Oct, general admission $13 Nov-Feb; ⌚ 9:30am-5pm Mar-Oct, 9:30am-4pm Nov-Feb), the country's oldest zoo, which has tigers, pumas, polar bears – you name it – in naturalistic habitats.

MANAYUNK

A compact residential neighborhood northwest of the city, with steep hills and Victorian row houses, Manayunk, from a Native American expression meaning 'where we go to drink,' is a lovely place for an afternoon and evening. Just be aware that thousands of others have the same idea on weekend nights, when this otherwise peaceful area overlooking the Schuylkill River has the feel of a raucous frat party. As well as drinking, visitors are also permitted to eat (see p224) and shop. Parking is near impossible to come by here on weekends, so cycling is a good option – there's a towpath that runs alongside the neighborhood.

GERMANTOWN & CHESTNUT HILL

An odd mix of blight and preserved grandeur, the Germantown historic district – a good 20-minute drive or ride north on the SEPTA (p226) 23 from central downtown Philly – has a handful of tiny museums and notable homes worth checking out. **Cliveden of the National Trust** (☎ 215-848-1777; www.cliveden.org; 6401 Germantown Ave; admission $10; ⌚ noon-4pm Thu-Sun) was the summer home of wealthy Benjamin Chew. It was built in 1760 and used as a de facto stronghold in the Battle of Germantown during the Revolutionary War in 1777. You can visit it, along with the **Deshler-Morris House** (☎ 215-597-7130; www.nps.gov/demo; 5442 Germantown Ave), where President Washington met with his cabinet in 1793, the **Germantown Historical Society** (☎ 215-844-1683; www.germantownhistory.org; 5501 Germantown Ave; admission $5; ⌚ 9am-1pm Tue, 1-5pm Thu & Sun), and the **Johnson House** (☎ 215-438-1768; www.johnsonhouse.org; 6306 Germantown Ave; ⌚ 10am-4pm Thu-Fri, 1-4pm Sat, tours at 1:30pm, 2:30pm & 3:30pm), the site of a 1768 station house for the Underground Railroad.

Just north of Germantown is **Chestnut Hill** (www.chestnuthillpa.com) with its quaint, small-town-like main strip of shops and eateries, and huge and historic residential homes and mansions.

Tours

Ed Mauger's Philadelphia on Foot (☎ 215-627-8680; www.ushistory.org/more/mauger; tours per person $20) Historian and author Ed Mauger offers walking tours with a variety of themes, including Exercise Your Rights (Conservatives Tour), Exercise Your Lefts (Liberals Tour) and Women in the Colony.

Mural Tours (☎ 215-389-8687; www.muralarts.org/tours; tours adult/child $25/15; ⌚ tours Wed, Sat & Sun Apr-Nov) Guided trolley tour of the city's diverse and colorful outdoor murals, the largest collection in the country.

Philadelphia Trolley Works & 76 Carriage Company (☎ 215-389-8687; www.phillytour.com; tours adult/child from $25/10) Tour part of the city or just about every last corner, either on a narrated trolley ride or quieter horse-drawn carriage.

Festivals & Events

Mummers' Parade (www.mummers.com) A very Philly parade, this is an elaborate celebration of costumes every New Year's Day (January 1).

Annual Jam on the River (www.jamontheriver.com) Excellent music lineup, from folkies to jam bands. Memorial Day weekend.

Manayunk Arts Festival (www.manayunk.com) It's the largest outdoor arts and crafts show in the Delaware Valley, with more than 250 artists from across the country each June.

Philadelphia Live Arts Festival & Philly Fringe (www.livearts-fringe.org) Catch the latest in cutting-edge performance each September.

Sleeping

Though the majority of places are found in and around Center City, there are alternatives sprinkled throughout the other neighborhoods. There's certainly no shortage of places to stay, but it's primarily national chains or B&Bs. Note that most hotels offer some kind of parking service, usually costing about $20 to $45 per day.

BUDGET & MIDRANGE

Chamounix Mansion Hostel (☎ 215-878-3676; www.philahostel.org; 3250 Chamounix Dr, West Fairmount Park; dm $23; 🅿 💻) Looking more like a B&B than hostel, the Chamounix really should only be considered by those with use of a car. It's in a lovely wooded area in Fairmount Park north of the city on the way to Manayunk. Despite the 19th-century-style parlor and large communal rooms, the dorms themselves are basic but clean.

Apple Hostels of Philadelphia (☎ 215-922-0222; www.applehostels.com; 32 S Bank St; dm $25-40, r from $75;) Formerly the HI Bank Street Hostel, this upgraded jewel is sparkling clean and in a safe neighborhood, just a short walk from major sights. Everything, from the bunk beds to dishes in the spacious kitchen, looks like it's straight out of an Ikea catalogue – not a bad thing. Very friendly and helpful staff and events such as walking tours and movie nights with free beer (Tuesday).

Thomas Bond House (☎ 215-923-8523; www.thomasbondhousebandb.com; 129 S 2nd St; r incl breakfast $115-190;) Much like staying at your grandparents – if you were living in the 18th century – this colonial-era B&B pays attention to traditional period detail. Perfect for sightseeing in Independence Park, the restored 1769 Georgian-style house is furnished with Chippendale period furnishings and working fireplaces.

Penn's View Hotel (☎ 215-922-7600; www.pennsviewhotel.com; cnr Front & Market Sts; r from $149-329;) Housed in three early-19th-century buildings overlooking the Delaware waterfront, Penn's View is ideal for exploring the Old City district. Quaint and full of character but not overly nostalgic or a prisoner to history, the rooms have marble bathrooms and modern conveniences. An authentic Italian trattoria and charming wine bar are part of the hotel.

our pick **Morris House Hotel** (☎ 215-922-2446; www.morrishousehotel.com; 225 S 8th St; r incl breakfast from $179;) If Benjamin Franklin were a hotelier he would have designed a place like the Morris House Hotel. Upscale colonial-era boutique, this Federal-era building has the friendly charm and intimacy of an elegant B&B and the professionalism and good taste of a designer-run 21st-century establishment.

TOP END

Hilton Inn at Penn (☎ 215-222-0200; www.theinnatpenn.com; 3600 Sansom St; r $200-250; P) Located away from the downtown hubbub but quickly accessible via the nearby SEPTA, this Hilton hotel sits on the U Penn campus. The modern, comfortable rooms still have a classy old-world vibe. Prices double on weekends that have any U Penn–related event.

Rittenhouse 1715 (☎ 215-546-6500; www.rittenhouse1715.com; 1715 Rittenhouse Sq; r $249-305, ste $309-699;) Just steps from Rittenhouse Sq, this is an elegant, top-notch choice. Housed in a 1911 mansion and infused with old-world sophistication, it's brimming with modern amenities – iPod docking stations, plasma TVs and rain showerheads. The friendly and efficient staff is also worth noting.

Other recommended places with excellent locations for exploring the city by foot are the **Lowes Philadelphia** (☎ 215-627-1200; 1200 Market St; r from $170; P), an art-deco building with original details and one of the first skyscrapers in Philly, and the **Sofitel Philadelphia** (☎ 215-569-8300; www.sofitel.com; 120 S 17th St; r $215-400; P), which boasts spacious rooms and a cool vibe near Rittenhouse Sq.

Eating

Philly is deservedly known for its cheesesteaks – you shouldn't leave without a sampling – the city's dining scene has grown exponentially, in part due to the contributions of the Starr and Garces groups, which have added a range of quality international eateries. Because of Pennsylvania's arcane liquor laws, many restaurants are Bring Your Own Bottle (BYOB).

OLD CITY

Franklin Fountain (☎ 215-627-1899; 116 Market St; noon-11pm Sun-Thu, to midnight Fri & Sat) One of the more romantic date spots in the city, especially on weekend nights, this very-old-school ice-cream parlor features locally grown fruit and top-flight sundaes.

our pick **Amada** (☎ 215-625-2450; 217 Chestnut St; tapas $6-20; 11:30am-10pm Mon-Thu, to midnight Fri, 5pm-midnight Sat, 4-10pm Sun) One of several Spanish tapas places to have opened in Philly in the last few years, Amada is run by renowned restaurateur Jose Garces – weekend dinner reservations are hard to come by. The long communal tables foster a bustling, happening and loud atmosphere and the combination of bold and traditional flavored dishes (try the crab-stuffed peppers) are phenomenal.

Cuba Libre (☎ 215-627-0666; www.cubalibrerestaurant.com; 10 S 2nd St; dinner $15-24; 11:30am-11pm Mon-Fri, from 10:30am Sat & Sun) Colonial America couldn't feel further away at this festive, multistoried Cuban eatery and rum bar. The creative and inspired menu includes

Cuban sandwiches, guava-spiced BBQ, and savory black beans and salads tossed with smoked fish.

La Locanda del Ghiottone (☎ 215-829-1465; 130 N Third St; mains $16; 🕑 5-11pm Tue-Sun) The name means 'the Place of the Glutton,' and Chef Giussepe and Joe the head waiter encourage overeating. Small and modestly designed, unlike other nearby trendy spots, this place the gnocchi, mushroom crepes and mussels are recommended. BYOB.

CENTER CITY & AROUND

Reading Terminal Market (☎ 215-922-2317; www.readingterminalmarket.org; cnr 12th & Arch Sts; dishes $3-10; 🕑 8am-6pm Mon-Sat, 9am-5pm Sun) At the budget end, this huge indoor market is the best you'll find. Take your pick, from fresh Amish cheeses and Thai desserts, to falafel, cheesesteaks, salad bars, sushi, Peking duck, great Mexican and cups of fresh-roasted java.

Mama Palmas (☎ 215-735-7357; 2229 Spruce St; pizzas $10; 🕑 4-10pm Mon-Thu, 11am-11pm Fri & Sat, 2-10pm Sun) Just off Rittenhouse Sq, this small BYOB place serves up some of the best thin-slice brick-oven pizza in the city. It does have a reputation for not tolerating little tykes – if they're rowdy.

La Viola (☎ 215-735-8630; 253 S 16th St, at Spruce St; mains $13; 🕑 11am-10pm Mon-Thu, to 11pm Fri & Sat, 4-10pm Sun) Facing off across the street from one another are the old and new La Violas – both BYOB. The former is a cramped and unpretentious dining room, while the latter is larger and more modern; the cuisine at both, however, is fresh and reasonably priced.

Le Bec-Fin (☎ 215-567-1000; 1523 Walnut St; prix fixe dinners $90-138; 🕑 11:30am-9pm Mon-Fri, 6-9:30pm Sat) Totally over-the-top in its old-world snooty splendor, Le Bec-Fin is rated by many gourmets as the country's best restaurant for its setting, service and superb French food. Expect top-notch service, stuffy diners and rich and sophisticated meat and seafood dishes.

Joe's (☎ 215-569-0898; 122 S 16th St) has some of the best pizza by the slice in the neighborhood, while **Mama's Vegetarian** (☎ 215-751-0477; 18 S 20th St; sandwiches $6; 🕑 11am-9pm Mon-Thu, to 3pm Fri, noon-7pm Sun; Ⓥ), a kosher Middle Eastern eatery, serves heaping falafel. North of Center City, within walking distance of the Rodin Museum, is the always bustling **Philly Flavors** (☎ 215-232-7748; 2004 Fairmount Ave, at 20th St; ices $; 🕑 11am-11pm Sun-Thu, to midnight Fri & Sat), which some say is the best place for Italian ices in the city; even the small kiddie size is large enough for most.

SOUTH STREET

Maoz Vegetarian (☎ 215-625-3500; 248 South St; dishes $5-7; 🕑 11am-1am Sun-Wed, 11am-3am Thu-Sat) This tiny storefront, actually an outpost of a chain from Amsterdam, is always packed with healthy hipsters wanting in on the cheap, fresh falafel sandwiches, which you can pile high with marinated veggies, toppings and sauces.

Jim's Steaks (☎ 877-313-5467; 400 South St, at 4th St; steak sandwiches $6-8; 🕑 10am-1am Mon-Thu, to 3am Fri & Sat, noon-10pm Sun) If you can brave the long lines – which bust out of the front door and snake around the side of the shiny art-deco building – you'll be in for a treat at this Philly institution, which serves mouthwatering cheesesteaks and hoagies (plus soups, salads and breakfasts).

Horizons (☎ 215-923-6117; 611 S 7th St; mains $15-20; 🕑 6-10pm Tue-Thu, 6-11pm Fri & Sat; Ⓥ) One of the few restaurants in Philly to satisfy the vegan gourmand, Horizons serves healthy, guilt-free dishes made of soy and veggies.

CHINATOWN

Rangoon (☎ 215-829-8939; 112 N 9th St; mains $6-15; 🕑 11:30am-9pm Sun-Thu, to 10pm Fri & Sat) Try this Burmese spot in Chinatown, offering a huge array of tantalizing specialties from spicy red-bean shrimp and curried chicken with egg noodles to coconut tofu.

Nanzhou Handdrawn Noodle House (☎ 215-923-1550; 927 Race St; mains $6; 🕑 11am-9pm) serves satisfying and inexpensive meat noodle soups, while **Banana Leaf** (☎ 215-592-8288; 1009 Arch St; mains $8; 🕑 11am-1am) specializes in Malaysian and Japanese cuisine. **Lee How Fook** (☎ 215-925-7266; 219 N 11th St; mains $9-13; 🕑 11:30am-10pm Tue-Sun) has excellent contemporary Chinese.

SOUTH PHILADELPHIA & ITALIAN MARKET

Paradiso (☎ 215-271-2066; 1627 E Passyunk Ave; mains $18-26; 🕑 11:30am-3pm & 5-10pm Mon-Thu, to 11pm Fri & Sat, 4-9pm Sun) An elegant airy part of South Philly's Restaurant Row, Paradiso turns out upscale Italian feasts such as pistachio-crusted lamb chops, homemade gnocchi and New York strip steak glazed with anchovy butter.

Local aficionados debate the relative merits of this city's legendary cheesesteak shops like they are biblical scholars parsing the meaning of Deuteronomy. **Geno's** (☎ 215-389-0659; 1219 S 9th St; sandwiches $7; 🕑 24hr) and **Pat's King of Steaks** (☎ 215-468-1546; cnr S 9th St & Passyunk Ave; sandwiches $7; 🕑 24hr), considered classic Philly, are frequented as much by tourists and inebriated patrons, possibly unaware of the level of grease they're ingesting, as diehard locals. Some swear by **Tony Luke's Old Philly Style Sandwiches** (☎ 215-551-5725; www.tonylukes.com; 39 E Oregon Ave; sandwiches $7; 6am-midnight Mon-Thu, to 2am Fri & Sat), especially the roast pork or roast beef with hot peppers; it's a typical spot out by the sports stadiums with picnic tables and an ordering window.

South Street Souvlaki (☎ 215-925-3026; 507 South St; mains $13-18; noon-9:30pm Tue-Thu, to 10pm Fri & Sat, to 9pm Sun) is one of the best places for Greek food in the city and **Sabrina's Cafe** (☎ 215-574-1599; 910 Christian St; mains $9; 8am-10pm Tue-Sat, to 4pm Sun & Mon) is an extremely popular brunch spot.

The area around the corner of Washington and 11th Sts is chockablock with tasty family-owned **Vietnamese restaurants**.

UNIVERSITY CITY

Satellite Coffee Shop (☎ 215-729-1211; 701 S 50th St; sandwiches $5; 7am-10pm) This Cedar Park vegetarian-friendly café is a hipster meeting ground. Try the bike-shop special, a bagel with cream cheese, pesto and roasted red pepper.

White Dog Cafe (☎ 215-386-9224; 3420 Sansom St; dinner mains $12-29; 11:30am-2:30pm Mon-Sat, 5-10pm Mon-Thu, to 11pm Fri & Sat, 10:30am-2:30pm & 5-10pm Sun) This 24-year-old institution is the kind of funky-yet-upscale place that college students get their visiting parents to take them to for special dinners or brunch. The local, largely organic menu offers creative interpretations of meat and fish dishes.

Pod (☎ 215-387-1803; 3636 Sansom St; dinner mains $14-29; 11:30am-11pm Mon-Thu, to midnight Fri, 5pm-midnight Sat, to 10pm Sun) Part of the restaurateur Stephen Starr's empire, this space-age-looking theme restaurant has pan-Asian treats including dumplings and some of the best sushi in Philly, plus plenty of quirky cocktails and original desserts.

For meat and chicken sandwiches, definitely the best in area is **Lee's Hoagie House** (☎ 215-387-0905; 4034 Walnut St; sandwiches $7; 10am-10pm Mon-Sat, 11am-9pm Sun). **Koreana** (☎ 215-222-2240; 3801 Chestnut St; mains $7; noon-10pm) satisfies students and others interested in good, inexpensive Korean fare; enter from the parking lot in the back of the shopping plaza. The vibrant pink and lime decor doesn't drown out the taste of the contemporary Mexican fare served at **Distrito** (☎ 215-222-1657; 3945 Chestnut St; mains $9-30; 11:30am-11pm Mon-Fri, 5-11pm Sat, to 10pm Sun).

MANAYUNK, ROXBOROUGH, GERMANTOWN & CHESTNUT HILL

Trolley Car Diner (☎ 215-753-1500; 7619 Germantown Ave; dinner mains $12-20; 11:30am-2:30pm Tue-Sat, 5-9pm Tue-Thu, 5-10pm Fri & Sat, 10am-2pm & 5-9pm Sun) Housed in a classic art-deco diner (moved here from its former site in Wilkes Barre, PA), this old-fashioned, family-style diner serves all the comfort food: club sandwiches, patty melts, fried shrimp, salads and a homemade, white-bean 'peanut butter' sandwich.

Cresheim Cottage (☎ 215-248-4365; 7402 Germantown Ave; dinner mains $12-20; 11:30am-9pm Mon-Thu, to 10pm Fri & Sat, 10am-9pm Sun) The Cottage is a local-sustainable adherent, and you can tell by the freshness of the delicious dishes, like seafood stew and the unique chicken meatloaf muffin for dinner.

Chabaa Thai (☎ 215-483-1931; 4371 Main St; mains $12-23; 5-9:30pm Mon-Thu & Sun, to 10pm Fri & Sat) is a warm BYOB place doing authentic and reasonably priced Thai. Cheesesteak snobs rave about **Dalessandro's Steaks** (☎ 215-482-5407; 600 Wendover St, Roxborough; sandwiches $6.50; 11am-midnight Mon-Sat) and **Chubby's** (☎ 215-487-2575; 5826 Henry Ave; sandwiches $6.50; 11am-1am Mon-Thu, to 2am Fri & Sat, to 11pm Sun) across the street; the latter has the better chicken sandwiches. **Kildare's Irish Pub** (☎ 215-482-7242; 4417 Main St; mains $9; 11am-2am Mon-Fri, from 10am Sat) is the place for chicken wings – grilled, fried and baked.

Drinking & Entertainment

BARS & NIGHTCLUBS

McGillin's Olde Ale House (☎ 215-735-5562; www.mcgillins.com; 1310 Drury St; 11am-2am Mon-Sat, to midnight Sun) Philadelphia's oldest continually operated tavern (since 1860) – it remained open as a speakeasy in the prohibition years. Great buffalo wings (Tuesday is special wing night) and karaoke on Wednesdays and Fridays. St Patty's Day is absolutely crazy here.

Standard Tap (☎ 215-238-0630; cnr 2nd & Poplar Sts; 4pm-2am) One of the pioneers in the gastropub movement, this Northern Liberties bar offers a great selection of local brews on tap, as well as burgers and steaks.

Urban Saloon (☎ 215-808-0348; 2120 Fairmount Ave; 5pm-2am Mon-Fri, 11am-2am Sat, 11am-midnight Sun) The young proprietors of this Fairmount bar live right around the corner, so it has a neighborhood feel. There's room for dancing on Friday nights, and a kid-friendly brunch on Sundays (the peanut burger can be recommended).

Shampoo (☎ 215-922-7500; Willow St, btwn N 7th & 8th Sts; cover $7-12; 🕑 9pm-2am) Home to foam parties, hot tubs and velvet seating, this giant nightclub's weekly repertoire includes an immensely popular gay night on Fridays, a long-standing Wednesday Goth night, and a conventional free-for-all on Saturdays.

An area that lies between Broad and 12th Sts and Walnut and Pine Sts, unofficially called 'gayborhood,' was dubbed Midtown Village in 2007 and permanently decked out with rainbow-flag-festooned street signs during a special ceremony. Because nights and venues change frequently, check out www.phillygaycalendar.com. **Bump** (☎ 215-732-1800; 1234 Locust St) is a trendy, modern lounge with a cozy back patio, while **Sisters** (☎ 215-735-0735; 1320 Chancellor St) is a huge nightclub and restaurant for the ladies. Show tunes and other old-school fun reign in the downstairs piano bar at **Tavern on Camac** (☎ 215-545-0900; 243 S Camac St), one of the older gay bars in Philly, while a small upstairs dance floor gets packed with dance-happy folks.

Other places to recommend in the burgeoning brewpub scene include **Earth Bread & Brewery** (☎ 215-242-6666; 7136 Germantown Ave), **Dock Street Brewery & Restaurant** (☎ 215-726-2337; 701 S 50th St) and **Nodding Head Brewery** (☎ 215-569-9525; 1516 Sansom St).

Continental Midtown (☎ 215-567-1800; 1801 Chestnut St) is a swank and pricey rooftop bar and **Brasil's** (☎ 215-413-1700; 112 Chestnut St; cover $10) is the place to bump and grind to Latin, Brazilian and Caribbean sounds, with DJ John Rockwell.

LIVE MUSIC

Chris' Jazz Club (☎ 215-568-3131; www.chrisjazzcafe.com; 1421 Sansom St; cover $10-20) Showcasing local talent along with national greats, this intimate space features a four o'clock piano happy hour Tuesday through Friday and good bands Monday through Saturday nights.

Ortlieb's Jazzhaus (☎ 215-922-1035; www.ortliebsjazzhaus.com; 847 N 3rd St; cover Tue-Thu, $10 Fri, $15 Sat, $3 Sun) A respectable jazz lineup with a house band jamming every Tuesday night and Cajun cuisine on the menu (mains $20).

Khyber (☎ 215-238-5888; 56 S 2nd St; cover $5-15) Trendy Old City stops at the door to this down-and-dirty old rock bar. Nightly music except Mondays, when karaoke takes over. The Strokes made it big while they were the Khyber's resident band.

Trocadero Theater (☎ 215-922-6888; www.thetroc.com; 1003 Arch St; cover up to $12) A rock-and-roll showcase in Chinatown housed in a 19th-century Victorian theater. Monday night is movie night, followed by the Monday Night Club, with a hodgepodge of musicians, spoken-word artists and comedians.

World Cafe Live (☎ 3025 Walnut St; www.worldcafelive.com; 3025 Walnut St; cover $10-40) Located on the eastern edge of University City, World Cafe Live has upstairs and downstairs performance spaces featuring a restaurant and bar and is home to the radio station WXPN. It hosts an eclectic variety of live acts.

THEATER & CULTURE

Kimmel Center for the Performing Arts (☎ 215-790-5800; www.kimmelcenter.org; cnr Broad & Spruce Sts) Philadelphia's most active center for fine music, the Kimmel Center organizes a vast array of performances, including those for many of the companies listed below.

Philadelphia Theatre Company (☎ 215-985-0420; www.phillytheatreco.com; Suzanne Roberts Theatre, 480 S Broad St, at Lombard St; tickets $35-70) This company, which produces quality contemporary plays with regional actors, has a high-end home in the heart of the arts district.

Pennsylvania Ballet (☎ 215-551-7000; www.paballet.org; 1819 John F Kennedy Blvd; tickets $25-130) An excellent dance company that performs in the beautiful Academy of Music and the next-door Merriam Theater.

Philadelphia Dance Company (☎ 215-387-8200; www.philadanco.org; 9 N Preston St; tickets $25-130) For almost 40 years this company has been providing top-shelf exhibitions of dance, blending ballet and modern as the resident company at the Kimmel Center.

Philadelphia Orchestra (☎ 215-893-1999; www.philorch.org; cnr Broad & Spruce Sts; tickets $10-130) The city's orchestra, founded in 1900, plays at the Kimmel Center, where it also resides.

SPORTS

Football is all about the **Philadelphia Eagles** (www.philadelphiaeagles.com), who play at state-of-the-art **Lincoln Field** (☎ 215-463-5500; S 11th St) from August through January, usually twice a month, on Sunday. The baseball team is the National League **Philadelphia Phillies** (www.phillies.mlb.com), who play 81 home games at **Citizen's Bank Park** (☎ 215-463-1000) from April to October. Finally, basketball comes courtesy of the **Philadelphia 76ers** (www.nba.com/sixers) at **Wachovia Center** (☎ 215-339-7600; 3601 S Broad St).

Getting There & Away

Philadelphia International Airport (PHL; ☎ 215-937-6937, 800-745-4283; www.phl.org; 8000 Essington Ave), 7 miles south of Center City, is served by direct international flights; domestically, it has flights to over 100 destinations in the USA. See below for information on getting to/from the airport.

Greyhound (☎ 215-931-4075; www.greyhound.com; 1001 Filbert St) and **Peter Pan Bus Lines** (☎ 800-343-9999; www.peterpanbus.com; 1001 Filbert St) are the major bus carriers. Greyhound connects Philadelphia with hundreds of cities nationwide, while Peter Pan concentrates on the northeast. A round-trip fare to New York City is about $46 (2½ hours one way), to Atlantic City $20 (1½ hours) and to Washington, DC, $54 (4½ hours). **NJ Transit** (☎ 215-569-3752, in New Jersey 800-772-2222; www.njtransit.com) carries you from Philly to various points in New Jersey. See p191 for less-expensive bus options to NYC.

Beautiful **30th St Station** (p220; www.30thstreetstation.com) is one of the biggest train hubs in the country. **Amtrak** (☎ 215-349-2222, 800-872-7245; www.amtrak.com) provides service from here to Boston (regional and Acela express service one way $97 to $206, five to 5¾ hours) and Pittsburgh (regional service $45, 7¼ hours). A cheaper but longer (adult/child $19/13; 2½ hours) way to get to NYC is to take the SEPTA R7 suburban train to Trenton in New Jersey. From there you can connect with **NJ Transit** (www.njtransit.state.nj.us) to Newark's Penn Station, then continue on NJ Transit to New York City's Penn Station.

Several interstate highways lead through and around Philadelphia. From the north and south, the I-95 (Delaware Expwy) follows the eastern edge of the city beside the Delaware River, with several exits for Center City. The I-276 (Pennsylvania Turnpike) runs east across the northern part of the city and over the river to connect with the New Jersey Turnpike.

Getting Around

The fare for a taxi to Center City from the airport is a flat fee of $28.50. The airport is also served by SEPTA's regional service using the R1 line. The R1 ($7) will drop you off in University City or in numerous stops in Center City.

Downtown distances are short enough to let you see most places on foot, and a train, bus or taxi can get you to places farther out relatively easily. See p1164 for car-rental advice.

SEPTA (☎ 215-580-7800; www.septa.org) operates Philadelphia's municipal buses, plus two subway lines and a trolley service. Though extensive and reliable, the web of bus lines (120 routes servicing 159 sq miles) is difficult to make sense of. The one-way fare on most routes is $2, for which you'll need exact change or a token. Many subway stations and transit stores sell discounted packages of two tokens for $2.90.

Cabs, especially around City Center, are easy to hail. The flag drop or fare upon entry is $2.70, then $2.30 per mile or portion thereof. All licensed taxis have GPS and some cabs accept credit cards.

The **Phlash** (☎ 215-474-5274; www.phillyphlash.com; ⌚ 10am-6pm) shuttle bus looks like an old-school trolley and loops between Penn's Landing and the Philadelphia Museum of Art (one way/all day $2/5). It runs approximately every 12 minutes.

AROUND PHILADELPHIA

New Hope & Lambertville

New Hope (www.newhopepa.com), about 40 miles north of Philadelphia and its sister town Lambertville (www.lambertville.org), across the Delaware River in NJ, sit equidistant from Philadelphia and New York City, and are a pair of quaint, artsy little towns. Both are edged with long and peaceful towpaths, perfect for runners, cyclists and strollers, and a bridge with a walking lane lets you crisscross between the two with ease. The towns draw a large number of gay folk; rainbow flags hanging outside various businesses demonstrate the town's gay-friendliness.

One of New Hope's unique offerings is the mule-drawn canalboat rides in the Delaware Canal, a leftover from the canal-building era of the mid-19th century. Stop by the **New Hope Canal Boat Company** (☎ 215-862-0758; www.onthecanal.net; 149 S Main St; adult/child $10/6; ⌚ tours noon May-Oct) for tickets. Or spend a few picturesque hours gliding downstream in a tube, raft or canoe, courtesy of **Bucks County River Country** (☎ 215-297-5000; www.rivercountry.net; 2 Walters Lane, Point Pleasant; tube $18-22, canoe $62;

rental 9am-2:30pm, return by 5pm), about 8 miles north of New Hope on Rte 32. The **Golden Nugget Antique Market** (609-397-0811; www.gnmarket.com; 1850 River Rd; 6am-4pm Wed, Sat & Sun), one mile south of Lambertville, has all sorts of finds, from furniture to clothing, from a variety of dealers.

Both towns have a plethora of cute B&Bs if you decide to make a weekend out of it. Try the **York Street House Bed & Breakfast** (609-397-3007; www.yorkstreethouse.com; 42 York St, Lambertville; r incl breakfast $125-260;), a 1909 mansion with cozy rooms and big breakfasts, or the **Mansion Inn** (215-862-1231; www.themansioninn.com; 9 South Main St, New Hope; r $155-275;) in the heart of town – an 1865 gingerbread mansion with elegant detailing.

When you get hungry, head four miles north to the town of Stockton to **Meil's Restaurant** (609-397-8033; cnr Main & Bridge Sts; mains $10-15; 8am-9pm Sun-Thu, to 10pm Fri & Sat) for large portions of satisfying comfort food. **Marsha Brown Creole Kitchen and Lounge** (215-862-7044; www.marshabrownrestaurant.com; 15 S Main St, New Hope; mains $15-22; 5-10pm Mon-Thu, to 11pm Fri, 2-11pm Sat, to 9pm Sun) in New Hope serves catfish, steaks and lobster.

Easton

The historic, picturesque and artsy town of Easton (www.easton-pa.com), home to Lafayette College, is in the Leheigh Valley, just over the New Jersey border and on the banks of the Delaware River, only 70 miles or so from both Philadelphia and New York City.

Strolling around the quaint main streets here is a lovely way to spend the afternoon, especially if you step into some of the many art galleries. The most popular reason to visit is the wonderful **Crayola Factory** (610-515-8000; www.crayola.com/factory; 30 Centre Sq; admission $9.50, includes National Canal Museum; 9:30am-3pm Tue-Fri, to 5pm Sat, noon-5pm Sun Sep-May, 9:30am-5pm Mon-Sat, from 11am Memorial Day–Labor Day;), home of the beloved crayons, where kids and curious adults can watch the crayons and markers get made, and get silly with hands-on exhibits. In the same complex with the same hours is the **National Canal Museum** (610-559-6625; www.canals.org), with exhibits explaining how canals helped create a national economy.

If you want to make an evening of it, grab a cozy room at the **Lafayette Inn** (610-253-4500; www.lafayetteinn.com; 525 W Monroe St; r incl breakfast $125-175, ste $225;), an 18-room Georgian-style mansion with antiques and big breakfasts.

Brandywine Valley

Straddling the Pennsylvania–Delaware border southwest of Philadelphia, the Brandywine Valley is a patchwork of rolling, wooded countryside, historic villages, gardens, mansions and museums. The **Chester County's Brandywine Valley Tourist Information Center** (800-228-9933; www.brandywinevalley.com; 300 Greenwood Ave; 10am-6pm Apr-Sep, to 5pm Oct-Mar) sits outside the gates of the spectacular **Longwood Gardens** (610-388-1000; www.longwoodgardens.org; Rte 1; admission $16; 9am-6pm Mon, Tue, Wed & Sun, to 10pm Thu, Fri & Sat;), near Kennett Sq, which has 1050 acres, 20 indoor gardens and 11,000 kinds of plants, with something always in bloom. There's also a Children's Garden with a maze, fireworks and illuminated fountains in summer, and festive lights at Christmas. The **Brandywine Valley Wine Trail** (www.bvwinetrail.com), meanwhile, is a lovely conduit between a handful of new vineyards, all with tasting rooms.

A showcase of American artwork, the **Brandywine River Museum** (610-388-2700; www.brandywinemuseum.org; cnr Hwy 1 & Rte 100; adult/child $10/6; 9:30am-4:30pm), at Chadd's Ford, includes the work of the 'Brandywine School' – Howard Pyle, NC Wyeths and Maxfield Parrish. One of the valley's most famous attractions, though, is **Winterthur** (302-888-4600, 800-448-3883; www.winterthur.org; Rte 52, Winterthur, DE; adult/child/senior & student $18/5/16; 10am-5pm Tue-Sun), actually in Delaware, an important museum of American furniture and decorative arts that was the country estate of Henry Francis du Pont until he opened it to the public in 1951.

Valley Forge

After being defeated at the Battle of Brandywine Creek and the British occupation of Philadelphia in 1777, General Washington and 12,000 continental troops withdrew to Valley Forge. Today, Valley Forge symbolizes Washington's endurance and leadership. The **Valley Forge National Historic Park** (610-783-1099; www.nps.gov/vafo; cnr N Gulph Rd & Rte 23; admission free; park grounds 6am-10pm, welcome center & Washington's Headquarters 9am-5pm) contains 5½ sq miles of scenic beauty and open space 20 miles northwest of downtown Philadelphia – a remembrance of where 2000 of George Washington's 12,000 troops perished from freezing temperatures, hunger and disease, while many others returned home. A 22-mile cycling path along the Schuylkill River connects Valley Forge to Philadelphia.

PENNSYLVANIA DUTCH COUNTRY

The core of Pennsylvania Dutch Country lies in the southeast region of Pennsylvania, in an area about 20 by 15 miles, east of Lancaster. The Amish (*ah*-mish), Mennonite and Brethren religious communities are collectively known as the 'Plain People.' All are Anabaptist sects, persecuted in their native Switzerland, who from the early 1700s settled in tolerant Pennsylvania. Speaking German dialects, they became known as 'Dutch' (from 'Deutsch'). Most Pennsylvania Dutch live on farms and their beliefs vary from sect to sect. Many do not use electricity, and most opt for horse-drawn buggies – a delightful sight, and sound, in the area. The strictest believers, the Old Order Amish, wear dark, plain clothing, and live a simple, Bible-centered life – but have, ironically, become a major tourist attraction, thus bringing busloads of gawkers and the requisite strip malls, chain restaurants and hotels that lend this entire area an oxymoronic quality, to say the least.

Information

To escape the busloads of tourists and learn about the region, use a map to navigate the back roads, avoiding main Rtes 30 and 340 at all costs, or simply visiting in winter when tourism is down. Even better, rent a bicycle from **Rails to Trail Bicycle Shop** (☎ 717-367-7000; www.railstotrail.com; 1010 Hershey Rd, Elizabethtown; rental per day $25; 🕑 10am-6pm) between Hershey and Lancaster, pack some food and hit the road. Some farm homes rent rooms for $50 to $100 – they welcome kids, provide home-cooked meals and offer a unique opportunity to experience farm life. The **Dutch Country Visitors Center** (☎ 800-723-8824; www.padutchcountry.com; 🕑 9am-6pm Mon-Sat, to 4pm Sun), off Rte 30 in Lancaster, offers comprehensive information.

Sights & Activities

On the western edge of Amish country, the pleasant town of **Lancaster** – a surprising mix of hip art galleries, eateries and preserved brick row houses – was briefly the US capital in September 1777, when Congress stopped here overnight. The bustling **Central Market** (☎ 717-291-4723; Penn Sq; 🕑 6am-3pm Tue, Fri & Sat) offers local produce, cheese, meats and Amish baked goods and crafts. Next door, the **Heritage Center Museum** (☎ 717-299-6440; www.lancasterheritage.com; 13 W King St; admission free; 🕑 9am-5pm Mon-Sat, 10am-3pm Sun) has a collection of 18th- and 19th-century paintings and period furniture, and gives an excellent overview of Amish culture. The monthly **First Friday** (www.lancasterarts.com) celebration brings out a friendly local crowd for gallery hops along artsy Prince St.

Probably named for its crossroads location, nearby **Intercourse** has heavily touristed shops selling clothing, quilts, candles, furniture, fudge and, of course, souvenirs with off-color jokes.

Bird-in-Hand has craft stores, restaurants and a **farmers market** (☎ 717-393-9674; 2710 Old Philadelphia Pike). The **Bird-in-Hand Bake Shop** (☎ 717-656-7947; 542 Gibbons Rd; 🕑 8am-5pm Mon-Sat), north of town, has a good selection of souvenirs, crafts and homemade pies and cakes. **Abe's Buggy Rides** (☎ 717-392-1794; 2596 Old Philadelphia Pike; 🕑 10am-5pm Mon-Sat; adult/child $10/5; 👪) does a fun but not-so-authentic 2-mile tour. In **Lititz**, visitors come for the **Sturgis Pretzel House** (☎ 717-626-4354; www.juliussturgis.com; Rte 772; admission $3; 🕑 9am-5pm Mon-Sat), the USA's first pretzel factory. The nearby **Ephrata Cloister** (☎ 717-733-6600; www.ephratacloister.org; 632 W Main St, Ephrata; adult/child $9/6; 🕑 9am-5pm Mon-Sat, from noon Sun) gives tours of its collection of medieval-style buildings, one of the country's earliest religious communities.

Sleeping & Eating

There's a slew of inns in Amish country, and you will find several cheap motels along the southeastern portion of Rte 462/Rte 30. **Beacon Hollow Farm** (☎ 717-768-8218; 130 Centreville Rd; r incl breakfast $75), a dairy farm in Gordonville, has a cozy cottage with two bedrooms, provides a country breakfast and lets you milk the cows. A slightly more upscale and modern (complete with cable TV) experience can be had at **Landis Farm** (☎ 717-898-7028; www.landisfarm.com; 2048 Gochlan Rd, Manheim; r incl breakfast $100), a 200-year-old stone home with pinewood floors. For a refreshingly hip and urban experience, make a beeline to the snazzy new **Lancaster Arts Hotel** (☎ 866-720-2787; www.lancasterartshotel.com; 300 Harrisburg Ave; r from $169; Ⓟ ⊠ ✖ 📶), housed in an old brick tobacco warehouse and featuring a groovy boutique-hotel ambience and locally grown, organic-centric restaurant **John J Jeffries** (☎ 717-431-3307; mains

$14-25; ⏲ 11:30am-2pm & 5:30-10pm Mon-Fri, noon-2pm & 5:30-10pm Sat, 5:30-9pm Sun).

To sample one of the famous family-style restaurants and hearty dishes of Amish country, including the famous, sticky-sweet dessert of shoofly pie, get prepared to rub elbows with lots of tourists. To avoid the tour-bus crush, try the **Family Cupboard Restaurant & Buffet** (☎ 717-768-4510; 3029 Old Philadelphia Pike; mains $11; ⏲ 7am-8pm Mon-Sat) in Bird-in-Hand, for mouthwatering specials such as hamloaf (yes, that's right) and chicken in gravy over waffles.

Getting There & Around

RRTA (☎ 717-397-4246; www.redrosetransit.com) local buses link the main towns, but a car is much more convenient for sightseeing. The **Capitol Trailways & Greyhound terminal** (☎ 717-397-4861; Lancaster train station) has buses to Philadelphia ($15, two hours 40 minutes) and Pittsburgh ($71, eight hours). The **Amtrak train station** (53 McGovern Ave, Lancaster) has trains to and from Philadelphia ($15 to $18, 70 minutes) and Pittsburgh ($44, six hours).

SOUTH CENTRAL PENNSYLVANIA

Hershey

Less than two hours from Philly is the fabled kids' favorite **Hershey** (www.hersheypa.com), home to a collection of attractions that detail, hype and, of course, hawk, the many trappings of Milton Hershey's chocolate empire. The pièce de résistance is **Hershey Park** (☎ 800-437-7439; www.hersheypark.com; 100 W Hersheypark Dr; adult/child $52/31; ⏲ 10am-10pm Jun-Aug, 9am-6pm or 8pm Sep-May), an amusement park with more than 60 thrill rides (not chocolate themed), plus various performances and frequent fireworks displays. **Hershey's Chocolate World** (☎ 717-534-4900; www.hersheys.com/chocolate world; 251 Park Blvd; 'Chocolate Experience' film adult/child $6/4, 'Chocolate Tasting Adventure' $10/7; ⏲ 9am-10pm Jun-Aug, 9am-6pm or 8pm Sep-May; 🚸) is a mock factory and massive candy store with over-stimulating features like singing characters and free chocolate galore. For a more low-key informational visit, try the **Hershey Story, The Museum on Chocolate Avenue** (☎ 717-534-3439; www.hersheymuseum.org; 111 W Chocolate Ave; adult/child $10/7.50; ⏲ 9am-8pm summer, to 5:30pm other times; 🚸), which explores the life and legacy of Mr Hershey through interactive history exhibits; try molding your own candy in the hands-on 'Chocolate Lab.'

Gettysburg

This tranquil, compact and history-laden town, 145 miles west of Philadelphia, saw one of the Civil War's most decisive and bloody battles. It's also where Lincoln delivered his Gettysburg Address. The area is anchored by the 8-sq-mile **Gettysburg National Military Park** (☎ 717-334-1124; www.nps.gov/gett; 1195 Baltimore Pike (Rte 97); park admission free, museum admission adult/child $7.50/5.50; ⏲ 8am-6pm Apr-Oct, 8am-5pm Nov-Mar), with a great visitor center, museum and bookstore. Here you can pick up a map that details a self-guided auto tour, with somber sights including the Wheatfield, which was strewn with more than 4000 dead and wounded after battle.

The **Gettysburg Convention & Visitors Bureau** (☎ 717-334-2100; www.gettysburg.com; 89 Steinwehr Ave; ⏲ 8:30am-5:30pm) also distributes a comprehensive list of town attractions, which include the **Eisenhower National Historic Site** (☎ 717-338-9114; 250 Eisenhower Farm Lane; adult/child $6.50/4; ⏲ 9am-4pm), which is Ike's former home, and the house that served as **General Lee's Headquarters** (☎ 717-334-3141; 401 Budford Ave; admission free; ⏲ 9am-5pm mid-Mar–Nov), now a museum.

The annual **Civil War Heritage Days** (recorded information ☎ 717-334-0853), a festival taking place from the last weekend of June through the first weekend of July, features living-history encampments, battle reenactments, a lecture series and book fair that draws war reenactment aficionados from near and wide. You can find other **reenactments** (www.gettysburg.com /livinghistory) throughout the year.

For accommodations, try the stately three-story Victorian **Brickhouse Inn** (☎ 717-338-9337; www.brickhouseinn.com; 452 Baltimore St; r $115-165; ⊠ 📶), c 1898, a wonderful B&B with charming rooms and an outdoor patio. For a meal in Gettysburg's oldest home, built in 1776, head to **Dobbin House Tavern** (☎ 717-334-2100; 89 Steinwehr Ave; mains $8-25; ⏲ 11:30am-9pm), which serves heaping sandwiches as well as more elaborate meat and fish meals; choose from one of six fairly kitschy themed dining rooms, including a bedroom.

NORTHEASTERN PENNSYLVANIA

Occupying the northeast corner of Pennsylvania is the famed **Poconos** (☎ 800-762-6667; www.800poconos.com) region, containing 2400 sq miles of mountains, streams, waterfalls, lakes and forests, making it a beautifully natural getaway at any time during the four seasons. Among the quaint (as well as tacky) towns is

IF YOU HAVE A FEW MORE DAYS

Central PA can be an interesting counterpoint to the more touristy parts of the region. The town of **Bethlehem**, from its initial founding by a small religious community to heavy industry center to its current incarnation as a gambling destination, retains a charming historic quality. No doubt the Moravians, a Protestant denomination with roots in 14th-century European traditions who established the town on Christmas Eve in 1741, wouldn't recognize their tight-knit collective in the **New Sands Casino** (☎ 877-726-3777; www.pasands.com; 77 Sands Blvd). Built on the site of the former Bethlehem Steel factory, which produced materials for the George Washington Bridge, Empire State Building and Rockefeller Center, the building takes design cues from its utilitarian past.

A few hours further south and west from here down Hwys 222 and 30, is the architecturally interesting and historic town of **Hanover**, a peaceful alternative base for visiting Gettysburg, just 10 miles east on Rte 116. While you're there, visit the lively **Amish Market** (E Chestnut St) on Saturday or tour one of two snack-food factories – famous pretzel-maker **Snyder's of Hanover** (☎ 800-233-7125; www.snydersofhanover.com; 1350 York St; tours free; 10am, 11am, 1pm Tue-Thu) or **UTZ Quality Foods** (☎ 800-367-7629; www.utzsnacks.com; 900 High St; tours free; 8am-4pm Mon-Thu), best known for its potato chips.

adorable **Milford** (www.pikechamber.com), home to the lovingly and luxuriously restored **Hotel Fauchere** (☎ 570-409-1212; www.hotelfauchere.com; 401 Broad St; r incl breakfast $170-350;).

For river fun, contact **Adventure Sports** (☎ 570-223-0505, 800-487-2628; www.adventuresport.com; Rte 209; per day canoe/kayak $40/44; 9am-6pm Mon-Fri, from 8am Sat & Sun May-Oct) in Marshalls Creek, Pennsylvania. There are several different put-in and take-out points that allow a variety of itineraries, from quick half-day trips to leisurely multiday adventures. Camping is allowed at many points along the way and is a great way to experience the beauty of the area. Also in Marshalls Creek is the **Pocono Mt Go-Karts & Play Park** (☎ 570-223-6299; Rte 209), which in addition to the aforementioned go-karts has paintball and archery.

A little further west in a tucked-away valley is **Jim Thorpe** (named for an athletic hero of the early 1900s who was buried here – but likely never visited – after town officials decided they needed a signature tourism sight), which offers a slew of mountain-biking trails and rafting runs (as well as the requisite outfitters); and the **Lehigh Gorge Scenic Railway** (☎ 570-325-8485; www.lgsry.com; adult/child $12/9; 11am, 1pm & 3pm), offering peaceful one-hour rides through the Lehigh Gorge State Park. A few miles east of Jim Thorpe is the family-run **Big Creek Vineyard** (☎ 610-681-3959; www.bigcreekvineyard.com; Keller Rd, Kresgeville; 1-5pm Sun-Thu, to 7pm Fri & Sat), worth a tasting tour when you're in the area.

North of here, where the Delaware River swings west, marking the border between Pennsylvania and New York, not far from the Catskills, are a number of small, primarily blue-collar towns with the occasional bistro that caters to weekending downstaters. **Lander's River Trips** (☎ 800-252-3925; www.landersrivertrips.com; per day canoe/kayak/tube $39/45/26) in Callicoon, NY and in Narrowsburg, NY, further down the river rents canoes, kayaks and tubes.

PITTSBURGH

Famous as an industrial center during the 19th century, to many Americans Pittsburgh still conjures stark images of billowing clouds emanating from steel and coal factories. Scottish-born immigrant Andrew Carnegie made his fortune here by modernizing steel production, and his legacy is still synonymous with the city and its many cultural and educational institutions. Production dipped during the Great Depression but rose again because of mass-produced automobiles in the 1930s. Today's city, however, despite continuing economic challenges, has a well-earned reputation for being one of the more livable metropolitan areas in the country. Hilly like San Francisco and boasting more bridges than any other city in the US, in terms of geography, at least, Pittsburgh has an almost European feel. Teeming with students from the many universities in town, it's a surprisingly hip and cultured city with top-notch museums, abundant greenery and several bustling neighborhoods with lively restaurant and bar scenes. When the economy and local steel industry took another major hit in the 1970s, the city's pride was buoyed by its local NFL football team: the Steelers achieved a remarkable run of four Super Bowl championships, a feat whose importance to the continuing psyche of some Pittsburghers can't be underestimated. After the steel industry's demise, Pittsburgh's economy has refocused on health care, technology and education and the city is home to several notable Fortune 500 companies, including Alcoa and Heinz.

Orientation

The city sits at the point where the Monongahela and Allegheny Rivers join the Ohio River, spreads out over the waterways and has neighborhoods connected by picturesque bridges (all with footpaths). It's large and not easily traversed on foot unless you're exploring one neighborhood at a time. The mystical-sounding Golden Triangle, between the converging Monongahela and Allegheny Rivers, is Pittsburgh's renovated downtown. Just northeast of here, the Strip offers warehouses, ethnic food stores and nightclubs and, across the Allegheny River, the North Side has big sports stadiums plus several museums. Across the Monongahela River is the South Side, whose Slopes rise up to Mt Washington; at the Flats, E Carson St bustles with clubs and restaurants. East of downtown is Oakland, the university area, and beyond that Squirrel Hill and Shadyside, residential neighborhoods with an elegant, small-town feel.

Rand McNally makes good laminated maps of Pittsburgh, available in the city's bookstores, while **Universal Map** (www.universalmap.com) makes an excellent paper street map of Greater Pittsburgh ($13).

Information

BOOKSTORES

Caliban Book Shop (☎ 412-681-9111; www.calibanbooks.com; 410 S Craig St; 🕑 11am-5:30pm Mon-Sat & 1-5:30pm Sun) Specializes in literary first editions, fine arts, poetry and travel.

City Books (☎ 412-481-7555; 1111 E Carson St; 🕑 11am-5pm Mon-Sat & 1-5pm Sun) On the South Side.

Joseph-Beth Booksellers (☎ 412-381-3600; www.josephbeth.com; 2705 E Carson St; 🕑 10am-9pm Mon-Thu, to 10pm Fri & Sat, 11am-7pm Sun) Part of a regional chain; massive selection.

University of Pittsburgh Book Center (☎ 412-648-1455; 4000 Fifth Ave; 🕑 8:30am-6:30pm Mon-Thu, 9am-5pm Fri & Sat) Tens of thousands of general titles, plus textbooks.

INTERNET ACCESS

The city offers free wi-fi access downtown (as does the Pittsburgh International Airport). In addition to cafés, several on the South Side, the **Carnegie Library of Pittsburgh** (☎ 412-622-3114; 4400 Forbes Ave; wi-fi) main branch (plus others) has free public access at terminals.

INTERNET RESOURCES

Citysearch (pittsburgh.citysearch.com) Nightlife, restaurant and shopping listings.

Hello Pittsburgh (www.hellopittsburgh.com) Comprehensive city listings.

Pittsburgh.net (www.pittsburgh.net) Listings, neighborhoods and events.

Pop City (www.popcitymedia.com) Weekly e-magazine highlighting arts and cultural events.

MEDIA

Pittsburgh City Paper (www.pghcitypaper.com) Free alternative weekly with extensive arts listings.

Pittsburgh's Out (www.outonline.com) Free monthly gay newspaper.

Pittsburgh Post-Gazette (www.post-gazette.com) A major daily.

Pittsburgh Tribune-Review (www.pittsburghlive.com) Another major daily.

WQED-FM: 90.5 Local National Public Radio affiliate.

WYEP-FM: 91.3 Local independent station with eclectic music.

MEDICAL SERVICES

Allegheny County Health Department (☎ 412-687-2243; 3333 Forbes Ave) Has a walk-in medical center.

Allegheny General Hospital (☎ 866-680-0004; 320 E North Ave; 🕑 24hr) Emergency room.

University of Pittsburgh Medical Center (☎ 412-647-8762; 200 Lothrop St; 🕑 24hr) Emergency, high-ranking medical care.

MONEY

You will find ATMs in delicatessens and grocery stores (where you may be charged up to a $3 fee) as well as in banks.

POST

Post office (☎ 412-642-0769; 700 Grant St) Main branch; call for other locations.

TOURIST INFORMATION

Greater Pittsburgh Convention & Visitors Bureau Main Branch (☎ 412-281-7711, 800-359-0758; www.visitpittsburgh.com; 30th fl, 425 Sixth Ave; 🕑 9am-4pm Mon-Fri, to 5pm Sat, 10am-3pm Sun); Pittsburgh International Airport (near baggage claim; 🕑 9am-5pm Mon-Fri, to 3pm Sat & Sun) Publishes the *Official Visitors Guide* and provides maps and tourist advice.

Sights & Activities

Points of interest in Pittsburgh are scattered everywhere, and the city's spread-out nature makes it a difficult place to cover thoroughly on foot. Driving can also be troublesome, due to the oddly laid-out streets, which confuse even locals. Public buses, luckily, are quite reliable (see p236 for more information). University of Pittsburgh, Carnegie-Mellon University, Duquesne University and several other smaller colleges are all large presences in town, with sprawling campuses and bustling academic crowds.

For pretty much any outdoor pursuit, the best option is the elaborate, 1700-acre system of the **Pittsburgh Parks Conservancy** (☎ 412-682-7275; www.pittsburghparks.org), which comprises **Schenley Park** (with a public swimming pool and golf course), **Highland Park** (with swimming pool, tennis courts and bicycling track), **Riverview Park** (sporting ball fields and horseback riding trails) and **Frick Park** (with hiking trails, clay courts and a bowling green), all with beautiful running, cycling and in-line skating trails.

Active types can find guidance at places such as the **Golden Triangle Bike & Blade Shop** (☎ 412-600-0675; www.goldentrianglebikenblade.com; Eliza Furnace Trail, under 1st Ave Transit Station; 🕑 11am-8pm Tue-Fri, from 10am Sat & Sun; rental per hr/day $8/30), which rents bikes and leads various tours of the city; there's even a continuous trail all the way to Washington, DC. **Venture Outdoors** (☎ 412-255-0564; www.wpfi.org; 304 Forbes Ave) is the prime source for outdoor recreation in the region, and sponsors cycling, hiking and kayaking tours in and around the city.

DOWNTOWN

Referred to as the 'Golden Triangle' only in official tourist brochures, downtown is where you'll find the **Allegheny County Courthouse** (☎ 412-350-5313; 436 Grant St; 🕑 9am-5pm Mon-Fri), a 19th-century Romanesque stone building that fills two city blocks. At the triangle's tip is the renovated and beautified waterfront **Point State Park**, which is popular during summer with strollers, cyclists, loungers and runners; for a longer run, head to the 11-mile gravel-paved **Montour Trail** (www.montourtrail.org), accessible by crossing the 6th St Bridge and catching the paved path at the Carnegie Science Center (opposite). The park's renovated **Fort Pitt Museum** (☎ 412-281-9284; www.fortpittmuseum.com; 101 Commonwealth Pl; admission $7; 🕑 9am-5pm Wed-Sun) commemorates the historic heritage of the French and Indian War. The nicely remodeled brick warehouse that is the **Senator John Heinz Pittsburgh Regional History Center** (☎ 412-454-6000; www.pghhistory.org; 1212 Smallman St; adult/child $10/5, includes admission to Sports Museum; 🕑 10am-5pm) offers a good take on the region's past, with exhibits on the French and Indian War, early settlers, immigrants, steel and the glass industry; it's also home to the **Western Pennsylvania Sports Museum** (☎ 412-454-6000; www.pghhistory.org; 1212 Smallman Ave; 🕑 10am-5pm), focusing on champs from Pittsburgh. In September 2009 the **August Wilson Center for African American Culture** (☎ 412-258-2700; www.augustwilsoncenter.org; 425 Sixth Ave) christened it's strikingly contemporary new building, which houses a museum, classrooms and performance space.

SOUTH SIDE & MT WASHINGTON

Youthful, funky and bustling like NYC's East Village, the South Side is bursting with shops, eateries and drinking spots. In the 10 blocks between the 10th St Bridge and Birmingham Bridge there are nearly 50 bars, not including little hole-in-the-wall joints. When sober and satiated, stop in at the **Society for Contemporary Art** (☎ 412-261-7003; www.contemporarycraft.org; 2100 Smallman St; 🕑 1-5pm Tue-Sat) for cutting-edge crafts and other art exhibitions.

To see the south side from above, ride either the **Monongahela Incline** (☎ 412-442-2000; www.portauthority.org; one way adult/child $2/1; 🕑 5:30am-12:45am Mon-Sat, 8:45am-midnight Sun) or **Duquesne Incline** (☎ 412-381-1665; www.incline.pghfree.net; one way adult/child $2/1; 🕑 5:30am-12:45am Mon-Sat, from 7am Sun), the historic funicular railroads that run up and down **Mt Washington**'s steep slopes and afford great city views. At the start of the Duquesne Incline is **Station Square** (☎ 800-859-8959; www.stationsquare.com; Station Sq Dr, at Fort Pitt Bridge), a group of beautiful, renovated railway buildings that now comprise what is essentially a big ol' mall. Rising up from the bustling South Side valley is the neighborhood called the **South Side Slopes**, a fascinating community of houses that seem perilously perched on the edge of cliffs, accessible via steep, winding roads and hundreds of stairs.

NORTH SIDE

While this part of town feels most populated when its PNC Park (p236) is filled with sports fans for a Pittsburgh Steelers game, rest assured that its many museums are hopping, too. The **Andy Warhol Museum** (☎ 412-237-8300; www.warhol.org; 117 Sandusky St; adult/child $15/8; ⏰ 10am-5pm Tue-Thu, Sat & Sun, to 10pm Fri) celebrates Pittsburgh's coolest native son, who became famous for his pop art, avant-garde movies, celebrity connections and Velvet Underground spectaculars. Exhibits include celebrity portraits, while the museum's theater hosts frequent film screenings and quirky performers. Friday-night cocktails at the museum are popular with Pittsburgh's gay community.

Also not to be missed is the **Mattress Factory** (☎ 412-231-3169; www.mattress.org; 500 Sampsonia Way; adult/child $10/free; ⏰ 10am-5pm Tue-Sat, 1-5pm Sun), hosting unique installation art and frequent performances.

Carnegie Science Center (☎ 412-237-3400; www.carnegiesciencecenter.org; 1 Allegheny Ave; adult/child $14/10, IMAX & special exhibits extra; ⏰ 10am-5pm Sun-Fri, to 7pm Sat; 👶), great for kids, is a cut above the average hands-on science museum, with innovative exhibits on subjects ranging from outer space to candy.

The **National Aviary** (☎ 412-321-4364; www.aviary.org; W Commons, Allegheny Sq; adult/child $10/8.50; ⏰ 10am-5pm, from 9am late May–early Sep; 👶) is another treat, with more than 600 exotic and endangered birds. Nearby in the northwest is the **Mexican War Streets** neighborhood, named after battles and soldiers of the 1846 Mexican War. The carefully restored row houses, with Greek Revival doorways and Gothic turrets lining the quiet streets, make for a peaceful, postmuseum stroll.

The **Pittsburgh Children's Museum** (☎ 412-322-5058; www.pittsburghkids.org; Allegheny Sq; adult/child $11/10; ⏰ 10am-5pm Mon-Sat, noon-5pm Sun; 👶) features loads of interactive exhibits, including a chance for kids to get under the hood of real cars and some child-friendly Warhol works.

OAKLAND & AROUND

The University of Pittsburgh and Carnegie Mellon University are here, and the surrounding streets are packed with cheap eateries, cafés, shops and student homes. Rising up from the center of the U Pitt campus is the soaring **Cathedral of Learning** (☎ 412-624-6000; 4200 Fifth Ave; admission free, tours $3; ⏰ 9am-3pm Mon-Sat, from 11am Sun), a grand, 42-story Gothic tower which, at 535ft, is the second-tallest education building in the world. It houses the elegant **Nationality Classrooms**, each representing a different style and period, with gorgeous details such as the red-velvet upholstered chairs of Austria; most are accessible only with a guided tour.

Nearby are two **Carnegie Museums** (☎ 412-622-3131; www.carnegiemuseums.org; 4400 Forbes Ave; adult/child to both $15/11; ⏰ 10am-5pm Tue-Sat, from noon Sun) – the **Carnegie Museum of Art**, with terrific exhibits of architecture, impressionist, postimpressionist and modern American paintings; and the **Carnegie Museum of Natural History**, featuring a complete Tyrannosaurus skeleton and exhibits on Pennsylvania geology and Inuit prehistory. East of Oakland, in Point Breeze, is the wonderful **Frick Art & Historical Center** (☎ 412-371-0600; www.frickart.org; 7227 Reynolds St; museum & grounds free, Clayton tours $10; ⏰ 10am-5pm Tue-Sun), which displays some of Henry Clay Frick's Flemish, French and Italian paintings in its Art Museum; assorted Frickmobiles like a 1914 Rolls Royce in the Car & Carriage Museum; more than five acres of grounds and gardens; and Clayton, the restored 1872 Frick mansion.

SQUIRREL HILL & SHADYSIDE

These upscale neighborhoods feature wide streets, excellent restaurants, chain stores and independent boutiques and bakeries (try the burnt-almond tortes, a classic Pittsburgh dessert). Squirrel Hill is home to Pittsburgh's large Jewish community, the city's best kosher eateries, butchers and Judaica shops; apartment buildings, duplexes and more modest housing are almost as common as the grand mansions the neighborhood is known for. **Temple Sinai** (☎ 412-421-9715; www.templesinaipgh.org; 5505 Forbes Ave) is a synagogue that's housed in the architecturally stunning Elizabethan-style former mansion of John Worthington. In Shadyside, Walnut St is the bustling main strip. The leafy campus of **Chatham University**, located between the two neighborhoods, is a nice place to stroll.

GREATER PITTSBURGH

Formerly gritty **Lawrenceville** has become the city's **Interior Design District** (www.1662designzone.com), comprising the stretch on and around Butler St from 16th to 62nd Sts. It's a long and spotty strip of shops, galleries, studios, bars and eateries that's on every hipster's radar, and runs into the gentrifying **Garfield** neighborhood, a good place for cheap ethnic eats. **Bloomfield**, a really little Little Italy, is a strip of groceries, Italian eateries and, of all things, a landmark Polish restaurant, the Bloomfield Bridge Tavern (see opposite).

Folks with kids to entertain might want to seek out the **Pittsburgh Zoo & PPG Aquarium** (412-665-3640; www.pittsburghzoo.com; 7340 Butler St; adult/child $12/10; 9am-5pm Apr–late May & early Sep–late Dec, to 4pm Jan–Mar, to 6pm late May–early Sep;), or for wet fun in the summer, the **Sandcastle Waterpark** (412-462-6666; www.sandcastlewaterpark.com; 1000 Sandcastle Dr; admission $28; 11am-6pm Jun-Sep;).

Tours

Alan Irvine Storyteller Tours (412-521-6406; www.alanirvine.com/walking_tour; tours $10-15) This historian brings the city's past to life in a journey through several neighborhoods.

Just Ducky Tours (412-402-3825; www.justducky tours.com; Station Sq; adult/child $19/15; Apr-Oct) General city tours in a WWII amphibious vehicle.

Pittsburgh History & Landmarks Foundation (412-471-5808; www.phlf.org; Station Sq; tours from $5) Specialized historic, architectural or cultural tours by foot or motor coach.

Festivals & Events

Hothouse (www.sproutfund.org/hothouse) Annual June night of eclectic performance, art and music supports Pittsburgh's creative side.

Three Rivers Art Festival (www.artsfestival.net) Showcasing the city's cultural credentials, this 10-day blowout in June features free concerts and outdoor visual and performance arts in Point State Park.

Pittsburgh Three Rivers Regatta (www.threerivers regatta.com) Speedboats race on the three rivers in July or August.

Step Trek (www.southsideslopes.org) A community climb up the 23,982 vertical feet of steps of the South Side Slopes in early fall.

Sleeping

Oakland has the straight-up chain hotels – Hampton Inn, Holiday Inn, Residence Inn and the like. The **Holiday Inn Express** (412-488-1130; www.hiexpress.com; 20 S 10th St; r from $160;) is only worth pointing out for its convenient location on the busy South Side. For more character, check in with the **Pittsburgh Bed & Breakfast Association** (www.pittsburghbnb.com).

Inn on the Mexican War Streets (412-231-6544; www.innonthemexicanwarstreets.com; 604 W North Ave; r incl breakfast $139-189;) This historic, gay-owned mansion on the North Side is near the museums and right on the bus line that takes you downtown. Expect hearty homemade breakfasts, charming hosts, stunning antique furnishings and an elegant porch, plus a martini lounge and the four-star restaurant Acanthus.

Morning Glory Inn (412-431-1707; www.gloryinn .com; 2119 Sarah St; r incl breakfast $145-190, ste $175-450;) An Italianate-style Victorian brick town house popular for weddings, the Morning Glory is in the heart of the busy South Side. The overall decor is slightly chintzy – think floral patterns, wicker furniture, four-poster beds – but you can relax in the charming backyard patio, and delicious breakfasts are a major plus.

Inn on Negley (412-661-0631; www.theinnson negley.com; 703 Negley Ave; r $180-235;) Formerly a pair of Shadyside inns, these two Victorian houses have been combined into one newly refurbished gem with a clean-line aesthetic that still bursts with romance. It features four-poster beds, handsome furniture and fireplaces, large windows and, in some rooms, hot tubs.

Sunnyledge (412-683-5014; www.sunnyledge .com; 5124 Fifth Ave; r/ste $189/275;) Though it refers to itself as a 'boutique hotel,' it would be more accurate to describe the Sunnyledge as a 'historic' one. Housed in an 1886 mansion in Shadyside, the atmosphere is one of traditional elegance, overwrought at times. The restaurant on premises gets mixed reviews.

Omni William Penn Hotel (412-281-7100; www.omnihotels.com; 530 William Penn Place; r from $200;) An old-school high-rise hotel in the downtown district – good for a Pirates or Steelers game but not nightlife – the Omni features a grand lobby and spacious rooms. Above-average service, a spa and several dining options as well.

Eating

BUDGET

Primanti Bros (412-263-2142; www.primantibros .com; 18th St, at Smallman St; sandwiches $6; 24hr) A Pittsburgh institution on the Strip, this always-packed place specializes in greasy and delicious hot sandwiches – from knockwurst and cheese to the 'Pitts-burger cheesesteak.' Other outlets are in Oakland, downtown and South Side.

Original Hot Dog Shop (☎ 412-621-7388; 3901 Forbes Ave; meals $3-5; ⏰ 10am-3:30am Mon-Thu, to 5am Fri & Sat) Affectionately nicknamed 'dirty Os' or 'the O' by locals, this is a favorite for its cheap dogs and mounds of crispy fries – especially after a night at the bars.

Quiet Storm Coffeehouse & Restaurant (☎ 412-661-9355; www.quietstormcoffee.com; 5430 Penn Ave; mains $6-11; ⏰ 8am-7pm Mon-Thu, 8am-10pm Fri, 10am-10pm Sat, 10am-4pm Sun; Ⓥ) This hipster-filled, multi-use café in Garfield specializes in veggie and vegan cuisine and hosts frequent readings and musical performances.

Kessab's (☎ 412-381-1820; 1207 Carson St; mains $6; ⏰ 10:30am-10pm Mon-Thu, to 11pm Fri & Sat), a Lebanese restaurant on the South Side, serves splendid baba ghanoush, and the tiny and popular **Pho Minh** (☎ 412-661-7443; 4917 Penn Ave; mains $5-7; ⏰ noon-9pm Wed, Thu & Sun, to 10pm Fri & Sat) does excellent Vietnamese noodle, soup and tofu dishes.

MIDRANGE & TOP END

Kaya (☎ 412-261-6565; 2000 Smallman Ave; dishes $9-25; ⏰ 11:30am-10pm Mon-Wed, to 11pm Thu-Sat, noon-9pm Sun) Sleek and funky – think bongo drums for bar stools – Kaya is a popular place serving up creative Caribbean-inspired dishes. Vegetarians are well catered for here as well.

Gypsy Café (☎ 412-381-4977; 1330 Bingham St; mains $14-19; ⏰ 11:30am-midnight) The purple floors and walls and brightly colored rugs make loyal patrons here as happy as the fresh, seasonal fare. Sample menu items include a smoked trout plate and a stew of shrimp, scallop and feta. Hours are changeable so call ahead

Dish Osteria Bar (☎ 412-390-2012; 128 S 17th St; mains $14-25; ⏰ 5pm-2am Mon-Sat) A tucked-away, intimate locals' fave. The simple wood tables and floors belie the at-times extravagant Mediterranean creations, which range from fresh sardines with caramelized onions to fettuccine with lamb *ragù*.

Cafe du Jour (☎ 412-488-9695; 1107 E Carson St; mains $15-35; ⏰ 11:30am-10pm Mon-Sat) Part of the raucous South Side 'hood, Cafe du Jour has a constantly changing menu of Mediterranean dishes. It does especially good soups and salads for lunch; try to get a seat in the small outside courtyard. It's BYOB.

Also recommended:

City Grill (☎ 412-431-1770; 2019 E Carson St; mains $10-25; ⏰ 11am-11pm Mon-Thu, to midnight Fri & Sat, 4-10pm Sun) On the South Side; known for mouthwatering burgers, considered one of the best in the city.

Double Wide Grill (☎ 412-390-1111; 2339 E Carson St; mains $14-27; ⏰ 11am-10pm Mon-Wed, to midnight Thu-Sat, 10am-10pm Sun) Does barbecue as well as interesting veggie options like pulled seitan and coconut tofu.

Drinking & Entertainment

BARS & NIGHTCLUBS

Most nightlife is centered on the South Side and the Strip. Carson St is ground zero for bar-hopping: a few worth including in your itinerary are **Smokin' Joe's** (☎ 412-431-6757; 2001 E Carson St) for its huge beer selection; **Dee's Cafe** (☎ 412-431-1314; 1314 E Carson St), a notable punk bar with Pabst on tap; **Z: Lounge** (☎ 412-481-2234; 2108 E Carson St), a mellow and trendy pub; and the **Hofbräuhaus** (☎ 412-224-2328; 2705 S Water St), an imitation of the famous Munich beer hall and only a block off Carson.

Last Chance (2533 Penn Ave), on the Strip, is a popular neighborhood pub for guys who can hold their liquor. **Bloomfield Bridge Tavern** (☎ 412-682-8611; 4412 Liberty Ave), 'the only Polish restaurant in Lil' Italy,' is a gritty pub serving beers with excellent sides of pierogi and the occasional indie rock band, while the **Church Brew Works** (☎ 412-688-8200; 3525 Liberty Ave), serving handcrafted beers in a massive former church space, is a standout in Lawrenceville.

You'll find several big, frenzied dance clubs, known 'meatmarkets,' clustered at the edge of the Strip district, including **Matrix** (☎ 412-261-2220; www.matrixpgh.com; 7 E Station Sq Dr), a sort of mall of nightclubs housing Club Exit ('80s classics), Club Liquid (techno and trance), Club Velvet (salsa and merengue) and Club Goddess (Top 40 pop).

Most gay bars are in a concentrated stretch of Liberty Ave downtown. They're hoppin' and plentiful, but perhaps the hippest, most frenzied gay spot is the off-the-beaten-path nightclub **Pittsburgh Eagle** (☎ 412-766-7222; www.pitteagle.com; 1740 Eckert St; ⏰ 9pm-2am Fri & Sat), which draws internationally known DJs and porn stars alike.

LIVE MUSIC

Shadow Lounge (☎ 412-363-8277; www.shadowlounge.net; 5972 Baum Blvd) is the place for catching hot hip-hop and house DJs, plus indie bands, readings and open mike nights. **Rex Theater** (☎ 412-381-6811; www.elkoconcerts.com; 1602 E Carson St) is a favorite South Side venue, a converted movie theater, for touring jazz, rock and indie bands; everyone from Edgar Winter to Ani DiFranco. On the South Side, **Club**

Café (☎ 412-431-4950; www.clubcafelive.com; 56-58 S 12th St) has live music nightly, mostly of the singer-songwriter type. Live concerts/ recordings of top jazz musicians are held at **Manchester Craftsman Guild** (☎ 412-323-4000; www.mcgjazz.org; 1815 Metropolitan St) on the north side of the city.

THEATER & CULTURE

Pittsburgh Cultural Trust (☎ 412-471-6070; www.pgharts.org; 803 Liberty Ave) promotes all downtown arts, from the Pittsburgh Dance Council and PNC Broadway in Pittsburgh to visual art and opera; the website has links to all main arts venues.

The restored **Harris Theater** (☎ 412-682-4111; 809 Liberty Ave) screens a wide variety of art-house films, often part of film festivals.

Gist Street Readings (www.giststreet.org; 3rd fl, 305 Gist St; readings $5) holds monthly readings from local and well-known national literary figures. Best to get there when doors open at 7:15pm, since turnout is typically large. Bring your own refreshments.

SPORTS

Pittsburgh is a big-time sports city. Fans will tell you they bleed black and gold, the colors of the hometown NFL franchise the **Steelers** who play at **Heinz Field** (☎ 412-323-1200; www.pittsburghsteelers.com). Also on the North Side, just by the Allegheny River, is **PNC Park** (☎ 412-323-5000; www.pirateball.com), where the Pittsburgh Pirates major-league baseball team bases itself. **Mellon Arena** (☎ 412-642-1800; www.penguins.nhl.com), just east of downtown, is where the NHL Pittsburgh Penguins, Stanley Cup finalists in 2008 and winners in 2009, play hockey. The University of Pittsburgh basketball team, the **Pitt Panthers** (☎ 412-648-7488; www.pittsburghpanthers.com), is a perennial top-ranked team with a rabid fan base.

Getting There & Away

Pittsburgh International Airport (PIT; ☎ 412-472-3525; www.pitairport.com), 18 miles west from downtown, has direct connections to Europe, Canada and major US cities via a slew of airlines.

Arriving in its station near the Strip, **Greyhound** (☎ 412-392-6513; cnr 11th St & Liberty Ave) has frequent buses to Philadelphia ($46, seven hours), New York ($54, 11 hours) and Chicago, IL ($62, 10 to 14 hours).

Pittsburgh is easily accessible via major highways, from the north or south on the I-76 or I-79, from the west on Rte 22 and from the east on the I-70. It's about an eight-hour drive from New York City and about three hours from Buffalo.

Amtrak (☎ 800-872-7245; 1100 Liberty Ave) is behind the magnificent original train station, with trains heading to cities including Philadelphia (from $47, seven to eight hours) and New York (from $63, nine to 11 hours).

Getting Around

The excellent **28X Airport Flyer** (☎ 412-442-2000; www.portauthority.org/PAAC.com; one way $2.60) public bus makes runs from the airport to Oakland and downtown every 20 minutes. Taxis are readily available and cost about $40 (not including tip) to downtown. Various shuttles also make downtown runs and cost $15 to $20 per person one way.

Driving around Pittsburgh can be extremely frustrating – roads end with no warning, one-way streets can take you in circles and there are various bridges to contend with. Get a good map or, even better, a copilot, and stop to ask locals for directions.

Port Authority Transit (☎ 412-442-2000; www.portauthority.org) operates an extensive bus system and a limited light-rail system, the 'T,' which is useful for going from downtown to the South Side. Bus and T fares range from free to $3, depending on the zone in which you're traveling.

For taxis, call **Yellow Cab Co of Pittsburgh** (☎ 412-321-8100), which charges by zone.

AROUND PITTSBURGH

A Frank Lloyd Wright masterpiece, **Fallingwater** (☎ 724-329-8501; www.fallingwater.org; adult/child $18/12; 🕒 8:30am-4:30pm Thu-Tue Mar-Nov, 11:30am-3pm Fri-Sun Dec, closed Jan & Feb) is south of Pittsburgh on Rte 381. Completed in 1939 as a weekend retreat for the Kaufmanns, owners of the Pittsburgh department store, the building blends seamlessly with its natural setting. To see inside you must take one of the hourly guided tours, and reservations are recommended. A more intensive two-hour tour, with photography permitted, is offered ($55; times vary depending on day and month, reservations required). The rather attractive forested grounds open at 8:30am.

Much less visited is **Kentuck Knob** (☎ 724-329-1901; www.kentuckknob.com; adult/child $16/10; 🕒 10am-5pm Tue-Sun, from noon Wed), another Frank Lloyd Wright house (designed in 1953), built into the side of a rolling hill. It's noted for its natural materials, hexagonal design and honeycomb skylights. House tours last about an hour and include a jaunt through the on-site sculpture garden, with works by Andy Goldsworthy, Ray Smith and others.

To spend a night or two in the area, opt for the historic mountaintop **Summit Inn** (☎ 724-438-8594; www.summitinnresort.com; 101 Skyline Dr; r $120-300) or the swank **Nemacolin Woodlands Resort & Spa** (☎ 724-329-8555; www.nemacolin.com; 1001 Lafayette Dr; r from $200), with a spa, golf course and dining rooms. Both are in Farmington.

NORTHWESTERN PENNSYLVANIA

The smallest of the Great Lakes, at 241 miles across and only 62ft deep, **Lake Erie** warms quickly in the summer and frequently freezes in the winter, making it a magnet for all sorts of recreation, from swimming to ice fishing (a popular sport here). Several wineries in the area, cultivating largely Concord grapes, the first native American grape, are found along the southern shore.

Surrounded by rural byways and small towns, the city of **Erie** (www.visitEriePA.com), the fourth largest in the state, is for the most part a neglected industrial center combined with a touristy, revitalized shop-filled **Bayfront District**. But the **Presque Isle State Park** (☎ 814-838-7424; www.presqueisle.org; park office on Peninsula Dr), which shoots north and then curves back down upon itself just like Cape Cod in Massachusetts, is a stunningly beautiful place to visit, no matter the season. It's a lovely sandy peninsula with dramatic, ocean-like vistas interspersed with wooded areas and cycling trails. The **Lady Kate** (☎ 800-988-5780; www.piboattours.com; adult/child $16/9), a ferry that leaves from Presque Isle's south shore, gives 90-minute narrated tours of Lake Erie's shoreline.

Though there is no camping allowed on Presque Isle, the nearby **Virginia's Beach** (☎ 814-922-3261; www.virginiasbeach.com; campsites $28-42, cottages $69-119;) has tent/RV sites and cottages right on Lake Erie. Standard chain accommodations are a dime a dozen in and around Erie and near the park's entrance. **Spencer House B&B** (☎ 814-454-5984; www.spencerhouse.net; 519 W Sixth St; $119-200;), in Erie itself, is an impressively maintained classic Victorian with elegant and stately common areas.

To the east, some 80-odd miles from Erie, nature-lovers can explore the 797-sq-mile ` (☎ 814-723-5150; www.fs.fed.us/r9/forests/allegheny), which encompasses several state parks and sprouting acres of hemlock, maple, white ash and the valuable Allegheny black cherry. It's an excellent place for camping and hiking, canoeing and fishing.

New England

New Englanders like to think this is where it all began. They did, after all, set off the American Revolution. Today Boston, the self-proclaimed 'Hub' of the region, still packs a wallop with history and culture aplenty, and is the perfect place to start your explorations. No place in New England is more than a day's drive from Boston, but the region's compactness belies its diversity. Along the coast you'll find age-old fishing villages raking in lobster, beaches begging for a dip and century-old schooners hoisting the sails. Revitalized urban gems such as Providence, Portland and Portsmouth boast uncrowded sights, palate-pleasing dining and microbreweries.

Ready to stretch your quads? Inland Maine, New Hampshire and Vermont are as rugged and rural as the mountains that run up their spines. Snowboard the slopes, hike off to your own swimming hole or just get lost on a scenic back road and count the covered bridges. If you're lucky enough to be here in the fall, when the mountains are ablaze with color, you're in for the finest foliage scenery in the USA.

So give yourself time to get a real taste of the region. Crack open a lobster and let the sweet juices run down your fingers, stroll the cobbled streets of Nantucket, sink your toes into the sands of Cape Cod. Go to Harvard and Yale, if just for a day, and rub shoulders with Ivy Leaguers in hip campus cafés. Arm yourself with a good map and ramble along country roads past rolling rivers and iconic New England villages with white-steepled churches on tidy greens.

HIGHLIGHTS

- Following in the footsteps of Colonial rebel rousers along **Boston's Freedom Trail** (p252).
- Feasting on fresh boiled lobster at one of the **lobster shacks** (p304) along New England's coast towns like Ogunquit.
- Driving the scenic **Kancamagus Highway** (p299) across the craggy White Mountains, stopping for waterfalls, trails and moose sightings.
- Romping across the dunes at **Cape Cod National Seashore** (p264).
- Digging into **Acadia National Park** (p310), hiking and cycling its carriage roads and relaxing over afternoon tea at Jordan Pond.
- Ogling the palatial mansions and basking in music at folk and jazz festivals in **Newport** (p276).
- Working off an organic lunch at one of **Burlington's** (p292) green cafés with a paddle around Lake Champlain.
- Treating yourself to dazzling fall foliage in the **Green Mountains** (p288 and p291), **Berkshires** (p273) and **Litchfield Hills** (p284).

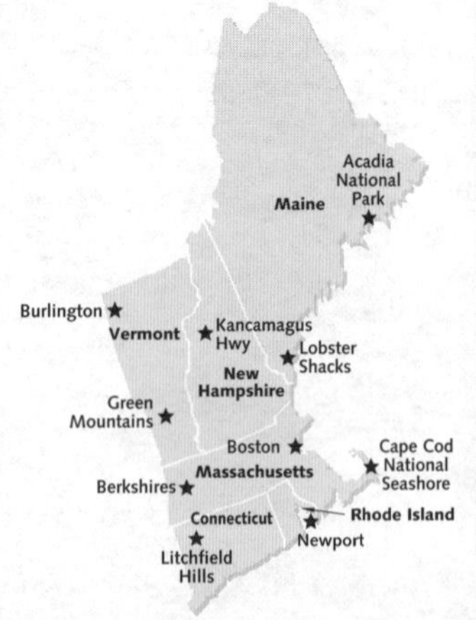

HISTORY

When the first European settlers arrived, much of New England was inhabited by native Algonquians who lived in small tribes, raising corn and beans, hunting game and harvesting the rich coastal waters.

English captain Bartholomew Gosnold landed at Cape Cod and sailed north to Maine in 1602 but it wasn't until 1614 that Captain John Smith, who charted the region's coastline for King James I, christened the land 'New England.' With the arrival of the Pilgrims at Plymouth in 1620, European settlement began in earnest. Over the next century the colonies expanded and thrived, often at the expense of the indigenous people.

Although subjects of the British crown, New Englanders governed themselves with their own legislative councils and they came to view their affairs as separate from those of England. In the 1770s King George III instituted policies intent on reining in the colonists' free-wheeling spirits and he imposed a series of costly taxes. The colonists, unrepresented in the English Parliament, revolted under the slogan 'no taxation without representation.' Attempts to squash the revolt resulted in the battles of Lexington and Concord, setting off the American Revolution that gave birth to the USA in 1776.

Following independence, New England became an economic powerhouse, its harbors booming centers for shipbuilding, fishing and trade. New England's famed Yankee Clippers plied ports from China to South America. The USA's first water-powered cotton-spinning mill was established in Rhode Island in 1793. In the years that followed New England's swift rivers became the engines of vast mills turning out clothing, shoes and machinery.

But no boom lasts forever. By the early 20th century many of the mills had moved south. The economy sprung back to life again during WWII. Today education, finance, biotechnology and tourism are linchpins of the regional economy.

LOCAL CULTURE

New Englanders tend to be reserved by nature, with a Yankee thriftiness of speech, which stands in marked contrast to the casual outgoing nature of, say, Californians. This taciturn quality shouldn't be confused with unfriendliness, as it's simply a more formal regional style.

Particularly in rural areas you'll notice the pride folks take upon themselves in their ingenuity and self-sufficient character. These New Englanders remain fiercely independent, from the fishing boat crews who brave Atlantic storms to the small Vermont farmers who fight to keep operating independently within America's gobble-up agribusiness economy.

Fortunately for the farmers and fishers, buy-local and go-organic movements have grown by leaps and bounds throughout New England. From bistros in Boston to small towns in the far north the menus are greening.

One place you won't find that ol' Yankee reserve is at the ball field. New Englanders are absolutely fanatical about sports. Attending a Red Sox game is as close as you'll come to a modern-day gladiators-at-the-coliseum scene – wild cheers and nasty jeers galore.

Generally regarded as a liberal enclave, New England's in the forefront on progressive political issues from gay rights (four of the five US states that have legalized gay marriage are in New England) to health care reform. Indeed the universal health insurance program in Massachusetts is now being touted as a model for a nationalized plan.

LAND & CLIMATE

New England's landscape has ample variety, with verdant valleys, rolling hills and vast forests. A spine of craggy mountains runs roughly from northeast to southwest; the highest point, Mt Washington in the White Mountains, tops out at 6288ft.

The coast is varied as well. In the north it's largely rocky, sculpted into coves and sprinkled with the occasional sandy beach, while the southern coastline's bounded by long swaths of sand and dunes.

The weather in New England is famously changeable. Muggy 90°F (32°C) days in July may be followed by a day of cool 65°F (18°C) weather. Precipitation averages about 3in per month year-round.

The beachy summer season is roughly June to mid-September. New England's brilliant fall foliage peaks from mid-September to mid-October.

PARKS

If you're ready to explore the great outdoors, New England provides plenty of options. Acadia National Park (p310), on the rugged,

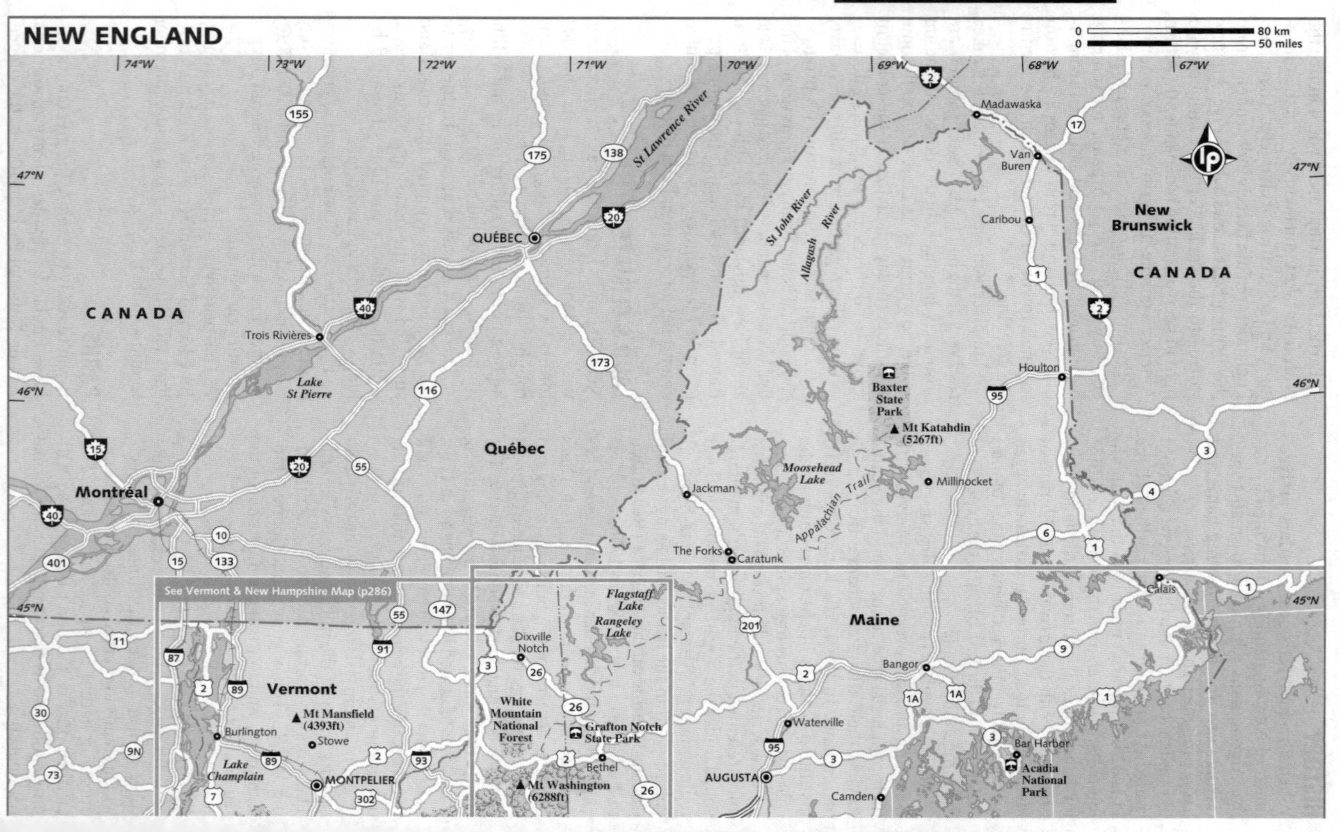
NEW ENGLAND
0 80 km
0 50 miles
74°W
73°W
72°W
71°W
70°W
69°W
68°W
67°W
47°N
46°N
45°N
St Lawrence River
QUÉBEC
CANADA
Trois Rivières
Lake St Pierre
Montréal
Québec
St John River
Allagash River
Madawaska
Van Buren
Caribou
New Brunswick
CANADA
Houlton
Baxter State Park
Mt Katahdin (5267ft)
Moosehead Lake
Appalachian Trail
Millinocket
Jackman
The Forks
Caratunk
Calais
Maine
Bangor
Waterville
AUGUSTA
Camden
Bar Harbor
Acadia National Park
See Vermont & New Hampshire Map (p286)
Flagstaff Lake
Rangeley Lake
Dixville Notch
White Mountain National Forest
Grafton Notch State Park
Bethel
Mt Washington (6288ft)
Vermont
Mt Mansfield (4393ft)
Burlington
Stowe
Lake Champlain
MONTPELIER

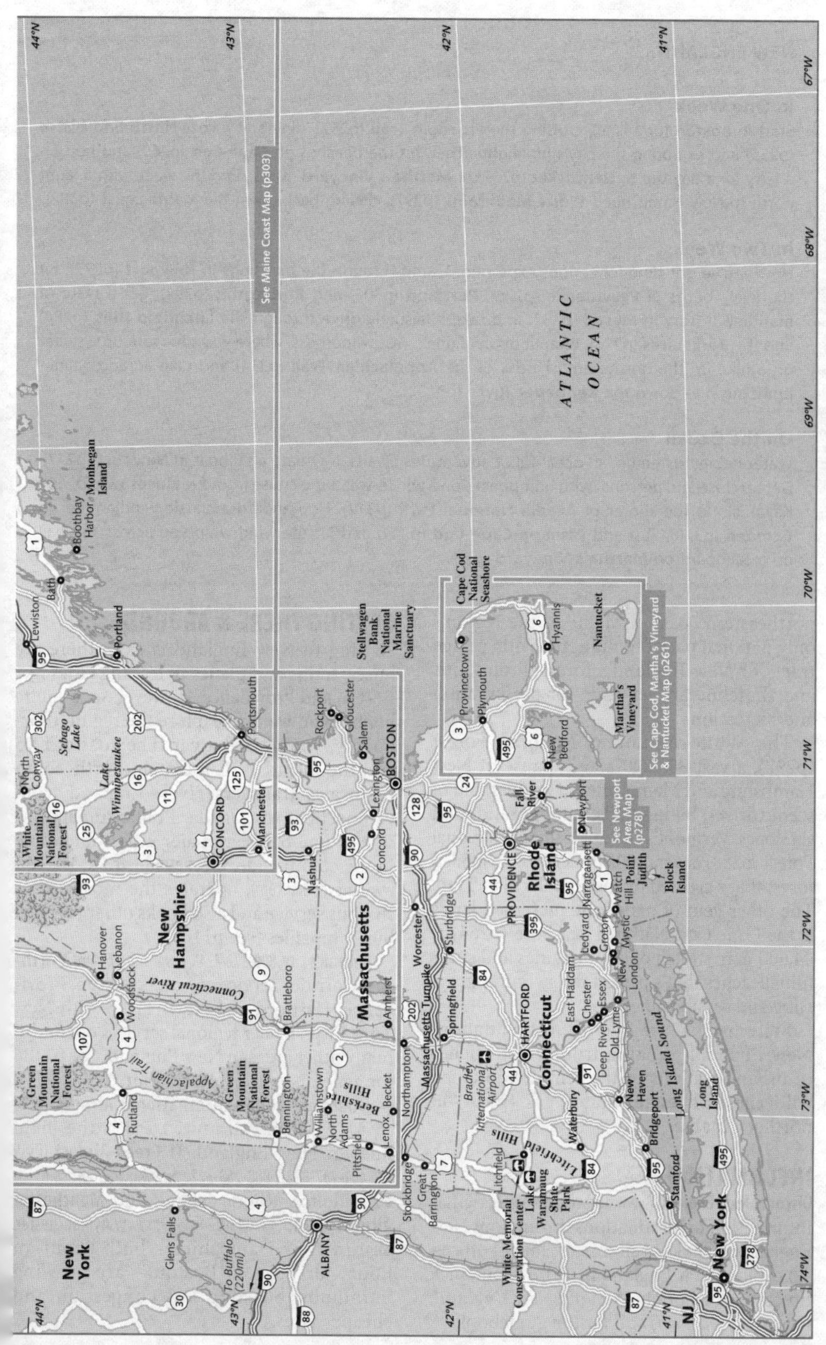
New York
New Hampshire
Massachusetts
Connecticut
Rhode Island
NJ
ATLANTIC OCEAN
See Maine Coast Map (p303)
See Cape Cod, Martha's Vineyard & Nantucket Map (p261)
See Newport Area Map (p278)
Green Mountain National Forest
White Mountain National Forest
Appalachian Trail
Connecticut River
Berkshire Hills
Litchfield Hills
Long Island Sound
Long Island
Lake Winnipesaukee
Sebago Lake
Stellwagen Bank National Marine Sanctuary
Cape Cod National Seashore
Massachusetts Turnpike
Bradley International Airport
White Memorial Conservation Center
Lake Waramaug State Park
To Buffalo (220mi)
ALBANY
Glens Falls
Rutland
Woodstock
Hanover
Lebanon
Bennington
Brattleboro
Williamstown
North Adams
Pittsfield
Lenox
Becket
Stockbridge
Great Barrington
Northampton
Amherst
Springfield
Worcester
Sturbridge
HARTFORD
East Haddam
Chester
Essex
Deep River
Old Lyme
New London
Groton
Ledyard
Mystic
Watch Hill
Point Judith
Block Island
Narragansett
Newport
PROVIDENCE
Fall River
New Bedford
Martha's Vineyard
Nantucket
Hyannis
Plymouth
Provincetown
BOSTON
Lexington
Concord
Salem
Gloucester
Rockport
Nashua
Manchester
CONCORD
Portsmouth
North Conway
Portland
Lewiston
Bath
Boothbay Harbor
Monhegan Island
Litchfield
Waterbury
New Haven
Bridgeport
Stamford
New York
44°N
43°N
42°N
41°N
74°W
73°W
72°W
71°W
70°W
69°W
68°W
67°W

NEW ENGLAND...

In One Week

Start in **Boston** (opposite), cruising the **Freedom Trail** (p252), dining at a cozy **North End bistro** (p255) and exploring the city's highlights. Then hit the beaches on **Cape Cod** (p260) and hop on a ferry for a day trip to **Nantucket** (p267) or **Martha's Vineyard** (p268). End the week with a jaunt north to New Hampshire's **White Mountains** (p297), circling back down the **Maine coast** (p302).

In Two Weeks

Now you've got time for serious exploring. Tramp through the mansions in **Newport** (p277), hit the lively burgs of **Providence** (p275), **Portland** (p305) and **Burlington** (p292), get a taste of maritime history in **Mystic** (p282) and take a leisurely drive through the **Litchfield Hills** (p284) and the **Berkshires** (p273). Wrap it up in Maine's vast wilderness, where you can work up a sweat on a hike up the northernmost peak of the **Appalachian Trail** (p314) and take an adrenaline-pumping ride down the **Kennebec River** (p313).

On the Ocean

Water babies, listen up: an oceanful of adventures awaits. Navigate a sailboat in **Newport** (p277). Get up close and personal with humpbacks on a whale-watching cruise from **Provincetown** (p266). Kayak along the shores of **Acadia National Park** (p312). Hop aboard a classic windjammer in **Camden** (p310). Surf and swim on **Cape Cod** (p264) and let the wind whip you across the bay on a sailboard on **Martha's Vineyard** (p270).

northeastern coast of Maine, is the region's only national park but numerous other large tracts of New England's forest, mountains and shoreline are set aside for preservation and recreation.

The White Mountain National Forest (p297), a vast 800,000-acre expanse of New Hampshire and Maine, offers a wonderland of scenic drives, hiking trails, campgrounds and ski slopes. Vermont's Green Mountain National Forest (p288) covers 400,000 acres of unspoiled forest that's crossed by the Appalachian Trail. The other gem of nationally preserved lands is the Cape Cod National Seashore (p264), a 44,600-acre stretch of rolling dunes and stunning beaches that's perfect for swimming, cycling and seaside hikes.

State parks are plentiful throughout New England, ranging from green niches in urban locations to the remote, untamed wilderness of Baxter State Park (p314) in northern Maine.

INFORMATION

Discover New England (www.discovernewengland.org) has information on destinations throughout New England and links to all six state tourist offices. To explore New England in more depth, pick up copies of Lonely Planet's *New England*, *New England Trips* and *Boston* guidebooks.

GETTING THERE & AROUND

Getting to New England is easy; there are buses, trains and planes to leading cities like Boston and Providence. However once you're here, if you want to explore the region thoroughly, you'll need a car. The coastal I-95 and the inland I-91, the main north–south highways, transverse New England from Connecticut to Canada. Public transportation is fine between major cities but scarce in the countryside. **Greyhound** (☎ 800-231-2222; www.greyhound.com), operates the most extensive bus service and also books other regional bus companies (see p1160).

Amtrak's (☎ 800-872-7245; www.amtrak.com) Northeast Corridor service connects Boston, Providence, Hartford and New Haven with New York City; smaller regional services operate in many other areas in New England. See p1166 for general Amtrak information.

Boston's **Logan International Airport** (BOS; ☎ 800-235-6426; www.massport.com) is the main hub for New England. **TF Green Airport** (PVD; ☎ 401-737-8222, 888-268-7222; www.pvdairport.com) in Providence, Rhode Island, and **Manchester Airport** (MHT; ☎ 603-624-6539; www.flymanchester.com) in New Hampshire – both about an hour's drive from Boston – are growing 'minihubs' boasting less congestion and cheaper fares.

Regional driving distances:
Boston to North Conway 165 miles
Boston to Acadia National Park 310 miles
New Haven to Burlington 270 miles

MASSACHUSETTS

New England's most populous state packs in appealing variety from the woodsy hills of the Berkshires to the sandy beaches of Cape Cod. Massachusetts' rich history oozes from almost every quarter: you can explore Plymouth, 'America's hometown;' walk the Freedom Trail in Boston, where the first shots of the American Revolution rang out; and hit the cobbled streets of the old whaling village of Nantucket. University-laden Boston offers all the accoutrements – from world-class museums to edgy nightlife – you'd expect of a great college town. Provincetown's a gay-extravaganza whirl like no other, Northampton's got the coolest café scene this side of New York, and Martha's Vineyard offers the perfect family vacation – just ask the Obamas and Clintons.

History

Massachusetts has played a leading role in American politics since the arrival of the first colonists. In the 18th century, spurred by a booming maritime trade, Massachusetts colonists revolted against trade restrictions imposed by Great Britain. British attempts to put down the revolt resulted in the 1770 Boston Massacre, which became a rallying cry to action. In 1773, angered by a new British-imposed tax on tea, colonists raided three British merchant ships and dumped their cargo of tea into Boston Harbor. Known as the Boston Tea Party, this tax revolt against the crown set the stage for the battles that started the American Revolution.

In the 19th century Massachusetts became the center of the world's whaling industry, bringing unprecedented wealth to the islands of Nantucket and Martha's Vineyard, whose ports are still lined with grand sea captains' homes.

MASSACHUSETTS FACTS

Nicknames Bay State, Old Colony
Population 6.5 million
Area 7840 sq miles
Capital city Boston (population 590,800)
Other cities Springfield (population 151,180)
Sales tax 6.25%
Birthplace of Agriculturalist Johnny Appleseed (1774–1845), inventor Benjamin Franklin (1706–90), five presidents including John F Kennedy (1917–63), authors Jack Kerouac (1922–69) and Henry David Thoreau (1817–62)
Home of Harvard University, Boston Marathon, Plymouth Rock
Famous for Boston Tea Party, Boston Red Sox, first state to legalize gay marriage
Most parodied accent Bostonians' *pahk the cah in Hahvahd Yahd*
Driving distances Boston to Provincetown 145 miles, Boston to Northampton 98 miles

Information

Boston Globe (www.boston.com) The region's main newspaper has a great online site.
Massachusetts Department of Conservation and Recreation (☎ 877-422-6762; www.mass.gov/dcr/recreate/camping.htm; campsites $10-26) Offers camping in 28 state parks.
Massachusetts Office of Travel & Tourism (Map pp248-9; ☎ 617-973-8500, 800-227-6277; www.massvacation.com; 10 Park Plaza, Suite 4510, Boston, MA 02116) Provides information on the entire state.

BOSTON

One of America's oldest cities is also one of its youngest. A score of colleges and universities add a fresh face to this historic capital and feed a thriving arts and entertainment scene. But don't think for a minute that Boston is all about the literati. Grab a seat in the bleachers at Fenway Park and join the fanatical fans cheering on the Red Sox. Wicked pissah (super cool), as they say here in the Hub.

History

When the Massachusetts Bay Colony was established by England in 1630, Boston became its capital. It's a city of firsts: Boston Latin School, the first public school in the USA, was founded in 1635, followed a year later by Harvard, the nation's first university. The first newspaper in the colonies was printed here in 1704, America's first labor union organized here in 1795 and the country's first subway system opened in Boston in 1897.

Not only were the first battles of the American Revolution fought here, but Boston was also home to the first African American

NEW ENGLAND

regiment to fight in the US Civil War. Waves of immigrants, especially Irish in the mid-18th century and Italians in the early 20th, have infused the city with European influences.

Today Boston remains at the forefront of higher learning and its universities have spawned world-renowned industries in biotechnology, medicine and finance.

Orientation

Boston retains an intimate scale that's best experienced on foot. Begin at Boston Common, where you'll find the tourist office and the start of the Freedom Trail. Everything radiates out from the Common, with historic sites, graceful parks and promenades around every corner.

Outlying attractions and the airport are easily accessible by MBTA (the 'T') subway trains (p259). The Park St station, a 'T' hub, is beneath the Common. Harvard Square, the epicenter of Cambridge, is about 5 miles northwest of the Common and served by the T's Red Line.

Information

BOOKSTORES

Barnes & Noble (Map pp248-9; ☎ 617-247-6959; www.barnesandnoble.com; 800 Boylston St; 9am-11pm Mon-Sat, 10am-9pm Sun) This Prudential Center branch is convenient and well stocked.

Coop (Map p251; ☎ 617-499-2000; 1400 Massachusetts Ave, Cambridge; 9am-10pm Mon-Sat, 10am-9pm Sun) Regional books, music and all sorts of souvenirs emblazoned with the Harvard logo.

Globe Corner Bookstore (Map p251; ☎ 617-497-6277; www.globecorner.com; 90 Mt Auburn St, Cambridge; 9:30am-9pm Mon-Sat, 11am-7pm Sun) An indie specializing in travel books and maps.

Out of Town News (Map p251; ☎ 617-354-7777; Harvard Sq, Cambridge; 6am-9pm) This National Historic Landmark sells major US and international newspapers.

INTERNET ACCESS

Boston Public Library (Map pp248-9; ☎ 617-536-5400; www.bpl.org; 700 Boylston St; 9am-9pm Mon-Thu, 9am-5pm Fri & Sat, 1-5pm Sun Oct-May) Free for 15 minutes, or get a visitor card at the circulation desk and sign up for longer terminal time.

Tech Superpowers & Internet Café (Map p245; ☎ 617-267-9716; www.techsuperpowers.com; 252 Newbury St; per 15min/1hr $3/5; 9am-8pm Mon-Fri, 10am-5pm Sat & Sun) Provides online computers, but if you have your own device wi-fi access is free throughout Newbury St.

INTERNET RESOURCES & MEDIA

Boston Globe (www.boston.com) New England's major daily newspaper provides a wealth of information online.

Boston Phoenix (www.thephoenix.com) Free alternative weekly with solid arts and entertainment coverage.

City of Boston (www.cityofboston.gov) The official website for the city government has links to visitor services.

MEDICAL SERVICES

CVS Pharmacy (Map pp248-9; ☎ 617-437-8414; 587 Boylston St; 24hr) Opposite the public library.

Massachusetts General Hospital (Map pp248-9; ☎ 617-726-2000; 55 Fruit St; 24hr) At the west side of the city center.

MONEY

You'll find ATMs throughout the city, including at most subway stations. Foreign currency can be exchanged at **Citizens Bank** (☎ 800-922-9999; State St Map pp248-9, 53 State St; Boylston St Map pp248-9; 607 Boylston St; Harvard Sq Map p251).

POST

Main post office (Map pp248-9; ☎ 800-275-8777; 25 Dorchester Ave; 6am-midnight) One block southeast of South Station. There are several other post offices around central Boston (Map pp248–9) and near Harvard Sq (Map p251).

TOURIST INFORMATION

Cambridge Visitor Information Booth (Map p251; ☎ 617-441-2884, 800-862-5678; www.cambridge-usa.org; 4 Brattle St; 9am-5pm Mon-Sat, 9am-1pm Sun) This Harvard Sq kiosk has the latest scoop on Cambridge.

Greater Boston Convention & Visitors Bureau (GBCVB; Map pp248-9; ☎ 617-426-3115, 888-733-2678; www.bostonusa.com) Boston Common (Map pp248-9; 148 Tremont St; 8:30am-5pm Mon-Fri, 9am-5pm Sat & Sun); Prudential Center (Map pp248-9; 800 Boylston St; 9am-6pm) Has oodles of brochures and info.

Sights & Activities

Slip on a good pair of walking shoes, and this city's yours. Most of Boston's main attractions are found in or near the city center, making it easy to ramble from one to the next.

BOSTON COMMON & PUBLIC GARDEN

The heart of Boston since 1634, the 50-acre **Boston Common** (Map pp248–9), bordered by Tremont, Beacon and Charles Sts, was the nation's first public park. In years past it was a pasture for cattle grazing, a staging ground for soldiers of the American Revolution and the site of chastising pillory-and-stocks for

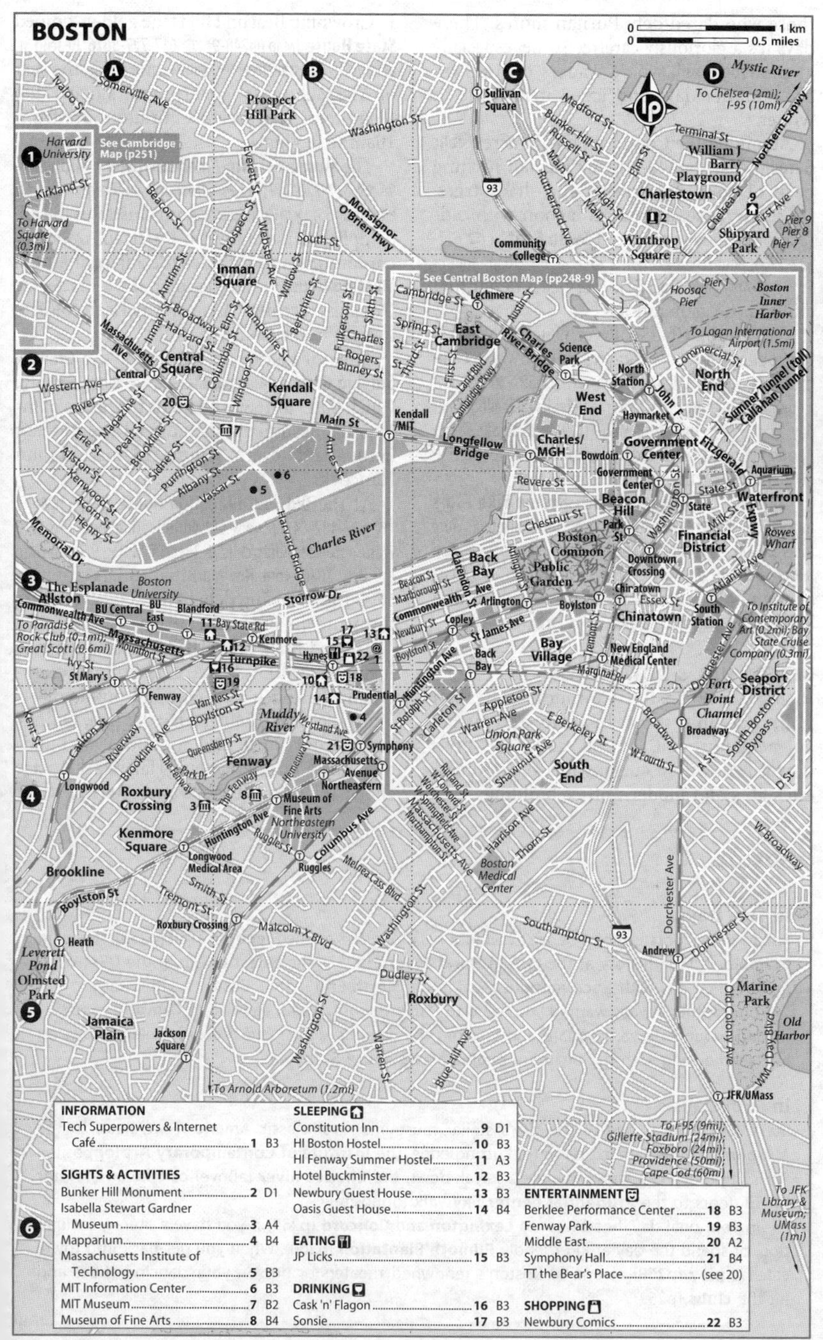
BOSTON
0 1 km
0 0.5 miles
See Cambridge Map (p251)
See Central Boston Map (pp248-9)
Harvard University
Kirkland St
To Harvard Square (0.3mi)
Prospect Hill Park
Sullivan Square
Mystic River
To Chelsea (2mi); I-95 (10mi)
Northern Expwy
William J Barry Playground
Charlestown
Shipyard Park
Pier 9
Pier 8
Pier 7
Winthrop Square
Community College
Monsignor O'Brien Hwy
Inman Square
Central Square
Kendall Square
Lechmere
East Cambridge
Charles River Bridge
Science Park
North Station
West End
North End
Boston Inner Harbor
To Logan International Airport (1.5mi)
Sumner Tunnel (toll)
Callahan Tunnel
Kendall /MIT
Longfellow Bridge
Charles/ MGH
Haymarket
Government Center
Bowdoin
Aquarium
Waterfront
Beacon Hill
State
Financial District
Rowes Wharf
Park St
Boston Common
Public Garden
Downtown Crossing
Chinatown
South Station
Charles River
Memorial Dr
The Esplanade
Allston
Boston University
BU Central
BU East
Blandford
Kenmore
Massachusetts Turnpike
Storrow Dr
Harvard Bridge
Back Bay
Arlington
Copley
Boylston
Bay Village
New England Medical Center
To Institute of Contemporary Art (0.2mi); Bay State Cruise Company (0.3mi)
Fort Point Channel
Seaport District
Broadway
To Paradise Rock Club (0.1mi); Great Scott (0.6mi)
St Mary's
Fenway
Hynes
Prudential
Muddy River
Symphony
Massachusetts Avenue
Northeastern
Museum of Fine Arts
Northeastern University
Longwood
Roxbury Crossing
Kenmore Square
Longwood Medical Area
Ruggles
Brookline
South End
Union Park Square
Boston Medical Center
Heath
Leverett Pond
Olmsted Park
Jamaica Plain
Jackson Square
Roxbury
Andrew
Marine Park
Old Harbor
JFK/UMass
To Arnold Arboretum (1.2mi)
To I-95 (9mi); Gillette Stadium (24mi); Foxboro (24mi); Providence (50mi); Cape Cod (60mi)
To JFK Library & Museum; UMass (1mi)
INFORMATION
Tech Superpowers & Internet Café 1 B3
SIGHTS & ACTIVITIES
Bunker Hill Monument 2 D1
Isabella Stewart Gardner Museum 3 A4
Mapparium 4 B4
Massachusetts Institute of Technology 5 B3
MIT Information Center 6 B3
MIT Museum 7 B2
Museum of Fine Arts 8 B4
SLEEPING
Constitution Inn 9 D1
HI Boston Hostel 10 B3
HI Fenway Summer Hostel 11 A3
Hotel Buckminster 12 B3
Newbury Guest House 13 B3
Oasis Guest House 14 B4
EATING
JP Licks 15 B3
DRINKING
Cask 'n' Flagon 16 B3
Sonsie 17 B3
ENTERTAINMENT
Berklee Performance Center 18 B3
Fenway Park 19 B3
Middle East 20 A2
Symphony Hall 21 B4
TT the Bear's Place (see 20)
SHOPPING
Newbury Comics 22 B3

those who dared defy Puritan mores. These days it's a gloriously carefree scene, especially at the **Frog Pond**, where waders cool off on hot summer days and ice-skaters frolic in winter.

Adjoining the Common, the 24-acre **Public Garden** (Map pp248–9) provides an inviting oasis of bountiful flowers and shady trees. Its centerpiece, a tranquil lagoon with old-fashioned pedal-powered **Swan Boats** (☎ 617-522-1966; adult/child 2-15yr $2.75/1.50; 🕑 10am-4pm or 5pm mid-Apr–early Sep;), has been delighting children for generations.

The nearby Charles River is action-central for joggers, cyclists, skaters and rowers. **Community Boating** (Map pp248-9; ☎ 617-523-1038; www.community-boating.org; The Esplanade; kayak/sailboat per day $35/75; 🕑 1pm-dusk Mon-Fri, 9am-dusk Sat & Sun Apr-Oct) rents boats from its boathouse at the south side of the Longfellow Bridge.

Cyclists can join up with **Boston Bike Tours** (Map pp248-9; ☎ 617-308-5902; www.bostonbiketours.com; tours $35-40; 🕑 10am & 2pm Sat & Sun mid-Apr–Jun, Sep & Oct, daily Jul & Aug), departing from Boston Common, to follow Paul Revere's ride, cruise Harvard Square or take in a brewery tour.

BEACON HILL & DOWNTOWN

Rising above Boston Common is Beacon Hill, Boston's most historic and affluent neighborhood. To the east is the city's downtown, with a curious mix of Colonial-era sights and modern office buildings.

Crowning Beacon Hill is the golden-domed **State House** (Map pp248-9; ☎ 617-727-3676; Beacon St, at Park St; admission free; 🕑 8am-6pm Mon-Fri), the seat of Massachusetts' government since 1798. Volunteers lead free 40-minute tours from 10am to 3:30pm.

The **Museum of Afro-American History** (Map pp248-9; ☎ 617-720-2991; www.afroammuseum.org; 46 Joy St; admission $5; 🕑 10am-4pm Mon-Sat) illustrates the accomplishments of Boston's African American community and includes the adjacent **African Meeting House**, where former slave Frederick Douglass recruited African American soldiers to fight in the Civil War.

Tons of history lie buried at the **Granary Burying Ground** (Map pp248-9; cnr Tremont & Park Sts), which dates to 1660 and holds the bones of influential Bostonians, including Revolutionary heroes Paul Revere, Samuel Adams and John Hancock.

At the **Old South Meeting House** (Map pp248-9; ☎ 617-482-6439; www.oldsouthmeetinghouse.org; 310 Washington St; adult/child 6-18yr $5/1; 🕑 9:30am-5pm Apr-Oct, 10am-4pm Nov-Mar), colonists met in 1773 for a rousing debate on taxation before throwing the Boston Tea Party.

The red-brick **Faneuil Hall** (Map pp248-9; Congress St), topped with its famed grasshopper weathervane, has been a market and public meeting place since 1740. Today the hall, Quincy Market and North and South Market buildings make up the Faneuil Hall Marketplace chock-full of small shops and eateries.

BOSTON...

In Two Days

Follow in the footsteps of America's revolutionary founders on the **Freedom Trail** (p252), stopping to imbibe a little history at the **Bell in Hand Tavern** (p257), the oldest tavern in the USA. Wrap up your first day with a scrumptious meal in the **North End** (p255), Boston's 'Little Italy.'

Your mother always wanted you to go to Harvard, right? Begin day two in **Cambridge** (p251) poking around Harvard Square and cruising the campus sights. End the day gallery browsing and schmoozing with the beautiful people on **Newbury St** (p258).

In Four Days

Start day three at one of the city's stellar museums – for classic American art, head to the **Museum of Fine Arts** (p250) or for cutting edge, the **Institute of Contemporary Art** (opposite). For sumptuous city views, paddle a kayak down the **Charles River** (above) or take an elevator up 50 floors to the **Prudential Center Skywalk** (opposite).

On your final day, head west to **Lexington** and **Concord** (p259) if you have a literary inclination, or spend the day at kid-friendly **Plimoth Plantation** (p260). When you get back into town, catch a **play** (p258) at one of Boston's renowned theaters or put on your dancing shoes and hit the **clubs** (p257).

NORTH END & CHARLESTOWN

An old-world warren of narrow streets, the Italian North End offers visitors an irresistible mix of colorful period buildings and mouth-watering eateries. Colonial sights spill across the river into Charlestown, home to America's oldest battleship.

Paul Revere House (Map pp248-9; ☎ 617-523-2338; www.paulreverehouse.org; 19 North Sq; adult/child 6-17yr $3.50/1; 🕒 9:30am-5:15pm mid-Apr–Oct, to 4:15pm Nov–mid-Apr) is the oldest (1680) house still standing in Boston. Even more significantly, it's the former home of Paul Revere, a leader of the colonial militia (the Minutemen) known for their ability to deploy rapidly. It was Revere who jumped on his horse and rode through the streets shouting the warning 'the British are coming.'

It was at the **Old North Church** (Map pp248-9; ☎ 617-523-6676; 193 Salem St; admission free; 🕒 9am-6pm Jun-Oct, 9am-5pm Nov-May), built c 1723, that two lanterns were hung in the steeple on that pivotal night of April 18, 1775, signaling to a waiting Paul Revere that British forces were setting out by sea ('one if by land, two if by sea').

Work off that North End lunch by clambering around the decks of the **USS Constitution** (Map pp248-9; ☎ 617-242-7511; admission free; 🕒 10am-6pm Tue-Sun Apr-Oct, 10am-4pm Thu-Sun Nov-Mar), centerpiece of the Charlestown Navy Yard. Built in 1797, the old warship's oak-timbered hull was so thick that cannonballs literally bounced off it, earning it the nickname 'Old Ironsides.'

The **Bunker Hill Monument** (Map p245; (☎ 617-242-5641; Monument Sq; admission free; 🕒 9am-4:30pm), a 221ft granite obelisk commemorates the American Revolution's first major battle.

BACK BAY

Extending west from Boston Common this well-groomed neighborhood boasts graceful brownstone residences, grand edifices and the tony shopping mecca of Newbury St.

Copley Square (Map pp248–9) is surrounded by handsome historic buildings, including the ornate French-Romanesque **Trinity Church** (☎ 617-536-0944; cnr Boylston & Clarendon Sts; adult/child under 16 $6/free; 🕒 9am-5:45pm Mon-Fri, 9am-5pm Sat, 1-5:45pm Sun), the masterwork of architect HH Richardson. Across the street, the classic **Boston Public Library** (☎ 617-536-5400; 700 Boylston St; 🕒 9am-9pm Mon-Thu, 9am-5pm Fri & Sat), America's first municipal library, lends credence to Boston's reputation as the 'Athens of America.'

For a stunning 360-degree bird's-eye view of the city, head to the **Prudential Center Skywalk** (Map pp248-9; ☎ 617-859-0648; 800 Boylston St; adult/child 4-12yr $12/8; 🕒 10am-10pm), the tower's 50th-floor observation deck.

If you've ever wanted to walk across the planet, the Christian Science Church's **Mapparium** (Map p245; ☎ 617-450-7000; 200 Massachusetts Ave; adult/child 6-17yr $6/4; 🕒 10am-4pm Tue-Sun), an enormous stained-glass globe with a bridge through its center, provides the easiest route.

BOSTON GOES GREEN

The hulking highway that once tore across the center of the city has morphed into a ribbon of green stretching from Chinatown to the North End. Known as the Rose Kennedy Greenway in honor of JFK's mother, this meandering green space reclaims land that was until a few years back the elevated section of I-93.

Completed in late 2008, the interconnecting pocket parks that comprise the greenway offer shady respites from the city bustle, replete with water fountains, artwork and sculpture gardens.

Incidentally, if you're wondering what happened to the highway, it's now buried in tunnels running beneath the city, thanks to the 'Big Dig,' the costliest highway project in US history.

WATERFRONT & SEAPORT DISTRICT

Boston's waterfront offers an ever-growing list of attractions, all connected by the Harborwalk, a dedicated pedestrian path.

The dazzling **Institute of Contemporary Art** (off Map p245; ☎ 617-478-3100; www.icaboston.org; 100 Northern Ave; adult/child under 18yr $12/free; 🕒 10am-5pm Tue, Wed, Sat & Sun, 10am-9pm Thu & Fri) snags rave exhibits by the likes of street artist Shepard Fairey. The building's striking cantilevered architecture defines modern, and its floor-to-ceiling glass walls pop with Boston's most dramatic harbor view. Admission's free after 5pm on Thursday.

The **New England Aquarium** (Map pp248-9; ☎ 617-973-5200; www.neaq.org; Central Wharf; adult/child 3-11yr $20/12; 🕒 9am-5pm Mon-Fri, 9am-6pm Sat & Sun; 👶) centers on a four-story tank teeming with sharks and colorful tropical fish but it's the cool penguin pool that kids go nuts over. Also popular are the aquarium's **whale-watching cruises** (adult/child under 11yr $40/32; 🕒 Apr-Oct), led by

NEW ENGLAND

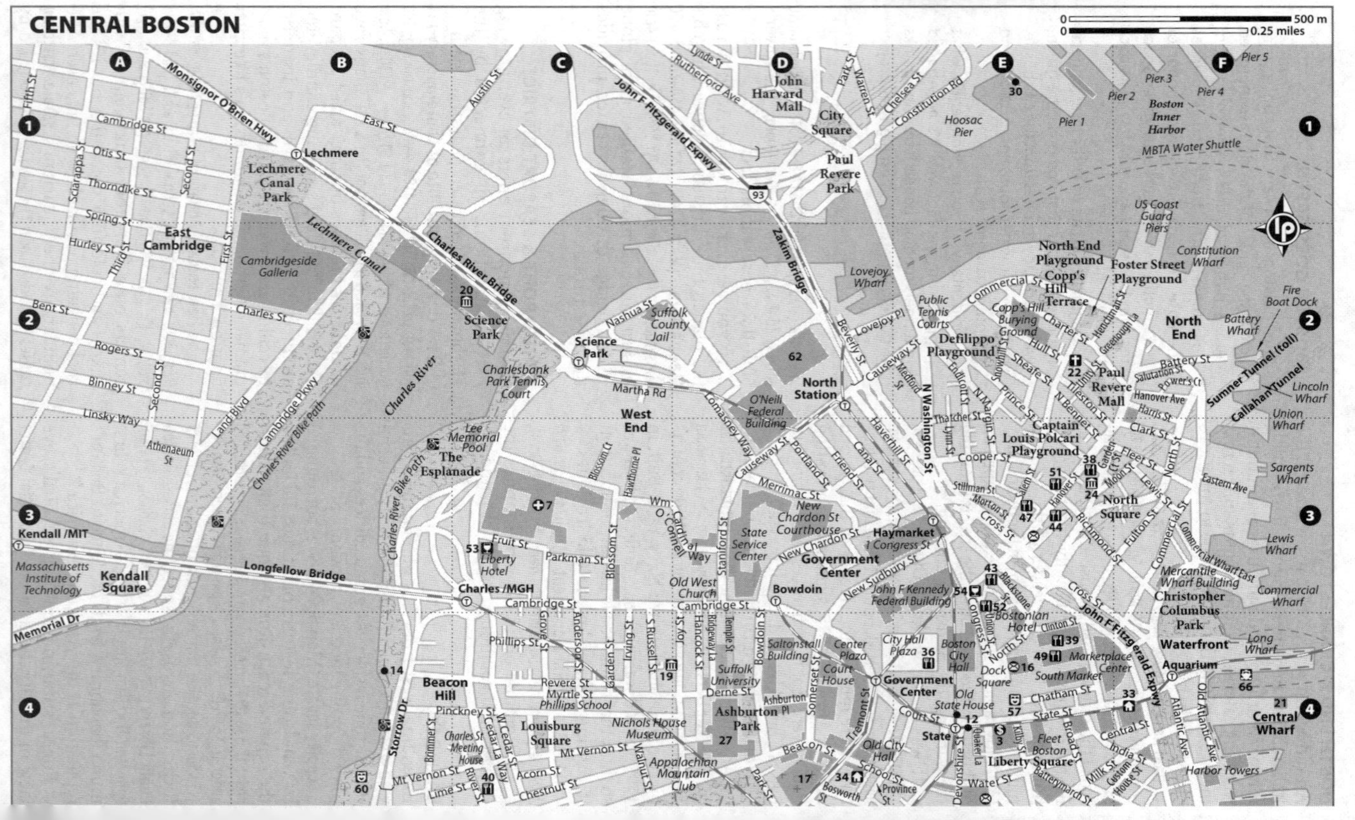
CENTRAL BOSTON
0 500 m
0 0.25 miles
A
B
C
D
E
F
1
2
3
4
Pier 1
Pier 2
Pier 3
Pier 4
Pier 5
Boston Inner Harbor
MBTA Water Shuttle
US Coast Guard Piers
Constitution Wharf
Battery Wharf
Fire Boat Dock
Sumner Tunnel (toll)
Callahan Tunnel
Lincoln Wharf
Union Wharf
Sargents Wharf
Lewis Wharf
Commercial Wharf
Long Wharf
Central Wharf
Hoosac Pier
Constitution Rd
Chelsea St
Warren St
Park St
City Square
Paul Revere Park
John Harvard Mall
Rutherford Ave
Lynde St
John F Fitzgerald Expwy
Zakim Bridge
Lovejoy Wharf
North Station
North End
Foster Street Playground
North End Playground
Copp's Hill Terrace
Copp's Hill Burying Ground
Defilippo Playground
Captain Louis Polcari Playground
Paul Revere Mall
North Square
N Washington St
Haymarket
Government Center
Bowdoin
New Chardon St Courthouse
State Service Center
O'Neill Federal Building
John F Kennedy Federal Building
Boston City Hall
City Hall Plaza
Center Plaza
Court House
Old State House
State
Old City Hall
Marketplace Center
South Market
Christopher Columbus Park
Waterfront
Aquarium
Mercantile Wharf Building
Atlantic Ave
Old Atlantic Ave
Harbor Towers
Liberty Square
Fleet Boston
Dock Square
Bostonian Hotel
Congress St
Cross St
Causeway St
Beverly St
Merrimac St
Cambridge St
Temple St
Ridgeway La
Hancock St
Joy St
S Russell St
Irving St
Garden St
Anderson St
Grove St
Phillips St
Bowdoin St
Suffolk University
Saltonstall Building
Ashburton Park
Appalachian Mountain Club
Nichols House Museum
Mt Vernon St
Louisburg Square
Beacon Hill
Beacon St
Tremont St
Somerset St
Park St
Old West Church
Wm Cardinal O'Connell Way
West End
Martha Rd
Lomasney Way
Suffolk County Jail
Nashua St
Science Park
Charles River Bridge
Charlesbank Park Tennis Court
Lee Memorial Pool
The Esplanade
Charles River Bike Path
Charles River
Storrow Dr
Charles /MGH
Liberty Hotel
Fruit St
Parkman St
Blossom St
Longfellow Bridge
Lechmere
Lechmere Canal
Lechmere Canal Park
Cambridgeside Galleria
Cambridge Pkwy
Land Blvd
Charles St
East St
Austin St
Monsignor O'Brien Hwy
East Cambridge
First St
Second St
Third St
Fifth St
Cambridge St
Otis St
Thorndike St
Spring St
Hurley St
Rogers St
Binney St
Linsky Way
Athenaeum St
Bent St
Kendall /MIT
Kendall Square
Massachusetts Institute of Technology
Memorial Dr

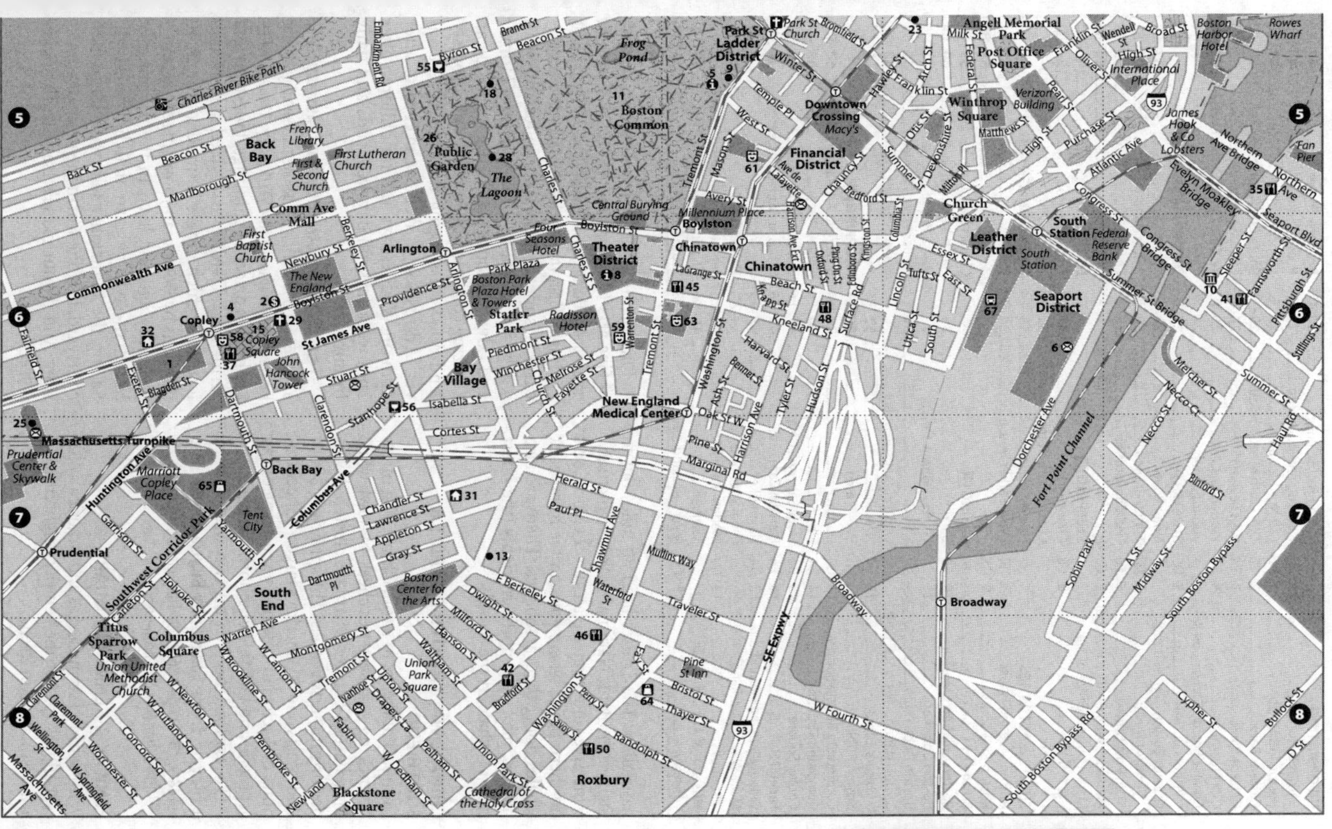
Charles River Bike Path
Back Bay
French Library
First Lutheran Church
First & Second Church
Comm Ave Mall
First Baptist Church
The New England
Public Garden
The Lagoon
Frog Pond
Boston Common
Central Burying Ground
Four Seasons Hotel
Park St Church
Park St Ladder District
Downtown Crossing
Macy's
Financial District
Angell Memorial Park
Post Office Square
Winthrop Square
Verizon Building
International Place
Boston Harbor Hotel
Rowes Wharf
Fan Pier
James Hook & Co Lobsters
Northern Ave Bridge
Evelyn Moakley Bridge
Church Green
Leather District
South Station
Federal Reserve Bank
Congress St Bridge
Summer St Bridge
Seaport District
Fort Point Channel
Theater District
Chinatown
Boylston
Arlington
Copley
Copley Square
John Hancock Tower
Park Plaza
Boston Park Plaza Hotel & Towers
Statler Park
Radisson Hotel
Bay Village
New England Medical Center
Massachusetts Turnpike
Prudential Center & Skywalk
Marriott Copley Place
Back Bay
Tent City
Prudential
Southwest Corridor Park
South End
Boston Center for the Arts
Titus Sparrow Park
Columbus Square
Union United Methodist Church
Union Park Square
Claremont Park
Blackstone Square
Cathedral of the Holy Cross
Roxbury
Broadway
SE Expwy
Commonwealth Ave
Columbus Ave
Huntington Ave
Beacon St
Back St
Marlborough St
Newbury St
Boylston St
St James Ave
Charles St
Tremont St
Washington St
Arlington St
Berkeley St
Clarendon St
Dartmouth St
Summer St
Dorchester Ave
A St
Midway St
South Boston Bypass
W Fourth St
Embankment Rd
NEW ENGLAND

INFORMATION
Barnes & Noble....(see 25)
Boston Public Library.... 1 A6
Citizens Bank.... 2 B6
Citizens Bank.... 3 E4
CVS Pharmacy.... 4 B6
Greater Boston Convention & Visitors Bureau.... 5 D5
Greater Boston Convention & Visitors Bureau....(see 25)
Main Post Office.... 6 E6
Massachusetts General Hospital... 7 C3
Massachusetts Office of Travel & Tourism.... 8 C6

SIGHTS & ACTIVITIES
African Meeting House....(see 19)
Boston Bike Tours.... 9 D5
Boston by Little Feet....(see 16)
Boston Children's Museum.... 10 F6
Boston Common.... 11 C5
Boston Duck Tours....(see 25)
Boston National Historical Park Visitors Center.... 12 E4
Boston Public Library....(see 1)
Community Bicycle Supply.... 13 C7
Community Boating.... 14 B4
Copley Square.... 15 B6
Faneuil Hall.... 16 E4
Granary Burying Ground.... 17 D4
Make Way for Ducklings Statues.... 18 C5
Museum of Afro-American History.... 19 C4
Museum of Science.... 20 C2
New England Aquarium.... 21 F4
Old North Church.... 22 E2
Old South Meeting House.... 23 E5
Paul Revere House.... 24 E3
Prudential Center.... 25 A7
Public Garden.... 26 B5
State House.... 27 D4
Swan Boats.... 28 C5
Trinity Church.... 29 B6
USS Constitution.... 30 E1

SLEEPING
Chandler Inn.... 31 C7
Charlesmark Hotel.... 32 A6
Harborside Inn.... 33 F4
Omni Parker House.... 34 D4

EATING
Barking Crab.... 35 F5
City Hall Plaza Farmers Market.... 36 E4
Copley Square Farmers Market.... 37 B6
Daily Catch.... 38 E3
Durgin Park.... 39 E4
Figs.... 40 C4
Flour Bakery & Cafe.... 41 F6
Franklin Café.... 42 C8
Haymarket.... 43 E3
Legal Sea Foods....(see 25)
Modern Pastry Shop.... 44 E3
Montien.... 45 D6
Myers + Chang.... 46 C8
Neptune Oyster.... 47 E3
Peach Farm.... 48 D6
Quincy Market.... 49 E4
South End Farmers Market.... 50 C8
Trattoria Il Panino.... 51 E3
Ye Olde Union Oyster House.... 52 E3

DRINKING
Alibi.... 53 C3
Bell in Hand Tavern.... 54 E3
Cheers.... 55 B5
Club Café.... 56 B6
Fritz....(see 31)
Top of the Hub....(see 25)

ENTERTAINMENT
BosTix.... 57 E4
BosTix.... 58 B6
Charles Playhouse.... 59 C6
Hatch Memorial Shell.... 60 B4
Opera House.... 61 D5
TD Banknorth Garden.... 62 D2
Wang Theatre.... 63 D6

SHOPPING
Bromfield Art Gallery.... 64 C8
Copley Place.... 65 A7
Out of Left Field....(see 16)
Shops at Prudential Center....(see 25)

TRANSPORT
Ferry to Boston Harbor Islands National Recreation Area.... 66 F4
South Station.... 67 E6

naturalists. The cruises head 30 miles out to Stellwagen Bank National Marine Sanctuary, a massive underwater plateau off Cape Cod's northern point, where you can see humpback whales doing their acrobatics. There are also minkes, pilots and northern rights (the rarest type of whale in the world).

CHINATOWN, THEATER DISTRICT & SOUTH END

Compact and easy to stroll, Chinatown offers up enticing Asian eateries cheek-by-jowl, while the adjacent Theater District is clustered with performing-arts venues. The sprawling South End boasts one of America's largest concentrations of Victorian row houses, a burgeoning art scene and terrific neighborhood cafés.

To explore the area on two wheels, rent a bicycle from **Community Bicycle Supply** (Map pp248-9; ☎ 617-542-8623; 496 Tremont St; per day $20-25; 🕑 10am-7pm Mon-Sat, noon-5pm Sun).

FENWAY & KENMORE SQUARE

With world-class museums and America's oldest ballpark (p258), the Fenway neighborhood is a destination in itself.

One of the country's finest, the **Museum of Fine Arts** (MFA; Map p245; ☎ 617-267-9300; www.mfa.org; 465 Huntington Ave; adult/child 7-17yr $17/6.50; 🕑 10am-4:45pm Thu-Tue, 10am-9:45pm Wed) showcases a superb American collection with works by artists such as Winslow Homer and Edward Hopper, as well as pieces by an amazing collection of French Impressionists. And don't miss seeing the Paul Revere silver. Admission is free for everyone after 4pm on Wednesdays and for children after 3pm weekdays, all day weekends and daily in summer.

The **Isabella Stewart Gardner Museum** (Map p245; ☎ 617-566-1401; www.gardnermuseum.org; 280 The Fenway; adult/child under 18yr $12/free; 🕑 11am-5pm Tue-Sun) houses priceless paintings, tapestries and furnishings. Gardner assembled her vast collection – which ranges from Rembrandts to portraits by Bostonian John Singer Sargent – a century ago and lived in the magnificent Venetian-style palazzo that houses it all. Seeing the mansion itself, with its garden courtyard, is alone worth the price of admission. And if your name's Isabella, the ticket is free!

CAMBRIDGE

On the north side of the Charles River lies politically progressive Cambridge, home to academic heavyweights Harvard University and Massachusetts Institute of Technology (MIT). Some 30,000 students make for a diverse, lively scene. Its central **Harvard Square** (Map p251) overflows with cafés, bookstores and street performers. Along Massachusetts Ave, opposite the Harvard T station, lies **Harvard University** (Map p251; www.harvard.edu), which counts dozens of Nobel laureates and eight US presidents among its graduates – for other chewy tidbits join a free student-led campus tour at the **Harvard University Information Center** (Map p251; ☎ 617-495-1573; 1350 Massachusetts Ave; 🕑 1hr tours 10am & 2pm Mon-Fri, 2pm Sat).

It should come as no surprise that the nation's oldest (1636) and wealthiest university has amassed incredible collections. The **Harvard Art Museum/Arthur M Sackler Museum** (☎ 617-495-9400; 485 Broadway; adult/child under 19yr $9/free; 🕑 10am-5pm Mon-Sat, 1-5pm Sun) showcases the artworks, which cover a broad gamut from Picasso to Islamic art. The **Harvard Museum of Natural History** (Map p251; ☎ 617-495-3045; 26 Oxford St; adult/child 3-18yr $9/6; 🕑 9am-5pm) and the interconnected **Peabody Museum of Archaeology & Ethnology** present outstanding Native American exhibits and an exquisite collection of 4000 hand-blown glass flowers. The admission price gets you into both.

Nerds rule ever so proudly at the **Massachusetts Institute of Technology** (MIT; Map

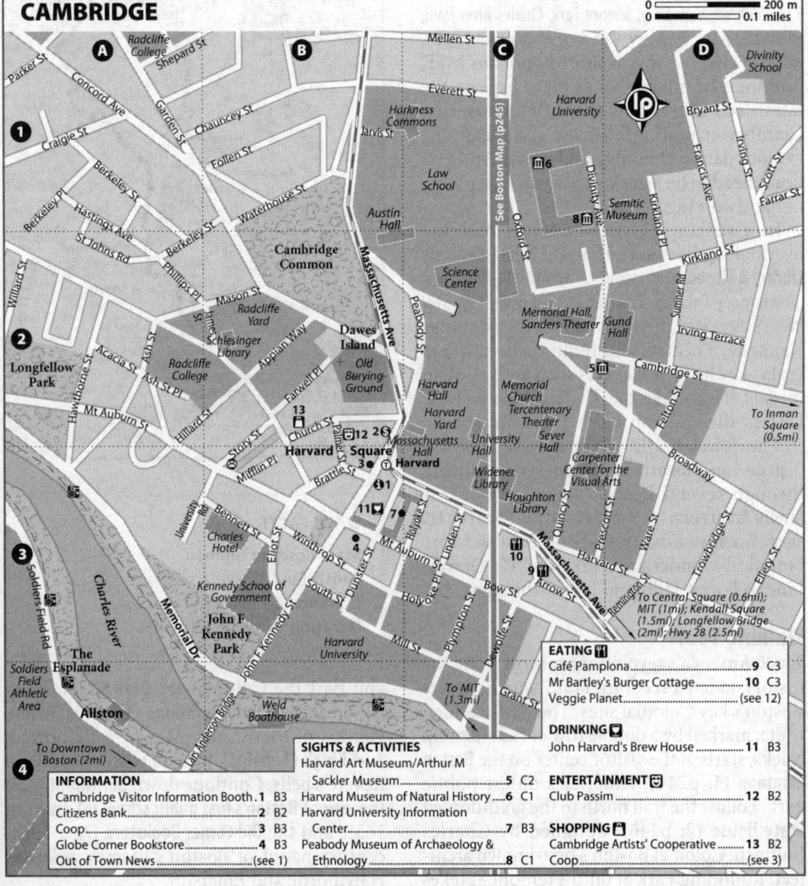

p245), America's foremost tech campus. Stop at the **MIT Information Center** (Map p245; ☎ 617-253-4795; www.mit.edu; 77 Massachusetts Ave; admission free; 🕑 90min tours 11am & 3pm Mon-Fri) for the scoop on where to see campus art, including Henry Moore bronzes, and cutting-edge architecture by the likes of Frank Gehry.

The **MIT Museum** (Map p245; ☎ 617-253-4444; 265 Massachusetts Ave, adult/child under 18yr $7.50/3; 🕑 10am-5pm) is packed with wow-'em exhibits like the world's largest holography collection, robots from MIT's Artificial Intelligence Laboratory and cool kinetic sculptures. Swing by between 10am and noon on Sundays and admission is free.

GREATER BOSTON

At the **Museum of Science** (Map pp248-9; ☎ 617-723-2500; www.mos.org; Science Park, Charles River Dam; adult/child 3-11yr $19/6; 🕑 9am-5pm Sat-Thu, 9am-9pm Fri, longer hours Jul-Aug; 🚸), a short hop from MIT, hundreds of interactive displays explore the latest tech trends and scientific discoveries. Clamber around a full-scale space capsule, explore nanotechnology and more. And you don't need to be a geek – kids will find plenty of hands-on fun.

In a striking IM Pei–designed building overlooking Boston Harbor, the **John F Kennedy Library & Museum** (off Map p245; ☎ 617-514-1600; www.jfklibrary.org; Columbia Point; adult/child under 13yr $12/free; 🕑 9am-5pm) provides an ode to all things Kennedy. Theaters and multimedia displays replay key historical events such as the Cuban missile crisis. Take the T's Red Line to JFK/UMass, then hop on a free 'JFK' shuttle bus.

The jewel of the Emerald Necklace, a 7-mile-long swath of green space cutting through several Boston neighborhoods, is **Arnold Arboretum** (off Map p245; ☎ 617-524-1718; 125 Arborway; admission free; 🕑 sunrise-sunset), a 265-acre botanical wonderland. Take the T's Orange Line to Forest Hills and follow the signs.

Walking Tour

Trace America's revolutionary birth along the history-laden Freedom Trail, which covers Boston's key Colonial sites. The well-trodden route, marked by a double row of red sidewalk bricks, starts at the visitor center on the **Boston Common** (1; p244), America's oldest public park. Follow the trail north to the gold-domed **State House** (2; p246), designed by Charles Bulfinch, Colonial Boston's best-known architect. Rounding Park St onto Tremont St takes

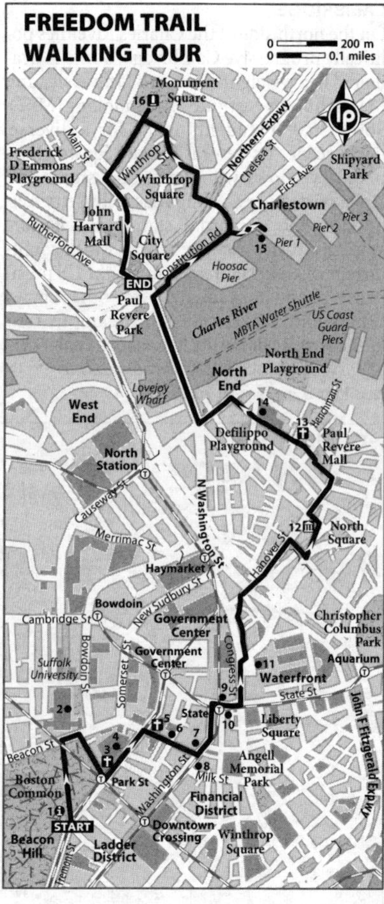

WALK FACTS

Start Boston Common
Finish Bunker Hill Monument
Distance 2.5 miles
Duration three hours

you past the Colonial-era **Park Street Church (3)**; the **Granary Burying Ground** (4; p246), where victims of the Boston Massacre lie buried; and **King's Chapel (5)**, topped with one of Paul Revere's bells. Continue down School St, past the site of **Boston's first public school (6)**, built in 1635, and the **Old Corner Bookstore (7)**, a 19th-century haunt of Boston's literary geniuses Hawthorne and Emerson.

A minute's detour south from the corner of School and Washington Sts leads to the **Old South Meeting House** (**8**; p246), where the nitty-gritty on the Boston Tea Party is proudly displayed. True diehards will find more Revolutionary exhibits at the **Old State House** (**9**; ☎ 617-720-1713; 206 Washington St; adult/child 6-18yr $7/3; 9am-5pm), Boston's oldest public building, erected in 1713. Nearby, a ring of cobblestones at the intersection of State, Devonshire and Congress Sts marks the **Boston Massacre site** (**10**), where the first victims of the American Revolution died. Next up is the landmark **Faneuil Hall** (**11**; p246), a public market since Colonial times.

Walk north on Union St and up Hanover St, the trattoria-rich heart of Boston's Italian enclave. Treat yourself to lunch before continuing to North Sq, where you can tour the **Paul Revere House** (**12**; p247), the Revolutionary hero's former home. Follow the trail onward to the **Old North Church** (**13**; p247), where a lookout in the steeple signaled to Revere that the British were coming, setting off his famous midnight gallop.

Continue northwest on Hull St, where you'll find more Colonial graves at **Copp's Hill Burying Ground** (**14**) before crossing the Charlestown Bridge to reach the **USS Constitution** (**15**; p247), the world's oldest commissioned warship. To the north lies **Bunker Hill Monument** (**16**; p247), the site of the first battle fought in the American Revolution, where your walk peaks after climbing 294 stairs (huff, huff) with a sweeping view of Boston.

Boston for Children

Boston's small scale makes it easy for families to explore. A good place to start is the **Public Garden** (p244), where fans of Robert McCloskey's classic Boston tale *Make Way for Ducklings* can visit bronze **statues** (Map pp248–9) of the famous mallards and paddle the lagoon in one of the Swan Boats. At the **Boston Common** (p244), kids can cool their toes in the Frog Pond and romp on playground swings and jungle gyms.

The **Boston Children's Museum** (Map pp248-9; ☎ 617-426-6500; www.bostonchildrensmuseum.org; 300 Congress St; adult/child 1-15yr $12/9; 10am-5pm Sat-Thu, 10am-9pm Fri;) offers oodles of fun for the younger ones, while the **Museum of Science** (opposite) thrills kids of all ages. Hits at the **New England Aquarium** (p247) include stroking creatures in the touch pool, watching seals being fed at the Animal Rescue Center and hopping aboard a whale-watching tour.

Boston by Little Feet (Map pp248-9; ☎ 617-367-2345; www.bostonbyfoot.com; 1hr tour $8; tours 10am Mon & Sat, 2pm Sun May-Oct;), departing from Dock Sq at Faneuil Hall, and designed for kids aged six to 12, offers a fun slice of the Freedom Trail from a child's perspective. And those quirky, quacky **Boston Duck Tours** (below) are always a hit.

Tours

Boston Duck Tours (Map pp248-9; ☎ 617-723-3825; www.bostonducktours.com; adult/child 3-11yr $30/20; every 30min 9am-dusk Apr-Nov;) offers ridiculously popular tours using WWII amphibious vehicles that cruise the downtown streets before splashing into the Charles River. Tours leave from the Prudential Center and the Museum of Science.

Knowledgeable guides from **Boston by Foot** (☎ 617-367-2345; www.bostonbyfoot.com; 90min tours $12; May-Oct) leads all sorts of architecture-focused walking tours, including one through the Italian-centric North End and another of literary landmarks.

Guides dressed in Colonial garb – think Ben Franklin – lead **Freedom Trail walking tours** (90min tours adult/child 5-12yr $12/6; every 30min) from the visitor bureau at Boston Common (p244). Or join one of the free, ranger-led Freedom Trail tours provided by the **Boston National Historical Park Visitors Center** (Map pp248-9; ☎ 617-242-5642; www.nps.gov/bost; 15 State St; 9am-5pm).

If you're traveling with an MP3 player, you can be your own guide by downloading a free walking tour of Cambridge (p251) at www.cambridge-usa.org and of the Harborwalk (p247) at www.bostonharborwalk.com.

Festivals & Events

Boston Marathon (www.bostonmarathon.com) One of the country's most prestigious marathons takes runners up Heartbreak Hill in a 26.2-mile race ending at Copley Sq on Patriots Day, a Massachusetts holiday on the third Monday in April.

Bunker Hill Day Redcoats and rebellious patriots reenact the first battle of the American Revolution at Bunker Hill Monument on June 16.

Fourth of July (www.bso.org) Boston hosts one of the biggest Independence Day bashes in the USA, with a free Boston Pops concert on the Esplanade and a fireworks display that's televised nationally.

Head of the Charles Regatta (www.hocr.org) Spectators line the banks of the Charles River on a weekend in mid-October to watch the world's largest rowing event.

IF YOU HAVE A FEW MORE DAYS

Designated a National Recreation Area, **Boston Harbor Islands** (www.bostonislands.com; admission free) consist of 34 islands with sandy beaches and hiking trails. Since the massive cleanup of Boston Harbor in the 1990s, these once-polluted islands, just a 45-minute boat ride from downtown Boston, have been transformed into sparkling natural assets.

Georges Island is the site of Fort Warren, a 19th-century fort and Civil War prison. Other popular destinations are Bumpkin Island, known for its slate beaches and wildflower fields; Grape Island, a haven for bird-watchers; and Lovells Island, with dunes and a wide swimming beach.

Harbor Islands Express (☎ 617-223-8666; round-trip adult/child under 12yr $12/7; May-Sep) runs ferries between Boston's Long Wharf (Map pp248–9) and Georges Island. From Georges Island free shuttle boats go to other islands in the chain.

Camping is allowed at primitive **campsites** (☎ 877-422-6762; www.reserveamerica.com; campsites $25; late Jun–early Sep) on Grape, Bumpkin and Lovells islands.

Sleeping

Boston has a reputation for high hotel prices, but affordable options and online discounts can lessen the sting at even high-end places. You'll typically find the best deals on weekends. The majority of hotels are in the downtown area and the Back Bay, both convenient to public transportation and sightseeing.

For places that book solely through agencies try **Bed & Breakfast Agency of Boston** (☎ 617-720-3540, 800-248-9262; www.boston-bnbagency.com; r $120-200, 2br $200-350, 3br $300-400), which represents around 100 B&Bs, studios and apartments.

BUDGET

HI Boston Hostel (Map p245; ☎ 617-536-9455; www.bostonhostel.org; 12 Hemenway St; dm incl breakfast $31-48, r incl breakfast $79-129) This terrific year-round Back Bay hostel offers dorm rooms with just four to six beds and lots of perks, from free use of linens to organized tours. It fills quickly, especially in summer, so book early.

HI Fenway Summer Hostel (Map p245; ☎ 617-267-8599; www.bostonhostel.org/fenway.shtml; 575 Commonwealth Ave; dm/r incl breakfast $39/99; Jun-Aug) A Boston University dormitory in winter, this Kenmore Sq hostel has dorms with just three beds each, as well as private rooms. Good dining and nightlife options are close at hand.

MIDRANGE

Oasis Guest House (Map p245; ☎ 617-267-2262, 800-230-0105; www.oasisgh.com; 22 Edgerly Rd; s/d with shared bath $99/119, r with private bath $169) On a tree-lined lane just beyond bustling Mass Ave, this guesthouse offers straightforward rooms simply furnished but clean and comfortable. Free wi-fi and morning snacks add to the appeal. One caveat: there are entertainment venues nearby, so on weekends street noise can be an issue.

Chandler Inn (Map pp248-9; ☎ 617-482-3450, 800-842-3450; www.chandlerinn.com; 26 Chandler St; r $115-185) For a delectable taste of the hip South End, book a room at this European-style boutique hotel within roaming range of some of Boston's hottest nightspots. The staff is friendly, the rooms small but tidy, and the price a fraction of any faceless chain hotel. Request one of the upper-floor rooms, which are fresh off a renovation.

Newbury Guest House (Map p245; ☎ 617-670-6000, 800-437-7668; www.newburyguesthouse.com; 261 Newbury St; s/d incl breakfast from $140/165) Stay on fashionable Newbury St in this pension-like B&B occupying three interconnected brownstones. Built in 1882, the buildings retain many of the original handcrafted details such as carved mantels and molded ceilings.

Hotel Buckminster (Map p245; ☎ 617-236-7050, 800-727-2825; www.bostonhotelbuckminster.com; 645 Beacon St; r $149-179) Built in 1897 by renowned architect Stanford White, this Kenmore Sq hotel is a mere baseball's toss from Fenway Park. Don't expect anything fancy – it's a faded dame, but the rooms are adequate and sport money-saving conveniences such as microwaves and refrigerators.

Constitution Inn (Map p245; ☎ 617-241-8400, 800-495-9622; www.constitutioninn.org; 150 Third Ave; r $149-189) Comfy digs and a classic setting in the historic Charlestown Naval Yard make this a great option if you don't mind being outside the city center. The modern rooms have all the expected amenities and the fitness center with Olympic-size pool puts facilities at the city's top-end hotels to shame.

Charlesmark Hotel (Map pp248-9; ☎ 617-247-1212; www.thecharlesmark.com; 655 Boylston St; r incl breakfast $169-219;) This smart boutique hotel packs it all from an unbeatable Copley Sq location to cheery rooms graced with artwork, Italian tile and high-tech amenities. Runners, take note: the Boston Marathon finish line is just outside the front door.

Harborside Inn (Map pp248-9; ☎ 617-723-7500; www.harborsideinnboston.com; 185 State St; r from $199;) This renovated 19th-century warehouse-turned-inn offers cozy rooms just steps from Faneuil Hall and Boston's waterfront. No two rooms are alike but period ambience, from the exposed brick walls to the hardwood floors, prevails throughout. Light sleepers should request an inside atrium room.

TOP END

our pick **Omni Parker House** (Map pp248-9; ☎ 617-227-8600; www.omniparkerhouse.com; 60 School St; r $299-419;) If the walls could talk, this historic hotel overlooking the Freedom Trail would fill volumes. Employees have included Malcolm X and Ho Chi Minh, the guest list Charles Dickens and JFK. Despite its well-polished elegance, dark woods and chandeliers, there's nothing stodgy about the place – you can be as comfortable here in a T-shirt as in a suit and tie. And you couldn't be more in the thick of things; it's just a stroll to many of Boston's top sights and best restaurants. Don't be dissuaded by the price; online discounts can slice rates in half.

Eating

No matter what your taste, Boston will tantalize your buds. Head to Chinatown for affordable Asian fare, or to the South End for the café scene. And when the sun sets, there's no place like the Italian North End, whose narrow streets are thick with trattorias and ristorantes.

BEACON HILL & DOWNTOWN

Quincy Market (Map pp248-9; off Congress & North Sts; 8am-9pm Mon-Sat, 8am-7pm Sun) For a quick eat along the Freedom Trail, stop at this market lined with dozens of food stalls selling everything from pizza slices (Regina's is best) to New England clam chowder in a bread bowl.

Durgin Park (Map pp248-9; ☎ 617-227-2038; 340 Faneuil Hall Marketplace; lunch mains $9-15, dinner mains $15-30; 11:30am-10pm Mon-Sat, 11:30am-9pm Sun) Forget nouvelle, climb the stairs to this storied eatery for a taste of good ole Colonial fare. Durgin Park's been dishing out New England staples like Yankee pot roast, Indian pudding and slow-cooked Boston baked beans since 1827.

Figs (Map pp248-9; ☎ 617-742-3447; 42 Charles St; mains $10-20; 11:30am-10pm) The brainchild of celebrity chef Todd English, Figs rakes 'em in with its innovative whisper-thin pizzas. For a real treat, order the signature fig and prosciutto pizza with gorgonzola. Equally delish are the sandwiches, salads and pastas.

Ye Olde Union Oyster House (Map pp248-9; ☎ 617-227-2750; 41 Union St; mains $16-25; 11am-9:30pm Sun-Thu, 11am-10pm Fri & Sat) Slurp up fresh-shucked oysters and a heaping of history at Boston's oldest (1826) restaurant. It's been a haunt of many prominent Bostonians including JFK, who had his own booth in the upstairs dining room. Forgo the meat dishes – this place is all about seafood.

NORTH END

Modern Pastry Shop (Map pp248-9; ☎ 617-523-3783; 257 Hanover St; snacks $2-4; 7am-10pm Sun-Fri, 7am-midnight Sat) It's not the biggest bakery on Hanover St, but it's the best. Fresh fruit tarts, chocolate-dipped biscotti and decadent cannoli filled to order in front of your eyes…oh so sweet!

Trattoria Il Panino (Map pp248-9; ☎ 617-720-1336; 11 Parmenter St; mains $15-25; 11am-10pm) In sunny weather, the café tables in the courtyard of this traditional trattoria are the place to be. On dreary days, the cozy candlelit dining

FARMERS MARKETS

Many neighborhoods in Boston have farmers markets that truck seasonal fruits and vegetables into the city from mid-May to November. The ultimate bonanza of ripe and ready produce is the **Haymarket** (Map pp248-9; Blackstone & Hanover Sts; 7am-5pm Fri & Sat), where more than 100 vendors line up along the street.

Other markets:

City Hall Plaza (Map pp248-9; City Hall Plaza; 11am-6pm Mon & Wed)

Copley Square (Map pp248-9; St James Ave; 11am-6pm Tue & Fri)

South End (Map pp248-9; 540 Harrison Ave; 10am-5pm Sun)

room will warm you up. Pasta and shellfish are the specialties but the menu covers a lot of ground, including sizzling steaks.

Daily Catch (Map pp248-9; ☎ 617-523-8567; 323 Hanover St; mains $18-26; 11:30am-9pm Sun-Thu, 11:30am-10:30pm Fri & Sat) It's an unassuming joint with the kitchen and dining tables squeezed into one small room, but you'll find superb Sicilian-style seafood as fresh as its name. The specialty is calamari in endless renditions from garlicky scampi to homemade squid-ink pastas. The only difficult catch is scoring a seat – arrive early.

Neptune Oyster (Map pp248-9; ☎ 617-742-3474; 63 Salem St; mains $20-30; 11:30am-11pm Sun-Thu, 11:30am-midnight Fri & Sat) Barely bigger than a clam, this snappy place has the best raw bar in the North End and serves up good hot Italian-style seafood as well. You *will* want to start with the oysters.

BACK BAY

JP Licks (Map p245; ☎ 617-236-1666; 352 Newbury St; cones $4; 11am-midnight) Go ahead, spoil your dinner. Cool off with a cone of Boston's favorite homemade ice cream.

Legal Sea Foods (Map pp248-9; ☎ 617-266-6800; Prudential Center, 800 Boylston St; mains $15-30; 11am-10:30pm Mon-Sat, noon-10pm Sun) Running with the motto 'If it isn't fresh, it isn't Legal,' this Boston establishment indeed serves top-of-the-line seafood – broiled, grilled or fried – and invariably draws a satisfied crowd.

WATERFRONT & SEAPORT DISTRICT

Barking Crab (Map pp248-9; ☎ 617-426-2722; 88 Sleeper St; mains $12-30; noon-10pm) A waterfront landmark, this brightly painted and ever-bustling seafood shack serves big buckets of steaming crabs, authentic New England clambakes and good ol' beer-battered fish and chips.

> **DON'T MISS**
>
> Certified green, **Flour Bakery & Cafe** (Map pp248-9; ☎ 617-338-4333; 12 Farnsworth St; light eats $3-10; 7am-7pm Mon-Fri, 8am-6pm Sat, 9am-5pm Sun) is all the buzz in leading gourmet magazines, and scrumptiously affordable. The pecan sticky buns are awesome, the sandwiches innovative, and the pizzas a revelation. Their motto is 'make life sweeter…eat dessert first.' No argument here.

CHINATOWN, THEATER DISTRICT & SOUTH END

Peach Farm (Map pp248-9; ☎ 617-482-1116; 4 Tyler St; mains $7-18; 11am-3am) Step into this basement restaurant with its Cantonese chatter and live fish tanks for the best seafood in Chinatown. The net's cast wide, from local flounder to abalone and eels. If you don't mind having your lunch stare back at you, try the savory fish-head soup.

our pick **Myers + Chang** (Map pp248-9; ☎ 617-542-5200; 1145 Washington St; mains $10-15; 11:30am-11pm Mon-Sat, 11:30am-10pm Sun) A marriage of two South End top chefs, this smokin' multiethnic joint dishes up the most eclectic taste treats, blending Thai, Chinese and Vietnamese influences with an urban New England tweak. Think shiitake-basil spring rolls, wok-roasted mussels and tea-smoked spareribs. No matter what you order, the spicy, fresh herbs carry the day. The food's local whenever possible, the scene's hip and casual.

Montien (Map pp248-9; ☎ 617-338-5600; 63 Stuart St; mains $10-16; 11:30am-10:30pm Mon-Sat, 4-10pm Sun) For a tasty meal before the opening curtain, head to this Thai restaurant in the midst of the theater district. Montien has wonderfully fragrant curries and other spicy counterparts, including scores of vegetarian options. The food's the real deal, so let the server know how much heat you can handle.

Franklin Café (Map pp248-9; ☎ 617-350-0010; 278 Shawmut Ave; mains $15-20; 5:30pm-1:30am) Search out this tiny South End haunt for New American comfort food with a gourmet twist. Everyone orders the roasted turkey meatloaf with cinnamon fig gravy and chive mashed potatoes – arguably the most famous meal in the South End. Just a half-dozen booths and a line of bar stools, so get there early.

CAMBRIDGE

Veggie Planet (Map p251; ☎ 617-661-1513; Club Passim, 47 Palmer St; mains $6-12; 11:30am-10:30pm; V) The crunchy granola crowd gravitates here for all things vegetarian. Creativity knows no bounds – vegans favor the coconut curry tofu pizza. Big organic salads and delicious homemade soups too.

Café Pamplona (Map p251; ☎ 617-492-0352; 12 Bow St; mains $8-15; 11am-1am Mon-Sat, 2pm-1am Sun) The menu of zesty options in this backstreet cellar café include a fab gazpacho, Spanish-style pressed sandwiches and heady coffee. With its low ceilings it can feel a bit claustrophobic

GAY & LESBIAN BOSTON

Naturally, the hub city of the first state to legalize gay marriage embraces gay travelers. You'll find openly gay communities throughout Boston and Cambridge, but the pulse of the action beats from Boston's South End.

The stalwart of the gay and lesbian scene is **Club Café** (Map pp248-9; ☎ 617-536-0966; 209 Columbus Ave; 🕒 2pm-2am), a convivial South End bar and entertainment venue. Also a gay landmark is **Fritz** (☎ 617-482-4428; 26 Chandler St; 🕒 noon-2am), a bustling, hustling watering hole in the South End that proudly proclaims itself 'Boston's gay sports bar.'

You'll find of slew of other LGBT gathering spots, as well as events and entertainment listings, at **Bay Windows** (www.baywindows.com), a weekly serving the gay and lesbian community, and at **Edge Boston** (www.edgeboston.com). The city's biggest gay and lesbian event, **Boston Pride** (www.bostonpride.org), includes a parade, a festival and block parties in mid-June.

but in warm weather you can dine on the sunny patio.

Mr Bartley's Burger Cottage (Map p251; ☎ 617-354-6559; 1246 Massachusetts Ave; burgers $9-13; 🕒 11am-9pm Mon-Sat) Join the Ivy Leaguers at this landmark joint serving juicy hamburgers with quirky names, like the Yuppie Burger topped with boursin cheese and bacon. The onion rings and sweet potato fries score an A-plus too.

Drinking & Entertainment

Boston's entertainment scene offers something for everyone. For up-to-the-minute listings, grab a copy of the free *Boston Phoenix*.

Half-price tickets to same-day theater and concerts are sold for cash only at the **BosTix kiosks** (Map pp248-9; www.bostix.org; 🕒 10am-6pm Tue-Sat, 11am-4pm Sun) Faneuil Hall (Congress St); Copley Sq (cnr Dartmouth & Boylston Sts).

BARS

Sonsie (Map p245; ☎ 617-351-2500; 327 Newbury St; 🕒 7am-1am) Overlooking the action on trendy Newbury St, Sonsie is where the beautiful people go to see and be seen. Chardonnay, anyone?

Top of the Hub (Map pp248-9; ☎ 617-536-1775; Prudential Center, 800 Boylston St; 🕒 11:30am-1am) A head-spinning city view is on tap at this chic restaurant-lounge on the 52nd floor of the Prudential Center. Live jazz nightly too.

Alibi (Map pp248-9; ☎ 617-244-0400; 215 Charles St; 🕒 5pm-midnight) The quirkiest place to have a drink in Boston is this bar in the former Charles Street Jail, now renovated into the upscale Liberty Hotel. The decor features slammin' remnants of its former life, such as iron cell bars.

Cheers (Map pp248-9; ☎ 617-227-9605; 84 Beacon St; 🕒 11am-1am) Only the exterior of this landmark bar appeared in the opening scenes of the *Cheers* sitcom and it serves so many tourists that nobody knows anybody's name, but what the heck.

John Harvard's Brew House (Map p251; ☎ 617-868-3585; 33 Dunster St, Cambridge; 🕒 11:30am-12:30am Sun-Thu, 11:30am-1:30am Fri & Sat) This subterranean Harvard Square microbrewery pours well-crafted brews in an inviting English-pub atmosphere; it has good pub grub too.

Bell in Hand Tavern (Map pp248-9; ☎ 617-227-2098; 45 Union St; 🕒 11:30am-2am) A gaggle of bars lines historic Union St, just north of Faneuil Hall, including this one, which opened in 1795, making it the oldest tavern in the USA.

Cask 'n' Flagon (Map p245; ☎ 617-536-4840; 62 Brookline Ave; 🕒 11:30am-2am) Sports bars pepper the neighborhood around Fenway Park, including this venerable place, which is wallpapered with classic Red Sox memorabilia and frenzied fans.

NIGHTCLUBS & LIVE MUSIC

Hours vary with the season and the act – call for schedules.

Paradise Rock Club (off Map p245; ☎ 617-562-8800; www.thedise.com; 967 Commonwealth Ave; cover $15-35) Top bands – like U2, whose first gig in the USA was on this stage – rock at this edgy landmark club.

Great Scott (off Map p245; ☎ 617-566-9014; www.greatscottboston.com; 1222 Commonwealth Ave; cover $5-15) The newest 'it' place for rock and indie, this cavernous club rarely gets uncomfortably crowded.

Club Passim (Map p251; ☎ 617-492-7679; www.clubpassim.org; 47 Palmer St; cover $5-25) Folkies flock to this venerable Harvard Sq club, which has been a haunt of up-and-coming folk singers since the days of Dylan and Baez.

Middle East (Map p245; ☎ 617-864-3278; www.mideastclub.com; 472 Massachusetts Ave; cover $10-20) Rock and indie bands rumble at this dual-stage club near Cambridge's Central Sq.

TT the Bear's Place (Map p245; ☎ 617-492-2327; www.ttthebears.com; 10 Brookline St, Cambridge; cover $8-15) Grungy, diehard rock joint played by local bands on the rise. Well, not all are on the rise – the music's hit or miss.

Berklee Performance Center (Map p245; ☎ 617-747-2261; www.berkleebpc.com; 136 Massachusetts Ave; cover $20-50) One of America's premier music schools hosts concerts by famed alumni and other renowned artists.

THEATER & CULTURE

Wang Theatre (Map pp248-9; ☎ 617-482-9393; www.citicenter.org; 270 Tremont St) One of New England's largest theaters, this lavish 1925 landmark hosts top dance and theater performances.

Symphony Hall (Map p245; ☎ 617-266-1492; www.bso.org; 301 Massachusetts Ave) The celebrated Boston Symphony Orchestra and Boston Pops perform here.

Charles Playhouse (Map pp248-9; ☎ 617-426-6912; 74 Warrenton St) Home to the ever-popular Blue Man Group, this dual-stage backstreet theater has an engaging underground ambience.

Opera House (Map pp248-9; ☎ 617-880-2442; 539 Washington St) Restored to its 1920s grandeur, this extravagant theater hosts Broadway productions.

Hatch Memorial Shell (Map pp248-9; Charles River Esplanade) Free summer concerts take place at this outdoor bandstand on the banks of the Charles River, including the Boston Pops' July 4 concert, Boston's biggest annual music event.

SPORTS

From April to September join the frenzied fans cheering on the **Boston Red Sox** (☎ 888-327-0100; www.redsox.com), at **Fenway Park** (Map p245; tickets $20-125), major-league baseball's oldest (1912) and most storied ballpark.

At the **TD Banknorth Garden** (Map pp248-9; 150 Causeway St) from October to April, the NBA **Boston Celtics** (☎ 617-523-3030; www.celtics.com; tickets $15-180) play basketball, and the NHL **Boston Bruins** (☎ 617-624-2327; www.bostonbruins.com; tickets $16-190) play ice hockey.

At the **Gillette Stadium** (off Map p245) in Foxboro, 25 miles south of Boston, the NFL **New England Patriots** (☎ 800-543-1776; www.patriots.com; tickets $50-145) play football from August to January and the MLS **New England Revolution** (☎ 877-438-7387; www.revolutionsoccer.net; tickets $20-40) play soccer from April to October.

Shopping

Head to fashionable Newbury St, Boston's version of New York's Fifth Ave, for the city's most interesting shopping stroll. Starting on its highbrow east end it's all Armani, Brooks Brothers and Cartier, but by the time you reach the west end you'll find offbeat shops and funky bookstores.

Get independent music CDs at **Newbury Comics** (Map p245; ☎ 617-236-4930; 332 Newbury St), Harvard-logo sweatshirts at the **Coop** (Map p251; Massachusetts Ave, Cambridge) and Red Sox paraphernalia at **Out of Left Field** (Map pp248-9; ☎ 617-722-9401; Congress St) at Faneuil Hall.

Good places to browse for arts and crafts are **Bromfield Art Gallery** (Map pp248-9; ☎ 617-451-3605; 450 Harrison Ave), Boston's oldest cooperative, and **Cambridge Artists' Cooperative** (Map p251; ☎ 617-868-4434; 59a Church St, Cambridge) at Harvard Sq.

Copley Place (Map pp248-9; 100 Huntington Ave) and the **Shops at Prudential Center** (Map pp248-9; 800 Boylston St), both in the Back Bay, are the city's main indoor malls.

Getting There & Away

Getting in and out of Boston is easy. The train and bus stations are conveniently side by side, and the airport is a short subway ride away.

Logan International Airport (BOS; ☎ 800-235-6426; www.massport.com/logan), just across Boston Harbor from the city center, is served by major US and foreign airlines and has full services including currency-exchange booths.

South Station (Map pp248-9; 700 Atlantic Ave) is the terminal for an extensive network of long-distance buses operated by **Greyhound** (☎ 617-526-1808, 800-231-2222; www.greyhound.com). In addition, **Fung Wah Bus Company** (☎ 617-345-8000; www.fungwahbus.com) runs buses between South Station and New York City for just $15 each way.

MBTA Commuter Rail (☎ 617-222-3200; www.mbta.com) trains connect Boston's North Station (Map pp248–9) with Concord and Salem and Boston's South Station (Map pp248–9) with Plymouth and Providence; fares vary with the distance, maxing out at $7.75.

The **Amtrak** (☎ 617-345-7460, 800-872-7245; www.amtrak.com) terminal is at South Station; trains to New York cost $62 (4¼ hours) or $93 on the speedier *Acela Express* (3½ hours).

Major car-rental companies have offices at the airport, and many have locations around the city. Bear in mind that driving in Boston is utterly confusing with lots of one-way streets and archaic traffic patterns. It's best to stick to public transportation within the city. If you're traveling onward by rental car, pick up your car at the end of your Boston visit.

Getting Around

Logan International Airport is connected to downtown Boston by the **MBTA** (☎ 617-222-3200; www.mbta.com; single ride $2, day/week pass $9/15), which operates the USA's oldest subway (the 'T'), started in 1897. Five color-coded lines – Red, Blue, Green, Orange and Silver – radiate from the downtown stations of Park St, Downtown Crossing and Government Center. 'Inbound' trains are headed for one of these stations, 'outbound' trains away from them. Trains operate from around 5:30am to 12:30am.

Taxis are plentiful; expect to pay between $10 and $25 between two points within the city limits. Flag taxis on the street, find them at major hotels or call **Metro Cab** (☎ 617-242-8000) or **Independent** (☎ 617-426-8700).

AROUND BOSTON

The historic towns rimming Boston make for fine day-tripping. If you don't have your own transportation, you can reach these places by MBTA (above) buses and rail.

Lexington & Concord

In 1775 the Colonial town of Lexington, 15 miles northwest of Boston, was the site of the first battle of the American Revolution. Following the battle, the British redcoats marched 10 miles west to Concord where they fought the American Minutemen at the town's North Bridge – the first American victory. You can revisit this momentous bit of history at **Minute Man National Historic Park** (☎ 978-369-6993; www.nps.gov/mima; 174 Liberty St, Concord; admission free; 🕑 9am-5pm Apr-Oct) and along the 5.5-mile **Battle Road Trail**, which is open to cyclists as well as hikers.

In the 19th century, Concord harbored a vibrant literary community. Next to the **Old North Bridge** is the **Old Manse** (☎ 978-369-3909; 269 Monument St; adult/child 6-12yr $8/5), former home of author Nathaniel Hawthorne. Within a mile of the town center are the **Ralph Waldo Emerson house** (☎ 978-369-2236; 28 Cambridge Turnpike; adult/child 7-17yr $8/6), Louisa May Alcott's **Orchard House** (☎ 978-369-4118; 399 Lexington Rd; adult/child 6-17yr $8/5) and the **Wayside** (☎ 978-369-6993; 455 Lexington Rd; adult/child under 16yr $5/free), where Alcott's *Little Women* was set.

Walden Pond, where Henry David Thoreau lived and wrote *Walden*, is 3 miles south of the town center; you can visit his cabin site and take an inspiring hike around the pond. All these authors are laid to rest in **Sleepy Hollow Cemetery** (Bedford St) in the town center. Admission is free to Walden Pond and the cemetery. **Concord Chamber of Commerce** (☎ 978-369-3120; www.concordchamberofcommerce.org; 58 Main St) has full details on sites, including opening hours for the homes, which vary with the season

Salem

Salem, 20 miles northeast of Boston, burned itself an infamous place in history with the 1692 hysteria that put innocent people to death for witchcraft (see the boxed text, below). The tragedy has proven a boon for

WITCH HUNTS

In early 1692 a group of Salem girls began to act strangely. The work of the devil? The girls, pressured to blame someone, accused a slave named Tituba of witchcraft. Under torture, Tituba accused others and soon accusations were flying thick and fast. By September, 55 had pleaded guilty and 19 who wouldn't 'confess' to witchcraft were hanged. The frenzy finally died down when the accusers pointed at the governor's wife.

The most poignant site in Salem is the **Witch Trials Memorial** (Charter St), a quiet park behind the Peabody Essex Museum, where simple stones are inscribed with the names and final words of the victims, decrying the injustice befallen them.

Best of Salem's other 'witchy' sites is the **Witch House** (☎ 978-744-8815; 310 Essex St; adult/child 6-14yr $8.25/4.25; 🕑 10am-4:45pm), the home of the magistrate who presided over the trials. To dig deeper, read Arthur Miller's *The Crucible,* which doubles as a parable to the 1950s anticommunist 'witch hunts' in the US Senate that resulted in Miller's own blacklisting.

operators of numerous Salem witch attractions, some serious, others just milking witchy-wacky-woo for all it's worth. **Destination Salem** (☎ 877-725-3662; www.salem.org; 1 New Liberty St) has full information on town sights.

The exceptional **Peabody Essex Museum** (☎ 978-745-9500; www.pem.org; East India Sq; adult/child under 17yr $15/free; 10am-5pm Tue-Sun) reflects Salem's rich maritime history. The museum was founded upon the art, artifacts and curios collected by Salem traders during their early expeditions to the Far East. As the exhibits attest, they had deep pockets and refined taste. In addition to world-class Chinese and Pacific Island displays, the museum boasts a fine Native American collection.

Salem was the center of a thriving clipper-ship trade with China and its preeminent trader, Elias Derby, became America's first millionaire. For a sense of those glory days, take a walk along Derby St and out to Derby Wharf, now the center of the **Salem Maritime National Historic Site**.

Plymouth

Proclaiming itself 'America's hometown,' Plymouth celebrates its heritage as the region's first permanent European settlement. **Plymouth Rock**, a weather-worn chunk of granite on the harborfront, is said to mark the place the Pilgrims came ashore in 1620. Don't expect anything monumental; the rock upon which America was built is indeed small – so diminutive that most visitors have to take a second look.

These days, people make their pilgrimage to **Plimoth Plantation** (☎ 508-746-1622; www.plimoth.org; MA 3A; adult/child 6-12yr $28/18; 9am-5pm mid-Mar–Nov;), an authentically re-created 1627 Pilgrim village. Everything – the houses, the crops, the food cooked over wood stoves and even the vocabulary used by the costumed interpreters – is meticulously true to the period. Equally insightful are the home sites of the Wampanoag tribe, who helped the Pilgrims through their first difficult winter. If you're traveling with kids, or you're a history buff, don't miss it. The admission price includes entry to the *Mayflower II*, a replica of the Pilgrims' ship, at Plymouth Harbor.

Destination Plymouth (☎ 508-747-7533; www.visit-plymouth.com; 170 Water St), opposite the harbor, has details on all sights. When hunger strikes, you'll find good seafood restaurants right at the harbor.

CAPE COD

Clambering across the National Seashore dunes, cycling the Cape Cod Rail Trail, eating oysters at Wellfleet Harbor – this sandy peninsula serves up a bounty of local flavor. Fringed with 400 miles of sparkling shoreline, 'the Cape,' as it's called by Cape Codders, rates as New England's top beach destination. But there's a lot more than just beaches here. When you've had your fill of sun and sand, get out and explore artist enclaves, take a cruise, or join the free-spirited street scene in Provincetown.

Cape Cod Chamber of Commerce (☎ 508-362-3225, 888-332-2732; www.capecodchamber.org; US 6, at MA 132, Hyannis; 8:30am-5pm Mon-Fri year-round, 9am-5pm Sat, 10am-2pm Sun summer) provides Cape-wide information.

HOT TOPIC: WINDMILLS ON THE HORIZON

Cape Wind wants to build the nation's largest offshore wind farm, consisting of 130 mega-turbines, in the waters off Cape Cod. You might think with the greening of America that everyone would be on board. But in fact, the issue has been slow to win over many local environmentalists.

The Cape Cod Commission, a regional planning board that's progressive on most issues, denied approval to the project in 2007 only to be overruled by a new state program bent on speeding along green energy projects. In May 2009, citing the state's Green Communities Act, Massachusetts approved a bundle of state and local permits. That leaves only a final go-ahead from the federal government, which seems an apparent shoe-in considering Barack Obama's support for wind energy.

Among the wind farm's supporters are national heavyweights like Greenpeace and the Sierra Club. The detractors are mostly local and heavily funded by wealthy oceanfront homeowners who don't want wind turbines to be part of their ocean vista. Situated just a few miles offshore, they will indeed be visible on the horizon, but whether it's a welcome sight or an eyesore is certainly a matter of perspective.

Sandwich

The Cape's oldest village wraps its historic center around a picturesque swan pond. Here you'll find the Cape's oldest house, **Hoxie House** (☎ 508-888-1173; 18 Water St; adult/child 5-12yr $3/2; ⏰ 10am-5pm Mon-Sat, 1-5pm Sun mid-Jun–mid-Oct) c 1640; the **Dexter Grist Mill** (☎ 508-888-5144; Water St; adult/child 5-12yr $3/2; ⏰ 10am-5pm Mon-Sat, 1-5pm Sun mid-Jun–Sep) c 1654, whose oak waterwheel stills grinds cornmeal; and the kiddy-geared **Thornton W Burgess Museum** (☎ 508-888-4668; 4 Water St; adult/child under 13yr $2/1; ⏰ 10am-4pm Mon-Sat, 1-4pm Sun late May–Oct; 👶), named for the Sandwich native who wrote the *Peter Cottontail* series.

Artfully displayed in the **Sandwich Glass Museum** (☎ 508-888-0251; www.sandwichglassmuseum.org; 129 Main St; adult/child 6-14yr $5/1.25; ⏰ 9:30am-5pm Apr-Dec, 9:30am-4pm Wed-Sun Feb-Mar) is the town's 19th-century glass-making heritage. Glass-blowing demonstrations are given on the hour.

The 76-acre **Heritage Museums & Gardens** (☎ 508-888-3300; www.heritagemuseumsandgardens.org; Grove St; adult/child 6-16yr $12/6; ⏰ 10am-5pm Apr-Oct; 👶) sports a terrific vintage automobile collection, folk-art exhibits and one of the finest rhododendron gardens in America. Kids will love riding the classic 1912 carousel.

If you're ready for salt spray, head to **Sandy Neck Beach** (Sandy Neck Rd), off MA 6A, a 6-mile dune-backed strand (parking $15) ideal for beachcombing and a bracing swim.

A 6-mile path perfect for cycling and in-line skating runs along the south side of the **Cape Cod Canal** starting at Sandwich Harbor.

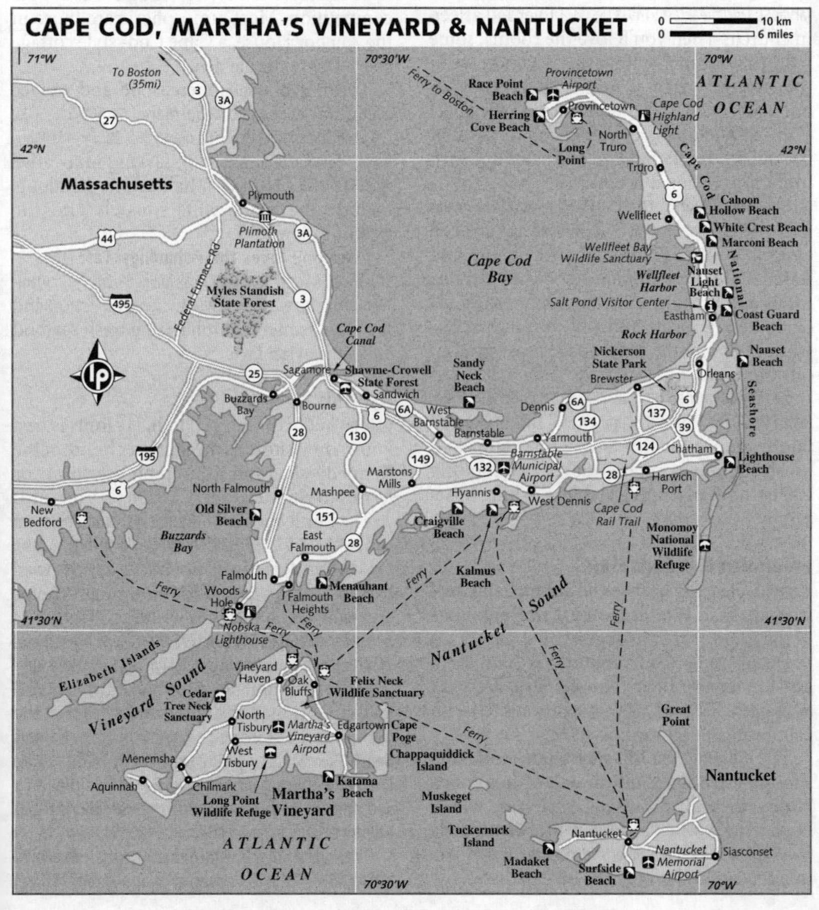

SCENIC DRIVE: MA 6A

When exploring the Cape, eschew the speedy Mid-Cape Hwy (US 6) and follow instead the Old King's Hwy (MA 6A), which snakes along Cape Cod Bay. The longest continuous stretch of historic district in the USA, it's lined with gracious period homes, antique shops and art galleries, all of which makes for good browsing en route.

SLEEPING & EATING

Shawme-Crowell State Forest (☎ 508-888-0351, 877-422-6762; www.reserveamerica.com; MA 130; campsites $14) You'll find 285 shady campsites in this 700-acre woodland, near MA 6A.

Belfry Inne (☎ 508-888-8550; www.belfryinn.com; 8 Jarves St; r incl breakfast $149-315; ⊠) Ever fall asleep in church? Then you'll love the rooms, some with the original stained-glass windows, in this creatively restored former church, now an upmarket B&B. If, however, having the angel Gabriel watching over you in bed seems a bit too quirky, Belfry has two adjacent inns with more conventional rooms.

Bee-Hive Tavern (☎ 508-833-1184; 406 MA 6A; mains $8-20; 🕑 11:30am-9pm Mon-Sat, 8:30am-9pm Sun) The agreeable mix of Colonial atmosphere and home-style New England cooking attracts locals and visitors alike. Lunch favorites include hearty salads and roll-up sandwiches, while at dinner the honey-sage roast chicken hits the spot.

Seafood Sam's (☎ 508-888-4629; Coast Guard Rd; mains $9-20; 🕑 11am-8:30pm; ♿) This is a good family choice for fish and chips, clams and lobster. Dine at picnic tables overlooking Cape Cod Canal and watch the fishing boats sail by.

Falmouth & Woods Hole

Crowd-pleasing beaches and the quaint seaside village of Woods Hole are the highlights of the Cape's second-largest town.

Deeply indented Falmouth has 70 miles of coastline, none finer than **Old Silver Beach** (off MA 28A, North Falmouth), a long, sandy stretch with calm waters; parking costs $20.

The **Shining Sea Bikeway** runs along the shoreline from Falmouth center to Woods Hole, rewarding cyclists with fine views of Martha's Vineyard en route. **Corner Cycle** (☎ 508-540-4195; 115 Palmer Ave; per day $17; 🕑 9am-6pm) rents bicycles near the bike path.

Woods Hole is the departure point for Martha's Vineyard ferries (p271) and home of the **Woods Hole Oceanographic Institution** (WHOI; www.whoi.edu), one of the world's most prestigious marine research facilities. You'll gain insights into WHOI's work at the **Ocean Science Exhibit Center** (☎ 508-289-2663; 15 School St; adult/child under 10yr $2/free; 🕑 10am-4:30pm Mon-Sat May-Oct). See more than a hundred species of sea creatures, including some in a kid-friendly touch tank, at **Woods Hole Science Aquarium** (☎ 508-495-2001; 166 Water St; admission free; 🕑 11am-4pm Tue-Sat Jun-Aug, Mon-Fri Sep-May; ♿).

Within walking distance of the beach and Vineyard ferry, all 28 rooms at **Falmouth Heights Motor Lodge** (☎ 508-548-3623, 800-468-3623; www.falmouthheightsmotel.com; 146 Falmouth Heights Rd; r incl breakfast from $149; ✻ ◙) are a cut above the competition. Most atmospheric are those in the Anchor House, a Cape Cod–style cottage overlooking the garden.

Top-notch atmosphere, food and service are in store at **La Cucina Sul Mare** (☎ 508-548-5600; 237 Main St; mains lunch $6-12, dinner $15-20; 🕑 11:30am-2:30pm Tue-Sun, 4:30-9pm daily), serving innovative renditions of Northern Italian fare. Standouts include the white-wine mussels and the rigatoni a la vodka.

Everyone loves the **Fishmonger Café** (☎ 508-540-5376; 56 Water St, Woods Hole; mains $8-26; 🕑 7:30am-10pm) for the water views in every direction and the eclectic menu emphasizing fresh seafood and vegetarian fare.

Hyannis

Cape Cod's commercial hub, Hyannis is best known to visitors as the summer home of the Kennedy clan and a jumping-off point for ferries to Nantucket and Martha's Vineyard.

The worthwhile **John F Kennedy Hyannis Museum** (☎ 508-790-3077; 397 Main St; adult/child 10-16yr $5/2.50; 🕑 9am-5pm Mon-Sat, noon-5pm Sun late May–Oct, varied hours Nov-Apr) celebrates JFK's life through photos and exhibits on the USA's 35th president.

Hy-Line Cruises (☎ 508-790-0696; www.hylinecruises.com; Ocean St Dock; adult/child 3-11yr $15/8; 🕑 mid-Apr–Oct) offers an hour-long harbor cruise aboard an old-fashioned steamer that circles past the compound of Kennedy family homes. **Kalmus Beach** (Ocean St) is popular for windsurfing, while **Craigville Beach** (Craigville Beach Rd) is the place to see and be seen for the college set; parking at either beach costs $15.

The rates are a bargain, but the little **SeaCoast Inn** (☎ 508-775-3828; www.seacoastcapecod.com; 33 Ocean

St; r incl breakfast $108-148;) is no Plain Jane. Rooms are spacious with perks aplenty, from free wi-fi to kitchenettes, and the central location is just minutes from everything in town.

Bright airy rooms with harbor-view balconies separate the family-run, boutique **Anchor-in** (☎ 508-775-0357; www.anchorin.com; 1 South St; r incl breakfast from $139-289;) from all the chains back on the highway. And if you're planning a day trip to Nantucket, the ferry is just a stroll away.

Come to **La Petite France Café** (☎ 508-775-1067; 349 Main St; sandwiches $7; 7am-3pm Mon-Sat) for flaky croissants, superb baguette sandwiches and homemade soup. Don't let the chef's French accent fool you – he does a nice job with New England–style clam chowder too.

With its dizzying array of options, **Ardeo** (☎ 508-790-1115; 644 Main St; mains $7-24; 11:30am-10pm;) is a perfect family choice with something for every taste. The menu ranges from pizza and Black Angus burgers to traditional Greek fare and seafood.

Brewster

Woodsy Brewster, on the Cape's bay side, makes a good base for outdoorsy types. The Cape Cod Rail Trail (see the boxed text, below) cuts clear across town and there are excellent options for camping, hiking and water activities.

The 2000-acre oasis of **Nickerson State Park** (☎ 508-896-3491; 3488 MA 6A; admission free; 8am-8pm) has it all: ponds with sandy beaches, boating, cycling and walking trails. You can rent canoes, kayaks and sailboats within the park at **Jack's Boat Rentals** (☎ 508-896-8556; Cliff Pond; rental per hr $20-30; 9am-6pm) and bicycles from **Barbara's Bike** (☎ 508-896-7231; half/full day $16/24; 9am-6pm) by the park entrance.

The **Cape Cod Museum of Natural History** (☎ 508-896-3867; www.ccmnh.org; 869 MA 6A; adult/child 3-12yr $8/3.50; 9:30am-4pm daily Jun-Sep, 11am-3pm Wed-Sun Oct-May;) has exhibits on the Cape's creatures and a cool boardwalk trail that tromps across a saltmarsh to a remote beach.

WHAT THE...?

Lobster mania takes a new twist at **Ben & Bill's Chocolate Emporium** (☎ 508-548-7878; 209 Main St, Falmouth; cones $4.50; 9am-11pm) where the crustacean has crawled onto the ice-cream menu. Forget plain vanilla. Step up to the counter and order a scoop of lobster ice cream. Now there's one you won't find with the old 31 flavors folks.

SLEEPING & EATING

Nickerson State Park (☎ 877-422-6762; www.reserveamerica.com; campsites $17-26) Head here for Cape Cod's best camping with 418 wooded campsites; it often fills, so reserve your spot early.

Old Sea Pines Inn (☎ 508-896-6114; www.oldseapinesinn.com; 2553 MA 6A; r incl breakfast with shared bath $85, with private bath $115-195;) A former girls' school dating to 1840, the inn's 21 rooms retain a simple yesteryear look. It's a bit like staying at grandma's house: antique fittings, floral wallpaper, clawfoot bathtubs. No TV, but rocking chairs await on the porch.

Cobies (☎ 508-896-7021; 3256 MA 6A; meals $8-20; 10:30am-9pm) Conveniently located near Nickerson State Park, this roadside clam shack dishes out fried seafood that you can crunch and munch at outdoor picnic tables.

our pick **Brewster Fish House** (☎ 508-896-7867; 2208 MA 6A; lunch $10-16, dinner $20-30; 11:30am-3pm & 5-9:30pm) Not an eye-catcher from the outside but inside you'll find some of the best seafood on the Cape. Start with the lobster bisque, naturally sweet with chunks of fresh lobster. From

CYCLING THE RAIL TRAIL

A poster child for the rails-to-trail movement, the **Cape Cod Rail Trail** follows a former railroad track for 22 glorious miles past cranberry bogs and along sandy ponds ideal for a dip. It's one of the finest cycling trails in all New England. There's a hefty dose of Olde Cape Cod scenery en route and you can detour into quiet villages for lunch or sightseeing. The path begins in Dennis on MA 134 and continues all the way to South Wellfleet. If you have time to do only part of the trail, begin at Nickerson State Park in Brewster and head for the Cape Cod National Seashore in Eastham. Bicycle rentals are available at the trailhead in Dennis, at Nickerson State Park and opposite the National Seashore's Salt Pond Visitor Center.

there it's safe to cast your net in any direction. Just 11 tables, and no reservations, so think lunch or early dinner to avoid long waits.

Chatham

Upscale inns and tony shops are a hallmark of the Cape's most genteel town, but some of Chatham's finest pleasures come free for the taking. Start your exploring on Main St, with its old sea captains' houses and cool art galleries. At **Chatham Fish Pier** (Shore Rd) watch fishermen unload their catch and spot seals basking on nearby shoals. A mile south on Shore Rd is **Lighthouse Beach**, an endless expanse of sea and sandbars that offers some of the finest beach strolling on Cape Cod. The 7600-acre **Monomoy National Wildlife Refuge** (www.fws.gov/northeast/monomoy) covers two uninhabited islands thick with shorebirds; to see it up close take the 1½-hour boat tour with **Outermost Harbor Marine** (☎ 508-945-5858; 83 Seagull Rd; adult/child $28/16).

Within walking distance of the town center and beach, the homey, **Bow Roof House** (☎ 508-945-1346; 59 Queen Anne Rd; r incl breakfast $95-105), built c 1780, is sweetly old-fashioned in both price and offerings. No frou-frou, mind you – except for the addition of private baths, the place looks nearly the same as it did in Colonial times. A rare budget traveler's find in upscale Chatham.

Join the townies at the ultra-casual **Larry's PX** (☎ 508-945-3964; 1591 Main St; mains $4-12; 🕑 5am-4pm Jun-Aug, 6am-2pm Sep-May) for omelets, burgers and service with a sassy smile. The sign on the door says 'Sorry, we're open.' Gotta love that.

The perky **Chatham Squire** (☎ 508-945-0945; 487 Main St; mains $7-20; 🕑 11:30am-10pm) pub is the busiest place in town. The menu's piled high with Monomoy steamers, raw oysters and other briny local delights. How fresh is the seafood? Just take one look at the fishermen hanging at the bar.

Cape Cod National Seashore

our pick **Cape Cod National Seashore** (www.nps.gov/caco) extends some 40 miles around the curve of the Outer Cape and encompasses most of the shoreline from Eastham to Provincetown. It's a treasure-trove of unspoiled beaches, dunes, salt marshes and forests. Thanks to President John F Kennedy, this vast area was set aside for preservation in the 1960s, just before a building boom hit the rest of his native Cape Cod. The **Salt Pond Visitor Center** (☎ 508-255-3421; Nauset Rd, at US 6, Eastham; admission free; 🕑 9am-5pm) is the place to start and has a great view to boot. Here you'll find exhibits and films on the area's ecology and the scoop on the park's numerous cycling and hiking trails, some of which begin right at the center.

You brought your board, didn't you? **Coast Guard Beach**, just down the road from the visitor center, is a stunner that attracts everyone from surfers to beachcombers. And the view of untouched Nauset Marsh from the dunes above the beach is nothing short of spectacular. **Nauset Light Beach**, running north from Coast Guard Beach, takes its name from the lighthouse perched above it; three other classic lighthouses are nearby. Summertime beach parking passes cost $15/45 a day/season and are valid at all Cape Cod National Seashore beaches including Provincetown (opposite).

Wellfleet

Art galleries, primo beaches and those famous Wellfleet oysters lure visitors to this little seaside town.

Birders flock to Massachusetts Audubon Society's **Wellfleet Bay Wildlife Sanctuary** (☎ 508-349-2615; www.wellfleetbay.org; West Rd; adult/child $5/3; 🕑 8:30am-5pm), off MA 6A, where trails cross 1100 acres of tidal creeks, salt marshes and sandy beaches. You can walk along the trails until dusk, but get there before 5pm to see the displays in the solar-powered nature center.

Marconi Beach has a monument to Guglielmo Marconi, who sent the first wireless transmission across the Atlantic from this site, and a beach backed by undulating dunes. The adjacent beaches of **White Crest Beach** and **Cahoon Hollow Beach** offer high-octane surfing.

About two dozen **art galleries** host receptions on summer Saturdays. For an evening of nostalgia, park at **Wellfleet Drive-In** (☎ 508-349-7176; 51 US 6; adult/child 4-11yr $8/5; 🕑 May–mid-Sep), one of a dwindling number of drive-in cinemas in the USA. **Wellfleet Flea Market** (☎ 508-349-0541; per car $3; 🕑 8am-3pm Wed, Thu, Sat & Sun in summer, Sat & Sun in spring & fall), at the Wellfleet Drive-In, hosts scores of dealers and makes an interesting diversion for bargain-hunters. The acclaimed **Wellfleet Harbor Actors Theater** (☎ 508-349-9428; www.what.org; 2357 US 6; tickets $10-30) produces edgy contemporary plays.

Historic without being cloying, the 1871 Victorian **Stone Lion Inn of Cape Cod** (☎ 508-349-9565; www.stonelioncapecod.com; 130 Commercial St; r incl breakfast $140-200;) is the finest place in Wellfleet to tuck in. Pine floors, antique decor and handcrafted furnishings set the tone. The location is handy for exploring town on foot.

Head to **Mac's Seafood** (508-349-9611; Wellfleet Town Pier; mains $7-16; 7:30am-11pm) for market-fresh seafood at bargain prices. Fried-fish standards are paired with snappy-fresh oysters harvested from nearby flats. Order at the window and chow down at picnic tables overlooking Wellfleet Harbor.

A former lifesaving station right on the beach, **Beachcomber** (508-349-6055; Cahoon Hollow Beach, Ocean View Dr), aka 'Da Coma,' is *the* place to have a drink and hit the dance floor.

Truro

Squeezed between Cape Cod Bay on the west and the open Atlantic on the east, narrow Truro abounds with water views and beaches. In North Truro, **Cape Cod Highland Light** (508-487-1121; Lighthouse Rd; admission $4; 10am-5:30pm mid-May–Oct) dates to 1797, casts the brightest light on the New England coastline, and offers a sweeping view. The adjacent **Highland House Museum** (508-487-3397; Lighthouse Rd; adult/child $4/free; 10am-4:30pm Mon-Sat & 1-4:30pm Sun Jun-Sep) is dedicated to the area's farming and fishing past.

Budget digs don't get much more atmospheric than at **HI Truro** (508-349-3889, 888-901-2086; www.capecodhostels.org; N Pamet Rd, North Truro; dm $32-35; mid-Jun–early Sep;), a former coast guard station dramatically sited amid beach dunes. Book early to avoid disappointment.

Provincetown

Go to the cabaret, set off on a whale watch, join the carnival street scene – there's no limit to what you can do on this outer reach of the Cape. Fringe writers and artists began making a summer haven in Provincetown a century ago. Today it's morphed into the hottest gay and lesbian destination in the Northeast. While the action throbs from the center of town, Provincetown also has quiet dunes and an untamed coastline with glorious beaches.

ORIENTATION & INFORMATION

The town's center runs along two parallel streets, the seaside Commercial St, with the lion's share of restaurants, galleries and shops, and Bradford St one block inland. Guesthouses line the narrow streets between Bradford and Commercial.

Provincetown Chamber of Commerce (508-487-3424; www.ptownchamber.com; 307 Commercial St; 9am-7pm Jun-Aug, 10am-3pm Mon-Sat Sep-May) At MacMillan Wharf; get tourist information here.
Provincetown Post Office (800-275-8777; 219 Commercial St)
Provincetown Public Library (508-487-7094; 356 Commercial St; 10am-5pm Mon & Fri, noon-8pm Tue & Thu, 10am-8pm Wed, 10am-2pm Sat, 1-5pm Sun) Allows 30 minutes of free internet access; see also the boxed text, p266.
Seamen's Bank (508-487-0035; 221 Commercial St)
Wired Puppy (508-487-0017; 379 Commercial St; 6:30am-10pm;) Free internet for the price of a cup of coffee.

SIGHTS & ACTIVITIES

Climb to the top of the USA's tallest all-granite structure, the 253ft-high **Pilgrim Monument** (508-487-1310; High Pole Rd; adult/child 4-14yr $7/3.50; 9am-5pm Apr-Nov, to 7pm Jun–mid-Sep), for a sweeping view of town and the surrounding coast. The monument commemorates the *Mayflower* Pilgrims, who landed in Provincetown in 1620 before moving on to Plymouth.

Established in 1914 to celebrate the town's thriving art community, the superb **Provincetown Art Association & Museum** (PAAM; 508-487-1750; www.paam.org; 460 Commercial St; adult/child under 12yr $5/free; 11am-8pm Mon-Thu, 11am-10pm Fri, 11am-5pm Sat & Sun Jun-Sep, noon-5pm Thu-Sun Oct-May) displays the works of artists who have found inspiration in Provincetown over the past century.

Provincetown hosts some of the finest **art galleries** in the region. For the best browsing begin at PAAM and start walking southwest along Commercial St. Over the next few blocks every second storefront harbors a gallery worth a peek.

On the wild tip of the Cape, **Race Point Beach** is a breathtaking stretch of sand with crashing surf and undulating dunes as far as the eye can see. It's the kind of beach where you could walk for miles and see no one but the occasional angler casting for bluefish. Swimmers favor the calmer though equally brisk waters of **Herring Cove Beach**; nude (though illegal) sunbathers head to the left, families to the right. Herring Cove faces west, the perfect place to be at sunset. Both beaches are part of Cape Cod National Seashore (opposite).

The National Seashore's **Province Lands Visitor Center** (508-487-1256; Race Point Rd; admission free; 9am-5pm May-Oct) has displays on dune ecology and leads dune walks. Don't miss the rooftop

WHAT THE...?

In a town of colorful buildings the **Provincetown Public Library** (p265) rules. Erected in 1860 as a church, it was turned into a museum a century later, complete with a replica of Provincetown's race-winning schooner *Rose Dorothea*. The museum went bust and the town converted the building to a library. One catch: the boat, which occupies the building's upper deck, was too big to remove. So it's still there, with bookshelves built around it. Pop upstairs and take a look.

observation deck with its eye-popping 360-degree view of the outermost reaches of Cape Cod; the deck stays open until midnight.

An exhilarating way to explore Provincetown's amazing dunes and beaches is along the National Seashore's 8 miles of paved bike trail. Several shops rent bikes, including **Ptown Bikes** (☎ 508-487-8735; 42 Bradford St; per day cruiser/mountain bike $17/22; 9am-6pm). Or explore the easy way with **Art's Dune Tours** (☎ 508-487-1950; 4 Standish St; adult/child $23/18), which provides hour-long 4WD tours through the dunes.

Provincetown is an ideal departure point for **whale-watching tours**, which cruise Stellwagen Bank National Marine Sanctuary. Extending north from Provincetown, the sanctuary is the summer feeding ground for humpback whales, awesome creatures with a flair for acrobatic breaching. They come surprisingly close to the boats, offering great photo ops. Other whales also frequent these waters, including many of the 300 remaining North Atlantic right whales, the world's most endangered whale species. The environmentally oriented **Dolphin Fleet Whale Watch** (☎ 508-240-3636, 800-826-9300; MacMillan Wharf; 3-4hr trips adult/child 5-12yr $39/31; Apr-Oct;) has several tours a day.

SLEEPING

Provincetown offers nearly 100 guesthouses without a single chain hotel to mar the view. In summer it's wise to book ahead, doubly so on weekends. If you arrive without a booking, the chamber of commerce (p265) can help.

Dunes' Edge Campground (☎ 508-487-9815; www.dunes-edge.com; 386 US 6; campsites $40;) Camp amid the dunes and shady pines at this family-friendly campground, between the National Seashore and town.

Christopher's by the Bay (☎ 508-487-9263, 877-476-9263; www.christophersbythebay.com; 8 Johnson St; r with shared/private bath from $105/155;) Tucked away on a quiet side street, this welcoming inn is top value. The 2nd-floor rooms are the largest and snazziest, but the 3rd-floor rooms, which share a bathroom, get the ocean view.

Fairbanks Inn (☎ 508-487-0386, 800-324-7265; www.fairbanksinn.com; 90 Bradford St; r incl breakfast $149-265;) The two women who run this place know how to make you feel at home. Choose between a new wing with fireplaces and kitchens, and old-fashioned rooms in the 1776 sea captain's home where sloping pine floors and antique wallpaper set the mood.

Race Point Lighthouse (☎ 508-487-9930; www.racepointlighthouse.net; Race Point; r $155-185;) Want to *really* get away? If unspoiled sand dunes and a 19th-century lighthouse sound like good company, book one of the three bedrooms in the old lightkeeper's house. Cool place – powered by solar panels and a wind turbine, and literally on the outer tip of the Cape.

Carpe Diem (☎ 508-487-4242, 800-487-0132; www.carpediemguesthouse.com; 12 Johnson St; r incl breakfast $195-309;) Sophisticated and relaxed, with smiling buddhas, orchid sprays and a European-style spa. Each guest room's decor is inspired by a different gay literary genius; the room themed on poet Raj Rao, for example, has sumptuous embroidered fabrics and hand-carved Indian furniture.

Brass Key Guesthouse (☎ 508-487-9005, 800-842-9858; www.brasskey.com; 67 Bradford St; r $210-400;) This adults-only boutique hotel sets the standard for gay travelers. The rooms fuse Victorian style with 21st-century comforts like Jacuzzi tubs, pillow-top mattresses and flat-screen TVs. Other features: an infinity pool, private sunbathing decks and wine-and-cheese evenings.

EATING

Hungry? Every third building on Commercial St houses some sort of eatery, so that's the place to start.

Portuguese Bakery (☎ 508-487-1803; 299 Commercial St; snacks $2-5; 7am-8pm) This Provincetown bakery has been serving up *malasadas* (sweet fried dough), *linguica* (Portuguese sausage) soups and sandwiches for more than a century. True local flavor.

Purple Feather (☎ 508-487-9100; 334 Commercial St; snacks $2-10; 8am-midnight) Head to this stylish café for killer panini sandwiches, blueberry gelato and decadent desserts all made from scratch. No better place in town for light eats.

Spiritus Pizza (☎ 508-487-2808; 190 Commercial St; pizza slices/pies $3/18; 11:30am-2am) The pizza's just middling, but this is nonetheless the favorite spot for a late-night bite and cruising after the clubs close.

Fanizzi's by the Sea (☎ 508-487-1964; 539 Commercial St; mains $8-22; 11:30am-10pm;) Consistent food, an amazing water view and reasonable prices make this restaurant at the east end of Provincetown a sure winner. The extensive menu has something for everyone, from fresh seafood to salads and fajitas – even a kids menu.

Bubala's by the Bay (☎ 508-487-0773; 183 Commercial St; mains $9-20; 11am-1am) Great people-watching and good food at this sidewalk café that bustles night and day. Fish and chips and focaccia sandwiches are the mainstays.

Mews Restaurant & Café (☎ 508-487-1500; 429 Commercial St; mains $10-16; 6-10pm) Want affordable gourmet? Skip the pricier restaurant here and go upstairs to the bar for a fab view, great martinis and scrumptious bistro fare. Perhaps the Angus gorgonzola burger?

Lobster Pot (☎ 508-487-0842; 321 Commercial St; mains $20-32; 11:30am-10pm) True to its name, this bustling fish house overlooking the ocean is *the* place for lobster. Keep it simple: order it boiled and sit on the deck.

DRINKING

PiedBar (☎ 508-487-1527; 193 Commercial St; 10am-11pm) sports a fine ocean view and attracts a mixed crowd. Many dining spots also have good bars, including **Ross' Grill** (☎ 508-487-8878; 236 Commercial St; 11:30am-10pm), another great choice for a water-view drink.

ENTERTAINMENT

Opening hours vary with the season and schedule.

Nightclubs

Provincetown is awash with gay clubs, drag shows and cabarets. And don't be shy if you're straight – everyone's welcome.

Crown & Anchor (☎ 508-487-1430; 247 Commercial St) The queen of the scene, this multiwing complex has a nightclub, a leather bar and a steamy cabaret that takes it to the limit.

DON'T MISS

Catch a world-class act at the **Provincetown Theater** (☎ 508-487-7487; www.newprovincetownplayers.org; 238 Bradford St). This stellar performing arts center hosts Provincetown's leading theater troupe, the New Provincetown Players. There's always something of interest to see.

Vixen (☎ 508-487-6424; 336 Commercial St) A favorite lesbian hangout, with everything from an intimate wine bar to comedy shows and dancing.

A-House (☎ 508-487-3821; 4 Masonic Pl) A hot weekend dance spot for gay men.

Theater

Provincetown boasts a rich theater history. Eugene O'Neill began his writing career here and several stars including Marlon Brando and Richard Gere performed on Provincetown stages before they hit the big screen.

SHOPPING

Scores of shops line up cheek-by-jowl along Commercial St selling everything from kitsch and tourist T-shirts to quality crafts and edgy clothing.

None attract more attention than **Shop Therapy** (☎ 508-487-9387; 346 Commercial St). Downstairs it's all patchouli and tie-dye clothing, but everyone gravitates upstairs, where the sex toys are wild enough to make an Amsterdam madam blush. Parents, use discretion: your teenagers *will* want to go inside.

GETTING THERE & AWAY

Plymouth & Brockton buses (☎ 508-746-0378) connect Boston and Provincetown ($30, 3½ hours). From mid-May to mid-October, **Bay State Cruise Company** (off Map p245; ☎ 617-748-1428; www.baystatecruises.com) runs a ferry (one way/round-trip $58/86, 1½ hours) three times a day between Boston's World Trade Center Pier and MacMillan Wharf.

NANTUCKET

Once home port to the world's largest whaling fleet, Nantucket's storied past is reflected in its period homes and cobbled streets. When whaling went bust in the mid-19th century the town plunged from riches to rags. The population dwindled, and its grand old houses

NEW ENGLAND

sat idle until wealthy urbanites discovered Nantucket made a fine place to summer. High-end tourism has been Nantucket's mainstay ever since. **Visitor Services** (☎ 508-228-0925; www.nantucket-ma.gov/visitor; 25 Federal St; 9am-5pm) has tourist information and maintains a kiosk at the ferry dock.

Sights & Activities

Step off the boat and you're in the only place in the USA where the entire town is a National Historic Landmark. It's a bit like stepping into a museum – wander around, soak up the atmosphere. A top sight is the evocative **Whaling Museum** (☎ 508-228-1894; www.nha.org; 13 Broad St; adult/child 6-17yr $15/8; 10am-5pm mid-May–Oct, shorter hours Nov–mid-May) in a former spermaceti (whale-oil) candle factory.

At the eastern end of the island sits Nantucket's only other village, picture-perfect **Siasconset** ('Sconset), known for its rose-covered cottages.

Then there are the gorgeous beaches. If you have young 'uns head to **Children's Beach**, right in Nantucket town, where the water's calm and there's a playground. **Surfside Beach**, 2 miles to the south, is where the college crowd heads for an active scene and bodysurfing waves. The best place to catch the sunset is **Madaket Beach**, 5.5 miles west of town.

No destination on the island is more than 8 miles from town and thanks to Nantucket's relatively flat terrain, cycling is an easy way to explore. Rent bikes at the ferry dock from **Nantucket Bike Shop** (☎ 508-228-1999; 4 Broad St; per day $30; 8am-6pm).

Sleeping & Eating

HI Nantucket (☎ 508-228-0433, 888-901-2084; www.capecodhostels.org; 31 Western Ave; dm $32-38;) Known locally as Star of the Sea, this atmospheric hostel in an 1873 lifesaving station has a million-dollar setting at Surfside Beach. As Nantucket's sole nod to the budget traveler, it books up well in advance.

Barnacle Inn (☎ 508-228-0332; www.thebarnacleinn.com; 11 Fair St; s/d incl breakfast with shared bath $90/150, private bath $115/195;) This is what old Nantucket is all about – folksy owners and simple accommodations that hearken to earlier times. Rooms in this century-old inn don't have TVs or air-con, but they do have good rates, particularly if you opt for shared bath.

Martin House Inn (☎ 508-228-0678; www.martinhouseinn.net; 61 Centre St; s incl breakfast $120, d incl breakfast $210-295;) For a stylish sleep, this elegant inn boasts soothing rooms with four-poster beds and period decor. It's a particularly good deal if you're traveling solo.

Even Keel Café (☎ 508-228-1979; 40 Main St; breakfast & lunch $5-15, dinner $12-25; 7am-10pm) If the weather's good, walk straight through the restaurant to the shady patio out back and order up the island's best cup o' joe. Other favorites: the ginger scones, the oversized omelets and the crab cakes.

Brotherhood of Thieves (☎ 508-228-2551; 23 Broad St; mains $7-24; 11:30am-1am) Nantucketers come here for the friendly tavern atmosphere – all brick and dark woods – and the island's best burgers. Good fresh seafood too, including sweet Nantucket scallops.

Sayle's Seafood (☎ 508-228-4599; 99 Washington St Extension; mains $8-22; 10am-8pm) For the island's best fried clams, cheapest lobster dinners and other seafood treats, head to this combo fish market and clam shack on the south side of town. It's all takeout but there's outdoor seating where you can enjoy your feast.

Getting There & Around

Cape Air (☎ 800-352-0714; www.flycapeair.com) flies from Boston, Hyannis, Martha's Vineyard and Providence to Nantucket Memorial Airport (ACK).

The **Steamship Authority** (☎ 508-477-8600; www.steamshipauthority.com; round-trip adult/child 5-12yr slow ferry $33/16, fast ferry $65/29) runs ferries throughout the day between Hyannis and Nantucket. The fast ferry takes an hour; the slow ferry 2¼ hours. The slow ferry takes cars, but the $380 round-trip fare aims to discourage visitors from adding to traffic congestion on Nantucket's narrow streets.

Getting around Nantucket is a snap. The **NRTA Shuttle** (☎ 508-228-7025; www.shuttlenantucket.com; rides $1-2, day pass $7; late May–Sep) operates buses around town and to 'Sconset, Madaket and the beaches. Buses have bike racks, so cyclists can bus one way and pedal back.

MARTHA'S VINEYARD

New England's largest island is a world unto itself. Home to 15,500 year-round residents, its population swells to 100,000 in summer. The towns are charming, the beaches good, the restaurants chef-driven. And there's something for every mood here – fine-dine in gentrified Edgartown one day and hit the cotton candy and carousel scene in Oak Bluffs the next.

EATING NEW ENGLAND: CHOW-DAH PLEASE

Feasting on New England's homegrown specialties can be an event in itself. Local culinary delights include the following:

- clam chowder – or, as Bostonians say, 'chow-dah,' this New England staple combines chopped clams, potatoes and clam juice in a milk base
- clambake – a meal of lobster, clams and corn on the cob, usually steamed
- cranberries – tart red berries grown in Massachusetts bogs, usually sweetened and used in juice, sauces and muffins
- frappe – whipped milk and ice cream, pronounced 'frap;' called a 'milk shake' in other regions, but known as a 'cabinet' in Rhode Island
- Indian pudding – baked pudding made of milk, cornmeal, molasses, butter, ginger, cinnamon and raisins
- littlenecks – small hard-shelled clams typically eaten raw on the half shell, or as clams casino with the meat dashed with hot sauce, wrapped in bacon and grilled
- lobster dinner – summer favorite featuring a hot boiled lobster, a crock of melted butter and a bib to keep you dry
- oysters – often served raw on the half-shell or, for the less intrepid, broiled or baked; the sweetest are Wellfleet oysters from Cape Cod
- quahogs – large hard-shelled clams (*ko-hogs*) that are cut into strips and fried, or chopped in chunks for chowder
- raw bar – a place to eat fresh-shucked live (raw) oysters and clams
- steamers – soft-shelled clams steamed and served in a bucket; extract the meat, swish it in broth to wash off any sand, dip it in melted butter and enjoy

Martha's Vineyard Chamber of Commerce (☎ 508-693-0085; www.mvy.com; Beach Rd, Vineyard Haven; 9am-5pm Mon-Fri, 9am-4pm Sat) has visitor information. There are also summertime visitor kiosks at the ferry terminals.

Oak Bluffs

This ferry-port village is likely to be your introduction to the island, as it's where most boats arrive. Oak Bluffs is the island's fun center – a place to wander with an ice-cream cone in hand, poke into souvenir shops and revel into the night. Oak Bluffs started out in the mid-19th century as a summer retreat by a revivalist church, whose members enjoyed a day at the beach as much as a gospel service. They first camped out in tents, but soon built some 300 cottages, each adorned with whimsical gingerbread trim. These brightly painted cottages surround the open-air **Trinity Park Tabernacle** (1879), where the lucky descendants of the Methodist Campmeeting Association still gather for events.

Take a nostalgic ride on the **Flying Horses Carousel** (☎ 508-693-9481; Circuit Ave, at Lake Ave; tickets $1.50; 10am-10pm;), which has been captivating kids of all ages since 1876. It's the USA's oldest merry-go-round: the antique horses have manes of real horse hair and if you stare into their glass eyes you'll see neat little silver animals inside.

A scenic **bike trail** runs along the coast connecting Oak Bluffs, Vineyard Haven and Edgartown – it's largely flat so makes a good pedal for families. Seasoned riders might want to bike the 20 miles to Aquinnah. Rent bicycles at **Anderson's Bike Rental** (☎ 508-693-9346; Circuit Ave Extension; per day $18; 9am-6pm) near the ferry terminal.

SLEEPING & EATING

Nashua House (☎ 508-693-0043, 888-343-0043; www.nashuahouse.com; 30 Kennebec Ave; r with shared bath $89-149;) The Vineyard the way it used to be – no phones, no TV, no in-room bath. Instead you'll find suitably simple and spotlessly clean accommodations at this small inn (1873) right in the center of town.

Narragansett House (☎ 508-693-3627, 888-693-3627; www.narragansetthouse.com; 46 Narragansett Ave; r incl breakfast $130-225;) On a quiet residential street, this inn occupies two adjacent

Victorian gingerbread-trimmed houses. It's pleasantly old-fashioned and unlike other places in this price range all the rooms have private bathrooms.

Slice of Life (☎ 508-693-3838; 50 Circuit Ave; mains $7-20; 🕑 7am-9pm) The look is casual, the fare is gourmet: portobello mushroom omelets, roasted cod with sun-dried tomatoes and luscious desserts.

Giordano's (☎ 508-693-0184; 107 Circuit Ave; mains $9-18; 🕑 11:30am-11pm; 👶) Established in 1930, this family-friendly eatery is famous for its fried clams and also serves good hand-tossed pizzas.

DRINKING & ENTERTAINMENT

Offshore Ale Co (☎ 508-693-2626; 30 Kennebec Ave; 🕑 10:30am-11:30pm) This popular microbrewery is the place to enjoy a pint of Vineyard ale and a good spot to hear live music on the weekends.

Lampost (☎ 508-696-9352; 6 Circuit Ave) Head to this combo bar and nightclub for the hottest dance scene on the island. Hours vary.

Vineyard Haven

A lovely harbor full of classic wooden sailboats, and streets lined with eye-catching restaurants and shops, lures visitors to this appealing town.

A vineyard on the Vineyard? But of course: about 3 miles southwest of town, **Chicama Vineyards** (☎ 508-693-0309; Stoney Hill Rd, West Tisbury; 🕑 11am-5pm Mon-Sat, 1-5pm Sun) offers free tasting tours at noon, 2pm and 4pm.

Wind's Up (☎ 508-693-4252; 199 Beach Rd; 🕑 9am-6pm) rents kayaks and boards. Windsurfing gear costs $50 to $78 per four hour, single and tandem kayaks $45 to $55.

Reserve early for one of the 72 beds at the **HI Martha's Vineyard** (☎ 508-693-2665; www.capecodhostels.org; Edgartown-West Tisbury Rd, West Tisbury; dm $32-38; 🕑 mid-May–mid-Oct; 💻), 8 miles from Vineyard Haven.

A mile and a half from the ferry terminal, the woodsy **Martha's Vineyard Family Campground** (☎ 508-693-3772; www.campmv.com; 569 Edgartown Rd; campsites $49, cabins $130-150) offers the island's only camping and has basic cabins that sleep four to six people.

Convenient to town and the ferry, the cheery **Crocker House Inn** (☎ 508-693-1151, 800-772-0206; www.crockerhouseinn.com; 12 Crocker Ave; r $185-415; ⊠ ❄ 📶) has eight well-appointed rooms, some with fireplaces and harbor views.

These days it's more famous for its T-shirts than its food, but the legendary **Black Dog Tavern** (☎ 508-693-9223; 20 Beach St Extension; mains $7-30; 🕑 7am-9pm), just a trot from the ferry, packs a crowd. Poke your wet nose in and see what catches your fancy, or just grab a muffin on the run from the bakery counter.

The place for breakfast and lunch is **Art Cliff Diner** (☎ 508-693-1224; 39 Beach Rd; mains $6-15; 🕑 7am-2pm Thu-Tue). Chef-owner Gina Stanley, a grad of the prestigious Culinary Institute of America, adds flair to everything she touches from the almond-encrusted pancakes to the fresh-fish tacos. Expect a line – it's worth the wait.

Edgartown

Perched on a fine natural harbor, Edgartown has a rich maritime history and a patrician air. At the height of the whaling era it was home to more than 100 sea captains whose fortunes built the grand old homes that line the streets today.

The **Martha's Vineyard Preservation Trust** (☎ 508-627-8619) manages a trio of vintage buildings clustered together on Main St: the **Dr Daniel Fisher House**, an 1840 mansion that once housed the island's wealthiest resident (no, he didn't make his fortune from his medical practice – he owned the whale-oil refinery); the **Old Whaling Church**, a classic Greek Revival building; and the 1672 **Vincent House**, built in traditional Cape style. Opening hours are irregular; call the trust for tour information. Entry prices depend on the tour taken, except Vincent House, where entry is $5.

For more insight into Edgartown's past, visit the **Martha's Vineyard Museum** (☎ 508-627-4441; 59 School St; adult/child 6-15yr $7/4; 🕑 10am-5pm Mon-Sat mid-Jun–mid-Oct, shorter hours mid-Oct–mid-Jun), where you'll find a fascinating collection of whaling paraphernalia and scrimshaw.

After exploring the town, hop on the **ferry** (☎ 508-627-9427; round-trip bicycle & rider $6, car & driver $12; 🕑 7am-midnight) for the five-minute jaunt to **Chappaquiddick Island**, where there are good beaches, including lovely **Cape Poge**, a wildlife refuge that runs along the entire east side of the island.

The Massachusetts Audubon Society's **Felix Neck Wildlife Sanctuary** (☎ 508-627-4850; Edgartown-Vineyard Haven Rd; adult/child 2-12yr $4/3; 🕑 sunrise-sunset) is a birder's paradise with 4 miles of trails skirting marshes and ponds. A magnificent barrier beach, **Katama Beach** (also called 'South Beach'), off Katama Rd, stretches for

IF YOU HAVE A FEW MORE DAYS

Known as **Up-Island**, the rural western half of Martha's Vineyard is a patchwork of rolling hills, small farms and open fields frequented by wild turkeys and deer. Feast your eyes and your belly at the picturesque fishing village of **Menemsha**, where you'll find seafood shacks with food so fresh the boats unload their catch at the back door. They'll shuck you an oyster and steam you a lobster while you watch and you can eat al fresco on a harbor-side bench.

The coastal **Clay Cliffs of Aquinnah**, also known as the Gay Head Cliffs, are so special they're a National Natural Landmark. These 150ft-high cliffs glow with an amazing array of colors that can be best appreciated in the late-afternoon light. You can hang out at **Aquinnah Beach**, just below the multihued cliffs, or walk a mile north along the shore to an area that's popular with nude sunbathers. Beach parking costs $15.

Cedar Tree Neck Sanctuary (☎ 508-693-5207; Indian Hill Rd, West Tisbury; admission free; 🕑 8:30am-5:30pm), off State Rd, has an inviting 2.5-mile hike across native bogs and forest to a coastal bluff with views of Cape Cod. **Long Point Wildlife Refuge** (☎ 508-693-7392; adult/child under 16 $3/free; 🕑 9am-5pm), off Edgartown–West Tisbury Rd, offers good birding and a mile-long trail to a lovely remote beach; parking costs $10.

3 miles; rough surf is the norm on the ocean side but there are protected salt ponds on the inland side.

SLEEPING & EATING

Edgartown Inn (☎ 508-627-4794; www.edgartowninn.com; 56 N Water St; r with shared bath $125, with private bath $170-275; ⊠ ❄) The inn's the best bargain in town with straightforward rooms spread across three adjacent buildings. The oldest dates to 1798 and claims Nathaniel Hawthorne and Daniel Webster among its early guests!

Victorian Inn (☎ 508-627-4784; www.thevic.com; 24 S Water St; r incl breakfast $245-425; ⊠ ❄ 📶) Four-poster beds, fresh-cut flowers and a gourmet multicourse breakfast are just part of the appeal at this upscale inn. And, yes, it is Victorian – listed on the National Register of Historic Places.

Among the Flowers Café (☎ 508-627-3233; 17 Mayhew Lane; mains $5-12; 🕑 8am-4pm) Join the townies on the garden patio for omelets, homemade soups and sandwiches. Although everything's served on paper plates, it's still kinda chichi.

Seafood Shanty (☎ 508-627-8622; 31 Dock St; mains $11-35; 🕑 11:30am-10pm) For a knockout harbor view this place reaches over the water with a wall of windows in all directions. Lunch focuses on burgers and fish sandwiches while dinner digs deeper into your pockets with the usual surf 'n' turf selections.

Getting There & Around

Martha's Vineyard has a small airport but most everyone arrives by ferry. The biggest ferry company, the **Steamship Authority** (☎ 508-477-8600; www.steamshipauthority.com; round-trip adult/child 5-12yr/bike/car $15/8/6/135) operates from Woods Hole to both Vineyard Haven (nine per day in summer) and Oak Bluffs (five per day), a 45-minute voyage. If you're bringing a car, book well in advance.

From Falmouth Harbor, the passenger-only ferry **Island Queen** (☎ 508-548-4800; www.islandqueen.com; 75 Falmouth Heights Rd; round-trip adult/child 4-12yr/bike $18/9/6) sails to Oak Bluffs at least seven times daily in summer.

From Hyannis, **Hy-Line Cruises** (☎ 508-778-2600, 800-492-8082; www.hylinecruises.com; Ocean St Dock; round-trip adult/child 5-12yr/bike slow ferry $43/22/12, fast ferry $69/48/12) operates a slow ferry (1½ hours) once daily to Oak Bluffs and a high-speed ferry (55 minutes) five times daily.

Martha's Vineyard Regional Transit Authority (☎ 508-693-9440; www.vineyardtransit.com; 1-/3-day pass $6/15) operates a bus network with frequent service between towns. It's a practical way to get around and you can even reach out-of-the-way destinations like the Clay Cliffs of Aquinnah.

CENTRAL MASSACHUSETTS

Poking around this central swath of Massachusetts, between big-city Boston and the fashionable Berkshires, provides a taste of the less-touristed stretch of the state. But it's no sleeper, thanks largely to a score of colleges that infuse a youthful spirit to the region.

The **Central Massachusetts Convention & Visitors Bureau** (☎ 508-753-2920; www.worcester.org) and the **Greater Springfield Convention & Visitors Bureau**

WHAT THE...?

Life-size bronze sculptures of the Cat in the Hat and other wonky characters look beseechingly at passers-by. Oh me, oh my. Welcome to the world of Theodor Seuss Geisel, Springfield's favorite native son. Your kids *will* insist on stopping at the **Dr Seuss National Memorial Sculpture Garden** (cnr State & Chestnuts Sts; admission free) in Springfield.

(☎ 413-787-1548; www.valleyvisitor.com) provide regional visitor information.

Worcester

The state's second-largest city (population 175,450) had its glory days in the 19th century. The industries that made the town rich went bust but the old barons left a legacy in Worcester's fine museums. The first-rate **Worcester Art Museum** (☎ 508-799-4406; www.worcesterart.org; 55 Salisbury St; adult/child under 17yr $10/free, Sat morning free; 11am-5pm Wed-Fri, 10am-5pm Sat, 11am-5pm Sun) showcases works by luminary French Impressionists and American masters like Whistler. The amazing **Higgins Armory Museum** (☎ 508-853-6015; www.higgins.org; 100 Barber Ave; adult/child 6-16yr $9/7; 10am-4pm Tue-Sat, noon-4pm Sun) is a military buff's heaven. It started as the private collection of a local steel tycoon who built a fanciful art-deco armory to house thousands of military collectibles including Corinthian helmets from ancient Greece and more than 100 full suits of armor.

Springfield

Workaday Springfield's top claim to fame is as the birthplace of the all-American game of basketball. The **Naismith Basketball Hall of Fame** (☎ 413-781-6500, www.hoophall.com; 1000 W Columbus Ave; adult/child 5-15yr $17/12; 10am-5pm;), south of I-91, celebrates the sport with exhibits and memorabilia from all the big hoop stars.

Northampton

The region's best dining, hottest nightlife and most interesting street scenes all await in this uber-hip burg known for its liberal politics and outspoken lesbian community. Easy to explore on foot, the eclectic town center is chockablock with cafés, funky shops and art galleries. **Greater Northampton Chamber of Commerce** (☎ 413-584-1900; www.explorenorthampton.com; 99 Pleasant St; 9am-5pm Mon-Fri) is information central.

The **Smith College** (☎ 413-584-2700; www.smith.edu) campus, covering 127 acres with lovely gardens, is well worth a stroll. Don't miss the **Smith College Museum of Art** (☎ 413-585-2760; Elm St at Bedford Tce; adult/child 6-12yr $5/2; 10am-4pm Tue-Sat, noon-4pm Sun), which boasts an impressive collection of 19th- and 20th-century European and North American paintings, including works by John Singleton Copley, Eastman Johnson and Claude Monet.

SLEEPING & EATING

Autumn Inn (☎ 413-584-7660; 259 Elm St/MA 9; r incl breakfast $99-139;) Despite its motel-like layout, this two-story place near Smith College sports an agreeable inn-like ambience and large, comfy rooms.

Hotel Northampton (☎ 413-584-3100; www.hotelnorthampton.com; 36 King St; r from $170;) Northampton's most upscale sleep since 1927, this 100-room hotel in the town center features period decor and well-appointed rooms.

Sylvester's (☎ 413-586-5343; 111 Pleasant St; mains $5-10; 7am-2pm) Follow the locals to this unassuming eatery for the best breakfast in town. Forget mixes – everything is from scratch, real maple syrup tops the pancakes, the home fries are loaded with sautéed onions and the omelets are however you like them.

Paul & Elizabeth's (☎ 413-584-4832; 150 Main St; mains $8-20; 11:30am-9:15pm) Fresh, local and organic ingredients highlight the menu at this stellar natural food café serving innovative vegetarian fare and Japanese-style fish dishes.

Spoleto (☎ 413-586-6313; 50 Main St; mains $15-25; 5-10pm Mon-Sat, 4-9pm Sun) Just-tweaked-enough Italian standards, like the cioppino swimming with New England seafood, attract the dinner crowd at this fine-dining ristorante.

DRINKING & ENTERTAINMENT

Haymarket Café (☎ 413-586-9969; 185 Main St; 7am-10pm;) Northampton's coolest hangout for bohemians and caffeine addicts.

Northampton Brewery (☎ 413-584-9903; 11 Brewster Ct; 11:30am-1am) On a sunny day you'll find half of Northampton chugging ales on the rooftop beer garden at New England's oldest microbrewery.

Iron Horse Music Hall (☎ 413-584-0610; 20 Center St; tickets $10-30) Nationally acclaimed folk and jazz artists line up to play in this intimate setting.

Calvin Theatre (☎ 413-584-0610; 19 King St; tickets $25-70) The venue for big-name performances for everything from hot rock and indie bands to comedy shows.

Amherst

This college town, a short drive from Northampton, is built around the mega **University of Massachusetts** (☎ 413-545-0111; www.umass.edu) and two small colleges, the liberal **Hampshire College** (☎ 413-549-4600; www.hampshire.edu) and the prestigious **Amherst College** (☎ 413-542-2000; www.amherst.edu). Contact them for campus tours and event information; there's always something happening. If hunger strikes, you'll find the usual bevy of college-town eateries radiating out from Main St in the town center.

The lifelong home of poet Emily Dickinson (1830–86), the 'belle of Amherst,' is open to the public as the **Emily Dickinson Museum** (☎ 413-542-8161; www.emilydickinsonmuseum.org; 280 Main St; adult/child 6-17yr $8/3; 🕑 11am-4pm Wed-Sun Mar-May & Sep-Dec, 10am-5pm Wed-Sun Jun-Aug). Admission includes a 40-minute tour.

THE BERKSHIRES

Tranquil towns and a wealth of cultural attractions are nestled in these cool green hills. For more than a century the Berkshires have been a favored retreat for wealthy Bostonians and New Yorkers. And we're not just talking Rockefellers – the entire Boston symphony summers here as well. One tip: weekends are busiest. You'll find fewer crowds and better room rates on weekdays. The **Berkshire Visitors Bureau** (☎ 413-443-9186, 800-237-5747; www.berkshires.org; 109 South St, Pittsfield; 🕑 9am-5pm) can provide information on the entire region.

Great Barrington

This up-and-coming town is hands-down the best place in the Berkshires to be at mealtime. Head straight to the intersection of Main (US 7) and Railroad Sts in the town center where you'll find an artful mix of galleries and eateries serving mouthwatering food – everything from bakeries to ethnic cuisines.

If you've got a hankering for breakfast at noon, go to **Martin's** (☎ 413-528-5455; 49 Railroad St; breakfasts $4-8; 🕑 6am-3pm). Families will love **Baba Louie's** (☎ 413-528-8100; 286 Main St; pizzas $9-16; 🕑 11:30am-9:30pm; 👶) for its organic wood-fired pizzas and $5 kids specials. For fine dining, **Allium** (☎ 413-528-2118; 42 Railroad St; mains $20-30; 🕑 5-10pm) offers innovative New American cuisine in a stylish setting.

Stockbridge

This timeless New England town, sans even a single traffic light, looks like something straight out of a Norman Rockwell drawing. Oh wait…it is! Rockwell (1894–1978), the most popular illustrator in US history, lived on Main St and used the town and its residents as subjects. At the evocative **Norman Rockwell Museum** (☎ 413-298-4100; www.nrm.org; 9 Glendale Rd/MA 183; adult/child under 18yr $15/free; 🕑 10am-5pm), Rockwell's slice-of-Americana paintings come to life when examined up close.

Lenox

The cultural heart of the Berkshires, the refined village of Lenox hosts one of the country's premier music series, the open-air **Tanglewood Music Festival** (☎ 617-266-1492, in summer 413-637-5165; www.tanglewood.org; admission $20-100; 🕑 Jul–early Sep), featuring the Boston Symphony Orchestra and guest artists like James Taylor and Yo-Yo Ma.

Shakespeare & Company (☎ 413-637-3353; www.shakespeare.org; 70 Kemble St; admission $12-60) performs the Bard's work throughout the summer. The renowned **Jacob's Pillow Dance Festival** (☎ 413-243-0745; www.jacobspillow.org; 385 George Carter Rd; admission $30-60; 🕑 late Jun–Aug), 10 miles east of Lenox in Becket, stages contemporary dance performances.

The **Mount** (☎ 413-551-5111; 2 Plunkett St, at US 7; adult/child under 12yr $16/free; 🕑 10am-5pm May-Oct), novelist Edith Wharton's former estate, offers hour-long tours of her mansion and inspirational gardens.

Charming period inns abound in Lenox. The senior of them, **Birchwood Inn** (☎ 413-637-2600; www.birchwood-inn.com; 7 Hubbard St; r incl breakfast $175-335; ⊠ 📶), registered its first guest in 1767 and continues to offer warm hospitality today.

You'll find stylish bistros along Church St in the town center, including **Bistro Zinc** (☎ 413-637-8800; 56 Church St; mains $15-30; 🕑 11:30am-3pm & 5:30-10pm) with hot postmodern decor and French-inspired New American fare.

Pittsfield

Just west of the town of Pittsfield is **Hancock Shaker Village** (☎ 413-443-0188; www.hancockshakervillage.org; US 20; adult/child under 13yr $16.50/free;

10am-5pm Jun–mid-Oct, 10am-4pm mid-Oct–May), a fascinating museum illustrating the lives of the Shakers, the religious sect that founded the village in 1783. The Shakers believed in communal ownership, the sanctity of work and celibacy, the latter of which proved to be their demise. Their handiwork – graceful in its simplicity – includes wooden furnishings and 20 buildings, the most famous of which is the round stone barn.

Williamstown & North Adams

Cradled by the Berkshire's rolling hills, Williamstown is a picture-perfect New England college town revolving around the leafy campus of Williams College. Williamstown and neighboring North Adams boast three outstanding art museums, each a worthy destination in itself.

SIGHTS & ACTIVITIES

The **Clark Art Institute** (☎ 413-458-2303; www.clarkart.edu; 225 South St, Williamstown; adult/child under 18yr Jun-Oct $12.50/free, Nov-May free to all; 10am-5pm, closed Mon Sep-Jun) focuses on 19th-century paintings with oodles of Renoirs and other French impressionists as well as a solid collection of American paintings by Winslow Homer, John Singer Sargent and others.

The **Williams College Museum of Art** (☎ 413-597-2429; www.wcma.org; 15 Lawrence Hall Dr, Williamstown; admission free; 10am-5pm Tue-Sat, 1-5pm Sun) showcases works by American luminaries such as Mary Cassett, Edward Hopper and Andy Warhol.

Mass MoCA (☎ 413-662-2111; www.massmoca.org; 87 Marshall St, North Adams; adult/child 6-16yr $15/5; 10am-6pm Jul–mid-Sep, 11am-5pm Wed-Mon mid-Sep–Jun;) has put once-sleepy North Adams on the map. Just a decade old, this contemporary art museum sprawls across an amazing 222,000 sq ft, making it the USA's largest. Bring your walking shoes! In addition to description-defying installation pieces, MoCA is a venue for cutting-edge theater and dance.

The first-rate **Williamstown Theatre Festival** (☎ 413-597-3400; www.wtfestival.org; 1000 Main St, Williamstown; tickets $25-60) stages contemporary and classic plays in July and August, often with notable casts.

Just south of North Adams, **Mt Greylock State Reservation** (☎ 413-499-4262; Rockwell Rd, Lanesborough) has trails up to Massachusetts' highest peak (3491ft), where there's a panoramic view of several ranges and, on a clear day, five different states.

SLEEPING & EATING

River Bend Farm (☎ 413-458-3121; www.riverbendfarmbb.com; 643 US 7; r incl breakfast with shared bath $120;) Step back to the 18th century in this Georgian Colonial B&B furnished with real-deal antiques and boasting five fireplaces.

Williams Inn (☎ 413-458-9371, 800-828-0133; www.williamsinn.com; 1090 Main St; r $180-295;) A favorite of visiting alumni, this oh-so-proper century-old establishment on the Williamstown green is the area's best hotel.

Tunnel City Coffee (☎ 413-458-5010; 100 Spring St; snacks $2-6; 6am-6pm;) Come to this student haunt near Williams College campus for potent espressos, light eats and sugar-laced desserts.

Chopsticks (☎ 413-458-5750; 412 Main St; mains $6-16; 11am-10:30pm) Can't agree on what to eat? Then head to this Asian eatery with everything from fiery Szechuan vegetarian dishes to Japanese sushi and Korean barbecue.

RHODE ISLAND

America's smallest state packs a lot into a compact package, more than making up for its lack of land with 400 miles of craggy coastline, deeply indented bays and lovely beaches. The state's engaging capital, Providence, is small enough to be friendly but big enough to offer top-notch dining and attractions. Newport, a summer haunt of the well-heeled, brims with opulent mansions, pretty yachts and world-class music festivals. Should you want to take it further afield, hopping on a ferry to Block Island makes a perfect day-trip.

History

The name Roger Williams (1603–83) gave to the community he founded in 1636 – nothing less than Providence! – spoke to the optimism his followers shared. A religious outcast from Puritanical Boston, Williams established the colony on the principle that all people were entitled to freedom of conscience. He was an early advocate of separation of religion and government, a concept that later became a foundation of the US Constitution. Progressive little Rhode Island became the first American colony to abolish slavery (1774) and the first to declare independence from Britain in 1776.

RHODE ISLAND FACTS

Nicknames Ocean State, Little Rhody
Population 1,051,000
Area 1045 sq miles
Capital city Providence (population 175,250)
Other city Newport (population 24,400)
Sales tax 7%
Birthplace of Broadway composer George M Cohan (1878–1942) and toy icon Mr Potato Head (b 1952)
Home of The first US tennis championships
Famous for being the smallest state
Official state bird A chicken? Why not. The Rhode Island Red revolutionized the poultry industry
Driving distances Providence to Newport 37 miles, Providence to Boston 50 miles

Information

Providence Journal (www.projo.com) The state's largest daily newspaper.
Rhode Island Parks (☎ 877-742-2675; www.riparks.com; campsites $20) Offers camping in five state parks.
Rhode Island Tourism Division (☎ 401-222-2601, 800-556-2484; www.visitrhodeisland.com; 1 W Exchange Pl, Providence, RI 02903; 🕑 8:30am-4:30pm Mon-Fri) Distributes visitor information on the whole state.

PROVIDENCE

The revitalization of Providence has turned this once-dreary capital into one of the finest small cities in the Northeast. Not only has it been infused with an artsy edge, but it's the only city in the USA to have its entire downtown on the National Register of Historic Places. From the period buildings in the city center to the café-laden streets embracing Brown University, everything about this town invites a closer look.

Orientation & Information

Exit 22 off I-95 deposits you downtown. The university area is a short walk to the east. The colorful Italian enclave of Federal Hill centers on Atwells Ave, a mile west of the city center.
Brown Bookstore (☎ 401-863-3168; 244 Thayer St; 🕑 9am-8pm Mon-Fri, 10am-8pm Sat, 11am-5pm Sun)
Post office (☎ 800-275-8777; 2 Exchange Tce; 🕑 8am-5pm Mon-Fri)
Providence Visitor Information Center (☎ 401-751-1177, 800-233-1636; www.goprovidence.com; Providence Convention Center, 1 Sabin St; 🕑 9am-5pm Mon-Sat)

Sights & Activities

Providence's focal point, the **State House** (☎ 401-222-3983; 82 Smith St; admission free; 🕑 8:30am-4:30pm Mon-Fri, free tours 9am, 10am & 11am Mon-Fri) is crowned with one of the world's largest self-supporting marble domes. Check out their Gilbert Stuart portrait of George Washington, then compare it to the $1 bill in your wallet.

The wonderfully eclectic **Rhode Island School of Design Museum** (RISD; ☎ 401-454-6500; www.risd.edu; 224 Benefit St; adult/child 5-18yr $10/3; 🕑 10am-5pm Tue-Sun) showcases everything from ancient Greek art to 20th-century American paintings and decorative arts. Pop in before 1pm Sunday and admission is free. On the hillside above RISD lies **Brown University** (☎ 401-863-2378; www.brown.edu; 71 George St), its eminently strollable campus awash in Ivy League charm.

The offbeat **Culinary Archives & Museum** (☎ 401-598-2805; www.culinary.org; 315 Harborside Blvd; adult/child 5-18yr $7/2; 🕑 10am-5pm Tue-Sun) contains collection of half-a-million items devoted to the history of dining – everything from ancient cookbooks to early-20th-century dining cars. It's at Johnson & Wales University; take I-95 exit 18, turn right on Allens Ave and follow the signs.

Roger Williams Park (☎ 401-785-3510; 1000 Elmwood Ave; admission free; 👪) has so many Victorian-era touches, such as its classic carousel, it's been cited by the National Trust for Historic Preservation as one of America's top urban parks. Among its varied sights are flowery botanical gardens and a **zoo** (adult/child 3-12yr $12/6; 🕑 9am-4pm; 👪) with snow leopards and elephants. From downtown, take I-95 south to exit 17.

Sleeping

Christopher Dodge House (☎ 401-351-6111; www.providence-hotel.com; 11 W Park St; r incl breakfast $130-180; ⊠ 💻) Cozy quilts and gas fireplaces add a warm glow at this inviting B&B overlooking the State House. If it's full, ask about its sister inn, the Mowry-Nicholson House, just a block away.

Edgewood Manor (☎ 401-781-0099; www.providence-lodging.com; 232 Norwood Ave; r incl breakfast $139-299; ⊠ 📶) If you're in a pampering mood, book a room in this elegant Greek Revival B&B bordering Roger Williams Park. The lavish lobby drips with museum-quality antiques, while the rooms boast four-poster mahogany beds and marble baths.

NEW ENGLAND

Providence Biltmore (☎ 401-421-0700, 800-294-7709; www.providencebiltmore.com; 11 Dorrance St; r/ste $189/209;) Entering the chandeliered lobby of this historic downtown hotel is like stepping back into the 1920s. The classic appeal continues in the rooms fitted with damask upholstered chairs, gilt mirrors and king beds.

Eating

Providence abounds with superb eateries. For the 'Little Italy' immersion, stroll the trattorias lining Atwells Ave on Federal Hill. For the café scene head to Thayer St, on the hill above Brown University.

Costantino's Venda Ravioli (☎ 401-421-9105; 265 Atwells Ave; meals $6-10; 8:30am-6pm Mon-Sat, 8:30am-4pm Sun) Grab one of the small tables lining this bustling deli for the most amazing dining experience on Federal Hill. Hanging salamis, crispy breads, every imaginable antipasto, real gelato – you'll think you're in Italy.

Caserta Pizzeria (☎ 401-621-3618; 121 Spruce St; pizza $7-16; 9:30am-10:30pm Tue-Thu & Sun, 9:30am-11:30pm Fri & Sat) This spartan eatery on the back side of Federal Hill serves the best Sicilian pizza in all Rhode Island. The secret: a sauce so spicy it'll make your mouth sing.

Meeting Street Café (☎ 401-273-1066; 220 Meeting St; mains $8-14; 8am-11pm) For thick sandwiches, tasty shish kabob and luscious desserts head to this perky café near Brown University. The meats are hormone-free, the veggies fresh and the servings so big that most everything feeds two.

Hemenway's (☎ 401-351-8570; 121 S Main St; meals $15-30; 11:30am-10pm Mon-Thu, 11:30am-11pm Fri & Sat, noon-9pm Sun) A standout among the city's excellent seafood restaurants, this stylish grill is within walking distance of the universities and downtown. If you're feeling romantic, start with the oyster bar.

Drinking & Entertainment

Trinity Brewhouse (☎ 401-453-2337; 186 Fountain St; 11:30am-1am Mon-Thu, noon-2am Fri-Sat) This microbrewery in the entertainment district brews terrific British-style beers. Don't miss the stouts.

Lupo's Heartbreak Hotel (☎ 401-331-5876; www.lupos.com; 79 Washington St; cover $10-35; hours vary) Providence's legendary music venue features top rock bands and indie acts.

AS220 (☎ 401-831-9327; www.as220.org; 115 Empire St; 5pm-1am) An alternative space abuzz with experimental bands, offbeat films, poetry slams – you never know what you'll find here.

Providence Performing Arts Center (☎ 401-421-2787; www.ppacri.org; 220 Weybosset St; tickets $33-70) Concerts, comedy and Broadway musicals take the stage at this beautifully restored 1928 art-deco theater.

WHAT THE...?

Move over, Christo. Providence has blazed onto the public art installation scene with **WaterFire** (www.waterfire.org), set on the river that meanders through the city center. Nearly 100 braziers poke above the water, each supporting a bonfire that roars after dark. Flames dance off the water, music plays, black-clad gondoliers glide by, and party-goers pack the riverbanks. A captivating blend of art and entertainment, WaterFire takes place about a dozen times between May and September, mostly on Saturday, from sunset to 1am.

Getting There & Away

TF Green Airport (PVD; ☎ 401-737-8222; www.pvdairport.com; I-95, exit 13, Warwick), 20 minutes south of downtown Providence, is served by major US airlines and car-rental companies.

Peter Pan Bus Lines (☎ 888-751-8800; www.peterpanbus.com) connects Providence with Boston ($10, 1¼ hours), Cape Cod ($30, 2¼) and New York ($45, 3½ hours). **Amtrak** (☎ 800-872-7245) trains also link cities in the Northeast with Providence.

The **Rhode Island Public Transit Authority** (RIPTA; ☎ 800-244-0444; www.ripta.com; one way $1.75, day pass $5) runs old-fashioned, trolley-style buses throughout the city from its downtown Kennedy Plaza hub; other RIPTA buses link Providence with Newport.

NEWPORT

The town's very name conjures up images of Great Gatsby mansions and unbridled wealth. In the 1890s Newport became *the* place for rich New Yorkers to summer. They built opulent seaside mansions, each successive one attempting to outdo the neighbors. These mansions – dubbed 'summer cottages' – are so dazzling that people still flock to Newport today just to ogle them. Newport, population 24,400, is also famous for its legendary music festivals and its active yachting scene.

Orientation & Information

Newport is easy to navigate, with most of the action on or near the waterfront.

Citizens Bank (☎ 401-847-4411; 8 Washington Sq)

Newport Gateway Transportation & Visitors Center (☎ 800-976-5122; www.gonewport.com; 23 America's Cup Ave; 9am-5pm) Newport's tourist office distributes a handy guide and tracks accommodation vacancies.

Newport Public Library (☎ 401-847-8720; 300 Spring St; 12:30-9pm Mon, 9:30am-9pm Tue-Thu, 9:30am-6pm Fri & Sat;) Two dozen online computers with free access.

Post office (☎ 800-275-8777; 320 Thames St; 8:30am-5:30pm Mon-Fri, 9am-1pm Sat)

Sights & Activities

Many of Newport's grandest mansions are managed by the **Preservation Society of Newport County** (☎ 401-847-1000; www.newportmansions.org; 5-site combination tickets adult/child 6-17yr $31/10, Breakers $16.50/4, Breakers plus 1 other mansion $23/6). Each mansion takes about 90 minutes to tour, and has varied off-season hours – call ahead. If you have time for only one, make it the **Breakers** (44 Ochre Point Ave; 9am-5pm Apr–mid-Oct), an extravagant 70-room, 1895 Italian Renaissance mega-palace built for Cornelius Vanderbilt II, patriarch of America's richest family. **Rosecliff** (548 Bellevue Ave; 10am-5pm), a 1902 masterpiece of architect Stanford White, resembles the Grand Trianon at Versailles; its immense ballroom had a starring role in Robert Redford's *Great Gatsby*. The palace of Versailles also inspired the 1892 **Marble House** (596 Bellevue Ave; 10am-5pm), posh with Louis XIV–style furnishings. The **Elms** (367 Bellevue Ave; 10am-5pm), built c 1901, is nearly identical to the Château d'Asnières near Paris, while the Victorian **Chateau-sur-Mer** (474 Bellevue Ave; 10am-5pm), built in 1852, was the first of Newport's palatial summer mansions.

Astors' Beechwood Mansion (☎ 401-846-3772; www.astorsbeechwood.com; 580 Bellevue Ave; adult/child 6-17yr $15/6; 10am-5pm most days May-Oct, varied hours off-season) takes a spirited living-history approach with costumed actors portraying the Astor clan and servants who once lived here. Mystery murder nights too.

For a glorious hike take the 3.5-mile **Cliff Walk**, which hugs the coast along the back side of the mansions. You'll not only enjoy the same dramatic ocean views once reserved for the filthy rich, but you'll get to gawk at their mansions en route. The Cliff Walk runs from Memorial Blvd to Bailey's Beach; a scenic place to start is at Ruggles Ave near the Breakers.

As you'd expect in the hometown of the prestigious America's Cup, the sailing in breezy Newport is phenomenal. If you can handle your own sails, **Sail Newport** (☎ 401-849-8385; 60 Fort Adams Rd; 9am-7pm) rents sailboats ($64 to $120 three hours). Otherwise, hop aboard the graceful schooner **Adirondack II** (☎ 401-847-0000; 1½hr cruise $27-35; 11am-7pm), which sails from Bowen's Wharf five times a day.

The **International Tennis Hall of Fame** (☎ 401-849-3990; www.tennisfame.com; 194 Bellevue Ave; adult/child under 16yr $10/5; 9:30am-5pm), the world's largest tennis museum, is housed in the club where America's first tennis championships took place in 1881. For $80 you can jump into your whites and play a game on those classic grass courts.

At the **Touro Synagogue National Historic Site** (☎ 401-847-4794; 85 Touro St; adult/child under 12yr $5/free; noon-2pm Sun-Fri), you can tour the oldest synagogue (c 1763) in the USA, an architectural gem that treads the line between austere and lavish.

Fort Adams State Park (☎ 401-367-0038; Harrison Ave; park admission free, fort tours adult/child 6-17yr $10/5; park sunrise-sunset, tours hourly 10am-4pm mid-May–Oct), site of the largest coastal fortification (c 1824) in the USA, borders Newport Harbor with expansive lawns ideal for picnicking. Swimming is okay at Fort Adams, but **Easton's Beach** (Memorial Blvd), also known as 'First Beach,' and **Sachuest (Second) Beach** (Purgatory Rd) are better.

Festivals & Events

Newport's summer music events draw large crowds, so plan ahead.

Newport Music Festival (☎ 401-849-0700; www.newportmusic.org; admission $35-40) A class act, with 17 days of chamber music held at various mansions in July.

our pick **Newport Folk Festival** (☎ 800-514-3849; www.folkfestival50.com; Fort Adams State Park; admission $69-75) Everybody who's anybody in the folk world has taken the stage at this hallmark festival, held the first weekend in August.

Newport Jazz Festival (☎ 800-514-3849; www.jazzfestival55.com; Fort Adams State Park; admission $69-75) The roster reads like a who's who of jazz, with the likes of Dave Brubeck and Etta James, on a weekend in mid-August.

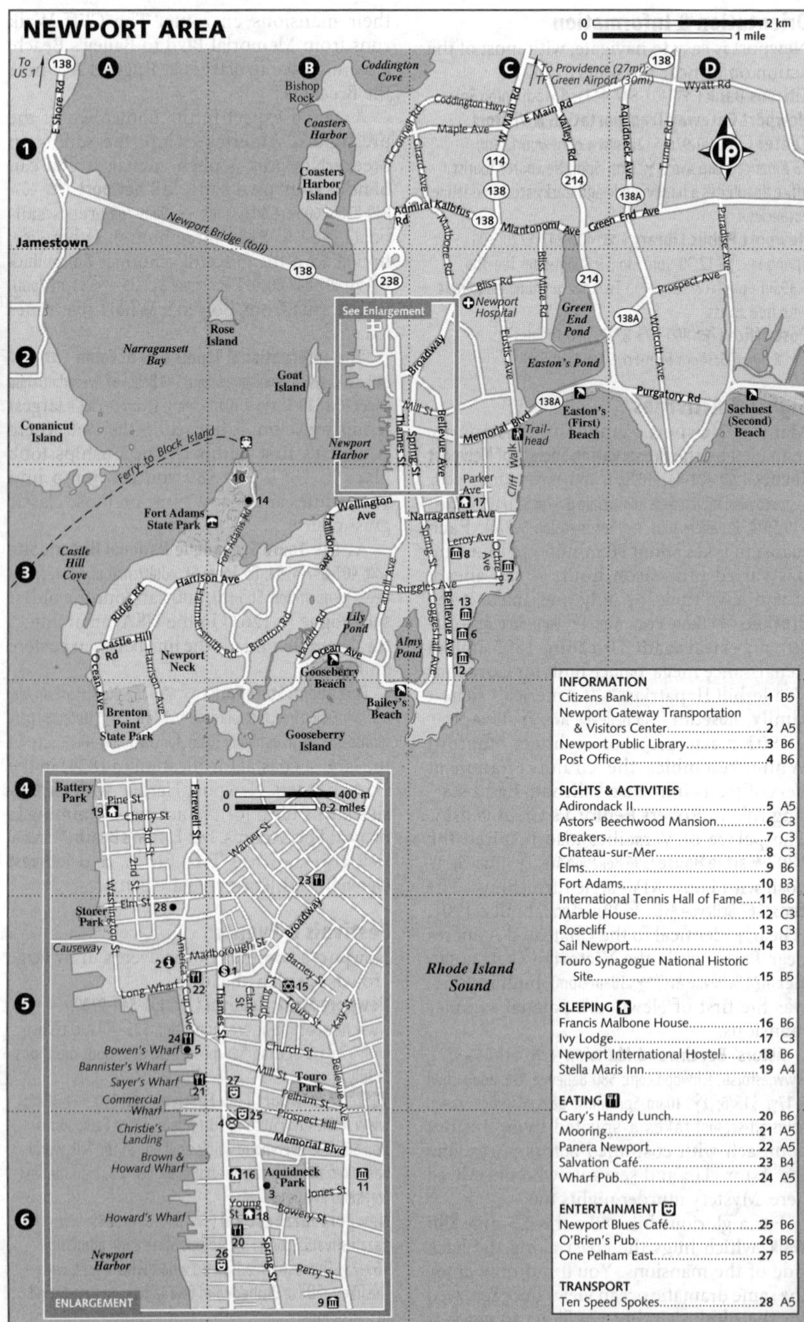
NEWPORT AREA
0 2 km
0 1 mile
To US 1
To Providence (27mi); TF Green Airport (30mi)
A
B
C
D
1
2
3
4
5
6
Bishop Rock
Coddington Cove
Coasters Harbor
Coasters Harbor Island
Jamestown
Narragansett Bay
Rose Island
Goat Island
Conanicut Island
Ferry to Block Island
Newport Harbor
Fort Adams State Park
Castle Hill Cove
Newport Neck
Brenton Point State Park
Gooseberry Beach
Gooseberry Island
Lily Pond
Almy Pond
Bailey's Beach
Green End Pond
Easton's Pond
Easton's (First) Beach
Sachuest (Second) Beach
Newport Hospital
Trailhead
Rhode Island Sound
See Enlargement
E Shore Rd
Newport Bridge (toll)
Coddington Hwy
Maple Ave
Admiral Kalbfus Rd
JT Connell Rd
Girard Ave
Malbone Rd
W Main Rd
E Main Rd
Valley Rd
Aquidneck Ave
Turner Rd
Wyatt Rd
Mlantonomi Ave
Green End Ave
Paradise Ave
Bliss Rd
Bliss Mine Rd
Prospect Ave
Wolcott Ave
Eustis Ave
Purgatory Rd
Memorial Blvd
Broadway
Mill St
Thames St
Spring St
Bellevue Ave
Cliff Walk
Parker Ave
Wellington Ave
Narragansett Ave
Halidon Ave
Fort Adams Rd
Leroy Ave
Ochre Pt Ave
Harrison Ave
Ridge Rd
Hammersmith Rd
Ruggles Ave
Carroll Ave
Brenton Rd
Hazard Rd
Coggeshall Ave
Castle Hill Rd
Ocean Ave
Harrison Ave
138
114
214
138A
238
ENLARGEMENT
0 400 m
0 0.2 miles
Battery Park
Pine St
Cherry St
3rd St
2nd St
Farewell St
Warner St
Washington St
Elm St
Storer Park
Causeway
America's Cup Ave
Marlborough St
Broadway
Barney St
Long Wharf
Thames St
Clarke St
Spring St
Touro St
Kay St
Bowen's Wharf
Bannister's Wharf
Sayer's Wharf
Commercial Wharf
Christie's Landing
Brown & Howard Wharf
Howard's Wharf
Church St
Mill St
Touro Park
Pelham St
Bellevue Ave
Prospect Hill
Memorial Blvd
Aquidneck Park
Jones St
Young St
Bowery St
Perry St
Newport Harbor
INFORMATION
Citizens Bank 1 B5
Newport Gateway Transportation & Visitors Center 2 A5
Newport Public Library 3 B6
Post Office 4 B6
SIGHTS & ACTIVITIES
Adirondack II 5 A5
Astors' Beechwood Mansion 6 C3
Breakers 7 C3
Chateau-sur-Mer 8 C3
Elms 9 B6
Fort Adams 10 B3
International Tennis Hall of Fame 11 B6
Marble House 12 C3
Rosecliff 13 C3
Sail Newport 14 B3
Touro Synagogue National Historic Site 15 B5
SLEEPING
Francis Malbone House 16 B6
Ivy Lodge 17 C3
Newport International Hostel 18 B6
Stella Maris Inn 19 A4
EATING
Gary's Handy Lunch 20 B6
Mooring 21 A5
Panera Newport 22 A5
Salvation Café 23 B4
Wharf Pub 24 A5
ENTERTAINMENT
Newport Blues Café 25 B6
O'Brien's Pub 26 B6
One Pelham East 27 B5
TRANSPORT
Ten Speed Spokes 28 A5

Sleeping

Newport International Hostel (☎ 401-369-0243; www.newporthostel.com; 16 Howard St; dm incl breakfast with shared bath $35-59; ☒ ☐) This central hostel in a period home has just a handful of beds, so book ahead. The friendly manager has tips aplenty for having a great time in Newport without breaking the bank.

Stella Maris Inn (☎ 401-849-2862; www.stellamarisinn.com; 91 Washington St; r incl breakfast $155-225; ☒) Grab a rocking chair on the porch and watch the sailboats breeze by at this comfortably old-fashioned inn occupying a former convent. High ceilings and heaps of dark wood set the mood. It's in a quiet neighborhoods but is just a stroll to the city center.

Ivy Lodge (☎ 401-849-6865, 800-834-6865; www.ivylodge.com; 12 Clay St; r incl breakfast $189-479; ☒ ☐ ☐) Treat yourself to the good life at this grand Victorian inn mere steps from Newport's sumptuous mansions. All rooms have antique furnishings, most have fireplaces, and if you need more romance, some have Jacuzzis.

Francis Malbone House (☎ 401-846-0392, 800-846-0392; www.malbone.com; 392 Thames St; r incl breakfast from $265; ☒ ☐ ☐) Cozy up inside this luxurious 1760 inn with its Colonial decor, crackling fireplaces and afternoon tea. Or just walk out the front door and you're smack in the heart of Newport's bustling Thames St.

Eating & Drinking

Panera Newport (☎ 401-324-6800; 49 Long Wharf Mall; mains $4-7; ⏰ 7am-7pm Sun-Thu, 7am-8pm Fri & Sat; ☐) Fresh-made pastries, good salads and sandwiches, and free wi-fi rake in a crowd at this café near the tourist office.

Gary's Handy Lunch (☎ 401-847-9480; 462 Thames St; mains $4-7; ⏰ 5am-3pm, to 8pm Fri) Newport's working folk kick-start their day over coffee and simple breakfast fare at this old-school diner.

Wharf Pub (☎ 401-846-9233; Bowen's Wharf; mains $9-17; ⏰ 11:30am-11pm) Come here for reasonable prices, good portions and fast service. Think sandwiches, fried calamari and burgers. Wash it down with a Newport Storm ale.

Salvation Café (☎ 401-847-2620; 140 Broadway; mains $10-25; ⏰ 5-11pm) A funky, eclectic decor and brilliant food are in store at this bohemian café. The multiethnic menu ranges far and wide, from pad thai to Moroccan spiced lamb, but seldom misses the mark.

our pick Mooring (☎ 401-846-2260; Sayer's Wharf; mains $10-35; ⏰ 11:30am-10pm) A harborfront setting and a menu brimming with fresh seafood make this an unbeatable combination for seaside dining. Tip: if it's packed, bypass the crowds, take the side entrance to the bar, grab a stool and order the meaty clam chowder and a 'bag of doughnuts' (tangy lobster fritters).

Entertainment

Newport Blues Café (☎ 401-841-5510; 286 Thames St; ⏰ 6pm-midnight) Intimate atmosphere and one of the best blues and R&B scenes this side of New York City.

One Pelham East (☎ 401-847-9460; 270 Thames St; ⏰ 3pm-1am) This romping bar has rock and indie bands several nights a week.

O'Brien's Pub (☎ 401-849-6623; 501 Thames St; ⏰ 11:30am-12:30am) The frat-house crowd comes here for live bands like Dogie & the Cowpie Poachers.

Getting There & Away

Peter Pan Bus Lines (☎ 888-751-8800) has several buses daily to Boston ($26, 1¾ hours). State-run **RIPTA** (☎ 800-244-0444; www.ripta.com) operates frequent buses (one way $1.75, day pass $5) from the visitor bureau to the mansions, beaches and Providence.

Rent bicycles at **Ten Speed Spokes** (☎ 401-847-5609; 18 Elm St; per hr/day $6/25; ⏰ 10am-8pm) near the visitors center.

RHODE ISLAND BEACHES

If you're up for a day at the beach, Rhode Island's southwestern coastal towns fit the bill. It is the Ocean State, after all.

The mile-long **Narragansett Town Beach** in Narragansett is the place to go for surfing. The nearby **Scarborough State Beach** is among Rhode Island's finest, with a wide beach, a glorious pavilion and inviting boardwalks. **Watch Hill** at the state's southwestern tip is a wonderful place to turn back the clock, with its Flying Horse Carousel and Victorian setting. The **South County Tourism Council** (☎ 800-548-4662; www.southcountyri.com) has details on the entire area.

CONNECTICUT

Sandwiched between sexy New York City and northerly New England's quainter quarters, Connecticut typically gets short shrift by travelers. Sure the brawny I-95 coastal corridor is largely industrial, but take a closer look and you're in for pleasant surprises. Seaside Mystic, with its nautical attractions, and the time-honored towns bordering the Connecticut River are a whole other world, and the Litchfield Hills, in the state's northwestern corner, are as charmingly rural as any place in New England.

Incidentally, the Connecticut River, which slices clear across Connecticut, gives the state its name. The word comes from the Mohegan mouthful *quinnehtukqut*, which means 'place of the long river.'

History

In 1633 the Dutch built a small settlement at current-day Hartford, but it was the English, arriving en masse in the following years, that shaped Connecticut.

Thanks to the industriousness of the citizenry, the Connecticut Yankee peddler became a fixture in early American society, traveling by wagon from town to town selling clocks and other manufactured gadgets. Connecticut etched a leading role in the Industrial Revolution when Eli Whitney built a New Haven factory in 1798 to produce firearms with interchangeable parts – the beginning of modern mass production.

In 1810 America's first insurance company opened in Hartford and by the 1870s the city boasted the highest per capita income in the USA. Two of America's leading literary figures, Harriet Beecher Stowe (1811–96) and Mark Twain (1835–1910), were Hartford neighbors for 17 years.

CONNECTICUT FACTS

Nicknames Constitution State, Nutmeg State
Population 3.5 million
Area 4845 sq miles
Capital city Hartford (population 124,500)
Sales tax 6%
Birthplace of Abolitionist John Brown (1800–59), circus man PT Barnum (1810–91), actress Katharine Hepburn (1909–2003)
Home of The first written constitution in the US; the first lollipop, Frisbee and helicopter
Famous for Starting the US insurance biz and building the first nuclear submarine
Quirkiest state song lyrics 'Yankee Doodle,' which entwines patriotism with doodles, feathers and macaroni
Driving distances Hartford to New Haven 40 miles, Hartford to Providence 75 miles

Information

There are welcome centers at the Hartford airport and on I-95 and I-84 when entering the state by car.

Connecticut State Parks (☎ 877-668-2267; www.ct.gov/dep/cwp; campsites $13-29) Offers camping in 13 state parks.

Connecticut Tourism Division (☎ 888-288-4748; www.ctvisit.com) Distributes visitor information for the entire state.

Hartford Courant (www.courant.com) The state's largest newspaper has entertainment listings online.

WORTH THE TRIP: BLOCK ISLAND

This unspoiled island, separated from the rest of Rhode Island by 12 miles of open ocean, offers simple pleasures: rolling farms, uncrowded beaches and miles of quiet hiking and cycling trails.

Ferries dock at Old Harbor, the main town, which has changed little since its gingerbread houses were built in the late 19th century. The beaches begin right at the north side of town. If you continue north 2 miles you'll come to the **Clay Head Nature Trail**, which follows high clay bluffs above the beach offering good bird-watching along the way. **Rodman Hollow**, a 100-acre wildlife refuge at the island's south end, is also laced with interesting trails.

A mere 7 miles long, Block Island begs to be explored by bicycle; several places near the ferry dock rent them for $25 a day. The **Block Island Chamber of Commerce** (☎ 800-383-2474; www.blockislandchamber.com), at the ferry dock, can help with accommodations, but be aware the island's four-dozen inns typically book out in summer and many require minimum stays.

The **Block Island Ferry** (☎ 866-783-7996; www.blockislandferry.com; adult round-trip slow/high-speed $22/36) runs high-speed (30 minutes) and slow (55 minutes) ferries from Galilee State Pier in Point Judith, each four to eight times a day, as well as once-daily slow ferries (two hours, July and August) from Fort Adams State Park in Newport. Children pay half price; bring a bicycle along for a $6 round-trip. Schedules are convenient for day-trippers, with morning departures and late-afternoon returns.

CONNECTICUT COAST

The Connecticut coast is not all of a piece. The western end is largely a bedroom community connected by commuter rail to New York City. By the time you get to New Haven, Connecticut's artsier side shines through. Maritime Mystic, at the eastern end of the state, spotlights tall ships and the siren call of the sea.

New Haven

For visitors New Haven is all about Yale. Head straight to New Haven Green, graced by old Colonial churches and Yale's hallowed ivy-covered walls. The city's top museums and best restaurants are all within a few blocks of the Green. The oldest planned city in America (1638), New Haven (population 124,000) is laid out in orderly blocks spreading out from the Green, making it a cinch to get around. The **Greater New Haven Convention & Visitors Bureau** (☎ 203-777-8550, 800-332-7829; www.visitnewhaven.com; 169 Orange St; 9am-4:30pm Mon-Fri) is two blocks east of the Green.

SIGHTS & ACTIVITIES

Yale University is not only the prestigious alma mater of five US presidents but it's one cool campus thick with Gothic buildings. Most impressive of the spires is **Harkness Tower**, from which a carillon peals at measured moments throughout the day. For campus tours or to pick up a campus map, drop by Yale's **visitor center** (☎ 203-432-2300; www.yale.edu/visitor; 149 Elm St; 9am-4:30pm Mon-Fri, 11am-4pm Sat & Sun) on the north side of the Green. There are free one-hour tours at 10:30am and 2pm weekdays, and at 1:30pm on weekends.

America's oldest university art museum, the **Yale University Art Gallery** (☎ 203-432-0600; 1111 Chapel St; admission free; 10am-5pm Tue-Sat, 1-6pm Sun), boasts American masterworks by Winslow Homer, Edward Hopper and Jackson Pollock, as well as a superb European collection that includes Vincent van Gogh's *The Night Café*.

Wannabe paleontologists will be thrilled by the dinosaurs at the **Peabody Museum of Natural History** (☎ 203-432-5050; 170 Whitney Ave; adult/child 3-18yr $7/5; 10am-5pm Mon-Sat, noon-5pm Sun;).

You may also want to pop into the **Yale Center for British Art** (☎ 203-432-2800; 1080 Chapel St; admission free; 10am-5pm Tue-Sat, noon-5pm Sun), which holds the most comprehensive British art collection outside the UK.

SLEEPING & EATING

Touch of Ireland Guest House (☎ 203-787-7997, 866-787-7990; www.touchofirelandguesthouse.com; 670 Whitney Ave; r incl breakfast $135-150;) Share tips with fellow travelers in the fireplaced den at this friendly B&B on the north side of the city. The four guest rooms sport an Irish theme and comfy down-home decor.

Study at Yale (☎ 203-503-3900; www.studyhotels.com; 1157 Chapel St; r from $229;) Ready for an Ivy League splurge? This sleek new boutique hotel right in the midst of the campus offers 124 ultra-mod rooms with featherbeds, soft leather chairs, flat-screen TVs and iPod docking stations.

Louis' Lunch (☎ 203-562-5507; 261 Crown St; hamburgers $5; 11am-4pm Tue & Wed, noon-2am Thu-Sat Sep-Jul) New Haven's classic hamburger joint invented America's iconic fast food in 1900 and it still broils burgers in the original cast-iron vertical grills. Some things have changed over the century – but you won't find them here. Don't even think of asking for ketchup.

Claire's Corner Copia (☎ 203-562-3888; 1000 Chapel St; mains $6-10; 8am-9pm Mon-Thu, 8am-10pm Fri & Sat, 9am-9pm Sun;) For the best vegetarian food in town, saunter over to this cheerful green restaurant opposite Yale. Claire Criscuolo cooks up her own time-honored recipes using fresh, organic ingredients – everything from thick peasant soups to luscious pastries.

Frank Pepe's (☎ 203-865-5762; 157 Wooster St; pizza $7-18; 4-10pm Mon, Wed & Thu, 11:30am-11pm Fri & Sat, 2:30-10pm Sun) New Haven's most famous eatery takes its name from the Italian immigrant who tossed America's first pizza a century ago. You'd best believe they've got the recipe down pat. For the ultimate, order Pepe's signature white pizza topped with garlicky fresh clams.

Sally's Apizza (☎ 203-624-5271; 237 Wooster St; pizza $7-16; 5-10:30pm Tue-Sun) If Pepe's is packed, as it often is, try this place nearby, a breakaway started by a relative of Pepe's in 1938. Like Pepe's, Sally's also specializes in terrific wood-fired thin-crust pizza.

DRINKING & ENTERTAINMENT

The free weekly **New Haven Advocate** (www.newhavenadvocate.com) lists current entertainment happenings.

Toad's Place (☎ 203-624-8623; www.toadsplace.com; 300 York St; admission $5-35) The hottest music scene this side of New York City. Everyone from Count Basie to Bob Dylan and U2 have taken the stage at this legendary venue.

New Haven has a first-rate theater scene. Catch a hit before it happens at the venerable **Shubert Theater** (☎ 203-562-5666, 888-736-2663; www.capa.com; 247 College St; tickets $15-70), which has been hosting Broadway musicals on their trial runs since 1914. New Haven also has two award-winning repertory theaters: **Yale Repertory Theatre** (☎ 203-432-1234; www.yale.edu/yalerep; 1120 Chapel St; tickets $20-65) and **Long Wharf Theatre** (☎ 203-787-4282, 800-782-8497; www.longwharf.org; 222 Sargent Dr; tickets $26-70).

GETTING THERE & AWAY

By train from New York City skip Amtrak and take **Metro North** (☎ 212-532-4900, 800-638-7646; one way $14-19), which has near-hourly services and the lowest fares. **Greyhound Bus Lines** (☎ 800-231-2222; www.greyhound.com) connects New Haven to scores of cities including Hartford ($14, one hour) and Boston ($36, four hours).

Mystic & Around

A centuries-old seaport, Mystic boasts a top-notch nautical museum, a stellar aquarium and attractive period accommodations. Yes, it gets inundated with summer tourists, but there's a good reason why everyone stops here, so get off the highway and check it out. Swing by on a weekday to avoid the worst of the crowds. The **Greater Mystic Chamber of Commerce** (☎ 860-572-1102; www.mysticchamber.org; 2 Roosevelt Ave; 🕑 10am-4pm), at the old train station, has visitor information.

SIGHTS & ACTIVITIES

America's maritime history springs to life at **Mystic Seaport** (☎ 860-572-5315; www.mysticseaport.org; 75 Greenmanville Ave/CT 27; adult/child 6-17yr $24/15; 🕑 9am-5pm Apr-Oct, 10am-4pm Nov-Mar; 🚸), where costumed interpreters ply their trades in a sprawling re-created 19th-century seaport village. You can scurry aboard several historic sailing vessels, including the *Charles W Morgan* (built in 1841), the last surviving wooden whaling ship in the world. And if you want to experience a little voyage yourself, the 1908 steamboat **Sabino** (☎ 860-572-5351; adult/child 6-17yr $5.50/4.50; 🕑 11:30am-3:30pm) departs hourly from 11.30am on jaunts up the Mystic River.

Mystic Aquarium (☎ 860-572-5955; www.mysticaquarium.org; 55 Coogan Blvd; adult/child 3-17yr $24/18; 🕑 9am-6pm; 🚸) is home to all manner of interesting sea creatures, and we're not talking just fish. The residents include penguins, sea lions and even a beluga whale! And where else can a kid pet a cownose ray?

In nearby Ledyard the extensive **Mashantucket Pequot Museum & Research Center** (☎ 800-411-9671; www.pequotmuseum.org; 110 Pequot Trail, off CT 214, Mashantucket; adult/child 6-15yr $15/10; 🕑 10am-4pm Wed-Sat) features a reconstructed 16th-century Native American village. The Mashantucket Pequot tribe also owns the mega-splash **Foxwoods Resort & Casino** (☎ 800-369-9663; www.foxwoods.com; CT 2, Ledyard), the largest gambling venue this side of Vegas.

SLEEPING, EATING & DRINKING

Whaler's Inn (☎ 860-536-1506, 800-243-2588; www.whalersinnmystic.com; 20 E Main St; r $159-259; ⊠ ✇ 💻 📶) By the drawbridge in the center of Mystic, this place offers a variety of comfy accommodations from traditionally decorated rooms in an 1865 Victorian house to modern rooms in motel-style buildings. It's an ideal location for walking to just about everything.

Old Mystic Inn (☎ 860-572-9422; www.oldmysticinn.com; 52 Main St, Old Mystic; r incl breakfast $165-215; ⊠ 📶) Canopy beds, cozy fireplaces and gourmet breakfasts set the tone at this romantic 1784 Colonial inn near the head of the Mystic River. Formerly a bookstore, its rooms are themed after American authors like Henry David Thoreau and Mark Twain.

Jamms Restaurant (☎ 860-536-2683; 8 Coogan Blvd; mains $8-23; 🕑 11:30am-midnight) Close to the aquarium, Jamms jams 'em in by offering something for everyone. The menu spans the gamut from burgers and leafy salads to pastas and steak.

S&P Oyster Co (☎ 860-536-2674; 1 Holmes St; mains $10-20; 🕑 11:30am-10pm) On a summer day, there's nothing better than dining on the waterfront. This reliable seafood eatery, famous for oysters on the half shell and hefty portions of fish and chips, is in the town center at the east side of the drawbridge.

Harp & Hound (☎ 860-572-7778; 4 Pearl St) This pub, in a historic building on the west side of the drawbridge, is the late-night place to grab a pint of Irish ale; decent pub grub and English football on the telly too.

LOWER CONNECTICUT RIVER VALLEY

Several Colonial-era towns grace the banks of the Connecticut River, offering up their rural charm at an unhurried pace. The **Central Regional Tourism District** (860-244-8181; 800-793-4480, visitctriver.com) provides information on the region.

Essex

The genteel riverside town of Essex, established in 1635, makes a good starting point for exploring the valley. The streets are lined with handsome Federal-period houses, the legacy of rum and tobacco fortunes made in the 19th century.

The **Connecticut River Museum** (☎ 860-767-8269; 67 Main St; adult/child 6-12yr $8/5; 10am-5pm Tue-Sun) exhibits regional history and includes a reproduction of the world's first submarine, a hand-propelled vessel built at this site in 1776.

The best way to see the river valley is hopping aboard the **Essex Steam Train & Riverboat** (☎ 860-767-0103; www.essexsteamtrain.com; 1 Railroad Ave; adult/child 2-11yr $17/9, with cruise $26/17; departs 11am, 12:30pm, 2pm & 3:30pm mid-Jun–Aug, Sat & Sun only in spring & fall;), an antique steam locomotive that runs 6 scenic miles to Deep River, where you can cruise on a Mississippi-style riverboat before returning by train.

The landmark **Griswold Inn** (☎ 860-767-1776; www.griswoldinn.com; 36 Main St; r incl breakfast $115-370;), in the town center, has been providing cozy Colonial comfort since 1776, making it one of the oldest inns in America. It's also a favorite place to dine on traditional New England cuisine in a historic setting.

Old Lyme

Set near the mouth of the Connecticut River, Old Lyme was home to some 60 sea captains in the 19th century. Today its claim to fame is its art community. In the early 1900s art patron Florence Griswold opened her estate to visiting artists, many of whom offered paintings in lieu of rent. Her Georgian mansion, now the **Florence Griswold Museum** (☎ 860-434-5542; 96 Lyme St; adult/child under 12yr $9/free; 10am-5pm Tue-Sat, 1-5pm Sun), exhibits 6000 works with solid collections of American Impressionist paintings, sculpture and decorative arts.

The prettiest place to lay your head is the classy **Bee & Thistle Inn** (☎ 860-434-1667, 800-622-4946; www.beeandthistleinn.com; 100 Lyme St; r $150-275;), a 1756 Dutch Colonial farmhouse with antique-filled rooms and four-poster beds.

East Haddam

Two intriguing attractions mark this small town on the east bank of the Connecticut River. The medieval-style **Gillette Castle** (☎ 860-526-2336; 67 River Rd; adult/child 6-12yr $5/2; 10am-4:30pm late May–mid-Oct) is a wildly eccentric stone-turreted mansion built in 1919 by actor William Hooker Gillette, who made his fortune playing Sherlock Holmes. The classic **Goodspeed Opera House** (☎ 860-873-8668; www.goodspeed.org; 6 Main St; tickets $26-66), an 1876 Victorian music hall known as 'the birthplace of the American musical,' still produces a full schedule of musicals.

HARTFORD

Connecticut's capital is best known as the hometown of America's insurance industry – not exactly a 'let's-rush-to-see-the-place' endorsement. But look beyond its backbone of office buildings and you'll find some worthwhile sights offering unique slices of Americana. The **Greater Hartford Welcome Center** (☎ 860-244-0253; www.enjoyhartford.com; 45 Pratt St; 9am-5pm Mon-Fri) distributes tourist information.

Sights & Activities

The former home of legendary author Samuel Langhorne Clemens, aka Mark Twain, is now the **Mark Twain House & Museum** (☎ 860-247-0998; www.marktwainhouse.org; 351 Farmington Ave; adult/child 6-16yr $14/8; 9:30am-5:30pm Mon-Sat, noon-5:30pm Sun). It was here that Twain penned many of his greatest works, including *A Connecticut Yankee in King Arthur's Court*. The house itself, a Victorian Gothic with fanciful turrets and gables, reflects Twain's quirky character.

Next door you'll find the **Harriet Beecher Stowe House** (☎ 860-522-9258; www.harrietbeecherstowe.org; 77 Forest St; adult/child 5-16yr $9/6; 9:30am-4:30pm Tue-Sat, noon-4:30pm Sun), which was home to the author of *Uncle Tom's Cabin*, a book which so rallied Americans against slavery that Abraham Lincoln once credited Stowe with starting the US Civil War.

America's oldest art museum, **Wadsworth Atheneum** (☎ 860-278-2670; www.wadsworthatheneum.org; 600 Main St; adult/child under 13yr $10/free; 11am-5pm Wed-Fri, 10am-5pm Sat & Sun), showcases outstanding collections of Hudson River School paintings and sculptures by renowned Connecticut artist Alexander Calder (1898–1976).

You can tour the **State Capitol** (☎ 860-240-0222; cnr Capitol Ave & Trinity St; admission free; 8am-5pm Mon-Fri), built in 1879 in such a hodgepodge of styles that it's sometimes dubbed 'the most beautiful ugly building in the world.' Below the capitol grounds, the 37-acre **Bushnell Park** features a working 1914 carousel, lovely gardens and summer concerts. The real prize

WHAT THE...?

Jaded museum browsers, don't turn your nose up at this one. Garbage goes green at the curious **Trash Museum** (☎ 860-757-7765, 211 Murphy Rd, Hartford; admission free; ⏲ noon-4pm Wed-Fri Sep-Jun, 10am-2pm Tue, 10am-4pm Wed-Fri Jul-Aug) smack in the midst of a trash facility. Run by the Connecticut Resources Recovery Authority (CRRA), it enlightens visitors on earth-friendly recycling techniques. A viewing platform overlooking the sorting operation takes center stage while cool sculptures made from trash and wormy composting displays plug the green side of it all. You'll also get the scoop on CRRA's trash-to-energy program that fuels a billion kilowatts of green electric power annually. To get to the museum take I-95 to exit 27, which dumps you right at the site.

of Connecticut's public buildings is the **Old State House** (☎ 860-522-6766; 800 Main St; adult/child 6-17yr $6/3; ⏲ 9am-5pm Mon-Fri), designed by famed Colonial architect Charles Bulfinch. Erected in 1796, it's one of the oldest capitol buildings in the USA.

Sleeping & Eating

Hilton Hartford (☎ 860-728-5151; www.hilton.com; 315 Trumbull St; r $89-179;) Within walking distance of the city's central sights, this modern hotel is Hartford's most conveniently located. The rooms are well appointed, and amenities include state-of-the-art fitness facilities. On weekends, when the lowest rates are offered, it's an unbeatable deal.

Pavilion at State House Square (cnr Main & State Sts; mains $4-12; ⏲ 10am-5pm) This handy food court opposite the Old State House draws a crowd for its variety of ethnic eateries, including several vegetarian options.

Peppercorn's Grill (☎ 860-547-1714; 357 Main St; mains $12-22; ⏲ 11:30am-10pm Mon-Wed, Thu-Sat 11:30am-11pm) Dine on contemporary Italian-American fare at Hartford's favorite restaurant, where you'll find plenty of tempting options from spicy clam cakes to lobster ravioli. Save room for the tiramisu.

Getting There & Away

The conveniently central **Union Station** (☎ 860-247-5329; 1 Union Pl) links Hartford by train to cities throughout the Northeast, including New Haven (one way $16, one hour) and New York City (one way $48, three hours).

LITCHFIELD HILLS

Laced with lakes, woodlands and vineyards, the rolling hill country of northwestern Connecticut provides rich opportunities for quiet escapes. The **Northwest Connecticut Visitors Bureau** (☎ 800-663-1273; www.litchfieldhills.com) has information on the entire region.

Litchfield

Founded in 1719, Litchfield prospered from the commerce brought by stagecoaches traveling between Hartford and Albany, and its many handsome period buildings are a testimony to that era. Stroll along North and South Sts to see the finest homes, including the 1773 **Tapping Reeve House & Law School** (☎ 860-567-4501; www.litchfieldhistoricalsociety.org; 82 South St; adult/child under 15yr $5/free; ⏲ 11am-5pm Tue-Sat, 1-5pm Sun mid-Apr–Nov), the USA's first law school, which trained 129 members of Congress. Included in the admission fee is the **Litchfield History Museum** (☎ 860-567-4501; 7 South St).

Haight-Brown Vineyard (☎ 860-567-4045; 29 Chestnut Hill Rd, off CT 118; ⏲ 11am-5pm Mon-Sat, noon-5pm Sun) is the state's first winery, and offers tours, tastings and self-guided vineyard walks.

If you're ready for a hike, Connecticut's largest wildlife preserve, the **White Memorial Conservation Center** (☎ 860-567-0857; US 202; admission free; ⏲ sunrise-sunset), 2.5 miles west of town, has 35 miles of inviting trails with good bird-watching.

Lake Waramaug

The most beautiful of the dozens of lakes and ponds in the Litchfield Hills is Lake Waramaug. As you make your way around the northern shore on North Shore Rd, stop at **Hopkins Vineyard** (☎ 860-868-7954; 25 Hopkins Rd; ⏲ 10am-5pm Mon-Sat, 11am-5pm Sun May-Dec) for wine tastings. It's next to the 19th-century **Hopkins Inn** (☎ 860-868-7295; www.thehopkinsinn.com; 22 Hopkins Rd, New Preston; r from $125;), which has lakeview accommodations and a well-regarded restaurant with Austrian-influenced country fare. **Lake Waramaug State Park** (☎ 860-868-0220; 30 Lake Waramaug Rd; campsites 1st/successive nights $22/13) has lakeside campsites, but book well in advance.

VERMONT

Artisanal cheeses, buckets of maple syrup, Ben & Jerry's ice cream…just try to get out of this state without gaining 10 pounds. Fortunately, there are plenty of ways to work it off: hike the trails of the Green Mountains, paddle a kayak on Lake Champlain or hit Vermont's snowy slopes.

Vermont gives true meaning to the word rural. Its capital would barely rate as a small town in other states and even its largest city, Burlington, has just 39,000 content souls. The countryside is a blanket of rolling green, with 80% of the state forested and most of the rest given over to some of the prettiest farms you'll ever see. So take your time, meander down quiet side roads, stop in those picturesque villages, and sample a taste of the good life.

History

Frenchman Samuel de Champlain explored Vermont in 1609 and in his ever-humble manner lent his name to Vermont's largest lake.

Vermont played a key role in the American Revolution in 1775 when Ethan Allen led a local militia, the Green Mountain Boys, to Fort Ticonderoga, capturing it from the British. In later years Allen took a friendlier stance toward the British, and considered petitioning the crown to make Vermont an independent British state. In 1791, two years after Allen's death, Vermont was finally admitted to the USA.

VERMONT FACTS

Nickname Green Mountain State
Population 621,270
Area 9250 sq miles
Capital city Montpelier (population 8035)
Other cities Burlington (population 38,358)
Sales tax 6%
Birthplace of Mormon leader Brigham Young (1801–77), folk painter Anna Mary 'Grandma' Moses (1860–1961), President Calvin Coolidge (1872–1933)
Home of More than 100 covered bridges
Famous for Ben & Jerry's ice cream
Sudsiest state Most microbreweries per capita in the USA
Driving distances Burlington to Bennington 116 miles, Burlington to Portland, Maine 194 miles

The state's independent streak is as long and deep as a vein of Vermont marble. Long a land of dairy farmers, Vermont is still largely agricultural and has the lowest population of any New England state.

Information

Vermont Dept of Tourism (☎ 802-828-3237, 800-837-6668; www.vermontvacation.com) Provides online information on Vermont by region, season and other user-friendly categories.

Vermont State Parks (☎ 888-409-7579; www.vtstateparks.com; campsites $18-26) Operates 40 state parks with camping.

SOUTHERN VERMONT

The southern swath of Vermont holds its oldest towns, the cool trails of the Green Mountain National Forest and plenty of scenic back roads just aching to be explored.

Brattleboro

Ever wonder where the 1960s counter-culture went? It's alive and well in this riverside burg overflowing with craft shops and more tie-dye per capita than any other place in New England.

SIGHTS & ACTIVITIES

Begin at Main St, which is lined with period buildings, including the handsome art deco Latchis Building, which houses a hotel and theater. The **Brattleboro Museum & Art Center** (☎ 802-257-0124; www.brattleboromuseum.org; 10 Vernon St; adult/child under 6yr $6/free; 11am-5pm Thu-Mon), in the old Union Station, showcases the multimedia works of regional artists.

Windham County, surrounding Brattleboro, boasts several **covered bridges**. Pick up a driving guide to them at the **Brattleboro Area Chamber of Commerce** (☎ 802-254-4565, 877-254-4565; www.brattleborochamber.org; 180 Main St; 9am-5pm Mon-Fri).

SLEEPING

Latchis Hotel (☎ 802-254-6300, 800-798-6301; www.latchis.com; 50 Main St; r $80-145;) You couldn't be more in the thick of things than at this restored art-deco hotel with 30 simply furnished rooms.

Forty Putney Road B&B (☎ 802-254-6268, 800-941-2413; www.fortyputneyroad.com; 40 Putney Rd; r incl breakfast $149-259;) This estate-home-turned-B&B is one sweet spot: classy rooms, beautiful grounds, river views, hot tub, billiards and a gourmet breakfast. The 'beer geek' owners

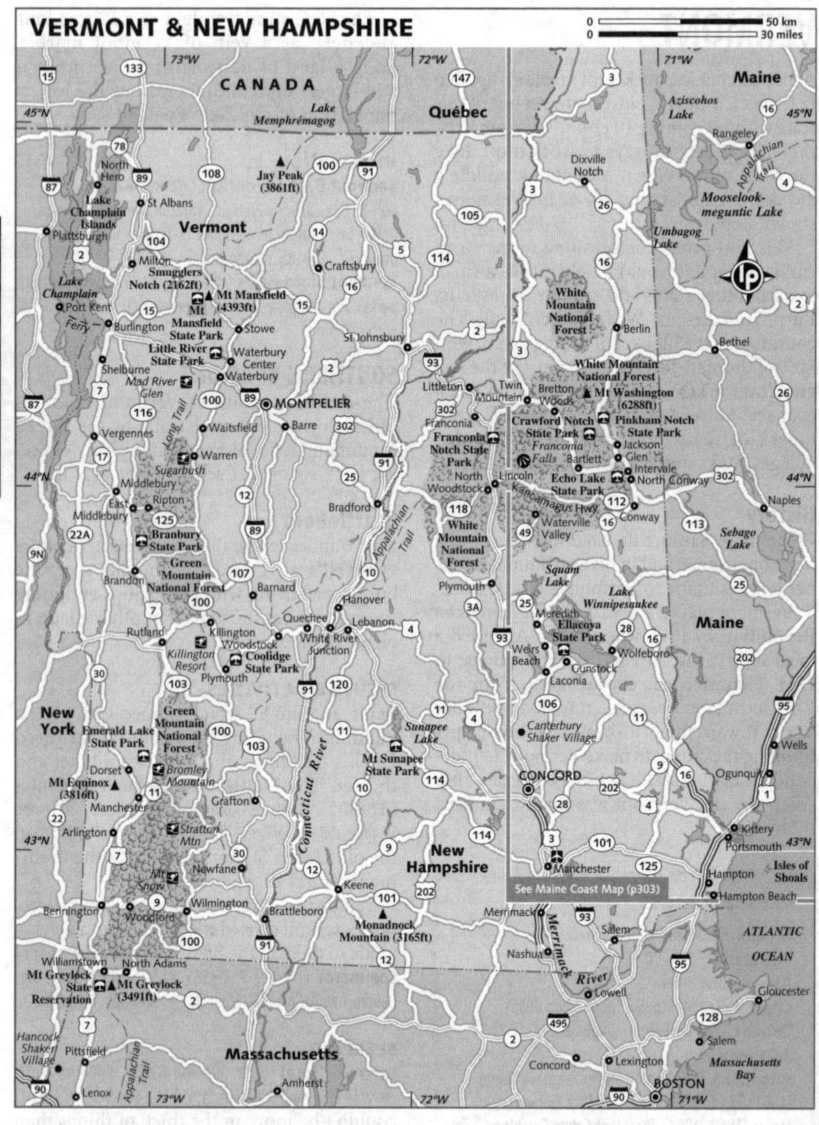

even have a pint-size pub perfect for sampling Vermont brews.

EATING & DRINKING

Brattleboro Food Co-op (☎ 802-257-0236; 2 Main St; 8am-9pm Mon-Sat, 9am-9pm Sun) Naturally this town has a big-league health-food store, with all the fixings for a locavore picnic.

Riverview Café (☎ 802-254-9841; 36 Bridge St; mains $6-18; 8am-8pm Sun-Thu, 8am-8pm Fri & Sat) Enjoy alfresco dining smack on the Connecticut River at this celebrated restaurant emphasizing fresh regional ingredients: wild blueberry pancakes topped with real maple syrup, homemade vegetable soups and juicy steaks.

McNeill's Brewery (☎ 802-254-2553; 90 Elliot St; 4pm-2am Mon-Thu, 2pm-2am Fri-Sun) This friendly brewpub flows with award-winning suds.

Wilmington & Mt Snow

Wilmington, midway between Brattleboro and Bennington, is the gateway to **Mt Snow** (☎ 802-464-3333, 800-245-7669; www.mountsnow.com; VT 100), a family-oriented skiing resort. When the snow melts, its lifts and trail system draw hikers and mountain bikers, including National Off-Road Bicycle Association championship events. The **Mt Snow Valley Chamber of Commerce** (☎ 802-464-8092, 877-887-6884; www.visitvermont.com; 21 W Main St; 10am-5pm) has information on accommodations and activities.

In Wilmington the **Nutmeg Country Inn** (☎ 802-464-7400, 800-277-5402; www.nutmeginn.com; 153 VT 9; r incl breakfast $109-215;), an 18th-century farmhouse, offers local hospitality including a full country breakfast. Just passing by? It also has a small bakery.

Bennington

A measure of how rural southern Vermont really is, cozy Bennington, with just 15,000 inhabitants, ranks as the region's largest town. You'll find an interesting mix of cafés and shops downtown along Main St, while the hillside area known as Old Bennington boasts age-old Colonial homes and a trio of covered bridges (see the boxed text, p288). A hilltop granite obelisk commemorating the 1777 Battle of Bennington towers above it all, making Bennington visible from miles around.

The **Bennington Area Chamber of Commerce** (☎ 802-447-3311, 800-229-0252; www.bennington.com; US 7; 9am-5pm Mon-Fri, 10am-4pm Sat & Sun), a mile north of downtown, provides visitor information.

SIGHTS & ACTIVITIES

Gracing the center of Old Bennington, the **Old First Church** (cnr Monument Ave & VT 9) is famous for its churchyard, which holds the bones of five Vermont governors and poet Robert Frost, who is buried beneath the inscription 'I Had a Lover's Quarrel with the World.'

Vermont's loftiest structure, the **Bennington Battle Monument** (☎ 802-447-0550; Monument Ave; adult/child $2/1; 9am-5pm Apr-Oct), offers an unbeatable 360-degree view of the countryside with peeks at covered bridges and across to New York. And you won't have to strain hamstrings climbing this 306ft obelisk – an elevator whisks you painlessly to the top.

The **Bennington Museum** (☎ 802-447-1571; www.benningtonmuseum.com; 75 Main St/VT 9; adult/child under 18yr $9/free; 10am-5pm Thu-Tue) showcases an array of early Americana crafts, but is most notable for having the world's largest collection of works by famed folk artist Anna Mary 'Grandma' Moses (1860–1961), who painted Vermont farm scenes until the age of 100.

You can tour the potters workshop at **Bennington Potters** (☎ 802-447-7531; 324 County St; admission free; 9:30am-6pm Mon-Sat, 10am-5pm Sun), where distinctive mottled-design stoneware has been made for more than a half-century. Should anything catch your fancy there's an on-site shop.

SLEEPING & EATING

Paradise Inn (☎ 802-442-8351, 800-575-5784; www.theparadisemotorinn.com; 141 W Main St; r $80-145;) Attractive rooms, a quiet yet central setting and a heated outdoor pool add up to good bang for the buck. Spend the extra for a premier room and enjoy your own little sauna and a Jacuzzi.

Henry House (☎ 802-442-7045, 888-442-7045; www.henryhouseinn.com; 1338 Murphy Rd; r incl breakfast $90-145;) Sit on the rocking chair and watch the traffic trickle across a covered bridge at this Colonial home built in 1769 by American Revolution hero William Henry. This is the real deal on 25 peaceful acres and dripping with so much original character you might expect long-gone Lieutenant Henry to walk down the hall.

Blue Benn Diner (☎ 802-442-5140; 314 North St; mains $5-12; 6am-5pm Mon-Fri, 7am-4pm Sat & Sun) It may be a classic 1950s-era diner, but it's no greasy spoon. The extensive menu includes breakfast all day and a healthy mix of American, Asian and Mexican fare – even vegetarian.

Izabella's (☎ 802-447-4949; 351 Main St; mains $6-9; 8:30am-3pm Tue-Fri, 8:30am-4pm Sat) This hip café in the center of town adds an innovative twist to American standards. For breakfast, take on the organic bacon and boursin cheese omelet. For lunch, the smoked turkey and cranberry chutney panini is a wower.

Madison Brewing Co (☎ 802-442-7397; 428 Main St; mains $8-20; 11:30am-9:30pm;) A family-style microbrewery? Yep, this perky pub-restaurant brews homemade root beer as well as heady malt ales. The food ranges from veggie burgers to juicy steaks and there's even a kids menu.

> **SCENIC DRIVE: COVERED BRIDGES**
>
> A 30-minute detour from Bennington takes you across three picture-perfect covered bridges spanning the Wallomsac River at the rural north side of town. To get started turn west onto VT 67A just north of the tourist office and continue 3.5 miles, turning left on Murphy Rd at the **Burt Henry Covered Bridge**. Exhale, slow down: you're back in horse and buggy days. As you pop out the back side of this 117ft-long bridge dating to 1840, curve to the left. Murphy Rd soon loops through the **Paper Mill Bridge**, which takes its name from the 1790 mill that once sat beneath the bridge (look along the river for the old gear works). Next turn right onto VT 67A, go half a mile and turn right onto Silk Rd where you'll soon cross the **Silk Road Bridge** (c 1840). If you continue along Silk Rd for 2 miles, bearing to the left at each turn, you'll reach the **Bennington Battle Monument** (p287).

Manchester

Sitting in the shadow of Mt Equinox, Manchester's been a fashionable summer retreat since the 19th century. The mountain scenery, the agreeable climate and the Batten Kill River – Vermont's best trout stream – continue to draw vacationers today.

The town has two faces, both likable. Manchester Center, at the north end, sports cafés and upscale outlet stores. To the south lies dignified Manchester Village, lined with marble sidewalks, stately homes and the posh Equinox hotel.

The **Manchester & the Mountains Regional Chamber of Commerce** (☎ 802-362-2100, 800-362-4144; www.manchestervermont.net; 5046 Main St, Manchester Center; 🕒 9am-5pm Mon-Fri) provides visitor information.

SIGHTS & ACTIVITIES

Anglers make pilgrimages to Manchester to visit the **American Museum of Fly Fishing** (☎ 802-362-3300; 4104 VT 7A; adult/child 5-14yr $5/3; 🕒 10am-4pm Tue-Sun), where rods used by Ernest Hemingway and other famed fishers are displayed; to shop at the adjacent **Orvis** (☎ 802-361-3750; VT 7A) flagship store, which is dedicated to outfitting fisher-folk; and to fly-fish for trout in the **Batten Kill River**.

BattenKill Canoe (☎ 802-362-2800; www.battenkill.com; 6328 VT 7A, Arlington; canoes $55-65, kayaks $35-40; 🕒 9:30am-5:30pm mid-April–Oct), 5 miles south of Manchester, rents canoes and kayaks for paddling the Batten Kill River. Rent a road or mountain bike from **Batten Kill Sports Bicycle Shop** (☎ 802-362-2734; US 7 & VT 11/30; per day $25; 🕒 9:30am-5:30pm).

The **Appalachian Trail**, which overlaps the **Long Trail** (p291) in Vermont, passes just east of Manchester. For trail maps as well as details on shorter day hikes, stop by the **Green Mountain National Forest office** (☎ 802-362-2307; 2538 Depot St, Manchester Center; 🕒 8am-4:30pm Mon-Fri).

Just south of Manchester, **Hildene** (☎ 802-362-1788; www.hildene.org; 1005 Hildene Rd/VT 7A; adult/child 6-14yr $12.50/5; 🕒 9:30am-4:30pm), a 24-room Georgian Revival mansion, was the country estate of Robert Todd Lincoln, son of President Abraham Lincoln. You can tour the mansion decorated with original Lincoln family furnishings and stroll its lovely gardens, though don't expect much to be in bloom before June.

For a view from the top, drive to the summit of **Mt Equinox** (3836ft). Take VT 7A south of Manchester to **Skyline Drive** (☎ 802-362-1114; car & driver $12, additional passenger $2; 🕒 9am-sunset May-Oct), a private 5-mile toll road.

SLEEPING & EATING

Aspen Motel (☎ 802-362-2450; www.theaspenatmanchester.com, 5669 Main St/VT 7A; r $80-140;) An affordable standout, this family-run hotel set back serenely from the road has 25 comfortable rooms and a convenient location within walking distance of Manchester Center.

Equinox (☎ 802-362-4700, 800-362-4747; www.equinoxresort.com; 3567 Main St; r $260-600;) Manchester's grande dame since 1769 boasts 195 rooms, its own 18-hole golf course, two pools, restaurants and a luxury spa. Despite modern upgrades its handsome period character prevails.

Spiral Press Café (☎ 802-362-9944; cnr VT 11 & 7A; mains $5-9; 🕒 7am-6pm Mon-Sat, 8am-6pm Sun;) Stop at this Manchester Center café attached to Northshire Bookstore for flaky croissants and delicious panini sandwiches. Good lattes too.

Little Rooster Café (☎ 802-362-3496; VT 7A; mains $5-10; 🕒 7am-2:30pm Thu-Tue) This popular little café, near the outlet stores in Manchester Center, serves home-style fare that really hits the spot. The eclectic menu ranges from leafy salads and thickly stacked sandwiches to grilled portobello focaccia.

Up for Breakfast (☎ 802-362-4204; 4935 Main St; mains $6-12; 🕑 7am-12:30pm Mon-Fri, 7am-1:30pm Sat & Sun) Search out this hole-in-the-wall 2nd-floor restaurant in Manchester Center for the best breakfast in town, anything from good ol' blueberry pancakes to smoked-salmon-and-caper omelets.

CENTRAL VERMONT

Nestled in the Green Mountains, central Vermont is classic small-town, big-countryside New England. Its time-honored villages and ski resorts have been luring travelers for generations.

Woodstock & Quechee

The archetypal Vermont town, Woodstock has streets lined with graceful Federal- and Georgian-style houses, and a river spanned by a covered bridge meanders right through the heart of town. Quechee (*kwee*-chee), its smaller cousin 7 miles to the northeast, abounds in rural scenery. The whole area invites you to slow down. The **Woodstock Area Chamber of Commerce** (☎ 802-457-3555, 888-496-6378; www.woodstockvt.com; 61 Central St; 🕑 8:30am-4:30pm Mon-Fri) provides visitor information.

SIGHTS & ACTIVITIES

Quechee Gorge, an impressive 170ft-deep gash cut by the Ottauquechee River, can be viewed from above or along walking trails that skirt the 3000ft-long chasm. Begin at the **Quechee Gorge Visitor Center** (☎ 802-295-6852; US 4, Quechee; 🕑 9am-5pm Jun-Oct, 10am-4pm Nov-May), at the east side of the gorge, where you can pick up a trail map.

VINS Nature Center (☎ 802-359-5000; www.vinsweb.org/nature-center; US 4, Quechee; adult/child 3-18yr $9/7; 🕑 10am-5pm May-Oct, 10am-4pm Wed-Sun Nov-Apr; 👶), a mile west of the gorge, rehabilitates injured bald eagles and other raptors. Get a close-up look at these magnificent birds, then enjoy a nature walk on the center's 47 acres.

See what 19th-century farm life was all about at **Billings Farm & Museum** (☎ 802-457-2355; www.billingsfarm.org; VT 12, at River Rd; adult/child 5-15yr $11/6; 🕑 10am-5pm May-Oct; 👶), a living-history museum and functioning dairy farm. The adjacent **Marsh-Billings-Rockefeller National Historical Park** (☎ 802-457-3368; www.nps.gov/mabi; admission free), occupying a former Rockefeller family estate, is the only national park to tell the story of America's conservation history and land stewardship. The 550-acre park is crisscrossed with shady trails that beg a stroll and it's just a mile north of Woodstock center.

> **WORTH THE TRIP: SUGARBUSH FARM**
>
> To get the scoop on traditional maple sugaring and cheese-making, and sample both, head to the family-run **Sugarbush Farm** (☎ 802-457-1757; www.sugarbushfarm.com; 591 Sugarbush Farm Rd; admission free; 🕑 8am-5pm Mon-Fri, 9am-5pm Sat & Sun). The sugaring season is from March to April, but you can tour the sugarhouse year-round. To get there take US 4 to Taftsville, 3.5 miles east of Woodstock, cross the Taftsville covered bridge and follow the signs.

SLEEPING

Quechee State Park (☎ 888-409-7579; www.vtstateparks.com; 5800 US 4, Quechee; campsites/lean-tos $18/25) Campers will find 45 pine-shaded campsites and seven lean-tos in this 600-acre park bordering Quechee Gorge.

Quechee Inn at Marshfield Farm (☎ 802-295-3133, 800-235-3133; www.quecheeinn.com; 1119 Main St, Quechee; r incl breakfast $90-250; ⊠ 👶) Dating to 1793, this classic country inn on the National Register of Historic Places offers cozy rooms with wide pine floors, four-poster beds and plenty of rural tranquility.

Ardmore Inn (☎ 802-457-3887; www.ardmoreinn.com; 23 Pleasant St, Woodstock; r incl breakfast $135-205; ⊠) This congenial inn, just a five-minute walk from Woodstock town center, occupies a stately 1867 Greek Revival building and features five antique-laden rooms with marble baths.

EATING

Alléchante (☎ 802-457-3300; 61 Central St, Woodstock; mains $6-12; 🕑 8am-5pm Mon-Fri, 7:30am-5:30pm Sat & Sun) A gourmet bakery-café, Alléchante makes everything from scratch, including organic artisanal breads, delectable pastries and a free-range chicken pot pie to die for. The best place in Woodstock for breakfast, bar none.

Farmers Diner (☎ 802-295-4600; 5573 Woodstock Rd/US 4, Quechee; mains $8-15; 🕑 7am-8pm) Grab a booth in this old-fashioned diner and feast on fresh Vermont-grown delights like maple syrup–laden pancakes, creamy organic milk shakes and juicy burgers. This cornerstone of the buy-local, eat-local movement is well worth seeking out.

our pick **Simon Pearce** (☎ 802-295-1470; 1760 Main St, Quechee; lunch mains $12-17, dinner mains $22-30; 11:30am-2:45pm & 6-9pm) Not only is Simon Pearce an unbeatable choice for an upscale meal but lunch is surprisingly affordable. Start by watching the artisans hand-blowing glass and throwing pottery in the basement workshops, then go upstairs and enjoy creative New American fare served on their handiwork. Very cool place – they even generate their own electricity from the waterfall the restaurant overlooks.

Killington

An hour's drive west of Woodstock, **Killington Resort** (☎ 802-422-3333, 800-621-6867; www.killington.com) is New England's answer to Vail, boasting 200 runs on seven mountains, a vertical drop of 3150ft and more than 30 lifts. And thanks to the world's most extensive snowmaking system, Killington has one of the longest seasons in the east. Come summer when the snow melts, mountain bikers and hikers claim the slopes.

There are more than a hundred places to stay in the Killington area, from cozy ski lodges to chain hotels. Most are along Killington Rd, the 6-mile road that heads up the mountain from US 4. The **Killington Chamber of Commerce** (☎ 802-773-4181, 800-337-1928; www.killingtonchamber.com; US 4; 9am-5pm Mon-Fri) has all the nitty-gritty.

Middlebury

This former factory town has converted its old water-driven mills into enticing riverside restaurants and galleries. Add the verdant campus of Middlebury College and you've got yourself a fine place to while away an afternoon. The small but diverse **Middlebury College Museum of Art** (☎ 802-443-5007; S Main St; admission free; 10am-5pm Tue-Fri, noon-5pm Sat & Sun) takes you on a world twirl beginning with an Egyptian sarcophagus and ending with Andy Warhol. The **Addison County Chamber of Commerce** (☎ 802-388-7951; www.addisoncounty.com; 2 Court St; 9am-5pm Mon-Fri) has area information.

On the National Register of Historic Places, the gracious, 1803 Federal-style **Inn on the Green** (☎ 802-388-7512, 888-244-7512; www.innonthegreen.com; 71 S Pleasant St; r incl breakfast $149-279;) has 11 attractive rooms that overlook the town green. Talk about pampering – they'll even serve you breakfast in bed.

For a slice of retro Americana, stop at the **A&W Drive-In** (☎ 802-388-2876; 1557 US 7; mains $3-5; 11am-8pm) where carhops – some on roller skates – deliver root beer floats, cheeseburgers, onion rings and other artery-clogging goodness directly to your car window.

Set directly above the river, smart **Tully & Marie's** (☎ 802-388-4182; 5 Bakery Lane; mains $10-22; 11:30am-9pm) serves New American fare with Asian influences, covering the gamut from vegetarian Thai noodles to Vermont-raised steaks. Brilliant food, service and atmosphere.

Warren & Waitsfield

The towns of Warren and Waitsfield boast two significant ski areas: **Sugarbush** and **Mad River Glen**, in the mountains west of VT 100. Opportunities abound for cycling, canoeing, horseback riding, kayaking, gliding and other activities. Stop at the **Mad River Valley Chamber of Commerce** (☎ 802-496-3409, 800-828-4748; www.madrivervalley.com; VT 100, Waitsfield; 8:30am-5pm Mon-Fri, 9am-noon Sat) for a mountain of details; brochures and restrooms are available 24/7 in the chamber's lobby.

NORTHERN VERMONT

The lushly green northern region of Vermont cradles the fetching state capital of Montpelier, the ski mecca of Stowe, the vibrant college town of Burlington and the state's highest mountains. It has some of the prettiest landscapes in the Northeast.

Montpelier

America's smallest capital, Montpelier is a thoroughly likable town full of period buildings and backed by verdant hills. It speaks to its village nature that you can walk in the front door of the gold-domed **State House** (☎ 802-828-2228; 115 State St; admission free; tours 10am-3:30pm Mon-Fri, 11am-2:30pm Sat Jul–mid-Oct), built c 1836, and exit out the back onto a forested trail. Tours run on the half hour. The **Vermont Chamber of Commerce** (☎ 802-223-3443; www.centralvt.com) has tourist information on Montpelier.

If you come through at mealtime, head for the intersection of State and Main Sts, where you'll find several restaurants. Don't even think junk food – Montpelier prides

SCENIC DRIVE: VT 100

Running up the rugged backbone of Vermont, VT 100 meanders through the rural heart of the state. This quintessential country road rambles past rolling pastures speckled with cows, through tiny villages with white-steepled churches and along green mountains crossed with hiking trails and ski slopes. It's the perfect side trip for those who want to slow down, inhale pine-scented air and soak up the bucolic country life that forms the very soul of Vermont. Think farm stands, century-old farmhouses converted to small inns, pottery shops, country stores and home-style cafés. The road runs north to south all the way from Massachusetts to Canada. It has some tranquil moments but never a dull one – jump on for a taste of it at any point.

itself on being the only state capital in the USA without a McDonald's! The bakery-café **La Brioche** (☎ 802-229-0443; 89 Main St; snacks $2-6; 6:30am-5pm Mon-Fri, 7am-5pm Sat), run by students from Montpelier's New England Culinary Institute, gets an A-plus for its quiches, sandwiches and pastries. Or make your way over to **Hunger Mountain Co-op** (☎ 802-223-8000; 623 Stone Cutters Way; buffet $7.50; 8am-8pm), a terrific health-food store and deli with café tables perched above a river.

Stowe & Around

With Vermont's highest peak, Mt Mansfield (4393ft), as its backdrop, Stowe ranks as Vermont's classiest ski destination. It packs all the Alpine thrills you could ask for – both cross-country and downhill skiing, with gentle runs for novices and challenging drops for pros. Cycling, hiking and kayaking take center stage in the summer. Lodgings and eateries are thick along VT 108 (Mountain Rd), which continues northwest from Stowe center to the ski resorts. The **Stowe Area Association** (☎ 802-253-7321, 877-317-8693; www.gostowe.com; 51 Main St; 9am-5pm Mon-Sat, longer hours midsummer) provides information.

SIGHTS & ACTIVITIES

Wintertime's action-central, the twin-peak **Stowe Mountain Resort** (☎ 802-253-3000, 800-253-4754; www.stowe.com; 5781 Mountain Rd) has a variety of terrains with ski runs suitable for all levels. Cross-country skiing is available at several places, including the **Trapp Family Lodge** (☎ 802-253-8511, 800-826-7000; www.trappfamily.com; 700 Trapp Hill Rd), run by the family whose life inspired *The Sound of Music*.

The 5.5-mile **Stowe Recreation Path**, a greenway running along the West Branch River northwest from the village center, is a great place for walking, jogging, cycling and skating. **AJ's Ski & Sports** (☎ 802-253-4593; 350 Mountain Rd; 10am-6pm), next to the path, rents bikes for $8 per hour or $27 per day.

Umiak Outdoor Outfitters (☎ 802-253-2317; 849 S Main St; 9am-6pm) rents canoes ($50 per day) and kayaks ($40) and also offers two-hour guided river trips ($39).

Get the inside scoop at **Ben & Jerry's Ice Cream Factory** (☎ 802-882-1240; www.benjerrys.com; VT 100, Waterbury; adult/child under 12yr $3/free; 9am-9pm Jul–mid-Aug, 9am-7pm mid-Aug–Oct, 10am-6pm Nov-Jun;), where tours and a moo-vie about the hippie founders are topped off with a taste tease of the latest flavor.

Vermont's **Long Trail**, which passes through Stowe, follows the crest of the Green Mountains and runs the entire length of Vermont with rustic cabins, lean-tos and campsites along the way. Its caretaker, the **Green Mountain Club** (☎ 802-244-7037; www.greenmountainclub.org; 4711 Waterbury-Stowe Rd, VT 100), has full details on the Long Trail and shorter day hikes around Stowe.

If the snow has cleared, be sure to take a drive through dramatic **Smugglers Notch**, northwest of Stowe on VT 108 (the road's closed in winter). This narrow pass slices through mountains with 1000ft cliffs on either side, and there are plenty of places where you can stop along the way to ooh and aah or take a short walk.

SLEEPING & EATING

Smugglers Notch State Park (☎ 802-253-4014; 6443 Mountain Rd; campsites/lean-tos $18/25; mid-May–mid-Oct) Camp at the base of Mt Mansfield, 9 miles northwest of downtown Stowe on VT 108.

Best Western Waterbury-Stowe (☎ 802-244-7822, 800-621-7822; www.bestwesternwaterburystowe.com; VT 100, I-89 exit 10; r incl breakfast $99-129;) Family-friendly and good value, this convenient hotel has a playground, a sunny atrium pool and fitness facilities a notch above the usual standards. And it's just a short drive from Ben & Jerry's.

NEW ENGLAND

Ye Olde England Inne (☎ 802-253-7558, 800-477-3771; www.englandinn.com; 433 Mountain Rd; r incl breakfast $109-189; ⊠) The English innkeepers here add Britannia accents like complimentary afternoon tea and an on-site pub serving UK ales. Rooms have canopied beds and some have Jacuzzis. Skip the food here, though – there are better options nearby.

Harvest Market (☎ 802-253-3800; 1031 Mountain Rd; 7am-5:30pm) Stop at this gourmet market for morning coffee and delicious pastries, Vermont cheeses and sandwiches before you head for the hills.

Pie-casso (☎ 802-253-4411; 1899 Mountain Rd; mains $8-20; 11am-9pm) This pizzeria goes far beyond the simple pie: organic arugula chicken salad, portobello paninis and hand-tossed pesto pizzas are just part of the menu. There's a bar and live music too.

Hen of the Wood (☎ 802-244-7300; 92 Stowe St, Woodbury; mains $20-30; 5-10pm Mon-Sat) Arguably the finest dining in northern Vermont, this chef-driven restaurant is just three years old but has already earned rave reviews from *Gourmet* and *Food & Wine* magazines for its innovative farm-to-table cuisine. Set in a historic grist mill, the ambience is as fine as the food, which features densely flavored dishes like smoked duck breast and sheep's milk gnocchi.

BURLINGTON

This hip college town on the shores of scenic Lake Champlain is one of those places that makes you think, wouldn't it be great to live here? The café and club scene is on par with a much bigger city, while the slow, friendly pace is pure small town. And where else can you walk to the end of Main St and paddle off in a kayak?

Orientation & Information

Vermont's largest city (population 38,358) is a manageable place with most of its cafés and pubs on or near Church St Marketplace, a brick-lined pedestrian mall, where half of Burlington hangs on a sunny day. The mall sits midway between the University of Vermont and Lake Champlain.

Crow Bookshop (☎ 802-862-0848; 14 Church St; 10am-9pm Mon-Wed, 10am-10pm Thu-Sat, noon-6pm Sun) Excellent selection of used and rare books.

Fletcher Allen Health Care (☎ 802-847-0000; 111 Colchester Ave; 24hr) Vermont's largest hospital.

Lake Champlain Regional Chamber of Commerce (☎ 802-863-3489, 877-686-5253; 60 Main St; www.vermont.org; 8am-5pm Mon-Fri) Also maintains a 24-hour visitor kiosk on Church St Marketplace.

Post office (☎ 800-275-8777; 11 Elmwood Ave; 8am-5pm Mon-Fri, 9am-1pm Sat)

Seven Days (www.7dvt.com) Free weekly with event and entertainment listings.

Sights & Activities

Ready for outdoor adventures? Head to the waterfront, where options include boating on **Lake Champlain** and cycling, in-line skating and walking on the 9-mile, shorefront **Burlington Bike Path**. Jump-off points and equipment rentals for all these activities are within a block of each other near the waterfront end of Main St. Rent bikes at **Local Motion** (☎ 802-652-2453; 1 Steele St; bikes per half-/full day $23/28; 10am-6pm). **Waterfront Boat Rentals** (☎ 802-864-4858; Perkins Pier; rentals per hr $10-16; 10am-5pm) rents canoes, kayaks and rowboats. For an inexpensive cruise of the lake, hop aboard the 115ft *Northern Lights* operated by **Lake Champlain Cruises** (☎ 802-864-7669; 1 King St; 1½hr trip adult/child 3-11yr $13/6). If you prefer a more intimate sail, opt for the 17-passenger *Friend Ship* (☎ 802-598-6504; 1 College St; 2hr trip adult/child $35/20), a classic schooner.

Crowning the highest hill in town is the handsome **University of Vermont** (UVM; ☎ 802-656-3131; www.uvm.edu; Main St/Rte 2), home to the **Fleming Museum** (☎ 802-656-2090; 61 Colchester Ave; adult/child 6-17yr $5/3; 9am-4pm Tue-Fri, 1-5pm Sat & Sun Sep-Apr, noon-4pm Tue-Fri, 1-5pm Sat & Sun May-Aug). This beautiful beaux arts–style building houses a 2000-item Native American gallery and works by American artists ranging from John James Audubon to Andy Warhol.

The **ECHO Lake Aquarium & Science Center** (☎ 802-864-1848; www.echovermont.org; 1 College St; adult/child 3-17yr $9.50/7; 10am-5pm;), on the waterfront, will delight youngsters with its aquatic habitats wriggling with creatures and hands-on interactive exhibits illuminating Lake Champlain's ecological wonders.

WHAT THE...?

Packrats, take note. The **world's tallest filing cabinet** – a 50ft-high shrine to dead letters – sits in a roadside field midway between downtown and Magic Hat Brewery. Turn west onto Flynn Ave off US 7/Shelburne Rd and go 700 yards+; it's on the right, adjacent to 208 Flynn Ave.

SCENIC DRIVE: LAKE CHAMPLAIN ISLANDS

If you have time to take your travels beyond Burlington, head north on US 2 to explore the unspoiled Lake Champlain Islands. Connected to the mainland by a causeway, these four islands (and a peninsula jutting down from Canada) are home to just 6500 year-round residents. Extending 30 miles from south to north they make a perfect day trip with fine rural scenery, lakeside beaches and small farms selling roadside produce. Should you want to stay overnight, information on campgrounds and B&Bs is available from **Lake Champlain Islands Chamber of Commerce** (☎ 802-372-8400, 800-262-5226; www.champlainislands.com; 3501 US 2, North Hero; 9am-4pm Mon-Fri year-round, plus 10am-2pm Sat & Sun Jun-Aug).

If you're up for a swim, head to **Oakledge Park** (Flynn Ave), near the south end of the Burlington Bike Path. In addition to the beach, the park has an awesome **tree house** at its south end and the **Burlington Earth Clock**, a cool Stonehenge-wannabe sun clock, at its north end.

The insanely popular **Magic Hat Brewery** (☎ 802-658-2739; www.magichat.net; 5 Bartlett Bay Rd, South Burlington; 10am-6pm Mon-Sat, noon-5pm Sun), off US 7, offers free tours of its brew operation – and of course they'll tip the tap to let you sample the art. Perhaps the coolest brewery you'll ever see.

On a 45-acre estate, 7 miles south of Burlington in Shelburne, the **Shelburne Museum** (☎ 802-985-3346; www.shelburnemuseum.org; US 7, Shelburne; adult/child 4-18yr $20/10; 10am-5pm May-Oct) boasts a stellar collection of American folk art, New England architecture and, well, just about everything. The wildly eclectic collection ranges from an early American sawmill to the Lake Champlain side-wheeler steamship *Ticonderoga*. How's that for lawn decor?

You can get a taste of Vermont farm life at **Shelburne Farms** (☎ 802-985-8686; www.shelburnefarms.org; 1611 Harbor Rd, Shelburne; adult/child 3-17yr $8/5; 9am-5:30pm mid-May–mid-Oct), a classic 1400-acre farm laid out by Frederick Law Olmsted, America's premier 19th-century landscape architect. Try your hand at milking a cow, feed the chickens, or hike the extensive nature trails through pastures and along Lake Champlain.

Sleeping

North Beach Campground (☎ 802-862-0942, 800-571-1198; www.enjoyburlington.com; 60 Institute Rd; campsites $25) This choice lakeside campground skirts the Burlington Bike Path and has a sandy beach with kayak and canoe rentals.

Lang House (☎ 802-652-2500, 877-919-9799; www.langhouse.com; 360 Main St; r incl breakfast $145-245) Little extras like cozy bathrobes and a home-cooked breakfast add to the appeal of this friendly Victorian inn. Situated between downtown and the university, it makes an ideal base for exploring Burlington.

Willard Street Inn (☎ 802-651-8710, 800-577-8712; www.willardstreetinn.com; 349 S Willard St; r incl breakfast $150-230) With marble floors and a solarium dining room, this gracious inn, a short walk from UVM, is a class act. The 14 rooms are comfy, some with lake views and gas fireplaces, and the gourmet breakfast will start your day in style.

Inn at Shelburne Farms (☎ 802-985-8498; www.shelburnefarms.org; 1611 Harbor Rd, Shelburne; r with shared bath $150-215, private bath $255-450) Vacation like a millionaire at this lakefront manor-house-turned-inn at Shelburne Farms (left). On the National Register of Historic Places, this former summer residence of the Vanderbilts has 24 antique-filled bedrooms and the air of a bygone era.

Eating

Muddy Waters (☎ 802-658-0466; 184 Main St; snacks $3-6; 7am-6pm Mon, 7am-11pm Tue-Sun) As much a chill-out spot as an eatery, this arty student haunt offers chili and hummus plates and a full array of drinks from espresso and smoothies to Vermont-brewed beers.

Stone Soup (☎ 802-862-7616; 211 College St; mains $5-10; 7am-7pm Mon, 7am-9pm Tue-Fri, 9am-7pm Sat) Don't let the bargain prices fool you. The food at this laid-back café is hearty and healthy, most of it vegetarian, much of it organic. Sandwiches, soups and a buffet bar of fresh salads and hot dishes shore up the menu.

Penny Cluse Café (☎ 802-651-8834; 169 Cherry St; mains $6-10; 6:45am-3pm Mon-Fri, 8am-3pm Sat & Sun) One block east of Church St Marketplace, Penny Cluse packs a perky college crowd with its southwestern accented dishes like ranchero-style omelets, fish tacos and freshly squeezed juices.

Magnolia Bistro (☎ 802-846-7446; 1 Lawson Lane; mains $7-10; 7am-3pm Mon-Fri, 8am-3pm Sat & Sun;) The hottest café in a hot-café town, Magnolia utilizes sustainable local ingredients from range-fed beef to leafy green salads, and is certified by the Green Restaurant Association. Specialties include the house-cured organic salmon and the Vermont maple sausage omelet.

L'Amante (☎ 802-863-5200; 126 College St; mains $20-28; 5:30-10pm Mon-Sat) Sleek yet engagingly informal, L'Amante serves upscale northern Italian cuisine such as squash-blossom fritters with truffle oil, and swordfish with saffron-encrusted risotto. Perfect for a memorable night out.

Drinking & Entertainment

Uncommon Grounds (☎ 802-865-6227; 42 Church St; items $2-5; 7am-8pm Mon-Thu, 8am-9pm Fri & Sat, 9am-6pm Sun;) With sidewalk tables right on the pedestrian mall, this café has people-watching that is as good as the organic fair-trade coffee and crispy croissants.

Vermont Pub & Brewery (☎ 802-865-0500; 144 College St; 11:30am-1am Sun-Wed, 11:30am-2am Thu-Sat) Vermont's oldest microbrewery attracts a crowd with its bustling outdoor beer garden and burly ales. Try the Dogbite Bitter and howl at the moon.

Radio Bean (☎ 802-660-9346; 8 N Winooski Ave; 8am-3am;) A social hub for the music scene, this bohemian coffeehouse serves fair-trade coffee by day and transforms after dark into an intimate venue for jazz and indie bands.

Nectar's (☎ 802-658-4771; 188 Main St) This is the place where the jam band Phish got its start; aspiring bands still take the stage at Nectar's hoping to be the next big thing. Maybe you'll catch a rising star.

Red Square (☎ 802-859-8909; 136 Church St) With a stylish Soho-like ambience, this is where the club crowd hangs to listen to Burlington's best roadhouse music, which spills onto the outdoor patio on warm nights.

Getting There & Away

Lake Champlain Ferries (☎ 802-864-9804; www.ferries.com; King St Dock; adult/child/car $4.95/2.20/12.55) runs ferries several times a day from mid-June to mid-October across the lake to Port Kent, NY (one hour).

NEW HAMPSHIRE

You're gonna like the scale of things in the Granite State: the towns are small and personable, the mountains majestic and rugged. The heart of New Hampshire is unquestionably the granite peaks of the White Mountain National Forest. Outdoor enthusiasts of all stripes flock to New England's highest range (6288ft at Mt Washington) for cold-weather skiing, summer hiking and brilliant fall foliage scenery. Oh, and don't be fooled by that politically conservative label that people stick on the state. The state mantra, 'Live Free or Die,' indeed rings from every automobile license plate, but truth be told residents here pride themselves on their independent spirit more than right-wing politics.

History

Named in 1629 after the English county of Hampshire, New Hampshire was one of the first American colonies to declare its independence from England in 1776. During the 19th-century industrialization boom, the state's leading city, Manchester, became such a powerhouse that its textile mills were the world's largest.

New Hampshire played a high-profile role in 1944 when president Franklin D Roosevelt gathered leaders from 44 Allied nations to remote Bretton Woods for a conference to rebuild global capitalism. It was at the Bretton Woods Conference that the World Bank and the International Monetary Fund emerged.

In 1963 New Hampshire, long famed for its antitax sentiments, found another way to raise revenue – by becoming the first state in the USA to have a legal lottery.

Information

Welcome centers are situated at major state border crossings, including ones open 24/7 at the north and south ends of I-93.

New Hampshire Division of Parks and Recreation (☎ 877-647-2757; www.nhparks.state.nh.us; campsites $23-25) offers camping in 19 state parks.

New Hampshire Division of Travel & Tourism Development (☎ 603-271-2665, 800-386-4664; www.visitnh.gov) Distributes visitor information on the state, as do the welcome centers.

Union Leader (www.unionleader.com) The state's largest newspaper.

PORTSMOUTH

America's third-oldest city (1623), Portsmouth wears its history on its sleeve. Its roots are in shipbuilding, but New Hampshire's sole coastal city also has a hip, youthful energy. The old maritime warehouses along the harbor now house cafés and boutiques. Elegant period homes built by shipbuilding tycoons have been converted into B&Bs. The **Greater Portsmouth Chamber of Commerce** (☎ 603-436-3988; www.portsmouthchamber.org; 500 Market St; 8:30am-5pm Mon-Fri, lobby 24hr) provides visitor information.

Sights & Activities

For the largest collection of historic sites, go straight to **Strawbery Banke Museum** (☎ 603-433-1100; www.strawberybanke.org; cnr Hancock & Marcy Sts; adult/child 5-17yr $15/10; 10am-5pm May-Oct), where an entire neighborhood of 40 period buildings comprise a living-history museum depicting the town's multilayered past. Visit the old general store, watch the potter throw his clay then treat yourself to a scoop of homemade ice cream.

Like a fish out of water, the 205ft-long **USS Albacore** (☎ 603-436-3680; 600 Market St; adult/child 7-17yr $5/3; 9:30am-5:30pm Jun–mid-Oct, 9:30am-4pm Thu-Mon mid-Oct–May) is now a beached museum on a grassy lawn. The decommissioned submarine, once the world's fastest, was launched from Portsmouth Naval Shipyard in 1953.

Portsmouth Harbor Cruises (☎ 603-436-8084, 800-776-0915; www.portsmouthharbor.com; 64 Ceres St Dock; adult $12-20, child $8-13) runs several trips around the historic harbor as well as inland river cruises that are particularly scenic during fall foliage season. **Isles of Shoals Steamship Company** (☎ 603-431-5500, 800-441-4620; www.islesofshoals.com; 315 Market St; adult/child 5-12yr $26/16;) provides cruises aboard a replica 1900s ferry that harkens back to more leisurely times. Its Shoals and Harbor Cruise takes in three lighthouses, nine islands and countless harbor sights. On Fridays, the cruise includes a lobster clambake (adult/child $66/36).

Sleeping

Inn at Strawbery Banke (☎ 603-436-7242, 800-428-3933; www.innatstrawberybanke.com; 314 Court St; r incl breakfast $160-170;) Friendly innkeepers, cozy rooms and a delicious homemade breakfast are the hallmarks of this Colonial-era B&B convenient to both the Strawbery Banke Museum and the city center.

NEW HAMPSHIRE FACTS

Nicknames Granite State, White Mountain State
Population 1.3 million
Area 8968 sq miles
Capital city Concord (42,378)
Other cities Manchester (population 109,497)
Sales tax None
Birthplace of America's first astronaut Alan Shepard (1923–98), *The Da Vinci Code* author Dan Brown (b 1964), Tupperware inventor Earl Tupper (1907–83)
Home of the highest mountains in northeastern USA
Famous For Being the first to vote in US presidential primaries, which gives the state enormous political influence for its size
Most extreme state motto 'Live Free or Die'
Driving distances Boston to Portsmouth 60 miles, Concord to Hanover 66 miles

Sise Inn (☎ 603-433-1200, 877-747-3466; www.siseinn.com; 40 Court St; r/ste incl breakfast $199/239;) Step back a century at this graceful 1881 Queen Anne–style inn that flawlessly fuses classic period decor with 21st-century amenities. Rooms are generously proportioned with the suites sleeping up to four guests.

Eating & Drinking

Head to the intersection of Market and Congress Sts, where restaurants and cafés are thick on the ground.

Breaking New Grounds (☎ 603-436-9555; 14 Market St; snacks $2-5; 6:30am-10pm;) Get your caffeine fix at this café smack in the heart of town. Plump muffins, crispy croissants and outdoor tables perfect for people-watching.

Blue Mermaid (☎ 603-427-2583; 409 The Hill; mains $8-20; 11:30am-9pm Sun-Thu, 11:30am-10pm Fri & Sat) If you need a break from New England seafood head here for a delectable mix of Caribbean-inspired fare. It's also a hopping place at night for its potent mojitos.

Jumpin' Jay's Fish Café (☎ 603-766-3474; 150 Congress St; mains $18-24; 5:30-10pm) Fish-fanciers book tables at this sleek contemporary seafooder, which features a wide range of fresh pan-seared fish spiced with delicious sauces.

Portsmouth Brewery (☎ 603-431-1115; 56 Market St;) This lively microbrewery serves specialty beers like Smuttynose Portsmouth Lager along with light eats, including the best fish sandwich in town.

NEW ENGLAND

MANCHESTER

A couple of colleges and an art school give this old mill town fresh vitality. New Hampshire's largest city, Manchester (population 109,497) became a manufacturing powerhouse in the 19th century by harnessing the ripping Merrimack River. The brick **Amoskeag Mills** (1838), which stretch along the Commercial St riverbanks for more than a mile, now house software companies and other 21st-century backbones of the city's economy.

Head to Elm St near the town green where you'll find the tourist office and the lion's share of eateries and pubs. The **Greater Manchester Chamber of Commerce** (☎ 603-666-6600; www.manchester-chamber.org; 889 Elm St; 🕑 8am-5pm Mon-Thu, 8:30am-4:30pm Fri) has visitor information.

The city's highlight, the **Currier Museum of Art** (☎ 603-669-6144; www.currier.org; 201 Myrtle Way; adult/child under 18yr $10/free, Sat morning free; 🕑 11am-5pm Sun, Mon, Wed & Fri, 10am-5pm Sat), showcases works by American artists Georgia O'Keeffe and Andrew Wyeth. It also operates the 1950 **Zimmerman House** (tours $15), the only home in New England designed by famed American architect Frank Lloyd Wright (1867–1959) open to the public.

I-93, US 3 and NH 101 all pass through Manchester. The **Manchester Airport** (MHT; ☎ 603-624-6539; www.flymanchester.com) is served by major US airlines, including discounter Southwest Airlines. **Greyhound** (☎ 800-231-2222; www.greyhound.com) provides bus services between Manchester and other New England cities.

CONCORD

History-laden Concord makes a refreshing break. Don't let the fact that it's a state capital throw you – think of it as a laid-back little town that just happens to have a capitol building gracing Main St, the way other communities this size would have a town hall. Everything radiates out from the State House – you'll find several delis and restaurants nearby.

The gold-domed, eagle-topped **State House** (☎ 603-271-2154; 107 N Main St; admission free; 🕑 8am-5pm Mon-Fri), built in 1819 of New Hampshire granite, houses the oldest legislative chamber in the US. Forget heavy-handed security, this is a remarkably relaxed affair – you can walk right in, check out the intriguing lobby display of battle-tattered Civil War flags, then head up to the 2nd floor to visit the chamber. The **Museum of New Hampshire History** (☎ 603-228-6688; www.nhhistory.org; 6 Eagle Sq; adult/child 6-18yr $5.50/3; 🕑 9:30am-5pm Mon-Sat, noon-5pm Sun, closed Mon Jan-Jun & Nov), opposite the State House, chronicles the history of the Granite State in more depth. **Pierce Manse** (☎ 603-225-4555; 14 Horseshoe Pond Lane; adult/child 6-18yr $5/2; 🕑 11am-3pm Tue-Fri mid-Jun–Aug), the home of Franklin Pierce (1804–69), the only US president to hail from New Hampshire, can be toured in summer. The **Greater Concord Chamber of Commerce** (☎ 603-224-2508; www.concordnhchamber.com; 40 Commercial St; 🕑 9am-5pm Mon-Fri, 9am-3pm Sat) maintains a tourist information kiosk on the sidewalk in front of the State House.

LAKE WINNIPESAUKEE

A popular summer retreat for families looking for a break from the city, New Hampshire's largest lake stretches 28 miles in length, contains 274 islands and offers abundant opportunities for swimming, boating and fishing.

Weirs Beach

This lakeside town dishes up a curious slice of honky-tonk Americana with its celebrated video arcades, mini-golf courses and go-cart tracks. The **Greater Laconia/Weirs Beach Chamber of Commerce** (☎ 603-524-5531; www.laconia-weirs.org; 383 S Main St, Laconia) supplies information on the area.

Mount Washington Cruises (☎ 603-366-5531; www.cruisenh.com; cruises $25-40) operates scenic lake cruises, the pricier ones with champagne brunch, from Weirs Beach aboard the old-fashioned MS *Mount Washington*. For a unique experience hop aboard the MV *Sophie C*, the oldest floating post office in the USA, on its two-hour **cruise** (adult/child 4-12yr $22/12) to deliver mail to the lake islands.

Winnipesaukee Scenic Railroad (☎ 603-279-5253; www.hoborr.com; adult/child 3-11yr $14/11) offers train rides along the shore of Lake Winnipesaukee.

Wolfeboro

On the opposite side of Lake Winnipesaukee, and a world away from the ticky-tacky commercialism of Weirs Beach, sits genteel Wolfeboro. Anointing itself 'the oldest summer resort in America,' the town's awash with graceful period buildings, including several that are open to the public. The friendly folks at the **Wolfeboro Chamber of Commerce** (☎ 603-569-2200, 800-516-5324; www.wolfeborochamber.com; 32 Central Ave; 🕑 10am-5pm Mon-Sat, 10am-3pm Sun), in the old

WORTH THE TRIP: CANTERBURY SHAKER VILLAGE

A traditional Shaker community from 1792, **Canterbury Shaker Village** (☎ 603-783-9511; www.shakers.org; 288 Shaker Rd, Canterbury; adult/child 6-17yr $17/8; ⌚ 10am-5pm mid-May–Oct) maintains the Shaker heritage as a living-history museum. Interpreters demonstrate the Shakers' daily lives, artisans create Shaker crafts, and walking trails invite pond-side strolls. The greening of America has deep roots here – for more than two centuries the Shakers' abundant gardens have been turning out vegetables, medicinal herbs and bountiful flowers the organic way. If you're ready for a soulful diversion you could easily spend half a day here on the farm, which covers nearly 700 acres. Take a little wholesomeness home with you – there's a store selling Shaker handicrafts, a farm stand and a superb restaurant serving the kind of food grandma used to make using heirloom veggies fresh picked from the garden. The village is 15 miles north of Concord; take I-93 to exit 18 and follow the signs.

train station, have the scoop on everything from boat rentals to lakeside beaches.

Wolfeboro is home to the **Great Waters Music Festival** (☎ 603-569-7710; www.greatwaters.org; Brewster Academy, NH 28; ⌚ Jul & Aug), where big-name folk, jazz and blues artists perform on the banks of Lake Winnipesaukee.

Off NH 28, about 4 miles north of town, is lakeside **Wolfeboro Campground** (☎ 603-569-9881; 61 Haines Hill Rd; campsites $27-30) with 50 wooded campsites.

The classic stay is the **Wolfeboro Inn** (☎ 603-569-3016, 800-451-2389; www.wolfeboroinn.com; 90 N Main St; r incl breakfast from $200), the town's principal lodging since 1812. Some of the rooms have balconies overlooking the lake.

The **Yum Yum Shop** (☎ 603-569-1919; 16 N Main St; snacks $1-7; ⌚ 6am-7pm), a Wolfeboro institution, is a family-run bakery selling flaky pastries, old-fashioned cream doughnuts and fresh-made sandwiches. **51 Mill** (☎ 603-569-3303, 51 Mill St; mains $8-22; ⌚ 11:30am-9pm) offers a varied menu, large portions and a fine lakeside setting; the crab cakes and grilled swordfish go nicely with the wine selections.

WHITE MOUNTAINS

What the Rockies are to Colorado the White Mountains are to New Hampshire. New England's loftiest mountain range is a magnet for adventurers, with boundless opportunities for everything from hiking and kayaking to skiing. Those who prefer to take it in from the comfort of a car seat won't be disappointed either, as scenic drives wind over rugged mountains ripping with waterfalls, sheer rock faces and sharply cut gorges.

You'll find information on the White Mountains at ranger stations throughout the **White Mountain National Forest** (www.fs.fed.us/r9/white) and chambers of commerce in the towns along the way.

Waterville Valley

In the shadow of Mt Tecumseh, Waterville Valley was developed as a resort community during the latter half of the 20th century, when hotels, condos, golf courses and ski trails were all laid out. It's very much a planned community and arguably a bit too groomed but there's plenty to do, including tennis, indoor ice skating, cycling and other family fun. The **Waterville Valley Region Chamber of Commerce** (☎ 603-726-3804, 800-237-2307; www.watervillevalleyregion.com; NH 49, Campton; ⌚ 9am-5pm Wed-Mon), off I-93 exit 28, has all the details.

Like many New England ski mountains, the **Waterville Valley ski area** (☎ 603-236-8311, 800-468-2553; www.waterville.com) is open in the summer for mountain biking and hiking.

Mt Washington Valley

Stretching north from the eastern terminus of the Kancamagus Hwy (see the boxed text, p299), Mt Washington Valley includes the towns of Conway, North Conway, Intervale, Glen, Jackson and Bartlett. Every conceivable outdoor activity is available. The area's hub and biggest town, North Conway, is also a center for outlet shopping, including some earthy stores like LL Bean. For information on the entire area contact the **Mt Washington Valley Chamber of Commerce** (☎ 603-356-5701, 877-948-6867; www.mtwashingtonvalley.org; 2617 White Mountain Hwy, North Conway; ⌚ 9am-5pm Mon-Fri).

SIGHTS & ACTIVITIES

Nostalgia at its finest, the **Conway Scenic Railroad** (☎ 603-356-5251, 800-232-5251; www.conwayscenic.com; NH 16, North Conway; adult $14-65, child 4-12yr $10-40;

daily mid-May–Oct, Sat & Sun Apr–mid-May & Nov-Dec;) runs an antique steam train on a variety of excursions from North Conway through Mt Washington Valley and dramatic Crawford Notch. It's a real stunner, especially during the fall foliage season.

Two miles west of North Conway off US 302, placid **Echo Lake State Park** rests at the foot of a sheer rock wall called White Horse Ledge. The park offers lakeside hiking, swimming and a scenic road up 700ft-high Cathedral Ledge.

Skiing areas include **Attitash** (603-374-2368, 877-677-7669; www.attitash.com; US 302, Bartlett), 5 miles west of Glen, which also operates America's longest Alpine slide in summer, and **Black Mountain Ski Area** (603-383-4490; www.blackmt.com; NH 16B, Jackson), a cross-country skiing mecca that offers summertime horseback riding.

If you're up for a water adventure, **Saco Bound** (603-447-2177; www.sacobound.com; 2561 E Main/US 302, Conway; rental per day from $25) rents canoes and kayaks and also offers guided tours ranging from placid lake paddles to day-long white-water outings.

SLEEPING

North Conway in particular is thick with sleeping options from resort hotels to cozy inns.

HI Albert B Lester Memorial Hostel (603-447-1001; www.conwayhostel.com; 36 Washington St, Conway; dm/r $23/58;) Perched on the edge of the White Mountain National Forest, off NH 16, this 45-bed hostel in a converted farmhouse is well situated for outdoor adventurers.

Cranmore Inn (603-356-5502, 800-526-5502; www.cranmoreinn.com; 80 Kearsarge St, North Conway; r incl breakfast $89-135;) With a convenient in-town location, this North Conway landmark has been operating as a country inn since 1863 and good-value, home-style comfort has been its key to success.

North Conway Grand Hotel (603-356-9300, 800-522-1793; www.northconwaygrand.com; NH 16, Settlers' Green, North Conway; r $99-219;) If you're looking for all the trappings of a resort hotel, this family-friendly place has commodious rooms with full amenities and extras like a free DVD library, tennis courts and children's programs.

Wyatt House Country Inn (603-356-7977, 800-527-7978; www.wyatthouseinn.com; NH 16, North Conway; r incl breakfast $120-179;) You'll be pampered with a candlelit gourmet breakfast, afternoon tea and evening sherry. Feeling really romantic? Request the Angel Wing, light the fireplace, slip into the two-person Jacuzzi and uncork the champagne.

The best camping options are **Cove Camping Area** (603-447-6734; www.covecamping.com; Cove Rd, Conway; campsites $25-50), off Stark Rd on Conway Lake; and **Saco River Camping Area** (603-356-3360; www.sacorivercampingarea.com; North Conway; campsites $25-35;) off NH 16 on the Saco River; both places have canoe rentals and beaches.

EATING

Peach's (603-356-5860; South Main St, North Conway; mains $6-10; 7am-2:30pm) This peachy place, a half-mile south of the chamber of commerce, really captures a small-town feel. Who can resist fruit-smothered waffles, hearty omelets and homemade soups served in somebody's cozy living room?

Café Noche (603-447-5050; 147 Main St, Conway; mains $10-15; 11:30am-9pm) For good Tex-Mex fare topped with real-deal salsas head to this festive central Conway spot. The margaritas, in a head-spinning variety of flavors, will rev up the appetite.

Flatbread Company (603-356-4470; 2760 White Mountain Hwy, North Conway; pizzas $10-18; 11:30am-9pm) A socially conscious pizzeria, Flatbread uses organic veggies and nitrate-free meats, and dishes up a portion of its profits to local environmental causes. The deliciously crispy pizzas are cooked in front of your eyes in a wood-fired clay oven built into the dining room.

North Woodstock & Lincoln

You'll pass right through the twin towns of Lincoln and North Woodstock on your way between the Kancamagus Hwy (see the boxed text, opposite) and Franconia Notch State Park, so it's a handy place to break for a bite or a bed. The towns straddle the Pemigewasset River at the intersection of NH 112 and US 3. If you're ready for some action, **Loon Mountain** (603-745-8111; www.loonmtn.com; Kancamagus Hwy, Lincoln) offers winter skiing and snowboarding, and in summer has mountain-bike trails, climbing walls and New Hampshire's longest gondola ride. Or ratchet the adrenaline up a notch by zipping 2000ft down a hillside while strapped to just a cable with **Alpine Adventures** (603-745-9911; 41 Main St, Lincoln; zips $85; 9am-4pm) treetop zip line. For more on the area, contact the **Lincoln-Woodstock Chamber of Commerce** (603-745-6621; www.lincolnwoodstock.com; Main St/NH 112, Lincoln; 9am-5pm Mon-Fri).

SCENIC DRIVE: KANCAMAGUS HIGHWAY

One of New England's finest, the 35-mile Kancamagus Hwy (NH 112) is a beauty of a road cutting through the **White Mountain National Forest** between Conway and Lincoln. Laced with excellent hiking trails, scenic lookouts and swimmable streams, this is as natural as it gets. There's absolutely no development along the entire highway, which reaches its highest point at **Kancamagus Pass** (2868ft).

You can pick up brochures and hiking maps at the **Saco Ranger District Office** (☎ 603-447-5448; 33 Kancamagus Hwy; 🕑 8am-4:30pm) at the eastern end of the highway near Conway and at the **Lincoln Woods Ranger Office** (☎ 603-630-5190; Kancamagus Hwy; 🕑 8am-5pm) at the western end near the Mile 29 marker.

Coming from Conway, 6.5 miles west of the Saco ranger station, you'll see **Lower Falls** on the north side of the road – stop here for the view and a swim. No trip along this highway is complete without taking the 20-minute hike to the breathtaking cascade of **Sabbaday Falls**; the trail begins at Mile 15 on the south side of the road. The best place to spot moose is along the shores of **Lily Pond**; stop at the roadside overview at Mile 18. At the Lincoln Woods ranger station, cross the suspension footbridge over the river and hike 3 miles to **Franconia Falls**, the finest swimming hole in the entire national forest, complete with a natural rock slide. Parking anywhere along the highway costs $3 per day (honor system) or $5 per week; just fill out an envelope at any of the parking areas.

The White Mountain National Forest is ideal for campers, and you'll find several campgrounds run by the forest service accessible from the Kancamagus Hwy. Most are on a first-come, first-served basis; pick up a list of them from one of the ranger stations that bookend the highway.

SLEEPING & EATING

Woodstock Inn (☎ 603-745-3951, 800-321-3985; www.woodstockinnnh.com; US 3, North Woodstock; r incl breakfast with shared bath $78-105, with private bath $95-200;) Spread across five historic houses in the heart of North Woodstock, this inn offers a variety of comfortable rooms, many furnished with antiques, some with fireplaces and Jacuzzi baths.

Wilderness Inn (☎ 603-745-3890, 800-777-7813; www.thewildernessinn.com; cnr US 3 & NH 112; r incl breakfast $95-175;) Gather round the fireplace with other guests at this century-old B&B with hardwood floors and country-style decor. Or if you want your own private space, swing for the cottage ($175) with a gas fireplace and oversized Jacuzzi tub. The multicourse breakfasts are marvelous.

Cascade Coffee House (☎ 603-745-2001; 115 Main St, North Woodstock; mains $4-8; 🕑 7am-3pm Mon-Fri, 7am-5pm Sat & Sun) This creative place in the center of town serves up luscious pastries, fresh smoothies and micro-roaster coffees. At lunch, you'll also find crispy panini sandwiches and innovative salads.

Woodstock Inn Station & Brewery (☎ 603-745-3951; US 3, North Woodstock; mains $8-22; 🕑 11:30am-10pm) If your family can't settle on what to eat, this brewpub satisfies an amazing range of food cravings with pub grub, steaks, pizza and Mexican fare. There's live entertainment on weekends in summer and frothy microbrewed ales year-round.

Franconia Notch State Park

Franconia Notch is the most celebrated mountain pass in New England, a narrow gorge shaped over the eons by a rushing stream slicing through the craggy granite. I-93, in places feeling more like a country road than a highway, runs straight through **Franconia Notch State Park** (admission free). The park **visitor center** (☎ 603-745-8391; www.franconianotchstatepark.com; I-93, exit 34A) is 4 miles north of North Woodstock at the side of the **Flume Gorge** (adult/child 6-12yr $12/8; 🕑 9am-5pm May-Oct), an awesome cleft in the granite bedrock. A 2-mile self-guided nature walk takes you right through the deep opening, which narrows to a mere 12ft, as water rushes at your feet.

The visitor center can give you details on other hikes in the park, ranging from short nature walks to day-long treks. For an enjoyable 20-minute stroll, stop at the **Basin** pull-off, between exits 34A and 34B, where a half-mile trail runs along a stream to a glacier-carved granite pool. The Basin is lovely. However, as swimming is not allowed here, to take a dip head to **Echo Lake Beach** (☎ 603-823-8800; adult/child $4/2; 🕑 10am-5:30pm),

NEW ENGLAND

exit 34C, where you can also rent kayaks, rowboats and canoes.

The **Cannon Mountain Aerial Tramway** (☎ 603-823-8800; I-93, exit 34B; round-trip adult/child 6-12yr $12/9; 9am-5pm late May–mid-Oct;) whisks you to the 4180ft summit for breathtaking views of Franconia Notch and the White Mountains.

Franconia Notch State Park's **Lafayette Place Campground** (☎ 603-823-9513, reservations 603-271-3628; campsites $25; late May–mid-Oct), a hub for hikers, has 97 wooded campsites, but they fill up early in summer, so it's best to reserve in advance.

A few miles north of Franconia Notch lies the **Frost Place** (☎ 603-823-5510; www.frostplace.org; Ridge Rd, Franconia; adult/child 6-18yr $5/3; 1-5pm Sat & Sun late May–Jun, 1-5pm Wed-Mon Jul–mid-Oct), the farm where poet Robert Frost (1874–1963) wrote his most famous poems, 'The Road Not Taken' and 'Stopping by Woods on a Snowy Evening.' It retains the simplicity and inspiration of Frost's day, free of flashy displays.

THE TENACIOUS OLD MAN

The Old Man of the Mountain is everywhere except on the mountain. This 40ft-tall natural rock profile that graced Franconia Notch for eons was the iconic image of the White Mountains for generations of visitors. And even though the old rock face collapsed and crumbled down the mountainside in 2003, this craggy symbol of the Granite State keeps appearing on brochures as if nothing ever happened. His stony face graces the commemorative New Hampshire quarter. He's plastered on state highway signs. And the old geezer's proud gaze still stares out from the 'Live Free or Die' license plates. Long live the Old Man.

Bretton Woods & Crawford Notch

Before 1944, Bretton Woods was known primarily as a low-key retreat for wealthy visitors who patronized the majestic Mt Washington Hotel. After President Roosevelt chose the hotel for the historic conference that established a new post-WWII economic order, the town's name took on worldwide recognition. The countryside, with Mt Washington looming above it, is as magnificent today as it was back then. The **Twin Mountain-Bretton Woods Chamber of Commerce** (☎ 800-245-8946; www.twinmountain.org; cnr US 302 & US 3, Twin Mountain) has details on the area.

The region's largest ski area, **Bretton Woods ski station** (☎ 603-278-3320; www.brettonwoods.com; US 302) offers both downhill and cross-country winter skiing.

US 302 heads south from Bretton Woods to Crawford Notch (1773ft) through stunning mountain scenery ripe with towering cascades. **Crawford Notch State Park** (☎ 603-374-2272; adult/child 6-11yr $4/2; mid-May–mid-Oct) maintains an extensive system of hiking trails, including short hikes around a pond and to a waterfall, and a longer trek up Mt Washington.

Inside Crawford Notch State Park, the **Dry River Campground** (☎ 603-271-3628; US 302; campsites $23; mid-May–mid-Dec) has 36 quiet sites and good facilities.

If walls could talk, the historic **Mt Washington Hotel** (☎ 603-278-1000, 800-314-1752; www.mountwashingtonresort.com; US 302; r $219-600;) could spin quite a tale. Opened in 1902, this grande dame of New England mountain resorts boasts 2600 acres of grounds, 27 holes of golf, 12 clay tennis courts, a pair of heated pools and an equestrian center.

Mt Washington

From Pinkham Notch (2032ft), on NH 16 about 11 miles north of North Conway, a system of hiking trails provides access to the natural beauties of the Presidential Range, including lofty **Mt Washington** (6288ft), the highest mountain east of the Mississippi and north of the Smoky Mountains. Hikers need to be prepared: Mt Washington's weather is notoriously severe and can turn on a dime. Dress warmly – not only does the mountain register New England's coldest temperatures (in summer, the average at the summit is 45°F) but unrelenting winds make it feel colder than the thermometer reading.

One of the most popular trails up Mt Washington begins at the AMC's Pinkham Notch Visitor Center and runs 4.2 strenuous miles to the summit, taking four to five hours to reach the top and a bit less on the way down. If your quads aren't up for a workout, the **Mt Washington Auto Road** (☎ 603-466-3988; www.mountwashingtonautoroad.com; car & driver $23, extra adult/child 5-12yr $8/6; mid-May–mid-Oct) offers easier summit access, weather permitting.

While purists walk, and the out-of-shape drive, the quaintest way to reach the summit is to take the **Mt Washington Cog Railway** (☎ 603-278-5404, 800-922-8825; www

.thecog.com; adult/child 4-12yr $59/39, ⌚ May-Oct). Since 1869, coal-fired steam-powered locomotives have followed a 3.5-mile track up a steep mountainside trestle for a jaw-dropping excursion.

The **Pinkham Notch Visitor Center** (☎ 603-466-2727; www.outdoors.org; NH 16; ⌚ 6:30am-10pm), run by the Appalachian Mountain Club (AMC), is the area's informational nexus for like-minded adventurers and a good place to buy hiking necessities, including topographic trail maps and the handy *AMC White Mountain Guide*.

The AMC runs the adjacent **Joe Dodge Lodge** (☎ 603-466-2727; dm incl breakfast & dinner $67). **Dolly Copp Campground** (☎ 603-466-2713, 877-444-6777; NH 16; campsites $20), a USFS campground 6 miles north of the AMC's Pinkham Notch facilities, has 176 simple campsites.

HANOVER

The archetypal New England college town, Hanover has a town green that is bordered on all four sides by the handsome brick edifices of Dartmouth College. Virtually the whole town is given over to this Ivy League school; chartered in 1769, Dartmouth is the nation's ninth-oldest college.

Main St, rolling down from the green, is bordered by perky pubs and cafés catering to the collegian crowd. **Hanover Area Chamber of Commerce** (☎ 603-643-3115; www.hanoverchamber.org; 53 S Main St; ⌚ 9am-5pm Mon-Fri) is a good place to start your visit. Parking is restricted on campus, but there's on-street parking along Main St.

Sights & Activities

Hanover is all about Dartmouth College, so hit the campus. If you'd like to join a free student-guided **campus walking tour** (☎ 603-646-2875; www.dartmouth.edu), see the calendar online for tour times. Or just pick up a map at the admissions office and head off on your own. Don't miss the **Baker-Berry Library** (☎ 603-646-2560; ⌚ 8am-10pm), splashed with the grand *Epic of American Civilization*, painted by the outspoken Mexican muralist José Clemente Orozco (1883–1949), who taught at Dartmouth in the 1930s.

The collections at Dartmouth's **Hood Museum of Art** (☎ 603-646-2808; Wheelock St; admission free; ⌚ 10am-5pm Tue & Thu-Sat, 10am-9pm Wed, noon-5pm Sun) cover a wide swath from Assyrian stone reliefs dating to 883 BC to contemporary American art by heavyweights Jackson Pollock and Edward Hopper.

Sleeping & Eating

Chieftain Motor Inn (☎ 603-643-2550; www.chieftaininn.com; 84 Lyme Rd/NH 10; r $99-140; ❄ 📶 🚭) In a riverfront setting on the north side of town, this rustic inn offers complimentary use of canoes, making it a good spot to combine an outing with a night's sleep.

Lou's (☎ 603-643-3321; 30 S Main St; mains $4-8; ⌚ 6am-3pm Mon-Fri, 7am-3pm Sat & Sun) A student haunt since 1947, Lou's has good sandwiches and pastries, but everybody comes to this simple diner for the hearty breakfasts served until closing.

Canoe Club Bistro (☎ 603-643-9660; 27 S Main St; mains $10-20; ⌚ 11:30am-11:30pm) This smart café does a fine job with grilled food – not just burgers and steaks, but also tasty treats like open-faced lamb pita. There's also live entertainment nightly – anything from acoustic to jazz.

Drinking & Entertainment

Murphy's on the Green (☎ 603-643-4075; 11 S Main St; ⌚ 11am-1am) At this classic Irish pub, students and faculty discuss weighty matters over pints of Irish ale.

Hopkins Center for the Arts (☎ 603-646-2422; www.hop.dartmouth.edu; Lebanon St) The 'Hop' is Dartmouth's refined venue for string quartets, modern dance and plays.

MAINE

Maine is New England's frontier – a land so vast it could swallow the region's five other states with scarcely a gulp. Its coast, with sandy beaches in the south and craggy mountains in the north, extends some 3500 miles, if you were to travel along its deeply indented shoreline. While time-honored fishing villages and seaside lobster joints are the fame of Maine, inland travel also offers ample reward. Maine's rugged interior is given over to rushing rivers, dense forests and lofty mountains just aching to be explored.

As a traveler in Maine, your choices are as spectacularly varied as the landscape. You can opt to sail serenely along the coast on a graceful schooner or rip through white-water rapids on a river raft, spend the night in an

MAINE FACTS

Nickname Pine Tree State
Population 1.3 million
Area 35,387 sq miles
Capital city Augusta (population 18,560)
Other cities Portland (population 63, 011)
Sales tax 5%
Birthplace of Poet Henry Wadsworth Longfellow (1807–82)
Home of Horror novelist Stephen King
Famous for Lobster, moose, blueberries, LL Bean
State drink Maine gave the world Moxie, America's first (1884) and spunkiest soft drink
Driving distances Portland to Acadia National Park 160 miles, Portland to Boston 150 miles

old sea captain's home-turned-B&B, or camp among the moose on a backwoods lake.

History

It's estimated that 20,000 Native Americans from several tribes known collectively as Wabanaki ('People of the Dawn') inhabited Maine before the arrival of Europeans. The French and English vied to establish colonies in Maine during the 1600s, but, deterred by the harsh winters, these settlements failed.

In 1652 Massachusetts annexed the territory of Maine to provide a front line of defense against potential attacks during the French and Indian Wars. And indeed Maine at times did become a battlefield between English colonists in New England and French forces in Canada. In the early 19th century, in an attempt to settle sparsely populated Maine, 100-acre homesteads were offered free to settlers willing to farm the land. In 1820 Maine broke from Massachusetts and entered the Union as a state.

In 1851 Maine became the first state to ban the sale of alcoholic beverages, the start of a temperance movement that eventually took hold throughout the United States. It wasn't until 1934 that Prohibition was finally lifted.

Information

If you're entering the state on the I-95 heading north, stop at the well-stocked visitor information center on the highway.

Maine Bureau of Parks and Land (☎ 800-332-1501; www.maine.gov/doc/parks; campsites $10-27) Offers camping in 12 state parks.

Maine Office of Tourism (☎ 888-624-6345; www.visitmaine.com) Will send out a handy 288-page magazine on Maine destinations.

Maine Tourism Association (☎ 207-623-0363; www.mainetourism.com) Links regional tourist offices throughout Maine.

SOUTHERN MAINE COAST

Maine's most touristed quarter, this seaside region lures visitors with its sandy beaches, resort towns and outlet shopping. The best place to stop for the latter is the southernmost town of Kittery, which is chockablock with outlet stores.

Ogunquit

Aptly named, Ogunquit means 'Beautiful Place by the Sea' in the native Abenaki tongue, and its 3-mile beach has long been a magnet for summer visitors. Ogunquit Beach, a sandy barrier beach, separates the Ogunquit River from the Atlantic Ocean, offering beachgoers the appealing option to swim in cool ocean surf or in the warmer, calmer cove.

As a New England beach destination, Ogunquit is second only to Provincetown for the number of gay travelers who vacation here. Most of the town lies along Main St (US 1), lined with restaurants, shops and motels. For waterfront dining and boating activities head to Perkins Cove at the south end of town.

The **Ogunquit Chamber of Commerce** (☎ 207-646-2939; www.ogunquit.org; 36 Main St; 9am-5pm) has visitor information.

SIGHTS & ACTIVITIES

A highlight is walking the scenic 1.5-mile **Marginal Way**, the coastal footpath that skirts the 'margin' of the sea from Shore Rd, near the center of town, to Perkins Cove. A sublime stretch of family-friendly coastline, **Ogunquit Beach**, also called Main Beach by locals, begins right in the town center at the end of Beach St.

Ogunquit Playhouse (☎ 207-646-5511; www.ogunquitplayhouse.org; 10 Main St;), which first opened in 1933, presents both showy Broadway musicals and children's theater each summer.

Finestkind Scenic Cruises (☎ 207-646-5227; www.finestkindcruises.com; Perkins Cove; adult/child from $15/8;) offers several boat cruises, including cool 50-minute voyages to pull up lobster traps.

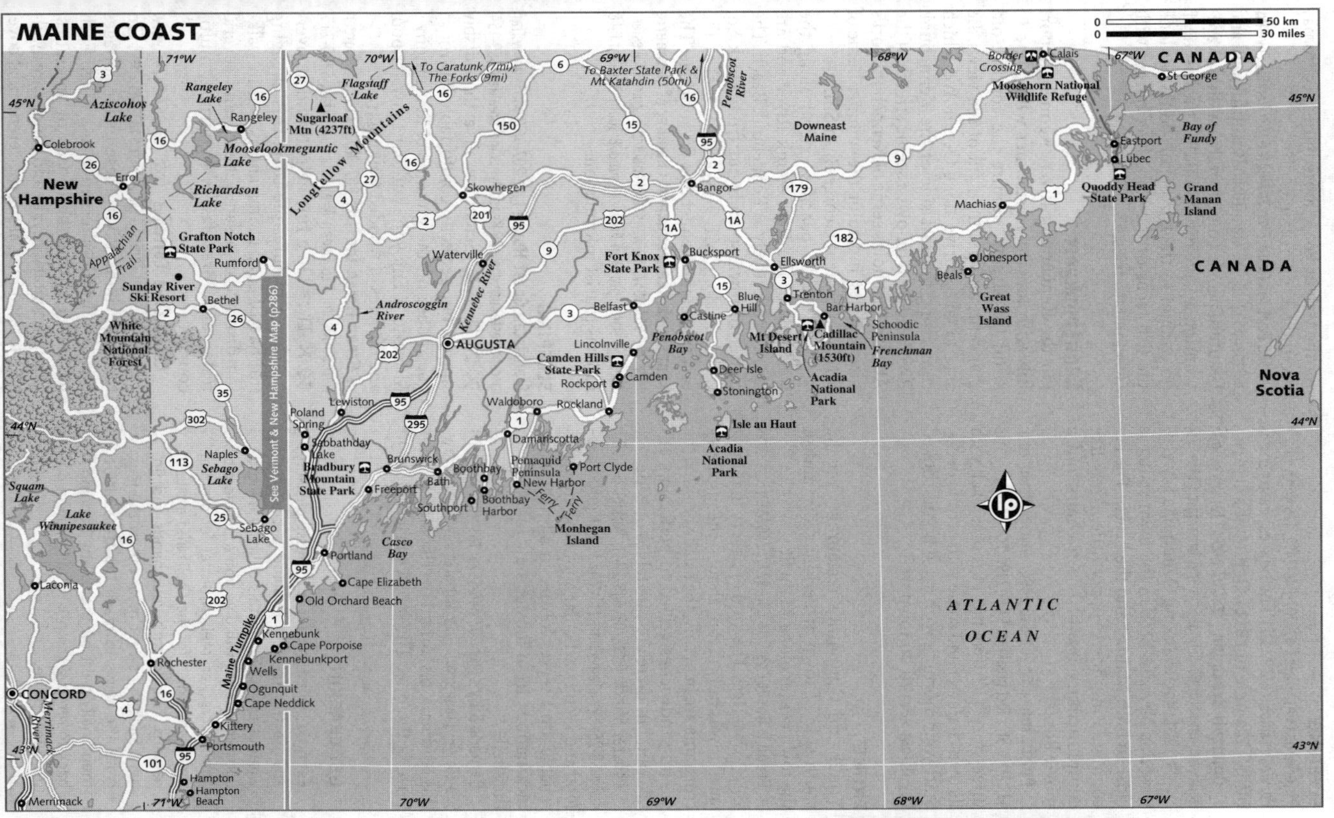
MAINE COAST
0 50 km
0 30 miles
CANADA
St George
Bay of Fundy
Grand Manan Island
CANADA
Nova Scotia
Eastport
Lubec
Quoddy Head State Park
Border Crossing
Calais
Moosehorn National Wildlife Refuge
Machias
Jonesport
Beals
Great Wass Island
ATLANTIC
OCEAN
Schoodic Peninsula
Frenchman Bay
Bar Harbor
Cadillac Mountain (1530ft)
Acadia National Park
Trenton
Mt Desert Island
Ellsworth
Downeast Maine
Blue Hill
Castine
Deer Isle
Stonington
Isle au Haut
Acadia National Park
Penobscot River
Bangor
Bucksport
Fort Knox State Park
Penobscot Bay
To Baxter State Park & Mt Katahdin (50mi)
Belfast
Lincolnville
Camden
Camden Hills State Park
Rockport
Rockland
Port Clyde
Pemaquid Peninsula
New Harbor
Ferry
Ferry
Monhegan Island
Damariscotta
Waldoboro
Boothbay
Boothbay Harbor
Southport
Bath
Brunswick
Freeport
Casco Bay
Cape Elizabeth
Portland
Old Orchard Beach
Kennebunk
Cape Porpoise
Kennebunkport
Wells
Ogunquit
Cape Neddick
Kittery
Portsmouth
Hampton
Hampton Beach
Maine Turnpike
AUGUSTA
Kennebec River
Waterville
Skowhegan
To Caratunk (7mi), The Forks (9mi)
Androscoggin River
Lewiston
Sabbathday Lake
Poland Spring
Bradbury Mountain State Park
Longfellow Mountains
Flagstaff Lake
Sugarloaf Mtn (4237ft)
Mooselookmeguntic Lake
Rangeley
Rangeley Lake
Richardson Lake
Grafton Notch State Park
Rumford
Bethel
Sunday River Ski Resort
See Vermont & New Hampshire Map (p286)
Sebago Lake
Naples
Sebago Lake
White Mountain National Forest
Appalachian Trail
Errol
Aziscohos Lake
Colebrook
New Hampshire
Lake Winnipesaukee
Squam Lake
Laconia
Rochester
CONCORD
Merrimack River
Merrimack
45°N
44°N
43°N
67°W
68°W
69°W
70°W
71°W

NEW ENGLAND

SLEEPING

Pinederosa Camping (☎ 207-646-2492; 128 North Village Rd, Wells; campsites $28;) The nearest camping is off US 1, a mile north of Ogunquit's center.

Ogunquit Beach Inn (☎ 207-646-1112; www.ogunquitbeachinn.com; 67 School St; r incl breakfast $119-179;) A favorite among Ogunquit's gay visitors, this pleasant B&B in the town center is close to both Main St and the beach. The accommodating hosts supply little extras like complimentary use of beach chairs and a movie library.

Puffin Inn (☎ 207-646-5496; www.puffininn.com; 433 Main St; r incl breakfast $119-219;) This three-story Victorian has 11 rooms, each with its own character and some with private decks. Start your morning with a full home-cooked breakfast served on the porch.

EATING

You'll find Ogunquit's restaurants on the south side of town at Perkins Cove and in the town center along Main St.

Bread & Roses (☎ 207-646-4227; 246 Main St; snacks $3-8; 7am-11pm) The kind of bakery that most small towns only dream about – the raspberry croissants are heavenly, the salads healthy, the panini sandwiches grilled to perfection. It's takeout, but there are café tables outside.

Lobster Shack (☎ 207-646-2941; Perkins Cove Rd; mains $8-25; 11am-8pm) If you want good seafood and aren't particular about the view, this reliable joint serves lobster in all its various incarnations from lobster stew to lobster in the shell.

Barnacle Billy's (☎ 207-646-5575; 183 Shore Rd; mains $10-35; 11am-9pm) For lobsters with a view, this landmark restaurant overlooking Perkins Cove is the one. The lobster prices depend on the weight you choose but expect to pay around $30 on average.

MC Perkins Cove (☎ 207-646-6263; Perkins Cove Rd; bar menu $12-20; 11am-10pm) Beautiful food and beautiful people come together at this award-winning seaside restaurant. For the best deal, go straight to the bar menu: don't overlook the fish tacos or the Kobe beef burger with sweet potato fries.

GET CRACKIN'

Eating a boiled lobster is a messy pleasure and no trip to New England is complete without experiencing this culinary delight. Lobster eateries will give you a plastic bib, a metal cracker, melted butter for dipping the meat, a dish for the shells and a pile of napkins. Tear in with your hands and fingers. Suck the sweet meat out of the legs, crack the claws to reach the treat inside, then finally twist off the tail by bending it back to remove the prized tail meat in one succulent piece.

Kennebunkport

On the Kennebunk River, Kennebunkport fills with tourists in summer who come to stroll the streets, admire the century-old mansions and get their fill of sea views. Be sure to take a drive along Ocean Ave, which runs along the east side of the Kennebunk River and then follows a scenic stretch of the Atlantic that holds some of Kennebunkport's finest estates, including the summer home of former president George Bush Snr.

Three public beaches extend along the west side of the Kennebunk River and are known collectively as Kennebunk Beach. The center of town spreads out from Dock Sq, which is along ME 9 (Western Ave) at the east side of the Kennebunk River bridge. The **Kennebunk/Kennebunkport Chamber of Commerce** (☎ 207-967-0857; www.visitthekennebunks.com; 17 Western Ave; 9am-5pm Mon-Fri year-round, 8:30am-3pm Sat Jul & Aug) has tourist information.

SLEEPING

Franciscan Guest House (☎ 207-967-4865; www.franciscanguesthouse.com; 26 Beach Ave; r incl breakfast $89-154;) Serenity awaits at this suitably simple, but perfectly comfortable, 50-room guesthouse on the grounds of St Anthony's Monastery. Enjoy the outdoor saltwater pool and 60 acres of wooded walking trails.

Green Heron Inn (☎ 207-967-3315; www.greenheroninn.com; 126 Ocean Ave; r incl breakfast $180-215;) In a fine neighborhood, overlooking a picturesque cove, this engaging inn has 10 cozy rooms and is within walking distance of a sandy beach and several restaurants. Breakfast is a gourmet, multicourse event.

Cabot Cove Cottages (☎ 207-967-5424; www.cabotcovecottages.com; 7 S Maine St; r $185-345;) On the Kennebunk River, these idyllic cottages offer a splendid alternative to a hotel. Each has a full kitchen and loads of amenities. Complimentary kayaks and canoes are available for paddling along the serene tidal cove.

EATING

Clam Shack (☎ 207-967-2560; 2 Western Ave; mains $7-20; 11am-9:30pm) By the bridge at the west side of the Kennebunk River, this simple joint is justifiably famous for its fried clams, but the lobster roll overflowing with succulent chunks of lobster is the ultimate prize here.

Hurricane (☎ 207-967-9111; 29 Dock Sq; lunch mains $10-20, dinner $20-40; 11:30am-9:30pm) Right on the water with great food and a wonderful sense of place. If you're not whizzing through and have time for a leisurely lunch, order the hand-picked Maine crabmeat sandwich on sourdough, a glass of wine and enjoy the view.

Bandaloop (☎ 207-967-4994; 2 Dock Sq; mains $17-23; 5-10pm) Local, organic and deliciously innovative, running the gamut from pork chops with Yukon gold potatoes to baked tofu with hemp-seed crust and seaweed salad. Whew!

PORTLAND

The 18th-century poet Henry Wadsworth Longfellow referred to his childhood city as the 'jewel by the sea,' and thanks to a hefty revitalization effort, Portland once again sparkles. Its lively waterfront, burgeoning gallery scene and manageable size (population 63,000) add up to great exploring. Foodies, rev up your taste buds: cutting-edge cafés and chef-driven restaurants have turned Portland into the hottest dining scene north of Boston.

Orientation & Information

Portland sits on a hilly peninsula surrounded on three sides by water: Back Cove, Casco Bay and the Fore River. It's easy to find your way around. Commercial St (US 1A) runs along the waterfront through the Old Port, while the parallel Congress St is the main thoroughfare through downtown, passing the art museum, city hall and banks.

Greater Portland Convention & Visitors Bureau (☎ 207-772-5800; www.visitportland.com; 14 Ocean Gateway Pier; 8:30am-5pm Mon-Fri, 10am-3pm Sat year-round, 10am-3pm Sun Jul-Aug) Pick up a free Portland guide here.

JavaNet Cafe (☎ 207-773-2469; 37 Exchange St; per 15min $2; 7am-9pm Mon-Fri, 8am-9pm Sat, 8am-5pm Sun;) Internet café with good java.

Maine Medical Center (☎ 207-662-0111; 22 Bramhall St; 24hr)

Portland Phoenix (www.thephoenix.com/portland) Free alternative weekly newspaper, covering events and entertainment.

DON'T MISS

- The Winslow Homer collection at the Portland Museum of Art (below)
- Blueberry cream scones at Standard Baking Co (p306)
- A pint of Black Fly stout at Gritty McDuff's (p307)

Portland Public Library (☎ 207-871-1700; 5 Monument Sq; 10am-7pm Tue-Thu, 10am-6pm Fri, 10am-5pm Sat;) Fifteen-minute free internet access.

Post office (☎ 800-275-8777; 400 Congress St; 8am-7pm Mon-Fri, 9am-1pm Sat)

Sights & Activities

OLD PORT

Portland's heart thumps from the **Old Port**, where salt-scented breezes, brick sidewalks and lamp-lit streets just beg for poking about. This restored waterfront district centers on the handsome 19th-century buildings lining Commercial St and the narrow side streets extending a few blocks inland. Once home to the brawny warehouses and merchant quarters of a bustling port, the focus has shifted from shipping to shopping. This gentrified neighborhood now houses many of Portland's finest restaurants, pubs, boutiques and galleries.

Head to waterfront Commercial St for an eclectic food and drink scene, to Exchange and Fore Sts for gallery row. Seek out **Maine Potters Market** (☎ 207-774-1633; 376 Fore St), a collective of 15 of Maine's best potters; **Abacus** (☎ 207-772-4880; 44 Exchange St) for jewelry, glass and lots of colorful gift items; and **Edgecomb Potters** (☎ 207-780-6727; 49 Exchange St), where contemporary pottery, glass and sculpture rules.

MUSEUMS & HISTORIC BUILDINGS

Works of Maine painters Winslow Homer, Edward Hopper and Andrew Wyeth are showcased at the **Portland Museum of Art** (☎ 207-775-6148; www.portlandmuseum.org; 7 Congress Sq; adult/child 6-17yr $10/4, 5-9pm Fri free; 10am-5pm Sat-Thu, 10am-9pm Fri, closed Mon mid-Oct–May). Maine's finest art museum also boasts solid contemporary collections; post-Impressionist works by Picasso, Monet and Renoir; and a brilliant collection of Portland art glass. If you enjoy period homes, be sure to stroll through the restored 1801 **McLellan House**, entered through the museum and included in the ticket price.

Folks with kids in tow should head for the **Children's Museum of Maine** (☎ 207-828-1234; www.childrensmuseumofme.org; 142 Free St; admission $8; 10am-5pm Mon-Sat, noon-5pm Sun, closed Mon Sep-May;). This house of fun is conveniently next to the Portland Museum of Art.

The **Longfellow House** (☎ 207-879-0427; 489 Congress St; adult/child 5-17yr $8/3; 10am-5pm Mon-Sat, noon-5pm Sun May-Oct), the childhood home of Henry Wadsworth Longfellow (1807–82), retains its original character, complete with the poet's family furnishings. Admission includes entry to the adjacent **Maine Historical Society Museum**, which has exhibits on the state's history.

History buffs won't want to miss the hilltop **Portland Observatory Museum** (☎ 207-774-5561; 138 Congress St; adult/child 6-16yr $7/4; 10am-5pm late May–early Oct), built in 1807 as a maritime signal station to direct ships entering the bustling harbor. Its function was roughly on par with that of an airport traffic control tower today. From the top of this observatory, the last of its kind remaining in the USA, you'll be rewarded with a sweeping view of Casco Bay.

AROUND PORTLAND

Up for a picnic in an unbeatable setting? Head 4 miles south of central Portland to Cape Elizabeth and the 90-acre **Fort Williams Park** (admission free; sunrise-sunset) where you'll find **Portland Head Light** (☎ 207-799-2661; 1000 Shore Rd, Cape Elizabeth; lighthouse museum adult/child 6-18yr $2/1; 10am-4pm Jun-Oct), New England's most photographed lighthouse and the oldest (1791) of Maine's more than 60 lighthouses.

For a whole different angle on Portland and Casco Bay, hop one of the boats offering narrated scenic cruises out of Portland Harbor. **Casco Bay Lines** (☎ 207-774-7871; www.cascobaylines.com; 56 Commercial St; adult $13-24, child 5-9yr $6-11) tours the Portland coast and Casco Bay islands on a variety of cruises that last from 1¾ to six hours. You can also have Casco Bay Lines drop you off at Peaks Island and then hook up with **Maine Island Kayak Company** (☎ 207-766-2373; www.maineislandkayak.com; 70 Luther St, Peaks Island, Portland; tour $65; May-Nov) for a half-day kayak tour of the bay. For a classy sail, the **Portland Schooner Company** (☎ 207-776-2500; www.portlandschooner.com; 56 Commercial St, Portland; adult/child 2-12yr $35/15; May-Oct) offers two-hour trips aboard a pair of elegant Maine-built, century-old wooden schooners.

Landlubbers can ride the rails on the antique steam trains of the **Maine Narrow Gauge Railroad Co & Museum** (☎ 207-828-0814; www.mngrr.org; 58 Fore St; adult/child 3-12yr $10/6; 11am-4pm mid-May–Oct, shorter hours low season;) for a journey departing on the hour along Casco Bay.

Sleeping

In addition to in-town choices, there are several chain hotels south of the city near the airport.

Inn at St John (☎ 207-773-6481, 800-636-9127; www.innatstjohn.com; 939 Congress St; r incl breakfast $69-129;) Built in 1897 to accommodate train passengers arriving at the old Union Station, this Victorian hotel retains its period character with style. One caveat: the location opposite the bus station and hospital can be noisy. Light sleepers should request room 102 – no windows and whisper quiet.

La Quinta Inn (☎ 207-871-0611; www.laquinta.com; 340 Park St; r incl breakfast $69-129;) The best value among the chain operations, La Quinta has well-maintained rooms and a good in-town location opposite the ballpark of the Portland Sea Dogs, a Boston Red Sox–affiliate team.

Inn at Park Spring (☎ 207-774-1059, 800-437-8511; www.innatparkspring.com; 135 Spring St; r incl breakfast $139-185;) Friendly innkeepers, comfortable rooms and a convenient location within easy walking distance of the port add to the appeal of this period B&B.

Eating

Standard Baking Co (☎ 207-773-2112; 75 Commercial St; snacks $2-4; 7am-6pm Mon-Fri, 7am-5pm Sat & Sun) For a sweet breakfast treat, head to this Old Port bakery and order a blueberry cream scone and chocolate croissant. Portland's best organic rustic breads are made here too.

Duckfat (☎ 207-774-8080; 43 Middle St; mains $6-10; 11am-9pm Mon-Sat, 10am-5pm Sun) If you have gourmet taste on a fast-food budget, this one-of-a-kind eatery won't disappoint. Try the innovative panini sandwiches, the duck confit salad, and, if you have a tolerance for grease, the signature fries crisped in duck fat with truffle-ketchup dip.

our pick **Green Elephant** (☎ 207-347-3111; 608 Congress St; mains $9-13; 11:30am-2:30pm & 5-9:30pm Tue-Sat; V) Even carnivores shouldn't miss the brilliant vegetarian fare at this Zen-chic, Thai-inspired café. Start with the crispy spinach wontons, then move on to one of the exotic soy creations like gingered 'duck' with shiitake mushrooms. Do save room for the incredible chocolate orange mousse pie.

Portland Lobster Co (☎ 207-775-2112; 180 Commercial St; mains $10-22; 🕑 11am-9pm) Lobster stew, lobster rolls and lobster dinners shore up the menu at this harborfront shack. Take your meal to the deck and watch the boats pull up as you get crackin'.

Hugo's (☎ 207-774-8538; 88 Middle St; mains $25-32; 🕑 5:30-9pm Tue-Thu, to 9:30pm Fri & Sat) If you have just one night to splurge let it be here. Owner-chef Rob Evans won the coveted James Beard Award in 2009 as the top chef in the Northeast. Trained at Napa Valley's elite restaurant French Laundry, Evans masterfully fuses California influences with fresh New England ingredients. Pistachio-encrusted lobster anyone?

Drinking & Entertainment

Gritty McDuff's (☎ 207-772-2739; 396 Fore St; 🕑 11am-1am) This Old Port brewpub has it all: harbor views, high energy, good pub grub and award-winning ales. Order up a robust pint of Black Fly stout and join the crowd.

North Star Music Café (☎ 207-699-2994; 225 Congress St) There's always something going on at this little café. The packed calendar features acoustic music, jazz nights, local singer-songwriters and open mike. Hours vary.

Styxx (☎ 207-828-0822; 3 Spring St; 🕑 4pm-1am) Drag shows, hot DJs and a huge dance floor make Styxx the top draw for the gay and lesbian community.

Getting There & Around

Portland International Jetport (PWM; ☎ 207-774-7301; www.portlandjetport.org) is served by domestic airlines, with nonstop flights to cities in the eastern US.

Greyhound (☎ 800-231-2222; www.greyhound.com) buses and **Amtrak** (☎ 800-872-7245; www.amtrak.com) trains connect Portland and Boston; both take about 2½ hours and charge $24 one way.

The local bus **Metro** (☎ 207-774-0351; www.gpmetrobus.com; fares $1.25), which runs throughout the city, has its main terminus at Monument Sq, the intersection of Elm and Congress Sts.

CENTRAL MAINE COAST

Midcoast Maine is where the mountains meet the sea. You'll find craggy peninsulas jutting deep into the Atlantic, alluring seaside villages and endless opportunities for hiking, sailing and kayaking.

Freeport

The fame and fortune of Freeport, 16 miles northeast of Portland, began a century ago when Leon Leonwood Bean opened a shop to sell equipment to hunters and fishers heading north into the Maine wilderness. Bean's good value earned him loyal customers, and over the years the **LL Bean store** (☎ 800-341-4341; www.llbean.com; Main St; 🕑 24hr) has expanded to add sportswear to its outdoor gear. Although a hundred other stores have joined the pack, the wildly popular LL Bean is still the epicenter of town.

Ironically, this former stopover for hardy outdoor types is now devoted entirely to city-style shopping, consisting of a mile-long Main St (US 1) lined with outlet stores that sell everything from dinnerware to shoes. **Freeport Merchants Association** (☎ 207-865-1212, 800-865-1994; www.freeportusa.com; 23 Depot St; 🕑 9am-5pm Mon-Fri) provides information.

Although 'shop till you drop' may be the town's motto, there's no need to stay on your feet all night – this town has some two dozen inns.

The innkeepers make you feel right at home at the beautifully restored **Kendall Tavern B&B** (☎ 207-865-1338, 800-341-9572; www.kendalltavern.com; 213 Main St; r incl breakfast $140-175; ⊠ ⁘), a farmhouse at the quieter north side of the town center. Blueberry pancakes or similar treats greet guests at breakfast.

A favorite with shoppers, **Lobster Cooker** (☎ 207-865-4349; 39 Main St; mains $8-22; 🕑 11am-7pm Sun-Fri, 11am-8pm Sat), just south of LL Bean, has generous fish sandwiches, homemade chowders and steamed lobsters.

For the best atmosphere, head to the casual, harbor-side **Harraseeket Lunch & Lobster Co** (☎ 207-865-4888; 36 Main St, South Freeport; mains $9-25; 🕑 11am-7:30pm, to 8:45pm Jul & Aug), 3 miles south of Freeport center, for its popular lobster dinners, steamers and fried seafood. Feast at picnic tables within spitting distance of the bay.

Bath

Bath has been renowned for shipbuilding since Colonial times and that remains the raison d'être for the town today. **Bath Iron Works**, one of the largest shipyards in the USA, builds steel frigates and other ships for the US Navy. The substantial **Maine Maritime Museum** (☎ 207-443-1316; 243 Washington St; adult/child

4-17yr $12/9; 9:30am-5pm), south of the ironworks on the Kennebec River, showcases the town's centuries-old maritime history, which included construction of the six-mast schooner *Wyoming*, the largest wooden vessel ever built in the USA.

Boothbay Harbor

On a fjord-like harbor, this achingly picturesque fishing village with narrow, winding streets is thick with tourists in the summer. Other than eating lobster, the main activity here is hopping on boats. **Balmy Days Cruises** (207-633-2284, 800-298-2284; www.balmydayscruises.com; Pier 8) runs one-hour harbor tours (adult/child aged three to 12 years $14/7) and day trips to Monhegan Island (adult/child $38/25). **Cap'n Fish's Boat Trips** (207-633-3244, 800-636-3244; www.mainewhales.com; Pier 1;) offers four-hour whale-watching trips (adult/child aged six to 10 years $38/25). **Tidal Transit** (207-633-7140; 18 Granary Way) leads three-hour kayak tours ($35 to $40) up coastal waters where wildlife abounds. The **Boothbay Harbor Region Chamber of Commerce** (207-633-2353; www.boothbayharbor.com; 192 Townsend Ave; 9am-5pm Mon-Fri, 10am-5pm Sat) provides visitor information.

SLEEPING & EATING

Gray Homestead (207-633-4612; www.graysoceancamping.com; 21 Homestead Rd, Southport; campsites $35) Fall asleep to the lull of the surf at this oceanside campground 4 miles south of Boothbay Harbor via ME 27 and 238.

Tugboat Inn (207-633-4434, 800-248-2628; www.tugboatinn.com; 80 Commercial St; r incl breakfast $99-169;) Wings of this hotel, literally hanging over the water, are on piers, offering the most amazing water views you'll ever experience without being on a boat. You could cast a fishing pole from your front door. The rooms themselves are straightforward, nothing fancy – this is all about the setting.

Topside Inn (207-633-5404, 877-486-7466; www.topsideinn.com; 60 McKown St; r incl breakfast $125-225;) Perched on a hilltop, this 19th-century sea captain's house turned B&B has 21 comfortable rooms, hospitable owners and a quiet location. Request an upper-floor room in the main house for a stunning panorama.

Blue Moon Cafe (207-633-2220; 54 Commercial St; mains $4-7; 7:30am-2:30pm) Get a $5 breakfast with a million-dollar view on the waterfront deck of this family-run café serving omelets, blueberry pancakes and sandwiches.

Lobster Dock (207-633-7120; 49 Atlantic Ave; mains $10-20; 11:30am-8:30pm) Boothbay Harbor crawls with lobster eateries. This is one of the best and cheapest. From chunky lobster stew to boiled lobster in the shell, this seaside place perfects everything that can be done with Maine's signature shellfish.

Monhegan Island

This small granite island with high cliffs and crashing surf, 9 miles off the Maine coast, attracts summer day-trippers, artists and nature-lovers who find inspiration in the dramatic views and agreeable isolation. Tidy and manageable, Monhegan is just 1.5 miles long and a half-mile wide. The website **Monhegan Commons** (www.monhegan.com) has island information and accommodation links. Rooms typically book out in summer, so plan ahead if you're not just visiting on a day trip.

In addition to its 17 miles of walking trails, there's an 1824 **lighthouse** with a small museum in the former keeper's house and several artists' studios that you can poke your head into.

The 28 rooms in the 1870 **Monhegan House** (207-594-7983; www.monheganhouse.com; s/d incl breakfast $85/150;) have shared baths but offer cheery ocean and lighthouse views. The café at the Monhegan House sells pizza, sandwiches and ice cream.

Departing from Port Clyde, the **Monhegan Boat Line** (207-372-8848; www.monheganboat.com; round-trip adult/child 2-12yr $32/18) runs three trips daily to Monhegan from late May to mid-October, once a day for the rest of the year. The **MV Hardy III** (800-278-3346; www.hardyboat.com; round-trip adult/child under 12yr $32/18; mid-Jun–Sep) departs for Monhegan twice daily from New Harbor, on the east side of the Pemaquid Peninsula. Both boats take approximately one hour and both have early morning departures and late-afternoon returns, perfect for day-tripping.

Camden

With rolling hills as a backdrop and a harbor full of sailboats, Camden is a gem. Home to Maine's justly famed fleet of windjammers (see the boxed text, p310), it attracts nautical-minded souls.

You can get a superb view of pretty Camden and its surroundings by taking the 45-minute climb up Mt Battie in **Camden Hills State Park** (207-236-3109; 280 Belfast Rd/US 1; adult/

WORTH THE TRIP: PEMAQUID PENINSULA

Adorning the southernmost tip of the Pemaquid Peninsula, **Pemaquid Point** is one of the most wildly beautiful places in Maine, with its tortured igneous rock formations pounded by treacherous seas. Perched atop the rocks in the 7-acre **Lighthouse Park** (☎ 207-677-2494; Pemaquid Point; adult/child under 12yr $2/free; 🕑 sunrise-sunset) is the 11,000 candle power Pemaquid Light, built in 1827. A climb to the top will reward you with a fine coastal view. A star of the 61 surviving lighthouses along the Maine coast, you may well be carrying an image of Pemaquid Light in your pocket without knowing it – it's the beauty featured on the back of the Maine state quarter. The keeper's house now serves as the **Fishermen's Museum** (🕑 9am-5:30pm mid-May–mid-Oct) displaying period photos, old fishing gear and lighthouse paraphernalia. Admission is included in the park fee.

Off the main highway, Pemaquid Point is bypassed by the masses today, but artists are still drawn here in great numbers and in summertime a small art museum opens on the grounds of Lighthouse Park. Pemaquid Peninsula is 15 miles south of US 1 via ME 130.

child 5-11yr $4.50/1; 🕑 7am-sunset) at the north side of Camden.

Lobster fanatics (and who isn't!) won't want to miss the **Maine Lobster Festival** (www.mainelobsterfestival.com), New England's ultimate homage to the crusty crustacean, held near the beginning of August in nearby Rockland.

The **Camden-Rockport-Lincolnville Chamber of Commerce** (☎ 207-236-4404, 800-223-5459; www.camdenme.org; 2 Public Landing; 🕑 9am-5pm Mon-Sat, 10am-4pm Sun), near the harbor, provides visitor information on the region.

SLEEPING & EATING

Camden Hills State Park (☎ 207-236-3109; 280 Belfast Rd/US 1; campsites $27; 🕑 mid-May–mid-Oct) This popular park has 107 forested campsites and 30 miles of scenic hiking trails; reservations are advised in midsummer.

Camden Maine Stay Inn (☎ 207-236-9636; www.camdenmainestay.com; 22 High St; r incl breakfast $130-290) This stately 1802 home has lovely gardens, an agreeable period ambience and a fine location, just a couple blocks from restaurants and the waterfront. The friendly owners offer eight nicely appointed rooms and can share a wealth of insights on the area.

Captain Swift Inn (☎ 207-236-8113, 800-251-0865; www.swiftinn.com; 72 Elm St; r incl breakfast $139-245; ⊠ ❄ 📶) Crème brûlée French toast? That gives you just a taste of what you're in for at this pampering B&B. Occupying an 1810 Federal-style home, the eight comfy rooms vary, but think hardwood floors, four-poster beds and a warm fireplace.

Camden Deli (☎ 207-236-8343; 37 Main St; mains $5-9; 🕑 7am-10pm) Family-run Camden Deli has a rooftop deck overlooking Camden Harbor and everything from Maine blueberry pancakes to Italian sub sandwiches piled high with salami and hot peppers. Come between 4pm and 7pm for free appetizers and $3 draft beers.

Cappy's (☎ 207-236-2254; 1 Main St; mains $6-15; 🕑 11am-11pm; 📶) The star of Cappy's is the award-winning clam chowder, sold by the cup, bowl or pint. You can also order burgers, fresh fish sandwiches and lobster rolls but definitely start off with the rich, creamy chowder. It's a good spot to pick up bakery items too.

Waterfront (☎ 207-236-3747; 40 Bayview St; mains $15-25; 🕑 11am-11pm) You're smack on the water at this harborfront eatery specializing in perfectly prepared seafood with just the right twist. Local rock crab and artichoke fondue, Cajun-blackened haddock, Maine lobster crêpes – yowza!

Blue Hill

Graced with period houses, Blue Hill is a charming coastal town that's home to artists and craftspeople. Start your exploration at Main St and the adjoining Union St, where you'll find several quality galleries selling Blue Hill pottery, sculptures and paintings.

Since 1902 the **Kneisel Hall Chamber Music Festival** (☎ 207-374-2203; www.kneisel.org; Pleasant St/ME 15; tickets $20-30; 🕑 Fri-Sun late Jun–late Aug) has attracted visitors from far and wide to its summer concert series. The **Blue Hill Peninsula Chamber of Commerce** (☎ 207-374-3242; www.bluehillpeninsula.org; 107 Main St; 🕑 9am-4pm Tue & Thu) has visitor information.

Evening hors d'oeuvres by the fireplace and a gourmet breakfast are just two of the perks at **Blue Hill Inn** (☎ 207-374-2844, 800-826-7415; www.bluehillinn.com; 40 Union St; r incl breakfast $155-205; ❄ 💻 📶), the town's landmark B&B since 1840.

NEW ENGLAND

HOIST THE SAILS

Feel the wind in your hair and history at your side aboard the gracious, multimasted sailing ships known as windjammers. The sailing ships, both historic and replicas, gather in the harbors at Camden and neighboring Rockland to take passengers out on day trips and overnight sails.

Day sails cruise for two hours in Penobscot Bay from June to October for around $30 and you can usually book your place on the day. On the Camden waterfront, look for the 86ft wooden tall-ship **Appledore** (☎ 207-236-8353; www.appledore2.com) and the two-masted schooner **Olad** (☎ 207-236-2323; www.maineschooners.com).

Other schooners make two- to six-day cruises, offer memorable wildlife viewing (seals, whales and puffins) and typically include stops at Acadia National Park, small coastal towns and offshore islands for a lobster picnic.

You can get full details on several glorious options in one fell swoop through the **Maine Windjammer Association** (☎ 800-807-9463; www.sailmainecoast.com), which represents 12 traditional tall ships, several of which have been designated National Historic Landmarks. Among them is the granddaddy of the schooner trade, the *Lewis R French,* America's oldest (1871) windjammer. Rates range from $400 for a two-day cruise to $1000 for a six-day voyage and are a bargain when you consider they include meals and accommodation. Reservations for the overnight sails are a must. Prices are highest in midsummer. June offers long days, uncrowded harbors and lower rates, though the weather can be cool. Late September, when the foliage takes on autumn colors, captures the scenery at its finest.

Every artists' enclave needs a top-notch natural food store, and in these hills it's the **Blue Hill Co-op** (☎ 207-374-2165; 4 Ellsworth Rd; mains $5-8; 8am-7pm Mon-Fri, 8am-6pm Sat, 9am-5pm Sun), which also serves good café fare including burritos, falafels and organic coffee.

ACADIA NATIONAL PARK

The only national park in New England, Acadia encompasses an unspoiled wilderness of undulating coastal mountains, towering sea cliffs, surf-pounded beaches and quiet ponds. The dramatic landscape offers a plethora of activities for both leisurely hikers and adrenaline junkies.

The park was established in 1919 on land that John D Rockefeller donated to the national parks system to save from encroaching lumber interests. Today you can hike and bike along the same carriage roads that Rockefeller once rode his horse and buggy on. The park covers over 62 sq miles, including most of mountainous Mt Desert Island and tracts of land on the Schoodic Peninsula and Isle au Haut, and holds a wide diversity of wildlife including moose, puffins and bald eagles.

Orientation & Information

Granite mountains and coastal vistas greet you upon entering **Acadia National Park** (www.nps.gov/acad). The park is open year-round, though Park Loop Rd and most facilities are closed in winter. An admission fee is charged from May 1 to October 31. The fee, which is valid for seven consecutive days, is $20 per vehicle between mid-June and early October, $10 at other times, and $5 on bike or foot.

Start your exploration at **Hulls Cove Visitor Center** (☎ 207-288-3338; ME 3; 8am-4:30pm mid-Apr–Jun & Oct, 8am-6pm Jul & Aug, 8am-5pm Sep), from where the 20-mile **Park Loop Road** circumnavigates the eastern portion of the park.

Sights & Activities

PARK LOOP ROAD

Park Loop Rd, the main sightseeing jaunt through the park, takes you to several of Acadia's highlights. If you're up for a bracing swim or just want to stroll Acadia's longest beach, stop at **Sand Beach**. About a mile beyond Sand Beach you'll come to **Thunder Hole**, where wild Atlantic waves crash into a deep narrow chasm with such force that it creates a thundering boom, loudest during incoming tides. Look to the south to see dramatic **Otter Cliffs**, a favorite rock-climbing spot that rises vertically from the sea. At **Jordan Pond** choose from a 1-mile nature trail loop around the south side of the pond or a 3.5-mile trail that skirts the entire pond perimeter. After you've worked up an appetite, reward yourself with a relaxing afternoon tea on the lawn of Jordan Pond House (opposite). Near the end of Park Loop Rd a side road leads up to Cadillac Mountain.

CADILLAC MOUNTAIN

The majestic centerpiece of Acadia National Park is Cadillac Mountain (1530ft), the highest coastal peak in the eastern US, reached by a 3.5-mile spur road off Park Loop Rd. Four **trails** lead to the summit from four directions should you prefer hiking boots to rubber tires. The panoramic 360-degree view of ocean, islands and mountains is a winner any time of the day, but it's truly magical at dawn when hardy souls flock to the top to watch the sun rise over Frenchman Bay.

OTHER ACTIVITIES

Some 125 miles of **hiking trails** crisscross Acadia National Park, from easy half-mile nature walks and level rambles to mountain treks up steep and rocky terrain. A standout is the 3-mile round-trip **Ocean Trail**, which runs between Sand Beach and Otter Cliffs and takes in the most interesting coastal scenery in the park. Pick up a guide describing all the trails at the visitor center.

The park's 45 miles of carriage roads are the prime attraction for **cycling**. You can rent quality mountain bikes, replaced new at the start of each season, at **Acadia Bike** (☎ 207-288-9605; 48 Cottage St, Bar Harbor; per day $22; 🕑 8am-8pm).

Rock climbing on the park's sea cliffs and mountains is breathtaking. Gear up with **Acadia Mountain Guides** (☎ 207-288-8186; www.acadiamountainguides.com; 198 Main St, Bar Harbor; half-day with instructor & equipment $80-125; 🕑 9am-8pm), a highly regarded and fully accredited climbing school.

Scores of **ranger-led programs**, including nature walks, birding talks and kids' field trips, are available in the park. The visitor center provides the daily schedule. For information on kayaking and other activities see Bar Harbor (right).

Sleeping & Eating

The park has two campgrounds, both wooded and with running water, showers and barbecue pits. The 214-site **Seawall Campground** (ME 102A; campsites $14-20; 🕑 late May–Sep), 4 miles south of Southwest Harbor, operates on a first-come, first-served basis. The 306-site **Blackwoods Campground** (☎ 877-444-6777; ME 3; campsites $20; 🕑 year-round), 5 miles south of Bar Harbor, accepts advance reservations. If these are full several commercial campgrounds can be found just outside Acadia National Park.

For a memorable afternoon break, head to **Jordan Pond House** (☎ 207-276-3316; afternoon tea $9, mains $10-25; 🕑 11:30am-8pm mid-May–Oct), sit on the lawn overlooking the pond and order the afternoon tea served with warm popovers and homemade strawberry jam. The park's sole restaurant also has lobster rolls at lunchtime and prime rib dinners.

There are scores of restaurants, inns and hotels in Bar Harbor (p312), just a mile beyond the park.

Getting There & Around

The convenient **Island Explorer** (☎ 207-667-5796; www.exploreacadia.com; rides free; 🕑 late Jun–early Oct) runs eight shuttle bus routes throughout Acadia National Park and to adjacent Bar Harbor, linking trailheads, campgrounds and accommodations.

BAR HARBOR

Set on the doorstep of Acadia National Park, this alluring coastal town once rivaled Newport, RI, as a trendy summer destination for wealthy Americans. Today many of the old mansions have been turned into inviting inns and the town has become a magnet for outdoor enthusiasts. The **Bar Harbor Chamber of Commerce** (☎ 207-288-5103, 800-345-4617; www.barharbormaine.com; 1201 Bar Harbor Rd/ME 3, Trenton; 🕑 8am-6pm late May–mid-Oct, 8am-5pm Mon-Fri mid-Oct–late May) has a convenient welcome center just before the bridge onto Mt Desert Island.

Sights & Activities

Abbe Museum (☎ 207-288-3519; 26 Mt Desert St; adult/child 6-16yr $6/2; 🕑 10am-6pm) has fascinating presentations on the four Native American tribes that hail from this region. The thousands of artifacts range from pottery and fishing implements dating back more than a millennium to contemporary woodcarvings and birch-bark containers.

Bar Harbor Whale Watch (☎ 207-288-2386; www.barharborwhales.com; 1 West St; adult $26-58, child 6-14yr $16-28; 🕑 mid-May–Oct; 👶), next to the town pier, offers a wide variety of sightseeing cruises, including whale-watching and puffin trips. It also offers a ranger-led tour to Baker Island, a 130-acre island that's part of Acadia National Park but reachable only by boat.

For a cruise in style, hop aboard the four-mast schooner *Margaret Todd* operated by **Downeast Windjammer Cruises** (☎ 207-288-4585;

NEW ENGLAND

www.downeastwindjammer.com; 27 Main St; adult/child 6-12yr $35/25), which sets sail three times a day.

Kayaking tours generally go to the islands in Frenchman Bay or the west side of Mt Desert Island, depending on which way the wind's blowing. **Coastal Kayaking Tours** (☎ 207-288-9605; www.acadiafun.com; 48 Cottage St; 2½/4hr tours $38/48; 8am-8pm) offers personalized tours, taking out a maximum of six kayaks at a time.

Sleeping

There's no shortage of sleeping options in Bar Harbor, ranging from period B&Bs to the usual chain hotels.

Bar Harbor Hostel (☎ 207-288-5587; www.barharborhostel.com; 321 Main St; dm/r $25/80;) This tidy hostel a mile from Acadia National Park has both men's and women's dorms each with 10 beds, as well as a private room that can sleep up to four people. Reservations are advised.

Holland Inn (☎ 207-288-4804; www.hollandinn.com; 35 Holland Ave; r incl breakfast $85-175;) Nine cheery rooms with frill-free decor, a hearty breakfast and innkeepers who make you feel at home are in store at this inn just a short stroll from the town center and waterfront.

Quimby House Inn (☎ 207-288-5811, 800-344-5811; www.quimbyhouse.com; 109 Cottage St; r $90-195;) Top value among Bar Harbor's small hotels, with comfortable rooms, helpful staff and a convenient downtown location. And if you're a stickler for clean, you'll love the way they keep this place spic and span.

Aysgarth Station Inn (☎ 207-288-9655; 20 Roberts Ave; www.aysgarth.com; r incl breakfast $110-145;) On a quiet side street near the town center, this 1895 B&B has six cozy rooms with homey touches. Request the Tan Hill room, which is on the 3rd floor, for a view of Cadillac Mountain.

Eating & Drinking

Cafe This Way (☎ 207-288-4483; 14½ Mt Desert St; mains breakfast $5-9, dinner $14-22; 7-11am Mon-Sat, 8am-1pm Sun, 5:30-9pm nightly) At *the* place in Bar Harbor for breakfast, the feather-light blueberry pancakes topped with real maple syrup melt in your mouth. Vegans will love the scrambled tofu chock-full of veggies, old-schoolers the eggs Benedict with smoked salmon. Solid seafood menu at dinner.

Rupununi (☎ 207-288-2886; 119 Main St; mains $7-25; 11am-1am) Enjoy an all-American menu of burgers, steaks and barbecued chicken. Rupununi also pours an amazing variety of Maine beers and has live music in the summer.

our pick **Trenton Bridge Lobster Pound** (☎ 207-667-2977; ME 3, Ellsworth; lobsters $10-15; 10:30am-8pm Mon-Sat) Sit at a picnic table and crack open a boiled lobster at this traditional lobster pound bordering the causeway that connects Mt Desert Island to mainland Maine. Run by the very folks who pull up the lobster traps, – this is as fresh as it gets.

McKays (☎ 207-288-2002; 231 Main St; mains $10-20; 4:30-9:30pm) One of Maine's buy-local and organic-when-possible restaurants, this pub-style eatery is a perfect choice for Maine crab cakes, farm-raised chicken and good ol' beer-battered fish and chips.

Havana (☎ 207-288-2822; 318 Main St; mains $18-35; 5-10pm) Maine goes Latin at this elegant dinner restaurant featuring the likes of lobster paella, coconut curried scallops and mojito cheesecake. The wine list is one of the finest in the state, the service superb.

DOWNEAST MAINE

The 900-plus miles of coastline running northeast from Bar Harbor are sparsely populated, slower-paced and foggier than southern and western Maine. Highlights include the **Schoodic Peninsula**, whose tip is a noncontiguous part of Acadia National Park; the lobster fishing villages of **Jonesport** and **Beals**; and **Great Wass Island**, a nature preserve with walking paths and good bird-watching, including the chance to see puffins.

Machias, with a branch of the University of Maine, is the center of commerce along this stretch of coast. **Lubec** is about as far east as you can go and still be in the USA; folks like to watch the sun rise at nearby **Quoddy Head State Park** so they can say they were the first in the country to catch the sun's rays.

Calais (*ka*-lus), at the northern end of US 1, is a twin town to St Stephen in New Brunswick, Canada. Southwest of Calais is the **Moosehorn National Wildlife Refuge** (☎ 207-454-7161; US 1, Baring; admission free; sunrise-sunset), which has hiking trails and offers opportunities to spot bald eagles, America's national bird.

INTERIOR MAINE

Sparsely populated northern and western Maine is rugged outdoor country. River rafting, hiking trails up Maine's highest mountain and the ski town of Bethel make the region a magnet for adventurers.

Augusta

In 1827 Augusta became Maine's capital, but it's small and, truth be told, not terribly interesting. The **Kennebec Valley Chamber of Commerce** (☎ 207-623-4559; www.augustamaine.com; 21 University Dr; 8:30am-5pm Mon-Fri) provides information on Augusta. If you're passing through, take a gander at the granite **State House** (1829), then stop at the adjacent **Maine State Museum** (☎ 207-287-2301; State House Complex, State St; adult/child 6-18yr $2/1; 9am-5pm Mon-Fri, 10am-4pm Sat), which traces the state's natural and cultural history.

Bangor

A boomtown during Maine's 19th-century lumbering prosperity, Bangor was destroyed by a sweeping fire in 1911. Today it's a modern, workaday town, perhaps most famous as the hometown of horror novelist Stephen King (look for his mansion – complete with bat-and-spider-web gate – among the grand houses along Broadway). The **Bangor Region Chamber of Commerce** (☎ 207-947-0307; www.bangorregion.com; 519 Main St; 9am-4pm Mon-Fri) has visitor information.

Sabbathday Lake

The nation's only active Shaker community is at Sabbathday Lake, 25 miles north of Portland. Founded in the early 18th century, a handful of devotees keep the Shaker tradition of simple living, hard work and fine artistry alive. You can tour several of their buildings on a visit to the **Shaker Museum** (☎ 207-926-4597; adult/child 6-12yr $6.50/2; 10am-4:30pm Mon-Sat late May–mid-Oct). To get there, take exit 63 off the Maine Turnpike and continue north for 8 miles on ME 26.

Bethel

The rural community of Bethel, nestled in the rolling Maine woods 12 miles east of New Hampshire on ME 26, offers an engaging combination of mountain scenery, outdoor escapades and good-value accommodations. **Bethel Area Chamber of Commerce** (☎ 207-824-2282, 800-442-5826; www.bethelmaine.com; 8 Station Pl; 9am-5pm Mon-Fri) provides information for visitors.

SIGHTS & ACTIVITIES

Bethel Outdoor Adventure (☎ 207-824-4224, 800-533-3607; www.betheloutdooradventure.com; 121 Mayville Rd/US 2; per day kayak/canoe $40/60; 8am-6pm), right on the banks of the Androscoggin River, rents canoes and kayaks; rates include a free shuttle upriver allowing you to paddle back at your own pace. They also rent bicycles, can set you up for fly-fishing and offer on-site camping.

If you're ready for a hike, head to **Grafton Notch State Park** (☎ 207-824-2912; ME 26), north of Bethel, which has pretty mountain scenery, waterfalls and lots of trails of varying lengths.

Sunday River Ski Resort (☎ 800-543-2754; www.sundayriver.com; ME 26;), 6 miles north of Bethel, is one of the best family-oriented ski centers in the region, with eight interconnected mountain peaks and 120 trails.

SLEEPING & EATING

White Mountain National Forest (☎ 877-444-6777; www.recreation.gov; campsites $18) The Maine portion of this national forest has several basic campgrounds near Bethel.

Chapman Inn (☎ 207-824-2657, 877-359-1498; www.chapmaninn.com; 2 Church St; incl breakfast dm $33, r $89-129;) A great place to share notes with fellow travelers, this friendly, central 1865 B&B has 10 country-style rooms as well as hostel-style dorm beds. A gourmet breakfast, billiards, darts and two saunas add to the fun.

Sudbury Inn & Suds Pub (☎ 207-824-2174, 800-395-7837; www.sudburyinn.com; 151 Main St; r incl breakfast $99-159;) The choice place to stay in downtown Bethel, this historic inn has 17 rooms, a pub with 29 beers on tap, pizza and live weekend entertainment. It also has an excellent dinner restaurant serving Maine-centric fare (mains $8 to $25).

Caratunk & The Forks

For white-water rafting at its best, head to the **Kennebec River**, below the Harris Dam, where the water shoots through a dramatic 12-mile gorge. With rapid names like Whitewasher and Magic Falls, you know you're in for an adrenaline rush.

The adjoining villages of Caratunk and The Forks, on US 201 south of Jackman, are at the center of the Kennebec River rafting operations. The options range from rolling rapids and heart-stopping drops to calmer waters where children as young as seven can join in. Rates vary with demand and which tour you choose, but range from $75 to $125 per person for a day-long outing. Multiday packages, with camping or cabin accommodations, can also be arranged.

A MAINE WOODS NATIONAL PARK?

The concept is as grand as Maine's vast north woods. Taking inspiration from John D Rockefeller, who donated land for Acadia National Park, Roxanne Quimby, founder of the organic personal-care company Burt's Bees, bought 77,000 acres of Maine woods bordering Baxter State Park, hoping to make it the cornerstone of a new national park. The goal is to grow it into a 3.2-million-acre park that would restore native ecosystems and cover a greater land area than Yellowstone and Yosemite national parks combined. Actor Robert Redford and other Hollywood celebs jumped on board to support the idea but a counter movement has thus far managed to put the proposed park on hold.

Concerned with the loss of timber jobs, as well as the possibility of losing access to hunting and snowmobiling in a new park, many folks in the surrounding towns became vocal opponents. Probably even more telling, some conservation groups came out against the park, worried that the backlash would hamper their efforts in other areas where public support is essential. Still, the vision is there and supporters are optimistic that its time will come. Check out their website at www.restore.org.

Reliable operators include the following:

Crab Apple Whitewater (☎ 800-553-7238; www.crabapplewhitewater.com)
Magic Falls Rafting (☎ 800-207-7238; www.magicfalls.com)
Northern Outdoors (☎ 800-765-7238; www.northernoutdoors.com)

Baxter State Park

Set in the remote forests of northern Maine, **Baxter State Park** (☎ 207-723-5140; www.baxterstateparkauthority.com; per car $13) centers on Mt Katahdin (5267ft), Maine's tallest mountain and the northern terminus of the 2175-mile **Appalachian Trail** (www.nps.gov/appa). This vast 204,733-acre park is maintained in a wilderness state – no electricity and no running water (bring your own or plan on purifying stream water) – and there's a good chance you'll see moose, deer and black bear. Baxter has extensive hiking trails, several leading to the top of Mt Katahdin, which can be hiked round-trip in a day as long as you're in good shape and get an early start.

Baxter's 10 campgrounds contain 1200 campsites ($10 per person per day) but they do fill up, so it's best to book in advance, which can be done online or by phone with a credit card.

At Millinocket, south of Baxter State Park, there are motels, campgrounds, restaurants and outfitters that specialize in white-water rafting and kayaking on the Penobscot River. Get information from the **Katahdin Area Chamber of Commerce** (☎ 207-723-4443; www.katahdinmaine.com; 1029 Central St, Millinocket).

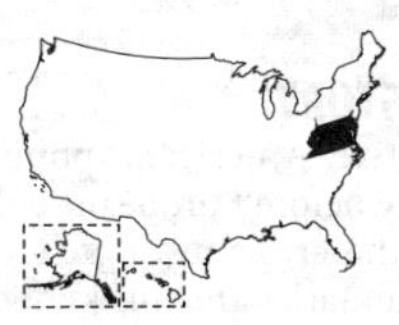

Washington, DC & the Capital Region

Washington, DC: its very name invokes power, politics and prose. It is arguably the most influential city in the world. The policy decisions made within the marbled halls of the nation's capital resonate around the world.

About 15 million visitors come to Washington, DC, every year to soak up the history, the world-class Smithsonian museums, the columned monuments and imposing government buildings. With some justification, DC has a reputation for being a stuffy city filled with political wonks, lobbyists and lawyers. But she is so much more – a multilayered, multifaceted city filled with great culture, restaurants, shopping, neighborhoods, nightlife and outdoor adventures.

Beyond the Beltway, the surrounding states of Maryland, Virginia, West Virginia and Delaware are a microcosm of the US. It's a culturally, ethnically and historically diverse region that is literally the birthplace of America, the grounds caked in blood from America's conception (Jamestown), birth (Williamsburg and Yorktown) and coming of age (Antietam and Appomattox).

The Mid-Atlantic region is also a place of unheralded natural beauty, from the rolling peaks of the Blue Ridge Mountains, to the marshlands of Chesapeake Bay and the sandy beaches of the Eastern Shore. Outdoor adventures include hiking, biking, skiing and white-water rafting. Get lost exploring the cobblestoned streets of colonial villages such as Williamsburg and Annapolis. Or drink your way through the vineyards of Virginia – America's fifth-largest wine producer.

HIGHLIGHTS

- Visit Washington, DC's, world-famous (and free!) **Smithsonian Institution museums** (p325), then watch the sunset from the steps of the **Lincoln Memorial** (p326).
- Trace America's roots at the living-history museum of **Colonial Williamsburg** (p368).
- Explore the region's nautical past with a pub crawl through the cobblestoned port-town neighborhood of **Fells Point, Baltimore** (p344).
- Take a Sunday drive and hike along **Skyline Drive** (p376), then camp under the stars in **Shenandoah National Park** (p375).
- Marvel at Thomas Jefferson's architectural masterpieces of **Monticello** (p373) and the **University of Virginia** (p374) in historic **Charlottesville** (p373).
- Stroll down the boardwalk and stop for a milk shake at **Royal Treat** (p356) in the family- and gay-friendly seaside resort of **Rehoboth Beach** (p355).
- Tackle the white-water rapids of **New River Gorge National River** (p383) in Fayetteville.

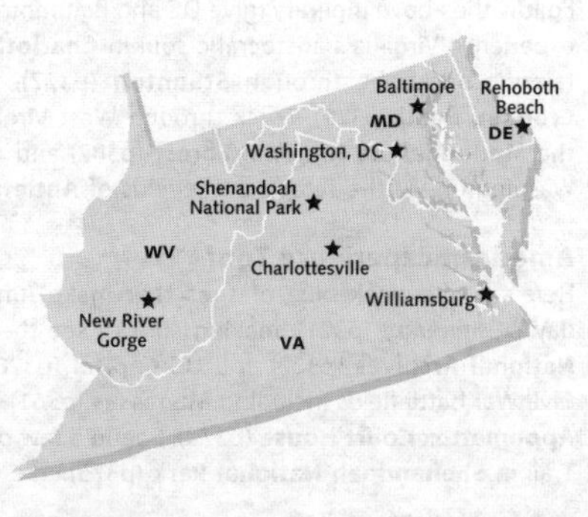

HISTORY

Native Americans populated this region long before European settlers arrived. Many of the area's most well-known geographic landmarks are still known by their Indian names, such as Chesapeake, Shenandoah, Appalachian and Potomac. In 1607 a group of 108 English colonists established the first permanent European settlement in the New World: Jamestown. During the early years, colonists battled harsh winters, starvation, disease and occasionally hostile Native Americans.

Jamestown survived, and the Royal Colony of Virginia came into being in 1624. Ten years later, fleeing the English Civil War, Lord Baltimore established the Catholic colony of Maryland at St Mary's City, where a Spanish-Jewish doctor treated a town council that included a black Portuguese sailor and Margaret Brent, the first woman to vote in North American politics. Delaware was settled as a Dutch whaling colony in 1631, practically wiped out by Native Americans, and later resettled by the British. Celts displaced from Britain filtered into the Appalachians, where they created a fiercely independent culture that persists today. Border disputes between Maryland, Delaware and Pennsylvania led to the creation of the Mason–Dixon line, which eventually separated the industrial North from the agrarian, slave-holding South.

The fighting part of the Revolutionary War finished here with the British surrender at Yorktown in 1781. Then, to diffuse regional tension, central, swampy Washington, District of Columbia (DC), was made the new nation's capital. But divisions of class, race and economy were strong, and this area in particular split along its seams during the Civil War: Virginia seceded from the Union while its impoverished western farmers, long resentful of genteel plantation owners, seceded from Virginia. Maryland stayed in the Union but her white slave-owners rioted against Northern troops, while thousands of black Marylanders joined the Union Army.

LOCAL CULTURE

The North–South tension long defined this area, but the region has also jerked between

THE CAPITAL REGION...

In One Week

Follow a version of the two-day DC itinerary (p321) and spend a day and a hard-partying night in **Baltimore** (p339) before exploring Maryland's gorgeous **Eastern Shore** (p350) and the **Delaware beaches** (p355). Head south and cross over the Chesapeake Bay bridge-tunnel and time-warp through Virginia's history, from her settlement and independence struggle in the **Historic Triangle** (p367) to her reconciliation with America at **Appomattox Court House** (p375). Swing north through **Richmond** (p362), where students, Dixie aristocracy and African Americans combine to form a fascinating whole, before rolling back (exhausted) into DC.

In Two Weeks

Follow the above itinerary (give DC and Baltimore a few more days while you're at it). Afterwards, experience Virginia's aristocratic soul in **Charlottesville** (p373) before driving down her mountainous backbone through **Staunton** (p377), **Lexington** (p377), **Roanoke** (p378) and the **Crooked Road** (p379). Truck through West Virginia, stopping to hike, mountain bike or ski in the **Monongahela National Forest** (p382) and rafting in New River Gorge before returning to Washington via the serene battlefields of **Antietam** (p353).

American Experience Tour

Here's a one-week blitz of sites that make America...well, simply America. Follow the two-day DC itinerary (p321), making sure to see the **Supreme Court** (p327), **White House** (p328), **National Archives** (p327) and **US Capitol** (p326). Take a scenic drive through Virginia's many Civil War battlefields including **Manassas** (p361), **Fredericksburg** (p361), **Petersburg** (p367) and **Appomattox Court House** (p375). Spend a few days hiking and camping along the Appalachian Trail in **Shenandoah National Park** (p375).

the aristocratic pretensions of upper-class Virginia, miners and watermen, immigrant boroughs and the ever-changing rulers of Washington, DC. Since the Civil War, local economies have made the shift from agriculture and manufacturing to high technology and servicing and staffing the federal government.

Many blacks settled this border region either as slaves or escapees running for Northern freedom. Today African Americans still form the visible underclass of major cities, but in the rough arena of the disadvantaged they compete with Latino immigrants, mainly from Central America. At the other end of the spectrum, ivory towers – in the form of world-class universities and research centers such as the National Institute of Health – attract intelligentsia from around the world. The local high schools are often packed with the children of scientists and consultants staffing some of the world's most prestigious think tanks.

All of this has spawned a culture that is, in turns, as sophisticated as a journalists' book club, as linked to the land as bluegrass festivals in Virginia and as hooked into the main vein of urban America as Tupac Shakur, go-go, Baltimore Club and DC Hardcore. And of course, there's always politics, a subject continually simmering under the surface here.

LAND & CLIMATE

Maryland describes herself as 'America in Miniature,' but the label could apply to the entire region.

Starting from the east of the region are the windy beaches of the Atlantic Shore and just a bit inland is Chesapeake Bay, the nation's largest estuary. Bay towns breathe the slow tidal respiration of a land married to water, and if you unfurled the clotted mass of rivers and streams here you'd get a coastline bigger than California's.

Further west the Atlantic coastal plain is studded with farms and suburbs, climbing through rolling hills to the increasingly developed Piedmont Plateau and finally, the hard, beautiful mountains of the Blue Ridge and Shenandoah.

Spring and fall are gorgeous and mild, while summer and winter suffer through thermometer extremes. The humidity of the summer in particular makes DC feel like Hanoi, Vietnam.

PARKS & WILDLIFE

Scenic grandeur here means the Appalachians, best explored from the Shenandoah Valley and West Virginia. The New River Gorge National River (p383) is utterly Eden-like and home to white-tailed deer and black bears. If you're fit enough, try hiking a bit of the Appalachian Trail, which runs through Shenandoah National Park (p375) and George Washington and Jefferson National Forests (p377).

Chesapeake Bay has a user-friendly, gentle charm: Assateague Island National Seashore (p353) and Chincoteague (p373) are awash with great blue herons, ospreys, blue crabs and wild horses.

Despite there being more than 30 parks in Virginia alone, a lot of protected land here is preserved for historical, rather than environmental properties. That doesn't mean all those old battlefields and houses aren't beautiful though; one of the weird paradoxes of old war sites is how peaceful they are today. Antietam (p353) and Manassas (p361) are particularly good examples of this phenomenon.

INFORMATION

A lot of conventions and conferences are held in this region and they can double or triple lodging prices: it's always best to call ahead. Smoking is banned in restaurants, bars and clubs in Maryland, Delaware and Washington, DC. Some local municipalities in Virginia and West Virginia, and an increasing number of private businesses, are also going smoke-free. Businesses that are smoke-free in these states are usually clearly marked.

GETTING THERE & AROUND

The region is served by three major airports: **Washington Dulles International Airport** (IAD; ☎ 703-572-2700), **Ronald Reagan Washington National Airport** (DCA; ☎ 703-417-8000) and **Baltimore/Washington International Thurgood Marshall Airport** (BWI; ☎ 410-859-7111, 800-435-9294). **Richmond International Airport** (RIC; ☎ 804-226-3000) is less frequently used. Bus (p1160) and Amtrak (p1166) information is listed for specific cities in this chapter. Major roads include the I-81 through Western Virginia, the I-495 (DC Beltway), the I-695 (Baltimore Beltway), the East Coast–connecting the I-95 and the I-66 (DC to Northern Virginia).

WASHINGTON, DC

The capital of the most powerful country in the world is, in many ways, a surprisingly neighborly, small town. We know that's not the DC of popular imagination, city of a thousand gleaming white marble buildings and guys in suits and smoky rooms and really important-sounding music playing as really important-looking people go through really big wooden doors. That DC does exist. But beyond the federal capital and all the iconography that makes America, well, America, is a city of neighborhoods and low-slung buildings: folks who've passed homes

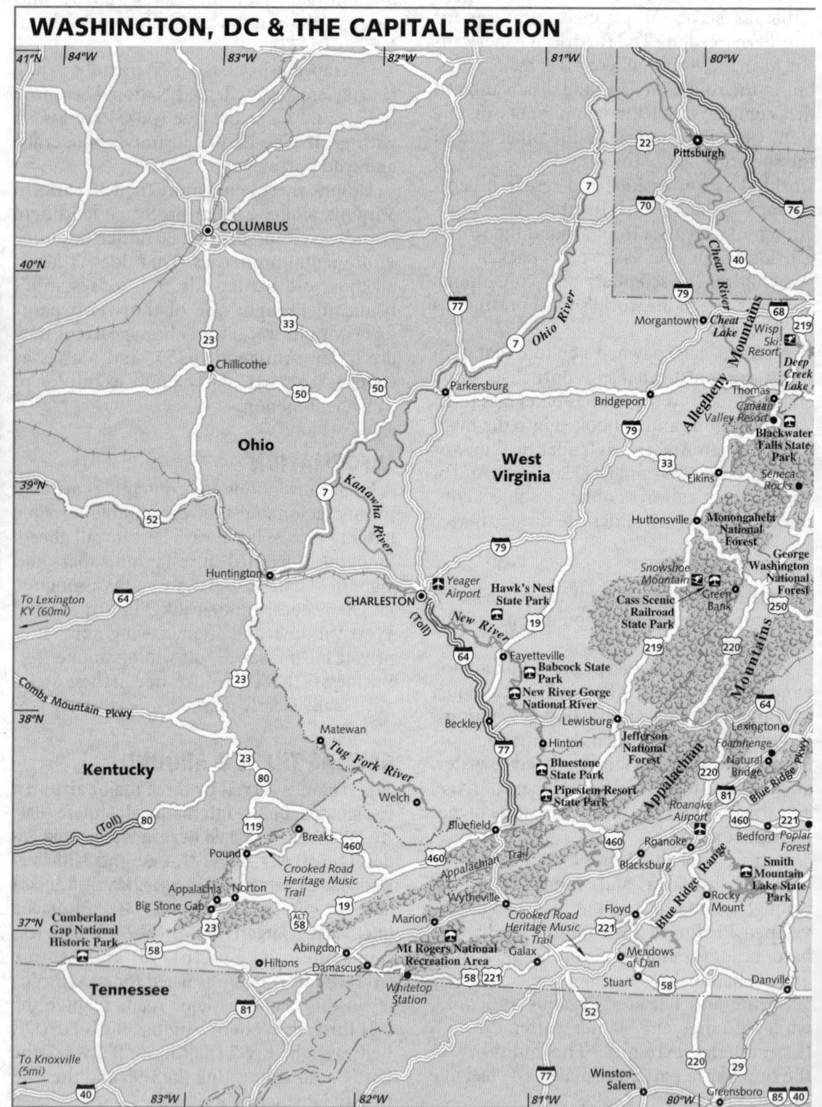

through the family over generations, and new immigrants from El Salvador; a crop of artists and creative types attracted by Washington's undeniable intellectual energy and more over-achieving, incredibly talented types than any city of this size deserves.

Yes, Washington is regal. But past the columns and the Capitol, she's small enough to share a beer and a shot with you, and smart enough to do so while parsing the Constitution.

HISTORY

Like a lot of American history, the District of Columbia (DC) story is one of compromise. In this case, the balance was struck

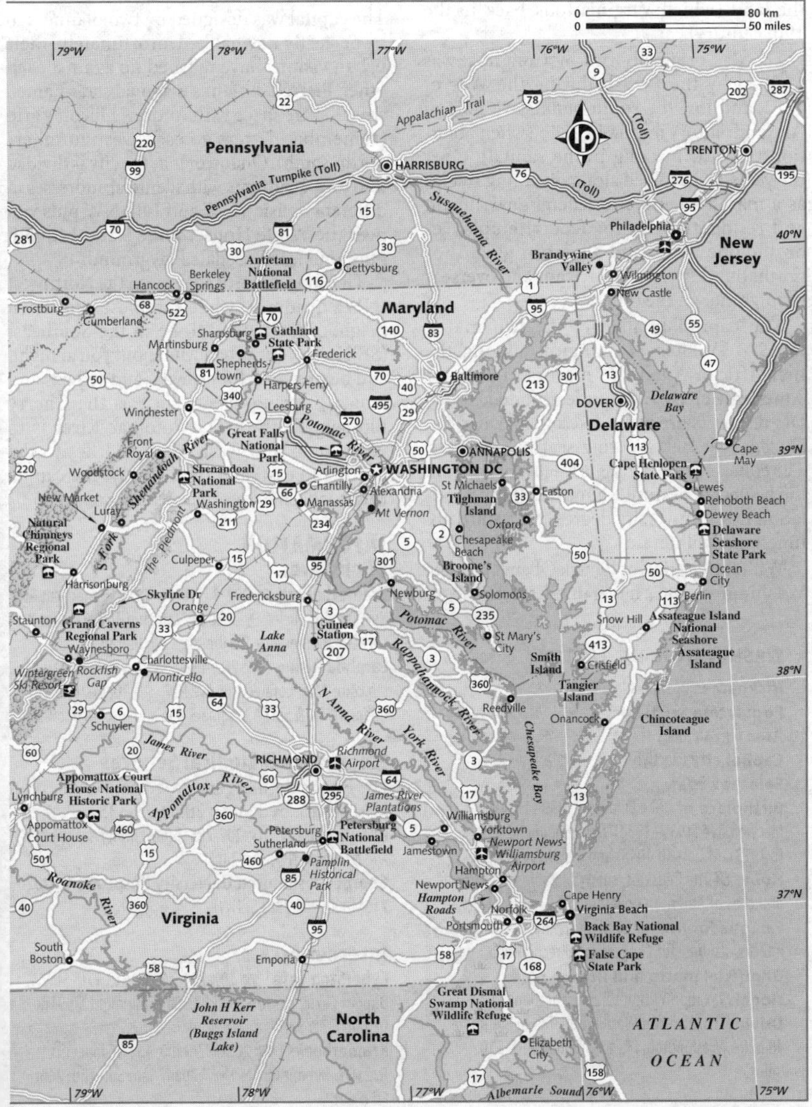

between Northern and Southern politicians who wanted to plant a federal city between their power bases. As potential capitals such as Boston, Philadelphia and Baltimore were rejected as too urban-industrial by Southern plantation owners, it was decided a new city would be carved at the 13 colonies' midway point, along the banks of the Potomac River. Maryland and Virginia donated the land (which Virginia took back in the 19th century).

DC was originally run by Congress, was torched by the British during the War of 1812, and lost the south-bank slave port of Alexandria to Virginia in 1846 (when abolition talk was buzzing in the capital). Over the years DC evolved along diverging tracks; as a marbled temple to federal government and residential city for federal employees on the one hand, and an urban ghetto for northbound African Americans and overseas immigrants on the other.

The capitol finally got its own mayor in 1973 (Walter Washington, among the first African American mayors of a major American city). Ever under-funded, today DC residents are taxed like other American citizens, yet lack a voting seat in Congress. The educated upper class is leagues away from the neglected destitute; almost half the population has a university degree, yet a third are functionally illiterate.

With the election of Barack Obama in 2008, Washington, DC, has gained a bit of cool cachet – New Yorkers are coming here now, instead of the other way around! President Obama's habit of playing pickup basketball and patronizing local restaurants has folks wondering if he's set to become that rarest of breeds: a president who doesn't just live in Washington, but is also a Washingtonian.

WASHINGTON, DC, FACTS

Nicknames DC, Chocolate City
Population 591,833
Area 68.3 sq miles
Capital city Exactly!
Sales tax 5.75%
Birthplace of Duke Ellington(1899–1974), Marvin Gaye (1939–1984), Dave Chappelle (b 1973), Al Gore (b 1948) and democracy, baby!
Home of The Redskins, cherry blossoms, all three branches of American government
Famous for National symbols, crime, partying interns, struggle for Congressional recognition
Unofficial motto and license plate slogan Taxation Without Representation
Driving distances Washington, DC, to Baltimore 40 miles, Washington, DC, to Virginia Beach 210 miles

ORIENTATION

The capital was designed by two planners to be perfectly navigable. Unfortunately, their urban visions have mashed up against each other. Pierre L'Enfant's diagonal state-named streets share space with Andrew Ellicott's grid (remember: letters go east–west, numbers north–south). On top of that the city is divided into four quadrants with identical addresses in different divisions – F and 14th NW puts you near the White House, while F and 14th NE puts you near Rosedale Playground.

The lion's share of sites are in the Northwest (NW) quadrant, while the most run-down neighborhoods tend to be in the Southeast (SE). Keep your urban wits about you at night, and be prepared for crowds (and crowds and *crowds*) during events such as the Cherry Blossom Festival. The Potomac River is to your south and west; Maryland lies to the north and east; and the Beltway, the capital ring road, encircles the entire package.

INFORMATION

Bookstores

Kramerbooks (☎ 202-387-1400; 1517 Connecticut Ave NW, Dupont Circle; 🕑 7:30am-1am Sun-Thu, 24hr Fri & Sat) The mother lode for the city's hip literati.

Lambda Rising (☎ 202-462-6969; www.lambdarising.com; 1625 Connecticut Ave NW; 🕑 10am-10pm, to midnight Fri & Sat) A landmark gay and lesbian bookstore.

Emergency & Medical Services

DC Fire and Emergency Medical Services can also be reached at ☎ 202-673-3331.

CVS Pharmacy (☎ 202-785-1466; cnr Massachusetts Ave & 20th St NW; 🕑 24hr)

George Washington University Hospital (☎ 202-715-4000; 900 23rd St NW)

Internet Access

CyberStop Café (☎ 202-234-2470; 1513 17th St NW, Dupont Circle; per hr $8; 🕑 7:30am-midnight Sun-Thu, to 2am Fri & Sat)

Kramerbooks (☎ 202-387-1400; 1517 Connecticut Ave NW, Dupont Circle; 🕑 7:30am-1am Sun-Thu, 24hr Fri & Sat)

WASHINGTON, DC...

In Two Days

Head for the **Capitol** (p326), feel the grandeur, then pop into the **Library of Congress** (p327). Now go Smithsonian-ing: try the **Air & Space Museum** (p325), **National Museum of Natural History** (p325) and the **National Museum of the American Indian** (p326). Wander down the **National Mall** (below); at the 'bottom,' soak up pride, love and loss at the **Lincoln Memorial** (p326) and **Vietnam Veterans Memorial** (p326). Hungry? **Dupont Circle** (p334) and **U Street** (p333) are both good for international eats.

Next day, head back to the Mall for the **US Holocaust Memorial Museum** (p325) and the **Arthur M Sackler Gallery** (p325) and the **Freer Gallery of Art** (p325), then see the **National Archives** (p327) and **Reynolds Center for American Art** (p328). Catch the illuminated **White House** (p328) and **FDR Memorial** (p327) at night.

In Four Days

Time to see the other side of DC: ride out to **Anacostia** (p329) and the **Anacostia Community Museum** (p330). Grab dinner in **Dupont Circle** (p334). On day four pick a site you haven't seen and live la dolce vita in **Georgetown** (p329) and/or **U Street** (p329).

Internet Resources & Media

88.5 WAMU National Public Radio (NPR) affiliate.
89.3 WPFW Local news and views.
93.9 FM WKYS Hip-hop.
101.1 FM WWDC Rawk.
103.1 WRNR Better rawk, but spotty signal.
1500AM Federal News Radio, for news and policy wonks.
Online visitor information (www.washington.org, www.thedistrict.com)
Washington City Paper (www.washingtoncitypaper.com) Free edgy weekly with entertainment and dining listings.
Washington Post (www.washingtonpost.com) Respected daily city (and national) paper. Its tabloid-format daily *Express* is free. Also check www.washingtonpost.com/gog for events listings.

Money

Currency exchange is available at the major airports and during weekday business hours at most banks, as well as **Travelex** (☎ 202-371-9220; Union Station, 50 Massachusetts Ave NE, Gate G booth; 🕑 9am-5pm Mon-Sat, noon-6pm Sun). Also has a location **downtown** (☎ 202-872-1428; 1880 K St NW; 🕑 9am-5pm Mon-Fri).

Post

Post office (2 Massachusetts Ave NE; 🕑 7am-midnight Mon-Fri, to 8pm Sat & Sun)

Tourist Information

DC Chamber of Commerce Information Center (☎ 866-324-7386; http://washington.org/; Ronald Reagan Bldg, 1300 Pennsylvania Ave NW; 🕑 9am-4:30pm Mon-Fri Sep–mid-Mar, 8:30am-5:30pm Mon-Fri, 9am-4pm Sat mid-Mar–Aug) Hotel reservation line and a film that gives an excellent overview of DC.
International Visitors Information Desk (☎ 703-572-2536; 🕑 9am-5pm Mon-Fri) Run by the Meridian International Center; staff at this desk (at the Arrivals Terminal at Washington-Dulles Airport) can answer questions in more than 40 languages.
Washington Convention & Visitors Association (☎ 202-789-7000; www.washington.org; 901 7th St NW, 4th fl, Washington, DC, 20005; 🕑 9am-5pm Mon-Fri)

For travelers with disabilities:
General information (☎ 202-789-7000) On hotels, restaurants and attractions.
Metrorail (☎ 202-637-7000; www.wmata.com)
Smithsonian access (☎ 202-633-2921, TTY 202-633-4353)

SIGHTS

National Mall

When someone says 'Washington, DC,' and you think of everything that symbolizes America – white buildings, big flags, Abe Lincoln and a reflecting pool – you're thinking of the National Mall. This is America's great public space, where citizens come to protest their government, chill in the sun, visit museums and soak up collective national symbolism. The 1.9-mile-long lawn is anchored at one end by the Lincoln Memorial, at the other by Capitol Hill, intersected by the reflecting pool and WWII memorial, and centered by the Washington Monument.

WASHINGTON, DC

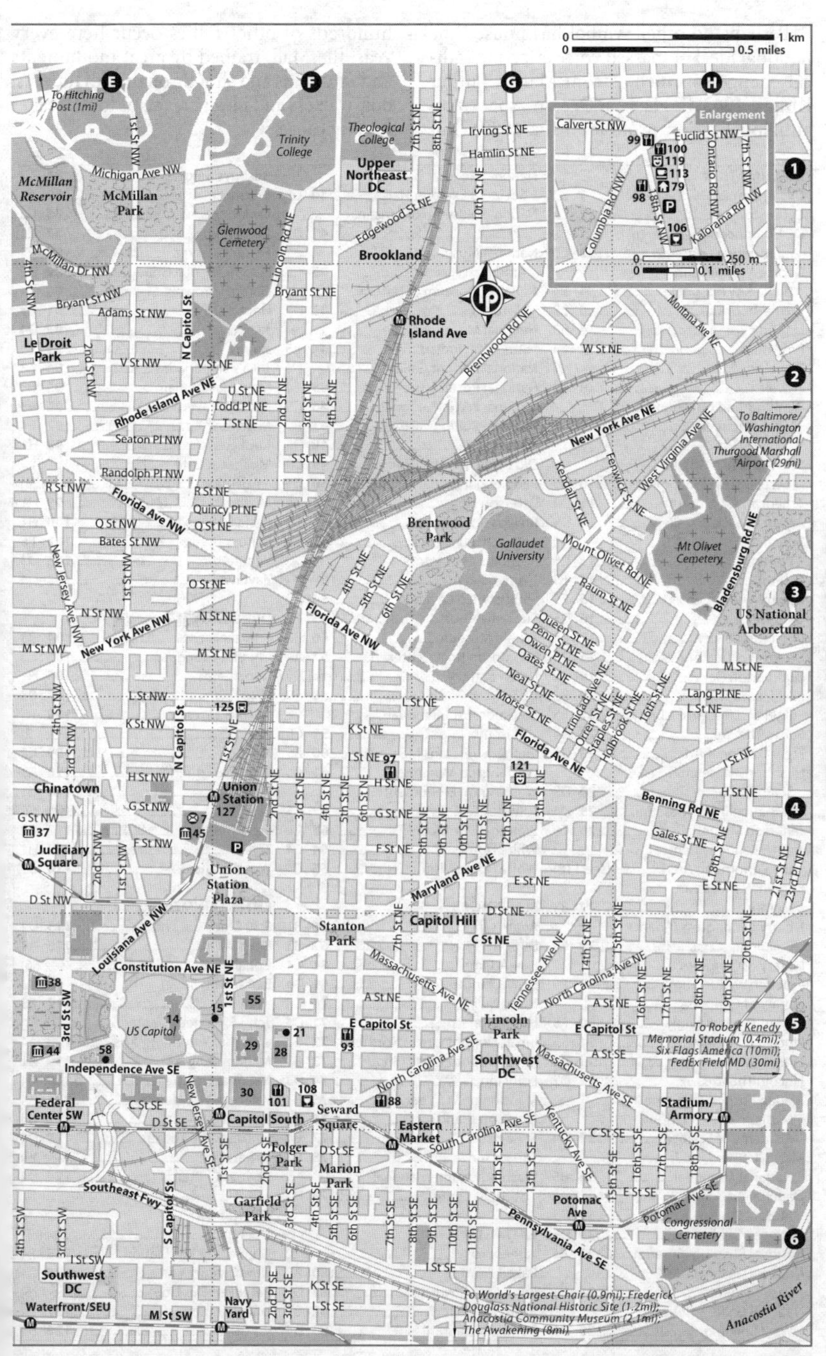

WASHINGTON, DC & THE CAPITAL REGION

Perhaps no other symbol has housed the national ideal of massed voice affecting radical change so much – from Martin Luther King's 1963 'I Have a Dream' speech to antiglobalization protests in the 1990s. But hundreds of other rallies occur here every year; the Mall, framed by great monuments and museums and shot through with tourists, dog-walkers and idealists, acts as loudspeaker for any cause.

INFORMATION

CVS Pharmacy	**1**	B3
CyberStop Café	**2**	C3
DC Chamber of Commerce Information Center	**3**	C5
George Washington University Hospital	**4**	B4
Kramerbooks	**5**	B3
Lambda Rising	**6**	B3
Post Office	**7**	E4
Travelex	(see 127)	
Travelex	**8**	B4
Washington Convention & Visitors Association	**9**	D4

SIGHTS & ACTIVITIES

Albert Einstein Monument	**10**	B5
American Art Museum	**11**	D4
Arthur M Sackler Gallery	**12**	D5
Bureau of Engraving & Printing	**13**	C5
Capitol	**14**	E5
Capitol Visitor Center	**15**	F5
Carousel	**16**	D5
Corcoran Gallery	**17**	C4
Discovery Theater	**18**	D5
Dumbarton Oaks	**19**	A2
FDR Memorial	**20**	B6
Folger Shakespeare Library	**21**	F5
Ford's Theatre	**22**	D4
Freer Gallery of Art	**23**	D5
Hirshhorn Museum & Sculpture Garden	**24**	D5
International Spy Museum	**25**	D4
Jefferson Memorial	**26**	C6
John F Kennedy Center for the Performing Arts	(see 118)	
Korean War Veterans Memorial	**27**	B5
Library of Congress (Adams Building)	**28**	F5
Library of Congress (Jefferson Building)	**29**	F5
Library of Congress (Madison Building)	**30**	F5
Lincoln Memorial	**31**	B5
Lincoln Museum	(see 22)	
Lincoln Theatre	**32**	D2
Marian Koshland Science Museum of the National Academy of Sciences	**33**	D4
Martin Luther King Jr National Memorial	**34**	B5
National Air & Space Museum	**35**	D5
National Archives	**36**	D5
National Building Museum	**37**	E4
National Gallery of Art - East Building	**38**	E5
National Gallery of Art - West Building	**39**	D5
National Geographic Society's Explorer Hall	**40**	C3
National Museum of African Art	**41**	D5
National Museum of American History	**42**	C5
National Museum of Natural History	**43**	D5
National Museum of the American Indian	**44**	E5
National Portrait Gallery	(see 11)	
National Postal Museum	**45**	E4
National WWII Memorial	**46**	C5
National Zoological Park	**47**	B1
Newseum	**48**	D5
Old Post Office Pavilion	**49**	D4
Paddleboat Rentals	**50**	C6
Peterson House	**51**	D4
Phillips Collection	**52**	B3
Renwick Gallery	**53**	C4
Reynolds Center for American Art	(see 11)	
Smithsonian Castle	**54**	D5
Supreme Court	**55**	F5
Textile Museum	**56**	B2
Thompson Boat Center	**57**	A4
Union Station	(see 127)	
US Botanic Garden	**58**	E5
US Holocaust Memorial Museum	**59**	C5
Vietnam Veterans Memorial	**60**	B5
Washington Monument	**61**	C5
Washington Monument Kiosk	**62**	C5
Watergate Complex	**63**	A4
White House	**64**	C4
White House Visitor Center	**65**	C4

SLEEPING

Adam's Inn	**66**	B1
Dupont Hotel	**67**	B3
Hay-Adams	**68**	C4
HI-Washington, DC	**69**	D4
Hotel Helix	**70**	C3
Hotel Monaco	**71**	D4
Inn at Dupont Circle (North)	**72**	C2
Inn at Dupont Circle (South)	**73**	B3
Lofty Inn	**74**	D3
Mansion on O Street	**75**	B3
Morrison-Clark Inn	**76**	D3
St Regis	**77**	C4
Tabard Inn	**78**	C3
Washington International Student Center	**79**	H1

EATING

Afterwords	(see 5)	
Baked & Wired	**80**	A3
Ben's Chili Bowl	**81**	D2
Bistro Du Coin	**82**	B2
Burma Restaurant	**83**	D4
Busboys & Poets	**84**	C2
Citronelle	**85**	A3
Cork	**86**	C2
Dos Gringos	**87**	C1
Eastern Market	**88**	F5
Florida Avenue Grill	**89**	D2
Georgia Brown's	**90**	C4
Hook	**91**	A3
Jaleo	**92**	D4
Jimmy T's	**93**	F5
Julia's Empanadas	**94**	C3
Malaysia Kopitiam	**95**	B3
Martin's Tavern	**96**	A3
Matchbox Pizza	**97**	F4
Meskerem	**98**	H1
Minibar at Café Atlantico	(see 123)	
Mixtec	**99**	H1
Pasta Mia	**100**	H1
Sonoma	**101**	F5
Vegetate	**102**	D3
Zaytinya	**103**	D4

DRINKING

Brickskellar	**104**	B3
Chi-Cha Lounge	**105**	C2
Dan's Café	**106**	H1
Halo	**107**	C3
Hawk & Dove	**108**	F5
JR's	(see 2)	
Marvin's	**109**	C2
Mie N Yu Lounge	**110**	A3
Raven	**111**	C1
Saloon	(see 32)	
Stetson's	**112**	C2
Tryst	**113**	H1
Wonderland	**114**	D1

ENTERTAINMENT

9:30 Club	**115**	D2
Blues Alley	**116**	A3
Cobalt	(see 86)	
Eighteenth Street Lounge	**117**	B3
John F Kennedy Center for the Performing Arts	**118**	A4
Madam's Organ	**119**	H1
National Theatre	**120**	C4
Palace of Wonders	**121**	G4
Science Club	**122**	B3
Shakespeare Theatre	**123**	D4
Ticketplace	(see 49)	
Verizon Center	**124**	D4

TRANSPORT

DC2NY	(see 1)	
Greyhound Bus Station	**125**	F4
New Century Bus	**126**	D4
Peter Pan Bus Lines	(see 125)	
Union Station	**127**	F4
WashNY	**128**	B3

SMITHSONIAN INSTITUTION MUSEUMS

If America was a quirky grandfather, these museums – as stimulating as a (free!) good book or lecture – would be his attic. An attic that happens to house a globally prestigious research unit, yes, but an attic nonetheless, where a rotating 1% of a staggering collection – the lunar lander, dinosaurs, great art and relics that weren't looted during the days of Empire (ahem, Europe) – is on display at any given time.

Englishman James Smithson (who never came to the USA) willed $4.1 million to the country to found an 'establishment for the increase and diffusion of knowledge' in 1826. Unfortunately, his intellectual baby badly needs (and is receiving) some expensive upkeep. It has been suggested the museums start charging for admission, but the powers that be won't hear of it, arguing that fees would fly in the face of the Smithsonian's mission. The museums will stay free if it kills them. And it just might. Currently, the **Arts & Industries Museum** (www.si.ed/ai; 900 Jefferson Dr, SW) is closed indefinitely.

The red-turreted **Smithsonian Castle** (Smithsonian Institution Bldg; ☎ 202-633-1000; www.si.edu/visit/infocenter/sicastle.htm; 1000 Jefferson Dr SW; 🕑 8:30am-5pm) is the visitor center for all museums, but is not that interesting in and of itself. Be prepared for lines and bag-checks. The following museums are free and open every day except Christmas Day from 10am to 5:30pm unless otherwise noted. Some have extended hours in summer. Note that not all Smithsonian museums are included here.

A favorite of the kids, the **National Museum of Natural History** (cnr 10th St & Constitution Ave SW) bounces between some sweet dinosaur skeletons, a fantastic archaeology/anthropology collection, the 45-carat Hope diamond and pretty damn near everything else under the sun.

The **National Air & Space Museum** (cnr 6th St & Independence Ave SW) is the most popular Smithsonian museum; everyone flocks to see the Wright brothers' flyer, Chuck Yeager's *Bell X-1*, Charles Lindbergh's *Spirit of St Louis* and the *Apollo 11* command module. An IMAX theater, planetarium and a ride simulator are all here (adult/child $8.50/7 each). Even more avionic goodness is in Virginia at the Steven F Udvar-Hazy Center (p361), an annex to hold this museum's leftovers.

The **National Gallery of Art** (☎ 202-737-4215; www.nga.gov; Constitution Ave, btwn 3rd & 4th Sts NW; admission free; 🕑 10am-5pm Mon-Sat, 11am-6pm Sun) is about as cultured as you'll get outside of NYC's Met (with a *très* IM Pei facade). An underground passage connects the double wings: the original, neoclassical west wing is primarily stuffed with European art from the Middle Ages to the early 20th century, with works by all the greats (including the continent's only Da Vinci); the east wing is a little more abstract, a lot more conceptual.

The **National Museum of American History** (http://americanhistory.si.edu; cnr Constitution Ave & 14th St NW) is accented with the daily bric-a-brac of the American experience – synagogue shawls, protest signs and cotton gins – plus an enormous display of the original Star-Spangled Banner and icons such as Dorothy's slippers and Kermit the Frog.

At times a grim summation of human nature, at others a fierce confirmation of basic goodness, the **US Holocaust Memorial Museum** (☎ 202-488-0400; www.ushmm.org; 100 Raoul Wallenberg Pl; 🕑 10am-5:20pm) is a must-see. The main exhibit (not recommended for under-11s, who can go to a separate, also-free on-site exhibit) gives visitors the identity card of a single Holocaust victim, narrowing the scope of suffering to the individual level while paying thorough, overarching tribute to its powerful subject. Only a limited number of visitors are admitted each day, so come early.

The doughnut-shaped **Hirshhorn Museum & Sculpture Garden** (cnr 7th St & Independence Ave SW; 🕑 garden 7:30am-dusk, museum 10am-5:30pm) houses a huge collection of modern sculpture, rotated regularly, including works by Rodin, Henry Moore and Ron Mueck, as well as paintings by O'Keeffe, Warhol, Man Ray and de Kooning.

The **National Museum of African Art** (950 Independence Ave SW) showcases masks, textiles and ceramics from the sub-Sahara, as well as ancient and contemporary art from all over the continent.

Poring over ancient manuscripts and Japanese silk screens is about as perfect a way to spend an afternoon as any at both the quiet **Arthur M Sackler Gallery** (1050 Independence Ave SW) and the **Freer Gallery of Art** (cnr Jefferson Dr & 12th St SW), which together comprise the National Museum of Asian Art. Slightly incongruously, they are also home to more than 1300 works by the American painter James Whistler.

The **National Museum of the American Indian** (cnr 4th St & Independence Ave SW) takes on a little too much and can feel scattered, but it is still worth visiting if you want to learn about America's indigenous people. One absolute success here is the regionally specialized menu of the Native Foods café on the ground floor.

MALL MONUMENTS & ATTRACTIONS

Oldest joke in DC: 'So, what part of Washington is his monument modeled on?' Yeah, that's right, America has a bigger… obelisk than you. Just peaking at 555ft (and 5in), the **Washington Monument** (☎ 202-426-6841; 🕒 9am-4:45pm) is the tallest building in the district. It took two phases of construction to complete; note the different hues of the stone. Tickets are free but must be reserved; or you can order in advance from http://reservations.nps.gov for $1.50. They're available from the **kiosk** (15th St, btwn Madison St & Jefferson Dr SW; 🕒 8am-4:30pm).

The following all have free admission unless otherwise noted.

The **Bureau of Engraving & Printing** (☎ 202-874-4114; cnr 14th & C Sts SW; 🕒 9am-2pm Mon-Fri), aka the most glorified print shop in the world, is where all the US paper currency is designed. Some $32 million of it rolls off the presses daily. Get in line early at the ticket kiosk on Raoul Wallenberg Pl.

'Poppa Abraham' looks out on the reflecting pool from the **Lincoln Memorial** (☎ 202-426-6895; 🕒 24hr), where the inscribed Gettysburg Address speaks to all the potential hopes of a nation that weathered the Civil War.

The **Vietnam Veterans Memorial** (☎ 202-462-6841; southeast of Lincoln Memorial, Constitution Gardens; 🕒 24hr) is the opposite of DC's usual white, gleaming marble. Instead it's a black, low-lying 'V,' a physical expression of the psychic scar wrought by the Vietnam War. The 58,000 names of dead soldiers chiseled into the dark, reflective wall, scattered with heartfelt mementos left by visitors, form the most powerful monument in DC (if not the nation).

The elaborate **Korean War Veterans Memorial** (southwest of Lincoln Memorial, Constitution Gardens; 🕒 8am-11:45pm) is centered around a patrol of ghostly steel soldiers marching by a wall of etched faces from that conflict; seen from a distance, the images on the wall form the outline of the Korean mountains.

Occupying one end of the reflecting pool (and controversially, the center of the Mall, the only war memorial to have that distinction) the **National WWII Memorial** (17th St, btwn Constitution & Independence Aves; 🕒 24hr) wants to be (and pretty much is) as stirring as one of the great quotes from that war. Consequently, those quotes are inscribed all over the memorial, which manages to avoid being over the top – just.

DC's oldest art museum, the **Corcoran Gallery** (☎ 202-639-1700; cnr 17th St & New York Ave NW; adult/child under 13 $10/8; 🕒 10am-5pm Wed-Sun, to 9pm Thu), has had a tough time standing up to the free, federal competition around the block, but this hasn't stopped it from maintaining one of the most eclectic exhibitions in the country.

Touted as 'the most interactive museum in the world,' the **Newseum** (☎ 888-639-7386; www.newseum.org; 555 Pennsylvania Ave; admission adult/child $20/10) gives too much of the worst cable news has to offer: lots of flash, little substance. It's also a bit of sloppy self-love on the part of journalists. Still, it's great for the kids, and the memorial to journos killed in pursuit of the truth and the exhibits on press freedoms and ethics are worth the price of admission.

Groundbreaking occurred on the **Martin Luther King Jr National Memorial** in November, 2006, in West Potomac Park, but at the time of research, the memorial's project foundation was seeking funds to secure construction permits.

Capitol Hill

The Capitol, appropriately, sits atop Capitol Hill (what L'Enfant called 'a pedestal waiting for a monument') across a plaza from the almost-as-regal Supreme Court and Library of Congress. Congressional office buildings surround the plaza. A pleasant residential district stretches from E Capitol St to Lincoln Park. Union Station, Capitol South and Eastern Market metro stations serve this area.

CAPITOL

Since 1800, this is where the legislative branch of American government – ie Congress – has met to write the country's laws. The lower House of Representatives (438 members) and upper Senate (100) meet respectively in the south and north wings of the building.

In 2008 work was finally completed on a **visitor center** (☎ 202-225-6827; www.aoc.gov; 1st St NE), which showcases the exhaustive background of a building that fairly sweats history. The center also provides free tours of the building –

be on the lookout for statues of two famous residents per state, plus some of the most stunning, baroque/neoclassical architecture in the nation. The interior of the building is as daunting as the exterior, if a little cluttered with the busts, statues and personal mementos of generations of Congress members.

To watch Congress in action, call ☎ 202-225-6827 for session dates. US citizens can request visitor passes from their representatives or senators (☎ 202-224-3121); foreign visitors show passports at the House gallery. Congressional committee hearings are actually more interesting (and substantive) if you care about what's being debated; check for a schedule, locations and to see if they're open to the public (they often are) at www.house.gov and www.senate.gov.

LIBRARY OF CONGRESS

To prove to Europeans that America was cultured, John Adams plunked the world's largest **library** (LOC; ☎ exhibitions 202-707-5000; www.loc.gov; 101 Independence Ave SE; admission free; 10am-5:30pm Mon-Sat) on Capitol Hill. The LOC's motivation is simple: 'universality,' the idea that all knowledge is useful. Stunning in scope and design, the building's baroque interior and neoclassical flourishes are set off by a Main Reading Room that looks like an ant colony constantly harvesting 29 million books. The visitor center and tours of the reading rooms are both located in the Jefferson Building, just behind the Capitol building.

SUPREME COURT

Even non–law students are impressed by the **highest court in America** (☎ 202-479-3030; 1 1st St NE; admission free; 9am-4:30pm Mon-Fri). Arrive early to watch arguments (Monday to Wednesday October to April) or bench sittings (Monday mid-May to June). You can visit the permanent exhibits and the building's seven-spiral staircase year-round.

UNION STATION & AROUND

Union Station (☎ 202-289-1908; www.unionstationdc.com; 50 Massachusetts Ave) greets train visitors to the capital with a gorgeous 1908 beaux-arts building. Its great hall was modeled on the Roman baths of Diocletian.

Also recommended in this area:

Folger Shakespeare Library (☎ 202-544-4600; 201 E Capitol St; admission free; 10am-4pm Mon-Sat) Houses the world's largest collection of Shakespeare materials.

National Postal Museum (☎ 202-633-8181; 2 Massachusetts Ave NE; admission free; 10am-5:30pm) Has the planet's largest stamp collection, antique mail plane and touching war letters.

US Botanic Garden (☎ 202-225-8333; 245 1st St SW; admission free; 10am-5pm) Hot, sticky, green and enormous: more than 26,000 different species of plants flower here.

Tidal Basin

It's magnificent to stroll around this man-made inlet and watch the monument lights wink across the Potomac, especially during the Cherry Blossom Festival (p331), the city's annual spring rejuvenation, when the basin bursts into a pink and white floral collage (thanks for the trees, Japanese ambassador from 1912). **Paddleboat rentals** (1501 Maine Ave, SW; 2-person boat per hr $7) are available at the boathouse.

The be-domed **Jefferson Memorial** (☎ 202-426-6822; 900 Ohio Drive, SW, south side of Tidal Basin; admission free; 8am-11:45pm), etched with the founding father's most famous writings, might win the 'best quotes on the inside of a DC memorial' award.

The **FDR Memorial** (Memorial Park; admission free; 24hr) is a 7.5-acre tribute to the longest-serving president in US history and the era he governed. In a thoughtful, well-laid-out path, visitors are taken through the Depression, the New Deal–era and WWII. It's best visited at night, when the interplay of rock, fountains and the lights of the Mall are enchanting.

Downtown

Downtown Washington began in what is now called Federal Triangle, but has since spread north and east, encompassing the area east of the White House to Judiciary Sq at 4th St, and from the Mall north to roughly M St. Hours of operation for the attractions listed here are 10am to 5:30pm daily, unless otherwise noted.

It's hard not to feel a little in awe of the big three documents in the **National Archives** (☎ 866-272-6272; www.archives.gov; 700 Constitution Ave; admission free; 10am-9pm summer, to 5:30pm rest of year). The Declaration of Independence, the Constitution and the Bill of Rights, plus one of four copies of the Magna Carta: taken together, it becomes clear just how radical the American experiment was for its time. The Public Vaults, a bare scratching of archival bric-a-brac, are a flashy rejoinder to the main exhibit – and speaking of which, do *not* use the flash on your camera here.

Don't miss the **Reynolds Center for American Art** (☎ 202-275-1500; cnr F St & 8th St NW; http://reynoldscenter.org; admission free), which combines the **National Portrait Gallery** with the **American Art Museum**. From haunting depictions of the inner city and rural heartland to the self-taught visions of itinerant wanderers, the center has dedicated itself to capturing the relentless optimism and critical self-appraisal of American art, and succeeds in a big way.

You like those bits in the Bond movies with Q? Then you'll like the immensely popular **International Spy Museum** (☎ 202-393-7798; www.spymuseum.org; 800 F St NW; adult/child 6-11 $18/15; 10am-6pm, slightly longer hours summer & weekends); all the undercover tools-of-the-trade on display make this place great for (secret) history buffs. Get there early. Hours change seasonally, so it's best to check online or call first.

Devoted to the architectural arts, the under-appreciated **National Building Museum** (☎ 202-272-2448; www.nbm.org; 401 F St NW; donations accepted; 10am-5pm Mon-Sat, from 11am Sun) is appropriately housed in an architectural jewel: the 1887 Old Pension Building. Four stories of ornamented balconies flank the dramatic 316ft-wide atrium, and the gold-colored Corinthian columns rise 75ft high. The various permanent and rotating exhibits on different aspects of architecture are sequestered in rooms off the atrium.

The **Marian Koshland Science Museum of the National Academy of Sciences** (☎ 202-334-1201; cnr 6th & E Sts; adult/child 5-18yr $5/3) is a big, kid-friendly complex of hands-on, educational fun.

The red-carpeted entrance and dignified Grand Salon of **Renwick Gallery** (☎ 202-633-7970; cnr 17th St & Pennsylvania Ave NW; admission free) is crammed with 19th-century paintings – a startling contrast to the wild, whimsical craftwork in the adjoining rooms. It's worth a visit just for Wendell Castle's *Ghost Clock*.

Grub out at the sweet international food court in the **Old Post Office Pavilion** (☎ 202-298-4224; www.oldpostofficedc.com; 1100 Pennsylvania Ave NW; admission free; 10am-8pm Mon-Sat, noon-7pm Sun Mar-Aug, 10am-7pm Mon-Sat, noon-6pm Sun Sep-Feb), which also happens to be an elegant 1899 Romanesque revival landmark. The 400ft observation tower gives great downtown panoramas.

On April 14, 1865, John Wilkes Booth assassinated Abraham Lincoln in his box seat at **Ford's Theatre** (☎ 202-347-4833; 511 10th St). The theater still operates today, with its threadbare, basement **Lincoln Museum** (admission free; 9am-5pm) devoted to the assassination. Across the street, **Peterson House** (516 10th St NW; admission free; 9am-5pm) is where Lincoln gave up the ghost the next morning.

White House & Foggy Bottom

An expansive park called the Ellipse borders the Mall; on the east side is the power-broker block of Pennsylvania Ave. Foggy Bottom was named for the mists that belched out of a local gasworks; now, as the home of the State Department and George Washington University, it's an upscale (if not terribly lively) 'hood crawling with students and professionals.

WHITE HOUSE

You can practically hear the theme to *The West Wing* as you walk by 1600 Pennsylvania Ave, and at night the grounds are so stately you'll want to snap off a salute. The White House has survived both fire (the Brits) and expansions in its day. Jacqueline Kennedy redecorated with her stylish touch, Franklin Roosevelt added a pool, Clinton a jogging track and George W Bush a T-ball field. Cars can no longer pass the White House on Pennsylvania Ave, clearing the area for posing school groups and round-the-clock peace activists.

A self-guided **tour** (☎ 202-456-7041; 7:30am-noon Tue-Sat) will lead you through the ground and 1st floors, but the 2nd and 3rd floors are off-limits. Unfortunately these tours are only available to groups of 10 or more and need to be arranged months in advance. Americans must apply via one of their state's members of Congress, and non-Americans must apply through either the US consulate in their home country or their country's consulate in DC. If that sounds like too much work, pop into the **White House visitor center** (☎ 202-456-7041; www.whitehouse.gov; Chamber of Commerce Bldg, cnr 15th & E Sts NW; 7:30am-4pm); it's not the real deal, but hey, there's executive paraphernalia scattered about.

The riverfront **Watergate complex** (2650 Virginia Ave NW) encompasses apartments, boutiques, and the office towers that made 'Watergate' a byword for political scandal after it broke that President Nixon's 'plumbers' had bugged the headquarters of the 1972 Democratic National Committee.

Adams Morgan, Shaw & U Street

If it's not party time in Adams Morgan, it's time to get a hangover-cure lunch from an Ethiopian or Central American diner. This multiethnic neighborhood (especially 18th St) becomes sin central on weekend nights. The area isn't easily metro-accessible; try to catch bus 98, which runs between Adams Morgan and U Street Metro stations.

To the east, Shaw stretches from around Thomas Circle to Meridian Hill Park and from N Capitol St to 15th St NW. Best known for its African American heritage, back in the 1930s the **Lincoln Theatre** (☎ 202-328-6000; 1215 U St NW) was a high point on the 'chitlin' circuit' of African American entertainment, hosting celebrities such as DC native Duke Ellington. Following the 1968 assassination of Dr Martin Luther King Jr, riots devastated the commercial district. This area has since undergone a renaissance; there are lots of excellent restaurants and bars around.

Dupont Circle

A well-heeled splice of gay community and DC diplomatic scene, this is city life at its best. Great restaurants, bars, bookstores, cafés, captivating architecture and the electric energy of a lived-in, happening neighborhood make Dupont worth a linger. The local historic mansions have largely been converted into embassies, and Embassy Row (on Massachusetts Ave), runs through DC's thumping gay heart.

The **Phillips Collection** (☎ 202-387-2152; www.phillipscollection.org; 1600 21st St NW; admission free Tue-Fri, special exhibitions vary; 🕒 10am-5pm Tue-Sat, 10am-8:30pm Thu summer, 11am-6pm Sun) was the first modern-art museum in the country; its main draw is whatever the special exhibition happens to be at the moment. Always first-rate.

Rotating exhibits on worldwide expeditions are found at the **National Geographic Society's Explorer Hall** (☎ 202-857-7588; 1145 17 St NW; admission free; 🕒 9am-5pm Mon-Sat, from 10am Sun).

Know your warp from your woof? Set in a quiet neighborhood, the oft-overlooked **Textile Museum** (☎ 202-667-0441; www.texttilemuseum.org; 2320 S St NW; requested donation $5; 🕒 10am-5pm Mon-Sat, from 1pm Sun) is the country's only museum devoted to the textile arts.

Georgetown

Georgetown is so damn regal it doesn't need public transportation. No, seriously, the Metro doesn't stop here, but thousands of the bright and beautiful, from Georgetown students to ivory-tower academics and diplomats call this leafy, aristocratic neighborhood home. At night, shop-a-block M St becomes congested with traffic, turning into a weird mix of high-school cruising night and high-street boutique.

Get a historical overview from the **visitor center** (☎ 202-653-5190; 1057 Thomas Jefferson St NW; 🕒 10am-4pm). Costumed guides lead visitors on a history-intensive, hour-long, mule-driven barge trip along the **C&O Canal towpath** (adult/child $8/5).

A museum featuring exquisite Byzantine and pre-Columbian art is housed within the historic mansion at **Dumbarton Oaks** (☎ 202-339-6401; cnr R & 31st Sts NW); the 10 acres of outstanding formal **gardens** (adult/child $8/5 Apr-Oct, free Nov-Mar; 🕒 2-6pm Tue-Sun) are a treat as well.

Bill Clinton went to school at **Georgetown University** (☎ 202-687-0100; 37th & O Sts), which should give you an idea of the student body: smart, hard-working party people.

The **Potomac Heritage National Scenic Trail** connects Chesapeake Bay to the Allegheny Highlands in a 700-mile corridor. It includes the C&O Canal towpath, the 17-mile Mt Vernon Trail (Virginia), and the 75-mile Laurel Highlands Trail (Pennsylvania). See p330 for bike-rental information.

Anacostia

The drive from Georgetown to Anacostia takes about 30 minutes and the patience to endure a world of income disparity. The neighborhood's smack-, crack- and brick row houses sitting mere miles from the Mall form one of DC's great contradictory panoramas, yet strong communities persist. More tourists started arriving on the first day of the baseball season in 2008, when Nationals Stadium opened, bringing with it double-edged gentrification. The impact of renovation dollars can already be seen at some spruced-up intersections.

Freedom fighter and man of letters Frederick Douglass' home is now the **Frederick Douglass National Historic Site** (☎ 202-426-5960; 1411 W St SE; admission free; 🕒 9am-4pm). Despite an awfully cheesy intro movie, the on-site rangers are fantastically helpful, and

OFFBEAT WASHINGTON, DC

Father Karras tumbled to his cinematic death down the staircase nowadays referred to as the **Exorcist Steps** (3600 Prospect St, Georgetown).

Those of timid stock better stick to the amputation kits and the bullet that killed Lincoln on display at the **National Museum of Health & Medicine** (☎ 202-782-2200; 6900 Georgia Ave, at Elder St NW; admission free; 🕒 10am-5:30pm), which remains open while its exhibits are moved to Bethesda, MD. The rest of us will be staring in horrified fascination at jars of elephantitis-stricken legs, conjoined twins and megacolons.

The Awakening is a spectacular statue of a man climbing out of the ground. His giant head, arm, knee and foot have delighted visitors for years. In 2007 the trapped giant finally freed himself when he was moved to National Harbor, a waterfront development project in Maryland 8 miles south of the city. From his new harbor home, developers say the giant will be clawing his way out of the banks of the Potomac.

In Anacostia, the **world's largest chair** towers over Martin Luther King Ave and V St.

The **Albert Einstein monument** (cnr Constitution Ave & 21st St NW) on the lawn of the National Academy of Sciences is a little-known statue of the frumpy physicist. His lap just begs to be climbed onto.

You may need binoculars to spot it, but that is indeed **Darth Vader's Head** on the west tower of the National Cathedral (below). Luke's dad shares space with a pig-tailed girl, a raccoon and an umbrella-toting man, all designs sent in by children for a cathedral-sponsored contest in the 1980s.

the house, with its commanding view over crumbling Anacostia, speaks to the heights that black America has reached and the wide gaps it has left to bridge.

The Smithsonian's **Anacostia Community Museum** (☎ 202-287-3306; 1901 Fort Pl SE; 🕒 10am-5pm) is surrounded by the community that is the subject of its educational mission, and houses good rotating exhibits on the African American experience in the USA. Call ahead, as the museum closes for about a month between installations.

Around Washington, DC

While plenty of DC buildings take a leaf from the 'inspire reverent awe' school of design, they're rarely religious in nature (unless you consider patriotism a religion). The Gothic **Washington National Cathedral** (☎ 202-537-6200; www.cathedral.org; cnr Massachusetts & Wisconsin Aves; admission free; 🕒 10am-5:30pm Mon-Sat, 8am-6:30pm Sun), as hushed and overwhelming as its European counterparts, breaks this rule. It's officially Episcopal, but serves as the 'national house of prayer for all people,' and is a common venue for First Family weddings and the like. The Bishop's Garden and the gargoyle tour are recommended. Fees vary.

ACTIVITIES

Under the auspices of the National Park Service (NPS), the 1775 acres of **Rock Creek Park** follow Rock Creek as it winds through the northwest of the city. There's miles of bicycling, hiking and horseback-riding trails, and even a few coyotes. The C&O Canal offers bicycling and hiking trails in canalside parks, and the lovely 11-mile **Capital Crescent Trail** (www.cctrail.org) connects Georgetown north to Silver Spring, MD, via some splendid Potomac River views. Fifteen miles north of DC, **Great Falls National Park** (www.nps.gov/grfa) is a fairly outstanding slice of wilderness, great for rafting or rock climbing some of the beautiful cliffs that hang over the Potomac.

Thompson Boat Center (☎ 202-333-9543; cnr Virginia Ave & Rock Creek Pkwy NW) at the Potomac River end of Rock Creek Park rents canoes (per hour $8), tandem kayaks (per hour $10) and bikes (per day $25). **Big Wheel Bikes** (☎ 202-337-0254; 1034 33rd St; per hr/day $7/25; 🕒 11am-7pm Tue-Fri, 10am-6pm Sat & Sun) is also a good bike-rental outfitter.

WASHINGTON, DC, FOR CHILDREN

Museums around the city will entertain and educate children of all ages. But if you – or they – tire of indoor attractions, there are plenty of parks and playgrounds, such as the **Guy Mason Playground** (3600 Calvert St NW) off Wisconsin Ave.

Many hotels offer babysitting services, but here are a few independent agencies:

Bring Along the Children (☎ 202-484-0889) Offers day and evening babysitting services and kid-oriented tours.

Mothers' Aides (☎ 703-250-0700, 800-526-2669; www.mothersaides.com)

The Mall

The wide-open spaces of the Mall are perfect for outdoor family fun, whether you want to throw a Frisbee, have a picnic, ride the world's oldest **carousel** (tickets $2) or stroll through museums.

Kids like things that go squish and/or make other things go squish; they can find both in the dinosaurs and insects of the National Museum of Natural History (p325). The John F Kennedy Center for the Performing Arts (p337) puts on entertaining shows for tots, and the National Air & Space Museum (p325), has moon rocks, IMAX films and a wild simulation ride.

The **Discovery Theater** (☎ 202-633-9700; www.discoverytheater.org; 1010 Jefferson Dr; tickets adult/child $6/5; performances 10am & 11:30am Jan-Jul), in the basement of the Ripley Center, stages magical theatrical performances.

The **National Theatre** (p337) offers free Saturday-morning performances from puppet shows to tap dancers (reservations required).

The **National Children's Museum** (☎ 202-675-4120; www.ncm.museum) will reopen its expanded doors in 2013 in the National Harbor Complex south of the city.

Off the Mall

The **National Zoological Park** (☎ 202-633-4800; 3000 Connecticut Ave NW; admission free; 10am-6pm Apr-Oct, to 5pm Nov-Mar) is home to some 2000 species in natural habitats. The 'Asia Trail' is an excellent open-air stroll by some of the most fascinating ecosystems (and their inhabitants) of the world's largest continent.

Located about 15 miles east of downtown in Largo, MD, **Six Flags America** (☎ 301-249-1500; adult/child over 3 $50/25; May-Oct) offers a full array of roller coasters and tamer kiddie rides.

TOURS

Bike the Sites (☎ 202-966-8662; www.bikethesites.com; adult/child under 13 $40/30; Mar-Nov) The three-hour 'Capital sites' tour is a favorite with families.

Scandal Tours (☎ 202-783-7212; www.gnpcomedy.com/ScandalTours.html; adult/student $30/20; tours 1pm Sat Apr-Sep) Run by comedy troupe Gross National Product, it dishes all the gossip about DC's infamous spots, covering George Washington to George Dubya.

City Segway Tours (☎ 202-626-0017; http://citysegwaytours.com/washington-dc) Extremely popular and relaxing way of seeing the major sites along the Mall and in Penn Quarter ($70).

Tourmobile Sightseeing (☎ 202-554-5100, 888-868-7707; www.tourmobile.com) An open-air trolley runs daily between the major sights. Tons of theme tours are offered, including the spectacular Washington-by-night 'Twilight Tour' (adult/child $27/13).

FESTIVALS & EVENTS

National Cherry Blossom Festival (☎ 877-442-5666; www.nationalcherryblossomfestival.org) Held late March to early April. DC at her prettiest.

Smithsonian's Folklife Festival (☎ 202-633-6440; www.festival.si.edu) This fun family event, held over two weekends in June and July, features distinctive regional folk art, crafts, food and music.

Independence Day Not surprisingly, a big deal here, celebrated on July 4 with the best freakin' fireworks ever.

SLEEPING

Washington DC Accommodations (☎ 202-289-2220, 800-503-3330; www.wdcahotels.com) provides assistance with lodging. For B&Bs citywide, contact **Bed & Breakfast Accommodations** (☎ 877-893-3233; www.bedandbreakfastdc.com). Parking costs constantly shift at the following properties; expect to pay $20 to $40 for in-and-out privileges.

Budget

Washington International Student Center (☎ 202-667-7681; www.washingtondchostel.com; 2451 18th St NW; dm $25; check-in 8am-11pm; P) Located well in the heart of Adams Morgan; you can basically stumble out of the club directly into your bed here. Decent dorms and free parking for your first night.

HI-Washington, DC (☎ 202-737-2333; www.hiwashingtondc.org; 1009 11th St NW, at K St; dm incl breakfast from $25;) If you're looking for an enormous (ie 270-room), friendly hostel full of fun, young international types, look no further than this budget institution. Non–HI members incur a $3 fee.

Lofty Inn (☎ 202-506-7106; www.dclofty.com; 1333 11th St NW; dm from $33;) Located in a crisp, clean house near the Convention Center, Lofty, with its brick walls and smooth wood floors, vaguely delivers on the implied hipness and semiluxury its name suggests. That said, the dorms are just dorms – nothing to go wild over.

Midrange

Dupont Collection (☎ 202-467-6777; http://thedupontcollection.com; r $95-230; P); Dupont North (1620 T St NW) Dupont South (1312 19th St NW) If you're craving a good range of B&B coziness in the heart of the capital, check out the four excellent heritage properties run by the Dupont Collection. Perhaps most convenient for the visitor are the inns at Dupont North and South; the former feels like the modernly appointed home of a wealthy friend, while the latter evokes much more of a chintz-and-lacy-linen sensibility. Other properties: Brookland Inn and the Jackson Guest House, both in the far northeast.

Adam's Inn (☎ 202-745-3600; www.adamsinn.com; 1746 Lanier Pl NW; r $109-159; P) It can be a struggle to get eye contact, let alone one-on-one service in DC, but this town-house B&B provides all of the above, plus fluffy linens and a central location.

Tabard Inn (☎ 202-785-1277; 1739 N St NW; r from $158; P) The Tabard is an elegant piece of work, but elegant in a slightly subdued way. From the pretty, antique-ed out guest rooms you could easily feel as if it were time to go fox hunting. Or wining and dining in the nearby urban jungle of Dupont Circle.

Hotel Helix (☎ 202-296-7700; www.hotelhelix.com; 1430 Rhode Island Ave NW; r from $180; P) Modish and highlighter bright, the Helix is playfully cool – the perfect hotel for the bouncy international set that makes up the surrounding neighborhood of Dupont Circle. Little touches suggest a youthful energy (Pop Rocks in the minibar) balanced with worldly cool, like the pop-punk decor – just camp enough to be endearing. Parking is $27.

Dupont Hotel (☎ 202-483-6000; www.doylecollection.com; 1500 New Hampshire Ave NW; r from $189; P) Part of the Doyle group, this spot is chic and glamorous, in a more contemporary and sleek fashion than the embassy row it sits near. The general vibe is somewhere between nightclub, art gallery and big box hotel.

Top End

Morrison-Clark Inn (☎ 202-898-1200; www.morrisonclark.com; 1015 L St NW; r from $200; P) The only hotel in town on the Register of Historic Places, this elegant inn has spacious rooms ranging from Victorian to neoclassical. Some come decked out with private balconies and marble fireplaces.

Hotel Monaco (☎ 202-628-7177, 800-649-1202; www.monaco-dc.com; 700 F St NW; r from $239; P) The neoclassical facade has aged with considerable grace at this marble temple to stylish glamour. Free goldfish on request and a geometric, deco-inspired interior helps polish the 1930s, cool-daddy-o vibe.

St Regis (☎ 202-638-2626; www.starwoodhotels.com; 923 16th & K St NW; r from $277; P) The St Regis is a tony downtown option that quite convincingly evokes all the pomp, circumstance, crystal chandeliers, tapestries and paintings in gilded frames you may associate with Washington, DC, lodging. The Regis is aristocratic and it knows it, and you'll feel the same after a night here.

Hay-Adams (☎ 202-638-6600; www.hayadams-dc.com; 800 16th St NW; r from $279; P) When you're right across the road from the White House, chances are you'll be swank and in style, as is the case with the Hay-Adams, one of the city's great heritage hotels. All the mod cons you could want are complimented by service and setting that is, cliché as it may be, fit for a head of state.

our pick **Mansion on O Street** (☎ 202-496-2020; www.omansion.com; 2020 O St NW; ste $550-4000; P) Enter this mansion and you've gone through the looking glass of the American hotel industry. Over 20 highly individualized suites pepper this property, ranging from the 'Graceland,' filled with Elvis and Marilyn Monroe kitsch, and the 'James Bond,' literally hidden behind a secret door. Each suite is gorgeously appointed and service is swift and discreet. The pinnacle of DC's sleeping stakes.

EATING

As you might expect of one of the world's most international cities, DC has an eclectic palette. No single culture defines its menu, although Southern Americans, Ethiopians, Asians and Latinos all try.

Capitol Hill

Eastern Market (225 7th St SE; 10am-6pm Tue-Fri, 8am-6pm Sat, 8am-4pm Sun) This covered arcade is more than a market – it's the focal point of residential Capitol Hill, the soul of the neighborhood without which this area might just be houses and roads. The oyster sandwich at the Market Lunch stall is divine.

Jimmy T's (☎ 202-546-3646; 501 E Capitol St; mains $6-10; 7am-3pm Tue-Sun) Jimmy's is a neighborhood joint of the old school, where folks cram in to read the *Post,* have a burger or an omelet or some coffee and basically be themselves. If you're hungover on Sunday and in Cap Hill, this is the place to cure yourself.

Sonoma (☎ 202-544-8088; 223 Pennsylvania Ave SE; mains $20-31; 🕑 11:30am-2:30pm Mon-Fri, 5:30-10pm Mon-Thu, 5:30-11pm Fri & Sat, 5:30-9pm Sun) Washington is a city that has embraced the wine bar genre with a vintner's passion, but there's a lot of mediocre executions of the genre about. Not Sonoma; there's great meat, great grape and great pairings thanks to friendly, knowledgeable staff.

Downtown & White House Area

Zaytinya (☎ 202-638-0800; 701 9th St NW; mezes $4-10; 🕑 11:30am-11:30pm Tue-Thu, to midnight Fri & Sat, to 10pm Sun & Mon) Good-looking waitstaff serve good-looking clientele Greek, Lebanese and Turkish meze against a sleek, spacious white, brown and Hellenic-blue backdrop.

Burma Restaurant (☎ 202-638-1280; 740 6th St NW; mains from $10; 🕑 11am-3pm Mon-Fri, 6-10pm daily) Actually, the cuisine is more Shan, but since no one knows the difference and the food is still great, who cares? The mango pork is reason alone to revel in this mortal coil.

Matchbox Pizza (☎ 202-289-4441; 713 H St NW; pizzas $13-20; 🕑 11am-10:30pm, to 1am Fri & Sat, to 10pm Sun) The pizza here rocketed into the DC gastronomic universe with a vengeance, and you can't come here now without finding the restaurant packed with the curious and the satisfied. What's so good about it? Fresh ingredients, a crust baked by angels, and more fresh ingredients.

Jaleo (☎ 202-628-7949; 480 7th St NW; tapas $6-10, dinner mains $16; 🕑 11:30am-11:30pm Tue-Thu, to midnight Fri & Sat, to 10pm Sun & Mon) The whole tapas thing has been done to death, but Jaleo helped start the trend in DC and still serves some of the best Spanish cuisine in town. The interior is an Iberian pastiche of explosive color and vintage mural-dom, which all underlines, rather than overpowers, the quality of the excellent food.

Georgia Brown's (☎ 202-393-4499; 950 15th St NW; mains $16-32; 🕑 11:30am-10pm Mon-Fri, 5-10pm Sat, 10am-2:15pm & 5-9:30pm Sun) Georgia Brown's treats the humble ingredients of the American South (shrimp, okra, red rice, grits and sausage) with the respect great French chefs give their provincial dishes. The result is consistently excellent regional American cuisine: high-class Southern food from the Carolina Lowcountry served in a warm, autumnal interior.

our pick Minibar at Café Atlantico (☎ 202-393-0812; tasting menu $120; 405 8th St NW; 🕑 6pm & 8:30pm, Tue-Sat) Atlantico's minibar is foodie nirvana, where the curious get wowed by animal bits spun into cotton candy and cocktails frothed into clouds, and all the conceptualization of food that says we, as a society, have a lot of time on our hands. The tasting menu, entirely determined by the chef, is often delicious, and at least original.

Adams Morgan, Shaw & U Street

Julia's Empanadas (☎ 202-328-6232; 2452 18th St NW; empanadas $3; 🕑 10:30am-10:30pm Mon-Thu, to 4am Fri & Sat, to 8pm Sun) In Europe, you soak up your beer with a kabob. Here, you go to Julia's, where the Salvadoran owner/namesake still rolls out meat-and-cheese pocket pastries that go down great even when you're stone-cold sober.

Florida Avenue Grill (☎ 202-265-1586; 1100 Florida Ave NW; mains $4-7; 🕑 8am-9pm Tue-Sat, to 4:30pm Sun) Your stomach will thank you, even if your heart decides to pack it in after feasting on the Grill's Southern standards of fried catfish and collard greens. This joint's been raking 'em in since 1944 and has the celebrity photos and neighborhood loyalty to prove it.

Ben's Chili Bowl (☎ 202-667-0909; 1213 U St NW; mains $4-8; 🕑 11am-2am Mon-Thu, to 4am Fri & Sat, noon-8pm Sun) Every night the lines stretch around the block from this institution, known as much for its welcoming atmosphere as its excellent food. Go for a half-smoked, DC's (better) version of your hot dog slathered in cheese and (what else?) chili.

Mixtec (☎ 202-797-1819; 1792 Columbia Rd NW; mains $5-10; 🕑 9am-10pm Sun-Thu, 10am-11pm Fri & Sat) Budget Mexican that eschews the taco/burrito/enchilada drabness of the genre, Mixtec is justifiably popular with Anglos and Latinos. The moles are freshly prepared, the meat authentically spiced (rumors say they use more than 200 seasonings) and the huevos rancheros are a great hangover cure.

Cork (☎ 202-265-2675; www.corkdc.com; 1720 14th St NW; small plates $5-14; 🕑 5pm-1am) This dark 'n' cozy wine bar manages to come off as foodie magnet and friendly neighborhood hangout all at once, which is a feat. Smart wine choices plus small plates equals culinary bliss – with this innovative menu (and excellent cheese selection) you generally can't go wrong, although those little dishes do add up on the wallet.

Busboys & Poets (☎ 387-7638; 2021 14th St NW; mains $6-15; 🕑 8am-midnight Mon-Fri, 9am-midnight Sat & Sun) In just a few years, Busboys (named for a Langston Hughes poem) has become a US stalwart, an African American–owned business where everyone seems to gather for coffee, wi-fi, café fare and a progressive vibe (and attached bookstore) that makes San Francisco feel conservative.

Vegetate (☎ 232-4585; 1414 9th St NW; mains $6-15; 6–10pm, to 11pm Fri, noon-11pm Sat; V) As you read, probably the best vegetarian food in town is being served here: blue cheese skillet bread and Bambi-friendly risottos, all prepped with ingredients culled from local farms. You enter, you eat, you leave, feeling good about your meal, your karma, your place in the circle of delicious life.

Pasta Mia (☎ 202-328-9114; 1790 Columbia Rd NW; mains $10-15; 6:30-10pm Mon-Sat) Even cold weather doesn't deter the faithful from lining up for their turn at affordable, monstrously portioned Italian on checkered tablecloths. No reservations or line-jumping bribes accepted.

Meskerem (☎ 202-462-4100; 2434 18th St NW; mains $10-20; noon-midnight Sun-Thu, to 3am Fri & Sat) A standby of the local Ethiopian scene, Meskerem is three floors of communal eating goodness smack in the African heart of Adams Morgan.

Dupont Circle

Malaysia Kopitiam (☎ 202-833-6232; 1827 M St NW; mains $5-12; 11:30am-10pm Mon-Thu, to 11pm Fri & Sat, noon-10pm Sun) If you're familiar with Malaysian food, this is as close as you get to a Penang street stall in Washington. If you're not, may we introduce you to: laksa, bowls of noodle soup cut with coconut milk and pillowy chunks of chicken, and spiced dried fish, plus anything cooked in a banana leaf. It's next door to Camelot, DC's most (in)famous stripper bar.

our pick **Bistro Du Coin** (☎ 202-234-6969; 1738 Connecticut Ave NW; mains $8-24; 11:30am-11pm Tue, Wed & Sun, 11:30am-1am Thu-Sat) Mon Dieu! Bistro has a reputation for serving roll-up-your-sleeves, American-sized portions of rustic French favorites such as *steak-frites* (grilled steak and French fries), cassoulet, rabbit stew, and tureens of its famous *moules* (mussels). This place is always packed, usually with happy European diplomats and other Old World expats.

Afterwords (☎ 202-387-1400; 1517 Connecticut Ave NW; mains $12-16; 7:30am-1am Sun-Thu, 24hr Fri & Sat) Not your average bookstore café, this spot attached to Kramerbooks will stimulate your palate as much as the novel you just bought stimulates your mind.

Georgetown

Baked & Wired (☎ 202-333-2500; 1052 Thomas Jefferson St NW; mains $3; 6am-7pm Mon-Fri, 9am-7pm Sat, 11am-5pm Sun) With one of the US's great universities only a latte away, you'd think Georgetown would have more hip coffee shops, but alas, there's a lack. B&W makes up for this with a studio-chic interior and, more importantly, great coffee and some of the best cupcakes in DC.

Martin's Tavern (☎ 202-333-7370; 1264 Wisconsin Ave NW; lunch mains $8-15, dinner mains $12-27; from 11:30am) Martin's is a favorite with Georgetown students and US presidents, who all enjoy the old-school darkened dining room and quite possibly the best cheeseburger in town.

Hook (☎ 202-625-4488; www.hookdc.com; 3241 M St NW; mains $26-30; 11:30am-2:30pm Tue-Fri, 5-10pm Sun-Tue, to 11pm Wed-Sat, 11am-2:30pm Sat & Sun) Simple and sexy, with a frosty white Zen interior, Hook is the fish bar of the future: locally sourced seafood prepped artful and uncomplicated, so the flesh of your flounder or rockfish is allowed to play, with just the right nudge in the direction of deliciousness.

Citronelle (☎ 202-625-2150; tasting menu from $105; 3000 M St NW; 6-9:30pm) Big name Michel Richard started this show, a split-level study in the most creative twists tweakable on the American palate. Shrimp wrapped in phyllo dough spun from a cloud is a good example of the above, but order anything, and if in doubt, give the tasting menu some love.

Columbia Heights & Around

More and more restaurants and bars are opening in Columbia Heights and Petworth, north on the Green Line. Palena is in Cleveland Park, northwest on the Red Line.

Dos Gringos (☎ 202-462-1159; www.dosgringoscafe.com; 3116 Mt Pleasant St NW; mains $3-7.25; 7:30am-8pm Tue-Thu, to 9pm Fri, 9am-9pm Sat, 9am-4pm Sun) Latinos and Anglos alike line up to order off a bilingual menu that includes fresh veg burritos, cheap cups of coffee, curry chicken salads and portobello sandwiches.

our pick **Hitching Post** (☎ 202-726-1511; 200 Upshur St NW; mains $12-18; 10:30am-10pm Tue-Sat) 'This is East Coast jazz,' says the owner behind the counter of this Petworth diner. 'No one listens to this anymore.' Another song comes up; the Drifters. Really? The Drifters and jazz in a diner so neighborly it should put on a cardigan and loafers when it comes inside? Let's try the fried chicken…which, oh-mygod, is seriously like a whole, freaking fried chicken.

GAY & LESBIAN BARS & CLUBS

There is a gay bar scene concentrated around Dupont Circle. The funny thing about **Halo** (☎ 202-797-9730; 1435 P St NW) is it looks like it should be a total den of douchebaggery, what with its super-sleek spaceship style furniture and Euro-I'm-too-cool-for-school vibe, but then you go inside and it's a totally friendly, even laid-back gay bar. The crowd is older and accommodating, and generally a joy to be around.

JR's (☎ 202-328-0090; 1519 17th St NW), a popular gay hangout, is frequented by the 20- and 30-something, work-hard and play-hard set. Some DC residents claim that the crowd at JR's epitomizes the conservative nature of the capital's gay scene; but even if you love to hate it, as many do, JR's is the happy-hour spot in town and is packed more often than not.

Cobalt (☎ 202-232-4416; 1639 R St NW; admission Sun-Thu free, Fri & Sat $5) pretty much rules the roost of the DC club scene. The music is great, the bartenders are ripped and sufficiently shirtless and the scene is equal parts all about the hookup and getting down to some good (if pounding) dance music.

Served with two sides. And another man comes in and the owner calls him by name and the customer asks, 'This the Chi-lites?', and we know we're in love.

W Domku (☎ 202-722-7475; 821 Upshur St NW; mains $12-18; 🕑 5-11pm Tue & Wed, 10am-11pm Thu, to midnight Fri & Sat, to 10pm Sun) As unexpected as…well, a hip, artsy coffee shop in the middle of a very local Petworth strip of churches, funeral homes and Caribbean takeouts, Domku is a gem. The interior is like Ikea on good drugs, the food an intriguing execution of Polish, Norwegian and Russian fare.

Palena (☎ 537-9250; 3529 Connecticut Ave NW; fixed menu from $58; 🕑 5:30-10pm Tue-Sat) Roll up to Cleveland Park and get ready for a culinary ride into innovative gastro-orgasm land. Palena's menu defies our conventions, deliciously; Swiss chard served in ink ravioli, sturgeon wrapped in pancetta, and pheasant consommé. The interior is warm but oddly modern in its crafted rusticity, but to see or eat any of the above, book early.

DRINKING & ENTERTAINMENT

See the *Washington City Paper* or *Washington Post* weekend section (p321) for comprehensive listings. Conveniently located at the Old Post Office Pavilion, **Ticketplace** (☎ 202-842-5387; www.ticketplace.org; 1100 Pennsylvania Ave, NW; 🕑 11am-6pm Tue-Fri, 10am-5pm Sat) sells same-day concert and show tickets at half-price. Closing time is generally 2am weekdays, 3am weekends.

Bars & Nightclubs

CAPITOL HILL & DOWNTOWN

Hawk & Dove (☎ 202-543-3300; 329 Pennsylvania Ave SE; 🕑 from 10am) The quintessential Capitol Hill bar is a hot spot for political junkies, with intimate corner booths perfect for sipping pints and creating the next District scandal.

Palace of Wonders (☎ 202-398-7469; 1210 H St NE; 🕑 6pm-2am) Damn but DC needed this place: a permanent freak show. Seriously; the Palace puts on fire-eating, sword-swallowing and flea circuses every week, performed by a cast of regulars and appreciated by a tattooed (or not) audience that sinks plenty of beers during intermission (and during shows too, come to think of it).

ADAMS MORGAN, SHAW & U STREET

Tryst (☎ 202-232-5500; 2459 18th St; 🕑 from 6:30am Mon-Sat, 8am-12:30am Sun; wi-fi) The hodgepodge of tables and cozy sofas at this Greenwich Village–style coffeehouse/lizard lounge harbors patrons so faithful they should probably pay rent. There's wi-fi, but surfing's a no-no on weekend nights – you should be striking up a conversation with that cute stranger next to you anyway.

Chi-Cha Lounge (☎ 202-234-8400; 1624 U St NW; 🕑 from 5:30pm) Slip through the double-sided mirror door, settle into a low settee and order up a hookah of fruit-flavored tobacco. In the midst of this Middle Eastern atmosphere, the trendy clientele is nibbling Ecuadorian tapas and sipping Peruvian drinks.

Dan's Café (☎ 202-265-9241; 2315 18th St NW; 🕑 from 7:30pm Sun-Thu) Dan's dive is all the more grotty for its location: smack in the middle of the 18th St skimpy skirt parade. Inside this barely signed bar is dim lighting, old locals, J Crew–looking types slumming it and flasks of whiskey, coke and a bucket of ice for under $12 (!).

Marvin's (☎ 202-797-7171; www.marvindc.com; 2007 14th St NW; 🕒 5:30pm-2am) One of our favorite watering holes is always good for playing hottie spotty, but it's hardly intimidating. The roof deck is great for rubbing shoulders and sparking conversation on summer nights or in the midst of winter, when folks huddle under roaring heat lamps and enjoy imported Belgian beer.

Stetson's (☎ 202-667-6295; 1610 U St NW; 🕒 5pm-2am) Stetson's is a political spot and not. There's a good chance you'll be hanging with Senate staffers, but folks don't flash congressional ID badges here: they come for beer, peanuts and fun times. The beer garden is a bonus.

Saloon (☎ 462-2640; 1207 U St NW; 🕒 11am-2am, 2pm-2am Sat) The Saloon takes a firm stand against packing patrons in like sardines, with posted rules against standing between tables. That's great, because the added elbow room better allows you to enjoy brew ordered off one of the most extensive beer menus in town.

Madam's Organ (☎ 202-667-5370; 2461 18th St NW; cover weekday/weekend $3/5; 🕒 5pm-2am Sun-Thu, to 3am Fri & Sat) The Organ is a well-loved standby (*Playboy* named it one of the best bars in the country) and still one of the rowdiest, sweatiest, All-American-iest joints to catch some power blues, power rock and power shots.

DUPONT CIRCLE

our pick **Brickskeller** (☎ 202-293-1885; 1523 22nd St NW; 🕒 from 11:30am Mon-Fri, from 6pm Sat & Sun) Let's make this simple: *The Guinness Book of World Records* says the 'Skeller has the biggest variety of beer available. *In the world*. See you there.

Science Club (☎ 202-775-0747; 1136 19th St NW; 🕒 from 5pm) Everyone, from the geeky types implied by the name to the DC power set, comes here to shake a tailfeather to the blend of hip-hop, funk and house that thumps across the dimly lit floors of this excellent club.

Eighteenth Street Lounge (☎ 202-466-3922; 1212 18th St NW; 🕒 from 9:30pm Tue, Wed & Sat, from 5:30pm Thu & Fri) You know what cool is? Listening to the best DJs in the city spin while sipping a strong drink and chatting up the gorgeous clientele in this beautiful club. That's cool.

GEORGETOWN

Tombs (☎ 202-337-6668; 1226 36 St, at P St NW; 🕒 from 11:30am Mon-Sat, from 9:30am Sun) If it looks familiar, think back to the '80s; this was the setting for *St Elmo's Fire*. Today this cozy, windowless bar is a favorite with Georgetown students and profs boozing under crew regalia.

Mie N Yu Lounge (☎ 202-333-6122; 3125 M St NW; 🕒 from 4pm) Mie N Yu (pronounced 'Me an you' – ugh) lays snob appeal and the Asian-fusion lounge thing on pretty thick, and the bar prices are frankly outrageous. But it's popular with the gorgeous Georgetown set, who love to look as good as the dark bamboo-and-silk interior.

COLUMBIA HEIGHTS & AROUND

Raven (☎ 202-387-9274; 3125 Mt Pleasant Ave NW; 🕒 from noon) A dive! Huzzah! A dirty, skuzzy, cheapo DC dive! The Raven, with a jukebox full of oldies and more attitude than a pissed-off Ramone, can kick your ass. Give it some respect and you'll agree this is the best bar for warm-up drinking (and postclub beers) in the capital.

Looking Glass Lounge (☎ 202-722-7669; 3634 Georgia Ave NW; 🕒 5pm-1:30am Mon-Thu, to 2:30am Fri & Sat) Here's who you expect to find when you look through the Looking Glass: an old guy, one who's owned his chair at the bar for decades, in a broad-brimmed cap clutching a highball of Jameson as if to prove it. But drinking next to him is a crowd of 20- and 30-somethings who respect his presence, even as they crank the music under dark chandelier-ish lighting and commiserate in the beer garden out back.

Red Derby (☎ 202-291-5000; www.redderby.com; 3718 14th St NW; 🕒 5pm-2am Mon-Thu, to 3am Fri, 11am-3am Sat & Sun) There's no sign – always a good sign – just the symbol of a red hat. Underneath that cap, a hipster-punk lounge where the bartenders know the names, the sweet-potato fries soak up the beer ordered off an impressively long menu and – why yes, that is *The Princess Bride* – movies play on a projector screen. The lighting is bloodred and sexy, natch; you can't help but look good under it.

our pick **Wonderland** (☎ 202-232-5263; 1101 Kenyon St NW; 🕒 from 5pm) We've got a lot of time for Wonderland, which manages to combine punk sensibility and affordable drinks with a welcoming beer garden where you can chat up strangers on some outsize wooden benches. That done, take your new friend to the upstairs dancefloor, where local DJs spin and just-met couples get close.

Live Music

Spacious dive **9:30 Club** (☎ 202-393-0930; 815 V St NW; 🕑 hours vary with gigs) features two floors and a midsize stage, and is the best place in town to see bands such as Wilco, the Pixies or Jack Johnson. **Blues Alley** (☎ 202-333-4141; 1073 Wisconsin Ave NW; 🕑 from 8pm), a classy Georgetown jazz supper club, attracts some big-name artists. Entrance is through the alley just south of the intersection of Wisconsin and M.

Verizon Center (☎ 202-628-3200; 601 F St NW) is DC's great big sports arena–cum-big-name-band venue.

Performing Arts

John F Kennedy Center for the Performing Arts (☎ 202-467-4600; www.kennedy-center.org; 2700 F St NW) One of the best places to catch a performance. It occupies a gorgeous, grandiloquent space on the Potomac. The National Symphony, Washington Chamber Symphony and Washington Opera perform here, while the center's Millennium Stage puts on free performances at 6pm daily.

Wolf Trap Farm Park for the Performing Arts (☎ 703-255-1900; www.wolftrap.org; 1645 Trap Rd, Vienna, Virginia) This outdoor park some 40 minutes from downtown DC hosts summer performances by the National Symphony and other highly regarded musical and theatrical troupes.

The **National Theatre** (☎ 202-628-6161; www.nationaltheatre.org; 1321 Pennsylvania Ave NW; tickets $40-90) is Washington's oldest continuously operating theater, though the **Shakespeare Theatre** (☎ 202-547-1122; www.shakespearedc.org; 450 7th St NW; tickets $23-70) has a more evocative venue. In summer outdoor performances are held at **Carter Barron Amphitheatre** (cnr 16th St & Colorado Ave NW).

Sports

The city's football team, the **Washington Redskins** (☎ 301-276-6050; www.redskins.com), plays at **FedEx Field** (☎ 301-276-6000; 1600 Fedex Way, Landover, MD; tickets $40-500), east of DC in Maryland. The **Washington Nationals** (☎ 202-397-7328; http://washington.nationals.mlb.com), DC's baseball team, plays at **Nationals Stadium** (☎ 888-632-6287; 1500 S Capitol St SE), along the Anacostia riverfront in southeast DC. Soccer teams **DC United** (☎ 202-587-5000) and the women's **Washington Freedom** (☎ 202-547-3137) play at **Robert F Kennedy (RFK) Memorial Stadium** (☎ 800-664-5056; 2400 East Capitol St). Washington stole Baltimore's lacrosse team in 2007; now the **Washington Bayhawks** (☎ 866-994-2957; www.washingtonbayhawks.com), who used to play at Harbin field at Georgetown University, have moved to **Navy-Marine Corps Memorial Stadium** (550 Talour Ave, Annapolis, MD) in Annapolis.

The **Verizon Center** (☎ 202-628-3200, 202-432-7328; 601 F St NW) hosts the NHL Washington Capitals ice-hockey team and NBA Washington Wizards, WNBA Washington Mystics and Georgetown University Hoyas basketball games.

GETTING THERE & AWAY

Air

Washington Dulles International Airport (IAD; ☎ 703-572-2700), 25 miles west of the city center, and **Ronald Reagan Washington National Airport** (DCA; ☎ 703-417-8000), 22 miles south, are the main airports serving DC, although **Baltimore/Washington International Thurgood Marshall Airport** (BWI; ☎ 410-859-7111, 800-435-9294), 30 miles to the northeast, is also an option. All three airports, particularly Dulles and National, are major hubs for flights from around the world.

Bus & Train

The main bus company is **Greyhound** (☎ 202-289-5141; www.greyhound.com; 1005 1st St NE), which provides nationwide service. **Peter Pan Bus Lines** (☎ 800-343-9999; www.peterpanbus.com), which travels to northeastern US, uses a terminal just opposite Greyhound's. This neighborhood is deserted after dark, and the nearest Metro station is several blocks south (via 1st St NE) at Union Station. Cabs are usually available at the bus station, and you should use one; don't walk across town from the bus station at night.

MARC train (Maryland Rail Commuter; ☎ 800-325-7245; www.mtamaryland.com), the regional rail service for the Washington DC–Baltimore metro area, runs trains frequently to Baltimore ($7) and other Maryland towns ($4 to $9). Amtrak trains also run from here to destinations around the country, including New York City ($49), Chicago ($82) and Richmond ($22).

There are numerous cheap bus services to New York, Philadelphia and Richmond. Most charge around $20 for a one-way trip (it takes four to five hours). Pick-up locations are scattered around town, but are always Metro-accessible. Tickets usually need to be bought online, but can also be purchased at the bus itself if there is room. Try **New Century** (☎ 202-789-8222; www.2000coach.com; 513 H Street NW), **DC2NY** (☎ 202-332-2691; www.dc2ny.com; 20th St & Massachusetts Ave NW) or **WashNY** (☎ 866-287-6932; www.washny.com; 1333 19th St NW).

GETTING AROUND

To/From the Airport

Door-to-door airport shuttles from downtown DC (www.washingtondcairportshuttles.com) cost $14 one way from National and $29 one way from Dulles. National airport has its own Metro rail station, which is by far the cheapest option into the city (around $2) and pretty quick too. For door-to-door van service between all three airports and downtown DC, the 5A **Metrobus** (☎ 202-637-7000; www.wmata.com; tickets $3) runs from the Dulles car-rental area to Rosslyn Metro station and central DC (L'Enfant Plaza; $3) once an hour, or try the more cushy and timely **Washington Flyer** (☎ 888-927-4359; www.washfly.com), which runs to West Falls Church Metro ($10), or **SuperShuttle** (☎ 800-258-3826; www.supershuttle.com; $27). Not much room for baggage.

Car

Car rentals include the following:

Budget (☎ Dulles airport 703-437-9559, Reagan airport 703-872-0320; www.budget.com)

Dollar (☎ Dulles airport 866-434-2226, 703-661-6630; www.dollar.com)

Thrifty (☎ 877-283-0898; www.thrifty.com)

Public Transportation

Metrobus (☎ 202-637-7000; www.wmata.com) operates buses throughout the city and suburbs (tickets from $1.20). **Metrorail** (☎ 202-637-7000; www.wmata.com) runs to most sights, hotel and business districts, and to the Maryland and Virginia suburbs. Trains operate from 5:30am to midnight weekdays and from 8am to 1am weekends. Machines inside stations sell computerized fare cards; fares cost from $1.20. All-day excursion passes cost $5.

Taxi

Try **Capitol Cab** (☎ 202-636-1600), **Diamond** (☎ 202-387-6200) or **Yellow Cab** (☎ 202-544-1212).

MARYLAND

Maryland is often described as 'America in Miniature,' and for good reason. This small state has the best bits of the country, from the Appalachian Mountains in the west to sandy white beaches in the east. A blend of Northern streetwise and Southern down-home gives this most osmotic of border states an appealing identity crisis. Her main city, Baltimore, is a sharp, demanding port town; the Eastern Shore jumbles artsy yuppies and working fishermen; while the DC suburbs are packed with government and office workers seeking green space, and the poor seeking lower rents. Yet it all works. Who cares about identity when you can kick back with a bushel of blue crabs, a case of Natty Boh beer and experience the beauty of Chesapeake country?

History

George Calvert set Maryland up as a refuge for persecuted English Catholics in 1634 when he purchased St Mary's City from the local Piscataway, whom he initially tried to coexist with. Puritan refugees drove both Piscataway and Catholics from control and shifted power to Annapolis; their harassment of Catholics produced the Tolerance Act, a flawed but progressive law that allowed freedom of any (Christian) worship in Maryland – a North American first.

That commitment to diversity has always characterized this state, despite a mixed record

MARYLAND FACTS

Nickname The Old Line State, The Free State

Population 5.63 million

Area 12,407 sq miles

Capital city Annapolis (population 36,603)

Sales tax 6%

Birthplace of Abolitionist Frederick Douglass (1818–95), baseball great Babe Ruth (1895–1948), actor David Hasselhoff (b 1952), filmmakers John Waters (b 1946) and Barry Levinson (b 1942), author Tom Clancy (b 1947), swimmer Michael Phelps (b 1985)

Home of 'The Star-Spangled Banner', Baltimore Orioles, TV crime shows *The Wire* and *Homicide: Life on the Street*

Famous for Blue crabs, lacrosse, Chesapeake Bay

State sport Jousting

Driving distances Baltimore to Annapolis 29 miles, Baltimore to Ocean City 147 miles on slavery. Although her loyalties were split during the Civil War, a Confederate invasion was halted here in 1862 at Antietam. Following the war, Maryland harnessed its black, white and immigrant work force, splitting the economy between Baltimore's industry and shipping, and later Washington, DC's need for services. Today the answer to 'What makes a Marylander?' is 'all of the above': the state mixes rich, poor, the foreign-born, urban sophisticates and rural villages like few others.

Information

Department of Natural Resources (www.dnr.maryland.gov) Administers Maryland's 55 state parks. Many offer camping or cabin accommodations for $30 per night; reservations can be booked online at http://reservations.dnr.state.md.us or by calling ☎ 888-432-2267.

Maryland Office of Tourism (☎ 866-639-3526; www.visitmaryland.org; 217 E Redwood St, Baltimore, MD 21202) Other welcome centers with maps and region-specific guides are scattered throughout Maryland.

BALTIMORE

Once one of the most important port towns in America, Baltimore – or 'Bawlmer' to locals – is a city of contradictions. On one hand, she retains something of the ugly duckling – a defiant, working-class, somewhat gritty city still tied to her nautical past. But in recent years, Baltimore (population 631,366) has grown into a beautiful swan, filled with world-class museums, trendy shops, ethnic restaurants, boutique hotels, culture and sports. She does this all with a twinkle in the eye and a wisecrack on the lips. After all, this is a quirky city that spawned Billie Holiday and John Waters. Yet she remains intrinsically tied to the water, from the Disney-fied Inner Harbor and cobblestoned streets of portside Fells Point to the shores of Fort McHenry, birthplace of America's National Anthem, 'The Star-Spangled Banner.' Baltimore lives up to her nickname, 'Charm City.'

History

Although Baltimore briefly served as national capital after the Revolution, her port defines this town. Besieged during the War of 1812 and riot-torn during the Civil War, Baltimore weathered both, dispatching Baltimore Clippers (the fastest sailing ships in the world) across the globe in her heyday.

DON'T MISS

- **National Aquarium of Baltimore** Recently renovated, the country's top aquarium is better than ever (p342).
- **Fort McHenry** Inspiration for America's national anthem, 'The Star-Spangled Banner' (p343).
- **Fell's Point/Canton** Join the happy crowds bar-hopping through old Baltimore (p347).

The slow erosion of shipping, the Great Depression and the loss of the steel industry in the 1970s all gutted Baltimore. The boom-and-bust cycle has carved this city's character, attracting and dispersing immigrants into Baltimore's ethnic enclave neighborhoods. The city is 70% African American, mixing persistent black poverty with an African American middle class that is one of the nation's oldest and most culturally significant.

During the 1980s the Inner Harbor was spruced up into the city's centerpiece. Gentrification projects remain a double-edged sword, carving out urban rot in some places while simultaneously pricing out the urban poor.

Orientation

From the Inner Harbor walk east (or go by water taxi) to the huddled intimacy of Little Italy and the party districts of Canton and Fell's Point (Salvadoran central these days). Baltimore St divides city streets into north and south; Charles St divides them east and west. Up north are kitschy Hampden, swish Mt Vernon, and Johns Hopkins University (surrounded by dodgy neighborhoods). The docks are to the southeast. Don't go too far west of Martin Luther King Jr Blvd, especially at night.

Information

BOOKSTORES

Atomic Books (☎ 410-662-4444; 3620 Falls Rd; 11am-7pm Mon-Sat, to 6pm Sun) Let's just say that John Waters loves this indie in Hampden. In fact, any John Waters fan mail should be sent care of them.

Barnes & Noble (☎ 401-385-1709; 601 E Pratt St, Power Plant, Inner Harbor; 9am-10pm Mon-Sat, 10am-9pm Sun) Will carry everything that Atomic doesn't and likely nothing Atomic does.

BALTIMORE

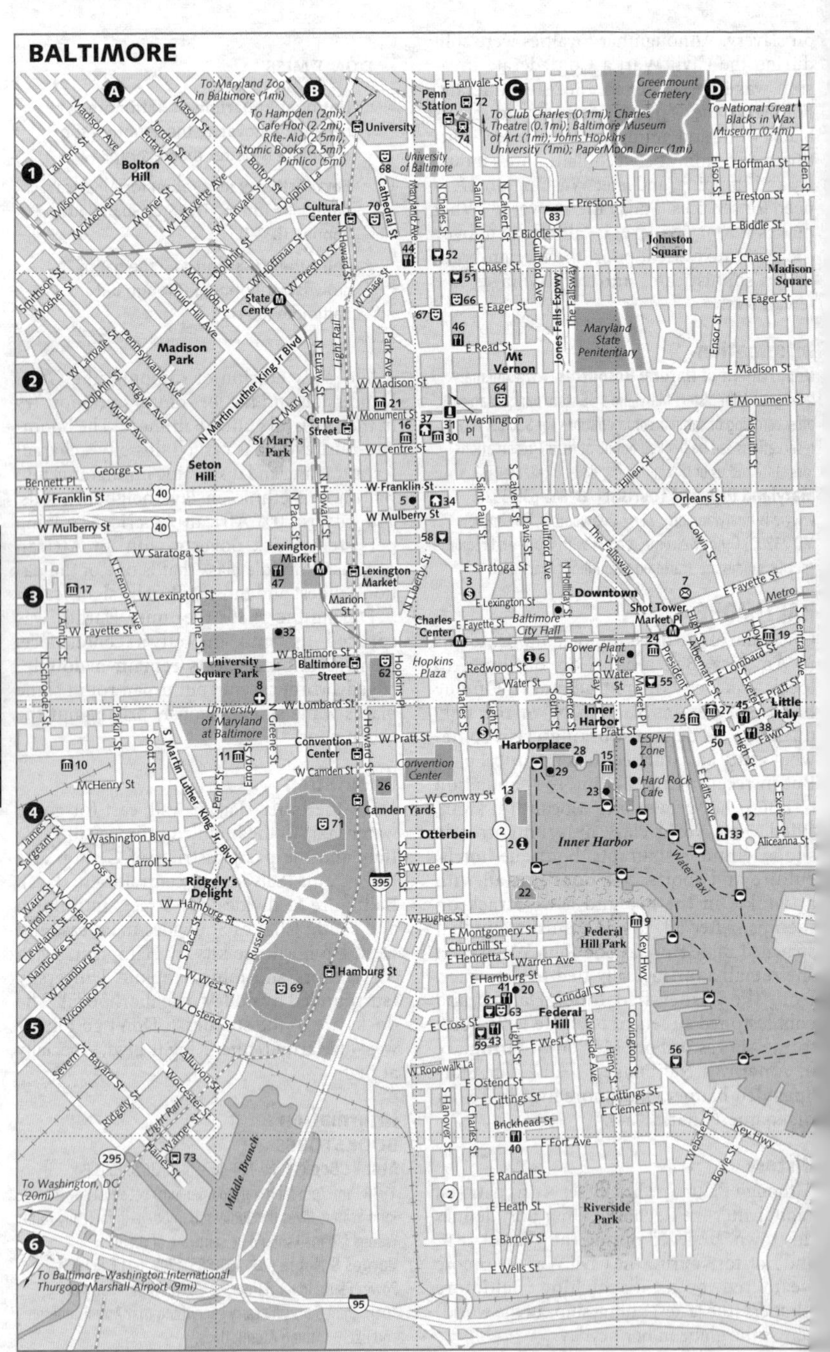

WASHINGTON, DC & THE CAPITAL REGION

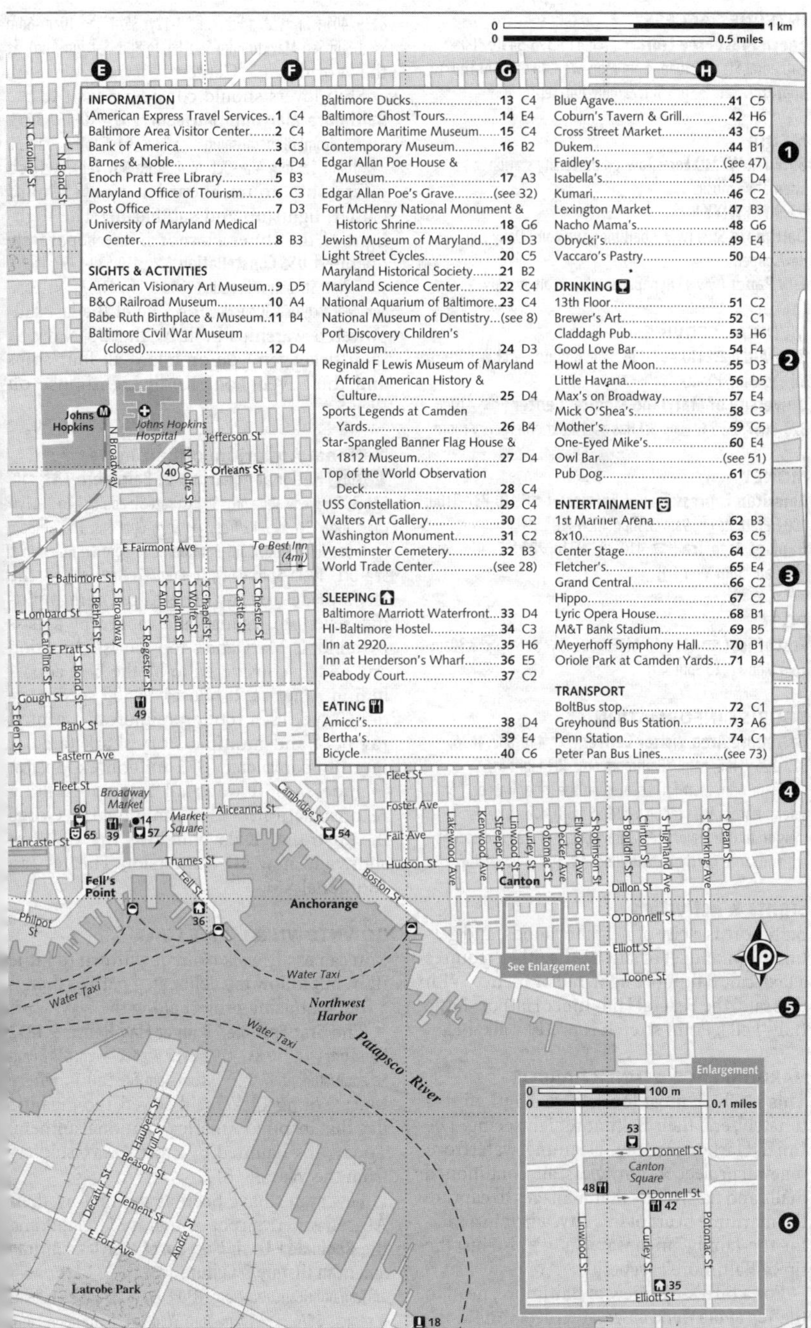

WASHINGTON, DC & THE CAPITAL REGION

INTERNET ACCESS

Enoch Pratt Free Library (☎ 410-396-5430; 400 Cathedral St; 10am-8pm Mon-Wed, to 5:30pm Thu, to 5pm Fri & Sat, 1-5pm Sun & daily Jun-Sep)

MEDIA

89.7 FM WTMD Local Towson University station; alternative music.
97.9 FM WIYY Rock.
Baltimore Sun (www.baltimoresun.com) Daily city newspaper.
City Paper (www.citypaper.com) Free alt-weekly.

MEDICAL SERVICES

Rite-Aid (☎ 410-467-3343; the Rotunda, 711 W 40th St; 8am-10pm)
University of Maryland Medical Center (☎ 410-328-8667; 22 S Greene St) Has a 24-hour emergency room.

MONEY

American Express Travel Services (☎ 410-837-3100; 100 E Pratt St; 9am-5:30pm Mon-Fri)
Bank of America (☎ 410-385-8310; 201 N Charles St; 9am-5pm Mon-Fri)

POST

Post office (☎ 410-347-4425; 900 E Fayette St; 8:30am-7pm Mon-Fri, to 5pm Sat)

TOURIST INFORMATION

Baltimore Area Visitor Center (☎ 410-837-4636, 877-225-8466; http://baltimore.org; 401 Light St; 9am-6pm Mon-Fri) Located on the Inner Harbor. Consider a Harbor Pass (adult/child $57/38), which gives admission to five major area attractions; get a 25% discount with advance purchase by calling ☎ 1-877-225-8466.

Sights & Activities

Baltimore is a city of neighborhoods, and getting from one set of sites to the other requires a taxi, car, Baltimore light-rail or metro. With that said, the Federal Hill–Inner Harbor–Little Italy-Fell's Point stretch is pretty walkable.

HARBORPLACE & INNER HARBOR

This is where most tourists start and, unfortunately, end their Baltimore sightseeing. The Inner Harbor is a big, gleaming waterfront renewal project of shiny glass, air-conditioned malls and flashy bars that manages to capture the maritime heart of this city, albeit in a safe-for-the-family kinda way. But it's also just the tip of Baltimore's iceberg.

For a bird's-eye view of Baltimore, head to the **Top of the World observation deck** (☎ 410-837-8439; 401 E Pratt St; adult/child 3-12yr $5/4; 10am-6pm Wed-Sun Sep-May, to 6pm Sun-Fri, to 8pm Sat Jun-Aug) at the World Trade Center.

Ship-lovers should consider a visit to the **Baltimore Maritime Museum** (☎ 410-369-3453; www.baltomaritimemuseum.org; Piers 3 & 5, off E Pratt St; 10am-5:30pm Mar-Oct, to 4:30pm Nov-Feb), which offers ship tours aboard a Coast Guard Cutter, lightship and submarine. The highlight of the Inner Harbor is the separately operated **USS Constellation** (☎ 410-539-1797; Pier 1, 301 E Pratt St; joint ticket adult/child 6-14yr $16/7; 10am-5pm Mar-Oct, to 4:30pm Nov-Feb), one of the last sail-powered warships built by the US Navy. A joint ticket gets you on board all four ships and the Seven Foot Knoll Lighthouse on Pier 5.

National Aquarium of Baltimore

our pick National Aquarium of Baltimore (☎ 410-576-3800; www.aqua.org; 501 E Pratt St; adult/child 3-11yr/child under 3yr $25/15/free; 9am-6pm Sun-Thu, to 8pm Fri & Sat Jul & Aug, 9am-5pm daily, to 8pm Fri Mar-Jun & Sep-Oct, 10am-5pm daily, to 8pm Fri Nov-Feb) is the city's pride and joy. The huge main building, seven stories high and capped by a glass pyramid, is Maryland's top tourist attraction and widely considered to be the best aquarium in America. It houses 16,500 specimens of 660 species, a rooftop rainforest, a central ray pool and multiple-story shark tank. A recently completed, $75-million expansion includes a 35ft waterfall and painstaking reconstruction of the Umbrawarra Gorge in Australia. Kids will love the dolphin show and new 4D Immersion Theater (an additional $5).

DOWNTOWN & LITTLE ITALY

You can easily walk from downtown to Little Italy, but follow the delineated path as there's a rough housing project along the way.

The **Star-Spangled Banner Flag House & 1812 Museum** (☎ 410-837-1793; www.flaghouse.org; 844 E Pratt St; adult/student $7/5; 10am-4pm Tue-Sat) is where Mary Young Pickersgill sewed the gigantic flag that inspired America's national anthem. Today, it's haunted by creepy wax soldiers from the War of 1812.

Few states have been as defined by their African American population as Maryland, and the **Reginald F Lewis Museum of Maryland African American History & Culture** (☎ 410-333-1130; www.africanamericanculture.org; 830 E Pratt St; adult/students & seniors $8/6; 10am-5pm Wed-Sat, from noon Sun) across the street from a pre–Civil War slave market, effectively tells their complex tale. In East Baltimore, the **National Great Blacks in Wax Museum** (☎ 410-563-3404; www.ngbiwm.com; 1601 E North Ave; adult/student/child 3-11yr $12/11/10; ⌚ 9am-5pm Tue-Sat, to 6pm Mar-Aug) surreally mixes religious leaders, activists, the Atlantic slave trade and the African American struggle for social justice with…Madame Tussaud's.

Maryland has also traditionally had one of the largest, most active Jewish communities in the country; their story is told at the **Jewish Museum of Maryland** (☎ 410-727-1539; www.jewishmuseummd.org; 15 Lloyd St; adult/student/child under 12 $8/4/3; ⌚ noon-4pm Sun & Tue-Thu), worth a visit for two of the best-preserved historical synagogues in America.

The **Babe Ruth Birthplace & Museum** (☎ 410-727-1539; www.baberuthmuseum.com; 216 Emory St; adult/child $6/3; ⌚ 10am-5pm, to 7pm during Orioles home games) celebrates the Baltimore native son who happens to be the greatest baseball player in history. Four blocks east, **Sports Legends at Camden Yards** (Camden Station, cnr Camden & Sharp Sts; adult/child $8/4) honors more Maryland athletes. The museums share hours and tickets for $12/5.

The Baltimore & Ohio railway was (arguably) the first passenger train in America, and the **B&O Railroad Museum** (☎ 410-752-2490; www.borail.org; 901 W Pratt St; adult/senior/child 2-12yr $14/12/8) is a loving testament to both that line and American railroading in general. Train spotters will be in heaven among more than 150 different locomotives, the most comprehensive collection in the country.

The first blood of the Civil War was shed on April 19, 1861, when Southern sympathizers rioted against Union soldiers at the President Street Railroad Station. The station housed the **Baltimore Civil War Museum** (☎ 410-385-5188; 601 S President St). Unfortunately the museum is now closed and its future is uncertain, but the building is still worth a look.

The **Edgar Allan Poe House & Museum** (☎ 410-396-7932; 203 N Amity St; adult/child under 13 $3/1; ⌚ noon-3:30pm Wed-Sat Apr-Nov) was home to Baltimore's most famous adopted son from 1832 to 1835. It was here that the macabre poet and writer first found fame after winning a $50 short-story contest. After moving around, Poe later returned to Baltimore in 1849, where he died in mysterious circumstances. His **grave** can be found in nearby **Westminster Cemetery** (cnr Fayette & Greene Sts; admission free). Take caution, the Poe House is located in a dodgy neighborhood.

The **National Museum of Dentistry** (☎ 410-706-0600; www.dentalmuseum.org; 31 S Greene St; adult/student & child over 6yr $6/4; ⌚ 10am-4pm Wed-Sat, 1-4pm Sun) is one of America's most unusual museums, an interactive museum tracing the history of dental care from ancient Egypt to today. See George Washington's dentures (ivory, not wood) and Queen Victoria's toothbrush!

Light Street Cycles (☎ 410-685-2234; 1124 Light St; rental per day $25-45; ⌚ 10am-8pm Mon-Fri, to 6pm Sat, 11am-3pm Sun) rents out everything from street to mountain bikes.

MT VERNON

Don't pass up the **Walters Art Gallery** (☎ 410-547-9000; www.thewalters.org; 600 N Charles St; admission free; ⌚ 10am-5pm Wed-Sun), which spans over 55 centuries, from ancient to contemporary, with excellent displays of Asian treasures, rare and ornate manuscripts and books, and a comprehensive French paintings collection.

So modern it's probably 'post,' the **Contemporary Museum** (☎ 410-783-5720; www.contemporary.org; 100 W Centre St; admission free; ⌚ noon-5pm Wed-Sun, to 7pm Thu) loves to ride the cutting edge of art. Auxiliary to the on-site exhibits is the museum's mission of bringing art to unexpected spots around the city. Call or check the website for the latest guerrilla art attack.

With more than 5.4 million artifacts, the **Maryland Historical Society** (☎ 410-685-3750; www.mdhs.org; 201 W Monument St; adult/student & child over 12 $4/3; ⌚ 10am-5pm Wed-Sun) houses one of the largest collections of Americana in the world, including Francis Scott Key's original manuscript of the 'Star-Spangled Banner.' A new permanent exhibit traces Maryland's maritime history.

For the best views of Baltimore, climb the 228 steps of the **Washington Monument** (☎ 410-396-0929; 699 Washington Pl; suggested donation $1; ⌚ 10am-5pm Wed-Sun), a 178ft-tall Doric column dedicated to America's founding father, George Washington. It was designed by Robert Mills, who also created DC's Washington Monument. The ground floor contains a museum about Washington's life.

FEDERAL HILL & AROUND

On a bluff overlooking the harbor, **Federal Hill Park** lends its name to the comfortable neighborhood that's set around Cross St Market and comes alive after sundown.

our pick **Fort McHenry National Monument & Historic Shrine** (☎ 410-962-4290; www.nps.gov/fomc;

2400 E Fort Ave; adult/child under 17 $7/free; ⌚ 8am-7:45pm summer, to 4:45pm rest of year) is the birthplace of America's national anthem. On September 13 and 14, 1814, the star-shaped fort successfully repelled a British navy attack during the Battle of Baltimore. After a long night of bombs bursting in air, prisoner Francis Scott Key saw, 'by dawn's early light,' the tattered flag still waving, inspiring him to pen 'The Star-Spangled Banner' (set to the tune of a popular drinking song).

The **American Visionary Art Museum** (☎ 410-244-1900; www.avam.org; 800 Key Hwy; adult/student & senior $12/8; ⌚ 10am-6pm Tue-Sun) is a showcase for self-taught (or 'outsider' art), a celebration of unbridled creativity utterly free of arts-scene pretension. Some of the work comes from asylums, others are created by self-inspired visionaries, but it's all totally captivating and well worth a long afternoon.

FELL'S POINT & CANTON

Once the center of Baltimore's shipbuilding industry, the historic cobblestoned neighborhood is now a gentrified mix of 18th-century homes and restaurants, bars and shops. The neighborhood has been the setting for several films and TV series, most notably *Homicide: Life on the Street*. Further east, the slightly more sophisticated streets of Canton fan out, with its grassy square surrounded by great restaurants and bars. On weekends, both neighborhoods can get quite crowded with bar-hoppers.

NORTH BALTIMORE

The 'Hon' expression of affection, an oft-imitated but never quite duplicated 'Bawlmerese' peculiarity, was born from **Hampden**, an urban neighborhood at the pinnacle of hipness. Spend a lazy afternoon browsing kitsch, antiques and eclectic clothing along the **Avenue** (aka W 36th St). To get to Hampden, take the I-83 N, merge onto Falls Road (northbound) and take a right onto the Avenue.

Close by, you'll find **Johns Hopkins University** (☎ 410-516-8171, main bldgs 3400 N Charles St), famed for its medical school. The **Baltimore Museum of Art** (☎ 410-573-1700; 10 Art Museum Dr, at 31st & N Charles Sts; admission free except for special exhibits; ⌚ 11am-5pm Wed-Fri, to 6pm Sat & Sun), with its massive collection (the early American, Asian and African galleries are particularly impressive) and a lovely sculpture garden, easily competes with its Smithsonian cousins to the south.

Baltimore for Children

This city loves kids and proves it with amazing museums, stroll-worthy waterfront promenades and family-friendly restaurants. Most attractions are centered on the Inner Harbor, including the National Aquarium of Baltimore (p342), perfect for pint-sized visitors. Kids can run wild o'er the ramparts of historic Fort McHenry National Monument & Historic Shrine (p343) too.

Swinging into a three-level jungle tree house, producing a TV show and solving riddles in the Mystery House are a sample of the interactive adventures at **Port Discovery Children's Museum** (☎ 410-727-8120; www.portdiscovery.org; Power Plant Live complex, 35 Market Pl; admission $11.75; ⌚ 10am-5pm Mon-Sat, noon-5pm Sun summer, 9:30am-4:30pm Tue-Fri, 10am-5pm Sat, noon-5pm Sun Oct-May), a cool kids' museum where even the adults have fun.

Lily-pad hopping, adventures with Billy the Bog Turtle and grooming live animals are all in a day's play at the **Maryland Zoo in Baltimore** (☎ 410-366-5466; www.marylandzoo.org; Druid Hill Park; adult/child/senior $15/10/12; ⌚ 10am-4pm). Get discounted tickets on the zoo's website.

The awesome **Maryland Science Center** (☎ 410-685-5225; www.mdsci.org; 601 Light St; adult/child 3-12yr $14/9.50; ⌚ 10am-6pm Sun-Thu, to 8pm Fri & Sat summer, 10am-5pm Tue-Thu, to 8pm Fri, to 6pm Sat, 11am-5pm Sun, closed Mon fall-spring) features a three-story atrium, tons of interactive exhibits on dinosaurs, asteroids and the human body, and the requisite IMAX theater. Hours change seasonally and it's best to check online or call ahead first.

Tours

Baltimore Ducks (☎ 877-887-8225; www.baltimoreducks.com; cnr Conway & Light Sts, Inner Harbor; adult/child 3-12yr $25/15) The quintessential tourist activity, a ride on an amphibious former-WWII military 'Duck' shows visitors the city via land and water.

Baltimore Ghost Tours (☎ 410-522-7400; www.baltimoreghosttours.com; departs from Max's on Broadway 731 S Broadway, Fells Point; adult/child under 13 $13/8; ⌚ tours 7pm Fri or Sat Mar-Nov) Delve into the spooky and bizarre side of a bawdy maritime area. Also offers a Fell's Point haunted pub tour for $20 (21 and older only).

Festivals & Events

Preakness (☎ 410-542-9400; www.preakness.com) Held on the third Sunday of every May, the 'Freakness' is the second leg of the Tripe Crown horse race.

Honfest (www.honfest.net) Put on your best 'Bawlmerese' accent and head to Hampden for this June celebration of kitsch, beehive hairdos, rhinestone glasses and other Baltimore eccentricities.

Artscape (☎ 410-752-8632; www.artscape.org) America's largest free arts festival takes place in mid-July and features art displays, live music, theater and dance performances, international food vendors and more.

Sleeping

Stylish and affordable B&Bs are mostly found in the downtown burbs of Canton, Fell's Point and Federal Hill.

our pick HI-Baltimore Hostel (☎ 410-576-8880; www.baltimorehostel.org; 17 W Mulberry St; HI members/nonmembers dm $25/28, r $60/63, all incl breakfast;) Located in a beautifully restored 1857 mansion, the HI-Baltimore has 49 beds, including a private double room. Helpful management, nice location and filigreed classical chic make this one of the best hostels we've seen in the region.

Best Inn (☎ 410-485-7900; www.bestinnhotel.com; 6510 Frankford Ave; r $67-78;) The Best doesn't excel in any areas, including price, although this is the main reason to stay at this otherwise nondescript hotel.

Inn at 2920 (☎ 410-342-4450; www.theinnat2920.com; 2920 Elliott St; r incl breakfast $155-225;) Housed in a former bordello, this boutique B&B has five individual rooms, high-thread-count sheets, sleek, avant-garde decor, beta fish roommates and the bohemian/boozapalooza neighborhood of Canton right outside your door. The Jacuzzis and the green sensibility of the owners are a nice touch.

Peabody Court (☎ 410-727-7101; www.peabodycourthotel.com; 612 Cathedral St; r from $159;) This European-style boutique hotel is smack in the middle of Mt Vernon. The friendly staff and all-marble bathrooms at the Peabody want to give you a big, luxurious hug. Valet parking is $29.

Inn at Henderson's Wharf (☎ 410-522-7777; www.hendersonswharf.com; 1000 Fell St; r $179-259;) A complimentary bottle of wine upon arrival sets the tone at this marvelously situated Fell's Point hotel, which began life as an 18th-century tobacco warehouse. Consistently one of the city's best lodges.

Baltimore Marriott Waterfront (☎ 410-385-3000; www.baltimoremarriottwaterfront.com; 700 Aliceanna St; r from $299;). From the moment you step into the luxurious lobby, you'll know you're in for a treat. The 31-story Marriott in the heart of the Inner Harbor has all the amenities you'd expect from a four-star hotel, including luxurious bedding, contemporary furnishings and fixtures, first-class service and great views of the city and harbor.

Eating

Look, this is an ethnically rich town that sits on top of the greatest seafood repository in the world, not to mention the fault line between the down-home South and cutting-edge innovation of the Northeast. Baltimore, in other words, knows how to eat. A great place to sample food is the city's famous markets – here are two favorites:

Cross Street Market (1065 Cross St, btwn Light & Charles Sts; 7am-7pm Mon-Sat)

our pick Lexington Market (☎ 410-685-6169; www.lexingtonmarket.com; 400 W Lexington St; 8:30am-6pm Mon-Sat) A Baltimore tradition since 1782. Don't miss the Faidley's Seafood stall for the absolute best crab cakes in town!

DOWNTOWN & LITTLE ITALY

Vaccaro's Pastry (☎ 410-685-4905; 222 Albemarle St; items $3-10; 9am-10pm Mon, to 11pm Tue-Thu & Sun, to 1am Fri & Sat) After a lovely Italian dinner, head to Vacarro's for the best desserts and coffee in town. The cannoli are to die for, and the gelato and tiramisu are divine.

Isabella's (☎ 410-962-8888; 221 S High St; sandwiches $7-9, pizzas $11-15; 11am-9pm Mon-Sat, to 4pm Sun) This new neighborhood pizza place is always crowded and for good reason. The brick-oven pizzas are probably the most authentically Italian pies in town.

Amicci's (☎ 410-528-1096; www.amiccis.com; 231 S High St; lunch mains $7-10, dinner mains $12-20; 11:30am-midnight Mon-Fri) This local icon serves up traditional Italian comfort food at reasonable prices. Seafood-lovers and vegetarians will be especially pleased.

MT VERNON

Kumari (☎ 410-547-1600; 911 N Charles St; mains $10-16; 11:30am-2:30pm & 5-10pm Sun-Thu, to 10:30pm Fri & Sat) If you haven't had Nepalese food, think heavier and creamier (and at this place, tastier) than your average curry. Kumari's $8.95 lunch buffet is great value. Tibetan and Indian dishes are also on offer.

Dukem (☎ 410-385-0318; 1100 Maryland Ave; mains $10-20; 11am-11pm, to later Fri & Sat) A satellite branch of DC's famous Ethiopian restaurant, Dukem serves up the same delicious menu, including spicy chicken, lamb and vegetarian dishes, all sopped up with spongy flatbread. Live music most evenings.

FEDERAL HILL & AROUND

Blue Agave (☎ 410-576-3938; 1032 Light St; mains $13-28; ⏰ from 5pm) Agave's does hip, upscale Mexican food, but it's not pretentious; a Midwestern family would feel as welcome here as a clique of New York socialites. The pork *carnitas* platter is heavenly and the margaritas could knock out a horse.

Bicycle (☎ 410-234-1900; 1444 Light St; mains $15-28; ⏰ 5:30-10pm Mon-Thu, to later Fri & Sat) Striking colored walls, a spacious interior and a hip art-gallery feel accent the French, South American and Asian fusion cuisine.

FELL'S POINT

Bertha's (☎ 410-327-5795; www.berthas.com; 734 S Broadway St; mains $10-22; ⏰ 11:30am-11pm Sun-Thu, to later Fri & Sat) Green bumper stickers across the state command you to 'Eat Bertha's Mussels.' You'll understand why after your first bivalve bite swimming in garlic butter. Seafood and pub grub make up the rest of the menu. Live music most evenings.

Obrycki's (☎ 410-732-6399; www.obryckis.com; 1727 E Pratt St; mains $15-29; ⏰ 11:30am-10pm Mon-Thu, to 11pm Fri, to 9pm Sun March-Nov) Despite its somewhat touristy reputation, Obrycki's remains one of the city's best seafood restaurants. The menu is heavy on Maryland's most famous critter: blue crabs (see boxed text, p351), including crab soup, crab balls, crab cakes, steamed crabs and soft-shelled crabs, meaning that Obrycki's is only open during crab season, ie March to November.

CANTON

Coburn's Tavern & Grill (410-342-0999; 2921 O'Donnell St; mains $7-23; ⏰ 11am-2am Mon-Fri, from 8am Sat & Sun) At first glance, Coburn's looks like any other British/Irish pub in Canton: hardwood floors, exposed brick, sports on TV. But that's where the similarities end. The food is delish, from the burgers to the fish and steak dishes. Our favorite was the Captain's Toast appetizer: shrimp and crab sautéed with tomatoes, cream and Old Bay seasoning.

HAMPDEN & NORTH BALITMORE

Cafe Hon (☎ 410-243-1230; http://cafehon.com; 1002 W 36th St; mains $6-16; ⏰ 7am-9pm Mon-Fri, from 9am Sat & Sun) You don't have to be sporting rhinestone-studded glasses and a bouffant hairdo to eat here, but you'll earn serious brownie points. The American comfort food at this veggie-friendly diner is as hearty as the café's attitude. After dinner slide over to adjacent Bar Hon.

our pick **PaperMoon Diner** (☎ 410-889-4444; 227 W 29th St; mains $7-14; ⏰ 7am-midnight Sun-Thu, to 2am Fri & Sat) Like a kaleidoscope dream, this brightly colored, quintessential Baltimore diner is decorated with thousands of old toys, creepy mannequins and other quirky knickknacks. The real draw here is breakfast – perfect eggs Benedict, fluffy pancakes and strong coffee.

Drinking & Entertainment

On weekends, Fell's Point and Canton turn into temples to alcoholic excess that would make a Roman emperor blush. Mt Vernon and North Baltimore are a little more civilized, but any one of Baltimore's neighborhoods houses a cozy local pub. The Power Plant Live complex is filled with chain-brand clubs. Unless otherwise noted, closing time is 2am.

BARS & NIGHTCLUBS

Downtown & Little Italy

Mick O'Shea's (☎ 410-539-7504; 328 N Charles St; ⏰ from 11:30am) Your standard paraphernalia-festooned Irish pub, with live Irish music Wednesday through Saturday. Maryland Governor (and former Baltimore mayor) Martin O'Malley used to play here.

Howl at the Moon (☎ 410-783-5111; 22 Market Pl, Power Plant Live complex; cover Thu $5, Fri & Sat $7; ⏰ from 7pm Wed-Thu, from 5pm Fri, from 5:30pm Sat) Howl stands out from the cookie-cutter clubs of Power Plant Live with its innovative theme: a call-in piano bar where the audience forces an ivory-masher/crooner to improvise the entertainment all night long.

Mt Vernon

Brewer's Art (☎ 410-547-9310; 1106 N Charles St; ⏰ from 4pm Mon-Sat, from 5pm Sun) This subterranean cave mesmerizes the senses with an overwhelming selection of beers. Its upstairs embodiment serves respectable dinners in its classy dining room.

our pick **Club Charles** (☎ 410-727-8815; 1724 N Charles St; ⏰ from 6pm) Filled with hipsters displaying the breed's usual skinny jeans/vintage T-shirt plumage, normals also flock to this 1940s art-deco cocktail lounge to enjoy good tunes and cheap drinks.

13th Floor (☎ 410-347-0888; 1 E Chase St; ⌚ from 5pm Wed-Fri, from 6pm Sat) This is one of the smoothest spots in the city to get your club on: atop the Gothic Belvedere Hotel, with fresh tracks, unbeatable views and a classy elevator ride waiting when you're ready to go home. Also in the Belvedere, the Owl Bar is a nostalgic throwback to '50s Baltimore, with a long wooden bar that attracts a martini-sipping crowd.

Federal Hill

Pub Dog (☎ 410-727-6077; pubdog.net; 20 E Cross St; ⌚ 5pm-2am) Marylanders really love drinking with their dogs. After you've made the rounds petting the canine clientele, grab a delicious brew (or two for $4) and try to snag the cozy fireside nook in the back. Excellent pizza, too.

Mother's (☎ 410-244-8686; 1113 S Charles St; ⌚ from 11am Mon-Fri, from 8am Sat & Sun) Here's a classic Baltimore neighborhood bar and grill where the drinks flow freely; you'll be called 'Hon' more than once and the Purple Patio is the meeting spot for wing specials and pre- and post-Ravens game discussions.

Little Havana (☎ 410-837-9903; 1325 Key Hwy; ⌚ 4:30pm-midnight Mon-Thu, from 11am Fri-Sun) A good after-work spot and a great place to sip mojitos on the waterfront deck, Little Havana attracts the sort of young professional who just *knows* there's a salsa goddess deep in their soul.

8x10 (☎ 410-625-2000; www.the8x10.com; 10 E Cross St; cover $10-20; ⌚ from 7pm) After a brief, ill-advised name change, Baltimore's premiere live music venue since 1983 has returned to its roots. It mixes big-name acts with strong local talent in a funky concert hall that feels intimate and expansive all at once.

Fell's Point & Canton

our pick **Good Love Bar** (☎ 410-534-4588; 2322 Boston St; ⌚ 8pm-2am Wed-Sat & Mon, to midnight Sun) Think dark, sexy lighting; think three floors of cushy, lounge-and-flirt furniture; think music that manages to mingle black and white clubbers like few other places in Baltimore, and you've thought up Good Love.

One-Eyed Mike's (☎ 410-327-9823; 708 S Bond St; ⌚ 11am-1am Mon-Sat) Yar! There be pirates at this seedy, drunk-as-a-sailor-on-shore-leave pub, and if ye want, they be stowing away a bottle of Grand Marnier for ye in a glass display case, which ye can drink from whenever ye return. Now walk the plank, or something.

Max's on Broadway (☎ 410-675-6297; 737 S Broadway; ⌚ from 11am; wi-fi) For beer-lovers, this Baltimore institution has one of the most extensive menus around, with 71 beers on tap and another 300 in bottles. The staff is friendly, the beer is cold, and there's pool and darts to pass the time. What more do you need?

Claddagh Pub (☎ 410-522-4220; 2918 O'Donnell St; ⌚ from 11am Mon-Fri, from 9am Sat & Sun) The crowds at Claddagh work hard to confirm ugly stereotypes about the Irish by trying to consume their volume in alcohol at this Disney-fied Dublin pub.

Fletcher's (☎ 410-558-1889; 701 S Bond St; cover $5; ⌚ from 4pm Mon-Thu, from 11am Fri-Sun) Inhale the dried-beer scent on the walls with the pretty youngsters and rough, amiable oldsters who come here, one of the best rock stages in town.

GAY & LESBIAN VENUES

Baltimore has one of the largest gay African American scenes in America, many on the 'down low.' In fact, Baltimore has a remarkably vibrant, multiracial gay scene. **Out in Baltimore** (www.outinbaltimore.com) has comprehensive listings. Plenty of straight folks go out in gay Baltimore to soak up the friendly, often outrageous vibe.

Hippo (☎ 410-547-0069; 1 W Eager St; ⌚ from 4pm) This is the city's largest gay club, with ladies' and men's tea, cabaret and crazy themed dance nights.

Grand Central (☎ 410-752-7133; 1001 N Charles St; ⌚ 4pm-2am Mon-Sat, to midnight Sun, from 3pm Sun) More of a complex than a club, whatever your taste, one of Central's areas (dancefloor, pub, video bar, and leather-and-Levi's club) is sure to suit your fancy.

PERFORMING ARTS & THEATER

The **Baltimore Symphony Orchestra** (☎ 410-783-8000) performs at the **Meyerhoff Symphony Hall** (1212 Cathedral St). The Baltimore Opera performs at the **Lyric Opera House** (☎ 410-685-5086; www.lyricoperahouse.com; 140 W Mt Royal Ave). Theater options include **Center Stage** (☎ 410-332-0033; 700 N Calvert St), which stages Shakespeare, Wilde, Miller and contemporary works, and **Charles Theatre** (☎ 410-727-3456; www.thecharles.com; 1711 N Charles St), screening the best art-house films in the city.

SPORTS

Whether it's touchdowns, home runs, goals or monster-truck shows, Baltimoreans love their sports. The town plays hard and parties even harder, with tailgating parties in parking lots and games on numerous televisions.

The **Baltimore Orioles** (www.orioles.com) play at **Oriole Park at Camden Yards** (☎ 410-547-6277; 333 W Camden St; 🕑 Apr-Oct), arguably the best ballpark in America. Daily tours ($7 to $9) of the stadium are offered during regular season. The **Baltimore Ravens** (www.baltimoreravens.com) play at **M&T Bank Stadium** (☎ 410-261-7283; 1101 Russell St; 🕑 Sep-Jan).

Maryland is lacrosse heartland, and its residents arguably the sport's most fanatic followers. With the loss of the Bayhawks, the best place to watch 'lax' is **Johns Hopkins University** (☎ 410-516-7490; hopkinssports.cstv.com; stadium at cnr University Pkwy & N Charles St). The National Indoor Soccer League team **Baltimore Blast** (☎ 410-732-5278; www.baltimoreblast.com; 🕑 Oct-Apr) plays at the **1st Mariner Arena** (☎ 410-321-1908; 201 W Baltimore St).

Horse racing is huge here, especially at **Pimlico** (www.pimlico.com), which hosts the Preakness (p344).

Getting There & Away

The **Baltimore-Washington International Thurgood Marshall Airport** (BWI; ☎ 410-859-7111, 800-435-9294) is located 10 miles south of downtown via I-295.

The **Greyhound Bus Station** and **Peter Pan Bus Lines** (☎ 410-752-7682; 800-343-9999; 2110 Haines St) has buses from Washington, DC (14 per day, roughly every 45 minutes, one hour, $11); from New York they cost $27 to $37 (11 per day, 4½ hours). The cheaper **BoltBus** (1610 St Paul St; www.boltbus.com) offers dirt-cheap rates to and from DC (1 hour)and New York (3½ hours). There are seven buses a day on the DC–Baltimore–NYC route. Tickets start at $1 if you book at least two weeks in advance.

Penn Station (☎ 410-291-4165; 1515 N Charles St) is in north Baltimore. MARC operates weekday commuter trains to/from Washington, DC (one way/round-trip $7/14). **Amtrak** (☎ 800-872-7245; www.amtrak.com) trains serve the entire East Coast and beyond.

Getting Around

Light Rail (☎ 410-539-5000; tickets $1.60; 🕑 6am-11pm Mon-Sat, 11am-7pm Sun & holidays) runs from BWI airport to Lexington Market and Penn Station. Train frequency is every five to 10 minutes. **MARC trains** (☎ 800-325-7245) run hourly between Penn Station and BWI airport on weekdays for $4. **SuperShuttle** (☎ 800-258-3826; www.supershuttle.com) provides a BWI-van service to the Inner Harbor for $21.

Check **Maryland Transit Administration** (MTA; www.mtamaryland.com) for all schedules and fares. **Baltimore Water Taxi** (☎ 410-563-3901; Inner Harbor; daily pass adult/child under 11 $9/4) docks at all harborside attractions and neighborhoods.

ANNAPOLIS

Annapolis is as charming as state capitals get. The Colonial architecture, cobblestones, flickering lamps and brick row houses are worthy of Dickens, but the effect isn't artificial; this city has preserved, rather than created, its heritage.

Perched on Chesapeake Bay, life in Annapolis (motto: 'Come Sail Away') revolves around her rich maritime traditions. It's home to the US Naval Academy, whose 'middies' (midshipmen students) stroll through town in their starched white uniforms. Sailing is not just a hobby, it's a way of life. The city docks are crammed with vessels of all shapes and sizes. For landlubbers, the food is great, and a beer on the pier cooled by a salty headwind is even better.

There's a **visitor center** (☎ 410-280-0445; www.visitannapolis.org; 26 West St; 🕑 9am-5pm) and a seasonal information booth at City Dock. A **Maryland Welcome Center** (☎ 410-974-3400; 350 Rowe Blvd; 🕑 9am-5pm) is inside the State House, and runs tours of the building twice daily.

Sights & Activities

Think of the State House as a wheel hub from which most attractions fan out, leading down to the City Dock and historic waterfront.

US NAVAL ACADEMY

The undergraduate college of the US Navy is one of the most selective universities in America. The **Armel-Leftwich visitor center** (☎ 410-293-8125; Gate 1 at the City Dock entrance; tours adult/senior/student $8.50/7.50/6.50; 🕑 9am-5pm, to 4pm Jan & Feb) is the place to book tours and immerse yourself in all things Academy. Come for the formation weekdays at 12:05pm sharp, when the 4000 midshipmen and midshipwomen conduct a 20-minute military marching display in the Yard. Photo ID is required upon entry. If you've got a thing for American naval history, go on and revel in the **Naval Academy Museum** (☎ 410-293-2108; 118 Maryland Ave; admission free; 🕑 9am-5pm Mon-Sat, from 11am Sun).

MARYLAND STATE HOUSE

The country's oldest state capitol in continuous legislative use, the stately 1772 **State House** (☎ 410-974-3400; 25 State Circle; admission free; ⏰ 9am-5pm Mon-Fri, 10am-4pm Sat & Sun) also served as national capital from 1733 to 1734. The Maryland Senate is in action here from January to April. The upside-down giant acorn atop the dome stands for wisdom. Photo ID is required upon entry.

DOWNTOWN ANNAPOLIS

Annapolis has more 18th-century buildings than any other city in America, including the homes of all four Marylanders who signed the Declaration of Independence. The highlights include the 18th-century **William Paca House & Garden** (☎ 410-267-7619; annapolis.org; adult/child 6-17yr $8/5; ⏰ 10am-5pm Mon-Sat, from noon Sun) and the **Chase-Lloyd House** (☎ 410-263-2723; 22 Maryland Ave; admission $2; ⏰ 2pm-4pm Mon-Sat), the latter still partially used as a home for elderly women.

Of the many historical homes in town, the nicest is the **Hammond-Harwood House** (☎ 410-263-4683; 19 Maryland Ave; www.hammondharwoodhouse.org; adult/child/student $6/3/5.50; ⏰ noon-5pm Tue-Sun Apr-Oct). Completed in 1774 by architect William Buckland, it is considered one of the finest existing British colonial homes in America.

Take a self-guided tour through the grounds of **St John's College** (☎ 410-263-2371; www.stjohnscollege.edu; cnr College Ave & King George St). Originally founded in 1696 as the King William's preparatory school, it's one of the oldest institutions of higher learning in the country.

At the City Dock, the **Kunta Kinte-Alex Haley Memorial** marks the spot where Kunta Kinte – ancestor of *Roots* author Alex Haley – was brought in chains from Africa. Haley received a 1977 special Pulitzer Prize Letters award for his epic.

Tours

A costumed docent will lead you on a **Three Centuries Walking Tour** (☎ 410-268-7601; adult/child under 12 $16/4), a great introduction to all things Annapolis. The 10:30am tour leaves from the visitor center and the 1:30pm tour leaves from the information booth at the City Dock; there's a slight variation in sights visited by each, but both cover the country's largest concentration of 18th-century buildings, influential African Americans and colonial spirits who don't want to leave. The associated **Pirates of the Chesapeake Cruise** (adult/child 3-11yr $16/13; ⏰ late May–Sep) is good 'yar'-worthy fun, especially for the kids.

The best way to explore the city's maritime heritage is on the water. **Watermark Cruises** (☎ 410-268-701; City Dock; adult/child 3-11yr $20/10), which operates the Three Centuries Walking Tour, offers a variety of cruise options.

The beautiful 74ft schooner **Woodwind** (☎ 410-263-7837; 80 Compromise St; sunset cruise adult/senior/child under 12 $37/35/22; ⏰ May-Oct) offers two-hour day and sunset cruises. Or splurge for the Woodwind 'boat & breakfast' package (rooms $289, including breakfast), one of the more unique lodging options in town.

Sleeping

Call ☎ 800-848-4748 for free accommodation reservations.

ScotLaur Inn (☎ 410-268-5665; www.scotlaurinn.com; 165 Main St; r $95-125; P ⊠ ≋) The folks from Chick & Ruth's Delly (below) offer 10 simple pink-and-blue rooms with private bath at their B&B (bed and bagel) above the deli.

Country Inn & Suites (☎ 800-456-4000, 410-571-6700; www.countryinns.com; 2600 Housley Rd, at Hwy 450; r from $119; P ⊠ ⊡) As charming as chains get, plus it has free shuttles to the historic district.

O'Callaghan Hotel (☎ 410-263-7700; www.ocallaghanhotels.com; 174 West St; r $130-300; P ⊠ ≋ ⊡) This Irish chain is a cushy if corporate-feeling big box that offers good luxury outside the B&B circuit.

1908 William Page Inn (☎ 410-263-6631; www.1908-williampageinn.com; 8 Martin St; r incl breakfast $205-295; P ⊠ ≋) For a romantic getaway, nothing beats this Victorian B&B. Beautifully decorated, comfortable rooms are capped with wonderful hospitality and delicious breakfast.

Eating & Drinking

As you might guess, the seafood here is superb. Annapolis also does excellent power grub (steaks, pizza etc), which makes sense, given all the politicians running around.

City Dock Café (☎ 410-269-0969; 18 Market Space; items $2-5; ⏰ 6:30am-10pm) We will swear by the café mocha here, which must be the tastiest rocket fuel we've ever imbibed.

Chick & Ruth's Delly (☎ 410-269-6737; 165 Main St; mains $6-10; ⏰ 6:30am-10pm Sun-Thu, to 11:30pm Fri & Sat) A cornerstone of Annapolis, the 'delly' is bursting with affable quirkiness and a stressfully large menu. Sandwiches are named after famous local folks – Maryland Senator Barbara Mikulski is the open-faced tuna.

Middleton Tavern (☎ 410-263-3333; www.middletontavern.com; 2 Market Space; mains $7-25; 11:30am-1:30am Mon-Fri, from 10am Sat & Sun) One of the oldest continuously operating pubs in the country. As you'd expect from a waterside pub, the menu features some of the freshest seafood around. Live music most nights.

Rams Head Tavern (☎ 410-268-4545; www.ramsheadtavern.com; 33 West St; mains $7-28; from 11am) The best bar in town serves good eats and tasty microbrews in an attractive oak-paneled setting, while hot live (tickets $11 to $60) acts burn up the stage.

our pick **Galway Bay** (☎ 410-263-8333; 63 Maryland Ave; mains $8-15; 11am-midnight Mon-Sat, from 10:30am Sun) The epitome of a power-broker bar, the Irish-owned and -operated restaurant-pub is the dark sort of hideaway where political deals go down over Jameson, stouts and mouth-watering seafood specialties.

Buddy's Crabs & Ribs (☎ 410-626-1100; 100 Main St; mains $14-28; 11:30am-9:30pm Mon-Thu, from 11am Fri & Sat, from 8:30am Sun;) The $12.95 all-you-can-eat weekday lunch buffet is the best value in town. Kids under five eat free, and kids aged six to 10 for half-price.

Getting There & Around

The C-60 bus route (service from 7am to 7pm Monday to Friday, $4) connects Annapolis with BWI airport. Greyhound runs buses to Washington, DC (once daily, from $6.50). **Annapolis Transit** (☎ 410-263-7964) provides local transport. **Dillon's Bus** (www.dillonbus.com; tickets $4.50) has 26 weekday-only commuter buses between Annapolis and Washington's Union Station.

EASTERN SHORE

Just across the Chesapeake Bay Bridge, a short drive from the urban sprawl of the Baltimore-Washington corridor, Maryland's landscape makes a dramatic about-face. Nondescript suburbs and jammed highways give way to unbroken miles of bird-dotted wetlands, serene waterscapes, endless cornfields, sandy beaches and friendly little villages. The coastal flat plains are ideal for bicycling. For the most part, the Eastern Shore retains its charm despite the growing influx of city-dwelling yuppies and day-trippers. This area revolves around the water. Working waterfront communities still survive off Chesapeake Bay and its tributaries. Boating, fishing, crabbing, kayaking are a part of local life. This is America at its most genuine.

St Michaels & Tilghman Island

St Michaels, the prettiest little village on the Eastern Shore, lives up to its motto as 'The Heart & Soul of Chesapeake Bay.' It's a mix of old Victorian homes, quaint B&Bs, boutique shops and working docks, where escape artists from Washington mix with salty-dog crabbers. On weekends, the village can get crowded with out-of-town boaters. During the War of 1812, inhabitants rigged up lanterns in a nearby forest and blacked out the town. British naval gunners shelled the trees, allowing St Michaels to escape destruction. The building now known as the **Cannonball House** (Mulberry St) was the only structure to have been hit.

At the lighthouse, the **Chesapeake Bay Maritime Museum** (☎ 410-745-2916; www.cbmm.org; Navy Point; adult/child 6-17yr $13/6; 10am-6pm summer, to 5pm spring & fall, to 4pm winter) delves into the deep ties between Shore folk and America's largest estuary. Narrated historic cruises aboard the **Patriot** (☎ 410-745-3100; Navy Point; adult/child under 13 $24.50/12.50) leave from the Crab Claw dock four times a day.

Laura Ashley's most lurid fantasies probably resemble the rooms in the red-brick **Parsonage Inn** (☎ 410-745-5519; www.parsonage-inn.com; 210 N Talbot St; r incl breakfast $100-195; P), which is run by a pair of lovely, awfully hospitable innkeepers.

From the oysters in champagne sauce to the pan-roasted rockfish, everything at **208 Talbot** (☎ 410-745-3838; 208 N Talbot St; mains $26-33; 5-9pm Sun-Thu, to 10pm Fri & Sat) is delicately prepared and delicious. The perfect date restaurant.

At the end of the road over the Hwy 33 drawbridge, tiny **Tilghman Island** still runs a working waterfront where local captains take visitors out on graceful oyster skipjacks; the historic **Rebecca T Ruark** (☎ 410-886-2176; www.skipjack.org; 2hr cruises adult/child under 12 $30/15), built in 1886, is the oldest certified vessel of its kind. Head to legendary **Harrison's Chesapeake House** (☎ 410-886-2121; 21551 Chesapeake House Dr; mains $8-22; 6am-9pm Mon-Fri, to 11pm Sat & Sun) for a massive 'no apologies, lots of butter' Eastern Shore seafood feast.

Berlin & Snow Hill

Imagine 'small-town, main street Americana, cute that vision up by a few points, and you've

EATING MARYLAND: BLUE CRABS

Eating at a crab shack, where the dress code stops at shorts and flip-flops, is the quintessential Chesapeake Bay foodie experience. Folks in these parts take their crabs seriously and can spend hours debating the intricacies of how to crack a crab, the proper way to prepare them and where to find the best crabs. There is one thing Marylanders can agree on: they must be blue crabs (scientific name: *Callinectes sapidus*), a critter indigenous to these parts and one of the Bay's most important economic products.

Steamed crabs are prepared very simply, using beer and Old Bay seasoning. One of the best crab shacks in the state is **Jimmy Cantler's Riverside Inn** (☎ 410-757-1311; 458 Forest Beach Rd, Annapolis; 11am-11pm Sun-Thu, to midnight Sun), where eating a steamed crab has been elevated to an art form – a hands-on, messy endeavor, normally accompanied by corn on the cob and ice-cold beer. The other great Maryland recipe is the crab cake. The best have the right amount of 'filler' to balance out lumpy crabmeat. Again, this is yet another source of debate but our favorites are at **Faidley's** (p345).

Sadly, the blue crab is slowly disappearing from Chesapeake Bay, due to overfishing and water pollution. Stocks are down 70% since 1991 and many restaurants now import inferior crabs from the Gulf of Mexico and Thailand. As a result, real Maryland crabs ain't cheap. Prices fluctuate wildly, but expect to pay about $35 per dozen; a bushel of about seven dozen will set you back $200.

come close to these Eastern Shore villages. Most of the buildings here are preserved or renovated to look preserved. If you love antique shops, die before you leave, because you will never find a greater concentration of porcelain knickknacks.

our pick **Globe Theater** (☎ 410-641-0784; 12 Broad St; lunch mains $6-12, dinner mains $10-28; 11am-11pm Mon-Thu, to midnight Fri & Sat, 10am-11pm Sun) in Berlin is a lovingly restored main stage that serves as a restaurant, bar, art gallery and theater for nightly live music; the kitchen is known for its Asian-meets-American menu. Don't miss the spicy cream-of-crab soup. The nearby, still-functioning **Hair Shop** (17 N Main St) was used as a location in the 1999 film *Runaway Bride*.

There are B&Bs galore overflowing with charm and doilies, but if you need an alternative try the **Atlantic Hotel** (☎ 410-641-3589; www.atlantichotel.com; 2 N Main St; r $85-155, d $105-245; P). This handsome, Gilded-era lodger gives guests the time-warp experience with all the modern amenities, and the attached **Drummer's Cafe** (lunch mains $8-13, dinner mains $15-33; 11am-3pm & 5-10pm Mon-Sat, 10am-3pm Sun) serves up local favorites.

A few miles from Berlin, Snow Hill is even tinier and cozier. Nearby **Furnace Town** (☎ 410-632-2032; Old Furnace Rd; adult/child $5/3; 10am-5pm Apr-Oct), off Rte 12, is a living-history museum that marks the old location of a 19th-century iron-smelting town. In Snow Hill itself, while away an odd, rewarding half-hour in the **Julia A Purnell Museum** (☎ 410-632-0515; 208 W Market St; adult/child under 12 $2/50¢; 10am-4pm Tue-Sat, from 1pm Sun Apr-Oct), a tiny structure that feels like an attic for the entire Eastern Shore. Staying in town? Check out the **River House Inn** (☎ 410-632-2722; 201 E Market St; www.riverhouseinn.com; r $190-250; P), which overlooks a breathtakingly pretty bend of the Pocomoke River.

OCEAN CITY

For better or worse, 'The OC' is where you'll experience the American seaside resort at its tackiest. The center of action is the 2.5-mile-long boardwalk, which stretches from the inlet to 27th St. Go for a spin on nausea-inducing thrill rides, buy a T-shirt with unprintably obscene slogans, drink to excess at cheesy theme bars, many run by European students on gap year. The beaches are beautiful, but it's nearly impossible to relax on the downtown beaches with the packs of roaming wild teenagers and noisy crowds; the beaches north of the boardwalk are much quieter.

The **visitor center** (☎ 410-723-8600; www.ococean.com; 9am-5pm) and **Ocean City Hotel-Motel-Restaurant Association** (☎ 410-289-6733; www.ocvisitor.com), in the convention center on Coastal Hwy at 40th St, can help you find lodging. In summer, the town's tiny year-round population of 7100 swells to over 150,000; traffic is jammed and parking scarce. When you tire of the crowds, Assateague Island (p353) and the Delaware Beaches (p355) are just a short drive away.

SCENIC DRIVE: MARITIME MARYLAND

Maryland and Chesapeake Bay have always been inextricable, but few parts of the state actually live off the water today. Here's a chance to see some towns that stubbornly cling to the ebb-and-rip clock of the tides.

About 150 miles south of Baltimore, at the edge of the Eastern Shore, is **Crisfield**, the top working water town in Maryland. Get visiting details at the **visitor center** (☎ 410-968-2501; 3 9th St; 10am-4pm Mon-Sat). Any seafood you eat here will be goooood, but for a true Shore experience, try some of the strip-the-paint strong coffee at **Gordon's** (☎ 410-968-0566; 831 W Main St; from 4am), where watermen flock in the early morning hours before heading out on their boats.

From here you can leave your car overnight (or take a day trip) and board the pedestrian **ferry** (☎ 410-425-5931/4471; $25 round-trip; departs noon & 5pm daily, evening service varies in winter) to **Smith Island**, the only offshore settlement in the state. Settled by fisherfolk from the English West Country some 400 years ago, the island's tiny population still speak with what linguists reckon is the closest thing to a 17th-century Cornish accent. The online visitors page (www.visitsmithisland.com) has information on island B&Bs, restaurants and activities. Ferries will take you back to the mainland and the present day at 3:30pm.

Sleeping

There are some 10,000 identical guest rooms (double beds, cable TV, kitchenette) in town. Prices listed here are for the high-season (summer), from Memorial Day to Labor Day. Many places have a two-night minimum. Many establishments are only open during temperate months; prices plummet out of season.

MIDRANGE

King Charles Hotel (☎ 410-289-6141; www.kingcharleshotel.com; 1209 Baltimore Ave, at 12th St; r $105-169; P) This place could be a quiet summer cottage, except it happens to be within spitting distance of the best boardwalk action.

Spinnaker Motel (☎ 410-289-5444; www.purnellproperties.com/spinnaker; cnr 18th St & Baltimore Ave; r from $166; P) Basically a bunch of boxes on the beach, but the boxes are comfy and cheaper than most waterfront hotels.

Hilton Suites Oceanfront (☎ 410-289-6444; www.oceancityhilton.com; 3200 North Baltimore Ave; r $189-235; P) Located just north of the boardwalk at 33rd St and the beach, this luxurious all-suites hotel is surprisingly affordable when you consider its amenities and location. The beachfront water park will keep kids busy.

TOP END

Lighthouse Club Hotel (☎ 410-524-5400, 888-371-5400; www.fagers.com/hotel; 201 60th St on the Bay; r incl breakfast $225-340; P) You might never make it to the beach when your buff-toned suite is equipped with a double Jacuzzi and romantic views of the bay.

Inn on the Ocean (☎ 410-289-8894; www.innontheocean.com; 1001 Atlantic Ave, at the Boardwalk; r $275-265 incl breakfast; P) This six-roomed B&B is an elegant escape from the usual OC lodging.

Eating & Drinking

Surf 'n' turf and all-you-can-eat deals are the order of the day. Dance clubs cluster around the boardwalk's southern tip.

Soriano's (☎ 410-289-6656; 310 S Baltimore Ave; breakfast $4-7, lunch $6-7; 8am-3pm) This local diner is a great place to start the day. Breakfast specialties include French toast and cream chipped beef.

our pick **Liquid Assets** (☎ 410-524-7037; www.la94.com; 9301 Coastal Hwy; mains $10-23; 11:30am-11pm Sun-Thu, to midnight Fri & Sat) Like a diamond in the rough, this bistro gem and wine shop complex is hidden in a strip mall in north OC. The menu is a refreshing mix of modern American cuisine with seasonal specialties.

Fager's Island (☎ 410-524-5500; 60th St; mains $19-36; from 11am) The food is hit-and-miss, but it's a great place for a drink – Tchaikovsky's 1812 Overture is cued up exactly 15 minutes and 34 seconds before sunset, to time the cannons with the sun hitting the horizon over the Isle of Wight Bay.

Seacrets (☎ 410-524-4900; cnr W 49th St & the Bay; from 11am) A water-laced, Jamaican-themed, rum-soaked bar straight out of MTV's *Spring Break*. You can drift around in an inner tube while sipping a drink and flirting with the hotties at OC's most famous meet-market.

Getting There & Around

Greyhound (☎ 410-289-9307; 12848 Ocean Gateway) buses run twice daily to and from Washington ($38) and once to Baltimore ($40).

Ocean City Coastal Highway Bus (☎ 410-723-1607; day pass $2) runs the length of the beach, 24 hours a day.

WESTERN MARYLAND

The western spine of Maryland is mountain country. The Appalachian peaks soar to 3000ft above sea level and the surrounding valleys are packed with rugged scenery and Civil War battlefields. This is Maryland's outdoor playground, where hiking, skiing, rock climbing and white-water rafting are just a short drive from Baltimore.

Frederick

Halfway between the battlefields of Gettysburg, PA, and Antietam, Frederick is a popular stop along the Civil War trail. Its 50-square-block historic district is filled with 18th- and 19th-century buildings in various states of renovation. The **visitor center** (☎ 301-663-8687; 19 E Church St, at Market St) conducts weekend walking tours in summer ($4.50); it validates parking from the garage next door.

The **National Museum of Civil War Medicine** (☎ 301-695-1864; www.civilwarmed.org; 48 E Patrick St; adult/student/child 10-16yr $6.50/5.50/4.50; 10am-5pm Mon-Sat, from 11am Sun) gives a fascinating, sometimes gruesome look at the health conditions soldiers and doctors faced during the war, as well as important medical advances that resulted from the conflict.

Hollerstown Hill B&B (☎ 301-228-3630; www.hollerstownhill.com; 4 Clarke Pl; r $125-135; P) has four pattern-heavy rooms, two resident terriers and an elegant billiards room.

The **Mudd Puddle** (☎ 301-620-4324; 124 S Carroll St; panini $5; 7am-5pm Mon, to 8pm Tue-Wed, to 9pm Thu & Fri, 8am-10pm Sat) is a warm, comfortable coffee and panini place that hosts live entertainment most weekends.

Frederick is accessible via **Greyhound** (☎ 301-663-3311; 100 S East St) and **MARC trains** (☎ 301-228-2888, 800-325-7245; 141 B&O Ave, at East Ave; Mon-Fri).

Antietam National Battlefield

The site of the bloodiest day in American history is, ironically, supremely peaceful, quiet and haunting, uncluttered save for plaques and statues. On September 17, 1862, General Robert E Lee's first invasion of the North was stalled here in a tactical stalemate that left 23,000 dead, wounded or missing – more casualties than America had suffered in all her previous wars combined. Poignantly, many of the battlefield graves are inscribed with German and Irish names, a roll call of immigrants who died fighting for their new homeland.

The **visitor center** (☎ 301-432-5124; State Rd 65; 3-day individual/family pass $4/6; 8:30am-6pm, to 5pm low season) offers self-guided driving tour pamphlets and audiotapes ($6).

Ten miles after the I-68 turns into I-70, the highway literally passes through **Sideling Hill**, an impressive rock exposure nearly 850ft high. Pull over to check out the **exhibit center** (☎ 301-842-2155; admission free; 9am-5pm) and the striated evidence of some 340 million

WORTH THE TRIP: ASSATEAGUE ISLAND

Just 8 miles south but a world away from Ocean City is Assateague Island seashore, a perfectly barren landscape of sand dunes and beautiful, secluded beaches. This undeveloped barrier island is populated by the only herd of wild horses on the East Coast, made famous in the book *Misty of Chincoteague*.

The island is divided into three sections. **Assateague State Park** (☎ 410-641-2120; Rte 611; admission $4; campsites $30; campground open late Apr-late Oct).

Assateague Island National Seashore (☎ 410-641-1441; Rte 611; www.nps.gov/asis/; admission $3, vehicle $15; campsites $20; visitors center 9am-5pm) is federally administered.

The former two are both in Maryland, while **Chincoteague National Wildlife Refuge** (p373) is in Virginia.

As well as swimming and sunbathing, recreational activities include birding, kayaking, canoeing, crabbing and fishing. There are no services on the Maryland side of the island, so you must bring all your own food and drink. Don't forget insect repellent; the mosquitoes and biting horseflies are pure evil!

years of geological history. Ten miles away off I-67 in **Burkittsville** is **Gathland State Park** (☎ 301-791-4767; admission free; 🕑 8am-sunset), site of the world's only **War Correspondents Memorial**. Burkittsville is also famous as the setting of *The Blair Witch Project*.

Cumberland

At the Potomac River, the frontier outpost of Fort Cumberland (not to be confused with the Cumberland Gap between Virginia and Kentucky) was the pioneer gateway across the Alleghenies to Pittsburgh and the Ohio River. Today Cumberland has expanded into the outdoor recreation trade to guide visitors to the region's rivers, forests and mountains.

C&O CANAL NATIONAL HISTORIC PARK

A marvel of engineering, the C&O Canal was designed to stretch alongside the Potomac River from Chesapeake Bay to the Ohio River – linking commercial centers in the east with frontier resources out west. Construction on the canal began in 1828 but was halted here in 1850 by the Appalachian Mountains. By then the first railroad had made its way to Cumberland, rendering the canal obsolete.

The **C&O Canal National Historic Park visitor center** (☎ 301-739-4200; 15 Canal Pl; 🕑 9am-5pm Mon-Fri) chronicles the importance of river trade in eastern seaboard history. The park's protected 185-mile corridor includes a 12ft-wide tow-path/hiking and bicycling trail and maintains six visitor centers, the first in Georgetown and the last one here.

Outside the **Allegheny County visitor center** (☎ 301-777-5132) passengers can catch steam-locomotive rides aboard the **Western Maryland Scenic Railroad** (☎ 800-872-4650; www.wmsr.com; adult/child $29/15), traversing forests and steep ravines to Frostburg, a three-hour round-trip.

There are plenty of reputable outfitters in the area. **Allegany Expeditions** (☎ 800-819-5170; www.alleganyexpeditions.com; 10310 Columbus Ave/Rte 2) leads tours to suit whatever adventure itch you've got, from spelunking to fly-fishing.

Deep in your heart, you know you should have been in *Grease*. The next best thing is chilling by the iconoclastic soda fountain and jukebox in the famous **Queen City Creamery & Deli** (☎ 301-777-0011; N Harrison St; mains $4-8; 🕑 7am-10pm, reduced hours winter).

Deep Creek Lake

In the extreme west of the panhandle, Maryland's largest freshwater lake is an all-seasons playground. The crimson and copper glow of the Alleghenies attracts thousands during the annual **Autumn Glory Festival** in October, rivaling New England's leaf-turning backdrops. The **Garrett County visitor center** (☎ 301-387-4386; www.garrettchamber.com), off US 219 on the north end, has information on all outdoor activities, including the state's only ski resort, **Wisp** (☎ 301-387-4911).

DELAWARE

Diminutive, delectable Delaware, the nation's second-smallest state (96 miles long and less than 35 miles across at its widest point) is overshadowed by her neighbors and overlooked by visitors to the Capital Region. And that's too bad, because Delaware has a lot more on offer than just tax-free shopping and chicken farms.

You may be pleasantly surprised to learn that Delaware is home to long, white sandy beaches, cute colonial villages, a cozy countryside and small-town charm. There's a whole state just waiting to be explored. Delaware still rides on her reputation as being the first state to ratify the US Constitution, hence her new slogan: 'It's Good Being First.'

History

In colonial days Delaware was the subject of an aggressive land feud between Dutch, Swedish and British settlers. The former imported classically northern European middle-class concepts, the latter a plantation-based aristocracy, which is partly why Delaware remains a typically mid-Atlantic cultural hybrid today.

DEFINING DELMARVA

The large peninsula east of Chesapeake Bay is known collectively as 'Delmarva,' an acronym for the three states that occupy it: the entire state of Delaware, Maryland's Eastern Shore and a tiny sliver of Virginia. Together, the Delmarva peninsula measures 180 miles by 60 miles, bordered by Chesapeake Bay, Delaware River, Delaware Bay and the Atlantic Ocean.

The little state's big moment came on December 7, 1787, when Delaware became the first state to ratify the US Constitution and thus the first state in the Union. It remained in that union throughout the Civil War, despite supporting slavery. During this period, as throughout much of the state's history, the economy drew on its chemical industry. DuPont, the world's second-largest chemical company, was founded here in 1802 as a gunpowder factory by French Immigrant Eleuthère Irénée du Pont. Low taxes drew other firms (particularly credit-card companies) in the 20th century, boosting the state's prosperity.

Information

Delaware Tourism Office (☎ 302-739-4271, 866-284-7489; www.visitdelaware.com; 99 King's Hwy, Dover, DE 19903)

Visitor center (☎ 302-737-4059; I-95, btwn exits 1 & 3)

DELAWARE BEACHES

Delaware's 28 miles of sandy Atlantic beaches are the best reason to linger. All businesses and services listed here are open year-round unless otherwise noted, and all prices are for the high season (June to August). Low-season bargains abound.

Lewes

In 1631 the Dutch gave this whaling settlement the pretty name of Zwaanendael, or valley of the swans, before promptly getting massacred by local Nanticokes. The name was changed to Lewes (pronounced LOO-iss) when William Penn gained control of the area. Today it's a cute seaside gem with a mix of English and Dutch architecture.

The **visitor center** (☎ 302-645-8073; www.leweschamber.com; 120 Kings Hwy; 9am-5pm Mon-Fri) directs you to sights such as the **Zwaanendael Museum** (☎ 302-645-1148; 102 Kings Hwy; admission free; 10am-4:30pm Tue-Sat, 1:30-4:30pm Sun), where the friendly staff explains the Dutch roots of this first state settlement.

You'll find many restaurant and hotel options in the small historic downtown including **Beacon Motel** (☎ 302-645-4888; 514 Savannah Rd; r $90-175; P), with large, quiet rooms and easy access to Rehoboth Beach and **Hotel Rodney** (☎ 302-645-6466; www.hotelrodneydelaware.com; 142 2nd St; r $190-250, ste $225-325; P), a charming boutique hotel with exquisite bedding and antique furniture.

> **DELAWARE FACTS**
>
> **Nickname** The First State
> **Population** 873,092
> **Area** 1982 sq miles
> **Capital city** Dover (population 35,811)
> **Sales tax** None
> **Birthplace of** Rock musician George Thorogood (b 1952), actress Valerie Bertinelli (b 1960), actor Ryan Phillippe (b 1974)
> **Home of** Vice President Joe Biden, the Du Pont family, DuPont chemicals, credit-card companies, lots of chickens
> **Famous for** Tax-free shopping, beautiful beaches
> **State bird** Blue Hen Chicken
> **Driving distances** Wilmington to Dover 52 miles, Dover to Rehoboth Beach 43 miles

Get acquainted with the Reubens and friendly waitstaff at the **Blue Plate Diner** (☎ 302-644-8400; 329 Savannah Rd; dishes $5; 8am-9pm, reduced hours winter). Located on the canal, the clapboard **Striper Bites Bistro** (☎ 302-645-4657; 107 Savannah Rd, mains $18-27; 11:30am-late Mon-Sat) specializes in local seafood dishes like rockfish and scallops.

The **Cape May–Lewes Ferry** (☎ reservations 800-643-3779, schedule 302-644-6030; www.capemaylewesferry.com; per vehicle $29.50 plus per adult/child passenger $7.50/3.75 Nov-Mar, per vehicle $36 plus per passenger $10/5 Apr-Oct) runs daily 80-minute ferries across Delaware Bay to New Jersey at the terminal 1 mile from downtown Lewes. For foot passengers, a seasonal shuttle bus operates between the ferry terminal and Lewes and Rehoboth Beach.

Cape Henlopen State Park

One mile east of Lewes, more than 4000 acres of dune bluffs, pine forests and wetlands are preserved at this lovely **state park** (☎ 302-645-8983) that's popular with bird-watchers and beachgoers ($6 per out-of-state car). You can see clear to Cape May from the observation tower. **North Shores beach** draws many gay and lesbian couples. **Camping** (☎ 877-987-2757; campsites $32; Mar-Nov) includes oceanfront or wooded sites.

Rehoboth Beach & Dewey Beach

As the closest beach to Washington, DC, (121 miles), Rehoboth is often dubbed 'The Nation's Summer Capital.' Founded in 1873 as a Christian seaside resort camp, Rehoboth is today a shining example of tolerance. It is both a family-friendly destination and one of the most gay-friendly cities on the East Coast. It has a particularly large lesbian community. There's even a gay beach – aka Poodle Beach – located, appropriately, at the end of Queen St.

Downtown Rehoboth is a mix of grand Victorian and gingerbread houses, tree-lined streets, boutique B&Bs and shops, posh restaurants, kiddie amusements and wide beaches fronted by a 1-mile-long boardwalk. Rehoboth Ave, the main drag, is lined with restaurants and the usual tacky souvenir shops; it stretches from the **visitor center** (☎ 302-227-2233; www.beach-fun.com; 501 Rehoboth Ave; 9am-5pm) at the traffic circle to the boardwalk. Outside of town, Rte 1 is a busy highway crammed with chain restaurants, hotels and outlet malls, where shoppers take advantage of Delaware's tax-free status.

Less than 2 miles south on Hwy 1 is the tiny hamlet of Dewey Beach. Unapologetically known as 'Do Me' beach for its wild singles (straight) scene and hedonistic nightlife, Dewey is the Mid-Atlantic region's biggest party beach.

SLEEPING

Prices listed below are for high season (June to August), when many hotels have a two- or three-night minimum. Prices skyrocket on weekends and July 4. Reservations are a must during summer, when the town's tiny population swells to 50,000. Cheaper lodging options are located on Rte 1.

Crosswinds Motel (☎ 302-227-7997; www.crosswindsmotel.com; 312 Rehoboth Ave; r $105-255; P) Located in the heart of Rehoboth Ave, this simple motel offers great value for your dollar, with such amenities as minifridge and flat-screen TV. Walk to the beach in 12 minutes.

our pick **Bellmoor** (☎ 302-227-5800; www.thebellmoor.com; 6 Christian St; incl breakfast r $155-395; ste $225-495; P) If money were no object, we'd splurge for a room at Rehoboth's most luxurious inn. With its English country decor, fireplaces, quiet garden and secluded setting, this is not your usual seaside resort. A full-service day spa caps the amenities.

Hotel Rehoboth (☎ 302-227-4300; www.hotelrehoboth.com; 247 Rehoboth Ave; incl breakfast r $179-329; ste $199-429; P) Opened in 2008, Rehoboth's newest boutique hotel has quickly gained a reputation for great service and luxurious amenities, including a free shuttle to the beach.

EATING & DRINKING

Cheap eats are available right on the boardwalk; you haven't been to Rehoboth until you've had Thrasher's fries, Grotto's pizza and Dolle's saltwater taffy. When you're ready for something with a little more substance, check out these favorites:

our pick **Royal Treat** (☎ 302-227-6277; 4 Wilmington Ave; items $2-9; 8-11:30am & 1-11:30pm May-Sep) There's a reason why there's always a line outside this landmark ice-cream parlor. Royal Treat serves up the best and thickest chocolate milk shakes we've ever tasted. The breakfast menu is only so-so.

Starboard (☎ 302-227-4600; 2009 Hwy 1, Dewey Beach; mains $5-15; 9am-late, Apr-Oct) A Dewey Beach tradition since 1960, the Starboard is the region's best bet for brunch. Order the Eggs Del marva – eggs Benedict topped with crab-meat. At night, Starboard transforms into the area's biggest beach party with wall-to-wall drunks and live entertainment.

Dogfish Head (☎ 302-226-2739; 320 Rehoboth Ave; mains $9-23; noon-late) When a place mixes its own brewery with some of the best live music on the Eastern Shore, you know you've got a winning combination.

Cultured Pearl (☎ 302-227-8493; 301 Rehoboth Ave; sushi $3-9, mains $13-32; 4:30pm-late) A locals' favorite, this wonderful Asian restaurant with traditional Japanese decor and rooftop deck has the area's best sushi.

our pick **La La Land** (☎ 302-227-3887; 22 Wilmington Ave; mains $26-33; from 6pm) Rehoboth's perfect date restaurant is a whimsical pink and purple dreamland featuring an acclaimed Asian-fusion menu, beautiful outdoor patio dining area and cloudlike back bar. Don't miss the lobster tail topped with crabmeat gratin.

GETTING THERE & AROUND

The **Jolly Trolley** (☎ 302-227-1197; one way $2, after midnight $3; 8am-2am summer) connects Rehoboth and Dewey and makes frequent stops along the way. Unfortunately, long-distance buses no longer serve Rehoboth. Your best bet is to take a **Greyhound bus** (www.greyhound.com) to Ocean City, MD (one or two per day, $19, 5½ hours), take the Coastal Highway Bus (every 10 to 15 minutes, $2, 30 minutes; runs 24 hours) to 144th St, then switch to DART bus route 208 (www.dartfirststate.com; $1.15; eight per day; 30 minutes).

Bethany Beach & Fenwick Island

Want to get away from it all? The seaside towns of Bethany and Fenwick, about halfway between Rehoboth and Ocean City, are known as 'The Quiet Resorts.' They share a tranquil, almost boring, family-friendly scene.

There are only a few restaurants and even fewer hotels here; most visitors stay in rented apartments and beach houses. For a nice change of pace from the usual seafood fare, **Bethany Blues BBQ** (☎ 302-537-1500; www.bethanyblues.com; mains $8-25; 4:30pm-late) has falling-off-the-bone ribs and pulled-pork sandwiches.

NORTHERN & CENTRAL DELAWARE

The grit of Wilmington is balanced by the rolling hills and palatial residences of the Brandywine Valley, particularly the soaring estate of Winterthur. Dover is cute, friendly, and gets a little lively after hours.

Wilmington

A unique cultural milieu (African Americans, Jews, Caribbeans etc) and an energetic arts scene make this a town (population 72,868) worth a visit. The central commercial district is along Market St, while Riverfront turns old warehouses and other industrial sites into shops, restaurants and museums. The **visitor center** (☎ 302-295-2210; www.visitwilmingtonde.com; 100 W 10th St; 9am-5pm Mon-Fri) is downtown.

The **Delaware Art Museum** (☎ 302-571-9590; www.delart.org; 800 S Madison St; adult/child $12/6, free Sun; 10am-4pm Wed-Sat, from noon Sun) exhibits work of the local Brandywine School, including Edward Hopper, John Sloan and three generations of Wyeths. The **Delaware Center for the Contemporary Arts** (☎ 302-656-6466; www.thedcca.org; 200 S Madison St; adult/student/child under 12 $5/3/free, free Sat morning & Wed; 10am-5pm Tue, Thu-Sat, from noon Wed & Sun) is bringing some mind-expanding culture to the burgeoning Riverfront district. Located in, of all things, an art-deco Woolworth's building, the **Delaware History Museum** (☎ 302-656-0637; www.hsd.org; 200 S Madison St; adult/student/child under 12 $4/3/free; 11am-4pm Wed-Fri, 10am-4pm Sat) proves the First State has done loads more than earn its nickname.

The premier hotel in the state, the **Hotel du Pont** (☎ 302-594-3100; www.hoteldupont.com; cnr Market & 11th Sts, r $130-430, ste $560-750; P) is luxurious and classy enough to satisfy its namesake (ie one of America's most successful industrialist families). **Leo & Jimmy's Deli** (☎ 302-656-7151; 728 Market St; mains $4-10; 5:30am-4pm Mon-Fri) is a Wilmington standby, well loved for its excellent sandwiches and service. For dessert, try the famously decadent chocolate at old-school **Govatos** (☎ 302-652-4082; 800 Market St; mains $4-9; 8am-5pm Mon-Fri year-round, to 3pm Sat Oct-Apr).

Wilmington is accessible by **Greyhound** or **Peter Pan Bus Lines** buses. A Greyhound bus to DC costs $15.50 (seven per day, 2¾ hours), and to New York $17 (five per day, 2¼ hours). Both bus lines serve the **Wilmington Transportation Center** (☎ 302-655-6111; 101 N French St). **Amtrak trains** (☎ 302-429-6527; 100 S French St) also run to Wilmington: to DC costs $32 (10 per day, 1½ hours), to Baltimore $26 (10 per day, 45 minutes), and to New York $39 (10 per day, 1¾ hours).

Brandywine Valley

After making their fortune the French-descended Du Ponts turned the Brandywine Valley into a sort of American Loire Valley, and it remains a nesting ground for the wealthy and ostentatious to this day. The **Brandywine Valley Tourist Information Center** (☎ 610-719-1730), outside Longwood Gardens in Kennett Square, PA, distributes information on the region's triple crown of **chateaux** and gardens: Winterthur, Longwood Gardens and Nemours (recently renovated – it reopened in May 2008).

Winterthur (☎ 302-888-4600; www.winterthur.org; Hwy 52; adult/student/child $20/18/10; 10am-5pm Tue-Sun), 6 miles northwest of Wilmington, is the 175-room country estate of industrialist Henry Francis du Pont and his collection of antiques and American arts, one of the world's largest.

Hagley Museum (☎ 302-658-2400; www.hagley.org; Hwy 141; adult/student/child $11/9/4; 9:30am-4:30pm Apr-Dec, Sat & Sun Jan-Mar) is another fascinating shrine to the Du Pont legacy. The sprawling outdoor museum includes the ruins of the original DuPont company mills, craftsmith demonstrations and exhibits on some of the DuPont company inventions such as nylon.

New Castle

New Castle is a web of cobblestoned streets and 18th-century buildings that's as colonially cute as a kitten in a powdered wig. The **visitor center** (42 The Strand; 9am-5pm Mon-Fri) arranges walking tours, or you can wander the compact old town on your own. Sights include the **Old Court House** (closed Mon), the **arsenal on the Green**, **churches** and **cemeteries** dating back to the 17th century, and **historic houses**.

The owner of the five-room **Terry House B&B** (☎ 302-322-2505; www.terryhouse.com; 130 Delaware St; r $90-110; P ⊠) will play the piano for you while you enjoy a full breakfast.

There are big, mouthwatering colonial dishes like roast duck and honey-drop biscuits, all heavy on butter, cream and the other things that make life worth living, at **Jessop's Tavern** (☎ 302-322-6111; 114 Delaware St; mains $12-22; 11am-3pm & 5-10pm Mon-Sat) and its classier sister, the **Arsenal at Old New Castle** (☎ 302-328-1290; 30 Market St; mains around $30; 11:30am-9pm Tue-Thu, to 10pm Fri & Sat).

Dover

You wouldn't think so, given how stately central Dover is, with her classic brick buildings and shady, tree-lined boulevards, but this little town is good fun. The 1792 Old State House, 1874 Court House, belly-stretching cheap eateries and cheerful bars dot the area around the central Green, and throb with happy crowds at night.

Walk beside the State House to find the state **visitor center** (☎ 302-739-4266; 406 Federal St; 8:30am-4:30pm Mon-Sat, from 1:30pm Sun) and history exhibits at the foot of a long plaza from the capitol.

NASCAR fans worldwide know Dover as the home of **Dover International Speedway** (☎ 302-883-6500; doverspeedway.com; 1131 N Dupont Hwy), considered one of the best tracks in the country. See its website for current race schedules and ticket information. At the same location is Dover's other major attraction, **Dover Downs Casino** (☎ 302-674-4600; doverdowns.com; 8am-4am Mon-Sat, from noon Sun), an 80,000-sq-ft entertainment complex with 3200 slot machines, horse racing, hotel, spa and concert venue.

The **Johnson Victrola Museum** (☎ 302-739-4266; cnr Bank & New Sts; admission free; 10am-3:30pm Tue-Fri, 9am-4:30pm Sat) honors 'talking machine' pioneer Eldridge Johnson, including an exhibit on the RCA Records trademark dog, Nipper. The **Delaware Agriculture Museum and Village** (☎ 302-734-1618; 866 N Dupont Hwy; adult/student $5/3; 10am-3pm Tue-Sat) is a living-history museum featuring a re-creation of an 1890s farming community.

Southeast of town, Dover Air Force Base is the country's largest air base and the first stop for America's returning war dead. There are no public ceremonies to mark their homecoming, but you can visit the **Air Mobility Command Museum** (☎ 302-677-5938; www.amcmuseum.org; cnr Hwys 9 & 1; admission free; 9am-4pm Tue-Sun), filled with vintage planes and other aviation artifacts.

WT Smithers (☎ 302-674-8875; 140 S State St; from 11am Mon-Sat) is a great neighborhood bar that's a mix of students and State House staff sharing buffalo wings and excellent beer on tap.

VIRGINIA

Beautiful, passionate, lovely Virginia is a state steeped in history. It's the birthplace of America, where English settlers established the first permanent colony in the New World in 1607. From there, the Commonwealth of Virginia has played a lead role in nearly every major American drama, from the Revolutionary and Civil Wars to the Civil Rights movement and September 11, 2001.

Virginia's natural beauty is as diverse as her history and people. Chesapeake Bay and the wide sandy beaches kiss the Atlantic Ocean. Pine forests, marshes and rolling green hills form the soft curves of the central Piedmont region. The rugged Appalachian Mountains and stunning Shenandoah Valley line her back.

The nation's invisible line between North and South is drawn here, somewhere around Richmond; you'll know it as soon as you hear the sweet southern drawl offering plates of biscuits and Virginia ham. With something for everyone, it's easy to appreciate the state's motto: 'Virginia is for Lovers.'

History

Humans have occupied Virginia for at least 5000 years. Several thousand Native Americans were already here in May 1607 when Captain James Smith and his crew sailed up Chesapeake Bay and founded Jamestown, the first permanent English colony in the New World. Named for the 'Virgin Queen' Elizabeth I, the territory originally occupied most of America's Eastern seaboard. By 1610 most of the colonists had died from starvation in their quest for gold, until colonist John Rolfe (husband of Pocahontas) discovered Virginia's real riches: tobacco.

A feudal aristocracy grew out of tobacco farming, and many gentry scions became Founding Fathers, including native son

VIRGINIA FACTS

Nickname Old Dominion
Population 7.77 million
Area 42,774 sq miles
Capital city Richmond (population 200,123)
Sales tax 4.5%
Birthplace of Eight US presidents including George Washington (1732–99), Confederate General Robert E Lee (1807–70), tennis ace Arthur Ashe (1943–93), author Tom Wolfe (b 1931), actor-siblings Warren Beatty (b 1937) and Shirley MacLaine (b 1934), actress Sandra Bullock (b 1964)
Home of The Pentagon, the CIA, more technology workers than any other state
Famous for American history, tobacco, apples, Shenandoah National Park
State beverage Milk
Driving distances Arlington to Shenandoah 113 miles, Richmond to Virginia Beach 108 miles

George Washington. In the 19th century the slave-based plantation system grew in size and incompatibility with the industrializing North; Virginia seceded in 1861 and became the epicenter of the Civil War. Following its defeat the state walked a tense cultural tightrope, accruing a layered identity that included older aristocrats, a rural and urban working class, waves of immigrants and today, the burgeoning tech-heavy suburbs of DC. The state revels in its history, yet still wants to pioneer the American experiment; thus, while Virginia only reluctantly desegregated in the 1960s, it today houses one of the most ethnically diverse populations of the New South.

Information

Virginia's **Division of Tourism** (☎ 800-321-3244; www.virginia.org; 901 E Byrd St, Richmond, VA 23219) produces a comprehensive state guide. There are 10 welcome centers throughout the state.

NORTHERN VIRGINIA

Hidden within its suburban sprawl exterior, 'NOVA' mixes small-town charm with metropolitan chic. Colonial villages and battlefields bump up against skyscrapers, shopping malls and world-class arts venues.

You'll discover unexpected green spaces like **Great Falls National Park** (☎ 703-285-2965; www.nps.gov/grfa; 🕑 7am-sunset), a wilderness space that somehow survives despite being mere minutes from a major urban nexus. The park is a gorgeous, well-maintained forest cut through by the Potomac River, which surges over a series of white-water rapids. Kayaking (experienced paddlers only), rock climbing, hiking and fishing are all popular activities.

Arlington

Just across the Potomac River from DC, Arlington County was once part of Washington until it was returned to Virginia in 1847. In recent years, the gentrified neighborhoods of Arlington have spawned some of the hottest dining and nightlife scenes in the capital area.

The county's most well-known attraction is **Arlington National Cemetery** (☎ 703-692-0931; www.arlingtoncemetery.org; admission free; 🕑 8am-7pm Apr 1–Sep 30, to 5pm rest of year), the somber final resting place for more than 300,000 military personnel and their dependents, with veterans of every US war from the Revolution to Iraq. The cemetery is spread over 612 hilly acres. Departing from the Visitor Center, **Tourmobiles** (☎ 202-554-5100; adult/child $7.50/3.75) are a handy way to visit the cemetery's memorials.

Much of the cemetery was built on the grounds of **Arlington House**, the former home of Robert E Lee and his wife Mary Anna Custis Lee, a descendant of Martha Washington. When Lee left to lead Virginia's army in the Civil War, Union troops confiscated the property to bury their dead. The **Tomb of the Unknowns** contains the remains of unidentified American servicemen from both World Wars and the Korean War; military guards retain a round-the-clock vigil and the changing of the guard (every half-hour, March to September, every hour October to February) is one of Arlington's most moving sights. An eternal flame marks the **grave of John F Kennedy**, next to those of Jacqueline Kennedy Onassis and two of her infant children. The **Women in Military Service for America Memorial** (☎ 800-222-2294; womensmemorial.org) is a museum honoring the two million women who have served in America's armed forces. Other points of interest include the **Pan Am Flight 103 cairn** and the **Space Shuttle Challenger memorial**.

Near Rosslyn Metro station, the **Marine Corps Memorial** depicts six soldiers raising the American flag on Iwo Jima. The Felix de Weldon-designed sculpture is based on an iconic photo by Associated Press photographer Joe Rosenthal.

South of Arlington Cemetery is the **Pentagon**, the largest office building in the world. It's not open to the public, but outside you may visit the **Pentagon Memorial** (www.whs.mil/memorial; admission free; 24hr); 184 illuminated benches honor each man, woman and child killed in the September 11, 2001 terrorist attack on the Pentagon. Nearby, the **Air Force Memorial's** (703-247-5805; www.airforcememorial.org) three soaring arcs invoke the contrails of jets.

Dozens of chic restaurants, bars and hotels are located along Clarendon and Wilson Blvds between Rosslyn and Clarendon Metro stations.

our pick **Whitlow's on Wilson** (703-276-9693; 2854 Clarendon Blvd; mains $5-20; 11am-2am Mon-Fri, 9am-2am Sat & Sun) has the neighborhood's best Sunday-brunch menu, plus weekday happy hour specials.

Ray's Hell-Burger (703-841-0001; 1713 Wilson Blvd; mains $8-20; noon-10pm Tue-Sun, from 5pm Mon) lives up to the hype and has attracted a legion of fans including President Barack Obama. **Iota** (703-522-8340; iotaclubanDCafe.com; 2832 Clarendon Blvd; cover free-$15; 5pm-2am) is Arlington's top spot to catch live local and national musicians nightly; Norah Jones and John Mayer have performed here.

Alexandria

The charming colonial village of Alexandria is just 5 miles and 250 years away from Washington. Once a salty port town, Alexandria – known as 'Old Town' to locals – is today a posh collection of red-bricked colonial homes, cobblestoned streets and flickering gas lamps, waterfront promenade, boutiques, outdoor cafés and neighborhood bars and restaurants. The **visitor center** (703-838-5005; www.visitalexandriava.com; 221 King St; 9am-5pm) issues parking permits and discount tickets to historic sights.

The 333ft-tall **George Washington Masonic National Memorial** (703-683-2007; www.gwmemorial.org; cnr King & Callahan Sts; admission free; 9am-5pm) is an imposing tower modeled after Egypt's Lighthouse of Alexandria and dedicated to America's first president, who was a member of the shadowy Freemasons. **Gadsby's Tavern Museum** (703-838-4242; 134 N Royal St; adult/child 11-17yr $4/2; 10am-5pm Tue-Sat, from 1pm Sun) has exhibits on colonial life and is still a working pub and restaurant; past guests included George Washington and Thomas Jefferson. Once a munitions factory, the **Torpedo Factory Art Center** (703-838-4565; www.torpedofactory.org; 105 N Union St; admission free; 10am-5pm) now houses arts space with some 150 galleries and studios.

It's a bit touristy and pricey, but you haven't been to Old Town until you've downed a giant schooner of beer and sampled the seafood at the **Fish Market** (703-836-5676; www.fishmarketva.com; 105 King St; mains $6-28; 11:15am-midnight).

our pick **Momo Sushi & Cafe** (703 299 9092; www.mymomosushi.com; 212 Queen St; sushi $4-6, mains $7-23; 11:30am-2:30pm & 4-10pm Mon-Fri, noon-10pm Sat, 4pm-10pm Sun) is tiny and has just 13 seats, but it serves some of the best sushi we've ever tasted. The Green Tea Roll is a MUST!

Roll up your sleeves for some good pub grub and free, live bluegrass music at **Tiffany Tavern** (703-836-8844; 1116 King St; lunch mains $6-13, dinner mains $9-18; 5pm-midnight, to 2am Fri & Sat, 11:30am-2:30pm Wed-Fri).

Just north of Old Town by the Braddock Rd Metro station is one of America's premier music halls, the **Birchmere** (703-549-7500; www.birchmere.com; 3701 Mt Vernon Ave; tickets $15-60). The legendary venue stages an eclectic range of acts, from Dave Matthews and kd lang to Linda Ronstadt and Mary Chapin Carpenter.

To get to Alexandria from downtown DC get off at the King St Metro station. Local buses cover the mile to the visitor center. On weekends the free DASH shuttle bus connects the station with the waterfront and points in between.

Mount Vernon

One of the most visited historic shrines in the nation, **Mount Vernon** (703-780-2000; www.mountvernon.org; adult/child 6-11yr $15/7; 9am-5pm, to 4pm Nov-Feb), was the beloved home of George and Martha Washington, who lived here from their marriage in 1759 until his death in 1799. Now owned and operated by the Mount Vernon Ladies Association, the estate offers glimpses of 18th-century farm life and the first president's life as a country planter. Mount Vernon does not gloss over the Founding Father's slave ownership; visitors can tour slave quarters and the burial ground.

Mount Vernon is 16 miles south of DC off the Mount Vernon Memorial Hwy. By public transportation, take Metro to Huntington, then switch to Fairfax Connector bus 101. **Tourmobile** (202-554-5100; www.tourmobile.com;

incl Mount Vernon adult/child $30/15) offers three trips a day to Mount Vernon from Arlington National Cemetery or the Washington Monument. Several companies offer seasonal boat trips from DC and Alexandria; the cheapest is **Potomac Riverboat Company** (☎ 703-548-9000; www.potomacriverboatco.com; incl Mount Vernon adult/child $38/20). A free and fit alternative is to take a gorgeous bike ride along the Potomac River from DC.

Manassas

On July 21, 1861, Union and Confederate soldiers clashed in the first major land battle of the Civil War. Expecting a quick victory, Union fans flocked here to picnic and watch the First Battle of Bull Run (known in the South as First Manassas). The surprise Southern victory erased any hopes of a quick end to the war. Union and Confederate soldiers again met on the same ground for the larger Second Battle of Manassas in August 1862; again the South was victorious. Today, **Manassas National Battlefield Park** is a curving green hillscape, sectioned into fuzzy fields of tall grass and wildflowers by split-rail wood fences. Start your tour at the **Henry Hill Visitor Center** (☎ 703-361-1339; www.nps.gov/mana; admission $3; 🕑 8:30am-5pm) to watch the orientation film and pick up park and trail maps.

Virginia Railway Express (VRE; ☎ 800-742-3873; www.vre.org; 9451 West St; per person $8.45; 🕑 5am-7pm Mon-Fri) trains roll between DC's Union Station and the historic Old Town Manassas Railroad Station; from there it's a 6-mile taxi ride to the park. There are several nice restaurants and bars around the Manassas train station, but the rest of the city is an ugly mess of strip malls and suburban sprawl.

> **WORTH THE TRIP: STEVEN F UDVAR-HAZY CENTER**
>
> The Smithsonian National Air & Space Museum's **Steven F Udvar-Hazy Center** (☎ 202-357-2700; 🕑 10am-5:30pm), located in Chantilly near Dulles airport, is a huge hangar filled with surplus planes and spacecraft that wouldn't fit at the museum's DC location. Highlights include the space shuttle *Enterprise*, the B-29 *Enola Gay*, SR-71 Blackbird and a Concorde supersonic airliner. While the museum is free, parking costs a ridiculous $15.

FREDERICKSBURG

Fredericksburg is a pretty town with a historical district that is almost a cliché of small-town Americana. George Washington grew up here, and the Civil War exploded in the streets and surrounding fields. Today, main street is a pleasant amble of bookstores, gastropubs and cafés.

Sights

More than 13,000 Americans were killed during the Civil War in four battles fought in a 17-mile radius covered by **Fredericksburg & Spotsylvania National Military Park**, maintained by the NPS. Don't miss the burial ground of Stonewall Jackson's amputated arm near the **Fredericksburg Battlefield visitor center** (☎ 540-373-6122; 1013 Lafayette Blvd; admission free, film $2; 🕑 9am-5pm).

The **visitor center** (☎ 540-373-1776; www.fredericksburgva.com; 706 Caroline St; 🕑 9am-5pm) offers a pass to historic Fredericksburg for nine local sights (adult/child six to 18 $32/10) including the ones described below. Unless otherwise noted, the following colonial attractions are open 9am to 5pm Monday to Saturday and 11am to 5pm Sunday March to November, and from 10am to 4pm Monday to Saturday and noon to 4pm Sunday in winter.

James Monroe Museum & Memorial Library (☎ 540-654-1043; 908 Charles St; adult/child 6-18yr $5/1; 🕑 10am-5pm Mon-Sat, from 1pm Sun, reduced hours winter) The museum's namesake was the nation's fifth president.

Mary Washington House (☎ 540-373-1569; 1200 Charles St; adult/child 6-18yr $5/2) Home of George Washington's mother.

Rising Sun Tavern (☎ 540-371-1494; 1304 Caroline St; adult/child 6-18yr $5/2) A museum with tavern wenches.

Sleeping & Eating

Richard Johnston Inn (☎ 540-899-7606; www.therichardjohnstoninn.com; 711 Caroline St; r $105-210; P ✖) Scores points for location, comfort and friendliness (especially from the two resident Scottie dogs). Most rooms have private bathrooms, and guests get full breakfast on weekends.

As well as serving a classy caffeine jolt, the **Griffin Bookshop & Coffee Bar** (☎ 540-899-8041; 106 Hanover St; 🕑 9am-5pm Mon-Wed, to 9pm Thu-Sat, noon-5pm Sun) may be the best bookstore between DC and Richmond.

You'll find dozens of restaurants and cafés along historic Caroline and William

SCENIC DRIVE: VIRGINIA'S HORSE COUNTRY

About 40 miles west of Washington, DC, suburban sprawl gives way to endless green farms, vineyards, quaint villages and palatial estates and ponies. This is 'Horse Country,' where wealthy Washingtonians pursue their equestrian pastimes. The following route is the most scenic drive to Shenandoah National Park. From DC, take Rte 50 West to **Middleburg**, a too-cute-for-words town of B&Bs, taverns, wine shops and boutiques. The **National Sporting Library** (☎ 540-687-6542; 102 The Plains Rd; ⌚ 10am-4pm Tue-Fri, from 1pm Sat) is a museum and research center devoted to horse and field sports like foxhunting, dressage, steeplechase and polo.

our pick **Griffin Tavern** (☎ 540-675-3227; 659 Zachary Taylor Hwy; mains $6-19; ⌚ 11:30am-11pm Sun-Thu, to 1am Fri & Sat) is a quintessential British pub with English and Irish food and beer; head southwest on Rtes 522 and 211 to Flint Hill.

Six miles down Rte 211 is **Little Washington**, another cute town that's home to one of the finest B&B restaurants in America, **The Inn at Little Washington** (☎ 540-675-3800; cnr Middle & Main Sts; r from $400). Further down the road at the foothills of Blue Ridge Mountains is **Sperryville** and its many galleries and shops, a must-stop for antique-lovers. Continue 9 miles west to reach the Thornton Gap entrance of **Skyline Drive** in **Shenandoah National Park** (p375).

Sts. One of our favorites is **Caroline Street Cafe** (☎ 540-654-9180; 1002 Caroline St; mains $6.50-7.25; ⌚ 11am-4pm Mon, Wed & Thu, 9am-5pm Fri & Sun, to 7pm Sat), with homemade soups, salads and sandwiches.

Getting There & Away

VRE ($10.30, 12 per day, 1½ hours) and **Amtrak** ($17, five per day, 1¼ hours) trains depart from the new Fredericksburg train station (200 Lafayette Blvd) with service to DC. Buses come into the **Greyhound/Trailways depot** (☎ 540-373-2103; 2217 Princess Ann St). **Greyhound** has five buses per day to/from DC (from $8.75, 1½ hours). There are two buses per day to Richmond ($8.75, one hour). (Trips beyond DC such as to Baltimore and NYC require a transfer in DC).

RICHMOND

Richmond has been the capital of the Commonwealth of Virginia since 1780. It was here during the American Revolution that patriot Patrick Henry gave his famous 'Give me Liberty, or give me Death!' speech. But Richmond is most notable for serving as the capital of the secessionist Confederate States of America during the Civil War from 1861 to 1865. Ironically, Richmond is now an ethnically diverse city, with one of the most vibrant African American communities in the country. Of course, the attractive veneer of diversity cracks soon enough into ugly income disparities; most African American neighborhoods seem depressed compared with upmarket areas on the East and West ends of the center. This town also grapples with memorializing its controversial history. But in the end Richmond is a welcoming, warm traditional Southern city that is slowly being absorbed into the international milieu of the Northeast Corridor.

Orientation & Information

The James River bisects Richmond, with most attractions to its north. Uptown residential neighborhoods include the Fan district, south of Monument Ave, and Carytown, in the west end. Downtown, Court End holds the capitol and several museums. On E Cary St between 12th and 15th Sts, converted warehouses in Shockoe Slip house shops and restaurants. Once you pass under the trestle-like freeway overpass, you're in Shockoe Bottom. Just north of Court End is the historic African American neighborhood of Jackson Ward. Keep in mind that Cary St is more than 5 miles long; E Cary St is downtown, while W Cary St is in Carytown.

BOOKSTORES

Carytown Books (☎ 804-359-4831; 2930 W Cary St; ⌚ 10am-7pm Mon-Sat, to 5pm Sun)

Fountain Bookstore (☎ 804-788-1594; 1312 E Cary St; ⌚ 10am-8pm Mon-Thu, to 9pm Fri & Sat, noon-5pm Sun)

MEDIA

90.1 FM WDCE University of Richmond station.

93.5 FM WBBC Country.

Richmond-Times Dispatch (www.timesdispatch.com) Daily newspaper.

WASHINGTON, DC & THE CAPITAL REGION

MEDICAL SERVICES

Johnston-Willis Hospital (☎ 804-330-2000; 1401 Johnston-Willis Dr)

Richmond Community Hospital (☎ 804-225-1700; 1500 N 28th St)

POST

Post office (700 E Main St; 7:30am-5pm Mon-Fri)

TOURIST INFORMATION

Richmond visitor center (☎ 804-783-7450; www.richmondva.org; 405 N 3rd St; 9am-5pm, to 6pm Jun-Aug)

Virginia State visitor center (☎ 804-786-4485; 101 N 9th St; 9am-5pm Mon-Fri) This statewide center is located in the Bell Tower on the grounds of the State Capitol.

Sights

our pick **Museum & White House of the Confederacy** (☎ 804-649-1861; www.moc.org; cnr 12th & Clay Sts; adult/senior/student/child under 7 $11/10/6/free; 10am-5pm Tue-Sat, from noon Sun) traces the history of the Confederate States of America with the country's largest collection of Confederate civilian and military artifacts. It's a must-see for any history and Civil War buff. The adjacent 1818 White House mansion was the home of CSA President Jefferson Davis.

American Civil War Center at Historic Tredegar (☎ 804-780-1865; www.tredegar.org; 490 Tredegar St; adult/concession/child 7-12yr/child under 7yr $8/6/2/free; 9am-5pm), located in an 1861 gun foundry, accurately and fairly explores the causes and course of the Civil War from the perspectives of Union, Confederate and African American experiences. The center is one of 13 protected area sites that make up **Richmond National Battlefield Park** (www.nps.gov/rich).

The **Virginia State Capitol** (☎ 804-698-1788; cnr 9th & Grace Sts, Capitol Sq; admission & tours free; 9am-5pm Mon-Sat, 1-4pm Sun), designed by Thomas Jefferson, was completed in 1788 and houses the oldest legislative body in the Western Hemisphere, the Virginia General Assembly, established in 1619.

Changing and permanent exhibits at the **Virginia Historical Society** (☎ 804-358-4901; 428 N Blvd; adult/concession/child under 18yr $5/3/free; 10am-5pm Tue-Sat, from 1pm Sat) traces the history of the Commonwealth from prehistoric to present times.

Monument Avenue, a tree-lined boulevard in northeast Richmond, holds **statues** of such revered Southern heroes as JEB Stuart, Robert E Lee, Matthew Fontaine Maury, Jefferson Davis, Stonewall Jackson and, controversially, African American tennis champion Arthur Ashe.

It was at **St John's Episcopal Church** (☎ 804-648-5015; 2401 E Broad St; tours adult/child $6/4; 10am-4pm, from 1pm Sun) that firebrand Patrick Henry uttered his famous battle cry, 'Give me Liberty, or give me Death!' during the rebellious 1775 Second Virginia Convention. His speech is reenacted at 2pm on Sunday in summer.

The **Virginia Holocaust Museum** (☎ 804-257-5400; www.va-holocaust.com; 2000 E Cary St; admission free; 9am-5pm Mon-Fri, from 11am Sat & Sun) is structured like an attic/diorama of the Holocaust survivors who settled here after WWII. It's occasionally kitschy but still powerful, due to the personalized nature of the exhibits.

Jackson Ward, an African American neighborhood that was known as Little Africa in the late 19th century, is now a national historic landmark district. It comes off as a tough neighborhood (which it is), but there's a deep cultural legacy here as well. The **Black History Museum & Cultural Center of Virginia** (☎ 804-780-9093; 3 E Clay St; adult/student/child under 13 $5/4/3; 10am-5pm Tue-Sat, from 11am Sun) highlights the achievements of African American Virginians and displays collections of African arts, textiles and artifacts.

The **Virginia Museum of Fine Arts** (☎ 804-340-1400; www.vmfa.state.va.us; 2800 Grove Ave; requested donation $5; 11am-5pm Wed-Sun) has a remarkable collection of European works, sacred Himalayan art and one of the largest Fabergé egg collections on display outside Russia.

The **Science Museum of Virginia** (☎ 804-367-0000; 2500 W Broad St; adult/child 4-12yr $10/9, incl IMAX adult/child $15/14; 9:30am-5pm Mon-Sat, 11:30am-5pm Sun) is an interactive, educational, entertaining way to distract the kids.

The **Poe Museum** (☎ 804-648-5523; www.poemuseum.org; 1914-16 E Main St; adult/student $6/5; 10am-5pm Tue-Sat, from 11am Sun) contains the world's largest collection of manuscripts and memorabilia of macabre poet Edgar Allan Poe, who lived and worked in Richmond.

Tranquil **Hollywood Cemetery** (☎ 804-648-8501; entrance cnr Albemarle & S Cherry Sts; free admission, tours $7; 8am-5pm, to 6pm summer), perched above the James River rapids, contains the gravesites of two US presidents (James Monroe and John Tyler), the only Confederate president (Jefferson Davis) and 18,000 Confederate soldiers.

The 1.25-mile waterfront **Canal Walk** between the James River and the Kanawha

RICHMOND

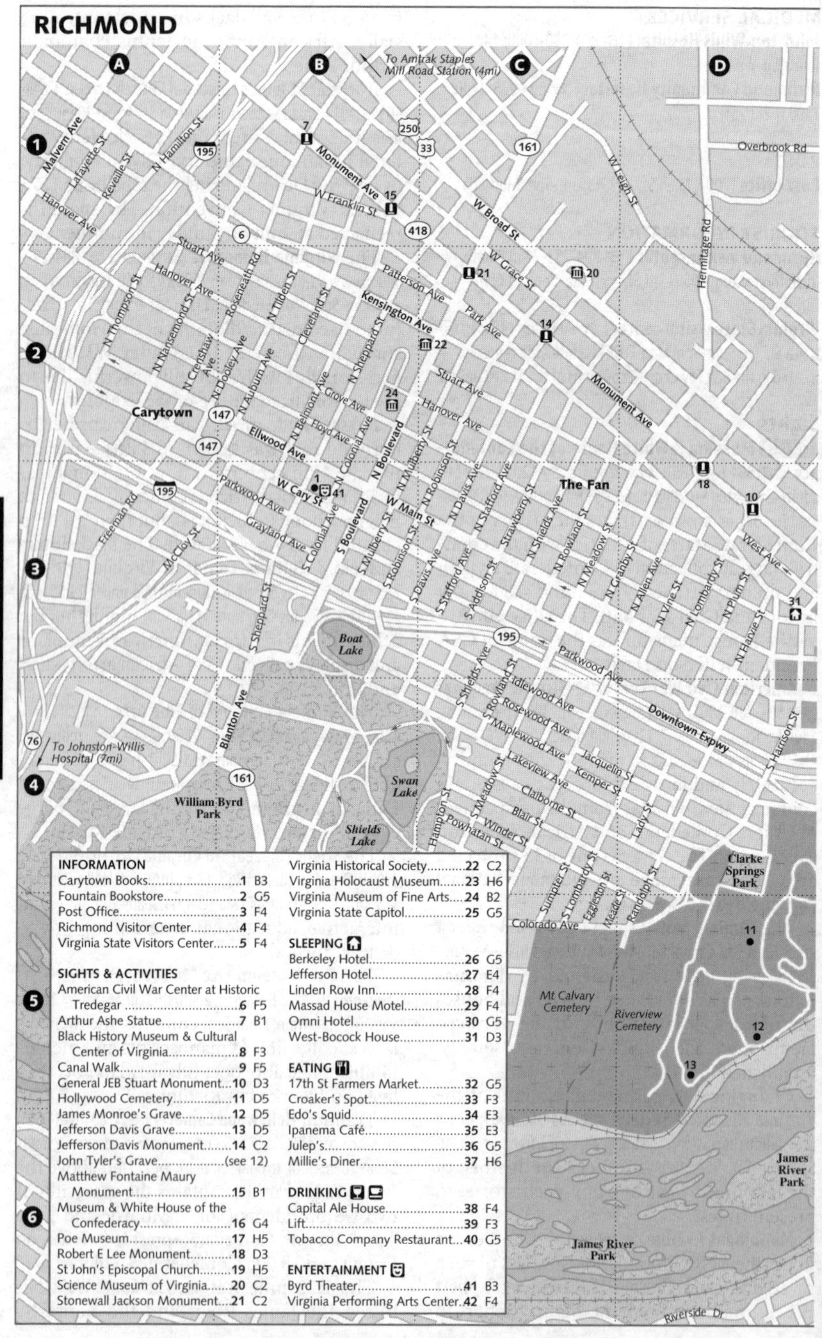

To Amtrak Staples Mill Road Station (4mi)
To Johnston-Willis Hospital (7mi)
Carytown
The Fan
Boat Lake
Swan Lake
Shields Lake
William Byrd Park
Clarke Springs Park
Mt Calvary Cemetery
Riverview Cemetery
James River Park
Monument Ave
W Broad St
W Grace St
W Franklin St
Kensington Ave
Patterson Ave
Park Ave
Stuart Ave
Hanover Ave
Grove Ave
Floyd Ave
Ellwood Ave
W Cary St
W Main St
Parkwood Ave
Grayland Ave
Downtown Expwy
N Boulevard
S Boulevard
Overbrook Rd
Hermitage Rd
W Leigh St
West Ave
Idlewood Ave
Rosewood Ave
Maplewood Ave
Lakeview Ave
Claiborne St
Blair St
Winder St
Powhatan St
Colorado Ave
Riverside Dr
Blanton Ave
INFORMATION
Carytown Books 1 B3
Fountain Bookstore 2 G5
Post Office 3 F4
Richmond Visitor Center 4 F4
Virginia State Visitors Center 5 F4
SIGHTS & ACTIVITIES
American Civil War Center at Historic Tredegar 6 F5
Arthur Ashe Statue 7 B1
Black History Museum & Cultural Center of Virginia 8 F3
Canal Walk 9 F5
General JEB Stuart Monument 10 D3
Hollywood Cemetery 11 D5
James Monroe's Grave 12 D5
Jefferson Davis Grave 13 D5
Jefferson Davis Monument 14 C2
John Tyler's Grave (see 12)
Matthew Fontaine Maury Monument 15 B1
Museum & White House of the Confederacy 16 G4
Poe Museum 17 H5
Robert E Lee Monument 18 D3
St John's Episcopal Church 19 H5
Science Museum of Virginia 20 C2
Stonewall Jackson Monument 21 C2
Virginia Historical Society 22 C2
Virginia Holocaust Museum 23 H6
Virginia Museum of Fine Arts 24 B2
Virginia State Capitol 25 G5
SLEEPING
Berkeley Hotel 26 G5
Jefferson Hotel 27 E4
Linden Row Inn 28 F4
Massad House Motel 29 F4
Omni Hotel 30 G5
West-Bocock House 31 D3
EATING
17th St Farmers Market 32 G5
Croaker's Spot 33 F3
Edo's Squid 34 E3
Ipanema Café 35 E3
Julep's 36 G5
Millie's Diner 37 H6
DRINKING
Capital Ale House 38 F4
Lift 39 F3
Tobacco Company Restaurant 40 G5
ENTERTAINMENT
Byrd Theater 41 B3
Virginia Performing Arts Center 42 F4

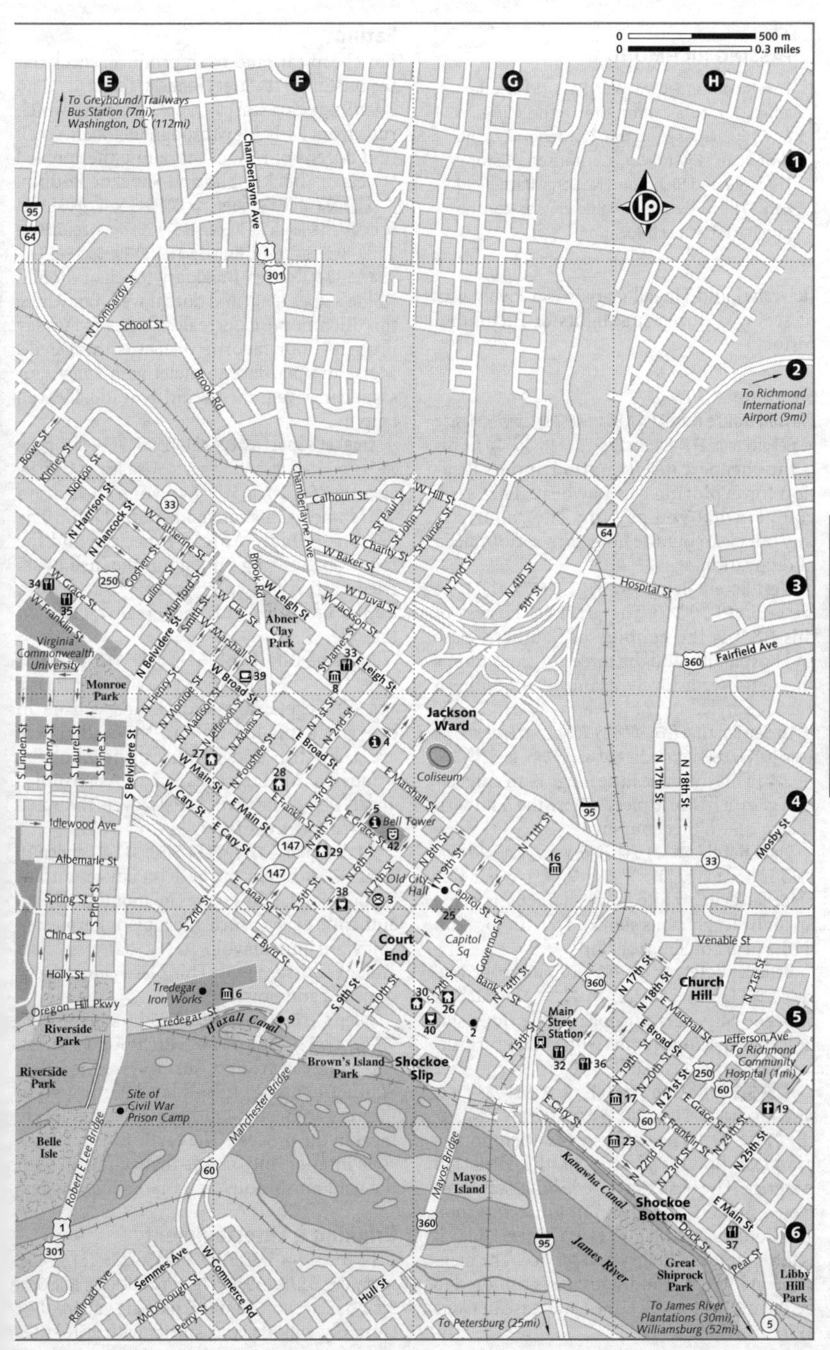
0 500 m
0 0.3 miles
E
F
G
H
1
2
3
4
5
6
To Greyhound/Trailways Bus Station (7mi); Washington, DC (112mi)
To Richmond International Airport (9mi)
To Richmond Community Hospital (1mi)
To James River Plantations (30mi); Williamsburg (52mi)
To Petersburg (25mi)
Chamberlayne Ave
N Lombardy St
School St
Brook Rd
Bowe St
Kinney St
Norton St
N Harrison St
N Hancock St
W Catherine St
Goshen St
Gilmer St
Munford St
W Grace St
W Franklin St
Virginia Commonwealth University
Monroe Park
N Belvidere St
S Belvidere St
Smith St
W Clay St
W Marshall St
W Broad St
W Leigh St
Abner Clay Park
N Henry St
N Monroe St
N Madison St
N Jefferson St
N Adams St
N Foushee St
W Main St
W Cary St
E Main St
E Cary St
E Canal St
E Byrd St
S 2nd St
S Linden St
S Cherry St
S Laurel St
S Pine St
Idlewood Ave
Albemarle St
Spring St
China St
Holly St
Oregon Hill Pkwy
Tredegar Iron Works
Tredegar St
Haxall Canal
Riverside Park
Belle Isle
Site of Civil War Prison Camp
Robert E Lee Bridge
Manchester Bridge
Brown's Island Park
Shockoe Slip
Mayos Bridge
Mayos Island
Calhoun St
W Hill St
St Paul St
St John St
St James St
W Charity St
W Baker St
W Duval St
W Jackson St
E Leigh St
N 1st St
N 2nd St
E Broad St
N 3rd St
N 4th St
E Franklin St
E Grace St
N 5th St
N 6th St
N 7th St
N 8th St
N 9th St
S 5th St
S 9th St
S 10th St
S 12th St
Jackson Ward
Coliseum
Bell Tower
Old City Hall
Capitol St
Capitol Sq
Court End
Governor St
Bank St
N 14th St
S 15th St
E Marshall St
N 11th St
N 2nd St
N 4th St
5th St
Hospital St
Fairfield Ave
N 17th St
N 18th St
Mosby St
Venable St
Church Hill
N 21st St
Main Street Station
E Broad St
N 19th St
N 20th St
N 21st St
E Grace St
E Franklin St
N 22nd St
N 23rd St
N 24th St
N 25th St
E Cary St
Kanawha Canal
Shockoe Bottom
Dock St
E Main St
Pear St
Jefferson Ave
Great Shiprock Park
Libby Hill Park
James River
Semmes Ave
McDonough St
W Commerce Rd
Railroad Ave
Perry St
Hull St
95
64
1
301
33
250
147
360
60
5
1
2
3
4
5
6
8
9
16
17
19
23
25
26
27
28
29
30
32
33
34
35
36
37
38
39
40
42

> **PASSING RICHMOND**
>
> The Richmond Civil War Pass ($15) offers admission to all three sites – the Museum & White House of the Confederacy, the American Civil War Center at Historic Tredegar and Richmond National Battlefield Park. These excellent-value passes can be purchased at each location.

(ka-naw) and Haxall Canals is a lovely way of seeing a dozen highlights of Richmond history.

Sleeping

Massad House Hotel (☎ 804-648-2893; www.massadhousehotel.com; 11 N 4th St; r $75-110; P ⊠ ⁘) This is the cheapest in-city option and its location for exploring can't be beat. That said, you get what you pay for. The rooms are tiny but clean but the hotel is in serious need of renovation.

West-Bocock House (☎ 804-358-6174; 1107 Grove Ave; r $85; P ⊠ ⁘) The gracious hostess of this B&B is the epitome of Southern class and hospitality, and the three gorgeous rooms she rents are a lovely example of Southern baroque style.

Linden Row Inn (☎ 804-783-7000; www.lindenrowinn.com; 100 E Franklin St; r incl breakfast $99-149, ste $239-269; P ⁘) This intimate little lodge is an antebellum gem, a historic piece where the Southern charm doesn't feel put on.

Omni Hotel (☎ 804-344-7000; www.omnihotel.com; 100 S 12th St; r $160-200; P ⁘) What this place lacks in architectural character is made up for by its gracious staff and terrific location in the heart of Shockoe Slip.

Berkeley Hotel (☎ 804-780-1300; www.berkeleyhotel.com; 1200 E Cary St; r $205-225; P ⁘) Located in Shockoe Slip, this European-style, four-star hotel has spacious rooms with cherry furnishings and gracious staff.

our pick **Jefferson Hotel** (☎ 804-788-8000; www.jeffersonhotel.com; 101 W Franklin St; r $260-360; P ⁘) The Jefferson is Richmond's grandest hotel and one of the finest in America. The beaux-arts-style hotel was completed in 1895, the vision of tobacco tycoon and Confederate Major Lewis Ginter. Today it is the epitome of luxury and service. The magnificent lobby's grand staircase is rumored to be the model for the famed staircase in *Gone With the Wind*.

Eating

For cheap eats and fresh produce, check out the bustling **17th Street Farmers Market** (cnr 17th & E Main Sts; 9am-4pm Thu-Sun, hours may vary), which runs from early May through October. You'll find dozens of restaurants along the cobbled streets of Shockoe Slip and Shockoe Bottom.

our pick **Millie's Diner** (☎ 804-643-5512; 2603 E Main St; breakfast & lunch $6-10, dinner $19-28; 11am-2:30pm & 5:30-10:30pm Tue-Fri, 10am-3pm & 5:30-10:30pm Sat, 9am-3pm & 5:30-9:30pm Sun) Breakfast, lunch or dinner, Millie's does it all, and does it well. But where this Richmond icon really shines is Sunday brunch – our favorite dish was the Devil's Mess, an open-faced omelet with spicy sausage, curry, veg, cheese and avocado. Heaven help us.

Croaker's Spot (☎ 804-421-0560; 119 E Leigh St; mains $8-17; 11am-9pm Mon-Wed, to 10pm Thu, to 11pm Fri, noon-11pm Sat, 1-7pm Sun) Everyone in Jackson Ward knows this soul and seafood joint. The decor is proudly African American and the food…angels sing on high of the 'fish boat': fried catfish drowning in spicy sauce with hunks of cornbread and creamy grits on the side.

Ipanema Café (☎ 804-213-0170; 917 W Grace St; mains $12-19; 11:30am-1pm Mon-Fri & 5:30-11pm Mon-Sat) Vegetarians and vegans will be in heaven at this hip hole-in-the-wall. There are a few fish and poultry dishes, but the wonderful Mediterranean- and Asian-influenced veg dishes will satisfy even the most hard-core carnivore.

Edo's Squid (☎ 804-864-5488; 411 N Harrison St; mains $12-30) Easily the best Italian restaurant in Richmond, Edo's serves up mouthwatering, authentic cuisine such as eggplant Parmesan, spicy shrimp diavolo pasta, daily specials and, of course, squid. This place can get very crowded and noisy.

Julep's (☎ 804-377-3968; 1719 E Franklin St; mains $17-27; 5:30-11pm Mon-Sat) Richmond's latest, and some say greatest, shrine to refined New Southern cuisine, Julep's is where you go to impress someone and have a swank, lovely meal in the process. The earth-toned, 1940s-style interior only makes that yellowfin with the wild mushroom orzo that much classier.

Drinking & Entertainment

Lift (☎ 804-344-5438; 218 W Broad St; coffees $1.50-4.50, sandwiches $3.75-7.50; 7am-7pm Mon-Fri, 9am-3pm Sat;) Part coffeehouse, part art gallery, Lift certainly will lift your spirits with stiff lattes and tasty breakfast sandwiches. A cuter café we dare you to find.

Tobacco Company Restaurant (☎ 804-782-9555; 1201 E Cary St; ⏰ from 11:30am) An embodiment of the era when tobacco was king, the atmosphere of this three-story, brothel-like restaurant-bar is more of a draw than the food. Have a drink instead.

Capital Ale House (☎ 804-780-2537; 623 E Main St; ⏰ 11am-1:30am Mon-Sat, from 10am Sun) Popular with political wonks from the nearby state capitol, this downtown pub has an awesome selection of beer (46 on tap and 250 bottled) and decent pub grub. The frozen trough on the bar keeps your drink ice-cold.

Byrd Theater (☎ 804-353-9911; www.byrdtheatre.com; 2908 W Cary St; tickets $1.99) You can't beat the price at this classic 1928 cinema, which shows second-run films. Wurlitzer-organ concerts precede the Saturday-night shows.

Virginia Performing Arts Center (☎ 804-343-0144; www.vapaf.com; cnr Grace & 6th Sts) In 2009, Richmond raised the curtain on the area's premiere venue for concerts, dance and theater, including touring Broadway productions.

Getting There & Around

The cab fare from **Richmond International Airport** (RIC; ☎ 804-226-3000), about 10 miles east of town, is about $25.

Amtrak (☎ 800-872-7245) Trains stop at the main station at 7519 Staples Mill Rd, 7 miles north of town. More convenient but less frequent trains stop downtown at the Main Street Station (1500 E Main St).

Greater Richmond Transit Company (GRTC; ☎ 804-358-4782; www.ridegrtc.com) Runs local buses (base fare $1.50, exact change only). Bus 27 runs to/from the downtown area.

Greyhound/Trailways bus station (☎ 804-254-5910; www.greyhound.com; 2910 N Blvd).

PETERSBURG

About 25 miles south of Richmond, the little town of Petersburg played a big role in the Civil War. It was a major railway junction, providing Confederate troops and supplies. Union troops laid a 10-month siege of Petersburg in 1864–65, the longest on American soil. The **Siege Museum** (☎ 804-733-2404; 15 W Bank St; adult/child $5/4, combo ticket with Blandford Church $11/9; ⏰ 10am-5pm) relates the plight of civilians during the siege. Several miles east of town, **Petersburg National Battlefield** (US 36; vehicle/pedestrian $5/3; ⏰ 9am-5pm) is where Union soldiers planted explosives underneath a Confederate breastwork, leading to the Battle of the Crater (novelized and cinematized in *Cold Mountain*). West of downtown in Pamplin Historical Park, the excellent **National Museum of the Civil War Soldier** (☎ 804-861-2408; adult/child 6-12yr $10/5; ⏰ 9am-5pm) illustrates the hardships faced by soldiers on both sides of the conflict. South of town, **Old Blandford Church** (☎ 804-733-2396; 319 S Crater St; adult/child $5/4; ⏰ 10am-5pm) has the largest collection of Tiffany glass windows in one place. Each exquisite pane is dedicated to one Confederate state and its war dead. More than 30,000 Confederate soldiers are buried on the church grounds.

HISTORIC TRIANGLE

This is America's birthplace. Nowhere else in the country has such a small area played such a pivotal role in the course of the nation's history. The nation's roots were planted in Jamestown, the first permanent English settlement in the New World. The flames of the American Revolution were fanned at the colonial capital of Williamsburg. America finally won her independence from Britain at Yorktown.

You'll need at least two days to give the Triangle any justice. A daily free shuttle travels between the Williamsburg visitor center, Yorktown and Jamestown. A variety of tickets and pass combinations can be purchased at the Williamsburg visitor center (p368) or online at www.historyisfun.org. The best deal is the America's Historic Triangle pass (adult/child six to 17 $80.25/33.25), allowing seven days of unlimited admission to Jamestown Settlement, Historic Jamestowne, Colonial Williamsburg, Yorktown Battlefield and the Yorktown Victory Center).

Williamsburg

If you visit only one historical town in Virginia, make it Williamsburg, home to Colonial Williamsburg, one of the most astounding and authentic living-history museums in the world. If any place is going to get kids into history, this is it, but it's plenty of fun for adults too.

The actual town of Williamsburg, Virginia's capital from 1699 to 1780, is a stately place. The prestigious campus of the College of William & Mary adds a decent dash of youth culture, with coffee shops, cheap pubs and fashion boutiques.

SIGHTS & ACTIVITIES

our pick **Colonial Williamsburg** (☎ 757-229-1000, 800-447-8679; www.colonialwilliamsburg.org; 9am-5pm), the restored capital of England's largest colony in the New World, is a must-see attraction for visitors of all ages. This is not some cheesy, fenced-in theme park; Colonial Williamsburg is a living, breathing, working history museum that transports visitors back to the 1700s. The 301-acre historic area contains 88 original 18th-century buildings and several hundred faithful reproductions, including homes, taverns, shops and public buildings. The British Union Jack flutters everywhere. Costumed townsfolk and 'interpreters' in period dress go about their colonial jobs as blacksmiths, apothecaries, printers, barmaids, soldiers and patriots, breaking character only long enough to pose for a snapshot. Costumed patriots like Patrick Henry and Thomas Jefferson stand on their soapbox outside taverns, delivering impassioned speeches for freedom and democracy. Children will love the interactive, hands-on exhibits and activities, and hilarious skits such as witch trials and tar and featherings.

Highlight buildings of Colonial Williamsburg include the reconstructed **Capitol Building** and **Governor's Palace**, the **Bruton Parish Church** and **Raleigh Tavern**. Walking around the historic district and patronizing the shops and taverns is free, but entry to building tours and most exhibits is restricted to ticket holders. Expect crowds, lines and petulant children, especially in summer.

To park and to purchase tickets, follow signs to the **visitor center** (☎ 757-229-1000; 8:30am-6pm), north of the historic district between Hwy 132 and Colonial Pkwy, where kids can get outfitted in period costumes for $20 (tri-cornered hat sold separately). Parking is free; shuttle buses run frequently to and from the historic district, or walk along the tree-lined footpath. Exhibitions are open 9am to 5pm.

One-day passes include:

Capital City Pass (adult/child 6-17yr $35/18) Covers orientation tour and entrance to all exhibition buildings and museums, minus the palace.

Governor's Key to the City (adult/child $45/23) Includes all exhibition buildings and museums plus the Governor's Palace.

You can also buy tickets at the **Merchants Square information booth** (9am-5pm) at the west end of Duke of Gloucester St, and the **Secretary's Office** (9am-5pm), near the capitol, at the east end.

Chartered in 1693, the **College of William & Mary** (☎ 757-221-1540; www.wm.edu) is the second-oldest college in the country and retains the oldest academic building in continued use in the USA, the Sir Christopher Wren Building. The school's alumni include Thomas Jefferson, James Monroe and comedian Jon Stewart.

Williamsburg Winery (☎ 757-229-0999; www.williamsburgwinery.com; 5800 Wessex Hundred; admission free; tasting tours $8, lunch $9-11; 10am-6pm Mon-Sat, from 11am Sun Apr-Oct, closes at 5pm Nov-Mar), four miles southwest of downtown, is the largest winery in Virginia, cranking out 60,000 cases a year and 25 varieties of the sweet nectar of the gods. Stay for lunch at the on-site Gabriel Archer Tavern, serving up tasty sandwich and wrap plates.

SLEEPING & EATING

You'll find many restaurants, cafés and pubs in **Merchants Square** (merchantssquare.org), adjacent to Colonial Williamsburg. The **Williamsburg Hotel & Motel Association** (☎ 800-446-9244; www.gowilliamsburg.com) at the visitor center will help find and book accommodations at no cost.

Williamsburg & Colonial KOA Resorts (☎ 800-562-1733; www.williamsburgkoa.com; 5210 & 4000 Newman Rd respectively, I-64 exit 234; campsites $20-35, cabins $50-65;) With two campgrounds rolled into one, you'll find superb amenities such as games rooms, movies, a pool and laundry facilities.

Governor's Inn (☎ 757-229-1000; www.colonialwilliamsburgresorts.com; 506 N Henry St; r $70-110; P) Williamsburg's official 'economy' choice is a big box by any other name, but there's nothing to complain about, and hey, it's central.

Williamsburg White House (☎ 757-229-8580, 866-229-8580; www.awilliamsburgwhitehouse.com; 718 Jamestown Rd; r $155-220; P) This romantic, beautifully furnished B&B decorated with red, white and blue bunting is located across the campus of William & Mary and just a few blocks walk to Colonial Williamsburg.

Williamsburg Inn (☎ 757-229-1000, ext 3089; 136 E Francis St; r from $330; P) Queen Elizabeth II has stayed here twice, so you know this place is palatial. Williamsburg's premier property is noted by its not-so-colonial price tag, but the pampering is nonstop at this classic resort.

Cheese Shop (☎ 757-220-0298; 410 Duke of Gloucester St, Merchants Sq; mains $5-6; 10am-8pm Mon-Sat, 11am-6pm Sun) Locals swear by this deli, with its wide assortment of sandwiches and a Paris-worthy cheese selection.

Trellis Cafe (☎ 757-229-8610; www.thetrellis.com; Merchants Sq; lunch mains $8-14, dinner mains $17-32; 11am-3pm & 5-9:30pm) A Virginia culinary landmark, the Trellis caters to burger-seeking tourists for lunch and nirvana-seeking foodies for dinner. Regional specialties, such as salmon fillet with country ham, shine.

King's Arms Tavern (☎ 757-229-2141; Duke of Gloucester St; lunch mains $12-14, dinner mains $27-35; 11am-3pm) Of the four restaurants located within Colonial Williamsburg, this is the most elegant, serving early American cuisine like game pie – venison, rabbit and duck braised in port.

GETTING THERE & AROUND

Williamsburg Transportation Center (☎ 757-229-8750, cnr Boundary & Lafayette Sts) Amtrak trains run from here twice a day to Washington, DC ($28, 3¾ hours), Richmond ($14, 50 minutes) and New York ($58, eight hours). Greyhound runs buses to Richmond ($7.50, one hour) five times daily. Buses to other destinations require a transfer in Richmond.

Bikes Unlimited (☎ 757-229-4620; 759 Scotland St; bike rental per hr from $14; 9:30am-6:30pm Tue-Fri, 10am-5pm Sat, noon-4pm Sun)

Triangle Theme Parks

Three miles east of Williamsburg on Hwy 60, **Busch Gardens** (☎ 800-343-7946; www.buschgardens.com; adult/child 3-9yr $60/50; Apr-Oct; P) is a European-themed park with some of the best roller coasters on the East Coast. Just down the road off Hwy 199 east of Williamsburg, **Water Country USA** (☎ 800-343-7946; www.watercountryusa.com; adult/child 3-9yr $39/32; May-Sep; P) is a kids' paradise, with twisty slides, raging rapids and wave pools. A three-day, combo ticket for both parks is $70. Parking is $12 at both places.

Jamestown

The first permanent English settlement in North America almost wasn't. On May 14, 1607, a group of 104 English men and boys settled on this swampy island with a charter from the Virginia Company of London to search for gold and other riches. Instead, they found starvation and disease. By January of 1608, only about 40 colonists were still alive. The colony survived the 'Starving Time' with the leadership of Captain James Smith and help from local Powhatans. In 1619, the elected House of Burgesses convened, forming the first democratic government in the Americas.

Historic Jamestowne (☎ 757-253-4838; adult/child under 17 $10/free, 5-day ticket incl Yorktown Battlefield; 9am-5pm), run by the NPS, is the original Jamestown site. Start your visit at the on-site museum and check out the statues of John Smith and Pocahontas. The original Jamestown ruins were rediscovered in 1994; visitors can watch the ongoing archaeological work at the site.

More child-friendly and cheesy, the state-run **Jamestown Settlement** (☎ 757-253-4838; adult/child 6-12yr $14/6.50; 9am-5pm) reconstructs the 1607 James Fort, a Native American village and full-scale replicas of the first ships that brought the settlers to Jamestown, along with living-history fun. A **combo ticket** (adult/child 6-12yr $19.25/9.25) that includes the Yorktown Victory Center is available.

Yorktown

On October 19, 1781, British General Cornwallis surrendered to George Washington here, effectively ending the American Revolution. The event was more of a whimper than a bang; the British were cut off from the sea by the French and confronted with massive American guns on land. Cornwallis' position was hopeless, his superiors indifferent and surrender inevitable.

Yorktown Battlefield (☎ 757-898-3400; incl Historic Jamestowne adult/child under 17 $10/free; 9am-5pm), run by the NPS, is the site of the last major battle of the American Revolution. Start your tour at the visitor center and check out the orientation film and the display of Washington's original tent. The 7-mile Battlefield Rd Tour takes you past the major highlights. Don't miss a walk through the last British defensive sites, Redoubts 9 and 10.

The state-run **Yorktown Victory Center** (☎ 757-253-4838; adult/child 6-12yr $8.75/4.50; 9am-5pm) is an interactive, living-history museum that focuses on reconstruction, reenactment, and the Revolution's impact on the people who lived through it.

The actual town of Yorktown is a pleasant waterfront village overlooking the York River with a nice range of shops, restaurants and pubs.

Carrot Tree (☎ 757-988-1999; 411 Main St; mains $8-13; lunch 11am-3:30pm daily, dinner 5-8:30pm Thu-Sat) is a good, affordable spot for lunch with silly-named sandwiches like the Lord Nelson BBQ.

Afterwards, grab a beer at the **Yorktown Pub** (☎ 757-886-9964; 112 Water St; mains $6-22; 🕑 11am-late). For a more upscale option, **Nick's Riverwalk Restaurant** (☎ 757-875-1522; www.riverwalkrestaurant.net; 323 Water St; lunch mains $9-15, dinner mains $17-30 🕑 11:30am-2:30pm & 5-9pm) offers waterfront dining and modern American cuisine.

James River Plantations

The grand homes of Virginia's slaveholding aristocracy were a clear sign of the era's class divisions. A string of them line scenic Hwy 5 on the north side of the river, though only a few are open to the public. The ones listed here run from east to west.

Sherwood Forest (☎ 804-829-5377; sherwoodforest.org), the longest frame house in the country, was the home of 10th US president John Tyler. Tours are available by appointment for $35 per person. The grounds (and a touching pet cemetery) are open to **self-guided tours** (adult/child $5/3; 🕑 9am-5pm).

Berkeley (☎ 804-829-6018; www.berkeleyplantation.com; adult/child 13-16yr/child 6-12yr $11/7.50/6; 🕑 9am-4:30pm) was the site of the first official Thanksgiving in 1619. It was the birthplace and home of Benjamin Harrison V, a signer of the Declaration of Independence, and his son William Henry Harrison, 9th US president.

Shirley (☎ 800-232-1613; www.shirleyplantation.com; adult/child 6-18 $11/7.50; 🕑 9am-5pm), situated picturesquely on the river, is Virginia's oldest plantation (1613) and is perhaps the best example of how a British-model plantation actually appeared, with its tidy row of brick service and trade houses – tool barn, ice house, laundry etc – leading up to the big house.

HAMPTON ROADS

The Hampton Roads (named not for asphalt, but the confluence of the James, Nansemond and Elizabeth Rivers and Chesapeake Bay) have always been prime real estate. The Powhatan Confederacy fished these waters and hunted the fingerlike protrusions of the Virginia coast for thousands of years before John Smith arrived in 1607. The pirate Blackbeard was killed here and had his head popped onto a pike, while navies from two continents littered the area with wreckage during the Revolutionary and Civil Wars. Today Hampton Roads is known for its horribly congested roads, as well as its cultural mishmash of history, the military and the arts.

Norfolk

Norfolk is home to the world's largest naval base. Not surprisingly, it had a reputation as a rowdy port town filled with drunken sailors. In recent years, Norfolk has worked had to clean up its image through development, gentrification and focusing on its burgeoning arts scene. It's now the state's second-largest city, with a diverse population of 234,000. But at the end of the day, the city still revolves around the US Navy, as evident by the frequent sights of mammoth warships offshore and sounds of screaming fighter jets above.

There are two visitor centers: **Interstate** (☎ 757-441-1852; I-64 exit 273; 🕑 9am-5pm) and **Downtown** (☎ 757-664-6620; 232 E Main St; 🕑 9am-5pm). The historic Ghent district, west of the city center, is where this town's refugee population of artsy types, foodies and cappuccino-lovers flocks.

SIGHTS

our pick Naval Station Norfolk (☎ 757-444-7955; www.cnic.navy.mil/norfolksta; 9079 Hampton Blvd; adults/child 3-11yr $10/5; 🕑 tour times vary), the world's largest navy base and one of the busiest airfields in the country, is a must-see. Depending on what ships are in port, you might see aircraft carriers, destroyers, frigates, amphibious assault ships and submarines. The 45-minute bus tours are conducted by naval personnel and must be booked in advance. Photo ID is required for adults. Alternatively, view the docks from a narrated, two-hour cruise aboard the **Victory Rover** (☎ 757-627-7406; www.navalbasecruises.com; adult/child 12yr & under $16.50/10; 🕑 Mar-Dec).

Nauticus (☎ 757-664-1000; adult/child 4-12yr $11/8.50; 🕑 10am-5pm May-Sep, 10am-5pm Tue-Sat, from noon Sun Oct-Apr; 👶) is an interactive maritime-themed museum. Use the Center entrance to access the more adult-oriented **Hampton Naval Museum** (☎ 757-322-2987; admission free), where you can explore the deck of the **USS Wisconsin**. Built in 1943, it was the largest (887ft long) and last battleship built by the US Navy.

The **Chrysler Museum of Art** (☎ 757-664-6200; 245 W Olney Rd; adult/child & student with university ID $7/free, free Wed; 🕑 10am-5pm Thu-Sat, to 9pm Wed, 1-5pm Sun) is a glorious setting for a spectacular and eclectic collection of artifacts from ancient Egypt to present day, including works by Monet, Matisse, Renoir, Warhol and a world-class collection of Tiffany blown glass.

The **MacArthur Memorial** (☎ 757-441-2965; MacArthur Sq; admission free; 🕑 10am-5pm Mon-Sat, from 11am Sun) houses the final resting place of WWII hero General Douglas MacArthur and his wife, Jean. The complex includes a museum, theater and exhibits of the general's military and personal artifacts.

SLEEPING & EATING

For waterfront digs, there are tons of budget to midrange options lining Ocean View Ave (which actually borders the bay). Two of the best dining strips are downtown's Granby St and Ghent's Colley Ave.

Best Western (☎ 757-583-2621; 1330 E Ocean Ave; r from $100; P ✗ ⚿) Overlooking Chesapeake Bay, this place is a reliable and comfortable option.

Tazewell Hotel (☎ 757-623-6200; www.thetazewell.com; 245 Granby St; r $110-200; ✗ ⚿) Attractive hotel in the heart of the Granby St pub and restaurant district, Tazewell is a friendly hotel with tiny but clean rooms.

Page House Inn (☎ 757-625-5033; www.pagehouseinn.com; 323 Fairfax Ave; r $150-230; P ⊠ ✗ ⚿) Opposite the Chrysler Museum of Art, this luxurious B&B is a cornerstone of Norfolk elegance.

Doumar's (☎ 757-627-4163; 919 Monticello Ave, at E 20th St, Ghent; mains $1.50-4; ⏲ 8am-late Mon-Sat) Since 1904, this slice of Americana has been the drive-up home of the world's original ice-cream-cone machine, plus great BBQ. Counter service available too. Cash only.

Todd Jurich's Bistro (☎ 757-622-3210; 150 W Main St; lunch mains $21-30, dinner mains $25-35; ⏲ 11:30am-2pm Mon-Fri, 5:30-10pm Mon-Sat) Jurich's is arguably the best upscale restaurant in Hampton Roads. This swish addition to the Norfolk dining scene gets solid reviews for mixing up Tidewater, Southern and global cuisines, like the scrumptious jumbo lump crab cakes with smoked gouda grits.

DRINKING & ENTERTAINMENT

Elliot's Fair Grounds (☎ 757-640-2899; 806 Baldwin Ave, Ghent; items $3-10 ⏲ 7am-late; ⚿ V) This tiny, funky coffeehouse attracts everyone from students to sailors. The menu also includes vegan and kosher items such as Boca Burgers.

Taphouse Grill at Ghent (☎ 757-627-9172; 931 W 21st St, Ghent) Good microbrews are served and good local bands jam at this warm little pub.

Scotty Quixx (☎ 757-625-0008; 436 Granby St; ⏲ 4pm-2am Mon-Sat) What do you do with a drunken sailor? Send him to Scotty's, which is packed with shore-leave Navy guys looking for a good time.

GETTING THERE & AROUND

Greyhound (☎ 757-625-7500; www.greyhound.com; 701 Monticello Ave) runs buses five times a day to Richmond ($18 to $23), Virginia Beach ($10 to $16) and Washington, DC ($30 to $44).

By plane, the region is served by **Norfolk International Airport** (NIA; ☎ 757-857-3351), located 7 miles northeast of downtown Norfolk.

Hampton Roads Transit (☎ 757-222-6100; www.hrtransit.org) serves the entire Hampton Roads region. Buses ($1.50) run from downtown throughout the city and to Newport News and Virginia Beach.

Norfolk Electronic Transit (NET) (⏲ 6:30am-11pm Mon-Fri, noon-midnight Sat, noon-8pm Sun) is a free bus service that connects Norfolk's major downtown sites, including Nauticus and the Chrysler Museum.

Newport News & Hampton

The city of Newport News comes off as a giant example of suburban sprawl, but it's unclear what it's sprawling from. There are several attractions here, most notably the amazing Mariner's Museum. But apart from that, the city is an ugly mess of strip malls and chain hotels and restaurants. For more charming lodgings and lively dining options, head south to Norfolk or north to Williamsburg. The **visitor center** (☎ 888-493-7386; 13560 Jefferson Ave, Newport News Park; ⏲ 9am-5pm) is at the north end off I-64 exit 250-B.

our pick **Mariners' Museum** (☎ 757-596-2222; www.mariner.org; 100 Museum Dr; adult/child 6-12 $14/12; ⏲ 10am-5pm Mon-Sat, from noon Sun) is one of the biggest, most comprehensive maritime museums in the world. The on-site **USS Monitor Center** (www.monitorcenter.org) houses the dredged carcass of the *Monitor*, one of the world's first ironclad warships, as well as a life-size replica of the real deal (which can be seen undergoing a long chemical bath, a single step in a lengthy preservation process). The **Virginia Living Museum** (☎ 757-247-8523; thevlm.org; 9285 Warwick Blvd, Huntington Park; adult/child 3-12yr $15/12; ⏲ 9am-5pm, reduced hours winter) is an educational extravaganza that comprises a petting zoo, planetarium and other interactive science-y stuff.

In nearby Hampton, the **Virginia Air & Space Center** (☎ 757-727-0900; 600 Settlers Landing Rd; adult/child 3-18yr $9.50/7.50; ⏲ 10am-5pm Mon-Wed, to 7pm Thu-Sun) will fascinate astronomy nuts with exhibits like the *Apollo 11* command module and a DC-9 passenger plane. IMAX films are an additional cost.

VIRGINIA BEACH

With 35 miles of sandy beaches, 3-mile concrete oceanfront boardwalk and a plethora of outdoor activities, it's no surprise that Virginia Beach is the largest city in the state (population 304,000) and a prime tourist destination. In recent years, the city has worked hard to shed its unfortunate reputation as a rowdy 'Redneck Riviera.' A recent $300-million investment project has given the city a much-needed facelift. The beach is wider, cleaner and better than ever, with dolphins frolicking off the shore. New hotels, restaurants and entertainment options are popping up on every corner. A giant statue of Neptune, more police and ever-present 'no profanity' signs keep watch over the new reborn resort.

The I-264 runs straight into the **visitor center** (☎ 800-822-3224; www.vbfun.com; 2100 Parks Ave; 9am-5pm) and the beach. Surfing is permitted at the beach's southern end near Rudee Inlet and alongside the 14th St pier.

Sights

If you want to see an aquarium done right, come to the **Virginia Aquarium & Marine Science Center** (☎ 757-385-3474; www.virginiaaquarium.com; 717 General Booth Blvd; adult/child 3-11 $12/8; 9am-5pm, to 6pm May-Sep), one of the country's best. Get up close and personal with marine life on one of the aquarium's dolphin- ($19, April to October) or whale-watching ($28, January to March) boat trips.

Mt Trashmore (☎ 757-473-5237; 310 Edwin Dr; admission free; 7:30am-dusk) is off I-64 exit 17B. Virginia Beach's only verticality was the creative solution to a landfill problem, and now serves as a prime picnicking and kite-flying venue. Tony Hawk has grinded in the renovated skate park.

Fort Story (cnr 89th St & Pacific Ave), an active army base at Cape Henry, is home to several attractions including the **First Landing Site** (admission free), where 1607 colonists first touched land after their voyage from London, and the 1791 **Old Cape Henry Lighthouse** (adult/child 3-12 $4/2), offering spectacular views of the surrounding area from its observation deck. All adults must have a photo ID to enter the base.

Edgar Cayce Association for Research & Enlightenment (☎ 800-333-4499; www.edgarcayce.org; admission free; 215 67th St; 9am-8pm Mon-Sat, from noon Sun), founded by the self-proclaimed psychic of the early 20th century, has an extensive library and bookstore (with shelving categories like 'Life after Life' and 'Intuitive Arts'), a full schedule of drop-in lectures and therapies such as massages, acupuncture, meditation and colonics.

The **Contemporary Arts Center of Virginia** (☎ 757-425-0000; 2200 Parks Ave; adult/child $7/5; 9am-5pm daily, to 9pm Mon) has excellent rotating exhibitions housed in a fresh, ultramodern building that lovingly focuses natural light onto an outstanding collection of local and international artwork.

WILDLIFE REFUGES

Back Bay National Wildlife Refuge (☎ 757-721-2412; www.fws.gov/backbay; per vehicle/pedestrian $5/2 Apr-Oct, free Nov-Mar) is an 8000-acre wildlife and migratory bird marshland habitat, most stunning during the December migration season. Some 30 miles southwest of Virginia Beach, the 109,000-acre **Great Dismal Swamp National Wildlife Refuge** (☎ 757-986-3705; admission free; sunrise-sunset), which straddles the North Carolina border, is rich in flora and fauna, including black bears, bobcats and more than 200 bird species.

Sleeping

All prices are for high season (Memorial Day to Labor Day); rates may drop significantly the rest of the year.

Angie's Guest Cottage & Hostel (☎ 757-491-1830; www.angiescottage.com; 302 24th St; dm $20-23, s/d $52-32, cottages from $600 per wk; P) Located just one block from the beach, Angie's HI-USA-affiliated hostel offers five dormitories, two private rooms and a communal kitchen.

First Landing State Park (☎ 757-412-2300; dcr.virginia.gov; Cape Henry; campsites $24-30, cabins $75-149) You couldn't ask for a prettier campground than the one at this bayfront state park, though cabins have no water view. The 2888-acre park offers a plethora of outdoor activity options including camping, hiking, biking, fishing, kayaking and swimming.

Cutty Sark Motel (☎ 757-428-2116; 3614 Atlantic Ave; r $165-240; P) Rooms at Cutty Sark have private balconies and kitchenettes, but check that the view you're promised doesn't look out onto a parking lot.

our pick **Hilton Virginia Beach Oceanfront** (☎ 800-445-8667; www.hiltonvb.com; 3001 Atlantic Ave; r $240-405; P) The premiere place to stay on the beach, the 21-story, 290-room hotel is super-luxurious. The oceanfront rooms are spacious, comfortable and packed with

SCENIC DRIVE: VIRGINIA'S EASTERN SHORE

Across the 17-mile Chesapeake Bay bridge-tunnel (fee $12), Virginia's isolated Eastern Shore, dotted with fishing villages and serene, low-lying natural refuges, has the feel of a remote, maritime escape. A drive up or down the peninsula takes a little over an hour. Tucked behind windswept Assateague Island (p353), the town of **Chincoteague** (shink-o-teeg), on the island of the same name, is Virginia's principal Eastern Shore destination. Chincoteague is famous for its oysters and late-July **wild pony swim**, when the small horses that inhabit Assateague are led across the channel for annual herd-thinning foal auctions. The **chamber of commerce** (☎ 757-336-6161; 6733 Maddox Blvd; 9am-4:30pm) has maps of hiking and bicycling trails up to and into the incredibly relaxing **Chincoteague National Wildlife Refuge** (☎ 757-336-6122; per vehicle $5; 6am-8pm), a lovely wetland repose for migratory waterfowl. Five miles west of Chincoteague, stop by **NASA Wallops Flight Facility** (☎ 757-824-2298; admission free; 10am-4pm Thu-Mon), where you can watch occasional rocket launches and enjoy exhibits of the facility's work.

amenities like huge flat-screen TVs, dreamy bedding and large balconies that open out to the beach and Neptune Park below.

Eating & Drinking

There is no shortage of restaurants along the boardwalk and Atlantic Ave, most geared towards local seafood. A bevy of interchangeable clubs and bars sit between 17th and 23rd Sts around Pacific and Atlantic Aves.

our pick **Mary's Restaurant** (☎ 757-428-1355; 616 Virginia Beach Blvd; mains $4-8; 6am-3pm) A local institution for more than 40 years, Mary's is a great place to start the day with a tasty, filling, cheap breakfast. We're huge fans of the fluffy, gooey, chocolate chip waffles.

Jewish Mother (☎ 757-422-5430; cnr 31st St & Pacific Ave; mains $5-14; 8am-2am) Get your nosh on here with packed deli sandwiches, 'penicillin soup' (chicken and matzo ball) and monster-sized pie. Excellent live music staged nightly.

Mahi Mah's (☎ 757-437-8030; www.mahimahs; 615 Atlantic Ave; sushi $1-3, mains $5-15; 5pm-late Mon-Fri, from 7am Sat & Sun) Located in the Ramada Inn, this oceanfront local has some fantastic sushi, which makes up for the snail-paced service. After dark, this is one of the most popular nightspots on the beach.

Catch 31 (☎ 757-213-3472; 3001 Atlantic Ave; mains $20-30; 7am-11pm, to 10pm low season, bar 11am-2am) Yes it's overpriced and a bit pretentious, but you're paying for the spectacular view from this oceanfront seafood restaurant. The outdoor patio is a great people-watching spot, with rocking chairs and roaring pit fires that help take the chill off the ocean breeze. Find it in the Hilton.

Getting There & Around

Greyhound (☎ 757-422-2998; www.greyhound.com; 1017 Laskin Rd) has several buses a day to Richmond ($15.50, five per day, 3½ hours), which also stop in Norfolk and Newport News; transfer in Richmond for services to Washington, DC, Wilmington, NYC and beyond. **Hampton Roads Transit** (☎ 757-222-6100; www.hrtransit.com) runs the Virginia Beach Wave trolley (tickets $1), which plies Atlantic Ave in summer.

THE PIEDMONT

Central Virginia's rolling green landscape separates the coastal lowlands from the mountainous frontier. The fertile valley gives way to dozens of wineries, country villages and grand colonial estates.

Charlottesville

Set in the shadow of the Blue Ridge Mountains, Charlottesville is regularly ranked as one of the country's best places to live. This culturally rich town of 41,000 is home to the University of Virginia, which attracts Southern aristocracy and artsy lefties in equal proportion. With the UVA grounds and pedestrian downtown area overflowing with attractive students, couples, professors and the occasional celebrity under a blanket of blue skies, 'C-ville' is practically perfect.

Two **Charlottesville/Albemarle Visitor Centers** (☎ 877-386-1103; www.charlottesvilletourism.org), on Hwy 20 south near I-64 exit 121a and at 610 E Main St, sell various block passes for area attractions.

MONTICELLO & AROUND

our pick **Monticello** (☎ 434-984-9822; adult/child 6-11 $20/8; 8am-5pm Mar-Oct, 9am-4:30pm Nov-Feb) is an architectural masterpiece designed and inhabited by Thomas Jefferson, Founding Father and third US President. 'I am as happy nowhere else and in no other society, and all my wishes end, where I hope my days will end, at Monticello,' wrote Jefferson, who spent 40 years building his dream home, finally completed in 1809. Today it is the only home in America designated a UN World Heritage site. Built in Roman neoclassical style, the house was the centerpiece of a 5000-acre plantation tended by 150 slaves. Monticello today does not gloss over Jefferson's role as a slave owner nor the likelihood that he fathered children with slave Sally Hemings, a complicated past of the man who declared that 'all men are created equal' in the Declaration of Independence. Jefferson and his family are buried in a small wooded plot near the home.

Visits to the house are conducted by guided tours only; you can take self-guided tours of the plantation grounds, gardens and cemetery. A wonderful new visitor center that opened in 2009 delves deeper into the lives of Jefferson and the free and enslaved people who lived and worked at Monticello. Frequent shuttles run from the visitor center to the hilltop house, or you can take the wooded footpath.

Tours are also offered of the nearby 1784 **Michie Tavern** (☎ 434-977-1234) and James Monroe's estate, **Ash Lawn-Highland** (☎ 434-293-9539), 2.5 miles east of Monticello. A combo ticket for all three is $34. Visit Michie Tavern during lunchtime, when its dining room, the **Ordinary** (meals $15; 11:15am-3:30pm), serves lunch buffets of Southern delights like fried chicken with biscuits.

UNIVERSITY OF VIRGINIA

One of the most beautiful college campuses in America, Thomas Jefferson's **University of Virginia** is another must-see. The classically designed buildings and grounds embody the spirit of communal living and learning that Jefferson envisioned. The centerpiece is the Jefferson-designed **Rotunda** (☎ 434-924-7969), a scale replica of Rome's Pantheon. Free, student-led tours of the Rotunda meet inside the main entrance daily at 10am, 11am, 2pm, 3pm and 4pm. The UVA **Art Museum** (☎ 804-924-3492; 155 Rugby Rd; admission free; 1-5pm Tue-Sun) has an eclectic and interesting collection of American, European and Asian arts.

SLEEPING

There's a good selection of budget and midrange chain motels lining Emmet St/US 29 north of town. If you're after a reservation service, try **Guesthouses** (☎ 434-979-7264; www.va-guesthouses.com; r from $155; 9am-2pm Mon-Fri; P ☒), which provides cottages and B&B rooms in private homes.

English Inn (☎ 434-971-9900; www.englishinncharlottesville.com; 2000 Morton Dr; r incl breakfast $100-150; P) British hospitality and furnishings and a Tudor facade accent this unique hotel.

Inn at Monticello (☎ 434-979-3593; www.innatmonticello.com; 1188 Scottsville Rd; r $160-245; P) Located across from Monticello, this Victorian B&B is set off against the Piedmont's rolling hillscape. Every one of the lodge's five rooms are cozy little testaments to colonial grandeur.

South Street Inn (☎ 434-979-0200; www.southstreetinn.com; 200 South St; r incl breakfast $170-255, ste $210-295; P) Located in the heart of downtown, this aged brick hotel was once a girl's finishing school and, later, a brothel.

White Pig B&B (☎ 434-831-1416; www.thewhitepig.com; 5120 Irish Rd, Schuyler; r $155-185; P V) Vegans and vegetarians should make a pilgrimage to the White Pig, about 22 miles southwest of Monticello. Located on the 170-acre Briar Creek Farm, this B&B/animal sanctuary has one of the most innovative vegan menus in the state.

EATING & DRINKING

The Downtown Mall, a pedestrian zone of 120 shops and 30 restaurants, is great for people-watching and outdoor dining when the weather is nice. At night, the bars along University Ave are the place to see and be seen.

Mudhouse (☎ 434-984-6833; mudhouse.com; 213 W Main St; 6:30am-10pm Mon-Thu, to 11pm Fri & Sat, 7am-7pm Sun;) Do as the cool kids do and come here for bracing espresso, wi-fi and daily artsy happenings.

our pick **Splendora's Gelato Cafe** (☎ 434-296-8555; www.splendoras.com; 317 E Main St, 7:30am-10pm;) The most authentic gelato this side of the Atlantic, Splendora's extensive menu includes exotic but wonderful flavors like Chinese Five Spice, Gianduia, Dulce de Leche and Thai Iced Tea. The morning crowd will find coffee, pastries and other Italian treats.

VINTAGE VIRGINIA

Now the fifth-biggest wine producer in the USA, Virginia has 140 vineyards around the state, many located in the pretty hills around Charlottesville. Three good options are listed below. For more information on Virginia wine, visit www.virginiawine.org.

- **Jefferson Vineyards** (☎ 800-272-3042; www.jeffersonvineyards.com) Known for consistent quality vintage, this winery harvests from its namesake's original 1774 vineyard site.
- **Keswick Vineyards** (☎ 434-244-3341; www.keswickvineyards.com) Keswick won a wave of awards for its first vintage and has since been distilling a big range of grapes off Rte 231.
- **Kluge Estate** (☎ 434-977-3895; www.klugeestateonline.com) Oenophiles regularly rate Kluge wine as the best in the state.

White Spot (☎ 434-295-9899; 147 University Ave; mains around $5; 8am-11pm, to 2:30am Fri & Sat) While in the commercial district, try a genuine C-ville concoction, the fried-egg-topped Gus Burger.

Christian's Pizza (118 W Main St; slices $2-4, pies $10; 434-977-9688; 11am-10pm) A C-ville institution in the Downtown Mall, Christian's serves up great pizza with perfect thin, crispy crust.

Rapture (☎ 434-293-9526; 303 E Main St; mains $6-10; 11:30am-2:30am) When the weather is perfect, this is one of the better outdoor dining spots in the Downtown Mall. The spicy grilled chicken sandwiches are amazing. At night, this place transforms into a hit-and-miss nightclub.

Zocalo (☎ 434-977-4944; 201 E Main St; mains $18-26; 5:30pm-2:30am Tue-Sun) Zocalo is cooler than you and kinda lets you know it. This sharp, metallic restaurant-bar serves the world's latest fusion cuisine, Pan-Piedmont Latin, and pulls the effort off nicely. The pretty people propping up the bar with their cocktails certainly make the food more enjoyable.

GETTING THERE & AROUND

A free trolley runs through the historic district.

Amtrak (☎ 434-296-4559; www.amtrak.com; 810 W Main St) Train services to Washington ($22, 2½ to three hours, two per day) and Lynchburg ($15, one hour, two per day).

Greyhound/Trailways terminal (☎ 434-295-5131; 310 W Main St) Runs buses several times a day to Richmond ($12, 1¼ hours, three per day) and Washington ($15, three hours, three per day).

Charlottesville Albemarle Airport (CHO; ☎ 434-973-8342; www.gocho.com) Ten miles north of downtown; offers regional flights.

Appomattox Court House & Around

At the McLean House in the town of Appomattox Court House, General Robert E Lee surrendered the Army of Northern Virginia to General Ulysses S Grant, in effect ending the Civil War. Instead of coming straight here, follow **Lee's retreat** (☎ 800-673-8732; www.varetreat.com) on a winding 25-stop tour that starts in Petersburg at Southside Railroad Station (River St and Cockade Alley) and cuts through some of the most attractive countryside in Virginia. Best take a detailed road map, as the trail is not always clearly marked. You'll finish at the 1300-acre **Appomattox Court House National Historic Park** (☎ 434-352-8987; www.nps.gov/apco; $4 summer, $3 Sep-May; 8:30am-5pm). Most of the 27 restored buildings are open to visitors.

SHENANDOAH VALLEY

Local lore says Shenandoah was named for a Native American word meaning 'Daughter of the Stars.' True or not, there's no question – this is God's country, one of the most beautiful places in America. The 200-mile-long valley and its flanking Blue Ridge Mountains hold amazing wonders at every turn, from small towns and wineries to battlefields and caverns. This was once the western border of colonial America, settled by Scots-Irish frontiersmen who were Highland Clearance refugees. The area offers an endless array of outdoor activities including hiking, camping, fishing, horseback riding and canoeing.

Shenandoah National Park

our pick **Shenandoah** (☎ 540-999-3500; www.nps.gov/shen/; week passes Mar-Nov $15 per car, $8 per pedestrian or bicyclist, cheaper winter), one of the most spectacular national parks in the country, is like a new smile from nature: in spring and summer the wildflowers explode, in fall the leaves burn bright red and orange and in winter a cold, starkly beautiful hibernation period sets in. White-tailed deer are a common sight and, if you're lucky, you might spot a black bear, bobcat or wild turkey. The park lies just 75 miles west of Washington, DC. Whatever your agenda, don't miss a visit to this amazing wonderland.

SIGHTS & ACTIVITIES

Skyline Drive, a 105-mile-long road running down the spine of the Blue Ridge Mountains, redefines the definition of 'Scenic Route.' You're constantly treated to an impressive view, but keep in mind the road is bendy, slow-going (35mph limit) and (in peak season) congested. On a good day it takes three hours to traverse the entire stretch.

There are two visitor centers in the park. **Dickey Ridge** (☎ 540-635-3566; Mile 4.6; 🕑 8:30am-5pm Apr 6–Oct 27) in the north and **Harry F Byrd** (☎ 540-999-3500; Mile 51; 🕑 8:30am-5pm Mar 31–Oct 27) in the south have maps, backcountry permits and information on horseback riding, hang gliding, bicycling (only on public roads) and other wholesome goodness.

Shenandoah has more than 500 miles of hiking trails, including 101 miles of the Appalachian Trail. These are just a few of the great hikes that await, listed from north to south:

Old Rag Mountain This is a tough, 8.8-mile trail that culminates in a rocky scramble only suitable for the physically fit. Your reward is the summit of Old Rag Mountain and, along the way, some of the best views in Virginia.

Skyland Four easy trails here, none exceeding 1.6 miles, with a few steep sections throughout. Stony Man Trail gives great views for not-too-strenuous trekking.

Big Meadows Very popular area, with four easy-to-midlevel difficulty hikes. The Lewis Falls and Rose River Trails run by the park's most spectacular waterfalls, and the former accesses the Appalachian Trail.

Bearfence Mountain A short trail leads to a spectacular 360-degree viewpoint. The circuit hike is only 1.2 miles, but it involves a strenuous scramble over rocks.

Riprap Three trails of varying difficulty. Blackrock Trail is an easy 1-mile loop that yields fantastic views. You can either hike the moderate 3.4-mile Riprap Trail to Chimney Rock, or detour and make a fairly strenuous 9.8-mile circuit that connects with the Appalachian Trail.

SLEEPING & EATING

Camping is available at five **NPS campgrounds** (☎ 877-444-6777; www.recreation.gov). The following prices are per day: **Mathews Arm** (Mile 22.1; campsites $15), **Big Meadows** (Mile 51.3; campsites $20), **Lewis Mountain** (Mile 57.5; campsites $15, no reservations), **Loft Mountain** (Mile 79.5; campsites $15) and **Dundo Group** (Mile 83.7; campsites $35, min 7 people, reservations required). Most are open mid-May to October. Camping elsewhere requires a free backcountry permit, available from any visitor center.

For not-so-rough lodging, stay at **Skyland Lodge** (Mile 41.7; r $87-200), **Big Meadows** (Mile 51.2; r $99-159) or **Lewis Mountain** (Mile 57.5; cabins from $76; ⊠), all open from early March to mid-November. Reservations can be made by calling ☎ 800-999-4714 or booking online at www.visitshenandoah.com.

Skyland and Big Meadows both have restaurants and taverns with nightly live music. Big Meadows is the prettiest and largest resort in the park and offers the most services, including gas, laundry and camp store. It's best to bring your own food into the park if you're going camping or on extended hikes.

GETTING THERE & AROUND

Amtrak trains run to Staunton, in the Shenandoah Valley, once a day from Washington, DC ($34), and twice a day from Richmond ($17). But you'll really need your own wheels to explore the length and breadth of the park, which can be easily accessed from several exits off I-81.

Front Royal & Around

The northernmost tip of Skyline Dr initially comes off as a drab strip of gas stations, but there's a friendly enough main street and some cool caverns nearby. Stop in at the **visitor center** (☎ 540-332-3971; 414 E Main St; 🕑 9am-5pm) and the **Shenandoah Valley Travel Association** (☎ 800-847-4878; www.visitshenandoah.org; US 211 W, I-81 exit 264; 🕑 9am-5pm) before heading 'up' (a reference to altitude, not direction) the valley.

Front Royal's claim to fame is **Skyline Caverns** (☎ 540-635-4545; www.skylinecaverns.com; US 340; adult/child 7-13yr $16/8; 🕑 9am-5pm Mon-Fri, to 6pm Sat, Sun & summer), which boasts rare, white-spiked anthodites – mineral formations that look like sea urchins.

Woodward House on Manor Grade (☎ 540-635-7010; www.acountryhome.com; 413 S Royal Ave/US 320; r $99-135, cottages $220; Ⓟ ⊠) is a cluttered B&B with eight cheerful rooms. Sip your coffee from the deck and don't let the busy street below distract from the Blue Ridge Mountain vista.

County Seat (☎ 540-636-8884; 104 S Royal Ave; mains $6-8; 🕑 7am-5pm Mon-Fri, 9am-4pm Sat) is a cuddly, colonial-style pub with Virginia ham sandwiches in the deli and Belgian beer on tap.

Jalisco's (☎ 540-635-7348; 1303 N Royal Ave; mains $8-15; 🕑 11am-10pm) has surprisingly good Mexican; the chili rellenos go down a treat.

Soul Mountain Cafe (☎ 540-636-0070; 1303 117 E Main St; mains $12-24; ⌚ noon-9pm Mon-Sat, to 4pm Sun), with its Bob Marley posters and African sculptures, is kinda incongruous, but when you're serving *andouille* (a spiced pork sausage) over penne and crabmeat-stuffed salmon, that's fine by us.

Some 25 miles north, in the town of Winchester, is the **Museum of the Shenandoah Valley** (☎ 888-556-5799; 901 Amherst St; adult/student $12/10; ⌚ 10am-4pm Tue-Sun), which does a good job of introducing you to Appalachian culture and history.

If you can only fit one cavern into your itinerary, head 25 miles south from Front Royal to the world-class **Luray Caverns** (☎ 540-743-6551; www.luraycaverns.com; I-81 exit 264; adult/child 7-13yr $21/10; ⌚ 9am-6pm, to 7pm summer, to 4pm Nov 1–Mar 31) and hear the 'Stalacpipe Organ,' hyped as the largest musical instrument on Earth.

George Washington & Jefferson National Forests

Stretching along the entire western edge of Virginia, these two mammoth **forests** (www.fs.fed.us/r8/gwj; campsites $5-16, primitive camping free) comprise more than 1562 sq miles of mountainous terrain bordering the Shenandoah Valley, and contain challenging to easy trail networks, which include 330 miles of the **Appalachian Trail** (www.appalachiantrail.org) and mountain-biking routes. Hundreds of developed campgrounds are scattered throughout. **USDA Forest Service headquarters** (☎ 540-265-5100; 5162 Valleypointe Pkwy), off the Blue Ridge Pkwy in Roanoke, oversees a dozen ranger stations along the ranges. You can also pick up information at the **Natural Bridge visitor center** (☎ 540-291-2121) across from the Natural Bridge entrance.

Staunton & Around

This pretty little town jumps out of the mountains with its cozy college (Mary Baldwin), old time-y avenues, and oddly enough, one of America's premier Shakespeare companies.

The **Frontier Culture Museum** (☎ 540-332-7850; overlooking I-81 exit 222; adult/child/student $10/6/9; ⌚ 9am-5pm mid-Mar–Nov, 10am-4pm Dec–mid-Mar) has authentic historic farm buildings from Germany, Ireland and England, which have been plunked here to provide a comparison to an on-site American frontier farm. Good if you're into history or farming or both. The town's **visitor center** (⌚ 9am-5pm) shares space with the museum.

Woodrow Wilson Presidential Library (☎ 540-885-0897; www.woodrowwilson.org; 18-24 N Coalter St; adult/student/child 6-12 $12/5/3; ⌚ 9am-5pm Mon-Sat, from noon Sun, to 4pm Nov-Feb) is a scholarly peek into the life of the 28th president and founder of the League of Nations, as well as the pre- and post-WWI era he emerged from. Don't leave without catching a show at the **Blackfriars Playhouse** (☎ 540-851-1733; 10 S Market St; tickets $20-30), where the American Shakespeare Center company performs in the world's only re-creation of Shakespeare's original indoor theater.

Right downtown, the thoroughly mauve and immensely welcoming **Frederick House** (☎ 540-885-4220, 800-334-5575; www.frederickhouse.com; 28 N New St; r incl breakfast $103-273; P ⊠ ⌘) consists of five historical residences with a combination of rooms and suites, all with private bathrooms and some with fireplaces and decks.

A valley tradition since 1947, **Mrs Rowe's** (☎ 540-886-1833; I-81 exit 222; mains $5-15; ⌚ 7am-8pm Mon-Sat, to 7pm Sun), offers Southern hospitality and home-cooked fare like fried chicken and hash browns topped with melted cheese.

Lexington & Around

This is the place to see Southern gentry at their stately best, as cadets from the Virginia Military Institute jog past the prestigious academics of Washington & Lee University. The **visitor center** (☎ 540-463-3777; 106 E Washington St; ⌚ 9am-5pm) has free parking.

You'll either be impressed or put off by the extreme discipline of the cadets at **Virginia Military Institute** (VMI; ☎ 540-464-7230; Letcher Ave; ⌚ 9am-5pm when campus & museums open), the only university to have sent its entire graduating class into combat (plaques to student war dead are touching and ubiquitous). A full-dress parade takes place most Fridays at 4:30pm during the school year. The school's **George C Marshall Museum** (☎ 540-463-7103; adult/child $5/free) honors the creator of the Marshall Plan for post-WWII European reconstruction. The **VMI Cadet Museum** (☎ 540-464-7334; admission free) houses the stuffed carcass of Stonewall Jackson's horse, a homemade American flag made by an alumnus prisoner of war in Vietnam, and a tribute to VMI students killed in the War on Terror.

Founded in 1749, colonnaded Washington & Lee University is one of the top small colleges in America. The **Lee Chapel & Museum** (☎ 540-458-8768; ⌚ 9am-4pm, from 1pm Sun) inters

Robert E Lee, while his horse Traveller is buried outside. One of the four Confederate banners surrounding Lee's tomb is set in an original flagpole, a branch a rebel soldier turned into a makeshift standard.

Historic Country Inns (☎ 540-463-2044; 11 N Main St; r $70-150, ste $130-180; P) operates two inns downtown and one outside town. All of the buildings have some historical significance to Lexington, and most of the rooms are individually decorated with period antiques. The charming, ecominded **Applewood Inn & Llama Trekking** (☎ 540-463-1962, 1-800-463-1902; r $115-150; P) offers a slew of outdoorsy activities on a farm a 10-minute drive away.

The **Southern Inn** (☎ 540-463-9498; 37 S Main St; lunch mains $7-12, dinner mains $15-30; 5-10pm Mon & Tue, 11:30am-10pm Wed-Sat, to 9pm Sun) has a no-nonsense, classy menu (think roast duck and stuffed trout) and the perfect ambience for a date between a VMI cadet and Washington & Lee sorority sister.

Natural Bridge

Yes, it's a kitschy tourist trap, and yes, vocal creationists who insist it was made by the hand of God are dominating the site, but the 215ft-high **Natural Bridge** (☎ 540-291-2121; www.naturalbridgeva.com; adult/child 6-15 $18/10; 8am-dusk), 15 miles from Lexington, is still pretty cool. It was surveyed by 16-year-old George Washington, who supposedly carved his initials into the wall, and was once owned by Thomas Jefferson.

BLUE RIDGE HIGHLANDS & SOUTHWEST VIRGINIA

The southwestern tip of Virginia is the most rugged part of the state. Turn onto the Blue Ridge Pkwy or any side road and you'll immediately plunge into dark strands of dogwood and fir, fast streams and white waterfalls. You're bound to see Confederate flags in the small towns, but there's a proud hospitality behind the fierce veneer of independence.

Blue Ridge Parkway

Where Skyline Dr ends, the **Blue Ridge Parkway** (www.nps.gov/blri/) picks up. The road is just as pretty and runs from the southern Appalachian ridge in Shenandoah National Park at Mile 0 to North Carolina's Great Smoky Mountains National Park at Mile 469. Wildflowers bloom in spring, and fall colors are spectacular, but watch out for foggy days; no guardrails can make for hairy driving. There are a dozen visitor centers scattered over the Pkwy, and any of them make a good kick-off point to start your trip. For more details, see p401.

SIGHTS & ACTIVTIES

There are all kinds of sights running along the Pkwy; these are a handful, listed from north to south:

Sherando Lake (☎ 540-291-2188, Mile 16) In George Washington National Forest (p377), this is a pretty blue dollop of pastel scenery and a nice place for a swim.

James River & Kanawha Canal (☎ 800-933-9535; Mile 63) A footpath here leads to the canal locks and, if you have time, a pleasant amble over local river bluffs.

Peaks of Otter (☎ 540-586-4357; Mile 86) You close a nice Capital Region circle by coming here; stones from the tops of these mountains (Sharp Top, Flat Top and Harkening Hill) are inside the Washington Monument. Shuttles run to the top of Sharp Top or you can try a fairly challenging hike to the summit.

Mabry Mill (☎ 276-952-2947; Mile 176) One of the most photographed buildings in the state, the Mill nests in such a fuzzy green vale you'll think you've entered the opening chapter of a Tolkien novel.

SLEEPING

Get in touch with the NPS beforehand if you're planning on sleeping along the Pkwy. There are nine local **campgrounds** (☎ 977-444-6777), four in Virginia; all campsites are $16 (cabins extra). Every year the staggered opening date of facilities changes, but sites are generally accessible from April to November. Two NPS-approved indoor facilities are on the Pkwy in Virginia: **Peaks of Otter** (☎ 540-586-1081; Mile 86, 85554 Blue Ridge Pkwy; r $100; P), a pretty, split-rail-surrounded lodge nestled between two of its namesake mountains, and **Rocky Knob Cabins** (☎ 540-593-5303; Mile 174, 256 Mabry Mill Rd; cabin with shared bath $59; P), set off in a secluded stretch of forest. Bring food, as eating options are limited along the Pkwy.

Roanoke & Around

Illuminated by the giant star atop Mill Mountain, Roanoke is the largest city in the valley and is the self-proclaimed 'Capital of the Blue Ridge.' It has a compact set of attractions based around the bustling indoor-outdoor **Historic City Market** (213 Market St; 7:30am-4:30pm Mon-Sat), a sumptuous farmers market loaded with temptations even for those with no access to a kitchen. For local information, check out the **Roanoke Valley Visitor Information Center** (☎ 540-342-6025, 800-635-5535; www.visitroanokeva.com; 101 Shenandoah Ave NE; 9am-5pm) in the old Norfolk & Western train station.

The **Taubman Museum of Art** (☎ 540-342-5760; www.taubmanmuseum.org; adult/student with ID/child 4-12yr $10.50/8.50/5.50; 10am-5pm Tue-Wed & Fri & Sat, to 7pm Thu, noon-5pm Sun), opened in 2008, is set in a futuristic glass-and-steel structure that was supposedly inspired by the valley's natural beauty. We don't get it, but inside you'll find a wonderful collection of classic and modern art.

Nearby, **Center in the Square** (☎ 540-342-5700; www.centerinthesquare.org; 1 Market Sq; 10am-5pm Tue-Sat, 1-5pm Sun) is the city's cultural heartbeat, with a science museum and planetarium (adult/child $8/6), local history museum (adult/child $3/2) and theater. The site of the **Harrison Museum of African American Culture** (☎ 540-345-4818; www.harrisonmuseum.com; 523 Harrison Ave; admission free; 10am-5pm Tue-Wed & Fri, to 7pm Thu, 1pm-5pm Sat), was the first public high school for African Americans in America, and has displays on local African American culture and traditional and contemporary African art.

About 30 miles east of Roanoke, the tiny town of Bedford suffered the most casualties per capita during WWII, and hence was chosen to host the moving **National D-Day Memorial** (☎ 540-586-3329; US 460 & Hwy 122; adult/child $5/3; 10am-5pm). Among its towering arch and flower garden is a cast of bronze figures reenacting the storming of the beach, complete with bursts of water symbolizing the hail of bullets the soldiers faced.

Mt Rogers National Recreation Area

This seriously beautiful district is well worth a visit from outdoor enthusiasts. Hike, fish or cross-country ski among ancient hardwood trees and the state's tallest peak. The **park headquarters** (☎ 276-783-5196), on Hwy 16 in Marion, offers maps and recreation directories. The NPS operates five campgrounds in the area; contact park headquarters for details.

Abingdon

One of the most photogenic towns in Virginia, Abingdon retains fine Federal and Victorian architecture in its historic district, and hosts the bluegrass **Virginia Highlands Festival** over the first half of August. The **visitor center** (☎ 800-435-3440; 335 Cummings St; 9am-5pm) has exhibits on local history.

Fields-Penn 1860 House Museum (☎ 276-676-0216; 208 W Main St; adult/child 6-12 $3/2; 11am-4pm Wed & Sat, 1-4pm Thu & Fri) has exhibits on 19th-century life in southwest Virginia. Founded during the Depression, **Barter Theatre** (☎ 540-628-3991; www.bartertheatre.com; 133 W Main St; performances from $20) earned its name from audiences trading food for performances. Actors Gregory Peck and Ernest Borgnine cut their teeth on Barter's stage.

The **Virginia Creeper Trail** (www.vacreepertrail.org), named for the railroad that once ran this route, travels 33 miles between Whitetop Station near the North Carolina border and downtown Abingdon. Several outfitters rent bikes, organize outings and run shuttles, including **Virginia Creeper Trail Bike Shop** (☎ 276-676-2552; 201 Pecan St; per 2hr $10; 9am-6pm) near the trailhead.

Martha Washington Inn (☎ 540-628-3161; 150 W Main St; r from $225; P), opposite the Barter, is the region's premier historic hotel, a Victorian sprawl of historical classiness and wrought-iron style.

Zazzy'z (☎ 276-698-3333; 380 E Main St; sandwiches $4.25; 7am-7pm Mon-Fri, 8am-6pm Sat, to 5pm Sun) serves cheap, filling sandwiches and strong coffee in a lovely old bookstore.

The Crooked Road

When Scots-Irish fiddle-and-reel married African American banjo-and-percussion, American mountain or 'old-time' music was born, with such genres as country and bluegrass. The latter genre still dominates the Blue Ridge, and the **Crooked Road** (www.thecrookedroad.org) takes you through nine sites associated with that history, and some eye-stretching mountain scenery. The trail is sad and beautiful; the traditions it tries to preserve always seem threatened by gentrification, but during a live show you'll witness the double joy of elders connecting to deep cultural roots and a new generation of musicians keeping that heritage alive and evolving. The following are only two stops on the Crooked Road.

FLOYD

Tiny, cute-as-a-postcard Floyd is nothing more than an intersection between Hwys 8 and 221, but life explodes on Friday nights at the **Floyd Country Store** (☎ 540-745-4563; www.floydcountrystore.com; 206 S Locust St; jamboree admission $4; 10am-10:30pm Fri, to 5:30pm Sat). Every Friday starting at 6:30pm, $4 gets you four bluegrass bands in four hours and the chance to watch happy crowds nod along to regional heritage. No smokin', no drinkin', but plenty of dancin' (of the jig-and-tap style) is the order of the day. Nearby **County Sales** (☎ 540-745-2001; Talley's Alley; 9am-4:30pm Mon-Fri) claims to be the world's first, and still largest, purveyor of bluegrass music.

Built in 2007 with ecofriendly materials and furnishings, **Hotel Floyd** (☎ 540-745-6080; www.hotelfloyd.com; 120 Wilson St; r $75-135; P) is one of the most 'green' hotels in Virginia and is a model of sustainability. Each of the 14 unique rooms were decorated by local artisans.

When you're all jigged out head for **Oddfella's** (☎ 540-745-3463; lunch mains $7-14, dinner mains $8-21; 11am-2:30pm & 5-9pm Wed-Sat, 10am-3pm Sun), which has a woodsy, organic menu.

our pick **Pine Tavern** (☎ 540-745-4482; 611 Floyd Hwy; mains $8-10; 4:30-9pm Thu-Sat, 11am-8pm Sun) Serving Blue Ridge Mountain cuisine since 1927, this tavern is the place to head for a real local vibe. With the family-style dinner, $12 gets you meat, veg, side dish, dessert and drink. Or go for the house specialties like the divine spicy grilled catfish with peppery mashed potatoes. Wash it down with a Rebel Ale from the local **Shooting Creek Farm Brewery** (www.shootingcreekbrewery.com). It was opened in 2004 by two friends, and their beer is based on recipes and methods brought to America by European settlers.

GALAX

Galax claims to be the world capital of mountain music, although it feels like any-where-else-ville outside of the immediate downtown area (on the National Register of Historic Places). The main attraction is the **Rex Theater** (☎ 276-236-5309; www.rextheatergalax.com; 113 E Grayson St), a musty, red-curtained belle of yore. Frequent bluegrass acts cross its stage, but the easiest one to catch is the free Friday-night live WBRF 98.1 show, which pulls in crowds from across the mountains.

Tom Barr of **Barr's Fiddle Shop** (☎ 276-236-2411; 105 S Main St) is the Stradivarius of the mountains, a master craftsman sought out by fiddle and mandolin aficionados from across the world. The **Old Fiddler's Convention** (www.oldfiddlersconvention.com) is held every year in Galax; it's one of the premier mountain music festivals in the world.

The **Doctor's Inn** (☎ 276-238-9998; thedoctorsinnvirginia.com; 406 W Stuart Dr; r $109-129; P) nicely fills the local 'let's stuff a historic building full of grandma's antiques and spoil our guests rotten' B&B niche.

The **Galax Smokehouse** (☎ 276-236-1000; 101 N Main St; mains $5-13; 11am-9pm Mon-Sat, to 3pm Sun) serves groaning platters of sweetly sauced Memphis-style BBQ.

WEST VIRGINIA

Wild and wonderful West Virginia is often overlooked by American and foreign travelers. It doesn't help that the state can't seem to shake its negative stereotypes. That's too bad, because West Virginia is one of the prettiest states in the Union. With its line of unbroken green mountains, raging white water rivers and snowcapped ski resorts, this is an outdoor-lovers' paradise.

Created by secessionists from secession, the people here still think of themselves as hardscrabble sons of miners, and that perception isn't entirely off. But the Mountain State is also gentrifying and, occasionally, that's a good thing: the arts are flourishing in the valleys, where some towns offer a welcome break from the state's constantly evolving outdoor activities.

History

Virginia was once the biggest state in America, divided between the plantation aristocracy of the Tidewater and the mountains of what is now West Virginia. The latter were settled by tough farmers who staked out independent freeholds across the Appalachians. Always resentful of their Eastern brethren and their reliance on cheap (ie slave) labor, the mountaineers of West Virginia declared their independence from Virginia when the latter tried to break off from America during the Civil War.

Yet the scrappy, independent-at-all-costs stereotype was challenged in the late 19th and early 20th centuries, when miners here formed into cooperative unions and battled employers in some of the bloodiest battles in American labor history. That odd mix of chip-on-the-shoulder resentment towards authority and look-out-for-your-neighbor community values continues to characterize West Virginia today, although the creeping blandness of suburbia threatens this unique regional culture.

Information

West Virginia Division of Tourism (☎ 304-558-2200, 800-225-5982; www.wvtourism.com.com) operates wel come centers at interstate borders and in **Harpers Ferry** (☎ 304-535-2482). Check www.adven turesinwv.com for info on the state's myriad adventure tourism opportunities.

Many hotels and motels tack on a $1 'safe' fee, refundable upon request at checkout. So if you didn't use that room safe, get your dollar back.

EASTERN PANHANDLE

The most accessible part of the state has always been and continues to be a mountain getaway for DC types.

Harpers Ferry

The center of this town is a maddeningly cute conglomeration of steep cobblestoned streets framed by the Shenandoah Mountains and River. Exhibits narrate the town's role at the forefront of westward expansion, American industry and, most famously, the slavery debate. In 1859 old John Brown tried to spark a slave uprising here and was hung for his efforts; the incident rubbed friction between North and South into the fires of Civil War. Historic buildings and museums are accessible to those with passes, which can be found, along with parking and shuttles, north of town at the **Harpers Ferry National Historic Park Visitor Center** (☎ 304-535-2482; www.nps.gov/hafe; 171 Shoreline Drive; vehicle/pedestrian $6/4; 8am-5pm) off Hwy 340. Parking is incredibly limited in Harpers Ferry proper.

SIGHTS & ACTIVITIES

Among the free sites in the historic district, the 1858 **Master Armorer's House** explains how rifle technology developed here revolutionized the firearms industry; the **Storer College building**, long ago a teachers' college for freed slaves, now traces the town's African American history. The laughably tacky **John Brown Museum** (168 High St; adult/child 6-12 $7/5; 9am-5pm) tells the story of Brown's life and raid in wax.

The 2160-mile Appalachian Trail is headquartered at the **Appalachian Trail Conference** (☎ 304-535-6331; www.atconf.org; cnr Washington & Jackson Sts; 9am-5pm Mon-Fri Apr-Oct), a tremendous resource for hikers. Day-hikers also scale the Maryland Heights Trail past Civil War fortifications or the Loudoun Heights Trail for river views.

> **WEST VIRGINIA FACTS**
>
> **Nickname** Mountain State
> **Population** 1.81 million
> **Area** 24,230 sq miles
> **Capital city** Charleston (population 50,478)
> **Sales tax** 6%
> **Birthplace of** Olympic gymnast Mary Lou Retton (b 1968), writer Pearl S Buck (1892–1973), pioneer aviator Chuck Yeager (b 1923), actor Don Knotts (1924–200)
> **Home of** The National Radio Astronomy Observatory, much of the American coal industry
> **Famous for** Mountains, John Denver's 'Take Me Home, Country Roads,' the Hatfield-McCoy feud
> **State slogan** 'Wild and Wonderful'
> **Driving distances** Harpers Ferry to Fayetteville 280 miles, Fayetteville to Morgantown 148 miles

Check with the visitor center about renting bikes to explore the **C&O Canal towpath**. To arrange rafting, kayaking, canoeing and tubing excursions, contact **River Riders** (☎ 800-326-7238; www.riverriders.com; 408 Alstadts Hill Rd).

SLEEPING & EATING

HI-Harpers Ferry Hostel (☎ 301-8347652; www.hi hostels.com; 19123 Sandy Hook Rd, Knoxville, MD; dm $20; P) Located 2 miles from downtown on the Maryland side of the Potomac River, this friendly hostel has plenty of amenities including a kitchen, laundry and lounge area with games and books.

Town Inn (☎ 304-702-1872, 877-489-2447; www.the townsinn.com; 179 High St; r $70-140) Smack in the middle of the historic district, this B&B feels like it's been built into the mountain, an illusion accented by the pretty slate bathroom in the largest room.

Anvil (☎ 304-535-2582; 1270 Washington St; lunch mains $6-10, dinner mains $13-22; 11am-9pm Wed-Sun) Local trout melting in honey-pecan butter and an elegant Federal dining room equals excellence at this restaurant, in next-door Bolivar.

GETTING THERE & AROUND

Amtrak (☎ 800-872-7245) and **MARC** (☎ 800-325-7245) trains run to Washington's Union Station (one daily, $11; five daily, $9).

Berkeley Springs

America's first spa town (George Washington relaxed here) is an odd jumble of spiritualism, artistic expression and pampering spa centers.

Farmers in pickups sporting Confederate flags and acupuncturists in tie-dye smocks regard each other with bemusement on the roads of Bath (still the official name).

Don't let the locker-room appearance deter you from the Berkeley Springs State Park's **Roman Baths** (☎ 304-258-2711; bath $40; ⏰ 10am-6pm); it's the cheapest spa deal in town. (Fill your water bottle with some of the magic stuff at the fountain outside the door.) For a more indulgent experience, try a mix-and-match of treatments across the green at the **Bath House** (☎ 800-431-4698; www.bathhouse.com; 21 Fairfax St; ⏰ 10am-5pm) such as a bath and hour's massage ($140) or chocolate-strawberry body wrap ($90).

Inn & Spa at Berkeley Springs (☎ 304-258-2210, 800-822-6630; www.theinnandspa.com; r $69-250; P ⊠), right next to the park, offers luxurious treatment plus lodging package deals at breathtaking prices. The holistic **Coolfont Resort** (☎ 304-258-4500; 3621 Cold Run Valley Rd; campsites $20-35, r per person $69-99, chalets per person $139-179; P ⊠) is like a wellness summer camp for adults (but popular with families, too).

Grab a yummy sandwich or daily blue plate specials at **Tari's** (☎ 304-258-1196; 123 N Washington St; lunch $5-8, dinner $15-25), or go gourmet at **Lot 12 Public House** (☎ 304-258-6264; 302 Warren St; mains $18-30; ⏰ from 5pm Wed-Sun), halfway up the hill.

MONONGAHELA NATIONAL FOREST

Almost the entire eastern half of West Virginia is marked green parkland on the map, and all that goodness falls under the auspices of this stunning national forest. Within its 1400 sq miles are wild rivers, caves and the highest peak in the state (Spruce Knob). More than 850 miles of trails include the 124-mile **Allegheny Trail**, for hiking and backpacking, and the 75-mile rails-to-trails **Greenbrier River Trail**, popular with bicyclists.

Elkins, at the forest's western boundary, is a good base of operations. The **National Forest Service Headquarters** (☎ 304-636-1800; 200 Sycamore St; campsites $5, RV sites $10-30, primitive camping free) distributes recreation directories for hiking, bicycling and camping.

Fat Tire Cycle (☎ 304-636-0969; 101 Randolph Ave; ⏰ 9am-5pm Mon-Fri, to 3pm Sat) rents gear and sponsors excursions. Stock up on trail mix, energy bars and hippie auras at **Good Energy Foods** (☎ 304-636-8808; 214 3rd St; ⏰ 9am-5:30pm Mon-Sat).

In the southern end of the forest, **Cranberry Mountain Nature Center** (☎ 304-653-4826; cnr Hwys 150 & 39/55; ⏰ 9am-4:30pm May-Oct) has scientific information on the forest.

The surreal landscapes at **Seneca Rocks**, 35 miles southeast of Elkins, attract rock climbers up its 900ft-tall sandstone strata. **Seneca Shadows Campground** (☎ 877-444-6777; campsites $11-30; ⏰ Apr-Oct) is 1 mile east.

An 8-mile portion of the Allegheny Trail links two full-service state parks 30 miles northeast of Elkins: **Canaan Valley Resort** (☎ 304-866-4121), a downhill ski resort, and **Blackwater Falls State Park** (☎ 304-259-5216), with backcountry ski touring. Further south, **Snowshoe Mountain** (☎ 877-441-4386; www.snowshoemtn.com; lift tickets adult/student with ID/child 6-12 $75/72/62) is the state's largest downhill ski and snowboard resort with a beautiful alpine-inspired, pedestrian village. Snowshoe is a popular mountain-biking center from spring to fall.

Nearby, the **Cass Scenic Railroad State Park** (☎ 304-456-4300; www.cassrailroad.com; excursions from $17) runs steam trains, from an old logging town to mountaintop overlooks, daily in summer and for peak fall foliage. Accommodations include **cottages** ($71-111) and **cabooses** ($83-209).

The **National Radio Astronomy Observatory** (☎ 304-456-2150; www.gb.nrao.edu; Green Bank; admission & tour free; ⏰ 8:30am-6pm summer, 10am-5pm Wed-Sun rest of year) is home to the 328ft Green Bank Telescope, the largest movable radio dish in the world. The center lies within the country's only federal radio-free zone, which is why your car won't pick up any stations within 25 miles of the center.

MORGANTOWN

Morgantown's been dubbed one of the best cities of its size in the country, and it's not hard to see why: it's nestled within a dramatic valley, has a thriving arts scene fed from local West Virginia University, drips with bars, cafés and restaurants, and houses a population that runs from South Asian immigrants to Appalachian mountain folk.

The students of enormous **West Virginia University** (WVU; ☎ 304-293-0111; www.wvu.edu) fuel much of the city's energy. **Mountaineer Field** (☎ 304-293-2294; 1 Rogers St) is (in)famous for housing some of the rowdiest fans in American collegiate sport. WVU is regularly ranked as the nation's top party school.

As always in this state, there are outdoor activities a stone's throw away; **Cheat Lake** (www.cheatlake.com) is an 8-mile-long reservoir east of town overflowing with hiker-bicyclist trails, ski routes and scenic overlooks. **Monongalia Arts Center** (☎ 304-282-3325; 107 High St; admission free; 10am-6pm Mon-Fri, to 4pm Sat) is one of the largest and best museum and gallery spaces in the mountains. Catch a show in the lovely old 1924 **Metropolitan Theatre** (☎ 304-291-4884; 369 High St), an elegant main-street anchor, and see the fascinating, if exhaustive glass collection of Mr Kurt Ly, a Vietnamese West Virginian, at the **Morgantown Glass Museum** (☎ 304-291-2957; 1628 Mileground Rd; 2-5pm Wed-Sat).

The **Hotel Morgan** (☎ 304-291-2517; 127 High St; r $80-150; P) is a gorgeously appointed historical building. The student-favorite **Blue Moose Café** (☎ 304-292-8999; 248 Walnut St; 7am-10pm Mon-Thu, to 11pm Fri; 8am-11pm Sat, to 10pm Sun) is a popular coffeehouse with occasional live music. **Maxwells** (☎ 304-292-0982; 1 Wall St; lunch mains $6-11, dinner mains $9-11; 11am-8:45pm Mon-Thu, to 9:45pm Fri & Sat, to 1:45pm Sun) is a dark, underground den of burgers and dinner and a popular Sunday brunch. For something more upscale, **Dragonfly** (☎ 304-241-4305; www.dragonflywv.com; 341 Chestnut St; sushi $2-6, mains $8-28; 4pm-late) is a posh Asian and sushi restaurant with fabulous contemporary decor and chill-out lounge music.

SOUTHERN WEST VIRGINIA

This part of the state has carved out a viable stake as adventure-sports capital of the Eastern seaboard.

New River Gorge National River

The New River is actually one of the oldest in the world, and the primeval forest gorge it runs through is one of the most breathtaking in the Appalachians. The NPS protects a stretch of the New River that falls 750ft over 50 miles, with a compact set of rapids up to Class V concentrated at the northernmost end.

Canyon Rim visitor center (☎ 304-574-2115; 9am-5pm), just north of the impressive gorge bridge, is the only one of five NPS visitor centers along the river that's open year-round, with information on river outfitters, gorge climbing, hiking and mountain biking, as well as white-water rafting to the north on the Gauley River. Rim and gorge trails offer beautiful views. There are four free basic camping areas.

Nearby **Hawks Nest State Park** offers views from its rim-top **lodge** (☎ 304-658-5212; r $53-78); in summer it operates an aerial tram (closed Monday) to the river, where you can catch a cruising boat ride.

> **WHAT THE...?**
>
> Oh my God, everything inside this madhouse *tilts at an angle!* See gravity and the known limits of tackiness defied at the **Mystery Hole** (☎ 304-658-9101; US 60, Mile 44; adult/child under 11 $5/4; 10:30am-6pm, call ahead for open days), one of the great attractions of roadside America.

Babcock State Park (☎ 304-438-3003; www.babcocksp.com) has hiking, canoeing, horseback riding, camping and cabin accommodations. The park's highlight is its photogenic Glade Creek Grist Mill.

Fayetteville & Around

Dubbed one of the coolest small towns in America, pint-sized Fayetteville acts as the jumping-off point for New River thrill-seekers. On the third Saturday in October, hundreds of base jumpers parachute from the 876ft-high New River Gorge Bridge for the **Bridge Day Festival**.

Among the many state-licensed rafting outfitters in the area, **Cantrell Ultimate Rafting** (☎ 800-470-7238; www.ultimaterafting.com; packages from $50) stands out for its white-water rafting trips. For rock climbers, **Hard Rock** (☎ 304-574-0735; www.hardrockclimbing.com; 131 South Court St; packages from $75) offers trips and training courses.

The **Beckley Exhibition Coal Mine** (☎ 304-256-1747; beckleymine.com; adult/child 4-12yr $20/12; 10am-6pm Apr-Nov) in nearby Beckley is a museum to the region's coal heritage. Visitors can descend 1500ft to a former coal mine. Bring a jacket, as it's cold underground!

River Rock Retreat Hostel (☎ 304-574-0394; www.riverrockretreatandhostel.com; Lansing-Edmond Rd; dm $22.50; P), located less than 1 mile north of the New River Gorge Bridge, has basic, clean rooms and plenty of common space. Owner Joy Marr is a wealth of local information. Two miles south of the bridge, **Rifrafters Campground** (☎ 304-574-1065; Laurel Creek Rd; campsites $11, cabins d/q $36/72) has primitive campsites, comfy cabins and hot-shower and bathroom facilities.

Start the day with breakfast and coffee under stained-glass windows at **Cathedral Café & Bookstore** (☎ 304-574-0202; 134 S Court St; mains $5-8; 8am-4pm;).

our pick Pies & Pints (☎ 304-574-2200; 219 W Maple Ave; pies $11-23; ⏰ 11am-10pm) has 18 kinds of pizza and a huge beer selection. Order the Thai shrimp pizza. You'll thank us later!

Greenbrier Valley

Tucked between the Allegheny Mountains, the eclectic Greenbrier Valley is home to breathtaking natural beauty and hot-spring spa towns, all anchored by the sophisticated artsy town of Lewisburg. The valley's star attraction is **Greenbrier** (☎ 800-624-6070; www.thegreenbrier.com; 300 W Main St, White Sulphur Springs; r from $275; P), an unparalleled, luxurious hotel and spa resort. Dubbed the Queen of the Southern Spas, it was originally built in 1778 to pamper wealthy Southerners. In the 20th century, the Greenbrier housed a more covert amenity: a **nuclear bunker**. In the 1950s during the height of the Cold War, the government built this massive bunker under Greenbrier to house Congress in the event of a nuclear holocaust. It remained a secret until 1992, when *The Washington Post* spilled the beans; the bunker shut down three years later. Today, visitors can take a guided **bunker tour** (adult/child 10-18yr $30/15, closed Jan-Mar) of this unique and fascinating bit of American lore.

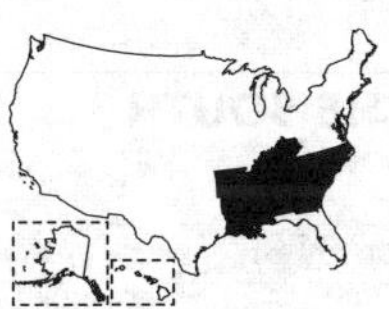

The South

More than any other part of the country, the South has an identity all its own – a musical way of speaking, a complicated political history and a pride in a shared culture that cuts across state lines. As a result, visiting the South feels more 'different' than visiting other parts of the country (and not just because you can't understand the accents!). While powerhouse cities such as Atlanta and Charlotte are in perpetual states of reinvention, some of the more historic cities – places like New Orleans and Savannah – are virtual shrines to their 19th-century former selves.

Nurtured by deep roots yet shaped by hardship, Southerners are often creative types – from William Faulkner all the way to Uncle Jimmy who likes to tell big-fish stories outside the Texaco station. The history of American music is the history of Southern music: jazz, the blues, bluegrass, country and rock and roll were all born in the South. Cooking is a creative art here as well: smoky barbecue, plump Gulf oysters, fluffy buttermilk biscuits, fried green tomatoes. Get ready to eat, eat, eat. Then loosen your belt and eat some more.

The South is truly a wonderful place to travel. It's the kind of place where you're likely to discover new things, merely because the people are so friendly. It's no wonder that Coca-Cola, bourbon and sweet tea – all things you can offer a guest while 'visiting' (chatting) on the porch – were invented in the South. People 'round here like an excuse to talk. Stay long enough and you'll no doubt be invited for dinner.

HIGHLIGHTS

- Donning a mask and joining the chaos of Mardi Gras in **New Orleans** (p481)
- Grasping the soul, rhythm, history and perseverance of the **Delta blues** (p466) in the museums and juke joints of Clarksdale, MS
- Exploring the caverns, mountains, rivers and forests of Arkansas' **Ozark Mountains** (p497), where folk music reigns
- Stompin' your boots at **Tootsie's Orchid Lounge** (p431) on Nashville's honky-tonk-lined Lower Broadway
- Hiking, camping and jaw-dropping in the magnificent **Great Smoky Mountains National Park** (p402)
- Driving windswept Hwy 12 down the length of North Carolina's **Outer Banks** (p391) and taking the ferry to funky little Ocracoke Island
- Touring the grand antebellum homes and cotton plantations of **Charleston** (p404)

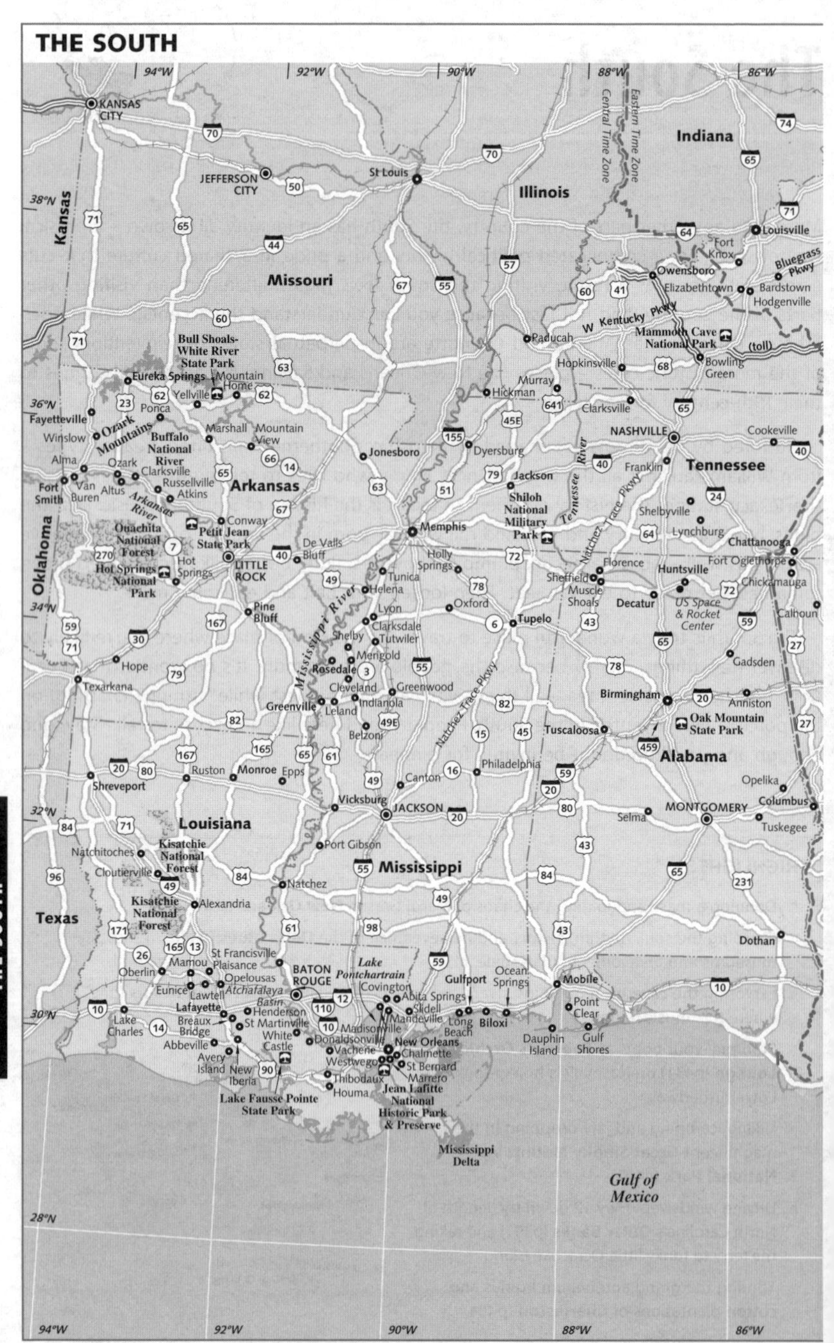

THE SOUTH
94°W
92°W
90°W
88°W
86°W
38°N
36°N
34°N
32°N
30°N
28°N
Central Time Zone
Eastern Time Zone
Kansas
Missouri
Illinois
Indiana
Oklahoma
Arkansas
Tennessee
Texas
Louisiana
Mississippi
Alabama
KANSAS CITY
JEFFERSON CITY
St Louis
Louisville
Fort Knox
Owensboro
Bluegrass Pkwy
Elizabethtown
Bardstown
Hodgenville
W Kentucky Pkwy
Paducah
Mammoth Cave National Park
(toll)
Hopkinsville
Bowling Green
Murray
Hickman
Clarksville
NASHVILLE
Cookeville
Franklin
Dyersburg
Jackson
Shiloh National Military Park
Tennessee River
Natchez Trace Pkwy
Shelbyville
Lynchburg
Chattanooga
Fort Oglethorpe
Chickamauga
Florence
Sheffield
Muscle Shoals
Huntsville
Decatur
US Space & Rocket Center
Calhoun
Gadsden
Birmingham
Anniston
Oak Mountain State Park
Tuscaloosa
Opelika
Columbus
MONTGOMERY
Selma
Tuskegee
Dothan
Bull Shoals-White River State Park
Eureka Springs
Mountain Home
Yellville
Ponca
Fayetteville
Ozark Mountains
Winslow
Buffalo National River
Marshall
Mountain View
Alma
Ozark
Clarksville
Fort Smith
Van Buren
Altus
Russellville
Atkins
Arkansas River
Conway
Petit Jean State Park
Ouachita National Forest
Hot Springs National Park
Hot Springs
LITTLE ROCK
De Valls Bluff
Jonesboro
Memphis
Holly Springs
Tunica
Helena
Mississippi River
Oxford
Tupelo
Lyon
Clarksdale
Tutwiler
Shelby
Mergold
Rosedale
Cleveland
Greenwood
Greenville
Leland
Indianola
Belzoni
Pine Bluff
Hope
Texarkana
Shreveport
Ruston
Monroe
Epps
Canton
Philadelphia
Vicksburg
JACKSON
Port Gibson
Natchez
Natchitoches
Kisatchie National Forest
Cloutierville
Alexandria
St Francisville
Mamou
Plaisance
Oberlin
Opelousas
Eunice
Lawtell
Atchafalaya Basin
Lafayette
Henderson
BATON ROUGE
Lake Pontchartrain
Covington
Abita Springs
Slidell
Mandeville
Madisonville
Lake Charles
Breaux Bridge
St Martinville
White Castle
Donaldsonville
Abbeville
Avery Island
New Iberia
Vacherie
Westwego
Thibodaux
Houma
New Orleans
Chalmette
St Bernard
Marrero
Jean Lafitte National Historic Park & Preserve
Lake Fausse Pointe State Park
Gulfport
Ocean Springs
Long Beach
Biloxi
Mobile
Point Clear
Dauphin Island
Gulf Shores
Mississippi Delta
Gulf of Mexico

THE SOUTH

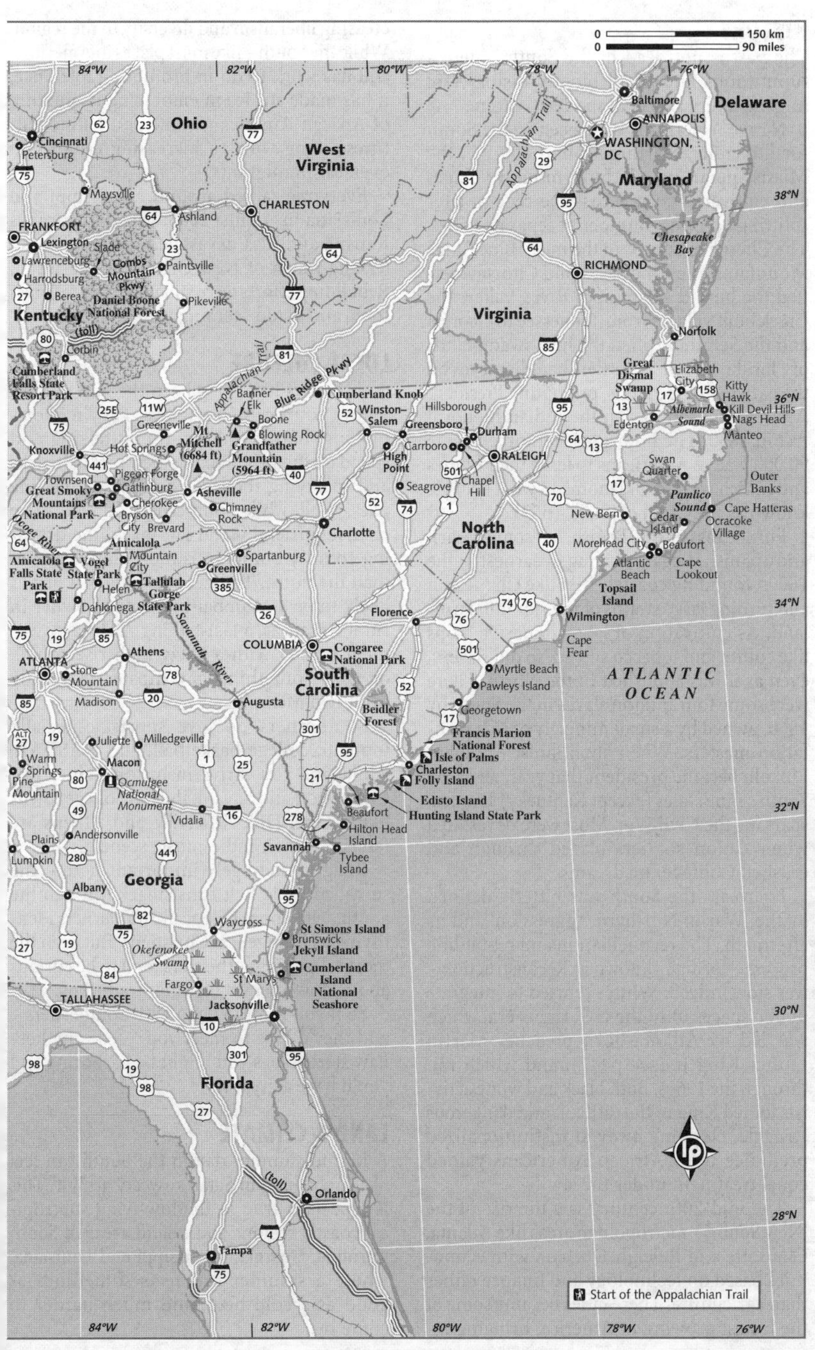
0 150 km
0 90 miles
84°W
82°W
80°W
78°W
76°W
38°N
36°N
34°N
32°N
30°N
28°N
Ohio
West Virginia
Kentucky
Virginia
Maryland
Delaware
North Carolina
South Carolina
Georgia
Florida
Cincinnati
Petersburg
Maysville
Ashland
CHARLESTON
FRANKFORT
Lexington
Slade
Lawrenceburg
Combs Mountain Pkwy
Harrodsburg
Paintsville
Berea
Daniel Boone National Forest
Pikeville
(toll)
Corbin
Cumberland Falls State Resort Park
Baltimore
ANNAPOLIS
WASHINGTON, DC
Appalachian Trail
Chesapeake Bay
RICHMOND
Norfolk
Great Dismal Swamp
Elizabeth City
Kitty Hawk
Kill Devil Hills
Nags Head
Manteo
Albemarle Sound
Edenton
Blue Ridge Pkwy
Cumberland Knob
Banner Elk
Boone
Blowing Rock
Mt Mitchell (6684 ft)
Grandfather Mountain (5964 ft)
Greeneville
Hot Springs
Knoxville
Townsend
Pigeon Forge
Gatlinburg
Great Smoky Mountains National Park
Cherokee
Bryson City
Brevard
Asheville
Chimney Rock
Winston-Salem
Greensboro
Hillsborough
Carrboro
Durham
Chapel Hill
RALEIGH
High Point
Seagrove
Charlotte
Swan Quarter
Outer Banks
Pamlico Sound
Cape Hatteras
Ocracoke Village
Cedar Island
New Bern
Morehead City
Beaufort
Atlantic Beach
Cape Lookout
Topsail Island
Wilmington
Cape Fear
Ocoee River
Amicalola
Mountain City
Amicalola Falls State Park
Vogel State Park
Helen
Tallulah Gorge State Park
Dahlonega
Spartanburg
Greenville
Savannah River
Florence
COLUMBIA
Congaree National Park
Myrtle Beach
Pawleys Island
Georgetown
ATLANTIC OCEAN
ATLANTA
Stone Mountain
Athens
Madison
Augusta
Beidler Forest
Francis Marion National Forest
Isle of Palms
Charleston
Folly Island
Edisto Island
Hunting Island State Park
Juliette
Milledgeville
Macon
Warm Springs
Pine Mountain
Ocmulgee National Monument
Vidalia
Beaufort
Hilton Head Island
Savannah
Tybee Island
Plains
Andersonville
Lumpkin
Albany
Waycross
St Simons Island
Brunswick
Jekyll Island
Okefenokee Swamp
Cumberland Island National Seashore
Fargo
St Marys
TALLAHASSEE
Jacksonville
(toll)
Orlando
Tampa
Start of the Appalachian Trail

HISTORY

The past is not dead in the South, where a tumultuous and often bloody history still informs every aspect of modern culture.

Native Americans have been in the South for millennia. Starting around 800 BC, the Mississippian people built mound villages and cultivated corn across the region, later splitting up into a number of separate tribes. The Cherokee hunted in the misty Blue Ridge Mountains, the Chickasaw and Choctaw settled the humid Mississippi River Valley, the Creek built villages from Tennessee to Georgia and the Seminole plied the lush swamplands of Florida. But white settlers had their eyes on the native people's lands, prompting President Andrew Jackson to sign the Indian Removal Act in 1830. The notorious Act forced some 90,000 Native Americans to leave their homes and march west to Oklahoma in what became known as the 'Trail of Tears' (p52).

Europeans (mostly British, but some French and Spanish) began arriving in earnest in the 1600s, founding coastal cities like Charleston and turning large swaths of interior into farmland. As cultivation of labor-intensive crops like cotton and tobacco spread, so did slavery, even as it was abolished in the North. There were some four million slaves in the South by 1860, owned by a small minority of rich plantation masters. When abolitionist Abraham Lincoln became president that year, all of the South's nine states (except Kentucky) seceded, sparking the Civil War. Most were devastated when Union soldiers blazed through and crushed Confederate dreams.

For years the South was bitterly defined by the 'War of Northern Aggression' and its aftermath. The reconciliation and rebuilding process – formally known as Reconstruction – was slow indeed. Whites refused to integrate public spaces until the civil rights era, which was led by Atlanta-born preacher Martin Luther King Jr (see p447), and which ran through the 1960s. Both black and white activists joined King in the difficult and dangerous struggle, chipping away at institutionalized prejudice until African Americans gained equal treatment under the law.

The mid-20th century saw the rise of the 'New South' – metropolitan areas like Atlanta, Charlotte and Raleigh-Durham with economies based on technology and finance rather than agriculture. These cities became some of the fastest growing in America, bringing increasing liberalism and diversity to the region. While the South – like most places in America – still has work to do in promoting tolerance, it has made strides in embracing its mixture of African American, white and Latino cultures, along with an increasing number of overseas immigrants.

Everyone rallied around Mississippi and Louisiana in August 2005, when Hurricanes Katrina and Rita devastated the Gulf Coast, leaving much of New Orleans under water. Rebuilding efforts were still under way at press time, and could seemingly go on forever.

LOCAL CULTURE

Southerners have long been the butt of their fellow countrymen's jokes. They're slow-moving, hard-drinking, funny-talking and spend all their time fixing their pickup trucks and marrying their cousins. Or so the line goes. Well, while Southerners do tend to be relatively friendly and laid-back, the drawling country bumpkin is more the exception than the norm. Today's Southerner is just as likely to be a Mumbai-born motel owner in rural Arkansas, a fast-talking Atlanta investment banker with a glitzy high-rise condo, or a 20-something gay hipster in trendy Midtown Memphis.

Southerners do love sports, especially football, college basketball, and NASCAR, while fine arts thrive in historic cities like Charleston and Savannah, and college towns like Chapel Hill, Knoxville and Athens are famed for their indie-music scenes.

Religion is hugely important here – the so-called Bible Belt runs smack through the South, with about half of all Southerners identifying as Evangelical Christians. But even the most religious Southerners tend to be curious about, and tolerant of, other traditions.

So if you want to hang with Southerners – and they'd love to meet you – lose any hee-haw stereotypes you might be harboring and you'll have a great time.

LAND & CLIMATE

A humid summer day in the South can feel like sunbathing in Satan's sweaty armpit. This is especially true in the low-lying subtropical coastal regions and inland areas of South Carolina, Georgia, Mississippi and Louisiana, where a summer breeze is sometimes as good as a cold beer, and much harder to come by.

In the northern part of the region, mountains cool and dry out the air and the mountain rivers trickle into the fertile lands, especially in Arkansas' Ozark and Ouachita Mountains, in Tennessee's Blue Ridge Mountains, and in North Carolina where the foothills of the Appalachian Mountains thrust northward.

Tourism in the region peaks from June to September. Mild weather and blossoming flowers make spring (May to June) a good time to visit, and fall colors decorate the landscape in September and October, especially in the mountain regions.

PARKS & WILDLIFE

Parks in the South run the gamut, from the black-water swamps of South Carolina's Congaree National Park (p415), to the heathery peaks of Great Smoky Mountains National Park (p434) to the, well, mammoth, caverns of Kentucky's Mammoth Cave National Park (p441). Some parks honor people (Martin Luther King Jr National Historic Site in Georgia, p447, the Wright Brothers National Memorial in North Carolina, p392), others preserve historic and scenic passages (Natchez Trace Parkway from Mississippi to Tennessee, p432, the Blue Ridge Parkway in North Carolina, p401), mark significant Civil War battles (the National Military Park in Vicksburg, MS, p468, Shiloh National Military Park, TN, p423), or promote good old-fashioned relaxation (Arkansas' Hot Springs National Park, p496).

Learn more at the **National Park Service** (NPS; www.nps.gov) website or contact the states' park systems directly (see each state's Information section).

INFORMATION

No central tourism agency covers the entire South, but each state runs helpful visitor centers located at state borders along major highways. These places are stocked with highway maps, brochures and coupon books. (They also have cleaner restrooms than you're likely to find in off-ramp gas stations.) Visit the individual states online for specific information to help plan your trip ahead of time (see each state's Information section for details).

GETTING THERE & AROUND

With the world's busiest airport, Atlanta, Georgia is the main air gateway to the region. Memphis, TN, New Orleans, LA, and Charlotte and Raleigh, NC, have large regional airports. **Greyhound** (☎ 800-231-2222; www.greyhound.com) buses are frequent (if sometimes slow) and can be a dependable way to get from city to city (see p1160). A number of **Amtrak** (☎ 800-872-7245; www.amtrak.com) train routes traverse the South (see p1166). Beyond the cities – and often within them – you really need a car to get around.

Fortunately, this region has some good drives. These include the Blue Ridge Pkwy, the Natchez Trace Pkwy and Hwy 12 along North Carolina's Outer Banks. I-10 runs along the Gulf Coast from Florida to New Orleans; I-20 links South Carolina with Louisiana via Georgia, Alabama and Mississippi; and I-40 goes from North Carolina to Arkansas via Tennessee. The chief north–south routes include I-95, I-75, I-65 and I-55.

NORTH CAROLINA

It's trailer parks next to McMansions in North Carolina, where the Old South stands shoulder-to-shoulder with the New South. From the ancient mountains in the west to the sandy barrier islands of the Atlantic you'll find a variety of cultures and communities not easy to stereotype.

The fast-growing state is a patchwork of the progressive and the Stone Age: Asheville was named the 'New Freak Capital of the US' by *Rolling Stone,* while cohabitation of unmarried couples was technically illegal until 2006. The Raleigh area has the highest concentration of PhDs in the country, yet North Carolina routinely ranks 48th in education. Important industries range from tobacco and hogs to finance and nanotechnology.

Though the bulk of North Carolinians live in the business-oriented urban centers of the central Piedmont region, most travelers tend to stick to the scenic routes along the coast and through the Appalachian Mountains.

So come on down, ya'll, grab a plate of 'cue and watch the Duke Blue Devils and the Carolina Tar Heels battle it out on the basketball court – college hoops rival Jesus for Carolinians' souls.

History

Native Americans have inhabited North Carolina for more than 10,000 years. Major tribes included the Cherokee, in the mountains, the

Catawba in the Piedmont and the Waccamaw in the Coastal Plain.

North Carolina was the second territory to be colonized by the British, named in memory of King Charles I (Carolus in Latin), but the first colony to vote for independence from the crown. Several important Revolutionary War battles were fought here.

The state was a sleepy agricultural backwater through the 1800s, earning it the nickname the 'Rip Van Winkle State.' Divided on slavery (most residents were too poor to own slaves), North Carolina was the last state to secede during the Civil War, but went on to provide more Confederate soldiers than any other state.

North Carolina was a civil rights hotbed in the mid-20th century, with highly publicized lunch counter sit-ins in Greensboro and the formation of the influential Student Nonviolent Coordinating Committee (SNCC) in Raleigh. The later part of the century brought finance to Charlotte, and technology and medicine to the Raleigh-Durham area, driving a huge population boom and widening cultural diversity.

Information

North Carolina Division of Tourism (☎ 919-733-8372, 800-847-4862; www.visitnc.com; 301N N Wilmington St, Raleigh) Sends out good maps and information, including its annual *Official Travel Guide*.

North Carolina State Parks (☎ 919-733-4181; www.ncparks.gov) Offers info on North Carolina's 40 state parks, some of which have camping (prices range from free to more than $20 a night).

NORTH CAROLINA COAST

Which one of the following does not belong? A) windswept barrier islands; B) dignified Colonial villages once frequented by pirates; C) laid-back beach towns full of locally owned ice-cream shops and mom 'n' pop motels; D) flashy resort areas with megamalls and beach-

THE SOUTH...

In One Week

Fly into the Big Easy and stretch your legs with a **walking tour** (p479) of the legendary French Quarter before devoting your remaining time to celebrating jazz history and partying the night away on **Bourbon Street** (p476). Then wind your way upward through the languid Delta, stopping in Clarksdale for a sultry evening of blues at the **juke joints** (p466) before alighting in **Memphis** (p416) to walk in the footsteps of the King at **Graceland** (p417). From here, head on down the Music Hwy to **Nashville** to see Elvis's gold Cadillac at the **Country Music Hall of Fame** (p426) and practice your line dancing at the honky-tonks of (country-music club) the **District** (p426).

In Two to Three Weeks

Head east to hike amid the craggy peaks and waterfalls of **Great Smoky Mountains National Park** (p434) before a revitalizing overnight in the arty mountain town of **Asheville** (p400) and a tour of the scandalously opulent **Biltmore Estate** (p401), America's largest private home. Plow straight through to the coast to loll on the sandy barrier islands of the isolated **Outer Banks** (opposite), then head down the coast to finish up in **Charleston** (p404), with decadent food and postcard-pretty architecture.

For Foodies

Southern food is a journey unto itself. New Orleans is foodie central, thanks to oyster-stuffed po'boys (sandwiches) at **Domilise's Po-Boys** (p484) and *muffuletta* sandwiches at **Central Grocery** (p483). Memphis' legendary chopped-pork sandwich reaches its zenith at **Payne's Bar-B-Q** (p422), but Nashville counters with the flamingly hot fried chicken at **Prince's Hot Chicken** (p429), where the lines stretch out into the parking lot of a shabby strip mall. Devouring huge steaks in tumbledown (but James Beard Award–winning) **Doe's Eat Place** (p467) in Greenville is an unbeatable Delta experience, though the pork-stuffed tamales at **Abe's** (p467) over in Clarksdale come close. Head to the South Carolina coast to stuff yourself with ridiculously perfect fried shrimp in an old bait warehouse at the **Wreck of the Richard & Charlene** (p409) or head into Charleston for haute pig's feet at **FIG** (p410), the centerpiece of the city's hot nouvelle Southern dining scene.

NORTH CAROLINA FACTS

Nickname Tar Heel State
Population 9.2 million
Area 48,711 sq miles
Capital city Raleigh (population 375,806)
Other cities Charlotte (population 630,478)
Sales tax 7%, plus an additional hotel-occupancy tax of up to 6%
Birthplace of President James K Polk (1795–1849), jazzman John Coltrane (1926–67), NASCAR driver Richard Petty (b 1937), singer-songwriter Tori Amos (b 1963)
Home of America's first state university, the Biltmore House, Krispy Kreme doughnuts
Famous for *The Andy Griffith Show*, first airplane flight, college basketball
Pet name Natives are called 'tar heels,' a nickname of uncertain origin but said to be related to their pine tar production *and* their legendary stubbornness
Driving distances Asheville to Raleigh 247 miles, Raleigh to Wilmington 131 miles

themed chain restaurants. If you answered 'D,' buy yourself a celebratory shrimp sandwich. The North Carolina coast is relatively undeveloped, so even the most touristy beaches still have a small-town vibe. If it's solitude you seek, head to the isolated Outer Banks (OBX), where fishermen still make their living hauling in shrimp and the older locals speak in an archaic British-tinged brogue. Further south, Wilmington is known as a center of film and TV production and its surrounding beaches are popular with local spring breakers and tourists.

Outer Banks

These fragile ribbons of sand trace the coastline for 100 miles, cut off from the mainland by various sounds and waterways. From north to south, the barrier islands of Bodie (pronounced 'Body'), Roanoke, Hatteras and Ocracoke, essentially large sandbars, are linked by bridges and ferries. The far-northern communities of **Corolla** (pronounced kur-*all*-ah, not like the car), **Duck** and **Southern Shores** are former duck-hunting grounds for the northeastern rich, and are quiet and upscale. The nearly contiguous Bodie Island towns of **Kitty Hawk**, **Kill Devil Hills** and **Nags Head** are heavily developed and more populist in nature, with fried-fish joints, outdoor bars, motels and dozens of sandals 'n' sunblock shops. **Roanoke Island**, west of Bodie Island, is home to tons of Colonial history and the quaint waterfront town of **Manteo**. Further south, **Hatteras Island** is a protected national seashore with a few teeny villages and a wild, windswept beauty. At the tail end of the banks, wild ponies run free and salty old Bankers shuck oysters and weave hammocks on **Ocracoke Island**, accessible only by ferry.

A meandering drive down Hwy 12, which connects much of the Outer Banks, is one of the truly great American road trips, whether you come during the stunningly desolate winter months, or the sunny summer.

ORIENTATION

Hwy 12, also called Virginia Dare Trail, or 'the coast road,' runs close to the Atlantic for the length of the Outer Banks. US 158, usually called 'the Bypass,' begins just north of Kitty Hawk and merges with US 64 as it crosses onto Roanoke Island. Most of the tourist attractions and facilities are along the 16-mile strip of Bodie Island that includes Kitty Hawk, Kill Devil Hills and Nags Head. Locations are usually given in terms of 'Mileposts' (Mile or MP), beginning with Mile 0 at the foot of the Wright Memorial Bridge at Kitty Hawk, where US 158 crosses to the mainland. Just past Mile 16, US 64/264 crosses the Nags Head–Manteo Causeway ('the Causeway') to Roanoke Island and from there goes to the mainland. Hwy 12 continues south to Hatteras Island and, by ferry, to Ocracoke Island. While desolate in winter, Hwy 12 can become a parking lot in summer.

INFORMATION

The best sources of information are at the main **visitor centers** (9am-5pm; Hatteras ☎ 252-441-5711; Apr-Oct; Kitty Hawk (☎ 252-261-4644; Manteo ☎ 252-473-2138, 877-629-4386; Ocracoke ☎ 252-928-4531. Many smaller centers are open seasonally. Also useful is www.outerbanks.org. Corolla's **public library** (1123 Ocean Trail/Hwy 12) has free

THE SOUTH

internet access and the entire Manteo waterfront has free wi-fi.

SIGHTS

The following sights are listed in order north to south.

Currituck Heritage Park

The sunflower-yellow, art nouveau–style **Whalehead Club** (☎ 252-453-9040; www.whaleheadclub.org; Corolla; tours $7; sunrise-sunset), built in the 1920s as a hunting 'cottage' for a Philadelphia industrialist, is the centerpiece of this manicured park in the village of Corolla. You can also climb the **Currituck Beach Lighthouse** (adult/child $7/free) and visit the Victorian lighthouse keeper's home, or check out the modern **Outer Banks Center for Wildlife Education** (☎ 252-453-0221; admission free; 9am-5pm) for an interesting film on area history, info on local hiking trails, and duck-decoy carving classes.

Wright Brothers National Memorial

This **historic site** (☎ 252-473-2111; www.nps.gov/wrbr; Kitty Hawk; admission $4; 9am-5pm, to 6pm summer) is located among the same windswept Kitty Hawk dunes where self-taught engineers Wilbur and Orville Wright launched the world's first successful airplane flight on December 17, 1903 (it lasted 12 seconds). A boulder now marks the take-off spot. Climb a nearby hill where the brothers conducted earlier glider experiments for fantastic views of sea and sound. The on-site **Wright Brothers Visitor Center** has a reproduction of the 1903 flyer and offers exhibits and lectures on aviation history.

Fort Raleigh National Historic Site

In the late 1580s, three decades before the Pilgrims landed at Plymouth Rock, a group of 116 British colonists disappeared without a trace from their Roanoke Island settlement. Were they killed off by drought? Did they run away with a Native American tribe? Did they try to sail home and capsize? The fate of the 'Lost Colony' remains one of America's greatest mysteries, and the **visitor center** (☎ 252-473-5772; www.nps.gov/fora; 1401 National Park Dr, Manteo; 9am-5pm, to 6pm summer) has exhibits, artifacts, maps and a free film to fuel the imagination. Look for the prints based on 1585 illustrations by colony leader John White, now some of the best-known depictions of pre-European North America. A small mound nearby is meant to re-create the earthworks of the original fort.

Attractions at the site include the **Lost Colony Outdoor Drama** (☎ 252-473-3414, 866-468-7630; www.thelostcolony.org; adult/child $18/10; 8pm Mon-Sat Jun-Aug). This beloved long-running musical from Pulitzer Prize–winning North Carolina playwright Paul Green dramatizes the fate of the colonists. It plays at the Waterside Theater throughout summer.

The 16th-century-style **Elizabethan Gardens** (☎ 252-473-3234; www.elizabethangardens.org; adult/child $8/5; 9am-8pm daily summer, shorter hours off-season) include a Shakespearian herb garden and rows of beautifully manicured flower beds.

Just south of Fort Raleigh, head to the **North Carolina Aquarium** (☎ 252-473-3494, 866-332-3475; www.ncaquariums.com/roanoke-island; 374 Airport Rd, Roanoke Island; adult/child $8/6; 9am-5pm;) to watch tiger sharks glide through the gloomy depths, chill by the gator pond or stroke the slimy bellies of (de-barbed) stingrays in the touch tank. Great for kids.

Cape Hatteras National Seashore

Extending some 70 miles from south of Nags Head to the south end of Okracoke Island, this fragile necklace of islands remains blissfully free of overdevelopment. Natural attractions include local and migratory water birds, marshes, woodlands, dunes and miles of empty beaches. Don't miss the 156ft striped **Bodie Island Lighthouse**, south of Nags Head. You can't climb it, but it's darn photogenic. Other attractions (from north to south) follow.

At the northern end of Hatteras Island, the 5834-acre **Pea Island National Wildlife Refuge** (☎ 252-987-2394; www.fws.gov/peaisland; admission free; 9am-4pm, to 5pm summer) is a bird-watcher's heaven, with nature trails and 13 miles of unspoiled beach.

Built in 1874, the **Chicamacomico Lifesaving Station** (☎ 252-987-1552; www.chicamacomico.net; Rodanthe village; adult/child $5/4; noon-5pm Mon-Fri Apr-Oct) was the first lifesaving station in the state, now a museum filled with pre–Coast Guard artifacts.

At 208ft, the black-and-white-striped **Cape Hatteras Lighthouse** (☎ 252-995-4474; www.nps.gov/caha; climbing tours adult/child $7/3.50; 9am-4:30pm, to 5:30pm summer) is the tallest brick lighthouse in the US and is one of North Carolina's most iconic images. Climb the 248 steps and check out the visitor center (open year-round).

Graveyard of the Atlantic Museum (☎ 252-986-2995; www.graveyardoftheatlantic.com; Hatteras; admission by donation; 10am-4pm) is all about preserving the Outer Banks' maritime history, with exhibits about shipwrecks, piracy and salvaged cargo.

Ocracoke Island

Accessed via the free Hatteras–Ocracoke ferry, **Ocracoke Village** (252-928-6711; www.ocracokevillage.com) sits at the south end of 14-mile-long Ocracoke Island. It's a funky little village that's crowded in summer and desolate in winter, where the older residents still speak in the 17th-century British dialect known as 'Hoi Toide' (their pronunciation of 'high tide') and refer to non-islanders as 'dingbatters.' Edward Teach, AKA Blackbeard the pirate, used to hide out in the area and was killed here in 1718. You can camp by the beach where the wild ponies run, have a fish sandwich in a local pub, ride a rented scooter around the village's narrow streets or visit the 1823 **Ocracoke Lighthouse**, the oldest one still operating in North Carolina.

ACTIVITIES

The same strong wind that helped the Wright brothers launch their biplane today propels windsurfers, sailors and hang gliders. Other popular activities include kayaking, fishing, cycling, horse tours and scuba diving – all well catered for in the northern resort areas. The usually calm coastal waters kick up between August and October, creating perfect conditions for bodysurfing.

Back Country Outfitters (252-453-0877; www.outerbankstours.com; 107c Corolla Light Town Center; 2hr tour adult/child $46/23) offers guided 4WD tours over the dunes and through the maritime forest to see the unique wild mustang ponies that roam the Outer Banks.

Kitty Hawk Kites (252-441-4124, 877-359-2447; www.kittyhawkkites.com; 3933 Croatan Hwy, Nags Head; bike/kayak rental per day $25/39) has locations all over the Banks offering beginners' kiteboarding lessons (three hours $200) and hang-gliding lessons at Jockey's Ridge State Park (from $89). It also rents kayaks, sailboats, bikes and in-line skates and has a variety of tours and courses.

Nags Head Diving (252-473-1356; www.nagsheaddiving.com; 406 Uppowoc St, Manteo; scuba class $295, open-water dives $225, beach dives $30) has NAUI-certified instructors who run everything from basic classes to guided dives of the shipwrecks of the Graveyard of the Atlantic.

SLEEPING

Crowds swarm the Outer Banks in summer, so reserve in advance. The area has few massive chain hotels, but hundreds of small motels, efficiencies and B&Bs; the visitor centers offer referrals. Also check www.outer-banks.com. The following are open year-round; rates are for high season.

Campgrounds (800-365-2267; www.nps.gov/caha/planyourvisit/campgrounds.htm; campsites $20; P) The National Park Service runs four summer-only campgrounds on the islands, which feature cold-water showers and flush toilets. They are located at Oregon Inlet, near Bodie Island Lighthouse, Cape Point and Frisco near Cape Hatteras Lighthouse and **Ocracoke** (800-365-2267; www.recreation.gov) on Ocracoke Island. Only sites at Ocracoke can be reserved; the others are first-come, first-served.

Adventure Bound Campground (252-255-1130, 877-453-2545; 1004 W Kitty Hawk Rd, Kitty Hawk; campsites for 2 adults $20, additional adult/child $5/2.50; P) In a pleasant but out-of-the-way interior island location, this welcoming campsite has a newly renovated bathhouse with hot water and flush toilets, badminton, volleyball and shuffleboard courts, free use of fishing equipment, and tent rental.

our pick **Island Inn** (252-928-4351, 877-456-3466; www.ocracokeislandinn.com; 25 Lighthouse Rd, Ocracoke; r $59-139, villas per week $1200-1500; P) In Ocracoke Village, this grand old turn-of-the-century clapboard inn is built entirely from shipwrecked wood, with shabby-chic rooms with mismatched bedspreads, spooky oil portraits and pedestal sinks. Two-story modern 'villas' across the street are bright and beachy.

Buccaneer Motel (252-261-2030, 800-442-4412; www.buccaneermotelouterbanks.com; Mile 5 Kitty Hawk; r from $99; P) One of many deliciously retro motor motels lining the Coast Rd, the Buccaneer has clean, tile-floor rooms with wooden pirate swords on the doors, at bargain-basement rates.

Sanderling Resort & Spa (252-261-4111, 877-650-4812; www.thesanderling.com; 1461 Duck Rd, Duck; r $349-459; P) The poshest digs in the Outer Banks has impeccably tasteful neutral-toned rooms with decks and flat-screen TVs, several restaurants and bars, and a spa offering luxe oceanside massage.

EATING & DRINKING

The main tourist strip on Bodie Island has the most restaurants and nightlife, but only in season. The following are all non-chain places open year-round.

Howard's Pub (☎ 252-928-4441; Hwy 12, Ocracoke Village; mains $6-16; 🕑 11am-10pm Mon-Thu, to midnight Fri & Sat) has been around in one incarnation or another since the 1850s. Listen to live music on the big wooden porch while snacking on a crab cake sandwich and sipping a mug of one of the 200 beers of tap.

Awful Arthur's Oyster Bar (☎ 252-441-5955; Mile 6; mains $11-18; 🕑 11am-10:30pm) Oysters go down easy at this friendly restaurant and raw bar (emphasis on the 'bar'), as do the excellent soft-shell crab sandwiches and sky-high, homemade key lime pie. Don't be shy about ordering a beer before noon; the locals aren't.

Jolly Roger (☎ 252-441-6530; Mile 6.5, Kill Devil Hills; mains $11-24; 🕑 6am-late) The atmosphere in this OBX institution could be described as 'pirate bordello,' with Christmas lights, mermaid murals and evening karaoke contests. Come for huuuuge Southern breakfasts, groaning platters of shrimp fettuccine, or late-night burgers at the bar.

Blue Point (☎ 252-261-8090; 1240 Duck Rd, Duck; mains $20-32; 🕑 11:30am-2pm & 5-9:30pm Tue-Sun, 5-9:30pm Mon) Overlooking Currituck Sound in the upscale town of Duck, this contemporary bistro serves refined Southern coastal cuisine – think seared sea scallops over arugula – and is considered by many to be the best fine dining on the Banks. At lunchtime, paninis and fancy salads are delicious and reasonably priced.

GETTING THERE & AWAY

If you're driving, access Hwy 12 (the main road along the cape) from Hwy 158 at Kitty Hawk or from Hwy 64/264, which leads over Roanoke Island to the park's northern entrance.

No public transportation exists to or on the Outer Banks. However, the **North Carolina Ferry System** (☎ 800-293-3779; www.outer-banks.com/ferry) operates several routes, including the free 40-minute Hatteras–Ocracoke car ferry, which runs at least hourly from 5am to 10pm; reservations aren't necessary. North Carolina ferries also run between Ocracoke and Cedar Island (one way $15, 2¼ hours) and Ocracoke and Swan Quarter on the mainland ($15, 2½ hours) every two hours or so; reservations are recommended in summer.

Crystal Coast

The southern Outer Banks are collectively called the 'Crystal Coast,' at least for tourist offices' promotional purposes. Less rugged than the northern beaches, they include several historic coastal towns, a number of sparsely populated islands, and some vacation-friendly beaches.

A rather unappealing industrial and commercial stretch of US 70 goes through **Morehead City**, with plenty of chain hotels and restaurants. Get information from the well-stocked **Crystal Coast Visitors Bureau** (☎ 252-726-8148; www.crystalcoastnc.org; 3407 Arendell St/Hwy 70; 🕑 9am-5pm Mon-Fri, from 10am Sat & Sun).

Postcard-pretty **Beaufort** (*bow*-fort), the third-oldest town in the state, has a charming boardwalk and mountains of B&Bs. The pirate Blackbeard was a frequent visitor to the area in the early 1700s – in 1996 the wreckage of his flagship, the *Queen Anne's Revenge*, was discovered at the bottom of Beaufort Inlet. See artifacts from the ship and meet modern shipbuilders at the **North Carolina Maritime Museum** (☎ 252-728-7317; www.ncmaritimemuseum.org; 315 Front St; admission free; 🕑 9am-5pm Mon-Sat, from 1pm Sun). Blackbeard himself is said to have lived in the Hammock House off Front St. You can't go inside, but some claim you can still hear the screams of the pirate's murdered wife at night.

Small ferries leave regularly from the Beaufort boardwalk for the isolated islands of the **Cape Lookout National Seashore** (www.nps.gov/calo; ferries $14-25). Highlights include **Shackleford Banks**, an uninhabited sandbar with spectacular seashells and herds of wild ponies, and the diamond-patterned **Cape Lookout Lighthouse**. Primitive camping is allowed in some areas – the coolest place to sleep is on **Portsmouth Island**, where you can wander an abandoned 18th-century settlement and sleep on the beach. Hire a private ferry from Beaufort or Ocracoke and bring plenty of bug spray – the mosquitoes are absolutely notorious. There are also rustic multiroom **cabins** (☎ South Core 252-241-6783, North Core 252-732-4424; www.nps.gov/calo; from $73) popular with fishermen.

The **Bogue Banks**, across the Sound from Morehead City via the Atlantic Beach Causeway, have several well-trafficked beach communities – try Atlantic Beach if you like the smell of coconut suntan oil and doughnuts. Pine Knoll Shores is home to the **North Carolina Aquarium** (☎ 252-247-4003;

www.ncaquariums.com; 1 Roosevelt Blvd; adult/child $8/5; 9am-5pm;), with an ultracool exhibit recreating local shipwrecks. In Atlantic Beach, **Fort Macon State Park** (252-726-3775; www.ncparks.gov; admission free; 8am-9pm in summer, shorter hours in winter) draws crowds to its reconstructed Civil War fort.

Wilmington

Wilmington may not have the name recognition of other antebellum tourist destinations like Charleston and Savannah, but eastern North Carolina's largest city has historic neighborhoods, azalea-choked gardens and cute cafés aplenty. All that plus reasonable hotel prices and a lack of crowds make Wilmington a hidden gem, in our book. At night the historic riverfront downtown becomes the playground for local college students, tourists and the occasional Hollywood type – there are so many movie studios here the town has earned the nickname 'Wilmywood'.

Wilmington sits at the mouth of the Cape Fear River, about 8 miles from the beach. The **visitor center** (910-341-4030, 800-222-4757; 24 N 3rd St; 8:30am-5pm Mon-Fri, 9am-4pm Sat, from 1pm Sun), in the 1892 courthouse building, has a walking-tour map. A **free trolley** (7:20am-9:20pm Mon-Fri, 11am-9:20pm Sat, 11am-6pm Sun) runs through the historic district.

SIGHTS

Wander beneath the wisteria at **Airlie Gardens** (910-798-7700; www.airliegardens.org; 300 Airlie Rd; adult/child $5/3; 9am-5pm, closed Sun winter), 67 acres of bewitching formal flower beds, lakes and trails.

Take a river taxi ($5 round-trip) or cross the Cape Fear Bridge to reach the **Battleship North Carolina** (910-251-5797; www.battleshipnc.com; adult/child $12/6; 8am-5pm, to 8pm summer). Self-guided tours take you through the decks of this 45,000-ton megaship, which earned 15 battle stars in the Pacific theater in WWII before being decommissioned in 1947.

Screen Gems Studios (910-343-3433; www.screengemsstudios.com; 1223 N 23rd St; adult/child $12/5; noon & 2pm Sat & Sun summer) offers a fun, one-hour, behind-the-scenes tour of the working studio where shows such as *Dawson's Creek* and *One Tree Hill* were filmed.

our pick **Cape Fear Serpentarium** (910-762-1669; www.capefearserpentarium.com; 20 Orange St; admission $8; 11am-5pm Mon-Fri, to 6pm Sat & Sun) is the place to go if you don't mind keeping reptilian company. You can gawk at yellow eyelash vipers, read about how it feels to die from the bite of the deadly bushmaster, and, at 3pm on Saturday and Sunday, watch gonzo herpetologist/ringmaster Dean Ripa hand-feed mice to his 100-plus species of beasties.

SLEEPING & EATING

There are numerous budget hotels and a Kampgrounds of America campground on Market St, just north of downtown. Restaurants directly on the waterfront can be crowded and mediocre; head a block or two inland for the best eats and nightlife.

Wilmingtonian (910-343-1800; www.thewilmingtonian.com; 101 S Second St; d from $140; P) Right downtown, cheery, tile-floored suites cluster around a humble courtyard. Rooms in the 1841 de Rosset House wing, across the street, are much more elegant.

Graystone Inn (910-763-2000; www.graystoneinn.com; 100 S 3rd St; r incl breakfast $169-379; P) Built as the home of a turn-of-the-century railroad magnate, this imposing Renaissance-style mansion has nine splendiferous guest rooms with period furnishings like claw-foot tubs, all walking distance from the downtown action.

Front Street Brewery (910-251-1935; 9 N Front St; mains $6-14; 11:30am-10pm Sun-Wed, to 2am Thu-Sat) This two-story downtown pub is madly popular for simple grub like drippy burgers and crab cakes, and for its microbrews. There are free beer tastings and brewery tours every Wednesday from 6pm to 8pm.

Deluxe (910-251-0333; 114 Market St; mains $23-32; 5:30-10pm daily, brunch 10:30am-2pm Sun) This arty little bistro, all exposed brick and antique wood, works magic with seafood. Think tempura lobster tail with wasabi cream, and curried mussels with sesame crostini.

THE TRIANGLE

In the central North Carolina region known as the Piedmont, the cities of Raleigh, Durham and Chapel Hill form a rough triangle. Three top research universities – Duke, University of North Carolina, and North Carolina State – are located here, as is the 7000-acre computer and biotech-office campus known as Research Triangle Park. Swarming with egghead computer programmers, bearded peace activists and hip young families, each town has its own unique personality, despite being only

WILMINGTON-AREA BEACHES

While riverfront Wilmington doesn't have its own beach, there are plenty of sandy stretches just a few minutes away.

From north to south:

Surf City A low-key beach town with good waves.

Topsail Beach Clean, white-sand beach, home to sea turtle rehab center.

Wrightsville Beach The closest beach to Wilmington, with plenty of fried-fish joints, sunglass shops and summer crowds.

Carolina Beach Warm water and boardwalk equal row upon row of beach umbrellas.

Kure Beach Popular fishing beach and home to the North Carolina Aquarium at Fort Fisher.

Southport Not a swimming beach, but a quaint town with tons of antique stores.

Bald Head Island Accessible by ferry from Southport, this secluded sea turtle sanctuary forbids cars, making travel difficult for those for who don't rent a golf cart.

Caswell Beach A quiet beach with nearby golf course.

Oak Island The largest beach community in North Carolina, with three piers.

a few miles apart. Come here in March to see everyone – we mean *everyone* – go crazy for college basketball.

GETTING THERE & AROUND

Raleigh-Durham International Airport (RDU; ☎ 919-840-2123; www.rdu.com), a significant hub, is a 25-minute drive northwest of downtown Raleigh. **Carolina Trailways/Greyhound** (Raleigh ☎ 919-834-8275; 314 W Jones St; Durham ☎ 919-687-4800; 820 W Morgan St) serve Raleigh and Durham. The **Triangle Transit Authority** (☎ 919-549-9999; www.triangletransit.org; adult $2) operates buses linking Raleigh, Durham and Chapel Hill, and all three to the airport.

Raleigh

Founded in 1792 specifically to serve as the state capital, Raleigh remains a rather staid government town with some major sprawl issues. Still, the handsome downtown has some neat (and free!) museums and galleries, and the food and music scene is on the upswing. The older, more interesting parts of town are referred to as 'Inside the Beltway.'

The **Raleigh Convention & Visitors Bureau** (☎ 866-724-8687; www.visitraleigh.com; 220 Fayetteville St; 🕑 10am-5pm Mon-Sat) hands out maps and other info.

SIGHTS

North Carolina Museum of Art (☎ 919-839-6262; www.ncartmuseum.org; 2110 Blue Ridge Rd; admission free; 🕑 9am-5pm Tue-Thu & Sat, 9am-9pm Fri, 10am-5pm Sun) is located on the western fringe of town and has a fine collection including works by masters from Raphael to Monet to Georgia O'Keeffe. Summer movies and concerts on the rolling lawn are delightful.

North Carolina Museum of History (☎ 919-807-7900; www.ncmuseumofhistory.org; 5 E Edenton St; admission free; 🕑 9am-5pm Mon-Sat, from noon Sun) has all kinds of artifacts, such as Civil War photos, Cherokee crafts, 19th-century costumes and a special exhibit on stockcar racing.

See Willo, the world's only dinosaur with a heart (it's fossilized), at the modern, airy **North Carolina Museum of Natural Sciences** (☎ 919-733-7450; www.naturalsciences.org; 11 W Jones St; admission free; 🕑 9am-5pm Mon-Sat, from noon Sun). There's also a unique and scary Acrocanthosaurus skeleton, five habitat dioramas and lots of well-done taxidermy.

SLEEPING & EATING

Downtown is pretty quiet on nights and weekends, except for the City Market area at E Martin and S Person Sts. Just to the northwest, the Glenwood South neighborhood hops with cafés, bars and clubs. You'll find plenty of moderately priced chain hotels around Exit 10 off I-440 and off I-40 near the airport.

William B Umstead State Park (☎ 919-571-4170; www.ncparks.gov; 8801 Glenwood Ave; campsites $18) Pitch your tent under the oaks at this 5439-acre suburban park, convenient to Raleigh, Durham and Chapel Hill.

Umstead Hotel & Spa (☎ 919-447-4000; www.theumstead.com; 100 Woodland Pond, Cary; r from $279; P ⊠ ✣ 💻 ᯤ 🏊) Computer chips embedded in the silver room-service trays alert bellboys to whisk away leftovers post haste at this lavish new boutique hotel. How's that for taking care of details? In a wooded suburban office park, the Umstead caters to visiting biotech CEOs with simple, sumptuous rooms and a Zen-like spa.

Poole's Downtown Diner (☎ 919-832-4477; 426 S McDowell St; mains $9-15; 6pm-midnight Wed-Sat, brunch 10:30am-3pm Sat) Chef Ashley Christensen sautés burgers in duck fat and bakes the world's most exquisitely creamy mac 'n' cheese at this new Southern diner–meets–Parisian bistro, the toast of the local food scene. Don't miss the haute takes on classic American pies like banana cream.

Durham

Home to world-class Duke University and Duke Hospital, Durham currently bills itself as the 'City of Medicine.' But 100 years ago it could just as easily have called itself 'City of Cigarettes.' Built on the fortunes of the Bull Durham and American Tobacco companies, its main industry collapsed when smoking began to go out of style in the 1960s, leaving behind acres of brick tobacco warehouses, now art galleries, cafés and condos. Though still fundamentally a working-class Southern city, Durham's making its name as a hot spot for foodies, gays and lesbians, lefty rabble-rousers and the rest of the 'creative class' set.

Hubs of activity include Brightleaf Sq and the American Tobacco Campus, downtown tobacco warehouses turned upscale pedestrian shopping and dining areas, and boutique-lined, New Agey Ninth St, near Duke campus.

The **visitor center** (☎ 919-687-0288, 800-446-8604; www.durham-nc.com; 101 E Morgan St; 8:30am-5pm Mon-Fri, 10am-2pm Sat) has information and maps.

SIGHTS

Endowed by the Duke family's cigarette fortune, **Duke University** (☎ 919-684-2572; www.duke.edu) has a Georgian-style East Campus and a neo-Gothic West Campus notable for its towering 1930s chapel. Heavenly **Sarah P Duke Gardens** (☎ 919-684-3698; www.hr.duke.edu/dukegardens; 426 Anderson St; admission free; 8am-dusk) include 55 acres of koi ponds, terraced rose gardens and magnolia groves, where students and visitors play Frisbee on warm afternoons. The university's **Nasher Museum of Art** (☎ 919-684-5135; www.nasher.duke.edu; 2001 Campus Dr; adult/child $5/free; 10am-5pm Tue-Sat, to 9pm Thu, from noon Sun) houses an impressive collection of international contemporary works in an even more impressive futuristic cube of a building.

our pick **Duke Lemur Center** (☎ 919-489-3364; www.lemur.duke.edu;) is the coolest of all, with the largest collection of endangered prosimian primates outside their native Madagascar. Only a robot could fail to melt at the sight of these big-eyed fuzzy-wuzzies. Call well in advance for tours, held Monday to Saturday by appointment only.

In 1865, Confederate general Joseph E Johnston surrendered 90,000 troops to Union general William T Sherman at the humble **Bennett Place** (☎ 919-383-4345; 4409 Bennett Memorial Rd; 9am-5pm Tue-Sat) farmstead, effectively ending the Civil War. Free guided tours start every half-hour.

Have a quintessentially American afternoon of beer and baseball watching the minor-league Durham Bulls (of 1988 Kevin Costner film *Bull Durham* fame), who play from April to September at the **Durham Bulls Athletic Park** (☎ 919-956-2855; www.dbulls.com; 409 Blackwell St; tickets $7-9;).

SLEEPING & EATING

There are plenty of cheap chain motels off I-85 in north Durham. Downtown's Brightleaf Square area, on W Morgan St, has several good coffee shops, restaurants and bars.

Duke Tower (☎ 919-687-4444, 866-385-3869; www.duketower.com; 807 W Trinity Ave; ste $85; P) For less than most local hotel rooms you can have a contemporary condo with hardwood floors, full kitchen and flat-screen TV, in Durham's historic downtown tobacco-mill district.

Guglhupf Bakery (☎ 919-401-2600; 2706 Durham-Chapel Hill Blvd; mains $5-10; 7am-6pm Tue-Sat, 9am-3pm Sun) Mornings, a tart cherry Danish and a cappuccino are the way to go at this superior German-style bakery and café. In the afternoon, try a Westphalian ham sandwich and a pilsner on the sunny patio.

our pick **Watts Grocery** (☎ 919-416-5040; 1116 Broad St; mains $14-18; 11am-2:30pm & 5:30-10pm Tue-Thu & Sun, 11am-2:30pm & 5:30pm-midnight Fri & Sat) Durham's hippest 'farm-to-table' joint serves upscale takes on local bounty (think bourbon-glazed pork belly, hand-cut buttermilk onion rings) in an airy renovated storefront. Sausage- and avocado-laden bowls of grits might be the best weekend brunch in town. The late-night menu features homemade ice-cream sandwiches. Magic.

Chapel Hill & Carrboro

The ultraconservative North Carolina senator Jesse Helms once famously said, 'Why build

IF YOU HAVE A FEW MORE DAYS

Ten miles north of Chapel Hill, the 18th-century village of **Hillsborough** (www.historichillsborough.org) is as scenic as they come, with several historic homes and schools open for tours.

An hour-and-a-half west of Durham in the city of Winston-Salem is **Old Salem** (☎ 336-721-7300; www.oldsalem.org; 924 S Main St; adult/child $17/10; 🕑 9:30am-4:30pm Tue-Sat, from 1pm Sun), a village settled in the late 1700s by Moravians, a Protestant sect originally from Central Europe. Today costumed interpreters make shoes, spin cotton and bake in the restored original buildings. The sugar bread and thin spice cookies baked in the real stone ovens at the Winkler Bakery are particularly popular.

An hour-and-a-half southwest of Chapel Hill is the town of **Seagrove** (www.discoverseagrove.com), a community of potters that dates back to the 1700s. Today you can wander studios looking at everything from heavy folk-art jugs to delicate hand-painted ceramic platters.

a zoo when we can just put a fence around Chapel Hill?' This funky, forward-thinking little college town took that as a compliment. The University of North Carolina (UNC) was founded here in 1789 as the first state university in the nation and has set the tone every since. Music, especially indie rock and alternative country, is huge, as is basketball – Michael Jordan leaped to fame during his tenure at UNC.

Chapel Hill's main drag is Franklin St, with shops, bars and restaurants on its north side and the UNC campus to the south; the same street enters the hip former mill town of **Carrboro** to the west. Here, the big lawn at **Weaver Street Market** (www.weaverstreetmarket.com) grocery co-op serves as an informal town square, with live music and free wi-fi.

Pick up good area information from the **Chapel Hill-Orange County Visitors Bureau** (☎ 919-968-2060, 888-968-2060; www.chocvb.org; 501 W Franklin St; 🕑 8:30am-5pm Mon-Fri, 10am-2pm Sat). Downtown Chapel Hill and Carrboro have free wi-fi.

SLEEPING & EATING

You'll find most restaurants and nightspots along Franklin St. Just to the west, Carrboro attracts post-college hippies and hipsters.

Inn at Celebrity Dairy (☎ 919-742-5176; www.celebritydairy.com; 144 Celebrity Dairy Way; r incl breakfast $90-150; P ⊠) Thirty miles west of town in rural Chatham County, this working goat dairy offers B&B accommodations in a Greek Revival farmhouse. Enjoy goat's-cheese omelets for breakfast then head out to the barn to pet the goat who provided the milk. You can also come for the Sunday lunch, served on the third Sunday of each month.

Allen & Son's Barbecue (☎ 919-942-7576; 6203 Millhouse Rd; mains $7-10; 🕑 10am-5pm Tue-Wed, to 8pm Thu-Sat) Owner Keith Allen splits his own hickory wood behind this cinder-block cabin to smoke what many consider the best pork BBQ in the state. Try it topped with slaw on a soft bun with a side of hush puppies (balls of fried cornmeal) and a slice of frozen peanut butter pie.

Crook's Corner (☎ 919-929-7643; 610 W Franklin St; mains $7-25; 🕑 5:30-10pm Tue-Sun, brunch 10:30am-2pm Sun) Topped by a folk-art sculpture of a pig, Crook's is a longtime institution for Southern food that ranges from the down-home (pit BBQ sandwiches) to the haute (T-bone with horseradish butter), and is always good for an elegant cocktail in the bamboo-shaded patio.

DRINKING & ENTERTAINMENT

For entertainment listings, pick up the free weekly **Independent** (www.indyweek.com).

Top of the Hill (☎ 919-929-8276; 100 E Franklin St) The second-story patio of this downtown restaurant and microbrewery is *the* place for the preppy set to see and be seen after football games.

Cat's Cradle (☎ 919-968-4345; www.catscradle.com; 300 E Main St, Carrboro) This place has been hosting the cream of the indie-music world for 32 years. The 600-capacity venue is smoke-free and most shows are all-ages.

CHARLOTTE

The largest city in North Carolina and the biggest US banking center after New York, Charlotte has the sprawling, sometimes faceless look of many New South suburban megalopolises. But although Queen City, as it's known, is primarily a business town, it's got a few good museums, stately old neighborhoods and lots of fine food.

Busy Tryon St cuts through skyscraper-filled 'uptown' Charlotte, home to banks, hotels, museums and restaurants. The renovated textile mills of the NoDa neighborhood (named for its location on N Davidson St) and the funky mix of boutiques and restaurants in the Plaza-Midwood area, just northeast of uptown, have a hipper vibe.

The downtown **visitor center** (☎ 704-331-2700, 800-231-4636; www.charlottesgotalot.com; 330 S Tryon St; 8:30am-5pm Mon-Fri, 9am-3pm Sat) publishes maps and a visitor's guide. The **public library** (☎ 704-336-2725; 301 N College St; 9am-9pm Mon-Thu, to 6pm Fri & Sat, from 1pm Sun) has 90 terminals with free internet. Check out the alt-weekly **Creative Loafing** (http://charlotte.creativeloafting.com) for entertainment listings.

Sights & Activities

The slick **Levine Museum of the New South** (☎ 704-333-1887; www.museumofthenewsouth.org; 200 E 7th St; adult/child $6/5; 10am-5pm Mon-Sat, from noon Sun) has an informative permanent exhibit on post–Civil War Southern history and culture, from sharecropping to sit-ins.

The **Mint Museum of Art** (☎ 704-337-2000; www.mintmuseum.org; 2730 Randolph Rd; adult/child $10/5; 10am-9pm Tue, 10am-5pm Wed-Sat, noon-5pm Sun) is housed in the imposing 19th-century US mint building. The hushed halls display historic maps, American paintings and an impressive number of gruesome Spanish Colonial bleeding saint statues. Your ticket also gets you into the **Mint Museum of Craft & Design** (200 N Tryon St), which chronicles the history of glass, wood, metal, and jewelry crafts.

Wander through a rainforest, peer inside a huge eyeball or sample liquid-nitrogen ice cream in the chemistry lab at the hands-on **Discovery Place** (☎ 704-372-6261; www.discoveryplace.org; 301 N Tryon St; adult/child $10/8; 9am-4pm Mon-Fri, 10am-6pm Sat, from noon Sun) science museum, complete with an **Omnimax cinema** (adult/child $11/9).

NASCAR races, a homegrown Southeastern obsession, are held at the visible-from-outer-space **Lowe's Motor Speedway** (☎ 704-455-3200; www.lowesmotorspeedway.com; tours $5; tours 9:30am-3:30pm Mon-Sat, from 1:30pm Sun), 12 miles northeast of town. For the ultimate thrill/near-death experience, ride shotgun at up to 165 miles per hour in a real stockcar with the **Richard Petty Driving Experience** (☎ 800-237-3889; www.1800bepetty.com; rides from $149).

Sleeping

Because so many uptown hotels cater to the business traveler, rates are often lower on weekends. Cheaper chains cluster off I-85 and I-77.

Blake Hotel (☎ 704-372-4100; www.theblakehotel.net; 555 South McDowell St; r from $129; P) All black leather, chrome and tiger print, this 308-room uptown hotel practically screams 'hey baby, what's your sign?'. Yes, that's a real lava lamp in the cocktail lounge.

Duke Mansion (☎ 704-714-4400; www.dukemansion.com; 400 Hermitage Rd; r from $169; P) Tucked away in an oak-shaded residential neighborhood, this stately, white-columned inn was the residence of 19th-century tobacco millionaire James B Duke and still retains the quiet, discreet feel of a posh private home. Most rooms have high ceilings and their own screened-in sleeping porches.

Eating & Drinking

Uptown eating and drinking options cater to the preppy young banker set; you'll see more tattoos at the laid-back pubs and bistros of NoDa.

Bar-B-Q King (☎ 704-399-8344; 2900 Wilkinson Blvd; mains $4-9; 10:30am-10:30pm Tue-Thu, 10am-11:30pm Fri & Sat) Wilkinson Blvd, the first four-lane highway in North Carolina, has several retro drive-ins, including this venerable place where carhops deliver minced-pork platters and perfectly-fried trout sandwiches to your driver's side window.

Price's Chicken Coop (☎ 704-333-9866; 1614 Camden Rd; mains $5-10; 10am-6pm Tue-Sat) A Charlotte institution, scruffy Price's regularly makes 'Best Fried Chicken in America' lists. Line up to order your 'dark quarter' or 'white half' from the army of white-jacketed cooks, then take your bounty outside – there's no seating.

Rí Rá (☎ 704-333-5554; 208 N Tryon St) A friendly mixed-age crowd downs Guinness and nibbles fish-and-chips at this cozy uptown pub, meticulously outfitted with worn brass and burnished wood to transport you to Victorian Ireland.

Getting There & Around

Charlotte Douglas International Airport (CLT; ☎ 704-359-4027; www.charmeck.org/departments/airport; 5501 Josh Birmingham Pkwy) is a US Airways hub with direct flights from Europe and the UK. Both the **Greyhound station** (☎ 704-375-3332; 601 W

Trade St) and **Amtrak** (☎ 704-376-4416; 1914 N Tryon St) are handy to Uptown. **Charlotte Area Transit** (☎ 704-336-3366; www.charmeck.org) runs local bus and light-rail services; its main station is at 310 E Trade St.

NORTH CAROLINA MOUNTAINS

Seekers of all sorts have been drawn to these ancient mountains for hundreds of years. The Cherokee came to hunt, Scots-Irish immigrants came in the 1700s looking for a better life, fugitives hid from the law in the deep forests, the ill came to take in the fresh air, and naturalists came to hike the craggy trails.

The Appalachians in the western part of the state include the Great Smoky, Blue Ridge, Pisgah and Black Mountain subranges. Carpeted in blue-green hemlock, pine and oak trees, these cool hills are home to cougars, deer, black bears, wild turkeys and great horned owls. Hiking, camping, climbing and rafting adventures abound, and there's another jaw-dropping photo opportunity around every bend.

High Country

The northwestern corner of the state is known as 'High Country.' Its main towns are Boone, Blowing Rock and Banner Elk, all short drives from the Blue Ridge Pkwy. **Boone** is a lively college town, home to Appalachian State University (ASU). **Blowing Rock** and **Banner Elk** are quaint tourist centers near the winter ski areas.

The High Country **visitor center** (☎ 828-264-1299, 800-438-7500; www.highcountryhost.com; 1700 Blowing Rock Rd, Boone; 9am-5pm) has info on accommodations and outdoors outfitters.

Hwy 321 from Blowing Rock to Boone is studded with gem-panning mines and other tourist traps. **Tweetsie Railroad** (☎ 828-264-9061; www.tweetsie.com; adult/child $30/22;), is a much-loved Wild West–themed amusement park – opening hours vary by season.

Grandfather Mountain (☎ 800-468-7325; www.grandfather.com; Blue Ridge Pkwy Mile 305; adult/child $15/7; 8am-6pm) rakes in car tourists who tiptoe across its vertigo-inducing mile-high suspension bridge. Lose the crowds on one of 11 hiking trails, the most difficult of which include steep hands-and-knees scrambles.

River and Earth Adventures (☎ 828-963-5491; www.raftcavehike.com; 1655 Hwy 105, Boone; half-/full-day rafting from $65/85) offers everything from family-friendly caving trips to rafting Class V rapids at Watauga Gorge. Ecoconscious guides even pack organic lunches. Bike and kayak rentals available.

SLEEPING & EATING

Chain motels abound in Boone. You'll find private campgrounds and B&Bs scattered throughout the hills.

Grandfather Mountain Campground (☎ 828-738-1111, 800-788-2582; www.grandfatherrv.com; Hwy 105N; campsites from $20, cabins from $50; P) Though popular with RVers, this roadside campground, just outside Banner Elk, is pleasant enough for tent campers and has clean bathhouses and good-value camping cabins.

Mast Farm Inn (☎ 828-963-5857, 888-963-5857; www.mastfarminn.com; 2543 Broadstone Rd, Blowing Rock; r/cottages from $149/200; P) In the achingly beautiful hamlet of Valle Crucis, this restored farmhouse defines rustic chic with worn hardwood floors, claw-foot tubs, and handmade toffees on your bedside table. The upscale mountain cuisine at the inn's restaurant, Simplicity, is worth a trip in itself.

Knights on Main (☎ 828-295-3869; 870 Main St, Blowing Rock; mains $7-17; 7am-8:30pm, to 2:30pm Sun) This wood-paneled family diner is *the* place to try livermush, a mountain specialty consisting of…well, you can guess.

Asheville

This Jazz Age gem of a city appears like a mirage out of the mists of the Blue Ridge Mountains. Long a vacation destination for moneyed East Coasters (F Scott Fitzgerald was a fan), the city now has a huge artist population and a highly visible contingent of hard-core hippies. The art-deco buildings of downtown remain much the same as they were in 1930, though the area is now hopping with decidedly modern boutiques, restaurants, vintage stores and record shops. Visit Asheville once, and you'll likely find yourself perusing local real-estate listings on the sly once you've returned home.

Downtown is compact and easy to negotiate on foot. West Ashville is an up-and-coming area, still gritty but very cool. The shiny new **visitor center** (☎ 828-258-6129; www.exploreasheville.com; 36 Montford Ave; 9am-5pm) is at I-240 exit 4C.

Malaprop's Bookstore & Cafe (☎ 828-254-6734; www.malaprops.com; 55 Haywood St; 8am-9pm Mon-Sat, to 7pm Sun) is beloved for its used books, cappuccino, and free wi-fi.

SCENIC DRIVE: THE BLUE RIDGE PARKWAY

Commissioned by president Franklin D Roosevelt as a Depression-era public-works project, the glorious Blue Ridge Pkwy traverses the southern Appalachians from Virginia's Shenandoah National Park (see p375 and p378) at Mile 0 to the Great Smoky Mountains National Park (p402) at Mile 469. North Carolina's piece of the parkway twists and turns for 262 miles of killer alpine vistas. The National Park Service **campgrounds and visitor centers** (☎ 877-444-6777; www.blueridgeparkway.org; tent sites $16) are open May to October. Parkway entrance is free; be aware that restrooms and gas stations are few and far between.

Parkway highlights and campgrounds include the following:

Cumberland Knob Mile 217.5 – NPS visitor center, easy walk to the knob.
Doughton Park Mile 241.1 – Gas, food, trails and camping.
Blowing Rock Mile 291.8 – Small tourist town, named for a craggy, commercialized cliff that offers great views, occasional updrafts and a Native American love story.
Moses H Cone Memorial Park Mile 294.1 – A lovely old estate with pleasant walks and a craft shop.
Julian Price Memorial Park Mile 296.9 – Camping.
Grandfather Mountain Mile 305.1 – Hugely popular for its mile-high pedestrian 'swinging bridge.'
Linville Falls Mile 316.4 – Short hiking trails to the falls, campsites.
Linville Caverns Mile 317 – Limestone cave with neat formations and underground streams; tours $7.
Little Switzerland Mile 334 – Old-style mountain resort.
Crabtree Meadows Mile 339.5 – Camping.
Mt Mitchell State Park Mile 355.5 – Highest peak east of the Mississippi (6684ft); hiking and camping.
Craggy Gardens Mile 364 – Hiking trails explode with rhododendron blossoms in summer.
Folk Art Center Mile 382 – Local crafts for sale.
Mount Pisgah Mile 408.8 – Hiking and camping.

The **public library** (☎ 828-250-4711; 67 Haywood Ave; 🕒 10am-8pm Mon-Thu, to 6pm Fri, 2-5pm Sat) has computers with free internet.

SIGHTS

With 43 bathrooms, 65 fireplaces and a private bowling alley, the Gilded Age **Biltmore Estate** (☎ 828-225-1333, 800-624-1575; www.biltmore.com; adult/child under 17 $50/free; 🕒 9am-4:30pm), is a veritable American Versailles. The country's largest private home and Asheville's number-one tourist attraction, it was built in 1895 for shipping and railroad heir George Washington Vanderbilt II, who modeled it after the grand chateaux he'd seen on his various European jaunts. Viewing the estate and its 250 acres of gorgeously manicured grounds and gardens takes several hours. There are numerous cafés, a gift shop the size of a small supermarket, a hoity-toity hotel, and an award-winning winery offering free tastings.

Downtown, *Look Homeward Angel* author Thomas Wolfe's childhood home is now the **Thomas Wolfe Memorial** (☎ 828-253-8304; www.wolfememorial.com; 52 N Market St; admission $1; 🕒 9am-5pm Tue-Sat, 10am-4pm winter, 1-5pm Sun), displaying artifacts from his brief life.

At **Chimney Rock Park** (☎ 828-625-9611; www.chimneyrockpark.com; adult/child $14/6; 🕒 8:30am-4:30pm), a 20-mile drive southeast of Asheville, the American flag flaps in the breeze atop this popular park's namesake 315ft granite monolith. An elevator takes visitors up to the chimney, but the real draw is the exciting hike around the cliffs to a 404ft waterfall.

SLEEPING

The **Asheville Bed & Breakfast Association** (☎ 877-262-6867; www.ashevillebba.com) handles bookings for numerous area B&Bs, from gingerbread cottages to alpine cabins.

Bon Paul & Sharky's Hostel (☎ 828-350-9929; www.bonpaulandsharkys.com; 816 Haywood Rd; campsites per person $13, dm/d $22/55; P) In the hip West Asheville residential neighborhood, this cottage has a friendly college-dorm vibe and sweet amenities like foosball, communal bikes, and backyard tent space.

our pick **Campfire Lodgings** (☎ 828-658-8012; www.campfirelodgings.com; 116 Appalachian Village Rd; tent sites $30, yurts from $105; P) All yurts should have flat-screen TVs, don't you think? Sleep like the world's most stylish Mongolian nomad in one of these furnished multiroom tents, on

THE SOUTH

the side of a hill with stunning valley views. Cabins and tent sites are also available.

ArtHaus Hostel (☎ 828-225-3278; www.aahostel.com; 16 Ravenscroft Dr; s $40; P ⊠ ⁘ ▭ ≋) Right downtown, this inconspicuous green bungalow has spartan private rooms, shared bathrooms and free waffles, but not much communal space.

Grove Park Inn Resort & Spa (☎ 828-252-2711, 800-438-5800; www.groveparkinn.com; 290 Macon Ave; r $155; P ⁘ ▭ ≋) Built in 1913, this titanic arts-and-crafts–style stone lodge clings to the side of the mountain like the castle of a goblin king. Inside is a mini-village of 510 richly appointed rooms, four restaurants, numerous shops and an underground grotto of a spa, complete with stone pools and an indoor waterfall.

EATING

Downtown has more than its fair share of great restaurants. Try the massive Gothic-style **Grove Arcade** (Page Ave) building for fancy groceries and produce.

Rosetta's Kitchen (☎ 828-232-0738; 116 N Lexington Ave; mains $7-9 ⏲ 11am-11pm Mon-Thu, to 3am Fri & Sat, to 9pm Sun; V) An institution among Asheville's dreadlocked set, where you can belly up to the counter for a bowl of peanut butter tofu (looks awful, tastes heavenly) at 2am.

Early Girl Eatery (☎ 828-259-9292; 8 Wall St; mains $7-11; ⏲ 7:30am-3pm & 5-9pm Mon-Fri, brunch 9am-3pm Sat & Sun) Order a tofu scramble or a plate of free-range roast chicken in this neighborhood café's sunny, crowded dining room, overlooking a small city park.

our pick **Salsa's** (☎ 828-252-9805; 6 Patton Ave; mains $13-17; ⏲ 11:30am-2:30pm & 5:30-9pm) Uh oh, Mexico and Jamaica just crashed into a farmer's market cart and landed on your plate! This tiny, brightly painted joint serves amazing, mutant Latin fusion cuisine – think lamb empanadas with goat's cheese and banana salsa or crab-jalapeño-saffron-fennel egg rolls. Beware huge crowds, unreasonably spicy appetizers and unannounced substitutions, and *always* order off the specials menu.

DRINKING & ENTERTAINMENT

Downtown Asheville has all types of bars and cafés, from frat-boy beer halls to hookah-n-sprout hippie holes-in-the-wall. West Asheville has a more laid-back townie vibe.

Westville Pub (☎ 828-225-9782; 777 Haywood Rd) This is a good place to bond with local 20- and 30-somethings over a bottle of organic ale.

Asheville Pizza and Brewing Company (☎ 828-254-1281; 675 Merrimon Ave; movies $3; ⏲ movies 1pm, 4pm, 7pm & 10pm) Catch a flick at the small theater inside this one-of-a-kind spot.

For live music, try the warehouse-sized **Orange Peel** (☎ 828-225-5851; www.theorangepeel.net; 101 Biltmore Ave; tickets $10-25) for big-name indie and punk, or the **Grey Eagle** (☎ 828-232-5800; www.thegreyeagle.com; 185 Clingman Ave; tickets $8-15) for bluegrass and jazz.

GETTING THERE & AROUND

Asheville Transit (☎ 828-253-5691; www.ashevilletransit.com; tickets $1) has 24 local bus routes running from 6am to 11:30pm Monday to Saturday. Twenty minutes south of town, **Asheville Regional Airport** (AVL; ☎ 828-684-2226; www.flyavl.com) has a handful of direct flights, including to/from Atlanta, Charlotte and New York. **Greyhound** (☎ 828-253-8451; www.greyhound.com; 2 Tunnel Rd) is just northeast of downtown.

Great Smoky Mountains National Park

More than 10 million visitors a year come through this majestic park, one of the world's most biodiverse areas. Landscapes range from deep, dim spruce forest to sunny meadows carpeted with daisies and Queen Anne's lace to wide, coffee-brown rivers. There's ample hiking and camping, and opportunities for horseback riding, bike rental and fly-fishing. The North Carolina side has less traffic than the Tennessee side, so even at the height of summer tourist season you'll still have room to roam. For more information about the Tennessee section of this park, see p434.

Newfound Gap Road/Highway 441 is the only thoroughfare that crosses Great Smoky Mountains National Park, winding through the mountains from Gatlinburg, TN, to the town of Cherokee and the busy **Oconaluftee Visitor Center** (☎ 865-436-1200; Hwy 441), in the southeast. Pick up your backcountry camping permits here. The Oconaluftee River Trail, one of only two in the park that allows leashed pets, leaves from the visitor center and follows the river for 1.5 miles.

Nearby attractions include the 1886 **Mingus Mill** (self-guided tours free; ⏲ 9am-5pm 15 Mar–1 Dec), 2 miles west of Cherokee, a turbine-powered mill that still grinds wheat and corn much as it always has. The on-site **Mountain Farm Museum** is a restored 19th-century farmstead, complete with barn, blacksmith shop and smokehouse (with real pig heads!), assembled from original

SMOKY MOUNTAIN DAY HIKES

These are a few of our favorite short hikes in the North Carolina side of the park:

Big Creek Trail Hike an easy 2 miles to Mouse Creek Falls or go another 3 miles to backcountry campground; the trailhead's near I-40 on the park's northeastern edge.

Boogerman Trail Moderate 7-mile loop passing old farmsteads; access via Cove Creek Rd.

Chasteen Creek Falls From Smokemont campground, this 4-mile round-trip passes a small waterfall.

Shustack Tower Starting at massive Fontana Dam, climb 3.5 miles for killer views from an old fire tower.

buildings from different parts of the park. A few miles away, the **Smokemont Campground** (www.nps.gov/grsm; campsites $17) is the only North Carolina campground open year-round.

To the east, remote **Cataloochee Valley** has several historic buildings to wander through and is a prime location for elk and black bears.

Southwestern North Carolina

The state's westernmost tip is blanketed in parkland and sprinkled with tiny mountain towns. The area has a rich but sad Native American history – many of the original Cherokee inhabitants were forced off their lands during the 1830s and marched to Oklahoma on the Trail of Tears. Descendants of those who escaped are known as the Eastern Band of the Cherokee, about 12,000 of whom now occupy the 56,000-acre Qualla Boundary territory at the edge of Great Smoky Mountains National Park.

The unlovely town of **Cherokee** anchors the Qualla Boundary with ersatz Native American souvenir shops, fast-food joints and **Harrah's Cherokee Casino** (☎ 828-497-7777; www.harrahs.com). The best sight is the modern **Museum of the Cherokee Indian** (☎ 828-497-3481; www.cherokeemuseum.org; cnr Hwy 441 & Drama Rd; adult/child $9/6; 🕑 9am-5pm), with an informative exhibit on the Trail of Tears and eerily realistic dioramas. In the hills behind the museum, Cherokees demonstrate traditional crafts in the 18th-century replica **Oconaluftee Indian Village** (☎ 866-554-4557; adult/child $15/6; 🕑 9am-5pm).

South of Cherokee, the contiguous **Pisgah** and **Nantahala National Forests** have more than a million acres of dense hardwood trees, windswept balds, and some of the country's best white water. Both contain portions of the Appalachian Trail. Pisgah highlights include the bubbling baths in the village of **Hot Springs** (www.hotspringsnc.org), the natural waterslide at Sliding Rock, and the 30-mile Art Loeb Trail, which skirts Cold Mountain of book and movie fame. Nantahala has several recreational lakes and dozens of roaring waterfalls, several of which can be easily accessed via the Mountain Waters Scenic Byway.

For plush accommodations try **Brevard**, a cute mountain town with tons of B&Bs on the east edge of Pisgah. Or head just north of Nantahala to quaint **Bryson City**, an ideal jumping-off point for outdoor adventures. It's home to the huge and highly recommended **Nantahala Outdoor Center** (☎ 828-488-2176, 828-586-8811; www.noc.com; 13077 Hwy 19/74; guided rafting trips $45-177), which specializes in wet and wild rafting trips down the Nantahala, French Broad, Pigeon and Ocoee Rivers, and rents out bikes, kayaks and more. It even has its own lodge and restaurant. From the Bryson City depot, the **Great Smoky Mountain Railroad** (☎ 800-872-4681; www.gsmr.com; Nantahala Gorge trip adult/child $34/19) runs scenic train excursions through the dramatic river valley.

SOUTH CAROLINA

Cross the border of South Carolina and plunge back in time. For a traveler heading down the eastern seaboard, venturing into South Carolina marks the beginning of the Deep South, where the air is hotter, the accents are thicker and traditions are clung to with even more fervor.

Starting at the silvery sands of the Atlantic Coast, the state climbs westward from the Coastal Plain and up through the Piedmont and into the Blue Ridge Mountains. Most travelers stick to the coast, with its splendid antebellum cities and palm tree–studded beaches. But the interior has a wealth of sleepy old towns, wild and undeveloped state parks and spooky black-water swamps just waiting to be explored by canoe. Along the sea islands you hear the sweet songs of the Gullah, a culture and language created by former slaves who held onto many West African traditions through the ravages of time.

SOUTH CAROLINA FACTS

Nickname Palmetto State
Population 4.5 million
Area 30,109 sq miles
Capital city Columbia (population 124,818)
Other cities Charleston (107,845)
Sales tax 5%, plus up to 10% extra tax on accommodations
Birthplace of Jazzman Dizzy Gillespie (1917–93), political activist Jesse Jackson (b 1941), boxer Joe Frazier (b 1944), *Wheel of Fortune* hostess Vanna White (b 1957)
Home of First US public library (1698), museum (1773) and steam railroad (1833)
Famous for Firing the first shot of the Civil War, from Charleston's Fort Sumter
Smelliest festival Chitlin' Strut festival in Salley, a celebration of the odiferous stuffed pig's intestine dish chitterlings, or chitlins, a dubious Southern delicacy
Driving distances Columbia to Charleston 115 miles, Charleston to Myrtle Beach 97 miles

Whether you're looking for a romantic weekend in genteel, gardenia-scented Charleston or a week of riotous fun at bright, tacky Myrtle Beach, South Carolina is a lovely, affordable destination.

History

More than 28 separate tribes of Native Americans have lived in what is now South Carolina, many of them Cherokee who were later forcibly removed during the Trail of Tears era.

The English founded the Carolina colony in 1670, with settlers pouring in from the royal outpost of Barbados, giving the port city known as Charles Towne a Caribbean flavor.

West African slaves were brought over to turn the thick coastal swamps into rice paddies and by the mid-1700s the area was deeply divided between the slave-owning aristocrats of the Lowcountry and the poor Scots-Irish and German farmers of the rural backcountry.

South Carolina was the first state to secede from the Union, and the first battle of the Civil War occurred at Fort Sumter in Charleston Harbor. The end of the war left much of the state in ruins.

South Carolina traded in cotton and textiles for most of the 20th century. It remains a relatively poor agricultural state, though with a thriving coastal tourism business.

Information

South Carolina Department of Parks, Recreation & Tourism (☎ 803-734-1700 www.discoversouthcarolina.com; 1205 Pendleton St, Room 505, Columbia) Sends out *South Carolina Smiles*, the state's official vacation guide.

South Carolina State Parks (☎ 888-887-2757; www.southcarolinaparks.com) This helpful website lists activities, hiking trails and allows online reservations for campsites (prices vary).

CHARLESTON

Put on your twinset and pearls or your seersucker suit, have a fortifying sip of sherry, and prepare to be thoroughly drenched in Southern charm. Charleston is a city for strolling, for admiring antebellum architecture, for long dinners on the verandah, for stopping to smell the blooming jasmine. Tooth-achingly romantic, everywhere you turn is another blushing bride standing on the steps of yet another charming church.

Named the 'Best-Mannered City in America' 11 years in a row, Charleston is one of the most popular tourist destinations in the Southeast. In the high season the scent of gardenia and honeysuckle mixes with the tang of horse from the innumerable carriage tours that clip-clop down the cobblestones day and night. In winter the weather is milder and the crowds thinner, making Charleston a great bet for off-season travel.

History

Well before the Revolutionary War, Charles Towne (named for Charles II) was one of the busiest ports on the eastern seaboard, the center of a prosperous rice-growing and trading colony. With influences from the West Indies and Africa, France and other European countries, it became a cosmopolitan city often compared to New Orleans.

The first shots of the Civil War rang out at Fort Sumter, in Charleston's harbor. After the war, as the labor-intensive rice plantations became uneconomical without slave labor, the city's importance declined. Natural disasters wrought more damage, with a major earthquake in 1886, several fires and storms, and devastating Hurricane Hugo in 1989. But much of the town's historic fabric remains, to the delight of four million tourists every year.

Orientation

The Charleston metropolitan area sprawls over a broad stretch of coastal plains and islands, but the historic heart is very compact, about 4 sq miles at the southern tip of a peninsula between the Cooper and Ashley Rivers. I-26 goes to North Charleston and the airport. Hwy 17, the main coastal road, cuts across the Charleston peninsula as the Crosstown Expwy. Soaring bridges connect west to James Island and West Ashley, and east to Mount Pleasant.

The most important north–south streets of the downtown peninsula are King, Meeting and E Bay. Market and Broad Sts cut east-west, with lots of shops and restaurants.

Information

BOOKSTORES

Blue Bicycle Books (☎ 843-722-2666; www.bluebicyclebooks.com; 420 King St; 10am-6pm Mon-Sat, 1-5pm Sun) This teeny indie favorite holds used and new titles on everything from antebellum Charleston to pop art.

EMERGENCY

Main police station (☎ 843-577-7434; 180 Lockwood Blvd)

INTERNET ACCESS

The City of Charleston maintains free public internet (wi-fi) access throughout the downtown area.

Public library (☎ 843-805-6801; www.ccpl.org; 68 Calhoun St; 9am-9pm Mon-Thu, to 6pm Fri & Sat, 2-5pm Sun) Free internet access.

MEDIA

Charleston City Paper (www.charlestoncitypaper.com) Published each Wednesday, this alt-weekly has good entertainment and restaurant listings.

Post & Courier (www.charleston.net) Charleston's daily newspaper.

MEDICAL SERVICES

University Hospital (MUSC; ☎ 843-792-2300; 171 Ashley Ave; 24hr) Emergency room.

POST

Post office (☎ 843-577-0688; 83 Broad St; 9am-5pm Mon-Fri)

TOURIST INFORMATION

Visitor center (☎ 843-853-8000; www.charlestoncvb.com; 375 Meeting St; 8:30am-5pm) Find help with accommodations and tours or watch a half-hour video on Charleston history in this spacious renovated warehouse.

Sights & Activities

The city itself is the main attraction, especially the part of the peninsula south of Hwy 17, with its magnolia-shaded avenues and winsome cobblestoned alleys.

HISTORIC DISTRICT

The quarter south of Beaufain and Hasell Sts has the bulk of the antebellum mansions, shops, bars and cafés. The historic **City Market** (Market St) is the crowded center of it all, with vendors hawking junky souvenirs from open-air stalls.

At the southernmost tip of the peninsula are the antebellum mansions of the Battery – take a seat in shady **White Point Park** and ponder whether 'filthy-rich merchant seaman' is still a viable career. Around the corner, a stretch of lower E Bay St known as **Rainbow Row** is one of the most photographed areas of town for its candy-colored houses.

Kids love the **Old Exchange & Provost Dungeon** (☎ 843-727-2165; www.oldexchange.com; 122 E Bay St; adult/child $7/3.50; 9am-5pm), built in 1771 as a customs house and later used as a dungeon prison for pirates. Costumed guides lead tours.

African men, women and children were once auctioned off at the **Old Slave Mart Museum** (☎ 843-958-6467; www.nps.gov/nr/travel/charleston/osm.htm; 6 Chalmers St; adult/child $7/5; 9am-5pm Mon-Sat), now a museum of South Carolina's shameful past. Text-heavy exhibits illuminate the slave experience; the few artifacts, like leg shackles, are especially chilling.

Gibbes Museum of Art (☎ 843-722-2706; www.gibbesmuseum.org; 135 Meeting St; adult/child $9/5; 10am-5pm Tue-Sat, 1-5pm Sun) houses a decent collection of American and Southern works; the most interesting way to visit is in conjunction with a two-hour **walking tour** (www.oldcharlestontours.com;

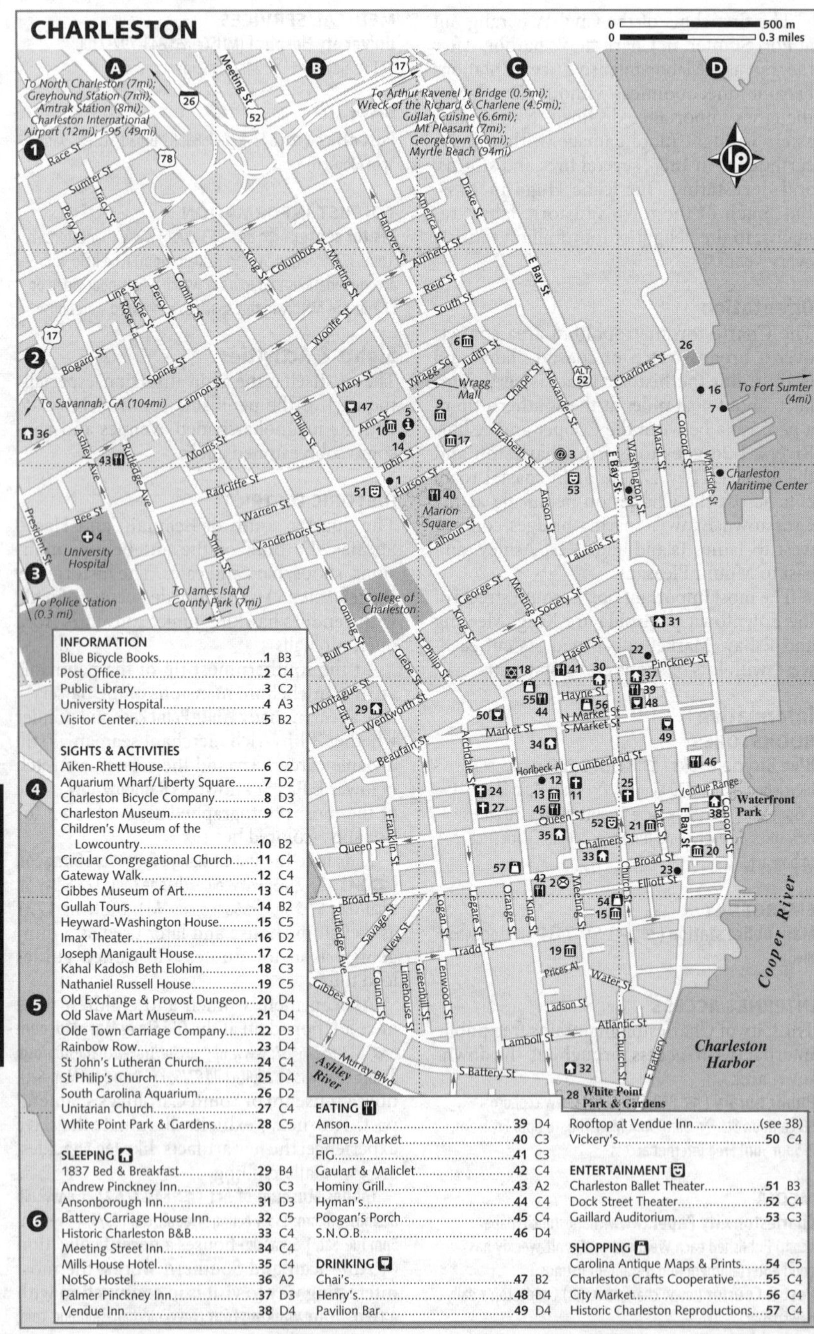
CHARLESTON
0 500 m
0 0.3 miles
A
B
C
D
1
2
3
4
5
6
To North Charleston (7mi); Greyhound Station (7mi); Amtrak Station (8mi); Charleston International Airport (12mi); I-95 (49mi)
To Arthur Ravenel Jr Bridge (0.5mi); Wreck of the Richard & Charlene (4.5mi); Gullah Cuisine (6.6mi); Mt Pleasant (7mi); Georgetown (60mi); Myrtle Beach (94mi)
To Savannah, GA (104mi)
To Fort Sumter (4mi)
To Police Station (0.3 mi)
To James Island County Park (7mi)
Race St
Sumter St
Tracy St
Perry St
Meeting St
King St
Columbus St
Hanover St
America St
Drake St
Amherst St
Reid St
South St
E Bay St
Line St
Ashe St
Rose La
Percy St
Coming St
Woolfe St
Bogard St
Spring St
Cannon St
Mary St
Wragg Sq
Wragg Mall
Judith St
Chapel St
Alexander St
Charlotte St
Ann St
Philip St
John St
Hutson St
Elizabeth St
Morris St
Ashley Ave
Rutledge Ave
Radcliffe St
Warren St
Vanderhorst St
Bee St
President St
Smith St
University Hospital
Marion Square
Calhoun St
Anson St
Washington St
Marsh St
Concord St
Wharfside St
Charleston Maritime Center
Laurens St
College of Charleston
George St
Society St
Bull St
Glebe St
St Philip St
Hasell St
Pinckney St
Montague St
Pitt St
Wentworth St
Hayne St
N Market St
S Market St
Market St
Beaufain St
Archdale St
Horlbeck Al
Cumberland St
Vendue Range
Waterfront Park
Queen St
Franklin St
Chalmers St
State St
Church St
Broad St
Elliott St
Savage St
New St
Logan St
Legare St
Orange St
Tradd St
Prices Al
Water St
Gibbes St
Council St
Limehouse St
Greenhill St
Lenwood St
Ladson St
Atlantic St
Lamboll St
E Battery
Murray Blvd
S Battery St
Ashley River
White Point Park & Gardens
Cooper River
Charleston Harbor

INFORMATION
Blue Bicycle Books....1 B3
Post Office....2 C4
Public Library....3 C2
University Hospital....4 A3
Visitor Center....5 B2

SIGHTS & ACTIVITIES
Aiken-Rhett House....6 C2
Aquarium Wharf/Liberty Square....7 D2
Charleston Bicycle Company....8 D3
Charleston Museum....9 C2
Children's Museum of the Lowcountry....10 B2
Circular Congregational Church....11 C4
Gateway Walk....12 C4
Gibbes Museum of Art....13 C4
Gullah Tours....14 B2
Heyward-Washington House....15 C5
Imax Theater....16 D2
Joseph Manigault House....17 C2
Kahal Kadosh Beth Elohim....18 C3
Nathaniel Russell House....19 C5
Old Exchange & Provost Dungeon....20 D4
Old Slave Mart Museum....21 D4
Olde Town Carriage Company....22 D3
Rainbow Row....23 D4
St John's Lutheran Church....24 C4
St Philip's Church....25 D4
South Carolina Aquarium....26 D2
Unitarian Church....27 C4
White Point Park & Gardens....28 C5

SLEEPING
1837 Bed & Breakfast....29 B4
Andrew Pinckney Inn....30 C3
Ansonborough Inn....31 D3
Battery Carriage House Inn....32 C5
Historic Charleston B&B....33 C4
Meeting Street Inn....34 C4
Mills House Hotel....35 C4
NotSo Hostel....36 A2
Palmer Pinckney Inn....37 D3
Vendue Inn....38 D4

EATING
Anson....39 D4
Farmers Market....40 C3
FIG....41 C3
Gaulart & Maliclet....42 C4
Hominy Grill....43 A2
Hyman's....44 C4
Poogan's Porch....45 C4
S.N.O.B....46 D4

DRINKING
Chai's....47 B2
Henry's....48 D4
Pavilion Bar....49 D4
Rooftop at Vendue Inn....(see 38)
Vickery's....50 C4

ENTERTAINMENT
Charleston Ballet Theater....51 B3
Dock Street Theater....52 C4
Gaillard Auditorium....53 C3

SHOPPING
Carolina Antique Maps & Prints....54 C5
Charleston Crafts Cooperative....55 C4
City Market....56 C4
Historic Charleston Reproductions....57 C4

THE SOUTH

DON'T MISS

- Eating fried shrimp in an old bait warehouse at the **Wreck of the Richard & Charlene** (p409)
- Ogling the oh-so-photogenic painted town houses of **Rainbow Row** (p405)
- Strolling past ancient churchyards abloom with flowers on the **Gateway Walk** (below)
- Peeking into the lives of the 19th-century Southern aristocracy at **Middleton Place** (p411)
- Watching the sun set in a blaze of orange over the river at the **Rooftop at Vendue Inn** (p410)

tours $20) that combines the museum with various artistically significant city sites.

About half a dozen majestic historic homes are open to visitors. Discounted combination tickets may tempt you to see more, but one or two will be enough for most people. Most houses are open from 10am to 5pm Monday to Saturday, 1pm to 5pm Sunday and run guided tours every half-hour. Admission is $10. Of the most interesting, **Aiken-Rhett House** (☎ 843-723-1159; www.historiccharleston.org; 48 Elizabeth St) is the only surviving urban plantation; it gives a fascinating look into antebellum life, including the role of slaves.

Heyward-Washington House (☎ 843-722-0354; www.charlestonmuseum.org; 87 Church St), built in 1772, belonged to Thomas Heyward Jr, a signer of the Declaration of Independence, and contains some lovely examples of Charleston-made mahogany furniture and the city's only preserved historic kitchen.

Built by a Rhode Islander, known in Charleston as 'the king of the Yankees,' the 1808 Federal-style **Nathaniel Russell House** (☎ 843-724-8481; www.historiccharleston.org; 51 Meeting St) is noted especially for its spectacular, self-supporting spiral staircase and lush English garden.

Long a culturally diverse city, Charleston gave refuge to persecuted French Protestants, Baptists, and Jews over the years, and earned the nickname the 'Holy City' for its abundance of houses of worship. The **Gateway Walk**, a little-known garden path between Archdale St and Philadelphia Alley, connects four of the city's most beautiful historic churches: the white-columned **St John's Lutheran Church**; the Gothic Revival **Unitarian Church**; the striking Romanesque **Circular Congregational Church**, originally founded in 1681; and **St Philip's Church**, with its picturesque steeple and 17th-century graveyard, parts of which were once reserved for 'strangers and transient white persons.'

Kahal Kadosh Beth Elohim (☎ 843-723-1090; Hasell St) is the oldest continuously used synagogue in the country. There are free tours by appointment.

MARION SQUARE

Formerly home to the state weapons arsenal, this 10-acre park is Charleston's living room, with various monuments and an excellent Saturday farmers market.

Founded in 1773, the **Charleston Museum** (☎ 843-722-2996; www.charlestonmuseum.org; 360 Meeting St; adult/child $10/5; ⌚ 9am-5pm Mon-Sat, from 1pm Sun) claims to be the country's oldest, with exhibits from various periods of Charleston's long and storied history, from prehistoric whale skeletons to slave tags and Civil War weapons.

The **Children's Museum of the Lowcountry** (☎ 843-853-8962; www.explorecml.org; 25 Ann St; admission $7; ⌚ 10am-5pm Tue-Sat, from 1pm Sun; 👶) has eight interactive exhibit areas, including a 30ft replica shrimp boat where kids can play captain.

The three-story **Joseph Manigault House** (☎ 843-722-2996; www.charlestonmuseum.org; 350 Meeting St) was once the showpiece of a French Huguenot rice planter. Don't miss the tiny neoclassical temple in the garden.

AQUARIUM WHARF

Aquarium Wharf surrounds pretty Liberty Sq and is a great place to stroll around and watch the tugboats guiding ships into the seventh-largest container port in the US. The wharf is the embarkation point for tours to Fort Sumter. Also here is the IMAX theater.

The massive, excellent **South Carolina Aquarium** (☎ 843-720-1990; www.scaquarium.org; 100 Aquarium Wharf; adult/child $17/10; ⌚ 9am-5pm, from noon Sun; 👶) showcases the state's diverse aquatic life, from the otters of the Blue Ridge Mountains to the loggerhead turtles of the Atlantic. The highlight is the 42ft Great Ocean Tank, which teems with sharks and alien-looking puffer fish.

The first shots of the Civil War rang out at **Fort Sumter**, on a pentagon-shaped island in the harbor. A Confederate stronghold, the fort was shelled to bits by Union forces from 1863 to 1865. A few original guns and fortifications give a feel for the momentous history. The only way to get here is by boat tour (☎ 843-883-3123; www.nps.gov/fosu; adult/child $16/10; ⏲ tours 9:30am, noon & 2:30pm summer, fewer in winter), which also depart from Patriot's Point in Mt Pleasant, across the river (p411).

Stretching across the Cooper River like some massive stringed instrument, the three-mile-long **Arthur Ravenel Jr Bridge** is a triumph of contemporary engineering. Biking or jogging across the protected no-car lane is one of active Charlestonians' go-to weekend activities. Rent a cruiser at **Charleston Bicycle Company** (☎ 843-407-0482; www.charlestonbicyclecompany.com; 334 M E Bay St; bikes per day $27; ⏲ 10am-6pm, from noon Sun).

Tours

Listing all of Charleston's walking, horse-carriage, bus and boat tours could take up this entire book. Ask at the visitor center for the gamut.

Culinary Tours of Charleston (☎ 800-918-0701; www.culinarytoursofcharleston.com; 2½hr tour $36) Sample grits, pralines, BBQ and more on this walking tour of Charleston's restaurants and markets.

Charleston Harbor Tours (☎ 800-344-4483; www.charlestonharbortours.com; 90min tours adult/child $16.25/11.50) Historical tours of town aboard the 80ft *Carolina Belle* depart from the Charleston Maritime Center.

Gullah Tours (☎ 843-763-7551; www.gullahtours.com; 43 John St; 2hr tour adult/child $18/12) A native Gullah speaker directs a bus exploration of the history of African American Charleston.

Olde Towne Carriage Company (☎ 843-722-1315; www.oldetownecarriage.com; 20 Anson St; 45min tour adult/child $20/12) Guides on this popular horse-drawn-carriage tour offer colorful commentary as you clip-clop around town.

Sleeping

Staying in the historic downtown is the most attractive option, but it's the most expensive, especially on weekends, in high season, and during special events. The rates below are for high season (spring and early summer). The chain hotels on the highways offer significantly lower rates.

One of the best ways to get to know Charleston is to stay at a small home where the owners serve up authentic Southern breakfasts and dole out great local information. They fill up fast, so try using an agency such as **Historic Charleston B&B** (☎ 843-722-6606; www.historiccharlestonbedandbreakfast.com; 57 Broad St).

BUDGET

NotSo Hostel (☎ 843-722-8383; www.notsohostel.com; 156 Spring St; dm/r $21/60; P ⊠ ⁂ 💻 ᯤ) On the north edge of downtown, three tottering old houses have been carved into dorms and private rooms, the verandahs decked with hammocks. Get local tips from friendly staff members during the shared morning breakfast.

James Island County Park (☎ 843-795-7275; www.ccprc.com; 871 Riverland Dr; tent/RV sites $23/41, 8-person cottages $159) Southwest of town, this park offers shuttle services downtown. Reservations are highly recommended.

MIDRANGE

1837 Bed & Breakfast (☎ 843-723-7166, 877-723-1837; www.1837bb.com; 126 Wentworth St; r incl breakfast $99-209; P ⊠ ⁂) Like staying at the home of your eccentric, antique-loving aunt, 1837 has nine charmingly over-decorated rooms, including three in the old brick carriage house. In the morning, the friendly proprietress serves up hearty egg and meat dishes in the yellow dining room.

Meeting Street Inn (☎ 843-723-1882, 800-842-8022; www.meetingstreetinn.com; 173 Meeting St; r incl breakfast from $129; ⊠ ⁂ ᯤ) Dark, antique-furnished rooms with four-poster beds contrast with the sunny, pink-stucco courtyard of this 56-room hotel, in the thick of the historic district. Parking costs $12.

Palmer Pinckney Inn (☎ 843-722-1733; www.pinckneyinn.com; 19 Pinckney St; r $150-300; P ⊠ ⁂ ᯤ) This bubble-gum-pink 'single house' (a narrow building style characteristic of Charleston) has five twee guest rooms tucked away on a Historic District side street.

Andrew Pinckney Inn (☎ 843-937-8800, 800-505-8983; www.andrewpinckneyinn.com; 40 Pinckney St; r $159-229; ⊠ ⁂ 💻 ᯤ) A pre-Colonial sugar baron would have been right at home breakfasting in the rooftop garden of this 32-room hotel. Sand-colored walls and botanical prints lend an upscale Caribbean vibe. The location, on a quiet bit of street right near the market, is excellent. Parking costs $14.

our pick **Ansonborough Inn** (☎ 800-522-2073; www.ansonboroughinn.com; 1 Maiden Ln; r $180-290; ⊠ ⁂ ᯤ) A central atrium done up with burnished pine, exposed beams and nautical-themed oil paintings makes this intimate Historic

District hotel feel like being inside an antique sailing ship. Droll neo-Victorian touches like the Persian-carpeted glass elevator and the closet-sized British pub add a sense of fun. Huge guest rooms mix old and new, with worn leather couches, high ceilings, and flat-screen TVs. Parking is $12.

Battery Carriage House Inn (☎ 843-727-3100; www.batterycarriagehouse.com; 20 S Battery; r $189-300; P ⊠ ✲ ⓦ) Step through the iron gates and into this secluded 11-room treasure, where an interior garden filled with roses and whimsically trimmed topiary hedges begs you to sit down for a cup of tea. A 'gentleman ghost' is said to wander the Victorian-style rooms at night.

TOP END

Mills House Hotel (☎ 843-577-2400, 800-874-9600; www.millshouse.com; 115 Meeting St; r $205-300; ⊠ ✲ ⓢ ⓦ) This grand old dame (150 years young, *merci*) has gotten an $11-million facelift, and is now one of the most opulent choices in the area. Gilded elevators lead from an enormous marble lobby to 214 lushly upholstered rooms. The sun has still not set on the British Empire inside the clubby, wood-paneled Barbadoes Room restaurant. Parking costs $20.

Vendue Inn (☎ 843-577-7970; www.vendueinn.com; 19 Vendue Range; r incl breakfast $205-325; ⊠ ✲ ⓦ) This teeny boutique hotel, in the part of downtown known as the French Quarter, is decked out in a trendy mix of exposed brick and eccentric antiques. Rooms have cool amenities like deep soaking tubs and gas fireplaces. Even cooler is the rooftop bar (p410). Parking costs $16.

Eating

From hearty, lard-heavy Lowcountry cuisine to nouvelle-French bistros, there are enough good restaurants in Charleston for a town three times its size. On Saturday, stop by the **farmers market** (Marion Sq; ⏲ 8am-1pm Sat Apr-Oct).

BUDGET & MIDRANGE

Gullah Cuisine (☎ 843-881-9076; 1717 Hwy 17 N, Mt Pleasant; mains $7-11; ⏲ 9am-3pm & 5-9:30pm) It's not much to look at, but this dowdy suburban café is the best place to taste South Carolina's West African–influenced Gullah cooking. We recommend the lunch buffet, groaning with red rice, okra gumbo (roux-based stew), oxtail stew and fried fish.

Hominy Grill (☎ 843-937-0930; 207 Rutledge Ave; mains $7-18; ⏲ 7:30am-9pm Mon-Fri, 9am-3pm Sat & Sun) Slightly off the beaten path, this neighborhood café serves modern, vegetarian-friendly Lowcountry cuisine in an old barbershop. Spoon up a bowl of shrimp and grits (ground corn), a classic Charleston fisherman's breakfast, on the shady patio.

Gaulart & Maliclet (☎ 843-577-9797; 98 Broad St; mains $8-15; ⏲ 8am-4pm Mon, 8am-10pm Tue-Thu, to 10:30pm Fri-Sun) Locals crowd around the shared tables at this tiny bistro, known as 'Fast & French,' to nibble on Gallic cheeses and sausages or nightly specials ($15) that include bread, soup, a main dish and wine.

Hyman's (☎ 843-723-6000; 215 Meeting St; mains $8-24; ⏲ 11am-11pm) Yeah, it's a tourist trap, but the famous she-crab soup, po'boy sandwiches and crispy flounder at this massive downtown institution are worth the wait, especially at lunch when the lines are not quite so long.

our pick **Wreck of the Richard & Charlene** (☎ 843-884-0052; 106 Haddrell St; mains $12-22; ⏲ 5:30-8:30pm Sun-Thu, to 9:30pm Fri & Sat) It's practically impossible to find, but don't give up! This unmarked warehouse, down a dirt road overlooking Shem Creek in suburban Mt Pleasant, has what many consider the best fried seafood in the state. Kick back in a plastic chair with a free bowl of boiled peanuts while you wait; finish with the key lime bread pudding. No credit cards.

Poogan's Porch (☎ 843-577-2337; 72 Queen St; mains $15-25; ⏲ 9am-3pm & 5-9:30pm) Dine on sherried crab soup and toast points in the dim, floral-patterned environs of this supposedly haunted Victorian mansion, tucked away on a downtown side street.

TOP END

S.N.O.B. (☎ 843-723-3424; 192 E Bay St; mains $18-34; ⏲ lunch Mon-Fri, dinner nightly) The cheeky name (it stands for 'slightly north of Broad,' as in Broad St) reflects the anything-goes spirit of this newcomer, which draws raves for its eclectic menu, filled with treats such as house-smoked salmon or sautéed squab breast over cheese grits. Exposed brick walls and an open kitchen lend a casual ambience.

Anson (☎ 843-577-0551; 12 Anson St; mains $23-31; ⏲ 5-10pm Mon-Thu, to 11pm Fri & Sat) The most upscale Lowcountry place around, in a dreamy pink-and-green carriage house straight out of central casting. Filet mignon and grouper in champagne cream are complemented by a well-edited wine list.

FIG (☎ 843-805-5900; 232 Meeting St; mains $25-31; 5:30-10:30pm Mon-Thu, to 11pm Fri-Sun) Foodies swoon over inspired nouvelle-Southern fare like crispy pig's trotters (that means 'feet' – local and hormone-free, of course) with celery-root remoulade in this rustic-chic dining room.

Drinking

Balmy Charleston evenings are perfect for lifting a cool cocktail or dancing to live blues. Check out the weekly *Charleston City Paper* and the 'Preview' section of Friday's *Post & Courier*. When things are busy, bars stay open until around 2am.

Chai's (☎ 843-722-7313; 462 King St) On rapidly gentrifying Upper King St, this slick tapas bar draws an attractive crowd.

Henry's (☎ 843-723-4363; 54 N Market St) The bar of choice for single, young (and not-so-young) professionals, with a large wood bar and sports on TV.

Pavilion Bar (☎ 843-723-0500; 225 E Bay St) The swimming pool at this sexy rooftop bar is for hotel guests only, but the luscious views of the Cooper River and downtown Charleston are free.

Rooftop at Vendue Inn (☎ 843-723-0486; 23 Vendue Range) This two-level rooftop bar has the best views of downtown, and the crowds to prove it. Enjoy afternoon nachos or late-night live blues.

Vickery's (☎ 843-577-5300; 15 Beaufain St) Locals flock to Vick's to heft ice-cold beers on the tiki-torchlit patio or chow down on Cuban sandwiches in the diner-style booths.

Entertainment

Dock Street Theater (☎ 843-965-4032; www.charlestonstage.com; 135 Church St) Reconstructed in 1936 from original 1736 blueprints, Dock Street is America's oldest live-performance theater. The busy venue hosts an array of community and professional music and theater groups.

Charleston Ballet Theater (☎ 843-723-7334; www.charlestonballet.com; 477 King St) The ballet puts on an eclectic mix of traditional and contemporary shows.

Charleston Symphony Orchestra (☎ 843-723-7528; www.charlestonsymphony.com) Since 1936, the symphony, now led by David Stahl, has performed in the **Gaillard Auditorium** (77 Calhoun St).

CHARLESTON FESTIVALS

Lowcountry Oyster Festival In January, oyster-lovers in Mt Pleasant feast on 65,000 pounds worth of the salty bivalves.

Charleston Food & Wine Festival This newish March event draws celebrity chefs and well-heeled foodies.

Spoleto USA This 17-day performing arts festival in May is Charleston's biggest event, with operas, dramas and musicals staged across the city, and artisans and food vendors lining the streets.

Charleston Harbor Fest In June, antique tall ships sail into town; visitors can take tours and sailing lessons.

MOJA Arts Festival Spirited poetry jams and gospel concerts mark this two-week September celebration of African-American culture.

Shopping

The historic district is clogged with overpriced souvenir shops and junk markets. The further north on King St you go, the hipper the shopping.

Carolina Antique Maps & Prints (☎ 843-722-4773; 91 Church St; 10am-5pm Tue-Sat) Buy a vintage map of Charleston or a magnolia-blossom botanical print at this crowded little shop, tucked away on a residential street.

Charleston Crafts Cooperative (☎ 843-723-2938; 87 Hasell St; 10am-5:30pm) A pricey, well-edited selection of contemporary South Carolina–made crafts like sweetgrass baskets, hand-dyed silks and wood carvings.

Historic Charleston Reproductions (☎ 843-723-8292; 105 Broad St; 10am-5pm Tue-Sat) This place showcases jewelry, home furnishings and furniture inspired by the city's historic homes, like earrings based on the cast-iron railings at the Aiken-Rhett House (p407).

Getting There & Around

Charleston International Airport (CHS; ☎ 843-767-7009; www.chs-airport.com; 5500 International Blvd) is 12 miles outside of town in North Charleston, with 124 daily flights to 17 destinations.

The **Greyhound station** (☎ 843-744-4247; www.greyhound.com; 3610 Dorchester Rd) and the **Amtrak train station** (☎ 843-744-8264; 4565 Gaynor Ave) are both in North Charleston.

CARTA (☎ 843-724-7420; www.ridecarta.com; single/day pass $1.50/5) runs citywide buses; the DASH streetcars do four loop routes from the visitor center.

AROUND CHARLESTON

North Charleston

ourpick **HL Hunley** (☎ 843-743-4865; www.hunley.org; 1250 Supply St; admission $12; 10am-5pm Sat, from noon Sun) submarine, in a faceless warehouse at a working dockyard north of downtown, rests in a 90,000-gallon tank of water like some strange top-secret science experiment. In 1864 the Confederate *Hunley* completed the world's first submarine mission by sinking the Union's USS *Housatonic*, only to vanish immediately afterwards. In 1995 it was discovered off Sullivan's Island and carefully brought to shore. On weekends you can visit the *Hunley* and see creepy facial reconstructions of her eight crew members.

Mt Pleasant

Across the Cooper River is the residential and vacation community of Mt Pleasant, originally a summer retreat for early Charlestonians, along with the slim barrier resort islands of **Isle of Palms** and **Sullivan's Island**. Though increasingly glutted with traffic and strip malls, the area still has some charm, especially in the historic downtown, called the **Old Village**. Some good seafood restaurants sit overlooking the water at **Shem Creek**, where it's fun to dine creekside at sunset and watch the incoming fishing-boat crews unload their catch. This is also a good place to rent kayaks to tour the estuary. Stop by the **Isle of Palms Visitors Center** (☎ 843-849-9172; 311 Johnnie Dodds Blvd/Hwy 17; 9am-5pm Mon-Fri) for information and maps.

Patriot's Point Naval & Maritime Museum (☎ 843-884-2727; www.patriotspoint.org; 40 Patriots Point Rd; adult/child $16/8; 9am-6:30pm) is home to the USS *Yorktown*, a giant aircraft carrier used extensively in WWII. You can tour the ship's flight deck, bridge and ready rooms and get a glimpse of what life was like for its sailors. There is also a small museum, submarine, naval destroyer, Coast Guard cutter and a re-created 'fire base' from Vietnam. You can also catch the Fort Sumter boat tour from here (p407).

Just 7 miles from Charleston on Hwy 17 N, **Boone Hall Plantation** (☎ 843-884-4371; www.boonehallplantation.com; 1235 Long Point Rd; adult/child $17.50/7.50; 9am-5pm Mon-Sat, 1-4pm Sun) claims to be America's most photographed plantation. It's famous for its magical Avenue of Oaks, planted by Thomas Boone in 1743. Boone Hall is still a working plantation, though strawberries, tomatoes and Christmas trees long ago replaced cotton as the primary crop.

Near Boone Hall, the **Charles Pinckney National Historic Site** (☎ 843-881-5516; 1254 Long Point Rd; admission free; 9am-5pm) sits on the remaining 28 acres of Snee Farm, once the expansive plantation of statesman Charles Pinckney. There are archaeological and historical exhibits in the 1820s cottage turned museum, and several walking trails meandering through the magnolias.

About 8 miles south of Charleston, **Folly Beach** is good for a day of sun and sand. **Folly Beach County Park** (☎ 843-588-2426; cars/pedestrians $5/free; 10am-6pm), on the west side, has public changing areas and beach-chair rentals. The other end of the island is popular with surfers.

Ashley River Plantations

Only 20 minutes' drive from Charleston, three spectacular plantations are worthy of a detour. You'll be hard-pressed for time to visit all three in one outing, but you could squeeze in two (allow at least a couple of hours for each). If you've only got time to visit one, choose Magnolia Plantation (a better bet with kids) or Middleton Place (a delight for the sheer mastery of its gardens). Ashley River Rd is also known as SC 61, which can be reached from downtown Charleston via Hwy 17.

The 1738 Palladian brick mansion of **Drayton Hall** (☎ 843-769-2600; www.draytonhall.org; 3380 Ashley River Rd; adult/child $14/8; 9am-4:30pm, shorter hours in winter) was the only structure on the Ashley River to survive the Revolutionary and Civil Wars and the great earthquake of 1886. Guided tours through the empty house will appeal to history and architecture buffs.

Magnolia Plantation (☎ 843-571-1266; www.magnoliaplantation.com; 3550 Ashley River Rd; adult/child $15/10, plus per additional sight $7; 8am-5:30pm), which sits on 500 acres owned by the Drayton family since 1676, will be enjoyed even by those who disdain 'boring historical stuff.' It's a veritable plantation theme park, with a nature train, boat tours, a swamp walk, a petting zoo, and an outdoor café full of wandering peacocks, in addition to the guided house tour. Don't miss the reconstructed cabins of the slaves who once tended the indigo, cotton, corn and sugarcane.

Designed in 1741, the vast gardens of **Middleton Place** (☎ 843-556-6020; www.middletonplace.org;

4300 Ashley River Rd; adult/child $25/5; 9am-5pm) are the oldest in the US. One hundred slaves spent a decade terracing the land and digging the precise geometric canals for the owner, wealthy South Carolina politician Henry Middleton. The grounds, now maintained by a nonprofit organization, are truly bewitching, a mix of classic formal French gardens and romantic woodland settings. Popular horse-drawn carriage tours ($15) take visitors to see real flooded rice paddies. Horse tours are $10. In contrast to the antebellum plantation house, the on-site **inn** (r incl plantation admission from $184) is a series of modernist glass boxes overlooking the Ashley River.

SEA ISLANDS

From just north of Charleston, the southern half of the South Carolina coast is a tangle of islands cut off from the mainland by inlets and tidal marshes. Here, descendants of West African slaves known as the Gullah maintain small communities in the face of resort and golf-course development. The landscape ranges from tidy stretches of shimmery, oyster-gray sand, to wild, moss-shrouded maritime forests. The following islands can all be reached by road.

Upscale rental homes and golf courses abound on **Kiawah Island**, just southeast of Charleston, while nearby **Edisto Island** (*ed*-is-tow) is a homespun family vacation spot without a single traffic light. At its southern tip, **Edisto Beach State Park** (☎ 843-869-2156; admission $4; campsites from $17, furnished cabins from $72) has a gorgeous, uncrowded beach and oak-shaded hiking trails and campgrounds.

Between Kiawah and Edisto, agricultural **Wadmalaw Island** is home to **Charleston Tea Plantation** (☎ 843-559-0383; www.bigelowtea.com/act; 6617 Maybank Hwy; trolley tours $10, factory tours free; 10am-4pm, from noon Sun), America's only working tea farm. Ride a trolley through the fields, or buy prettily packaged Plantation Peach and Island Green teas in the gift shop.

On Port Royal Island, the darling colonial town of **Beaufort** (byoo-furt) is often used as a set for Hollywood films about the South. The streets of the historic district are lined with antebellum homes and magnolias dripping with Spanish moss, and the riverfront downtown has gobs of linger-worthy cafés and galleries. The **visitor center** (☎ 843-986-5400, 800-638-3525; www.beaufortsc.org; 1106 Carteret St; 9am-5:30pm) has maps and info on boat, carriage and walking tours.

South of Beaufort, some 20,000 young men and women go through boot camp each year at the **Marine Corps Recruit Depot** on Parris Island, made notorious by Stanley Kubrick's *Full Metal Jacket.* The fascinating base **museum** (www.pimuseum.com; admission free; 10am-4:30pm) has antique uniforms and weaponry. Come for Friday graduations to see newly minted marines parade proudly in front of weeping family and friends.

East of Beaufort, the Sea Island Pkwy/Hwy 21 connects a series of marshy, rural islands, including **St Helena Island**, considered the heart of Gullah country. Once one of the nation's first schools for freed slaves, the **Penn Center** (☎ 843-838-2432; www.penncenter.org; adult/child $4/2; 11am-4pm Mon-Sat) has a small museum of Gullah culture and is a good place to get info for further exploration. Further down the road, **Hunting Island State Park** (☎ 843-838-2011; www.huntingisland.com; adult/child $4/2; campsites from $17, cabins from $89) has acres of spooky maritime forest, tidal lagoons, and empty, bone-white beach. The Vietnam War scenes from *Forrest Gump* were filmed in the marsh, a nature-lover's dream. Campgrounds fill up quickly in summer.

Across Port Royal Sound, tony **Hilton Head Island** is South Carolina's largest barrier island and one of America's top golf spots. There are literally dozens of courses, many enclosed in posh private residential communities called 'plantations.' Though summer traffic and miles of stoplights make it hard to see the forest (or a tree) along Hwy 278, there are some lush nature preserves and wide white beaches

WHAT THE...?

Yes, that's a giant sombrero rising above I-95 on the North Carolina–South Carolina state line. *Bienvenidos* to **South of the Border**, a Mexican-flavored monument to American kitsch. Begun in 1950s as a fireworks stand – pyrotechnics are illegal in North Carolina – it's since morphed into a combo rest stop, souvenir mall, motel and (mostly defunct) amusement park, promoted on hundreds of billboards by a wildly stereotypical Mexican cartoon character named Pedro. Stop for a photo, some taffy, and a key chain that pees when you squeeze it.

GULLAH CULTURE

Many parts of the US resemble the European cities from which the founding settlers emigrated, but only on remote islands along the Georgia and South Carolina coast can the same claim be given to Africa. From the region known as the Rice Coast (Sierra Leone, Senegal, The Gambia and Angola), African slaves were transported across the Atlantic to a landscape that was shockingly similar – swampy coastlines, tropical vegetation and hot, humid summers.

These new African Americans were able to retain many of their homeland traditions, even after the fall of slavery and well into the 20th century. The resulting Gullah (also known as Geechee) culture has its own language, an English-based Creole with many African words and sentence structures, and many traditions, including fantastic storytelling, art, music and crafts. The Gullah culture is celebrated annually with the energetic **Gullah Festival** (☎ 843-525-0628; www.gullahfestival.org) in Beaufort. As many as 70,000 people gather on the last weekend in May to enjoy music, dance and crafts, including the famous Gullah sweetgrass baskets, and to eat traditional foods such as fried whiting, candied yams and okra gumbo.

hard enough to ride a bike on. At the entrance to the island is the **visitor center** (☎ 800-523-3373; 9:30am-5pm), with a small museum and info on accommodations and, well, golf.

NORTH COAST

The coastline from the North Carolina border to the city of Georgetown is known as the Grand Strand, with some 60 miles of fast-food joints, beach resorts and three-story souvenir shops. What was once a laid-back summer destination for working-class people from across the Southeast has become some of the most overdeveloped real estate in the country. Whether you're ensconced in a behemoth resort or sleeping in a tent at a state park, all you need to enjoy your stay is a pair of flip-flops, a margarita and some quarters for the pinball machine.

Myrtle Beach

Love it or hate it, Myrtle Beach means summer vacation, American-style.

Bikers take advantage of the lack of helmet laws to let their graying ponytails fly in the wind, bikini-clad teenagers play Pac-Man and eat hot dogs in smoky arcades, and whole families roast like chickens on the white sand.

North Myrtle Beach, actually a separate town, is slightly lower-key, with a thriving culture based on the 'shag' (no, not that kind of shag) – a jitterbug-like dance invented here in the 1940s.

It ain't for nature-lovers, but with enormous outlet malls and innumerable mini-golf courses, water parks, daiquiri bars and T-shirt shops, it's a rowdy good time.

There's internet access at **Chapin Memorial Library** (☎ 843-918-1275; 400 14th Ave N; 9am-6pm Mon-Thu, to 5pm Fri & Sat) and loads of maps and brochures at the **visitor center** (☎ 843-626-7444, 800-496-8250; www.myrtlebeachinfo.com; 1200 N Oak St; 8:30am-5pm Mon-Fri, 10am-2pm Sat).

SIGHTS & ACTIVITIES

The beach itself is pleasant enough – wide, hot and crowded with umbrellas. Beachfront Ocean Blvd has the bulk of the hamburger stands and seedy gift shops. Hwy 17 is utterly choked with mini-golf courses, boasting everything from animatronic dinosaurs to faux volcanoes spewing lurid-pink water.

Several amusement park/shopping mall hybrids teem with people at all hours. **Broadway at the Beach** (☎ 843-444-3200; www.broadwayatthebeach.com; 1325 Celebrity Circle), with shops, restaurants, nightclubs, rides and an IMAX theater, is the largest.

Family Kingdom (☎ 843-626-3447; www.family-kingdom.com; combo pass $33) is an old-fashioned amusement-and-water-park combo overlooking the ocean. Hours vary by season; it's closed in winter.

Go parasailing or rent jet skis or speed boats at **Myrtle Beach Water Sports** (☎ 843-497-8848; www.myrtlebeachwatersports.com; 17th Ave S, North Myrtle Beach; jet ski rental per hr/half-day $60/95).

Sixteen miles south of town on Hwy 17 S, magical **Brookgreen Gardens** (☎ 843-235-6000; www.brookgreen.org; adult/child $12/5; 9:30am-5pm) are home to the largest collection of American sculpture in the country, set amid 9000 acres of rice plantation turned subtropical garden paradise.

SLEEPING

Hundreds of hotels, ranging from retro family-run motor inns to vast resort complexes, have prices that vary widely by season; a room might cost $30 in January and more than $150 in July. The following lists summer high-season rates.

Myrtle Beach State Park (☎ 843-238-5325; www.southcarolinaparks.com; campsites $23-25, cabins & apts $54-124; P) Most campgrounds are veritable parking lots catering to families with RVs, but the best camping is found in the shady sites of this state park, 3 miles south of central Myrtle Beach.

Landmark Resort (☎ 843-448-9441; www.landmarkresort.com; 1501 S Ocean Blvd; d $95-165; P) Didn't get to go to summer camp as a kid? This family-oriented behemoth will make up for it, with a full menu of activities from beach kickball to tie-dying, the 'South's largest indoor pool complex,' and bright, modern rooms.

Breakers (☎ 800-952-4507; www.breakers.com; 2006 N Ocean Blvd; d $129-289; P) This long-standing megaresort has three towers of crisp, summery-yellow suites, with only-in-Myrtle-Beach amenities like a pirate-ship swimming pool and a pirate-themed bar.

EATING

The thousands of restaurants are mostly high-volume and middlebrow – think buffets longer than bowling alleys, and 24-hour doughnut shops. Ironically, good seafood is hard to come by; locals go to the nearby fishing village of Murrells Inlet. North Myrtle Beach has some cute retro-style ice-cream and hamburger stands.

Prosser's BBQ (☎ 843-357-6146; 3750 Business Hwy 17; buffets $6) Your best bet on Murrells Inlet's 'restaurant row,' homey Prosser's has a gut-busting buffet of fried fish and chicken, sweet potatoes, mac 'n' cheese, and vinegary pulled pork. Hours vary by season. Worth the drive.

Duffy Street Seafood Shack (☎ 843-281-9840; 202 Main St, North Myrtle Beach; mains $7-15; 4pm-late) This place has a divey, peanut-shells-on-the-floor ambience and a raw bar 'happy hour' with 30¢ shrimp.

DRINKING & ENTERTAINMENT

our pick **Fat Harold's Beach Club** (☎ 843-249-5779; 212 Main St, North Myrtle Beach) It's a gas to watch the graying beach bums groove to doo-wop and old-time rock 'n' roll at this North Myrtle institution, which calls itself 'Home of the Shag.' The dance, that is. Free shag lessons are offered at 7pm every Tuesday.

The **Carolina Opry** (☎ 843-913-1400; www.thecarolinaopry.com; 8901a Business 17 N; tickets from $35; 8pm Mon-Sat) has glittery musicals and variety shows, but **Dolly Parton's Dixie Stampede** (☎ 800-433-4401; www.dixiestampede.com; 8901 Hwy 17 N; admission incl dinner $42) out-glitters them all with a nightly dinner theater extravaganza involving herds of buffalo and flag-waving stunt riders.

GETTING THERE & AROUND

The traffic coming and going on Hwy 17 Business/Kings Hwy can be infuriating. To avoid 'the Strand' altogether, stay on the Hwy 17 bypass, or take Hwy 31/Carolina Bays Pkwy, which parallels Hwy 17 between Hwy 501 and Hwy 9.

Myrtle Beach International Airport (MYR; ☎ 843-448-1589; 1100 Jetport Rd) is located within the city limits, as is the **Greyhound** (☎ 843-448-2472; 511 7th Ave N) station.

Around Myrtle Beach

Fifteen minutes down I-17 is **Pawleys Island**, a narrow strip of pastel sea cottages that's worlds away from the neon of Myrtle Beach. There's not much to do here but kayak and fish, but that's just fine. Another 15 minutes will bring you to mellow **Georgetown**, South Carolina's third-oldest city. Have lunch on Front St, with photogenic 19th-century storefronts overlooking the water, or use it as a quiet jumping-off point for exploring the Francis Marion National Forest (see the boxed text, opposite).

COLUMBIA

South Carolina's state capital is a quiet place, with wide, shady streets and the kind of old-fashioned downtown where pillbox hats are still on display in the windows of family-run department stores. The University of South Carolina adds a youthful vibe, and college students whoop it up over basketball wins in campus-side bars. Though Columbia is a pleasant stop, most visitors, like General Sherman's troops, charge on through to the coast.

The **visitor center** (☎ 803-545-0002; www.columbiacvb.com; 1101 Lincoln St; 8am-6pm Mon-Fri, 8am-4pm Sat, 1pm-6pm Sun) has information about four historic houses open for tours, including

EXPLORING SOUTH CAROLINA SWAMPS

Inky-black water, dyed with tannic acid leached from decaying plant matter. Bone-white cypress stumps like the femurs of long-dead giants. Spanish moss as dry and gray as witches' hair. There's nothing like hiking or canoeing through one of South Carolina's unearthly swamps to make you feel like a character in a Southern Gothic novel.

About 45 minutes from Charleston, **Beidler Forest** (☎ 843-462-2150; www.beidlerforest.com; 336 Sanctuary Rd, Harleyville; ⏲ 9am-5pm Tue-Sun; adult/child $7/3.50) is a spooky 1800 acres of cypress swamp managed by the Audubon Society, who lead springtime weekend canoe trips (adult/child $30/15).

Near Columbia, the 22,000-acre **Congaree National Park** (☎ 803-776-4396; www.nps.gov/cosw; 100 National Park Rd, Hopkins; ⏲ 8:30am-5pm), America's largest contiguous, old-growth floodplain forest, has camping and free ranger-led canoe trips (reserve in advance). Casual day-trippers can wander the 2.4-mile elevated boardwalk.

Between Charleston and Myrtle Beach, **Francis Marion National Forest** (☎ 843-928-3368; 5821 Hwy 17 N, Awendaw) has 259,000 acres of black-water creeks, camping, and hiking trails, including the 42-mile Palmetto Trail, which runs along old logging routes. Charleston-based **Nature Adventures Outfitters** (☎ 843-568-3222; www.natureadventuresoutfitters.com; adult/child half-day $55/39) leads kayak and canoe trips.

Woodrow Wilson's boyhood home (closed for renovations at the time of research).

The grand, Corinthian-columned **State House** (☎ 803-734-2430; www.scstatehouse.gov; 1100 Gervais St; admission free; ⏲ 9am-5pm Mon-Fri, from 10am Sat) has bronze stars on its west side to mark the impacts from Northern troops' cannonballs.

The **South Carolina State Museum** (☎ 803-898-4921; www.museum.state.sc.us; 301 Gervais St; adult/child $7/3; ⏲ 10am-5pm Tue-Sat, from 1pm Sun) is housed in an 1894 textile factory building, one of the world's first electrically powered mills. Exhibits on science, technology and the state's cultural and natural history make a nice activity for a rainy day.

For eating and entertainment, head down Gervais St to the Vista, a hip renovated warehouse district popular with young professionals. For coffee and cheap ethnic food, mingle with USC students in Five Points, where Harden, Greene and Devine Sts meet Saluda Ave. There are plenty of chain hotels off I-26. In Five Points, the 28-room **Inn at Claussen's** (☎ 803-765-0440; www.theinnatclaussens.com; 2003 Greene St; r $125-145) gamely attempts a boutique art deco look, with modest success.

TENNESSEE

Most states have one official state song. Tennessee has seven. And that's not just a random fact – Tennessee has music deep within its soul. Here, the folk music of the Scots-Irish in the eastern mountains combined with the bluesy rhythms of the African Americans in the western Delta to give birth to the modern country music that makes Nashville famous.

These three geographic regions, represented by the three stars on the Tennessee flag, have their own unique beauty: the heather-colored peaks of the Great Smoky Mountains descend into lush green valleys in the central plateau around Nashville and then onto the hot, sultry lowlands near Memphis.

In Tennessee, you can hike shady mountain trails in the morning, and by evening whoop it up in a Nashville honky-tonk or walk the streets of Memphis with Elvis' ghost.

From country churches where snake handlers still speak in tongues to modern cities where record execs wear their sunglasses even at night, Tennesseans are a zesty lot.

History

Spanish settlers first explored Tennessee in 1539 and French traders were plying the rivers by the 17th century. Virginian pioneers soon established their own settlement and fought the British in the American Revolution. Tennessee joined the United States as the 16th state in 1796, taking its named from the Cherokee town of Tanasi.

The Cherokee themselves were brutally booted from their homes, along with many other Tennessee tribes, in the mid-1800s and marched west along the Trail of Tears.

Tennessee was the second-to-last Southern state to secede during the Civil War, and many important battles were fought here. Immediately following the war, six Confederate veterans from the town of Pulaski formed the infamous Ku Klux Klan to disenfranchise and terrorize the newly free blacks.

Major industries today are textiles, tobacco, cattle and chemicals, with tourism, especially in Nashville and Memphis, raking in hundreds of millions of dollars a year.

Information

Department of Environment & Conservation (☎ 888-867-2757; www.state.tn.us/environment/parks) Check out this well-organized website for camping (prices range from free to $27 or more), hiking and fishing info for Tennessee's more than 50 state parks.

Department of Tourist Development (☎ 615-741-2159, 800-462-8366; www.tnvacation.com; 312 8th Ave N, Nashville) Has welcome centers at the state borders.

MEMPHIS

Memphis doesn't just attract tourists. It draws pilgrims. Music-lovers come to lose themselves amid the throb of blues guitar on Beale St. Barbecue connoisseurs come to stuff themselves sick on smoky pulled pork and dry-rubbed ribs. Elvis fanatics fly in from London and Reykjavik and Osaka to worship at the altar of the King at Graceland. You could spend days hopping from one museum or historic site to another, stopping only for a spot o' barbecue, and leave happy.

But once you get away from the lights and the tourist buses, Memphis is a different place entirely. Named after the capital of ancient Egypt, it has a certain baroquely ruined quality that's both sad and beguiling. Poverty is rampant – Victorian mansions sit next to tumbledown shotgun shacks (small houses found throughout Southern cities), college campuses lie in the shadow of eerie abandoned factories, and whole neighborhoods seem to have been nearly reclaimed by kudzu and honeysuckle vines.

But Memphis' wild river-town spirit reveals itself to visitors willing to look. Keep your eyes open and you'll find some of the country's strangest museums, most deliciously oddball restaurants (barbecued spaghetti, anyone?), spookiest cemeteries and craziest dive bars.

History

Originally home to members of the native Mississippian culture, the area that would become Memphis was occupied by the French in the 18th century. It became part of the new state of Tennessee in 1796 and quickly prospered on the expanding cotton trade of the Mississippi Delta.

Union troops occupied the city during the Civil War, but the postwar collapse of the cotton trade was far more devastating. After a yellow fever outbreak caused most whites to flee the city, Memphis was forced to declare bankruptcy. The African American community revived the town, led by Robert Church, a former slave. By the early 1900s Beale St was the hub of black social and civic activity, becoming an early center for what became known as blues music. In the '50s and '60s, local recording companies cut tracks for blues, soul, R & B and rockabilly artists like Al Green, Johnny Cash and Elvis, cementing Memphis' place in the American music firmament.

TENNESSEE FACTS

Nickname Volunteer State
Population 6.2 million
Area 41,217 sq miles
Capital city Nashville (population 590,807)
Major city Memphis (population 670,902)
Sales tax 7%, plus local taxes of up to about 15%
Birthplace of Frontiersman Davy Crockett (1786–1836), soul diva Aretha Franklin (b 1942), singer Dolly Parton (b 1946), former vice president Al Gore (b 1948)
Home of Graceland, *Grand Ole Opry*, Jack Daniel's distillery
Famous for 'Tennessee Waltz,' country music, Tennessee walking horses
Odd law In Tennessee, it's illegal to fire a gun at any wild game, other than whales, from a moving vehicle
Driving distances Memphis to Nashville 213 miles, Nashville to Great Smoky Mountains National Park 223 miles

Orientation

Downtown Memphis lies along the east bank of the Mississippi. The principal tourist district is a bit inland, roughly bounded by Union Ave and Beale St, and Main and 4th Sts. A bit south, the S Main Arts District has some funky bars and restaurants. Further east, Midtown Memphis has several hip neighborhoods with shopping and dining, especially around Overton Sq (off N Cooper St) and Cooper-Young (the intersection of Cooper St and Young Ave). Graceland is 3 miles south of town on US 51, also called 'Elvis Presley Blvd.'

Information

EMERGENCY & MEDICAL SERVICES

Police station (☎ 901-543-2677; 545 S Main St)
Regional Medical Center (☎ 901-545-7100; 877 Jefferson Ave) Has the only level-one trauma center in the region.

INTERNET ACCESS

Public library (☎ 901-526-1712; 33 S Front St; 🕑 10am-5pm Mon-Fri) Computers with free internet access.
Quetzal Cafe (☎ 901-521-8388; 668 Union Ave; 🕑 7:30am-10pm Mon-Wed, to 3am Fri & Sat, to 3pm Sun) Has both wi-fi and public terminals in a trendy brick storefront.

MEDIA

Commercial Appeal (www.commercialappeal.com) Daily newspaper.
Memphis Flyer (www.memphisflyer.com) Free weekly distributed on Thursday; has entertainment listings.
Triangle Journal News (www.tjmemphis.com) Free monthly for the gay community.

POST

Main post office (☎ 901-521-2559; 555 S 3rd St; 🕑 8:30am-5pm Mon-Fri)

TOURIST INFORMATION

Tennessee State Visitor Center (☎ 901-543-5333, 888-633-9099; www.memphistravel.com; 119 N Riverside Dr; 🕑 9am-5pm Nov-Mar, to 6pm Apr-Oct) Stocked with brochures for the whole state.

Sights & Activities

GRACELAND

Though born in Mississippi, Elvis Presley was a true son of Memphis, raised in the Lauderdale Courts public housing projects, inspired by the blues in the Beale St clubs, and discovered at Sun Studio (p418) on Union Ave. In the spring of 1957, the already-famous 22-year-old spent $100,000 on a Colonial-style mansion called **Graceland** (☎ 901-332-3322, 800-238-2000; www.elvis.com; Elvis Presley Blvd/US 51; house-only tour adult/child $28/12, full tour $33/15; 🕑 9am-5pm Mon-Sat, to 4pm Sun, shorter hours & closed Tue winter). Priscilla Presley (who divorced Elvis in 1973) opened Graceland to tours in 1982, and now millions come here to pay homage to the King and gawk at the infamous decor. The King himself had the place redecorated in 1974; with a 15ft couch, fake waterfall, yellow vinyl walls and green shag-carpet ceiling – it's a virtual textbook of ostentatious '70s style. Elvis died here in 1977, killed by heart failure in the upstairs bathroom. Throngs of fans still weep at his grave, next to the swimming pool out back.

You begin your tour at the high-tech visitor plaza on the other side of seedy Elvis Presley Blvd. Book ahead in the busy season to ensure a prompt tour time. The basic self-guided mansion tour comes with a headset audio narration with the voices of Elvis, Priscilla and Lisa Marie. Buy a package to see the entire estate, or pay extra for additional attractions: the 'Elvis in Hollywood' memorabilia collection, the car museum, and two custom airplanes. Parking costs $6. Nondrivers can take bus 43 from downtown, or hop on the free Sun Studio shuttle (p418).

NATIONAL CIVIL RIGHTS MUSEUM

Housed in the Lorraine Motel, where the Reverend Dr Martin Luther King Jr was fatally shot on April 4, 1968, is the gut-wrenching **National Civil Rights Museum** (☎ 901-521-9699; www.civilrightsmuseum.org; 450 Mulberry St; adult/child $12/8.50; 🕑 9am-5pm Mon & Wed-Sat, 1pm-5pm Sun Sep-May, to 6pm Jun-Aug). Five blocks south of Beale St, this museum's extensive exhibits, detailed timeline and accompanying audioguide chronicle the ongoing struggles for African American freedom and equality in the US. Both Dr King's cultural contribution and his assassination serve as prisms for looking at the Civil Rights movement, its precursors and its indelible and continuing impact on American life. The turquoise exterior of the 1950s motel and two preserved interior rooms remain much as they were at the time of King's death, and serve as pilgrimage points in their own right.

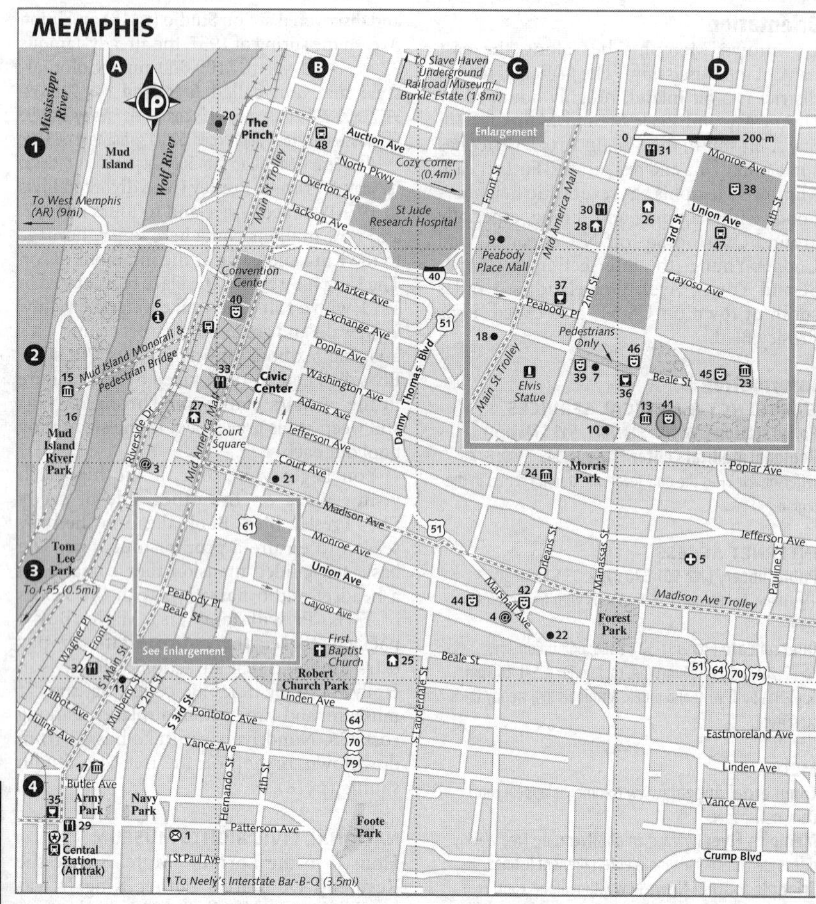

MUSIC SIGHTS

ourpick Sun Studio (☎ 901-521-0664, 800-441-6249; www.sunstudio.com; 706 Union Ave; adult/child $12/free; 🕑 10am-6pm) doesn't look like much from outside, but this dusty storefront is ground zero for American rock and roll music. Starting in the early 1950s, Sun's Sam Phillips recorded blues artists such as Howlin' Wolf, BB King and Ike Turner, followed by the rockabilly dynasty of Jerry Lee Lewis, Johnny Cash, Roy Orbison and, of course, the King himself (who started here in 1953). Today packed 40-minute guided tours through the tiny studio offer a chance to hear original tapes of historic recording sessions. Guides are witty and full of anecdotes; many are musicians themselves. Pose for photos in the old recording studio on the 'X' where Elvis once stood, or buy a CD of the 'Million Dollar Quartet,' Sun's spontaneous 1956 jam session between Elvis, Johnny Cash, Carl Perkins and Jerry Lee Lewis.

From here, you can hop on the studio's free shuttle (hourly, starting at 11:15am), which does a loop between Sun Studio, Beale St and Graceland.

Wanna get funky? Head directly to Soulsville USA, where the 17,000-sq-ft **Stax Museum of American Soul Music** (☎ 901-946-2535; www.staxmuseum.com; 926 E McLemore Ave; adult/child $10/7; 🕑 9am-4pm Mon-Sat, 1-4pm Sun Mar-Oct, 10am-4pm Mon-Sat, 1-4pm Sun Nov-Feb) sits on the site of the old Stax recording studio. This venerable spot was soul music's epicenter in the 1960s,

when Otis Redding, Booker T and the MGs and Wilson Pickett recorded here. Dive into soul-music history with photos, displays of '60s and '70s peacock clothing and, above all, Isaac Hayes' 1972 Superfly Cadillac outfitted with shag-fur carpeting and 24-karat-gold exterior trim.

If you're in town on a Sunday, put on your least-wrinkled pants and head to services at South Memphis' **Full Gospel Tabernacle Church** (☎ 901-396-9192; www.algreenmusic.com; 787 Hale Rd; services 11:30am & 4pm Sun), where soul music legend turned reverend Al Green presides over a powerful choir. Visitors are welcome, and usually take up about half the pews. Join in the whooping 'hallelujahs,' but don't forget to tithe (about $1 is fine).

BEALE STREET

The pedestrian-only stretch of Beale St is a 24-hour carnival zone, where you'll find deep-fried funnel cakes, to-go beer counters, and music, music, music. Although locals don't hang out here much, visitors tend to get a kick out of the ribald, party-happy atmosphere.

Originally built for vaudeville, the **Orpheum Theatre** (☎ 901-525-7800; www.orpheum-memphis.com; 203 S Main St) has been restored to its glittering 1928 glory. Today you can catch big comedy and Broadway shows, but beware; the ghost of a pigtailed little girl named Mary is said to giggle eerily between acts.

The original **A Schwab's** (☎ 901-523-9782; 163 Beale St; 9am-5pm Mon-Sat) dry-goods store has three floors of voodoo powders, $1 neckties and Elvis shot glasses.

On the corner of 4th St, the **WC Handy House Museum** (☎ 901-522-1556; 352 Beale St; adult/child $3/2; 11am-4pm Tue-Sat, later in summer) is a shotgun shack once belonging to the composer called the 'father of the blues.'

The Smithsonian's **Memphis Rock 'n' Soul Museum** (☎ 901-205-2533; www.memphisrocknsoul.org; cnr Lt George W Lee Ave & 3rd St; adult/child $9/6; 10am-7pm), next to FedEx Forum, examines how African American and white music mingled in the Mississippi Delta to create modern sound. The audio tour has more than 100 songs.

Take the fascinating 45-minute tour of the enormous **Gibson Beale Street Showcase** (☎ 901-544-7998; www.gibson.com; 145 Lt George W Lee Ave; admission $10, no children under 5; tours 11am-4pm Mon-Sat, noon-4pm Sun) to see master craftspeople transform solid blocks of wood into legendary Gibson guitars. Tours leave on the hour.

MISSISSIPPI RIVER & MUD ISLAND

A monorail ($4, or free with museum admission) and elevated walkway cross the Wolf River Lagoon to **Mud Island River Park** (☎ 901-576-7241; www.mudisland.com; 125 N Front St; 10am-5pm Tue-Sun, later in summer;). Jog, rent bikes, or wade in the park's awesome scale model of the Mississippi, which empties into a 1.3-million-gallon 'Gulf of Mexico' where visitors tool around in pedal boats. The **Mississippi River Museum** (☎ 901-576-7241; www.mudisland.com; adult/child $8/5; 10am-5pm Apr-May & Sep-Oct, to 6pm Jun-Aug, closed Mon) has a cool full-size replica of a packet boat and other historical displays.

MUSEUMS & HISTORIC HOMES

The 'Victorian Village' district on Adams Ave, east of downtown, has several stunning historic homes, though some are in rather Gothic states of decay. Not so the grand 1870 **Woodruff-Fontaine House** (☎ 901-526-1469; www.woodruff-fontaine.com; 680 Adams Ave; adult/child $10/free; noon-4pm Wed-Sun), which carefully preserves Victorian clothing and furnishings. Docents tell ghost stories.

Slave Haven Underground Railroad Museum/ Burkle Estate (☎ 901-527-3427; 826 N 2nd St; adult/ child $6/4; 10am-1pm Mon-Sat), in an unimposing clapboard house, is thought to have been a way station for runaway slaves on the Underground Railroad, complete with trapdoors and tunnels.

The **Center for Southern Folklore** (☎ 901-525-3655; www.southernfolklore.com; 119 S Main St; admission free; 11am-6pm Mon-Sat, to 5pm in winter), is a well-tended community space with a café, craft gallery and frequent (free!) local music performances and film screenings.

Children's Museum of Memphis (☎ 901-458-2678; www.cmom.com; 2525 Central Ave; admission $9; 9am-5pm Mon-Sat, from noon Sun;) gives the kids a chance to let loose and play in, on and with exhibits such as an airplane cockpit, weaving loom and waterwheel.

The 1923 **Pink Palace Museum & Planetarium** (☎ 901-320-6320; www.memphismuseums.org; 3050 Central Ave; adult/child $8.75/6.25, free Tue afternoon; 9am-5pm Mon-Sat, from noon Sun) was built as a residence for Piggly Wiggly founder Clarence Saunders and opened in 1996 as a natural- and cultural-history museum. It mixes fossils, Civil War exhibits and an exact replica of the original 1916 Piggly Wiggly, the world's first self-service grocery store. It also has an IMAX theater.

OVERTON PARK

Stately homes surround the rolling acres of **Overton Park** (Poplar Ave), where the **Levitt Shell** (☎ 901-272-5159; www.levittshell.org) was the site of Elvis' first concert, in 1954. Today the newly reopened band shell hosts free concerts all summer.

Also within the park, the world-class **Memphis Zoo** (☎ 901-276-9453; www.memphiszoo.org; 2000 Prentiss Pl; adult/child $13/8; 9am-4pm Mar-Oct, to 4pm Nov-Feb;) hosts two giant panda stars, Ya Ya and Le Le, in a $16-million exhibit on native Chinese wildlife and habitat. The Northwest Passage section is home to polar bears, sea lions and eagles. Other residents include the full gamut of monkeys, penguins, African wildlife, etc. Imagine an animal, the zoo probably has it.

At the park's edge is the **Brooks Museum of Art** (☎ 901-544-6200; www.brooksmuseum.org; 1934 Poplar Ave; adult/child $7/3; 10am-4pm Wed-Sat, to 8pm Thu, 11:30am-5pm Sun), with an excellent permanent collection encompassing everything from Renaissance sculpture to Impressionists like Renoir to abstract expressionists like Robert Motherwell.

Tours

Blues City Tours (☎ 901-522-9229; www.bluescity tours.com; adult/child from $24/16) A variety of bus tours, including an Elvis tour.

HOT TOPIC: ABANDONED MEMPHIS

Memphis has struggled with money since the Civil War, leaving it with more than its share of abandoned buildings. What to do with these 'big empties' remains a matter of intense debate among citizens. Here are some of the most bizarre, fascinating and photogenic ruins you'll encounter:

Hotel Chisca (1913 S Main St) Legendary DJ Dewey Phillips first put Elvis on the airwaves from the WHBQ studio in the mezzanine of this hotel, vacant since the 1990s.

Sears Crosstown (N Watkins St) Blotting out the Midtown sun like something from a Tim Burton film, this 1.4-million-sq-ft department store headquarters is too expensive to redevelop or to tear down. Built in 1927, it's been abandoned since 1993.

Sterick Building (8 N 3rd St) Towering over AutoZone Park, this Gothic 1929 office building was once called the 'Queen of Memphis.' It's been empty since the 1980s.

Tennessee Brewery (Tennessee St) This castlelike Victorian complex, built in 1890 overlooking the river, was one of the South's most venerable breweries until it closed its doors a half-century ago. Renovation talks are ongoing.

The Pyramid The 321ft-high Pyramid was meant to be the city's version of the Eiffel Tower, dominating the downtown riverfront since 1991. But the money never came through and, after years as a sports and concert arena, it has sat empty since 2007.

Carriage Tours of Memphis (☎ 901-527-7542; www.carriagetoursofmemphis.com; per 30min $45) Horse carriages depart from Beale St or the Peabody Hotel.

Memphis Riverboats (☎ 901-527-5694, 800-221-6197; www.memphisriverboats.net; adult/child from $20/17) Sightseeing and dinner cruises on the Mississippi.

Memphis Rock Tours (☎ 901-359-3102; www.shangrilaprojects.com; 2-person tour $75) Quirky custom tours of music sites and local restaurants.

Festivals & Events

International Blues Challenge (www.blues.org) Sponsored by the Blues Foundation, each January/February blues acts do battle in front of a panel of judges.

Memphis in May (www.memphisinmay.org) Every Friday, Saturday and Sunday in May, something's cookin', whether it's the Beale St Music Festival, the barbecue contest or the grand finale sunset symphony.

Mid-South Fair (www.midsouthfair.org) Since 1856, folks come out each September to this combo amusement park and agricultural fair.

Sleeping

Cheap and ultracheap chain motels lie off I-40, exit 279, across the river in West Memphis, AR.

Pilgrim House Hostel (☎ 901-273-8341; 1000 S Cooper St; dm/r $15/25; P ⊠ 💻 📶) Yes, it's in a church. No, no one will try to convert you. But the chatty young live-in staff may well invite you for a beer down the street, in Midtown's trendy Cooper-Young neighborhood. An international crowd plays cards and chats (no alcohol) in a sunny, open common area resembling an IKEA catalog. Dorms and private rooms are clean and spare. All guests must do a brief daily chore, like taking out the trash.

Memphis Graceland RV Park & Campground (☎ 901-396-7125; www.elvis.com; 3691 Elvis Presley Blvd; campsites/cabins from $23/42; P 🏊 📶) Next to Graceland and owned by Elvis Presley Enterprises, keep Lisa Marie in business when you camp out or sleep in the no-frills log cabins (with shared bathrooms).

Days Inn Graceland (☎ 901-346-5500; www.daysinn.com; 3839, Elvis Presley Blvd; r from $85; P ⊠ 📶) With a guitar-shaped pool, 24-hour Elvis channel, and neon Cadillacs on the roof, the Days Inn manages to out-Elvis the neighboring Heartbreak Hotel. Guest rooms themselves are clean but nothing special.

Sleep Inn at Court Square (☎ 901-522-9700; www.sleepinn.com; 400 N Front St; r from $94; ⊠ 📶) One of the cheapest downtown options, this stubby stucco box has pleasant modern rooms, with sage-green walls, sparkling shower-only baths, and flat-screen TVs. Parking is $12.

Heartbreak Hotel (☎ 901-332-1000, 877-777-0606; www.elvis.com/epheartbreakhotel/; 3677 Elvis Presley Blvd; d from $112; P ⊠ ⊠ 💻 📶 🏊) At the end of Lonely St (seriously) across from Graceland, this basic hotel is tarted up with all things Elvis. Ramp up the kitsch with one of the themed suites, like the red-velvet monstrosity that is the Burnin' Love room.

Inn at Hunt Phelan (☎ 901-525-8225; www.huntphelan.com; 533 Beale St; ste from $129; P ⊠ ⊠ 📶) Outside the gates are dystopian warehouses and vacant lots. But inside the gates, it's still 1828, the year this aristocratic mansion was built. Sip complimentary evening cocktails

THE SOUTH

by the courtyard fountain and wander the 4.5-acre gardens before retiring to your four-poster bed (or heading to the Beale St bars, just down the road).

our pick **Talbot Heirs** (☎ 901-527-9772, 800-955-3956; www.talbothouse.com; 99 S 2nd St; ste from $130;) More like studio apartments than hotel rooms, each suite has individually chosen furniture and each kitchen is stocked with snacks. Kilim rugs, local artwork, and warm sunlight and staff make this cheerful brownstone smack in the middle of downtown both convenient and comfy. Parking costs $10.

Peabody Hotel (☎ 901-529-4000, 800-732-2639; www.peabodymemphis.com; 149 Union Ave; r from $199;) This grande dame has been Memphis' premier hotel since the 1930s. It's a social center, with a spa, superb restaurants and a classy lobby bar. It also boasts its own quirky tradition: every day for 85 years, at 11am sharp, the hotel's 10 ducks file from the elevator across the red-carpeted lobby, accompanied by their red-coated Duckmaster. The birds cavort in the fountain until 5pm, when they retire to their penthouse. Parking is $21.

Eating

Locals come to blows over which of the city's chopped-pork sandwiches or dry-rubbed ribs are the best. Barbecue joints are scattered across the city; the ugliest exteriors often yield the tastiest goods. Hip young locals head to the S Main Arts District, or Cooper-Young for dinner and drinks.

BUDGET

Payne's Bar-B-Q (☎ 901-942-7433; 1393 Elvis Presley Blvd; mains $4-6; 11am-6:30pm Tue-Sat) We'd say this smudgy South Memphis storefront has the best chopped-pork sandwich in town, but we don't want to have to fight anyone. Decide for yourself.

Gus's World Famous Fried Chicken (☎ 901-527-4877; 310 S Front St; mains $5-9; 11am-9pm Sun-Thu, to 10pm Fri & Sat) Fried chicken connoisseurs across the globe twitch in their sleep at night, dreaming about the gossamer-light fried chicken at this downtown concrete bunker.

Leonard's (☎ 901-528-0875; 103 N Main St; mains $5-12; 11am-2pm Mon & Tue, 11am-2pm & 5-8pm Wed-Fri) The lunch buffet here is popular with downtown office workers, though lord knows how they get any work done afterwards. Pile on the turnip greens, corn pudding, hot-buttered peaches and – oh! – the most succulent, aggressively spiced ribs.

our pick **Cozy Corner** (☎ 901-527-9158; 745 N Pkwy; mains $5-16; 10:30am-5pm Tue-Sat, later in summer) Slouch in a torn vinyl booth and devour an entire barbecued Cornish game hen, the house specialty at this pug-ugly cult favorite.

Neely's Interstate Bar-B-Q (☎ 901-775-1045; 2265 S 3rd St; mains $5-16; 11am-11pm Sun-Thu, to midnight Fri & Sat) Two words: barbecued spaghetti. It's just as weird as it sounds, but not half bad. Jim Neely's ribs and chopped-shoulder sandwiches are superb, and the atmosphere is homey and family-friendly.

Arcade (☎ 901-526-5757; 540 S Main St; mains $6-8; 7am-3pm, plus dinner Fri) Elvis used to eat at this ultraretro diner, Memphis' oldest. Crowds still pack in for sweet potato pancakes and cheeseburgers.

MIDRANGE & TOP END

Charlie Vergos' Rendezvous (☎ 901-523-2746; www.hogsfly.com; 52 S 2nd St; mains $7-18; 4:30-10:30pm Tue-Thu, 11am-11pm Fri & Sat) Tucked in an alleyway off Union Ave, this subterranean institution sells an astonishing 5 tons of its exquisite dry-rubbed ribs weekly. Friendly service and walls plastered with historic memorabilia make eating here an event.

Automatic Slim's Tonga Club (☎ 901-525-7948; 83 S 2nd St; mains $17-26; 11am-late) This sleek, artsy bistro has fusion fare like jerk duck and coconut shrimp, and huge, crayon-colored cocktails.

Restaurant Iris (☎ 901-590-2828; 4146 Monroe Ave; mains $22-34; 5-10pm Tue-Sat, 11am-3pm Sun) Chef Kelly English richly deserved his *Food & Wine Magazine* 2009 Best New Chef award. Since opening Iris in 2008, his avant-garde Creole menu has been sending foodies into paroxysms of delight with playful entries like a 'ham and cheese' of fried Camembert and *tête de cochon* (roast pig head). The setting, in a green cottage on a residential Midtown block, is so low-profile it feels like a speakeasy.

Drinking & Entertainment

Many Memphis restaurants and bars mix food, drinks and music, so it's easy to turn a meal into a party. Beale St is the obvious spot for live blues, country, rock and jazz. Cover for most clubs is free or only a few bucks. Beale St warms up early, and its bars are open all day, while neighborhood clubs tend to start filling up around 10pm. Last call for alcohol is 3am, but bars sometimes close earlier on quiet nights. Hip locals head to the Cooper-Young neighborhood for everything from margarita bars to Irish pubs. To find out what live acts are playing, check www.livefrommemphis.com.

BARS

ourpick Earnestine & Hazel's (☎ 901-523-9754; 531 S Main St) One of the world's greatest dive bars has a second floor full of rusty bedsprings and claw-foot tubs, remnants of its brothel past.

Silky O'Sullivan's (☎ 901-522-9596; 183 Beale St) Party-happy youth swill 'divers' out of yellow plastic buckets while goats graze in the courtyard of this massive bizarro tavern.

Silly Goose (☎ 901-435-6917; 100 Peabody Pl) Beautiful people sip fancy house cocktails (think handmade syrups, rosemary garnishes) at this swank new downtown lounge.

Young Avenue Deli (☎ 901-278-0034; 2119 Young Ave) This Midtown hipster favorite has food, occasional live music, and a laid-back vibe.

LIVE MUSIC

BB King's (☎ 901-524-5464; 143 Beale St) A full restaurant serving ribs and Southern favorites, BB's is better known for its friendly fun-seeking crowd and great live music.

Hi-Tone Cafe (☎ 901-278-8663; www.hitonememphis.com; 1913 Poplar Ave) Near Overton Park, this funky little dive balances pool-shooting with live music.

Kudzu's (☎ 901-525-4924; 603 Monroe Ave) Near downtown, this well-loved pub gets jumping with live bands (Friday and Saturday) and Thursday-night guitar-pickin' jam sessions.

Rum Boogie (☎ 901-528-0150; www.rumboogie.com; 182 Beale St) Huge, popular and noisy, this Cajun-themed Beale club hops every night to the tunes of the house blues band.

THEATER & CULTURE

Orpheum Theatre (☎ 901-525-7800; www.orpheum-memphis.com; 203 S Main St) On Beale, this theater has Broadway shows and big concerts.

New Daisy Theater (☎ 901-525-8971; www.newdaisy.com; 330 Beale St) This groovy place hosts everything from kickboxing to Prince tribute bands.

Cannon Center for Performing Arts (☎ 901-576-1269, 800-726-0915; www.thecannoncenter.com; 255 N Main St) This 2100-seat centre hosts the Memphis Symphony Orchestra and ballet, opera and jazz concerts.

Hattiloo Theatre (☎ 901-525-0009; www.hattilootheatre.org; 656 Marshall Ave) Memphis' African American repertory theatre stages musicals, Shakespeare and modern drama.

SPORTS

Memphis Redbirds (☎ 901-721-6000; www.memphisredbirds.com; tickets $5-18) This American Automobile Association (AAA) minor-league affiliate of the St Louis Cardinals baseball team plays at AutoZone Park April to August.

Memphis Grizzlies (☎ 901-888-4667, 866-648-4667; www.grizzlies.com) The NBA's Grizzlies bring on the basketball action at FedEx Forum from October to April.

Getting There & Around

Memphis International Airport (MEM; ☎ 901-922-8000; www.memphisairport.org; 2491 Winchester Rd) is 12 miles southeast of downtown via I-55; taxis to downtown cost $27. **Memphis Area Transit Authority** (MATA; ☎ 901-274-6282; www.matatransit.com; 444 N Main St; fares $1.50) operates local buses; 2A and 32A go to the airport. MATA's vintage trolleys ($1, every 12 minutes) ply Main St and Front St downtown. **Greyhound** (☎ 901-523-1184; 203 Union Ave) is right downtown, as is **Central Station** (☎ 901-526-0052; 545 S Main St), the Amtrak terminal.

SHILOH NATIONAL MILITARY PARK

'No soldier who took part in the two days' engagement at Shiloh ever spoiled for a fight again,' said one veteran of the bloody 1862 battle, which took place among these lovely fields and forests. During the fight 3400 soldiers died, and the Confederate forces were eventually repelled by the Union.

The **Shiloh National Military Park** (☎ 731-689-5696; www.nps.gov/shil; park entry $3; 8am-5pm) is located just north of the Mississippi border near the town of Crump, TN. The visitor center gives out maps and shows a video about the battle, and sells an audio tour.

The vast park can only be seen by car. Sights along the route include the Shiloh National Cemetery, an overlook of the Cumberland River where Union reinforcement troops arrived by ship, and various markers and monuments.

NASHVILLE

Imagine you're an aspiring country singer, arriving in downtown Nashville after days of hitchhiking, with nothing but your battered guitar on your back. Gaze up at the neon lights of Lower Broadway, take a deep breath of smoky, beer-perfumed air, feel the boot-stompin' rumble from deep inside the crowded honky-tonks, and say to yourself 'I've made it.'

For country-music fans and wannabe songwriters all over the world, a trip to Nashville is the ultimate pilgrimage. Think of any song involving a pickup truck, a bottle of booze, a no-good woman, or a late, lamented hound dog, and chances are it came from Nashville. Since the 1920s the city has been attracting musicians who have taken the country genre from the 'hillbilly music' of the early 20th century to the slick 'Nashville sound' of the 1960s to the punk-tinged alt-country of the 1990s.

Nashville has many attractions to keep you busy, from the Country Music Hall of Fame and the revered Grand Ole Opry House to rough blues bars, historic buildings and big-name sports. It also has friendly people, a lively university community, excellent fried chicken and an unrivaled assortment of tacky souvenirs.

History

Originally inhabited by the Shawnee, the city was settled by Europeans in 1779 and named Fort Nashborough after Revolutionary War hero Francis Nash.

By the beginning of the Civil War, Nashville was prospering as a river port and railway center, only to be hammered down by Union troops. The Tennessee Centennial Exposition in 1897 and its concurrent building boom signaled the city's recovery – the lovely Victorian-style brick buildings of downtown are a legacy of this period.

From 1925, Nashville became known for its live-music radio program *Barn Dance*, later nicknamed the *Grand Ole Opry*. Its popularity soared, the city proclaimed itself the 'country-music capital of the world' and recording studios sprang up in Music Row.

Today Nashville is the second most populous city in Tennessee, with more than a dozen colleges and universities and an economy based on music, tourism, health care and publishing.

Orientation

Nashville sits on a rise beside the Cumberland River, with the state capitol situated at the highest point. The compact downtown area slopes south to Broadway, the city's central artery. Briley Pkwy forms a ring around the city and connects to I-40 to take you out of town.

Downtown, the entertainment area called 'the District' runs along Broadway from 2nd Ave to 5th Ave, with divey honky-tonks rubbing up against tourist-grabbers like the Hard Rock Cafe. Across the Cumberland River is the up-and-coming East End, where gritty commercial stretches alternate with historical residential neighborhoods. The West End is a lively area around Vanderbilt University, with funky shops and restaurants along Broadway, West End Ave, and Elliston Pl. Ten minutes northeast of downtown off Briley Pkwy, Music Valley is a tourist zone full of budget motels, franchise restaurants and outlet stores built around the Grand Ole Opry.

Information

BOOKSTORES

Elder's Bookstore (☎ 615-327-1867; www.eldersbookstore.com; 2115 Elliston Pl; 🕑 10am-4:30pm Mon-Fri, to 4pm Sat) This excellent used-book shop has been around since the 1930s.

EMERGENCY & MEDICAL SERVICES

Baptist Hospital (☎ 615-284-5555; 2000 Church St)
Main police station (☎ 615-862-8600; 310 1st Ave S)
Vanderbilt University Medical Center (☎ 615-322-5000; 1211 22nd Ave S)

INTERNET ACCESS

Centennial Park (2600 W End Ave; wi-fi) Has free wi-fi, as do all locations of Tennessee's homegrown fast-food chain, Krystal Burger.
Public library (☎ 615-862-5800; www.library.nashville.org; 615 Church St; 🕑 9am-8pm Mon-Thu, 9am-6pm Fri, 9am-5pm Sat, 2-5pm Sun) Free internet access.

INTERNET RESOURCES & MEDIA

InsideOut (www.insideoutnashville.com) A weekly covering the local gay and lesbian scene.
Metromix (www.nashville.metromix.com) A useful entertainment and music listings website.
Nashville Convention & Visitors Bureau (www.nashvillecvb.com) Has a great online visitors' guide and hotel booking portal.
Nashville Scene (www.nashvillescene.com) Free alternative weekly with entertainment listings.
Tennessean (www.tennessean.com) Nashville's daily newspaper.

POST

Post office (☎ 800-275-8777; 1718 Church St; 🕑 8am-5:30pm Mon-Fri)

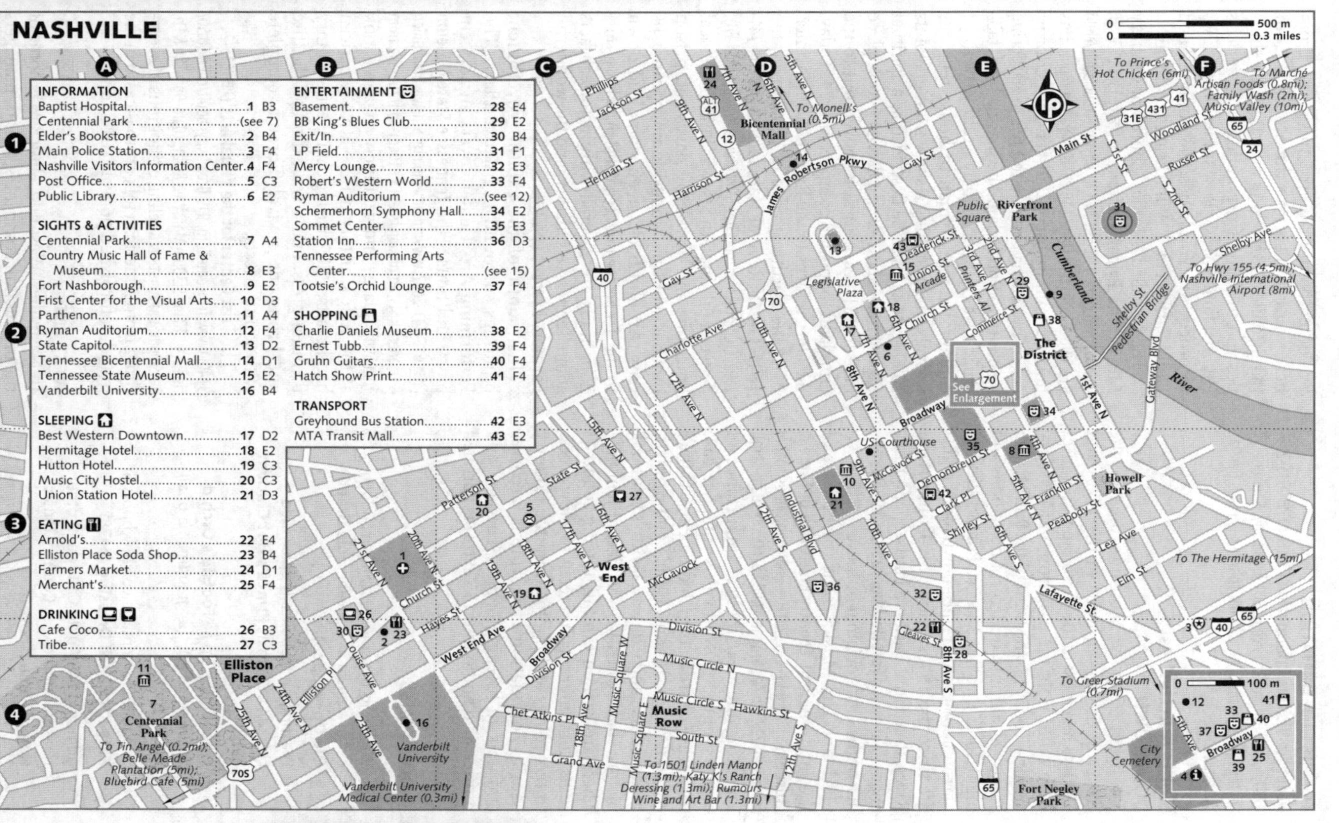
NASHVILLE
0 500 m
0 0.3 miles
INFORMATION
Baptist Hospital 1 B3
Centennial Park (see 7)
Elder's Bookstore 2 B4
Main Police Station 3 F4
Nashville Visitors Information Center 4 F4
Post Office 5 C3
Public Library 6 E2
SIGHTS & ACTIVITIES
Centennial Park 7 A4
Country Music Hall of Fame & Museum 8 E3
Fort Nashborough 9 E2
Frist Center for the Visual Arts 10 D3
Parthenon 11 A4
Ryman Auditorium 12 F4
State Capitol 13 D2
Tennessee Bicentennial Mall 14 D1
Tennessee State Museum 15 E2
Vanderbilt University 16 B4
SLEEPING
Best Western Downtown 17 D2
Hermitage Hotel 18 E2
Hutton Hotel 19 C3
Music City Hostel 20 C3
Union Station Hotel 21 D3
EATING
Arnold's 22 E4
Elliston Place Soda Shop 23 B4
Farmers Market 24 D1
Merchant's 25 F4
DRINKING
Cafe Coco 26 B3
Tribe 27 C3
ENTERTAINMENT
Basement 28 E4
BB King's Blues Club 29 E2
Exit/In 30 B4
LP Field 31 F1
Mercy Lounge 32 E3
Robert's Western World 33 F4
Ryman Auditorium (see 12)
Schermerhorn Symphony Hall 34 E2
Sommet Center 35 E3
Station Inn 36 D3
Tennessee Performing Arts Center (see 15)
Tootsie's Orchid Lounge 37 F4
SHOPPING
Charlie Daniels Museum 38 E2
Ernest Tubb 39 F4
Gruhn Guitars 40 F4
Hatch Show Print 41 F4
TRANSPORT
Greyhound Bus Station 42 E3
MTA Transit Mall 43 E2
To Prince's Hot Chicken (6mi)
To Marché Artisan Foods (0.8mi); Family Wash (2mi); Music Valley (10mi)
To Monell's (0.5mi)
To Hwy 155 (4.5mi); Nashville International Airport (8mi)
To The Hermitage (15mi)
To Greer Stadium (0.7mi)
To 1501 Linden Manor (1.3mi); Katy K's Ranch Deressing (1.3mi); Rumours Wine and Art Bar (1.3mi)
Vanderbilt University Medical Center (0.3mi)
To Tin Angel (0.2mi); Belle Meade Plantation (5mi); Bluebird Cafe (5mi)
Bicentennial Mall
Riverfront Park
Public Square
Cumberland River
The District
See Enlargement
Howell Park
Legislative Plaza
US Courthouse
West End
Elliston Place
Centennial Park
Vanderbilt University
Music Row
City Cemetery
Fort Negley Park
0 100 m

THE SOUTH

TOURIST INFORMATION

Nashville Visitors Information Center (☎ 615-259-4747; www.visitmusiccity.com; 501 Broadway, Sommet Center; 8:30am-5:30pm) Pick up free city maps here at the glass tower.

Sights & Activities

DOWNTOWN

The historic 2nd Ave N business area was the center of the cotton trade in the 1870s and 1880s, when most of the Victorian warehouses were built; note the cast-iron and masonry facades. Today it's the heart of the **District**, with shops, restaurants, underground saloons and nightclubs. Two blocks west, **Printers Alley** is a narrow cobblestoned lane known for its nightlife since the 1940s. Along the Cumberland River, Riverfront Park is a landscaped promenade featuring **Fort Nashborough**, a 1930s replica of the city's original outpost.

'Honor Thy Music' is the catchphrase of the monumental **Country Music Hall of Fame & Museum** (☎ 615-416-2001; www.countrymusichalloffame.com; 222 5th Ave S; adult/child $22/15; 9am-5pm), reflecting the near-biblical importance of country music to Nashville's soul. See case upon case of artifacts including Patsy Cline's cocktail gown, Johnny Cash's guitar, Elvis' gold Cadillac and Conway Twitty's yearbook picture (back when he was Harold Jenkins). There are written exhibits tracing country's roots, computer touch screens to allow access to recordings and photos from the Country Music Foundation's enormous archives and walk-in listening booths. The fact- and music-filled audio tour ($5 extra) is narrated by contemporary country musicians. From here you can also take the Studio B Tour (adult/child $13/11, one hour), which shuttles you to Radio Corporation of America's (RCA's) famed Music Row studio, where Elvis recorded 'Are You Lonesome Tonight?' and Dolly Parton cut 'I Will Always Love You.'

The so-called 'Mother Church of Country Music,' the **Ryman Auditorium** (☎ 615-889-3060; www.ryman.com; 116 5th Ave N; daytime tour adult/child $12.50/6.25, incl backstage $16.25/10; 9am-4pm) has hosted a laundry list of 20th-century performers, from Martha Graham to Elvis to Katherine Hepburn to Bob Dylan. The soaring brick tabernacle was built in 1890 by wealthy riverboat captain Thomas Ryman to house religious revivals, and watching a show from one of its 2000 seats can still be described as a spiritual experience. The *Grand Ole Opry* took place here for 31 years, until it moved out to the Opryland (opposite) complex in 1974. Today, the *Opry* returns to the Ryman during winter.

At the northeast edge of downtown, the 1845 Greek Revival **state capitol** (☎ 615-741-2692; Charlotte Ave; tours free; tours 9am-4pm Mon-Fri), between 6th and 7th Sts, was built from local limestone and marble by slaves and prison inmates working alongside European artisans. Around back, steep stairs lead down to the **Tennessee Bicentennial Mall**, whose outdoor walls are covered with historical facts about Tennessee's history, and the wonderful Farmers Market (p429).

Just south of the capitol, government buildings surround Legislative Plaza. The Performing Arts Center covers an adjacent block and houses the **Tennessee State Museum** (☎ 615-741-2692; www.tnmuseum.org; 5th Ave, btwn Union & Deaderick Sts; admission free; 10am-5pm Tue-Sat, from 1pm Sun), a large and genuinely engaging look at the state's history, with Native American handicrafts, a life-size log cabin, 18th-century printing press, and a walk-through 'hellfire and brimstone' revival diorama, complete with sound effects.

The **Frist Center for the Visual Arts** (☎ 615-244-3340; www.fristcenter.org; 919 Broadway; adult/child $8.50/free; 10am-5:30pm Mon-Wed & Sat, 10am-9pm Thu & Fri, 1-5:30pm Sun) hosts traveling exhibitions of everything from American folk art to Picasso in the grand, refurbished post office building.

WEST END

In Nashville's West End, **Music Row** is home of the production companies, agents, managers

DON'T MISS

- Watching the singin', stompin', fiddlin' extravaganza at the venerable **Grand Ole Opry** (opposite)
- Feasting on diabolically spicy fried chicken at 3am at **Prince's Hot Chicken** (p429)
- Whooping it up at **Tootsie's Orchid Lounge** (p431), the grandmama of all honky-tonks
- Shopping for vintage cowboy boots at **Katy K's Ranch Dressing** (p428)
- Admiring Elvis' gold Caddy and other treasures at the vast **Country Music Hall of Fame** (above)

NASHVILLE...

In Two Days

Grab a meat-and-three (we like the roast beef) at **Arnold's** (p429) and go ogle Elvis' gold Cadillac at the **Country Music Hall of Fame** (opposite). See who's stompin' the stage at **Tootsie's Wild Orchid Lounge** (p431) and wander the smoky honky-tonks of the **District** (opposite) until dawn.

The next day, explore the tacky wonderland of **Music Valley** (below) and take in a show at the venerable **Grand Ole Opry House** (p431). Swing up to north Nashville for some late-night eats at deadly delicious **Prince's Hot Chicken** (p429).

In Four Days

In addition to the two-day itinerary: suck down an old-fashioned milk shake at **Elliston Place Soda Shop** (p429) and go check out the vintage cowboy boots at **Katy K's Ranch Dressing** (p428) in the funky 12th Ave S neighborhood. Book a table at **Bluebird Cafe** (p430) to see some of the best singer-songwriters play at a strip mall hole-in-the-wall.

The next morning, hang out with Vandy students in Centennial Park and visit the hilarious reproduction **Parthenon** (below) before strolling over to punky **Elliston Place** (below) for a brunch of pie at all-night **Cafe Coco** (p430). Then experience 19th-century plantation life first-hand at the **Hermitage** (below), the home of seventh US president Andrew Jackson.

and promoters who run Nashville's country-music industry. There's not much to see, but you can pay to cut your own record at some of the smaller studios (about $25 to $100 an hour). 'World's Greatest Love Songs on the Kazoo,' anyone?

Elliston Place is an enclave of bohemia anchored by the ancient Elliston Place Soda Shop (p429) and Elder's Bookstore (p424).

Almost 12,000 students attend the prestigious **Vanderbilt University**, founded in 1883 by railway magnate Cornelius Vanderbilt, who wanted to give the South a world-class university. The 330-acre campus buzzes with students, who eat, shop and drink along 21st Ave N, Broadway and West End Ave.

Yes, that is indeed a reproduction Athenian **Parthenon** (☎ 615-862-8431; www.parthenon.org; 2600 West End Ave; adult/child $6/3.50; 🕑 9am-4:30pm Tue-Sat, plus Sun in summer) sitting in **Centennial Park**. Originally built in 1897 for Tennessee's Centennial Exposition and rebuilt in 1930 due to popular demand, the full-scale plaster copy of the 438-BC original now houses an art museum with a collection of American paintings and a 42ft statue of the Greek goddess Athena.

MUSIC VALLEY

This suburban tourist zone is about 10 miles northeast of downtown at Hwy 155/Briley Pkwy exits 11 and 12B, and also reachable by bus.

The **Grand Ole Opry House** (☎ 615-871-6779; www.opry.com; 2802 Opryland Dr; tours $10) seats 4400 fans in a squarish modern building for the *Grand Ole Opry* on Friday and Saturday from March to November (see p431). Guided backstage tours are offered daily by reservation. The **Grand Ole Opry Museum** (☎ 615-889-3060; 2802 Opryland Dr; admission free; 🕑 10:30am-6pm Mar-Dec) across the plaza tells the story of the *Opry* with wax characters, colorful costumes and dioramas. Check out the model of Marty Robbins' 1970s Nashville office, all orange shag carpet and cowboy prints. Next door, the **Opry Mills Mall** (☎ 615-514-1100; 🕑 10am-9:30pm Mon-Sat, to 7pm Sun) houses an IMAX theater, theme restaurants and the **Gibson Bluegrass Showcase** (☎ 615-514-2200, ext 2231; www.gibson.com; 161 Opry Mills Dr; 🕑 10am-9:30pm Mon-Sat, to 7pm Sun), where you can see banjos, mandolins and resonator guitars being made through the glass.

PLANTATIONS

The former home of seventh president Andrew Jackson, the **Hermitage** (☎ 615-889-2941; www.thehermitage.com; 4580 Rachel's Lane; adult/child $17/7; 🕑 8:30am-5pm Apr-Oct, 9am-4:30pm Oct-Mar) lies 15 miles east of downtown. The 1000-acre plantation is a peek into what life was like for a Mid-South gentleman farmer in the 19th century. Tour the Federal-style brick mansion, now a furnished house museum with costumed interpreters, and see Jackson's original 1804 log cabin and the

VIVA NASHVEGAS!

Brash, glittery Nashville is proud to have earned the nickname NashVegas. So put on your rhinestone cowboy boots and explore the city's weird and wild side of town.

'Outlaw Country' star Willie Nelson sold all his worldly goods to pay off $16.7 million in unpaid taxes in the early 1990s. You can see them at the **Willie Nelson Museum** (McGavock Pike, Music Valley), which might as well be called the Everything-But-Willie-Nelson's-Used-Toothbrush Museum. Up the street is the **Music City Wax Museum** (2515 McGavock Pik), with eerie, corpse-like statues of country stars dead and alive.

The Tuesday-night **Doyle and Debbie** show at the Station Inn (p430) is a cult-hit parody of a washed-up country-music duo.

Printer's Alley, once the epicenter of NashVegas vice, has cleaned up but still has at least one bar advertising **nude karaoke**. That's all we have to say about that.

Also downtown, the **Charlie Daniels Museum** (110 2nd Ave N) is less museum and more gift shop, hawking everything from bacon-scented air fresheners to T-shirts bearing the likeness of 'Devil Went Down to Georgia' singer Daniels, who looks like a chicken-fried Santa Claus.

In the quirky 12th Ave S neighborhood, a former stylist to New York City's drag queens stocks bouffant wigs, vintage cowboy boots, and handmade bolo ties at **Katy K's Ranch Dressing** (2407 12th Ave S).

old slave quarters (Jackson was a lifelong supporter of slavery, at times owning up to 150 slaves; a special exhibit tells their stories). The arcadian gardens and grounds are lovely to wander, though somewhat marred by the highway passing nearby.

Six miles west of Nashville is **Belle Meade Plantation** (☎ 615-356-0501; www.bellemeadeplantation.com; 5025 Harding Pike; adult/child $15/7; 9am-5pm Mon-Sat, from 11am Sun), where the Harding-Jackson family began raising thoroughbreds in the early 1800s. Every horse entered in the Kentucky Derby in the past five years is a descendant of Belle Meade's studly sire, Bonnie Scotland, who died in 1880. The 1853 mansion is open to visitors, as are various interesting outbuildings, including a model slave cabin.

THE SOUTH

Tours

Ask at the visitor center for a list of the many theme tours available in Nashville.

General Jackson Showboat (☎ 615-458-3900; www.generaljackson.com; tours from $14) Sightseeing cruises of varying length on the Cumberland River, some with music and food.

Gray Line (☎ 615-883-5555, 800-251-1864; www.graylinenashville.com; tours from $40) Offers a variety of bus tours, including a Homes of the Stars tour.

our pick **NashTrash** (☎ 800-342-2132, 615-226-7300; www.nashtrash.com; 900 8th Ave N) The big-haired 'Jugg Sisters' offer a campy frolic ($32, 1½ hours) through the risqué side of Nashville history while guests sip BYO booze.

Festivals & Events

CMA Music Festival (☎ 800-262-3378; www.cmafest.com) Draws tens of thousands of country-music fans to town each June.

Tennessee State Fair (☎ 615-862-8980; www.tennesseestatefair.org) Nine days of racing pigs, mule-pulls and cake bake-offs every September.

Sleeping

Bargain-bin chain motels cluster on all sides of downtown, along I-40 and I-65. Rooms are usually cheaper midweek, and pricier in summer. Be aware: hotel tax in Nashville adds 14.25%.

DOWNTOWN

Best Western Downtown (☎ 615-242-4311, 800-627-3297; www.bestwesterntennessee.com; 711 Union St; r from $125; P) This beige box has 101 clean, basic motel-style rooms. The cheapest rates in downtown Nashville plus free parking make up for the total lack of charm.

our pick **Union Station Hotel** (☎ 615-726-1001; www.unionstationhotelnashville.com; 1001 Broadway; r from $188;) This soaring Romanesque stone castle was once a train station and is now the city's grandest hotel. The vaulted lobby is dressed in peach and gold with inlaid marble floors and a stained-glass ceiling. Rooms are tastefully modern, with flat-screen TVs and deep soaking tubs. Parking costs $18.

Hermitage Hotel (☎ 615-244-3121, 888-888-9414; www.thehermitagehotel.com; 231 6th Ave N; r from $339;) Nashville's first million-dollar hotel was a hit with the socialites when it opened in 1910. The lobby feels like a Czar's palace, every surface covered in rich tapestries and ornate carvings. Rooms are generic upscale, with plush beds and mahogany furniture. Parking costs $18.

WEST END

Music City Hostel (☎ 615-692-1277; www.musiccityhostel.com; 1809 Patterson St; dm/r $25/70; P ✲ 💻 wi-fi) These squat brick bungalows are less than scenic, but Nashville's only hostel is lively and welcoming, with bike rental, common kitchen, a computer and free wi-fi. The crowd is young, international and fun – you can almost guarantee an evening jam session in the courtyard. Many fun West End bars are within walking distance.

1501 Linden Manor (☎ 615-298-2701; www.nashville-bed-breakfast.com; 1501 Linden Ave; r from $125; P ✲ wi-fi) The husband-and-wife owners have filled this yellow Victorian cottage with antiques collected through their world travels – Persian rugs, Asian carvings, old Victrolas. Have homemade egg soufflés for breakfast in the sunny dining room, or dip your hand into the 'bottomless cookie jar' anytime.

Hutton Hotel (☎ 615-340-9333; www.huttonhotel.com; 1808 West End Ave; r from $189; P ✲ 💻 wi-fi) Nashville's newest hotel is also its slickest, riffing on mid-Century Modern design with bamboo-paneled walls and grown-up beanbags in the lobby. Rust- and chocolate-colored rooms have miniature cactus gardens and a number of ecofriendly touches.

MUSIC VALLEY

Nashville KOA Kampground (☎ 615-889-0282, 800-562-7789; www.koa.com; 2626 Music Valley Dr; campsites $39, cabins from $60, lodges $129; P wi-fi) Popular with RVers, this well-manicured, wholesome campground also has tent sites, cabins, and lodges with kitchenettes, all set back from the road. Amenities include a pool, game room, and snack bar.

Gaylord Opryland Hotel (☎ 615-889-1000, 866-972-6779; www.gaylordhotels.com; 2800 Opryland Dr; r from $189; P ⊠ ✲ 💻 wi-fi) This whopping 2881-room hotel is a universe unto itself. Why set foot outdoors when you could ride a paddleboat along an artificial river, eat sushi beneath a faux waterfall in an indoor garden, shop for bolo ties in a model 19th-century town, or sip Scotch in an antebellum-style mansion, all *inside* the hotel's three massive glass atriums.

Eating

The classic Nashville meal is the 'meat-and-three' – a heaping portion of fried chicken, meatloaf, etc with your choice of three home-style sides. But there are plenty of options, from steakhouses popular with Music Row powerbrokers to quirky West End bistros. Many of the restaurants in the District are high-volume tourist traps and should be avoided.

BUDGET

Farmers Market (☎ 615-880-2001; 900 8th Ave N, at Jackson St; 🕑 9am-6pm) This daily market has fresh produce and a covered food court serving tacos, gyros, jerk chicken, po'boys and more.

Elliston Place Soda Shop (☎ 615-327-1090; 2111 Elliston Pl; mains $3-6; 🕑 7am-7pm Mon-Sat) This eatery has served fountain Cokes and meat-and-threes to Vandy students since the 1930s, and the decor hasn't changed much since.

Prince's Hot Chicken (☎ 615-226-9442; 123 Ewing Dr; mains $4-8; 🕑 noon-10pm Tue-Thu, noon-4am Fri & Sat) Cayenne-rubbed 'hot chicken,' fried to succulent perfection and served on a piece of white bread with a side of pickles, is Nashville's unique contribution to the culinary universe. Tiny, faded Prince's, in a northside strip mall, is a local legend. In mild, medium, hot and death-defying extra hot, its chicken will burn a hole in your stomach and you'll come back begging for more.

Arnold's (☎ 615-256-4455; 605 8th Ave S; mains $5-8; 🕑 6am-2:30pm Mon-Fri) Grab a tray and line up with college students, garbagemen, and country-music stars at Arnold's, king of the meat-and-three. Slabs of drippy roast beef are the house specialty, along with fried green tomatoes, cornbread two ways, and big gooey wedges of chocolate cream pie.

Family Wash (☎ 615-226-6070; 2038 Greenwood Ave; mains $9-15; 🕑 6pm-midnight Tue-Sat) This East Nashville neighborhood gastropub is the kind of place where you can eat a sublime roast-garlic shepherd's pie and nurse a microbrew while watching the bartender shoot the breeze with the regulars and kids play with toy cars on the floor. Live music gets rolling on the small stage around 9pm most nights.

MIDRANGE & TOP END

Tin Angel (☎ 615-298-3444; 3201 West End Ave; mains $10-19; 🕑 11am-10pm Mon-Fri, 5-10pm Sat, 11am-3pm Sun) This West Nashville bistro serves Tennessee-meets-Paris fare (think steak frites, pecan torte) in a cute corner space with exposed-brick walls and pressed-tin ceilings.

Monell's (☎ 615-248-4747; 1235 6th Ave N; all-you-can-eat $15; 🕑 10:30am-2pm Mon, 10:30am-2pm & 5-8:30pm Tue-Fri, 8:30am-1pm & 5-8:30pm Sat, 8:30am-4pm Sun) In an old brick house just north of the District, Monell's is beloved for down-home Southern food served communally, meaning you sit with strangers and pass the food around the table yourselves. This being Nashville, you'll all be friends before you're done with your fried catfish.

Marché Artisan Foods (☎ 615-262-1111; 1000 Main St; mains $12-16; 🕑 8am-9pm Tue-Fri, brunch 9am-4pm Sat & Sun) In rapidly gentrifying East Nashville, this airy new bistro has a veggie-friendly menu of light French- and Italian-inflected fare, made with seasonal local ingredients. Drop in for a cinnamon brioche at breakfast, or a plate of homemade gnocchi with sweet corn for dinner.

Merchant's (☎ 615-254-1892; 401 Broadway; mains $20-39; 🕑 11am-11pm Mon-Thu, 11am-midnight Fri & Sat, 4-9pm Sun) In a renovated 19th-century hotel in the heart of the District, this clubby bistro has gleaming parquet floors, white tablecloths and a mahogany bar overlooking Broadway. Splurge on ritzy, old-school fare such as *steak au poivre* (pepper steak) and chicken Louis. The downstairs Grille has cheaper, more casual eats.

Drinking & Entertainment

Nashville has the nightlife of a city three times its size, and you'll be hard-pressed to find a place that *doesn't* have live music. College students, bachelor party–goers, Danish backpackers and conventioneers all rock out downtown, where neon-lit Broadway looks like a country-fried Las Vegas. Bars and venues west and south of downtown tend to attract more locals, with many places clustered near Vanderbilt University. Last call is at 3am, so many bars stay open until then when it's busy.

BARS & NIGHTCLUBS

Cafe Coco (☎ 615-321-2626; 210 Louise Ave; 🕑 24hr) In a ramshackle old cottage just off Elliston Pl, Cafe Coco is like an especially groovy frat house, with a 24-hour whirl of action. People snack on sandwiches and cake in the front parlor, smoke on the large patio, drink at the bar, and tap away on laptops in the old bedrooms (there's free wi-fi).

Tribe (☎ 615-329-2912; 1517 Church St) Ultra-friendly Tribe caters to a largely gay and lesbian crowd, though everyone is welcome to sip martinis, watch music videos and dance the night away at this slick, modern club.

Rumours Wine and Art Bar (☎ 615-292-9400; 2404 12th Ave S; 🕑 5pm-midnight Mon-Sat) If you need a rest from neon NashVegas, head to the hip but low-key 12th Ave S neighborhood for a glass of Malbec at this arty hangout.

LIVE MUSIC

Nashville's opportunities for hearing live music are unparalleled. As well as the big venues, many talented country, folk, bluegrass, Southern-rock and blues performers play smoky honky-tonks, college bars, coffee shops and organic cafés for tips. Many places are free Monday to Friday or if you arrive early enough.

Bluebird Cafe (☎ 615-383-1461; www.bluebirdcafe.com; 4104 Hillsboro Rd; cover free-$15; 🕑 shows 6pm & 9:30pm) It's in a strip mall in suburban South Nashville, but don't let that fool you: some of the best original singer-songwriters in country music have graced this tiny stage. Steve Earle, Emmylou Harris, and the Cowboy Junkies have all played the Bluebird, which was the setting for the 1993 Sandra Bullock and River Phoenix movie *The Thing Called Love*. Try your luck at Monday open mike nights.

BB King's Blues Club (☎ 615-256-2727; www.bbkingbluesclub.com; 152 2nd Ave N) Watch live jazz and blues in this downtown cathedral of sound, complete with stained-glass windows and folk-art portraits of the 'saints': Johnny Cash, Miles Davis, Elvis. The kitchen serves soul food like ribs, fried chicken and catfish.

Robert's Western World (☎ 615-244-9552; www.robertswesternworld.com; 416 Broadway) Buy a pair of boots, a beer or a burger at Robert's, a longtime favorite on the strip. Music starts at 11am and goes all night; Brazilbilly, the house band, rocks it after 10pm on weekends.

Ryman Auditorium (☎ tickets 615-458-8700, info 615-889-3060; www.ryman.com; 116 5th Ave) The Ryman's excellent acoustics, historic charm and large seating capacity have kept it the premier venue in town (p426). The *Opry* returns for winter runs (opposite).

Station Inn (☎ 615-255-3307; www.stationinn.com; 402 12th Ave S) South of downtown, this unassuming stone building is the best place in town for serious bluegrass.

OUR PICK **Tootsie's Orchid Lounge** (☎ 615-726-7937; www.tootsies.net; 422 Broadway) The most venerated of the downtown honky-tonks, Tootsie's vibrates with boot-stompin' every night of the week. In the 1960s, club owner and den mother 'Tootsie' Bess nurtured the likes of Willie Nelson, Kris Kristofferson and Waylon Jennings. Now, up-and-coming country musicians play the two tiny stages and it's not unusual for big stars to stop by for an impromptu jam session.

Tired of country? On Elliston Pl, **Exit/In** (☎ 615-321-3340; www.exitin.com; 2208 Elliston Pl), opened in 1971, does indie rock, hip-hop, and more. Beneath Grimey's Records, the **Basement** (☎ 615-254-8006; www.thebasementnashville.com; 1604 8th Ave S) has intimate alt-rock and folk shows. Up the street is **Mercy Lounge** (☎ 615-251-3020, www.mercylounge.com; 1 Cannery Row) with arty rock and roll shows in an old brick cannery.

THEATER

Grand Ole Opry (☎ 615-871-6779; www.opry.com; 2802 Opryland Dr, Music Valley; adult $36-53, child $26-53) Though you'll find a variety of country shows throughout the week, the performance to see is the *Grand Ole Opry,* a lavish tribute to classic Nashville country music, every Tuesday, Friday and Saturday night. Shows return to the Ryman from November to February.

Nashville Symphony (☎ 615-687-6500; 1 Symphony Pl; www.nashvillesymphony.org) Hosts maestros and pop stars in the shiny new Schemerhorn Symphony Hall.

Tennessee Performing Arts Center (☎ 615-782-4000; www.tpac.org; 505 Deaderick St) With three great stages, this center is home to the Nashville Ballet, the Nashville Opera, and the Tennessee Repertory Company.

SPORTS

Tennessee Titans (☎ 615-565-4200; www.titansonline.com) The NFL Tennessee Titans play at LP Field, across the river from downtown, from August to December.

Nashville Sounds (☎ 615-242-4371; www.nashvillesounds.com) A minor-league AAA baseball affiliate for the Pittsburgh Pirates, the Sounds play at Greer Stadium, south of town.

Nashville Predators (☎ 615-770-2300; www.nashvillepredators.com) For NHL hockey, catch the Nashville Predators at the Sommet Center from September through April.

IF YOU HAVE A FEW MORE DAYS

About 20 miles south of Nashville off I-65, the historic town of **Franklin** (www.historicfranklin.com) has a charming downtown and beautiful B&Bs. Stop off at **Puckett's Grocery** (☎ 615-794-5527; 120 4th Ave S; mains $10-20; ⏰ 6am-6pm Sun-Thu, to late Fri & Sat) for a fried-catfish sandwich and some bluegrass. About an hour further south via the scenic US-41, **Shelbyville** (www.shelbyvilletn.com) is the epicenter of the high-stepping, head-bobbing Tennessee walking horse.

Shopping

Ernest Tubb (☎ 615-255-7503; 417 Broadway) Marked by a giant neon guitar sign, this is the best place to shop for country and bluegrass records. Open late.

Gruhn Guitars (☎ 615-256-2033; 400 Broadway) This renowned vintage instrument store has expert staff.

Hatch Show Print (☎ 615-256-2805; 316 Broadway) One of the oldest letter-print shops in the US. Using old-school cut-blocks, Hatch began making posters to promote early vaudeville and circus shows. The company has produced graphic ads and posters for almost every country star since.

Getting There & Around

Nashville International Airport (BNS; ☎ 615-275-1675; www.nashintl.com), 8 miles east of town, is not a major air hub. MTA bus 18 links the airport and downtown; the **Gray Line Airport Express** (☎ 615-275-1180; www.graylinenashville.com; one way/return $12/20; ⏰ 5am-11pm) serves major downtown and West End hotels. Taxis charge a flat rate of $25 to downtown or Opryland.

Greyhound (☎ 615-255-3556; 200 8th Ave S) is less than a mile from downtown.

The **Metropolitan Transit Authority** (MTA; ☎ 615-862-5950; www.nashvillemta.org; fares $1.60) operates city bus services based downtown at **Transit Mall** (cnr Deaderick St & 4th Ave N). Express buses go to Music Valley.

EASTERN TENNESSEE

Dolly Parton, Eastern Tennessee's most famous native, loves her home region so much she has made a successful career out of singing about girls who leave the honeysuckle-scented embrace of the Smoky Mountains for the false glitter of the city. They're always sorry.

SCENIC DRIVE: NATCHEZ TRACE PARKWAY

About 25 miles southwest of Nashville off Hwy 100, drivers pick up the **Natchez Trace Pkwy** (☎ 800-305-7417), which leads 444 miles southwest to Natchez, Mississippi (p470). This northern section is one of the most attractive stretches of the entire route, with broad-leafed trees leaning together to form an arch over the winding road. There are three primitive campsites along the way, free and available on a first-come, first-served basis. Near the parkway entrance, stop at the landmark **Loveless Cafe**, a 1950s roadhouse famous for its biscuits with homemade preserves, country ham, and ample portions of Southern fried chicken.

Largely a rural region of small towns, rolling hills and river valleys, the eastern third of the state has friendly folks, hearty country food and pastoral charm to make most anyone feel at home.

The lush, heather-tinted Great Smoky Mountains are great for hiking, camping and rafting, while the region's two main urban areas, Knoxville and Chattanooga, are easygoing riverside cities with lively college populations and kicking music scenes.

Chattanooga

Named 'the dirtiest city in America' in the 1960s, Chattanooga was shamed into cleaning up rampant industrial pollution and focusing on downtown revitalization. Today the city is recognized as being one of the country's greenest, with miles of well-used waterfront trails, free electric buses, and pedestrian bridges crossing the Tennessee River. With world-class rock climbing, hiking, biking and water-sports opportunities, it's one of the South's best cities for outdoorsy types.

The city was once a major railway hub throughout the 19th and 20th centuries, hence the *Chattanooga Choo-Choo,* which was originally a reference to the Cincinnati Southern Railroad's passenger service from Cincinnati to Chattanooga and later the title of a 1941 Glen Miller song.

Downtown is on the south side of the river, with the bulk of the museums. Directly across the water, the North Shore is rapidly becoming the city's go-to spot for bars and restaurants.

The **visitor center** (☎ 423-756-8687, 800-322-3344; www.chattanoogafun.com; 2 Broad St; 🕑 8:30am-5:30pm) is huge and modern, with friendly staff. The Bluff View Art District at High and E 2nd Sts has upscale shops and restaurants overlooking the river.

SIGHTS & ACTIVITIES

On the North Shore, **Coolidge Park** is a good place to start a riverfront stroll. There's a carousel, well-used playing fields, and a 50ft climbing wall attached to one of the columns supporting the **Walnut Street Bridge**. Hop on the pedestrian-only bridge to cross into downtown. Below you you'll notice the grass-covered 'living roof' of **Outdoor Chattanooga** (☎ 423-643-6888; www.outdoorchattanooga.com), a city-run agency promoting active recreation. It leads hiking, kayaking and biking trips – call or check the website for schedules. It's also a good resource for outdoor info and trail suggestions.

That glass pyramid looming over the riverside bluffs is the wonderful **Tennessee Aquarium** (☎ 800-262-0695; www.tnaqua.org; 1 Broad St; adult/child $22/15; 🕑 10am-6pm; ♿), the world's largest freshwater aquarium. Climb aboard the aquarium's high-speed catamaran for two-hour excursions through the Tennessee River Gorge (adult/child $29/22). While here, check out a show at the attached **IMAX theater** (adult/child $8.50/6).

East of the aquarium is the equally striking glass lobby of the **Hunter Museum of American Art** (☎ 423-267-0968; www.huntermuseum.org; 10 Bluff View; adult/child $10/5; 🕑 10am-5pm Mon, Tue & Thu-Sat, noon-5pm Wed & Sun), which has a fantastic 19th- and 20th-century collection.

Chattanooga African-American Museum (☎ 423-266-8658; www.caamhistory.com; 200 Martin Luther King Jr Blvd; adult/child $5/2; ☎ 10am-5pm Mon-Fri, noon-4pm Sat) has a special exhibit on 'Empress of the Blues' singer Bessie Smith, a Chattanooga native.

Some of Chattanooga's oldest and best-known attractions are 6 miles outside the city at **Lookout Mountain** (☎ 423-821-4224; www.lookoutmtnattractions.com; 827 East Brow Rd; adult/child $44/23; ♿). Admission price includes the Incline Railway, which chugs up a steep incline to the top of the mountain; the world's longest underground waterfall, Ruby Falls; and Rock City, a garden with a dramatic clifftop overlook; opening hours vary by season. The mountain is also a popular hang-gliding location. The folks at **Lookout Mountain Flight Park** (☎ 800-688-5637; www.hanglide.com; 7201 Scenic Hwy, Rising Fawn, GA; intro tandem flight $199) give lessons.

SLEEPING & EATING

You can find many budget motels around I-24 and I-75.

Harrison Bay State Park (☎ 423-344-7966; 8411 Harrison Bay Rd; campsites $25) On the banks of Chickamauga Lake, about 40 minutes northeast of downtown, this park has a campground popular with boaters and fishermen.

Bluff View Inn (☎ 423-265-5033; www.bluffviewartdistrict.com; 411 E 2nd St; r from $105; P ✖ 💻 📶) Overlooking the river, this hotel has three separate houses – an English Tudor, a Colonial Revival and a Victorian, each with its own unique character and cozy, antique-furnished rooms.

Chattanooga Choo-Choo Holiday Inn (☎ 423-266-5000, 800-872-2529; www.choochoo.com; 1400 Market St; r from $126, railcars $184; P ✖ 💻 📶 🏊) The city's grand old railway terminal has been transformed into a bustling hotel. There's a train-car restaurant, a retro '40s-style bar, numerous shops and a small railroad museum. You'll sleep like a turn-of-the-century aristocrat in one of the Choo-Choo's 48 authentic Victorian railcars, outfitted for the modern age with double beds and TVs. Standard rooms and suites, in separate buildings, are clean but ordinary.

Aretha Frankenstein's (☎ 423-265-7685; 518 Tremont St; mains $5-9; ⏰ 7am-midnight) This turquoise cottage, tucked away on a residential street in the hip North Shore area, is tops for all-day pancakes and omelets, burritos and BLTs, or enjoying a beer on the sprawling patio.

Big River Grille & Brewing Works (☎ 423-267-2739; 222 Broad St; mains $9-20; ⏰ 11am-midnight Sun-Thu, to 2am Fri & Sat) A lively crowd drinks beer and chows down on crowd-pleasing upmarket pub grub – burgers, calamari, barbecue chicken pizza – in a warehouse-y downtown space with a big front patio. There's live music and pool at night.

GETTING THERE & AROUND

Chattanooga's modest **airport** (CHA; ☎ 423-855-2202; www.chattairport.com; 1001 Airport Rd) is just east of the city. The **Greyhound station** (☎ 423-892-1277; 960 Airport Rd) is just down the road.

For access to most downtown sites, ride the free electric shuttle buses that ply the center. The visitor center has a route map.

With an utter lack of nostalgia, Amtrak does not serve Chattanooga.

Knoxville

Once known as the 'underwear capital of the world' for its numerous textile mills, Knoxville is now home to the University of Tennessee and a number of high-tech industries. Downtown is full of ornate, slightly crumbling 19th-century buildings and lovely outdoor cafés shaded by pear trees.

The **visitor center** (☎ 865-523-7263, 800-727-8045; www.knoxville.org; 301 S Gay St; ⏰ 9am-5pm Mon-Sat, from 1pm Sun) has locations downtown and near the riverfront. Most restaurants and nightlife are in the arty, renovated warehouses of Old City, near the train station, and Market Square, in central downtown. Concerts and University of Tennessee sports teams play at **Neyland Stadium** (☎ 865-974-0953; 1600 Stadium Dr).

The city's visual centerpiece is the **Sunsphere**, a gold orb atop a tower that's the main remnant of the 1982 World Fair. You can take the elevator up to the (usually deserted) viewing deck to see the skyline and a dated exhibit on Knoxville's civic virtues.

You can't miss the massive orange basketball that marks the **Women's Basketball Hall of Fame** (☎ 865-633-9000; www.wbhof.com; 700 Hall of Fame Dr; adult/child $8/6; ⏰ 10am-5pm Mon-Sat summer,

THE SOUTH

WORTH THE TRIP: JACK DANIEL'S DISTILLERY

The irony of the **Jack Daniel's Distillery** (☎ 931-759-6180; www.jackdaniels.com; Rte 1, Lynchburg; tours free; ⏰ 9am-4:30pm) being in a 'dry county' is lost on no one – local liquor laws dictate that no hard stuff can be sold within county lines, thus the distillery cannot give out samples of its famous whiskey. But it can give hour-long free tours, where visitors are encouraged to take long sniffs of the golden brew. It's the oldest registered distillery in the US: the folks at Jack Daniels have been dripping whiskey through layers of charcoal then aging it in oak barrels since 1866. The distillery is located off Hwy 55 in the diminutive town of Lynchburg, which freely admits that all visitors are either here to see the distillery or they are lost.

from 11am Tue-Sat winter), a nifty look at the sport from the time when women were forced to play in full-length dresses.

If you're spending the night, try **Hotel St Oliver** (☎ 865-521-0050; 407 Union Ave; r from $75; P ✕). This 28-room downtown gem has an eccentric rococo ambience, like staying at the home of your very rich but slightly dotty great aunt. Rooms have antique four-poster beds and wet bars; the downstairs library has Victorian fainting couches and sinister-looking oil paintings.

Great Smoky Mountains National Park

The Cherokee called this territory Shaconage (shah-*cone*-ah-jey), meaning roughly 'land of the blue smoke,' for the heather-colored mist that hangs over the ancient peaks. The Southern Appalachians are the world's oldest mountain range, with mile upon mile of cool, humid deciduous forest.

The 815-sq-mile park is the country's most visited, and while the main arteries and attractions can get crowded, studies have shown that 95% of visitors never venture further than 100yd from their cars, so it's easy to leave the teeming masses behind.

Unlike most other national parks, Great Smoky charges no admission fee, nor will it ever; this proviso was written into the park's original charter as a stipulation for a $5-million Rockefeller family grant. Stop by a visitor center to pick up a park map and the free park newspaper, *Smokies Guide*. For more information about the North Carolina section of this park, see p402.

ORIENTATION & INFORMATION

Great Smoky Mountains National Park straddles the North Carolina–Tennessee border, which zigzags diagonally through the heart of the park. The north–south **Newfound Gap Road/Highway 441** spans the park, connecting the gateway towns of Gatlinburg, TN, on the north-central border and Cherokee, NC, on the south-central border.

The park's three interior visitor centers are **Sugarlands Visitor Center** (☎ 865-436-1291; 8am-4:30pm, to later spring & summer), at the park's northern entrance near Gatlinburg; **Cades Cove Visitor Center** (☎ 877-444-6777; 9am-4:30pm, to later spring & summer), halfway up Cades Cove Loop Rd, off Hwy 441 near the Gatlinburg entrance; and Oconaluftee Visitor Center (p402), at the park's southern entrance near Cherokee, NC.

SIGHTS & ACTIVITIES

The remains of the 19th-century settlement at **Cades Cove** are some of the park's most popular sights, as evidenced by the teeth-grinding summer traffic jams on the loop road. **Mt LeConte** has some of the park's best hikes, as well as the only non-camping accommodation, **LeConte Lodge** (☎ 865-429-5704; www.leconte-lodge.com; cabins $70 per person, dinner & breakfast $35). Though the only way to get to the lodge's rustic, electricity-free cabins is via an 8-mile uphill hike, it's so popular you need to reserve up to a year in advance. You can drive right up to the dizzying heights of **Clingmans Dome**, the third-highest mountain east of the Mississippi, with a futuristic observation tower.

CAMPING

With 10 developed campgrounds offering about 1000 campsites, you'd think finding a place to pitch would be easy. Not so in the busy summer season: your best bet is to plan ahead. You can make **reservations** (☎ 800-365-2267; www.nps.gov/grsm) for some sites; others are first-come, first-served. Camping fees are $14 to $23 per night. Of the park's 10 campgrounds, only Cades Cove and Smokemont are open year-round; others are open March to October.

Backcountry camping is an excellent option. A (free) permit is required; you can make **reservations** (☎ 865-436-1231) and get permits at the ranger stations or visitor centers.

Gatlinburg

Wildly kitschy Gatlinburg sits at the entrance of the Great Smoky Mountains National Park,

> **WHAT THE...?**
>
> **Dollywood** (☎ 865-428-9488, 800-365-5996; www.dollywood.com; 1020 Dollywood Lane; adult/child $53/42; Apr-Dec) is a self-created ode to the patron saint of East Tennessee, the big-haired, bigger-bosomed country singer Dolly Parton. The park features Appalachian-themed rides and attractions, from the Mystery Mine roller coaster to the bald eagle sanctuary to the faux one-room chapel named after the doctor who delivered Dolly.

waiting to stun hikers with the scent of fudge and cotton candy. Tourists flock here to ride the ski lifts, shop for Confederate-flag undershorts, get married at the many wedding chapels, and play hillbilly-themed mini-golf. The city has three **visitor centers** (☎ 865-436-0519, 800-343-1475; www.gatlinburg.com; 8am-6pm, to 8pm Fri & Sat, to 10pm summer), at the third and fifth stoplights and 2 miles north of town on US 441.

Ten miles north of Gatlinburg, **Pigeon Forge** (www.mypigeonforge.com) is a tacky complex of motels, outlet malls and country-music theaters and restaurants, all of which have grown up in the shadow of **Dollywood** (see the boxed text, opposite).

KENTUCKY

With an economy based on bourbon, horse racing and tobacco, you might think Kentucky would rival Las Vegas as Sin Central. Well, yes and no. For every whiskey-soaked Louisville bar there's a dry county where you can't get anything stronger than ginger ale. For every racetrack there's a Catholic monastery or a Southern Baptist church.

Kentucky's full of strange juxtapositions like that. A geographic and cultural crossroads, the state combines the friendliness of the South, the rural frontier history of the West, the industry of the North, and the aristocratic charm of the East.

Every corner of the state is easy on the eye. In spring, the pastures of central Kentucky bloom with tiny azure buds, earning it the moniker 'Bluegrass State.' There are few sights more heartbreakingly beautiful than the rolling limestone hills of horse country, where thoroughbred breeding is a multimillion-dollar industry. Even the mountains, often maligned as 'hillbilly country,' blaze with color and culture.

KENTUCKY FACTS

Nickname: Bluegrass State
Population 4.3 million
Area 39,728 sq miles
Capital city Frankfort (pop 27,098)
Other cities Louisville (pop 554,496), Lexington (pop 270,789)
Sales tax 6%
Birthplace of 16th US president Abraham Lincoln (1809–65), 'gonzo' journalist Hunter S Thompson (1937–2005), boxer Muhammad Ali (b 1942), actress Ashley Judd (b 1968)
Home of Kentucky Derby, Louisville Slugger, bourbon
Famous for Horses, bluegrass music, fried chicken, caves
Interesting place names Monkeys Eyebrow, Chicken Bristle, Shoulderblade, Hippo, Petroleum
Driving distances Louisville to Lexington 77 miles, Lexington to Mammoth Cave National Park 135 miles

History

British and French forces battled for control of Kentucky in the mid-1700s, recognizing the value of the fertile land that was once used by Native Americans as a hunting ground.

Legendary frontiersman Daniel Boone blazed a trail through the Cumberland Gap and the British began pouring over the Appalachians in 1775. The state became a battleground during the Revolutionary War, with local Shawnee allying with the crown.

Though a slave state, Kentucky was bitterly divided during the Civil War, with 30,000 fighting for the Confederacy and 64,000 for the Union. Both the Union president Abraham Lincoln and Confederacy president Jefferson Davis were Kentucky-born.

After the war, Kentucky built up its economy on railways, tobacco and coal-mining. Today its motto, 'Unbridled Spirit,' reflects the dominance of scenic horse country.

Information

The boundary between Eastern and Central time goes through the middle of Kentucky.

Kentucky State Parks (☎ 800-255-7275; www.parks.ky.gov) Offers info on hiking, caving, fishing, camping and more in Kentucky's 52 state parks. So-called 'Resort Parks' have more upscale options, like lodges, while 'Recreation Parks' are all about roughin' it.

Kentucky Travel (☎ 502-564-4930, 800-225-8747; www.kentuckytourism.com) Sends out a detailed booklet on the state's attractions.

LOUISVILLE

Best known as the home of the Kentucky Derby, Louisville (or Louahvul, as the locals say) is a handsome, underrated city. A major Ohio River shipping center during the days of westward expansion, Kentucky's largest city now has a lively, working-class vibe, with corner pool halls, punk-rock bars, and drive-through chili restaurants. It's a fun place to spend a day or two, checking out the museums, wandering the old neighborhoods, drinking a little bourbon.

The downtown area lies along the banks of the Ohio River, opposite Indiana. Just south of downtown is Old Louisville, with the largest collection of Victorian homes in the country. The Highlands area, centered on Bardstown and Baxter Rds, is where locals come to play, with cafés and bars galore. A series of pretty parks laid out by Frederick Law Olmsted in the 1890s encircle the city, along with an inner (I-264) and outer (I-265) ring road.

The **visitor center** (☎ 502-582-3732, 888-568-4784; www.gotolouisville.com; 301 S 4th St; 10am-6pm Mon-Sat, noon-5pm Sun) has a free exhibit about that great Kentucky icon, KFC founder Colonel Sanders. Surf the web free at the **public library** (☎ 502-574-1611; 301 York St; 9am-9pm Mon-Thu, to 5pm Fri & Sat) downtown.

Sights

Look for the 120ft baseball bat leaning against the **Louisville Slugger Museum** (☎ 877-775-8443; www.sluggermuseum.org; 800 W Main St; adult/child $10/5; 9am-5pm Mon-Sat, from noon Sun;) – ya can't miss it. Hillerich & Bradsby Co have been making the famous Louisville Slugger baseball bat here since 1884. The admission fee includes a plant tour, a hall of baseball memorabilia such as Babe Ruth's bat, a batting cage and a free mini slugger. Customized bats are sold in the lobby. Note: bat production halts on Sunday, as well as on Saturday in the winter.

Across the street, the state-of-the-art **Frazier International History Museum** (☎ 502-412-2280; www.fraziermuseum.org; 829 W Main St; adult/child $12/9; 9am-5pm Mon-Sat, from noon Sun) covers 1000 years of history with grisly battle dioramas and costumed interpreters demonstrating swordplay and staging mock debates.

our pick **Muhammad Ali Center** (☎ 502-584-9254; www.alicenter.org; 144 N 6th St; adult/child $9/4; 9:30am-5pm Mon-Sat, from noon Sun) is a love offering to the city from its most famous native. Self-guided tours include a stirring film on Ali's life and video projections of his most famous fights, as well as exhibits about the racial segregation and humanitarian issues that so vexed the outspoken man once known as the 'Louisville Lip.'

Speed Art Museum (☎ 502-634-2700; www.speedmuseum.org; 2035 S 3rd St; admission free; 10:30am-4pm Tue, Wed & Fri, to 8pm Thu, to 5pm Sat, noon-5pm Sun) is a handsome Greek Revival–style building with more than 12,000 pieces of art, from classical sculptures to Kentucky mint julep cups.

A shallow part of the river exposes fossils from an ancient sea at the **Falls of the Ohio State Park** (☎ 812-280-9970; www.fallsoftheohio.org; W Riverside Dr, Clarksville, IN; adult/child $4/1; 9am-5pm Mon-Sat, from 1pm Sun;). Kids will love the big aquariums in the visitors center.

The Victorian-era **Old Louisville** neighborhood, just south of downtown, is well worth a drive or stroll. There are several wonderful **historic homes** (☎ 502-899-5079; www.historichomes.org) open for tours, including Thomas Edison's old shotgun cottage.

CHURCHILL DOWNS

On the first Saturday in May, a who's who of upper-crust America puts on their pinstripe suits and most flamboyant hats and descends upon **Churchill Downs** (☎ 502-636-4400, 800-283-3729; www.churchilldowns.com; 700 Central Ave) for the 'greatest two minutes in sports,' the Kentucky Derby. After the race, the crowd sings 'My Old Kentucky Home' and watches as the winning horse is covered in a blanket of roses. Then they party.

To be honest, they've been partying for a while. The **Kentucky Derby Festival** (☎ 502-584-6383; www.kdf.org), which includes a balloon race and the largest fireworks display in North America, starts two weeks before the big event.

Most seats at the derby are by invitation only or they've been reserved years in advance. On Derby Day, $40 gets you into the paddock party scene (no seat) if you arrive early, but it's so crowded you won't see much of the race. Don't fret, though. From April through to November, you can get a $3 seat at the Downs for many exciting races, often warm-ups for the big events.

On the grounds, the **Kentucky Derby Museum** (☎ 502-637-7097; www.derbymuseum.org; Gate 1, Central Ave; adult/child $12/5; 8am-5pm Mon-Sat, from 11am Sun) has exhibits on derby history, including a peek into the life of jockeys and a roundup of the most illustrious horses. There is a 360-degree audiovisual about the race, and a behind-the-scenes track tour ($10) that leads you through the jockey's quarters and posh VIP seating areas.

WORTH THE DRIVE: INTERNATIONAL BLUEGRASS MUSIC MUSEUM

Kentuckian Bill Monroe is considered the founding father of bluegrass music; his band, the Blue Grass Boys, gave the genre its name. Bluegrass has its roots in the old-time mountain music, mixed with the fast tempo of African songs and spiced with lashings of jazz. Any banjo picker or fiddle fan will appreciate the historic exhibits at the **International Bluegrass Music Museum** (☎ 270-926-7891; www.bluegrass-museum.org; 207 E 2nd St; admission $5; 10am-5pm Tue-Sat, 1-4pm Sun) in Owensboro. The pretty Ohio River town, about 100 miles west of Louisville, also hosts the **ROMP Bluegrass Festival** (www.bluegrass-museum.org/riverofmusic) in June.

Sleeping & Eating

Chain hotels cluster near the airport off I-264. The Highlands area is the spot for locally owned cafés and bars. Downtown's 'Fourth Street Live' is a rather contrived 'entertainment district' of casual shopping and dining; there are better pickings in the area, so don't be afraid to wander.

Rocking Horse B&B (☎ 502-583-0408, 888-467-7322; www.rockinghorse-bb.com; 1022 S 3rd St; r incl breakfast $105-195; P) On a stretch of 3rd St once known as Millionaire's Row, this 1888 Romanesque mansion has six guest rooms decorated with Victorian antiques and splendid stained glass. Guests can eat their two-course breakfast in the English country garden or sip complimentary port in the parlor.

Brown Hotel (☎ 502-583-1234; www.brownhotel.com; 335 West Broadway; r from $139) Opera stars, queens and prime ministers have trod the marble floors of this storied downtown hotel, now restored to all its 1920s gilded glamour with 293 comfy rooms and a swank bar. Parking is $18.

our pick **21c** (☎ 502-217-6300; www.21chotel.com; 700 W Main St; r from $159) This contemporary art museum/hotel would be edgy anywhere; in laid-back Louisville, it's practically in a different dimension. Video screens project your distorted image on the wall as you wait for the elevator. Chandeliers made from scissors dangle weirdly in the hallways. Sexually suggestive sculptures in the lobby make even normally unflappable guidebook authors blush. Urban loft–like rooms have iPod docks and mint julep kits in the mini-fridge. Parking is $18.

Lynn's Paradise Cafe (☎ 502-583-3447; 984 Barret Ave; mains $7-15; 7am-10pm Mon-Fri, from 8am Sat & Sun) It's breakfast anytime at this psychedelic diner, marked by the 10ft-tall teapot outside. Don't miss the homemade biscuits with sorghum butter, or the Hot Brown sandwich, a Louisville classic invented in the 1920s at the Brown Hotel.

Lilly's Bistro (☎ 502-451-0447; 1147 Bardstown Rd; mains $19-26; 11am-3pm Tue-Sat, 5:30-10pm Tue-Thu, 5:30-11pm Fri & Sat) Chef Kathy Cary creates 'Kentucky tapas' (think catfish spring rolls, chorizo spoonbread) at this eclectic upscale eatery, a longtime Bardstown Rd favorite. The three-course lunch menu ($15) is a steal.

Drinking & Entertainment

The free weekly **Leo** (www.leoweekly.com) lists gigs and entertainment. You'll have no problem finding a watering hole in the Highlands area. Try **Cahoots** (☎ 502-454-6687; 1047 Bardstown Rd), one of Bardstown's classic rock and roll dives, or **Molly Malone's** (☎ 502-473-1222; 933 Baxter Ave), a lively Irish pub with a big patio.

Rudyard Kipling (☎ 502-636-1311; 422 W Oak St) In Old Louisville, this place is loved by arty locals for its intimate indie-bluegrass shows and Kentucky bar food (try the 'snappy cheese').

Actors Theatre of Louisville (☎ 502-584-1205; www.actorstheatre.org; 504 W Main St) This highly regarded theater performs everything from Shakespeare to contemporary musicals and has premiered several Pulitzer Prize–winning plays.

Getting There & Around

Louisville's International Airport (SDF; ☎ 502-367-4636; www.flylouisville.com) is 5 miles south of town on I-65. Get there by cab (around $18) or local bus 2. The **Greyhound station** (☎ 502-585-3331; 720 W Muhammad Ali Blvd) is just west of downtown. **TARC** (☎ 502-585-1234; 1000 W Broadway) runs local buses from the Union Station depot.

BLUEGRASS COUNTRY

Drive through northeast Kentucky's Bluegrass Country on a sunny day, and you'll get an idea of what the ancient Greeks were imagining when they wrote about the elysian fields of paradise. Horses graze in the brilliant-green hills dotted with ponds, poplar trees and handsome estate houses. These once-wild woodlands and meadows have been a center of horse breeding for almost 250 years – the region's natural limestone deposits are said to produce especially nutritious grass. The area's principal city, Lexington, is known as 'Horse Capital of the World.'

Lexington

Even the prison looks like a country club in Lexington, home of million-dollar houses and multimillion-dollar horses. Once the wealthiest and most cultured city west of the Allegheny Mountains, it was called 'the Athens of the West,' and today is home to the University of Kentucky and the heart of the thoroughbred-racehorse industry. The small downtown has some pretty Victorian neighborhoods, but most of the attractions are in the countryside outside the metro area.

Pick up maps and area information from the **visitor center** (☎ 859-233-7299, 800-845-3959; www.visitlex.com; 301 E Vine St; 8:30am-5pm Mon-Fri, 10am-4pm Sat). The **public library** (140 E Main St; 10am-5pm Tue-Fri, from noon Sat & Sun;) has free internet access and free wi-fi for those with laptops.

SIGHTS & ACTIVITIES

Downtown Lexington has several **historic homes** (www.nps.gov/history/nr/travel/lexington) open for tours. The following are $7 each, or $15 for all four with a combination ticket – available at the visitor center or at Ashland.

Just 1.5 miles east of downtown, **Ashland** (☎ 859-266-8581; www.henryclay.org; 120 Sycamore Rd; 10am-4pm Tue-Sat, 1-4pm Sun) was the Italianate estate of statesman Henry Clay (1777–1852). **Hunt-Morgan House** (☎ 859-253-0362; www.bluegrasstrust.org; 201 N Mill St; 1-4pm Wed-Fri & Sun, 10am-3pm Sat) is a fine Federal-style mansion (c 1814) with a small Civil War museum. The 1806 **Mary Todd-Lincoln House** (☎ 859-233-9999; www.mtlhouse.org; 578 W Main St; 10am-4pm Mon-Sat) has articles from the first lady's childhood and her years as Abe's wife. **Waveland** (☎ 859-272-3611; http://parks.ky.gov/findparks/histparks/wl; 225 Waveland Museum Lane; 9am-4pm) is a 19th-century plantation.

our pick **Headley-Whitney Museum** (☎ 859-255-6653; www.headley-whitney.org; 4435 Old Frankfort Pike; adult/child $7/5; 10am-5pm Tue-Fri, from noon Sat & Sun), marvellously old, holds the private collection of the late George Headley, a jewelry designer whose gemstone trinkets and handmade dollhouses are on display, along with a truly bizarre garage turned 'seashell grotto.'

An educational theme park and equestrian sports center, the **Kentucky Horse Park** (☎ 859-233-4303, 800-678-8813; www.kyhorsepark.com; 4089 Iron Works Pkwy; adult/child $15/8; 9am-5pm daily mid-Mar–Oct, Wed-Sun Nov–mid-Mar;) sits on 1200 acres just north of Lexington. Horses representing 50 different breeds live in the park and participate in special live shows. Also included, the international **Museum of the Horse** has neat dioramas of the horse through history, from the tiny prehistoric 'eohippus' to the pony express mail carriers. Seasonal horseback riding costs $15 with park ticket, $22 without. The adjacent **American Saddlebred Museum** focuses on America's first registered horse breed – for hard-core enthusiasts only.

Most farms are closed to the public, but you can see working racehorses up close at the **Thoroughbred Center** (☎ 859-293-1853; www.thethoroughbredcenter.com; 3380 Paris Pike; adult/child $10/5; tours 9am Mon-Sat Apr-Oct, Mon-Fri Nov-Mar), with tours of the stables, practice tracks and paddocks.

Watch 'em run at the **Keeneland Race Course** (☎ 859-254-3412, 800-456-3412; www.keeneland.com; 4201 Versailles Rd; tickets $5), which has races in April and October and horse sales throughout the year. From March to November, you can watch the champions train from sunrise to 10am. Or head to the **Red Mile** (☎ 859-255-0752; www.theredmile.com; 1200 Red Mile Rd) to see harness racing, where jockeys are pulled behind horses in special two-wheeled carts. Live races are in the fall, but you can watch and wager on simulcasts of races from around the world year-round.

Several working ranches around Lexington offer **horseback riding** to both newbies and experienced riders. Call to arrange guided trail rides at **Whispering Woods** (☎ 502-570-9663; www.whisperingwoodstrails.com; 265 Wright Lane; trail rides per hr $25; Mar-Nov), in bucolic Georgetown.

SLEEPING & EATING

There are several downtown cafés and bars with outdoor seating around Main and Limestone Sts. S Limestone, across from the UK campus, has student-friendly nightlife.

Kentucky Horse Park (☎ 859-259-4257, 800-370-6416; www.kyhorsepark.com; 4089 Iron Works Pkwy; paved/unpaved campsites from $22/15;) has 260 paved sites open year-round. There are showers, laundry, a grocery, playgrounds and more. Primitive camping is also available.

WHAT THE...?

Fact: nearly half of Americans don't believe in evolution. Hence the popularity of Petersburg, Kentucky's new multimillion-dollar **Creation Museum** (☎ 888-582-4253; www.creationmuseum.org; 2800 Bullittsburg Church Rd; adult/child $22/12; ⌚ 10am-6pm Mon-Sat, from noon Sun), an interactive tour through a biblical interpretation of history. The scientific-minded will fume at what may be seen as an anti-rational message. But that doesn't mean they won't enjoy the walk-through Noah's Ark, animatronic dinosaurs (creationists believe they coexisted with humans), and the zonkeys (zebra-donkey hybrids) in the petting zoo.

Gratz Park Inn (☎ 859-231-1777, 800-752-4166; www.gratzparkinn.com; 120 W 2nd St; r from $169; P) On a quiet downtown street, this 40-room hotel feels like a genteel hunt club, with mahogany furnishings and Old World oil paintings in heavy frames. The attached restaurant, Jonathan's, serves fine regional cuisine.

Billy's Hickory Pit Bar-B-Q (☎ 859-269-9593; 101 Cochran Rd; mains $6-15; ⌚ 11am-10pm Mon-Sat, 11:30am-9pm Sun) Even the green beans have meat in them at homey Billy's, an institution known for its Kentucky-style smoked pork, beef and mutton and its burgoo, a regional chili-like stew.

Holly Hill Inn (☎ 859-846-4732; www.hollyhillinn.com; 426 N Winter St, Midway; mains $15-35; ⌚ 5:30-10pm Thu & Fri, 11am-2pm & 5:30-10pm Sat, 11am-2pm Sun, plus lunch May-Jul) Guests dine in the converted bedrooms and parlors of an elegant old farmhouse, just west of Lexington in the town of Midway. The husband-and-wife owners serve local bounty with a deft touch – lamb with scallion ravioli, farmstead egg custard with fiddlehead ferns.

GETTING THERE & AROUND

Blue Grass Airport (LEX; ☎ 859-425-3114; www.bluegrassairport.com; 4000 Terminal Dr) is west of town, with about a dozen domestic nonstops. **Greyhound** (☎ 859-299-8804; 477 W New Circle Rd) is 2 miles from downtown. **Lex-Tran** (☎ 859-253-4636; www.lextranonthemove.org) runs local buses (bus 6 goes to the Greyhound station).

Frankfort

A pretty little postcard of a town, all red brick and gingerbread trim, Kentucky's diminutive capital lies 26 miles west of Lexington on the banks of the Kentucky River. There are some notable historic buildings, including the **old state capitol** (☎ 502-564-1792; admission free; ⌚ 10am-5pm Tue-Sat), which functioned from 1827 to 1910. Nearby is the handsome **Kentucky History Center** (☎ 502-564-1792; www.history.ky.gov; 100 W Broadway St; admission free; ⌚ 8am-4pm Tue-Sat), for those truly interested in state history. Daniel Boone is buried in the **Frankfort Cemetery** (E Main St).

CENTRAL KENTUCKY

The Bluegrass Pkwy runs from I-65 in the west to Rte 60 in the east, passing through some of the most luscious pasturelands in Kentucky.

About 40 miles south of Louisville is **Bardstown**, the 'Bourbon Capital of the World' (see the boxed text, p440). The historic downtown comes alive in September for the **Kentucky Bourbon Festival** (☎ 800-638-4877; www.kybourbonfestival.com). Have a meal, some bourbon, and a good night's sleep in the dim limestone environs of **Old Talbott Tavern** (☎ 502-348-3494; www.talbotts.com; 107 W Stephen Foster Ave; r from $59; P), welcoming guests like Abraham Lincoln and Daniel Boone since the late 1700s.

Follow Hwy 31 southwest and turn left at Monks Rd to visit the ascetically beautiful **Abbey of Gethsemani**, a Trappist monastery once home to famed Catholic thinker Thomas Merton. You can buy monk-made fudge at the **gift shop** (⌚ 9am-5pm Mon-Fri). Continue on Hwy 31 to **Hodgenville** and the **Abraham Lincoln Birthplace** (☎ 270-358-3137; www.nps.gov/abli; admission free; ⌚ 8am-4:45pm, to 6:45pm summer), a faux Greek temple constructed around an old log cabin. Ten minutes away is Honest Abe's boyhood home at Knob Creek, with hiking trails.

Thirty minutes southwest of Lexington is **Shaker Village at Pleasant Hill** (☎ 800-734-5611; www.shakervillageky.org; 3501 Lexington Rd, Harrodsburg; adult/child $15/5; ⌚ 10am-5pm), home to a community of the Shaker religious sect until the early 1900s. Tour 14 impeccably restored buildings, set amid buttercup meadows and winding stone paths. There's an inn and restaurant, and a gift shop selling the Shakers' famous handicrafts.

Forty miles south of Lexington is **Berea**, famed for its folk art. The **Kentucky Artisan Center** (☎ 859-985-5448; www.kentuckyartisancenter.ky.gov; Exit 77, off Hwy 75; ⌚ 8am-8pm) has a large variety of handcrafts and food.

THE BOURBON TRAIL

Silky, caramel-colored bourbon whiskey was likely first distilled in Bourbon County, north of Lexington, around 1789. Today 90% of all bourbon is produced here in Kentucky (no other state is allowed to put its own name on the bottle). Good bourbon must contain at least 51% corn, and must also be stored in charred oak barrels for a minimum of two years. While most connoisseurs drink it straight or with water, you must try a mint julep, the archetypal Southern drink made with bourbon, sugar syrup and crushed mint.

The **Oscar Getz Museum of Whiskey History** (☎ 502-348-2999; www.whiskeymuseum.com; 114 N 5th St; donations appreciated; 🕒 10am-4pm Mon-Sat, from noon Sun), in Bardstown, tells the bourbon story with old moonshine stills and other artifacts.

Most of Kentucky's distilleries, which are centered on Bardstown and Frankfort, offer free tours. Call for times.

Distilleries

Near Bardstown:

Heaven Hill (☎ 502-348-3921; www.bourbonheritagecenter.com; 1311 Gilkey Run Rd, Bardstown) Not a distillery tour, but an interactive Bourbon Heritage Center, with a tasting room inside a giant barrel.

Jim Beam (☎ 502-543-9877; www.jimbean.com; 149 Happy Hollow Rd, Clermont) Watch a film about the Beam family and sample small-batch bourbons at the country's largest bourbon distillery.

Maker's Mark (☎ 270-865-2099; www.makersmark.com; 3350 Burks Spring Rd, Loretto) This restored Victorian distillery is like a bourbon theme park, with an old gristmill and a gift shop where you can seal your own bottle in red wax.

Tom Moore (☎ 502-348-3774; www.1792bourbon.com; 300 Barton Rd, Bardstown) Connoisseur-quality 1792 Ridgemont Reserve is produced at this small distillery, the only one within Bardstown city limits.

Near Frankfort/Lawrenceburg:

Buffalo Trace (☎ 502-696-5926; www.buffalotrace.com; 1001 Wilkinson Blvd, Frankfort) The nation's oldest continuously operating distillery has highly regarded tours and free tastings.

Four Roses (☎ 502-839-3436; www.fourroses.us; 1224 Bonds Mills Rd, Lawrenceburg) One of the most scenic distilleries, in a riverside Spanish Mission–style building. Free tastings.

Wild Turkey (☎ 502-839-4544; www.wildturkey.com; Hwy 62 E, Lawrenceburg) Master distiller Jimmy Russell has been making this extra-dark bourbon since 1954. The factory is more industrial than scenic.

Woodford Reserve (☎ 859-879-1812; www.woodfordreserve.com; 7855 McCracken Pike, Versailles) The historic site along a creek is restored to its 1800s glory; the distillery still uses old-fashioned copper pots.

Daniel Boone National Forest

These 707,000 acres of rugged ravines and gravity-defying sandstone arches cover much of the Appalachian foothills of eastern Kentucky. The forest has numerous state- and federal-run areas; the main **ranger station** (☎ 859-745-3100; www.fs.fed.us/r8/boone) is in Winchester.

An hour southeast of Lexington is the **Red River Gorge** area, whose cliffs and natural arches make for some of the best rock climbing in the country. **True North Outfitters** (☎ 606-668-3745; www.truenorthoutfitters.com; 20 Sky Bridge Rd, Pine Ridge; full-day guided climb $200) sells gear and offers guided climbing and hiking trips, plus hostel beds ($18). Climbers can also pay $2 to camp out behind **Miguel's Pizza** (☎ 606-663-1975; 1890 Natural Bridge Rd, Slade; mains $10-14; 🕒 7am-10pm Mon-Thu, to 11pm Fri & Sat) in the hamlet of Slade.

Bordering Red River Gorge is the **Natural Bridge State Resort Park** (☎ 606-663-2214; www.parks.ky.gov; 2135 Natural Bridge Rd, Slade), notable for its gravity-defying 78ft-high sandstone arch. It's a family-friendly park, with camping, a variety of short hiking trails, and a lake with an island known as 'hoedown island' for its occasional clogging performances.

Further south, the **Cumberland Falls State Resort Park** (☎ 606-528-4121; admission free; campsites $19) is one of the few places in the world to see a moonbow, a rainbow that sometimes forms in the fall's mist at night. The park has a rustic lodge (from $99) and campgrounds. While you're there, head over to the adjacent **Natural Arch Scenic Area** to see the 90ft sandstone arch and hike the half-dozen trails. The nearby town of **Corbin** has the original Kentucky Fried

Chicken restaurant, with a rather disturbing life-size statue of the Colonel.

Mammoth Cave National Park

With the longest cave system on earth, **Mammoth Cave National Park** (☎ 270-758-2328; www.nps.gov/maca; Exit 53, off I-65; 8:45am-5:15pm) has some 300 miles of surveyed passageways. Mammoth is at least three times bigger than any other known cave, with vast interior cathedrals, bottomless pits, and strange, undulating rock formations. The caves have been used for prehistoric mineral gathering, as a source of saltpeter for gunpowder and as a tuberculosis hospital. Tourists started visiting around 1810 and guided tours have been offered since the 1830s. The area became a national park in 1926 and now brings nearly two million visitors each year.

The only way to see the caves is on the excellent **ranger-guided tours** (☎ 800-967-2283; adult $12-48), and it's wise to book ahead, especially in summer. Tours range from subterranean strolls to strenuous, day-long spelunking adventures. The history tour is especially interesting.

In addition to the caves, the park contains 70 miles of trails for hiking, horseback riding and mountain biking. There are also three campsites with restrooms, but no electricity or water hookups ($12 to $30), 12 free backcountry campsites, and the **Mammoth Cave Hotel** (☎ 270-758-2225; www.mammothcavehotel.com; r $89, cottages from $59; P), next to the visitors center, which has standard hotel rooms and, in spring and summer, rustic cottages. There is a gas station and convenience store near the visitor center. But to be honest, we prefer to drive down to shabby Cave City to sleep in the giant concrete tipis at the **Wigwam Village Inn** (☎ 270-773-3381; www.wigwamvillage.com; 601 N Dixie Hwy, Cave City; wigwams $35-70; P), a 1937 chunk of pure American kitsch.

GEORGIA

Vastly different at each of its edges, Georgia – the largest state east of the Mississippi River – is in many ways the perfect distillation of everything the South has to offer. It's a state of wild geographic and cultural extremes: right-leaning Republican politics rub against liberal idealism, small towns merge with gaping cities, northern mountains rise to the clouds and produce roaring rivers, while coastal marshlands teem with fiddler crabs and swaying cordgrass.

Atlanta is the state capital and the region's transportation hub, a sprawling metropolis with friendly neighborhoods alongside multinational corporations such as UPS and Coca-Cola. So start your trip in the city known as 'the ATL,' then road-trip across the state to fall under the spell of Savannah's live oaks, seafood, antebellum homes and humid nights. From here you're close to the coastal barrier islands – bring your tuxedo to Jekyll Island and your hiking boots to Cumberland Island.

History

Permanent English settlement dates from 1733, when James Edward Oglethorpe founded Savannah. By the time of the Revolutionary War, almost half the population was made up of slaves. Georgia held two crucial battlefronts in the latter part of the Civil War:

THE SOUTH

WORTH THE DRIVE: OTHER CAVE COUNTRY CAVES

By the early 20th century, Mammoth Cave had become such a popular attraction that owners of smaller local caves began diverting travelers heading to Mammoth by claiming it was flooded or quarantined. The inevitable conflicts became known as the 'Cave Wars.' Today, you'll still see plenty of billboards beseeching you to visit other caves around Mammoth. Here are a few that are actually worth the drive:

Cub Run Cave One of the 'newest' caves, discovered in 1950, with tons of colorful formations.

Diamond Caverns Has guided one-hour tours (adult/child $16/8) of its vast cathedrals dripping stalactites and draped in pearly flowstone.

Hidden River Cave A cave museum and a one-hour tour that takes you by the ruins of a turn-of-the-century hydroelectric system. Special off-trail adventure tours can be arranged in advance during summer.

Lost River Cave Offers a family-friendly 25-minute boat ride through an underground river. There are 2 miles of hiking trails on-site.

Chickamauga, where Union troops were defeated, and Atlanta, which they conquered and burned. Atlanta, the South's major transportation hub, was rebuilt with startling speed.

In the 20th century the state vaulted to national prominence on the back of an eclectic group of events and images: the wildly popular novel and film *Gone With the Wind;* Reverend Martin Luther King Jr and civil rights protests; 39th US President Jimmy Carter; and Atlanta's rise as a global media and business center, culminating in the 1996 Summer Olympics. Since then, Georgia's capital has become known as the 'Motown of the South' thanks to its sizzling hip-hop and R & B scene.

GEORGIA FACTS

Nickname Peach State
Population 9.7 million
Area 57,906 sq miles
Capital city Atlanta (population metro area 5 million)
Other cities Savannah (population 127,889)
Sales tax 7%
Birthplace of Baseball legend Ty Cobb (1886–1961), president Jimmy Carter (b 1924), civil rights leader Martin Luther King Jr (1929–68), singer Ray Charles (1930–2004)
Home of Coca-Cola, the world's busiest airport, the world's biggest aquarium
Famous for Peaches
Driving distances Atlanta to St Marys 343 miles, Atlanta to Dahlonega 75 miles

Information

For statewide tourism information, contact the **Georgia Department of Economic Development** (☎ 800-847-4842; www.exploregeorgia.org). For information on state parks, contact the **Georgia Department of Natural Resources** (☎ 800-864-7275; www.gastateparks.org), where you can find information on camping and activities in parks statewide. Forty-one parks offer tent-only and RV-site camping for around $23 per night. Most parks have laundry facilities.

Cars are the most convenient way to move around Georgia. (Atlanta has a citywide train system called Marta, but service is limited. Some cyclists brave the city streets.) I-75 bisects the state running north–south; I-20 runs east–west.

You can expect to pay an additional 6% tax on hotel accommodations in Georgia.

ATLANTA

With five million residents in the metro and outlying areas, the so-called capital of the South continues to experience explosive growth thanks to southbound Yankees and international immigrants alike. It's also booming as a tourist destination thanks to two glitzy 21st-century attractions – the Georgia Aquarium and the World of Coca-Cola – plus giant panda exhibits at Zoo Atlanta. Beyond the attractions you'll find a constellation of superlative restaurants, two luxury megamalls, ample Civil War lore, miles of walking trails and a plethora of African American history.

Without natural boundaries to control development, Atlanta keeps growing – sometimes up, but mostly out. Suburban sprawl has turned Atlanta into an almost endless city. Increased car dependence creates horrendous traffic and pollution.

For all this suburbanization, Atlanta is a pretty city covered with trees and elegant homes. Distinct neighborhoods are like friendly small towns. Racial tensions are minimal in 'the city too busy to hate,' which prides itself as hometown to the civil rights titan Martin Luther King Jr.

History

Born as a railroad junction in 1837, Atlanta became a major Confederate transportation and munitions center for General William T Sherman, whose Union forces blazed through Georgia in 1864. When they left they burned everything, leaving more than 90% of Atlanta's buildings in ruins.

After the war, Atlanta became the epitome of the 'New South,' a concept that entailed reconciliation with the North, the promotion of industrialized agriculture, and a progressive business outlook. Segregation ended relatively painlessly here, compared with other Southern cities, and President John F Kennedy lauded this transition as a model for other communities facing integration.

Atlanta earned a moment in the international spotlight when it hosted the 1996 Summer Olympic Games. The city put on her prettiest debutante gown, and CNN beamed her picture worldwide. People took notice, the moving trucks came rolling down the freeways and, like summer weeds, condos sprouted everywhere. Since then, the city has focused its development energy on the downtown and midtown neighborhoods, both of which have flourished in recent years.

Orientation

The Atlanta metropolitan area sits inside a highway loop called I-285 or, locally, 'the Perimeter.' I-20 travels east–west, while I-75 and I-85 run north–south. Atlanta's rapid transit system is known as **Marta** (Metropolitan Atlanta Rapid Transit Authority; www.itsmarta.com), and it's extremely handy for getting to and from the airport. Unfortunately, its destinations around the city aren't as plentiful as urban explorers might hope.

In the city, Ponce de Leon Ave (known in town as 'Ponce') is a key east–west surface road. Peachtree St and Piedmont Ave are the main north–south arteries, but be forewarned: you'll find lots of other streets, roads and avenues also called Peachtree. Many streets also change names suddenly. W Peachtree St divides east from west and Martin Luther King Jr Dr/Edgewood Ave divides north from south.

Business-oriented downtown Atlanta has a few worthwhile attractions, but you'll have to venture out to see everything. East of downtown, Sweet Auburn attractions pay homage to Martin Luther King Jr. Little Five Points (L5P) and East Atlanta cater to Atlanta's alternative set. Yuppie central Virginia-Highland boasts restaurants, boutique shopping and taverns. Decatur – a quaint independent city just east of Atlanta – offers several good restaurants and nightspots. Turner Field and Grant Park are south of downtown. North of downtown, midtown is a bustling entertainment and nightlife area.

Information

BOOKSTORES

A Cappella Books (☎ 404-681-5128, 866-681-5128; www.acappellabooks.com; 484c Moreland Ave NE; ⏲ 11am-8pm Mon-Thu, to 9pm Fri & Sat, noon-8pm Sun) A bit of an anarchist spirit pervades in this L5P haunt, which hosts many readings and musical performances. The store has a particularly well-stocked music section.

EMERGENCY & MEDICAL SERVICES

Atlanta Medical Center (☎ 404-265-4000; 303 Pkwy Dr NE)

Emory University Hospital (☎ 404-778-7777; 1364 Clifton Rd NE)

Main police station (☎ 404-546-2374; 675 Ponce de Leon Ave) At City Hall East.

Piedmont Hospital (☎ 404-605-5000; 1968 Peachtree Rd NW)

INTERNET ACCESS

Central Library (☎ 404-730-1700; 1 Margaret Mitchell Sq; ⏲ 9am-9pm Mon-Thu, to 6pm Fri & Sat, 2-6pm Sun) Many branches of the public library offer free internet, including this main branch.

Maasty Computers Internet Cafe (☎ 404-294-8095; 736 Ponce de Leon Ave; per 15min $2.50; ⏲ 8am-11pm Mon-Thu, to midnight Fri & Sat, to 10pm Sun) Near City Hall East, Maasty supplements its computer café with repair services and electronics sales. It's a dark little place with a vaguely industrial vibe and a menu that uses computer slang to indicate sizes.

INTERNET RESOURCES

Access Atlanta (www.accessatlanta.com) A great place to find out about Atlanta news and upcoming events.

Atlanta Travel Guide (www.atlanta.net) Official site of the Atlanta Convention & Visitors Bureau with excellent links to shops, restaurants, hotels and upcoming events.

MEDIA

Atlanta (www.atlantamagazine.com) A monthly general-interest magazine covering local issues, arts and dining.

Atlanta Daily World (www.atlantadailyworld.com) The nation's oldest continuously running African American newspaper (since 1928).

Atlanta Journal-Constitution (www.ajc.com) Atlanta's major daily newspaper, with a good travel section on Sunday.

Creative Loafing (www.atlanta.creativeloafing.com) For hip tips on music, arts and theater, this free alternative weekly comes out every Wednesday.

POST

For general postal information call ☎ 800-275-8777.

Post office Downtown (41 Marietta St); Federal Center (☎ 404-521-9843; 41 Marietta St NW); Little Five Points (455 Moreland Ave NE); North Highland (1190 N Highland Ave NE)

TOURIST INFORMATION

Atlanta Convention & Visitors Bureau (☎ 404-521-6600; www.atlanta.net; 233 Peachtree St; ⏲ 8:30am-5:30pm Mon-Fri) Has an online neighborhood guide, a restaurant guide and a link to info for gay and lesbian travelers. Its website also lets you buy a CityPass, a tremendous money saver that bundles admission to five attractions for the discounted price of $89.

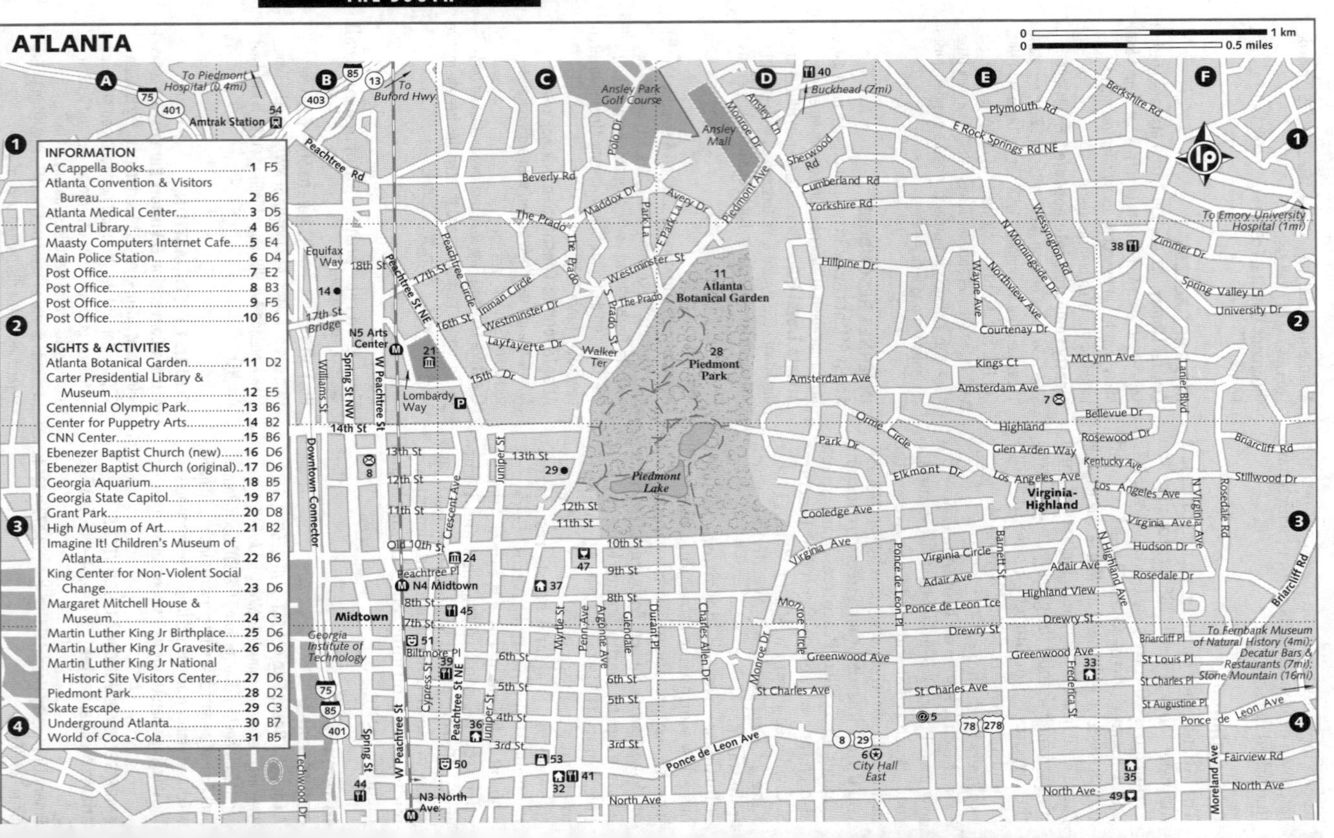
THE SOUTH
ATLANTA
0 1 km
0 0.5 miles
INFORMATION
A Cappella Books....1 F5
Atlanta Convention & Visitors Bureau....2 B6
Atlanta Medical Center....3 D5
Central Library....4 B6
Maasty Computers Internet Cafe....5 E4
Main Police Station....6 D4
Post Office....7 E2
Post Office....8 B3
Post Office....9 F5
Post Office....10 B6
SIGHTS & ACTIVITIES
Atlanta Botanical Garden....11 D2
Carter Presidential Library & Museum....12 E5
Centennial Olympic Park....13 B6
Center for Puppetry Arts....14 B2
CNN Center....15 B6
Ebenezer Baptist Church (new)....16 D6
Ebenezer Baptist Church (original)....17 D6
Georgia Aquarium....18 B5
Georgia State Capitol....19 B7
Grant Park....20 D8
High Museum of Art....21 B2
Imagine It! Children's Museum of Atlanta....22 B6
King Center for Non-Violent Social Change....23 D6
Margaret Mitchell House & Museum....24 C3
Martin Luther King Jr Birthplace....25 D6
Martin Luther King Jr Gravesite....26 D6
Martin Luther King Jr National Historic Site Visitors Center....27 D6
Piedmont Park....28 D2
Skate Escape....29 C3
Underground Atlanta....30 B7
World of Coca-Cola....31 B5
To Piedmont Hospital (0.4mi)
Amtrak Station
To Buford Hwy
Buckhead (7mi)
Ansley Park Golf Course
Ansley Mall
Atlanta Botanical Garden
Piedmont Park
Piedmont Lake
N5 Arts Center
N4 Midtown
N3 North Ave
Midtown
Georgia Institute of Technology
Virginia-Highland
City Hall East
To Emory University Hospital (1mi)
To Fernbank Museum of Natural History (4mi); Decatur Bars & Restaurants (7mi); Stone Mountain (16mi)
Downtown Connector
Peachtree St NE
Ponce de Leon Ave
N Highland Ave

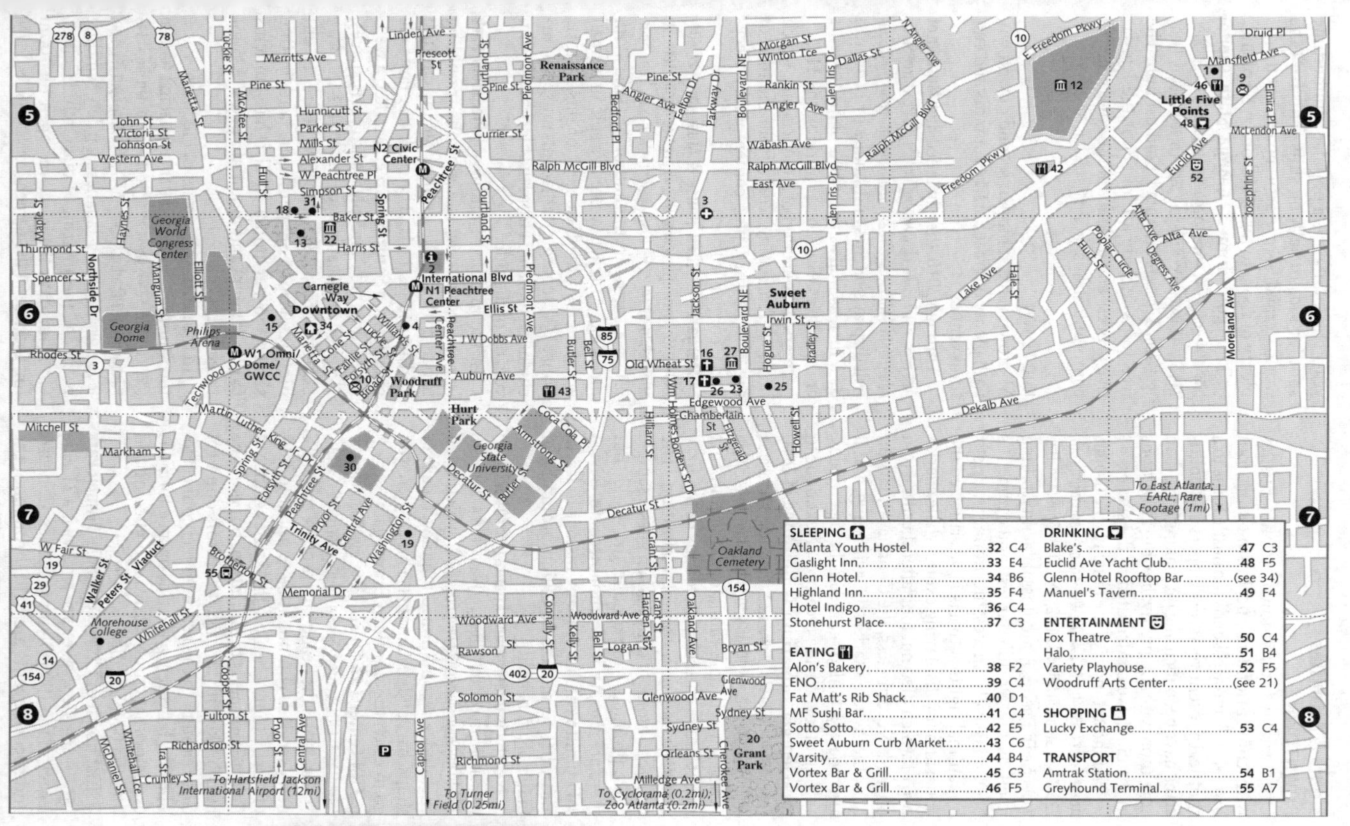
SLEEPING
Atlanta Youth Hostel.....32 C4
Gaslight Inn.....33 E4
Glenn Hotel.....34 B6
Highland Inn.....35 F4
Hotel Indigo.....36 C4
Stonehurst Place.....37 C3
EATING
Alon's Bakery.....38 F2
ENO.....39 C4
Fat Matt's Rib Shack.....40 D1
MF Sushi Bar.....41 C4
Sotto Sotto.....42 E5
Sweet Auburn Curb Market.....43 C6
Varsity.....44 B4
Vortex Bar & Grill.....45 C3
Vortex Bar & Grill.....46 F5
DRINKING
Blake's.....47 C3
Euclid Ave Yacht Club.....48 F5
Glenn Hotel Rooftop Bar.....(see 34)
Manuel's Tavern.....49 F4
ENTERTAINMENT
Fox Theatre.....50 C4
Halo.....51 B4
Variety Playhouse.....52 F5
Woodruff Arts Center.....(see 21)
SHOPPING
Lucky Exchange.....53 C4
TRANSPORT
Amtrak Station.....54 B1
Greyhound Terminal.....55 A7
To East Atlanta; EARL; Rare Footage (1mi)
To Hartsfield Jackson International Airport (12mi)
To Turner Field (0.25mi)
To Cyclorama (0.2mi); Zoo Atlanta (0.2mi)
Downtown
Sweet Auburn
Little Five Points
Renaissance Park
Woodruff Park
Hurt Park
Grant Park
Georgia World Congress Center
Georgia Dome
Philips Arena
Georgia State University
Oakland Cemetery
Morehouse College
N2 Civic Center
N1 Peachtree Center
W1 Omni/Dome/GWCC

Sights & Activities

DOWNTOWN

On weekdays, downtown Atlanta bustles with conventioneers and businessfolk, but by nightfall and weekends the bustle turns to a shuffle. In recent years, developers and politicians have been focusing on making the urban core more vibrant and livable. Big attractions in the city have contributed to the success.

The showstopper of the bunch is the **Georgia Aquarium** (☎ 404-581-4000; www.georgiaaquarium.com; 225 Baker St; adult/child $24/18; 🕑 10am-5pm Mon-Thu, 9am-6pm Fri-Sun; 🚸), a colossal facility billing itself as the world's largest aquarium. It's been massively successful among tourists, but animal rights activists have criticized the aquarium for displaying exotic whale sharks, two of which died not long after the attraction opened. Nevertheless, the Georgia Aquarium has other whale sharks still swimming, and it also boasts a tank of gorgeous beluga whales, among other marine creatures. Next door to the Georgia Aquarium is the **World of Coca-Cola** (☎ 404-676-5151; www.woccatlanta.com; 121 Baker St; adult/child $15/10; 🕑 10am-6:30pm Sun-Thu, 9am-6:30pm Fri & Sat), a self-congratulatory museum that might prove entertaining to fans of the fizzy beverage and rash commercialization. The climactic moment comes when guests sample Coke products from around the world. But there are also Andy Warhol pieces to view, a 4-D film to catch, company history to learn, and what seems like 20 billion promotional materials to behold.

Nearby is **Underground Atlanta** (☎ 404-523-2311; www.underground-atlanta.com; cnr Peachtree & Alabama Sts; 🕑 10am-9pm Mon-Sat, 11am-6pm Sun), which is an enclosed, air-conditioned multilevel maze of shops, bars and restaurants. This is where you go to catch the shuttle to Braves games.

CNN Center (☎ 404-827-2300; www.cnn.com/tour/atlanta; 1 CNN Center; 50min tour adult/child $13/10; 🕑 9am-5pm) is the headquarters of the cable-TV news service. You might be tempted to take the CNN tour, a behind-the-scenes glance at the 24-hour news organization, but don't be heartbroken if you miss it. Visitors don't get close enough to the action to feel connected. They do, however, get to ride on an enormous escalator that climbs above a food court and into the CNN facility.

Just north of CNN, **Centennial Olympic Park** (☎ 404-223-4412; www.centennialpark.com) is a 21-acre legacy of the 1996 Olympic Games. Concerts and special events are held throughout the year. The fountain is a popular summertime spot for kids in bathing suits. This isn't the world's grandest or grassiest park, but there's plenty of room to toss a ball or have a picnic.

The gold-domed **Georgia State Capitol** (☎ 404-463-4536; www.sos.ga.gov/archives/state_capitol; 214 State Capitol; 🕑 8am-5pm Mon-Fri, tours 10am, 11am, 1pm, 2pm & 3pm) is Atlanta's political hub. The free tours include a film about the legislative process and a glance at the government's communications facility.

MIDTOWN

Midtown is like a hipper, second downtown, with plenty of great bars, restaurants and cultural venues.

Through 2010, the expanded **High Museum of Art** (☎ 404-733-4444; www.high.org; 1280 Peachtree St NE; adult/child $18/11; 🕑 10am-5pm Tue-Sat, noon-5pm Sun) will display sketches and studies by Leonardo da Vinci, as well as the works of his students and teachers. But don't overlook the High's permanent collection of American art, which includes fascinating works from the turn of the 20th century, plus contemporary pieces and Georgian folk art.

Margaret Mitchell House & Museum (☎ 404-249-7015; www.gwtw.org; 990 Peachtree St, at 10th St; adult/child $12/9; 🕑 10am-5:30pm Mon-Sat, from noon Sun) is a shrine to the author of *Gone With the Wind*. Mitchell wrote her epic in a small apartment in the basement of this historic house. A separate, adjacent museum includes memorabilia from the blockbuster film version of the title.

In the middle of midtown, **Piedmont Park** (www.piedmontpark.org) is a glorious, rambling urban park and the setting of many cultural and music festivals. The park has fantastic bike paths, a Saturday Green Market, a well-loved dog area and pleasant green spaces. Neighboring **Skate Escape** (☎ 404-892-1292; www.skateescape.com; 1086 Piedmont Ave NE) rents out bicycles (from $6 per hour) and in-line skates ($6 per hour). It also has tandems ($12 per hour) and mountain bikes ($25 for three hours).

In the northwest corner of Piedmont Park, the stunning 30-acre **Atlanta Botanical Garden** (☎ 404-876-5859; www.atlantabotanicalgarden.org; 1345 Piedmont Ave NE; adult/child $15/12; 🕑 9am-6pm Tue-Sun, to 7pm summer) has a Japanese garden, winding paths and the amazing Fuqua Orchid Center. On Thursdays the garden is open till 10pm for **Cocktails in the Garden** (admission $15; 🕑 Thu

THE SHORT LIFE OF A CIVIL RIGHTS GIANT

Martin Luther King Jr, the quintessential figure of the American Civil Rights movement, was born in 1929, the son of an Atlanta preacher. His lineage was significant, not only because he followed his father to the pulpit of Ebenezer Baptist Church, but because his political speeches rang out with a preacher's inflections.

In 1955 King led the 'bus boycott' in Montgomery, AL. After a year of boycotting, the US Supreme Court removed laws that enforced segregated buses. From this successful beginning, King emerged as an inspiring moral voice in civil rights.

His nonviolent approach to racial equality and peace makes the irony of his death all the more cruel: he was assassinated on a Memphis hotel balcony in 1968, four years after receiving the Nobel Peace Prize and five years after giving his legendary 'I Have a Dream' speech in Washington, DC.

King remains one of the most recognized and respected figures of the 20th century. In a span of 10 years, he led a movement that essentially ended a system of statutory discrimination in existence since the country's founding. The Martin Luther King Jr National Historic Site (below) and the King Center for Non-Violent Social Change (below) in Atlanta are testaments to his moral vision, his ability to inspire others and his lasting impact on the fundamental fabric of American society.

May-Sep) that pairs a drink with a particular flower and area of the garden. There is a DJ and snacks.

SWEET AUBURN

Auburn Ave was the thumping commercial and cultural heart of African American culture in the 1900s. Today, a collection of sights is associated with Sweet Auburn's most famous son, Martin Luther King Jr, who was born on Auburn and preached on Auburn and whose grave now looks onto the street. Although the neighborhood seems dilapidated, new development suggests an imminent Sweet Auburn revival.

The historic **Martin Luther King Jr National Historic Site** commemorates the life, work and legacy of the civil rights lodestar. The center takes up several blocks. A stop by the excellent bustling **visitor center** (☎ 404-331-5190; www.nps.gov/malu; 450 Auburn Ave NE; admission free; ⏰ 9am-5pm, to 6pm in summer) will help you get oriented with a map and brochure of area sites and exhibits. From here, free guided tours leave for the **Martin Luther King Jr Birthplace** (501 Auburn Ave). If you miss the tour, a film in the visitor center tells about King's life in the house.

Across from the visitor center, the **King Center for Non-Violent Social Change** (☎ 404-526-8900; www.thekingcenter.org; 449 Auburn Ave NE; ⏰ 9am-5pm, to 6pm summer) has more information on King's life and work, and a few of his personal effects, including his Nobel Peace Prize. His **gravesite**, between the church and center, is surrounded by a long, reflecting pool and can be viewed anytime.

Ebenezer Baptist Church (☎ 404-688-7263; www.historicebenezer.org; 407 Auburn Ave NE; admission free; ⏰ tours 9am-6pm Mon-Sat, from 1:30pm Sun) was the preaching ground for King Jr, his father and grandfather, who were all pastors here. This is also where King Jr's mother was murdered in 1974. You can take a free tour of the original church, but Sunday services are now held at a new Ebenezer across the street.

All of the King sites are a few blocks' walk from Marta's King Memorial station.

GRANT PARK

A large oasis of green situated on the edge of the city center, **Grant Park** (www.grantpark.org) is home to **Zoo Atlanta** (☎ 404-624-5600; www.zooatlanta.org; adult/child $19/14; ⏰ 9:30am-5:30pm Mon-Fri, to 6:30pm Sat & Sun; 👪), which features flamingos, elephants, kangaroos and the odd tiger. But the zoo's pride and joy are the giant pandas. They tend to have cubs that slaughter you with cuteness. Be prepared to wait to see the cubs.

For history buffs, on the south side of Grant Park is the **Cyclorama** building that houses the gigantic mural *Battle of Atlanta,* which visually recounts the history of the fight.

LITTLE FIVE POINTS & EAST ATLANTA

These two bohemian neighborhoods are close to one another, but miles away from mainstream Atlanta's genteel sensibilities. They're young, hipster neighborhoods with a definite

GAY & LESBIAN ATLANTA

Atlanta – or 'Hotlanta' as some might call it – is one of the few places in Georgia, perhaps in the South, with a noticeable and active gay and lesbian population. Midtown is the center of gay life; the epicenter is around Piedmont Park and the intersection of 10th St and Piedmont Ave. The town of Decatur, east of downtown Atlanta, has a significant lesbian community. For news and information, grab a copy of the *Southern Voice* newspaper; also check out www.gayatlanta.com.

Atlanta Pride Festival (☎ 404-929-0071; www.atlantapride.org) is a massive annual celebration of the city's gay and lesbian community. Held at the end of June in and around Piedmont Park, it attracts people from all over the country.

alternative edge. Both are dominated by a main drag – **Euclid Ave** in L5P and **Flat Shoals Ave** in East Atlanta – and both are anchored by popular music venues, Variety Playhouse and the EARL, respectively (see p450). These neighborhoods offer Atlanta's most dense concentration of funky local boutiques; the stretch of Moreland Ave separating the two 'hoods is equally dense with big chain stores. Both neighborhoods are well explored on foot, and both are jammed with restaurants.

VIRGINIA-HIGHLAND

Atlanta's preppiest neighborhood is populated by adorable homes (with big price tags) and beautiful boutiques (with big price tags). Highland Ave runs through the heart of the neighborhood, and makes for a pleasant stroll.

POINTS EAST & DECATUR

Located on a hilltop overlooking downtown, the **Carter Presidential Library & Museum** (☎ 404-865-7100; www.jimmycarterlibrary.org; 441 Freedom Pkwy; adult/child $8/free; 9am-4:45pm Mon-Sat, from noon Sun) features exhibits highlighting Jimmy Carter's 1977–81 presidency, including a replica of the Oval Office. Carter's Nobel Prize is also on display. Don't miss the tranquil Japanese garden out back. The museum underwent a recent redesign, which was completed in October 2009.

Fernbank Museum of Natural History (☎ 404-929-6300; www.fernbankmuseum.org; 767 Clifton Rd NE; adult/child $15/13; 10am-5pm Mon-Sat, from noon Sun) makes other museums seem hopelessly dull. It covers the natural world from seashells to giant lizards, and it has an **IMAX theater** (adult/child $11/9). A righteous night out is had on Martinis & IMAX Friday (5:30pm to 10pm January to November), when the lobby turns into a cocktail lounge and live jazz echoes through the bones of a 123ft dinosaur.

Atlanta for Children

Atlanta has plenty of activities to keep children entertained, delighted and – perhaps against their will – educated.

Center for Puppetry Arts (☎ 404-873-3391; www.puppet.org; 1404 Spring St NW; museum $8; 9am-3pm Tue-Fri, 9am-5pm Sat, 11am-5pm Sun) is a wonderland for visitors of all ages, and hands-down one of Atlanta's most unique attractions. The museum houses a treasury of puppets, some of which you get to operate yourself. Separate tickets are required for the performances.

Imagine It! Children's Museum of Atlanta (☎ 404-659-5437; www.childrensmuseumatlanta.org; 275 Olympic Centennial Park Dr NW; admission $12.50; 10am-4pm Mon-Fri, to 5pm Sat & Sun) is a hands-on museum geared toward kids aged eight and under. Adults aren't allowed in without a youngster in tow.

Festivals & Events

Atlanta Jazz Festival (www.atlantafestivals.com) A city-sponsored month-long event culminating in live concerts in Piedmont Park on Memorial Day weekend in late May.

Atlanta Pride Festival (www.atlantapride.org) End of June (see the boxed text above).

National Black Arts Festival (☎ 404-730-7315; www.nbaf.org) Artists from across the country converge on Atlanta for this festival celebrating African American music, theater, literature and film. Held in July at various locations.

Sleeping

Rates at downtown hotels tend to fluctuate wildly depending on whether there is a large convention in town. Weekends are often cheaper in hotels away from downtown, but in the city, rates are higher on weekends.

BUDGET

A cheap option is to stay somewhere along the Marta line outside downtown, and take the train into the city for sightseeing. There are plenty of chain hotels.

THE SOUTH

Atlanta Youth Hostel (☎ 800-473-9449; www.hostel-atlanta.com; 223 Ponce de Leon Ave, at Myrtle St; dm/r $25/59; P ⊠ ✻ 💻 📶) In a white-brick Midtown mansion, this lively hostel has private beds and dorm rooms. On one hand, it wins accolades both for its cleanliness and for its sweet location. On the other, readers have given it some mixed reviews. If you don't mind sharing a room, ask for room 36, which has a massive balcony.

MIDRANGE & TOP END

Highland Inn (☎ 404-874-5756; www.thehighlandinn.com; 644 N Highland Ave; r & ste incl breakfast $87-106; P ⊠ ✻ 📶) This European-style inn has a great location in the middle of Virginia-Highland. Appealing to touring musicians over the years and with its own casual music venue, the Ballroom Lounge, on the bottom floor, this ragged but clean hotel has lyrical personality.

Gaslight Inn (☎ 404-875-1001; www.gaslightinn.com; 1001 St Charles Ave NE; r incl breakfast $125-215; P ⊠ ✻ 📶) If you're looking for a homey B&B saddled up next to the shops and restaurants of Highland Ave this is your place. Some rooms feature a Jacuzzi or steam room.

Hotel Indigo (☎ 404-874-9200; www.hotelindigo.com; 683 Peachtree St; r $129-179; ⊠ ✻ 💻 📶) A boutique-style hotel that's actually part of a chain, the Indigo has a boisterous blue color scheme and a sunny personality. More important is the outstanding midtown location, across the street from restaurants and entertainment and within walking distance of a Marta stop. Parking costs $18.

Glenn Hotel (☎ 404-521-2250; www.glennhotel.com; 110 Marietta St NW; r from $140; ✻ ⊠ 📶) Painstakingly hip, the Glenn feels more like a discreet nightclub than a slick hotel, but (with a swanky rooftop bar for guests and locals alike) it's actually a bit of both. Boutique hotels are surprisingly rare in Atlanta, and this place seems to relish its exclusivity. Parking will be around $21 per day.

our pick Stonehurst Place (☎ 404-881-0722; www.stonehurstplace.com; 923 Piedmont Ave NE; r $139-400; P ⊠ ✻ 💻 📶) Built in 1896 by the Hinman family, this elegant, almost Parisian, B&B has all the modern amenities one could ask for and is fully updated with ecofriendly water treatment and heating systems. Plus, Trenell, the innkeeper, makes you feel right at home. Smack in the middle of midtown, this is truly an exceptional place to stay in Atlanta.

Eating

Food culture in Atlanta is nothing short of obsessive. Hot new restaurants are instantly mobbed and lines at local favorites stretch out the door. The options range from haute cuisine to humble Southern staples, and the quality can be absolutely magnificent at both ends of the spectrum.

DOWNTOWN & MIDTOWN

Varsity (☎ 404-881-1706; 61 North Ave, at Spring St; dogs from $1.35; 🕑 10am-11:30pm Mon-Thu, to 12:30am Fri & Sat) The world's largest drive-in restaurant and an Atlanta institution since 1928, the Varsity is a glorified fast-food joint, but it's always packed with folks ordering walk-a-dogs (hot dogs), gussied-up steaks (hamburgers) and bags of rags (fries).

Fat Matt's Rib Shack (☎ 404-607-1622; 1811 Piedmont Ave NE; sandwiches from $3.95; 🕑 11:30am-11:30pm Mon-Fri, to 12:30am Sat, 1-11:30pm Sun) Less than a mile north of Piedmont Park, a much more down-home choice is divey Fat Matt's, a shrine to two great Southern traditions: barbecue and the blues. Take special note of the Brunswick stew, a delicious side dish best described as barbecue soup.

MF Sushi Bar (☎ 404-815-8844; 265 Ponce de Leon Ave; special rolls $7-17.50; 🕑 lunch 11:30am-2:30pm Mon-Fri, dinner 5:30-10:30pm Mon-Thu, to 11:30pm Fri, 6-10pm Sun) A fresh rose on your table and a hot towel for your face are your preambles to sushi glory. The ultimate treat is to order *omakase,* an off-the-menu move that allows the chef total control over your meal. Yet, the standard rolls and fish pieces are above par as well. The MF, by the way, stands for Magic Fingers.

our pick ENO (☎ 404-685-3191; 800 Peachtree St NE; mains from $18; 🕑 11:30am-2:30pm & 5-11pm Tue-Thu, 11:30am-2:30pm & 5pm-midnight Fri, 5pm-midnight Sat) This Mediterranean-style wine bar has delectable, fine dishes, each paired with a suggested glass of wine. Better yet, proprietor Doug Strickland prioritizes local, sustainable and organic fare and libations. The interior boasts contemporary art exhibits and the exterior has a lovely sidewalk patio.

SWEET AUBURN

Sweet Auburn Curb Market (☎ 404-659-1665; www.sweetauburncurbmarket.com; 209 Edgewood Ave SE; 🕑 8am-6pm Mon-Sat) Like the Reading Terminal Market in Philadelphia or the Ferry Building in San Francisco (but, frankly, not as nice as either), the Curb Market allows foodies to browse countless stalls for cooking ingredients or hot meals served on the premises.

LITTLE FIVE POINTS

Vortex Bar & Grill (☎ 404-688-1828; 438 Moreland Ave; burgers from $6.45; 11am-midnight Sun-Thu, to 3am Fri & Sat) Walk through the gaping jaws of a giant skull and enter the Vortex, a scrappy joint with a snarky menu boasting '140 styles of gourmet burgers,' an ideal meal before hitting the L5P bar scene. Ages 18 and up only. There's also a branch in midtown (878 Peachtree St).

VIRGINIA-HIGHLAND

Alon's Bakery (☎ 404-872-6000; 1394 N Highland Ave; sandwiches from $6.30; 7am-8pm Mon-Fri, 8am-8pm Sat, 9am-4pm Sun) At this revered bakery you'll find stellar components for a sumptuous European picnic – include gourmet cheeses, wine, pâté, roasted vegetables, and all manner of brioche.

our pick **Sotto Sotto** (☎ 404-523-6678; 313 N Highland Ave NE; dishes $16-32; 5:30-11:30pm Mon-Thu, to midnight Fri & Sat, to 10pm Sun) Known for its authenticity, this lively, trendy restaurant has crisp service and risotto that is heaven on earth. Reservations suggested.

DECATUR

Watershed (☎ 404-378-4900; www.watershedrestaurant.com; mains $12-34; 11am-10pm Mon-Sat, 10am-3pm Sun) Simply outstanding (and outstandingly simple), this is the place for traditional Southern food done up with just a touch of class. Tuesday night is fried-chicken night; get there early or the birds will be gone. Any other night, order the veggie plate – you've never had a better one. The James Beard Award–winning chef Scott Peacock is nothing less than a local hero.

Drinking

Atlanta likes to drink. The following spots, a few of many, include a local institution, a swanky hotel bar and a great dive.

Manuel's Tavern (☎ 404-525-3447; 602 N Highland Ave; 11am-2am Mon-Sat, to midnight Sun) A longtime political hangout that draws a good, conversational beer-drinking crowd.

Euclid Avenue Yacht Club (☎ 404-688-2582; 1136 Euclid Ave; 3pm-2am Mon-Thu, noon-3am Fri & Sat, noon-midnight Sun) A divey bar ideal for grabbing a drink before a show at the nearby Variety Playhouse. Smokers and nonsmokers get separate rooms.

Glenn Hotel rooftop bar (☎ 404-521-2250; 110 Marietta St NW; 5:30pm-12am Mon-Thu, to 2am Fri & Sat, to 11pm Sun) If you're facing the reception desk, head through the unmarked door to the right and take the elevator to the roof. Then, feast your eyes on the skyline.

Blake's (☎ 404-892-5786; www.blakesontheparkatlanta.com; 227 10th St NE; 11am-3am Mon-Sat, 12.30pm-midnight Sun) Right on Piedmont Park, Blake's bills itself as 'Atlanta's favorite gay bar since 1987.'

Entertainment

Atlanta has big-city nightlife, with lots of live music and cultural events. Check out the free *Creative Loafing* for weekly listings. Also check out **Atlanta Coalition of Performing Arts** (www.atlantaperforms.com), which has info and links about the city's music, film, dance and theater scene. The **Atlanta Music Guide** (www.atlantamusicguide.com) maintains a live-music schedule, plus a directory of local venues and links to online ticketing.

THEATER

Fox Theatre (☎ 404-881-2100; www.foxtheatre.org; 660 Peachtree St NE) A spectacular 1929 movie palace with fanciful Moorish and Egyptian designs. It hosts Broadway shows, and concerts in an auditorium holding more than 4500 people.

Woodruff Arts Center (☎ 404-733-4200; www.woodruffcenter.org; 1280 Peachtree St NE, at 15th St) An arts campus hosting the High Museum, the Atlanta Symphony Orchestra and the Alliance Theatre.

LIVE MUSIC & NIGHTCLUBS

Cover charges at the following vary nightly. Check their respective websites for music calendars and ticket prices.

EARL (☎ 404-522-3950; www.badearl.com; 488 Flat Shoals Ave) The indie rocker's pub of choice – a smoky restaurant with surprisingly good food; it's also a bar and a busy live-music venue.

Eddie's Attic (☎ 404-377-4976; www.eddiesattic.com; 515b N McDonough St, Decatur; ☒) One of the city's best venues to hear live folk and acoustic music, in a nonsmoking atmosphere seven nights a week.

Halo (☎ 404-962-7333; www.halolounge.com; 817 W Peachtree St) If you can find this sexy industrial lounge, which is tucked into the north side of the Biltmore building, you're cool enough to chill on the space-age furniture, and to drink at a glowing marble bar that resembles hot lava.

IF YOU HAVE A FEW MORE DAYS

About 20 miles east of Atlanta, a giant mount of granite, **Stone Mountain**, juts into the Georgia sky. You'll visit the mountain through **Stone Mountain Park** (☎ 770-498-5690; www.stonemountainpark.com; Hwy 78 E, exit 8; per car $8; park 6am-midnight, attractions from 10am), which combines natural splendor with a creepy Confederate nostalgia – Confederate laser light show anyone? (The rebel flag, for instance, still flies at the mountain's base, and the trio of Robert E Lee, Stonewall Jackson and Jefferson Davis are carved into the mountain's side.) If you're up for a climb, skip the Crossroads area (a tourist-trap cluster of old-timey shops) and hike to the summit for a lovely city view. Camping and basic hotel accommodations are available in the park.

Variety Playhouse (☎ 404-524-7354; www.variety-playhouse.com; 1099 Euclid Ave NE) A smartly booked and well-run concert venue for a variety of touring artists.

SPORTS

Order tickets to sporting events through **Ticketmaster** (☎ 404-249-6400; www.ticketmaster.com).

The Major League Baseball (MLB) team **Atlanta Braves** (☎ 404-522-7630; www.atlantabraves.com; tickets $1-60) plays at Turner Field.

Shopping

Atlantans love to shop. There are gigantic malls in Buckhead, and Virginia-Highland has a unique selection of boutique shops. Find vintage and secondhand threads in Little Five Points or at the smartly stocked **Lucky Exchange** (☎ 404-817-7715; 212 Ponce de Leon Ave; 11:30am-6pm Mon-Sat, noon-5pm Sun). The teeny East Atlanta boutique **Rare Footage** (☎ 404-215-2188; 493 Flat Shoals Ave; noon-8pm Mon-Sat, to 6pm Sun) sells limited-edition sneakers.

Getting There & Away

Atlanta's huge **Hartsfield-Jackson International Airport** (ATL; ☎ 800-897-1910; www.atlanta-airport.com), 12 miles south of downtown, is a major regional hub and an international gateway. It's the busiest airport in the world in overall passenger traffic.

The **Greyhound terminal** (☎ 404-584-1728; 232 Forsyth St) is next to the Marta Garnett station. Some destinations include Nashville, TN (five hours), New Orleans, LA (10½ hours), New York (20 hours), Miami, FL (16 hours) and Savannah, GA (4¾ hours).

The **Amtrak station** (☎ 404-881-3062; 1688 Peachtree St NW, at Deering Rd) is just north of downtown.

Getting Around

The **Metropolitan Atlanta Rapid Transit Authority** (Marta; ☎ 404-848-4711; www.itsmarta.com; fares $2.25) rail line travels to/from the airport to downtown, along with a few less-useful routes used mostly by commuters.

The **Atlanta Airport Shuttle** (☎ 404-524-3400; one-way tickets $16.50-20.50) also transports passengers to hotels all over the city (from 6am to midnight). The shuttle and car-rental agencies have desks in the airport situated at the baggage-claim level.

Driving in Atlanta can be infuriating. You'll often find yourself sitting in traffic jams, and it's easy to get disoriented – a road map is invaluable.

NORTH GEORGIA

The southern end of the great Appalachian Range extends some 40 miles into Georgia's far north, providing some superb mountain scenery and wild white-water rivers. The landscape is unlike anywhere else in Georgia. The fall colors emerge late here, peaking in October.

A few days are warranted to see sites like the 1200ft-deep **Tallulah Gorge** (☎ 706-754-7970), the mountain scenery and hiking trails at **Vogel State Park** (☎ 706-745-2628) and **Unicoi State Park** (☎ 706-878-2201), and the interesting collection of Appalachian folk arts at the **Foxfire Museum** (☎ 706-746-5828; www.foxfire.org; adult/child $5/free; 9am-4pm Mon-Fri) in Mountain City.

One traveler described the town of **Helen** as 'NASCAR meet Disneyland.' This faux Swiss-German, head shop–studded, mountain village is definitely hokey. It's the result of business leaders attempting to transform the dreary lumber town into a tourist attraction.

The **visitor center** (☎ 800-858-8027; www.helenga.org; 726 Brukenstrasse; 9am-5pm Mon-Sat, 10am-4pm Sun) is on the southern side of town. **Oktoberfest**, from mid-September to early November, is a popular event but only serves cheap American beer. In summer, you'll see hundreds of folks **Shooting the Hooch** – going down the slow-moving Chattahoochee River on inner tubes.

Dahlonega

In 1828 Dahlonega was the site of the first gold rush in the USA. The boom these days, though, is in tourism. It's an easy excursion from Atlanta and is a fantastic destination if you want to get away to the mountains.

Walking around the historic main square is an event in itself. Many offbeat shops compete for tourist dollars. The **visitor center** (☎ 706-864-3711; www.dahlonega.org; 13 S Park St; 9am-5:30pm) has plenty of information on area sites and activities (including hiking, canoeing, kayaking, rafting and mountain biking).

Amicalola Falls State Park (☎ 706-265-4703; www.amicalolafalls.com), 18 miles west of Dahlonega on Hwy 52, features the 729ft **Amicalola Falls**, the highest waterfall in Georgia. The park offers spectacular scenery, a lodge, and excellent hiking and mountain biking trails.

The **cycling** (www.cyclenorthgeorgia.com) was fantastic enough for Lance Armstrong to train here. **Dalhonega Wheelworks** (☎ 706-867-0228; www.wheelworksga.com; 24 Alicia Lane; 11am-6pm Mon-Fri, 9am-5pm Sat) is a nice bike shop in town with mountain and road bike rentals, bike guides, and daily rides offered at the shop. The 35-mile **Three Gap** cycling loop is spectacular, but bring your climbing legs.

There are a number of wineries near Dahlonega that actually produce some tasty products, but it's especially worth going to hang out at the gorgeous vineyards. **Frogtown Cellars** (☎ 706-865-0687; www.frogtownwine.com; 700 Ridge Point Dr; noon-5pm Fri, to 6pm Sat, 12:30-5pm Sun) is a beautiful winery and has a killer deck on which to sip libations and nibble cheese.

our pick Hiker Hostel (☎ 770-312-7342; hikerhostel@yahoo.com; 7693 Hwy 19N; dm $16, private r $38; P), on Hwy 19N near the Three Gap Loop, is owned by an avid couple of cycling and outdoors enthusiasts, so there's always a place to hang an adventurous head here. Plus, the hostel is newish, wonderfully kept, provides hearty breakfasts, and has its own chickens. All in all, an awesome deal.

Cedar House Inn and Yurts (☎ 770-867-9446; www.georgiamountaininn.com; 6463 Highway 19N; r from $85, yurts from $95; P V) offers eco-friendly accommodations and organic fare. The composting toilets don't lend to the yurt's atmosphere; staying in a room is suggested. Stay midweek, as the weekend prices are a bit much.

THE SOUTH

CENTRAL GEORGIA

Central Georgia is a kind of catch-all for everything that's not metro Atlanta, mountainous north Georgia or swampy Savannah-centric south Georgia. The remaining area feels rustic and Southern. You're likely to see open fields and red-clay earth.

Athens

A beery, artsy and laid-back college town roughly 70 miles east of Atlanta, Athens has an extremely popular football team (the University of Georgia Bulldogs), a world-famous music scene (which has launched artists including the B-52's, REM and Widespread Panic) and a burgeoning restaurant culture. The university drives the culture of Athens and ensures an ever-replenishing supply of young bar-hoppers and concertgoers. The pleasant, walkable downtown offers a plethora of funky choices for eating, drinking and shopping. At least three routes run from Atlanta to Athens (Hwy 316, Hwy 129 and Hwy 78), each with relative pluses and minuses.

The **Athens Welcome Center** (☎ 706-353-1820; www.athenswelcomecenter.com; 280 E Dougherty St; 10am-6pm Mon-Sat, from noon Sun), in a historic antebellum house at the corner of Thomas St, provides maps and information on local tours – these include a Civil War tour and the 'Walking Tour of Athens \Music History.'

SIGHTS & ACTIVITIES

Truly gorgeous, with winding outdoor paths and a sociohistorical edge to boot, Athens' **State Botanical Garden of Georgia** (☎ 706-542-1244; www.uga.edu/~botgarden; 2450 S Milledge Ave; suggested donation $2; 8am-6pm, to 8pm summer) rivals Atlanta's. Signs provide smart context for its amazing collection of plants, which runs the gamut from rare and threatened species to a tantalizing watermelon patch.

Oconee Forest Park (http://warnell.forestry.uga.edu/ofp/facilities.htm; cnr College Station Rd & Alumni Dr), located at the back of the university's expansive Recreational Sports Complex, has wooded hiking trails and an enormous off-leash dog area.

SLEEPING & EATING

Athens does not have an awesome variety of places to stay. There are a number of standard chains just out of town on W Broad St.

Travelodge (☎ 706-549-5400; www.travelodge.com; 898 W Broad Street; r from $55; P) The price and the amiable staff is what this place have going for it. The rooms are feeling their years.

Foundry Park Inn & Spa (☎ 706-549-7020; www.foundryparkinn.com; 295 E Dougherty St; r $99-145; P) An upscale, non-corporate choice right in the middle of the city, this place will pamper you. In addition to its on-site spa, the hotel campus includes a restaurant and the Melting Point, a cozy music venue.

Jittery Joe's (☎ 706-227-4291; www.jitteryjoes.com; 780 E Broad Street; 7am-6pm Mon-Fri, from 8am Sat & Sun;) This Georgia coffee chain serves a good cup. As photos in the café indicate, it sponsors a professional cycling team, and also provides a tranquil space to get online or hang out with a book.

Grit (☎ 706-543-6592; www.thegrit.com; 199 Prince Ave; mains $6-8; 11am-10pm Mon-Fri, 10am-3pm & 5-10pm Sat & Sun; V) This popular vegetarian joint riffs on traditional Southern fare, plus serves hot noodle bowls and falafel.

our pick **Farm 255** (☎ 706-549-4659; www.farm255.com; 255 W Washington St; 5:30-10pm Tue-Thu, to 10:30pm Fri & Sat, 11am-2pm & 5:30-9:30pm Sun) Like a hippy dressed up in his Sunday's best, this stylish, light-filled bistro gets much of its meat and vegetables from its own 5-acre, organic/biodynamic Blue Moon Farms outside of Athens. The chefs prepare the scrumptious fare in the open-air kitchen. The operative word here is *fresh*.

Five & Ten (☎ 706-546-7300; www.fiveandten.com; 1653 S Lumpkin St; mains $16-31; 5:30-10pm Sun-Thu, to 11pm Fri & Sat, 10:30am-2:30pm Sun) Driven by superior ingredients (as opposed to showy technique), Five & Ten ranks among the South's best restaurants. Its menu is earthy and slightly gamey: sweatbreads, hand-cut pasta, North Carolina trout and frogmore stew (stewed corn, sausage and potato). Brunch is sensational. If you want a table for dinner, you'd best call ahead.

DRINKING & ENTERTAINMENT

40 Watt Club (☎ 706-549-7871; www.40watt.com; 285 W Washington St) It has lounges, a tiki bar, $2 PBR beers, and indie rock on stage. It's where the big hitters in town play. No wonder it's legendary.

Trappeze Pub (☎ 706-543-8997; www.trappezepub.com; 269 W Washington St; drafts $4-8; 11:30am-2am Mon-Fri, from noon Sat, to midnight Sun) Those 'beer weirdos,' as one local put it, flock here to enjoy a choice of 38 beers on tap and 215 by the bottle. It has an above-average pub menu.

283 (283 E Broad St; to 2am Mon-Sat) Locals hang out next to students who hang out next to you, in any given order. The scene in this little bar is jovial and laid-back.

Ciné (☎ 706-353-7377; www.athenscine.com; 234 W Hancock Ave) A smart two-screen art-house movie theater with a little bar in the lobby.

Macon

Macon is a pleasant little city with a few interesting sights. The town was established in 1823 and prospered as a cotton port on the Ocmulgee River. Many antebellum houses remain today. In fact, it has more structures on the National Register of Historic Places (5500) than any other Georgian city.

The **convention & visitors bureau** (☎ 478-743-1074; www.maconga.org; 450 Martin Luther King Jr Blvd) has a website with a downloadable visitors guide.

Georgia Music Hall of Fame (☎ 888-427-6257; www.georgiamusic.org; 200 Martin Luther King Jr Blvd; adult/child $8/3.50; 9am-5pm Mon-Sat, from 1pm Sun) showcases the multitude of musical talent that has bloomed in Georgia, including REM, James Brown, Little Richard, Ray Charles and the Allman Brothers.

Held in the third week of March, Macon's **Cherry Blossom Festival** (☎ 478-751-7429; www.cherryblossom.com) celebrates the blossoming of 250,000 flowering Japanese Yoshino cherry trees.

Ocmulgee National Monument (☎ 478-752-8257; www.nps.gov/ocmu; 1207 Emery Hwy; admission free; 9am-5pm), just east of town, is an archaeological site with Native American burial mounds, artifacts and an ancient earth lodge.

SAVANNAH

Like a Southern belle who wears hot pants under her skirt, this grand historic town revolves around formal antebellum architecture and the revelry of local students from Savannah College of Art & Design. It sits alongside the Savannah River, about 18 miles from the coast, amid Lowcountry swamps and mammoth live oak trees dripping with Spanish moss. With its gorgeous mansions, cotton warehouses, wonderfully beautiful squares, and Colonial public buildings, Savannah preserves its past with pride, and grace. However, unlike its sister city of Charleston, SC, which retains its reputation as a dignified and refined cultural center, Savannah isn't clean-cut – the town has been described as 'a beautiful lady with a dirty face.'

The city's massive St Patrick's Day celebration is a legendary rite of spring and there is an entire cottage industry catering to those tourists who have heard that Savannah is haunted – curious ghost-hunters can arrange to take tours of the city in a chauffeured hearse.

Orientation

Savannah's Historic District is a rectangle bounded by the Savannah River, Forsyth Park, E Broad St and Martin Luther King Jr Blvd (MLK). Almost everything of interest to visitors lies either within or just outside this area. In converted cotton warehouses situated along the Savannah River, you will find a touristy commercial district of bars, restaurants and shops. City Market is an equally touristy district of shops and restaurants near Franklin Sq, and W Broughton St is a cosmopolitan shopping drag with cafés and restaurants. There are hip enclaves around town: on busy MLK by the college and E Park Ave by Forsyth Park.

Each of the 21 remaining of Savannah's original 24 squares marks a truly exquisite place to relax among flower gardens, shade trees and – usually – a monument to some notable person who is buried in the square.

Information

BOOKSTORES

E Shaver, Bookseller (☎ 912-234-7257; 326 Bull St; 9am-6pm Mon-Sat) Shelves are stocked with tomes on local and regional history and the collected works of Paula Deen.

EMERGENCY

Main police station (☎ 912-232-4141)

INTERNET ACCESS

Main Library (☎ 912-652-3600; 2002 Bull St, btwn 36th & 37th Sts; 9am-9pm Mon-Thu, to 6pm Fri & Sat, 2-6pm Sun; wi-fi) Offers free internet and wi-fi access.

MEDICAL SERVICES

Candler Hospital (☎ 912-819-6000; 5353 Reynolds St)
CVS Pharmacy (☎ 912-238-1494; cnr Bull & W Broughton Sts)

MONEY

There are plenty of ATMs throughout the city. For full service, head to Johnson Sq, where there are several major banks.

POST

Post office (☎ 912-235-4653) Historic District (111 E Liberty St; 8am-5pm Mon-Fri); Main (1 E Bay St; 8am-5:30pm Mon-Fri, 9am-1pm Sat)

TOURIST INFORMATION

Visitor center (☎ 912-944-0455; www.savannahvisit.com; 301 Martin Luther King Jr Blvd; 8:30am-5pm Mon-Fri, from 9am Sat & Sun) Excellent resources and services are available in this center, based in a restored 1860s train station. Many privately operated city tours start here and there's tons of information about various city tours, from carriage to bus.

Sights & Activities

A great way to enjoy Savannah is to lollygag in one of the verdant squares and watch the world go by. Another, more robust way to see the city is by bike. Rentals are available at **Bicycle Link** (☎ 912-233-9401; www.bicyclelinksav.com; 408 Martin Luther King Jr Blvd; half-/full day $15/20; 10am-6pm Mon-Sat).

MUSEUMS & PARKS

The Central Park of Savannah is a sprawling rectangular green space called **Forsyth Park**, which has lots of room for jogging, tossing Frisbees and walking dogs. The park's beautiful fountain is a quintessential photo op.

Along with silver from the 1800s and a colossal oil painting depicting a scene from the Hundred Years War, Sylvia Shaw's famous 1936 *Bird Girl* sculpture – the one on the cover of *Midnight in the Garden of Good and Evil* – stands inside the **Telfair Museum of Art** (☎ 912-232-1177; www.telfair.org; 121 Barnard St; multi-venue ticket adult/child $15/5; noon-5pm Mon, 10am-5pm Tue-Sat, 1-5pm Sun). The $15 multi-venue ticket allows discounted admission to two affiliated museums, the Jepson and the Owens-Thomas House.

The **Jepson Center for the Arts** (JCA; ☎ 912-790-8800; www.telfair.org; 207 W York St; multi-venue ticket adult/child $15/5; 10am-5pm Mon & Wed-Sat, noon-5pm Sun) is fresh off a 2006 opening and is looking pretty darn space-age by Savannah's standards. The JCA focuses on 20th- and 21st-century art. Its contents are modest in size, but intriguing. There's also a neat interactive area for kids.

On the outskirts of the historic district is the **Ralph Mark Gilbert Civil Rights Museum** (☎ 912-231-8900; 460 Martin Luther King Jr Blvd; 9am-5pm Mon-Sat). Leaving the larger history of the movement to the Civil Rights Institute in Birmingham, Savannah's museum focuses on the local history of segregated schools, hotels, hospitals, jobs and lunch counters. It's definitely a must-see if you want a full understanding of the city.

HISTORIC HOMES

Completed in 1819 by British architect William Jay, the **Owens-Thomas House** (☎ 912-233-9743; 124 Abercorn St; adult/child $10/4; 🕑 noon-5pm Mon, 10am-5pm Tue-Sat, 1-5pm Sun) exemplifies Regency architecture, which is known for its symmetry. The guided tour is fussy, but it delivers interesting trivia about the number of coats of paint on the walls (22) and the number of years by which this mansion preceded the White House in getting running water (about 20).

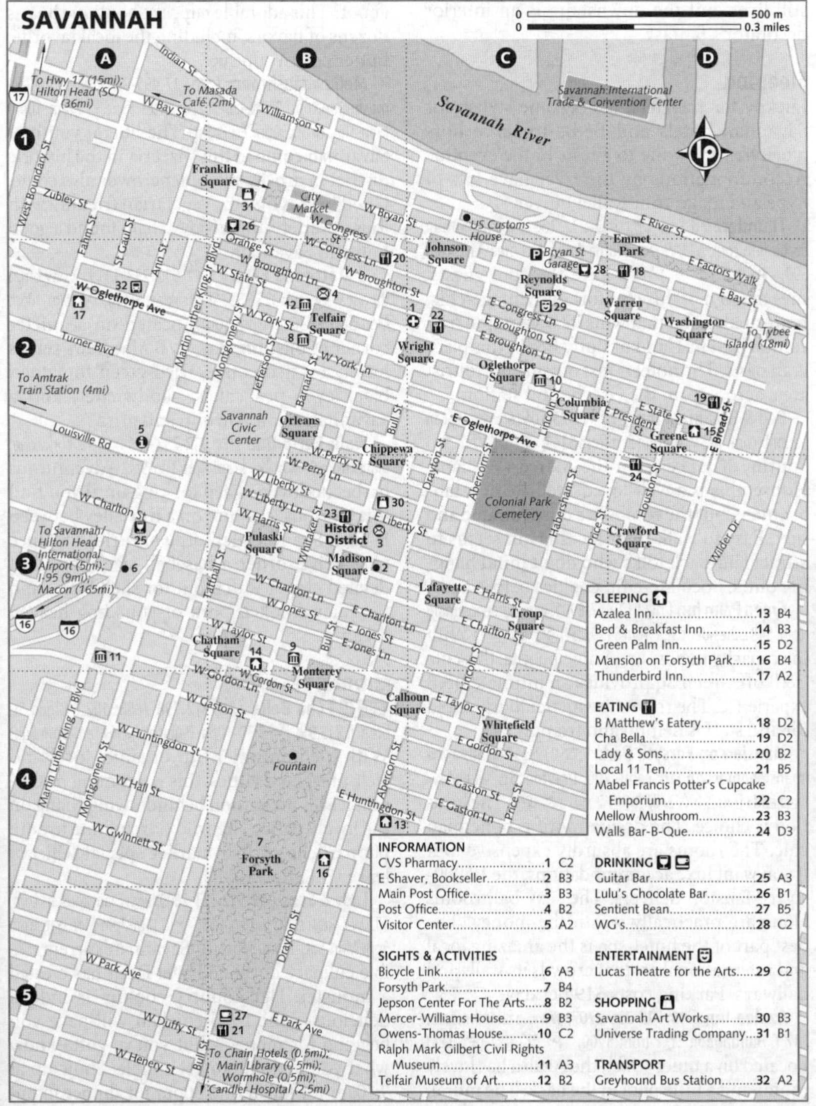

Consider seeing the **Mercer-Williams House** (☎ 912-236-6352; www.mercerhouse.com; 429 Bull St; adult/child $12.50/8). Although Jim Williams, the Savannah art dealer portrayed by Kevin Spacey in the film version of *Midnight in the Garden of Good and Evil,* died back in 1990, his infamous mansion didn't become a museum until 2004. You're not allowed to see the upstairs, where Williams' family still lives, but the downstairs is an interior decorator's fantasy.

Sleeping

Luckily for travelers, it's become stylish for Savannah hotels and B&Bs to serve hors d'oeuvres and wine to guests in the evening. Accommodations by the river have lots of hype and make your wallet quiver.

Thunderbird Inn (☎ 912-232-2661; www.thethunderbirdinn.com; 611 W Oglethorpe Ave; r incl breakfast from $99; P ⊠ ✺ ≋) 'We have the cool guests' says the sign of this comfortable vintage-chic, renovated motel that wins its own popularity contest. But in a land of stuffy B&Bs, this place is an oasis. The hotel is just outside the tourist area, across from the Greyhound station.

Bed & Breakfast Inn (☎ 912-238-0518; www.savannahbnb.com; 117 W Gordon St; r from $149; P ⊠ ✺ ≋) Spittin' distance from the Mercer-Williams House, this is a well-loved, well-worn establishment, but the rooms are crisp, unique and tidy. Easy to walk right by, this inn seems to attract laid-back folks who don't mind hanging out. Chocolate-chip cookies before bed.

Green Palm Inn (☎ 912-447-8901; www.greenpalminn.com; 548 E President St; r from $159; P ⊠ ✺ ≋) With the capacity to host up to nine people, this cute B&B off Green Sq provides an intimate B&B experience. The rooms are meticulously cared for and staff is helpful and friendly.

Mansion on Forsyth Park (☎ 912-238-5158; www.mansiononforsythpark.com; 700 Drayton St; weekday/weekend r from $190/270; ⊠ ✺ ☐ ≋ ☒) The location is choice. The design motif is bohemian chic. The rooms are absurdly expensive. But if you want luxe accommodations, the 18,000-sq-ft Mansion delivers. The sexy bathrooms alone are practically worth the money. The best part of the hotel-spa is the amazing local and international art that crowds its walls and hallways. Parking costs $19 per day.

Azalea Inn (☎ 912-236-2707; www.azaleainn.com; 217 E Huntingdon St; r from $200; P ⊠ ✺ ≋ ☒) Located on a quiet street, the Azalea has lovely rooms and a little pool in the back. The mural, created by art students, in the dining room is a highlight.

Eating

BUDGET

Mabel Francis Potter's Cupcake Emporium (☎ 912-341-8014; 6 E State St; cupcakes $1.50; ⏲ 10:30am-6pm Mon-Sat, noon-5pm Sun) How can one be sad with the aroma of fresh-baked cupcakes wafting about? This adorable cupcake boutique boasts dozens of flavors, including the local favorite: butter cream cupcake.

Mellow Mushroom (☎ 912-495-0705; www.mellowmushroom.com; 11 W Liberty St; slices $3; ⏲ 11am-10pm Mon-Thu, to 10:30pm Fri & Sat) The liberal youth of Savannah come to this pizzeria in the historic district in droves, but older crowds also come. Good beer is on tap. Vegetarian friendly with tons of variety, this groovy chain found a good home in Savannah.

B Matthews Eatery (☎ 912-233-1319; www.bmatthewseatery.com; 325 E Bay St; breakfast $5-10; ⏲ 8am-10pm Mon-Sat, 11:30am-3pm Sun) Located on a quieter corner of bustling Bay St, B Matthews serves locally roasted coffee, fried green tomatoes, black-eyed-pea cakes, sandwiches, and a Savannah staple: shrimp and grits.

Walls Bar-B-Que (☎ 912-232-9754; 515 E York Lane; plates from $6.40; ⏲ 11am-9pm Thu-Sat) Adventurous barbecue-lovers, keep looking until you find this glorious 'cue hut' on a tiny alley between E York St and Oglethorpe off Price St. Once you arrive, order a baseball-size mound of deviled crab – watch out for shell bits – and the juicy smoked pork of your hog-heaven dreams.

MIDRANGE

our pick **Cha Bella** (☎ 912-790-7888; 102 E Broad St; brunch $15.95; ⏲ 5:30-10pm daily, brunch 11am-3pm Sun) With a commitment to organic, local and well-presented vittles, this welcoming restaurant leaves pretention behind: swings hang on the lovely patio. The wild porcini mushroom pappardelle or fish market special will not leave you unpleased.

Lady & Sons (☎ 912-233-2600; www.ladyandsons.com; 102 W Congress St; buffets $18; ⏲ 11am-3pm Mon-Sat, from 5pm Mon-Sat, 11am-5pm Sun) Savannah's irrepressible culinary doyenne Paula Deen has created a monster. Her country cookin' is indeed delicious – the fried chicken will have you begging for mercy – but you've gotta know what you're doing to get a table. Show up at 9:30am for lunch or 3:30pm for dinner to put your name on the list. 'Sho-nuff Vegetable Sandwich' meets vegetarian needs.

TOP END

Local 11 ten (☎ 912-790-9000; www.local11ten.com; 1110 Bull St; mains $25; ⏰ 5-10pm Mon-Sat) Upscale, sustainable, local, fresh: a combination of elements that creates a monumental experience in an elegant, well-run restaurant. If Carolina yellowfin tuna Oscar or five-spice lacquered duck breast sound tempting, go here. The truffle parmesan fries will make you a fiend.

Drinking

our pick **Lulu's Chocolate Bar** (☎ 866-461-8681; www.luluschocolatebar.net; 42 Martin Luther King Jr Blvd; martinis from $10; ⏰ 5pm-midnight Mon-Wed, 5pm-1am Thu-Sat, 11:30am-11pm Sun) The heavenly signature Lulutini here is pure chocolate decadence – we weren't afraid to lick the glass. This adorable yet chic neighborhood martini and dessert bar is comfortable and has outdoor seating. Sometimes there's live music. On Sundays it serves brunch with shrimp and grits and has a Bloody Mary bar.

Sentient Bean (☎ 912-232-4447; www.sentientbean.com; 13 E Park Ave; baked goods $1.50; ⏰ 7am-10pm; 📶 V) Come one and all to nurture your inner hipster. The vibe is friendly: this place cares about coffee and community. Plus, it has vegan treats, organic café fare, and live music or performance art on its stage.

Guitar Bar (☎ 912-236-5190; 348 Martin Luther King Jr Blvd) Dubbed as 'a musician's lounge,' this appears to be a chilled-out neighborhood bar where you can grab cheap beer next to cool-looking people. There may be music or karaoke, depending on the night.

WG's (☎ 912-236-7696; 17 Lincoln St) Feeling more like a hobbit house than a bar, this rustic-chic dive bar will put you in the company of thirsty locals, not rowdy tourists. Order an unusual beer (Celebrator, anyone?) and head out to the cozy verandah. Or shoot pool.

Entertainment

Wormhole (www.wormholebar.com; 2307 Bull St; ⏰ from 6pm Mon-Thu, 8pm-3am Fri & Sat; 📶) Embracing a broad scope of the alternative-music scene, this new dive bar and venue is in the seedier part of town but will let you experience how alternative Savannah kicks it.

Lucas Theatre for the Arts (☎ 912-525-5040; www.scad.edu/venues/lucas; 32 Abercorn St) Hosting concerts (guitarist Jonny Lang), plays *(Guys and Dolls)* and films *(The Day the Earth Stood Still)* in a historic building dating from 1921.

Shopping

Savannah Art Works (☎ 912-443-9331; www.savannahartworks.com; 240 Bull St; ⏰ 11am-6pm Mon-Sat, 1-5pm Sun) Come here for vivacious folk art with a positive vibe, like a big ol' heart made from empty Coke and Pabst Blue Ribbon cans.

Universe Trading Company (☎ 912-233-1585; 27 Montgomery St) 'Bric-a-brac' doesn't begin to cover the contents of this cluttered salvage and antiques emporium. Walking through this place is like taking the world's deepest dumpster dive. The wares include lawn ornaments, used shoes, vinyl records, cigar-store Indians, life-size Blues Brothers statues and a fake shark head with '$185 firm' on the price tag.

Getting There & Around

The visitor center runs shuttles from the airport to Historic District hotels for $25 round-trip. You won't need a car. It's best to park it and walk or take tours. Another Earth-friendly and entertaining way to get around is by bike taxi with **Savannah Pedicab** (☎ 912-232-7900; www.savannahpedicab.com; 30-/60min $25/45, full day $150). More traditionally, **Chatham Area Transit** (CAT; ☎ 912-233-5767) operates local buses, including a free shuttle that makes its way around the Historic District and stops within a couple of blocks of nearly every major site.

The **Savannah/Hilton Head International Airport** (SAV; ☎ 912-964-0514; www.savannahairport.com) is about 5 miles west of downtown off I-16.

Greyhound (☎ 912-232-2135; 610 W Oglethorpe Ave) has connections to Atlanta (about five hours), Charleston, SC (about two hours), and Jacksonville, FL (2½ hours).

The **Amtrak station** (☎ 800-872-7245; 2611 Seaboard Coastline Dr) is just a few miles west of the Historic District.

BRUNSWICK & THE GOLDEN ISLES

Georgia is blessed with a string of islands running down the coast. The islands have very different characters, and provide experiences ranging from the rustic to the spoiled rotten.

With its large shrimp-boat fleet and downtown historic district shaded beneath lush live oaks, **Brunswick** dates from 1733 and has

IF YOU HAVE A FEW MORE DAYS

About 18 miles east of Savannah at the end of US Hwy 80, **Tybee Island** (☎ visitor center 912-786-5444; www.tybeevisit.com; 1st St/US Hwy 80; 9:30am-5pm) is a sleepy beach community with 3 miles of wide, sandy beach, good for swimming and castle building. The 154ft-tall **Tybee Island Lighthouse** (☎ 912-786-5801; www.tybeelighthouse.org; adult/child $7/5; 9am-5:30pm Wed-Mon) is the oldest in Georgia. The strenuous 178 steps to the top reward you with magnificent views. The admission also gets you into neighboring **Tybee Island Museum**.

charms you might miss when sailing by on I-95 or the Golden Isle Pkwy (US Hwy 17). During WWII, Brunswick shipyards constructed 99 Liberty transport ships for the navy. Today, a new 23ft scale model at **Mary Ross Waterfront Park** (Bay St) stands as a memorial to those ships and their builders. Also, check out the International Youth Hostel **Forest Hostel** (☎ 912-264-9738; www.foresthostel.com; Hwy 82; per person $25; P) if you're up for staying in little nature-loving tree houses (sans air or heat) on an ecofriendly, sustainable campus. It's 10 miles outside Brunswick; phone reservations only.

Brunswick-Golden Isles Visitors Bureau (☎ 912-265-0620; www.bgivb.com; Hwy 17, St Simons Causeway; 8:30am-5pm Mon-Fri) has loads of practical information about all the Golden Isles.

St Simons Island

Famous for its golf courses, resorts and majestic live oaks, St Simons Island is the largest and most developed of the Golden Isles. It lies 75 miles south of Savannah and just 5 miles from Brunswick. While the southern half of the island is a thickly settled residential and resort area, the northern half and adjacent **Sea Island** (www.explorestsimonsisland.com) and **Little St Simons** offer tracts of coastal wilderness amid a tidewater estuary.

Jekyll Island

An exclusive refuge for millionaires in the late 19th and early 20th centuries, Jekyll Island is a 4000-year-old barrier island with 10 miles of beaches. Today it's an unusual clash of wilderness, historically preserved buildings, modern hotels and a massive campground (complete with wi-fi). It's an easily navigable place – you can get around by car, horse or bicycle, but there's a $3 parking fee per day. The posh **Jekyll Island Club Hotel** (☎ 800-535-9547; www.jekyllclub.com; 371 Riverview Dr; d/ste $189/399; P) looms large on this island. It's a great place for a drink after a sunset seafood dinner at nearby waterfront restaurant **Latitude 31** (☎ 912-635-3800; www.crossoverjekyll.com; from 11am Tue-Sat, from 1pm Sun), located right on the wharf. An endearing attraction is the **Georgia Sea Turtle Center** (☎ 912-635-4444; www.georgiaseaturtlecenter.org; Hopkins Rd; adult/child $6/4; 9am-5pm Sun-Tue, 10am-2pm Mon), a conservation center and turtle hospital where the patients are on view for the public.

Cumberland Island & St Marys

An unspoiled paradise, a backpacker's fantasy, a site for day trips or extended stays – it's clear why the Carnegie family used Cumberland as a retreat long ago. Most of this southernmost barrier island is now occupied by the **Cumberland Island National Seashore** (☎ 912-882-4336; www.nps.gov/cuis; admission $4). Almost half of its 36,415 acres consists of marsh, mudflats and tidal creeks. On the ocean side are 16 miles of wide, sandy beach that you might have all to yourself. The island's interior is characterized by a maritime forest. Ruins from the Carnegie estate **Dungeness** are astounding, as are the wild turkeys, tiny fiddler crabs and beautiful butterflies. Feral horses roam the island and are a common sight.

The only public access to the island is via boat to/from the quirky, lazy town of **St Marys** (www.stmaryswelcome.com). A convenient and pleasant **ferry** (☎ 912-882-4335; adult/child $17/12; departures 9am & 11:45am) leaves from the mainland at the St Marys dock. Reservations are staunchly recommended well before you arrive, and if you show up without them, be at the dock an hour before the boat leaves. December through February, the ferry does not operate on Tuesday or Wednesday.

St Marys caters to tourists visiting Cumberland. This tiny, lush one-horse town has a number of comfortable B&Bs that conveniently usher people in and out of the area. One lovely one is **Emma's Bed and Breakfast** (☎ 912-822-4199; www.emmasbedandbreakfast.com; 300 W Conyers St; r from $119; P), which is right off the main street on a quiet road. The decorations are thankfully not of the common Southern frilly variety and the staff is helpful. Ask for a midweek special. For something cheap and in the 'action' by the dock, the tattered **Riverview Hotel** (☎ 912-882-3242; www.riverviewhotelstmarys.com; 105 Osborne St; r from $53; P ✕) might be worth braving to save a dime. Its attached bar **Seagles Saloon** (☎ 912-882-1807) is a most interesting local dive bar that's worth a visit just to say hello to Cindy, the bartender. Make sure you're up to date on expletives.

On Cumberland Island, the only private accommodations are at the **Greyfield Inn** (☎ 904-261-6408; www.greyfieldinn.com; d & ste incl meals $475-595), a mansion built in 1900 with a two-night minimum stay. Camping is available at **Sea Camp Beach** (☎ 912-882-4335; per person $4), a campground set among magnificent live oaks.

Note: there are no stores or wastebins on the island. Eat before arriving or bring lunch, and keep your trash with you.

Okefenokee National Wildlife Refuge

Established in 1937, the **Okefenokee National Wildlife Refuge** (☎ 912-496-7366; www.fws.gov/okefenokee) is a national gem, encompassing 396,000 acres of bog in a giant saucer-shaped depression that was once part of the ocean floor. The swamp is home to an estimated 9000 to 15,000 alligators, 234 bird species, 49 types of mammal and 60 amphibian species. The **Okefenokee Swamp Park** (☎ 912-283-0583; www.okeswamp.com; US 1 South, Waycross; admission $12; 9am-5:30pm) maintains around 3000 acres of the refuge and captive bears and gators on-site, or you can explore the swamp in a canoe or on a boat tour. The ultimate experience is a multiday canoe trip on the swamp's 120 miles of waterways. Call the US Fish & Wildlife Service's **Okefenokee National Wildlife Refuge Wilderness Canoe Guide** (☎ 912-496-7836; www.fws.gov/okefenokee) if you're considering a trip. Guided boat trips are also available if the water levels are high enough.

ALABAMA

Obsessed with football and race – two things Southerners never stop discussing – Alabama has been home to one of gridiron's most legendary coaches (Paul 'Bear' Bryant), and Jefferson Davis, the first president of the Confederacy in 1861, the year the Civil War began. Nearly 100 years later, an African American woman named Rosa Parks galvanized the Civil Rights movement when she refused to budge on a bus.

ALABAMA FACTS

Nickname The Heart of Dixie
Population 4.7 million
Area 50,744 sq miles
Capital city Montgomery (population 220,000)
Other cities Birmingham (population 229,424)
Sales tax 4%, but up to 11% with local taxes
Birthplace of Author Helen Keller (1880–1968), civil rights activist Rosa Parks (1913–2005), musician Hank Williams (1923–53)
Home of US Space & Rocket Center
Famous for Rosa Parks and the Civil Rights movement
Bitterest rivalry University of Alabama vs Auburn University
Driving distances Montgomery to Birmingham 91 miles, Mobile to Dauphin Island 38 miles

In the 1950s and '60s, Alabama led the way for civil rights triumphs throughout the country and continues to deal with its reputation and legacy of rebels, segregation, discrimination and wayward politicians – in the face of both progress and setbacks. Exploring Alabama provides a powerful insight into the racial dynamic and history in the USA.

Geographically, Alabama has a surprising diversity of landscapes, from foothills in the north and a gritty city in the middle to the subtropical Gulf Coast down south. Visitors come to see the heritage of antebellum architecture, to celebrate the country's oldest Mardi Gras, in Mobile, and to learn about the civil rights struggle. Every fall, the University of Alabama Crimson Tide and the Auburn University Tigers continue one of college football's greatest rivalries.

History

Alabama was among the first states to secede in the Civil War. Montgomery was the first Confederate capital. Alabama lost around 25,000 soldiers in the war, and reconstruction came slowly and painfully.

Racial segregation and Jim Crow laws survived into the mid-20th century, when the Civil Rights movement campaigned for desegregation of everything from public buses to private universities, a notion that Governor George Wallace viciously opposed. In perhaps the most famous moment in civil rights history, an African American woman named Rosa Parks refused to give up her bus seat to a white passenger and was thus arrested; the ensuing uproar sparked a bus boycott and began to turn the tide in favor of racial equality. Alabama saw brutal repression and hostility, but federal civil rights and voting laws eventually prevailed. At a political level, reform has seen the election of dozens of African American mayors and representatives.

Information

Alabama Bureau of Tourism & Travel (☎ 334-242-4169, 800-252-2262; www.800alabama.com) Sends out a vacation guide and has a website with extensive tourism options.

Alabama State Parks (☎ 888-252-7272; www.alapark.com) Alabama has 23 parks statewide with camping facilities ranging from primitive ($14) to RV hookups ($23). Making advanced reservations for weekends and holidays is suggested.

BIRMINGHAM

No one can ignore Birmingham's checkered past – civil rights violence earned it the nickname 'Bombingham.' Even though that was decades ago, invisible racial boundaries are still evident and smack of the city's history. Yet, this midsize, blue-collar city has made progress, can show you a good time, has a surprising amount of culture to offer, and has integrated its civil rights struggle into the tourist experience.

Birmingham's urban core is mostly a business district, and only a few attractions sit beneath the skyscrapers. There are four highlight neighborhoods: lively Five Points, near the University of Alabama Birmingham; funky Lakeview; charming Homewood, an upscale shopping strip with a pedestrian-friendly layout; and the must-see Civil Rights District, an unforgettable cluster of attractions at the edge of downtown.

THE SOUTH

Orientation & Information

The streets in downtown Birmingham run north–south, and the avenues run east–west. The primary attractions and cool neighborhoods are all relatively close, but seeing the city with a car or bike is convenient. The hip Lakeview and Five Points neighborhoods are on the city's south side, and the civil rights attractions and main art museum are north.

You can find tourist information at the **Greater Birmingham Convention & Visitors Bureau** (☎ 205-458-8000, 800-458-8085; www.sweetbirmingham.com; 2200 9th Ave N; 8:30am-5pm Mon-Fri).

Sights & Activities

Birmingham Civil Rights Institute (☎ 205-328-9696, 866-328-9696; www.bcri.org; 520 16th St N; adult/child $11/3, free Sun; 10am-5pm Tue-Sat, 1-5pm Sun) is the most worthwhile sight in town. Its moving audio, video and photography exhibits tell the story of racial segregation in the USA, from WWI and the Civil Rights movement to racial and human-rights issues around the world today, and it reveals the complicated and shocking layers of Birmingham's history. The media lab is a fantastic resource for further inquiry.

Across the street in **Kelly Ingram Park**, 1960s civil rights protesters are depicted in sculptures that are both proud and harrowing.

The **16th Street Baptist Church** (☎ 205-251-9402; cnr 16th St & 6th Ave N; ministry tours 10am-4pm Tue-Fri) became a gathering place for meetings and protests in the 1950s and '60s. When Ku Klux Klan (KKK) members bombed the church in 1963, killing four girls, the city was flung into a whirlwind of social change. Today, the rebuilt church is a memorial and a house of worship (services 11am Sunday).

Birmingham Museum of Art (☎ 205-254-2565; www.artsbma.org; 2000 Rev Abraham Woods Jr Blvd; admission free; 10am-5pm Tue-Sat, noon-5pm Sun) collects work from Asia, Africa, Europe and the Americas. Don't miss Rodin's striking work in the outdoor sculpture garden.

Art-deco buildings in trendy **Five Points South** house shops, restaurants and nightspots. Equally noteworthy is the **Homewood** community's quaint commercial drag on 18th St S.

You gotta love hippies who have it together. Cross on over the invisible racial lines to **Nomad Supply** (☎ 205-252-9359; www.nomadsupply.com; 916 23rd St; 7am-10pm;) where you can buy vegan cookies, use the internet for free, and buy peace-loving, ecofriendly wares.

Visible from all over the city thanks to the country's second-largest statue, the nearby **Vulcan Park** (☎ 205-933-1409; www.visitvulcan.com; 1701 Valley View Dr; 7am-10pm) offers fantastic views for free, and an **observation tower** (adult/child $6/4).

The Carver Performing Arts Center houses the **Alabama Jazz Hall of Fame** (☎ 205-254-2731; www.jazzhall.com; 1631 4th Ave N; self-guided/guided tours $2/3; 10am-5pm Tue-Sat), which celebrates jazz musicians such as Dinah Washington, Nat King Cole and Duke Ellington.

If you want to amp up your Alabama experience, go rock climbing with seasoned guide **David Hemphill** (☎ 205-253-0691; dvhemp@yahoo.com; climbs per person $70-200), who will rent equipment and take you to some little-known, yet stellar, climbing sites nearby.

Twelve miles south of town, off I-65 exit 246, **Oak Mountain State Park** (☎ 205-620-2524; admission $3; ⌚ sunrise-sunset) is Alabama's largest state park, where you can hike, camp, boat or chill out on the lakeside beach.

Sleeping

Cobb Lane Bed and Breakfast (☎ 205-918-9090; www.cobblanebandb.com; 1309 19th St S; r from $89; P ⊠ ❄ ᯤ) It's the weird Southern aunt of B&Bs. It aims for the traditional frilliness of Southern B&Bs, but ends up with a giant stuffed peacock in the fireplace and life-size carousel horse in the main window. A lodging choice with personality.

Hotel Highland (☎ 205-271-5800; www.thehotelhighland.com; 1023 20th St S; r from $106; P ⊠ ❄ 💻 ᯤ) Birmingham does swanky, and it succeeds. Nuzzled right up next to the lively Five Points district, this colorful, slightly trippy, modern hotel manages to be very comfortable and a good deal.

Redmont Hotel (☎ 205-324-2101; www.theredmont.com; 2101 5th Ave N; r from $119; ⊠ ❄ 💻 ᯤ) Born in the roaring '20s, the hotel's piano and chandelier in the lobby lend a certain historical, old-world feel throughout. The Redmont was undergoing a renovation at the time of research. Parking is available ($15).

Eating & Drinking

For such a small Southern city, student-tilted Birmingham has a wide variety of eateries and cafés, from ethnic to local, for all budgets. If you want live music, most likely you'll find it at one of the numerous venues in town.

Pete's Famous Hot Dogs (☎ 205-252-2905; 1925 2nd Ave N; hot dogs $1.80; ⌚ to 6pm) This closet-size downtown joint has been serving since 1915 and makes a good choice for inexpensive but tasty fare. Wolf down your dogs on a nearby park bench.

Sakura (☎ 205-933-1025; 1025 20th St S; rolls $6-9; ⌚ 11:30am-2pm Mon-Fri, plus 5-9:30pm Mon-Wed, to midnight Thu, to 2am Fri & Sat) Crawfish avocado rolls: man, you have to love sushi in the South. But, for real, this sushi is pretty good.

Sol Y Luna (☎ 205-322-1186; 2811 7th Ave S; tapas $9-12; ⌚ 5-10pm Mon-Wed, to midnight Thu-Sat) Thirsty patrons can order tequila flights (and then a taxi) at this inviting Mexican restaurant-cantina, which specializes in small plates and has a fabulous patio.

Moe's Original BBQ and Blues Revue (☎ 205-252-5888; www.moesoriginalbbq.com; 731 29th St S; platters $10; ⌚ from 11am Mon-Sat, to late Thu-Sat) One of nine in the chain, Moe's prides itself on serving the freshest food possible – dinner is served till it runs out – and has live blues music Thursday and Friday. The patio is a total plus.

J Clyde (☎ 205-939-1312; www.jclyde.com; 1312 Cobb Lon S; ⌚ 3pm-midnight Sun-Mon, to 2am Tue-Thu & Sat, to 4am Fri) Some preppie types come, some not-so-preppie types come, but they are in their 20s and 30s. Since the Gourmet Beer Bill just passed, it will have over 70 beers on draft. There's outdoor seating and live music sometimes.

Getting There & Around

The **Birmingham International Airport** (BHM; ☎ 205-595-0533; www.flybirmingham.com) is located about 5 miles northeast of downtown. **Greyhound** (☎ 205-253-7190; www.greyhound.com; 618 19th St N), north of downtown, serves cities including Huntsville, Montgomery, Atlanta, GA, Jackson, MS, and New Orleans, LA (10 hours). **Amtrak** (☎ 205-324-3033; www.amtrak.com; 1819 Morris Ave), downtown, has trains daily to New York and New Orleans.

Birmingham Transit Authority (☎ 205-521-0101; www.bjcta.org; adult $1.25) runs local buses.

AROUND BIRMINGHAM

North of Birmingham, the aerospace community of **Huntsville** hosts the US space program that took off and attracted international aerospace-related companies. The **US Space & Rocket Center** (☎ 1-800-637-7223; www.spacecamp.com/museum; I-565, exit 15; adult/child museum $20/15, with IMAX $25/20; ⌚ 9am-5pm; 👶) is a combination science museum and theme park. It's a great place to take a kid, or to become one again. The center has IMAX films, exhibits, rides and video presentations.

East of Huntsville in **Scottsboro**, you'll find the infamous **Unclaimed Baggage Center** (☎ 256-259-1525; www.unclaimedbaggage.com; 509 W Willow St; ⌚ 9am-6pm Mon-Fri, from 8am Sat) that draws pilgrims from far and wide who peruse the now-for-sale belongings of unfortunate air travelers who have lost their baggage irrevocably down the dark annals of fate. Sucks for them, fabulous deals for you.

Four cities on the Tennessee River make up the area known as 'the Shoals': **Florence**, **Sheffield**, **Tuscumbia** and **Muscle Shoals**. You'll find yourself up to your elbows in rural Alabama here. To find your way around, grab one of the free and extremely useful maps located at the **Colbert County visitor center** (☎ 256-383-0783; www.colbertcountytourism.org; 719 Hwy 72W, Tuscumbia; 8:30am-5pm Mon-Fri year-round, 9am-4pm Sat summer).

The area has some acclaim for music history, and the cheesy-cool **Alabama Music Hall of Fame** (☎ 1-800-239-2643; www.alamhof.org; 617 Hwy 72 W, Tuscumbia; adult/child $8/5; 9am-5pm Mon-Sat, from 1pm Sun summer) immortalizes both Hank Williams and Lionel Richie. An original spectacle indeed, the **Key Underwood Coon Dog Cemetery** (☎ 256-383-7481; off Hwy 247; sunrise-sunset), near Cherokee, pays homage to over 185 trusty beasts who have so loyally guided their masters. **Tennessee River Guide Service** (☎ 256-383-7481; 1114 N Main St, Tuscumbia; full day from $200) will take you to the lakes of Tennessee River to catch some smallmouth and crappie.

MONTGOMERY

The explosion of the Civil Rights movement happened here in 1955, when a black seamstress named Rosa Parks refused to give up her seat to a white man on a city bus, launching a bus boycott and galvanizing the Civil Rights movement nationwide. Montgomery has commemorated that incident with a museum, which (along with an excellent Shakespeare program) is the main reason to visit.

Although it's Alabama's capital city, Montgomery feels more like a sleepy little city with a dead downtown. To its credit, Montgomery covers both fine and folk arts well, with a terrific Shakespeare festival and a museum devoted to country-music legend Hank Williams.

Sights & Activities

The **Montgomery Chamber of Commerce** (☎ 334-261-1100; www.visitingmontgomery.com; 300 Water St; 8am-5pm Mon-Sat, noon-4pm Sun) has tourist information and a helpful website.

A tribute to Mrs Parks (who died in October 2005), the **Rosa Parks Museum** (☎ 334-241-8661; http://montgomery.troy.edu/rosaparks/museum; 251 Montgomery St; adult/child $5.50/3.50; 9am-5pm Mon-Fri, 9am-3pm Sat;) features a sophisticated and wacky (but cool) video re-creation of Montgomery's history of racial conflict and also the bus-seat protest. There's a separate children's area that covers African American history pre-1955. A must-see.

The **Scott & Zelda Fitzgerald Museum** (☎ 334-264-4222; 919 Felder Ave; donation requested; 10am-2pm Wed-Fri, 1-5pm Sat & Sun), the writers' home from 1931 to '32, now houses first editions, translations, and original artwork including a mysterious self-portrait of Zelda in pencil.

The superb **Alabama Shakespeare Festival** (☎ 334-271-5353, 800-841-4273; www.asf.net; tickets $26-42) delivers live summertime performances at a lovely facility in Blount Cultural Park. Get thyself there if you have the opportunity.

The **Hank Williams Museum** (☎ 334-262-3600; www.thehankwilliamsmuseum.com; 118 Commerce St; adult/child $8/3; 10am-4:30pm Mon-Sat, 1-4pm Sun) pays homage to the country-music giant and Alabama native, a pioneer who effortlessly fused hillbilly music with African American blues.

Sleeping & Eating

OK, so Montgomery may not be known for its restaurants and accommodations, but there are a couple of finds.

Lattice Inn (☎ 334-262-3388; www.thelatticeinn.com; 1414 S Hull St; r from $85; P) Most definitely this cute little B&B in the Garden District is a lovely alternative to chain hotels in Montgomery's downtown and outskirts. It's not fancy-pants, but well executed and homey. There's a pool to boot and a hot tub on the way.

Chris' Hot Dog (☎ 334-265-6850; www.chrishotdogs.com; 138 Dexter Ave; hot dogs $2; 10am-7pm Mon-Sat, to 8pm Fri) Served on pillow-soft buns, the dogs have made this funky joint a Montgomery institution since 1917. Order your dog 'all the way' and see if you can guess what's in the special house sauce.

Montgomery Brewing Co (☎ 334-834-2739; www.montgomerybrewpub.com; 12 W Jefferson St; dinner $10-16; 11am-2pm Mon-Fri, plus 5:30-9pm Mon-Thu, 5:30-10pm Fri & Sat) A lively hub of activity, the MBC is located in a neat little warehouse district by the ballpark. Try the house-made Montgomery Blonde brew with a burger or alligator tail.

Getting There & Around

Montgomery Regional Airport (MGM; ☎ 334-281-5040; www.montgomeryairport.org; 4445 Selma Hwy) is about 15 miles from downtown and is served by daily flights from Atlanta, Charlotte, Cincinnati, Houston and Memphis. **Greyhound** (☎ 334-286-0658; 950 W South Blvd) also serves the city. The **Montgomery Area Transit System** (☎ 334-241-2200;

www.montgomerytransit.com; tickets $1) operates the city buses.

SELMA

On Bloody Sunday, March 7, 1965, the media captured state troopers and deputies beating and gassing African Americans and white sympathizers near the Edmund Pettus Bridge. Led by Martin Luther King Jr, the crowd was marching to the state capital (Montgomery) to demonstrate for voting rights. This was the culmination of two years of violence, which ended when President Johnson signed the Voting Rights Act of 1965. Today Selma is a quiet town, and though its attractions are few, they do provide an excellent insight into the voting rights protests that were at the crux of the Civil Rights movement.

Selma's key attraction, the **National Voting Rights Museum** (☎ 334-418-0800; www.nvrm.org; 1012 Water Ave; adult/senior & student $6/4; 9am-5pm Mon-Fri, 10am-3pm Sat), near the Edmund Pettus Bridge, is an important stop as it honors the movement's 'foot soldiers' – the unsung heroes who marched for freedom.

MOBILE

Wedged between Mississippi and Florida, the only real Alabama coastal town is Mobile (mo-*beel*), a seaport with green spaces, shady boulevards and four historic districts. It's ablaze with azaleas in early spring, and festivities are held throughout February for **Mardi Gras** (www.mobilemardigras.com), which has been celebrated here for nearly 200 years. It culminates on Fat Tuesday (the Tuesday before Ash Wednesday). Mobile can be fun like New Orleans, only the volume and brightness are turned way down. The Dauphin St historic district is where you'll find many bars and restaurants, and it's where much of the Mardi Gras action takes place. Unlike the Mississippi Gulf Coast, which is still devastated by Hurricane Katrina, downtown Mobile looks as though the storm never happened.

Government St, near downtown, makes for a lovely drive thanks to its mansions and tree canopy. The **Leinkauf Historic District** has more great homes.

USS Alabama (☎ 251-433-2703, 800-426-4929; www.ussalabama.com; 2703 Battleship Pkwy; adult/child $12/6; 8am-6pm Apr-Sep, 8am-4pm Oct-Mar) is a 690ft behemoth famous for escaping nine major WWII battles unscathed. It's a worthwhile self-guided tour for its awesome size and might. While there, you can also tour a submarine and get up close and personal with military aircraft. Parking's $2.

During the Civil War, the 40-room **Malaga Inn** (☎ 251-438-4701, 800-235-1586; www.malagainn.com; 359 Church St; r from $94; P) used to be two town houses owned by brothers. Nicely placed near the historic district, the well-done rooms open onto balconies overlooking the courtyard or street.

For dinner, slurp up some slimy suckers at the oyster bar at **Wintzell's** (☎ 251-432-4605; www.wintzellsoysterhouse.com; 605 Dauphin St; 11am-10pm Sun-Thu, 11am-11pm Fri & Sat), an iconic and historic restaurant serving fresh bivalves 'fried, stewed, or nude.'

DAUPHIN ISLAND

Alabama has an island? Yes, but many write it off because oil rigs grace its horizon, and it's still recovering from Katrina. However unsung it may be, it's a worthwhile destination. The whole 14-mile-long, 1¾-mile-wide island is a designated bird sanctuary, with 6 miles for public use and 8 miles of private property. Though it has its fair share of traditional beach-vacation kitsch and the water is not sparkly turquoise, it's still pretty nice. Plus, the white-blonde beaches are stellar and prices reasonable. The island is accessed from the north by Hwy 193 and from the east by **ferry** (☎ 251-861-3000; www.mobilebayferry.com) shuttling from Fort Morgan.

For helpful maps and information, contact the **Dauphin Island Chamber of Commerce** (☎ 251-861-5524; www.dauphinislandcoc.com).

The biggest highlight is the **Dauphin Island Bird Sanctuary** (☎ 251-861-2120; www.coastalbirding.org), where you'll find what many people consider to be some of the best birding in the southeast. In addition, you'll encounter uncrowded beaches accessed only by hiking paths, placards explaining the flora and fauna, and several miles of winding trails.

Seafood shacks and a couple of eateries line the street as you enter from the highway, but BYO if you want to eat really well.

Though many people rent condos, check out **Gulf Breeze Motel** (☎ 1-800-286-0296, 251-861-7344; gulfinfo.com/gulfbreezemotel; 1512 Cadillac Ave; high/low season r from $89/59; P). Right across from the public beach, clean rooms and wallet-friendly prices make this family-owned-and-operated motel a beautiful option for a budget beach getaway.

MISSISSIPPI

One of the USA's most misunderstood (and yet most mythologized) states, Mississippi is home to gorgeous country roads, shabby juke joints, crispy catfish, hallowed authors and acres of cotton. Most people feel content to malign Mississippi, long scorned for its lamentable civil rights history and its low ranking on the list of nearly every national marker of economy and education, without ever experiencing it firsthand. But unpack your bags for a moment and you'll glimpse the real South. It lies somewhere amid the Confederate defeat at Vicksburg, the literary legacy of William Faulkner in bookish Oxford, the birthplace of the blues in the Mississippi Delta and the humble origins of Elvis Presley in Tupelo.

The state seems proud of its rural nature and small pleasures, with no lament for the lack of urban glitz. Being a spread-out place, there's opportunity for drives through awe-inspiring cotton country and the winding, wooded Natchez Trace Pkwy.

History

Stay in Mississippi long enough, and you'll hear folks refer to a time 'when cotton was king.' That time dates back at least to 1860, when Mississippi was the country's leading cotton producer and one of the 10 wealthiest states. The Civil War wrecked Mississippi's economy, and reconstruction was traumatic. And the state's racist history – from slavery through the civil rights era – has left deep scars. (One of the most famous incidents came in 1962, when violence erupted as student James Meredith became the first African American to attend the University of Mississippi.)

Today, though Mississippi is still a poor state, people have come to realize that the blues of the Delta – one of America's richest and most distinctive art forms – are worth celebrating. And that Mississippi has been disproportionately blessed with literary luminaries. Therefore, the state has developed a tourist industry revolving around its proud cultural history, as well as its waterfront casinos.

MISSISSIPPI FACTS

Nickname The Magnolia State
Population 2.9 million
Area 46,906 sq miles
Capital city Jackson (population 176,600)
Sales tax 7%
Birthplace of Author Eudora Welty (1909–2001), musicians Robert Johnson (1911–38) and Elvis Presley (1935–77), puppeteer Jim Henson (1936–90)
Home of The blues
Famous for Cotton fields
Kitschiest souvenir Elvis lunchbox in Tupelo
Driving distances Jackson to Clarksdale 187 miles, Jackson to Ocean Springs 176 miles

Information

The legendary north–south Hwy 61 runs the length of the Delta. I-55 is the main north–south highway down the heart of the state, and I-20 bisects Mississippi going east–west. A small portion of the state's southern tip – the Gulf Coast – touches the Gulf of Mexico.

Mississippi Division of Tourism Development (☎ 601-359-3297; www.visitmississippi.org) Has a directory of visitor bureaus.

Mississippi Wildlife, Fisheries, & Parks (☎ 1-800-467-2757; www.mississippistateparks.reserveamerica.com) Camping costs $11 to $22, depending on the facilities, and some parks have cabins for rent.

TUPELO

Unless you have an unhealthy Elvis obsession or want to pick up the Natchez Trace Pkwy, you probably shouldn't plan to spend a long time in Tupelo. But an afternoon pop-in is rewarding indeed if you are a fan of the King.

Elvis Presley's Birthplace (☎ 662-841-1245; www.elvispresleybirthplace.com; 306 Elvis Presley Blvd; adult/child $7/3.50; 9am-5:30pm Mon-Sat, 1-5pm Sun) is east of downtown off Hwy 78. The 15-acre park complex contains the two-room shack Elvis lived in as a boy, a museum displaying personal items, a modest chapel and a massive gift shop.

OXFORD

A refreshingly sophisticated little town that's bustling and prosperous, Oxford was named after the English city by colonists who hoped it would open a school as revered as its namesake. The University of Mississippi (Ole Miss) opened in 1848, and provides Oxford's heartbeat. (You know a town has an intellectual bent when its favorite native son is a literary lion like William Faulkner. But former Ole Miss quarterback Archie Manning runs a close second; the speed limit here on campus is 18mph, in deference to his old uniform number.)

Social life in Oxford revolves around 'the Square,' a series of downtown blocks dotted with shops and eateries.

Sights & Activities

Square Books (☎ 662-236-2262; www.squarebooks.com; 160 Courthouse Sq; 9am-9pm Mon-Thu, to 10pm Fri & Sat, 9am-6pm Sun), one of America's great independent bookstores, is the epicenter of Oxford's lively literary scene and a frequent stop for traveling authors. There's a café and balcony upstairs, along with an immense section devoted to Faulkner.

University of Mississippi Museum (☎ 662-915-7073; University Ave, at 5th St; www.olemiss.edu/depts/u_museum; admission free; 9:30am-4:30pm Tue-Sat, 1-4:30pm Sun) houses fine arts, folk arts, a Confederate uniform and a plethora of science-related marvels, including a microscope and electromagnet from the 19th century.

Literary pilgrims head directly to **Rowan Oak** (☎ 662-234-3284; off Old Taylor Rd; adult/child & student $5/free; 10am-4pm Tue-Sat, 1-4pm Sun), the graceful 1840s home of William Faulkner, who authored so many brilliant and dense novels set in Mississippi, and whose work is celebrated in Oxford with an annual conference in July. Tours of Rowan Oak – where Faulkner lived from 1930 until he died in 1962 – are self-guided. The staff can also provide directions to **Faulkner's grave**, which is located in St Peter's Cemetery, northeast of the Square.

For a serene stretch of the legs, head to **Lamar Park** (cnr Old Sardis & Country Club Rds) just outside of town where you can get in a good jog or casual stroll by the manicured artificial lake.

Sleeping & Eating

The cheapest accommodations are on the outskirts of town at chain hotels. But there are some other choices with more personality. A number of high-quality restaurants dot Oxford Sq.

Inn at Ravine (☎ 662-234-4555; www.oxfordravine.com; 53 County Rd 321; r from $99;) The lovely restaurant Ravine (see right) offers two B&B-style guest rooms above the restaurant and a cabin for those wanting a peaceful stay on Oxford's green fringes.

(5) Twelve (☎ 662-234-8043; 512 Van Buren Ave; r from $105;) Formerly the Oliver Britt House (now under new management), this six-room B&B has an antebellum-style exterior, modern interior, and Southern breakfasts to order. It's an easy walk from shops and restaurants at Oxford Sq.

Bottletree Bakery (☎ 662-236-5000; 923 Van Buren; cinnamon rolls $3.25; 7am-4pm Tue-Fri, 9am-4pm Sat, 9am-2pm Sun;) Saucer-sized, sweet, sticky cinnamon rolls are the source of this bakery's acclaim. But it also has sandwiches, espresso drinks, and 'humble pie.'

Taylor Grocery (☎ 662-236-1716; www.taylorgrocery.com; 4 County Rd 338 A, Taylor; dishes $8-14; 11am-2pm Mon-Fri, 6-10pm Thu-Sat, to 9pm Sun) Be prepared to wait – and to tailgate in the parking lot – at this splendidly rusticated catfish haunt. You'll be glad you did. Get your cat fried or grilled, and bring a marker to sign your name on the wall. The joint is about 15 minutes' drive from downtown Oxford, south on Old Taylor Rd.

our pick **Ravine** (☎ 662-234-4555; www.oxfordravine.com; 53 County Rd 321;) About 3 miles outside the city, this unpretentious, cozily elegant restaurant nuzzles up to the forest. Chef Joel Miller picks and pulls much of the produce and herbs from his garden outside and buys locally and organically when he can. The result is simply wonderful food and a delicious experience. A BYOB rule was in place at the time of research, folks, but Ravine is negotiating its dry county's red tape.

Entertainment

Proud Larry's (☎ 662-236-0050; www.proudlarrys.com; 211 S Lamar Blvd) On Oxford Sq, this iconic music venue hosts some of the bigger names passing through town.

Rooster's Blues House (☎ 662- 236-7970; 114 Courthouse Sq) Also on the square, this is where you'll find that soulful crooning on the weekends.

MISSISSIPPI DELTA

One of the most mythical places in the USA, the Delta is a panoramic agricultural expanse that thrums with historic significance. Its vernacular food culture ranks as one of America's great folk arts, but even the grub is trumped by the Delta's other great cultural export: blues music. David L Cohn, Greenville native and author of *God Shakes Creation*, devised a geo-cultural definition of the region. He wrote that 'the Delta begins in the lobby of the Peabody Hotel in Memphis and ends on Catfish Row in Vicksburg.'

VISITING JUKE JOINTS

It's believed that 'juke' is a West African word that survived in the Gullah language, the Creole-English hybrid spoken by isolated African Americans in the US. The Gullah 'juke' means 'wicked and disorderly.' Little wonder, then, that the term was applied to the roadside sweatboxes of the Mississippi Delta, where secular music, suggestive dancing, drinking and, in some cases, prostitution were the norm. The term 'jukebox' came into vogue when recorded music, spun on automated record-changing machines, began to supplant live musicians in such places, as well as in cafés and bars.

Most bona-fide juke joints are African American neighborhood clubs, and outside visitors can be a rarity. Many are mostly male hangouts. There are very few places that local women, even in groups, would turn up without a male chaperone. Otherwise, women can expect a lot of persistent, suggestive attention.

For a taste of the juke joint scene, we recommend **Ground Zero** (☎ 662-621-9009; www.groundzerobluesclub.com; 0 Blues Alley, Clarksdale; 🕑 11am-2pm Mon-Tue, to 11pm Wed & Thu, to 1am Fri & Sat), a huge and friendly hall with a dancefloor surrounded by tables. By contrast, **Red's** (☎ 662-627-3166; 395 Sunflower Ave, Clarksdale), which is usually open on Friday and Saturday nights, looks a little scary to first-timers, but it is one of Clarksdale's best jukes. If the pit's smoking, order whatever's cooking.

Clarksdale

If you come here for anything, come for the love of music. Clarksdale is the real deal. It hosts a healthy blues-lovin' tourist industry and also caters to moneyed patrons, but what keeps Clarksdale genuine is its residents: they adore music. It's no surprise that big-name blues bands still honor Clarksdale on the weekends and that music museums sprinkle the area. Over the twists and turns of its intriguing past, this little juke-jointed Delta town continues to navigate contradictions: wealth, poverty, white culture, black culture and blues culture.

LEGEND OF THE BOTTLE TREES

If you choose to explore the fascinating landscapes of Mississippi, you're bound to run across an odd-looking tree with old, different-colored bottles stuck on the branches. It's not just creative recycling, it's a bottle tree. Originally, the supplanted slaves from the Congo in Africa began this tradition because they believed the bottle trees protected their homes from evil spirits. Supposedly the indignant spirits from their ancestral homes were trapped inside the bottles. Eventually, bottle trees became a general talisman of good luck and protection. Though less common these days, the tradition is still upheld in certain places around rural Mississippi.

Juke Joint Festival (www.jukejointfestival.com) and **Sunflower River Blues & Gospel Festival** (www.sunflowerfest.org) are two bluesy throwdowns, the former in April and the latter in August. The juke fest is more about the venues than the headliners; Sunflower draws bigger names.

SIGHTS & ACTIVITIES

Friendly St Louis carpetbagger Roger Stolle runs **Cat Head Delta Blues & Folk Art** (☎ 662-624-5992; 252 Delta Ave; 🕑 10am-5pm Mon-Sat), a colorful, all-purpose, blues emporium. The shelves are jammed with books, face jugs, local art and blues records. Stolle seems to know everyone in the Delta; skip the Chamber of Commerce and stop here for the lowdown.

A small but excited and well-done collection of memorabilia is on display at the **Delta Blues Museum** (☎ 662-627-6820; www.deltabluesmuseum.org; 1 Blues Alley; adult/child $7/5; 🕑 9am-5pm Mon-Sat), including Charlie Musselwhite's harmonica and BB King's guitar, Lucille. There's also a shrine to Delta legend Muddy Waters, local art exhibits, and a gift shop.

Theo's Rock and Roll Museum (☎ 901-605-8662; www.rockmuseum.biz; 113 E Second St; admission $5; 🕑 10am-5pm Thu-Sun) is a recent addition to Clarksdale's lineup of tributes to music and the blues. Theo, a jovial Swiss supplant and blues fanatic, has on display an impressive personal collection of records, memorabilia, and artifacts from local artists to the Beatles. He'll open outside hours by appointment.

Quapaw Canoe Company (☎ 662-627-4070; www.island63.com; 291 Sunflower Ave) is an outfitter in town who can take you down the Mississippi River in a canoe or kayak (day or multiday trips available). Trips cost between $55 and $150 per day, depending on the number of participants, and include a shuttle, gear and meals.

SLEEPING & EATING

our pick **Shack Up Inn** (☎ 662-624-8329; www.shackupinn.com; r $50-75; P ⊠ ✤ ≈) This is a self-titled 'beer and breakfast.' At the cheeky Hopson Plantation, 2 miles south on the west side of Hwy 49, guests stay in refurbished sharecropper cabins or the creatively renovated cotton gin. The cabins have covered porches and are filled with old furniture and musical instruments. The old commissary, the Juke Joint Chapel (equipped with pews), is an atmospheric venue for live-music performances, and the owners Guy and Bill are jovial and helpful.

Riverside Hotel (☎ 662-624-9163; www.cathead.biz/riverside; 615 Sunflower Ave; r $65; P ✤) In business since 1944, this worn hotel is soaked in blues history and has hosted many an artist in its day. The friendly proprietor Rat continues to charm folks from all over with his hospitality and prices.

Abe's (☎ 662-624-9947; 616 State St; mains $4-12; 9:30am-9pm Mon-Sat, 10:30am-2pm Sun) At the Crossroads – the famous intersection of Hwys 61 and 49, where bluesman Robert Johnson supposedly sold his soul to the devil – look for the tall sign with the happy pig in a bow tie. Abe's has served zesty pork sandwiches, vinegary slaw, and slow-burning tamales since 1924.

Hicks (☎ 622-624-9887; 305 S State St; 11am-7pm Mon-Thu, to 11pm Fri & Sat) This is a small, modest drive-through that's been here forever on the outskirts of town. It arguably has the best Delta hot tamales in town (half a dozen for $5), a special genre of hot tamale that is HOT.

Madidi (☎ 662-627-7770; www.madidires.com; 164 Delta Ave; mains $27-35; 6-9pm Tue-Sat) Handsome and refined, just like cofounder Morgan Freeman, this upscale eatery has a menu including cornmeal oysters, rib-eye steak and wild-mushroom risotto. Reservations requested.

Around Clarksdale

For such a poor, flat part of the country, the Delta has a surprisingly deep list of funky little towns with food, gambling and history to offer.

GREENVILLE

The Delta's largest city, Greenville is roughly midway between Clarksdale and Vicksburg. It was here that the levee broke during the catastrophic Great Flood of 1927. Today it has some riverboat gambling and not much else. But in September, Greenville hosts the **Mississippi Delta Blues & Heritage Festival** (☎ 662-335-3523; www.deltablues.org) near the intersection of Hwys 454 and 1. Also, the James Beard Award–winning dive **Doe's Eat Place** (☎ 662-334-3315; www.doeseatplace.com; 502 Nelson St; 5-9pm Mon-Sat) serves world-class steaks in the middle of a poor neighborhood. It used to be you paid a kid a dollar 'to watch your car,' ie not break into it. Now there's a security guard outside. Souped-up SUVs and polo shirts mill around a block of run-down houses. Come early or make a reservation.

LELAND

East of Greenville, Hwy 82 heads out of the Delta. The **Highway 61 Blues Museum** (☎ 662-686-7646; www.highway61blues.com; 400 N Broad St; 10am-5pm Mon-Sat), in the Old Temple Theater, hosts four modest, but interesting, rooms that venerate local bluesmen. Local music is sold here. **Leland** (www.lelandms.org) hosts the **Highway 61 Blues Festival** in June as well as the **Crawfish Festival** at the beginning of May. The **Jim Henson Exhibit** (☎ 662-686-7383; donations encouraged; 10am-4pm Mon-Sat), on the bank of Deer Creek, 1.5 miles west of the intersection of Hwys 82 and 61, is a small building that honors Muppet-man Jim Henson, who was born in Leland. It proudly displays a range of memorabilia, including the original Kermit from *The Muppet Movie*.

INDIANOLA

Stopping in this tiny Delta town is well worth it to visit the incredible, modern **BB King Museum and Delta Interpretive Center** (☎ 662-887-9539; www.bbkingmuseum.org; 400 Second St; adult/student/child $10/5/free; 10am-6pm Tue-Sat, 1-5pm Sun). Situated in between Greenville and Greenwood on Hwy 82, this center, filled with interactive displays, video exhibits, and an amazing array of blues and BB King artifacts, effectively communicates the history and legacy of the blues while shedding light on the soul of the Delta.

GREENWOOD

Greenwood is a poor Delta town furnished with one block of opulence due to Viking

Range Corporation's investment (its headquarters is here). Visitors are usually wealthy patrons or splurging travelers who want to take advantage of the Alluvian hotel, its restaurant, and cooking school, all owned by Viking.

The tourist beacon of Greenwood, the **Alluvian** (☎ 662-453-2114; www.thealluvian.com; 318 Howard St; r from $185; P ⊠ ✿ 🖳 📶) is a luxurious boutique hotel equipped with a high-class spa, gourmet restaurant, Giardina's (locally pronounced 'Gardinia's'), and an unbelievably outfitted cooking school. If you feel like splurging, this might be the place, though some find the oasis of wealth a disturbing contrast to the poverty of the surrounding town.

As an alternative to the Alluvian, 3 miles north of Greenwood, **Tallahatchie Flats** (☎ 662-453-1854; www.tallahatchieflats.com; 58458 County Rd 518; shacks $65-85; P ⊠ ✿) is a compound of shacks simulating rural homes that once dotted the area. They're now outfitted for guests.

Vicksburg

Vicksburg is famous for its strategic location in the Civil War, thanks to its position on a high bluff overlooking the Mississippi River, and history buffs dig it. General Ulysses S Grant besieged the city for 47 days, until its surrender on July 4, 1863, at which point the North gained dominance over North America's greatest river.

The major sights are readily accessible from I-20 exit 4B (Clay St). The **visitor center** (☎ 601-636-9421; www.visitvicksburg.com; 3300 Clay St; 🕑 9am-5pm Mon-Fri) hands out indispensable free maps that mark color-coded scenic driving paths into and out of the city.

The old, slow downtown stretches along several cobblestoned blocks of Washington St, and **historic-house museums** cluster in the Garden District. Vicksburg's stretch of the **Mississippi River** has casinos. Down by the water is a block of murals depicting the history of the area, and a Children's Art Park.

National Military Park (☎ 601-636-0583; www.nps.gov/vick; Clay St; per car $8; 🕑 8am-7pm), north of I-20 is a massive battlefield, Vicksburg's main attraction for Civil War buffs. A 16-mile driving tour passes historic markers explaining battle scenarios and key events. You can buy an audiotape tour on cassette or CD in the visitor center gift shop, or drive through on your own using the free map distributed on-site (but plan for at least 90 minutes). If you have your bike, cycling is a fantastic way to tour the place. Locals use the scenic park for walking and running, too. The cemetery contains some 17,000 Union graves, and a museum houses the ironclad gunboat USS *Cairo*. **Civil War reenactments** are held in May and July.

For non–history buffs, there are a couple of hidden jewels that might entice you to visit Vicksburg. Cloistered on top of the Highway 61 Coffeehouse (below) is the **Attic Gallery** (☎ 601-638-9221; www.atticgallery.net; 1101 Washington St; 🕑 10am-5pm Mon-Sat), which is a must-see if you want to appreciate some impressive and quirky work by local artists. Make sure to look at Kennith Humphrey's crazy-awesome paintings. Head north out of town on 61 a number of miles past the Port of Vicksburg and you'll hit a bona-fide, fire-and-brimstone, see-it-to-understand-it, gigantic piece of **living folk art**. Clue: the painted bus is the church.

SLEEPING & EATING

Battlefield Inn (☎ 601-638-5811; www.battlefieldinn.org; 4137 N I-20 Frontage Rd; r incl breakfast from $65; P ⊠ ✿ 📶 🏊) Robert E Lee meets David Lynch in this hotel, which is surreal in the extreme. The Battlefield Inn has a talking parrot in the entryway, a karaoke bar inside the hotel, a wet bar by the swimming pool and cannons on the property.

Corners Mansion (☎ 601-636-7421; www.thecorners.com; 601 Klein St; r from $125; P ⊠ ✿ 📶) The best part of this Old South B&B could be looking over the Yazoo and Mississippi Rivers from your rocking-chair vantage point. The gardens and Southern breakfast don't hurt either.

our pick Walnut Hills (☎ 601-638-4910; 1214 Adams St; 🕑 11am-9pm Mon-Sat, 11am-2pm Sun) For a dining experience that brings you back in time, head to this eatery where you can enjoy the utterly delectable, down-home Southern food elbow-to-elbow, family-style at a round table from 11am to 2pm. Try the blue-plate special ($9).

Highway 61 Coffeehouse (☎ 601-638-9221; www.61coffee.com; 1101 Washington St; 🕑 7am-5pm Mon-Fri, 9am-5pm Sat; 📶) This surprisingly excellent coffee shop has live music on Thursdays and is a minuscule epicenter of artsy-ness.

JACKSON

Mississippi's capital and largest city is victim to the common car-culture phenomenon of a dead downtown surrounded by plush suburbs. However, interesting areas like the

THE SOUTH

funky Fondren District, along with a cluster of well-done museums and historic sites, give insight into the culture of Mississippi and make Jackson a worthwhile stopover.

The **convention & visitors bureau** (☎ 601-960-1891; www.visitjackson.com; 111 E Capitol St, Suite 102; 9am-5pm Mon-Fri) has free information.

The one fantastic attraction is the **Mississippi Museum of Art** (☎ 601-960-1515; www.msmuseumart.org; 380 South Lamar St; admission free; 10am-5pm Tue-Sat, from noon Sun), which got new digs in June 2007. The museum's collection of Mississippi art – a permanent exhibit dubbed 'The Mississippi Story' – is nothing less than superb.

Also worth a stop, though completely different in its feel and scope, is the **Agriculture & Forestry Museum** (☎ 601-713-3365; 1150 Lakeland Dr; adult/child $4/2; 9am-5pm Mon-Sat;). This rustic attraction is actually spread among several buildings designed to resemble a small Mississippi town, complete with a blacksmith's shop and general store. In the main exhibit hall, you can learn about catfish farming 'from the egg to the plate.'

Southern-literature buffs should make a reservation to tour the **Eudora Welty House** (☎ 601-353-7762; www.mdah.state.ms.us/welty; 1119 Pinehurst St; tours 9am, 11am, 1pm & 3pm Wed-Fri). Welty, the Pulitzer Prize–winning author, lived in this Tudor Revival house for more than 75 years, and it's preserved to look as it did in the 1980s. The garden out back is lovely, too.

Tucked way back in Lefleur's Bluff State Park is the **Museum of Natural Science** (☎ 601-354-7303; www.msnaturalscience.org; 2148 Riverside Dr; adult/child $5/3; 8am-5pm Mon-Fri, from 9am Sat, from 1pm Sun;). It houses exhibits on the natural beasts of Mississippi and has aquariums inside and a nice walking trail outside.

The **Smith Robertson Museum** (☎ 601-960-1457; 528 Bloom St; adult/child $4.50/1.50; 9am-5pm Mon-Fri, 10am-1pm Sat, 2-5pm Sun), housed in Mississippi's first public school for African American kids, is the alma mater of author Richard Wright. It offers insight and explanation into the pain and perseverance of the African American legacy in Mississippi.

The **Old Capitol Museum** (☎ 601-576-6920; http://mdah.state.ms.us/museum; 100 State St; admission free; 8am-5pm Mon-Fri, 9:30am-4:30pm Sat, 12:30-4:30pm Sun), which was the state's capital from 1839 to 1903, is newly opened after major renovations and houses a museum that covers Mississippi's history from prehistoric to modern times.

Sleeping & Eating

our pick **Old Capitol Inn** (☎ 601-359-9000; www.oldcapitolinn.com; 226 N State St; r from $99; P) A heck of a deal, this 24-room boutique hotel, near museums and restaurants, has up-to-date rooms that are comfortably and uniquely furnished. The rooftop deck, complete with hot tub, overlooks a courtyard and pool. It serves a full Southern breakfast, and the thoughtful service is exemplified by details such as handwritten weather reports brought to your room.

Fairview Inn (☎ 601-948-3429; www.fairviewinn.com; 734 Fairview St; r/ste from $139/199; P) For a colonial estate experience, the Fairview Inn will not let you down when it comes to Southern formality and traditions, including a grits-and-bacon kind of breakfast. It also has a full spa.

Walker's Drive-In (☎ 601-982-2633; www.walkersdrivein.com; 3016 N State St; mains $24-32; 11am-2pm Mon-Fri, plus from 5:30pm Tue-Sat) This truly outstanding restaurant calls itself a drive-in, but it's really a gussied-up diner that serves lusciously tweaked Southern staples. And it serves things like heavenly barbecued oysters dolloped with brie, and incredible fish dishes. The wine menu is good, service impeccable, and creativity turned-up.

Mayflower (☎ 601-355-4122; 123 W Capitol St; 11am-2:30pm & 4:30-9:15pm Mon-Fri, 4:30-9:30pm Sat) This is a Jackson tradition. The Southern fare is incredible. Try the red fish topped with broiled oysters. It's also famous for its comeback dressing, which is guaranteed to make you come back. Sources citywide say use the bathroom before you come.

Fondren District is the budding artsy, boho area of town, ie fun restaurants, art galleries and cafés dot a strip of traffic-heavy road. Keifers, a Greek café with awesome outdoor seating and cheap beer, and the Pizza Shack attract young and old. High Noon Cafe is situated in the Rainbow Co-op, where you can order a mushroom burger and stock up on healthy groceries.

Entertainment

Hal & Mal's (☎ 601-948-0888; www.halandmals.com; 200 S Commerce St; 11am-2am Mon-Sat) This Jackson nightlife staple has Mississippi-made beer on tap and, oftentimes, live music in the air.

9:30 Blues Cafe (☎ 601-948-0888; www.jesdablues.com; 200 S Commerce St; 11am-2am Mon-Sat) Run by a Delta born-and-raised man, this club carries on the Delta blues tradition in its juke-joint atmosphere replete with artifacts from the owner's family farm and local art. There's blues every night starting at 9:30pm, barring Sunday. The upstairs patio is quite nice.

Getting There & Away

At the junction of I-20 and I-55, it's easy to get in and out of Jackson. Its international **airport** (JAN; ☎ 601-939-5631; www.jmaa.com) is 10 miles east of downtown. **Greyhound** (☎ 601-353-6342; 300 W Capitol St) buses serve Birmingham, AL, Memphis, TN, and New Orleans, LA. Amtrak's *City of New Orleans* stops at the station.

NATCHEZ

A tiny dollop of cosmopolitan in MS, quirky Natchez stews together a wide variety of folks, from gay log-cabin republicans, to intellectual liberals, to down-home folks. Perched on a bluff overlooking the Mississippi, it's the oldest town on the river and attracts tourists in search of antebellum history and architecture. It's also the end (or the beginning!) of the scenic 444-mile Natchez Trace Pkwy (p432), the state's cycling and recreational jewel.

The **visitor and welcome center** (☎ 601-446-6345; www.natchezms.com; 640 S Canal St; 8:30am-5pm Mon-Sat, 9am-4pm Sun) is a large, well-done tourist resource with little exhibits of area history and a ton of information on local sites. Tours of the historic downtown and antebellum mansions leave here. During the 'pilgrimage' seasons in spring and fall, local mansions are opened to visitors. For a well-rounded experience of the area's history, stop at the **African American Museum** or **Forks of the Road**, the site of the second-largest slave market in the South.

Along with opulent, old buildings, wonderful B&Bs sprinkle the tiny town. There is a helpful list on the visitor center's website, or just drop by.

Staying at classic Natchez B&B **Historic Oak Hill Inn** (☎ 601-446-2500; www.historicoakhill.com; 409 S Rankin St; r from $110; P ⊠ ✱ ⌔) you'll get a taste of antebellum aristocratic living, from period furniture to china. A high-strung staff makes for an immaculate experience. But a real treat, with more modern fixings, is the **Sunset View Guest Cottages** (☎ 601-870-2662; www.asunsetview.com; 26 Cemetery Rd; cottages $135-185; P ⊠ ✱ ⌔). The warmly decorated cottages, adorned with flowers 'only to be described as pornographic,' have private, stunning views of the Mississippi River. Tom, the owner, is a historian of Southern lore who can tell you anything you'd like to know about the area or point you to a book in the cottages' extensive libraries.

Economy options are limited here, but there is camping at **Natchez State Park** (☎ 601-442-2658; www.mississippistateparks.reserveamerica.com; 230 Wickcliff Rd B; camping $11-16, cabins $67-87). It's 1 mile east of the parkway on Hwy 61, 10 miles north of Natchez. Within the park is Emerald Mound, the second-largest Native American ceremonial mound of its type in the United States.

To get your fill of Southern eats, head to the **Pig Out Inn** (☎ 601-422-8050; 116 S Canal St; pulled pork sandwich $4.75; 11am-9pm Mon-Sat, to 3pm Sun), where some people say you'll find the best ribs in town. Alternatively, you can pick up something healthier or more high-falutin' at the **Uptown Market** (☎ 601-445-9111; 531 S Canal St; 11am-7pm Mon-Fri, to 3pm Sun), where you can buy a salad, sparkling water, prosciutto, or build-your-own sandwich.

GULF COAST

In the backyard of New Orleans, the Gulf Coast's economy, traditionally based on the seafood industry, got a shot of adrenaline in the 1990s when big Vegas-style casinos muscled in alongside the sleepy fishing villages. So it's an interesting mix down here: you've got Southern-speaking Vietnamese and Irish fishermen playing blackjack alongside bigwigs who have jetted in from big cities. The casinos in Biloxi have been rebuilt since Hurricane Katrina swept through. The nearby town of Gulfport, however, has still not fully recovered.

Keep track of what's open for business through the **Mississippi Gulf Coast Convention & Visitors Bureau** (☎ 228-896-6699; www.gulfcoast.org; 11975 Seaway Rd, Gulfport), which has a website that lists openings and reopenings.

Ocean Springs is one of the coolest, non-destroyed places on the Mississippi coast. Its **visitor center** (☎ 228-875-4424; www.oceanspringschamber.com; 1000 Washington St; 9am-4pm Mon-Fri) is at the head of Washington St, where you'll find a slew of cute shops, restaurants and coffee houses.

our pick **Walter Anderson Museum** (☎ 228-872-3164; www.walterandersonmuseum.org; 510 Washington

St; 9:30am-4:30pm Mon-Sat, from 12:30pm Sun) is a highlight of the city (and probably the state). A consummate artist and lover of Gulf Coast nature, Anderson had his fair share of turmoil and love that spurred his talent to great heights. After he died, the beachside shack where he lived was found to be completely covered in mind-blowing murals, which are now transplanted to the museum. Walter, his father, and his two brothers ran **Shearwater Pottery** (228-875-7320; www.dreamingincIay.com; 102 Shearwater Dr; 9am-5:30pm Mon-Sat, from 1pm Sun). The pottery shop is still run today by the family, even after it was destroyed by Hurricane Katrina.

If you have your bicycle or just want to tootle, the **Live Oaks Bike Path** is a lovely way to check out the area. It's a 15.5-mile loop starting at the train depot downtown, to the Davis Bayou Area of Gulf Islands National Seashore, and back. Maps are at the visitor center.

Hotels line the highway, or stay at **Oak Shade B&B** (888-875-4711; oakshade@cableone.net; 1017 La Fontaine Ave; r from $95-140;). A visit here is very similar to just being a guest in a friend's home: comfy and relaxed. There's a lovely courtyard to boot. Marion, the owner, is laid-back and loves to help you do whatever you want to do in the area. Nice camping (and a visitor center) can be found at **Gulf Islands National Seashore Park** (228-875-3962; www.nps.gov/guis), which is a little bit out of town.

LOUISIANA

In the words of William Faulkner: 'The past is never dead. It's not even past.' Nowhere is that as true in the US as it is in Louisiana. Nostalgia for times long gone and recognition of hardships endured are found at every turn. This leads to a dynamic sense of place – natives are rooted here, and embrace what makes them unique. This is a state where black cowboys strap washboards to their chests and strum the distinctive clicking sound of zydeco, and where gators lurk in swamps and are hunted by French-speaking Cajuns. Different cultures coexist – after all, don't we all just want to eat well and dance?

In the rolling hills and pine forests of northern Louisiana, the mostly Protestant population shares similar traits with other Southern states. But the world becomes a different place amid the swamps of southern Louisiana and the debauched streets of New Orleans – where jazz and Afro-Caribbean sounds are thick in the sultry air and make you unable to resist the urge to let loose.

History

The lower Mississippi River area was dominated by the Mississippian mound-building culture until around 1592 when Europeans arrived and decimated the Native Americans with the usual combination of disease, unfavorable treaties and outright hostility.

The land was then passed back and forth between France, Spain and England. After the American Revolution, the whole area passed to the USA in the 1803 Louisiana Purchase, and Louisiana became a state in 1812.

Steamboats opened a vital trade network across the continent. New Orleans became a major port, and Louisiana's slave-based plantation economy kept up a flowing export of rice, tobacco, indigo, sugarcane and especially cotton. After the Civil War, Louisiana was readmitted to the Union in 1868, and the next 30 years saw political wrangling, economic stagnation and renewed discrimination against African Americans.

In the 1920s, industry and tourism developed, but the tradition of unorthodox and sometimes ruthless politics continues today. Race and economics are ongoing sources of struggle: witness the post-Katrina rebuilding process (p476). The 2005 hurricane and the flooding in its aftermath have reshaped

LOUISIANA FACTS

Nicknames Bayou State, Pelican State, Sportsman's Paradise
Population 4.4 million
Area 43,561 sq miles
Capital city Baton Rouge (population 229,500)
Major city New Orleans (population 223,388)
Sales tax 4%, plus local city and county taxes
Birthplace of Jazz, naturalist John James Audubon (1785–1851), trumpeter Louis 'Satchmo' Armstrong (1901–71), author Truman Capote (1924–84), musician Antoine 'Fats' Domino (b 1928), pop star Britney Spears (b 1981)
Home of Tabasco sauce, chef Emeril Lagasse
Official state reptile Alligator
Driving distances New Orleans to Lafayette 137 miles, New Orleans to St Francisville 112 miles

southern Louisiana. Locals have negotiated the tricky path through redevelopment, the return of displaced peoples, wetland restoration and outsider involvement. Though revitalization has been more successful in some areas, progress has been painfully slow in others, especially the poorer areas.

Information

Thirteen welcome centers dot freeways throughout the state, or contact the **Louisiana Office of Tourism** (☎ 225-342-8119, 800-633-6970; www.louisianatravel.com).

Louisiana State Parks (☎ 888-677-1400; www.lastateparks.com) Louisiana has 20 state parks that offer camping ($1 primitive and backpack camping, $18 for premium campsites). Some parks offer lodge accommodations and cabins. Reservations can be made on the internet, phone, or on a drop-in basis if there's availability.

NEW ORLEANS

New Orleans gets called 'The Big Easy' in all its promotional material, and this city does take it easy, to some degree. It's rare in America to see folks hold up traffic for the sake of pulling over and calling out, 'Yo Dante, wassup,' and rarer still for the people behind them to accept the above nonchalantly and find another way around.

But when it comes to having a good time, New Orleanians are kind of like Manhattanites on a deadline. Just one more beer? Nah son, have a shot with that. You want a burger? How's about we put peanut butter and bacon on top? And throw in a huge baked potato with sour cream on the side. And hell, some crawfish.

At the mouth of the Mississippi, remember the three 'I's. The first two, indulgence and immersion, are easy to pick up on. Its brown sugar on bacon instead of oatmeal for breakfast; a double served neat instead of light beer; sex in the morning instead of being early for work ('My streetcar was down'). But the biggest 'I' here is *intermixing*. Tolerating everything and learning from it is the soul of this city. Social tensions and divisions of race and income keep New Orleans jittery, but when its citizens aspire to that great Creole ideal – a mix of all influences into something better – we get: jazz; Nouveau Louisiana cuisine; storytellers from African *griots* to Seventh Ward rappers to Tennessee Williams; French town houses a few blocks from Foghorn Leghorn mansions groaning under sweet myrtle and bougainvillea; Mardi Gras celebrations that mix pagan mysticism with Catholic pageantry. Just don't forget the indulgence and immersion, because that Creole-ization gets watered down when folks don't live life to its intellectual and epicurean hilt.

New Orleans may take it easy, but it takes it. The whole hog. Stuffed with rice and crawfish. Ya hear?

History

The town of Nouvelle Orléans was founded as a French outpost in 1718 by Jean-Baptiste Le Moyne de Bienville. Early settlers arrived from France, Canada and Germany, and the French imported thousands of African slaves. The city became a central port in the slave trade; due to local laws some slaves were allowed to earn their freedom and assume an established place in the Creole community as *les gens de couleur libres* (free people of color).

The Spanish were largely responsible for building the French Quarter as it still looks today because fires in 1788 and 1794 decimated the earlier French architecture. The influx of Anglo-Americans after the Louisiana Purchase led to an expansion of the city into the Central Business District (CBD), Garden District and Uptown. By 1840 New Orleans was the nation's fourth-largest city, with more than 100,000 people.

New Orleans survived the Civil War intact after an early surrender to Union forces, but the economy languished with the end of the slavery-based plantations. In the early 1900s, New Orleans was the birthplace of jazz music (p76). Many of the speakeasies and homes of the jazz originators have been destroyed through neglect, but the cultural claim was canonized in 1994 when the NPS established the New Orleans Jazz National Historical Park (opposite) to celebrate the origins and evolution of America's most widely recognized indigenous musical art form. Oil and petrochemical industries developed in the 1950s, and today, tourism is the other lifeblood of the local economy.

In 2005, a man-made disaster occurred when Katrina, a relatively weak Category 3 hurricane, overwhelmed New Orleans' federal flood protection system in over 50 places. Some 80% of the city was flooded, over 1800 people lost their lives, and the entire city was evacuated. Today, the population level stands at only two-thirds of pre-Katrina levels.

Although much of the city has rebuilt and tourists are back with a bead-throwing vengeance, the city has irrevocably changed, in ways good and bad; see boxed text, p476.

Orientation

New Orleans is wedged between the Mississippi River to the south and Lake Pontchartrain to the north. The historic French Quarter (Vieux Carré), encircling Jackson Sq, runs from Esplanade Ave to Canal St. Canal St separates the Quarter from the CBD and Warehouse District, which extends to the freeway.

Continuing upriver along St Charles Ave are the Lower Garden District, a ramshackle neighborhood with a bohemian enclave, and the lovely Garden District, well known for its historic mansions. St Charles Ave follows the hooked course of the river into Uptown and the Riverbend area, anchored by Tulane and Loyola universities.

The Tremé, across N Rampart St from the French Quarter, is a historically rich, predominantly African American residential neighborhood. Downriver from the French Quarter, the streets of Faubourg Marigny, a diverse and especially gay-friendly community, form a triangle bisected by lively Frenchmen St. The artsy Bywater neighborhood lies downriver.

Though the quaint Algiers District sits across the river, it is also part of New Orleans. Neighborhoods closer to the sites of the levee breaches, such as Lakeview, Gentilly and the Lower 9th Ward, were hard-hit by post-hurricane flooding, and are best explored only by car.

Maps are available at the New Orleans Welcome Center in Jackson Sq (right).

Information

BOOKSTORES

Faulkner House Books (☎ 504-524-2940; www.faulknerhousebooks.net; 624 Pirate's Alley; 🕑 10am-5:30pm) The erudite owner of this former residence of author William Faulkner sells rare first editions and new titles.

Maple Street Book Shop (☎ 504-866-4916; www.maplestreetbookshop.com; 7523 Maple St; 🕑 9am-7pm Mon-Sat, 11am-5pm Sun) A mainstay independent bookstore in Uptown, with a children's bookstore (p480) next door.

EMERGENCY & MEDICAL SERVICES

Medical Center of Louisiana (☎ 800-256-2311; www.mclno.org; 2021 Perdido St; 🕑 24hr) Has an emergency room.

INTERNET ACCESS

There's pretty good wi-fi coverage in the CBD, French Quarter, Garden and Lower Garden Districts and Uptown. Almost every coffee shop in the city has wi-fi coverage. Libraries have free internet access for cardholders.

Zotz (☎ 504-861-2224; 8210 Oak St; per 30min $3; 🕑 9am-2am) Appropriately funky coffee shop in Riverbend neighborhood, popular with Tulane types.

INTERNET RESOURCES & MEDIA

Gambit Weekly (www.bestofneworleans.com) Free weekly hot sheet of music, culture, politics and classifieds.

NOLA Fun Guide (www.nolafunguide.com) Great website for up-to-date info on gigs, gallery openings and the like.

Offbeat Magazine (www.offbeat.com) Free monthly specializing in music.

Times-Picayune (www.nola.com) New Orleans' daily newspaper has an entertainment calendar, and 'Lagniappe,' a more extensive guide, is included every Friday.

WWOZ 90.7 FM (www.wwoz.org) Tune in here for Louisiana music and more.

POST

Post office CBD (610 S Maestri Pl; 🕑 8:30am-4:30pm Mon-Fri); Main branch (☎ 504-599-9983; 701 Loyola Ave; 🕑 7am-7pm Mon-Fri, 8am-5pm Sat) Mail sent General Delivery, New Orleans, LA 70112, goes to the main branch. Postboxes in outlying areas are not necessarily reliable since Katrina. A private business, the post office (207 N Peters St, Suite 200; 🕑 8:30am-4:30pm Mon-Fri) in the French Quarter offers shipping and caters to post-related needs, as well as selling stationery.

TOURIST INFORMATION

The city's official visitor website is www.neworleansonline.com.

Jean Lafitte National Historic Park and Preserve Visitor Center (☎ 504-589-2636, 504-589-3883; www.nps.gov/jela; 419 Decatur St; 🕑 9am-5pm) Operated by the NPS, with exhibits on local history, guided walks and daily live music. There's not much in the park office itself, but educational musical programs are held on most days of the week. Many of the park rangers are musicians and knowledgeable lecturers, and their presentations discuss musical developments, cultural changes, regional styles, myths, legends and musical techniques in relation to the broad subject of jazz. At some point, the center is supposed to relocate to a permanent headquarters in Louis Armstrong Park.

New Orleans Welcome Center (French Quarter) (☎ 504-589-2636; www.neworleanscvb.com; 419 Decatur St; 🕑 9am-5pm) Provides lots of free information and maps.

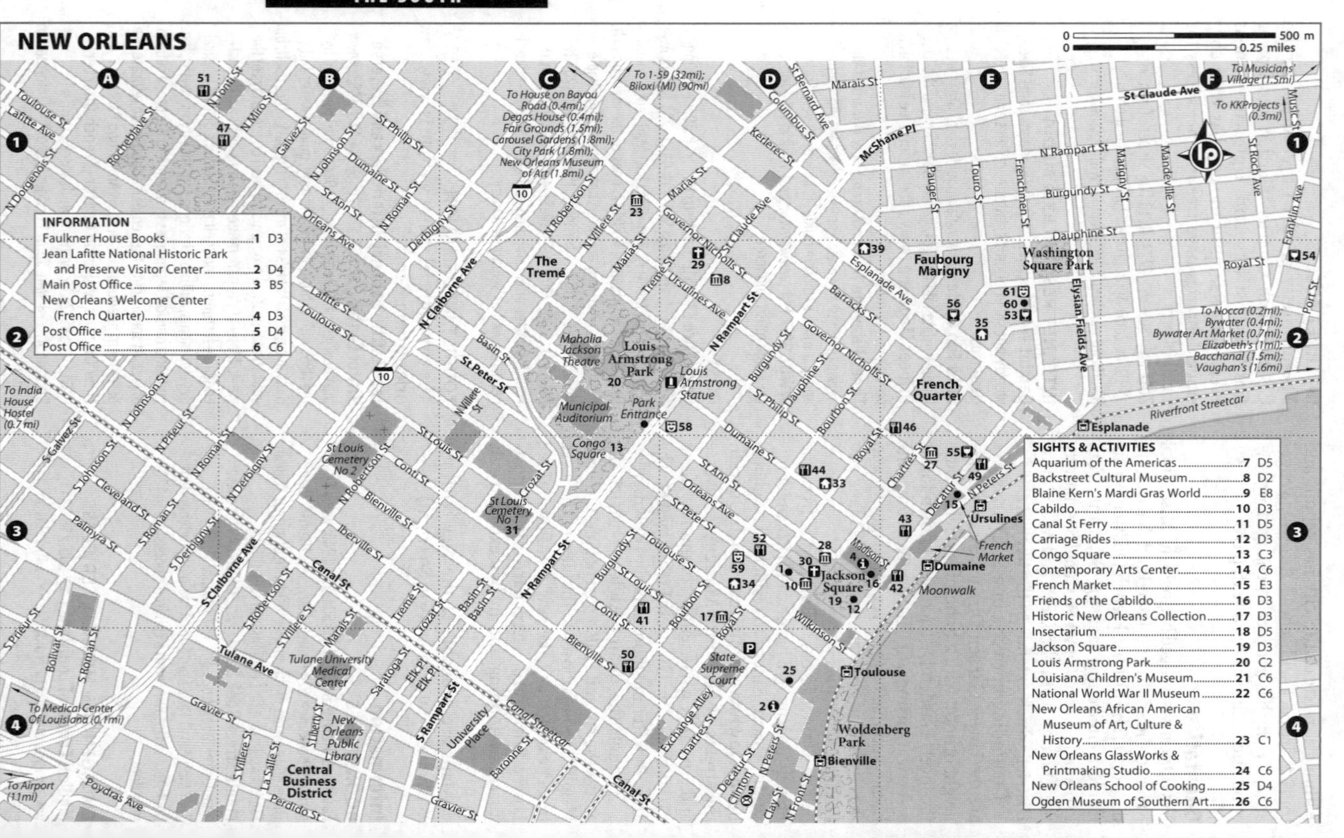
NEW ORLEANS
0 500 m
0 0.25 miles
INFORMATION
Faulkner House Books 1 D3
Jean Lafitte National Historic Park and Preserve Visitor Center 2 D4
Main Post Office 3 B5
New Orleans Welcome Center (French Quarter) 4 D3
Post Office 5 D4
Post Office 6 C6
SIGHTS & ACTIVITIES
Aquarium of the Americas 7 D5
Backstreet Cultural Museum 8 D2
Blaine Kern's Mardi Gras World 9 E8
Cabildo 10 D3
Canal St Ferry 11 D5
Carriage Rides 12 D3
Congo Square 13 C3
Contemporary Arts Center 14 C6
French Market 15 E3
Friends of the Cabildo 16 D3
Historic New Orleans Collection 17 D3
Insectarium 18 D5
Jackson Square 19 D3
Louis Armstrong Park 20 C2
Louisiana Children's Museum 21 C6
National World War II Museum 22 C6
New Orleans African American Museum of Art, Culture & History 23 C1
New Orleans GlassWorks & Printmaking Studio 24 C6
New Orleans School of Cooking 25 D4
Ogden Museum of Southern Art 26 C6
To Musicians' Village (1.5mi)
To KKProjects (0.3mi)
To Nocca (0.2mi); Bywater (0.4mi); Bywater Art Market (0.7mi); Elizabeth's (1mi); Bacchanal (1.5mi); Vaughan's (1.6mi)
To House on Bayou Road (0.4mi); Degas House (0.4mi); Fair Grounds (1.5mi); Carousel Gardens (1.8mi); City Park (1.8mi); New Orleans Museum of Art (1.8mi)
To I-59 (32mi); Biloxi (MI) (90mi)
To India House Hostel (0.7 mi)
To Medical Center Of Louisiana (0.1mi)
To Airport (11mi)
Faubourg Marigny
French Quarter
The Tremé
Washington Square Park
Louis Armstrong Park
Jackson Square
Woldenberg Park
Central Business District
Riverfront Streetcar
Canal Streetcar
Esplanade
Ursulines
Dumaine
Toulouse
Bienville
Moonwalk
St Louis Cemetery No 1
St Louis Cemetery No 2
Congo Square
Municipal Auditorium
Mahalia Jackson Theatre
Louis Armstrong Statue
Park Entrance
French Market
State Supreme Court
Tulane University Medical Center
New Orleans Public Library
University Place
St Claude Ave
Elysian Fields Ave
Esplanade Ave
McShane Pl
N Rampart St
S Rampart St
N Claiborne Ave
S Claiborne Ave
Canal St
Tulane Ave
Poydras Ave
Decatur St
Chartres St
Royal St
Bourbon St
Dauphine St
Burgundy St
Frenchmen St

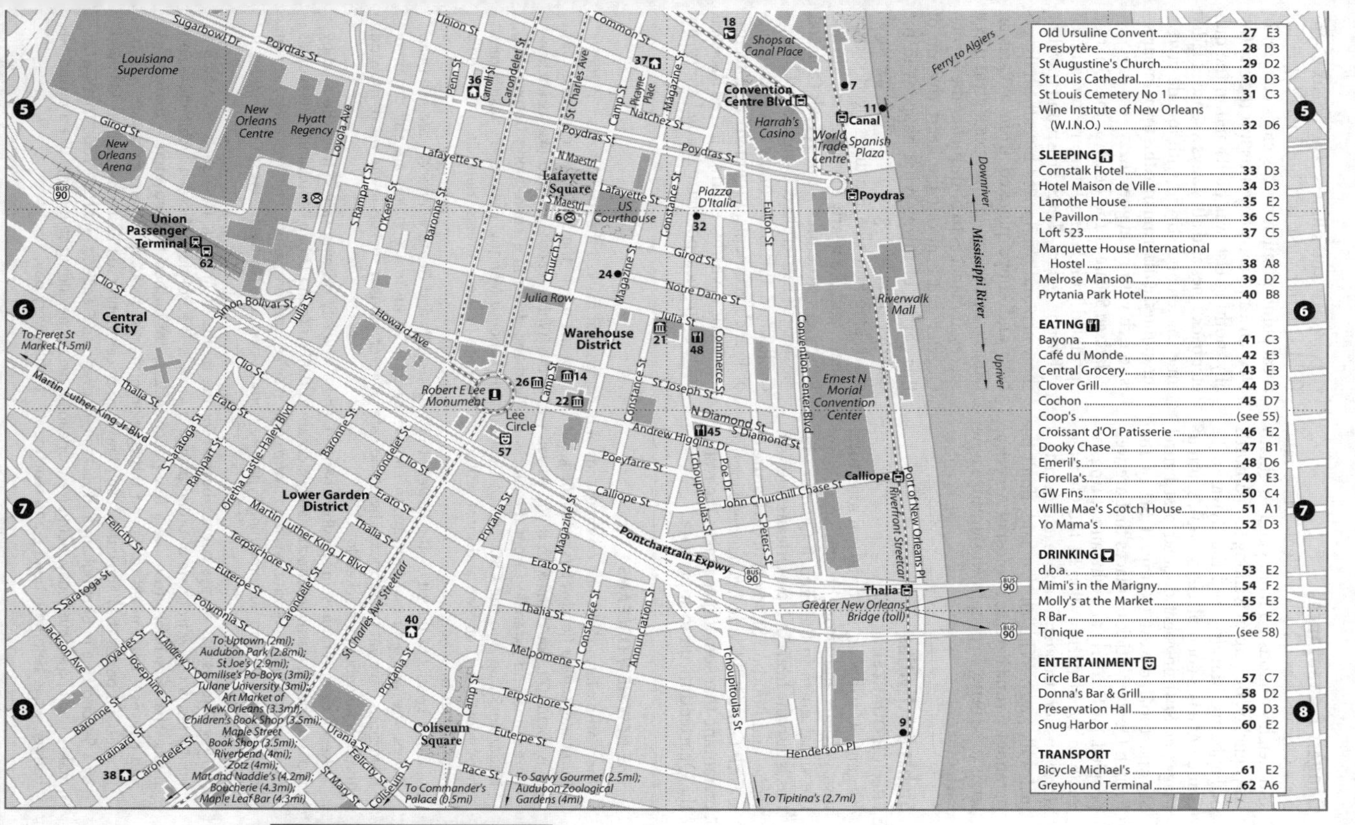
Old Ursuline Convent 27 E3
Presbytère 28 D3
St Augustine's Church 29 D2
St Louis Cathedral 30 D3
St Louis Cemetery No 1 31 C3
Wine Institute of New Orleans (W.I.N.O.) 32 D6
SLEEPING
Cornstalk Hotel 33 D3
Hotel Maison de Ville 34 D3
Lamothe House 35 E2
Le Pavillon 36 C5
Loft 523 37 C5
Marquette House International Hostel 38 A8
Melrose Mansion 39 D2
Prytania Park Hotel 40 B8
EATING
Bayona 41 C3
Café du Monde 42 E3
Central Grocery 43 E3
Clover Grill 44 D3
Cochon 45 D7
Coop's (see 55)
Croissant d'Or Patisserie 46 E2
Dooky Chase 47 B1
Emeril's 48 D6
Fiorella's 49 E3
GW Fins 50 C4
Willie Mae's Scotch House 51 A1
Yo Mama's 52 D3
DRINKING
d.b.a. 53 E2
Mimi's in the Marigny 54 F2
Molly's at the Market 55 E3
R Bar 56 E2
Tonique (see 58)
ENTERTAINMENT
Circle Bar 57 C7
Donna's Bar & Grill 58 D2
Preservation Hall 59 D3
Snug Harbor 60 E2
TRANSPORT
Bicycle Michael's 61 E2
Greyhound Terminal 62 A6
Mississippi River
Downriver
Upriver
Ferry to Algiers
Riverwalk Mall
Ernest N Morial Convention Center
Harrah's Casino
Shops at Canal Place
Convention Centre Blvd
Canal
Poydras
Calliope
Thalia
World Trade Centre
Spanish Plaza
Piazza D'Italia
Lafayette Square
US Courthouse
Warehouse District
Julia Row
Lee Circle
Robert E Lee Monument
Lower Garden District
Coliseum Square
Central City
Louisiana Superdome
New Orleans Arena
New Orleans Centre
Hyatt Regency
Union Passenger Terminal
Riverfront Streetcar
St Charles Ave Streetcar
Pontchartrain Expwy
Greater New Orleans Bridge (toll)
To Tipitina's (2.7mi)
To Freret St Market (1.5mi)
To Commander's Palace (0.5mi)
To Savvy Gourmet (2.5mi); Audubon Zoological Gardens (4mi)
To Uptown (2mi); Audubon Park (2.8mi); St Joe's (2.9mi); Domilise's Po-Boys (3mi); Tulane University (3mi); Art Market of New Orleans (3.3mi); Children's Book Shop (3.5mi); Maple Street Book Shop (3.5mi); Riverbend (4mi); Zotz (4mi); Mat and Naddie's (4.2mi); Boucherie (4.3mi); Maple Leaf Bar (4.3mi)

THE SOUTH

Dangers & Annoyances

New Orleans has a high violent-crime rate, and neighborhoods go from good to ghetto very quickly. Be careful walking too far north of Faubourg Marigny and the Bywater (St Claude Ave is a good place to stop), south of Magazine St (things get dodgier past Laurel St) and too far west (Rampart St) of the French Quarter. Stick to places that are well peopled, particularly at night, and spring for a cab to avoid dark walks. In the Quarter, street hustlers frequently approach tourists – just walk away. With all that said, don't be paranoid. Crime here, as in most of America, tends to be between people who already know each other.

Sights & Activities

FRENCH QUARTER

Elegant, Caribbean-colonial architecture, lush gardens and wrought-iron accents are the visual norm in the French Quarter. But this is also the heart of New Orleans' tourism scene, and Bourbon St, a sort of caricature of a 'Girls Gone Wild' video, generates a loutish membrane that sometimes makes the rest of the Quarter difficult to appreciate.

Look past said silliness. The 'Vieux Carré' (Old Quarter, first laid out in 1722) is the focal point of much of this city's culture. In New Orleans' early days this *was* the city (really; nothing else was built) and in the quieter back lanes and alleyways a sense of faded time shaken and stirred with joie de vivre – the quintessential romance this town imparts – is so rich your head goes fuzzy.

Jackson Square is the heart of the Quarter. Sprinkled with lazing loungers, surrounded by fortune-tellers, sketch artists and traveling showmen and overlooked by cathedrals, offices and shops plucked from a Parisian fantasy, this is one of America's great green spaces. It manages to both anchor the French Quarter and beat out the heart-rhythm of this corner of town. What happens in the Quarter usually begins here. The identical, block-long Pontalba Buildings overlook the square, and the nearly identical Cabildo and Presbytère structures flank **St Louis Cathedral**, the square's masterpiece. Designed by Gilberto Guillemard, this is one of the finest examples of French ecumenical (church) architecture in America. Nearby, the river levee's **Moonwalk** (named for local politician Moon Landry, not

THE NEW NEW ORLEANS

The 'Katrina Tattoo,' the line on thousands of buildings that marked the top elevation of 2005's Hurricane Katrina floodwaters, has faded, but that doesn't mean 'the Storm,' as everyone calls it, is spent. Oh, you'd think so if you stayed within the 'White Teapot,' shaped like its kitchenware name and extending from the blocks of Riverbend down in a curve along Uptown and Magazine St, up into the CBD, French Quarter and Faubourg Marigny. Few people lost homes here, most are Caucasian and most visitors concentrate in these streets. Here, life is not only normal, but thriving.

Other swaths of the city – the Lower 9th Ward, Gentilly and Gentilly Terrace – are still Dead Zones. The welcome mat remains an emergency-crew 'X.' Insurance claims are still disputed. Road signs have yet to reappear. There's no cute '504ever' bumper stickers in the weeds growing through Milneburg's cracked lots.

New Orleans endures, irreversibly changed, and a new city is being carved from the mud by thousands of new arrivals, affectionately nicknamed YURPs – Young, Urban Rebuilding Professionals (they've even got a website: www.nolayurp.com). It's like Freedom Summer all over again, except the idealistic 20- and 30-something types are from all over: the Northeast, West Coast, Midwest and, yes, the South.

New Orleans has always been a beacon for the misfits of America. Now she's becoming a litmus test for new frontiers of urban planning as well. The frontiers of green architecture and public charter schools, to name a few policy sectors, are pushed by innovators – transplants and natives – determined to defend this bastion of freaks, geeks, madmen, musicians, misfits, foodies and poets. They know they can't find drag queen/bunny suit Easter pub crawls followed by a Second Line in Birmingham and Jackson, or even San Francisco and New York. That's what makes this home, and today, being New Orleanian means defending said home like a pissed-off badger, while helping rebuild – and redefine it – a little every day.

the Michael Jackson dance) makes a great spot to sit and dip beignets in *café au lait* while watching the riverboats meander by.

The **Louisiana State Museum** (☎ 504-568-6968; http://lsm.crt.state.la.us; adult/child per bldg $6/free; 10am-4:30pm Tue-Sun) operates several institutions across the state. The standouts here include the 1911 **Cabildo** (701 Chartres St), on the left of the cathedral, a Louisiana history museum located in the old city hall where Plessy vs Ferguson (which legalized segregation) was argued. The huge amount of exhibits inside can easily eat up half a day, the remainder of which can be spent in the Cabildo's sister building, on the right of the church, the 1813 **Presbytère** (751 Chartres St;). Inside is an excellent Mardi Gras museum, with displays of costumes, parade floats and royal jewelry that explain the deep historical, even mystical, roots Mardi Gras has in New Orleans.

Ensconced in several exquisitely restored buildings, the **Historic New Orleans Collection** (☎ 504-523-4662; www.hnoc.org; 533 Royal St; admission free, home tour $5; 9:30am-4:30pm Tue-Sat, from 10:30am Sun) displays thoughtfully curated exhibits with an emphasis on archival materials, such as the original transfer documents of the Louisiana Purchase. It's one of the best quick introductions to the city's history on offer.

In 1728, 12 Ursuline nuns arrived in New Orleans to care for the French garrison's 'miserable little hospital' and to educate the young girls of the colony. Between 1745 and 1752, the French colonial army built the **Old Ursuline Convent** (☎ 504-529-3040; 1112 Chartres St; adult/senior/child $5/4/2, child under 8 free; tours 10am, 11am, 1pm, 2pm & 3pm Tue-Fri, 11:15am, 1pm & 2pm Sat & Sun), now the oldest structure in the Mississippi River Valley and the only remaining French building in the Quarter. Originally a Native American trading post, the **French Market** (☎ 504-522-2621; www.frenchmarket.org; N Peters St, btwn St Ann & Barracks Sts; 9am-5pm;) is the US' oldest public market.

THE TREMÉ

The oldest African American neighborhood in the city is obviously steeped in a lot of history.

Louis Armstrong Park encompasses **Congo Square**, an American cultural landmark. Now a brick open space, it was the one place where enslaved people were allowed to congregate and play the music they had carried over the seas – a practice outlawed in most other slave-holding societies. The preservation of this musical heritage helped lay the groundwork for rhythms that would eventually become jazz.

The 1824 **St Augustine's Church** (☎ 504-525-5934; www.staugustinecatholicchurch-neworleans.org; 1210 Governor Nicholls St) is the second-oldest African American Catholic church in the US; many jazz funeral processions originate here. Call ahead to try to arrange a visit, as the church is still in a rebuilding process post-Katrina. Across the street is the **Backstreet Cultural Museum** (☎ 504-303-9058; www.backstreetmuseum.org; 1116 St Claude Ave; suggested donation $5; 10am-5pm Tue-Sat). This is the place to see one facet of this town's distinctive customs – its African American side – and how they're expressed in daily life. The term 'backstreet' refers to New Orleans' 'back o' town,' or the poor black neighborhoods. If you have any interest in Mardi Gras Indian suits (African Americans who dress up in Carnival-esque Native American costume), second lines and the activities of social aid and pleasure clubs (the local black community version of civic associations), you need to stop by.

The **New Orleans African American Museum of Art, Culture & History** (☎ 504-566-1136; 1418 Governor Nicholls St; adult/child $5/3; 11am-4pm Wed-Sat) exhibits local artists and hit-and-miss rotating displays in a tidy Creole cottage with terraced grounds.

St Louis Cemetery No 1 (Basin St; 8am-3pm;) received the remains of most early Creoles. The shallow water table necessitated above-ground burials, with bodies placed in the family tombs you see to this day. The supposed grave of voodoo queen Marie Laveau is here, scratched with 'XXX's from spellbound devotees – this is graffiti you shouldn't add to, per the request of the family that owns the tomb.

FAUBOURG MARIGNY & THE BYWATER

North of the French Quarter are the Creole suburbs ('faubourgs,' which more accurately means 'neighborhoods') of the Marigny and the Bywater. The Marigny is the heart of the local gay scene; **Frenchman St**, which runs through the center of the 'hood, is a fantastic strip of live-music goodness. The Bywater is an edgier area, where a good mix of white, black, working class and artists are straddling the edge of urban cool. A lot of new New Orleanians have moved into this area, bringing a bit of gentrification along with some decent funkiness to the pretty rows of shotgun shacks.

There's some good examples of post-Katrina rebuilding work north of this area, but you'll want to drive or taxi to the following two sites. **KKProjects** (☎ 504-218-8701; www.kkprojects.org; 2448 N Villere St; 10am-4pm Sat & Sun) has taken, as of this writing, six abandoned homes and, with the input of the local community, turned them into studios/galleries/structures/works of art in their own right. Examples include a house floored and roofed with sod and turf that looks like a hobbit hole in the middle of the ghetto, community gardens and greenhouses. Open outside hours by appointment.

Musicians' Village (www.nolamusiciansvillage.com; btwn North Roman, Alvar & North Johnson Sts) encompasses an 8-acre tract of some 81 houses, built primarily for musicians, a vital component of the city's cultural and economic landscape. While mainly intended for musicians, it is not exclusively inhabited by them – non-musicians live here as well. If you visit, please bear in mind this is a living neighborhood; folks can get understandably tetchy if you take pictures of them or their property without asking permission or even getting out of your car. The brightly painted houses lighten up the surrounding neighborhood like a spilled pack of Skittles.

CBD & WAREHOUSE DISTRICT

The CBD and Warehouse District comprise the commercial section established after the Louisiana Purchase. Today, several outstanding museums anchor the Warehouse District, and local art galleries cluster along Julia St, holding openings on the first Saturday evening of each month.

Aquarium of the Americas (☎ 504-581-4629; www.audubоninstitute.org; 1 Canal St; adult/child $18/11; 9:30am-5pm Tue-Sun) simulates an eclectic selection of watery habitats – look for the rare white alligator. You can buy combination tickets to the IMAX theater next door, the Audubon Zoo in Uptown (opposite) and the **Insectarium** (☎ 504-410-2847; www.auduboninstitute.org; 423 Canal St; adult/child/senior $14/9/11; 10am-5pm Tue-Sun), a supremely kid-friendly learning center that's a joy for budding entomologists, or anyone with a bit of interest in biology. The Japanese garden dotted with whispering butterflies is particularly beautiful.

The **Canal Street Ferry** (pedestrian & cyclist/car free/$1; 6am-8:45pm), departing from the foot of Canal St, is a fast and fabulous ride across the Mississippi to Algiers, an attractive historic neighborhood just across the river, and back.

One of our favorite museums in the city, the **Ogden Museum of Southern Art** (☎ 504-539-9600; www.ogdenmuseum.org; 925 Camp St; adult/child $10/6; 11am-4pm Thu-Sun) manages to be beautiful, educating and unpretentious all at once. New Orleans entrepreneur Roger Houston Ogden has assembled one of the finest collections of Southern art anywhere – far too large to keep to himself – which includes huge galleries ranging from Impressionist landscapes to outsider folk-art quirkiness to contemporary installation work. There's free live music from 6pm to 8pm Thursday.

Across the street, the **Contemporary Arts Center** (☎ 504-528-3805; www.cacno.org; 900 Camp St; admission varies; 11am-4pm Thu-Sun) maintains airy galleries filled with rotating avant-garde shows.

The extensive, heart-wrenching **National World War II Museum** (☎ 504-527-6012; www.nationalww2museum.org; 945 Magazine St; adult/child $14/6; 9am-5pm Tue-Sun) should satisfy the historical curiosity of anyone who possesses even a passing interest in WWII. The museum presents an admirably nuanced and always thorough analysis of the biggest war of the 20th century. Of particular note is the D-Day exhibition, arguably the most in-depth of its type in the country. The oral history sections are fascinating and a gaggle of expansions that includes pavilions dedicated to every major campaign America participated in during the war are upcoming; some of this work is being directed by actor Tom Hanks.

The garish and good-fun **Blaine Kern's Mardi Gras World** (☎ 504-361-7821; www.mardigrasworld.com; 1380 Port of New Orleans Pl; adult/child $18/11; tours 9:30am-5:30pm) houses (and constructs) many of the greatest floats used in Mardi Gras parades. You can see them being built or on display any time of the year by popping by the facilities, located just behind the southern end of the Convention Center. After a short film on Mardi Gras history, the tour takes you through the giant workshops where artists create elaborate floats for New Orleans krewes (marching clubs), Universal Studios and Disney World.

GARDEN DISTRICT & UPTOWN

The main architectural division in New Orleans is between the elegant town houses of the Creole and French northeast and the magnificent mansions of the American district, settled after the Louisiana Purchase. These huge structures, plantationesque in their appearance, are most commonly found in the Garden District and Uptown. Magnificent oak trees arch over St Charles Ave, which cuts through the heart of this sector and where the **St Charles Avenue streetcar** (per ride $1.25;) runs. The boutiques and galleries of **Magazine Street** form the best shopping strip in the city.

Further west, Tulane and Loyola universities occupy adjacent campuses alongside expansive **Audubon Park**. Tulane was founded in 1834 as a medical college in an attempt to control repeated cholera and yellow fever epidemics. Today the verdant campuses offer a welcome respite from city streets, while the universities host plenty of concerts and lectures.

Among the country's best zoos, the **Audubon Zoological Gardens** (504-861-2537; www.auduboninstitute.org; 6500 Magazine St; adult/child $13/8; 9am-5pm Tue-Sun) contains the ultracool Louisiana Swamp exhibit, full of alligators, bobcats, foxes, bears and snapping turtles.

CITY PARK & MID-CITY

The **Canal streetcar** makes the run from the CBD to City Park. Three miles long, 1 mile wide, stroked by weeping willows and Spanish moss and dotted with museums, gardens, waterways, bridges, birds and the occasional alligator, **City Park** (504-482-4888; www.neworleanscitypark.com) is the nation's fifth-largest urban park (bigger than Central Park in NYC) and New Orleans' prettiest green lung. It's ridiculously picturesque and a perfect expression of a local 'park,' in the sense that it is an only slightly tamed expression of the Louisiana wetlands and forest that are the natural backdrop of the city.

Inside the park, the elegant **New Orleans Museum of Art** (504-658-4100; www.noma.org; 1 Collins Diboll Circle; adult/child $8/4; noon-8pm Wed, 10am-5pm Thu-Sun) was founded in 1910 and is well worth a visit both for its local exhibitions and top-floor galleries of African, Asian, Native American and Oceanic art. Its **sculpture garden** (admission free; 10am-4:30pm Wed-Sun) contains a cutting-edge collection in lush, meticulously planned grounds.

Besides hosting the regular horse-racing season, the **Fair Grounds** (1751 Gentilly Blvd, btwn Gentilly Blvd & Fortin St) are also home to the huge springtime New Orleans Jazz & Heritage Festival (p481).

Walking Tour

The Quarter's elegant 18th-century Spanish Colonial architecture lines narrow streets, seducing with bright colors and minimalist beauty. A leisurely stroll, peeking inside iron gates and browsing the shops and galleries, is the best way to soak up the vibe.

Begin your walk at the **Presbytère** (**1**; p477) on Jackson Sq and head down Chartres St to the corner of Ursulines Ave and the **Old Ursuline Convent** (**2**; p477).

Directly across Chartres St, at No 1113, the 1826 **Beauregard-Keyes House (3)** combines Creole and American-style design. Civil War General PGT Beauregard rented rooms here, and author Frances Parkinson Keyes lived here from 1942 to 1970.

Walk along Ursulines Ave to Royal St, perhaps stopping for a quick *café au lait* and delectable pastry at **Croissant D'Or Patisserie** (**4**; p483). The soda fountain at the **Royal Pharmacy (5)** is a preserved relic from halcyon malt-shop days; the owners of the pharmacy feel it's too classic to pull out.

Continue up Ursulines Ave and then turn left onto Bourbon St. The ramshackle one-story structure on the corner of St Philip St is a salty little tavern and National Historic Landmark called **Lafitte's Blacksmith Shop (6)**. Head down St Philip back to Royal St and take a right.

When it comes to quintessential New Orleans postcard images, Royal St takes the prize. Cast-iron galleries grace the buildings and a profusion of flowers garland the facades. Take it slowly and appreciate the details.

At No 915 the **Cornstalk Hotel** (**7**; p482) stands behind one of the most frequently photographed fences anywhere. At Orleans Ave, stately magnolia trees and lush tropical plants fill **St Anthony's Garden (8)**, behind **St Louis Cathedral** (**9**; p476).

Alongside the garden, Pirate's Alley is an inviting, shaded walkway that calls for a little detour. The first buildings to the right, Nos 622 to 624 Pirate's Alley, are just two of the **Labranche Buildings (10)**. Note the original wrought-iron balconies, some of the finest in town, which date from the 1840s. At 624 Pirate's Alley, charming **Faulkner House Books** (**11**; p473), is named for its most famous resident, William Faulkner.

Turn right down Cabildo Alley and then right up St Peter St, toward Royal St. Tennessee Williams shacked up at No 632 St Peter, the

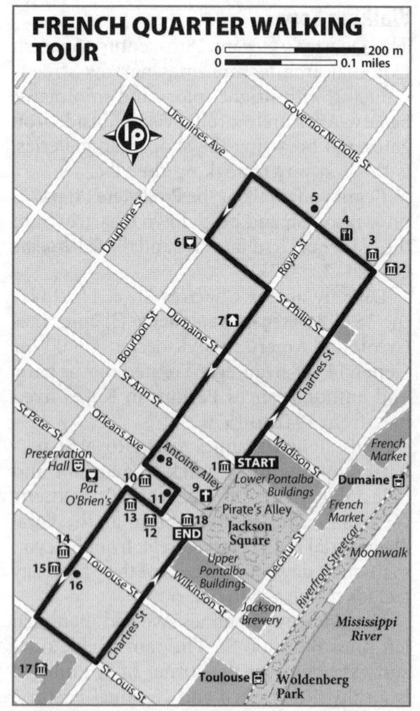

WALK FACTS

Start Presbytère
Finish Cabildo
Distance 1 miles
Duration About 90 minutes

Avart-Peretti House (12), in 1946–47 while he wrote *A Streetcar Named Desire*.

At the corner of Royal, the **LeMonnier Mansion (13)**, at No 640, is commonly known to be New Orleans' first 'skyscraper.' If you kept going up St Peter, you'd reach **Pat O'Brien's**, where the famous 'Hurricane' cocktail is served, and the rustic facade of **Preservation Hall** (p485).

Turn left on Royal St. At the corner of Royal and Toulouse Sts stands a pair of houses built by Jean François Merieult in the 1790s. The **Court of Two Lions (14)**, at 541 Royal St, opens onto Toulouse St and next door is the **Historic New Orleans Collection** (**15**; p477). Across the street, at No 520, a carriageway leads to the picturesque **Brulatour Courtyard (16)**.

On the next block, the massive 1909 **State Supreme Court Building (17)** was the setting for many scenes in director Oliver Stone's movie *JFK*. The white-marble and terracotta facade stands in attractive contrast with the rest of the Quarter.

Head down St Louis St to Chartres St and turn left. As Jackson Sq comes into view, you'll reach the Presbytère's near-identical twin, the **Cabildo** (**18**; p477). Kick back on the benches in front with the buskers or whip your palm out for a future foretold.

Courses

New Orleans GlassWorks & Printmaking Studio (☎ 504-529-7277; www.neworleansglassworks.com; 727 Magazine St; from $135) Try your hand at glassblowing (really!) or printmaking during weekend or six-week courses (September to May).

New Orleans School of Cooking (☎ 504-525-2665; www.neworleansschoolofcooking.com; 524 St Louis St; classes from $27) Menus rotate daily, but rest assured you'll be snacking on creations such as gumbo, jambalaya and pralines at the end of class.

Savvy Gourmet (☎ 504-895-2665; www.savvygourmet.com; 4519 Magazine St; classes $15-75) Whether you're looking to learn wine history, knife skills or hands-on seafood prep, Savvy's got it. Check the website for the schedule.

Wine Institute of New Orleans (W.I.N.O.) (☎ 324-8000; www.winoschool.com; 610 Tchoupitoulas St; from classes $35) The 'institute' runs classes on wine tasting, food pairing and the like, aimed at both amateur enthusiasts and folks looking to get professionally employed in the wine and spirit industry.

New Orleans for Children

Many of New Orleans' daytime attractions are well suited for kids: the Audubon Zoological Gardens (p479), Aquarium of the Americas (p478) and Mardi Gras World (p478), for example. Also check out the 'kid stuff' listings in the *Times-Picayune* 'Living' section on Monday.

Carousel Gardens (☎ 504-483-9382; www.neworleanscitypark.com; admission $3; ⌚ 10am-3pm Tue-Fri, 11am-6pm Sat & Sun; 🚸) The 1906 carousel is a gem of vintage carny-ride happiness.

Children's Book Shop (☎ 504-861-2105; www.maplestreetbookshop.com; 7529 Maple St; ⌚ 10am-6pm Mon-Sat; 🚸) Cozy storytelling next door to the Maple Street Book Shop (p473).

Louisiana Children's Museum (☎ 504-523-1357; www.lcm.org; 420 Julia St; admission $7.50; ⌚ 9:30am-4:30pm Tue-Sat, from noon Sun; 🚸) Great hands-on exploratory exhibits and toddler area. Children under 16 must be accompanied by an adult.

THE SOUTH

Tours

Tours, tours everywhere! Check the *New Orleans Official Visitors Guide* for a full selection of the myriad offerings. Some companies now give post-Katrina devastation tours. The Jean Lafitte National Historic Park and Preserve Visitor Center (p473) leads free walking tours of the French Quarter at 9:30am (get tickets at 9am).

Carriage ride (Jackson Sq; www.neworleanscarriages.com; 4 people per 30min from $60; to midnight) A mule-drawn ride through the Quarter gives a relaxing glimpse of the narrow streets at a gentle pace while the driver spins fanciful yarns.

Friends of the Cabildo (504-523-3939; 1850 House Museum Store, 523 St Ann St; adult/child/student $15/free/10; tours 10am & 1:30pm Tue-Sun) Volunteers lead the best available walking tours of the Quarter.

Historic New Orleans Tours (504-947-2120; www.tourneworleans.com; adult/child/student & senior from $20/7/15) Runs a wide variety of tours, from haunted house crawls to rebuilding house trips to areas hurt by the Storm.

Festivals & Events

New Orleans never needs an excuse to party – whether in commemoration of shrimp and petroleum or the mighty mirliton (a kind of squash), there's almost always some celebration in town. Just the wee-est of listings follow; check www.neworleanscvb.com for more.

Mardi Gras In February or early March, Fat Tuesday marks the orgasmic finale of the Carnival season.

St Patrick's Day March 17 and its closest weekend see parades of cabbage-wielding Irishfolk.

St Joseph's Day – Super Sunday March 19 and its nearest Sunday bring 'gangs' of Mardi Gras Indians out into the streets in all their feathered, drumming glory. The Super Sunday parade usually begins around noon at Bayou St John and Orleans Ave, but follows no fixed route.

Tennessee Williams Literary Festival (www.tennesseewilliams.net) In March, five days of literary panels, plays and parties celebrate the author's work.

French Quarter Festival (www.fqfi.org) The second weekend of April; free music on multiple stages.

Jazz Fest The last weekend of April and the first weekend of May; a world-renowned extravaganza of music, food, crafts and good living.

Essence Music Festival (www.essence.com) Independence Day weekend in early July sees star-studded performances at the Superdome.

Southern Decadence (www.southerndecadence.net) A huge gay, lesbian and transgender festival, including a leather block party, on Labor Day weekend (first weekend in September).

Sleeping

Rates peak during Mardi Gras and Jazz Fest, and fall in the hot summer months. Book early and call or check the internet for special deals. Hotel sales tax is 13%, plus $1 to $3 per person per night. Parking in the Quarter costs $15 to $25 per day.

BUDGET

India House Hostel (504-821-1904; www.indiahousehostel.com; 124 S Lopez St; dm/d $20/45;) In Mid-City, this place has a free-spirited party atmosphere. A large aboveground swimming pool and cabana-like patio add ambience to the three well-used old houses that serve as dorms. Ask about the private Cajun shacks out back, which come with pet alligators. Guests can use the washer and dryer, and log onto the internet. Children are not permitted.

Marquette House International Hostel (504-523-3014; www.neworleansinternationalhostel.com; 2249 Carondelet St; dm $25, s/d from $44/53; office 7am-noon & 5-10pm; P) A sprawling compound of both dorms and private rooms (with refrigerators and microwaves) near the Garden District. Serviceable, but certainly not luxurious, the rooms are upstaged by the lush garden area, perfect for hanging out and meeting fellow travelers.

MIDRANGE

Prytania Park Hotel (504-524-0427, 888-498-7591; www.prytaniaparkhotel.com; 1525 Prytania St; r from $90; P) Really a complex of three separate hotels, the Prytania Park's small honey-colored rooms are a bit dingy. The Prytania Oaks is sleeker (rooms from $119) and the Queen Anne is an exquisite boutique hotel, newly renovated and bedecked with antiques (rooms from $130). Perfect spot for bouncing between the Quarter and the Garden District or Uptown, and parking is free.

Lamothe House (504-947-1161, 800-367-5858; www.lamothehouse.com; 621 Esplanade Ave; r & ste incl breakfast from $99;) Grand mansion rooms fuse royal with bordello: gilt accents and rococo carvings compete with delicate oil paintings. Starker rooms in the outbuildings adjoin easily for families, and the spacious courtyard lets you all spread out.

Le Pavillon (504-581-3111, 800-535-9095; 833 Poydras Ave; r/ste from $100/340;) Built in 1907, this elegant European-style hotel's opulent marble lobby, plush, modern rooms and rooftop pool are a steal. Decadent suites

ART FOR EVERY WEEKEND

You can discover local art and meet local artists every weekend in New Orleans.

New Orleans Arts District Art Walk (www.neworleansartsdistrict.com; Julia St) The first Saturday of each month beginning at 6pm until close (whenever, really) the fine art galleries in New Orleans Art District celebrate the opening night of month-long feature artist exhibitions.

Freret Street Market (www.freretmarket.org; cnr Freret St & Napoleon Ave) A combination farmers, flea and art show, this market offers a great mix of local culture. Held the first Saturday of the month (except for July and August) from noon to 5pm.

Saint Claude Arts District Gallery Openings (www.scadnola.com) New Orleans' newest arts district, this growing collective of art exhibition spaces span Faubourg Marigny and the Bywater, home to some of New Orleans' more eclectic artists. Ask locals for weekend recommendations and you may be rewarded with a fire-eating display or impromptu collective installations at a secret, hidden art space.

Bywater Art Market (www.art-restoration.com/bam; cnr Royal & Piety Sts) Known as New Orleans' original art market, this market takes pride in a strict jurying process and features original artists' work. Held on the third Saturday of the month from 9am to 4pm.

Art Market of New Orleans (www.artscouncilofneworleans.org; Palmer Park, cnr Carrolton & Claiborne Aves) Last Saturday of every month. Featuring hundreds of the area's most creative local artists, this monthly market is juried for quality and always features local food, music and kids' activities. Perfect on warm-weather days.

With thanks to Lindsay Glatz, Arts Council of New Orleans.

might prevent you from ever leaving the building. If booking a queen room, request a bay window. Parking costs $25.

Cornstalk Hotel (☎ 504-523-1515, 800-759-6112; www.cornstalkhotel.com; 915 Royal St; r incl breakfast $135-200;) Pass through the famous cast-iron fence and into a plush, antiqued B&B where the serenity sweeps away the whirl of the busy streets outside. Gemlike rooms are all unique and luxurious. Parking's available for $15.

our pick House on Bayou Road (☎ 504-945-0992, 800-882-2968; www.houseonbayouroad.com; 2275 Bayou Rd; r incl breakfast from $135; P) The gem of Esplanade Ridge is this 1798 plantation house, which oozes sultry atmosphere, with wide galleries and French doors that open onto thick tropical gardens. Screened porches make it possible to enjoy the chirp of crickets at night without being slaughtered by mosquitoes, and a large swimming pool will keep you cool. Antiques in the three main houses are splashed with natural light from tall windows.

Melrose Mansion (☎ 504-524-3900, 800-776-3901; www.melrosemansion.com; 937 Esplanade Ave; r from $140;) If you were a millionaire with a New Orleans pied-à-terre, this could be it. It's austerely elegant with hand-selected antiques sitting alongside the freshest modern art, and during high season you'll be regaled with a home-baked breakfast and evening wine and cheese in the chic parlor. Before the Storm, prices were twice the current rates.

Degas House (☎ 504-821-5009; www.degashouse.com; 2306 Esplanade Ave; r incl breakfast from $149;) Edgar Degas, the famed French Impressionist, lived in this 1852 Italianate house when visiting his mother's family in the early 1870s. Arty rooms recall the painter's stay with reproductions of his work and period furnishings. The suites have balconies and fireplaces, while the less-expensive garret rooms are the cramped top-floor quarters that once housed the Degas family's servants.

Loft 523 (☎ 504-200-6523; www.loft523.com; 523 Gravier St; r from $179;) Top design magazines have recognized the hip industrial-minimalist style of Loft 523's 16 lodgings. Whirligig-shaped fans circle over low-lying Mondo beds and polished concrete floors. The best use of your freestanding half-egg-shaped tub is ordering a milk bath in-room spa service and listening to a mixed jazz CD in surround sound (or switching on the plasma screen).

TOP END

Hotel Maison de Ville (☎ 561-5858; www.hotelmaisondeville.com; 727 Toulouse St; ste from $230;) The one- and two-bedroom Audubon Cottage suites (where artist John J Audubon stayed and painted while in town) overflow with elegant touches: goose-down featherbeds, Gilchrist &

DON'T MISS

- **Boucherie** (p484)
- **Mat and Naddie's** (p485)
- **Bacchanal** (p484)
- **Fiorella's** (right)
- **Domilise's Po-Boys** (p485)

Soames bath products and Egyptian-cotton robes are just a few. These suites surround a lushly landscaped courtyard; the pool is rumored to be the oldest in the Quarter (from the late 1700s). At the time of writing, the sumptuous 19th-century main town house hotel itself is still being renovated. But if genteel Southern comfort and polished charm are what you're after, it's worth looking into when it does.

Eating

Louisiana may have the greatest native culinary tradition in the USA – not necessarily by dint of the quality of food (although quality is very high) but the long history that lies behind dishes that are older than most American states. Also: people here just *love to eat*. It's beautifully democratic how everyone in this city, from Garden District mansion dwellers to St Roch tenement residents, goes crazy when fecal-eating, sewage-dwelling mudbugs (crawfish, y'all) come into season.

FRENCH QUARTER

Café du Monde (☎ 800-772-2972; 800 Decatur St; beignets $2; 24hr;) Du Monde is overrated, but you're probably gonna go there, so here goes: the coffee is decent and the beignets (square, sugar-coated fritters) are inconsistent. The atmosphere is off-putting: you're a number forced through the wringer, trying to shout over Bob and Fran while they mispronounce 'jambalaya' and a street musician badly mangles John Lennon's 'Imagine.' At least it's open 24 hours – you might be able to capture some measure of noir-ish cool as the drunks stumble past in the Edward Hopper–esque wee hours.

Croissant D'Or Patisserie (☎ 504-524-4663; 617 Ursulines Ave; meals $3-5; 7am-2pm Wed-Mon) This ancient and spotlessly clean pastry shop is where many Quarter locals start their day. Bring a paper, order coffee and a croissant and bliss out. On your way in, check out the tiled sign on the threshold that says 'ladies entrance' – a holdover from pre-feminist days that is no longer enforced.

Clover Grill (☎ 504-598-1010; 900 Bourbon St; dishes $5-8; 24hr) Gay greasy spoon? Yup. It's all slightly surreal, given this place otherwise totally resembles a '50s diner, but nothing adds to the Americana like a prima-donna-ish argument between an out-of-makeup drag queen and a drunk club kid, all likely set to blaring disco music. The food is dependable diner fare and good for a hangover, or for those who can see the hangover approaching.

Central Grocery (☎ 504-523-1620; 923 Decatur St; half/full muffuletta $7/13; 9am-5pm Tue-Sat) A Sicilian immigrant invented the world-famous *muffuletta* sandwich – a round, seeded loaf of bread stuffed with ham, salami, provolone and marinated olive salad that's roughly the size of a manhole cover – here in 1906. Today, this is still the best place in town to get one.

Yo Mama's (☎ 522-1125; www.yomamasbarandgrill.com; 727 St Peters St; burgers $7-14; 11am-3am) Let us lay it on the line: peanut butter and bacon burger. Sorry; scrape the brains back into your ear, because we just *blew your mind*. That's right: looks like a cheeseburger, but that ain't melted cheddar on top. Honestly, it's great: somehow the stickiness of the peanut butter compliments the char-grilled edge of the meat and, if you've got the backbone, a heaping mound of sour cream, butter and bacon bits on the accompanying baked potato. There's lots of other awesome burgers on the menu, but it is incumbent on you, dear traveler, to eat the native cuisine of a city. In Hanoi, that's pho, in Marrakech, tagine, and in New Orleans: peanut butter and bacon burger.

Fiorella's (☎ 523-2155; 1136 Decatur St; mains $7-15; 11am-midnight Sun-Thu, 11am-2am Fri & Sat) If you need to eat right in the Quarter for under $20 a head, Fiorella's and nearby **Coop's** (☎ 525-9053; 1109 Decatur St; mains $8-17.50; 11am-3am) are as good as it gets. Coop's is a Cajun country shack, hipstered up – try the rabbit and sausage jambalaya for a taste of Cajun heaven. Fiorella's is a Sicilian café, all red-checkered cloth, but run through a similar punk-rock wringer. The food is quintessential Italian New Orleans: pastas, pizzas, veal cutlets and, arguably, the best fried chicken in town. Some find the latter too salty; we say it's just right, especially with a bit of hot sauce.

GW Fins (☎ 504-581-3467; www.gwfins.com; 808 Bienville St; mains $22-35; 5-10pm Sun-Thu, to 10:30pm

Fri & Sat) Fins focuses, almost entirely, on fish: fresh caught and prepped so the flavor of the sea is always accented and never overwhelmed. For New Orleans this is light, almost delicate dining – you'll still find the crabmeat stuffing and tasso (Cajun smoked pork) toppings, but Fins also knows how to serve a rare yellowtail with a bit of air-fine sticky rice. It's a refreshing breath of salty air if you're getting jambalaya-ed out.

Bayona (☎ 504-525-4455; 430 Dauphine St; mains $24-30; ⏲ 11:30am-2pm Mon-Fri, 6-10pm Mon-Thu, 6-11pm Fri & Sat) Bayona is, for our money, the best splurge in the Quarter. It's rich but not overwhelming, classy but unpretentious, innovative without being precocious and all-round excellent. Thank chef Susan Spicer and her army of line cooks – they all seem to have a genuine love of what they do and commitment to their craft. The menu changes regularly, but expect fish, fowl and game done up in what we'd describe as 'surprisingly pleasant' style – the tastes make you raise an eyebrow, than smile like you've discovered comfort food gone classy.

THE TREMÉ

Willie Mae's Scotch House (☎ 504-822-9503; 2401 St Ann St; mains $6-13; ⏲ 11am-3pm Mon-Fri) The fried chicken at Willie Mae's is good. Very good. But it's not the best in the world, despite being named an 'American Classic' by the James Beard foundation in 2005 (eight weeks before Katrina and a subsequent huge community effort at reopening the restaurant, which makes the place even more irresistible). In a little white house in a low-income neighborhood you'll see cars from California, Canada and New York seeking the best, but honestly and objectively, we'd score the fried chicken here 7 out of 10.

Dooky Chase (☎ 504-821-0600; 2301 Orleans Ave; mains $6-15; ⏲ 11am-2:30pm Tue-Fri) Ray Charles wrote 'Early in the Morning,' about Dooky's, local civil rights leaders used the spot as an informal headquarters in the 1960s and Barack Obama ate here when he visited New Orleans after his inauguration. This soul-food spot is a neighborhood backbone and serves perhaps the best meal for any vegetarian visiting New Orleans: gumbo z'herbes. Served on Thursdays during Lent, its green and gorgeous with mustards, beet tops, spinach, kale, collards and Lord knows what else.

FAUBOURG MARIGNY & THE BYWATER

Bacchanal (☎ 504-948-9111; http://bacchanalwine.com; 600 Poland Ave; sandwiches $11, cheese per piece from $5; ⏲ 11am-9pm) One of the best wine and cheese selections in New Orleans sits just across the water from the Lower 9th Ward. Let the folks behind the counter prep your *fromage* into a work of art, which is devoured in a backyard of overgrown garden green scattered with rusted-out lawn chairs and tatty foldouts. On chef Sundays, cooks from around the city are invited to guest-star in Bacchanal's kitchen and let loose with whatever their talented hearts desire.

Elizabeth's (☎ 504-944-9272; www.elizabeths-restaurant.com; 601 Gallier St; mains $11-27; ⏲ 11am-2:30pm Tue-Fri, 6-10pm Tue-Sat, 8am-2:30pm Sun; 🚸) Elizabeth's is deceptively divey. It looks like – hell it is – a neighborhood joint. But it tastes as good as the best haute New Orleans chefs can offer. Be sure to order some praline bacon: fried up in brown sugar and, as far as we can tell, God's own cooking oil. It's probably an utter sin to consume, but y'know what? Consider us happily banished from the garden.

CBD & WAREHOUSE DISTRICT

Cochon (☎ 504-588-2123; www.cochonrestaurant.com; 930 Tchoupitoulas St; mains $14-24; ⏲ 11am-10pm Mon-Fri, from 5:30pm Sat) James Beard Award–winning chef Donald Link's fabulous brasserie serves up gourmet Southern comfort food such as rabbit and dumplings and wood-fired roast oysters. House-made *boucherie* and a fearless willingness to pair the simply succulent with the exceptionally extravagant catapult this laid-back spot into the echelons of truly unique cuisine.

Emeril's (☎ 504-528-9393; www.emerils.com; 800 Tchoupitoulas St; dinner mains $27-39; ⏲ 11:30am-2pm Fri, 6-10pm nightly) Chef Emeril Lagasse's flagship restaurant lives up to all the hype. His protégés rustle up consistently scrumptious bam!-worthy fare under the modern glass arch looking out on the main dining room, and an attentive staff sees to your every need.

GARDEN DISTRICT & UPTOWN

Boucherie (☎ 504-862-5514; www.boucherie-nola.com; 8115 Jeannette St; small plates $6-12, mains $11-15; ⏲ 11am-3pm & 5:30-9pm Tue-Sat) Can you improve upon a Krispy Kreme doughnut? We didn't think so, but along comes Boucherie's Krispy Kreme bread pudding. That heavy bread pudding becomes airy yet drool-tastically fattening when married to a honey glazed, drowning in syrup…oh man. For dinner, barbecued shrimp-and-grits cakes are darkly sweet and savory, garlic parmesan fries are gloriously stinky and gooey and duck confit with a truffled baby salad is just magic.

Domilise's Po-Boys (☎ 504-899-9126; 5240 Annunciation St; po'boys $8-13; 🕒 11am-7pm Mon-Sat) Domilise's is everything that makes New Orleans great: a dilapidated white shack by the river serving Dixie beer, staffed by folks who've worked here for decades, and prepping, if not the best po'boys in the city, at least the best seafood sandwich around. Cash only.

our pick **Mat and Naddie's** (☎ 504-861-9600; www.matandnaddies.com; 937 Leonidas St; mains $17-29; 🕒 11am-2pm Mon-Fri, 5:30-9:30pm Thu-Sat & Mon;) Set in a beautiful riverfront shotgun house with a Christmas lights–bedecked patio in the back, M&N's is rich, innovative, even amusing: try food like duck-fat-fried chicken with waffles and pecan sweet potato pie (all crazy delicious). It's kind of weird, it's high quality topped with quirkiness, and honestly, it's one of our favorite splurges in the city.

Commander's Palace (☎ 504-899-8221; www.commanderspalace.com; 1403 Washington Ave; mains lunch $29-42; 🕒 11:30am-2pm Mon-Fri, to 1pm Sat, 10:30am-1:30pm Sun, 6-10pm Mon-Sat) One of New Orleans' grandes dames, Commander's is a formal but friendly mainstay of impeccable Creole cooking and knowledgeable, friendly service, in the heart of the gorgeous Garden District. Pop in for the lunchtime 25¢ martinis and a cup of the signature turtle soup ($6.50), or a *prix fixe* extravaganza. No shorts allowed.

Drinking

New Orleans is a drinking town. Heads up: Bourbon St sucks. Get into the neighborhoods and experience some of the best bars in America. The kinder, gentler strip runs along Frenchmen St in Faubourg Marigny.

Most bars open every day, often by noon, get hopping around 10pm, and can stay open all night. There's no cover charge unless there's live music. It's illegal to have open glass liquor containers in the street, so all bars dispense plastic 'go cups' when you're ready to wander.

d.b.a. (☎ 504-942-3731; 618 Frenchmen St) Mellow until it fills up for live music and late-night partying; the extensive drinks menu and window seats will keep you busy while you wait.

St Joe's (☎ 504-899-3744; 5535 Magazine St) Awesome neighborhood bar with great mojitos, a cool back courtyard and friendly ambience.

Tonique (☎ 504-324-6045; 820 Rampart St) Excellent cocktails poured by expert bartenders in a classic French Quarter pad with a god garden in the back.

Molly's at the Market (☎ 504-525-5169; 1107 Decatur St) A young, bohemian hipster crowd swills the Guinness and mingles out onto the sidewalk.

R Bar (☎ 504-948-7499; 1431 Royal St) Somewhere between a dive and a neighborhood joint; a beer and a shot runs you $5. 'Nuff said.

Mimi's in the Marigny (☎ 504-872-986; 2601 Royal St) Neighborhood joint with pool and tapas.

Entertainment

What's New Orleans without live local music? Almost any weekend night you can find something for every taste: jazz, blues, brass band, country, Dixieland, zydeco, rock or Cajun. Free shows in the daytime abound. Check *Gambit*, *Offbeat* (p473) or www.nolafunguide.com for schedules.

Snug Harbor (☎ 504-949-0696; 626 Frenchmen St; cover $5-25) In the Marigny, the city's best contemporary jazz venue is all about world-class music and a good variety of acts.

Donna's Bar & Grill (☎ 504-596-6914; 800 N Rampart St) Shoulder up to the bar, grab a plate of red beans and rice and groove to jazz, blues or brass bands in this homey room on the edge of the Quarter.

Preservation Hall (☎ 504-522-2841; 726 St Peter St; cover $5-8) A veritable museum of traditional and Dixieland jazz, Preservation Hall is a pilgrimage. But like many religious obligations, it ain't necessarily easy, with no air-conditioning, limited seating and no refreshments (you can bring your own water, that's it).

Tipitina's (☎ 504-895-8477; 501 Napoleon Ave; cover $10-30) Always drawing a lively crowd, this legendary Uptown club rocks out like the musical mecca it is: local jazz, blues, soul and funk stop in, as well as national touring bands.

Circle Bar (☎ 504-588-2616; 1032 St Charles Ave) A bar that looks like a New Orleanian vampire's mansion run through a drug den, with casual folk and indie shows most nights.

Maple Leaf Bar (☎ 504-866-9359; 8316 Oak St; cover $5-10) Riverbend's pride and joy – its pressed-tin ceiling and close atmosphere get especially heated late. Rebirth Brass Band plays Tuesday.

Vaughan's (☎ 504-947-5562; 800 Lesseps St; cover $7-10) A great Bywater neighborhood bar that hosts local favorite and awesome trumpeter Kermit Ruffins on Thursday nights.

Getting There & Away

Louis Armstrong New Orleans International Airport (MSY; ☎ 504-464-0831; www.flymsy.com; 900 Airline Hwy), 11 miles west of the city, handles primarily domestic flights.

The **Union Passenger Terminal** (☎ 504-299-1880; 1001 Loyola Ave) is home to **Greyhound** (☎ 504-525-6075, 800-231-2222; 5:15am-1pm & 2:30-6pm) which has regular buses to Baton Rouge ($8to $20.25, two hours), Memphis, TN ($40 to $90, 11 hours) and Atlanta, GA ($83, 12 hours). **Amtrak** (☎ 504-528-1610, 800-872-7245; ticketing 5:45am-10pm) trains also operate from the Union Passenger Terminal, running to Jackson, MS; Memphis, TN; Chicago, IL. Birmingham, AL; Atlanta, GA; Washington, DC; New York City; Los Angeles, CA; and Miami, FL.

Getting Around

TO/FROM THE AIRPORT

There's an information booth at the airport's A&B concourse. The **Airport Shuttle** (☎ 504-522-3500; one way per person $15) runs to downtown hotels. The **Jefferson Transit** (☎ 504-818-1077; adult $1.60) airport route E2 picks up outside entrance 7 on the airport's upper level; it stops along Airline Hwy (Hwy 61) on its way into town (final stop Tulane and Loyola Aves). After 7pm it only goes to Tulane and Carrollton Aves in Mid-City; a solid 5 miles through a dreary neighborhood to get to the CBD, from here you must transfer to a Regional Transit Authority (RTA) bus – a haphazard transfer at best, especially with luggage.

Taxis downtown cost $28 for one or two people, $12 more for each additional passenger.

CAR & MOTORCYCLE

Bringing a car is a useful way of exploring beyond the Quarter; just be aware that parking in the Quarter is a hassle. Garages charge about $5 for the first hour and $20 for 24 hours.

PUBLIC TRANSPORTATION

The **Regional Transit Authority** (RTA; ☎ 504-248-3900; www.norta.com) runs the local bus service. Bus and streetcar fares are $1.25, plus 25¢ for transfers; express buses cost $1.50. Exact change is required. RTA Visitor Passes for one/three days cost $5/12.

The RTA also operates three streetcar lines. The historic St Charles streetcar is running only a short loop in the CBD due to hurricane damage to the Uptown tracks. The Canal streetcar makes a long journey up Canal St to City Park, with a spur on Carrollton Ave. The Riverfront line runs 2 miles along the levee from the Old US Mint, past Canal St, to the upriver convention center and back.

For a taxi, call **United Cabs** (☎ 504-522-9771) or **White Fleet Cabs** (☎ 504-822-3800).

Rent bicycles at **Bicycle Michael's** (☎ 504-945-9505; www.bicyclemichaels.com; 622 Frenchmen St; rentals per day $25; 10am-7pm Mon, Tue & Thu-Sat, to 5pm Sun), in Faubourg Marigny.

AROUND NEW ORLEANS

Leaving gritty, colorful New Orleans quickly catapults you into a world of swamps, bayous, antebellum plantation homes and laid-back small communities. A foray into these lesser-known environs makes for an off-the-beaten-path adventure.

The North Shore

Bedroom communities sprawl along **Lake Ponchartrain's** north shore, but head north of Mandeville, and you'll reach the bucolic village of **Abita Springs**, which was popular in the late 1800s for its curative waters. Today, the springwater still flows from a fountain in the center of the village, but the primary liquid attraction here is the **Abita Brew Pub** (☎ 985-892-5837; www.abitabrewpub.com; 7201 Holly St; tours free; 11am-9pm Tue-Fri, to 10pm Sat), where you can choose from nine Abita beers on tap that are made a mile west of town at **Abita Brewery** (☎ 985-893-3143; www.abita.com; 21084 Hwy 36; tours free; tours 2pm Wed-Fri, 11am, noon & 1pm Sat).

Other local libations can be found on Hwy 1082, where you'll encounter Louisiana's finest wines at **Ponchartrain Vineyards** (☎ 985-892-9742; www.pontchartrainvineyards.com; 81250 Old Military Rd; tasting room noon-4pm Wed-Sun). It's a pleasant surprise that tends to diverge from the syrupy sweet wines usually produced down South. To the south, **Covington** has a worthwhile downtown with funky antique shops.

The 31-mile **Tammany Trace trail** (www.tammanytrace.org) connects north shore towns, beginning in Covington, passing through Abita Springs and **Fontainebleau State Park** (☎ 504-624-4443), on the lakeshore near Mandeville, and

SWAMP TOURS

You haven't experienced Louisiana unless you've been out on its waterways, and the easiest way to do it is to join a swamp tour. Arrange them from New Orleans or go on your own and contract directly with a bayou-side company.

Annie Miller's Son's Swamp & Marsh Tours (985-868-4758; www.annie-miller.com; 3718 Southdown Mandalay Rd, Houma; adult/child $15/10;) The son of legendary swamp guide Annie Miller has taken up his mom's tracks.

Westwego Swamp Adventures (504-581-4501; www.westwegoswampadventures.com; 501 Laroussini St, Westwego; adult/child with transport $48/24;) One of the closest to New Orleans, it can pick you up in the Quarter.

terminating in Slidell. This converted railroad makes for a lovely bike ride that drops you into each town's center. In Mandeville, you can rent bikes at the **Kick Stand Café and Bike Rental** (985-626-9300; www.kickstand.bz; 690 Lafitte St; 8am-3pm Mon & Wed-Sat).

Barataria Preserve

This section of the **Jean Lafitte National Historical Park & Preserve**, south of New Orleans near the town of Marrero, provides the easiest access to the dense swamplands that ring New Orleans. The 8 miles of platform trails are a stunning way to tread lightly through the fecund, thriving swamp where you can check out gators and other fascinating plant life and creatures. The preserve is home to alligators, nutrias, tree frogs and hundreds of species of birds. It is well worth taking a ranger-led walk to learn about the many ecosystems that make up what are often lumped together as 'wetlands.'

Start at the **NPS Visitors Center** (504-589-2330; Hwy 3134; admission free; 9am-5pm;), 1 mile west of Hwy 45 off the Barataria Blvd exit, where you can pick up a map or join a guided walk or canoe trip (most Saturday mornings and monthly on full-moon nights; call to reserve a spot). The center has informational exhibits and a 25-minute documentary on swampland habitats. To rent canoes or kayaks for a tour or an independent paddle, go to **Bayou Barn** (504-689-2663; www.bayoubarn.net; canoes per person $20, 1-person kayak per day $25; 10am-6pm Thu, Fri & Sun, from 8:45am Sat) on the Bayou de Familles just outside the park entrance. This pleasantly funky restaurant compound of tin-topped buildings hosts occasional Sunday Cajun or zydeco dances (admission $5).

River Road

Elaborate plantation homes dot the east and west banks of the Mississippi River between New Orleans and Baton Rouge. First indigo, then cotton and sugarcane, brought great wealth to these plantations, many of which are open to the public. Most tours focus on the lives of the plantation owners, the restored architecture and the ornate gardens of antebellum Louisiana, and they skip over the story of plantation slaves who made up the majority of the plantations' population. It's easy to explore the area by car or organized tour. For a funky, truly entertaining tour, hook up with Mark Armstrong of **Tiger Taxi and Tours** (225-921-9199). He's 'always on the prowl.'

Destrehan (985-764-8785; www.destrehanplantation.org) and **San Francisco** (985-535-2341; www.sanfranciscoplantation.org) plantations on the east bank are closest to New Orleans, but far and away the most dynamic and informative tour is at **Laura Plantation** (225-265-7690; www.lauraplantation.com; 2247 Hwy 18; adult/child $15/5; 10am-4pm) in Vacherie on the west bank. This ever-evolving and popular tour teases out the distinctions between Creole, Anglo and African American antebellum life via meticulous research and the written records of the Creole women who ran the place for generations.

Also in Vacherie, the most impressive aspect of **Oak Alley Plantation** (225-265-2151; www.oakalleyplantation.com; 3645 Hwy 18; adult/child $10/5; 9am-4:40pm) is its canopy of 28 majestic live oaks lining the entry to the grandiose Greek Revival–style house. The tour is relatively staid, but there are guest cottages and a restaurant on-site.

Be sure to flesh out any plantation tour with a visit to the **River Road African American Museum** (225-474-5553; www.africanamericanmuseum.org; 406 Charles St; museum $4; 10am-5pm Wed-Sat, from 1pm Sun), 25 miles further along in Donaldsonville. This excellent museum preserves the important history of African Americans in the rural communities along the Mississippi. Exhibits chronicle plantation slavery; the journey to freedom via the Underground Railroad, and the lives of free African American people. **Donaldsonville** itself was a prosperous city for African Americans after the Civil War and the site of the original African American Mardi Gras.

Closer to Baton Rouge, in White Castle, the striking **Nottoway Plantation** (☎ 225-545-2730; www.nottoway.com; 30970 Hwy 405; adult/child $10/5; 9am-5pm) is the largest plantation house in the South. The high ceilings, entirely white ballroom, and lavish furnishing time-warp you straight back to opulent antebellum days. Staying overnight, you essentially get the run of this intriguing place after the last tour. Rooms in the mansion proper are grandest (doubles in mansion from $195, singles/doubles in outbuildings from $155/180); rates include a gigantic breakfast and a tour.

Baton Rouge

In 1699, French explorers named this area *baton rouge* (red stick) when they came upon a reddened cypress pole that Bayagoulas and Houma Native Americans had staked in the ground to mark the boundaries of their respective hunting territories. An industrial town with a bustling port and the state capital, formerly lethargic Baton Rouge has swollen in size as relocated New Orleanians settle post-Katrina. Visitors are mostly drawn to Baton Rouge for Louisiana State University (LSU) and Southern University (the largest historically African American university in the country).

Most attractions are downtown, off I-110 which intersects I-10 near the river. The downtown **visitor center** (☎ 800-527-6843; www.visitbatonrouge.com; 358 3rd St; 8am-5pm) has maps, brochures of local attractions, and festival schedules.

THE SOUTH

SIGHTS & ACTIVITIES

The art-deco skyscraper looming over town is the **Louisiana State Capitol** (☎ 225-342-7317; tours free; 8am-4:30pm) on aptly named State Capitol Dr. Built at the height of the Great Depression to the tune of $5 million, it's populist governor 'Kingfish' Huey Long's most visible legacy. The 27th-floor **observation deck** has a great view. The neo-Gothic, pink fairy-tale-castle-like **Old State Capitol** (☎ 225-342-0500; 100 North Blvd; admission free; 9am-4:30pm Mon-Sat, from noon Sun) makes you think Governor Bobby Jindal is going to 'throw down his long hair' to Louisianans. It houses exhibits about the state's colorful political history. Across the street, the **LSU Museum of Art** (☎ 225-389-7200; www.lsumoa.com; 100 Lafayette St; adult/child $8/4; 10am-5pm Tue-Sat, to 8pm Thu, 1-5pm Sun) holds a small exhibit, the highlight being about Louisiana 'Old and New.'

The **Louisiana Arts & Science Museum** (☎ 225-344-5272; www.lasm.org; 100 S River Rd; adult/child $6/5, with planetarium show $8/7; 10am-4pm Tue-Fri, to 8pm Sat, 1-5pm Sun;) houses interesting arts and natural-history installations and offers planetarium shows. If you just want a good stretch of the legs, there's a pleasant **pedestrian/bike path** along the Mississippi River, stretching 2.5 miles from the downtown promenade to LSU.

Just east of town at I-10 and Highland Rd, kids will love the respective amusement and water park, **Dixie Landin** and **Blue Bayou** (☎ 225-753-3333; www.bluebayou.com; adult/child $35/28;); check the online calendar for opening hours.

SLEEPING & EATING

Stockade Bed & Breakfast (☎ 225-769-7358; www.thestockade.com; 8860 Highland Rd; r incl breakfast from $150; P) Chain hotels line the sides of I-10, but for a more intimate stay, try this homey place, which manages to be comfortable and elegant at the same time. Book ahead on weekends, especially during football season.

Main Street Market (501 Main St; mains $6; 7am-4pm Mon-Fri, to 2pm Sat) Head here for an array of fresh, organic sandwiches, salads, sushi and pastries. Good range for vegetarians. A few local artisans sell their work here as well.

Schlittz & Giggles (☎ 225-218-4271; www.schlittz.com; 301 3rd St; pizzas $17; 11am-2am Mon-Sat, to midnight Sun) The name has so many layers of wrongness, but people crowd this downtown, late-night joint for well-touted pizza and cheap beer.

Buzz Café (☎ 225-706-1236; www.thebuzzcafe.org; 340 Florida St; 7:30am-3pm Mon-Fri;) For an awesome cup of joe at a funky coffee shop in a historic building, try the Buzz.

ENTERTAINMENT

Varsity Theatre (☎ 225-383-7018; www.varsitytheatre.com; 3353 Highland Rd; 8pm-2am) At the gates of LSU, you'll find live music here, often on weeknights. The attached restaurant boasts an extensive beer selection and a raucous college crowd.

Boudreaux and Thiboudeux (☎ 225-636-2442; www.myspace.com/boudreauxdowntown; 214 3rd St) Try this place downtown for live music and a great upstairs patio.

GETTING THERE & AROUND

Baton Rouge lies 80 miles west of New Orleans on I-10. **Baton Rouge Metropolitan Airport** (BTR; ☎ 225-355-0333; www.flybtr.com) is north of town off I-110. **Greyhound** (☎ 225-383-3811; 1253 Florida Blvd, at N 12th St) has regular buses to New Orleans, Lafayette and Atlanta, GA. **Capitol Area Transit System** (CATS; ☎ 225-389-8282; www.brcats.com) operates buses around town.

St Francisville

North of Baton Rouge, the lush town of St Francisville and its neighboring plantations have historically been, and continue to be, a lovely respite from the heat of the Delta. During the antebellum decade, it was home to plantation millionaires, and much of their architecture is still intact. Its lazy tree-lined streets are worthy of a stroll.

Tourist Information (☎ 225-635-4224; www.stfrancisville.us; 11757 Ferdinand St) provides helpful information about the numerous plantations open for view in the area, many of which offer B&B services.

SIGHTS & ACTIVITIES

Myrtles Plantation (☎ 225-635-6277, 800-809-0565; www.myrtlesplantation.com; 7747 US Hwy 61 N; 9am-4:30pm, tours 6pm, 7pm & 8pm Fri & Sat) is an especially notable B&B because supposedly it's haunted, and it has night mystery tours on the weekend. We heard secondhand corroboration of the supernatural presence, so it might be fun to stay overnight (rooms from $115) to commune with the other world. In town, stroll down historic **Royal St** to catch a glimpse of antebellum homes and buildings turned homes. The visitor center has pamphlets that lead you on self-guided tours.

Tunica Falls (☎ 225.635.4221; tourism@stfrancisville.us), which is technically called Clark Creek Nature Area, is about half an hour away from St Francisville. The pleasant, hilly trails wind you past lovely waterfalls. Crude maps can be found at the visitor center and also at the general store in Pond, MS (at Hwys 24 and 969), the town in which you park, where the trailhead is located.

SLEEPING & EATING

our pick **Tourist Court** (☎ 225-721-7003; 5689 Commerce St; 1-/2-bed cabins $75/150; P) One of the oldest motor inns in the United States (started in the 1930s and on the National Register of Historic Places), these five units bring you back to simpler times. Rooms have period decorations and fixtures, but are comfy and almost adorable. Plus, the price is fantastic for St Francisville, and the location, next to the Magnolia Café, can't be beat.

Shadetree Inn Bed and Breakfast (☎ 225-635-6116; www.shadetreeinn.com; 5695 Commerce St; r from $145; P) Sidled up against the historic district and a bird sanctuary, this well-reputed B&B has a gorgeous flower-strewn, hammock-hung courtyard for its guests. Appetizers, cocktails and a deluxe continental breakfast can all be served in your room.

Magnolia Café (☎ 225-635-6502; www.themagnoliacafe.com; 5687 Commerce St; 11am-4pm Sun-Wed, to 9pm Thu-Sat) The nucleus of what's happening in St Francisville, the Magnolia Café used to be a health-food store/VW bus repair shop. Now it's where people go to eat, socialize and dance to live music on Friday night.

Birdman Coffee and Books (☎ 225-635-3665; 5695 Commerce St; 7-11am Mon-Fri, from 8am Sat & Sun, coffeehouse to 6pm daily) Right in front of the Magnolia Café lies the Birdman, which is known for its breakfasts (old-fashioned yellow grits, homemade pastries, etc) and nice folks.

CAJUN COUNTRY

One of the truly unique parts of the US, Acadiana is named for French settlers exiled from L'Acadie (now Nova Scotia, Canada) by the British in 1755. As they lived alongside Native Americans and Creoles, 'Acadian' eventually morphed into 'Cajun.' The harrowing journey to Louisiana and the fight for survival in its swamplands are points of cultural pride for modern-day Cajuns, and do a lot to explain their combination of toughness and absolute ease.

Cajuns are the largest French-speaking minority in the US – prepare to hear it on radios and in the sing-song lilt of their English. While Lafayette is the nexus of Acadiana, getting out and around the waterways, villages and ramshackle roadside taverns really drops you straight into Cajun living. It's hard to find a bad meal here; jambalaya (rice-based dish with tomatoes, sausage and shrimp) and crawfish étouffée (a thick Cajun stew) are prepared slowly with pride (and cayenne!), and if folks aren't fishing, then they are probably dancing. Don't expect to sit on the sidelines…*allons danson* (let's dance).

Lafayette

Lafayette is an unsung jewel, especially if you like to shake your moneymaker. Surprisingly, its incredibly vibrant music scene remains relatively under the radar. Around town, bands are rocking most any night, and you'll drink a beer next to genuine, life-lovin', laid-back folks looking for a dance or to kick back and appreciate the show. Although Lafayette has been blighted by sprawl and its accompanying traffic, the historic downtown and surrounding small-town Acadiana also add to Lafayette's appeal.

At the free and fabulous **Festival International de Louisiane** (www.festivalinternational.com), hundreds of local and international artists rock out for five days in April.

From I-10, exit 103A, the Evangeline Thruway (Hwy 167) goes to the center of town via the **visitor center** (☎ 337-232-3737, 800-346-1958; www.lafayettetravel.com; 1400 NW Evangeline Thruway; 🕒 8:30am-5pm Mon-Fri, from 9am Sat & Sun).

SIGHTS & ACTIVITIES

In the heart of downtown, the **Acadiana Center for the Arts** (☎ 337-233-7060; www.acadianacenterforthearts.org; 101 W Vermilion St; adult/child/student $5/2/3; 🕒 10am-5pm Tue-Fri, to 6pm Sat) maintains three chic galleries and hosts dynamic theater, lectures and special events.

The best NPS museum in Cajun Country is the **Acadian Cultural Center** (☎ 337-232-0789; 501 Fisher Rd; admission free; 🕒 8am-5pm), near the airport. Next door, tranquil **Vermilionville** (☎ 337-233-4077; www.vermilionville.org; 300 Fisher Rd; adult/student $8/5; 🕒 10am-4pm Tue-Sun; ♿), a restored/re-created 19th-century Cajun village, wends along the bayou. Friendly, costumed docents explain Cajun, Creole and Native American history; local bands perform most Sundays. They also offer very affordable Cajun **cooking classes**, and rangers guide **boat tours** (☎ 337-233-4077; adult/child $11/8; 🕒 10:30am & noon Tue-Sat Mar-May & Sep-Nov) of Bayou Vermilion.

Just south of Girard Park, the sleek **University Art Museum** (☎ 337-482-1369; museum.louisiana.edu; 710 E St Mary Blvd; adult/youth $5/3; 🕒 10am-5pm Tue-Sat) hosts beautifully curated exhibits, often with an educational bent.

SLEEPING & EATING

Chains clump near exits 101 and 103, off I-10 (doubles from $65). Head to Jefferson Street in downtown to take your choice of bars and restaurants, from sushi to Mexican.

Blue Moon Guest House (☎ 337-234-2422, 877-766-2583; www.bluemoonguesthouse.com; 215 E Convent St; dm $18, r $70-90; P ⊠ ✵ 💻 wi-fi) Not for the faint of heart, a bed in this tidy old home, which is walking distance from downtown, includes admission to Lafayette's popular down-home music venue, located in the backyard. The friendly owners, full kitchen, and camaraderie among guests create a casual hangout environment. Prices skyrocket during festival time.

Juliet (☎ 337-261-2225; www.juliethotel.com; 800 Girard Jefferson; r from $125; P ⊠ ✵ 💻 wi-fi) Right in the heart of Lafayette's downtown resides this new boutique hotel that has simple, elegant rooms that focus on comfort, not show. Great deal.

Pamplona Tapas Bar (☎ 337-232-0070; www.pamplonatapas.com; 631 Jefferson St; tapas from $3; 🕒 8am-10pm Mon-Fri, 9am-7pm Sat) A bit more upscale, this place has an amazing Spanish wine selection and delicious plates, like flatbread topped with roasted pig, figs, shallots and blue cheese.

Artmosphere (☎ 337-233-3331; www.myspace.com/artmosphere; 902 Johnston St; mains $5-8; 🕒 5pm-2am Mon-Sat, to midnight Sun; wi-fi) Your place if you're jonesing for vegan/vegetarian food, or even just a hookah. There is a variety of live music every night.

Old Tyme Grocery (☎ 337-235-8165; 218 W St Mary St; po'boys $7; 🕒 8am-10pm Mon-Fri, 9am-7pm Sat) Has famous shrimp or roast beef po'boys (sandwiches).

ENTERTAINMENT

To find out what's playing around town, pick up the free weekly **Times** (www.thetimesofacadiana.com) or **Independent** (www.theind.com).

our pick **Blue Moon Saloon** (☎ 337-234-2422, 877-766-2583; www.bluemoonpresents.com; 215 E Convent St; cover $5-8) The employees are happy, the patrons are happy, the musicians are happy, the dancers are happy. What don't you love about this small, welcoming spot?

Lafayette specializes in big ol' dance halls that offer one-stop entertainment, dancing and local cuisine. Standout Cajun music and dance joints include **Mulate's** (☎ 337-

THE SOUTH

332-4648; 325 Mills Ave, Breaux Bridge) on the way to Breaux Bridge, **Randol's** (☎ 337-981-7080; www.randols.com; 2320 Kaliste Saloom Rd, Lafayette; 🕑 5-10pm Sun-Thu, to 11pm Fri & Sat), south of town, and **Prejean's** (☎ 337-896-3247; www.prejeans.com; 3480 NE Evangeline Thruway/I-49, North Lafayette), 2 miles north of town.

GETTING THERE & AWAY

Greyhound (☎ 337-235-1541; 315 Lee Ave) operates from a hub beside the central commercial district, making 12 runs daily to New Orleans (3½ hours) and Baton Rouge (one hour). **Amtrak's** (133 E Grant St) *Sunset Limited* goes to New Orleans three times a week.

Cajun Wetlands

In 1755, *le Grande Dérangement,* the British expulsion of the rural French settlers from Acadiana, created a homeless population of Acadians who searched for decades for a place to settle. In 1785, seven boatloads of exiles arrived in New Orleans. By the early 19th century, 3000 to 4000 Acadians occupied the swamplands southwest of New Orleans. Native American tribes such as the Attakapas helped them learn to eke out a living based upon fishing and trapping, and the aquatic way of life is still the backdrop to modern living.

East and south of Lafayette, the **Atchafalaya Basin** is the preternatural heart of the Cajun wetlands. Stop in to the **Atchafalaya Welcome Center** (☎ 337-228-1094; Butte La Rose; 🕑 8:30am-5pm), at Exit 121 from I-10, to learn how to penetrate the dense jungle protecting these swamps, lakes and bayous from the casual visitor. They'll fill you in on camping in **Indian Bayou** and exploring the **Sherburne Wildlife Management Area**, as well as the exquisitely situated **Lake Fausse Pointe State Park**.

Eleven miles east of Lafayette in the sleepy town of **Breaux Bridge**, you'll find **Café des Amis** (☎ 337-332-5273; 140 E Bridge St; lunch $12-15, dinner $14-22; 🕑 11am-2pm Tue, to 9pm Wed & Thu, 7:30am-9:30pm Fri & Sat, 8am-2:30pm Sun), where you can relax amid funky local art, as waiters trot out sumptuous breakfasts. If you just want good coffee, friendly folks, and wi-fi, the **Coffee Break** (☎ 337-342-3334; 109 N Main St; 🕑 7am-7pm; wi-fi) is your place.

Check out the friendly **Tourist Center** (☎ 337-332-8500; www.breauxbridgelive.com; 318 E Bridge St; 🕑 8am-4pm Mon-Fri, to noon Sat), who can hook you up with one of numerous B&Bs in town, like tidy **Maison des Amis** (☎ 337-507-3399; www.maisondesamis.com; 111 Washington St; r $100-125; P ⊠ ✤ wi-fi) right along Bayou Teche. If you're in town the first week of May, don't miss the gluttony of music, dancing, and Cajun food at the **Crawfish Festival** (www.bbcrawfest.com).

Tiny **St Martinville** (www.stmartinville.org), 15 miles southeast of Lafayette, packs a mighty punch. Within one block of the bayou in the town center, visit the **African American Museum & Acadian Memorial** (☎ 337-394-2258; www.acadianmemorial.org; adult/child $3/free; 🕑 10am-4pm) to learn about the diasporas of both Cajuns and African Americans.

One mile north of the town center, **Longfellow-Evangeline State Historic Site** (☎ 337-394-3754; 1200 N Main St; adult/child $2/free; 🕑 9am-5pm) explains the nuances of Creole and Acadian history, and gives tours of its restored Creole cottage and farmstead.

Drive southwest of New Iberia along Hwy 329 through cane fields to lush and lovely **Avery Island**, home of **McIlhenny Tabasco** (☎ 337-365-8173; tours free; 🕑 9am-5pm) and its excellent **wildlife sanctuary** (adult/child $6.25/4.50). The beautiful, manicured paths around the island actually cover a salt dome that extends 8 miles below the surface. Even though the air smells lightly of Tabasco, alligators and egrets bask in the protected sunshine – bring a lunch and mosquito repellant.

Historic **Abbeville**, 21 miles southwest of Lafayette, carries the mantle of best oysters in Louisiana. If you are a devotee of the fat, salty bivalve, make the pilgrimage to **Dupuy's Oyster Shop** (☎ 337-893-2339; www.dupuysoystershop.com; 108 S Main St; 🕑 11am-2pm & 5-9pm Tue-Thu, 11am-2pm & 5-10pm Fri, 5-10pm Sat) or one of its worthy rivals.

If you happen to be on Hwy 90, **Thibodaux** (pronounced ti-ba-doh) has another NPS museum, the **Wetlands Acadian Cultural Center** (☎ 985-448-1375; 314 St Mary St; admission free; 🕑 9am-7pm Mon-Tue, to 6pm Wed-Thu, to 5pm Fri & Sat). Exhibits cover virtually every aspect of wetlands life, from music to the environmental impacts of oil exploration. Musicians jam here Monday evenings (5:30pm) and rangers guide seasonal boat tours.

Cajun Prairie

Think: dancing cowboys! Cajun and African American settlers to the higher, drier terrain north of Lafayette developed a culture based around animal husbandry and farming, and the ten-gallon hat still rules. It's also the hotbed of Cajun and zydeco music (and thus accordions), and crawfish farming.

Opelousas squats sleepily alongside Hwy 49, and its historic downtown is home to the esoteric **Museum & Interpretive Center** (☎ 337-948-2589; 315 N Main St; admission free; ⏲ 9am-5pm Mon-Sat); check out the doll collection.

The top zydeco joints in Acadiana, **Slim's Y-Ki-Ki** (☎ 337-942-6242; www.slimsykiki.com; Hwy 182 N), a few miles north on Main St, across from the Piggly Wiggly, and **Richard's** (☎ 337-543-8233; 11178 Hwy 190), 8 miles west in Lawtell, strike it up most weekends. Wear your dancing shoes and don't be afraid to sweat!

Plaisance, northwest of Opelousas, hosts the grassroots, fun-for-the-family **Southwest Louisiana Zydeco Festival** (☎ 337-232-7672; www.zydeco.org) in August.

In **Eunice** (www.eunice-la.com) there's the Saturday-night 'Rendez-Vous des Cajuns' at the **Liberty Theater** (☎ 337-546-0007; 200 Park Ave; adult/child $5/3), which is broadcast on local radio. In fact, visitors are welcome all day at **KBON** (☎ 337-546-0007; www.kbon.com; 109 S 2nd St), 101.1FM. Browse the capacious Wall of Fame, signed by visiting musicians. Two blocks away, the **Cajun Music Hall of Fame & Museum** (☎ 337-367-1526; www.cajunfrenchmusic.org) caters to the die-hard music buff, and the NPS runs the **Prairie Acadian Cultural Center** (☎ 337-457-8490; cnr 3rd St & Park Ave; admission free; ⏲ 8am-5pm Tue-Fri, to 6pm Sat) with interesting exhibits on swamp life and Cajun culture, and showing a variety of documentaries explaining the history of the area.

If all this leaves you in need of a respite, try centrally located **Potier's Cajun Inn** (☎ 337-457-0440; 110 W Park Ave; r $65, incl breakfast $75; P ⊠ ✜) for a simple, down-home-Cajun-style cozy room with a kitchenette, or **Ruby's Café** (☎ 337-550-7665; 221 W Walnut Ave; meals $4-7; ⏲ 6am-2pm Mon-Fri, from 7am Sun) for popular plate lunches in a '50s diner setting.

Though **Mamou** has a great name, the main thing the town's got going for it is **Fred's Lounge** (☎ 337-468-5411; 420 6th St), with its Saturday-morning live Cajun band and charming country waltzes.

CANE RIVER COUNTRY

The central part of the state is a crossroads of Louisiana's distinct cultures, politics and religions, with bilingual French Catholic and Franco African people along the Cane River, and monolingual, chiefly Protestant residents to the north. Hwy 119 meanders alongside the Cane River. You'll pass locals dipping fishing poles into the lazy water or whiling away the day on front-porch rockers.

Melrose Plantation (☎ 318-379-0055; I-49, exit 119; adult/child $7/3; ⏲ noon-4pm Tue-Sun) is a complex of interesting buildings built by a family of free people of color headed by Marie Therese Coincoin. The early-20th-century owner, Cammie Henry, housed artists and writers such as William Faulkner and Sherwood Anderson in the 1796 Yucca House. Congo-style Africa House contains a vivid 50ft mural depicting plantation life by Clementine Hunter, the renowned folk artist. Hunter had been a field hand and cook at Melrose before picking up a paintbrush at age 50. The nearby **Kate Chopin House** (☎ 318-379-2233; 243 Hwy 495, Cloutierville) was the author's residence while she wrote *The Awakening*.

Natchitoches

A bit further north you'll find French architecture in historic Natchitoches (mysteriously pronounced *nak*-id-esh), which is split scenically by the Cane River and is the oldest permanent settlement in the Louisiana Purchase. It gained significant notoriety after Hollywood filmmakers arrived in 1988 to film the blockbuster movie *Steel Magnolias*. Head to the **Visitor Bureau** (☎ 800-259-1714; www.natchitoches.net; 781 Front St; adult/child $7/3; ⏲ noon-4pm Tue-Sun) for information about the tours of Creole plantation estates and the numerous B&Bs in town.

Not to be missed is the Natchitoches meat pie famously served by **Lasyone's** (☎ 318-352-3353; www.lasyones.com; 622 Second St; meat pies $3.50; ⏲ 7am-3pm Mon-Sat). The meat pie's heritage dates back to the 1800s when African American youngsters sold them from street corners. Today this crispy fried savory remains ever-popular, with Lasyone's at the epicenter. Don't overlook the crawfish pies or other delectable Southern dishes on the menu.

If you don't want to stay in one of the many B&Bs in town, the 20-room **Church Street Inn** (☎ 318-238-8890; www.churchstinn.com; 120 Church St; r incl breakfast from $99; P ⊠ ✜ ☰) is a solid option. From here, you can stroll to downtown eateries and shops then cozy up in your room or do yoga on the communal balcony.

Right in the thick of this densely forested and sparsely populated part of Louisiana, just a short drive from Natchitoches, is the gorgeous **Kisatchie National Forest** (☎ 318-352-2568), 937 sq miles of hilly Southern yellow pine and hardwood. Trails aren't incredibly well maintained, as they are mostly used by hunters in the hunting season, but there are opportunities to mountain bike, hike, swim, and go on scenic drives. It's especially splendid during the shoulder seasons. Bring repellent in summer.

NORTHERN LOUISIANA

Make no mistake: the rural, oil-industry towns along the Baptist Bible Belt make northern Louisiana as far removed from New Orleans as Paris, TX, is from Paris, France. Even in the commercial center of Shreveport, in the far northwest corner of Louisiana, this is a region battling to find self-definition after decades of decline.

Captain Henry Shreve cleared a 165-mile logjam on the Red River and founded the river-port town of **Shreveport**, in 1839. The city boomed with oil discoveries in the early 1900s, but declined after WWII. Some revitalization came in the form of huge Vegas-sized casinos and a riverfront entertainment complex. The **visitor center** (☎ 318-222-9391, 800-458-4748; www.shreveport-bossier.org; 629 Spring St; ⌚ 8am-5pm Mon-Fri, 10am-2pm Sat) is downtown. If you're a rose-lover, it would be a shame to miss the **Gardens of the American Rose Center** (☎ 318-938-5402; www.ars.org; 8877 Sefferson Paige Rd; adult/child $4/$1.50; ⌚ 8am-5pm Mon-Fri, 10am-2pm Sat), which contains more than 65 individual gardens designed to show how roses can be grown in a home garden – take Exit 5 off the I-20. **Columbia Cafe** (☎ 318-425-3862; www.columbiacafe.com; 3030 Creswell St; ⌚ 7am-10pm Mon-Fri, from 10am Sat, 10am-2pm Sun) might entice you to stop and grab a bite. Eat outside on the patio or inside among local art. The Southern-influenced food is uncomplicated, nicely presented, and yummy.

About 50 miles northeast of Monroe on Hwy 557 near the town of Epps, the **Poverty Point State Historic Site** (☎ 318-926-5492, 888-926-5492; www.crt.state.la.us; 6859 Hwy 577, Pioneer; adult/child $2/free; ⌚ 9am-5pm) has a remarkable series of earthwork and mounds along what was once the Mississippi River. A two-story observation tower gives a view of the site's six concentric ridges. Around 1000 BC this was the hub of a civilization comprising hundreds of communities, with trading links as far north as the Great Lakes.

ARKANSAS

Tucked smack in the center of the US, hiding out between the Midwest and the Deep South, Arkansas is America's overlooked treasure. The natural areas are off the hook: the worn slopes of the Ozarks and the Ouachita (wash-*ee*-tah) mountains; clean, gushing rivers; and lakes bridged by crenellated granite and limestone outcroppings. The entire state is dotted with exceptionally well-done state parks and tiny, empty roads crisscrossing dense forests that let out onto surprising, sweeping vistas and gentle pastures dotted with grazing horses. Plus, the rural towns of Mountain View and Eureka Springs hold quirky charm. Don't be fooled by talk of Wal-Mart or backwoods culture. Though they all have a place here, it would be a shame to pass up an opportunity to visit this state.

History

Caddo, Osage and Quapaw Native Americans had permanent settlements here when Spaniard Hernando de Soto visited in the mid-1500s. Frenchman Henri de Tonti founded the first white settlement in 1686. After the 1803 Louisiana Purchase, Arkansas became a US territory, and slave-holding planters moved into the Delta to grow cotton. Poorer immigrants from Appalachia settled in the Ozark and Ouachita plateaus.

On the edge of the frontier, lawlessness persisted until the Civil War. Reconstruction was difficult, and development only came after 1870 with the expansion of railroads. Racial tension peaked in 1957, when the governor and irate whites tried to prevent nine African American students from attending Central High School in Little Rock. The federal government finally intervened, sending in the army.

The state has one of the lowest per-capita incomes in the US, with many poor African Americans in the Delta and poor whites in the Ozarks.

Information

Arkansas State Parks (☎ 888-287-2757; www.arkansasstateparks.com) Arkansas' well-reputed park system has 52 state parks, 28 offering camping ($10 to $27 depending on the amenities of the facility). A number of the parks offer lodge and cabin accommodations. Due to popularity, at many times reservations on weekends and holidays require multiday stay commitments.

Department of Parks & Tourism (☎ 501-682-7777, 800-628-8725; www.arkansas.com; 1 Capitol Mall, Little Rock) Sends out a vacation planning kit; ask for the excellent annual *State Parks Guide* and *Adventure Guide*.

LITTLE ROCK

Downtown Little Rock, strangled in the last several decades by parking lots and bad city planning, is now perking up a bit with the burgeoning River Market district. Across the river, North Little Rock, with a growing enclave of shops and restaurants, stretches alongside the extensive riverfront park. This conservative city definitely has some worthwhile things going on, but you just have to know where to look or it all might blur in strip-mall whiplash.

The town's **visitor center** (☎ 501-371-0075, 877-220-2568; www.littlerock.com; 615 E Capitol Ave; 7:30am-6:30pm) is housed in 1842 Curran Hall.

Sights

The best stroll is in the **River Market district** (☎ 501-375-2553; www.rivermarket.info), an area of shops, galleries, restaurants and pubs on W Markham St and President Clinton Ave along the riverbank. **Ottenheimer Market Hall** (btwn S Commerce & S Rock Sts; 7am-6pm Mon-Sat) houses an eclectic collection of food stalls and shops.

Just northwest of downtown, **Riverfront Park** rolls pleasantly along the Arkansas River and both pedestrians and cyclists take advantage of this fantastic city park daily. You can't miss the **Big Dam Bridge** (www.bigdambridge.com;), which is the largest bridge built specifically for pedestrians and cyclists in the United States; it connects 15 miles of multi-use trails in Little Rock and North Little Rock. For a proper perusal of Riverfront Park rent a bike (or tandem) from **River Trail Rentals** (☎ 501-374-5505; www.rivertrailrentals.com; 200 S Olive St; per hr/day from $6.50/30; 8-11am Mon-Fri, 1-8pm Tue, Thu, Fri & Sun) – outside opening hours you can call for a reservation. Otherwise **Chainwheel** (☎ 501-224-7651; www.chainwheel.com; 10300 Rodney Parham Rd; 10am-7pm Mon-Fri, to 5pm Sat) is the best bike shop in town and can rent higher-end road or mountain bikes, depending on availability.

The **Hillcrest Neighborhood** toward west Little Rock is a tiny epicenter of cafés and funky shops and is a communing ground for minority strains of counterculture in the city.

> **ARKANSAS FACTS**
>
> **Nickname** Natural State
> **Population** 2.9 million
> **Area** 52,068 sq miles
> **Capital city** Little Rock (population 184,450)
> **Other cities** Fayetteville (population 58,000)
> **Sales tax** 6%, plus 2% visitors tax and local taxes
> **Birthplace of** General Douglas MacArthur (1880–1964), musician Johnny Cash (1932–2003), former President Bill Clinton (b 1946), author John Grisham (b 1955), actor Billy Bob Thornton (b 1955)
> **Home of** Wal-Mart
> **Famous for** Football fans 'calling the Hogs'
> **Official state instrument** Fiddle
> **Driving distance** Little Rock to Eureka Springs 182 miles, Eureka Springs to Mountain View 123 miles

The **William J Clinton Presidential Center** (☎ 501-374-4242; www.clintonpresidentialcenter.com; 1200 President Clinton Ave; adult/child $7/3; 9am-5pm Mon-Sat, from 1pm Sun) houses the largest archival collection in presidential history, including 80 million pages of documents and two million photographs. Peruse the full-scale replica of the Oval Office, the exhibits on all stages of Clinton's life or the gifts from visiting dignitaries (such as Lance Armstrong's yellow jersey). The entire complex is built to environmentally friendly 'green' standards.

The **Old State House Museum** (☎ 501-324-9685; www.oldstatehouse.com; 300 W Markham St; admission free; 9am-5pm Mon-Sat, from 1pm Sun), the state capitol from 1836 to 1911, now holds impressively restored legislative chambers and displays on Arkansas history and culture.

Sleeping & Eating

Because of government and convention-center traffic, it's difficult to find inexpensive hotels in downtown, and rates fluctuate wildly. Budget motels lie off the interstates.

Rosemont (☎ 501-374-7456; www.rosemontoflittlerock.com; 515 W 15th St; s/d incl breakfast from $89-225;) In an 1880s restored farmhouse near the Governor's mansion, this place drips with cozy character.

Peabody Little Rock (☎ 501-906-4000, 800-723-2639; www.peabodylittlerock.com; 3 Statehouse Plaza; r from $149;) Sister to the famous Peabody Hotel in Memphis, TN, this one boasts a sleek marble lobby and luxed-out rooms overlooking the river. The hotel also re-creates the

Memphis Peabody's tradition of the Duck March (p422).

Ottenheimer Market Hall (☎ 501-375-2553; www.rivermarket.info; btwn S Commerce & S Rock Sts; 🕑 7am-6pm Mon-Sat) Trawl the stalls for some good-value breakfast or lunch – you'll find everything from fresh fruits and pastries, to sushi, burgers and BBQ.

Homer's (☎ 501-374-1400; www.homersrestaurant.com; 2001 East Roosevelt) Businessmen smoking stogies rub elbows with hunters in overalls and Air Force officers on break in this country-cooking venue famous for the under-the-table deals hatched under its roof. The chicken and dumplings and veggie plate are to die for.

Madea's Home Cooking (☎ 501-664-2230; 2801 W 7th St; 🕑 7am-6pm Mon-Sat; 🕑 11am-2pm Mon-Fri) It's the real deal. This tiny, bare-bones luncheonette serves delectable home-cooked chitterlings, purple-hull peas, and fried chicken, among other regional favorites.

Acadia (☎ 501-603.9630; www.acadiahillcrest.com; 3000 Kavanaugh Blvd; mains from $18; 🕑 5:30-10pm Mon-Sat) Situated in the Hillcrest neighborhood, Acadia's multilevel, twinkle-lighted patio is a fabulous place to enjoy fancy-shmancy Southern dishes like smoked Gouda mac 'n' cheese.

Getting There & Around

Little Rock National Airport (LIT; ☎ 501-372-3439; www.lrn-airport.com) lies just east of downtown. The **Greyhound station** (☎ 501-372-3007; 118 E Washington St), in North Little Rock, serves Hot Springs (one to two hours), Memphis, TN (2½ hours), and New Orleans, LA (18 hours). Amtrak occupies **Union Station** (☎ 501-372-6841; 1400 W Markham St). **Central Arkansas Transit** (CAT; ☎ 501-375-6717; www.cat.org) runs local buses; a trolley makes a loop on W Markham St and President Clinton Ave (adult/child 50/25¢).

HOT SPRINGS

It's a wonder that the little city of Hot Springs, with its strip malls, mini-golf suburbs and gasping downtown, hosted the vacationing elite of New York City's organized crime. At full throttle in the 1930s, the city was a hotbed of gambling, bootlegging, prostitution, opulence, and dangerous thugs. Yet it was also a spot of truce between warring gangs, a place where it was decreed that all criminals could be gluttonous hedons in peace. When gambling was squelched, so was the city's economy.

Though it still hasn't recovered from that blow, the healing waters have always drawn people, everyone from the Native American populations to present-day pilgrims. Elaborate restored bathhouses, where you can still get old-school spa treatments, line Bathhouse Row behind shady magnolias on the east side of Central Ave. Opposite, galleries, shops and restaurants pack 19th-century commercial buildings.

The other big draws are the horse races at **Oaklawn** (www.oaklawn.com; 🕑 Jan-Apr), close-by hiking opportunities, and water sports on nearby Lake Hamilton. For city information or to pick up a map of Clinton-related sites, go to the city's **visitor center** (☎ 501-321-2277, 800-772-2489; www.hotsprings.org; 629 Central Ave; 🕑 9am-6pm).

Sights & Activities

See the intriguing underbelly of Hot Springs' history at the **Gangster Museum** (☎ 501-318-1717; www.tgmoa.com; 113 Central Ave; admission $8; 🕑 10am-5pm Sun-Thu, to 8pm Fri & Sat), which explains the

LITTLE ROCK'S PUNK SCENE (YES, PUNK SCENE)

Starting in the '80s and cresting in the mid-'90s, Little Rock – much to the surprise and incredulity of everyone – nurtured a thriving, inclusive punk scene unlike any in the nation. Little Rock gave kids who didn't fit into the status quo ample boundaries and restrictions to rebel against, and they subsequently chose a screamingly creative outlet to express themselves. Though the movement has changed, the legacy and passion of musical ingenuity is still present today in this small community.

Check out music at **Max Recordings** (☎ 501-580-4341; www.maxrecordings.com; 1109 North Tyler), a record label started by then-16-year-old Burt Taggart, one of the originals of the movement. Its intention was to give voice to the bands and songwriters of Little Rock. Go to his website for info on music and shows in town, many of whom are at the **White Water Tavern** (☎ 501-375-8400; 2500 W 7th St; admission free; 🕑 to late Mon-Sat). Or check out the documentary **Towncraft** (www.towncraftmovie.com), which follows the Little Rock punk scene from its emergence to the present.

sin-filled glory days of Hot Springs when this small town in the middle of nowhere turned into a pinpoint of lavish wealth.

On Bathhouse Row in the 1915 Fordyce bathhouse, the **NPS visitor center** (☎ 501-624-2701; 369 Central Ave; ⏰ 9am-6pm) and **museum** (admission free) have exhibits about the park's history first as a Native American free-trade zone, and later as a turn-of-the-19th-century European spa.

A promenade runs through the park around the hillside behind Bathhouse Row, where some springs survive intact, and a network of trails covers Hot Springs' mountains. On the top of Hot Springs Mountain, the 216ft **Hot Springs Mountain Tower** (☎ 501-623-6035; adult/child $6/3; ⏰ 9am-9pm Apr-Oct, 9am-5pm Nov-Mar) has spectacular views of the surrounding mountains covered with dogwood, hickory, oak and pine – lovely in the spring and fall.

To test the curative waters, visit one of the resort hotels' spas, or **Buckstaff Bathhouse** (☎ 501-623-2308; www.buckstaffbaths.com; 509 Central Ave; thermal bath $24, with 20min massage $55; ⏰ 7-11:30am & 1:15-2:45pm Mon-Sat, 8-11:30am Sun), just south of the Fordyce. Note that spa service Hot Springs style is not usually a 'foofy' experience. No-nonsense Southern men and women whip you through the baths, treatments, and massages, just as in the 1930s.

National Park Duck Tours (☎ 501-321-2911; www.rideaduck.com; 418 Central Ave; adult/child $15/10; 👶) offers 75-minute amphibious-boat tours.

Sleeping & Eating

Chain motels line highways around town; the visitor center has a list of lakeside rental properties and area B&Bs. Some restaurants congregate along the Central Ave tourist strip and offer ho-hum food.

Gulpha Gorge Campground (☎ 501-620-6715; campsites $10) Two miles northeast of downtown off Hwy 70B, this campground offers attractive NPS campsites (no showers, hookups or reservations).

Alpine Inn (☎ 501-624-9164; www.alpine-inn-hot-springs.com; 741 Park Ave/Hwy 7 N; s/d from $50/60; P ⊠ ❄ 📶 🏊) The friendly owner of this inn, less than a mile from Bathhouse Row, tidily maintains a row of themed rooms like the golf room or the country-western room. Some have kitchenettes.

Arlington Resort Hotel & Spa (☎ 501-623-7771, 800-643-1502; www.arlingtonhotel.com; 239 Central Ave; r/ste from $80/$175; P ⊠ ❄ 📶 🏊) This imposing historic hotel tops Bathhouse Row and constantly references its glory days. The grand lobby tries to set the tone for the antique in-house spa and aging rooms. Catch a foxtrot on the weekend when there might be a live band.

McClard's (☎ 501-623-9665; www.mcclards.com; 505 Albert Pike; mains $6-14; ⏰ 11am-8pm Tue-Sat) Southwest of the center, Bill Clinton's favorite boyhood BBQ joint dishes up succulent ribs, slow-cooked beans and creamy slaw. This could be some of the South's best BBQ.

Cajun Boilers (☎ 501-767-5695; 2806 Albert Pike Rd; mains $8-20; ⏰ 11am-10pm Mon-Sat, to 9pm Sun) Right on Lake Hamilton, you can boat in or drive up. The outdoor patio is a fabulous setting to tear into the famous crawfish boil or a plate of frog's legs.

Getting There & Away

Greyhound (☎ 501-623-5574; 1001 Central Ave) has buses heading to Little Rock (1½ hours, twice daily).

AROUND HOT SPRINGS

The wild, pretty **Ouachita National Forest** (☎ 501-321-5202; welcome center 100 Reserve St, Hot Springs; ⏰ 8am-4:30pm) is studded with lakes and draws hunters, fisherfolk, mountain bikers and boaters. The small roads through the mountains unfailingly bring hidden nooks and wonderful views. The Ouachita boasts two designated National Forest Scenic Byways: Arkansas Scenic Highway 7 and Talimena Scenic Byway navigating mountain ranges from Arkansas into Oklahoma.

Nearby **Hot Springs National Park** (www.nps.gov/hosp; admission free), a tiny preserve, has thermal waters in and around that spout a million gallons of 143°F (62°C) water daily from 47 natural springs, and attract modern-day pilgrims that bathe in or sip its waters.

Clinton buffs might stop at **Hope**, where the ex-Pres spent his first seven years, but there's not much to see other than the spiffy **Hope Visitor Center & Museum** (☎ 870-722-2580, 800-233-4673; www.hopearkansas.net; 100 E Division St; ⏰ 8:30am-5pm Mon-Fri, from 9am Sat, 1-3pm Sun), in the old depot, and his boyhood home.

If you're wanting to test your luck and diamond-spotting skills, head to **Crater of Diamonds State Park** (☎ 870-285-3113; www.craterofdiamondsstatepark.com; 209 State Park Rd; ⏰ 8:30am-5pm Mon-Fri, from 9am Sat, 1-3pm Sun), where you can scour the diamond field in which three- to 40-carat diamonds have been found, and where valuable diamonds continue to be found today.

ARKANSAS RIVER VALLEY

The Arkansas River cuts a swath across the state from Oklahoma to Mississippi. Folks come to fish, canoe and camp along its banks and tributaries.

The excellently maintained trails of **Petit Jean State Park** (☎ 501-727-5441; www.petitjeanstatepark.com;), west of Morrilton, wind past a lush 95ft waterfall, romantic grottoes, expansive vistas, and dense forests. There's a rustic stone lodge, reasonable cabins (per night $75), and campgrounds. Another stellar state park is **Mount Magazine** (☎ 479-963-8502; www.mountmagazinestatepark.com; 16878 Hwy 309 S, Paris), which maintains 14 miles of trails around Arkansas' highest point. Outdoor enthusiasts enjoy stellar hang gliding and rock climbing here as well as hiking.

Arkansas has both a pickle capital (not surprising – **Atkins**), and a wine capital (surprising – **Altus**), which is at the center of Arkansas' Germanic wine-growing region. In Altus, you'll find a smattering of wineries that let you taste their sticky-sweet concoctions, like muscadine wine, that were heaven-sent during Prohibition. Two of the most notable for tastings are **Post Familie Vineyard** (☎ 479-468-2741; 1700 St Mary's Mountain Rd; 9:30am-6pm Mon-Sat, noon-5pm Sun) and **Wiederkehr Wine Cellars** (☎ 479-468-9463; 3324 Swiss Family Dr; 8:30am-9pm Mon-Sat, noon-6pm Sun), which has an attached restaurant where the servers were described by one tourist as 'depressed grandmothers stuffed into lederhosen.'

While you're in town, **Kelt's** (☎ 479-468-2413; 115 W Main St; mains $15-24; 11am-10pm Mon-Sat, 11am-3:30pm Sun) might be the better bet, with its full line of rich beers, and spoken menu of, among other things, home-cooked rib-eye steaks. It's a self-declared 'guilt-free zone.'

The spectacular **Highway 23/Pig Trail Byway**, lined with wild echinacea and lilies, climbs up through **Ozark National Forest** (☎ 479-968-2354) and into the mountains; an excellent way to reach Eureka Springs (p498).

The **Arkansas and Missouri Railway** (☎ 479-751-8600, 800-687-8600; www.arkansasmissouri-rr.com; adult/child from $31/16; Fri & Sat Apr-Sep, Sat Oct-Nov) offers a 70-mile trip through the Boston Mountain Range from **Van Buren** to **Winslow** and back.

OZARK MOUNTAINS

Stretching from northwest and central Arkansas into Missouri, the **Ozark Mountains** (☎ 870-404-2741, 800-544-6867; www.ozarkmountainregion.com) are an ancient range, once surrounded by sea and now well worn by time. Verdant rolling mountains give way to misty fields, and dramatic karst formations line sparkling lakes, meandering rivers and scenic back roads. Though some of the towns bank on kitschy hillbilly culture, scratch below the surface to find the unique cultural traditions, such as acoustic folk music and home-cooked hush puppies and catfish.

Mountain View

Detour east of US 65 or along Hwy 5 to this wacky Ozark town, known for its tradition of informal music-making at Courtsquare. Creeping commercialism is taking its toll, as the **Chamber of Commerce** (☎ 870-269-8068; www.yourplaceinthemountains.com; 107 N Peabody Ave; 9am-4:30pm Mon-Fri, 10am-2pm Sat) promotes the place as the 'Folk Music Capital of the World,' but loads of live folk-music and bizarre festivals keep it real, including the **Championship Outhouse Races**, where crowds cheer on their favorite 'people-powered potty' racing to the finish line – it usually takes place around the last week in October.

Ozark Folk Center State Park (☎ 870-269-3851; auditorium adult/child $10/6; 10am-5pm Wed-Sat, to 5:30pm Sat & Sun), just north of town, hosts ongoing craft demonstrations, a traditional herb garden, as well as nightly live music that brings in an avid, older crowd. Mountain View is known for its impromptu hill music, gospel, and bluegrass jam sessions in the **Courtsquare** by the Stone County Courthouse, especially on Saturday night.

The spectacular **Blanchard Springs Caverns** (☎ 888-757-2246; off Hwy 14; adult/child $10/5, wild cave tour $75; 9am-6pm Apr-Sep;), located 15 miles northwest of Mountain View, were carved by an underground river and rival those at Carlsbad (see p908). It's another little-known, mind-blowing spot in Arkansas. Three Forest Service guided tours range from disabled-accessible to adventurous three- to four-hour spelunking sessions. **Wildflower B&B** (☎ 870-269-4383; www.arkansas-inn.com; 100 Washington; r from $85; P) is right on the Courtsquare with a rocking chair–equipped wraparound porch, cozy down-home trappings and a $20 midweek discount. **Tommy's Famous Pizza**

ARKANSAS IS A FAT-TIRE DESTINATION

If you are partial at all to mountain biking, make sure you have your ride when you arrive in Arkansas. Though there's very little pretension around it, world-class trails, both flowy and technical, marble this hillbilly country. Your recovery meal might be BBQ, but that's not so bad is it? The **Mountain Bike Arkansas** (www.mtbark.com) and **Bike Arkansas Directory** (www.bikearkansas.com) websites provide trail, shop and logistical info.

Some of the epic Arkansas trails:

Lake Leatherwood Eureka Springs – 18 miles of looped single track for all levels with great views and fun descents.

The Syllamo Near Mountain View – 50 miles of looped single track. It's hard. Really.

The Womble Mt Ida, near Mena – The prize trail of the Ouachita Mountains that's 35 miles one way, accessed by numerous trailheads.

and BBQ (☎ 870-269-3278; cnr Carpenter & W Main Sts; mains $7-15; from 3pm) is run by the friendliest bunch of backwoods hippies you could ask for. The BBQ pizza marries Tommy's specialties indulgently.

Eureka Springs

Near the northwestern corner of the state, artsy Eureka Springs perches in a steep valley and is one of the coolest towns in the state. Victorian buildings line crooked streets and a crunchy local population welcomes all – it's one of the most explicitly gay-friendly towns in the Ozarks. On the surface, art galleries and shops compete with commercialized country music and the 70ft **Christ of the Ozarks** statue for your attention. But bend a local's ear and find out who's playing at the nearest pub or the location of their favorite swimming hole and this idiosyncratic village will take on new dimensions. Furthermore, hiking, biking, and horseback-riding opportunities abound.

The **visitor center** (☎ 479-253-8737, 800-638-7352; www.eurekaspringschamber.com; 516 Village Circle, Hwy 62 E) has information about lodging, activities, tours and local attractions, such as the rockin' **Blues Festival** (www.eurekaspringsblues.com) at the end of May. The old **ES & NA Railway** (☎ 479-253-9623; www.esnarailway.com; 299 N Main St; adult/child $12/6; Tue-Sat) puffs through the Ozark hills on an hour-long tour four times a day.

our pick **Thorncrown Chapel** (☎ 479-253-7401; www.thorncrown.com; 12968 Hwy 62 West; donation suggested; 9am-5pm Apr-Nov, 11am-4pm Mar & Dec) is a magnificent sanctuary made of glass, with its 48ft-tall wooden skeleton holding 425 windows. There's not much between your prayers and God's green earth here. It's just outside of town in the woods.

If your budget can stand it, bypass the cheap motels on the rim of the canyon and splurge on lodging in the town center. Right in the historic downtown is the super-comfortable and historic **New Orleans Hotel and Suchness Spa** (☎ 479-253-8667; www.neworleanshotelandspa.com; 63 Spring St; r $84-199; P), which sends you reeling back in time, except that it houses a spa with a menu fully loaded for your body and chakra needs. **Treehouse Cottages** (☎ 479-253-8630; www.treehousecottages.com; 165 W Van Buren St; from $145; P) offers gorgeous sunlit, Jacuzzi-armed tree houses (that are more like cottages on stilts) in the woods.

Right across the street is **Bubba's BBQ** (☎ 479-253-7706; www.bubbasbarbecueeurekasprings.com; 166 W Van Buren St; half rack $13; 11am-9pm Mon-Sat), which is a genuine Southern meat joint in a town that has its fair share of tourist contrivance. At **Mud Street Cafe** (☎ 479-253-6732; www.mudstreetcafe.com; 22 G South Main St; 8am-3pm Thu-Tue) in downtown you can find some healthier options, like hummus salad. The coffee drinks and breakfasts are renowned.

Buffalo National River

Yet another under-acknowledged Arkansas gem, this 135-mile river flows beneath dramatic bluffs through unspoiled Ozark forest. The upriver section tends to have most of the white water, while the lower reaches ease lazily along – perfect for a float. The **Buffalo National River** (☎ 870-741-5443; www.nps.gov/buff) has 13 campgrounds and three designated wilderness areas; the most accessible is through the **Tyler Bend visitor center** (☎ 870-439-2502; 8am-5pm May-Sep, 8:30am-4:30pm Oct-Apr), 11 miles north of Marshall on Hwy 65.

Evidence of human occupation here dates back some 10,000 years, but this wild and naturally bountiful area kept even modern Ozark settlers isolated and self-sufficient. They developed a distinct dialect, along with unique craftsmanship and musical traits. Thanks to its National River designation in 1972, the Buffalo is one of the few remaining unpolluted, free-flowing rivers in the country.

The best way to tour the park and see the gargantuan limestone bluffs is by canoe or raft. Outfitters such as **Wild Bill's** (☎ 800-554-8657; www.ozark-float.com; 23 Hwy 268 E;) in Yellville and **Buffalo Outdoor Center** (☎ 800-221-5514; www.buffaloriver.com; cnr Hwys 43 & 74;) in Ponca arrange canoes or rafting trips (from $40 per person), tubes ($5), hiking tours, fishing trips and horseback rides. For weekend trips, reserve in advance.

ARKANSAS DELTA

Roughly 120 miles east of Little Rock, the Great River Rd follows the west bank of the Mississippi River through the Arkansas Delta. Blues town of yesteryear, **Helena** is now a depressed little Arkansas town. However, it explodes for its annual **Arkansas Blues & Heritage Festival** (www.bluesandheritage.com; admission free), formerly the King Biscuit Blues Festival, when blues musicians and 100,000 fans take over downtown for three days in early October. Food stalls sell home-cooked soul food and BBQ.

Year-round, blues fans and history buffs should visit the **Delta Cultural Center** (☎ 870-338-4350; www.deltaculturalcenter.com; 141 Cherry St; admission free; 9am-5pm Mon-Sat), which is in two buildings: the Train Depot and the Visitor Center. The museum displays all manner of blues memorabilia such as Albert King's and Sister Rosetta Tharpe's guitars, and John Lee Hooker's signed handkerchief.

The world's longest-running blues radio program, *King Biscuit Time,* is broadcast here (12:15pm Monday to Friday), and *Delta Sounds* (1pm Monday to Friday) often has live musicians. Other than that, music in Helena is not to be found.

Florida

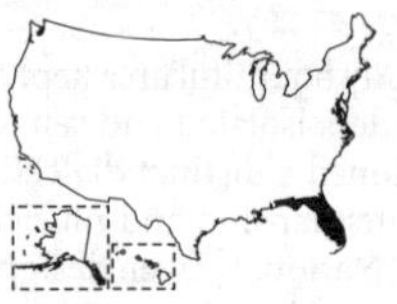

One thing you'll never catch Florida doing is taking itself too seriously: it's too busy basking in its nearly year-round sunshine. It's weird, delightful, wacky, wonderful. And it just wants you to have fun. A crazy protuberance of land, Florida puts as much space between itself and the other states as it can, like a runaway teenager, or a retiree heading to the Keys to spend the kids' inheritance. It doesn't have to try to be different. And that's why we love it. We count on it for glitzy theme parks and campy roadside attractions. For alligator farms and mermaid shows. For being an endless parade of the unusual, the garish and the superlative.

But beyond the giddy delights of manmade attractions are the natural wonders scattered about the state. Not just a few here and there, but a near-constant barrage of beaches, springs and forests. Florida boasts a ridiculous amount of shoreline, and you're never more than 60 miles from the beach. The Keys have crystal-clear water, and the only living coral reef in the continental US teems with brightly colored fish. The Everglades is the largest subtropical wilderness in the US, boasting amazing biodiversity. You might find yourself turning into a bird-watcher, as herons, osprey, pelicans and ibis put on an air show. Nature preserves, springs bubbling from underground caverns and wild beaches are liberally applied throughout the state.

So whether you're looking for natural attractions or entirely unnatural ones, the ridiculously beautiful or the beautifully ridiculous, Florida is the place to find it.

HIGHLIGHTS

- Marveling at the sheer number of deco gems in Miami Beach's **Art Deco Historic District** (p507)
- Cooling off with a key lime milk shake while feeding baby goats at **Robert is Here** (p522)
- Paddling quietly past manatees and alligators in the Everglades' **10,000 Islands** (p522)
- Hearing legends of ghosts, pirates and six-toed cats in **Key West** (p527)
- Feeling the earth rumble beneath your feet during a rocket launch at the **Kennedy Space Center** (p533)
- Exploring the Lightner Museum and the world's most opulent girls' dorm in **St Augustine** (p536)
- Seeing circus memorabilia – or confronting your fear of clowns – at the Sarasota **Ringling Museum Complex** (p543)
- Pondering the symbolism of ants at the **Salvador Dalí Museum** (p542), St Petersburg
- Discovering the mysteries of the world's deepest freshwater spring at **Edward Ball Wakulla Springs State Park** (p552)

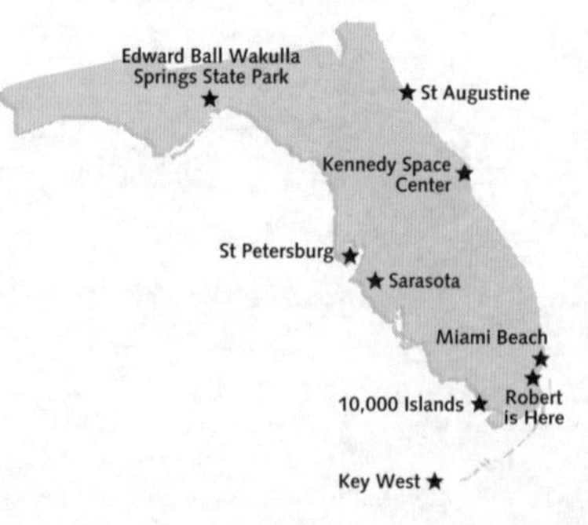

FLORIDA FACTS

Nickname Sunshine State
Population 18.3 million
Area 53,927 sq miles
Capital city Tallahassee (population 168,979)
Other cities Miami city (population 404,048), Tampa (population 332,888), Orlando (population 220,186)
Sales tax 6% (some towns and cities add another 9.5% to 11.5% to accommodations and meals)
Birthplace of Author Zora Neale Hurston (1891–1960), musician Jim Morrison (1943–71), actor William H Macy (b 1950), author Carl Hiaasen (b 1953), actor Eva Mendes (b 1974)
Home of Cuban Americans, manatees, Mickey Mouse, retirees, key lime pie
Famous for Theme parks, beaches, alligators, art deco
Notable local invention Suntan lotion (1944)
Driving distances Miami to Key West 160 miles, Tallahassee to Orlando 258 miles

HISTORY

There were, of course, already Native Americans living in Florida when it was 'discovered,' and they'd already been there for thousands of years. Imagine their surprise in 1513, those Apalachee, Timucuan and Calusa Indians, when Spanish explorer Juan Ponce de León hopped off his boat and onto the shores of what would become St Augustine, gestured grandly to the land he saw before him, and then, rather than asking what they called this place, declared it *Pascua Florida* for the Easter Feast of Flowers.

Other explorers soon followed. Pensacola was settled by Tristán de Luna y Arellano in 1559, making it the first European settlement in the US, but it was quickly abandoned with the help of a hurricane. The first European settlement to stick was St Augustine, settled in 1565 by Ponce de León's compatriot Pedro Menéndez de Avilés – making it the oldest continuously occupied city in the US.

Florida was admitted to the Union on March 3, 1845. Sixteen years later, at the onset of the Civil War, it seceded. It was readmitted in 1868, but still had a definite separateness from the states due to geography. But one Mr Henry Flagler solved that problem in the late 1800s when he constructed a railroad linking the east coast of Florida to the rest of the country, bringing traincarloads of people and unlocking Florida's tourism potential.

Because of its strategic location, new naval stations brought an influx of residents during the Spanish-American War and WWI, and post-WWII Florida thrived with the first wave of retirement communities and a fledgling aerospace industry. After the 1959 Cuban Revolution, many Cuban citizens settled in Miami, and thousands more would follow here as refugees, particularly as a result of the Mariel Boatlift (a mass exodus of Cubans from Mariel Harbor in Cuba) in the early 1980s.

No history of Florida would be complete without mentioning the opening of Walt Disney World here in 1971, which spawned hundreds of thousands of tourism-related jobs. Although the state was savaged in 2004 by four major hurricanes in six weeks, and was heavily impacted by the nation's economic meltdown in late 2008, Florida's appeal as a tourist destination remains unstoppable.

LOCAL CULTURE

There is no such thing as a typical Floridian. What unites them all is their lack of unity: everyone just goes on their merry way. Diversity thrives here, whether it is bikers, Cubans, retirees, gays, fishermen, environmentalists, Christian fundamentalists or circus performers. People are more likely to put on hip boots or a Goofy costume than they are to don a suit and tie. And Florida has a tourism-based economy, expect everyone to be welcoming of both you and your money.

LAND & CLIMATE

It doesn't get much flatter than Florida. Coastal lowlands, wetlands and reclaimed swampland typify most of the state, and in the center and north of the state you'll find gently inclining hills. The coasts are protected by barrier islands and, in the south,

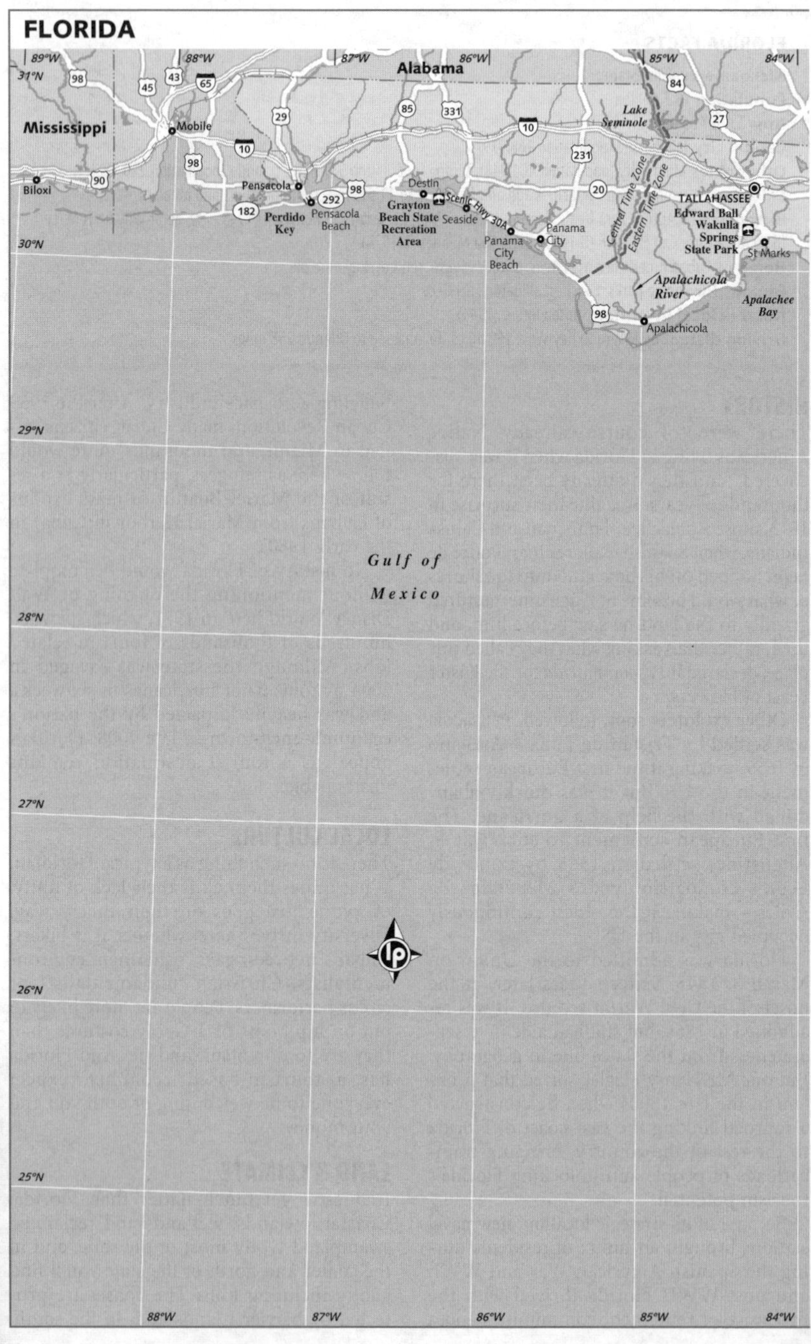
FLORIDA
Alabama
Mississippi
Mobile
Biloxi
Pensacola
Perdido Key
Pensacola Beach
Destin
Grayton Beach State Recreation Area
Seaside
Scenic Hwy 30A
Panama City Beach
Panama City
Lake Seminole
Central Time Zone
Eastern Time Zone
TALLAHASSEE
Edward Ball Wakulla Springs State Park
St Marks
Apalachicola River
Apalachee Bay
Apalachicola
Gulf of Mexico

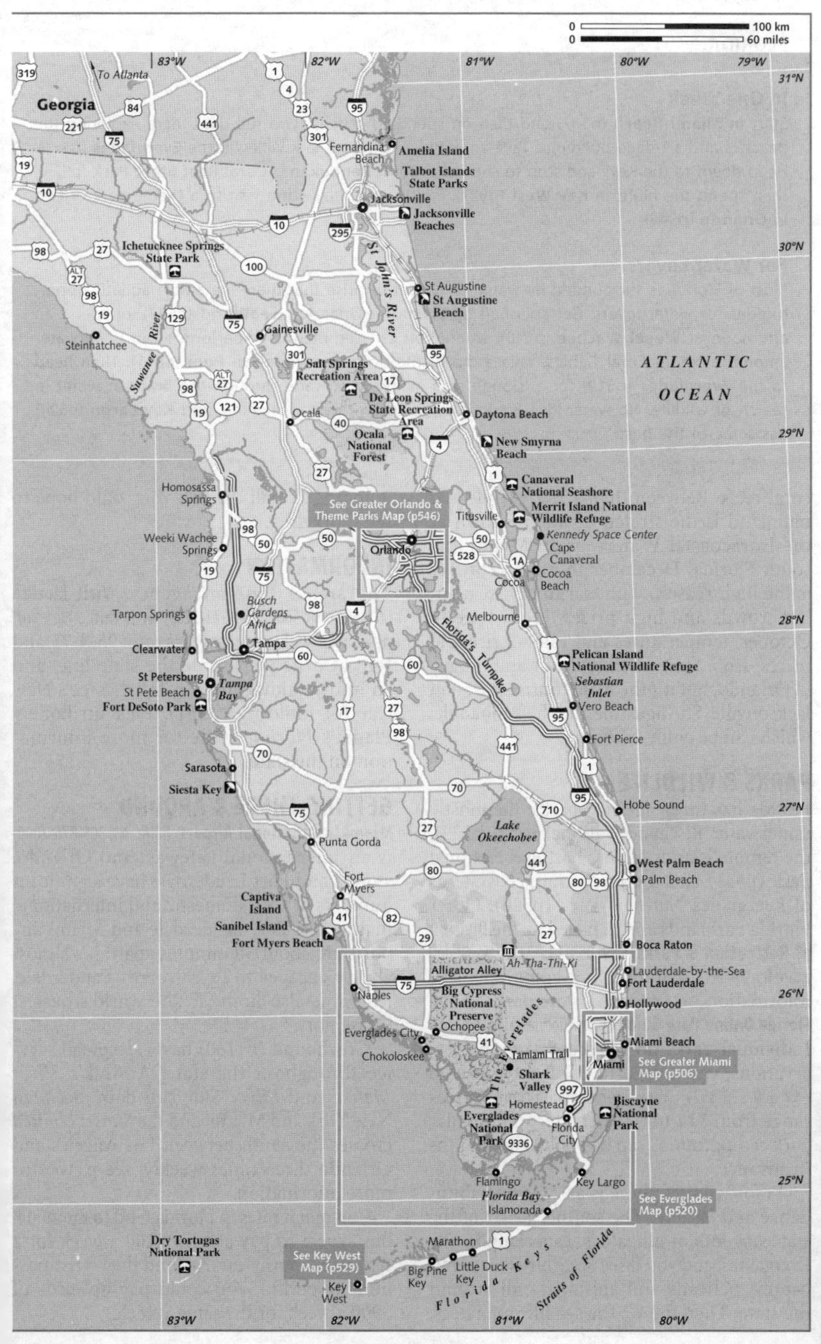

ATLANTIC OCEAN
Georgia
To Atlanta
Amelia Island
Fernandina Beach
Talbot Islands State Parks
Jacksonville
Jacksonville Beaches
Ichetucknee Springs State Park
St John's River
St Augustine
St Augustine Beach
Gainesville
Steinhatchee
Suwanee River
Salt Springs Recreation Area
De Leon Springs State Recreation Area
Ocala
Ocala National Forest
Daytona Beach
New Smyrna Beach
Canaveral National Seashore
Merrit Island National Wildlife Refuge
Kennedy Space Center
Cape Canaveral
Titusville
Homosassa Springs
Weeki Wachee Springs
See Greater Orlando & Theme Parks Map (p546)
Orlando
Cocoa
Cocoa Beach
Busch Gardens Africa
Tarpon Springs
Melbourne
Clearwater
Tampa
Florida's Turnpike
St Petersburg
Tampa Bay
St Pete Beach
Fort DeSoto Park
Pelican Island National Wildlife Refuge
Sebastian Inlet
Vero Beach
Fort Pierce
Sarasota
Siesta Key
Hobe Sound
Lake Okeechobee
Punta Gorda
West Palm Beach
Palm Beach
Fort Myers
Captiva Island
Sanibel Island
Fort Myers Beach
Boca Raton
Ah-Tha-Thi-Ki
Alligator Alley
Lauderdale-by-the-Sea
Fort Lauderdale
Naples
Big Cypress National Preserve
Hollywood
Ochopee
The Everglades
Everglades City
Miami Beach
Chokoloskee
Tamiami Trail
Miami
See Greater Miami Map (p506)
Shark Valley
Homestead
Biscayne National Park
Everglades National Park
Florida City
Flamingo
Key Largo
Florida Bay
Islamorada
See Everglades Map (p520)
Dry Tortugas National Park
Marathon
See Key West Map (p529)
Big Pine Key
Little Duck Key
Key West
Florida Keys
Straits of Florida
0 100 km
0 60 miles
83°W
82°W
81°W
80°W
79°W
31°N
30°N
29°N
28°N
27°N
26°N
25°N
FLORIDA

FLORIDA...

In One Week

Start in **Miami Beach** (p507) and plan on spending at least two full days there exploring the beaches and art-deco buildings. Take an easy day trip to Shark Valley in the **Everglades** (p521). Head down to the Keys and stop to snorkel at **John Pennekamp Coral Reef State Park** (p524), then spend the night in **Key West** (p527). Finish your trip with a visit to a theme park or two in **Orlando** (p545).

For Water Lovers

Most of Florida is surrounded by water, so it's no surprise that there are ample aquatic opportunities for water lovers. Get splashed by Shamu at Orlando's **SeaWorld** (p547), or spend an afternoon at **Weeki Wachee** (p540), where you can see mermaids perform in an underwater amphitheatre. In Coral Gables, take a dip in the gorgeous **Venetian Pool** (p511). Then head to the **Everglades** (p519) for a 'slough slog' where you wade through the brackish water in search of wildlife. No water-lover's trip is complete without snorkeling, and **Key Largo** (p524) has some of the best.

coral reefs. Between the barrier islands and mainland is the stretch of water known as the Intracoastal Waterway. In Miami and south Florida, December through February is the high season, with warm, dry weather, big crowds and high prices. From June to October, temperatures and rainfall rise and prices drop. Summertime is hot and muggy in Orlando, but it's the main tourist season in Jacksonville, St Augustine and the Panhandle, which can be chilly in winter.

PARKS & WILDLIFE

Florida has three national parks: the mostly underwater Biscayne National Park (p522), the remote islands of Dry Tortugas National Park (p531) and the fascinating ecosystems of Everglades National Park (p520). Other Florida parklands are managed by the **Division of Recreation & Parks** (☎ 850-245-2157; www.dep.state.fl.us/parks). You can find comprehensive information on the many state parks in the **Florida Online Park Guide** (www.floridastateparks.org). Individual parks don't accept camping reservations; you'll need to call **Reserve America** (☎ 800-326-3521; www.reserveamerica.com). Prices range from $12 to $28 per site, and popular park campgrounds can be booked up months in advance.

As for wildlife, there is an amazing abundance and variety. The southern part of the state has lots of alligators, especially in the Everglades, and you'll see large birds – herons, osprey, pelicans and anhinga – all around the state. Then there's the sea life: manatees, dolphins and all the fish you could hope to see snorkeling.

INFORMATION

The state's tourism agency, **Visit Florida** (☎ 850-488-5607, 866-972-5280; www.visitflorida.com), operates welcome centers on I-95, I-75 and I-10 at exits just inside the state line, and an information center in Tallahassee's New Capitol Building (p551). Pick up Lonely Planet's *Florida* guide for more information on the state.

GETTING THERE & AROUND

Miami International Airport (MIA; ☎ 305-876-7000) is an international gateway, and Orlando, Tampa and Fort Lauderdale have significant numbers of both domestic and international flights. The Fort Lauderdale and Miami airports are about 30 minutes apart; it's almost always cheaper to fly into Fort Lauderdale. Miami is also home to the world's busiest cruise port.

Greyhound (p1160) has widespread service throughout the state. Amtrak's *Silver Meteor* and *Silver Star* run daily between New York and Miami, and the *Sunset Limited* crosses the south between Los Angeles and Orlando three times weekly; see p1166 for more information.

Car-rental rates in Florida tend to fluctuate, but expect to pay at least $200 a week for a typical economy car. Around the Christmas-holiday period, you could pay upwards of $900 a week for the same vehicle.

SOUTH FLORIDA

As varied as the state of Florida is, you'd think you'd at least be able to generalize about the regions within it. But South Florida is made up of three wildly diverse areas that bear little resemblance to each other: Miami and Fort Lauderdale represent the sophisticated cities by the sea; the Everglades is a subtropical wilderness full of wildlife; and the Keys are a chain of islands with a laid-back vibe. The fact that they're just an hour or two apart gives you a great opportunity for a multidimensional vacation.

MIAMI

How does one city get so lucky? Most cities content themselves with one or two admirable attributes, but Miami seems to have it all. Let's just start with the fact that it's a world-class city, but also manages to have a perfectly gorgeous beach. It's got the sun, sand and surf you'd expect from a tropical island, but with the art, food and nightlife that only urban cities enjoy. On top of all that, Miami has arguably the best-looking people in the US. You know the glamorous model types you always see on TV but don't really exist in real life? Oh, they exist. They're all in Miami Beach, in-line skating down Ocean Ave in thongs. (Seriously, that's not just a stereotype.)

Tourism spearheaded Miami's stratospheric rise when the first passenger-train service reached there in 1896, and Miami's Cuban population swelled following the 1959 Castro coup. Today, crowned by the cruise-ship industry, a glittering entertainment scene and international business connections (not all of them wholly legitimate), Miami thrives almost as a nation unto itself, with 5.4 million residents in the metro area. More than 60% of the population speaks predominantly Spanish, and in many spots you're unlikely to hear English spoken at all. Well over half the population is Latino – the vast majority Cuban – which influences everything from politics to cocktails and infuses the city with a sexiness and style unlike any other.

Orientation

Greater Miami is a sprawling metropolis that includes suburbs such as Coral Gables and Coconut Grove, and neighborhoods such as Little Havana and Little Haiti. Miami is on the mainland, while Miami Beach lies 4 miles east across Biscayne Bay.

Downtown Miami operates on a fairly normal grid system. Streets run east–west, and avenues and courts run north–south. Flagler St divides NE and NW streets from SE and SW streets – with street numbers counting up as you move away from it in either direction – and Miami Ave divides NE and SE streets from NW and SW streets. (In other words, be sure to double-check whether that innocent-looking address on 1st is on NE 1st Ave, NW 1st Ave, SE 1st St or SW 1st St.)

In Miami Beach, streets also run east–west and avenues north–south. South Beach (SoBe) is the heart of the action and runs from 5th St up to 21st St.

If you're planning to spend some time checking out south Florida, pick up a copy of Lonely Planet's guide to *Miami & the Keys*.

Information

BOOKSTORES

Books & Books Coral Gables (Map p506; ☎ 305-442-4408; 265 Aragon Ave); Miami Beach (Map p508; ☎ 305-532-3222; 927 Lincoln Rd)

Downtown Book Center (Map p510; ☎ 305-377-9939; 247 SE 1st St)

Lambda Passages Bookstore (Map p506; ☎ 305-754-6900; 7545 Biscayne Blvd) Gay and lesbian bookstore.

EMERGENCY

Beach Patrol (☎ 305-673-7714; 24hr)

INTERNET ACCESS

See p1142 for websites that list wi-fi hot spots.

Miami-Dade Public Library Downtown (Map p510; ☎ 305-375-2665; www.mdpls.org; 101 W Flagler St;); Miami Beach (Map p508; ☎ 305-535-4219; 227 22nd St;) Free access as available.

MEDIA

El Nuevo Herald (www.elnuevoherald.com, in Spanish) Spanish daily published by the *Miami Herald*.

Miami Herald (www.miamiherald.com) The city's major English-language daily. Entertainment section on Friday.

New Times (www.miaminewtimes.com) Edgy, alternative weekly with good listings of restaurants, clubs, bars and theater.

MEDICAL SERVICES

Mount Sinai Medical Center (Map p506; ☎ 305-674-2121; 4300 Alton Rd) The area's best emergency room. Also has a 24-hour visitor's medical line (☎ 305-674-2222).

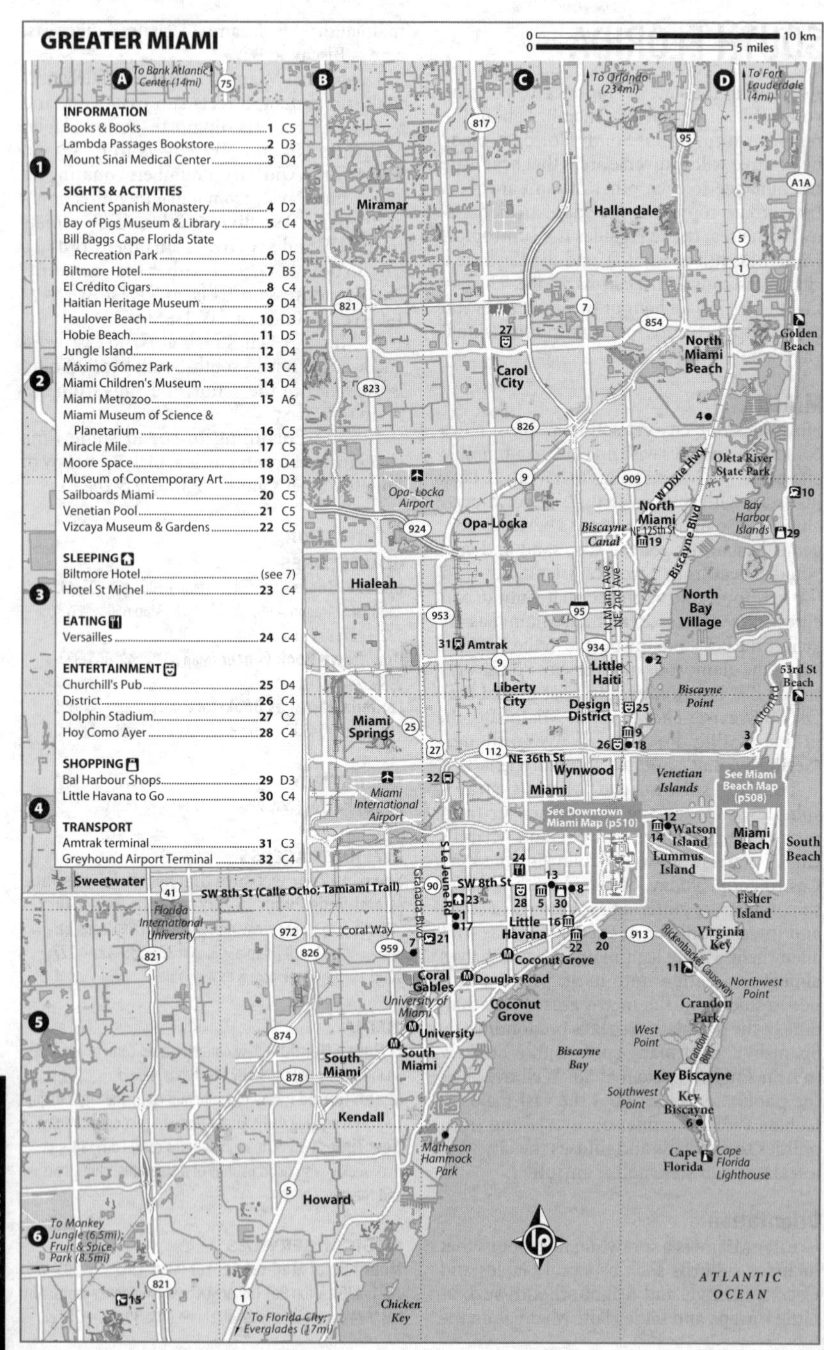
GREATER MIAMI
0 10 km
0 5 miles
INFORMATION
Books & Books 1 C5
Lambda Passages Bookstore 2 D3
Mount Sinai Medical Center 3 D4
SIGHTS & ACTIVITIES
Ancient Spanish Monastery 4 D2
Bay of Pigs Museum & Library 5 C4
Bill Baggs Cape Florida State Recreation Park 6 D5
Biltmore Hotel 7 B5
El Crédito Cigars 8 C4
Haitian Heritage Museum 9 D4
Haulover Beach 10 D3
Hobie Beach 11 D5
Jungle Island 12 D4
Máximo Gómez Park 13 C4
Miami Children's Museum 14 D4
Miami Metrozoo 15 A6
Miami Museum of Science & Planetarium 16 C5
Miracle Mile 17 C5
Moore Space 18 D4
Museum of Contemporary Art 19 D3
Sailboards Miami 20 C5
Venetian Pool 21 C5
Vizcaya Museum & Gardens 22 C5
SLEEPING
Biltmore Hotel (see 7)
Hotel St Michel 23 C4
EATING
Versailles 24 C4
ENTERTAINMENT
Churchill's Pub 25 D4
District 26 C4
Dolphin Stadium 27 C2
Hoy Como Ayer 28 C4
SHOPPING
Bal Harbour Shops 29 D3
Little Havana to Go 30 C4
TRANSPORT
Amtrak terminal 31 C3
Greyhound Airport Terminal 32 C4
To Bank Atlantic Center (14mi)
To Orlando (234mi)
To Fort Lauderdale (4mi)
Miramar
Hallandale
Golden Beach
North Miami Beach
Carol City
Oleta River State Park
Opa-Locka Airport
Opa-Locka
North Miami
Biscayne Canal
NE 125th St
W Dixie Hwy
Biscayne Blvd
Bay Harbor Islands
Hialeah
N Miami Ave
NE 2nd Ave
North Bay Village
Amtrak
Little Haiti
Liberty City
Design District
Biscayne Point
53rd St Beach
Alton Rd
Miami Springs
NE 36th St
Wynwood
Miami
Venetian Islands
See Miami Beach Map (p508)
Miami International Airport
See Downtown Miami Map (p510)
Watson Island
Lummus Island
Miami Beach
South Beach
S Le Jeune Rd
Granada Blvd
Sweetwater
SW 8th St (Calle Ocho; Tamiami Trail)
SW 8th St
Florida International University
Coral Way
Little Havana
Fisher Island
Virginia Key
Rickenbacker Causeway
Coconut Grove
Coral Gables
Douglas Road
Northwest Point
University of Miami
Coconut Grove
Crandon Park
University
West Point
South Miami
South Miami
Biscayne Bay
Crandon Blvd
Key Biscayne
Southwest Point
Key Biscayne
Kendall
Matheson Hammock Park
Cape Florida
Cape Florida Lighthouse
Howard
To Monkey Jungle (6.5mi); Fruit & Spice Park (8.5mi)
ATLANTIC OCEAN
Chicken Key
To Florida City; Everglades (17mi)
FLORIDA

MONEY

Abbot Foreign Exchange (Map p510; ☎ 305-374-2336; 230 NE 1st St, Downtown Miami)

Citibank (Map p508; ☎ 305-604-0220, 800-627-3999; 1685 Washington Ave, Miami Beach; 9am-4pm Mon-Thu, 9am-6pm Fri, 9am-1pm Sat) There's also a branch in downtown Miami (2001 Biscayne Blvd).

POST

Post Office Main Branch (Map p510; 500 NW 2nd Ave); Miami Beach (Map p508; 1300 Washington Ave)

TOURIST INFORMATION

Greater Miami & the Beaches Convention & Visitors Bureau (Map p510; ☎ 305-539-3000, 800-933-8448; www.miamiandbeaches.com; 701 Brickell Ave, 27th fl; 8:30am-5pm Mon-Fri)

Miami Beach Chamber of Commerce (Map p508; ☎ 305-673-7400; www.miamibeachguestservices.com; 1920 Meridian Ave; 9am-6pm Mon-Fri)

Dangers & Annoyances

Like all big cities, Miami has a few areas that locals consider dangerous: Liberty City, in northwest Miami, Little Haiti and stretches of the Miami riverfront and Biscayne Blvd (after dark). Deserted areas below 5th St in South Beach are riskier at night. In downtown, use caution near the Greyhound station and the shantytowns around causeways, bridges and overpasses.

Sights

MIAMI BEACH

Miami Beach has some of the best beaches in the country, with white sand and warm, blue-green water that rivals the Bahamas. But there's so much happening on shore, it's easy to think of the beaches more as a backdrop than as the main attraction. South Beach (or 'SoBe' if you're in a rush) is world-famous, but more for its people-watching than for its waves and sunshine.

Then there's the art-deco architecture. If you've never been to Miami Beach, you might think the **Art Deco Historic District** is just a cluster of pretty buildings, but it's actually the largest concentration of deco anywhere in the world, with approximately 1200 buildings lining the streets around Ocean Dr and Collins Ave. Learn more at the **Art Deco Welcome Center** (Map p508; ☎ 305-672-2014, 305-531-3484; 1001 Ocean Dr; 10am-7:30pm Mon-Sat, 10am-6pm Sun).

In the evening, stroll down **Española Way**, a *trés* European strip lined with restaurants and cafés representing most of the romance-language-speaking countries. Just a few blocks north, a section of **Lincoln Road** is blocked off to make a pedestrian mall, which draws people day and night with its stores, restaurants and bars.

You might be unfazed by the bare flesh on the beach, but there is likely to be something that will get your attention at the **World**

MIAMI...

In Two Days

Start your first day with a walking tour through the **Art Deco Historic District** (above), then head to the beach for swimming, sunning and people-watching. If they're in season, join the crush lining up for stone crabs at **Joe's Stone Crab Restaurant** (p515). While away the evening with swanky cocktails at **Skybar** (p515), or, for a low-key brew, head to the **Room** (p516). Stop by the **World Erotic Art Museum** (p509), which is open till midnight. The next morning, head into the city and shop for Cuban music and clothes along Little Havana's **Calle Ocho** (p509), followed up by classic Cuban cuisine at **Versailles** (p514). Afterwards, go for a stroll at **Vizcaya Museum & Gardens** (p511) then cool off with a dip at the **Venetian Pool** (p511). End with dinner and cocktails at **Novecento** (p515).

In Four Days

Follow the two-day itinerary, then head to the **Everglades** (p519) on day three, which will take up most of your day. For your last day, immerse yourself in art and design in the **Design District** (p511) followed by a visit to the **Miami Art Museum** (p509) or the **Museum of Contemporary Art** (p511), or enjoy your proximity to the ocean with **kayaking** or **windsurfing** (p512) off Key Biscayne. In the evening, check out live blues and rock and roll at Miami's oldest bar, **Tobacco Road** (p516).

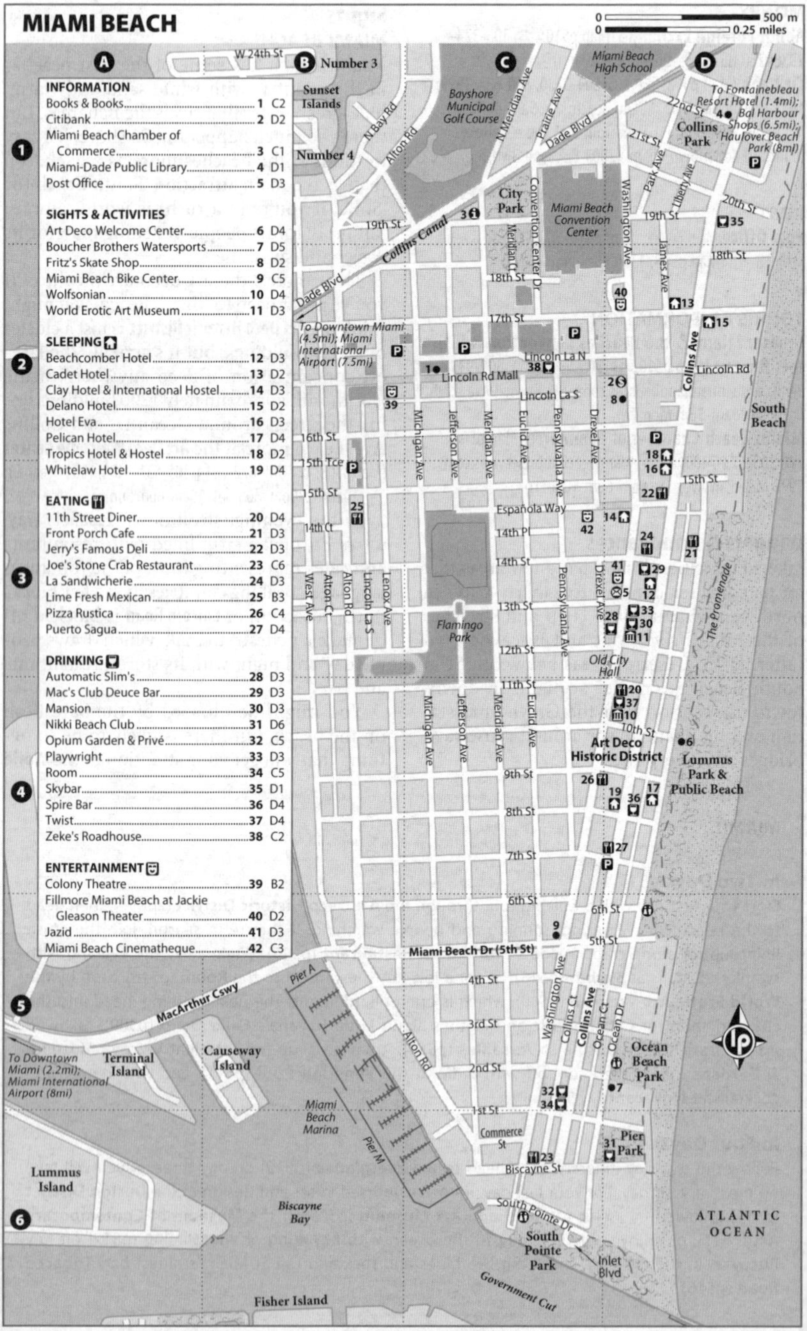
MIAMI BEACH
0 500 m
0 0.25 miles
A
B
C
D
1
2
3
4
5
6
INFORMATION
Books & Books 1 C2
Citibank 2 D2
Miami Beach Chamber of Commerce 3 C1
Miami-Dade Public Library 4 D1
Post Office 5 D3
SIGHTS & ACTIVITIES
Art Deco Welcome Center 6 D4
Boucher Brothers Watersports 7 D5
Fritz's Skate Shop 8 D2
Miami Beach Bike Center 9 C5
Wolfsonian 10 D4
World Erotic Art Museum 11 D3
SLEEPING
Beachcomber Hotel 12 D3
Cadet Hotel 13 D2
Clay Hotel & International Hostel 14 D3
Delano Hotel 15 D2
Hotel Eva 16 D3
Pelican Hotel 17 D4
Tropics Hotel & Hostel 18 D2
Whitelaw Hotel 19 D4
EATING
11th Street Diner 20 D4
Front Porch Cafe 21 D3
Jerry's Famous Deli 22 D3
Joe's Stone Crab Restaurant 23 C6
La Sandwicherie 24 D3
Lime Fresh Mexican 25 B3
Pizza Rustica 26 C4
Puerto Sagua 27 D4
DRINKING
Automatic Slim's 28 D3
Mac's Club Deuce Bar 29 D3
Mansion 30 D3
Nikki Beach Club 31 D6
Opium Garden & Privé 32 C5
Playwright 33 D3
Room 34 C5
Skybar 35 D1
Spire Bar 36 D4
Twist 37 D4
Zeke's Roadhouse 38 C2
ENTERTAINMENT
Colony Theatre 39 B2
Fillmore Miami Beach at Jackie Gleason Theater 40 D2
Jazid 41 D3
Miami Beach Cinematheque 42 C3
W 24th St
Number 3
Sunset Islands
Number 4
N Bay Rd
Alton Rd
Bayshore Municipal Golf Course
N Meridian Ave
Prairie Ave
Dade Blvd
Miami Beach High School
To Fontainebleau Resort Hotel (1.4mi); Bal Harbour Shops (6.5mi); Haulover Beach Park (8mi)
22nd St
21st St
Collins Park
Park Ave
Liberty Ave
Washington Ave
Convention Center Dr
City Park
Miami Beach Convention Center
Meridian Ct
19th St
20th St
18th St
17th St
James Ave
Collins Canal
To Downtown Miami (4.5mi); Miami International Airport (7.5mi)
Lincoln La N
Lincoln Rd Mall
Lincoln La S
Lincoln Rd
Collins Ave
South Beach
Michigan Ave
Jefferson Ave
Meridian Ave
Euclid Ave
Pennsylvania Ave
Drexel Ave
16th St
15th Tce
15th St
14th Ct
Española Way
14th Pl
14th St
13th St
12th St
11th St
10th St
West Ave
Alton Ct
Lincoln La S
Lenox Ave
Flamingo Park
Old City Hall
The Promenade
Art Deco Historic District
Lummus Park & Public Beach
9th St
8th St
7th St
6th St
5th St
Miami Beach Dr (5th St)
4th St
3rd St
2nd St
1st St
Commerce St
Biscayne St
Washington Ave
Collins Ct
Ocean Ct
Ocean Dr
Ocean Beach Park
Pier Park
MacArthur Cswy
Pier A
Pier M
Terminal Island
Causeway Island
To Downtown Miami (2.2mi); Miami International Airport (8mi)
Miami Beach Marina
Lummus Island
Biscayne Bay
South Pointe Dr
South Pointe Park
Inlet Blvd
Government Cut
Fisher Island
ATLANTIC OCEAN

FLORIDA

Erotic Art Museum (Map p508; ☎ 305-532-9336; 1205 Washington Ave; www.weam.com; adults over 18 $15; ⏰ 11am-midnight), with an amazingly extensive collection of naughty and erotic art, decorative items and even furniture depicting all sorts of parts and acts.

Just down the street, the **Wolfsonian** (Map p508; ☎ 305-531-1001; www.wolfsonian.org; 1001 Washington Ave; adult/child $7.50/5.35; ⏰ noon-6pm Sat-Tue, to 9pm Thu & Fri) has a fascinating collection that spans transportation, urbanism, industrial design, advertising and political propaganda from the late 19th to mid-20th century.

DOWNTOWN MIAMI

Unless you're there on business, you probably won't spend a lot of time downtown among the skyscrapers, but the **Metro-Dade Cultural Center Plaza** (Map p510; 101 W Flagler St) is home to two worthwhile museums, and $6 gets you a combo ticket that's good for both. The **Historical Museum of Southern Florida** (Map p510; ☎ 305-375-1492; www.hmsf.org; adult/child $5/2, Sat & 3rd Thu after 5pm free; ⏰ 10am-5pm Mon-Sat, noon-5pm Sun, noon-9pm 3rd Thu) has exhibits spanning Native American culture to the 1930s tourism boom. And **Miami Art Museum** (MAM; Map p510; ☎ 305-375-3000; www.miamiartmuseum.org; 101 W Flagler St; adult/child under 12 $8/free, 2nd Sat free; ⏰ 10am-5pm Tue-Fri, noon-5pm Sat & Sun) is home to permanent and rotating exhibits, as well as the JAM@MAM happy hour on the third Thursday of each month from 5pm to 9pm. The MAM won't be there indefinitely; it's planning a move to Bicentennial Park, scheduled at the time of research for late 2012.

Near the marina, **Bayside Marketplace** (Map p510; ☎ 305-577-3344; www.baysidemarketplace.com; 401 Biscayne Blvd; ⏰ 10am-10pm Mon-Thu, to 11pm Fri & Sat, 11am-9pm Sun) is a buzzy if touristy shopping and entertainment hub.

LITTLE HAVANA

As SW 8th St heads away from downtown, it becomes **Calle Ocho** (pronounced *kah*-yeh *oh*-cho, Spanish for 'Eighth Street'). That's when you know you've arrived in Little Havana, the most prominent community of Cuban Americans in the US. But this is no Cuban theme park; it's a real neighborhood where real live people live and work. One of the best times to experience it is the last Friday of the month during **Viernes Culturales** (www.viernesculturales.com; ⏰ 6-11pm), or 'Cultural Fridays,' a street fair showcasing Latino artists and musicians.

Pick up some Cuban-style cigars after watching *tabaqueros* hand-roll them at **El Crédito Cigars** (Map p506; ☎ 305-858-4162; 1106 SW 8th St/Calle Ocho; ⏰ 8:30am-5pm Mon-Fri, 9am-4pm Sat). And get a taste of old Cuba at **Máximo Gómez Park** (cnr Calle Ocho & SW 15th Ave). It's also known as 'Domino Park,' and you'll understand why when you see the old-timers throwing bones. History buffs can stop by the **Bay of Pigs Museum & Library** (Map p506; ☎ 305-649-4719; www.bayofpigsmuseum.org; 1821 SW 9th St; admission free; ⏰ 9am-4pm Mon-Sat) to learn more about the ill-fated Cuban invasion and pay tribute to the 2506 Brigade.

GUIDE TO MIAMI BEACHES

The beaches around Miami are some of the best in the country. The water is clear and warm and the imported white sand is relatively white. The beaches are also informally zoned into areas with their own unique crowds by tacit understanding so that everyone can enjoy them at their own speed.

Scantily-Clad Beaches In South Beach (Map p508) between 5th St and 21st St, modesty is in short supply.

Nude Beaches Nude bathing is legal at Haulover Beach Park (Map p506) in Sunny Isles. North of the lifeguard tower is predominantly gay; south is straight.

Gay Beaches All of South Beach (Map p508) is gay-friendly, but a special concentration seems to hover around 12th St.

Family-Fun Beaches North of 21st St is where you'll find the more family-friendly beaches, and the beach at 53rd St (Map p506) has a playground and public toilets.

Latino Beaches Latino families, predominantly Cuban, congregate between 5th St and South Pointe (Map p508).

Windsurfing Beaches Hobie Beach (Map p506), along the Rickenbacker Causeway on the way to Key Biscayne, is actually known as 'Windsurfing Beach.'

Surfing In Miami Beach, South Pointe Park (Map p508) is your best bet, but better yet is heading up to Haulover Beach or anywhere north of 70th St.

DOWNTOWN MIAMI

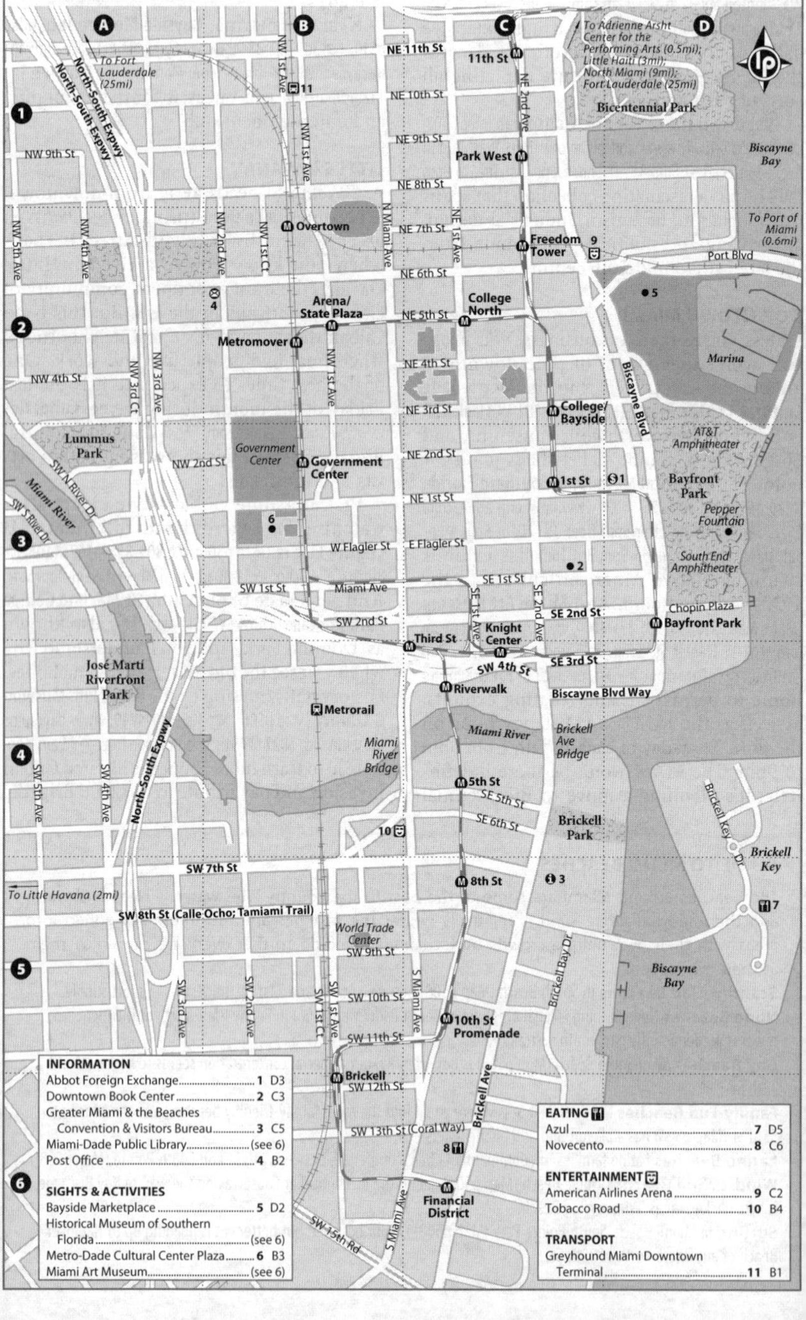

0 — 400 m
0 — 0.2 miles

To Adrienne Arsht Center for the Performing Arts (0.5mi); Little Haiti (3mi); North Miami (9mi); Fort Lauderdale (25mi)

To Fort Lauderdale (25mi)

To Port of Miami (0.6mi)

To Little Havana (2mi)

INFORMATION

- Abbot Foreign Exchange 1 D3
- Downtown Book Center 2 C3
- Greater Miami & the Beaches Convention & Visitors Bureau 3 C5
- Miami-Dade Public Library .... (see 6)
- Post Office 4 B2

SIGHTS & ACTIVITIES

- Bayside Marketplace 5 D2
- Historical Museum of Southern Florida .... (see 6)
- Metro-Dade Cultural Center Plaza 6 B3
- Miami Art Museum .... (see 6)

EATING

- Azul 7 D5
- Novecento 8 C6

ENTERTAINMENT

- American Airlines Arena 9 C2
- Tobacco Road 10 B4

TRANSPORT

- Greyhound Miami Downtown Terminal 11 B1

FLORIDA

DESIGN DISTRICT, WYNWOOD & LITTLE HAITI

Proving that SoBe doesn't hold the lease on hip, these two trendy areas north of downtown – all but deserted 25 years ago – aren't just rebounding; they're ensconcing themselves as bastions of art and design. The **Design District** (Map p506; www.miamidesigndistrict.net) is mecca for interior designers, home to dozens of galleries and contemporary furniture, fixture and design showrooms. Just south of the Design District, **Wynwood** (Map p506) is making a name for itself as an arts district, with myriad galleries and art studios housed in abandoned factories and warehouses.

The second Saturday of the month is the absolute best time to visit, when both neighborhoods hold evening gallery walks with art, music, food and wine.

In the absence of a gallery walk, stop by the Design District's experimental gallery **Moore Space** (Map p506; ☎ 786-543-7707; www.themoorespace.org; 4040 NE 2nd Ave; 🕑 10am-5pm Wed-Sat) to catch the zeitgeist. Then explore the 18-block area that goes from NE 36th St to 41st St, between NE 2nd Ave and N Miami Ave, or head down below 36th St to check out Wynwood.

The home of Miami's Haitian refugees, **Little Haiti** is defined by brightly painted homes, markets and botanicas (voodoo shops), and it's also home to the **Haitian Heritage Museum** (Map p506; ☎ 305-371-5988; 4141 NE 2nd Ave; www.haitianheritagemuseum.org; 10am-5pm Tue-Fri). which showcases Haitian art and history.

CORAL GABLES & COCONUT GROVE

For a slower pace and a more European feel, head inland. Designed as a 'model suburb' by George Merrick in the early 1920s, Coral Gables is a Mediterranean-style village that's centered around the shops and restaurants of the **Miracle Mile** (Map p506), a four-block section of Coral Way between Douglas and LeJeune Rds.

'Swimming pool' doesn't even begin to describe the spring-fed **Venetian Pool** (Map p506; ☎ 305-460-5306; www.coralgablesvenetianpool.com; 2701 DeSoto Blvd; adult/child $10/6.75; 🕑 11am-7:30pm Mon-Fri, 10am-4:30pm Sat & Sun), made by filling in the limestone quarry used to build Coral Gables. With waterfalls, grottos and an Italianate feel, it looks like where rich mermaids would go on vacation. You can peek, but most of it's hidden behind stucco walls, wrought iron fences and bougainvillea – best to dive right in.

WHAT THE...?

Out in the middle of Biscayne Bay, seven houses hover on pilings over the shallow waters, the remnants of the historic community of **Stiltsville**. It started in the early 1930s, when 'Crawfish' Eddie Walker built an off-shore shack where he could entertain his fishing buddies. At Stiltsville's peak there were 27 structures but, as hurricanes came and went, many of the buildings went with them. Slated to be torn down in 1999, the buildings were saved by a petition with 75,000 signatures. And while the Stiltsville Trust is now making plans for the buildings' future, a hurricane may get the final vote.

Architecturally speaking, the crown jewel of Coral Gables is the **Biltmore Hotel** (Map p506; ☎ 305-445-1926; www.biltmorehotel.com; 1200 Anastasia Ave; 🕑 tours Sun at 1:30pm, 2:30pm & 3:30pm), a magnificent edifice that once housed a speakeasy run by Al Capone. Even if you don't stay there, drop by for afternoon tea, a free Sunday tour or a gawk at the pool.

In nearby Coconut Grove, immerse yourself in the loveliness of **Vizcaya Museum & Gardens** (Map p506; ☎ 305-250-9133; www.vizcayamuseum.org; 3251 S Miami Ave; adult/child $15/6; 🕑 museum 9:30am-5pm, gardens to 5:30pm). The Italian Renaissance–style villa has 70 rooms full of centuries-old furnishings and art. The formal gardens, fountains and grottos make a gorgeous backdrop – expect to see at least one bride with a photographer in tow.

The **Miami Museum of Science & Planetarium** (Map p506; ☎ 305-646-4200; www.miamisci.org; 3280 S Miami Ave; adult/child $18/13; 🕑 10am-6pm; ♿) is a Smithsonian affiliate with a planetarium and wildlife center. Most of the museum is usually taken up with one major exhibit; call to see what's current.

GREATER MIAMI

North of downtown, the **Museum of Contemporary Art** (Map p506; ☎ 305-893-6211; www.mocanomi.org; 770 NE 125th St; adult/student $5/3; 🕑 11am-5pm Tue & Thu-Sat, 1-9pm Wed, noon-5pm Sun) has frequently changing exhibitions focusing on international, national and emerging artists.

In contrast, the peaceful **Ancient Spanish Monastery** (☎ 305-945-1461; www.spanishmonastery.com; 16711 W Dixie Hwy; adult/child $5/2; 🕑 9am-5pm Mon-Sat, 2-5pm Sun) is firmly rooted in the past.

Said to be the oldest building in the Western Hemisphere, it was built in Segovia, Spain, in 1411 and shipped here (much later) by William Randolph Hearst. Score one for crazy tycoons everywhere.

Thirty miles south of downtown, **Fruit & Spice Park** (off Map p506; ☎ 305-247-5727; www.fruitandspicepark.org; 24801 SW 187 Ave; adult/child $5/1.50; 9am-5pm) shows what you can do with trees when you have a tropical climate at your disposal, which is to grow more than 500 varieties of fruit, spice, vegetable and nut. (Bet you never knew there were 125 kinds of mango.)

KEY BISCAYNE

Serene beaches and stunning sunsets are just across the Rickenbacker Causeway (toll $1) at Key Biscayne, where you'll find the boardwalks and bike trails of the beachfront **Bill Baggs Cape Florida State Recreation Park** (Map p506; ☎ 305-361-5811; 1200 S Crandon Blvd; pedestrians & cyclists $1, vehicles 1-/2+ occupants $3/5; 8am-dusk). From the southern shore of the park you can catch a glimpse of **Stiltsville** (see boxed text, p511).

Activities

BICYCLING & IN-LINE SKATING

Skating or bicycling the strip along Ocean Dr in South Beach is pure Miami.

Fritz's Skate Shop (Map p508; ☎ 305-532-1954; 1620 Washington Ave; 10am-10pm) Rent bikes, skates and more by the hour, day or week.

Miami Beach Bike Center (Map p508; ☎ 305-531-4161; 601 5th St; per hr/day $8/24; 10am-7pm Mon-Sat, 10am-5pm Sun) Convenient bike rentals in the heart of SoBe.

WATER SPORTS

Boucher Brothers Watersports (Map p508; ☎ 305-535-8177; www.boucherbrothers.com; 161 Ocean Dr; 10:30am-4:30pm) Rentals and lessons for all sorts of water-related activities: kayaking, water-skiing, windsurfing, parasailing, waverunners & boats.

Sailboards Miami (Map p506; ☎ 305-361-7245; www.sailboardsmiami.com; 1 Rickenbacker Causeway; kayaks single/double per hr $15/20, windsurfing per hr $30) The waters off Key Biscayne are perfect for windsurfing, kayaking & kiteboarding; get your gear and lessons here.

Walking Tour

There are excellent walking tours available for the Art Deco Historic District – both guided and self-guided – but if you just want to hit the highlights, you can follow this quick and easy path. Start at the **Art Deco Welcome Center** (**1**; p507) at the corner of Ocean Dr and 10th St and step inside for a taste of deco style in its gift shop. Next, head north on Ocean. Between 12th and 14th Sts, you'll see three classic examples of deco hotels: the **Leslie (2)**, with classic 'eyebrows' and a typically boxy shape; the **Carlyle (3)**, which was featured in the film *The Birdcage;* and the graceful **Cardozo Hotel (4)**, featuring sleek, rounded edges. At 14th St, peek inside the **Winter Haven Hotel (5)**

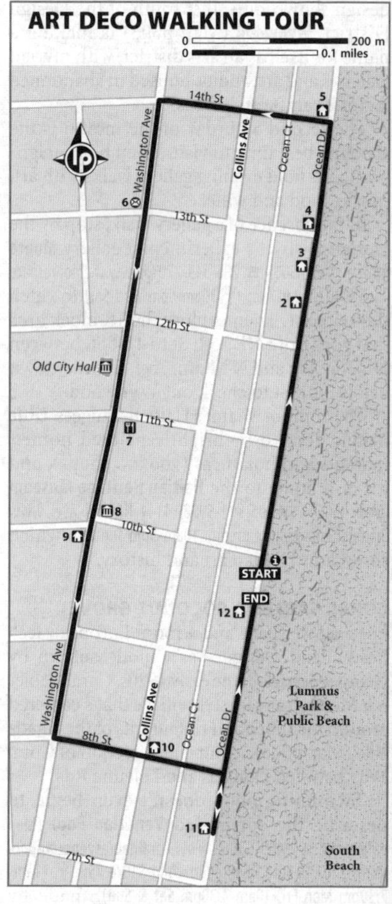

WALK FACTS

Start Art Deco Welcome Center
Finish Edison Hotel
Distance 1.2 miles
Duration 30 minutes

to see its fabulous terrazzo floors. Turn left and head along 14th St to Washington Ave, and turn left again to find the **US Post Office (6)** at 13th St. Step inside to admire the domed ceiling and marble stamp tables, and try whispering into the domed ceiling. Two blocks down on your left is the **11th St Diner** (**7**; p515), a gleaming aluminum deco-style Pullman car where you can also stop for lunch if you're hungry. At 10th St, you'll find the **Wolfsonian** (**8**; p509), an excellent museum with many deco-era treasures, and across the street is the beautifully restored **Hotel Astor (9)**. Turn left on 8th St and head one block east to Collins Ave. On the corner, you'll see **The Hotel (10)** – originally Tiffany Hotel and still topped by a deco-style neon spire bearing that name. Continue to Ocean Dr and turn right to see the **Colony Hotel (11)** and its famous neon sign, then double back to find the 1935 **Edison Hotel (12)**, another creation of deco legend Henry Hohauser, half a block past 9th St.

Miami for Children

The best beaches for kids are north of 21st St, especially at 53rd St, which has a playground and public toilets, and the dune-packed beach around 73rd St. Also head south to Matheson Hammock Park (Map p506), which has calm artificial lagoons.

Watson Island, between downtown Miami and Miami Beach, is home to two major children's attractions. The **Miami Children's Museum** (Map p506; ☎ 305-373-5437; www.miamichildrensmuseum.org; 980 MacArthur Causeway, Watson Island; admission $15; ⏲ 10am-6pm; 🚼) is a hands-on museum with fun music and art studios, as well as some branded 'work' experiences that make it feel a tad corporate. On the other side of MacArthur Causeway is **Jungle Island** (Map p506; ☎ 305-400-7000; www.jungleisland.com; 1111 Parrot Jungle Trail, Watson Island; adult/child 3-10yr $30/24; ⏲ 10am-6pm; 🚼), which used to be Parrot Jungle, but they added so many animal attractions a name change seemed in order.

Two more children's attractions are located in far South Miami: **Miami Metrozoo** (Map p506; ☎ 305-251-0400; www.miamimetrozoo.com; 12400 SW 152nd St; adult/child 3-12yr $16/12; ⏲ 9:30am-5:30pm, last admission 4pm; 🚼) has exotic elephants, tigers and Komodo dragons. The Amazon-like **Monkey Jungle** (off Map p506; ☎ 305-235-1611; www.monkeyjungle.com; 14805 SW 216th St; adult/child 3-9yr $30/24; ⏲ 9:30am-5pm, last admission 4pm; 🚼) is like an inside-out zoo, with you enclosed in screened-in trails and the simian species running free.

Tours

Learn about art deco and its icons on a 90-minute walking tour with the Miami Design Preservation League. Tours leave from the **Art Deco Welcome Center** (Map p508; ☎ 305-531-3484; 1001 Ocean Dr; guided tours adult/students $20/15) at 10:30am Friday through Wednesday and 6:30pm Thursday. DIY travelers can dial up an audio tour from their cell phone anytime (☎ 786-312-1229; $10).

Historian extraordinaire **Dr Paul George** (☎ 305-375-1621; www.hmsf.org/programs-adult.htm; tours $25-44) leads fascinating bike, boat, coach and walking tours, and offers a close-up peek at Stiltsville. Look online for a full menu of options.

Tour South Beach on two wheels with **South Beach Bike Tours** (☎ 305-673-2002; www.southbeachbiketours.com; half-day tour per person $59), a three-hour exploration that covers a lot of ground.

Festivals & Events

Calle Ocho Festival (www.carnavalmiami.com) This massive street party in March is the culmination of Carnaval Miami, a 10-day celebration of Latin culture.

Winter Music Conference (www.wmcon.com) The SXSW of dance music and electronica takes place every March.

Miami Gay & Lesbian Film Festival (www.mglff.com) This April event screens amateur and professional films at different venues around town.

Art Basel (www.artbaselmiamibeach.com) An art show held each December that includes parties and crossover events – a sister event to Art Basel Switzerland.

Sleeping

So little time, so many great places to stay. Miami Beach is home to dozens of small boutique hotels in renovated art-deco buildings. To find them and other stylish options, check out www.miamiboutiquehotels.com. Oceanfront rooms are usually the most expensive and often the noisiest. Rates vary widely by season – all bets are off during spring break, when a $79 room can go for $500 – and the low end of the range usually applies to the slower summer months. Hotels with free parking are rare; expect to pay $20 to $35 a night.

BUDGET

Clay Hotel & International Hostel (Map p508; ☎ 305-534-2988, 800-379-2529; www.clayhotel.com; 1438

Washington Ave; dm $24-29, r $58-190;) Nestled right off Española Way and just blocks from the beach, this century-old Spanish-style building has an illustrious history and clean, affordable rooms.

Tropics Hotel & Hostel (Map p508; ☎ 305-531-0361; www.tropicshotel.com; 1550 Collins Ave; dm $27-34, r $90-150;) This friendly, sunny hostel provides a taste of that Miami vibe you came here to be part of in a centrally located deco building surrounding an Olympic-size pool. Bring your passport; it's required.

MIDRANGE

Whitelaw Hotel (Map p508; ☎ 305-398-7000, 877-762-3477; www.whitelawhotel.com; 808 Collins Ave; r $99-249;) With a decor that can only be classified as 'brothel nouveau,' this deco hotel is all done up in bright red and white, from the lobby to the rooms.

Hotel Eva (Map p508; ☎ 305-673-1199; www.hotelevamiamibeach.com; 1506 Collins Ave; r $99-299;) Eva's suites are kind of like staying at a friend's apartment: maybe not as stylish, but roomy and a bargain.

Beachcomber Hotel (Map p508; ☎ 305-531-3755, 888-305-4683; www.beachcombermiami.com; 1340 Collins Ave; r $99-149;) Inside the green-banana-colored exterior, the Beachcomber has 29 cozy rooms.

Cadet Hotel (Map p508; ☎ 305-672-6688, 800-432-2338; www.cadethotel.com; 1701 James Ave; r $125-300;) This unassuming little boutique with clean, crisp rooms is close to everything but manages to remain an oasis of calm.

Hotel St Michel (Map p506; ☎ 305-444-1666, 800-848-4683; www.hotelstmichel.com; 162 Alcazar Ave; r $135-229;) You could conceivably think you're in Europe in this vaulted place at Coral Gables, with inlaid floors, old-world charm and just 28 rooms.

Biltmore Hotel (Map p506; ☎ 305-445-1926, 800-915-1926; www.biltmorehotel.com; 1200 Anastasia Ave; r $159-349; P) This 1926 hotel is a National Historic Landmark. Swimmers take note: it has a fabulous pool – the largest hotel pool in the country – and is just half a mile from the Venetian Pool (p511).

our pick **Pelican Hotel** (Map p508; ☎ 305-673-3373, 800-773-5422; www.pelicanhotel.com; 826 Ocean Dr; r $160-475;) The name and deco facade don't hint at anything unusual, but the decorators went wild inside with great themes such as 'Best Whorehouse,' 'Executive Zebra,' and 'Big Bamboo.'

TOP END

Delano Hotel (Map p508; ☎ 305-672-2000, 800-697-1791; www.delano-hotel.com; 1685 Collins Ave; r Jan-Apr $345-575;) The rooms at this grand boutique are minimalist-chic, and the indoor/outdoor lobby is all billowing curtains and pillars with occasional *Alice in Wonderland* touches.

Fontainebleau Resort Hotel (off Map p508; ☎ 305-538-2000; www.fontainebleau.com; 4441 Collins Ave; r from $279;) After a spectacular $1 billion renovation, this enormous landmark hotel, which has lured the rich and famous since the 1950s, is as resplendent as ever.

Eating

As Florida's most international city, Miami has the most international food choices, with Cuban, 'Floribbean' and seafood always in abundance.

BUDGET

Pizza Rustica (Map p508; ☎ 305-674-8244; 863 Washington Ave; slices $3-5; 11am-6pm) Big square slices that are a meal in themselves – when you're wandering around hungry, there's nothing better. Also at 1447 Washington Ave and 667 Lincoln Rd.

La Sandwicherie (Map p508; ☎ 305-532-8934; 229 14th St; mains $6-8; 10am-5am) Counter service at this casual walk-up just blocks from the beach includes salads, smoothies, shakes – and, of course, sandwiches.

Lime Fresh Mexican (Map p508; ☎ 305-532-5463; 1439 Alton Rd; mains $6-10; 11am-10pm) Pig out on Mexican food Miami Beach–style: with the low-fat 'skinny burrito' or low-carb 'South Beach burrito.' (Regular fattening food is also available if you don't have a thong to worry about.)

MIDRANGE

Puerto Sagua (Map p508; ☎ 305-673-1115; 700 Collins Ave; mains $6-25; 7am-2am) Pull up to the counter for authentic, tasty and inexpensive *ropa vieja* (shredded beef), black beans and *arroz con pollo* (rice with chicken) – plus some of the best Cuban coffee in town – at this beloved Cuban diner.

our pick **Versailles** (Map p506; ☎ 305-444-0240; 3555 SW 8th St; mains $8-20; 8am-2am Mon-Thu, 8am-3:30am Fri, 8am-4:30am Sat, 9am-2am Sun) *The* Cuban restaurant in town is not to be missed. It finds room for everybody in the large, cafeteria-style dining rooms.

EATING FLORIDA: CUBAN FOOD

You're bound to run across some Cuban food in south Florida, but what to order? If you don't know your plantains from your *ropa vieja*, here's a good place to start:

The Cuban sandwich layers sliced pickles, roast Cuban pork, ham and Swiss cheese between two slices of buttered Cuban white bread, then the whole thing is pressed till melty. If you're in the mood for a main course, try the *ropa vieja*. It literally translates to 'old clothes' in Spanish, but it's much more delicious, made from shredded flank steak cooked in tomatoes and peppers.

As for side dishes, you've got your plantains, a cousin to the banana that's often served fried or baked in butter and cinnamon. And most mains are served with Cuban black beans and yellow rice, or a *mixto*, which combines the two.

Front Porch Cafe (Map p508; ☎ 305-531-8300; 1418 Ocean Drive; mains $10-18; 🕑 8am-10:30pm) Pull up a chair on the front porch of the Penguin Hotel for great breakfasts, huge portions and reasonable prices, all overlooking the ocean.

11th St Diner (Map p508; ☎ 305-534-6373; 1065 Washington Ave; mains $8-16; 🕑 24hr) This deco diner housed inside a gleaming Pullman train car sees round-the-clock activity and is especially popular with people staggering home from clubs.

Jerry's Famous Deli (Map p508; ☎ 305-532-8030; www.jerrysfamousdeli.com; 1450 Collins Ave; mains $10-18; 🕑 24hr) Jerry's does it all – from pastrami melts to Chinese chicken salad to fettuccine Alfredo – and does it all day long. It also does it big, with huge portions served in a large, open, deco space.

Novecento (Map p510; ☎ 305-403-0900; 1414 Brickell Ave; mains $10-25; 🕑 11am-midnight Mon-Thu, 11am-1am Fri, 10am-1am Sat, 10am-midnight Sun) Dark wood lends an authentic ambience to this dimly-lit Argentine restaurant. It's noisy, thanks to the bar, and you'll probably be there a while – no one's in any hurry – but it's a cool downtown scene nonetheless.

TOP END

Joe's Stone Crab Restaurant (Map p508; ☎ 305-673-0365; 11 Washington Ave; mains $20-60; 🕑 11:30am-2pm Tue-Sat, dinner 5-10pm Sun-Thu, to 11pm Fri & Sat mid-Oct–mid-May, call for summer schedule) The wait is long, the prices high. But if those aren't deal-breakers, queue up to don a bib in Miami's most famous restaurant and enjoy deliciously fresh stone crab claws.

Azul (Map p510; ☎ 305-913-8288; 500 Brickell Key Dr; mains $33-65; 🕑 7am-4pm & 7pm-midnight) Be pampered, coddled even, at this terrific restaurant on Brickell Key with a stellar Asian fusion menu created by Chef Clay Conley. In addition to a massive wine list and waterfront views of downtown, you'll get to experience some of the best service in all of Miami.

Drinking & Entertainment

You'd have to try hard to be bored in Miami. The party goes on till the wee hours, with most bars staying open till 5am. There's also a cornucopia of theater and cultural performances as well as sporting events for every season. Check out www.miamiandbeaches.com for a calendar of events or www.cooljunkie.com for info on clubs, bars, galleries and more.

BARS & NIGHTCLUBS

To increase your chances of getting into the major nightclubs, call ahead to get on the guest list. Having gorgeous, well-dressed females in your group doesn't hurt either (unless you're going to a gay bar). There are tons of bars along Ocean Dr; wander around during happy hour for repeated offers of half price drinks.

Skybar (Map p508; ☎ 305-695-3900; Shore Club, 1901 Collins Ave) Sip chic cocktails on the alfresco terrace – they're too expensive to guzzle. Or, if you're 'somebody,' head for the exclusive indoor red room. Both have a luxurious Moroccan theme and beautiful people-watching.

Mansion (Map p508; ☎ 305-532-1525; 1235 Washington Ave; cover from $20; 🕑 Thu-Sun) This massive, 40,000-sq-ft nightclub complex has multiple dance floors, clubs, music styles and events. Be prepared for some quality time with the velvet rope and wear your nicest shoes.

Twist (Map p508; ☎ 305-538-9478; 1057 Washington Ave; admission free) This gay hangout has serious staying power and a little bit of something for everyone (except the religious right), including dancing, drag shows and go-go dancers.

Nikki Beach Club (Map p508; ☎ 305-538-1111; 1 Ocean Dr; cover from $25) Lounge on beds or inside your own tipi in this beach-chic outdoor space that's right on the sand.

Spire Bar (Map p508; ☎ 305-531-7700; 801 Collins Ave) The neon 'Tiffany' sign stands watch over this Todd Oldham–designed rooftop bar where you can keep an eye on most of Miami Beach.

Mac's Club Deuce Bar (Map p508; ☎ 305-531-6200; 222 14th St) Cough, cough. Is that your lung on the floor? No matter; quaff a cheap beer and revel in the gloriously seedy vibe in this, the beach's oldest bar, which has been pouring drinks since 1926.

Automatic Slim's (Map p508; ☎ 305-695-0795; 1216 Washington Ave) Rockers and rocker wannabes – tattoos are optional – come together at this rockabilly-light bar for theme nights and general rowdiness.

Room (Map p508; ☎ 305-531-6061, 100 Collins Ave) It's dark, atmospheric and low-key. It's also small – thus the name – which is a nice contrast to some of Miami's more grandiose offerings.

Zeke's Roadhouse (Map p508; ☎ 305-672-3118; 625 Lincoln Rd; Wed-Sun) Cheap beer and lots of it is the big draw; the outdoor seating on Lincoln Rd doesn't hurt either.

Playwright (Map p508; ☎ 305-534-0667; 1265 Washington Ave) An affable Irish pub with a vast selection of imported beers, where you can actually hold a conversation.

District (Map p506; ☎ 305-576-7242; 35 NE 40th St) One of those 'is it a restaurant, is it a nightspot?' places in the Design District, with loungey live jazz and cocktails.

Opium Garden & Privé (Map p508; ☎ 305-531-5535; 136 Collins Ave; cover from $25) An open-sky bar with a lantern-strewn Asian decor and more action upstairs. House and dance reign supreme.

LIVE MUSIC

Tobacco Road (Map p510; ☎ 305-374-1198; www.tobacco-road.com; 626 S Miami Ave; tickets from $10) With a roadhouse feel and the oldest liquor license in Miami-Dade County, this rockin' joint has been around since 1912 and is often the scene of impromptu jams by well-known rockers.

Other recommendations:

Hoy Como Ayer (Map p506; ☎ 305-541-2631; www.hoycomoayer.us; 2212 SW 8th St; cover $8-25; from 9pm Wed-Sat) Authentic Cuban music.

Jazid (Map p508; ☎ 305-673-9372; www.jazid.net; 1342 Washington Ave; cover $10 Fri & Sat) Quality jazz in a candlelit lounge.

Churchill's Pub (Map p506; ☎ 305-757-1807; www.churchillspub.com; 5501 NE 2nd Ave; cover $10-15) The best of indie music – as well as UK football broadcasts.

FLORIDA

THEATER & CULTURE

Colony Theater (Map p508; ☎ 305-674-1040; 1040 Lincoln Rd) Everything – from off-Broadway productions to ballet and movies – plays in this renovated 1934 art-deco showpiece.

Fillmore Miami Beach at Jackie Gleason Theater (Map p508; ☎ 305-673-7300; 1700 Washington Ave) Miami Beach's premier showcase for Broadway shows, headliners and the Miami City Ballet.

Adrienne Arsht Center for the Performing Arts (off Map p510; ☎ 305-949-6722; www.arshtcenter.org; 1300 Biscayne Blvd) Showcases jazz from around the world, as well as theater, dance, music, comedy and more.

Miami Beach Cinematheque (Map p508; ☎ 305-673-4567; www.mbcinema.com; 512 Española Way) Screens documentaries, international films and kitschy classics.

SPORTS

Dolphin Stadium (Map p506; 2269 NW 199th St, North Dade) is home to the NFL football team **Miami Dolphins** (☎ 305-620-2578; www.miamidolphins.com; tickets from $29; season Aug-Dec) and the Major League baseball team **Florida Marlins** (☎ 305-626-7400; www.marlins.mlb.com; tickets from $9; season May-Sep).

Miami Heat (☎ 786-777-4667; www.nba.com/heat; tickets from $10; season Nov-Apr) plays NBA basketball at **American Airlines Arena** (Map p510; 601 Biscayne Blvd).

Florida Panthers (☎ 954-835-7000; http://panthers.nhl.com; tickets from $15; season mid-Oct–mid-Apr) plays NHL hockey at the **Bank Atlantic Center** (off Map p506; 1 Panther Pkwy, Sunrise).

Shopping

Browse for one-of-a-kind and designer items at the South Beach boutiques around Collins Ave between 6th and 9th Sts and along Lincoln Rd mall. For unique items, try Little Havana (p509) and the Design District (p511). **Little Havana to Go** (Map p506; ☎ 305-857-9720; 1442 SW 8th St/Calle Ocho) stocks authentic Cuban goods and clothing.

Scads of malls include Miami's most elegant, **Bal Harbour Shops** (Map p506; ☎ 305-866-0311; www.balharbourshops.com; 9700 Collins Ave).

Getting There & Away

Miami International Airport (MIA; Map p506; ☎ 305-876-7000; www.miami-airport.com) is about 6 miles west of downtown and is accessible by **SuperShuttle** (☎ 305-871-2000; www.supershuttle.com), which costs about $15 to downtown or $20 to South Beach.

Greyhound destinations within Florida include Fort Lauderdale ($7.75, 45 minutes), Key West ($37, four hours) and Orlando ($45, five to six hours). Main terminals are the **Airport terminal** (Map p506; ☎ 305-871-1810; 4111 NW 27th St) and **Miami Downtown terminal** (Map p510; ☎ 305-374-6160; 1012 NW 1st Ave).

Amtrak (Map p506; ☎ 305-835-1222; 8303 NW 37th Ave) has a main Miami terminal. The **Tri-Rail** (☎ 800-874-7245; www.tri-rail.com) commuter system serves Miami (with a free transfer to Miami's transit system) and MIA, Fort Lauderdale and its airport ($8.45 round-trip), plus West Palm Beach and its airport ($11.55 round-trip).

Getting Around

Metro-Dade Transit (☎ 305-770-3131; www.miamidade.gov/transit) runs the local Metrobus and Metrorail ($2), as well as the free **Metromover** monorail serving downtown.

FORT LAUDERDALE

Fort Lauderdale was once known as spring break party central. But, like the drunken teens who once littered the beach, the town has graduated and moved on: It's now a stylish, sophisticated city known more for museums and open-air cafes than wet tee-shirt contests and beer bongs. It's also popular among the yacht crowd for its lovely, Venice-style waterways that many people don't even realize exist. Of course, there's still a great beach; it's just settled down since its party days.

Like the rest of south Florida, Fort Lauderdale is a major gay and lesbian destination, bringing a welcome new meaning to *Where the Boys Are*. Head to the **visitor bureau** (☎ 954-765-4466, 800-227-8669; www.sunny.org; 100 E Broward Blvd, Suite 200; 8:30am-5pm Mon-Fri), which also has information for gay and lesbian travelers (www.sunny.org/rainbow).

The **Museum of Art** (☎ 954-525-5500; www.moafl.org; 1 E Las Olas Blvd; admission adult/under 5/child $10/free/7; 11am-5pm Tue-Sat, to 8pm Thu, noon-5pm Sun) is leading the revitalization of downtown, and is known for its William Glackens collection (among Glackens fans) and its exciting exhibitions (among everyone else).

A 52ft kinetic-energy sculpture greets you at the **Museum of Discovery & Science** (☎ 954-467-6637; www.mods.org; 401 SW 2nd St; adult/child/senior $15/12/14; 10am-5pm Mon-Sat, noon-6pm Sun;). Fun exhibits include Gizmo City and Runways to Rockets – where it actually *is* rocket science. Admission to the IMAX theater is included.

Nostalgic car-lovers motor over to the **Fort Lauderdale Antique Car Museum** (☎ 954-779-7300; www.antiquecarmuseum.org; 1527 SW 1st Ave; adult/child under 12 $8/free; 10am-4pm Mon-Sat), features 22 vintage Packards and lots of auto memorabilia.

Add some green to your travel diet with the **Bonnet House Museum & Gardens** (☎ 954-563-5393; www.bonnethouse.org; 900 N Birch Rd; adult/under 6/child $20/free/16; 10am-4pm Tue-Sat, noon-4pm Sun, last house tour 2:30pm). Wandering the 35 acres of lush, subtropical gardens, you might just spot the resident Brazilian squirrel monkeys.

Explore the 'Venice of America' with a romantic **gondola ride** (☎ 877-926-2467; www.gondolaman.com; ride $125; by appointment) that takes you up and down the canals of the rich and famous. Or, for the best unofficial tour of the city, hop on the **Water Bus** (☎ 954-467-6677; www.watertaxi.com; day pass adult/child under 12 $13/10, general admission $7 after 7pm; 10:30am-midnight), whose drivers offer a lively narration of the passing scenery. Get off and on at different stops around town; call or check online for locations.

Sleeping

The area from Rio Mar St at the south to Vistamar St at the north, and from Hwy A1A at the east to Bayshore Dr at the west, offers the highest concentration of accommodations in all price ranges. Check out Superior Small Lodgings at www.sunny.org/ssl.

Deauville Hostel & Crewhouse (☎ 954-568-5000; www.deauvillehostel.com; 2916 N Ocean Blvd; dm $25, s/d $59/89; P) This spiffy hostel just a few blocks from the ocean is cute, clean, friendly and professional – not to mention a steal.

A Little Inn by the Sea (☎ 954-772-2450; www.alittleinn.com; 4546 El Mar Dr; incl breakfast r $109-159, ste $189-239; P) The bright, breezy rooms here have standard Florida beach decor – tiled floors, wicker and tropical prints – but you also get breakfast, bikes and the beach, plus a quieter, out-of-the-way location in Lauderdale-by-the-Sea.

Riverside Hotel (☎ 954-467-0671, 800-325-3280; www.riversidehotel.com; 620 E Las Olas Blvd; r $139-239; P) This Fort Lauderdale landmark – fabulously located downtown on Las Olas – has three room types: more modern rooms in the newer tower, restored rooms in the original property and the more old-fashioned 'classic' rooms.

Pelican Grand (☎ 954-568-9431, 800-525-6232; www.pelicangrandresort.com; 2000 N Ocean Blvd; r $209-379;

) Like staying in a comfy but upscale beach house – that just happens to be 11 stories tall. This oceanfront resort is right on the beach and includes a lazy river ride for freshwater fun.

Gay and lesbian travelers have a plethora of gay-friendly properties to choose from; browse your option at www.sunny.org/rainbow or www.gayfortlauderdale.com. Among the choices is the all-male **Schubert Resort** (954-763-7434; www.schubertresort.com; 855 NE 20th Ave; ste $99-309;). The exterior is motel-chic, the suites are spacious and lovely, and their clothing-optional policy means no one need ever feel encumbered by clothing.

Eating

Floridian (954-463-4041; 1410 E Las Olas Blvd; mains $5-12; 5:30-10pm Tue-Sun;) 'The Flo' satisfies with good diner food including outstanding breakfasts served round the clock. A 1930s classic diner, it keeps up with the times by offering free wi-fi.

Shuck N Dive (954-462-0088; 650 N Federal Hwy; mains $7-20; 11am-11pm) A cluttered shrine to Louisiana State University and the New Orleans Saints, this unassuming strip-mall restaurant serves up a mean Cajun menu.

Le Tub (954-921-9425; 1100 N Ocean Dr, Hollywood; mains $9-27; noon-4am) Head to Hollywood (about 10 miles south) for Le Tub's funky ambience and juicy burgers, which have garnered nationwide buzz.

Casablanca Cafe (954-764-3500; 3049 Alhambra St; mains $10-38; 11:30am-1am Sun-Tue, to 2am Wed-Sat) Try to score a seat on the upstairs balcony of this Moroccan-style home where they serve Mediterranean-inspired food and Florida-style ocean views. For just a taste of the ambience, drop by for happy hour.

Sublime Restaurant & Bar (954-539-9000; 1431 N Federal Hwy; mains $15-19; 5:30-10pm Tue-Sun; V) Shrugging off the alfalfa-sprout image, this chic restaurant serves such inventive and delicious dishes that even carnivores won't miss the meat.

Chima (954-712-0580; 2400 E Las Olas Blvd; all-you-can-eat dinner $49.50; 5:30-9:30pm Mon-Thu, to 10pm Fri, to 10:30pm Sat, 4pm-9pm Sun) Gaucho-costumed servers herd a never-ending cavalcade of meats from table to table in this Brazilian *churrasco*-style steakhouse. And while that may sound campy, it's not: Chima's upscale locale is one of the nicest on Las Olas.

Drinking & Entertainment

Bars generally stay open until 4am on weekends and 2am during the week; check out **Metromix** (southflorida.metromix.com) for listings. Meander the **Riverwalk Arts & Entertainment District** (www.riverwalk-ae.com) along the New River, where you'll find the **Las Olas Riverfront** (954-522-6556; SW 1st Ave at Las Olas Blvd), with stores, restaurants, a movie theater and entertainment. During the winter season, 2nd St is periodically closed off for a giant street party.

There's live music nightly at **O'Hara's Pub & Jazz Cafe** (954-524-1764; 722 E Las Olas Blvd) and the **Poor House** (954-522-5145; 110 SW 3rd Ave). Featured in the movie *Where the Boys Are*, **Elbo Room** (954-463-4615; 241 S Fort Lauderdale Beach Blvd) hangs onto its somewhat seedy reputation as one of the oldest and diviest bars around.

Laid-back **Lulu's Bait Shack** (954-463-7425; 17 S Fort Lauderdale Beach Blvd) lures 'em in with buckets of beer, bowls of mussels and fishbowl drinks for all, right on the edge of the ocean.

Getting There & Around

The **Fort Lauderdale-Hollywood International Airport** (FLL; 954-359-1200; www.fll.net) is served by more than 35 airlines, some with nonstop flights from Europe. A taxi from the airport to downtown costs around $20.

The **Greyhound station** (954-764-6551; 515 NE 3rd St at Federal Hwy) is five blocks from Broward Central Terminal, with multiple daily services. The **train station** (954-587-6692; 200 SW 21st Tce) serves **Amtrak** (800-872-7245; www.amtrak.com), and the **Tri-Rail** (800-874-7245; www.tri-rail.com) has services to Miami and Palm Beach.

Hail a **Sun Trolley** (954-761-3543; www.suntrolley.com; per ride 50¢; Thu-Sun) for rides between downtown, the beach, Las Olas and the Riverfront, Thursday through Sunday.

PALM BEACH & AROUND

Palm Beach isn't all yachts and mansions – but just about. This area, 45 miles north of Fort Lauderdale, is where railroad baron Henry Flagler built his winter retreat, and it's also home to Donald Trump's **Mar-a-Lago** (cnr Southern & S Ocean Blvds). In other words, if you're looking for a beach town or Florida kitsch, keep driving. Contact the Palm Beach County **Convention & Visitor Bureau** (561-233-3000, 800-833-5733; www.palmbeachfl.com; 1555 Palm Beach Lakes Blvd; 8:30am-5:30pm Mon-Fri) in West Palm Beach for area information and maps.

Boca Raton

Halfway between Fort Lauderdale and Palm Beach is this largely residential stretch of picturesque coast that's been preserved from major development. The main reason to stop is the outstanding **Boca Raton Museum of Art** (☎ 561-392-2500; www.bocamuseum.org; 501 Plaza Real, Mizner Park; adult/child under 12 $8/free; ⏲ 10am-5pm Tue, Thu & Fri, to 9pm Wed, noon-5pm Sat & Sun), which has a permanent collection of works by Picasso, Matisse and Warhol, and more than 1200 photographic images. Special exhibitions have a higher admission cost. The museum is in **Mizner Park** (www.miznerpark.org; cnr US 1 & Mizner Blvd), which isn't really a park so much as a ritzy outdoor mall with stores, restaurants and regular free concerts. While there, stop by the **Dubliner** (☎ 561-620-2540; mains $12-23; ⏲ 4pm-2am), where you can have your beer and eat it too, thanks to the Guinness fondue appetizer.

Palm Beach

About 30 miles north of Boca Raton are Palm Beach and West Palm Beach. The two towns have flip-flopped the traditional beachland hierarchy: Palm Beach, the beach town, is more upscale, while West Palm Beach on the mainland is younger and livelier. Because Palm Beach is an enclave of the ultrawealthy, especially during its winter 'social season,' most travelers just window-shop the oceanfront mansions and boutiques lining the aptly named **Worth Avenue**.

But it's worth a drive across the causeway to visit the resplendent **Henry Morrison Flagler Museum** (☎ 561-655-2833; www.flaglermuseum.com; 1 Whitehall Way; adult/child/youth $15/3/8; ⏲ 10am-5pm Tue-Sat, noon-5pm Sun) housed in the railroad magnate's winter estate, Whitehall Mansion. Admission includes the house, special exhibits, Flagler's personal train car and an excellent acoustic guide. Call about afternoon tea ($18), served during winter in the lovely glassed-in pavilion.

Modeled after Rome's Villa Medici, Flagler's opulent oceanfront 1861 hotel, **Breakers** (☎ 561-655-6611, 888-273-2537; www.thebreakers.com; 1 S County Rd; r from $195; P ⊠ ⁂ ☰ ☒) is a super-luxurious world unto itself, encompassing two golf courses, 10 tennis courts, a three-pool Mediterranean beach club and a trove of restaurants.

Watch the well-heeled try to navigate their messy condiments (and be sure to grab something for yourself) at the anachronistically casual **Hamburger Heaven** (☎ 561-655-5277; 314 S County Rd; mains $6-11; ⏲ 7:30am-3pm Mon-Sat, 7:30am-8pm winter). Or, kick it Formica-style with an egg cream and a low-cal platter at **Green's Luncheonette** (☎ 561-832-4443; 151 N County Rd; mains $3-11; ⏲ 7am-3pm Mon-Sat, to 2pm Sun) inside Green's Pharmacy.

West Palm Beach

Inland from Palm Beach is West Palm Beach, with a more relaxed vibe that's not so painstakingly tasteful. Start your visit at the well-regarded **Norton Museum of Art** (☎ 561-832-5196; www.norton.org; 1451 S Olive Ave; admission adult/child 12yr & under/student $8/free/3; ⏲ 10am-5pm Mon-Sat, 1-5pm Sun Oct-May, closed Mon May-Oct), housing American and European modern masters and impressionists, along with a large Buddha head presiding over an impressive Asian art collection.

If the kids are bored by all the opulence, treat them to the planetarium, aquarium and interactive exhibits at the **South Florida Science Museum** (☎ 561-832-1988; www.sfsm.org; 4801 Dreher Trail N; adult/child museum $9/6, planetarium extra $4/2; ⏲ 10am-5pm Mon-Fri, to 6pm Sat, noon-6pm Sun; ♿).

The coolest lodging in town is **Hotel Biba** (☎ 561-832-0094; www.hotelbiba.com; 320 Belvedere Rd; r $99-215; P ⁂ ☰ ☒). The retro-funky exterior looks like a cute, 1950s motel in honeydew-melon green, but the rooms have a modern boutique style that would be right at home in Miami's SoBe.

Much of the action centers around **CityPlace** (www.cityplace.com; 700 S Rosemary Ave), a European village-style alfresco mall with splashing fountains and a slew of dining and entertainment options. **Clematis Street** also has several worthy bars and restaurants to recommend it. Try **Rocco's Tacos & Tequila Bar** (☎ 561-650-1001; 24 Clematis St; mains $9-19; ⏲ 11:30am-11pm Sun & Mon, to midnight Tue-Wed, to 1am Thu-Sat) for, well, tacos and tequila. Make that 175 different kinds of tequila – no wonder it's so loud in here!

Admirably servicing its migration of snowbirds, **Palm Beach International Airport** (PBI; ☎ 561-471-7420; www.pbia.org), 2.5 miles west of downtown West Palm Beach, can be a good alternative gateway to the south Florida region. The downtown **Tri-Rail station** (☎ 800-874-7245; 201 S Tamarind Ave) also serves as the **Amtrak station** (☎ 561-832-6169).

THE EVERGLADES

To the uninitiated, the Everglades might appear to be nothing more than a big swamp full of alligators and the place where they occasionally find dead bodies on *CSI: Miami*. First of all, it's not a swamp; it's a wet prairie. This may be splitting hairs, but swamps have trees, whereas the Everglades only have tree islands. It's also not stagnant, as some people believe, but creeps slowly – verrry slowly – towards the ocean. You *will* see alligators, although they won't be wearing chef hats or driving airboats as the campy roadside signs will have you believe.

The Everglades is an incredible, unique ecosystem, a subtropical wilderness that supports creatures such as endangered American crocodiles, bottlenose dolphins, manatees, snowy egrets, bald eagles and ospreys. And amid the mangroves, cypress, hardwood hammocks and miles of sawgrass, there are endless opportunities for hiking, bicycling, canoeing, kayaking, boating, camping and fishing.

The Everglades has two seasons: the wet season and the dry season. And it makes a big difference which it is when you visit. The winter dry season – from December to April – is the prime time to visit: the weather is mild and pleasant and the wildlife is out in abundance. In the summer wet season – May through November – it's hot and humid and there are frequently afternoon thunderstorms. The animals disperse, but the bugs don't, and they'll be looking for you. The one upside to visiting in the wet season is that you won't be sharing your experience with as many tourists.

Everglades National Park

While the Everglades have a history dating back to prehistoric times, the park wasn't founded until 1947. It's the only national park preserved not for its stunning beauty, but because someone had the foresight to recognize its ecological importance. It's considered the most endangered national park in the USA, but the Comprehensive Everglades Restoration Plan (see the boxed text, opposite) has been enacted to undo some of the damage done by draining and development.

ORIENTATION & INFORMATION

The only road taking you south into the heart of the park is Rte 9336. Rte 997 takes you north–south along the park's eastern edge. Running east–west, the Tamiami Trail (a contraction of Tampa–Miami) is a breathtaking

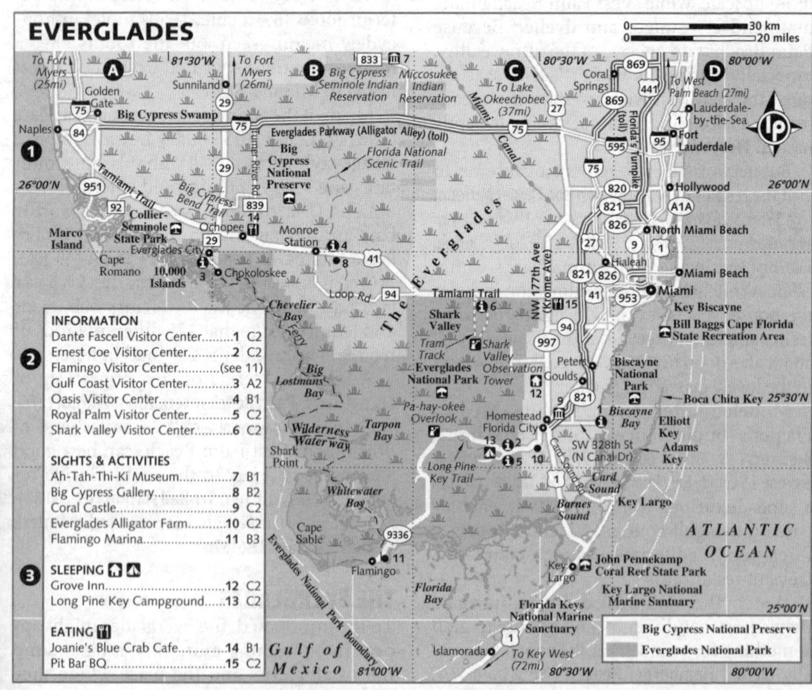

HOT TOPIC: SAVING THE EVERGLADES

A hundred years ago, politicians occupied themselves with how to drain the Everglades. Now, environmentalists and even politicians are working hard to bring the water back.

The Everglades was once a vibrant 100-mile-long river that flowed from Lake Okeechobee to the southern tip of Florida. In order to control flooding and reclaim the land, dikes were built and canals were dug. In 1906, the thirsty, non-native melaleuca tree was even introduced to help suck up all the water.

It all worked too well. The Everglades shrank to a fraction of their original size. The delicate ecosystem – which provides fresh water to the region and supports several endangered species – was on the verge of collapse. Today, water levels are a constant concern, as is water quality.

Now, the Corps of Engineers along with federal, state, local and tribal governments are coming together to carry out the Comprehensive Everglades Restoration Plan, approved as part of the Water Resources Development Act in 2000. It will take 30 years and billions of dollars, but the plan involves filling in canals, taking out levees and restoring the water flow.

For a thorough and fascinating look at how this story has unfolded over time, visit the excellent website, www.theevergladesstory.org.

drive between the coasts. It runs parallel to the northern (and far less scenic) Alligator Alley, or I-75.

The main park entry points have visitor centers where you can get maps, camping permits and ranger information. You only need to pay the entrance fee (per car/pedestrian $10/5 for seven days) once to access all points.

Even in winter it's almost impossible to avoid mosquitoes, but they're ferocious in summer: bring *strong* repellent. Alligators are also prevalent. As obvious as it sounds, don't provoke them or even feed them: it's important that they don't learn to associate humans with food, and anyway, they can't tell where the food ends and the human begins. Although you're not likely to see them, poisonous snakes here include the diamondback and pigmy rattlesnakes, cottonmouth or water moccasin (which swims along the surface of water), and coral snakes; wear long, thick socks and lace-up boots.

SIGHTS & ACTIVITIES

If you're just driving out from Miami to take a quick peek, the best use of your time is to head straight to **Shark Valley Visitor Center** (☎ 305-221-8776; Tamiami Trail; ⏲ 8:30am-6pm), where you can take an excellent two-hour **tram tour** (☎ 305-221-8455; adult/child 3-12yr $16.25/10) along a 15-mile asphalt trail where you'll see copious numbers of alligators in the winter months. Not only do you get to experience it from the shady comfort of a breezy tram, but it's narrated by knowledgeable park rangers who give a fascinating overview of the Everglades and its inhabitants. Halfway along the trail you'll come to a 50ft-high observation tower, an out-of-place concrete structure that offers a dramatic panorama of the park. You can also walk in or **bicycle** (bike rental per hr $7); guided full-moon bike tours are offered from January to April; call the main number for more info.

For people who have more than a couple of hours to spare, head south to the **Ernest Coe Visitor Center** (☎ 305-242-7700; www.nps.gov/ever; Hwy 9336; ⏲ 8am-5pm, from 9am in summer), which is packed with information about trails and other activities and has excellent, museum-like exhibits. Call for a schedule of fun ranger-led programs, including the 'slough slog,' a two-hour wet walk through the slow-moving grassy river. Most programs start at the nearby **Royal Palm Visitor Center** (☎ 305-242-7700; Hwy 9336; ⏲ 8am-4:15pm), where you can also catch two short trails. The Anhinga Trail is great for wildlife spotting, especially alligators and especially in winter, and the Gumbo-Limbo showcases plants and trees.

From here, you can drive 38 miles to the coast and the **Flamingo Visitor Center** (☎ 239-695-3094; ⏲ 7:30am-5pm Dec-Apr, hrs vary May-Nov), which has maps of canoeing and hiking trails. If you've been to the area before, you might notice the conspicuous absence of the Flamingo Lodge and restaurant – the only lodging and eating options in the park – which were wiped out by hurricanes in 2005. However, the **Flamingo Marina** (☎ 239-695-3101; ⏲ 7am-7pm Mon-Fri, 6am-7Pm Sat & Sun) still offers boat rentals and tours, plus a store where you can buy food and supplies.

For a completely different perspective, visit the park from the opposite side. At the northwestern edge of the Everglades is the **Gulf Coast Visitor Center** (239-695-3311; 815 Oyster Bar Lane off Hwy 29, Everglades City; 9am-4:30pm). From here, the **10,000 Islands** mangroves and waterways offer incredible canoeing and kayaking opportunities – including short trips to sandy beaches and shallow, brackish lagoons – and the 99-mile **Wilderness Waterway**, which runs along the park's southern edge from here to Flamingo. Rangers lead canoe trips and walks, and a **concessionaire** (239-695-2591; boat tours adult/child 5-12yr $26.50/13.25, canoe rental per day $25) offers 90-minute boat tours plus canoe rentals.

Think of the Everglades and you might think of airboats (those flat-bottom crafts with a giant fan on the back), but actually they're forbidden in the park proper. The best place to take a 30- to 45-minute ride is at the family-owned **Everglades Alligator Farm** (305-247-2628; www.everglades.com; 40351 SW 192 Ave, Homestead; adult/child $23/15.50; 9am-6pm), where you can also hold baby alligators.

SLEEPING

Sleep tight, and don't let the alligators bite. The Everglades has developed **campsites** (239-695-0124, 800-365-2267; www.recreation.gov; campsites $14; Sep-May) inside the park and at Long Pine Key, 7 miles from the main entrance. They're free during the brutally hot months (lucky you) but the rest of the year there's a fee and you'll need reservations.

Camping elsewhere in the park includes beach sites, ground sites and chickees (covered wooden platforms above the water) in the backcountry along the Wilderness Waterway. **Backcountry camping** (tent sites $10) is permitted throughout the park but a permit from the visitor center is required.

AROUND THE EVERGLADES

Coming from Miami, the gateway towns of Homestead and Florida City on the east side of the park make an ideal base, especially if you're headed for the Keys. Comprehensive information about the region is available at www.evergladesonline.com.

Biscayne National Park

Just south of Miami (and east of Homestead and Florida City) is this national park that's 95% water. But the 5% of land is some of the most serene and secluded waterfront you'll find. Here you can see manatees and sea turtles in four diverse ecosystems (keys, coral reef, mangrove forest and bay). Get general park information from **Dante Fascell Visitor Center** (305-230-7275; 9700 SW 328th St, Homestead; 9am-5pm). A park **concessionaire** (305-230-1100; www.biscayneunderwater.com) runs three-hour glass-bottom boat tours, snorkel trips, and dive trips, all of which require reservations, and also rents canoes and kayaks.

WHERE'S ROBERT?

Hot? Hungry? Heading towards the Everglades? You must – must! – stop at **Robert is Here** (305-246-1592; 19200 SW 344th St, Homestead; 8am-7pm Nov-Aug;) for a key lime milk shake (unless it's September or October, in which case you'll just have to stare longingly at the sign). This roadside fruit stand has local produce and a bevy of milk shake flavors. But it's one of the few places in the world where you'll find a key-lime–flavored milk shake, which has the perfect sweet-to-tart ratio and will have you perky and refreshed in no time.

Florida City & Homestead

A favored kitschy tourist stop in Homestead is **Coral Castle** (305-248-6345; www.coralcastle.com; 28655 S Dixie Hwy, Homestead; adult/child $9.75/5; 8am-6pm Sun-Thu, 8am-9pm Fri & Sat), which isn't a castle at all but a delightfully weird sculpture garden and monument to lost love.

The Homestead-Florida City area has no shortage of chain motels and fast-food restaurants, but there are some gems worth searching out, including the **Everglades International Hostel & Tours** (800-372-3874, 305-248-1122; www.evergladeshostel.com; 20 SW 2nd Ave, Florida City; dm/r $28/75;). Even if you're not staying here, one of the best ways to see the park is with the hostel's **canoe & slough slog tour** (all day incl meals $60-100), led by wilderness guides from November to March. You can also rent canoes ($30) and bikes ($15) to explore on your own. North of town, **Grove Inn** (305-247-6572; www.groveinn.com; 22540 SW Krome Ave, Miami; r $99-109) lets you escape the fast-paced Homestead lifestyle for more rural delights. Enjoy a tropical garden, homey rooms, and a full country breakfast.

Not just a restaurant but a bit of a social center, as well, the always-lively **White Lion**

Cafe (☎ 305-248-1076; 146 NW 7th St, Homestead; mains $7-22; 🕑 11am-3pm Mon-Sat, 5pm 'till the fat lady sings' Tue-Sat) has BBQs, patio parties and karaoke, and the inside is still cute enough to bring your grandmother for lunch. The diverse menu includes a $200 peanut-butter-jelly sandwich served with a complimentary bottle of Dom Perignon. For middle-of-the-night cravings, the dependable **Mario's Latin Cafe** (☎ 305-247-2470; 1090 N Homestead Blvd, Homestead; mains $5-14; 🕑 24hr) is open all night and even delivers from 10am to 10pm.

Tamiami Trail

On the north edge of Everglades National Park – just across the Tamiami Trail – is the 1139-sq-mile **Big Cypress National Preserve** (www.nps.gov/bicy). Residents include alligators, snakes, Florida panthers (rarely seen), wild turkeys and many impressively large birds. Great bald cypress trees are nearly gone from the area, but dwarf pond cypress thrive. Thirty-one miles of the **Florida National Scenic Trail** (☎ 352-378-8823; www.florida-trail.org) cut through Big Cypress. Get information from the **Oasis Visitor Center** (☎ 239-695-1201; 🕑 9am-4:30pm), about 20 miles west of Shark Valley. The preserve's four no-fee primitive **campgrounds** (☎ 239-695-1201) are along the Tamiami Trail and Loop Rd; **Monument Lake Campground** (campsites $16) has more developed facilities.

Half a mile east of the visitor center, drop into the **Big Cypress Gallery** (☎ 239-695-2428; www.clydebutcher.com; 52388 Tamiami Trail, Ochopee; 🕑 10am-5pm Wed-Mon Dec-Apr, Fri-Mon May-Nov), displaying Clyde Butcher's work; his large-scale B&W landscape photographs spotlight the region's unusual beauty.

North of Alligator Alley (Hwy 75) **Ah-Tah-Thi-Ki Museum** (☎ 863-902-1113; www.ahtahthiki.com; Big Cypress Seminole Indian Reservation, Hwy 8333; adult/child $9/6; 🕑 9am-5pm Tue-Sun) has a 1.5-mile, wheelchair-accessible nature trail that takes you through a 60-acre cypress dome to a re-created Seminole village.

A good pit stop as you're heading to or from Miami is the **Pit Bar BQ** (☎ 305-226-2272; 16400 SW 8th St, Miami; mains $7-12; 🕑 11am-10pm, closing hr vary), a screened-in roadside place with checkered table clothes and homemade BBQ sauce.

Everglades City

This small town at the edge of the park warrants a mention mostly as a good base for exploring 10,000 Islands or the Wilderness Waterway. You don't have to be a big-time hunter-gatherer to bunk at the **Rod & Gun Lodge** (☎ 239-695-2101; www.evergladesrodandgun.com; 200 Riverside Dr; r $95-140; P ✱ 🏊). Even though it was built as a hunting lodge, it still has wraparound porches, cozy rooms and a tranquil riverside setting. The **Ivey House Bed & Breakfast** (☎ 239-695-3299; www.iveyhouse.com; 107 Camellia St; r $60-145; P ⊠ ✱ 🏊) lets you choose between basic accommodations in the lodge (a former boarding house) or somewhat sprucer rooms in the inn.

A bright spot in the local dining scene, **JT's Island Grill & Gallery** (☎ 239-695-3633; 238 Mamie St, Chokoloskee; mains $4-12; 🕑 11am-3pm late Oct-May) sits on the edge of town, serving up lunch in a restored 1890 general store with kitsch and charm to spare.

For dinner, try the **Everglades Seafood Depot** (☎ 239-695-0075; 102 Collier Ave; mains $12-28), a seafood joint serving everything that swims in an atmosphere best described as 1970s nautical.

East of Everglades City – and just east of Ochopee – is the quintessential 1950s-style swamp shack, **Joanie's Blue Crab Cafe** (☎ 239-695-2682; 39395 Tamiami Trail; mains $9-15; 🕑 10am-5pm Wed-Mon), with open rafters, colorful, shellacked picnic tables and a swamp dinner of gator nuggets and fritters.

FLORIDA KEYS

Before Henry Flagler completed his railroad in 1912, which connected the Keys to the mainland, this 126-mile string of islands was just a series of untethered bumps of land accessible only by boat. (Little surprise, then, that their early economies were built on piracy, smuggling, ship salvaging and fishing). Flagler's railroad was destroyed by a hurricane in 1935, but what remained of its bridges allowed the Overseas Hwy to be completed in 1938. Now, streams of travelers swarm down from the mainland to indulge in the alluring jade-green waters, laid-back island lifestyle, great fishing and idyllic snorkeling and diving.

The Upper Keys – from Key Largo to Islamorada – are cluttered with touristy shops and motels, and from the highway you can't even see the water. But as you go farther south into the Middle Keys, the land starts to open up, offering the startling realization that you're actually driving from island to island. Trailing off like ellipses, the islands get smaller as you reach the Lower Keys, which is everything from Little Duck Key on. But far from petering out, the keys reach their grand finale at the end of the highway in Key West – the favorite key of all for many visitors.

Many addresses in the Keys are noted by their proximity to mile markers (indicated as MM), which start at MM126 in Florida City and count down to MM0 in Key West. They also might indicate whether they're 'oceanside,' which is the south side of the highway, or 'bayside,' which is north.

The **Florida Keys & Key West Visitors Bureau** (☎ 800-352-5397; www.fla-keys.com) has information on the entire area.

Key Largo

There are high expectations as you come over the Overseas Hwy onto Key Largo. You've heard of it your whole life. Made famous in film by Bogie and Bacall, it's been immortalized in song by musicians from the Beach Boys to Sade to Bertie Higgins. It sounds so romantic. And then you get there.

OK, it may be time to re-adjust. It's just a sleepy island and the views from the highway aren't even all that good. But there are water sports galore and some of the best snorkeling and diving around, thanks to the only living coral reef in the continental US. For maps and brochures, visit the **chamber of commerce** (☎ 305-451-4747, 800-822-1088; www.keylargo.org; MM 106 bayside; 🕑 9am-6pm).

Diving is best at **John Pennekamp Coral Reef State Park** (☎ 305-451-1202; www.pennekamppark.com; MM 102.5 oceanside; vehicle $3.50, with 2 passengers $6, each additional passenger 50c, pedestrian $1.50), the first underwater park in the US. In addition to a live coral reef, you can see the underwater **Christ of the Deep**, a 9ft algae-covered bronze statue that's a replica of Italy's Christ of the Abyss.

If you want to stay dry, you can view the dazzling fish and coral during a 2½-hour **glass-bottom boat tour** (adult/child $24/17; 🕑 9:15am, 12:15pm & 3pm). Or you can dive right in with a **snorkeling trip** (adult/child $30/25 plus gear rental; 🕑 9am, noon & 3pm), or a two-location, two-tank **diving trip** ($60 plus gear rental; 🕑 departs 9:30am & 1:30pm). You can also rent **canoes or kayaks** (per hr single/double $12/17) to journey through a 3-mile network of canoe trails. Call ☎ 305-451-6300 for all excursions.

Dozens of private outfitters take snorkelers and scuba divers out to the reef; half-day trips leave twice daily, usually around 9am and 1pm. **Horizon Divers** (☎ 305-453-3535, 800-984-3483; www.horizondivers.com; 100 Ocean Key, off MM 100 oceanside; trips snorkel $50, scuba $80) has a friendly crew and offers rentals, dive trips and even scuba instruction.

For off-park paddling, **Florida Bay Outfitters** (☎ 305-451-3018; www.kayakfloridakeys.com; MM 104 bayside; kayak rental per half-day $40) has kayak and canoe rentals, as well as kayak tours – including a full-moon paddle – starting at $60. You can also rent camping equipment here.

SLEEPING & EATING

In addition to luxe resorts, Key Largo has loads of bright, cheery motels and camping.

John Pennekamp Coral Reef State Park (☎ 800-326-3521; www.pennekamppark.com; campsites $26) Sleep with the fishes – or at least near them – at one of the 47 coral-reef-adjacent sites here. Camping's poplar; reserve well in advance by phone or at www.reserveamerica.com.

our pick **Largo Lodge** (☎ 305-451-0424; www.largolodge.com; MM 101.7 bayside; cottages $95-195; P) These charming, sunny cottages with their own private beach – family owned since the '50s – are surrounded by palm trees, tropical flowers and lots of roaming birds, for a taste of Florida in the good old days. (Over 16s only, please.)

Sunset Cove Beach Resort (☎ 877-451-0705; www.sunsetcovebeachresort.com; MM 99.5 bayside; r & cottages incl breakfast $120-180; ♿) Huge fiberglass sculptures of dinosaurs, zebras and swans play host at this funky place where, along with your room, you get continental breakfast and free use of canoes, kayaks and chickee huts.

Mrs Mac's Kitchen (☎ 305-451-3722; MM 99.4 bayside; mains $5-17; 🕑 7am-9:30pm Mon-Sat) This cute roadside diner bedecked with rusty license plates serves classic highway food such as burgers and fish baskets.

Alabama Jacks (☎ 305-248-8741; 58000 Card Sound Rd; mains $5-25; 🕑 11am-7pm) On the back road between Key Largo and Florida City, this funky open-air joint draws an eclectic crowd hungry for fish dishes washed down with local beer. Try the conch fritters; they're rave-worthy.

Hideout Restaurant (☎ 305-451-0128; MM 103.5 oceanside, end of Transylvania Ave; mains $6-9; 🕑 7am-2pm daily, 5-9pm Fri) Try to blend in; this place has cheap food and a suspicious attitude toward strangers. During Friday-night fish fries, eat as much as you like for $10.95.

Key Largo Conch House (☎ 305-453-4844; MM 100.2 oceanside; mains $7-25; 🕑 7am-10pm) Now *this* feels like the islands: conch architecture, tropical foliage, a parrot, and crab and conch dishes help ease you off the mainland.

RESPONSIBLE SNORKELING

Coral reefs are fragile ecosystems, and the more we appreciate them, the more we're in danger of losing them. Just being aware of the risks can go a long way when you're snorkeling or diving:

- Look at but don't touch the reef or its inhabitants.
- Don't take anything from the reef (like shells) or leave anything behind (like trash).
- 'Leave only footprints' is a good motto on land, but in the water you shouldn't even do that: take care not to stand on or accidentally kick the reef, and be aware of tides that could push you into it.
- Choose biodegradable sunblock that's less harmful to marine life, and go light on personal care products that will wash off in the water. (The fish don't care how you look.)
- Move slowly so you don't stress the fish, who might see you as a large predator, and don't chase them. In other words, try to blend in.

Fish House (☎ 305-451-4665; MM 102.4 oceanside; lunch mains $8-16, dinner mains $12-27; 11:30am-10pm) Fish nets (not the sexy kind), sea shells and a ship-like interior form the backdrop for you to enjoy fish, fish and more fish. (Try the fish.)

Islamorada

It sounds like an island, but Islamorada is actually a string of several islands, the epicenter of which is Upper Matecumbe Key. Several little nooks of beach are easily accessible here, providing scenic rest stops. Housed in an old red caboose, the **chamber of commerce** (☎ 305-664-4503, 800-322-5397; www.islamoradachamber.com; MM 83.2 bayside; 9am-5pm Mon-Fri, 9am-4pm Sat, 9am-3pm Sun) has information about the area.

Billed as 'The Sportfishing Capital of the World,' Islamorada is a good place to catch fish, look at fish, feed the fish and eat fish – it's almost Gumplike in its variety. Catering the buffet of options is **Robbie's Marina** (☎ 305-664-9814, 877-664-8498; www.robbies.com; MM 77.5 bayside), which offers fishing charters, jet skiing, and ecotours, and rents kayaks, boats and even houseboats. Even if you don't need watercraft, do stop to feed the tarpon. These huge fish swarm impatiently under the dock waiting for you to hand feed them from a $3 bucket of baitfish.

You'll need a boat to visit Islamorada's two greatest treasures – neither one is accessible by car. On the ocean side a few hundred yards offshore, **Indian Key Historic State Park** (☎ 305-664-2540; www.floridastateparks.org; 8am-sunset) is a peaceful little island with the crumbling foundations of a 19th-century settlement that was wiped out by Native Americans (who, to be fair, were there first). On the bay side, the isolated **Lignumvitae Key Botanical State Park** (☎ 305-664-2540; www.floridastateparks.org; 8am-dusk) has virgin tropical forests and Matheson House, which was built in 1919. Robbie's Marina helps get you there with shuttles and boat rentals; call for schedules and prices.

Dolphins and sea lions perform in an intimate, close-up setting at **Theater of the Sea** (☎ 305-664-2431; www.theaterofthesea.com; MM 84.5 oceanside; adult/child 3-10yr $26/19; 9:30am-5pm), and for an extra fee you can meet or swim with them.

Check out layer after layer of geological history in the quarry at **Windley Reef State Geologic Site** (☎ 305-664-2540; www.floridastateparks.org; MM 85.5 oceanside; call for schedule), with 8ft walls of fossilized coral. For public beach access and shaded picnic tables, try **Anne's Beach** (MM 73.5 oceanside; admission free) on the oceanside boardwalk (the beach disappears at high tide). Area dive shops include **Holiday Isle Dive Shop** (☎ 305-664-3483, 800-327-7070; www.diveholidayisle.com; MM 84.5 oceanside; half-day snorkeling/diving $30/50, plus equipment rental $9/40), with half-day trips departing at 9am and 1pm.

SLEEPING & EATING

Long Key State Recreation Area (☎ 305-664-4815; www.floridastateparks.org; MM 67.5; campsites $31.49) Book as far ahead as possible for 60 coveted oceanfront campsites in a shady, 965-acre park.

Ragged Edge Resort (☎ 305-852-5389; www.ragged-edge.com; 243 Treasure Harbor Rd; r $62-169, ste $160-249; P) Swim off the docks at this happily unpretentious oceanfront complex off MM 86.5, with spotless motel rooms, efficiencies and two-bedroom family suites.

Lime Tree Bay Resort Motel (☎ 305-664-4740, 800-723-4519; www.limetreebayresort.com; MM 68.5 bayside;

r $89-117, ste $125-295; P ⊠ ⁂ ≋ ⚐) A plethora of hammocks and lawn chairs provide front-row seats for the spectacular sunsets at this 2.5-acre waterfront hideaway.

Casa Morada (☎ 305-664-0044, 888-881-3030; www.casamorada.com; 136 Madeira Rd; ste incl breakfast summer $239-499, winter $329-659; P ⊠ ⁂ ⚐) Twelve Miami-stylish suites make the most of their oceanside location with a sandy beach and secluded pool; yoga and breakfast are included.

Island Grill (☎ 305-664-8400; MM 85.5 oceanside; mains $8-28; ⏲ 11am-10pm Sun-Thu, to 11pm Fri & Sat) Just under Snake Creek Bridge, this hidden spot has a lovely wooden deck made from a sunken houseboat that was raised and restored. The menu is eclectic, but mostly involves fish.

Hog Heaven (☎ 305-664-9669; MM 83 oceanside; mains $10-18; ⏲ 11am-3:30am) From bar food to sandwiches and salads to T-bone steaks, their diverse menu rocks. Come during happy hour (4pm to 8pm) and bring a designated driver; the drinks are practically free.

our pick **Morada Bay** (☎ 305-664-0604; MM 81.6 bayside; lunch mains $11-15, dinner mains $24-33; ⏲ 11:30am-10pm) Grab a table under a palm tree on the white-sand beach and sip a rum drink with your fresh seafood, or dance under the stars at their monthly full-moon party.

Pierre's (☎ 305-664-3225; MM 81.6 bayside; mains $34-40; ⏲ 5:30-10pm Sun-Thu, to 11pm Fri & Sat) Pierre's occupies a two-story waterfront colonial house next door to Morada Bay and pays attention to detail, right down to the hand-cut, hand-placed wooden bar, gourmet seafood and fine wine list.

Marathon

As you drive towards Marathon, you'll start seeing some spectacular ocean views. Halfway between Key Largo and Key West, Marathon has sizable marinas and is a hub for commercial fishing and lobster boats. Get local information at the **visitor center** (☎ 305-743-5417, 800-262-7284; www.floridakeysmarathon.com; MM 53.5 bayside; ⏲ 9am-5pm).

SIGHTS & ACTIVITIES

At the southwest city limit, the **Seven Mile Bridge** is the longest of the 40-plus bridges that link the island chain. Running parallel on the north side are remnants of the original Seven Mile Bridge, built as part of the railroad to Key West. **Pigeon Key National Historic District** (☎ 305-743-5999; www.pigeonkey.net; adult/child $11/8.50; ⏲ 9:30am-4pm, last admission 2:30pm) on the Marathon side of the bridge served as a camp for the workers who toiled 14 hours a day – thus the name 'Marathon' – to build the Overseas Hwy after the hurricane took down the railroad in the early 1900s. You can reach it by ferry (departs 10am to 2:30pm, call for schedule), which is included in your admission, or walk the 2.5 miles over the expanse of original bridge. Once there, you have access to the century-old buildings and a museum chronicling the lives of the men who lived and worked there.

If all those ocean views make you want to pull over and feel the sand between your toes, make your way to **Sombrero Beach** (Sombrero Beach Rd, off MM 50 oceanside; admission free) to sample the surf.

Escape all the development at the 63-acre **Crane Point Museums & Nature Center** (☎ 305-743-9100; www.cranepoint.net; MM 50.5 bayside; admission adult/child 6-12yr $11/7; ⏲ 9am-5pm Mon-Sat, noon-5pm Sun), where you'll find a vast system of nature trails and mangroves, a raised boardwalk, a rare early-20th-century Bahamian-style house, exhibits on pirates and wrecking, and a walk-through coral reef tunnel.

Marathon Kayak (☎ 305-743-0561; www.marathonkayak.com; 6363 Overseas Hwy/MM 50 oceanside; single/double half-day rental $35/50, full day $50/65) provides kayak instruction, plus three-hour guided mangrove ecotours and three-hour sunset tours (each tour per person $45).

SLEEPING & EATING

Conch Key Cottages (☎ 305-289-1377, 800-330-1577; www.conchkeycottages.com; MM 62.3 oceanside, Conch Key; efficiency $115-199, cottages $199-449; P ⁂ ≋ ⚐) This collection of cheery cottages and studios hidden away off the road features charmingly cozy decor, kayaks and grills, and a mess of bougainvillea.

Rainbow Bend Fishing Resort (☎ 305-289-1505, 800-929-1505; www.rainbowbend.com; MM58 oceanside; r $150-180, ste $165-280; P ⁂ ⚐) A stay here includes the half-day use of a motorboat, sailboat, paddleboat, canoe or kayak, and breakfast to fuel your adventures.

7 Mile Grill (☎ 305-743-4481; MM 47.5 bayside; mains $5-11; ⏲ 7am-9pm) The stopping point along the Overseas Hwy when there was nothing else here, this local favorite has served up reliable cheap eats since 1954.

Keys Fisheries Restaurant (☎ 305-743-4353; at the end of 35th St, off MM 49 bayside; mains $6-19; ⏲ 11:30am-9pm)

Shoo the seagulls from your picnic table on the deck and dig in to fresh seafood in a down-and-dirty dockside atmosphere.

Island Fish Co (☎ 305-743-4191; MM 54 bayside; mains $16-24; 11:30am-11pm) Grab a spicy bowl of conch chowder and a seat overlooking the water at this huge, open-air tiki hut that has a raw bar and copious fish specialties.

Lower Keys

Key West notwithstanding, the Lower Keys (MM 46 to MM 0) are the least developed of the island chain. The **chamber of commerce** (☎ 305-872-2411, 800-872-3722; www.lowerkeyschamber.com; MM 31; 9am-5pm Mon-Fri, 9am-3pm Sat) is on Big Pine Key.

The Keys' most acclaimed beach – known for its shallow, warm and eminently wade-able water – is at **Bahia Honda State Park** (☎ 305-872-3210; www.bahiahondapark.com; MM 37 oceanside; admission per 1-/2-/additional person $3.50/6/50¢), a 524-acre park with nature trails, ranger-led programs and water-sports rentals.

Drive slowly: along the highway in Big Pine Key is the 84,000-acre **National Key Deer Refuge**. Stop by or contact the **visitors center** (☎ 305-872-0774; nationalkeydeer.fws.gov; MM30.5 bayside; 8am-5pm Mon-Fri) at Big Pine Shopping Center to learn more about these endangered, dog-size deer and the trails where you can view them; they're easiest to spot at dusk and dawn.

Looe Key teems with colorful tropical fish and coral; try **Looe Key Dive Center** (☎ 305-872-2215, 800-942-5397; www.diveflakeys.com; MM 27.5 oceanside) on Ramrod Key for day trips departing at 10am and returning at 3pm. This three-tank/three-location dive is $80 plus gear for scuba divers, $40 plus gear for snorkelers, and $25 for 'bubblewatchers' who want to come along for the ride.

There are two good reasons we can think of to spend the night in the lower keys instead of heading on in to Key West: a splendid beach and a private island. Camping at **Bahia Honda State Park** (☎ 800-326-3521; campsites $31.50, cabins $136) is sublime, but highly sought after so book ahead; there are also six waterfront cabins. If luxury and seclusion is more your idea of paradise, try **Little Palm Island** (☎ 305-872-2524; www.littlepalmisland.com; Little Torch Key; r $690-1290;), where there are 30 thatched cottages on a private island that can be reached only by boat.

It's hard to miss the jumbo shrimp statue that marks your arrival at the **Good Food Conspiracy** (☎ 305-872-3945; MM 30 oceanside; mains $7-10; 9:30am-7pm Mon-Sat, to 5pm Sun), where you'll find healthy hippie food along with your photo op.

The proprietors at the **No Name Pub** (☎ 305-872-9115; N Watson Blvd off MM 30.5 bayside; mains $8-20; 11am-11pm), 1.5 miles north of US 1 on Big Pine Key, know where their retirement is coming from: the approximately $60,000 in $1 bills stapled to the walls by customers; stop by for pizza and beer.

Key West

Anyone will tell you Key West is a little kooky – and darn proud of it. In the words of one local: 'It's like they shook the United States and all the nuts fell to the bottom.'

The town's funky, laid-back vibe has long attracted artists, renegades and free spirits. Part of that independent streak is rooted in its physical geography: barely connected to the USA, Key West is closer to Cuba than to the rest of the States. There's only one road in, and it's not on the way to anywhere. In other words, it's an easy place to do your own thing.

Because of its handy proximity to absolutely nothing, it's been immune to corporate interference. Chickens and six-toed cats have their run of the island. Bicycles are the favored means of transportation. And few people work nine to five.

Originally called 'Cayo Hueso' – Spanish for 'Bone Island' – Key West was named for all the skeletons that early explorers found littering the beach. Since then, the island has enjoyed a long and colorful history that includes pirates, sunken treasures, literary legends and lots of ghosts.

These days, people flock to Key West to soak up the sun, the mellow atmosphere and more than a little booze. They listen to tales of the past. They snorkel the crystal-clear water. And they find their internal clocks set to 'island time.'

But the town's popularity is like catnip to frisky developers, and they've started snapping up real estate – of which, on an island this small, there's not much. The town still clings to its funky charm, but the whole place is in danger of becoming a giant condo complex with a faint memory of mystique. In other words, go now so that in 10 years you can shake your head and say, 'You shoulda seen it 10 years ago.'

ORIENTATION & INFORMATION

When most people think of Key West, they think of Old Town, the western end of the island and the heart of the action, with inns, eateries and boisterous bars. The main drags are Duval St, which at the north end has a bit of a giant souvenir shop feel, and Truman Ave (US 1). New Town – known by most as the part of town you drive through to get to Old Town – is primarily residential.

A great trip-planning resource is www.fla-keys.com/keywest. Once in town, you'll find maps and brochures at the **Key West Chamber of Commerce** (☎ 305-294-2587, 800-527-8539; www.keywestchamber.org; 402 Wall St, Mallory Sq; 🕑 8am-6:30pm Mon-Fri, 9am-6pm Sat & Sun).

Gay and lesbian visitors can get information (and free internet is available for anyone) at the **Gay & Lesbian Community Center** (☎ 305-292-3223; www.glcckeywest.org; 513 Truman Ave).

The best internet café (and best coffee) in town is **Coffee Plantation** (☎ 305-295-9808; 713 Caroline St; per min 20¢; 🕑 7am-6pm; wi-fi), which has free wi-fi.

SIGHTS & ACTIVITIES

On an island this small, you have to work pretty hard to avoid the over-the-top tourist action at **Mallory Square** at the northwestern end of Duval St. Near where the cruise ships vomit out their daily load, it's hardly the real Key West, but the nightly sunset celebration is a fun ritual to indulge in, however briefly, with jugglers, fire-eaters and street performers of every stripe.

Pirates and Hemingway make up much of the island's lore and legend, so it's no surprise there are museums dedicated to both. The **Ernest Hemingway Home & Museum** (☎ 305-294-1136; www.hemingwayhome.com; 907 Whitehead St; adult/child $12/6; 🕑 9am-5pm) offers tours every half-hour, during which bearded docents spin yarns of Papa. You'll see his studio, hear about his unusual pool, and witness scores of descendents of his six-toed cats languishing in the sun, on furniture, and pretty much wherever they feel like.

Dedicated to all things swashbuckling, **Pirate Soul** (☎ 305-292-1113; www.piratesoul.com; 524 Front St; adult/child 4-10yr $14/8; 🕑 9am-7pm; family-friendly) has an impressive collection of pirate paraphernalia, glammed up with special effects that make it either exciting or a little cheesy, depending on your perspective.

Hear an impressive tale of tenacity and treasure hunting at the **Mel Fisher Maritime Heritage Museum** (☎ 305-294-2633; www.melfisher.org; 200 Greene St; adult/child $12/6; 🕑 9:30am-5pm) and gawk at the treasures salvaged from the *Atocha,* a Spanish galleon that sank nearby almost 400 years ago.

Offering a more low-key, less swashbuckling version of Key West history, the **Museum of Art & History at the Custom House** (☎ 305-295-6616; www.kwahs.com/customhouse.htm; 281 Front St; adult/child $10/5; 🕑 9:30am-4:30pm) is an interesting collection of folklore, artwork and historical exhibits housed in the impressive former Customs House.

Even if you have only the faintest interest in butterflies, you'll find yourself entranced by the sheer quantity flittering all around you at the **Key West Butterfly & Nature Conservatory** (☎ 305-296-2988; www.keywestbutterfly.com; 1316 Duval St; adult/child $12/8.50; 🕑 9am-5pm; family-friendly). Further your nature kick at the **Florida Keys Eco-Discovery Center** (☎ 305-809-4750; 35 East Quay Rd; admission free; 🕑 9am-4pm Tue-Sat), which will help you appreciate the plants, animals and habitats that make up the Keys' unique ecosystem.

Don't come to Key West for its beaches; they range from rocky to algae-covered to funny-smelling. You'll find better just about everywhere else in Florida. That said, **Fort Zachary Taylor** (☎ 305-292-6713; www.fortzacharytaylor.com; vehicle $3.50, with 2 passengers $6, each additional passenger 50¢, pedestrian $1.50; 🕑 8am-sunset) is good for sunsets and picnics, and **Smathers Beach** on S Roosevelt Blvd provides sandy shores and sunrises.

Because pollution and boating activity have damaged the inner reefs, **snorkeling** is best a little farther out. Dive companies are easy to find, and **Sunny Days Catamaran** (☎ 305-296-5556, 800-236-7937; 201 Elizabeth St; www.sunnydayskeywest.com; adult/child $35/22) runs a top-notch trip.

Now divers have a whole new reason to visit the Keys: the artificial reef created from the **USS Vandenberg**. Sunk in 2009, the massive WWII ship is nearly two football fields in length; check with **Dive Key West** (☎ 305-296-3823; www.divekeywest.com) or **Subtropic Dive Center** (☎ 305-296-9914; www.subtropic.com) to plan your visit.

TOURS

You might just find out your guesthouse is haunted during the **Original Ghost Tours** (☎ 305-294-9255; www.hauntedtours.com; La Concha Hotel, 430 Duval St; adult/child $15/10 🕑 8pm & 9pm), and you'll hear all about the creepy antics that got Robert the haunted doll confined to East Martello.

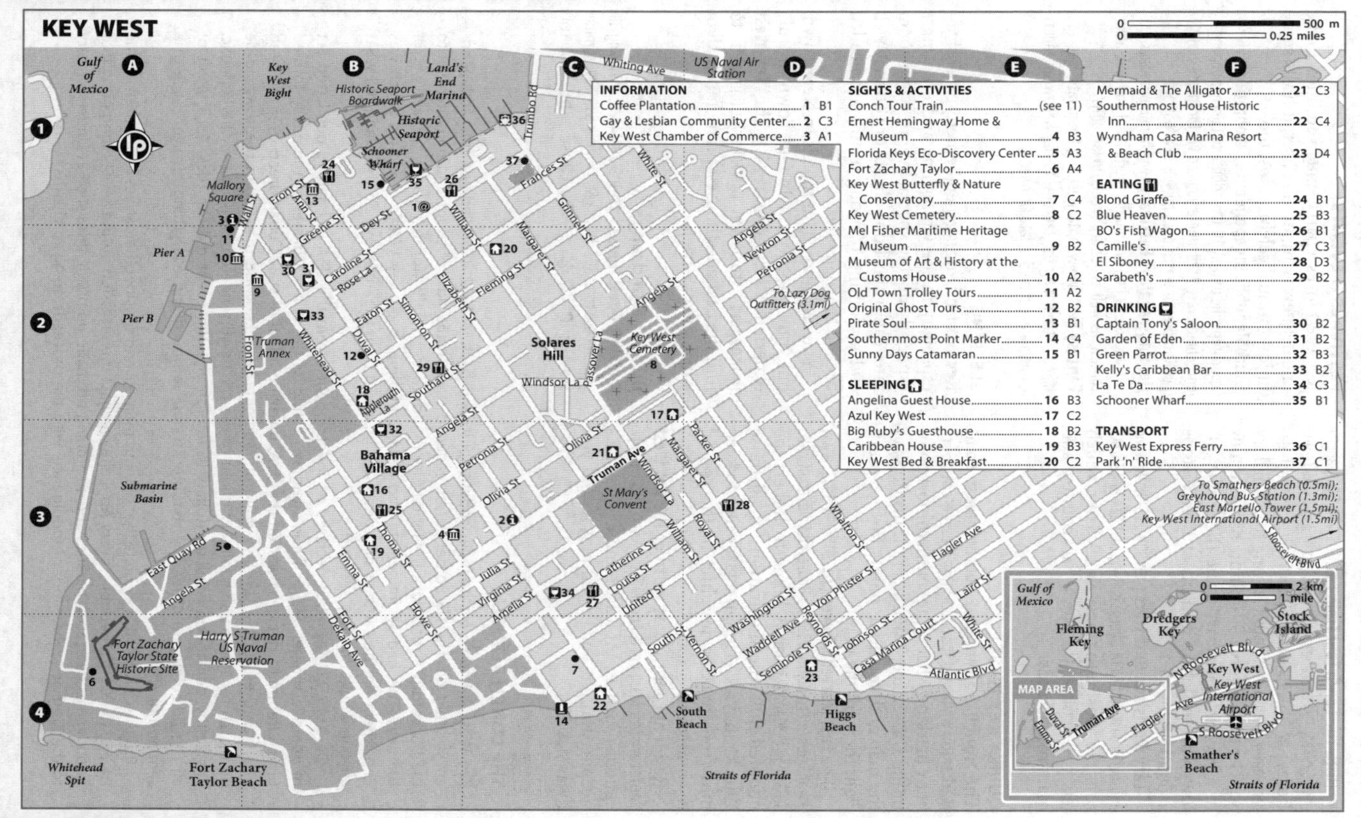
KEY WEST
0 500 m
0 0.25 miles
INFORMATION
Coffee Plantation 1 B1
Gay & Lesbian Community Center 2 C3
Key West Chamber of Commerce 3 A1
SIGHTS & ACTIVITIES
Conch Tour Train (see 11)
Ernest Hemingway Home & Museum 4 B3
Florida Keys Eco-Discovery Center 5 A3
Fort Zachary Taylor 6 A4
Key West Butterfly & Nature Conservatory 7 C4
Key West Cemetery 8 C2
Mel Fisher Maritime Heritage Museum 9 B2
Museum of Art & History at the Customs House 10 A2
Old Town Trolley Tours 11 A2
Original Ghost Tours 12 B2
Pirate Soul 13 B1
Southernmost Point Marker 14 C4
Sunny Days Catamaran 15 B1
SLEEPING
Angelina Guest House 16 B3
Azul Key West 17 C2
Big Ruby's Guesthouse 18 B2
Caribbean House 19 B3
Key West Bed & Breakfast 20 C2
Mermaid & The Alligator 21 C3
Southernmost House Historic Inn 22 C4
Wyndham Casa Marina Resort & Beach Club 23 D4
EATING
Blond Giraffe 24 B1
Blue Heaven 25 B3
BO's Fish Wagon 26 B1
Camille's 27 C3
El Siboney 28 D3
Sarabeth's 29 B2
DRINKING
Captain Tony's Saloon 30 B2
Garden of Eden 31 B2
Green Parrot 32 B3
Kelly's Caribbean Bar 33 B2
La Te Da 34 C3
Schooner Wharf 35 B1
TRANSPORT
Key West Express Ferry 36 C1
Park 'n' Ride 37 C1
Gulf of Mexico
Key West Bight
Land's End Marina
Historic Seaport Boardwalk
Historic Seaport
Schooner Wharf
Mallory Square
Pier A
Pier B
Truman Annex
Submarine Basin
US Naval Air Station
Whiting Ave
Trumbo Rd
Solares Hill
Bahama Village
St Mary's Convent
To Lazy Dog Outfitters (3.1mi)
To Smathers Beach (0.5mi); Greyhound Bus Station (1.3mi); East Martello Tower (1.5mi); Key West International Airport (1.5mi)
Fort Zachary Taylor State Historic Site
Harry S Truman US Naval Reservation
Whitehead Spit
Fort Zachary Taylor Beach
South Beach
Higgs Beach
Straits of Florida
Truman Ave
Duval St
Whitehead St
Simonton St
Atlantic Blvd
S Roosevelt Blvd
Gulf of Mexico
Fleming Key
Dredgers Key
Stock Island
Key West
Key West International Airport
N Roosevelt Blvd
Smather's Beach
MAP AREA
0 2 km
0 1 mile
Straits of Florida

FLORIDA

Both the **Conch Tour Train** (☎ 305-294-5161; adult/child $29/14; ⌚ tours depart 9am-4:30pm) and **Old Town Trolley** (☎ 305-296-6688; adult/child $29/14; ⌚ tours depart 9am-4:30pm) offer tours leaving from Mallory Sq. The train offers a 90-minute narrated tour in a breezy, open car, while the trolley allows you to get on and off at twelve stops around town.

Lazy Dog Island Outfitters (☎ 305-295-9898; www.mosquitocoast.net; 5114 Overseas Hwy; tour 2/4 hr $35/60) runs the Mosquito Coast Kayak Tour, which lets you explore the Keys' backcountry and mangrove islands.

QUIRKY KEY WEST

The much-ballyhooed **Southernmost Point Marker** (cnr Whitehead St & South St) is a large concrete buoy marking what is the southernmost point in the USA. Except that it's not. Just look at the map and you'll see points further south right there on the island.

The **East Martello Tower** (☎ 305-296-3913; www.kwahs.com/martello.htm; 3501 S Roosevelt Blvd; adult/child $6/3; ⌚ 9:30am-4:30pm) is home to Robert the haunted doll, the inspiration for all those Chucky movies. (He's in a glass case to keep him from making mischief in the rest of the museum.)

Residents get the last word at the **Key West Cemetery** (cnr Margaret & Angela Sts), with eccentric epitaphs such as, 'At least I know where he's sleeping tonight,' or the famous 'I told you I was sick.'

FESTIVALS & EVENTS

Key West loves a party, and in addition to the one held every night at sunset, it hosts some unique annual celebrations, too.

Conch Republic Independence Celebration (www.conchrepublic.com) A 10-day tribute to Conch Independence, held every April where you can vie for (made-up) public offices or watch drag queens in a footrace.

Hemingway Days Festival (www.hemingwaydays.net) Includes a bull run, marlin tournament and look-alike contest, as well as literary events, in late July.

Fantasy Fest (www.fantasyfest.net) Room rates get hiked to the hilt for this raucous, 10-day Halloween-meets-Carnivale event held in late October.

SLEEPING

Key West lodging is generally pretty expensive – especially in the wintertime and even *more* especially during special events, when room rates can triple. Book ahead, or you may well end up joining the long traffic jam headed back to the mainland.

You can find chain motels in New Town, but you've got to stay in Old Town to truly experience Key West. Visit the **Key West Innkeepers Association** (www.keywestinns.com) to find the best guesthouses, pretty much all of which are gay-friendly.

Budget & Midrange

Angelina Guest House (☎ 305-294-4480; www.angelinaguesthouse.com; 302 Angela St; r winter $99-179, summer $69-119; P ⊠ ❄ 📶 🏊) Close – but not too

THE CONCH REPUBLIC

Key West is known for its independent spirit, and back in 1982 it proved just how independent it could be. The US Border Patrol, eager to staunch the flow of drugs and immigrants into the US, set up a roadblock in Florida City that backed up traffic for miles both into and out of the Keys. This had an immediate and devastating impact on Key West's economy, which was dependent on the carloads of tourists driving down from the mainland. So the island did what anyone would do: they seceded.

On April 23, Key West declared its independence from the USA in a highly publicized act of guerrilla theater. Mayor Dennis Ludlow, acting as the Prime Minister of the newly formed Conch Republic, declared war on the USA, breaking a loaf of stale Cuban bread over the head of a man dressed in a US Navy uniform. Moments later, knowing that Cuban bread would be no match for the massive military might of the US, he surrendered on behalf of the Republic. Then they demanded a billion dollars in foreign aid. The event did the trick. As a result of all the ridiculous publicity, the roadblocks were removed and everything reverted back to a seminormal state.

But the Conchs still celebrate that glorious moment and consider themselves dual citizens of the US and the Conch Republic. Every April, they reenact the secession during a week-long party that also involves bed races, parades and auctioning off made-up public titles such as Undersecretary to the King or Ambassador of Indulgence, with the proceeds going to charity.

WORTH THE TRIP: DRY TORTUGAS

Seventy miles west of the Keys but feeling like the middle of nowhere, **Dry Tortugas National Park** (☎ 305-242-7700; www.nps.gov/drto) is America's most inaccessible national park. Reachable only by boat, it rewards you for your effort in getting there with amazing snorkeling, diving, bird-watching and star-gazing.

Ponce de León – a big fan of discovering and naming places – christened the area Tortugas (tor-*too*-guzz) after the sea turtles he found here, and the 'Dry' part was added later to warn about the absence of fresh water on the island. But this is more than just a pretty cluster of islands with no drinking water. The never-completed Civil War–era **Fort Jefferson** provides a striking hexagonal centerpiece of red brick rising up from the emerald waters on **Garden Key** – meaning along with your bottled water and seasickness pills, you should definitely bring your camera.

So how do you get there? **Sunny Days Catamaran** (☎ 305-296-5556, 800-236-7937; www.sunnydayskeywest.com; adult/children 3-16 $145/$100) leaves Key West at 8am, arrives around 10am, and gives you 4½ hours to enjoy the island before returning. Round-trip fares include continental breakfast, lunch, snorkeling gear and a 40-minute tour of the fort (but not the $5 park admission fee).

If you really want to enjoy the isolation, stay overnight at one of Garden Key's 13 **campsites** (per person $3, plus extra $30 boat fare). Reserve early and bring everything you need, because once that boat leaves, you're on your own.

close – to Duval St, this is great value for the money. You'd never know from its yellow-and-blue country-chic decor that it was once a bordello. There are no phones or TVs; children must be over 12.

our pick Key West Bed & Breakfast (☎ 305-296-7274, 800-438-6155; www.keywestbandb.com; 415 William St; r winter $99-285, summer $79-175;) Sunny, airy and full of artistic touches: hand-painted pottery here, a working loom there – is that a ship's masthead in the corner? There are also a range of rooms to fit every budget.

Caribbean House (☎ 305-296-0999; www.geocities.com/caribbeanhousekw; 226 Petronia St; r summer/winter $85/125;) Rooms are tiny, but they're clean, cozy and cheery. That and the welcoming hosts add up to something that's a rare find in Key West: a bargain.

Big Ruby's Guesthouse (☎ 305-296-2323, 800-477-7829; www.bigrubys.com; 409 Appelrouth La; r winter $191-312, summer $112-182;) Catering to a gay clientele, this guesthouse is straight-friendly (not to mention clothing-optional) with a beach-fabulous decor and lavish breakfast.

Wyndham Casa Marina Resort & Beach Club (☎ 305-296-3535, 888-303-5717; www.casamarinaresort.com; 1500 Reynolds St; r $149-289; P) This opulent 311-room hotel was built in the 1920s by railroad magnate Henry Flagler. The lobby still retains its old-world splendor, but the recently renovated rooms are thoroughly modern.

Azul Key West (☎ 305-296-5152; www.azulkeywest.com; 907 Truman Ave; r winter $219-259, summer $159-199; P) Overloading on rattan furniture and Tommy Bahama prints? This boutique has a serene, spa-like atmosphere that's as cool and smooth as the sea glass they leave for each guest.

Top End

Southernmost House Historic Inn (☎ 305-296-3141, 866-764-6633; www.southernmosthouse.com; 1400 Duval St; r winter $240-380, summer $210-350; P) What's that big peach and green thing? Why, that's your hotel, with a grandly garish facade but dignified, antique-laden rooms. It also has one of the nicest pools in town.

Mermaid & The Alligator (☎ 305-294-1894, 800-773-1894; www.kwmermaid.com; 729 Truman Ave; r winter $218-318, summer $148-198; P) Book way ahead: with only nine rooms, this place's charm exceeds its capacity. It's chock-a-block with treasures collected from the owners' travels, giving it a worldly flair that's simultaneously European and Zen.

EATING

You aren't technically allowed to leave the island without sampling the conch fritters – like hushpuppies, but made with conch – or the key lime pie, made with key limes, sweetened condensed milk, eggs and sugar on a Graham-cracker crust.

Blond Giraffe (☎ 305-296-9174; www.blondgiraffe.com; 107 Simonton St; slice of key lime pie $4.95; 9am-8pm) Stacks of awards proclaim this shop to have the best key lime pie in town; visit one of their five locations to sample for yourself.

El Siboney (☎ 305-296-4184; 900 Catherine St; mains $5-15; 🕑 11am-9:30pm) Key West is only 90 miles from Cuba, so this awesome corner establishment is quite literally the closest you can get to real Cuban food in the US. Cash only.

BO's Fish Wagon (☎ 305-294-9272; 801 Caroline St; mains $7-14; 🕑 11am-8pm Mon-Sat, 11pm-5pm Sun) This looks like the backyard shed of a crazy old fisherman (but in a good way). Fried fish, conch fritters and cold beer – not to mention great prices – will win over any scaredy-cats in your group.

Sarabeth's (☎ 305-293-8181; 530 Simonton St; mains $7-25; 🕑 8am-3pm & 6pm-close, Wed-Sun) On nice days, the patio of this historic building is the place to be, with good food and a laid-back atmosphere that invites you to linger.

our pick **Blue Heaven** (☎ 305-296-8666; 305 Petronia St; mains $10.50-30; 🕑 8am-3pm & 5-10pm) The outdoor dining can be a bit like eating in a barnyard, but a funky, eclectic barnyard, with creative, well-executed dishes. Waiting in line to enjoy a nice meal with chickens scratching under your table? Welcome to Key West.

Camille's (☎ 305-296-4811; 1202 Simonton St; mains $14-25; 🕑 8am-3pm & 4-10:30pm) Ditch Duval St and dine with the locals at Camille's; its inventive menu ranges from French toast with Godiva liqueur to tasty chicken salad.

DRINKING

The 'Duval Crawl' – hopping (or staggering) from one bar to the next – is a favorite pastime here in the Conch Republic, and there are plenty of options for your drinking pleasure.

our pick **Green Parrot** (☎ 305-294-6133; 601 Whitehead St) With tenure as the island's oldest bar (since 1890) this fabulous dive draws a lively mix of locals and out-of-towners; if you don't meet someone interesting, move over a seat.

Captain Tony's Saloon (☎ 305-294-1838; 428 Greene St) This former icehouse, morgue and Hemingway haunt is built around the town's old hanging tree. The eclectic decor includes emancipated bras and signed dollar bills.

Garden of Eden (☎ 305-296-4565; upstairs at 224 Duval St) Make like Adam and Eve at this clothing-optional rooftop bar where even the fig leaf is optional.

Kelly's Caribbean Bar (☎ 305-293-8484; 301 Whitehead St) A good place to sip a cool drink in a laid-back, patio atmosphere.

Schooner Wharf (☎ 305-292-3302; 202 William St) Happiness abounds with three happy hours a day (8am to noon, 5pm to 7pm and 2am to 4am).

La Te Da (☎ 305-296-6706; 1125 Duval St) Look for drag queens to mark your arrival at this complex that has three bars and a cabaret space famous for its drag shows.

Getting There & Around

The easiest way to travel the Keys is by car, though traffic along the one major route, US 1, can be maddening during the winter high season. **Greyhound** (Map p510; ☎ 800-229-9424; 1012 NW 1st Ave, Miami) serves the Keys along US Hwy 1, departing from downtown Miami. If you fly into Fort Lauderdale or Miami, the **Keys Shuttle** (☎ 888-765-9997) provides door-to-door service to most of the Keys from around $90 one way. Reserve at least 24 hours in advance.

You can fly into Key West International Airport (EYW; ☎ 305-296-5439; www.keywestinternationalairport.com) with frequent flights from major cities, most going through Miami; or **Marathon Airport** (MTH; ☎ 305-743-2155), which has less frequent, more expensive flights. Or, take a fast catamaran from Fort Myers or Miami; call the **Key West Express Ferry** (☎ 888-539-2628; www.keywestshuttle.com) for schedules and fares.

If you need to ditch your car, finding street parking can be a challenge. Give up? Head to the 24-hour **Park 'n' Ride** garage (☎ 305-293-6426; 300 Grinnell St), where you can park for $2 per hour or $13 all day.

ATLANTIC COAST

Part of the allure of Florida's East Coast is that things go fast: from the rockets blasting out of Cape Canaveral to the high-energy surfing all along the coast to the NASCAR International Speedway. By contrast, St Augustine and Amelia Island have been around for centuries, so they're in no hurry at all, and there are miles of undeveloped beaches and wetlands for a steady, back-to-nature pace.

SPACE COAST

They call the Titusville–Cocoa Beach–Melbourne area the Space Coast because it's home to NASA, but it could just as easily be referring to the miles of undeveloped beaches and protected national parkland, where space is one thing you can find plenty of. Once the fictional home of NASA astronaut Major

IF YOU HAVE A FEW MORE DAYS

Head south towards Vero Beach to see the nation's very first wildlife refuge, **Pelican Island** (☎ 772-562-3909; www.fws.gov/pelicanisland), designated by Theodore Roosevelt in 1903. Nesting season is from late November to late July. Although the island is closed off to us featherless types, you can get close enough to witness the avian action from the observation tower or on a kayak tour (around $50 per paddler).

Nelson in the iconic 1960s TV series *I Dream of Jeannie*, the Space Coast is the real-life home to the Kennedy Space Center, with its massive visitor complex and gut-rumbling shuttle launches. It's also a magnet for surfers, with Florida's best waves. Visitor information is available through **Florida's Space Coast Office of Tourism** (☎ 321-433-4470; www.space-coast.com; 430 Brevard Ave, Suite 150, Cocoa Village).

Sights & Activities

Houston, we have an attraction. It was perhaps inevitable that, considering its proximity to Orlando, the **Kennedy Space Center Visitor Complex** (☎ 321-449-4444; www.kennedyspacecenter.com; adult/child 3-11yr $38/28; 9am-5:30pm, closing times vary;) would have to come up with a ride, and thus **Shuttle Launch Experience** officially achieved lift-off. Reaching a top 'speed' of 17,500mph – vertically – this spookily realistic simulator ride was designed by an astronaut to feel just like taking off in a space shuttle but without all the teary goodbyes.

Your ticket to the complex – good for two days – includes a two-hour tour, a 45-minute IMAX film, live-action stage shows, exhibits on subjects such as early space exploration and encounters with astronauts. It also includes (or you can visit separately for $17/13) the **Astronaut Hall of Fame**, where you'll experience the G-Force Trainer and other simulator rides.

Add-on options abound, depending how serious you are about your astronaut experience (they're popular – book in advance). **NASA Up Close** (extra $21/15) is an in-depth tour led by an expert, and **Cape Canaveral: Then & Now** (☎ 321-449-4400; extra $21/15) is a guided tour focusing on the early days of space travel. Hungry space enthusiasts can have **Lunch with an Astronaut** (extra $23/16), and the one- or two-day **Astronaut Training Experience** (price depending on program) prepares you for spaceflight, should the opportunity ever arise.

To view a **rocket or space shuttle launch** up close, you have to pay an extra $15 to get bussed to a prime viewing area. Tickets go on sale a month prior to launch and sell out fast; check the website for schedules. Viewing's also good from the Visitor Complex, or head to the popular **Jetty Park Campgrounds** (☎ 321-783-7111; www.jettypark.org; 400 Jetty Park Dr, Cape Canaveral; per car $7), or Cherie Down Park, Rotary Riverfront Park or Brewer Pkwy bridge in Titusville. Be prepared for inevitable launch delays – and heavy traffic after it's over.

You'll have a better chance of seeing something in the sky at the 140,000-acre **Merritt Island National Wildlife Refuge** (☎ 321-861-0667; www.fws.gov/merrittisland; SR 402, Titusville; admission free; visitor center 8am-4:30pm Mon-Fri, 9am-5pm Sat & Sun, closed Sun Apr-Oct), one of the country's best birding spots, especially from October to May (early morning and after 4pm). More endangered and threatened species of wildlife inhabit the swamps, marshes and hardwood hammocks here than at any other site in the continental US. The best viewing is on **Black Point Wildlife Drive**, and **Village Outfitters** (☎ 321-633-7245; www.villageoutfitters.com; 113 Brevard Ave, Cocoa; half-day trip per person $30) offers kayak tours for groups of four or more. Be aware that the refuge closes in the days preceding a launch.

The 25 miles of pristine, windswept beaches at **Canaveral National Seashore** (☎ 321-267-1110; www.nps.gov/cana; adult/child under 16 $3/free; 6am-6pm Nov-Mar, to 8pm Apr-Oct) comprise the longest stretch of undeveloped beach on Florida's east coast. They include family-friendly **Apollo Beach** on the north end with its gentle surf, pristine **Klondike Beach** in the middle – a favorite of campers and nature lovers – and **Playalinda Beach** at the south end, which is surfer central.

Sleeping & Eating

Rates skyrocket (hee hee) during space launches. Titusville is convenient to the Kennedy Space Center, but Cocoa has more charm and better dining options.

Canaveral National Seashore (☎ 386-428-3384; www.nps.gov/cana; 7611 S Atlantic Ave, New Smyrna Beach; 1-5/6 or more people $10/20; 9am-5pm) Backcountry beach and island camping's available at designated sites. Reservations are essential; bring everything you need including drinking water.

Fawlty Towers Motel (☎ 321-784-3870; www.fawltytowersresort.com; 100 E Cocoa Beach Causeway, Cocoa Beach; r $79-149; P ⊠ ❄ ≋ ☒) Beneath the gloriously garish and extremely pink exterior – highlighted with bright teal, no less – lie fairly straightforward rooms with an unbeatable beachside location.

Inn at Cocoa Bach (☎ 321-799-3460; www.theinnatcocoabeach.com; 4300 Ocean Beach Blvd, Cocoa Beach; r $135-295; P ⊠ ❄ ☐ ≋ ☒) Not ones to rest on their oceanfront laurels, this inn also offers beautifully decorated rooms (usually hard to find with sand so close by), plus free breakfast and wine-and-cheese socials every evening.

Ron Jon Resort Cape Caribe (☎ 321-799-4900; www.ronjonresort.com; 1000 Shorewood Dr, Cape Canaveral; r $130-500; P ❄ ☐ ≋ ☒ ♿) Activities such as mini-golf, movies, a lazy river and a 248ft waterslide make this more than just a place to lay your head for the night. Their 'villas' – fancy-talk for 'condos' – sleep four to 12 people.

Ossorio (☎ 321-639-2423; 316 Brevard Ave, Cocoa; mains $7-9, ⏲ 8am-8:30pm Mon-Sat, 9am-6pm Sun) Fuel up pre- or post-beach at this sunny café in Cocoa Village, serving sandwiches, flatbread pizza, ice cream and coffee drinks.

Coconuts on the Beach (☎ 321-784-1422; 2 Minutemen Causeway, Cocoa Beach; mains $8-18; ⏲ 11am-10pm, bar open to 2am) Coconuts isn't just a name; it's a favored ingredient. The oceanfront 'party deck' hosts regular live music, so head indoors if you're seeking a family atmosphere.

Café Margaux (☎ 321-639-8343; 220 Brevard Ave, Cocoa; mains $9-35; ⏲ 11am-3pm & 5-9:30pm Mon-Sat) Ditch the flip-flops and enjoy French-inspired cuisine and an extensive wine list in a sophisticated atmosphere that's perhaps just ever so slightly stuffy.

Dixie Crossroads (☎ 321-268-5000; 1475 Garden St, Titusville; mains $9-45; ⏲ 11am-9pm Sun-Thu, to 10pm Fri & Sat) Smiling shrimp statues welcome you to a riot of murals, sculptures, fishponds and fountains – all paying homage to the fresh, local seafood. Want a lot? All-you-can-eat rock shrimp is $45 a person.

Getting There & Away

From Orlando take Hwy 528 east, which connects with Hwy A1A. Greyhound (p1160) has services from West Palm Beach and Orlando to Titusville.

DAYTONA BEACH

With big signs and glossy pamphlets, they bill Daytona Beach as 'The World's Most Famous Beach.' But if that sets up some sort of expectation in your head, remember that the title caught on in the 1920s and its accuracy is a matter of (not much) debate.

It certainly hasn't been the same since *Girls Gone Wild* left. Most people welcome the change, though some locals lament the decline in spring-break party action. (Can't a girl find a wet T-shirt contest *anywhere*?) In fact, because of a crackdown in partying, along with efforts to position Daytona as a family destination, the college kids don't flock in for body shots, all-night dancing and doing tangible harm to their futures the way they used to. Of course, whether families will step in remains to be seen, but the bikers already have, roaring into town every March for **Bike Week**.

One thing that's not going anywhere (except around in circles) is NASCAR, which was born here in 1947. As early as 1902, pioneers in the auto industry would drag race down the beach's hard-packed sands to test their inventions. That gave way to stock-car racing, which paved the way for Bill France, Sr, who ran the Daytona Beach Race Course, to formalize the event and move it to the Daytona International Speedway.

The **Daytona Beach Convention & Visitors Bureau** (☎ 386-255-0415, 800-544-0415; www.daytonabeach.com; 126 E Orange Ave; ⏲ 9am-5pm Mon-Fri) has a **visitor center** (☎ 386-253-8669; 1801 W International Speedway Blvd; ⏲ 8.30am-7pm) in the lobby of

> **SURF'S UP IN THE SUNSHINE STATE**
>
> Despite all the sunshine and shoreline, Florida is no *Endless Summer*. The water around Miami tends to stay flat, and much of the Gulf Coast is too protected to get much of a swell. You'll find surfable waves along the mid- to north Atlantic coast. For webcams, forecasts and info on the best spots in the state (and the country), check out www.surfline.com.
>
> The best surf school in Cocoa Beach for all ages and levels is the state's largest, **Ron Jon Surf School** (☎ 321-868-1980; www.ronjonsurfschool.com; 150 W Columbia Lane; semiprivate/private lessons per hr $50/65) run by ex-pro surfer and Kelly Slater coach, Craig Carroll.

Daytona 500 Experience (below). Information for gay and lesbian travelers is available at www.gaydaytona.com.

Sights & Activities

During daylight hours – tide permitting – you can still drive sections of the former race track on **Daytona Beach** (☎ 386-239-7873) at a top speed of 10mph. Car access to the beach costs $5 ($3 after 3pm) and is free during December and January.

The Holy Grail of raceways is the **Daytona International Speedway** (☎ box office 800-748-7467; www.daytonaintlspeedway.com; 1801 W International Speedway Blvd; tickets from $20). Ticket prices accelerate rapidly for the big races headlined by the **Daytona 500** in February, but you can wander the massive stands for free on nonrace days. Adjoining the speedway, **Daytona 500 Experience** (☎ 386-681-6800; www.daytona500experience.com; adult/child 6-12yr $24/19; 10am-6pm) is a superbly flashy shrine to the sport, including 3-D IMAX films, motion simulators and a 30-minute tram tour of the racetrack and pits. Real fanatics might want to indulge in the **Richard Petty Driving Experience**, where you can either ride shotgun ($135) or take the wheel ($525 to $2199) for laps around the track.

The **Museum of Arts & Sciences** (☎ 386-255-0285; www.moas.org; 352 S Nova Rd; adult/student $13/7; 9am-5pm Tue-Sat, 11am-5pm Sun) has a wonderful mishmash of everything from Cuban art to Coca-Cola relics to a 13ft giant sloth skeleton. About 6 miles south of Daytona Beach, you can walk the 203 steps up to the top of **Ponce Inlet Lighthouse** (☎ 386-761-1821; www.ponceinlet.org; 4931 S Peninsula Dr; adult/child $5/1.50; 10am-6pm winter, to 9pm summer) and congratulate yourself: it's Florida's tallest. In this auto-obsessed town where cars are a religion, you can pull right up for church at the **Daytona Beach Drive-In Church** (☎ 386-767-8761; www.driveinchurch.net; 3140 S Atlantic Ave; 8:30am & 10am Sun), a former drive-in movie theater where you attach a speaker to your car to hear the sermon.

Sleeping

The 2004 triple-hurricane action blew the roof off properties and left the beach a general shambles. Some hotels completely renovated and others shut down, with lots of condos springing up in their place. Prices soar during events; book well ahead.

our pick **Tropical Manor** (☎ 386-252-4920; www.tropicalmanor.com; 2237 S Atlantic Ave; r $65-80, ste from $120; P) With the same owner for more than 50 years, this is one of those wonderful little gems that's disappearing way too fast. The property includes motel rooms, efficiencies and cottages, all blanketed in a frenzy of murals and bright pastels.

Sun Viking Lodge (☎ 386-252-6252; www.sunviking.com; 2411 S Atlantic Ave; r $77-285; P) Just plain fun for families, with two pools, beach access, a 60ft waterslide and, of course, a Viking theme. Most rooms have kitchenettes, so just hanging at the hotel is easy to do.

August 7 Inn (☎ 386-248-8420; www.A7Inn.com; 1209 S Peninsula Dr; r $125-185; P) The innkeepers of this gorgeous B&B have a thorough appreciation for small details and have created the perfect haven from NASCAR, Bike Week and spring break madness.

Shores (☎ 386-767-7350; www.shoresresort.com; 2637 N Atlantic Ave; r $159-369; P) Suffering from beach-decor overkill? Check in to this chic, beachfront boutique with hand-striped walls, a full-service spa and a sophisticated color palette.

Eating & Drinking

Pasha Middle East Cafe (☎ 386-257-7753; 919 W International Speedway Blvd; mains $5-14; 10am-7pm Mon-Sat, noon-6pm Sun) Chow on falafel, kabob, hummus, tabbouleh – and of course baklava – in a casual, family-run café and deli.

Zen Bistro (☎ 386-248-0453; 112 Bay St; mains $6-11; 11am-3pm & 4:30-9pm Mon-Fri, 5-9pm Sat) You'd think a place this tiny would be easy to dress up a bit, but the no-frills atmosphere is a small price to pay for the yummy Thai curries and noodles.

Aunt Catfish's on the River (☎ 386-767-4768; 4009 Halifax Dr; mains $8-25; 11:30am-9pm) Oh, seafood, how do I eat thee? Let me count the ways…

Billy's Tap Room & Grill (☎ 386-672-1910; 58 E Granada Blvd, Ormond Beach; lunch $7-12, mains $12-25; 11:30am-10pm Mon-Fri, 5-10pm Sat) Dating back to 1926, this tavern-style restaurant in Ormond Beach has a solid maple bar, historic photographs and grouper served 24 different ways.

Entertainment

Razzles (☎ 386-257-6236; 611 Seabreeze Blvd; 8pm-3am) is the reigning high-octane dance club, with rope lines, cover charges and a permanent thumping sound emanating from within. **Rumors Nite Club & Bar** (☎ 386-252-3776; 1376 N Nova Rd; 2pm-2am) hosts drag shows, karaoke and pool for gay and gay-friendly revelers. And at **Froggy's Saloon** (☎ 386-254-8808; 800 Main St; 7am-3am) it's bike week all year long; plus, they're open 20 hours a day so you can keep the liver damage rolling. Just want a low-key spot to enjoy a beer? Chill over drafts and darts at **McK's Tavern** (☎ 386-238-3321; 218 S Beach St; 11am-2am).

Getting There & Around

Daytona Beach International Airport (DAB; ☎ 386-248-8069; www.flydaytonafirst.com) is just east of the Speedway, and the **Greyhound bus station** (☎ 386-255-7076; 138 S Ridgewood Ave) is the starting point for services around Florida.

Daytona is close to the intersection of two of Florida's major interstates: I-95 is the quickest way to Jacksonville (about 70 miles) and Miami (200 miles), and I-4 will get you to Orlando in about an hour.

Votran (☎ 386-761-7700; www.votran.com; adult/child 6-17yr $1.25/60¢) runs buses and trolleys throughout the city.

ST AUGUSTINE

The first this, the oldest that… St Augustine was founded by the Spanish in 1565, which means it's chock-full of age-related superlatives. Tourists flock here to stroll the ancient streets, and horse-drawn carriages clip-clop past townsfolk dressed in period costume around the National Historic Landmark District.

At times it screams, 'Hey, everyone, look how quaint we are!' but it stops just short of being cloying, because, well, what more would you really expect from the oldest permanent settlement in the US? The historical significance of the town occasionally comes into sharp focus while you're walking on the cobblestoned streets or standing on the (approximate) spot where Juan Ponce de León landed in 1513. The main **visitor center** (☎ 904-825-1000, 800-653-2489; www.visitoldcity.com; 10 Castillo Dr; 8:30am-5:30pm) screens a 45-minute film on the town's history told through archival footage.

Sights & Activities

The town's two Henry Flagler buildings shouldn't be missed. His former Hotel Alcazar (1888) is now home to the wonderful **Lightner Museum** (☎ 904-824-2874; www.lightnermuseum.org; 75 King St; adult/child under 12/child 12-18yr $10/free/5; 9am-5pm), with a little bit of everything from ornate Gilded Age furnishings to collections of marbles and cigar-box labels. Across the street is the gorgeous former **Hotel Ponce de León** (☎ 904-823-3378; 74 King St; tours adult/child 12yr & under $7/1; 10am & 2pm, additional tours summer), which was built in the 1880s and is now the world's most gorgeous dormitory, belonging to Flagler College. Take a guided tour – or at least step inside to gawk at the lobby for free.

History buffs will enjoy the oldest house in the US, the **Gonzalez-Alvarez House** (☎ 904-824-2872; www.oldesthouse.com; 14 St Francis St; adult/student $8/4; 9am-5pm), which claims continuous occupancy from the early 17th century, as well as the **Oldest Wooden School House** (☎ 904-824-0192; 14 St George St; adult/child 6-12yr $3.50/2.50; 9am-5pm Sun-Thu, 9am-6pm Fri & Sat), peopled by animatronic teachers and students. See how they did things back in the 18th century at the **Colonial Spanish Quarter Living History Village** (☎ 904-825-6830; 53 St George St; adult/child 6-17yr $7/4.25; 9am-5:30pm), a re-creation of Spanish-colonial St Augustine complete with craftspeople demonstrating blacksmithing, leather working and other trades.

Almost 500 years old (but not looking a day over 450) the **Fountain of Youth** (☎ 904-829-3168, 800-356-8222; 11 Magnolia Ave; adult/child $8/5; 9am-5pm) was the original tourist attraction, drawing Spanish explorer Juan Ponce de León for a visit in 1513. It still serves the nasty sulfur water in tiny paper cups – and that's absolutely as much as you'll want – but this is more than a five-minute pit stop. Educational exhibits, gorgeous grounds and the approximate spot where the explorer came ashore make it more than just a tourist trap – OK, well a *little* more, anyway.

Another monument to longevity is the country's oldest masonry fort, **Castillo de San Marcos National Monument** (☎ 904-829-6506; btwn San Marcos Ave & Matanzas River; adult/child under 15 $6/free; 8:45am-4:45pm) built by the Spanish between 1672 and 1695. Park rangers lead programs hourly and volunteers shoot off cannons most weekends.

Locals escape the tourist hordes at the nearby **Anastasia State Recreation Area** (☎ 904-461-2033; 1340 Hwy A1A; car/pedestrian $5/1, campsites $25) which has a terrific beach, a campground and rentals for all kinds of water sports.

Tours

Two companies provide convenient jump-on, jump-off tours with 20 stops on open-air trams: **Old Town Trolley Tours** (☎ 904-829-3800, 800-213-2474; www.trolleytours.com; 167 San Marco Ave; 3-day ticket adult/child 6-12yr $23/10) and **St Augustine Sightseeing Trains** (☎ 800-226-6545; www.redtrains.com; 19 San Marco Ave; adult/child 6-12yr $17/8).

Discover the town's spirited past with **Ghost Tours of St Augustine** (☎ 904-461-1009; www.ghosttoursofstaugustine.com; walking tours $12; tours 8pm daily, 9:30pm Fri & Sat winter, daily summer).

Sleeping

More than two dozen atmospheric B&Bs can be found at www.staugustineinns.com. St Augustine is a popular weekend escape; expect room rates to rise about 30% on Friday and Saturday. Inexpensive motels and chain hotels line San Marco Ave, near where it meets US Hwy 1.

Pirate Haus (☎ 904-808-1999; www.piratehaus.com; 32 Treasury St; dm $18, r $50-85; P) Yar, if ye don't be needing anything fancy, this family-friendly European-style guesthouse-hostel has an unbeatable location and includes a pirate pancake breakfast.

Inn at Camachee Bay (☎ 904-825-0003; www.camacheeinn.com; 201 Yacht Club Dr; r $119-179, ste $159-199; P) Historic inns are easy enough to find, but a pet-friendly suite with marina views and a pool? That's a real find.

Cedar House Inn (☎ 904-829-0079, 800-845-0012; www.cedarhouseinn.com; 79 Cedar St; r $129-229, ste $169-299; P) Victorian flourishes abound, but the beds are pure modern comfort.

Casa Monica (☎ 904-827-1888, 800-648-1888; www.casamonica.com; 95 Cordova St; r $179-369;) Built in 1888, this is *the* luxe hotel in town, with turrets and fountains adding to the Spanish Moorish castle feel. Parking is available for $21.

Eating & Drinking

Eateries in St Augustine are surprisingly inexpensive, and cheap eateries abound on St George St. Note that restaurants often close a bit earlier or later than the hours listed.

Spanish Bakery (☎ 904-471-3046; 42½ St George St; dishes $1-3; 9:30am-3pm) Behind Whetstone Chocolates in a picnic-table-strewn courtyard, this historic stone kitchen bakes up empanadas and smoked-sausage rolls. Five dollars gets you one of the above plus a drink, roll and cookie.

Scarlett O'Hara's (☎ 904-824-6535; 70 Hypolita St; mains $5-14; 11am-1am). Leave your hoop skirt at home. This rowdy place is not so much 'fiddle dee dee' as 'Frankly, my dear, I don't give a damn,' but it's a fine spot for beer and pub grub.

Gypsy Cab Co (☎ 904-824-8244; 828 Anastasia Blvd; mains $15-21, lunch $7-12; 11am-3pm Mon-Sat, brunch 10:30am-3pm Sun, 4:30-10pm Sun-Thu, to 11pm Fri & Sat) A local favorite, its excellent menu is all over the place, with influences from German to 'Floribbean'.

Harry's Seafood, Bar & Grill (☎ 904-824-7765; 46 Avenida Menendez; mains $8-23; 11am-10pm Sun-Thu, to 11pm Fri & Sat) It may pride itself on its Cajun food, but the hopping patio and Mardi Gras atmosphere is the real draw.

Taberna del Gallo (☎ 904-825-6830; 53 St George St; noon-5pm Wed-Thu, noon-9pm Fri & Sat, 1pm-5pm Sun) Flickering candles provide the only light at this 1736 stone tavern.

AIA Ale Works (☎ 904-829-6824; 1 King St; mains $10-25). If you love beer, then you owe it to beer to show it your appreciation. As a bonus you get decent bar food and a great view of the Bridge of Lions.

Getting There & Around

The **Greyhound bus station** (☎ 904-829-6401; 1711 Dobbs Rd) is a few miles from the heart of things, but once you're in Old Town, you can get almost everywhere on foot.

JACKSONVILLE

Are we there yet? Have we left yet? It's hard to tell, because Jacksonville sprawls out over a whopping 840 sq miles, making it the largest city by area in the continental US (eclipsed only by Anchorage, AK). Jacksonville Beach, known locally as 'Jax Beach', is about 17 miles east of the city center and is where you'll find white sand and most of the action. Information is available from the **convention & visitors bureau** (☎ 800-733-2668; www.visitjacksonville.com).

Sights & Activities

Enjoy a free tour (and free beer if you're over 21) at **Anheuser-Busch Brewery** (☎ 904-696-8373; www.budweisertours.com; 111 Busch Dr; admission free; 10am-4pm Mon-Sat). Packing kids? Maybe the **Museum of Science & History** (☎ 904-396-6674; www.themosh.org; 1025 Museum Circle; adult/child $9/7; 10am-5pm Mon-Fri, to 6pm Sat, 1-6pm Sun) is more your speed, with dinosaur fun and educational exhibits on Jacksonville's pre-Columbian history (but no beer). Small, but one of the best cultural offerings in town, the **Museum of Contemporary Art**

(☎ 904-366-6911; www.mocajacksonville.org; 333 N Laura St; adult/child $8/5; ⏰ 10am-4pm Tue-Sat, to 8pm on Thu, noon-4pm Sun) focuses on 1960 to the present.

Sleeping & Eating

The cheapest rooms are along I-95 and I-10, where the lower-priced chains congregate. Beach lodging rates often rise in summer.

Omni Jacksonville Hotel (☎ 904-355-6664, 800-843-6664; 245 Water St; r $89-199; P ⊠ ✻ ≋ ≋) Sure, it's a chain, but the plush, amenity-laden rooms are anything but generic, making it a great place to stay if you're downtown.

Inn at Oak Street (☎ 904-379-5525; www.innatoakstreet.com; 2114 Oak St; r $135-225; P ⊠ ✻ ≋) This place combines luscious decor, high-tech amenities and gourmet breakfast, all near downtown.

Casa Marina (☎ 904-270-0025; www.casamarinahotel.com; 691 N 1st St, Jacksonville Beach; r $139-159, ste $189-279; P ⊠ ✻ ≋) Not your typical beach digs, this charming historical hotel from the 1920s has retained its romantic, old-world flair.

Riverdale Inn (☎ 904-354-5080, 866-808-3400; www.riverdaleinn.com; 1521 Riverside Ave; r $149-189; P ⊠ ✻ ≋) In the early 1900s, this was one of 50 or so mansions lining Riverside. Now there are only two left, and you're invited to enjoy its lovely rooms with full breakfast.

Ellen's Kitchen (☎ 904-246-1572; 1824 3rd St, Jacksonville Beach; mains $4-9 ⏰ 7am-2pm) A Jax Beach staple for over 40 years, Ellen's keeps the locals happy with dependable breakfasts and lunches, both of which are served till 2pm.

our pick **European Street Cafe** (☎ 904-398-9500; 1704 San Marco Blvd; mains $5-12; ⏰ 10am-10pm) Decisions, decisions. If you just don't know what you want, this place has a lengthy menu, enormous bakery case and over 150 kinds of beer. Other locations include 2753 Park St, 5500 Beach Blvd and 992 Beach Blvd in Jax Beach.

River City Brewing Company (☎ 904-398-2299; 835 Museum Circle; lunch $9-10, dinner $17-33; ⏰ 11am-3pm & 5-10pm Mon-Thu, to 11pm Fri & Sat, 10:30am-2:30pm Sun) The perfect place to quaff a microbrew and enjoy some coconut shrimp overlooking the water.

Bistro Aix (☎ 904-398-1949; 1440 San Marco Blvd; mains $10-25; ⏰ 11am-10pm Mon-Thu, to 11pm Fri, 5-11pm Sat, 5-9pm Sun) Foodies find few havens in Jacksonville, but this chic San Marcos eatery will make them feel right at home.

Drinking & Entertainment

Downtown's **Jacksonville Landing** (☎ 904-353-1188; www.jacksonvillelanding.com; 2 Independent Dr) has restaurants, shops and bars, and free outdoor entertainment. At the beach, the **Freebird Live Cafe** (☎ 904-246-2473; www.freebirdlive.com; 200 N 1st St; ⏰ 8pm-2am) is a rocking music venue and home of the band Lynyrd Skynyrd.

Getting There & Around

North of the city, **Jacksonville International Airport** (JAX; ☎ 904-741-4902; www.jia.aero) has rental cars. **Greyhound** (☎ 904-356-9976; 10 N Pearl St) serves numerous cities, and **Amtrak** (☎ 904-766-5110; 3570 Clifford Lane) has trains from the north and south. The **Jacksonville Transportation Authority** (☎ 904-630-3100; www.ridejta.net) runs the **Skyway monorail** (per ride 50¢) and **city buses** (per local ride $1, to Jax Beach $1.50).

AMELIA ISLAND

Residents are quick to tell you: Amelia Island is just as old as that braggart St Augustine – they just can't prove it. Unfortunately, no Ponce de León, no plaque, so they have to content themselves with being a pretty little island and home to **Fernandina Beach**, a shrimping village with 40 blocks of historic buildings and romantic B&Bs. Pick up walking-tour maps and information at the **visitor center** (☎ 904-277-0717; 102 Centre St; ⏰ 9:30am-4pm Mon-Sat, noon-4pm Sun).

To learn about Amelia Island's intricate history, which has seen it ruled under eight different flags starting with the French in 1562, check out the **Amelia Island Museum of History** (☎ 904-261-7378; www.ameliamuseum.org; 233 S 3rd St; adult/student $7/4; ⏰ 10am-4pm Mon-Sat, 1-4pm Sun). Admission includes tours at 11am and 2pm. The museum also offers a Friday **ghost tour** (801 Atlantic Ave; adult/student $10/5; ⏰ 6pm Fri), leaving from the parking lot of St Peters Episcopal church.

Take a half-hour horse-drawn carriage tour with the **Old Towne Carriage Co** (☎ 904-277-1555; www.ameliacarriagetours.com; adult/child 3-13yr $15/7.50) or **Amelia Island Carriages** (☎ 904-556-2662; adults/child 5-14yr $15/7). Or, if you'd rather a carriage didn't come between you and your horse, **Kelly's Seahorse Ranch** (☎ 904-491-5166; www.kellyranchinc.com; ride per hr $60) offers beachfront trail rides for riders aged 13 and over.

Capping the north end of the island, the Spanish moss-draped **Fort Clinch State Park** (☎ 904-277-7274; pedestrian/car $1/5; ⏰ 8am-dusk) has beaches, camping, bike trails and a commanding Civil War-era **fort** (admission $2; ⏰ 9am-5pm), with reenactments taking place the first full weekend of every month. Amelia Island is part of the **Talbot Islands State Parks** (☎ 904-251-2320; pedestrian/car $1/4; 8am-dusk), which includes the pristine shoreline at **Little Talbot Island** and the 'boneyard beach' at **Big Talbot Island State Park**, where silvered tree skeletons create a dramatic landscape. Both are south of Amelia Island down the First Coast Hwy.

Fernandina does beat out St Augustine with two key 'oldests': Florida's oldest bar, the **Palace Saloon** (☎ 904-261-6320; 113 Centre St), and Florida's oldest hotel, **Florida House Inn** (☎ 904-261-3300, 800-258-3301; www.floridahouseinn.com; 20 & 22 S 3rd St; r $119-299; P), which stays modern with beautifully restored rooms, wi-fi and free use of zippy, red scooters.

Just around the corner, **Hoyt House** (☎ 904-277-4300, 800-432-2085; www.hoythouse.com; 804 Atlantic Ave; r $145-230; P) is another lovely inn with lavish breakfasts and a pool (a rarity among Amelia B&Bs). And out at the beach, **Elizabeth Pointe Lodge** (☎ 904-277-4851; www.elizabethpointelodge.com; 98 S Fletcher Ave; r $205-330; P) looks like an old Nantucket-style sea captain's house with wraparound porches, gracious service and beautifully-appointed rooms.

Start your day with **Bright Mornings** (☎ 904-491-1771; 105 S 3rd St; mains $5-10; 7:30am-2pm Mon-Tue & Thu-Fri, 8am-2pm Sat & Sun), a supremely pleasant café serving heaping portions of breakfast and lunch. Small plates and mains live happily side by side at the tiny, stylish bistro **29 South** (☎ 904-277-7919; 29 S 3rd St; small plates $5-12, mains $18-30; 11am-2pm & 5:30-9pm Tue-Sat, 10am-2pm Sun). And rounding out your dining options is **Beech Street Grill** (☎ 904-277-3662; 801 Beech St; mains $17-30, brunch $7-10; 6pm-close daily, 11:30am-2pm Sun), with whatever kind of seafood your heart desires at dinner, not to mention a killer brunch.

Hwy A1A links the island to the mainland, but there's no public transportation. Rent bikes at **Pipeline Surfshop** (☎ 904-277-3717; 2022 1st Ave; per hr/business day $5/12; 10am-6pm).

WEST COAST

If Henry Flagler's railroad made the east coast of Florida what it is today, his non-attention to the rest of the state similarly affected the west coast. Things are calmer here, with fewer tourist hordes and more room for nature to amuse us with shelling beaches, swamp lands and nature preserves. The west coast has front-row seats to flame-red sunsets emblazoned over the Gulf of Mexico, as well as adrenaline-pumping roller coasters, hand-rolled cigars and lip-synching mermaids.

TAMPA

Florida's third-largest city is all business. Well, mostly business. Chains and oversized office parks line the highways and it's not immediately apparent what there is to do here, other than get a nine-to-five job. But Tampa's revitalized historic district Ybor City and a few downtown museums absolutely reward a stop. Information is available from the **convention & visitors bureau** (☎ 813-223-2752, 800-448-2672; www.visittampabay.com; 615 Channelside Dr; 9:30am-5:30pm Mon-Sat, 11:30am-5pm Sun).

Sight & Activities

DOWNTOWN TAMPA

Check out the **Henry B Plant Museum** (☎ 813-254-1891; www.plantmuseum.com; 401 W Kennedy Blvd; adult/child $5/2; 10am-4pm Tue-Sat, noon-4pm Sun) if for no other reason than to wander around the landmark Victorian building it's housed in. Formerly a luxury hotel, it's easily the most beautiful building in town.

At the time of research, the **Tampa Museum of Art** (☎ 813-274-8130; www.tampamuseum.org; 120 Gasparilla Plaza; adult/child $7/3; 10am-5pm) was putting the finishing touches on a brand new, 66,000-sq-ft building – which should be open by the time you read this – to house their paintings, sculptures, and Greek and roman antiquities.

Kids can challenge the laws of physics as well as their fear of heights at the **Museum of Science & Industry** (☎ 813-987-6100; www.mosi.org; 4801 E Fowler Ave; adult/child $20/16; 9am-5pm Mon-Fri, to 6pm Sat & Sun), where you can ride a bike across a highwire 30ft in the air and learn about dinosaurs, hurricanes and the human body.

At **Florida Aquarium** (☎ 813-273-4000; www.flaquarium.org; 701 Channelside Dr; adult/child $20/15; 9:30am-5pm) you can get your hands wet with touch tanks or dive into the shark tank (scuba divers $150).

YBOR CITY

This cobblestoned 19th-century historic district preserves a strong Cuban-Spanish heritage while embracing a hip, happening nightlife scene. About two miles from

MARCY TERRY

For more than 10 years Marcy Terry has delighted audiences with underwater mermaid performances at Weeki Wachee Springs. Marcy now holds the dual title of Underwater Theatre Manager and Head Mermaid.

What's your favorite thing about being a mermaid? I just love the environment. My office is a beautiful underwater spring; I get to swim and get paid; I interact with children who believe in mermaids and they're just so happy to be here.

How long does it take to become a mermaid? First we have to get scuba-certified, then we learn to breathe through air hoses, which is different from regular scuba diving. Then we start learning how to swim in a tail and learning the choreography, so it takes three to six months.

Other than Weeki Wachee, what's your favorite Florida tourist attraction? I would have to say Disney. I just love the magic there, and I have a two-year-old and she loves going there. I love seeing her little eyes light up. Everybody's happy and all the little kids believe all that stuff so you can't help but feel that way also.

If you had visitors from out of state, where would you take them? First I would bring them here. Then, the beaches are beautiful; we'd probably go to a beach. Of course we'd hit Disney. And, I don't know, I think the small roadside attractions need all the tourists they can get, so I'd probably do those.

downtown, Ybor (rhymes with Eeyore) City was established by the owner of a cigar factory who drew hundreds of Cuban, Spanish and Italian immigrant workers to the area, and that diversity has bestowed more charm on this area than the whole rest of Tampa put together. The **visitor center** (☎ 813-241-8838; www.ybor.org; 1600 E 8th Ave; 🕑 10am-6pm Mon-Sat, noon-6pm Sun) provides an excellent introduction with walking-tour maps and info. Centered around a seven-block stretch of 7th and 8th Aves, everything is within walking distance.

You can still pick up a close-to-Cuban cigar and watch master cigar rollers at work at several different shops, including **La Herencia de Cuba** (☎ 813-248-9620, 800-324-9803; www.ramirezcigars.com; 1817 E 7th Ave) and **Gonzalez y Martinez** (☎ 813-248-8210; www.gonzalezymartinez.com; 2103 E 7th Ave) in the Columbia Restaurant building.

The **Ybor City Museum State Park** (☎ 813-247-6323; www.ybormuseum.org; 1818 E 9th Ave; admission $3; 🕑 9am-5pm) chronicles the history of cigar-making in interesting if text-heavy exhibits, and historic **walking tours** (incl museum admission $6) depart from the museum at 10:30am each Saturday.

BUSCH GARDENS & ADVENTURE ISLAND

Is it a theme park with animals or a zoo with rides? **Busch Gardens Africa** (☎ 813-987-5000; www.buschgardens.com; 10000 McKinley Dr; adult/child $70/60; 🕑 9am-6pm with seasonal variations; P ♿) is both – and way more exciting than Disney's Animal Kingdom (p548), thanks to all the rides. Cool off at **Adventure Island** (☎ 813-987-5660, 888-800-5447; www.adventureisland.com; 10001 McKinley Dr; adult/child $40/36; 🕑 10am-5pm with seasonal variations; ♿), a water park with slides and rides galore. Discounts and combination tickets are available online; parking costs $12 at Busch Gardens and $10 at Adventure Island.

WEEKI WACHEE SPRINGS

Since 1947 tourists have been lured up the coast by the siren song of **Weeki Wachee Springs** (☎ 352-596-2062; www.weekiwachee.com; 6131 Commercial Way, Weeki Wachee; adult/child $25/17; 🕑 10am-4pm, with seasonal variations; ♿), one of Florida's original roadside attractions. Elvis Presley and Esther Williams were among the guests who flocked here to watch glamorous long-haired mermaids perform in an underwater grotto. The mermaids are the main attraction, but there's also a river cruise, plus swimming and water slides at the adjoining Buccaneer Bay water park. (Hint: admissions are reduced in the off-season when the water park is closed.)

Sleeping

Chains abound near Busch Gardens, along Fowler Ave/Morris Bridge Rd (Hwy 582) and Busch Blvd (Hwy 580).

Gram's Place Hostel (☎ 813-221-0596; www.grams-inn-tampa.com; 3109 N Ola Ave; campsites $15, dm $23, r 25-70; P ⊠ ⌘ 💻 📶) Rooms at this rockin' hostel are themed by music genre, and the jukebox spins more than 400 CDs.

Tahitian Inn (☎ 800-876-1397; www.tahitianinn.com; 601 S Dale Mabry Hwy; r $69-149; P ⊠ ⌘ 📶 🏊)

Once a classic roadside motel, this family-owned and -operated place built in 1954 got a major facelift that's kept it looking smart.

our pick **Don Vicente de Ybor Historic Inn** (☎ 813-241-4545, 866-206-4545; www.donvicenteinn.com; 1915 Republica de Cuba; r $119-249; P) Built in 1895 by Ybor City's founder, this atmospheric B&B exudes history right down to its original marble staircase.

Casitas de la Verdad (☎ 813-654-6087; www.yborcityguesthouse.com, 1609 6th Ave; house $180-250; P) Right on the fringe of Ybor City you can rent an entire two-bedroom 1908 cigar-maker's cottage that's been artfully restored with a colorful whimsy.

Eating

Downtown is a desert for dining, but Ybor City is an oasis. Keep an eye out for places popping up in Tampa's SoHo area (South of Houston Ave).

Nicko's Fine Foods (☎ 813-234-9301; 4603 N Florida Ave, Tampa; mains $4-10; 6am-9pm Mon-Fri, 7am-9pm Sat, 7am-2pm Sun) The lure of cheap eats in a classic diner atmosphere has kept people coming here for decades, including Elvis back in 1956.

La Teresita (☎ 813-879-4909; 3246 W Columbus Dr, Ybor City; mains $5-7; 5am-midnight Mon-Thu, 24hr Fri & Sat, 5am-10pm Sun) Skip the restaurant and head for the cafeteria counters to eat your fill of plantains, yellow rice, black beans, Cuban bread and coffee.

Columbia Restaurant (☎ 813-248-4961; 2117 E 7th Ave, Ybor City; lunch mains $9-18, dinner $17-29; 11am-10pm Mon-Thu, to 11pm Fri & Sat, noon-9pm Sun) See that enormous building covered in hand-painted tiles? That's the famous Columbia, serving Spanish and Cuban specialties since 1920. Reservations and $6 gets you seating for flamenco performances.

Bella's Italian Cafe (☎ 813-254-3355; 1413 S Howard Ave, Tampa; mains $9-27; 11:30am-11:30pm Mon-Wed, to 12:30am Thu, to 1:30am Fri & Sat, 4-11:30pm Sun) Go simple or go fancy; this cute Italian place has enough options to fulfill all your carb cravings.

Bern's Steakhouse (☎ 813-251-2421; 1208 S Howard Ave, Tampa; mains $21-70; 5-10pm Sun-Thu, to 11pm Fri & Sat) Start with one of 20 kinds of caviar then move on to steak prepared to the most exacting tastes and specifications at this over-the-top homage to indulgence.

Drinking & Entertainment

Find out what's happening from the *Weekly Planet*, and *Tampa Tribune*'s 'Friday Extra.' When it comes to nightlife, just head for Ybor City's 7th Ave. Start at the pirate ship-like bar **Gaspar's Grotto** (☎ 813-248-5900; 1805 7th Ave; 11:30am-3am) then wander till you find the right scene.

Experience art in action at the **Tampa Bay Performing Arts Center** (☎ 813-229-7827, 800-955-1045; www.tbpac.org; 1010 MacInnes Pl), a sprawling, multi-venue complex where you can see touring Broadway shows, concerts, opera and more. For independent and classic films, try the elaborate 1926 **Tampa Theatre** (☎ 813-274-8981; www.tampatheatre.org; 711 N Franklin St; tickets $9).

Sports are big in Tampa. Catch Major League Baseball at **Tropicana Field** (☎ 888-326-7297; www.tampabayrays.com; 1 Tropicana Dr, St Petersburg; tickets from $8) with the **Tampa Bay Rays**, watch the **Buccaneers** play NFL football at **Raymond James Stadium** (☎ 800-795-2827; www.buccaneers.com; 4201 Dale Mabry Hwy; tickets from $30), or enjoy professional hockey at **St Pete Times Forum** (☎ 813-301-6600; http://lightning.nhl.com; 401 Channelside Dr; tickets from $8) with **Tampa Bay Lightning**.

Spring training for numerous Major League teams is a great way to see baseball stars up close in a spontaneous atmosphere. Tickets are around $30. Try **George M Steinbrenner Field** (☎ 813-879-2244; www.steinbrennerfield.com; 3802 W Dr ML King Jr Blvd) to watch the New York Yankees practice.

Getting There & Around

Tampa International Airport (TPA; ☎ 813-870-8700; www.tampaairport.com) has car-rental agencies inside. **Greyhound** (☎ 813-229-2174; 610 E Polk St) has numerous services. Trains run south to Miami and north through Jacksonville at the **Amtrak station** (☎ 813-221-7601; 601 Nebraska Ave). **HARTline** (☎ 813-254-4278; www.hartline.org; single/day pass $1.75/3.75) runs the old-style streetcars.

ST PETERSBURG

You know how in some families there's a sophisticated older sibling who wears suits and has an Important Job, and then there's the younger sibling who's kind of artsy and easier to hang out with? In this particular metaphor, Tampa is the former, and St Pete is the latter. Perched on a peninsula along the west side of Tampa Bay, St Pete is a cultured and tourist-friendly town that is in easy proximity to the beaches. For the scoop on local sights, stop by the **information booth** (☎ 727-821-6164) at the over-hyped **St Petersburg Pier** (☎ 727-821-6443; www.stpetepier.com; 800 2nd Ave N; 10am-8pm Mon-Thu,

WHAT THE...?

Of course St Petersburg was the logical place to put a museum dedicated to Salvador Dalí, the eccentric Spanish artist who painted melting clocks, grew an exaggerated handlebar mustache to look like King Philip, and once filled a Rolls Royce with cauliflower. Right? In fact, the **Salvador Dalí Museum** (☎ 727-823-3767; www.salvadordalimuseum.org; 1000 3rd St S; adult/child 5-9yr $17/4; 🕑 10am-5:30pm Mon-Sat, to 8pm Thu, noon-5:30pm Sun) is the largest Dalí collection outside of Spain. So how did that happen exactly?

In 1942, A Reynolds Morse and his wife Eleanor bought their first Dalí painting – the start of what would become the largest private Dalí collection in the world. When it came time to find a permanent home for the collection, they had one stipulation: that the collection had to stay together. Only three cities could agree to the terms, and St Petersburg won out for its waterfront location. The museum doesn't have *the* melting clocks, but it does have *some* melting clocks, as well as paintings with titles such as *The Ghost of Vermeer of Delft Which Can Be Used as a Table.*

to 9pm Fri & Sat, 11am-7pm Sun), which also houses tchotchke shops, restaurants and an observation deck. Advance planners can check out www.floridasbeach.com for information.

The recently expanded and twice-as-big **Museum of Fine Arts** (☎ 727-896-2667; www.fine-arts.org; 255 Beach Dr NE; adult/child 7-18 $12/6; 🕑 10am-5pm Tue-Sat, 1-5pm Sun) spans pre-Columbian to impressionism to modern. **St Petersburg Museum of History** (☎ 727-894-1052; www.spmoh.org; 335 2nd Ave NE; adult/child 7-17 $9/5; 🕑 10am-5pm Tue-Sat, 1-5pm Sun, summer hr vary) has interesting mementos of early Florida, plus a funky 3000-year-old mummy.

Hikers, cyclists and skaters can head north on the paved, 34-mile-long **Pinellas Trail** (☎ 727-464-8200; 🕑 sunrise-sunset), starting at 34th St and Fairfield Ave and ending in Tarpon Springs. A free booklet with mile-by-mile information is available at visitor centers.

One of the finest beaches in Florida – partly because of excellent amenities such as lots of shady picnic tables – is at **Fort DeSoto Park** (☎ 727-582-2267; www.pinellascounty.org/park; 3500 Pinellas Bayway S; admission free; 🕑 sunrsie-sunset), with a fishing pier, historic trail, water sports, camping and a fort built in 1898.

Sleeping & Eating

Fort DeSoto Park Campground (☎ 727-582-2267; www.pinellascounty.org/park; 3500 Pinellas Bayway S; campsites $30-35; P) Book way ahead for sites at the waterfront campground; the beaches here make it all worthwhile.

Dickens House (☎ 727-822-8622; www.dickenshouse.com; 335 8th Ave NE; r $109-235; P) This gorgeous craftsman home, convenient to downtown, offers Jacuzzis and gourmet breakfasts.

Renaissance Vinoy Resort (☎ 727-894-1000; www.marriott.com; 501 5th Ave NE; r from $139; P) This historic behemoth has been providing superposh pink lodging in downtown St Pete since the 1920s.

Loew's Don CeSar Beach Resort (☎ 727-360-1881; www.doncesar.com; 3400 Gulf Blvd, St Pete Beach; r from $194; P) Like the Vinoy, it's historical, posh and pink, but this one's located out at the beach.

our pick **Ceviche Tapas Bar** (☎ 727-209-2302; 10 Beach Dr SE; small plates $7-15; 🕑 5-10pm Sun & Mon, to midnight Tue-Thu, to 1am Fri & Sat) The flavors are amazing and, with over 100 different options, your foraging experience is limited only by your time and budget. Tuesday happy hour is a bargain.

Moon Under Water (☎ 727-896-6160; 332 Beach Dr NE; mains $7-20; 🕑 11am-11pm Sun-Thu, to 1am Fri & Sat) Get your fill of fish-and-chips, *tikka masala* and cold pints at this British-style pub with a lovely front patio.

Cafe Alma (☎ 727-502-5002; 260 1st Ave S; mains $7-24; 🕑 11am-10pm Mon-Thu, to 11pm Fri & Sat, to 8pm Sun) This cute subterranean café is a little hidden away but worth finding, serving sophisticated salads and sandwiches at lunch and small plates and mains at dinner.

Gratzzi Ristorante (☎ 727-822-7769; 199 2nd Ave N in Baywalk Mall; lunch $8-12, dinner $13-27; 🕑 11:30am-10pm Mon-Thu, to 11pm Fri & Sat, noon-10pm Sun) Don't be fooled by its mall location; the food is amazing, with presentation that will leave you agog.

Getting There & Around

St Petersburg-Clearwater International Airport (PIE; ☎ 727-453-7800; www.fly2pie.com) has several major carriers serving the US and Canada.

It also has car rentals. **Greyhound** (☎ 727-898-1496; 180 9th St N) services include to Tampa ($7, 35 minutes). Amtrak trains don't go to St Petersburg, but there is a bus link from Tampa.

Pinellas Suncoast Transit Authority (PSTA; ☎ 727-540-1900; www.psta.net; day pass/concession $4/1.75) operates PSTA buses citywide and the Suncoast Beach Trolley that links the beaches from Clearwater to Pass-a-Grille. The **Looper trolley** (per ride 25¢; 🕑 10am-5pm Sun-Thu, to midnight Fri & Sat) links the museums and St Petersburg Pier on a 30-minute narrated loop.

SARASOTA

Artists, writers, musicians, entertainers – artsy types have flocked to Sarasota since the 1920s, with John Ringling leading the way (see the boxed text, below). Today you can find cultural performances and arts venues – not to mention bookstores – all over town. The **visitor bureau** (☎ 941-957-1877, 800-522-9799; www.sarasotafl.org; 701 N Tamiami Trail; 🕑 10am-4pm Mon-Sat) has local information.

That big, fantastical purple building – some might say 'obnoxious' – is the **Van Wezel Performing Arts Hall** (☎ 941-953-3368, 800-826-9303; www.vanwezel.org; 777 N Tamiami Trail), purveyor of symphony, dance and theater. The **Sarasota County Arts Council** (☎ 941-365-5118; www.sarasota-arts.org; 1226 N Tamiami Trail, Suite 300) has information about a variety of upcoming local performances.

Wander about a cluster of colorful galleries and studios at **Towles Court Art District** (www.towlescourt.com; 1938 Adams Lane; 🕑 noon-4pm Tue-Sat). Independent films screen at the **Burns Court Cinema** (☎ 941-955-3456; 506 Burns Ct); call or visit www.filmsociety.org for schedules.

Right over the Ringling Causeway (which circus elephants helped build) on Lido Key is **St Armands Circle**, a roundabout that also serves as a social hub, with a proliferation of stylish shops and restaurants. **Mote Aquarium** (☎ 941-388-4441; www.mote.org; 1600 Ken Thompson Pkwy; adult/child 4-12yr $17/12; 🕑 10am-5pm; 🚸), a research center and rehabilitation facility, has touch pools, a manatee habitat, the fun Shark Attack Theater and, of course, fish.

Many of the beautiful beaches are private. The best public-access beach is **Siesta Key Beach**, about 5 miles south of downtown on Siesta Key, with wide, white strips of sugary quartz sand for your sunning pleasure.

Sleeping & Eating

Aloha Kai (☎ 941-349-5410; www.alohakai.net; 6020 Midnight Pass Rd; r $135-150; P ❄ 📶 🏊) The glorious Siesta Key sand is right at the end of the parking lot from your motel room, studio or retro apartment.

Cypress (☎ 941-955-4683; www.cypressbb.com; 621 Gulfstream Ave; r $150-279, ste 180-289; P ⊠ ❄ 📶) Beneath palm and mango trees sits this romantic – if occasionally frilly – B&B on the mainland.

Yoders (☎ 941-955-7771; 3434 Bahia Vista St; mains $5-12; 🕑 6am-8pm Mon-Sat) Not just home-cooking, but Amish home-cooking, and what could be homier than that? Finish off with a slice of their famous pie.

Broken Egg (☎ 941-346-2750; 140 Avenida Messina, Siesta Key; mains $6-12; 🕑 7:30am-2:30pm) This breakfast institution on Siesta Key, known for its pancakes and hash browns, has a new location and scored a great patio in the move.

Bijou Café (☎ 941-366-8111; 1287 1st St; lunch $9-19, dinner $17-29; 🕑 11:30am-2pm Mon-Fri, 5pm-close

CLOWNING AROUND AT THE RINGLING COMPLEX

Who doesn't love the circus? Well...people who are afraid of clowns. But a little coulrophobia isn't necessarily a deal-breaker at the **Ringling Museum Complex** (☎ 941-359-5700; www.ringling.org; 5401 Bayshore Rd; adult/child 6-17yr $20/7; 🕑 10am-5:30pm). On the grounds of the 66-acre complex are three separate museums, all included in your admission and each one a worthy attraction on its own. Railroad, real-estate and circus baron John Ringling and his wife Mabel put down roots here, building a Venetian Gothic waterfront mansion called **Ca d'Zan**. You can wander the ground floor at your own pace, or take a guided tour – totally worth it – which grants you access to the upstairs bedrooms. Also on the grounds, the **John & Mabel Museum of Art** is an excellent art museum with impressive high ceilings, intimidatingly large paintings and a recreated room from the Astor mansion. But the real standout here – the one you might want to avoid if you saw Stephen King's *It* – is the one-of-a-kind **Museum of the Circus**, which lets you relive the excitement of the big-top era with costumes, props, posters, antique circus wagons and an extensive miniature model.

Mon-Sat & Sun in high season) Indulge in the excellent French-inspired cuisine at this intimate downtown café.

FORT MYERS

Just a sleepy resort town in 1885, Fort Myers was pretty enough to entice Thomas Edison to build his winter home here. Among his many visions was palm-lined avenues, which he kicked off with a gift of more than 800 trees. His arboreal legacy lives on, and today 14 miles of McGregor Blvd are lined with more than 2000 palms. It's a nice introduction to what's still a fairly sleepy town; would that the rest of it were as impressive. The **visitor & convention bureau** (☎ 239-338-3500; www.fortmyers-sanibel.com) has visitor information; call or check online.

See how the early innovators lived at the **Edison & Ford Winter Estates** (☎ 239-334-7419; www.efwefla.org; 2350 McGregor Blvd; adult/child 6-12yr $20/11; 🕒 9am-5:30pm). In addition to Edison's winter home, you'll see his laboratory, gardens and a museum dedicated to his work, as well as the estate Henry Ford bought next door and the largest banyan tree in the continental US. Forty-minute guided tours leave every half-hour until 4pm.

Just north of Fort Myers, take a 90-minute swamp-buggy wildlife excursion through pinewoods, freshwater marsh and cypress swamp, led by **Babcock Wilderness Adventure** (☎ 800-500-5583; www.babcockwilderness.com; 8000 SR 31, Punta Gorda; adult/child 3-12yr $20/13; 🕒 tours vary, call for times).

For American bistro food try the cute **McGregor Cafe** (☎ 239-936-1771; 4305 McGregor Blvd; lunch $8-12, dinner $15-25; 🕒 lunch 11am-3pm Mon-Sun, dinner 5-9pm Tue-Sat), in a converted home with a shady patio under a huge live oak. Impress your date (or Mom, or client) with the regional specialties at the lovely **Veranda** (☎ 239-332-2065; 2122 Second St, Fort Myers; mains lunch $8-14, dinner $28-39; 🕒 11am-2pm Mon-Fri, 5:30-10pm Mon-Sat) located in a turn-of-the-century residence in downtown Fort Myers.

Getting There & Around

Regional, national and international flights service **Southwest Florida International Airport** (RSW; ☎ 239-590-4800; http://flylcpa.com). **Greyhound** (☎ 239-334-1011; 2250 Peck St) has regular services.

LeeTran (☎ 239-533-8726; www.rideleetran.com; single/all day $1.50/2.50) gets you from downtown to Summerlin Square, from where you can catch a beach-bound trolley. Check online for maps and schedules.

FORT MYERS BEACH

Fifteen miles south of Fort Myers, Fort Myers Beach is a cute if touristy party town on Estero Island. Look for blue, white and yellow flags marking beach access between houses. It's a good base for exploring nearby **Lovers Key State Recreation Area** (☎ 239-463-4588; pedestrian & cyclist $1, car $3-5; 🕒 8am-dusk), a bird and wildlife haven with gorgeous beaches where you can rent bikes, canoes and kayaks. You can also catch a ferry for a day trip to **Key West** (p527) via the **Key West Express** (☎ 888-539-2628; www.keywestshuttle.com; 2200 Main St; round trip adult/child $145/75).

Silver Sands Villas (☎ 239-463-6554; www.silversands-villas.com; 1207 Estero Blvd, Fort Myers Beach; r $89-199; P 🅧 🅧) is a sunny cluster of beach cottages painted with fresh, bright, tropical colors. Sunsets and sandy beaches are right downstairs from your room at the **Outrigger Beach Resort** (☎ 239-463-3131, 800-655-8997; www.outriggerfmb.com; 6200 Estero Blvd; r $105-225, ste $115-330; P 🅧 🅧 🅧). Snag some terrific fresh seafood and waterfront views at **Snug Harbor** (☎ 239-463-4343; San Carlos Blvd, Fort Myers Beach; mains $8-24; 🕒 4-9pm Tue-Fri, 11:30am-9pm Sat & Sun).

SANIBEL & CAPTIVA ISLANDS

Shaped like a fish hook trying to lure Fort Myers, these two slivers of barrier island lie just across a 2-mile causeway (toll $6). Remarkably undeveloped and free from condo-fever, they're as lush and green as Hawaii. Even the houses are hidden by foliage, giving the islands a wild, tropical feel.

The islands are famed for shell-collecting. S top just over the causeway at the extremely helpful **chamber of commerce visitor center** (☎ 239-472-1080; www.sanibel-captiva.org; 1159 Causeway Rd) for information about the islands – including where and at what time the shells will show themselves that day (an hour before or after low tide). The **Bailey-Matthews Shell Museum** (☎ 239-395-2233; www.shellmuseum.org; 3075 Sanibel-Captiva Rd; adult/child 5-16yr $7/4; 🕒 10am-5pm) helps you identify your shell finds, and is a nice place to wait out an afternoon shower.

Bike trails run all over the island, and you can rent bikes (4 hours $9) and more at **Finnimore's Bike & Beach Rentals** (☎ 239-472-5577; www.finnimores.com; behind 2353 Periwinkle Way, Sanibel; 🕒 9am-4pm). This is an especially good way to experience the marvelous, 5-mile **wildlife drive** (pedestrian/cyclist $1, car $5; 🕒 7:30am-sunset Sat-

Thu) at the bird-filled 6300-acre **JN 'Ding' Darling National Wildlife Refuge** (☎ 239-472-1100; www.fws.gov/dingdarling; 1 Wildlife Dr, Sanibel; 🕑 9am-4pm, to 5pm Jan-Apr). You can also experience the refuge with a guided tram, kayak or canoe tour through **Tarpon Bay Explorers** (☎ 239-472-8900; www.tarponbayexplorers.com; 900 Tarpon Bay Rd, Sanibel); call ahead for schedules.

Lodging on the islands is more expensive than on the mainland, but **Kona Kai Motel & Cottages** (☎ 239-472-1001, 800-820-2385; 1539 Periwinkle Way, Sanibel; r $100-160, ste $130-200; P ⊠ ⁂ ≋ ⛶) is great value, with lush gardens and clean, cute rooms. The lovely beachfront **Casa Ybel** (☎ 239-472-3145; www.casaybelresort.com; 2255 West Gulf Dr, Sanibel; r from $279; P ⊠ ⁂ ≋ ⛶) has casually elegant suites and its own bird sanctuary. You can find more lodging options at www.sanibelsmallinns.com.

Start your day at **Amy's Over Easy** (☎ 239-472-2625; 630 Tarpon Rd, Sanibel; mains $5-10; 🕑 7am-2:30pm), where you can still have breakfast even if it's lunchtime. Take a break at **Island Cow** (☎ 239-472-0606; 2163 Periwinkle Way, Sanibel; mains $8-20; 🕑 7am-9pm), a colorful island café, with tons of options from paella to po'boys to steaks. Or fancy it up at **Dolce Vita** (☎ 239-472-5555; 1244 Periwinkle Way, Sanibel; mains $17-36; 🕑 5:30-10:30pm), with an eclectic menu including wild boar saddle and Bahamian lobster tail.

On Captiva, the historic **'Tween Waters Inn Beach Resort** (☎ 239-472-5161; www.tween-waters.com; 15951 Captiva Dr, Captiva; r $180-290, ste $230-710; P ⊠ ⁂ ≋ ⛶) has a vast selection of rooms and cottages, plus tennis courts, spa, full-service marina and three restaurants. Don't miss the spectacularly kitschy **Bubble Room** (☎ 239-472-5558; 15001 Captiva Dr, Captiva; lunch $9-14, dinner $19-28; 🕑 11:30am-3pm & 4:30-9pm), with Christmas collectibles and memorabilia from the 1930s and '40s crammed into every corner.

CENTRAL FLORIDA

With such beautiful sand and water, it's no surprise that people gravitate to the coasts, leaving much of the middle part of the state a hollow, under-populated core. The exception is Orlando, the beating heart of tourism and the largest inland city. Tourists from around the world make the pilgrimage here, drawn to the oodles of family-lovin' theme parks. Central Florida also has a slew of gorgeous natural springs bubbling up from deep beneath the earth, offering yet another reason to leave behind the beaches for a couple of days inland.

ORLANDO

One of the top family destinations in the world, Orlando seems destined to always be mentioned in the same breath as theme parks. In fact, the parks seem to have permeated every corner, reaching their glossy, over-produced tentacles to restaurants and hotels across the city. Where are the dive bars? The hole-in-the-wall restaurants? Why are the waiters costumed and why does there always have to be something fiberglass hanging overhead? It's all Walt Disney's fault. The Magic Kingdom was so successful that it spawned a whole empire and attracted a slew of like-minded attractions; nowadays you can go to a different theme park every day of the week.

Of course, there are other things to do in Orlando. Many people are surprised to find that there's a stylish downtown district, a thriving nightlife scene, and even some residents who don't dress up like pirates during the day.

Orientation & Information

So many attractions compete for tourist dollars that it's easy to get overwhelmed. Good multilingual guides and maps are available from the **visitor bureau** (☎ 407-363-5872, 800-972-3304; www.orlandoinfo.com; 8723 International Dr; 🕑 8:30am-6:30pm); also check **Visit Orlando** (www.visitorlandoonline.com).

I-4 is the main north–south connector, though it's confusingly labeled east–west. To go north, take I-4 east (toward Daytona); to go south, get on I-4 west (toward Tampa). The main east–west roads are Hwy 50 and Hwy 528 (the Bee Line Expwy, a toll road), which connect Orlando to the Space Coast. The Bee Line Expwy accesses Orlando International Airport.

Sights & Activities

DOWNTOWN & LOCH HAVEN PARK

A good place to get 'It's a Small World' out of your head is in and around downtown's **Loch Haven Park**, a cluster of culture with nary a theme in sight.

Start with the **Orlando Museum of Art** (☎ 407-896-4231; www.omart.org; 2416 N Mills Ave; adult/child

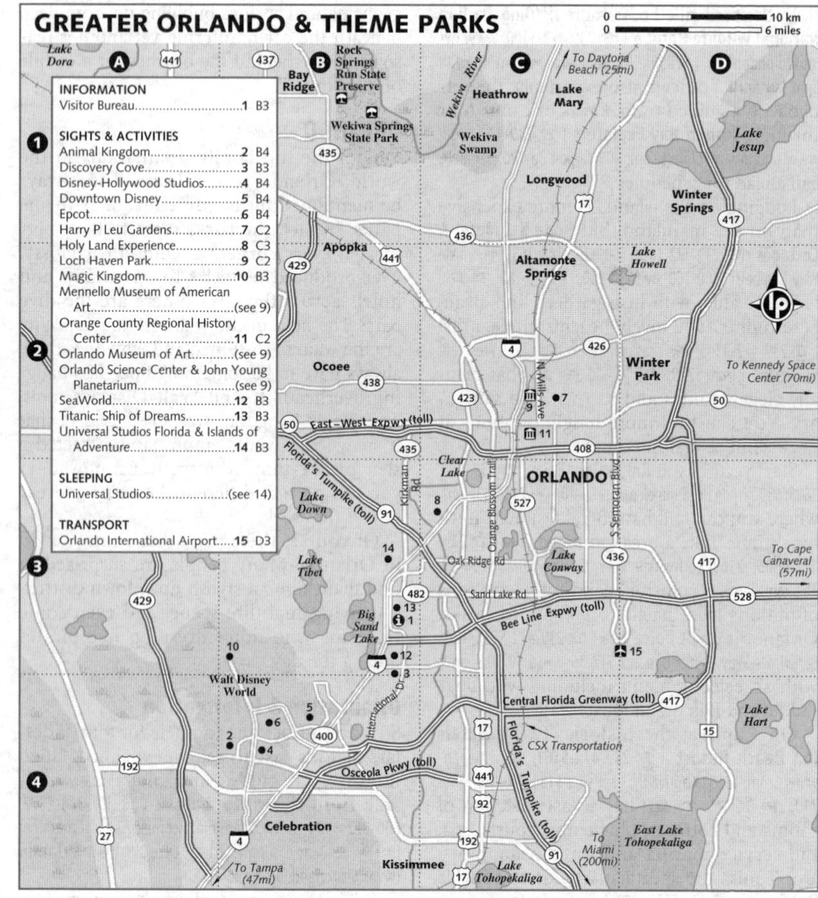

4-17yr $8/5; ⏲ 10am-4pm Tue-Fri, from noon Sat & Sun), spotlighting American and African art as well as unique traveling exhibits. The **Mennello Museum of American Art** (☎ 407-246-4278; www.mennellomuseum.org; 900 E Princeton St; adult/child under 12 $4/free; ⏲ 10:30am-4:30pm Tue-Sat, from noon Sun) features fascinating traveling exhibitions. Right across the street is the family-friendly **Orlando Science Center & John Young Planetarium** (☎ 407-514-2000; www.osc.org; 777 E Princeton St; adult/child 3-11yr $17/12; ⏲ 10am-5pm Sun-Fri, to 10pm Sat). One mile east of Loch Haven Park is the 50-acre **Harry P Leu Gardens** (☎ 407-246-2620; www.leugardens.org; 1920 N Forest Ave; adult/child 6-18yr $5/1; ⏲ 9am-5pm), a tranquil escape from all the gloss.

Pre-mouse Orlando is featured at the **Orange County Regional History Center** (☎ 407-836-8500; www.thehistorycenter.org; 65 E Central Blvd; adult/child 5-12yr $9/6; ⏲ 10am-5pm Mon-Sat, noon-5pm Sun) in a series of permanent and traveling exhibits showcasing the region.

INTERNATIONAL DRIVE

There are so many themed attractions, themed restaurants and themed hotels surrounding **International Drive** (I-Dr) that it's a quasi-theme park itself (with a theme of, well, themes). Two attractions attempt to add some gravitas to I-Dr's giddiness: **Titanic: Ship of Dreams** (☎ 407-248-1166; www.titanicshipofdreams.com; 8445 International Dr, at the Mercado; adult/child 6-11yr $17/12; ⏲ 10am-8pm) immerses you in replicas and relics from the doomed ship. And just north of I-Dr, **Holy Land Experience** (☎ 407-872-2272;

www.holylandexperience.com; 4655 Vineland Rd; adult/child 6-12yr $35/20; 10am-6pm Mon-Sat) is like a fun day in ancient Jerusalem, complete with lots of lessons from the bible.

UNIVERSAL ORLANDO

Universal is giving Disney a run for its money with this mega-complex that features two theme parks, a water park, three hotels and an entertainment district. But where Disney is all happy and magical, Universal's shtick is 'action, thrills and excitement.'

Universal Studios Florida (407-363-8000; www.universalorlando.com; 1000 Universal Studios Plaza; adult/child 3-9yr $75/65; from 9am, closing times vary;) has a Hollywood backlot feel with celluloid-inspired rides. Don't miss the *Back to the Future* time-travel simulator, or the fun 4-D *Shrek* show. Universal's **Islands of Adventure** (single day adult/child 3-9yr $67/56;) is a favorite with coaster-lovers, and is divided into five 'islands': Marvel Super Hero Island, featuring The Amazing Adventures of Spider Man; the dino-happy Jurassic Park; the ersatz-mystical Lost Continent; and the kid-friendly Toon Lagoon and Seuss Landing.

Look online for ticket deals, such as multi-day park-hopper passes. Parking at Universal costs $12.

SEAWORLD & DISCOVERY COVE

A not-altogether-logical blend of marine animals and thrill rides, **SeaWorld** (888-800-5447; www.seaworld.com; 7007 SeaWorld Dr; adult/child 3-9yr $75/65 from 9am, closing times vary; P) is home to both Shamu the killer whale and Kraken the floorless roller coaster. Journey to Atlantis tries to bring both concepts together: it's an oceanic water-coaster with a 60ft vertical drop. Feedings and shows take place at scheduled times, so plan your day to make sure you don't miss out. Parking costs $12.

Sister park **Discovery Cove** (407-370-1280, 877-557-7404; 6000 Discovery Cove Way; per person with/without dolphin swim $289/189; 9am-5:30pm, check-in from 8am; P) is like an exclusive tropical resort, complete with beaches, a fish-filled reef and an aviary. The price is steep, but everything is included: lunch, towels, parking, even a day pass to SeaWorld. Plus, they only admit 1000 guests per day – and that's worth a lot.

Sleeping

In addition to the Walt Disney World resorts (p549), Orlando has countless lodging options. Most are clustered around I-Dr, US 192 in Kissimmee and I-4. The **Central Reservation Service** (800-548-3311) operates a free service in conjunction with the visitor bureau to assist in making hotel reservations. **Universal Studios** (888-273-1311; r $199-439) has three hotels, and guests zoom straight to the front of the line for rides.

Magic Castle Inn & Suites (407-396-2212, 800-446-5669; www.magicorlando.com; 5055 W Hwy 192, Kissimmee; r $35-45; P) Garish exterior and serviceable rooms, but what the heck: it's super cheap, and just 3.5 miles from Walt Disney World.

Sheraton Safari Hotel (407-239-0444, 888-354-1356; www.sheratonsafari.com; 12205 Apopka Vineland Rd; r $99-159; P) Families can find a happy compromise at this well-located, safari-themed hotel that's fun for kids but not annoying for adults. The lavish pool area includes a 79ft python waterslide.

Veranda Bed & Breakfast (407-849-0321; www.theverandabandb.com; 115 N Summerlin Ave; r $99-209; P) Ideal for wandering Thornton Park and Lake Eola, this European style B&B has big antique beds and is a lovely retreat from all the bustle.

our pick **Courtyard at Lake Lucerne** (407-648-5188, 800-444-5289; www.orlandohistoricinn.com; 211 N Lucerne Circle E; r $99-225; P) This complex of four inns in a secluded enclave near downtown is a real find. Choices include art-deco suites in a refurbished apartment building and grand Victorian rooms in the Dr Phillips House, including cocktails and breakfast.

EO Inn & Spa (407-481-8485; www.eoinn.com; 227 N Eola Dr; r $119-189; P) Sleek and understated, this downtown boutique inn overlooks Lake Eola, with neutral-toned rooms that are elegant in their simplicity. It's mostly child-free.

Hyatt Regency Orlando Airport Hotel (407-825-1234; 9300 Airport Blvd; r from $159; P) Right inside the main terminal, this hotel has quite nice (and soundproof) rooms with balconies looking down on the hubbub below, plus easy access to airport shopping, dining and people-watching.

Grand Bohemian (407-313-9000; 325 S Orange Ave; r $169-459 P) No theme here, just lots of style, comfort, luxury and attentive service (if you like that sort of thing). Check out their art gallery; it's no sub for a museum, but it's a nice touch.

Eating

On and around I-Dr you'll find an explosion of chains; Sand Lake Rd has upscale dining.

Sea Thai (☎ 407-895-0985; 3812 E Colonial Dr; mains $6.50-16; ⏰ 11am-2:30pm, 5pm-9:30pm, to 10pm Fri & Sat) Hidden in a strip mall is this surprisingly chic restaurant serving what could well be the best Thai in Orlando.

Dexter's (☎ 407-648-2777; 808 E Washington St; mains $8-25; ⏰ 11am-10pm Mon-Thu, to 11pm Fri & Sat, 10am-10pm Sun) If you're craving low-key, head for this neighborhood café in fashionable Thornton Park on the edge of downtown.

Hot Olives (☎ 407-629-1030; 463 W New England Ave, Winter Park; lunch $9-14, dinner $18-37; ⏰ 11am-10pm, closed Sun & Mon during summer) Sandwiches and big salads at lunch, tropical seafood at dinner, all enjoyed on a breezy lanai.

Seasons 52 (☎ 407-354-5212; 7700 Sand Lake Rd; mains $11-27; ⏰ 11:30am-2:30pm & 5-10pm Mon-Fri, 11:30am-11pm Sat, 11:30am-10pm Sun) For a little *under*-indulgence, try this fresh-food grill that eschews butter, espouses low-cal and still pulls off a tasty meal.

Le Coq au Vin (☎ 407-851-6980; 4800 S Orange Ave; mains $12-29; ⏰ 5:30-10pm Tue-Sat, 5-9pm Sun) Known for its namesake, this immensely popular restaurant serves superb but hard-to-pronounce French specialties.

Combine dinner with a show and you usually end up with some lesser version of both; however, a lot of people find the combination fun enough that they don't mind. (Hint: you probably already have a pretty good idea if you're a dinner show type of person or not.) Good choices include the rollicking **Pirate's Dinner Adventure** (☎ 407-248-0590, 800-866-2469; www.piratesdinneradventure.com; 6400 Carrier Dr; adult/child $56/36) and the equestrian delight **Arabian Nights** (☎ 407-239-9223, 800-553-6116; www.arabian-nights.com; 6225 W Hwy 192; adult/child $53/29).

Drinking & Entertainment

Orlando Weekly (www.orlandoweekly.com) is the best source for entertainment listings, but there's plenty to do downtown, where there's a happening bar district around Orange Ave between Church St and Jefferson St. Find cheap drinks and a rockin' jukebox at the delightfully divey **Bar BQ Bar** (☎ 407-648-5441; 64 N Orange Ave). Check out great live music at the **Social** (☎ 407-246-1419; 54 N Orange Ave; cover varies). Or unwind upstairs at **Latitudes** (☎ 407-649-4270; 33 W Church St) in a pleasant, open-air setting. Whatever else you're looking for could be found at one of the eight bars constituting **Wall St Plaza** (☎ 407-849-0471; www.wallstplaza.net; 18 Wall St Plaza) or the six gay bars that make up **Parliament House** (☎ 407-425-7571; www.parliamenthouse.com; 410 N Orange Blossom Trail; cover varies).

Universal Studio's **CityWalk** (☎ 407-363-8000; www.citywalkorlando.com; ⏰ 11am-2am) has a concentration of movies, restaurants and clubs, and a $12 CityWalk Party Pass gives you access to most clubs. Venues include **CityJazz** (☎ 407-224-2189; cover $7) and **Hard Rock Live Orlando** (☎ 407-351-5483; www.hardrocklive.com; tickets from $20; ⏰ box office 10am-9pm).

Getting There & Around

Orlando International Airport (MCO; ☎ 407-825-2001; www.orlandoairports.net) has buses and taxis to major tourist areas for around $40 to $60. And **Meares Transportation** (☎ 407-423-5566; www.mearstransportation.com) provides shuttles for around $20 per person. **Greyhound** (☎ 407-292-3424; 555 N John Young Pkwy) serves numerous cities. **Amtrak** (☎ 407-843-7611; 1400 Sligh Blvd) offers daily trains south to Miami ($36) and north to New York City ($154).

Orlando's bus network is operated by **Lynx** (☎ 407-841-5969; www.golynx.com; single ride/day pass $1.50/3.50). **I-Ride Trolley** (www.iridetrolley.com; adult/child under 12/senior $1.25/free/25¢, exact change required; ⏰ 8am-10:30pm) buses run along I-Dr.

WALT DISNEY WORLD

At over 20,000 acres, Walt Disney World (WDW) is the largest theme park resort in the world. It includes four parks, two water parks, six golf courses, a couple dozen hotels, numerous restaurants and a mega-Disney entertainment district – proving that it's not such a small world, after all. At times it feels ridiculously crowded and corporate, but if you have kids in tow, you won't be able to inoculate yourself against their highly infectious enthusiasm. Even without kids, anyone who isn't scared off by the thought of life-sized costumed characters can easily end up drunk on Disney and clapping their hands because they do believe in fairies – they *do*! – and wandering home with bags full of souvenirs wondering what overtook them.

Orientation & Information

Walt Disney World (☎ 407-934-7639; www.waltdisneyworld.com; single-park admission adult/child 3-9yr $75/63, multiday discounts available; 👪) is 20 miles southwest of downtown Orlando and 4 miles northwest of Kissimmee.

To avoid lines for park admission, buy your tickets in advance online, by phone or from a Disney store. For an extra $50 a day, upgrade to a Park Hopper pass, which allows you to hop between all four WDW parks in the same day.

Crowds can sap the magic right out of the Magic Kingdom. Holidays aside (see p1141), WDW is least crowded in January, February, mid-September through October and early December. During the summer, weekends are the least crowded days; the rest of the year it's the other way round. Late fall tends to have the best weather, since frequent downpours dampen the hot, humid months of June, July and August.

Sights & Activities

MAGIC KINGDOM

It's the centerpiece of WDW and home of **Cinderella's Castle**. **Pirates of the Caribbean** has gotten some snazzed-up special effects with a dash of Johnny Depp, and **Haunted Mansion** and **Space Mountain** are still going strong. **Mickey's Toontown Fair** and **Fantasyland** are a hit with smaller kids, but anyone over 12 will want to keep walking. Fireworks displays light up the sky nightly and many nights end with a parade.

DISNEY HOLLYWOOD STUDIOS

Formerly Disney-MGM Studios, this park caters to the post-fairytale crowd and is also a working studio. Hands-down the most exciting rides are the spooky and unpredictable elevator in the **Twilight Zone Tower of Terror**, and the **Rock 'n' Roller Coaster**, where your stretch limo races through the streets of LA after dark. Wannabes can audition for the **American Idol Experience**, where casting agents determine which park guests will go on to perform onstage.

EPCOT

An acronym for 'Experimental Prototype Community of Tomorrow,' Epcot was Disney's vision of a high-tech city when it opened in 1982. It's divided into two halves: **Future World**, with corporate-sponsored journeys through not-very-cutting-edge technology, and **World Showcase**, which gives you an interesting toe-dip into the cultures of 11 different countries. (They were originally intended to be two separate parks, which explains a lot.) Epcot isn't the kids' paradise that the Magic Kingdom is, but the new **Soarin'** ride is a winner, and **Mission: SPACE** is good for getting the adrenaline pumping after one too many educational exhibits.

ANIMAL KINGDOM

Light on attractions, bigger on animals, this park lets you see wild things in re-created 'natural' environments through assorted experiences, including the 110-acre **Kilimanjaro Safari** (best early in the day). The iconic **Tree of Life** houses the fun **It's Tough to Be a Bug!** show, and **Expedition Everest** plummets you through an old mountain railway.

Sleeping

There are more than two dozen exceedingly family-friendly places to stay on Disney property, all offering free transportation to the parks and extended park hours. A **central reservation line** (☎ 407-934-7639) handles bookings and information.

Four properties make up Disney's 'value' segment, offering thousands of basic rooms. Beyond the themes, they're interchangeable, with over-the-top exteriors and wall-to-wall children common to all. Three **All-Star Resorts** (r $82-141; P) let you take your pick between movie, music and sports themes; and **Pop Century Resort** (r $82-141; P) tackles pop culture by the decade, with bowling pins and Mr Potato Head living side-by-side.

In the 'moderate' segment, **Port Orleans Resort** (r $149-199; P) is divided into the Southern-style Riverside Resort and the French Quarter Resort, which pulls off a pretty good facsimile of New Orleans architecture. And **Coronado Springs Resort** (r $149-199; P) has a Southwestern vibe that's low-key if not entirely authentic.

One of our favorite 'deluxe' resorts is the Yosemite-style **Wilderness Lodge** (r $240-420; P); the 'rustic opulence' theme includes erupting geysers, a lakelike swimming area and bunk beds for the kids.

Eating

Dining with Mickey and friends is insanely popular (and only available to park guests).

If you have your heart set on a particular restaurant, make reservations two to six months out with **central reservations** (☎ 407-939-3463). The hottest character dinner in all four parks is the usually-frenzied **Cinderella's Royal Table** (adult/child $32-40/$22-25; 🚼), where guests dine with Disney princesses in Cinderella's Castle.

Also in the Magic Kingdom, the old-timey **Plaza Restaurant** (Main St; sandwiches $10-13; 🚼) is a great option for sandwiches and banana splits. **Crystal Palace** (Main St; adult/child 3-9yr buffet $19-29/$11-14; 🚼) serves a lavish buffet with Pooh and friends at breakfast, lunch and dinner – tops in both quality and quantity.

At Disney Hollywood Studios, nostalgia rules at the **Sci-Fi Dine-In Theater** (by Star Tours; mains $12-22, kids meals $7.50; 🚼), where you dine in a Cadillac while watching B-movies (and traffic is bumper to bumper).

Each pavilion in Epcot's World Showcase has a sit-down restaurant that will set you back $14 to $30 per main, but it's more fun to snack your way around the world with the considerably cheaper counter-service options.

You can feast on Disney outside the parks, as well. Make a reservation at one of the resort restaurants, such as **California Grill** (☎ 407-939-3463; Disney's Contemporary Resort, 4600 North World Drive, Lake Buena Vista, mains $19-44) which pairs upscale eats with great views of the fireworks. Or wander **Downtown Disney's** many restaurants till you find what you're looking for. On Sundays, feed your soul at gospel brunch at Downtown Disney's **House of Blues** (☎ 407-934-2583; adult/child 3-9yr $33.50/17.25), serving an all-you-can-eat buffet that's fun and filling.

Drinking & Entertainment

Disney wouldn't dream of leaving you with non-Disney downtime, so it built Downtown Disney as a slightly overwhelming evening entertainment complex full of restaurants, shops and entertainment. The best live show in all of Disney World is **Cirque du Soleil** (☎ 407-939-7600; www.cirquedusoleil.com; adult $53-117, child 3-9yr $43-94; 🕑 6pm & 9pm Tue-Sat), featuring exquisitely theatrical acrobatics, and **House of Blues** (☎ 407-934-2583; www.hob.com; cover varies) hosts live music acts. Catch a movie at the 24-screen **AMC Pleasure Island** (☎ 888-262-4386), or enjoy five floors of virtual reality and arcade games at **DisneyQuest** (adult/child 3-9yr $40/34; 🕑 11:30am-10pm Sun-Thu, to 11pm Fri & Sat).

Getting There & Around

Most hotels in Kissimmee and Orlando – and all Disney properties – offer free transportation to WDW. Disney-owned resorts also offer free transportation from the airport. Drivers can reach all four parks via I-4 and park for $12. The Magic Kingdom lot is huge; you might need to catch a tram just to get to the entrance.

Within WDW, a complex network of monorails, boats and buses can get you anywhere you want to go, including resorts and Downtown Disney. Pick up a map at your resort or at Guest Relations (just inside the ticket turnstiles) to better understand your options.

AROUND CENTRAL FLORIDA

Hundreds of natural springs gush billions of gallons of crystal-clear water every day throughout the state, offering a plethora of outdoor pursuits. The water at **Salt Springs Recreation Area** (☎ 352-685-2048; 14152 SR 19N, Salt Springs; admission $4.25, camp-/RV sites $17/20; 🕑 8am-dusk) in the Ocala National Forest is rumored to have curative powers; either way, the swimming is sublime and there are fantastic opportunities for hiking, biking, canoeing, kayaking and camping.

At **Ichetucknee Springs State Park** (☎ 386-497-4690; 12087 SW US Hwy 27, Fort White; car $5, tubing $5; 🕑 8am-dusk), you can lie back on an inner tube or raft and gently float downstream on the crystal-clear waters through unspoiled wilderness as otters swim right up beside you.

In Volusia County, **De Leon Springs State Recreation Area** (☎ 386-985-4212; 601 Ponce DeLeon Blvd, De Leon Springs; pedestrian & cyclist $1, car $5; 🕑 8am-dusk) has a huge swimming area, and you can also explore the springs by canoe or kayak (per hour/day $10/$28). The springs flow into the Lake Woodruff National Wildlife Refuge, with 18,000 acres of lakes, creeks and marshes.

FLORIDA PANHANDLE

The beaches up here are lovely, with translucent aquamarine seas lapping against white sugar-sand formed by quartz crystal from the Appalachians. Known as the Emerald Coast, the area from Pensacola to Panama City has also earned the nickname 'Redneck Riviera' for its proximity to the southern states whose residents flock here.

There is indeed a Southern feel to the area that doesn't quite trickle down to the rest of Florida. Hwy 10 – the clothesline from which the whole state is hung – is lined with wooded forest for a scenic welcome to the Sunshine State.

TALLAHASSEE

Given how little resemblance it bears to the rest of the state, Tallahassee seems like an unlikely spot for the state capital. More Southern than Floridian, more forest than beach, it's a montage in the style of Margaret Mitchell's *Gone With the Wind*, with moss-draped oaks, rolling hills and sprawling plantations.

It was chosen as the capital in 1824, not so much for its representative qualities, but because they just couldn't pick between St Augustine and Pensacola, the two largest cities at the time. In a King Solomon–like move, they cut the baby in half, as it were, and put the capital approximately midway between the two. Still, it's a lovely place to visit and plays the gracious Southern host to anyone who drops by for a visit. Information and walking-tour maps are available from the **visitor center** (850-413-9200, 800-628-2866; www.seetallahassee.com; 106 E Jefferson St; 8am-5pm Mon-Fri, 9am-1pm Sat).

Sights & Activities

To learn about the people and events that shaped Florida, head to the museum in the **Florida Historic Capitol** (850-487-1902; www.flhistoriccapitol.gov; 400 S Monroe St; admission free; 9am-4:30pm Mon-Fri, 10am-4:30pm Sat, noon-4:30pm Sun & holidays), a grand, columned building with an art-glass dome and candy-striped awnings. Hovering behind it, with considerably less architectural charm, is the current **Florida State Capitol** (850-488-6167; cnr Pensacola & Duval Sts), a 22-story concrete slab where the state legislature meets for 60 days a year. The top floor has an observation deck and art gallery, and the ground floor has visitor information for the whole state.

The site of a 17th-century Spanish and Apalachee Indian mission, **Mission San Luis** (850-487-3711; www.missionsanluis.org; 2020 W Mission Rd; admission free; 10am-4pm Tue-Sun) has several convincingly re-created buildings, including the impressive Council House, for a fascinating look at what the area was like 300 years ago.

If the above elicited moans of boredom and shuffling of feet among the younger travelers in your party, make it up to them at the kid-friendly **Mary Brogan Museum of Art & Science** (850-513-0700; www.thebrogan.org; 350 S Duval St; adult/child 3-17yr $6/3.50; 10am-5pm Mon-Sat, 1-5pm Sun;), which has diverse collections ranging from folk art to hands-on science exhibits.

A treat for runners, skaters and cyclists, **Tallahassee–St Marks Historic Railroad State Trail** (877-822-5208; admission free; 8am-dusk) starts 100 yards south of the intersection of Capital Circle (Hwy 319) and Woodville Hwy (Hwy 363), and heads south for 16 flat, paved miles to the town of St Marks.

Sleeping & Eating

Accommodation rates can spike during football-game weekends and legislative sessions. Chains are clumped at exits along I-10 and along Monroe St between I-10 and downtown.

Doubletree Hotel (850-224-5000; 101 S Adams St; r $79-259;) This downtown hotel has homogenously nice rooms and is wired for business, making it a good base for the business traveler.

Inn at Park Avenue (850-544-2192; www.innatparkave.com; 323 E Park Ave; r $139-199;) Stay in grand Tallahassee style at this historic downtown inn, a stately home that's been in the same family for over 160 years.

Governors Inn (850-681-6855; www.thegovinn.com; 209 S Adams St; r $139-219, ste $179-299;) In a stellar downtown location, this warm, inviting inn has everything from single rooms to two-level loft suites, plus a daily cocktail hour.

Hopkins Eatery (850-386-4258; 1700 N Monroe; mains $7-10; 11am-9pm Mon-Fri, to 5pm Sat) These people will put anything between bread – and we mean that in a good way. Their creative combinations elevate the sandwich to new heights.

Po' Boys Creole Café (850-224-5400; 224 E College Ave; mains $7-15; 11am-9pm Sun & Mon, to 10pm Tue, Wed & Sat, to 11pm Thu & Fri, to 10pm Sat) Crawfish, jambalaya, red beans and blackened fish – not to mention an outdoor bar with a great happy hour – make this place a favorite among students and legislators alike.

Andrew's Capital Grill & Bar (850-222-3444; 228 S Adams St; mains $8-15; 11:30am-10pm Mon-Thu, to 11pm Fri & Sat, 11am-2pm Sun) Politicians spill onto sidewalk tables for salads and burgers named after themselves, and you can fuel up at the lunch buffet for only $10.

Urbane (☎ 850-422-2221; 115 E Park Ave; mains $16-32; ⌚ 5:30-10pm Tue-Sat) The vibe is chic, and the menu is creative. (Antelope? Really?) Make this your big night out, or stop by for small plates during happy hour.

Entertainment

Bradfordville Blues Club (☎ 850-906-0766; www.bradfordvilleblues.com; 7152 Moses Lane off Bradfordville Rd; tickets from $10; ⌚ call for schedule) Down the end of a dirt road lit by tiki torches, you'll find a bonfire raging under the live oaks at this hidden-away juke joint that hosts excellent national blues acts.

Getting There & Around

The **Tallahassee Regional Airport** (TLH; ☎ 850-891-7800) is about 5 miles southwest of downtown, off Hwy 263, and the **Greyhound station** (☎ 850-222-4249; 112 W Tennessee St; ⌚ 24hr) is right downtown. **Star Metro** (☎ 850-891-5200; http://talgov.com/starmetro; adult/child $1.25/60¢) provides a local bus service. Rent bikes at **Great Bicycle Shop** (☎ 850-224-7461; 1909 Thomasville Rd; bikes per 24hr $30; ⌚ 10am-6pm Mon-Fri, 10am-5pm Sat, noon-4pm Sun).

PANAMA CITY BEACH

There's no mistaking Panama City Beach for anything other than what it is: a beach town. Spring breakers and summer vacationers flock here for the beautiful white-sand beaches, and mile after mile of high-rise condos insist on disrupting the view. Stop by the **visitor bureau** (☎ 850-233-5070, 800-722-3224; www.thebeachloversbeach.com; 17001 Panama City Beach Pkwy; ⌚ 8am-5pm) for more information.

A renowned wreck-diving site, the area around Panama City Beach has dozens of natural, historic and artificial reefs. **Dive Locker** (☎ 850-230-8006, 888-612-7968; 106 Thomas Dr; ⌚ 8am-6pm Mon-Sat) has dives from $79 plus gear rental. Get inspiration at the **Man in the Sea Museum** (☎ 850-235-4101; www.maininthesea.org; 17314 Panama City Beach Pkwy; adult/child under 7 $5/free; ⌚ 10am-4pm Tue-Sun), showcasing the history of diving.

St Andrews State Recreation Area (☎ 850-233-5140; 4607 State Park Lane; pedestrian & cyclist/vehicle $1/5) is graced with nature trails and swimming beaches (one of the best places to swim with children is the 4ft-deep water near the jetties). Just offshore, **Shell Island** has fantastic snorkeling, and **shuttles** (☎ 850-233-0197, trip plus gear for adult/child $22/17) depart every 30 minutes in summer.

Mini-golf is *big* in Panama City Beach. Nostalgic favorite **Goofy Golf** (☎ 850-234-6403; 12206 Front Beach Rd; per round $7; ⌚ 9am-10pm or later Mar-Sep; 👶) was built in 1959 – look for the supersize sphinx.

Sleeping & Eating

Summer is the high season for Panhandle beaches.

Sandpiper Beacon Beach Resort (☎ 800-488-8828; www.sandpiperbeacon.com; 17403 Front Beach Rd; beachfront r $49-229, ste $209-269; P ✱ ≋ ⛝ 👶) With a tiki bar, lazy river, waterslides, mini-golf and even a grocery store, there's just not much need to leave the premises of this beachfront extravaganza.

Flamingo (☎ 850-234-2232; www.flamingomotel.com; 15525 Front Beach Rd; r $49-174, ste $54-219; P ✱ ⛝ 👶) Most of the immaculate rooms at this family-run, kid-friendly place on the beach have ocean views and kitchens.

Wisteria Inn (☎ 850-234-0557; wisteria-inn.com; 20404 Front Beach Rd; r $69-149; P ⊠ ✱ ≋ ⛝) More sophisticated than your average beach digs, the larger rooms are lightly themed and there are economical doubles in the back.

Mike's Diner (☎ 850-234-1942; 17554 Front Beach Rd; mains $4-11; ⌚ 8am-3pm) Cheap beach fuel can be found at this friendly, unassuming place with a little bit of everything.

DON'T MISS

Just 15 miles south of Tallahassee is the world's deepest freshwater spring at **Edward Ball Wakulla Springs State Park** (☎ 850-224-5950; 550 Wakulla Park Drive; cyclist/car $1/4, boat tours per adult/child $6/4; ⌚ 8am-dusk; 👶). The springs flow from massive underwater caves that are an archeologist's dream, with fossilized bones including a mastodon that was discovered around 1850. These days you can swim in the icy springs or enjoy them from a glass-bottom boat. You can also take a boat tour of the wildlife-filled Wakulla River, which was used as a movie set for several *Tarzan* movies, as well as *Creature from the Black Lagoon*. Overnighters can stay in the park at the **Wakulla Springs Lodge** (☎ 850-224-5950; r $85-105; P ⊠ ✱), a grand Spanish-style lodge built in 1937, where an 11ft stuffed alligator named 'Old Joe' keeps an eye on things.

SCENIC DRIVE: HIGHWAY 30A

Along the Panhandle coast between Panama City Beach and Destin, skip the main highway (Hwy 98) in favor of one of the most enchanting drives in Florida: Scenic Hwy 30A. This 18-mile stretch of road hugs what's referred to as the Emerald Coast for its almost fluorescent, gem-colored waters lapping brilliant white beaches of ground-quartz crystal.

Leading off Scenic Hwy 30A are pristine, wild parklands like **Grayton Beach State Recreation Area** (☎ 850-231-4210; 357 Main Park Rd, Santa Rosa Beach; pedestrian/vehicle $2/5). You also get to escape the high rises that obstruct the views in the more populated areas. But the best reason to make the detour is to visit the little village of **Seaside** (www.seasidefl.com).

If you saw the movie *The Truman Show*, you'll remember the town it was set in, with unnervingly friendly neighbors and candy-colored cottages clustered around a model town square. Turns out that that was no Hollywood backlot. It was Seaside. Stop for lunch in the slightly surreal planned community and wander the shops and galleries.

Good online resources are www.30-a.com, which has updated listings of all public beach access, and the website for the **South Walton Chamber of Commerce** (www.waltoncountychamber.com).

Firefly (☎ 850-249-3359; 535 Beckrich Rd; mains $12-35; 5-9:30pm) The food is fabulous, but it's the ambience that won us over, with drinks in the Library Lounge and dinner under a twinkle-lit oak tree.

Pineapple Willy's (☎ 850-235-0928; 9875 S Thomas Dr; mains $15-22; 11am-late) Ask for a table on the restaurant pier for breezy beachside dining. Famed for its signature drinks and its house special: Jack Daniels BBQ ribs.

Drinking & Entertainment

Billing itself as the 'last local beach club,' **Schooners** (☎ 850-235-3555; www.schooners.com; 5121 Gulf Dr; 11am-late) is good for a low-key beer on the beach. The two mega nightclubs are **Spinnaker** (☎ 850-234-7892; www.spinnakerbeachclub.com; 8795 Thomas Dr; 10am-4am) and the enormous, multiroom **Club La Vela** (☎ 850-234-3866; www.lavela.com; 8813 Thomas Dr; 10am-4am), which boasts activities such as Bon Jovi tribute nights and bikini beach parties. Covers apply – and vary – at both.

Getting There & Around

The **Panama City International Airport** (PFN; ☎ 850-763-6751; www.pcairport.com) is served by a handful of major and minor airlines.

The **Greyhound Station** (☎ 850-785-6111; 917 Harrison Ave) is in Panama City, and the limited **Bay Town Trolley** (☎ 850-769-0557; $1.25/60¢) will get you around town weekdays from 6am to 6pm.

PENSACOLA

Right next door to Alabama, Pensacola welcomes visitors driving in from the west. People are drawn not just by Pensacola's relative proximity, but by its white-sand beaches. In 2004 Hurricane Ivan smashed through the city; clean-up and regeneration is a lengthy process, but things are relatively back to normal and the local highway system got a major overhaul as an added bonus. The **visitor bureau** (☎ 850-434-1234, 800-874-1234; www.visitpensacola.com; 1401 E Gregory St; 8am-5pm Mon-Fri, 9am-4pm Sat, 11am-4pm Sun) has maps and free internet access.

The Spanish tried to colonize this stretch of the Panhandle in 1559, but the hurricane-plagued settlement was abandoned after two years, leaving St Augustine to claim the title of longest continuous European settlement in the country. Pensacola's harbor and geographical position have been key in its development as a military city.

Sights & Activities

Pensacola says 'take that!' to St Augustine with the **Historic Pensacola Village** (☎ 850-595-5985; www.historicpensacola.org; Zaragoza St, btwn Tarragona St & Adams St; adult/child 4-16yr $6/3; 10am-4pm Tue-Sat, tours at 11am, 1pm & 2:30pm), a self-contained enclave of historic homes and museums. Admission is good for one week and includes a guided tour and entrance to each building. The nearby **TT Wentworth Museum** (☎ 850-595-5990; 330 S Jefferson St; admission free; 10am-4pm Tue-Sat) has two floors of Florida history and one floor of Wentworth's collection of oddities, including his famous (and disgusting) petrified cat.

The Pensacola Naval Air Station (NAS) is home to both the **National Museum of Naval Aviation** (☎ 850-452-3604; www.naval-air.org; 1750 Radford Blvd; admission free; 9am-5pm)

WHAT THE...?

Every April, locals gather around the Florida–Alabama state line on Perdido Key for the **Interstate Mullet Toss**. This probably bears some explaining. 'Interstate' refers not to an interstate highway, but the fact that it involves two different states. 'Mullet' refers not to a redneck hairdo, but to a type of fish. And 'Toss,' well, that's pretty self-explanatory. Put them all together, and you've got contestants vying to see who can throw their dead fish furthest into Alabama. Organized by the **Flora-Bama Lounge & Package Store** (www.florabama.com), the mullet-toss has become a time-honored tradition, as well as a great excuse for a party.

and the elite **Blue Angels** squadron. You can watch the Blue Angels practice their death-defying air show at 8:30am most Tuesdays and Wednesdays through the summer and fall (check website).

To enjoy the area's lovely white sands, head to the easy-access Pensacola Beach or the neighboring **Gulf Islands National Seashore** (☎ 850-934-2600; www.nps.gov/guis; pedestrian or cyclist per 7 days $3, vehicle $8; ⏰ sunrise-sunset), part of a 150-mile stretch of undeveloped beach. After five years of closure due to Hurricane Ivan, the seashore's road to **Fort Pickens** has finally reopened, so you can once again picnic under the shadow of the imposing Civil War–era brick fort that once held Geronimo as a prisoner.

In 2006, a 910ft-long aircraft carrier was intentionally sunk off the coast of Pensacola to make the world's largest artificial reef. Now dubbed 'The Great Carrier Reef,' the **USS Oriskany** sits in the sand 210ft below the surface, with its flight deck at 137ft. **Viking Diving** (☎ 850-916-3483, 888-848-3483; 4612a Bellview Ave) and **Scuba Shack** (☎ 850-433-4319, 888-659-3483; 711 S Palafox St) can take you there.

Sleeping & Eating

Paradise Inn (☎ 850-932-2319, 800-301-5925; www.paradiseinn-pb.com; 21 Via de Luna; r $69-180; P ✠ ♒) Bringing a boutique feel to a motel format – we'll call it 'motel nouveau' – this Pensacola Beach inn is walking distance to the beach.

New World Inn (☎ 850-432-4111; www.newworldlanding.com; 600 S Palafox St; r $99-129; P ⊠ ✠ ☰) Peek under the lid of this former box factory and you'll find surprisingly lovely rooms with luxe bedding and real carpeting (a beach-town luxury).

our pick **Noble Manor** (☎ 850-434-9544, 877-598-4634; www.noblemanor.com; 110 W Strong St; r $125, ste $165; P ⊠ ✠ ♒) This B&B has the prettiest rooms in town; 'Bacall' would be opulent enough for its namesake.

Jerry's Drive-In (☎ 850-433-9910; 2815 E Cervantes St; mains $6-13; ⏰ 10am-10pm Mon-Fri, 7am-10pm Sat; ♿) No longer a drive-in or owned by Jerry, but this greasy spoon is always packed – possibly because you can hardly eat for less. Cash only.

Peg Leg Pete's Oyster Bar (☎ 850-932-4139; 1010 Fort. Pickens Rd; mains $8-20; ⏰ 11am-10pm) Raw? Rockefeller? Casino? Get your oysters the way you like 'em at this popular beach hangout that also serves lunch, dinner and plenty of cold beer.

Dharma Blue (☎ 850-433-1275; 300 S Alcaniz St; lunch mains $9-12, dinner $11-28; ⏰ lunch 11am-4pm Mon-Sat, dinner from 5pm nightly) Where else can you get both fried green tomatoes and sushi rolls? The menu may be a mishmash, but everyone leaves happy.

Jackson's Restaurant (☎ 850-469-9898; 400 S Palafox St; lunch mains $12-17, dinner $26-35; ⏰ lunch 11am-2pm Tue-Fri, dinner 5:30-10pm Tue-Sat, to 10:30pm Fri & Sat) Not your typical white-tablecloth restaurant; this one adds rustic touches and a stellar menu for dignified dining.

Drinking & Entertainment

Check out the *Pensacola News Journal's* Friday 'Weekender' section for entertainment listings. If you're not sure what you're after, head to **Seville Quarter** (☎ 850-434-6211), an entertainment complex with lots of options. Other good choices are **McGuire's Irish Pub** (☎ 850-433-6789; 600 E Gregory St) and gay dance club **Emerald City** (☎ 850-433-9491; 406 E Wright St).

Getting There & Around

Five miles northeast of downtown, **Pensacola Regional Airport** (PNS; ☎ 850-436-5000; www.flypensacola.com) is served by major airlines. The **Greyhound station** (☎ 850-476-4800; 505 W Burgess Rd) is nine miles north of downtown.

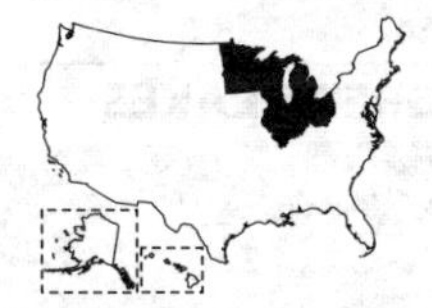

Great Lakes

Here's how it's going to go down. You're planning your USA trip; you unfurl the map and gravitate immediately to the coasts. Mountains! Oceans! Metropolises! Movie stars! But the middle of the country – what's the middle ever good for? Middle management, middle child, middle of nowhere. It's nothing to strive for.

Fine. Be that way. You'll miss out on surfing beaches and Tibetan temples, car-free islands and the green-draped night-lights of the aurora borealis. You'll forgo the only region in which you can sip a fresh-from-the-dairy-farm milk shake for lunch, and then take part in a five-way in the city for dinner. Are you sure you want to pass it up?

Roll call for the Midwest's cities starts with soaring Chicago, which shoots up the country's mightiest skyline. Milwaukee keeps the beer-and-Harley flame burning, while Minneapolis shines a hipster beacon out over the cornfields. Detroit rocks, plain and simple.

The Great Lakes themselves are huge, like inland seas, offering beaches, islands, dunes, resort towns and lots of lighthouse-dotted scenery. Dairy farms and fruit orchards blanket the region, meaning fresh pie and ice cream await hungry road-trippers. Thirsty travelers can indulge in the Midwest's beers – the cities here have long been known for suds crafting, thanks to their German heritage, and several microbreweries maintain the tradition.

Most visitors come in summer when the weather is fine for hiking, biking, canoeing and kayaking in the local lakes and forests. Snowmobiling and cross-country skiing take over in the butt-freezing winter (as do eating and drinking in warm taverns). Whatever the season, you're guaranteed a true slice of America here in the heartland.

HIGHLIGHTS

- Absorbing the skyscrapers, museums, festivals and foodie bounty of **Chicago** (p559)
- Beach lounging, berry eating and surfing on Michigan's **Gold Coast** (p619)
- Slowing down for clip-clopping horses and buggies in **Amish Country** (p596 and p603)
- Polka dancing at a Friday-night fish fry in **Milwaukee** (p627)
- Paddling the **Boundary Waters** (p648) and sleeping under a blanket of stars

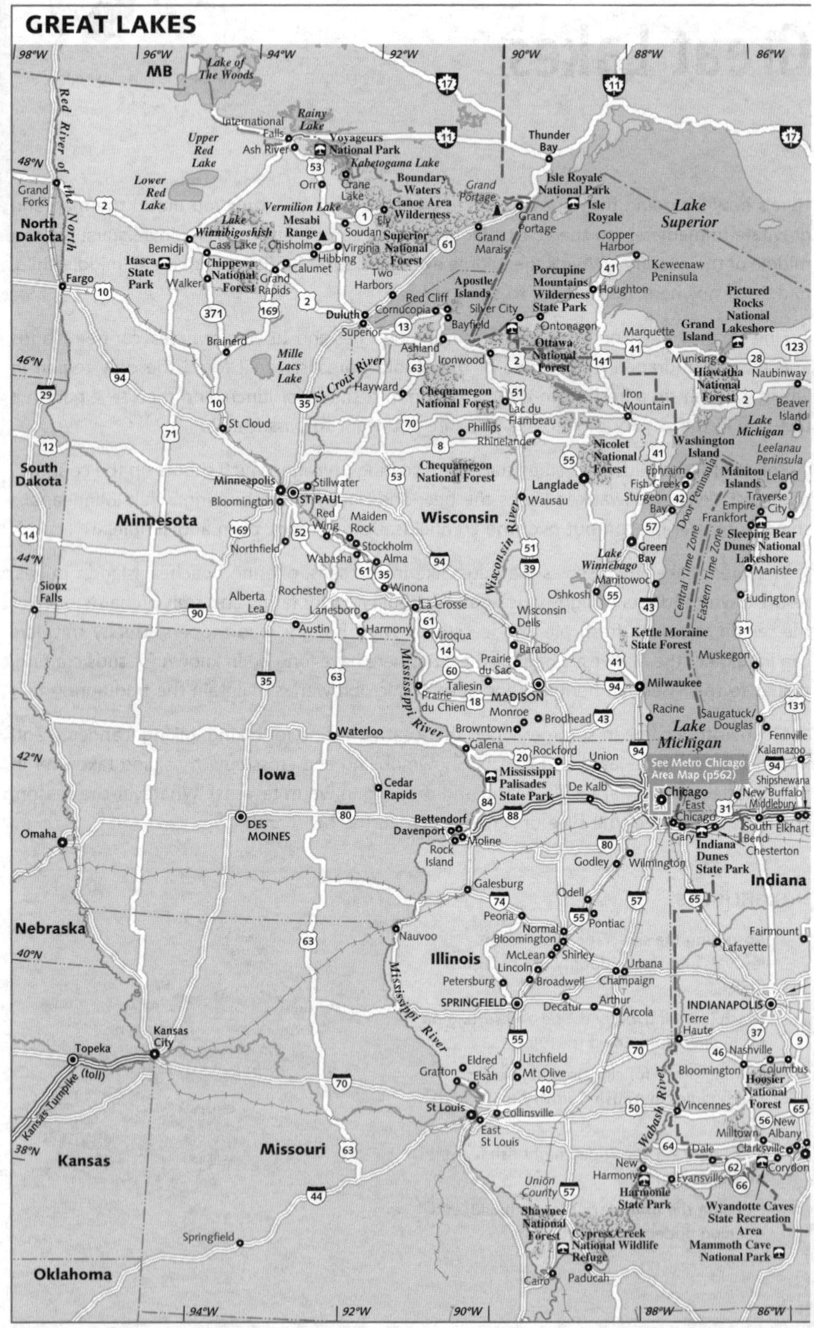
GREAT LAKES
98°W
96°W
94°W
92°W
90°W
88°W
86°W
MB
Lake of The Woods
Red River of the North
Rainy Lake
International Falls
Ash River
Voyageurs National Park
Upper Red Lake
Lower Red Lake
Kabetogama Lake
Thunder Bay
48°N
Grand Forks
Crane Lake
Orr
Boundary Waters Canoe Area Wilderness
Grand Portage
Isle Royale National Park
Isle Royale
Lake Superior
Vermilion Lake
Ely
Soudan
Mesabi Range
Lake Winnibigoshish
Cass Lake
Chisholm
Virginia
Hibbing
Superior National Forest
Grand Marais
North Dakota
Bemidji
Itasca State Park
Chippewa National Forest
Calumet
Grand Rapids
Walker
Two Harbors
Copper Harbor
Keweenaw Peninsula
Porcupine Mountains Wilderness State Park
Houghton
Apostle Islands
Red Cliff
Cornucopia
Silver City
Bayfield
Ontonagon
Fargo
Duluth
Superior
Pictured Rocks National Lakeshore
Grand Island
Marquette
Brainerd
Mille Lacs Lake
Ashland
Ironwood
Ottawa National Forest
Munising
Naubinway
46°N
St Croix River
Hayward
Chequamegon National Forest
Hiawatha National Forest
Iron Mountain
Lac du Flambeau
Beaver Island
St Cloud
Phillips
Rhinelander
Lake Michigan
Nicolet National Forest
Washington Island
Leelanau Peninsula
South Dakota
Minneapolis
Stillwater
ST PAUL
Bloomington
Chequamegon National Forest
Langlade
Wausau
Ephraim
Fish Creek
Sturgeon Bay
Manitou Islands
Leland
Traverse City
Empire
Frankfort
Door Peninsula
Minnesota
Red Wing
Maiden Rock
Wisconsin
Wisconsin River
Sleeping Bear Dunes National Lakeshore
Northfield
Stockholm
Wabasha
Alma
Green Bay
Lake Winnebago
Manistee
44°N
Central Time Zone
Eastern Time Zone
Sioux Falls
Rochester
Winona
Manitowoc
Oshkosh
Ludington
Alberta Lea
Lanesboro
La Crosse
Wisconsin Dells
Austin
Harmony
Viroqua
Kettle Moraine State Forest
Mississippi River
Baraboo
Prairie du Sac
Muskegon
Taliesin
Prairie du Chien
MADISON
Milwaukee
Monroe
Brodhead
Racine
Saugatuck/ Douglas
Browntown
Waterloo
Galena
Rockford
Union
Lake Michigan
Fennville
Kalamazoo
42°N
Iowa
See Metro Chicago Area Map (p562)
Mississippi Palisades State Park
De Kalb
Shipshewana
Cedar Rapids
Chicago
New Buffalo
Middlebury
East Chicago
Bettendorf
DES MOINES
Davenport
Moline
Gary
South Bend
Elkhart
Omaha
Rock Island
Indiana Dunes State Park
Chesterton
Godley
Wilmington
Galesburg
Indiana
Odell
Peoria
Pontiac
Nebraska
Nauvoo
Normal
Bloomington
Fairmount
Lafayette
40°N
Illinois
McLean
Shirley
Lincoln
Urbana
Petersburg
Broadwell
Champaign
Mississippi River
SPRINGFIELD
Decatur
Arthur
Arcola
INDIANAPOLIS
Terre Haute
Kansas City
Topeka
Nashville
Eldred
Litchfield
Grafton
Elsah
Mt Olive
Bloomington
Columbus
Kansas Turnpike (toll)
Hoosier National Forest
Vincennes
Wabash River
St Louis
Collinsville
East St Louis
New Albany
Milltown
38°N
Kansas
Missouri
Dale
Clarksville
New Harmony
Corydon
Harmonie State Park
Evansville
Union County
Shawnee National Forest
Wyandotte Caves State Recreation Area
Cypress Creek National Wildlife Refuge
Mammoth Cave National Park
Springfield
Oklahoma
Cairo
Paducah

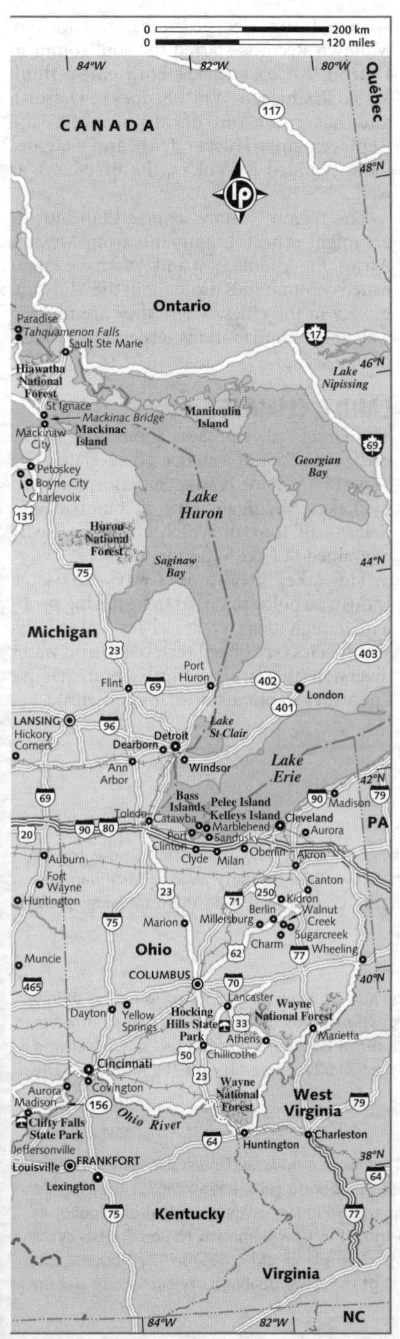

HISTORY

The region's first residents included the Hopewell (around 200 BC) and Mississippi River mound builders (around AD 700). Both left behind mysterious piles of earth that were tombs for their leaders and possibly tributes to their deities. You can see remnants at Cahokia (p590) in Illinois, and Mound City (p606) in Ohio.

The mound-building cultures began to decline around AD 1000, and over the next centuries the Miami, Shawnee and Winnebago moved in.

French voyageurs (fur traders) arrived in the early 17th century and established missions and forts. The British turned up soon after that. The rivalry spilled over into the French and Indian Wars (Seven Years' War, 1754–61), after which Britain gained all of the land east of the Mississippi. Following the Revolutionary War, the Great Lakes area became the new USA's Northwest Territory, which soon was divided into states.

Settlers flocked in after the region developed its impressive canal and railroad network. But conflicts erupted between the newcomers and the Native Americans here, including the 1811 Battle of Tippecanoe in Indiana; the bloody 1832 Black Hawk War in Wisconsin, Illinois and around, which forced indigenous people to move west of the Mississippi; and the 1862 Sioux uprising in Minnesota.

Industries sprang up and grew quickly, fueled by resources of coal and iron and cheap transport on the lakes. The work available brought huge influxes of immigrants from Ireland, Germany, Scandinavia and southern and eastern Europe. For decades after the Civil War, a great number of African Americans also migrated to the region's urban centers from the South.

The area prospered during WWII and throughout the 1950s. Then came 20 years of social turmoil and economic stagnation. Manufacturing industries declined, walloping Rust Belt cities like Detroit and Cleveland with high unemployment and 'white flight' (ie white middle-class families who fled to the suburbs).

The 1980s and '90s brought urban revitalization. The region's population picked up, notably with newcomers from Asia and Mexico. Growth in the service and high-tech sectors resulted in a better economic balance. But manufacturing industries like car making and steel still played a big role, and when the economic crisis hit in 2008, Great Lakes towns felt the pinch first and foremost.

LOCAL CULTURE

The Great Lakes region – aka the Midwest – is the USA's solid, sensible heartland. Folks here shrug at the brash glitz of the East Coast and flaky sex appeal of the West Coast, happy instead to be in the plain-speaking middle. It's no surprise that novelist Ernest Hemingway hailed from this part of the country, where words are seldom wasted.

Regional pride manifests at every turn in the road. It's evident in Wisconsin's freshly painted barns, the tidiness of family-owned motels in Michigan's Upper Peninsula, even in Rockford, Illinois' Sock Monkey Festival (p587).

If the Midwest had a mantra, it might be to work hard, go to church, and stick to the straight and narrow…unless there's a sports game happening, and then it's OK to slather on the body paint and dye your hair purple (or whatever team colors dictate). Baseball, football, basketball and ice hockey are all hugely popular, with the big cities sponsoring pro teams for each sport.

Music has always been a big part of local culture. Muddy Waters and Chess Records spawned the electric blues in Chicago. Motown Records started the soul sound in Detroit. Alt rock shakes both cities (think Wilco in Chicago, White Stripes in Detroit), and has come out of Minneapolis (the Replacements, Hüsker Dü), and Dayton, Ohio (Guided By Voices, the Breeders), as well.

The region is more diverse than outsiders might expect. Immigrants from Mexico, Africa, the Middle East and Asia have established communities throughout the Midwest, mostly in the cities, where they are making welcomed contributions, especially to local dining scenes.

LAND & CLIMATE

The Great Lakes possess about 20% of the earth's and 95% of America's fresh water. The largest by volume is Lake Superior, followed by Lakes Michigan, Huron, Ontario and Erie, – all four of which could be easily contained in Lake Superior.

The lakes' health is always an issue. Industrial pollution used to be the big problem, though today it takes a back seat to invasive species (see boxed text, p568) and water diversion (that is, exporting water in massive quantities to other states or countries).

GREAT LAKES…

In Five Days

Spend the first two days in **Chicago** (opposite). On your third day, make the 1½-hour trip to **Milwaukee** (p627) for culture, both high- and lowbrow. Take the ferry over to Michigan and spend your fourth day beaching in **Saugatuck** (p620). Come back via northern Indiana's **sand dunes** (p597) or **Amish community** (p596).

In 10 Days

After two days in Chicago, on day three make for **Madison** (p630) and its surrounding quirky sights. Spend your fourth and fifth days at the **Apostle Islands** (p635), and then head into the Upper Peninsula to visit **Marquette** (p625) and **Pictured Rocks** (p625) for a few days, followed by **Sleeping Bear Dunes** (p620) and the wineries around **Traverse City** (p621). Return via the galleries, pies and beaches of Saugatuck (p620).

Active Endeavors

The region offers activities to match a variety of weather moods and personal tastes. Visitors can **surf** (p619) in New Buffalo, **rock climb** (p605) at Hocking Hills, **kayak** (p635) the Apostle Islands, **canoe** (p648) amid moose and wolves in the Boundary Waters, **houseboat** (p650) in remote Voyageurs National Park, **mountain bike** (p635) in Chequamegon Nation Forest, **cycle rails-to-trail** (p627) through Wisconsin's cow-dotted farmland, **ski** (p626) in the Porkies, and **backcountry hike** (p625) on Isle Royale. Almost all of these are doable by beginners, so get up off your duff and get moving.

The Ohio and Mississippi Rivers are the major riverways. Most of the region's larger cities lie along them or on the lakeshores.

Winters can last from late November well into April, with plenty of snow, icy winds and subfreezing temperatures (eg Chicago and Minneapolis each average about 20°F (-7°C) in January, the coldest month). By June the sun is out and temperatures start to rise, and in July and August it can be downright hot and sticky. Spring and autumn fit in around the edges, and are wonderful times to visit – particularly autumn, when leaves are at their peak of color.

PARKS & WILDLIFE

Hiking, kayaking and sand-dune climbing are on tap at the region's national parks and lakeshores, including Isle Royale (p625), Sleeping Bear Dunes (p620) and Pictured Rocks (p625) in Michigan; the Apostle Islands (p635) in Wisconsin; Indiana Dunes (p597) in Indiana; and Voyageurs National Park (p649) in Minnesota.

Wide swaths of state park land also crisscross the Great Lakes; see each state's Information section for details.

Black bears, moose and wolves are the wildlife stars, though you'll have to travel to the dense northern forests to see them. Bald eagles fly in huge numbers in Minnesota and along the Mississippi River. Not as fun to encounter are insects, which can be a real pain the further north you go, specifically blackflies in the spring and mosquitoes in summer. It's therefore a good idea to pack bug repellent.

INFORMATION

The **Great Lakes Information Network** (www.great-lakes.net) is a web resource with info aplenty on the region's environment, economy and tourism, much of it culled from local news sources.

GETTING THERE & AROUND

Chicago's O'Hare International Airport (ORD) is the main air hub for the region. Detroit, Cleveland and Minneapolis also have busy airports.

Greyhound (p1160) connects many local cities and towns. Upstart **Megabus** (☎ 877-462-6342; www.megabus.com/us) provides an efficient alternative between major Great Lakes cities. Note that Megabus has no bus terminals (drop-off and pick-up are at various street corners), and all purchases must be made in advance online (you cannot buy a ticket from the driver). Most Megabus vehicles have wi-fi, though service can be sketchy.

If you are traveling on major interstate highways, such as I-80 in Ohio or I-90 in Illinois, piles of change are useful for the tolls.

Two car/passenger ferries sail across Lake Michigan, providing a shortcut between Wisconsin and Michigan. The *Lake Express* (p620) crosses between Milwaukee and Muskegon. The older *SS Badger* (p620) crosses between Manitowoc and Ludington.

The national railroad network centers on Chicago, from which Amtrak (p1166) runs trains regularly to cities throughout the region and the rest of the USA.

ILLINOIS

Chicago dominates the state with its sky-high architecture, lakefront beaches and superlative museums, restaurants and music clubs. But venturing further afield reveals Hemingway's hometown of 'wide lawns and narrow minds,' scattered shrines to local hero Abe Lincoln, and a trail of corn dogs, pies and drive-in movie theaters down Route 66. A cypress swamp and prehistoric World Heritage Site make appearances in Illinois too.

Information

Illinois Bureau of Tourism (☎ 800-226-6632; www.enjoyillinois.com)

Illinois highway conditions (☎ 800-452-4368; www.gettingaroundillinois.com)

Illinois state park information (☎ 217-782-6752; www.dnr.state.il.us) State parks are free to visit. Campsites cost $6 to $35; some accept reservations (fee $5).

CHICAGO

Loving Chicago is 'like loving a woman with a broken nose: you may well find lovelier lovelies, but never a lovely so real.' Writer Nelson Algren summed it up well in *Chicago: City on the Make*. There's something about this cloud-scraping city that bewitches. Well, maybe not during the six-month winter, when the 'Windy City' gets slapped by snowy blasts; however, come May, when the weather warms and everyone dashes for the outdoor festivals, ballparks, lakefront beaches and beer gardens – ahh, nowhere tops Chicago. And we mean it

CHICAGO...

In Two Days

On your first day take an **architectural tour** (p577) and look up at the city's skyscrapers. Look down from the **John Hancock Center** (p568), one of the world's tallest buildings. See 'the Bean' reflect the skyline, and splash with Crown Fountain's human gargoyles at **Millennium Park** (p563). Hungry after all the walking? Chow down on a deep-dish pizza at **Giordano's** (see boxed text, p580).

Make the second day a cultural one: explore the **Art Institute of Chicago** (p563) or **Field Museum of Natural History** (p567). Browse boutiques and grab a stylish dinner in **Wicker Park** (p581). Then head north to Al Capone's gin joint, the **Green Mill** (p584), for an evening of jazz.

In Four Days

Follow the two-day itinerary and then on your third day, rent a bicycle, dip your toes in Lake Michigan at **North Avenue Beach** (p569) and cruise through **Lincoln Park** (p569), making stops at the zoo and conservatory. If it's baseball season, head directly to **Wrigley Field** (p569) for a Cubs game. A smoky blues club, such as **Buddy Guy's Legends** (p584), is a fine way to finish the day (or start the morning).

Pick a neighborhood on your fourth day to eat, shop and soak up the culture: murals and mole sauce in **Pilsen** (p572), pagodas and Vietnamese sandwiches in **Uptown** (p569), or Obama and the Nuclear Energy sculpture in **Hyde Park** (p574). Then see a play at one of Chicago's 200 theaters, or a comedy at **Second City** (p585).

literally as the Willis Tower is here, the USA's tallest building.

Beyond its mighty architecture, Chicago is a city of Mexican, Polish, Vietnamese and other ethnic neighborhoods to eat and wander through. It's a city of blues, jazz and rock clubs any night of the week, and a full-fledged foodie scene that extends even to gourmet hot dogs.

Thanks to the election of local boy Barack Obama to the White House, Chicago has jumped into the spotlight and been 'discovered' for its low-key, cultured awesomeness. It's a wonder it took so long.

History

In the late 17th century, the Potawatomi gave the name Checagou – meaning wild onions – to the once-swampy environs, and the city was on its way. Its pivotal moment happened on October 8, 1871. That's when Mrs O'Leary's cow kicked over the lantern that started the Great Chicago Fire (or so the story goes). It torched the entire inner city and left 90,000 people homeless.

'Damn,' said the city planners. 'Guess we shouldn't have built everything from wood. It's flammable.' So they rebuilt with steel and created space for bold new structures, like the world's first skyscraper, which popped up in 1885.

Workers fought against factories' poor conditions in the late 1800s, and after violent strikes, the world's labor movement was born in Chicago (so thank the city for your lunch break).

Al Capone's gang more or less ran things during the 1920s and corrupted the city's political system. Local government has had issues ever since, with 30 city council members going to jail since 1970.

The 'Democratic Machine,' as City Hall is often referred to by the press, has been helmed by the Daleys for 40-plus years, namely Richard J Daley, Chicago's mayor from 1955 to 1976, and his son Richard M Daley, Da Mayor since 1989.

Orientation

The central downtown area is known as the Loop, a hub of skyscrapers and Chicago Transit Authority (CTA) trains. The city's streets are laid out on a grid and numbered; Madison and State Sts are the grid's center. As you go north, south, east or west from here, each increase of 800 in street numbers corresponds to 1 mile. At every increase of 400, there is a major arterial street. For instance, Division St (1200 N) is followed by North Ave (1600 N) and Armitage Ave (2000 N), at which point you're 2.5 miles north of downtown.

Information

Chicago's sales tax – from 10.25% to 11.25% – is the nation's highest.

BOOKSTORES

Borders (Map pp570-1; ☎ 312-573-0564; 830 N Michigan Ave) You name it, they've got it.
Quimby's (Map p562; ☎ 773-342-0910; 1854 W North Ave) Ground Zero for comics, zines and underground culture.
Women & Children First (Map p573; ☎ 773-769-9299; 5233 N Clark St) Women-penned books.

EMERGENCY & MEDICAL SERVICES

Northwestern Memorial Hospital (Map pp564-5; ☎ 312-926-5188; 251 E Erie St) Well-respected hospital downtown.
Rape crisis (☎ 888-293-2080)
Stroger Cook County Hospital (Map p562; ☎ 312-864-1300; 1969 W Ogden Ave) Public hospital serving low-income patients.
Walgreens (Map pp564-5; ☎ 312-664-8686; 757 N Michigan Ave; 24hr)

INTERNET ACCESS

Public libraries remain the best bet for free wired and wireless internet access. Bars and restaurants in Lincoln Park, Bucktown and Near North often have free wi-fi, as does the Chicago Cultural Center (p567) downtown.

INTERNET RESOURCES

The local media (right) websites and free downloadable audio tours (p577) are also good resources.

Chicagoist (www.chicagoist.com) Quirky take on news, food, arts and events.
Gaper's Block (www.gapersblock.com) News and events site with Chicago attitude.
Huffington Post Chicago (www.huffingtonpost.com/chicago) Amalgamates news from major local sources.
Mayor Daley's Channel (www.gapersblock.com) Da Mayor spouts on YouTube.
Vegchicago (www.vegchicago.com) Vegetarian/vegan dining guide.

LIBRARIES

Harold Washington Library Center (Map pp564-5; ☎ 312-747-4300; 400 S State St; 9am-9pm Mon-Thu, 9am-5pm Fri & Sat, 1-5pm Sun) A grand, art-filled building with free wi-fi throughout and 3rd-floor internet terminals.

MEDIA

Chicago's National Public Radio (NPR) affiliate is WBEZ-FM 91.5. For alternative music, tune into WXRT-FM 93.1.

Chicago Reader (www.chicagoreader.com) Free alternative newspaper with comprehensive arts and entertainment listings.
Chicago Sun-Times (www.suntimes.com) The *Tribune's* daily, tabloidesque competitor.
Chicago Tribune (www.chicagotribune.com) The city's stalwart daily newspaper; its younger, trimmed-down, freebie version is *RedEye*.

MONEY

ATMs are plentiful downtown, with many near Chicago and Michigan Aves. To change

ILLINOIS FACTS

Nicknames Prairie State, Land of Lincoln
Population 12.8 million
Area 57,900 sq miles
Capital city Springfield (population 116,500)
Other cities Chicago (population 2,833,321)
Sales tax 6.25%
Birthplace of Author Ernest Hemingway (1899–1961), animator Walt Disney (1901–66), jazz musician Miles Davis (1926–91), actor Bill Murray (b 1950)
Home of Cornfields, Route 66 starting point
Famous for Skyscrapers, corn dogs, Abe Lincoln sights
Official snack food Popcorn
Driving distances Chicago to Milwaukee 92 miles, Chicago to Springfield 200 miles

DON'T MISS

The Midwest is ready to pour you a cold one thanks to its German heritage. Yes, Budweiser and Miller are based here, but that's not what we're talking about. Far more exciting is the region's cache of craft brewers. Keep an eye on the taps for these slurpable brewers, available throughout the area:

Bell's Kalamazoo, MI
Capital Madison, WI
Founder's Grand Rapids, MI
Goose Island Chicago, IL
Great Lakes Cleveland, OH
Lakefront Milwaukee, WI
New Holland Holland, MI
Summit St Paul, MN
Three Floyds Munster, IN
Two Brothers Warrenville, IL

METRO CHICAGO AREA
0 4 km
0 2 miles
See Andersonville & Wrigleyville Map (p573)
See Gold Coast & Lincoln Park Map (pp570-1)
See Downtown Chicago (The Loop), Museum Campus & Near North Side Map (pp564-5)
Lake Michigan
To O'Hare International Airport (6mi)
To Oak Park (2mi)
Rosehill Cemetery
Logan Square
Bucktown
Wicker Park
Humboldt Park
Ukrainian Village
Douglas Park
Chinatown
Bronzeville
Bridgeport
Cicero
Hawthorne Race Track
Fuller Park
Kenwood
Sherman Park
Hyde Park
Chicago Midway Airport
Marquette Park
Granville
Thorndale
Bryn Mawr
Devon Ave
W Peterson Ave
N Lincoln Ave
W Foster Ave
W Montrose Ave
W Irving Park Rd
W Addison St
W Belmont Ave
W Diversey Ave
W Fullerton Ave
W Armitage Ave
W North Ave
W Division St
W Augusta Blvd
W Chicago Ave
W Grand Ave
W Madison St
W Roosevelt Rd
W Cermak Rd
W Ogden Ave
W 31st St
W 35th St
W Pershing Rd
W 47th St
W 55th St
W 59th St
W 63rd St
W Marquette Rd
Adlai Stevenson Expwy
Chicago Skyway
Clybourn Station (Metra)
27th St Station (Metra)
47th St Station (Metra)
51st-53rd St Station (Metra)
55th-56th-57th St Station (Metra)
59th St Station (Metra)
63rd St Station (Metra)

INFORMATION
Quimby's 1 B3
Stroger Cook County Hospital 2 B4

SIGHTS & ACTIVITIES
Capone's Chicago Home 3 C6
DuSable Museum of African American History 4 C6
Frank Lloyd Wright Row Houses 5 C5
Hyde Park Art Center 6 D5
Hyde Park Hair Salon 7 D5
Illinois Institute of Technology 8 C5
Leather Archives & Museum 9 B1
Museum of Science & Industry 10 D6
National Museum of Mexican Art 11 B4
Nelson Algren's House 12 B3
Nuclear Energy Sculpture 13 C6
Obama's House 14 D5
Robie House 15 D6
University of Chicago 16 C6

SLEEPING
Wicker Park Inn (see 32)

EATING
Don Pedro Carnitas 17 B4
Feed 18 B3
Handlebar Bar & Grill 19 B3
Hot Chocolate 20 B3
Hot Doug's 21 B2
Lula Cafe 22 B2

DRINKING
Danny's 23 B3
Map Room 24 B3

ENTERTAINMENT
Darkroom 25 B3
Double Door 26 B3
Empty Bottle 27 B3
Lava 28 B3
Lee's Unleaded Blues 29 D6
New Checkerboard Lounge 30 D5
Old Town School of Folk Music 31 B1
Phyllis' Musical Inn 32 B3
Redmoon Theater 33 B3
Rosa's 34 A3
United Center 35 B3
US Cellular Field 36 C5
Windy City Rollers 37 B4

money, try Terminal 5 at O'Hare International or the following places in the Loop:

Travelex (Map pp564-5; ☎ 312-807-4941; 19 S LaSalle St)

World's Money Exchange (Map pp564-5; ☎ 312-641-2151; 203 N LaSalle St)

POST

Post office (Map pp564-5) Fort Dearborn (☎ 312-644-0485; 540 N Dearborn St) Main (☎ 312-983-8182; 433 W Harrison St; 7:30am-midnight Mon-Thu, Sat & Sun, to 5pm Fri)

TOURIST INFORMATION

The **Chicago Office of Tourism** (☎ 312-744-2400, 877-244-2246; www.explorechicago.org) operates two well-staffed and -stocked visitors centers:

Chicago Cultural Center Visitors Center (Map pp564-5; 77 E Randolph St; 8am-7pm Mon-Thu, 8am-6pm Fri, 9am-6pm Sat, 10am-6pm Sun)

Water Works Visitors Center (Map pp570-1; 163 E Pearson St; 8am-7pm Mon-Thu, 8am-6pm Fri, 10am-6pm Sat, 10am-4pm Sun)

Sights

Chicago's main attractions are found mostly in or near the city center, though visits to distant neighborhoods, like Pilsen and Hyde Park, can also be rewarding. Purchase the lump-sum **CityPass** (☎ 888-330-5008; www.citypass.com; adult/child 3-11yr $69/59) and save on admission fees to five top attractions: the Shedd Aquarium (p567), Field Museum of Natural History (p567), Adler Planetarium (p567), Museum of Science & Industry (p574), and the Hancock (p568) or Willis Tower (p566) observatories. Students with ID often receive reduced admission. Look for additional discounts at www.chicagoofficeoftourism.org/chicagocoupons.

For a more in-depth exploration of the Windy City, pick up Lonely Planet's *Chicago* city guide or *Chicago Encounter* guide.

THE LOOP

The city center and financial district is named for the elevated train tracks that lasso its streets. It's busy all day, though not much happens at night other than in the Theater District, near the intersection of N State and W Randolph Sts.

Route 66 buffs should note the Mother Road starts in the Loop. Look for the **Route 66 sign** (Map pp564–5) on Adams St's north side, between Michigan and Wabash Aves.

Art Institute of Chicago

The second-largest museum in the country, the **Art Institute** (Map pp564-5; ☎ 312-443-3600; www.artic.edu/aic; 111 S Michigan Ave; adult/child/student 14-18yr $18/free/12, admission free 5-9pm Thu & Fri; 10:30am-5pm Mon-Wed, to 9pm Thu & Fri, 10am-5pm Sat & Sun Jun-Aug, 10:30am-5pm Mon-Wed & Fri, to 8pm Thu, 10am-5pm Sat & Sun Sep-May) houses treasures and masterpieces from around the globe, including a fabulous selection of both Impressionist and post-Impressionist paintings. Georges Seurat's pointillist *A Sunday on La Grande Jatte* is here, so is Grant Wood's *American Gothic*. The new Modern Wing, dazzling with natural light, hangs Picassos and Miros on its 3rd floor (added bonus: the mod, pedestrian Nichols Bridgeway arches from here into Millennium Park). Allow two hours to browse the museum's highlights; art buffs should allocate much longer. Ask at the front desk about free talks and tours once you're inside.

Millennium Park & Grant Park

Grant Park (Map pp564-5; Michigan Ave btwn 12th & Randolph Sts) is the sprawling green space that forms a playful buffer between the Loop and Lake Michigan. **Millennium Park** (Map pp564-5; Michigan Ave btwn Monroe & Randolph Sts) is Grant's crown jewel, sparkling in the northwest corner. Here, Frank Gehry's 120ft-high swooping silver band shell, aka **Pritzker Pavilion** (Map pp564–5), anchors what is, in essence, an outdoor modern-design gallery. It includes Jaume Plensa's 50ft-high fountain that projects video images of locals spitting out water gargoyle-style, a Gehry-designed bridge (his first) that spans Columbus Dr and offers great skyline views, and a winter ice-skating rink (p575). But the thing that has become the park's biggest draw is the Bean – Anish Kapoor's 110-ton, ridiculously smooth silver-drop sculpture, officially titled **Cloud Gate** (Map pp564–5). Visitors swarm it to see their reflection and that of the city skyline.

Free activities fill both parks in summer. Millennium's pavilion hosts free concerts at 6:30pm (new music on Mondays, world music on Thursdays and classical music on other days). Each Saturday free exercise classes take place on the Great Lawn (tai chi at 8am, yoga at 9am, Pilates at 10am and dance at 11am). And the Family Fun Tent provides free kids' activities daily between

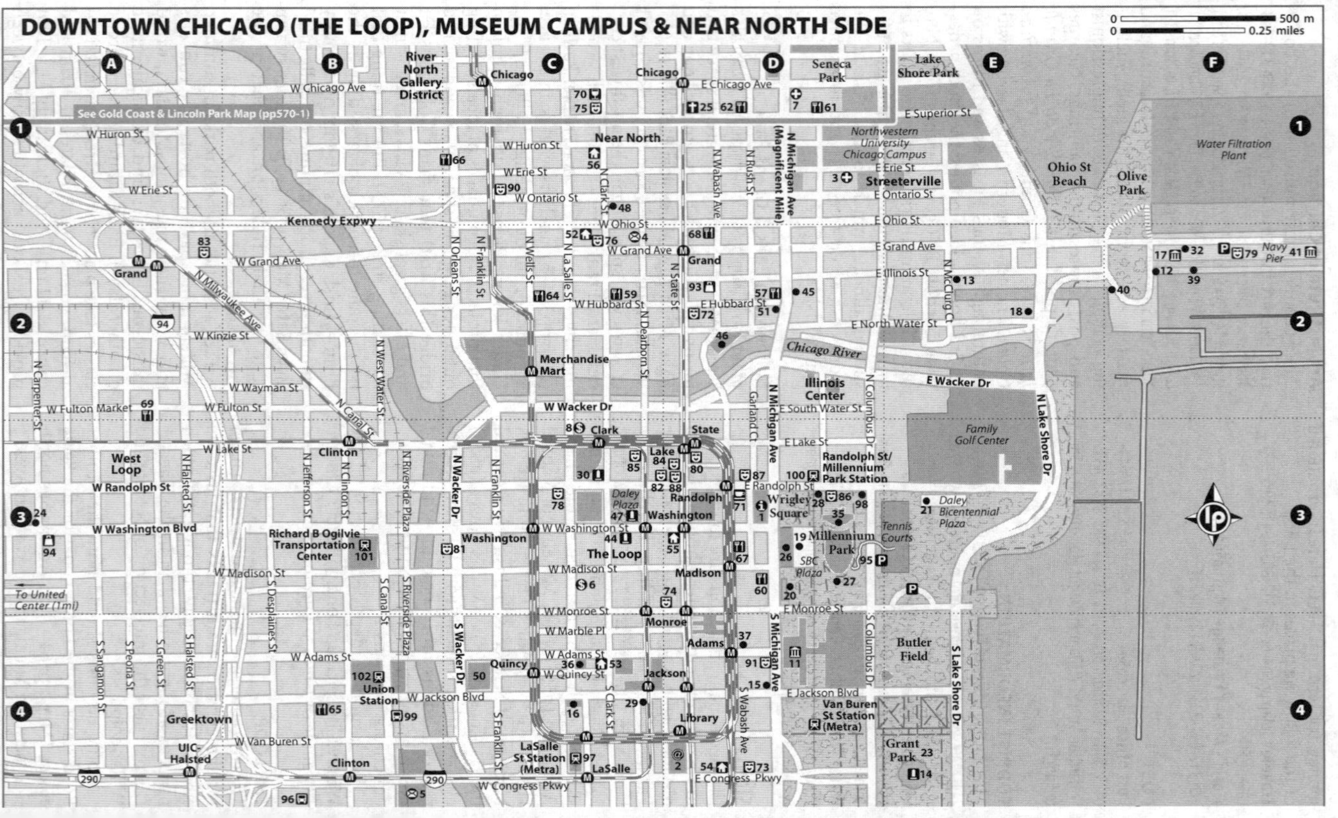
DOWNTOWN CHICAGO (THE LOOP), MUSEUM CAMPUS & NEAR NORTH SIDE
0 500 m
0 0.25 miles
See Gold Coast & Lincoln Park Map (pp570-1)
River North Gallery District
Near North
Seneca Park
Lake Shore Park
Northwestern University Chicago Campus
Streeterville
Ohio St Beach
Olive Park
Water Filtration Plant
Navy Pier
Chicago River
Illinois Center
Family Golf Center
Merchandise Mart
Randolph St/ Millennium Park Station
Wrigley Square
Millennium Park
SBC Plaza
Tennis Courts
Daley Bicentennial Plaza
Daley Plaza
The Loop
Butler Field
Grant Park
Van Buren St Station (Metra)
LaSalle St Station (Metra)
Richard B Ogilvie Transportation Center
Union Station
West Loop
Greektown
UIC-Halsted
To United Center (1mi)
Kennedy Expwy
W Chicago Ave
E Chicago Ave
E Superior St
W Huron St
W Erie St
E Erie St
W Ontario St
E Ontario St
W Ohio St
E Ohio St
W Grand Ave
E Grand Ave
E Illinois St
W Hubbard St
E Hubbard St
W Kinzie St
E North Water St
N Milwaukee Ave
N Canal St
N West Water St
W Wayman St
W Fulton Market
W Fulton St
W Wacker Dr
E Wacker Dr
E South Water St
W Lake St
E Lake St
W Randolph St
E Randolph St
W Washington Blvd
W Washington St
W Madison St
W Monroe St
E Monroe St
W Marble Pl
W Adams St
W Quincy St
W Jackson Blvd
E Jackson Blvd
W Van Buren St
W Congress Pkwy
E Congress Pkwy
N Carpenter St
N Halsted St
N Jefferson St
N Clinton St
N Riverside Plaza
N Wacker Dr
N Orleans St
N Franklin St
N Wells St
N La Salle St
N Clark St
N Dearborn St
N State St
N Wabash Ave
N Rush St
N Michigan Ave (Magnificent Mile)
N Michigan Ave
Garland Ct
N McClurg Ct
N Columbus Dr
N Lake Shore Dr
S Sangamon St
S Peoria St
S Green St
S Halsted St
S Desplaines St
S Canal St
S Riverside Plaza
S Wacker Dr
S Franklin St
S Clark St
S Wabash Ave
S Michigan Ave
S Columbus Dr
S Lake Shore Dr
Chicago
Grand
Clinton
Clark
State
Lake
Randolph
Washington
Madison
Monroe
Adams
Quincy
Jackson
Library
LaSalle
94
290

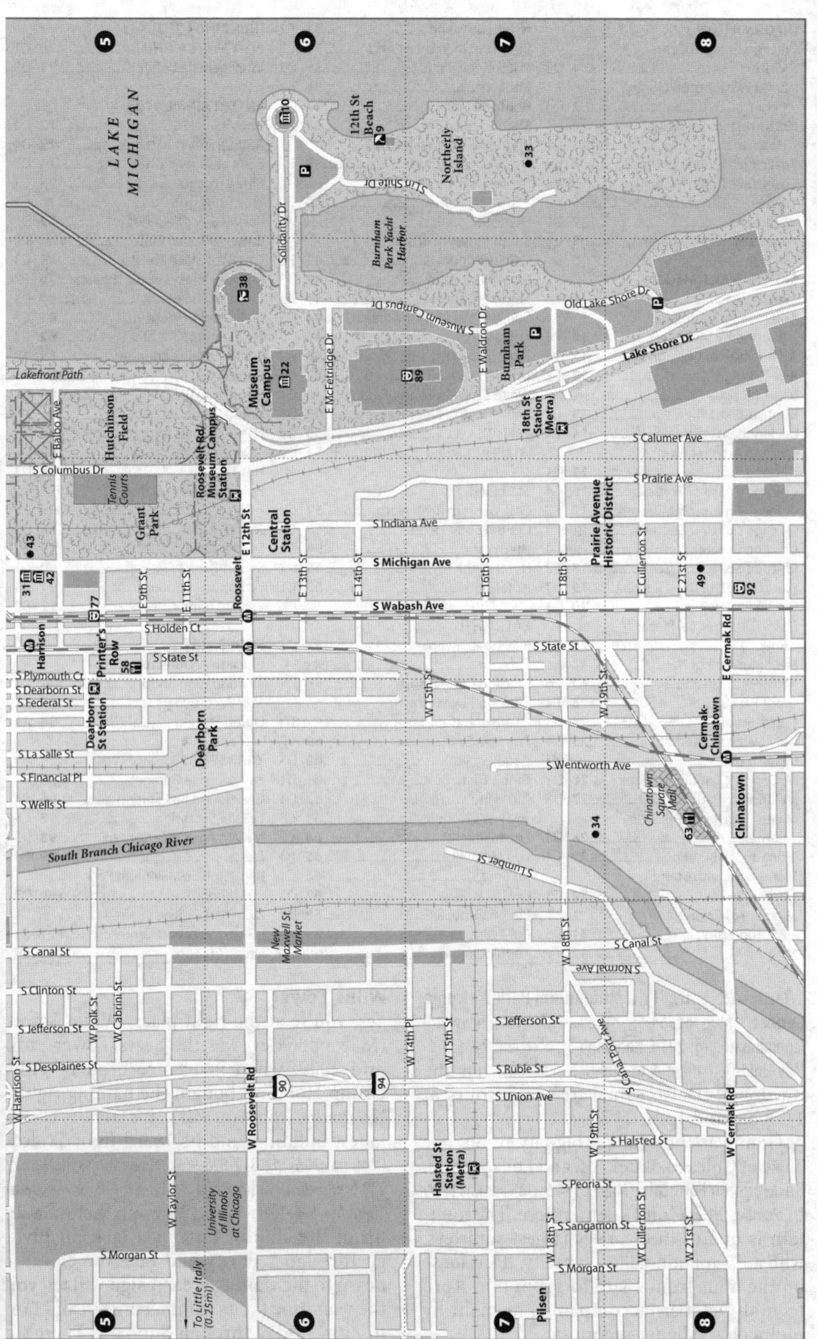

LAKE MICHIGAN
Lakefront Path
E Balbo Ave
Hutchinson Field
S Columbus Dr
Tennis Courts
Grant Park
Roosevelt Rd/Museum Campus Station
Museum Campus
22
38
Solidarity Dr
10
12th St Beach
9
S Linn White Dr
Northerly Island
33
Burnham Park Yacht Harbor
S Museum Campus Dr
E McFetridge Dr
89
E Waldron Dr
Burnham Park
Old Lake Shore Dr
Lake Shore Dr
18th St Station (Metra)
S Calumet Ave
S Prairie Ave
Prairie Avenue Historic District
S Indiana Ave
Central Station
E 12th St
43
31
42
S Michigan Ave
E 9th St
E 11th St
E 13th St
E 14th St
E 16th St
E 18th St
E Cullerton St
E 21st St
49
92
77
Roosevelt
S Wabash Ave
E Cermak Rd
Harrison
Printer's Row
58
S Holden Ct
S State St
S Plymouth Ct
S Dearborn St
S Federal St
Dearborn St Station
Dearborn Park
W 15th St
W 19th St
Cermak-Chinatown
S La Salle St
S Financial Pl
S Wells St
S Wentworth Ave
Chinatown Square Mall
63
Chinatown
34
South Branch Chicago River
S Lumber St
New Maxwell St Market
S Canal St
W 18th St
S Normal Ave
S Clinton St
W Polk St
W Cabrini St
S Jefferson St
S Desplaines St
W Harrison St
W Roosevelt Rd
90
94
W 14th Pl
W 15th St
S Canalport Ave
S Ruble St
S Union Ave
W 19th St
S Halsted St
W Cermak Rd
Halsted St Station (Metra)
W Taylor St
University of Illinois at Chicago
S Peoria St
S Sangamon St
W 18th St
W Cullerton St
W 21st St
S Morgan St
To Little Italy (0.25mi)
Pilsen
5
6
7
8

INFORMATION

Chicago Cultural Center Visitors Center	1	D3
Harold Washington Library Center	2	D4
Northwestern Memorial Hospital	3	D1
Post Office (Fort Dearborn)	4	C2
Post Office (Main Branch)	5	B4
Travelex	6	C3
Walgreens	7	D1
World's Money Exchange	8	C3

SIGHTS & ACTIVITIES

12th St Beach	9	F6
Adler Planetarium & Astronomy Museum	10	F6
Art Institute of Chicago	11	D4
Bike Chicago	12	F2
Bike Chicago	(see 98)	
Bobby's Bike Hike	13	E2
Buckingham Fountain	14	E4
Chicago Architecture Foundation	15	D4
Chicago Board of Trade	16	C4
Chicago Children's Museum	17	F2
Chicago Cultural Center	(see 1)	
Chicago Greeter	(see 1)	
Chicago Spire	18	E2
Cloud Gate	19	D3
Crown Fountain	20	D3
Daley Bicentennial Plaza Rink	21	E3
Field Museum of Natural History	22	E6
Grant Park	23	E4
Harpo Studios	24	A3
Holy Name Cathedral	25	D1
InstaGreeter	(see 1)	
McCormick Tribune Ice Rink	26	D3
Millennium Park	27	D3
Millennium Park Welcome Center	28	D3
Monadnock Building	29	C4
Monument with Standing Beast	30	C3
Museum of Contemporary Photography	31	D5
Navy Pier	32	F2
Northerly Island	33	F7
Ping Tom Memorial Park	34	C7
Pritzker Pavilion	35	D3
Rookery	36	C4
Route 66 Sign	37	D4
Shedd Aquarium	38	E6
Shoreline Lake Water Taxi to Museum Campus	39	F2
Shoreline River Water Taxi to Willis Tower	40	F2
Skydeck	(see 50)	
Smith Museum of Stained Glass Windows	41	F2
Spertus Museum	42	D5
SummerDance	43	D5
Sun, the Moon & One Star	44	C3
Tribune Tower	45	D2
Trump Tower	46	D2
Untitled	47	C3
Weird Chicago Tours	48	C1
Willie Dixon's Blues Heaven	49	D8
Willis Tower	50	C4
Wrigley Building	51	D2

SLEEPING

Best Western River North	52	C2
Central Loop Hotel	53	C4
HI-Chicago	54	D4
Hotel Burnham	55	D3
Hotel Felix	56	C1

EATING

Billy Goat Tavern	57	D2
Cafecito	(see 54)	
Chicago Curry House	58	D5
Chicago's Downtown Farmstand	(see 87)	
Frontera Grill	59	C2
Gage	60	D3
Gino's East	61	D1
Giordano's	62	D1
Joy Yee's Noodles	63	C8
Lou Malnati's	64	C2
Lou Mitchell's	65	B4
Mr Beef	66	C1
Oasis	67	D3
Pizzeria Uno	68	D2
Publican	69	A2
Topolobampo	(see 59)	

DRINKING

Clark Street Ale House	70	C1
Intelligentsia Coffee	71	D3

ENTERTAINMENT

Andy's	72	D2
Auditorium Theater	73	D4
Bank of America Theater	74	D3
Blue Chicago	75	C1
Blue Chicago	76	C2
Buddy Guy's Legends	77	D5
Butterfly Social Club	(see 83)	
Cadillac Palace Theater	78	C3
Chicago Shakespeare Theater	79	F2
Chicago Theater	80	D3
Civic Opera House	81	C3
Ford Center/Oriental Theater	82	C3
Funky Buddha Lounge	83	A2
Gene Siskel Film Center	84	D3
Goodman Theatre	85	C3
Harpo Studios	(see 24)	
Harris Theater for Music and Dance	86	D3
Hot Tix	87	D3
Hubbard Street Dance Chicago	(see 86)	
Joffrey Ballet	88	D3
Soldier Field	89	E7
Sound-Bar	90	C1
Symphony Center	91	D4
Velvet Lounge	92	D8

SHOPPING

Chicago Architecture Foundation Shop	(see 15)	
Jazz Record Mart	93	D2
Oprah Store	94	A3

TRANSPORT

East Monroe Garage	95	D3
Greyhound Bus Station	96	B4
LaSalle St Station	97	C4
McDonalds Cycle Center	98	D3
Megabus	99	B4
Randolph St/Millenium Park Station	100	D3
Richard B Ogilvie Transportation Center	101	B3
Union Station	102	B4

10am and 3pm. The **Millennium Park Welcome Center** (Map pp564-5; ☎ 312-742-1168; www.millenniumpark.org; 201 E Randolph St; 9am-7pm mid-May–mid-Oct, 10am-4pm mid-Oct–mid-May) has the lowdown; it also offers free park tours at 11:30am and 1pm.

Grant Park hosts all the big-city events, like Taste of Chicago, Blues Fest and Lollapalooza. **Buckingham Fountain** (Map pp564-5; cnr Congress Pkwy & Columbus Dr) is Grant's centerpiece. The fountain is one of the world's largest squirters, with a 1.5-million-gallon capacity. It lets loose on the hour from 10am to 11pm mid-April to mid-October, accompanied at night by multicolored lights and music.

Willis Tower

Yes, you're at the right place. Willis Tower (Map pp564–5) was the Sears Tower until mid-2009, when insurance broker Willis Group Holdings bought the naming rights. No matter what you call it, it's still the USA's tallest building, and its 103rd-floor **Skydeck** (Map pp564-5; ☎ 312-875-9696; www.the-skydeck.com; 233 S Wacker Dr; adult/child 3-11yr $15/10.50; 9am-10pm Apr-Sep, 10am-8pm Oct-Mar) puts visitors way up in the clouds. Enter via Jackson Blvd, go through security and take the elevator down to the waiting area. A sign will tell you the wait time (at its summertime peak 11am to 4pm Friday through Sunday). There's a factoid-filled film to watch while queuing, and then the 70-second ride to the top. Step onto the glass-floored Ledge for a feeling of mid-air suspension and view straight down. For those who prefer a drink with their vista, the John Hancock Center (p568) is a better choice.

Chicago Cultural Center

The exquisite interior of the **Cultural Center** (Map pp564-5; ☎ 312-744-6630; www.chicagocultural center.org; 78 E Washington St; admission free; 8am-7pm Mon-Thu, 8am-6pm Fri, 9am-6pm Sat, 10am-6pm Sun) features rooms modeled on the Doge's Palace in Venice and Palazzo Vecchio in Florence, and is notable for the 3rd floor's stained-glass Tiffany dome and sparkling mosaics. Free exhibits and lunchtime concerts are ongoing; there's also free wi-fi.

Architecture & Public Art

Ever since it presented the world with the first skyscraper, Chicago has thought big with its architecture and pushed the envelope of modern design. The Loop is a fantastic place to roam and gawk at these ambitious structures.

The Chicago Architecture Foundation (p577) runs tours that explain the following buildings and more.

The **Chicago Board of Trade** (Map pp564-5; 141 W Jackson Blvd) is a 1930 art-deco gem. Inside, manic traders swap futures and options – a mysterious process that has something to do with corn. A small **visitors center** (☎ 312-435-3590; admission free; 8am-4pm Mon-Fri) tries to explain it. Or stay outside and check out the mondo statue of Ceres, the goddess of agriculture, that tops the building.

The 1888 **Rookery** (Map pp564-5; 209 S LaSalle St) looks fortresslike outside, but this office building is light and airy inside thanks to Frank Lloyd Wright's atrium overhaul. Pigeons used to roost here, hence the name.

Architectural pilgrims get weak-kneed when they see the **Monadnock Building** (Map pp564-5; 53 W Jackson Blvd), which is two buildings in one. The north is the older, traditional design from 1891, while the south is the newer, mod half from 1893. See the difference? The Monadnock remains true to its original purpose as an office building.

Chicago has commissioned several head-scratching public sculptures throughout the decades. The Loop's triumvirate of puzzlement includes Pablo Picasso's **Untitled** (Map pp564-5; 50 W Washington St), which everyone just calls 'the Picasso;' Joan Miro's the **Sun, the Moon and One Star** (Map pp564-5; 69 W Washington St), which everyone just calls 'Miro's Chicago;' and Jean Dubuffet's **Monument with Standing Beast** (Map pp564-5; 100 W Randolph St), which everyone just calls 'Snoopy in a Blender.'

SOUTH LOOP

The South Loop, which includes the lower ends of downtown and Grant Park, along with the historic Printer's Row neighborhood of rare bookshops, soared recently from dereliction to development central. The Museum Campus is the lakefront area south of Grant Park, where three top attractions huddle.

Field Museum of Natural History

The mammoth **Field Museum** (Map pp564-5; ☎ 312-922-9410; www.fieldmuseum.org; 1400 S Lake Shore Dr; adult/child 3-11yr $15/10; 9am-5pm;) houses everything but the kitchen sink – beetles, mummies, gemstones, Bushman the stuffed ape. The collection's rockstar is Sue, the largest *Tyrannosaurus rex* yet discovered. She even gets her own gift shop. Special exhibits cost extra.

Shedd Aquarium

Top draws at the kiddie-mobbed **Shedd Aquarium** (Map pp564-5; ☎ 312-939-2438; www.shed daquarium.org; 1200 S Lake Shore Dr; adult/child 3-11yr $25/18; 9am-6pm Jun-Aug, to 10pm some Thu, reduced Sep-May;) include the Oceanarium, with its beluga whales and frolicking white-sided dolphins, and the shark exhibit, where there's just 5in of Plexiglas between you and two dozen fierce-looking swimmers. The 4-D theater costs $4 extra. For admission to just the plain ol' fish tanks, ask for the unadvertised 'aquarium only/general admission' fee (adult/child $8/6).

Adler Planetarium & Astronomy Museum

Space enthusiasts will get a big bang (pun!) out of the **Adler Planetarium** (Map pp564-5; ☎ 312-922-7827; www.adlerplanetarium.org; 1300 S Lake Shore Dr; adult/child 3-17yr $10/6; 9:30am-6pm Jun-Aug, 10am-4pm Sep-May). Cosmic films show in the digital theaters and cost $9 extra. A real bonus is if you're here the first Friday night of the month, when the Adler's staff bring out their telescopes and let you view the skies with them (adult/child $20/17).

HOT TOPIC: THE FISH WHO ATE THE GREAT LAKES

The title sounds like a bad sci-fi movie. The scary thing is, it has the potential to become reality.

The ravenous fish causing all the trouble is the Asian carp. Fish farms in the southern USA imported these creatures in the 1960s and '70s to eat away pesky algae. Floods washed them into the Mississippi River and they swam north. Though they only eat plankton, they chow phenomenal quantities – up to 40% of their body weight daily. The result is a 3ft-long, 50lb bully that's wiping out the food base for native species.

The carp are now in the Illinois River, which connects to Lake Michigan and the waters beyond. The fear is that if the fish enter, they'll wipe out the Great Lakes ecosystem. And since the lakes contain 20% of the world's fresh water…well, you get the scope of the problem.

So engineers built an electric barrier 50 miles southwest of Chicago that has kept the fish at bay – for now. The barrier has experienced all kinds of problems, from funding shortages to safety issues regarding electrocution risk.

Meanwhile, the fish wait hungrily at the gate, hoping it lets down its guard.

Around the Museum Campus

A path runs south from the planetarium to **12th St Beach** (Map pp564–5), where you'll have good views of the lake and fishermen casting there. Nearby **Northerly Island** (Map pp564–5) hosts big-name summer concerts (which you can hear from 12th St Beach for free), trails and bird-watching.

In addition to the big-ticket museums, the small **Museum of Contemporary Photography** (Map pp564-5; ☎ 312-663-5554; www.mocp.org; Columbia College, 600 S Michigan Ave; admission free; 🕑 10am-5pm Mon-Sat, to 8pm Thu, noon-5pm Sun) is worth exploring. Next door the **Spertus Museum** (Map pp564-5; ☎ 312-322-1700; www.spertus.edu; 610 S Michigan Ave; adult/child 5-18yr $7/5; 🕑 call for hours) has Jewish cultural exhibits on its 9th and 10th floors.

NEAR NORTH

The area north of the Chicago River to Chicago Ave encompasses several points of interest. Between the river and Oak St, the **Magnificent Mile** (Map pp564-5; N Michigan Ave) is the much-touted upscale shopping strip, where Bloomingdales, Neiman's and Saks will lighten your wallet.

The white terra-cotta exterior of the **Wrigley Building** (Map pp564-5; 400 N Michigan Ave) glows day or night. Take a close look when passing by the gothic **Tribune Tower** (Map pp564-5; 435 N Michigan Ave) to see chunks of the Taj Mahal, Parthenon and other famous structures embedded in the lower walls. The Donald's 1360ft **Trump Tower** (Map pp564-5; 401 N Wabash Ave) is now Chicago's second-tallest building, though architecture critics have mocked its 'toothpick' look. The **Chicago Spire** (Map pp564-5; 400 N Lake Shore Dr) is poised to rise above Trump and everything else in the country, though progress has been slow.

Navy Pier

Once the city's municipal wharf, **Navy Pier** (Map pp564-5; ☎ 312-595-7437; www.navypier.com; 600 E Grand Ave; admission free; 🕑 from 10am, closing times vary seasonally from 7pm-midnight), which is a half-mile long, is now covered with a Ferris wheel (per ride $6), an IMAX theater, numerous shops and gimmicky chain restaurants. Locals groan over its commercialization, but its lakefront view and cool breezes can't be beat. The fireworks displays on Wednesday (9:30pm) and Saturday (10:15pm) are a treat too.

The Chicago Children's Museum (p576) and gorgeous **Smith Museum of Stained Glass Windows** (Map pp564-5; ☎ 312-595-5024; admission free; 🕑 same as pier) are also on the pier, as are several boat-cruise operators. Try the **Shoreline water taxi** (Map pp564-5; 🕑 10am-6pm May-Aug) for a useful and economic ride to the Museum Campus (adult/child $7/3) or Willis Tower ($6/4).

GOLD COAST

Starting in 1882, Chicago's wealthy flocked to this neighborhood flanking the lake between Chicago and North Aves. Within 40 years most of the Gold Coast was covered with mansions.

Today the neighborhood giant is the 1127ft-tall **John Hancock Center** (Map pp570-1; ☎ 888-875-8439; www.hancock-observatory.com; 875 N Michigan Ave; adult/child 4-11yr $15/10; 🕑 9am-11pm), which has a great 94th-floor observatory that's often less crowded than the one at Willis Tower. Better yet, skip the observatory and head straight up to the 96th-floor Signature Lounge (p582), where the view is free if you buy a drink ($7 to $14). Time it to coincide with Navy Pier's fireworks (opposite) and you're stylin'.

The 154ft-tall, turreted **Water Tower** (Map pp570-1; cnr Chicago & Michigan Aves) is a defining city landmark: it was the sole downtown survivor of the 1871 Great Fire.

The **Museum of Contemporary Art** (Map pp570-1; ☎ 312-280-2660; www.mcachicago.org; 220 E Chicago Ave; adult/student 13-18yr $12/7, admission free Tue; ⏰ 10am-8pm Tue, 10am-5pm Wed-Sun) displays head-scratching works by Franz Kline, René Magritte, Cindy Sherman and Andy Warhol. Consider it the Art Institute's brash, rebellious sibling.

Oak Street Beach (Map pp570-1; 1000 N Lake Shore Dr) packs in bodies beautiful at the edge of downtown.

To sample the Gold Coast's former grandeur, saunter down the 1300 and 1400 blocks of N Astor St, where gems include Frank Lloyd Wright's **Charnley-Persky House** (Map pp570-1; ☎ 312-915-0105; www.charnleyhouse.org; 1365 N Astor St; tours free-$15; ⏰ Wed & Sat, call for times), which he proclaimed the 'first modern building.' One block west is a first of another kind – the **First Playboy Mansion** (Map pp570-1; 1340 N State St). Hugh Hefner began wearing his all-day jammies here, when the rigors of magazine production and heavy partying prevented him from getting dressed. The building contains condos now, but a visit still allows you to boast, 'I've been to the Playboy mansion.'

LINCOLN PARK & OLD TOWN

Lincoln Park is an urban oasis spanning 1200 leafy acres; its widest swath is between North Ave and Diversey Pkwy. 'Lincoln Park' is also the name for the abutting neighborhood. Both are alive day and night with people skating, walking dogs, pushing strollers and driving in circles looking for a place to park.

The **Lincoln Park Zoo** (Map pp570-1; ☎ 312-742-2000; www.lpzoo.org; 2200 N Cannon Dr; admission free; ⏰ 10am-4:30pm Nov-Mar, 10am-5pm Apr-Oct, 10am-6:30pm Sat & Sun Jun-Aug; 🚸) is popular with families, who stroll by the habitats of gorillas, lions, tigers and other exotic creatures. Pick up a free map at the Gateway Pavilion (the main entrance), which provides times and locations of when zookeepers give free discussions about various animals, as well as feeding times and training demonstrations.

Near the zoo's north entrance, the magnificent 1891 **Lincoln Park Conservatory** (Map pp570-1; ☎ 312-742-7736; 2391 N Stockton Dr; admission free; ⏰ 9am-5pm) coaxes palms, ferns and orchids to flourish despite Chicago's brutal weather.

The **Peggy Notebaert Nature Museum** (Map pp570-1; ☎ 773-755-5100; www.naturemuseum.org; 2430 N Cannon Dr; adult/child 3-12yr $9/6, admission free Thu; ⏰ 9am-4:30pm Mon-Fri, 10am-5pm Sat & Sun) has a year-round butterfly park and other natural wonders.

The **Chicago History Museum** (Map pp570-1; ☎ 312-642-4600; www.chicagohs.org; 1601 N Clark St; adult/child under 13yr/child 13-22yr $14/free/12, admission free Mon; ⏰ 9:30am-4:30pm Mon-Sat, noon-5pm Sun) covers the Great Fire well, among other storied events. Ask for the free audio tour.

North Avenue Beach (Map pp570-1; 1600 N Lake Shore Dr) is Chicago's most popular and amenity-laden stretch of sand. You can rent bikes, volleyballs and lounge chairs, as well as eat and drink at the beach house.

Old Town rests at the southwest foot of Lincoln Park. The intersection of North Ave and Wells St is the epicenter, with restaurants, bars and Second City (p585) fanning out from here.

LAKE VIEW & WRIGLEYVILLE

North of Lincoln Park, these neighborhoods can be enjoyed by ambling along Halsted St, Clark St, Belmont Ave or Southport Ave, which are well supplied with restaurants, bars and shops. Ivy-covered **Wrigley Field** (Map p573; 1060 W Addison St) is named after the chewing-gum guy and is home to the adored but perpetually losing Chicago Cubs. If they're playing a game, you can peep in the 'knothole,' a garage door–sized opening on Sheffield Ave, to watch the action for free. For ticket information, see above.

ANDERSONVILLE & UPTOWN

Creative types, lesbians, gays and yuppies occupy most of walkable, bar-filled Andersonville (Map p573), which was once heavily Swedish. Take the CTA Red Line to the Berwyn stop and walk west for about a mile.

Get off one stop south at the pagoda-like Argyle St station, and you're in Uptown's 'Little Saigon' area with its abundant Vietnamese, Chinese and Thai restaurants and shops.

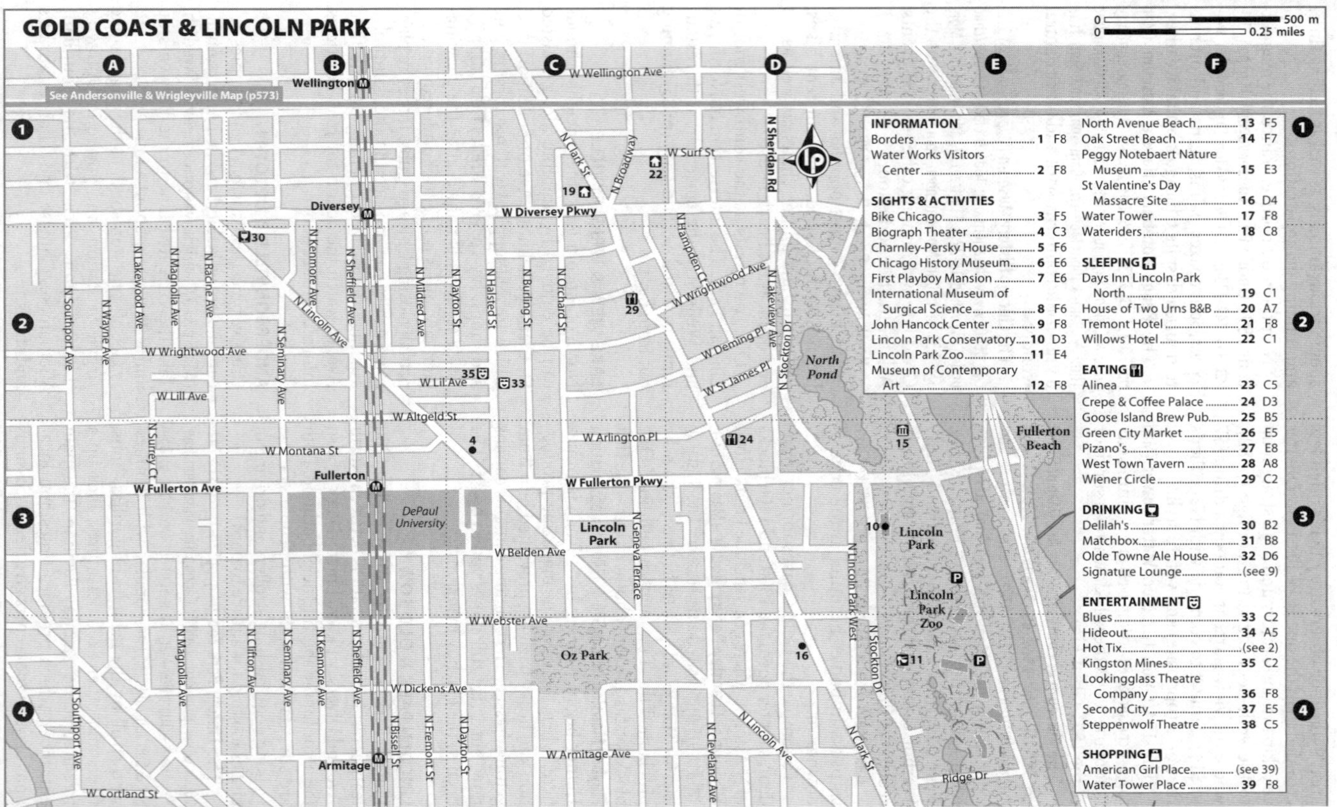

GOLD COAST & LINCOLN PARK
0 500 m
0 0.25 miles
See Andersonville & Wrigleyville Map (p573)
INFORMATION
Borders 1 F8
Water Works Visitors Center 2 F8
SIGHTS & ACTIVITIES
Bike Chicago 3 F5
Biograph Theater 4 C3
Charnley-Persky House 5 F6
Chicago History Museum 6 E6
First Playboy Mansion 7 E6
International Museum of Surgical Science 8 F6
John Hancock Center 9 F8
Lincoln Park Conservatory 10 D3
Lincoln Park Zoo 11 E4
Museum of Contemporary Art 12 F8
North Avenue Beach 13 F5
Oak Street Beach 14 F7
Peggy Notebaert Nature Museum 15 E3
St Valentine's Day Massacre Site 16 D4
Water Tower 17 F8
Wateriders 18 C8
SLEEPING
Days Inn Lincoln Park North 19 C1
House of Two Urns B&B 20 A7
Tremont Hotel 21 F8
Willows Hotel 22 C1
EATING
Alinea 23 C5
Crepe & Coffee Palace 24 D3
Goose Island Brew Pub 25 B5
Green City Market 26 E5
Pizano's 27 E8
West Town Tavern 28 A8
Wiener Circle 29 C2
DRINKING
Delilah's 30 B2
Matchbox 31 B8
Olde Towne Ale House 32 D6
Signature Lounge (see 9)
ENTERTAINMENT
Blues 33 C2
Hideout 34 A5
Hot Tix (see 2)
Kingston Mines 35 C2
Lookingglass Theatre Company 36 F8
Second City 37 E5
Steppenwolf Theatre 38 C5
SHOPPING
American Girl Place (see 39)
Water Tower Place 39 F8
Wellington
Diversey
Fullerton
Armitage
W Wellington Ave
W Diversey Pkwy
W Fullerton Pkwy
W Fullerton Ave
W Belden Ave
W Webster Ave
W Dickens Ave
W Armitage Ave
W Cortland St
W Wrightwood Ave
W Lill Ave
W Altgeld St
W Montana St
W Arlington Pl
W Deming Pl
W St James Pl
W Surf St
N Sheridan Rd
N Clark St
N Broadway
N Hampden Ct
N Lakeview Ave
N Stockton Dr
N Lincoln Park West
N Lincoln Ave
N Geneva Terrace
N Cleveland Ave
N Orchard St
N Burling St
N Halsted St
N Dayton St
N Mildred Ave
N Fremont St
N Bissell St
N Sheffield Ave
N Kenmore Ave
N Seminary Ave
N Clifton Ave
N Racine Ave
N Magnolia Ave
N Lakewood Ave
N Wayne Ave
N Southport Ave
N Surrey Ct
Ridge Dr
North Pond
Fullerton Beach
Lincoln Park
Lincoln Park Zoo
Oz Park
DePaul University

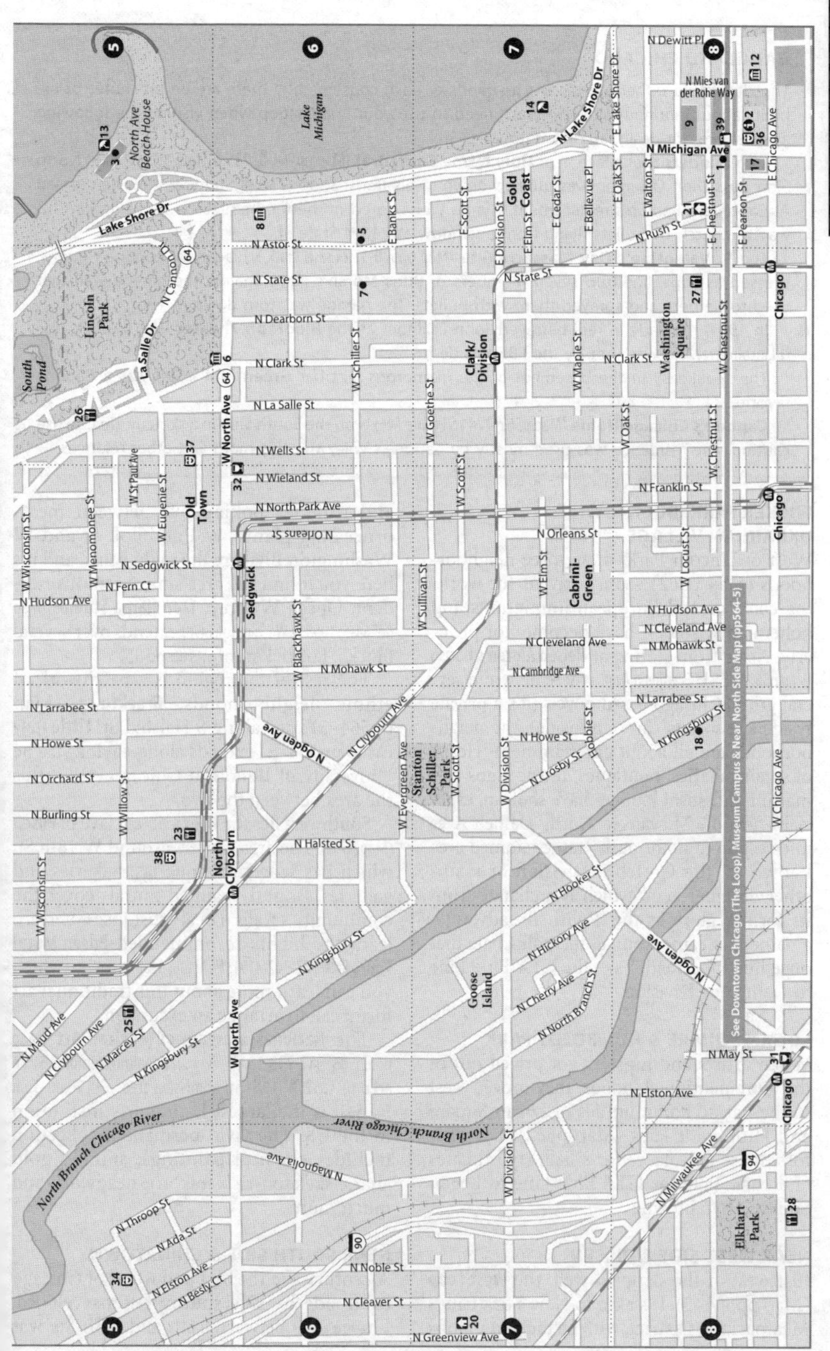
Lake Michigan
North Ave Beach House
Lake Shore Dr
N Lake Shore Dr
E Lake Shore Dr
Lincoln Park
South Pond
La Salle Dr
N Cannon Dr
Old Town
Gold Coast
Washington Square
Cabrini-Green
Stanton Schiller Park
Goose Island
Elkhart Park
North Branch Chicago River
N Dewitt Pl
N Mies van der Rohe Way
N Michigan Ave
E Chicago Ave
E Pearson St
E Chestnut St
W Chestnut St
E Walton St
E Oak St
W Oak St
E Bellevue Pl
E Cedar St
E Elm St
W Elm St
E Division St
W Division St
E Scott St
W Scott St
E Banks St
W Goethe St
W Schiller St
N Rush St
N Astor St
N State St
N Dearborn St
N Clark St
N La Salle St
N Wells St
N Wieland St
N North Park Ave
N Orleans St
N Sedgwick St
N Franklin St
N Hudson Ave
N Cleveland Ave
N Mohawk St
N Cambridge Ave
N Larrabee St
N Kingsbury St
N Howe St
N Crosby St
Hobbie St
N Orchard St
N Burling St
N Halsted St
N Hooker St
N Hickory Ave
N Cherry Ave
N North Branch St
N Ogden Ave
N Clybourn Ave
N Fern Ct
W Maple St
W Locust St
W Sullivan St
W Blackhawk St
W Evergreen Ave
W Chicago Ave
W North Ave
W Wisconsin St
W Menomonee St
W St Paul Ave
W Eugenie St
W Willow St
N Maud Ave
N Marcey St
N May St
N Elston Ave
N Magnolia Ave
N Milwaukee Ave
N Throop St
N Ada St
N Besly Ct
N Noble St
N Cleaver St
N Greenview Ave
Clark/Division
Sedgwick
North/Clybourn
Chicago
See Downtown Chicago (The Loop), Museum Campus & Near North Side Map (pp564-5)

GANGLAND CHICAGO

The city would rather not discuss its gangster past; consequently there are no brochures or exhibits about infamous sites. So you'll need to use your imagination when visiting the following as most are not designated as notorious.

Two murders took place near **Holy Name Cathedral** (Map pp564-5; 735 N State St). In 1924 North Side boss Dion O'Banion was gunned down in his florist shop (738 N State St) after he crossed Al Capone. O'Banion's replacement, Hymie Weiss, fared no better. In 1926 he was killed on his way to church by bullets flying from a window at 740 N State St.

The **St Valentine's Day Massacre Site** (Map pp570-1; 2122 N Clark St) is where Capone's goons, dressed as cops, lined up seven members of Bugs Moran's gang against the garage wall that used to be here and sprayed them with bullets. The garage was torn down in 1967.

In 1934, the 'lady in red' betrayed John Dillinger at the **Biograph Theater** (Map pp570-1; 2433 N Lincoln Ave). He was shot by the FBI outside it.

The speakeasy in the basement of the glamorous jazz bar **Green Mill** (p584) was a Capone favorite.

Capone's Chicago Home (Map p562; 7244 S Prairie Ave) is on the South Side in a sketchy area, so use caution. The residence was used mostly by Capone's wife, Mae, his mom and other relatives.

WICKER PARK, BUCKTOWN & UKRAINIAN VILLAGE

West of Lincoln Park, these three neighborhoods (Map p562) – once havens for working-class, central European immigrants and bohemian writers – have become hot property. Aside from staring at **Nelson Algren's house** (Map p562; 1958 W Evergreen Ave), where he wrote several gritty, Chicago-based novels (it's a private residence, so you can't go inside), the neighborhoods are all about entertainment. Heaps of small galleries, boutiques, music clubs and martini-and-sushi lounges have shot up, especially near the Milwaukee–North–Damen Aves intersection (a notoriously traffic-jammed area known as 'the Crotch'). Division St is another designer vein, which is a change from its former glory as the 'Polish Broadway' – a name that came from all the polka bars that once lined the road. Take the CTA Blue Line to Damen or Division.

LOGAN SQUARE & HUMBOLDT PARK

When artists and hipsters got priced out of the aforementioned 'hoods, they moved west to the Latino communities of Logan Square and Humboldt Park (Map p562). For visitors, these are places for small, stylish cafés and bars. Take the CTA Blue Line to Logan Square or California.

NEAR WEST SIDE & PILSEN

Just west of the Loop is, well, the **West Loop** (Map pp564–5). It's akin to New York City's Meatpacking District, with restaurants, clubs and galleries poking out between meat-processing plants. W Randolph St and W Washington Blvd are the main veins, and it's here you'll find the area's most famous resident, Oprah Winfrey. Her **Harpo Studios** (Map pp564-5; 1058 W Washington Blvd) extends over several blocks. For ticket info, see p585.

The rest of the region is a patchwork of ethnic neighborhoods. **Greektown** (Map pp564–5) runs along S Halsted St. **Little Italy** (Map pp564–5) extends along Taylor St. The University of Illinois at Chicago (UIC) fills the area between the two.

Southwest lies the Mexican enclave of **Pilsen** (Map p562). The area centers around W 18th St, which has scores of taquerías, bakeries and galleries. Brightly painted murals cover the community's walls. Local artist Jose Guerrero leads the highly recommended **Pilsen Mural Tours** (☎ 773-342-4191; 1½hr tour $100), during which you can learn more about this traditional art form; call to arrange an excursion.

The **National Museum of Mexican Art** (Map p562; ☎ 312-738-1503; www.nationalmuseumofmexicanart.org; 1852 W 19th St; admission free; ⏰ 10am-5pm Tue-Sun) is the largest Latino arts institution in the US. The vivid permanent collection includes classical paintings, shining gold altars, skeleton-rich folk art, beadwork and much more.

NEAR SOUTH SIDE & CHINATOWN

A century ago the best and worst of Chicago lived side by side south of Roosevelt Rd. Prairie Ave between 16th and 20th Sts was

Millionaire's Row, while the Levee District, four blocks to the west, was packed with saloons, brothels and opium dens. When the millionaires moved north, the neighborhood declined and mansions were demolished for industry. Now the neighborhood is on the upswing again.

The main (if modest) attraction is a building on Michigan Ave, where the Chess brothers started a recording studio in 1957. Bluesmen Muddy Waters, Howlin' Wolf and Bo Diddley cut tracks here first, and paved the way for rock 'n' roll with their sick licks and amped-up sound. Chuck Berry and the Rolling Stones arrived soon after that. The studio is now called **Willie Dixon's Blues Heaven** (Map pp564-5; ☎ 312-808-1286; www.bluesheaven.com; 2120 S Michigan Ave; tours $10; 11am-4pm Mon-Fri, noon-2pm Sat), and it holds a collection of blues memorabilia. Dixon was the guy who wrote most of the label's hits and the one who summed up the genre best: 'Blues is the roots, and everything else is the fruits.'

Chinatown's charm is best enjoyed by going bakery to bakery, nibbling chestnut cakes and almond cookies, and then shopping for Hello Kitty items in the small shops. Wentworth Ave, south of Cermak Rd, is the retail heart of old Chinatown; Chinatown Sq, along Archer Ave north of Cermak, is the newer commerce district. **Ping Tom Memorial Park** (Map pp564-5; 300 W 19th St) offers dramatic city and railroad-bridge views. Take the CTA Red Line to Cermak-Chinatown.

HYDE PARK, BRONZEVILLE & SOUTH SIDE

The South Side is the generic term applied to Chicago's myriad neighborhoods roughly to the south of 25th St; many are defined by their poverty and significant African American populations.

Hyde Park and abutting Kenwood are the South Side's stars, vaulted into the spotlight by local boy Barack Obama. Hefty security means you can't get close to **Obama's house** (Map p562; 5046 S Greenwood Ave), but you can visit his barber Zariff and the bulletproof glass–encased presidential barber chair at the **Hyde Park Hair Salon** (Map p562; 5234 S Blackstone Ave).

Obama taught law at the **University of Chicago** (Map p562; 5801 S Ellis Ave), at which the faculty and students have racked up 80-plus Nobel prizes (the economics and physics departments lay claim to most). It's also where the nuclear age began: Enrico Fermi and his Manhattan Project cronies built a reactor and carried out the world's first controlled atomic reaction on December 2, 1942. The **Nuclear Energy sculpture** (Map p562; S Ellis Ave btwn E 56th & E 57th Sts), by Henry Moore, marks the spot where it blew its stack.

The vast **Museum of Science & Industry** (Map p562; ☎ 773-684-1414; www.msichicago.org; cnr 57th St & S Lake Shore Dr; adult/child 3-11yr $13/11; ⏲ 9:30am-4pm Mon-Sat, 11am-4pm Sun, to 5:30pm Jun-Aug) will overstimulate the serenest of souls with its myriad (and often loud) exhibits. Highlights include a WWII German U-boat nestled in an underground display ($6 extra to tour it) and the 'body slices' exhibit. Special exhibits cost extra. The museum is revamping through 2011, though it should remain open throughout.

Of the numerous buildings that Frank Lloyd Wright designed around Chicago, none is more famous or influential than **Robie House** (Map p562; ☎ 773-834-1847; www.wrightplus.org; 5757 S Woodlawn Ave; adult/child 4-17yr $15/12). The resemblance of its horizontal lines to the flat landscape of the Midwestern prairie became known as the Prairie style. Inside are 174 art glass windows and doors. Robie offers hour-long tours from 11am to 3pm, Friday through Sunday; frequency varies by season.

The **DuSable Museum of African American History** (Map p562; ☎ 773-947-0600; www.dusablemuseum.org; 740 E 56th Pl; adult/child 6-12yr $3/1, admission free Sun; ⏲ 10am-5pm Tue-Sat, noon-5pm Sun) has artworks and exhibits on African Americans from slavery to the Civil Rights era.

All of the these sights are in or near Hyde Park, easily reached via Metra Electric Line trains from Randolph St/Millennium Park station downtown to the 55th-56th-57th St station. Bicycle tours (below) cruise by the highlights. InstaGreeter (p577) offers free one-hour walking tours from the **Hyde Park Art Center** (Map p562; 5020 S Cornell Ave; ⏲ 10am & 3pm Jun-Aug).

Bronzeville is another South Side neighborhood of note. Radiating from 35th St and Martin Luther King Jr Dr, it was the center of Chicago's African American culture from 1920 to 1950, comparable to Harlem in New York. Many of the area's grand houses are being restored, especially on Calumet Ave between 31st and 33rd Sts – this was once a high-crime neighborhood, and while it's gentrified to a great extent now, some elements linger, so visitors should still use caution. Note the stylish architecture of the **Frank Lloyd Wright row houses** (Map p562; 3213-3219 S Calumet Ave). Architecture buffs can explore further at the **Illinois Institute of Technology** (IIT; Map p562; ☎ 312-567-5014; www.mies.iit.edu; 3201 S State St; 90min tour $5; ⏲ 10am & 1pm), where famed architect Ludwig Mies van der Rohe designed all the modern buildings. To reach the area, take the CTA Green Line to 35th St-Bronzeville-IIT.

Activities

Tucked away in Chicago's 552 parks are public golf courses, ice rinks, swimming pools and more. Activities are free or low cost, and the necessary equipment is usually available for rent. Contact the **Chicago Park District** (☎ 312-742-7529; www.chicagoparkdistrict.com); there's a separate number for **golf information** (☎ 312-245-0909).

CYCLING

Riding along the 18.5-mile lakefront path is a great way to see the city. Two companies rent wheels. The cost is $18 to $35 per half day or $25 to $40 per full day; booking online nabs a discount. Both companies also offer two- to four-hour tours ($30 to $45, including bikes) that cover themes like the lakefront, nighttime fireworks or Obama sights (highly recommended!). **Bobby's Bike Hike** (Map pp564-5; ☎ 312-915-0995; www.bobbysbikehike.com; Ogden Slip at River East Docks, 465 N McClurg Ct; ⏲ 9am-7pm Jun-Aug, 9am-5pm Mar-May & Sep-Nov) is the eager upstart. **Bike Chicago** (☎ 888-245-3929; www.bikechicago.com) is more corporate, with multiple locations:

Millennium Park (Map pp564–5; 239 E Randolph St; ⏲ 6:30am-8pm Mon-Fri & 8am-8pm Sat & Sun Jun-Aug,

6:30am-7pm Mon-Fri & 9am-7pm Sat & Sun Apr-May & Sep-Oct, 6:30am-6:30pm Mon-Fri Nov-Mar)
Navy Pier (Map pp564–5; 600 E Grand Ave; 8am-10pm Jun-Aug, 9am-7pm Apr-May & Sep-Oct, closed Nov-Mar)
North Avenue Beach (Map pp570-1; 1603 N Lake Shore Dr; 8am-8pm Jun-Aug, 9am-7pm May & Sep, closed Oct-Apr)

The **Active Transportation Alliance** (www.activetrans.org) lists bike events around town. For more information, see p586.

ICE SKATING

The **Park District** (☎ 312-742-7529; www.chicagoparkdistrict.com) operates the **McCormick Tribune Ice Rink** (Map pp564-5; ☎ 312-742-5222; 55 N Michigan Ave; skate rental $10; 10am-8pm), with great views from Millennium Park, and the less-crowded **Daley Bicentennial Plaza Rink** (Map pp564-5; ☎ 312-742-7650; 337 E Randolph St; skate rental $5; 10am-3:30pm & 7-9:30pm Mon-Fri, 8:30am-noon Sat & Sun). Admission is free to both.

RUNNING & INLINE SKATING

Runners and inline skaters crowd onto the lakefront path alongside cyclists. Bike Chicago (opposite) rents inline skates for prices similar to its two-wheelers.

WATER SPORTS

Chicago sits by a big lake and river, so it's no surprise that water sports rule the waves here.

Take a dip, build a sand castle or loaf in the sun at any of Chicago's 30-plus beaches, operated by the Chicago Park District (above). All beaches are staffed with lifeguards during the summer. **North Avenue Beach** (Map pp570-1; 1600 N Lake Shore Dr) and **Oak Street Beach** (Map pp570-1; 1000 N Lake Shore Dr), both close to downtown, are particularly body-filled. Brace yourself as the water remains butt-numbing well into July.

For a remarkable view of downtown, where you'll slither through a canyon of glass and steel, kayak the Chicago River with **Wateriders** (Map pp570-1; ☎ 312-953-9287; www.wateriders.com; 950 N Kingsbury St; 3hr tours $50-60). Tours take in architectural sights and gangster spots. Beginners are welcome. Call for the schedule.

YOGA & PILATES

Center yourself with Millennium Park's free yoga, Pilates and tai chi classes on summer Saturdays (p563).

Walking Tour

This tour swoops through the Loop, highlighting Chicago's revered art and architecture, with a visit to Al Capone's dentist thrown in for good measure.

Start at the **Chicago Board of Trade** (**1**; p567), where guys in Technicolor coats swap corn (or something like that) inside a cool art-deco building. Step into the nearby **Rookery** (**2**; p567) to see Frank Lloyd Wright's handiwork in the atrium.

Head east on Adams St to the **Art Institute** (**3**; p563), one of the city's most-visited attractions. The lion statues out front make a classic keepsake photo. Walk a few blocks north to avant-garde **Millennium Park** (**4**; p563), and saunter in to explore 'the Bean' sculpture,

CHICAGO WALKING TOUR

WALK FACTS

Start: Chicago Board of Trade
Finish: Billy Goat Tavern
Distance: 3 miles
Duration: About two hours

human-gargoyle fountains and other contemporary designs.

When you depart Millennium Park, head west on Washington St to **Hotel Burnham** (**5**; p579). It's housed in the Reliance Building, which was the precursor to modern skyscraper design; Capone's dentist drilled teeth in what's now room 809. Just west, the **Untitled** (**6**; p567), created by Mr Abstract himself, is ensconced in Daley Center Plaza. Bird, dog, woman? You decide. Then go north on Clark St to **Monument with Standing Beast** (**7**; p567), another head-scratching sculpture.

Walk east on Randolph St through the theater district. Pop into the **Cultural Center** (**8**; p567) to get a soda in the café and maybe catch a free concert. Refreshed? Now go north on Michigan Ave and cross the Chicago River. Just north of the bridge you'll pass the **Wrigley Building** (**9**; **p568**), glowing as white as the Double Mint twins' teeth, and the nearby Gothic, eye-popping **Tribune Tower** (**10**; p568).

To finish your tour, visit **Billy Goat Tavern** (**11**; p580), a vintage Chicago dive that spawned the Curse of the Cubs. Just look around and you'll get the details, but in short: the tavern's owner, Billy Sianis, once tried to enter Wrigley Field with his pet goat. The smelly creature was denied entry, so Sianis called down a mighty curse on the baseball team in retaliation. They've had futile World Series attempts ever since.

Chicago for Children

Chicago is a kid's kind of town. Most museums have special areas to entertain and educate wee ones. A good resource is *Chicago Parent* (www.chicagoparent.com), a free publication available at libraries, the Children's Museum and elsewhere. Also check www.chicagokids.com.

CHILDREN'S THEATER

The **Children's Theatre Company** (☎ 773-227-0180; www.chicagochildrenstheatre.org) is one of the few, fully-fledged kids' theater troupes in the country. Performances take place at various venues around town; ticket prices and times vary.

For a theatrical experience of a different kind, take the youngsters to a taping of **Chic-A-Go-Go** (www.myspace.com/chicagogoshow), a cable-access TV show that's like a kiddie version of *Soul Train* – it's a dance party with children and adult hipsters groovin' to eclectic tunes and live bands. Check the website for taping dates and locations, which vary.

CHICAGO CHILDREN'S MUSEUM

This **museum** (Map pp564-5; ☎ 312-527-1000; www.chicagochildrensmuseum.org; 700 E Grand Ave; admission $10, free Thu evening; 10am-5pm, to 8pm Thu;) is on Navy Pier. Kids can climb a schooner, excavate dinosaur bones and generate hydroelectric power. It's fun – really! Follow up with an expedition down the pier itself, including spins on the Ferris wheel and carousel.

OTHER SIGHTS

Shedd Aquarium (p567) is drenched with whales, sharks and weird-looking fish and always pleases the young. The Field Museum of Natural History (p567) offers lots and lots of those perennial kid favorites – dinosaurs! **Lincoln Park Zoo** (p569) has a children's area and farm where tykes can touch the animals.

Other kid-friendly activities include an El ride (see p586) around the Loop; get on the Brown Line at Merchandise Mart (Map pp564–5) and go to Clark St, which takes you on a leisurely trip through the thick of downtown's tall buildings. In July and August, take a lakefront swim at North Avenue Beach (p569), where there's soft sand, lifeguards, a snack bar and bathrooms.

Girls visiting Chicago will want to head directly to **American Girl Place** (Map pp570-1; ☎ 877-247-5223; 835 N Michigan Ave;). In addition to purveying dolls from bygone eras, the store has a café in which dolls are seated and treated as part of the family.

American Childcare Services (☎ 312-644-7300; per hr $18.50, plus agency fee $20) provides professional babysitters who will come to your hotel; it's a four-hour minimum service.

Quirky Chicago

Sure, your friends will listen politely as you describe your trip to the Willis Tower's tip, but you'll stop them mid-yawn when you unleash stories of how you boozed with roller babes and honed your cornhole strategy. Chicago has a fine collection of unusual sights and activities to supplement its standard attractions.

First thing to know: locals love **cornhole** (www.chicagocornhole.com). C'mon, get your mind out of the gutter; we're not talking porn here. We mean a game in which small corn-filled bags (aka beanbags) are tossed into a sloped box with a hole in it. Cornhole is a game! Several bars have leagues and tournaments.

The **International Museum of Surgical Science** (Map pp570-1; ☎ 312-642-6502; www.imss.org; 1524 N Lake Shore Dr; adult/student $10/6, admission free Tue; ⌚ 10am-4pm Tue-Sun May-Sep, closed Sun Oct-Apr) has a bloodletting exhibit and fine collection of 'stones' (as in kidney stones and gallstones). For those who've always wanted to see an iron lung, here's your chance.

The bang-em-up sport of roller derby was born in Chicago in 1935, and the battlin' babes of the **Windy City Rollers** (Map p562; www.windycityrollers.com; UIC Pavilion, 525 S Racine Ave; tickets $20-40) will show you how it's played, bruises and all. Matches take place monthly.

Who knew Ben Franklin liked to be flogged and Egypt's Queen Hatshepsut had a foot fetish? The **Leather Archives & Museum** (Map p562; ☎ 773-761-9200; www.leatherarchives.org; 6418 N Greenview Ave; admission $5; ⌚ 11am-7pm Thu & Fri, to 5pm Sat & Sun) reveals these facts and more in its displays of leather, fetish and S&M subcultures.

Weird Chicago Tours (below) drives by kinky and spooky spots. And Chic-A-Go-Go (opposite) isn't just for kids: you, too, can shake it on the dancefloor with Miss Mia and Ratso.

Tours

For highly recommended architectural tours by foot, boat or bus, contact the **Chicago Architecture Foundation** (Map pp564-5; ☎ 312-922-3432; www.architecture.org; 224 S Michigan Ave; tours $5-40; ⌚ year-round). The $5 lunchtime tours Monday through Thursday are a bargain, as are the $15 Rise of the Skyscraper tours. Departure points and times vary.

The **Chicago History Museum** (Map pp570-1; ☎ 312-642-4600; www.chicagohs.org; 1601 N Clark St; tours $10-45; ⌚ year-round) counts pub crawls, kayak jaunts and cemetery walks among its tour arsenal. Departure points and times vary.

The three-hour **Weird Chicago Tours** (Map pp564-5; ☎ 888-446-7859; www.weirdchicago.com; cnr Clark & Ontario Sts; tours $30; ⌚ tours 7pm Thu-Sat) go by bus to ghost, gangster and red-light sites. Departure is from the Hard Rock Cafe.

Foodies can graze through various neighborhoods with **Chicago Food Planet Tours** (☎ 212-209-3370; www.chicagofoodplanet.com; tours $42; ⌚ year-round). Tickets must be prepurchased online or by telephone. Departure points and times vary.

Chicago Greeter (Map pp564-5; ☎ 312-744-8000; www.chicagogreeter.com; ⌚ year-round) pairs you with a local city dweller who takes you on a personal free two- to four-hour tour customized by theme (architecture, history, gay and lesbian and more) or neighborhood. Travel is by foot and/or public transportation; reserve seven business days in advance. **InstaGreeter** (Map pp564-5; ⌚ 10am-4pm Fri-Sun) is the quicker version, offering free on-the-spot one-hour tours from the visitors center at 77 E Randolph St and from Hyde Park (p574). For free Millennium Park tours, see p566.

The Activities section has information on bicycle tours (p574) and kayak tours (p575).

And you can always do it yourself with free downloadable audio tours. Try www.downloadchicagotours.com for jaunts like a Buddy Guy–narrated blues tour, or www.onscreenillinois.com for a tour of Chicago's famous movie sites.

Festivals & Events

Chicago has a full events calendar year-round, but the biggies are held in the summer. **SummerDance** (Map pp564-5; ☎ 312-742-4007; www.chicagosummerdance.org; 601 S Michigan Ave; admission free; ⌚ from 6pm Thu-Sat, from 4pm Sun mid-June–mid-Aug) has bands playing rumba, samba and other world music preceded by fun dance lessons.

The following events are free and are held downtown on a weekend, unless noted otherwise. For exact dates and other details, you can contact the city's **Office of Special Events** (☎ 312-744-3315; www.cityofchicago.org/specialevents).

St Patrick's Day Parade Mid-March. The local plumbers union dyes the Chicago River shamrock green; a big parade follows.

Blues Festival Early June. It's the biggest free blues fest in the world, with three days of the music that made Chicago famous.

Taste of Chicago Late June to early July. This 10-day food festival in Grant Park includes bands and a huge July 3 concert with fireworks.

Pitchfork Music Festival (www.pitchforkmusicfestival.com; day pass $35) Mid-July. Indie bands strum for three days in Union Park.

Lollapalooza (www.lollapalooza.com; day pass around $100) Early August. For three days, 130 bands take over Grant Park.

Air and Water Show Mid-August. People flock to North Avenue Beach to see daredevil displays by boats and planes.

Jazz Festival Early September. Top names on the national jazz scene play over Labor Day weekend.

Gay & Lesbian Chicago

Chicago has a flourishing gay and lesbian scene; for details, check the weekly free publications of *Chicago Free Press* (www.chicagofreepress.com) or *Windy City Times* (www.windycitymediagroup.com).

The **Chicago Area Gay & Lesbian Chamber of Commerce** (Map p573; ☎ 773-303-0167; www.glchamber.org; 3656 N Halsted St; 9:30am-6pm Mon-Fri) provides useful visitor information. Chicago Greeter (see Tours, p577) offers personalized sightseeing trips.

The biggest concentration of bars and clubs is in Wrigleyville on N Halsted St between Belmont Ave and Grace St, an area known as 'Boys' Town.' Massive **Sidetrack** (Map p573; ☎ 773-477-9189; 3349 N Halsted St) thumps dance music and show tunes and is prime for people watching.

Andersonville, aka 'Girls' Town,' is another area with many choices. Despite the name, both men and women frequent **Big Chicks** (Map p573; ☎ 773-728-5511; 5024 N Sheridan Rd;), with its weekend DJs, art displays and next-door organic restaurant **Tweet** (Map p573; ☎ 773-728-5576; 5020 N Sheridan Ave; 9am-3pm, closed Tue;), where weekend brunch is a major gay scene. Both sexes also hang out at **T's** (Map p573; ☎ 773-784-6000; 5025 N Clark St), a casual bar with good grub, and **Marty's** (Map p573; ☎ 773-561-6425; 1511 W Balmoral Ave), a martini bar attracting older, professional types.

The edgy party **Chance's Dances** (www.chancesdances.org) rocks in Wicker Park twice monthly; check the website for locations and times.

The late-June **Pride Parade** (☎ 773-348-8243; www.chicagopridecalendar.org; admission free) winds through Boys' Town and attracts close to 400,000 people.

Sleeping

Chicago lodging doesn't come cheap. The best way to cut costs is to use a bidding site like Priceline or Hotwire (look for 'River North' or 'Mag Mile' locations). On weekends and when the frequent big conventions trample through town, your options become much slimmer, so plan ahead to avoid unpleasant surprises. The prices we've listed are normal midweek rates in summer, the high season. Taxes add 15.4%.

B&Bs give a nice bang for the midrange buck. Contact the **Chicago Bed & Breakfast Association** (www.chicago-bed-breakfast.com; r $100-229), which represents 18 guesthouses. Many properties have two- to three-night minimum stays. Vacation rentals in local apartments are also a good deal here. Try **VacationsFRBO** (www.vacationsfrbo.com) or **Craigslist** (www.chicago.craigslist.org).

Hotels in the Loop are convenient to Grant Park, the museums and business district, but the area is pretty dead come nightfall. Accommodations in the Near North and Gold Coast are most popular, given their proximity to eating, shopping and entertainment venues. Rooms in Lincoln Park, Lake View and Wicker Park entice because they're often cheaper than rooms downtown; they are also near swingin' nightlife.

All properties listed here have free wi-fi.

BUDGET

HI-Chicago (Map pp564-5; ☎ 312-360-0300; www.hichicago.org; 24 E Congress Pkwy; dm incl breakfast $29-38; P) Chicago's best hostel is immaculate, centrally located in the Loop, and offers bonuses like a staffed information desk, free volunteer-led tours and discount passes to museums and shows. The simple dorm rooms have six to 12 beds and attached bathrooms. Parking costs $27.

MIDRANGE

Central Loop Hotel (Map pp564-5; ☎ 312-601-3525, 866-744-2333; www.centralloophotel.com; 111 W Adams St; r $119-171; P) The Central Loop has a good location (the name doesn't lie) and good prices if you're stuck paying rack rates. It's accessorized for business folk, though not so useful for families given the rooms' smallish size. A fine pub pours drinks downstairs. Parking costs $30.

Days Inn Lincoln Park North (Map pp570-1; ☎ 773-525-7010, 888-576-3297; www.lpndaysinn.com; 644 W Diversey Pkwy; r incl breakfast $120-180; P) Don't let the blah exterior put you off: this well-maintained chain hotel in Lincoln Park is a family favorite, with well-kept rooms, good service and perks like free health club access. It's an easy amble to the lakefront's parks and beaches, and a 15-minute bus ride to downtown. Parking costs $22.

House of Two Urns B&B (Map pp570-1; ☎ 773-235-1408, 877-896-8767; www.twourns.com; 1239 N Greenview Ave; r incl breakfast $129-199; P) Artists own these two houses at mod Wicker Park's edge, so it's no surprise both places are fancifully furnished with odd antiques and original art. Some rooms share a bathroom. Take the CTA Blue Line to Division.

Tremont Hotel (Map pp570-1; ☎ 312-751-1900, 800-621-8133; www.tremontchicago.com; 100 E Chestnut St; r incl breakfast $129-249; P ✖ ≋) The worn but mannerly Tremont, near the Water Tower, is good value if you find a room at the lower end of its price spectrum. The old-world, European-esque rooms are spacious but without many amenities. Mustachioed football hero Mike Ditka owns the attached bar and steakhouse. Parking costs $49.

our pick **Hotel Felix** (Map pp564-5; ☎ 312-447-3440; 877-848-404; www.hotelfelixchicago.com; 111 W Huron St; r $139-189; P ⊠ ✖ 💻 ≋) Opened in 2009 in the Near North, the 225-room, 12-story Felix is downtown's first hotel to earn eco-friendly LEED certification (Silver status, to be exact). The earth-toned, mod-furnished rooms are small but efficiently and comfortably designed. Parking costs $42 (if you drive a hybrid, it's free).

Willows Hotel (Map pp570-1; ☎ 773-528-8400, 800-787-3108; www.cityinns.com; 555 W Surf St; r/ste incl breakfast from $149/169; P ⊠ ✖ ≋) Small and stylish, this Lake View hotel wins an architectural gold star. The chic little lobby provides a swell refuge of overstuffed chairs by the fireplace. The 55 rooms, done up in shades of peach, cream and soft green, evoke a 19th-century French countryside feel. Parking is $22.

Wicker Park Inn (Map p562; ☎ 773-486-2743; www.wickerparkinn.com; 1329 N Wicker Park Ave; r incl breakfast $149-199; P ⊠ ✖ ≋) This six-room B&B lets you stay in a classic brick row house in Wicker Park. The location puts you a few blocks from Chicago's nouveau eating, drinking and shopping epicenter, while downtown is a mere 10-minute train ride. Take the CTA Blue Line to Damen.

Best Western River North (Map pp564-5; ☎ 312-467-0800, 800-727-0800; www.rivernorthhotel.com; 125 W Ohio St; r $169-235; P ✖ ≋ 🏊) Its large, vaguely Asian-flaired rooms, coupled with a marvy Near North location, indoor pool and sundeck overlooking the city, are unusual benefits in this price bracket. Free parking seals the deal.

The owners of the Willows Hotel have two other similarly styled and priced properties in the neighborhood: **City Suites Hotel** (Map p573; ☎ 773-404-3400, 800-248-9108; 933 W Belmont Ave), near the CTA Red/Brown Line Belmont station, which is a bit noisier than its counterparts; and the **Majestic Hotel** (Map p573; ☎ 773-404-3499, 800-727-5108; 528 W Brompton Ave), which lies east toward the lake and is more remote than its counterparts.

TOP END

Hotel Burnham (Map pp564-5; ☎ 312-782-1111, 877-294-9712; www.burnhamhotel.com; 1 W Washington St; r incl breakfast from $200; P ⊠ ✖ 💻 ≋) The proprietors brag that the Burnham has the highest guest return rates in Chicago; it's easy to see why. Housed in the Loop's landmark 1890s Reliance Building (precedent for the modern skyscraper), its super-slick decor woos architecture buffs. The bright rooms are lavishly furnished with mahogany writing desks and chaise lounges. There's complimentary wine to sip each evening. Parking costs $45.

Eating

For years epicures wrote off Chicago as a meaty backwater. Then a funny thing happened: the city won a heap of James Beard awards, and foodie magazines like *Saveur* ranked it as the nation's top restaurant scene. Highlights include ethnic eats, locavore fare and 'molecular gastronomy.' Food fanatics can fill up on anything from Nepali dumplings to Cuban sandwiches; from $225, 24-course meals to $2 hot dogs. Prices listed are for dinner mains, unless specified otherwise.

THE LOOP & SOUTH LOOP

It gets lonely here come nighttime as most Loop eateries are geared to lunch crowds of office workers.

Cafecito (Map pp564-5; ☎ 312-922-2233; 26 E Congress Pkwy; sandwiches $4-6; 🕑 6am-9pm Mon-Fri, 10am-6pm Sat & Sun; ≋) Attached to the hostel and perfect for the hungry, thrifty traveler, Cafecito serves kick-ass Cuban sandwiches layered with citrus-garlic-marinated roasted pork and ham. Strong coffee and hearty egg sandwiches make a fine breakfast.

Oasis (Map pp564-5; ☎ 312-443-9534; 21 N Wabash Ave; mains $5-7; 🕑 10am-5pm Mon-Fri, 11am-3pm Sat) Walk past diamonds, gold and other bling in the jewelers' mall before striking it rich at the café in back. Creamy hummus, crisp falafel, grilled chicken kebabs and other Middle Eastern favorites fill plates at bargain prices. Eat in or carry out to the nearby parks.

Chicago Curry House (Map pp564-5; ☎ 312-362-9999; 899 S Plymouth Ct; mains $10-19; 🕑 11am-10pm) The Nepali dishes rock harder than the Indian dishes. Standouts include *aloo tama bodi* (potatoes and black-eyed peas) and *khasi ko*

EATING CHICAGO: THE HOLY TRINITY

Chicago cooks up three beloved specialties. Foremost is deep-dish pizza, a hulking mass of crust that rises two or three inches above the plate and cradles a molten pile of toppings. One gooey piece is practically a meal. A large pizza averages $20 at the following places:

Pizzeria Uno (Map pp564-5; ☎ 312-321-1000; 29 E Ohio St; 🕑 11am-1am Mon-Thu, 11am-2am Fri & Sat, 11am-11pm Sun) Where the deep-dish concept originated in 1943; sister outlet Due is one block north.

Gino's East (Map pp564-5; ☎ 312-266-3337; 162 E Superior St; 🕑 11am-10pm Mon-Sat, to 9pm Sun) Write on the walls while you wait for your pie.

Lou Malnati's (Map pp564-5; ☎ 312-828-9800; 439 N Wells St; 🕑 11am-11pm Mon-Thu, 11am-midnight Fri & Sat, noon-10pm Sun) Famous for its butter crust.

Giordano's (Map pp564-5; ☎ 312-951-0747; 730 N Rush St; 🕑 11am-11pm Sun-Thu, 11am-midnight Fri & Sat) Perfectly tangy tomato sauce.

Pizano's (Map pp570–1; ☎ 312-751-1766; 864 N State St; 🕑 11am-2am Sun-Fri, to 3am Sat) Oprah's favorite.

No less iconic is the Chicago hot dog – a wiener that's been 'dragged through the garden' (ie topped with onions, tomatoes, shredded lettuce, bell peppers, pepperoncini and sweet relish, or variations thereof, but never ketchup), and then cushioned on a poppy-seed bun. Hot Doug's (p582) does it right.

The city is also revered for its spicy, drippy, only-in-Chicago Italian beef sandwiches. Mr Beef (below) serves the gold standard.

maasu (goat meat on the bone). Sample them during the lunch buffet ($11). Several menu items are vegetarian; a full bar helps wash it all down.

Gage (Map pp564-5; ☎ 312-372-4243; 24 S Michigan Ave; mains $16-32; 🕑 11am-2am Mon-Fri, 10am-3am Sat, 10am-midnight Sun) This gastropub dishes Irish-tinged grub with a fanciful twist, from Guinness-battered fish and chips and fries smothered in curry gravy to spicy mustard chicken livers. Ask the knowledgeable servers which beers from the solid list best accompany your food.

NEAR NORTH

Loads of restaurants and cafés pack the Near North's streets.

Billy Goat Tavern (Map pp564-5; ☎ 312-222-1525; lower level, 430 N Michigan Ave; burgers $3-6; 🕑 6am-2am Mon-Fri, 10am-2am Sat & Sun) Scruffy like the titular animal, this subterranean bar and burger joint is the legendary haunt of *Tribune* and *Sun-Times* reporters. Only the dimmest of bulbs orders fries with their cheezborger (remember John Belushi's famous *Saturday Night Live* skit: 'No fries – chips!').

Mr Beef (Map pp564-5; ☎ 312-337-8500; 666 N Orleans St; sandwiches $4-7; 🕑 8am-7pm Mon-Thu, to 5am Fri, 10:30am-3:30pm & 10:30pm-5am Sat) A Chicago specialty, the Italian beef sandwich stacks up like this: thin-sliced, slow-cooked roast beef that's sopped in natural gravy and *giardiniera* (spicy, pickled vegetables), and then heaped on a hoagie roll. Mr Beef serves the best at its picnic-style tables.

Frontera Grill (Map pp564-5; ☎ 312-661-1434; 445 N Clark St; small plates $7-9, mains $18-29; 🕑 11:30am-2:30pm Tue-Fri, 10:30am-2:30pm Sat, 5:30-9:30pm Tue-Thu, to 10:30pm Fri & Sat) Perhaps you've seen chef Rick Bayless on TV, stirring up pepper sauces and other jump-off-the-tongue Mexican creations. His isn't your typical taco menu: Bayless uses seasonal, sustainable ingredients for flavor-packed fare. No wonder it's a fave of President Obama. Sister restaurant Topolobampo, in an adjoining room, is sleeker and pricier, with similar hours.

LINCOLN PARK & OLD TOWN

Halsted, Lincoln and Clark Sts are the main veins teeming with restaurants and bars. Parking is frightful, but it's handy to the CTA train stops at Armitage and Fullerton.

Wiener Circle (Map pp570-1; ☎ 773-477-7444; 2622 N Clark St; items $2-5; 🕑 10:30am-4am Sun-Thu, 10:30am-5am Fri & Sat) As famous for its unruly, foul-mouthed ambience as its char-dogs and cheddar fries, the Wiener Circle is *the* place for late-night munchies. It helps to be shnockered before entering.

Crepe & Coffee Palace (Map pp570-1; ☎ 773-404-1300; 2433 N Clark St; mains $6-9; 🕑 9am-9pm Mon-Thu, 9am-10pm Fri, 8am-10pm Sat, 8am-9pm Sun) It's OK – delicious, in fact – to make a meal of pancakes. This Algerian eatery serves 'em sweet or savory (stuffed with chicken, smoked salmon or escargot).

Goose Island Brew Pub (Map pp570-1; ☎ 312-915-0071; 1800 N Clybourn Ave; mains $8-15; 🕑 11am-10pm) Goose Island's grub often incorporates its specialty beer into its dishes, like Belgian beef stew and ale-roasted chicken. Suds enthusiasts can swill from 24 drafts on tap, or get a four-beer flight (each 5oz) for $8. Crisp Honker's Ale remains a crowd favorite.

Alinea (Map pp570-1; ☎ 312-867-0110; 1723 N Halsted St; multicourse tastings $145-225; 🕑 5:30-9:30pm Wed-Sun) Grant Achatz is the guy behind Alinea's 'molecular gastronomy.' If you secure a coveted reservation, prepare for roughly 12 to 24 courses of mind-bending, space-age cuisine. Dishes may emanate from a centrifuge or be pressed into a capsule. *Gourmet* magazine recently ranked it the USA's number-one restaurant.

LAKE VIEW & WRIGLEYVILLE

Clark, Halsted, Belmont and Southport are fertile streets. Parking is near impossible, so take the CTA train to the Belmont, Southport or Addison stops.

Ian's Pizza (Map p573; ☎ 773-525-4580; 3463 N Clark St; slices $2.75-3.75; 🕑 5pm-2am Tue-Fri, noon-2am Sat & Sun) Need to soak up all those brewskis post Cubs game? Ian's can help. Crazy slices topped by macaroni and cheese (most popular), guacamole taco, barbecue chicken and about 20 other items are in high demand late night, so prepare to queue for the pleasure.

Mia Francesca (Map p573; ☎ 773-281-3310; 3311 N Clark St; mains $13-27; 🕑 5-10pm Sun-Thu, to 11pm Fri & Sat) Local chain Mia's buzzes with regulars who come for the trattoria's Italian standards, such as seafood linguine, spinach ravioli and mushroom-sauced veal medallions, all prepared with simple flair.

ANDERSONVILLE & UPTOWN

These northern neighborhoods burst with casual restaurants and bars. 'Little Saigon' is nearby on Argyle St. Take the CTA Red Line to Argyle or Berwyn.

Ba Le Bakery (Map p573; ☎ 773-561-4424; 5018 N Broadway; sandwiches $3-4.25; 🕑 7:30am-8pm) Ba Le serves sandwiches Saigon-style, called *banh mi*, with steamed pork, shrimp cakes or meatballs on fresh baguettes made right dang here.

Kopi Traveler's Café (Map p573; ☎ 773-989-5674; 5317 N Clark St; items $5-9; 🕑 8am-11pm Mon-Fri, 9am-midnight Sat, 10am-11pm Sun) Kopi has an Asian trekker-lodge vibe, from the pile of cushions to sit on and the healthy sandwiches to the bulletin board on which travelers post flyers.

WICKER PARK, BUCKTOWN & UKRAINIAN VILLAGE

Trendy restaurants open almost every day. Take the CTA Blue Line to Chicago, Damen or Western.

Handlebar Bar & Grill (Map p562; ☎ 773-384-9546; 2311 W North Ave; mains $9-14; 🕑 10am-midnight Mon-Thu, to 2am Fri & Sat, 10am-11pm Sun) Handlebar peddles (pun intended, since the decor is

FARM TO FORK FARE

These entities provide unique ways to eat local, sustainable foods:

- The outdoor **Green City Market** (Map pp570-1; ☎ 773-880-1266; www.chicagogreencitymarket.org; 1750 N Clark St; 🕑 7am-1pm Wed & Sat mid-May–late Oct) offers heirloom veggies, homemade pies, chef demos and much more at Lincoln Park's south end.
- **Chicago's Downtown Farmstand** (Map pp564-5; ☎ 312-742-8419; 66 E Randolph St; 🕑 11am-7pm Tue-Fri, to 4pm Sat) sells locally made honey, pastries and produce. Farmers come in to share stories on Fridays at noon.
- **Clandestino** (www.clandestinodining.com; multicourse meals $65-85) is an underground, 'community dining project,' where chef Efrain Cuevas serves sustainable meals in changing locations, like galleries or lofts. Sign up for the online mailing list, and grab a spot when he sends out event invitations.
- **City Provisions** (☎ 773-293-2489; www.cityprovisions.com; tours $125) takes foodies to area farms for dining amid the fields. The price includes transportation on a biodiesel bus from Chicago, food and beer pairings.

bicycle oriented) West African groundnut stew, wasabi-baked tofu and other energizing dishes; quaff the excellent beer selection on the patio.

Hot Chocolate (Map p562; ☎ 773-489-1747; 1747 N Damen Ave; sandwiches $10-15, mains $16-30; 🕑 11:30am-2pm Wed-Fri, 10am-2pm Sat & Sun, 5:30-10pm Tue-Sun) The pastry-chef owner whips up tasty mains, say walleye fish with pea-and-mint puree. But you're really here for dessert, so save room for the hot fudge.

West Town Tavern (Map pp570-1; ☎ 312-666-6175; 1329 W Chicago Ave; mains $19-25; 🕑 5-10pm Mon-Sat) Mmm, contemporary comfort foods – pot roast, pasta with turkey meatballs, mushroom chowder – all served in a warm, exposed-brick old row house.

LOGAN SQUARE & HUMBOLDT PARK

Several eats and drinks ring the intersection of Milwaukee, Logan and Kedzie Blvds. Take the CTA Blue Line to Logan Square.

our pick **Hot Doug's** (Map p562; ☎ 773-279-9550; 3324 N California Ave; mains $2.50-8; 🕑 10:30am-4pm Mon-Sat) Doug's the man to fulfill all your hot-dog fantasies. He serves multiple dog styles (Polish, bratwursts, Chicago) cooked multiple dog ways (char-grilled, deep-fried, steamed). Confused? He'll explain it all. Doug also makes gourmet 'haute dogs,' say blue-cheese pork with cherry cream sauce.

Feed (Map p562; ☎ 773-489-4600; 2803 W Chicago Ave; mains $6-12; 🕑 8am-10pm Mon & Wed-Fri, 9am-10pm Sat, 9am-9pm Sun) Folksy Feed serves a small menu of down-home chow such as rotisserie chicken, mac-n-cheese, mashed potatoes, corn pudding, fried okra and bulging fruit pies. Bring your own booze; cash only.

Lula Cafe (Map p562; ☎ 773-489-9554; 2537 N Kedzie Blvd; mains $17-26; 🕑 9am-10pm Mon & Wed-Thu, to 11pm Fri & Sat, closed Tue) Slow-food lovers crowd in for Lula's locally sourced menu, which changes with the seasons. Prior dishes include striped bass with pine nut–peppered orzo, and pasta with Moroccan cinnamon and feta.

NEAR WEST SIDE & PILSEN

Greektown extends along S Halsted St (take the Blue Line to UIC-Halsted), Little Italy is along Taylor St, and the Mexican Pilsen enclave centers around W 18th St (take the Pink Line to 18th). The West Loop holds several stylish eateries along Randolph and Washington Sts, and is most easily reached by taxi (about $8 from downtown).

Don Pedro Carnitas (Map p562; ☎ 312-829-4757; 1113 W 18th St; tacos $1.50-2; 🕑 6am-6pm Mon-Fri, 5am-5pm Sat, to 3pm Sun) At this no-frills Pilsen meat hive, a man with a machete salutes you at the front counter. He awaits your command to hack off pork pieces, and then wraps the thick chunks with onion and cilantro in a fresh tortilla. Goat stew and tripe add to the meaty menu. Cash only.

Lou Mitchell's (Map pp564-5; ☎ 312-939-3111; 565 W Jackson Blvd; mains $4-9; 🕑 5:30am-3pm Mon-Sat, 7am-3pm Sun) Lou's sprang up in Route 66's heyday. There's a queue to get in for the famed breakfasts, but staff give out free Milk Duds to ease the wait.

Publican (Map pp564-5; ☎ 312-733-9555; 837 W Fulton Market; mains $15-30; 🕑 3:30-10:30pm Mon-Thu, to 11:30pm Fri & Sat, 10am-2pm & 5-10pm Sun) Set up like a swanky beer hall, Publican specializes in oysters, hams and fine suds – all from small family farms and microbrewers. There's a four-course special ($45) Sunday nights.

NEAR SOUTH SIDE & CHINATOWN

Take the CTA Red Line to Harrison, Roosevelt or Cermak-Chinatown.

Joy Yee's Noodles (Map pp564-5; ☎ 312-328-0001; 2139 S China Pl; mains $7-12; 🕑 11am-10:30pm) Joy Yee's roaring blenders mix more than 100 types of fruit drinks and tapioca bubble teas, which make a fine accompaniment to the pan-Asian dishes such as udon (thick, wheat-based noodles) and chow mein.

Drinking

During the long winters, Chicagoans count on bars for warmth. The usual closing time is 2am, but some places stay open until 4am or 5am. In summer many bars boast beer gardens.

THE LOOP & NEAR NORTH

Intelligentsia Coffee (Map pp564-5; ☎ 312-920-9332; 53 E Randolph St; 🕑 6am-8pm Mon-Thu, 6am-9pm Fri, 7am-9pm Sat, 7am-7pm Sun) This local chain roasts its own beans and percolates good strong stuff. One of its baristas recently won the national latte-making championship.

Signature Lounge (Map pp570-1; ☎ 312-787-7230; John Hancock Center, 875 N Michigan Ave) Have the Hancock Observatory view without the Hancock Observatory admission price. Shoot straight up to the 96th floor and order a beverage while looking out over the city. Ladies: don't miss the bathroom view.

Clark Street Ale House (Map pp564-5; ☎ 312-642-9253; 742 N Clark St) Do as the retro sign advises and 'Stop & Drink Liquor.' Midwestern microbrews are the main draw; order a three-beer sampler for $5.

LINCOLN PARK & OLD TOWN

Olde Towne Ale House (Map pp570-1; ☎ 312-944-7020; 219 W North Ave) There are no pretenses at this longtime favorite: you'll mingle with beautiful people and not-so-beautiful people (they're the ones face down at the bar). It is across from Second City.

Delilah's (Map pp570-1; ☎ 773-472-2771; 2771 N Lincoln Ave) Delilah's is where underground rockers come to drink from the lengthy whiskey list.

WRIGLEYVILLE & ANDERSONVILLE

Ginger Man (Map p573; ☎ 773-549-2050; 3740 N Clark St) The pierced-and-tattooed patrons, pool tables and good beer selection make Ginger Man wonderfully different from the surrounding Wrigley sports bars.

Harry Caray's (Map p573; ☎ 773-327-7800; 3551 N Sheffield Ave) Across from Wrigley and named after its famed announcer, Harry Caray's caters to pre- and post–Cubs game guzzlers. The 60ft-6in bar is the same distance as the pitcher's mound to the home plate.

Hopleaf (Map p573; ☎ 773-334-9851; 5148 N Clark St) You've hit the mother lode of beer selection when you walk into this beauty – there are 200 types available (30 on tap) and a Belgian eatery upstairs.

DIY: HOW TO FIND A REAL CHICAGO BAR

While we can't list every watering hole in town – which is too bad because we'd enjoy the research process – we can give you the tools to go out and discover classic, character-filled bars on your own. Look for the following:

- an 'Old Style' beer sign swinging out front
- a well-worn dart board and/or pool table inside
- patrons wearing Cubs-, White Sox– or Bears-logoed ballcaps
- bottles of brew served in buckets of ice
- sports on TV (with the latter being a 1974 Zenith, not some fancy flat-screen thing).

WICKER PARK, BUCKTOWN & UKRAINIAN VILLAGE

Map Room (Map p562; ☎ 773-252-7636; 1949 N Hoyne Ave) At this map-and-globe-filled 'travelers' tavern,' artsy types sip coffee by day and suds from the 200-strong beer list by night. There's free ethnic food on Tuesdays at 7pm.

Danny's (Map p562; ☎ 773-489-6457; 1951 W Dickens Ave) Danny's comfortably dim and dog-eared ambience is perfect for conversations over a pint. A poetry-reading series and occasional DJs add to the scruffy artiness.

Matchbox (Map pp570-1; ☎ 312-666-9292; 770 N Milwaukee Ave) Lawyers, artists and bums all squeeze in for retro cocktails. It's small as – you got it – a matchbox, with about 10 barstools; everyone else stands against the back wall.

Entertainment

Check the *Reader* and other local media (see p561).

Hot Tix (www.hottix.org; ⏰ 10am-6pm Tue-Sat, 11am-4pm Sun) sells same-day theater tickets for half-price, either online, or at the branches: **Randolph** (Map pp564-5; 72 E Randolph St) or **Pearson** (Map pp570-1; 163 E Pearson St). Cover charges at music and dance clubs range from nil to $20 or more, depending on who's playing and the day of the week.

CLUBS

The club scene ranges from snooty places to casual joints where all you do is dance.

Funky Buddha Lounge (Map pp564-5; ☎ 312-666-1695; 728 W Grand Ave; ⏰ closed Mon-Wed) The Buddha shakes with hip-hop and house music.

Butterfly Social Club (Map pp564-5; ☎ 312-666-1695; 722 W Grand Ave) Next door to Funky Buddha, the ecohip Butterfly serves all-organic cocktails while DJs spin and patrons dance.

The Wicker Park-Ukie Village area has several clubs that tend to be more casual than those elsewhere. **Lava** (Map p562; ☎ 773-342-5282; 1270 N Milwaukee Ave) blasts music from the underground, while the **Darkroom** (Map p562; ☎ 773-276-1411; 2210 W Chicago Ave) welcomes everyone from Goths to reggae-heads with its eclectic spins.

The Near North's clubs are more cavernous and luxurious (with dress codes), such as **Sound-Bar** (Map pp564-5; ☎ 312-787-4480; 226 W Ontario St; ⏰ Fri & Sat only).

LIVE MUSIC

Blues and jazz both have deep roots in Chicago, and world-class performers appear at myriad venues nightly.

Blues

Buddy Guy's Legends (Map pp564-5; ☎ 312-427-0333; 754 S Wabash Ave) This place gets the top acts in town, including the venerable Mr Guy himself.

Rosa's (Map p562; ☎ 773-342-0452; 3420 W Armitage Ave; closed Sun & Mon) Rosa's is a real-deal venue that brings in top local talent and dedicated fans to a somewhat dodgy Logan Sq block.

Lee's Unleaded Blues (Map p562; ☎ 773-493-3477; 7401 S South Chicago Ave; closed Tue & Wed) Far off the tourist path and buried deep on the South Side, Lee's is a genuine juke joint. The local crowd dresses in their finest threads, and everyone jams until dawn.

Blue Chicago (Map pp564-5; ☎ 312-642-6261; 536 & 736 N Clark St) This is a pair of friendly clubs downtown.

New Checkerboard Lounge (Map p562; ☎ 773-684-1472; 5201 S Harper Ct) The Checkerboard was a renowned Bronzeville dump for decades. Then it moved to Hyde Park and slicked up. But the songs remain the same: blues or jazz nightly.

Noisy, hot, sweaty and crowded are **Blues** (Map pp570-1; ☎ 773-528-1012; 2519 N Halsted St) and **Kingston Mines** (Map pp570-1; ☎ 773-477-4646; 2548 N Halsted St). Both are conveniently located in Lincoln Park and are popular drawcards for the holiday-making 4am crowd.

Jazz

Green Mill (Map p573; ☎ 773-878-5552; 4802 N Broadway) The noble Green Mill earned its notoriety as Al Capone's favorite speakeasy (the tunnels in which he hid the booze are still underneath the bar), and you can feel his ghost urging you on to another martini. Top-flight local and national artists perform six nights per week; Sundays are for the nationally acclaimed poetry slam.

Velvet Lounge (Map pp564-5; ☎ 312-791-9050; 67 E Cermak Rd; closed Mon) The intimate Velvet Lounge is a jazz musician's jazz club, with avant-garde notes wafting from the saxophones.

Andy's (Map pp564-5; ☎ 312-642-6805; 11 E Hubbard St) Andy's is affordable and mixed, from its multiage clientele to its fusion of swing, bop and Afro-pop.

Rock & Folk

Metro (Map p573; ☎ 773-549-3604; 3730 N Clark St) Local bands and big names looking for an 'intimate' venue play here.

Old Town School of Folk Music (Map p562; ☎ 773-728-6000; 4544 N Lincoln Ave) It's a superb room offering an eclectic line-up of world music and, yes, folk music.

Hideout (Map pp570-1; ☎ 773-227-4433; 1354 W Wabansia Ave) Tucked behind a factory, Hideout is as hard to find as the name implies, but it is worth it for the laid-back, indie atmosphere and nightly rock, folk and country tunes (and sometimes theater).

Phyllis' Musical Inn (Map p562; ☎ 773-486-9862; 1800 W Division St) One of the all-time great dives, this former Polish polka bar features scrappy up-and-coming bands nightly.

Double Door (Map p562; ☎ 773-489-3160; 1572 N Milwaukee Ave) and **Empty Bottle** (Map p562; ☎ 773-276-3600; 1035 N Western Ave) epitomize the edgy Chicago rock scene. The Bottle hosts free shows on Mondays.

THEATER

Chicago's reputation for stage drama is well deserved. These are the city's main companies:

Chicago Shakespeare Theater (Map pp564-5; ☎ 312-595-5600; www.chicagoshakes.com; 800 E Grand Ave) Will's comedies and tragedies at Navy Pier.

Goodman Theatre (Map pp564-5; ☎ 312-443-3800; www.goodmantheatre.org; 170 N Dearborn St) Known for both new and classic works.

Steppenwolf Theatre (Map pp570-1; ☎ 312-335-1650; www.steppenwolf.org; 1650 N Halsted St) Drama club of Malkovich, Sinise and other Hollywood stars.

Some first-rate smaller companies:

Lookingglass Theatre Company (Map pp570-1; ☎ 312-337-0665; www.lookingglasstheatre.org; 821 N Michigan Ave) Improv-based works, often incorporating acrobatics.

Neo-Futurists (Map p573; ☎ 773-275-5255; www.neofuturists.org; 5153 N Ashland Ave) Original works that make you ponder and laugh simultaneously.

Redmoon Theater (Map p562; ☎ 312-850-8440; www.redmoon.org; 1463 W Hubbard St) Puppet-oriented productions.

Major venues for touring shows mostly cluster at State and Randolph Sts:

Auditorium Theater (Map pp564-5; ☎ 312-922-2110; 50 E Congress Pkwy)

Bank of America Theater (Map pp564-5; ☎ 312-977-1700; 18 W Monroe St)

Cadillac Palace Theater (Map pp564-5; ☎ 312-977-1700; 151 W Randolph St)

Chicago Theater (Map pp564-5; ☎ 312-462-6300; 175 N State St)

Ford Center/Oriental Theater (Map pp564-5; ☎ 312-977-1700; 24 W Randolph St)

COMEDY

Improv comedy began in Chicago, and the city still nurtures the best in the business.

Second City (Map pp570-1; ☎ 312-337-3992; www.secondcity.com; 1616 N Wells St) The cream of the crop – it's the place where John Belushi, Bill Murray and many others honed their wit.

iO Improv (Map p573; ☎ 773-880-0199; www.ioimprov.com; 3541 N Clark St) Many Saturday Night Livers were fostered here.

TELEVISION & CINEMA

Oprah Winfrey Show (Map pp564-5; ☎ tickets 312-591-9222, studio 312-633-1000; www.oprah.com; 1058 W Washington Blvd) The self-help queen's TV show is extremely popular and the free tickets are difficult to come by. Try the studio number if the ticket number isn't working. Last-minute tickets sometimes surface on the website.

Music Box Theatre (Map p573; ☎ 773-871-6604; www.musicboxtheatre.com; 3733 N Southport Ave) Patrons hear live organ music and see clouds roll across the ceiling prior to their art films at this old movie palace.

Gene Siskel Film Center (Map pp564-5; ☎ 312-846-2800; www.siskelfilmcenter.org; 164 N State St) This small theater screens offbeat films.

PERFORMING ARTS

Symphony Center (Map pp564-5; ☎ 312-294-3000; www.cso.org; 220 S Michigan Ave) The Chicago Symphony Orchestra makes music in this beautiful facility.

Civic Opera House (Map pp564-5; ☎ 312-332-2244; www.lyricopera.org; 20 N Wacker Dr) The Lyric Opera of Chicago, one of the country's best, performs in the grand venue here.

Grant Park Orchestra (☎ 312-742-7638; www.grantparkmusicfestival.com) The orchestra puts on free classical concerts in Millennium Park (p563) throughout the summer.

Joffrey Ballet (Map pp564-5; ☎ 312-386-8905; www.joffrey.com; 10 E Randolph St) The ballet practices in swanky new digs downtown, though it typically performs at the Auditorium Theater (opposite).

Modern **Hubbard Street Dance Chicago** (☎ 312-850-9744; www.hubbardstreetdance.com) performs at the **Harris Theater for Music and Dance** (Map pp564-5; ☎ 312-334-7777; 205 E Randolph St).

SPORTS

The **Cubs** (☎ 773-404-2827; www.cubs.com) last won the World Series in 1908, but their fans still pack baseball's most charming stadium, **Wrigley Field** (Map p573; 1060 W Addison St), which dates from 1914 and is known for its ivy-walled field, classic neon sign and men's trough urinals. Tickets are tough to procure. Try the box office about three hours before game time as tickets sometimes appear. Or you can buy 'em from street hustlers for big bucks. If all else fails, peer in the ballpark's 'knothole' on Sheffield Ave. Take the CTA Red Line to Addison; it's 4.5 miles north of the Loop.

The **White Sox** (☎ 312-674-1000; www.whitesox.com) are the Cubs' South Side rivals and play in the more modern 'Cell,' the **US Cellular Field** (Map p562; 333 W 35th St). Tickets are usually cheaper and easier to get than at Wrigley. Take the CTA Red Line to the Sox-35th-station; it's 4.5 miles south of the Loop.

The **Bulls** (☎ 800-462-2849; www.nba.com/bulls) play basketball in the huge **United Center** (Map p562; 1901 W Madison St), which is also used by the **Blackhawks** (☎ 312-559-1212; www.chicagoblackhawks.com) for ice hockey. It's about 2 miles west of the Loop. CTA runs special buses on game days; it's best not to walk here.

Soldier Field (Map pp564-5; 425 E McFetridge Dr) is where Chicago's NFL team, the **Bears** (☎ 847-615-2327; www.chicagobears.com), tackles. It stirred huge controversy when it was renovated from a classical facade to its current flying-saucer look; it is referred to as 'the mistake on the lake.'

Shopping

Easy-to-obtain local souvenirs include sports-logoed gear and jazz or blues CDs.

The shoppers' siren song emanates from N Michigan Ave, along the Magnificent Mile (p568). **Water Tower Place** (Map pp570-1; 835 N Michigan Ave) is among the large vertical malls here. Moving onward, boutiques fill Bucktown (mod), Lincoln Park (tony), Lake View (countercultural) and Andersonville (all three).

Chicago Architecture Foundation Shop (Map pp564-5; ☎ 312-922-3432; 224 S Michigan Ave) Skyscraper playing cards, Frank Lloyd Wright note cards and many more unusual gifts for those with an edifice complex.

Jazz Record Mart (Map pp564-5; ☎ 312-222-1467; 27 E Illinois St) It's thoroughly stocked with Chicago blues and jazz CDs.

Oprah Store (Map pp564-5; ☎ 312-633-2100; 37 N Carpenter St) Pick up a passion journal, 'live your own dreams' coffee cup or pair of Manolo Blahnik pumps – just like Oprah wears!

Getting There & Away

O'Hare International Airport (ORD; off Map p562; ☎ 800-832-6352; www.flychicago.com) is among the world's busiest. Most non-US airlines and international flights use Terminal 5 (except Lufthansa and flights from Canada).

The smaller **Chicago Midway Airport** (MDW; Map p562; ☎ 773-838-0600; www.flychicago.com) is used mostly by domestic carriers, like Southwest, which often have cheaper flights than airlines serving O'Hare.

The main **Greyhound station** (Map pp564-5; ☎ 312-408-5800; www.greyhound.com; 630 W Harrison St) is two blocks from the CTA Blue Line Clinton stop. Buses run frequently to Cleveland ($34 to $53, 7½ hours), Detroit ($26 to $41, seven hours) and Minneapolis ($29 to $63, nine hours), as well as small towns throughout the USA.

Megabus (Map pp564-5; ☎ 877-462-6342; www.megabus.com/us; southeast cnr Canal St & Jackson Blvd) travels only to major Midwestern cities. Prices are often less, and quality and efficiency are better than Greyhound on these routes.

Chicago's classic **Union Station** (Map pp564-5; 225 S Canal St) is the hub for **Amtrak's** (☎ 800-872-7245; www.amtrak.com) national and regional service. Seven trains a day go to Milwaukee ($22, 1½ hours). Other connections:

Detroit ($29 to $41, 5½ hours, three trains daily)
Minneapolis/St Paul ($56 to $125, eight hours, one train daily)
New York ($84 to $137, 20½ hours, two trains daily)
San Francisco (Emeryville) ($182 to $227, 53 hours, one train daily)
St Louis ($23, 5½ hours, five trains daily)

Getting Around

TO/FROM THE AIRPORT

O'Hare International Airport is 17 miles northwest of the Loop. The cheapest, and often the quickest, way to/from O'Hare is by the CTA Blue Line ($2.25), but the station is a long walk from the flight terminals. Airport Express shuttles run between the airport and downtown hotels (per person $27). Cabs to/from downtown cost about $45.

Chicago Midway Airport is 11 miles southwest of the Loop, connected via the CTA Orange Line ($2.25). Other options include shuttles (per person $22) and cabs ($25 to $35).

BICYCLE

Chicago has 120 miles of bike lanes. Request a free map from the city's **transportation department** (☎ 312-742-2453; www.chicagobikes.org). Bike racks are plentiful; the biggest, with showers, is at **McDonalds Cycle Center** (Map pp564-5; ☎ 888-245-3929; 239 E Randolph St). Lock it or lose it. For bike-rental information, see p574.

CAR & MOTORCYCLE

Be warned: street and garage/lot parking are expensive. If you must, try **East Monroe Garage** (Map pp564-5; Columbus Dr btwn Randolph & Monroe Sts; per 12hr $14). Chicago's rush-hour traffic is abysmal.

PUBLIC TRANSPORTATION

The **Chicago Transit Authority** (CTA; ☎ 888-968-7282; www.transitchicago.com) operates the city bus and train network, including both elevated (El) and subway trains. CTA buses go everywhere from early morning until late evening. Two of the eight color-coded train lines – the Red Line, and the Blue Line to O'Hare International Airport – operate 24 hours a day. The other lines run from about 5am to midnight daily. During the day, you shouldn't have to wait more than 15 minutes for a train (although track renovations can create lengthier lags). Get free maps at any station.

The standard fare per train is $2.25; per bus, it is $2. Transfers cost 25¢. On buses, you can use a fare card (called a Transit Card) or pay with exact change. On the train, you must use a Transit Card, which is sold from vending machines at train stations. Day passes (one-/three-day pass $5.75/14) provide excellent savings, but they can be purchased only at airports or downtown currency exchanges.

Metra commuter trains (☎ 312-836-7000; www.metrarail.com) have 12 routes serving the suburbs from four terminals ringing the Loop (LaSalle St Station, Randolph St/Millennium Park Station, Richard B Ogilvie Transportation Center and Union Station – all on Map pp564–5). Some lines run daily, while others operate only during weekday rush hours. Metra fares cost $2.15 to $7 or more. An all-weekend pass costs $5.

PACE (☎ 847-364-7223; www.pacebus.com) runs the suburban bus system that connects with city transport.

TAXI

Cabs are plentiful in the Loop, north to Andersonville and west to Bucktown. In other areas, call **Yellow Cab** (☎ 312-829-4222) or **Flash Cab** (☎ 773-561-1444). Flagfall is $2.25, plus $1.80 per mile and $1 per extra passenger; a 15% tip is expected. Venture outside city limits and you'll pay one and a half times the fare.

AROUND CHICAGO

Evanston & North Shore

Evanston, 14 miles north of the Loop and reached via the CTA Purple Line, combines sprawling old houses with a compact downtown. It's also home to Northwestern University.

Beyond are Chicago's northern lakeshore suburbs, which became popular with the carriage set in the late 19th century. A classic 30-mile drive follows Sheridan Rd through various tony towns to the socioeconomic apex of Lake Forest. Attractions include the **Baha'i House of Worship** (☎ 847-853-2300; www.bahai.us/bahai-temple; 100 Linden Ave, Wilmette; admission free; 🕑 6am-10pm), a glistening white architectural marvel, and the **Chicago Botanic Garden** (☎ 847-835-5440; www.chicagobotanic.org; 1000 Lake Cook Rd, Glencoe; admission free; 🕑 8am-dusk), with hiking trails, 255 bird species and weekend cooking demos by well-known chefs. Parking costs $20.

Inland lies the **Illinois Holocaust Museum** (☎ 847-967-4800; www.ilholocaustmuseum.org; 9603 Woods Dr, Skokie; adult/child 5-11yr $8/5; 🕑 10am-5pm Mon-Fri, to 8pm Thu, 11am-4pm Sat & Sun). Besides its excellent videos of survivors' stories from WWII, the museum contains thought-provoking art about genocides in Armenia, Rwanda, Cambodia and others.

Oak Park

Located west of the Loop and easily reached on the CTA Green Line, Oak Park spawned two famous sons: novelist Ernest Hemingway was born here, and architect Frank Lloyd Wright (see boxed text, p92) lived and worked here from 1889 to 1909.

During Wright's 20 years in Oak Park, he designed a helluva lot of houses. Stop at the **visitors center** (☎ 888-625-7275; www.visitoakpark.com; 158 N Forest Ave; 🕑 10am-5pm) and ask for the architectural site map (a free, photocopied page), which gives their locations. To actually get inside a Wright-designed dwelling, you'll need to tour the **Frank Lloyd Wright Home & Studio** (☎ 708-848-1976; www.wrightplus.org; 951 Chicago Ave; adult/child 4-17yr $15/12; 🕑 11am-3pm Mon-Fri, to 4pm Sat & Sun). Tour frequency varies seasonally, from every two hours in winter to every 20 minutes on summer weekends.

Despite Hemingway calling Oak Park a 'village of wide lawns and narrow minds,' the town still pays homage to him at the **Ernest Hemingway Museum** (☎ 708-848-2222; www.ehfop.org; 200 N Oak Park Ave; adult/child $8/6; 🕑 1-5pm Sun-Fri, 10am-5pm Sat). Admission also includes access to **Hemingway's Birthplace** (339 N Oak Park Ave).

NORTHERN ILLINOIS

The highlight is the hilly northwest, where cottonwood trees, grazing horses and twisty roads over old stagecoach trails fill the pocket around Galena.

En route is Union, where the **Illinois Railway Museum** (☎ 815-923-4000; www.irm.org; US 20 to Union Rd; adult $8-12, child 3-11yr $4-8 depending upon season; 🕑 hours vary Apr-Oct) sends trainspotters into fits of ecstasy with 200 acres of locomotives. Thirty miles farther west is Rockford, which birthed the sock knitting machine and subsequent Sock Monkey stuffed toy. Early March brings the **Sock Monkey Festival** (☎ 815-397-9112; www.midwayvillage.com; adult/child $7/4), complete with monkey-making workshops.

Galena

Though just a speck on the map, Galena is the area's main attraction and a popular excursion from Chicago. The town spreads across wooded hillsides near the Mississippi River and is perfectly preserved, despite a slew of tourist-oriented antique shops and restaurants.

Galena's heyday was the mid-19th century, when industrial demands fueled the need for lead, which the region's mines had in spades. Galena (whose name means 'lead sulfide ore') became a center for the industry, and businesses, hotels and mansions shot up. The boom ended abruptly after the Civil War, and Galena remained all but deserted until restoration began in the 1960s.

The **visitors center** (☎ 815-777-4390, 877-464-2536; www.galena.org; 101 Bouthillier St; 🕑 9am-5pm) is on the eastern side of the Galena River, in the 1857 train depot. Get a map, leave your car in the lot ($3 per day) and explore on foot.

Elegant old Main St curves around the hillside and the historic heart of town. Among numerous sights is the **Ulysses S Grant Home** (☎ 815-777-3310; www.granthome.com; 500 Bouthillier

St; adult/child $4/2; 9am-4:45pm Wed-Sun Apr-Oct, reduced hrs Nov-Mar), which was a gift from local Republicans to the victorious general at the Civil War's end. Tours are provided (sometimes conducted by a guy who pretends he 'is' Grant). The elaborate Italianate **Belvedere Mansion** (815-777-0747; 1008 Park Ave; adult/child $12/6; 11am-4pm Sun-Fri, to 5pm Sat late May-Oct) hangs the green drapes from *Gone With the Wind*.

Outdoors enthusiasts should head to **Fever River Outfitters** (815-776-9425; www.feverriveroutfitters.com; 525 S Main St; 10am-5pm, closed Tue-Thu early Sep-late May), which rents canoes, kayaks, bicycles and snowshoes. It also offers guided tours, such as two-hour kayak trips ($45 per person, equipment included) on the Mississippi River's backwaters.

On weekend evenings, set out on the hokey but fun **Annie Wiggins Ghost Tour** (815-777-0336; www.anniewiggins.com; 1004 Park Ave; 1hr tour $10.75; Fri & Sat evenings May-Oct). Or visit local bison ranches, artisanal cheesemakers and herb farms on a culinary tour with **Learn Great Foods** (866-240-1650; www.learngreatfoods.com; tours $50-105). Excursions vary; check online for the schedule and locations.

Galena brims with old-school B&Bs. Most cost $100 to $200 nightly and fill up during weekends. The visitors center website provides contact information. Otherwise, there's **Grant Hills Motel** (877-421-0924; www.granthills.com; 9372 US 20; s/d $69/79;), a no-frills option 1.5 miles east of town, with countryside views and a horseshoe pitch. Presidential types can be like Grant and Lincoln and stay in the well-furnished rooms at **DeSoto House Hotel** (815-777-0090; www.desotohouse.com; 230 S Main St; r $128-200;), which dates from 1855.

Clarks Again (815-777-4407; 200 N Main St; mains $4-8; 6am-1:30pm) is ideal for biscuit-and-gravy breakfasts or lunchtime sandwiches. **111 Main** (815-777-8030; 111 N Main St; mains $13-24; 11am-9pm Sun-Thu, to 10pm Fri & Sat) makes meatloaf, pork-and-beans and other Midwestern favorites using ingredients sourced from local farms.

Quad Cities

South of Galena along a pretty stretch of the **Great River Road** (www.greatriverroad-illinois.org) is scenic **Mississippi Palisades State Park** (815-273-2731), a popular rock-climbing, hiking and camping area; pick up trail maps at the north entrance park office.

> **SCENIC DRIVES: STAGECOACH TRAIL & BLACKJACK RD**
>
> Two pretty drives roll out of Galena. The Stagecoach Trail, which morphs from Field St downtown, is a 26-mile ride on a narrow, twisty road en route to Warren. And yes, it really was part of the old stagecoach route between Galena and Chicago. Blackjack Rd is a hilly, 16-mile ridge road that ambles between Galena and Hanover, passing farms, cottonwood trees, cows and horses along the way. Take Fourth St from downtown, which becomes Blackjack Rd.

Further downstream, the **Quad Cities** (563-322-3911; www.visitquadcities.com) – Moline and Rock Island in Illinois, and Davenport and Bettendorf across the river in Iowa – make a surprisingly good stop. Rock Island has an appealing downtown (based at 3rd Ave and 18th St), with a couple of cafés, a lively pub and music scene, and a paddle wheeler casino. On the edge of town, **Black Hawk State Historic Site** (309-788-0177; www.blackhawkpark.org; 1510 46th Ave; sunrise-10pm) is a huge park with trails by the Rock River. Its **Hauberg Indian Museum** (309-788-9536; 1510 46th Ave, Watch Tower Lodge; admission free; 9am-noon & 1-5pm Wed-Sun) outlines the sorry story of Sauk leader Black Hawk and his people.

Out in the Mississippi River, the actual island of **Rock Island** once held a Civil War–era arsenal and POW camp. It now maintains an impressive arms museum, Civil War cemetery, national cemetery and visitor center for barge viewing. All are free, but bring photo ID as the island is still an active army facility.

Moline is the home of John Deere, the international farm machinery manufacturer, which has a museum/showroom in town. For Iowa-side attractions, see p671.

CENTRAL ILLINOIS

Abraham Lincoln and Route 66 sights are sprinkled liberally throughout central Illinois, which is otherwise farmland plain. East of Decatur, Arthur and Arcola are Amish centers.

Springfield

The small state capital has a serious obsession with Abraham Lincoln, who practiced law here from 1837 to 1861. Its Abe-related sights offer an in-depth look at the man and his turbulent times, which only some cynics find overdone. Many of the attractions are walkable downtown and cost little to nothing. Get your bearings with a map from the **visitors center** (☎ 800-545-7300; www.visitspringfieldillinois.com; 109 N 7th St; 🕑 8:30am-5pm Mon-Fri).

SIGHTS & ACTIVITIES

To visit the top-draw **Lincoln Home**, you must first pick up a ticket at the **Lincoln Home Visitors Center** (☎ 217-492-4150; www.nps.gov/liho; 426 S 7th St; admission free; 🕑 8:30am-5pm). A tour guide will then take you through the house where Abraham and Mary Lincoln lived from 1844 until they moved to the White House in 1861. You'll see considerably more than just the home, as the whole block has been preserved.

The **Lincoln Presidential Library & Museum** (☎ 217-558-8844; www.alplm.org; 212 N 6th St; adult/child 5-15yr $10/4; 🕑 9am-5pm) contains the most complete Lincoln collection in the world. Real-deal artifacts like Abe's shaving mirror and briefcase join whiz-bang exhibits and Disneyesque holograms that keep the kids agog.

After his assassination, Lincoln's body was returned to Springfield, where it lies today. The impressive **Lincoln's Tomb** sits in **Oak Ridge Cemetery** (☎ 217-782-2717; admission free; 🕑 9am-5pm Mar-Oct, to 4pm Nov-Feb), north of downtown. The gleam on the nose of Lincoln's bust, created by visitors' light touches, indicates the numbers of those who pay their respects here.

Standing a block apart are the noteworthy **Old State Capitol** (☎ 217-785-7960; cnr 5th & Adams Sts; suggested donation adult/child $4/2; 🕑 9am-5pm, closed Sun & Mon early Sep–mid-May) and **Lincoln-Herndon Law Offices** (cnr 6th & Adams Sts; same cost & hours). Both offer detailed tours covering Lincoln's early political life; the former takes in his dramatic pre–Civil War debates with Stephen Douglas.

Lincoln-free attractions include the pristine 1904 **Dana-Thomas House** (☎ 217-782-6776; www.dana-thomas.org; 301 E Lawrence St; adult/child $5/3; 🕑 9am-4pm Wed-Sun), one of Frank Lloyd Wright's Prairie-style masterworks, with an insightful tour; **Shea's Gas Station Museum** (☎ 217-522-0475; 2075 Peoria Rd; admission $2; 🕑 8am-4pm Tue-Fri, to noon Sat), with Route 66 pumps and signs; and the **Route 66 Drive In** (☎ 217-698-0066; www.route66-drivein.com; 1700 Recreation Dr; adult/child 4-12yr $6/4; 🕑 nightly Jun-Aug, weekends mid-Apr–May & Sep), with first-run flicks under the stars.

SLEEPING & EATING

Statehouse Inn (☎ 217-528-5100; www.thestatehouseinn.com; 101 E Adams St; r incl breakfast $95-145; P ❄ 💻 📶) It looks concrete-drab outside, but inside, the Statehouse shows its style. Comfy beds, large baths and free wired internet access fill the rooms; a mod bar and free wi-fi fill the lobby.

Inn at 835 (☎ 217-523-4466; www.innat835.com; 835 S 2nd St; r incl breakfast $125-175; P ❄) This 10-room B&B in an historic home offers the classiest digs in town.

Cozy Dog Drive In (☎ 217-525-1992; 2935 S 6th St; items $2-4; 🕑 8am-8pm Mon-Sat) All must stop to hail the corn dog's birthplace at the Cozy Dog. It's a Route 66 legend, with memorabilia and souvenirs in addition to the deeply fried main course.

Trout Lilly Cafe (217-391-0101; 218 S Sixth St; mains $4-6; 7am-4:30pm Mon-Fri, 9am-3pm Sat; 📶) Arty Trout Lilly serves quiche and muffins for breakfast, soups and sandwiches for lunch, and coffee anytime.

D'Arcy's Pint (217-492-8800; 661 W Stanford Ave; mains $6-12; 🕑 11am-10pm Mon-Thu, to 11pm Fri & Sat) This pub concocts Springfield's best 'horseshoe,' a local sandwich that consists of fried meat on toasted bread, mounded with french fries and smothered in melted cheese. It's 3 miles south of downtown.

GETTING THERE & AROUND

The downtown **Amtrak station** (☎ 217-753-2013; cnr 3rd & Washington Sts) has four to five trains daily to/from St Louis ($13 to $25, two hours) and Chicago ($18 to $50, 3½ hours).

Petersburg

When Lincoln first arrived in Illinois in 1831, he worked variously as a clerk, storekeeper and postmaster in the frontier village of New Salem before studying law and moving to Springfield. In Petersburg, 20 miles northwest of Springfield, **Lincoln's New Salem State Historic Site** (☎ 217-632-4000; www.lincolnsnewsalem.com; Hwy 97; suggested donation adult/child $4/2; 🕑 9am-5pm, closed Mon & Tue mid-Sep–Apr) reconstructs the village with building replicas, historical displays and costumed performances – a pretty informative and entertaining package.

SOUTHERN ILLINOIS

A surprise awaits near Collinsville, 8 miles east of East St Louis: classified as a Unesco World Heritage Site with the likes of

ROUTE 66: GET YOUR KICKS IN ILLINOIS

America's 'Mother Road' kicks off in Chicago on Adams St, just west of Michigan Ave. Before embarking, fuel up at Lou Mitchell's (p582) diner near Union Station. After all, it's about 300 miles from the start of Route 66 to the Missouri state line.

Sadly, most of the original Route 66 has been superseded by I-55 in Illinois, though the old road still exists in scattered sections often paralleling the interstate. Follow the brown 'Historic Route 66' signs to keep on track.

A true route highlight pops up soon after Joliet. Leave I-55 at Joliet Rd, following Hwy 53 southbound to Wilmington. Here pay your respects to the 28ft fiberglass spaceman known as the **Gemini Giant** outside the **Launching Pad Drive-In** (☎ 815-476-6535; 810 E Baltimore St; 10am-9:30pm). Motor 33 miles onward to **Odell** and its preserved **service station** (☎ 815-998-2133; 400 S West St; 11am-3pm most days), which doubles as a Route 66 souvenir shop.

Next come Pontiac and the tchotchke-and-photo-filled **Route 66 Hall of Fame** (☎ 815-844-4566; 110 W Howard St; admission free; 11am-3pm Mon-Fri, 10am-4pm Sat). Cruise by Bloomington-Normal and stop off 12 miles later in Shirley at **Funk's Grove** (☎ 309-874-3360; call for seasonal hrs), a pretty 19th-century maple syrup farm and nature preserve.

The state capital of Springfield harbors a trio of sights: **Shea's Gas Station Museum** (p589), the **Cozy Dog Drive In** (p589) and **Route 66 Drive In** (p589).

Further south, a good section of old Route 66 parallels I-55 through Litchfield. Grab a meal and piece of pie at the 1924 **Ariston Cafe** (☎ 217-324-2023; N Old Rte 66; mains $7-15; 11am-9pm Tue-Fri, 4-10pm Sat, 11am-8pm Sun). In Mt Olive, the 1926 **Soulsby Shell Station** is the route's oldest gas pump and is in the slow process of becoming a museum.

Finally, before driving west over the Mississippi River and into Missouri, detour off I-70 at exit 3. Follow Hwy 203 south, turn right at the first stoplight and drive west to the 1929 **Chain of Rocks Bridge** (sunrise-sunet). Only open to pedestrians and cyclists, this mile-long bridge has a historically famous 22-degree angled bend.

For more information, contact the **Route 66 Association of Illinois** (www.il66assoc.org) or **Illinois Route 66 Heritage Project** (www.illinoisroute66.org). Detailed driving directions are at www.historic66.com/illinois.

Stonehenge, the Acropolis and the Egyptian pyramids is **Cahokia Mounds State Historic Site** (☎ 618-346-5160; www.cahokiamounds.com; Collinsville Rd; suggested donation adult/child $4/2; visitors center 9am-5pm, grounds 8am-dusk). Cahokia protects the remnants of North America's largest prehistoric city (20,000 people, with suburbs), dating from AD 1200. While the 65 earthen mounds, including the enormous Monk's Mound and the 'Woodhenge' sun calendar, are not overwhelmingly impressive in themselves, the whole site is worth seeing. If you're approaching from the north, take exit 24 off I-255 S; if approaching from St Louis, take exit 6 off I-55/70.

Grafton lies at the confluence of the Illinois and Mississippi Rivers. The time-forgotten town of **Elsah**, a few miles east, makes a worthy stop. The Great River Road in this area is edged with cliffs and is especially scenic. Guests at **Bluffdale Vacation Farm** (☎ 217-983-2854; www.bluffdalevacationfarm.com; off Hwy 108; per person all-inclusive $99-122;) help with chores like grooming horses, collecting eggs and feeding ducks. It's a kid-friendly family favorite located in Eldred, north of Grafton.

An exception to the state's flat farmland is the green southernmost section, punctuated by rolling **Shawnee National Forest** (☎ 618-253-7114) and rocky outcroppings. The area has numerous state parks and recreation areas good for hiking, swimming, fishing and canoeing, particularly around **Little Grassy Lake** and **Devil's Kitchen**. And who would think that Florida-like swampland, complete with bald cypress trees and croaking bullfrogs, would be here? But it is, at **Cypress Creek National Wildlife Refuge** (☎ 618-634-2231; www.fws.gov/midwe st/cypresscreek).

Union County, near the state's southern tip, has wineries and orchards. Sample the wares on the 35-mile **Shawnee Hills Wine Trail** (☎ 618-967-4006; www.shawneewinetrail.com), which connects 12 vineyards. At little **Cairo**, on the Kentucky border, the Mississippi and Ohio Rivers converge.

INDIANA

The state revs up around the Indy 500 race, but otherwise it's about slow-paced pleasures in corn-stubbled Indiana: pie-eating in Amish Country, meditating in Bloomington's Tibetan temples and admiring the big architecture in small Columbus. For the record, folks have called Indianans 'Hoosiers' since the 1830s, but the word's origin is unknown. One theory is that early settlers knocking on a door were met with 'Who's here?' which soon became 'Hoosier.' It's certainly something to discuss with locals, perhaps over a traditional pork tenderloin sandwich.

Information

Indiana highway conditions (☎ 800-261-7623; www.in.gov/indot)
Indiana Office of Tourism (☎ 888-365-6946; www.visitindiana.com)
Indiana state park information (☎ 800-622-4931; www.in.gov/dnr/parklake) Park entry costs $2 per day by foot or bicycle, $5 to $10 by vehicle. Campsites cost $6 to $38; reservations accepted (☎ 866-622-6746; www.camp.in.gov).

INDIANAPOLIS

Clean-cut Indianapolis (aka Indy) won't win any excitement contests, but it is a perfectly pleasant place to ogle racecars and take a spin around the renowned speedway. The art museum and White River State Park have their merits, as do the Mass Ave and Broad Ripple 'hoods for eating and drinking.

INDIANA FACTS

Nicknames Hoosier State, Crossroads of America
Population 6.3 million
Area 36,420 sq miles
Capital city Indianapolis (population 795,460)
Sales tax 7%
Birthplace of Author Kurt Vonnegut (1922–2007), actor James Dean (1931–55), *Brady Bunch* mom Florence Henderson (b 1934), TV host David Letterman (b 1947), king of pop Michael Jackson (1958–2009)
Home of Farmers, corn
Famous for Indy 500 motor race, winning basketball teams, pork tenderloin sandwich
Official pie Sugar cream
Driving distances Indianapolis to Chicago 185 miles, Indianapolis to Bloomington 53 miles

History

The location of Indiana's capital, on flat cornfields in the geographical center of the state, was the result of a legislative compromise in 1820 between agricultural and industrial regions. Many early carmakers opened shop in the city, but were eclipsed by the Detroit giants. They did leave a lasting legacy though – a 2.5-mile test track, which became the site for the first Indianapolis 500 race in 1911 (won at an average speed of 75mph).

Orientation

Indianapolis is geometrically laid out with diagonal avenues superimposed on a grid layout. Everything radiates from the massively impressive Monument Circle. Meridian St divides streets east from west; Washington St divides them north from south. The Broad Ripple neighborhood is 6 miles north at College Ave and 62nd St.

Information

BOOKSTORES

Borders (☎ 317-972-8595; 11 S Meridian St; 🕑 8am-7pm Mon-Thu, to 8pm Fri & Sat, 11am-6pm Sun)

EMERGENCY & MEDICAL SERVICES

CVS (☎ 317-923-1491; 1744 N Illinois St; 🕑 24hr) Pharmacy.
Indiana University Medical Center (☎ 317-274-4705; 550 N University Blvd)

INTERNET ACCESS

The visitors center at the Artsgarden has free wi-fi, as do most coffeehouses.
Indianapolis Central Library (☎ 317-275-4100; 40 E Saint Clair St; 🕑 9am-9pm Mon-Thu, to 6pm Fri, to 5pm Sat, 1-5pm Sun) Log on for free downtown.

INTERNET RESOURCES & MEDIA

WFBQ-FM 94.7 is the main rock channel; NPR sits on the dial at WFYI-FM 90.1.
Gay Indy (www.gayindy.org) Gay and lesbian news and entertainment listings.
Indianapolis Star (www.indystar.com) The city's daily newspaper.
Nuvo (www.nuvo.net) Free, weekly alternative paper with the arts and music low-down.

TOURIST INFORMATION

Visitors center (☎ 317-624-2563, 800-323-4639; www.visitindy.com; Artsgarden Bldg, cnr Washington & Illinois Sts; 🕑 10am-9pm Mon-Sat, noon-6pm Sun)

Sights & Activities

Who knew you could hike in Indy? The **Indianapolis Hiking Club** (www.indyhike.org) leads free, 5- to 8-mile jaunts around downtown, Broad Ripple, rugged Eagle Creek Park and elsewhere. Check the website for times and departure points.

INDIANAPOLIS MOTOR SPEEDWAY

The Speedway, home of the **Indianapolis 500** motor race, is Indy's supersight. The **Hall of Fame Museum** (☎ 317-492-6784; www.indianapolismotorspeedway.com; 4790 W 16th St; adult/child 6-15yr $3/1; 🕑 9am-5pm) features 75 racing cars (including former winners), a 500lb Tiffany trophy and a track tour ($3 extra). OK, so you're on a bus for the latter and not even beginning to burn rubber at 37mph, but it's still fun to pretend. **Tickets** (☎ 317-484-6700, 800-822-4639; www.imstix.com; $25-150) are hard to come by for the big event, which is held on Memorial Day weekend and attended by 450,000 crazed fans. Tickets for pre-race trials and practices are more likely (and cheaper). Other races at the Speedway are the NASCAR **Brickyard 400** in late July and **Indianapolis MotoGP** in late August. It's located 7.5 miles northwest of downtown.

The city celebrates the Indy 500 throughout May with the **500 Festival** (☎ 317-614-6400; www.500festival.com; tickets from $7). Events include a parade comprised of racecar drivers and a community shindig at the racetrack.

WHITE RIVER STATE PARK

Sprawling White River State Park, located at the edge of downtown, contains several worthwhile sights. The adobe **Eiteljorg Museum of American Indians & Western Art** (☎ 317-636-9378; www.eiteljorg.org; 500 W Washington St; adult/child 5-17yr $8/5; 🕑 10am-5pm Tue-Sat, noon-5pm Sun, plus Mon in summer) features Native American basketry, pots and masks, as well as a realistic/romantic Western painting collection with works by Frederic Remington and Georgia O'Keeffe.

The **NCAA Hall of Champions** (☎ 800-735-6222; www.ncaahallofchampions.org; 700 W Washington St; adult/child 6-18yr $5/3; 🕑 10am-5pm Tue-Sat, noon-5pm Sun, plus Mon in summer) reveals the country's fascination with college sports. The NCAA renovated the museum recently, making it much more interactive, so you can now shoot free throws or climb onto a swimming platform à la Michael Phelps. You'll probably find most Hoosiers hovering around the basketball exhibits, as locals are renowned hoop-ball fanatics.

Other park highlights include gardens, a zoo, a canal walk and a military Medal of Honor Memorial.

A few miles further west, at the **Indiana Medical History Museum** (☎ 317-635-7329; www.imhm.org; 3045 Vermont St; adult/child under 19yr $5/1; 🕑 10am-4pm Thu-Sat), a guide leads visitors through century-old pathology labs. The highlight, especially for zombies, is the room full of brains in jars. There's also a healing herb garden to walk through.

INDIANAPOLIS MUSEUM OF ART

This **museum** (☎ 317-920-2660; www.imamuseum.org; 4000 Michigan Rd; admission free; 🕑 11am-5pm Tue-Sat, to 9pm Thu & Fri, noon-5pm Sun) has a terrific collection of European art (especially Turner and some post-Impressionists), African tribal art, South Pacific art and Chinese works. The museum is linked to **Oldfields – Lilly House & Gardens** (🕑 same as museum), the 26-acre estate of the Lilly pharmaceutical family, and **Fairbanks Art & Nature Park**, which will feature sculptures and audio installations amid 100 acres of woodlands when it opens in mid-to-late 2010.

MONUMENTS

At Monument Circle, the city center is marked by the jaw-dropping 284ft **Soldiers & Sailors Monument**. For a bizarre (and cramped) experience, take the elevator ($1) to the top. Beneath is the **Civil War Museum** (☎ 317-232-7615; admission free; 🕑 10:30am-5:30pm Wed-Sun), which neatly outlines the conflict and Indiana's abolition position. A few blocks north, the **World War Memorial** (cnr Vermont & Meridian Sts) is another impressively beefy monument.

Sleeping

Hotels cost more and are usually full during race weeks in May, July and August. Add 16% tax to the prices listed here. Look for low-cost motels off I-465, the freeway that circles Indianapolis.

Indy Hostel (☎ 317-727-1696; www.indyhostel.us; 4903 Winthrop Ave; weekday/weekend dm $25/29, r $58/64; P 💻 Wi-Fi) This small, friendly hostel offers two dorm rooms (one six-bed coed room, and one four-bed female room) and a private room. The Monon Trail runs nearby (bike rental per day $5). It's located 6 miles from downtown, by Broad Ripple.

Stone Soup (☎ 866-639-9550; www.stonesoupinn.com; 1304 N Central Ave; r incl breakfast $85-145; P ⊠ ❄ Wi-Fi) This nine-room B&B sprawls throughout a rambling house filled with antiques and stained glass. The less-expensive rooms share a bath.

Hampton Inn (☎ 317-261-1200; www.hamptondt.com; 105 S Meridian St; r incl breakfast $139-169; P ✕ 💻 📶) Handsome-looking public areas, good amenities, plush beds and the prime downtown location add value to the cookie-cutter rooms. Parking is $14.

Conrad Indianapolis (☎ 317-713-5000; www.conradindianapolis.com; 50 W Washington St; r from $200; P ✕ 💻 📶 🏊) This is Indy's top address: a 241-room beauty near the sports venues. Spa services, 42-inch plasma screen TVs and bath telephones are part of the package. Wi-fi costs $12.95, and parking is $32.

Eating

Central Massachusetts Ave ('Mass Ave' to locals) is bounteous when the stomach growls. The Broad Ripple area, 6 miles north at College Ave and 62nd St, has pubs and eateries of numerous nationalities. At lunch it's hard to beat the cheap eats at the old **City Market** (222 E Market St; 🕑 6am-6pm Mon-Fri, 11am-3pm Sat), which is two blocks east of Monument Circle, and filled with ethnic food stalls and local produce vendors.

Mug 'N' Bun (☎ 317-244-5669; 5211 W 10th St; mains $3-5; 🕑 10:30am-10pm Mon-Sat, 11am-10pm Sun) The mugs are frosted and filled with a wonderful home-brewed root beer. The buns contain burgers, chili dogs and juicy pork tenderloins. And don't forget the fried macaroni-and-cheese wedges. At this vintage drive-in near the Speedway, you are served – where else? – in your car.

Monon Coffee Company (☎ 317-255-0510; 920 E Westfield Blvd; items $3-6; 🕑 6:30am-8pm Mon-Thu, to 10pm Fri, 7am-10pm Sat, 8am-8pm Sun; 📶) This locally owned, art-infused shop takes its lattes seriously, as well as its fruit smoothies, sandwiches and baked goods. It's located in Broad Ripple, just off the Monon Trail.

Shapiro's Deli (☎ 317-631-4041; 808 S Meridian St; sandwiches $8-12; 🕑 6:30am-8pm; 📶) Chomp into a towering corned beef or peppery pastrami sandwich on homemade bread, and then chase it with fat slices of chocolate cake or fruit pie.

Bazbeaux (☎ 317-636-7662; 334 Massachusetts Ave; sandwiches $6-9, large pizza $19-23; 🕑 11am-10pm Sun-Thu, to 11pm Fri & Sat) A local favorite, Bazbeaux offers an eclectic pizza selection, like the 'Tchoupitoulas,' topped with Cajun shrimp and andouille sausage. Muffalettas, stromboli and Belgian beer are some of the other unusual offerings.

Drinking & Entertainment

Downtown and Mass Ave have some good watering holes; Broad Ripple has several.

BARS & NIGHTCLUBS

Slippery Noodle Inn (☎ 317-631-6974; 372 S Meridian St) Downtown's Noodle is the oldest bar in the state, and has seen action as a whorehouse, slaughterhouse, gangster hangout and Underground Railroad station; currently, it's one of the best blues clubs in the country. There's live music nightly, and it's cheap.

Rathskeller (☎ 317-636-0396; 401 E Michigan St) Quaff German brews at the outdoor beer garden's picnic tables in summer, or at the deer-head–lined indoor beer hall once winter strikes. The six-beer sampler gets you acquainted with the wares. It is located in the historic Athenaeum building near Mass Ave.

Plump's Last Shot (☎ 317-257-5867; 6416 Cornell Ave) Bobby Plump inspired the iconic movie *Hoosiers*. He's the kid who swished in the last-second shot, so his tiny school beat the 'big city' school in the 1950s state basketball championship. There's sports memorabilia everywhere, and sometimes Bobby himself is on site. It's located in a big house in Broad Ripple overlooking the Monon Trail – great for people-watching and sipping a cold one on the dog-friendly patio.

SPORTS

The motor races aren't the only coveted spectator events. The NFL's Colts win football games under a huge retractable roof at **Lucas Oil Stadium** (☎ 317-262-3389; www.colts.com; 500 S Capitol Ave). Basketball is huge in Indiana, and **Conseco Fieldhouse** (☎ 317-917-2500; www.nba.com/pacers; 125 S Pennsylvania St) is ground zero, where the NBA's Pacers make it happen.

Getting There & Around

The new **Indianapolis International Airport** (IND; ☎ 317-487-7243; www.indianapolisairport.com; 7800 Col H Weir Cook Memorial Dr) is 16 miles southwest of town. The Washington bus (8) runs between the airport and downtown ($1.75, 50 minutes); the Green Line bus does it quicker ($7, 20 minutes). A cab to downtown costs about $30.

Greyhound (☎ 317-267-3076; www.greyhound.com) shares **Union Station** (350 S Illinois St) with Amtrak.

RONALD AUKERMAN

Ronald Aukerman, age 93, a retired grain-storage company owner and lifelong resident of Amboy, Indiana (population 400). He passed away shortly after this interview.

What's the biggest change in your town over the years? The stores on Main St are all gone now. Small towns like ours are having trouble. Kids can't get jobs out here, and they have to move away. Or join the army. It's all old men and old women left now, like a retirement community.

What's the most defining characteristic about people from Indiana? We're halfway between hillbillies and city people, though some of the farmers are pretty sharp. My friend Wendell, he's always got 5000 hogs on his farm. Slaughter time comes around, he sells them, buys 5000 more. That's a lot of money. And the price of corn is going up because of ethanol. A bunch of little towns around here now have ethanol plants. They buy up about a third of the corn crop. Of course, that means there's less corn to feed the hogs, so the farmers have to pay more to get their feed, and so the price of meat goes up.

You've been to India, the Middle East and all over Europe. When you travel, what do you miss most about home? Sometimes I think, 'I can't wait to get home to see some grain growing or green pasture fields.'

It goes to Cincinnati ($18 to $26, two hours) and Chicago ($25 to $38, 3½ hours). **Megabus** (☎ 877-462-6342; www.megabus.com/us) stops at 200 E Washington St, and is often cheaper.

IndyGo (☎ 317-635-3344; www.indygo.net; fares $1.75) runs the local buses. Bus 17 goes to Broad Ripple. The Red Line shuttle circles the downtown sights. Service is minimal during weekends.

Amtrak (☎ 317-263-0550; www.amtrak.com) chugs into **Union Station** (350 S Illinois St). One train daily goes to Chicago ($19 to $24, five hours), and three trains a week go to Cincinnati ($21 to $30, 3½ hours).

For a taxi, call **Yellow Cab** (☎ 317-487-7777).

AROUND INDIANAPOLIS

Bluegrass music, architectural hot spots, Tibetan temples and James Dean all furrow into the farmland around here.

Fairmount

This small town, north on Hwy 9, is the birthplace of James Dean, one of the original icons of cool. Fans should head directly to the **Historical Museum** (☎ 765-948-4555; www.jamesdeanartifacts.com; 203 E Washington St; admission free; ⏲ 10am-5pm Mon-Sat, noon-5pm Sun, closed Dec-Feb) to see Dean's bongo drums, among other artifacts. This is also the place to pick up a free map that will guide you to sites like the farmhouse where Jimmy grew up and his red-lipstick–kissed grave site. The museum sells Dean posters, zippo lighters and other memorabilia, and sponsors the annual **James Dean Festival** (admission free; late Sep), when as many as 50,000 fans pour in for four days of music and rebelry. The privately owned **James Dean Gallery** (☎ 765-948-3326; www.jamesdeangallery.com; 425 N Main St; admission free; ⏲ 9am-6pm) has more memorabilia a few blocks away.

If James Dean was the embodiment of cool, surely his polar opposite is Dan Quayle, who resided a mere 30 miles north on Hwy 9 in Huntington. The USA's 44th vice president (you spell potato, he spells potatoe) is treated reverentially, along with the country's other second fiddles, at the **Dan Quayle Center & Vice Presidential Museum** (☎ 260-356-6356; www.quaylemuseum.org; 815 Warren St; adult/child 7-17yr $3/1; ⏲ 9:30am-4:30pm Mon-Fri). Indiana is called 'the mother of vice presidents' for the five veeps it has spawned.

Columbus

When you think of the USA's great architectural cities – Chicago, New York, Washington DC – Columbus, Indiana, doesn't quite leap to mind, but it should. Located 40 miles south of Indianapolis on I-65, Columbus is a remarkable gallery of physical design. Since the 1940s the city and its leading corporations have commissioned some of the world's best architects, including Eero Saarinen, Richard Meier and IM Pei, to create both public and private buildings. Stop at the **visitors center** (☎ 812-378-2622, 800-468-6564; www.columbus.in.us; 506 5th St; ⏲ 9am-5pm Mon-Sat, noon-4pm Sun Mar-Nov, closed Sun Dec-Feb) to pick up a self-guided tour map ($2) or join a bus tour (adult/student/child $12/7/3); tours begin at 10am Monday to Friday, 10am and 2pm Saturday, and 1pm

Sunday. Over 70 notable buildings and pieces of public art are spread over a wide area (car required), but about 15 diverse works can be seen on foot downtown. **Hotel Indigo** (☎ 812-375-9100; www.hotelindigo.com; 400 Brown St; r from $117-159;), also downtown, offers the chain's trademark mod, cheery rooms, plus a fluffy white dog who works as the lobby ambassador (he even has his own email address).

Nashville

Gentrified and antique-filled, this 19th-century town west of Columbus on Hwy 46 is now a bustling tourist center, at its busiest in fall when leaf-peepers pour in. The **visitors center** (☎ 800-753-3255; www.browncounty.com; 10 N Van Buren St; 9am-6pm Mon-Thu, to 8pm Fri & Sat, 10am-5pm Sun) provides maps and online coupons.

Beyond gallery browsing, Nashville is the jump-off point to **Brown County State Park** (☎ 812-988-6406; www.browncountystatepark.com; campsites $13-26, cabins from $69), a 15,700-acre stand of oak, hickory and birch trees, where trails give hikers, mountain bikers and horseback riders access to the area's green hill country.

Among several B&Bs, central **Artists Colony Inn** (☎ 812-988-0600, 800-737-0255; www.artistscolonyinn.com; 105 S Van Buren St; r incl breakfast $100-170;) stands out for its spiffy rooms and rooftop hot tub. The **dining room** (mains $8-15; 7:30am-8pm Sun-Thu, to 9pm Fri & Sat) offers traditional Hoosier fare, such as catfish and pork tenderloins.

As with Nashville (p423), Tennessee, Nashville, Indiana, enjoys country music, and bands play regularly at several venues. To shake a leg, mosey into **Mike's Music & Dance Barn** (☎ 812-988-8636; www.thedancebarn; 2277 Hwy 46; Thu-Mon). The **Bill Monroe Museum** (☎ 812-988-6422; 5163 Rte 135 N, Bean Blossom; adult/child under 13yr $4/free; 9am-5pm daily May-Oct, 10am-4pm Tue-Sat Nov-Apr) hails the bluegrass hero 5 miles north of town.

Bloomington

Lively and lovely Bloomington, 53 miles south of Indianapolis via Hwy 37, is the home of Indiana University. The town centers on Courthouse Sq, surrounded by restaurants, bars, bookshops and the historic facade of Fountain Sq Mall. The super-stocked **visitors center** (☎ 812-334-8900; www.visitbloomington.com; 2855 N Walnut St; 8:30am-5pm Mon-Fri, 9am-4pm Sat) is a few miles north of the town center. Nearly everything else is walkable.

On the expansive campus, the **Art Museum** (☎ 812-855-5445; www.indiana.edu/~iuam; 1133 E 7th St; admission free; 10am-5pm Tue-Sat, noon-5pm Sun, reduced hours summer), designed by IM Pei, has an excellent collection of African art, as well as European and US paintings.

The colorful, prayer flag–covered **Tibetan Cultural Center** (☎ 812-331-0014; www.tibetancc.com; 3655 Snoddy Rd; admission free; 10am-4pm) and stupa, as well as the **Dagom Gaden Tensung Ling Monastery** (☎ 812-339-0857; www.dgtlmonastery.org; 102 Clubhouse Dr; admission free; 9am-6pm), indicate Bloomington's significant Tibetan presence. Both offer free teachings and meditation sessions; check the websites for weekly schedules.

If you arrive in mid-April and wonder why an extra 20,000 people are hanging out in town, it's for the **Little 500** (☎ 812-855-1103; www.iusf.indiana.edu; tickets $25). Lance Armstrong called the bike race, where amateurs ride one-speed Schwinns for 200 laps around a quarter-mile track, 'the coolest event I ever attended.' Look for cheap lodgings along N Walnut St near Hwy 46. **Grant Street Inn** (☎ 800-328-4350; www.grantstinn.com; 310 N Grant St; r incl breakfast $129-189;) fluffs up 24 rooms in a Victorian house and annex near campus.

For a town of its size, Bloomington offers a mind-blowing array of ethnic restaurants – everything from Burmese to Eritrean to Mexican. Browse Kirkwood Ave and E 4th St. **Anyetsang's Little Tibet** (☎ 812-331-0122; 415 E 4th St; mains $9-11; 11am-9:30pm, closed Tue) offers specialties from the Himalayan homeland. Pubs on Kirkwood Ave, close to the university, cater to the student crowd. **Nick's English Hut** (☎ 812-332-4040; 423 E Kirkwood Ave) pours not only for students and professors but also for Kurt Vonnegut, Dylan Thomas and Barack Obama.

SOUTHERN INDIANA

The pretty hills, caves, rivers and utopian history of southern Indiana mark it as a completely different region from the flat and industrialized north.

Ohio River

The Indiana segment of the 981-mile Ohio River marks the state's southern border. From tiny Aurora, in the southeastern corner of the state, Hwys 56, 156, 62 and 66, known collectively as the **Ohio River Scenic Route**, wind through a varied landscape.

Coming from the east, a perfect place to stop is little **Madison**, a well-preserved river settlement from the mid-19th century where architectural beauties beckon genteelly from the streets. At the **visitors center** (☎ 812-265-2956; www.visitmadison.org; 601 W First St; 9am-5pm Mon-Fri, 9am-4pm Sat, 11am-4pm Sun), pick up a walking tour brochure, which includes the James Lanier Mansion, a designated landmark overlooking the river.

Madison has motels around its edges, as well as several B&Bs; the visitors center can help with bookings. Large, wooded **Clifty Falls State Park** (☎ 812-273-8885; campsites $17-26), off Hwy 56 and a couple of miles west of town, has camping, hiking trails, views and waterfalls. Main St, with its numerous antique stores, also has places for a bite. **Cafe Camille** (☎ 812-265-5626; 149 E Main St; mains $3-7; 7am-3pm Mon-Thu, to 4pm Fri-Sun) is ideal for breakfast or lunch.

In Clarksville, **Falls of the Ohio State Park** (☎ 812-280-9970; www.fallsoftheohio.org; 201 W Riverside Dr) has only rapids, no falls, but is of interest for its 386-million-year-old fossil beds. The **interpretive center** (adult/child $4/1, plus $1 Fri-Sun; 9am-5pm Mon-Sat, 1-5pm Sun) explains it all. The rest of town and adjacent New Albany, the largest Indiana town in the region, aren't much, with one exception: **Rich O's Public House/New Albanian Brewing Company** (☎ 812-949-2804; 3312 Plaza Dr, New Albany; from 3pm Mon-Thu, from 1pm Fri & Sat) and its fine suds selection.

Scenic Hwy 62 heads west and leads to the Lincoln Hills and southern Indiana's limestone caves. A plunge into **Wyandotte Caves** (www.wyandottecaves.com; 7315 S Wyandotte Cave Rd; Mar-Oct), near Leavenworth, is highly recommended – though at the time of writing they were undergoing renovation and closed for tours; check the website for updates. **Marengo Cave** (☎ 812-365-2705, 888-702-2837; www.marengocave.com; 9am-6pm year-round), north on Hwy 66, is another standout. It offers a 40-minute tour (adult/child four to 12 years $12.75/6.75), 70-minute tour ($14.50/7.50) and combination tour ($21/11) walking past stalagmites and other ancient formations. The same group operates **Cave Country Canoes** (☎ 812-365-2705, 888-702-2837; www.cavecountrycanoes.com; May-Oct) in nearby Milltown, with half-day ($22), full-day ($25) or longer trips on the scenic Blue River; keep an eye out for river otters and rare hellbender salamanders.

Four miles south of Dale, off I-64, is the **Lincoln Boyhood National Memorial** (☎ 812-937-4541; www.nps.gov/libo; adult/child $3/free; 8am-5pm), where young Abe lived from age seven to 21. This isolated but good site also includes admission to a working **pioneer farm** (8am-5pm mid-Apr–Sep). Further west, on the Ohio River, **Evansville** is one of the state's largest cities; its Riverside Historic District retains many early 19th-century mansions.

Wabash River

In southwest Indiana, the Wabash River forms the border with Illinois. Beside it, south of I-64, captivating **New Harmony** is the site of two early communal-living experiments and is worth a visit. In the early 19th century a German Christian sect, the Harmonists, developed a sophisticated town here while awaiting the Second Coming. Later it was acquired by the British utopian Robert Owen. Learn more and pick up a walking tour map at the angular **Atheneum Visitors Center** (☎ 812-682-4488, 800-231-2168; www.newharmony.org; cnr North & Arthur Sts; 9:30am-5pm).

Today New Harmony retains an air of contemplation, if not otherworldliness, which you can experience at its newer attractions, such as the templelike Roofless Church and the Labyrinth, a maze symbolizing the spirit's quest. The town has a couple of guesthouses and camping at **Harmonie State Park** (☎ 812-682-4821; campsites $17-25). Pop into **Main Cafe** (☎ 812-682-3370; 508 Main St; mains $4-7; 5:30am-1pm Mon-Fri) for a ham-bean-and-cornbread lunch, but save room for the coconut cream pie.

NORTHERN INDIANA

The truck-laden I-80/I-90 tollways cut across Indiana's northern section. Parallel US 20 is slower and cheaper, but not much more attractive. Classic car connoisseurs should dip south on I-69 to the town of **Auburn**, where the Cord Company produced the USA's favorite cars in the 1920s and '30s. The **Auburn Cord Duesenberg Museum** (☎ 260-925-1444; www.automobilemuseum.org; 1600 S Wayne St; adult/child $10/6; 9am-5pm) has a wonderful display of early roadsters in a beautiful art-deco setting. Next door are the vintage rigs of the **National Automotive and Truck Museum** (☎ 260-925-9100; www.natmus.org; 1000 Gordon Buehrig Pl; adult/child $7/4; 9am-5pm).

Amish Country

Northwest of Auburn, around Shipshewana and Middlebury, is the USA's third-largest Amish community. Horses and buggies clip clop by, and long-bearded men hand-plow the tidy fields. Get situated with maps from the **Elkhart County CVB** (☎ 800-517-9739; www.amishcountry.org). Better yet, simply pick a backroad and head down it. Often you'll see families selling beeswax candles, quilts and fresh produce on their porch, which beats the often-touristy shops and restaurants on the main roads.

our pick Village Inn (☎ 574-825-2043; 105 S Main St; pie $2, mains $3-7; 5am-8pm Mon-Fri, to 2pm Sat), in Middlebury, sells real-deal pies; bonneted women in pastel dresses come in at 4:30am to bake the flaky wares. It's best to arrive early. Note most places close on Sunday.

South Bend

The city of South Bend is another ex-carmaker. Stop at the **Studebaker National Museum** (☎ 574-235-9714; www.studebakermuseum.org; 201 S Chapin St; adult/child 7-18yr $8/5; 10am-5pm Mon-Sat, noon-5pm Sun) and take a gander at the gorgeous 1956 Packard and many other classic beauties. South Bend is better known as the home of the University of Notre Dame, which is famous for its 'Fighting Irish' football team. To tour the pretty campus with its gold-domed administration building, Lourdes Grotto Replica and *Touchdown Jesus* painting, start at the **visitors center** (☎ 574-631-5726; www.nd.edu/visitors; 111 Eck Center; 8am-5pm Mon-Fri, noon-4pm Sat & Sun). US residents especially will be interested in seeing the downtown **College Football Hall of Fame** (☎ 574-235-9999; www.collegefootball.org; 111 S St Joseph St; adult/child 5-12yr $12/5; 10am-5pm Mon-Thu, 9am-6pm Fri & Sat, 9am-5pm Sun Jun-Nov, 10am-5pm daily Dec-May).

Indiana Dunes

Hugely popular on summer days with sunbathers from Chicago and South Bend, **Indiana Dunes National Lakeshore** (☎ 219-926-7561, 800-959-9174; www.nps.gov/indu; campsites $15; beaches 7am-sunset, park 7am-11pm) stretches along 21 miles of Lake Michigan shoreline. In addition to its beaches, the area is noted for its plant variety: everything from cactus to pine trees sprouts here. Hiking trails crisscross the dunes and woodlands, winding by a peat bog, a still-operating 1870s farm and a blue heron rookery, among other payoffs. Mt Baldy is the top dune to climb. Oddly, all this natural bounty lies smack-dab next to smoke-belching factories, which you'll also see at various vantage points. Stop at the **Dorothy Buell Visitor Center** (☎ 219-926-7561, 800-959-9174; Hwy 49; 8:30am-6:30pm Jun-Aug, to 4:30 Sep-May) for beach details, a schedule of ranger-guided walks and activities, and to pick up hiking, biking and birding maps. Or contact the **Porter County Convention & Visitors Bureau** (☎ 800-283-8687; www.indianadunes.com) to order the guides ahead of time.

Indiana Dunes State Park (☎ 219-926-1952; www.dnr.in.gov/parklake; per walk-in/car $2/10, campsites $17-28; beaches 9am-sunset, park 7am-11pm) is a 2100-acre, shoreside pocket within the national lakeshore; it's located at the end of Hwy 49, near Chesterton. It has more amenities, but it's also more regulated and crowded – and charges an entry fee. Wintertime brings out the cross-country skiers; summertime brings out the hikers. Seven trails zigzag over the landscape; No 4 up Mt Tom rewards with Chicago skyline views.

It's easy to reach the Dunes from Chicago. Driving takes one hour. The South Shore Metra train (see p586) departs from Randolph St/Millennium Park station downtown, and it's about 1¼ hours to the Dune Park or Beverly Shores stops (note both stations are a 1½-mile walk from the beach).

Other than a couple of beachfront snack bars, you won't find much to eat in the parks, so stop at homey, Italian **Lucrezia** (☎ 219-926-5829; 428 S Calumet Rd; mains $17-27; 11am-10pm Sun-Thu, to 11pm Fri & Sat) in Chesterton or the sophisticated foodie favorite **Miller Bakery Cafe** (☎ 219-938-2229; 555 Lake St; lunch $11-16, dinner mains $18-29; 11:30am-2pm Tue-Fri, 5-9pm Tue-Thu, to 10pm Fri & Sat, 4-8pm Sun) in Miller Beach.

Near Illinois, the steel cities of **Gary** and **East Chicago** present some of the bleakest urban landscapes anywhere. Taking the train (Amtrak or South Shore line) through here will get you up close and personal with the industrial underbelly.

OHIO

All right, time for your Ohio quiz. In the Buckeye State you can 1) watch butter churn on an Amish farm; 2) party your ass off at an island resort; 3) lose your stomach on one of the world's fastest roller coasters; 4) rock climb among streams and caves; 5) suck down a dreamy creamy milk shake fresh from a working dairy; or 6) examine a mondo, mysterious snake built into the earth.

OHIO FACTS

Nickname Buckeye State
Population 11.5 million
Area 44,825 sq miles
Capital city Columbus (population 747,755)
Other cities Cleveland (population 444,313), Cincinnatti (population 332,252)
Sales tax 5.5%
Birthplace of Inventor Thomas Edison (1847–1931), author Toni Morrison (b 1931), entrepreneur Ted Turner (b 1938), filmmaker Steven Spielberg (b 1947)
Home of Cows, roller coasters, aviation pioneers Wright Brothers
Famous for First airplane, first pro baseball team, deciding the outcome of presidential elections
State rock song 'Hang On Sloopy'
Driving distances Cleveland to Columbus 142 miles, Columbus to Cincinnati 108 miles

And the answer is…all of these. It hurts locals' feelings when visitors think the only thing to do here is tip over cows. C'mon, give Ohio a chance. Besides these activities, you can partake in a five-way in Cincinnati and rock out in Cleveland.

Information

Ohio Division of Travel and Tourism (☎ 800-282-5393; www.discoverohio.com)
Ohio highway conditions (www.buckeyetraffic.org)
Ohio state park information (☎ 614-265-6561; www.ohiodnr.com/parks) State parks are free to visit; some have free wi-fi. Campsites cost $18 to $35; reservations accepted (☎ 866-644-6727; www.ohio.reserveworld.com; fee $8.25).

CLEVELAND

Does it or does it not rock? That is the question. Drawing from its roots as a working man's town, Cleveland has toiled hard in recent years to prove it does. Step one was to control the urban decay/river-on-fire thing – the Cuyahoga River was once so polluted that it actually burned. Check. Step two was to bring a worthy attraction to town, say the Rock and Roll Hall of Fame. Check. Step three was to get grub beyond steak-and-potatoes. Check. So can Cleveland finally wipe the sweat from its brow? Check.

History

Surveyed in 1796, Cleveland boomed after the Civil War by using iron from the upper Great Lakes and coal transported along the Cuyahoga River to become one of the USA's top steel producers. Later, industrial wealth (think Rockefeller) bankrolled cultural aspirations, and the city still surprises with its world-class museums and performing arts.

Like neighboring Detroit, Cleveland has had its share of urban blight and industrial woes over the years. The recent global economic crisis hit it hard, and one out of every 13 houses stood vacant at the time of writing.

Orientation & Information

Cleveland's center is Public Sq, dominated by the conspicuous Terminal Tower. Ontario St is the east–west dividing line.

Most of Cleveland's attractions are downtown or at University Circle (the area around Case Western Reserve University, Cleveland Clinic and other institutions). Ohio City and Tremont, near downtown, are good neighborhoods for eating and drinking, as are Little Italy and Coventry, near the university.

Information

BOOKSTORES

Mac's (☎ 216-321-2665; 1820 Coventry Rd, Coventry; 🕒 10am-9pm Mon-Thu, to 10pm Fri & Sat, 11am-8pm Sun) Attached to Tommy's (p601).

EMERGENCY & MEDICAL SERVICES

MetroHealth Medical Center (☎ 216-778-7800; 2500 MetroHealth Dr)
Rape crisis (☎ 216-619-6192)

INTERNET ACCESS

Many of Cleveland's public places have free wi-fi, such as Public Sq and University Circle.

INTERNET RESOURCES & MEDIA

Tune into WCPN-FM 90.3 for NPR, or WNCX-FM 98.5 for rock.

Gay People's Chronicle (www.gaypeopleschronicle.com) A weekly publication with entertainment listings, distributed free throughout town.
Plain Dealer (www.cleveland.com) The city's daily newspaper, with a good Friday entertainment section.
Scene (www.clevescene.com) A weekly entertainment paper; out on Wednesday.

TOURIST INFORMATION

The **Cleveland CVB** (☎ 800-321-1001; www.positivelycleveland.com) operates a visitors center in the

Higbee Building (☎ 216-875-6680; 100 Public Sq, Suite 100; 9am-5pm Mon-Fri, plus 10am-3pm Sat & Sun Jun-Aug).

Sights & Activities

There's not a ton to do sight-wise; the Rock and Roll Hall of Fame and art museum are the big attractions.

DOWNTOWN

Cleveland's top attraction, the **Rock and Roll Hall of Fame & Museum** (☎ 216-781-7625, 888-764-7625; www.rockhall.com; 1 Key Plaza; adult/child 9-12yr $22/13; 10am-5:30pm, to 9pm Wed year-round, to 9pm Sat Jun-Aug) is more than a collection of memorabilia, though it does have Jimi Hendrix' Stratocaster, Janis Joplin's psychedelic Porsche and Ray

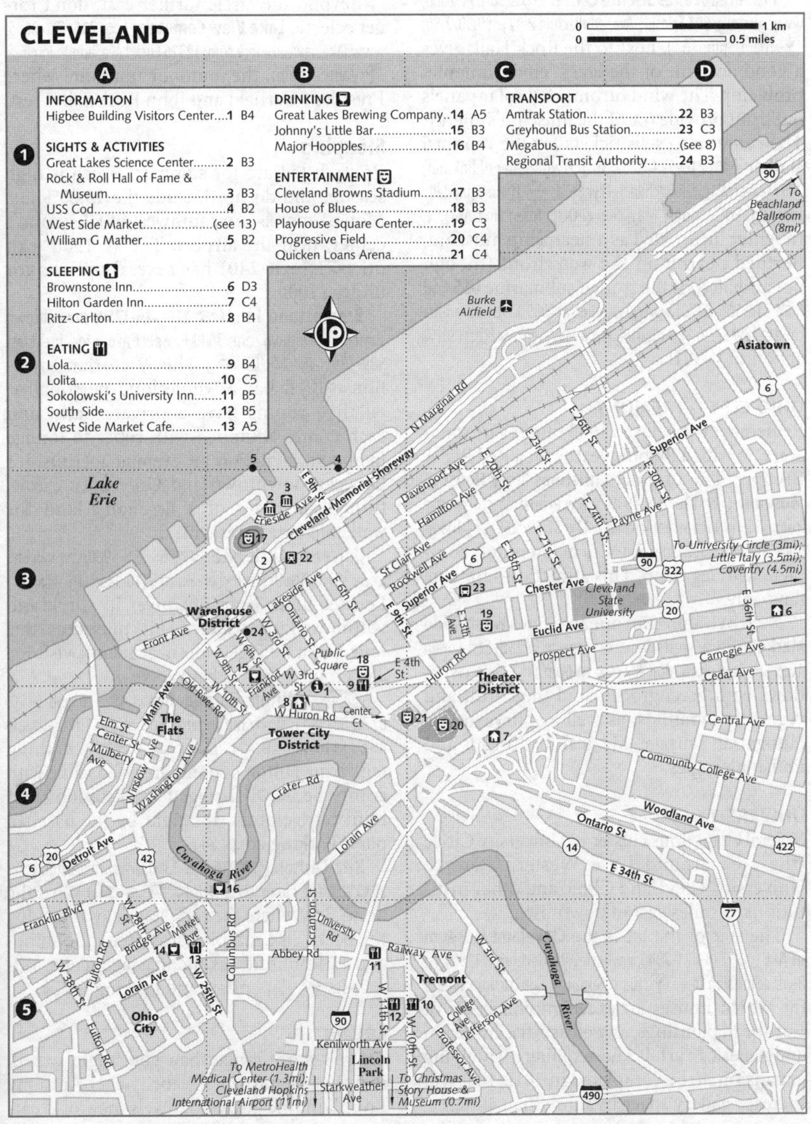

Charles' sunglasses. Interactive multimedia exhibits trace the history and social context of rock music and the performers who created it. Why is the museum in Cleveland? Because this is the hometown of Alan Freed, the disk jockey who popularized the term 'rock 'n' roll' in the early 1950s, and because the city lobbied hard and paid big. Be prepared for crowds.

The **Great Lakes Science Center** (☎ 216-694-2000; www.glsc.org; 601 Erieside Ave; adult/child 2-17yr $9.50/7.50; 🕑 10am-5pm; 👶), next to the Rock Hall, gives a good account of the lakes' environmental problems. The wind turbine and solar panels out front provide 6% of the museum's energy. The center also sells tickets for the **William G Mather** (☎ 216-574-6262; http://wgmather.nhlink.net; 305 Mather Way; adult/child 5-17yr $6/4; 🕑 10am-5pm daily Jun-Aug, Fri-Sun only May, Sep & Oct, closed Nov-Apr), a freighter incarnated as a steamship museum. Berthed nearby on the waterfront (though not affiliated) is the storied submarine **USS Cod** (☎ 216-566-8770; www.usscod.org; 1089 E 9th St; adult/child 6-18yr $7/4; 🕑 10am-4:30pm May-Sep), which saw action in WWII.

OHIO CITY & TREMONT

Remember the beloved 1983 film *A Christmas Story*, in which Ralphie yearns for a Red Ryder BB gun? The original **Christmas Story House & Museum** (☎ 216-298-4919; www.achristmasstoryhouse.com; 3159 W 11th St; adult/child 7-12yr $7.50/5.50; 🕑 10am-5pm Thu-Sat, noon-5pm Sun) sits in Tremont, complete with leg lamp. This attraction's for true fans only.

Nearby the European-style **West Side Market** (www.westsidemarket.org; cnr W 25th St & Lorain Ave; 🕑 7am-4pm Mon & Wed, to 6pm Fri & Sat) overflows with greengrocers and their fruit and vegetable pyramids, as well as purveyors of Hungarian sausage, Mexican flat breads and Polish pierogies.

UNIVERSITY CIRCLE

Several attractions cluster in University Circle (the area around Case Western Reserve University, Cleveland Clinic and other institutions) 5 miles east of downtown.

The star of the lot is the **Cleveland Museum of Art** (☎ 216-421-7340; www.clevelandart.org; 11150 East Blvd; admission free; 🕑 10am-5pm Tue-Sun, to 9pm Wed & Fri), which houses an excellent collection of European paintings, as well as African, Asian and American art. It's undergoing a whopping expansion, to be completed in 2012, that will increase gallery space by more than 40%.

The lovely **Cleveland Botanical Garden** (☎ 216-721-1600; www.cbgarden.org; 11030 East Blvd; adult/child 3-12yr $7.50/3; 🕑 10am-5pm Tue-Sat, noon-5pm Sun, to 9pm Wed Jun-Aug) has a Costa Rican cloud forest and Madagascan desert exhibits. An ice-skating rink opens nearby in winter; skate rentals cost $3. Parking costs $5 to $10 per day and gives access to all the museums here.

Beyond the circle further east, don't forget eclectic **Lake View Cemetery** (☎ 216-421-2665; www.lakeviewcemetery.com; 12316 Euclid Ave; admission free; 🕑 7am-5:30pm), the 'outdoor museum' where President Garfield and John Rockefeller rest.

Sleeping

Prices listed are for summer, which is high season, and do not include the 15.25% tax. Modest motels are southwest of Cleveland's center, near the airport. The W 150th exit off I-71 (exit 240) has several options for under $100.

Brownstone Inn (☎ 216-426-1753; www.brownstoneinndowntown.com; 3649 Prospect Ave; r incl breakfast $89-139; P ✕ 💻 wi-fi) This Victorian townhouse B&B has a whole lotta personality. All five rooms have a private bath, and each comes equipped with robes to lounge in and an invitation for evening aperitifs. It's between downtown and University Circle, though in a bit of a no-man's-land for walkable entertainment.

University Circle B&B (☎ 866-735-5960; www.ucbnb.com; 1575 E 108th St; r incl breakfast $110-145; P ✕ wi-fi) Located in the heart of University Circle and within walking distance of its museums, this four-room B&B gets lots of academic visitors. Two rooms share a bath.

our pick **Hilton Garden Inn** (☎ 216-658-6400, 877-782-9444; www.hiltongardeninn.com; 1100 Carnegie Ave; r $110-169; P ✕ 💻 wi-fi 🏋) While nothing fancy, the Hilton's rooms are good value with comfy beds, wi-fi-rigged workstations and mini refrigerators. It's right by the baseball park. Parking costs $16.

Ritz-Carlton (☎ 216-623-1300; www.ritzcarlton.com; 1515 W 3rd St; r from $229; P ✕ 💻 wi-fi 🏋) What the heck? Stay where the rock stars stay and enjoy the perks, like marble baths, free shoe shines and a 24-hour fitness and massage center. Wi-fi costs $9.95 per day, and parking is $24.

Eating

There's more range than you might expect in a Rust Belt town. Celebrity chef Anthony Bourdain (the guy who travels the world eating snake blood and whatnot) even filmed a 'No Reservations' episode here.

DOWNTOWN

The Warehouse District, between W 6th and W 9th Sts, jumps with trendy restaurants. Off the beaten path and east of the city center, Asiatown (bounded by Payne and St Clair Aves, and E 30th and 40ths Sts) has several Chinese, Vietnamese and Korean eateries.

Lola (☎ 216-621-5652; 2058 E 4th St; lunch mains $9-19, dinner mains $18-29; 🕑 11:30am-2:30pm Mon-Fri, 5-10pm Mon-Thu, to 11pm Fri & Sat) Famous for his piercings, Food Channel TV appearances and multiple national awards, local boy Michael Symon has put Cleveland on the foodie map with Lola. The lunch dishes are the most fun, say coconut-and-lime-tinged scallop ceviche or the showstopper – an egg-and-cheese-topped fried bologna sandwich.

OHIO CITY & TREMONT

Ohio City and Tremont, which straddle I-90 south of downtown, are areas with lots of new establishments popping up.

West Side Market Cafe (☎ 216-579-6800; 1995 W 25th St; mains $6-9; 🕑 7am-4pm Mon-Thu, to 9pm Fri & Sat, 9am-3pm Sun) This is a smart stop if you're craving well-made breakfast and lunch fare, and cheap fish and chicken mains. The café is inside West Side Market itself, which overflows with fresh produce and prepared foods that are handy for picnicking or road-tripping.

Sokolowski's University Inn (☎ 216-771-9236; 1201 University Rd; mains $6-14; 🕑 11am-3pm Mon-Fri, 5-9pm Fri, 4-9pm Sat) The portions are huge, enough to fuel the hungriest steelworker. It's cafeteria style, so grab a tray and fill it with plump pierogi, cabbage rolls and other rib-sticking Polish fare.

our pick **South Side** (☎ 216-937-2288; 2207 W 11 St; sandwiches $9-11, mains $14-19; 🕑 11am-2am; wi-fi) Local athletes, blue-collar electricians and everyone in between pile into this sleek Tremont establishment to drink at the winding granite bar. They come for the food too, like the grouper sandwich, veggie reuben, Kobe burger and chicken and waffles (brunch only).

Lolita (☎ 216-771-5652; 900 Literary Rd; mains $9-17; 🕑 5-11pm Tue-Thu, to 1am Fri & Sat, 4-9pm Sun) It's the lighter-fare sister of Lola (above). Munch on Iowa prosciutto, mussels and Neapolitan-style pizzas with cold local beer. Five-dollar food specials rock happy hour (5pm to 6:30pm, and after 9:30pm or so).

LITTLE ITALY & COVENTRY

These two neighborhoods make prime stops for refueling after hanging out in University Circle. Little Italy is closest: it's along Mayfield Rd, near Lake View Cemetery (look out for the Rte 322 sign). Alternatively, relaxed Coventry Village is a bit further east off Mayfield Rd.

Presti's Bakery (☎ 216-421-3060; 12101 Mayfield Rd; items $2-5; 🕑 6am-9pm Mon-Thu, to 10pm Fri & Sat, to 6pm Sun) Try Presti's for its popular sandwiches, stromboli and divine pastries.

Tommy's (☎ 216-321-7757; 1823 Coventry Rd; mains $5-9; 🕑 9am-9pm Sun-Thu, to 10pm Fri, 7:30am-10pm Sat) This is a neighborhood standout, with a broad, veggie-heavy menu; don't miss the Mary Lynn spinach pie.

Drinking

The downtown action centers on the Warehouse District (around W 6th St), and around E 4th St's entertainment venues. Tremont is also chockablock with chic bars. Most places stay open until 1am; some to 2:30am.

Major Hoopples (☎ 216-575-0483; 1930 Columbus Rd; 🕑 closed Sun) Look over the bar for Cleveland's best skyline view from this friendly, eclectic watering hole. There's free live music some nights.

Great Lakes Brewing Company (☎ 216-771-4404; 2516 Market Ave; 🕑 closed Sun) Great Lakes wins numerous prizes for its brewed-on-the-premises beers. Added historical bonus: Eliott Ness got into a shootout with criminals here; ask the bartender to show you the bullet holes.

Johnny's Little Bar (☎ 216-861-2166; 614 Frankfort Ave) One of the Warehouse District's more casual, compact offerings. The hard-to-find entrance is on Frankfort Ave, a side street.

Entertainment

LIVE MUSIC

Check *Scene* and Friday's *Plain Dealer* for listings.

House of Blues (☎ 216-523-2583; www.hob.com; 308 Euclid Ave) The chain brings in medium- and top-tier bands.

Beachland Ballroom (☎ 216-383-1124; www.beachlandballroom.com; 15711 Waterloo Rd) Hip young bands play at this venue east of downtown.

Grog Shop (☎ 216-321-5588; www.grogshop.gs; 2785 Euclid Hts Blvd) Up-and-coming rockers thrash at this longtime Coventry music house.

THEATER & CULTURE

Playhouse Square Center (☎ 216-771-4444; www.playhousesquare.com; 1501 Euclid Ave) This elegant center hosts theater, opera and ballet. Check the website for $10 'Smart Seats.'

Severance Hall (☎ 216-231-1111; www.clevelandorch.com; 11001 Euclid Ave) Near University Circle, Severance Hall is where the acclaimed Cleveland Symphony Orchestra holds its season (August to May). The orchestra's summer home is Blossom Music Center in Cuyahoga Valley National Park, about 22 miles south.

SPORTS

Cleveland is a serious jock town with three modern downtown venues.

Progressive Field (☎ 866-488-7423; www.indians.com; 2401 Ontario St) Pro baseball's Indians (aka 'the Tribe') hit here. Great sightlines and a fun atmosphere make it a top park to see a game.

Quicken Loans Arena (☎ 800-820-2287; www.nba.com/cavaliers; 1 Center Ct) The Cavaliers play basketball at 'the Q,' which doubles as an entertainment venue.

Cleveland Browns Stadium (☎ 440-891-5000; www.clevelandbrowns.com; 1085 W 3rd St) The NFL's Browns pass the football on the lakefront.

Getting There & Around

Eleven miles southwest of downtown, **Cleveland Hopkins International Airport** (CLE; ☎ 216-265-6030; www.clevelandairport.com; 5300 Riverside Dr) is linked by the Regional Transit Authority (RTA) Red Line train ($2). A cab to downtown costs about $29.

From downtown, **Greyhound** (☎ 216-781-0520; 1465 Chester Ave) offers frequent departures to Chicago ($34 to $53, 7½ hours) and New York ($59 to $72, 13 hours). **Megabus** (☎ 877-462-6342; www.megabus.com/us) also goes to Chicago, often for lower fares; it departs from the corner of W 3rd St and W Huron Rd.

The **Regional Transit Authority** (RTA; ☎ 216-621-9500; www.riderta.com; 1240 W 6th St) operates the Red Line train that goes to both the airport and Ohio City. It also runs the HealthLine bus that motors along Euclid Ave from downtown to University Circle's museums. Fares are $2; day passes are $4.50.

Amtrak (☎ 216-696-5115; 200 Cleveland Memorial Shoreway) runs once daily to Chicago ($49 to $96, seven hours) and New York City ($67 to $126, 13 hours).

For cab service, call **Americab** (☎ 216-429-1111).

AROUND CLEVELAND

Thirty miles south of Cleveland, **Akron** was a small village until Dr BF Goodrich established the first rubber factory in 1869. Akron became the 'rubber capital,' and it still produces more than half the country's tires.

Further south in **Canton**, the birthplace of the NFL, the popular **Pro Football Hall of Fame** (☎ 330-456-8207; www.profootballhof.com; 2121 George Halas Dr; adult/child 6-14yr $18/12; 🕑 9am-8pm Jun-Aug, 9am-5pm rest of year) is a shrine for the gridiron-obsessed. Look for the football-shaped tower off I-77.

West of Cleveland, attractive **Oberlin** is an old-fashioned college town, with noteworthy architecture by Cass Gilbert, Frank Lloyd Wright and Robert Venturi. Further west, just south of I-90, the tiny town of **Milan** is the birthplace of Thomas Edison. His home, restored to its 1847 likeness, is now a small **museum** (☎ 419-499-2135; www.tomedison.org; 9 Edison Dr; adult/child 6-12yr $7/4; 🕑 1-4pm Wed-Sun winter, extended hours Tue-Sun summer, closed Jan) outlining his inventions, like the light bulb and phonograph.

Still further west, on US 20 and surrounded by farmland, is **Clyde**, which bills itself as the USA's most famous small town. It got that way when native son Sherwood Anderson published *Winesburg, Ohio* in 1919. It didn't take long for the unimpressed residents to figure out where the fictitious town really was. Stop at the **Clyde Museum** (☎ 419-547-7946; www.clydeheritageleague.org; 124 W Buckeye St; admission free; 🕑 1-4pm Thu Apr-Sep & by appointment) in the old church for Anderson tidbits or at the library, a few doors down.

ERIE LAKESHORE & ISLANDS

In summer this good-time resort area is one of the busiest – and most expensive – places in Ohio. The season lasts from mid-May to mid-September, and then just about everything shuts down. Pre-book your accommodations.

Sandusky, long a port, now serves as the jump-off point to the Erie Islands and the world's roller-coaster capital (see boxed text, p604). The **visitors center** (☎ 419-625-2984; www.shoresandislands.com; 4424 Milan Rd; 🕑 8:30am-5:30pm Mon-Fri, plus evenings & weekends in summer) provides lodging and ferry information. Scads of chain motels line the roads heading into town.

New Sandusky Fish Company (☎ 419-621-8263; 235 E Shoreline Dr; items $4-6; 🕑 11am-7pm Mon-Thu, to 8pm Fri-Sun) makes waiting for the ferry easier. It fries up lightly breaded local lake perch and clams just east of the dock.

WORTH THE VISIT: CHILLIN' WITH ICE WINE

Hey, if the guys across the border in Canada can do it, so can Ohio. Ten state wineries, most along Lake Erie, began making ice wine a few years ago, and they're reaping big praise. The local weather – long autumns, followed by winters cold enough to freeze the grapes but not so cold that the vines die – results in a sweet dessert wine with hints of melon and apricot. Tour and try samples at **Debonne Vineyards** (☎ 440-466-3485; www.debonne.com; 7743 Doty Rd; 8-sample tasting $6; ⏰ noon-6pm Tue, to 11pm Wed & Fri, to 8pm Thu & Sat year-round, 1-6pm Sun Apr-Oct) in Madison, east of Cleveland.

Bass Islands

In the war of 1812's Battle of Lake Erie, Admiral Perry met the enemy English fleet near **South Bass Island**. His victory ensured that all the lands south of the Great Lakes became US, not Canadian, territory. While that's nice, history is all but forgotten on a summer weekend in packed Put In Bay, the island's main town and a party place full of restaurants and shops. Move beyond it, and you'll find a winery and opportunities for camping, fishing, kayaking and swimming. A singular attraction is the 352ft Doric column commemorating Perry's victory in the Battle of Lake Erie – you can climb up to the observation deck ($3) for views of the battle site and, on a good day, Canada.

The **Chamber of Commerce** (☎ 419-285-2832; www.visitputinbay.com; 148 Delaware Ave; ⏰ 10am-4pm Mon-Fri, to 5pm Sat & Sun) has information on activities and lodging, which starts at $90 in summer. **Ashley's Island House** (☎ 419-285-2844; www.ashleysislandhouse.com; 557 Catawba Ave; r incl breakfast $90-165, weekend $120-175; ⊠) is a 13-room B&B, where naval officers stayed in the late 1800s. The **Beer Barrel Saloon** (☎ 419-285-2337; Delaware Ave; ⏰ 11am-1am) has plenty of space for imbibing – its bar is 406ft long.

Cabs and tour buses serve the island, though cycling is a fine way to get around. **Jet Express** (☎ 800-245-1538; www.jet-express.com) leaves Port Clinton on the mainland for Put In Bay (round-trip adult/child six to 12 years $28/4, no cars), and also departs from Sandusky ($36/10, no cars); leave your car in the lot (per day $10). **Miller Boatline** (☎ 800-500-2421; www.millerferry.com) from Catawba is cheapest (round-trip adult/child six to 11 years $13/3, car $30).

Middle Bass Island, a good day trip by ferry from South Bass, offers nature and quiet; Miller Boatline will get you there.

Kelleys Island

Quiet and green, Kelleys Island is a popular weekend escape, especially for families. It has pretty 19th-century buildings, Native American pictographs, a good beach and glacial grooves raked through its landscape. Even its old limestone quarries are scenic.

The **Chamber of Commerce** (☎ 419-746-2360; www.kelleysislandchamber.com; Seaway Marina Bldg; ⏰ 10am-4pm, closed Wed), by the ferry dock, has information on accommodations and activities – hiking, camping, kayaking and fishing are popular. The Village, the island's small commercial center, has places to eat, drink, shop and rent bicycles – the recommended way to sightsee.

Kelleys Island Ferry Boat Line (☎ 419-798-9763; www.kelleysislandferry.com) departs frequently from the Marblehead dock (round-trip adult/child five to 11 years $18/12, car $30). The crossing takes about 20 minutes and leaves hourly (more frequently in summer). **Jet Express** (☎ 800-245-1538; www.jet-express.com) departs from Sandusky (round-trip adult/child six to 12 years $28/8, no cars) and also goes onward to Put In Bay on South Bass Island (island-hopping round-trip $40/12, no cars).

Pelee Island

Pelee, the largest Erie island, is a ridiculously green, quiet wine-producing and bird-watching destination that belongs to Canada. **Pelee Island Transportation** (☎ 800-661-2220; www.ontarioferries.com) runs a ferry (one way adult/child six to 12 years $13.75/6.75, car $30) from Sandusky to Pelee and onward to Ontario's mainland. Check www.pelee.org for lodging and trip planning information.

AMISH COUNTRY

The Amish have resisted modernity for centuries, and visiting here is like entering a time warp. Wayne and Holmes counties, between Cleveland and Columbus (immediately east of I-71), have the USA's densest Amish concentration, followed by areas in Pennsylvania and Indiana.

DON'T MISS

For the world's greatest concentration of roller-coasters, head to **Cedar Point Amusement Park** (☎ 419-627-2350; www.cedarpoint.com; adult/child $44/20; ⌚ from 10am mid-May–Aug, closing times vary, Fri-Sun evenings only Sep-Oct), 6 miles from Sandusky. The Top Thrill Dragster drops 420ft high and whips around at 120mph (one of the world's tallest and fastest), while the Maverick drops at a 95° angle (that's steeper than straight down) and rolls over eight hills, causing riders to feel weightless. If those and the 15 other coasters aren't enough, the surrounding area has a nice beach, a water park and a slew of tacky, old-fashioned attractions. Parking is $10.

Descendants of conservative Dutch–Swiss religious factions who migrated to the USA during the 18th century, the Amish continue to follow the *ordnung* (way of life), in varying degrees. Many adhere to rules prohibiting the use of electricity, telephones and motorized vehicles. They wear traditional clothing, farm the land with plow and mule, and go to church in horse-drawn buggies. Others are not so strict.

Unfortunately, what would surely be a peaceful country scene is often disturbed by behemoth tour buses. Many Amish are happy to profit from this influx of outside dollars, but don't equate this with free photographic access – the Amish typically view photographs as taboo. Drive carefully as roads are narrow and curvy, and there's always the chance of pulling up on a slow-moving buggy just around the bend. Many places are closed Sunday.

Contact the **Holmes County Chamber of Commerce** (☎ 877-643-8824; www.visitamishcountry.com) for information and maps online or via snail mail.

Kidron, on Rte 52 just north of US 250, is worth a stop on Thursday, when the **Kidron Auction** takes place at the livestock barn. Hundreds of buggies line up along the roadside, and an interesting flea market rings the barn. Across the street, **Lehman's Store** (☎ 888-438-5346; ⌚ 8am-5:30pm Mon-Sat) is an absolute must-see. It's the Amish community's main purveyor of modern-looking products that use no electricity. Ogle the wind-up flashlights and nonelectric waffle irons, and then take a pie break at the café inside.

To the south, on Hwy 39 between Walnut Creek and Sugarcreek, check out the **Amish Flea Market** (☎ 330-852-0181; ⌚ 9am-5pm Thu-Sat), where you can find new or used knickknacks, crafts, quilts, produce, antiques and delicious baked goods. Just north of Walnut Creek, along Hwy 515, **Yoder's** (☎ 330-893-2541; ⌚ 10am-5pm Mon-Sat mid-Apr–Oct) is an Amish farm that's open to visitors. Tours (adult/child $11/7) include a buggy ride.

Nearby, US 62 connects Berlin and Millersburg, the area's side-by-side 'big' towns. The historic **Hotel Millersburg** (☎ 330-674-1457; www.hotelmillersburg.com; 35 W Jackson St; r $65-95; ✖ 📶) has basic, reasonably priced rooms, as well as a modern tavern and dining room on the ground floor. Atmospheric **Boyd & Wurthmann Restaurant** (☎ 330-893-3287; Main St; mains $7-13; ⌚ 5:30am-8pm Mon-Sat) in Berlin serves home-style cooking that attracts locals and tourists alike. Amish specialties, like ham loaf and wedding steak (ground meat in mushroom sauce), join familiar American fare on the menu.

To get further off the beaten path, take Rte 557 through the countryside to wee Charm, 4 miles south of Berlin. The peaceful **Guggisberg Swiss Inn** (☎ 877-467-9477; www.guggisbergswissinn.com; r incl breakfast $75-110; ✖ 📶) has a cheese-making facility and horses on the grounds.

COLUMBUS

Columbus is like the blind date your mom arranges – average looking, restrained personality, but solid and affable. Better yet, she's easy on the wallet, an influence from Ohio State University's 50,000-plus students (the uni is the nation's largest).

There's a **visitors center** (☎ 866-397-2657; www.experiencecolumbus.com; 277 W Nationwide Blvd; ⌚ 8am-5pm Mon-Fri) in the Arena District.

The *Columbus Dispatch* (www.dispatch.com) is the city's daily newspaper. The free, weekly *Alive* (www.columbusalive.com) has entertainment listings. *Outlook* (www.outlookmedia.com) is a monthly gay and lesbian publication.

Sights & Activities

The remarkably large, all-brick **German Village**, a half mile south of downtown, is a restored 19th-century neighborhood with cobbled streets and Italianate and Queen Anne architecture. The **German Village Society** (☎ 614-221-8888; www.germanvillage.com; 588 S 3rd St; 9am-4pm Mon-Fri, 10am-2pm Sat) has self-guided walking-tour information. Just north of downtown, the browse-worthy **Short North** is a redeveloped strip of High St that holds contemporary art galleries, restaurants and jazz bars.

North of downtown, the university area has many casual storefronts. The campus's **Wexner Center for the Arts** (☎ 614-292-3535; www.wexarts.org; cnr 15th & N High Sts; gallery admission $5; 11am-6pm Tue, Wed & Sun, to 8pm Thu-Sat) offers cutting-edge art exhibits, films and performances.

Sleeping & Eating

Add 16.75% tax to hotel rates. German Village and the Short North provide fertile grazing and guzzling grounds. The Arena District (the area around the Nationwide Arena hockey stadium) bursts with mid-range chains and brewpubs. Around the university and along N High St from 15th Ave onward, you'll find everything from Mexican to Ethiopian to sushi, plus quality coffee shops.

Red Roof Inn (☎ 614-224-6539; 111 E Nationwide Blvd; r incl breakfast $85-129; P) Located in the Arena District, it's one of the classiest-looking Red Roofs you'll ever see. Parking is $10.

Short North B&B (☎ 614-299-5050, 800-516-9664; www.columbus-bed-breakfast.com; 50 E Lincoln St; r incl breakfast $129-149; P) These seven well-maintained rooms are steps away from the eponymous neighborhood's scene.

Blue Danube (☎ 614-261-9308; 2439 N High St; mains $5-9; 11am-1am) The D'ube's neon-lit booths (and cheap beer) endure as a campus favorite. Meals are late-night booze-absorbers, like gravy-smothered fries and gyros.

Schmidt's (☎ 614-444-6808; 240 E Kossuth St; mains $8-15; 11am-10pm Tue-Thu, to 11pm Fri & Sat, to 9pm Sun & Mon) In German Village, shovel in Old Country staples like sausage and schnitzel, but save room for the whopping half-pound cream puffs. Oompah bands play Wednesday to Saturday.

Drinking & Entertainment

The Ohio State Buckeyes football team packs a rabid crowd into legendary, horseshoe-shaped **Ohio Stadium** (☎ 800-462-8257; www.ohiostatebuckeyes.com; 411 Woody Hayes Dr) for its games, held on Saturdays in the fall. The National Hockey League's Columbus Blue Jackets slap the puck at downtown's **Nationwide Arena** (☎ 614-246-2000; www.bluejackets.com; 200 W Nationwide Blvd). The popular Columbus Crew pro soccer team plays in **Crew Stadium** (☎ 614-447-2739; www.thecrew.com), which is north off I-71 and 17th Ave, from March to October.

Getting There & Around

The **Port Columbus Airport** (CMH; ☎ 614-239-4000; www.port-columbus.com) is 10 miles east of town. A cab to downtown costs about $25.

Greyhound (☎ 614-221-4642; www.greyhound.com; 111 E Town St) buses run at least six times daily to Cincinnati ($15 to $24, two hours) and Cleveland ($18 to $30, 2½ hours). Often cheaper, **Megabus** (☎ 877-462-6342; www.megabus.com/us) runs once daily to Cincinnati and twice daily to Chicago. Check the website for exact locations.

SOUTHEASTERN OHIO

Ohio's southeastern corner cradles most of its forested areas, as well as the rolling foothills of the Appalachian Mountains and scattered farms.

Around Lancaster, southeast of Columbus, the hills lead gently into **Hocking County**, a region of streams and waterfalls, sandstone cliffs and cavelike formations. It's splendid to explore in any season, with miles of trails for hiking and rivers for canoeing, as well as abundant campgrounds and cabins at **Hocking Hills State Park** (☎ 740-385-6165; 20160 Hwy 664; campsites/cottages from $24/105). **Old Man's Cave** is a scenic winner for hiking. **Hocking Valley Canoe Livery** (☎ 740-385-8685; www.hockinghillscanoeing.com; 31251 Chieftain Dr; 2hr tours $42; 9am-5pm Apr-Oct) lets you paddle by moonlight and tiki torch from nearby Logan. **Earth-Water-Rock: Outdoor Adventures** (☎ 740-664-5220; www.ewroutdoors.com; half-day tour $85-110) provides thrills with guided rock climbing and rappelling trips; beginners are welcome.

Athens makes a lovely base for seeing the region. Situated where US 50 crosses US 33, it's set among wooded hills and built around the Ohio University campus (which comprises half the town). The **visitors center** (☎ 800-878-9767; www.athensohio.com; 667 E State St; 9am-5pm Mon-Fri) has good regional information. Nearby the **Village Bakery & Cafe** (☎ 740-594-7311; 268 E State St; mains $4-8; 7:30am-8pm Tue-Sat, 9am-2pm Sun) uses organic veggies, grass-fed meat and farmstead cheeses in its pizzas, soups and sandwiches. Student cafés and pubs line Court St, Athens' main road.

Further south, the Ohio River marks the state boundary and flows through many scenic stretches. It's a surprisingly quiet, undeveloped area.

The area south of Columbus was a center for the fascinating prehistoric Hopewell people, who left behind huge geometric earthworks and burial mounds from around 200 BC to AD 600. For a fine introduction visit the **Hopewell Culture National Historical Park** (☎ 740-774-1126; www.nps.gov/hocu; Hwy 104 north of I-35; admission free; 🕒 8:30am-6pm Jun-Aug, to 4:30pm Sep-May), 3 miles north of Chillicothe. Stop in the visitors center, and then wander about the variously shaped ceremonial mounds spread over 13-acre **Mound City**, a mysterious town of the dead. **Serpent Mound** (☎ 937-587-2796; www.ohiohistory.org; 3850 Hwy 73; per vehicle $7; 🕒 10am-5pm Fri-Sun Jun-Aug), southwest of Chillicothe and 4 miles northwest of Locust Grove, is perhaps the most captivating site of all. The giant, uncoiling snake stretches over a quarter of a mile and is the largest effigy mound in the USA.

DAYTON & YELLOW SPRINGS

Dayton has the aviation sights, but little Yellow Springs (18 miles northeast on US 68) has much more personality for accommodation and places to eat.

Sights & Activities

The huge **National Museum of the US Air Force** (☎ 937-255-3286; www.nationalmuseum.af.mil; 1100 Spaatz St; admission free; 🕒 9am-5pm) is at the Wright-Patterson Air Force Base, 6 miles northeast of Dayton. It's got everything from a Wright Brothers exhibit and Sopwith Camel (WWI biplane) to a Stealth bomber. Don't miss the annex with its collection of presidential planes; a free shuttle bus takes you over to the hangar (which you'll need a passport or driver's license to enter). Expect your visit to take three or more hours.

There are numerous Wright attractions. Among them, **Carillon Historical Park** (☎ 937-293-2841; www.daytonhistory.org; 1000 Carillon Blvd; adult/child 3-17yr $8/5; 🕒 9:30am-5pm Mon-Sat, noon-5pm Sun) has the 1905 Wright Flyer III biplane and a replica of the Wright workshop. The **Dayton Aviation Heritage National Historical Park** (☎ 937-225-7705; www.nps.gov/daav; 16 S Williams St; admission free; 🕒 8:30am-5pm), which includes Wright Cycle Company Complex, is where the brothers developed bikes and aviation ideas.

Sleeping & Eating

The following listings are located in Yellow Springs, a top-notch place to experience down-home Ohio.

Morgan House B&B (☎ 937-767-1761; www.arthurmorganhouse.com; 120 W Limestone St; r incl breakfast $90-125; ⊠ 📶) The six comfy rooms have super-soft linens and private baths. Breakfasts are organic, with free-trade African coffee.

Winds Cafe (☎ 937-767-1144; 215 Xenia Ave; mains $18-25; 🕒 11:30am-2pm & 5-10pm Tue-Sat, 10am-2pm Sun) A hippie co-op 30 years ago, the Winds has grown up to become a sophisticated foodie favorite plating seasonal dishes like fig-sauced asparagus crepes and rhubarb halibut.

our pick **Young's Jersey Dairy** (☎ 937-325-0629; 6880 Springfield-Xenia Rd) is a working dairy farm with two restaurants: the **Golden Jersey Inn** (mains $9-14; 🕒 lunch & dinner Mon-Fri, plus breakfast Sat & Sun), serving dishes like buttermilk chicken; and the **Dairy Store** (sandwiches $3.50-6.50; 🕒 6am-9pm Sun-Thu, to 10pm Fri & Sat, later in summer), serving sandwiches, dreamy ice cream and Ohio's best milk shakes. There's also minigolf, batting cages and opportunities to watch the cows get milked.

CINCINNATI

Cincinnati splashes up the Ohio River's banks. Its prettiness surprises, as do its haunted music-club mansions, its twisting streets to hilltop Mt Adams and locals' unashamed ardor for a five-way (see boxed text, p610. Amid all that action, don't forget to catch a baseball game, stroll the riverfront and visit the free art museum.

History

Thanks to its riverfront real estate, Cincinnati, founded in 1788, became an early commerce hub. German immigrants flocked in, drawn to the landscape that reminded them of their Rhine Valley homeland. The town soon became known as 'Porkopolis' because of its many meat-packing plants. These factories provided enough leftover lard for Messrs Procter and Gamble to become one of the world's largest soap makers (and eventual corporate conglomerate). The city was also an important center for the Underground Railroad and antislavery movement.

In the 1970s Cincy had a mayor named Jerry Springer (yes, *that* Jerry Springer), who got in trouble – then was re-elected – after getting caught paying for a hooker with a check, which he admitted to in a televised press conference. It was a colorful time for a city that takes its knocks for being fogyish.

Orientation

Downtown streets are laid out on a grid radiating from Fountain Sq. Vine St is the east–west dividing line; east and westbound streets are numbered, while north and southbound streets are named. The snaking Ohio River forms the city's southern boundary, and Kentucky is just across the water. The Northside neighborhood, north of where I-74 and I-75 intersect, is 5 miles north of downtown.

Information

BOOKSTORES

Barnes & Noble (☎ 859-581-2000; Newport on the Levee; 🕑 10am-10pm Sun-Thu, to 11pm Fri & Sat)

EMERGENCY & MEDICAL SERVICES

University Hospital (☎ 513-584-1000; 234 Goodman St)

INTERNET ACCESS

FedEx (☎ 513-241-3366; 51 E 5th St; per 30min $6; 🕑 24hr)

INTERNET RESOURCES & MEDIA

Cin Weekly (www.cinweekly.com) *Enquirer*'s weekly entertainment freebie.
Cincinnati Enquirer (www.enquirer.com) Daily newspaper.
CityBeat (www.citybeat.com) Free alternative weekly paper with good entertainment listings.

TOURIST INFORMATION

Cincinnati USA Regional Tourism Network (☎ 800-344-3445; www.cincinnatiusa.com) Call or go online for a visitor's guide.

Sights & Activities

DOWNTOWN

The elegant 1876 **Roebling Suspension Bridge** was a forerunner of John Roebling's famous Brooklyn Bridge in New York. At its foot is the **National Underground Railroad Freedom Center** (☎ 513-333-7500; www.freedomcenter.org; 50 E Freedom Way; adult/child 6-12yr $9/6; 🕑 11am-5pm Tue-Sat), with exhibits on how slaves escaped to the north; Cincinnati was a prominent stop on the railroad and a center for abolitionist activities led by residents, such as Harriet Beecher Stowe.

Fountain Square (cnr 5th & Vine Sts) is the city's centerpiece, a public space with a seasonal ice rink, chess tables, free wi-fi and the fancy old 'Spirit of the Waters' fountain. Just north, the **Rosenthal Center for Contemporary Arts** (☎ 513-721-0390; www.contemporaryartscenter.org; 44 E 6th St; adult/child 3-13yr $7.50/4.50, admission free Mon evening; 🕑 10am-9pm Mon, 10am-6pm Wed-Fri, 11am-6pm Sat & Sun) displays modern art in an avant-garde building designed by Iraqi architect Zaha Hadid. The structure and its artworks are a pretty big deal for traditionalist Cincy.

Indoor–outdoor **Findlay Market** (☎ 513-665-4839; www.findlaymarket.org; 1801 Race St; 🕑 9am-6pm Tue-Fri, 8am-6pm Sat, 10am-4pm Sun, reduced hours in winter) greens the somewhat blighted area at downtown's northern edge. It's a good stop for fresh produce, meats, cheeses and baked goods. The Belgian waffle guy will wow your taste buds.

A stroll along the riverfront will take you through several parks; one of them, **Bicentennial Commons at Sawyer Point**, features whimsical monuments and flying pigs. The pedestrian-only **Purple People Bridge** provides a unique crossing from Sawyer Point to Newport, Kentucky's entertainment district.

COVINGTON & NEWPORT

Covington and Newport, Kentucky, are sort of suburbs of Cincinnati. Newport is to the east and known for its massive **Newport on the Levee** restaurant and shopping complex. The development also contains the well-regarded **Newport Aquarium** (☎ 859-491-3467; www.newportaquarium.com; One Aquarium Way; adult/child 2-12yr $20/13; 🕑 9am-7pm Jun-Aug, 10am-6pm Sep-May), where you can meet Sweet Pea the shark ray, parading penguins and more.

Covington lies to the west. Funky restaurants and bars have opened in the neighborhood's 19th-century brick row houses. Antebellum mansions fringe Riverside Dr, and old paddle-wheel boats tie up along the water's edge.

MT ADAMS

It might be a bit of a stretch to compare Mt Adams, immediately east of downtown, to Paris's Montmartre, but this hilly 19th-century enclave of narrow, twisting streets, Victorian town houses, galleries, bars and restaurants is certainly a pleasurable surprise. Two big attractions here are the **Cincinnati Art Museum** (☎ 513-721-5204; www.cincinnatiartmuseum.org; 953 Eden Park Dr; admission free; 🕑 11am-5pm Tue-Sun, to 9pm Wed), with an emphasis on Middle Eastern

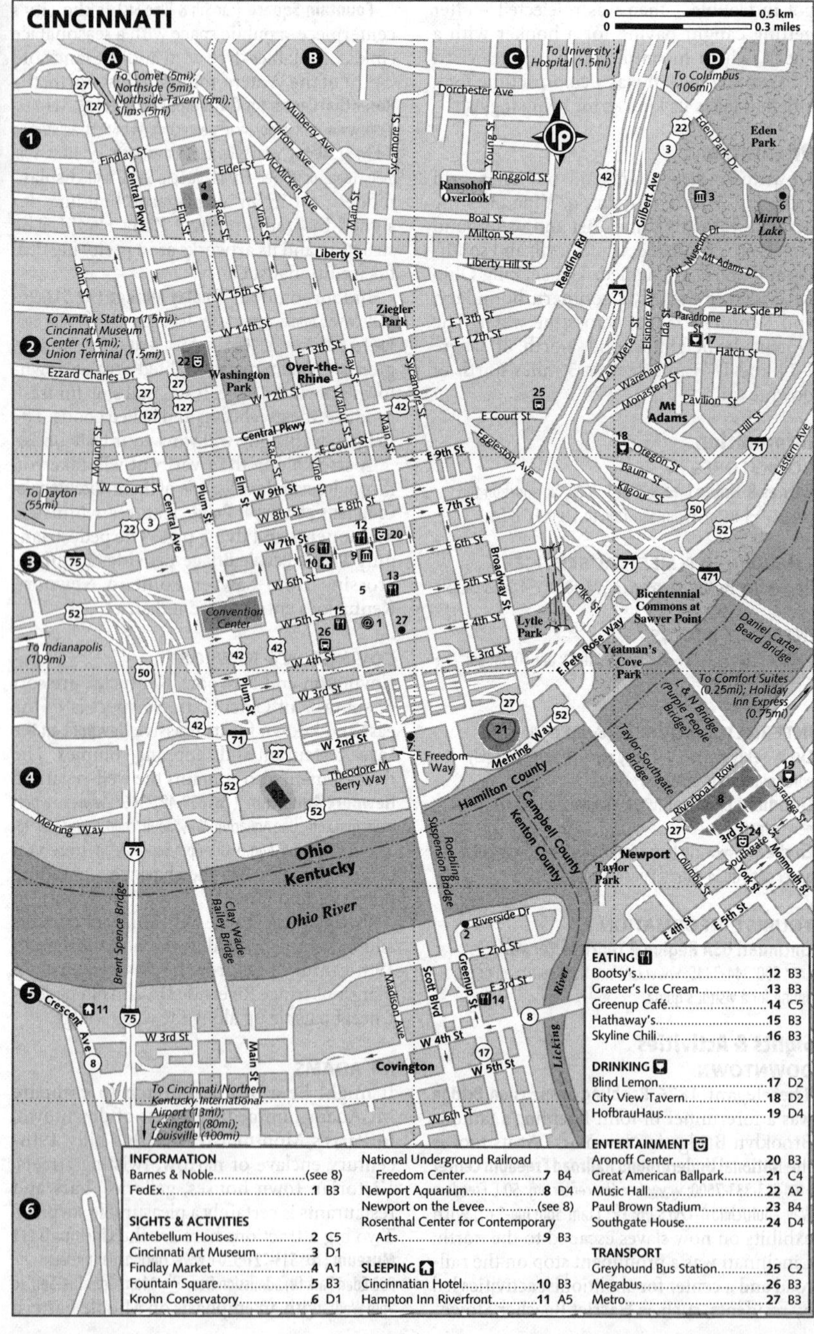
CINCINNATI
0.5 km
0.3 miles
To University Hospital (1.5mi)
To Columbus (106mi)
To Comet (5mi); Northside (5mi); Northside Tavern (5mi); Slims (5mi)
To Amtrak Station (1.5mi); Cincinnati Museum Center (1.5mi); Union Terminal (1.5mi)
To Dayton (55mi)
To Indianapolis (109mi)
To Comfort Suites (0.25mi); Holiday Inn Express (0.75mi)
To Cincinnati/Northern Kentucky International Airport (13mi); Lexington (80mi); Louisville (100mi)
Dorchester Ave
Young St
Ringgold St
Ransohoff Overlook
Boal St
Milton St
Liberty St
Liberty Hill St
Findlay St
Elder St
Central Pkwy
Elm St
Race St
Vine St
Mulberry Ave
Clifton Ave
McMicken Ave
Main St
Sycamore St
John St
W 15th St
W 14th St
E 13th St
E 12th St
W 12th St
Ziegler Park
Washington Park
Over-the-Rhine
Clay St
Walnut St
Ezzard Charles Dr
Mound St
W Court St
E Court St
E 9th St
W 9th St
E 8th St
W 8th St
E 7th St
W 7th St
E 6th St
W 6th St
E 5th St
W 5th St
E 4th St
W 4th St
E 3rd St
W 3rd St
W 2nd St
Central Ave
Plum St
Convention Center
Broadway St
Eggleston Ave
Lytle Park
E Pete Rose Way
Pike St
Bicentennial Commons at Sawyer Point
Yeatman's Cove Park
Daniel Carter Beard Bridge
L & N Bridge (Purple People Bridge)
Taylor-Southgate Bridge
E Freedom Way
Theodore M Berry Way
Mehring Way
Hamilton County
Campbell County
Kenton County
Ohio
Kentucky
Ohio River
Roebling Suspension Bridge
Clay Wade Bailey Bridge
Brent Spence Bridge
Reading Rd
Gilbert Ave
Eden Park Dr
Eden Park
Mirror Lake
Art Museum Dr
Mt Adams Dr
Van Meter St
Elsinore Ave
Ida St
Paradrome St
Park Side Pl
Hatch St
Wareham Dr
Monastery St
Pavilion St
Mt Adams
Hill St
Eastern Ave
Oregon St
Baum St
Kilgour St
Riverboat Row
Saratoga St
3rd St
Southgate St
York St
Monmouth St
Columbia St
Newport
Taylor Park
E 4th St
E 5th St
Licking River
Riverside Dr
E 2nd St
E 3rd St
Greenup St
Scott Blvd
Madison Ave
W 4th St
W 5th St
W 6th St
Covington
Crescent Ave
W 3rd St
Main St
INFORMATION
Barnes & Noble (see 8)
FedEx 1 B3
SIGHTS & ACTIVITIES
Antebellum Houses 2 C5
Cincinnati Art Museum 3 D1
Findlay Market 4 A1
Fountain Square 5 B3
Krohn Conservatory 6 D1
National Underground Railroad Freedom Center 7 B4
Newport Aquarium 8 D4
Newport on the Levee (see 8)
Rosenthal Center for Contemporary Arts 9 B3
SLEEPING
Cincinnatian Hotel 10 B3
Hampton Inn Riverfront 11 A5
EATING
Bootsy's 12 B3
Graeter's Ice Cream 13 B3
Greenup Café 14 C5
Hathaway's 15 B3
Skyline Chili 16 B3
DRINKING
Blind Lemon 17 D2
City View Tavern 18 D2
HofbrauHaus 19 D4
ENTERTAINMENT
Aronoff Center 20 B3
Great American Ballpark 21 C4
Music Hall 22 A2
Paul Brown Stadium 23 B4
Southgate House 24 D4
TRANSPORT
Greyhound Bus Station 25 C2
Megabus 26 B3
Metro 27 B3

and European arts, as well as local works, and the **Krohn Conservatory** (☎ 513-421-4086; www.cincinnatiparks.com/krohn-conservatory; 1501 Eden Park Dr; admission free; 10am-5pm), a vast greenhouse with a rainforest, desert flora and glorious seasonal flower shows. Most visitors just ascend the hill for a look around, a drink and a pause to enjoy the view from the hilltop Catholic church.

To get here, follow 7th St east of downtown to Gilbert Ave, bear northwest to Elsinore Ave, and head up the hill.

AROUND CINCINNATI

Two miles northwest of downtown, the **Cincinnati Museum Center** (☎ 513-287-7000; www.cincymuseum.org; 1301 Western Ave; 10am-5pm Mon-Sat, 11am-6pm Sun;) occupies the 1933 Union Terminal, an art-deco jewel still used by Amtrak. The interior has fantastic murals made of Rookwood tiles. The Museum of Natural History (adult/child three to 12 years $8/6) is mostly geared to kids, but it does have a limestone cave with real bats inside. A history museum, Omnimax theater and children's museum round out the offerings. Discounted combination tickets are available. Parking costs $5.

Tours

Architreks (☎ 513-721-4506; www.cincinnatipreservation.org/architreks; tours adult/child $10/5; May-Oct) Guided walking tours of various neighborhoods, including downtown, Mt Adams and Northside. Departure points and days/times vary.

Festivals & Events

Oktoberfest (www.oktoberfest-zinzinnati.com; admission free) German beer, brats and mania; held mid-September.

Midpoint Music Festival (www.mpmf.com; 3-day pass $29) Indie bands flood various venues in late September.

Sleeping

Hotel tax is cheaper on the Kentucky side at 11.3%, versus the 17% charged in Cincinnati. Tax is not included in the following prices.

Three similar midrange options on the Kentucky riverfront are **Comfort Suites** (☎ 859-291-6700; www.choicehotels.com; 420 Riverboat Row; r incl breakfast $105-170; P), with a morning waffle bar; **Hampton Inn Riverfront** (☎ 859-581-7800; 200 Crescent Ave; r incl breakfast $129-169; P), with a small indoor pool; and **Holiday Inn Express** (☎ 859-957-2320; www.ichotelsgroup.com; 110 Landmark Dr; r incl breakfast $111-150; P), with a hot breakfast *and* small indoor pool. All are near the Newport–Covington attractions and bus stops for the quick trip to downtown Cincy.

Cincinnatian Hotel (☎ 513-381-3000, 800-942-9000; www.cincinnatianhotel.com; 601 Vine St; r $129-240; P) The Cincinnatian is in a magnificent 1882 Victorian building; the spacious rooms have fluffy towels, silk-soft sheets and huge round bathtubs. Rates drop to the lower range during weekends. Parking costs $28.

Eating

In addition to downtown, dining options concentrate along the Kentucky riverfront and in Northside.

Graeter's Ice Cream (☎ 513-381-4191; 511 Walnut St; dishes $2-4; 6:30am-9pm Mon-Fri, 7am-9pm Sat, 11am-7pm Sun) It's a local delicacy, with scoop shops around the city. The flavors that mix in the gargantuan, chunky chocolate chips top the list.

Hathaway's (☎ 513-621-1332; Carew Tower, 441 Vine St; mains $5-8; 6:30am-4pm Mon-Fri, 8am-3pm Sat) Hathaway's hasn't changed its retro dinette tables, or apron-wearing waitresses, since it started feeding hungry businesspeople 30-plus years ago. Try the *goetta* (pork, oats, onions and herbs) for breakfast – it's a Cincy specialty. The milk shakes will please sweet tooths.

Greenup Café (☎ 859-261-3663; 308 Greenup St; mains $8-11; 8am-2pm Tue-Fri, 9:30am-2:30pm Sat & Sun) Greenup's French owner has imported the flavors of his homeland to this cheerful, bohemian bistro in an old brick warehouse. Get your croissants and *croque monsieur* (egg and ham sandwich) for breakfast; meatloaf hoagies and black-bean burgers for lunch; and pastries anytime.

Slims (☎ 513-681-6500; 4046 Hamilton Ave; mains $17-18; 5:30-9:30pm Thu-Sat) This bright, simple Northside restaurant serves organic and seasonal dishes – maybe a Chilean vegetarian stew or citrus-braised pork belly – at long communal tables from 5:30pm 'until the food runs out.' Cash only; bring your own vino.

Bootsy's (☎ 513-241-0707; 631 Walnut St; tapas $5-11, mains $15-23; 11am-2pm Mon-Fri, 5-10pm Mon-Thu, to 11pm Fri & Sat) True, it's trendy. And loud. But you gotta love a place vibed after Bootsy Collins, a Cincy boy done good as the funk bassist for James Brown and George Clinton. Check out Bootsy's gold records and other

JOIN IN A FIVE-WAY

Don't worry – you can keep your clothes on for this experience, though you may want to loosen your belt. A 'five-way' in Cincinnati has to do with chili, which is a local specialty. It comprises meat sauce (spiced with chocolate and cinnamon) ladled over spaghetti and beans, then garnished with cheese and onions. Although you can get it three-way (minus onions and beans) or four-way (minus onions *or* beans), you should go the whole way – after all, life's an adventure. **Skyline Chili** (☎ 513-241-2020; 643 Vine St; items $3.50-7.50; ⏰ 10:30am-8pm Mon-Fri, 11am-4pm Sat) has a cultlike following devoted to its version. There are outlets throughout town; this one is downtown.

memorabilia while sipping mojitos and noshing on sushi, paella and duck tacos.

Drinking

Both Mt Adams and Northside are busy nightspots.

Blind Lemon (☎ 513-241-3885; 936 Hatch St) Head down the passageway to enter this atmospheric old speakeasy. It has an outdoor courtyard in summer, with a fire pit added in winter, and there's live music nightly.

Comet (☎ 513-541-8900; 4579 Hamilton Ave) The casual Comet, in Northside, has the city's best jukebox and bar food; try the burrito.

City View Tavern (☎ 513-241-8439; 403 Oregon St) The city sparkles out in front of you at this unassuming boozer.

HofbrauHaus (☎ 859-491-7200; 200 E 3rd St) The legendary Munich beer hall fills steins in Newport.

Entertainment

Scope for free publications like *CityBeat* and *Cin Weekly* for current listings. The free *GLBT News* (www.greatercincinnatiglbtnews.com) has a club guide.

LIVE MUSIC

Southgate House (☎ 859-431-2201; www.southgatehouse.com; 24 E 3rd St; ⏰ from noon) Big and small, touring and local bands alike play in this 1814 haunted mansion, which also happens to be the birthplace of the tommy gun.

Northside Tavern (☎ 513-542-3603; www.northside-tavern.com; 4163 Hamilton Ave) Local bands plug in their amps here, and it's always free.

THEATER & CULTURE

Music Hall (☎ 513-721-8222; www.cincinnatiarts.org; 1241 Elm St) The acoustically pristine Music Hall is Cincy's classical music venue, where the symphony orchestra, pops orchestra, opera and ballet hold their seasons. This is not the best neighborhood, so be cautious and park nearby.

Aronoff Center (☎ 513-621-2787; www.cincinnatiarts.org; 650 Walnut St) The mod Aronoff hosts touring shows.

SPORTS

Great American Ballpark (☎ 513-765-7000; www.cincinnatireds.com; 100 Main St) Home to the Reds (pro baseball's first team), Cincy is a great place to catch a game thanks to its bells-and-whistles riverside ballpark.

Paul Brown Stadium (☎ 513-621-3550; www.bengals.com; 1 Paul Brown Stadium) The Bengals pro football team scrimmages a few blocks west of the ballpark.

Getting There & Around

The **Cincinnati/Northern Kentucky International Airport** (CVG; ☎ 859-767-3501; www.cvgairport.com) is actually in Kentucky, 13 miles south. To get downtown, take the TANK bus ($1.75) from near Terminal 1 or 3; a cab costs about $27.

Greyhound (☎ 513-352-6012; www.greyhound.com; 1005 Gilbert Ave) buses travel daily to Louisville ($18 to $30, two hours), Indianapolis ($15 to $26, 2½ hours) and Columbus ($15 to $24, two hours). Often cheaper and quicker, **Megabus** (☎ 877-462-6342; www.megabus.com/us) runs once daily to Columbus (2½ hours) and twice daily to Chicago (six hours). It departs from downtown Cincy at 4th and Race Sts.

Metro (☎ 513-621-4455; 120 E 4th St; www.go-metro.com) runs the local buses ($1.50) and links with the **Transit Authority of Northern Kentucky** (TANK; ☎ 859-331-8265; www.tankbus.org), which charges $1.50 to $1.75 per trip.

Amtrak (☎ 513-651-3337; www.amtrak.com) choo-choos into **Union Terminal** (1301 Western Ave) thrice weekly en route to Chicago ($35 to $75, 9½ hours) and Washington, DC ($55 to $121, 14½ hours), departing in the middle of the night.

MICHIGAN

More, more, more – Michigan is the Midwest state that cranks it up. It sports more beaches than the Atlantic seaboard. More than half the state is covered by forests. And more cherries and berries get shoveled into pies here than anywhere else in the USA. Plus its gritty city Detroit is the Midwest's rawest of all – and we mean that in a good way. Of course, there's more unemployment in Michigan than any other state, but we digress…

Michigan occupies prime real estate, surrounded by four of the five Great Lakes – Superior, Michigan, Huron and Erie. Islands freckle its coast – Mackinac, Beaver and Isle Royale – and make top touring destinations. Surfing beaches, colored sandstone cliffs and trekkable sand dunes also woo visitors.

The state consists of two parts split by water: the larger Lower Peninsula, shaped like a mitten; and the smaller, lightly populated Upper Peninsula, shaped like a slipper. They are linked by the gasp-worthy Mackinac Bridge, which spans the Straits of Mackinac (pronounced *mac*-in-aw).

MICHIGAN FACTS

Nicknames Great Lakes State, Wolverine State
Population 10.1 million
Area 96,720 sq miles
Capital city Lansing (population 114,300)
Other cities Detroit (population 871,121)
Sales tax 6%
Birthplace of Industrialist Henry Ford (1863–1947), filmmaker Francis Ford Coppola (b 1939), musician Stevie Wonder (b 1950), singer Madonna (b 1958), tennis player Serena Williams (b 1984)
Home of Auto assembly plants, freshwater beaches
Famous for Cars, Cornflakes, tart cherries, Motown music
State reptile Painted turtle
Driving distances Detroit to Traverse City 255 miles, Detroit to Cleveland 168 miles

Information

Michigan highway conditions (☎ 800-381-8477; www.michigan.gov/mdot)
Michigan state park information (☎ 800-447-2757; www.michigan.gov/dnr) Park entry requires a vehicle permit (per day/year residents $6/24, nonresidents $8/29). Campsites cost $16 to $33; reservations accepted (www.midnrreservations.com; fee $8). Some parks have wi-fi.
Travel Michigan (☎ 800-644-2489; www.michigan.org)

DETROIT

Tell any American that you're planning to visit Detroit, and then watch their eyebrows shoot up quizzically. They'll ask 'Why?' and warn you about the off-the-chart homicide rates, boarded-up buildings with trash swirling at their bases, and whoppingly high foreclosure rates where homes sell for $1. 'Detroit's a crap-hole. You'll get killed there.'

Clearly, the Motor City has an image problem. While the aforementioned attributes are true, and while the city does waft a sort of bombed-out, apocalyptic vibe, it's these same qualities that fuel a raw urban energy you won't find anywhere else. And that manifests in the city's arts and music scene. They shred a mean guitar in 'the D.' Very mean.

Once the pride of the nation for its carmaking savvy, Detroit fell to pieces as the auto industry tanked. Its constant struggles to recover make it a fascinating, if eerie, place to visit.

History

French explorer Antoine de La Mothe Cadillac founded Detroit in 1701. Sweet fortune arrived in the 1920s. That's when Henry Ford began churning out cars. He didn't invent the automobile, as so many mistakenly believe, but he did perfect assembly-line manufacturing and mass-production techniques. The result was the Model T, the first car the USA's middle class could afford to own.

Detroit quickly became the motor capital of the world. General Motors (GM), Chrysler and Ford were all headquartered in or near Detroit (and still are). The 1950s were the city's heyday, when the population exceeded two million and Motown music hit the airwaves. But racial tensions in 1967, and Japanese car competitors in the 1970s, shook the city and its industry. Detroit entered an era of deep decline, losing about two-thirds of its population.

The D resurged somewhat in the mid-2000s. Then the global economic crisis of 2008–9 crushed the auto industry. GM and Chrysler filed for bankruptcy, and thousands of blue- and white-collar workers lost their jobs. The city is currently 'restructuring.'

DON'T MISS

- **Detroit Institute of Arts** – Diego Rivera murals and more (right)
- **Henry Ford Museum** – American history's greatest hits (p617)
- **Heidelberg Project** – Polka-dotted neighborhood (p614)
- **Lafayette Coney Island** – Chili-slathered hot dogs (p615)
- **Funk Night** – All-night, get-down dance party (p616)

Orientation

Downtown revolves around the riverfront Renaissance Center and nearby Hart Plaza. Woodward Ave, the city's main boulevard, heads north from here to Midtown (containing the Cultural Center and its museums, plus Wayne State University) and on to architecturally rich New Center. Victorian-era, bar-filled Corktown sits west of downtown. The Mile Roads are Detroit's major east–west arteries; 8 Mile forms the city–suburbs boundary. Across the Detroit River lies Windsor, Canada.

The area between the sports arenas north to around Willis Rd is pretty deserted and best avoided on foot come nighttime.

Information

BOOKSTORES

John King Books (☎ 313-961-0622; 901 W Lafayette Blvd; 9:30am-5:30pm Mon-Sat) Second-hand bookstore.

EMERGENCY & MEDICAL SERVICES

Crisis hotline (☎ 313-224-7000)

CVS (☎ 313-833-0201; 350 E Warren Ave; 24hr) Pharmacy.

Detroit Receiving Hospital (☎ 313-745-3000; 4201 St Antoine St)

INTERNET ACCESS

You'll find free wi-fi in many cafés and bars, as well as the Renaissance Center (RenCen) lobby.

Detroit Main Library (☎ 313-833-1000; 5201 Woodward Ave; noon-8pm Tue & Wed, 10am-6pm Thu-Sat) Free internet terminals.

INTERNET RESOURCES

Forgotten Detroit (www.forgottendetroit.com) A website devoted to Detroit's 'ruins' (ie decaying buildings).

Model D (www.modeldmedia.com) Weekly e-zine about local developments and food/entertainment options, broken down by neighborhood.

MEDIA

WDET-FM 101.9 is the local NPR affiliate. WCSX-FM 94.7 blasts rock.

Between the Lines (www.pridesource.com) Free, weekly gay and lesbian paper.

Detroit News (www.detnews.com) Daily.

Detroit Free Press (www.freep.com) Daily.

Metro Times (www.metrotimes.com) Free alternative weekly that is the best guide to the entertainment scene.

MONEY

ATMs are plentiful in and near the RenCen. Metro Airport's McNamara Terminal has a couple of currency exchanges.

POST

Post office (☎ 313-226-8075; 1401 W Fort St; 6am-midnight)

TOURIST INFORMATION

Detroit Convention & Visitors Bureau (☎ 313-202-1800, 800-338-7648; www.visitdetroit.com; 10th fl, 211 W Fort St; 9am-5pm Mon-Fri)

Sights & Activities

Don't forget: top-notch attractions are also in Detroit's suburbs, like the Henry Ford Museum (p617) in Dearborn. Sights are commonly closed on Monday and Tuesday.

MIDTOWN & CULTURAL CENTER

Several museums cluster in the area known as the Cultural Center, by Woodward and Warren Aves. The cream of the crop is the **Detroit Institute of Arts** (☎ 313-833-7900; www.dia.org; 5200 Woodward Ave; adult/child 6-17yr $8/4; 10am-4pm Wed & Thu, 10am-10pm Fri, 10am-5pm Sat & Sun), which is lauded for its American collection. The centerpiece is Diego Rivera's mural *Detroit Industry*, which fills an entire room and reflects the city's blue-collar labor history.

The **Wright Museum of African American History** (☎ 313-494-5800; www.maah-detroit.org; 315 E Warren Ave; adult/child 3-12yr $8/5; 9am-5pm Tue-Sat, 1-5pm Sun) holds less than it would seem from the impressive exterior, though it's worth a look inside. The full-scale model of slaves chained up on a dark, creaking slave ship will leave you chilled.

The **Museum of Contemporary Art Detroit** (MOCAD; ☎ 313-832-6622; www.mocadetroit.org; 4454 Woodward

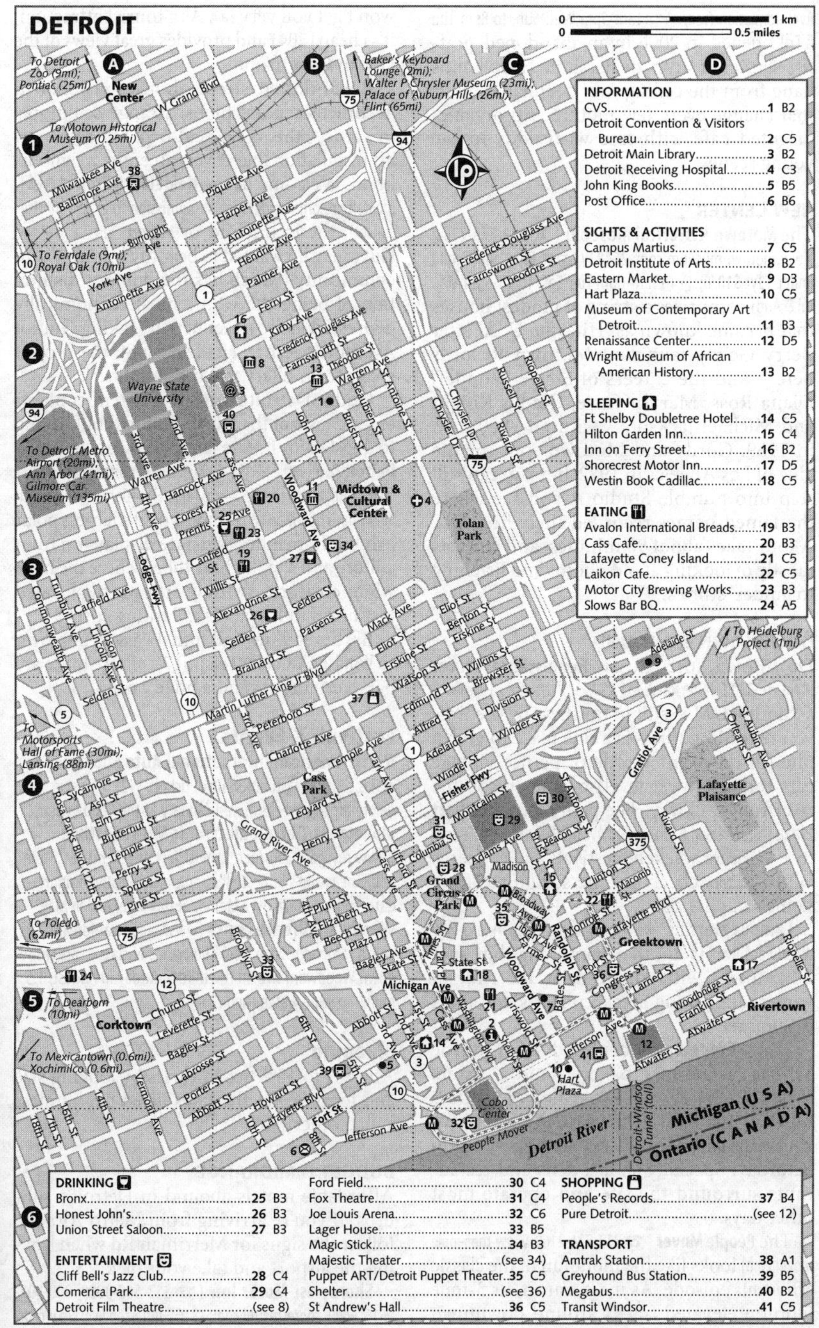
DETROIT
0 1 km
0 0.5 miles
A
B
C
D
1
2
3
4
5
6
To Detroit Zoo (9mi); Pontiac (25mi)
New Center
Baker's Keyboard Lounge (2mi); Walter P Chrysler Museum (23mi); Palace of Auburn Hills (26mi); Flint (65mi)
To Motown Historical Museum (0.25mi)
To Ferndale (9mi); Royal Oak (10mi)
To Detroit Metro Airport (20mi); Ann Arbor (41mi); Gilmore Car Museum (135mi)
To Motorsports Hall of Fame (30mi); Lansing (88mi)
To Toledo (62mi)
To Dearborn (10mi)
To Mexicantown (0.6mi); Xochimilco (0.6mi)
To Heidelburg Project (1mi)
Wayne State University
Midtown & Cultural Center
Tolan Park
Cass Park
Grand Circus Park
Lafayette Plaisance
Greektown
Rivertown
Corktown
Cobo Center
Hart Plaza
People Mover
Detroit River
Detroit-Windsor Tunnel (toll)
Michigan (U S A)
Ontario (C A N A D A)
W Grand Blvd
Milwaukee Ave
Baltimore Ave
Piquette Ave
Harper Ave
Antoinette Ave
Hendrie Ave
Palmer Ave
Burroughs Ave
York Ave
Ferry St
Kirby Ave
Frederick Douglass Ave
Farnsworth St
Theodore St
Warren Ave
Beaubien St
St Antoine St
John R St
Brush St
Chrysler Dr
Russell St
Riopelle St
Rivard St
Woodward Ave
Cass Ave
2nd Ave
3rd Ave
4th Ave
Lodge Fwy
Hancock Ave
Forest Ave
Prentis Ave
Canfield St
Willis St
Alexandrine St
Selden St
Parsons St
Brainard St
Martin Luther King Jr Blvd
Peterboro St
Charlotte Ave
Temple Ave
Park Ave
Mack Ave
Eliot St
Benton St
Erskine St
Watson St
Edmund Pl
Alfred St
Adelaide St
Winder St
Wilkins St
Brewster St
Division St
Fisher Fwy
Montcalm St
Columbia St
Adams Ave
Beacon St
Madison St
Clinton St
Macomb St
Gratiot Ave
St Aubin Ave
Orleans St
Trumbull Ave
Commonwealth Ave
Garfield Ave
Gibson St
Lincoln Ave
Sycamore St
Ash St
Elm St
Butternut St
Temple St
Perry St
Spruce St
Pine St
Rosa Parks Blvd (12th St)
Grand River Ave
Ledyard St
Henry St
Clifford St
Plum St
Elizabeth St
Beech St
Plaza Dr
Bagley Ave
State St
Times Sq
Park Pl
Broadway Ave
Library Ave
Farmer St
Randolph St
Monroe St
Lafayette Blvd
Fort St
Congress St
Larned St
Woodbridge St
Franklin St
Atwater St
Jefferson Ave
Michigan Ave
Washington Blvd
Griswold St
Shelby St
Bates St
Brooklyn St
Church St
Leverette St
Bagley St
Labrosse St
Porter St
Abbott St
Howard St
Lafayette Blvd
6th St
5th St
1st St
10th St
8th St
14th St
16th St
17th St
18th St
Vermont Ave

INFORMATION
CVS....1 B2
Detroit Convention & Visitors Bureau....2 C5
Detroit Main Library....3 B2
Detroit Receiving Hospital....4 C3
John King Books....5 B5
Post Office....6 B6
SIGHTS & ACTIVITIES
Campus Martius....7 C5
Detroit Institute of Arts....8 B2
Eastern Market....9 D3
Hart Plaza....10 C5
Museum of Contemporary Art Detroit....11 B3
Renaissance Center....12 D5
Wright Museum of African American History....13 B2
SLEEPING
Ft Shelby Doubletree Hotel....14 C5
Hilton Garden Inn....15 C4
Inn on Ferry Street....16 B2
Shorecrest Motor Inn....17 D5
Westin Book Cadillac....18 C5
EATING
Avalon International Breads....19 B3
Cass Cafe....20 B3
Lafayette Coney Island....21 C5
Laikon Cafe....22 C5
Motor City Brewing Works....23 B3
Slows Bar BQ....24 A5
DRINKING
Bronx....25 B3
Honest John's....26 B3
Union Street Saloon....27 B3
ENTERTAINMENT
Cliff Bell's Jazz Club....28 C4
Comerica Park....29 C4
Detroit Film Theatre....(see 8)
Ford Field....30 C4
Fox Theatre....31 C4
Joe Louis Arena....32 C6
Lager House....33 B5
Magic Stick....34 B3
Majestic Theater....(see 34)
Puppet ART/Detroit Puppet Theater..35 C5
Shelter....(see 36)
St Andrew's Hall....36 C5
SHOPPING
People's Records....37 B4
Pure Detroit....(see 12)
TRANSPORT
Amtrak Station....38 A1
Greyhound Bus Station....39 B5
Megabus....40 B2
Transit Windsor....41 C5

Ave; admission free; 11am-5pm Wed-Sun, to 8pm Thu & Fri) opened in 2006 in an abandoned, graffiti-slathered auto dealership. Heat lamps hang from the ceiling over peculiar exhibits that change every few months. An organic-oriented café with free wi-fi adds to the young scene.

NEW CENTER

The **Motown Historical Museum** (313-875-2264; www.motownmuseum.com; 2648 W Grand Blvd; adult/child under 13yr $10/8; 11am-6pm Tue-Sat, 10am-6pm Mon Jul & Aug) comprises a string of modest houses that became known as 'Hitsville USA' after Berry Gordy launched Motown Records here – and the careers of Stevie Wonder, Diana Ross, Marvin Gaye, Gladys Knight and Michael Jackson – with an $800 loan in 1959. Gordy and Motown split for the glitz of Los Angeles in 1972, but you can still step into humble Studio A and see where the famed names recorded their first hits. A tour takes about 90 minutes, and consists mostly of looking at old photos and listening to guides' stories.

DOWNTOWN & AROUND

Downtown, the glossy **Renaissance Center** (RenCen; 330 E Jefferson Ave), GM's headquarters – assuming GM is still in business by the time you're reading this – is a fine place to grab a bite (in the Wintergarden), peruse vintage cars (on the lower level) or embark on the riverfront walkway. The path ambles to **Hart Plaza** (cnr Jefferson & Woodward Aves), the site of many free, summer weekend festivals and concerts. While there, check out the sculpture of Joe Louis's mighty fist.

Campus Martius (www.campusmartiuspark.org; 800 Woodward Ave) is another communal hot spot downtown, with an outdoor ice rink in winter, and eating areas, concerts and films in summer.

Busy **Greektown** (centered on Monroe St) has restaurants, bakeries and a casino. Produce, cheese, spice and flower vendors fill the large halls at the **Eastern Market** (www.detroiteasternmarket.com; Gratiot Ave & Russell St) on Saturday. Specialty shops, delis and restaurants surround the site and operate most other days.

The **People Mover** (313-224-2160; www.thepeoplemover.com) looks like the monorail in the classic *Simpsons* episode. As mass transit, its 3-mile loop on elevated tracks around downtown won't get you very far. As a tourist attraction, it's cheap (50¢) and provides great views of the city and riverfront.

Polka-dotted streets, houses covered in Technicolor paint blobs, strange sculptures in yards – this is no acid trip, but rather an art installation that covers an entire neighborhood. Welcome to the **Heidelberg Project** (www.heidelberg.org; Heidelberg St; admission free; sunrise-sunset), the brainchild of street artist Tyree Guyton, who wanted to beautify his run-down community (which has the dubious distinction of being the USA's most economically depressed 'hood). Get here by taking Gratiot Ave northwest to Heidelberg St; the project spans from Ellery to Mt Elliott Sts.

Oddly, Detroit is one of the premier places to get a taste of the North Pole without having to dogsled for it. The Arctic Ring of Life at the **Detroit Zoo** (248-398-0900; www.detroitzoo.org; 8450 W 10 Mile Rd; adult/child 2-14yr $11/7; 10am-5pm Apr-Oct, 10am-4pm Nov-Mar;) is the world's largest polar exhibit. It includes first-rate displays on Inuit culture and a 'polar bear tube,' where the huge white creatures swim overhead. It's located just north in Royal Oak. Parking costs $5.

Border junkies will find it easy to pop over to **Windsor, Canada** (see p617), where there are bars, restaurants and a huge casino.

Festivals & Events

North American International Auto Show (www.naias.com; 1 Washington Blvd; tickets $12) It's autos galore for two weeks in mid-January at the Cobo Center.

Movement/Detroit Electronic Music Festival (www.myspace.com/detroitmusicfest; weekend pass from $40) The world's largest electronic music festival congregates in Hart Plaza over Memorial Day weekend in May.

Woodward Dream Cruise (www.woodwarddreamcruise.com; admission free) Thousands of classic cars cruise down Woodward Ave on the third Saturday in August; 1.5 million people watch them.

Sleeping

Add 9% to 15% tax (it varies by lodging size and location) to the rates listed here, unless stated otherwise.

BUDGET & MIDRANGE

Affordable motels abound in Detroit's suburbs. If you're arriving from Metro Airport, follow the signs for Merriman Rd when leaving the airport and take your pick.

Shorecrest Motor Inn (313-568-3000, 800-992-9616; www.shorecrestmi.com; 1316 E Jefferson Ave; s/d incl tax from $79/99; P) You'll get what you pay for at downtown's lowest-priced digs – good location and free parking, but pretty darn shabby, no-frills rooms.

Ft Shelby Doubletree Hotel (313-963-5600, 800-222-8733; http://doubletree1.hilton.com; 525 W Lafayette Blvd; ste $126-169;) This new hotel fills an historic beaux-arts building downtown. All rooms are suites, with both the sitting area and bedroom equipped with HDTV and free wi-fi. Pets under 20lb can stay for $50 extra. Parking costs $20, and there's free shuttle service around downtown.

Hilton Garden Inn (313-967-0900; www.hiltongardeninn.com; 351 Gratiot Ave; d $129-239;) The Hilton offers standard-issue digs, but it's comfortable and close to Comerica Park, Ford Field and Greektown. Parking costs $20.

our pick **Inn on Ferry Street** (313-871-6000; www.innonferrystreet.com; 84 E Ferry St; r incl breakfast from $149; P) Forty guest rooms fill a row of Victorian mansions right by the art museum. The lower-cost rooms are small but have deliciously soft bedding; the larger rooms feature plenty of antique wood furnishings. The healthy hot breakfast and shuttle to downtown are nice touches.

TOP END

Westin Book Cadillac (313-442-1600; www.bookcadillacwestin.com; 1114 Washington Blvd; r weekend/weekday from $179/299;) Opened in 2008, 'the Book' swooped into a 1924 landmark building and took over as the top address in town. It has all the amenities you'd expect at a swanky, 453-room hotel. In-room wi-fi costs $9.95 per day; parking costs $20.

Eating

Two nearby suburbs also have caches of hip restaurants and bars: walkable Ferndale at 9 Mile Rd and Woodward Ave, and Royal Oak just north of Ferndale on 10 Mile Rd.

MIDTOWN & CULTURAL CENTER

Avalon International Breads (313-832-0008; 422 W Willis St; items $1.50-5; 6am-6pm Tue-Sat, 7am-3pm Sun) Detroit's earthy types huddle round the hearth at Avalon, where its fresh-baked bread (like scallion dill or country Italian) makes an excellent base for the sandwiches it serves.

Cass Cafe (313-831-1400; 4620 Cass Ave; mains $6-14; 11am-11pm Mon-Thu, 11-1am Fri & Sat, 5-10pm Sun;) The Cass is a bohemian art gallery fused with a bar and restaurant serving soups, sandwiches and veggie beauties, like the lentil-walnut burger. Service can be fickle.

Motor City Brewing Works (313-832-2700; 470 W Canfield St; pizzas $6-9; 11am-midnight Mon-Thu, to 1am Fri & Sat, noon-midnight Sun;) Motor City fires up crisp-crusted pizzas in its brick oven, though you might be tempted to make a meal of house-brewed beer (Ghettoblaster wins praise) or the local cheese plate. For maximum effect, consume them on the rooftop patio.

DOWNTOWN

Fertile grazing grounds include Monroe St in Greektown and the RenCen fast-food court.

Lafayette Coney Island (313-964-8198; 118 Lafayette Blvd; items $2.50-4; 7:30-4am Mon-Thu, to 5am Fri & Sat, 9:30-4am Sun) The 'coney' – a hot dog smothered with chili and onions – is a Detroit specialty. When the craving strikes (and it will), take care of business at Lafayette. The minimalist menu consists of burgers, fries, pies, donuts and beer, in addition to the signature item. Cash only.

Laikon Cafe (313-963-7058; 569 Monroe St; mains $9-14; 11am-10pm Sun-Thu, to midnight Fri & Sat, closed Tue) Chef-owner Kostas has cooked staples like lamb and flaming cheese in his homey, old-school Greek restaurant for decades.

CORKTOWN & MEXICANTOWN

Xochimilco (313-843-0179; 3409 Bagley St; mains $5-12; 11-2am) Xochimilco is one of many places in Mexicantown, along Bagley St, that offers a solid, inexpensive line-up of burritos and other Mexican standards.

our pick **Slows Bar BQ** (313-962-9828; 2138 Michigan Ave; mains $12-20, half-rack ribs $16; 11am-11pm Mon-Thu, to midnight Fri & Sat, noon-11pm Sun) Mmm, slow-cooked southern-style barbecue in Corktown. Carnivores can carve into the three-meat combo plate (brisket, pulled pork and chicken). Vegetarians have options from okra fritters and mac 'n' cheese to a faux-meat barbecue sandwich.

Drinking

our pick **Bronx** (313-832-8464; 4476 2nd Ave;) There's not much inside Detroit's best boozer besides a pool table, dim lighting and a couple of jukeboxes filled with ballsy rock and soul. But that's the way the hipsters, slackers and rockers (the White Stripes used to hang here) like their dive bars. They're also fond of the beefy burgers served late at night and cheap beer selection.

FROM MOTOWN TO ROCK CITY

Motown Records and soul music put Detroit on the map in the 1960s. The thrashing punk rock of the Stooges and MC5 was the response to that smooth sound. By 1976, Detroit had been dubbed 'Rock City' by a Kiss song (though – just Detroit's luck – the tune was eclipsed by its B-side, 'Beth'). In recent years it has been hard-edged rock – aka whiplash rock 'n' roll – that has pushed the city to the music scene forefront. Homegrown stars include the White Stripes, Von Bondies and Dirtbombs. Rap (thank you, Eminem) and techno are Detroit's other renowned genres. Many music aficionados say the city's blight is what produces such a beautifully angry explosion of sound, and who's to argue? Scope free publications like the *Metro Times* and *Real Detroit Weekly,* or blogs like 'Motor City Rocks' (www.motorcityrocks.com), for current show and club listings.

Honest John's (☎ 313-832-5646; 488 Selden St; 7am-2am;) There really is a John and he's a Detroit classic, as is his unassuming bar where cops, nurses and other local workers toss back a cold one postshift.

Union Street Saloon (☎ 313-831-3965; 4145 Woodward Ave) This place has been around since the early 1900s and attracts a mod crowd.

Entertainment

LIVE MUSIC

St Andrew's Hall (☎ 313-961-6358; www.livenation.com; 431 E Congress St) It's a legendary alternative band venue in an old church. Downstairs is Shelter, a smaller music/dance club.

Lager House (☎ 313-961-4668; www.pjslagerhouse.com; 1254 Michigan Ave) This Corktown punk-underground club is dingy in an atmospheric way, with scrappy bands or DJs playing most nights.

Cliff Bell's Jazz Club (☎ 313-961-2543; www.cliffbells.com; 2030 Park Ave) With its dark wood, candlelight and art-deco decor, Bell's evokes 1930s elegance. Local jazz bands and poetry readings attract a diverse young audience nightly.

Baker's Keyboard Lounge (☎ 313-345-6300; www.bakerskeyboardlounge.com; 20510 Livernois Ave) Everyone from Miles Davis to Thelonious Monk to Nina Simone has let loose at the self-proclaimed 'world's oldest jazz club' on Detroit's far northwest side. It's rumored that the historic lounge may shutter due to financial constraints, so get here while you can.

Funk Night (www.myspace.com/funknightdetroit; rotating venues; admission $5) Dance your ass off at this all-night throw-down, which is held the last Friday of each month, when the owner of People's Records (see opposite) spins old funk tunes.

Magic Stick (☎ 313-833-9700; www.majesticdetroit.com; 4120 Woodward Ave) and the larger **Majestic Theater** (☎ 313-833-9700; 4140 Woodward Ave) are side-by-side concert halls where indie rockers and rap DJs perform. The complex also has bowling, billiards, a pizza joint and a café.

THEATER & CULTURE

Fox Theatre (☎ 313-983-6611; 2211 Woodward Ave) It's a gloriously restored 1928 venue that large touring shows occupy.

Puppet ART/Detroit Puppet Theater (☎ 313-961-7777; www.puppetart.org; 25 E Grand River Ave; adult/child $10/5;) Soviet-trained puppeteers perform beautiful shows in this 70-person theater; a small museum displays puppets from different cultures. Shows are typically held on Saturday afternoons.

Detroit Film Theatre (☎ 313-833-3237; 5200 Woodward Ave; tickets $7.50) Watch art flicks at the Detroit Institute of Arts (p612).

SPORTS

Palace of Auburn Hills (☎ 248-377-0100; www.nba.com/pistons; 5 Championship Dr) The Palace hosts the Pistons pro basketball team. It's about 30 miles northwest of downtown; take I-75 to exit 81.

Joe Louis Arena (☎ 313-396-7575; www.detroitredwings.com; 600 Civic Center Dr) The much-loved Red Wings play pro ice hockey at this arena where, if you can wrangle tickets, you might witness the strange octopus-throwing custom.

Ford Field (☎ 313-262-2003; www.detroitlions.com; 2000 Brush St) The Lions pro football team plays here.

Comerica Park (☎ 313-471-2255; www.detroittigers.com; 2100 Woodward Ave) Next door to Ford Field, the Tigers (in case you hadn't guessed from the giant stone animals roaring over the entrance) play pro baseball here. The park is particularly kid friendly, with a small Ferris wheel and carousel inside.

Shopping

Pure Detroit (☎ 313-259-5100; www.puredetroit.com; Renaissance Center, Level 1 of Wintergarden; 🕑 10:30am-5:30pm Mon-Fri, 11am-5pm Sat) Local artists create stylish products for Pure Detroit that celebrate the city's fast-cars-and-rock-music culture. This auto-centric outlet in GM's headquarters offers clocks made out of pistons and handbags cut from Camaro upholstery.

People's Records (☎ 313-831-0864; 3161 Woodward Ave; 🕑 10am-6pm Mon-Sat) Calling all crate-diggers: DJ-owned People's Records is your vinyl Valhalla. Used 45s are the specialty, with more than 80,000 jazz, soul and R & B titles filling bins.

Getting There & Around

Detroit Metro Airport (DTW; ☎ 734-247-7678; www.metroairport.com) is about 20 miles southwest of Detroit. Transport options from the airport to the city are few: you can take a cab for about $45; or you can take the 125 SMART bus ($1.50), but it takes one to 1½ hours to get downtown.

Greyhound (☎ 313-961-8005; 1001 Howard St) runs to various cities in Michigan and beyond. **Megabus** (☎ 877-462-6342; www.megabus.com/us) runs to/from Chicago (five hours) daily; departures are from downtown (at the Grand Circus Park People Mover station) and Wayne State University (corner off Cass and Warren Aves).

Amtrak (☎ 313-873-3442; 11 W Baltimore Ave) trains go thrice daily to Chicago ($29 to $41, 5½ hours). You can also head east – to New York ($78 to $152, 16½ hours) or destinations en route – but you'll first be bused to Toledo.

Transit Windsor (☎ 519-944-4111; www.citywindsor.ca/transitwindsor) operates the Tunnel Bus to Windsor, Canada. It costs $3.75 (American or Canadian) and departs by Mariner's Church (corner of Randolph St and Jefferson Ave) near the Detroit–Windsor Tunnel entrance, as well as other spots downtown. Bring your passport.

The **Detroit Department of Transportation** (DDOT; ☎ 888-336-8287; www.ridedetroittransit.com) handles the pokey local bus service ($1.50). The **Suburban Mobility Authority for Regional Transportation** (SMART; ☎ 866-962-5515; www.smartbus.org) handles service to the 'burbs ($1.50 to $2). For information on the People Mover city-rail line, see p614.

If you need a cab service, call **Checker Cab** (☎ 313-963-7000).

AROUND DETROIT

Stunning Americana and good eatin' lie just down the road from Detroit.

Dearborn

Dearborn is 10 miles west of downtown Detroit and home to two of the USA's finest museums. The indoor **Henry Ford Museum** (☎ 313-982-6001; www.thehenryford.org; 20900 Oakwood Blvd; adult/child 5-12yr $15/11; 🕑 9:30am-5pm) contains a fascinating wealth of American culture, such as the chair Lincoln was sitting in when he was assassinated, the presidential limo in which Kennedy was killed, the hot-dog-shaped Oscar Mayer Wienermobile (photo op!) and the bus on which Rosa Parks refused to give up her seat. Don't worry: you'll get your vintage car fix here too. Parking is $5. The adjacent, outdoor **Greenfield Village** (☎ 313-982-6001; adult/child 5-12yr $22/16; 🕑 9:30am-5pm daily mid-Apr–Oct, 9:30am-5pm Fri-Sun Nov & Dec) features historic buildings shipped in from all over the country, reconstructed and restored, such as Thomas Edison's laboratory from Menlo Park and the Wright Brothers' airplane workshop. Plus you can add on the **Rouge Factory Tour** (☎ 313-982-6001; adult/child 5-12yr $15/11; 🕑 9:30am-3pm Mon-Sat) and see F-150 trucks roll off the assembly line where Ford first perfected his self-sufficient, mass-production techniques.

All of these three attractions are separate, but you can get a combination ticket for Henry Ford and Greenfield Village (adult/child five to 12 years $32/24). Plan on at least one very full day at the complex.

Dearborn has the nation's greatest concentration of people of Arab descent, so it's no surprise that the **Arab American National Museum** (☎ 313-582-2266; www.arabamericanmuseum.org; 13624 Michigan Ave; adult/child 6-12yr $6/3; 🕑 10am-6pm Wed-Sat, to 8pm Thu, noon-5pm Sun) popped up here. It's a noble concept, located in a pretty, bright-tiled building, but it's not terribly exciting unless actor Jamie Farr's *MASH* TV-show script wows you. The thousand-and-one Arabian eateries lining Michigan Ave provide a more engaging feel for the culture. Cavernous **La Pita** (☎ 313-563-7482; 22681 Newman St; sandwiches $3.75-4.75, mains $10-19; 🕑 10am-11pm Mon-Sat, 11am-10pm Sun) is a classic; it's a block south of Michigan Ave, tucked into one of the many strip malls along the road.

Ann Arbor

Forty-odd miles west of Detroit, liberal and bookish Ann Arbor is home to the University of Michigan. The walkable downtown, which

CLASSIC CARS IN MICHIGAN

More than sand dunes, beaches and Mackinac Island fudge, Michigan is synonymous with cars. While the connection hasn't been so positive in recent years, the state commemorates its glory days via several auto museums. The following fleets are within a few hours' drive from the Motor City.

Henry Ford Museum (p617) This Dearborn museum is loaded with vintage cars, including the first one Henry Ford ever built. In adjacent Greenfield Village you can ride in a Model T that rolled off the assembly line in 1923.

Automotive Hall of Fame (☎ 313-240-4000; www.automotivehalloffame.org; 21400 Oakwood Blvd, Dearborn; adult/child 5-12yr $8/4; 9am-5pm late May-Oct, closed Mon & Tue Nov-Apr) Next door to the Henry Ford Museum, the interactive Auto Hall focuses on the people behind famed cars, such as Mr Ferdinand Porsche and Mr Soichiro Honda.

Motorsports Hall of Fame (☎ 800-250-7223; www.mshf.com; Novi Rd, Novi; adult/child under 12yr $5/3; 10am-5pm Tue-Sun) In the Novi Expo Center just off I-96, the Motorsports Hall has three-dozen vehicles that were driven by legendary racers.

Walter P Chrysler Museum (☎ 248-944-0001; www.chryslerheritage.com; 1 Chrysler Dr, Auburn Hills; adult/child 6-12yr $8/4; 10am-5pm Tue-Sat, noon-5pm Sun) This museum at Chrysler's headquarters (take exit 78 off I-75) has 70 beauties on display, including rare Dodge, DeSoto, Nash and Hudson models.

Sloan Museum (☎ 810-237-3450; www.sloanmuseum.com; 1221 E Kearsley St, Flint; adult/child 3-11yr $6/4; 10am-5pm Mon-Fri, noon-5pm Sat & Sun) The Sloan has two buildings housing more than 60 cars, including the oldest production-model Chevrolet in existence and a 1910 Buick 'Bug' raced by Louis Chevrolet.

Gilmore Car Museum (☎ 269-671-5089; www.gilmorecarmuseum.org; 6865 Hickory Rd, Hickory Corners; adult/child 7-15yr $9/7; 9am-5pm Mon-Fri, to 6pm Sat & Sun, closed Nov-Apr) North of Kalamazoo along Hwy 43, this museum complex offers 22 barns filled with 120 vintage autos, including 15 Rolls Royces dating back to a 1910 Silver Ghost.

RE Olds Transportation Museum (☎ 517-372-0529; www.reoldsmuseum.org; 240 Museum Dr, Lansing; adult/child 5-18yr $5/3; 10am-5pm Tue-Sat year-round, noon-5pm Sun Apr-Oct) Twenty vintage cars sit in the old Lansing City Bus Garage, including the first Oldsmobile, which was built in 1897.

abuts the campus, is loaded with free-trade coffee shops, bookstores, brewpubs and independent record stores. The **Ann Arbor CVB** (☎ 800-888-9487; www.annarbor.org) has the town lowdown.

The university provides the main sights. The **Matthaei Botanical Gardens** (☎ 734-647-7600; www.mbgna.umich.edu; 1800 Dixboro Rd; admission free; sunrise-sunset) offers 300-plus acres criss-crossed by walking paths, plus a cacti-filled **conservatory** (adult/child 5-18yr $5/2; 10am-4:30pm Tue-Sun, to 8pm Wed); it's about 5 miles east of downtown. The 'Arb' – **Nichols Arboretum** (☎ 734-647-7600; 1610 Washington Heights; admission free; sunrise-sunset) – is another oasis of greenery for walking, jogging and Frisbee throwing; it's on the campus' east side. The university also has groovy free art and archaeology museums.

If you happen to arrive on a fall weekend and wonder why 110,000 people – the size of Ann Arbor's entire population, more or less – are crowding into the school's stadium, the answer is football. Tickets are nearly impossible to purchase, especially when nemesis Ohio State is in town. You can try by calling the **U of M Ticket Office** (☎ 734-764-0247; www.mgoblue.com /ticketoffice).

There are several B&Bs within walking distance of downtown. Hotels tend to be about 5 miles out, with several clustered south on State St. The CVB website has contact details.

All these things are fine and dandy, but let's be frank: the real reason to visit Ann Arbor is the donut sundae.

our pick **Zingerman's Roadhouse** (☎ 734-663-3663; 2501 Jackson Ave; burgers $10-16, mains $17-27; 7am-10pm Mon-Thu, to 11pm Fri & Sat, to 9pm Sun) makes the glorious, bourbon-caramel-sauced dessert, as well as traditional American dishes like Carolina grits, Iowa pork chops and Massachusetts oysters using sustainably produced ingredients; it's 2 miles west of downtown. **Zingerman's Delicatessen** (☎ 734-663-3354; 422 Detroit St; sandwiches $10-15.50; 7am-10pm) piles local, organic and specialty ingredients onto towering sandwiches in downtown proper. **Jerusalem Garden** (☎ 734-995-5060; 307 S 5th Ave; mains $4-9; 10am-9pm Mon-Thu, to 9:30pm Fri & Sat, noon-8pm Sun) plates Middle Eastern dishes.

When darkness falls, head to the **Blind Pig** (☎ 734-996-8555; www.blindpigmusic.com; 208 S 1st St) for rock and blues, or the folk-oriented **Ark** (☎ 734-761-1800; www.a2ark.org; 316 S Main St). Handcrafted beer, like crisp Sacred Cow IPA, is found at **Arbor Brewing Company** (☎ 734-213-1393; 114 E Washington St).

CENTRAL MICHIGAN

Michigan's heartland, plunked in the center of the Lower Peninsula, alternates between fertile farms and highway-crossed urban areas.

Lansing

Smallish Lansing is the state capital; a few miles east lies East Lansing, home of Michigan State University. The **Greater Lansing CVB** (☎ 888-252-6746; www.lansing.org) has information on both.

Between Lansing's downtown and the university is the **River Trail**, which extends 8 miles along the shores of Michigan's longest river, the Grand. The paved path is popular with cyclists, joggers and inline skaters, and links a number of attractions, including a children's museum, zoo and fish ladder.

Downtown, the **Michigan Historical Museum** (☎ 517-373-3559; 702 W Kalamazoo St; admission free; 🕒 9am-4:30pm Mon-Fri, 10am-4pm Sat, 1-5pm Sun) features 26 permanent galleries, including a replica UP copper mine you can walk through. The **RE Olds Transportation Museum** (see boxed text, opposite) will please car buffs.

Lansing's downtown hotels feed off politicians and lobbyists, so they're fairly expensive. It's best to head to East Lansing's **Wild Goose Inn** (☎ 517-333-3334; www.wildgooseinn.com; 512 Albert St; r incl breakfast $139-159; ⊠ 📶), a six-room B&B one block from Michigan State's campus. All rooms have fireplaces and most have Jacuzzis.

Kewpee's (☎ 517-482-8049; 118 S Washington Sq; mains $3-7; 🕒 8am-6pm Mon-Fri, 11am-2pm Sat) has been feeding folks olive burgers and crisp onion rings by the capitol for more than 85 years. For breakfast, **Golden Harvest** (☎ 517-485-3663; 1625 Turner St; breakfast $7-9; 🕒 8am-2pm) is a loud, punk-rock-meets-hippie diner serving the sausage-and-French-toast Bubba Sandwich and hearty omelets. Abundant restaurants, pubs and nightclubs also fill Michigan State's northern campus area.

Grand Rapids

The second-largest city in Michigan, Grand Rapids is known for office-furniture manufacturing, a conservative Dutch Reform attitude and the fact that it's only 30 miles from Lake Michigan's Gold Coast. The **Grand Rapids CVB** (☎ 800-678-9859; www.visitgrandrapids.org) provides maps, coupons and any other information you'll need.

The downtown **Gerald R Ford Museum** (☎ 616-254-0400; www.fordlibrarymuseum.gov; 303 Pearl St NW; adult/child 6-18yr $7/3; 🕒 9am-5pm) is dedicated to the country's only Michigander president (though he was born with a different name in Nebraska). Ford stepped into the Oval Office after Richard Nixon and his vice president, Spiro Agnew, resigned in disgrace. It's an intriguing period in US history, and the museum does an excellent job of covering it, right down to displaying the burglary tools used in the Watergate break-in. Ford died in 2006 and is buried on a hillside on the museum's grounds.

The 118-acre **Frederik Meijer Gardens** (☎ 616-957-1580; www.meijergardens.org; 1000 E Beltline NE; adult/child 5-13yr $12/6; 🕒 9am-5pm Mon-Sat, to 9pm Tue, noon-5pm Sun) features impressive blooms and sculptures by Auguste Rodin, Henry Moore and others. It is 5 miles east of downtown via I-196.

Downtown's **Days Inn** (☎ 616-235-7611; www.dayshotelgrandrapids.com; 310 Pearl St NW; r $89-139; P ⊠ 💻 📶 🏊) is a good-value, well-located sleeping option. But if you come to Grand Rapids with time for only one stop, make it **Founders Brewing Company** (☎ 616-776-1195; 235 Grandville Ave SW; sandwiches $6-8; 🕒 11am-2am Mon-Sat, 3pm-2am Sun). The ruby-tinged Dirty Bastard Ale is good swillin', and there's meaty (or vegetable-y, for vegetarians) deli sandwiches to soak it up.

LAKE MICHIGAN SHORE

They don't call it the Gold Coast for nothing. Michigan's 300-mile western shoreline features endless stretches of beach, coastal parks, wineries, orchards and small towns that boom during the summer – and shiver during the snow-packed winter. Note all state parks listed here take **campsite reservations** (☎ 800-447-2757; www.midnrreservations.com; fee $8) and require a vehicle permit (day/year $8/29), unless specified otherwise.

Harbor Country

Harbor Country refers to a group of eight small, lake-hugging towns just over the Michigan border. Yep, they've got your requisite beaches, wineries and antique shops; however, they've got a couple of big surprises too. The **Harbor Country Chamber of Commerce** (☎ 269-469-5409; www.harborcountry.org) has the basics.

First up, surfing. Believe it, people: you can surf Lake Michigan, and the VW bus-driving dudes at **Third Coast Surf Shop** (☎ 269-932-4575; www.thirdcoastsurfshop.com; 22 S Smith St; 11am-6pm Jun-Aug, reduced hours Sep-May) will show you how. They provide wetsuits and boards for surfing, skim boarding and paddle boarding. For novices, they offer 1½-hour lessons right from the public beach Thursday to Sunday from June through to August (and Saturdays in September). Board rentals cost $15/25 per half-/full day. Wet suits cost $10/15 per half-/full day. Lessons (equipment included) cost $45/65 for group/private instruction. The surf shop is in New Buffalo, Harbor Country's biggest town.

Three Oaks is the only Harbor community that's inland (6 miles in, via US 12). Here Green Acres meets Greenwich Village in a funky farm-and-arts blend. By day, rent bikes at **Dewey Cannon Trading Company** (☎ 269-756-3361; 3 Dewey Cannon Ave; bike per day $15; 10am-4pm Sun-Fri, to 9pm Sat) and cycle lightly used rural roads past orchards and wineries. By eve, catch a provocative play or art-house flick at Three Oaks' theaters.

Hungry? Get a wax paper–wrapped cheeseburger, spicy curly fries and cold beer at **Redamak's** (☎ 269-469-4522; 616 E Buffalo St; burgers $4.50-9; noon-10:30pm, closed Nov-Feb) in New Buffalo.

Saugatuck & Douglas

Saugatuck is one of the Gold Coast's most popular resort areas, known for its strong arts community, numerous B&Bs and gay-friendly vibe. Douglas is its twin city a mile or so south, and they've pretty much sprawled into one. The **Saugatuck/Douglas CVB** (☎ 269-857-1701; www.saugatuck.com) provides maps and more.

The best thing to do in Saugatuck is also the most affordable. Jump aboard the **Saugatuck Chain Ferry** (one way $1; 9am-9pm late May-early Sep) at the foot of Mary St and the operator will pull you across the Kalamazoo River. On the other side, walk to the dock's left and soon you'll come to **Mt Baldhead**, a 200ft-high sand dune. Huff up the stairs to see the grand view, and then race down the north side to beautiful **Oval Beach**.

Galleries and shops proliferate downtown on Water and Butler Sts; galleries and antique shops also line the Blue Star Hwy running south from Saugatuck. Blueberry U-pick farms share the road here and make a juicy stop.

Several frilly B&Bs are tucked into the Saugatuck's century-old Victorian homes, with most ranging from $125 to $300 a night per couple in the summer high season. Try the **Bayside Inn** (☎ 269-857-4321; www.baysideinn.net; 618 Water St; r incl breakfast $110-200;), a 10-room former boathouse with an outdoor tub on Saugatuck's waterfront, or the retro-cool **Pines Motorlodge** (☎ 269-857-5211; www.thepinesmotorlodge.com; 56 Blue Star Hwy; r incl breakfast $129-189;), with rooms amid the firs in Douglas.

For eats, **Marro's Italian Restaurant** (☎ 269-857-4248; 147 Water St; pizzas $19-23; 5-10pm Tue-Sun) gets props for its pizzas. **Saugatuck Brewing Company** (☎ 269-857-7222; 2948 Blue Star Hwy; 11am-11pm Sun-Thu, to midnight Fri & Sat) gets praise for its beers and local clientele hangin' out. And for dessert, nothing beats the bulging fruit pies at **Crane's Pie Pantry** (☎ 269-561-2297; 6054 124th Ave; 9am-8pm Mon-Sat, 11am-8pm Sun May-Oct, reduced hours Nov-Apr). It's 3 miles south of Saugatuck–Douglas on the Blue Star, and then 4 miles inland on Hwy 89 in Fennville.

Muskegon & Ludington

These towns are jump-off points for the two ferries that sail across the lake, providing a shortcut between Michigan and Wisconsin. The **Lake Express** (☎ 866-914-1010; www.lake-express.com; May-Oct) crosses between Muskegon and Milwaukee (one way adult/child five to 17 years $81/47.50, car/bicycle $90/12, 2½ hours). The older **SS Badger** (☎ 888-337-7948; www.ssbadger.com; mid-May–mid-Oct) crosses from Ludington to Manitowoc (one way adult/child five to 15 years $74/29, car/bicycle $77/6, four hours).

The towns themselves aren't much, but the **Muskegon Winter Sports Complex** (☎ 231-744-9629; www.msports.org; 442 Scenic Dr; Nov-Mar) kicks ass with its full-on luge track, ice-skating rinks and cross-country ski trails. And lakeside **Ludington State Park** (☎ 231-843-8671; campsites $16-27; year-round), beyond the city limits on M-116, is one of Michigan's largest and most popular playlots. It has a top-notch trail system, a renovated lighthouse to visit (or live in, as a volunteer lighthouse keeper) and miles of beach.

Sleeping Bear Dunes National Lakeshore

This national park stretches from north of Frankfort to just before Leland, on the

Leelanau Peninsula. Stop at the park's **visitors center** (☎ 231-326-5134; www.nps.gov/slbe; 9922 Front St; 8:30am-6pm Jun-Aug, to 4pm Sep-May) in Empire for information, trail maps and vehicle entry permits (week/annual $10/20).

Attractions include the famous **Dune Climb** along Hwy 109, where you trudge up the 200ft-high dune and then run or roll down. Gluttons for leg-muscle punishment can keep slogging all the way to Lake Michigan, a strenuous 1½-hour trek one way; bring water. There are also plenty of easier hikes; ask at the visitors center. Short on time or stamina? Take the 7-mile, one-lane, picnic area–studded **Pierce Stocking Scenic Drive**, perhaps the best way to absorb the stunning lake vistas.

Those seeking an overnight wilderness adventure should head to **North Manitou Island** or day-trip to **South Manitou Island** on the **ferry** (☎ 231-256-9061; www.leelanau.com/manitou; Leland). A round-trip costs $32/18 per adult/child under 13 years, with two to seven departures per week from May to mid-October. The ride takes about 1½ hours. On South Manitou, the 7-mile hike to the Valley of the Giants, a towering stand of old cedar trees, rewards with mystical silence.

Feeling lazy? Plop your butt in an inner tube and float down the Platte River with **Riverside Canoe Trips** (☎ 231-325-5622; www.canoemichigan.com; 5042 Scenic Hwy, Honor; tube/kayak/canoe $18/28/39; May–mid-Oct) back on the mainland.

Traverse City

Michigan's 'cherry capital' is the largest city in the northern half of the Lower Peninsula. It's got a bit of urban sprawl, but it's still a happenin' base from which to see the Sleeping Bear Dunes, Mission Peninsula wineries, U-pick orchards and other area attractions.

Stop at the downtown **visitors center** (☎ 231-947-1120, 800-872-8377; www.visittraversecity.com; 101 W Grandview Pkwy; 9am-6pm Mon-Sat, 11am-3pm Sun Jun–mid-Oct, 9am-5pm Mon-Fri, 9am-3pm Sat mid-Oct–May) for maps and the do-it-yourself foodie tour brochure (also available online). Or kick it up a notch and take a guided jaunt to local farms and cherry orchards with **Learn Great Foods** (☎ 866-240-1650; www.learngreatfoods.com; tours $50-105). Excursions vary; some include alfresco dinner on the farm. Check online for the schedule and locations.

Traverse City State Park (☎ 231-922-5270; 1132 US 31 N; campsites $27) is a popular place to get your beach on, with 700ft of sugary sand. It's about 2 miles east of downtown, and dozens of resorts, motels, jet-ski rental shops and parasail operators fill the space in between.

Wineries are all over, but the most popular drive is to head north from Traverse City on Hwy 37 for 20 miles to the end of Mission Peninsula. Stop at **Chateau Grand Traverse** (☎ 231-223-7355; www.cgtwines.com; 10am-7pm Mon-Sat, noon-6pm Sun Jun-Aug, reduced hours Sep-May) or **Chateau Chantal** (☎ 800-969-4009; www.chateauchantal.com; 11am-8pm Mon-Sat, noon-5pm Sun mid-Jun–Aug, reduced hours Sep–mid-Jun) and sample their Chardonnay or Pinot Noir. **Peninsula Cellars** (☎ 231-933-9787; www.peninsulacellars.com; 10am-6pm Mon-Sat, noon-5pm Sun May-Oct, reduced hours Nov-Apr), which is in an old schoolhouse, is often less crowded and makes fine whites. Buy any local bottle; you can take it out to Lighthouse Park beach, at the peninsula's tip, and enjoy it with the waves licking your toes.

Back in the city, **Brick Wheels** (☎ 231-947-4274; www.brickwheels.com; 736 E 8th St; per day $30; 9am-6pm Tue-Thu, to 8pm Mon & Fri, 9am-4:30pm Sat, 11am-4pm Sun) rents bicycles; visitors can immediately jump onto the **Traverse Area Recreation Trail** (TART), an 11-mile paved path along the bay. Those with more ambition (and money) can learn to kiteboard with the outfitter **Broneah** (☎ 231-392-2212; www.broneah.com; 207 Grandview Pkwy; full-day lesson $450).

If you arrive in mid-July, be sure to drive north on US 31 toward Elk Rapids and beyond for roadside stands selling cherries and pies and for U-pick farms. Actually, they pop up throughout the region. We mean it literally when we say take your pick.

Traverse City lodgings are often full – and more expensive – during weekends; the visitors center website has contact details. Most resorts overlooking the bay cost $150 to $250 per night. The aforementioned Chantal and Grand Traverse wineries also double as B&Bs and fit into this price range.

Guests can rent jet skis and enjoy nightly bonfires at **Park Shore Resort** (☎ 877-349-8898; www.parkshoreresort.com; 1401 US 31 North; r incl breakfast weekday/weekend from $150/190;). Motels on the other side of US 31 (away from the water) are more moderately priced, such as **Mitchell Creek Inn** (☎ 231-947-9330, 800-947-9330; www.mitchellcreek.com; 894 Munson Ave; r/cottages from $99/150), near the state park beach.

After a day of fun in the sun, refresh with sandwiches at gastronome favorite **Folgarelli's**

(☎ 231-941-7651; 424 W Front St; sandwiches $6-9; 🕑 9:30am-6:30pm Mon-Fri, 9:30am-5:30 Sat) and cold, handcrafted beer and root beer at **North Peak Brewing Company** (☎ 231-941-7325; 400 W Front St).

Charlevoix & Petoskey

These two towns provide Hemingway sights and island excursions (see boxed text, below). They're also where Michigan's upper-crusters maintain summer homes. The downtown areas of both places have gourmet restaurants and high-class shops, and the marinas are filled with yachts.

In Petoskey, **Stafford's Perry Hotel** (☎ 231-347-4000; www.staffords.com; Bay at Lewis St; r $129-259; ❄ 💻 📶) is a grand historic place in which to stay. **Petoskey State Park** (☎ 231-347-2311; 2475 M-119; campsites $27-29; 🕑 year-round) is north along M-119 and has a beautiful beach. Look for indigenous Petoskey stones, which are honeycomb-patterned fragments of ancient coral. Or look for mushrooms. Inland at Boyne City, hundreds of fungus lovers forage at the **National Morel Mushroom Festival** (www.morelfest.com; 🕑 mid-May).

STRAITS OF MACKINAC

This region, between the Upper and Lower Peninsulas, features a long history of forts and fudge shops. Car-free Mackinac Island is Michigan's premier tourist draw.

One of the most spectacular sights in the area is the 5-mile-long **Mackinac Bridge** (known locally as 'Big Mac'), which spans the Straits of Mackinac. The $3 toll is worth every penny as the views from the bridge, which include two Great Lakes, two peninsulas and hundreds of islands, are second to none in Michigan.

And remember: despite the spelling, it's pronounced *mac*-in-aw.

Mackinaw City

At the south end of Mackinac Bridge, bordering I-75, is touristy Mackinaw City. It serves mainly as a jump-off point to Mackinac Island, but it does have a couple of interesting sights.

Next to the bridge (its visitors center is actually beneath the bridge) is **Colonial Michilimackinac** (☎ 231-436-5563; www.mackinacparks.com; adult/child 5-17yr $10.50/6.50; 🕑 9am-6pm Jun-Aug, to 4pm May & Sep–mid-Oct), a National Historic Landmark that features a reconstructed stockade first built in 1715 by the French. Some 3 miles southeast of the city on US 23 is **Historic Mill Creek** (☎ 231-436-4226; www.mackinacparks.com; adult/child 5-17yr $8/4.75; 🕑 9am-5pm Jun-Aug, to 4pm May & Sep–mid-Oct), which has an 18th-century sawmill, historic displays and nature trails. A combination ticket for both sights, along with Fort Mackinac (opposite), is available at a discount.

If you can't find lodging on Mackinac Island – which should be your first choice – motels line I-75 and US 23 in Mackinaw City. Most cost $100-plus per night. Try **Days Inn** (☎ 231-436-8961; www.daysinnbridgeview.com; 206 N Nicolet St; r incl breakfast $110-160; ❄ 📶 🏊).

PAPA'S FOOTPRINTS

A number of writers have ties to northwest Michigan, but none are as famous as Ernest Hemingway, who spent the summers of his youth at his family's cottage on Walloon Lake. Hemingway buffs often tour the area to view the places that made their way into his writing.

In Petoskey, you can see the Hemingway collection at the **Little Traverse History Museum** (☎ 231-347-2620; www.petoskeymuseum.org; 100 Depot Ct; admission $2; 🕑 10am-4pm Mon-Fri, 1-4pm Sat Jun–mid-Oct), including rare 1st-edition books that the author autographed for a friend when he visited in 1947. Afterward, visit **City Park Grill** (☎ 231-347-0101; 432 E Lake St; 🕑 11:30am-11pm Mon-Fri, to midnight Sat & Sun), where Hemingway, with his famous drinking habit, was a regular.

Next, head south on US 31 toward Charlevoix. Just before entering town, turn east onto Boyne City Rd. It skirts beautiful Lake Charlevoix and eventually arrives at the **Horton Bay General Store**, which appears in Hemingway's short story 'Up in Michigan.' Built in 1876 with 'a high false front,' the store's most prominent feature is its large porch, with benches and stairs at either end. Hemingway idled away some youthful summers on that porch and fished at nearby Horton Creek for trout. His fishing buddy was Vollie Fox, whose family owned the **Red Fox Inn** adjacent to the store. Fox's grandson now runs a Hemingway bookstore there.

The **Michigan Hemingway Society** (www.michiganhemingwaysociety.org) provides further information for self-guided tours. It also hosts a **Hemingway festival** for a weekend every October.

IF YOU HAVE A FEW MORE DAYS

Those looking for an alternative to Mackinac Island's fudgey hullabaloo can sail from downtown Charlevoix to **Beaver Island** (www.beaverisland.org), which is a quiet, Irish-influenced enclave of 600 people. The **ferry** (☎ 231-547-2311, 888-446-4095; www.beaverislandboatcompany.com) makes one to four trips daily from May to mid-September, less often in April and mid-September through to mid-December. The two-hour journey costs $24/75 one way per person/car.

Once on the island, **Inland Seas Kayaking** (☎ 231-448-2221; www.inlandseaskayaking.com; half-day tour $65) offers rewarding kayaking or snorkeling trips; the latter visit shipwrecked schooners. The island has a handful of hotels and B&Bs. You'll need to stay overnight if you go kayaking or snorkeling. The **Emerald Isle Hotel** (☎ 231-448-2376; www.emeraldislehotel.com; 37985 Kings Hwy; d $104-130, ste $149-169; wi-fi) is basic but pleasant.

St Ignace

At the north end of Mackinac Bridge is St Ignace, the other departure point for Mackinac Island and the second-oldest settlement in Michigan – Père Jacques Marquette founded a mission here in 1671. As soon as you've paid your bridge toll, you'll pass a huge **visitors center** (☎ 906-643-6979; I-75N; 8am-6pm summer, 9am-5pm rest of year) with racks of statewide information.

Mackinac Island

From either Mackinaw City or St Ignace you can catch a ferry to Mackinac Island, Michigan's top crowd-puller. The island's location in the straits between Lake Michigan and Lake Huron made it a prized port in the North American fur trade, and a site the British and Americans battled over many times.

The most important date on this 3.8-sq-mile island was 1898 – the year cars were banned to encourage tourism. Today all travel is by horse or bicycle; even the police use bikes to patrol the town. The crowds of tourists – called Fudgies by the islanders – can be crushing at times, particularly during summer weekends. But when the last ferry leaves in the evening and clears out the day-trippers, Mackinac's real charm emerges and you drift back into another, slower era.

The **visitors center** (☎ 800-454-5227; www.mackinacisland.org; Main St; 9am-5pm), by the Arnold Line ferry dock, has maps for hiking and cycling. Eighty percent of the island is state parkland. Not much stays open between November and April.

SIGHTS & ACTIVITIES

Edging the island's shoreline is Hwy 185, the only Michigan highway that doesn't permit cars. The best way to view the incredible scenery along this 8-mile road is by bicycle; bring your own or rent one in town at one of the many outfitters for $7 to $8 per hour. You can loop around the flat road in about an hour.

The two best attractions – **Arch Rock** (a huge limestone arch that sits 150ft above Lake Huron) and **Fort Holmes** (the island's other fort) – are both free. You can also ride past the **Grand Hotel**, which boasts a porch stretching halfway to Detroit. Unfortunately if you're not staying at the Grand (minimum $235 per night per person), it costs $10 to stroll its long porch. Best to admire from afar.

Fort Mackinac (☎ 906-847-3328; www.mackinacparks.com; adult/child 5-17yr $10/6; 9:30am-6pm Jun-Aug, 9:30am-4:30pm May & Sep–mid-Oct) sits atop limestone cliffs near downtown. The British built it in 1780, and it's one of the best-preserved military forts in the country. Stop into the fort's tearoom for a bite and million-dollar view of downtown and the Straits of Mackinac from the outdoor tables.

The fort admission price is also good for six other museums in town, including the Dr Beaumont Museum (where the doctor performed his famous digestive tract experiments) and Benjamin Blacksmith Shop. The Indian Dormitory Art Museum, housing Native American and other arts, is scheduled to open in 2010.

SLEEPING

Rooms are booked far in advance during summer weekends; July to mid-August is peak season. The visitors center website has lodging contacts. Camping is not permitted anywhere on the island.

Most hotels and B&Bs charge at least $175 for two people. Exceptions include the four-room **Bogan Lane Inn** (☎ 906-847-3439;

www.boganlaneinn.com; Bogan Lane; r incl breakfast $85-125; year-round;); the 11-room **Cloghaun B&B** (906-847-3885; www.cloghaun.com; Market St; r incl breakfast $105-190; mid-May–late Oct;) and the eight-room **Hart's B&B** (906-847-3854; www.hartsmackinac.com; Market St; r incl breakfast $145-175;). All are walkable to downtown.

EATING & DRINKING

Fudge shops are the island's best-known eateries; resistance is futile when they use fans to blow the aroma out onto Huron St. Hamburger and sandwich shops abound downtown.

JL Beanery Coffeehouse (906-847-6533; Huron St; mains $6-13; 7am-7pm;) Read the newspaper, sip a steaming cup of joe and gaze at the lake at this waterside café. It serves dandy breakfasts, sandwiches and soups.

Horn's Bar (906-847-6154; Main St; mains $10-18; 11am-2am) Horn's saloon serves American burgers and south-of-the-border fare, and there's live entertainment nightly.

Village Inn (906-847-3542; Hoban St; mains $18-23; 8am-10pm) Planked whitefish, pan-fried perch and other fresh-from-the-lake fish, meat and pasta dishes stuff diners at this year-round local hangout with a bar and outdoor seating.

GETTING THERE & AROUND

Three ferry companies – **Arnold Line** (800-542-8528; www.arnoldline.com), **Shepler's** (800-828-6157; www.sheplersferry.com) and **Star Line** (800-638-9892; www.mackinacferry.com) – operate out of both Mackinaw City and St Ignace, and charge the same rates: round-trip adult $24, bicycle $8, child five to 12 years $12. The ferries run several times daily from May to October; Arnold Line runs longer, weather permitting. The trip takes about 15 minutes. Once you're on the island, horse-drawn cabs will take you anywhere. Better yet, rent a bicycle.

UPPER PENINSULA

Rugged and isolated, with hardwood forests blanketing 90% of its land, the Upper Peninsula (UP) is a Midwest highlight. Only 45 miles of interstate highway slice through the trees, punctuated by a handful of cities, of which Marquette (population 20,000) is the largest. Between the small towns lie miles of undeveloped shoreline on Lakes Huron, Michigan and Superior; scenic two-lane roads; and pasties, which are the local meat-and-vegetable pot pies brought over by Cornish miners 150 years ago.

You'll find it's a different world up north. Residents of the UP, aka 'Yoopers,' consider themselves distinct from the rest of the state – they've even threatened to secede in the past.

Sault Ste Marie & Around

Founded in 1668, Sault Ste Marie (Sault is pronounced 'soo') is the oldest city in Michigan and the third oldest in the USA. The town is best known for its locks that raise and lower 1000ft-long freighters between the different lake levels. **Soo Locks Park & Visitors Center** (906-253-9101; admission free; 9am-9pm mid-May–mid-Oct) is on Portage Ave in the heart of downtown. It features displays, videos and neato observation decks from which you can watch the boats leap 21ft from Lake Superior to Lake Huron.

Spiffy **Askwith Lockview Motel** (906-632-2491, 800-854-0745; www.lockview.com; 327 W Portage Ave; r incl breakfast $75-81; May–mid-Oct) sits across from the locks and within walking distance of belly-filling Irish pubs, saloons and cafés on Portage Ave.

An hour's drive west of Sault Ste Marie, via Hwy 28 and Hwy 123, is the eastern UP's top attraction: lovely **Tahquamenon Falls**, with tea-colored waters tinted so by upstream hemlock leaves. The Upper Falls in **Tahquamenon Falls State Park** (906-492-3415; per vehicle $8) are 200ft across with a 50ft drop, making them some of the largest falls east of the Mississippi River. The Lower Falls are a series of smaller cascades best viewed by renting a boat (per person $4) and rowing across the river to an island. The large state park also has camping (campsites $16 to $23), great hiking and – bonus – a brewpub near the park entrance.

North of the park, beyond the little town of Paradise, is the fascinating **Great Lakes Shipwreck Museum** (906-635-1742; www.shipwreckmuseum.com; 18335 N Whitefish Point Rd; adult/child 6-17yr $12/8; 10am-6pm May-Oct); its intriguing displays include items trawled up from sunken ships. More than 300 vessels – including the *Edmund Fitzgerald* that Gordon Lightfoot crooned about – have sunk in the area's congested sea lanes and unpredictable weather, earning it such nicknames as the 'Shipwreck Coast' and 'Graveyard of the Great Lakes.'

Hwy 123 leads to Paradise, where family-owned **Cloud Nine Cottages** (906-492-3434; Hwy 123; cabins $75-100) provides four beachside abodes decked out with full kitchens, DVD players and outdoor grills; there's a two-night minimum stay. Numerous other well-kept mom-and-pop motels also line this stretch of highway.

Pictured Rocks National Lakeshore

Sitting roughly mid-peninsula on the Lake Superior shoreline, Munising is the gateway to **Pictured Rocks National Lakeshore** (www.nps.gov/piro), a 110-sq-mile national park to the east that holds the namesake colored sandstone bluffs. Most people view the 200ft-high cliffs on a 2½-hour boat tour with **Pictured Rock Cruises** (☎ 906-387-2379; www.picturedrocks.com; adult/child 6-12yr $33/10). Boats depart from downtown Munising hourly between 10am and 5pm (except for 11am and 4pm) in July and August; they go less often from mid-May to June and September to mid-October. You also can drive to **Miners Castle Overlook**, 12 miles east of Munising off Rte 58, for a good view. The most scenic backpacking adventure in Michigan is the **North Country National Scenic Trail** (www.nps.gov/noco), a four- to five-day, 42-mile trek from Grand Marais to Munising through the heart of the park. Stop in at the **Hiawatha National Forest/Pictured Rocks Visitors Center** (☎ 906-387-3700; www.nps.gov/piro; 400 E Munising Ave; 🕑 8am-6pm mid-May–mid-Oct, 9am-4:30pm Mon-Sat rest of year) at the corner of Hwy 28 and Rte 58 for maps, backcountry permits and other details.

Just offshore is **Grand Island**, part of Hiawatha National Forest. Hop aboard the **Grand Island Ferry** (☎ 906-387-3503; www.grandislandmi.com; 🕑 late May–mid-Oct) to get there (round-trip adult/child six to 12 years $15/10) and rent a mountain bike (per day $25) from the ferry company to zip around, or take the three-hour bus tour ($22). The ferry dock is on Hwy 28, which is about 4 miles west of town.

Munising has lots of motels, such as the recommended **Alger Falls Motel** (☎ 906-387-3536; www.algerfallsmotel.com; Hwy 28 E; r $48-68; ⊠ ☰). **Falling Rock Cafe & Bookstore** (☎ 906-387-3008; 104 E Munising Ave; sandwiches $5-9; 🕑 9am-8pm Sun-Fri, to 10pm Sat) has sandwiches, pasties and live music.

Marquette

From Munising, Hwy 28 heads west and hugs Lake Superior. This beautiful stretch of highway has lots of beaches, roadside parks and rest areas where you can pull over and enjoy the scenery. Within 45 miles you'll reach Marquette, a city that abounds with outdoor recreation opportunities – and snow. It's the USA's second-snowiest city.

Stop at the log-lodge **visitors center** (☎ 906-249-9066; www.marquettecountry.org; 2201 US 41; 🕑 9am-5pm) as you enter the city for brochures on local hiking trails and waterfalls.

The easy **Sugarloaf Mountain Trail** and the harder, wilderness-like **Hogsback Mountain Trail** offer panoramic views. Both are reached from County Rd 550, just north of Marquette. In the city, the high bluffs of **Presque Isle Park** make a great place to catch the sunset.

The **Noquemanon Trail Network** (www.noquetrails.org) is highly recommended for mountain biking and cross-country skiing. Check the website for equipment rental and day pass (per day $8) purchase locations.

Marquette is the perfect place to stay put for a few days to explore the central UP. Budgeteers can bunk at **Value Host Motor Inn** (☎ 906-225-5000; www.valuehostmotorinn.com; 1101 US 41 W; r incl breakfast $55-65; ⊠ ☰) a few miles west of town. Downtown's **Landmark Inn** (☎ 906-228-2580; www.thelandmarkinn.com; 230 N Front St; r $124-149; ⊠ ☰) fills a historic lakefront building and has a couple of resident ghosts.

Sample the local meat-veggie pie specialty at **Jean Kay's Pasties & Subs** (☎ 906-228-5310; 1639 Presque Isle Ave; items $3-4; 🕑 11am-9pm Mon-Fri, to 8pm Sat & Sun).

Those craving creative fish and meat dishes, crepes or chicken-pear-brie panini can warm up in **Coco's** (☎ 906-228-2680; 911 Lakeshore Blvd; sandwiches $7-10, mains $11-15; 🕑 8am-8pm Tue-Sat, to 2pm Sun). Michigan berry pie and house-crafted Belgian chocolates sweeten the lengthy dessert menu.

UpFront and Company (☎ 906-228-5200; 102 E Main St; mains $13-19; 🕑 11am-10pm Mon-Fri, 2-10pm Sat, closed Mon in winter) fires up the wood oven for pizzas, the taps for hearty beers and the amps for live music.

Isle Royale National Park

Totally free of vehicles and roads, **Isle Royale National Park** (www.nps.gov/isro; user fee per day $4; 🕑 mid-May–Oct), a 210-sq-mile island in Lake Superior, is certainly the place to go for peace and quiet. It gets fewer visitors in a year than Yellowstone National Park gets in a day, which means the packs of wolves and moose creeping through the forest are all yours.

The island is laced with 165 miles of hiking trails that connect dozens of campgrounds along Superior and inland lakes. You must be totally prepared for this wilderness adventure, with a tent, camping stove, sleeping bags, food and water filter. Or say 'to hell with that crap' and shell out the dough for the **Rock Harbor Lodge** (☎ 906-337-4993; www.isleroyaleresort.com; r/cottages $216-248). The **park headquarters** (☎ 906-482-0984; 800 E Lakeshore Dr; 🕑 8am-6pm Mon-Fri, 11am-6pm Sat Jun & Jul, 8am-4:30pm Mon-Fri, 2-4pm Sat Aug–mid-Sep, 8am-4:30pm Mon-Fri rest of year) in Houghton can provide information.

From the dock outside the headquarters in Houghton, the **Ranger III** (☎ 906-482-0984) departs at 9am on Tuesday and Friday for the six-hour boat trip (one way adult/child seven to 12 years $60/20) to Rock Harbor, at the east end of the island. **Royale Air Service** (☎ 877-359-4753; www.royaleairservice.com) offers a quicker trip, flying from Houghton County Airport to Rock Harbor in 30 minutes (one way $190). Or head 50 miles up the Keweenaw Peninsula to Copper Harbor (a beautiful drive) and jump on the **Isle Royale Queen** (☎ 906-289-4437; www.isleroyale.com) for the 8am three-hour crossing (one way adult/child under 12 years $64/32). Days of departure vary, so call for the schedule. You can also access Isle Royale from Grand Portage, Minnesota (p648). Bringing a kayak or canoe on the ferry costs an additional $25 each way.

Porcupine Mountains Wilderness State Park

Michigan's largest state park, with 90 miles of trails, is another UP winner, and it's a heckuva lot easier to reach than Isle Royale. 'The Porkies,' as they're called, are so rugged that loggers bypassed most of the range in the early 19th century, leaving the park with the largest tract of virgin forest between the Rocky Mountains and Adirondacks.

From Silver City, head west on Hwy 107 to reach the **Porcupine Mountains visitors center** (☎ 906-885-5275; www.porcupinemountains.com; 412 S Boundary Rd; 🕑 10am-6pm mid-May–mid-Oct), where you buy vehicle entry permits (per day/year $8/29) and backcountry permits (one to four people per night $14). Continue to the end of Hwy 107 and climb 300ft for the stunning view of **Lake of the Clouds**.

Winter is also a busy time at the Porkies, with downhill skiing (a 787ft vertical drop) and 26 miles of cross-country trails on offer; check with the **ski area** (☎ 231-420-5405, 906-289-4105; www.skitheporkies.com) for conditions and costs.

The park rents **rustic cabins** (☎ 906-885-5275, 800-447-2757; www.mi.gov/porkies; cabins $60) perfect for wilderness adventurers, as you have to hike in 1 to 4 miles, boil your own water and use a privy. **Sunshine Motel & Cabins** (☎ 906-884-2187; www.ontonagon.net/sunshinemotel; 24077 Hwy 64; r $55, cabins $60-75), 3 miles west of Ontonagon, provides another good base.

WISCONSIN

Wisconsin is cheesy and proud of it. The state pumps out 2.4 billion pounds of cheddar, gouda and other smelly goodness – a quarter of America's hunks – from its cow-speckled farmland per year. Local license plates read 'The Dairy State' with udder dignity. Folks here even refer to themselves as 'cheeseheads' and emphasize it by wearing novelty foam rubber cheese-wedge hats for special occasions (most notably during Green Bay Packers football games).

So embrace the cheese thing, because there's a good chance you'll be here for a while. Wisconsin has heaps to offer: exploring the craggy cliffs and lighthouses of Door County (p634), kayaking through sea caves at Apostle Islands National Lakeshore (p635), cow chip throwing along US 12 (p632), mountain biking in Chequamegon National Forest (p635) and soaking up beer, art and festivals in Milwaukee and Madison.

WISCONSIN FACTS

Nicknames Badger State, America's Dairyland
Population 5.6 million
Area 65,500 sq miles
Capital city Madison (population 228,775)
Other cities Milwaukee (population 573,358)
Sales tax 5%
Birthplace of Author Laura Ingalls Wilder (1867–1957), architect Frank Lloyd Wright (1867–1959), painter Georgia O'Keeffe (1887–1986), Senator Joseph McCarthy (1908–57), actor Orson Welles (1915–85)
Home of 'Cheesehead' Packer fans, dairy farms, water parks
Famous for Breweries, artisanal cheese, first state to legislate gay rights
Official dance Polka
Driving distances Milwaukee to Minneapolis 336 miles, Milwaukee to Madison 80 miles

Information

Travel Green Wisconsin (www.travelgreenwisconsin.com) Certifies businesses as ecofriendly by grading them on waste reduction, energy efficiency and seven other categories.

Wisconsin B&B Association (☎ 715-539-9222; www.wbba.org)

Wisconsin Department of Tourism (☎ 800-432-8747; www.travelwisconsin.com) Produces loads of free guides on subjects like bird-watching, biking, golf and rustic roads.

Wisconsin highway conditions (☎ 511; www.511wi.gov)

Wisconsin Milk Marketing Board (☎ 608-836-8820; www.eatwisconsincheese.com) Provides a free statewide map of cheesemakers titled *A Traveler's Guide to America's Dairyland*.

Wisconsin state park information (☎ 608-266-2181; www.wiparks.net) Park entry requires a vehicle permit (per day/year residents $7/25, nonresidents $10/35). Campsites cost from $12 to $22; reservations accepted (☎ 888-947-2757; www.wisconsinstateparks.reserveamerica.com; fee $10).

MILWAUKEE

Here's the thing about Milwaukee: it's cool, but for some reason everyone refuses to admit it. Yes, the reputation lingers as a working man's town of brewskis, bowling alleys and polka halls. But attractions like the Calatrava-designed art museum, bad-ass Harley-Davidson Museum and stylish eating and shopping 'hoods have turned Wisconsin's largest city into a surprisingly groovy place. In summertime, festivals let loose revelry by the lake almost every weekend. And where else on the planet will you see racing sausages?

History

Milwaukee was first settled by Germans in the 1840s. Many started small breweries, but a few decades later the introduction of bulk brewing technology turned beer production into a major industry here. Milwaukee earned its 'Brew City' and 'Nation's Watering Hole' nicknames in the 1880s when Pabst, Schlitz, Blatz, Miller and 80 other breweries made suds here. Today, only Miller and a few microbreweries remain. Later, waves of Italians, Poles, Irish, African Americans and Mexicans added to Milwaukee's varied culture.

Orientation

Lake Michigan sits to the east of the city, and is rimmed by parkland. The Riverwalk is a system of redeveloped walking paths along both sides of the Milwaukee River downtown. Wisconsin Ave divides east–west streets; north–south streets are usually numbered and increase as they head west from the lake.

Information

BOOKSTORES

Renaissance Books (☎ 414-271-6850; 834 N Plankinton Ave) Dusty used bookstore for bibliophiles.

EMERGENCY & MEDICAL SERVICES

Froedtert Hospital (☎ 414-805-3000; 9200 W Wisconsin Ave)

Walgreens (☎ 414-272-2171; 1400 E Brady St; 🕑 24hr) Pharmacy.

INTERNET ACCESS

The East Side neighborhood near the University of Wisconsin-Milwaukee boasts several coffee shops with free wi-fi.

Milwaukee Central Library (☎ 414-286-3000; 814 W Wisconsin Ave; 🕑 9am-7pm Mon & Tue, to 5:30pm Wed-Sat, 1-5pm Sun, closed Sun May-Sep) Free internet terminals.

INTERNET RESOURCES & MEDIA

Tune into WUWM-FM 89.7 for NPR, or WHQG-FM 102.9 for rock.

MOVING & GROOVING BY BICYCLE

Wisconsin has converted an amazing number of abandoned railroad lines into paved, bike-only paths. They go up hills, through old tunnels, over bridges and alongside pastures. Wherever you are in the state, there's likely a sweet ride nearby. Check www.trailsfromrails.com and the **Department of Tourism's Bike Path Directory** (www.travelwisconsin.com/bike_path_and_touring_directory.aspx).

Bike rentals are available in gateway towns, and you can buy trail passes (per day/year $4/20) at area businesses or trailhead drop-boxes.

Because this is Wisconsin, where cycling is almost as beloved as cheese, it's no surprise you can combine the two passions. That's right, the Wisconsin Milk Marketing Board provides **maps** (www.wisdairy.com/getmoving) highlighting cheese stores and dairy farms along various bike trails.

Milwaukee Journal Sentinel (www.jsonline.com) The city's daily newspaper.
On Milwaukee (www.onmilwaukee.com) Online site for traffic and weather updates, plus restaurant and entertainment reviews.
Quest (www.quest-online.com) GLBT entertainment resource.
Shepherd Express (www.expressmilwaukee.com) Free alternative weekly paper.

MONEY
US Bank (☎ 414-765-4035; 777 E Wisconsin Ave) ATM and foreign currency exchange is available.

POST
Post office (☎ 800-275-8777; 345 W St Paul Ave)

TOURIST INFORMATION
Visitors center (☎ 800-554-1448; www.visitmilwaukee.org; 1st fl, 500 N Harbor Dr, in Discovery World; 🕑 9am-5pm) Better information online than on-site.

Sights & Activities
MILWAUKEE ART MUSEUM
Even those who aren't usually museum-goers will be struck by this lakeside **museum** (☎ 414-224-3200; www.mam.org; 700 N Art Museum Dr; adult/child 13-18yr $12/10; 🕑 10am-5pm Tue-Sun, to 8pm Thu), which features a stunning winglike addition by Santiago Calatrava. It soars open and closed every day at noon, which is wild to see. There's a permanent display on architect Frank Lloyd Wright, and fabulous folk and outsider art galleries.

HARLEY-DAVIDSON MUSEUM & PLANT
In 1903 local schoolmates William Harley and Arthur Davidson built and sold their first Harley-Davidson motorcycle. A century later the big bikes are a symbol of American manufacturing pride. The **Harley-Davidson Museum** (☎ 877-436-8738; www.h-dmuseum.com; 400 W Canal St; adult/child 5-17yr $16/10; 🕑 9am-6pm, to 8pm Tue-Thu May-Oct, 10am-6pm Mon-Fri, 9am-6pm Sat & Sun Nov-Apr) pays homage in a sprawling industrial building just south of downtown. Hundreds of bikes show styles through the ages, but even non-Harley owners will like the scene – who doesn't jones to see the bikes of Elvis and Evel Knievel?

Hog-heads can get another fix at the **Harley-Davidson plant** (☎ 414-343-7850, 877-883-1450; www.harley-davidson.com; 11700 W Capitol Dr; admission free; 🕑 9:30am-2pm Mon-Fri, 10am-1pm Sat in summer), in the suburb of Wauwatosa, a 20-minute drive west of downtown. This is where the engines are built (body assembly goes on in York, Pennsylvania, and Kansas City, Missouri.) The one-hour tours are kind of technical, but the ultimate payoff comes when you get to sit in the saddle of a vintage bike. No open shoes are permitted.

BREWERIES
Pabst and Schlitz have moved on, but **Miller Brewing Company** (☎ 414-931-2337; www.millercoors.com; 4251 W State St; admission free; 🕑 10:30am-3:30pm Mon-Sat) preserves Milwaukee's beer legacy. Join the legions of drinkers lined up for the free tours. Though the mass-produced beer may not be your favorite, the factory impresses with its sheer scale: you'll visit the packaging plant where 2000 cans are filled each minute, and the warehouse where a half-million cases await shipment. And then there's the generous tasting session at the tour's end, where you can down three full-size samples. Don't forget your ID.

Well-loved **Lakefront Brewery** (☎ 414-372-8800; www.lakefrontbrewery.com; 1872 N Commerce St; 1hr-long tours $6; 🕑 Mon-Sat), across the river from Brady St, has afternoon tours, but the swellest time to visit is on Friday nights when there's a fish fry, 16 beers on tap and a polka band in the attached banquet hall. Tour times vary throughout the week, but there's usually at least a 2pm and 3pm show.

For more swills, head to **Sprecher Brewing Company** (☎ 414-964-2739; www.sprecherbrewery.com; 701 W Glendale Ave; tours $4; 🕑 4pm Mon-Fri, noon-2pm Sat & Sun). The small microbrewery's tour includes a museum of memorabilia from long-gone Milwaukee suds-makers and a beer garden replete with oompah music. It's 6 miles north of downtown; reservations are required.

OTHER MUSEUMS
The **Eisner Museum of Advertising and Design** (☎ 414-847-3290; www.eisnermuseum.org; 208 N Water St; adult/child 12-18yr $5/3; 🕑 11am-5pm Wed-Fri, to 8pm Thu, noon-5pm Sat, 1-5pm Sun) presents excellent exhibits on how the media influence today's culture.

Discovery World at Pier Wisconsin (☎ 414-765-9966; www.discoveryworld.org; 500 N Harbor Dr; adult/child 3-17yr $17/13; 🕑 9am-4pm Tue-Fri, 10am-5pm Sat & Sun; ♿) is the city's mondo, lakefront science and technology museum. It's primarily a kid-pleaser, with freshwater and saltwater aquariums (where you can touch sharks and sturgeon) and a dockside, triple-masted Great Lakes schooner to climb aboard.

LAKEFRONT PARK

The parkland edging Lake Michigan is prime for walking, cycling and in-line skating. For the latter, try **Milwaukee Bike & Skate Rental** (☎ 414-273-1343; www.milwbikeskaterental.com; Veteran's Park; per hr skates/bicycle $6/10; 10am-7pm Jun-Aug), just north of the art museum. Also here is Bradford Beach, which is good for swimming and lounging.

Festivals & Events

Summerfest (www.summerfest.com; day pass $15) is dubbed 'the world's largest music festival,' and indeed hundreds of rock, blues, jazz, country and alternative bands swarm its 10 stages over 11 days in late June/early July. The scene totally rawks; it is held at downtown's lakefront festival grounds.

There's also **PrideFest** (www.pridefest.com), held in mid-June, **Polish Fest** (www.polishfest.org), held in late June, **German Fest** (www.germanfest.com), held in late July, **Irish Fest** (www.irishfest.com), held in mid-August and a host of others. Call the visitors center for details.

Sleeping

Rates in this section are for summer, the peak season, when you should book in advance. Tax (14.6%) is not included. For cheap chain lodging, try Howell Ave, south near the airport. The first three places listed here are well-located downtown near the lakefront (and near each other).

Astor Hotel (☎ 414-271-4220, 800-558-0200; www.theastorhotel.com; 924 E Juneau Ave; r incl breakfast $99-139; P) The 1918 Astor is your back-up plan when other lodgings are sold out. Though faded in its glory, the old place is slowly renovating its rooms and the result is decent value. Parking costs $5.

Comfort Inn & Suites Downtown Lakeshore (☎ 414-276-8800, 800-328-7275; www.choicehotels.com; 916 E State St; r incl breakfast $110-170; P) Check in here and you'll be laying low in the same digs as touring indie bands who come to town. The free wi-fi, breakfast buffet and shuttle bus to local sights supplement the contemporary rooms. Parking costs $10.

County Clare Irish Inn (☎ 414-272-5273, 888-942-5273; www.countyclare-inn.com; 1234 N Astor St; r incl breakfast $139-179; P) Rooms have that snug Irish-cottage feel, with four-post beds, white wainscot walls and whirlpool baths. There's free parking and an on-site Guinness-pouring pub, of course.

our pick **Iron Horse Hotel** (☎ 888-543-4766; www.theironhorsehotel.com; 500 W Florida St; r from $179; P) This boutique hotel near the Harley Museum is geared toward motorcycle enthusiasts, with covered parking for bikes. Most of the loft-style rooms retain the post-and-beam, exposed-brick interior of what was once a bedding factory. Parking costs $25.

Eating

Good places to scope for eats include N Old World 3rd St downtown; the fashionable East Side by the University of Wisconsin-Milwaukee; hip, Italian-based Brady St by its intersection with N Farwell Ave; and the gentrified Third Ward, anchored along N Milwaukee St south of I-94.

The Friday night fish fry is a highly social tradition observed throughout Wisconsin and all over Milwaukee. Try it at Lakefront Brewery (opposite), which complements its fish with microbrews and a polka band.

Another Milwaukee specialty is frozen custard, which is like ice cream only smoother and richer. **Leon's** (☎ 414-383-1784; 3131 S 27th St; 11am-midnight) and **Kopp's** (☎ 414-961-2006; 5373 N Port Washington Rd, Glendale; 10:30am-11:30pm) are popular purveyors.

Milwaukee Public Market (☎ 414-336-1111; 400 N Water St; 10am-8pm Mon-Fri, 8am-6pm Sat, 10am-6pm Sun) Browse this Third Ward market for fresh and prepared foods, cheeses and chocolates – everything is local.

Trocadero (☎ 414-272-0205; 1758 N Water St; mains $7-17; 11am-11pm Mon-Fri, from 9am Sat & Sun) Let's see – a glorious wine list, cheese plates, crepes, baguettes with jam, mussels and frites. We're in Paris, *oui?* Nope, we're near Brady St at Trocadero, a romantic coffeehouse-restaurant-bar with a year-round patio (it's heated in winter).

Roots Restaurant and Cellar (☎ 414-374-8480; 1818 N Hubbard St; small plates $8-15, mains $19-36; 11am-2pm Mon-Fri, 5-9pm Mon-Thu, to 10pm Fri & Sat, 10am-2pm Sun) The Slow Food chefs host two options for dining. Upstairs is the sleek, pricier main room with entrees like soy-grilled tilapia. The funky downstairs (evening hours only) offers small plates, like the butterbean-peanut corn dog. The outdoor patio with views is prime for cocktails. It is located across the river from Brady St.

Drinking & Entertainment

BARS

Several bars tap kegs around N Water and E State Sts downtown, in the Third Ward and along Brady St between Astor and Farwell Sts. Drinkeries stay open to 2am.

Von Trier (☎ 414-272-1775; 2235 N Farwell Ave) The German Von Trier is a long-standing, real-deal favorite, with plenty of good stuff on tap and a biergarten.

Sugar Maple (☎ 414-481-2393; 441 E Lincoln Ave; ⊠) Located in an old Sikh temple in the south-side neighborhood of Bay View, the Sugar Maple sports an endless line of taps spurting 50 small-craft beers.

Kochanski's Concertina Beer Hall (☎ 414-837-6552; 1920 S 37th St; ⏲ closed Sun & Mon; ᯤ) Live polka music rules at kitschy Kochanski's, with beers from Schlitz to Polish drafts to Wisconsin craft labels. It's 5 miles southwest of downtown.

SPORTS

Miller Park (☎ 414-902-4000; www.milwaukeebrewers.com; 1 Brewers Way) The Milwaukee Brewers play baseball at top-notch Miller Park, which has a retractable roof, real grass and racing sausages (see right). It's located near S 46th St.

Bradley Center (☎ 414-227-0400; www.nba.com/bucks; 1001 N 4th St) The NBA's Milwaukee Bucks dunk here.

Getting There & Around

General Mitchell International Airport (MKE; ☎ 414-747-5300; www.mitchellairport.com) is 8 miles south of downtown. Take public bus 80 ($2) or a cab ($25).

The **Lake Express ferry** (☎ 866-914-1010; www.lake-express.com) sails from downtown (the terminal is located a few miles south of the city center) to Muskegon and Michigan; and provides easy access to Michigan's beach-lined Gold Coast. See p620 for details.

Greyhound (☎ 414-272-2156; 606 N James Lovell St) runs frequent buses to Chicago ($10 to $20, two hours) and Minneapolis ($39 to $61, seven hours). Across the street, **Badger Bus** (☎ 414-276-7490; www.badgerbus.com; 635 N James Lovell St) goes to Madison ($19, 1½ hours).

> **WHAT THE...?**
>
> It's common to see strange things after too many stadium beers. But a group of giant sausages sprinting around Miller Park's perimeter – is that for *real*? It is if it's the middle of the 6th inning. That's when the famous 'Racing Sausages' (actually people in meat costumes) waddle onto the field to give the fans a thrill. Folks here take their sausage seriously.

Megabus (☎ 877-462-6342; www.megabus.com/us) runs express to Chicago (two hours) and Minneapolis (six hours), often for lower fares than Greyhound.

The **Milwaukee County Transit System** (☎ 414-344-6711; www.ridemcts.com; 1942 N 17th Ave) provides an efficient local bus service ($2). Bus 31 goes to Miller Brewery; bus 90 goes to Miller Park.

Amtrak (☎ 414-271-0840; 433 W St Paul Ave) runs the *Hiawatha* train seven times a day to/from Chicago ($22, 1½ hours); catch it downtown or at Amtrak's airport train station.

If you're after a taxi service, call **Yellow Cab** (☎ 414-271-1800).

MADISON

Madison reaps a lot of kudos – most walkable city, best road-biking city, most vegetarian friendly, gay friendly, environmentally friendly, and just plain all-round friendliest city in the USA. Ensconced on a narrow isthmus between Mendota and Monona Lakes, it's a pretty combination of small, grassy state capital and liberal, bookish college town.

The **visitors center** (☎ 608-255-2537, 800-373-6376; www.visitmadison.com; 615 E Washington Ave; ⏲ 8am-5pm Mon-Fri) is six blocks east of Capitol Sq. You'll also find info at the University of Wisconsin's Memorial Union (see opposite).

Sights & Activities

The X-shaped **State Capitol** (☎ 608-266-0382; admission free; ⏲ 8am-6pm Mon-Fri, to 4pm Sat & Sun), the largest outside Washington, DC, marks the heart of downtown. Tours are available on the hour most days. On Saturday, the **Dane County Farmers Market** (www.dcfm.org; ⏲ 6am-2pm late Apr-early Nov) takes over Capitol Sq. It's one of the nation's largest markets, famed for its artisanal cheeses and cheese curds. Can't get enough of that dairy goodness (or arriving on a nonmarket day)? Walk around the corner to **Fromagination** (☎ 608-255-2430; www.fromagination.com; 12 S Carroll St; 9:30am-6pm Mon-Fri, 8am-4pm Sat), which specializes in small-batch and hard-to-find local, artisanal hunks.

State Street runs from the capitol west to the University of Wisconsin. The lengthy avenue is lined with free-trade coffee shops, parked bicycles and incense-wafting stores selling hacky sacks and flowy Indian skirts. State St also holds the impressive **Museum of Contemporary Art** (☎ 608-257-0158; www.mmoca.org; 227 State St; admission free; noon-5pm Tue-Thu, to 8pm Fri, 10am-8pm Sat, noon-5pm Sun), displaying works by Frida Kahlo, Claes Oldenburg and others. There's also a rooftop sculpture garden, cinema and martini lounge. The museum connects to the **Overture Center for the Arts** (☎ 608-258-4141; www.overturecenter.com; 201 State St), home to jazz, opera, dance and other performing arts.

The campus has its own attractions, including the 1260-acre **Arboretum** (☎ 608-263-7888; 1207 Seminole Hwy; admission free; 7am-10pm), dense with lilac, and the **Memorial Union** (☎ 608-265-3000; 800 Langdon St), with its festive outdoor bar and free live music, films and internet access.

It'd be a shame to leave town without taking advantage of the city's lakes and 120 miles of trails. For wheels, head to **Budget Bicycle Center** (☎ 608-251-8413; 1230 Regent St; rental per day $20; 9am-9pm Mon-Fri, to 7pm Sat, 10am-7pm Sun), about 1½ miles from Capitol Sq, near the university and good trails. For water-faring craft, try **Rutabaga Paddlesports** (☎ 608-223-9300, 800-472-3353; www.rutabaga.com; 220 W Broadway; canoe/kayak rental per half-/full day $25/40; 10am-8pm Mon-Fri, to 6pm Sat, 11am-5pm Sun), about 5 miles southeast of Capitol Sq and right on the water.

Festivals & Events

World's Largest Brat Fest (www.bratfest.com; admission free; late May) At this festival, 208,000 bratwursts go down the hatch, plus rides and bands.

Great Taste of the Midwest Beer Festival (www.mhtg.org; tickets $35; early Aug) Tickets sell out fast for this festival where 120 craft brewers pour their elixirs.

Sleeping & Eating

Moderately priced motels can be found off I-90/I-94 (about 6 miles from the town center), off Hwy 12/18 and along Washington Ave.

A global smorgasbord of restaurants peppers State St amid the pizza, sandwich and cheap-beer joints; many places have inviting patios. Cruising Williamson ('Willy') St turns up good Lao, Jamaican, Caribbean and other eateries.

HI Madison Hostel (☎ 608-441-0144; www.madisonhostel.org; 141 S Butler St; dm $22, r $49; P) This convenient hostel is a short walk from the State Capitol. The office is open from 8am to 11am and 5pm to 9pm, with continuous hours in summer. Parking is $5.

University Inn (☎ 608-285-8040, 800-279-4881; www.universityinn.org; 441 N Frances St; r $89-129; P) The rooms are fine, though nothing special; the inn's greatest asset is its handy location right by the State St and university action. Rates are highest at weekends.

Arbor House (☎ 608-238-2981; www.arbor-house.com; 3402 Monroe St; r incl breakfast weekday $110-175, weekend $150-230) Arbor House was an old tavern back in the mid-1800s. Now it's a wind-powered, energy-efficient-appliance-using, vegetarian-breakfast-serving B&B. It's located about 3 miles southwest of the State Capitol but accessible to public transportation. The owners will lend you mountain bikes too.

Weary Traveler Free House (☎ 608-442-6207; 1201 Williamson St; mains $7-11; 4pm-2am Mon, 11:30am-2am Tue-Sun) It's global comfort food at this dark-wood pub, including Hungarian goulash and vegan chili. Local brewers Capital and New Glarus provide the accompanying suds.

Himal Chuli (☎ 608-251-9225; 318 State St; mains $8-15; 11am-9pm Mon-Sat, noon-8pm Sun) Cheerful and cozy Himal Chuli serves up homemade Nepali fare, including lots of vegetarian dishes.

Cafe Soleil & L'Etoile (☎ 608-251-0500; 25 N Pinckney St; café mains $8-10, restaurant mains $29-42; closed Sun) The chefs here are Slow Food pioneers who've created their local, seasonal menu for 30-plus years. Dishes at L'Etoile (the restaurant, open from 6pm to 8:30pm Tuesday to Thursday, 5:30pm to 9:45pm Friday, and from 5pm to 9:45pm on Saturday) might include red snapper with summer squash or eggplant napoleon. But the best chow is found in the attached café (open 7am to 2:30pm Monday to Saturday), serving scrumptious sandwiches like trout salad with fresh-baked honey oatbread and Wisconsin grilled cheeses on whole grain bread.

Drinking & Entertainment

Bars stay open to 2am. *Isthmus* (www.thedailypage.com) is the free entertainment paper.

WORTH THE TRIP: QUIRKY US 12

Unusual sights huddle around US 12, all easy to experience on a northerly day trip from Madison.

About 27 miles up the road is the town of Prairie du Sac. If you happen to be driving through the first weekend in September, you can watch the annual **Cow Chip Throw** (☎ 608-643-4317; www.wiscowchip.com; admission free), where 800 competitors fling dried manure patties as far as the eye can see; the record is 248ft.

Seven miles onward is **Dr Evermor's Sculpture Park** (admission free; 🕑 9am-5pm Mon & Thu-Sat, noon-5pm Sun). The doc welds old pipes, carburetors and other salvaged metal into a hallucinatory world of futuristic creatures and structures. The crowning glory is the giant, egg-domed Forevertron, once cited by *Guinness World Records* as the globe's largest scrap metal sculpture. The good doctor himself – aka Tom Every – is often around and happy to chat about his birds, dragons and other pieces of folk art. Finding the entrance is tricky. Look for the Badger Army Ammunition Plant, and then a small sign leading you into a driveway across the street.

Baraboo, 42 miles northwest of Madison, was once the winter home of the Ringling Brothers Circus. **Circus World Museum** (☎ 608-356-8341, 866-693-1500; www.wisconsinhistory.org/circusworld; 550 Water St; adult/child 5-11yr summer $15/8, winter $7/3.50; 🕑 9am-6pm summer, reduced hours winter) preserves a nostalgic collection of wagons, posters and equipment from the touring big-top heyday. In summer, admission includes clowns, animals and acrobats doing the three-ring thing.

Continue north another 12 miles to the **Wisconsin Dells** (☎ 800-223-3557; www.wisdells.com; 👪), a megacenter of kitschy diversions, including 21 water parks, water-skiing thrill shows and super-minigolf courses. It's a jolting contrast to the natural appeal of the area, with its scenic limestone formations carved by the Wisconsin River. To appreciate the original attraction, take a boat tour or walk the trails at Mirror Lake or Devil's Lake state parks.

Memorial Union (☎ 608-265-3000; 800 Langdon St) Sit on the lakeside terrace to sip at this all-ages university hangout.

Great Dane Pub (☎ 608-284-0000; 123 E Doty St) Big, friendly and rambling like its namesake dog, the Dane is a popular brewpub with occasional live music.

Getting There & Around

The central **Greyhound station** (☎ 608-257-3050; 2 S Bedford St) is also used by **Badger Bus** (☎ 414-255-6771; www.badgerbus.com) for trips to Milwaukee ($19, 1½ hours).

SOUTHERN WISCONSIN

This part of Wisconsin has some of the prettiest landscapes, particularly the hilly southwest. Architecture fans can be unleashed at Taliesin (opposite), the Frank Lloyd Wright ubersight, and Racine, where two of his other works stand. Dairies around here cut a lot of cheese.

Racine

Racine is an unremarkable industrial town 30 miles south of Milwaukee, but it has two key Frank Lloyd Wright sights, both of which offer 45-minute tours that must be prebooked. The first, the **Johnson Wax Company Administration Building** (☎ 262-260-2154; 1525 Howe St; admission free; 🕑 tours at 9am, 10am, 11am, 1:45pm & 3pm Fri), dates from 1939 and is a magnificent space with tall, flared columns. The second is the lakeside **Wingspread** (☎ 262-681-3353; 33 E Four Mile Rd; admission free; 🕑 9:30am-2:30pm Tue-Fri), the last and largest of Wright's Prairie houses.

Green County

This pastoral area holds the nation's greatest concentration of cheesemakers, and **Green County Tourism** (☎ 888-222-9111; www.greencounty.org) will introduce you to them. Monroe is a fine place to start sniffing. Follow your nose to **Roth Käse** (☎ 608-328-2122; www.rothkase.com; 657 Second St; 🕑 9am-6pm Mon-Fri, to 5pm Sat, 10am-5pm Sun), a store and factory where you can watch cheesemakers in action from the observation deck (weekday mornings only). Bite into a fresh limburger-and-raw-onion sandwich at **Baumgartner's** (☎ 608-325-6157; 1023 Sixteenth Ave; sandwiches $4-7; 🕑 8am-11pm), an old Swiss tavern on the town square. At night, catch a flick at the local drive-in movie theater, and then climb into bed at **Inn Serendipity** (☎ 608-329-7056; www.innserendipity.com; 7843 County Rd P; r incl breakfast $105-120), a two-room, wind-and-solar-powered B&B on a 5-acre organic farm in Browntown, 8 miles west of Monroe.

The small town of Brodhead, 16 miles east, is another good base, especially for cyclists. **Earth Rider Hotel** (☎ 608-897-8300, 866-245-5276; www.earthridercycling.com; 929 W Exchange St; r incl breakfast $80-130;) offers five rooms with mod furnishings made from recycled bike gear. It's a delicious soft landing after riding the nearby, 23-mile **Sugar River Trail**. You can also rent bikes (per day $18) at the attached bike shop, and the owner will design a backroad route to your specification, taking in dairies, Amish businesses and/or emu farms.

For more on local dairy producers and plant tours, pick up the **Traveler's Guide to America's Dairyland map** (☎ 608-836-8820; www.eatwisconsincheese.com). For cheese-and-cycling routes, see p627.

Spring Green

Forty miles west of Madison and 3 miles south of the small town of Spring Green, **Taliesin** was the home of native son Frank Lloyd Wright for most of his life and is the site of his architectural school. It's now a major pilgrimage destination for fans and followers. The house was built in 1903, the Hillside Home School in 1932, and the **visitors center** (☎ 608-588-7900; www.taliesinpreservation.org; Hwy 23; 9am-5:30pm May-Oct) in 1953. A wide range of guided tours ($16 to $80) cover various parts of the complex; reservations are a good idea for the lengthier ones. The one-hour Hillside Tour ($16) provides a nice introduction to Wright's work.

A few miles south of Taliesin is the **House on the Rock** (☎ 608-935-3639; www.thehouseontherock.com; 5754 Hwy 23; adult/child 4-17yr $12.50/7.50; 9am-6pm May-Aug, to 5pm Sep & Oct, weekends only Nov-Apr), one of Wisconsin's busiest attractions. The strange 'house,' one man's obsession, was built atop a rock column and sprawled to become a monument of the imagination. The house is broken into three parts with a different tour exploring the objects and wonderments of each. Or you can experience the whole shebang for adult/child $28.50/15.50, which takes around three overwhelming hours.

Spring Green has a B&B in town and half a dozen motels strung along Hwy 14, north of town. Small **Usonian Inn** (☎ 877-876-6426; www.usonianinn.com; E 5116 Hwy 14; r $65-89;) was designed by a Wright student. Check www.springgreen.com for more options.

The **Spring Green General Store** (☎ 608-588-7070; 137 S Albany St; items $5-7; 9am-6pm Mon-Fri, 8am-6pm Sat, 8am-4pm Sun) serves sandwiches and earthy lunch specials.

The **American Players Theatre** (☎ 608-588-2361; www.playinthewoods.org) stages classical productions at an outdoor amphitheater by the Wisconsin River.

ALONG THE MISSISSIPPI RIVER

The Mississippi River forms most of Wisconsin's western border, and alongside it run some of the most scenic sections of the **Great River Road** (www.wigreatriverroad.org) – the designated route that follows Old Man River from Minnesota to the Gulf of Mexico.

From Madison, head west on US 18. You'll hit the River Rd (aka Hwy 35) at **Prairie du Chien**. Founded in 1673 as a French fur-trading post, the town's name quaintly honors the prairie dogs that once populated the area.

North of Prairie du Chien, the hilly riverside wends through the scene of the final battle in the bloody Black Hawk War. Historic markers tell part of the story, which finished at the Battle of Bad Ax when Native American men, women and children were massacred trying to flee across the Mississippi. At Genoa, Hwy 56 leads inland for 20 miles to the trout fishing mecca of **Viroqua** (☎ 608-637-2575; www.viroqua-wisconsin.com), a pretty little town surrounded by organic farms and round barns.

Back riverside and 18 miles upstream, **La Crosse** has a historic center nestling restaurants and pubs. Grandad Bluff offers grand views of the river. It's east of town along Main St (which becomes Bliss Rd); follow Bliss Rd up the hill and then turn right on Grandad Bluff Rd. For area information, stop by the **visitors center** (☎ 608-782-2366, 800-658-9424; www.explorelacrosse.com; 410 Veteran's Memorial Dr; 8am-5pm Mon-Fri, extended hours in summer). To bed down, try the friendly, English-owned **Guest House Motel** (☎ 608-784-8840, 800-274-6873; www.guesthousemotel.com; 810 S 4th St; r $60-100;).

For destinations on up the road, see Southern Minnesota (p645).

EASTERN WISCONSIN

Rocky, lighthouse-dotted Door County draws crowds in summer, while Green Bay draws crazed football fans in the freakin' freezing winter.

Green Bay

Founded in the 1660s as a fur-trading post, Green Bay boomed as a Lake Michigan port and later as a terminus for Midwest railroads. Processing and packing agricultural products became a major industry, and gave name to the city's legendary pro football team: the Green Bay Packers. The franchise is unique as the only community-owned nonprofit team in the NFL; perhaps pride in ownership is what makes the fans so die-hard (and wear foam-rubber cheese wedges on their head).

The **visitors center** (☎ 920-494-9507, 888-867-3342; www.greenbay.com; 1901 S Oneida St; 🕑 8am-4:30pm Mon-Fri) is by Lambeau Field (the football stadium), just off Lombardi Ave, south of downtown. The town core is on the east side of the Fox River around Walnut St.

While tickets are nearly impossible to obtain, you can always get into the spirit by joining a pregame tailgate party, where fans fire up grills and set up tables by their cars. The generous flow of alcohol has led to Green Bay's reputation as a 'drinking town with a football problem.' Or visit the **Green Bay Packer Hall of Fame** (☎ 920-569-7512; www.lambeaufield.com; adult/child 6-11yr $10/5; 🕑 9am-6pm Mon-Sat, 10am-5pm Sun, hours vary during home games), which is indeed packed with memorabilia. It has football movies and interactive exhibits, plus stadium tours.

The **National Railroad Museum** (☎ 920-437-7623; www.nationalrrmuseum.org; 2285 S Broadway; adult/child 4-12yr $9/6.50 May-Sep; 🕑 9am-5pm Mon-Sat, 11am-5pm Sun, closed Mon Jan-Apr) features some of the biggest steam and diesel locomotives ever to haul freight into Green Bay's vast yards; train rides ($1) are offered in summer.

Tidy, bare-bones **Bay Motel** (☎ 920-494-3441; www.baymotelgreenbay.com; 1301 S Military Ave; r $52-75; 📶) is a mile from Lambeau Field.

Door County

With its rocky coastline, picturesque lighthouses, cherry orchards and small 19th-century villages, you have to admit Door County is pretty damn lovely. The area spreads across a narrow peninsula jutting 75 miles into Lake Michigan, and visitors usually loop around on the county's two highways. Hwy 57 runs beside Lake Michigan and goes through Jacksonport and Baileys Harbor; this is known as the more scenic 'quiet side.' Hwy 42 borders Green Bay and passes through (from south to north) Egg Harbor, Fish Creek, Ephraim and Sister Bay; this side is more action oriented. The fishing hamlet of Gills Rock perches at the peninsula's tip, decorated by a string of islands. No public buses serve the peninsula, and only about half the businesses stay open from November to April.

Sturgeon Bay is the gateway and biggest town. As you enter it stop at the **visitors center** (☎ 920-743-4456, 800-527-3529; www.doorcounty.com; 1015 Green Bay Rd; 🕑 8am-5pm Mon-Fri, 10am-4pm Sat & Sun mid-May–mid-Oct, reduced hours rest of year), which is an excellent resource with special-interest brochures on art galleries, biking, lighthouses and much more.

Parkland blankets the county. Bayside **Peninsula State Park** is the largest, with bluff-side hiking and biking trails and a beach for kayaking and sailing. In winter, cross-country skiers and snowshoers take over the trails. On the lake side, secluded **Newport State Park** offers trails, backcountry camping and solitude. **Whitefish Dunes State Park** has sandscapes and a wide beach (beware of riptides). Adjacent **Cave Point Park** is known for its sea caves and kayaking. Multiactivity outfitters include **Bayshore Outdoor Store** (☎ 920-854-9220; www.kayakdoorcounty.com; Sister Bay) and **Nor Door Sport & Cyclery** (☎ 920-868-2275; www.nordoorsports.com; Fish Creek).

The bay side has the most lodging. Prices listed are for July and August, the peak season; many places have minimum-stay requirements. **Peninsula State Park** (☎ 920-868-3258; campsites $17-22; Fish Creek) has amenity-laden camping. Right by the park, **Julie's Park Cafe and Motel** (☎ 920-868-2999; www.juliesmotel.com; Fish Creek; r $79-120; ⊠ ❄ 📶) is tidy and relatively low cost (meals $7 to $14). All rooms at **Egg Harbor Lodge** (☎ 920-868-3115, 920-868-3215; www.eggharborlodge.com; Egg Harbor; r $155–195; ⊠ ❄ 📶 🏊) have a water view and free bike use.

Many local restaurants host a 'fish boil,' a regional specialty started by Scandinavian lumberjacks, in which whitefish, potatoes and onions are cooked in a cauldron. It's sedate, until the chef douses the flames with kerosene, and then whoosh! A fireball creates the requisite 'boil over' (which gets rid of the fish oil), signaling dinner is ready. Finish with Door's famous cherry pie.

Village Cafe (☎ 920-868-3342; Egg Harbor; sandwiches $6.50-8.50, mains $14-16; 🕑 7am-8pm summer, 8am-2pm winter) serves tasty breakfast, lunch and dinner. For drinks, hang with the young boater types at **JJ's** (☎ 920-854-4513; Sister Bay; 🕑 11am-2am, closed

Sun-Tue in winter), a good-time pub attached to a Mexican restaurant.

From the peninsula's tip near Gills Rock, daily **ferries** (☎ 920-847-2546; www.wisferry.com; Northport Pier) go every half hour to **Washington Island** (round-trip adult/child 6-11yr/bike/car $11.50/5.50/4/24), which has 700 Scandinavian descendants, a couple of museums, beaches, bike rentals and carefree roads for cycling. Accommodations and camping are available. More remote is lovely **Rock Island**, a state park with no cars or bikes at all. It's a wonderful place for hiking, swimming and camping. Get there via the eponymous **ferry** (☎ 920-535-0122), which departs Jackson Harbor on Washington Island (round-trip adult/child $9/5).

NORTHERN WISCONSIN

The north is a thinly populated region of forests and lakes, where folks paddle and fish in summer, and ski and snowmobile in winter. The cliffy, windswept Apostle Islands steal the show.

Northwoods & Lakelands

Nicolet National Forest is a vast, wooded district ideal for outdoor activities. The simple crossroads of **Langlade** is a center for white-water river adventures. **Wolf River Guides** (☎ 715-882-3002; www.wolfriverguides.com) provides half-day kayak-paddling classes followed by a half-day trip on the water (per person $110), while **Wolf River Lodge** (☎ 715-882-2182; www.wolfriverlodge.com; r incl breakfast $100;) provides accommodation where you can dry off, get warm and celebrate your accomplishments in the on-site bar.

In winter, **Granite Peak Ski Resort** (☎ 715-845-2846; www.skigranitepeak.com; day pass adult/child $56/44), Wisconsin's largest, perks up in **Wausau**, offering 275 skiable acres and a 700ft vertical drop.

North on Hwy 13, folk artist and retired lumberjack Fred Smith's **Concrete Park** (www.friendsoffredsmith.org; admission free; sunrise-sunset) in Phillips is extraordinary, with 200-plus whimsical, life-size sculptures.

West on Hwy 70, **Chequamegon National Forest** offers exceptional mountain biking with 300 miles of off-road trails. Contact the **Chequamegon Area Mountain Bike Association** (☎ 715-798-3599; www.cambatrails.org) for trail maps and bike rental information. The season culminates in mid-September with the **Chequamegon Fat Tire Festival** (☎ 715-798-3594; www.cheqfattire.com), when 1700 strong-legged men and women peddle 40 grueling miles through the woods. The town of **Hayward** (☎ 715-634-8662; www.haywardareachamber.com) makes a good base.

Apostle Islands

The 21 rugged Apostle Islands, floating in Lake Superior and freckling Wisconsin's northern tip, are a state highlight. Jump off from **Bayfield**, a humming resort town with hilly streets, Victorian-era buildings, apple orchards and nary a fast-food restaurant in sight. The **Chamber of Commerce** (☎ 715-779-3335; www.bayfield.org; 42 Broad St; 8:30am-5pm Mon-Fri) has an attached information center, accessible 24/7, with maps and the town lowdown.

Before exploring the Apostle Islands National Lakeshore, as it's officially called, drop by its **visitors center** (☎ 715-779-3397; www.nps.gov/apis; 410 Washington Ave; 8am-4:30pm Jun-Sep, closed Sat & Sun Oct-May). Campers can pick up the required camping permit (per night $10) here. The forested islands have no facilities, and walking is the only way to get around. Various companies offer seasonal charter, sailing and ferry trips to and around the islands, and kayaking is very popular. Try **Living Adventure** (☎ 715-779-9503; www.livingadventure.com; Hwy 13; half-/full-day tour $59/99; Jun-Sep) for a guided paddle through arches and sea caves; beginners are welcome. If you prefer a motor to power your explorations, climb aboard the **Apostle Islands Cruise Service** (☎ 715-779-3925; www.apostleisland.com; mid-May–mid-Oct) boat. It departs at 10am from Bayfield's City Dock for a three-hour narrated trip past sea caves and lighthouses (adult/child $40/24). Other trips call at islands to drop off/pick up campers and their kayaks, which avoids the long, possibly rough paddle.

Inhabited **Madeline Island** (☎ 715-747-2801; www.madelineisland.com), a fine day trip, is reached by a 20-minute **ferry** (☎ 715-747-2051; www.madferry.com) from Bayfield (round-trip adult/child/bicycle/car $11.50/5.50/5.50/24). Its walkable village of La Pointe has some mid-priced places to stay, and restaurants for a nosh. Bus tours are available, and you can rent bikes and mopeds – everything is near the ferry dock. **Big Bay State Park** (☎ 715-747-6425; campsites $15-17, vehicle $10) has a beach and trails.

Back in Bayfield, there are loads of B&Bs, cottages and other lodging, but reserve ahead in summer; see www.bayfield.org for options. Most rooms at no-frills **Seagull Bay**

Motel (☎ 715-779-5558; www.seagullbay.com; 325 S 7th St; r $70-100; ☒ ☐) have decks; ask for a lake view. Going upscale: **Pinehurst Inn** (☎ 877-499-7651; www.pinehurstinn.com; 83645 State Hwy 13; r incl breakfast $119-195; ☒ ☐) is a carbon-neutral, solar-heated, eight-room B&B.

Ecoconscious **Big Water Cafe** (☎ 715-779-9619; 117 Rittenhouse Ave; mains $4-7; 7am-4pm Mon-Fri, to 5pm Sat, 8am-4pm Sun) serves sandwiches, local farmstead cheeses and area microbrews. Kitschy, flamingo-themed **Maggie's** (☎ 715-779-5641; 257 Manypenny Ave; mains $7-16; 11:30am-9pm Sun-Thu, to 10pm Fri & Sat) is the place to sample local lake trout and whitefish; there's pizza and burgers too.

The **Big Top Chautauqua** (☎ 888-244-8368; www.bigtop.org) is a major regional summer event with big-name concerts and musical theater; call for schedule and prices.

MINNESOTA

Is Minnesota really the land of 10,000 lakes, as so often advertised? You betcha. Actually, in typically modest style, the state has undermarketed itself – there are 11,842 lakes. Which is great news for travelers. Intrepid outdoorsfolk can wet their paddles in the Boundary Waters (p648), where nighttime brings a blanket of stars and the lullaby of wolf howls. Those wanting to get further off the beaten path can journey to Voyageurs National Park (p649), where there's more water than roadway. If that all seems too far-flung, stick to the Twin Cities of Minneapolis and St Paul, where you can't swing a moose without hitting something cool or cultural. And for those looking for middle ground – a cross between the big city and big woods – the dramatic, freighter-filled port of Duluth (p646) beckons.

TALK LIKE A LOCAL

Admit it: you're puzzled by how to pronounce town names like Prairie du Chien and Lac du Flambeau. Lucky for you, the website www.misspronouncer.com provides recordings of how to say it in Wisconsinese. The site covers 190 cities, 1260 towns and heaps of famous locals' names. Soon you'll be chattering on about your visit to Rio *(rye-o)* or Chequamegon *(sheh wom again)* with confidence.

SCENIC DRIVE: HIGHWAY 13

After departing Bayfield, Hwy 13 takes a fine route around the Lake Superior shore, past the Ojibwa community of **Red Cliff** and the Apostle Islands' mainland segment, which has a beach. Tiny **Cornucopia**, looking every bit like a seaside village, has great sunsets. The road runs on through a timeless countryside of forest and farm reaching US 2 for the final miles back to civilization at Superior.

Information

Minnesota highway conditions (☎ 511; www.511mn.org)
Minnesota Office of Tourism (☎ 888-868-7476; www.exploreminnesota.com)
Minnesota state park information (☎ 888-646-6367; www.dnr.state.mn.us/state_parks) Park entry requires a vehicle permit (for residents and nonresidents per day/year $5/25). Campsites cost $12 to $24; reservations accepted (☎ 866-857-2757; www.stayatmnparks.com; fee $8.50).

MINNEAPOLIS

Minneapolis is the biggest and artiest town on the prairie, with all the trimmings of progressive prosperity – swank art museums, rowdy rock clubs, organic and ethnic eateries, and enough theaters to be nicknamed Mini-Apple (second only to the Big Apple, New York City). It's always happenin', even in winter.

But there's no attitude to go along with the abundance. It's the kind of place where homeless people are treated kindly at the coffee shops, where the buses are kept immaculately clean, and where the public workers tell everyone to 'Have a nice day,' rain or shine (or snow). No wonder the city recently topped the list as the most charitable place in America.

History

Timber was the city's first boom industry, and water-powered sawmills rose along the Mississippi River in the mid-1800s. Wheat from the prairies also needed to be processed, so flour mills churned into the next big business. The population boomed in the late 19th century with mass immigration, especially from Scandinavia and Germany. Today Minneapolis' Nordic heritage is evident, whereas twin city St Paul is more German and Irish-Catholic.

MINNESOTA FACTS

Nicknames North Star State, Gopher State
Population 5.2 million
Area 86,940 sq miles
Capital city St Paul (population 277,250)
Other cities Minneapolis (population 372,833)
Sales tax 6.875%
Birthplace of Author F Scott Fitzgerald (1896–1940), songwriter Bob Dylan (b 1941), filmmakers Joel Coen (b 1954) and Ethan Coen (b 1957)
Home of Lumberjack legend Paul Bunyan, Spam, walleye fish, Hmong and Somali immigrants
Famous for Niceness, funny accents, snowy weather, 10,000 lakes
Official muffin Blueberry
Driving distances Minneapolis to Duluth 153 miles, Minneapolis to Boundary Waters 245 miles

Orientation

Downtown Minneapolis is a modern grid of glassy high-rise buildings, many linked by enclosed overhead walkways called 'skyways' (very welcome in winter). The Mississippi River flows northeast of downtown. Despite the name, Uptown is actually southwest of downtown, with Hennepin Ave as its main axis. Minneapolis' twin city, St Paul, is 10 miles east.

Information

BOOKSTORES

Birchbark Books (☎ 612-374-4023; 2115 21st St W; ⏲ 9am-6pm Mon-Fri, 10am-5pm Sat, 11am-5pm Sun) Writer Louise Erdrich's unique store of Native American books and arts.

EMERGENCY & MEDICAL SERVICES

Fairview/University of Minnesota Medical Center (☎ 612-273-6402; 2450 Riverside Ave)
Victim crisis line (☎ 612-340-5400)
Walgreens (☎ 612-377-3308; 2426 Hennepin Ave S; ⏲ 24hr)

INTERNET ACCESS

Minneapolis Public Library (☎ 612-630-6000; www.hclib.org; 300 Nicollet Mall; ⏲ 10am-8pm Tue & Thu, to 6pm Wed, Fri & Sat, noon-5pm Sun) Mod facility with free internet.

INTERNET RESOURCES & MEDIA

KNOW-FM 91.1 broadcasts NPR. Community station KFAI-FM 90.3 provides eclectic music and talk.

City Pages (www.citypages.com) Weekly entertainment freebie.
Pioneer Press (www.twincities.com) St Paul's daily.
Star Tribune (www.startribune.com) Minneapolis' daily.
Vita.MN (www.vita.mn) The *Star Tribune*'s weekly entertainment freebie.

MONEY

Wells Fargo Bank (☎ 612-667-7990; cnr 6th St S & Marquette Ave) Offers foreign exchange, as well as an ATM and regular bank services.

POST

Post office (☎ 800-275-8777; 100 1st St S)

TOURIST INFORMATION

Visitors Center (☎ 612-335-6000, 888-676-6757; www.minneapolis.org; 1301 2nd Ave S; ⏲ 8am-4:30pm) In the Convention Center by the spiral staircase (near Ballroom A).

Sights & Activities

Most attractions are closed Monday; many stay open late Thursday.

DOWNTOWN & LORING PARK

Nicollet Mall is the pedestrian-friendly portion of Nicollet Ave in the heart of downtown, dense with stores, bars and restaurants. It's perhaps most famous as the spot where Mary Tyler Moore (of '70s TV fame) threw her hat into the air during the show's opening sequence. A cheesy **MTM statue** (8th St S & Nicollet Mall) depicts our girl doing just that. A **farmer's market** (⏲ 6am-6pm) takes over the mall on Thursdays from May to November.

The first-class **Walker Art Center** (☎ 612-375-7622; www.walkerart.org; 725 Vineland Pl; adult/child 13-18yr $10/6, admission free Thu evening; ⏲ 11am-5pm

DON'T MISS

- **Minneapolis Institute of Arts** – a heckuva lot of free art (p640)
- **Lake Calhoun** – biking and boating with the locals (p640)
- **Guthrie Theater** – peek out from the 'Endless Bridge' (p642)
- **Northeast neighborhood** – art galleries, dive bars and meat (p639)
- **International Marketplace** – Hmong food and wares (p645)

Tue-Sun, to 9pm Thu) has a strong permanent collection of 20th-century art and photography, including big-name US painters and great US pop art.

Beside the Walker is the 7-acre **Minneapolis Sculpture Garden** (admission free; 6am-midnight), studded with contemporary works, like the oft-photographed *Spoonbridge & Cherry* by Claes Oldenburg. The garden is connected to attractive Loring Park by a sculptural pedestrian bridge over I-94.

RIVERFRONT DISTRICT

At the north edge of downtown at the foot of Portland Ave is the **St Anthony Falls Heritage Trail**, a recommended 2-mile path that provides both interesting history (placards dot the route) and the city's best access to the banks of the Mississippi River. View the cascading falls from the car-free **Stone Arch Bridge**. On the north side of the river, Main St SE has a stretch of redeveloped buildings housing restaurants and bars. From here you can walk down to **Water Power Park** and feel the river's frothy spray.

Pick up a free trail map at the **Mill City Museum** (612-341-7555; www.millcitymuseum.org; 704 2nd St S; adult/child 6-17yr $10/5; 10am-5pm Tue-Sat, noon-5pm Sun, open Mon Jul & Aug). The building is indeed a former mill, and highlights include a ride inside an eight-story grain elevator ('the Flour Tower'), Betty Crocker exhibits and a baking lab. It's a bit dull unless you're really into milling history. The **Mill City Farmer's Market** (www

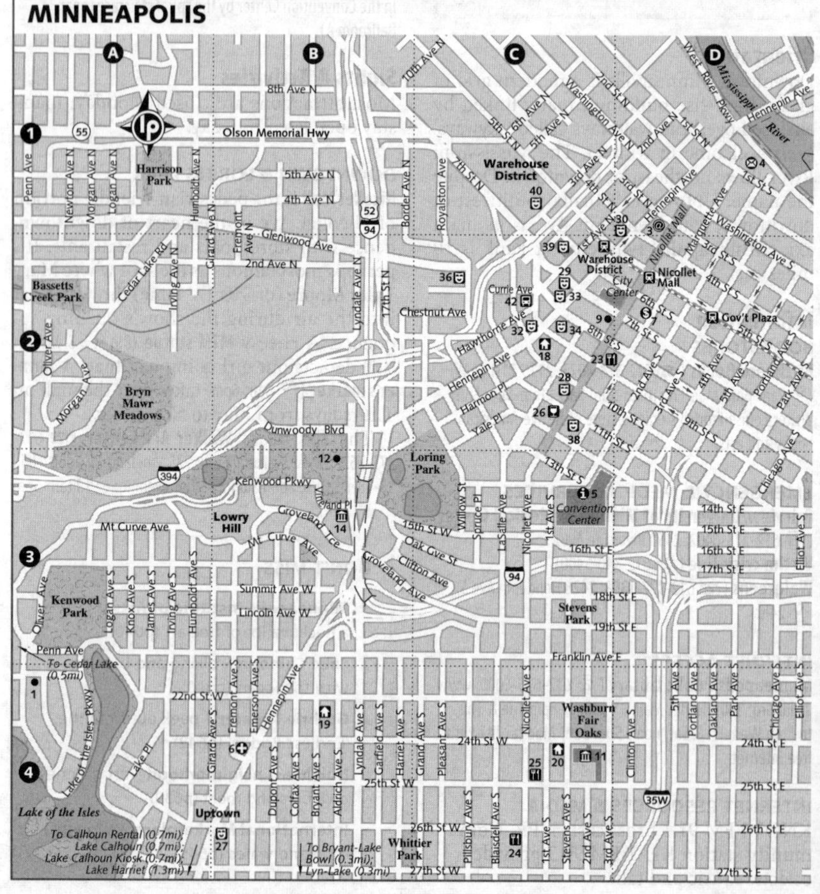

.millcityfarmersmarket.org; 8am-1pm Sat mid-May–mid-Oct) takes place in the museum's attached train shed; cooking demos fire up at 10am.

Definitely head next door to the cobalt-blue Guthrie Theater (p642) and make your way up to its '**Endless Bridge**,' a cantilevered walkway overlooking the river. You don't need a theater ticket – it's intended as a public space – though see a show if you can as the Guthrie is one of the Midwest's finest companies. **Gold Medal Park** spirals next door.

NORTHEAST

Once a working-class Eastern European neighborhood, Northeast (so named because of its position to the river) is where urbanites and artists now work and play. They appreciate the dive bars pouring microbrews along with Pabst, and boutiques selling ecogifts next to companies grinding sausage. Hundreds of craftsfolk and galleries fill historic industrial buildings. They fling open their doors the first Thursday of each month when the **Northeast Minneapolis Arts Association** (612-788-1679; www.nemaa.org) sponsors a gallery walk. Heady veins include 4th St NE and 13th Ave NE.

UNIVERSITY AREA

The **University of Minnesota**, by the river southeast of Minneapolis' center, is one of the USA's largest campuses, with over 50,000 students. Most of the campus is in the **East Bank** neighborhood. A uni (and city) highlight is the expanding **Weisman Art Museum** (612-625-9494;

www.weisman.umn.edu; 333 River Rd E; admission free; 10am-5pm Tue-Fri, to 8pm Thu, 11am-5pm Sat & Sun), which occupies a swooping silver structure by architect Frank Gehry. Works inside include early 20th-century American paintings. **Dinkytown**, based at 14th Ave SE and 4th St SE, is dense with student cafés and bookshops. A small part of the university is on the **West Bank** of the Mississippi River, near the intersection of 4th St S and Riverside Ave. This area has a few restaurants, some student hangouts and a big Somali community.

UPTOWN, LYN-LAKE & WHITTIER

These three neighborhoods are south of downtown. The fabulous **Minneapolis Institute of Arts** (612-870-3131; www.artsmia.org; 2400 3rd Ave S; admission free; 10am-5pm Tue-Sat, to 9pm Thu, 11am-5pm Sun) houses a veritable history of art, with a whopping modern and contemporary collection. The Prairie School and Asian galleries are also highlights.

Uptown, based around the intersection of Hennepin Ave S and Lake St, is a punk-yuppie collision of shops and restaurants that stays lively until late. **Lyn-Lake** abuts Uptown to the east and sports a similar urban-cool vibe; it's centered on Lyndale and Lake Sts. (Get the name?)

Uptown is a convenient jump-off point to the '**Chain of Lakes**' – Lake Calhoun, Lake of the Isles, Lake Harriet and Cedar Lake. It seems all of Minneapolis is out frolicking by the water – not surprising, really, since this is known as the 'city of lakes.' Paved cycling paths (which double as cross-country ski trails in winter) meander around the four lakes, where you can go boating in summer or ice skating in winter. Rent bikes and blades at **Calhoun Rental** (612-827-8231; 1622 W Lake St; per half-/full day $25/40; 10am-7pm Mon-Thu, to 8pm Fri & Sat, 9am-7pm Sun Apr-Oct) in Uptown; credit card and driver's license are required. A few blocks west, the **Lake Calhoun kiosk** (612-823-5765; base of Lake St; per hr $15; 10am-9pm late May-Aug, weekends only Sep & Oct) rents canoes, kayaks and paddleboats. It's a busy spot as there's also a patio restaurant and sailing school here.

Further around Lake Calhoun, Thomas Beach is popular for swimming. Cedar Lake's freewheeling Hidden Beach (aka East Cedar Beach) brings out the nudists, though you're welcome to keep your clothes on when visiting.

Minneapolis for Children

The local **Children's Theatre Company** (612-874-0400; www.childrenstheatre.org; 2400 3rd Ave S;) is so good it won a Tony award for 'outstanding regional theater.'

Note that many of the top sights for wee ones are in St Paul (p644), at the Mall of America (p645) and at Fort Snelling (p645). You'll also have to travel a ways to get to the respected **Minnesota Zoo** (952-431-9500; www.mnzoo.org; 13000 Zoo Blvd; adult/child 3-12yr $14/8; 9am-6pm summer, 9am-4pm winter;) in suburban Apple Valley, which is 20 miles south of town. It has naturalistic habitats for its 400-plus species, with an emphasis on cold-climate creatures. Parking is $5. And if the rides at the Mall of America aren't enough, drive out to **Valleyfair** (952-445-7600, 800-386-7433; www.valleyfair.com; 1 Valleyfair Dr; adult/child $38/17; from 10am daily mid-May–Aug, weekends only Sep, closing times vary;), a full-scale amusement park 25 miles southwest in Shakopee. Parking costs $10.

Festivals & Events

Minneapolis Aquatennial (612-376-7669; www.aquatennial.org; admission free) Ten days celebrating the ubiquitous lakes in mid-July.

Holidazzle (612-376-7669; www.holidazzle.com; admission free) Parades, lights and lots of good cheer downtown throughout December.

Sleeping

B&Bs offer the best value – they've got budget prices but are solidly midrange in quality. Tax adds 13.4% to prices.

BUDGET

Minneapolis International Hostel (612-522-5000; www.minneapolishostel.com; 2400 Stevens Ave S; dm $28-33, r $39;) This homey hostel beside the Institute of Arts has antique furniture, wood floors and fluffy quilts on the beds. Reservations are recommended.

MIDRANGE

Wales House (612-331-3931; www.waleshouse.com; 1115 5th St SE; r with/without shared bath, incl breakfast from $60/70;) This cheery 10-bedroom B&B often houses scholars from the nearby University of Minnesota. Curl up with a book on the season-round porch, or lounge by the fireplace. A two-night minimum stay is required.

Evelo's B&B (612-374-9656; 2301 Bryant Ave S; r with shared bath, incl breakfast $75-95;) Evelo's

GAY & LESBIAN MINNEAPOLIS

Minneapolis has the country's second-highest percentage of gay, lesbian, bisexual and transgender (GLBT) residents – only San Francisco has more – and the city enjoys strong GLBT rights. **Outfront Minnesota** (☎ 612-822-0127; www.outfront.org) provides information on GLBT-friendly local businesses; check the website for bar and restaurant information. Or pick up the free, biweekly magazine *Lavender* (www.lavendermagazine.com) at coffee shops around town.

For nightlife, **Gay Nineties** (☎ 612-333-7755; www.gay90s.com; 408 Hennepin Ave S) has dancing, dining and drag shows that attract both gay and straight clientele.

The late-June **Pride Festival** (☎ 952-852-6100; www.tcpride.com; admission free), one of the USA's largest, draws about 400,000 revelers.

four rooms creak and charm in this polished-wood-filled Victorian home. They're close quartered, but the B&B's strategic location between the Walker Art Center and Uptown compensates.

Aloft (☎ 612-455-8400; www.starwoodhotels.com/aloft; 900 Washington Ave S; r $109-149; P) Aloft's compact, efficiently designed, industrial-toned rooms draw a younger clientele. The clubby lobby has board games, a cocktail lounge and 24-hour snacks. There's a tiny pool and decent fitness room. Parking costs $15.

TOP END

Chambers Hotel (☎ 612-767-6900, 877-767-6990; www.chambersminneapolis.com; 901 Hennepin Ave S; r weekend/weekday from $179/265; P) It's an art gallery – no, it's a hotel. Actually, it's both, with 200 artworks (including Damien Hirst's floating bull's head at the front desk) spread throughout, and 60 minimalist rooms with luxury touches, like heated bathroom floors. Parking costs $24.

Eating

Minneapolis has ripened into a rich dining scene known for its many restaurants that use local, sustainable ingredients.

DOWNTOWN & NORTHEAST

Nicollet Mall is loaded with eateries.

Mayslack's (☎ 612-789-9862; www.mayslacksbar.com; 1428 4th St NE; sandwiches $7-9, mains $10-15; 11am-midnight) It's hard to beat their meat. Mayslack's has been slicing garlicky roast beef onto sandwiches and pouring icy brewskis since 1955. Walleye, pizza and breakfast omelets also make appearances, as do local rock bands thrashing Thursday through Saturday.

Hell's Kitchen (☎ 612-332-4700; 80 9th St S; mains $10-15; 6:30am-10pm Mon-Thu, 7:30am-11pm Fri & Sat, 7:30am-10pm Sun) Descend the stairs to Hell's devilish lair, where spirited waitstaff bring you uniquely Minnesotan foods, like the walleye bacon-lettuce-tomato sandwich, bison burger and lemon-ricotta hotcakes. Happy hour (3pm to 6pm) at the bar is a dandy deal.

Red Stag Supper Club (☎ 612-767-7766; 509 1st Ave NE; bar menu $8-13, mains $18-27; 11am-2am Mon-Fri, 9am-2am Sat & Sun) The exposed-beam Northwoods lodge look belies Red Stag's LEED-certified architecture. The locally sourced arugula-and-pine-nut flatbread sandwiches, smelt fries, smoked trout and cassoulet soothe the stomach. There are good deals for Sunday brunch and Tuesday dinner.

UNIVERSITY AREA

Low-priced eateries cluster in the campus area by Washington Ave and Oak St.

Al's Breakfast (☎ 612-331-9991; 413 14th Ave SE; mains $4-7; 6am-1pm Mon-Sat, 9am-1pm Sun) It's the ultimate hole-in-the-wall: 14 stools at a tiny counter. Whenever a customer comes in, everyone picks up their plates and scoots down to make room for the newcomer. Fruit-full pancakes are the big crowd-pleaser.

UPTOWN, LYN-LAKE & WHITTIER

Vietnamese, Greek, African and other ethnic restaurants line Nicollet Ave S between 14th and 29th Sts – aka 'Eat Street.'

Spyhouse Coffee (☎ 612-871-3177; 2451 Nicollet Ave S; items $2-5; 6:30am-midnight Mon-Fri, 8am-midnight Sat & Sun) Join the artists, business types and cabbies who are here for the coffee and baked goods.

our pick **Bryant-Lake Bowl** (☎ 612-825-3737; 810 W Lake St; sandwiches $7-9, mains $11-16; 8am-12:30am) A workingman's bowling alley meets epicurean food at the BLB. Artisanal cheese plates, mock duck rolls, cornmeal-crusted walleye strips and organic oatmeal melt in the mouth. A lovely list of local suds washes it all down. The on-site theater always has something intriguing and odd going on too.

Peninsula (☎ 612-871-8282; 2608 Nicollet Ave S; mains $9-15; 🕒 11am-10pm Sun-Thu, to 11pm Fri & Sat) Malaysian dishes – including *achat* (tangy vegetable salad in peanut dressing), red curry hot pot, spicy crab and fish in banana leaves – rock the palate in this contemporary restaurant.

Drinking & Entertainment

With its large student population and thriving performing-arts scene, Minneapolis has an active nightlife. Check *Vita.MN* and *City Pages* for current goings on.

BARS & NIGHTCLUBS

Bars stay open until 2am.

Brit's Pub (☎ 612-332-3908; 1110 Nicollet Mall) A lawn bowling green carpets the roof, and Brit's sweeping selection of Scotch, port and beer is sure to unleash skills in the sport you never knew you had.

Grumpy's (☎ 612-789-7429; 2200 4th St NE) Grumpy's is the Northeast's classic dive, with cheap (but good) beer and an outdoor patio. Sample the specialty 'hot dish' on Tuesdays for $1.

LIVE MUSIC

Minneapolis rocks; everyone's in a band, it seems. Acts such as Prince and post-punkers Hüsker Dü and the Replacements cut their chops here.

First Avenue & 7th St Entry (☎ 612-338-8388; www.first-avenue.com; 701 1st Ave N) This is the bedrock of Minneapolis' music scene, and it still pulls in top bands and big crowds.

Triple Rock Social Club (☎ 612-333-7499; www.triplerocksocialclub.com; 629 Cedar Ave) Triple Rock is a popular punk-alternative club.

Lee's Liquor Lounge (☎ 612-338-9491; www.leesliquorlounge.com; 101 Glenwood Ave) Rockabilly and country-tinged alt bands twang here.

Dakota Jazz Club (☎ 612-332-1010; www.dakotacooks.com; 1010 Nicollet Mall) The Dakota is a classy venue that gets big-name jazz acts.

Nye's Polonaise Room (☎ 612-379-2021; 112 E Hennepin Ave) The World's Most Dangerous Polka Band lets loose Thursday through Saturday. It's smashing fun, and enhanced if you find yourself an old-timer to twirl you around the room.

THEATER & CULTURE

They don't call it Mini-Apple for nothing, with 100-plus theater groups here. The Guthrie and other venues put unsold tickets on sale 10 minutes before showtime for $15 to $25.

Brave New Workshop Theatre (☎ 612-332-6620; www.bravenewworkshop.com; 2605 Hennepin Ave S) An established venue for musical comedy, revue and satire.

Guthrie Theater (☎ 612-377-2224; www.guthrietheater.org; 818 2nd St S) Minneapolis' top-gun theater troupe, with the jumbo facility to prove it.

Historic Pantages, State & Orpheum Theatres (☎ 612-339-7007; www.hennepintheatredistrict.org) The main venues for Broadway shows and touring acts, all in a row on Hennepin Ave S at street Nos 710, 805 and 910, respectively.

Orchestra Hall (☎ 612-371-5656; www.minnesotaorchestra.org; 1111 Nicollet Mall) Superb acoustics for concerts by the acclaimed Minnesota Symphony Orchestra.

SPORTS

Minnesotans love their sports teams. Note that ice hockey (p645) happens in St Paul.

Hubert H Humphrey Metrodome (☎ 612-338-4537; www.vikings.com; 900 5th St S) The Vikings pro football team passes in the 'Dome.

Target Center (☎ 612-337-3865; www.nba.com/timberwolves; 600 1st Ave N) This is where the Timberwolves pro basketball team lays 'em up.

Target Field (☎ 612-338-9467; www.minnesotatwins.com; 3rd Ave N btwn 5th & 7th Sts N) It's the brand spankin' new stadium for the Twins pro baseball team.

Getting There & Around

The **Minneapolis-St Paul International Airport** (MSP; ☎ 612-726-5555; www.mspairport.com) is between the two cities to the south. It's the home of Northwest Airlines, which operates several direct flights to/from Europe.

The cheapest way into Minneapolis is via the Hiawatha light-rail line (regular/rush-hour fare $1.75/2.25, 25 minutes). To reach St Paul, take bus 54 (same fare, 25 minutes).

Greyhound (☎ 612-371-3325; www.greyhound.com; 950 Hawthorne Ave) runs frequent buses to Milwaukee ($39 to $61, seven hours), Chicago ($29 to $63, nine hours) and Duluth ($20 to $36, three hours). **Megabus** (☎ 877-462-6342; www.megabus.com/us) runs express to Milwaukee (six hours) and Chicago (eight hours), often for lower fares. It departs from both downtown and the university; check the website for exact locations.

Metro Transit (☎ 612-373-3333; www.metrotransit.org) runs frequent, spic-n-span buses (regular/rush-hour fare $1.75/2.25) throughout the area, as well as the excellent Hiawatha light-rail line (same fare) between downtown and the Mall of America. Express bus 94 (regular/rush-hour fare $2.25/3) connects Minneapolis to St Paul; it departs from 6th St N's south side, just west of Hennepin Ave. A day pass ($6) is available from any rail station or bus driver.

The **Amtrak station** (☎ 651-644-6012; www.amtrak.com; 730 Transfer Rd), off University Ave SE, is between Minneapolis and St Paul. Trains go daily to Chicago ($56 to $125, eight hours) and Seattle ($150 to $270, 37 hours). The ride east to La Crosse ($24 to $53, three hours), Wisconsin, is beautiful, skirting the Mississippi River and offering multiple eagle sightings.

If you need a taxi service, call **Yellow Cab** (☎ 612-824-4444).

At the time of writing, Minneapolis was set to launch the nation's largest bike-share program in May 2010. **Nice Ride** (www.niceridemn.com) is placing 1000 bikes in 80 self-serve kiosks around the city. Users pay a subscription fee (per day/week $5/15) online or at the kiosk, plus a small fee per half-hour of use. Bikes can be returned to any kiosk.

ST PAUL

Smaller and quieter than its twin city Minneapolis, St Paul has retained more of a historic character. Walk through F Scott Fitzgerald's old stomping grounds, trek the trails along the mighty Mississippi River, or slurp some Lao soup.

The **visitors center** (☎ 651-292-3225, 800-627-6101; www.visitstpaul.com; 75 W 5th St; 9am-4pm Mon-Fri, 10am-3pm Sat, noon-3pm Sun), in the Landmark Center, makes a good first stop for maps and DIY walking tour info. Pick up the *St Paul Cultural Pass* brochure for local discounts.

Sights & Activities

The **Cathedral of St Paul** (☎ 651-228-1766; www.cathedralsaintpaul.org; 239 Selby Ave; admission free; 7am-7pm Sun-Fri, to 9pm Sat) presides over the city from its hilltop perch and marks the attractive **Summit-Selby** neighborhood. This wealthy 19th-century district, now ethnically mixed, is well worth an afternoon stroll. Follow **Summit Avenue**, which has a fine string of Victorian houses, including the palatial **James J Hill House** (☎ 651-297-2555; www.mnhs.org/hillhouse; 240 Summit Ave; adult/child 6-17yr $8/4; 10am-3:30pm Wed-Sat, 1-3:30pm Sun), a railroad magnate's former mansion, now open for tours.

Writer F Scott Fitzgerald once lived at the privately owned **599 Summit Avenue**, and authors Garrison Keillor and Sinclair Lewis have also called the area home. Literature buffs can pick up the *Fitzgerald Homes and Haunts* map at the visitors center (below).

A visit to the privately owned **Julian H Sleeper House** (☎ 651-225-1505; www.julianhsleeperhouse.com; 66 S St Albans St; tours $7; by appointment) lets you see how the upper crust really lived. The place is filled with chandeliers, oriental carpets and decorative arts from the late 19th century. The owner is a colorful storyteller and will show you his antique postcard collection and other weird stuff.

Downtown, the turreted 1902 **Landmark Center** contains a couple of small museums in addition to the visitors center. The **Schubert Club Museum** (☎ 651-292-3267; www.schubert.org; 75 W 5th St; admission free; 11am-3pm Mon-Fri, 1-5pm Sun) has a brilliant collection of old pianos and harpsichords – some tickled by Mozart, Beethoven and the like – in the basement. It displays old manuscripts and letters from famous composers on the 2nd floor. A free wood-turning museum (it's a decorative form of woodworking) is also on the 2nd floor.

The **Science Museum of Minnesota** (☎ 651-221-9444; www.smm.org; 120 W Kellogg Blvd; adult/child 4-12yr $11/8.50; 9:30am-5pm Sun-Wed, to 9pm Thu-Sat, 8:30am-10pm daily mid-Jun–early Sep) has the usual hands-on kids' exhibits and Omnimax theater ($5 extra). Adults will be entertained by the wacky quackery of the 4th floor's 'questionable medical devices.' In the museum lobby is the National Park Service's **Mississippi River Visitors Center** (☎ 651-293-0200; www.nps.gov/miss; 9:30am-5pm Sun-Thu, to 9pm Fri & Sat). Definitely stop by to pick up trail maps and see what sort of free ranger-guided walks and bike rides are going on. Most take place at 10am on Wednesday, Thursday and Saturday in summer. In winter, the centers hosts ice-fishing and snowshoeing jaunts.

Revitalized **Harriet Island**, running south off Wabasha St, is a lovely place to meander; it has a park, river walk, concert stages and fishing dock. **Padelford Packet Boat Co** (☎ 651-227-1100; www.riverrides.com; adult/child 3-12yr $16/8) operates 1½-hour paddle-boat tours from the dock. Tours begin at noon and 2pm from June to August

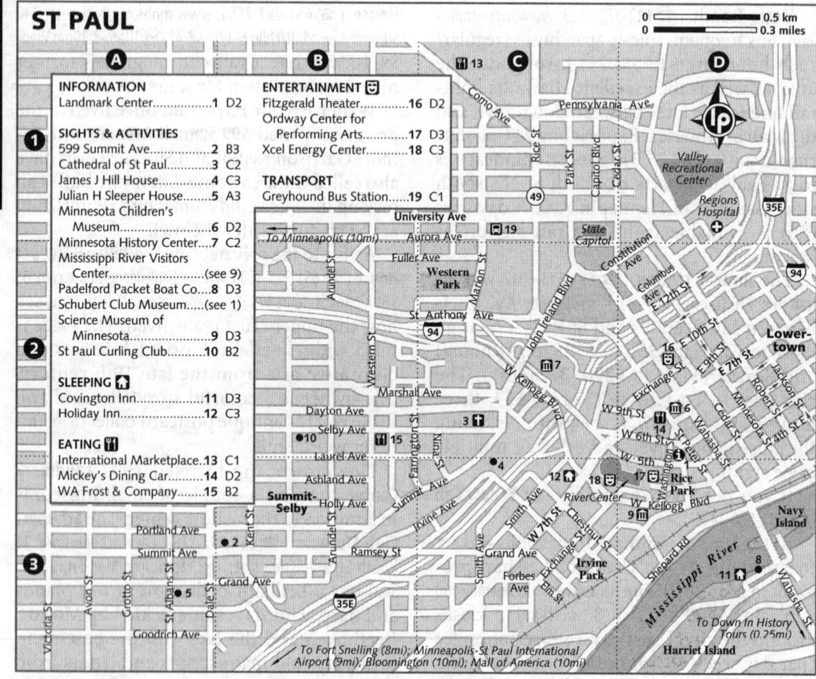

every day except Monday, and at 2pm Saturday and Sunday only in September and October.

From November to March, stop in and watch the action at the **St Paul Curling Club** (☎ 651-224-7408; www.stpaulcurlingclub.org; 470 Selby Ave). For those uninitiated in northern ways, curling is a winter sport that involves sliding a hubcap-sized 'puck' down the ice toward a bull's-eye.

St Paul for Children

The **Minnesota Children's Museum** (☎ 651-225-6000; www.mcm.org; 10 W 7th St; admission $9; 9am-5pm Tue-Sun, to 8pm Fri, open Mon Jun-Aug;) has the usual gamut of hands-on activities, as well as a giant anthill to burrow through, and the 'One World' intercultural community where kids can shop and vote.

The **Minnesota History Center** (☎ 651-259-3000; www.mnhs.org/historycenter; 345 W Kellogg Blvd; adult/child 6-17yr $10/5, admission free Tue evening; 10am-8pm Tue, 10am-5pm Wed-Sat, noon-5pm Sun;) educates with its 'A to Z' treasure hunt and climbable boxcar, while the Science Museum of Minnesota (p643) pleases kids with its laser show and Omnimax.

Tours

Down In History Tours (☎ 651-292-1220; www.wabashastreetcaves.com; 215 S Wabasha St) Tour St Paul's underground caves ($5), which gangsters once used as a speakeasy. The company offers other fun, offbeat tours too. Times vary.

Festivals & Events

St Paul Winter Carnival (☎ 651-223-4700; www.winter-carnival.com; admission varies depending on event) Ten days of ice sculptures, ice skating and ice fishing in January.

Sleeping

You'll find a bigger selection in Minneapolis.

Holiday Inn (☎ 651-225-1515; www.holiday-inn.com/stpaulmn; 175 W 7th St; r $99-159;) The rooms are the usual decent quality you expect from the Holiday Inn chain; the perks are the location adjacent to the RiverCentre, a small pool and an on-site Irish pub. Parking is $14.

Covington Inn (☎ 651-292-1411; www.covingtoninn.com; 100 Harriet Island Rd; r incl breakfast $150-235;) This four-room, Harriet Island B&B is on a tugboat floating in the Mississippi River; watch the river traffic glide by while sipping your morning coffee.

Eating & Drinking

Grand Ave between Dale and Victoria Sts is a worthy browse, with cafés, foodie shops and ethnic eats in close proximity.

Mickey's Dining Car (☎ 651-222-5633; 36 W 7th St; mains $4-8; 24hr) Mickey's is a downtown classic; the kind of place where the friendly waitress calls you 'honey' and satisfied regulars line the bar with their coffee cups and newspapers. The food has timeless appeal too: burgers, malts and apple pie.

our pick **International Marketplace** (☎ 651-487-3700; 217 Como Ave; items $4-8; 9am-7pm) The nation's largest enclave of Hmong immigrants live in the Twin Cities, and this market delivers their favorite Vietnamese, Lao and Thai dishes at its humble food court. Find the West Building and head to the back where vendors ladle hot-spiced papaya salad, beef ribs, sticky rice and curry noodle soup. Then stroll the market, where you can fix your dentures or buy a cockatoo or brass gong.

WA Frost & Company (☎ 651-224-5715; 374 Selby Ave; sandwiches $9-11, mains $16-32; 11am-10pm Sun-Thu, to 11pm Fri & Sat) Frost's tree-shaded, ivy-covered, twinkling-light patio is right out of a Fitzgerald novel, perfect for a glass of wine, beer or gin. The restaurant locally sources many ingredients for dishes like the artisanal cheese plate, glazed tofu steak and cardamom-glazed duck.

Entertainment

Fitzgerald Theater (☎ 651-290-1221; www.fitzgeraldtheater.org; 10 E Exchange St) Where Garrison Keillor tapes his *Prairie Home Companion* radio show.

Ordway Center for Performing Arts (☎ 651-224-4222; www.ordway.org; 345 Washington St) Chamber music and the Minnesota Opera fill the hall here.

Xcel Energy Center (☎ 651-222-9453; www.wild.com; 199 Kellogg Blvd) The Wild pro hockey team skates at Xcel.

Getting There & Around

St Paul is served by the same transit systems as Minneapolis; see p643 for details. Greyhound bus routes serving Minneapolis usually stop at the **St Paul station** (☎ 651-222-0507; 166 W University Ave) too.

AROUND MINNEAPOLIS–ST PAUL

Mall of America

In Bloomington, the **Mall of America** (☎ 952-883-8800; www.mallofamerica.com; off I-494 at 24th Ave; 10am-9:30pm Mon-Sat, 11am-7pm Sun) is the USA's largest shopping center. Yes, it's just a mall, filled with the usual stores, movie theaters and eateries. But there's also a wedding chapel inside. And an 18-hole **minigolf course** (☎ 952-883-8777; adult/child 4-12yr $9/7). And an amusement park, aka **Nickelodeon Universe** (☎ 952-883-8600; www.nickelodeonuniverse.com;), with 24 rides, including a couple of scream-inducing roller coasters. To walk through will cost you nothing; a one-day, unlimited-ride wristband is $30; or you can pay for rides individually ($3 to $6). What's more, the state's largest aquarium, **Underwater Adventures** (☎ 952-883-0202; www.sharky.tv; adult/child 3-12yr $19/12;) – where children can touch sharks and stingrays – is in the mall too. Combination passes are available to save dough. The Hiawatha light-rail runs to/from downtown.

Fort Snelling

East of the mall, **Fort Snelling** (☎ 612-726-1171; www.mnhs.org/fortsnelling; cnr Hwys 5 & 55; adult/child 6-17yr $10/5; 10am-5pm Mon-Sat, noon-5pm Sun Jun-Aug, Sat & Sun only May, Sep & Oct) is the state's oldest structure, established in 1820 as a frontier outpost in the remote Northwest Territory. Guides in period dress show restored buildings and reenact pioneer life.

SOUTHERN MINNESOTA

Some of the scenic southeast can be seen on short drives from the Twin Cities. Better is a loop of a few days' duration, following the rivers and stopping in some of the historic towns and state parks.

Just east of St Paul, the **St Croix River** forms the border with Wisconsin. Northeast of the city along US 61, then east on US 8, attractive Taylors Falls marks the upper limit of navigation. Take a walk along the gorge in Interstate Park. Due east of St Paul, on Hwy 36, touristy **Stillwater**, on the lower St Croix, is an old logging town with restored 19th-century buildings, river cruises and antique stores. It's also an official 'booktown,' an honor bestowed upon a few small towns worldwide that possess an extraordinary number of antiquarian bookshops. What's more, the town is filled with classy historic B&Bs; the **chamber of commerce** (☎ 651-439-4001; www.ilovestillwater.com) provides listings.

Larger **Red Wing**, to the south on US 61, is a similar but less-interesting restored town, though it does offer its famous Red Wing Shoes – actually more like sturdy boots – and salt glaze pottery.

The prettiest part of the **Mississippi Valley** area begins south of here. To drive it and see the best bits, you'll need to flip-flop back and forth between Minnesota and Wisconsin.

From Red Wing, cross the river on US 63. **Maiden Rock**, on Wisconsin Hwy 35 (aka the Great River Rd), is downstream and offers views from its 400ft Indian-legend namesake. A bit further south, a great stretch of Hwy 35 edges beside the bluffs around **Stockholm** (population 90). It's worth a stop here at **Bogus Creek Cafe** (☎ 715-442-5017; Spring St; mains $7-11; ⌚ 10am-4pm Mon-Thu, 9am-5pm Fri-Sun) for the sweetastic French toast cut from croissants, and fresh bread and Swedish pastries.

Continuing south, cross back over the river to **Wabasha** in Minnesota, which has a historic downtown and large population of bald eagles that congregate in winter. To learn more, visit the **National Eagle Center** (☎ 651-565-4989; www.nationaleaglecenter.org; 50 Pembroke Ave; adult/child $6/4; ⌚ 10am-5pm).

On the Wisconsin side again, Hwy 35 is scenic heading south to **Alma**, offering superlative views from Buena Vista Park. Cross back to Minnesota further downstream at **Winona**, where there are fine views from lofty Garvin Heights Park, with eagle sightings an added bonus in winter.

Inland and south, the Bluff Country is dotted with limestone bluffs, southeast Minnesota's main geological feature. **Lanesboro** is a gem for rails-to-trails cycling and canoeing. Seven miles westward on County Rd 8 (call for directions) is **Old Barn Resort** (☎ 507-467-2512; www.barnresort.com; dm/r $25/50, camp-/RV site $28/36; ⌚ Apr-mid-Nov; 🅧), a pastoral hostel-cum campground-restaurant-outfitter. **Harmony**, south of Lanesboro, is the center of an Amish community and another welcoming town.

> **WHAT THE...?**
>
> Behold the **World's Largest Ball of Twine** (☎ 320-693-7544; www.darwintwineball.com; 1st St; admission free; ⌚ 24hr) in Darwin, 62 miles west of Minneapolis on US 12. To be specific, it's the 'Largest Built by One Person' – Francis A Johnson wrapped the 17,400lb whopper on his farm over the course of 29 years. Gawk at it in the town gazebo. Better yet, visit the **museum** (⌚ 1-4pm Apr-Sep, by appointment Oct-Mar) beside it and buy your own twine ball starter kit in the gift shop.

Head north on US 52 to **Rochester**, home of the famed **Mayo Clinic** (☎ 507-284-2511; www.mayoclinic.org; 200 1st St SW), which attracts medical patients and practitioners from around the world. Free 90-minute tours (at 10am weekdays) and a film outline the Mayo brothers' story and describe how the clinic developed its cutting-edge reputation.

NORTHERN MINNESOTA

Northern Minnesota is where you come to 'do some fishing, do some drinking,' as one resident summed it up.

Duluth

At the Great Lakes' westernmost end, Duluth (with its neighbor, Superior, Wisconsin) is one of the busiest ports in the country, sporting over 40 miles of wharf and waterfront. The town's dramatic location spliced into a cliff makes it a fab place to see changeable Lake Superior in action. The water, along with the area's trails and natural splendor, has earned Duluth a reputation as a hot spot for outdoors junkies.

A seasonal **visitors center** (☎ 218-722-6024, 800-438-5884; www.visitduluth.com; 350 Harbor Dr; ⌚ 9:30am-7:30pm mid-May–Aug, reduced hours Sep–mid-Oct) is in the Duluth Entertainment Convention Center (DECC), opposite the Vista dock.

SIGHTS & ACTIVITIES

The waterfront area is distinctive. Mosey along the Lakewalk trail and around Canal Park. Look for the Aerial Lift Bridge, which rises to let ships into the port; about a thousand ships a year pass through here. Check the computer screens outside the **Maritime Visitors Center** (☎ 218-720-5260; www.lsmma.com; 600 Lake Ave S; admission free; ⌚ 10am-9pm Jun-Aug, reduced hours Sep-May) to learn when the big ones come and go. The first-rate center also has exhibits on Great Lakes' shipping and shipwrecks.

To continue the nautical theme, walk the mighty **William A Irvin** (☎ 218-722-7876; www.williamairvin.com; 350 Harbor Dr; adult/child $9/free; ⌚ 9am-7pm Jun-Aug, 10am-4pm May, Sep & Oct), a 610ft Great Lakes freighter. The hour-long tour also includes a look aboard a Coastguard ice cutter (although this may become a separate attraction with its own admission fee in the near future).

The **Great Lakes Aquarium** (☎ 218-740-3474; www.glaquarium.org; 353 Harbor Dr; adult/child 3-16yr $14.50/8.50; ⌚ 10am-6pm) is one of the coun-

WHAT THE...?

Lookin' for a little sweet pork magic? Hop on I-90 heading southwest from Rochester and pull off in Austin. Here, friends, lies the **Spam Museum** (☎ 800-588-7726; www.spam.com; 1101 N Main St; admission free; ⏲ 10am-5pm Mon-Sat, noon-4pm Sun May-Aug, closed Mon Sep-Apr), an entire institution devoted to the peculiar, revered blue tins of meat. Who knew canned hog could be so much fun?

try's few freshwater aquariums. Highlights include the daily stingray feedings at 2pm and the otter tanks.

The 1½-hour harbor cruises from **Vista Fleet** (☎ 218-722-6218; www.vistafleet.com; 323 Harbor Dr; adult/child $14/6; ⏲ mid-May–Oct) will get you out on the water. Or do it yourself by paddling a kayak with the **University of Minnesota Duluth's outdoor program** (☎ 218-726-7128; www.umdrsop.org; 1216 Ordean Ct; 4hr tour $45-50). It also offers rock climbing, paddleboarding and snowkiting programs; beginners are welcome for all activities.

Skiing and snowboarding are big pastimes come winter, and **Spirit Mountain** (☎ 218-628-2891; www.spiritmt.com; 9500 Spirit Mountain Pl; per day adult/child 7-12yr $45/35; ⏲ 9am-8pm Sun-Thu, to 9pm Fri & Sat mid-Nov–Mar), 10 miles south of Duluth, is the place to go; rentals are available.

For a spectacular view of the city and harbor, climb the rock tower in **Enger Park** (Skyline Pkwy), located a couple miles southwest by the golf course.

Back in town, **Leif Erikson Park** (cnr London Rd & 14th Ave E) is a lakefront sweet spot with a rose garden, replica of Leif's Viking ship and free outdoor movies each Friday night in summer. Take the Lakewalk from Canal Park (about 1½ miles) and you can say you hiked the Superior Trail (p649), which traverses this stretch.

SLEEPING & EATING

Duluth has several B&Bs; rooms cost at least $125 in the summer. Check **Duluth Historic Inns** (www.duluthbandb.com) for listings. The town's accommodations fill up fast in summer, which may mean you'll have to try your luck across the border in Superior, Wisconsin (where it's cheaper too). Note that most restaurants and bars reduce their hours in winter.

Willard Munger Inn (☎ 218-624-4814, 800-982-2453; www.mungerinn.com; 7408 Grand Ave; r incl breakfast peak weekends $90-136; ⊠ 💻 📶) Family-owned Munger Inn offers a fine variety of rooms (budget to Jacuzzi suites), along with perks for outdoor enthusiasts, such as hiking and biking trails right outside the door, free use of bikes and canoes and a fire pit. It's near Spirit Mountain.

Fitger's Inn (☎ 218-722-8826, 888-348-4377; www.fitgers.com; 600 E Superior St; r incl breakfast $99-209; ⊠ 💻 📶) Fitger's carved its 62 large rooms, each with slightly varied decor, from an old brewery. Located on the Lakewalk, the pricier rooms have great water views. The free shuttle to local sights is handy.

The Canal Park waterfront area has eateries of all price ranges. In the **DeWitt-Seitz Marketplace** (394 Lake Ave S), **Amazing Grace** (☎ 218-723-0075; sandwiches $6-10; ⏲ 7am-10pm) serves sandwiches in a hippyish café with folk music some evenings, while **Taste of Saigon** (☎ 218-727-1598; mains $7-12; ⏲ 11am-8:30pm Sun-Thu, to 9:30pm Fri & Sat) cooks Vietnamese meals, including vegetarian dishes like mock duck.

Earthy, pinewood-boothed **Chester Creek Cafe** (☎ 218-723-8569; 1902 E 8th St; mains $7-14; ⏲ 7am-9pm Mon-Sat, 7:30am-4pm Sun) plates omelets, tempeh reubens, thai tofu curry and fish and meat dishes. Organic wines and thick, double-crusted pie slices appear too. It's in the university area, about 2 miles from downtown.

Fully licensed **Pizza Luce** (☎ 218-727-7400; 11 E Superior St; large pizza $20-22; ⏲ 8am-1:30am Sun-Thu, to 2:30am Fri & Sat) is renowned for its gourmet pizzas, vegetarian options and late-night vibe. It's also plugged into the local music scene and hosts bands.

GETTING THERE & AROUND

Greyhound (☎ 218-722-5591; 4426 Grand Ave) has a couple of buses daily to Minneapolis ($20 to $36, three hours) and Milwaukee ($65 to $98, 12 hours).

North Shore

Heading northeast to Canada, Hwy 61 (see boxed text, p648) edges Lake Superior and passes numerous state parks, waterfalls, hiking trails and mom-and-pop towns. Lots of weekend, summer and fall traffic makes reservations essential.

Two Harbors has a museum, lighthouse and B&B. Actually, the latter two are one and the same, with the **Lighthouse B&B** (☎ 218-834-4814, 888-832-5606; www.lighthousebb.org; r incl breakfast $135-155) being a unique place to spend the night if you can snag one of its four rooms. Just beyond town is the **Houle Information Center** (☎ 800-777-7384; www.twoharborschamber.com; 1330 Hwy 61; 9am-5pm Mon-Fri, to 6pm Sat, 10am-5pm Sun), which provides area information.

Route highlights north of Two Harbors are Gooseberry Falls, Split Rock Lighthouse and Palisade Head. About 110 miles from Duluth, artsy little **Grand Marais** makes an excellent base for exploring the Boundary Waters (right) and environs. For Boundary permits and information, visit the **Gunflint Ranger Station** (☎ 218-387-1750; 7am-5pm May-Sep), just south of town. The **visitors center** (☎ 218-387-2524; www.grandmarais.com; 13 N Broadway St; 9am-5pm Mon-Thu, to 6pm Fri & Sat, 10am-2pm Sun Jul-Oct, reduced hours rest of year) is also a good resource.

Do-it-yourself enthusiasts can learn to build boats, tie flies or brew beer at the **North House Folk School** (☎ 218-387-9762; www.northhouse-folkschool.com; 500 Hwy 61). Classes start at $35, and the course list is phenomenal

Grand Marais' lodging options include camping, resorts and motels, like the **Harbor Inn** (☎ 218-387-1191; www.bytheharbor.com; 207 Wisconsin St; r $95-135;) in town or rustic, trail-encircled **Naniboujou Lodge** (☎ 218-387-2688; www.naniboujou.com; 20 Naniboujou; r $90-110), which is 8 miles outside town. **Sven and Ole's** (☎ 218-387-1713; 9 Wisconsin St; sandwiches $4-7.50; 11am-8pm, to 9pm Thu-Sat) is a classic for sandwiches and pizza; beer flows at the attached Pickled Herring Pub. Ecofriendly **Angry Trout Cafe** (☎ 218-387-1265; 416 Hwy 61; mains $19-25; 11am-8:30pm May–mid-Oct) grills fresh-plucked lake fish in a converted fishing shanty.

Hwy 61 continues to **Grand Portage National Monument**, beside Canada, where the early voyageurs had to carry their canoes around the Pigeon River rapids. This was the center of a far-flung trading empire, and the reconstructed 1788 trading post is well worth seeing. **Isle Royale National Park** in Lake Superior is reached by daily **ferries** (☎ 218-475-0024; www.isleroyaleboats.com; day trip adult/child 4-11yr $63/42) from May to October. (The park is also accessible from Michigan; see p625.)

Boundary Waters

From Two Harbors, Hwy 2 runs inland to the legendary **Boundary Waters Canoe Area Wilderness (BWCAW)**. This pristine region has more than a thousand lakes and streams in which to dip a paddle. It's possible to go just for the day, but most people opt for at least one night of camping. If you're willing to dig in and canoe for a while, you'll lose the crowds. Camping then becomes a wonderfully remote experience where it will be you, the howling wolves, the moose who's nuzzling the tent and the aurora borealis' greenish light filling the night sky. Beginners are welcome, and everyone can get set up with gear from local lodges and outfitters. **Permits** (☎ 877-550-6777; www.recreation.gov; adult/child under 18yr $16/8, plus $12 reservation fee) are required for overnight stays. Day permits, though free, are also required. Call **Superior National Forest** (☎ 218-626-4300; www.fs.fed.us/r9/forests/superior/bwcaw) for details; the website has a useful trip planning guide. Try to plan ahead, if possible, as permits are quota restricted and sometimes run out.

Many argue the best BWCAW access is via the engaging town of **Ely**, northeast of the Iron Range area, which has accommodations, restaurants and scores of outfitters. The **Chamber of Commerce** (☎ 800-777-7281; www.ely.org; 1600 E Sheridan St; 9am-5pm Mon-Sat, noon-3pm Sun) has general information and lodging assistance. Don't miss the **International Wolf**

SCENIC DRIVE: HWY 61

Hwy 61 conjures a headful of images. Local boy Bob Dylan mythologized it in his angry 1965 album *Highway 61 Revisited*. It's the fabled 'Blues Highway' clasping the Mississippi River en route to New Orleans (see p37 and p48). And in northern Minnesota, it evokes red-tinged cliffs and forested beaches as it follows Lake Superior's shoreline.

But let's back up and get a few things straight. The Blues Highway is actually US 61, and it starts just north of the Twin Cities. Hwy 61 is a state scenic road, and it starts in Duluth. To confuse matters more, there are two 61s between Duluth and Two Harbors: a four-lane expressway and a two-lane 'Old Hwy 61' (also called Scenic 61, Country Rd 61 and North Shore Scenic Drive). Whatever the name, take it. After Two Harbors, it's one wonderfully scenic strip of pavement all the way to the Canadian border. For more information, check the North Shore Scenic Drive at www.superiorbyways.com.

WORTH THE TREK: SUPERIOR HIKING TRAIL

The 205-mile **Superior Hiking Trail** (☎ 218-834-2700; www.shta.org) follows the lake-hugging ridgeline between Two Harbors and the Canadian border. Along the way it passes dramatic red-rock overlooks and the occasional moose and black bear. Trailheads with parking lots pop up every 5 to 10 miles, making it ideal for day hikes. The **Superior Shuttle** (☎ 218-834-5511; www.superiorhikingshuttle.com; $15-30; Fri-Sun mid-May–mid-Oct) makes life even easier, picking up trekkers from 17 stops along the route. Overnight hikers will find 81 backcountry campsites and several lodges to cushion the body come nightfall; the trail website has details. The whole footpath is free, with no reservations or permits required. Duluth also sports 39 miles of the trail, which should be connected to Two Harbors by 2012.

Center (☎ 218-365-4695; www.wolf.org; 1369 Hwy 169; adult/child 3-12yr $8.50/4.50; 10am-5pm), which offers intriguing exhibits and wolf-viewing trips. Across the highway from the center, **Kawishiwi Wilderness Station** (☎ 218-365-7561; 7am-5pm May-Aug, 8:30am-4:30pm Sep) provides expert camping and canoeing details, trip suggestions and required permits.

In winter, Ely gets mushy – it's a renowned dogsledding town. Outfitters such as **Wintergreen Dogsled Lodge** (☎ 218-365-6022, 877-753-3386; www.dogsledding.com; 4hr tour $125) and **Boundary Country Trekking** (☎ 800-322-8327; www.boundarycountry.com; 2-night trip $325) offer numerous packages.

Iron Range District

An area of red-tinged scrubby hills rather than mountains, Minnesota's Iron Range District consists of the Mesabi and Vermilion Ranges, running north and south of Hwy 169 from roughly Grand Rapids northeast to Ely. Iron was discovered here in the 1850s, and at one time more than three-quarters of the nation's iron ore was extracted from these vast open-pit mines. Visitors can see working mines and the terrain's raw, sparse beauty all along Hwy 169.

In **Calumet**, a perfect introduction is the **Hill Annex Mine State Park** (☎ 218-247-7215; 880 Gary St; tours adult/child 5-12yr $10/6; 9am-5:30pm Wed-Sat), with its open-pit tours and exhibit center. Tours are held in summertime only, from Wednesday to Saturday at 12:30pm and 3pm; there's also a fossil tour at 10am.

An even bigger pit sprawls in **Hibbing**, where a must-see **viewpoint** (admission free; 9am-5pm mid-May–mid-Sep) north of town overlooks the 3-mile Hull-Rust Mahoning Mine. Bob Dylan lived at 2425 E 7th Ave as a boy and teenager; the **Hibbing Public Library** (☎ 218-362-5959; www.hibbing.lib.mn.us; 2020 E 5th Ave; 9am-8pm Mon-Thu, to 5pm Fri) has well-done Dylan displays and a free walking tour map that takes you past various sites, like the place where Bobby had his bar mitzvah. **Zimmy's** (☎ 218-262-6145; 531 E Howard St; sandwiches $7-9, mains $12-24; 11am-1am) has more memorabilia, plus drinks and pub grub. For a bed, try **Hibbing Park Hotel** (☎ 218-262-3481; www.hibbingparkhotel.com; 1402 E Howard St; r $88-93;).

Chisholm has **Ironworld Discovery Center** (☎ 218-254-7959; www.ironworld.com; Hwy 169; adult/child 6-18yr $8/6; 10am-5pm Tue-Sun, to 9pm Thu), a theme park featuring open-pit mine tours and area ethnic displays.

Further east is **Virginia**, with more mine sites plus a giant loon, Minnesota's state bird. The **Pine View Inn Motel** (☎ 218-741-8918; www.pineviewinnmotel.com; 903 N 17th St; r incl breakfast $59-99;) could be the cleanest in the state. The Virginia area also has the Range's best restaurant selection. The **Whistling Bird Cafe** (☎ 218-741-7544; 101 N Broadway Ave; mains $15-23; 5-9pm Mon-Thu, 4-9pm Fri-Sun), a few miles south in Gilbert, serves Jamaican food.

Soudan sports the area's only **underground mine** (☎ 218-753-2245; www.soudan.umn.edu; 1379 Stuntz Bay Rd; adult/child 5-12yr $10/6; 10am-4pm late May-early Sep), which is available for touring; wear warm clothes.

Voyageurs National Park

In the 17th century, French-Canadian fur traders, or voyageurs, began exploring the Great Lakes and northern rivers by canoe. **Voyageurs National Park** (www.nps.gov/voya) covers part of their customary waterway, which became the border between the USA and Canada.

It's all about water up here. Most of the park is accessible only by hiking or motorboat – the waters are mostly too wide and too rough for canoeing, though kayaks are becoming popular. A few access roads lead to campgrounds and lodges on or near Lake

THE ROOTBEER LADY

So you've been hanging out in the remoter portions of the Boundary Waters, thinking you're a real wilderness stud. Sorry, that honor belongs to Dorothy Molter, who lived for 56 years in a cabin smack in the middle of nowhere, 18 miles from the nearest road. Dorothy paddled, hiked, fished, skied and snowshoed around the Boundary Waters – and served her homemade root beer to anyone who happened to drop by – cementing her reputation as a colorful north woods character. She died at age 79, and her friends hauled her homestead by dogsled to Ely. It's now a **museum** (☎ 218-365-4451; www.rootbeerlady.com; adult/child 6-12yr $6/4; 🕑 10am-5:30pm Mon-Sat, noon-5:30pm Sun Jun-Aug, weekends only May & Sep), which is located on the south side of Hwy 169; a guided tour is included in the admission and is well worth your time.

Superior, but these are mostly used by people putting in their own boats.

The visitors centers are car accessible and good places to begin your visit. Twelve miles east of International Falls on Hwy 11 is **Rainy Lake Visitors Center** (☎ 218-286-5258; 🕑 9am-5pm Jun-Sep, closed Mon & Tue Oct-May), the main park office. Ranger-guided walks and boat tours are available here. Seasonal visitors centers are at **Ash River** (☎ 218-374-3221; 🕑 9am-5pm Jun-Sep) and **Kabetogama Lake** (☎ 218-875-2111; 🕑 9am-5pm Jun-Sep). These areas have outfitters, rentals and services, plus some smaller bays for canoeing.

Houseboating is the region's rage. Outfitters such as **Ebel's** (☎ 888-883-2357; www.ebels.com; 10326 Ash River Trail, Orr) and **Voyagaire Houseboats** (☎ 800-882-6287; www.voyagaire.com; 7576 Gold Coast Rd, Crane Lake) can set you up. Rentals range from $260 to $685 per day, depending on boat size. Novice boaters are welcome and receive instruction on how to operate the vessels.

For sleeping, your choices are pretty much camping or resorts. The 12-room, shared-bath **Kettle Falls Hotel** (☎ 218-240-1724; www.kettlefallshotel.com; r incl breakfast $50-70; 🕑 May–mid-Oct) is an exception, located in the park's midst and accessible only by boat; make arrangements with the owners for pick-up (per person round-trip $45). **Nelson's Resort** (☎ 800-433-0743; www.nelsonsresort.com; 7632 Nelson Rd; cabins from $180) at Crane Lake is a winner for hiking, fishing and relaxing under blue skies.

While this is certainly a remote and wild area, those seeking wildlife, canoeing and forest camping in all their glory are best off in the Boundary Waters (p648).

Chippewa National Forest Area

This area is synonymous with outdoor activities and summer fun. Campsites and cottages abound, and almost everybody is fishing-crazy.

Attractive **Walker** has a beach and makes a good spot for a break. For information on hiking, canoeing and camping, check in at the **Chippewa National Forest office** (☎ 218-547-1044; 201 Minnesota Ave E; 🕑 8am-4:30pm Mon-Fri) either here, or in the town of Cass Lake, to the north.

Northwest of Walker, **Itasca State Park** (☎ 218-266-2100; off Hwy 71 N; campsites $16-24) is an area highlight. You can walk across the tiny headwaters of the mighty Mississippi River, rent canoes or bikes, hike the trails and camp. The log **HI Mississippi Headwaters Hostel** (☎ 218-266-3415; www.himinnesota.org; dm $24-27, r $80-130; ⊠ 📶) is in the park; winter hours vary, so call ahead. Or if you want a little rustic luxury, try the venerable **Douglas Lodge** (☎ 866-857-2757; r $69-115), run by the park, which also has cabins and two good dining rooms.

On the western edge of the forest, tidy **Bemidji** is an old lumber town with a well-preserved downtown and a giant statue of legendary logger Paul Bunyan and his faithful blue ox, Babe. The **visitors center** (☎ 800-458-2223; www.visitbemidji.com; 300 Bemidji Ave N; 🕑 8am-5pm Mon-Fri, 9am-5pm Sat, noon-4pm Sun Jun-Aug, reduced hours Sep-May) displays Paul's toothbrush. Stay by the lake and fish at **Taber's Log Cabins** (☎ 218-751-5781; www.taberslogcabins.com; 2404 Bemidji Ave N; cabins $69-79; 🕑 May-Oct). **Raphael's Bakery Cafe** (☎ 218-759-2015; 319 Minnesota Ave; items $3-5; 🕑 6am-5:30pm Mon-Fri, 6am-2pm Sat) has fine light lunches, coffee and wild-rice bread.

Great Plains

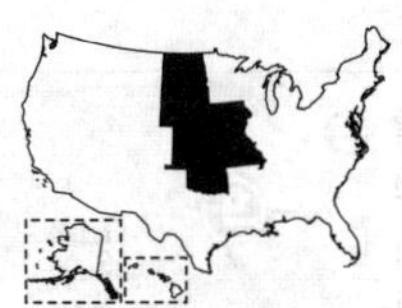

To best appreciate this vast and under-appreciated region in the heart of the US, you need to split the name. The first word, great, is easy. Great food, great scenery, great tornadoes, great people, great surprises all apply. The problem is with plains. Humdrum and flat are just two of the words that come to mind. Neither applies.

True, the Great Plains rarely head anybody's holiday plans but they should. Really. There are the endless horizons and raw drama of the settler experience in North Dakota; the dramatic peaks, valleys and monuments of South Dakota's respective Black Hills, Badlands and Mt Rushmore; and Iowa, which surprises with small towns and friendly folks that exude a creative charm that outclasses the snoots boasting of flying over.

Nebraska is much more than I-80. It captures the majestic sweep of the continent's center and has everything from the unexpected joys of arty Omaha to the miles of sand dunes in the middle. Missouri is bookended by two great cities, St Louis and Kansas City, which each have a unique and strong local vibe. In between is lots of lushly forested countryside.

Kansas has rural drives aplenty through scenery both bucolic and evocative of the Old West, while Oklahoma has more Native American culture than any other state.

So 'great' yes, 'plain' no. Possibly the biggest impediment to enjoying this enormous region is the great distances: the sites and attractions are scattered. In this chapter, many places are organized around important roads: the interstates and the more-intriguing two-laners. More far-flung points of interest and scenic drives are listed in a 'Detours & Extras' box for each state.

HIGHLIGHTS

- Going from mountain highs in the **Black Hills** (p680) to death valley lows in the **Badlands** (p679)
- Gaping at the otherworldly landscapes of **Theodore Roosevelt National Park** (p675)
- Eating yourself silly on the amazing barbecue in **Kansas City** (p668)
- Finding your own rhythms in quietly beautiful **Chase County, Kansas** (p694)
- Veering off the interstates for beguiling alternate routes such as old Route 66 through **Missouri** (p666), **Kansas** (p694) and **Oklahoma** (p696)

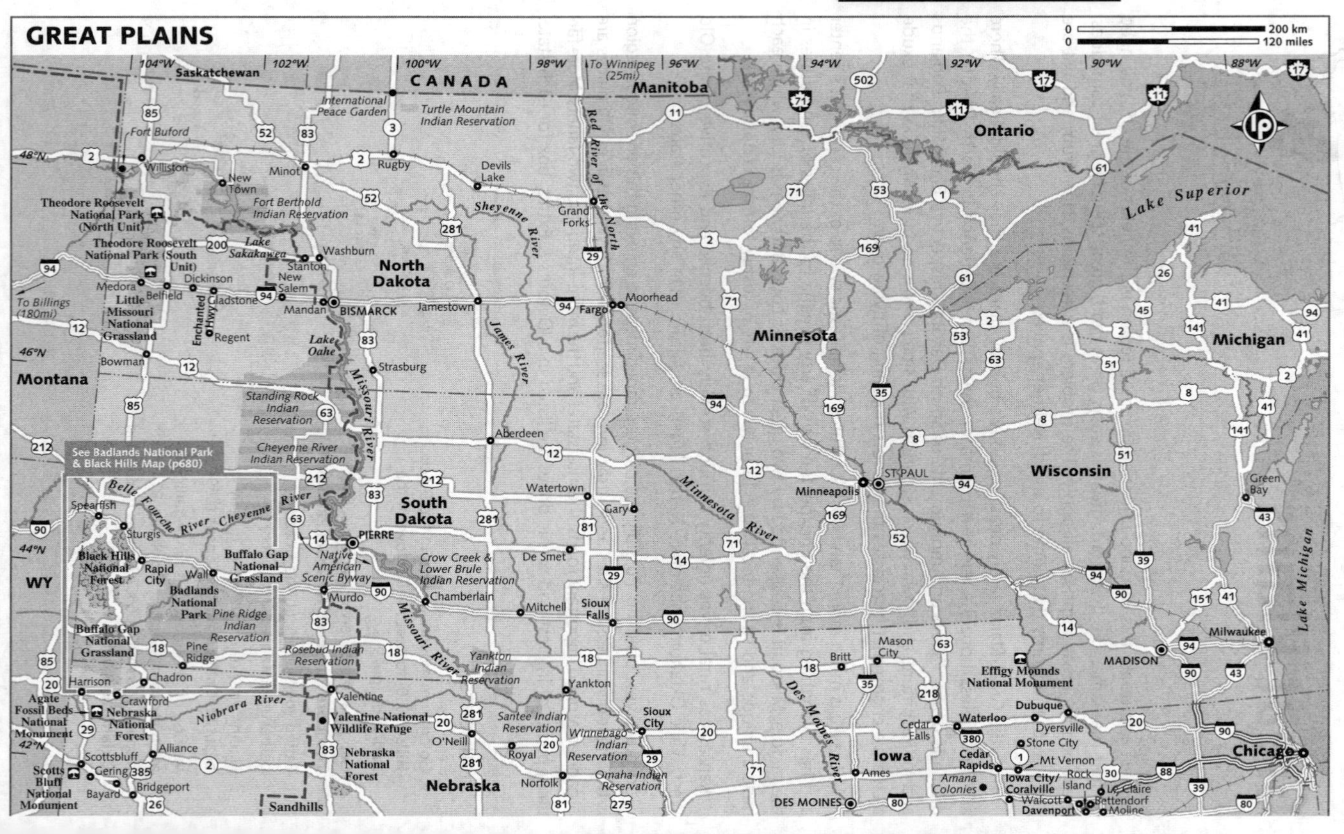
GREAT PLAINS
0 200 km
0 120 miles
CANADA
Saskatchewan
Manitoba
Ontario
Michigan
Wisconsin
Minnesota
North Dakota
South Dakota
Iowa
Nebraska
Montana
WY
Lake Superior
Lake Michigan
Red River of the North
Sheyenne River
James River
Missouri River
Minnesota River
Des Moines River
Cheyenne River
Belle Fourche River
Niobrara River
Lake Sakakawea
Lake Oahe
To Winnipeg (25mi)
To Billings (180mi)
International Peace Garden
Turtle Mountain Indian Reservation
Fort Berthold Indian Reservation
Theodore Roosevelt National Park (North Unit)
Theodore Roosevelt National Park (South Unit)
Little Missouri National Grassland
Enchanted Hwy
Standing Rock Indian Reservation
Cheyenne River Indian Reservation
Crow Creek & Lower Brule Indian Reservation
Native American Scenic Byway
Buffalo Gap National Grassland
Badlands National Park
Pine Ridge Indian Reservation
Rosebud Indian Reservation
Yankton Indian Reservation
Santee Indian Reservation
Winnebago Indian Reservation
Omaha Indian Reservation
Valentine National Wildlife Refuge
Nebraska National Forest
Sandhills
Black Hills National Forest
Agate Fossil Beds National Monument
Scotts Bluff National Monument
Effigy Mounds National Monument
Amana Colonies
See Badlands National Park & Black Hills Map (p680)
Fort Buford
Williston
New Town
Minot
Rugby
Devils Lake
Grand Forks
Fargo
Moorhead
Jamestown
BISMARCK
Mandan
Washburn
Stanton
New Salem
Gladstone
Dickinson
Regent
Belfield
Medora
Bowman
Strasburg
Aberdeen
Watertown
Gary
De Smet
Mitchell
Sioux Falls
Chamberlain
PIERRE
Murdo
Wall
Rapid City
Sturgis
Spearfish
Pine Ridge
Chadron
Crawford
Harrison
Alliance
Scottsbluff
Gering
Bridgeport
Bayard
Valentine
O'Neill
Norfolk
Royal
Yankton
Sioux City
Minneapolis
ST PAUL
Mason City
Britt
Ames
DES MOINES
Cedar Falls
Waterloo
Cedar Rapids
Iowa City/Coralville
Mt Vernon
Stone City
Dyersville
Dubuque
Rock Island
Moline
Davenport
Bettendorf
Walcott
Le Claire
MADISON
Milwaukee
Green Bay
Chicago
104°W
102°W
100°W
98°W
96°W
94°W
92°W
90°W
88°W
48°N
46°N
44°N
42°N

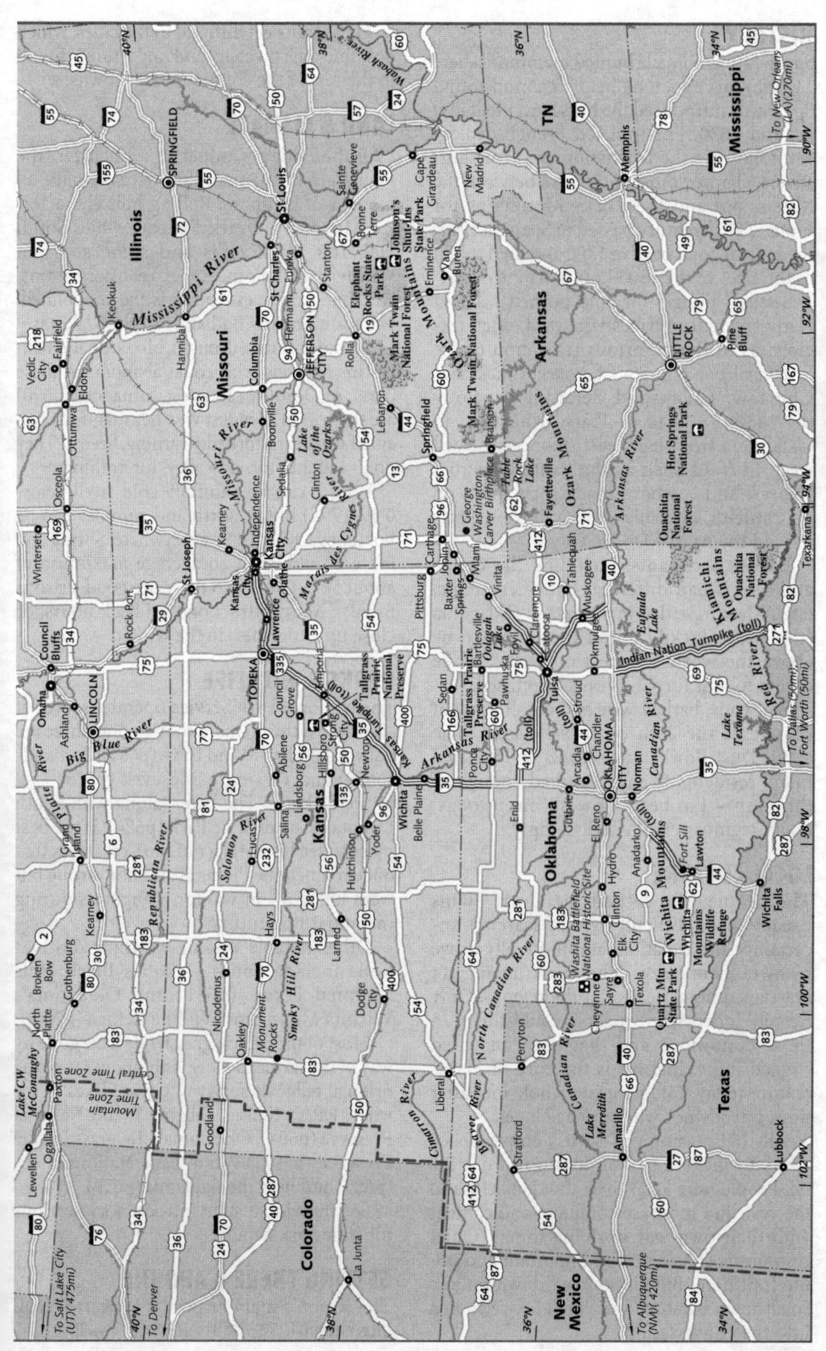

GREAT PLAINS

HISTORY

Spear-toting nomads hunted mammoths here 11,000 years ago, long before cannon-toting Spaniards introduced the horse (accidentally) around 1630. Fur-frenzied French explorers, following the Mississippi and Missouri Rivers, claimed most of the land between the Mississippi and the Rocky Mountains for France. The territory passed to Spain in 1763, the French got it back in 1800 and then sold it to the USA in the 1803 Louisiana Purchase.

Settlers' hunger for land pushed resident Native American tribes westward, often forcibly, as in the notorious relocation of the Five Civilized Tribes – Cherokee, Chickasaw, Choctaw, Creek and Seminole – along the 1838–39 'Trail of Tears,' which led to Oklahoma from back east. Pioneers blazed west on trails such as the Santa Fe across Kansas, and cowboys made their myth on the cattle-drivin' Chisholm Trail from Texas to wild towns like Dodge City.

Earlier occupants, including the Osage and Sioux, had different, but often tragic, fates. Many resettled in pockets of Oklahoma (the Osage luckily found their plots to be above the world's richest oil wells), while others fought for lands once promised.

Railroads, barbed wire and oil all brought change as the 20th century hovered. The 1930s Dust Bowl ruined farms and spurred many residents to say: 'I've had enough of this crap – I'm heading west.' Even today, many regions remain eerily empty.

LOCAL CULTURE

The people who settled the Great Plains usually faced difficult lives of scarcity, uncertainty and isolation; and it literally drove many of them crazy. Others gave up and got out (failed homesteads dot the region). Only fiercely independent people could thrive in those conditions and that born-and-bred rugged individualism is the core of Plains culture today. Life here is a whole lot easier now, but it's not without challenges.

All that staring out across empty space tends to make a person look inward a little. People here keep their thoughts close to the vest, and most are confident and content with their own way of doing things. Quiet restraint is considered an important and polite trait here. But sit yourself down on any small-town barstool and you'll be welcomed into the conversation.

These traits get diffused in the cities, which host the same diversity and opportunity found in the rest of the country's large towns.

LAND & CLIMATE

Like the dodgy product of a huckster, the Plains are misnamed; they actually have all manner of contours. Rolling hills characterize Missouri's Ozark Plateau, while South Dakota's Black Hills and some spots in southern Oklahoma sport real mountains. Another bumpy exception is the convoluted, below-the-plains Badlands of the Dakotas.

Thunderstorms, drought, blizzards and hailstorms all brew with equal abandon in these parts. As Dorothy can attest, tornadoes (p690) are the region's wildest weather manifestation and if you hear a tornado warning, heed it. They don't call this 'tornado alley' for nothing.

Winter can be painfully cold (well below 0°F/-17°C) in the north and summer can be hot (above 90°F/32°C) everywhere. Spring and fall are mild, with an average maximum of about 50°F (10°C), so these are good seasons to visit. Many attractions cut back hours, or close up altogether, in the winter.

PARKS & WILDLIFE

The National Park Service operates scores of sites across the plains, although only three are national parks – Wind Cave (p685), Badlands (p679) and Theodore Roosevelt (p675) – all in the Dakotas. The latter, along with South Dakota's Custer State Park (p684), is the best place to see bison (aka buffalo), creatures that once roamed the Plains 60-million strong but were killed off in wanton slaughters during the mid-19th century.

Other notable wildlife-watching destinations include South Dakota's Black Hills National Forest (p681) and Oklahoma's Wichita Mountains Wildlife Refuge (p700).

Most of the prairie grasslands have gone by way of the farmer's plow: only about 1% of the original tallgrass survives. Great places to see what's left are Kansas' Tallgrass Prairie National Preserve (p694), Oklahoma's Tallgrass Prairie Preserve (p702), Wind Cave National Park (p685) and near the Badlands (p679).

See individual state introductory sections for state park details.

GETTING THERE & AROUND

The region's main airport is **Lambert-St Louis International** (STL; ☎ 314-426-8000; www.flystl.com), but it only has a few direct international flights from Canada. Visitors from abroad will be better off flying to Chicago (p586) or Dallas (p740) and then connecting to one of the region's myriad airports.

The car- or motorcycle-less brave will miss a lot of the Plains. Greyhound buses only cover some interstates and don't enter much of the region at all, but **Jefferson Lines** (☎ 800-451-5333; www.jeffersonlines.com) and **Burlington Trailways** (☎ 800-992-4618; www.burlingtontrailways.com), a smaller carrier that specializes in Great Plains routes, take up the slack, getting you to most major towns and many smaller ones. They both honor Greyhound's Discovery passes.

A few other companies have limited service including **Megabus** (☎ 877-462-6342; www.megabus.com), linking Kansas City to Chicago via St Louis for as little as $15.

Unlike the rest of the US, you can actually get somewhat of a feel for the region from the interstate, since the wide-open spaces know no bounds. But the real joy of the region are the oodles of two-lane roads. Substantial stretches of Route 66 survive and are covered in the Missouri (p666), Kansas (p694) and Oklahoma (p696) sections.

Numerous daily **Amtrak** (☎ 800-872-7245; www.amtrak.com) routes across the Plains make getting here by train easy, but getting around by rail is impractical.

California Zephyr Between Chicago and San Francisco via Iowa (including Osceola, south of Des Moines) and Nebraska (including Omaha and Lincoln).
Empire Builder Between Chicago and Seattle via North Dakota.
Heartland Flyer Between Fort Worth and Oklahoma City.
Lincoln Service Between Chicago and St Louis.
Missouri River Runner Between St Louis and Kansas City.
Southwest Chief Between Chicago and Los Angeles via Missouri (including Kansas City) and Kansas (including Topeka and Dodge City).
Texas Eagle Between Chicago and San Antonio via St Louis.

MISSOURI

The most-populated state in the Plains, Missouri likes to mix things up, serving visitors ample portions of both sophisticated city life and down-home country sights. St Louis and Kansas City are vibrant cities that are destinations in their own right. But, with more forest and less farm field than neighboring states, Missouri also cradles plenty of wild places and wide-open spaces, most notably the rolling Ozark Mountains where the winding valleys invite adventurous exploring or just some laid-back meandering behind the steering wheel. Maybe you'll find an adventure worthy of Hannibal-native Mark Twain as you wander the state.

MISSOURI FACTS

Nickname Show-Me State
Population 5.8 million
Area 69,710 sq miles
Capital city Jefferson City (population 39,600)
Other cities St Louis (population 347,181), Kansas City (population 447,306)
Sales Tax 4.23%
Birthplace of author Samuel Clemens (Mark Twain; 1835–1910), scientist George Washington Carver (1864–1943), author William S Burroughs (1914–97), author Maya Angelou (b 1928), singer Sheryl Crow (b 1962)
Home of Budweiser, Chuck Berry
Famous for Gateway Arch, Branson
Official dance Square dance
Driving distances St Louis to Kansas City 250 miles, St Louis to Chicago 300 miles

History

Claimed by France as part of the Louisiana Territory in 1682, Missouri had only a few small river towns by the start of the 19th century when the land passed to American hands and Lewis and Clark pushed up the Missouri River. Missouri was admitted to the Union as a slave state in 1821, per the Missouri Compromise (which permitted slavery in Missouri but prohibited it in any other part of the Louisiana Territory above the 36°30′ parallel), but abolitionists never compromised their ideals, and bitter feelings were stoked along the Missouri–Kansas border by Civil War time.

The state's 'Show-Me' nickname is attributed to Congressman Willard Duncan Vandiver, who said in an 1899 speech, 'I come from a state that raises corn and cotton and cockleburs and Democrats, and frothy eloquence neither convinces nor satisfies me. I am from Missouri. You have got to show me.' The name now implies a stalwart, not-easily-impressed character.

Information

Bed & Breakfast Inns of Missouri (www.bbim.org)
Missouri Division of Tourism (☎ 800-519-2100; www.visitmo.com)
Missouri state parks (☎ 800-334-6946; www.mostateparks.com) State parks are free to visit. Site fees range from $10 to $24 and some sites may be reserved in advance.

GREAT PLAINS

ST LOUIS

Slide into St Louis and revel in the unique vibe of the largest city in the Great Plains. Beer, bowling and baseball are some of the top attractions, but history and culture, much of it linked to the Mississippi River, are a vital part of the fabric. And, of course, there's the iconic Gateway Arch that you have seen in a million pictures; it's even more impressive in person. Many music legends, including the likes of Scott Joplin, Chuck Berry, Tina Turner and Miles Davis, got their start here and the bouncy live music venues keep the flame burning.

History

Fur-trapper Pierre Laclede knew prime real estate when he saw it, so he put down stakes at the junction of the Mississippi and Missouri rivers in 1764. The hustle picked up considerably when prospectors discovered gold in California in 1849 and St Louis became the jump-off point (aka 'Gateway to the West') for get-rich-quick dreamers.

St Louis became known as a center of innovation after hosting the 1904 World's Fair. Aviator Charles Lindbergh furthered the reputation in 1927 when he flew the first nonstop, solo transatlantic flight in the 'Spirit of St Louis,' named for the far-sighted town that funded the aircraft. Grand plans have always been part of the city's self-assurance and you'll find no chips on local shoulders.

GREAT PLAINS...

In One Week

Spend your first two or three days in either **St Louis** (above) or **Kansas City** (p665) and the next two or three exploring the small town standouts of Nebraska and Iowa, such as **Lincoln** (p687) or **Iowa City** (p671). Try scenic routes like the **Loess Hills Scenic Byway** (p673) or the **Great River Road** (p673) at either end of Iowa. Then head north to South Dakota where the gorgeous **Black Hills** (p680) and **Badlands National Park** (p679) will vie for your remaining time.

In Two Weeks

With two weeks behind the wheel, you can take a big bite out of the Plains. Do the trip as above. But then head south from South Dakota along eastern Nebraska, stopping at fascinating, isolated sites like the **Agate Fossil Beds National Monument** (p689), **Carhenge** (p689) and **Scotts Bluff** (p689).

Meander into Kansas and pick up **US 50** (p694) heading east. Stop at the amazing, astonishing **Cosmosphere** (p693) in Hutchinson. Head south to Oklahoma and join historic **Route 66** (p696) going northeast for sights like the **Will Rogers Memorial Museum** (p702). Follow the road into Missouri and finish your trip at either of the major cities you skipped on the way out.

For Nature-lovers

Skip straight out of Oklahoma City for the mixed-grass prairie and wildlife of the **Wichita Mountains Wildlife Refuge** (p700). Leave the fields for the forest to paddle and hike in **The Ozarks** (p664) in Missouri and then head up to Nebraska, stopping in Kansas' Flint Hills to see the **Tallgrass Prairie National Preserve** (p694) on the way.

Between February and April along the **Platte River** (p688), near Grand Island, view half a million sandhill cranes. Head northwest through the awesome Sandhills to the **Valentine National Wildlife Refuge** (p689). Take a canoe trip on the **Niobrara River** (p689) and then drive through more Sandhills scenery on the **Bridges to Buttes Byway** (p688).

Go north to South Dakota's spectacular **Black Hills** (p680) and on to North Dakota's **Theodore Roosevelt National Park** (p675) where the badlands are even more beautiful than South Dakota's.

Orientation & Information

The landmark Gateway Arch rises right along the Mississippi River. Downtown runs west of the arch while the Laclede's Landing entertainment district sits just to the north.

The reighborhoods of most interest radiate out from this core. These include the posh Central West End abutting Forest Park; the buzzing-all-night Loop northwest of the park; the Hill, an Italian-American neighborhood; the Bohemian but gentrifying Grand South Grand; Soulard, the city's Irish-Cajun-blues entertainment quarter; and finally, nearby, historic but increasingly trendy Lafayette Sq.

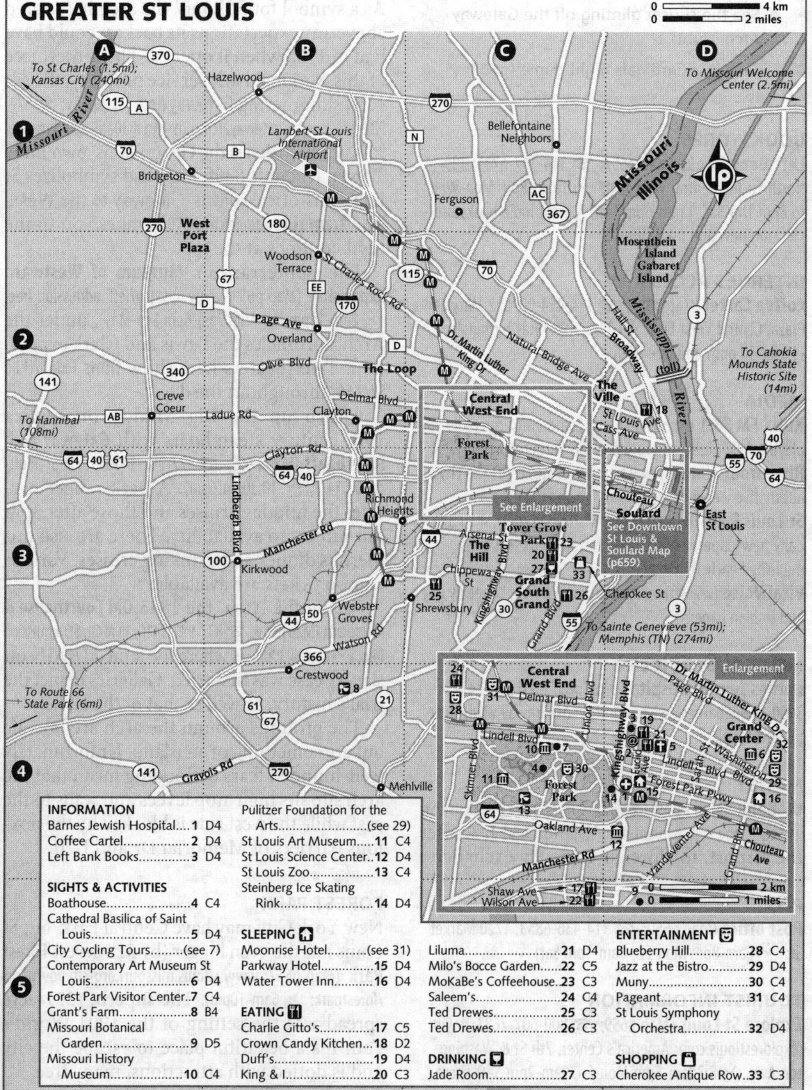

DON'T MISS

- Get pumped at the morning at the fun-filled city museum (p660).
- Lick your lunch at a Ted Drewes Frozen Custard stand (p662).
- Laze away the afternoon in Forest Park (right).
- See the sunset glinting off the Gateway Arch (right).
- Take in a Cardinals night game (p663).

BOOKSTORES

Left Bank Books (Map p657; ☎ 314-367-6731; 399 North Euclid, Central West End; 10am-8pm Mon-Wed, to 8pm Thu-Sat, 11am-6pm Sun) A great indie bookstore stocking new and used titles.

INTERNET ACCESS

Coffee Cartel (Map p657; ☎ 314-454-0000; 2 Maryland Plaza, Central West End; 24/7;) Has terminals ($5 for 50 min) and free wi-fi.

MEDIA

KDHX FM 88.1 (www.kdhx.org) Community-run radio playing folk, blues, odd rock and local arts reports.

Riverfront Times (www.riverfronttimes.com) The city's alternative weekly.

St Louis Post-Dispatch (www.stltoday.com) St Louis' daily newspaper; its *Get Out* entertainment section is published each Thursday.

Vital Voice (www.thevitalvoice.com) A free, biweekly gay and lesbian paper.

MEDICAL SERVICES

Barnes Jewish Hospital (Map p657; ☎ 314-747-3000; www.barnesjewish.org; N Kingshighway Blvd) Next to Forest Park.

MONEY

US Bank (Map p659; ☎ 314-418-2803; 721 Locust St; exchange dept 8:30am-4pm Mon-Fri) Best bet, after the airport, for foreign-currency exchange.

POST

Post office (Map p659; ☎ 314-436-6853; 1720 Market St; 8am-8pm Mon-Fri, 8am-1pm Sat)

TOURIST INFORMATION

Explore St Louis (Map p659; ☎ 800-607-2683; www.explorestlouis.com; America's Center, 7th St & Washington Ave; 8:30am-5pm Mon-Fri, 9am-2pm Sat) There are other branches in Kiener Plaza at 6th and Chestnut and at the airport.

Missouri Welcome Center (☎ 314-869-7100; www.visitmo.com; I-270 exit 34; 8am-5pm, closed Sun Nov-Mar)

Sights & Activities

JEFFERSON NATIONAL EXPANSION MEMORIAL

As a symbol for St Louis, the arch has soared above any expectations its backers could have had in 1965 when it opened. The centerpiece of this National Park Service property, the silvery, shimmering **Gateway Arch** (Map p659; ☎ 877-982-1410; www.gatewayarch.com; 8:30am-9pm Jun-Aug, 9:30am-5pm Sep-May) is the Great Plains' own Eiffel Tower. It stands 630ft high and symbolizes St Louis' historical role as 'Gateway to the West.' The **tram ride** (adult/child $10/5) takes you to the tight confines at the top.

The subterranean **Museum of Westward Expansion** (Map p659; www.nps.gov/jeff; admission free; 8am-10pm Jun-Aug, 9am-6pm Sep-May), under the Arch, chronicles the Lewis and Clark expedition. Two theaters here show **films** (adult/child $7/2.50) throughout the day.

Churn up the Big Muddy on replica 19th-century steamboats with **Gateway Arch Riverboats** (Map p659; ☎ 877-982-1410; 1hr tour adult/child $14/8; 10:30am-6pm). A park ranger narrates the midday cruises and those after 3pm sail subject to availability. There are also numerous dinner and drinking cruises. Various combo tickets are available.

Facing the Arch, the 1845 **Old Courthouse & Museum** (Map p659; ☎ 877-982-1410; 11 N 4th St; admission free; 8am-4:30pm) is where the famed Dred Scott slavery case was first tried. Galleries depict the trial's history, as well as that of the city.

The grounds around the arch are bucolic but are something of an island. Unfortunately well-founded fears of flooding mean that the arch site sits high atop levees and walls to the east while the west side is blocked by the noxious barriers of Memorial Dr and I-70.

FOREST PARK

New York City may have Central Park, but St Louis has the even bigger (by 528 acres) **Forest Park** (Map p657; www.stlouis.missouri.org/citygov/parks/forestpark; 6am-10pm). The superb, 1371-acre spread was the setting of the 1904 World's Fair. It's a beautiful place to escape the city and is dotted with attractions, many free.

The **visitor center** (Map p657; ☎ 314-367-7275; www.forestparkforever.org; 5595 Grand Dr; 🕑 6am-8pm Mon-Fri, 6am-7pm Sat & Sun) is in an old street car pavilion and has a café.

In warm weather, sail over to the **Boathouse** (Map p657; ☎ 314-367-2224; 6101 Government Dr; boat rental per hr $15; 🕑 10am-sunset) to paddle over Post- Dispatch Lake. In cooler weather, make for the **Steinberg Ice Skating Rink** (Map p657; ☎ 314-367-7465; off N Kingshighway Blvd; adult/child $6.50/5.50, skates $2.50; 🕑 10am-9pm Sun-Thu, 10am-midnight Fri & Sat Nov-Mar).

In the grounds is the grand beaux arts **St Louis Art Museum** (Map p657; ☎ 314-721-0072; www.slam.org; 1 Fine Arts Dr; admission free; 🕑 10am-5pm Tue-Sun, to 9pm Fri), originally built for the fair.

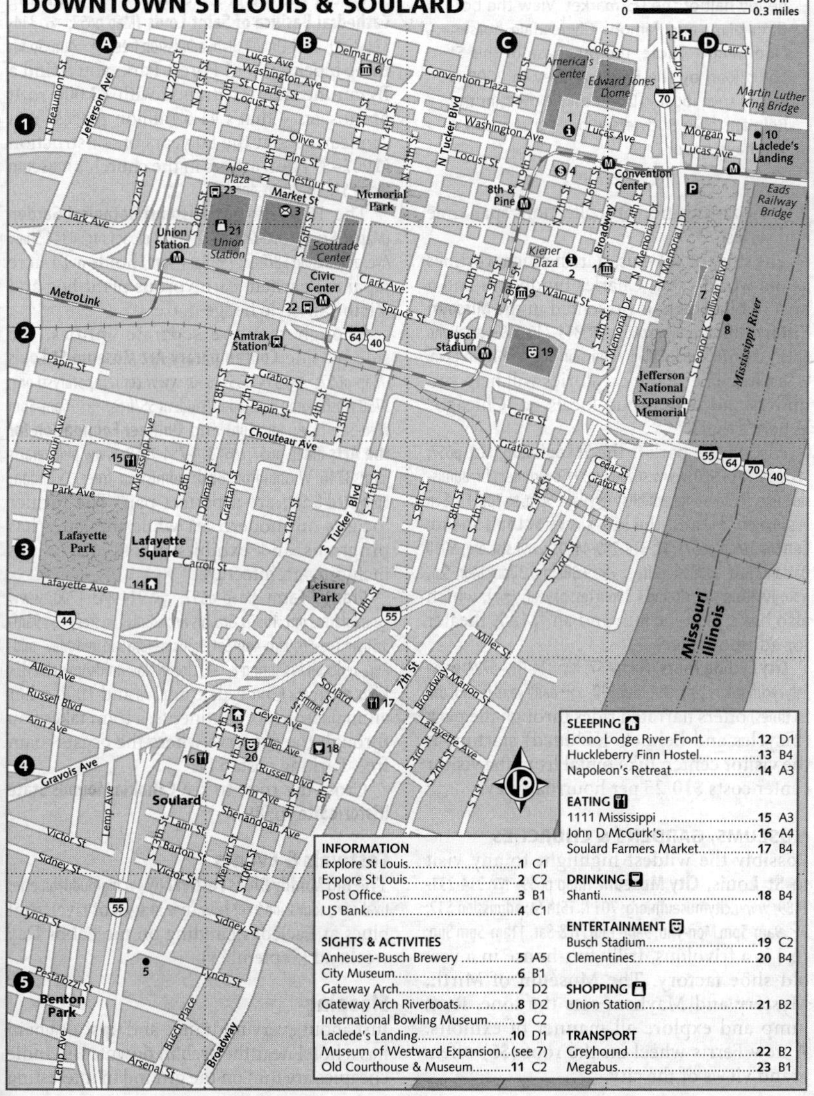

YOUR BELGIAN BUD

The world's largest beer plant, the historic **Anheuser-Busch Brewery** (Map p659; ☎ 314-577-2626; www.budweisertours.com; 12th & Lynch Sts; admission free; 9am-4pm Mon-Sat, 11:30am-4pm Sun, to 5pm Jun-Aug, start 10am Nov-Feb), gives the sort of marketing-driven tours you'd expect from the company with nearly half of the US market. View the bottling plant and famous Clydesdale horses. One thing to note, the purchase of this St Louis icon by the Belgian InBev in 2008 is a sore spot locally. Don't ask: 'Now that the Belgians own Budweiser, does that mean it will have flavor?'

A storied institution, its collections span time and styles.

The story of St Louis, starring such worthies as the world's fair, Charles Lindbergh and a host of bluesmen, is presented in the **Missouri History Museum** (Map p657; ☎ 314-746-4599; www.mohistory.org; 5700 Lindell Blvd; admission free; 10am-6pm, to 8pm Tue). The rich local stories will help you understand why proud locals go 'Chicago? Where's that?'

Also in the park is the **St Louis Zoo** (Map p657; ☎ 314-781-0900; www.stlzoo.org; 1 Government Dr; admission free, fee for some exhibits; 9am-5pm, to 7pm Fri-Sun in summer;) and the kid-savvy **St Louis Science Center** (Map p657; ☎ 314-289-4400; www.slsc.org; 5050 Oakland Ave; admission free; 9:30am-5:30pm Mon-Sat, from 10:30am Sun, closing 4:30pm rest of year;), which also has a planetarium and an IMAX theater for additional fees.

City Cycling Tours (Map p657; ☎ 314-616-5724; www.citycyclingtours.com; 3hr tour $30; daily year-round, call for times) offers narrated rides through the park (bicycles and helmets included) starting at the visitor center. Bike rental from the visitor center costs $10/25 per hour/half-day.

MUSEUMS, GARDENS & CHURCHES

Possibly the wildest highlight to any visit to St Louis, **City Museum** (Map p659; ☎ 314-231-2489; www.citymuseum.org; 701 N 15th St; admission $12; 9am-5pm Mon-Thu, 9am-1am Fri & Sat, 11am-5pm Sun;) is a frivolous, frilly fun-house in a vast old shoe factory. The Museum of Mirth, Mystery and Mayhem sets the tone. Run, jump and explore all manner of exhibits. A new Ferris wheel on the roof ($5) offers grand views of the city.

Nobody knows if they designated beer frames, but there is some evidence the ancient Romans and Egyptians bowled. Learn this and much more at the **International Bowling Museum** (Map p659; ☎ 314-231-6340; www.bowlingmuseum.com; 111 Stadium Plaza; adult/child $7.50/6; 9am-5pm Apr-Sep, to 6:30pm during Cardinals games, 11am-4pm Tue-Sat Oct-Mar) and then bowl free frames at the lanes below.

Under the big green dome of the stunning **Cathedral Basilica of Saint Louis** (Map p657; ☎ 314-373-8200; 4431 Lindell Blvd; admission free; 7am-5pm), three blocks east of Forest Park, you'll find a Byzantine interior draped with 83,000 sq ft of mosaics – that's 41.5 million pieces. You can learn about the 80 years of construction (1907–87) downstairs in the church's **museum** (entry $1; 10am-4pm).

The 150-year-old **Missouri Botanical Garden** (Map p657; ☎ 800-642-8842; www.mobot.org; 4344 Shaw Ave; adult/child $8/free; 9am-5pm) holds a 14-acre Japanese garden, carnivorous plant bog and Victorian-style hedge maze.

Though they are separate entities, the side-by-side **Contemporary Art Museum St Louis** (Map p657; ☎ 314-535-4660; www.contemporarystl.org; 3750 Washington Blvd; adult/student $5/free; 10am-5pm Wed-Sat, 11am-4pm Sun) and **Pulitzer Foundation for the Arts** (Map p657; ☎ 314-754-1850; www.pulitzerarts.org; 3716 Washington Blvd; admission free; noon-5pm Wed & Sat) are a perfect pair. The former focuses on modern art while the latter has programs and exhibits across disciplines including architecture.

Grant's Farm (Map p657; ☎ 314-843-1700; www.grantsfarm.com; 10501 Gravois Rd; admission free; 9am-3:30pm Tue-Fri, 9am-4pm Sat, 9:30am-4pm Sun mid-May–mid-Aug, reduced hrs spring & fall, closed Nov–mid-Apr) thrills kids with its Clydesdale horses and 1000 other animals from six continents; a tram takes you through the preserve where the beasts roam free. Parking costs $11.

Cross the river to see **Cahokia Mounds State Historic Site** (p589).

Festivals & Events

The **Big Muddy Blues Festival** (www.bigmuddybluesfestival.com; admission free) has five stages of riverfront blues at Lacledes Landing on the Labor Day weekend (September).

Sleeping

Just about every midrange and upscale chain has a hotel near the arch in downtown. Indie cheapies are thin on the ground in interesting areas but you'll find plenty near the airport and you can ride the MetroLink light rail into the city. Upscale Clayton at exit 1F on I-170 also has rail access and a cluster of chains.

BUDGET

Huckleberry Finn Hostel (Map p659; ☎ 314-241-0076; www.huckfinnhostel.com; 1908 S 12th St, Soulard; dm $25; closed Jan & Feb;) In two old town houses, this independent hostel is a bit ragged, but it's a friendly gathering spot with a piano in the lounge/kitchen and free lockers. Its Soulard location is ideal. Reserve ahead.

Econo Lodge River Front (Map p659; ☎ 314-421-6556; www.econolodge.com; 1100 N 3rd St; r from $70; P) When you're sleeping in one of the barebones but clean rooms here, you can't see just what a charmless place this is. But the Lacledes Landing location is ideal, as are the prices.

MIDRANGE

Water Tower Inn (Map p657; ☎ 314-977-7500; www.slu.edu/x27017.xml; Saint Louis University, 3545 Lafayette Ave; r $80-100; P) Right in the middle of Saint Louis University and near the interesting Central West End, the 62 rooms here are clean and modern.

Napoleon's Retreat (Map p659; ☎ 314-772-6979, 800-700-9980; www.napoleonsretreat.com; 1815 Lafayette Ave; r $100-175, 2-night min weekends;) A lovely 2nd French Empire home in beautiful and historic Lafayette Sq, this B&B has five bold and beautiful rooms, each with private bath and antique furnishings. Michael and Jeff are excellent hosts.

Parkway Hotel (Map p657; ☎ 314-256-7777, 866-314-7700; www.theparkwayhotel.com; 4550 Forest Park Blvd; r $90-200; P) Right in the midst of the upscale fun of the Central West End, this indie 8-story hotel has 220 modern rooms. Standards are high and you simply can't beat the location.

Moonrise Hotel (Map p657; ☎ 314-721-1111, 877-872-1122; www.moonrisehotel.com; 6177 Delmar Blvd; r $140-220; P) Easily the city's most cutting-edge hotel, the Moonrise has a high-profile amidst the high-energy of the Loop neighborhood. Rooms are sleekly decorated with just enough whimsy to slow things down to comfy.

Eating

St Louis boasts the region's most diverse selection of food. The monthly magazine **Sauce** (www.saucemagazine.com) is full of reviews.

The **Soulard Farmers Market** (Map p659; 7th St, Soulard; 8am-5pm Wed-Sat) is a local treasure with a range of vendors selling the best organic regional produce and foodstuffs. Picnic or nosh yourself silly.

DOWNTOWN

Laclede's Landing, along the riverfront next to the historic Eads Railway Bridge, has several restaurants, though generally people pop down here for the atmosphere – cobblestoned streets, converted brick buildings and free-flowing beer – rather than the food.

Crown Candy Kitchen (Map p657; ☎ 314-621-9650; 1401 St Louis Ave; mains $3-10; 11am-8pm Sun-Thu, 11am-10pm Fri & Sat) An authentic family-run soda fountain that's been making families smile for decades. Malts come with spoons, the floats, well, float, and you can snack on chili dogs where the wiener groans under the toppings. Homemade candies top it off.

SOULARD & LAFAYETTE SQUARE

Restaurants and pubs occupy most corners in Soulard, with plenty of live blues and Irish music. Just go and wander. Lafayette Sq, 1 mile northwest, has a growing number of trendy spots.

John D McGurk's (Map p659; ☎ 314-776-8309; 1200 Russell Blvd, Soulard; mains $7-20; 11am-1:30am Mon-Sat, 3pm-midnight Sun) The city's favorite pub oozes charm inside, where there's live Irish music many nights, but you can't beat the backyard garden. The steaky menu is a cut above pub fare.

1111 Mississippi (Map p659; ☎ 314-241-9999; 1111 Mississippi Ave, Lafayette Sq; mains $9-22; 11am-10pm Mon-Thu, to midnight Fri & Sat;) Supplying the food and drink to help the local revival continue, this wildly popular bistro and wine bar fills an old shoe factory. Options on the seasonal menu include sandwiches, pizzas, steaks and many veggie options. Excellent wine bar.

GRAND SOUTH GRAND

Running along South Grand Blvd, this young, Bohemian area near beautiful Tower Grove Park has a slew of excellent ethnic restaurants, many with outside terraces.

King & I (Map p657; ☎ 314-771-1777; 3157 S Grand Blvd; mains $7-15; 11:30am-9:30pm Tue-Sun) Fiery and authentic Thai food draws in locals who appreciate the weeknight-friendly prices. The decor has a bit of Royal Thai pomp.

EATING ST LOUIS: LOCAL SPECIALTIES

Try these local specialties:

- **Toasted ravioli** They're filled with meat, coated in breadcrumbs, then deep fried. **Charlie Gitto's** (below) probably started it all, but practically every restaurant on the Hill serves them.
- **St Louis pizza** Its thin-crusted, square-cut, Provolone cheese–based pizzas are really addictive. Local chain **Imo's** (www.imospizza.com; large special $16), with over 70 locations across the metro, bakes 'the square beyond compare.'
- **ourpick** **Frozen custard** Don't dare leave town without licking yourself silly on this super-creamy ice cream-like treat at historic **Ted Drewes** (Map p657; ☎ 314-481-2652; 6726 Chippewa St; cone $0.50-2.50; 🕒 11am-11pm or so Feb-Dec). There's a smaller summer-only branch at 4224 S Grand Blvd. Rich and poor rub elbows enjoying a 'concrete.'
- **Schlafly beer** This sign in the window speaks well of the bar; the only locally brewed beer (a fine ale) still owned locally.

GREAT PLAINS

THE HILL

This tiny-housed Italian neighborhood has innumerable pasta joints. Stroll the tidy streets and stop for a coffee at an Italian café or deli.

ourpick **Milo's Bocce Garden** (Map p657; ☎ 314-776-0468; 5201 Wilson Ave; mains $6-14; 🕒 11am-1am) Enjoy sandwiches, pizzas and pastas out on the vast outdoor courtyard. Watch and join the regulars on the busy bocce ball courts.

Charlie Gitto's (p657 ☎ 314-772-8898; 26 Shaw Ave; mains $16-40; 🕒 5-10pm Mon-Thu, 5-11pm Fri & Sat, 4-10pm Sun) Legendary Charlie Gitto's makes a strong claim to having invented St Louis' famous toasted ravioli. On any night the weather allows, dine under the huge tree on the patio. Classy but casual.

CENTRAL WEST END & THE LOOP

Sidewalk cafés rule Euclid Ave in this posh and trendy old neighborhood. 'The Loop,' near Washington University, runs along Delmar Blvd (embedded with the St Louis Walk of Fame) and has many bars and ethnic restaurants catering to a hipster crowd.

Saleem's (Map p657; ☎ 314-721-7947; 6501 Delmar Blvd, The Loop; mains $7-18; 🕒 5-10pm Mon-Sat, to 11pm Fri & Sat) 'Where garlic is king' is the alluring motto, and the favored flavor shows up in Saleem's kabobs, kofte, silky hummus and other Persian dishes. Portions are huge.

Duff's (Map p657; ☎ 314-361-0522; 392 N Euclid Ave, Central West End; mains $8-18; 🕒 11am-10pm Sun-Thu, to midnight Fri & Sat) The hippies who once tossed back cheap Chablis here are now enjoying the many fine wines on the long list. Duff's has gentrified with the neighborhood and serves an eclectic fusion menu of sandwiches, salads and more ambitious fare. Score a sidewalk table outside under the trees.

Liluma (Map p657; ☎ 314-361-7771; 238 N Euclid Ave, Central West End; mains $10-30; 🕒 11am-9pm Mon-Thu, to 10pm Fri & Sat; ⊠) Amidst the buzzy outdoor cafés of the Maryland and Euclid Aves hot spot, this bistro serves up fresh seasonal fare with a strong Italian accent.

Drinking & Entertainment

BARS & NIGHTCLUBS

Check the **Riverfront Times** (www.riverfronttimes.com) for updates on entertainment options around town. Laclede's Landing and Soulard are loaded with pubs and bars, many with live music. Most bars close at 1:30am, though some have 3am licenses.

Blueberry Hill (Map p657; ☎ 314-727-0880; www.blueberryhill.com; 6504 Delmar Blvd, The Loop) St Louis native Chuck Berry still rocks the small basement bar here at least one Wednesday a month. The $30 tickets sell out very quickly. The venue hosts smaller-tier bands on the other nights.

Jazz at the Bistro (Map p657; ☎ 314-531-1012; www.jazzatthebistro.com; 3536 Washington Ave, Grand Center; ⊠) Big names often play this serious little club.

Jade Room (Map p657; ☎ 314-664-2020; 3131 S Grand Blvd, Grand South Grand; 🕒 5pm-late) One of several good bars and clubs here, the Jade Room is ideal for sitting outside on a balmy night with a brew and planning your next move.

Pageant (Map p657; ☎ 314-726-6161; www.thepageant.com; 6161 Delmar Blvd, The Loop) A big venue for touring bands.

Shanti (Map p659; ☎ 314-241-4772; www.theshanti.com; 825 Allen Ave, Soulard; 🕒 10am-1:30am Mon-Sat)

Meaning 'peace' in Sanskrit, Shanti is the Bohemian heart of Soulard. It hosts a popular Tuesday open mike and folk-bluegrass-rock acts most other nights.

PERFORMING ARTS

Grand Center, west of downtown, is the heart of St Louis' theater scene and home of the **St Louis Symphony Orchestra** (Map p657; ☎ 800-232-1880; www.slso.org; 718 N Grand Blvd), which has 50 free tickets for most performances.

Muny (Map p657; ☎ 314-361-1900; www.muny.com) The Municipal Opera (aka 'Muny') hosts nightly summer musicals outdoors in Forest Park; some of the 12,000 seats are free.

Purchase tickets for most venues through **MetroTix** (☎ 800-293-5949; www.metrotix.com).

GAY & LESBIAN VENUES

The Central West End is the GLBT community's hub, but Soulard and Grand South Grand also have hangouts.

Overlooking Tower Grove Park, **MoKaBe's Coffeehouse** (Map p657; ☎ 314-865-2009; 3606 Arsenal St, Grand South Grand; ⏰ 8am-midnight Mon-Sat, 9am-midnight Sun) caters to women. Men in leather to Levis will enjoy **Clementines** (Map p659; ☎ 314-664-7869; 2001 Menard St; ⏰ 10am-1:30am Mon-Sat, 11am-midnight Sun), a long-running favorite with good bar food.

Peruse the **Vital Voice** (www.thevitalvoice.com) or **St Louis Gay Guide** (www.stlouisgayguide.com) for more.

SPORTS

Busch Stadium (Map p659; ☎ 314-345-9000; www.stlcardinals.com; Broadway & Clark Ave) The Cardinals baseball team won the World Series in 2006, the same year this fun, retro-style stadium opened.

Shopping

The Loop and Central West End have the best mix of shops. If you love antiques, you'll love **Cherokee Antique Row** (Map p657; Cherokee St, east of Jefferson Ave) in the appropriately historic Cherokee-Lemp neighborhood. The shops in the reconstructed **Union Station** (Map p659; 1820 Market St) cover the chain gang.

Getting There & Around

Lambert-St Louis International Airport (Map p657; STL; ☎ 314-426-8000; www.lambert-stlouis.com) is the Great Plains' hub, with flights to many US cities. The airport is 12 miles northwest of downtown and is connected by the light-rail MetroLink ($3.75), taxi (about $35) or **Trans Express** (☎ 800-844-1985; $15) shuttles, which can drop you off at downtown hotels.

Greyhound (Map p659; ☎ 314-231-4485; 430 S 15th St) buses depart several times daily to Chicago ($40, six to seven hours), Memphis ($50, six hours), Kansas City ($45, 4½ hours) and many more cities. The station is near Amtrak downtown.

The low-cost **Megabus** (Map p659; ☎ 877-462-6342; www.megabus.com) runs services to Chicago and Kansas City from as little as $15 one way; it stops next to Union Station.

Metro (☎ 314-231-2345; www.metrostlouis.org; single/day-pass $2.25/7.50) runs local buses and the MetroLink light-rail system. Bus 93 connects most points of interest, including Soulard, downtown and the Central West End.

If you need a taxi, call **St Louis County Cabs** (☎ 314-993-8294).

The **Amtrak** (Map p659; ☎ 314-331-3304; 551 S 16th St) *Lincoln Service* travels five times daily to Chicago (from $23, 5½ hours). Two daily *Missouri River Runner* trains go to/from Kansas City (from $26, six hours). There is also an Amtrak bus link to Memphis and the daily *Texas Eagle* to Dallas (16 hours).

AROUND ST LOUIS

Several appealing and historic river towns north and south of St Louis on the Mississippi and just west on the Missouri make popular weekend excursions for St Louisans, including the historic pair of St Charles and Hannibal. If you're looking for some grand meeting of the two great rivers however, don't. The two muddies meet in a swirl of mud and are surrounded by many square miles of – you guessed it – often muddy and inaccessible floodplains.

St Charles

This Missouri River town, founded in 1769 by the French, is just 20 miles northwest of St Louis. The cobblestoned Main St anchors a well-preserved downtown where you can visit the **first state capitol** (☎ 636-940-3322; 200 S Main St; admission free, tours adult/child $2.50/1.50; ⏰ 9am-4pm Mon-Sat, 11am-5pm Sun, closed Mon Jan-Mar). Ask at the **visitor center** (☎ 800-366-2427; www.historicstcharles.com; 230 S Main St; ⏰ 8am-5pm Mon-Fri, 10am-5pm Sat, noon-5pm Sun) about tours, which pass some rare French colonial architecture in the **Frenchtown neighborhood** just north.

Lewis and Clark began their epic journey in St Charles on May 21, 1804 and their encampment is reenacted annually at that time. The **Lewis & Clark Boathouse and Nature Center** (☎ 636-947-3199; www.lewisandclarkcenter.org; 1050 Riverside Dr; adult/child $3/1.50; 10am-5pm Mon-Sat, noon-5pm Sun) has a handful of displays about the duo.

For cyclists, St Charles is the eastern gateway to **Katy Trail State Park** (☎ 800-334-6946; www.katytrailstatepark.com), a superb 225-mile trail that cuts across Missouri to Clinton, 65 miles southeast of Kansas City, along the former Missouri–Kansas–Texas railroad (the 'Katy'). The trail's eastern two-thirds snake between high bluffs and the Missouri River. **Momentum Cycles** (☎ 636-946-7433; 104 S Main St; 1hr/day from $6/30) rents out bikes.

Hotels are spread along St Charles' four I-70 exits. St Charles also has several historic B&Bs, including **Boone's Colonial Inn** (☎ 888-377-0003; www.boonescolonialinn.com; 322 S Main St; r weekday $150-250;). The three rooms in the 1820 stone row houses are posh.

Hannibal

When the air is sultry in this old river town, you almost expect to hear the whistle of a paddlewheel. Mark Twain's boyhood home, 100 miles northwest of St Louis, has some authentically vintage sections and plenty of sites where you can get a sense of the muse and his creations Tom Sawyer and Huck Finn.

The **Mark Twain Boyhood Home & Museum** (☎ 573-221-9010; www.marktwainmuseum.org; 415 N Main St; adult/child $9/4; 9am-7pm, reduced in winter) presents eight buildings, including two homes Twain lived in and that of Laura Hawkins, the real-life inspiration for Becky Thatcher. Afterward, float down the Mississippi on the **Mark Twain Riverboat** (☎ 573-221-3222; www.marktwainriverboat.com; Center St; 1hr sightseeing cruise adult/child $14/11; Apr-Nov, schedule varies). **National Tom Sawyer Days** (around Jul 4th weekend) features frog jumping and fence painting contests and much more.

Many of Hannibal's historic homes are now B&Bs. The **Hannibal Visitors Bureau** (☎ 866-263-4825; www.visithannibal.com; 505 N 3rd St; 8am-5pm Mon & Wed, 8am-6pm Tue, Thu & Fri, 9am-6pm Sat, 10am-5pm Sun) keeps a list. **Garden House B&B** (☎ 573-221-7800, 866-423-7800; www.gardenhousebedandbreakfast.com; 301 N 5th St; r $150-240;), in a Victorian house, lives up to its name. Some rooms share bathrooms.

THE OZARKS

Ozark hill country spreads across southern Missouri and extends into northern Arkansas and eastern Oklahoma.

One of the best Ozark escapes is the **Ozark Trail** (☎ 573-436-0540; www.ozarktrail.com), a 350-mile hiking route mostly through the Mark Twain National Forest.

At massive **Johnson's Shut-Ins State Park** (☎ 573-546-2450; www.mostateparks.com/jshutins.htm), 8 miles north of Lesterville on Hwy N, the swift Black River swirls through canyon-like gorges (shut-ins). The park reopened in 2009, much improved after floods in 2005. Little **Elephant Rocks State Park** (☎ 573-546-3454), next to Graniteville on Hwy 21, has enormous billion-year-old rocks – most far larger than any pachyderm. Some stand end-to-end like circus elephants.

North of US 60, in the state's southcentral region, the **Ozark National Scenic Riverways** (☎ 573-323-4236; www.nps.gov/ozar) – the Current and Jack's Fork Rivers – boast 134 miles of splendid canoeing and inner-tubing. Weekends often get busy and boisterous. The headquarters, along with outfitters and motels, is in **Van Buren**. **Eminence** also makes a good base. There are many campgrounds along the rivers. Hwy 19 through here is a scenic gem.

Branson

Hokey Branson is a cheerfully shameless tourist resort in the tradition of Blackpool or Atlantic City. The main attractions are the more than 50 theaters hosting 100-plus country music, magic and comedy shows. The neon-lit '76 Strip' (Hwy 76) packs in miles of motels, restaurants, wax museums, shopping malls, fun parks and theaters. As Bart Simpson once said: 'It's like Vegas; if it were run by Ned Flanders.'

During the summer and again in November and December, the SUV-laden traffic often crawls. It's often faster to walk than drive, although few others have this idea.

The **Branson Lakes Area Convention & Visitors Bureau** (☎ 800-214-3661; www.explorebranson.com; 269 Hwy 248; 8am-5pm Mon-Sat, 10am-4pm Sun), just west of the US 65 junction, has town and lodging information. It has a second location north of town at the junction of US 65 and Hwy 160. The scores of 'Visitor Information' centers around town (even the 'official' ones) are fronts for time-share sales outfits. Sit through a pitch, however, and you can get free tickets to a show.

Popular **theater shows** feature performers you may have thought were dead. However, Branson has been the salvation for scores of entertainers young and old whose careers collapsed after the death of variety shows on TV (who knew there were still bird acts?). Patriotic themes are a stock part of every show; the official singer of the Republican Party, Lee Greenwood, seems to have a lifetime contract. Fundamentalist Christian themes are also common; expect dancers wearing enough fabric to outfit all of their counterparts in Vegas for a year. And while fudge is available in copious quantities, irony is not: when we drove by a much-hyped Titanic attraction, the sign implored people to come in and 'renew your wedding vows'. Expect a lot of Elvis.

Theaters usually run afternoon and evening shows, and sometimes morning ones. Prices range from about $25 to $50 a head, but you rarely need to pay full price. Pick up any of the many coupon books around town or stop by **Branson 2 for 1 Tickets** (☎ 417-336-0241; www.branson2for1tickets.com; 1100 W Hwy 76), which does business with, as the sign says, 'No Bull.' Reserve a week in advance during peak seasons.

Two attractions, opened in 1959 and 1960 respectively, spurred the Branson boom. The **Baldknobbers Jamboree** (☎ 888-734-1935; www.baldknobbers.com; 2835 W Hwy 76; adult/child $34/18), a cornball country music and comedy show; and **Silver Dollar City** (☎ 800-831-4386; www.silverdollarcity.com; adult/child $50/40; 9:30am-7pm summer, shorter hr other times), a huge amusement park west of town.

There are dozens of indie and chain motels (starting at around $30) along Hwy 76 on the strip. **Meloday Lane Inn** (☎ 417-338-8598; 2821 W Hwy 76; r from $60;) is a large old property with good-sized rooms and pool and actual large trees with shade out front (a Strip rarity). Nicer places are off the Strip in quieter locales. **Table Rock Lake**, snaking through the hills southwest of town, is a deservedly popular destination for boating, fishing, camping and other outdoor activities, and it also has good value lodging. Try unassuming **Indian Trails Resort** (☎ 417-338-2327; www.indiantrailsresort.com; Indian Point Rd; cottages $95-185;), on the lake 9 miles south of Branson.

Branson cuisine consists almost entirely of fast food, junk food and all-you-can-eat buffets (most priced $5 to $10).

KANSAS CITY

Wide open and inviting, Kansas City (KC) is famed for its BBQ (100-plus joints smoke it up), fountains (over 200; on par with Rome) and jazz. The latter serves as an anchor for a vibrant African American community. Attractive neighborhoods abound and you can easily run aground for several days as you enjoy the local vibe, which ranges from buff to boho.

History

KC began life in 1821 as a trading post but really came into its own once westward expansion began. The Oregon, California and Santa Fe trails all met steamboats loaded with pioneers here.

Jazz exploded in the early 1930s under Mayor Tom Pendergast's Prohibition-era tenure, when he allowed alcohol to flow freely. At its peak, KC had more than 100 nightclubs, dance halls and vaudeville houses swinging to the beat (and booze). The roaring good times ended with Pendergast's indictment on tax evasion (the same way they got Capone) and the scene had largely faded by the mid-1940s.

KC was a bustling farm-distribution and industrial center for generations – a serious cowtown, though its giant stockyards closed in 1991.

Orientation

State Line Rd divides KC Missouri and KC Kansas (a conservative suburban sprawl with little to offer travelers). KC Missouri has some distinct areas, including the fun and historic River Market (still home to a large farmers market) immediately north of downtown; the gallery-filled Crossroads Arts District around Baltimore and 20th Sts; and the historic 18th and Vine Historic Jazz District (on the upswing, but still rough).

Westport, on Westport Rd just west of Main St; 39th St West, just west of Westport by the Kansas border; and the upscale Country Club Plaza (often shortened to 'the Plaza'), centered on Broadway and 47th Sts, are ideal for eating, drinking and shopping.

Information

BOOKSTORES

Barnes & Noble (☎ 816-753-1313; 420 W 47th St; 9am-10pm Sun-Thu, 9am-11pm Fri & Sat) At the Plaza.

Prospero's Books (☎ 816-531-9673; 1800 W 39th St; 10am-9pm) Funky used bookstore in a vibey part of town. Great recommendations, live poetry and even a few bands.

GREAT PLAINS

GREAT PLAINS

INTERNET ACCESS

Westport Coffeehouse (☎ 816-756-3222; 4010 Pennsylvania St; 8am-11pm Mon-Thu, to midnight Fri & Sat, 10am-10pm Sun;) Computers (per hr $5). Free wi-fi for customers (also see opposite).

INTERNET RESOURCES & MEDIA

Arts Council of Metropolitan Kansas City (www.artskc.org) Has details on culture high and low.
Bar Scoop (www.barscoop.com) Helps boozers plot their evening.
Kansas City Star (www.kansascity.com) KC's daily paper; its *Preview* entertainment section comes out on Thursday.
Pitch (www.pitch.com) The free alt-weekly newspaper.

MEDICAL SERVICES

University of Kansas Medical Center (☎ 913-588-5000; 3901 Rainbow Blvd) In Kansas, just across the border from 39th St West.

POST

Post office (☎ 816-374-9180; 300 W Pershing; 7am-6pm Mon-Fri, 7:30am-3:30pm Sat) In Union Station.

TOURIST INFORMATION

Greater Kansas City Visitor Center (☎ 816-221-5242, 800-767-7700; www.visitkc.com; 22nd fl, 1100 Main St in City Center Sq; 8:30am-5pm Mon-Fri) A desk is also staffed daily in Union Station.
Missouri Welcome Center (☎ 816-889-3330; www.visitmo.com; I-70, exit 9; 8am-5pm) Statewide maps and information.

Sights & Activities

Quality Hill, downtown around W 10th St and Broadway, has grand, restored buildings from the 1920s. Just north, the **Arabia Steamboat Museum** (☎ 816-471-1856; www.1856.com; 400 Grand Blvd; adult/child $12.50/4.75; 10am-5:30pm Mon-Sat, noon-5pm Sun) is home to 200 tons of salvaged 'treasure' from a riverboat that sunk in 1856 (one of hundreds claimed by the river). It's in City Market, which is an attraction itself (opposite).

South of downtown, **Crown Plaza** is a 1970s development anchored by several major hotels and Hallmark (yes, the greeting card company is located right here). Uphill, the sobering **National WWI Museum** (☎ 816-784-1918; www.nww1.org; 100 W 26th St; adult/child $8/4; 10am-5pm Tue-Sun) sits under the towering **Liberty Memorial** (observation deck adult/child $4/3; last ticket sold 4:15pm).

The **Museums at 18th & Vine** (☎ 816-474-8463; 1616 E 18th St; adult for 1/2 museums $6/8, child $2.50/4;

ROUTE 66: GET YOUR KICKS IN MISSOURI

The Show-Me state will show you a long swath of Mother Road. Meet the route in **St Louis** (p656), where **Ted Drewes Frozen Custard** (p662) has been serving generations of Roadies from its Route 66 location on Chippewa St. There are a couple of well-signed historic routes through the city.

Follow I-44 (the interstate is built over most of Route 66 in Missouri) west to **Route 66 State Park** (☎ 636-938-7198; www.mostateparks.com/route66.htm; exit 266; 7am-30min after sunset), with its visitor center and **museum** (admission free; 9am-4:30pm) inside a 1935 roadhouse. Although the displays show vintage scenes from around St Louis, the real intrigue here concerns the town of Times Beach, which once stood on this very site. It was contaminated with dioxin and in the 1980s the government had to raze the entire area.

Speed southwest on I-44 to Stanton, then follow the signs to family-mobbed **Meramec Caverns** (☎ 800-676-6105; www.americascave.com; adult/child $18/9; 8:30am-7:30pm summer, reduced hr rest of year), as interesting for the Civil War history and hokey charm as for the stalactites; and the conspiracy-crazy **Jesse James Museum** (☎ 573-927-5233; adult/child $6/2.50; 9am-6pm Jun-Aug, 9am-5pm Sat & Sun Sep-Oct), which posits that James faked his death and lived until 1951.

The **Route 66 Museum & Research Center** (☎ 417-532-2148; www.lebanon-laclede.lib.mo.us; 915 S Jefferson St; admission free; 8am-8pm Mon-Thu, 8am-5pm Fri & Sat) at the library in Lebanon has memorabilia past and present. Ready for a snooze? Head to the 1940s **Munger Moss Motel** (☎ 417-532-3111; www.mungermoss.com; 1336 E Rte 66; r from $40;). It's got a monster of a sign and Mother Road–loving owners.

Ditch the interstate west of Springfield, taking Hwy 96 to Civil War–era **Carthage**'s historic town square and **66 Drive-In Theatre** (☎ 417-359-5959; www.66drivein.com; 17231 Old 66 Blvd; adult/child $6/3; Fri-Sun Apr-Oct). In **Joplin** get on State Hwy 66, turning onto old Route 66 (the pre-1940s route), before the Kansas state line.

The **Route 66 Association of Missouri** (www.missouri66.org) has loads of info on its website.

9am-6pm Tue-Sat, noon-6pm Sun) are must-stops. You'll learn about different styles, rhythms, instruments and musicians – including KC native Charlie Parker – at the interactive **American Jazz Museum** (www.americanjazzmuseum.org). The **Negro Leagues Baseball Museum** (www.nlbm.com) covers African American teams (eg the KC Monarchs and New York Black Yankees) that flourished until baseball became fully integrated.

Giant badminton shuttlecocks (the building represents the net) surround the encyclopedic **Nelson-Atkins Museum of Art** (816-751-1278; www.nelson-atkins.org; 4525 Oak St; admission free; 10am-5pm Wed & Sat, 10am-9pm Thu-Fri, noon-5pm Sun), which has standout European painting, photography and Asian art collections. Its luminescent and cock-free Bloch Building, designed by Steven Holl, has earned rave reviews. The nearby **Kemper Museum of Contemporary Art** (816-753-5784; www.kemperart.org; 4420 Warwick Blvd; admission free; 10am-4pm Tue-Thu, 10am-9pm Fri & Sat, 11am-5pm Sun) is smaller, but edgier. Both museums are near Country Club Plaza.

Festivals & Events

The **American Royal Barbecue** (www.americanroyal.com) is the world's largest BBQ contest (500 teams); it takes place in the old stockyards the first weekend in October.

Sleeping

Downtown accommodations are costly and not well suited for optimal eats and drinks. Westport and the Plaza are better options. For something cheap, you'll need to head out on the interstate: north on I-35 and I-29 and east on I-70 are good places to look.

Econo Lodge Inn (816-531-9250, 877-424-6423; www.econolodge.com; 3240 Broadway; r from $60;) Ideally located and convenient to everything, this basic 52-room motel has inside corridors and a pool big enough for a small family.

Q Hotel (816-931-0001, 800-942-4233; www.theqhotel.com; 560 Westport Rd; r from $110;) Formerly called the Quarterage, this environmentally conscious indie hotel is centrally located in Westport. All 125 rooms have a bright, new color scheme that seems as fresh as spring. Free breakfasts include fair-trade coffee.

Southmoreland on the Plaza (816-531-7979; www.southmoreland.com; 116 E 46th St; r incl breakfast $135-200, ste $250;) The 13 rooms at this posh B&B are furnished like the home of your rich country club friends. It's a big old mansion between the art museums and the Plaza. Extras include Jacuzzis, decks, sherry, fresh flowers and more.

Eating & Drinking

Westport, 39th St West and Country Club Plaza are your best bets for clusters of atmospheric local food and drink places. Don't leave town without hitting a few barbecue joints (p668).

The glam new **Power & Light District** (www.powerandlightdistrict.com) is a vast urban development centered on Grand Blvd and W 12th St. It has dozens of mostly upscale chain restaurants and bars plus live performance venues.

Be sure to try a locally brewed Boulevard Beer; bars close between 1:30am and 3am.

our pick **City Market** (www.thecitymarket.org; W 5th St & Grand Blvd) Everything the Power & Light District is not, City Market is a haven for small local businesses selling an idiosyncratic range of foods and other items. Ethnic groceries abound and there is a farmers market for regional producers on weekends. Little ethnic eateries and greasy spoons do big business from breakfast through dinner.

Westport Coffeehouse (816-756-3222; 4010 Pennsylvania St; sandwiches $5.50-6.50; 8am-11pm Mon-Thu, to midnight Fri & Sat, 10am-10pm Sun;) This laid-back place off the main drag has good coffee and specialty teas. Look for live music, comedy, art films and more at night.

Eden Alley (816-561-5415; 707 W 47th St; mains $6-12; 11am-2:30pm Mon & Tue, to 9pm Wed-Sat;) Healthy eating never tasted better. The 'ultimate grilled cheese sandwich' is a work of art with four cheeses bubbling under an aioli sauce. Other options handle every variation on veggie eating and range from salads to falafel.

Le Fou Frog (816-474-6060; City Market, 400 E 5th St; mains $15-25; 5-10pm Tue-Sun) Take a trip to Paris without leaving the prairie at this small bistro that's authentic right down to the at-times brusque service. The food is superb, especially hearty stalwarts like cassoulet. Tables outside are to be cherished.

JJs (816-561-7136; 910 W 48th St; mains $10-30; 11am-10pm, from 5pm Sat & Sun) A long-running steak house in the Plaza that stays busy by serving nearly flawless timeless classics like French onion soup and perfectly grilled meats. The bar buzzes with local glitterati,

GREAT PLAINS

EATING KANSAS CITY: BBQ

Savoring hickory-smoked brisket, pork, chicken or ribs at one of the BBQ joints around town is a must for any visitor. The local style is pit-smoked and slathered with heavily-seasoned vinegar-based sauces. You may well swoon for 'burnt ends,' the crispy ends of smoked pork or beef brisket. Amazing.

Arthur Bryant's (☎ 816-231-1123; 1727 Brooklyn Ave; 🕑 10am-9:30pm Mon-Thu, 10am-10pm Fri & Sat, 11am-8pm Sun) Not far from the Jazz District, this famous institution serves up piles of superb BBQ in a somewhat slick setting. The sauce is silky and fiery.

LC's (☎ 816-923-4484; 5800 Blue Pkwy; 🕑 11am-8pm) Oddly located and utterly inauspicious, LC's saves its grandeur for its savory beef and pork. Little details are taken into account, like the handcut fries that work as a sauce delivery system.

and the wine list sparkles with hundreds of choices.

Entertainment

The **Pitch** (www.pitch.com) has the top cultural calendar.

Live music venues are scattered across the city:

Davey's Uptown (☎ 816-753-1909; www.daveysuptown.com; 3402 Main St) Since 1925, local and regional alternative acts have been playing nearly nightly.

Jardine's (☎ 816-561-6480; www.jardines4jazz.com; 4536 Main St) This mannered club near the Plaza has jazz seven nights a week, plus Saturday afternoons.

Mutual Musicians Foundation (☎ 816-471-5212; 1823 Highland Ave) Also at 18th & Vine, this little spot has hosted after-hours jams since 1930. Nowadays they take place on Friday and Saturday nights and don't kick off until about 1am.

Locals are passionate about Major League Baseball's **Royals** (☎ 816-921-8000; www.kcroyals.com) and the NFL's **Chiefs** (☎ 816-931-3330; www.kcchiefs.com). Both play at gleaming side-by-side stadiums in the **Truman Sports Complex** (I-70 exit 9).

Shopping

Historic Country Club Plaza is KC's top shopping destination (its lavish architecture is modeled on Seville, Spain and dates to 1923), though it's mostly upscale national chains. Westport and 39th St West have more eclectic shops. Over 60 galleries call Crossroads Art District home.

Zebedee's (☎ 816-960-6900; www.zebedeesrpm.com; 1208 W 39th St; 🕑 11am-8pm Mon & Wed-Sat, noon-5pm Sun) has a great vinyl collection, including lots of old jazz.

Getting There & Around

KC International Airport (KCI; ☎ 816-243-5237; www.flykci.com) is 16 miles northwest of downtown. A taxi to downtown/Plaza costs about $40/45; call **Yellow Cab** (☎ 888-471-6050). Or take the cheaper **Super Shuttle** (☎ 800-258-3826; downtown/Plaza $17/18).

Greyhound (☎ 816-221-2835; www.greyhound.com) sends buses daily to St Louis ($45, 4½ hours) and Denver ($100, 11 hours) while **Jefferson Lines** (☎ 800-451-5333; www.jeffersonlines.com) heads to Omaha ($45, 3¼ to four hours) and Minneapolis ($85, 9½ to 10 hours). Both use the city's inconveniently located main bus station at 1101 Troost St. **Megabus** (☎ 877-462-6342; www.megabus.com; 10th & Main Sts) goes to St Louis and Chicago right from downtown for as low as $15.

Amtrak (☎ 816-421-3622; www.amtrak.com), in majestic Union Station, has two daily *Missouri River Runner* trains to St Louis (from $26, six hours). The *Southwest Chief* stops here daily on its runs between Chicago and LA.

Local transport is with **Metro buses** (☎ 816-221-0660; www.kcata.org; adult fare $1.50). A one-/three-day unlimited ride-pass costs $3/10. The convenient MAX express bus runs regularly between City Market and Country Club Plaza.

AROUND KANSAS CITY

Independence

Just east of Kansas City, picture-perfect Independence was the home of Harry S Truman, US president from 1945 to 1953. The **Truman Presidential Museum & Library** (☎ 800-833-1225; www.trumanlibrary.org; 500 W US 24; adult/child $7/3; 🕑 9am-5pm Mon-Sat, noon-5pm Sun year-round, to 9pm Thu summer) exhibits thousands of objects, including the famous 'The BUCK STOPS here!' sign, from the man who led the US through one of its most tumultuous eras.

See the simple life Harry and Bess lived in the charming **Truman Home** (www.nps.gov/hstr; 219 N Delaware St; adult/child $4/free), furnished with original belongings. He lived here from 1919 to 1972; it was refurbished in 2009. Tour tickets are sold at the **visitor center** (☎ 816-254-9929; 223 N Main St; 8:30am-5pm). Ask for directions to the Truman farm where the future president 'got his common sense'.

The excellent 2.7-mile **Truman Historic Walking Trail**, starting at the visitor center, leads to dozens of other Truman-related sites, including the courthouse where he began his political career and **Clinton's Soda Fountain** (☎ 816-833-2046; 100 W Maple Ave; mains $4-8; 8:30am-6pm Mon-Thu, 8:30am-8pm Fri & Sat;) where he landed his first job.

The **National Frontier Trails Museum** (☎ 816-325-7575; www.ci.independence.mo.us/nftm; 318 W Pacific St; adult/child $5/3; 9am-4:30pm Mon-Sat, 12:30-4:30pm Sun) gives a good look at life for the pioneers along the Santa Fe, California and Oregon Trails; many began their journey in Independence.

Stay across from the Truman House at the **Higher Ground Hotel** (☎ 816-836-0292, 888-342-1112; www.olivebranchinn.us; 200 N Delaware; r from $70;), a modern place that looks like a school. The 30 rooms are commodious and comfortable.

St Joseph

The first Pony Express set out, carrying mail from 'St Jo' 2000 miles west to California, in 1860. The service, making the trip in as little as eight days, lasted just 18 months before telegraph lines made the riders redundant. The **Pony Express National Museum** (☎ 800-530-5930; www.ponyexpress.org; 914 Penn St; adult/child $4/2; 9am-5pm Mon-Sat, 1-5pm Sun) tells the story of the Express and its riders, who were mostly orphans due to the dangers.

St Jo, 50 miles north of Kansas City, was also home to outlaw Jesse James. He was killed at what is now the **Jesse James Home Museum** (☎ 816-232-8206; 12th & Penn Sts; adult/child $3/1.50; 10am-5pm Mon-Sat, 1-5pm Sun, weekends only Nov-Mar). The fateful bullet hole is still in the wall.

Housed in the former 'State Lunatic Asylum No 2,' the **Glore Psychiatric Museum** (☎ 816-364-1209; 3406 Frederick Ave; adult/child $3/1; 10am-5pm Mon-Sat, 1-5pm Sun) gives a frightening and fascinating look at lobotomies, the 'bath of surprise' and other discredited treatments. Tickets also include entrance to several other museums.

Get details on the town's many museums at the **visitor center** (☎ 800-785-0360; www.stjomo.com; 502 N Woodbine Rd; 9am-4pm Mon-Sat) near I-29 exit 47, where most hotels are located.

IOWA

Instead of two girls for every guy, Iowa has eight pigs for every person. But there's a lot more to do here than roll in the mud. The towering bluffs on the Mississippi River and the soaring Loess Hills lining the Missouri River bookend the state; in between you'll find the writers' town of Iowa City, the commune-dwellers of the Amana Colonies and lots of little towns full of highlights.

In fact, Iowa surprises in many ways. It makes or breaks presidential-hopefuls: the Iowa Caucus opens the national election battle and in 2008 Barrack Obama stunned many pundits with a win here. In 2009 the state shirked its staid image by allowing same-sex marriages.

History

After the 1832 Black Hawk War pushed local Native Americans westward, immigrants flooded into Iowa from all parts of the world and hit the ground farming. Some established experimental communities such as the Germans of the Amana Colonies (p672). Others spread out and kept coaxing the soil (95% of the land is fertile) until Iowa attained its current status as a leading grain producer (bio-fuel has caused a boomlet) and the US leader in hogs and corn (much of the latter ends up as syrup in junk food).

Information

Iowa Bed & Breakfast Guild (☎ 800-743-4692; www.ibbg.com)

IOWA FACTS

Nickname Hawkeye State
Population 3 million
Area 56,275 sq miles
Capital city Des Moines (population 200,000)
Sales Tax 6%
Birthplace of painter Grant Wood (1891–1942), actor John Wayne (1907–79), author Bill Bryson (b 1951)
Home of Madison County's bridges
Famous for Iowa Caucus that opens the presidential election season
Official flower Wild rose
Driving distances Dubuque to Chicago 180 miles, Des Moines to Rapid City 625 miles

GREAT PLAINS

Iowa state parks (☎ 515-281-5918; www.iowadnr.com) State parks are free to visit. Half of the park campsites are reservable; fees range from $6 to $20 per night.

Iowa Tourism Office (☎ 888-472-6035; www.travel iowa.com)

DES MOINES

Des Moines, meaning 'of the monks' not 'in the corn' as the surrounding fields might suggest, is Iowa's snoozy capital. The town really is rather dull, but does have one of the nation's best state capitols and state fairs. Pause, but then get out and see the state.

Orientation & Information

The Des Moines River slices through downtown. The Court Ave Entertainment District sits just west, while East Village, at the foot of the capitol, and (yes) east of the river, is home to some up-and-coming art and design galleries, eateries and a few gay bars.

The **visitor center** (☎ 800-451-2625; www.seedes moines.com; 400 Locust St, Suite 265; 8:30am-5pm Mon-Fri) is downtown.

Sights & Activities

The bling-heavy **State Capitol** (☎ 515-281-5591; E 9th St & Grand Ave; 8am-4:30pm Mon-Fri, 9am-3pm Sat) must have been Liberace's favorite government building. Its every detail, from the sparkling gold dome to the spiral staircases and stained glass in the law library, seems to strive to outdo the other. Join a free tour and you can climb halfway up the dome.

The engaging **State Historical Museum** (☎ 515-281-5111; 600 E Locust St; admission free; 9am-4:30pm Mon-Sat, noon-4:30pm Sun), at the foot of the capitol, features first person accounts from people who lived through a particular historical era or event.

Much more than just country music and butter sculpture, the **Iowa State Fair** (www.iowa statefair.org; adult/child $10/4;) draws a million visitors over its 10-day mid-August run. They enjoy the award-winning farm critters and just about every food imaginable that can be shoved on a stick. It's the setting for the Rogers and Hammerstein musical *State Fair* and the 1945 film version.

Sleeping

Chains of all flavors congregate on I-80 at exits 121, 124, 131 and 136.

Hotel Fort Des Moines (☎ 515-243-1161, 800-532-1466; www.hotelfortdesmoines.com; 1000 Walnut St; r $90-160;) Everyone from Mae West to JFK has spent the night in this old-world hotel. It retains its 1917 elegance and the 204 rooms spread across 11 floors are well-equipped.

Eating & Drinking

Downtown's Court Ave and East Village (Grand Ave and Locust St) are good for browsing restaurants.

Java Joe's (☎ 515-288-5282; 214 4th St; mains $3-7; 7am-11pm Mon-Thu, 7am-midnight Fri & Sat, 9am-10pm Sun;) The small menu covers a lot of ground: breakfast pastries, sandwiches, Indian dishes (lotsa lentils) and, of course, cupfuls of coffee. There's live local music many nights.

House of Bricks (☎ 515-727-4370; 525 E Grand Ave; meals $10-15; 11am-late) A gritty live music legend in the East Village, it serves up tasty, beer-absorbent chow.

MISSOURI: EXTRAS & DETOURS

The state's backbone, I-70 is a congested dud (with a surprising number of porn and sex shops); whenever possible, leave the interstate.

- **Hwy 94** Following the Missouri river from Jefferson City east to St Louis, Hwy 94 passes through a beautiful region of wineries and forests. It's a good I-70 detour.
- **Sainte Genevieve, Missouri** This petite, French-founded Mississippi River town oozes history. Many of the restored 18th- and 19th-century buildings are now B&Bs and gift shops.
- **George Washington Carver** accomplished a lot more than just experimenting with peanuts. The **birthplace** (☎ 417-325-4151; Diamond; admission free; 9am-5pm) of this African American renaissance man is near Joplin. Take exit 11A off I-44, then follow US 71 4.5 miles south to Hwy V, then go east.

AROUND DES MOINES

Madison County

This scenic county, about 30 miles southwest of the capital, slumbered for half a century until Robert James Waller's block-buster, tear-jerking novel *The Bridges of Madison County* and its Clint Eastwood–Meryl Streep movie version brought in scores of fans to check out the covered bridges where Robert and Francesca fueled their affair. Pick up (or download) a map to all six bridges and other movie sets at the **Chamber of Commerce** (☎ 800-298-6119; www.madisoncounty.com; 73 Jefferson St; 9am-5pm Mon-Fri, 10am-4pm Sat, noon-4pm Sun) in Winterset.

The humble **birthplace of John Wayne** (☎ 515-462-1044; www.johnwaynebirthplace.org; 216 S 2nd St, Winterset; adult/child $4/1; 10am-4:30pm), aka Marion Robert Morrison, is now a museum.

Eldon

Grab a 'tool' out of your trunk and make your very own parody of Grant Wood's iconic painting *American Gothic* (1930) in tiny Eldon, about 90 miles southeast of Des Moines. The original house is at 301 American Gothic St, though it's not open to the public. An **interpretive center** (☎ 641-652-3352; admission free; 10am-5pm Tue-Sat, 1-4pm Sun-Mon summer, 10am-4pm Tue-Fri, 1-4pm Sat-Mon rest of year) sits across the street. The actual painting is in the Art Institute of Chicago (p563). Wood spent much of his time in tiny Stone City, a cute little burg 14 miles north of Mt Vernon, off Hwy 1.

ALONG I-80

Most of Iowa's attractions are within an easy drive of bland I-80, which runs east–west across the state's center. Des Moines is midway along the road. Much more interesting alternatives are US 20 (p672) and US 30 (p672).

Quad Cities

Four cities straddle the Mississippi River by I-80: Davenport and Bettendorf in Iowa and Moline and Rock Island in Illinois. See p588 for Illinois-side details. The **visitor center** (☎ 800-747-7800; www.visitquadcities.com; 102 S Harrison St, Davenport; 8:30am-5pm year-round, 10am-4pm Sat & Sun summer) have bike rentals ($10 per hour) for a ride along the Big Muddy.

The **Iowa 80 Truckstop** (☎ 563-284-6961; www.iowa80truckstop.com; I-80 exit 284 in Walcott; 24hr) is the world's biggest, complete with a **trucking museum** (10am-6pm Wed-Sun) displaying actual rigs. The gift shop contains some of the tackiest merchandise imaginable. Stock up.

You can cruise the gorgeous Mississippi on the Victorian-style riverboat **Twilight** (☎ 800-331-1467; www.riverboattwilight.com; $330 per person double, incl hotel & meals), which runs two-day round-trips to Dubuque from nearby Le Claire.

Motels are found at I-74 exit 2 and I-780 exit 295A.

Iowa City

The youthful, artsy vibe here is courtesy of the **University of Iowa campus** (www.uiowa.edu), home to good art and natural history museums. It spills across both sides of the Iowa River; to the east it mingles with charming downtown's restaurants and bars. In summer (when the student-to-townie ratio evens out) the city mellows somewhat, but there is always something happening. The **visitor center** (☎ 800-283-6592; www.iowacitycoralville.org; 900 1st Ave; 8am-5pm Mon-Fri) is in neighboring Coralville.

The cute gold-domed building at the heart of campus is the **Old Capitol** (☎ 319-335-0548; admission free; 10am-3pm Tue-Wed & Fri, 10am-5pm Thu & Sat, 1-5pm Sun). Built in 1840, it was the seat of government until 1857 when Des Moines grabbed the reins. It's now a museum with galleries and furnishings from back in its heyday.

Chain motels line 1st Ave in Coralville (I-80 exit 242) like hogs at the trough. Beer and cheap chow abound downtown.

our pick **Alexis Park Inn & Suites** (☎ 319-337-8665, 888-925-3947; www.alexisparkinn.com; 1165 S Riverside Dr; r $75-110;), locally owned, is a modest apartment complex that has been converted into an extraordinary motel. The large rooms have kitchens and, reflecting the interests of the owners, each is decorated with an aerospace theme, such as the Apollo room, the Pan Am Clipper room etc (those seeking romance may wish to avoid the Piper Cub room). Four-poster beds and other antiques adorn Mark and Bob's **Brown Street Inn** (☎ 319-338-0435; www.brownstreetinn.com; 430 Brown St; r $85-165;), a six-room 1913 Dutch Colonial that's an easy walk from downtown.

The hallmark at lovely little bistro **Motley Cow Café** (☎ 319-688-9177; 160 N Linn St; mains $10-20; 5-10pm Mon-Sat;) is organic regional fare on a seasonal menu. **Dave's Foxhead Tavern** (☎ 319-351-9824; 402 E Market St) is popular with the U of I's revered Iowa Writers' Workshop crowd, who debate gerunds in

GREAT PLAINS

this tiny boozer (brilliantly satirized in Jane Smiley's *Moo;* alums include 16 Pulitzer prize winners).

Amana Colonies

These seven villages, just northwest of Iowa City, are stretched along a 17-mile loop. All were established as German religious communes between 1855 and 1861 by inspirationists who, until the Great Depression, lived a Utopian life with no wages paid and all assets communally owned. Unlike the Amish and Mennonite religions, Inspirationists embrace modern technology.

Today the seven well-preserved (and well-organized) villages, completely devoid of chain businesses, offer a glimpse of this unique culture, and there are lots of arts, crafts, cheeses, baked goods and wines to buy. Stop at the grain-elevator-shaped **visitor center** (☎ 800-579-2294; www.amanacolonies.com; 622 46th Ave, Amana; 🕑 9am-5pm Mon-Sat, 10am-5pm Sun Apr-Oct, 10am-4pm rest of year) for the essential guide-map. It also has audio tours on CD ($10) and bike rental ($15 per day).

Six museums are sprinkled throughout the villages, including the insightful **Amana Heritage Museum** (☎ 319-622-3567; 4310 220th Trail, Amana; 🕑 9am-5pm Mon-Sat, noon-4pm Sun Apr-Oct, Sat only Mar & Nov-Dec). The others are open summers only. An $8/free adult/child pass gets you into them all. Another popular stop is the privately owned **Barn Museum** (☎ 319-622-3058; 220th Trl, South Amana; adult $3.50, child $1.25-1.75; 🕑 9am-5pm Apr-Oct), which has miniature versions of buildings found across rural America.

The villages have many good-value B&Bs and historic inns including **Zuber's Homestead Hotel** (☎ 319-622-3911, 888-623-3911; www.zubershomesteadhotel.com; 2206 44 Ave, Homestead; r $85-110; ⊠ ❄ 📶) with 15 individually decorated rooms in an 1890s brick building.

One of the Amanas' top draws is the hefty-portioned, home-cooked German cuisine dished out at various humble dining spots. Keep an eye out for Millsteam wheat beer, brewed in Amana.

ALONG US 30

Like a clichéd needlepoint come to life, US 30 passes through fertile fields dotted with white-washed farmhouses and red-hued barns. It parallels I-80 an average of 20 to 30 miles to the north before dropping down to Nebraska near Omaha.

The real attraction here is just enjoying the succession of small towns. **Mt Vernon** may be only two blocks long but there's a lot here. Most noteworthy is the foodie favorite **Lincoln Café** (☎ 319-895-4041; 117 1st St; mains $6-15; 🕑 11am-2pm & 5-9pm Tue-Sat, 10am-2pm Sun), which serves amazing versions of local foods (try the burger with Maytag blue cheese.

Ames, 25 miles north of Des Moines, is home to Iowa State University and has lots of good motels and undergrad dives.

ALONG US 20

US 20 stretches from Dubuque on the Mississippi River to Sioux City on the Missouri River. It has offered up charms similar to those on US 30 to generations of travelers seeking new lives, adventure or just a new farm implement.

Dubuque

Dubuque makes a great entry to Iowa from Illinois: 19th-century Victorian homes line its narrow and lively streets between the Mississippi River and seven steep limestone hills. Get information from the **visitor center** (☎ 800-798-4748; www.traveldubuque.com; 300 Main St; 🕑 9am-5pm Mon-Sat, 9am-3pm Sun summer, 9am-4pm Mon-Sat, 9am-1pm Sun rest of year).

The **4th Street Elevator** (☎ 563-582-6496; www.dbq.com; 4th St & Fenelon; adult/child round-trip $2/1; 🕑 8am-10pm Apr-Nov), built in 1882, climbs a steep hill for huge views. Ring the bell to begin the ride. Learn about life (of all sorts) on the Mississippi at the impressive **National Mississippi River Museum & Aquarium** (☎ 563-557-9545; www.rivermuseum.com; 350 E 3rd St; adult/child $11/8; 🕑 9am-5pm summer, 10am-5pm rest of year). Nearby, the **Spirit of Dubuque** (☎ 563-583-8093; www.dubuqueriverrides.com; 3rd St, at Ice Harbor; adult/child from $18/12; 🕑 Apr-Oct, call for schedule) offers a variety of Mississippi sightseeing and dining cruises on a mock-paddleboat.

The historic **Hotel Julien** (☎ 563-556-4200, 800-798-7098; www.hoteljuliendubuque.com; 200 Main St; r $120-200; ❄ 📶) was built in 1914 and was once owned by Al Capone. A recent lavish renovation has turned it upscale and it's a real antidote for chains.

Main St is lined with good eateries grand and humble.

Waterloo & Around

Home to five **John Deere tractor factories,** Waterloo is the place to get one of those

IOWA: DETOURS & EXTRAS

- **Effigy Mounds National Monument** (☎ 563-873-3491; www.nps.gov/efmo; admission $3; 🕑 8am-4:30pm) Hundreds of Native American burial mounds sit in the bluffs high above the Mississippi River in far northeast Iowa.
- **Hobo Museum** (☎ 641-843-9104; www.hobo.com; 51 Main Ave S; 🕑 10am-5pm Mon-Fri summer) The only museum of its kind and located in northcentral Britt; hosts the National Hobo Convention the second weekend in August.
- **Loess Hills Scenic Byway**, a 220-mile network of roads running along Iowa's western edge, is named for the rare loess, a windblown glacier-ground soil that began piling up about 24,000 years ago. Steep, terraced bluffs are the result today. The most dramatic scenery is between Council Bluffs and Sioux City. Download a detailed map at www.byways.org.
- **Great River Road** (see also p48) has an Iowa route that hugs the Mississippi and passes through some isolated towns and some verdant, rural scenery. Burlington has an excellent visitor center and is good for a break. Download a detailed map at www.byways.org.
- **Fairfield & Vedic City**, on US 34 in the southeast, are home to the Maharishi University of Management, founded by the Maharishi Mahesh Yogi (he who taught the Beatles transcendental meditation in India). In hippie-trippy Vedic City all homes face east and have small domes on top.

prized green-and-yellow caps you've seen across middle America. Fun and free tractor-driven **Tractor Assembly Tours** (☎ 319-292-7668; 3500 E Donald St; 🕑 8am, 10am, 1pm Mon-Fri) and **Engine Works Tours** (☎ 319-292-5347; 3801 Ridgeway Ave; 🕑 9:30am, 1pm Mon-Fri) show how these vehicles are made. The minimum age is 13 and reservations are required.

NORTH DAKOTA

Magnificent desolation. Buzz Aldrin used it to describe the moon and it applies just as well in North Dakota. Fields of grain – green in the spring and summer, bronze in the fall and white in winter stretch beyond every horizon. Except the rugged 'badlands' of the far west, geographic relief is subtle. More often it is the collapsing remains of a failed homestead that break up the vistas.

Isolated far to the north, North Dakota is the least visited state in the US. But that just means that there's less traffic as you whiz along at the usual legal limit of 75mph. This is a place to get lost on remote two-lane routes and to appreciate the magnificence of raw land.

History

During their epic journey, Lewis and Clark spent more time in what is now North Dakota than any other state, meeting up with Shoshone guide Sacagawea on their way west. In the mid-19th century, smallpox epidemics came up the Missouri River, decimating the Arikara, Mandan and Hidatsa tribes, who affiliated and established the Like-a-Fishhook Village around 1845. When the railroad arrived in North Dakota in the 1870s, thousands of settlers flocked in to take up allotments under the Homestead Act. By 1889 the state population was more than 250,000, half foreign-born (one in eight were from Norway).

Young Theodore Roosevelt came here to ditch his city-slicker image. As president, inspired by his time in North Dakota, he earned the title 'The Father of Conservation' for his work creating national forests and parks.

Despite those seemingly endless summer fields of grain, the state's economy is tied to large oil deposits in the west. During the recent recession, the state was barely affected.

Information

North Dakota Bed & Breakfast Association (☎ 888-271-3380; www.ndbba.com)

North Dakota state parks (☎ 701-328-5357; www.ndparks.com) Vehicle permits cost $5/25 per day/year. Nearly half of the park campsites are reservable; fees range from $8 to $20 per night.

North Dakota Tourism Division (☎ 800-435-5663; www.ndtourism.com)

NORTH DAKOTA FACTS

Nickname Peace Garden State
Population 643,000
Area 70,705 sq miles
Capital city Bismarck (population 63,000)
Sales Tax 5%
Birthplace of Legendary Shoshone woman Sacagawea (1788–1812), cream of wheat (1893), bandleader Lawrence Welk (1903–92), singer-writer of westerns Louis L'Amour (1908–88)
Home of world's largest bison, turtle and Holstein statues
Famous for the movie *Fargo*
Official fish Northern pike
Driving Distances Fargo to Bismarck 193 miles

ALONG I-94

Arrowing across North Dakota, I-94 provides easy access to most of the state's top attractions although it would not be the road of scenic choice (US 2 is more atmospheric).

Fargo

Named for the Fargo of Wells Fargo Bank, North Dakota's biggest city has been a fur-trading post, a frontier town, a quick-divorce capital and a haven for folks in the Federal Witness Protection Program; not to mention the namesake of the Coen Brothers' film *Fargo* – though the movie was set across the Red River in Minnesota. Still, expect to hear a lot of accents similar to Frances McDormand's brilliant version in the film.

The grain elevator–shaped **visitor center** (☎ 800-235-7654; www.fargomoorhead.org; 2001 44th St; 7:30am-6pm Mon-Fri, 10am-4pm Sat & Sun summer, 8am-5pm Mon-Fri rest of year) is off I-94 exit 348.

The modern, ambitious **Plains Art Museum** (☎ 701-232-3821; www.plainsart.org; 704 1st Ave N; adult/child $5/free; 10am-5pm Tue-Sat, 1-5pm Sun, to 8pm Thu) features sophisticated programming in a renovated warehouse. The permanent collection includes contemporary work by Native American artists.

Just across the river in Moorhead, Minnesota, the **Heritage Hjemkomst Interpretive Center** (☎ 218-299-5511; www.hjemkomst-center.com; 202 1st Ave; adult/child $7/5; 9am-5pm Mon-Sat, to 8pm Tue, noon-5pm Sun) has a Norwegian stave church and 76ft replica of a 9th-century Viking ship with a heart-warming history.

Chain motels cluster at exits 64 on I-29 and 348 on I-94. A good indie choice is **Prairie Rose Inn** (☎ 701-235-3141, 800-437-0044; www.fargoponyexpress.com; 1340 21st Ave S; r from $80). Its 116 rooms are on nice grounds and the pool is indoors, away from the blizzards.

Hotel Donaldson (☎ 701-478-1000, 888-478-8768; www.hoteldonaldson.com; 101 Broadway; r from $190) is a stylish and swank revamp of a flophouse. The 17 luxurious suites are each decorated by a local artist. The chic restaurant and rooftop bar are worth stopping in for a dine or a drink.

Widman's Candy Shop (☎ 701-281-8664; 4325 13th Ave S; snacks $1-5; 9:30am-7pm Mon-Fri, to 5pm Sat) has been run by the same family since 1885. Their unique recipes are legendary and include chocolate-covered potato chips and flax seed.

Bismarck

Like the surrounding plains of wheat, Bismarck, North Dakota's capital, has a quick and bountiful summer. Otherwise, it's a compact place that hunkers down for the long winters where the low averages -4°F (-20°C).

The Bismarck-Mandan **Visitor Center** (☎ 800-767-3555; www.discoverbismarckmandan.com; 1600 Burnt Boat Dr, Bismarck; 7:30am-7pm Mon-Fri, 8am-6pm Sat, 10am-5pm Sun summer, 8am-5pm Mon-Fri rest of year) is just off I-94 exit 157.

The stark 1930s **State Capitol** (☎ 701-328-2480; N 7th St; 8am-4pm Mon-Fri, tours hourly except noon plus 9am-4pm Sat & 1-4pm Sun summer) is often referred to as the 'skyscraper of the prairie' and looks something like a Stalinist school of dentistry from the outside, but has some art-deco flourishes inside. There's an observation deck on the 18th floor.

Behind the Sacagawea statue, the huge **North Dakota Heritage Center** (☎ 701-328-2666; www.history.nd.gov; Capitol Hill; admission free; 8am-5pm Mon-Fri, 10am-5pm Sat & Sun) has details on everything from Norwegian bachelor farmers to the scores of nuclear bombs perched on missiles in silos across the state.

On River Rd, below the I-94 bridge, there's a replica of the 55-foot **keelboat** Lewis and Clark used on this part of their journey.

Fort Abraham Lincoln State Park (☎ 701-667-6340; $5 per vehicle, plus adult/child $6/4 to tour historical sites), 7 miles south of Mandan on SR 1806, is well worth the detour. Its **On-A-Slant Indian Village** has five re-created Mandan earth lodges, while the fort, with several replica buildings, is where Custer departed from for the Battle of Little Bighorn.

HOT TOPIC: TOO MUCH WATER

In the winter of 2009 Fargo was hit by record floods that taxed dikes protecting the city from the Red River. Much of the community turned out to fill over 2 million sandbags and while there was destruction a much worse calamity was averted. Downriver, Grand Forks was also threatened and memories of a disastrous flood in 1997 were reawakened.

A plethora of late storms in March, coupled with colder than average conditions that kept the ground frozen and unable to absorb water, meant that these largely flat lands were easily inundated. And these problems are not unique to North Dakota. Floods are becoming more common throughout the Great Plains; eastern Iowa had devastating floods in 2008.

Climate change, which has caused the weather to be colder and wetter, is responsible, as is the predilection of people to settle in historic flood plains. There's a growing sense that it will be impossible to build dikes to keep up with the rising water levels. All the states are busily debating what to do next.

In Bismarck, chain motels congregate around I-94 exit 159. Closer to the center, **Best Western Ramkota Hotel** (☎ 701-258-7700; www.bismarck.ramkota.com; 800 S Third St; r $80-130;) has 306 rooms around an indoor pool with a 150ft slide (whee!).

Locally made candy bars star at **Lindy Sue's** (☎ 701-663-5311; 316 W Main St, Mandan; snacks $3-5; 9am-6pm Mon-Sat;), an authentic soda fountain with fine root beer floats. **Little Cottage Cafe** (☎ 701-223-4949; 2513 E Main Ave; mains $5-12; 6am-9pm) is down near the train tracks near the center and is a classic diner with hearty local food (bring on the meatloaf!). Free newspapers lay about and the timeless waitresses (honey!) never let coffee cups empty.

Around Bismarck

North of Bismarck are several worthwhile attractions near the spot where Lewis and Clark wintered with the Mandan in 1804–05. The best is the **North Dakota Lewis & Clark Interpretive Center** (☎ 701-462-8535; www.fortmandan.com; adult/child $7.50/5; 9am-5pm daily year-round, from noon Sun in winter), 38 miles away in Washburn, where you can learn about the duo's epic expedition and the Native Americans who helped them. The same ticket gets you into **Fort Mandan** (CR 17), a replica of the fort built by Lewis and Clark, 2.5 miles west (10 miles downstream from the flooded original site).

West of Bismarck on I-94, stop and see **Sue, the World's Largest Holstein Cow** at New Salem (exit 127). At exit 72, there's a unique detour south along the Enchanted Hwy (p676). In Dickinson, another hour west, the **Dakota Dinosaur Museum** (☎ 701-225-3466; www.dakotadino.com; I-94 exit 61; adult/child $7/4; 9am-5pm May-Sep) has oodles of dinosaur fossils and statues, most found in the state.

Theodore Roosevelt National Park

A tortured land known as the 'badlands' and whose colors seem to change with the moods of nature, **Theodore Roosevelt National Park** (☎ 701-623-4466; www.nps.gov/thro; 7-day pass per vehicle $10) is the state's natural highlight. Bizarre rock formations, streaked with a rainbow of red, yellow, brown, black and silver minerals, are framed by green prairie. Most visitors opt for the 36-mile scenic drive in the South Unit, near I-94 at Medora. The more rugged North Unit, 68 miles north on US 85, has far fewer visitors and a 14-mile drive to the beautiful **Oxbow Overlook**. The verdant surrounds are protected as the **Little Missouri National Grassland**.

The park has three visitor centers, including the **Medora visitor center** (☎ 701-623-4466; 8am-6pm Mon-Thu, 8am-8pm Fri-Sun summer, 8am-4:30pm rest of year), with Theodore Roosevelt's old cabin out back. Roosevelt described this area as 'a land of vast, silent spaces, of lonely rivers, and of plains where the wild game stared at the passing horsemen,' and it's hard to describe the place better even today.

Wildlife is still everywhere: mule deer, wild horses, bighorn sheep, elk, bison, around 200 species of bird and, of course, sprawling subterranean prairie dog towns.

Hikers can explore 85 miles of backcountry trails. For a good adventure, hike or cycle the 96-mile **Maah Daah Hey Trail** between the park units. Driving, continue north on US 85 to Fort Buford (p676).

Accommodations in Medora include several motels. The most fun choice, however,

NORTH DAKOTA: DETOURS & EXTRAS

- **International Peace Garden** (☎ 888-432-6733; www.peacegarden.com; per vehicle $10) Around 150,000 flowers and several monuments sit symbolically on the North Dakota–Manitoba border on US 281.
- The **Enchanted Highway** (www.enchantedhighway.net) has huge whimsical metal sculptures of local folks and critters by local artist Gary Greff. It runs for 32 miles straight south to Regent from exit 72 on I-94.
- **Knife River Indian Villages** (☎ 701-745-3300; www.nps.gov/knri; CR 37; admission free; 🕑 8am-6pm summer, 8am-4:30pm rest of year) feature the sites of three Hidatsa and Mandan villages that were occupied for at least 900 years and a re-created earth lodge. Sacagawea joined Lewis and Clark from here. The sites are just north of Stanton (20 miles west of Washburn) on Hwy 200, which runs through verdant rolling prairie for 110 miles between US 83 and US 85.

is the **Rough Riders Hotel** (☎ 701-623-4444, 800-633-6721; www.medora.com/rough-riders; 301 3rd Ave; r $90-180;), which dates back to 1885. Recent renovations made the eight original rooms dude-worthy and 68 more will be ready from 2010. The park itself has two simple **campgrounds** (campsites $10) and free backcountry camping (permit required).

ALONG US 2

US 2 is the more interesting alternative to I-94. The endless sky vistas stretch even further than the seas of golden grain. **Grand Forks** is a stolid city, while **Devils Lake** is one of the top waterfowl hunting destinations in the country. The entire area is subject to the flood-prone Red River (p675).

Amtrak's *Empire Builder* parallels the road on the legendary Great Northern route.

Rugby

Rugby is about halfway down the highway, but its more notable location identity is as the **geographical center of North America**. The **Prairie Village Museum** (☎ 701-776-6414; www.prairievillagemuseum.com; 102 US 2 SE; adult/child $7/1; 🕑 8am-7pm Mon-Sat, 1-7pm Sun May-Sep) recreates Great Plains life through the decades.

Minot

North Dakota's fourth largest city seriously celebrates its Scandinavian roots. **Scandinavian Heritage Park** (1020 S Broadway) contains northern European icons like a Norwegian stave church and Finnish sauna plus Minot's **visitor center** (☎ 800-264-2626; www.visitminot.org; 🕑 8am-7pm Mon-Fri, 10am-4pm Sat, noon-4pm Sun summer, 8am-5pm Mon-Fri rest of year;). October's **Norsk Høstfest** (www.hostfest.com) is promoted as the world's largest Scandinavian festival.

Minot has a full range of modest chain and indie motels along US 2, 52 and 83.

West to Montana

West of Minot the horizon is dotted with forlorn little settlements slipping back into the prairie soil. Twenty-two miles southwest of Williston along SR 1804, **Fort Buford** (☎ 701-572-9034; adult/child $5/2.50; 🕑 8am-6pm mid-May–mid-Sep) is the bleak Army outpost where Sitting Bull surrendered. The adjacent **Missouri-Yellowstone Confluence Interpretive Center** (🕑 8am-6pm mid-May–mid-Sep, 9am-4pm Wed-Sun rest of year) includes the fort's visitor center. Swing by the boat landing in May to see anglers reeling in paddlefish.

About 2 miles west, on the Montana–North Dakota border, the more evocative **Fort Union Trading Post** (☎ 701-572-9083; www.nps.gov/fous; admission free; 🕑 8am-8pm Central Time summer, 9am-5:30pm rest of year) is a reconstruction of the American Fur Company post built in 1828.

SOUTH DAKOTA

Gently rolling prairies through shallow fertile valleys mark much of this endlessly attractive state. But head southwest and hell breaks loose – in a good way. The Badlands are the geologic equivalent of fireworks. The Black Hills are like opera: majestic, challenging, intriguing and even frustrating. Mt Rushmore matches the Statue of Liberty for five-star icon status. Throughout the state are important Native American sites and interesting towns big and small.

History

When the USA acquired South Dakota with the 1803 Louisiana Purchase, the region was the domain of the Sioux and a few fur trappers. It wasn't until the 1850s that the rich Dakota soil attracted the interest of settlers.

The 1868 Fort Laramie Treaty between the USA and the Sioux promised the Sioux a 60-million-acre reservation that stretched from the Missouri River in the east to the Bighorn Mountains in the west. The treaty was broken in 1874 after Lt Col George Custer led an expedition into the Black Hills in search of gold. Unfortunately for the Sioux, he found it.

Miners and settlers soon streamed in illegally and the Sioux retaliated in the biggest of the Indian Wars. The Battle of Little Bighorn in 1876, in which the great Crazy Horse defeated Custer and killed every last soldier, was the Plains Indians' last major victory over the invaders. Faced with overwhelming force, the tribes split up. Sitting Bull fled to Canada, Crazy Horse turned in his gun in 1877, and the railroads and settlers continued the march west. The final decimation of Sioux resistance came at Wounded Knee in 1890 (see p680). Decades later, in 1973, Oglala Sioux loyal to the American Indian Movement and opposed to their tribal leaders occupied Wounded Knee and kept federal officers at bay for 71 days.

Information

Bed & Breakfast Innkeepers of South Dakota (☎ 888-500-4667; www.southdakotabnb.com)

South Dakota Dept of Tourism (☎ 800-732-5682; www.travelsd.com)

South Dakota state parks (☎ 605-773-3391; www.sdgfp.info) Vehicle permits cost $6/28 per day/year. Most park campsites are reservable; fees range from $8 to $25 per night. Cabins start at $35.

SIOUX FALLS

South Dakota's largest city (population 152,000) has some historic buildings and a sculpture walk downtown, but it will always just be a gigantic rest stop for travelers.

The city's namesake splashes along the Big Sioux River at **Falls Park** off Phillips Ave north of downtown. The park has a **visitor center** (☎ 605-367-7430; www.siouxfallscvb.com; ⏰ 9am-9pm daily Apr-Oct, reduced winter hr) with city-wide information and an observation tower. The huge pink quartzite **Old Courthouse Museum** (☎ 605-367-4210; www.siouxlandmuseums.com; 200 W 6th St; admission free; ⏰ 8am-5pm Mon-Fri, 9am-5pm Sat, noon-5pm Sun, to 9pm Thu), a restored 1890s building, has three floors of changing exhibits on the region.

Sioux Falls has thickets of chain motels at I-29 exits 77 to 83. For hearty fare look for the brilliant sign outside otherwise humble **Bob's Cafe** (☎ 605-336-7260; 1312 W 12th St; mains $4-9; ⏰ 7am-8pm). Inside you'll usually find the real Bob cooking up the best breakfasts, burgers and roast chicken in the region.

AROUND SIOUX FALLS

Dedicated *Little House on the Prairie* fans should head to Laura Ingalls Wilder's former home, **De Smet**. You can pick up a free drive-by tour-map of various sites from her and her family's life at the **Laura Ingalls Wilder Memorial Society** (☎ 800-880-3383; www.discoverlaura.org; 105 Olivet Ave; ⏰ 9am-5:30pm Mon-Sat & 10am-5:30pm Sun summer, 9am-4pm Mon-Sat May & Sep, 9am-4pm Mon-Fri Oct-Apr) office and gift shop. The society leads hour-long tours inside two original **Wilder homes** (adult/child $8/4) – the one where the Wilders spent the first winter and the home Michael Landon, er, 'Pa' built. A melodramatic **outdoor play** (www.desmetpageant.org; adult/child $8/5) is performed on some July weekends.

ALONG I-90

Easily one of the least interesting stretches of interstate highway, I-90 across South Dakota does have some worthy stops along the way. For driving alternatives such as US 14, see p684.

SOUTH DAKOTA FACTS

Nickname Mt Rushmore State

Population 805,000

Area 77,125 sq miles

Capital city Pierre (population 14,100)

Sales Tax 4%

Birthplace of Sitting Bull (c 1831–90), Crazy Horse (c 1840–77) and Black Elk (c 1863–1950), all of Little Bighorn fame, and genial broadcaster Tom Brokaw (b 1940)

Home of Mt Rushmore, the Sioux

Famous for HBO show *Deadwood*, Wounded Knee Massacre

Official animal Coyote

Driving distances Sioux Falls to Rapid City 341 miles, Sioux Falls to Des Moines 283 miles

IF YOU HAVE A FEW MORE DAYS

Large swaths of South Dakota are unchanged since the 19th century when the Native Americans and the US Army clashed. See the land as it was then along the **Native American Scenic Byway**, which begins in Chamberlain (below) on Hwy 50 and meanders 100 crooked miles northwest to Pierre along Hwy 1806, following the Missouri River through rolling, rugged countryside, including the Crow Creek and the Lower Brule Indian reservations. This stretch makes a good detour off I-90. For the full effect follow the entire length by first going west from Pierre on US14 and then meandering north on Hwy 63 through the remote Standing Rock and Cheyenne River Indian reservations. Buttes and grasslands seem to go on forever and you can fully get caught up in their spectre over two or three days and 300 miles.

Mitchell

Every year, half a million people pull off I-90 (exit 332) to see the Taj Mahal of agriculture, the all-time-ultimate roadside attraction, the **Corn Palace** (☎ 866-273-2676; www.cornpalace.org; 604 N Main St; admission free; 8am-9pm daily summer, reduced hr rest of year). Close to 300,000 ears of corn are used each year to create a tableaux of murals on the outside of the building. Ponder the scenes and you may find a kernel of truth or just say 'aw shucks.'

At night, thrill to a double feature at the **Starlite Drive-In Theatre** (☎ 605-996-4511; www.loganmovie.com; 4601 N Main St; adult/child $8/free; Apr-Sep), where it still seems to be 1965.

Chamberlain

In a picturesque site where I-90 crosses the Missouri River, Chamberlain (exit 263) is home to the excellent **Akta Lakota Museum & Cultural Center** (☎ 800-798-3452; www.aktalakota.org; 1301 N Main St; admission free; 8am-6pm Mon-Sat, 9am-5pm Sun summer, 8am-5pm Mon-Sat rest of year) at St Joseph's Indian School. It has Lakota cultural displays and contemporary art from numerous tribes.

History buffs should pop into the hilltop rest stop, south of town, where the **Lewis & Clark Information Center** (☎ 605-734-4562; admission free; 8am-6pm May-Oct) has exhibits on the intrepid band.

Pierre

Pierre (pronounced *'peer'*) is just too small (population 14,100) and ordinary to feel like a seat of power. Small-town Victorian homes overlook the imposing **State Capitol** (☎ 605-773-3765; 500 E Capitol Ave; 8am-10pm) with its black copper dome. The best reason to detour off I-90 here is because it lies along the **Native American Scenic Byway** and lonely, stark **US 14** (see p684).

Exhibits at the ecologically groundbreaking **South Dakota Cultural Heritage Center** (☎ 605-773-3458; www.sdhistory.org; 900 Governor's Dr; adult/child $4/free; 9am-6:30pm Mon-Sat, 1-4:30pm Sun summer, closes at 4:30pm rest of year) include a bloody Ghost Dance shirt from Wounded Knee.

At a bend on the Missouri River, **Framboise Island** has several hiking trails and plentiful wildlife. It's across from where the Lewis and Clark expedition spent four days and was nearly derailed when they inadvertently offended members of the local Brule tribe. The Pierre **visitor center** (☎ 800-962-2034; www.pierre.org; 800 W Dakota Ave; 8am-5pm Mon-Fri) is nearby.

Most hotels lie along US 83. The **Pierre Inn & Suites** (☎ 605-224-5981; www.pierreinnsuites.com; 200 W Pleasant Dr; r from $60;) has solid motel-style rooms with fridges and microwaves. It's close to the cute center of Pierre, with shops that include a bookstore.

Minuteman Missile National Historic Site

In the 1960s and 1970s, 450 Minutemen II intercontinental ballistic missiles, always at the ready in underground silos, were just 30 minutes from their targets in the Soviet Union. The missiles have since been retired (more modern ones are still lurking in silos across the northern Great Plains). The first national park dedicated to the Cold War preserves a silo and its underground launch facility (Map p680).

At the small temporary **headquarters** (☎ 605-433-5552; www.nps.gov/mimi; I-90 exit 131; 8am-4:30pm Mon-Fri plus Sat in summer), you can take tours (free) of the launch complex where two people stood ready around the clock to turn keys launching missiles from this part of South Dakota. Visits are limited to six people per tour and there are only one or two per day. Call far in advance to secure a place.

The **silo** (I-90 exit 116; 8am-4pm) can be viewed without a reservation through a glass cover. Note that from here west, Mountain Time is used, which is one hour earlier.

Wall

Hyped for hundreds of miles, **Wall Drug** (605-279-2275; www.walldrug.com; 510 Main St; 6:30am-6pm, extended summer hr) is a surprisingly worthy stop. They really do have 5¢ coffee, free ice water and enough diversions and come-ons to warm the heart of schlock-lovers everywhere. But amidst the fudge in the faux frontier complex is a superb bookstore with the best selection of regional titles we've seen.

The highly recommended **Wounded Knee Museum** (605-279-2573; www.woundedkneemuseum.org; I-90 exit 110; adult/child $5/free; 8:30am-5:30pm Apr-Oct, extended summer hr) tells the story of the massacre from the Lakota perspective using photos and narratives. It's more insightful than anything at the actual site (see p680).

The namesake town of the drug store is a good place for an overnight pause. It's compact and walkable, there are tasty and cheap cafés and bars, and several good indie motels, including **Sunshine Inn** (605-279-2178; www.sunshineinnatwallsd.com; 608 Main St; r 50-80;), which has a genial owner and 22 sparkling rooms.

Badlands National Park

This otherworldly landscape, oddly softened by its fantastic rainbow hues, is a spectacle of sheer walls and spikes stabbing the dry air. It was understandably named *mako sica* (badland) by Native Americans. Looking over the bizarre formations from the corrugated walls surrounding the Badlands is like seeing an ocean someone boiled dry.

The park's north unit (Map p680) gets the most visitors; the Hwy 240 loop road is easily reached from I-90 (exits 110 and 131) and you can drive it in an hour if you're in a hurry (and not stuck behind an RV). Lookouts and vistas abound.

Much less visited is the portion west of Hwy 240 along the gravel Sage Creek Rim Rd. There are stops at prairie dog towns and this is where most backcountry hikers and campers go. There is nearly no water or shade here, so don't strike out into the wilderness unprepared. The less-accessible south units are in the Pine Ridge Indian Reservation and see few visitors.

The **Ben Reifel Visitor Center** (605-433-5361; www.nps.gov/badl; Hwy 240; 7am-7pm summer, 8am-5pm Apr-May & Sep-Oct, 8am-4pm rest of year) has good exhibits and advice for ways to ditch your car to appreciate the geologic wonder. The **White River Visitor Center** (605-455-2878; Hwy 27; 10am-4pm summer) is small. A seven-day pass costs $15 for cars and $7 for cyclists.

Neither the developed **Cedar Pass Campground** (campsites $10) or primitive **Sage Creek Campground** (campsites free) takes reservations. Hotels can be found on I-90 in Kadoka and Wall, or stay at a cozy cabin inside the park at **Cedar Pass Lodge** (605-433-5460; www.cedarpasslodge.com; Hwy 240; cabins $85-110; May-Oct). There is a restaurant and shops.

The national park (Map p680), along with the surrounding **Buffalo Gap National Grassland**, protects the country's largest prairie grasslands, several species of Plains mammal (including bison and black-footed ferret), prairie falcons and lots of snakes. The **National Grasslands Visitors Centre** (605-279-2125; www.fs.fed.us/grasslands; 798 Main St; 8am-4:30pm) in Wall has good displays on this under-appreciated and complex ecosystem. Rangers can map out backroad routes that will let you do looping tours of the Badlands and the grasslands without ever touching I-90. Hwy 44 to Rapid City is also a fine alternative to the interstate.

Pine Ridge Indian Reservation

Home to the Lakota Oglala Sioux, the Pine Ridge reservation south of the Badlands is one of the nation's poorest 'counties,' with over half the population living below the poverty line. Despite being at times a jarring dose of reality, it is also a place welcoming to visitors.

In 1890 the new Ghost Dance religion, which the Lakota followers believed would bring back their ancestors and eliminate the white man, became wildly popular. This struck fear into the area's soldiers and settlers and the frenetic circle dances were outlawed. The 7th US Cavalry rounded up a band of Lakota under Chief Big Foot and brought them to the small village of Wounded Knee. On December 29, as the soldiers began to search for weapons, a shot was fired (nobody knows by who) leading to the massacre of more than 250 men, women and children, most of them unarmed. It's one of the most infamous atrocities in US history. Twenty-five soldiers also died.

Today, the **Wounded Knee Massacre Site**, 16 miles northeast of Pine Ridge town, is marked by a faded roadside sign and craft vendors. The mass grave, often frequented by young men looking for handouts, sits atop the hill. The nearby visitor center has little to offer: stop at the museum in Wall (p679) instead.

Four miles north of Pine Ridge town at the Red Cloud Indian School is the **Red Cloud Heritage Center** (☎ 605-867-5491; www.redcloudschool.org; Hwy 18; admission free; 🕓 8am-6pm Mon-Fri, 8am-5pm Sat, 11am-5pm Sun summer, 8am-5pm Mon-Fri rest of year), a well-curated art museum with traditional and contemporary work and a craft shop. You can get here by Hwy 27 from the Badlands.

Tune in to what's happening on KILI (90.1 FM), 'the voice of the Lakota nation,' which broadcasts community events and sometimes plays traditional music.

The farmhouse **Wakpamni B&B** (☎ 605-288-1800; www.wakpamni.com; r from $60; ⊠ ❄ 📶), 21 miles east of Pine Ridge town off US 18, has regular rooms and tipis. The owners have a superb Lakota craft shop and can arrange horseback riding (from $50), sweat-lodge ceremonies and other cultural activities.

BLACK HILLS

This stunning region on the Wyoming–South Dakota border lures oodles of visitors with its winding canyons and wildly eroded 7000ft peaks. The region's name – the 'Black' comes from the dark Ponderosa pine-covered slopes – was conferred by the Lakota Sioux.

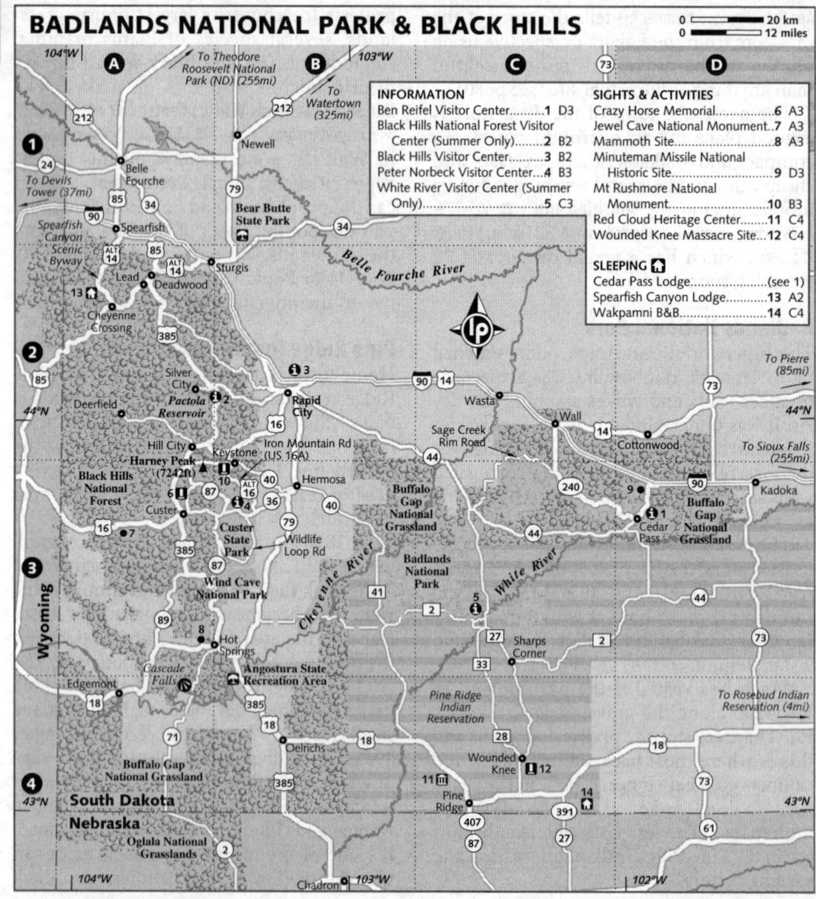

In the 1868 Fort Laramie Treaty, they were assured that the hills would be theirs for eternity, but the discovery of gold changed that and the Sioux were shoved out to low-value flatlands only six years later. *Dances With Wolves* covers some of this period.

You'll need several days to explore the area. Throughout are bucolic back-road drives, caves, bison herds, forests, Mt Rushmore and Crazy Horse monuments and outdoor activities (ballooning, cycling, rock climbing, boating, fishing, hiking, downhill skiing, gold-panning etc). Like fool's gold, gaudy tourist traps lurk in corners and keep things lively.

Orientation & Information

I-90 skirts the north of the Black Hills providing access to the gateway towns of Rapid City, Sturgis, Spearfish and Deadwood. US 385 (initially US 85), the Black Hills Pkwy, runs north–south the length of the hills; along with east–west US 16 (and US 16A) out of Rapid City, it provides access to the more scenically situated, but also more touristy and expensive, south Hills towns of Keystone, Hill City and Custer, plus most of the top attractions like Mt Rushmore and Custer State Park. No matter where you stay, nothing is more than a couple of hours away.

There are hundreds of hotels and campgrounds across the hills; still, during the summer, room rates shoot up like geysers and reservations are essential. Avoid visiting during the Sturgis motorcycle rally (p682) when hogs rule the roads and fill the rooms. Much is closed October to April.

Visitor centers and reservations:

Black Hills Central Reservations (☎ 866-601-5103; www.blackhillsvacations.com) Accommodation reservations and last-minute deals.

Black Hills Visitor Center (☎ 605-355-3700; www.blackhillsbadlands.com; I-90 exit 61, Rapid City; 🕑 8am-8pm summer, to 5pm rest of year)

Black Hills National Forest

The majority of the Black Hills lie within this 1875-sq-mile mixture of protected and logged forest, perforated by pockets of private land along most roads. The scenery is fantastic, whether you get deep into it along the 450 miles of hiking trails or just drive the many scenic byways and gravel fire roads. The 111-mile **Centennial Trail** meanders across the Black Hills linking Sturgis p682) to Wind Cave National Park (p685).

The 109-mile **George S Mickelson Trail** (www.mickelsontrail.com; daily/annual fee $3/15) cuts through much of the forest, running from Deadwood through Hill City and Custer to Edgemont on an abandoned railway line. There are bike rentals at various trailside towns.

The forest **headquarters** (☎ 605-673-9200; www.fs.fed.us/bhnf; 25041 US 16; 🕑 7:30am-5pm Mon-Fri) is in Custer and a modern summer-only **visitor center** (☎ 605-343-8755; US 385, near Hwy 44; 🕑 8:30am-6pm) sits on the Pactola Reservoir between Hill City and Rapid City.

Good camping abounds in the forest. There are 30 basic (no showers or electricity) **campgrounds** (☎ 877-444-6777; campsites free-$25) and backcountry camping is allowed just about anywhere (free; no open fires). Reservations are recommended during summer.

Rapid City

A worthy capital to the region, 'Rapid' has a beautiful, lively and walkable downtown. Well-preserved brick buildings, filled with quality shopping and dining, makes it a good urban base. Look for life-size **statues of presidents** throughout the center (Nixon is suitably shifty). The **visitor center** (☎ 866-727-4324; www.rapidcitycvb.com; 444 Mt Rushmore Rd; 🕑 8am-5pm Mon-Fri) is in the civic center.

SIGHTS

Looking like an ICBM launch site, the **Journey Museum** (☎ 605-394-6923; www.journeymuseum.org; 222 New York St; adult/child $7/free; 🕑 9am-6pm summer, 10am-5pm Mon-Sat, 1-5pm Sun rest of year) takes you on a trip through 2½ billion years of the history of the Black Hills with lots of space given to the Lakota Sioux and dinosaurs.

You can see more dinosaur bones and some stellar fossils at the **Museum of Geology** (☎ 605-394-2467; http://sdmines.sdsmt.edu/museum; 501 E St Joseph St, O'Harra Bldg; admission free; 🕑 9am-5pm Mon-Fri, 10am-5pm Sat, noon-5pm Sun summer, 9am-4pm Mon-Fri, 10am-4pm Sat rest of year) at the South Dakota School of Mines & Technology.

Two sure-fire hits with kids are the life-size concrete statues at **Dinosaur Park** (940 Skyline Dr; admission free; 🕑 6am-10pm; 🚸) and the character-filled playground at **Storybook Island** (off Hwy 44 W; admission free; 🕑 9am-7pm summer; 🚸).

GREAT PLAINS

GREAT PLAINS

SLEEPING & EATING

Indie motels line North St between I-90 and downtown and US16 south of town. Main St has scores of eateries and bars.

Gold Star Motel (☎ 605-341-7051, 800-681-7051; www.blackhillsmotels.com/rapidcity/goldstarmotel.html; 801 E North St; r $50-90; ⊠ ❄ ≋) A classic yet clean 26-room motel on a shady site.

our pick **Hotel Alex Johnson** (☎ 605-342-1210, 800-888-2539; www.alexjohnson.com; 523 6th St; r $70-250; ❄ ◻ ≋) The design of this 1927 classic magically blends Germanic Tudor architecture and traditional Lakota Sioux symbols – note the lobby's painted ceiling and the chandelier made of war lances. The 127 rooms are modern and quite comfortable but the real appeal here is that it hasn't been turned into a boutique hotel. Its timeless qualities include a portrait of guest Al Capone near the front desk.

our pick **Tally's** (☎ 605-342-7621; 530 6th St; meals $4-8; ⏲ 7am-3pm Mon-Sat) With prices that don't seem to have changed since Reagan was president (his statue is out front), Tally's is not only a bargain but the food at this timeless coffee shop is superb.

Corn Exchange (☎ 605-343-5070; www.cornexchange.com; 727 Main St; mains $13-21; ⏲ 5-9pm Tue-Sat; ⊠) Seasonal menus, local and organic produce and a talented kitchen make this small bistro a standout. Dishes use simple preparations that emphasize the inherent flavors of the food. But don't get carried away: desserts are dreamy.

Firehouse Brewing Co (☎ 605-348-1915; 610 Main St; mains $5-12; ⏲ 4pm-midnight) Microbrews and plenty of tasty pub grub are served year-round. In summer there's live music in the beer garden.

Sturgis

Fast food, Christian iconography and billboards for glitzy biker bars featuring dolled up models unlikely to ever be found on the back of a hog are just some of the cacophony of images of this tacky small town on I-90 (exits 30 and 32). Things get even louder for the annual **Sturgis Motorcycle Rally** (☎ 605-720-0800; www.sturgismotorcyclerally.com; ⏲ early Aug), when around 500,000 riders, fans and curious onlookers take over the town. Temporary campsites are set up and motels across the region unmuffle their rates. Check the rally website for vacancies. The **chamber of commerce** (☎ 605-347-2556; www.sturgis-sd.org; 2040 Junction Ave; ⏲ 8am-5pm Mon-Fri) also has info.

The **Sturgis Motorcycle Museum** (☎ 605-347-2001; www.sturgismuseum.com; 999 Main St; adult/child $5/free; ⏲ 9am-5pm Mon-Fri, to 4pm Sat & Sun) houses dozens of bikes, including many classics. A 'freedom fighters' exhibit honors those who have fought for the rights of bikers.

Spearfish

At the start of gorgeous **Spearfish Canyon Scenic Byway** (US 14A), Spearfish is lined with motels. The **chamber of commerce** (☎ 800-626-8013; www.spearfishchamber.org; 106 W Kansas; ⏲ 8am-5pm Mon-Fri) has a self-guided tour of the byway and hiking trail maps.

Chain hotels cluster around I-90 exit 14 and aging indie motels are downtown. For a rural retreat, the **Spearfish Canyon Lodge** (☎ 605-584-3435, 877-975-6343; www.spfcanyon.com; US 14A; r from $150; ⊠ ❄ ≋) is 13 miles south of Spearfish near trails and streams. The massive lobby fireplace adds charm and the 54 modern piney rooms are cozy.

Deadwood

'No law at all in Deadwood, is that true?' So began the eponymous HBO series. Today things have changed, although the glitzy gambling halls would no doubt put a sly grin on the faces of the hard characters who founded the town.

Settled illegally by eager gold rushers in the 1870s, Deadwood is now a National Historic Landmark. Its atmospheric streets are lined with gold rush-era buildings restored with casino dollars. Its storied past is easy to find (and surprisingly in-line with the TV series). There's eternal devotion to Wild Bill Hickok, who was shot in the back of the head here in 1876 while gambling.

SIGHTS

The splendid **Deadwood History & Information Center** (☎ 800-999-1876; www.deadwood.org; Pine St; ⏲ 8am-7pm summer, 9am-5pm rest of year), in the restored train depot, has tons of info, plus exhibits and photos of the town's history. Ask about tours led by local history buffs. Downtown is walkable, but the fake **trolley** (per ride $1) can be handy for getting between attractions, hotels and parking lots.

Actors reenact famous **shootouts** (⏲ 4pm & 6pm daily) on Main St during summer. **Hickok's murder** (⏲ 1pm, 3pm, 5pm & 7pm) is acted out in Saloon No 10 (opposite). A **trial** (⏲ 8pm) of the killer takes place in the Masonic Temple (Main St).

The **Adams Museum** (☎ 605-578-1714; www.adamsmuseumandhouse.org; 54 Sherman St; adult/child $7/2; ⏲ 9am-5pm daily summer, 10am-4pm Tue-Sat rest of year) does an excellent job of capturing the town's colorful past.

Calamity Jane (born Martha Canary, 1850–1903) and Hickok (1847–76) rest side by side up on Boot Hill at the very steep **Mount Moriah Cemetery** (adult/child $1/50¢; 8am-8pm summer, 8am-5pm rest of year). Entertaining bus tours ($8) leave hourly from Main St.

SLEEPING & EATING

Casinos offer up buffets with plenty of cheap chow. Wander the streets for better choices. There are scores of places to stay right in the center.

Deadwood Dick's (605-578-3224, 877-882-4990; www.deadwooddicks.com; 51 Sherman St; r $60-200) These homestyle and idiosyncratic rooms feature furniture from the owner's antique shop and range in size from small doubles to large suites with kitchens.

Bullock Hotel (605-578-1745, 800-336-1876; www.historicbullock.com; 633 Main St; r from $105;) Fans of the TV show will recall the conflicted but upstanding sheriff Seth Bullock. This hotel was opened by the real Bullock in 1895. The 28 rooms are modern and comfortable while retaining the period charm of the building.

Saloon No 10 (605-578-3346; 657 Main St; 8am-2am) Dark paneled walls and sawdust on the floor are features of this storied bar. The original, where Hickok literally lost big-time, stood across the street, but the building burned to the ground and the owners brought the bar over here.

Midnight Star (605-578-1555; 677 Main St) Owned by actor Kevin Costner, this attractive boozer has costumes and photos from his movies. The restaurant serves pricey steaks.

Lead

Just uphill from Deadwood, Lead (pronounced *leed*) has an unrestored charm and still bears plenty of scars from the mining era. Peek at the 1250ft-deep **Homestake gold mine** (605-584-3110; 160 W Main St; admission free; 24hr) to see what open-pit mining can do to a mountain. Nearby are the same mine's shafts, which plunge more than 1.5 miles below the surface and are now being used for physics research.

The **Main Street Manor Hostel** (605-717-2044; www.mainstreetmanorhostel.com; 515 W Main St; dm $20-25; closed Dec-Jan;) is a gem in its own right. Guests get use of the kitchen, garden and laundry at this very friendly place.

US 385

The scenic spine of the Black Hills, US 385 runs 90 miles from Deadwood to Hot Springs and beyond. Beautiful meadows and dark stands of conifers are interspersed with roadside attractions that include kangaroos, mistletoe and, of course, Elvis.

Hill City (www.hillcitysd.com) is an attractive old town with a certain dignity not found at places like Keystone. It's a good base in the hills and is the western terminus of the **1880 Train** (866-367-1880; www.1880train.com; 222 Railroad Ave; adult/child round-trip $22/12; May-Oct), a classic steam train running through rugged country to Keystone. The **Lantern Inn** (605-574-2582, 800-456-0520; www.lanterninn.com; 580 E Main St; r $55-130;) is an 18-room motel-style place spread over two stories fronting attractive grounds.

Mount Rushmore

Fans of *North by Northwest* may remember the charmingly piney and low-key visitor center where Cary Grant gets 'plugged.' That was then (1959). Today the public areas around Mt Rushmore seem devilishly designed to rob visitors of any enjoyment from their visit. Yes, the amazing mountainside sculpture is still there. George Washington, Thomas Jefferson, Abraham Lincoln and Theodore Roosevelt are each in their own 60ft-tall glory. But trying to appreciate one of the most iconic American images is just that: trying.

A bunker-like multilevel parking garage greets visitors followed by bombastic entrances that obscure the memorial. You pass through an over-wrought avenue of all 50 state flags before reaching a terrace, underneath which is the **visitor center** (605-574-3198; www.nps.gov/moru; admission free, parking $10; 8am-

WHAT THE...?

Only four presidents on Mt Rushmore right? Well, maybe not. Nature may have provided a fifth. Drive 1.5 miles northwest from the Mt Rushmore parking entrance (away from Keystone) on Hwy 244 and look for a sheer rock face that's the backside of Mt Rushmore. Pull over safely and then decide just which president might be honored by the rather lurid shape on the rockface. Which head of state it represents may depend on your politics.

GREAT PLAINS

10pm summer, 8am-5pm rest of year). Displays here are aimed at short attention spans and give little feel for the massive physical effort of the team (led by sculptor Gutzon Borglum) who created the memorial between 1927 and 1941.

Fortunately, with a little walking, you can escape the crowds and commercialism and fully appreciate this magnificent work. The **Presidential Trail** loop leads near the monument for some fine nostril views and past the fascinating sculptors' studio. A **nature trail** to the right as you face the entrance connects the viewing and parking areas, passing through a pine forest.

Keystone

The nearest lodging and restaurants to Mt Rushmore are in Keystone, a one-time mining town now solely devoted to milking the monument. Gaudy motels vie with fudgeries for your attention.

Crazy Horse Memorial

The world's largest monument, the **Crazy Horse Memorial** (☎ 605-673-4681; www.crazyhorsememorial.org; US 385; person/carload $10/27; 🕑 7am-dusk summer, 8am-5pm rest of year) is, as author Ian Frazier describes, 'a ruin, only in reverse.' Onlookers at the 563ft-tall work-in-progress can gawk at what will be the Sioux leader astride his horse, pointing to the horizon saying, 'My lands are where my dead lie buried.'

Never photographed or persuaded to sign a meaningless treaty, Crazy Horse was chosen for a monument that Lakota Sioux elders hoped would balance the presidential focus of Mt Rushmore. In 1948 a Boston-born sculptor, the indefatigable Korczak Ziolkowski, started blasting granite. His family continue the work since his death in 1982. (It should also be noted that many Native Americans oppose the monument as desecration of sacred land.)

No one is predicting when the sculpture will be complete (the face was dedicated in 1998). A rather thrilling **laser-light show** that tells the story of the monument and what it represents is splashed across the rock face on summer evenings.

The huge **visitor center** includes a Native American museum, a cultural center where you can see artisans at work and Ziolkowski's studio. A bus ($4) takes you to the base of the mountain and during the Volksmarch (first weekend of June) you can climb up to the face.

You can sleep in a tipi in view of Crazy Horse's profile at the hokey but cute **Heritage Village** (☎ 605-673-5005; www.heritage-village.com; tent/tipi/cabin $16/23/42), 1 mile south.

SOUTH DAKOTA: DETOURS & EXTRAS

- **Hwy 14** runs across the middle of the state, crossing I-29 at Brookings (exit 133), then west to Pierre (p678) and on to Wall (p679). It meanders through a sea of grassland under big skies colored by long sunsets stretching across the broad horizon.
- Historic **Yankton**, a county seat on the Missouri River, has a well-preserved old center with cafés and stores selling second-hand books.

Custer State Park

The only reason 111-sq-mile **Custer State Park** (☎ 605-255-4515; www.custerstatepark.info; 7-day pass per person/carload $5/12) isn't a national park is that the state grabbed it first. It boasts one of the largest free-roaming bison herds in the world (about 1500), the famous 'begging burros' (donkeys seeking handouts) and more than 200 species of bird. Other wildlife include elk, pronghorns, mountain goats, bighorn sheep, coyotes, prairie dogs, mountain lions and bobcats.

The **Peter Norbeck Visitor Center** (☎ 605-255-4464; US 16A; 🕑 8am-8pm summer, 9am-5pm rest of year), on the east side of the park, has good exhibits and offers activities like gold-panning demonstrations and guided nature walks. The nearby **Black Hills Playhouse** (☎ 605-255-4141; www.blackhillsplayhouse.com; tickets $20-25) hosts summer theater.

Meandering over awesome stone bridges and across sublime Alpine meadows, the 18-mile Wildlife Loop Rd and the incredible 14-mile Needles Hwy (SD 87) are two superb drives in the park. The latter links with US 385 at either end.

Hiking through the pine-covered hills and prairie grassland (keep an eye out for rattlesnakes) is a great way to see wildlife and rock formations. The Sylvan Lake Shore, Sunday Gulch, Cathedral Spires and French Creek Natural Area trails are all highly recommended. Another rewarding hike is up the state's tallest mountain, **Harney Peak** (7242 ft). Swimming, fishing and boating on the park's lakes and climbing on its jagged rock spires are also popular.

You can pitch a tent in eight **campgrounds** (☎ 800-710-2267; www.campsd.com; campsites $16-22) around the park. At four, you can rent a well-equipped camping cabin for $45 per night. Reservations are vital in summer.

Backcountry camping ($4 per person per night) is allowed in the French Creek Natural Area. The park also has four impressive **resorts** (☎ 800-658-3530; www.custerresorts.com) with a mix of lodge rooms and cabins starting at $95 and going much higher. Book well ahead. The town of Custer, the main gateway into the park, has plenty of hotels and restaurants.

Wind Cave National Park

This park, protecting 44 sq miles of grassland and forest, sits just south of Custer State Park. The central feature is, of course, the cave, which has 132 miles of mapped passages. The cave's foremost feature is its 'boxwork' calcite formations (95% of all that are known exist here), which look like honeycomb and date back 60 to 100 million years. The strong gusts, felt at the entrance, but not inside, give the cave its name. Call the **visitor center** (☎ 605-745-4600; www.nps.gov/wica; 🕒 8am-7pm summer, reduced hr rest of year) for details on the variety of **tours** (adult $7-23, child $3.50-4.50) offered.

Hiking is a popular activity in the park, where you'll find the southern end of the 111-mile **Centennial Trail** to Sturgis (see p682); the visitor center has good info. The **campground** (campsites $6-12) rarely fills and backcountry camping (free with permit) is allowed in limited areas.

Jewel Cave National Monument

Another of the Black Hills' many fascinating caves is Jewel Cave, 13 miles west of Custer on US 16, so named because calcite crystals line nearly all of its walls. Currently 145 miles have been surveyed, making it the second longest known cave in the world, but it is presumed to be the longest. **Tours** (☎ 605-673-8300; adult $4-27, child free-$4) range in length and difficulty; reservations are recommended. Make arrangements at the **visitor center** (☎ 605-673-2288; www.nps.gov/jeca; 🕒 8am-5:30pm). If you'll only visit one Black Hills cave, this would be a good choice.

Hot Springs

This surprisingly attractive town, south of the main Black Hills circuit, boasts ornate 1890s red sandstone buildings and warm mineral springs feeding the Fall River.

You can fill your waterbottles at **Kidney Springs**, just south of the **visitor center** (☎ 800-325-6991; www.hotsprings-sd.com; 630 N River St; 🕒 7am-7pm summer) or swim at **Cascade Falls**, which is 71°F (22°C) all year, 11 miles south on US 71. The water at **Evans Plunge** (☎ 605-745-5165; www.evansplunge.com; 1145 N River St; adult/child $11/9; 🕒 10am-9pm summer, reduced hr rest of year), a giant indoor geothermal springs waterpark, is always 87°F (30.5°C).

The remarkable **Mammoth Site** (☎ 605-745-6017; www.mammothsite.com; 1800 US 18 bypass; adult/child $7.50/5.50; 🕒 8am-8pm May 15-Aug 15, reduced hrs rest of year) is the country's largest left-as-found mammoth fossil display. Hundreds of animals perished in a sinkhole here about 26,000 years ago. In July you can join paleontologists digging for more bones.

Red Rock River Resort (☎ 605-745-4400, 800-306-8921; www.redrockriverresort.com; 603 N River St; r $85-170; ⊠) has cozy and stylish rooms in a beautiful 1891 downtown building plus spa facilities (day passes for nonguests $20).

NEBRASKA

Those who just see Nebraska as 480 miles of blandness along I-80 are missing out on a lot. The Cornhusker state (they do grow a lot of the stuff) has beautiful river valleys and an often stark bleakness that is entrancing. Its links to the past – from vast fields of dinosaur remains to Native American culture to the toils of hardy settlers – provides a dramatic storyline. Dotted with cute little towns, Nebraska's two main cities, Omaha and Lincoln, are vibrant and artful.

The key to enjoying this long stoic stretch of country is to take the little roads, whether it's US 30 instead of I-80, US 20 to the Black Hills or the lonely and magnificent US 2.

History

Lewis and Clark followed the Missouri along Nebraska's eastern fringe and met with Native Americans here in 1804. Some 20 years later, trappers latched onto the Platte River. Then in 1841, the first covered wagon passed through on its way to Oregon. The Platte Valley was soon swarming with hopeful settlers (around

NEBRASKA FACTS

Nickname Cornhusker State
Population 1.8 million
Area 77,360 sq miles
Capital city Lincoln (population 225,600)
Other cities Omaha (population 419,545)
Sales Tax 5.5%
Birthplace of dancer Fred Astaire (1899–1987), actors Marlon Brando (1924–2004) and Hilary Swank (b 1974), civil rights leader Malcolm X (1925–65)
Home of Air Force generals
Famous for only unicameral state legislature, corn
Official beverage milk
Driving distances Omaha to the Wyoming border on I-80 480 miles, Omaha to Kansas City 186 miles

400,000), all looking to start a new life in the mythical West.

Transcontinental railroads such as the Union Pacific made covered wagons irrelevant and the trail ruts succumbed to pasture as more settlers rushed in after the 1862 Homestead Act. The rich soils and abundant grasslands helped Nebraska develop into a productive agricultural state.

Information

Nebraska Association of Bed & Breakfasts (☎ 877-223-6222; www.nabb1.com)
Nebraska state parks (☎ 800-826-7275; www.outdoornebraska.org) Vehicle permits cost $4/21 per day/year. Some campsites at popular parks are reservable; fees overall range from $7 to $25 per night.
Nebraska Travel & Tourism Division (☎ 877-632-7275; www.visitnebraska.org)

OMAHA

Be careful if you're planning a quick pit-stop in Omaha. Home to the vibrant brick-and-cobblestoned Old Market neighborhood downtown, a lively music scene and several quality museums, this town can turn a few hours into a few days. After all, billionaire Warren Buffet lives here and when is he ever wrong?

Omaha grew to prominence as a transport hub. Its location on the Missouri River and proximity to the Platte made it an important stop on the Oregon, California and Mormon Trails, and later the Union Pacific Railroad stretched west from here. These days Omaha is in the nation's top 10 for billionaires and Fortune 500 companies per capita.

Information

City Weekly (www.omahacityweekly.com) Free weekly newspaper with a good entertainment calendar.
Visitor center (☎ 866-937-6624; www.visitomaha.com; 1001 Farnam St; 🕒 9am-6pm Mon-Sat) Has a good coffee bar.

Sights & Activities

It's easy to spend much of your Omaha visit in **Old Market** on the river edge of downtown. This revitalized warehouse district, full of nightclubs, restaurants and funky shops, easily holds its own when it comes to aesthetics, energy and sophistication. Nearby parks boast fountains and waterside walks.

The much-admired and architecturally imposing **Joslyn Art Museum** (☎ 402-342-3300; www.joslyn.org; 2200 Dodge St; adult/child $7/4; 🕒 10am-4pm Tue-Sat, noon-4pm Sun) houses a great collection of 19th- and 20th-century European and American art and has a good selection of Western-themed works plus a new sculpture garden.

Another landmark, the art-deco Union Station train depot, is now the **Durham Museum** (☎ 402-444-5071; www.durhammuseum.org; 801 S 10th St; adult/child $7/5; 🕒 10am-8pm Tue, 10am-5pm Wed-Sat, 1-5pm Sun). It covers local history from the Lewis and Clark expedition to the Omaha stockyards. The soda fountain still serves hot dogs and phosphates.

Across the river in Council Bluffs, Iowa, the **Union Pacific Railroad Museum** (☎ 712-329-8307; www.uprr.com; 200 Pearl St; admission by donation; 🕒 10am-4pm Tue-Sat) tells the story of the company that rammed the transcontinental railroad west from here in the 1860s and continues today as one of the world's busiest railways.

After WWII Omaha's Offutt Air Force Base was home to the US Air Force Strategic Air Command, the force of nuclear bombers detailed in Stanley Kubrick's *Dr Strangelove*. This legacy is documented at the cavernous **Strategic Air & Space Museum** (☎ 402-827-3100; www.strategicairandspace.com; I-80 exit 426, Ashland; adult/child $8.50/4; 🕒 9am-5pm), which boasts a huge collection of bombers, from the B-52 to the B-17. Don't expect exhibits looking at the wider implications of bombing. It's 30 miles southwest of Omaha, well within the kill radius of a 1-megaton bomb.

Sleeping

There is a good mix of midrange and budget hotels along US 275 near 60th St, at I-80 exits 445 and 449 and across the river in Council Bluffs, Iowa at I-29 exit 51.

Omaha Magnolia Hotel (☎ 402-341-2500, 888-915-1110; www.magnoliahotelomaha.com; 1615 Howard St; r $110-200;) Not far from Old Market, the Magnolia is a new boutique hotel housed in a gorgeous 1923 Italianate highrise. The 145 rooms have a vibrant, modern style. Rates include a full buffet breakfast and bedtime milk and cookies.

Embassy Suites Omaha (☎ 402-346-9000, 800-445-8667; 555 South 10th St; r $120-200; P) This large 249-room modern hotel is in the middle of Old Market. The rooms are of the usual large size for this chain and extras include a full breakfast.

Eating & Drinking

The best thing you can do is just wander Old Market and see what you find.

our pick **Urban Wine Company** (☎ 402-934-0005; 1037 Jones St; small plates $4-9; 3pm-late Tue-Sat, noon-9pm Sun;) A real Old Market find. Sample glasses from a vast wine list and enjoy dishes such as a smoked salmon platter and prosciutto lavosh. The sumptuous lobster bisque is $4(!).

Upstream Brewing Company (☎ 402-344-0200; 514 S 11th St; mains $10-30; 11am-1am;) In a big old firehouse, the beer here is also big on flavor. The Caesar salads have enough garlic to propel you over the Missouri to Iowa. Steaks are thick and up to local standards. There are sidewalk tables, a rooftop deck and a huge bar.

Mister Toad's (☎ 402-345-4488; 1002 Howard St; noon-1am) Sit out front on benches under big trees or nab a corner table inside while you work through the beer and cocktail list. It's woodsy, worn and flirting with dive bar status. There's live jazz Sunday nights.

Getting There & Away

Amtrak's *California Zephyr* stops in Omaha on its run between Northern California and Chicago.

LINCOLN

Home to the historic Haymarket District and a lively bar scene thanks to the huge downtown campus of the University of Nebraska, Lincoln makes a good overnight stop. Nebraska's capital city is a very livable place and has more parks per capita than any other similarly sized US city.

The **visitor center** (☎ 800-423-8212; www.lincoln.org; 201 N 7th St, Haymarket; 9am-8pm Mon-Fri, 8am-2pm Sat, noon-4pm Sun) is inside Lincoln Station, where Amtrak's *California Zephyr* stops.

Sights & Activities

From the outside, Nebraska's remarkable 1932 400ft-high **State Capitol** (☎ 402-471-0448; 1445 K St; hourly tours free; 8am-5pm Mon-Fri, 10am-5pm Sat, 1-5pm Sun) represents the apex of phallic architecture (like many tall buildings in the Plains, it's often called the penis on the prairie), while the symbolically rich interior curiously combines classical and art-deco motifs. A 14th-floor observation deck is open to the public.

The **Museum of Nebraska History** (☎ 402-471-4754; www.nebraskahistory.org; 131 Centennial Mall N; admission free; 9am-4:30pm Mon-Fri, 1-4:30pm Sat & Sun) follows the Cornhusker State's story, starting with a large First Nebraskans room.

The **University of Nebraska** (www.unl.edu) has its main campus right downtown. The campus is as practical as a farmer and lacks real highlights but is an interesting stroll. However, you'll have more excitement than you can handle if you're in town on one of the six fall Saturdays when the Cornhuskers football team plays at home. Passions run high, especially as the team tries to overcome a recent streak of disappointments. The school lends much culture to Lincoln, including the following:

Sheldon Memorial Art Gallery (☎ 402-472-2461; www.sheldon.unl.edu; N 12th & R Sts; admission free; 10am-8pm Tue, to 5pm Wed-Sat, noon-5pm Sun) Focuses on American art from the 19th century to the present.

State Museum (☎ 402-472-2642; www.museum.unl.edu; N 14th & Vine Sts, Morrill Hall; adult/child $5/3; 9:30am-4:30pm Mon-Sat, 1:30-4:30pm Sun, to 8pm Thu) Covers natural history and anthropology with many hands-on dinosaur exhibits for children.

Sleeping

Most hotels are near I-80. Those around exit 403 are mostly midrange, while there are budget motels aplenty at exit 399.

Embassy Suites Hotel (☎ 402-474-1111, 800-362-2779; 1040 P St; ste incl breakfast from $129; P) This downtown Haymarket-handy hotel has 252 spacious rooms around a nine-story atrium. A full breakfast is included.

Anniversary Mansion B&B (☎ 402-438-4900, 877-907-4900; www.amansion.com; 1149 S 17th St; r $110-180;

GREAT PLAINS

) One of several elegant B&Bs in old mansions near downtown and the capitol, this one was built in 1902 and has an opulent wood interior and a grand colonnaded exterior. Extras like a 24-hour pantry abound.

Eating & Drinking

Lincoln's Haymarket District, a rejuvenated six-block warehouse area dating from the early 20th century, has numerous cafés, restaurants, coffeehouses and bars. If you're after falafel sandwiches followed by beer and body shots, follow the undergrads down O St to 14th St.

our pick **Indigo Bridge** (402-477-7770; 701 P St, Haymarket; meals $0-5; 8am-10pm;) Fantastic bookstore with a fine café serving coffees and snacks through the day. At lunch weekdays, enjoy hearty organic soup and bread and pay what you can afford.

Magnolia (402-477-5888; 301 N 8th St, Haymarket; mains $9-30; 11:30am-2pm, 5-9pm Mon-Sat;) One of Lincoln's best restaurants features a varied menu of seasonal specials and hearty standards like steaks. There's a long list of veggie options and foods are sourced locally and are often organic. The owner is a gracious charmer.

ALONG I-80

Shortly after Lincoln, I-80 runs an almost razor-straight 83 miles before hugging the Platte River. Several towns along its route to Wyoming make up for its often monotonous stretches. Whenever possible, use US 30 which bounces from one interesting burg to the next (Gothenburg, exit 211 is especially attractive), following the busy Union Pacific (UP) mainline the entire way.

Grand Island

The amazing **Stuhr Museum of the Prairie Pioneer** (308-385-5316; www.stuhrmuseum.org; I-80 exit 312; adult/child $8/6; 9am-5pm Mon-Sat, noon-5pm Sun) combines museum exhibits with a vast outdoor living museum. Note how conditions dramatically improved from the homes in 1860 to 1890 thanks to riches made possible by the railroad.

Upstream of Grand Island, the Platte hosts 500,000 sandhill cranes (80% of the world population) and 15 million waterfowl during the spring migration (mid-February to early April). **Wings Over the Platte Visitor Center** (308-382-4400; www.wingsovertheplatte.com; I-80 exit 305; tours $8-30; Mar-Apr) is a good place to break out the binoculars.

Kearney

The **Great Platte River Road Archway Monument** (877-511-2724; www.archway.org; adult/child $10/3; 9am-6pm summer, 9am-4pm rest of year) arches unexpectedly over I-80 east of Kearney near exit 272. The multimedia exhibits tell an engaging story of the people who've passed this way, from those riding wagon trains to those zipping down the Interstate.

Like all the I-80 towns, Kearney has no shortage of motels. The compact downtown, near US 30, has good cafés and bars including **Platte River Brewery** (308-237-0751; 14 E Railroad St; mains $4-10; noon-midnight), which has a beer garden over-looking the busy UP mainline.

North Platte

North Platte, a rail-fan mecca, is home to the **Buffalo Bill Ranch State Historical Park** (308-535-8035; www.ngpc.state.ne.us/parks; carload $4; 9am-5pm daily summer, 9am-4pm Mon-Fri Apr-May & Sep-Oct), 2 miles north of US 30. Once the home of Bill Cody, the father of rodeo and the famed Wild West Show, it's now a fun museum that reflects his colorful life.

Enjoy sweeping views of Union Pacific's **Bailey Yard**, the world's largest rail classification yard, from the **Golden Spike Tower** (308-532-9920; 1249 N Homestead Rd; adult/child $6/4; 9am-7pm Mon-Sat, from 1pm Sun summer, to 5pm rest of year), an eight-story observation tower with indoor and outdoor decks. From I-80, take exit 177.

ALONG US 20

The further west you go on US 20, the more space you'll see between towns, trees and pickup trucks. The western side of the

SCENIC DRIVE: HIGHWAY 2

Nebraska's **Hwy 2** branches northwest from I-80 and Grand Island through Broken Bow 272 miles to Alliance in the panhandle. It crosses the lonely and lovely **Sandhills** – 19,000 sq miles of sand dunes covered in grass – one of the country's most isolated areas. With the wind whistling in your ears, the distant call of a hawk and the biggest skies imaginable, this is pure iconic Great Plains travel.

NEBRASKA: DETOURS & EXTRAS

- **Carhenge** (☎ 308-762-1520; www.carhenge.com; Alliance; admission free) is a Stonehenge replica assembled from 38 discarded cars. The faithful reproduction, along with other car-part art, rises out of a field 3 miles north of town along Hwy 87, east of US 385, the road to the Black Hills.
- **Scotts Bluff National Monument** has been a beacon to travelers for centuries. Rising 800 feet above the flat plains of western Nebraska, it was an important waypoint on the Oregon Trail in the mid-19th century. You can still see wagon ruts today in the park. The **visitor center** (☎ 308-436-9700; www.nps.gov/scbl; Gering; per vehicle $5; 8am-7pm summer, to 5pm other times) has displays and can guide you to walks and drives. It's off US 26 south of Scottsbluff town.
- Here's Johnny! **Norfolk**, a mid-sized town in eastern Nebraska at the junction of US 81 and 275, was home to America's most popular late-night TV entertainer. The **Elkhorn Valley Museum** (☎ 402-371-3886; www.elkhornvalleymuseum.org; 515 Queen City Blvd; adult/child $6/3; 10am-5pm Tue-Sat) traces Johnny Carson's career.

road, known as the **Bridges to Buttes Byway**, is very beautiful.

Royal

Watch paleontologists work at **Ashfall Fossil Beds** (☎ 402-893-2000; www.ashfall.unl.edu; 86930 517th Ave; adult/child $5/3 plus vehicle permit $4; 9am-5pm Mon-Sat, 11am-5pm Sun, reduced hr May & Sep–mid-Oct), 8 miles northwest of town. You can see unearthed prehistoric skeletons of hundreds of animals, including rhinoceroses, buried 12 million years ago by ash from a Pompeii-like explosion in what is now Idaho.

Valentine

'America's Heart City' sits on the edge of the Sandhills and is a great base for canoeing, kayaking and inner-tubing the winding canyons of the federally protected **Niobrara River** (☎ 402-376-1901; www.nps.gov/niob). The river crosses the **Fort Niobrara National Wildlife Refuge** (☎ 402-376-3789; www.fws.gov/fortniobrara), home to hundreds of bison and elk plus a few waterfalls.

The hearts-and-flowers-themed **visitor center** (☎ 402-376-2969; www.visitvalentine.com; 253 N Main St; 9am-7pm Mon-Sat summer, 9am-5pm Mon-Fri rest of year) can steer you to one of many local outfitters for a river adventure.

Twenty miles south of town, the **Valentine National Wildlife Refuge** (☎ 402-376-1889; Hwy 83) has some superb Sandhills scenery and lots of lakes.

The classic red-brick **Trade Winds Motel** (☎ 402-376-1600, 888-376-1601; www.tradewindslodge.com; US 20 & 83; r $60-85;) has 32 comfy and clean rooms with fridges and microwaves.

Northern Panhandle

Get a feel for the tough lives led by early residents at the **Museum of the Fur Trade** (☎ 308-432-3843; www.furtrade.org; adult/child $5/free; 8am-5pm May-Oct), 3 miles east of Chadron, which includes the restored sod-roofed Bordeaux Trading Post, which swapped pelts for guns, blankets and whiskey from 1837 to 1876.

Fort Robinson State Park (☎ 308-665-2900; admission per vehicle $4; sunrise-sunset), 4 miles west of Crawford, is where Crazy Horse was killed in 1877 while in captivity.

At Harrison, detour 23 miles south on pastoral Hwy 29 to reach **Agate Fossil Beds National Monument** (☎ 308-668-2211; www.nps.gov/agfo; person/carload $3/5; 8am-6pm summer, 8am-4pm rest of year), a rich source of unusual fossils dating back 20 million years. The Native American artifact display is small but excellent.

KANSAS

Wicked witches and yellow-brick roads, hot-air balloons over fields of sunflowers and tornadoes powerful enough to pulverize entire towns are some of the gaudier images of Kansas. But the common image – amber waves of grain from north to south and east to west is closer to reality. But there's much more to the state than 13 billion loaves of bread and strands of spaghetti in the making.

There's a simple beauty to the green rolling hills and limitless horizons. Places such as Chase County beguile those who value

CHASING THE BIG BLOW

Much of the Great Plains is prone to severe weather, including violent thunderstorms, hail the size of softballs, spectacular lightening storms and more. But the real stars of these metrological nightmares are tornados. Far less benign than the cyclones that carried Dorothy off to Oz, tornados cause death and destruction from the Great Plains east across the central US. With winds of 300 mph or more, tornadoes are both awesome and terrifying. Still, each year many people visit the region hoping to spot a funnel cloud, drawn by the sheer spectacle and elemental drama.

Tour companies use gadget-filled vans to chase storms across multiple states, with no guarantee that you'll actually see a storm. Costs average $200 to $400 a day and May to August offer the best spotting. Operators include: **Cloud 9 Tours** (☎ 405-323-1145; www.cloud9tours.com), **Silver Lining Tours** (☎ 832-717-4712; www.silverliningtours.com) and **Tempest Tours** (☎ 817-274-9313; www.tempesttours.com).

For a completely over-hyped look at the world of storm spotters – in the best Hollywood tradition – check out the 1996 movie *Twister*. Read the recollections of veteran tornado chaser Roger Hill in *Hunting Nature's Fury*.

understatement. Gems abound, from the amazing space museum in Hutchinson to the indie music clubs of Lawrence. Most importantly, follow the Great Plains credo of ditching the interstate for the two-laners and make your own discoveries. The website, www.kansassampler.org, is a brilliant resource for finding the best the state has to offer.

History

Kansas' history has been pretty tumultuous. The state played a key role in sparking the Civil War when the Kansas–Nebraska Act of 1854 allowed settlers in these territories to vote on whether slavery would exist in each state. Immediately, swarms of settlers on both sides of the question flooded the territories, hoping to swing the vote in their favor. Election fraud was rampant and clashing views led to widespread violence. Known as 'Bleeding Kansas,' this volatile era lasted until January 1861, when Kansas was admitted as a free state. The Civil War began 10 weeks later.

Growing pains continued: early settlers wiped out herds of bison and expelled the Native Americans (even the state's namesake Kansa relocated to Oklahoma in 1873). Before long – partly due to prohibitionist Carrie Nation, who swept through Kansas in 1900 wielding her axe against the evils of drink – the Sunflower State was transformed from rip-roaring open range into some of the world's most productive wheatlands. The children of Mennonites who emigrated from the steppes of Russia during the 1870s brought with them handfuls of the now-famous 'Turkey Red' wheat, which made itself thoroughly at home.

Over the last decade religious fanatics in Kansas have fought to teach creationism in schools instead of evolution. However, for the time being, biology curriculums still only contain science.

Information

Kansas Bed & Breakfast Association (☎ 888-572-2632; www.kbba.com)

Kansas state parks (☎ 620-672-5911; www.kdwp.state.ks.us) Per vehicle per day/year $4.20/24.70. Campsites cost $7.50 to $11.

Kansas Travel & Tourism (☎ 785-296-2009; www.travelks.com)

WICHITA

From its early cowtown days at the head of the Chisholm Trail in the 1870s to its current claim as Air Capital of the World (thanks to about half the world's general aviation aircraft being built here by the likes of Cessna *et al.*), Kansas' largest city has always been a prosperous place. It's a worthwhile stopover but not at the expense of the rest of the state.

Orientation & Information

Wichita's historic, all-brick Old Town, good for shopping, eating and drinking, is on the east side of downtown while the park-like Museums on the River district fills a triangle of green space between the Big and Little Arkansas Rivers to the west.

The **visitor center** (☎ 800-288-9424; www.visitwichita.com; 100 S Main; ⏰ 8am-5pm Mon-Fri) is geared towards conventions.

Sights

The Museums on the River district includes the first three places in the following section plus botanical gardens and a science museum aimed at kids.

Guarded by Wichita artist Blackbear Bosin's 44-foot statue 'Keeper of the Plains,' the **Mid-America All-Indian Center** (☎ 316-262-5221; www.theindiancenter.org; 650 N Seneca St; adult/child $7/3; ⏰ 10am-4pm Tue-Sat) has exhibits of Native American art and artifacts and a traditional Wichita-style grass lodge.

The **Wichita Art Museum** (☎ 316-268-4921; www.wichitaartmuseum.org; 1400 W Museum Blvd; adult/child $5/2, free Sat; ⏰ 10am-5pm Tue-Sat, noon-5pm Sun) is home to a good collection of American art, including pieces by Frederick Remington and Mary Cassatt.

Old Cowtown (☎ 316-660-1871; www.oldcowtown.org; 1865 Museum Blvd; adult/child $8/5.50; ⏰ 10am-5pm Fri, Sat & Mon, noon-5pm Sun Jun-Oct; ♿) is an open-air museum that recreates the Wild West (as seen on TV…). Pioneer-era buildings, staged gunfights and guides in cowboy costumes thrill kids.

With a complete T-Rex, Egyptian mummies, Greek pottery, Abraham Lincoln's walking cane, military relics, a sports hall of fame and much more, Old Town's **Museum of World Treasures** (☎ 888-700-1311; www.worldtreasures.org; 835 E 1st St; adult/child $9/7; ⏰ 10am-5pm Mon-Sat, noon-5pm Sun) has something for everyone.

Sleeping

Hotbeds for chains include I-135 exit 1AB, I-35 exit 50 and the Hwy 96 Rock Rd and Webb Rd exits. Broadway north of the center offers a mixed bag of indie cheapies.

Cambridge Suites (☎ 316-263-1061, 866-822-6274; www.cambridge-suites.com; 711 S Main St; r $80-140; P ❄ 📶 🏊) On the south edge of downtown, suites here range up to two-bedroom in size and have kitchens. It's modern and commodious, perfect for families or quarreling couples.

Hotel at Old Town (☎ 316-267-4800, 877-265-3869; www.hotelatoldtown.com; 830 1st St; r $120-200; P ❄ 💻 📶) In the midst of nightlife, this restored 1906 hotel is the pick compared to some nearby upscale chains. All rooms are suites and have kitchenettes.

Eating & Drinking

Wichita is the home of Pizza Hut, but that's far from the pinnacle of the city's dining options. For some real-deal Mexican or Vietnamese, drive north on Broadway and take your pick. Old Town has a fun **Farmers Market** (⏰ 7am-noon Sat May-Oct).

Nu Way Cafe (☎ 316-267-1131; 1416 W Douglas Ave; mains $2-5; ⏰ 11am-9pm) Frosty glasses of homemade root beer are among the highlights at this west-of-downtown outlet of a beloved Wichita chain. Old-style Formica is a backdrop for delicate onion rings, loose meat sandwiches and much more.

our pick **Doc's Steak House** (☎ 316-264-4735; 1515 N Broadway; mains $5-12; ⏰ 11am-9pm) Once owned by the brother of the genius that started Wall Drugs (p679), this local institution is home to the wildly addictive garlic salad (trust us, plunge in, order a double). Steaks, chicken-fried steak and pork chops are amazing bargains.

Club Indigo (☎ 316-265-6760; 126 N Mosley; ⏰ 4pm-late) A vibey Old Town joint popular with local scenesters (such as they are); the rooftop deck is a fine place for a frilly cocktail on a balmy evening.

ALONG I-70

What it lacks in glamour, Kansas' 420-mile 'Main Street' makes up for in efficiency, quickly shuttling you from Kansas City to the Colorado border. The scenery can be monotonous, but there are many interesting stops along the way. West of Salina, the landscape around I-70 stretches into rolling, wide-open plains, with winds sometimes strong enough to knock over 18-wheelers. US 50 (p694) and US 56 (p694) are intriguing alternatives.

KANSAS FACTS

Nickname Sunflower State
Population 2.8 million
Area 82,282 sq miles
Capital city Topeka (population 122,400)
Other cities Wichita (population 357,698)
Sales Tax 5.3%
Birthplace of aviator Amelia Earhart (1897–1937), temperance crusader Carrie Nation (1846–1911), TV talker Dr Phil (b 1950), Pizza Hut (established 1958), singer-songwriter Melissa Etheridge (b 1961)
Home of Dorothy and Toto (of *Wizard of Oz* fame)
Famous for wheat
Official state song 'Home on the Range'
Driving distances Wichita to Kansas City 200 miles, Dodge City to Abilene 188 miles

KANSAS: DETOURS & EXTRAS

- **Nicodemus** is the only surviving town in the west built by emancipated slaves from the south after the Civil War. A national park **visitor center** (☎ 785-839-4233; www.nps.gov/nico; admission free; 8:30am-5pm) recounts the town's history and the experience of African Americans in the west. The town is on US 24 about 35 miles north of I-70 via US 183 or US 283.
- **Monument Rocks** are 80ft-tall pyramid-shaped chalk formations that look like a Jawa hangout in *Star Wars*. Go 25 miles southeast of Oakley via US 83 off I-70 exit 76.
- **Lindsborg** flaunts its Swedish roots while brick streets and lots of art galleries boost the appeal. The **Old Mill Museum** (☎ 785-227-3595; 120 Mill St; adult/child $2/1; 9am-5pm Mon-Sat, 1-5pm Sun) is inside an 1898 flour mill. Enjoy lots of dishes made with berries in summer. The town is just west of I-135 exit 72.
- **Legendary fried chicken** is a hallmark of six restaurants in far southeastern Crawford County. Try **Chicken Mary's** (☎ 620-231-9510; 1133 E 600th Ave, Pittsburg; meals from $6; 11am-8pm), which isn't far from where Route 66 crosses into Kansas.

Lawrence

Lawrence, 40 miles west of Kansas City, has been an oasis of progressive politics from the start. Founded by abolitionists in 1854 and an important stop on the Underground Railroad, it became a battlefield in the clash between pro- and antislavery factions. In 1863, the Missouri 'Bushwhackers' of William Clarke Quantrill raided Lawrence, killing nearly 200 people and burning much of it to the ground. The city survived, however, and so did its free-thinking spirit, which is fitting for the home of the **University of Kansas** (KU; www.ku.edu).

The **Visitor Information Center** (☎ 888-529-5267; www.visitlawrence.com; 402 N 2nd St; 8:30am-5:30pm Mon-Sat, 1-5pm Sun summer, 9am-5pm Mon-Sat, 1-5pm Sun rest of year) offers self-guided and iPod tours of Lawrence's antislavery heritage and sites.

The walkable downtown, where townies and students merge, centers on **Massachusetts Street**, one of the most pleasant streets in this part of the country for a stroll. KU's **Spencer Museum of Art** (☎ 785-864-4710; www.spencerart.ku.edu; 1301 Mississippi St; admission free; 10am-4pm Tue-Sat, noon-4pm Sun, to 8pm Thu) isn't large, but has a collection encompassing work by Western artist Frederic Remington and many European masters.

SLEEPING & EATING

Lawrence's motels cluster at the junction of US 40 and US 59 south of I-70.

Halcyon House B&B (☎ 785-841-0314, 888-441-0314; www.thehalcyonhouse.com; 1000 Ohio St; r $55-99; P ⊠ ✻ ≈) The nine cute bedrooms (some share bathrooms) have lots of natural light, and there's a landscaped garden and home-made baked goods for breakfast. Downtown is a short walk.

Eldridge Hotel (☎ 785-749-5011, 800-527-0909; www.eldridgehotel.com; 701 Massachusetts St; r from $140; P ⊠ ✻ ▣ ≈) The modern two-room suites at this historic 1926 downtown hotel have antique-style furnishings. The bar and restaurant are stylish; the ghost misunderstood (rumors abound).

our pick **Local Burger** (☎ 785-856-7827; 714 Vermont St; mains $4-8; 11am-9pm Mon-Sat, 11am-8pm Sun; ⊠) Just like Lawrence meeting Kansas, New Age meets the burger joint here. The veggie burger is amazing and there are scores of healthy and organic options. But you can also chow down on a damn fine bacon cheeseburger.

Free State Brewing (☎ 785-843-4555; 636 Massachusetts St; mains $6-15; 11am-late) One of many good places en masse downtown, this is the first brewery in Kansas since Carrie Nation got one closed in 1880. A cut above brew-pub standards, the beers are excellent. The food is much-loved as well, leaning towards cheesy thirst-inducing classics.

The music scene is up to college town standards and the **Bottleneck** (☎ 785-841-5483; www.bottlenecklive.com; 737 New Hampshire) usually has the best of the newest.

Topeka

Kansas and its vital role in America's race relations is symbolized in the otherwise humdrum state capital of Topeka.

It took real guts to challenge the segregationist laws common in the US in the 1950s and the stories of these courageous men and women are told at the **Brown vs Board of**

Education National Historic Site (☎ 785-354-4273; www.nps.gov/brvb; 1515 SE Monroe St; admission free; ⌚ 9am-5pm). It's set in Monroe Elementary School, one of Topeka's African American schools at the time of the landmark 1954 Supreme Court decision that banned segregation in US schools. Displays cover the whole Civil Rights movement.

The city's **visitor center** (☎ 800-235-1030; www.visittopeka.travel; 1275 SW Topeka Blvd; ⌚ 8am-5pm Mon-Thu, 8am-4:30pm Fri) can guide you to other sites that include the domed, DC-wannabe **State Capitol** (☎ 785-296-3966; 300 SW 10th St; ⌚ 8am-5pm daily, tours 9am-3pm Mon-Fri). Don't miss the fiery John Steuart Curry mural of abolitionist John Brown.

From a Cheyenne war lance to Carrie Nation's hammer, the engaging **Kansas History Center** (☎ 785-272-8681; www.kshs.org; 6425 SW 6th Ave; adult/child $5/3; ⌚ 9am-5pm Tue-Sat, 1-5pm Sun) is packed with stories of the state.

Abilene

In the late 19th century, Abilene was a rowdy cowtown at the end of the Chisholm Trail. Today its compact core of historic brick buildings and well-preserved residential neighborhoods seems perfectly appropriate for the birthplace of Dwight D Eisenhower (1890–1969), president and WWII general.

The **visitor center** (☎ 800-569-5915; www.abilenekansas.org; 201 NW 2nd St; ⌚ 8am-6pm Mon-Sat, 10am-4pm Sun summer, reduced hr rest of year) has free samples of Mamie Eisenhower's sugar cookies.

The **Eisenhower Center** (☎ 785-263-6700; www.dwightdeisenhower.com; 200 SE 4th St; museum adult/child $8/1, other sites free; ⌚ 8am-5:45pm summer, 9am-4:45pm rest of year) includes Ike's boyhood home, a museum and library, and his and Mamie's graves. Displays will help you put the Eisenhower era (1953–61) and its formative role for modern America in context.

The **Brookville Hotel** (☎ 785-263-2244; meals $14; ⌚ 11am-2pm & 4-7.30pm Wed-Sun) has been serving fried chicken since Ike graduated from West Point (1915). Cream-style corn, fresh biscuits and much more come with every meal.

Lucas

'Outsider art,' meaning works created outside the bounds of traditional culture, has blossomed in tiny Lucas. Samuel Dinsmoor began it all in 1907 by filling his yard with enormous concrete sculptures espousing his eccentric philosophies. His **Garden of Eden** (☎ 785-525-6395; www.garden-of-eden-lucas-kansas.com; 301 2nd St; adult/child $6/1; ⌚ 10am-5pm May-Oct, 1-4pm Mar-Apr, 1-4pm Sat & Sun Nov-Feb) is visible from the sidewalk, but paid admission lets you hear some wonderful stories and see his remains in a glass-topped coffin.

The phenomenal **Grassroots Art Center** (☎ 785-525-6118; www.grassrootsart.net; 213 S Main St; adult/child $6/2; ⌚ 10am-5pm Mon-Sat, 1-5pm Sun May-Sep, 10am-4pm Mon & Thu-Sat, 1-4pm Sun Oct-Apr) has gathered works made of materials such as buttons, barbed wire, pull-tabs and strange machines by self-taught, self-motivated artists from around Kansas.

The best way to reach Lucas is along the **Post Rock Scenic Byway**, a scenic 18-mile jaunt past Wilson Lake starting at exit 206.

Hays

The town of Hays grew up around its namesake fort, built in the 1860s to protect railroad workers from Native Americans, but most people stop today for a look much further into the past at the domed **Sternberg Museum of Natural History** (☎ 877-332-1165; www.fhsu.edu/sternberg; 3000 Sternberg Dr; adult/child $8/5; ⌚ 9am-7pm

WORTH THE TRIP: HUTCHISON

Possibly the most surprising sight in Kansas, the amazing **Cosmosphere & Space Center** (☎ 800-397-0330; www.cosmo.org; 1100 N Plum St; all-day pass adult/child $13/10.50, museum only $8/7.50; ⌚ 9am-9pm Mon-Sat, noon-9pm Sun summer, closing 6pm Sun-Thu rest of year) captures the race to the moon better than any museum on the planet. Absorbing displays and artifacts like the Apollo 13 command module will enthrall you for hours.

All puns aside, the museum's isolated location in Hutchinson might as well be the Moon, but if you're making a day trip from Witchita or just stopping off in this small city of huge grain elevators, see what flour can do in the homemade tortillas at **Anchor Inn** (☎ 620-669-0311; 128 S Main St; meals $5-9; ⌚ 11am-8pm), a family-run Mexican restaurant that draws people from several counties to its fresh fare.

Tue-Sat, 1-7pm Sun). It houses many unusual fossils, including its famous fish-within-a-fish, and animated dinosaurs.

ALONG US 50

Fabled US 50 splits off from I-35 at Emporia and follows the old Santa Fe mainline west through classic Kansas vistas. Along the way it passes through two places no Kansas visitor should miss.

Chase County

Nearly a perfect square, this is the county William Least Heat-Moon examined mile by mile in his best-selling *Prairyerth*.

The beautiful Flint Hills roll through here and are home to two-thirds of the nation's remaining tallgrass prairie. The 10,894-acre **Tallgrass Prairie National Preserve** (☎ 620-273-8494; www.nps.gov/tapr; admission free; 9am-4:30pm), 2 miles northwest of Strong City and US 50, is a perfect place to hike the prairie and revel in its ever-changing colorful flowers. Rangers offer tours of the preserved ranch and **bus tours** (adult/child $5/3; 11am, 1pm & 3pm May-Oct) of the prairie.

The rangers also have maps of some evocative remote drives in the county as well as a tour of sights on Moon's book. Don't miss the show-stopping **County Courthouse** in Cottonwood Falls, 2 miles south of Strong City. Completed in 1873, it is a fantasy of French Renaissance style.

ALONG US 56

US 56 follows the old Santa Fe Trail to Dodge City through the heart of the heartland. Most sights along here are also easily reached from US 50.

The large Mennonite communities around **Hillsboro** are descendants of Russian immigrants who brought the 'Turkey Red' strain of wheat to the Plains, where it thrived despite harsh conditions. The **Mennonite Settlement Museum** (☎ 620-947-3775; www.hillsboro-museums.com; 501 S Ash St; adult/child $3/1; 10am-noon & 1:30-4pm Tue-Fri, 2-4pm Sat & Sun, closed Jan-Feb) preserves a Russian clay brick house, one-room schoolhouse and replica windmill.

A further 110 miles west in **Larned**, the **Santa Fe Trail Center Museum** (☎ 620-285-2054; www.santafetrailcenter.org; 1349 Hwy 156; adult $4, child $1.50-2.50; 9am-5pm, closed Mon Sep-May) details the vital route linking the US and Mexico for much of the 19th century. Six miles west of town on Hwy 156, **Fort Larned National Historic Site** (☎ 620-285-6911; www.nps.gov/fols; admission free; 8:30am-4:30pm) is a remarkably well-preserved Santa Fe Trail fort.

Dodge City

Dodge City, where famous lawmen Bat Masterson and Wyatt Earp tried, sometimes successfully, to keep law and order, had a notorious reputation during the 1870s and 1880s. The long-running TV series *Gunsmoke* (1955–75) spurred tourism and big crowds have got the heck *into* Dodge ever since. Geared towards families, historical authenticity here plays a distant second fiddle to fun and frolic.

Tours (adult/child $6/4; 9:30am, 10:45am, 1:30pm & 3pm summer) on fake trolleys start at the **visitor center** (☎ 800-653-9378; www.visitdodgecity.org; 400 W Wyatt Earp Blvd; 8am-6:30pm summer, 8:30am-5pm Mon-Fri Sep-Apr). Expect to hear a lot of well-spun apocryphal yarns. Self-guided audio

ROUTE 66: GET YOUR KICKS IN KANSAS

Only 13 miles of Route 66 pass through the southeast corner of Kansas, but it's a good drive.

The first town you hit after Joplin, **Galena**, has been in the decline since even before the last of the area's lead and zinc mines closed in the 1970s.

Three miles down the road is **Riverton**, where you might consider a detour 20 miles north to Pittsburg for some famous fried chicken (p692).

Cross US 400 and stay on old Route 66 to the 1923 **Marsh Rainbow Arch Bridge**, the last of its kind.

From the bridge, it's less than 3 miles south to **Baxter Springs**, the site of a Civil War massacre and numerous bank robberies. The multifaceted **Baxter Springs Heritage Center** (☎ 620-856-2385; www.baxterspringsmuseum.org; 740 East Ave; admission free; 10am-4:30pm Mon-Sat, 1-4:30pm Sun Apr-Oct, closed Mon-Wed Nov-Mar) has helped restore a 1939 Phillips 66 gas station into the **Kansas Route 66 Visitor Center** (☎ 620-856-2066; 10am-5pm Mon-Sat). Military Ave (US 69A) takes you into Oklahoma.

tours and free maps let you visit on your own schedule.

The studio-backlot-like **Boot Hill Museum** (☎ 620-227-8188; www.boothill.org; adult/child summer $8/7.50, rest of year $7/6.50; 8am-8pm summer, 9am-5pm Sep-Apr) includes a cemetery, jail and saloon, where gunslingers re-enact high-noon shootouts while Miss Kitty and her dancing gals do the cancan.

Escape the schmaltz and view surviving **Santa Fe Trail wagon-wheel ruts** about 9 miles west of town on US 50. The site is well marked.

Chain and indie motels line Business US 50, aka Wyatt Earp Blvd.

OKLAHOMA

Oklahoma gets its name from the Choctaw name for 'Red People.' One look at the state's vividly red earth and you'll wonder if the name is more of a sartorial than an ethnic comment. Still, with 39 tribes located here, it is a place with deep Native American significance. Museums, cultural displays and more abound.

The other side of the Old West coin, cowboys, also figure prominently in the Sooner State. Although pickups have replaced horses, there's still a great sense of the open range, interrupted only by urban Oklahoma City and Tulsa. Oklahoma's share of Route 66 (see p696) links some of the Mother Road's iconic highlights and there are myriad atmospheric old towns. And just when it seems the vistas go on forever, mountains in the south and far west add texture.

History

Early on, Wichita, Arapaho, Comanche and Osage people populated or used this land. By 1834 it (minus the panhandle) had been declared autonomous Indian Territory and tribes from across the nation were relocated here, often at gunpoint. In one of the most dramatic examples, more than 4000 of 15,000 Cherokee perished of cold and hunger while marching the 'Trail of Tears' to the territory in the winter of 1838–39.

In the 1880s, before the US gave the go-ahead to take over Native American lands yet again, eager homesteaders (Sooners) crossed territory lines to stake claims. That's right: the Sooner State is named for lawbreakers. In April 1889, settlement to non-Native Americans was officially opened and towns emerged overnight in the Great Land Rush.

Statehood in 1907 was followed by another boom when oil was discovered in the 1920s, but the Depression and soil erosion hurt the state badly. Thousands of 'Okie' farmers migrated west on Route 66 to find a better life. The state's agricultural industry eventually rebounded, due to greater care for the fragile Plains environment. The oil and gas industries continue to be major employers.

OKLAHOMA FACTS

Nickname Sooner State
Population 3.65 million
Area 69,900 sq miles
Capital city Oklahoma City (population 550,000)
Other cities Tulsa (population 382,872)
Sales Tax 4.5%
Birthplace of humorist Will Rogers (1879–1935), athlete Jim Thorpe (1888–1953), folk musician Woody Guthrie (1912–67), parking meters (invented 1935), actor Brad Pitt (b 1963)
Home of the band Flaming Lips
Famous for 1930s dust bowl, Carrie Underwood
Official state meal okra, chicken fried steak and 10 more dishes
Driving distances Oklahoma City to Tulsa 104 miles, Kansas to Texas following historic Route 66 426 miles

Information

Oklahoma Bed & Breakfast Association (☎ 866-676-5522; www.oklabedandbreakfast.com)
Oklahoma Dept of Tourism (☎ 800-652-6552; www.travelok.com)
Oklahoma state parks (☎ 800-654-8240; www.touroklahoma.com) Most parks are free for day-use; campsites average $10 per night, cabins are more. Campsites cost $10 to $26 per night; some are reservable.

OKLAHOMA CITY

Often abbreviated to OKC, Oklahoma City is nearly dead-center in the state and is the cultural and political capital. It has worked hard over the years to become more than just a cowtown, all without turning its back on its cowboy heritage. It makes a good pause on your Route 66 travels and has numerous attractions plus good restaurants that offer more than just chicken fried steak.

ROUTE 66: GET YOUR KICKS IN OKLAHOMA

Oklahoma's connection with America's Main Street runs deep: the road's chief proponent, Cyrus Avery, came from here; John Steinbeck's *Grapes of Wrath* told of the plight of Depression-era Okie farmers fleeing west on Route 66; and Oklahoma has more miles of the original alignment than any other state. The **Oklahoma Route 66 Association** (www.oklahomaroute66.com) puts out an excellent 88-page booklet that you can pick up from most visitor centers along the road or download off the web. It's vital because so many of the brown-and-white Historic Route 66 signs have been stolen for souvenirs and the original road goes by a variety of monikers, including OK 66, US 69, US 270 etc.

Shortly after you enter the state from Kansas on US 69A you'll come to Miami. Continue south through town on Main St and 2.5 miles after crossing the Neosho River turn right at the T-intersection. This will take you to the first of two original and very rough 9ft wide alignments. The second, E 140 Rd (turn west) comes soon after the first, just before I-44.

You'll cross I-44 twice before rolling into Vinita. **Clanton's** (☎ 918-256-9053; 319 E Illinois Ave; mains $4-10; 🕑 5:30am-8pm Mon-Fri, to 2pm Sat & Sun) dates back to 1927 and is the place for chicken fried steak and calf fries (don't ask).

Thirty miles further on, Foyil is worth a 4-mile detour on Hwy 28A to the massive and colorful concrete sculptures of **Totem Pole Park** (☎ 918-342-9149; www.rchs1.org; admission free; 🕑 24/7)

Another 10 miles brings you to Claremore (p702), former home of Will Rogers.

Next up at the port city of Catoosa, just before Tulsa, is one of the most photographed Route 66 landmarks, the 80ft-long **Blue Whale** (2680 N Hwy 66).

East 11th St takes you into and right through art deco–rich Tulsa; be sure to look for the neon wonder of the restored **Meadow Gold sign** at S Quaker Ave. Southwest Blvd takes you across the river and out of town.

The rural route from Tulsa to Oklahoma City is one of the longest continuous stretches of Mother Road remaining (110 miles), a fine alternative to the I-44 tollway that it snakes around. At Chandler, 60 miles southwest of Tulsa, the **Route 66 Interpretive Center** (☎ 405-258-1300; 400 E Rte 66; adult/child $5/4; 🕑 10am-5pm Tue-Sat) recreates the experience of driving the road through the decades.

In Arcadia, 23 miles northeast of downtown OKC, stop at the cavernous, red **Round Barn** (☎ 405-396-0824; www.arcadiaroundbarn.org; admission free; 🕑 10am-5pm daily summer, closed Mon winter); its restoration by volunteers is a good story.

Route 66 follows US 77 into Oklahoma City and beyond that, it's unmarked. Take Kelley Ave south, head over to Lincoln Blvd at 50th St and turn west on NW 23rd St at the capitol. You'll leave OKC by turning north on May Ave and west on NW 39th St where **Ann's Chicken Fry House** (see p699) and the **66 Bowl** (☎ 405-946-3966; 3810 NW 39th St) are fun and photogenic. Beyond this, the route follows Business I-40.

El Reno, 20 miles west of OKC, is home to the fried onion burger (average $3), a road food classic. Among several historic drive-ins and dives, try **Jobe's** (☎ 405-262-0194; 1220 W Sunset) or **Robert's** (☎ 405-262-1262; 300 S Bickford Ave). Ground beef is combined with raw onions and then cooked and caramelized on the grill. Both are open 11am to 9pm.

Another 30 miles west, **Lucille's**, a 1929 gas station fronting the freeway just west of Hydro, was run by the same woman for 59 years.

In Clinton, walk through six decades of history, memorabilia and music at the spiffy **Route 66 Museum** (☎ 580-323-7866; www.route66.org; 2229 W Gary Blvd; adult/child $3/1; 🕑 9am-7pm Mon-Sat, 1-6pm Sun summer, closed at 5pm rest of year, closed Sun-Mon Dec-Jan). Fuel up at iconic **Jiggs Smokehouse** (☎ 580-323-5641; meals $5-10; 🕑 11am-7pm Tue-Fri, 11am-5pm Sat), a haven for lovers of smoked meats at the Exit 62 on I-40, 3 miles west of town.

Thirty miles further west in Elk City, the **National Route 66 Museum** (☎ 580-225-6266; adult/child $5/4; 🕑 9am-7pm Mon-Sat, 1-5pm Sun summer, 9am-5pm Mon-Sat, 2-5pm Sun rest of year) has old cars, photos and is part of a re-created pioneer town and a farm museum.

Route 66 spills into Texas at **Texola**, which is just a dust devil away from being a ghost town.

The city is forever linked to the 1995 bombing of the Alfred P Murrah Federal Building and the memorials to this tragedy are moving and worthy stops.

History

Oklahoma City literally sprang up overnight after unassigned Indian Territory lands were opened to white settlement on April 22, 1889. More than 10,000 land claimants rushed into the wilderness and staked out their piece of the pie around the Santa Fe railroad station. The city yanked capital honors out from under Guthrie in 1910 and was catapulted into wealth in 1928 when OKC's first gusher erupted above a vast oil field.

Information

Full Circle Bookstore (☎ 405-842-2900; in 50 Penn Pl mall; 🕑 10am-9pm Mon-Thu, 10am-10pm Fri & Sat, noon-5pm Sun; 📶) Superb independent bookstore that stocks many Route 66 books and has a café.
Oklahoma City Visitors Center (☎ 800-225-5652; www.visitokc.com; 189 W Sheridan Ave; 🕑 8:30am-5pm Mon-Fri)
Oklahoma Welcome Center (☎ 405-478-4637; www.travelok.com; 1-35 exit 137; 🕑 8:30am-5pm) Has city info too.
OU Medical Center (☎ 405-271-4700; 700 NE 13th St) Has a 24hr emergency room.
Post office (☎ 405-232-2198; 305 NW 5th St; 🕑 7am-9pm Mon-Fri, 8am-5pm Sat)
Ronald J Norick Downtown Library (☎ 405-231-8650; 300 Park Ave; 🕑 9am-9pm Mon-Thu, 9am-6pm Fri, 9am-5pm Sat, 1-6pm Sun; 📶) One-hour free internet with photo ID.

Sights

The story of America's worst incident of domestic terrorism is told at the engrossing **Oklahoma City National Memorial Museum** (☎ 888-542-4673; www.oklahomacitynationalmemorial.org; 620 N Harvey Ave; adult/student $8/6; 🕑 9am-6pm Mon-Sat, 1-6pm Sun, box office closes 1hr earlier). The outdoor **Symbolic Memorial** (N Harvey Ave; admission free; 🕑 24hr) has 168 empty chair sculptures for each of the people killed in the attack (the 19 small ones are for the children who perished in the day care center). It's next to a reflecting pool in the former building's footprint. People tie simple yet heart-breaking memorials to the fence on Harvey St.

Also downtown, the **Oklahoma City Museum of Art** (☎ 405-236-3100; www.okcmoa.com; 415 Couch Dr; adult/child $12/10; 🕑 10am-5pm Tue-Sat, to 9pm Thu, noon-5pm Sun) displays good 20th-century American art.

Only the smells are missing at the **National Cowboy & Western Heritage Museum** (☎ 405-478-2250; www.nationalcowboymuseum.org; 1700 NE 63rd St; adult/child $10/4.50; 🕑 9am-5pm), which covers both art and history. Even if you come for just one, you're sure to be enthralled by the other. The excellent collection of Western painting and sculpture features many works by Charles M Russell and Frederic Remington while the historical galleries range from barbed wire to rodeos to cowboy hats.

You'll brush up against real cowboys in **Stockyards City** (www.stockyardscity.org; Agnew Ave & Exchange Ave), southwest of downtown, either in the shops and restaurants that cater to them or at the **Oklahoma National Stockyards** (🕑 auctions 9am Mon-Tue), the world's largest stocker and feeder cattle market.

The vast **Oklahoma History Center** (☎ 405-522-5248; www.okhistorycenter.org; 2401 N Laird Ave; adult/child $5/3; 🕑 9am-5pm Mon-Sat, noon-5pm Sun) makes people the focus as it tells the story of the Sooner state. It's across the street from the **State Capitol** (☎ 405-522-0836; 2300 N Lincoln Blvd; 🕑 7am-7pm Mon-Fri, 9am-4pm Sat & Sun), which was built in 1917, but only got its dome in 2002.

Festivals & Events

Red Earth Native American Cultural Festival (☎ 405-427-5228; www.redearth.org; adult/child from $10/7.50) Native Americans come from across the nation to celebrate and compete in early June.
State Fair Park (☎ 405-948-6704; www.okstatefairpark.com; I-44 & NW 10th St) The fairgrounds host frequent horse- or rodeo-related events. (The state fair itself is a dud.)

Sleeping

Many older motels line I-35 south of town; newer chain properties stack up along I-44 and the NW Expwy.

Carlyle Motel (☎ 405-946-3355; 3600 NW 39th St; r from $40; P ✖) Little has changed (other than the sheets) since the 1950s at this simple 15-room place, which is popular with Route 66 buffs.

Hampton Inn & Suites (☎ 405-232-3600, 800-426-7866; 300 E Sheridan Ave; r $100-140; P ✖ 📶 ♿) This new 200-room hotel in Bricktown is across from the ballpark. Built in a traditional style, the rooms are very comfortable and modern.

Colcord Hotel (☎ 405-601-4300, 866-781-3800; www.colcordhotel.com; 15 N Robinson Ave; r from $149, ste $279; P ✖

GREAT PLAINS

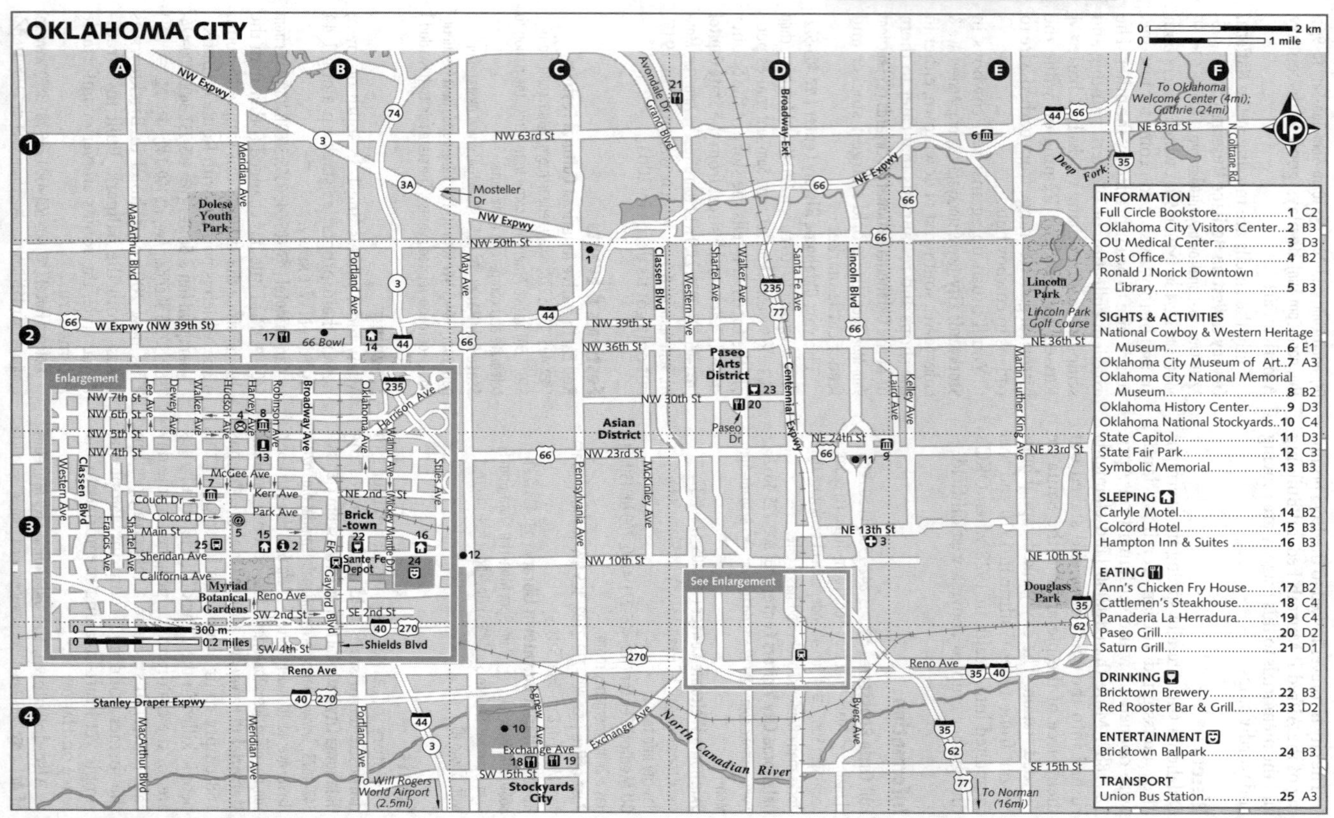
OKLAHOMA CITY
INFORMATION
Full Circle Bookstore 1 C2
Oklahoma City Visitors Center 2 B3
OU Medical Center 3 D3
Post Office 4 B2
Ronald J Norick Downtown Library 5 B3
SIGHTS & ACTIVITIES
National Cowboy & Western Heritage Museum 6 E1
Oklahoma City Museum of Art 7 A3
Oklahoma City National Memorial Museum 8 B2
Oklahoma History Center 9 D3
Oklahoma National Stockyards 10 C4
State Capitol 11 D3
State Fair Park 12 C3
Symbolic Memorial 13 B3
SLEEPING
Carlyle Motel 14 B2
Colcord Hotel 15 B3
Hampton Inn & Suites 16 B3
EATING
Ann's Chicken Fry House 17 B2
Cattlemen's Steakhouse 18 C4
Panaderia La Herradura 19 C4
Paseo Grill 20 D2
Saturn Grill 21 D1
DRINKING
Bricktown Brewery 22 B3
Red Rooster Bar & Grill 23 D2
ENTERTAINMENT
Bricktown Ballpark 24 B3
TRANSPORT
Union Bus Station 25 A3
To Oklahoma Welcome Center (4mi); Guthrie (24mi)
To Norman (16mi)
To Will Rogers World Airport (2.5mi)
See Enlargement
Enlargement
Lincoln Park
Lincoln Park Golf Course
Douglass Park
Paseo Arts District
Asian District
Dolese Youth Park
Stockyards City
Brick-town
Myriad Botanical Gardens
Sante Fe Depot
North Canadian River
Deep Fork
Martin Luther King Ave
Lincoln Blvd
Broadway Ext
Centennial Expwy
Classen Blvd
NW Expwy
W Expwy (NW 39th St)
NE Expwy
Stanley Draper Expwy
Meridian Ave
MacArthur Blvd
Portland Ave
May Ave
Pennsylvania Ave
Reno Ave
Shields Blvd
66 Bowl

) OKC's first skyscraper, built in 1910, is now a 12-story boutique hotel. Many original flourishes, like the marble-clad lobby, survive while the 108 rooms have a stylish, contemporary touch. The hotel is walking distance to Bricktown.

Eating

Bunches of eateries cluster in Bricktown, line Western Ave between 41st and 82nd Sts, and anchor the Asian District (around 23rd St and Classen Blvd) with reasonable Vietnamese, Chinese and Thai noodle houses.

Panaderia La Herradura (405-232-3502; 2235 SW 14th St; snacks $1-5; 6am-4pm) A classic Mexican bakery in the heart of the Stockyards District. Grab a pair of tongs and load up your platter with any of 100 different breads and pastries made fresh daily.

Ann's Chicken Fry House (405-943-8915; 4106 NW 39th St; mains $4-12; 11am-8:30pm Tue-Sat;) Part real diner, part tourist attraction, Ann's is a Route 66 veteran known for its – you guessed it – chicken fried steak. Okra and cream gravy also star.

Saturn Grill (405-843-7114; 6432 Avondale Dr; mains $8-10; 11am-9pm Mon-Sat) Locally beloved for its fresh and inventive menu, Saturn has a wide-ranging fusion charm at amazing prices. Lots of vegetarian choices and splendid pizzas, salads and much more.

our pick **Cattlemen's Steakhouse** (405-236-0416; 1309 S Agnew Ave; breakfasts $3-7, lunch $4-25, dinners $10-25; 6am-10pm Sun-Thu, 6am-midnight Fri & Sat) OKC's most storied restaurant, this Stockyards City institution has been feeding cowpokes and city slickers slabs of beef and lamb's fries (that's a polite way of saying gonads) since 1910. Deals are still cut at the counter and back in the luxe booths.

Paseo Grill (405-601-1079; 2909 Paseo Dr; mains $12-35; 11am-10pm Mon-Sat) On a balmy night (common in OKC) the patio at this southwestern restaurant is the place to be. Blackened steaks and seafood and fresh treats like gazpacho keep people returning again and again.

Drinking & Entertainment

For listings, pick up the free weekly **Oklahoma Gazette** (www.okgazette.com) or just head to the renovated warehouses in the **Bricktown District**, which contain many restaurants and bars. To make a complete night of it in the district, watch the Triple A Redhawks play at **Bricktown Ballpark** (405-218-1000; www.oklahomaredhawks.com; 2 Mickey Mantle Dr).

The heart of gay Oklahoma is the **39th Street Strip** (west of Pennsylvania Ave).

Red Rooster Bar & Grill (405-525-7631; 3100 N Walker Ave; noon-1am) Classic OKC dive bar with a cheap beer-only line-up (and good burgers) and enough cigarette smoke to give nonsmokers the habit.

Bricktown Brewery (405-232-2739; 1 N Oklahoma Ave; 11am-1am) A large microbrewery in Bricktown, with revelers splayed out across large rooms enjoying pool, darts and just being spectators. Always hopping and has a decent food menu.

Shopping

The **Paseo Arts District** isn't much more than Paseo Dr itself, but there are several art galleries and boutiques in the Spanish colonial buildings. You can buy all forms of Western wear and gear in **Stockyards City**.

Getting There & Around

Will Rogers World Airport (OKC; 405-680-3200; www.flyokc.com) is 5 miles southwest of downtown. With **Yellow Cab** (405-232-6161) it costs about $20 to get downtown.

The Amtrak *Heartland Flyer* train goes from OKC's **Santa Fe Depot** (800-872-7245; 100 S EK Gaylord Blvd) to Fort Worth ($36, 4¼ hours). Buy your ticket on the train; there's no office here.

Greyhound buses depart daily from the **Union Bus Station** (405-235-6425; 427 W Sheridan Ave) for Dallas ($39, five hours), Wichita ($29, 2¾ hours) and Tulsa ($25, two hours, four daily), among other destinations.

Oklahoma Spirit (405-235-7433; www.gometro.org) fake trolleys connect downtown and Bricktown sights for a quarter per ride. Regular city bus fares are $1.25.

AROUND OKLAHOMA CITY

Guthrie

Brick-and-stone Victorian buildings line street after street of Oklahoma's first capital, 25 miles north of Oklahoma City. The well-preserved downtown contains shops, museums and eateries, and during much of the year the **Guthrie Gunfighters** (1-5pm Sat) stage shootouts hourly at 2nd St and Harrison Ave.

The **Guthrie Information Center** (405-282-1947; www.guthrieok.com; 212 W Oklahoma Ave; 9am-5pm Mon-Fri) can point out the small museums (banjo, frontier drugstore, art, history and more) in town. Let the **Bed & Breakfast Association of Guthrie** (www.guthriebb.com) put you in one of a dozen historic inns.

WESTERN OKLAHOMA

West of Oklahoma City toward Texas the land opens into expansive prairie fields; nowhere as beautifully as in the Wichita Mountains, which, along with some Route 66 attractions (see p696) and Native American sites, make this prime road-trip country.

Anadarko

Sixty miles southwest of OKC, Anadarko and the surrounding area are home to 64 Native American tribes. The town hosts powwows and other events almost monthly. Get a schedule from the Anadarko Visitor Center inside the **National Hall of Fame for Famous American Indians** (☎ 405-247-5555; www.anadarko.org; Hwy 62, east of town; admission free; 9am-5pm Mon-Sat, 1-5pm Sun), which has a park with 42 bronze busts. Next door is the **Southern Plains Indian Museum** (☎ 405-247-6221; Hwy 62; admission free; 9am-5pm Tue-Sat) with crafts from Kiowa, Cheyenne, Wichita and other western Oklahoma tribes.

Take a guided tour of seven typical tribal lodgings (Navajo, Apache, Wichita, Kiowa, Caddo, Pawnee and Pueblo) re-created on a hillside at **Indian City USA** (☎ 800-433-5661; www.indiancityusa.com; Rte 8, 2 miles south of town). It was closed for renovations at the time of research.

Going north from town, US 281 runs through a beautiful area of multihued sandstone canyons and bluffs.

Fort Sill & Lawton

Established in 1869 as an outpost against Native Americans, Fort Sill remains an active army base and includes relics from 140 years of war. The original stone structures, which were built by buffalo soldiers, are remarkably well preserved and the **Fort Sill Museum** (☎ 580-442-5123; 437 Quanah Rd; admission free; 8:30am-5pm Tue-Sat) fills several of them. It includes a barracks furnished as it was in the 1870s and the guardhouse where Geronimo was detained after he had celebrated a little too much in nearby Lawton. Many old weapons are displayed nearby. Ask for a map to **Geronimo's grave**, which is located a couple of miles away.

The stockaded Red River Trading Post at the **Museum of the Great Plains** (☎ 580-581-3460; www.museumgreatplains.org; 601 NW Ferris Ave; adult/child $6/2.50; 10am-5pm Mon-Sat, 1-5pm Sun) in Lawton is a faithful reproduction of those found in the area from the 1830s to 1840s. There's a prairie dog town where you can watch the sociable critters cavort.

Wichita Mountains

Some 600 bison and a herd of longhorns roam the **Wichita Mountains Wildlife Refuge** (☎ 580-429-3222; http://wichitamountains.fws.gov; visitor center, Hwy 49 & Hwy 115; 8am-6pm), 15 miles northwest of Lawton along the north side of Fort Sill. The mixed-grass prairie and lake areas are superb for hiking and wildlife spotting. Drive up Mt Scott (2464ft) for great views and listen for coyotes and screech owls while sleeping at the refuge's first-come, first-served **campground** ($6-16) or in the backcountry (permit required). Hwy 49 runs for a very scenic 20 miles west of I-44.

TULSA

Self-billed as the 'Oil Capital of the World', Tulsa has never dirtied its hands much on the black gold that oozes out elsewhere in the state. Rather, it is the home to scores of energy companies that make their living drilling for oil, selling it or supplying those who do. The steady wealth this provides helped create Tulsa's beautiful art-deco downtown. That said, Tulsa (population 390,000) is not the most charming Great Plains town: suburban sprawl has dispersed its appeal and much life seems to center on the malls and chains gathered at highway interchanges.

The **Tulsa Visitor Center** (☎ 800-558-3311; www.visittulsa.com; William Center Towers II, 2 W 2nd St; 8am-5pm Mon-Fri) will help you find the city's elusive charms.

Sights & Activities

Downtown Tulsa has so much art-deco architecture it was once known as the 'Terra-Cotta City.' The **Philcade Building** (511 S Boston), with its glorious T-shaped lobby, and **Boston Avenue United Methodist Church** (☎ 918-583-5181; 1301 S Boston; 8:30am-5pm Mon-Fri, 8am-5pm Sun, guided tour noon Sun), rising at the end of downtown, are two exceptional examples. The *Downtown Tulsa Self-Guided Historic Walking Tour* map, free from the visitor center, will lead you to dozens more.

Northwest of downtown, off Hwy 64, the superb **Gilcrease Museum** (☎ 888-655-2278; www

.gilcrease.org; 1400 Gilcrease Museum Rd; adult/child $8/free; 10am-5pm Tue-Sun) sits on the estate of a Native American who discovered oil on his allotment. The impressive collection of American Western, Native American, and Central and South American fine art and archaeology is surrounded by some fine formal gardens.

South of town, another oil magnate's converted Italianate villa, also ringed by fabulous foliage, houses the eclectic **Philbrook Museum of Art** (918-749-7941; www.philbrook.org; 2727 S Rockford Rd, east of Peoria Ave; adult/child $7.50/5.50; 10am-5pm Tue-Sun, to 8pm Thu). The Native American works stand out; look for *Navajo Woman on Horseback* by Gerald Nailor.

Greenwood Cultural Center (918-596-1020; www.greenwoodculturalcenter.com; 322 N Greenwood Ave; admission free; 9am-5pm Mon-Fri) displays photos of the historic African American Greenwood District, which was the scene of America's worst race riot in 1921 when whites killed scores of African Americans and burned the neighborhood, leaving over 10,000 homeless.

Tulsa's beautiful Union Station has new life as the **Oklahoma Jazz Hall of Fame** (918-281-8600; www.okjazz.org; 111 E 1st St; admission free; 9am-5pm Mon-Fri, call to confirm). For most of the year there are Sunday concerts at 5pm.

With a 200ft UFO-like **Prayer Tower** (918-495-6262; 7777 S Lewis Ave; admission free; 10am-3:30pm Tue-Sat, 12:30-3:30pm Sun) at its heart, the campus of financially troubled **Oral Roberts University** is as idiosyncratic as its televangelist founder.

Sleeping

Chain motels aplenty line Hwy 244 and I-44, especially at the latter's exits 229 and 232.

our pick Desert Hills Motel (918-834-3311; www.deserthillstulsa.com; 5220 E 11th St; r from $40; P) One of several low-cost Route 66 classics on the east side of town, but the neon cactus sign sets this one apart. The 50 spotless rooms have microwaves and fridges.

Inn at Woodward Park (918-712-9770, 888-712-9770; www.innatwoodwardpark.com; 1521 E 21st St; r $100-140; P) In a historic neighborhood south of the center, this elegant 1920s B&B has three themed rooms surrounded by lavish gardens. Rooms have DVD players and queen-size beds. The Philbrook Museum is a short walk through a beautiful park.

Hotel Ambassador (918-587-8200, 888-408-8282; www.hotelambassador-tulsa.com; 1324 S Main St; r from $220; P) Look in the hallway for the photos of this 1929 nine-story hotel before the recent opulent renovation. Public spaces are suitably grand; the 55 rooms have a contemporary feel that helps the somewhat close quarters seem a tad larger. It is close to the center.

Eating & Drinking

Look for dining options in the Brookside neighborhood, on Peoria Ave between 31st and 51st Sts; on Historic Cherry St (now 15th St) just east of Peoria Ave; and the artsy Brady District, centered on Brady and Main Sts immediately north of downtown.

Gypsy Coffee House (918-295-2181; www.gypsycoffee.com; 303 N Cincinnati Ave; meals $3-8; noon-midnight Sun-Thu, noon-3am Fri & Sat) An all-around great hangout in the Brady District with couches, board games and live music (open mike Tuesdays, bands weekends).

Full Moon Café (918-583-6666; www.eatfullmoon.com; 1525 E 15th St; meals $6-12; 11am-midnight Mon-Fri, 9am-2am Sat & Sun) Quesadillas, burgers and salads line the menu, while dueling rock and roll pianos Thursday through Saturday assault the ears; there's live music other nights too.

Elmer's (918-742-6702; 4130 S Peoria St; mains $5-10; 11am-8pm Tue-Sat) A legendary barbecue joint where the star of the menu is the potentially deadly 'Badwich,' a bun-crushing combo of superbly smoked sausages, ham, beef, pork and more. The dining room is bare-bones, as is the service (and the ribs after you're through).

our pick Ri Le's (918-496-2126; Suite 102, 4932 E 91st St; mains $5-12; noon-9pm) Tulsa has a vibrant Vietnamese community that dates back to the 1970s. Among the many fine eateries is this absolute gem. The namesake owner wanders the tables ensuring diners are not just happy but thrilled.

Entertainment

Pick up the free **Urban Tulsa Weekly** (www.urbantulsa.com) to learn what's going on.

Cain's Ballroom (918-584-2306; www.cainsballroom.com; 423 N Main St) Rising rockers grace the same boards where Bob Wills played Western swing in the 1930s and the Sex Pistols caused confusion in 1978.

Discoveryland! (918-245-6552; www.discoverylandusa.com; 19501 W 41st St, Sand Springs; adult/child $20/free; 7pm Mon-Sat summer) Whether you're a boy or a girl you won't be able to say no to this high energy outdoor production of *Oklahoma!* A Western musical revue and Native American dancers kick things off, and a pre-show dinner is available. It's 10 miles west of Tulsa.

Getting There & Around

Tulsa International Airport (TUL; ☎ 918-838-5000; www.tulsaairports.com), situated off Hwy 11, is northeast of downtown. **Greyhound** (☎ 918-584-4428; 317 S Detroit Ave) has daily buses bound for Oklahoma City ($20, two hours) and St Louis ($81, eight hours). Almost all local **Tulsa Transit** (☎ 918-582-2100; www.tulsatransit.org; one-day pass $3.25) buses originate downtown at 319 S Denver Ave.

GREEN COUNTRY

Subtle forested hills interspersed with iconic red dirt and lakes cover Oklahoma's northeast corner, aka **Green Country** (www.greencountryok.com), which includes Tulsa. The area has a strong Native American influence as it is where several of the Five Civilized Tribes (Cherokee, Choctaw, Chickasaw, Creek and Seminole) were relocated in the 1820s and '30s.

Don't miss Totem Pole Park and the Blue Whale along Route 66 (see p696).

Bartlesville

Oklahoma's first commercial oil well was dug in Bartlesville, 50 miles north of Tulsa, and soon after in 1905 Frank Phillips, of Phillips 66 fame, arrived to dig more. You can relive these rough and tumble days at the **Phillips Petroleum Company Museum** (☎ 918-661-8687; 410 S Keeler Ave; admission free; ⏲ 10am-4pm Mon-Sat) right in town.

Phillips' vast county estate, **Woolaroc** (☎ 918-336-0307; www.woolaroc.org; Rte 123, 12 miles southwest of town; adult/child $8/free; ⏲ 10am-5pm Wed-Sun, open Tue summer), is now an excellent museum of southwestern art and culture, and a wildlife refuge with buffalo. (Maybe it's us, but Phillips looks like the ultimate city dude in the photos of him in Western wear.)

Thirty miles west of Bartlesville and just north of Pawhuska, some 2500 bison roam across 44,645 acres at the **Tallgrass Prairie Preserve** (☎ 918-287-4803; www.nature.org) the world's largest patch of protected tallgrass prairie. There are nature trails here.

You can tour the only Frank Lloyd Wright–designed skyscraper ever built, the 1956, 221ft **Price Tower Arts Center** (☎ 918-336-4949; www.pricetower.org; 510 Dewey Ave; adult/child $4/free, tours $10/5; ⏲ 10am-5pm Tue-Sat, noon-5pm Sun, tours 11am & 2pm Tue-Sat plus noon & 1pm Fri & Sat, 2pm Sun). Inside and out it is like *Architectural Digest* meets the *Jetsons*. Wright shopped the design around for 30 years before he found clients willing to build it here.

You can stay in one of 19 Wright-inspired rooms in the **Inn at Price Tower** (☎ 918-336-1000, 877-424-2424; r from $145; ⊠ ✣). The 15th-floor bar, Cooper, has sweeping views of the prairie (fitting for a Wright building).

Much more down to earth, **Murphy's Steak House** (☎ 918-336-4789; 1625 W Frank Phillips Blvd; mains $6-16; ⏲ 11am-8pm) has steaks but the cognoscenti opt for the 'hot hamburger,' a meaty plate of goodness that's best with gravy over all.

Claremore

This was the setting for the 1931 play *Green Grow the Lilacs*, which went on to become the hugely popular musical *Oklahoma!*, which chronicles *highly* fictionalized events in 1906.

Born in a log cabin just north of town in 1879, Will Rogers was a cowboy, a hilarious homespun philosopher, star of radio and movies, and part Cherokee. The hilltop **Will Rogers Memorial Museum** (☎ 918-341-0719; www.willrogers.com; 1720 W Will Rogers Blvd; admission free; ⏲ 8am-5pm), 30 miles northeast of Tulsa off Route 66, is an entertaining tribute to a man good for quotes like this: 'My ancestors didn't come over on the Mayflower, but they met the boat.'

More than 20,000 guns, knives, swords and other tools of mayhem are on display at **J M Davis Arms and Historical Museum** (☎ 918-341-5707; www.thegunmuseum.com; 333 N Lynn Riggs Blvd; admission free; ⏲ 8:30am-5pm Mon-Sat, 10am-5pm Sun). The beer stein collection adds irony.

Tiny **Dot's Café** (☎ 918-341-9718; 310 W Will Rogers Blvd; breakfasts $4-10; ⏲ 7am-2pm Mon-Sat, to 8pm Thu) is a good place to at least hum – if not sing – 'Oh What a Beautiful Mornin'.'

Trail of Tears Country

The area southeast of present-day Tulsa was, and to some degree still is, Creek and Cherokee land. This is an excellent place to learn about Native American culture, especially before the 1800s.

Namesake of Merle Haggard's 1969 hit 'Okie from Muskogee?', **Muskogee** ('where even squares can have a ball') is 49 miles southeast of Tulsa, and is home to the **Five**

OKLAHOMA: DETOURS & EXTRAS

Following Route 66 through Oklahoma can seem like one long detour and can offer days of exploration. But there are many more options in various corners of the state.

- **Okmulgee**, off US 75, 30 miles south of Tulsa, looks like the set of a 1950s film featuring an idealized small town America. It has good Native American museums.
- **Washita Battlefield National Historic Site** (www.nps.gov/waba; Hwy 47A, 2 miles west of Cheyenne; admission free; sunrise-susnet) is where George Custer's troops launched an 1868 attack on the peaceful village of Chief Black Kettle. The **visitor center** (580-497-2742; admission free; 8am-5pm) has a good museum. There's a self-guiding trail or you can take a free ranger-led tour (hourly 9am-4pm Jun-Aug). The scenery is both stark and bucolic; much of the area is part of the Black Kettle National Grasslands. It is 25 miles north of Route 66/I-40.
- The **Pioneer Woman Museum** (580-765-6108; Ponca City; adult/child $3/2; 9am-5pm Mon-Sat, 1-5pm Sun) honors the people who did the real work in the Old West, while the men hung around towns waiting for shoot-outs or getting liquored up in saloons. At least that's how it seems in the movies. It's 15 miles east of I-35 in northern Oklahoma.

Civilized Tribes Museum (877-587-4237; www.fivetribes.org; Agency Hill, Honor Heights Dr; adult/student $3/1.50; 10am-5pm Mon-Sat, 1-5pm Sun) inside an 1875 Union Indian Agency house. It recalls the cultures of the Native Americans forcibly moved here from America's southeast. Bacone College's **Ataloa Lodge Museum** (918-781-7283; www.bacone.edu/ataloa; 2299 Old Bacone Rd; adult/student $3/1.50; 8.30am-5.30pm Mon-Sat, 1-5pm Sun), east of town on US 62, is renowned for artifacts that include Hopi and Navajo kachina dolls and pottery.

Twenty miles east on Hwy 62 is **Tahlequah** (tal-*ah*-quaw), the Cherokee capital since 1839. The excellent **Cherokee Heritage Center** (888-999-6007; www.cherokeeheritage.org; 21192 Keeler Rd, Park Hill; adult/child $8.50/5; 10am-5pm Mon-Sat, 1-5pm Sun, closed Jan, last tour 3.30pm) features Native American–led tours through a re-creation of a pre-European contact woodland village. A log cabin town represents Cherokee life during the mid-19th century and the museum focuses on the Trail of Tears.

Scenic Hwy 10 follows the Illinois River north of Tahlequah. Outfitters, including **War Eagle Floats** (800-722-3834; www.wareagleresort.com; 13020 N Hwy 10), offer two-hour to two-day trips, campgrounds, cabins and more.

Texas

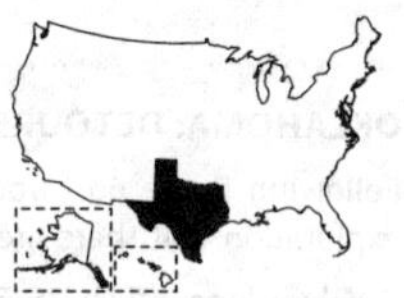

If you thought 'Don't mess with Texas' was the official state motto, not just an antilitter campaign, you'd be forgiven for misunderstandin'. A certain chest-puffin' pride does seem to go with being from the Lone Star State. It probably has as much to do with a leftover independent spirit (locals are mighty proud of Texas having once been its own country) as it does with all that bigness (the state *is* larger than Germany, England, Scotland, Ireland, Northern Ireland, Belgium and the Netherlands combined). Nevertheless, the Wild West lives on today, for the most part, in attitude alone. If you're thinkin' you'll run into cowboys dusty from the trail just anywhere, you're about as sharp as a heapa mashed potaters. Computer-geek millionaires outnumber rich cattlemen here, and you're as likely to see an uptown fashionista as a good ol' gal in her tight-fittin' jeans.

Sure you can (and might oughta) do some two-steppin' in a 100-year-old dance hall, but you should also rock out at the *hundreds* of live-music venues in Austin and pulse to a mariachi beat in ol' San Antone. If what you really want to do is some ropin' and ridin', mosey on over to Fort Worth's historic stockyards or get your giddy-up on at Bandera's dude ranches. But don't forget about the bright lights of them big cities Dallas and Houston.

Nature-lovers should know that Texas ain't all just tumblin' tumbleweeds. Here you can also explore the tall pine forests of east Texas, walk along miles of undeveloped southern Gulf Coast beach or catch sight of winter snow in the 8000ft-plus Guadalupe Mountains. Wherever you do go, most folks are just as friendly as pie. Can you blame 'em? They're from Texas.

HIGHLIGHTS

- Sinking your teeth into smoked brisket at a central Texas BBQ joint, like Luling's **City Market** (p718)
- Grooving live-music clubs in the state's incredibly cool capital, **Austin** (p715)
- Floating down Santa Elena Canyon in **Big Bend National Park** (p746)
- Going country at the National Cowgirl Museum by day and the rodeo by night in **Fort Worth** (p742)
- Trying a *tripas* (tripe) taco while listening to a Tejano band during **Fiesta San Antonio** (p723)
- Boot-scootin' at **Gruene Hall** (p717), reputedly the oldest dance hall in Texas

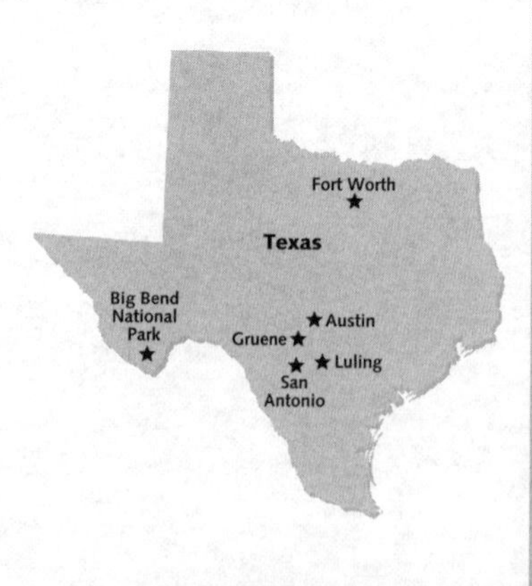

TEXAS FACTS

Nickname Lone Star State
Population 24.3 million
Area 261,797 sq miles
Capital city Austin (population 743,000)
Other cities San Antonio (population 1,351,305), Houston (population 2,242,193), Dallas (population 1,279,910), El Paso (population 613,190)
Sales tax 6.25%
Birthplace of Singer Buddy Holly (1936–59), entrepreneur Howard Hughes (1905–76), rocker Janis Joplin (1943–70), country singer George Strait (b 1952), actor Matthew McConaughey (b 1969)
Home of Dr Pepper, corny dogs and two President Bushes
Famous for Cowboys and The Cowboys (football), great BBQ
Best souvenir 'Don't mess with Texas' toilet paper
Driving distances Austin to San Antonio 78 miles, Houston to Dallas 237 miles, Dallas to El Paso 622 miles, Brownsville to Houston 350 miles

HISTORY

Given that the conquerors' diseases wiped out much of the indigenous population, it seems a bit ironic that the Spaniards named the territory Tejas (*tay*-has) – a corruption of the Caddo word for 'friend.' Caddo, Apache and Karankawa were among the tribes that Spanish explorers encountered when they arrived to map the Gulf coast in 1519.

Spain's rule of the territory continued until Mexico won its independence in 1821. That same year, Mexican general Antonio López de Santa Anna eliminated the state federation system, outlawed slavery and curtailed immigration. None of this sat well with independent-minded 'Texians' (US- and Mexico-born Texans) who had been given cheap land grants and Mexican citizenship. Clashes escalated into the Texas War for Independence (1835–36). A month after Santa Anna's forces massacred survivors of the siege in San Antonio, Sam Houston's rebels routed the Mexican troops at San Jacinto with the cry – let's all say it – 'Remember the Alamo!' (see boxed text, p722). And thus the Republic of Texas was born. The nation's short life ended nine years later when, by treaty, Texas opted to become the 28th state of the Union.

The last battle of the Civil War (Texas was on the Confederate side) was reputedly fought near Brownsville in May of 1865 – one month after the war had ended. Cattle-ranching formed the core of Texas' postwar economy, but it was the black gold that spewed up from Spindletop in 1910 that really changed everything. From then on, for better or worse, the state's economy has run on oil. Texans – who were the biggest domestic oil supplier and had many of the nation's largest refineries – laughed all the way to the bank during the energy crisis of the 1970s when gasoline prices quadrupled. Boom time was big, but the bust in the 1980s was just as spectacular. A worldwide glut devastated the oil industry and towns in Texas were deserted overnight.

Diversification became the buzzword in the 1990s. South-central Texas established itself as a high-tech corridor, Houston invested in the space and medical industries, and the North American Free Trade Agreement (NAFTA) encouraged trade with neighboring Mexico from across the state. Former Texas governor George W Bush was elected to two terms as 43rd president of the United States (2001–2009), which must have made his father, George Bush Sr (the 41st US president), mighty proud. Those still involved in the oil industries had long joked: 'Lord, give me just one more boom and I promise I won't piss it away.'

Crude oil prices rose dramatically in the early 2000s, and it looked like their dreams just may have come true – until the global economic crisis began in 2008. Texas took a hit, but the state economy remained one of only 10 outperforming the country as a whole, according to an April 2009 study by the Nelson A Rockefeller Institute of Government. Maybe those oil revenues helped out some after all.

LOCAL CULTURE

Trying to typify Texas culture is like tryin' to wrestle a pig in mud – it's awful slippery. In vast generalization, Austin is alternative Texas,

TEXAS

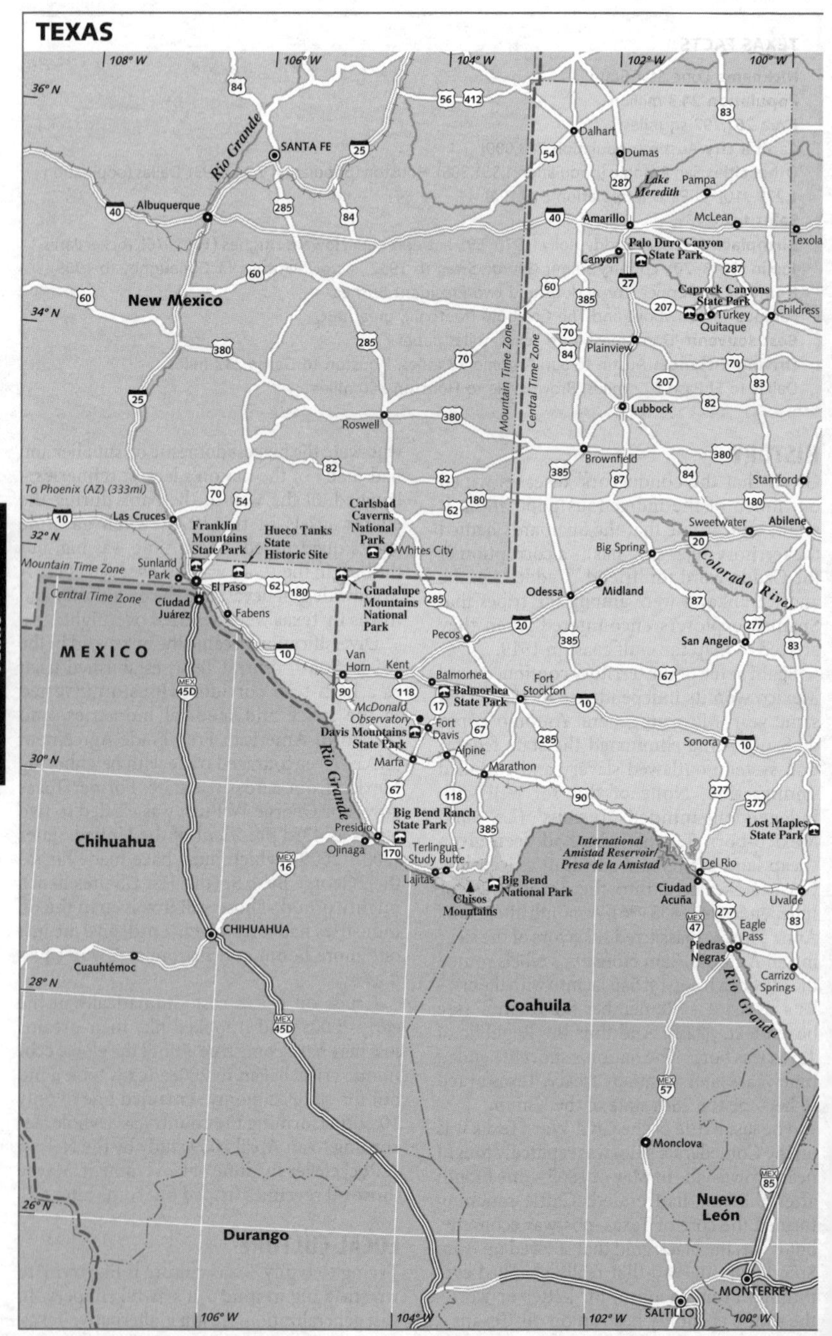

New Mexico
MEXICO
Chihuahua
Coahuila
Durango
Nuevo León
SANTA FE
Albuquerque
Rio Grande
Roswell
Las Cruces
To Phoenix (AZ) (333mi)
Franklin Mountains State Park
Hueco Tanks State Historic Site
Carlsbad Caverns National Park
Whites City
Guadalupe Mountains National Park
Sunland Park
El Paso
Ciudad Juárez
Fabens
Mountain Time Zone
Central Time Zone
Dalhart
Dumas
Lake Meredith
Pampa
Amarillo
McLean
Texola
Palo Duro Canyon State Park
Canyon
Caprock Canyons State Park
Turkey
Quitaque
Childress
Plainview
Lubbock
Brownfield
Stamford
Sweetwater
Abilene
Big Spring
Colorado River
Odessa
Midland
Pecos
San Angelo
Van Horn
Kent
Balmorhea
Balmorhea State Park
Fort Stockton
McDonald Observatory
Fort Davis
Davis Mountains State Park
Alpine
Marfa
Marathon
Sonora
Big Bend Ranch State Park
Presidio
Ojinaga
Terlingua - Study Butte
Lajitas
Chisos Mountains
Big Bend National Park
International Amistad Reservoir/ Presa de la Amistad
Del Rio
Ciudad Acuña
Lost Maples State Park
Uvalde
Eagle Pass
Piedras Negras
Carrizo Springs
CHIHUAHUA
Cuauhtémoc
Monclova
SALTILLO
MONTERREY
108° W
106° W
104° W
102° W
100° W
36° N
34° N
32° N
30° N
28° N
26° N

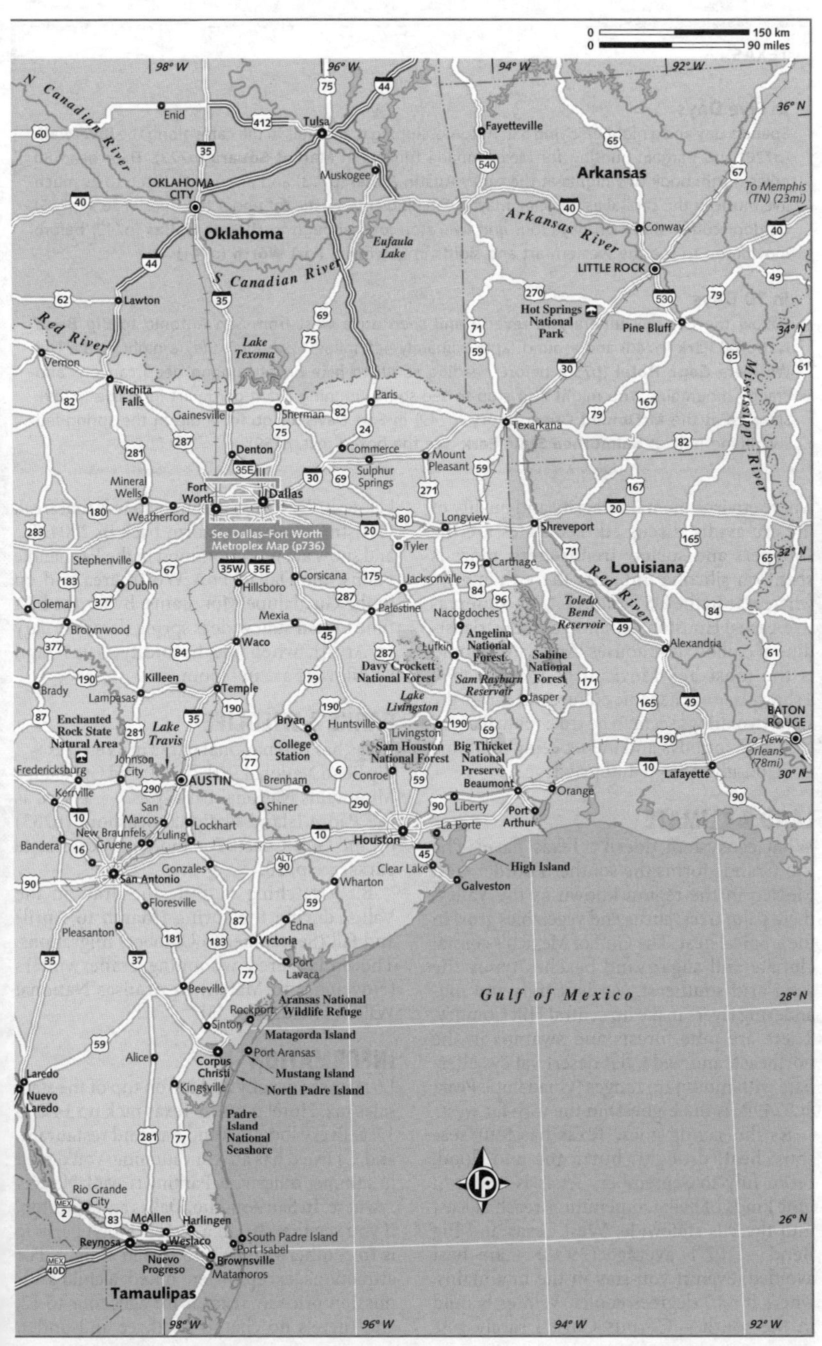

150 km
90 miles
Oklahoma
Arkansas
Louisiana
Tamaulipas
OKLAHOMA CITY
Tulsa
Enid
Muskogee
Lawton
Fayetteville
Conway
LITTLE ROCK
Pine Bluff
Hot Springs National Park
To Memphis (TN) (23mi)
Texarkana
Shreveport
Alexandria
BATON ROUGE
To New Orleans (78mi)
Lafayette
Vernon
Wichita Falls
Gainesville
Sherman
Paris
Denton
Commerce
Sulphur Springs
Mount Pleasant
Mineral Wells
Fort Worth
Dallas
Weatherford
See Dallas–Fort Worth Metroplex Map (p736)
Longview
Tyler
Carthage
Stephenville
Dublin
Hillsboro
Corsicana
Jacksonville
Palestine
Nacogdoches
Mexia
Coleman
Brownwood
Waco
Lufkin
Angelina National Forest
Davy Crockett National Forest
Sabine National Forest
Sam Rayburn Reservoir
Toledo Bend Reservoir
Jasper
Brady
Killeen
Temple
Lampasas
Lake Livingston
Enchanted Rock State Natural Area
Lake Travis
Bryan
College Station
Huntsville
Livingston
Sam Houston National Forest
Big Thicket National Preserve
Beaumont
Orange
Port Arthur
Fredericksburg
Johnson City
AUSTIN
Brenham
Conroe
Kerrville
San Marcos
Lockhart
Shiner
Liberty
New Braunfels
Gruene
Luling
Bandera
Houston
La Porte
High Island
Clear Lake
Galveston
San Antonio
Gonzales
Wharton
Floresville
Edna
Pleasanton
Victoria
Port Lavaca
Beeville
Aransas National Wildlife Refuge
Rockport
Sinton
Matagorda Island
Port Aransas
Alice
Corpus Christi
Mustang Island
North Padre Island
Kingsville
Laredo
Nuevo Laredo
Padre Island National Seashore
Rio Grande City
McAllen
Harlingen
Reynosa
Weslaco
South Padre Island
Port Isabel
Nuevo Progreso
Brownsville
Matamoros
Gulf of Mexico
N Canadian River
S Canadian River
Arkansas River
Red River
Mississippi River
Eufaula Lake
Lake Texoma
98° W
96° W
94° W
92° W
36° N
34° N
32° N
30° N
28° N
26° N

TEXAS...

In Five Days

Spend a day and a night enjoying San Antonio, sipping margaritas in the cafés along the **Riverwalk** (p720) and bargain-hunting for Mexico-made trinkets in **Market Square** (p722). Then head 80 miles north: book two nights at the funky **Austin Motel** (p713) and arrange to listen to as much live music in the capital as you can, maybe catching an acoustic set under the trees at **Jo's** (p715) outdoor coffee shop. On days four and five, stop long enough to shop in **Dallas** (p740) before moving on to see the western art and sights in Cowtown, **Fort Worth** (p741).

In 10 Days

Follow the five-day itinerary in reverse and then drive west from San Antonio to **Big Bend National Park** (p746) and around (approximately 440 miles, 6½ hours). Stay a night at the Old West–era **Gage Hotel** (p750) before heading south to hike or raft among deep canyons and craggy mountains. You might also stop to see some stunning avant-garde art in **Marfa** (p749), stargaze at the **McDonald Observatory** (p749) in Fort Davis, or go for a dip in the spring-fed swimming hole at **Balmorhea State Park** (see the boxed text, p750).

where environmental integrity and quality of life are avidly discussed. Dallasites are the shoppers and society trendsetters; more is spent on silicone implants there than anywhere else in the US besides LA. In conservative, casual Houston, oil-and-gas industrialists dine at clubby steakhouses. And San Antonio is the most Tex-Mexican of the bunch – a showplace of Hispanic culture. All across the state, two things seem to be true: football is sacred and, for boys and men, peeing outdoors is a God-given right and privilege.

LAND & CLIMATE

What ecosystem doesn't Texas have? The Rio Grande forms the southern border with Mexico in the region known as the Valley; there palm trees, citrus and vegetables grow in the tropical heat. The Gulf of Mexico's coastal climate and sugar-sand beaches typify the semi-arid southeast. Verdant hills and meandering rivers make up central Hill Country. There are pine forests and swamps in the northeast, and wide, flat desert valleys alternate with mountain ranges (Guadalupe Peak, at 8749ft, is the highest) in the way-far west.

As the saying goes, Texas has four seasons: heat, drought, hurricane and flood. From July to September, Texas is hotter 'n nine kinds of hell: temperatures reach at least into the 90s statewide. West Texas and Big Bend – 102°F average (39°C) – are best avoided, even if you stay in the mountains, where it's 10 degrees cooler. Winter is mild in the south – Corpus Christi rarely gets below 40°F (4°C), though there was that freak Christmas Eve snowstorm back in 2004. Ice and snow are more common in the Panhandle Plains, the Dallas–Fort Worth area and up in the Guadalupe Mountains. By far the best time to visit statewide is spring (late February to April), when the humidity is low and wildflowers are in bloom.

PARKS & WILDLIFE

Texas has two national parks in West Texas – Big Bend National Park (p746) and Guadalupe Mountains National Park (p753) – as well as the Padre Island National Seashore (p733) on the Gulf Coast. For more on Texas state parks, see p710.

Bird-watching is quite the draw in the Valley during the spring (March to April) and fall (September to October) migrations. The endangered whooping crane winters (November to March) in Aransas National Wildlife Refuge (p733).

INFORMATION

Local taxes usually add 2% on top of the state sales tax. Hotel taxes in Texas rack up 14% to 17%. Every lodging (and bar, and restaurant, and…) listed has air-conditioning; you'd melt in summer otherwise. Parking is available everywhere. In San Antonio, Dallas and Houston, if you see the 'P' in a review, hotel parking is free; otherwise it's $15 to $30 a night. For attractions, except where noted, a child's admission price in Texas is for ages four to 12, and there's no charge for three and under.

In Houston and Dallas, you must dial all 10 digits in a telephone number, even for local calls. Otherwise, you can drop the area code if you're calling locally.

Request the free, booklike annual *Texas State Travel Guide* from **Texas Tourism** (☎ 800-888-8839; www.traveltex.com), or get it at one of its 12 Texas Travel Information Centers. The extensive website has lodging listings also.

Read more about the state in the following glossy mags:

Best in Texas Music Magazine (www.bestintexasonline.com) Monthly home-grown concert listings.
Texas Highways (www.texashighways.com) Road-trip through the state's landscape, history and culture.
Texas Monthly (www.texasmonthly.com) In-depth features on personalities, food and current events.
Texas Music Magazine (www.txmusic.com) Follow the latest up-and-coming musicians.
Texas Parks & Wildlife Magazine (www.tpwmagazine.com) All things outdoorsy.
This Week in Texas (www.thisweekintexas.com) Gay and lesbian news and entertainment.

GETTING THERE & AROUND

The main international gateways to the state are Houston's George Bush Intercontinental Airport (IAH), Dallas–Fort Worth International Airport (DFW) and San Antonio International Airport (SAT). Austin and El Paso also have major airports.

Amtrak (p1166) runs the *Sunset Limited* train between Orlando, Florida and Los Angeles three times a week, with stops including Houston, San Antonio and El Paso. The *Texas Eagle* runs between Chicago and San Antonio daily, with stops in Dallas–Fort Worth and Austin. Note that trains often have late-night arrivals or departures in Texas.

Greyhound (p1160) and its partner **Kerrville Bus Lines** (☎ 800-231-2222; www.iridekbc.com) serve all but the tiniest towns, though it may take several transfers and twice as long as by car.

Given the distances, traveling by car is all but necessary in Texas – if you're hiring, make sure you opt for unlimited rental mileage. To avoid one-way drop-off fees, you could catch a cheap intra-Texas flight between cities, from where it's easy to rent a car. Cut-rate carrier Southwest Airlines serves Houston, Dallas, San Antonio, Austin, El Paso, Midland–Odessa, Lubbock, Corpus Christi and Harlingen (South Padre Island). In-Texas hops can cost as little as $49 to $99 one way if you book ahead. Houston-based Continental and Dallas-based American Airlines often match Southwest's sales. For airline contact details, see p1159.

Note that passports are required for all people (US citizens included) crossing in from the border with Mexico. For more details see p1152.

SOUTH-CENTRAL TEXAS

So what if the hills are more mole-size than mountainous; they – and the rivers that flow through them – still define south-central Texas. To the north is the state capital of Austin, where music, music and more music are on the schedule, day or night. Eighty miles south, the major metropolitan centre of San Antonio is home to the Alamo (p720) and the festive Riverwalk (p720) bars and restaurants. Between and to the west of the two towns is the Hill Country (p717). Here you can eat great BBQ, dance across an old wooden floor, or spend a lazy day floating on the river in small Texas-y towns that show the influence of early German and Czech settlers. If you want to get to the heart of Texas in a short time, south-central Texas is the way to go.

AUSTIN

On show is an eclectic pick-a-mix of retro-funk and New Age entrepreneurial spirit. In Austin, a musician resembling a punked-out Lucille Ball might live side by side with an internet millionaire. Heck, they may even be the same person. This mystic soup of social consciousness and capitalist development has fostered quite the city-supported active lifestyle. Buttoned-down businessmen take off to jog along Lady Bird Lake trails or bike through town on cycle-only lanes. And every night at one of 200-plus venues, they (and you) can listen to live indie rock, jazz-funk, Tejano trumpets, techno pop, alt-country, punk ska, acoustic rhythms, Latin sambas, world beat drums…shall we go on? Just don't think that all this coolness has gone unnoticed. Residents are rightly concerned about 'Keeping Austin Weird' as more people migrate in. The restaurant selection has noticeably improved; but not to worry, for now Austin is still the kind of place you'll see 'Jesus is Coming' painted on a rear windshield above a 'Marijuana is king' bumper sticker, or you'll run into someone

DID YOU KNOW?

Texas has more than 125 state parks, historic sites and natural areas. Highlights are listed in this chapter, but there's so much more to explore. You could seek out the unique ecosystem at swampy Caddo Lake, watch bats fly out of Devil's Sinkhole, or see where the Texas Declaration of Independence was signed (in 1836; Texas hasn't seceded – yet). Some parks are remote and rustic; others are downright fancy. Bastrop State Park, in Hill Country, has a swimming pool and golf course to go with its well-equipped cabins. Campsites cost between $3 and $20 per night depending on the facilities, cabins from $40 to $120 for two people. Peruse the free guide, in print and online, put out by **Texas Parks & Wildlife** (☎ 800-792-1112, central reservations 512-389-8900; www.tpwd.state.tx.us) to start creating your own adventure.

leaving their motel room in the morning with giant sparkly-striped Hula-hoops. Really, we swear, it happened.

History

The second president of the Republic of Texas, Mirabeau Lamar, chose the bend in the Colorado River (which would become Austin) to be the capital in 1839. The city in large part took shape because of the University of Texas (UT), founded here in 1883. (All those longhorn tattoos and car-window stickers you see? Those are Bevo, the UT mascot – 'Hook 'em horns!') Musically speaking, the 1960s and '70s were *big* locally. Beer joints launched the likes of rock diva Janis Joplin and cosmic cowboy Willie Nelson. Though folk, country and rockabilly roots run deep, there are just as many local artists and venues pounding out punk and indie rock these days.

Orientation

Downtown centers on north–south Congress Ave, below Martin Luther King Jr Blvd. E 6th St, between Congress Ave and I-35, is notorious for nighttime entertainment. Lady Bird Lake, which is really a dammed stretch of the Colorado River, is the southern edge of downtown and the northern boundary of South Austin. Quirky stores, cool restaurants and hip hotels line S Congress Ave (SoCo). North of downtown is UT; Guadalupe St ('the Drag'), with its cheap eats, bars and bookstores, parallels Congress Ave alongside the university. Mopac Expwy (Loop 1) is west of downtown; roads to other area lakes lead off that.

DON'T MISS

- **Continental Club** – live music, sometimes twice, nightly (p715)
- **SoCo boutiques** – 'Hey Cupcake,' Allen Boots and lots of quirky shopping (p716)
- **Barton Springs Pool** – dip in a real cool pool (p712)
- **Amy's Ice Cream** – Austin's original scoop since 1984 (p715)

Information

Austin indoors is nonsmoking, period (bars, too). A vast wi-fi network blankets downtown. For other hot spots check out www.austinwirelesscity.org. City of Austin libraries (www.ci.austin.tx.us) have free internet.

Austin American-Statesman (www.statesman.com) Daily newspaper.

Austin Visitor Information Center (☎ 512-478-0098; www.austintexas.org; 209 E 6th St; 9am-5pm Mon-Fri, to 6pm Sat & Sun) Tour and performance tickets sold; general info on hand.

Birds Barbershop (☎ 512-442-8800; 2110 S Lamar Blvd; 9am-11pm) Hippest haircut in town; mohawks $15.

Book People Inc (☎ 512-472-5050; 603 N Lamar Blvd; 9am-11pm) A bookstore as independent as Austin.

FedEx Office (☎ 512-472-4448; 327 Congress Ave; 7am-11pm Mon-Fri, 10am-7pm Sat & Sun) Internet access 30¢ a minute.

KLRU TV (www.klru.org) PBS affiliate with local programming that includes the popular music show *Austin City Limits* at 9:30pm Friday.

Post office (☎ 512-494-2206; 510 Guadalupe St)

Sights

Don't limit yourself to the sights; Austin is about the experience. Bars, restaurants, even grocery stores and the airport have live music. And there are outdoor activities galore. A full day might also include shopping for some groovy vintage clothes and getting a J-Bird haircut with a pink highlight.

TEXAS

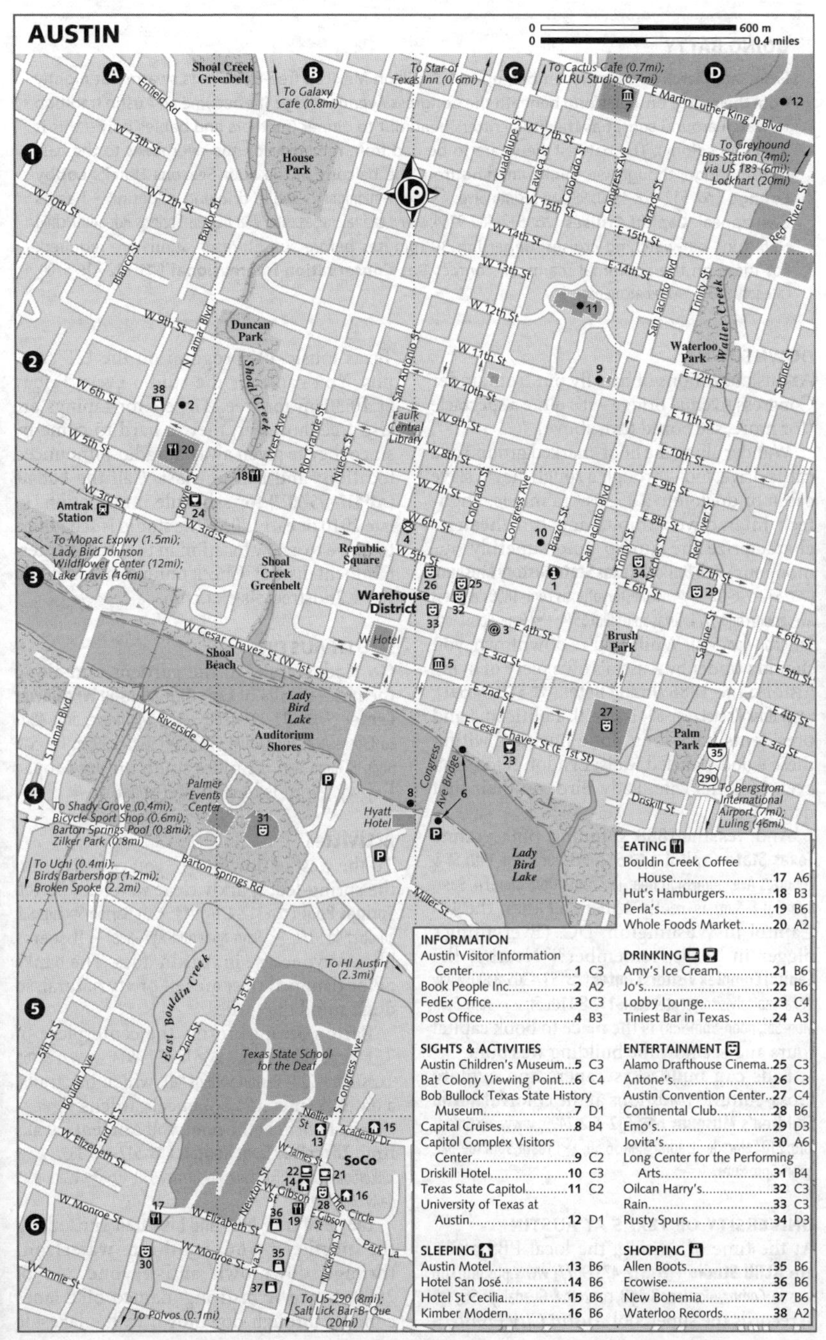
AUSTIN
0 600 m
0 0.4 miles
To Galaxy Cafe (0.8mi)
To Star of Texas Inn (0.6mi)
To Cactus Cafe (0.7mi); KLRU Studio (0.7mi)
To Greyhound Bus Station (4mi); via US 183 (6mi); Lockhart (20mi)
To Mopac Expwy (1.5mi); Lady Bird Johnson Wildflower Center (12mi); Lake Travis (16mi)
To Shady Grove (0.4mi); Bicycle Sport Shop (0.6mi); Barton Springs Pool (0.8mi); Zilker Park (0.8mi)
To Uchi (0.4mi); Birds Barbershop (1.2mi); Broken Spoke (2.2mi)
To HI Austin (2.3mi)
To Bergstrom International Airport (7mi); Luling (46mi)
To US 290 (8mi); Salt Lick Bar-B-Que (20mi)
To Polvos (0.1mi)
Shoal Creek Greenbelt
House Park
Duncan Park
Waterloo Park
Republic Square
Warehouse District
Brush Park
Palm Park
Shoal Beach
Lady Bird Lake
Auditorium Shores
Palmer Events Center
Hyatt Hotel
W Hotel
Faulk Central Library
Amtrak Station
Texas State School for the Deaf
SoCo
INFORMATION
Austin Visitor Information Center 1 C3
Book People Inc 2 A2
FedEx Office 3 C3
Post Office 4 B3
SIGHTS & ACTIVITIES
Austin Children's Museum 5 C3
Bat Colony Viewing Point 6 C4
Bob Bullock Texas State History Museum 7 D1
Capital Cruises 8 B4
Capitol Complex Visitors Center 9 C2
Driskill Hotel 10 C3
Texas State Capitol 11 C2
University of Texas at Austin 12 D1
SLEEPING
Austin Motel 13 B6
Hotel San José 14 B6
Hotel St Cecilia 15 B6
Kimber Modern 16 B6
EATING
Bouldin Creek Coffee House 17 A6
Hut's Hamburgers 18 B3
Perla's 19 B6
Whole Foods Market 20 A2
DRINKING
Amy's Ice Cream 21 B6
Jo's 22 B6
Lobby Lounge 23 C4
Tiniest Bar in Texas 24 A3
ENTERTAINMENT
Alamo Drafthouse Cinema 25 C3
Antone's 26 C3
Austin Convention Center 27 C4
Continental Club 28 B6
Emo's 29 D3
Jovita's 30 A6
Long Center for the Performing Arts 31 B4
Oilcan Harry's 32 C3
Rain 33 C3
Rusty Spurs 34 D3
SHOPPING
Allen Boots 35 B6
Ecowise 36 B6
New Bohemia 37 B6
Waterloo Records 38 A2
TEXAS

GOING BATTY

From late March to early November, up to 1.5 million Mexican free-tailed bats swarm out nightly from their roost on a platform beneath the Congress Avenue Bridge. It's become an Austin tradition to watch around sunset as the little critters head out to dinner (mothers and babies only – this is a mating colony). The battiest views are to be had from the lawns on the riverbanks to the east of the bridge, though we think watching from the balcony of the Four Seasons Hotel's **Lobby Lounge** (☎ 512-478-4500; 98 San Jacinto Blvd; noon-midnight) – while drinking a 'batini' – has its own appeal. **Capital Cruises** (☎ 512-480-9264; www.capitalcruises.com; 208 Barton Springs Rd; adult/child $8/6) runs bat-watching cruises, departing 30 minutes before sunset; reservations are required. For more on the nocturnal mammal, contact **Bat Conservation International** (☎ 512-416-5700, category 3636; www.batcon.org).

DOWNTOWN

At dusk bazillions of bats fly out from under Congress Avenue Bridge – it's quite a spectacle (for more, see boxed text, above).

Wander along the hoof-marked ground of a cattle drive, look through a rough-hewn slave cabin or duck into a 1930s-era movie. High-tech interactive exhibits and fun theatrics characterize the superb (and superbly humongous) **Bob Bullock Texas State History Museum** (☎ 512-936-8746; www.thestoryoftexas.com; 1800 Congress Ave; adult/child $7/4, Texas Spirit film $5/4; 9am-6pm Mon-Sat, noon-6pm Sun). While you're downtown, you should wander by Austin's own piece of living history: the 1886 **Driskill Hotel** (☎ 512-474-5911; www.driskillhotel.com; 604 Brazos St). Politicians and presidents have long done business within these wood-paneled walls; Lyndon B Johnson even took his wife, Lady Bird, on their first date here.

And, yes, the 1888, stunning, pink-granite **Texas State Capitol** (☎ 512-463-0063; cnr 11th St & Congress Ave; admission free; 7am-10pm Mon-Fri, 9am-8pm Sat & Sun) is really 15ft taller than the US Capitol in Washington, DC. (Everything's bigger in Texas, remember?) Nearby, the **Capitol Complex Visitors Center** (☎ 512-305-8400; www.texascapitolvisitorscenter.com; 112 E 11th St; 9am-5pm Mon-Sat, noon-5pm Sun) is the place to book capital tours and see how the building was built.

Kids can build skyscrapers and explore cross-cultural traditions at the colorful **Austin Children's Museum** (☎ 512-472-2499; www.austinkids.org; 210 Colorado St; admission $6.50; 10am-5pm Tue-Sat, noon-5pm Sun).

UNIVERSITY OF TEXAS AT AUSTIN

At the time of writing, the local PBS affiliate **KLRU Studio** (☎ 512-475-9077; www.pbs.org/klru/austin; Communications Bldg B, cnr 26th & Guadalupe Sts, 6th fl) records the supercool *Austin City Limits*, a Texas music-TV program on the UT campus. You can tour the studio every Friday at 10:30am for free. Tickets for tapings are also free; however, they're hard to come by since they're given away at radio-announced locations and run out fast. Call the **hotline** (☎ 512-475-9077) for schedule information. In late 2010 or early 2011, the studio is scheduled to move to a new location in the 2nd St entertainment district. Check online for updates at www.2ndstreetdistrict.com.

SOUTH AUSTIN

Go Kodak crazy in the gardens and along the nature trails of **Lady Bird Johnson Wildflower Center** (☎ 512-292-4200; www.wildflower.org; 4801 La Crosse Ave; adult/child $7/3; 9am-5:30pm Tue-Sat, noon-5:30pm Sun), 12 miles south on the Mopac Expwy. April is bluebonnet season.

Activities

To the west of downtown, you can dive into the spring-fed, sparkly clear waters of **Barton Springs Pool** (☎ 512-476-9044; 2201 Barton Springs Rd; adult/child $3/2; 9am-8pm mid-Apr–Sep) – it seems like everyone else in Austin does. The banks of the dammed river are left pretty natural, so don't mind the turtles.

Barton Springs forms the centerpiece of 351-acre **Zilker Park** (☎ 512-472-4914; www.ci.austin.tx.us/zilker; 2201 Barton Springs Rd), which has trails, a nature center and botanical gardens. Creekside just north of the pool, you can rent kayaks from **Zilker Park Boat Rentals** (☎ 512-478-3852; www.zilkerboats.com; Zilker Park; per hr/day $10/40; 10am-dark daily May-Oct).

Lady Bird Lake hike and bike trail runs along the northern and southern waterfront through downtown and beyond. As of 2009, Lance Armstrong–named bike lanes connect through downtown to the lakeside paths. Park near the Congress Avenue Bridge and take a walk; or reserve ahead and rent a bike (from $22 a day) at **Bicycle Sport Shop** (☎ 512-477-3472; http://bicyclesportshop.com; 517 S Lamar Blvd; ⏲ 10am-8pm Mon-Fri, 9am-6pm Sat, 11am-5pm Sun). A free PDF map brochure of all bicycle routes in Austin is available online at www.cityofaustin.org/bicycle.

Festivals & Events

South by Southwest (SXSW; ☎ 512-467-7979; www.sxsw.com) One of the American music industry's biggest gatherings, held in mid-March (see the boxed text, p715).

Austin City Limits Music Festival (☎ 512-389-0315; www.aclfestival.com; 3-day pass $185) The locals' favorite: more than 130 bands play on eight stages for three days in September.

Sleeping

SoCo has some quirky and cool digs. Hotels downtown are high-rent, but you don't have to go far to find reasonable motels.

BUDGET

Chain motels line up all along I-35; south of town, a whole slew of them congregate near the Oltorf St intersection (including a Howard Johnson, Days Inn and a Red Roof Inn).

HI Austin (☎ 512-444-2294; www.hiaustin.org; 2200 S Lakeshore Blvd; dm members/nonmembers $19/22; ⊠ ⁂ 💻 📶) Two-story views of the lake from the sunny great room – complete with fish tank, guitar and comfy couches – might make even nonhostelers consider a stay. Bus it or rent a bike ($10 a day) for the 2.5-mile trek to downtown. Power at this green-friendly hostelry comes from solar collectors. Cat on-site.

our pick **Austin Motel** (☎ 512-441-1157; www.austinmotel.com; 1220 S Congress Ave; r $69-110; P ⁂ 📶 🏊) Decorated with a waterfall mural or retro polka dots, each room is individually fun or funky. Random, savvy-thrift-shopper furniture makes this old motor-court motel oddly appealing. The least expensive rooms are shoeboxes; the poolside pads are palatial.

MIDRANGE

Note that at the time of writing, a shiny new W Hotel (www.whotels.com) was under construction on 2nd St in downtown.

Star of Texas Inn (☎ 512-472-6700; www.staroftexasinn.com; 611 W 22nd St; r incl breakfast $95-200; ⊠ ⁂ 💻 📶) Make yourself at home in a rambling-old-house B&B near UT. The hip young owners (and dog and cats) couldn't be friendlier.

Hotel San José (☎ 512-444-7322; www.sanjosehotel.com; 1316 S Congress Ave; r with shared bath $105, with bath $160-240; P ⊠ ⁂ 📶 🏊) Cherry platform beds float beneath pendant lights, and meditation nooks punctuate native Texas gardens – Hotel San José just oozes sleek and simple sophistication. The courtyard bar is known for its celebrity-spotting potential.

TOP END

Kimber Modern (☎ 512-912-1046; www.kimbermodern.com; 110 The Circle; r incl breakfast $250-350; P ⊠ ⁂ 📶) Staying in one of the five rooms at the architecturally adept Kimber does indeed seem like sleeping in a minimalist art museum – one with a Frake espresso machine and Egyptian cotton linens.

Hotel St Cecilia (☎ 512-852-2400; www.hotelstcecilia.com; 112 Academy Dr; r $300-500; P ⊠ ⁂ 💻 📶 🏊) Named in honor of the patron saint of music, here you can check out a record from the lobby's vinyl collection to play on your room's turntable. Studios, in an old Austin arts-and-crafts house, are classic in style; the sleek poolside bungalows are all mod and moody.

Eating

The hip-and-trendy but fun S Congress Ave eateries (south of Nellie St/Academy Dr) have been discovered. Those in the know go instead to S 1st St (1400 to 2100 blocks), where Mexican herbalists and tattoo parlors alternate with trailer-park food courts and organic cafés. Barton Springs Rd (east of Lamar Blvd) also has a number of interesting eateries, and Guadalupe St by UT is the place to look for cheap eats. Some great meat-market BBQ is available in nearby central Texas; see the boxed text, p718.

DOWNTOWN

Hut's Hamburgers (☎ 512-472-3050; 807 W 6th St; meals $5-9; ⏲ 11am-10pm) Choose from regular beef, natural grass-fed cattle or buffalo meat for your burger at this Austin roadhouse (it was opened in 1939). Southern mains, like chicken-fried steak, are pretty good too.

Whole Foods Market (☎ 512-476-1206; www.wholefoods.com; 525 N Lamar Blvd; sandwiches $6-9, mains $6-15; ⏲ 8am-10pm; 📶) The flagship of the Austin-founded Whole Foods Market is a gourmet grocery and café with restaurant counters and a staggering takeaway buffet, including

TASTES BORN IN TEXAS

- **Corny dogs** – cornbread-batter-dipped hot dogs on a stick were created in 1948 by Neil Fletcher for the State Fair of Texas (p737); Fletcher's still sells 'em there; now available with jalapeño cornbread too.
- **Shiner Bock** – the state's favorite amber ale came to be when Kosmos Spoetzl brought Bavarian brewing to Shiner, Texas, in 1914. Available countrywide, it's still brewed at **Spoetzl Brewery** (☎ 361-594-3383; www.shiner.com; 603 E Brewery St, Shiner; admission free; gift shop 9am-5pm Mon-Fri, 10am-3pm Sat, tours 11am & 1:30pm).
- **Chicken-fried bacon** – you've heard of steak coated and deep-fried like chicken, but the taste (and heart-attack factor) was taken to new heights when **Sodolak's** (☎ 979-272-6002; 9711 Fm 60 E, Snook; mains $6-15; 11am-10pm), near Bryan-College Station, started cooking bacon the same way in the early 1990s.
- **Dr Pepper** – a pharmacist in a Waco drugstore–soda shop invented this aromatic cola in the 1880s. Taste the original sugarcane formula at the first bottling plant, **Dublin Dr Pepper** (☎ 888-398-1024; www.olddocs.com; 105 E Elm St, Dublin; museum free, tours adult/child $2.50/2; 10am-5pm). Don't forget to pick up some Dr Pepper cake mix at the gift-and-ice-cream shop.

self-made salads, global mains, deli sandwiches and more.

SOUTH AUSTIN

The latest food trend in Austin is the Airstream-trailer food court. In several south Austin lots, vendors have arranged their Silver Bullets aside one another, selling crepes, tacos, pizza – whatever ('Hey Cupcake' is a favorite). They're open roughly noon to 8pm, from Tuesday to Sunday. Two of the best locations are in the 1600 block of S Congress Ave and the 1300 block of S 1st St; the latter has shade and tables.

Bouldin Creek Coffee House (☎ 512-416-1601; 1501 S 1st St; meals $5-7; 7am-midnight Mon-Fri, 9am-midnight Sat & Sun; V) You can get your veggie chorizo scrambler or organic oatmeal with apples all day long at this eclectic vegan/vegetarian eatery. Dishes like Italian fajitas (with portobello and zucchini strips) are quite hearty.

Polvos (☎ 512-441-5446; 2004 S 1st St; breakfast $5-8, mains $9-16; 8am-11pm) Fun, festive and just a little divey, Polvos serves central-Mexican food that always packs in a crowd. Try some of the dozen or so salsa varieties with one of the fierce margaritas.

Uchi (☎ 512-916-4808; 801 S Lamar Blvd; small plates $9-16; 5:30-10pm Sun-Thu, to 11pm Fri & Sat) Artisanal Japanese-fusion food and slap-your-face fresh sushi at this modern Asian restaurant rival that of New York's finest. Book well ahead if you hope to experience the wonder.

Perla's (☎ 512-291-7300; 1400 S Congress Ave; lunch $11-15, dinner mains $18-26; 11:30am-3pm & 5-10pm) Beautiful people lounge about the outdoor sofas and tables at this see-and-be-seen fish house on the SoCo strip. Reservations are essential.

AROUND TOWN

Galaxy Cafe (☎ 512-478-3434; 1000 W Lynn St; breakfasts & sandwiches $6-9, dinner specials $11; 7am-10pm) Oh, that flourless chocolate cake! Or is it the sweet-potato french fries with the blue-cheesey burger? Or maybe it's the retro self-serve diner decor (in a former laundromat) that keeps 'em coming back.

Salt Lick Bar-B-Que (☎ 512-894-3117; www.saltlickbbq.com; 18300 FM 1826, Driftwood; mains $10-16; 11am-10pm) It's worth the 20-mile drive just to see the massive outdoor barbecue pits at this park-like place off US 290. It's a bit of a tourist fave, but the crowd-filled experience still gets our nod. BYOB.

Drinking

The frat-boy brawl that is E 6th St gets started evenings when middle-aged tourists fill the dozens of similarly pubby bars. As the night progresses, the crowd gets younger and rowdier than a pig in heat. It's not necessarily the best Austin has to offer, but it is something to see. Start at Congress Ave and crawl your way east or west.

The lounges around the Warehouse District (near the intersection of W 4th and Colorado Sts) are a bit more upscale and attract a more sophisticated crowd. Far W 6th St (from Lamar Blvd to Congress Ave) is the newest eat-and-drink destination: the fun-loving **Tiniest Bar in Texas** (☎ 512-391-6222; 817 W 5th St; ⏲ 2pm-2am) has a Wii game inside and a huge patio outside.

SoCo caters to the more offbeat in eclectic Austin. Grab a homemade shake at the Austin-original **Amy's Ice Cream** (☎ 512-440-7488; 1301 S Congress Ave; ⏲ 11am-10pm) or a table and coffee across the street at **Jo's** (☎ 512-444-3800; 1300 S Congress Ave; ⏲ 7am-10pm;), an outdoor-only café, and then watch as the local tattoo art walks by.

Entertainment

LIVE MUSIC

Now you're talking – music is the reason to come to Austin. More than a hundred clubs host jam sessions throughout the week, and that doesn't include the restaurants, grocery stores (like Whole Foods), record shops and city hall that also have live music. The free weekly *Austin Chronicle* (www.austinchronicle.com) and the 360 entertainment section in Thursday's *Austin American-Statesman* (www.austin360.com) newspaper both have listings. Remember, even clubs are nonsmoking. The most concentrated of the music 'hoods is Red River St, a pretty hard-core scene in which indie, ska and metal prevail. Otherwise clubs are spread through the drinking districts (listed above) and beyond.

Continental Club (☎ 512-441-2444; www.continentalclub.com; 1315 S Congress Ave) Beret-wearing beatniks, suburban housewives and backpack-toting tourists come together at this granddaddy of all Austin clubs. The two nightly shows might be any kind of music.

Broken Spoke (☎ 512-442-6189; www.brokenspokeaustintx.com; 3201 S Lamar Blvd; ⏲ 11am-midnight Tue-Thu, to 2am Fri & Sat) With sand-covered wood floors and wagon-wheel chandeliers that George Strait once hung from, Broken Spoke is a true Texas honky-tonk. Look for local country acts like Dale Watson and Gary Nunn.

Cactus Cafe (☎ 512-475-6599; www.myspace.com/cactuscafeaustin; Texas Union, cnr 24th & Guadalupe Sts; ⏲ 3pm-midnight Mon-Thu, to 1am Fri & Sat) Listen to acoustic up close and personal at this intimate club on the UT campus.

Antone's (☎ 512-320-8424; www.antones.net; 213 W 5th St) This is the blues greats' swanky first choice when they stop in Austin. If Texas-native Marcia Ball is playing – go.

Emo's (☎ 512-477-3666; www.emosaustin.com; 603 Red River St) Emo's leads the pack in the punk and indie scene along Red River St.

Jovita's (☎ 512-447-7825; www.jovitas.com; 1619 S 1st St; ⏲ 11am-11pm Tue-Sun) Shows start at 6pm or 8pm at Jovita's restaurant, which has a huge stage for live Tex-Mex music.

THEATER & CINEMA

Long Center for the Performing Arts (☎ 512-457-5100; www.longcenter.org; 701 W Riverside Dr) This state-of-the-art theater opened in late 2008 as part

TEXAS

THE MUSIC FESTIVAL TO END ALL MUSIC FESTIVALS

Nearly 10,000 musicians and fans converge on Austin for five days in mid-March for **South by Southwest** (SXSW; ☎ 512-467-7979; http://sxsw.com), the mecca of music festivals. The roughly 1700 acts that play around town represent every genre of music – metal funk, indie ska, baseline jazz, rock, acoustic… And there are scads more unofficial bands playing at unofficial venues. Then there are the parties, both private and public (some are listed at www.austinist.com). This is the best (for indie music-lovers) or worst (for crowd-haters) time to be in Austin. Hotels are often booked a year in advance.

Buying a Platinum Badge ($850 to $1145, depending how far ahead you buy) allows access to all three trade shows (music, film and internet), conferences, talks, film screenings, clubs and VIP lounges. A Music Badge ($550 to $695) gains entry to the music conference, trade show and nightly gigs (both badges are sold online starting in September). The cheapest way to get into the clubs, however, is to buy a wristband ($180). The surprise sale date – usually in late February or early March – is announced by same-day text message. For details, check online at http://wristbands.sxsw.com. Note that those with badges gain entry before those with wristbands; and capacity controls are strictly enforced, which means that everyone may not get in. If your heart's set on seeing a certain group, go early and wait through a couple of acts. Research pays: the same showcase bands that sell out nights also play day parties and in-store gigs. Check the *Austin Chronicle* (www.austinchronicle.com) for SXSW event listings.

GAY & LESBIAN AUSTIN

The **Austin Gay & Lesbian Chamber of Commerce** (☎ 512-472-4422; www.aglcc.org) sponsors the Pride Parade in June, as well as smaller events throughout the year. The *Austin Chronicle* (www.austinchronicle.com) runs a gay event column among the weekly listings, and the glossy *L Style/G Style* (www.lstylegstyle.com) magazine has a dual gal/guy focus.

A relative newcomer to the GLBT scene, **Rusty Spurs** (☎ 512-482-9002; www.rustyspurs.com; 405 E 7th St) is part country-and-western dance club, part patio bar and part cabaret. A few doors apart in the Warehouse District are two popular gay dance clubs: **Oilcan Harry's** (☎ 512-320-8823; www.oilcanharrys.com; 211 W 4th St) raves on with loud house music and a raucous crowd; and **Rain** (☎ 513-494-1190; www.rainon4th.com; 217 W 4th St) is a bit more laid-back, with a pool table and patio in addition to a dancefloor.

Outside town, at Lake Travis, Hippie Hollow (opposite) is a clothing-optional, gay-friendly beach. First Splash and Last Splash parties (the first Sunday in May and September, respectively) draw big crowds.

of a waterfront redevelopment along Lady Bird Lake. The multistage venue hosts drama, dance, concerts and comedians.

Alamo Drafthouse Cinema (☎ 512-867-1839; www.originalalamo.com; 409 Colorado St; admission $7) Eat dinner, down a brewski, and watch cult classics and independent films at a downtown theater. The quote-along *Princess Bride* showings are pretty hilarious.

TEXAS

Sports

Get ready to rumble – it's roller-derby night and the Hellcat women skaters are expected to kick some Cherry Bomb ass. No matter who wins, the **TXRD Lonestar Rollergirls** (www.txrd.com) league always puts on a good show, usually at the **Austin Convention Center** (☎ 512-404-4000; www.austinconventioncenter.com; 500 E Cesar Chavez St).

Shopping

Find something fun at all the kitsch candy and costume shops, vintage-clothing stores and cool boutiques on S Congress Ave. On the first Thursday of every month, stores stay open late and restaurants host bands on the patios.

Allen Boots (☎ 512-447-1413; 1522 S Congress Ave) Need new fire-red lizard boots with orange flames licking up the side? Allen Boots stocks thousands of the best pairs of attention-grabbing boots – just ask local celebrity Sandra Bullock.

Waterloo Records (☎ 512-474-2500; www.waterloorecords.com; 600 N Lamar Blvd; 9am-10pm) Austin's one-stop music central shop hosts concerts, sells tickets and generally acts as *the* source for local music info – in addition to selling CDs.

New Bohemia (☎ 512-326-1238; 1606 S Congress Ave; noon-10pm) When it comes to retro thrift shops, New Bohemia is the place to look for vintage jewelry and clothing.

Ecowise (☎ 512-326-4474; 1110 W Elizabeth St) Earth-friendly gifts, toys and housewares are for sale off SoCo.

Getting There & Around

Austin-Bergstrom International Airport (AUS; ☎ 512-530-2242; www.ci.austin.tx.us/austinairport) is off Hwy 71, southeast of downtown. The Airport Flyer (bus 100, $1.50) runs to downtown (7th St and Congress Ave) and UT (Congress Ave and 18th St) every 40 minutes or so. **SuperShuttle** (☎ 512-258-3826; www.supershuttle.com) charges $16 from the airport to downtown. A taxi between the airport and downtown costs from $20 to $25. Most of the national rental-car companies are represented at the airport.

The **Greyhound Bus Station** (☎ 512-458-4463; www.greyhound.com; 916 E Koenig Lane) is located on the north side of town off I-35; take bus 7 (Duval; $1.50) to downtown. More than 10 buses a day leave for San Antonio (from $16, 1½ hours).

The *Texas Eagle*, heading from San Antonio to Chicago, stops at Austin's **Amtrak Station** (☎ 512-476-5684; www.amtrak.com; 250 N Lamar Blvd).

Capital Metro (☎ 512-474-1200; www.capmetro.org) runs a citywide service, including the tourist-oriented Dillo trolleybus (50¢ per ride). The Congress Dillo line runs north–south on the namesake avenue, connecting the capitol with 6th St. The 6th St Dillo runs west through town on 6th and back east on 5th St.

AROUND AUSTIN

Northwest of Austin along the Colorado River are the six Highland Lakes. Though recent years have seen serious droughts, one of the most popular lakes for recreation – when there's water – is the 19,000-sq-acre **Lake Travis**. Rent boats and jet skis at the associated marina, or overnight in the posh digs at **Lakeway Resort and Spa** (☎ 512-261-6600; www.dolce-lakeway-hotel.com; 101 Lakeway Dr; r from $169;), off Hwy 71. **Lake Austin Spa Resort** (☎ 512-372-7300; www.lakeaustin.com; 1705 S Quinlan Park Rd, off FM 2222; 3-night packages from $1600;) is the premier place to be pampered in the state. And Lake Travis has Texas' only official nude beach. **Hippie Hollow** (www.hippiehollow.com; day pass $10; 9am-dusk Sep-May, 8am-dusk Jun-Aug) is a popular gay hangout with regular events – naked yoga, anyone? To get there from FM 2222, take Rte 620 south 1.5 miles to Comanche Trail and turn right. The entrance is 2 miles ahead on the left.

HILL COUNTRY

Detour down dirt roads in search of fields of wildflowers, check into a dude ranch to live the cowboy life, float along the Guadalupe River on a lazy day or twirl around an old dance-hall floor. Most of the small towns in the rolling hills and valleys to the west and between Austin and San Antonio are easy day trips – from either city. More than a century ago, German and Czech immigrants settled these towns; look for their influence in the local names and food offerings.

Gruene

False-front wood buildings and old German homes make this the quintessential rustic Texas town. All of Gruene (pronounced *green*) is on the National Historic Register – and boy, do day-trippers know it. You won't be alone wandering among the arts-and-crafts and knickknack shops in search of the perfect straw cowboy hat. However, dancing at the place that stakes claim to being Texas' oldest dance hall (c 1878), **Gruene Hall** (☎ 830-606-1281; www.gruenehall.com; 1280 Gruene Rd; 11am-9pm Mon-Wed, 10am-midnight Thu & Fri, 10am-1am Sat, 10am-9pm Sun), makes it all worthwhile. Country, Cajun or folk-rock bands play nightly in summer, and at least three nights a week the rest of the year. If you go in on a weekend afternoon, you don't have to pay a cover.

Lonestar Music Store (☎ 830-627-1992; 1243 Gruene Rd; 10am-7pm Sun-Thu, to 9pm Sat & Sun) has a great Texas-music selection and also hosts concerts some Sunday afternoons.

Launch in Gruene to float lazily downriver in an inner tube, which is a Texas summer tradition. Rent what you need at **Rockin' R River Rides** (☎ 830-629-9999; www.rockinr.com; 1405 Gruene

TEXAS

AUSTIN LOUNGE LIZARDS

For more than 20 years the **Austin Lounge Lizards** (www.austinloungelizards.com) have been playing Texas clubs and poking some serious fun at subjects from passion to politics in a bevy of musical genres, including folk, country, bluegrass and surfers' rock. Founding member, and native Texan, Conrad Deisler plays guitar and contributes to the wacky, wordsmithy lyrics. He answered some of our questions.

A lot of your songs, such as the repetitively redundant ballad 'Big Rio Grande River,' deal with Texas topics... Texas is so rife with outrages both legendary and banal that a whole raft of songwriters could mine its veins for decades without bumping into each other.

What do you consider best/worst about the state? Does your 'Stupid Texas Song' ('Our accents are the drawliest, our howdies are the y'alliest, our Lone Star flag's the waviest, our fried steak's the cream-graviest...') have anything to do with it? If you spend a little time here, you'll quickly learn to place the hype in proper perspective. It's almost like an inside joke – everybody knows that Texas is huge, hot, flat and prone to natural disasters and venomous snakes, but come on down and we will show you a good time!

Immigration is always a hot topic – thoughts? Our song 'Teenage Immigrant Welfare Mothers on Drugs' gets timelier by the moment. We didn't write it, but we enhanced it with Lee Goland's permission. After one show, a Mexican immigrant approached me – his wife and friend were quite upset. He said he'd been in this country for seven years and thought he understood the song as satire. I told him that, indeed, we were depicting those who express bitter opposition to the influx of foreign workers while profiting from their labor. He seemed relieved. We shook hands.

THE BEST BBQ

People take their BBQ pretty personally in Texas. Every few years *Texas Monthly* stirs the pot by publishing its picks for the best 'Q (most recently in 2008). Central Texas has a strong meat-market tradition that dates back to German and Czech settlers' influence.

Arguably the BBQ capital of Texas, Lockhart (20 miles southeast of Austin on US 183) has four places to get your fix. The two most frequented are barnlike **Kreuz Market** (☎ 512-398-2361; 619 N Colorado St; 10:30am-8pm Mon-Sat), where the ribs taste like peppery jerky on the outside and juicy tenderloin inside – ham, beans and such are also served. **Smitty's** (☎ 512-398-9344; 208 S Commerce St; 7am-6pm Mon-Sat, 9am-3pm Sun) is the real deal: the blackened pit room and homely dining room are all original (knives used to be chained to the tables). Ask them to trim off the fat on the brisket if you're particular about that.

But judging from our unscientific but extensive tasting, it's nearby Luling's **City Market** (☎ 830-875-9019; 633 E Davis; 7am-6pm Mon-Sat) that wins all-round best BBQ in the state. Years of smoke blacken the pit room, the brisket is always succulent, the sausage is made on-site and a tart-and-tangy sauce adds a lot. Besides, everybody knows everybody here – it's a real slice of small-town life. Don't ask for utensils or plates: there haven't been any since it opened in the 1930s. Why fix what ain't broke? Your hands and butcher paper will do just fine.

For more tasty bits, check out Robb Walsh's *Legends of Texas Barbecue Cookbook* and *Follow the Smoke: 14,783 Miles of Great Texas Barbecue* by John DeMers.

Rd; tubes per day $17; 8am-2:30pm). The outfitter buses you up the Guadalupe and you float the three to four hours back to base. Put a plastic (not Styrofoam) cooler full of adult beverages (cans, no bottles) in a bottom-fortified tube next to you and you have a day.

If you can still stand afterwards, you could dine out on the decks overlooking the river at **Gristmill Restaurant** (☎ 830-625-0684; 1287 Gruene Rd; mains $15-22; 11am-11pm), an open-air place sort of contained in an old mill ruin.

What with all the BBQ pits, volleyball nets, tube rental and grassy riverfront lawn, the rustic, removed **Gruene Outpost River Lodge** (☎ 830-625-7772; www.grueneoutpostlodge.com; 1273 River Tce; r $85-125;) feels a bit like summer camp. The more central, innlike **Gruene Apple Bed & Breakfast** (☎ 830-643-1234; www.grueneapple.com; 1235 Gruene Rd; r incl breakfast $195-235;) is a bit more swish – with a movie-screening room, individually decorated guest quarters and elaborate breakfasts.

Gruene is just off I-10 and Rte 46, 45 miles south of Austin and 25 miles northeast of San Antonio.

Fredericksburg

Victorian town houses filled with boutiques line the main street of the region's largest old German-settled town (c 1870). This extremely busy street is the six-lane US 290, which detracts from the town's quaintness. However, it doesn't seem to deter the parade of retirees who come to shop here. So if you like precious B&Bs and cute crafts, you've found your spot – just ask the **Fredericksburg Convention & Visitors Bureau** (☎ 830-997-6523; www.fredericksburg-texas.com; 302 E Austin St; 9am-5pm Mon-Sat, noon-5pm Sun). Be aware that not much German is spoken (or food cooked well) here anymore.

WWII Pacific fleet commander Admiral Chester Nimitz grew up in Fredericksburg. His family's old hotel contains part of the well-detailed **National Museum of the Pacific War** (☎ 830-997-4379; www.nimitz-museum.org; 100 Legacy Dr; adult/child $7/4; 9am-5pm), which has some larger artillery and tons of soldiers' mementos.

In and around the area are 15 wineries. Pick up a **wine-trail map** (www.texaswinetrail.com) at the visitor center or stop at **Fredericksburg Winery** (☎ 830-990-8747; www.fbgwinery.com; 247 W Main St; 10am-5:30pm Mon-Thu, to 7:30pm Fri & Sat, noon-5:30pm Sun) for an in-town tasting.

Eighteen miles north of Fredericksburg, **Enchanted Rock State Natural Area** (☎ 325-247-3903; www.tpwd.state.tx.us; Rte 965; adult/child $6/free; 8am-10pm) is a 425ft-high, big pink rock that sure looks out of place. If you want to climb it, go early; gates close when the daily attendance quota is reached.

Nearly 300 B&Bs do business in this county; **Gastehaus Schmidt Reservation Service** (☎ 830-997-5612; www.fbglodging.com) helps sort them out. National newsman Dan Rather came from Fredericksburg; his star-chef daughter Rebecca runs **Rather Sweet Bakery**

& Café (☎ 830-990-0498; 249 E Main St; sweets $2-5, sandwiches $6-9; 🕑 8am-5pm Mon-Sat).

Fredericksburg is 78 miles west of Austin on Hwy 281, and 70 miles north of San Antonio (via I-10 and US 87). **Kerrville Bus Co** (☎ 800-231-2222; www.iridekbc.com; Golden Convenience Store, 1001 S Adams St) sends two daily buses to and from San Antonio (from $27, two hours); none to Austin.

Luckenbach

Calling Luckenbach a town is a bit of an exaggeration. The handful of creaky wooden buildings here includes a dance hall, a concession stand, a hat shop and the **General Store & Luckenbach Bar** (☎ 830-997-3224; www.luckenbachtexas.com; 🕑 9am-10pm Mon-Sat, noon-10pm Sun). Part fun Western mercantile, part post office and part beer joint, this oddball place has been a country-music shrine ever since Hondo Crouch bought the 'town' in 1970 and invited friends like Waylon and Willie to hang out. Pickers and singers still play most afternoons (1pm), either inside the store or out under the oak trees. Check online for events; frequent festivals take over the place. From Fredericksburg, follow US 290 east to FM 1376 and turn south about 3 miles.

Bandera

Cowboy up! Bandera's worked hard to keep its Old West character – no McDonald's are allowed in this town, pardner. Here you see horses regularly tied up on the main street, and numerous local saloons are goin' strong. From the false-front buildings, stores sell Western duds or rustic antiques, and a few cafés serve up hearty grub. There's always something doin': strolling minstrels and cowboy demonstrations entertain on the main street from 1pm to 4pm each Saturday, April though November; cowboy Christmas events take over after that.

But the main reason why wannabe cowpokes come is to saddle up at the dozen or so outlying dude ranches. The friendly folks at **Bandera County Visitors Bureau** (☎ 800-364-3833; www.banderacowboycapital.com; 1206 Hackberry St; 🕑 9am-5pm Mon-Fri, 10am-4pm Sat) will gladly help figure out which dude ranch suits you. At most, lodging (cabins or rooms), meals (cookouts or buffets) and at least a one-hour horseback ride per day are included for an average of $95 to $150 per person, per night. There may also be hay rides, kids' programs, ropin' lessons, swimming and such, depending on the place.

At **Silver Spur Guest Ranch** (☎ 830-796-3037; www.ssranch.com; 9266 Bandera Creek Rd), in addition to overnightin', you can do nonguest day rides – one hour on horseback plus a campfire-cooked breakfast costs about $50. **Twin Elm Ranch** (☎ 830-796-3628; www.twinelmranch.com; cnr Rte 470 & Hwy 16; rodeo nonguests/guests $6/free; 🕑 8pm Fri May-Aug) has lots of family-friendly activities, including river tubing, and hosts open-to-the-public rodeos on Fridays in season. Serious riders should check into **Hill Country Equestrian Lodge** (☎ 830-796-7950; www.hillcountryequestlodge.com; 1580 Hay Hollar Rd), a smaller (pricier) operation that dotes on its horses, won't take more than five people out on a ride at a time and only offers breakfast.

Digging into a big steak-and-eggs breakfast at **OST Restaurant** (☎ 830-796-3836; 305 Main St; breakfast $4-7, mains $7-14; 🕑 6am-10pm) before a ride just seems right. For entertainment after the sun goes down, mosey over to the patio at **11th Street Cowboy Bar** (☎ 830-796-4849; 307 11th St; 🕑 10am-midnight Mon-Fri, to 1am Sat, noon-midnight

SCENIC DRIVE: WILDFLOWER TRAILS

You know spring has arrived in Texas when you see cars pulling up roadside and families climbing out to take the requisite picture of their kids surrounded by bluebonnets – the state flower. From March to April in Hill Country, orange Indian paintbrushes, deep-purple winecups and white-to-blue bluebonnets are at their peak. To see vast cultivated fields of color, there's **Wildseed Farms** (☎ 800-848-0078; www.wildseedfarms.com; 100 Legacy Dr; general admission free, botanical garden $5; 🕑 9am-6:30pm), which is 7 miles east of Fredericksburg on US 290. Or for a more do-it-yourself experience, check with TXDOT's **Wildflower Hotline** (☎ 800-452-9292) to find out what's blooming where. Taking Rte 16 and FM 1323, north from Fredericksburg and east to Willow City, is usually a good route. Then again you might just set to wandering – most backroads host their own shows daily.

Sun). Hank Williams Sr used to play at **Arky Blue's Silver Dollar Saloon** (☎ 830-796-8826; 308 Main St; 🕑 10am-2am); look for the table into which he carved his name. Both bars have live country crooners from Friday to Sunday.

From Austin, Bandera is about 100 miles (via I-35 and Rte 46); it's 27 miles northwest of San Antonio's outskirts on Rte 16 (or Bandera Rd).

SAN ANTONIO

More than 2.5 million tourists a year cry 'Remember the Alamo!' as they stampede ol' San Antone's central mission, the site of the infamous battle/massacre. Crowds come for the history, and to party along the tree-shaded Riverwalk – which has more cafés and clubs than a dog has fleas. The volume of visitors is daunting (as is the amount of commercial crap that's developed around the Alamo – Davy Crockett's wild amusement ride?), but the lively Tex-Mex culture (about 60% of the 1.35 million residents have Hispanic heritage) is worth experiencing. Sure, see the Alamo and the Riverwalk, but go beyond them. Drink an *agua fresca* (fruit-infused water) at the *mercado* (marketplace) and then hear country music at an old country store – here you can *fiesta* one day and rodeo the next.

TEXAS

History

In the 18th century the Spanish established a string of missions in the area for territorial defense and the religious conversion of the indigenous people. By 1724 the Mission San Antonio de Valero (now known as the Alamo) had been moved to the current site. The town became the seat of the Tejas state government in an independent Mexico. A few years later, a large influx of German immigrants arrived post–US statehood. The city's growth in the 20th century was due in large part to local military bases – and tourist dollars.

Orientation

The intersection of Commerce and Losoya Sts is the very heart of downtown and the Riverwalk, which runs in a U shape below street level. Signs point out access stairways, but a 3-D map bought at the info center is the best way to get oriented. Southtown and the King William Historic District lie south along the river.

Information

Visitor center 'amigos' (in turquoise shirts and straw hats) roam the downtown core offering direction.

Alamo Bookstore (☎ 210-225-1391; www.thealamo.org; Alamo, 300 Alamo Plaza; 🕑 9am-5:30pm Mon-Sat, 10am-5:30pm Sun, to 7pm daily Jun-Aug) Amazing array of area history books.

Good Bytes Café (☎ 210-444-2233; www.goodbytescafe.org; 418 W Commerce St; 🕑 7am-7pm Mon-Fri, 11am-5pm Sat) Free internet for a cause (proceeds from food sales go to Goodwill and local job training).

Out in San Antonio (www.outinsanantonio.com) Local gay and lesbian info online.

Post office (☎ 210-220-5331; 100 W Houston St)

San Antonio Express-News (www.mysa.com) Daily news and travel info on web.

San Antonio Public Library (www.mysapl.org) Branch locations provide free internet access across the city.

Visitor Information Center (☎ 210-207-6748; www.sanantoniovisit.com; 317 Alamo Plaza; 🕑 9am-5pm) Free coupon booklets and souvenirs for sale, but don't expect restaurant recommendations – they aren't allowed to make 'em.

Sights & Activities

In addition to what's listed here, there are flashy diversions downtown (rides, laser-tag mazes, believe-it-or-not freak shows…) and two amusement parks (Fiesta Texas and SeaWorld) on Loop 1604.

THE ALAMO

A 17-minute film and exhibits in the Long Barrack Museum at the **Alamo** (☎ 210-225-1391; www.thealamo.org; 300 Alamo Plaza; admission free; 🕑 9am-5:30pm Mon-Sat, 10am-5:30pm Sun, to 7pm daily Jun-Aug) tell the full story of the 13 days in 1836 when Mexican general Santa Anna laid siege to this occupied garrison. A few wall fragments and the mission church (its iconic facade dates from 1846) are all that remain of the original structure. The contemporary appellation of the mission is probably derived from the name of one of the early troops stationed there: the *Compañia de Alamo de Parras*. For more on the history of the siege, see the boxed text, p722.

RIVERWALK

Stroll past landscaped hotel gardens, eat at riverside cafés, stop into souvenir shops and cruise the waterway: the Riverwalk is an essential part of the San Antonio experience. Restaurant after restaurant, and bar after bar,

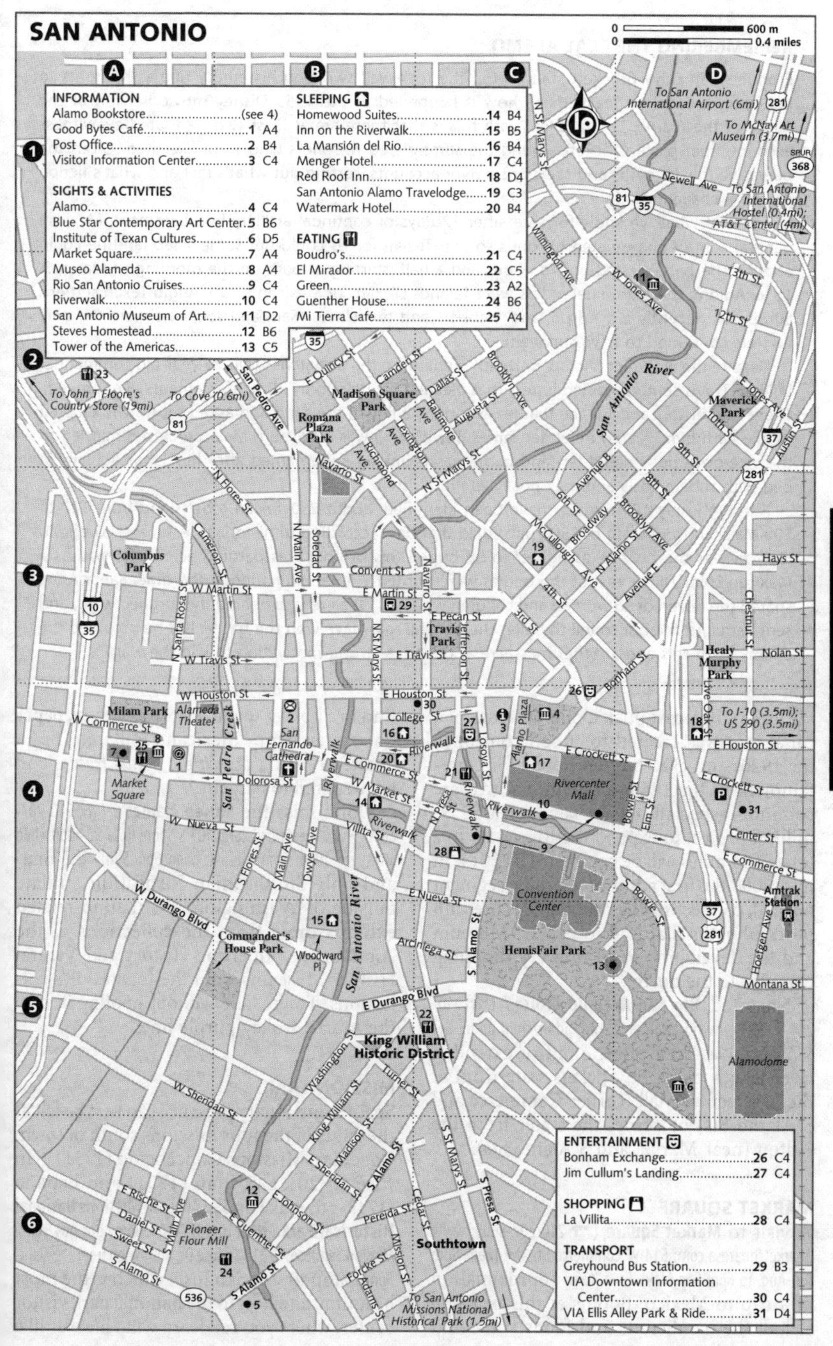
SAN ANTONIO
INFORMATION
Alamo Bookstore (see 4)
Good Bytes Café 1 A4
Post Office 2 B4
Visitor Information Center 3 C4
SIGHTS & ACTIVITIES
Alamo 4 C4
Blue Star Contemporary Art Center 5 B6
Institute of Texan Cultures 6 D5
Market Square 7 A4
Museo Alameda 8 A4
Rio San Antonio Cruises 9 C4
Riverwalk 10 C4
San Antonio Museum of Art 11 D2
Steves Homestead 12 B6
Tower of the Americas 13 C5
SLEEPING
Homewood Suites 14 B4
Inn on the Riverwalk 15 B5
La Mansión del Rio 16 B4
Menger Hotel 17 C4
Red Roof Inn 18 D4
San Antonio Alamo Travelodge 19 C3
Watermark Hotel 20 B4
EATING
Boudro's 21 C4
El Mirador 22 C5
Green 23 A2
Guenther House 24 B6
Mi Tierra Café 25 A4
ENTERTAINMENT
Bonham Exchange 26 C4
Jim Cullum's Landing 27 C4
SHOPPING
La Villita 28 C4
TRANSPORT
Greyhound Bus Station 29 B3
VIA Downtown Information Center 30 C4
VIA Ellis Alley Park & Ride 31 D4
To San Antonio International Airport (6mi)
To McNay Art Museum (3.7mi)
To San Antonio International Hostel (0.4mi); AT&T Center (4mi)
To John T Floore's Country Store (19mi)
To Cove (0.6mi)
To I-10 (3.5mi); US 290 (3.5mi)
To San Antonio Missions National Historical Park (1.5mi)
Madison Square Park
Romana Plaza Park
Maverick Park
Columbus Park
Travis Park
Healy Murphy Park
Milam Park
Alameda Theater
San Fernando Cathedral
Market Square
Rivercenter Mall
Convention Center
HemisFair Park
Commander's House Park
King William Historic District
Southtown
Alamodome
Amtrak Station
Pioneer Flour Mill
San Antonio River
San Pedro Creek
TEXAS

REMEMBERING THE REAL ALAMO

Frontiersman Davy Crockett stands atop the rock wall swinging his empty rifle as he fights to his dying breath…at least, that's how it happened in the 1955 Disney movie version of the battle of the Alamo. The problem with this is that there are at least two translated eyewitness accounts that place Crockett among the surrendered prisoners who were executed. Given the pervasive movie myths and sketchy survivor accounts, sorting out what's fact and what's fiction can be a challenge.

Some of what we know for sure: after 12 days of continual artillery bombardment, Mexican general Santa Anna quieted his guns so that Texian forces could get some sleep (and he could attack). The battle lasted only an hour and a half, starting at 5am on the morning of March 3, 1836. Among the Alamo defenders were Tejanos (Texans of Mexican birth), Anglo-Texan settlers, Europeans, recently arrived US land-grabbers and two slaves (Sam and Joe, who were the only fighters confirmed to have survived).

Despite the eloquent 'Victory or Death' signatures, the dispatches that 26-year-old commander William Travis sent contained letters that pleaded for help (only 30 reinforcements ever arrived). There's no historical evidence that he ever drew a line in the sand and asked those who crossed to 'die with him.' Alamo defender James Bowie, who was a US-born Mexican citizen married to the vice-governor's daughter (and had a nasty-looking knife named after him), was actually in bed with tuberculosis and may not have fired a shot.

Although only 189 remains have been identified, about 250 Texian rebels (and from 120 to 500 Mexican troops out of 1500-plus) died that day, according to historians' estimates. Gregorio Esparza was the only Texas fighter to be buried (his brother was battling across the wall as a Mexican soldier); the rest of the bodies were burned – an abomination at the time. Santa Anna spared the dozen or so women and children who had taken refuge behind the fortified walls, and sent Sam and Joe out to tell the tale. The general may have won the battle, but he provided the enemy, with this and another massacre at Goliad, a strong motivation to win the war.

vie for your tourist buck along the sides of a canal that was created for flood control in the 1920s and '30s, but developed for entertainment in the 1940s and '50s. Crowds are common, especially on weekends. The $259-million project to expand the Riverwalk to a total of 14 miles will be completed by 2014. In mid-2009 the first additional 2-mile segment opened, connecting the commercial core with peaceful paths that lead to the Art Museum and the developing Pearl Brewery shopping complex to the north.

Narrated **Rio San Antonio Cruises** (☎ 210-244-5700; www.riosanantonio.com; adult/child under 5yr $8.50/2; 🕑 9am-9pm) ply the entire extended river length daily. Buy tickets waterfront at the Rivercenter Mall (corner Commerce and S Alamo Sts) or across the water from the Hilton (near Market and S Alamo Sts).

MARKET SQUARE

A visit to **Market Square** (☎ 210-207-8600; www.marketsquaresa.com; 514 W Commerce St; 🕑 10am-8pm Jun-Aug, to 6pm Sep-May) is a fair approximation of a trip to Mexico. Booths at this *mercado* sell all the handicrafts and foods you could find in a border town: Talavera pottery, paper flowers, authentic Mexican vanilla, etc. Buy a Tecate beer or a pineapple *aguas frescas* and be prepared to bargain.

Don't miss the **Museo Alameda** (☎ 210-207-8600; www.thealameda.org; 101 S Santa Rosa St; adult/child $8/3; 🕑 10am-6pm Tue-Sat, noon-6pm Sun), the one-and-only Smithsonian Institution affiliate outside of Washington, DC. Latino-related exhibits draw from the collections of the Air & Space, American History and Natural History Museums from the Institution's collections. To get here without hoofing it, take the tourist trolley purple line.

MISSION TRAIL

Spain's missionary presence can best be felt at the ruins of the four missions south of town. Together, Missions Concepción (1731), San José (1720), San Juan (1731) and Espada (1745–56) make up **San Antonio Missions National Historical Park** (☎ 210-932-1001; www.nps.gov/saan; Mission San José, 6701 San José Dr; admission free; 🕑 9am-5pm). Stop first at San José, which is the most beautiful, and host to the national park visitor center, where you can learn what life was like here from an informative film and a few exhibits. Free tours are offered at each mission. From the Alamo, take S St Marys St to Mission Rd. Bus 42 serves some of the Mission Trail from downtown (Navarro and Villita Sts).

AROUND DOWNTOWN

Thirty cultures, including Native American and Mexican, have made Texas what it is; explore them at the museum of the **Institute of Texan Cultures** (☎ 210-458-2300; www.texancultures.utsa.edu; 801 S Bowie St; adult/child $7/4; 10am-6pm Tue-Sat, noon-5pm Sun). Afterwards you can ride up to the observation deck of the 750ft **Tower of the Americas** (☎ 210-223-3101; www.toweroftheamericas.com; HemisFair Park; adult/child $11/9; 9am-10pm Sun-Thu, to 11pm Fri & Sat). Admission includes a glitzy, Texas-themed 3-D theater ride.

Late 19th- to early-20th-century colonial-revival mansions and Queen Anne cottages inhabit the **King William Historic District** (www.saconservation.org) near E Durango Blvd and S St Mary St. The only home regularly open to the public is the **Steves Homestead** (☎ 210-225-5924; 509 King William St; adult/child $6/free; 10am-3:30pm).

Across S Alamo St to the east is **Southtown** (www.southtown.net), a small arts district. On the first Friday of every month, galleries stay open late and restaurants host entertainment. A 1920s warehouse contains the **Blue Star Contemporary Art Center** (☎ 210-227-6960; www.bluestarartspace.org; 116 Blue Star; admission free; noon-6pm Wed-Sun) and its fiber arts, photography and contemporary studio spaces.

Way more traditional is the **San Antonio Museum of Art** (SAMA; ☎ 210-978-8100; www.samuseum.org; 200 W Jones Ave; adult/child $8/3; 10am-5pm Tue-Sat, noon-6pm Sun), which has a good collection of Spanish Colonial, folk-Mexican and pre-Columbian works. In late 2008 the **McNay Art Museum** (☎ 210-824-5368; www.mcnayart.org; 600 N New Braunfels Ave; adult/child $8/free; 10am-5pm Tue-Sat, noon-5pm Sun) opened a 45,000-sq-ft addition to its original mansion home, set on 23 acres.

Festivals & Events

San Antonio Stock Show & Rodeo (☎ 210-225-5851; www.sarodeo.com) Big-name concerts follow each night's rodeo; 16 days in mid-February.

Fiesta San Antonio (☎ 210-227-5191; www.fiesta-sa.org) Over 10 days in mid-April there are river parades, carnivals, Tejano music, dancing and tons of food in a mammoth, citywide party.

Sleeping

San Antonio has at least 10 gazillion-trillion hotel rooms, so you have plenty of choices right downtown. Unlike more business-oriented Texas towns, high rates here are on weekends, not weekdays.

BUDGET

San Antonio International Hostel (☎ 210-223-9426; 621 Pierce St; dm $18, r incl breakfast $59-89; P) With stuffy barrackslike bunk rooms, this place wouldn't be much worth mentioning – except it's the only hostel in town and there is a pool. The associated B&B rooms occupy an antique-filled house. Pierce St is off Grason St, northeast of downtown.

Several standard chain motels have outlets just a few blocks from Rivercenter Mall, including the exterior-access **San Antonio Alamo Travelodge** (☎ 210-222-1000; www.travelodge.com; 405 Broadway; r $59-99; P) and the high-rise **Red Roof Inn** (☎ 210-229-9973; www.redroof.com; 1011 E Houston St; r $65-99; P). Free parking at both is a real plus.

MIDRANGE

Menger Hotel (☎ 210-223-4361; www.historicmenger.com; 204 Alamo Plaza; r $129-179) President Teddy Roosevelt once gathered his Rough Riders in the bar, and Confederate general Robert E Lee rode his horse into the lobby. This living-museum-cum-luxury-hotel is so welcoming that several spirits never left.

Inn on the Riverwalk (☎ 210-225-6333; www.innonriver.com; 129 Woodward Pl; r incl breakfast $129-239; P) Cottage rooms with Jacuzzi tubs, riverview rooms, multiroom rooms: all 16 decorator-designed digs are different, spread among three old houses-turned-B&B. This peaceful stretch of the river is just an eight-minute walk from the party.

Homewood Suites (☎ 210-222-1515; www.homewoodsuites.com; 432 W Market St; r $169-219) Free breakfast and light happy-hour meals with drinks (Monday to Thursday) come standard at this all-suite property. The two-story gathering-room windows frame the Riverwalk nicely.

TOP END

La Mansión del Rio (☎ 210-518-1000; www.lamansion.com; 112 College St; r $199-249) Rustic beams adorn ceilings, dark-wood French doors open to riverfront patios and balconies;

Spanish-colonial élan drips from every terracotta fountain here.

Watermark Hotel (☎ 210-396-5800; www.watermarkhotel.com; 212 W Crockett St; r $299-379;) The Watermark is like a sigh: deeply serene and timeless. Neutral neoclassical designs include cool marble beneath your feet – in the lobby, in the bathrooms, but best yet, in parts of the rooftop spa.

Eating & Drinking

Trip on the Riverwalk and you'll bump into a bar-restaurant (or fall in the water). S St Marys and S Alamo Sts in the Southtown–King William districts also host a good number of eateries. Look for hole-in-the-wall Mexican joints scattered the length of N Flores St.

Green (☎ 210-320-5865; 1017 N Flores St; meals $6-9; 9am-9pm Sun-Fri; V) San Antonio's only 100% vegetarian restaurant (think eggplant enchiladas) is solar powered and community oriented; there's a farmers market here two Sundays a month.

El Mirador (☎ 210-225-4444; 722 S St Marys St; mains $6-11; 6am-3pm Mon, 6am-10pm Tue-Sat, 9am-2pm Sun) Impossibly tender *carne asada* (marinated, grilled flank steak) is always on the menu at this traditional Mexican haunt, but changing soups like *caldo de rez* (beef and cabbage) are the specialty.

Guenther House (☎ 210-227-1061; 205 E Guenther St; meals $7-9; 7am-3pm) Enjoy some of the sweetest, light waffles ever at the café in the historic home to former owners of Pioneer Flour Mill (next door).

Mi Tierra Café (☎ 210-225-1262; 218 Produce Row, Market Sq; breakfast $7-10, mains $7-15; 24hr) Red-velvet booths, colorful streamers, guitar-playing troubadours, a colorful *pan dulce* (sweet pastry) counter – this Market Sq veteran is touristed, but tops for pageantry *à la Mexicana.*

Boudro's (☎ 210-224-8484; 421 E Commerce St; lunch $7-14, dinner mains $22-32; 11am-11pm) Boudro's is the locals' riverside favorite for upscale Texas tastes. Try the quail stuffed with poblano peppers, apricots and corn.

> **WORTH THE TRIP: FLOORE'S COUNTRY STORE**
>
> This terrific old bar and dance hall first opened in 1942 as a store run by a friend of Willie Nelson. (Willie used to play here nightly; the sign still says so.) Today at **John T Floore's Country Store** (☎ 210-695-8827; www.liveatfloores.com; 14492 Bandera Rd, Helotes; tickets $10-30; 11am-9pm Sun & Tue-Thu, to 12:30am Fri & Sat), whether in the outdoor stage yard or by the fire in the rustic building, this is the true way to hear Texas country music on a Friday or Saturday night. Bandera Rd is off Hwy 16.

Entertainment

For listings of local music and cultural events, pick up the free weekly *San Antonio Current* (www.sacurrent.com).

LIVE MUSIC & NIGHTCLUBS

Dick's Last–Ugly–Hard Rock – the Riverwalk's many chain clubs blur together even before you've started drinking. Perhaps the best thing to do is take a margarita taste-test tour (if you're walking); or can you find the place that has the 42oz gulper, or the 'horni'est on the walk?

Cove (☎ 210-227-2683; 606 W Cypress St; 11am-11pm Tue-Thu, to midnight Fri, to 1am Sat;) Jazz, bluegrass, roots and rock – they play it all. The Cove is an incredibly unique combo of food stand/café/laundromat/car wash, with a kiddie playground (you read right).

Jim Cullum's Landing (☎ 210-223-7266; www.landing.com; 123 Losoya St) Listen to area jazz legends here and everyone will think you're a local.

Bonham Exchange (☎ 210-271-3811; www.bonhamexchange.com; 411 Bonham St) A stalwart brick building conceals San Antonio's premier, multifloor gay dance club.

SPORTS

Four-time NBA champions the **San Antonio Spurs** (☎ 210-554-7787; www.nba.com/spurs) shoot hoops at the **AT&T Center** (☎ 210-444-5000; 1 AT&T Center Pkwy & Walters St), off I-35. Purchase tickets through **Ticketmaster** (☎ 210-224-9600; www.ticketmaster.com).

Shopping

A few artisan craft shops exist among the tourist-T-shirt-filled Riverwalk. The old buildings of the city's first neighborhood, **La Villita** (www.lavillita.com; La Villita St), house the largest concentration of galleries and boutiques.

Getting There & Away

You can reach 28 US and Mexican cities nonstop from **San Antonio International Airport** (SAT; ☎ 210-207-3411; www.sanantonio.gov/airport),

TEXAS

8 miles north of the Riverwalk off I-410, east of Hwy 281. VIA city bus 5 ($1) runs from the airport to downtown about every 30 minutes, or you can take a **SATrans** (☎ 210-281-9900; www.saairportshuttle.com) shuttle bus for $17. A taxicab ride will cost about $25. Major car-rental agencies all have offices at the airport.

From the **Greyhound Bus Station** (☎ 210-270-5824; www.greyhound.com; 500 N St Marys St), you can get to all the big cities in the state (and lots of the small ones). For example, Houston is 3½ hours (from $24) away.

The *Sunset Limited* (Florida–California) and *Texas Eagle* (San Antonio–Chicago) trains stop a few days a week (usually late at night) at the **Amtrak Station** (☎ 210-223-3226; www.amtrak.com; 350 Hoefgen Ave).

Getting Around

The extremely tourist-friendly downtown trolleybus routes ($1.10 one way) are the best way to cover any distance around downtown. Buy a day pass ($4) at **VIA Downtown Information Center** (☎ 210-362-2020; www.viainfo.net; 260 E Houston St; 🕒 9am-6pm Mon-Fri, to 2pm Sat).

Parking-garage fees in San Antonio really add up. You can park free at the **VIA Ellis Alley Park & Ride** (☎ 210-362-2020; btwn E Crockett & Center Sts; 🕒 ticket office 7am-6pm Mon-Fri, 9am-2pm Sat), a quick two stops from the Alamo. Ask for a parking transfer on the bus and put it in the slot to 'pay' when you exit.

HOUSTON

Concrete superhighways may blind you to Houston's good points when you first zoom into the sprawling town. But, look around. The nation's fourth-largest city (2.2 million in the city proper, 5.8 million in the metro area) is really a multicultural, zoning-free hodgepodge in which you see both world-class paintings and funky folk art. In one strip mall there might be a Vietnamese grocery, a Venezuelan empanada stand and a high-priced Texas meat market. And outside of town are Space Center Houston (p731) and the Gulf of Mexico beaches on Galveston Island (p731). The interest's here; you just have to drive a little to get to it.

Houston absorbed hundreds of thousands of new residents when Hurricane Katrina pummeled neighboring Louisiana. Three years later in 2008, Galveston and Houston took a direct hit from Hurricane Ike. Inland areas did fairly well compared with the island, where recovery continues.

DON'T MISS

- **Menil Collection** – exceptional contemporary art and a 13th-century Cypriot fresco chapel (p726)
- **Orange Show Center for Visionary Art** – funky folk-art orange and beer-can houses (p728)
- **Space Center Houston** – Apollo rockets and interactive spaceman fun (p731)
- **Breakfast Klub** – dig into wings-and-waffles or catfish 'n' grits (p729)

Orientation

Where I-45 (northwest–southeast), I-59 (southwest–northeast) and I-10 (east–west) meet forms downtown Houston. The light-rail system line starts along Main St downtown and zooms south to the Museum District, Hermann Park, the Texas Medical Center and on to the behemoth Reliant Stadium. Mid-town begins immediately southwest of downtown. The eclectic Montrose neighborhood is a little further west of the center. Westheimer (local street names don't always have modifiers like Rd or Dr) runs from it to wealthy River Oaks and out to the Galleria at I-610.

Information

Brazos Bookstore (Map p727; ☎ 713-523-0701; 2421 Bissonnet St) Independent bookseller, author events.
Chase Bank (Map p728; ☎ 713-216-4865; 712 Main St) Currency exchange and ATM.
Greater Houston Convention & Visitors Bureau (Map p728; ☎ 713-437-5200; www.visithoustontexas.com; cnr Walker & Bagby Sts; 🕒 9am-4pm Mon-Sat, 11am-4pm Sun) Free parking on Walker St.
Houston Public Library (Map p728; ☎ 713-236-1313; www.hpl.lib.tx.us; 500 McKinney St; 🕒 9am-9pm Mon-Thu, 9am-6pm Fri & Sat, 1-5pm Sun) Free internet computers and wi-fi.
KUHT 88.7 Classical music and NPR (National Public Radio) from the University of Houston.
Memorial Hermann Hospital (Map p727; ☎ 713-704-4000; 6411 Fannin St) Part of the Texas Medical Center megacomplex.
Police station (Map p727; ☎ 713-529-3100; 802 Westheimer; 🕒 24hr)
Post office (Map p728; ☎ 713-226-3161; 401 Franklin St)

Sights & Activities

In addition to the sights listed below, there are small museums on the Holocaust, printing history, funerary tradition and firefighters. Don't miss the day trips (see p731).

Local philanthropists John and Dominique de Menil's 15,000 artworks form the core of the impressive **Menil Collection** (Map p727; ☎ 713-525-9400; www.menil.org; 1515 Sul Ross St; admission free; 🕒 11am-7pm Wed-Sun). The couple's taste ran from the medieval to the surreal – several rooms in the main building are devoted to the likes of René Magritte and Max Ernst. The **Cy Twombly Gallery** (Map p727; ☎ 713-525-9450; 1501 Branard St; admission free; 🕒 11am-7pm Wed-Sun) annex contains very abstract art. And Menil's importation of a complete 13th-century Cypriot fresco almost caused an international incident. But in the end Dominique custom-built the stunning **Byzantine Fresco Chapel Museum** (Map p727; ☎ 713-521-3990; 4011 Yupon Dr; admission free; 🕒 11am-6pm Fri-Sun) to fit the ceiling art, which is to be held in trust for 99 years. Fourteen large abstract-expressionist Mark Rothko paintings anchor the much more modern sanctuary, **Rothko Chapel** (Map p727; ☎ 713-524-9839; www.rothkochapel.org; 3900 Yupon Dr; admission free; 🕒 10am-6pm).

French-Impressionism and post-1945 European and American painting are particularly well represented at the wide-ranging **Museum of Fine Arts, Houston** (Map p727; ☎ 713-639-7300; www.mfah.org; 1001 Bissonnet St; adult/child $7/3.50, free Thu; 🕒 10am-5pm Tue & Wed, 10am-9pm Thu, 10am-7pm Fri & Sat, 12:15-7pm Sun). Across the street, admire the talents of luminaries like Rodin and Matisse in the **Cullen Sculpture Garden** (Map p727; cnr Montrose Blvd & Bissonnet St; admission free).

Delve into excellent traveling shows, often with shiny themes like Treasures of Ancient Afghanistan etc, at the **Houston Museum of Natural Science** (Map p727; ☎ 713-639-4629; www.hmns.org; 1 Hermann Circle; adult/child $15/10; 🕒 9am-5pm Mon-Sat, 11am-9pm Sun). Dinosaurs, fossils, gems and mineral exhibits – plus an IMAX, a planetarium and a tropical-butterfly conservatory – are permanent exhibits. The museum is celebrating a 100-year history by making expansion plans.

And now for something funky: the warehouselike **Art Car Museum** (off Map p727; ☎ 713-861-5526; www.artcarmuseum.com; 140 Heights Blvd; admission free; 🕒 11am-6pm Wed-Sun) contains more than 15 vehicles that have been tricked out and turned into things like psychedelic, buglike and Mad Max–esque wonders. All have taken part in the 250-car-strong annual spring Art Car Parade. Rotating exhibits are also offbeat: they've included subjects like road refuse and bone art. This is one of several quirky local collections (see also boxed text, p728).

Houston for Children

Young 'uns gettin' restless? Since mid-2008, there's been a new place to play – right downtown. The 10-acre **Discovery Green** (Map p728; www.discoverygreen.com; Avenida de las Americas; 👪) park has a lake, playground, play fountains, art, restaurants and an outdoor performance space. The entire park was constructed to strict Leadership in Energy and Environmental Design (LEED) 'gold level' standards.

In the museum district, **Hermann Park** (Map p727; www.hermannpark.org; 600 Fannin St; 👪) is home to playgrounds, a lake with paddleboats, the **Hermann Park Miniature Train** (Map p727; ☎ 713-529-5216; per ride $2.75; 🕒 10am-6pm; 👪) and the **Houston Zoo** (Map p727; ☎ 713-533-6500; www.houstonzoo.org; 1513 N MacGregor Dr; adult/child $10/6; 🕒 9am-5pm, to 6pm Jun-Aug; 👪).

Walking distance from the park is the activity-filled **Children's Museum of Houston** (Map p727; ☎ 713-522-1138; www.cmhouston.org; 1500 Binz St; admission $7; 🕒 9am-5pm Tue-Sat, to 8pm Thu, noon-5pm Sun; 👪), where little ones can make tortillas in a Mexican village or draw in an open-air art studio.

Festivals & Events

Houston Livestock Show & Rodeo (☎ 832-667-1000; www.hlsr.com) Twenty days in March of midway rides, prize bulls and a nightly rodeo, followed by a concert.

Art Car Parade & Festival (www.orangeshow.org; Allen Parkway) Wacky arted-out automobiles roll on by on the second Sunday in May.

Sleeping

Chain motels line all the major freeways. If you are visiting the Space Center and Galveston, consider staying on I-45 south.

BUDGET

Houston International Hostel (Map p727; ☎ 713-523-1009; www.houstonhostel.com; 5302 Crawford St; dm $18; P 🅧 💻 📶) Semipermanent residents and

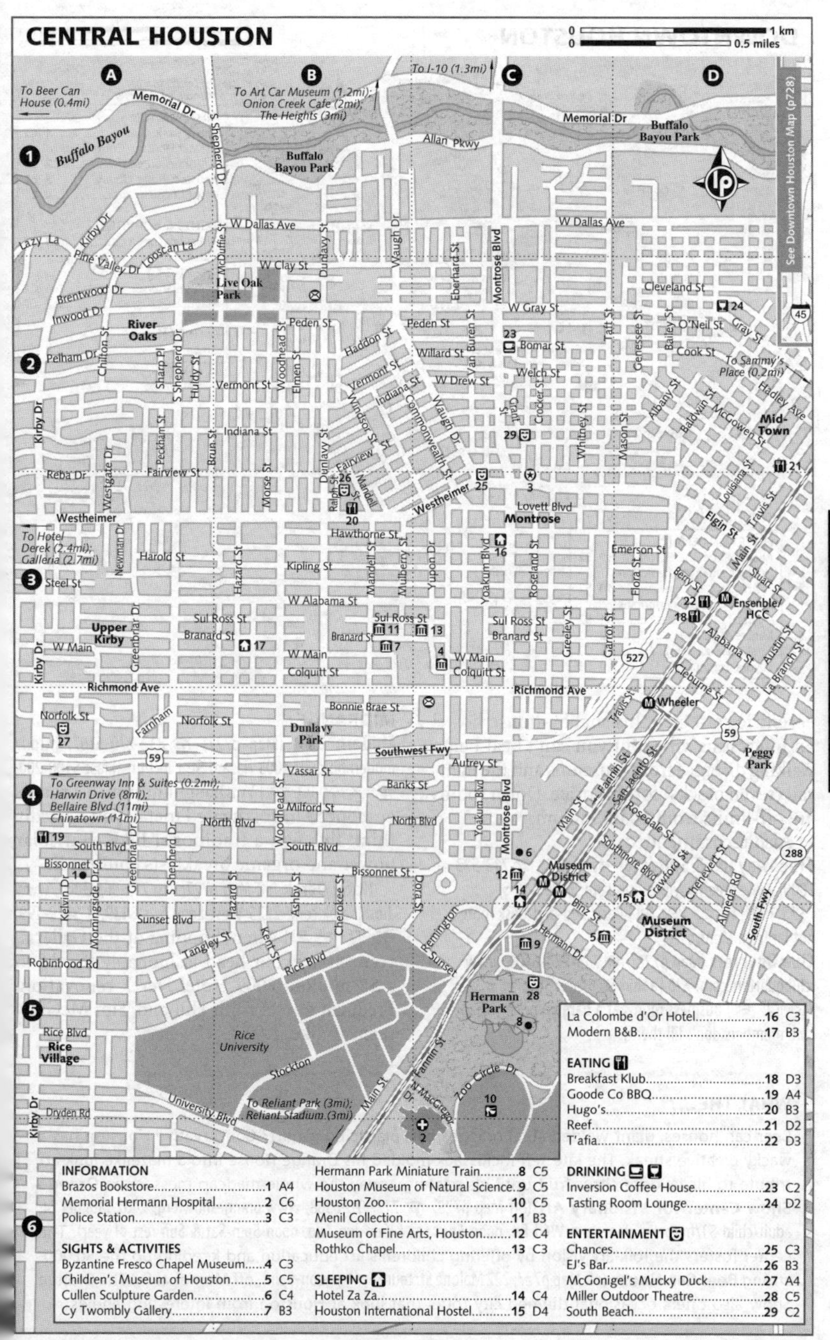
CENTRAL HOUSTON
0 1 km
0 0.5 miles
A
B
C
D
1
2
3
4
5
6
To Beer Can House (0.4mi)
To Art Car Museum (1.2mi); Onion Creek Cafe (2mi); The Heights (3mi)
To I-10 (1.3mi)
See Downtown Houston Map (p728)
Memorial Dr
Buffalo Bayou
Buffalo Bayou Park
Allan Pkwy
S Shepherd Dr
W Dallas Ave
Lazy La
Kirby Dr
Pine Valley Dr
Looscan La
McDuffie St
W Clay St
Dunlavy St
Waugh Dr
Eberhard St
Montrose Blvd
Brentwood Dr
Inwood Dr
Live Oak Park
River Oaks
Peden St
Cleveland St
W Gray St
O'Neil St
Gray St
Bomar St
Cook St
To Sammy's Place (0.2mi)
Pelham Dr
Chilton St
Sharp Pl
Huldy St
Woodhead St
Elmen St
Haddon St
Willard St
Van Buren St
Welch St
Taft St
Genessee St
Bailey St
Vermont St
Indiana St
W Drew St
Hadley Ave
Albany St
Baldwin St
McCowen St
Mid-Town
Windsor St
Commonwealth St
Grant St
Crocker St
Whitney St
Mason St
Peckham St
Brun St
Westgate Dr
Reba Dr
Fairview St
Morse St
Mandell St
Ralph St
Westheimer
Lovett Blvd
Montrose
Louisiana St
Travis St
Elgin St
To Hotel Derek (2.4mi); Galleria (2.7mi)
Newman Dr
Harold St
Hawthorne St
Emerson St
Main St
Kipling St
Yupon Dr
Mulberry St
Yoakum Blvd
Roseland St
Flora St
Berry St
Stuart St
Steel St
Hazard St
W Alabama St
Ensemble/HCC
Upper Kirby
Greenbriar Dr
Sul Ross St
Branard St
Greeley St
Garrott St
Alabama St
Austin St
W Main
Colquitt St
Cleburne St
La Branch St
Richmond Ave
Wheeler
Norfolk St
Farnham
Bonnie Brae St
Dunlavy Park
Southwest Fwy
Peggy Park
Autrey St
Vassar St
Banks St
To Greenway Inn & Suites (0.2mi); Harwin Drive (8mi); Bellaire Blvd (11mi) Chinatown (11mi)
Milford St
North Blvd
South Blvd
Fannin St
San Jacinto St
Rosedale St
Southmore Blvd
Bissonnet St
Kelvin Dr
Morningside Dr
Ashby St
Cherokee St
Dora St
Museum District
Crawford St
Chenevert St
Almeda Rd
South Fwy
Sunset Blvd
Binz St
Tangley St
Kent St
Remington
Hermann Dr
Robinhood Rd
Rice Blvd
Sunset
Hermann Park
Rice Village
Rice University
Stockton
Zoo Circle Dr
N MacGregor Dr
University Blvd
To Reliant Park (3mi); Reliant Stadium (3mi)
Dryden Rd
45
59
527
288
INFORMATION
Brazos Bookstore....1 A4
Memorial Hermann Hospital....2 C6
Police Station....3 C3
SIGHTS & ACTIVITIES
Byzantine Fresco Chapel Museum....4 C3
Children's Museum of Houston....5 C5
Cullen Sculpture Garden....6 C4
Cy Twombly Gallery....7 B3
Hermann Park Miniature Train....8 C5
Houston Museum of Natural Science....9 C5
Houston Zoo....10 C5
Menil Collection....11 B3
Museum of Fine Arts, Houston....12 C4
Rothko Chapel....13 C3
SLEEPING
Hotel Za Za....14 C4
Houston International Hostel....15 D4
La Colombe d'Or Hotel....16 C3
Modern B&B....17 B3
EATING
Breakfast Klub....18 D3
Goode Co BBQ....19 A4
Hugo's....20 B3
Reef....21 D2
T'afia....22 D3
DRINKING
Inversion Coffee House....23 C2
Tasting Room Lounge....24 D2
ENTERTAINMENT
Chances....25 C3
EJ's Bar....26 B3
McGonigel's Mucky Duck....27 A4
Miller Outdoor Theatre....28 C5
South Beach....29 C2

TEXAS

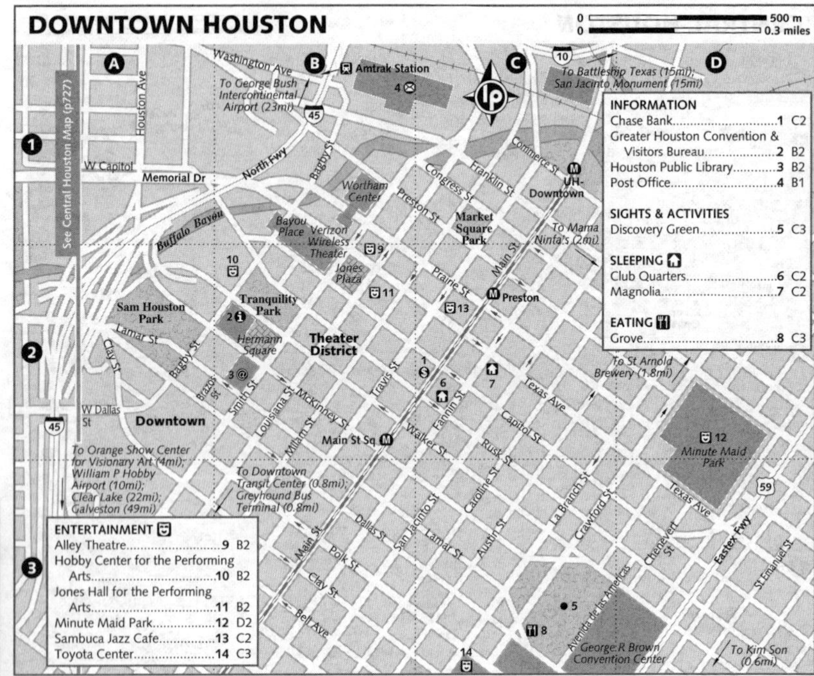

eccentric staff give this shabby-house hostel an interesting vibe. But you can't beat being walking distance from museums and the light-rail (seven blocks) for this price. Dorm rooms are off-limits from 10am to 5pm.

Also recommended:

Greenway Inn & Suites (off Map p727; ☎ 713-523-1009; www.greenwayinnsuites.com; 2929 I-59 S; r $73-100; P ✲ ᯤ) Basic bed-and-desk motel, not far from Montrose.

Club Quarters (Map p728; ☎ 713-224-6400; www.clubquarters.com; 720 Fannin St; r from $89; ✲ ▢ ᯤ) Business rooms at a bargain price (when club members don't fill them).

MIDRANGE

Modern B&B (Map p727; ☎ 832-279-6367; http://modernbb.com; 4003 Hazard St; r incl breakfast $100-200; P ✲ ▢ ᯤ) With eight minimalist rooms ensconced in corrugated metal, you'd hardly think this was a traditional B&B. But solar power and organic breakfasts confirm it.

Hotel Derek (off Map p727; ☎ 713-961-3000; www.hotelderek.com; 2525 West Loop S; s $139, d $179-199; ✲ ▢ ᯤ) After shopping at the Galleria, you can lay your head fashionably thanks to a $2 million, 2009 Hotel Derek renovation. Frequent guests Faith Hill and Tim McGraw seem to like it.

WHAT THE...?

Beer-can houses, giant welded-steel oranges and plastic flower art? Conservative Houston has a wacky creative streak. The late Jeff McKissack molded his Orange House into a mazelike junk-art tribute to his favorite citrus fruit until his passing; today the whole madcap mess is the **Orange Show Center for Visionary Art** (off Map p728; ☎ 713-926-6368; www.orangeshow.org; 2402 Munger St; adult/child $1/free; ⏲ 9am-1pm Wed-Fri, noon-5pm Sat & Sun Jun-Aug, noon-5pm Sat & Sun rest of year). The center fosters the folk-art vision by offering children's art education and keeping up the 50,000-strong **Beer Can House** (off Map p727; 222 Malone St; tour $5; ⏲ noon-5pm), off Memorial Dr. The Orange Show also offers occasional themed city tours that look at Houston from interesting angles.

IF YOU HAVE A FEW MORE DAYS

History-lovers, drive 15 miles west of downtown to see where Texas nationhood was won on April 21, 1836. The 570ft **San Jacinto Monument** (off Map p728; ☎ 281-479-2421; www.tpwd.state.tx.us; 3523 Hwy 134, La Porte; adult/child $12/8; 9am-6pm) looks like the Washington Monument but has a cement star on top (which makes it 12ft taller). Tour the museum, watch the movie and then ride up to the observation deck to look over the 1000-acre battlefield, where Texan forces under General Sam Houston shouted 'Remember the Alamo' while whooping Mexican general Santa Anna's forces. You can tour the still-afloat 1912 **Battleship Texas** (off Map p728; adult/child $10/5; 10am-5pm), also part of the park.

Magnolia (Map p728; ☎ 713-221-0011; www.magnoliahotelhouston.com; 1100 Texas Ave; r $141-225;) Dressed in deep woods and modern neutrals, rooms at this downtown hotel are both stylish *and* comfortable.

TOP END

Hotel Za Za (Map p727; ☎ 713-526-1991; www.hotelzaza.com; 5701 Main St; r $205-270;)It's see-and-be-seen at this flamboyantly hip Museum District hotel. Imagine silk brocade, plus animal prints and leather.

La Colombe d'Or Hotel (Map p727; ☎ 713-524-7999; www.lacolombedor.com; 3410 Montrose Blvd; r $225-525;) Sotheby-quality antiques and rare oil paintings fill six suitelike rooms in a 1923 Montrose mansion.

Eating

Montrose and Upper Kirby are two of the principal eating enclaves, but the downtown is improving; check out the restaurants clustered around Main and McKinney Sts and the new-in-2009 Pavillions complex at Fannin & Dallas Sts. Steak is huge in Houston; most all of the national heavy hitters – Ruth's Chris, the Palm etc – are on Westheimer near the Galleria.

DOWNTOWN

Kim Son (Map p728; ☎ 713-222-2461; 2001 Jefferson St; lunch specials $6-10, mains $10-18; 11am-11pm) For more than 25 years, Kim Son has been a local legend with a booklike Vietnamese menu (300-plus items).

Grove (Map p728; ☎ 713-337-7321; 1611 Lamar St; sandwiches $7-19, mains $12-27; 11am-10pm) Free-range chicken potpie, rosemary french fries…the American classics get a modern metropolitan update at the Grove.

MID-TOWN

our pick **Breakfast Klub** (Map p727; ☎ 713-528-8561; www.thebreakfastklub.com; 3711 Travis St; mains $4-10; 7am-2pm Mon-Fri, 8am-2pm Sat) Down-home cookin' with soul. Whether it's wings 'n' waffles for breakfast or red beans and rice for lunch, expect a wait at this funky coffeehouselike place.

Reef (Map p727; ☎ 713-526-8282; 2600 Travis St; lunch $11-19, dinner mains $19-29; 11am-10pm Mon-Fri, 5-11pm Sat) Gulf Coast seafood is served in a sleek and sophisticated dining room with a skyline-view raw bar. The chef has won oodles of awards.

T'afia (Map p727; ☎ 713-524-6922; 3701 Travis St; mains $15-22; 5:30-10pm Tue-Thu, to 10:30pm Fri & Sat) Chef Monica Pope is committed to using top-quality local and organic ingredients in her new American cuisine. A farmers market is held here 8am to noon each Saturday.

MONTROSE & UPPER KIRBY

Goode Co BBQ (Map p727; ☎ 713-522-2530; 5109 Kirby Dr; mains $7-10; 11am-10pm) Belly up to piles of beef brisket, jalapeño sausages and smoked duck in a big ol' barn or out back on picnic tables.

Hugo's (Map p727; ☎ 713-524-7744; 1600 Westheimer; lunch $14-19, dinner mains $18-28; 11am-10pm Sun-Thu, to 11pm Fri & Sat) Chef Hugo Ortega is known for his inspired interior-Mexican regional cuisine, like squash-blossom crepes and Veracruz snapper with olives and capers.

Drinking

For eclectic (and expensive) cocktails with downtown views, head to the patio bar at the Grove (left). Market Square Park, downtown at Congress and Milam Sts, has a good dive bar or two.

Tasting Room Lounge (Map p727; ☎ 713-528-6402; 114 Gray St) More than 100 wines are available by the glass. Bring your dog for 'yappy' hour on the patio.

St Arnold Brewery (off Map p728; ☎ 713-686-9494; 2000 Lyons Ave; tours $5; 1pm Sat) If you take the 40-minute tour, you're invited for free

GAY & LESBIAN HOUSTON

Montrose has been the town's gathering place for gay men and women for decades. That's not to say the town isn't conservative: public displays of affection will probably turn heads. Every June, the **Pride Committee of Houston** (☎ 713-529-6979; www.pridehouston.org) sponsors a huge gay-pride parade; related events and festivals take place all month. KPFT 90.1 FM is the home of Queer Voices radio. The *Houston Voice* (www.houstonvoice.com) is the gay and lesbian newspaper, and *Out Smart Magazine* (www.outsmartmagazine.com) has loads of local info.

Enjoy a tasty cup o' Joe with the boys at **Inversion Coffee House** (Map p727; ☎ 713-523-4866; 1953 Montrose Blvd; 6:30am-midnight Mon-Sat, 7:30am-10:30pm Sun;). Several clubs line Pacific St; the high-tech sound and dancefloor lights help make **South Beach** (Map p727; ☎ 713-529-7623; www.southbeachthenightclub.com; 810 Pacific St) the busiest and best. **EJ's Bar** (Map p727; ☎ 713-527-9071; www.ejsbar.com; 2517 Ralph St) puts some hunky eye candy on display during regular amateur strip shows.

You have three different stages and styles to choose from at the popular lesbian dance bar **Chances** (Map p727; ☎ 713-523-7217; www.chancesbar.com; 1100 Westheimer) – country and western, dance or live chick-band music. Note that parking is limited (avoid Hollywood Video's lot: they tow).

tasting of Texas-only microbrews in the beer garden until 3pm. Bringing bag lunches is encouraged.

The corner of White Oak and Studemont in the Heights has a few funky little bars, including a roadhouse, a tiki bar and a live music club in an old house. A few blocks further, **Onion Creek Cafe** (off Map p727; ☎ 713-880-0768; 3106 White Oak; 7am-2am) is a great neighborhood hangout with a big patio; open from early-morning coffee to late-night cocktails.

Entertainment

There's a fair bit of nightlife around the Preston and Main Street Square stops downtown. Montrose and Mid-town have clubs, but they're spread around. Look for listings in the independent weekly *Houston Press* (www.houstonpress.com) and in the Thursday edition of the *Houston Chronicle* (www.chron.com).

NIGHTCLUBS & LIVE MUSIC

McGonigel's Mucky Duck (Map p727; ☎ 713-528-5999; www.mcgonigels.com; 2425 Norfolk St) Listen nightly to live acoustic, Irish, folk and country performers in pubby surrounds.

Sammy's Place (Map p727; ☎ 713-751-3101; www.sammysat2016main.com; 2016 Main St) Live your rock-star dream, karaoke-ing on nights there's a live band accompanying. Other evenings may be Motown music, '80s cover bands or a DJ.

Sambuca Jazz Cafe (Map p728; ☎ 713-224-5299; www.sambucarestaurant.com; 900 Texas Ave) A swanky supper club, Sambuca serves live jazz accompanied by an eclectic menu.

THEATER & PERFORMING ARTS

The Houston Grand Opera, the Society of the Performing Arts, Houston Ballet, Da Camera chamber orchestra and the Houston Symphony all perform downtown in the **Theater District** (www.houstontheaterdistrict.org). From the district's website, you can purchase tickets and view all schedules. Venues include the following:

Alley Theatre (Map p728; ☎ 713-228-8421; 615 Texas Ave)

Hobby Center for the Performing Arts (Map p728; ☎ 713-315-2525; 800 Bagby St)

Jones Hall for the Performing Arts (Map p728; ☎ 713-227-3974; 615 Louisiana St)

Miller Outdoor Theatre (Map p727; ☎ 281-373-3386; www.milleroutdoortheatre.com; 100 Concert Dr) Hermann Park's outdoor theater is a great place to lay out a blanket on a summer night and enjoy a free play, musical or concert.

SPORTS

Reliant Stadium (off Map p727; ☎ 832-667-1400; www.reliantpark.com; 1 Reliant Park) is home to the **Houston Texans** (☎ 877-635-2002; www.houstontexans.com) football team. The **Houston Astros** (☎ 713-259-8000; www.astros.com) play pro baseball downtown at **Minute Maid Park** (Map p728; 501 Crawford St). The **Toyota Center** (Map p728; ☎ 713-758-7200; www.houstontoyotacenter.com; 1510 Polk St) is home to the **Houston Rockets** (☎ 713-627-3865; www.houstonrockets.com) NBA basketball team.

Shopping

A huge conglomeration of shops collides in and near the mazelike **Galleria** (off Map p727; ☎ 713-

622-0663; www.simon.com; 5075 Westheimer), which is off I-610. Macy's, Foley's and Nordstrom anchor nearly 400 mall stores.

Along 19th St (between Yale and Shepherd) in the **Heights** (www.heightsfirstsaturday.com), Houston's first neighborhood, you'll find unique antiques, clever crafts, artsy furniture stores and cafés. On the first Saturday of every month, the street takes on a carnival-like air with outdoor booths and entertainment. North of I-10, Waugh Dr turns into Heights Blvd.

If you're looking for a sari, head to the Little India shops along **Harwin Drive** (Southwest Fwy), southwest of town off I-59; Houston's **Chinatown** (www.chinatownmap.com), and its scattered shops and restaurants, surround Bellaire Blvd at Beltway 8.

Getting There & Around

Houston Airport System (www.fly2houston.com) has two airports. Twenty-two miles north of the city center, **George Bush Intercontinental** (IAH; off Map p728; ☎ 281-230-3100; btwn I-45 & I-59 N), home base for Continental Airlines, serves cities worldwide through many carriers – one of the newest nonstop connections is Dohar, Qatar. Twelve miles southeast of town, **William P Hobby Airport** (HOU; off Map p728; ☎ 713-640-3000), off I-45 S, is a major hub for Southwest Airlines and domestic travel. Read your ticket closely: some airlines, like Delta, fly out of both airports. Wi-fi is available at both facilities.

The Hobby airport bus (88) connects to downtown (and to the Downtown Transit Center light-rail stop) from Monday to Saturday, 6am to 11pm ($1.25). The Airport Direct nonstop bus runs between the Downtown Transit Center and Bush Intercontinental ($15) daily from 5:30am to 8:30pm. **SuperShuttle** (☎ 800-258-3826; www.supershuttle.com) provides service from both Bush ($23) and Hobby ($19) airports. A taxi to IAH/HOU airports from downtown is about $40/25.

Long-distance buses arrive at the **Greyhound Bus Terminal** (off Map p728; ☎ 713-759-6565; www.greyhound.com; 2121 Main St), which is located between downtown and the Museum District, and two blocks from the Downtown Transit Center light-rail stop.

The *Sunset Limited* train stops at the **Amtrak Station** (Map p728; ☎ 713-224-1577; www.amtrak.com; 902 Washington Ave) three times a week.

Houston's **Metropolitan Transit Authority** (Metro; ☎ 713-635-4000; www.ridemetro.org) runs the convenient light-rail system; $1.25 gets you a one-way ride. Most of the in-town sights are along the Downtown–Museum District–Reliant Park light-rail corridor. If you want to venture further, you'll need to rent a car; the bus system is mostly inefficient for visitors' needs. Every major national car-rental agency can be found at either airport.

AROUND HOUSTON

Clear Lake Area

Dream of a landing on the moon? You can't get any closer (without years of training) than at **Space Center Houston** (☎ 281-244-2100; www.spacecenter.org; 1601 NASA Rd 1, Clear Lake; adult/child $20/16; 🕑 10am-5pm Mon-Fri, 10am-7pm Sat & Sun), off I-45 S, the official visitor center and museum of NASA's Johnson Space Center. Interactive exhibits let you try your hand at picking up an object in space or landing the shuttle. Be sure to enter the short theater films, because you exit past Apollo capsules and history exhibits. The free tram tour covers the center at work – shuttle training facilities, zero-gravity labs and the original mission control ('Houston, we have a problem').

Clear Lake's marinas, 22 miles from downtown, are Houston's recreational boating port of call. **Bay Area Houston Convention & Visitors Bureau** (☎ 281-338-0333; www.visitbayareahouston.com; 20710 I-45, Webster; 🕑 9am-5pm Mon-Fri) lists water-sports operators on its website. East on Galveston Bay, the **Kemah Boardwalk** (☎ 877-285-3624; www.kemah.com; cnr Bradford & 2nd Sts, Kemah; 🚸) took a beating in Hurricane Ike; however, the kid-savvy waterfront entertainment complex, with theme restaurants, shops, amusement rides, carnival games and a jet-boat ride, is up and running.

Galveston

Part genteel Southern lady, part sunburned beach bunny, Galveston Island is Houston's favorite playmate. In 2008 the old gal was ravaged by a direct hit from Hurricane Ike. The islandwide cleanup has continued for years and will go on, but many of the gingerbread-covered Victorian homes in the historic districts have been restored. Parts of waterfront 61st St may still be boarded up; nevertheless, shops are once again filling the old brick buildings on the Strand. At the time of writing, an ambitious beach restoration project was underway – refurbishing the depleted sands along the Gulf of Mexico.

The island (at the southeastern end of I-45, 49 miles from Houston) is 30 miles long but no more than 3 miles wide. From the highway, 61st St leads to Seawall Blvd along the Gulf. The Mechanic and 22nd Sts intersection centers the historic shopping district, the Strand. Ask at **Galveston Island Visitors Center** (☎ 409-763-4311; www.galveston.com; Ashton Villa, 2328 Broadway; 9am-5pm) for loads more dining and activity info.

Ike doesn't hold a candle to the killer hurricane that hit Galveston in 1921, submerging the island and claiming an estimated 8000 victims – still the country's worst natural disaster in terms of lives lost. Experience the Great Storm, narrated with entries from survivors' diaries, in the multimedia presentation at **Pier 21 Theatre** (☎ 409-763-8808; www.galveston.com/pier21theatre; cnr Pier 21 & Harborside Dr; adult/child $5/4; 11am-6pm Sun-Thu, to 8pm Fri & Sat). Next door, you can tour the *Elissa*, a beautiful 1877 Scottish tall ship, and investigate the town's 19th-century shipping heyday at the **Texas Seaport Museum** (☎ 409-763-1877; www.tsm-elissa.org; cnr Harborside Dr & 21st St; adult/child $7/5; 10am-5pm).

TEXAS

Small, free beaches lie between the Gulf and Seawall Blvd; follow that road to organized beach parks at the northeastern end of the island. At the time of writing, **Galveston Island State Park** (☎ 409-737-1222; www.tpwd.state.tx.us; cnr FM 3005 & 13 Mile Rd; admission free; 9am-5pm Sat & Sun), on the quieter southwestern end, has limited access.

Kids seem to love all the activity stuffed in and around the pastel glass pyramids of **Moody Gardens** (☎ 409-744-4673; www.moodygardens.com; 1 Hope Blvd; adult/child under 3yr $47/free; 10am-6pm;) – aquariums, a penguin encounter, a butterfly rain forest, swimming beach, theater rides…The ginormous, indoor–outdoor **Schlitterbahn Waterpark** (2026 Lockheed St; www.schlitterbahn.com; day pass adult/child $38/30; 10am-8pm Jun–mid-Aug;) further adds to the island's amusements; off-season hours vary.

It's easy to make Galveston a day trip from Houston. If you decide to stay over, the **Beachcomber Inn** (☎ 409-744-7133; www.galvestoninn.com; 2825 61st St; r $59-80;), a block from the beach, is a neat and clean bargain. Or you can bask in palm-fringed Spanish-colonial luxury in the historic **Hotel Galvez** (☎ 409-765-7721; www.galveston.com/galvez; 2024 Seawall Blvd; r $161-259;), where the pool deck has a lovely Gulf view and the full-service spa came back online mid-2009.

So close to the Gulf, it's no surprise that sea is the primary food source in Galveston; fish restaurants (mostly chains) line the bayside piers near the Strand. At the laid-back **Shrimp N Stuff** (☎ 409-763-2805; cnr 39th Blvd & Ave O; mains $7-12; 11am-10pm), the fried shrimp are hand-breaded and sauces are homemade. A local boy made good by buying and running the **Spot** (☎ 409-621-5237; 3204 Seawall Blvd; mains $10-19; 11am-10pm Sun-Thu, to 11pm Sat & Sun); the three old houses containing the restaurant–tiki bar–ice-cream parlor are a favorite local hangout, with a great Gulf-view patio.

Kerrville Bus Company (☎ 800-231-2222; www.iridekbc.com; 3825 Broadway) runs a morning bus and an evening bus (from $20, one hour) to Houston. Ike knocked the around-town **Galveston Island Rail Trolley** (www.islandtransit.net) clear off its tracks; when (if?) it will be running again is uncertain.

Piney Woods

In Piney Woods, northeast Texas, 100ft-plus-tall trees outnumber people. Nature is the attraction, but don't expect breathtaking vistas; here you'll find quiet trails and varied ecosystems. At **Big Thicket National Preserve** (☎ 409-246-2337; www.nps.gov/bith; cnr US 69 & Rte 420; admission free; visitor center 9am-5pm), coastal plains meet desert sand dunes, and cypress swamps stand next to pine and hardwood forests. If you're lucky, you may run across one of 20 species of small wild orchids while hiking the 45 miles of trail. The eight disparate park units are 100 miles northwest of Houston.

SOUTHERN GULF COAST

Sparkling bays, small harbors filled with shrimp boats and more than 60 miles of protected beaches, a trip to the Southern Gulf Coast can't help but focus on the water – you'll want to anyway, because the scrubby mesquite trees and prickly-pear cactus inland don't make for the prettiest of landscapes. From the region's largest town, Corpus Christi, you can tour a huge aircraft carrier and visit a national seashore. Further south, the climate becomes a bit more tropical. Once you're in the Valley, you're just about to Mexico.

ARANSAS NATIONAL WILDLIFE REFUGE

Back in 1951 only 31 whooping cranes remained in the world; today there are more than 500, thanks in large part to the preservation efforts at their wintering ground, the 70,504-acre **Aransas National Wildlife Refuge** (☎ 361-286-3559; www.fws.gov/southwest/refuges/texas/aransas.html; FM 744; per car $5; park sunrise-sunset, visitor center 8:30am-4:30pm), off Hwy 35. These giant white birds can stand 5ft tall (with a 7ft wingspan); from the observation tower you can usually spot one or two. Otherwise, to see the cranes you have to board a boat tour 35 miles south of the refuge in the town of **Rockport** (www.rockport-fulton.org). Captain Tommy with **Rockport Birding & Kayak Adventures** (☎ 877-892-4737; www.whoopingcranetours.com; tours $35; 7:30am & 1pm Mar-Nov) has a relatively small, shallow-drafting boat, and so can get you into back bays that larger charters can't reach.

CORPUS CHRISTI & AROUND

The salt breezes and palm tree–lined bay are quite pleasant in this 'city by the sea,' whose population numbers 285,000. Downtown has a waterfront promenade and a few museums, but there's not too much in town to entice visitors – and the city council seems to like it that way. Trip out to Padre Island and the National Seashore for a beachy break, though don't expect the windblown surf to be azure blue. To the north, Port Aransas is a bustling little fishing town with tons of restaurants and boat charters.

Shoreline Dr, in downtown Corpus, has a small beach; the street continues south as Ocean Dr, which has bayfront playgrounds and parks, as well as some serious mansions lining it. **Corpus Christi Convention & Visitors Bureau** (☎ 800-766-2322; www.corpuschristi-tx-cvb.org; 1823 N Chaparral; 9am-5pm Tue-Sat) has helpful coupons online.

Across the harbor bridge from downtown, by Corpus Christi Beach, see the foldable-winged airplanes that still cover the deck of the 900ft aircraft carrier **USS Lexington Museum** (☎ 361-888-4873; www.usslexington.com; 2914 N Shoreline Blvd; adult/child $13/8; 9am-6pm Jun-Aug, to 5pm rest of year). Next-door, exhibits at the **Texas State Aquarium** (☎ 361-881-1200; www.texasstateaquarium.org; 2710 N Shoreline Blvd; adult/child $15.50/10.50; 9am-6pm) focus on the Gulf of Mexico aquatic life and more.

Twenty miles east of downtown, off Hwy 358 (SPID), the sugar-sand beaches of **Padre Island** beckon. (Technically, this is 'North' Padre Island, but locals just call it 'the island.') Public access is easy – you can drive (15mph) and park on the packed sand at the water's edge (not on the dunes behind). No environmental groups seem to be protesting, but there is also a parking lot at **Bob Hall Pier** (15820 Park Rd 22) that you can use instead.

Downtown, there are several waterfront hotels; **Bayfront Inn** (☎ 361-883-7271; www.bayfrontinncc.com; 601 N Shoreline Blvd; r $60-110;) has the best basic-motel deals with a view of the bay. Numerous condos are for short-term rent on the island (see the visitors bureau website), and **Holiday Inn Sunspree Resort** (☎ 361-949-8041; www.ichotelsgroup.com; 15202 Windward Dr; r from $85;) sits right on the sand; plus it has a complimentary kids' club from Memorial Day through to Labor Day.

Bars and restaurants cluster on the streets surrounding Chaparral and Water Sts downtown – there are few restaurants on the island. Eat a fried-shrimp wrap from a surfboard table at longtime fave **Executive Surf Club** (☎ 361-884-7873; www.executivesurfclub.com; 309 N Water St; mains $6-10; 11am-11pm Sun-Wed, to midnight Thu-Sat). **Brewster St Icehouse** (☎ 361-884-2739; 1724 N Tancahua St; mains $7-16; 11am-2am;) has country-fried everything, cold brews, live country music (Thursday to Saturday nights) – and a playground for the kiddies.

Padre Island National Seashore

The 60 southern miles of 'North' Padre Island that lie outside Corpus Christi city limits are all a protected part of the **Padre Island National Seashore** (☎ 361-949-8068; www.nps.gov/pais; Park Rd 22; per car $10; visitor center 8:30am-4:30pm, to 6pm Jun-Aug). Four-wheel drive is necessary to see the extent of the park, but if you hike even a short distance from the visitor center, you'll be free of the crowds. The constant wind not only creates and moves dunes, it also attracts kite- and windsurfers to the inland-side Bird Island Basin area. Watch for the endangered Kemp Ridley sea turtles that nest in the park, and are closely protected. If you're visiting in late summer, you might be able to take part in a turtle release; call the **Hatchling Hotline** (☎ 361-949-7163) for information. Camping is available at the semideveloped, paved Malaquite campground ($8), or go primitive – beach camping is free with a permit.

WORTH THE TRIP: PORT ARANSAS

Driving north, Padre Island morphs imperceptibly into Mustang Island, at the tip of which (20 miles along) is **Port Aransas** (www.portaransas.org). This bustling little fishing and vacation village is worth a stop. From divey to divine, there are lots of places to eat seafood – look for names like Fin's, Hook's, Trout Street. Gulf fishing charters depart from here; **Fisherman's Wharf** (☎ 361-749-5448; www.wharfcat.com; 900 N Tarpon St; 5hr trip adult/child $60/30) has regular deep-sea excursions and runs jetty boats to outer islands (adult/child $12/6).

SOUTH PADRE ISLAND

Want to parasail, bungee jump and drink yourself silly? This condo-crammed island has beach activities and bars galore. **South Padre Island Visitor Center** (☎ 956-761-6433; www.sopadre.com; 600 Padre Blvd; 9am-5pm) website has a comprehensive list of mini-golf courses, rowdy restaurants, condo rentals and beachfront hotels. The tours and feeding presentations every 30 minutes at **Sea Turtle Inc** (☎ 956-761-4511; www.seaturtleinc.com; 6617 Padre Blvd; adult/child $3/1; 10am-4pm Tue-Sun) rescue facility are refreshingly educational entertainment.

If you want to experience a hard-core fisherman's life, stop in Port Isabel (before you cross the bridge) to eat or stay at **Marchan's White Sands Motel, Marina & Restaurant** (☎ 956-943-2414; www.the-white-sands.com; 418 W Hwy 100; breakfast $4-8, mains $7-16, r $69-109; 6am-9pm Tue-Sat, to 2pm Mon;).

THE VALLEY

Way down here in the Rio Grande Valley (known simply as 'the Valley'), you're spittin' distance from Mexico. Citrus tree plantations are gradually giving way to new subdivisions, but there are enough remaining to supply the roadside stands at which you can pick up fresh local grapefruits and oranges (harvested November through May).

Nuevo Progreso (www.shop-progreso.com), Mexico, is probably the border shopping town least affected by drug-cartel violence. We have friends who still visit regularly; nonetheless, we're urging caution. See boxed text, p752.

Weslaco (www.weslaco.com), 58 miles west of South Padre Island, is a farming community known for its sweet onions. It is the closest US town with services to the crossing. Both the **Best Western Palm Aire** (☎ 956-969-2411; www.bestwesternpalmaire.com; 415 Rte 1015, Weslaco; r $59-72;), with a tropical pool and hot tub, and the **Blue Onion** (☎ 956-447-0067; 423 Rte 1015, Weslaco; mains $5-11; 11am-9pm), with locally loved homemade meals and flatbread, are on the road to Mexico.

Birders flock to the Valley's parks associated with the **World Birding Center** (www.worldbirdingcenter.org). Migrating avian masses, including thousands of hawks, pass through this natural corridor along the main North–South American fly route from March to April and September to October. Twenty miles or so west of Weslaco, the visitor and educational center at **Bentsen-Rio Grande Valley State Park** (☎ 956-585-1107; 2800 FM 2062, Mission; adult/child $5/free; park 7am-10pm, center 8am-5pm) is a model of sustainable, green-driven architecture, including rainwater collection. Rent a bike (from $5 a day) or take the tram the 2 miles into the park. There, alligators and birds roam the wetlands, and you may spot a javelina (wild pig) or a horny toad on your way to the hawk-observation tower.

Twenty-seven miles southwest of South Padre in **Brownsville** (www.brownsville.org), the southernmost town in Texas, **Gladys Porter Zoo** (☎ 956-546-2177; www.gpz.org; 500 Ringgold St; adult/child $9/6; 9am-dusk;) is a lush tropical botanical garden with a conservation bent. It specializes in breeding endangered animals like Komodo dragons and Philippine crocodiles.

Both Brownsville and Harlingen (30 miles east of Weslaco, 50 miles northwest of South Padre) have regional airports and national car rental.

DALLAS–FORT WORTH

Dallas and Fort Worth are as different as a Beemer-driving yuppie and a rancher in a Dodge dually pickup truck – the proverbial city slicker and his country cousin. Just 30 miles apart, the two towns anchor a giant megalopolis of six million people known as the Metroplex. Go see the excesses of the Big D and then day-trip to Fort Worth – the cowboy and Western sights and museums there might be the state's best-kept secret.

DALLAS

Big hair, big egos and big guns – flashy TV-show millionaires and heroic/criminal Cowboy football players are what outsiders

TEXAS

think of Dallas. The reality is not unrelated. Hairstyles may have tamed, but the city is still highly image-conscious. An upscale ethos in this town of 1.3 million makes for an amazing dining scene (you can tell which place is hot by the caliber of cars the valet leaves out front) and the shopping is world-class. There is also a handful of interesting museums – history buffs should not miss the memorials of President John F Kennedy's assassination. Add to that the emerging performing-arts district, and it's plenty to keep you entertained for a couple of days. Though don't try to scratch the surface too deep – you may be disappointed.

Orientation

Downtown Dallas is east of the junction of I-30 and I-35 E; take the Commerce St exit off I-35. Uptown – with smart, trendy bars, restaurants and hotels – is north of downtown; follow Harwood St (or St Paul St, if you're taking the trolley) to McKinney Ave. Bars line Greenville Ave, northeast of downtown off Ross Ave. Deep Ellum, at the eastern end of Elm St, is a bit gritty, but it's the nucleus of Dallas' small live-music scene. The Bishop Arts District is just west of downtown, south of I-20, which connects to Fort Worth, 30 miles to the west.

Information

Bank of America (Map p738; ☎ 214-508-6881; 1401 Elm St) Foreign currency exchange.

Borders Books (Map p738; ☎ 214-219-0512; 3600 McKinney Ave; 🕑 10am-10pm)

Central Library (Map p738; ☎ 214-670-1700; 1515 Young St; 🕑 9am-9pm Mon-Thu, to 5pm Fri & Sat, noon-5pm Sun) Get a free internet card at the desk.

Dallas CVB Visitor Center (Map p738; ☎ 214-571-1300; www.visitdallas.com; Old Red Courthouse, 100 S Houston St; 🕑 8am-5pm Mon-Fri, 9am-5pm Sat & Sun) Free 20-minute internet access.

Dallas Morning News (www.dallasnews.com) The city's daily newspaper.

Parkland Memorial Hospital (Map p736; ☎ 214-590-8000; 5201 Harry Hines Blvd)

Police station (off Map p738; ☎ 214-670-4413; 334 S Hall St)

Post office (Map p738; ☎ 214-468-8270; 400 N Ervay St)

Sights

DOWNTOWN

President John F Kennedy's downtown assassination sent the city reeling in November 1963. The shooting was followed by a chaotic manhunt and gunman Lee Harvey Oswald's eventual assassination. The fascinating and highly audiovisual **Sixth Floor Museum** (Map p738; ☎ 214-747-6660; www.jfk.org; Book Depository, 411 Elm St; adult/child under 5yr $13.50/free; 🕑 10am-6pm Tue-Sun, noon-6pm Mon) narrates in minute-by-minute detail what happened where. Eyewitness photos and actual video and audio clips add depth to the experience. Even the myriad twisted assassin conspiracy theories are succinctly summarized. From Dealey Plaza, walk along Elm St beside the infamous grassy knoll, and look for the white 'X' in the road that marks the exact spot where the president was shot. Turn around and look up at the top floor of the Texas School Book Depository – now the museum – where Oswald pulled the trigger. Across N Market St is the **Kennedy Memorial** (Map p738), a simple but profound sculpture by architect Phillip Johnson.

The 1892 Old Red Courthouse that houses the **Old Red Museum** (Map p738; ☎ 214-757-1949; www.oldred.org; 100 S Houston St; adult/child $8/6; 🕑 9am-5pm) is almost as interesting as the museum's interactive exhibits on Dallas county history. Entry includes the free building tour (2pm daily).

Modern-art installations shine both outside and in at the fabulous glass-and-steel **Nasher Sculpture Center** (Map p738; ☎ 214-242-5100; www.nashersculpturecenter.org; 2001 Flora St; adult/child $10/free; 🕑 11am-5pm Tue-Sun). The **Dallas Museum of Art** (Map p738; ☎ 214-922-1200; www.dallasmuseumofart.org; 1717 N Harwood St; adult/child $10/free; 🕑 11am-5pm Tue-Sun) is a high-caliber world tour of decorative and fine art befitting a big city. Both are set amid numerous theaters, part of the developing Arts District, and are open free to the public 5pm to 9pm on Thursday.

Among the flora and fauna of 14 countries, you can explore the watery Mayan world of a Central American jungle at the **Dallas World Aquarium** (Map p738; ☎ 214-720-2224; 1801 N Griffin St; www.dwazoo.com; adult/child $19/11; 🕑 10am-5pm; 👶).

SOUTHFORK RANCH

Who shot JR? Locals certainly no longer care (the TV drama *Dallas* was cancelled in 1992), but that doesn't stop interstate and international visitors from driving 20 miles north from Dallas to **Southfork Ranch** (off Map p738; ☎ 972-442-7800; www.southfork.com; 3700 Hogge Rd/FM 2551, Plano; adult/child $9.50/7; 🕑 9am-5pm). If you are expecting to see Miss Ellie's kitchen

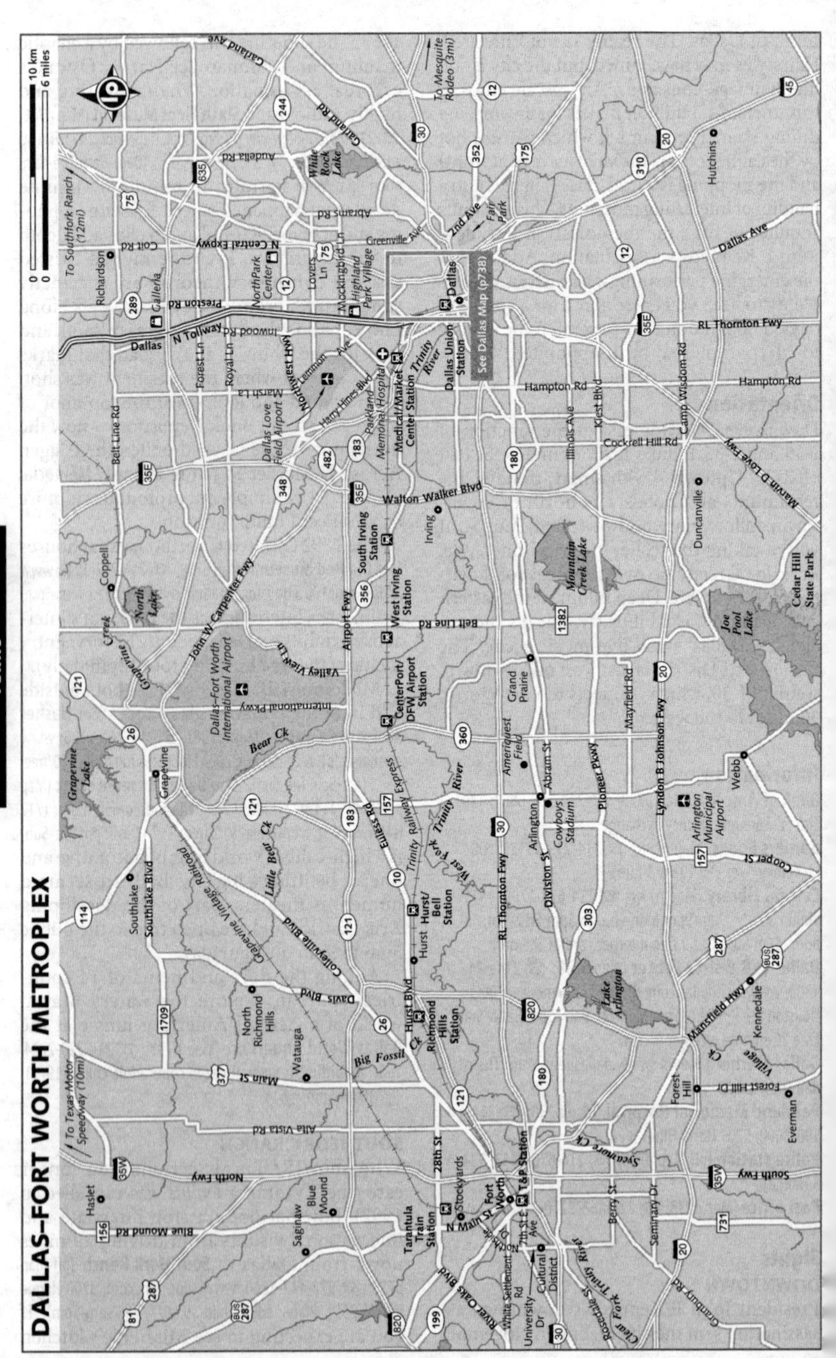
DALLAS–FORT WORTH METROPLEX
0 10 km
0 6 miles
To Southfork Ranch (12mi)
To Mesquite Rodeo (3mi)
To Texas Motor Speedway (10mi)
See Dallas Map (p738)
Dallas
Richardson
Galleria
NorthPark Center
Highland Park Village
White Rock Lake
Fair Park
Dallas Love Field Airport
Parkland Memorial Hospital
Medical/Market Center Station
Dallas Union Station
Trinity River
Irving
South Irving Station
West Irving Station
CenterPort/DFW Airport Station
Dallas–Fort Worth International Airport
Coppell
North Lake
Grapevine Creek
Grapevine Lake
Grapevine
Bear Ck
Grand Prairie
Mountain Creek Lake
Duncanville
Joe Pool Lake
Cedar Hill State Park
Hutchins
Ameriquest Field
Arlington
Cowboys Stadium
Arlington Municipal Airport
Webb
Southlake
Little Bear Ck
Grapevine Vintage Railroad
Trinity Railway Express
West Fork Trinity River
Hurst
Hurst/Bell Station
Richmond Hills Station
North Richmond Hills
Watauga
Big Fossil Ck
Lake Arlington
Kennedale
Village Ck
Forest Hill
Everman
Sycamore Ck
Haslet
Saginaw
Blue Mound
Tarantula Train Station
Stockyards
Fort Worth
T&P Station
Cultural District
Clear Fork Trinity River
Garland Ave
Garland Rd
Audelia Rd
Abrams Rd
Greenville Ave
2nd Ave
Coit Rd
N Central Expwy
Lovers Ln
Mockingbird Ln
Preston Rd
Dallas N Tollway
Inwood Rd
Forest Ln
Royal Ln
Northwest Hwy
Lemmon Ave
Marsh La
Harry Hines Blvd
Belt Line Rd
Hampton Rd
Illinois Ave
Kiest Blvd
Cockrell Hill Rd
Camp Wisdom Rd
RL Thornton Fwy
Marvin D Love Fwy
Dallas Ave
Walton Walker Blvd
John W Carpenter Fwy
Airport Fwy
Valley View Ln
International Pkwy
Mayfield Rd
Lyndon B Johnson Fwy
Pioneer Pkwy
Abram St
Division St
Euless Rd
Cooper St
Colleyville Blvd
Southlake Blvd
Davis Blvd
Hurst Blvd
Main St
Alta Vista Rd
North Fwy
28th St
Blue Mound Rd
N Main St
Mansfield Hwy
Forest Hill Dr
South Fwy
Berry St
Seminary Dr
Granbury Rd
River Oaks Blvd
White Settlement Rd
University Dr
7th St E
Rosedale St
635
75
244
30
12
352
175
20
45
310
289
35E
180
482
348
183
356
1382
121
26
360
157
114
10
303
287
1709
26
820
377
35W
156
81
199
731
BUS 287

DON'T MISS

- **Sixth Floor Museum** – relive JFK's fateful assassination in multimedia surround sound (p735)
- **Uptown eats** – a chichi neighborhood chockablock with tasty eateries (p739)
- **Arts District** – museums, theaters, restaurants and some stunning modern architecture (p735)
- **NorthPark Center mall** – a massive monument to conspicuous consumption (p740)

or JR's bedroom, don't. The ranch was used for exterior filming only; interior shots were filmed on a Hollywood set. The family who owned the ranch during the TV-show era lived there fulltime – until the show became so popular that they woke up to fans camped around their pool. The house is now an event center. You have to take a tour to see it and the tiny museum, including props like Lucy's wedding dress.

FAIR PARK

The art-deco buildings of **Fair Park** (off Map p738; ☎ 214-421-9600; www.fairpark.org; 1300 Cullum Blvd; adult/child passport $24/14), which were created for the 1936 Texas Centennial Exposition, today contain seven museums that focus on science, railroads, African American and women's history. The neighborhood is not the best, but it's perfectly safe.

Tours

Dramatic and committed conspiracy theorist–historian **John Nagle** (☎ 214-674-6295; www.jfktours.com; tours $20; by appointment Sat & Sun) guides 1¼-hour walking tours of JFK assassination sights.

Festivals & Events

The 52ft Big Tex statue towers – and talks – over Fair Park from late September to October, during the **State Fair of Texas** (☎ 214-565-9931; www.bigtex.com; Fair Park, 1300 Cullum Blvd). Come ride one of the tallest Ferris wheels in North America, eat corny dogs (this is where they were invented), and browse among the prize-winning cows, sheep and quilts.

Sleeping

Staying uptown, you're closest to restaurants and nightlife, but hotels there can get pricey. The further you get from the center, the cheaper the highway chain motels get.

BUDGET

Dallas Irving Backpackers Stop (off Map p738; ☎ 214-682-9636; 214 W 6th St, Irving; dm $20;) This big, clean, family-run house is a pleasant place to stay – big kitchen, living room, four-bed rooms, super owners. But it is way out in a dry town (no alcohol sold), and the bus (20 minutes or less to Dallas) is a 10-minute walk away.

Best Western City Place Inn (off Map p738; ☎ 214-827-6080; www.bestwestern.com; 4150 N Central Expwy; r $69-99;) A funky 24-hour diner on-site gives soul to this otherwise standard motel. You can't beat the value-to-uptown-proximity ratio; the McKinney Ave trolley is just a 15-minute walk away.

MIDRANGE

Hotel Lawrence (Map p738; ☎ 214-761-9090; www.hotellawrencedallas.com; 302 S Houston St; r $89-169;) Neoclassical earth-tone designs don't make the 1900s downtown hotel rooms seem bigger – asking for a corner room does. Check online: packages and internet specials make rates exceptionally reasonable.

our pick **Hotel Belmont** (off Map p738; ☎ 866-870-8010; www.belmontdallas.com; 901 Fort Worth Ave; r $109-179;) You could just imagine Marlene Dietrich walking down the terra-cotta stairs in this stylish 1940s bungalow hotel. The garden rooms – with soaking tubs, Moroccan-blue tile work, kilim rugs and some city views – are tops.

Joule (Map p738; ☎ 214-748-1300; www.starwoodhotels.com; 1530 Main St; r from $149;) A ceiling-height, moving, cog-and-wheel construction in the stylish lobby hints at the building's industrial-revolution-era beginnings. Urbane elegance continues throughout. The rooftop pool – cantilevered over Main St – had everyone talking when this place opened in 2009.

TOP END

Mansion on Turtle Creek (Map p738; ☎ 214-559-2100; www.rosewoodhotels.com; 2821 Turtle Creek Blvd; r $200-490;) Step into a life of ease, where for every two guests there's one staff member attending. Fresh flowers sit atop hand-carved

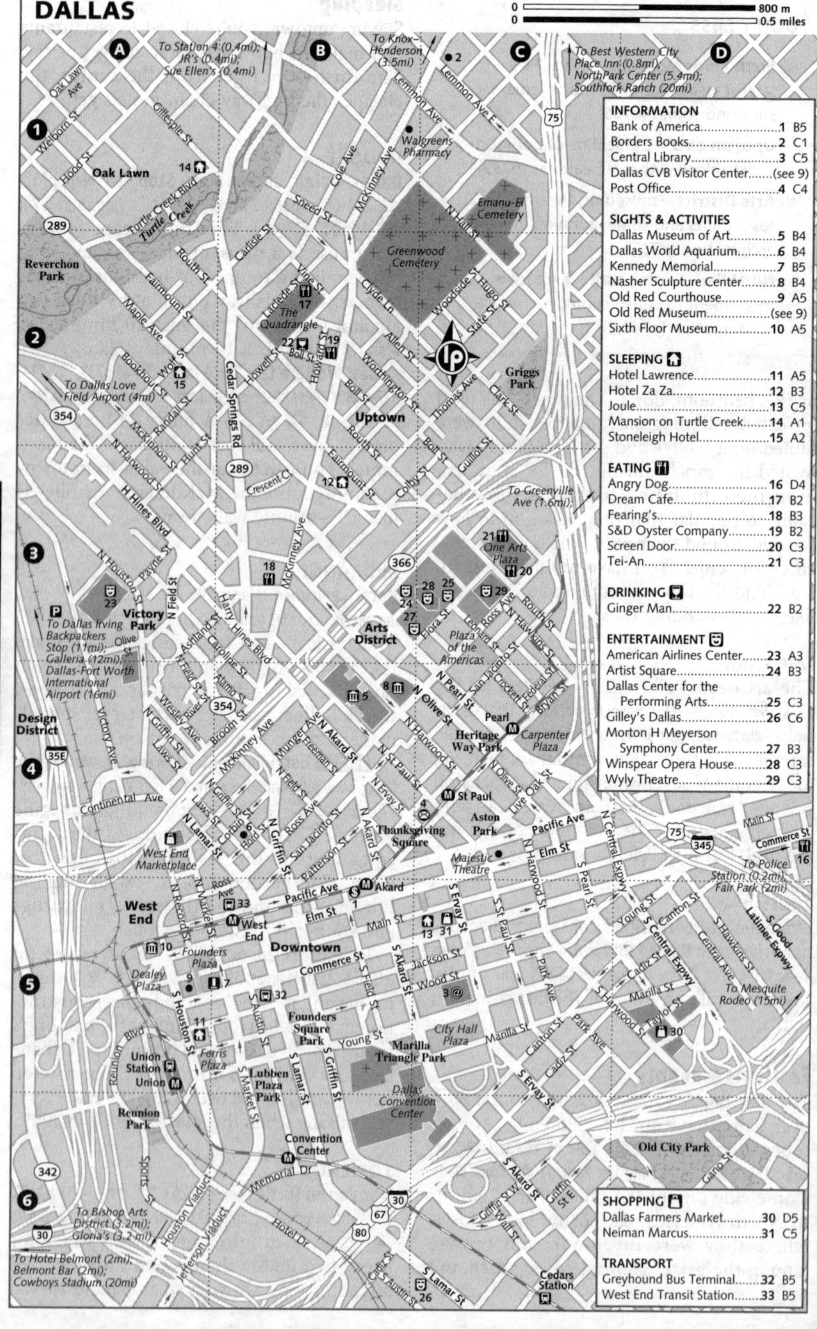
DALLAS
0 800 m
0 0.5 miles
INFORMATION
Bank of America 1 B5
Borders Books 2 C1
Central Library 3 C5
Dallas CVB Visitor Center (see 9)
Post Office 4 C4
SIGHTS & ACTIVITIES
Dallas Museum of Art 5 B4
Dallas World Aquarium 6 B4
Kennedy Memorial 7 B5
Nasher Sculpture Center 8 B4
Old Red Courthouse 9 A5
Old Red Museum (see 9)
Sixth Floor Museum 10 A5
SLEEPING
Hotel Lawrence 11 A5
Hotel Za Za 12 B3
Joule 13 C5
Mansion on Turtle Creek 14 A1
Stoneleigh Hotel 15 A2
EATING
Angry Dog 16 D4
Dream Cafe 17 B2
Fearing's 18 B3
S&D Oyster Company 19 B2
Screen Door 20 C3
Tei-An 21 C3
DRINKING
Ginger Man 22 B2
ENTERTAINMENT
American Airlines Center 23 A3
Artist Square 24 B3
Dallas Center for the Performing Arts 25 C3
Gilley's Dallas 26 C6
Morton H Meyerson Symphony Center 27 B3
Winspear Opera House 28 C3
Wyly Theatre 29 C3
SHOPPING
Dallas Farmers Market 30 D5
Neiman Marcus 31 C5
TRANSPORT
Greyhound Bus Terminal 32 B5
West End Transit Station 33 B5
To Station 4 (0.4mi); JR's (0.4mi); Sue Ellen's (0.4mi)
To Knox-Henderson (3.5mi)
To Best Western City Place Inn (0.8mi); NorthPark Center (5.4mi); Southfork Ranch (20mi)
To Dallas Love Field Airport (4mi)
To Greenville Ave (1.6mi)
To Dallas Irving Backpackers Stop (11mi); Galleria (12mi); Dallas-Fort Worth International Airport (16mi)
To Police Station (0.2mi); Fair Park (2mi)
To Mesquite Rodeo (15mi)
To Bishop Arts District (3.2mi); Gloria's (3.2 mi)
To Hotel Belmont (2mi); Belmont Bar (2mi); Cowboys Stadium (20mi)
Oak Lawn
Reverchon Park
Turtle Creek
The Quadrangle
Greenwood Cemetery
Emanu-El Cemetery
Walgreens Pharmacy
Uptown
Griggs Park
Victory Park
Arts District
One Arts Plaza
Plaza of the Americas
Design District
Heritage Way Park
Carpenter Plaza
Pearl
St Paul
Aston Park
Thanksgiving Square
Majestic Theatre
West End Marketplace
West End
Akard
Downtown
Founders Plaza
Dealey Plaza
Founders Square Park
City Hall Plaza
Marilla Triangle Park
Union Station
Union
Ferris Plaza
Lubben Plaza Park
Dallas Convention Center
Reunion Park
Convention Center
Old City Park
Cedars Station

TEXAS

European guest-room furnishings, and dinner is served in the original, 1925 marble-clad Italianate villa.

More options:

Stoneleigh Hotel (Map p738; ☎ 800-921-8498; www.stoneleighhotel.com; 2927 Maple Ave; r $200-450;) A $36 million makeover in 2008 upped the art-deco quotient.

Hotel Za Za (Map p738; ☎ 214-468-8399; www.hotelzaza.com; 2332 Leonard St; r $229-395;) Hip, over-the-top eclectic rooms.

Eating

The stretch of Main near Akard St has some interesting food options, but downtown in general is pretty quiet. For those living in **uptown** (www.uptowndallas.net), dining out nightly is de rigueur, so there are plenty of options. You'll also do well eating just about anywhere along Knox–Henderson Sts, to the north.

UPTOWN & KNOX–HENDERSON

Dream Cafe (Map p738; ☎ 214-954-0486; 2800 Routh St; mains $6-15; 7am-9pm Sun-Thu, to 10pm Fri & Sat;) Imagine a healthy, organic diner – one with quirky decor, a huge patio and a playground for kids – and you've got the picture.

S&D Oyster Company (Map p738; ☎ 214-880-0111; 2701 McKinney Ave; mains $12-20; 11am-10pm) An uptown staple for ages – the no-frills decor and great fried seafood keep 'em coming back. Try the BBQ shrimp.

our pick **Fearing's** (Map p738; ☎ 214-922-4848; Ritz-Carlton Hotel, 2121 McKinney Ave; lunch mains $16-24, dinner mains $30-50; 11am-2:30pm & 6-10:30pm Mon-Sat, 11:15am-3pm & 6-10pm Sun) Press accolades have poured in for chef Dean Fearing's four-star, four-dining room restaurant in the Ritz-Carlton. No need to dress up to enjoy the upscale Texas cuisine. Choose to sup in the lively open-kitchen room, a glass-enclosed conservatory, a tropical courtyard or the white-tableclothed 'gallery.'

BISHOP ARTS DISTRICT

Gloria's (off Map p738; ☎ 214-948-3672; 600 W Davis St; lunch specials $7-9, mains $9-15; 11:30am-10pm) Plantains, black beans and yucca are big players on the El Salvadorian Mexican menu. Gloria's has done so well that it's expanded to several local venues.

DOWNTOWN & DEEP ELLUM

Angry Dog (Map p738; ☎ 214-741-4406; 2726 Commerce St; mains $5-9; 11am-midnight Sun-Thu, to 2am Fri & Sat) Workers crowd in at lunchtime for the unbeatable burgers at this saloon.

One Arts Plaza, at 1722 Routh St, hosts five restaurants (Italian, Southern, Japanese and wine bars); **Tei-An** (Map p738; ☎ 214-220-2828; mains $11-20; 11am-2pm & 5:30-10pm) is most interesting because it specializes in laboriously handmade Japanese soba noodle dishes. **Screen Door** (Map p738; ☎ 214-720-9111; lunch $17-22, dinner mains $22-36; 11am-2pm & 5-10pm Mon-Fri, 5-11pm Sat, 10:30am-2pm Sun) serves an artistic interpretation of Southern mainstays.

Drinking

Numerous pubs with outdoor patios are to be found in uptown along not only McKinney Ave (in the 2500 to 2800 blocks especially), but also Knox St near Willis Ave. Note that bars and clubs in Dallas (at least mostly) have succumbed to the indoor smoking ban.

Belmont Bar (off Map p738; ☎ 866-870-8010; www.belmontdallas.com; Hotel Belmont, 901 Fort Worth Ave) Sip your adult beverage on a stylish terrace overlooking the city. Sometimes the bar screens B-grade flicks on the white stucco wall in the garden.

Ginger Man (Map p738; ☎ 214-754-8771; 2718 Boll St; 11am-2am Wed-Fri, 1pm-2am Sat-Tue) An appropriately spice-colored house is home to this always-busy neighborhood pub. The bar has multilevel patios and porches, out front and back.

Entertainment

For entertainment listings, check the weekly alternative newspaper *Dallas Observer* (www.dallasobserver.com) or *Guide Live* (www.guidelive.com), which appears in Friday's *Dallas Morning News.*

LIVE MUSIC & NIGHTCLUBS

During lunch hour, office workers crowd into the bars and restaurants of downtown's **Deep Ellum** (www.deepellumtexas). The scene at night is definitely grittier, almost scary, but this is still live-music central. Most of the clubs are hard-core, but you'll occasionally find country or jazz. The bars and clubs of Lower Greenville Ave (1500 to 2200 blocks) cater to a crowd temperament somewhere between the uptown yuppies and downtown grunge set. Victory Park, near American Airlines Center (Map p738), has yet to really take off as an entertainment neighborhood,

GAY & LESBIAN DALLAS

Dallas' gay and lesbian scene centers on Cedar Springs Rd and Oak Lawn Ave, north of uptown. The Dallas Gay & Lesbian Alliance's **Resource Center of Dallas** (☎ 214-528-9254; www.resourcecenterdallas.org) can refer you to points of interest and gay-owned businesses in town, and many more business listings can be found at the website of the **Cedar Springs Merchant Association** (http://dallascrossroads.com). The *Dallas Voice* newspaper (www.dallasvoice.com) is the town's gay and lesbian advocate.

A number of the hottest clubs are within a few steps of each other: **Station 4** (off Map p738; ☎ 214-559-0650; 3911 Cedar Springs Rd) dance club hosts the Rose Room drag show on Friday and Saturday nights at 11pm. **JR's** (off Map p738; ☎ 214-528-1004; 3923 Cedar Springs Rd; 11am-2am) is a fun boys' bar with darts and pool, food and wi-fi. And **Sue Ellen's** (off Map p738; ☎ 214-559-0650; 3903 Cedar Springs Rd) is Dallas' biggest lesbian club.

but there are a number of chain bars and clubs (think Hard Rock, House of Blues).

Gilley's Dallas (☎ 214-421-2021; www.gilleysdallas.com; 1135 S Lamar St; 8pm-2am Fri & Sat) Boot-scoot around the floor or ride the mechanical bull from the movie *Urban Cowboy* at this longtime country-and-western fave.

SPORTS

Mesquite Rodeo (off Map p738; ☎ 972-285-8777; www.mesquiterodeo.com; 1818 Rodeo Dr; tickets $15-30; 8pm Fri & Sat May-Sep) Bronc-bustin', bull-ridin' cowboys square off at weekend rodeos broadcast nationwide. Take I-30 15 miles east to Hwy 80.

The **Dallas Cowboys** (www.dallascowboys.com) got the nickname 'America's Team' after they won three US football championships in the 1990s. Their snazzy new, retractable-roof home, **Cowboys Stadium** (Map p736; ☎ 817-892-8687; http://stadium.dallascowboys.com; 925 N Collins St, Arlington; stadium tours adult/child $15/12; 9am-6pm Mon-Sat, 11am-6pm Sun), opened in mid-2009.

The **American Airlines Center** (Map p738; ☎ 214-222-3687; www.americanairlinescenter.com; 2500 Victory Ave) in Victory Park hosts megaconcerts and is home to the **Dallas Stars** (☎ 214-467-8277; www.dallasstars.com) ice-hockey team and the **Dallas Mavericks** (☎ 214-747-6287; www.dallasmavericks.com) pro basketball team.

THEATER & CULTURE

With the opening of the multibillion-dollar **Dallas Center for the Performing Arts** (Map p738; ☎ 214-880-0202; www.dallasperformingarts.org; 2403 Flora St) in October 2009, Dallas now has four new, architecturally noteworthy performance venues: 2000-seat Winspear Opera House (Map p738), 1500-seat Wyly Theatre (Map p738) and an open-air stage, Artist Square (Map p738). Classical concerts will continue to be held at the **Morton H Meyerson Symphony Center** (Map p738; ☎ 214-670-3600; www.meyersonsymphonycenter.com; 2301 Flora St), which is also in the Arts District.

Shopping

You can find some interesting gifts of arty housewares, like vintage Fiestaware plates, in the quirky, but small, **Bishop Arts District** (www.bishopartsdistrict.com). On the northern end of uptown (at Lemmon and McKinney Aves), the **West Village** (www.westvil.com) neighborhood has a collection of chain stores and individual boutiques, like 'Cowboy Cool.'

Dallas Farmers Market (Map p738; ☎ 214-670-5880; www.dallasfarmersmarket.org; cnr Marilla Blvd & S Harwood St; 7am-6pm) Buy produce directly from the growers, or shop for flowers and antiques at this multibarn market.

Neiman Marcus (Map p738; ☎ 214-741-6911; www.neimanmarcus.com; 1618 Main St) A downtown landmark, this six-story behemoth was the first Neiman Marcus store in the country.

NorthPark Center (Map p736; ☎ 214-361-6345; www.northparkcenter.com; 1030 NorthPark Center, Northwest Hwy at US 75) Almost 2 million sq ft of retail space, Northpark is shopping nirvana for Dallasites.

Galleria (Map p736; ☎ 972-702-7100; www.galleriadallas.com; 13355 Noel Rd) The Galleria is another mega shopping mall, a favorite with out-of-towners – maybe it's the ice-skating rink in the center?

Getting There & Away

American Airlines' home port is **Dallas–Fort Worth International Airport** (DFW; Map p736; ☎ 972-973-8888; www.dfwairport.com), 16 miles northwest of the city via I-35 E. Great Britain and Mexico are among the nonstop international destinations. Southwest Airlines uses smaller **Dallas Love Field Airport** (DAL; Map p736; ☎ 214-670-6073; www.dallas-lovefield.com), just northwest of downtown; take Inwood Rd northeast from Harry Hines Blvd and turn left on Cedar Springs.

Greyhound buses make runs all over the country from the **Greyhound Bus Terminal** (Map p738; ☎ 214-655-7085; www.greyhound.com; 205 S Lamar St). Direct Greyhound buses connect Dallas with cities such as Austin ($32, 3½ hours) and Houston ($37, 4½ hours).

Amtrak's San Antonio–Chicago *Texas Eagle* stops at downtown's **Union Station** (Map p738; ☎ 214-653-1101; www.amtrak.com; 401 S Houston St).

Getting Around

TO/FROM THE AIRPORT

From Monday to Saturday you can ride the **Trinity Railway Express** (www.trinityrailwayexpress.org) between downtown's Union Station and the Center Port/DFW Airport stop ($2.50 one way), which is actually in a parking lot; free shuttle buses take you to the terminals. Daily, DART bus 39 ($1.50) travels between downtown's **West End Transit Station** (Map p738; 800 Pacific Ave) and Dallas Love Field, but service is limited on weekends.

It's often easiest to take a shared-ride shuttle: **Yellow Checker Shuttle** (☎ 817-267-5150; www.yellowcheckershuttle.com) and **SuperShuttle** (☎ 817-329-2000; www.supershuttle.com) both run from DFW or Dallas Love Field to downtown for $19. A taxi between either airport and central Dallas should cost about $40 to $50.

Every major rental-car company has an office at DFW, and many are at Dallas Love Field too.

BUS & LIGHT RAIL

Dallas Area Rapid Transit (DART; ☎ 214-979-1111; www.dart.org) operates buses and an extensive light-rail system that connects Union Station and other stops downtown with outlying areas (single trip $2.50). Day passes ($5) are available from the store at the **Akard Station** (Map p738; 1401 Pacific Ave; 🕑 7:30am-5:30pm Mon-Fri). Travel to uptown from downtown on the free **McKinney Ave Trolley** (☎ 214-855-0006; www.mata.org; 🕑 7am-10pm Mon-Thu, to midnight Friday, 10am-midnight Sat, to 10pm Sun), which runs from the corner of Ross Ave and St Paul St, near the Dallas Museum of Art, and up McKinney Ave to Hall St.

CAR & MOTORCYCLE

If you do rent a car, be warned that rush-hour freeway traffic is bad and there's little free parking downtown. Public garages cost from $12 per day.

AROUND DALLAS

Northeast Texas is full of small towns organized around courthouse squares, where spring and fall festivals and rodeos are big doggone deals. Check the **Texas Highways** (www.texashighways.com) listings to find one that suits you. For example, **Tyler** (www.tylertexas.com; cnr I-20 & US 69), 100 miles east of Dallas, is known for its October Rose Festival and the 14-acre municipal garden (in bloom April to November).

FORT WORTH

Yee-haw, Fort Worth is one Texas town that still has its twang. The place first became famous during the great open-range cattle drives of the late 19th century, when more than 10 million head of cattle tramped through the city on the Chisholm Trail. Today you can see a mini–cattle drive in the morning and a rodeo on Saturday night. Don't forget to go honky-tonkin' at Billy Bob's after all that ropin' and ridin'. Down in the Cultural District, tour the Cowgirl Museum and others, including three amazing art collections. Then, after you've meditated on minimalism, Sundance Square's restaurants and bars call you downtown. With a population of 702,000, the town is a more user-friendly size than Dallas, not to mention greener and cleaner. There's a lot to do here, without a whole lotta pretense.

Orientation & Information

Fort Worth is fairly compact and easy to drive around: I-30 runs east–west through downtown, and I-35 W runs to the south. Downtown, the Cultural District and the Stockyards form a lopsided triangle. North Main St runs between downtown and the Stockyards, 7th St E Ave connects downtown to the Cultural District, and University and Northside Drs connect the Cultural District to North Main St near the Stockyards.

Central Library (☎ 817-871-7701; 500 W 3rd St; 🕑 10am-6pm Mon, Wed, Fri & Sat, noon-8pm Tue & Thu, 1-5pm Sun) Free internet access.

Fort Worth Convention & Visitors Bureau (www.fortworth.com) Cultural District (☎ 817-882-8588; 3401 W Lancaster Ave; 🕑 10am-5pm Mon-Sat); Downtown (☎ 817-698-3300; 501 N Main St; 🕑 10am-6pm

DON'T MISS

- **Billy Bob's Texas** – live bull-riding and Texas two-stepping (p744)
- **National Cowgirl Museum** – ride 'em, cowgirl (right)!
- **Amon Carter Museum** – wild western art (right)
- **Love Shack** – Food Network star chef; low, low prices (opposite)

Mon-Sat); Stockyards (☎ 817-624-4741; 130 E Exchange Ave; 9am-6pm Mon-Sat, noon-5pm Sun) The most together tourist board in the state; ask for the spiffy free 3-D maps.

Sights & Activities

The Stockyards are cowboy central; most area museums call the leafy Cultural District home.

STOCKYARDS NATIONAL HISTORIC DISTRICT

Westernwear stores and knickknack shops, saloons and steakhouses occupy the Old West–era buildings of the **Stockyards** (www.fortworthstockyards.org; Exchange Ave). What used to be a livestock industry center has turned tourist trade. City-paid cowboys on horseback roam the district, answering questions and posing for photos. Twice a day, at 11:30am and 4pm, they drive a small herd (16 to 20 beasts) of Texas longhorns down the block in front of the visitor center. It's a *goll-dang* Kodak moment, pardner. See a real live rodeo at **Cowtown Coliseum** (☎ 817-625-1025; www.stockyardsrodeo.com; 121 E Exchange Ave; adult/child rodeo $15/10, Wild West Show $12/8) at 8pm on Friday and Saturday nights year-round. From June to August, horses and riders show off at Pawnee Bill's Wild West Show (2:30pm and 4:30pm on Saturday and Sunday).

In addition to all the shops here, there and yonder, the former sheep and hog pens of **Stockyards Station** (140 E Exchange Ave; www.stockyardsstation.com) house a mall of sorts. It's also the depot of the **Grapevine Vintage Railroad** (☎ 817-625-7245; www.tarantulatrain.com; adult/child $10/6; 3:30pm Thu-Sat), from where you can catch an hour-long 'Trinity River' tourist train ride, but the scenery's dismal. It's more fun – and free – to gather with the others by the roundhouse a few minutes before scheduled departure, put your penny on the track and pick it up after you watch the steam locomotive smash it.

CULTURAL DISTRICT

Five major museums and the Will Rogers Memorial Center are part of the parklike **Cultural District** (www.fwculture.com). At the **Amon Carter Museum** (☎ 817-738-1933; www.cartermuseum.org; 3501 Camp Bowie Blvd; admission free; 10am-5pm Tue-Sat, noon-5pm Sun), you can see displays of pre-1945 American art, including one of the country's best compilations of work by western artists Frederic Remington and Charles M Russell. There's also an extensive photography collection.

At the **Modern Art Museum of Fort Worth** (☎ 817-738-9215; www.themodern.org; 3200 Darnell St; adult/child $10/free; 10am-5pm Tue-Sat, 11am-5pm Sun) you round a corner from womblike, concrete galleries to be confronted by a two-story wall of glass looking out at the city skyline. Noteworthy art in the collection includes work by Picasso and Mark Rothko. European, pre-Colombian and other international art are in focus at the **Kimbell Art Museum** (☎ 817-332-8451; www.kimbellart.org; 3333 Camp Bowie Blvd; general admission free; 10am-5pm Tue-Thu & Sat, noon-8pm Fri, noon-5pm Sun).

The **National Cowgirl Museum** (☎ 817-336-3375; www.cowgirl.net; 1721 Gendy St; adult/child $8/7; 9am-5:30pm Mon-Thu, to 8pm Fri & Sat, 11:30am-5:30pm Sun) rides high with state-of-the-art exhibits. Mount a slow-mo electronic bucking bronc and video magic makes it look like you're in a fast-action rodeo. Four small theaters focus on different personalities – one is about Jessie in Pixar's *Toy Story* – but the museum overall is more rugged-frontiers-woman than about anything 'girly.'

Your Cowgirl ticket also gets you into the **Museum of Science & History** (☎ 817-255-9300; www.fwmuseum.org; 1501 Montgomery St; adult/child $8/7; 9am-5pm Mon-Thu, to 8pm Fri & Sat, 11:45am-5pm Sun;), which brims with fossils, dinosaurs and kid-friendly stuff to do – like the planetarium and an Omni IMAX theater. A huge expansion, completed in late 2009, immerses you in today's cattle-breeding and cowboy industry.

DOWNTOWN

Colorful architecture, an art gallery or two, and a host of shops, bars, restaurants and hotels make the 14-block **Sundance Square** (www.sundancesquare.com), near Main and 3rd Sts, supremely strollable. The area is more than safe:

IF YOU HAVE A FEW MORE DAYS

Have yourself a NASCAR experience at **Texas Motor Speedway** (☎ 817-215-8500; www.texasmotorspeedway.com; cnr Hwy 114 & I-35). The annual stock-car race is in November, but year-round you can ride along at more than 150mph (four laps $125) or go to driving school (10 laps $345) with **Team Texas** (☎ 940-648-1043; www.teamtexas.com). The speedway is 20 miles north of downtown, on I-35 W. Four miles away **Babe's Fried Chicken House** (☎ 817-491-2900; 104 North Oak St, Roanoke; meals $11; 11am-2pm & 5-10pm Mon-Fri, 11am-10pm Sat & Sun), where all the down-home dishes and sides are served family-style, makes an excellent pit stop on the way to or from the park.

it's downright friendly, day or night. Parking garages are free after 5pm and on weekends.

All the works at the **Sid Richardson Collection of Western Art** (☎ 817-332-6554; www.sidrichardsonmuseum.org; 309 Main St; admission free; 9am-5pm Mon-Sat, noon-5pm Sun) were once privately held.

Festivals & Events

The town's biggest event is the **Fort Worth Stock Show & Rodeo** (☎ 817-877-2400; www.fwstockshowrodeo.com), which is held in late January or early February each year at **Will Rogers Coliseum** (1 Amon Carter Sq) in the Cultural District.

Sleeping

It's also easy to do a day trip to Fort Worth from Dallas…

Holiday Inn Express – Fort Worth Downtown (☎ 817-698-9595; www.hiexpress.com; 1111 W Lancaster Ave; r $99-150) A retro vibe pervades the newish (opened late 2008) HI Express, 1 mile southwest of downtown. What surprising stylishness from a chain.

Hyatt Place Stockyards (☎ 817-626-6000; http://stockyards.place.hyatt.com; 132 E Exchange Ave; r $135-179) Upscale granite and neutral color schemes keep things businessy, but staying here you're stumblin' distance to the fun of the Stockyards' bars and attractions.

Stockyards Hotel (☎ 817-625-6427; www.stockyardshotel.com; 109 E Exchange Pl; r $189-229) First opened in 1907, this place clings to its cowboy past with Western-themed art, individual cowboyed-out rooms with lots of leather and a steakhouse on-site.

Yet more options:

Texas White House B&B (☎ 817-923-3597; www.texaswhitehouse.com; 1417 Eighth St; r incl breakfast $125-235) Large historic home, contemporary Texas style – near downtown.

Ashton Hotel (☎ 866-327-4866; www.theashtonhotel.com; 610 Main St; r $208-290) A 39-room boutique hotel in an 1890 and a 1915 building off Sundance Square.

Eating

Put on the feed bag at the numerous cafés and restaurants in Sundance Square and in the Stockyards (the latter is a tad touristy, but all good fun). Note that steak prices around town are weighty, but then so is the portion of beef.

our pick Love Shack (☎ 817-740-8812; 110 E Exchange Ave; burgers $4-6; 11:30am-8pm Sun-Wed, to 11pm Thu, to 1am Fri & Sat) Native son and Food Network iron chef Tim Love (www.cheftimlove.com) has almost as many restaurants in town as he does accolades. The best bargain is his tenderloin-and-brisket burgers, some topped with a quail egg, here at Love Shack. Don't miss the home-cut fries or Parmesan chips – oh, and those double-thick milk shakes…yum. Live local music plays on Saturdays at 8pm.

Angelo's Barbecue (☎ 817-332-0357; 2533 White Settlement Rd; plates $6-12; 10am-10pm Mon-Sat) They've been smokin' brisket, ribs and sausage at this BBQ joint north of the Cultural District since 1958.

Joe T Garcia's (☎ 817-626-4356; 2201 N Commerce St; lunch & brunch mains $6-12, dinner mains $12-14; 11am-10pm Mon-Thu, to 11pm Fri & Sat, 10am-10pm Sun) Eat inside, or outdoors in the walled courtyard, where Mexican-tile fountains bubble among the tropical foliage. Lunch is à la carte, but for dinner you choose between chicken or beef enchiladas and fajitas served family-style. On weekends the line to get in here (they don't take reservations) often stretches around the block.

8.0 Restaurant & Bar (☎ 817-336-0880; 111 E 3rd St, Sundance Sq; mains $8-15; 11am-11pm Tue-Sat, 3-10pm Sun) 'Mom's Meatloaf' and Mexican enchiladas are both on the mixed-up but lovable menu. A large patio under the trees with live music on Wednesdays and DJs on weekends (from Memorial Day to Labor Day) makes this a favorite place to kick back.

Taverna (☎ 817-885-7502; 450 Throckmorton St; lunch $9-10, dinner mains $12-19; 🕑 11am-10pm) Young professionals rave about the quality pasta here. But frequent specials, such as half-price hand-tossed pizza in the bar (3:30pm to 7pm daily), are even more praise-worthy.

Reata (☎ 817-336-1009; 310 Houston St; lunch $9-18, dinner mains $16-39; 🕑 11am-10pm) The proprietors also own their own cattle ranch, so the sizable steaks are worth their weight. But you might also try the Texas specialties such as tenderloin tamales and jalapeño-cheddar grits.

Drinking

Rahr & Sons Brewing Co (☎ 817-810-9266; www.rahrbrewing.com; 701 Galveston Ave, at S Main St; admission $5) While out on the town, ask for local microbrews from Rahr & Sons, or take a tour of the place from 1pm to 3pm on Saturdays – tasting and live music included.

All the restaurants in and around Sundance Square have popular bars attached, and then there are the stand-alone favorites like **Flying Saucer Emporium** (☎ 817-336-7470; 111 E 4th St; 🕑 11am-1am Mon-Wed, to 2am Thu-Sat, noon-midnight Sun), which is made for craft beer–lovers (77 brews on tap). You definitely won't go thirsty 'round here.

Entertainment

On weekend evenings, country music becomes common in the Stockyards District, and a variety of live bands play in and around Sundance Square. Look for listings in *Fort Worth Weekly* (www.fwweekly.com).

LIVE MUSIC

our pick **Billy Bob's Texas** (☎ 817-624-7117; www.billybobstexas.com; 2520 Rodeo Plaza, Stockyards; 🕑 11am-2am Mon-Sat, noon-2am Sun) Top country-and-western stars, house bands and country DJs play on two stages at Texas' largest honky-tonk. Just having a mechanical bull isn't good enough here – on Friday and Saturday night a live bull-riding competition takes place at an indoor arena. Pool tables and games help make this a family place; under 18s are welcome with a parent.

White Elephant Saloon (☎ 817-624-1887; www.whiteelephantsaloon.com; 106 E Exchange Ave; 🕑 2pm-midnight Mon-Thu, to 2am Fri, noon-2am Sat, noon-midnight Sun) Stockyards cowboys have been bellying up to this bar since 1887 (now Tim Love owns it too). Local singers and songwriters are showcased nightly.

THEATER & PERFORMING ARTS

Bass Performance Hall (☎ 817-212-4325; www.basshall.com; 555 Commerce St) The glittery Bass Hall's theaters host everything from Mingo Fishtrap to the Will Rogers Follies. The symphony, ballet and opera also make their home here.

Getting There & Around

From Monday to Saturday you can ride the **Trinity Railway Express** (www.trinityrailwayexpress.org) between Fort Worth's **T&P Station** (☎ 817-215-8654; 221 W Lancaster Ave) and the Center Port/DFW Airport stop ($1.50 one way); free shuttle buses take you from the train parking lot to the terminals. If you're coming into Dallas Love Field, you'll have to transfer through in downtown Dallas.

Eleven buses a day make the one-hour trip (from $6.60) from the downtown Fort Worth **Greyhound Bus Terminal** (☎ 817-429-3089; www.greyhound.com; 901 Commerce St) to Dallas.

The **Fort Worth Transit Authority** (The T; ☎ 817-215-8600; www.the-t.com) runs bus 1 to the Stockyards and bus 2W to the Cultural District, departing from the ITC Transfer Center at Jones and 9th Sts. The single fare is $1.50.

The *Texas Eagle* stops at the **Amtrak Station** (☎ 817-332-2931; www.amtrak.com; 1001 Jones St) en route to San Antonio or Chicago. Monday to Saturday the **Trinity Railway Express** (TRE; ☎ 817-215-8600; www.trinityrailwayexpress.com; T&P Station, 1600 Throckmorton St) connects downtown Fort Worth with downtown Dallas ($2.50, 1¼ hours).

PANHANDLE PLAINS

Angry black clouds gather on the horizon, and seemingly seconds later hail, thunder and lightning are flashing down in a darn-good imitation of judgment day. The endlessly flat landscape, punctuated only by utility poles and windmills, produces some phenomenal weather, oil and not a whole lot else. The little bit that's left of old Route 66 scoots through Amarillo on its way west.

AMARILLO

Little remains of this once-fabled stop on Route 66, but there are a few quirky sights and the Big Texan Steak Ranch is as kitsch as they come. The town is a convenient overnight stop for those driving across the US. To the south, Palo Duro Canyon seems awfully surprising in this flat land. Remember that this is cattle country: if the wind is blowing just right, that's the stockyards you smell.

There are a few small Western museums in town; get oriented at the **Visitor Information Center** (☎ 806-374-8474; www.visitamarillotx.com; 401 S Buchanan St; 9am-6pm Mon-Fri, 10am-4pm Sat & Sun). Old Route 66 here is most character-filled along W 6th Ave, also known as the San Jacinto District. Shopfronts from the 1920s sell everything from burgers and beer to books, hardware and antiques.

On Rte 1541, 25 miles south of downtown Amarillo, nature really shows off at **Palo Duro Canyon State Park** (☎ 806-488-2227; www.paloduro canyon.com; Hwy 217; adult/child $5/free). A fork of the Red River carved its way through multicolor caprock to create the second-largest canyon in the US. A good paved road leads down to the floor and around the scenic 16-mile loop with hiking trails. An amphitheater carved into the canyon is the site of the **Texas Show** (☎ 806-655-2181; www.texas-show.com; tickets $10-30, dinner adult/child $17/13; 8:30pm Tue-Sun Jun–mid-Aug), a cowboy-pioneer, singing-dancing-acting musical extravaganza; a cowboy camp meal is served.

our pick Big Texan Steak Ranch & Motel (☎ 800-657-7177; www.bigtexan.com; 7700 I-40 E, exit 74; mains $15-35;), along I-40 Amarillo has every chain hotel and restaurant you can think of, and then some (those west of town are newest). And in contrast, stretch-Cadillac limos with steer-horn hood ornaments wait out front, marquee lights blink above, a shooting arcade pings inside the saloon, and a big, tall Tex road sign welcomes you to the Big Texan Steak Ranch & Motel. This cheesy roadside attraction built on historic Route 66 is a love-it-or-hate-it kinda place. A Texas-shaped cement pond (aka swimming pool) completes the over-the-top Old West theme at the motel (singles $60, doubles $70 to $80). Billboards start advertising the 'free 72oz steak' in Oklahoma; however, be warned: if you take the challenge and can't eat all the steak – and all the side dishes – in an hour, that 'free' steak costs $72. For such a kitschy place, the beef is surprisingly good and tender. And who doesn't want cowboy troubadours serenading you while you eat?

Greasy-spoon **Golden Light Café** (☎ 806-374-0097; 2908 W 6th Ave; sandwiches $3-7; 11am-10pm Mon-Wed, to 11pm Thu-Sat) has been serving burgers, home-cut fries and cold beer to travelers on Route 66 from this same spot since 1946.

Amarillo is a long way from most anywhere in Texas, but coaches leave from the **Greyhound Bus Terminal** (☎ 806-374-5371; www.greyhound.com; 700 S Tyler St) for places like Dallas (from $82, six hours). Southwest and Continental Airlines fly into Amarillo International Airport, located on the eastern edge of town north of I-40 via exit 76.

WEST TEXAS

Tumbleweeds roll across dusty ground, cacti bloom in desert sands, endless skies contain shimmering heat: West Texas is the stuff of Hollywood screen-maker dreams. Drive west along I-10 and there's a whole lotta nothin' to see. Turn south off the interstate and it's a different story. Big Bend National Park

ROUTE 66: GET YOUR KICKS IN TEXAS

The Mother Road crosses Texas for a mere 178 miles, most of which is paved under I-40. The state's claim to Route 66 fame is that it contains the road's center point. We figure it probably also has the greatest number of cars stuck in the dirt as art.

Once you pass into Texas from Oklahoma, McLean is about 35 miles west of Texola. There the **Devil's Rope Museum** (☎ 806-779-2225; www.barbwiremuseum.com; 100 Kingsley St, McLean; admission free; 10am-4pm Tue-Sat) has a Route 66 – and barbed-wire – museum (it has an excellent Texas Route 66 map online).

Forty-five miles west of McLean, stop in Conway to spray-paint your name on one of the VW Beetles planted nose down at Bug Ranch (see boxed text, p746). As you approach Amarillo, 18 miles later, it's hard to miss the giant cowboy waving from the Big Texan Steak Ranch & Motel (above). Downtown's W 6th St is a short, but entirely original, Mother Road segment. And just outside of town to the west, more car art is buried nose-deep at Cadillac Ranch (see the boxed text, p746).

Though nearby Vega contests this, when you reach Adrian, 50 miles west of Amarillo on I-40, you're halfway between Chicago and Los Angeles.

WHAT THE...?

In 1974 the late, local eccentric millionaire Stanley Marsh planted 10 Cadillacs (vintage 1949 to 1963) headlights down in a deserted stretch of dirt outside Amarillo – and then moved them further out in 1997 because of town encroachment. The reason? He said he constructed what has come to be known as **Cadillac Ranch** (I-40, btwn exits 60 & 62) in a salute to Route 66, using cars he considered to represent the golden age of car travel. The accepted practice today is to leave your own mark on the art by drawing on the cars. Bring spray paint in case other visitors haven't left any around. Occasionally the cars get a makeover, like when they were all painted pink in honor of breast-cancer awareness. To get here, park along the south feeder road, a couple of miles west of Loop 335, and walk the well-worn path. As cool as it sounds, there's a sort of forlorn feel to the place.

The ground around here seems to be fertile for growing cars – 18 miles east of Amarillo in Conway, there are five stripped-down VW bugs sprouting on **Bug Ranch** (Hwy 207 access road). The story goes that in 2002 the owners of a now-defunct convenience-souvenir store at the highway interchange wanted to attract customers and so built the roadside attraction in parody of the classic Cadillac Ranch. It didn't save the store, and the family has moved off, but the slug bugs in the dirt do attract attention. Again, feel free to leave your spray-painted signature. Both sights are visible from 1-40 and accessible 24/7.

TEXAS

(right) is a moonscape of desert mountains and deep arroyos on the Mexican border – a river-running, mountain-hiking paradise. Around the park, more mountains and small-town surprises await, like cutting-edge art installations and historic hotels. North of I-10, the state's tallest peaks rise from Guadalupe Mountains National Park (p753), near Carlsbad, NM. And way far west, El Paso is a town in a whole different time zone from the rest of Texas.

BIG BEND

Look at a Texas map. See the western elbow of land poking into Mexico? That's the Big Bend area following the curve of the Rio Grande, and the border. You can tell you're in the middle of nowhere – gasoline is extra expensive, cell-phone coverage is virtually nonexistent and internet connections are rare. What you come across instead is a national and state park filled with the interesting vegetation of Chihuahuan desert and limestone canyons. An hour and a half north of the parks are several more state parks with great old Civilian Conservation Corps (CCC) lodgings, towns with thriving art colonies, eclectic hotels and an astronomical observatory.

The Big Bend region has been likened to the 'devil's playground' in summer – 102°F (39°C) average temperature in July – but winter in the mountains can see snow. The best times to visit are February to April and October to November. Midland–Odessa (150 miles northeast of Alpine) and El Paso (220 miles northwest) are the closest major airports. Alpine, 95 miles north of the Big Bend National Park entrance, is the main base for gas and groceries. For more info, check out **Visit Big Bend** (www.visitbigbend.com).

Big Bend National Park

The Chisos Mountains rise up at the center of **Big Bend National Park** (☎ 432-477-2251; www.nps.gov/bibe; 7-day pass per vehicle $20; 24hr). To the west, the dramatic mesas and rock formations are the result of ancient volcanic activity. To the east of the mountains stretches desert habitat. The diverse geography in the park's 800,000 acres supports mountain lions and black bears, though you're more likely to see some of the 56 species of reptiles and 100 bird types. The park runs along the Rio Grande, but there's no legal access to Mexico here. River-rafting and other outdoor outfitters are based outside the park (see boxed text, p748). The **Panther Junction Visitors Center** (☎ 915-477-2251; 8am-6pm) is along the main park road, 29 miles from the Persimmon Gap entrance gate, south of Marathon, and 26 miles from the Maverick entrance at Study Butte. Gasoline is sold nearby.

The park puts out pamphlets, but the best trail resource is *Hiking Big Bend* by Laurence Parent. Most of the 150-plus miles of hiking paths are in the Chisos Mountains, where the 14-mile **Rim Trail** has some challenging ascents, rewarded by mountain panoramas. Ten to 20°F hotter down on the desert floor, the 1.5-mile **Santa Elena Canyon Trail** (40 miles southwest of Panther Junction) is one of the most popular treks because of the stunning rock and river views. It's rated easy, but you have to wade through a stream and climb stairs in the canyon wall. The adventurous (and ecoconscious) might convince the rangers to direct them to the trail that's left off maps. Hint: there are falls and abundant vegetation for a desert. Twenty miles southeast of the main visitor center, you can hike around old bathhouse buildings, along the river to the **hot springs** (0.75 miles from the parking lot). The waters are channeled into an old building foundation that forms a kind of hot tub above the riverbanks.

Stone-and-wooden-beam cottages at **Chisos Mountains Lodge** (☎ 877-386-4383; http://chisosmountainslodge.com; lodge & motel r $116-120, cottages $150) are the most secluded of several lodging options (cottage 103 has the best view). The all-together standard motel rooms have thin walls. Restaurant food here is so-so; better to pack a cooler ahead of time. The complex has a **visitor center** (🕑 9am-4:30pm) and a **camp store** (🕑 9am-9pm) with basic supplies. The mountain climate at **Chisos Basin Campground** (☎ 877-444-6777; www.recreation.gov; campsites $14) attracts the most campers in the park.

The abundant cottonwood trees shading the desert **Rio Grande Village Campground** (☎ 877-444-6777; www.recreation.gov; campsites $14) are quite unexpected – unless you know that this was once part of a pioneer's farm and the irrigation canals are still in use. Continue past the turnoff for the hot springs to the village.

Terlingua–Study Butte

Three miles east of the park boundary, two dusty little towns run together at the junction of Hwy 118 and Route 170. Outfitters, a couple of motels and a few restaurants lie along both routes.

DON'T MISS

- **Hot Springs Trail, Big Bend National Park** – hike along the Rio Grande to a natural hot tub (left)
- **McDonald Observatory, Fort Davis** – an evening party among the stars (p749)
- **Marfa** – engaging modern art, and aliens (p749)
- **Wyler Aerial Tramway, El Paso** – an almost 6000ft-high overview of Texas, NM, and Mexico (p751)
- **Gage Hotel, Marathon** – right out of a dime-store Old West novel (p750)

In the **Terlingua Ghost Town** (www.historic-terlingua.com; Rte 170 W), hippies and hard-core desert dwellers have turned the clay brick–built former mining shanties into minihomes. **Terlingua Trading Company** (☎ 432-371-2234; Ivey St) sells a walking-tour map of the few old buildings, local arts and crafts, and books on sustainable living (most residents don't have electricity or running water). Buy a beer inside the store and hang out on the porch with locals at sunset; it's the thing to do. (Though there are two bars nearby.)

We'd stay in a park, a town to the north or Lajitas instead, but the bare-bones-basic **Chisos Mining Company Motel** (☎ 432-371-2554; www.cmcm.cc; Rte 170; s $57, d $75-95) is the cheapest sleeping in Terlingua–Study Butte.

Next to the store, **Starlight Theatre** (☎ 432-371-2326; Ivey St; mains $15-20; 🕑 5-10pm) has been resurrected as an event as much as a restaurant – complete with twinkly lights, mural-covered walls, live music playing and chicken-fried antelope. Part food stand, part roadside attraction, **Kathy's Kosmic Kowgirl Kafe** (☎ 432-371-2164; Rte 170; BBQ & sandwiches $4-9; 🕑 6:30am-3pm Thu-Sun) is a hot-pink trailer

DETOUR: BUDDY HOLLY CENTER

You're a big fan of rock and roll? Buddy Holly's birth (and burial) place, Lubbock, is 125 miles south of Amarillo. The **Buddy Holly Center** (☎ 806-767-2686; www.buddyhollycenter.org; 1801 Ave G; adult/child $5/2; 🕑 10am-5pm Tue-Sat, 1-5pm Sun) highlights the career of not only the rocker, whose plane went down in an Iowa snowstorm in 1959, but also his contemporaries. Fans leave guitar picks at **Buddy Holly's grave** (Lubbock City Cemetery, cnr 31st St & Teak Ave). Take a right when you get into the cemetery; the modest headstone is on the left by the side of the road.

Otherwise, maybe Mac Davis had it right when he sang, 'Happiness is Lubbock in my rearview mirror…'

TEXAS

OUTDOOR ACCESS

Most people see Big Bend from a road or a trail, but there are some captivating perspectives you can only get with an outfitter's help. Several companies based in Terlingua–Study Butte lead multihour to multiday, multisport trips in the region. River-rafting (in high enough water) or canoeing through the canyons are the most popular options. (The river flows principally in fall and winter; in the summer it can be just a trickle.) For a short trip, float through Santa Elena Canyon (half-day from $140). If you have four days, the remote, 33-mile Bouquillas Canyon trip (from $685 with meals and tents) is a guider's favorite – no other people, just great rock formations and hiking.

The guides at **Big Bend River Tours** (☎ 432-371-3033; www.bigbendrivertours.com; Rte 170), just west of Hwy 118, have run the river more than a time or two themselves. They also combine rafting with horseback-riding expeditions. Active, do-it-yourself types should check out **Desert Sports** (☎ 432-371-2727; www.desertsportstx.com; Rte 170), 5 miles west of Hwy 118; the dedicated staff rents canoes ($50 per day), bikes ($35) and inflatable kayaks ($40) and will shuttle you in your car or theirs to river-launch and pick-up points ($25 to $105). Hike, bike and float tours are also available. **Far Flung Outdoor Center** (☎ 432-371-2633; www.farflungoutdoorcenter.com; Rte 170 at Hwy 118) is a bit more motor-oriented. Three-hour Jeep (from $65) and ATV (from $125) tours are on offer, in addition to the requisite rafting trips.

about a mile west of Hwy 118. It sometimes shows movies and has campfires at night.

On the Thursday through Sunday surrounding the first Saturday in November, the whole place goes crazy with the **Terlingua International Chili Cook-Off** (www.abowlofred.com; admission $30). Nightly entertainment, ugly-hat contests and, of course, tastings are all part of the spicy fun held annually for more than 40 years.

Lajitas to Presidio

Leaving Terlingua to the west, you come to **Lajitas** (☎ 877-525-4827; www.lajitas.com; r $195-330; ⊠ ⊠ ⊠), which looks like a town but is actually all one resort. On-site outfitters arrange adventures – overnight horse riding/posh camping trips, Colt 45 target shooting, etc. Afterwards you can rejuvenate at the spa, dine on upscale Tex-Mex and listen to live music on weekends at the Thirsty Goat. A new golf course is scheduled to open in mid-2010.

Lajitas Stables (☎ 432-371-2212; www.lajitasstables.com; Rte 170; 2hr rides $60), 3 miles west of the resort, guides riders along mesas and mountains outside area parks.

Big Bend Ranch State Park (☎ 432-229-3416; www.tpwd.state.tx.us; off Rte 170; day use $3) is much less explored than its big brother, but the easily accessed turnouts for hiking or picnicking along the river road shouldn't be ignored. Make the easy 0.7-mile trek into narrow **Closed Canyon**, where the cliffs rise above you, blocking out the sun. Camping is off Casa Piedra Rd, but you have to register at the **Fort Leaton State Historic Site** (☎ 432-229-3613; www.tpwd.state.tx.us; Rte 170; camping $3, fort admission $2; 🕒 8:30am-4:30pm), which is past the park.

Alpine

Primarily a pit stop, this university town has no real attractions of note. But it is the most sizable population (5700) in Big Bend – and the only place with big-name chain motels, numerous restaurants, grocery stores, more than one gas station and public transportation. From here, the national park is 90 miles south, Marfa is 20 miles west, Marathon is 18 miles east and Fort Davis is 17 miles northwest. People do visit to hear tall tales told at Sul Ross State University's annual **Cowboy Poetry Gathering** (☎ 432-364-2490; www.cowboy-poetry.org) in February. You can get regionwide information at the **Alpine Chamber of Commerce** (☎ 432-837-2326; www.alpinetexas.com; 106 N 3rd St; 🕒 9am-5pm Mon-Fri, 10am-2pm Sun).

Antelope Lodge (☎ 432-837-2451; www.antelopelodge.com; 2310 W Hwy 90; s $49-54, d $54-59; ⊠) may just be the best deal in Big Bend. Compact rooms in white-stucco-and-red-tile cottages circle around a grassy lawn in true (renovated) 1930s motor-court style. **Maverick Inn** (☎ 432-837-0628; www.themaverickinn.com; 1200 E Holland Ave; r $85-145; ⊠), also an old adobe motor court, is definitely more upscale, with rooms dressed in rustic Southwestern style.

Look for grocery stores along Holland Ave and Ave E in the town center. You can dig into superfresh pizzas and pastas, or just order an espresso or *michelada* (margarita-tasting beer) and use the wi-fi at the friendly **La Trattoria** (☎ 432-837-2200; 202 W Holland Ave; breakfasts $4-8, mains $8-16; 🕑 8:30am-3pm & 5-10pm Tue-Sun; wi-fi).

The town has a limited **Greyhound** (☎ 800-231-2222; www.greyhound.com; Quick Stop, 2305 E Hwy 90) bus service. The Florida–California *Sunset Limited* stops at the **Amtrak Station** (☎ 800-872-7245; www.amtrak.com; 102 W Holland St). Buy tickets on board; there's no ticket office. Arrivals are often delayed by freight traffic until the middle of the night. If you want to rent a car, you're stuck with **Alpine Auto Rental** (☎ 432-837-3463; www.alpineautorental.com; 414 E Holland Ave; per day from $35).

Marfa

The unlikely home to art and aliens (maybe), Marfa was named by a pioneer settler after a character in the book she was reading, Fyodor Dostoevsky's *Brothers Karamazov*, when she arrived. The town's fame first emerged when James Dean, Elizabeth Taylor and Rock Hudson filmed *Giant*, a Texas movie classic, here in 1955. The cast and crew stayed at the 1930s-era **Hotel Paisano** (☎ 866-729-3669; www.hotelpaisano.com; 207 N Highland Ave). Look for the movie memorabilia in a room off the lobby, near the shops. James Dean's room was pretty standard; Rock Hudson's was a suite (yes, you can book them for $99 to $249). Also off the lobby, the **Marfa Chamber of Commerce** (☎ 432-729-4942; www.marfacc.com; 🕑 9am-5pm) has more info on the movie and the town.

New York–born artist Donald Judd created a modern-art mecca when he constructed the sprawling **Chinati Foundation** (☎ 432-729-4362; www.chinati.org; off Hwy 67; adult/child $10/5; 🕑 tours 10am & 2pm Wed-Sat) complex a mile south of town in 1986. Different sections are shown morning and afternoon; Judd's original 'boxes' and building are on the 10am tour.

The Chamber of Commerce keeps tabs on art openings and has a list of all the small galleries in town, but the majority are on San Antonio St (W and E). Then there are those alien lights so many have claimed to see off US 90, complete with a viewing platform from which to watch for them (see also boxed text, p750).

If mod is your mode, you'll want to stay at the **Thunderbird** (☎ 432-729-1984; www.thunderbirdmarfa.com; US 90 W; r $130-175; ⊠ ✻ 🅿), a 'cowboy Zen' motel – think platform beds and faux-cowskin rugs. The **Cochineal** (☎ 432-729-3300; 107 W San Antonio St; breakfasts $5-11, mains $22-34; 🕑 6-10pm Wed & Thu, 8am-noon & 6-10pm Fri-Tue) restaurant is also appropriately minimalist for a town that art built – with surprisingly sublime food for the middle of nowhere. Owners Tom and Toshi call it 'global home cooking.'

Padre's (☎ 432-729-4425; 209 W El Paso St; sandwiches $5-10; 🕑 11:30am-midnight Wed & Thu, 11:30am-1am Fri & Sat) sells burgers and dogs, but mostly it's a cool bar with live music on weekends. Pinball machines and pool tables are in the game room on the way to the patio.

Pop into **Marfa Book Company** (☎ 429-729-2906; 105 S Highland Ave; 🕑 9am-9pm) to have a coffee and look for local titles.

Fort Davis

False-front wooden buildings, an old fort and a stellar observatory make Texas' tallest town (elevation 5000ft) a Big Bend must-see. The temperature can be a delightful 10°F to 20°F (6°C to 12°C) cooler here than in the national park, 120 miles to the south.

Atop Mt Locke (6791ft), **McDonald Observatory** (☎ 432-426-3640; www.mcdonaldobservatory.org;

SCENIC DRIVE: ROUTE 170

West of Lajitas, Rte 170 hugs the Rio Grande through some of the most spectacular and remote scenery in Big Bend country. This river road takes you up and down through a rugged landscape of low desert arroyos, sweeping vistas and stony mountains – at one point there's a 15% grade, the maximum allowable. Keep going past Presidio (50 miles, 1½ hours) and 35 miles west, just past Ruidoso, and you'll come to the turnoff for **Chinati Hot Springs** (☎ 432-229-4165; www.chinatihotsprings.com; Hot Springs Rd; baths $12.50; 🕑 sunrise-sunset). Locals love the isolation of the outdoor tubs, campgrounds (campsites $15, bathing included) and cabins ($75 to $115).

Turn north at Presidio, and Marfa is 60 miles up US 67. If you plan to go back the way you came, at least travel as far as Colorado Canyon (20 miles from Lajitas) for the best scenery.

WHAT THE...?

It's a bird! It's a plane! It's a super alien! No one really knows what the famous Marfa lights are (or aren't, for that matter). The mysterious glowballs in the sky appear occasionally to dance in the distance. The first sighting was recorded in 1883 (before car headlights), and scientists have been tracking the phenomenon to no avail ever since. Attempt to check it out at the freely accessible **Marfa Lights Viewing Site**, 8 miles east of town on US 90. Be prepared to wait all night: there's no schedule (the balls have been spotted anytime between susnet and sunrise) and no guarantees. Buying alien knickknacks and watching a 'famous Marfa lights' film at a local gift shop may have to do.

Hwy 118; adult/child $8/7; 10am-5:30pm) has a perfect vantage point for seeing stars. The daytime tour and solar viewing are nothing compared with the evening **star party** (adult/child $10/8; 7:30pm Tue, Fri & Sat Apr-Aug, 9:30pm Nov-Mar), where constellations are laser-pointed out from an amphitheater and you can gaze at celestial objects through as many as eight huge telescopes. The observatory is 16 steep miles northwest of town. On the way, 2 miles west of town, 24 intact buildings from the 1880s make up **Fort Davis National Historic Site** (432-426-3224; www.nps.gov/foda; Hwy 118; 7-day pass $3; 8am-5pm).

You can hike (or drive) the 3 miles further west from there to **Davis Mountains State Park** (432-426-3337; www.tpwd.state.tx.us; Hwy 118; day pass adult/child $5/free, campsites $10-20). Here the 1930s adobe buildings at **Indian Lodge** (432-426-3254; www.tpwd.state.tx.us; Hwy 118; r $75-90;) were built as part of a Depression-era CCC project. Rooms have been renovated, with pine-log ceilings complementing burgundy and green Southwestern hues.

A few shops line the main street in town, and **Hotel Limpia** (432-426-3237; www.hotellimpia.com; Town Sq, Hwy 118; r $89-180;) sprawls across several of the buildings. Across from the courthouse, **Murphy's Pizzeria & Cafe** (432-426-2020; Hwy 118; mains $5-10; 11am-9pm Mon-Sat) serves light meals and good thin-crust pizzas.

Marathon

The tiny town of Marathon (population 400) isn't much more than a main street with a few cafés and a historic hotel, 58 miles north of Big Bend National Park.

our pick **Gage Hotel** (432-386-4205; www.gagehotel.com; 101 US 90, Marathon; r $115-260;), built in 1902, seems straight out of Old West pulp fiction. Wide wooden blinds cover the windows, and saddle blankets drape across the raised log beds in the historic building rooms. There are earplugs for the few 1st-floor, shared-bathroom rooms ($97, no TV or phone) for a reason. Old wood floors reverberate, and the rich and ranchlike lobby in which guests congregate is just down the hall. Adjacent adobe suites – with Saltillo-tile floors, kiva fireplaces and *latilla* (branch-and-beam) ceilings – ring a lush Mexican-style courtyard with flowers and fountain. The associated **Café Cenzio** (mains $20-30; 6-10pm) whips up gourmet renditions of Texas faves well worth traveling for – chicken-fried venison with jalapeño cream sauce, anyone?

The **Famous Burro** (432-386-4100; cnr Hwy 90 & Post St; mains $12-22; restaurant 6-10pm Wed-Sun, bar 5pm-midnight Wed-Sat), a bar-restaurant in a funky old filling station, changes its upscale comfort food menu weekly. Sometimes there's live music; sometimes it's movie night.

There are a number of authors from the region; pick up their works at **Front Street Books** (915-386-4249; 145 US 90), where you can also procure some of those old Western novels.

DETOUR: BALMORHEA STATE PARK

Native Americans have known about the springs at modern-day **Balmorhea State Park** (432-375-2370; Hwy 17, off I-10; www.tpwd.state.tx.us; day pass $7;), 37 miles north of Fort Davis, since ancient times. In the 1930s the CCC came along and created a mighty-fine swimming hole by walling off some of the flow to make a 72°F to 76°F (22°C to 24°C) pool. What a perfect temperature for a summer-day dip. The CCC also built an adobe motel (rooms $60 to $80) that is still in operation. At the time of writing a new wetland area was under construction, expanding on the one that was built at the park's inception.

EL PASO

Well, you've made it. You're just about as far west in Texas as you can go. Here you're closer to Santa Fe than Austin. Mexico – New and old – holds more sway than that Texas capital anyhow. For centuries the mountain pass for which the city is named has been a key route across the Americas. (Mexican revolutionary Pancho Villa holed up here for a time.) There's still a fair bit of commerce: just over the Rio Grande from this town of 613,190 (82% Hispanic), 1.6 million more people live in sister city Ciudad Juárez, Mexico.

Escalating gang- and drug-related violence across the border has kept gringo tourists on the Texas side in recent years (for more, see boxed text, p752). But there are still shops to haunt and sights to see even if you don't day-trip into Mexico. The Franklin Mountains are always dramatic, rising from the desert flatlands, and developers have spiffed up areas of downtown near museums. So ride the gondola to a mountain peak, buy handcrafted boots, visit an exhibit and, by all means, eat some of the city's famous red enchiladas – bicultural El Paso awaits.

Orientation & Information

The Franklin Mountains pin the downtown area against the border and cleave the rest of the city along I-10 into the eastern, airport area and the western side near the University of Texas at El Paso (UTEP) and New Mexico. Note that El Paso is in the mountain time zone, one hour behind the rest of the state. Downtown, **El Paso Public Library** (☎ 915-544-6772; 501 N Oregon; ⏲ 9am-8pm Mon-Thu, to 6pm Fri & Sat, 1-5pm Sun) has free internet access. The **El Paso Visitors Center** (☎ 915-534-0601; www.visitelpaso.com; 1 Civic Center Plaza; ⏲ 8am-5pm Mon-Sat) stocks racks and racks of brochures, and the staff is quite helpful.

Sights & Activities

The soul of El Paso is downtown by the border. Streets surrounding San Jacinto Plaza are crowded with discount clothing stores and people waiting for buses. And the Plaza Theatre is once again beating as the city's cultural heart. Check out the still-expanding **El Paso Museum of History** (☎ 915-351-4345; www.elpasotexas.gov/history; 510 N Santa Fe St; admission free; ⏲ 10am-5pm Tue-Sat, noon-5pm Sun) for a long-range outlook on the area's development.

You'll get an entirely different kind of overview if you ride the **Wyler Aerial Tramway** (☎ 915-566-6622; www.tpwd.state.tx.us; 1700 McKinley Ave; adult/child $7/4; ⏲ noon-6pm Mon, Thu & Sun, to 8pm Fri & Sat) up 5632ft-tall Ranger Peak. At the top, a panorama of sprawling Juárez, the Franklin Mountains and New Mexico lays out before you. It's part of **Franklin Mountains State Park** (☎ 915-566-6441; www.tpwd.state.tx.us; Transmountain Rd; day pass $3; ⏲ 8am-5pm Mon-Fri, to 8pm Sat & Sun Apr-Oct), which also has 118 miles of hiking trails threading through the desert hills.

It's not so set up for tourists, but history buffs might enjoy the lower valley's **Mission Trail**. The driving route southeast of town connects three churches of early Spanish missions. Start at the **Tigua Indian Cultural Center** (☎ 915-859-7700; www.ysletadelsurpueblo.org; 305 Yaya Ln; admission by donation; ⏲ 10am-4pm Wed-Sat), where there's a small museum. Call ahead; some Saturdays it has native dance or bread-baking demonstrations.

Sleeping

Most of El Paso's lodging is in characterless chain motels found along I-10; choose your desired location first – the places are pretty much the same.

La Hacienda Travelodge (☎ 915-772-4231; www.travelodge.com; 6400 Montana Ave; r $47-85; ❄ 💻 📶 🏊) Barrel-tile roofs, courtyard greenery and wooden-plank doors provide loads of Spanish character at this motel. Street noise leaks into some rooms; all have microwaves and mini-fridges.

Hilton Garden Inn (☎ 915-351-2121; www.hiltongardeninn.com; 111 W University Ave; r $80-109; ⊠ ❄ 💻 📶 🏊) Opened at the edge of UTEP, the Garden Inn was built to blend with campus architecture. So, of course, it resembles a Bhutanese *dzong*, or religious fortress – what else? (Architects thought the style fit the desert mountain landscape.) The interior is more nice-chain-hotel than exotic monastery.

Eating & Drinking

Clearly, Mexican is the food of choice in El Paso: the town's known for a special bright-red chili-and-tomato sauce used on enchiladas.

H&H Car Wash (☎ 915-533-1144; 701 E Yandell Ave; mains $3-7; ⏲ 7am-3pm) This tiny hole-in-the-wall Mexican diner is attached to a hand car wash. Go for the breakfast tacos; stay to get your car cleaned.

L&J Café & Bar (☎ 915-566-8418; 3622 E Missouri; mains $5-12; ⏲ kitchen 10am-8pm, bar to 2am) The town's best salsa and fresh chips start you off, but everything served at this friendly Tex-Mex bar is tasty.

2900 (☎ 915-772-0066; 2900 N Mesa St; lunch $9-16, dinner mains $16-26; 11am-4pm & 5-10pm Tue-Sat) Hot and hip, chefs here use the seasonally changing menu to highlight ingredients, like hormone-free beefsteak, and to invent new-American dishes such as fried chicken-and-waffle sandwiches (with maple sauce).

Outside the city:

Ardovino's Desert Crossing (☎ 505-589-0653; 1 Ardovino Dr, Sunland Park, NM; mains $10-20; 5-10:30pm Wed-Fri, 11am-3pm & 5-10:30pm Sat, 3-9pm Sun) Vintage landmark restaurant (and bar, live-music venue and farmers market) across the other (New Mexico) border.

Cattleman's Steakhouse (☎ 915-544-3200; Indian Cliffs Ranch, I-10 E, exit 49, Fabens; mains $15-30; 5-10pm Mon-Fri, 12:30-10pm Sat & Sun) On a ranch that's used as an Old West movie set.

Entertainment

El Paso's mini-entertainment district is two blocks of restaurants and bars around Cincinnati St, between Mesa and Stanton, not far from UTEP. For cultural and music listings, pick up the free weekly *El Paso Scene* (www.epscene.com) or the Friday 'Tiempo' supplement to the *El Paso Times* (www.elpasotimes.com).

Garage Tequila Bar (☎ 915-328-4445; 4025 N Mesa St) More than 100 tequilas are on the menu at this fun and casual drinkery. Live music plays Thursday through Sunday.

Plaza Theatre (☎ 915-534-0600; www.theplazatheatre.org; 125 Pioneer Plaza) This elaborate theater under the stars is all indoors: pinpoint lights replicate stars, and vines cling to faux Spanish courtyard walls. Plays, concerts and shows are staged at this 1930 downtown landmark.

Shopping

On I-10 east of town, several warehouse-like shops sell all the goodies you can find in Mexico – pottery, blankets, silver – at similar prices. And then there are all those boots to buy (see boxed text, opposite)…

Getting There & Around

El Paso International Airport (☎ 915-780-4749; www.elpasointernationalairport.com), 8 miles northeast of downtown off I-10, services 16 US and two Mexican cities. Numerous chain rental-car companies are on-site (you really need a car here).

Amtrak's Florida–California *Sunset Limited* stops at **Union Depot** (☎ 915-545-2247; www.amtrak.com; 700 San Francisco Ave). The **Greyhound Bus Station** (☎ 915-532-2365; www.greyhound.com; 200 W San Antonio St) sends coaches to Albuquerque, NM, (from $38, 4½ hours) several times daily.

HUECO TANKS STATE HISTORIC SITE

About 32 miles east of El Paso off US 62/180, the Hueco Tanks (pronounced *wey*-co) have attracted humans for as many as 10,000 years – as evidenced by area pictographs. Three small granite mountains are pocked with depressions (*hueco* is Spanish for 'hollow') that hold rainwater, creating an oasis in the barren desert. Today the 860-acre park is a magnet for rock climbers. **Park Headquarters** (☎ 915-849-6684, central reservations 512-389-8900; www.tpwd.state.tx.us; Rte 2775; day pass $5, campsites $12-16; 8am-6pm) has a small gift shop, a nearby interpretive center and 20 campsites (17 with electricity and water). To minimize human impact, a daily visitor quota is enforced; make reservations 24 hours in advance to gain entry. You can explore the North Mountain area by yourself, but to hike deeper into the park – where the more interesting pictographs are –

HOT TOPIC: BORDERLANDS

Que paso? Nada, man. All across the state, Tex mixes with Mex and gringos readily use Mexican phrases. Locals continue to casually cross into Mexico proper. But according to US State Department reports, more than 1800 people were killed in Ciudad Juárez from January 2008 to February 2009 (and there were 17,000 car thefts). In March 2009, Mexican president Filipe Calderon sent troops into that city to quell drug-cartel-related violence. The state department urges caution when visiting *all* border towns in Mexico – as do we. Crime continues in border towns like Nuevo Laredo as well. Ciudad Juárez was not a stranger to violence before President Calderon started trying to clean up the cartels. An earlier wave of murders involved Mexican women disappearing (*The Daughters of Juarez,* by Teresa Rodriguez, is a provocative read), but didn't affect travelers.

TEXAS

GIVE 'EM THE BOOT

Savvy shoppers from around the globe – not to mention Julia Roberts and Dwight Yoakam – fly in to El Paso to get their feet custom-measured for some fine-fittin' leather. You may not be able to round up the $800 to $3000 a custom pair costs, but make an appointment to visit **Rocketbuster Boots** (☎ 915-541-1300; www.rocketbuster.com; 115 S Antony St; ⏰ by appointment) and you'll see what all the fuss is about. The creative concordance of vintage-inspired art – '50s-era pin-up cowgirls, smiling Day of the Dead skeletons – with hand-worked leather is stunning. This is no shop: it's a museum of Americana (with the record-holding 'World's Biggest Boots' on display). Owner–designer Nevena Christi will gladly show you around. You can pick up leather pillows and boot-shaped Christmas stockings for just $75 to $300.

Numerous other custom boot-makers work around town, including **Caboots** (☎ 915-544-1855; www.caboots.com; 501 S Cotton St; ⏰ 9am-5pm Mon-Fri), which also sells a few pre-made pairs (about $300). Bargain shopping? Check out the local outlet centers along I-10, such as **Justin Boots** (☎ 915-779-5465; I-10 E, at Hawkins) and **Cowtown Boots** (☎ 915-593-2929; 11401 Gateway W).

you have to reserve and join one of the free **pictograph** or **bouldering/hiking tours** (⏰ tours 9am & 11am Wed-Sun May-Sep, 10:30am & 2pm daily Oct-Apr).

GUADALUPE MOUNTAINS NATIONAL PARK

At 8749ft, remote Guadalupe Peak is the highest point in Texas. McKittrick Canyon has the state's best autumn foliage, and impressive spring wildflower displays in April. Winter vistas of snow-covered succulents seem incongruous and amazing. Though beautiful, this is one of the nation's least-visited national parks – it's not so easy to reach from Texas, and there aren't many services. You'll find the closest motels in Whites City, about 35 miles to the north in New Mexico, near Carlsbad Caverns National Park (p908). El Paso is 120 miles to the west.

The **Headquarters Visitors Center** (☎ 915-828-3251; www.nps.gov/gumo; 7-day pass $5, campsites $8; ⏰ 8am-6pm Jun-Aug, to 4:30pm rest of year), off US 62/180 at Pine Springs, also has camping. Of the 80 miles of trails, the most rewarding trek is strenuous – from the visitor-center parking lot to **Guadalupe Peak**, it's an 8.5-mile round-trip that gains 3000ft in elevation. A fairly easy day hike is **McKittrick Canyon Trail** (⏰ 8am-4:30pm), a 6.8-mile round-trip. The trailhead is off US 62/180, 11 miles northeast of the visitor center.

To get to the park's even more remote northern segment, **Dog Canyon**, you have to take Hwy 137 into New Mexico. Ten backcountry campsites (permit required) dot the section. No water is available in the backcountry. No gasoline, food or beverages are sold anywhere in the park.

Rocky Mountains

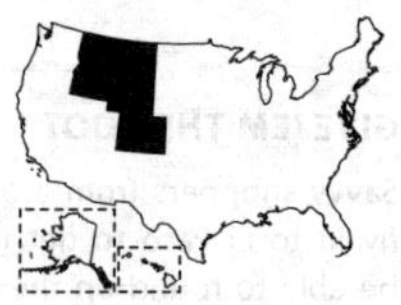

One hundred years ago a vacation in the Rocky Mountains was the doctor's first-choice tonic for curing everything from tuberculosis to fatigue and mental illness. Perhaps today's practitioners should take a lesson from their predecessors and start writing prescriptions to 'Go West' for dealing with stress.

The states in this region are such amazing natural healers it only takes a few blissful days road-tripping around them before your worries are lost in a babbling brook; your stress swept away in a cloudless blue sky. For how can one stay depressed in a place where the sun is always shining? Where the snowcapped peaks, wildflower meadows and misty ponderosa forests are so beautiful, they inspire artists to paint masterpieces and songwriters to pen classic tunes?

Everything about the Rockies – from the bears to the beers to the fried bull's testicles – feels big, larger than life. Nature-lovers will dig big national parks like Yellowstone, Grand Teton, Rocky Mountain and Glacier, where America's 'Big Five' (grizzly, moose, buffalo, mountain lion and wolf) still roam. Adrenaline junkies get their fix off a supersized big-thrill menu – heli-skiing steep powder chutes in Telluride's backcountry, paddling the Middle Fork's wild rapids, spending a week camping under the stars 100 miles from anywhere.

Wherever you go, you're in for a hell of a good trip. Climb a mountain, ski a glacier, get buzzed on local brews and savor your first chewy bite of seasoned bull balls. It doesn't take long; you'll slip right into that sweet, pine-scented nirvana they call the Rocky Mountain high.

HIGHLIGHTS

- Scouting for geysers and grizzlies in **Yellowstone National Park** (p793), one of America's greatest natural treasures
- Shredding powder with rock stars in **Sun Valley** (p812), the Rocky Mountains' least pretentious wealthy winter playground
- Rafting wild white water and camping under the stars on a week-long **Middle Fork of the Salmon** (p815) rafting adventure
- Slurping down happy-hour margaritas at a sidewalk café in neo-hippie, utopian **Boulder** (p770), a college town where growing up doesn't seem mandatory
- Discovering **Silverton** (p786), a true Wild West town with unpaved streets and stupendous 4WDing
- Hiking past frozen blue lakes and snowfields in **Glacier National Park** (p808) while you still can – at the moment the park's glaciers are losing the global warming battle

HOT TOPIC: DENVER'S MOMENT IN HISTORY

Serving as the stage for the history-making 2008 Democratic National Convention, Denver is proud of the role she played in electing America's first African American president. On a surprisingly sweltering August 28, 2008, at the city's famous INVESCO Field at Mile High football stadium, history was made when Barack Obama became the first African American to accept his party's nomination to run for President. He accepted the nomination in front of a cheering, celebrity-heavy crowd of 70,000+ after a day of star-studded build up. Coincidentally, the event took place exactly 45 years after Martin Luther King Jr made his own history belting out 'I Have a Dream' on the National Mall in Washington, DC; even though the convention was planned long before an African American man had swept the Democratic primaries.

HISTORY

Before the late 18th century when French trappers and Spaniards stepped in, the Rocky Mountain area was a land of many tribes, including the Nez Percé, the Shoshone, the Crow, the Lakota and the Ute.

Meriwether Lewis and William Clark claimed their enduring fame after the USA bought almost all of present-day Montana, Wyoming and eastern Colorado in the Louisiana Purchase in 1803. The two explorers set out to survey the land, covering 8000 miles in three years. Their success urged on other adventurers, and soon the migration was in motion. Wagon trains voyaged to the mountainous lands right into the 20th century, only temporarily slowed by the completion of the Transcontinental Railroad across southern Wyoming in the late 1860s.

To accommodate settlers, the USA purged the western frontier of the Spanish, British and, in a truly shameful era, most of the Native American population. The government signed endless treaties to defuse Native American objections to increasing settlement, but always reneged and shunted tribes onto smaller reservations. Gold-miners' incursions into Native American territory in Montana and the building of US Army forts along the Bozeman Trail ignited a series of wars with the Lakota, Cheyenne, Arapaho and others.

Gold and silver mania preceded Colorado's entry to statehood in 1876. Statehood soon followed for Montana (1889), Wyoming (1890) and Idaho (1890). Along with miners, white farmers and ranchers were the people with power in the late 19th century.

Mining, grazing and timber played major roles in the area's economic development, sparking the growth of cities and towns to provide financial and industrial support. They also subjected the region to boom-and-bust cycles by unsustainable use of resources and left a legacy of environmental disruption.

After the economy boomed post-WWII, the national parks started attracting vacationers. Tourism is now a leading industry in all four states, with the military placing a close second – there is a major presence in Colorado especially.

LOCAL CULTURE

The Rocky Mountain states are the kind of places where red-blooded, pistol-toting libertarians can sit down and have a few pints with stoned-out trustafarians, and no one gets hurt. The clientele in Montana and Wyoming's Wild West saloons is a mix of leathery old cowboys and New Agers – heavy on the crystal pendants and karmic evolutionary talks. Coloradoans are split on whether they vote red or blue, but nearly all believe the government shouldn't tell them what to do. Residents proved this in 2000, when voters legalized marijuana to treat certain chronic medical conditions, and did so not just with a law, but with a constitutional amendment. In 2009 Colorado remained the only state in the nation to have a marijuana law written directly into its constitution.

In trendy après-ski boozing holes you'll still find plenty of rich kids decked out in Burton's latest snow gear, toting Chanel and Vuitton on their gym-toned shoulders, sipping microbrews and swapping ski stories, but even the wealthiest Rocky Mountain towns, like Aspen, Vail, Jackson and Ketchum took a big hit when the financial system collapsed at the end of 2008. Only Boulder seems to have escaped the economic crisis unscathed. While boarded-up buildings and 'for sale' signs are prominent realities in nearly every other Rocky Mountain town these days, in Boulder the bubble has yet to burst. Restaurants remain packed on

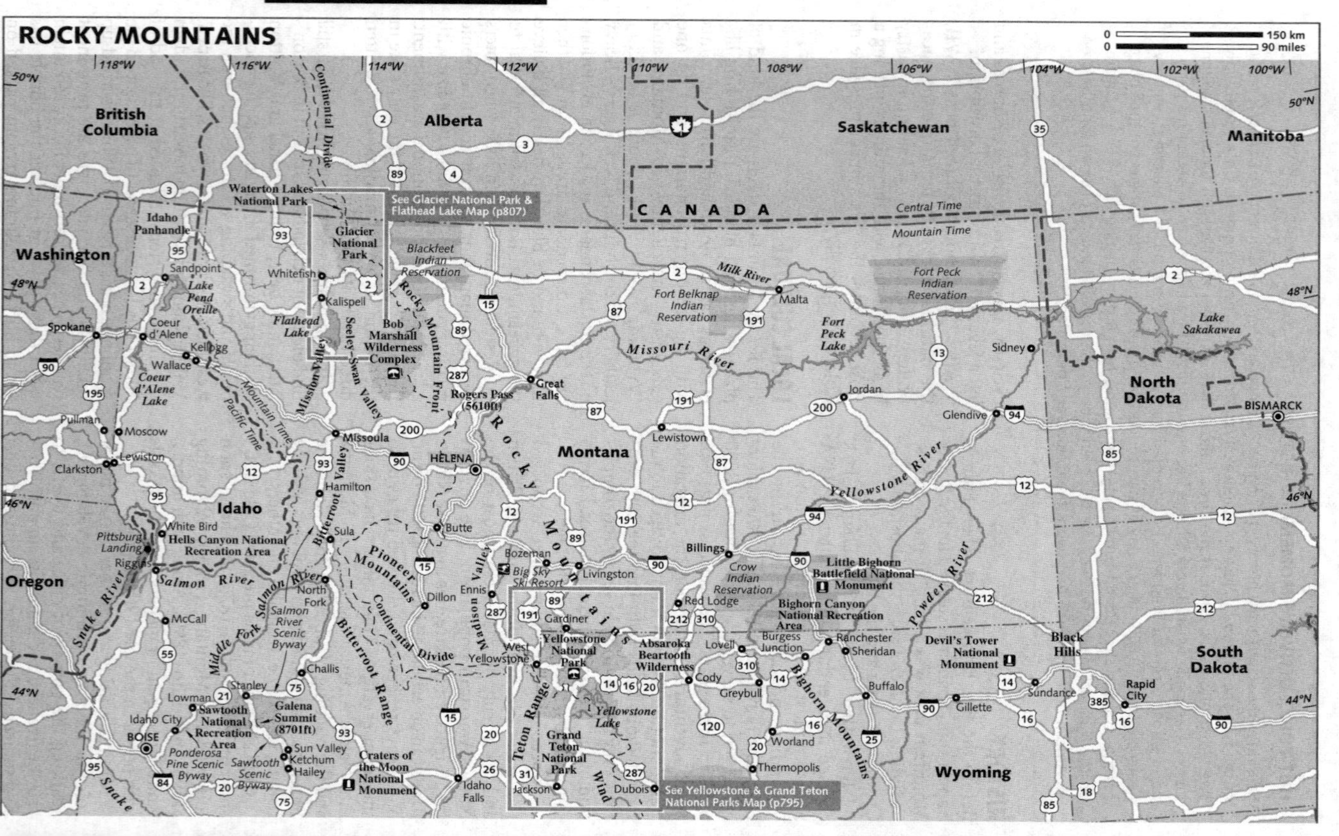
ROCKY MOUNTAINS
0 150 km
0 90 miles
118°W
116°W
114°W
112°W
110°W
108°W
106°W
104°W
102°W
100°W
50°N
48°N
46°N
44°N
British Columbia
Alberta
Saskatchewan
Manitoba
CANADA
Central Time
Mountain Time
Pacific Time
Washington
Idaho
Oregon
Montana
North Dakota
South Dakota
Wyoming
Idaho Panhandle
Waterton Lakes National Park
See Glacier National Park & Flathead Lake Map (p807)
Glacier National Park
Blackfeet Indian Reservation
Continental Divide
Whitefish
Kalispell
Flathead Lake
Seeley-Swan Valley
Bob Marshall Wilderness Complex
Rocky Mountain Front
Mission Valley
Sandpoint
Lake Pend Oreille
Spokane
Coeur d'Alene
Kellogg
Wallace
Coeur d'Alene Lake
Pullman
Moscow
Clarkston
Lewiston
Missoula
Bitterroot Valley
Hamilton
Sula
HELENA
Great Falls
Rogers Pass (5610ft)
Rocky Mountains
Milk River
Malta
Fort Belknap Indian Reservation
Fort Peck Indian Reservation
Fort Peck Lake
Missouri River
Lewistown
Jordan
Sidney
Glendive
Lake Sakakawea
BISMARCK
Yellowstone River
Butte
Bozeman
Big Sky Ski Resort
Livingston
Ennis
Madison Valley
Dillon
Pioneer Mountains
Continental Divide
Bitterroot Range
White Bird
Hells Canyon National Recreation Area
Pittsburg Landing
Riggins
Salmon River
Snake River
North Fork
Salmon River Scenic Byway
Middle Fork Salmon River
McCall
Challis
Stanley
Lowman
Sawtooth National Recreation Area
Galena Summit (8701ft)
Idaho City
BOISE
Ponderosa Pine Scenic Byway
Sawtooth Scenic Byway
Sun Valley
Ketchum
Hailey
Craters of the Moon National Monument
Idaho Falls
Snake
Gardiner
Yellowstone National Park
West Yellowstone
Absaroka Beartooth Wilderness
Yellowstone Lake
Teton Range
Grand Teton National Park
Jackson
Wind
Dubois
See Yellowstone & Grand Teton National Parks Map (p795)
Billings
Crow Indian Reservation
Red Lodge
Little Bighorn Battlefield National Monument
Bighorn Canyon National Recreation Area
Powder River
Lovell
Burgess Junction
Ranchester
Sheridan
Cody
Greybull
Bighorn Mountains
Buffalo
Worland
Thermopolis
Devil's Tower National Monument
Black Hills
Gillette
Sundance
Rapid City

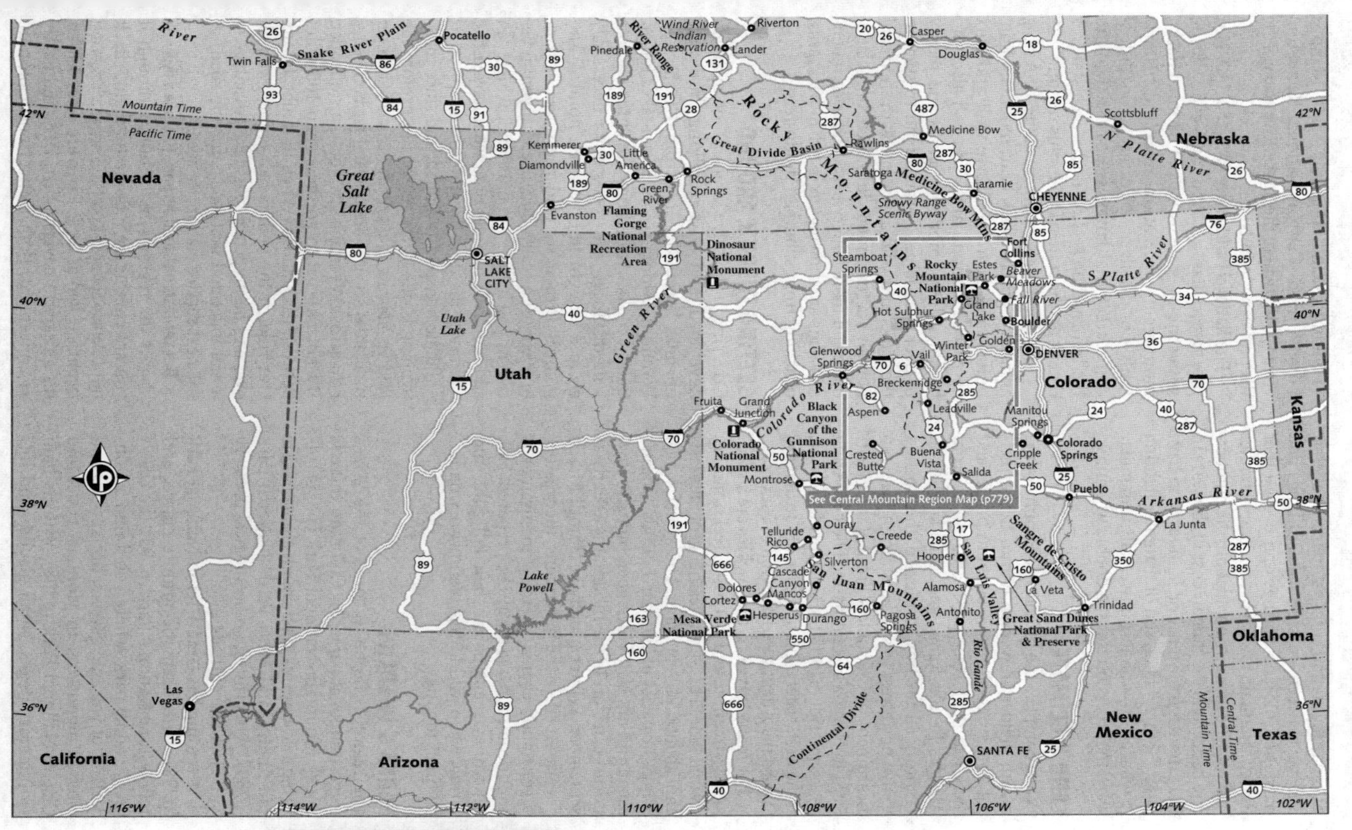

ROCKY MOUNTAINS

Tuesday nights and empty storefronts are few and far between. In blue-collar Billings and patriotic Colorado Springs and every other Rocky Mountain town where military families make up the majority population, the number-one concern is the human cost of the wars in Iraq and Afghanistan. For families who have lost a mother, father, son or daughter fighting in what are now almost universally unpopular wars, the recession is just a double whammy.

LAND & CLIMATE

While complex, the physical geography of the region divides conveniently into two principal features: the Rocky Mountains proper and the Great Plains (see p651). Extending from Alaska's Brooks Range and Canada's Yukon Territory all the way to Mexico, the Rockies sprawl northwest to southeast, from the steep escarpment of Colorado's Front Range westward to Nevada's Great Basin. Their towering peaks and ridges form the Continental Divide: to the west, waters flow to the Pacific; to the east, toward the Atlantic and the Gulf of Mexico.

For many travelers, the Rockies are a summer destination, and it starts to feel summery around June. The warm weather generally lasts until about mid-September. The winter, which brings in packs of powder hounds, doesn't usually hit until late November, though snowstorms can start in the mountains as early as September. Winter usually lasts until March or early April. In the mountains, the weather is constantly changing (snow in summer is not uncommon), so always be prepared. Fall, when the aspens flaunt their fall gold, and spring, when wildflowers bloom, are wonderful times to visit.

PARKS & WILDLIFE

The region is home to some of the USA's biggest national parks. In Colorado there is Rocky Mountain National Park (p774), offering awesome hiking through alpine forests and tundra, and Mesa Verde National Park (p789), primarily an archaeological preserve with elaborate cliffside dwellings.

Wyoming has Grand Teton National Park (p798), with dramatic granite spires, and Yellowstone National Park (p793), the USA's first national park, where you'll find a wonderland of volcanic geysers, hot springs and forested mountains. In Montana you'll find Glacier National Park (p808), with its high sedimentary peaks, small glaciers and lots of wildlife, including grizzly bears. Idaho is home to Hells Canyon National Recreation Area (p815), where the Snake River carves the deepest canyon in North America.

The **National Park Service** (NPS; ☎ 303-969-2500; www.nps.gov) has a comprehensive website with state-by-state listings of national parks, monuments, recreation areas and historic trails. For details about camping on all federal recreational lands, see p1132. Look to the Information section under each state for details on the state parks in this region.

The Rockies are home to all the USA's big animals – grizzly, black bear, mountain lion, buffalo and even the elusive wolf and lynx all roam the mountains. You will also find bighorn sheep, mountain goats and plenty of deer. The larger animals tend to stick to the parks and wild areas, but with the rapid human encroachment into their homeland, more and more hungry bears and even mountain lions are showing up in urban backyards, poaching from suburban dumpsters.

GETTING THERE & AROUND

Covering a massive amount of sparsely developed land – we're talking thousands of miles here – driving around Colorado, Wyoming, Montana and Idaho takes longer than it looks. Attractions are spread across long distances, and roads don't necessarily go in a straight line between point A and point B. If there's a wilderness area or park or even just a really long, deep canyon in between, you'll have to go around, which can add hundreds of miles onto what looked like a connect-the-dots drive on the map.

Public transport is limited, and since road-tripping is one of *the* reasons to explore the Rockies, touring in a private vehicle is best. In rural areas services are few and far between – I-80 across Wyoming is a notorious offender. It's not unusual to go more than 100 miles between gas stations. When in doubt, fill up. Our rule? If the tank is half-empty, we pull over and pump petrol (plus take advantage of a real toilet and grab sodas for the road) at the next service station we see.

Denver International Airport (DIA; www.flydenver.com) is the region's main hub, although if you are coming on a domestic flight, check out **Colorado Springs Airport** (COS; www.springsgov.com/airportindex.aspx) as well. Fares are often lower, it's quicker to navigate than DIA, and nearly as convenient. Both Denver and Colorado

ROCKY MOUNTAINS…

In Two Weeks

Start your Rocky Mountain odyssey in the **Denver** (p760) area. Go tubing, vintage-clothes shopping or biking in outdoor-mad, totally boho **Boulder** (p770), then sit outside, at a sidewalk café and soak up the ultra-liberal atmosphere. Enjoy the vistas of the **Rocky Mountain National Park** (p774) before heading west on I-70 to play in the mountains around **Breckenridge** (p778), which also has the best beginner slopes in Colorado. Go to **Steamboat Springs** (p777) before crossing the border into Wyoming.

Your first stop in the state should be **Lander** (p793) – rock-climbing destination extraordinaire. Continue north to chic **Jackson** (p799) and fabulous **Grand Teton National Park** (p798) before hitting **Yellowstone National Park** (p793). Save at least three days for exploring this geyser-packed wonderland.

Cross the state line into 'big sky country' and slowly make your way northwest through Montana, stopping in funky **Bozeman** (p801) and lively **Missoula** (p805) before visiting **Flathead Lake** (p806). Wind up your trip in Idaho. Get your outdoor fix in **Hells Canyon National Recreation Area** (p815) before continuing to up-and-coming **Boise** (p810). End your trip with a few days skiing **Sun Valley** and partying in **Ketchum** (p812). The town and ski resort, despite being *the* winter playground du jour for today's Hollywood set, are refreshingly unpretentious and affordable.

In One Month

With a month on your hands, you can really delve into the region's off-the-beaten-path treasures. Follow the itinerary above for two weeks, but dip southwest in Colorado – an up-and-coming wine region – before visiting Wyoming. Ride the 4WD trails around **Ouray** (p786). Be sure to visit **Mesa Verde National Park** (p789) while in this area.

In Montana, you'll want to get lost backpacking in the **Bob Marshall Wilderness Complex** (p806) and visit **Glacier National Park** (p808) before the glaciers disappear altogether. In Idaho, spend more time playing in **Sun Valley** (p812) and make sure to explore the shops, pubs and yummy organic restaurants in delightful little **Ketchum** (p812). With a one-month trip, you also have time to drive along a few of Idaho's fantastically remote scenic byways. Make sure you cruise Hwy 75 from Sun Valley north to **Stanley** (p813). Situated on the wide banks of the Salmon River, this stunning mountain hamlet is completely surrounded by national forest land and wilderness areas and is the only spot in America where three scenic byways collide. Wild good looks withstanding, Stanley is also blessed with world-class trout fishing and mild to wild rafting. Take **Highway 21 from Stanley to Boise** (p814). This scenic drive takes you through miles of dense ponderosa forests, and past some excellent, solitary riverside camping spots – some of which come with their own natural hot-springs pools.

For Powder Hounds

Where to start? Well, we suppose in Colorado. Head to Summit County, where you can sleep in **Breckenridge** (p778) – the liveliest town of the bunch – and still ski at four different resorts on just one combo lift ticket. The pass includes **Vail** (p780), one of America's most famous resorts (and our favorite powder bowls), **Arapahoe Basin Ski Area** (p778), which, at more than 13,000ft, has a totally different, very local and laid-back vibe and stays open into June! The other ski area included in the pass is Keystone Ski Resort, across from **Arapahoe Inn** (p778).

From this region you can head south and ski the slopes at **Telluride** (p788) or **Aspen** (p781). Both are true old gold towns, and have a bit more attitude than Vail. Be sure to devote at least a few hours to exploring Aspen's glitzy shops and Telluride's down-to-earth bars for a real local vibe in a historic Wild West setting.

From Aspen catch a local flight up to **Jackson Hole Mountain Resort** (p800) to do some real vertical powder riding in the Grand Tetons.

Springs offer flights on smaller planes to major small towns around the region – Jackson, WY, Boise, ID, Bozeman, MT, and Aspen, CO, are just a few options. Salt Lake City (p873) also has connections with destinations in all four states.

For public transport, **Greyhound** (☎ 800-231-2222; www.greyhound.com) has fixed routes throughout the Rockies, and offers the most comprehensive bus service. The following **Amtrak** (☎ 800-872-7245; www.amtrak.com) services run to and around the region:

California Zephyr Daily between Emeryville, CA (in San Francisco Bay Area), and Chicago, IL, with six stops in Colorado, including Denver, Fraser-Winter Park, Glenwood Springs and Grand Junction.

Empire Builder Runs daily from Seattle, WA, or Portland, OR, to Chicago, IL, with 12 stops in Montana (including Whitefish and East and West Glacier) and one stop in Idaho at Sandpoint.

COLORADO

Colorado was cool with the college crowd long before MTV's cameras caught on. Neither the seven strangers on the reality-TV show *The Real World Denver* nor Heidi Montag and Spencer Pratt on MTV's even bigger hit, *The Hills*, were the first to dig this funky Rocky Mountain high.

Their contemporaries have been flocking to the Centennial State for decades to participate in a uniquely Colorado coming-of-age ritual: the act of ski-bumming (definition: living in a mountain ski-resort town such as Breckenridge, working in the service industry and riding as much fresh powder as possible in between). And it's not just the college crowd. Colorado has been catching Californians, New Yorkers and Washingtonians faster than a fly-fisher can snare a cutthroat trout on the Platte River.

Simply said, Colorado is a great place to live and play, and common knowledge among the locals is that once you taste that 'Rocky Mountain High' John Denver used to croon about, you'll get so addicted to the atmosphere, altitude and attitude you'll never leave. Where else can you spend the morning in an office, the afternoon on the mountain bike and the evening sipping a hopped-up, local beer at a brewpub with friends?

Information

Colorado Road Conditions (☎ 877-315-7623; www.state.co.us) Highway advisories.

Colorado State Parks (☎ 303-470-1144, 800-678-2267; www.parks.state.co.us) Tent sites cost from $8 to $18 per night, depending on facilities, while RV hook-ups are $22 per night. Advance reservations for specific campsites are taken, but subject to an $8 nonrefundable booking fee. At the time this book went to print, the Colorado State Parks Board was considering increasing park fees – including reservation charges – by $2 across the board, so check the prices when booking.

Colorado Travel & Tourism Authority (☎ 800-265-6723; www.colorado.com) State-wide tourism information.

Denver Post (www.denverpost.com) Denver's major daily newspaper.

DENVER

Where in the country does the city's mayor also own some of the state's most popular microbreweries? Why, Denver, of course. Mayor John Hickenlooper was famous for

COLORADO FACTS

Nickname Centennial State
Population 4.9 million
Area 104,247 sq miles
Capital city Denver (population 566, 974)
Other cities Boulder (population 103,100), Colorado Springs (population 402,417)
Sales tax 2.9% state tax, plus individual city taxes
Birthplace of Florence Sabin (1871–1953), one of the first prominent female scientists; silent-film star Douglas Fairbanks (1883–1939); 'King of Jazz' Paul Whiteman (1890–1967)
Home of Ski slopes, hot springs, bighorn sheep, family of Heidi Montag from *The Hills*
Famous for Hosting the 2008 Democratic National Convention nominating Barack Obama, MTV's *The Real World Denver*, skiing
Weird food Rocky Mountain oysters (fried bull's testicles)
Driving distances Denver to Telluride 331 miles, Boulder to Colorado Springs 95 miles

> **WHAT THE...?**
>
> So you just get into Denver and you have a few beers at the pub and suddenly your head is swirling. What the heck is going on? You're not that much of a lightweight, right? Wrong. In the Rocky Mountains, where the elevation is usually at least a mile high, your body takes in less oxygen. This means that until you get adjusted, you will get drunk much quicker! This may be a good thing, especially if you come from a country with a weaker currency... But locals sure do like to laugh at those not smart enough to heed our warning.

owning Front Range brewpubs (including the city's beloved Wynkoop) long before he got into politics. This trivia is just one of Denver's many eccentric quirks. Whether it's making pop culture (hosting the 18th season of the USA's first and longest-running reality-TV show, MTV's *The Real World*) or textbook-worthy history (hosting the 2008 Democratic National Convention nominating America's first African American president), Denver is quite the newsmaker.

Sitting at exactly 5280ft or 1 mile high (hence the nickname 'Mile High City'), this one-time Wild West railway town is a cool place to acclimatize. Low on humidity and high on sunshine, the city is compact and friendly. Take a stroll down the pedestrian-only 16th St Mall or plop down at a chic sidewalk café in the trendy LoDo neighborhood, which dates back to its 1865 beginnings, to soak up the effortless blend of cosmopolitan and Old West vibe.

Orientation

Most of Denver's sights are in the downtown district, which comprises a square defined to the south and east by Colfax Ave and Broadway. The 16th St Mall is the focus of most retail activity, while Lower Downtown (LoDo), which includes historic Larimer Sq, is the heart of Denver's nightlife scene. To access LoDo and the 16th St Mall, exit I-25 at Speer Blvd.

If you're arriving in Denver by bus, you'll be dropped off at Denver Bus Station on 19th St. From here it's an easy walk to the 16th St Mall. Turn right on Curtis St and follow it to 16th St.

Information

BOOKSTORES

For the beloved Tattered Cover Bookstore, see p766.

EMERGENCY & MEDICAL SERVICES

In the event of a citywide emergency, radio station KOA (850 AM) is a designated point of information.

Police Headquarters (☎ 720-913-2000; 1331 Cherokee St) For life-threatening emergencies, call ☎ 911.

University Hospital (☎ 303-399-1211; 4200 E 9th Ave; 24hr) Emergency services.

MEDIA

The mainstream newspaper is the **Denver Post** (www.denverpost.com). The best source for local events is the free weekly **Westword** (www.westword.com). Monthly glossy mag *5280* has a comprehensive dining guide.

POST

Post office (☎ 303-296-4692; 951 20th St; 8am-6:30pm Mon-Fri, 9am-6:30pm Sat) Main branch.

TOURIST INFORMATION

Denver Visitor Center (☎ 303-892-1505, 800-233-6837; www.denver.org; 918 16th St; 9am-5pm Mon-Fri)

Sights & Activities

The **16th Street Mall**, a pedestrian-only strip of downtown, is lined with shops, restaurants and bars, and is a great place to stretch your legs or people-watch from an outdoor café. Another not-to-be-missed area is funky **LoDo**, around Larimer Sq. This is the place to have a drink or browse the boutiques.

The $110-million Frederic C Hamilton wing at the **Denver Art Museum** (☎ 720-865-5000; www.denverartmuseum.org; 100 W 14th Ave; adult/student $13/10; 10am-5pm Tue & Thu-Sat, 10am-9pm Wed, noon-5pm Sun), designed by Daniel Libeskind, is a strange, angular, fan-like edifice, which resembles the Sydney Opera House on speed. It's mesmerizing, but slightly torturous on the eyes. If you think the place looks weird from the outside, look inside: here shapes shift with each turn thanks to a combination of design and uncanny natural-light tricks. The museum is home to one of the largest Native American art collections in the USA, and puts on special avant-garde multimedia exhibits. The latest, entitled 'The Psychedelic Experience,' was a sensory extravaganza using music, video, lights and even activities designed to transport

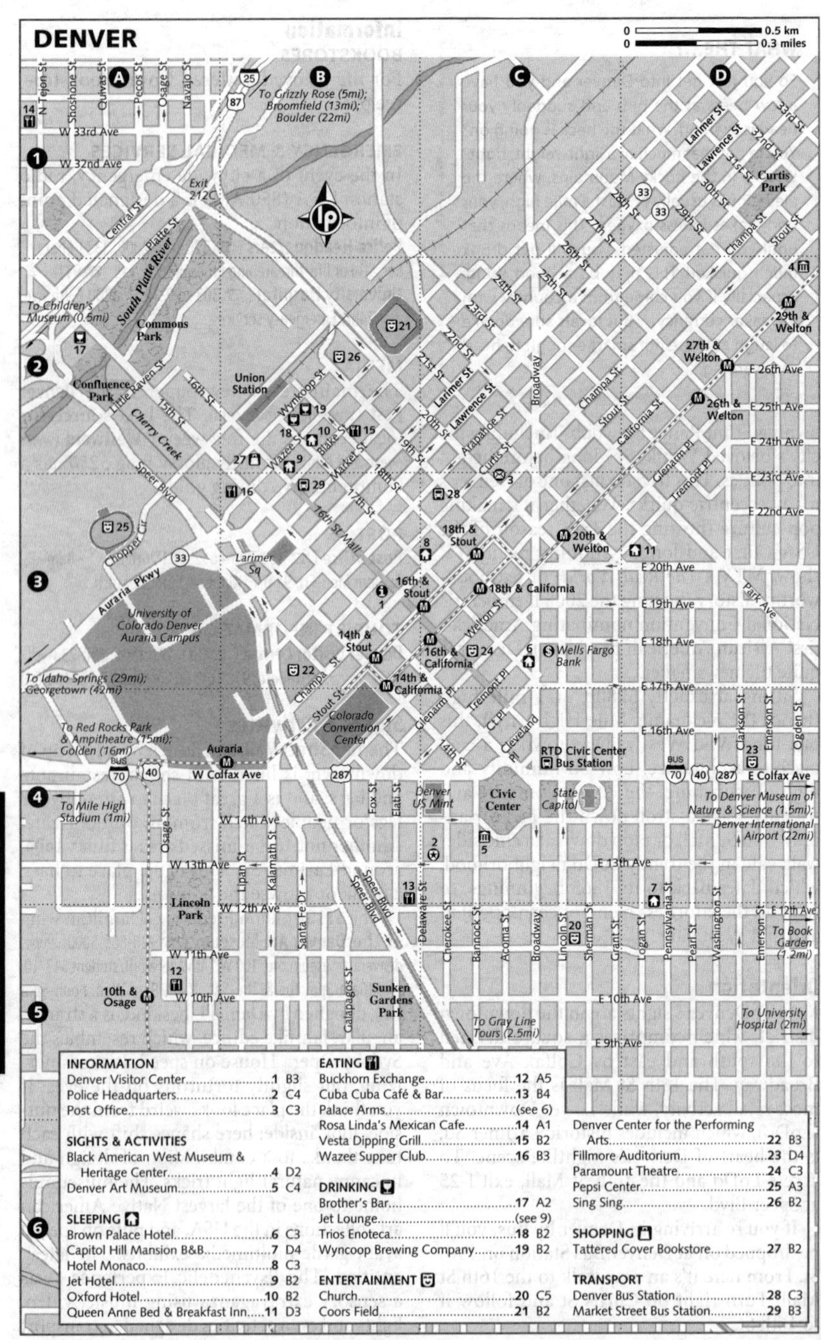
DENVER
0 0.5 km
0 0.3 miles
To Grizzly Rose (5mi); Broomfield (13mi); Boulder (22mi)
To Children's Museum (0.5mi)
South Platte River
Commons Park
Confluence Park
Union Station
Cherry Creek
Curtis Park
Larimer Sq
University of Colorado Denver Auraria Campus
To Idaho Springs (29mi); Georgetown (42mi)
To Red Rocks Park & Ampitheatre (15mi); Golden (16mi)
To Mile High Stadium (1mi)
Colorado Convention Center
Auraria
RTD Civic Center Bus Station
Wells Fargo Bank
Denver US Mint
Civic Center
State Capitol
To Denver Museum of Nature & Science (1.5mi); Denver International Airport (22mi)
Lincoln Park
Sunken Gardens Park
10th & Osage
To Gray Line Tours (2.5mi)
To Book Garden (1.2mi)
To University Hospital (2mi)
29th & Welton
27th & Welton
26th & Welton
20th & Welton
18th & Stout
18th & California
16th & Stout
16th & California
14th & Stout
14th & California
ROCKY MOUNTAINS
INFORMATION
Denver Visitor Center....1 B3
Police Headquarters....2 C4
Post Office....3 C3
SIGHTS & ACTIVITIES
Black American West Museum & Heritage Center....4 D2
Denver Art Museum....5 C4
SLEEPING
Brown Palace Hotel....6 C3
Capitol Hill Mansion B&B....7 D4
Hotel Monaco....8 C3
Jet Hotel....9 B2
Oxford Hotel....10 B2
Queen Anne Bed & Breakfast Inn....11 D3
EATING
Buckhorn Exchange....12 A5
Cuba Cuba Café & Bar....13 B4
Palace Arms....(see 6)
Rosa Linda's Mexican Cafe....14 A1
Vesta Dipping Grill....15 B2
Wazee Supper Club....16 B3
DRINKING
Brother's Bar....17 A2
Jet Lounge....(see 9)
Trios Enoteca....18 B2
Wyncoop Brewing Company....19 B2
ENTERTAINMENT
Church....20 C5
Coors Field....21 B2
Denver Center for the Performing Arts....22 B3
Fillmore Auditorium....23 D4
Paramount Theatre....24 C3
Pepsi Center....25 A3
Sing Sing....26 B2
SHOPPING
Tattered Cover Bookstore....27 B2
TRANSPORT
Denver Bus Station....28 C3
Market Street Bus Station....29 B3

observers to the time of swingin' 1960s San Francisco. Admission to the museum is free on the first Saturday of each month.

Denver is also home to the excellent **Black American West Museum & Heritage Center** (☎ 303-482-2242; www.blackamericanwestmuseum.com; 3091 California St; adult/child $8/6; ⏲ 10am-2pm Mon-Fri, 10am-5pm Sat & Sun, closed Mon & Tue winter), dedicated to 'telling history how it was.' It provides an intriguing look at the contributions of African Americans (from cowboys to rodeo riders) during the pioneer era – according to museum statistics, one in three Colorado cowboys were African American.

Red Rocks Park & Amphitheatre (☎ 303-640-2637; www.redrocksonline.com; 16352 County Rd 93; park admission free; ⏲ 5am-11pm) is set between 400ft-high red sandstone rocks 15 miles southwest of Denver. Acoustics are so good many artists record live albums here. The 9000-seat theater offers stunning views and draws big-name bands all summer.

If you've got the kids, check out the **Children's Museum** (☎ 303-433-7444; www.mychildsmuseum.org; 2121 Children's Museum Dr; admission $7.50; ⏲ 9am-4pm Mon-Fri, 10am-5pm Sat & Sun; 🚸), which is full of excellent interactive exhibits. A particularly well-regarded section is the kid-size grocery store, where your little consumerists can push a shopping cart of their very own while learning about food and health. In the 'Arts à la carte' section kids can get creative with crafts that they can take home – all use recycled materials.

The **Denver Museum of Nature & Science** (☎ 303-322-7009; www.dmns.org; 2001 Colorado Blvd; museum adult/child $11/6, museum & IMAX $16/10; ⏲ 9am-5pm; 🚸), 3.5 miles east of downtown, has an IMAX theater and absorbing exhibits for all ages.

Festivals & Events

These are just a few highlights of Denver's festival-laden year. Ask the visitor center for a complete schedule.

Cinco de Mayo (☎ 303-534-8342; http://cincodemayodenver.com) Salsa music and margaritas at one of the country's biggest Cinco de Mayo celebrations; first weekend in May.

Great American Beer Festival (☎ 303-447-0816; www.beertown.org) A whole gamut of brews served in early September.

Taste of Colorado (☎ 303-295-6330; www.atasteofcolorado.com; 🚸) More than 50 restaurants cook up their specialties at food stalls; there's also booze, live music, and arts-and crafts-vendors at this Labor Day festival.

Sleeping

Besides the places mentioned here, there are chain and independent motels throughout the city, with rooms starting at $50. Check out Lonely Planet Hotels & Hostels (www.lonelyplanet.com/hotels), with a range of sleeping options in the Denver 'burbs. Those on a budget should consider the very clean **Boulder International Youth Hostel** (p771) in nearby Boulder, as both Denver's hostels were catering more to transients than backpackers when we dropped by.

Jet Hotel (☎ 303-572-3300; www.thejethotel.com; 1612 Wazee St; r $99-169; P ✖ 💻 📶) Priced for partying, this slick minimalist boutique in the heart of LoDo is all about fun, especially on weekends. That's when Denver's beautiful people come for the slumber-party-with-bottle-service experience – you can dance all night in the swank first floor lounge, then stumble up to your Zen quarters, burrow under the thick white comforters and sleep until brunch. Stay

EATING COLORADO: ROCKY MOUNTAIN OYSTERS

When it comes to Colorado lingo, there is one definition you really should know: Rocky Mountain Oyster. It's not likely to be what you think. These regional delicacies don't come on a half-shell garnished with lemon; they are served deep-fried. And although the chewiness is similar to that of an oyster, the breaded ball in the wax-paper basket is made from 100% beef. So what is a Rocky Mountain Oyster exactly? Good old-fashioned bull testicles, seasoned and deep-fried. It's a Western ranching specialty that never died. Hey, if you believe in reusing everything, think of eating these seasoned balls as another form of recycling – to some the taste is similar to that of overcooked calamari, while others equate them with lean fried chicken. We'll even go as far as to give you props for going green. If you dare to try the testicles, the **Buckhorn Exchange** (☎ 303-534-9505; 1000 Osage St; testicles $8.75; ⏲ 11am-2pm & 5:30pm-9:30pm) serves them as the house special. The restaurant does a mean basket of crispy fried bulls balls, which is exactly what one should expect from Denver's oldest steakhouse. In operation since 1893, it's had more than a century to perfect the art of testicle frying.

on a weekday if you want a posh central hotel room without the boozy party scene and accompanying noise. When we stopped by, Jet was set to open a new lobby restaurant, XO, featuring a healthy Asian fusion menu (perfect for kicking last night's hangover).

Capitol Hill Mansion B&B (☎ 303-839-5221, 800-839-9329; www.capitolhillmansion.com; 1207 Pennsylvania St; r incl breakfast $115-200; P ⊠ ✤ 💻 wi-fi) Stained-glass windows, original 1890s woodwork and turrets make this gorgeous, gay- and family-friendly Romanesque mansion a special place to stay. Rooms are elegant, uniquely decorated and come with different special features – one has a solarium, another boasts Jacuzzi tubs.

our pick **Queen Anne Bed & Breakfast Inn** (☎ 303-296-6666; www.queenannebnb.com; 2147 Tremont Pl; r incl breakfast $165-215; P ⊠ ✤) Soft chamber music wafting through public areas, fresh flowers, manicured gardens and evening wine tastings create a romantic ambience at this eco-conscious B&B in two late-1800s Victorian homes. Featuring period antiques, private hot tubs and exquisite hand-painted murals, each room has its own personality, but all are green. Mattresses are made from recycled coils and green-tea insulation, fabrics are organic (and so is the delicious full breakfast) and products and produce are purchased from local merchants when possible. It even encourages you to take the house bikes out rather than your car. Check online for special rates.

Hotel Monaco (☎ 303-296-1717, 800-990-1303; www.monaco-denver.com; 1717 Champa St; r from $169; P ✤ 💻 wi-fi) An ultrastylish boutique joint that's a favorite with the celebrity set. Modern rooms blend French and art-deco styles – think bold colors and those fabulous European-style feather beds. Don't miss the evening 'Altitude Adjustment Hour,' when guests enjoy free wine and five-minute massages. The place is 100% pet-friendly; staff will even deliver a named goldfish to your room upon request. Discounts are routinely offered online.

Oxford Hotel (☎ 303-628-5400, 800-228-5838; www.theoxfordhotel.com; 1600 17th St; r from $180; P ⊠ ✤ 💻 wi-fi) Marble walls, stained-glass windows, frescoes and sparkling chandeliers adorn the public spaces of this classy hotel in a red sandstone building. Rooms are large and decked out with imported English and French antiques. The art-deco Cruise Room Bar is one of Denver's swankiest cocktail lounges. Rates vary dramatically based on season and demand; check the website for the best rates and packages.

Brown Palace Hotel (☎ 303-297-3111, 800-321-2599; www.brownpalace.com; 321 17th St; r from $199; P ✤) This distinguished historic landmark is *the* place to stay in Denver. Within walking distance of restaurants and nightlife, the Brown Palace is elegantly decorated and provides old-world atmosphere and excellent service. It has hosted everyone over the years, from the Beatles to Winston Churchill. Have afternoon tea in the lobby.

Eating

Cheap street meals are found on the 16th St Mall. The pedestrian mall and LoDo are full of restaurants catering to all budgets and continents, and many of them have great sidewalk seating in the summer months.

our pick **Rosa Linda's Mexican Cafe** (☎ 303-455-0608; 2005 W 33rd Ave; mains $6-12; 🕑 11:30am-10pm; 👶) For more than 20 years the Aguirre family has been serving Denver reasonably priced authentic Mexican comfort fare with a side of old-fashioned hospitality. Winner of numerous awards – including Top 15 nachos in the nation by the *Wall Street Journal* – Rosa Linda's also does excellent *chiles rellenos* and *mole*. The menu includes plenty of vegetarian and health-conscious choices (check out the wholewheat grilled-cactus burrito).

Wazee Supper Club (☎ 303-623-9518; 1600 15th St; mains $6-9, pizzas $10-18; 🕑 11am-1am Mon-Sat) Once you step into Wazee, on Denver's most historic street, there's little chance you'll turn around – it smells so delicious. Known for some of the best pizza and *stromboli* in the city, this longtime local favorite is a buzzing place day and night, with the kitchen open until 1am.

Cuba Cuba Café & Bar (☎ 303-605-2882; 1173 Delaware St; mains $10-22; 🕑 11am-11pm) We get dreamy just thinking about the mango mojito (rum-based cocktail) at this swanky Cuban joint serving finger-lickin' BBQ spareribs, flavor-packed fried yucca and a sumptuous coconut-crusted tuna. The back patio offers fantastic sunset city views; the bright blue-walled environs emit an island vibe.

Vesta Dipping Grill (☎ 303-296-1970; 1822 Blake St; mains $15-25; 🕑 5-10:30pm) Pick a type of meat, then choose from 30 different sauces to dip it into. It's a simple concept that works exceedingly well. The melt-in-your mouth quality of the creative dishes – many Asian inspired – makes Vesta one of Denver's favorite restaurants. The atmosphere is relaxed and funky.

Palace Arms (☎ 303-297-3111; Brown Palace Hotel, 321 17th St; mains from $20; ⏲ 5:30pm-late) The patriotic pioneer decor inside the Brown Palace's award-winning restaurant dates back to the 1700s – check out the silver centerpiece the British royal family commissioned. The food is as impressive as the old-world ambience, and the wine list features 900 bottles. Signature dishes include Kobe rib-eye steak and seared bison tenderloin.

Drinking

Most bars and nightspots are in LoDo and around Coors Field. The biweekly gay newspaper *Out Front,* found in coffee shops and bars, has entertainment listings. Many of the venues listed under Eating (opposite) are also bars.

Wynkoop Brewing Company (☎ 303-297-2700; 1634 18th St) Mayor Hickenlooper's brewery is a good place to come for a pint and a game of pool. Big and breezy, with more than 20 billiard tables, Wynkoop is arguably the city's most rocking pub. It serves juicy burgers to soak up its award-winning microbrews.

Jet Lounge (☎ 303-572-3300; Jet Hotel, 1612 Wazee St) Designed to blend into the Jet Hotel's lobby, this lounge is the place to see and be seen in Denver. There is a bedroom-meets-house-party vibe – candles, cozy couches, a weekend DJ and lots and lots of beautiful people. Jet Lounge was a favorite with the *Real World Denver* housemates. Order bottle service, sit back and melt into the party.

Trios Enoteca (☎ 303-293-2887; 1730 Wynkoop St) Art-glass lampshades, bare brick walls and old pinups from the 1920s create the speakeasy atmosphere in this sleek LoDo wine bar with excellent live jazz. If you are hungry order a wood-oven pizza from the varied bar menu. The kitchen stays open late.

Brother's Bar (☎ 303-445-9991; 2376 15th St) Classic rock and roll, lacquered booths and tables made from old wood barrels greet you inside Denver's oldest bar. Grab a seat on the leafy patio if it's nice outside. The bar is on a popular cycle path, and has been a local institution since it opened.

Entertainment

To find out what's happening with music, theater and other performing arts, pick up a free copy of *Westword.*

our pick Grizzly Rose (☎ 303-295-1330; 5450 N Valley Hwy; cover $5-10) This is one kick-ass honky-tonk, attracting real cowboys from as far as Cheyenne – the Country Music Association (CMA) has called it the best country bar in America. If you've never experienced line dancing, there's no better place to put on the boots, grab the Stetson and let loose. Just north of the city limits off I-25 (you'll have to drive or cab it), the Grizzly is famous for bringing in huge industry stars – Willie Nelson, Lee Ann Rimes – and only charging $10 per ticket.

Church (☎ 303-832-3538; 1160 Lincoln St; cover $10) There's nothing like ordering a stiff drink inside an old cathedral. Yes, this club, which draws a large and diverse crowd, is in a former house of the Lord. Lit by hundreds of altar candles and flashing blue strobe lights, the Church has three dancefloors, a couple of lounges and even a sushi bar! Arrive before 10pm Friday through Sunday to avoid the cover charge.

Sing Sing (☎ 303-291-0880; 1735 19th St; cover $7) This lively dueling piano bar is very popular with bachelorette parties. Sing Sing fills quickly; arrive around 6:30pm to score a table near the pianos. It's pretty noisy (don't expect much talking) but the atmosphere is really fun. Song requests are taken (and usually accompanied by $5), but many folks request the same songs, so you could just sit back, sip from the famous Long Island iced-tea buckets and listen. Beware when drunken brides-to-be get up on stage to dance.

Denver Center for the Performing Arts (☎ 303-893-4100; www.denvercenter.org; 1245 Champa St) Covering four city blocks, this complex is the world's second-largest performing-arts center. It hosts resident Colorado Symphony Orchestra, Opera Colorado, Denver Center Theater Company, Colorado Ballet and touring Broadway shows.

In town, the main music venues for national acts are the **Paramount Theatre** (☎ 303-534-8336; www.denverparamount.com; 1621 Glenarm Pl) and **Fillmore Auditorium** (☎ 303-837-0360; 1510 Clarkson St).

Denver is a city known for manic sports fans, and boasts five pro teams. The **Colorado Rockies** (☎ 303-762-5437; http://colorado.rockies.mlb.com) play baseball at the highly rated **Coors Field** (2001 Blake St). The **Pepsi Center** (☎ 303-405-1111; www.pepsicenter.com; 1000 Chopper Circle) hosts the Denver Nuggets basketball team and the Colorado Avalanche hockey team. The much-lauded **Denver Broncos**

football team (☎ 720-258-3333; www.denverbroncos.com) and the **Colorado Rapids soccer team** (☎ 303-299-1599; www.coloradorapids.com) play at **Mile High Stadium** (☎ 720-258-3000; www.invescofieldatmilehigh.com; 1805 S Bryant St), 1 mile west of downtown. **Public Regional Transit District** (RTD; ☎ 303-299-6000; www.rtd-denver.com) buses run from points around Denver and Boulder directly to the sports stadiums and back on game nights. The cost is $3 one way. Check RTD's website for details.

Shopping

The pedestrian-only 16th St Mall and the boutiques of LoDo are the city's main downtown shopping areas.

ourpick **Tattered Cover Bookstore** (☎ 303-436-1070; 1628 16th St; 6:30am-9pm Mon-Fri, 9am-9pm Sat, 10am-6pm Sun) Denver's most loved bookstore is in this main shopping area. By far the coolest shop in Denver, it's massive and bursting with books. The armchair-travel section is wonderful – curl into the comfy chairs scattered around the shop and read about Kathmandu. And if you need a new writing journal, well this is where we come to stock up before our research trips. The selection is fabulous!

Getting There & Away

Denver International Airport (DIA; www.flydenver.com; 8500 Peña Blvd) is served by around 20 airlines and offers flights to nearly every major US city. Located 24 miles east of downtown, DIA is connected with I-70 exit 238 by 12-mile-long Peña Blvd.

Tourist and airport information is available at a **booth** (☎ 303-342-2000) in the terminal's central hall.

Greyhound buses stop at **Denver Bus Station** (☎ 303-293-6555; 1055 19th St), which runs services to Boise (from $140, 18 hours), Billings (from $105, 14 hours) and Los Angeles (from $150, 20 hours).

Amtrak's *California Zephyr* runs daily between Chicago and San Francisco via Denver. Trains arrive and depart from **Union Station** (☎ 303-825-2583; cnr 17th & Wynkoop Sts). For recorded information on arrival and departure times, call ☎ 303-534-2812. **Amtrak** (☎ 800-872-7245; www.amtrak.com) can also provide schedule information and train reservations.

Getting Around

TO/FROM THE AIRPORT

All transportation companies have booths near the baggage-claim area. **Public Regional Transit District** (RTD; ☎ 303-299-6000; www.rtd-denver.com) runs a SkyRide service to the airport from downtown Denver hourly ($10, one hour). RTD also goes to Boulder ($12, 1½ hours) from the **Market Street Bus Station** (cnr 16th & Market Sts). Taxis to downtown Denver charge a flat $45, excluding tip. **SuperShuttle** (☎ 303-370-1300, 800-258-3826) offers van services (from $22) between the Denver area and the airport.

CAR & MOTORCYCLE

Street parking can be a pain, but there are slews of pay garages in downtown and LoDo. Nearly all the major car-rental agencies have counters at DIA, though only a few have offices in downtown Denver.

PUBLIC TRANSPORTATION

RTD provides public transportation throughout the Denver and Boulder area. Local buses cost $1.15 for local services, $2.50 for express services. Useful free shuttle buses run along the 16th St Mall.

RTD also operates a light-rail line serving 16 stations on a 12-mile route through downtown. Fares are the same as for local buses.

TAXI

For 24-hour cab service, call:

Freedom Cab (☎ 303-292-8900)
Metro Taxi (☎ 303-333-3333)
Yellow Cab (☎ 303-777-7777)

FRONT RANGE

Home to Colorado Springs, Boulder and fabulous Rocky Mountain National Park (as well as Denver, the hub city), the Front Range is Colorado's most populated region and where most people's Rocky Mountain odyssey begins. I-25 is the north–south artery along the Front Range (which is just a name for this part of the Rocky Mountains), with Colorado Springs and Denver, 65 miles apart, both sitting on this highway.

Northwest of Denver, accessed via US 36, is Mork and Mindy's hometown, Boulder. It's a hippie utopia where the word 'recession' does not appear to exist. Continuing north on Hwy 36 from Boulder takes you to Estes Park, one of the Rocky Mountain National Park's two gateway towns. Grand Lake, 100 miles from Denver, is the other. It's accessed from Denver via I-70 to I-40, where you'll also find two favorite local ski resorts – Winter Park and Steamboat Springs.

A GOOD PLACE TO BE A DOG

If you're traveling with pooch, he or she will wag a tail over a visit to Colorado Springs. Home to 402,417 people and 87,055 canines – that's one dog for every two households – it's possibly the nation's most canine-friendly city. Whether they are playing catch in one of the five city dog parks, hitting the trails with their guardians in Garden of the Gods, one of many off-leash hiking havens, or accompanying their humans on a shopping trip to Pottery Barn or Banana Republic at the pro-dog Promenade Shops at Briargate (in the northwest corner of town), Colorado Springs is a good place to be a canine. Dogs can even take in a minor-league ballgame at pet-friendly SkySox stadium! If you're visiting, the five-star posh and historic Broadmoor hotel (see p768) caters to your furry best friend with in-room beds and doggie room service).

Colorado Springs

In a picture-perfect location below famous Pikes Peak, Colorado Springs offers a runaway train of listed attractions: hike through Garden of the Gods' strange red rock formations, take a ride on the cog railway or stroll down the Tejon Strip.

Evangelical conservatives, libertarians, tourists and military installations comprise the bizarre demographics of Colorado's second-largest city. It's home to a large military base, the US Air Force Academy and the North American Radar Air Defense (the command center monitoring US and Canadian airspace in a hollowed-out mountain, it's where the president would weather a nuclear-missile strike). But it's also the place where evangelical mega-church pastor Ted Haggard's headline-making sex and drugs scandal played out. And where this century's most notorious band of fugitive outlaws – the Texas 7 – were captured.

ORIENTATION & INFORMATION

I-25 bisects the sprawling metropolitan area. To the east is the main 'downtown' business district, centered on Tejon St between Kiowa St to the north and Colorado Ave to the south. Here you will find restaurants, bars, clubs and shops. To the west of the I-25 are Old Colorado City, Garden of the Gods and Manitou Springs.

The **Colorado Springs Visitor Center** (☎ 719-635-7506; www.coloradosprings-travel.com; 515 S Cascade Ave; 🕑 8:30am-5pm) has all the usual tourist information.

SIGHTS & ACTIVITIES

The bewitching red sandstone formations at **Garden of the Gods** (the rocks are smack in the middle of town and seem so out of place you won't quite believe your eyes) draw around two million visitors each year to see highlights such as Balanced Rock, High Point and Central Garden. Soak up the beauty on one of the park hiking trails.

Travelers have been making the trip on the **Pikes Peak Cog Railway** to the summit of Pikes Peak (14,110ft) since 1891. Katherine Lee Bates was so impressed by her 1893 trip to the summit that she was inspired to write 'America the Beautiful.' Swiss-built trains smoothly make the round-trip in 3¼ hours, which includes 40 minutes at the top. Trains depart from the **Manitou Springs depot** (☎ 719-685-5401; www.cograilway.com; 515 Ruxton Ave, Manitou Springs; round-trip $33; 🕑 Apr-Jan; 🚸), 6 miles west of Colorado Springs on US 24 in eccentric little Manitou Springs.

You can also reach the summit on foot, via the tough 12.5-mile **Barr Trail**. From the trailhead, just above the Manitou Springs depot, the path climbs 7300ft. Fit hikers should reach the top in about eight hours. Leave in the early morning, as afternoon thunderstorms can prove deadly. Make sure your body is acclimatized to the altitude before setting out. It's easy to hitch a ride down the mountain once you reach the top.

Practically falling into a crumbly red rock canyon, **Manitou Springs** is one of the nation's quirkiest small towns, hosting a slew of unusual festivals. Don't miss the famous fruitcake toss around Christmas, when locals make homemade slingshots to catapult the suckers (the cake that goes furthest wins). The costumed coffin races down the main street at Halloween are another beloved tradition. The games still work at the historic **penny arcade** in the heart of downtown. The old-fashioned emporium is truly worth a wander, no matter your age, for the goose-bumps-inducing nostalgia.

From the town of Divide, west of Manitou Springs on US 24, you can drive the **Pikes Peak**

Toll Road (per person/car $10/35; ⌚ 9am-3pm winter, 7am-7pm summer) to the summit. It's sometimes closed in winter due to bad weather. If it's open, and you have a set of skis or a snowboard and at least three people – one driver and two riders – there is some great (free, after you pay the toll) backcountry powder skiing with easy drop-in and pick-up points along the serpentine road. The locals would kill us for listing mile-markers, so you'll have to drive the highway and look for tracks.

SLEEPING

There are cheap 1950s-style independent motels on Nevada Ave about 1 mile north and 1 mile south of the central business district. For the more upscale chains, like Holiday Inn and Best Western, try the Fillmore, Garden of the Gods and Circle Ave exits off I-25.

Garden of the Gods Campground (☎ 719-475-9450; www.coloradocampground.com; 3704 W Colorado Ave; campsites $33, cabins/r from $45/60;) For camping close to town you could do worse than here. There are only a few trees, and most of the area is paved, but the pool is refreshing and the basic cabins and bunkhouse rooms are quite good value.

El Colorado Lodge (☎ 719-685-5485; www.pikes-peak.com/elcolorado; 23 Manitou Ave; cabins $50-100;) On the outskirts of Manitou Springs, El Colorado is a pink Southwestern-style lodge c 1926. Accommodations are in comfortable adobe cabins set among blue spruce and pine trees. Most come with fireplaces and cute little decks equipped with picnic tables.

Avenue Hotel (☎ 719-685-1277; www.avenuehotelbandb.com; 711 Manitou Ave; r incl breakfast $80-130;) This Victorian mansion on a hill in downtown Manitou Springs began as a boarding house in 1886. One hundred years later, it reopened as the city's first B&B. Decorated in warm colors, the seven rooms have claw-foot tubs, lush fabrics and canopy-topped wrought-iron beds. They are reached via a fantastic three-floor, open turned staircase. Families should ask about the bigger Carriage House, which has a private kitchen.

Broadmoor (☎ 719-634-7711; www.broadmoor.com; 1 Lake Ave; r from $250;) One of the top five-star resorts in the USA, the Broadmoor sits in a picture-perfect location against the blue-green slopes of Cheyenne Mountain. Everything about the property is exquisite: acres of lush grounds and a shimmering lake to stroll past, world-class golf, ornately decorated grandiose public spaces, myriad bars and restaurants, a fantastic spa and uber-comfortable European-style guest rooms.

EATING

The Tejon Strip downtown is the place to eat.

Pike's Perk Coffee & Teahouse (☎ 719-635-1600; 14 S Tejon St; espressos & snacks from $2; ⌚ 6am-10pm Mon-Thu, to 11pm Fri, 7am-11pm Sat, to 8pm Sun) With a fantastic rooftop boasting unobstructed views of Colorado Springs' signature mountain, Pikes Perk is our all-time-favorite regional coffee shop. Read a magazine, write a novel or just a chat with friends in the cozy 2nd floor lounge or on the aforementioned deck when the weather's nice. Pike's Perk serves the usual range of espresso drinks, all excellent quality, as well as a range of pastries, bagels, breakfast burritos and other light meals.

Western Omelette (☎ 719-636-2286; 16 S Walnut St; mains $4-8; ⌚ 7am-2pm;) If you're hung over after a big night, do as the locals do and head here for a green chili cure. The Mexican breakfast dishes, such as huevos rancheros (with green chili, of course), are greasy-spoon fare. It's a big place completely lacking in character, which oddly gives it its charm.

Trinity Brewing Co (☎ 719-634-0029; www.trinitybrew.com; 1466 Garden of the Gods Rd; mains $5-8; ⌚ 11am-midnight Thu-Sat, 11am-10pm Sun-Wed) Inspired by Belgium's beer cafés, the ecofriendly Trinity Brewing Co is an extremely cool addition to the Colorado Springs pub scene. Owned by two self-admitted beer geeks, it serves 'artisanal beers' (made from rare ingredients and potent amounts of alcohol) and has a menu focused on creating a 'Slow Food dining experience based on…environmental sustainability.' The vegan BBQ sandwich, spicy Thai curry soup, vegetarian 'chicken wings' and other healthy, organic choices are definitely a departure from usual pub fare. But don't fret, carnivores: there is some meat on offer. If you're still hungry after dinner, wash your tofu down with a beer float. A 10% discount is given for arriving on foot or bike. Look for the brewery in a strip mall one block west of Centennial Blvd. It's about a 15-minute bike ride northwest of downtown.

Phantom Canyon Brewing Co (☎ 719-635-2800; 2 E Pikes Peak Ave; mains $7-18; ⌚ 11am-late;) In an old exposed warehouse building, this local brewery serves a variety of pints and American cuisine in a casual atmosphere. The appetizers can be large enough for a meal, and the

DON'T MISS

A Colorado Springs institution for decades now, **Poor Richard's** (320-324 N Tejon St; 9am-9pm Sun-Thu, to midnight Fri & Sat;), owned by local politico Richard Skorman, is a unique one-stop combo shopping experience, with four very different businesses under one roof.

Got a hankering to get lost in an aisle of old books? No problem. **Poor Richard's Bookstore** (719-578-0012) is the city's most revered secondhand bookseller. Traveling with family? The attached **Little Richard's Toy Store** (719-578-3072;) mesmerizes kids with a large collection of toys. Parents can be stoked too, because toys sold here are specifically designed to foster imagination, creativity and cognitive development in children. Ringing ahead to speak with a trained shopkeeper about your child's specific needs is encouraged.

When you've finished shopping, hit up **Poor Richard's Restaurant** (719-632-7721; mains $5-10, pizza slices/pies from $3.65/14.50;) for an additive-free meal. The casual restaurant is well-known for its delicious, hand-tossed, New York–style pizzas made from crispy white, wheat or spelt crust ,as well as fresh build-your-own salads with more than 30 ingredient choices. Kids will dig the indoor playground in the back.

Between the restaurant and the toy store, **Rico's Coffee, Chocolate & Wine Bar @ Poor Richard's** (719-630-7723) serves a European café menu of the ham-and-cheese croissant and fresh pastry variety, but really people come here for the espresso, chocolate (served hot and cold) and wine (more than 20 by-the-glass choices). Oh, and there's live jazz many nights.

downstairs dining room is family-friendly. Locals flock to the upstairs bar for pool and socializing at night.

Blue Star (719-632-1086; 1645 S Tejon St; mains $10-25; 5:30-9pm Sun-Thu, to 10pm Fri & Sat) One of Colorado Springs' most popular gourmet eateries, the Blue Star is in a quiet neighborhood just south of downtown. The menu at this landmark spot changes regularly, but always involves fresh fish, top-cut steak and inventive chicken dishes, flavored with Mediterranean and Pacific Rim rubs and spices. The colorful bar area, with metal and sleek wood decor and booth or high-top tables, is more social than the open-kitchen dining room in the back. There's live jazz on Mondays and dancing on weekends, and the menu is slightly less expensive. There is an impressive 8500-bottle wine cellar here that includes organic varietals.

DRINKING & ENTERTAINMENT

The Tejon Strip, between Platte and Colorado Sts, is where most of the after-dark action happens. Also check out the burgeoning SoDo (South Downtown). For now it's just a block-long strip of S Tejon St between E Cimarron St and E Moreno St, but crammed into this recently gentrified small space is the city's dance club du jour, **SoDo**.

Hotel Bar (719-577-5733; Broadmoor Hotel, 1 Lake Ave) On a warm summer afternoon there's no better spot for a drink with a view than this bar overlooking a private lake. Order a chilled glass of wine and a cigar, and sit back and watch the ducks pass by. When the weather turns cool the outdoor stone fireplaces are lit.

Cowboys Nightclub (719-596-1212; www.worldfamouscowboys.com; 25 N Tejon St; cover $3-8; 5pm-2am Wed-Thu, 4pm-2am Fri-Sun) Voted the best nightclub in the city by the readers of its daily newspaper, Cowboys is loud, brash and 100% country and western. In the heart of the Tejon Strip, it's a great place to just cut loose and dance. From karaoke to two-step lessons to live concerts, this club is always packed and always buzzing. There are plans to open a bowling alley upstairs. Across the street from Cowboys – and owned by the same people – is the city's other megahot nightlife venue, **Rum Bay**, with eight clubs in one.

GETTING THERE & AROUND

Colorado Springs Municipal Airport (COS; 719-550-1900; 7770 Drennan Rd) offers a viable alternative to Denver International Airport. The **Yellow Cab** (719-634-5000) fare from the airport to the city center is between $25 and $30.

Greyhound buses between Cheyenne, WY, and Pueblo, CO, stop daily at the **depot** (719-635-1505; 120 Weber St). The **transportation center** (719-385-7433; 127 E Kiowa St; 8am-5pm Mon-Fri) offers schedule information and route maps for all local buses.

WORTH THE TRIP: GOING DOWN TO CRIPPLE CREEK

Just an hour from Colorado Springs, yet worlds away, a visit to Cripple Creek is like stepping back into the Wild West of lore. The booze still flows and gambling still thrives, but yesteryear's saloons and brothels have been converted into tasteful casinos. Despite the flashing neon signs, Cripple Creek manages to retain a lot of its old charm, with most casinos tucked inside original century-old buildings.

At the beginning of the 20th century, the city was one of the most important in the state – producing $340 million worth of gold between 1891 and 1916, and a staggering $413 million worth by 1952.

These days, Cripple Creek is a wonderful day trip from Colorado Springs. The road climbs quickly as you head west into the mountains and the last 18 miles, especially in the fall when the trees turn golden, are quite breathtaking.

Cripple Creek is 50 miles southwest of Colorado Springs on Hwy 67. Catch the **Ramblin' Express** (☎ 719-590-8687; www.ramblinexpress.com; tickets $22-25) from Colorado Springs. The bus departs hourly between 7am and 10pm from the 8th St Depot and leaves from JP McGills casino hourly between 8:30am and 2:10am.

Boulder

A model example of a functioning utopian society, the People's Republic of Boulder (as the locals say) is a liberal university town with a yuppie crunch attitude and a mad crush on the outdoors – in 1967 Boulder became the first US city to tax itself specifically to preserve open space. Packs of cyclists whip up and down the main streets, and the endless city parks those taxpayer dollars purchased bustle with happy hikers and their dogs. The pedestrian-only Pearl St Mall, bursting with shops, sidewalk cafés and street performers, is lively, clean and perfect for strolling. At night, head to the Hill, home of the 30,000-student University of Colorado, a legendary American party school.

In many ways it is Boulder, not Denver, that is the region's tourist hub. The city is about the same distance from Denver International Airport, and staying in Boulder puts you 45 minutes closer to the big ski resorts west on I-70 and Rocky Mountain National Park. Plus the locale, up against the strange jagged rock formations called the Flatirons, is picture-perfect.

ORIENTATION

Boulder's two areas to see and be seen are the downtown Pearl St Mall and the University Hill district (next to campus), both off Broadway. Overlooking the city from the west are the Flatirons, an eye-catching rock formation. Boulder is north of Denver. From I-25 exit at Hwy 36 (it's a left-hand exit); follow this road for about 20 miles into town.

INFORMATION

Boulder Bookstore (☎ 303-447-2074; 1107 Pearl St) Boulder's favorite indie bookstore has a huge travel section downstairs, along with all the hottest new fiction and nonfiction.

Boulder Visitor Center (☎ 303-442-2911, 800-444-0447; www.bouldercoloradousa.com; 2440 Pearl St; 🕒 8:30am-5pm Mon-Thu, 8:30am-4pm Fri) Offers information and internet access.

SIGHTS & ACTIVITIES

The main feature of downtown Boulder is the **Pearl Street Mall**, a vibrant pedestrian zone filled with bars, galleries and restaurants. However, Boulder's most famous feature is the striking iron-like mountains along the southwest flank.

Hiking and mountain biking are both huge in Boulder, and luckily there's plenty of space for everyone to practice both (the city has dedicated huge chunks of land to public open space).

From the popular Chautauqua Park, at the west end of Baseline Rd, **hiking** trails head in many directions, including up to the Flatirons. Locals and their canine companions dig the 3.2-mile (round-trip) calf-buster up **Mt Sanitas**. Rocky outcroppings grace the summit and make great focal points for pictures. The views across Boulder and onto the plains to the east are stupendous. To reach the trailhead, take Broadway Ave to Mapleton Ave and head west toward the mountains for about five blocks. You can park just past the hospital in a lot on the north side where the trail begins.

The 16-mile **Boulder Creek Trail** is the main **bicycling** route in town and leads west on an unpaved streamside path to Four Mile Canyon. Challenge-seekers can also ride 4 miles up Flagstaff Rd to the top of Flagstaff Mountain. Bike rentals, maps and information are available from **University Bicycles** (☎ 303-444-4196; 839 Pearl St) and **Full Cycle** (☎ 303-440-7771; 1211 13th St).

Eldorado Canyon State Park (☎ 303-494-3943; visitor center 9am-5pm) is one of the country's most favored rock-climbing areas, offering Class 5.5 to 5.12 climbs. The park entrance is on Eldorado Springs Dr, west of Hwy 93. Information is available from **Boulder Rock Club** (☎ 303-447-2804; www.totalclimbing.com; 2829 Mapleton Ave).

During winter, city buses leave from the corner of 14th and Walnut Sts (round-trip $11) and take you to **Eldora Mountain Resort** (☎ 303-440-8700; www.eldora.com; Hwy 130; lift ticket adult/child $62/37), where you can spend the day skiing and snowboarding on decent terrain.

On hot summer days, cool off like the locals do – riding an inner tube down the Boulder Creek's white water at the west end of town. It just might be the best urban do-it-yourself tubing trip in the country! Rapids range from mild to slightly wild, depending on water levels. There are a few waterfalls sure to flip your tube, plus some good swimming holes to relax in after they do.

Most people start their run north of the parking lot at Eben G Fine Park between Arapahoe and Canyon Aves – head west on Canyon until you see the pull-off. There are usually vendors renting out tubes for about $8 here, but if you want to purchase your own rubber, visit the **Conoco Gas Station** (☎ 303-442-6293; 1201 Arapahoe Ave; tubes $15; 9am-5pm). If the water feels too rough, the creek gets milder further south; try riding from the picnic tables in Eben G Fine down to the library.

If you'd rather paddle, the stretch of creek running parallel to the bike path and Canyon Rd (just north of the park) doubles as one of Colorado's holiest of **white-water kayak parks**. Built by a local, Gary Lacy, who has made quite a name for himself in the quickly growing white-water kayaking industry, the highlight is a steep drop below the last bridge before you hit Eben G Fine – it leads into a sticky hydraulic. The park is perfect for kayakers looking to practice eddy turns and cartwheels.

SLEEPING

Boulder has dozens more hotels than we have space to list – drive down Broadway or Hwy 36 to take your pick. Booking online usually scores the best discounts. Check the hotel websites for special packages, which can include everything from spa treatments to meal coupons or champagne.

Boulder Mountain Lodge (☎ 303-444-0882; www.bouldermountainlodge.com; 91 Four Mile Canyon Rd; campsites $24, r from $94) Set in a shady canyon 4 miles west of Boulder off Hwy 119, this family-owned and -operated lodge in the mountains is gorgeously placed amid pines and cottonwood trees. It offers shady camping, as well as clean, motel-style rooms with kitchenettes. The kids' fishing pond is a plus.

Boulder International Youth Hostel (☎ 303-442-0522; www.boulderhostel.com; 1107 12th St; dm $27, r with shared bath from $55) Located amid the fraternity houses on hip University Hill, this hostel has been meeting the needs of travelers for nearly half a century (it opened in 1961). Dorms and private rooms are clean and warm, and the facilities are infinitely better than those in Denver's hostels. Bring bedding or rent linen for $7 per stay.

Boulder Outlook Hotel & Suites (☎ 303-443-3322; www.boulderoutlook.com; 800 28th St; r from $99) Calling itself the 'cure for the common hotel,' the totally green (zero-waste) Boulder Outlook is colorful and energetic, and includes amenities like an indoor 11ft-high rock-climbing boulder (and a mini one for kids), a heated chlorine-free pool and live music in the bar overlooking it all. Traveling with a dog? No problem. Call ahead to book one of the 'Fido rooms.'

Hotel Boulderado (☎ 303-442-4344, 800-433-4344; www.boulderado.com; 2115 13th St; r from $150) Celebrating a century of service in 2009, the charming Boulderado is a National Register landmark and a wonderfully romantic place to spend the night. Full of Victorian elegance and wonderful public spaces, each antique-filled room is uniquely decorated and boasts luxurious amenities.

EATING

Lucille's Creole Cafe (☎ 303-442-4743; 2142 14th St; mains $4-8; 8am-2pm) Lines form early at Boulder's favorite wake-up joint, but the wait is worth it. This New Orleans diner has perfected breakfast, and the Creole egg dishes (served over a bed of creamy spinach, alongside cheesy grits

DON'T MISS

If you're on a budget in Boulder you are in luck – this is one of the best cities in the country for happy-hour hopping. Between 3:30pm and 6:30pm nearly every restaurant in the city features some kind of amazing food and drink specials. And since Boulder is jam-packed with some of Colorado's top restaurants, this means you can eat like a king even if your wallet says you are a pauper. We're talking a full meal's worth of gourmet appetizers and a couple of top-shelf martinis for less than $20, folks. Best of all, since no one in Boulder appears to work in an office, happy hours here are as crowded as dinner, which means you get to experience the ambience at bargain-basement prices too. Don't miss it.

or next to perfectly blackened trout) are what to order. Start with a steaming mug of chai or chicory coffee and an order of beignets. The powder-sugar-drenched French Cajun doughnuts are the house specialty.

Sink (☎ 303-444-7465; 1165 13th St; mains $5-10; 🕑 11:30am-10:30pm) The Sink is a Hill classic that's been satisfyingly feeding hungry college kids and their professors since it opened in 1923. A pizza and burger dive with the most amazing graffiti art all over its dim-lit cavernous interior, it's almost worth visiting just to read the writing on the walls. We said almost. Once you've sunk your teeth into the legendary Sink burger and swallowed it with a slug of a deliciously hoppy Colorado microbrew, you'll be glad you stuck around. Live music on select nights.

Rio Grande Cafe (☎ 303-444-3690; 1101 Walnut St; dishes $8-15; 🕑 11am-11pm; 🚸) Always packed, this Tex-Mex institution consistently delivers potent margaritas, sumptuous beef fajitas and the most addictive queso dip. Loud and chaotic, with a buzzing bar scene and kid-friendly restaurant, the Rio appeals to first-date couples and families alike. Visit the awesome uncovered rooftop patio in summer.

our pick **Boulder Dushanbe Teahouse** (☎ 303-442-4993; 1770 13th St; mains $8-20; 🕑 8am-10pm) No visit to Boulder is complete without a meal at this incredible Tajik work of art. A gift from Boulder's sister city (Dushanbe, Tajikistan), incredible craftsmanship and meticulous painting envelop the vibrant multicolored interior. The international fare ranges from Amazonian to Mediterranean to, of course, Tajik. Outside, in the quiet gardens, is a lovely, shaded full-service patio. It's an intimate place to grab cocktails or dinner with friends on a warm summer day.

Zolo Southwestern Grill (☎ 303-449-0444; 2525 Arapahoe Ave; mains $8-20; 🕑 11am-late; 🅿) Zolo has been delighting residents with award-winning Southwestern fare and easy parking (it has its own lot) for 15 years now. The menu is a Colorado take on classic Mexican. Perennial favorites include *fundido* (warm goat Oaxaca cheese fondue with red pepper jam, roasted garlic, flour tortillas), chicken enchiladas and the tortilla-crusted ahi tuna. Whatever you do, don't skip the tequila. There are more than 150 choices, which can be served neat or blended into what many argue are Boulder's best margaritas. Look for Zolo about 11 blocks southeast of the Pearl St Mall, tucked into a quiet shopping center.

Boulder Cafe (☎ 303-444-4884; 1247 Pearl St; mains $8-25; 🕑 11:30am-10:30pm) Score a sidewalk table and check out the street performers on the Pearl St Mall while waiting for your oysters and ice-cold beer. The perennially popular Boulder Cafe does a great raw bar, along with a host of eclectic appetizers such as classic Swiss fondue. Mains include pastas, steaks, sandwiches and salads. From 3pm to 6pm, all appetizers (including the raw bar) and drinks are half-price. It's the best deal in town.

Kitchen (☎ 303-544-5973; 1039 Pearl St; mains $10-30; 🕑 8am-2pm & 5:30pm-late Mon-Fri, 9am-2pm & 5:30pm-late Sat & Sun) It's gourmet, green and has a 750-bottle-strong wine list. Do you need to hear more? OK. This relative newbie on the national foodie circuit is also a contender for greenest restaurant in the West. Electricity is generated by wind-power and almost all waste is either reused or recycled. The mouth watering fare is nouveau American meets French bistro with a flavor of Italy, and it evolves with the seasons. There are two dining rooms. The one on the 2nd floor is bright and modern, and attracts a chic crowd. Don't miss the nightly tasting hour, between 5:30pm and 6:30pm, when there are excellent small-plate and drink specials.

BOULDER'S TOP FIVE ROOFTOP BARS

Rooftop watering holes define Boulder's bar scene in the warmer months. The city is home to dozens of these wonderful, breezy establishments, and bar-hopping between them is a cherished summer ritual. Usually part of the restaurant downstairs, some rooftops are covered by awnings, others open to the night sky, but all come with heat lamps for those chilly mountain nights and most come with fantastic views of the Flatirons.

The following are our top five picks, but we're just giving you the basics. You'll have to visit to find out why.

- **West End Tavern** (☎ 303-444-3535; 926 Pearl St)
- **Bacaro Venetian Taverna** (☎ 303-444-4888; 921 Pearl St)
- **Foundry** (☎ 303-447-1803; 1109 Walnut St)
- **K's China** (☎ 303-413-0000; 1325 Broadway)
- **Lazy Dog Sports Bar & Grill** (☎ 303-440-3355; 1346 Pearl St)

DRINKING & ENTERTAINMENT

The blocks around the Pearl St Mall and the Hill are party central, with many restaurants doubling as bars or turning into all-out dance clubs come 10pm – see Eating (p771) for even more choices.

Mountain Sun Pub & Brewery (☎ 303-546-0886; 1535 Pearl St) Boulder's favorite brewery serves a rainbow of brews from chocolaty to fruity, and packs in an eclectic crowd of yuppies, hippies and everyone in between. Walls are lined with tapestries, there are board games to amuse you and the pub grub (especially the burgers) is delicious. There's usually live music of the bluegrass and jam-band variety at night.

Pearl Street Pub (☎ 303-939-9900; 1108 Pearl St) Sorrows are drowned with multiple pints at the scarred wooden bar upstairs, where the vibe is shabby chic meets Old West. Downstairs, 20-something locals pound shots by the pool tables, soaking up the beer-drenched atmosphere at this town's favorite trendy dive. Come for Friday-night happy hour, when there is often live music at the packed upstairs bar.

Catacombs Bar (☎ 303-443-0486; 2115 13th St) A cavernous pool and beer joint underneath the Boulderado Hotel, Catacombs lures a young and rowdy crowd with ultracheap drink specials. The dimly lit rooms are perfect for mingling, and the place has a good singles bar reputation.

'Round Midnight (☎ 303-442-2176; 1005 Pearl St) One of Boulder's hottest dance clubs, it spins underground dub, dance-hall and hip-hop late in a basement space right on the Pearl St Mall. There's free pool during happy hour.

SHOPPING

Boulder has the most varied shopping in the region, in the prettiest environs. Shops are either on the Pearl St Mall or surrounding streets or on the brand-new 29th St Mall, just off 28th St between Canyon and Pearl St about a mile east of the Pearl St Mall. It is a similar al fresco shopping experience, but looks decidedly generic and planned (which it was). There's also a big Cineplex theater here, and a couple of restaurants.

Momentum (☎ 303-440-7744; www.ourmomentum.com; 1625 Pearl St; 🕑 10am-6pm Tue-Sat, 11am-5pm Sun) Owned by Kevin and Jenny Napatow, an enthusiastic young couple committed to socially responsible and environmentally friendly business practices, Momentum is one of those shops that makes you feel good about spending money. It sells the kitchen sink of unique global gifts – from recycled bottlecap earrings to embroidered aprons and intricate sari blankets – all handcrafted and purchased at fair value from disadvantaged artisans all over the world. Every item purchased provides a direct economic lifeline to the artists.

Common Threads (☎ 303-449-5431; www.commonthreadsboulder.com; 2707 Spruce St) Vintage shopping at its most haute couture, this fun place is where to go for secondhand Choo's and Prada purses. Prices are higher than your run-of-the-mill shop, but clothes, shoes and bags are always in good condition, and the designer clothing is guaranteed authentic. The consignment shop itself is a pleasure to browse, with clothing organized by color and type on visually aesthetic racks, just like a big-city boutique.

GETTING THERE & AROUND

Boulder has fabulous public transportation, with services extending as far away as Denver and its airport. Ecofriendly buses are run by **RTD** (☎ 303-299-6000; www.rtd-denver.com) and cost $1.25 per ride. Maps are available at **Boulder Station** (cnr 14th & Walnut Sts). RTD buses (route B) operate between Boulder Station and Denver's Market St Bus Station ($3.50, one hour). RTD's SkyRide bus (route AB) heads to Denver International Airport ($12, 1½ hours, hourly). **SuperShuttle** (☎ 303-444-0808) provides hotel ($22) and door-to-door ($28) shuttle service from the airport.

Rocky Mountain National Park

Rocky Mountain National Park is a must-visit, boasting all the classic Colorado scenery that people croon over – serene blue mountain lakes and jagged snowcapped peaks, wildflowers, alpine tundra and aspen glades. It's so alluring, in fact, that more than three million visitors mosey in annually. Breathe in crisp mountain air, hike through grassy meadows, gasp at snowcapped peaks and keep an eye out for elk, bighorn sheep, moose, marmots and bear. Most visitors stay near Trail Ridge Rd (open from the last Monday in May to mid-October), which winds through spectacular alpine tundra environments. Those who prefer communing with nonhuman nature should venture on foot away from the road corridor; the reward is quiet, superlative scenery.

ORIENTATION & INFORMATION

Trail Ridge Rd (US 34) is the only east–west route through the park; the US 34 eastern approach from I-25 and Loveland follows the Big Thompson River Canyon. From Boulder, the most direct route follows US 36 through Lyons to the east entrances. Another approach from the south, mountainous Hwy 7, provides access to campsites and trailheads (including Longs Peak) on the east side of the Continental Divide. Winter closure of US 34 through the park makes access to the west side dependent on US 40 at Granby.

Two entrance stations are on the east side: at Fall River (US 36) and Beaver Meadows (US 34). The Grand Lake station (US 34) is the sole entry on the west side.

There are five visitor centers associated with Rocky Mountain National Park, although only two are actually inside the park's boundaries. All are well sign-posted. You'll find the headquarters at the **Beaver Meadows Visitor Center** (☎ 970-586-1206; www.nps.gov/romo; US 36; 🕑 8am-6pm Jun-Aug, 8am-5pm rest of year), on US 36 just east of the entrance.

Entry to the park (vehicles $25, hikers and cyclists $15) is valid for seven days. Backcountry permits ($25) are required for overnight trips.

ACTIVITIES

The bustling Bear Lake Trailhead offers easy **hikes** to several lakes and beyond. Another busy area is Glacier Gorge Junction Trailhead. The free Glacier Basin–Bear Lake shuttle services both.

Forested Fern Lake, 4 miles from the Moraine Park Trailhead, is dominated by craggy Notchtop Peak. You can complete a loop to the Bear Lake shuttle stop in about 8.5 miles for a rewarding day hike. The strenuous **Flattop Mountain Trail** is the only cross-park trail, linking Bear Creek on the east side with either Tonahutu Creek Trail or the North Inlet Trail on the west side.

Families might consider the moderate hikes to **Calypso Cascades** in the Wild Basin or to **Gem Lake** in the Lumpy Ridge area.

Trail Ridge Rd crosses the Continental Divide at Milner Pass (10,759ft), where trails head 4 miles (and up 2000ft!) southeast to Mt Ida, which offers fantastic views.

WORTH THE TRIP: NEW BELGIUM BREWING CO

It's worth driving 30 miles north of Boulder on I-25 – especially if you're heading to Wyoming anyway – to pay a visit to the famous **New Belgium Brewing Co** (☎ 800-622-4044; 500 Lined St; 🕑 guided tours 2pm & 4pm Mon-Fri, 11am-4pm Sat) in the college town of Fort Collins (home to another party-hearty college, Colorado State University). Here you can choose your own destiny with a self-guided tour and complimentary tasting of the flagship and specialty brews. Recognized as one of the world's most environmentally conscious breweries, New Belgium was the first totally wind-powered operation thanks to a 100,000-kilowatt turbine. It's best known for the Fat Tire Amber Ale, but other good brews to try are the Loft, Trippell or Sunshine Wheat.

SUMMIT THIS!

Colorado has 52 fourteeners (mountains over 14,000ft), and many residents make it a mission to summit all of them. We don't expect you to be quite so fierce, but climbing to the top of at least one should earn you some major bragging rights back home.

Longs Peak, in Rocky Mountain National Park, stands at 14,255ft and is one of Colorado's most popular climbs. There is only one nontechnical (meaning you don't need ropes and climbing experience) route to the summit, the Keyhole Route, and it usually doesn't open until July. You'll want to begin your hike around 3am so you can get off the summit by 10am, which should allow enough time to reach the bottom before afternoon thunderstorms roll in. The trailhead begins at the Longs Peak ranger station. The first 6 miles aren't difficult, but save some reserves for the final 1½ miles, which is an intense 4850ft scramble through a field of small boulders to the summit.

Do not attempt this hike if you are not used to the altitude, don't have enough water or have little hiking experience – the terrain is harsh, and you can expect sudden snowstorms in any month. That said, when it comes to trying your first fourteener, Longs Peak is a good starter mountain (it's in a national park, which means you can register with the rangers before setting out, and if you get into trouble, help comes a lot faster).

Trails on the west side of the park are quieter and less trodden than those on the east side. Try the short and easy East Inlet Trail to **Adams Falls** (0.3 miles) or the more moderate 3.7-mile Colorado River Trail to the **Lulu City** site.

Before July, many of the trails are snowbound, and high water runoff makes passage difficult. On the east side, the Bear Lake and Glacier Gorge Junction Trailheads offer good routes for **cross-country skiing** and **snowshoeing**. **Backcountry skiing** is also possible; check with the visitor centers.

SLEEPING & EATING

The only overnight accommodations in the park are at campgrounds; the majority of motel or hotel accommodations are around Estes Park (right) or Grand Lake (p776).

The park has five formal campgrounds. All have a seven-day limit during summer and all but Longs Peak take RVs (no hookups). Fees are $20 per site per night.

Aspenglen (54 sites) Five miles west of Estes Park on US 34.
Glacier Basin (150 sites) Seven miles west of Beaver Meadows Visitor Center.
Longs Peak (26 sites) Twelve miles south of Estes Park on Hwy 7; provides Longs Peak hikers with an early trail start.
Moraine Park (247 sites) Two-and-a-half miles from Beaver Meadows Visitor Center.
Timber Creek (100 sites) Seven miles north of Grand Lake.

When it comes time for eating, you'll need to head to Estes Park (p776) or Grand Lake (p776).

GETTING AROUND

A free shuttle bus provides frequent summer service from the Glacier Basin parking area to Bear Lake. Another shuttle operates between Moraine Park campground and the Glacier Basin parking area. Shuttles run daily from mid-June to early September, and thereafter at weekends only until mid-October.

Estes Park

The primary gateway to Rocky Mountain National Park, Estes Park has enough cheesy T-shirt shops and ice-cream parlors to prove it. In the summer season the population skyrockets, and the place is filled with camera-toting tourists and meandering elk (yes, they do just wander down the street sometimes).

Try the **Estes Park Visitor Center** (☎ 970-577-9900, 800-443-7837; www.estesparkresortcvb.com; 500 Big Thompson Ave; 🕑 9am-8pm Jun-Aug, 8am-5pm Mon-Fri, 9am-5pm Sat, 10am-4pm Sun Sep-May), just east of the US 36 junction, for help with lodging; note that many places close in winter.

SLEEPING

Estes Park has dozens of hotels; we have space for only a special few. Most of the budget and midrange motels are east of town along US 34 or Hwy 7.

YMCA of the Rockies Estes Park Center (☎ 970-586-3341; www.ymcarockies.org; 2515 Tunnel Rd; r & cabins $99-229;) On a peaceful 860-acre plot just outside town, this is a great family choice. Accommodations are in lodge rooms sleeping up to six, or rustic multibedroom cabins (online reservations are essential for both). It also runs quality, wholesome weekend or weeklong outdoor camps for families who want to teach conservation in a fun way. Check the website for specific info.

our pick **Mary's Lake Lodge** (☎ 970-577-9495; www.maryslakelodge.com; 2625 Marys Lake Rd; r & cabins from $140) This atmospheric old wooden lodge, perched on a ridge looking over its namesake lake, is an utterly romantic place to slumber. Built from polished pine logs, it reeks of Wild West ambience and has an amazing covered front porch with panoramic Rocky Mountain views. The rooms and cabins are a blend of modern and historic, and many of the latter have private hot tubs. Both the saloon-style Tavern (mains $7 to $20; open 11am to 11pm) and fine-dining Chalet Room (mains $12 to $20; open 5pm to 10pm) serve delicious fresh lake fish (and flown-in seafood), and have seating on the heated porch. A big hot tub under the stars, fire pit and live music five nights per week round out amenities, while an on-site spa takes care of gritty hiking feet and sore muscles. Mary's is 3 miles south of Estes Park off Hwy 7.

Stanley Hotel (☎ 970-586-4964; www.stanleyhotel.com; 333 Wonderview Ave; r from $159;) Stephen King was inspired to write *The Shining* after staying at this glittering-white, supposedly haunted monolith on a hill overlooking Estes. The grand dame of northern Colorado historic resort hotels, its rooms are posh modern with 42in flat-screen TVs, neutral colors and plush duvets. It also boasts mountain views, splendid dining and after-dark building ghost tours ($13). Book room 401 to increase your chances of spotting a ghost – staff consider it the 'most haunted.'

EATING

Estes Park Brewery (☎ 970-586-6409; 2470 Colorado 66; mains $7-16; 11am-late) The town's brewpub serves pizza, burgers and wings, and at least eight different house beers, in a big, boxy room, resembling a cross between a classroom and a country kitchen. Pool tables and outdoor seating keep the place rocking late into the night.

Ed's Cantina & Grill (☎ 970-586-2919; 390 E Elkhorn Ave; mains $10-25; 11am-late daily, from 8am Sat & Sun) With an outdoor patio right on the river, Ed's is a great place to kick back with a margarita and one of the daily $3 blue plate specials (think flautas with shredded pork and guacamole). Serving Mexican and American staples, the restaurant is in a retro mod space with leather booth seating and a bold primary-color scheme. The bar is in a separate room with light-wood stools featuring comfortable high backs.

GETTING THERE & AWAY

From Denver International Airport, **Estes Park Shuttle** (☎ 970-586-5151; www.estesparkshuttle.com) runs four times daily to Estes Park ($45, 1¾ hours).

Grand Lake

The other gateway to Rocky Mountain National Park, Grand Lake, 102 miles northwest of Denver and 33 miles from Boulder, is less chaotic than Estes Park, although it still rakes in summer tourists by the thousands. The downtown is pleasant, the namesake lake handsome. The **Grand Lake Visitor Center** (☎ 970-627-3402, 800-531-1019; www.grandlakechamber.com; 9am-5pm) is at the junction of US 34 and W Portal Rd.

The **Arapaho National Forest**, to the west of town, has some good mountain-biking trails; get a map from the **Grand Lake Metro Recreation District** (☎ 970-627-8328; 928 Grand Ave, Suite 204; 8am-5pm Mon-Fri). **Rocky Mountain Sports** (☎ 970-627-8124; 900 Grand Av) rents and sells outdoor equipment. Several Rocky Mountain National Park **hiking** trailheads are just outside the town limits, including those to the Tonahutu Creek Trail and the Cascade Falls/North Inlet Trail, both near Shadowcliff Lodge.

Overlooking Grand Lake, the nonprofit **HI Shadowcliff Lodge** (☎ 970-627-9220; www.shadowcliff.org; 405 Summerland Park Rd; dm/d/cabin $23/60/125; 25 May–30 Sep) is an ecofriendly mountain resort in a beautiful setting. Rooms and dorms are simple, but clean. Reservations are essential. A two-night minimum stay is required for rooms.

EG's Garden Grill (☎ 970-627-8404; 1000 Grand Ave; dishes $10-20; 11:30am-10pm) serves good grub from salads to seafood; its fish tacos make a very satisfying lunch.

Grand Lake is 102 miles northwest of Denver via I-70 west to I-40 west. Be careful crossing Berthoud Pass. The town is 35 miles north of Winter Park (opposite), a popular ski destination. If you don't have your own wheels, **Home James Transportation Services** (☎ 970-726-5060; www.homejamestransportation.com) runs door-to-door shuttles to Denver International Airport ($85, 2½ hours). Reservations are required.

Winter Park

Located less than two hours from Denver, unpretentious Winter Park is a favorite ski resort with Front Rangers, who flock here from as far as Colorado Springs to ski fresh tracks each weekend. Beginners can frolic on miles of powdery groomers while experts test their skills on Mary Jane's world-class bumps. The congenial town is a wonderful base for year-round romping. Most services are along US 40 (the main drag), including the **visitor center** (☎ 970-726-4118, 800-903-7275; www.winterpark-info.com; 78841 Hwy 40; 8am-5pm Mon-Fri, 9am-5pm Sat & Sun).

South of town, **Winter Park Resort** (☎ 970-726-5514; www.skiwinterpark.com; lift ticket adult/child $92/48) covers four mountains and has a vertical drop of more than 2600ft. It also has 45 miles of lift-accessible **mountain-biking** trails connecting to a 600-mile trail system running through the valley. Other fine rides in the area include the road up to **Rollins Pass**.

The **Vintage Resort & Conference Center** (☎ 970-726-8801; www.vintagehotel.com; 100 Winter Park Dr; r from $120;) is right at the base of the mountain. Standard rooms are smallish, but have high ceilings, big windows and comfortable decor. The on-site restaurant and bar serves decent food. Service is efficient and very friendly.

Locals park their dogs out front of the funky **Base Camp Bakery** (☎ 970-726-5530; 78437 Hwy 40; mains $5-12), then head inside the packed little joint for delicious breakfast sandwiches, rich, creamy lattes, and healthy bison burgers or veggie sandwiches on home-baked bread. Paintings by resident artists grace the cozy stonewashed walls, and seating is at tables with benches.

Steamboat Springs

Steamboat has always been, and remains, a ranchers' town at heart. Its historic area features restaurants serving tasty, down-home American cooking, and plenty of old mountain bars where the twang of live rockabilly rattles old wood dancefloors well into the night. It doesn't have the looks of Aspen or the soul of Telluride, but what Steamboat lacks in Wild West charm, it more than compensates for in snow – and lots of it.

Steamboat Springs' two major areas are Old Town and, 5 miles south, the curving streets at Steamboat Village, centered on the ski resort. Through town, US 40 is called Lincoln Ave.

Visit the **Steamboat Springs Visitor Center** (☎ 970-879-0880, 877-754-2269; www.steamboat-chamber.com; 1255 S Lincoln Ave; 8am-5pm Mon-Fri, 10am-3pm Sat) to get oriented.

Steamboat is known for skiing and hot springs. To check out the town's consistently rocking powder, head to the **Steamboat Ski Area** (☎ 970-879-6111; www.steamboat.com; lift ticket adult/child $91/56). With a 3600ft vertical drop, it offers trails for all levels.

For something a bit warmer, try the **Old Town Hot Springs** (☎ 970-879-1828; www.steamboathotsprings.org; cnr 3rd St & Lincoln Ave; adult/child from $10/6.50; 5:30am-9.45pm Mon-Fri, 7am-8.45pm Sat, 8am-8.45pm Sun) smack in the center of town. Known by the Ute Indians as the 'medicine springs,' the mineral waters here are said to have special healing powers. The springs recently underwent a $5-million renovation that built a new pool, a pair of 230ft-long waterslides and, perhaps coolest of all, an aquatic climbing wall!

Steamboat's favorite hot springs are actually outside city limits. The **Strawberry Park Hot Springs** (☎ 970-879-0342; www.strawberryhotsprings.com; 44200 County Rd; campsites/cabins/covered wagons/cabooses $50/55/65/110;) offer great back-to-basics relaxation. Choose from covered wagons with a double mattress on the floor (quite unique) or rustic cabins. There's no electricity – but you do get gas lanterns – and you'll need your own linens. Be sure to reserve. Weekend reservations require a two-night stay.

The emphasis at Strawberry Park is really on the hot pools (admission included if you stay overnight, even for campers). There is a cool creek, waterfalls and massage therapists to tend to your whims. The sandy-bottomed, rock-lined soaking pools are fantastic on moonlit evenings; clothing is optional after dark. If you just want to soak, the springs are open daily from 10am to 10:30pm; admission is $10 for adults, $5 for children. Vehicles without 4WD are required to use chains from November to April for the 3-mile steep road up to the resort. Credit cards are not accepted for the pools; bring cash.

There are plenty of places to sleep in Steamboat itself. The elegant **Hotel Bristol** (☎ 970-879-3083; www.steamboathotelbristol.com; 917 Lincoln Ave; r from $89-199;) has small but sophisticated Western digs, with dark-wood and brass furnishings and Pendleton wool blankets on the beds. There's a ski shuttle, a six-person indoor Jacuzzi and a cozy restaurant.

Locals flock to the **Old Town Pub & Restaurant** (☎ 970-879-2101; cnr 6th St & Lincoln Ave; mains $9-16; 🕑 11am-late) for dinner and dancing. The Wild West pub – check out the bullet holes in the phone booth in the bar area – serves tasty gourmet pub fare including lots of pasta selections. It hosts live bands most weekends. Arrive after 9pm and the old wood floors will be rocking. Order a margarita; they're delish!

Harwigs/L'Apogee at 911 Lincoln Ave (☎ 970-879-1919; 911 Lincoln Ave; mains from $25; 🕑 5-10pm) is the town's best fine-dining option, serving Asian-influenced French fare in elegant, candlelit environs.

Greyhound's US 40 service between Denver and Salt Lake City stops at the **Stockbridge Center** (☎ 970-870-0504; 1505 Lincoln Ave), about half a mile west of town. **Steamboat Springs Transit** (☎ 970-879-3717) runs free buses between Old Town and the ski resort year-round. Steamboat is 166 miles northwest of Denver via US 40.

CENTRAL MOUNTAIN REGION

Colorado's central and northern mountains are well known for their plethora of ski resorts – including world-famous Aspen and Vail, family-friendly Breckenridge and never-summer A-Basin.

Breckenridge & Around

With its 19th-century mining vibe, it is hard to resist fun-loving 'Breck' – a town as appealing to family vacationers as it is to college grads partaking in that great Colorado coming-of-age ritual affectionately called 'ski-bumming.' Breck has a reputation for partying, but boozing aside, it also makes a great base for regional explorations. Four of Colorado's best ski resorts are less than an hour's drive away.

The **visitor center** (☎ 970-453-6018, 888-251-2417; www.gobreck.com; 309 N Main St; 🕑 9am-5pm) has information on accommodations.

ACTIVITIES

In winter, it's all about the snow. **Breckenridge Ski Area** (☎ 800-789-7669; www.breckenridge.snow.com; lift ticket adult/child $92/49) spans four mountains and features some of the best beginner and intermediate terrain in the state (the green runs are flatter than most in Colorado), as well as killer steeps and chutes for experts, and a renowned snowboard park.

North America's highest resort, **Arapahoe Basin Ski Area** (☎ 970-468-0718; www.arapahoebasin.com; lift ticket adult/child $65/39), about 12 miles from Breck, is smaller, less commercial and usually open until at least mid-June! Full of steeps, walls and backcountry terrain, it's a local favorite because it doesn't draw herds of package tourists. The outdoor bar is a great place to kick back with a cold microbrew, and people are always grilling burgers and socializing at impromptu tailgate parties in the parking lot (known as 'the beach').

Just because the snow melts, it doesn't mean the mountain closes. In summer the **Peak 8 Fun Park** (half-/full-day pass $50/65; 🕑 9am-5pm) opens with a laundry list of made-for-thrills activities, including a big-air trampoline, climbing wall, mountain-bike park and the resort's most celebrated warm weather attraction, the **SuperSlide** (per ride adult/child $12/10). Here you slide down a luge-like course on a sled at exhilaration-inducing speeds. Experienced riders should try the giant slalom track. It has multiple dips built into it, allowing your sled to catch some serious big air and your stomach to seriously drop. The adrenaline rush is well worth the $12 ticket.

If you'd rather be pedaling, take the chairlift (per ride/day $15/30) to the 11,059ft summit and cruise (or fly, depending on the run) down one of the designated cycle trails. To practice tricks and catch air, stop at the mountain-bike park on the way down. **Breckenridge Sports** (☎ 970-496-7546; bike rental $31-51), at the bottom of Peak 8, hooks you up with full-suspension bike rentals. It also has the scoop on 200 miles of off-road trails in the area.

SLEEPING

Rates skyrocket the week between Christmas and New Year. Expect to pay about 25% more than what's quoted here. That's if you can get a room. Most places book out months in advance.

Fireside Inn B&B & Hostel (☎ 970-453-6456; www.firesideinn.com; 114 N French St; dm $28-38, r incl breakfast $88-160; 💻) One of the best-value places in town, this is a clean, welcoming hostel and B&B with friendly staff and a hot tub for après-ski (or slide) soaks.

Arapahoe Inn (☎ 970-513-9009; www.arapahoeinn.com; 22859 Hwy 6; r $90-150; ⊠ 📶) This hotel across from Keystone Ski Resort, 10 miles north of Breck via Hwy 9, is a dependable, pet-friendly

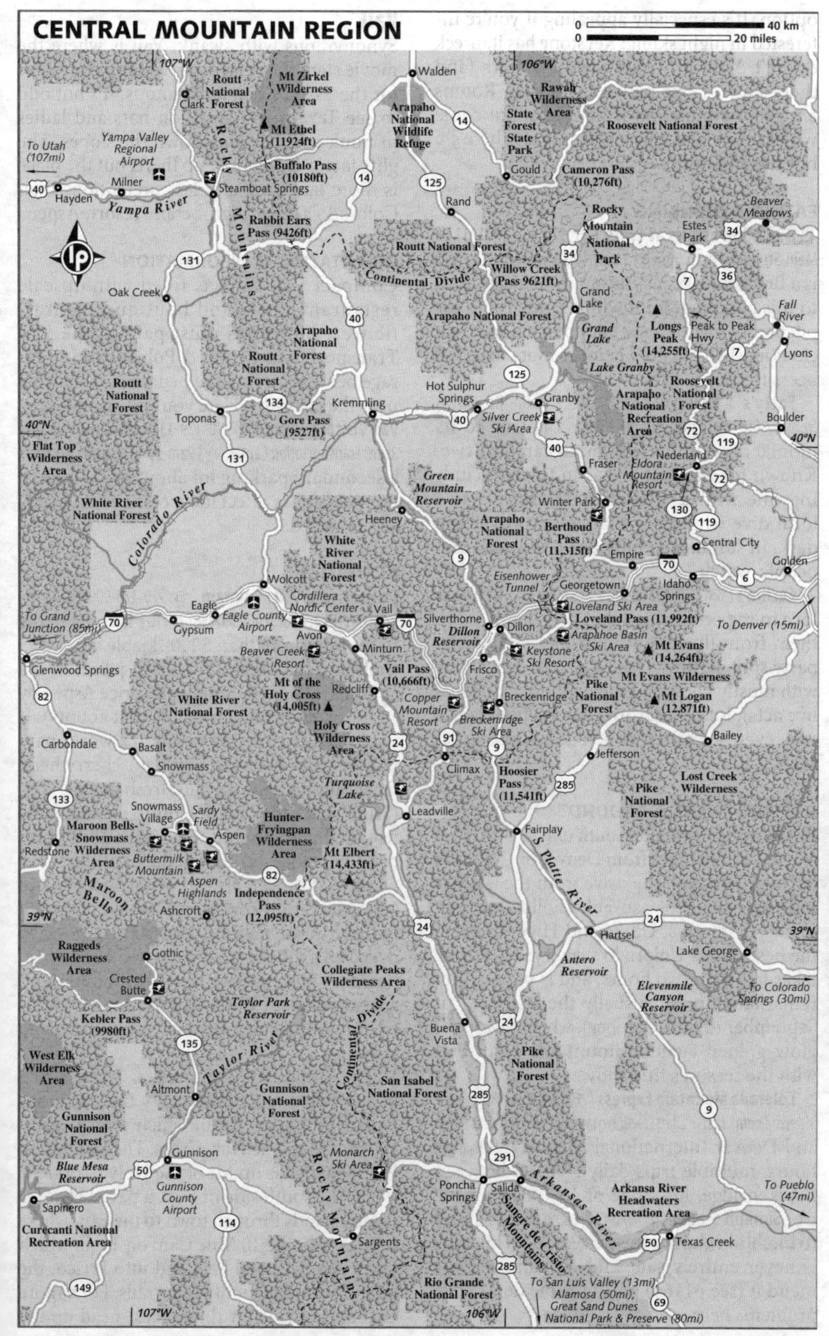
CENTRAL MOUNTAIN REGION
0 40 km
0 20 miles
107°W
106°W
40°N
39°N
Routt National Forest
Clark
Mt Zirkel Wilderness Area
Mt Ethel (11924ft)
Walden
Arapaho National Wildlife Refuge
Rawah Wilderness Area
State Forest State Park
Roosevelt National Forest
Gould
Cameron Pass (10,276ft)
To Utah (107mi)
Yampa Valley Regional Airport
Buffalo Pass (10180ft)
Milner
Hayden
Steamboat Springs
Yampa River
Rocky Mountains
Rabbit Ears Pass (9426ft)
Rand
Rocky Mountain National Park
Estes Park
Beaver Meadows
Routt National Forest
Continental Divide
Willow Creek (Pass 9621ft)
Oak Creek
Grand Lake
Grand Lake
Longs Peak (14,255ft)
Peak to Peak Hwy
Fall River
Lyons
Arapaho National Forest
Arapaho National Forest
Routt National Forest
Lake Granby
Roosevelt National Forest
Routt National Forest
Hot Sulphur Springs
Granby
Arapaho National Recreation Area
Kremmling
Silver Creek Ski Area
Boulder
Toponas
Gore Pass (9527ft)
Flat Top Wilderness Area
Fraser
Nederland
Eldora Mountain Resort
Green Mountain Reservoir
White River National Forest
Colorado River
Winter Park
Heeney
Arapaho National Forest
Berthoud Pass (11,315ft)
White River National Forest
Central City
Empire
Golden
Wolcott
Eisenhower Tunnel
Georgetown
Idaho Springs
Eagle
Cordillera Nordic Center
Vail
Loveland Ski Area
Loveland Pass (11,992ft)
To Grand Junction (85mi)
Gypsum
Eagle County Airport
Avon
Silverthorne
Dillon Reservoir
Dillon
To Denver (15mi)
Arapahoe Basin Ski Area
Glenwood Springs
Beaver Creek Resort
Minturn
Keystone Ski Resort
Mt Evans (14,264ft)
Vail Pass (10,666ft)
Frisco
Mt Evans Wilderness
Mt of the Holy Cross (14,005ft)
Redcliff
Pike National Forest
White River National Forest
Copper Mountain Resort
Breckenridge
Mt Logan (12,871ft)
Breckenridge Ski Area
Holy Cross Wilderness Area
Carbondale
Basalt
Bailey
Snowmass
Climax
Jefferson
Hoosier Pass (11,541ft)
Turquoise Lake
Lost Creek Wilderness
Pike National Forest
Snowmass Village
Sardy Field
Hunter-Fryingpan Wilderness Area
Leadville
Maroon Bells-Snowmass Wilderness Area
Aspen
Fairplay
Redstone
Buttermilk Mountain
Mt Elbert (14,433ft)
S Platte River
Aspen Highlands
Independence Pass (12,095ft)
Maroon Bells
Ashcroft
Hartsel
Lake George
Ragged Wilderness Area
Gothic
Antero Reservoir
Crested Butte
Collegiate Peaks Wilderness Area
Elevenmile Canyon Reservoir
To Colorado Springs (30mi)
Taylor Park Reservoir
Kebler Pass (9980ft)
Buena Vista
West Elk Wilderness Area
Taylor River
Pike National Forest
Continental Divide
San Isabel National Forest
Altmont
Gunnison National Forest
Gunnison National Forest
Gunnison
Monarch Ski Area
Blue Mesa Reservoir
Gunnison County Airport
Poncha Springs
Salida
Arkansas River
Arkansa River Headwaters Recreation Area
To Pueblo (47mi)
Sapinero
Curecanti National Recreation Area
Sangre de Cristo Mountains
Sargents
Rocky Mountains
Texas Creek
Rio Grande National Forest
To San Luis Valley (13mi); Alamosa (50mi); Great Sand Dunes National Park & Preserve (80mi)
ROCKY MOUNTAINS

option. It's especially appealing if you're interested in night skiing: Keystone has it, Breck doesn't. Your lift ticket is good at both (and there's a free bus between resorts). Rooms are generic motel no-frills affairs, but come with fridges and microwaves. Plus there's a hot tub and sauna.

EATING & DRINKING

our pick **Downstairs at Eric's** (☎ 970-453-1401; 111 S Main St; mains from $6; ⏰ 11am-10:30pm; 👶) Eric's is a Breckenridge institution. And locals flock to this basement joint with a game room for pitchers of microbrews, juicy burgers and delicious mashed potato. There are more than 120 beers to choose from.

Fatty's (☎ 970-453-9802; 106 S Ridge Rd; pizzas from $7.50; ⏰ 11am-10pm) Fatty's is true to its moniker: even the 10in pizza can feed two. Known for the best pizzas in town, including one with a Sicilian-style crust, it is a local dive with a bar that gets rowdy come dark. In summer sit outside on the patio and people-watch.

Cecilia's (☎ 970-453-2243; 520 S Main St) Ski bums love to rag on Cecilia's, but that doesn't stop them from flocking to this long-established party spot nightly. There's a large dancefloor with mostly DJ-spun grooves (and occasional live acts), lots of martini choices, pool tables and even a corner couch for some quiet kissing.

GETTING THERE & AROUND

Breckenridge is 9 miles south of I-70 on Hwy 9 and about 100 miles from Denver or Colorado Springs, although the drive from the latter is infinitely more pleasurable. Following secondary highways, US 24 and Hwy 9, covers the best classic Colorado scenery. This drive takes less than two hours, and is particularly remarkable in fall (usually the last week of September to mid-October), when the aspens glow golden against mountains garnished with the season's first snow.

Colorado Mountain Express (☎ 970-926-9800; www.ridecme.com) runs shuttles between Breckenridge and Denver International Airport ($90, two hours, multiple trips daily). To get between Breckenridge, Keystone or Vail, hop on the free **Summit Stages** (☎ 970-668-0999) bus. It's easy to hitchhike during the ski season. While this is never entirely safe, and we can't recommend it (see p1165), most people don't have problems here.

Vail

Synonymous with swank, Vail is where the movie stars ski. A favorite winter playground for the world's rich and famous, it's not odd to see Texans in ten-gallon hats and ladies in mink coats zipping down the slopes. The glitz factor is certainly up there, but the place is more laid-back and less pretentious than Colorado's other high-octane resort, Aspen.

ORIENTATION & INFORMATION

Compact Vail Village, filled with upscale restaurants, bars and boutiques, is traffic free. Motorists must park at the Vail Transportation Center & Public Parking garage before entering the pedestrian mall area near the chairlifts. Here you will also find the **Vail Visitor Center** (☎ 970-479-1385; www.visitvailvalley.com; Transportation Center; ⏰ 9am-5pm). Lionshead is a secondary parking lot about half a mile to the west. It has direct lift access and is usually less crowded.

ACTIVITIES

For terrain, **Vail Mountain** (☎ 970-476-9090; vail.snow.com; lift ticket adult/child $97/58) is our favorite in the state, with more than 5200 skiable acres, 193 trails and the highest lift-ticket prices in the country (OK, so they only out-price Aspen by $1, but still, it's the principle that counts). If you're a Colorado ski virgin, it's worth paying the extra bucks to pop your cherry here. Especially on a sunny, blue, fresh powder day. (Hint: check the parking lots to see if anyone needs a buddy to split their 2-for-1 lift ticket coupon before paying top dollar at the ticket window. You can also try King Soopers and City Market grocery stores, which often sell reduced-price tickets). Experts will go gaga over Vail's shoots, tree glades and wide-open, powdery fresh back bowls. The mountaintop **Adventure Ridge** (☎ 970-476-9090; 👶) has child-friendly winter and summer sports including laser tag.

The Holy Cross Wilderness Area is rich with **hiking** opportunities. Try the strenuous Notch Mountain Trail, which affords great views of Mt of the Holy Cross. The Half Moon Pass Trail leads up Mt of the Holy Cross.

On the south side of I-70, a paved **bicycling** route extends through town to the east, where it links with the 10 Mile Canyon Trail, which takes you over Vail Pass and into Frisco, the hub of Summit County bike trails. For a more challenging ride on singletrack, head up the

Two Elk trail and down towards the town of Minturn. Look for the trailhead east of town near the Gore Creek Campground (see Sleeping, below).

SLEEPING

Budget is not a word in Vail's vocabulary, but visit during the off-season and you can expect rates to drop exponentially. Avoid the week between Christmas and New Year, when rooms book out months in advance and prices rise by at least 25%.

Gore Creek Campground (☎ 970-945-2521; Bighorn Rd; campsites $12; 🕑 Memorial Day–Labor Day) This primitive campground at the end of Bighorn Rd has 25 first-come, first-served tent sites with picnic tables and fire grates nestled in the woods by Gore Creek. There is excellent fishing near here. Try the Slate Creek or Deluge Lake trails; the latter leads to a fish-packed lake. The campground is 6 miles east of Vail Village via the East Vail exit off I-70.

Tivoli Lodge (☎ 970-476-5615; www.tivolilodge.com; 386 Hanson Rd; r $140-600;) Resembling a Swiss or Austrian castle, it's a palatial place that caters to the Euro crowd. Rooms are understated, but incredibly posh with luxurious rich-colored duvets and white walls trimmed in deep-brown wood. Visit in the off-season, when even the walk-in rate is a steal.

Vail Cascade Resort & Spa (☎ 970-476-7111; www.vailcascade.com; 1300 Westhaven Dr; r from $260;) An award-winning swanky property, this is the place to go for luxurious pampering. Rooms feature lots of cherrywood furnishings and marble vanities. Two movie theaters show first-run films, and a restaurant, athletics club and full spa complete the package. Rates drop dramatically in summer.

EATING & DRINKING

Joe's Famous Deli (☎ 970-479-7580; 288 Bridge St; dishes $5-8; 🕑 8am-9:30pm) A casual, counter-service joint, Joe's does a great sandwich – if you don't like one of the 20 grilled and cold varieties, create your own. Kids will delight in the ice-cream possibilities.

Sweet Basil (☎ 970-476-0125; 193 E Gore Creek Dr; lunch mains $15, dinner mains $30; 🕑 11:30am-2:30pm & 5:30pm-close) Sweet Basil is still churning out what many critics argue is the best food in the state. The menu changes seasonally, but the eclectic American fare, which usually includes favorites such as Colorado leg of lamb with white bean ratatouille, is consistently good. The ambience is also fantastic.

Tap Room & Sanctuary (☎ 970-479-0500; 333 Bridge St) A favorite stop with hipsters on the bar-hopping circuit, the Tap Room has a giant selection of beers, fabulous margaritas and a cigar lounge. Upstairs, the Sanctuary is a hot club that's popular with a fashionable, younger crowd.

GETTING THERE & AROUND

From December to early April only, the **Eagle County Airport** (EGE; ☎ 970-524-9490), 35 miles west of Vail, has direct jet services to destinations across the country.

Colorado Mountain Express (☎ 970-926-9800; www.cmex.com) shuttles to/from Denver International Airport ($100, three hours). Greyhound buses stop at the **Vail Transportation Center** (☎ 970-476-5137; 241 S Frontage Rd) en route to Denver ($30, 2¼ hours) or Grand Junction ($25, 3¼ hours).

Vail's free **buses** (☎ 970-477-3456; http://vailgov.com/transit) stop in West Vail, East Vail and Sandstone; most have bike racks.

Aspen

Immodestly posh Aspen is Colorado's glitziest high-octane resort, playing host to some of the wealthiest skiers in the world. The handsome, historic red-brick downtown is as alluring as the glistening slopes, but Aspen's greatest asset is its magnificent scenery. The stunning alpine environment – especially during late September and October, when the aspen trees put on a spectacular display – just adds extra sugar to an already sweet cake.

Aspen Visitor Center (☎ 970-925-1940, 800-670-0792; www.aspenchamber.org; 425 Rio Grande Pl; 🕑 8am-5pm Mon-Fri) has all the usual information.

ACTIVITIES

OK, the top winter activity is pretty much a given: snow riding, and lots of it. The **Aspen Skiing Company** (☎ 970-925-1220; www.aspensnowmass.com; lift ticket adult/child $96/57) operates the area's four ski resorts. **Aspen** (or Ajax) is an athlete's mountain, offering more than 3000ft of steep vertical drop. **Aspen Highlands** has outstanding extreme skiing and breathtaking views. **Buttermilk Mountain** provides gentle slopes for beginners and intermediate skiers. **Snowmass** offers mixed terrain and boasts the longest vertical drop in the USA (4400ft).

The best cross-country skiing in the area is at **Ashcroft** (☎ 970-925-1971), in the beautiful Castle Creek Valley, with 20 miles of groomed trails passing through a ghost town.

When the snow melts, hit the **hiking trail**. The fall is especially stunning for walking, when the yellow leaves of the aspen trees provide a fantastic contrast to the purple hue of the Maroon Bells mountain range. The Hunter Valley Trail leads through wildflower meadows and into the Hunter-Fryingpan Wilderness Area. Hot springs are the reward after 8.5 miles of moderate climbing on the Conundrum Creek Trail. The stunningly beautiful Maroon Bells–Snowmass Wilderness Area is another awesome area to hike.

Mountain biking is also popular, with loads of routes plying Aspen and Smuggler Mountains. The Montezuma Basin and Pearl Pass rides offer extreme bicycling experiences, well above the timberline, south of town from Castle Creek Rd. The **Hub** (☎ 970-925-7970; 315 E Hyman Ave) rents out bikes.

SLEEPING

Book through an online consolidator for the best deals. Avoid the week between Christmas and New Year when prices skyrocket. The **USFS White River National Forest's Aspen Ranger District** (☎ 970-925-3445; 806 W Hallam; 8am-4:30pm Mon-Fri winter, plus 8am-4:30pm Sat summer) operates nine **campgrounds** (campsites $12).

St Moritz Lodge (☎ 970-925-3220; www.stmoritzlodge.com; 334 W Hyman Ave; dm $36-43, r incl breakfast $80-182;) Yes, it's a lot of cash to pay for a dorm room, but then again it's Aspen, and everything is inflated here. That understood, St Moritz is the best no-frills deal in town. The European-style lodge offers a wide variety of options, from quiet dorms to two-bedroom condos. A continental breakfast is included, and the pool and steam-room are open to all guests. The cheapest rooms share baths.

our pick **Annabelle Inn** (☎ 970-925-3822; www.annabelleinn.com; 232 W Main St; r incl breakfast from $210;) Personable and unpretentious, the newly renovated Annabelle Inn resembles an old-school European-style ski lodge in a central location. Rooms are cozy without being too cute and come with flat-screen TVs and warm duvets. We dug the after-dark ski video screenings from the upper-deck hot tub (one of two on the property).

Little Nell (☎ 970-920-4200; www.thelittlenell.com; 675 E Durant Ave; r from $285;) Beautiful and relaxing, Little Nell exudes elegant European ambience. Gas-burning fireplaces, high-thread-count linens and rich color schemes make up the bedroom decor. The Greenhouse Bar is perfect for some après-ski unwinding.

EATING & DRINKING

Main St Bakery (☎ 970-925-6446; 201 E Main St; mains $6-10; 7am-3pm) It's a hit, especially at breakfast time, for its gamut of sweet and savory goods – from granola and pancakes to chicken pot pie – in its convivial room and outdoor patio.

J-Bar (☎ 877-412-7725; 330 E Main St; mains $8-15; 11:30am-1am) Aspen's premier saloon since 1889, the J-Bar, inside the Jerome Hotel, is full of historic charm and packed with everyone from local shopkeepers to Hollywood stars. Order the signature cocktail, the Aspen Crud, if you're in the mood for something sweet. It's a delicious blend of bourbon and ice cream! The tarter J-Rita is equally delicious. The menu features gourmet American pub fare that's nearly as tasty as the drinks.

Woody Creek Tavern (☎ 970-923-4285; 2 Woody Creek Plaza; mains $11-20; 5-11pm) Enjoying a 100% agave tequila and fresh-lime margarita at the late, great gonzo journalist Hunter S Thompson's favorite watering hole is well worth the 8-mile trek from Aspen. The walls at this rustic funky tavern, a local haunt for decades now, are plastered with newspaper clippings and paraphernalia (mostly dedicated to Thompson). The menu features organic salads, low-fat but still juicy burgers and plenty of alcohol.

our pick **Jimmy's** (☎ 970-925-6020; 205 S Mill St; mains $15-50; 11:30am-10pm) Jimmy's is a tequila-, crab- and steakhouse with attitude that attracts a very A-list crowd. Settle into a booth and check out the writing on the wall in the main dining room. No, we're not being cryptic: Jimmy's idea of decorating is covering the walls with guest graffiti. Bring a pen. You're paying a king's ransom to dine with the rich and famous, so you may as well leave your mark! A cheaper menu and 105 types of tequila and mescal are served in the perpetually packed bar. Thursday nights are devoted to the crab – with king crab legs going for just $12.50.

Double Diamond (☎ 970-920-6905; 450 S Galena St; admission from $5) When live-music acts – from rock and blues to salsa and reggae – come to town, they rock this spacious club. It's seen George Clinton, G-Love and many others. Shows get started around 10pm.

GETTING THERE & AROUND

Four miles north of Aspen on Hwy 82, **Sardy Field** (ASE; ☎ 970-920-5380) has commuter flights from Denver, and nonstops to Phoenix, Los Angeles, San Francisco, Minneapolis and Memphis. **Colorado Mountain Express** (☎ 970-947-0506; www.cmex.com) runs frequent shuttles to/from Denver International Airport ($100, three hours).

Roaring Fork Transit Agency (☎ 970-920-1905; www.rfta.com) buses connect Aspen with the ski areas.

Buena Vista & Salida

Buena Vista and Salida won't stick in your mind after you leave, but shooting the Arkansas River's rapids or soaking in hot springs under the stars sure will.

For rafting, stop by **Wilderness Aware Rafting** (☎ 719-395-2112; www.inaraft.com; trips $50-115). You'll want to run Brown's Canyon (Class III to IV), the Narrows (III to IV) or the Numbers (IV to V), and the earlier in the season the better (try for late April or early May, when the river is bloated with snow runoff and the rapids are much more intense). The company is located at the junction of Hwys 285 and 24 at Johnson Village, 2 miles south of Buena Vista.

After a day on the river, forget the soreness with a soak at **Cottonwood Hot Springs Inn & Spa** (☎ 719-395-6434; www.cottonwood-hot-springs.com; 18999 County Rd 306; admission $1). The five pools are rustic with fantastic views (the stars can be amazing). The hot springs are about 6 miles south of Buena Vista. You can spend the night in one of the simple dorms ($35), rooms (from $97) or cabins (from $165) – the latter come with a private soaking pool. Even campsite rates ($35) include use of the public pools. The cabins are pet-friendly for an extra $10 to $15 per night, depending on dog size.

You'll need a car to get to this area south of Leadville on US 24.

Crested Butte

Remote and beautiful, Crested Butte feels real. Despite being one of Colorado's best ski resorts (some say *the* best), it doesn't put on airs. There's nothing haughty, or even glossy, about the town – just lovely fresh mountain air, a laid-back attitude and friendly folk.

Most everything in town is on Elk Ave, including the **visitor center** (☎ 970-349-6438; www.crestedbuttechamber.com; 601 Elk Ave; 9am-5pm).

Crested Butte Mountain Resort (☎ 970-349-2222; www.skicb.com; lift ticket adult/child $82/41) sits 2 miles north of the town at the base of the impressive mountain of the same name. Surrounded by forests, rugged mountain peaks, and the West Elk, Raggeds and Maroon Bells–Snowmass Wilderness Areas, the scenery is wet-your-pants beautiful. It caters mostly to intermediate and expert riders.

Crested Butte is also a **mountain-biking** mecca, full of excellent high-altitude singletrack trails. For maps, information and mountain-bike rentals, visit the **Alpineer** (☎ 970-349-5210; 419 6th St).

If you are looking for the privacy of a hotel with the lively ambience of a hostel, then grab a room at the newly renovated **Crested Butte International Hostel** (☎ 970-349-0588; www.crestedbuttehostel.com; 615 Teocalli Ave; dm $25-31, r $65-99;), one of Colorado's nicest. The best private rooms have their own baths. Dorm bunks come with reading lamps and lockable drawers. The communal area is mountain rustic with a stone fireplace and comfortable couches. Rates vary dramatically by season, with fall being cheapest.

The **Timberline Restaurant** (☎ 970-349-9831; cnr Second St & Elk Ave; pizzas $12-25; 5:30-10pm;) was popular in the Butte before Heidi Montag and MTV's cameras made it famous. Owned and run by Montag's mother and stepfather, the family bistro serves a seasonal mostly American and Italian menu – think double-cut pork chops and BBQ *frites* or shrimp, basil pesto and tomato linguini.

Crested Butte has an interesting music scene year-round. Check out the lively **Eldo** (☎ 970-349-6125; 215 Elk Ave), one of the town's most popular microbreweries, which doubles as the club where most out-of-town bands play. Check out the great outdoor deck.

Crested Butte's air link to the outside world is **Gunnison County Airport** (☎ 970-641-2304), 28 miles south of the town. **Alpine Express** (☎ 970-641-5074) meets all commercial flights in winter, but requires reservations in summer. The fare to Crested Butte is $25.

The free **Mountain Express** (☎ 970-349-7318) connects Crested Butte with Mt Crested Butte every 15 minutes in winter, less often in other seasons; check times at bus stops.

SOUTHERN COLORADO

Home to the dramatic San Juan and Sangre de Cristo mountain ranges, Colorado's bottom half is just as pretty as her top and is filled with stuff to see and do.

Great Sand Dunes National Park

Landscapes collide in a shifting sea of sand at **Great Sand Dunes National Park** (☎ 719-378-2312; www.nps.gov/grsa; 11999 Hwy 150; admission $3; visitor center 9am-5pm), making you wonder whether a spaceship has whisked you to another planet. The 30-sq-mile dune park – the tallest sand peak rises 700ft above the valley floor – is squeezed between the jagged 14,000ft peaks of the Sangre de Cristo and San Juan Mountains and flat, arid scrub-brush of the San Luis Valley.

Plan a visit to this excellent-value national park (at just $3, admission is a steal) around a full moon. Stock up on supplies, stop by the visitor center for your free backcountry camping permit and hike into the surreal landscape to set up camp in the middle of nowhere. You won't be disappointed.

There are numerous **hiking trails**, or the more adventuresome can try **sandboarding** (where you ride a snowboard down the dunes). You'll need your own equipment, but Colorado is jam-packed with snowboard rental shops. Spring is the best time for boarding, when the dunes are at their most moist. For the slickest boarding, arrive a few hours after it rains – when the dunes are wet underneath, but dry on top. Try riding down Star Dune, roughly 750ft high. It's a strenuous 3-mile hike from the Dunes parking lot. The High Dune, about 650ft tall, is another option. Be sure to bring lots of water. Walking in loose sand is difficult, and summer temperatures on the dunes can exceed 130°F (54°C).

There is a **campground** (campsites $12) in the preserve. Otherwise, just south of the entrance you'll find tent and RV sites at the **Great Sand Dunes Oasis** (☎ 719-378-2222; 5400 Hwy 150; tent/RV sites $18/28, cabin r $50, motel r $90; May-Oct) along with super rustic camper cabins and slightly more upscale motel rooms with queen beds and cable TV. A restaurant and grocery store are also on-site. Horseback riding can be arranged.

The national park is about 35 miles northeast of Alamosa and 250 miles south of Denver. From Denver, take I-25 south to Hwy 160 west and turn onto Hwy 150 north. There is no public transportation.

Durango

The darling of this region, Durango is nothing short of delightful. It's an archetypal old mining town, filled with graceful hotels, Victorian-era saloons and mountains dominating the periphery as far as the eye can see. As you walk aroundit , Durango seems frozen in the century before last – just look at the waitress, dressed straight out of the late 1800s, slinging drinks at the scarred old saloon, or the musician pounding ragtime on worn ivory at an antique-laden Wild West inn with swinging wood doors.

If the town's yesteryear charm doesn't whet your appetite, dipping into Durango's goody bag of adventures is guaranteed to get the glands salivating. Meander through the historic district and listen for a shrill whistle, then watch the steam billow as the old train pulls in. Rent a bicycle and explore the trails, or get out the skis and head up the road for mile upon mile of powdery white bowls and tree-lined glades.

ORIENTATION & INFORMATION

Most visitor facilities are along Main Ave, including the 1882 Durango & Silverton Narrow Gauge Railroad Depot (at the south end of town). Motels are mostly north of the town center.

The **visitor center** (☎ 800-525-8855; www.durango.org; 111 S Camino del Rio) is south of town at the Santa Rita exit from US 550.

SIGHTS & ACTIVITIES

Riding the steam-drive choo-choo down the **Durango & Silverton Narrow Gauge Railroad** (☎ 970-247-2733, 888-872-4607; www.durangotrain.com; adult/child $75/45;) is a Durango must. These vintage locomotives have been making the scenic 45-mile trip north to Silverton (3½ hours each way) for more than 125 years. The dazzling journey allows two hours for exploring Silverton. This trip operates only from May through October. Check online for different winter options.

Durango Mountain Resort (☎ 970-247-9000; www.durangomountainresort.com; lift ticket adult/child$72/44), 25 miles north on US 550, is Durango's winter highlight. The resort, also known as Purgatory, offers 1200 skiable acres of varying difficulty and boasts 260in of snow per year. Two ter-

ROCKY MOUNTAINS

rain parks offer plenty of opportunities for snowboarders to catch big air. Check local grocery stores and newspapers for promotions and 2-for-1 lift tickets and other promotional ski season specials before purchasing directly from the ticket window.

If winter is about the snow, summer is all about the bikes. From steep single-track to scenic road rides, Durango has hundreds of exhilarating **mountain biking trails** to choose from. Some are well advertised, others locals like to keep secret (much in the manner of surf spots), and you'll have to do a bit of snooping if you want to hit pay dirt. For an easy ride try the **Old Railroad Grade Trail**, a 12.2-mile loop that uses both US Hwy 160 and a dirt road following the old railway tracks. From Durango take Hwy 160 west through the town of Hesperus. Turn right into the Cherry Creek Picnic Area, where the trail starts. For something a bit more technical, try **Dry Fork Loop**, accessible from Lightner Creek just west of town. It has some great drops, blind corners and vegetation. There are quite a few sports shops on Main Ave that rent out mountain bikes.

SLEEPING

Durango's best sleeping deals are found at the independent motels just north of town on Hwy 550 (Main Ave), with the greatest concentration between 18th and 32nd Sts. Rooms go for around $40 in winter, and $65 in summer.

Day's End (☎ 970-259-3311; www.daysenddurango.com; 2202 N Main Ave; r from $42;) The best budget bet, it's on a small creek just north of town. Rooms are well maintained and many have king-size beds. In winter, it offers discounts for skiing at Purgatory. There's an indoor hot tub and BBQ grill by the creek. Pets are welcome.

General Palmer Hotel (☎ 970-247-4747; www.generalpalmer.com; 567 Main Ave; r from $110;) A Victorian landmark from 1898, the hotel features pewter four-poster beds, quality linens and even a teddy bear for snuggling. Rooms are small but elegant, and if you tire of TV there's a collection of board games at the front desk. Check out the cozy library or the relaxing solarium.

Rochester House (☎ 970-385-1920; www.rochesterhotel.com; 721 E 2nd Ave; r $120-180;) Influenced by old Westerns (movie posters and marquee lights adorn the hallways), the Rochester is a little bit of old Hollywood in the New West. Rooms are spacious with high ceilings. Two formal sitting rooms where you're served cookies, and a breakfast room in an old train car are other perks at this pet-friendly establishment.

our pick **Strater Hotel** (☎ 970-247-4431; www.strater.com; 699 Main St; r $200;) The interior of this lovely, old-world hotel is museum worthy – check out the Stradivarius violin or the gold-plated commemorative Winchester in the lobby. Romantic rooms feature antiques, crystal and lace. Beds are heavenly and comfortable with impeccable linens. The hot tub is a major romantic plus – it can be reserved by the hour – as is the summertime melodrama (theater) the hotel runs. In winter, rates drop by more than 50%, making it a virtual steal. Look online.

EATING & DRINKING

From the budget diner to the top-end steakhouse to mouthwatering microbreweries, Durango offers a surprisingly diverse collection of restaurants for a town its size.

Steamworks (☎ 970-259-9200; 801 E 2nd Ave; mains $10-15; 11am-late) Industrial meets ski lodge at this popular microbrewery, with high sloping rafters and metal pipes. There's a large bar area, as well as a separate dining room with a Cajun-influenced menu. At night there are DJs and live bands.

Ore House (☎ 970-247-5707; 147 E College Dr; dishes $20-30; 5-10pm;) The best steakhouse in town, with food served in casual and rustic environs. Order a hand-cut aged steak, or try the steak, crab leg and lobster combo known as the Ore House Grubsteak ($40). It's easily big enough for two people. There's also a large wine cellar.

Ska Brewing Company (☎ 970-247-5792; 545 Turner Dr) Big on flavor and variety, these are the best beers in town. Although the small, friendly tasting-room bar was once mainly a production facility, over the years it's steadily climbed in the popularity charts. Today it is usually jam-packed with friends meeting for an after-work beer. Despite the hype, the place remains surprisingly laid-back and relaxed. Ska does weekly BBQs with live music and free food. Call for dates – they are never fixed.

Diamond Belle Saloon (☎ 970-376-7150; 699 Main Ave) An elegant and cozy period place right down to the waitress dressed in Victorian-era fishnets and garter with a feather in her hair.

The piano player pumps out ragtime tunes and takes requests. There are half-price appetizers and drink specials from 4pm to 6pm.

Lady Falconburgh's (☎ 970-582-9664; 640 Main Ave) With the largest selection of microbrews and imports in the Four Corners region, it's no secret that this place is popular. There's a brick and brass theme with original murals on the walls and more than 100 beers on offer – 38 of which are on tap.

GETTING THERE & AROUND

Durango–La Plata County Airport (DRO; ☎ 970-247-8143) is 18 miles southwest of Durango via US 160 and Hwy 172. Greyhound buses run daily from the **Durango Bus Center** (☎ 970-259-2755; 275 E 8th Ave), north to Grand Junction and south to Albuquerque, NM.

Durango is at the junction of US 160 and US 550, 42 miles east of Cortez, 49 miles west of Pagosa Springs and 190 miles north of Albuquerque.

Silverton

A dozen odd years ago, when the last mine shut down, it seemed that Silverton was destined to fade into historical obscurity. And for a while it did: tourists riding the Durango & Silverton Narrow Gauge Railroad were greeted with long-abandoned storefronts and shabby restaurants. You'd hardly believe that ghost town is the Silverton of today. Whether you're into snowmobiling, mountain biking, fly-fishing or just basking in sunshine, this boom-bust-boom town produces.

Silverton is a two-street city, and only one, Greene St, is paved. On it you'll find most of the town's businesses. Unpaved Blair St runs parallel to Greene and is a blast from the past. During the silver rush, Blair St was considered 'notorious' and home to thriving brothel and boozing establishments.

In summer most people rent jeeps to explore the fabulous 4WD trails in the region (see the boxed text, opposite). Try the **Red Mountain Motel & RV Park** (☎ 970-382-5512; www.redmtnmotelrvpk.com; 664 Greene St; cabins from $65, r $75), which rents out jeeps for $140 per day. This pet-friendly place stays open year-round, and runs snowmobile tours in the winter. The micro log cabins (they really are tiny, especially if you try to sleep four) stay warm and cozy and make good use of their limited space – ours came with a double bed, a bunk, tiny TV with HBO and even a fully outfitted little kitchenette. The river, with good fishing, is just a few minutes' walk away.

To start the day with a morning latte and a breakfast burrito, visit **Mobius Cycles & Café** (☎ 970-387-0770; 1321 Greene St; coffees & mains $3-5; 8am-5pm;), which does the best espresso drinks in town– try the frozen ones. Ask the proprietor, a young man named Winston Churchill, about the best mountain biking in the area. He also does bicycle repairs.

Right next door to Mobius Cycles & Café, the **Pride of the West** (☎ 970-387-5150; 1323 Greene St) is Silverton's best bar. A gigantic creaking no-frills place, it is the kind of spot where locals gather late into the night, shooting the shit at the long bar, or playing a game of pool upstairs.

Silverton is 50 miles north of Durango and 24 miles south of Ouray off US 550.

Ouray

No matter how many times you visit, Ouray's views slam you in the face every time. Sandwiched between imposing peaks, tiny Ouray just might be that little bit of paradise John Denver waxes lyrical about in 'Rocky Mountain High.' Here the mountains don't just tower over you, they actually embrace you – the peaks leave barely quarter of a mile of valley floor in town!

The **visitor center** (☎ 970-325-4746, 800-228-1876; www.ouraycolorado.com; 1220 Main St; 9am-5pm) is at the hot-springs pool.

SIGHTS & ACTIVITIES

Ouray's stunning scenery isn't the only ace up the town's sleeve. For a healing soak, try the **Ouray Hot Springs** (☎ 970-325-4638; 1220 Main St; admission $9; 10am-10pm Jun-Aug, call for hours rest of year). The crystal-clear natural springwater is free of the sulphur smells plaguing other hot springs around here, and the giant pool features a variety of soaking areas at temperatures from 96°F (36°C) to 106°F (41°C). It is definitely one of the nicest public mineral springs that you will find in the region.

Climbing the face of a frozen waterfall can be a sublime experience. Head to the **Ouray Ice Park** (☎ 970-325-4061; www.ourayicepark.com; admission free; 7am-5pm mid-Dec–Mar) to try it yourself. This park spans a 2-mile stretch of the Uncompagre Gorge that has been dedicated to public ice climbing. The park is the world's first, and draws enthusiasts from around the globe to try their hand on climbs for all skill

SCENIC DRIVE: THE MILLION DOLLAR HIGHWAY & OVERTON PASS 4WD DRIVE ROUTE

To really get a feel for the rugged majesty of this region – we would argue it's one of the state's most dramatic areas – take a drive from Ouray to Telluride. Fall, when the aspen trees turn the mountainsides into yellow seas, is particularly brilliant.

The following drive starts in Ouray, loops through Silverton and ends in Telluride. If you have at least a Subaru (keep reading and you'll understand) you can make the entire journey in summer, but know that Overton Pass is not paved and is considered a 4WD route.

If you don't feel comfortable, or don't have the right vehicle, it is still worth driving the Million Dollar Hwy (US 550) between Ouray and Silverton (the pass is paved and open all year). This 24-mile stretch of pavement gets its name because the roadbed fill contains valuable ore.

The road is only a silver lining in this golden cloud. This is easily one of the most spectacular drives in America, and would qualify as heaven in John Denver's book. The road clings to the side of the crumbly mountains, passing old minehead frames and big alpine scenery. At some points, in fact, the jagged peaks seem close enough to snatch you.

Five miles south of Ouray town limits, on the way to Silverton, you'll pass the **Alpine Loop Backcountry Byway** (www.co.blm.gov/gra). If you have a properly equipped vehicle, it's definitely worth detouring to ride at least a portion of this classic 4WD trail. The path leads through ghost towns such as Animas Forks, forgotten stagecoach stops and trails to five fourteeners. It's worth stopping at the trailhead, regardless of your vehicle, to snap a picture. Canyons are juxtaposed against mountains that remain snowcapped even in July.

Spend a night in Silverton and then get an early start on Overton Pass to Telluride. Silverton local Doug Wall says they call it 'Subaru Pass' because 'going from Silverton to Ouray in the summer you can get by in a Subaru. Coming back's a bit more technical, but it's a beautiful drive.'

It sure is. If you're into exhilarating 4WD tracks, this is arguably one of the best (and certainly the most famous) in the state. It's especially appealing because it doesn't require super expertise, and relative beginners can conquer it when starting in Silverton.

The pass is open in summer only.

levels. For information on its festival, see below. **San Juan Mountain Guides** (☎ 970-325-4925; www.ourayclimbing.com; 2-day courses from $320) offers a weekend two-day introduction course. All equipment is included, but check out the website for dates.

FESTIVALS & EVENTS

The **Ouray Ice Festival** (☎ 970-325-4288; www.ourayicefestival.com) features four days of climbing competitions, dinners, slide shows and clinics in January. You can watch the competitions for free, but to check out the various evening events you will need to make a $15 donation to the ice park. Once inside you'll get free brews from popular Colorado microbrewer New Belgium.

SLEEPING & EATING

Some of Ouray's lodges are destinations in themselves.

Box Canyon Lodge & Hot Springs (☎ 970-325-4981; www.boxcanyonouray.com; 45 3rd Ave; r from $80) Spacious and accommodating geothermal-heated rooms. The real treat here is four wooden springs-fed hot tubs perfect for a romantic stargazing soak.

Beaumont Hotel (☎ 970-325-7000; www.beaumonthotel.com; 505 Main St; r $180-350) Ouray's classiest lodging option, this small hotel offers 12 rooms elegantly appointed with period furnishings. Established in 1886, the hotel was closed for more than 30 years before undergoing extensive renovations and reopening in 2002. It also boasts a spa and three unique boutiques.

Silver Nugget Café (☎ 970-325-4100; 746 Main St; dishes $7-20; 🕑 8am-9pm) A busy, contemporary eatery in a historic building, Silver Nugget features a very large breakfast menu as well as deli-style sandwiches at lunch. Dinner offerings include deep-fried Rocky Mountain rainbow trout, and liver and onions.

Tundra Restaurant at the Beaumont (☎ 970-325-7040; 505 Main St; dishes from $20; 🕑 5-10pm) This elegant restaurant has won several awards for its wine cellar and does Thursday-evening tastings. Billing itself as serving 'High Altitude' cuisine, it focuses on regional specialties with great results.

GETTING THERE & AROUND

Ouray is 24 miles north of Silverton along US 550 and best reached by private vehicle.

Telluride

It's hard not to dig Telluride. Once an old Ute hunting ground and then a saloon-swinging mining town, Telluride offers great skiing, mountain biking and festivals. She's a good-looking babe – an archetypical Wild West mountain village with a well-preserved Victorian downtown, laid-back residents and fabulous mountain views.

Colorado Ave, also known as Main St, is where you'll find most businesses. From downtown you can reach the ski mountain via two lifts and the gondola. The latter also links Telluride with Mountain Village, the true base for the Telluride Ski Area. Located 7 miles from town along Hwy 145, Mountain Village is a 20-minute drive east, but only 12 minutes away by gondola (free for foot passengers). Check with the **visitor center** (☎ 970-728-3041, 888-353-5473; www.telluride.com; 398 W Colorado Ave; 9am-5pm) for area info.

SIGHTS & ACTIVITIES

Covering three distinct areas, **Telluride Ski Resort** (☎ 970-728-6900; www.tellurideskiresort.com; lift ticket adult/child$76/43) is served by 16 lifts. Much of the terrain is for advanced and intermediate skiers, but there's still ample choice for beginners.

Experienced cross-country skiers will appreciate the **San Juan Hut Systems'** (☎ 970-626-3033; www.sanjuanhuts.com; huts per night $25) series of crude huts along a 206-mile route stretching from Telluride west to Moab, UT. In summer these huts, equipped with bunks and cooking facilities, are popular with mountain bikers. Book well in advance, as huts fill quickly.

While on the subject, **mountain biking** is big news in Telluride. The surrounding peaks offer awesome single-track routes and, of course, stupendous scenery. Beginners should try the easy and smooth gravel **River Trail** that connects Town Park with Hwy 145 for a total trail distance of about 2 miles. If you want a bit more of a workout, continue up **Mill Creek Trail**, west of the Texaco gas station near where the River Trail ends. After the initial climb, the trail follows the contour of the mountain and ends at the Jud Wiebe Trail (hikers only), where you'll have to turn back. To rent some gear, visit **Easy Rider Mountain Sports** (☎ 970-728-4734; 101 W Colorado Ave), which has a variety of bikes to choose from, as well as maps and information.

Hiking is also popular. The **Bear Creek Trail** is slightly more than 2 miles and ascends 1040ft to a beautiful cascading waterfall. From here you can access the strenuous **Wasatch Trail**, a 12-mile loop that heads west across the mountains to **Bridal Veil Falls** – Telluride's most impressive waterfalls. The Bear Creek trailhead is at the south end of Pine St, across the San Miguel River.

FESTIVALS & EVENTS

Telluride has two giant festivals each year:

Telluride Bluegrass Festival (☎ 800-624-2422; www.planetbluegrass.com; 4-day pass $175) Held in late June, this festival attracts thousands for a weekend of top-notch rollicking alfresco bluegrass. Stalls sell all sorts of food and local microbrews to keep you happy, and acts continue well into the night. Camping out for the four-day festival is very popular. Check out the website for info on sites, shuttle service and combo ticket-and-camping packages – it's all very organized!

Telluride Film Festival (☎ 603-433-9202; www.telluridefilmfestival.com; admission $20-650) Held in early September. National and international films are premiered throughout town, and the event attracts big-name stars. For more information on the relatively complicated pricing scheme, visit the film festival website.

SLEEPING

Telluride's lodgings can fill quickly, and for the best rates it's best to book online. Unless you're planning to camp, however, don't expect much in the budget category. Telluride's activities and festivals keep it busy year-round.

Telluride Town Park Campground (☎ 970-728-2173; 500 W Colorado Ave; campsites $10; mid-May–mid-Sep) Right in the center of town, it has 20 sites with shower access ($1.50 for a hot shower). It fills up quickly in the high season. There are many other campgrounds within 10 miles of town; check with the visitor center for more info.

Victorian Inn (☎ 970-728-6601; www.tellurideinn.com; 401 W Pacific Ave; r from $99;) One of Telluride's better deals, it offers comfortable rooms (some with kitchenettes) and a hot tub and dry sauna, and best off all, fantastic lift ticket deals for guests. Kids 12 and under stay free, and you can't beat the downtown location.

ROCKY MOUNTAINS

Hotel Columbia (☎ 970-728-0660; www.columbiatelluride.com; 300 San Juan Ave; r from $145; ⓟ) Each room at this charismatic place has a balcony, fireplace and a mountain view. Baths are larger than average, and breakfast is included. Other highlights include a rooftop hot tub and fitness room. The hotel is right across the street from the gondola and it's pet-friendly.

EATING & DRINKING

Telluride's main street (Colorado Ave) is packed with bars and eateries.

Baked in Telluride (☎ 970-728-4775; 127 S Fir St; mains $6-10; ⏰ 5:30am-10pm) It has become a Telluride institution over the last 25 years, and this is where everyone now heads for a fill-up on pizza, sandwiches, salads and calzones. The front deck is where to sit if you're looking to see or be seen; the atmosphere is more than casual.

Excelsior Cafe (☎ 970-728-4250; 200 W Colorado Ave; mains $16-40; ⏰ 5-10pm) One of Telluride's hottest restaurants, Excelsior gets rave reviews for its Parisian café meets jazzy wine bar vibe. The menu features a little bit of everything, from Moroccan lamb chops to Montana buffalo short ribs. If you are short on cash, order from the less expensive, but equally tantalizing, bar menu.

Cosmopolitan (☎ 970-728-0660; www.columbiatelluride.com; 300 San Juan Ave; mains from $20) The on-site restaurant at the Hotel Columbia is one of Telluride's most respected for fine modern dining with a twist – can you resist Himalayan yak rib-eye or lobster corn dogs?

Smugglers Brewpub & Grille (☎ 970-728-0919; 225 South Pine St; ⏰ 11am-late) Beer-lovers will feel right at home at casual Smugglers, a great place to hang out in any season. With at least seven beers on tap, this brewpub is big on variety. Try the chocolaty Two Plank Porter or the Smugglers' Scottish Strong Ale. The menu of American pub fare (mains $5 to $10) features burgers, fries, salads and sandwiches.

Fly Me to the Moon Saloon (☎ 970-728-6666; 132 E Colorado Ave) Let your hair down and kick up your heels to the tunes of live bands at this saloon, the best place in Telluride to groove.

GETTING THERE & AROUND

Commuter aircraft serve the mesa-top **Telluride Airport** (TEX; ☎ 970-778-5051; www.tellurideairport.com), 5 miles east of town – weather permitting. At other times, planes fly into Montrose, 65 miles north. **Telluride Express** (☎ 970-728-6000; www.tellurideexpress.com) runs shuttles to Montrose airport (adult/child $42/20); call to arrange pickup.

Mesa Verde National Park

Shrouded in mystery, Mesa Verde is a fascinating, if slightly eerie, national park to explore. It is here that a civilization of Ancestral Pueblo Indians appears to have vanished in AD 1300, leaving behind a complex civilization of cliff dwellings. Mesa Verde is unique among parks for its focus on preserving this civilization's cultural relics so that future generations may continue to interpret the puzzling settlement, and subsequent abandonment, of the area.

Mesa Verde rewards travelers who set aside a day or more to take the ranger-led tours of Cliff Palace and Balcony House, explore Wetherill Mesa or participate in one of the campfire programs. But if you only have time for a short visit, check out the Chapin Mesa Museum and walk through the Spruce Tree House, where you can climb down a wooden ladder into the cool chamber of a kiva.

The park entrance is off US 160, midway between Cortez and Mancos. From the entrance it is 21 miles to the **park headquarters** (☎ 970-529-4461; www.nps.gov/meve; 7-day park entry per vehicle $10, bicyclists, hikers & motorcyclists $5), which has road information and the word on park closures (many areas are closed in winter).

SIGHTS & ACTIVITIES

The **Chapin Mesa Museum** (☎ 970-529-4631; admission free; ⏰ 8am-6:30pm, 8am-5pm winter) is near the park headquarters. Along the way are panoramic **Park Point** (10 miles from the entrance) and the **Far View Visitor Center** (☎ 970-529-5034; ⏰ 8am-5pm), 15 miles from the entrance, where visitors must buy tickets ($2.50) for tours of the magnificent Cliff Palace or Balcony House.

The largest concentration of Ancestral Puebloan sites is at **Chapin Mesa**, where you'll see the densely clustered Far View Site and the large Spruce Tree House. At **Wetherill Mesa**, the second-largest concentration, visitors may enter stabilized surface sites and two cliff dwellings, including the Long House, open from late May through August. South from Park Headquarters, the 6-mile **Mesa Top Road** connects excavated mesa-top sites, accessible cliff dwellings and vantages of inaccessible dwellings from the mesa rim.

The park concessionaire, **Aramark Mesa Verde** (☎ 970-529-4421; www.visitmesaverde.com; adult/child from $36/25), offers guided tours to excavated pit homes, cliff dwellings and the Spruce Tree House daily from May to mid-October.

SLEEPING & EATING

The nearby towns of Cortez and Mancos have plenty of midrange places to stay; inside the park there's camping and a lodge.

Morefield Campground (☎ 970-529-4421; campsites $20, canvas tents from $40; May–mid-Oct;) Gourmet campers will dig the big canvas tents kitted out with two cots and a lantern here. The park's camping option, located 4 miles from the entrance gate, also has 445 regular tent sites on grassy grounds conveniently located near Morefield Village, which has a general store, gas station, restaurant, showers and laundry. Free evening campfire programs take place nightly from Memorial Day (May) to Labor Day (September) at the Morefield Campground Amphitheater.

Far View Lodge (☎ 970-529-4421; r $100; mid-Apr–Oct;) Perched on a mesa-top 15 miles inside the park entrance, this tasteful Pueblo-style lodge has 150 Southwestern rooms, some with kiva fireplaces. Don't miss sunset over the mesa from your private balcony. You can even bring Fido for an extra $10 per night.

Metate Room (☎ 970-529-4421; Far View Lodge; mains $15-25; 5-10pm) This restaurant has an innovative menu inspired by Native American food and flavors. Palates are titillated by oven-roasted chicken breast with green chili stuffing and buffalo fajitas.

WYOMING

Galloping with rodeos and pageants, the pioneer past is alive and kicking in the 'Cowboy State.' With much of its beauty derived from its romantic emptiness, sparsely populated Wyoming is the kind of place you'd expect to find that lonesome cowboy riding the range, whistling a melancholy tune and embracing the solitude.

Wyoming's greatest bounty lies in its northwestern corner, which is home to two of the USA's most magnificent national parks: geyser-packed Yellowstone and the majestic Grand Tetons. Gateway towns, such as chic Jackson and progressive Lander, are ideal launchpads for epic hiking, camping, climbing and skiing adventures in the region. To really get off the beaten path, spend a few days wandering through Wyoming's less touristy towns and windswept prairies – places such as Laramie and Cheyenne are hardly on many travelers' radar, but do give a taste of modern Wyoming reality. Be warned: it can feel a bit isolated and depressing.

Information

You haven't experienced wind until you've driven across the plains of Wyoming. Distances are long, with gas stations few and far between. Other driving hazards include frequent high gusty winds and fast-moving snow squalls that can create whiteout blizzard conditions in a matter of minutes. Don't worry: when the weather gets too rough, the

BARGAIN BASEMENT HELI-SKIING

Heli-skiing is no longer reserved solely for the Richard Bransons of the adventure world. Thanks to a trip by **Telluride Helitrax** (☎ 970-728-8377; www.helitrax.net; guided trips $285; Jan-May), even backpackers can afford the thrill of riding virgin powder above the tree line. Called the Bear Creek Descent, this guided trip is more affordable – heli-skiing can cost into the thousands for a single day – because it makes use of a remote yet easily accessible area right outside town. Plus, the trip only includes a single lift in the chopper.

One's all you need. After the bird leaves you hovering at 13,200ft on a ridge of Silver Mountain, take a few minutes to admire the views around you – you'll be able to see nine fourteeners in Colorado and mountains as far away as Utah. Then it's time to take the plunge. The guided 4300-vertical-foot descent takes you on an exhilarating ride – this is an expert-only trip – that flies into an alpine bowl, over a sheer face, down two couloirs and through the glades before dropping you directly into downtown Telluride. Rates include the rental of extra-fat skis, which allow you to cut through waist-high powder with ease. Snowboarders will need their own gear – you'll definitely want to bring a wide powder board or you'll be sure to get stuck. The best snow is usually found in April – strange we know, but typical of Colorado. Helitrax usually begins trips in January, but this varies depending on snow levels and avalanche danger, so check the website.

WYOMING FACTS

Nicknames Equality State, Cowboy State
Population 532,688
Area 97,100 sq miles
Capital city Cheyenne (population 55,314)
State tax 7%
Birthplace of Abstract expressionist artist Jackson Pollock (1912–56)
Home of Former Vice President Dick Cheney
Famous for Yellowstone, homes where buffalo roam, agriculture, dude ranches
Best souvenir A piece of coal – the state is the USA's biggest producer
Driving distances Cheyenne to Jackson 440 miles, Cheyenne to Denver 100 miles

highway patrol will shut the entire interstate until it clears.

Wyoming Road Conditions (☎ 307-772-0824, 888-996-7623)

Wyoming State Parks & Historic Sites (☎ 877-996-7275; www.wyo-park.com) Wyoming has 12 state parks. There is a daily admission fee of $6 per person. If you wish to spend the night in a campground, the fee is $17 per person, inclusive of the tent site and daily use fee. Reservations are taken online or over the phone through September 15.

Wyoming Travel & Tourism (☎ 800-225-5996; www.wyomingtourism.org; cnr I-25 & College Dr, Cheyenne)

CHEYENNE

Many a country tune has been penned about the cowboy town of Cheyenne, which doubles as Wyoming's state capital and largest city. With the exception of July's Frontier Days festival, this town on the edge of the prairie doesn't offer much for visitors (it's the kind of place people live in, rather than travel to). But its location at the junction of I-25 and I-80 makes it an obvious pit stop.

The **Cheyenne Visitor Center** (☎ 307-778-3133, 800-426-5009; www.cheyenne.org; 1 Depot Sq; ⏰ 8am-5pm Mon-Fri, 9am-5pm Sat, 11am-5pm Sun, closed Sat & Sun winter) is a great resource.

Sights & Activities

The **Cheyenne Gunslingers** (☎ 307-635-1028; cnr Lincolnway & Carey Ave; admission free; ⏰ Jun & Jul) is a nonprofit group of actors who puts on a lively, if not exactly accurate Old West show – from near hangings to slippery jailbreaks. Stars include corrupt judges, smiling good guys and, of course, the bad-ass villains. Show times are 6pm daily as well as noon on Saturdays.

For a peek into the pioneer past, visit the lively **Frontier Days Old West Museum** (☎ 307-778-7290; 4601 N Carey Ave; adult/child $7/free; ⏰ 8am-6pm Mon-Fri, 9am-5pm Sat & Sun summer, 9am-5pm Mon-Fri, 10am-5pm Sat & Sun winter) at I-25 exit 12. It is chock-full of rodeo memorabilia – from saddles to trophies.

Festivals & Events

Beginning in late July, the city stages Wyoming's largest celebration, **Cheyenne Frontier Days** (☎ 307-778-7222; 4501 N Carey Ave; admission varies). It is 10 days of rodeos, concerts, dances, air shows, chili cook-offs and other shindigs that draw big crowds from across the Rockies.

Sleeping & Eating

Reservations are a must during Frontier Days, when rates double and everything within 50 miles is booked. A string of cheap motels line noisy Lincolnway (I-25 exit 9).

Lincoln Court (☎ 307-638-3302; 1720 W Lincolnway; r from $50;) With decent rooms, this is the best-value motel in summer, when it shares facilities with the pricier Best Western next door, including an indoor pool, fitness room and Jacuzzi.

Nagle Warren Mansion Bed & Breakfast (☎ 307-637-3333; www.naglewarrenmansion.com; 222 E 17th St; r from $125;) This lavish spread is a fabulous find. In a quickly-going-hip neighborhood, it offers very luxurious abodes decked out with late-19th-century regional antiques. Spacious and elegant, the mansion also boasts a small health club, Jacuzzi and massage treatments. Considering the glitz factor, it's a great deal.

HOT TOPIC: STAYING LOCAL

Today Wyoming remains a rural state where most folk either work on the family ranch or have jobs in the energy agency. One of the hottest issues in the state pertains to trying to keep the younger generation from moving away following university – indeed, recent census numbers show Wyoming's under-50-year-old population is quickly declining. To entice people to stay, or to interest other 20-somethings to move to the state, politicians are offering cheap plots of land if residents agree to live and work in small towns for a set number of years. The state is also concentrating on boosting tourism revenues.

It also does mystery dinner packages – check the website.

Sanford's Grub & Pub (☎ 307-634-3381; 115 E 17th St; mains $8-16; 🕑 11am-10pm) The walls are aflutter with sports bric-a-brac and road signs, and this fun place gets consistently good reviews for its novella-length menu of tasty eats, including burgers, chicken and even a range of 'porker' dishes. Beer is served in ice-cold glasses.

Getting There & Around

Cheyenne Airport (CYS; ☎ 307-634-7071; www.cheyenneairport.com; 200 E 8th Ave) has daily flights to Denver. Greyhound and Powder River buses depart from the **bus depot** (☎ 307-634-7744; 222 E Deming Dr) daily for Billings, MT ($90, 11 hours), and Denver, CO ($29, three hours), among other destinations.

On weekdays, the **Cheyenne Transit Program** (CTP; ☎ 307-637-6253; 🕑 8am-5pm Mon-Fri) operates six local bus routes ($1).

LARAMIE

Home to the state's only four-year university, Laramie radiates a kind of boisterous vibe missing from most Wyoming prairie towns. The small historic downtown is a lively five-block grid of attractive two-story brick buildings with hand-painted signs and murals pushed up against the railroad tracks. Beware of the legendary blustery winds that always seem to blow here; they're strong enough to nearly sweep you off your feet.

For an infusion of culture, check out one of the museums on the **University of Wyoming** (UW; ☎ 307-766-4075) campus. If you're traveling with the kids (or just feel like one), stop by the **Wyoming Territorial Prison & Old West Park** (☎ 307-745-616; www.wyoprisonpark.org; 975 Snowy Range Rd; adult/child $11/free; 🕑 9am-6pm May-Oct, 10am-5pm Sat & Sun Nov-Mar, closed Apr; 👪); it's a curious restoration of an early prison and frontier town.

There are numerous cheap sleeps off I-80 at exit 313. In town, the **Gas Lite Motel** (☎ 307-742-6616; 960 N 3rd St; r $70;) relies on an outrageous kitsch setup to sell its well-priced digs. Plastic horses keep watch over the lawn, while plastic roosters languish on the roof. A greenhouse encloses a swimming pool adorned with cowboy murals. The spick-and-span rooms in a U-shaped log-cabin-style building are pet-friendly and dressed with playful Wild West touches.

Everyone eats at **Jeffrey's Bistro** (☎ 307-742-7046; 123 Ivinson Ave; mains $8-20; 🕑 11am-8pm Mon-Wed, 11am-9pm Thu-Sat; 👪), a long-established downtown spot with a zesty menu of fresh and innovative salads, sandwiches and pasta dishes. Check out the cheap cocktails – martinis and margaritas are just $3.75.

For live country music and beers, you'll want to head to the **Old Buckhorn Bar** (☎ 307-742-3554; 114 Ivinson St). Established in 1900, it's Laramie's oldest standing bar and a fantastic example of what a good Wild West saloon should look like in this century – check out the hand-scratched graffiti and half-century-old condom dispenser in the bathroom. The Buckhorn is smoker-friendly, but boxy and ventilated enough to not smell too bad.

Located 4 miles west of town via I-80 exit 311, **Laramie Regional Airport** (☎ 307-742-4164) has daily flights to Denver. **Greyhound** (☎ 307-742-5188) buses stop at the **Tumbleweed Express gas station** (4700 Bluebird Lane) at the east end of town (I-80 exit 316). Fill up your tank (and tummy) in Laramie; heading west on I-80, the next services aren't for 75 miles.

CODY

Raucous Cody capitalizes on its Wild West image (it's named after legendary William F 'Buffalo Bill' Cody). With a streak of yee-haw, the town happily relays yarns (not always the whole story, mind you) about its past. Summer is high season, and Cody puts on quite an Old West show for the throngs of visitors making their way to Yellowstone National Park, 52 miles to the west. From Cody, the approach to geyserland is dramatic to say the least. President Teddy Roosevelt once said this stretch of pavement was 'the most scenic 50 miles in the world.'

The **visitor center** (☎ 307-587-2777; www.codychamber.org; 836 Sheridan Ave; 🕑 8am-6pm Mon-Sat, 10am-3pm Sun Jun-Aug, 8am-5pm Mon-Fri Sep-May) is the logical starting point.

Cody's major tourist attraction is the superb **Buffalo Bill Historical Center** (☎ 307-587-4771; www.bbhc.org; 720 Sheridan Ave; adult/child $15/6; 🕑 7am-8pm Jun-Aug, 10am-3pm Tue-Sun Sep-May). A sprawling complex of five museums, it showcases everything Western: from posters, grainy films and other lore pertaining to Buffalo Bill's world-famous Wild West shows, to galleries showcasing frontier-oriented artwork to museums dedicated to Native Americans. Its Draper Museum of Natural History explores

ROCKY MOUNTAINS

PIT STOP: COAL CREEK COFFEE CO

If you're craving a pick-me-up espresso to get you through the windy long-haul drive across Wyoming's endless plains, you'd do well to get off I-80 in Laramie and pay ecofriendly **Coal Creek Coffee Co** (☎ 307-745-7737; 110 E Grand Ave; mains $3-6; 6am-10pm;) a visit. Serving a fair-trade caffeine buzz, Coal Creek makes a mean iced vanilla latte. The organic sandwiches are healthy and equally delicious. We thought the blue cheese and portobello panini was the best we'd tasted – it came out tangy, fresh and crisped just right. If you need to just chill, there are a number of tables good for lounging and it stays open late. Talk about an awesome pit stop. Look for Coal Creek off Grand Ave by the University of Wyoming campus next to the Hilton Garden Inn.

the Yellowstone region's ecosystem with excellent results. Also popular is the **Cody Nite Rodeo** (☎ 307-587-2992; Stampede Park, 421 W Yellowstone Ave; adult/child from $12/6), which giddy-ups nightly from June to August.

Built by ol' Mr Bill in 1902, **Irma Hotel** (☎ 307-587-4221; www.irmahotel.com; 1192 Sheridan Ave; r from $99;) offers historic rooms in the main building or more modern, less expensive motel-style rooms. Don't miss the on-site Silver Saddle Saloon; the ornate cherrywood bar was a gift from Queen Victoria. Gunfights break out nightly at 6pm in front of the hotel from June through September.

The **Silver Dollar Bar** (☎ 307-527-7666; 1313 Sheridan Ave; mains $5-12) is a historic watering hole with lots of TV screens and live music nightly. It serves yummy burgers and has pool tables. Thursdays are 25¢ beer nights, and there's a daily special served on the deck.

Yellowstone Regional Airport (COD; ☎ 307-587-5096; www.flyyra.com) is 1 mile east of Cody and runs daily flights to Salt Lake City and Denver.

LANDER

Lander just might be the coolest little one-street town in Wyoming. Just a stone's throw from the Wind River Indian Reservation, it's a rock-climbing and mountaineering mecca attracting folks the region over.

Despite its growing popularity, Lander remains refreshingly unpretentious. Playing in the outdoors is of paramount importance to locals, and when the day's climbing activities finish, impromptu celebrations take place over brews at the town's only bar.

The **Lander Visitor Center** (☎ 307-332-3892, 800-433-0662; www.landerchamber.org; 160 N 1st St; 9am-5pm Mon-Fri) is a good source of general information. If you've come to hike, camp or climb, you're best popping into **Wild Iris Mountain Sports** (☎ 307-332-4541; 333 Main St). The shop has the inside scoop on Lander's best spots for all three. If you want to check out the singletrack trails outside town, head down the street to **Freewheel Ski & Cycle** (☎ 307-332-6616; 378 W Main St).

Sinks Canyon State Park, 6 miles south of Lander on Sinks Canyon Rd (Hwy 131), is a beautiful park with perplexing natural features. The Middle Fork of the Popo Agie River flows through the narrow canyon and disappears into the soluble Madison limestone called the Sinks, and pops up faster and warmer a quarter of a mile downstream in a pool called the Rise. The summer-only **visitor center** (☎ 307-332-3077; 3079 Sinks Canyon Rd; 9am-6pm Jun-Aug) is near two scenic **campgrounds** (campsites $8), which come highly recommended by locals.

For lodging, one of the better returns for your money is **Pronghorn Lodge** (☎ 307-332-3940; www.pronghornlodge.com; 150 Main St; r incl breakfast from $65;), which has faultless spacious rooms, plus a hot tub one block from downtown.

Pizza, sandwiches and salads go down well on the outdoor deck or inside the big wooden barnlike place called the **Lander Bar** (☎ 307-332-8228; 126 Main St; mains $6-9; 11am-late). A Lander institution, it not only serves filling fare (although ask for your sandwiches with the dressing on the side), it's also the place to go for climbing and mountain-biking gossip. There's live music many nights.

Wind River Transportation Authority (☎ 307-856-7118; www.wrtabuslines.com) provides scheduled Monday-to-Friday service between Lander, Riverton, Dubois, Rock Springs and Riverton Regional Airport ($20).

YELLOWSTONE NATIONAL PARK

They grow their mammals and geysers big up in Yellowstone, America's first national park and Wyoming's flagship attraction. From shaggy grizzlies to giant moose, this park boasts the lower 48's most motley concentration of wildlife. Plus, it is home to half the world's geysers. And when you factor in the plethora of alpine lakes, rivers and waterfalls you'll quickly realize you've stumbled across one of Mother Nature's most fabulous creations. This natural cornucopia attracts up to 30,000 visitors daily in summer and three million gatecrashers annually. To escape the crowds, take a hike.

When John Colter became the first white man to visit the area in 1807, the only inhabitants were Tukadikas, a Shoshone Bannock people who hunted bighorn sheep. Colter's reports of the soaring geysers and boiling mudholes (at first dismissed as tall tales) brought in expeditions and tourism interest. The park was established in 1872 to preserve Yellowstone's spectacular geography: the geothermal phenomena, the fossil forests and Yellowstone Lake.

Orientation

The 3472-sq-mile park is divided into five distinct regions (clockwise from the north): Mammoth, Roosevelt, Canyon, Lake and Geyser Countries.

Of the park's five entrance stations, only the North Entrance, near Gardiner, MT, is open year-round. The others, typically open May to October, are the Northeast Entrance (Cooke City, MT), the East Entrance (Cody), the South Entrance (north of Grand Teton National Park) and the West Entrance (West Yellowstone, MT). The park's main road is the 142-mile Grand Loop Rd scenic drive.

Information

The park is open year-round, but most roads close during winter. Park entrance permits (hiker/vehicle $12/25) are valid for seven days for entry into both Yellowstone and Grand Teton National Parks. Summer-only visitor centers are evenly spaced every 20 to 30 miles along Grand Loop Rd. The **Albright Visitors Center & Park Headquarters** (☎ 307-344-2263; www.nps.gov/yell; Mammoth; 🕑 8am-7pm Jun-Aug, 9am-5pm Sep-May) serves as park headquarters.

Sights & Activities

Just sitting on the porch of the Old Faithful Lodge with a cocktail in one hand and a book in the other waiting for the geyser to erupt could be considered an activity by itself. While it's perfectly acceptable – and really quite encouraged – this better not be the only thing you do in this fabulous national park. No, get your butt off the bench and go for a hike.

Yellowstone is split into five regions, representing the five distinct ecosystems found inside the park's boundaries. And we encourage you to explore them all. You'll be given a map upon entering the national park (and your admission to Grand Teton is good here, so you can go back and forth at leisure without paying twice), and all the lodges have helpful information desks. Don't be scared to ask a park ranger for a trail recommendation; many will go out of their way to help you tailor a hike to your tastes, from great photo spots to best chance at spotting bear.

Geyser Country has the most geothermal features in the park. Upper Geyser Basin contains 180 of the park's 200 to 250 geysers. The most famous is **Old Faithful**, which spews from 3700 to 8400 gallons of water 100ft to 180ft into the air every 1½ hours or so. The Firehole and Madison Rivers offer superb fishing and wildlife viewing. For an easy walk, check out the well-marked, very easy gravel and paved walking trail around Old Faithful and other smaller geysers; it begins just outside Old Faithful Lodge.

Known for its fossil forests and geothermal areas at Mammoth Hot Springs and Norris Geyser Basin, **Mammoth Country** is North America's most volatile and oldest-known continuously active (115,000 years) thermal area. The peaks of the Gallatin Range rise to the northwest, towering above the area's lakes, creeks and numerous hiking trails.

Fossil forests, the commanding Lamar River Valley and its tributary trout streams, Tower Falls and the Absaroka Mountains' craggy peaks are the highlights of **Roosevelt Country**, the park's most remote, scenic and undeveloped region. Several good hikes begin near Tower Junction.

A series of scenic overlooks and a network of the Grand Canyon of the Yellowstone rim trails highlight the beauty of **Canyon Country**. South Rim Dr leads to the canyon's most spectacular overlook, at Artist Point. Mud Volcano is Canyon Country's primary geothermal area. Yellowstone Lake, the centerpiece of **Lake Country** and one of the world's largest alpine lakes, is also home to the country's largest inland population of cutthroat trout. Rising east and southeast of the lakes, the oft snowcapped Absaroka Mountains make for a dramatic

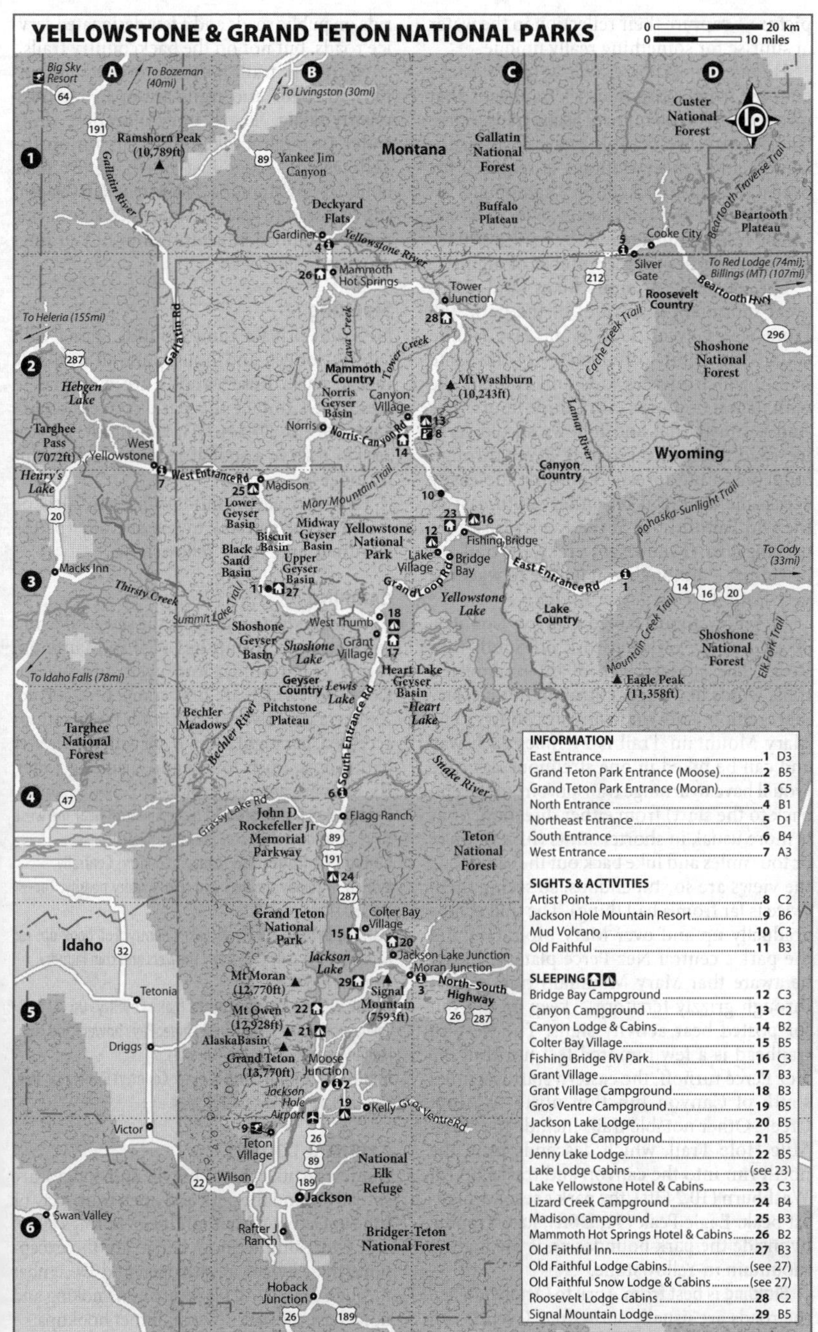
YELLOWSTONE & GRAND TETON NATIONAL PARKS
0 20 km
0 10 miles
Big Sky Resort
To Bozeman (40mi)
To Livingston (30mi)
Ramshorn Peak (10,789ft)
Yankee Jim Canyon
Montana
Gallatin National Forest
Custer National Forest
Buffalo Plateau
Deckyard Flats
Gallatin River
Gardiner
Yellowstone River
Cooke City
Beartooth Traverse Trail
Beartooth Plateau
Silver Gate
To Red Lodge (74mi); Billings (MT) (107mi)
Beartooth Hwy
Mammoth Hot Springs
Tower Junction
Roosevelt Country
To Helena (155mi)
Gallatin Rd
Lava Creek
Tower Creek
Cache Creek Trail
Shoshone National Forest
Hebgen Lake
Mammoth Country
Mt Washburn (10,243ft)
Norris Geyser Basin
Canyon Village
Lamar River
Targhee Pass (7072ft)
West Yellowstone
Norris
Norris-Canyon Rd
Wyoming
Henry's Lake
West Entrance Rd
Madison
Mary Mountain Trail
Canyon Country
Lower Geyser Basin
Midway Geyser Basin
Yellowstone National Park
Pahaska-Sunlight Trail
Fishing Bridge
Black Sand Basin
Biscuit Basin
Upper Geyser Basin
Lake Village
Bridge Bay
To Cody (33mi)
Macks Inn
East Entrance Rd
Thirsty Creek
Grand Loop Rd
Yellowstone Lake
Summit Lake Trail
Lake Country
West Thumb
Shoshone Geyser Basin
Shoshone Lake
Grant Village
Mountain Creek Trail
Elk Fork Trail
Heart Lake Geyser Basin
To Idaho Falls (78mi)
Geyser Country
Lewis Lake
Eagle Peak (11,358ft)
Bechler Meadows
Pitchstone Plateau
Heart Lake
Targhee National Forest
Bechler River
South Entrance Rd
Snake River
Grassy Lake Rd
John D Rockefeller Jr Memorial Parkway
Flagg Ranch
Teton National Forest
Grand Teton National Park
Colter Bay Village
Idaho
Jackson Lake
Jackson Lake Junction
Moran Junction
Mt Moran (12,770ft)
Signal Mountain (7593ft)
North-South Highway
Tetonia
Mt Owen (12,928ft)
Alaska Basin
Driggs
Grand Teton (13,770ft)
Moose Junction
Jackson Hole Airport
Kelly
Gros Ventre Rd
Victor
Teton Village
National Elk Refuge
Wilson
Jackson
Swan Valley
Rafter J Ranch
Bridger-Teton National Forest
Hoback Junction
INFORMATION
East Entrance 1 D3
Grand Teton Park Entrance (Moose) 2 B5
Grand Teton Park Entrance (Moran) 3 C5
North Entrance 4 B1
Northeast Entrance 5 D1
South Entrance 6 B4
West Entrance 7 A3
SIGHTS & ACTIVITIES
Artist Point 8 C2
Jackson Hole Mountain Resort 9 B6
Mud Volcano 10 C3
Old Faithful 11 B3
SLEEPING
Bridge Bay Campground 12 C3
Canyon Campground 13 C2
Canyon Lodge & Cabins 14 B2
Colter Bay Village 15 B5
Fishing Bridge RV Park 16 C3
Grant Village 17 B3
Grant Village Campground 18 B3
Gros Ventre Campground 19 B5
Jackson Lake Lodge 20 B5
Jenny Lake Campground 21 B5
Jenny Lake Lodge 22 B5
Lake Lodge Cabins (see 23)
Lake Yellowstone Hotel & Cabins 23 C3
Lizard Creek Campground 24 B4
Madison Campground 25 B3
Mammoth Hot Springs Hotel & Cabins 26 B2
Old Faithful Inn 27 B3
Old Faithful Lodge Cabins (see 27)
Old Faithful Snow Lodge & Cabins (see 27)
Roosevelt Lodge Cabins 28 C2
Signal Mountain Lodge 29 B5

picture – capture their reflection in the water at sunrise for something really unique.

Hikers can explore Yellowstone's backcountry from more than 85 trailheads that give access to 1200 miles of **hiking** trails. A free backcountry-use permit, available at visitor centers and ranger stations, is required for overnight trips. Backcountry camping is allowed in 300 designated sites, 60% of which can be reserved in advance by mail; a $20 fee applies regardless of the number of nights.

One of the best family hikes (and also a great mountain-bike ride) in the park, the Lone Star Geyser Trail is an easy 5-mile round-trip jaunt to the geyser of the same name, which pleases kids and adults alike with its watery burps every three hours. The trail is mostly flat and follows an old service road along the Firehole River through lodgepole pine forests. Look for the easily accessible trailhead 3.5 miles south east of the Old Faithful Inn at the Keplar Cascades parking area. If you've got a bike, the trail can be ridden – although you'll have to walk the very last bit to the geyser itself.

In Yellowstone's famed Canyon Country, check out the trail network off South Rim Road. The spidery web of interconnected trails winds like fingers through the spectacular, remote and wild canyon country. The Mary Mountain Trail is 21 miles each way and can be hiked in one strenuous day hike (you'll have to arrange transport from the end back to the start) from either direction, or as is more usual, in shorter stints (hike in three or four miles and hike back out the same way; the views are so stupendous, so seeing them twice is far from a bad thing). The trail climbs gradually up and over Mary Mountain and the park's central Nez Percé plateau. Please be aware that Mary Mountain trail crosses through grizzly territory – keep an eye-out for posted bear activity signs. The western trailhead is a few hundred feet north of the Nez Percé turnoff, the eastern start is 4 miles south of Canyon Junction north of Alum Creek. Other notable trails include the Seven Mile Hole Trail, which descends from the north rim into the canyon and tracks up Mt Washburn (10,243ft), the park's second-highest peak. Eagle Peak (11,358ft), just scraping by inside the park boundaries, is the highest mountain in Yellowstone.

Bicycling is best from April to October, when the roads are usually snow-free. Cyclists can ride on public roads and a few designated service roads, but not on the backcountry trails.

Most park trails are not groomed, but unplowed roads and trails are open for **cross-country skiing**. There is exhilarating white water through Yankee Jim Canyon on the Yellowstone River just north of the park boundary in Montana. **Yellowstone Raft Company** (☎ 800-858-7781; www.yellowstoneraft.com) offers a range of guided adventures out of Gardiner starting in late May.

Sleeping

NPS and private campgrounds, along with cabins, lodges and hotels, are all available in the park. Reservations are essential in summer. Contact the park concessionaire **Xanterra** (☎ 307-344-7311; www.travelyellowstone.com) to reserve a spot at its campsites, cabins or lodges.

Plentiful accommodations can also be found in the gateway towns of Cody (p792), Gardiner and West Yellowstone.

CAMPING

The best budget options are the seven NPS-run campgrounds (campsites $14) in Mammoth (open year-round), Roosevelt and Geyser Countries, which are first-come, first-served. Xanterra runs five campgrounds (reservations accepted, per night $18.50), all with cold-water bathrooms, flush toilets and drinking water. RV sites are also available.

Bridge Bay Campground (Lake Country) Near the west shore of Yellowstone Lake. There are 425 sites.

Canyon Campground (Canyon Country) Centrally located, with pay showers and coin laundry nearby. There are 250 sites.

Fishing Bridge RV Park (Lake Country) Full hook-ups for hard-shell RVs only ($35). Pay showers and coin laundry. There are 325 sites.

Grant Village Campground (Lake Country) On Yellowstone Lake's southwest shore. Pay showers and coin laundry nearby. There are 400 sites.

Madison Campground (Geyser Country) Generator-free, tent-only area. There are 250 sites.

CABINS & LODGES

Xanterra-run cabins, hotels and lodges are spread around the park and open from May or June to October. Mammoth Hot Springs Hotel and Old Faithful Snow Lodge are the exceptions; these lodges are also open mid-December through March. All places are nonsmoking and none have air con, TV or internet hookups.

WHERE THE BIG BEARS & BISON ROAM…

Along with the big mammals – grizzly, black bear, moose and lynx – Yellowstone is home to elk, pronghorn antelope and bighorn sheep. Despite some grumblings from worried farmers just outside park boundaries, wolves (see p124) and bison have been reintroduced into the national park with great success. Both species are native to the area, but by the end of the last century hunting and human habitation had sent their populations spiraling toward extinction. In the last decade, the numbers have once again risen, which has ecologists and rangers alike excited.

Hayden Valley, in Yellowstone's heart, is your best all-round bet for wildlife viewing. Check along the Yellowstone River between Yellowstone Lake and Canyon Village. For the best chances of seeing wildlife, get up early or stay out late (dawn and dusk are the best times to see the furry creatures). You can pull over anywhere off Grand Loop Rd and stage a stakeout. Have enough patience (and a pair of binoculars handy) and a bear just might wander into your viewfinder, or perhaps you'll spy a rutting elk or hear the bugle of a solitary moose before it dips its mighty head into the river for a drink.

Lamar Valley, in the north of the park, is ground zero for spotting wolves – it's where these magnificent beasts are being reintroduced. Ask rangers where the action is at the moment; at the time of research, wolves were often seen between Tower Junction and Yellowstone's northeast entrance. Catching even a fleeting glimpse of these wild and shaggy giant dogs, once almost gone forever, is a refreshing and magical experience that reminds us there are parks in the USA wild enough to just get lost looking for wolves and to take a poop with the bear in the wilderness.

Roosevelt Lodge Cabins (Roosevelt Country; cabins $68-113) These cabins are good for families. With a cowboy vibe, the place offers nightly 'Old West dinner cookouts.' Guests travel by horse or wagon to a large meadow 3 miles from the lodge for open-air buffets.

Lake Lodge Cabins (Lake Country; cabins $70-160) The main lodge boasts a large front porch with lakeside mountain views and a cozy great room with two fireplaces. Choose from rustic 1920s wooden cabins or more modern motel-style modules.

Old Faithful Snow Lodge & Cabins (Geyser Country; r $99-201) The newest sleeping option in the park is built to resemble a great Old Western lodge (think lots of timber). Wildlife-themed, the place tries to incorporate classic park motifs. Rooms are stylish and modern.

our pick **Old Faithful Inn** (Geyser Country; r $100-240) Built right next to the signature geyser, it's little surprise Old Faithful is the most requested lodging in the park. A national historic landmark, it embodies everything a national park lodge should. The immense timber lobby, with its huge stone fireplaces and sky-high knotted-pine ceilings, is the sort of place you'd imagine Teddy Roosevelt lingering. Rooms come in all price ranges, and the cheapest share baths (hint: stay two nights, enjoy the atmosphere and get your money's worth). Even if you're in one of the lovely 'premium rooms,' don't count on spending much time in it – the public areas are alluring enough that cabin fever is not an option!

Lake Yellowstone Hotel & Cabins (Lake Country; cabins $135, r $151-227) Oozing grand 1920s Western ambience, this historic hotel is a classy option. It has Yellowstone's most divine lounge, which was made for daydreaming; it offers big picture windows with lake views, lots of natural light and a live string quartet serenading in the background. Rooms are well appointed, cabins more rustic.

Grant Village (Lake Country; r $145-151) Near the southern edge of the park, it offers attractive motel-style rooms. Two nearby restaurants have fabulous lake views and provide easy access to sustenance.

Also recommended:

Old Faithful Lodge Cabins (Geyser Country; cabins $69-113) Views of Old Faithful; simple, rustic cabins.

Canyon Lodge & Cabins (Canyon Country; cabins $74-157, r $173) Clean and tidy in a central locale.

Mammoth Hot Springs Hotel & Cabins (Mammoth Country; cabins $79-222, r $90-450) Wide variety of sleeping options; elk are often seen grazing on the front lawn.

Eating

Snack bars, delis, burger counters and grocery stores are scattered around the park. In addition, most of the lodges offer breakfast buffets, salad bars, and lunches and dinners in formal dining rooms. Food, while not always exceptional, is quite good considering how many people the chef is cooking for, and not too overpriced for the exceptional views. The **Old Faithful Inn** (☎ 307-545-4999; lunch mains $7-10, dinner mains $17-30; 🕒 11:30am-2:30pm & 5-10pm) is our favorite restaurant. It has a more innovative menu, serving a selection of nouveau American West cuisine – think seasoned game meat paired with eclectic sauces.

Getting There & Away

The closest year-round airports are: Yellowstone Regional Airport (COD) in Cody (52 miles); Jackson Hole Airport (JAC) in Jackson (56 miles); Gallatin Field Airport (BZN) in Bozeman, MT (65 miles); and Idaho Falls Regional Airport (IDA) in Idaho Falls, ID (107 miles). The airport (WYS) in West Yellowstone, MT, is usually open June to September. It's often more affordable to fly into Salt Lake City, UT (390 miles), or Denver, CO (563 miles), then rent a car.

No public transportation exists to or within Yellowstone National Park.

GRAND TETON NATIONAL PARK

It's hard to stop gawking at the jagged granite spires of the Teton Range, the centerpiece of spectacular Grand Teton National Park, sitting directly south of Yellowstone. Twelve glacier-carved summits rise above 12,000ft, crowned by the singular Grand Teton (13,770ft). Less crowded than Yellowstone, Grand Teton has plenty of places to get lost in the tranquility of the mountains. Soak up the solitude and beauty on hiking trails winding through alpine meadows, past roaring streams and ending at a mirror lake, where the translucent water perfectly reflects the toothy smile of the jagged granite peaks above. Bear, elk and moose roam this 40-mile-long range; the chance of spotting wildlife is good.

ROCKY MOUNTAINS

Orientation

The park has two entrance stations: Moose (south), on Teton Park Rd west of Moose Junction; and Moran (east), on US 89/191/287 north of Moran Junction. The park is open year-round, although some roads and entrances close from around November to May 1, including part of Moose-Wilson Rd, restricting access to the park from Teton Village.

Information

Park entrance permits (hiker/vehicle $12/25) are valid for seven days for entry into both Yellowstone and Grand Teton National Parks. It's easy to stay in one park and explore the other in the same day.

Park Headquarters (☎ 307-739-3600; www.nps.gov/grte; 🕒 8am-7pm Jun-Aug, 8am-5pm rest of year) shares a building with **Moose Visitor Center** (☎ 307-739-3399, for backcountry permits 307-739-3309; Teton Park Rd; 🕒 8am-7pm Jun-Aug, 8am-5pm rest of year), half a mile west of Moose Junction.

Activities

First up: there's 200 miles of **hiking trails** here, and you can't really go wrong with any of them. So pick up a map at the visitor center, and take a hike. A free backcountry-use permit, also available at visitor centers, is required for overnight trips. If that's not your style, fine. Climb a mountain instead. The Tetons are known for excellent short-route **rock climbs** as well as classic longer routes to summits like Grant Teton, Mt Moran and Mt Owen. The **Jenny Lake Ranger Station** (☎ 307-739-3343; 🕒 8am-6pm Jun-Aug) is ground zero for climbing information. For instruction and guided climbs, contact **Exum Mountain Guides** (☎ 307-733-2297; www.exumguides.com).

Fishing is another draw. Several species of whitefish and cutthroat, lake and brown trout thrive in local rivers and lakes. Get a license at the Moose Village store, Signal Mountain Lodge or Colter Bay Marina.

Cross-country skiing and **snowshoeing** are the best ways to take advantage of park winters. Pick up a brochure detailing routes at Moose Visitor Center.

Sleeping

CAMPING

The **NPS** (☎ 800-628-9988) operates the park's five **campgrounds** (Bridge Bay, Canyon, Grant Village, Madison & Fishing Bridge RV Park; camp sites $12), all first-come, first-served. Demand for sites is high from early July to Labor Day. Most campgrounds fill by 11am (Jenny Lake fills much earlier; Gros Ventre rarely fills up). Colter Bay and Jenny Lake have tent-only sites reserved for backpackers and cyclists.

CABINS & LODGES

Most of the park's private lodges and cabins are run by ecofriendly **Grand Teton Lodge Company** (☎ 307-543-3100; www.gtlc.com). The park concessionaire pushes sustainable energy, water conservation and recycling – you'll see bins around the park. It's best to reserve ahead, as nearly everything is completely booked by early June. It's worth calling about last-minute cancellations, however. Each lodge features an activity desk.

Colter Bay Village (☎ 307-543-3100; www.gtlc.com; tent sites per person $7, cabins with shared bath $55, cabins $100-200; ⏰ Jun-Sep; 👪) A good family option with rustic one- and- two-bedroom cabins on the shores of Jackson Lake. Two restaurants, a marina and a grocery store complete the picture.

Signal Mountain Lodge (☎ 307-543-2831; www.signalmtnlodge.com; r $160-230, cabins $181-273; ⏰ May–mid-Oct) At the edge of Jackson Lake, this spectacularly located place offers cozy well-appointed cabins and rather posh rooms with stunning lake and mountain views.

Jackson Lake Lodge (☎ 307-543-3100; www.gtlc.com; r & cabins $210-320; ⏰ Jun-Sep; 📶 🏊) With its sky-high ceilings and 60ft picture windows showcasing perfect Teton views, the grand lobby is the centerpiece of this full-service resort featuring 365 cottage-style rooms perched on a bluff overlooking Jackson Lake. This is the most popular lodge in the park, and fills quickly; definitely reserve.

Jenny Lake Lodge (☎ 307-543-3100; www.gtlc.com; cabins incl full board $585; ⏰ Jun-Sep) In a gorgeous wooded locale, Jenny Lake Lodge is the Grand Teton's most exclusive lodging option. Digs are in 37 historic Western-styled cabins. Each is beautifully decorated with thick down comforters and handmade quilts. Rates include breakfast, a five-course dinner, horseback riding and mountain biking.

Eating

Several reasonably priced restaurants are in and around Colter Bay Village, Jackson Lake Lodge and Moose Junction. The lodges all have restaurants of some sort.

Pioneer Grill (☎ 307-543-1911; Jackson Lake Lodge; mains $7-15; ⏰ 7am-9pm; 👪) This 1950s-style soda fountain offers service at countertops that snake around the room in a serpentine. The food is nothing special – burgers and grilled cheese – but reasonably priced. Kids will love the ice-cream sundaes ($6).

Mural Room (☎ 307-543-1911; Jackson Lake Lodge; mains $15-40; ⏰ 7am-9pm) The butter comes shaped like a moose and the in-your-face Teton views justify the buffalo tenderloin's $36 price tag at the Jackson Lake Lodge's most upscale dining choice. The wine list is moderately priced; service is stellar.

Jenny Lake Lodge Dining Room (☎ 307-543-3352; breakfast dishes $19, lunch mains $10-30, dinner mains $60; ⏰ 7am-9pm) Dinner is an intimate five-course experience served in a quaint room. Breakfast is also a fixed-price affair – you can choose up to 10 items from the menu. The à la carte lunch is the best value (especially if you're mainly coming for the views). Dinner and breakfast reservations are required; jackets are suggested for men at dinner. The porch is perfect for cocktails. All these meals are included if you stay at this lodge (see Sleeping, left).

JACKSON

Jackson is as jet-setting as Wyoming gets. The handsome town – which many people incorrectly call Jackson Hole (the 'Hole' actually refers to the entire valley) – is set against a stellar Teton backdrop. It's the kind of place where cowboy meets couture, where moose, elk and bison cruise the valley floor and powder hounds swish down world-class ski slopes. The vibe is playful and slightly glam, but never pretentious. Wander into the Mangy Moose Saloon, packed with ski bums, tourists, hipsters, ranchers and even the occasional movie star, and you'll get the idea. Jackson buzzes year-round, and summer visitors can hike, bike, raft and roam to their heart's content.

Orientation & Information

Most of the area's amenities are concentrated in the town of Jackson. Teton Village, 12 miles northwest of Jackson, is home to the wintertime mecca of Jackson Hole Mountain Resort.

Jackson Hole Wyoming (www.jacksonholenet.com) A good website for information on the area.

Valley Bookstore (☎ 307-733-4533; 125 N Cache St) Superb selection of books and regional maps.

Visitor center (☎ 307-733-3316; www.jacksonhole chamber.com; 532 N Cache Dr; ⏰ 9am-5pm)

Sights

Downtown Jackson has a handful of **historic buildings** and, in summer, the **town square shoot-out** (admission free; 👪), which is a hokey tourist draw that takes place at 6:15pm Monday to Saturday. For more substance, visit the **National Elk Refuge** (☎ 307-733-9212; www.nation alelkrefuge.fws.gov; Hwy 89; admission free; ⏰ 8am-5pm Sep-May, 8am-7pm Jun-Aug), about 2 miles northeast of town via Elk Refuge Rd. It protects thousands of wapiti from November to March. A 45-minute **horse-drawn sleigh ride** (adult/child

$18/14; 10am-4pm mid-Dec–Mar) is a highlight of a winter visit to the refuge. The magical rides take you across sparkling-white frozen fields strewn with elk, and the photo opportunities are awesome.

Activities

One of the USA's top ski destinations, **Jackson Hole Mountain Resort** (307-733-2292; www.jacksonhole.com; lift ticket adult/child from $59/32), known as 'the Village,' boasts the USA's greatest continuous vertical rise – from the 6311ft base at Teton Village to the 10,450ft summit of Rendezvous Mountain. The terrain is mostly advanced, boasting lots of fluffy powder and rocky ledges made for jumping. When the snowmelts, the resort runs a plethora of summertime activities; check the website.

Sleeping

Jackson has plenty of lodging options, both in town and around the ski hill. Reservations are essential in summer and winter, when the place fills quickly.

Anvil Motel (307-733-3668; www.anvilmotel.com; 215 N Cache Dr; r $55-125;) Easily the best value in town, the Anvil offers queen rooms done up with a Western motif and equipped with fridges and microwaves in a super central location. The best perk is the available passes to the nearby rec center, which has an indoor pool, waterslide, hot tub, workout room and our personal favorite – the dry sauna.

Virginian Lodge (307-733-2792; www.virginianlodge.com; 750 W Broadway; winter/summer r from $120/200;) This cheerful place is another good-value motel. In winter, including ski season, rates drop dramatically.

Snake River Lodge (307-732-6000; www.snakeriverlodge.com; 7710 Granite Loop Rd; r $175-450;) In a gorgeous spot at the bottom of Jackson Hole Mountain Resort, Snake River has a beautiful pool, spa facilities and a fitness room with a view. Wooden walls, stone slab floors and big fireplaces create the vibe. Rooms are well stocked with down comforters, exposed wood-beamed ceilings and lots of other luxury trappings.

Eating & Drinking

Jackson is home to Wyoming's most sophisticated food. Many of our favorite restaurants here double as bars.

Bubba's Bar-B-Que (307-733-2288; 515 W Broadway Ave; mains $5-15; 7am-10pm) Get the biggest, fluffiest breakfast biscuits for miles at this friendly and energetic bring-your-own-bottle (BYOB) eatery. Later on, it's got a decent salad bar, and serves up a ranch of ribs and racks.

Snake River Brewing Co (307-739-2337; 265 S Millward St; mains $6-15; 11:30am-midnight;) Popular with the local ski crowd, Snake River's pub grub (think wood-fired pizza and juicy burgers) stands up well to the smooth homemade microbrews.

Rendezvous Bistro (307-739-1100; 380 S Broadway; mains $15-30; 5:30-10pm Mon-Sat) Locals love this bustling, unpretentious bistro that serves the best-value top-end food in town – from steak to lobster. Environs are intimate and smart, and the service excellent.

Mangy Moose Saloon (307-733-9779; Teton Village) This lively Jackson institution hosts a wide variety of live shows, from free local bands to big-name artists. A favorite après-ski spot, it attracts hordes of locals and tourists. It's an intimate venue where the stage is visible from two levels.

Million Dollar Cowboy Bar (307-733-2207; 25 N Cache Dr) There's no way you can miss the entrance to this town landmark – the neon sign is too big. It's kitschy West all right, but it is also pretty entertaining.

Getting There & Around

Jackson Hole Airport (JAC; 307-733-7682) is 7 miles north of Jackson off US 26/89/189/191 within Grand Teton National Park. Daily flights serve Denver, Salt Lake City, Dallas and Houston, while weekend flights connect Jackson with Chicago.

Alltrans' Jackson Hole Express (307-733-1719; www.jacksonholebus.com) buses depart at 6:30am daily from Jackson's Exxon Station (cnr Hwy 89 S and S Park Loop Rd) for Salt Lake City (around $65, 5½ hours).

MONTANA

Warning: Montana is addictive. There's nothing quite like that first Montana soul-soothing experience that words can't explain. Maybe it's the sky, which seems bigger and bluer here than anywhere else. Maybe it's the air, intoxicatingly crisp, fresh and scented with pine. Maybe it's the way the mountains melt into undulating grasslands, or the sight of a shaggy grizzly sipping from an ice-blue glacier lake.

Maybe it's the frontier spirit, wild and free and oh-so-wonderfully American, that earned Montana its 'live and let live' state motto. Whatever the cause, Montana's the kind of place that remains with you long after you've left its beautiful wilds behind.

Information

Montana Fish, Wildlife & Parks (☎ 406-444-2535; www.fwp.state.mt.us) Camping in Montana's 24 state parks costs between $12 and $15 per night, while RV hookup sites (where available) cost an additional $5. Reservations are not taken; all camping is first come, first served.

Montana Road Conditions (☎ 800-226-7623, within Montana 511; www.mdt.state.mt.us)

Travel Montana (☎ 800-847-4868; www.visitmt.com)

BOZEMAN

In a gorgeous locale, surrounded by rolling green hills and pine forests and framed by snowcapped peaks, dog-friendly Bozeman is the coolest town in Montana. The historic Main St district is retro cowboy funky with low brick buildings housing trendy boutiques, Bohemian wine bars and bustling sidewalk cafés serving global fare. The location, up against the Bridger Mountains, means there's plenty of outdoor activities to keep you busy. Bumped up against the Bridger Mountains, Bozeman is also blessed with plenty of outdoor adventure opportunities.

The **visitor center** (☎ 406-586-5421; www.bozemanchamber.com; 1003 N 7th Ave; 8am-5pm Mon-Fri) can provide information on lodging and attractions in the area.

Montana State University's **Museum of the Rockies** (☎ 406-994-2251; www.museumoftherockies.org; 600 W Kagy Blvd; adult/child $10/7; 8am-8pm;) is the most entertaining natural history museum in Montana, with dinosaur exhibits, early Native American art and laser shows.

Only in Montana would you find a nonprofit ski resort. But the excellent community-owned **Bridger Bowl Ski Area** (☎ 406-587-2111; www.bridgerbowl.com; 15795 Bridger Canyon Rd; day lift ticket adult/child under 12yr $45/16), 16 miles north of Bozeman, is just that. It's known for its fluffy, light powder and unbeatable prices – especially for children under 12.

Located in the same geothermal ecosystem as Yellowstone, the area around Bozeman is home to around a dozen of Montana's 61 hot springs. Soak away your aches and pains in the pools, sauna and steam-room at **Bozeman Hot Springs** (☎ 406-586-6492; admission $5; 8am-1pm Sun-Thu, 8am-midnight Fri & Sat), 8 miles west of town off US 191.

Sleeping

The full gamut of chain motels lies north of downtown on 7th Ave, near I-90. There are more options east of downtown on Main St. Depending on the season, rooms cost

IF YOU HAVE A FEW MORE DAYS

Wyoming is full of great places to get lost, sadly too many for us to elaborate on in this guide, but we'll prime you with a taster.

- **Bighorn Mountains** With vast grassy meadows, seas of wildflowers and peaceful conifer forests, the Bighorn Mountains in north-central Wyoming are truly awe-inspiring. Factor in gushing waterfalls and abundant wildlife and you've got a stupendous natural playground with hundreds of miles of marked trails.
- **Devil's Tower National Monument** Rising a dramatic 1267ft above the Belle Fourche River, this nearly vertical monolith is an awesome site. Known as Bears Lodge by some of the 20-plus Native American tribes who consider it sacred, it's a must-see if you are traveling between the Black Hills (on the Wyoming–South Dakota border) and the Tetons and Yellowstone.
- **Medicine Bow Mountains & Snowy Range** West of Laramie, the lofty national forest stretching across both mountain ranges is a wild and rugged place, perfect for multinight hiking and camping trips.
- **Sheridan** Nestled in the shadow of the Bighorn Mountains, Sheridan boasts century-old buildings, once home to Wyoming cattle barons, and is popular with adventure fanatics who come to play in the Bighorns.

between $35 and $65; some places have pools, others take pets.

Bear Canyon Campground (☎ 800-438-1575; www.bearcanyoncampground.com; tent/RV sites $21/29; 🕑 May-Oct; 🏊) Three miles east of Bozeman off I-90 exit 313, Bear Canyon Campground is on top of a hill with great views of the surrounding valley. There's even a pool.

Bozeman Backpackers Hostel (☎ 406-586-4659; www.bozemanbackpackershostel.com; 405 W Olive St; dm/d $20/42) In a beautiful yellow-painted Victorian house built in 1890 (trivia: it was once home to actor Gary Cooper when he attended school in town), this independent hostel's casual approach means a relaxed vibe, friendly folk and no lockout. It's *the* place to rendezvous with active globe-stompers.

Lewis & Clark Motel (☎ 406-586-3341; www.lewisandclarkmotel.net; 824 W Main St; r $75; ❄ 📶 🏊) For a drop of Vegas in your Montana, stay at this flashy motel with casino games and cold beers in the lobby. The large rooms have floor-to-ceiling front windows, and there's a 60ft-long indoor heated swimming pool, Jacuzzi and on-site sauna.

Eating & Drinking

As a college town, Bozeman has no shortage of student-oriented cheap eats and enough watering holes to quench an army's thirst. Nearly everything is located on Main St.

La Tinga (☎ 406-586-3341; 12 E Main St; mains $1.50-8; 🕑 11am-close) Simple and cheap, La Tinga is no-frills dining at its tastiest. The tiny order-at-the-counter taco joint makes a delicious version of the Mexican pork dish it is named after, and lots of freshly made tacos starting at just $1.50 (there's also a lunch combo deal for less than $7). No wonder one of Bozeman's newer restaurants is packed all the time.

Burger Bob's (☎ 406-585-0800; 39 W Main St; mains $5-10; 🕑 11:30am-9pm, to 10pm Fri & Sat) This Old West greasy spoon has been serving cold beer and loaded burgers long enough to be considered a Bozeman institution. The menu features dozens of burgers topped with pretty much everything, other sandwich staples and a mixture of domestic and small-batch beer on draft.

Plonk (☎ 406-587-2170; 29 E Main St; mains $10-30; 🕑 11:30am-10pm) Where to go for a drawn-out three-martini, gossipy lunch, Plonk serves an innovative nouveau American meets French bistro menu. Dishes look and taste great, and are made from local organic products when possible. In summer the entire front opens up, letting light and cool breezes enter the long building, which also has a shotgun bar and pressed-tin ceilings. The sidewalk seating in the sun is equally lovely.

John Bozeman's Bistro (☎ 406-388-1100; Belgrande, 27 E Main St; mains $10-30; 🕑 5-10pm) This local landmark with a fabulous wine list offers more sophistication than a typical Montana roadhouse. Located 8 miles west of town, the menu is meat-oriented with juicy steaks featured prominently. Sleek booths, old cowboy photos and a mounted longhorn head create the ambience. Those on a budget will appreciate the cheaper bar menu; vegetarians can chow down on a daily meatless plate.

Molly Brown (☎ 406-586-9903; S 8th St) Popular with students, this noisy dive bar offers 20 beers on tap and eight pool tables for getting your game on.

Zebra Cocktail Lounge (☎ 406-585-8851; 15 N Rouse St) Inside the Bozeman Hotel, this place is the epicenter of the local live music scene.

MONTANA FACTS

Nickname Treasure State

Population 967,440

Area 145,552 sq miles

Capital city Helena (population 30,000)

Other cities Billings (population 89,850), Missoula (100,000)

Sales tax Montana has no state sales tax

Birthplace of Hollywood movie star Gary Cooper (1901–61), legendary motorcycle daredevil Evel Knievel (1938–2007)

Famous for Big sky, fly-fishable rivers, snow, rodeos, bears

Random fact Some Montana highways didn't have a set speed limit until the 1990s!

Driving distances Bozeman to Denver 695 miles, Missoula to Whitefish 136 miles

Getting There & Away

Gallatin Field Airport (BZN; ☎ 406-388-6632) is 8 miles northwest of downtown. **Karst Stage** (☎ 406-388-2293; www.karststage.com) runs buses daily, December to April, from the airport to Big Sky (around $35, one hour) and West Yellowstone (around $50, two hours); summer service is by reservation only.

Greyhound buses depart from the **bus depot** (☎ 406-587-3110; 1205 E Main St), half a mile from downtown, and service all Montana towns along I-90.

TROUT FISHING IN MONTANA

Ever since Robert Redford and Brad Pitt made it look sexy in the 1992 classic, *A River Runs through It*, Montana's visitors have had a love affair with fly-fishing. For good reason. Montana has more miles of wild trout rivers than any other state in the lower 48. Whether you are just learning or a world-class trout wrangler, this land of big skies and wide, fast rivers is always spectacularly beautiful and filled with fish. FYI movie buffs: although the film – and book it is based on – is set in Missoula and the nearby Blackfoot River, the movie was actually shot around Bozeman and the fishing scenes filmed mostly on the Yellowstone and Gallatin Rivers. Which is the area we focus on here.

For DIY trout fishing, the Gallatin River, 8 miles west of Bozeman along Hwy 191, has the most accessible, consistent angling spots. Novices will have a field day on this river, as there are lots of wild rainbow and brown trout waiting to bite. The Yellowstone River, 25 miles east of Bozeman, is also full of trout, and truly is one of Montana's most beautiful fishing spots.

For the scoop on everything trout – as well as flies, rods and a Montana fishing license – visit the **Bozeman Angler** (☎ 406-587-9111; 23 E Main St; 🕑 9:30am-5:30pm Mon-Sat, 10am-3pm Sun). Owned by a local couple for more than a decade, the downtown shop runs a great introduction-to-fishing class. The day-long adventure teaches you the casting, lures and fish basics, feeds you, then sets you loose on the river (with a guide of course) to practice your newly minted skills. If you know what you're doing, but don't know where the best fishing holes are, contact the shop about a guided trip, which they'll customize to your experience and interest.

GALLATIN & PARADISE VALLEYS

Outdoor enthusiasts can explore the expansive beauty around the Gallatin River, running through the Gallatin and Paradise Valleys, for days. **Big Sky Resort** (☎ 800-548-4486; www.bigskyresort.com; lift ticket adult $78), with multiple mountains, 400in of annual powder and Montana's longest vertical drop (4350ft), is the valley's foremost destination for skiing. Lift tickets cost less here than at many Rocky Mountain resorts, and if you are traveling with kids then Big Sky is too good a deal to pass up – children under 10 ski free, while even your teenager saves $20 off the adult ticket price. In summer it offers gondola-served hiking and mountain biking. For backpacking and backcountry skiing, head to the **Lee Metcalf Wilderness Complex**. It covers 389 sq miles of Gallatin and Beaverhead National Forest land west of US 191. Numerous scenic USFS campgrounds snuggle up to the Gallatin Range on the east side of US 191.

Twenty miles south of Livingston, off US 89 en route to Yellowstone, unpretentious **Chico Hot Springs** (☎ 406-333-4933; www.chicohotsprings.com; r from $50-355; 🕑 8am-midnight; 📶) has garnered quite a following in the last few years – now attracting celebrity guests from Hollywood. They, along with many regular folks, come to this relaxed place to soak in the two suave open-air mineral pools (admission for nonguests $8.50). The larger pool is the perfect temperature for floating (93°F or 34°C); the smaller pool is hotter (103°F or 54°C), but still not too hot to stay in long enough for wrinkles. The lively bar hosts swinging country-and-western dance bands on weekends. The on-site restaurant (mains $20 to $30) is known for fine steak and seafood.

ABSAROKA BEARTOOTH WILDERNESS

The fabulous, vista-packed Absaroka Beartooth Wilderness covers more than 943,377 acres and is perfect for a solitary adventure. Thick forests, jagged peaks and marvelous, empty stretches of alpine tundra are all found in this wilderness, saddled between Paradise Valley in the west and Yellowstone National Park in the south. The thickly forested Absaroka Range dominates the area's west half and is most easily reached from Paradise Valley or the Boulder River Corridor. The Beartooth Range's jagged peaks are best reached from Hwy 78 and US 212 near Red Lodge. Because of its proximity to Yellowstone, the Beartooth portion gets two-thirds of the area's traffic.

A picturesque old mining town with fun bars and restaurants and a good range of places to stay, **Red Lodge** offers great day hikes, backpacking and, in winter, skiing right near town. The **Red Lodge Visitor Center** (☎ 406-446-1718; 601 N Broadway Ave; 🕑 9am-5pm Jun-Aug,

WORTH THE TRIP: LITTLE BIGHORN BATTLEFIELD

Ensconced within the boundless prairies and pine-covered hills of Montana's southwest plains, the Crow Indian Reservation is home to the **Little Bighorn Battlefield National Monument** (☎ 406-638-3224; admission per car $12; ⌚ 8am-6pm). One of the USA's best-known Native American battlefields, this is where General George Custer made his famous 'last stand.' Custer, and 272 soldiers, messed one too many times with Native Americans (including Crazy Horse of the Lakota Sioux), who overwhelmed the force in a frequently painted massacre. A visitor center tells the tale. The entrance is a mile east of I-90 on US 212.

9:30am-4:30pm Mon-Fri Sep-May) has accommodation information.

The awesome **Beartooth Highway** (US 212; ⌚ Jun–mid-Oct) connects Red Lodge to Cooke City and Yellowstone's north entrance by an incredible 68-mile journey that passes soaring peaks and wildflower-sprinkled tundra. There are five USFS campgrounds (reservations accepted) along the highway, within 12 miles of Red Lodge.

BILLINGS

It's hard to believe laid-back little Billings is Montana's largest city. The friendly oil and ranching center is not a must-see, but makes for a good overnight pit stop. The historic downtown, with squat brown buildings, wide streets, cozy cafés and interesting little knickknack shops, is hardly cosmopolitan, but emits a certain endearing charm.

Road-weary travelers will appreciate the convenient **Billings Hotel & Convention Center** (☎ 800-537-7286; www.billingshotel.net; 1223 Mullowney Lane; r from $85;). It has comfortable rooms, a restaurant and bar on the premises and best of all – especially if you're road-tripping with the little ones – two huge waterslides at the indoor pool!

Fuel up at the chipper **McCormick Cafe** (☎ 406-255-9555; 2419 Montana Ave; meals $4-7; ⌚ 7am-4pm Mon-Fri, 8am-3pm Sat;), where you can get a steaming cup of coffee and heaped plates of bacon and eggs. Soups, salads and pizza are served at lunch. It's a down-home no-frills dining experience.

Logan International Airport (BIL; ☎ 406-238-3420), 2 miles north of downtown, has direct flights to Salt Lake City, Denver, Minneapolis, Seattle, Phoenix and destinations within Montana. The **bus depot** (☎ 406-245-5116; 2502 1st Ave N; ⌚ 24hr) has services to Bozeman ($35, three hours) and Missoula ($60, eight hours).

HELENA

Luring politicians, outdoor enthusiasts and artists, Montana's state capital is an agreeable city at the foot of the Rockies with trendy galleries and interesting restaurants. During the week it's a bustling place where politicos and lobbyists pound out legislation. At weekends it becomes a veritable ghost town, as almost everyone seems to take to the mountains for a little playtime.

For information, visit the **Helena Visitor Center** (☎ 406-442-4120, 800-743-5362; www.helenachamber.com; 225 Cruse Ave; ⌚ 8am-5pm Mon-Fri).

Many of Helena's sites are free, including the neoclassical **state capitol** (☎ 406-444-4789; cnr Montana Ave & 6th St; ⌚ 8am-6pm Mon-Fri); the elegant old buildings along Last Chance Gulch (Helena's pedestrian shopping district); and the **Holter Museum of Art** (☎ 406-442-6400; www.holtermuseum.org; 12 E Lawrence St; ⌚ 10am-5pm Mon-Sat Jun-Aug, 11:30am-5pm Tue-Fri, noon-5pm Sat & Sun Sep-May), which exhibits modern pieces by Montana artists.

Nine **hiking** and **mountain-biking** trails wind through Mt Helena City Park, including one that takes you to the 5460ft-high summit of Mt Helena.

East of downtown near I-15 is a string of chain motels. Most rooms are $60 to $85, and come with free continental breakfast, pool and Jacuzzi.

The **Sanders** (☎ 406-442-3309; www.sandersbb.com; 328 N Ewing St; r incl/breakfast $130;) is an historic B&B with seven elegant guest rooms, a wonderful old parlor and a breezy front porch. Each bedroom is unique and thoughtfully decorated.

Fire Tower Coffee House (☎ 406-495-8840; 422 Last Chance Gulch; mains $7; ⌚ 7am-late;) is where to go for coffee, light meals and live music on Friday evening. The breakfast menu features a couple of different types of egg-based burritos, while lunch has a wholesome and interesting sandwich selection.

Two miles north of downtown, **Helena Regional Airport** (HNL; ☎ 406-442-2821; www.helenaairport.com) operates flights to most other air-

ROCKY MOUNTAINS

ports in Montana, as well as to Salt Lake City, Spokane and Minneapolis. Rimrock Stages leave from Helena's **bus depot** (☎ 406-442-5860; 3100 E Hwy 12), 7 miles east of town on US 12, where at least daily buses go to Missoula ($25, 2¼ hours), Billings ($42, 4¾ hours) and Bozeman ($22, two hours).

MISSOULA

Missoula is the kind of place where you can hike through a wilderness area, fly-fish a blue-ribbon stream and attend the symphony in a day. Montana's most culturally diverse city is an urban oasis in a pastoral wilderness. Sitting at the convergence of five valleys on the banks of the Clark River, there are seven different wilderness areas within 100 miles of here. Plus it's spittin' distance from three major rivers, it's filled with sophisticated restaurants and galleries and just down the road from a ski area with one of the country's steepest vertical drops. It's no wonder folks passionate about play are racing to relocate here. Home to the University of Montana, Missoula is also a college town, and the dreadlocked students, global import shops and dive bars around the university add extra buzz.

Information

Trail Head (☎ 406-543-6966; www.trailheadmontana.net; 110 E Pine St; ⌚ 9:30am-8pm Mon-Fri, 9am-6pm Sat, 11am-6pm Sun) Maps, abundant advice, camping and kayaking rental gear.

Visitor center (☎ 406-532-3250, 800-526-3465; www.missoulacvb.org; 1121 E Broadway; ⌚ 8am-5pm Mon-Fri)

Sights & Activities

Seven miles west of downtown, the **Smokejumper Visitor Center** (☎ 406-329-4900; W Broadway; admission free; ⌚ 10am-4pm Jun-Aug) is the active base for the heroic men and women who parachute into forests to combat raging wildfires. Its visitor center has thought-provoking audio and visual displays that do a great job illustrating the life of the Western firefighter.

One of the area's most accessible **hikes** is along the south side of Clark Fork from McCormick Park (west of the Orange St bridge) into Hellgate Canyon. At sunset join the steep pilgrimage from the football stadium to the 'M' on 5158ft Mt Sentinel for spectacular views.

Advanced skiers love **Snowbowl Ski Area** (☎ 406-549-9777; www.montanasnowbowl.com; lift ticket $35), 17 miles north of Missoula, for its 2600ft vertical drop – one of the steepest in the USA.

Montana and **fly-fishing** go together like peanut butter and jelly – this is where Montana's most famous movie, *A River Runs Through It*, was set (although it was filmed outside Bozeman, see p803) and the area around Missoula has some of the best angling in the state. Rock Creek, 21 miles east of Missoula, is a designated blue-ribbon trout stream and the area's best year-round fishing spot. Fishing with the kids? Try the child-friendly Beavertail Hill Pond east of Missoula on I-90 (take the Beavertail exit).

Sleeping & Eating

Most lodging is on Broadway between Van Buren and Orange Sts, within walking distance of the campus and downtown.

Campus Inn (☎ 406-549-5134; www.campusinnmissoula.com; 744 E Broadway; r from $85;) This solid-value place has spacious rooms with ample amenities. Some rooms are inside the main building; others are motel-style. There are two hot tubs.

Goldsmith's Bed & Breakfast (☎ 406-728-1585; www.goldsmithsinn.com; 809 E Front St; r from $130;) This delightful B&B, with comfy rooms, is a pebble's toss from the river. The outdoor deck overlooking the water is the perfect place to kick back with a good novel. Rooms are attractive, featuring Victorian furniture. Some come with private sitting rooms, fireplaces and reading nooks.

Bernice's Bakery (☎ 406-728-1358; 190 S 3rd St; mains $3-6; ⌚ 7am-midnight) Fabulous organic coffee and tea, sink-your-teeth-into-'em sweets and yummy breakfasts are all staples at this revered Missoula institution. Don't miss the homemade granola.

Depot (☎ 406-728-7007; 201 W Railroad Ave; mains $13-35; ⌚ 11:30am-9pm) The Depot has a reputation for consistently good steaks served in upscale cowboy contemporary environs. Grab a seat at the welcoming brick bar looking out onto the active rail line. The beef menu is almost as long as the wine list, but there are other options. For something cheesy and creamy, try the scallop-and-mushroom casserole, a house specialty.

Iron Horse Brewpub (☎ 406-728-8866; 501 N Higgins St; ⌚ 11:30am-late) It's undergone a multimillion-dollar expansion, and now includes a swank, smoke-free upstairs bar known as 501 (yes, you can still smoke in Montana bars), complete with a saltwater aquarium. Students flock to the outdoor patio to sip microbrews and chow down on American pub food.

Getting There & Around

Missoula County International Airport (MSO; ☎ 406-728-4381) is 5 miles west of Missoula on US 12 W.

Greyhound buses serve most of the state, and stop at the **depot** (☎ 406-549-2339; 1660 W Broadway), 1 mile west of town.

FLATHEAD LAKE

Thanks to picture-pretty bays and 128 miles of wooded shoreline, fish-filled Flathead Lake is one of Montana's most favored attractions. The **Flathead Lake Marine Trail** makes paddling from one access point to another a fun way to travel; two marine **campsites** (☎ 406-751-4577; tent sites from $10) are available. You can easily drive around the lake in four hours. Be sure to spend time lingering along the shores and stopping at roadside fruit stands.

On the Indian Reservation at the lake's south end, **Polson** (☎ visitor center 406-883-5969; www.polsonchamber.com; 4 2nd Ave E; 8am-4pm Mon-Fri, 9am-4pm Sat, 10am-3pm Sun Jun-Aug, 10am-2pm Sep-May Mon-Fri) is the region's biggest service center, with several gas stations, fast-food restaurants and motels.

The mind-boggling **Miracle of America Museum** (☎ 406-883- 6804; 58176 Hwy 93; adult/child $3/1; 8am-8pm Jun-Aug, 8:30am-5pm Mon-Sat, 1:30-5pm Sun Sep-May), located just 2 miles south of Polson, is worth seeing. At turns random and fascinating, it consists of 5 acres cluttered with the leftovers of American history. Wander past weird artifacts including the biggest buffalo (now stuffed) ever recorded in Montana.

At the opposite end of the lake, **Bigfork** (☎ visitor center 406-837-5888; www.bigfork.org; 8155 Hwy 35; 9am-5pm Jun-Aug, 10am-2pm Mon-Fri Sep-May) is an artsy village with good grub and funky shops.

Between Polson and Bigfork are lakefront campgrounds, summer camp–style resorts and, on the lake's east side, orchards festooned with plump cherries. In either town you can join a boat tour to visit **Wild Horse Island**, where wild mares and steeds roam. Watch for Flathead Nessie, who has been lurking around since the 1930s and is said to be a distant cousin of Scotland's Loch Ness Monster.

BOB MARSHALL WILDERNESS COMPLEX

Let's just say, if the state had a perfume, its essence would be bottled from the wilds around Bob Marshall. Running roughly from the southern boundary of Glacier National Park in the north to Rogers Pass (on Hwy 200) in the south, there are three designated wilderness areas within the complex. A medley of geology, plants and wildlife, Great Bear, Bob Marshall and Scapegoat are scintillating. National-forest lands girding the complex offer campgrounds, road access to trailheads and quieter country when 'the Bob' hosts hunters in fall. The core lands encompass 2344 sq miles, with 3200 miles of trails and sections that are a 40-mile slog from the nearest road.

Accessing the Bob Hwy 200 in the south just got a heck of a lot easier, thanks to a four-year renovation; the park service has opened rustic **Monture Guard Station Cabin** (cabins $60), on the Bob's perimeter, to the public. To reach it you'll need to drive 7 miles north of Ovando and snowshoe or hike the last mile to your private abodes at the edge of the gorgeous Lewis and Clark Range. Contact the forest service about reservations.

Other Bob access points include the Seeley-Swan Valley in the west, Hungry Horse Reservoir in the north and the Rocky Mountain Front in the east. The easiest (and busiest) access routes are from the Benchmark and Gibson Reservoir trailheads in the Rocky Mountain Front.

Trails generally start steep, reaching the wilderness boundary after around 7 miles. It takes another 10 miles or so to really get into the Bob's heart. Good day hikes run from all sides. Two USFS districts tend to the Bob:

Flathead National Forest Headquarters (☎ 406-758-5204; www.fs.fed.us/r1/flathead; 1935 3rd Ave E, Kalispell; 8am-4:30pm Mon-Fri)

Lewis & Clark National Forest Supervisors (☎ 406-791-7700; www.fs.fed.us/r1/lewisclark; 1101 15th St N, Great Falls; 8am-4:30pm Mon-Fri)

WHITEFISH

If you just think of Whitefish as the main gateway to Glacier National Park, you'll be missing out. This hip New West town – filled with cool boutiques and tasty restaurants, and sitting in the shadow of a great, largely undiscovered ski resort – is a destination in itself. The resort formerly known as Big Mountain, **Whitefish Mountain Resort** (☎ 406-862-2900;

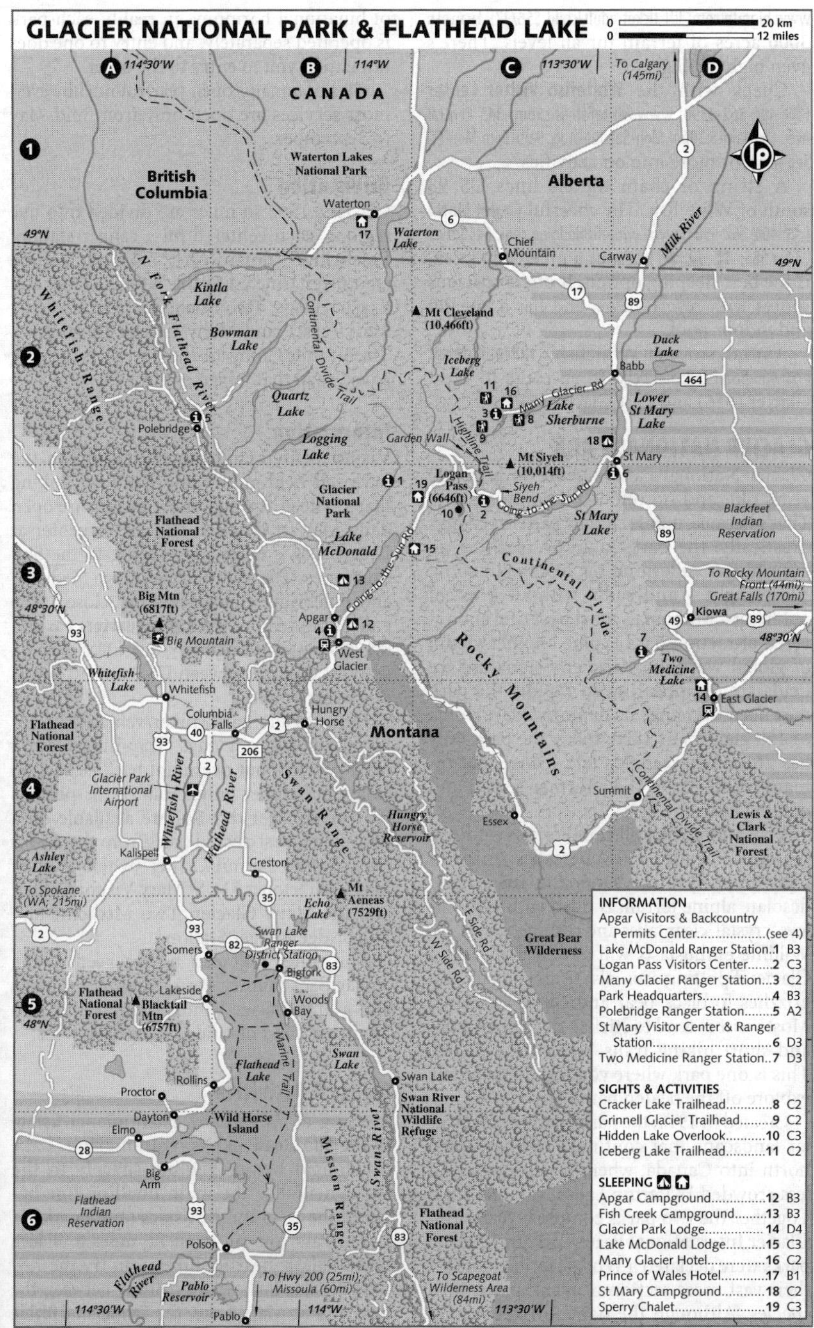
GLACIER NATIONAL PARK & FLATHEAD LAKE
0 20 km
0 12 miles
CANADA
British Columbia
Waterton Lakes National Park
Alberta
Waterton
Waterton Lake
Chief Mountain
Carway
Milk River
49°N
Kintla Lake
Bowman Lake
Quartz Lake
Logging Lake
Whitefish Range
N Fork Flathead River
Continental Divide Trail
Mt Cleveland (10,466ft)
Iceberg Lake
Duck Lake
Babb
Many Glacier Rd
Lake Sherburne
Lower St Mary Lake
Polebridge
Garden Wall
Highline Trail
Mt Siyeh (10,014ft)
St Mary
Logan Pass (6646ft)
Siyeh Bend
Going-to-the-Sun Rd
Glacier National Park
Flathead National Forest
Lake McDonald
St Mary Lake
Blackfeet Indian Reservation
Continental Divide
To Rocky Mountain Front (44mi); Great Falls (170mi)
Big Mtn (6817ft)
Big Mountain
48°30'N
Apgar
West Glacier
Kiowa
Rocky Mountains
Two Medicine Lake
East Glacier
Whitefish Lake
Whitefish
Columbia Falls
Hungry Horse
Montana
Glacier Park International Airport
Whitefish River
Flathead River
Swan Range
Hungry Horse Reservoir
Summit
Essex
Lewis & Clark National Forest
Ashley Lake
Kalispell
Creston
To Spokane (WA; 215mi)
Echo Lake
Mt Aeneas (7529ft)
E Side Rd
W Side Rd
Great Bear Wilderness
Swan Lake Ranger District Station
Somers
Bigfork
Lakeside
Woods Bay
Flathead National Forest
Blacktail Mtn (6757ft)
48°N
Flathead Lake
Rollins
Swan Lake
Proctor
Dayton
Wild Horse Island
Swan River National Wildlife Refuge
Elmo
Big Arm
Mission Range
Swan River
Flathead Indian Reservation
Polson
Flathead River
Pablo Reservoir
Pablo
To Hwy 200 (25mi); Missoula (60mi)
To Scapegoat Wilderness Area (84mi)
To Calgary (145mi)
114°30'W
114°W
113°30'W

INFORMATION
Apgar Visitors & Backcountry Permits Center (see 4)
Lake McDonald Ranger Station 1 B3
Logan Pass Visitors Center 2 C3
Many Glacier Ranger Station 3 C2
Park Headquarters 4 B3
Polebridge Ranger Station 5 A2
St Mary Visitor Center & Ranger Station 6 D3
Two Medicine Ranger Station 7 D3

SIGHTS & ACTIVITIES
Cracker Lake Trailhead 8 C2
Grinnell Glacier Trailhead 9 C2
Hidden Lake Overlook 10 C3
Iceberg Lake Trailhead 11 C2

SLEEPING
Apgar Campground 12 B3
Fish Creek Campground 13 B3
Glacier Park Lodge 14 D4
Lake McDonald Lodge 15 C3
Many Glacier Hotel 16 C2
Prince of Wales Hotel 17 B1
St Mary Campground 18 C2
Sperry Chalet 19 C3

www.bigmtn.com; lift ticket adult/child $56/27) boasts 3000 acres of terrain for all levels. There's even night skiing.

Check with the **Whitefish Visitor Center** (☎ 406-862-3390; www.whitefishvisit.com; 343 Central Ave; 9am-5:30pm Mon-Sat Jun-Aug, 9am-5pm Mon-Fri Sep-May) for more info on activities.

A string of chain motels lines US 93 south of Whitefish. The cheerful **Chalet Motel** (☎ 406-862-5581; www.whitefishlodging.com; 6430 Hwy 93 S; r $85;), about a mile from town, is the best sleeping option. It offers spacious rooms with resort views, and has a hot tub and indoor pool.

Amtrak stops at Whitefish's **railroad depot** (☎ 406-862-2268; 500 Depot St) en route to West Glacier ($16) and East Glacier ($32).

GLACIER NATIONAL PARK

Glacier National Park is about to turn 100 years old, and no one is planning a party. That's because unless climate patterns change drastically, the park could be reaching an even bigger milestone by 2030: extinction. Alarmingly – and sadly without a lot of publicity – Montana's most beautiful and revered attraction has become another victim of global warming. Glacier's signature ice fields are disappearing so rapidly the park may need to change its name by 2030. Home to 150 glaciers in 1850, today the park only has 26 named icefields left. Those that remain are shells of their former selves, and melting fast.

Visit while you still can. For now at least, the park's beauty still supersedes its seemingly doomed future. Dramatic, rugged and desolate alpine terrain is filled with lush valleys, crystal-clear lakes and rushing waterfalls. Wildlife enthusiasts will have a field day in Glacier. Spotting animals, from cougars and grizzlies to black bear and elk, is common. Most visitors tend to stick to developed areas and short hiking trails, which is a shame. This is one park where you should definitely explore off the beaten path.

Created in 1910, the park boasts a spectacular landscape that continues uninterrupted north into Canada, where it is protected in less crowded Waterton Lakes National Park. Together the two parks comprise Waterton-Glacier International Peace Park. In 1995 the parks were declared a World Heritage site for their vast cross section of plant and animal species. Although the name evokes images of binational harmony, in reality each park is operated separately, and entry to one does not entitle you to entry to the other.

Glacier remains open year-round; however, most services are open only from mid-May to September.

Orientation

Glacier's 1562 sq miles are divided into five regions, each centered on a ranger station: Polebridge (northwest); Lake McDonald (southwest), including the West Entrance and Apgar village; Two Medicine (southeast); St Mary (east); and Many Glacier (northeast). The 50-mile Going-to-the-Sun Rd is the only paved road that traverses the park.

Information

Visitor centers and ranger stations in the park sell field guides and hand out hiking maps. Those at Apgar and St Mary are open daily May to October; the visitor center at Logan Pass is open when Going-to-the-Sun Rd is open. The Many Glacier, Two Medicine and Polebridge Ranger Stations close at the end of September. **Park headquarters** (☎ 406-888-7800; www.nps.gov/glac; 8am-4:30pm Mon-Fri), in West Glacier between US 2 and Apgar, is open year-round.

Entry to the park (hiker/vehicle $12/25) is valid for seven days. Day-hikers don't need permits, but overnight backpackers do (May to October only). Half of the permits (per person per day $4) are available on a first-come, first-served basis from the Apgar Backcountry Permit Center (which is open May 1 to October 31), St Mary Visitor Center, and the Many Glacier, Two Medicine and Polebridge Ranger Stations.

The other half can be reserved at the Apgar Backcountry Permit Center, St Mary and Many Glacier Visitor Centers and Two Medicine and Polebridge Ranger Stations.

Sights & Activities

Starting at Apgar, the phenomenal **Going-to-the-Sun Road** skirts shimmering Lake McDonald before angling sharply to the Garden Wall – the main dividing line between the west and east sides of the park. At Logan Pass you can stroll 1.5 miles to **Hidden Lake Overlook**; heartier hikers can try the 7.5-mile **Highline Trail**. About halfway between the pass and St Mary Lake, the **Continental Divide**

WORTH THE TREK: ICEBERG LAKE HIKE

Considering the rate at which Glacier is losing its glaciers, it's now more important than ever to undertake the five- to six-hour 9-mile day **Iceberg Lake hike**, a classic favorite.

Enclosed by stunning 3000ft vertical headwalls on three sides, it's one of the most impressive glacial lakes in North America. The 1200ft ascent is gentle and the approach is mostly at or above the tree line, affording awesome views. Wildflower fiends will delight in the meadows around the lake.

Iceberg Lake was named in 1905 by George Grinnell, who saw icebergs calving from the glacier at the foot of the headwalls. The glacier is no longer active, but surface ice and avalanche debris still provide sizable flotillas of bergs as the lake melts in early summer. Scientists predict that if global climate-warming trends continue, all of the park's 50-some moving ice masses will be completely melted by 2030, so there's no better time than the present to see this ancient ice. The hike begins and ends at Iceberg Lake trailhead near the Many Glacier Ranger Station.

Trail crosses the road at Siyeh Bend, a good starting point for multiday hikes.

Busier routes include the 5-mile **Grinnell Glacier Trail**, which climbs 1600ft to the base of the park's most visible glacier, and the 6-mile **Cracker Lake Trail**, a 1400ft climb to some of the park's most dramatic scenery. For more solitude, try trails in the North Fork or Two Medicine areas. North of the Canadian border, the approaches to spectacular hikes are much shorter.

Glacier Park Boat Co (☎ 406-257-2426; www.glacierparkboats.com) rents out kayaks and canoes, and runs popular guided tours (adult/child $22/11) from five locations in Glacier National Park.

Sleeping

There are 13 **NPS campgrounds** (☎ 406-888-7800; http://reservations.nps.gov; camp sites $15) and seven historic lodges in the park, which operate between mid-May and the end of September. Of the sites, only Fish Creek and St Mary can be reserved in advance (up to five months). Sites fill by midmorning, particularly in July and August.

Glacier also has seven historic lodges from the early 1800s.

Lake McDonald Lodge (☎ 406-888-5431; www.lakemcdonaldlodge.com; Lake McDonald Valley; r from $120; 🕒 Jun-Sep; ⊠) Built in 1913, this old hunting lodge is adorned with stuffed-animal trophies and exudes relaxed ambience. The 100 rooms are in lodge-, chalet- or motel-style digs. Nightly park ranger talks and lake cruises are popular activities. There's an on-site restaurant and pizzeria.

Glacier Park Lodge (☎ 406-226-5600; www.glacierparkinc.com; East Glacier; r from $140; 🕒 late May–Sep; ⊠) The park's flagship lodge is a graceful, elegant place featuring interior balconies supported by Douglas fir timbers and a massive stone fireplace in the lobby. It's an aesthetically appealing, historically charming and very comfortable place to stay. Pluses include nine holes of golf and cozy reading nooks.

Many Glacier Hotel (☎ 406-732-4411; www.manyglacierhotel.com; Many Glacier Valley; r from $145; 🕒 mid-Jun–mid-Sep; ⊠) Modeled after a Swiss chalet, this national historic landmark on Swiftcurrent Lake is the park's largest hotel, with 208 rooms featuring panoramic views. Evening entertainment, a lounge and fine-dining restaurant specializing in fondue all add to the appeal.

Prince of Wales Hotel (☎ 403-859-2231; www.princeofwaleswaterton.com; Prince of Wales Rd, Waterton townsite, Waterton Lakes National Park; r from C$350; 🕒 mid-May–Sep; ⊠) On the Canadian side, the venerable Prince of Wales Hotel is a national historic site perched on a rise overlooking the lake. Though photogenic from a distance (we're talking cover-model material), up close the hotel looks smaller and much more genteel. Nevertheless, the views alone are worth the price.

Eating

In summer there are grocery stores with limited camping supplies in Apgar, Lake McDonald Lodge, Rising Sun and at the Swiftcurrent Motor Inn. Most lodges have on-site restaurants, although the quality of food varies.

Dining options in East or West Glacier are unexciting. If you can, head to Whitefish.

Getting There & Around

Amtrak's Empire Builder stops at East Glacier (Glacier Park Station) and West Glacier (Belton Station). **Glacier Park, Inc** (☎ 406-892-2525) runs shuttles over Going-to-the-Sun Rd, including the unreservable Hiker's Shuttle ($12 to $26), which originates in West Glacier or Many Glacier.

IDAHO

Once could argue that with more protected wilderness areas and national forest than any state except Alaska, the beguiling blue-green backcountry wonderland that is Idaho is the lower 48's last great wild place. Wedged into the space where the Pacific Northwest's lush, green curves and the Rocky Mountain's craggy glacier-capped peaks meet at the far western edge of the Mountain time zone, sunsets here seemingly last forever. Summer twilight stretches on toward 11pm, and even in winter Boise gets dark a full hour later than Denver.

Yet despite all the blue-ribbon trout fishing, extreme white-water rafting, first-class skiing (with a ritzy movie-star crowd to boot) and scenic drives galore, Idaho is left off most conventional Rocky Mountain road-trip itineraries. In fact, one could argue that this state, which gets more press for its potatoes, neo-Nazi groups and Bruce Willis ties than it does for ravishing natural beauty and boundless outdoor adventure options, is America's best-kept secret backcountry playground.

Information

Idaho Road Conditions (☎ 208-336-6600, within Idaho 888-432-7623)

Idaho State Parks & Recreation (☎ 208-334-4199; www.idahoparks.org) Camping in Idaho state parks costs between $9 (for a primitive, no facilities, tent site) and $22 (full-service campground with RV hookups). There are also cabins and yurts available for rent in some parks. Reservations for campsites, cabins and yurts in all parks can be made online or over the phone (☎ 888-922-6743).

Idaho Tourist Information (☎ 800-635-7820; www.visitid.org)

IDAHO FACTS

Nickname Gem State
Population 1.5 million
Area 82,747 sq miles
Capital city Boise (population 198,650)
Sales tax 6%, plus up to 3% city tax
Birthplace of Sacagawea (1787–1812), Shoshone woman who guided the Lewis and Clark expedition; Gutzon Borglum (1867–1941), sculptor of Mt Rushmore; Picabo Street (b 1971), Olympic skiing medalist
Home of Bruce Willis, Demi Moore, Ashton Kutcher
Famous for Spuds (potatoes), wilderness, white water, hunting
Movie trivia The smash indie flick *Napoleon Dynamite* was set and filmed in eastern Idaho
Driving distances Boise to Boulder 890 miles, Sun Valley to Los Angeles 981 miles

BOISE

Boise is positively buzzing these days. Not only is it Idaho's largest city and capital, it's also young, hip and fun. With an outdoors slant and hippie-trendy vibe, this city boasts a mixture of Basque and Western architecture where the desert meets the mountains. It's a lively town, where cafés and restaurants stay open late, and crowds from nightspots spill onto the streets on hot summer nights. Locals consider Boise a gay-friendly city, and it has an active gay and lesbian community. And in recent years more than a few magazines have named it as one of America's top places to live.

Orientation & Information

Delve into the main business district, bounded by State, Grove, 4th and 9th Sts. Restaurants and nightspots are found downtown in the brick-lined pedestrian plaza of the Grove, the gentrified former warehouse district between 8th St and Idaho Ave.

WORTH THE TREK: SPERRY CHALET

It's worth trekking nearly 7 miles one way to sleep at the 17-room **Sperry Chalet** (☎ 888-345-2649; www.sperrychalet.com; s/d incl meals $170/285; ⌚ Jul 7–Sep 8) for the views alone. This is the heart of the high country, where wildflower-strewn meadows, jagged peaks and babbling brooks make the place feel like nirvana. Factor in a chance to sleep away from it all in a rustic Swiss-style chalet (which just happens to serve hot meals) on the edge of a ridge staring down at Lake McDonald, and the deal gets even sweeter. Rates include meals, and you can hire a mule to carry your gear for an extra $130 – check out www.mule-shoe.com for reservations.

Stop by the **visitor center** (☎ 208-344-5338, 800-635-5240; www.boise.org; 850 Front St; 🕒 10am-5pm Mon-Fri, 10am-2pm Sat Jun-Aug, 9am-4pm Mon-Fri Sep-May).

Sights & Activities

Boise has the largest population of Basque descendants outside Europe's Basque country. Along Grove St between 6th St and Capitol Blvd, the Basque Block has sites commemorating early Basque pioneers.

Boise is bursting with outdoor adventures, from hiking to skiing to swimming. In the foothills above town, hit the **Ridge to Rivers Trail System** (www.ridgetorivers.org), offering 75 miles of scenic to strenuous hiking and mountain-biking routes.

In summer everyone loves to float down the Boise River. Rent tubes or rafts at **Barber Park** (☎ 208-343-6564; Warm Spring Rd; tube rental $8) and float 5 miles downstream. A shuttle bus ($5) runs from the take-out point.

Festivals & Events

Boise River Festival (☎ 208-338-8887; www.boiseriverfestival.org) Parades, sporty fun and lots for kids; held the last weekend in June.

Snake River Stampede (☎ 208-466-8497; www.snakeriverstampede.com) Action-packed pro rodeo in Nampa; held late July.

Art in the Park (☎ 208-345-8330) Outdoor art fest held the weekend after Labor Day.

Sleeping

Hostel Boise (☎ 208-467-6858; 17322 Canada Rd, Nampa; www.hostelboise.com; dm/s/d $20/35/45; 💻 📶 🚸) This country hostel just outside town has dorms with a maximum of four beds, as well as private rooms. There's a BBQ on the back patio, and lots of yard space for lying around and digesting after grilling up those tasty Boca Burgers. Lifts from the airport cost $10 each way, and advance notice is required.

Hotel 43 (☎ 800-243-4622; www.hotel43.com; 981 Grove St; r $85-270; ❄ 📶) Named after the latitude (Boise sits on the 43rd parallel) and in honor of Idaho being the 43rd state, this is an urban cozy boutique hotel in the heart of downtown. The 112 rooms and suites are artfully laid out and feature views of the state capitol and surrounding foothills. The swanky on-site Chandlers Restaurant and Martini Bar (mains from $15) is one of Boise's most popular watering and eating holes.

Grove Hotel (☎ 208-333-8000; www.grovehotelboise.com; 245 S Capital Blvd; r from $125; ❄ 📶 🏊) Its outside looks bland, but Boise's only four-star hotel feels more than classy inside. The European-influenced decor features cherry-paneled walls, warm tones and neoclassical chandeliers. With cocktail lounges, restaurants and cozy public areas, this is one of Boise's best bets for upscale accommodations.

Eating & Drinking

Eat your way around the globe on one block. Most of Boise's bars and restaurants are found along N 8th St between Idaho and Grove Sts. Offerings include everything from French to Greek and Mexican. Have a wander. There are many more good options than we have room to print.

Piehole (☎ 208-344-7783; 205 N 8th St; pizza slices from $1.85; 🕒 11am-late; 📶) For cheap pizza by the slice and an ice-cold Pabst, you can't beat this Boise dive. There are four loaded pizza slice specials each day (along with the usual assortment of made-to-order pies). These rotate, but always include unique topping combos.

Bittercreek Ale House & Red Feather Lounge (☎ 208-345-1813; 246 N 8th St; mains $7-15; 🕒 11:30am-late) These adjoining restaurants (owned by the same people) have lively sidewalk patios, intimate environs and lots of personality. They also serve wholesome, usually locally produced food with an emphasis on sustainable growth. The nouveau American menu at Bittercreek features a good selection of vegetarian options (it does organic Idaho black bean burgers on request). Order one of the whiskey cocktails made using an old-fashioned preprohibition-era recipe. Try the bourbon sour with lemon, whiskey, egg whites and sugar (c 1860). The Red Feather is slightly more upscale, and does delicious wood-oven pizza and a set three-course menu for two (per person $23).

our pick **8th Street Wine Co** (☎ 208-426-9463; 405 S 8th St; mains $8-15; 🕒 11am-11pm) This trendy BoDo warehouse wine bar is gaining national attention – *Food & Wine Magazine* recently called it one of America's best wine experiences. There are more than 1000 bottles to choose from, including 50 by the glass. Along with wine, there are microbrews, sweet cocktails and delicious food in light and airy environs.

Bardenay (☎ 208-426-0538; 610 Grove St) One of Boise's most unique watering holes, Bardenay was the USA's very first 'distillery-pub,' and remains a one-of-a-kind. Today it serves its own home-brewed vodka, rum and gin in casual, airy environs. It gets consistently good reviews.

Getting There & Around

Boise Municipal Airport (BOI; ☎ 208-383-3110; I-84 exit 53) has daily flights to Denver, Las Vegas, Phoenix, Portland, Salt Lake City, Seattle and Spokane. Greyhound services depart from the **bus station** (☎ 208-343-3681; 1212 W Bannock St). **Boise Urban Stages** (BUS; ☎ 208-336-1010) operates local buses, including an airport route (bus 13).

KETCHUM & SUN VALLEY

In one of Idaho's most stunning natural locations, Ketchum sits inside a volcanic crater surrounded by igneous rocks resembling ashy rippled potato chips that stick straight up from the valley floor. The town's stunning scenery is only the icing on the cake. Thanks to the highly rated Sun Valley ski resort just 1 mile away, little Ketchum is also Idaho's most popular destination. A longtime favorite with high rollers, Sun Valley frequently takes top honors as one of the best ski resorts in the USA. Trophy homes of the truly rich and famous dot the hilltops, and it's not uncommon to see a shining Hollywood face cruising down a slope.

Despite the swank appeal, Ketchum feels polished rather than pretentious. Easy on the eyes and heart, it's more like the au naturel girl next door than the perfectly coiffed, big-city diva. The quaint downtown is meticulously maintained, and a delightful place to stroll – filled with organic juice shops, wonderful bookstores and unique shops.

Orientation & Information

Main St between 1st and 5th Sts is where you'll find nearly all the businesses. The turnoff for Sun Valley is at the north end of town. Twelve miles south of Ketchum, also on Hwy 75, is Hailey, another small town. This is where most of the seasonal workers and many locals live. It has a lively bar scene.

For info, try the **Sun Valley/Ketchum Visitors Center** (☎ 208-726-3423, 866-305-0408; www.visitsunvalley.com; 411 Main St; 9am-6pm).

Activities

Famous for its light, fluffy powder and celebrity guests, **Sun Valley Resort** (☎ 800-786-8259; www.sunvalley.com) is comprised of advanced-terrain **Bald Mountain** (lift ticket $55-80) and easier-on-the-nerves **Dollar Mountain** (lift ticket adult $32-38, child $16-30). The USA's first destination ski resort, built by Averell Horriman, chairman of the Union Pacific railroad, Sun Valley has been a success from the day it opened in 1936. Dollar Mountain also has a **tubing hill** (adult/child $10/5). In summer, take the chairlift to the top of either mountain, and hike or cycle down. There are numerous other **hiking** and **mountain biking** trails around Ketchum and Sun Valley, as well as excellent **fishing** spots.

> **STARS IN YOUR EYES**
>
> Nobel Prize–winning author (and avid sportsman) Ernest Hemingway (1899–1961) was a frequent visitor to Sun Valley, and spent his last years in Ketchum, where he's buried. Nearby Hailey is half-owned, and partially lived in, by Bruce Willis and assorted family members.

Sleeping

Lift Tower Lodge (☎ 208-726-5163; 703 S Main St; r $65-100) This friendly small motel in downtown Ketchum offers free continental breakfasts and a hot tub. It sits next to a landmark exhibition chairlift c 1939 and is the best budget bet in town.

Tamarack Lodge (☎ 208-726-3344; www.tamaracksunvalley.com; 500 E Sun Valley Rd; r $120) Tasteful rooms complete with fireplace, balcony and many amenities are offered at this well-maintained lodge. The Jacuzzi and indoor pool are definite assets. Discounts are often available midweek and off-season.

Sun Valley Lodge (☎ 208-622-2001; 1 Sun Valley Rd; r from $150) Hemingway completed *For Whom the Bell Tolls* here, and although the place is fading slightly from its original luxurious sheen, it still remains one of the most popular top-end hotels, getting good marks for its old-fashioned elegance. Rooms are comfortable, although some are a tad cramped. Amenities include a fitness facility, game room, bowling alley and sauna. It runs a ski shuttle and has a children's program.

Eating & Drinking

Rickshaw (☎ 208-726-8481; 460 Washington Ave N; small plates & mains $5-12; 5:30-10pm Tue-Sat, 11:30am-2pm Fri) This supercool painted shack just off Main St does delicious tapas. The menu is Asian fusion – creative, fresh small plates inspired by the cuisine of Vietnam, Thailand, China and Indonesia, which the chef refers to as 'Asian

ROCKY MOUNTAINS

street food.' Be careful how much you order. Most portions are small, and it's easy to spend a fortune before you feel stuffed. The exception is the special Friday lunch menu, when full meals cost less than $10.

Desperado's (☎ 208-726-3068; 211 4th St; mains $7-10; 🕑 11:30am-10pm Mon-Sat) Despo's is a bright, busy and colorful eatery specializing in reasonably priced Mexican food. Fill up on burritos, chimichangas and tacos; wash them down with a margarita.

Ketchum Grill (☎ 208-726-4660; 520 East Ave; mains $10-20; 🕑 5:30pm-close) A local favorite, Ketchum Grill boasts a creative menu bursting with fresh fare. The elegant offerings include lots of seafood, along with plenty of veggie options.

Whiskey Jacques (☎ 208-726-5297; 251 Main St; cover up to $5; 🕑 4pm-2am) Sun Valley's top nightspot is purported to have been one of Ernest Hemingway's favorite watering holes. A rustic, Old West saloon-style spot, it's where to go for smooth cocktails, a game of pool, dancing and live music.

Getting There & Around

The region's airport **Friedman Memorial Airport** (☎ 208-788-4956) in Hailey, 12 miles south of Ketchum. **A-1 Taxi** (☎ 208-726-9351) offers rides to the airport from Ketchum ($22).

Ketchum Area Rapid Transit (KART; ☎ 208-726-7576; 🕑 8am-6pm Mon-Fri) operates free daily bus service between Ketchum and Sun Valley.

HWY 75: KETCHUM TO STANLEY

Following the Salmon River, Hwy 75 north from Ketchum to Stanley is part of the nationally designated **Sawtooth Scenic Byway**. The 60-mile drive is gorgeous, winding through a misty, thick ponderosa pine forest – where the air is crisp and fresh and smells like rain and nuts – before ascending the 8701ft **Galena Summit**. From the overlook at the top, there are views of the glacially carved Sawtooth Mountains, part of the 1180-sq-mile **Sawtooth National Recreation Area** (☎ 208-727-5000; Hwy 75; 🕑 8am-4:30pm Sep-May, to 5pm Jun-Aug). It is home to 40 peaks over 10,000ft, over 300 high-alpine lakes, 100 miles of streams and 750 miles of trails.

STANLEY

Tiny Stanley (population 100) just might be the most scenic small town in America. Surrounded entirely by protected wilderness and national-forest land, the remote outpost is nestled into the crook of Salmon River, miles from anywhere. It's the kind of place where peaceful high summer twilight stretches on past 10pm, and you fall asleep to the river's melodic roar.

The US Department of Transportation thinks as highly of Stanley's beauty too. When deciding which of the country's two-lane highways were worthy of earning national scenic byway status, all three roads into Stanley made the cut (it's the only place in the USA where this happens). Considering there are only 125 such roads in the country, it means 2.4% of American's prettiest pavement runs through bucolic Stanley.

Activities

There is epic trout fishing on the Salmon and in surrounding mountain lakes from March until November, with late June to early October the best time for dry-fly fishing. **Sawtooth Fishing Guides** (☎ 208-774-TROUT; www.sawtoothfishingguides.com) does custom trips to remote river spots only accessible via drift

ROCKY MOUNTAINS

SOMETHING DIFFERENT – GETTING JUICED ON BOOKS

For something different, pay a visit to **Chapter One Bookstore** (☎ 208-726-5425; 160 N Main St), which has been delighting locals and tourists with its wide selection of books – including out-of-print titles – for more than 30 years. Check out the special fiction section dedicated to books about or by authors from Idaho and the Pacific Northwest. It also features lots of spirituality and wellness titles. When you've finished browsing, head to **Ashaka Organics**, the old-school hippie juice bar in the back of the store, for a revitalizing smoothie. The fruit, root and spice concoctions are delightfully refreshing and meant to fuel everything from mental awareness to immunity. Ask for a potion that fits how you feel – we loved the citrus blast ($6.50, and worth every penny). The small café, stocked with herbs and tinctures, also does a limited menu of organic veggie sandwiches, pizza and something called an 'energy ball.' The latter tastes like a fibrous, coconut-flavored doughnut hole, but is surprisingly delicious and provided the promised energy boost.

boat or float tube. There are no less than eight species of trout in these waters, including the mythical Steelhead. Measuring up to 40in, these fish swim east about 900 miles from the Pacific Ocean at the end of winter, arriving near Stanley in March and April.

Stanley is the jumping-off point for rafting the legendary Middle Fork of the Salmon (see the boxed text, opposite). For more affordable, albeit slightly less dramatic, white-water action, do a **DIY float trip** down the Main Fork of the Salmon. There's 8 miles of quiet water starting in Stanley, with views of the Sawtooth Mountains you can't see from the road. Bring fishing gear. Float trips in inflatable kayaks (from $25) or inner tubes ($7) can be arranged through the Riverside Motel (see below), which also runs a shuttle service from the take-out ($20 per load).

Sleeping & Eating

There are about half a dozen hotels in Stanley, all done in traditional pioneer log-cabin style. During the short summer season (June to September) a couple of restaurants open up. There is a grocery and liquor store at the junction of Hwys 75 and 21.

our pick **Riverside Motel** (☎ 208-774-3409; www.riversidemotel.biz; Hwy 75; r & cabins $95-145; ⊠ ⊞ ᯤ) Oh the views… Perfectly perched above the Salmon, this family-run log cabin motel features well-appointed rooms with kitchenettes; pay extra for one of the eight with a river view. These have awesome private decks overlooking the rushing Salmon – grab a couple of cold beers and sit on yours long enough, and you'll surely reach a hypnotic state. The stripped-pine beds are ultra comfy, kitted out with nonscratchy linens and a big stuffed animal of some species for lights-out cuddles.

Bridge St Grill (☎ 208-774-2208; Hwy 75, Lower Stanley; 🕑 11:30am-close Jun-Aug) Right on the river, this is one of only a very few dining options in Stanley, and locals swear it's the best. Only open during the summer, Bridge St manages to serve tasty steaks, seafood, burgers and cold beer to a packed house nightly. Don't expect fast service. It's not that kind of place. Look for it about 1 mile north of Stanley proper.

HWY 21: STANLEY TO BOISE

The **Ponderosa Pine Scenic Byway** (Hwy 21) between Stanley and Boise is so beautiful, it's hard to reach your destination – you'll want to stop so much. From Stanley, the trees increase in density, until you find yourself enveloped in a sweetly scented cloak of pine. The look is different from the rest of the region, more Pacific Northwest than classic Rockies. Blue skies and wide open spaces are replaced with opaque grey skies. Fast-moving clouds bring frequent bursts of rain and the roadway can feel dangerous, its sides strewn with near-missed fallen boulders and giant logs. Mountains peak out of the thick fog cloak, and even in late May the snowfields stretch right down to the highway.

There are a number of designated camping areas along this byway. The primitive **Kikham Creek Hot Springs** (self-pay campsites $16), 6 miles east of Lowman, is our favorite. It's set by one of this geothermal region's natural hot springs, this one boiling out of the creek. Seeing the hot springs through a veil of summer rain, when the mist rises off the silver water, is magical. Stepping into the soothing heat is even better.

The **Southfork Lodge** (☎ 208-259-3871; www.southforklodge.biz; 7236 Hwy 21; r & cabins $89-125; ᯤ ♿) on Lowman's western edge is a good choice if you want to sleep near the hot springs, but aren't game to sacrifice the comforts of pillowtop mattress slumber. The nine rooms are spotless and quiet. Horseback riding can be arranged, and nearby Clear Creek has excellent fly-fishing. The restaurant (mains $6 to $25) has riverside patio seating, and kids will dig the ice-cream shop. Pets can stay for $10.

From Lowman the road follows a series of switchbacks up and over Mores Creek Pass before sliding into **Idaho City**. Once a rip-roaring 1860s gold-mining town, today

DON'T MISS

A one-hour drive southeast of Ketchum, **Craters of the Moon National Monument** (☎ 208-527-3257; vehicle/hiker or cyclist $4/2, 🕑 8am-4:30pm Sep-May, to 6pm Jun-Aug) is an 83-sq-mile volcanic showcase. Lava flows and tubes and cinder cones are found along the 7-mile **Crater Loop Rd**, accessible by car or bicycle from April to November. In winter it's popular with skiers and snowshoers. Short trails lead from Crater Loop Rd to crater edges, onto cinder cones and into tunnels and lava caves. A surreal **campground** (campsites $10) near the entrance station has running water only in summer.

FEEL THE RUSH: RAFTING THE MIDDLE FORK OF THE SALMON

From the first stomach-churning drop, a trip down the **Salmon's Middle Fork** is a river rat's wet dream. Averaging a 28ft descent per mile, the Middle Fork is considered one of the world's most exhilarating white-water trips (billed the 'last wild river,' it is part of the longest undammed river system outside Alaska). The 106-mile canyon boasts 300 rapids (from mild Class II rollers to raging Class IV+ waterfalls) and a 3000ft vertical descent. The action starts at the Boundary Creek put-in, just north of Stanley. From here, the Middle Fork worms through a deep canyon into the primeval heart of the majestic 2.4-million-acre Frank Church/River of No Return Wilderness Area. By the time you are a day into the journey, you'll be deep in a canyon, more than 100 miles from any type of road. Life stays this way until the river empties into the Main Fork of the Salmon at the end of the six-day adventure.

Trips aren't just about white water. Hikes to well-preserved art sites, fishing for native cutthroat and rainbow trout in gin-clear riffles, and just sitting back and soaking a white-water pummeled body in a bubbling riverside hot spring, are all part of the experience. Camping in a canyon a hundred miles from anywhere can prove nearly as thrilling as running the roller-coaster rapids. Even if you're not used to roughing it, there's something alluring about falling asleep to the roar of the river under a blanket of bright stars.

The Middle Fork is run between June and September. Early season (early to mid-June) features peak snowmelt and the season's most thrilling (though chilly) white water. **Solitaire River Trips** (☎ 800-396-1776; www.rivertrips.com; Mountain Village Lodge, Hwy 21, Stanley), owned by Al and Jeana Burkowsky (one or both always accompany all guests on trips), is one established outlet running trips down the Middle Fork. It gets consistently good reviews. Trips start and end at the Mountain Village Lodge, at the junction of Hwys 21 and 75, in Stanley. All-inclusive rates (including transport) start at around $1800 per person (six days).

If you know how to run rivers, the cheaper way to raft the Middle Fork is to **do it yourself**. You'll need to arrange the necessary river permit, but you need not worry about having gear. The Riverside Motel (see Sleeping & Eating, opposite) in Stanley rents out 13ft self-bailer rafts, including life jackets, oars, repair kit, dry bags, rope and even a cooler, for $425 per week.

it's less rowdy, but still a trip to visit. Pause for a photo in front of the pest house and county jail. In 1867 they were housed in the same dark timber and corrugated-tin roof building. Around the block is the most insane piece of Americana property we've ever laid eyes on. Covered from top to bottom with old signs, toilet seats and other random junk, the private residence can be viewed from the outside only, but should not be missed. To truly understand, we challenge you to visit.

The **Idaho City Visitor Center** (☎ 208-392-4159; www.idahocitychamber.com) has the scoop on the half-dozen restaurants and saloons in town. From Idaho City the pine slopes gently ease into rolling green hills covered in sage. From here it's less than 40 miles to Boise (p810).

HELLS CANYON NATIONAL RECREATION AREA

Plunging down 8913ft from Mt Oore's He Devil Peak on the east rim to the Snake River at Granite Creek, awe-inspiring Hells Canyon is North America's deepest gorge – thousands of feet deeper than the Grand Canyon. The remote 652,488-acre Hells Canyon National Recreation Area is one of the state's premier natural attractions, a must-see on any Idaho itinerary. Fishing, swimming, camping and dramatic views of the gorge and surrounding mountains are just a few of the highlights. The **Snake National Wild & Scenic River** winds through the canyon and is a favorite spot for rafting and jet boat trips. Nearly 900 miles of **hiking** trails traipse by riverbanks, past mountain peaks and along canyon walls decorated with ancient petroglyphs. Wildflowers color area meadows, and much wildlife resides here.

The Hells Canyon NRA spans the Idaho–Oregon state line, but the Oregon section is not readily accessible from Idaho. US 95 parallels its eastern boundary; a few unpaved roads lead from US 95 between the tiny towns of Riggins (a big rafting center) and White Bird into the NRA. Only one road leads from US 95 to the Snake River itself, at Pittsburg Landing.

Hells Canyon NRA Riggins (☎ 208-628-3916; 8am-5pm Mon-Fri) has maps and information on campgrounds, roads, trails and fishing.

Travelers with time (and high-clearance vehicles) can drive to the canyon rim on unpaved roads for dramatic views: USFS Rd 517 (open July to October), a quarter-mile south of the Hells Canyon Riggins office on US 95, climbs 17 miles to the rim and ends 2 miles later at the breathtaking **Heaven's Gate Lookout**.

IDAHO PANHANDLE

The long skinny spoon handle tipping north toward Canada was never supposed to belong to Idaho, but a land dispute with Montana ended with the state claiming the Panhandle. Still, in both looks and attitude this area differs from the rest of Idaho. An alluring region of seemingly impenetrable deep-green forests, rolling byways, rain and mist, it feels more like the Pacific Northwest than the Rockies.

Although it's specked with some pleasant resorts, lots and lots of lakes (and the accompanying water sports), the Panhandle is more of a local holiday spot than the kind of place one needs to go out of the way to see. But should you be driving across its narrow body anyway, there are a few places worth visiting. The Panhandle has a reputation – often inflated by the media – as a base for neo-Nazi, white-supremacist groups. However, you're far more likely to meet wildlife than wildly irrational people.

The **Coeur d'Alene Visitors Center** (☎ 208-665-2350; 115 Northwest Blvd; 10am-3pm Tue-Sat, to 5pm Jun-Aug) is a good regional info starting point.

Sandpoint, in a gorgeous wilderness locale surrounded by mountains, is the nicest of the Panhandle's towns. **Coeur d'Alene**, on the Washington border, is the largest town, but is overdeveloped with a rather tacky boardwalk waterfront. It's not really worth stopping here unless it's late and you need to sleep, in which case go straight to the darling pink-doored **Flamingo Motel** (☎ 208-664-2159; 718 Sherman Ave; r $80-100; ⊠), a retro 1950s throwback.

Further north in Sandpoint, the waterfront **Lakeside Inn** (☎ 208-263-3717; lakeside@televar.com; 106 Bridge St; r $65-95;), featuring comfortable rooms and a Jacuzzi, is a solid option.

The old silver-mining town of **Wallace** exudes preserved Western flavor, and is a Panhandle attraction worth pausing for. The 60 lakes within 60 miles of Coeur d'Alene, including Hayden, Priest and Pend Oreille, all surrounded by campgrounds, are also good places to get lost.

ROCKY MOUNTAINS

Southwest

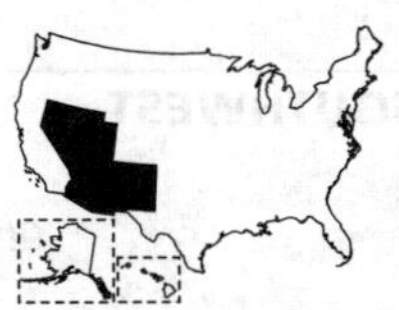

The Southwest is an awe-inspiring place, earning its reputation as the USA's land of adventure with plunging canyons, colossal buttes and towering mountains that beg to be explored. Slick brochures and adventure mags add to the allure, urging you to set out for the wild, test your limits, ponder the big picture or even bet the mortgage while living like a king. But really, much of the Southwest's charm comes from its 'do-able' adventures: slurping that first spoonful of green chili stew, riding a steam train to the Grand Canyon's rim, catching a new flick at the Sundance Film Festival or sliding down a sand dune on a big plastic disc.

The best part is, most of these adventures require a road trip, and if you're going to be traveling by car there's no better place than here. Two-lane roads and a handful of interstate highways connect a diverse range of forests and parks stretching from Utah's Wasatch Mountains to Monument Valley, the Grand Canyon and south to Carlsbad Caverns. Others loop lazily to nowhere, unfurling between quirky museums, remote gourmet restaurants and hideouts of Billy the Kid. The human population has the same variety, with Anglo, Native American and Hispanic residents forming a unique tricultural mix.

What more can we say? Find your keys, hop in the car and grab your piece of adventure – no matter how big or how small.

HIGHLIGHTS

- Hiking to panoramic views at the **Grand Canyon** (p851) and **Canyonlands** (p880)
- Gaping at monolithic red buttes from your balcony in **Monument Valley Navajo Tribal Park** (p858)
- Living the high life on the **Las Vegas Strip** (p822)
- Sledding the dunes at **White Sands** (p905)
- Slicing down the slopes of **Park City** (p874)
- Marveling at the Big Room inside **Carlsbad Caverns** (p908)
- Sliding and splashing over red rocks at **Oak Creek Canyon** (p849)
- Climbing into mysterious cliffside abodes at **Bandelier** (p898) or **Gila Cliff Dwellings** (p905)
- Enjoying a family-friendly float on the San Juan River in **Bluff** (p880) or on the Rio Grande outside **Santa Fe** (p900)
- Becoming a citizen of Black Rock City during the **Burning Man** (p835) festival

SOUTHWEST

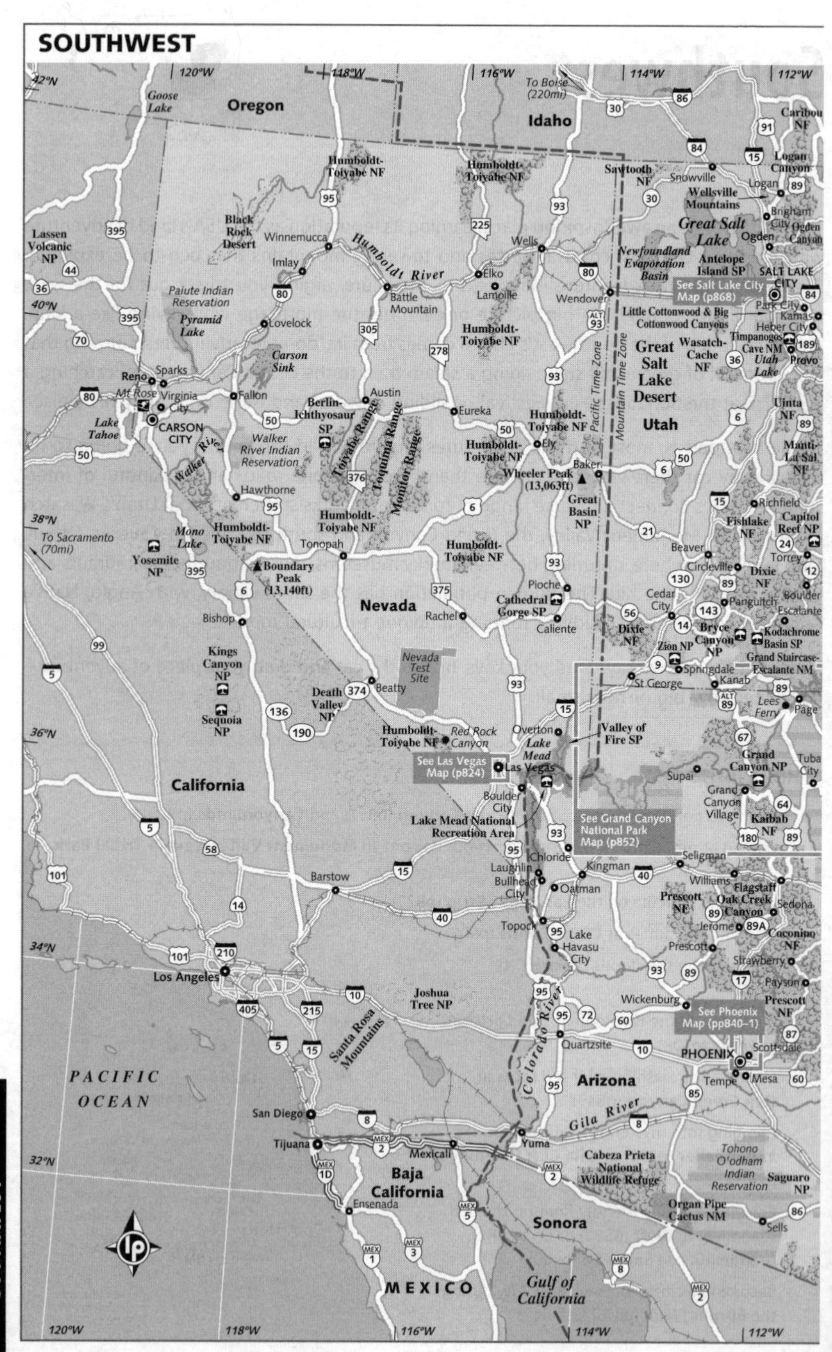

42°N
120°W
118°W
116°W
114°W
112°W
Goose Lake
Oregon
To Boise (220mi)
Idaho
Caribou NF
Logan Canyon
Humboldt-Toiyabe NF
Sawtooth NF
Snowville
Logan
Wellsville Mountains
Brigham City
Ogden Canyon
Great Salt Lake
Ogden
Black Rock Desert
Winnemucca
Humboldt River
Wells
Newfoundland Evaporation Basin
Antelope Island SP
SALT LAKE CITY
See Salt Lake City Map (p868)
Lassen Volcanic NP
Imlay
Elko
Lamoille
Wendover
Park City
Kamas
Heber City
Battle Mountain
Paiute Indian Reservation
Pyramid Lake
Lovelock
Little Cottonwood & Big Cottonwood Canyons
Timpanogos Cave NM
Utah Lake
Provo
40°N
Great Salt Lake Desert
Wasatch-Cache NF
Carson Sink
Pacific Time Zone
Mountain Time Zone
Sparks
Reno
Mt Rose
Virginia City
Fallon
Austin
Berlin-Ichthyosaur SP
Uinta NF
Lake Tahoe
CARSON CITY
Eureka
Utah
Walker River
Walker River Indian Reservation
Toiyabe Range
Toquima Range
Monitor Range
Ely
Manti-La Sal NF
Wheeler Peak (13,063ft)
Baker
Great Basin NP
Hawthorne
Richfield
38°N
To Sacramento (70mi)
Mono Lake
Yosemite NP
Fishlake NF
Capitol Reef NP
Tonopah
Beaver
Torrey
Boundary Peak (13,140ft)
Circleville
Dixie NF
Boulder
Pioche
Cedar City
Panguitch
Escalante
Cathedral Gorge SP
Nevada
Rachel
Caliente
Bryce Canyon NP
Kodachrome Basin SP
Bishop
Zion NP
Kings Canyon NP
Nevada Test Site
Springdale
Grand Staircase-Escalante NM
St George
Kanab
Beatty
Death Valley NP
Lees Ferry
Page
Sequoia NP
36°N
Red Rock Canyon
Overton
Valley of Fire SP
Lake Mead
Grand Canyon NP
Tuba City
See Las Vegas Map (p824)
Las Vegas
Supai
California
Boulder City
Grand Canyon Village
Lake Mead National Recreation Area
See Grand Canyon National Park Map (p852)
Kaibab NF
Chloride
Seligman
Kingman
Laughlin
Williams
Flagstaff
Barstow
Bullhead City
Oatman
Prescott NF
Oak Creek Canyon
Sedona
Jerome
Topock
Lake Havasu City
Coconino NF
34°N
Prescott
Strawberry
Los Angeles
Payson
Joshua Tree NP
Wickenburg
See Phoenix Map (pp840–1)
Prescott NF
Santa Rosa Mountains
Colorado River
Quartzsite
Scottsdale
PHOENIX
PACIFIC OCEAN
Arizona
Tempe
Mesa
San Diego
Gila River
Tijuana
Mexicali
Yuma
Tohono O'odham Indian Reservation
32°N
Baja California
Cabeza Prieta National Wildlife Refuge
Saguaro NP
Ensenada
Organ Pipe Cactus NM
Sonora
Sells
MEXICO
Gulf of California

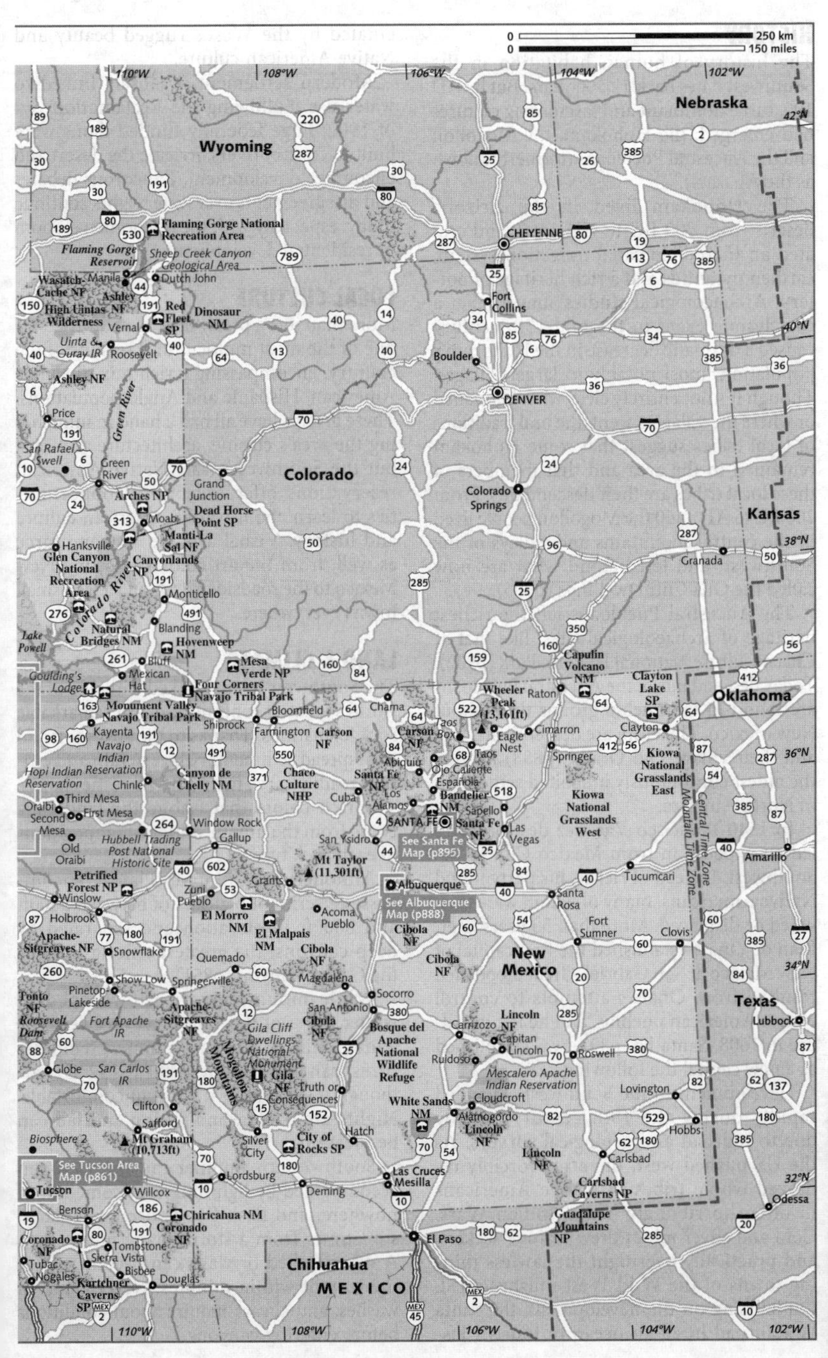
0 250 km
0 150 miles
110°W
108°W
106°W
104°W
102°W
42°N
40°N
38°N
36°N
34°N
32°N
Wyoming
Nebraska
Colorado
Kansas
Oklahoma
Texas
New Mexico
Chihuahua
MEXICO
CHEYENNE
DENVER
Fort Collins
Boulder
Colorado Springs
Grand Junction
Granada
Flaming Gorge National Recreation Area
Flaming Gorge Reservoir
Sheep Creek Canyon Geological Area
Manila
Dutch John
Wasatch-Cache NF
Ashley NF
High Uintas Wilderness
Red Fleet SP
Dinosaur NM
Vernal
Uinta & Ouray IR
Roosevelt
Ashley NF
Green River
Price
San Rafael Swell
Green River
Arches NP
Moab
Dead Horse Point SP
Manti-La Sal NF
Hanksville
Glen Canyon National Recreation Area
Canyonlands NP
Colorado River
Monticello
Blanding
Natural Bridges NM
Lake Powell
Hovenweep NM
Bluff
Mexican Hat
Goulding's Lodge
Mesa Verde NP
Four Corners Navajo Tribal Park
Monument Valley Navajo Tribal Park
Shiprock
Bloomfield
Farmington
Kayenta
Navajo Indian Reservation
Hopi Indian Reservation
Canyon de Chelly NM
Chinle
Third Mesa
Oraibi
Second Mesa
First Mesa
Old Oraibi
Hubbell Trading Post National Historic Site
Window Rock
Gallup
Chaco Culture NHP
Carson NF
Chama
Taos Box
Wheeler Peak (13,161ft)
Eagle Nest
Taos
Cimarron
Raton
Capulin Volcano NM
Clayton Lake SP
Clayton
Springer
Kiowa National Grasslands East
Kiowa National Grasslands West
Abiquiu
Ojo Caliente
Española
Santa Fe NF
Los Alamos
Bandelier NM
Cuba
SANTA FE
Santa Fe NF
Sapello
Las Vegas
See Santa Fe Map (p895)
San Ysidro
Mt Taylor (11,301ft)
Grants
Albuquerque
See Albuquerque Map (p888)
Tucumcari
Santa Rosa
Amarillo
Central Time Zone
Mountain Time Zone
Petrified Forest NP
Winslow
Holbrook
Zuni Pueblo
El Morro NM
El Malpais NM
Acoma Pueblo
Cibola NF
Fort Sumner
Clovis
Apache-Sitgreaves NF
Snowflake
Quemado
Show Low
Springerville
Pinetop-Lakeside
Magdalena
Socorro
San Antonio
Tonto NF
Roosevelt Dam
Fort Apache IR
Apache-Sitgreaves NF
Gila Cliff Dwellings National Monument
Mogollon Mountains
Gila NF
Bosque del Apache National Wildlife Refuge
Carrizozo
Lincoln NF
Capitan
Lincoln
Roswell
Ruidoso
Mescalero Apache Indian Reservation
Lubbock
Globe
San Carlos IR
Truth or Consequences
Clifton
Safford
White Sands NM
Cloudcroft
Alamogordo
Lovington
Hobbs
Biosphere 2
Mt Graham (10,713ft)
Silver City
City of Rocks SP
Hatch
Carlsbad
Carlsbad Caverns NP
See Tucson Area Map (p861)
Tucson
Lordsburg
Deming
Las Cruces
Mesilla
Willcox
Benson
Chiricahua NM
Coronado NF
Coronado NF
Tombstone
Sierra Vista
Bisbee
Tubac
Nogales
Kartchner Caverns SP
Douglas
El Paso
Guadalupe Mountains NP
Odessa

HISTORY

The history of human habitation in the Southwest dates back 12,500 years. But by AD 100, three dominant and fascinating cultures had emerged: the Hohokam, the Mogollon and the Ancestral Puebloans (formerly known as the Anasazi).

The Hohokam lived in the Arizona deserts from 300 BC to AD 1450, and created an incredible canal irrigation system, earthen pyramids and a rich heritage of pottery. Archaeological studies suggest that a cataclysmic event in the mid-15th century caused a dramatic decrease in the Hohokam's population, most notably in larger villages. Though it's not entirely clear what happened or where the villagers went, the oral traditions of local tribes suggest that some Hohokam remained in the area and that members of these local tribes are their descendants. From 200 BC to AD 1450 the Mogollon people lived in the central mountains and valleys of the Southwest, and left behind what are now called the Gila Cliff Dwellings (p905).

The Ancestral Puebloans left the richest heritage of archaeological sites, like that at Chaco Culture National Historic Park (p902). Today descendants of the Ancestral Puebloans are found in the Pueblo groups throughout New Mexico. The Hopi are descendants, too, and their village Old Oraibi (p858) may be the oldest continuously inhabited settlement in North America.

In 1540 Francisco Vásquez de Coronado led an expedition from Mexico City to the Southwest. Instead of riches, his party found Native Americans, many of whom were then killed or displaced. More than 50 years later, Juan de Oñate established the first capital of New Mexico at San Gabriel. Great bloodshed resulted from Oñate's attempts to control Native American pueblos, and he left in failure in 1608. Santa Fe (p892) was established as a new capital the following year.

Development in the Southwest expanded rapidly during the 19th century, mainly due to railroad and geological surveys. As the US pushed west, the army forcibly removed whole tribes of Native Americans in often horrifyingly brutal Indian Wars. Gold and silver mines drew fortune seekers, and practically overnight the lawless mining towns of the Wild West mushroomed. Capitalizing on the development, the Santa Fe Railroad lured an ocean of tourists fascinated by the West's rugged beauty and Native American culture.

Modern settlement is closely linked to water use. Following the Reclamation Act of 1902, huge federally funded dams were built to control rivers, irrigate the desert and encourage development. Rancorous debates and disagreements over water rights continue today, especially with the phenomenal boom in residential development.

LOCAL CULTURE

More than just a pretty face, the Southwest is one of the most multicultural regions of the country, encompassing a rich mix of Native American, Hispanic and Anglo populations. These groups have all had a hand in influencing the area's cuisine, architecture and arts, but the Southwest's vast Native American reservations offer exceptional opportunities to learn about Native American culture and history. Visual arts are a strong force as well, from the art colonies dotting New Mexico to the roadside kitsch on view in small towns everywhere.

LAND & CLIMATE

The Southwest is jam-packed with one of the world's greatest concentrations of remarkable rock formations. Thanks to the area's soft and widespread sedimentary layers, rain and erosion readily carve them into fantastic shapes. The rich colors that imbue the landscape come from the unique mineral compositions of each rock type.

Although the Colorado Plateau encompasses a series of plateaus of between 5000ft and 8000ft in elevation and separated by deep canyons, the greatest among them is the Grand Canyon (p851).

While mountains are snowcapped in winter, most of the Southwest receives little annual rainfall. During summer, temperatures can soar to over 90°F (32°C); although it's dry heat, it's still uncomfortable. Nights are cooler, and spring and fall can be pleasant.

Southwestern summer rainstorms, often accompanied by lightning, can come out of nowhere, and flash floods occur regularly, sometimes from a storm many miles away. A dry riverbed or wash can become a raging torrent within minutes. Never camp in washes, and always inquire about conditions before entering canyons.

PARKS

The Southwest has *the* most fabulous concentration of national parks and monuments in North America. But keep in mind that a number of less crowded state parks are worth visiting.

One of the national park system's most deservedly popular destinations is the Grand Canyon National Park (p851) in Arizona. Other Arizona parks include Monument Valley Navajo Tribal Park (p858), a desert basin with towering sandstone pillars and buttes; Canyon de Chelly National Monument (p858), with ancient cliff dwellings; Petrified Forest National Park (p859), with its odd mix of Painted Desert and fossilized logs; and Saguaro National Park (p862), with pristine desert and giant cacti.

The southern red-rock Canyon Country in Utah includes five national parks: Arches (p879), Canyonlands (p880), Zion (p884), Bryce (p883) and Capitol Reef (p881), which offers exceptional wilderness solitude. Grand Staircase-Escalante National Monument (p882) is a mighty region of undeveloped desert.

New Mexico boasts both Carlsbad Caverns National Park (p908) and the mysterious Chaco Culture National Historic Park (p902). Nevada's only national park is Great Basin (p837), a rugged and remote mountain oasis.

For further information, check out the **National Park Service** (NPS; www.nps.gov) website. For information on the region's state parks, see p822 for Nevada, p839 for Arizona, p867 for Utah and p886 for New Mexico.

INFORMATION

American Southwest (www.americansouthwest.net) Arguably the most comprehensive site for national parks and natural landscapes of the Southwest.

American West Travelogue (www.amwest-travel.com) A selective reading list, photographs and more.

Notes from the Road (www.notesfromtheroad.com) Click on 'Desert Southwest' for travel writing on the region.

GETTING THERE & AROUND

Phoenix' Sky Harbor International Airport (p846) and Las Vegas' McCarran International Airport (p833) are the region's busiest airports, followed by the airports serving Salt Lake City, Albuquerque and Tucson. For domestic airlines, see p1159.

Long-distance buses (p1160), including Greyhound, can get you to major points within the region but don't serve all national parks or important, off-track tourist towns such as Moab. Be aware that bus terminals can be in less safe areas of town.

Private vehicles are often the only means to reach out-of-the-way towns, trailheads and swimming spots. For information on renting a car, see p1164.

Train service with Amtrak (p1166) is much more limited than the bus system, although it does link many major Southwestern towns and offers bus connections to other towns (including Santa Fe and Phoenix). The *California Zephyr* traverses Utah and Nevada; the *Southwest Chief* stops in Arizona and New Mexico; and the *Sunset Limited* cuts through southern Arizona and New Mexico.

NEVADA

A vast and mostly empty stretch of desert, a few former mining towns that have traded pickaxes for the levers of slot machines, and the mother lode, Las Vegas – this is where people still catch gold fever.

The first state to legalize gambling, Nevada is loud with the chime of slot machines singing out from gas stations, supermarkets and hotel lobbies. Pockets of licensed brothels dot the landscape. There's no legally mandated closing time for bars, so get ready to see grandmas in the casino, beers in hand, at 2am. Nevada banks on what people *really* want.

At the fringes of this grown-up play land, artists in search of cheap digs and lots of space have been staking their claim. Witness the peaceful riot of self-expression at Burning Man or spend time exploring Reno's thriving art scene, and the state never feels quite the same.

History

Nevada's first inhabitants were the Paiute and Ancestral Puebloan people. Though claimed by Spain, Nevada was scarcely touched by Europeans until the 1820s, when trappers ventured into the Humboldt River Valley. Most 19th-century emigrants passed straight through Nevada to the California goldfields. But in 1859 the Comstock Lode – the largest silver deposit ever mined – was discovered south of Reno.

THE SOUTHWEST...

In One Week

Swoop down on **Phoenix** (p839) to check out the burgeoning arts scene then cruise over to **Scottsdale** (p842) for top-notch shopping and gallery-hopping in the Old Town district. Next up is **Sedona** (p849) for spiritual recharging before pondering the immensity of the **Grand Canyon** (p851). Detour onto the largest surviving stretch of **Route 66** (p860), then brave the jarring road to the Hualapai Nation's spectacular **Grand Canyon Skywalk** (p856). For your last few days, indulge your fantasies in **Las Vegas** (below) or earmark one day for the high life and spend the rest on an out-and-back visit to **Zion National Park** (p884).

In Two Weeks

Try your luck in **Las Vegas** (below) before kicking back in funky **Flagstaff** (p847) and peering into the abyss at **Grand Canyon National Park** (p851). Check out collegiate **Tucson** (p860) or frolic among the cacti at **Saguaro National Park** (p862). Watch the high-noon gunslinging in **Tombstone** (p865) before settling into Victorian **Bisbee** (p865).

Head east to the blinding dunes of **White Sands National Monument** (p905), then sink into **Santa Fe** (p892), a magnet for art-lovers. Explore a pueblo in **Taos** (p899) and watch the sunrise at awesome **Monument Valley Navajo Tribal Park** (p858). Head into Utah for the red-rock national parks, **Canyonlands** (p880) and **Arches** (p879). Savor a fresh fruit pie at **Capitol Reef** (p881) and do the hoodoos at **Bryce Canyon** (p883). Pay your respects at glorious **Zion** (p884), before returning to Las Vegas.

As the Comstock Lode was mined out, the population of Nevada declined. In the early 20th century, new mineral discoveries temporarily revived the state's fortunes, but the Great Depression brought an end to those dreams. So in 1931 the state government legalized gambling and created agencies to tax it, turning an illegal activity into a revenue source and tourist attraction. Today the state thrives on tourism, with most revenues coming from the ubiquitous casinos.

Information

Prostitution is illegal in Clark County (which includes Las Vegas) and Washoe County (which includes Reno), although there are legal brothels in many of the smaller counties.

TOP FIVE PARKS IN THE SOUTHWEST

- Grand Canyon National Park (p851)
- Monument Valley Navajo Tribal Park (p858)
- Arches National Park (p879)
- Zion National Park (p884)
- Carlsbad Caverns National Park (p908)

Nevada is on Pacific Standard Time and has two areas codes: Las Vegas and vicinity is ☎ 702, while the rest of the state is ☎ 775.

Nevada Commission on Tourism (☎ 775-687-4322; www.travelnevada.com; 401 N Carson St, Carson City) Sends free books, maps and information on accommodations, campgrounds and events.

Nevada Department of Transportation (☎ 877-687-6237; www.nvroads.com) For up-to-date road conditions.

Nevada Division of State Parks (☎ 775-684-2770; www.parks.nv.gov; 901 S Stewart St, 5th fl, Carson City) Camping in state parks ($10 to $15 per night) is first-come, first-served.

LAS VEGAS

The only place in the world you can see ancient hieroglyphics, the Eiffel Tower, Brooklyn Bridge and the canals of Venice in a few short hours. Sure, they're all reproductions, but in a slice of desert that's transformed itself into one of the most lavish places on earth, you can bet that the fakery is slicker than a card shark dealing from the bottom of the deck. Nothing is halfway here, even the illusions.

A neon-clad metropolis catering to the unruffled high roller, college kids in search of cheap debauchery and easy hookups, and everyone in between, Sin City aims to infatuate, and its reaches are all-inclusive. Hollywood bigwigs gyrate at A-list ultralounges, while grandparents whoop it up at the penny slots. You can sip designer martinis as you sample the apex of world-class cuisine or wander the casino floor with a 3ft-high cocktail tied around your neck.

If that sounds more like hell than heaven, Las Vegas has its share of resorts that somehow manage to marry the glamour and excitement of gaming with the beauty of Nevada's great outdoors. If you can dream up the kind of vacation you want, it's already a reality here.

Vegas is Hollywood for the everyman, where you play the role instead of watching it – welcome to the dream factory.

NEVADA FACTS

Nicknames Silver State, Sagebrush State
Population 2.6 million
Area 109,826 sq miles
Capital city Carson City (population 55,000)
Other cities Las Vegas (population 552,539), Reno (population 210,255)
Sales tax 6.5%
Birthplace of First Lady Thelma 'Pat' Nixon (1912–93), tennis pro Andre Agassi (b 1970)
Home of Nevada Test Site, Burning Man festival
Famous for Las Vegas, the Comstock Lode near Virginia City, legal prostitution
Best souvenir Life-size cardboard likeness of Liberace at Liberace Museum, Las Vegas
Driving distances Las Vegas to Boulder City (Hoover Dam) 32 miles, Las Vegas to Reno 500 miles

History

Contrary to Hollywood legend, there was much more at the dusty crossroads than a gambling parlor and some tumbleweeds the day mobster Ben 'Bugsy' Siegel rolled in and erected a glamorous tropical-themed casino, the Flamingo, under the searing sun.

Speared into the modern era by the completion of a railroad that linked up Salt Lake City to Los Angeles in 1902, Las Vegas boomed in the 1920s thanks to federally sponsored construction projects. The legalization of gambling in 1931 then carried Vegas through the Great Depression. WWII brought a huge air-force base and big aerospace bucks, plus a paved highway to Los Angeles. Soon after, the Cold War justified the Nevada Test Site. It proved to be a textbook case of 'any publicity is good publicity': monthly above-ground atomic blasts shattered casino windows downtown, while the city's official Miss Mushroom Cloud mascot promoted atomic everything in tourism campaigns.

A building spree sparked by the Flamingo in 1946 led to mob-backed tycoons upping the glitz ante at every turn. Big-name entertainers, like Frank Sinatra, Liberace and Sammy Davis Jr, arrived on stage at the same time as topless French showgirls.

The high-profile purchase of the Desert Inn in 1966 by eccentric billionaire Howard Hughes gave the gambling industry a much-needed patina of legitimacy. The debut of the MGM Grand in 1993 signaled the dawn of the era of the corporate megaresort.

An oasis in the middle of a final frontier, Sin City continues to exist chiefly to satisfy the desires of visitors. Hosting 37.5 million people a year, until recently Las Vegas was the engine of North America's fastest-growing metropolitan area. The housing crisis hit residents here especially hard, but if history is any judge, the city will double-down and resume its winning streak in no time.

Orientation

The Strip, aka Las Vegas Blvd, is the center of gravity in Sin City. Roughly four miles long, this is where you'll find most of the massive (2000 sleeping rooms on the small end) hotel-casinos and all of the big stage shows. Circus Circus Las Vegas caps the north end of the Strip and Mandalay Bay is on the south end near the airport. It can take more than 15 minutes to drive from one end to the other, and even longer in traffic, which is atrocious most of the time.

Distances are deceiving, and a walk to what looks like a nearby casino usually takes longer than expected. Walking is a crowded, sometimes hot affair, and the always-under-construction Strip has plenty of pedestrian bottlenecks.

Downtown Las Vegas is the original town center and home to the city's oldest hotels and casinos. Its main drag is Fremont St, four blocks of which are a covered pedestrian mall that runs a groovy light show every night.

More casinos are found east of the Strip along Paradise Rd, and just west of I-15 near the intersection of Flamingo Rd and Valley View Blvd. The Chinatown district is west of the Strip on Spring Mountain Rd.

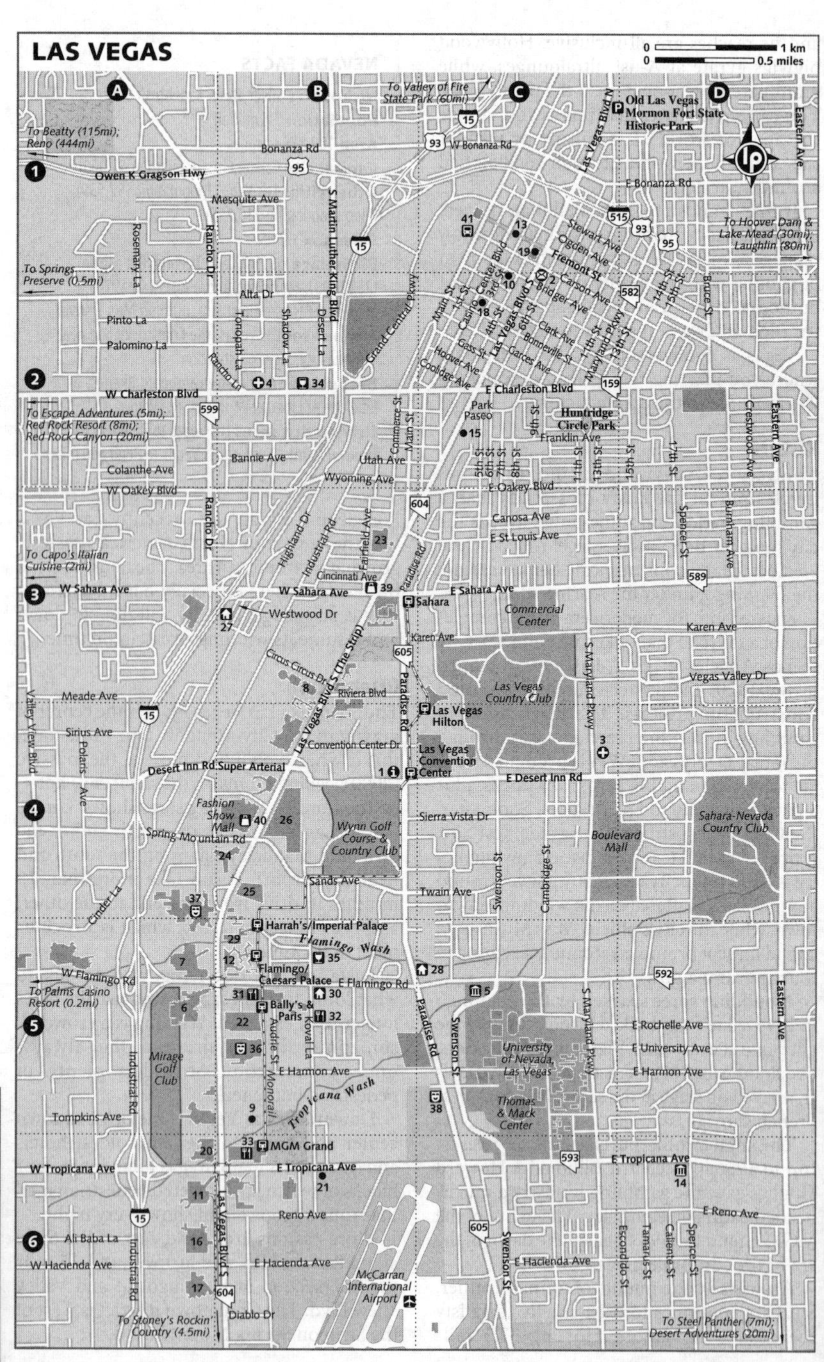
LAS VEGAS
0 1 km
0 0.5 miles
To Valley of Fire State Park (60mi)
Old Las Vegas Mormon Fort State Historic Park
To Beatty (115mi); Reno (444mi)
Bonanza Rd
W Bonanza Rd
Owen K Gragson Hwy
Las Vegas Blvd N
E Bonanza Rd
Eastern Ave
Mesquite Ave
S Martin Luther King Blvd
Rosemary La
Rancho Dr
To Hoover Dam & Lake Mead (30mi); Laughlin (80mi)
Stewart Ave
Ogden Ave
Fremont St
Carson Ave
Bridger Ave
To Springs Preserve (0.5mi)
Alta Dr
Tonopah La
Shadow La
Desert La
Grand Central Pkwy
Pinto La
Palomino La
Rancho Ln
Main St
1st St
Casino Center Blvd
3rd St
4th St
Las Vegas Blvd S
6th St
Clark Ave
Bonneville St
Garces Ave
Gass St
Hoover Ave
Coolidge Ave
11th St
Maryland Pkwy
13th St
14th St
15th St
Bruce St
W Charleston Blvd
E Charleston Blvd
To Escape Adventures (5mi); Red Rock Resort (8mi); Red Rock Canyon (20mi)
Park Paseo
Huntridge Circle Park
Franklin Ave
Commerce St
Crestwood Ave
Bannie Ave
Utah Ave
Colanthe Ave
Wyoming Ave
W Oakey Blvd
E Oakey Blvd
5th St
6th St
7th St
8th St
9th St
17th St
Canosa Ave
E St Louis Ave
Highland Dr
Industrial Rd
Fairfield Ave
Paradise Rd
Spencer St
Burnham Ave
To Capo's Italian Cuisine (2mi)
Cincinnati Ave
W Sahara Ave
E Sahara Ave
Sahara
Westwood Dr
Commercial Center
Karen Ave
Circus Circus Dr
Las Vegas Blvd S (The Strip)
Las Vegas Country Club
Vegas Valley Dr
S Maryland Pkwy
Meade Ave
Riviera Blvd
Las Vegas Hilton
Valley View Blvd
Sirius Ave
Polaris Ave
Convention Center Dr
Las Vegas Convention Center
Desert Inn Rd Super Arterial
E Desert Inn Rd
Fashion Show Mall
Wynn Golf Course & Country Club
Sierra Vista Dr
Sahara-Nevada Country Club
Boulevard Mall
Spring Mountain Rd
Sands Ave
Twain Ave
Swenson St
Cambridge St
Cinder La
Harrah's/Imperial Palace
Flamingo Wash
Flamingo/Caesars Palace
W Flamingo Rd
E Flamingo Rd
To Palms Casino Resort (0.2mi)
Bally's & Paris
Audrie St
Koval La
E Rochelle Ave
E University Ave
E Harmon Ave
Mirage Golf Club
Industrial Rd
Monorail
Tropicana Wash
University of Nevada, Las Vegas
Thomas & Mack Center
Tompkins Ave
MGM Grand
W Tropicana Ave
E Tropicana Ave
Reno Ave
E Reno Ave
Ali Baba La
W Hacienda Ave
E Hacienda Ave
Las Vegas Blvd S
Escondido St
Tamarus St
Caliente St
Diablo Dr
McCarran International Airport
To Stoney's Rockin' Country (4.5mi)
To Steel Panther (7mi); Desert Adventures (20mi)

INFORMATION
American Express .... (see 40)
Borders Express .... (see 40)
Las Vegas Visitor Information Center 1 B4
Post Office 2 C2
Sunrise Hospital & Medical Center 3 C4
University Medical Center 4 B2

SIGHTS & ACTIVITIES
Adventuredome .... (see 8)
Atomic Testing Museum 5 C5
Bellagio 6 A5
Bellagio Conservatory & Botanical Gardens .... (see 6)
Bellagio Gallery of Fine Art .... (see 6)
Bodies…The Exhibition .... (see 16)
Caesars Palace 7 A5
Circus Circus 8 B3
CityCenter 9 B5
Commisioner of Civil Marriages 10 C2
Dick's Last Resort .... (see 11)
Encore .... (see 26)
Excalibur 11 A6
Flamingo 12 B5
Fremont Street Experience 13 C1
Liberace Museum 14 D6
Little White Wedding Chapel 15 C2
Luxor 16 A6
Madame Tussauds .... (see 25)
Mandalay Bay 17 A6
Mandalay Bay Wedding Chapel .... (see 17)
Manhattan Express Rollercoaster .... (see 20)
Marriage Bureau 18 C2
Midway .... (see 8)
Minus 5 Ice Lounge .... (see 17)
Neon Museum 19 C1
Neonopolis .... (see 19)
New York-New York 20 A6
New York-New York .... (see 20)
Papillon Helicopter Tours 21 B6
Paris-Las Vegas 22 B5
Shark Reef .... (see 17)
Sirens of Treasure Island .... (see 24)
Stratosphere 23 B3
Stratosphere Tower .... (see 23)
Titanic: The Artifact Exhibition .... (see 16)
Treasure Island 24 B4
Venetian 25 B4
Wildlife Habitat .... (see 12)
Wynn Las Vegas 26 B4

SLEEPING
Bill's Gamblin' Hall & Saloon .... (see 12)
Blue Moon Resort 27 B3
Caesars Palace .... (see 7)
Candlewood Suites Extended Stay 28 C5
Encore .... (see 26)
Flamingo .... (see 12)
Imperial Palace 29 B5
Luxor .... (see 16)
Mandalay Bay .... (see 17)
Paris-Las Vegas .... (see 22)
Platinum Hotel 30 B5
THEhotel .... (see 17)

EATING
Bally's Steakhouse 31 B5
Border Grill .... (see 17)
Cypress Street Marketplace .... (see 7)
Ellis Island Casino & Brewery 32 B5
Fammia .... (see 33)
House of Blues .... (see 17)
Joël Robuchon .... (see 33)
L'Atelier de Joël Robuchon .... (see 33)
Red Square .... (see 17)
Society Café .... (see 26)
Victorian Room .... (see 12)
'wichcraft 33 B6

DRINKING
Frankie's Tiki Room 34 B2
O'Sheas 35 B5

ENTERTAINMENT
Bank .... (see 6)
CatHouse .... (see 16)
Criss Angel Believe .... (see 16)
Ka .... (see 33)
Krave 36 B5
LAX .... (see 16)
LOVE 37 A4
Mystère .... (see 24)
O .... (see 6)
Piranha 38 C5
Tix 4 Tonight .... (see 12)
Zumanity .... (see 20)

SHOPPING
Bonanza Gifts 39 B3
Fashion Show Mall 40 B4
Forum Shops .... (see 7)
Grand Canal Shoppes .... (see 25)
Mandalay Place .... (see 17)
Miracle Mile Shops .... (see 36)
Wynn Esplanade .... (see 26)

TRANSPORT
Greyhound 41 C1

Major tourist areas are safe. However, Las Vegas Blvd between downtown and the Strip gets shabby, and Fremont St east of downtown is rather unsavory.

Information

BOOKSTORES

Borders Express (☎ 702-733-1049; 3200 Las Vegas Blvd S) Inside the Fashion Show Mall.

EMERGENCY & MEDICAL SERVICES

Gamblers Anonymous (☎ 702-385-7732) Assistance with gambling concerns.
Police (☎ 702-828-3111)
Sunrise Hospital & Medical Center (☎ 702-731-8000; 3186 S Maryland Pkwy)
University Medical Center (☎ 702-383-2000; 1800 W Charleston Blvd)

INTERNET ACCESS

Wi-fi is available in most hotel rooms ($13 to $17 per day) and there are internet kiosks with attached printers in most hotel lobbies ($5 per five minutes).

INTERNET RESOURCES & MEDIA

Las Vegas Review-Journal (www.lvrj.com) Daily paper with a weekend guide, *Neon*, on Friday.
Las Vegas Tourism (www.onlyinvegas.com) Official tourism website.
Las Vegas Weekly (www.lasvegasweekly.com) Free weekly with good entertainment and restaurant listings.
Las Vegas.com (www.lasvegas.com) Travel services.
Lasvegaskids.net (www.lasvegaskids.net) The lowdown on what's up for the wee ones.
Vegas.com (www.vegas.com) Travel information with booking service.

MONEY

Every hotel-casino and bank and most convenience stores have an ATM. The ATM fee at most casinos is around $5. Best to stop at off-Strip banks if possible.

American Express (☎ 702-739-8474; Fashion Show Mall, 3200 Las Vegas Blvd S; 🕑 10am-9pm Mon-Fri, 10am-8pm Sat, noon-6pm Sun) Changes currencies at competitive rates.

POST

Post office (☎ 702-382-5779; 201 Las Vegas Blvd S) Downtown.

DON'T MISS

- **Bellagio fountains** – dancing spurt and spray in the evening (below)
- **Stoney's Rockin' Country** – friendliness in the Wild West (p832)
- **Fremont Street Experience** – street canopy of sound and art (opposite)
- **Cirque du Soleil** – artsy acrobatic circus (p832)
- **Liberace Museum** – king of bling (p828)
- **Joël Robuchon** – ultimate gourmet experience (p831)
- **CatHouse** – sassy, sultry, sexy…meow (p832)

TOURIST INFORMATION

Las Vegas Visitor Information Center (☎ 702-892-7575; www.visitlasvegas.com; 3150 Paradise Rd; 🕑 8am-5pm) Free local calls, internet access and maps galore.

Sights

CASINOS

A slice of the French Riviera in Las Vegas – and classy enough to entice any of the Riviera's regulars – Steve Wynn has upped the wow factor, and the skyline, yet again with the late-2008 opening of **Encore** (☎ 702-770-8000; www.encorelasvegas.com; 3121 Las Vegas Blvd S). Filled with indoor flower gardens and a definite butterfly motif, it's an oasis of bright beauty. **Botero**, the restaurant headed by Mark LoRusso, is centered on a large sculpture by Fernando Botero himself. Encore is attached to its sister property, the $2.7-billion **Wynn Las Vegas** (☎ 702-770-7100; www.wynnlasvegas.com; 3131 Las Vegas Blvd S). The entrance is obscured from the Strip by a $130-million artificial mountain, which rises seven stories tall in some places. Inside, the Wynn resembles a natural paradise – with mountain views, tumbling waterfalls, fountains and other special effects.

The **Bellagio** (☎ 702-693-7111, 888-987-6667; www.bellagio.com; 3600 Las Vegas Blvd S) dazzles with Tuscan architecture and an 8-acre artificial lake, complete with choreographed dancing fountains (3pm to midnight weekdays, noon to midnight weekends; on the half-hour until 8pm and then every 15 minutes). The lobby features an 18ft ceiling adorned with a back-lit glass sculpture composed of 2000 hand-blown flowers. The **Bellagio Gallery of Fine Art** (☎ 702-693-7871; admission $15; 🕑 10am-6pm Sun-Thu, 10am-7pm Fri & Sat) showcases temporary exhibits by top-notch artists. The **Bellagio Conservatory & Botanical Gardens** (admission free; 🕑 daily) has changing exhibits throughout the year.

Quintessentially Las Vegas, **Caesars Palace** (☎ 702-731-7110; www.caesarspalace.com; 3570 Las Vegas Blvd S) is a Greco-Roman fantasyland featuring marble reproductions of classical statuary, including a not-to-be-missed 4-ton Brahma shrine near the front entrance. Towering fountains, goddess-costumed cocktail waitresses and the swanky haute-couture Forum Shops (p833) all ante up the glitz.

Another quintessentially Vegas hotel is the **Flamingo** (☎ 702-733-3111; www.flamingolasvegas.com; 3555 Las Vegas Blvd S). Weave through the slot machines to the **Wildlife Habitat** (admission free; 🕑 daily) to see the flock of Chilean flamingos that call these 15 tropical acres home. Check out the shrub maze near the wedding chapel to see the plaque that commemorates the exploits of the Flamingo's founder, Bugsy Siegel – it's one of the rare nods to the past in this city.

Hand-painted ceiling frescoes, roaming mimes and full-scale reproductions of famous Venice landmarks are found at the romantic **Venetian** (☎ 702-414-1000; www.venetian.com; 3355 Las Vegas Blvd S; gondola rides adult/private $16/64). To do some hobnobbing with wax likenesses of celebrities, stop by **Madame Tussauds** (☎ 702-862-7800; www.madametussauds.com; adult/child/child under 6 $25/15/free; 🕑 10am-9pm) and snap pics of Hugh Hefner or Zac Efron. The complex also has an on-site wedding chapel.

Not trying to be any one fantasy, the tropically themed **Mandalay Bay** (M-Bay; ☎ 702-632-7777; www.mandalaybay.com; 3950 Las Vegas Blvd S) is worth a walkthrough. Standout attractions include the multilevel **Shark Reef** (☎ 702-632-4555; www.sharkreef.com; adult/child $17/11; 🕑 10am-11pm; 🚸), an aquarium home to thousands of submarine beasties with a shallow pool where you can pet pint-sized sharks. Certified Scuba divers can take the half-day **Dive with Sharks Experience** (per diver/pair $650/$1000) in a 1.3 million gallon tank.

Though traces of the original swashbuckling skull-and-crossbones theme linger at **Treasure Island** (TI; ☎ 702-894-7111; www.treasureisland.com; 3300 Las Vegas Blvd S), the resort now strives for a sassy adults-only Caribbean feel. The spiced-up **Sirens of Treasure Island** (admission free; 🕑 daily) is a mock sea battle featuring salty lasses fighting bare-chested swashbucklers for their share of

GOING TO THE CHAPEL, GOING TO GET MARRIED

More than 122,000 couples say their vows in Las Vegas each year. Whether it's a planned affair or a spur-of-the-moment decision, there are loads of places to tie the knot. You just have to be at least 18 years old and show up at the **Marriage Bureau** (☎ 702-671-0600; 201 E Clark Ave; license $60; 8am-midnight). Once you have the certificate, it's off to the chapel, and there are plenty of touts with chapel brochures waiting outside the marriage bureau.

If all you want is a civil ceremony, walk three blocks to the **Commissioner of Civil Marriages** (☎ 702-671-0600; Regional Justice Center, 309 S 3rd St; ceremony $50; 8am-10pm). The bride and groom take their vows under a small white gazebo with fake leaves, but it looks OK in pictures. Cash (exact change) and a witness are required; it's possible to pinch the latter from the waiting room.

One of the classiest places to get hitched is at the **Mandalay Bay Wedding Chapel** (☎ 702-632-7490; www.mandalaybay.com; 3950 Las Vegas Blvd S; packages $1100-8450; 11am-4pm Sun-Thu, 11am-6pm Fri, 11am-8pm Sat).

The **Little White Wedding Chapel** (☎ 702-382-5943; www.littlewhitechapel.com; 1301 Las Vegas Blvd S; 24hr) has welcomed thousands of couples since opening in 1946 and is a favorite spot for celebs (Bruce Willis and Demi Moore, Frank Sinatra and Mia Farrow) to tie the knot. Drive-through rates start at $40 and à la carte weddings in the chapel start at $55.

booty. You can see it every 90 minutes from 7pm to 11:30pm.

Evoking the gaiety of the City of Light, **Paris-Las Vegas** (☎ 702-946-7000; www.parislasvegas.com; 3655 Las Vegas Blvd S) strives to capture the essence of the grand dame by recreating her landmarks. Fine likenesses of the Opéra, the Arc de Triomphe, the Champs-Élysées and even the Seine frame the property. The signature attraction is the ersatz Eiffel Tower.

New York-New York (☎ 800-689-1797; www.nynyhotelcasino.com; 3790 Las Vegas Blvd S) is a mini metropolis featuring scaled-down replicas of the Empire State Building (47 stories or 529ft), the Statue of Liberty, ringed by a September 11 memorial, and the Brooklyn Bridge.

The focus at **Luxor** (☎ 702-262-4444; www.luxor.com; 3900 Las Vegas Blvd S) is its 30-story pyramid cloaked in black glass from base to apex. The exterior still has realistic copies of hieroglyphics but a few years ago the new owners gave the public spaces a massive remodel and lost much of the Egypt theme; hard to do when living in a pyramid and all. It's gotten a touch classier and is still worth a visit because of two long-term exhibits: **Bodies...The Exhibition** (☎ 702-262-4400; adult/child $31/23; 10am-10pm) features stunning specimens of the human body sliced up and filled with dyes of various colors to show how the whole bag of bones works, and **Titanic: The Artifact Exhibition** (☎ 702-262-4400; adult/child $27/20; 10am-10pm) is a spooky and cool experience that's surprisingly moving.

At 1149ft, the white, three-legged $550-million **Stratosphere** (☎ 702-380-7777; www.stratospherehotel.com; 2000 Las Vegas Blvd S) is capped with indoor and outdoor viewing decks with spectacular 360-degree panoramas.

OTHER ATTRACTIONS

At the **Atomic Testing Museum** (☎ 702-794-5161; www.atomictestingmuseum.org; 755 E Flamingo Rd; adult/child $12/9; 9am-5pm Mon-Sat, 1-5pm Sun), the quality is what you'd expect of a Smithsonian Institution affiliate. The Atomic Age exhibit has a neat timeline that shows how popular culture (in the form of lunchboxes, toys, movies) reacted to the nuclear arms race. Don't skip the deafening Ground Zero Theater, which mimics a concrete test bunker.

A four-block pedestrian mall topped by an arched steel canopy and filled with computer-controlled lights, the **Fremont Street Experience** (www.vegasexperience.com; Fremont St; hourly 7pm-midnight), between Main St and Las Vegas Blvd, has brought life back to downtown. Every evening, the canopy is transformed into a six-minute light-and-sound show enhanced by 550,000 watts of wraparound sound. It doesn't hurt that the table limits are lower in this part of town and the free drinks seem to appear a little faster.

The **Neon Museum** (☎ 702-387-6366; www.neonmuseum.org; cnr Fremont & 4th Sts; displays free, guided tours $15; displays 24hr, guided tours noon & 2pm Tue-Sat) isn't really a museum at all, but a walking tour that begins at the Neonopolis shopping center at Las Vegas Blvd and extends to the 3rd St cul-de-sac adjacent to the Fremont Street Experience. Contact them for appointment-only tours ($15) of the 'Neon boneyard,' where old signs go to die.

Site of the spring where early Native Americans got their water, the **Springs Preserve** (☎ 702-822-7700; www.springspreserve.org; 333 S Valley View Blvd; adult/child $19/11; 10am-5pm;) is about 5 miles north of the Center Strip. The 180-acre space is dedicated to the original people, and landscape, of Las Vegas. Indoor and outdoor exhibits include a cool ecodwelling called the Desert Living Center and a (free) 1.8-mile walking trail through the desert.

Activities

For Las Vegas at high altitude and nearby natural wonders, float like a butterfly over to **Papillon Helicopter Tours** (☎ 702-736-7243; www.papillon.com; 275 E Tropicana Ave; tours from $245). Helicopter trips to the Grand Canyon range from flyovers to a champagne toast at the bottom of the canyon with some time for exploration.

With Lake Mead and Hoover Dam just a few hours' drive away, would-be river rats should check out **Desert Adventures** (☎ 702-293-5026; www.kayaklasvegas.com; 1647 Nevada Hwy, Suite A, Boulder City; trips from $120) for lots of half-, full- and multiday kayaking adventures. Hiking trips, too.

Escape Adventures (☎ 702-596-2953; www.escapeadventures.com; 8221 W Charleston Blvd; trips incl bike from $120) is the source for guided mountain-bike tours of Red Rock Canyon State Park (p833). Rentals, too.

A small taste of the New York of old, when your life would flash before your eyes on a regular basis, the **Manhattan Express Rollercoaster** (☎ 800-689-1797; www.nynyhotelcasino.com; New York-New York, 3790 Las Vegas Blvd S; admission $14, re-ride $7; 11am-11pm Sun-Thu, 10:30am-midnight Fri & Sat;) is twisty fun.

At the **Stratosphere Tower** (☎ 702-380-7777; www.stratospherehotel.com; Stratosphere, 2000 Las Vegas Blvd S; elevator adult/child $14/10, per ride $13; 10am-1am Sun-Thu, 10am-2am Fri & Sat;), the Big Shot shoots passengers straight up 160ft until they are 1081ft above the Strip and the X-Scream and Insanity rides both spin riders over the edge of the tower, 866ft above the ground.

Las Vegas for Children

Few places in Vegas bill themselves as family-friendly. State law prohibits people under 21 from loitering in gaming areas.

The **Circus Circus** (☎ 702-734-0410; www.circuscircus.com; 2880 Las Vegas Blvd S;) hotel complex is all about the kids, and its **Adventuredome** (☎ 702-794-3939; adult/child $25/15; 10am-7pm Sun-Thu, 10am-midnight Fri & Sat;) is a 5-acre indoor theme park with fun ranging from laser tag to bumper cars and a roller coaster. The **Midway** (admission free; 11am-midnight;) features animals, acrobats and magicians performing on center stage; shows are held every 30 minutes.

Excalibur (☎ 702-597-7777; www.excalibur.com; 3050 Las Vegas Blvd S;) weighs in as well, with a video arcade and shopping at themed stores like Dragon's Lair, for all your dragon and wizard sculpture needs.

Quirky Las Vegas

Check out artifacts from the original king of bling at the **Liberace Museum** (☎ 702-798-5595; www.liberace.org; 1775 E Tropicana Ave; adult/child over 10 $12.50/8.50; 10am-5pm Tue-Sat, noon-4pm Sun). The home of 'Mr Showmanship' houses the flamboyant art cars, ornate pianos and the most outrageous costumes concocted outside a Halloween parade.

Cool your heels at **Minus 5 Ice Lounge** (☎ 702-632-7777; www.mandalaybay.com; Mandalay Bay, 3950 Las Vegas Blvd S; admission & 1 drink before/after 6pm $30/40; 10am-3am), a bar where the entire room, including tables and chairs, is made completely of ice – you even sip cocktails out of one-use ice goblets. A warm coat and gloves come with admission.

For an adults-only, off-color good time, **Dick's Last Resort** (☎ 702-597-7991; www.dickslastresort.com; Excalibur, 3050 Las Vegas Blvd S) is an eating and drinking place where staff dish out a heaping helping of verbal abuse. It's not for the faint of heart: diners have to wear dunce caps with personalized, obscene insults. When we say adults-only, we mean it.

Sleeping

There's something for everyone's budget or credit-card-bruising splurge. Rates rise and fall dramatically depending on demand, with weekends and convention traffic driving up rates. Downtown hotels are generally less expensive than those on the Strip. Most hotel websites have handy calendars with day-by-day room rates listed. Options are categorized here by lowest possible standard room rates, but prices can easily be double that.

BUDGET

Imperial Palace (☎ 702-731-3311, 800-351-7400; www.imperialpalace.com; 3535 Las Vegas Blvd S; r from $45;) As affordable as they come for such a central location, but more for those looking for a place to sleep than a fine hotel experience. The celebrity-impersonator 'Dealertainers' make it more fun than usual to negotiate the casino floor.

Candlewood Suites Extended Stay (☎ 888-299-2208; 4034 Paradise Rd; r $65-120;) Set just a mile from the Strip. The free wi-fi, free laundry machines and a kitchenette in every room to save on food costs more than makes up for the occasional taxi ride for big nights out. With lots of business travelers calling this place home, count on quiet nights.

Bill's Gamblin' Hall & Saloon (☎ 702-737-2100, 866-245-5745; www.billslasvegas.com; 3595 Las Vegas Blvd S; r $65-150;) Set smack bang mid-Strip with affordable rooms nice enough to sport plasma TVs, Bill's is great value, so book far ahead. Rooms feature Victorian-themed decor, and guests can use the pool next door at the Flamingo without charge.

Luxor (☎ 702-262-4444, 877-386-4658; www.luxor.com; 3900 Las Vegas Blvd S; r from $65-190;) It's a bit jarring to leave the shiny Luxor lobby and discover a rather tatty Pyramid room; those who don't like loud music pulsing in the lobby until late at night should try to get a tower room. It houses a few of the hottest nightspots in Las Vegas, including CatHouse (p832) and LAX (p832), and has indoor walkways to the classy Mandalay Bay and the downmarket but lots of fun Excalibur.

New York-New York (☎ 866-815-4365; www.nynyhotelcasino.com; 3790 Las Vegas Blvd S; r from $75;) The rooms are a nice surprise, especially for the price. Basic but not ratty, and relatively quiet considering how close you feel to the casino floor. A definite rock-and-roll, unpretentious vibe at the clubs and bars here.

MIDRANGE

Flamingo (☎ 702-733-3111; www.flamingolasvegas.com; 3555 Las Vegas Blvd S; r from $90;) Try to get one of the newly outfitted GO rooms, a sleek homage to the hotel's glory days that feel like luxury accommodations at midrange prices. At the epicenter of all the action; the location is second to none.

Paris-Las Vegas (☎ 702-946-7000, 877-603-4386; www.parislasvegas.com; 3655 Las Vegas Blvd S; r from $90;) Nice rooms with a nod to classic French design; the newer Red Rooms are a study in sumptuous class. The more expensive rooms with a view of the faux Eiffel Tower are good for special occasions.

Caesars Palace (☎ 866-227-5938; www.caesarspalace.com; 3570 Las Vegas Blvd S; r from $90;) Send away the centurions and decamp in style – Caesars' standard rooms are some of the most luxurious you will find in town. The menu of dining, shopping and amenities is a mile long, with the complex sometimes feeling as large as Rome itself.

Mandalay Bay (☎ 702-632-7777, 877-632-7800; www.mandalaybay.com; 3950 Las Vegas Blvd S; r from $130;) The ornately appointed rooms have a South Seas theme, and amenities include floor-to-ceiling windows and luxurious bathrooms. Swimmers will swoon over the sprawling pool complex, with a sand-and-surf beach and wave machine and the adults-only Moorea Beach Club.

our pick **Platinum Hotel** (☎ 702-365-5000, 877-211-9211; www.theplatinumhotel.com; 211 E Flamingo Rd; r from $130;) A favorite of business travelers and locals who want to be near the Strip but not on it. The coolly modern rooms at this spiffy, relatively new property are comfortable and full of nice touches – many have fireplaces and they all have kitchens and Jacuzzi tubs. There is no gaming here.

TOP END

Luxury comes cheaper here than almost anywhere else in the world, and sometimes internet-only specials can knock up to 50% off the prices listed following. If you rain fistfuls of cash around the casino, expect to be comped a sumptuous suite.

THEhotel (☎ 702-632-7777, 877-632-7800; www.thehotelatmandalaybay.com; Mandalay Bay, 3950 Las Vegas Blvd S; ste $130-500;) The service and style at this all-suites boutique hotel with a contemporary NYC vibe make people want to live here. The spacious rooms come tricked out with wet bars and large plasma TVs.

Palms Casino Resort (☎ 702-942-7777, 866-942-7777; www.palms.com; 4321 W Flamingo Rd; r $149-500;) Off-Strip and originally aimed at young locals, the post–*Real World* Palms now attracts a flashier, MTV-influenced crowd and is a favorite with celebrity partiers like Paris Hilton and Britney Spears. Standard rooms are generous, and upper floors have a Strip view. The pool here is the place to see

CITYCENTER: MODERN VEGAS, LIKE IT OR NOT

Despite shaky finances and a rash of on-site construction deaths, the newest big gamble in Vegas was set to open in phases beginning in late 2009. The future of the project is greatly in flux and things may shut down completely, so take the following as a best-case scenario. **CityCenter** (www.citycenter.com) is an $11-billion city-within-a-city of hotels, residences, the 4000-room **ARIA** casino-resort, restaurants and retail shops that takes up a city block (67 acres) on the Strip across from the MGM Grand. Some say it brings an urban core to Las Vegas that puts it on par with other global centers of tourism. Others say that despite the kitsch factor of the many themed hotels here, you at least know you're in Vegas. Critics also say that with plummeting room rates, more inventory will only hurt other hotels. CityCenter was designed by A-list architects, but it's the **Veer Towers** – ultramodern skyscrapers that lean in opposite directions – that promise to become the visual shorthand of modern Las Vegas. One of the towers houses a **Mandarin Oriental** hotel – white-glove luxury in the heart of the Strip.

and be seen, and the on-site recording studio lets anyone live the diva dream.

Red Rock Resort (☎ 702-797-7878; www.redrocklasvegas.com; 11011 W Charleston Blvd; r $200-625;) Red Rock touts itself as the first off-Strip billion-dollar gaming resort, and most people who stay here eschew the Strip forever more. There's free transportation between the Strip, and hiking and biking outings to the nearby Red Rocks State Park and beyond. Rooms are well appointed and comfy.

Encore (☎ 702-770-8000; www.encorelasvegas.com; 3121 Las Vegas Blvd S; r $250-850;) Classy and playful more than overblown and opulent – even people cheering at the roulette table clap with a little more elegance. There's a definite French Riviera colorful theme in the public spaces, but the rooms themselves are studies in subdued luxury.

Eating

Sin City is an unmatched eating adventure. Since Wolfgang Puck brought Spago to Caesars in 1992, celebrity chefs have taken up residence in nearly every megaresort. Cheap buffets and loss-leader meal deals still exist, mostly downtown, but the gourmet quotient is high, with prices to match. Reservations are a must for fancier restaurants; book far in advance. Every major casino has a 24-hour café and at least a couple of restaurants.

BUDGET

Just west of the Strip, the Asian restaurants on Spring Mountain Rd in Chinatown are also good budget options, with lots of vegetarian choices. On the Strip itself, cheap eats beyond fast-food joints are hard to find.

Cypress Street Marketplace (☎ 702-893-4800; Caesars Palace, 3500 Las Vegas Blvd S; mains $5-10; 11am-11pm) In the Forum Shops connected to Caesars Palace, this glorified food court has a wide variety of decent food at good prices.

'wichcraft (☎ 702-891-3199; MGM Grand, 3799 Las Vegas Blvd S; sandwiches $7-9; 10am-5pm) Conveniently located beside the monorail entrance, this designy little sandwich shop can set you up with a breakfast or lunch bite on the fly. Brainchild of celebrity chef Tom Colicchio, this is the best place to taste gourmet on a budget.

Ellis Island Casino & Brewery (☎ 702-733-8901; 4178 Koval Lane; mains $7-14; 24hr) Get steamed clams, pasta dishes and sandwiches in the restaurant any time, but if it's between 4pm and 10pm hit the nightly barbecue on the brewery patio for a full rack of baby back ribs ($12) and wash it down with one of the tasty and cheap ($1.50) beers made in those big vats you can see from the casino floor. Slices at the on-site pizza parlor start at $2.50.

Victorian Room (☎ 702-737-2100; Bill's Gamblin' Hall & Saloon, 3595 Las Vegas Blvd S; mains $8-20; 24hr) A hokey old-fashioned San Francisco theme belies one of the best deals in sit-down restaurants in Las Vegas. The prime rib or New York steak specials ($14.95) are delicious around the clock.

MIDRANGE

House of Blues (☎ 702-632-7600; Mandalay Bay, 3950 Las Vegas Blvd S; dishes $13-20; 7:30am-midnight Sun-Thu, 7:30am-1am Fri & Sat) The BBQ, burgers and salads at this Southern juke joint are enhanced by funky folk art and free live music on nights a ticketed concert isn't playing. The reservations-only Sunday Gospel Brunch ($20 to $50; at 10am and 1pm) has buffets of biscuits, Creole chicken and shrimp jambalaya – a spiritual experience.

Society Café (☎ 702-248-3463, 888-352-3463; Encore, 3121 Las Vegas Blvd S; mains $14-30; ⏰ 7am-midnight Sun-Thu, 7am-3am Fri & Sat) A slice of reasonably priced culinary heaven in the midst of Encore's loveliness. The basic café here is equal to fine dining at other joints. The sliders are a good appetizer or light meal, and the lobster roll club sandwich makes eating with your hands classy again.

Border Grill (☎ 702-632-7403; Mandalay Bay, 3950 Las Vegas Blvd S; mains $17-30; ⏰ 11:30am-10pm Mon-Thu, 11:30am-11pm Fri, 11am-11pm Sat, 11am-10pm Sun) With Mexican food at its best, an outdoor patio that's nice for people-watching and margarita-sipping during the day, and dishes like green chicken poblano enchiladas, made by the women known as the 'too hot tamales' on the Food Network, it's worth making a trip here for dinner.

Capo's Italian Cuisine (☎ 702-364-2276; 5675 W Sahara Ave; mains $17-40; ⏰ 5pm-midnight) The gangster theme starts when you enter through the rear and someone peeks through a peephole to let you in. It's a shtick, for sure, but it's not overdone and just makes the meal – fit for Don Corleone himself – more fun. Psst, here's a tip: any of the house specialties is good, but the Maker's Mark New York steak is worth bustin' outta' jail for.

TOP END

Depending on the state of the economy, chances are many of the top-end restaurants will have prix-fixe tasting menus that give a 30% to 40% discount over ordering à la carte.

Bally's Steakhouse (☎ 702-967-7999; Bally's, 3645 Las Vegas Blvd S; dishes $25-40; ⏰ 9:30am-2:30pm Sun, 5:30-10:30pm daily) Indulge in the best – and most expensive – Sunday brunch ($85) in town. Ice sculptures and lavish flower arrangements abound at the Sterling Brunch, as do food stations featuring roast duckling, beef tenderloin and fresh sushi.

Red Square (☎ 702-632-7407; Mandalay Bay, 3950 Las Vegas Blvd S; dishes $30-45; ⏰ restaurant 5-10:30pm, bar 5pm-2am Sun-Thu, 4pm-4am Fri & Sat) A headless Lenin invites you to join your comrades to live like czars behind the red curtain in this postmodern Russian restaurant. Imbibers here have got rubles to spare for exquisite stroganoff, salmon *kulebyaka* or clams topped with caviar. Don a Russian army coat to sip vodka in the subzero vault.

Fammia (☎ 702-891-7600; MGM Grand, 3799 Las Vegas Blvd S; meals $50–60; ⏰ 5:30pm-10pm Sun-Thu, 5:30pm-11pm Fri & Sat) Fammia is set in a row of outstanding restaurants at MGM Grand, but what sets it apart is that it's a top-tier dining experience you won't be paying off for the next decade. You haven't had spaghetti until you've had Fammia's take on it, made with Kobe beef meatballs.

our pick **Joël Robuchon** (☎ 702-891-7925; MGM Grand, 3799 Las Vegas Blvd S; menu per person $250-385; ⏰ 5:30-10pm Sun-Thu, to 10:30pm Fri & Sat) A once-in-a-lifetime culinary experience; block off a solid three hours and get ready to eat your way through the six- or 16-course seasonal menu of traditional French fare (garlic-roasted lobster, frog's legs, foie gras). This intimate little restaurant has garnered a veritable constellation of stars from foodie organizations, and many a celeb has called this red and gold palace of opulence home for an evening. L'Atelier de Joël Robuchon, next door, is where you can belly up to the counter for a slightly more economical but still delicious meal.

Drinking

For those who want to mingle with the locals and drink for free, check out **SpyOnVegas** (www.spyonvegas.com). It arranges an open bar at a different venue every weeknight.

ghostbar (☎ 702-942-6832; Palms Casino Resort, 4321 W Flamingo Rd; admission $10-25; ⏰ 8pm-late) Think sleek, space age and saucy. The 55th-floor aerie casts an otherworldly glow, with industrial chain-mail drapes and radiant purple-tinted banquettes. Mix it up with the bold-face names and admire the drop-dead views from the outdoor patio prow.

O'Sheas (☎ 702-697-2711; www.osheaslasvegas.com; 3555 Las Vegas Blvd S; drinks from $2; ⏰ 24hr) Right in the heart of the action. Luckily for the thirsty among us, O'Sheas has a 24-hour happy hour and 'bottle service' that gets you a bottle of Jack Daniel's or Smirnoff vodka and a mixer for $45.

Frankie's Tiki Room (☎ 702-385-3110; www.frankiestikiroom.com; 1712 W Charleston Blvd; all drinks $8; ⏰ 24hr) At the only round-the-clock tiki bar in the US, the drinks are rated in strength by skulls and the top tiki sculptors and painters in the world have their work on display.

Entertainment

Las Vegas has no shortage of entertainment on any given night, and **Ticketmaster** (☎ 702-474-4000; www.ticketmaster.com) sells tickets for pretty much everything.

Tix 4 Tonight (☎ 877-849-4868; www.tix4tonight.com; Bill's Gamblin' Hall & Saloon, 3595 Las Vegas Blvd S; 🕑 10am-8pm) offers half-price tix for a limited lineup of same-day shows and small discounts on 'always sold-out' shows. Of its six locations in Las Vegas, Bill's Gamblin' Hall is the most central. It also does half-price dinner at select restaurants.

NIGHTCLUBS & LIVE MUSIC

Admission prices to nightclubs vary wildly based on the mood of doorstaff, male to female ratio, and how crowded the club is that night.

Stoney's Rockin' Country (☎ 702-435-2855; www.stoneysrockincountry.com; 9151 Las Vegas Blvd S; cover local/out-of-state $5/10; 🕑 7pm-late Thu-Sun) An off-Strip place worth the trip. Friday and Saturday has $20 all-you-can-drink draft beer and free line dancing lessons from 7:30pm to 8:30pm. The mechanical bull is a blast.

Bank (☎ 702-693-8300; Bellagio, 3600 Las Vegas Blvd S; cover men from $30, women free-$30; 🕑 10:30pm-4:30am) Service and an upscale vibe are what sets this place apart. Spring for VIP treatment (starting at $475) and you will be treated like a celebrity.

CatHouse (☎ 702-262-4228; www.cathouselv.com; Luxor, 3900 Las Vegas Blvd S; cover Fri & Sat men/women $30/20, less other days; 🕑 10:30pm-4am Mon & Thu-Sun, 1am-4am Wed) An ultralounge that looks like a 19th-century French bordello where people get up and dance, or not; a sexy place and good vibe that's loads of fun. Good dinner before the club opens, we hear.

LAX (☎ 702-262-4529; www.laxthenightclub.com; Luxor, 3900 Las Vegas Blvd S; cover men from $40, women free-$40; 🕑 10pm-4am Wed-Sat) With celebrity investors like Christina Aguilera and a stream of hard-partying stars who host events there, it's probably the hottest club in Vegas and the near-riot outside its front doors every night proves it.

Moon (☎ 702-942-7000; www.n9negroup.com; Palms Casino Resort, 4321 W Flamingo Rd; cover weekday/weekend $20/$40; 🕑 10:30pm-4am Tue & Thu-Sun) A rooftop spot stylishly outfitted like a nightclub in outer space. Admission includes entry to the only Playboy Club in the world, attached to Moon via escalator. When the retractable roof opens, there's nothing like dancing to pulsating beats under the stars.

PRODUCTION SHOWS

There are hundreds of shows to choose from in Vegas.

LOVE (☎ 702-792-7777; tickets $99-150) at the Mirage is a popular addition to the Cirque du Soleil lineup and locals who have seen many a Cirque production come and go say it's the best one yet. Still a favorite is Cirque du Soleil's aquatic show, **O** (☎ 702-796-9999; tickets $99-150), performed at the Bellagio. Cirque du Soleil also presents **Mystère** (☎ 702-796-9999; tickets $60-110) at Treasure Island (aka TI), the adult-themed **Zumanity** (☎ 702-740-6815; tickets $69-129) at New York-New York, and **Ka** (☎ 702-796-9999; tickets $69-150) at MGM Grand. Love him or hate him, the eponymous front man at **Criss Angel Believe** (☎ 702-262-4400; tickets $59-160) puts on a trippy, dark (probably disturbing for kids) Cirque show at Luxor.

GAY & LESBIAN NIGHTS OUT: LAS VEGAS

Fabrice Marino, an Italian journalist who knows where the boys and girls are in Las Vegas, says that it's a great city for gay travelers *if* you know where to look. His starter-kit recommendations:

Krave (☎ 702-836-0830; www.kravelasvegas.com; 3663 Las Vegas Blvd S; cover $5-20; 🕑 10pm-late Sun-Thu, 11pm-late Fri & Sat) A super-happening gay club especially good for after-hours partying. Crowded during special events and can be very touristy. Every Saturday night is CandyBar, the biggest and best party of the week for Sin City's lesbian set. Enter off Harmon Ave outside Desert Passage.

Piranha (☎ 702-791-0100; www.piranhavegas.com; 4633 Paradise Rd; cover $5-10; 🕑 midnight-late) Where the locals go, it's packed, in a good way, Thursday to Sunday night and is the best place for meetups. Ask a regular about the handful of nearby gay spots.

Blue Moon Resort (☎ 702-784-4500; www.bluemoonlv.com; 2651 Westwood Dr; r incl breakfast $126-80;) Owned by gay men and catering exclusively to gay men, Blue Moon has 45 stylish rooms appointed in chic dark leather and wood. The pool area is the place to be, with a 10-man Jacuzzi and loads of special events. It adds up to men men men and fun fun fun.

Steel Panther (☎ 702-617-7777; www.greenvalleyranchresort.com; Green Valley Resort, 2300 Paseo Verde Pkwy, Henderson; admission free; 🕑 11pm-late Fri), a hair-metal tribute band, makes fun of the audience, themselves and the 1980s with sight gags, one-liners and many a drug and sex reference. At their Los Angeles shows they've gotten celebs like Pink and Billy Ray Cyrus on stage to belt out tunes.

Shopping

Bonanza Gifts (☎ 702-385-7359; 2440 Las Vegas Blvd S) The best place for only-in-Vegas kitsch souvenirs.

Fashion Show Mall (☎ 702-369-0704; 3200 Las Vegas Blvd S) Nevada's biggest and flashiest mall.

Forum Shops (☎ 702-893-4800; Caesars Palace, 3500 Las Vegas Blvd S) From Abercrombie & Fitch to Versace, it's got it all.

Grand Canal Shoppes (☎ 702-414-4500; Venetian, 3355 Las Vegas Blvd S) Italianate indoor luxury mall with gondolas.

Mandalay Place (☎ 702-632-9333; 3930 Las Vegas Blvd S) On the sky bridge between the Mandalay Bay and the Luxor. An airy promenade with unique, fashion-forward boutiques.

Miracle Mile Shops (☎ 702-866-0710; Planet Hollywood, 3663 Las Vegas Blvd S) A staggering 1.5 miles long; get a tattoo, drink and duds.

Wynn Esplanade (☎ 702-770-7000; Wynn Las Vegas, 3131 Las Vegas Blvd S) A 75,000-sq-ft showcase of upscale consumer bliss.

Getting There & Around

Just south of the major Strip casinos and easily accessible from I-15, **McCarran International Airport** (LAS; ☎ 702-261-4636; www.mccarran.com) has direct flights from most US cities, and some from Canada and Europe. **Bell Trans** (☎ 702-739-7990; www.bell-trans.com) offers a shuttle service ($6.50) between the airport and the Strip. Fares to downtown destinations are slightly higher. At the airport, exit door 9 near baggage claim to find the Bell Trans booth.

The **Greyhound bus station** (☎ 702-383-9792; www.greyhound.com; 200 S Main St), downtown, has regular buses to and from Los Angeles ($40 to $57, six hours), San Diego ($47 to $62, nine hours) and San Francisco ($60 to $93, 15 hours). **Amtrak** (☎ 800-872-7245; www.amtrak.com) does not run trains to Las Vegas, although it does offer a connecting bus service from Los Angeles ($50, six hours).

All of the attractions in Vegas have free self-parking and valet parking available (tip $2). Fast, fun and fully wheelchair accessible, the **monorail** (☎ 702-699-8299; www.lvmonorail.com) connects the Sahara to the MGM Grand, stopping at major Strip megaresorts along the way, and operating from 7am to 2am Monday to Thursday and until 3am Friday through Sunday. A single ride is $5, a 24-hour pass is $12, and a three-day pass is $28. The **Deuce** (☎ 702-228-7433; www.rtcsouthernnevada.com), a local double-decker bus, runs frequently 24 hours daily between the Strip and downtown (one ride/24-hour pass $3/7).

AROUND LAS VEGAS

Red Rock Canyon

This dramatic **park** (☎ 702-515-5350; www.redrockcanyonlv.org; entry $5; 🕑 6am-dusk) is the perfect anecdote to Vegas' artificial brightness. A 20-mile drive west of the Strip, the canyon is actually more like a valley, with the steep, rugged red-rock escarpment rising 3000ft on its western edge. There's a 13-mile scenic loop with access to hiking trails and first-come, first-served **camping** (campsites $10) 2 miles east of the visitor center.

Lake Mead & Hoover Dam

Lake Mead and Hoover Dam are the most-visited sites within the **Lake Mead National Recreation Area** (☎ 702-293-8906; www.nps.gov/lame), which encompasses 110-mile-long Lake Mead, 67-mile-long Lake Mohave and many miles of desert around the lakes. The excellent **Alan Bible Visitors Center** (☎ 702-293-8990; 🕑 8:30am-4:30pm), on Hwy 93 halfway between Boulder City and Hoover Dam, has information on recreation and desert life. From there, North Shore Rd winds around the lake and makes a great scenic drive.

Straddling the Arizona–Nevada border, the graceful curve and art-deco style of the 726ft **Hoover Dam** (www.usbr.gov/lc/hooverdam) contrasts superbly with the stark landscape. Visitors can either take the 30-minute **power plant tour** (adult/child $11/6; 🕑 9:15am-5:15pm, to 4:15pm winter) or the more in-depth, one-hour **Hoover Dam tour** (no children under 8, tour $30).

Tickets for both tours are sold at the **visitor center** (☎ 702-494-2517, 866-730-9097; 🕑 9am-6pm; exhibits adult/child $8/free). Tickets for the power plant tour only can be purchased online. Note that commercial trucks and buses are not allowed to cross the dam, and pedestrians cannot walk on the dam after dark. All vehicles crossing the dam are subject to search. A highway that will bypass the dam traffic choke point is in the works, with a scheduled opening date of June 2010.

Valley of Fire State Park

A masterpiece of desert scenery filled with psychedelically shaped sandstone outcroppings, this **park** (www.parks.nv.gov/vf.htm; admission $6) is a great escape 55 miles from Vegas. Hwy 169 runs right past the **visitor center** (☎ 702-397-2088; 8:30am-4:30pm), which has hiking and **camping** (campsites $14) information and excellent desert-life exhibits.

Laughlin

On the banks of the Colorado River, Laughlin is the poor man's Vegas. The casinos lining the strip sport familiar names – Flamingo, Harrah's – but the look is more blue jeans than bling. Laughlin's a down-home gambling type of place – think burgers, Budweiser and penny slots. It attracts an older, more sedate crowd.

One reason Laughlin has become so popular is that it boasts some of the cheapest hotel rates in the West – and while rooms are fairly bland, these are no fleapits. Try the **Tropicana Express** (☎ 702-298-4200, 800-243-6846; www.tropicanax.com; 2121 S Casino Dr; r from $22;); the recently renovated rooms draw rave reviews from travelers. And, for rail fans, there's a working locomotive that chugs around the 27-acre resort. Right on the river, the **Golden Nugget** (☎ 702-385-7111, 800-846-5336; www.goldennugget.com; 2300 S Casino Dr; r $25-60;) has nice rooms with a tropical theme. Riverview rooms show Laughlin at its prettiest right around sunset.

WESTERN NEVADA

A vast and mostly undeveloped sagebrush steppe, the western corner of the state is carved by mountain ranges and parched valleys. The place where modern Nevada began with the discovery of the famous Comstock silver lode in and around Virginia City, these days this part of the state lures visitors with outdoor adventure in the form of hiking, biking, and skiing on the many mountains; quaint historic towns full of grand homes built by silver barons; and, of course, the gambling mecca of Reno. For information about the Nevada side of Lake Tahoe, see p1004.

Reno

Those who don't judge a book by its cover often leave 'The Biggest Little City in the World' thoroughly charmed. A walkable downtown at the edge of the Sierra Nevada mountain range, a thriving arts scene, a year-round white-water kayaking park in the center of the city and nearby outdoor adventure add up to a jackpot of good times.

Reno's downtown is north of the Truckee River and south of I-80. Most of the casino action is along N Virginia St, between 1st and 6th Sts. The River Walk district along W 1st St is the best place for noncasino entertainment and food.

South of downtown, you'll find a **visitor center** (☎ 775-827-7600, 800-367-7366; www.visitrenotahoe.com; Reno Town Mall, 4001 S Virginia St; 8am-5pm Mon-Fri).

SIGHTS & ACTIVITIES

Casinos

Few of Reno's casinos have the flash of Vegas, though some do try.

Eldorado (☎ 775-786-5700; www.eldoradoreno.com; 345 N Virginia St) This hotel-casino complex is a small city under one roof.

Grand Sierra Resort (☎ 775-789-2000; www.grandsierraresort.com; 2500 E 2nd St) A champagne lounge, concerts and a small theme park packed with thrill rides.

Peppermill (☎ 775-826-2121; www.peppermillreno.com; 2707 S Virginia St) A snazzy Vegas-quality place. November 2008 saw the opening of a muscle-melting 30,000-sq-ft spa.

Siena (☎ 775- 327-4362; www.sienareno.com; 1 S Lake St) Right on the Truckee River, it's an upscale, friendly place to game or spa.

Silver Legacy (☎ 775-329-4777; 407 N Virginia St) A 19th-century streetscape plus sound-and-light shows inside a 120ft dome. Lots of antiques displays from the silver-mining days.

Other Attractions

The **Truckee River Whitewater Park** (☎ 775-334-2262; cnr Sierra & 1st Sts) injects action into the middle of downtown with year-round kayaking. There's a mellow beginner's area, but most of the park is Class II or III rapids. Located on the valet level of Silver Legacy, **Wild Sierra Adventures** (☎ 866-323-8928; www.wildsierra.com; 407 N Virginia St), run by the affable Jim Bell, offers tons of adventure: kayaking, tubing, mountain biking, skiing, horseback riding and snowmobiling.

In winter, Lake Tahoe (p1004) ski resorts are close by, and **Mt Rose** (☎ 775-849-0704; www.mtrose.com; lift ticket adult/child $64/17) is a mere 25 minutes away.

The **National Automobile Museum** (☎ 775-333-9300; www.automuseum.org; 10 S Lake St; adult/child $10/4; 9:30am-5:30pm Mon-Sat, 10am-4pm Sun; P) has an

GREAT BALLS OF FIRE!

For the week straddling the end of August and the beginning of September, **Burning Man** (www.burningman.com; admission $195-280) explodes onto the sunbaked Black Rock Desert and Nevada sprouts a third major population center – Black Rock City. It's an experiential art party (and alternative universe) that climaxes in the immolation of a towering stick figure.

impressive collection of one-of-a-kind vehicles, like a 24-karat gold-plated DeLorean, and some cool celebrity rides like Elvis' 1973 Cadillac.

The **Nevada Museum of Art** (☎ 775-329-3333; www.nevadaart.org; 160 W Liberty St; adult/child $10/1; 🕒 10am-5pm Wed-Sun, to 8pm Thu) has striking sculptures on the outside and permanent collections inside that include more than 600 photographs of landscapes, paintings from regional artists, and a good sampling of contemporary and pop art.

Run by the Historic Reno Preservation Society, most **historic walking tours** (☎ 775-747-4478; www.historicreno.org; tours $10; 🕒 tours 6pm Tue, 10am Sat) begin at the Riverside Artist Lofts on the corner of the Truckee River and Virginia St.

SLEEPING

Wildflower Village (☎ 775-747-8848; 4395 W 4th St; www.wildflowervillage.com; r from $50; 💻) This artists colony on the edge of town has a tumbledown yet creative vibe. Individual murals decorate the facade of each room, and you can hear the freight trains rumble on by.

Silver Legacy (☎ 775-325-7401, 800-687-8733; www.silverlegacyreno.com; 407 N Virginia St; r $50-100; ❄ 💻 📶 🏊) All pretty in leather and lace, this large, central hotel-casino has Victorian-themed rooms that are surprisingly classy and comfortable. Topped by a huge dome (a faux silver mine and restaurants are underneath), the place is a local landmark.

Siena Hotel Spa Casino (☎ 775-327-4362, 877-743-6233; www.sienareno.com; 1 S Lake St; r from $90-170; 🚭 ❄ 💻 📶 🏊) This boutique hotel is one of Reno's most luxurious addresses, with cozy, nicely appointed riverside rooms. All rooms are nonsmoking.

EATING

Jungle Java & Jungle Vino (☎ 775-329-4484; www.javajunglevino.com; 246 W 1st St; sandwiches $6; 🕒 6am-midnight; 📶) A side-by-side coffee shop and wine bar with a cool mosaic floor, an internet café and free wi-fi all rolled into one.

Golden Flower (☎ 775-323-1628; 205 W 4th St; meals $6-9; 🕒 10am-9pm) Walk in on a Sunday to see the place packed with Vietnamese families – a positive omen. Everything is good, but the pho and fresh spring rolls are especially fresh and tasty.

Peg's Glorified Ham & Eggs (☎ 775-329-2600; 420 S Sierra St; dishes $7-10; 🕒 6:30am-2pm) Widely cited as the best breakfast place in the city, if not the state, Peg's offers tasty grill food that's not too greasy. It's the perfect place to sit outside and read the Sunday paper while munching on an overstuffed omelet. Kid-friendly.

Louis' Basque Corner (☎ 775-323-7203; 301 E 4th St; lunch menu adult/child $12/7, dinner menu adult/child $24/12; 🕒 11:30am-2:30pm Tue-Sat, 5-9:30pm daily) Get ready to dine on lamb, rabbit, sweet breads and more lamb at a big table full of people you've never met before. A different set-course menu is offered every day, posted in the window.

Wild River Grille (☎ 775-284-7455; www.wildrivergrille.com; 17 S Virginia St; lunch mains $12, dinner mains $30; 🕒 11am-11pm Sun-Thu, 11am-midnight Fri & Sat) Chic ambience and good eats right on the river. The crab and salmon cakes ($9.50) are divine, and on weekend nights you may be lucky enough to be serenaded by local chanteuse Kate Cotter.

DRINKING & ENTERTAINMENT

210 North (☎ 775-786-6210; www.210north.com; 210 N Sierra St; free before 10pm, cover $10-20; 🕒 Thu-Sat) When Reno folk want to flaunt it, they end up here. A pulsing-hot dance club and down-tempo lounge that would feel right at home in Vegas.

Davidson's Distillery (☎ 775-324-1917; 219 E 4th St; 🕒 noon-late) Yes, that's a vending machine with cigarettes and spare parts for Harley-Davidson motorcycles. As long as you come in with a live-and-let-live attitude you'll have a blast at this rocking locals bar with a heavy biker contingent. A tattoo and a Harley shop share the building, if you get inspired.

Shooter's (☎ 775-329-9646; 434 N Virginia St; 🕒 noon-late) It ain't easy being sleazy and this dark bar right across from the big casinos on Virginia St does it oh so well. No gambling and a heavy-metal jukebox seal the deal.

GETTING THERE & AROUND

Reno-Tahoe International Airport (RNO; ☎ 775-328-6400; www.renoairport.com; 📶) is a few miles southeast of downtown and has free wi-fi. **Greyhound** (☎ 775-322-2970; www.greyhound.com; 155 Stevenson St; ⏰ 5am-10pm) has frequent buses to San Francisco ($39, six hours) and Los Angeles ($66 to $93, 10½ to 15 hours), and two daily to Las Vegas ($63 to $105, 18 to 20 hours). **Amtrak** (☎ 775-329-8638; www.amtrak.com; 280 N Center St; ⏰ 7:45am-5pm) has one daily run to Sacramento at 9:36am ($42, five hours); note that this route often has major delays and uses buses. One train leaves eastbound daily at 4:06pm with stops in Salt Lake City, UT ($58, 13 hours), and Denver, CO ($96, 29 hours).

Many hotels offer free shuttles to and from the airport. Local bus system **Citifare** (☎ 775-348-7433) covers the metropolitan area (adult/child $2/1.25); the main transfer station is at E 4th and Center Sts. The free yellow Sierra Spirit bus (called the pinwheel bus by locals) plies Virginia St from the University of Nevada to the river from 7am to 7pm and is a roving wi-fi hot spot.

Pyramid Lake

A piercingly blue expanse in an otherwise barren landscape 25 miles north of Reno on the Paiute Indian Reservation, Pyramid Lake is popular for recreation and fishing. Permits for **camping** (primitive campsites per vehicle per night $9) and **fishing** (per person $9) are available at area gas stations, at outdoor suppliers and the Long's Drug Store locations in Reno, and at the **ranger station** (☎ 775-476-1155; www.plpt.nsn.us; ⏰ 8am-6pm Mon-Thu) on Hwy 446 in Sutcliffe.

Carson City

It's easy to enjoy a quick stop at this quiet, old-fashioned place where pretty historic buildings and pleasant tree-lined streets offer a refreshing change of pace. The casinos are sedate and there are a few worthwhile historical museums to discover.

Hwy 395/Carson St is the main drag. The **visitor center** (☎ 775-687-7410; www.visitcarsoncity.com; 1900 S Carson St; ⏰ 9am-5pm Mon-Fri, gift store only 10am-3pm Sat), a mile south of downtown, gives out a local map with interesting historical walking and driving tours. For hiking and camping information, stop by the United States Forest Service (USFS) **Carson Ranger District Office** (☎ 775-882-2766; 1536 S Carson St; ⏰ 8am-4:30pm Mon-Fri).

Train buffs shouldn't miss the **Nevada State Railroad Museum** (☎ 775-687-6953; 2180 S Carson St; admission $4; ⏰ 8:30am-4:30pm), which displays some 30 train cars and engines from the 1800s to the early 1900s.

There is a handful of casino properties in town, but for a taste of the old Carson City check into the restored 1914 **Bliss Bungalow** (☎ 775-883-6129; www.blissbungalow.com; 408 W Robinson St; r incl breakfast from $85; ⊠ 📶) in the leafy historic district and call out 'howdy neighbor' to passers-by as you sit a spell on the spacious front porch. Each of the five rooms oozes charm.

RTC Intercity (☎ 775-348-7433; www.rtcwashoe.com) has a weekday commuter service between Carson City and Reno ($4, one hour). The buses have free wi-fi.

Virginia City

During the 1860s gold rush, Virginia City was a high-flying, rip-roaring Wild West boomtown. Newspaperman Samuel Clemens, alias Mark Twain, spent some time in this raucous place during its heyday; years later his eyewitness descriptions of mining life were published in a book called *Roughing It*.

The high-elevation town is a National Historic Landmark, with a main street of Victorian buildings, wooden sidewalks and some hokey but fun museums. The main drag is C St; check out the **visitor center** (☎ 775-847-4386; www.virginiacity-nv.org; 86 S C St; ⏰ 10am-4pm).

The **Virginia City International Camel Races** celebrated 50 years of camels battling toward the finish line in 2009. Expect enormous crowds for this popular September event – emus and ostriches race here too. Contact the visitor center for dates.

One of the town's star attractions is the quirky **Way It Was Museum** (☎ 775-847-0766; 113 N C St; admission $3; ⏰ 10am-6pm). It's a fun, old-fashioned place offering good background information on mining the lode. To see how the mining elite lived, stop by the **Mackay Mansion** (D St) and the **Castle** (B St).

Virginia City has a number of places to sleep, including a large RV park. A more luxurious choice, the historic **Chollar Mansion B&B** (☎ 775-847-9777, 877-246-5527; www.chollarmansion.com; 565 S D St; r incl breakfast $135; ⊠) used to be the town mine office. The best food in Virginia City is probably at **Cafe del Rio** (☎ 775-847-5151; 394 S C St; meals from $12; ⏰ 11am-8pm Wed-Sat, 10am-8pm Sun), serving a nice blend of *nuevo* Mexican and good café food, including breakfast.

NEVADA GREAT BASIN

A trip across Nevada's Great Basin is a serene, almost haunting experience. But those on the quest for the 'Great American Road Trip' will relish the fascinating historic towns and quirky diversions tucked away along lonely desert highways.

Along I-80

Heading east from Reno, **Winnemucca**, 150 miles to the northeast, is the first worthwhile stop. It boasts a vintage downtown, shops and numerous motels and restaurants. There's a number of Basque restaurants here, and the city has a yearly Basque festival. For information, stop by the **chamber of commerce** (☎ 775-623-2225; 30 W Winnemucca Blvd; 8:30am-5pm Mon-Fri, 9am-4pm Sat, 11am-4pm Sun June 1–mid-Sept). Plan to spend some time checking out the displays here: a buckaroo (cowboy) and big-game museum call the visitor center home.

The culture of the American West is most diligently cultivated in **Elko**. Aspiring cowboys and cowgirls should visit the **Western Folklife Center** (☎ 775-738-7508; www.westernfolklife.org; 501 Railroad St; exhibit admission adult/child $5/1; 10am-5:30pm Mon & Wed-Fri, 10:30am-5:30pm Tue, 10am-5pm Sat), which offers art and history exhibits and also hosts the popular **Cowboy Poetry Gathering** each January. There's also a **National Basque Festival**, held every 4th of July, with games, traditional dancing and a 'Running of the Bulls' event. At the town center, **Stockmen's Casino & Hotel** (☎ 775-738-5141, 800-648-2345; www.stockmenscasinos.com; 340 Commercial St; r/ste from $45/80;) is a good place to stay, with clean rooms.

Along Highway 50

Towns are few and far between, the only sounds the hum of the engine or the whisper of wind. Once part of the Lincoln Hwy, lonesome Hwy 50 follows the route of the Overland Stagecoach, the Pony Express and the first transcontinental telegraph line.

Fallon, 60 miles east of Reno, is an agricultural and military town, and home to a naval air base. If you're heading east this is your last chance to get gas for 110 miles. **Fallon Lodge** (☎ 775-423-4648; www.fallonlodge.com; 390 W Williams Ave; r from $35;) has clean, simple rooms with kitchenettes.

Heading east, the next substantial town is **Austin**, smack-dab in the middle of Nevada. It's become run-down since its 1880s heyday but is still interesting. The mountainous area around it is lovely, and Austin's **USFS office** (☎ 775-964-2671; 100 Midas Rd; 7:30am-4:30pm Mon-Fri), just off Hwy 50, can recommend hikes and driving loops. **Mountain biking** is phenomenal here; the website of the **chamber of commerce** (☎ 775-964-2200; www.austinnevada.com) lists good bike routes.

During the late 19th century, $40 million worth of silver was extracted from the hills near **Eureka**. The town is now fairly well preserved, possessing a handsome courthouse, the interesting **Eureka Sentinel Museum** (☎ 775-237-5010; 10 S Bateman St; admission free; 10am-6pm daily May-Oct, 10am-6pm Tue-Sat Nov-Apr), a beautifully restored 1880 opera house and a few well-kept motels.

Near the Nevada–Utah border is the awesome, uncrowded **Great Basin National Park**. It encompasses 13,063ft Wheeler Peak, rising abruptly from the desert. Hiking trails near the summit take in superb country with glacial lakes, ancient bristlecone pines and even a permanent ice field. Admission is free; the park **visitor center** (☎ 775-234-7331; www.nps.gov/grba; 8am-5:30pm), just north of the town of **Baker**, is the place to get oriented on everything the park has to offer.

For a 60- or 90-minute guided tour of the caves here that are richly decorated with rare limestone formations, head to the **Lehman Caves** (☎ 775-234-7331; www.nps.gov/grba; admission $8-10; 8:30am-4pm) five miles outside of Baker. There are first-come, first-served developed **campgrounds** (campsites $12) in the park.

Along Highway 95

Hwy 95 runs roughly north–south through the western part of the state; the southern section is starkly scenic as it passes the Nevada Test Site (where more than 720 nuclear weapons were exploded in the 1950s). Five miles north of Beatty, **Bailey's Hot Springs & RV Park** (☎ 775-553-2395; tent/RV sites $18/21), a 1906 former railroad depot, has three private hot springs in antique bathhouses, open from 8am to 8pm daily. Overnight guests get complimentary usage, and day-trippers pay $5 per person for a 30-minute soak.

Off Hwy 374, a few miles southwest of Beatty, the **Goldwell Open Air Museum** (☎ 702-870-9946; www.goldwellmuseum.org; admission free; 24hr) is a rather mysterious 8-acre outdoor sculpture site surrounded by desert.

Along Highways 375 & 93

Hwy 375 is dubbed the 'Extraterrestrial Hwy' because of the huge amount of UFO sightings along this stretch of concrete and because it intersects Hwy 93 near top-secret **Area 51**, part of Nellis Air Force Base and a supposed holding area for captured UFOs. In the tiny town of **Rachel**, on Hwy 375, **Little A'Le'Inn** (☎ 775-729-2515; www.aleinn.com; r from $45) accommodates earthlings and aliens alike, and sells extraterrestrial souvenirs. Probings not included.

Continuing east, Hwy 93 passes through a gorgeous Joshua-tree grove before arriving in **Caliente**, a former railroad town with a 1923 Mission-style depot. Area attractions include **Cathedral Gorge State Park**, with first-come, first-served **campsites** ($14) set amid badlands-style cliffs. Twenty miles north, **Pioche** is an attractive mining town overlooking beautiful Lake Valley.

ARIZONA

Every state tourism brochure claims a huge amount of diversity, but Arizona has the bona fides. You can visit ancient cities hewn into high cliffs and a self-sufficient city of the future in one half-day outing, and in winter you can ski in the morning and go hiking in shorts in the afternoon. Mostly, though, it's the landscape that gets people, and the space. Armies of saguaro cactus stand at attention along nearly every roadway. Bushes, trees and cacti in all sorts of gnarly shapes and colors spread out on rolling sandy hills for as far as the eye can see.

In the heart of Arizona is Phoenix and its suburbs, the aptly named Valley of the Sun. This is one of the biggest metro areas in the Southwest and has the eating, sights and glorious spas you'd expect in a spot that stakes its claim on rest and renewal. Tucson is the funky, artsy gateway to southern Arizona's astronomical and historical sights, and the last major stop until Nogales, a city that straddles the Mexican border.

Up north is Flagstaff, a cool mountain town where locals seek relief from the searing summer heat and people come to play on the nearby San Francisco Peaks all year long. Lying on the northern edge of the state like the crown that it is, the Grand Canyon is Arizona's star attraction. Carved over eons by the mighty Colorado River, the greatest hole on earth draws visitors from around the world.

ARIZONA FACTS

Nickname Grand Canyon State
Population 6.5 million
Area 113,637 sq miles
Capital city Phoenix (population 1.5 million)
Other cities Tucson (population 519,000), Flagstaff (population 60,000), Sedona (population 11,400)
Sales tax 5.6%
Birthplace of Apache chief Geronimo (1829–1909), political activist Cesar Chavez (1927–93), singer Linda Ronstadt (b 1946)
Home of Sedona New Age movement, mining towns turned art colonies
Famous for Grand Canyon, saguaro cacti
Best souvenir Pink cactus-shaped neon lamp from roadside stall
Driving distances Tucson to Sedona 230 miles, Phoenix to Grand Canyon Village 235 miles

History

The Pueblo, Mogollon and Hohokam tribes inhabited Arizona for centuries before Spanish explorer Francisco Vasquez de Coronado launched a Southwest expedition here from Mexico City in 1540. Settlers and missionaries followed in his wake, and by the mid-19th century the US controlled Arizona. The Indian Wars, in which the US Army battled Native Americans to 'protect' settlers and claim land for the government, officially ended in 1886 with the surrender of Apache warrior Geronimo.

Railroad and mining expansion grew. In 1912 President Theodore Roosevelt's support for damming the territory's rivers led to Arizona becoming the 48th state.

Today Arizona is in transition. Fifty years of rapid growth have taken a toll on the state's limited natural resources. Scarcity of water remains among the foremost issues for Arizona lawmakers, who continue the desperate search for the water needed to supply the burgeoning cities. An influx of new residents, many from places with a more liberal and less libertarian bent, are slowly changing the political makeup of the place.

Information

Arizona is on Mountain Standard Time but is the only western state that does not observe daylight saving time from spring to early fall. The exception is the Navajo Reservation, which *does* observe daylight saving time.

Generally speaking, lodging rates in southern Arizona (including Phoenix, Tucson and Yuma) are much higher in winter and spring, which are considered the state's 'high season.' Great deals are to be had in the hot areas in the height of summer.

Arizona Office of Tourism (☎ 602-364-3700, 866-891-3640; www.arizonaguide.com; 1110 W Washington, Suite 155, Phoenix) Free state information.

Arizona Public Lands Information Center (☎ 602-417-9300; www.publiclands.org; 1 N Central Ave, Suite 102, Phoenix) Information about USFS, NPS, Bureau of Land Management (BLM) and state lands and parks.

Arizona State Parks (☎ 602-542-4174; www.azstateparks.com; 1300 W Washington St, Phoenix) Camping ($10 to $30 per vehicle per night) is first-come, first-served at all but two state parks, Buckskin Mountain and Roper Lake.

PHOENIX

Covering almost 2000 sq miles, Phoenix is easily the largest metropolis in the Southwest. At first glance it can seem like a limitless sprawl of beige and strip malls, but look a little harder and there's an interesting mix of upscale pampering and sunbaked weirdness.

In the midst of a revitalization, downtown Phoenix has signs of life at night now, with the up-and-coming Roosevelt District finally bringing together what were lonely pockets of arts and culture before. Add to this the spiffy new light-rail system that runs past some of the best museums and eateries in the state, and a reborn Phoenix is more than marketing hype.

Phoenix is the center of gravity for a family of interconnected cities in the Valley of the Sun. Think of Scottsdale as the always stylish big sister who married up, Tempe like the good-natured but occasionally rowdy college kid, and Mesa like the brother who wanted nothing more than a quiet life in the suburbs.

Reveling in more than 300 days of sunshine a year, Phoenix is crazy-hot in summer – above 110°F (43°C) – but pleasant days prevail in winter.

The city is a major transportation hub, and is often used as a jumping-off point for further-flung adventures.

Orientation

Most of the valley sits approximately 1100ft above sea level, though it's ringed by mountains that range from 2500ft to more than 7000ft in elevation. Central Ave runs north–south through Phoenix, dividing west addresses from east addresses; Washington St runs west–east, dividing north addresses from south addresses.

Scottsdale, Tempe and Mesa are east of the airport. Scottsdale Rd runs north–south between Scottsdale and Tempe. The airport is 3 miles southeast of downtown.

Avoid the grungy stretch of Van Buren St between downtown and the airport; motels here are run-down and popular with prostitutes.

Information

BOOKSTORES

Bookman's (☎ 602-433-0255; www.bookmans.com; 8034 N 19th Ave; wi-fi) Aisle after aisle of used books; free in-store wi-fi.

Wide World of Maps (☎ 602-279-2323; 2626 W Indian School Rd; 9am-6pm Mon-Fri, to 5pm Sat) Dedicated to maps and guidebooks.

EMERGENCY & MEDICAL SERVICES

Banner Good Samaritan Medical Center (☎ 602-239-2000; 1111 E McDowell Rd; 24hr emergency)

Police (☎ 602-262-7626; 620 W Washington St)

INTERNET ACCESS

Burton Barr Central Library (☎ 602-262-4636; www.phoenixpubliclibrary.org; 1221 N Central Ave; 11am-7pm Mon, Wed & Fri, 9am-5pm Tue, Thu & Sat, 1-5pm Sun) Free internet access.

INTERNET RESOURCES & MEDIA

Arizona Republic (www.azcentral.com) Arizona's largest newspaper; publishes a free entertainment guide, *Calendar,* every Thursday.

craigslist (http://phoenix.craigslist.org) The active local branch of the popular bulletin board, with info on ride shares, events etc.

Phoenix New Times (www.phoenixnewtimes.com) The major free weekly; lots of event and restaurant listings.

MONEY

Foreign exchange is available at the airport and major bank branches.

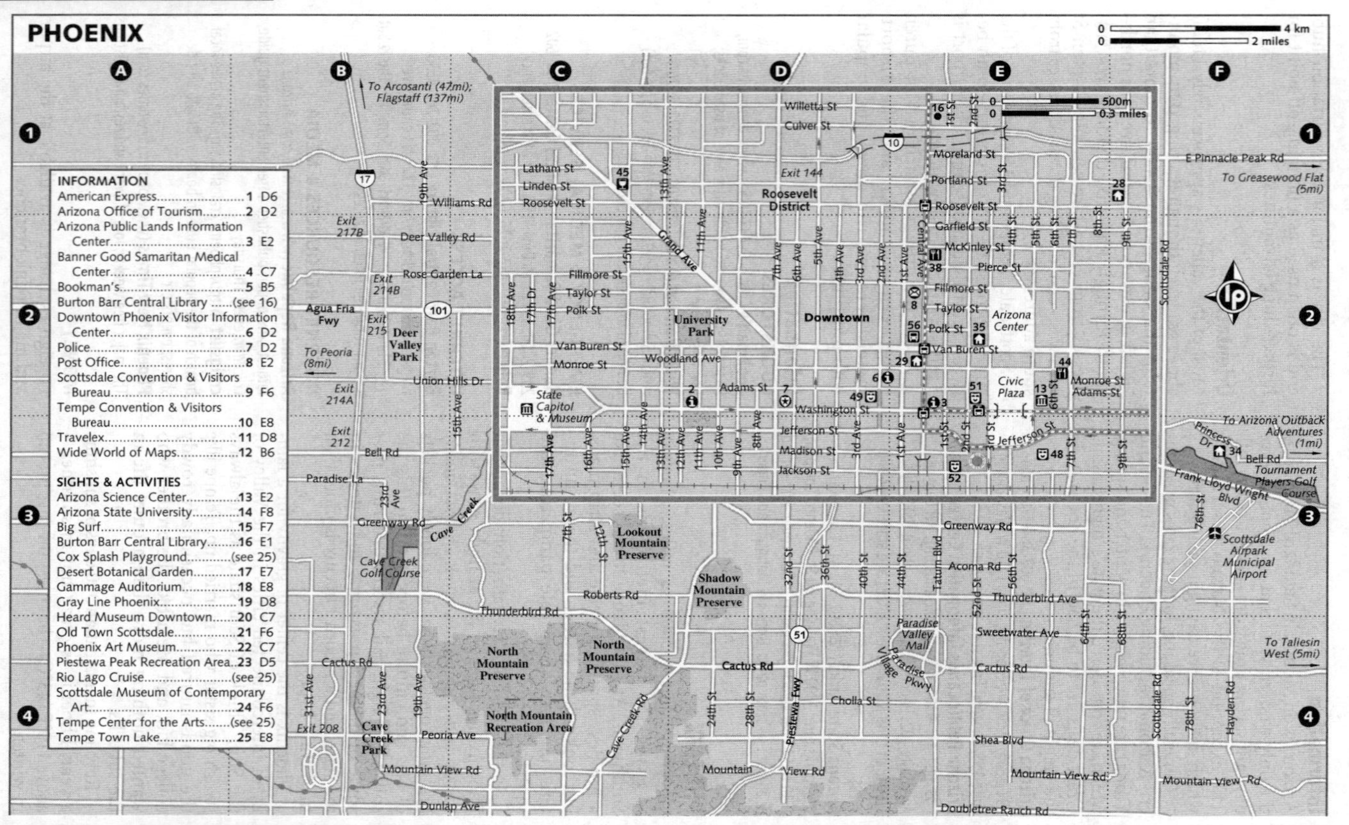
PHOENIX
INFORMATION
American Express....1 D6
Arizona Office of Tourism....2 D2
Arizona Public Lands Information Center....3 E2
Banner Good Samaritan Medical Center....4 C7
Bookman's....5 B5
Burton Barr Central Library....(see 16)
Downtown Phoenix Visitor Information Center....6 D2
Police....7 D2
Post Office....8 E2
Scottsdale Convention & Visitors Bureau....9 F6
Tempe Convention & Visitors Bureau....10 E8
Travelex....11 D8
Wide World of Maps....12 B6
SIGHTS & ACTIVITIES
Arizona Science Center....13 E2
Arizona State University....14 F8
Big Surf....15 F7
Burton Barr Central Library....16 E1
Cox Splash Playground....(see 25)
Desert Botanical Garden....17 E7
Gammage Auditorium....18 E8
Gray Line Phoenix....19 D8
Heard Museum Downtown....20 C7
Old Town Scottsdale....21 F6
Phoenix Art Museum....22 C7
Piestewa Peak Recreation Area....23 D5
Rio Lago Cruise....(see 25)
Scottsdale Museum of Contemporary Art....24 F6
Tempe Center for the Arts....(see 25)
Tempe Town Lake....25 E8
0 4 km
0 2 miles
0 500m
0 0.3 miles
To Arcosanti (47mi); Flagstaff (137mi)
To Greasewood Flat (5mi)
To Peoria (8mi)
To Arizona Outback Adventures (1mi)
To Taliesin West (5mi)
Roosevelt District
Downtown
University Park
Arizona Center
Civic Plaza
State Capitol & Museum
Deer Valley Park
Cave Creek Golf Course
Lookout Mountain Preserve
Shadow Mountain Preserve
North Mountain Preserve
North Mountain Recreation Area
Cave Creek Park
Paradise Valley Mall
Scottsdale Airpark Municipal Airport
Tournament Players Golf Course
Agua Fria Fwy
Piestewa Fwy
Grand Ave
Scottsdale Rd
Greenway Rd
Thunderbird Rd
Cactus Rd
Bell Rd
Shea Blvd
Mountain View Rd
Frank Lloyd Wright Blvd

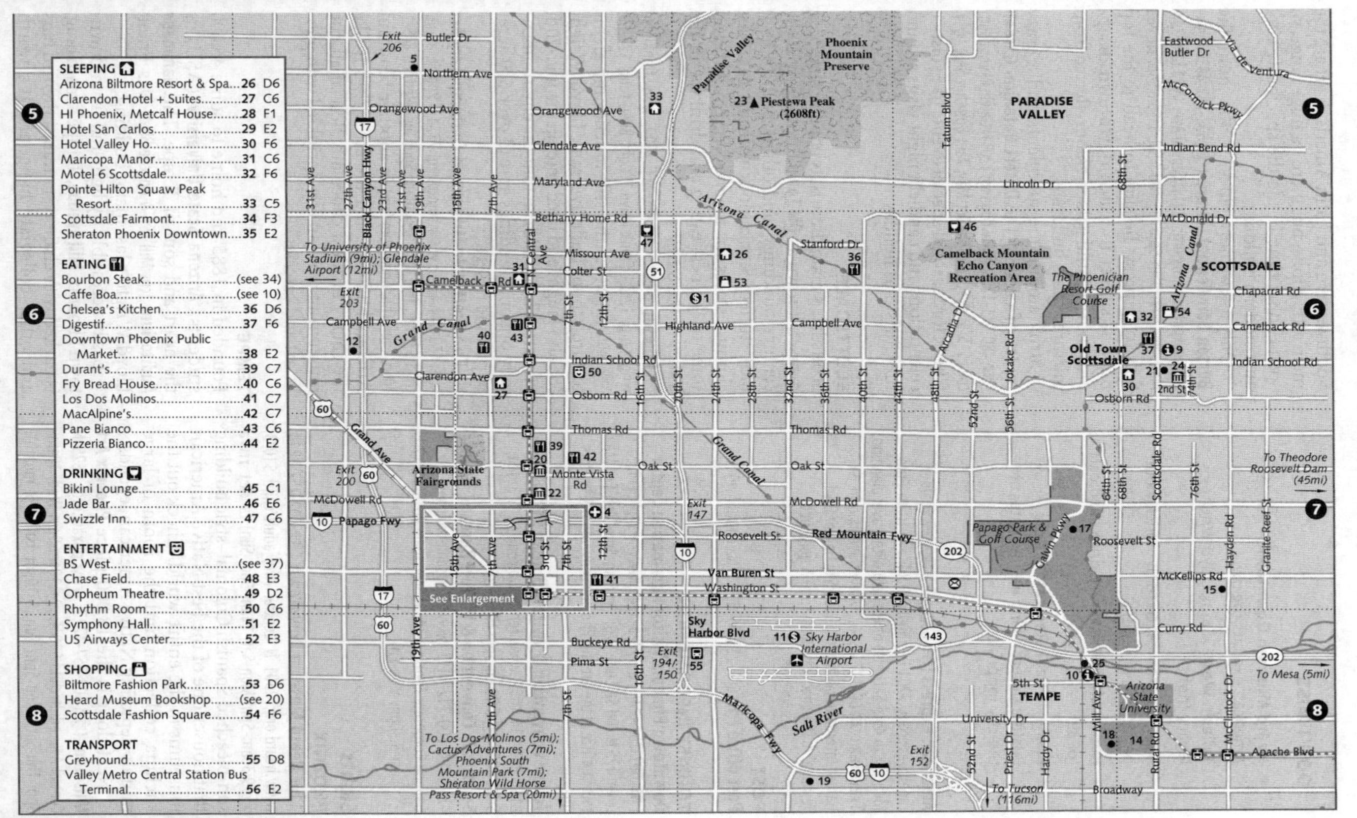
SLEEPING
Arizona Biltmore Resort & Spa...26 D6
Clarendon Hotel + Suites...27 C6
HI Phoenix, Metcalf House...28 F1
Hotel San Carlos...29 E2
Hotel Valley Ho...30 F6
Maricopa Manor...31 C6
Motel 6 Scottsdale...32 F6
Pointe Hilton Squaw Peak Resort...33 C5
Scottsdale Fairmont...34 F3
Sheraton Phoenix Downtown...35 E2
EATING
Bourbon Steak...(see 34)
Caffe Boa...(see 10)
Chelsea's Kitchen...36 D6
Digestif...37 F6
Downtown Phoenix Public Market...38 E2
Durant's...39 C7
Fry Bread House...40 C6
Los Dos Molinos...41 C7
MacAlpine's...42 C7
Pane Bianco...43 C6
Pizzeria Bianco...44 E2
DRINKING
Bikini Lounge...45 C1
Jade Bar...46 E6
Swizzle Inn...47 C6
ENTERTAINMENT
BS West...(see 37)
Chase Field...48 E3
Orpheum Theatre...49 D2
Rhythm Room...50 C6
Symphony Hall...51 E2
US Airways Center...52 E3
SHOPPING
Biltmore Fashion Park...53 D6
Heard Museum Bookshop...(see 20)
Scottsdale Fashion Square...54 F6
TRANSPORT
Greyhound...55 D8
Valley Metro Central Station Bus Terminal...56 E2
Phoenix Mountain Preserve
Piestewa Peak (2608ft)
PARADISE VALLEY
Paradise Valley
Camelback Mountain Echo Canyon Recreation Area
The Phoenician Resort Golf Course
SCOTTSDALE
Old Town Scottsdale
Arizona State Fairgrounds
Papago Park & Golf Course
Sky Harbor International Airport
TEMPE
Arizona State University
Arizona Canal
Grand Canal
Salt River
Black Canyon Hwy
Papago Fwy
Red Mountain Fwy
Maricopa Fwy
Grand Ave
See Enlargement
To University of Phoenix Stadium (9mi); Glendale Airport (12mi)
To Los Dos Molinos (5mi); Cactus Adventures (7mi); Phoenix South Mountain Park (7mi); Sheraton Wild Horse Pass Resort & Spa (20mi)
To Tucson (116mi)
To Mesa (5mi)
To Theodore Roosevelt Dam (45mi)

> **DON'T MISS**
>
> - **Heard Museum Downtown** – Native American exhibits (below)
> - **Taliesin West** – Frank Lloyd Wright legacy (right)
> - **Desert Botanical Garden** – prickly but perfect stroll (right)
> - **Roosevelt District** – art, drinks and eats (p839)
> - **Piestewa Peak Recreation Area** – Pristine desert hiking in the center of the city (opposite)

American Express (☎ 602-468-1199; www.americanexpress.com; 2201 E Camelback Rd; ⏰ 10am-6pm Mon-Fri, to 4pm Sat) Also offers help with travel planning.
Travelex (☎ 602-275-8767; www.travelex.com; Sky Harbor International Airport, 3800 Sky Harbor Blvd, Terminal 4, Phoenix; ⏰ 8am-8pm) A good bet.

POST

Post office (☎ 602-253-9648; 522 N Central Ave)

TOURIST INFORMATION

Downtown Phoenix Visitor Information Center (☎ 602-254-6500, 877-225-5749; www.visitphoenix.com; 125 N 2nd St, Suite 120; ⏰ 8am-5pm Mon-Fri) Main tourist office of the Greater Phoenix Convention & Visitors Bureau.
Tempe Convention & Visitors Bureau (☎ 480-894-8158, 866-914-1052; www.tempecvb.com; 51 W 3rd St, Suite 105; ⏰ 8:30am-5pm Mon-Fri)
Scottsdale Convention & Visitors Bureau (☎ 480-421-1004, 800-712-1117; www.scottsdalecvb.com; Galleria Corporate Centre, 4343 N Scottsdale Rd, Suite 170; ⏰ 8am-5:30pm Mon-Fri)

Sights

PHOENIX

The **Heard Museum Downtown** (☎ 602-252-8848; www.heard.org; 2301 N Central Ave; adult/child $10/3; ⏰ 9:30am-5pm Mon-Sat, 11am-5pm Sun) is set in a sun-bleached Spanish Colonial–style building that houses one of the best Native American museums in the entire world. Check out the kachina collection and the room of large murals depicting Native American legends.

Next door is the 18,000-piece **Phoenix Art Museum** (☎ 602-257-1222; www.phxart.org; 1625 N Central Ave; adult/child $10/4; ⏰ 10am-9pm Wed, 10am-5pm Thu-Sat, noon-5pm Sun, 6-10pm 1st Fri of month). Southwestern and Latin American art are the main attractions, but there's a huge range, so spend some time inside the spaciously cool and modern building.

Only a few more blocks to the south, the **Burton Barr Central Library** (☎ 602-262-4636; www.phoenixpubliclibrary.org; 1221 N Central Ave; ⏰ 11am-7pm Mon, Wed & Fri, 9am-5pm Tue, Thu & Sat, 1-5pm Sun) never fails to impress. Be sure to head to the top floor at sunset to watch downtown disappear into a wistful golden color reflected from mirrored-glass buildings.

Stroll among the succulents and a crazy forest of cacti at the **Desert Botanical Garden** (☎ 480-941-1225; www.dbg.org; 1201 N Galvin Pkwy; adult/child $15/5; ⏰ 8am-8pm Oct-May, 7am-8pm Jun-Sep; 👪). Check for seasonal special events like solstice celebrations and candlelit night visits around the Christmas holiday.

SCOTTSDALE

Scottsdale's main draw is its popular shopping district, known as **Old Town** for its early 20th-century buildings (and others built to look old) stuffed chockablock with art galleries, clothing stores for the modern cowgirl, and some of the best eating and drinking in the Valley of the Sun.

Taliesin West (☎ 480-860-2700; www.franklloydwright.org; 12621 Frank Lloyd Wright Blvd; tours $27-60; ⏰ hours variable) is the still-functioning architecture school built by Frank Lloyd Wright (he also taught and lived here) in the mid-20th century. The public can tour the environmentally organic buildings spread over 600 acres of pristine desert.

The **Scottsdale Museum of Contemporary Art** (☎ 480-874-4666; www.smoca.org; 7374 E 2nd St; adult/child $7/free, free Thu; ⏰ 10am-5pm Tue-Wed, Fri & Sat, 10am-8pm Thu, noon-5pm Sun) is another beautiful Arizona building, and the art within is like the cherry inside a chocolate. Best of all, the museum anchors an area sprinkled with public art and eateries.

TEMPE

Founded in 1885 and home to some 46,000 students, **Arizona State University** (ASU) is the heart and soul of Tempe. The **Gammage Auditorium** (cnr Mill Ave & Apache Blvd) was Frank Lloyd Wright's last major building.

Easily accessible by light-rail from downtown Phoenix, **Mill Avenue**, Tempe's main drag, is packed with chain restaurants, themed bars and other collegiate hangouts. It's worth checking out while visiting **Tempe Town Lake**, an artifical lake with boat rides and paths perfect for strolling or biking its fringes.

The **Tempe Center for the Arts** (☎ 480-350-2829; www.tempe.gov/tca; 700 W Rio Salado Pkwy; admission free; 🕑 10am-6pm Tue-Fri, 11am-6pm Sat), set right on the lake, has a sculpture garden and infinity pool outside of the curved-steel building. Inside, there's a theater for the performing arts and a 3500-sq-ft gallery.

Activities

Phoenix South Mountain Park (☎ 602-495-0222; www.phoenix.gov/parks/hikesoth.html; 10919 S Central Ave) offers more than 40 miles of trails to hike or bike, where civilization feels thousands of miles away, as well as dozens of Native American petroglyph sites. Drive to the top along small crazy-curving roads and you're rewarded with a view of the valley below. Horseback riding is also available.

Just a quick quarter-mile pedal from South Mountain Park is **Cactus Adventures** (☎ 480-940-7433; www.cactusadventures.com; 4747 Elliot Rd, Suite 21; half-day rental from $30; 🕑 9am-7pm Mon-Sat, 9am-5pm Sun), for mountain-bike rental. It also rents road bikes and beach cruisers.

For fabulous desert views, especially at sunset, head to **Piestewa Peak Recreation Area** (☎ 602-262-7901; Piestewa Peak Dr). The trek to the 2608ft summit of Piestewa Peak is one of Phoenix' most popular outdoor endeavors. The easier circumference trail begins at the very last parking lot and offers a more Zen experience.

Stop by **Rio Lago Cruise** (☎ 480-517-4050; www.riolagocruise.com; boat rental per hr from $10; 🕑 9am-noon & 6-9pm Tue-Sun May-Sep, 11am-7pm Tue-Sun Oct-Apr) at Tempe Town Lake to rent your own pedal-powered or motorboat.

Phoenix for Children

If the kiddies are wilting in the heat, visit Tempe's **Big Surf** (☎ 480-947-2477; 1500 N McClintock Rd; adult/child under 2/child $26/3/19.50; 🕑 11am-6pm Sat & Sun, May-Sep; 🚼), with two wave pools, many a twisty waterslide and a mellow cove for toddlers.

For a quick few hours of slippery fun, visit Tempe Beach Park's **Cox Splash Playground** (🕑 10am-7pm April-Sep; 🚼), where kids can frolic in their bathing suits in all sorts of oversized sprinkler fun.

At the popular **Arizona Science Center** (☎ 602-716-2000; www.azscience.org; 600 E Washington St; adult/child $12/10; 🕑 10am-5pm; 🚼), play with 300-odd hands-on exhibits, watch live demonstrations or take in the mysteries of the universe at the planetarium.

ART SMART

Every Thursday evening more than 100 of Scottsdale's galleries keep their doors open until 9pm for **Art Walk** (www.scottsdalegalleries.com), centered on Marshall Way and Main St. On the first Friday evening of every month, downtown Phoenix kicks up the gritty and fun factor a few notches for **First Fridays** (www.artlinkphoenix.com), and the happening Roosevelt District is packed with bicyclists and pedestrians moseying between galleries and bars.

Tours

Arizona Detours (☎ 866-438-6877; www.detoursaz.com) Offers day tours to far-flung locations like Tombstone (adult/child $140/70) and the Grand Canyon (adult/child $145/80), and five-hour city tours (adult/child $75/40).

Arizona Outback Adventures (☎ 480-945-2881; www.aoa-adventures.com; 16447 N 91st St, Scottsdale) Offers day trips for hiking ($55, minimum two people), biking ($75, minimum two people), and other active outings.

Gray Line Phoenix (☎ 602-437-3484; www.graylinephoenix.com; 4001 S 34th St) Offers four-hour city tours (adult/child $52/27.50), as well as a 10-hour Sedona tour (adult/child $95/50.50).

Festivals & Events

Phoenix' most popular event is the **Tostitos Fiesta Bowl football game** (☎ 480-350-0911; www.fiestabowl.com), held in the first days of January at the University of Phoenix Stadium in Glendale. It's preceded by massive celebrations and parades.

Sleeping

From basic motels to ritzy resorts, the valley's hundreds of places to stay have one thing in common: prices plummet in summer when the mercury rises. Peak-season rates are quoted here.

BUDGET

Chain hotels clustered around the airport and in the West Valley city of Peoria often have great deals, especially on weekends when business travelers leave.

HI Phoenix, Metcalf House (602-254-9803; www.home.earthlink.net/~phxhostel; 1026 N 9th St, Phoenix; dm $18-25, r $30-45; 5-10pm check-in;) Chalked thank-you notes grace the facade of this homey hostel in a residential neighborhood. Kitchen and common areas close during the day, and the whole place shuts down for July and August.

Motel 6 Scottsdale (480-946-2280; www.motel6.com; 6848 E Camelback Rd, Scottsdale; s/d $38/56;) Yes, it's a standard chain, but this motel is conveniently located smack-dab in the middle of upscale Scottsdale, only a quick drive from the Old Town.

MIDRANGE

Hotel San Carlos (602-253-4121; www.hotelsancarlos.com; 202 N Central Ave, Phoenix; r $83-110;) A historic property in the heart of downtown Phoenix, this 1928 gem sports smallish but clean rooms, friendly staff and lots of old-school charm. It's set across the street from a light-rail station.

Hotel Valley Ho (480-248-2000; www.hotelvalleyho.com; 6850 E Main St, Scottsdale; r $99-600) A stylish Rat Pack–era hotel that reopened just a few years ago, this property is near the gourmet food and drink action of Scottsdale's Southbridge area. The rooms are groovy paeans to mid-Century Modern style and have modern comforts like huge flat-screen and luscious beds. You can get your tiki-style bowl of rum drink at the on-site Trader Vic's. Check it out, hep cat.

our pick **Clarendon Hotel + Suites** (602-252-7363; www.theclarendon.net; 401 W Clarendon Ave, Phoenix; r/ste incl breakfast $110/200;) Modern yet lusciously retro, this blue pinstriped boutique hotel features cool contemporary art and groovy touches like painted sliding window blinds. Throw in complimentary phone use (including long distance), wi-fi and a superhip rooftop bar, and you're living large.

Maricopa Manor (602-274-6302, 800-292-6403; www.maricopamanor.com; 15 W Pasadena Ave, Phoenix; r incl breakfast from $150;) This small, elegant place right near tree-lined Central Ave has seven beautiful suites, many with French doors onto a deck overlooking the pool, garden and fountain areas. Although it's a B&B, privacy is paramount.

Sheraton Phoenix Downtown (602-262-2500, 800-323-3535; www.sheratonphoenixdowntown.com; 340 N 3rd St, Phoenix; r from $170;) One of the newest additions to downtown Phoenix properties. The hotel's facade, designed to keep cooling costs down, belies an especially attractive interior full of pieces from regional artists. It's mainly a business hotel during the week, but on First Friday and on weekends the hotel's bar and restaurant is a popular hangout chock-full of local art and art-lovers. Rooms are modern and comfy, and the rooftop pool has great views.

TOP END

The resorts are the most elegant and expensive places to stay. Not just places to sleep, they are destinations within themselves, and some make an entire vacation out of it.

Pointe Hilton Squaw Peak Resort (602-997-2626, 800-947-9784; www.pointehilton.com; 7677 N 16th St, Phoenix; r from $180;) With plenty of pools, water slides, a tubing 'river' and a kids' camp – as well as a concierge for kids' activities – this all-suite resort is the most family-friendly spot in town.

Scottsdale Fairmont (480-585-4848, 866-540-4495; www.fairmont.com/scottsdale; 7575 E Princess Dr, Scottsdale; r from $240;) Beautiful, well-appointed rooms, excellent service and dining that's basically par for the course at Arizona's luxury resorts. But, in the quest for the best spa, this is the winner.

Sheraton Wild Horse Pass Resort & Spa (602-225-0100, 888-625-5144; www.wildhorsepassresort.com; 5594 W Wild Horse Pass Blvd, Chandler; r from $273;) Designed by the Gila River tribe as a luxurious place to soak up the best of Native American healing and wisdom, this place has comfortable rooms, spacious common areas, fine dining and plenty of programs to educate the well-cared-for guests.

Arizona Biltmore Resort & Spa (602-955-6600, 800-950-0086; www.arizonabiltmore.com; 2400 E Missouri Ave, Phoenix; r from $380;) At the Biltmore, built in 1929 as one of Arizona's first super-luxe resorts, the class and history nearly oozes from the deco walls. It's close to the upscale Camelback Corridor, but with an on-site golf course, a spa, tennis courts, bike rentals and property tours, it's hard to leave.

Eating

The Phoenix-Scottsdale area has the largest selection of restaurants in the Southwest.

UNDER THE STARS, STAR WARS–STYLE

The brainchild of groundbreaking architect and urban planner Paolo Soleri, **Arcosanti** (☎ 928-632-7135; www.arcosanti.org; Cordes Junction; s/d from $30/40, Sky Suite incl breakfast $100) is a desert outpost based on 'acrology': architecture meets ecology. This cross between a kibbutz and design school 65 miles north of Phoenix looks like a village on Luke Skywalker's home planet. Radical when conceived in the 1960s, Soleri's ideas now seem cutting-edge in this age of urban sprawl and global warming. Arcosanti is good for a day trip or a long stay – there are week- and month-long seminars, a café, one-hour tours, concerts and other events. Basic accommodation is available, and the Sky Suite is designed for great views of a dark desert night.

BUDGET

Downtown Phoenix Public Market (www.phoenixpublicmarket.com; 721 N Central Ave, Phoenix; 4-8pm Wed, 8am-noon Sat) It's hard to beat this farmers market for quality and price. Specialty gourmet foods and local bands are just one more reason to stop by. Market happens rain or shine.

Fry Bread House (☎ 602-351-2345; 4140 N 7th Ave, Phoenix; mains $4-7; 10am-7pm Mon-Sat) The Native American treat known as an elephant ear or Navajo taco is a flat piece of fried dough topped with meat, beans and veggies, or, for dessert, smeared with honey. This small place gets packed to the gills with nearby office workers at lunchtime, so try to avoid the rush.

MacAlpine's (☎ 602-252-5545; 2303 N 7th St, Phoenix; dishes from $5; 11am-7pm Sun-Thu, 11am-8pm Fri & Sat) The oldest diner in Phoenix serves basic salads and sandwiches, but it's the old-timey soda fountain that's the real attraction – nothing like a malted milk to chase those blues away. There's an attached antique store.

Pane Bianco (☎ 602-234-2100; 4404 N Central Ave, Phoenix; sandwiches $8; 11am-3pm Tue-Sat) A café from the Pizzeria Bianco group, here you taste the same goodness being served at the flagship location for a fraction of the price. Savor the flavor with a salad or sandwich, or just nibble on pastries while sipping java.

MIDRANGE

Los Dos Molinos (☎ 602-243-9113; 8646 S Central Ave, Phoenix; mains from $8-15; 11am-2:30pm & 5-9pm Tue-Fri, 11am-9pm Sat) Near the foot of South Mountain in a Spanish Mission–style house, this is the mecca of New Mexican cuisine in Phoenix. The menu sticks to the basics – tacos, enchiladas, fajitas – with plenty of green chili. There's also a location downtown (1010 E Washington St; same menu and hours).

Pizzeria Bianco (☎ 602-258-8300; 623 E Adams St, Phoenix; pizzas $11-14; 5-10pm Tue-Sat) James Beard Award–winner Chris Bianco makes the best pizza in town and maybe even in all of America. A hopping spot – be prepared to wait on the patio, drink in hand.

Chelsea's Kitchen (☎ 602-957-2555; 5040 N 40th St, Phoenix; dishes $12-25; 11am-10pm Mon-Wed, 11am-11pm Thu, 11am-midnight Fri & Sat, 10am-9pm Sun) Set in a converted mid-Century Modern home alongside a canal in Phoenix' quietly upscale Arcadia district. Get a platter of tacos or some ribs and you won't be disappointed; it's comfort food (yes, in the Southwest tacos are comfort food) gone gourmet.

Caffe Boa (☎ 480-968-9112; 398 S Mill Ave, Tempe; mains $16-22; 11am-10pm Mon-Wed, 11am-11pm Thu-Sat, noon-10pm Sun) Caffe Boa was serving bistro-style food with fresh ingredients long before that became the hip thing to do; the wine menu and jazz nights cement its status as an oasis of cool on Tempe's Mill Ave.

TOP END

Digestif (☎ 480-425-9463; 7114 E Stetson Dr, Scottsdale; dinner mains $18-28; 11am-midnight) A blend of Italian and California cuisine in the happening Southbridge area of Scottsdale – think freshly made ravioli stuffed with farm-fresh pureed pumpkin. Grab a porch seat to people-watch and be sure to check out the listening booth stocked with local bands, near the restroom.

Durant's (☎ 602-264-5967; 2611 N Central Ave, Phoenix; mains from $20; 11am-10pm Mon-Thu, 11am-11pm Fri & Sat, 4:30-10pm Sun) If the vibe of the red leather dining room is more Rat Pack Vegas than downtown Phoenix, that's because the original owner was friends with mobsters who made their fame and fortune in the Nevada gambling mecca. The martinis and steaks here are heaven.

Bourbon Steak (☎ 480-513-6002; Scottsdale Fairmont, 7575 E Princess Dr, Scottsdale; mains $30-70; 5:30-11pm) Along came celebrity chef Michael Mina to raise the culinary bar in Scottsdale even further with the 2008 opening of this aptly named steak and bourbon joint. The meat is prepared in more delicious ways than an avid carnivore stuck on a meat-free deserted island could ever dream of.

Kai (☎ 602-385-5726; Sheraton Wild Horse Pass Resort & Spa, 5594 W Wild Horse Pass Blvd, Chandler; mains $40-50, 8-course tasting menu with wine pairings $280; 6-10pm Tue-Sat) One of the most highly rated restaurants in Arizona, where simple ingredients from mainly Native American farms and ranches are turned into something extraordinary. The grilled buffalo from the Cheyenne River tribe is a must-try. The restaurant closes for one month from early August.

Drinking

Scottsdale has the greatest concentration of trendy bars and clubs; Tempe attracts the student crowd; and Phoenix has a slew of longstanding dive bars that are in again.

Bikini Lounge (☎ 602-252-0427; 1502 Grand Ave, Phoenix; 6pm-late) There are a few good places to drink in the artsy Roosevelt District but the Lounge is the king of divey-cool. Rusty pickups and BMWs share the small parking lot, and inside, bamboo and carved tiki totems rule the roost.

Greasewood Flat (☎ 480-585-9430; www.greasewoodflat.net; 27375 N Alma School Pkwy, Scottsdale; 11am-1am) This outdoor drinking place is a cash-only affair and at night the stars really are big and bright. On cold nights the fire pits are blazed up and on weekends you can count on a country band and plenty of whooping it up on the dancefloor. Burgers and other greasy goodness available.

Jade Bar (☎ 480-948-2100; Sanctuary on Camelback Mountain, 5700 E McDonald Dr, Paradise Valley) A swanky hotel bar on the side of Camelback Mountain, it's shaped like a long patio so that as many people as possible can marvel at the fiery red sky as the sun sinks low on the horizon.

Swizzle Inn (☎ 602-277-7775; 5835 N 16th St, Phoenix; 5pm-late) Swizzle in…stagger out, or so proclaims a sign on the door. The best dive bar in the state, it's set in a strip mall and used to cater to sisters of Sappho. Now, all types – from hipster to oldster – call it theirs until closing time.

Entertainment

BS West (☎ 480-945-9028; www.bswest.com; 7125 E 5th Ave, Scottsdale; 2pm-2am) This gay bar and dance club in the Old Town has pool tables, a small dancefloor, Rock Band video gaming on Monday nights and karaoke some nights.

Rhythm Room (☎ 602-265-4842; www.rhythmroom.com; 1019 E Indian School Rd, Phoenix; cover $4-30; Tue-Sun) Lots of R & B, jazz and rocky funk fuel the boogie at the rib shack in the parking lot. It attracts an eclectic crowd looking for a good time.

Orpheum Theatre (☎ 602-262-7272; 203 W Adams St, Phoenix; tickets from $50) A splendid, restored movie house downtown used by highbrow touring shows and the symphony. It's chock-full of history; in the days when movie stars toured the cities their movies were playing in they'd often grab a soda in the now-defunct café (owned by this writer's grandparents).

Both the **Arizona Opera** (☎ 602-266-7464; www.azopera.com; tickets $30-130) and the **Phoenix Symphony Orchestra** (☎ 602-495-1999; tickets $20-70) perform at **Symphony Hall** (☎ 602-262-7272; 75 N 2nd Ave, Phoenix).

The men's basketball team, the **Phoenix Suns** (☎ 602-379-7867; www.nba.com/suns), and the women's team, the **Phoenix Mercury** (☎ 602-252-9622; www.wnba.com/mercury), play at the US Airways Center. The **Arizona Cardinals** (☎ 602-379-0101; www.azcardinals.com) football team plays at the new University of Phoenix Stadium in Glendale. The **Arizona Diamondbacks** (☎ 602-462-6500; http://arizona.diamondbacks.mlb.com) play baseball at Chase Field.

Shopping

The **Heard Museum Bookshop** (☎ 602-252-8344; www.heard.org; 2301 N Central Ave, Phoenix) has the best range of books about Native Americans, and the most reliable and expansive selection of Native American arts and crafts.

The valley has several notable shopping malls. For more upscale shopping, visit the **Scottsdale Fashion Square** (cnr Camelback & Scottsdale Rds) and the even more exclusive **Biltmore Fashion Park** (cnr Camelback Rd & 24th St).

Getting There & Around

Phoenix' **Sky Harbor International Airport** (PHX; ☎ 602-273-3300; http://phoenix.gov/aviation) is 3 miles southeast of downtown. There is a free bus that runs between the light-rail station on the southwest corner of 44th and Washington Sts and the airport during normal light-rail operating hours.

Greyhound (☎ 602-389-4200; www.greyhound.com; 2115 E Buckeye Rd, Phoenix) runs regular buses to Tucson ($23, two hours), Flagstaff ($25, three hours), Los Angeles ($54, eight hours) and other destinations.

Parking is plentiful nearly everywhere in Phoenix, save for days of special events.

The **light-rail system** (☎ 602-253-5000; www.metrolightrail.org; fares $1.25, 3-day pass $7.50) started running in late 2008 and links the Central Ave corridor, downtown Phoenix and the eastern suburbs of Tempe and Mesa. For the first time, it's possible to see much of what the valley has to offer without needing to rent a car.

Valley Metro (☎ 602-253-5000; www.valleymetro.org) operates buses ($1.25) all over the valley. On weekdays it also runs the free Flash service around the ASU area and the free Dash service around downtown Phoenix. The free and frequent **Scottsdale Trolley** (☎ 480-421-1004; www.scottsdaletrolley.com) covers the Old Town area and runs to a number of good shopping areas. Catch it from 11am to 9pm.

CENTRAL ARIZONA

This part of Arizona draws people year-round for outdoor fun and is an oasis for summer visitors searching for cooler climes. After Phoenix, the land gains elevation, turning from high rolling desert to jagged hills covered in scrubby trees. Farther north still, mountains punctuate thick stands of pine. The outdoorsy college town of Flagstaff, set on the historic Route 66, is here. Williams, the launching point for a train ride to the Grand Canyon, is a tiny town that keeps the spirit of Route 66 alive. Sedona is famous for beautiful towering red rocks and as a center of New-Age spiritual energy, and is one of the state's biggest draws. Jerome is a former mining town turned artsy redoubt. Prescott brings Arizona's frontier days alive.

Flagstaff

A noisy reminder of Flagstaff's past, approximately 100 freight trains barrel through this fine mountain city each day, blowing their horns with spirited abandon. A funky, vibrant town filled with students attending Northern Arizona University (NAU), Flagstaff boasts cool mountain air, ponderosa pines and even a mountain to ski, and is the favored summer retreat for Phoenix folk. Microbreweries, interesting hotels and hip restaurants are housed in historic brick buildings a hop, skip and jump from historic Route 66. Nearby hiking and biking trails are abundant. A two-hour drive from the Grand Canyon, and by far the largest town in the region, Flagstaff makes a great base.

The **visitors center** (☎ 928-774-9541, 800-842-7293; www.flagstaffarizona.org; 1 E Rte 66; 🕑 8am-5pm) is inside the historic Amtrak train station.

SIGHTS

If you have time for only one sight in Flagstaff, head to the **Museum of Northern Arizona** (☎ 928-774-5213; www.musnaz.org; 3101 N Fort Valley Rd; adult/student $7/4; 🕑 9am-5pm). It features exhibits on local Native American archaeology, history and customs, as well as geology, biology and the arts.

The **Lowell Observatory** (☎ 928-233-3211; www.lowell.edu; 1400 W Mars Hill Rd; adult/child $6/3; 🕑 9am-5pm Apr-Oct, noon-5pm Nov-Mar, varied night hours) witnessed the first sighting of Pluto in 1920; before this many scientists thought the existence of 'Planet X' was a crackpot theory. Weather permitting, there's nightly stargazing, helped by the fact that Flagstaff is the first International Dark Sky city in the world. During the day 30-minute tours are offered hourly between 1:15pm and 4:15pm.

The Sinagua cliff dwellings at **Walnut Canyon National Monument** (☎ 928-526-3367; www.nps.gov/waca; admission $5; 🕑 9am-5pm Nov-Apr, 8am-5pm May-Oct) are set in the nearly vertical walls of a small limestone butte amid a forested canyon. A short hiking trail descends past many cliff-dwelling rooms. The monument is 11 miles southeast of Flagstaff off I-40 exit 204. Occasional rock falls can close the paths, so call ahead.

ACTIVITIES

If you want to say you've skied Arizona, head to the small but lofty **Arizona Snowbowl** (☎ 928-779-1951; www.arizonasnowbowl.com; Snowbowl Rd; half-/full day $38/48). Four lifts service 32 runs and a snowboarding park at elevations between 9200ft and 11,500ft. You can also ride the chairlift (adult/child $10/8) in summer, and the main lodge turns into a daytime hangout spot where you can watch disc golf matches. For a snow report, call ☎ 928-779-4577.

Arizona's highest mountain, the 12,663ft **Humphreys Peak**, is a reasonably straightforward, though strenuous, hike in summer. The trail begins at the Arizona Snowbowl and winds through forest, eventually coming out above the tree line, a beautifully barren, extremely windy place. The total distance is 4.5 miles one way; allow six to eight hours round-trip.

Get the rundown on nearby hiking, bike rental, rock climbing and cross-country skiing at **Peace Surplus** (☎ 928-779-4521; www.peacesurplus.com; 14 W Rte 66; 🕑 8am-9pm Mon-Fri, 8am-8pm Sat, 8am-6pm Sun). It's one of the best places for outdoor and travel gear in the city, and the friendly, helpful staff is more than willing to share their knowledge.

SLEEPING

Flagstaff provides the widest variety of lodging choices in the region. Unlike in southern Arizona, summer is high season here. Take note that Route 66 is right next to the train tracks, and those freight trains run all night long. All of the properties following are within a short walk of Flagstaff's eating and drinking options.

Grand Canyon International Hostel (☎ 928-779-9421, 888-442-2696; www.grandcanyonhostel.com; 19½ S San Francisco St; dm/r incl breakfast from $18/38; 💻 ⊠) Run by friendly people in a historic building, dorms are clean and small. There's a kitchen, laundry facilities and a host of tours to the Grand Canyon and Sedona, and you'll be fetched from the Greyhound for free.

Dubeau Hostel (☎ 928-774-6731, 800-398-7112; www.grandcanyonhostel.com; 19 W Phoenix Ave; incl breakfast dm $18-20, r $41-48) Run by the Grand Canyon International Hostel folks. The private rooms are like basic hotel rooms, but at half the price. With a jukebox, things can get a little loud here.

our pick Weatherford Hotel (☎ 928-779-1919; www.weatherfordhotel.com; 23 N Leroux St; r $65-79, ste $125; ⊠) Flagstaff's most historic hotel is fantastic value, keeping its rates year-round. Eight snug, low-frills rooms (three share one bathroom) and two larger, spiffy suites have a turn-of-the-19th-century feel (with no TVs or telephones except in the suites).

Monte Vista Hotel (☎ 928-779-6971, 800-545-3068; www.hotelmontevista.com; 100 N San Francisco St; r $70-170; ⊠ ⊠ ≋) Many of the 50 rooms and suites here are named after the film stars who slept in them – rooms are clean and not claustrophobic, but these days this place definitely banks on its historic charm and stellar location more than its value for the buck. Ask for a quiet room if you're afraid of the live music at the downstairs Monte Vista Lounge.

EATING

Wander around downtown and you'll stumble on plenty of eating options.

Bun Huggers (☎ 928-779-3743; 901 S Milton Rd; meals under $8; 🕑 10:30am-10pm) After a day on the nearby mountains it's a local tradition to stop here and refuel, and it's a college-crowd favorite because of the cheap prices. Meat-lovers adore the mesquite-grilled burgers and the ice-cold beer on tap is widely appreciated, too.

our pick Mountain Oasis (☎ 928-214-9270; 11 Aspen Ave; mains from $10; 🕑 11am-9pm) Come in your mountain-biking shorts for lunch and nice jeans for dinner – the class factor rises when the sun sets. More than an oasis of good food and drink, this place is a UN of flavors: dishes range from Mediterranean to Japanese to Thai, with weekend-only cuts of prime rib cooked just right.

Brix Restaurant & Wine Bar (☎ 928-213-1021; 413 N San Francisco St; dishes $24-32; 🕑 11am-2pm & 5-9:30pm Mon-Sat, 5-9:30pm Sun) Housed in a gently modernized building from the 1900s, this contemporary and casual American eatery showcases fresh food made with produce from local farms and ranches and wine from small producers.

DRINKING & ENTERTAINMENT

Museum Club (☎ 928-526-9434; 3404 E Rte 66; 🕑 11am-2am) Yee-haw! Kick up your heels at this honky-tonk roadhouse where the country dancing is nightly. Inside what looks like a huge log cabin you'll find a large wooden dancefloor and a sumptuous elixir-filled mahogany bar.

Flagstaff Brewing Company (☎ 928-773-1442; www.flagbrew.com; 16 E Rte 66; 🕑 11am-2am Mon-Sat, 11am-midnight Sun) A low-key place with a fun outdoorsy vibe, handcrafted brews, live music and lots of Scotch just a stumble away from downtown. The pub grub – pizza, burgers, soup and salads – is quite good.

Orpheum Theater (☎ 928-556-1580; www.orpheumpresents.com; 15 W Aspen St; tickets from $15) A grand old-style movie house from 1911, this theater is now a fine-looking music venue that hosts top regional and national bands and the occasional movie night.

> **WHAT THE...?**
>
> Nearly a mile across and 600ft deep, the second most impressive hole in Arizona was formed by a fiery meteor that screamed into the atmosphere about 50,000 years ago, when giant sloths lived in these parts. **Meteor Crater** (☎ 928-289-2362; www.meteorcrater.com; I-40 exit 233; adult/child/senior $15/7/13; 🕑 7am-7pm Jun–mid-Sep; 👶), 40 miles east of Flagstaff, is an out-of-this-world site for those with a thimbleful of imagination. There are lookout points around the crater's edge but no hiking to the bottom. Check out the fun, informative visitor center.

GETTING THERE & AROUND

From the **Greyhound bus station** (☎ 928-774-4573; www.greyhound.com; 399 S Malpais Lane; 6am-2:30am) buses run frequently to Las Vegas, NV ($67, six hours), Los Angeles, CA ($66 to $75, 12 hours), and Phoenix ($26 to $35, three hours). **Open Road Tours** (☎ 928-226-8060; www.openroadtours.com; 1 E Rte 66) has shuttles from the Amtrak station to the Grand Canyon ($27), Phoenix Sky Harbor International Airport ($42) and, depending on the season, Sedona ($25). Call to reserve.

Operated by **Amtrak** (☎ 928-774-8679; www.amtrak.com), the *Southwest Chief* stops in Flagstaff on its daily runs between Chicago, IL, and Los Angeles, CA.

Williams

Williams, 60 miles south of Grand Canyon Village and 35 miles west of Flagstaff on I-40, is a splendid place to base a Grand Canyon South Rim adventure. Plenty of classic Route 66 motels and bargain chain hotels are here, and the old-school homes and train station charm the socks off visitors.

Most tourists visit to ride the turn-of-the-19th-century **Grand Canyon Railway** (☎ 800-843-8724; www.thetrain.com; Railway Depot, 233 N Grand Canyon Blvd; round-trip adult/child from $70/40;) to the South Rim (departs Williams 9:30am). Even if you're not a train buff, a trip is a scenic stress- and traffic-free way to visit the Grand Canyon. Characters in period costumes provide historical and regional narration, and banjo folk music sets the tone. There's also a wildly popular *Polar Express* service (adult/child from $29/14) from November through January, ferrying pajama-clad kids to the 'North Pole' to visit Santa.

The **Red Garter Bed & Bakery** (☎ 928-635-1484, 800-328-1484; www.redgarter.com; 137 Railroad Ave; r incl breakfast $120-145;) is an 1897 bordello turned B&B where the ladies used to hang out the windows to flag down customers. The four rooms have nice period touches and the downstairs bakery has good coffee. The funky little **Grand Canyon Hotel** (☎ 928-635-1419, 877-635-1419; www.thegrandcanyonhotel.com; 145 W Rte 66; dm $23, r with shared/private bath $60/75;) has small themed rooms, a six-bed dorm room, and even an on-site Thai restaurant.

Route 66 fans will dig the eclectic decor at **Cruiser's Cafe' 66** (☎ 928-635-2445; 233 W Rte 66; mains $8-16; 11am-11pm Mar 1–Jan 15, 3pm-11pm Jan 15–March 1, bar open to 2am year-round). It's a fun place, serving tasty microbrews, BBQ and other American fare inside a 1930s filling station.

Open Road (☎ 928-226-8060; www.openroadtours.com; Railway Depot, 233 N Grand Canyon Blvd) offers two daily shuttles to the Grand Canyon ($22, plus $6 park entrance fee) and Flagstaff ($17).

Sedona

Native tribes have long considered the Sedona area – where the red rocks glow so bright they look like they're about to explode – a sacred place with its spindly towers, grand buttes and flat-topped mesas carved in crimson sandstone. Today, it's one of the top New Age destinations in the world, and a supposed hot spot of spiritually charged vortexes. Regardless of what you believe, 'Red Rock Country' is one of the most beautiful places in Arizona, full of art galleries, gourmet restaurants, resorts and many a New Age healer.

In the middle of town, the 'Y' is the landmark junction of Hwys 89A and 179. Businesses are spread along both roads. The **visitors center** (☎ 928-282-7722, 800-288-7336; www.visitsedona.com; 331 Forest Rd; 8am-5pm Mon-Sat, 9am-3pm Sun) has tourist information and vortex maps.

SIGHTS & ACTIVITIES

New Agers believe Sedona's rocks, cliffs and rivers radiate Mother Earth's mojo. The world's four best-known vortexes are here, and include **Bell Rock** near Village of Oak Creek east of Hwy 179, **Cathedral Rock** near Red Rock Crossing, **Airport Mesa** along the Airport Rd, and **Boynton Canyon**. Airport Rd is also a great location for watching the Technicolor sunsets.

The best way to explore the area is by hiking, biking or horseback riding in the surrounding **Coconino National Forest** (☎ 928-203-2900; www.redrockcountry.org/recreation). Most day use and parking areas require a Red Rock Pass ($5/15 per day/week), which can be purchased at most area stores and lodging and at a number of self-serve kiosks at the parking lot of the most popular sites. The most scenic spots in Coconino National Forest are along Hwy 89A north of Sedona, which snakes alongside Oak Creek through the heavily visited **Oak Creek Canyon**.

If it's a warm day and you want to cool down, visit Oak Creek Canyon's star attraction, **Slide Rock State Park** (☎ 928-282-3034; www.azstateparks.com; 6871 N Hwy 89A; per vehicle $10; 8am-7pm Jun-Aug, 8am-6pm Mar-Apr & Sep-Oct, 8am-5pm Nov-Feb) to swoosh down big rocks into the cool creek water. Or, walk the hiking trails. Call for water-quality reports.

Many companies offer 4WD tours, but **Pink Jeep Tours** (☎ 928-382-5000, 800-873-3662; www.pinkjeep.com; 204 N Hwy 89A; tours from $68) has a great reputation and a vast variety of outings. **Earth Wisdom Jeep Tours** (☎ 928-282-4714; www.earthwisdomtours.com; 293 N Hwy 89A; tours $68-98) offers vortex tours that are even fun for nonbelievers. For close encounters of another kind, the astronomers at **Evening Sky Tours** (☎ 928-203-0006; www.eveningskytours.com; adult/child $60/$20; after sunset nightly) take you across the universe via their huge telescopes from the serenity of remote Sedona at night.

Bike & Bean (☎ 928-284-0210; www.bike-bean.com; 6020 Hwy 179; 2hr/day from $25/40) is a mountain-bike rental place with hiking, mellow biking and vortex-gazing.

SLEEPING

Sedona hosts many beautiful B&Bs, creekside cabins, motels and full-service resorts.

Coconino National Forest Campgrounds (☎ 928-203-2900; www.redrockcountry.org/recreation; campsites $15-20) There are eight campsites in the area, mainly north of Sedona along Hwy 89A. Some offer good hiking and views while others afford laid-back creekside camping. Most have a mix of reservable and first-come, first-served spots to pitch a tent or pull up the RV.

White House Inn (☎ 928-282-6680; www.sedonawhitehouseinn.com; 2986 W Hwy 89A; r $60-100) Not quite fit for a president, but the friendly management makes this good-value basic motel in the quieter, western part of Sedona, that much better. Long-term visitors should ask about weekly rates.

Garland's Oak Creek Lodge (☎ 928-282-3343; www.garlandslodge.com; 8067 N Hwy 89A; cabins $235-290; Apr–mid-Nov) Set along an especially scenic stretch of Oak Creek, the stand-alone cabins are often booked solid months in advance for good reason; in addition to rates including breakfast, count on a scrumptious four-course dinner each night of your stay.

EATING & DRINKING

New Frontiers Natural Market & Deli (☎ 928-282-6311; 1420 W Hwy 89A; sandwiches $5; 8am-8pm) Stock up on healthy groceries, good cheese and nice wines. There's also a deli with good sandwiches and snacks on hand for picnickers.

D'lish Very Vegetarian (☎ 928-203-9393; 3190 W Hwy 89A; dishes $6-12; 11am-8pm; V) Delicious food and attitude- and animal-free dining add up to a solid meal. The food will impress even die-hard meat-eaters.

our pick **Sedona Airport Restaurant** (☎ 928-282-3576; 1185 Airport Rd; lunch mains from $7, dinner mains $12-25; 7am-8pm) Try to land here on a Thursday (and make reservations): fresh crab is flown in. All-you-can-eat snow crab is only $17.95. The stellar view atop Airport Mesa, the food, the red rocks glowing like the embers of a dying fire – truly, life is good.

Cowboy Club (☎ 928-282-4200; 241 N Hwy 89A; lunch mains $9-16, dinner mains $15-25; 11am-10pm) Home of the prickly pear margarita, only-in-Arizona cocktails, dishes like fried cactus strips and an appetizer platter that includes snake brochettes (tastes like chicken, really). The lineup includes plenty of sandwich, steak and salad standards. There's both a kid-friendly and adult-oriented section.

GETTING THERE & AROUND

The **Sedona-Phoenix Shuttle** (☎ 928-282-2066; www.sedona-phoenix-shuttle.com) runs between Phoenix Sky Harbor International Airport and Sedona eight times daily ($50). Call to make reservations. The free city-run **Sedona Roadrunner** (☎ 928-282-0938; www.sedonaroadrunner.com) shuttles between Hillside and the Uptown area north of the 'Y' from 9am to 6:30pm daily; trolleys arrive three to six times hourly.

Jerome

Shabbily chic, this old mining town and resurrected ghost town perched on a hillside exudes an untouristy and altogether romantic feel – especially once the weekend day-trippers clear out. It was known as the 'Wickedest Town in the West' during its late 1800s mining heyday, but today its historic buildings have been lovingly restored and turned into galleries, restaurants, saloons and B&Bs.

The **chamber of commerce** (☎ 928-634-2900; www.jeromechamber.com; 310 Hull Ave; 11am-3pm), located in a small trailer, offers information on the local attractions and arts scene.

A restored 1898 building with 12 rooms, the rooms at the **Connor Hotel** (☎ 928-634-5006, 800-523-3554; www.connorhotel.com; 164 Main St; r $90-165;) are a nice surprise; checking-in at the gift shop cash register is rarely a good sign, but, plump beds, skylights and beautiful Victorian furnishings delight. The popular **Spirit Room Bar** (☎ 928-634-5006; 164 Main St; 10am-2am), the town's liveliest watering hole, is downstairs, and makes hotel rooms 1 to 4 a trifle noisy because of live music on weekends and some weeknights.

Grapes (☎ 928-634-8477; 111 Main St; mains from $10; ⏰ 8am-9pm) serves top-drawer pizza, pasta and steak in an upscale but lively environment. Everything on the menu has a wine-pairing suggestion.

Prescott

With a historic Victorian-era downtown and a colorful Wild West history, Prescott, Arizona's first territorial capital and home of the world's oldest rodeo, feels like the Midwest meets cowboy country. Residents are a diverse mix of retirees, artists and families looking for a taste of yesteryear's wholesomeness. The town boasts over 500 buildings on the National Register of Historic Places. Along the plaza is **Whiskey Row**, an infamous strip of old saloons that still serve up their fair share of booze and host an interesting mix of not-so-fresh locals and whooping-it-up visitors.

The **chamber of commerce** (☎ 928-445-2000; www.prescott.org; 117 W Goodwin; ⏰ 9am-5pm Mon-Fri, 10am-2pm Sat & Sun) has tourist information.

Right in the thick of Whiskey Row, the historic **Hotel St Michael** (☎ 928-776-1999, 800-678-3757; www.stmichaelhotel.com; 205 W Gurley St; r incl full breakfast $60-120; 💻) has basic rooms in a dynamite location. The early hours of the free breakfast aren't convivial for Whiskey Row enthusiasts. The restored **Hassayampa Inn** (☎ 928-778-9434, 800-322-1927; www.hassayampainn.com; 122 E Gurley St; r incl full breakfast $99-139; 🚭 📶) features a vintage hand-operated elevator, original furnishings, hand-painted wall decorations and a lovely dining room.

For a bite to eat, the burgers, Mexican food and pizzas are nearly as good as the microbrews at **Prescott Brewing Company** (☎ 928-771-2795; 130 W Gurley St; ⏰ 11am-late), and that's a compliment of the highest order. The 'brew poo' platter gives a nice sampling of tasty apps.

On Whiskey Row, the **Palace** (☎ 928-541-1996; 120 S Montezuma St; ⏰ 11am-11pm) is an atmospheric place to sit and sip; you enter through a swinging saloon door into a big room full of Old West memorabilia. **Bird Cage Saloon** (☎ 928-771-1913; 148 Whiskey Row; ⏰ 10am-2am) is a divey, fun bar full of stuffed birds, and merits a look-see.

Prescott Transit Authority (☎ 928-445-5470, 800-445-7978; www.prescotttransit.com; 820 E Sheldon St) has shuttles to Phoenix and the Sky Harbor airport ($34, two hours, 16 daily).

GRAND CANYON NATIONAL PARK

Whatever you want to call it – the greatest hole on earth, the crown jewel of Arizona, or one of the seven natural wonders of the world – you really have to see the Grand Canyon, cleaving a mile deep and averaging 10 miles across, and ponder the eons it took to make it, to get it. Even the most jaded traveler comes away with a touch more appreciation for our ancient, ever-changing planet.

Snaking along its floor are 277 miles of the Colorado River, which has carved the canyon over the past six million years and exposed rocks up to two billion years old – half the age of the earth.

The two rims of the Grand Canyon offer quite different experiences; they lie more than 200 miles apart by road and are rarely visited on the same trip. Most visitors choose the South Rim with its easy access, wealth of services and vistas that don't disappoint. The quieter North Rim has its own charms; at 8200ft elevation (1000ft higher than the South Rim), its cooler temperatures support wildflower meadows and tall, thick stands of aspen and spruce.

Orientation

The park's most developed area is Grand Canyon Village, 6 miles north of the South Rim Entrance Station. The only entrance to the North Rim lies 30 miles south of Jacob Lake on Hwy 67. The North Rim and South Rim are 215 miles apart by car, 21 miles on foot through the canyon, or 10 miles as the condor flies.

Information

The entrance ticket for the **park** (vehicles/cyclists & pedestrians $25/12) is valid for seven days and can be used at both rims.

Grand Canyon Visitor Center (☎ 928-638-7644; www.nps.gov/grca; Grand Canyon Village; ⏰ 8am-5pm) The main visitor center is only accessible by free shuttle bus that runs along the main roads inside the park, a one-mile walk or bicycle ride from Market Plaza on the Greenway Trail, or a short walk from Mather Point.

National Geographic Visitor Center (☎ 928-638-2468; www.explorethecanyon.com; Hwy 64, Tusayan; ⏰ 8am-10pm) Stop in Tusayan, 7 miles south of Grand Canyon Village, to pay your $25 vehicle entrance fee and spare yourself what could be a 30-minute wait at the entrance of the park in the summer months. There's a neat IMAX film about the canyon here.

SOUTHWEST

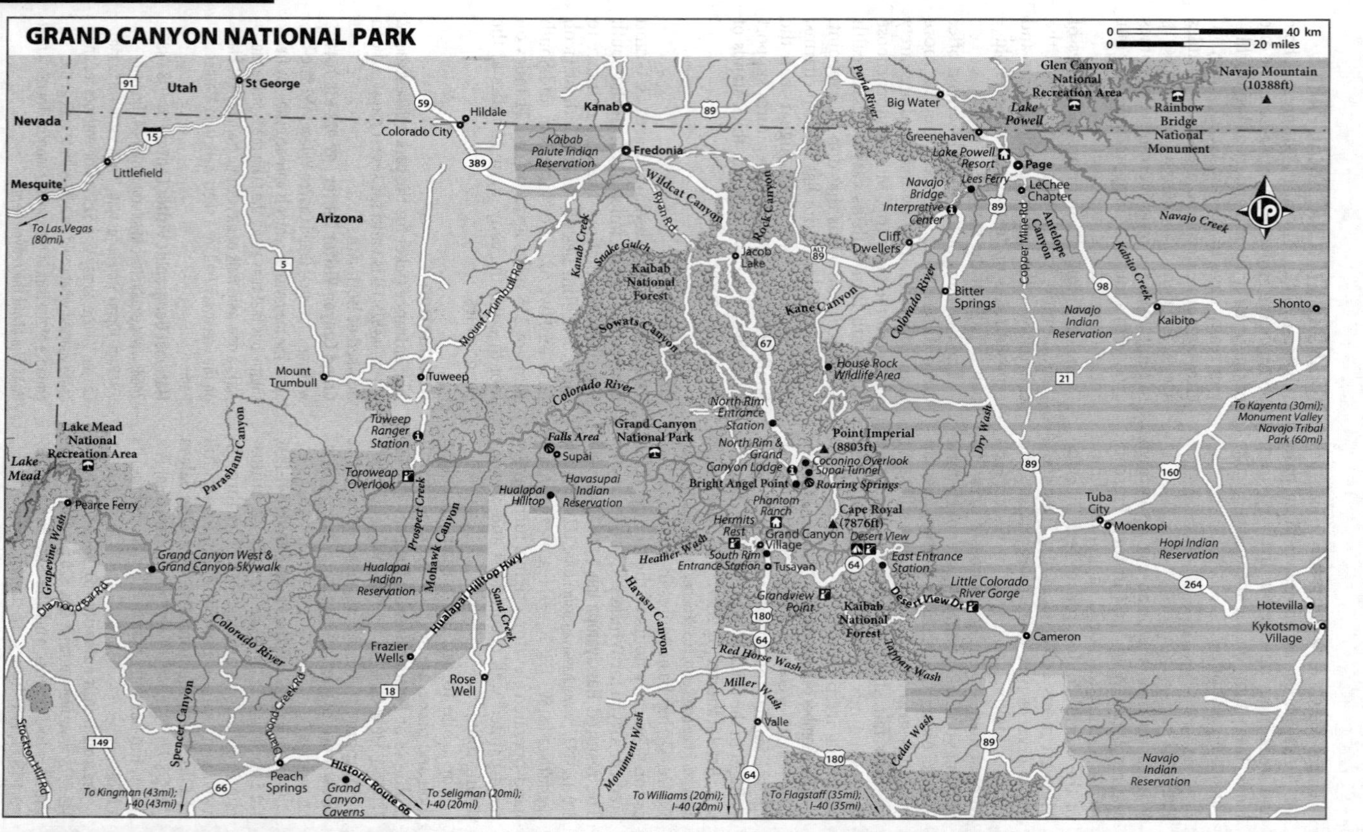
GRAND CANYON NATIONAL PARK
0 40 km
0 20 miles
Utah
Nevada
Arizona
St George
Mesquite
Littlefield
To Las Vegas (80mi)
Hildale
Colorado City
Kanab
Fredonia
Kaibab Paiute Indian Reservation
Wildcat Canyon
Ryan Rd
Rock Canyon
Kanab Creek
Snake Gulch
Kaibab National Forest
Sowats Canyon
Mount Trumbull Rd
Mount Trumbull
Tuweep
Tuweep Ranger Station
Toroweap Overlook
Prospect Creek
Mohawk Canyon
Parashant Canyon
Lake Mead National Recreation Area
Lake Mead
Pearce Ferry
Grapevine Wash
Diamond Bar Rd
Grand Canyon West & Grand Canyon Skywalk
Colorado River
Spencer Canyon
Diamond Creek Rd
Peach Springs
Historic Route 66
Grand Canyon Caverns
Stockton Hill Rd
To Kingman (43mi); I-40 (43mi)
To Seligman (20mi); I-40 (20mi)
Hualapai Indian Reservation
Frazier Wells
Rose Well
Hualapai Hilltop Hwy
Sand Creek
Hualapai Hilltop
Falls Area
Supai
Havasupai Indian Reservation
Havasu Canyon
Monument Wash
To Williams (20mi); I-40 (20mi)
Colorado River
Grand Canyon National Park
Jacob Lake
Kane Canyon
House Rock Wildlife Area
North Rim Entrance Station
North Rim & Grand Canyon Lodge
Point Imperial (8803ft)
Coconino Overlook
Supai Tunnel
Bright Angel Point
Roaring Springs
Phantom Ranch
Cape Royal (7876ft)
Hermits Rest
Grand Canyon Village
Desert View
Heather Wash
South Rim Entrance Station
Tusayan
East Entrance Station
Grandview Point
Kaibab National Forest
Desert View Dr
Little Colorado River Gorge
Red Horse Wash
Tappan Wash
Miller Wash
Valle
Cedar Wash
To Flagstaff (35mi); I-40 (35mi)
Paria River
Big Water
Greenehaven
Lake Powell
Glen Canyon National Recreation Area
Navajo Mountain (10388ft)
Rainbow Bridge National Monument
Lake Powell Resort
Page
Lees Ferry
Navajo Bridge Interpretive Center
LeChee Chapter
Copper Mine Rd
Antelope Canyon
Cliff Dwellers
Colorado River
Bitter Springs
Navajo Creek
Kaibito Creek
Kaibito
Shonto
Navajo Indian Reservation
Dry Wash
To Kayenta (30mi); Monument Valley Navajo Tribal Park (60mi)
Tuba City
Moenkopi
Hopi Indian Reservation
Cameron
Hotevilla
Kykotsmovi Village
Navajo Indian Reservation
91
15
59
389
89
5
ALT 89
67
98
21
89
160
264
64
180
18
149
66

North Rim Visitor Center (☎ 928-638-7888; www.nps.gov/grca; 🕑 8am-6pm) Adjacent to the Grand Canyon Lodge.

Verkamp's Visitor Center (www.nps.gov/grca; Grand Canyon Village; 🕑 8am-5pm) More accessible South Rim visitor center, across from El Tovar Hotel. Has an information desk, exhibits on the history of Grand Canyon Village, maps for self-guided walking tours of the village, a bookstore and a meeting point for ranger-led walks and talks.

WHEN TO GO

June is the driest month, July and August the wettest. January has average overnight lows of 13°F (-11°C) to 20°F (-7°C) and daytime highs around 40°F (4°C). Summer temperatures inside the canyon regularly soar above 100°F (38°C). While the South Rim is open year-round, most visitors come between late May and early September. The North Rim is open from mid-May to mid-October.

BACKCOUNTRY PERMITS

All overnight hikes and backcountry camping in the park require a permit. The **Backcountry Information Center** (☎ 928-638-7875; www.nps.gov/grca; Grand Canyon Village; 🕑 8am-noon & 1-5pm, phone staffed 1-5pm Mon-Fri) accepts applications for backpacking permits ($10, plus $5 per person per night) for the current month and following four months only. Your chances are decent if you apply early (four months in advance for spring and fall) and provide alternative hiking itineraries.

If you arrive without a permit, don't despair. Head to the office, by Maswik Lodge, to get on the waiting list. Show up every morning to hear the 8am callout of accepted wait-listers. If you're not on the list, this is when you'll receive a number for the next day. You'll likely get a permit within one to four days depending on the season and itinerary.

South Rim

Every summer, camera-toting visitors throng the park's most popular rim, though most stay only long enough to ogle from the easily accessible scenic viewpoints. To dodge the crowds, visit during fall or winter, especially on weekdays.

SIGHTS & ACTIVITIES

A **scenic route** follows the rim along the west side of the village along **Hermit Road**. Closed to private vehicles, the road is serviced by the free park shuttle bus and bicycling is encouraged because of the relatively light traffic. Stops along the way offer spectacular views, and interpretive signs explain canyon features and geology.

Hiking along the South Rim is among park visitors' favorite pastimes, with options for every skill level. The **Rim Trail** is the most popular, and easiest, walk in the park. It dips in and out of the scrubby pines of Kaibab National Forest and connects a series of scenic points and historical sights over 12 miles; portions are paved. Every viewpoint is accessed by one of the three shuttle routes. There's a spiffy new 3-mile paved western extension of the trail that's open to cyclists between **Monument Creek Vista** and **Pima Point**.

While on Hermit Rd, keep an eye peeled for one of 18 numbered signs that indicate a point in the **audio tour** (☎ 928-225-2907). Do yourself a favor and hit option 4 while gazing at the clear night sky for a sky tour.

Desert View Drive starts to the east of Grand Canyon village and follows the canyon rim for 26 miles to Desert View, the east entrance of the park. Pullouts along the way offer spectacular views, and interpretive signs explain canyon features and geology.

The most popular of the corridor trails is the beautiful **Bright Angel Trail**. The steep and scenic 8-mile descent to the Colorado River is punctuated with four logical turnaround spots. Summer heat can be crippling; day hikers should either turn around at one of the two resthouses (a 3- to 6-mile round-trip) or hit the trail at dawn to safely make the longer hikes to Indian Garden and Plateau Point (9.2 and 12.2 miles round-trip respectively). Hiking to the river in one day is not an option. The trailhead is at Grand Canyon Village.

The **South Kaibab** is arguably one of the park's prettiest trails, combining stunning scenery and unobstructed 360-degree views with every step. Steep, rough and wholly exposed, summer ascents can be dangerous, and during this season rangers discourage all but the shortest day hikes – otherwise it's a 6-mile, grueling round-trip. Turn around at **Cedar Ridge**, perhaps the park's finest short day hike.

Individuals and groups who want a more in-depth experience of the park while giving something back can apply for programs with **Grand Canyon Volunteers** (☎ 928-774-7488; www.gcvolunteers.org). One- and multiday programs include wildlife monitoring, native plant restoration and forest surveying.

TOURS

Park tours are run by **Xanterra** (☎ 303-297-2757, 888-297-2757; www.xanterra.com), which has information desks at the visitor centers and Bright Angel, Maswik and Yavapai Lodges. Various daily bus tours (tickets from $19) are offered.

Mule trips into the canyon depart daily from the corral west of Bright Angel Lodge. Choose from the seven-hour day trip ($162) or the overnight trip ($477), which includes lodging at Phantom Ranch and all meals. Riders must be at least 4ft 7in tall, speak fluent English, weigh less than 200lbs (90kg) and not be pregnant. Keep in mind that this is no carnival ride – these journeys are hot, dusty and bumpy.

SLEEPING

Advance or same-day reservations are required for the South Rim's six lodges, which are operated by **Xanterra** (☎ 888-297-2757; www.grandcanyonlodges.com) – use this phone number to make advance reservations (highly recommended) at any of the places (including Phantom Ranch) listed here. For same-day reservations or to reach a guest, call the **South Rim switchboard** (☎ 928-638-2631). If you can't find accommodations in the national park, try Tusayan (at South Rim Entrance Station), Valle (31 miles south), Cameron (53 miles east) or Williams (about 60 miles south).

Desert View Campground (campsites $12; ⏲ mid-May–mid-Oct) Near the East Entrance Station, 26 miles east of Grand Canyon Village, this first-come, first-served campground is a quieter alternative to Mather. A small cafeteria-snack shop serves meals.

Mather Campground (☎ 877-444-6777; www.recreation.gov; Grand Canyon Village; campsites $18-50) Well-dispersed, relatively peaceful sites amid piñon and juniper trees. There are pay showers and laundry facilities nearby, drinking water, toilets, grills and a small general store. First-come, first-served during winter months.

Phantom Ranch (dm/cabins $42/92) At the bottom of the canyon, the ranch has basic cabins sleeping four to 10 people, and segregated dorms. Most cabins are reserved for overnight mule tours, but hikers may make reservations if there's space – you can book up to 13 months ahead. The ranch serves meals ($12 to $41) – reserve well in advance. If you lack a sleeping reservation, show up at the Bright Angel Lodge transportation desk at 6am to snag a canceled bunks. Also offered is baggage transport by mule ($65).

Bright Angel Lodge (Grand Canyon Village; r & cabins $79-174; ⊠ ❄) Built in 1935, the log-and-stone Bright Angel offers historic charm and refurbished rooms, the cheapest of which have shared bathrooms. Don't expect a TV in these very basic rooms (think dorm room from university), but rim cabins have better views than any boob tube and the cabins with fireplaces are magical.

El Tovar Hotel (Grand Canyon Village; d/ste $205/426; ⊠ ❄) Wide inviting porches wreathe the rambling wooden structure, offering pleasant spots to people-watch and admire canyon views. Even if you're not a guest, stop by to relax with a book on the porch swing or a drink on the patio. The public spaces show the lodgelike, genteel elegance of the park's heyday. The standard rooms are small but first-class. Suites are fantastic.

Also recommended:

Trailer Village (Grand Canyon Village; tent & RV sites $32) Camp here if everywhere else is full. You can reserve well in advance or same-day.

Maswik Lodge (Grand Canyon Village; r $90-170, cabins $90; ⊠ ❄) Set away from the rim, but with a sports bar and cafeteria.

Yavapai Lodge (Grand Canyon Village; r $97-126; ⏲ mid-Feb–mid-Nov; ⊠) Basic lodging amid peaceful piñon and juniper forest.

Kachina Lodge & Thunderbird Lodge (Grand Canyon Village; r $170-180; ⊠ ❄) Decent motel-style rooms in a central location. Some rooms have canyon views.

EATING & DRINKING

Bright Angel Lounge (Bright Angel Lodge, Grand Canyon Village; dishes $8-13; ⏲ 11am-11pm) Perfect for those who want to relax with a burger and a beer (or similar pub food and drink) without cleaning up too much; a fun place to sit and relax at night when the lack of windows and dark decor aren't a big deal. If you're lucky, Terry Rickard will be working his guitar magic for the crowd.

Arizona Room (Bright Angel Lodge, Grand Canyon Village; dishes $9-26; ⏲ 11:30am-3pm & 4:30-10pm Mar-Oct, 4:30-10pm Nov & Dec) Striking a wonderful balance between casual and upscale, this restaurant is a solid option. Antler chandeliers hang from the ceiling and picture windows overlook the canyon. Mains include steak, chicken and fish dishes. No reservations; there's often a wait.

El Tovar Dining Room (☎ 928-638-2631; El Tovar Hotel, Grand Canyon Village; dishes $12-35; ⏲ 6:30am-2pm & 5-10pm) Set a stone's throw away from the canyon's edge, it has the best views of any restaurant of the state, if not the country. If you don't get a table with a view – you can request it in advance but it won't be guaranteed – the grand stone and dark oak dining room warms the soul like an upscale lodge of yore, and the food, especially the steaks, makes the trip worthwhile. Head to the verandah of the El Tovar Lounge afterwards for a guaranteed Grand Canyon vista.

Also recommended:

Canyon Village Marketplace (Grand Canyon Village; 8am-7pm, 7am-8pm Jul & Aug) Stock up on groceries or hit the deli (sandwiches and warm snacks from $5).

Canyon Cafe at Yavapai Lodge (Yavapai Lodge, Grand Canyon Village; dishes $5-9; 6am-10pm) Cafeteria food, service and seating.

Maswik Cafeteria (Maswik Lodge, Grand Canyon Village; dishes $5-9; 6am-10pm) Another cafeteria-style place.

GETTING THERE & AROUND

Most people arrive at the canyon in private vehicles or on a tour. Be advised that finding parking can be a chore in Grand Canyon Village. **Open Road Tours** (☎ 928-226-8060; www.openroadtours.com) runs shuttles from Flagstaff ($27, two daily) and Williams ($22, two daily). It can also arrange helicopter tours (from $145) over the canyon.

Free **park shuttles** operate along three routes: around Grand Canyon Village, west along Hermits Rest Route and east along Kaibab Trail Route. Buses run at least twice per hour, starting from one hour before sunset to one hour afterwards.

A free shuttle from Bright Angel Lodge during the summer months, the **Hiker's Express** (7am, 8am & 9am Mar, 6am, 7am & 8am Apr, 5am, 6am & 7am May) has pickups at the Backcountry Information Center and Grand Canyon Visitor Center, and then heads to the South Kaibab trailhead.

For the free **Tusayan Route** (8am-9:30pm mid-May–mid-Sep) riders must purchase a park entrance pass in Tusayan at one of a number of locations before boarding the bus – the **National Geographic Visitor Center** (p851) is convenient because it's a shuttle stop. The trip takes 20 minutes, and the last bus to Tusayan leaves the Grand Canyon Visitor Center at 9:30pm.

North Rim

Head here for blessed solitude in nature's bountiful bosom; only 10% of park visitors make the trek. Meadows are thick with wildflowers and dense clusters of willowy aspen and spruce trees, and the air is often crisp, the skies big and blue.

Facilities on the North Rim are closed from mid-October to mid-May, although you can drive into the park and stay at the campground until the first snow closes the road from Jacob Lake.

SIGHTS & ACTIVITIES

North Rim Visitor Center (☎ 928-638-7888; www.nps.gov/grca; 8am-6pm), next to the Grand Canyon Lodge (p856), is the place to get information on the park and the starting point for ranger-led nature walks and evening programs.

The short and easy paved trail (0.5 miles) to **Bright Angel Point** is a canyon must. Beginning from the back porch of Grand Canyon Lodge, it goes to a narrow finger of an overlook with fabulous views.

The **North Kaibab Trail** is the North Rim's only maintained rim-to-river trail and connects with trails to the South Rim. The first 4.7 miles are the steepest, dropping 3050ft to **Roaring Springs** – a popular all-day hike. If you prefer a shorter day hike below the rim, walk just 0.75 miles down to **Coconino Overlook** or 2 miles to the **Supai Tunnel** to get a flavor for steep inner-canyon hiking. The 28-mile round-trip to the Colorado River is a multiday affair.

Canyon Trail Rides (☎ 435-679-8665; www.canyonrides.com; Grand Canyon Lodge) offers one-hour mule trips ($40) along the rim and half- or full-day trips into the canyon. The full-day, seven-hour trip ($165, minimum age 12 years) departs at 7:30am. Lunch and water are provided. Half-day trips ($75, minimum age 10 years) leave at 7:30am and 12:30pm. Make arrangements at Grand Canyon Lodge.

SLEEPING

Accommodations within the North Rim are limited to one lodge and one campground. If these are booked, try your luck 80 miles north in Kanab, UT, or 84 miles northeast in Lees Ferry. There are also campgrounds in the Kaibab National Forest north of the park.

North Rim Campground (☎ 877-444-6777; www.recreation.gov; campsites $18) This campground, 1.5 miles north of Grand Canyon Lodge, offers pleasant sites on level ground blanketed in pine needles. There is water, a store, a snack bar and coin-operated showers and laundry facilities, but no hookups. Hikers and cross-country skiers can use the campground during winter months if they have a backcountry permit (p853). Reservations accepted.

Grand Canyon Lodge (☎ 877-386-4383; www.foreverlodging.com; r & cabins $112-170; mid-May–mid-Oct;) This lodge made of wood, stone and glass is the kind of place you imagine should be perched on the rim. Rustic yet modern cabins make up the majority of accommodations. The most expensive cabins offer two rooms, a porch and beautiful rim views. The canyon views from the Sun Room are stunning, the lobby regal. Reserve far in advance.

EATING & DRINKING

Grand Canyon Lodge Dining Room (☎ 928-638-2611; Grand Canyon Lodge; lunch mains $6-15, dinner mains $14-31; 6:30am-10am, 11:30am-2:30pm & 4:45-9:45pm) The windows are so huge that you can sit anywhere to get a good view. The menu includes several vegetarian options and unexpected treats like shrimp cocktail and bison flank steak. Dinner reservations are required, and it's neighbors with the atmospheric Rough Rider Saloon, full of memorabilia from the country's most adventurous president ever.

Grand Canyon Cookout Experience (☎ 928-638-2611; Grand Canyon Lodge; adult/child $35/22; 6pm;) This chuck-wagon-style cookout featuring beef brisket and biscuits is more of an event than a meal. Kids love it, and there's no better way to feel like a well-fed, well-cared-for pioneer. Make arrangements at the Grand Canyon Lodge.

GETTING THERE & AROUND

The **Transcanyon Shuttle** (☎ 928-638-2820; www.trans-canyonshuttle.com; one way/round-trip $80/150; 7am mid-May–mid-Oct) departs daily from Grand Canyon Lodge for the South Rim (five hours) and is perfect for rim-to-rim hikers. Reserve at least one or two weeks in advance. A **hikers' shuttle** (first person $8, each additional person $5) to the North Kaibab Trail departs at both 5:20am and 7:20am from Grand Canyon Lodge. Reservations must be made at least 24 hours in advance.

AROUND THE GRAND CANYON

Havasu Canyon

Even after the massive flooding that hit the area in August 2008 and closed it down for 10 months, Havasupai is still one of the most beautiful places in the canyon.

On the Havasupai Indian Reservation, about 195 miles west of the South Rim, the valley around Havasu Canyon has spring-fed waterfalls and sparkling swimming holes. The falls lie 10 miles below the rim, accessed via a moderately challenging hiking trail, and trips require an overnight stay in the nearby village of Supai.

Supai offers two sleeping options and reservations must be secured before starting out. There's a $35 entrance fee ($17 for children) for all overnight guests. The **Havasupai Campground** (☎ 928-448-2174; adult/child $17/8.50), 2 miles north of Supai, has primitive campsites along a creek. In addition, every camper must pay a $5 environmental fee, refunded if you pack out trash. The **Havasupai Lodge** (☎ 928-448-2111; www.havasupaitribe.com/lodge.html; r $145;) has motel rooms with canyon views and no phones or TVs. Be sure to check in by 5pm, when the lobby closes. A village café serves meals and accepts credit cards.

After a night in Supai, continue through Havasu Canyon to the waterfalls and blue-green swimming holes. If you don't want to hike to Supai, call the lodge or campground to arrange for a mule or horse ($187 round-trip) to carry you there. Rides depart from Hualapai Hilltop, where the hiking trail begins. The road to Hualapai Hilltop is 7 miles east of Peach Springs off Route 66. Look for the marked turnoff and follow the road for 62 miles.

Grand Canyon West

The **Grand Canyon Skywalk** (☎ 702-878-9378, 877-716-9378; www.destinationgrandcanyon.com; Diamond Bar Rd; admission incl tour $75; sunrise-sunset year-round) is a slender see-through glass horseshoe bridge that levitates over a 4000ft chasm of the Grand Canyon.

Run by the Hualapai Nation, the remote site is 70 miles northeast of Kingman (and 215 driving miles from Grand Canyon Village), and the last 14 miles are rough, unpaved and unsuitable for RVs. Environmentalists have decried the Skywalk as an eyesore desecrating an otherwise pristine landmark.

NORTHEASTERN ARIZONA

Some of Arizona's most photogenic landscapes lie in the northeastern corner of the state. Between the red brooding buttes of Monument Valley, the cool blue waters of Lake Powell and the fossilized logs of the Petrified Forest National Park are lands locked in ancient history. Inhabited by Native Americans for centuries, this region is largely made up of reservation land called Navajo Nation, which spills into surrounding states. There's a Hopi reservation here as well, completely surrounded by Navajo land.

Lake Powell

The country's second-largest artificial reservoir and part of the **Glen Canyon National Recreation Area** (☎ 928-608-6200; www.nps.gov/glca; admission vehicle/boat $15/16), Lake Powell stretches between Utah and Arizona. Set amid striking red-rock formations, sharply cut canyons and dramatic desert scenery, it's water-sports heaven. South of the lake and looking out over a scenic stretch of the Colorado River, **Lees Ferry** (campsites $12) is a pleasant stopover, with same-day and advance reservations.

The region's central town is **Page**, and Hwy 89 forms the main strip. The **Carl Hayden Visitor Center** (☎ 928-608-6404; 8am-7pm late May–early Sep, 8am-4pm early Sep–late May) is located at the Glen Canyon Dam, 2.5 miles north of Page. **Tours** (☎ 928-608-6072; adult/child $5/2.50) run by the Glen Canyon Natural History Association take you inside the dam. In high season tours run every half-hour, in low season every two hours.

To visit photogenic **Antelope Canyon** (www.navajonationparks.org/htm/antelopecanyon.htm), a stunning sandstone slot canyon with two main parts, you must join a tour. **Upper Antelope Canyon** is easier to navigate and more touristed. **Antelope Canyon Slot Tours** (☎ 928-645-5594; www.antelopeslotcanyon.com; 55 S Lake Powell Blvd; tours adult/child $32/20) is recommended, and runs stargazing outings as well.

The more strenuous **Lower Antelope Canyon** sees much smaller crowds. If you've already gone on an Upper Antelope Canyon tour that day show your receipt to avoid paying the $6 Navajo Permit Fee again. After parking in a well-signed dirt lot, arrange a tour at the welcome kiosk, starting at $20 per person. Visitors with the trappings of serious photographers can pay the fee and wander at will.

Chain hotels line Hwy 89 in Page and a number of independent places line 8th Ave. One inexpensive and longtime reliable indie choice is **Bashful Bob's Motel** (☎ 928-645-3919; www.bashfulbobsmotel.com; 750 S Navajo Dr; r $39;), which was constructed to house Glen Canyon Dam builders. All 13 rooms are more like apartments, with full kitchens.

Six miles north of Page and with a direct view of the lake, the **Lake Powell Resort** (☎ 928-645-2433, 800-528-6154; www.lakepowell.com; 100 Lake Shore Dr; RV sites $43, d $160-260;) offers rooms, camping, houseboat rentals and a dining room with panoramic views.

For breakfast in Page, the **Ranch House Grille** (☎ 928-645-1420; 819 N Navajo Dr; dishes $6-11; 6am-3pm) has good food, huge portions and fast service. The portions are large and the drinks cold at **Fiesta Mexican** (☎ 928-645-4082; 125 S Powell Blvd; mains $8-17; 11am-9pm), walking distance from most of the independent hotels.

Navajo Nation

The wounds are healing but the scars remain, a testament to the uprooting and forced relocation of thousands of Native Americans to reservations.

Amid the isolation is some of North America's most spectacular scenery, including Monument Valley. Cultural prides remain strong, and many still speak Navajo as their first language. The Navajo rely heavily on tourism; visitors can help keep their heritage alive by staying on reservation land or purchasing their renowned crafts. Stopping at roadside stalls is a nice way to make purchases for personal interaction and making sure money goes straight into the artisan's pocket.

Unlike Arizona, the Navajo Nation observes Mountain daylight saving time. During summer, the reservation is one hour ahead of Arizona.

CAMERON

Cameron is the gateway to the east entrance of the Grand Canyon's South Rim, but the other reason people come here is for **Cameron Trading Post** (www.camerontradingpost.com), just north of the Hwy 64 turnoff to the Grand Canyon. Food, lodging, a gift shop and even a post office are in this historic settlement. It's one of the few worthwhile places to stop and wander on Hwy 89 between Flagstaff and Page.

WINDOW ROCK

The tribal capital is at Window Rock, a bustling little place at the intersection of Hwys 264 and 12. The **Navajo Nation Museum Library & Visitors Center** (☎ 928-871-7941; www.navajonationmuseum.org; cnr Hwy 264 & Post Office Loop Rd; admission by donation; 8am-5pm Mon, 8am-8pm Tue-Fri, 9am-5pm Sat) features an information kiosk, a gift shop, a snack bar and permanent art collections and changing shows.

Rooms at the **Quality Inn Navajo Nation Capital** (☎ 928-871-4108, 800-662-6189; www.qualityinnwindowrock.com; 48 W Hwy 264; r incl breakfast $72-90;)

WORTH THE TRIP: HOPI NATION

Descendants of the Ancestral Puebloans, the Hopi are one of the most untouched tribes in the United States and their village of Old Oraibi may be the oldest continuously inhabited settlement in North America. Come for a rare peek into a present with close ties to the past – the people here live in one of 12 traditional villages, each self-governing.

Hopi land is surrounded by Navajo Nation. Hwy 264 runs past the three mesas (First, Second and Third Mesa) that form the heart of the Hopi reservation.

There are no banks, and except at the **Hopi Cultural Center Restaurant & Inn** (☎ 928-734-2401; www.hopiculturalcenter.com; r $95-99, dishes $7-9; 🕐 7am-8pm Nov-Feb, 6am-9pm March-Oct; ❄), cash is king. Photographs, sketching and recording are not allowed.

Get oriented at the **tourist office** (☎ 928-737-2262) in the tiny village of Walpi (c 1600). To reach Walpi, look for signs to First Mesa from Hwy 264 (around Mile 392).

are the clean, comfy, basic accommodations you'd expect from a reputable mid-tier brand. The on-site restaurant serves Navajo and American fare.

HUBBELL TRADING POST NATIONAL HISTORIC SITE

Thirty miles west of Window Rock in the town of Ganado, this is the oldest operating **trading post** (☎ 928-755-3475; www.nps.gov/hutr; admission free; 🕐 8am-6pm May-Sep, to 5pm Oct-Apr) on the Navajo Nation. Local artisans sell local crafts and jewelry, including top-quality Navajo weavings.

CANYON DE CHELLY NATIONAL MONUMENT

This many-fingered canyon (pronounced *duh-shay*) contains several beautiful Ancestral Puebloan sites important to Navajo history, including ancient cliff dwellings. Families still farm the land, wintering on the rims, then moving to hogans on the canyon floor in spring and summer. The canyon is private Navajo property administered by the NPS. Enter hogans only with a guide and don't photograph people without their permission.

Most of the bottom of the canyon is off-limits to visitors unless you hire a guide. The **Thunderbird Lodge** (☎ 928-674-5841; www.tbirdlodge.com; d $105-155; ❄) is the place to book a tour (from $46/35 per adult/child) into the canyon. The lodge also boats comfortable rooms, an ATM and an inexpensive cafeteria serving tasty Navajo and American meals ($6 to $12).

The Canyon de Chelly **visitor center** (☎ 928-674-5500; www.nps.gov/cach; 🕐 8am-5pm) is three miles from Rte 191 in the small village of Chinle. Near the visitor center, the **campground** (campsites free) has 93 large sites on a first-come, first-served basis, with water but no showers.

FOUR CORNERS NAVAJO TRIBAL PARK

Don't be shy: do a spread eagle for the folks on top of the **four corners marker** (☎ 928-871-6647; www.navajonationparks.org; admission $3; 🕐 8am-5pm Oct-May, 7am-8pm Jun-Sep) that signifies you're in four states at once. It makes a good photograph, even if it's not 100% accurate – an April 2009 news story had government surveyors admitting that the marker is almost 2000ft east of where it should be, but that the marker is a legally recognized border point, regardless. Put a foot into Arizona and plant the other in New Mexico. Slap a hand in Utah and place the other in Colorado.

MONUMENT VALLEY NAVAJO TRIBAL PARK

With flaming-red buttes and impossibly slender spires bursting to the heavens, the Monument Valley landscape has starred in countless Hollywood Westerns and looms large in many a road-trip daydream.

Great views can be had from along Hwy 163, but to really get up close and personal you'll need to visit the **Monument Valley Navajo Tribal Park** (☎ 435-727-5874; www.navajonationparks.org; entry per person $5; 🕐 6am-8pm May-Sep, 8am-4:30pm Oct-Apr). The visitor center houses exhibits and a huge gift shop. From the visitor center, a rough and unpaved scenic driving loop covers 17 miles of stunning valley views. You can drive it in your own vehicle or take a tour ($65, 2½ hours) through one of the kiosks in the parking lot (tours enter areas private vehicles can't).

Inside the tribal park is the **View Hotel at Monument Valley** (☎ 435-727-5555; www.monumentvalleyview.com; Hwy 163; r $180; ⊠ ❄ 💻). Just how sweet is the View? Very. Built in harmony with the landscape, the sandstone-colored hotel blends naturally with its surroundings and most of the 96 rooms have private balconies facing the monuments. Though the Navajo-based specialties at the adjoining restaurant (mains $9 to $12; no alcohol) won't knock your socks off, the red-rock panorama will tug your tennis shoes toward the door. Visitors can also overnight in the park's de facto **campground** (per vehicle $10). It's basically just a parking lot, but the awesome sunrise view makes up for the lack of amenities.

Goulding's Lodge (p881) is just across the border in Utah. The surprisingly stylish, well-appointed **Hampton Inn** (☎ 928-697-3170; www.monumentvalleyonline.com; junction Hwys 160 & 163; r incl breakfast $130-180;) is in the town of Kayenta, a popular base for Monument Valley trips that's just 20 miles from the park. Neighboring an interesting **visitor center** (☎ 928-697-3572; junction Hwys 160 & 163; 10am-5pm), the hotel has a good restaurant and a handful of fast-food places and gas stations with snacks are nearby.

Winslow

'Standing on a corner in Winslow, Arizona, such a fine sight to see…' Sound familiar? Thanks to the Eagles' twangy 1970s tune 'Take It Easy,' otherwise nondescript Winslow has earned its wings in pop-culture heaven. A small plaza on Route 66 at Kinsley Ave pays homage to the band.

Just 50 miles east of Petrified Forest National Park, Winslow makes a good regional base. About a dozen old motels are found along Route 66 and eateries sprinkle the downtown. The 1929 hacienda-style **La Posada** (☎ 928-289-4366; www.laposada.org; 303 E 2nd; r $99-169;) is the town's most famous building.

Petrified Forest National Park

The multicolored Painted Desert here is strewn with fossilized logs predating the dinosaurs. This **national park** (☎ 928-524-6228; www.nps.gov/pefo; entry per vehicle $10) is an extraordinary site. The hard-to-miss **visitor center** (7am-7pm) is just half a mile north of I-40 and has maps and information on guided tours and science lectures.

The park straddles I-40 at exit 311, 25 miles east of Holbrook. From this exit, a 28-mile paved park road offers a splendid **scenic drive**. There are no campsites, but a number of short trails, ranging from less than a mile to two miles, pass through the best stands of petrified rock and ancient Native American dwellings in the park. Those prepared for rugged backcountry camping need to pick up a free permit at the visitor center.

SCENIC DRIVE: RIM COUNTRY

The section of eastern Arizona south of Winslow, formed by the southern edge of the Colorado Plateau, is called Rim Country by locals and is where they go for scenic drives and weekends in rented cabins during the summer months. Colorful little towns like **Show Low** (won in a poker game), **Strawberry** and **Snowflake** (named by Erastus Snow and William Jordan Flake) dot twisty roads lined by pines. Check out www.wmonline.com or www.paysonrimcountry.com.

WESTERN ARIZONA

The Colorado River is alive with sun-worshippers at Lake Havasu City, while Route 66 offers well-preserved stretches of classic highway near Kingman. South of I-10, the wild, empty landscape is among the most barren in the West. If you're already here there are some worthwhile sites, but nothing worth shaping an itinerary around unless you're a serious Route 66 or boating fanatic.

Kingman & Around

Faded motels and gas stations galore grace Kingman's main drag, but several turn-of-the-19th-century buildings remain. If you're following the Route 66 trail (aka Andy Devine Ave here) or looking for cheap lodging, it's worth a stroll.

Pick up self-guided walking-tour maps at the historic **Powerhouse Visitor Center** (☎ 928-753-6106; www.kingmantourism.org; 120 W Andy Devine Ave; 8am-5pm), which has an impressive **Route 66 museum** (☎ 928-753-9889; admission $4; 9am-5pm).

The atmospheric 1909 **Hotel Brunswick** (☎ 928-718-1800; www.hotel-brunswick.com; 315 E Andy Devine Ave; incl breakfast r $35-66, ste $95-175;) is in the heart of Kingman and has rock-bottom-budget cowboy/girl rooms with single beds and shared baths, as well as nicer digs with larger beds, TVs and private baths. The on-site **Hubbs Brunswick Bistro** (dishes $20-30; 11am-2pm & 5-9pm Mon-Fri, 5-9pm Sat) is a fabulous gourmet bistro serving pasta, steaks and seafood.

Lake Havasu City

When the city of London auctioned off its 1831 bridge in the late 1960s, developer Robert McCulloch bought it, took it apart, shipped it, and then reassembled it at Lake Havasu City,

ROUTE 66: GET YOUR KICKS IN ARIZONA

Route 66 enthusiasts will find 400 miles of pavement stretching across Arizona – including the longest uninterrupted portion of old road left in the country, between Seligman and Topock. The Mother Road connects the dots between Winslow's windblown streets, Williams' 1940s-vintage downtown, Kingman's mining settlements and gunslinging Oatman, each a glimpse of a bygone era. Unpaved dirt segments give a taste of old-school motoring. For more info contact the **Historic Route 66 Association of Arizona** (☎ 928-753-5001; www.azrt66.com).

which sits along a dammed-up portion of the Colorado River. The place attracts hordes of young spring-breakers and weekend warriors who come to play in the water and party hard. An 'English Village' of pseudo-British pubs and tourist gift shops surrounds the bridge.

The **visitor center** (☎ 928-453-3444; www.golakehavasu.com; 420 English Village; 🕑 9am-5pm Mon-Sat) has information on tours and boat rentals.

With pools, popular nightclubs, a bar, hot tubs, restaurants and a lakeside location, **London Bridge Resort & Convention Center** (☎ 928-855-0888, 866-331-9231; www.londonbridgeresort.com; 1477 Queens Bay; ste $140-359;) attracts a playful crowd. Units feature either one or two bedrooms with kitchenettes.

Thanks to the college crowd there are plenty of affordable places to eat, drink and be merry, but **Mudshark Brewing Co** (☎ 928-453-2981; 210 Swanson Ave; dishes $8-20; 🕑 11am-10:30pm Sun-Thu, 11am-11:30pm Fri & Sat) is a favorite for casual dining, killer microbrews and quality food. There are many weeknight food specials: ribs, cheap happy-hour bites etc.

TUSCON

Arizona's second-largest city is set in the Sonoran Desert, full of rolling, sandy hills and crowds of cacti. The vibe here is ramshackle-cool and cozy compared with the shiny vastness of Phoenix. A college town, Tucson (the 'c' is silent) is home turf to the 36,000-strong University of Arizona (U of A) and was an artsy, dress-down kind of place before that was the cool thing to be. Eclectic shops and scores of funky restaurants and bars flourish in this arid ground.

Tucsonans are proud of the city's geographic and cultural proximity to Mexico (the southern neighbor is only 65 highway miles to the south), and more than 35% of the population is of Mexican or Central American descent. Spanish slides easily off most tongues and high-quality Mexican restaurants abound. The gateway for many attractions and little towns that get stranger and more beautiful the further afield you go, Tucson is a great base.

Orientation

Downtown Tucson and the historic district are east of I-10 exit 258. About a mile northeast of downtown is the U of A campus; 4th Ave is the main drag here, packed with cafés, bars and interesting shops.

With a number of downtown redevelopment construction projects happening, driving can be a bit confusing in this part of town, but with patience and caution you can get to wherever you need.

Information

BOOKSTORES

Bookman's (☎ 520-325-5767; 1930 E Grant Rd; 🕑 9am-10pm) Great selection of used books, music and magazines.

EMERGENCY & MEDICAL SERVICES

Police (☎ 520-791-4444; 270 S Stone Ave)

Tucson Medical Center (☎ 520-327-5461; 5301 E Grant Rd; 🕑 24hr emergency)

INTERNET ACCESS

Joel D Valdez Main Library (☎ 520-791-4393; 101 N Stone Ave; 🕑 9am-8pm Mon-Wed, to 6pm Thu, to 5pm Fri, 10am-5pm Sat, 1-5pm Sun) Free internet access.

MEDIA

Arizona Daily Star (www.azstarnet.com) The Tucson region's daily newspaper.

Tucson Weekly (www.tucsonweekly.com) A free weekly full of entertainment and restaurant listings.

MONEY

ATMs are abundant. Foreign exchange is available at most banks; $5 is charged if you don't have an account. Tucson International Airport doesn't exchange currency.

POST

Tucson Downtown post office (☎ 520-903-1958, 800-275-8777; 141 S 6th Ave; 🕑 9am-5pm Mon-Fri)

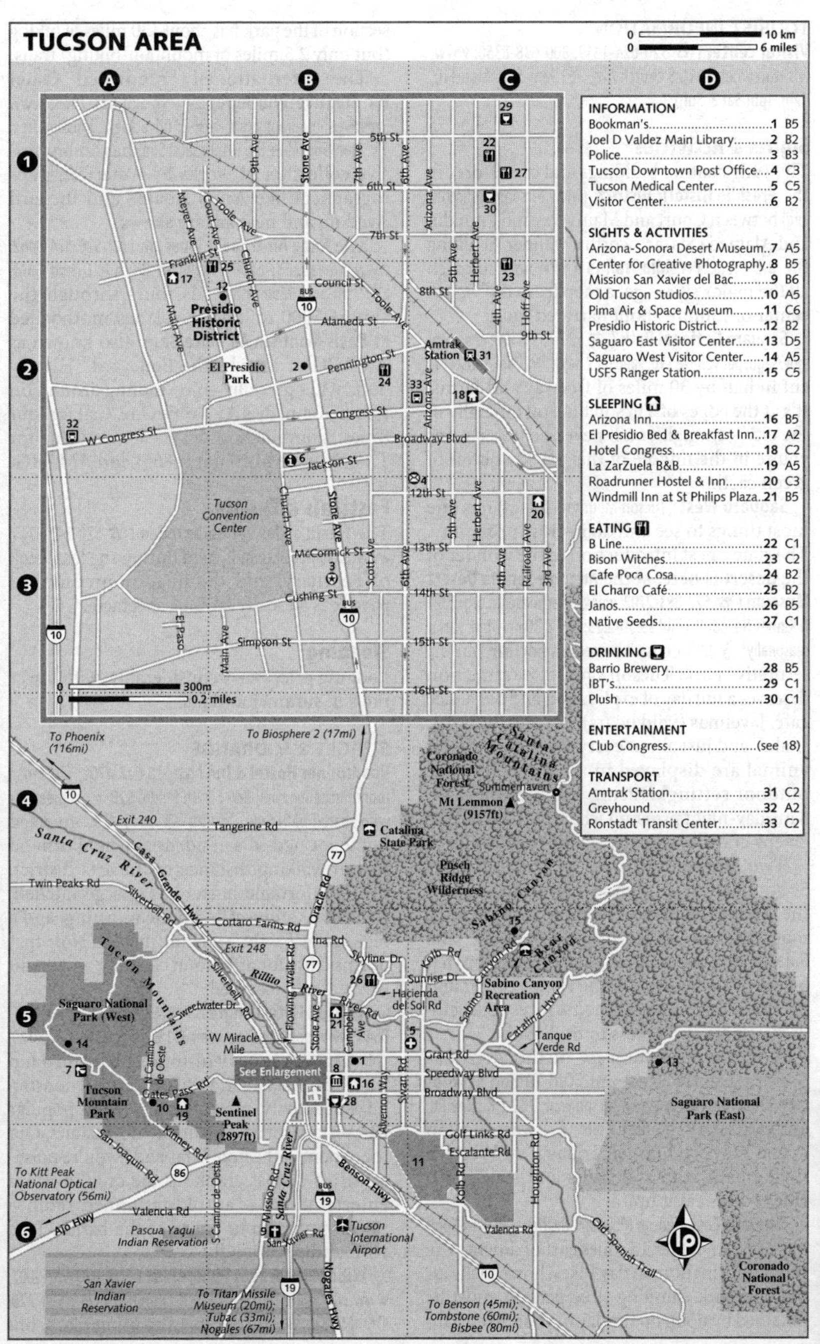
TUCSON AREA
0 10 km
0 6 miles
A
B
C
D
1
2
3
4
5
6
INFORMATION
Bookman's...1 B5
Joel D Valdez Main Library...2 B2
Police...3 B3
Tucson Downtown Post Office...4 C3
Tucson Medical Center...5 C5
Visitor Center...6 B2
SIGHTS & ACTIVITIES
Arizona-Sonora Desert Museum...7 A5
Center for Creative Photography...8 B5
Mission San Xavier del Bac...9 B6
Old Tucson Studios...10 A5
Pima Air & Space Museum...11 C6
Presidio Historic District...12 B2
Saguaro East Visitor Center...13 D5
Saguaro West Visitor Center...14 A5
USFS Ranger Station...15 C5
SLEEPING
Arizona Inn...16 B5
El Presidio Bed & Breakfast Inn...17 A2
Hotel Congress...18 C2
La ZarZuela B&B...19 A5
Roadrunner Hostel & Inn...20 C3
Windmill Inn at St Philips Plaza...21 B5
EATING
B Line...22 C1
Bison Witches...23 C2
Cafe Poca Cosa...24 B2
El Charro Café...25 B2
Janos...26 B5
Native Seeds...27 C1
DRINKING
Barrio Brewery...28 B5
IBT's...29 C1
Plush...30 C1
ENTERTAINMENT
Club Congress...(see 18)
TRANSPORT
Amtrak Station...31 C2
Greyhound...32 A2
Ronstadt Transit Center...33 C2
Presidio Historic District
El Presidio Park
Tucson Convention Center
Amtrak Station
0 300m
0 0.2 miles
To Phoenix (116mi)
To Biosphere 2 (17mi)
Coronado National Forest
Santa Catalina Mountains
Summerhaven
Mt Lemmon (9157ft)
Catalina State Park
Pusch Ridge Wilderness
Sabino Canyon
Bear Canyon
Sabino Canyon Recreation Area
Santa Cruz River
Casa Grande Hwy
Tucson Mountains
Saguaro National Park (West)
Tucson Mountain Park
Sentinel Peak (2897ft)
See Enlargement
Saguaro National Park (East)
To Kitt Peak National Optical Observatory (56mi)
Pascua Yaqui Indian Reservation
San Xavier Indian Reservation
Tucson International Airport
To Titan Missile Museum (20mi); Tubac (33mi); Nogales (67mi)
To Benson (45mi); Tombstone (60mi); Bisbee (80mi)
Coronado National Forest

TOURIST INFORMATION

Visitor center (☎ 520-624-1817, 800-638-8350; www.visittucson.org; 110 S Church Ave; 🕑 9am-5pm Mon-Fri, 9am-4pm Sat & Sun)

Sights & Activities

The 19th-century buildings and craft stores in the **Presidio Historic District**, (www.tucsonpresidiotrust.org) between Court and Main Aves and Franklin and Alameda Sts, are worth a wander. Walking the 2.5-mile **Presidio Trail** is a fun way to catch all the major sites – get a map from the visitor center or inquire about narrated tours.

Saguaro National Park (☎ 520-733-5100; www.nps.gov/sagu; per vehicle $10, valid for 7 days; 🕑 7am-sunset) is cut in half by 30 miles of freeway and farms. It's at the edges of Tucson but still officially in the city – though you'll never believe it once you're in the middle of this prickly ocean of green cacti.

Saguaro West (Tucson Mountain District) has the most things to see and do in close proximity. The state's best introduction to the wonder of the desert is here, at the **Arizona-Sonora Desert Museum** (☎ 520-883-2702; www.desertmuseum.org; 2021 N Kinney Rd; adult/child $9.50/2.25; 🕑 8:30am-5pm, varies seasonally; ♿). A cross between a zoo and an interpretive park, Tucson's must-see attraction deserves a full day of exploration and has a nice café. Javelinas (wild boars), coyotes, bobcats, snakes and just about every other local desert animal are displayed in a natural-looking outdoor setting. During summer there's a Saturday-night program where you can see the creepy crawlies who live on the night shift.

Two miles northwest of the Arizona-Sonora Desert Museum (follow the signs) is the **Saguaro West Visitor Center** (🕑 9am-5pm), with maps and ranger-led programs galore. The **Bajada Loop Drive** is an unpaved 6-mile loop that begins 1.5 miles west of the visitor center and provides fine views of cactus forests, several picnic spots and access to trailheads.

A few miles southeast of the Arizona-Sonora Desert Museum, **Old Tucson Studios** (☎ 520-883-0100; www.oldtucson.com; 201 S Kinney Rd; adult/child $17/11; 🕑 10am-6pm; ♿) was once an actual Western film set. Today it's a Western theme park with shootouts and stagecoach rides – kids eat it up.

Saguaro East (Rincon Mountain District; 🕑 9am-5pm) has a visitor center 15 miles east of downtown. It has information on day hikes, horseback riding and park camping (free permits must be obtained by noon on the day of your hike). This section of the park has about 130 miles of hiking (but only 2.5 miles of mountain-biking) trails.

The internationally renowned **Center for Creative Photography** (☎ 520-621-7968; www.creativephotography.org; 1030 N Olive Ave; admission free; 🕑 9am-5pm Mon-Fri, 1-4pm Sat & Sun) has an impressive collection of works by American photographers like Ansel Adams and Richard Avedon, and neat gallery shows.

The **Pima Air & Space Museum** (☎ 520-574-0462; www.pimaair.org; 6000 E Valencia Rd; adult/child $6/3; 🕑 9am-5pm Mon-Fri) leads tours through the almost 5000 military airplanes mothballed at **Davis-Monthan Air Force Base**, also known as AMARG or simply 'the Boneyard.' History buffs will especially enjoy tooling around on John F Kennedy's Air Force One. Call for tour times. Combination tickets are available for Titan Missile Museum (p865) and AMARG.

Festivals & Events

The **Fiesta de los Vaqueros rodeo** (☎ 520-741-2233; www.tucsonrodeo.com) is held during the last week of February, and the huge nonmotorized parade is a locally famous spectacle.

Sleeping

Lodging prices vary considerably, with lower rates in summer and fall.

BUDGET & MIDRANGE

Roadrunner Hostel & Inn (☎ 520-628-4709; www.roadrunnerhostelinn.com; 346 E 12th St; dm $20, r incl breakfast with shared bath $40; ⊠ ❄ 💻 📶) A converted home located in a residential neighborhood within walking distance of the arts district, this comfortable hostel has a large kitchen, free coffee and waffles in the morning, and a big-screen TV for watching movies. Note that dorms close for afternoon cleaning and credit cards aren't accepted.

our pick **Hotel Congress** (☎ 520-622-8848, 800-722-8848; www.hotelcongress.com; 311 E Congress St; r $79-120; ❄ 💻 📶) A groovy historic hotel with a hip rock-and-roll flavor, the Congress is a nonstop buzz of activity, mostly because of its popular bar, restaurant and nightclub downstairs. Opt for a room at the hotel's far end if you're noise-sensitive or just crank up the only in-room entertainment – an old-fashioned radio – for an impromptu battle of the bands. Free wi-fi and pet-friendly.

Windmill Inn at St Philips Plaza (☎ 520-577-0007; www.windmillinns.com; 4250 N Campbell Ave; r $80-220; ⊠ ❄ 💻 📶 ♿) Set in a shopping plaza, but

HOT TOPIC: IMMIGRATION FROM MEXICO

Immigration issues continue to fan the flames in the Southwest, especially in southern Arizona. High unemployment at home and higher wages in the US mean that Mexican immigrants continue to come north in large numbers. Increased border enforcement in California and Texas and vigilante groups like the Minutemen have driven this human traffic to the most inhospitable and dangerous portions of the Sonoran Desert, with a subsequent spike in fatalities from hypothermia and exposure. When people are ill-prepared for the journey, or *coyotes* (paid smuggling guides) abandon them, the heat kills quickly yet painfully.

Distraught over a death toll of more than 100 a year, regional humanitarian and religious groups have approached it as an issue of human rights. Working within the law, they maintain emergency water stations in known crossing areas, in the hope that no one will die to cross a border.

don't let that deter you from the exceptional value on offer: all of the rooms are enormous suites. Kids under 18 and pets stay free. Free bike rentals, wi-fi and board games, too.

El Presidio Bed & Breakfast Inn (☎ 520-623-3860; www.bbonline.com/az/elpresidio; 297 N Main Ave; r incl breakfast $120-150; ☒ ❄ 💻 📶) In Tucson's Presidio District, the 'Victorian Adobe' features four rooms that mix the genteel of yesteryear with Spanish Colonial. Rooms feature antique furniture and a private entrance. A gourmet breakfast and afternoon drinks and treats are included. Children over 13 only, and check-in is between 4pm and 6pm.

TOP END

Tucson's ranches and resorts are often destinations in themselves. Rates drop dramatically in the summer.

Arizona Inn (☎ 520-325-1541, 800-933-1093; www.arizonainn.com; 2200 E Elm St; r from $220; ❄ 💻 🏊) Exuding grace and old-Arizona charm on 14 manicured acres, this is where in-the-know locals go for the weekend if they want a sumptuous 'staycation.' Depending on the season, enjoy the afternoon tea service or poolside ice-cream social. Free internet and bicycle use, as well.

La ZarZuela B&B (☎ 520-884-4824, 888-848-8225; www.zarzuela-az.com; 455 N Camino de Oeste; r $285-325; 🕐 Oct-Jun; ☒ ❄ 💻 📶 🏊) If you entertain fantasies of escaping to a remote and luxurious hideaway, this is your place. A gorgeous adults-only mansion in the foothills west of the city, it has five colorful casitas with wide-open terrace and porch views. Quiet and luxury abound.

Eating

For an inexpensive meal, stop into any little taqueria; they have to be at least decent to survive.

BUDGET

Your best bet for great food at good prices is 4th Ave; following are some of the standouts.

Native Seeds (☎ 520-622-5561; 526 N 4th Ave; mixes $6-10; 🕐 10am-5pm Mon-Sat, noon-4pm Sun) Snacks like prickly pear cactus lollipops are the only things ready to eat, but mixes for cooking at home are plentiful.

Bison Witches (☎ 520-740-1541; 326 N 4th Ave; sandwiches $7; 🕐 11am-midnight) Dive into a bread bowl at this lively hangout for college students and the occasional hipster. It's all about the sandwiches; the beef and brie is exactly what it sounds like. The music is boisterous, there are myriad TVs and drinks from the full bar are served till 2am.

B Line (☎ 520-882-7575; 621 N 4th Ave; mains $7-11; 🕐 7:30am-9pm Mon-Thu, 7:30am-10pm Fri & Sat, 7:30am-8pm Sun) Breakfast burritos and stacks of crepes in the AM, and a lunch and dinner menu with Mexican standards, pasta and salads. A small but exceptionally well-chosen wine and beer menu.

MIDRANGE & TOP END

El Charro Café (☎ 520-622-1922; 311 N Court Ave; dishes $9-18; 🕐 11am-9pm) With its famous *carne seca*, this is probably the most revered Mexican eatery in Tucson, if not the state. The food is innovative, mouthwatering and fresh, making it popular with tourists and locals alike. There are four other area locations, but this is the original.

Cafe Poca Cosa (☎ 520-622-6400; 110 E Pennington St; dinner mains $19-26; 🕐 11am-9pm Tue-Thu, 11am-10pm Fri & Sat) The excellent food incorporates many regions of Mexico, and it's freshly prepared, innovative and beautifully presented. If you want to catch a glimpse of Tucson's big-shot politicians and businesspeople, come here for lunch.

our pick **Janos** (☎ 520-615-6100; Westin La Paloma, 3770 E Sunrise Dr; mains $28-50, tasting menu/wine pairing $75/115; 5:30-9pm Mon-Sat) The James Beard Award winner Janos Wilder is a chef-magician who teases flavors that you didn't know existed out of meat. One of the most scenic spots for a romantic dinner or special meal in Tucson, the dining room at the Westin La Paloma overlooks the desert valley. Try the New York strip steak rubbed with coffee, molasses and Mexican chocolate. The attached J Bar is good for an after-steak drink.

Drinking & Entertainment

Downtown 4th Ave, near 6th St, is the happening bar-hop spot, and there are a number of nightclubs on downtown Congress St. Clubs showcase everything from DJs to live music.

Barrio Brewery (☎ 520-791-2739; www.barriobrewing.com; 800 E 16th St; 11am-1am) Set near train tracks in an industrial part of town – whenever a freight train rolls by pints are $3 and this locomotive goodness is sometimes met with cheers. It's roomy inside with a long porch on the front, and the food (snacks $3 to $7) is two notches above usual bar fare.

Club Congress (☎ 520-622-8848; 311 E Congress St; cover $3-10) Live and DJ music are found at this very popular place that's sometimes a rock hangout and sometimes a dance club. The crowd really depends on the night, but it's almost always a happening place.

IBT's (☎ 520-882-3053; www.myspace.com/ibtstucson; 616 N 4th Ave) The daddy of Tucson's gay bars. Every night has a different theme, from karaoke to dance to barbecue.

Plush (☎ 520-798-1298; www.plushtucson.com; 340 E 6th St; cover $5-10) A balm to the manic 4th Ave scene, the front of this club has a downtempo atmosphere with lounging aplenty on funky furniture.

Getting There & Around

Tucson International Airport (TUC; ☎ 520-573-8000; www.tucsonairport.org) is 10 miles south of downtown. **Arizona Stagecoach** (☎ 877-782-4355; www.azstagecoach.com) runs shared van service with fares from $23 between downtown and the airport. **Greyhound** (☎ 520-792-3475; www.greyhound.com; 471 W Congress St; 7am-11pm) runs buses to Phoenix (from $21, two hours, daily) and Nogales (from $11, one hour, daily) among other destinations in the US and Mexico. Don't be fooled by the Greyhound's street address, it's on the western end of Congress St, three miles from downtown.

Amtrak (☎ 520-623-4442, 800-872-7245; www.amtrak.com; 400 E Toole Ave) is across from Hotel Congress and has trains to Los Angeles (from $38, 10 hours, three weekly) and other locations.

The **Ronstadt Transit Center** (cnr Congress St & 6th Ave) is the major downtown transit hub. From here **Sun Tran** (☎ 520-792-9222; www.suntran.com) buses serve metropolitan Tucson (day pass $2).

AROUND TUSCON

The places listed following are less than 1½ hours' drive from town and make great day trips.

North of Tuscon

About 35 miles away from downtown via backcountry roads, **Biosphere 2** (☎ 520-838-6200; www.b2science.org; 32540 S Biosphere Rd, Oracle; adult/child $20/13; 9am-4pm;) is a 3-acre glassed dome housing seven separate microhabitats – a jungle, a desert, a swamp – designed to be self-sustaining. In 1991 eight bionauts entered Biosphere 2 for a two-year tour of duty, during which they were physically cut off from the outside world. They emerged thinner, but in fair shape. Although this experiment could be used as a prototype for future space stations, it was privately funded and controversial. The massive glass structure is now a University of Arizona–run earth science research institute. Visits are by guided tour only, but they start often, and if you're lucky your guide will let you stand in the huge, kind of scary artificial 'lung' of the place.

West of Tuscon

From Tucson, Hwy 86 heads west into some of the driest and emptiest parts of the Sonoran Desert. West of Sells, the **Kitt Peak National Optical Observatory** (☎ 520-318-8726; www.noao.edu/kpno; Hwy 86; visitor center admission by donation, observing program adult/student/senior $41/36/36; Sep–mid-Jul) features the largest collection of optical telescopes in the world. Guided tours (adult/child $4/2.50; at 10am, 11:30am and 1:30pm) last about an hour. Book two to four weeks in advance for the worthwhile nightly observing program (adult/child $46/41; no programs from July 1 to September 15 because of monsoon season) – clear, dry skies equal an awe-inspiring glimpse of the cosmos. Dress warmly, gas up the car in Tucson (the nearest gas station is 30 miles from the observatory) and note that children under eight are not allowed, for safety reasons. The picnic area draws amateur astronomers at night.

South of Tucson

South of Tucson, I-19 is the main route to Nogales and Mexico. Along the way are several interesting stops.

Mission San Xavier del Bac (☎ 520-294-2624; www.sanxaviermission.org; 1950 W San Xavier Rd; admission by donation; ⌚ 8am-5pm) is Arizona's oldest European building still in use. Dark and moody inside, it's a graceful blend of Moorish, Byzantine and late Mexican Renaissance architecture. It's nine miles south of downtown Tucson.

At exit 69, 16 miles south of the mission, the **Titan Missile Museum** (☎ 520-625-7736; www.titanmissilemuseum.org; 1580 W Duval Mine Rd, Sahuarita; adult/child/senior $9.50/6/8.50; ⌚ tours 9am-4pm) features an underground launch site for Cold War–era intercontinental ballistic missiles. Tours are chilling, informative and leave frequently. Look into combo tickets for Pima Air & Space Museum (p862).

If history and/or shopping for crafts interest you, head 48 miles south of Tucson to the small village of **Tubac** (I-19 exit 34), with more than 80 galleries.

Nogales

Arizona's most important gateway into Mexico sees a constant flow of foot and vehicle traffic sliding across the border separating Nogales, AZ, from Nogales, Sonora, Mexico. The US State Department warns travelers that because of violent drug cartels along border cities, visitors should exercise caution. There can be delays for cars crossing into the US; check online (http://apps.cbp.gov/bwt) for waiting times, updated hourly.

The **chamber of commerce** (☎ 520-287-3685; www.nogaleschamber.com; 123 W Kino Park Way; ⌚ 9am-5pm Mon-Fri) has all the usual tourist information. There is also a **Mexican Consulate** (☎ 520-287-2521/3381; 571 N Grand Ave; ⌚ Mon-Fri).

Chain motels are found off I-19 at exit 4. Mariposa Rd has the usual assortment of fast-food restaurants and a supermarket.

Crucero USA/Greyhound (☎ 520-287-5628; 35 N Terrace Dr) is located less than a mile from the border and has regular service to Tucson (from $11, one hour, daily). Five daily buses go to Hermosillo, Mexico ($19, four hours), where there are frequent connections to points deeper in Mexico with **Estrella Blanca** (www.estrellablanca.com.mx).

Drivers into Mexico can obtain car insurance from friendly, helpful **Sanborn's** (☎ 520-281-1865, 800-222-0158; www.sanbornsinsurance.com; 850 W Shell Rd; ⌚ 8am-5pm Mon-Fri, varies Sat & Sun). The cost is determined by the value of the car and the length of your stay, with rates starting at $30 per day.

SOUTHEASTERN CORNER

Chockablock with places that loom large in the history of the Wild West, southern Arizona is home to the wonderfully preserved mining town of Bisbee, the OK Corral in Tombstone, and beautiful wonderlands of stone spires at Chiricahua National Monument

Kartchner Caverns State Park

Nine miles south of town, **Kartchner Caverns State Park** (☎ 502-586-4100; www.explorethecaverns.com; Hwy 90; entry $5; ⌚ park 7:30am-6pm, tours 8:40am-4:40pm) is a 2.5-mile-long wet limestone fantasia of rocks that look like everything from impossibly long soda straws to huge ice-cream cones. Two tours (from $17/9 per adult/child) are offered and these can sell out weeks in advance, so reserve ahead.

Chiricahua National Monument

The remote **Chiricahua National Monument** (☎ 520-824-3560; www.nps.gov/chir; adult/child $5/free), in the Chiricahua Mountains is full of towers of rock sometimes rising hundreds of feet high that often look like they're on the verge of tipping over. The **Bonita Canyon Scenic Drive** takes you 8 miles to Massai Point at 6870ft and there are numerous hiking trails. The monument is 36 miles southeast of Willcox off Hwy 186/181.

Tombstone

In Tombstone's 19th-century heyday as a booming mining town the whiskey flowed and six-shooters blazed over disputes large and small, most famously at the OK Corral. Now a National Historic Landmark, it attracts hordes of tourists to its old Western buildings, stagecoach rides and nonstop gunfight reenactments. The **Visitor & Information Center** (☎ 520-457-3929; www.tombstone.org; cnr 4th & Allen Sts; ⌚ 9am-4pm) has good walking maps and local recommendations.

Bisbee

Oozing old-fashioned ambience, Bisbee is a former copper-mining town that's now a delightful mix of aging bohemians, elegant buildings, sumptuous restaurants and charming hotels.

Most businesses are found in the Historic District (Old Bisbee), along Subway and Main Sts. The **visitor center** (☎ 520-432-3554, 866-224-7233; www.discoverbisbee.com; 2 Copper Queen Plaza; 9am-5pm Mon-Fri, 10am-4pm Sat & Sun) is a good place to start.

To burrow under the earth in a tour led by the retired miners who worked here, take the **Queen Mine Tour** (☎ 520-432-2071; 478 Dart Rd; adult/child $12/5; 9am-3:30pm). Right outside of town, check out the **Lavender Pit**, an ugly yet impressive testament to strip mining. On the **Historic Walking Tour** led by cowboy-attired Michael London, ask to see the historic photograph that shows the mountain where Lavender Pit now lies. The tour costs $10 and leaves every hour on the hour from outside the visitor center.

Rest your copper-heavy head at **Shady Dell RV Park** (☎ 520-432-3567; www.theshadydell.com; 1 Douglas Rd; trailers $50-130;), kitschy trailer park extraordinaire. Everything's done up with retro furnishings and stocked with period movies. There's an on-site diner that serves breakfast and lunch.

our pick **Copper Queen Hotel** (☎ 520-432-2216; www.copperqueen.com; 11 Howell Ave; r $80-180;), built in 1902, is still charming as heck and a number of rooms are themed after the famous personalities that stayed in them, including John Wayne. The rooms and halls are bewitched by lovely copper lamps, and supposedly ghosts wander here. The downstairs restaurant and patio bar, which often has live piano music, draw locals and tourists alike.

Caffeinate at **Bisbee Coffee Company** (☎ 520-432-7879; 2 Copper Queen Plaza; snacks $3-6; 11am-9pm) in the morning and come back later in the day for a quiche, sandwich, salad or dessert. Root around Copper Queen Plaza for other, more expensive, dining options.

UTAH

The rugged terrain of this little-populated state comes ready-made for adventure, and opportunities for biking, hiking, skiing and rafting roll into view after every scenic bend on the road. Its dazzling display of geographic grandeur leaves visitors a bit awestruck and dumbfounded. The temptation to sit still and watch the ever-changing kaleidoscope runs in opposition to hiking where no one (literally) has hiked before. This haunting topography is *that* vast.

The southern Utah landscape is defined by five national parks, featuring towering mountain peaks, plunging canyons, sweeping sandstone domes and seemingly endless expanses of undulating desert. Northern Utah is marked by the Great Salt Lake, forested mountains in the snow-covered Wasatch Range (where the 2002 Winter Olympic Games were held) and the wild Uinta Mountains.

Utah is also defined by modern Mormons, whose social and political influence reverberates statewide. When the Mormon pioneers reached the area in 1847, they, too (like the Native Americans 7000 years before them), felt a spiritual response and claimed it as their new home (their Zion). No matter what your belief system, the magical landscape of Utah will feel like heaven on earth.

UTAH FACTS

Nicknames Beehive State, Mormon State
Population 2.7 million
Area 84,900 sq miles
Capital city Salt Lake City (population 180,650)
Sales tax 4.7%
Birthplace of Entertainers Donny (b 1957) and Marie (b 1959) Osmond, beloved bandit Butch Cassidy (1866–1908)
Home of 2002 Winter Olympic Games
Famous for Mormons, red-rock canyons
Best souvenir T-shirt for Wasatch Brewery's Polygamy Porter – 'Why have just one?'
Driving distances Salt Lake City to Moab 235 miles, St George to Park City 304 miles

History

Utah gets its name from the nomadic Ute people who, along with the Paiute and Shoshone, lived in the Great Basin Desert more than 8000 years ago. Europeans arrived as early as 1776, but Native Americans inhabited the region freely until the mid-19th century. Led by Brigham Young, the Mormons fled to Utah to escape religious persecution, establishing Salt Lake City on July 24, 1847. They called their state Deseret, meaning 'honeybee,' according to the Book of Mormon.

After the US acquired the Utah Territory from Mexico, the Mormons petitioned Congress for statehood six times. Their petitions were consistently rejected because of Mormon polygamy (the practice of having more than one spouse at the same time), which was outlawed by the US government. Tensions grew between the Mormons and the federal government until 1890, when Mormon Church president Wilford Woodruff announced that God had told him that Mormons should abide by US law. Polygamy was discontinued and, soon afterward, Utah became the 45th state in 1896. Today Mormons remain in the majority in Utah and continue to exert a powerful conservative influence here.

Information

It's difficult to change currency outside Salt Lake City (p869). Where opening hours are listed by season (not month), readers should call first, as hours can fluctuate based on weather, budgets and level of custom.

Natural Resources Map & Bookstore (Map p868; ☎ 801-537-3320, 888-882-4627; www.mapstore.utah.gov; 1594 W North Temple, Salt Lake City; 🕑 7am-6pm Mon-Thu) Look online or inside the store for detailed maps of all the stellar places to explore.

Utah Office of Tourism (Map p868; ☎ 801-538-1030, 800-200-1160; www.utah.com; Capitol Hill, 300 N State St, Salt Lake City; 🕑 9am-6pm Mon-Fri, 10am-5pm Sat & Sun) Links on lodging, camping and outdoor activities. Website has information in six languages. Publishes the free *Utah Travel Guide;* the bookstore sells guides and maps.

Utah Pride Center (Map p868; ☎ 801-539-8800, 888-874-2743; www.utahpridecenter.org; 361 N 300 West, Salt Lake City; 🕑 administrative offices 10am-6pm Mon-Fri, coffee shop (p873) and library 7am-9pm Mon-Fri, 8am-9pm Sat, 10am-9pm Sun) Helpful gay and lesbian center offers advice, activities and classes.

Utah State Parks & Recreation Department (Map p868; ☎ 801-538-7220, 877-887-2757; www.stateparks.utah.gov; 1594 W North Temple, Salt Lake City; 🕑 7am-6pm Mon-Thu) In the same building as the Natural Resources Map & Bookstore, this separate office sells state park permits and arranges camping reservations (campsites cost $10 to $25 per night). State-park camping reservations are also available through **Reserve America** (☎ 800-322-3770; www.reserveamerica.com).

SALT LAKE CITY

Ushered into the spotlight by the 2002 Winter Olympic Games, Salt Lake City (SLC) has built on the momentum ever since. It's modern, with charming anachronisms and a mountain setting – its location prompted pioneer Mormon leader Brigham Young to inform his weary band of emigrant settlers, 'This is the place.'

SLC is the headquarters of the Mormon Church, though only about half its citizens are Latter-Day Saints (LDS; see p870). It surprises many that the city is politically progressive (compared with the rest of the state) and has a sizable gay and lesbian community.

The proximity of the Wasatch Mountains is a huge lure for outdoor enthusiasts year-round. World-class hiking, climbing and snow sports await less than an hour away, and it seems like the soaring peaks loom over you from all points in the city. Add in a thriving university, wildly eclectic restaurants and a flourishing arts scene, and you might second Brigham Young's pronouncement.

Orientation

SLC is laid out in a grid with streets aligned north–south or east–west. Everything radiates from Temple Sq: the corner of S Temple (east–west) and Main St (north–south) is the zero point for streets and addresses. Eight blocks equals one mile. The streets were originally built 132ft wide so that four oxen pulling a wagon could turn around.

Two major interstates cross at SLC: I-15 runs north–south and I-80 east–west. I-215 loops the city.

Information

BOOKSTORES

Sam Weller Books (☎ 801-328-2586, 800-333-7269; 254 S Main; 🕑 10am-7pm Mon-Sat) The city's biggest

HOT TOPIC: LIFTING THE ZION CURTAIN

Thanks to the efforts of Governor Jon Huntsman (now US ambassador to China), it just got easier to order a drink in Utah. What was the problem? For 40 years, Utah bars operated as private clubs. Visitors could enter only as a member's guest or as a temporary member after garnering sponsorship and paying a $5 fee. Bars were required to install partitions, or curtains, between bartenders and guests, and beer was all low-alcohol.

While it was not impossible to get a drink, the laws slowed things down – the goal when introduced by the Mormon-led legislature. But times change, and Utah's $6-billion tourism industry became a power player. Together with Huntsman, it persuaded the legislature to rescind the private club rule, and the change went into effect on July 1, 2009. Details are still being worked out, so a few unusual practices may linger.

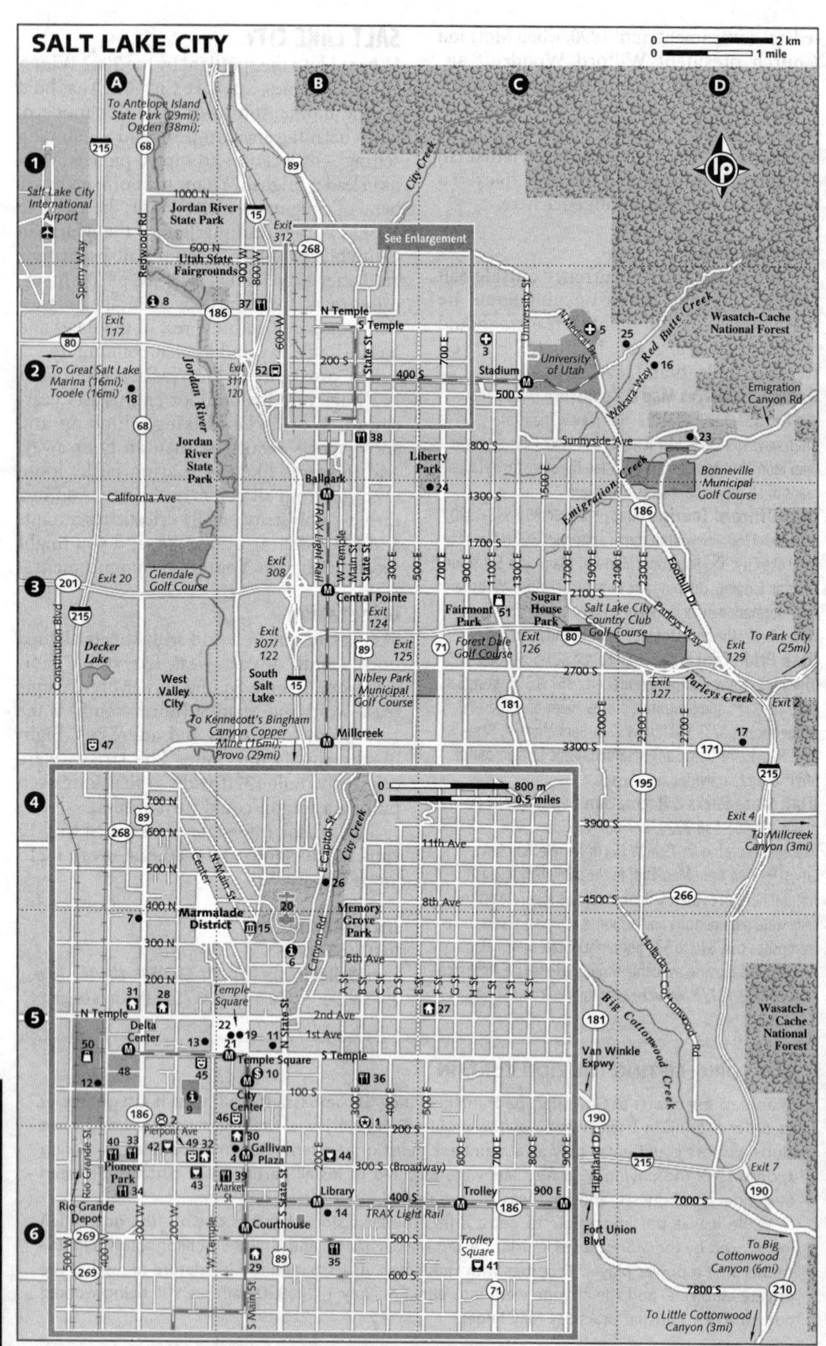
SALT LAKE CITY
To Antelope Island State Park (29mi); Ogden (38mi);
Salt Lake City International Airport
Jordan River State Park
Utah State Fairgrounds
See Enlargement
Wasatch-Cache National Forest
University of Utah
Stadium
To Great Salt Lake Marina (16mi); Tooele (16mi)
Jordan River
Emigration Canyon Rd
Sunnyside Ave
Bonneville Municipal Golf Course
Liberty Park
Ballpark
California Ave
TRAX Light Rail
Glendale Golf Course
Central Pointe
Fairmont Park
Sugar House Park
Salt Lake City Country Club Golf Course
Forest Dale Golf Course
Decker Lake
West Valley City
South Salt Lake
Nibley Park Municipal Golf Course
To Park City (25mi)
To Kennecott's Bingham Canyon Copper Mine (16mi); Provo (29mi)
Millcreek
To Millcreek Canyon (3mi)
Marmalade District
Memory Grove Park
Temple Square
Delta Center
City Center
Gallivan Plaza
Pioneer Park
Rio Grande Depot
Library
Trolley
Courthouse
Trolley Square
Van Winkle Expwy
Holladay
Big Cottonwood Creek
Cottonwood Rd
Fort Union Blvd
To Big Cottonwood Canyon (6mi)
To Little Cottonwood Canyon (3mi)

INFORMATION
Main Library ......(see 14)
Natural Resources Map & Bookstore......(see 8)
Police......1 B5
Post Office......2 A5
Public Lands Information Center......(see 17)
Salt Lake Regional Medical Center......3 C2
Sam Weller Books......4 B6
University Hospital......5 C2
Utah Office of Tourism......6 B5
Utah Pride Center......7 A5
Utah State Parks & Recreation Department......8 A2
Visitor Information Center......9 A5
Wells Fargo......10 B5

SIGHTS & ACTIVITIES
Beehive House......11 B5
Discovery Gateway......12 A5
Family History Library......13 A5
Main Library......14 B6
Pioneer Memorial Museum......15 B5
Red Butte Gardens......16 D2
REI......17 D4
Salt Lake City Parks & Recreation Department......18 A2
Salt Lake Temple......19 B5
State Capitol......20 B4
Tabernacle......21 B5
Temple Square......22 B5
This Is The Place Heritage Park......23 D2
Tracy Aviary......24 C3
University of Utah Outdoor Recreation Program......25 D2
Utah Heritage Foundation......26 B4

SLEEPING
Avenues Hostel......27 C5
City Creek Inn......28 A5
Grand America......29 B6
Hotel Monaco......30 B6
Howard Johnson Express Inn......31 A5
Peery Hotel......32 A6

EATING
Cucina Toscana......33 A6
Downtown Farmers Market......34 A6
Les Madeleines Patisserie & Café......35 B6
One World Everybody Eats......36 B5
Red Iguana......37 B2
Tacos Don Rafa......38 B2
Takashi......39 B6
Tony Caputo's Market & Deli......40 A6

DRINKING
Café Marmalade......(see 7)
Green Street Social Club......41 C6
Red Rock Brewing Company......42 A6
Squatter's Pub Brewery......43 A6
Tavernacle Social Club......44 B6

ENTERTAINMENT
Abravanel Hall......45 A5
Capitol Theater......46 B5
E Center......47 A4
EnergySolutions Arena......48 A5
Rose Wagner Performing Arts Center......49 A6

SHOPPING
Gateway......50 A5
Sugarhouse......51 C3

TRANSPORT
Greyhound......52 B2
Union Pacific Rail Depot (Amtrak)......(see 52)

independent bookstore. At press time, Weller's was looking for a new home downtown.

EMERGENCY & MEDICAL SERVICES

Police (☎ 801-799-3000; 315 E 200 South)
Salt Lake Regional Medical Center (☎ 801-350-4111; 1050 E South Temple; 24hr emergency)
University Hospital (☎ 801-581-2121; 50 N Medical Dr; 24hr emergency)

INTERNET ACCESS

Main Library (☎ 801-524-8200; www.slcpl.org; 210 E 400 South; 9am-9pm Mon-Thu, 9am-6pm Fri & Sat, 1-5pm Sun) Free wireless and internet access. Excellent periodicals, including foreign.

INTERNET RESOURCES & MEDIA

City Weekly (www.cityweekly.net/utah) Free alternative weekly with good restaurant and entertainment listings.
Downtown SLC (www.downtownslc.org) Arts, entertainment and business information about the downtown core.
Salt Lake Convention & Visitors Bureau (www.visitsaltlake.com) SLC's official tourist-information website.
Salt Lake Tribune (www.sltrib.com) Utah's largest-circulation paper.

MONEY

Wells Fargo (☎ 801-246-2677; 79 S Main St) Currency-exchange services. Call ahead to confirm specific currency available.

POST

Post office (☎ 800-275-8777; www.usps.com; 230 W 200 South; 8am-5:30pm Mon-Fri, 9am-2pm Sat)

TOURIST INFORMATION

Public Lands Information Center (☎ 801-466-6411; www.publiclands.org; 3285 E 3300 South; 10:30am-5:30pm Mon-Fri, 9am-1pm Sat) Recreation information on the Wasatch-Cache National Forest; located inside the REI store.
Visitor Information Center (☎ 801-534-4900/4902, 800-541-4955; www.visitsaltlake.com; 90 S West Temple; 9am-6pm Mon-Fri, 9am-5pm Sat & Sun) Within the Salt Palace Convention Center; publishes the free *Destination: Salt Lake* visitors guide.

Sights

TEMPLE SQUARE

The city's most famous sight, the 10-acre **Temple Square** (☎ 801-240-2534, 800-537-9703; www.visittemplesquare.com; admission free; 9am-9pm) is certainly awe-inspiring, but it's the disarming helpfulness of the square's Mormon volunteers and docents that will leave the biggest impression. Docents can be found at the visitor centers inside the two entrances (on S and N Temple); they give free 30-minute tours of the grounds.

The egg-shaped 1867 **Tabernacle** (admission free; 9am-9pm) is again the highlight after the completion of an extensive seismic retrofit and renovation in 2007. Some preservationists grumbled about the replacement of its pine pews, but a few rows of the originals were left in the back. To show off its fabled acoustics, pin drops are held every 15 minutes – the sound can be heard all the way in the back, more than 200ft away. It's also home to the world-renowned Mormon Tabernacle Choir, and visitors can drop in on **rehearsals** (8pm Thu, choir broadcast 9:15am Sun) accompanied by the 11,000-pipe organ.

Lording it over the square, the 210ft **Salt Lake Temple** is topped with a golden statue of the angel Moroni, who appeared to LDS founder Joseph Smith. Temple ceremonies are secret and open only to LDS 'in good standing.'

Brigham Young lived in the **Beehive House** (801-240-2671; 67 E South Temple; admission free; tours 9am-9pm Mon-Sat) until his death in 1877, and the house has been meticulously maintained with period furnishings and artwork.

Research your genealogy at the **Family History Library** (801-240-2584, 800-346-6044; www.familysearch.org; 35 N West Temple; 8am-5pm Mon, 8am-9pm Tue-Sat). The library holds genealogical records for more than 3 billion deceased people from around the world. Searching its vast resources is free.

THIS IS THE PLACE

The members of the **Church of Jesus Christ of Latter-Day Saints** (LDS; www.lds.org, www.mormon.org) – Mormons – prize family above all else, and Mormon families tend to be large. Hard work and strict obedience to church leaders are very important. Smoking and drinking alcohol, tea or coffee are forbidden. Women are forbidden to take leadership roles, as were African Americans until 1978.

The faith considers missionary service important, and many young adults travel the world spreading the word. Women are called Sisters during their service and the men are called Elders. There are now around 12 million Mormons worldwide.

DOWNTOWN

Daughters of Utah Pioneers (DUP) museums are located throughout Utah, but the **Pioneer Memorial Museum** (801-532-6479; www.dupinternational.org; 300 N Main St; admission free; 9am-5pm Mon-Sat year-round, plus 1-5pm Sun Jun-Aug) is by far the best, a vast four-story treasure trove of thousands of pioneer artifacts.

The grand **State Capitol** (801-538-1800; www.utahstatecapitol.utah.gov; 8am-8pm Mon-Fri, 8am-6pm Sat & Sun) rises majestically from a hill north of Temple Sq. Inside, colorful Works Progress Administration (WPA) murals of pioneers, trappers and missionaries adorn a portion of the building's dome. Outside, views of the city and the Wasatch Range are fantastic. Free tours (from 9am to 4pm) start hourly at the 1st-floor visitor center.

Also worth a stop is Moshe Safdie's architecturally stunning **Main Library** (801-524-8200; www.slcpl.org; 210 E 400 South; 9am-9pm Mon-Thu, 9am-6pm Fri & Sat, 1-5pm Sun), a gently curved glass-and-steel structure complete with sleek glass elevator, rooftop views of the city and loads of natural light. There's also a gallery, coffee shop and deli.

BEYOND DOWNTOWN

In the nearby Wasatch foothills, the lovely 150-acre **Red Butte Gardens** (801-585-0556; www.redbuttegarden.org; 300 Wakara Way; adult/child & senior $6/4; 9am-9pm Mon-Sat & 9am-5pm Sun May-Aug, 9am-7:30pm Mon-Sat & 9am-5pm Sun Apr & Sep, 10am-5pm daily Oct-Mar) has trails, 25 acres of gardens and gorgeous valley views. In summer, during its popular outdoor concert series, check online to see who's playing – from Neko Case to Deathcab for Cutie.

Dedicated to the 1847 arrival of the Mormons, **This Is the Place Heritage Park** (801-582-1847; www.thisistheplace.org; 2601 E Sunnyside Ave/800 South; park admission free, village adult/child $8/6 May-Sep; 9am-5pm;) covers 450 acres and marks the spot where Brigham Young uttered the

NAVIGATING UTAH: WHERE'S MAPLE STREET?

Throughout Utah, towns and cities use the same street layout. The system is more complicated to explain than learn, but once learned, you can use it all over Utah.

Normally, there's a zero point in the town center, at the intersection of two major streets (often called Main St and Center St). Addresses and street names radiate out from this zero point, rising by 100 with each city block. Thus, an address of 500 South 400 East will be at the intersection of 500 South St and 400 East St, or five blocks south and four blocks east of the zero point. The first cardinal point is usually abbreviated, but the second cardinal point is abbreviated less frequently – 500 S 400 East would be the most likely designation.

SOUTHWEST

fateful words, 'This is the place.' The centerpiece is **Heritage Village**, a living-history museum where, June through August, costumed docents depict life in the mid-19th century. Guests can wander the village at a cheaper price (adult/child $5/3) the rest of the year.

Activities

Millcreek, Big Cottonwood and Little Cottonwood Canyons, all on the east side of the Wasatch Range and in easy reach of SLC, offer excellent opportunities for hiking, mountain biking, camping and cross-country skiing. For directions as well as articles about activities in the canyons, visit www.utah.com. Peak-baggers looking for a moderate workout with big views can hike to **Grandeur Peak** (admission $3; 6 miles round-trip) in Millcreek Canyon off Wasatch Blvd (drive 3 miles east on 3800 S to Church Creek Picnic Area). It's a pet-friendly trail.

Salt Lake City Parks & Recreation Department (☎ 801-972-7800; www.slcgov.com; 1965 W 500 South; 8am-5pm Mon-Fri) has tons of information about city parks.

REI (☎ 801-486-2100; www.rei.com/stores/19; 3285 E 3300 South) rents camping equipment, climbing shoes, kayaks and most winter-sports gear, as does the **University of Utah Outdoor Recreation Program** (☎ 801-581-8516; www.utah.edu/campusrec; 2140 E Red Butte Canyon Rd; 8am-6pm Mon-Fri), which also rents mountain bikes ($20 per day).

Salt Lake City for Children

Consider purchasing a one- to three-day **Visit Salt Lake Connect Pass** (www.visitsaltlake.com/visit/activities/connect_pass) if you plan to visit a few attractions.

Discovery Gateway (☎ 801-456-5437; www.discoverygateway.org; 444 W 100 South; admission $8.50; 10am-6pm Mon-Thu, 10am-8pm Fri & Sat, noon-6pm Sun;) is an enthusiastic, hands-on children's museum and possibly the best city attraction for families. The mock network-news desk in the media zone looks particularly cool for budding journos.

The **Tracy Aviary** (☎ 801-596-8500; 589 E 1300 South; adult/child $5/3; 9am-6pm;), located in the southwest corner of Liberty Park, delights bird-lovers with winged creatures from all over the world. Kids can feed pelicans and mohawk-sportin' guira cuckoos.

Tours

City Sights (☎ 801-534-1001; www.saltlakecitytours.org) Offers tours of SLC and the Great Salt Lake. They collect you from your accommodations.

Utah Heritage Foundation (☎ 801-533-0858; www.utahheritagefoundation.com; 485 N Canyon Rd) Gives tours of SLC's historic landmarks and distributes free self-guided walking-tour brochures.

Festivals & Events

Crowds come for the **Utah Arts Festival** (www.uaf.org) in late June. **Days of '47** (☎ 801-254-4656; www.daysof47.com), the 'Mormon Mardi Gras,' from mid to late July has everything from a rodeo to an enormous parade.

Sleeping

SLC's lodgings are primarily chain properties, many clustered on W North Temple near the airport and along S 200 West near 500 South and 600 South. Rates are lowest during spring and fall, and spike when there's a convention. At top-end hotels, rates are lowest at weekends. Summertime prices plunge at ski resorts (p874), about 45 minutes' drive from downtown. High-season rates are listed here:

BUDGET

Avenues Hostel (☎ 801-359-3855, 801-539-888; www.saltlakehostel.com; 107 F St; dm $17, s/d with shared bath $31/35, with private bath $40-46; P) This standard hostel is in a quiet residential neighborhood.

City Creek Inn (☎ 801-533-9100, 866-533-4898; www.citycreekinn.com; 230 W North Temple; s $69-79, d $85-95; P) Monochromatic walls and patterned red chairs add a splash of style to the 33 revamped rooms at this family-run motel, one of the city's best budget options. The one-story, U-shaped motel isn't far from Temple Sq and the Gateway mall.

Howard Johnson Express Inn (☎ 801-521-3450, 800-541-7639; www.hojo.com; 121 N 300 West; r incl breakfast $79-89; P) The exterior looks a little forlorn at this national chain, but the rooms are clean, the staff professional, and the choices aplenty at the continental breakfast. The delicious Red Iguana (p872) is a short, straight-shot west.

MIDRANGE & TOP END

Peery Hotel (☎ 801-521-4300, 800-331-0073; www.peeryhotel.com; 110 W 300 South; r $119-219;) This stately historic hotel is modernized with grace. The E-shaped building ushers in tons of natural light, and the impeccably maintained rooms have gilt-framed mirrors, heavy wooden furniture and thick bedspreads (atop

Tempur-Pedic mattresses). Small but up-to-date bathrooms come with pedestal sinks and aromatherapy soaps. Parking is $10.

Hotel Monaco (☎ 801-595-0000, 877-294-9710; www.monaco-saltlakecity.com; 15 W 200 South; r $209-219, ste $239-259;) At this sassy boutique hotel, circus tent meets beach cabana in a conflagration of colors, stripes and plush leopard-print bathrobes. The front desk is a touch cooler-than-thou but hey, they'll loan you a goldfish if you miss your pet. There's also an evening wine hour with free chair massages. Valet parking is $15.50 per day, and wi-fi costs $10 per day but is free if you join the no-cost Kimpton InTouch program.

Grand America (☎ 801-258-6000, 800-621-4505; www.grandamerica.com; 555 S Main St; r $299-329;) Rooms in SLC's only true luxury hotel are decked out with Italian marble bathrooms, English wool carpeting, tasseled damask draperies and other cushy touches. If that's not enough to spoil you, there's always afternoon high tea ($16 to $30). Parking is $10.

Eating

Foodies will love SLC. Almost anything you crave can be found here, and there's a bountiful assortment of ethnic and vegetarian restaurants.

BUDGET

Downtown Farmers Market (Pioneer Park, cnr 300 South & 300 West; 8am-1pm Sat Jun-Oct) In warmer months, this market showcases locally grown produce and tasty ready-to-eat goodies.

Tacos Don Rafa (State St bwn Sears & 800 South; 9am-8pm) For a hot meal on the go, visit this cart on State St just south of Sears. You get two savory tacos – with a cooler-full of toppings – for $1.50. *Salt Lake* magazine calls its *cabrito* (goat kid meat) taco one of Utah's top 100 foods.

One World Everybody Eats (☎ 801-519-2002; 41 S 300 East; 11am-9pm) Until recently, diners at this organic, ecominded eatery could decide how much they'd pay for their meal. Unfortunately, a few cheapskates abused the system so the owner reversed the process – now you tell the server how much you *can* pay and an appropriate-sized portion is prepared. The welcoming staff will gladly explain the process to newbies, and they'll also show you the day's mains (salads, pastas, stir-fries).

Tony Caputo's Market & Deli (☎ 801-531-8669; 314 W 300 South; sandwiches $7.10-8.25; 9am-6pm Mon-Fri, 9am-5pm Sun) The line moves fast at this old-fashioned Italian deli where a short but satisfying sandwich menu includes meatball, prosciutto, and mozzarella with tomato. The adjoining gourmet market has a chocolate bar and a cheese cave.

Les Madeleines Patisserie & Cafe (☎ 801-355-2294; 216 E 500 South; mains under $10; 8am-6pm Mon-Fri, 8am-4pm Sat) OMG! What was that? Crunchy, buttery, fluffy, caramelized. I've never had anything like it. And now I want another one. Yep, just another convert to the *kouign amann* pastry, originally from Brittany, and the house specialty at this stylish but cheerful bakery that's an easy stroll from the main library. The *kougin amann* is $5 (it's made in only a handful of US bakeries) but croissants and scones are more traditionally priced. Sandwiches available at lunch.

MIDRANGE & TOP END

Takashi (☎ 801-519-9595; 18 W Market St; lunch mains $7-14, dinner mains $8-25; 11:30am-2pm Mon-Fri, 5:30-10pm Mon-Thu, 5:30-11pm Fri & Sat) Even LA sushi snobs rave about the excellent rolls at ever-so-chic Takashi, one of the top spots for a first date in SLC. But solos never fear, you'll do just fine at the friendly but professional sushi bar.

our pick **Red Iguana** (☎ 801-322-1489; 736 W North Temple; mains $8-15; 11am-10pm Mon-Thu, 11am-11pm Fri, 10am-11pm Sat, 10am-9pm Sun) You'll be offered a plate of sample moles if you can't decide which of the seven chili- or chocolate-based sauces sounds best. But really, you can't go wrong at this exceptional, family-run Mexican restaurant, a great choice for thoughtfully flavored Mexican food, tasty margaritas and festive good times. The *puntas de filete a la norteña* (sirloin tips with almond mole sauce) is a super-savory delight.

Cucina Toscana (☎ 801-328-3463; 307 W Pierpont Ave; mains $15-31; 5:30-10pm Mon-Sat) Be seated at a convivial Tuscan trattoria and possibly the best dinner party you've ever unwittingly attended. Charismatic owner-manager Valter Nassi flits between the tables in the elegant yellow room, making sure your gnocchi is delightful and your evening one to remember.

Drinking & Entertainment

With the closing of the infamous Port O'Call in 2009, the downtown club scene got a whole lot quieter, but the bustling microbreweries seem to be picking up the slack. The brewpubs listed here serve lunch and dinner. Most open by 11am and close between 11pm and midnight.

Red Rock Brewing Company (☎ 801-521-7446; www.redrockbrewing.com; 254 S 200 West) Can't make up your mind between the oats beer or the nut brown? Order a sampler flight and see what suits your fancy. The upscale pub grub inside this spacious former dairy building draws kudos too.

Squatter's Pub Brewery (☎ 801-363-2739; www.squatters.com; 147 W Broadway) Sampler flights arrive on a cut-off ski at lofty, brick-walled Squatter's.

Tavernacle Social Club (☎ 801-519-8900; 201 E Broadway) From dueling pianos to karaoke to $1 drafts Sundays and Tuesdays, there's always something happening at this neighborhood club.

Green Street Social Club (☎ 801-532-4200; 602 E 500 South) Twenty-somethings flock to this popular bar in Trolley Sq.

Café Marmalade (☎ 801-539-8800; www.utahpridecenter.com; 361 N 300 West; 7am-9pm Mon-Fri, 8am-9pm Sat, 10am-9pm Sun) This upbeat coffee shop, inside the Utah Pride Center (p867), has open mike nights, weekend BBQs and concerts, and the largest GLBT library in the state.

The Salt Lake City Arts Council provides a complete cultural events calendar on its website (www.slcgov.com/arts/calendar.pdf). The historic **Capitol Theater** (☎ 801-355-2787; 50 W 200 South), dramatic **Rose Wagner Performing Arts Center** (☎ 801-355-2787; 138 W 300 South) and acoustically rich **Abravanel Hall** (☎ 801-533-6683; 123 W South Temple) are the city's primary venues. Reserve through **ArtTix** (☎ 801-355-2787, 888-451-2787; www.arttix.org).

Utah Jazz (www.nba.com/jazz), the men's professional basketball team, plays at **EnergySolutions Arena** (☎ 801-325-2000; www.energysolutionsarena.com; 301 W South Temple). The International Hockey League's **Utah Grizzlies** (☎ 801-988-7825; www.utahgrizzlies.com) play at the **E Center** (☎ 801-988-8800; www.theecenter.com; 3200 S Decker Lake Dr, West Valley City).

Shopping

The best downtown major-label shopping is at the indoor-outdoor **Gateway** (☎ 801-456-0000; www.shopthegateway.com; btwn 200 S & N Temple, 400 W & 500 W; 10am-9pm Mon-Sat, noon-6pm Sun). The **Sugarhouse neighborhood** (2100 South, btwn 900 East & 1300 East) looks like Main St, USA, and has a good mix of indie shops and mall stores.

Getting There & Around

Salt Lake City International Airport (SLC; ☎ 801-575-2400, 800-595-2442; www.slcairport.com; 776 N Terminal Dr) is 5 miles northwest of downtown. **Express Shuttle** (☎ 800-397-0773; www.xpressshuttleutah.com) runs from the airport to downtown for $8, while **Yellow Cab** (☎ 801-521-2100) will cost you around $23. **UTA** (☎ 801-743-3882, 888-743-3882; www.rideuta.com; one way $2) bus 550 travels downtown from the parking structure between terminals 1 and 2.

There are several daily buses with **Greyhound** (☎ 801-355-9579; www.greyhound.com; 300 S 600 West) south through Provo and St George to Las Vegas, NV ($70, eight hours); west to San Francisco, CA ($106, 16 hours); east to Denver, CO ($74, 10 hours); and north to Seattle, WA ($153, 20 to 26 hours).

UTA (☎ 801-743-3882, 888-743-3882; www.rideuta.com; one way $2) buses serve SLC and the Wasatch Front area until about midnight, with limited service on Sunday. TRAX, UTA's light-rail system, runs east from EnergySolutions Arena to the university and south to Sandy. The center of downtown SLC is a free-fare zone. During ski season UTA serves the four local resorts near Provo (all $7 round-trip).

Amtrak's *California Zephyr* stops daily at the **Union Pacific Rail Depot** (☎ 801-322-3510, 800-872-7245; www.amtrak.com; 340 S 600 West) going east to Chicago, IL ($163, 34¼ hours), and west to Oakland/Emeryville, CA ($68, 18¾ hours). Schedule delays can be substantial.

AROUND SALT LAKE CITY

Great Salt Lake

Once part of prehistoric Lake Bonneville, the Great Salt Lake today covers 2000 sq miles and is far saltier than the ocean; you can easily float on its surface.

The pretty, 15-mile-long **Antelope Island State Park** (☎ 801-773-2941; www.stateparks.utah.gov; I-15 exit 332; per vehicle $9; 7am-sunset), 40 miles northwest of SLC, has nice hiking and the best beaches for lake swimming (though they're occasionally stinky). It's also home to one of the largest bison herds in the country. A basic **campground** (campsites $13) is open year-round. Six of the 26 sites are available first-come, first-served, the rest by reservation. For larger parties, check the website for information about separate group sites.

Kennecott's Bingham Canyon Copper Mine

The view into this century-old **mine** (☎ 801-204-2025; www.kennecott.com; Hwy 111; per vehicle $5;

8am-8pm Apr-Oct) is slightly unreal, with massive haulage trucks (some more than 12ft tall) looking no larger than toys as they wind up and down the world's largest factitious excavation. The 2.5-mile-wide and 0.75-mile-deep gash, which is still growing, is in the Oquirrh Mountains west of SLC. The pit is visible from space, and there's a picture from *Apollo* 11 inside the museum to prove it. Overall, it's a fascinating stop.

Ski Resorts

Within 40 minutes' drive of SLC are four world-class resorts in Little Cottonwood and Big Cottonwood Canyons. Consider purchasing a **Super Pass** (www.visitsaltlakecity.com/ski/superpass; 2-6 day pass $114-336). It requires reservations at one of the 80-plus area lodgings but offers discounted access to all four resorts plus round-trip transportation from SLC.

Alta Ski Area (801-359-1078; www.alta.com; Little Cottonwood Canyon; adult/child $66/34) A laid-back choice for skiers. No snowboarding.

Brighton Ski Area (801-532-4731, 800-873-5512; www.brightonresort.com; Big Cottonwood Canyon; adult/child $58/25)

Snowbird Ski Area (801-933-2222; www.snowbird.com; Little Cottonwood Canyon; adult/child under 7yr/child 7-12yr $72/15/39) Excellent snowboarding.

Solitude Ski Area (801-534-1400; www.skisolitude.com; Big Cottonwood Canyon; adult/senior/child $61/40/39)

WASATCH MOUNTAINS & NORTH

Utah has awesome skiing, some of the best anywhere in North America. Its fabulous low-density, low-moisture snow – between 300in and 500in annually – and thousands of acres of high-altitude terrain helped earn Utah the honor of hosting the 2002 Winter Olympics. This mountainous region, within 55 miles of SLC, is home to 11 ski resorts and offers abundant hiking, camping, fly-fishing and mountain biking.

Park City

A mere 35 miles east of SLC via I-80, Park City (elevation 6900ft) skyrocketed to international fame when it hosted the downhill, jumping and sledding events at the 2002 Winter Olympics. Not only is Park City the Southwest's most popular ski town, it's also home to the US ski team. Come spring, the town (population 8100) gears up for hiking and mountain-biking season in the high peaks nearby.

A silver-mining community during the 19th century, the city has an attractive and remarkably well-preserved Main St, lined with upscale galleries, shops, hotels, restaurants and bars. And despite the spread of prefab housing across the valley and surrounding hills, the town remains relatively charming.

The biggest and most star-studded event is the annual **Sundance Film Festival** (institute 801-328-3456, festival 435-658-3456; www.sundance.org) each January. Independent films and their makers, stars and fans fill the town to bursting for two weeks, and tickets often sell out in advance.

There's one **Visitor Information Center** (435-658-4541, 800-453-1360; www.parkcityinfo.com; cnr Hwy 224 & Olympic Blvd; 9am-7pm Mon-Sat, 11am-4pm Sun Jun-Sep, closes earlier Oct-May) in the northern Kimball Junction area; the other is the **Main Street Visitor Center** (435-615-9559; 518 Main St, inside the Park City Museum) in downtown Park City which was moving to a new location at press time. Call ahead to confirm opening hours.

ACTIVITIES

Park City boasts three of Utah's preeminent ski resorts. An in-town chairlift whisks skiers to **Park City Mountain Resort** (435-649-8111, 800-222-7275; www.parkcitymountain.com; adult/child under 6 $83/free), host of the 2002 Winter Olympics giant slalom and snowboarding events. In summer it has zip-line rides ($19). Posh **Deer Valley Resort** (435-649-1000, 800-558-3337; www.deervalley.com; adult/senior/child $83/59/50) is for skiers only, and **Canyons** (435-649-5400; www.thecanyons.com; adult/child & senior $79/46) is Utah's largest resort. All three host summer activities like mountain biking and hiking.

Olympians may be long gone from **Utah Olympic Park** (435-658-4200; www.utaholympicpark.com; 3419 Olympic Pkwy, off Hwy 224; admission & self-guided tours free, guided tours adult/child $7/5; 9am-6pm), but you can tour the facilities where it all happened and, if you're lucky, watch the pros practice (call for rates, schedules and reservations). From January to March (possibly earlier), Park City's most thrilling offering is a 70–80mph **bobsled ride** (tickets $200) with an incredible 4Gs of centrifugal force – some liken it to an out-of-body experience. The risk-averse can check out the free Alf Engen Ski Museum and the Olympic Museum.

The **Historic Union Pacific Rail Trail** (http://stateparks.utah.gov/stateparks/parks/historic-union, www.mountaintrails.org) is a 28-mile multiuse trail that's also a state park. Pick it up at Bonanza Dr just south of Kearns Blvd. Maps are available at the Park City Visitor Information Center.

SLEEPING

There are more than 100 condo complexes, upscale hotels and B&Bs in Park City, and while the winter rates quoted here are very high, prices drop by half in summer. Rates go through the roof for the Sundance Film Festival.

Chateau Après Lodge (☎ 435-649-9372, 800-357-3556; www.chateauapres.com; 1299 Norfolk Ave; dm $40, r incl breakfast $105-155;) Located near the ski lifts, this reasonably priced 1963 lodge – with a 1st-floor dorm – is deservedly popular with budget travelers. Private rooms are basic and comfortably sleep one to four. Best to reserve; caters to groups outside wintertime.

Washington School Inn (☎ 435-649-3800, 800-824-1672; www.washingtonschoolinn.com; 543 Park Ave; r incl breakfast $185-440, ste $285-690;) These sumptuous rooms are located in a restored schoolhouse that survived the infamous Park City fire of 1898. In the evenings it has fresh house-baked cookies, and a spread of hors d'oeuvres in the winter months. For history and charm, you won't find better. Usually a four- or five-night minimum stay in ski season.

Best Western Landmark Inn (☎ 435-649-7300, 800-548-8824; www.bwlandmarkinn.com; 6560 N Landmark Dr; r incl breakfast $219-239;) Not the quietest place, but it's cheaper than most and the hot breakfast is substantial. At checkout, if you didn't use the in-room safe, ask to have the $1.50 fee for its use removed from your bill. Rooms from $70 in summer.

Treasure Mountain Inn (☎ 435-655-4501, 800-344-2460; www.treasuremountaininn.com; 255 Main St; r from $250;) Park City's first member of the Green Hotel Association is a committed eco-friendly property. The privately owned units here range from studios to suites and all have kitchens. Recent improvements include granite countertops and pillow-top mattresses.

EATING

Park City has dining options to suit any palate, with many upscale choices. Some of the hottest new eateries are opening in the Redstone development in Kimball Junction.

Maxwell's (☎ 435-647-0304; 1456 New Park Blvd; pizza slices from $3, mains $10-20; 11am-9pm Sun-Thu, 11am-10pm Fri & Sat) The buzz is strong for this new pizza, pasta and beer joint tucked in a back corner of the stylish outdoor mall at Redstone. The crispy-crusted Fat Boy pizza is the big draw and slices never linger for long on the tables. So far the scene is loud, local and upbeat. Check it out.

Wasatch Brew Pub (☎ 435-649-0900; 250 Main St; lunch mains $7-12, dinner mains $10-20; 11am-9:30pm mid-Apr–mid-Dec, 11am-10pm mid-Dec–mid-Apr) The Polygamy Porter and First Amendment Lager go down easy with hearty pub grub. There's a full restaurant downstairs and a cantina upstairs (with billiards) that's usually open later.

Morning Ray Café & Bakery (☎ 435-649-5686; 255 Main St; mains $8-12; 7:30am-1:30pm, sometimes longer hours in winter) A popular place that serves strong coffee and veggie scrambles.

Loco Lizard Cantina (☎ 435-645-7000; 1612 Ute Blvd; lunch mains $8-14, dinner mains $9-15; 11:30am-10pm Mon-Fri, 11am-10pm Sat & Sun) The bright, bold colors of this bustling Mexican eatery will lure you in, but it's the salsas and moles that will have you returning with friends. One local calls the *enchiladas suizas* with green chili sour-cream sauce 'mind-numbingly good.' Chips and salsa made in-house.

Zoom (☎ 435-649-9108; 660 Main St; mains $20-36; 11:30am-2:30pm & 5-9pm, may be open later Nov–mid-Apr) Co-owner Robert Redford is easy to spot at this upscale American restaurant – just look for his big artsy portrait above the register. But really, it works, fitting in comfortably with the Sundance Film Festival photos splashed across the walls inside this rehabbed train depot. Most of the beef, chicken and fish mains come grilled, roasted or crusted.

Purple Sage (☎ 435-655-9505; 434 Main St; mains $21-42; from 5:30pm) Enjoy an intimate dinner in a restored 1895 telephone office along historic Main St. The American Western menu includes dishes like butternut-squash ravioli and cornmeal-fried rainbow trout, with desserts like bread pudding with raisins and pine nuts topped with cinnamon ice cream.

ENTERTAINMENT

Main St is where it's at, with half a dozen swinging nightclubs and bars.

O'Shucks (☎ 435-645-3999; 427 Main St; 10am-2am) This hard-partyin' dive bar is fun, especially on Tuesdays when it packs 'em in with $3 schooners (32oz beers). A carpet of peanut shells crunches underfoot.

No Name Saloon (☎ 435-649-6667; 447 Main St; 11am-1am) There's a motorcycle hanging from the ceiling, Johnny Cash's 'Jackson' playing on the stereo, and a waitress who might be lying about the history of this memorabilia-filled bar. We like it here.

Cisero's (☎ 435-649-6800; 306 Main St; 5pm-2am) Cisero's basement nightspot is happening seven days a week, with live music, karaoke and a dancefloor tricked out with lasers.

Egyptian Theatre Company (☎ 435-649-9371; www.egyptiantheatrecompany.org; 328 Main St) The restored 1926 theater is a primary venue for Sundance; the rest of the year it hosts plays, musicals and concerts.

GETTING THERE & AROUND

Several companies run vans from Salt Lake City International Airport and hotels to Park City; make reservations. **Park City Transportation** (☎ 435-649-8567, 800-637-3803; www.parkcitytransportation.com) operates frequent shared rides ($37), while **Powder for the People** (☎ 435-649-6648, 888-482-7547; www.powderforthepeople.com) has private-charter vans ($89 for one to three people, $132 for four, then $33 each additional passenger).

Park City Transit (☎ 435-615-5350; www.parkcity.org/citydepartments/transportation) runs free trolleys one to six times an hour from 8am to 11pm depending on location (reduced frequency in summer). The excellent system covers most of Park City, including the three ski resorts, and makes it easy not to need a car. There's a downloadable route map online.

Heber City & Around

About 45 miles southeast of SLC, Heber City is fairly utilitarian, but it's an affordable base for exploring the Wasatch Mountains. Most businesses are on Hwy 40 (Main St).

The 1904 **Heber Valley Historic Railroad** (☎ 435-654-5601; www.hebervalleyrr.org; 450 S 600 West; adult/child $30/20; late May–Oct) offers family-friendly scenic trips through gorgeous **Provo Canyon**. For information on camping and hiking in the Uinta National Forest, contact the **Heber Ranger Station** (☎ 435-654-0470; 2460 S Hwy 40; 8am-4:30pm Mon-Fri).

Consider driving the attractive 20-mile route known as the **Alpine Scenic Loop**. From Hwy 189, head north onto narrow and twisting Hwy 92, which leads to Robert Redford's **Sundance Resort** (☎ 801-225-4107, 800-892-1600; www.sundanceresort.com; 9521 Alpine Loop Rd, Provo; r $319, ste $429-549, 3-/4-bedroom house $1229-1429;), an elegant, rustic and environmentally conscious getaway located in a wilderness setting, with excellent skiing, a year-round arts program, a spa, summer hiking and mountain biking.

Three beautiful caves in **Timpanogos Cave National Monument** (☎ 801-756-5238; www.nps.gov/tica; Alpine Scenic Loop; per vehicle $6; May-Oct) are accessible on ranger-led tours (adults $7, children $3 to $5); call ahead to reserve.

Heber City motels are basic but far cheaper than those in Park City. Or you can camp in the surrounding forest and nearby state parks. The flower-bedecked **Swiss Alps Inn** (☎ 435-654-0722; www.swissalpsinn.com; 167 S Main; r $69-99;) is one of the best motels in town.

It's not every day you can nibble a pork lettuce wrap at a bistro sharing a roof with Texaco, but that's part of the charm at **Spin Cafe** (☎ 435-654-0251; 220 N Main St; lunch mains $7-13, dinner mains $10-18; 11:30am-9pm Mon-Sat, 11:30am-8pm Sun), a contemporary oasis scoring kudos from *Salt Lake* and *Sunset* magazines.

Tucked behind a Wild West shoot-'em-up facade is **Snake Creek Grill** (☎ 435-654-2133; 650 W 100 South; mains $20-26; 5:30-9:30pm Wed-Sun), one of northern Utah's best restaurants. Hospitable chef Dean Hottle serves Southwest-style American dishes like corn-tortilla-crusted sustainable red trout and maple mustard BBQ baby back ribs.

Word of warning for party hounds: the city isn't known for its nightlife.

NORTHEASTERN UTAH

Despite being hyped as 'Utah's Dinosaurland,' the main attraction of this area is actually the high wilderness terrain. All towns are a mile above sea level, and the rugged Uinta Mountains make for great trips.

Mirror Lake Highway

This alpine route (Hwy 150) begins in **Kamas**, about 12 miles east of Park City, and covers 65 miles as it climbs to elevations of more than 10,000ft into Wyoming. The highway provides breathtaking vistas of the western Uinta Mountains, while passing by scores of lakes, campgrounds and trailheads. Portions may be closed to cars in winter due to heavy snowfall. Contact the **ranger station** (☎ 435-783-4338; 50 E Center St, Kamas; 8am-4:30pm Mon-Fri) for general information on the Wasatch-Cache National Forest.

Vernal

The capital of Utah's dinosaur country, Vernal welcomes visitors with a large pink dino-buddy and plenty of services. The **Travel Board of Northeastern Utah** (☎ 800-477-5558; www.dinoland.com) can provide information, and the good **natural history museum** (☎ 435-789-3799; 496 E Main St; adult/child $6/3; 🕑 9am-5pm) helps walk-ins and has driving-tour brochures. The Red Cloud Loop and Petroglyphs tour is a highlight. Check out the museum's garden full of life-size dinosaurs. The **Vernal Ranger Station** (☎ 435-789-1181; 355 N Vernal Ave; 🕑 8am-5pm Mon-Fri) has details on camping and hiking.

Twelve miles northeast of Vernal, **Red Fleet State Park** (☎ 435-789-4432; www.stateparks.utah.gov; Hwy 191; per vehicle $7, campsites $13) offers boating, camping and an easy hike to a series of fossilized dinosaur tracks (best visited when the reservoir isn't full). Campsites are a mix of reservable and and first-come, first-served.

The Green and Yampa Rivers have satisfying rapids for white-water enthusiasts, as well as calmer areas for gentler floats. **Hatch River Expeditions** (☎ 435-789-4316, 800-342-8243; www.donhatchrivertrips.com, www.oars.com; 221 N 400 East; 🕑 May-Sep), now partnered with OARS, runs a variety of one- to five-day trips.

Flaming Gorge National Recreation Area

Named for its fiery red sandstone, the gorge area (day use $5) has 375 miles of reservoir shoreline, fly-fishing and rafting on the Green River, trout fishing, hiking and cross-country skiing. Visit the **Flaming Gorge Headquarters** (☎ 435-784-3445; www.fs.fed.us/r4/ashley/recreation; 25 W Hwy 43; 🕑 8am-5pm Mon-Fri) or **Flaming Gorge Dam Visitors Center** (☎ 435-885-3135; Hwy 191; 🕑 8am-6pm mid-May–Aug, 9am-5pm Sep–mid-Oct, 10am-4pm Fri-Mon mid-Oct–mid-May).

Sheep Creek Canyon Geological Loop (www.utah.com/vernal), a dramatic 13-mile paved (but rutted) loop through the Sheep Creek Canyon Geological Area, leaves Hwy 44 about 15 miles west of Greendale Junction.

The **campgrounds** (☎ 877-444-6777; www.recreation.gov; campsites $9-15) in and around Flaming Gorge are generally open mid-May to mid-September; reserve ahead. **Red Canyon Lodge** (☎ 435-889-3759; www.redcanyonlodge.com; 2450 W Red Canyon Lodge, Dutch John; cabins $105-145, available nightly mid-Mar–mid-Oct, weekends mid-Oct–mid-Mar; 📶) provides rustic and luxury cabins without TVs or phones. Wi-fi is available in the restaurant. **Flaming Gorge Resort** (☎ 435-889-3773; www.flaminggorgeresort.com; 1100 E Flaming Gorge Resort, Dutch John; r $119, ste $159-249; ⊠ ❄ 📶) rents motel rooms and suites.

Dinosaur National Monument

One of the largest dinosaur fossil beds in North America was discovered here in 1909. The **dinosaur quarry** was enclosed and hundreds of bones were exposed but left in the rock. The visitor center surrounding the quarry closed in 2006 because of dangerous structural problems. The reopening is planned for 2011.

In the meantime, the **monument** (☎ 435-781-7700; www.nps.gov/dino; per vehicle $10; 🕑 8:30am-4:30pm daily, guided ranger tours daily Jun-Aug) is still accessible, with a scaled-back, temporary visitor center. You can drive, hike, backpack and raft through the dramatic and starkly eroded canyons. Budding scientists can walk through seven different periods of geologic history, and see a few bones on the Fossil Discovery Hike. The monument straddles the Utah–Colorado state line. The Utah portion of the park is about 15 miles east of Vernal via Hwys 40 and 149.

SOUTHEASTERN UTAH

Nicknamed 'Canyon Country,' this desolate corner of Utah is home to soaring snow-blanketed peaks towering over plunging red-rock river canyons – so inhospitable that it was the last region to be mapped in the continental US.

Over 65 million years, water carved serpentine, sheer-walled gorges along the course of the Colorado and Green Rivers, which define the borders of Canyonlands National Park, Utah's largest. Nearby Arches National Park encompasses more rock arches than anywhere else in the world. Between the parks lies Moab, the state's premier destination for mountain biking, river running and 4WDing. South of Moab, Ancestral Puebloan sites are scattered among wilderness areas and parks, most notably Monument Valley, which extends into Arizona (see p858).

This section is organized roughly north to south, beginning with the town of Green River, on I-70, and following Hwy 191 into the southeastern corner of the state.

Green River

The 'World's Watermelon Capital,' Green River offers a good base for river running on the Green and Colorado Rivers, or exploring the nearby San Rafael Swell, an eroded 80-mile dome of rock created by a massive geologic upheaval 40 to 60 million years ago.

The legendary one-armed Civil War veteran, geologist and ethnologist John Wesley Powell first explored these rivers in 1869 and 1871. Learn about his amazing travels at the **John Wesley Powell River History Museum** (☎ 435-564-3427;

www.jwprhm.com; 1765 E Main St; adult/child $4/1; 8am-7pm Apr-Oct, 8am-5pm Tue-Sat Nov-Mar), which also has exhibits on the Fremont Native Americans, geology and local history. The museum serves as the local visitor center.

Local outfitters run day-long **white-water rafting day trips** (adult/child from $55/40), including lunch and transportation; ask about multiday excursions. Call **Holiday Expeditions** (435-564-3273, 801-266-2087; www.holidayexpeditions.com) or **Moki Mac River Expeditions** (435-564-3361, 800-284-7280; www.mokimac.com).

Robbers Roost Motel (435-564-3452; www.rrmotel.com; 325 W Main St; s $31-33, d $40-43;) is a basic but clean one-story family-owned motel. At **Best Western River Terrace** (435-564-3401, 800-528-1234; www.bestwestern.com; 880 E Main St; r incl breakfast $110-106;) many rooms overlook the river. **Ray's Tavern** (435-564-3511; 25 S Broadway; mains $8-26; 11am-10pm) is far and away the best place to eat in town.

There are daily **Greyhound** (435-564-3421, 800-231-2222; www.greyhound.com; 525 E Main St) buses to SLC ($48, 3¾ hours) and Las Vegas, NV ($82, 7½ hours); buses stop at the Rodeway Inn. **Amtrak** (800-872-7245; www.amtrak.com; 250 S Broadway) runs the daily *California Zephyr* to Denver, CO ($58, 10¾ hours). Green River is the only stop in southeastern Utah.

Moab

Mountain bikes, microbrews and red rocks about sums it up for this outdoorsy town that stays busy almost year-round. Encircled by stunning orange mountains and the snow-topped La Sal Mountains, Moab is southeastern Utah's largest community and an often-mobbed gateway for alfresco adventures. Moab bills itself as Utah's recreation capital, and it delivers.

INFORMATION

Most businesses are along Hwy 191, also called Main St. Bibliophiles rejoice: there are two great indie bookstores across the street from each other.

Arches Book Company (435-259-0782; 78 N Main St; 7:30am-8pm Jun-Aug, 8am-5pm Sep-May) Good fiction selection. Also has coffee shop and wi-fi.

Back of Beyond (435-259-5154; 83 N Main St; 9am-9pm Apr-Sep, 9am-6pm Oct-Mar) Excellent downtown bookstore with extensive regional selection.

Bureau of Land Management (BLM; 435-259-2100; www.blm.gov/utah/moab; 82 E Dogwood Ave; 7:45am-4:30pm Mon-Fri) Has camping information and takes reservations for group campsites. Canoeists and kayakers, stop here for river permit information.

Moab Area Travel Council (435-259-8825, 800-635-6622; www.discovermoab.com; 8am-5pm Mon-Fri) Dispenses visitor information over the phone and through the mail.

Moab Information Center (cnr Main & Center Sts; 8am-7pm Mon-Sat & 9am-6pm Sun Apr-Sep, 9am-5pm Oct-Mar) This helpful place serves walk-in visitors only. It carries books, maps and comprehensive information on everything from area campgrounds and permits to current river conditions. There's a fantastic series of free activities brochures.

ACTIVITIES

Outfitters take care of everything, from permits to food to setting up camp to transportation. Among the best:

Adrift Adventures (435-259-8594, 800-874-4483; www.adrift.net; 378 N Main St) Leads trips by raft, jeep and horseback.

Canyon Voyages (435-259-6007, 800-733-6007; www.canyonvoyages.com; 211 N Main St) Come here for rafting, kayaking and hiking.

OARS (435-259-5919, 800-342-5938; www.oars.com; 2540 S Hwy 191) Overnight rafting adventures are OARS specialty.

Sheri Griffith Expeditions (435-259-8229, 800-332-2439; www.griffithexp.com; 2231 S Hwy 191) Rafting and kayaking with 'a touch of class.'

SLEEPING

Despite tons of hotels, B&Bs and campgrounds, the town is packed from spring to fall; reservations are advised. Individual **BLM campsites** (www.blm.gov; campsites $8-12) in the area are first-come, first-served. In peak season, check with the Moab Information Center to see which sites are full.

Adventure Inn Moab (435-259-6122, 866-662-2466; www.adventureinnmoab.com; 512 N Main St; s/d incl breakfast $65/80; Mar-Oct;) Family owned and incredibly friendly, this standard motel has a homey feel, a shaded front yard and a laundry. Room 10 is a smidgen larger than the rest.

our pick **Redstone Inn** (435-259-3500, 800-772-1972; www.moabredstone.com; 535 S Main St; r $79-99;) From the ranch-style exterior and big gas grill to the pine-paneled walls and chunky wood furniture, this place looks like Moab. And that's without mentioning the red-rock monoliths that are the ever-present backdrop. Walls are a bit thin at this 52-room motel but after a hard day on the trail, sleep will probably come easy. There's a hot tub on-site and guests have pool privileges at Bighorn Lodge across the street. Look for $20-off discount coupons at visitor centers.

Gonzo Inn (☎ 435-259-2515, 800-791-4044; www.gonzoinn.com; 100 W 200 South; r $159, ste $205-339, incl breakfast in season;) The lizard looks a wee bit tired at this funky, gecko-themed hotel, but that's not surprising considering the number of cyclists who churn through. The retro splashes of color and eclectic furniture are still fun, and the ample suites can comfortably sleep four, with kitchenettes and spacious patio or balcony areas to boot. There's a bicycle wash and repair station as well as a laundry.

EATING

There's no shortage of places to fuel up in Moab, from backpacker coffeehouses to gourmet dining rooms. Some restaurants close earlier in winter, so call ahead.

Love Muffin (☎ 435-259-6833; 139 N Main St; mains under $10; 7:30am-2pm;) You gotta grab your love muffin fast at this breezy new bakery, because early-rising moms, gnarly adventure chicks and on-the-ball seniors nab the best ones – raspberry-blueberry, chocolate vegan – before most people get out of bed. But no worries: the breakfast menu also offers burritos, waffles, and honey yogurt with granola. Gourmet salads and sandwiches are served at lunch.

Moab Brewery (☎ 435-259-6333; 686 S Main St; mains $7-20; 11:30am-10pm Mon-Thu, 11:30am-11pm Fri & Sat, may close earlier Nov-Feb) At Moab's only on-site microbrewery restaurant you can see the vats just behind the bar area. It serves a range of burgers, seafood, steak and chicken, all to better accompany a pint of Derailleur or Dead Horse Ale. Natural, house-made gelato is sold on the front porch.

Miguel's Baja Grill (☎ 435-259-6546; 51 N Main St; dishes $11-20; 5-10pm) Dine on Baja fish tacos in the sky-lit breezeway patio lined with brightly painted walls. Fajitas, *chilis rellenos* and seafood mains are good sized, and the portobello salad is excellent. Refreshingly honest staff will tell you yes, they do have margaritas, but they may not be the best in town.

Center Café (☎ 435-259-4295; 60 N 100 West; mains $19-32; from 4pm) Ready to trade your spandex and bike clips for a sundress and strappy shoes? Leave Main St behind and stroll over to stylish Center Café, consistently named southern Utah's best restaurant. The chef-owner cooks with confidence, drawing inspiration from American, Mediterranean and Asian cuisines. Lighter tapas menu ($4 to $12) served 4pm to 6pm.

GETTING THERE & AROUND

Twice daily Monday through Friday, **Great Lakes Airlines** (☎ 800-554-5111; www.flygreatlakes.com) flies from Denver, CO, to **Canyonlands Airport** (CNY; www.moabairport.com), 16 miles north of town via Hwy 191. There's one flight on Saturday and Sunday.

Bighorn Express (☎ 801-417-5191, 888-655-7433; www.bighornexpress.com) operates a scheduled van service to and from SLC ($69 one way) and Green River ($59 one way), while **Roadrunner Shuttle** (☎ 435-259-9402; www.roadrunnershuttle.com) operates an on-demand service to Moab airport as well as hiker-biker and river shuttles. **Coyote Shuttle** (☎ 435-260-2097, 435-259-8656; www.coyoteshuttle.com) also does the full range of recreational shuttles.

Arches National Park

One of the Southwest's most gorgeous parks, **Arches** (☎ 435-719-2299; www.nps.gov/arch; per vehicle $10; visitor center 7:30am-6:30pm Apr-Oct, 8am-4:30pm Nov-Mar) boasts the world's greatest concentration of sandstone arches. Just 5 miles north of Moab on Hwy 191, the park is always packed in summer. Consider a moonlight exploration, when it's cooler and the rocks feel ghostly. Many arches are easily reached by paved roads and relatively short hiking trails.

Highlights include **Balanced Rock**, oft-photographed **Delicate Arch** (best captured in the late afternoon), spectacularly elongated **Landscape Arch**, and popular, twice-daily ranger-led trips into the **Fiery Furnace** (adult/child $10/5; mid-Mar–Oct), for which reservations are recommended.

Because of water scarcity and the heat, few visitors backpack, though it is allowed with free permits (available from the visitor center). The scenic **Devils Garden Campground** (☎ 518-885-3639, 877-444-6777; www.recreation.gov; Hwy 191; campsites $20) is 18 miles from the visitor center and fills up March to October. Twenty-four sites available on a first-come, first-served basis, 52 sites by reservation. For the former, stop by the entrance station or visitor center after 7:30am.

Dead Horse Point State Park

A tiny but stunning **state park** (☎ 435-259-2614; www.stateparks.utah.gov; Hwy 313; per vehicle $10; park 6am-10pm, visitor center 8am-5pm), Dead Horse Point has been the setting for numerous movies, including the opening scene from *Mission Impossible II* and the finale of *Thelma & Louise*. Located just off Hwy 313 (the road to Canyonlands), the park has canyons rimmed with white cliffs and walloping, mesmerizing views of the Colorado River, Canyonlands National Park and the distant La Sal Mountains. The 21-site **Kayenta Campground** (☎ 801-322-3770, 800-322-3770; www.stateparks.utah.gov; Hwy 313; campsites $20) provides limited water (bringing your own is highly recommended) and RV facilities. Four campsites are available first-come, first-served, the rest by reservation.

Canyonlands National Park

Covering 527 sq miles, **Canyonlands** (☎ 435-719-2313; www.nps.gov/cany; per vehicle $10) is Utah's largest and wildest park. Indeed, parts of it are as rugged as almost anywhere on the planet. Arches, bridges, needles, spires, craters, mesas, buttes – Canyonlands is a crumbling, decaying beauty, a vision of ancient earth.

You can hike, raft and 4WD (Cataract Canyon offers some of the wildest white water in the West), but be sure that you have plenty of gas, food and water. Difficult terrain and lack of water render this the least developed and visited of the major Southwestern national parks.

The canyons of the Colorado and Green Rivers divide the park into three districts. **Island in the Sky** is most easily reached and offers amazing views. There's a helpful **visitor center** (☎ 435-259-4712; www.nps.gov/cany/island; Hwy 313; 9am-4:30pm Nov-Apr, extended hours Mar-Oct) and some excellent short hikes. Our favorite is the half-mile loop to oft-photographed **Mesa Arch**, a slender, cliff-hugging span framing a picturesque view of Washer Woman Arch and Buck Canyon. Drive a bit further to reach the **Grand View Overlook** trailhead. The path follows the canyon's edge and ends at a praise-your-maker precipice. This park section is 32 miles south of Moab; head north along Hwy 191 then west on Hwy 313.

Needles, the second district, is on Hwy 211, which heads west from Hwy 191, 40 miles south of Moab; you'll find more great views here and a smaller **visitor center** (☎ 435-259-4711; www.nps.gov/cany/needles; Hwy 211; 9am-4:30pm Nov-Feb, 8am-6pm Mar-May, 8am-5pm Jun-Oct). And then there's the **Maze**, one of the wildest and most remote areas in the Southwest, accessible by 4WD only. Within **Horseshoe Canyon**, along the 32-mile road from Hwy 24 to the Maze, you'll find Great Gallery, with superb life-size rock art left by prehistoric Native Americans.

In addition to entrance fees, permits ($5 to $30) are required for overnight backcountry and mountain-biking camping, 4WD trips and river trips. Reserve at least two weeks ahead, by fax or mail only, with the **Canyonlands NP Reservations Office** (☎ 435-259-4351; fax 435-259-4285; www.nps.gov/cany/permits.htm; 2282 S West Resource Blvd, Moab, UT 84532), or just show up, although reservations are recommended in spring and fall. For more reservation information, visit www.nps.gov/cany/planyourvisit/reservations.htm.

Natural Bridges National Monument

Forty miles west of Blanding via Hwy 95, this **monument** (☎ 435-692-1234; www.nps.gov/nabr; Hwy 275; per vehicle $6; visitor center 8:30am-6:30pm Apr-Sep, 8:30am-4:30pm Oct-Mar, sometimes later, park open 24hr) became Utah's first NPS land in 1908. The highlight is a dark-stained, white-sandstone canyon containing three easily accessible natural bridges. The oldest, the Owachomo Bridge, spans 180ft but is only 9ft thick. The flat 9-mile Scenic Drive loop is ideal for biking. The monument's 13 basic **campsites** ($10) are available on a first-come, first-served basis.

Hovenweep National Monument

Beautiful, little-visited **Hovenweep** (☎ 970-562-4282; www.nps.gov/hove; Hwy 262; per vehicle $6; visitor center 8am-6pm Apr-Sep, 8am-5pm Oct-Mar, park & trails sunrise-sunset), meaning 'deserted valley' in the Ute language, contains six sets of prehistoric Ancestral Puebloan sites, five accessed by long hikes. You'll find a visitor center, ranger station and basic **campground** (campsites $10), but no facilities. The 31 campsites are first-come, first-served, but there's no need to rush because the campground rarely fills up.The main access is east of Hwy 191 on Hwy 262 via Hatch Trading Post, more than 40 miles from Bluff or Blanding.

Bluff

Surrounded by red rock, tiny Bluff was founded by Mormon pioneers in 1880 and makes a comfortable, laid-back base for regional exploring. It sits at the junction of Hwys 191 and 163, along the San Juan River. Hwy 191 through town is also called Main St. For up-close views of rock art, cliff dwellings and fossils, try **Wild Rivers Expeditions** (☎ 435-672-2244, 800-422-7654; www.riversandruins.com; 101 Main St; Mar-Oct). This history-and-geology-minded outfitter has been leading river trips since 1957 (day trips adult/child $165/123). Vaughn Hadenfeldt, owner of **Far Out**

SCENIC DRIVE: MOKI DUGWAY & MULE POINT

The Moki Dugway (Hwy 261) heads south from Hwy 95 to connect with Hwy 163 at Mexican Hat. Along the way is a turnoff to Mule Point Overlook – don't miss this cliff-edge viewpoint, one of the country's most sweeping, encompassing Monument Valley and other landmarks.

Back on Hwy 261, the pavement ends and the Moki Dugway suddenly descends a whopping 1100ft along a series of fist-clenching hairpin turns on a narrow, mostly dirt road with no guardrails. At the bottom, a dirt road heads east into the Valley of the Gods, a 17-mile drive through mind-blowing sandstone monoliths.

Expeditions (☎ 435-672-2294; www.faroutexpeditions.com; cnr 7th & Mulberry Sts), arranges off-the-beaten-track trips to Monument Valley and archaeological sites. Lodging is available in the company's guesthouse (rooms from $90).

Another good choice is the hospitable **Recapture Lodge** (☎ 435-672-2281; www.bluffutah.org/recapturelodge; Hwy 191; r incl breakfast $60-80;), a rustic, cozy property pleasantly shaded between the highway and the river. Also nice are the spacious rooms inside the fancy-timbered **Desert Rose Inn** (☎ 435-672-2303; www.desertroseinn.com; 701 W Main St; r $99-109, cabins $119;).

Just across the street, **Comb Ridge Coffee** (☎ 435-672-9931; Hwy 191; mains $2-6; 7am-3pm Wed-Sun, may vary seasonally;) serves espresso, muffins and blue-corn pancakes inside a timber and adobe café. For lunch and dinner, the organic-minded **San Juan River Kitchen** (☎ 435-672-9956; 75 E Main St; lunch mains $8-13, dinner mains $9-20; 11am-9pm Tue-Sun) offers regionally sourced and inspired American and Mexican dishes including salads made with produce from a garden shared with Wild Rivers Expeditions.

Monument Valley

From the village of **Mexican Hat** (named for an easy-to-spot sombrero-shaped rock), Hwy 163 winds southwest and enters the Navajo Indian Reservation and, after about 30 miles, **Monument Valley Navajo Tribal Park** (see p858), where a 17-mile unpaved driving loop circles the massive formations.

For years, **Goulding's Lodge** (☎ 435-727-3231; www.gouldings.com; Hwy 163; r $180;) was the only area hotel, luring tourists with million-dollar views of the colossal red buttes. The full-service property still has a lot to offer – a restaurant, museum, gas station and campground (tent/RV sites $25/42) – but with the 2008 opening of Navajo-owned View Hotel at Monument Valley (p858), it's time to suit up for serious competition.

SOUTH-CENTRAL & SOUTHWESTERN UTAH

Locals call it 'color country,' but the cutesy label hardly does justice to the eye-popping hues that saturate the landscape. The deep-crimson canyons of Zion, the delicate pink-and-orange minarets at Bryce Canyon, the swirling yellow-white domes of Capitol Reef – the land is so spectacular that it encompasses three national parks and the gigantic Grand Staircase-Escalante National Monument.

This section is organized roughly northeast to southwest, following the highly scenic Hwy 12 and Hwy 89 from Capitol Reef National Park to Zion National Park.

Capitol Reef National Park

Not as crowded as its fellow parks but equally scenic, Capitol Reef contains much of the 100-mile **Waterpocket Fold**, created 65 million years ago when the earth's surface buckled up and folded, exposing a cross section of geologic history that is downright painterly in its colorful intensity. Hwy 24 cuts grandly through the park, but take the park's own scenic drive ($5) starting from the **visitor center** (☎ 435-425-3791; www.nps.gov/care; cnr Hwy 24 & Scenic Dr; 8am-4:30pm mid-fall–spring, to 6pm spring–mid-fall), where there's grassy, first-come, first-served **campsites** ($10) that fill fast spring through fall. A legacy of the Mormon settlement of Fruita, the park also encompasses amazing **orchards** (www.nps.gov/care/historyculture/orchardscms.htm) where visitors can pick cherries, peaches and apples in season. In summer, stop by the historic **Gifford Farmhouse** south of the visitor center for preserves or a fruit-filled minipie ($5).

Torrey

This little village makes a good stopping point for lodging and provides surprisingly great meals. The **travel council** (☎ 435-425-3365, 800-858-7951; www.capitolreef.org) has good information.

The slightly larger-than-average rooms at the Western-themed **Austin's Chuck Wagon Lodge** (☎ 435-425-3335; www.austinschuckwagonmotel.com;

12 W Main St; r from $75, cabins $135; mid-Mar–Oct;) are very clean with basic but sturdy furniture and lots of bathroom counter space. Grab supplies and food at the on-site general store.

Pecan chicken. Mayan tamales. Fire-roasted pork tenderloin. It's all devil-icious at the inviting **Café Diablo** (435-425-3070; 599 W Main St; mains $21-29; 5-10pm Apr–mid-Oct;), one of southern Utah's best eateries. The highly stylized Southwestern fare – which includes 10 mains and a diverse selection of small plates – bursts with flavor and towers on the plate. Feeling adventurous? Try the award-winning rattlesnake cakes.

Boulder

Tiny Boulder is 32 miles south of Torrey on Hwy 12. From here, the attractive **Burr Trail** heads east as a paved road across the northeastern corner of the Grand Staircase-Escalante National Monument, winding up at Bullfrog Marina on Lake Powell. To explore the canyons, consider taking a one-day, child-friendly excursion with knowledgeable **Earth Tours** (435-691-1241; www.earth-tours.com), which offers half-/full-day tours for $75/100, or a multiday backcountry trek with the equally recommended **Escalante Canyon Outfitters** (435-691-3037, 888-326-4453; www.ecohike.com; late Mar–early Nov). The ecocommitted company, which powers its office with a hydro-turbine, offers four-to six-day all-inclusive treks and archeo-hikes for $1225 to $1620. Guests enjoy in-season organic produce from the company garden.

The sturdy-but-stylish rooms at **Boulder Mountain Lodge** (435-335-7460, 800-556-3446; www.boulder-utah.com; 20 N Hwy 12; r $99-175, ste $190;) are among the nicest accommodations along Hwy 12. The outdoor hot tub with mountain views is a particularly scenic spot to soak off trail-earned aches and pains. Wi-fi is available in the lobby. The lodge's must-visit **Hell's Backbone Grill** (435-335-7464; Boulder Mountain Lodge, 20 N Hwy 12; breakfast dishes $8-10, dinner mains $16-34; 7-11:30am & 5:30-9:30pm) serves soulful, earthy preparations of regionally inspired and sourced cuisine.

Escalante

This gateway town of 750 people is the closest thing to a metropolis for 75 miles. It's also a good place to stock up and map it out before heading into the adjacent Grand Staircase-Escalante National Monument.

The **Escalante Interagency Office** (435-826-5499; www.ut.blm.gov/monument; 775 W Main St; 7:30am-5:30pm mid-Mar–Oct, 8am-4:30pm Nov–mid-Mar) is a superb resource center with complete information on all area public lands. Fifteen miles east on Hwy 12, **Calf Creek Recreation Area** (435-826-5499; www.ut.blm.gov/monument; per vehicle $2) has 13 basic but fast-filling campsites ($7) and a recommended 3-mile hike to Lower Calf Creek Falls.

Escalante Outfitters, Inc (435-826-4266; 310 W Main St; 8am-9pm;) is a great travelers' oasis, selling maps, books, camping supplies, liquor, espresso and the best homemade pizza ($17 to $23, no slices) you'll find in Utah – no kidding.

Motels fill up fast in Escalante in high season, but the 50-room **Prospector Inn** (435-826-4653; www.prospectorinn.com; Hwy 12; r $55-65;) may have a few units – basic but spacious and very clean – at the last minute. View-loving guests here settle into their balcony chairs to watch the sun go down.

Grand Staircase-Escalante National Monument

This 2656-sq-mile **monument** (www.ut.blm.gov/monument), established in 1996, is tucked between Bryce Canyon National Park, Capitol Reef National Park and Glen Canyon National Recreation Area. Tourist infrastructure is minimal, leaving a vast, remote desert for adventurous travelers who have the time and necessary outdoor equipment to explore.

Roads get slick and impassable when wet. Wilderness camping is allowed with a required free permit. Before heading out, obtain current road and travel information from the Escalante Interagency Office (above), the visitor centers in Kanab (opposite) or **Cannonville** (435-826-5640; 10 Center St, Cannonville; 8am-4:30pm Mar-Nov but hours may vary).

Kodachrome Basin State Park

Dozens of red, pink and white sandstone chimneys highlight this colorful **state park** (435-679-8562; www.stateparks.utah.gov; Cottonwood Canyon Rd; per vehicle $6), named for its photogenic landscape by the National Geographic Society. The Grand Parade Trail has the best views of sand pipes and other formations; there's also a **campground** (801-322-3770, 800-322-3770; campsites $16). Three campsites are first-come, first-served, 24 are available by reservation. Spring and fall are the busiest seasons.

THE MYSTERY OF EVERETT RUESS – SOLVED?

In November 1934, 20-year-old artist Everett Ruess walked into the Escalante backcountry, well prepared to explore, paint and experience the stunningly beautiful wilderness. Before leaving, he wrote to his brother, 'As to when I shall visit civilization, it will not be soon, I think…I prefer the saddle to the streetcar and star-sprinkled sky to a roof, the obscure and difficult trail, leading into the unknown, to any paved highway, and the deep peace of the wild to the discontent bred by the cities.' This was Ruess' last contact with his family, and he never returned from this trip.

The mystery of his disappearance grew into legend with the publication of several books examining his possible fate. In 2008, writer David Roberts and guide Vaughn Hadenfeldt (p880), acting on a tip that Ruess was murdered, found human remains in a crevice along desolate Comb Ridge. Although DNA tests seem to confirm that they belonged to Ruess, state archaeologists aren't 100% convinced.

Either way, it's clear today that Ruess' romantic idealism will live on in songs, books, an art festival (www.everettruessdays.org) and his own collected letters.

Bryce Canyon National Park

The Grand Staircase, a series of steplike uplifted rock layers stretching north from the Grand Canyon, culminates at this very popular **national park** (☎ 435-834-5322; www.nps.gov/brca; Hwy 63; per vehicle $25; ⏰ visitor center 8am-8pm May-Sep, 8am-4:30pm Nov-Mar, 8am-6pm Oct & Apr) in the Pink Cliffs formation. It's full of wondrous pinnacles and points, steeples and spires, and odd formations called 'hoodoos.' The 'canyon' is actually an amphitheater eroded from the cliffs.

From Hwy 12, Hwy 63 heads 4 miles south to Rim Rd Dr (8000ft), an 18-mile dead-end road that follows the rim of the canyon, passing the visitor center, lodge, viewpoints (don't miss Inspiration Point) and trailheads, ending at Rainbow Point at 9115ft elevation. The park's only licensed outfitter is **Canyon Trail Rides** (☎ 435-679-8665; www.canyonrides.com; Hwy 63; 2hr/half-day $50/75), which operates out of Bryce Canyon Lodge (below).

The two campgrounds, **North Campground** (☎ 877-444-6777; www.recreation.gov; campsites $15) and **Sunset Campground** (campsites $15; ⏰ late spring–fall), both have toilets and water. Sunset is more wooded, but has fewer amenities and doesn't accept reservations. For laundry, showers and groceries, visit North Campground. During summer, sites fill by noon.

The 1920s **Bryce Canyon Lodge** (☎ 435-834-8700, 888-297-2757; www.brycecanyonlodge.com; Hwy 63; lodge r $130-179, hotel r $165, cabins $175; ⏰ Apr-Oct; ⊠) exudes rustic mountain charm. Rooms are in satellite buildings and range from modern hotel-style units with up-to-date furnishings and balconies to romantic, slightly dated, cabins with gas fireplaces and front porches. No TVs.

Kanab

Vast expanses of rugged desert surround remote Kanab, and until the advent of roads it was an isolated Mormon community. Filmmakers arrived in the 1920s to shoot Hollywood Westerns and Kanab soon earned the nickname 'Utah's Little Hollywood.'

Today, Hwy 89 snakes through town, passing a good selection of motels and restaurants. The **Kanab Visitor Center** (☎ 435-644-4680; www.ut.blm.gov/monument; 745 E Hwy 89; ⏰ 8am-5pm Nov-Mar, 8am-4:30pm Dec-Feb) provides road, trail and weather updates for Grand Staircase-Escalante National Monument (opposite). For area information, visit the **Kane County Office of Tourism** (☎ 435-644-5033, 800-733-5263; www.kaneutah.com; 78 S 100 E; ⏰ 10am-7pm Mon-Fri, 10am-5pm Sat, 10am-4pm Sun mid-May–Oct, 10am-5pm Mon-Sat Nov–mid-May).

John Wayne, Maureen O'Hara and Gregory Peck are a few Hollywood notables who slumbered at **Parry Lodge** (☎ 435-644-2601, 888-289-1722; www.parrylodge.com; 89 E Center St; r $73-84, ste $92-102;). Today you can sleep in the same rooms they did (hotel records confirm room numbers). Units are well kept – if tired – and you'll find a hot tub, restaurant and bar onsite. Wi-fi is available in some units. **Laid Back Larry's** (☎ 435-644-3636; 98 S 100 East; sandwiches $2-5; ⏰ 7am-2pm Thu-Tue) serves lunch and breakfast sandwiches, and it has good coffee.

St George

Nicknamed 'Dixie' for its warm weather and southern location, St George is a spacious Mormon town with wide streets, an eye-catching temple and pioneer buildings. St George, a city of 71,100, is popular with retirees and visitors to Zion and other nearby parks. The main source for town information is the **chamber of commerce** (☎ 435-628-1658; www.stgeorgechamber.com; 97 E St George Blvd; 9am-5pm Mon-Fri). The **Interagency Information Center** (☎ 435-688-3246; 345 E Riverside Dr; 7:45am-5pm Mon-Fri, 10am-3pm Sat) provides information on USFS and BLM lands, state parks and the Arizona Strip.

Nine miles north of town, 7400-acre **Snow Canyon State Park** (☎ 435-628-2255; www.stateparks.utah.gov; Hwy 18; per vehicle $5) is a great spot to stretch your legs and soak in stellar scenery: sandstone cliffs, volcanic landscapes and petroglyphs. Scope out lava caves and abundant wildlife from the hiking trails.

St George has the biggest selection of accommodations in southern Utah; most are chains, though, and many line St George Blvd. For a stylish budget abode with a great breakfast – that's close to the Interagency Information Center and Snow Canyon – try the hospitable **Ambassador Inn** (☎ 435-673-7900, 877-373-7900; www.ambassadorinn.net; 1481 Sunland Dr; r incl breakfast $65-75;) just off I-15 Exit 6.

Animal pelts and timber set a frontiersman's tone at **Gun Barrel Steak & Game House** (☎ 435-652-0550; 1091 N Bluff St; lunch mains $8-12, dinner mains $8-32; 11:30am-2pm Mon-Fri, 5-9pm Mon-Thu, 5-9:30pm Fri & Sat), a vibe perfectly in sync with the game-heavy menu. That said, solo female travelers will do just fine. For a scrumptious, meal-sized appetizer, try the buffalo wrap layered with onions, peppers, cheese and spicy chipotle mayo. For coffee, omelets and oatmeal, everybody heads to family-friendly **Bear Paw Coffee Company** (☎ 435-634-0126; 75 N Main St; mains $5-11; 7am-3pm).

Greyhound (☎ 435-673-2933, 800-231-2222; www.greyhound.com; 1235 S Bluff St) departs from the local McDonald's, with buses to SLC ($52, 5½ hours) and Las Vegas, NV ($23, two hours).

Springdale

Many travelers to Zion National Park pass through here, as Springdale sits along Hwy 9 just outside the park's southern entrance. It's a pleasant, relaxed community, catering mostly to park visitors. The **regional visitors bureau** (☎ 888-518-7070; www.zionpark.com) does not have a physical office. Call for a travel planner or check the website for information about lodging, restaurants and shopping.

Springdale has an abundance of good restaurants and nice lodging options, including the 22 recently revamped rooms – tile floors, monochromatic colors – at the pleasant **Canyon Ranch Motel** (☎ 435-772-3357; www.canyonranchmotel.com; 668 Zion Park Blvd; s $84-94, d $94-99, r with kitchenette $114-125;) Located half a mile south of the park, it has a nice shaded lawn with picnic tables.

Grab a coffee, breakfast burrito or turkey panini at scruffy **Mean Bean** (☎ 435-772-0654; 932 Zion Park Blvd; mains under $10; 7am-noon Mon-Fri, 7am-1pm Sat & Sun;), a hiker-and-biker haven in the heart of downtown. Unless it's really busy, the place closes by noon on weekdays, and lunches are made to go. For dinner, you don't have to gussy up too much for the **Spotted Dog** (☎ 435-772-0700; 428 Zion Park Blvd; breakfast $8, mains $11-24; 7-11am & 5-10pm Mon-Fri, 7-11:30am & 5-10pm Sat & Sun, to 9pm off-season, may close Jan) but it might be nice to look fresh while people-watching on the patio. The seasonal, mostly regional menu has included wild game meatloaf and golden rainbow trout. There's also a breakfast buffet. For drinks, the **Bit & Spur Restaurant & Saloon** (☎ 435-772-3498; 1212 Zion Park Blvd) is a local institution and the liveliest spot in town, offering up a large selection of microbrews and occasional live music.

Zion National Park

If possible, enter **Zion** (☎ 435-772-3256; www.nps.gov/zion; Hwy 9; per vehicle $25) from the east, following Hwy 9 west from Hwy 89. The route is jaw-droppingly scenic as it rolls through colorful red rocks and a gallery-dotted tunnel before switchbacking 3.5 miles into the canyon.

More than 100 miles of trails offer everything from leisurely strolls to wilderness backpacking and camping. The most famous backpacking trip is through the **Narrows**, 16 miles of walking and wading in the Virgin River through dramatic canyons (June to September). Prepare to get wet or your spirits dampened if there's a flash-flood warning. The **Angels Landing Trail** is a strenuous vertigo-inducer, but the views of Zion Canyon are phenomenal. It's 5 miles round-trip.

From April through October, the park operates frequent free shuttles which are the only vehicles allowed into the canyon (except for guests at the lodge). Two linked shuttle loops depart from the visitor center from 6:45am to 10pm daily. One loop picks up and drops off passengers along Zion Park Blvd in Springdale and the other stops at trailheads within the park. To avoid the hefty $25 vehicle entrance fee, ride the shuttle from town and pay the walk-in rate ($12 per person).

Motorhome drivers may have to pay a $15 escort pass to drive – or squeeze – large vehicles through the 1.1-mile Zion-Mt Carmel tunnel at the east entrance.

The **Zion Canyon Visitor Center** (☎ 435-772-3256; www.nps.gov/zion; 8am-8pm summer, 8am-6pm fall, 8am-5pm winter & spring) has books, maps and park recreation information. Ask about ranger-led activities, which include nature walks and interpretive talks on flora, fauna, ecology and geology. The center also houses the **backcountry desk** (☎ 435-772-0170; 7am-8pm Jun-Aug, 7am-6pm Sep–mid-Oct, 8am-4:30pm mid-Oct–May), which dispenses 25% of its backcountry permits to walk-ins either the day before, or the day of, a hike. To reserve a backcountry permit for a specific area (permits for popular areas like The Narrows go fast), call or reserve online well ahead of your arrival date (www.nps.gov /zion/planyour visit/index.htm)

At the south gate, two **campgrounds** (☎ 877-444-6777; www.recreation.gov; campsites $16-20), South and Watchman, have almost 300 campsites. Fewer than half of these campsites can be reserved, so come early for the first-come, first-served spots. Smack in the middle of Zion Canyon, **Zion Lodge** (☎ reservations same day 435-772-7700, advance 888-297-2757; www.zionlodge .com; r/cabins/ste $160/173/183;) has 81 well-appointed motel rooms and 40 cabins with gas fireplaces. All have wooden porches with stellar views. There are no TVs, but there's a good restaurant. Reservations are accepted up to 13 months in advance, or try your luck with same-day booking.

NEW MEXICO

Explaining New Mexico's undeniable allure in mere words is no easy task. Maybe it's the juxtaposition of art and landscape, with bleached cattle skulls hanging from sky-blue walls and silhouetted crosses topping centuries-old missions. Or maybe it's the fact that ancient pueblos, 300-year-old haciendas and stylish modern buildings stand in easy proximity, a testament to the three dominant cultures – Native American, Hispanic and Anglo – which intersect so pointedly here. Beyond that, there's crisp mountain air, chili-smothered enchiladas, national monuments and a welcoming populace. What's not to love?

But then, just when you think you've finally pinned it down, New Mexico turns to show a completely different side. Creatures from outer space lurk in Roswell. Billy the Kid is trumpeted like a hero. Museums honor the atomic age. Bats plumb the ethereal corners of Carlsbad Caverns. Seems there's a little more to it than turquoise and Taos. Maybe New Mexico's elusive, contradictory charm is best expressed in the captivating paintings of Georgia O'Keeffe, the state's patron artist. She herself exclaimed, on her very first visit: 'Well! Well! Well!…This is wonderful! No one told me it was like this.'

But seriously, how could they?

History

People roamed the land here as far back as 10,500 BC, but by Coronado's arrival in the 16th century, Pueblos were the dominant communities found here. Santa Fe was established as the colonial capital in 1610, after which Spanish settlers and farmers fanned out across northern New Mexico and missionaries began their often violent efforts to convert the area's Puebloans to Catholicism. Following on from a successful revolt, Native Americans then occupied Santa Fe until 1692, when Diego de Vargas recaptured the city.

In 1851 New Mexico became US territory. Native American wars, settlement by cowboys and miners, and trade along the Santa Fe Trail further transformed the region, and the arrival of the railroad in the 1870s created an economic boom.

Painters and writers set up art colonies in Santa Fe and Taos in the early 20th century. In 1943 a scientific community descended on Los Alamos and developed the atomic bomb (see p898). Big issues include water rights (whoever owns the water has the power) and immigration.

Information

Where opening hours are listed by season (not month), readers should call first, as hours can fluctuate based on weather, budgets and level of custom.

New Mexico CultureNet (www.nmcn.org) Listings for upcoming concerts, readings and openings in northern New Mexico.**New Mexico Magazine** (www.nmmaga zine.com) Good guide to the state with sections on destinations, diversions and comforts.

NEW MEXICO FACTS

Nickname Land of Enchantment
Population 1.9 million
Area 121,599 sq miles
Capital city Santa Fe (population 72,000)
Other cities Albuquerque (population 507,800), Las Cruces (population 86,200), Roswell (population 45,600), Alamogordo (population 36,000), Carlsbad (population 25,400)
Sales tax 5%
Birthplace of Outlaw William Bonney, aka Billy the Kid (1859–81); national icon Smokey Bear
Home of International UFO Museum & Research Center (Roswell), Julia Roberts
Famous for Chilies, ancient pueblos, the first atomic bomb (1945)
State question 'Red or green?' (chili sauce, that is)
Driving distances Albuquerque to Carlsbad 275 miles, Las Cruces to Taos 352 miles

New Mexico Route 66 Association (www.rt66nm.org) Information on the famous path through the state.
New Mexico State Parks Division (Map p895; ☎ 505-476-3355, 888-667-2757; www.emnrd.state.nm.us; 1220 South St Francis Dr, Santa Fe) Camping ($8 to $18 per night) is available by reservation (☎ 877-664-7787; www.newmexico.reserveworld.com) at some parks.
New Mexico Tourism Department (☎ 505-827-7400, 800-545-2040; www.newmexico.org) Order a free *Vacation Guide,* download a Scenic Byways map or research activities and accommodations.
Public Lands Information Center (☎ 877-851-8946; www.publiclands.org) Camping and recreation information.

ALBUQUERQUE

This bustling crossroads has a sneaky charm, one based more on its locals than big-city sparkle. The citizens here are proud of their city, and folks are more than happy to share history, highlights and must-try restaurants – which makes the state's most populous city much more than a dot on the Route 66 map.

Centuries-old adobes line the lively Old Town area, and downtown Central Ave has a densely packed nightlife district that's easy to navigate on foot. Ancient petroglyphs cover rocks just outside town while modern museums explore space and nuclear energy. There's a distinctive and vibrant mix of university students, Native Americans, Hispanics, gays and lesbians. You'll find square dances and yoga classes flyered with equal enthusiasm, and ranch hands and real-estate brokers chow down at hole-in-the-wall taquerias and retro cafés.

Orientation

Albuquerque's major boundaries are Paseo del Norte Dr to the north, Central Ave to the south, Rio Grande Blvd to the west and Tramway Blvd to the east. Central Ave is the main artery (aka old Route 66) – it passes through Old Town, downtown, the university and Nob Hill. The city is divided into four quadrants (NW, NE, SW and SE), and the intersection of Central Ave and the railroad tracks just east of downtown serves as the center point of the city.

Information

BOOKSTORES

Page One (Map p888; ☎ 505-294-2026; www.page1book.com; 11018 Montgomery Blvd NE, Juan Tabo Plaza; ⏲ 9am-9pm Mon-Sat, 9am-7pm Sun) Huge and comprehensive; also buys and sells used books.

EMERGENCY & MEDICAL SERVICES

Police (Map p888; ☎ 505-242-2677; 2501 Carlisle Blvd)
Presbyterian Hospital (Map p888; ☎ 505-841-1234; 1100 Central Ave SE; ⏲ 24hr emergency)
UNM Hospital (Map p888; ☎ 505-272-2411; 2211 Lomas Blvd NE; ⏲ 24hr emergency) Head here if you don't have insurance.

INTERNET ACCESS

FedEx Office (Map p888; ☎ 505-255-9673; 2706 Central Ave SE; per min 20¢; ⏲ 24hr Mon-Thu, midnight-11pm Fri, 9am-9pm Sat, 9am-midnight Sun)
Main Library (Map p890; ☎ 505-768-5141; 501 Copper Ave NW; ⏲ 10am-6pm Mon & Thu-Sat, 10am-7pm Tue & Wed) Free internet access after purchasing a $3 SmartCard. Wi-fi available for free but must obtain access card.

INTERNET RESOURCES

Albuquerque Online (www.abqonline.com) Exhaustive listings and links for local businesses.
Albuquerque.com (www.albuquerque.com) Attractions, hotels and restaurants.
Alibi (☎ 505-346-0660; www.alibi.com) Free weekly with entertainment listings.

City of Albuquerque (www.cabq.gov) Information on public transportation, area attractions and more.

POST

Post office (Map p890; ☎ 505-346-1256; 201 5th St SW)

TOURIST INFORMATION

The **Albuquerque Convention & Visitors Bureau** (www.itsatrip.org) has three visitor centers:

Downtown (Map p890; ☎ 505-842-9918, 800-284-2282; 20 First Plaza NW at cnr 2nd St & Copper Ave; 🕑 9am-4pm Mon- Fri)

Old Town (Map p890; ☎ 505-243-3215; 303 Romero St NW; 🕑 10am-5pm Oct-May, 10am-6pm Jun-Sep)

Sunport (Albuquerque International Airport) At the lower-level baggage claim.

Sights

OLD TOWN

From its foundation in 1706 until the arrival of the railroad in 1880, the plaza was the hub of Albuquerque; today Old Town is the city's most popular tourist area.

You may want to tiptoe past the fangs, scales and rattling tails that inhabit the informative – but slightly unnerving – **Rattlesnake Museum** (Map p890; ☎ 505-242-6569; www.rattlesnakes.com; 202 San Felipe St NW; adult/child/senior $5/3/4; 🕑 11:30am-5:30pm Mon-Fri, 10am-6pm Sat, 1pm-5pm Sun) southeast of the plaza. From eastern diamondbacks to canebrakes, you won't find more species of rattlesnakes coiled anywhere else in the world. Get a 'certificate of bravery' with admission.

Conquistador armor and weaponry are highlights at the **Albuquerque Museum of Art & History** (Map p890; ☎ 505-243-7255; www.cabq.gov/museum; 2000 Mountain Rd NW; adult/child 4-12yr/senior $4/1/2, 1st Wed of month & 9am-1pm Sun free; 🕑 9am-5pm Tue-Sun) where visitors can study the city's tricultural Native American, Hispanic and Anglo past. Works by New Mexico artists also featured.

Also in the Old Town are ¡Explora! Children's Museum (p888) and the New Mexico Museum of Natural History & Science (p889).

AROUND TOWN

The University of New Mexico (UNM) area (Map p890) has loads of good restaurants, casual bars, offbeat shops and hip college hangouts. The main drag is Central Ave between University and Carlisle Blvds. Just east is trendy Nob Hill, a pedestrian-friendly neighborhood lined with indie coffee shops, stylish boutiques and patio-wrapped restaurants.

Operated by New Mexico's 19 pueblos, the **Indian Pueblo Cultural Center** (Map p888; ☎ 505-843-7270; www.indianpueblo.org; 2401 12th St NW; adult/child & student/senior $6/3/5.50; 🕑 9am-5pm) is a must for anyone visiting pueblos. The museum traces the development of Pueblo cultures, exhibits customs and crafts, and features changing exhibits. The restaurant serves Pueblo fare.

In 2009 the National Atomic Museum moved across town and changed its name to the **National Museum of Nuclear Science & History** (off Map p888; ☎ 505-245-2137; www.nuclearmuseum.org; 601 Eubank Blvd SE; adult/child & senior $8/4; 🕑 9am-5pm). Exhibits examine the Manhattan Project, the history of arms control and the use of nuclear energy as an alternative energy source. Docents here are retired military, and they're very knowledgeable about the exhibits. Take a moment to read the provocative and soul-searching comments in the visitors' journal beside the Hiroshima and Nagasaki display.

More than 20,000 rock etchings are found inside the **Petroglyph National Monument** (Map p888; ☎ 505-899-0205; www.nps.gov/petr; per vehicle at Boca Negra Canyon Mon-Fri $1, Sat & Sun $2) northwest of town. Stop by the visitor center to determine which of three viewing trails – in different sections of the park – best suits your schedule and hiking ability. Boca Negra, which has petroglyphs dating back 3000 years, works well if you're short on time. Note: smash-and-grab thefts have been reported at some trailhead parking lots, so don't leave valuables in your vehicle. Head west on I-40 across the Rio Grande and take exit 154 north.

The 2.7-mile **Sandia Peak Tramway** (Map p888; ☎ 505-856-7325; www.sandiapeak.com; Tramway Blvd; vehicle entrance fee $1, adult/youth 13-20 & senior/child $17.50/15/10; 🕑 9am-8pm Wed-Mon, 5-8pm Tue Sep-May, 9am-9pm Jun-Aug) starts in the desert realm of cholla cactus and soars to the pines atop 10,678ft Sandia Peak.

Activities

The omnipresent Sandia Mountains and the less crowded Manzano Mountains offer outdoor activities, including hiking, skiing (downhill and cross-country), mountain biking and camping. The **Sandia Ranger Station** (off Map p888; ☎ 505-281-3304; 11776 Hwy 337, Tijeras; 🕑 8am-4:30pm Mon-Fri Oct-May, to 5pm Mon-Fri, 8:30am-5pm Sat Jun-Sep), off I-40 exit 175 south, has maps and information. Best to call before visiting to confirm station is open. For equipment, try **REI** (Map p888; ☎ 505-247-1191; 1550 Mercantile Ave NE).

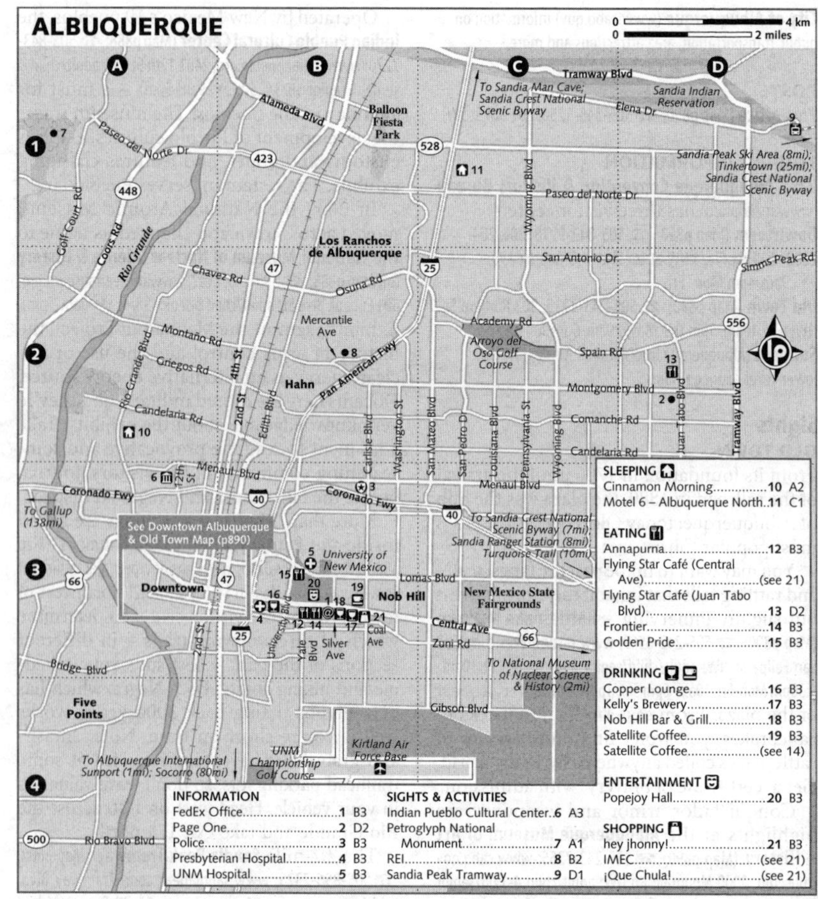

Reach the top of the Sandias via the eastern slope along the lovely **Sandia Crest National Scenic Byway** (I-40 exit 175 north), which passes several trailheads. Alternatively, take the Sandia Peak Tramway (p887) or Hwy 165 from Placitas (I-25 exit 242), a dirt road through Las Huertas Canyon that passes the prehistoric dwelling of **Sandia Man Cave**.

Atop the Sandia Peak Tramway, the **Sandia Peak Ski Area** (☎ 505-242-9052; www.sandiapeak.com; half-/full-day lift tickets adult $36/48, teen $30/38, child & senior $28/35) remains open during summer weekends and holidays (June to September) for mountain bikers. You can rent a bike at the base facility ($48 with $350 deposit) or ride the chairlift to the top of the peak with your own bike ($18).

Several companies offer rides over the city and the Rio Grande, including **Discover Balloons** (Map p890; ☎ 505-842-1111; www.discoverballoons.com; 205c San Felipe NW; adult/child under 12 $160/100). Flights last about an hour, and many are offered early in the morning to catch optimal winds and the sunrise.

Albuquerque for Children

The gung-ho **¡Explora! Children's Museum** (Map p890; ☎ 505-224-8300; www.explora.us; 1701 Mountain Rd NW; adult/child under 12/senior $7/3/5; 🕑 10am-6pm Mon-Sat, noon-6pm Sun; 🚼) will captivate your kiddies for hours. From the lofty high-wire bike to the leaping waters to the arts-and-crafts workshop, there's a hands-on exhibit for every type of child (don't miss the elevator). Not traveling with kids? Check the website to see if you're in town for the popular 'Adult Night.' Typically hosted by an acclaimed local scientist, it's become one of the hottest tickets in town.

The teen-friendly **New Mexico Museum of Natural History & Science** (Map p890; ☎ 505-841-2800; www.nmnaturalhistory.org; 1801 Mountain Rd NW; adult/child under 13/senior $7/4/6; 9am-5pm;) features an Evolator (evolution elevator), which transports visitors through 38 million years of New Mexico's geologic and evolutionary history. The new Space Frontiers exhibit highlights the state's contribution to space exploration, from ancient Chaco observatories to an impressive, full-scale replica of the Mars Rover. The museum also houses the huge-screen **DynaTheater** (adult/child 3-12yr/senior $7/4/6).

Tours

From mid-March to mid-December, the Albuquerque Museum of Art & History (p887) offers informative, guided **Old Town walking tours** (11am Tue-Sun) of historically significant structures. It takes about 45 minutes to an hour and is free with museum admission.

Festivals & Events

The **New Mexico Gay Rodeo Association** (www.nmgra.com) hosts the **Zia Regional Rodeo** during the second weekend of August. In early October, 900,000 spectators are drawn to magical hot-air-balloon ascensions at the **International Balloon Fiesta** (☎ 888-422-7277; www.balloonfiesta.com).

Sleeping

BUDGET

Motel 6 – Albuquerque North (Map p888; ☎ 505-821-1472; www.motel6.com; 8510 Pan American Fwy NE; r from $42; P) Yeah, it's a chain, and it's a few miles north of downtown, but this one is cheap, clean, just off I-25 and has a laundry. Wi-fi costs $3 per night.

Hotel Blue (Map p890; ☎ 505-924-2400, 877-878-4868; www.thehotelblue.com; 717 Central Ave NW; r incl breakfast $62-99; P) Well positioned beside a park and downtown, the art-deco 140-room Hotel Blue has Tempur-Pedic beds and a free airport shuttle. Bonus points awarded for the good-sized pool and 40in flat-screen TVs.

MIDRANGE & TOP END

Mauger Estate B&B (Map p890; ☎ 505-242-8755, 800-719-9189; www.maugerbb.com; 701 Roma Ave NW; r incl breakfast $99-193, ste $164-204; P) This restored Queen Anne mansion (Mauger is pronounced 'major') has comfortable rooms with down comforters, stocked fridges and freshly cut flowers. Kids are welcome and there's one dog-friendly room complete with Wild West decor and a small yard ($20 extra).

Cinnamon Morning (Map p888; ☎ 505-345-3541; www.cinnamonmorning.com; 2700 Rio Grande Blvd NW; r $109-225; P) Travelers looking for an easygoing spot to blog, twitter or check their e-mails will fall hard for this wired B&B's welcoming back patio. Bright, Southwestern-themed rooms – choose from the main house, casita or guesthouse – maintain the hospitable vibe. In summer, breakfast is cooked on the patio's Mexican-style kitchen. Pets and children welcome.

our pick **Böttger Mansion** (Map p890; ☎ 505-243-3639, 800-758-3639; www.bottger.com; 110 San Felipe St NW; r incl breakfast $124-179; P) A friendly and informative proprietor gives this well-appointed Victorian-era B&B an edge over some tough competition. The eight-bedroom mansion, built in 1912, is close to Old Town Plaza, top-notch museums and several in-the-know New Mexican restaurants like Duran's Central Pharmacy (1815 Central Ave; cash only). The honeysuckle-lined courtyard is a favorite with bird-watchers. Famous past guests in the home include Elvis, Janis Joplin and Machine Gun Kelly.

Eating

our pick **Golden Crown Panaderia** (Map p890; ☎ 505-243-2424; 1103 Mountain Rd NW; mains under $10; 7am-8pm Tue-Sat, 10am-8pm Sun) Who doesn't love a friendly neighborhood bakery? Especially one with gracious staff, fresh-from-the-oven bread, fruit-filled empanadas, smooth coffee and the frequent free cookie. Make time in your schedule to sample the goodies inside this beloved adobe oasis, and call ahead to reserve a loaf of quick-selling green chili bread.

Frontier (Map p888; ☎ 505-266-0550; 2400 Central Ave SE; dishes $3-10; 24hr;) An Albuquerque tradition, the Frontier boasts enormous cinnamon rolls, addictive green chili stew, and the best huevos rancheros ever. The food and people-watching are outstanding, and students love the low prices on the 24/7 breakfast, burgers and Mexican food.

Golden Pride (Map p888; ☎ 505-242-2181; 1830 Lomas Blvd NE; most dishes under $10; 6am-10pm) For breakfast burritos and fried chicken this popular minichain (Frontier's sister restaurant) is great for hungry travelers on the go.

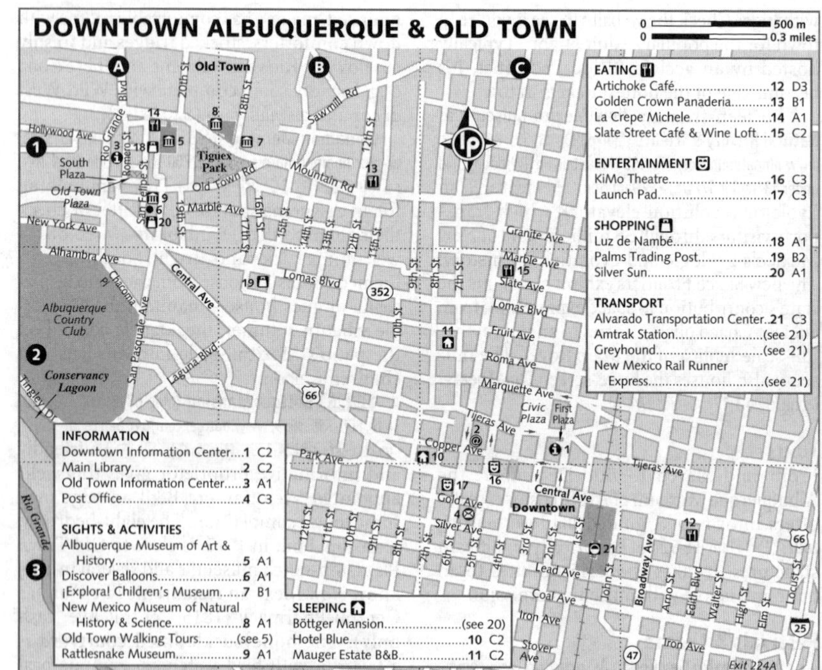

Annapurna (Map p888; ☎ 505-262-2424; 2201 Silver Ave SE; mains $7-12; 🕒 7am-8pm Mon-Wed, 7am-9pm Thu-Sat, 10am-8pm Sun; 📶 V) For some of the freshest, tastiest health food in town, grab a seat within the bright, mural-covered walls of Annapurna. The delicately spiced ayurvedic dishes are all vegetarian or vegan, but they're so delicious that even carnivores will find something to love.

Flying Star Café (Map p888; mains $8-11; Central Ave ☎ 505-255-6633; 3416 Central Ave SE; 🕒 6am-11pm Sun-Thu, 6am-midnight Fri & Sat; Juan Tabo Blvd ☎ 505-275-8311; 4501 Juan Tabo Blvd NE; 🕒 6am-10pm Sun-Thu, 6am-11pm Fri & Sat) With seven constantly packed locations, this is the place to go for homemade soups, muffins, bread, innovative main dishes, desserts and ice cream.

Slate Street Café & Wine Loft (Map p890; ☎ 505-243-2210; 515 Slate Ave NW; breakfast dishes $8-12, lunch mains $9-15, dinner mains $13-25; 🕒 7:30am-3pm Mon-Fri, 9am-2pm Sat & Sun, 5-9pm Tue-Thu, 5-10pm Fri & Sat, wine bar 4-10pm Tue-Sat) This downtown establishment in the burgeoning Route 66 Art District is usually packed with people who come to sample the clever Southwestern fare in the café and drink Merlot in the upstairs wine loft. A great new addition to downtown.

La Crepe Michele (Map p890; ☎ 505-242-1251; 400 San Felipe St; lunch mains $8-14, dinner mains $9-25; 🕒 11:30am-2pm Tue-Sun, 6-9pm Tue-Sat) Tucked in the corner of an adobe courtyard near Old Town Plaza, this intimate restaurant is the place to enjoy a quiet romantic dinner. A variety of crepes are served for lunch and dinner, while French specialties, ranging from beef Wellington to barramundi au champagne, change nightly.

Artichoke Café (Map p890; ☎ 505-243-0200; 424 Central Ave SE; lunch mains $8-16, dinner mains $17-30; 🕒 11am-2:30pm Mon-Fri, 5-9pm Mon & Sun, 5:30-10pm Tue-Sat) Voted an Albuquerque favorite many times over, this place takes the best from Italian, French and American cuisine.

Drinking & Entertainment

Satellite Coffee (Map p888; ☎ 505-254-3800; 2300 Central Ave NE) Don't be put off by the hip, space-age appearance. The staff is welcoming and seats filled with all manner of laptop-viewing, java-swilling locals. There are eight locations scattered across town; also try the one in Nob Hill (3513 Central Ave NE).

Copper Lounge (Map p888; ☎ 505-242-7490; 1504 Central Ave SE, 2nd fl; 🕒 Mon-Sat) If a parking lot filled with pickup trucks spells the word 'fun' in your party dictionary, then pull over for the red-brick Copper Lounge where baseball caps and cowboy hats sip beer, play pool and scope the ladies.

Kelly's Brewery (Map p888; ☎ 505-262-2739; 3226 Central Ave SE) Grab a seat at a communal table then settle in for a convivial night of people-watching and beer-drinking at this former Ford dealership and gas station. On warm spring nights, it seems everyone in town is chilling on the sprawling patio.

Nob Hill Bar & Grill (Map p888; ☎ 505-266-4455; 3128 Central Ave SE) Though this place is just up the block from Kelly's Brewery, the mood here is a tad more refined, with fancy cocktails getting all the attention. Try the Berries and Bubbles martini – a dry-ice infusion gives this drink a burbling kick.

Launch Pad (Map p890; ☎ 505-764-8887; www.launchpadrocks.com; 618 Central Ave SW) Indie, reggae, punk and country bands rock the house most nights (though not at the same time). Look for the spaceship on Central Ave.

Popejoy Hall (Map p888; ☎ 505-277-3824, tickets 505-277-4569; www.popejoyhall.com; cnr Central Ave & Cornell St SE) and the historic **KiMo Theatre** (Map p890; ☎ 505-768-3544; 423 Central Ave NW) are the primary venues for big-name national acts, local opera, symphony and theater.

Shopping

If you're looking for Native American crafts and informed salespeople who can give you advice, stop by the **Palms Trading Post** (Map p890; ☎ 505-247-8504; 1504 Lomas Blvd NW; 🕑 9am-5:30pm Mon-Sat). Nearby, just off Old Town Plaza, look for discounted and famed Nambe ware at **Luz de Nambé** (Map p890; ☎ 505-242-5699; 328 San Felipe St NW; 🕑 10am-6pm Mon-Sat, 11am-5pm Sun). Just south, **Silver Sun** (Map p890; ☎ 505-246-9692; 2011 Central Ave NW; 🕑 9am-4:30pm) is a reputable spot for turquoise.

For eclectic gifts, head to Nob Hill, east of the university. Park on Central Ave SE or one of the college-named side streets, then take a stroll past the inviting boutiques and specialty stores. **¡Que Chula!** (Map p888; ☎ 505-255-0515; 3410 Central Ave SE) sells bright and funky Mexican imports while **hey jhonny!** (Map p888; ☎ 505-256-9244; 3418b Central Ave SE) displays sophisticated home furnishings and accessories. Around the corner, you'll find artistic fine jewelry at **IMEC** (Map p888; ☎ 505-265-0114; 101 Amherst SE).

Getting There & Around

AIR

Though the **Albuquerque International Sunport** (ABQ; off Map p888; ☎ 505-244-7700; www.cabq.gov/airport; 2200 Sunport Blvd SE) is New Mexico's biggest airport, it's still relatively small. Most major US airlines service Albuquerque, though **Southwest** (☎ 800-435-9792; www.southwest.com) has the largest presence. Cabs to downtown cost $17 to $20; try **Albuquerque Cab** (☎ 505-883-4888) or **Yellow Cab** (☎ 505-247-8888).

BUS

The **Alvarado Transportation Center** (Map p890; 100 1st St SW, cnr Central Ave) houses **ABQ RIDE** (☎ 505-243-7433; www.cabq.gov/transit; 🕑 8am-5pm), the public bus system. It covers most of Albuquerque on weekdays and hits the major tourist spots daily (adult/child $1/35¢; one-day pass $2). Most lines run until 6pm. ABQ RIDE Route 50 connects the airport with downtown (last bus at 8pm weekdays; limited service Saturday). Check website for maps and exact schedules. Route 36 stops near Old Town and the Indian Pueblo Cultural Center.

Greyhound (Map p890; ☎ 505-243-4435, 800-231-2222; www.greyhound.com, 320 1st St SW) is next door, and serves destinations throughout New Mexico. Two buses run daily to Santa Fe ($17) and one daily for Taos ($40 to $44).

Sandia Shuttle (☎ 505-474-5696, 888-775-5696; www.sandiashuttle.com) runs daily shuttles from Albuquerque to many Santa Fe hotels between 9am and 11pm (one way/round-trip $25/45).

TRAIN

The *Southwest Chief* stops daily at Albuquerque's **Amtrak station** (Map p890; ☎ 505-842-9650, 800-872-7245; www.amtrak.com; cnr 1st St & Central Ave), heading east to Kansas City, MO ($131, 17½ hours), and beyond, or west through Flagstaff, AZ ($86, five hours), to Los Angeles, CA (from $98, 16½ hours). Service to Santa Fe ($36, 1½ hours) involves transferring to a bus in Lamy (25 minutes), 18 miles south of Santa Fe.

A commuter line, the **New Mexico Rail Runner Express** (Map p890; www.nmrailrunner.com), shares the station, with eight departures for Santa Fe weekdays (one way/day pass $6/8) and six departures on Saturday (one way/day pass $4/6). The trip takes about 1½ hours.

ALONG I-40

Although you can zip between Albuquerque and Flagstaff, AZ, in less than five hours, the national monuments and pueblos along the way are well worth a visit. For a scenic loop, take Hwy 53 southwest from Grants, which leads to all the following sights, except Acoma. Hwy 602 brings you north to Gallup.

Acoma Pueblo

The dramatic mesa-top 'Sky City' sits 7000ft above sea level and 367ft above the surrounding plateau. One of the oldest continuously inhabited settlements in North America, this place has been home to pottery-making people since the later part of the 11th century. Guided **tours** (adult/senior/child $20/15/10; hourly 8am-3pm mid-Oct–mid-Apr, 8am-5pm mid-Apr–mid-Oct) focusing on their craft leave from the **visitor center** (800-747-0181; http://sccc.acomaskycity.org; photo permit $10) at the bottom of the mesa and take 1¼ hours. From I-40, take exit 102, which is about 60 miles west of Albuquerque, then drive 12 miles south.

El Morro National Monument

The 200ft sandstone outcropping at this **monument** (505-783-4226; www.nps.gov/elmo; adult/child $3/free; 8am-7pm Jun-Aug, 9am-6pm Sep-Oct & Apr-May, 9am-5pm Nov-Mar), also known as 'Inscription Rock,' has been a travelers' oasis for millennia. Thousands of carvings – from petroglyphs in the pueblo at the top (c 1275) to elaborate inscriptions by the Spanish conquistadors and the Anglo pioneers – offer a unique means of tracing history. It's about 38 miles southwest of Grants via Hwy 53.

Zuni Pueblo

The Zuni are known worldwide for their delicately inlaid silverwork, which is sold in stores lining Hwy 53. Inside the **pueblo** (505-782-7238; www.zunitourism.com; 1239 Hwy 53; visitor center free, tours of pueblo $10; 8:30am-5:30pm Mon-Fri, 10:30am-4pm Sat, noon-4pm Sun), walk past stone houses and beehive-shaped mud ovens to the massive **Our Lady of Guadalupe Mission**, featuring impressive kachina murals. The **A:shiwi A:wan Museum & Heritage Center** (505-782-4403; www.ashiwi-museum.org; Ojo Caliente Rd; admission by donation; 9am-5pm Mon-Fri) displays early photos and other tribal artifacts.

The friendly, eight-room **Inn at Halona** (505-782-4547, 800-752-3278; www.halona.com; 23b Pia Mesa Rd; r incl breakfast $79;), decorated with local Zuni arts and crafts, is the only place to stay on the pueblo.

Gallup

Because Gallup serves as the Navajo and Zuni peoples' major trading center, you'll find many trading posts, pawnshops, jewelry stores and crafts galleries in the historic district. It's arguably the best place in New Mexico for top-quality goods at fair prices. Gallup is another classic Route 66 town, with loads of vintage motels and businesses. Contact the **chamber of commerce** (505-722-2228, 800-380-4989; www.thegallupchamber.com; 103 W Hwy 66; 8:30am-5pm Mon-Fri, 10am-4pm Sat) for details.

The town's lodging jewel is **El Rancho** (505-863-9311, 800-543-6351; www.elranchohotel.com; 1000 E Hwy 66; r $76-138, ste $138-148; P). Many of the great actors of the 1940s and '50s stayed here. El Rancho features a superb Southwestern lobby, a restaurant, a bar and an eclectic selection of simple rooms. There's wi-fi in the lobby.

SANTA FE

In Santa Fe, the state capital, it's all about the art. A sizable number of painters, sculptors and photographers live here, hundreds of galleries have set up shop, and more than a dozen museums thrive. The renowned Indian Market has been celebrated for more than 80 years. Against the dramatic backdrop of the Sangre de Cristo range, Santa Fe oozes sophistication, its cosmopolitan stature belying its size. It boasts gourmet restaurants, spas, an opera company and even a ski resort.

Orientation

Cerrillos Rd (I-25 exit 278), a 6-mile strip of hotels and fast-food restaurants, enters town from the south; Paseo de Peralta circles the center of town; St Francis Dr (I-25 exit 282) forms the western border of downtown and turns into Hwy 285, which heads north toward Los Alamos and Taos. Guadalupe St is the main north–south street through downtown. Most downtown restaurants, galleries, museums and sites are either on or east of Guadalupe St and within walking distance of the plaza, in the center of town.

Information

BOOKSTORES

Collected Works (505-988-4226; 202 Galisteo St) A good selection of regional travel books.

Travel Bug (505-992-0418; www.mapsofnewmexico.com; 839 Paseo de Peralta;) Huge selection of guidebooks and maps.

EMERGENCY & MEDICAL SERVICES

Police (☎ 505-428-3700; 2515 Camino Entrada)
St Vincent's Hospital (☎ 505-983-3361; 455 St Michael's Dr; 24hr emergency)

INTERNET ACCESS

New Mexico Tourism Department (☎ 505-827-7400; www.newmexico.org; 491 Old Santa Fe Trail; 8:30am-5:30pm) Free internet access.
Santa Fe Public Library (☎ 505-955-6781; 145 Washington Ave) Reserve up to an hour of free access.
Travel Bug (☎ 505-992-0418; www.mapsofnewmexico.com; 839 Paseo de Peralta;) Free wi-fi and internet access from onsite terminals.

INTERNET RESOURCES

New Mexican (☎ 505-983-3303; www.santafenewmexican.com) Daily paper with breaking news.
Santa Fe Chamber (www.santafechamber.com) Listings and links for local businesses.
Santa Fe Information (www.santafe.org) Official online visitors guide.
Santa Fe Reporter (☎ 505-988-5541; www.sfreporter.com) Free alternative weekly; culture section has thorough listings of what's going on.

POST

Post office (☎ 505-988-2239; 120 S Federal Pl)

TOURIST INFORMATION

New Mexico Tourism Department (☎ 505-827-7400, 800-545-2070; www.newmexico.org; 491 Old Santa Fe Trail; 8:30am-5:30pm) Has brochures, a hotel reservation line, free coffee and free internet access.
Public Lands Information Center (☎ 505-438-7542, 505-954-2002; www.publiclands.org; 301 Dinosaur Trail, just south of the intersection of Cerillos Rd and I-25; 8:30am-4:30pm Mon-Fri) Lots of maps and information.

Sights

Art enthusiasts coming for the weekend may want to arrive early on Friday to take advantage of the evening's free admission policies at many museums.

Possessing the world's largest collection of her work, the **Georgia O'Keeffe Museum** (☎ 505-946-1000; www.okeeffemuseum.org; 217 Johnson St; adult/senior/child $10/8/free, free Fri 5-8pm; 10am-5pm, to 8pm Fri) features the artist's paintings of flowers, bleached skulls and adobe architecture. Tours of O'Keeffe's house (p899) require advance reservations.

Canyon Road (www.canyonroadarts.com) is the epicenter of the city's upscale art scene. More than 100 galleries, studios, shops and restaurants line the narrow – but long – road. Look for Santa Fe School masterpieces, rare Native American antiquities and wild contemporary work. The area buzzes with activity during early-evening art openings on Friday.

The **Museum of New Mexico** (www.museumofnewmexico.org; 1 museum $9, 4-day pass to all 4 museums $20, children under 16 free, free Fri 5-8pm; 10am-8pm Fri, 10am-5pm Sat-Thu, closed Mon winter), which celebrated its centennial in 2009, administers four museums around town. On the plaza, the adobe **Palace of the Governors** (☎ 505-476-5100; 105 W Palace Ave) – dating from the 1600s – displays a handful of regional relics, but most of its holdings are now shown in an adjacent exhibit space called the **New Mexico History Museum** (113 Lincoln Ave), a glossy, 96,000-sq-ft expansion that opened in 2009. Inside, you can press handprints on a mock cliff wall to hear Native American stories or stop by a 1950s-era office to learn 'classified' info about the once-secret city of Los Alamos. Just down the street, there's fine art at the third of New Mexico's four museums, the **New Mexico Museum of Art** (☎ 505-476-5072; 107 W Palace Ave), while a short drive to Museum Hill leads to the enlightening **Museum of Indian Arts & Culture** (☎ 505-476-1250; 710 Camino Lejo) and the fascinating **Museum of International Folk Art** (☎ 505-476-1200; 706 Camino Lejo).

St Francis Cathedral (☎ 505-982-5619; 131 Cathedral Pl; 8:30am-5pm) houses the oldest Madonna statue in North America.

In 1937, Mary Cabot established the **Wheelwright Museum of the American Indian** (☎ 505-982-4636; www.wheelwright.org; 704 Camino Lejo; admission free; 10am-5pm Mon-Sat, 1-5pm Sun), part of Museum Hill, to showcase Navajo ceremonial art. While its strength continues to be Navajo exhibits, it now includes contemporary Native American art and historical artifacts as well.

Activities

The Pecos Wilderness and Santa Fe National Forest, east of town, have over 1000 miles of **hiking** trails, several of which lead to 12,000ft peaks. Summer storms are frequent, so prepare for hikes by checking weather reports. For maps and details, contact the Public Lands Information Center (left).

The **Santa Fe Ski Area** (☎ 505-982-4429, snow report 505-983-9155; www.skisantafe.com; lift ticket adult/child $58/46; 9am-4pm) is a half-hour drive from the plaza up Hwy 475. From the 12,000ft summit

SCENIC DRIVES: NEW MEXICO'S BEST

The following four drives are accessible, historically and culturally significant, and all exude a certain undeniable awesomeness. For details and a map, see www.newmexico.org/explore/scenic_byways/index.php.

Billy the Kid Scenic Byway (www.billybyway.com) This mountain-and-valley loop in southeastern New Mexico swoops past Billy the Kid's stomping grounds, Smokey Bear's gravesite and the orchard-lined Hondo Valley. From Roswell, take Hwy 380 west.

Santa Fe Trail to Enchanted Circle (www.byways.org, www.enchantedcircle.org) This geographically diverse, if indirect, route from Santa Fe to Taos offers rolling plains, the Santa Fe Trail, hot springs, Wild West towns, a mountain lake, towering mountains and a final cruise past Kit Carson's one-time digs. From Santa Fe, take I-25 north, following it 140 miles to Hwy 58. Follow Hwy 58 west through Cimarron, continuing into the mountains. Pick up Hwy 64 south to Taos.

Trail of the Mountain Spirits (www.tmsbyway.com) The highlight of this southwestern New Mexico trip is a twisting drive from spurs-and-boots Silver City through the Gila National Forest, anticipation building as you approach the mysterious Gila Cliff Dwellings. From Deming, take Hwy 180 north to Silver City then continue north on Hwy 15.

Turquoise Trail (www.turquoisetrail.org) The Turquoise Trail, a scenic back route between Tijeras, near Albuquerque, and Santa Fe, was a major trade route for several thousand years. Today it rolls past art galleries, shops (with turquoise jewelry) and a mining museum. From I-40, follow Hwy 14 north to I-25.

you can admire 80,000 sq miles of desert and mountains.

Busloads of people head up to the Taos Box (p900) for white-water river running, but there are also mellow float trips throughout New Mexico and overnight guided rafting trips. Contact **New Wave River Trips** (☎ 505-984-1444, 800-984-1444; www.newwaverafting.com) and stay cool on trips through the Rio Grande Gorge (adult/child half-day $52/42, full day $90/75), the wild Taos Box (full day $115), or the Rio Chama Wilderness (three days $500).

The Japanese-style **10,000 Waves** (☎ 505-982-9304; www.tenthousandwaves.com; 3451 Hyde Park Rd; communal tubs $19, private tubs per person $29-49; 🕑 2pm-10:30pm Tue, 9am-10:30pm Wed-Mon Jul-Oct, varies slightly Nov-Jun), with landscaped grounds concealing eight attractive tubs in a smooth Zen design, offers waterfalls, cold plunges, and hot and dry saunas.

Mellow Velo (☎ 505-995-8356; 638 Old Santa Fe Trail) rents bikes, has information about regional trails and does guided rides.

Courses

If you develop a love for New Mexican cuisine, try cooking lessons at the **Santa Fe School of Cooking** (☎ 505-983-4511; www.santafeschoolofcooking.com; 116 W San Francisco St). Classes, with over 25 options including traditional New Mexican and Southwestern breakfast, are typically between 1½ and three hours long and cost $42 to $80, including the meal.

Santa Fe for Children

The **Santa Fe Children's Museum** (☎ 505-989-8359; www.santafechildrensmuseum.org; 1050 Old Pecos Trail; admission $9; 🕑 10am-5pm Wed & Sat, noon-8pm Thu, 9am-5pm Fri, noon-5pm Sun Sep-May, 10am-5pm Tue Jun-Aug; 👶) features hands-on exhibits on science and art for young children. The museum runs daily programs tackling subjects like solar energy and printmaking.

The **Santa Fe Southern Railway** (☎ 505-989-8600; www.thetraininsantafe.com; 410 S Guadalupe St; 👶) runs excursions on restored railcars. Its four-hour daytime trips (adult/child from $32/18), departing 11am Friday and Saturday, venture through the high desert and are pulled by working freight trains. Reservations are recommended.

Festivals & Events

Santa Fe's biggest festivals:

Spanish Market (☎ 505-982-2226; www.spanishmarket.org) In late July, traditional Spanish colonial arts, from *retablos* (paintings on wooden panels) and *bultos* (wooden carvings of religious figures), to handcrafted furniture and metalwork, make this juried show an artistic extravaganza.

Santa Fe Indian Market (☎ 505-983-5220; www.swaia.org) Typically held the weekend after the third Thursday in August, this event draws the country's finest Native American artisans to the plaza – and tens of thousands of visitors.

Santa Fe Fiestas (☎ 505-988-7575) Two weeks of events in early September, including concerts, dances and parades.

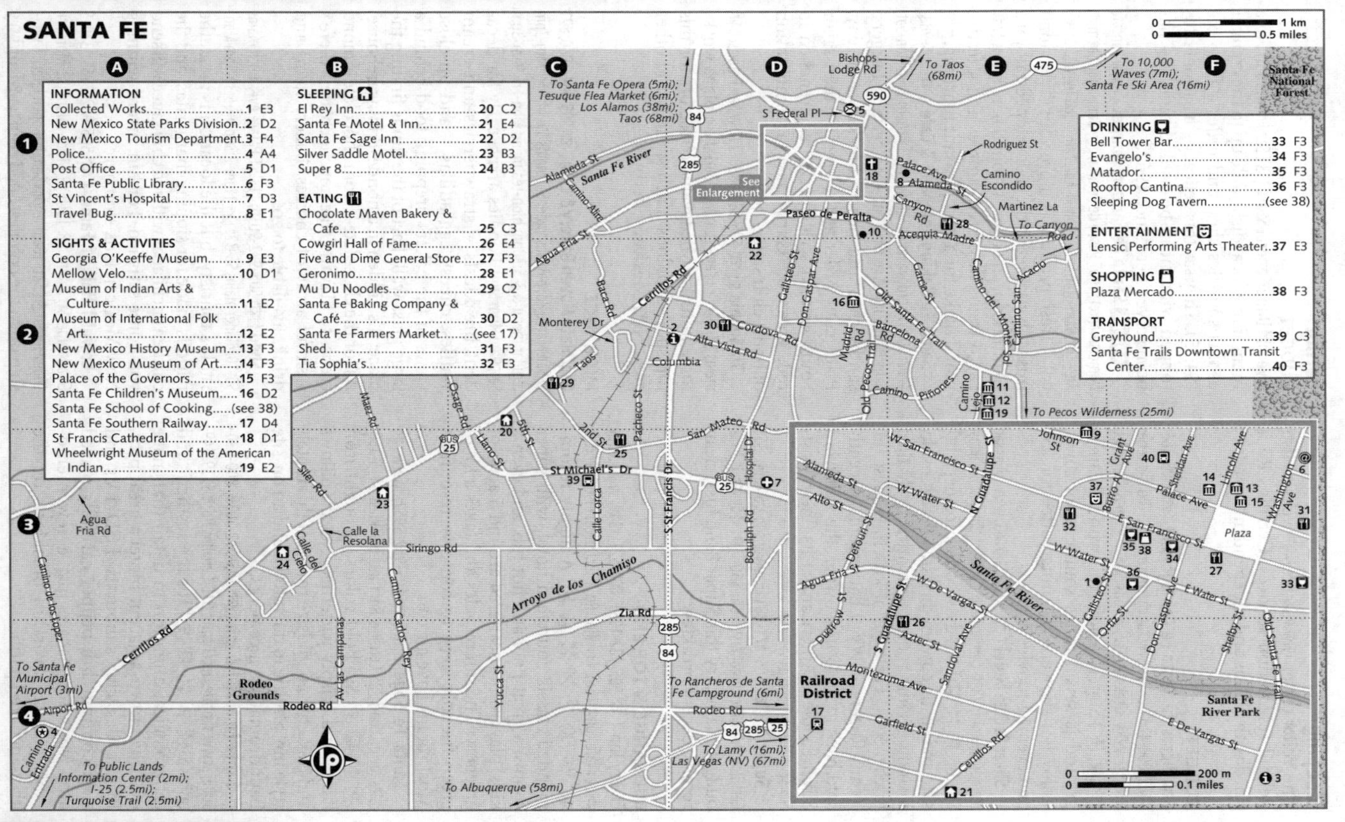
SANTA FE
INFORMATION
Collected Works 1 E3
New Mexico State Parks Division 2 D2
New Mexico Tourism Department 3 F4
Police 4 A4
Post Office 5 D1
Santa Fe Public Library 6 F3
St Vincent's Hospital 7 D3
Travel Bug 8 E1
SIGHTS & ACTIVITIES
Georgia O'Keeffe Museum 9 E3
Mellow Velo 10 D1
Museum of Indian Arts & Culture 11 E2
Museum of International Folk Art 12 E2
New Mexico History Museum 13 F3
New Mexico Museum of Art 14 F3
Palace of the Governors 15 F3
Santa Fe Children's Museum 16 D2
Santa Fe School of Cooking (see 38)
Santa Fe Southern Railway 17 D4
St Francis Cathedral 18 D1
Wheelwright Museum of the American Indian 19 E2
SLEEPING
El Rey Inn 20 C2
Santa Fe Motel & Inn 21 E4
Santa Fe Sage Inn 22 D2
Silver Saddle Motel 23 B3
Super 8 24 B3
EATING
Chocolate Maven Bakery & Cafe 25 C3
Cowgirl Hall of Fame 26 E4
Five and Dime General Store 27 F3
Geronimo 28 E1
Mu Du Noodles 29 C2
Santa Fe Baking Company & Café 30 D2
Santa Fe Farmers Market (see 17)
Shed 31 F3
Tia Sophia's 32 E3
DRINKING
Bell Tower Bar 33 F3
Evangelo's 34 F3
Matador 35 F3
Rooftop Cantina 36 F3
Sleeping Dog Tavern (see 38)
ENTERTAINMENT
Lensic Performing Arts Theater 37 E3
SHOPPING
Plaza Mercado 38 F3
TRANSPORT
Greyhound 39 C3
Santa Fe Trails Downtown Transit Center 40 F3
To Santa Fe Opera (5mi); Tesuque Flea Market (6mi); Los Alamos (38mi); Taos (68mi)
To Taos (68mi)
To 10,000 Waves (7mi); Santa Fe Ski Area (16mi)
Santa Fe National Forest
To Pecos Wilderness (25mi)
To Canyon Road
To Rancheros de Santa Fe Campground (6mi)
To Lamy (16mi); Las Vegas (NV) (67mi)
To Albuquerque (58mi)
To Public Lands Information Center (2mi); I-25 (2.5mi); Turquoise Trail (2.5mi)
To Santa Fe Municipal Airport (3mi)
See Enlargement
Santa Fe River
Arroyo de los Chamiso
Rodeo Grounds
Railroad District
Plaza
Santa Fe River Park
Cerrillos Rd
S St Francis Dr
Paseo de Peralta
Old Santa Fe Trail
Old Pecos Trail
Canyon Rd
Camino del Monte Sol
Rodeo Rd
Airport Rd
Camino Carlos Rey
Siringo Rd
Zia Rd
Yucca St
St Michael's Dr
Guadalupe St
Alameda St
Agua Fria St
Galisteo St
Don Gaspar Ave
Cordova Rd
Alta Vista Rd
Palace Ave
Washington Ave
Lincoln Ave

Sleeping

The **visitor center** (www.santafe.org) website lists helpful reservation services. Cerrillos Rd is lined with chains and independent motels.

BUDGET

Rancheros de Santa Fe Campground (☎ 505-466-3482, 800-426-9259; www.rancheros.com; 736 Old Las Vegas Hwy; tent/RV sites $21/37, cabins $45; mid-Mar–Oct;) Superfriendly, this wooded campground is seven miles southeast of town. Enjoy hot showers, morning coffee for 25¢ and evening movies.

Silver Saddle Motel (☎ 505-471-7663; www.silversaddlemotelllc.com; 2810 Cerrillos Rd; r incl continental breakfast $40-63;) Shady wooden arcades outside and rustic cowboy-inspired decor inside, including some rooms with attractively tiled kitchenettes. For a bit of kitsch, request the Kenny Rogers or Wyatt Earp rooms. Recently sold back to its former owner, the well-worn Silver Saddle is Americana at its finest. Costs $5 for Fido to stay.

Super 8 (☎ 505-471-8811; www.super8.com; 358 Cerrillos Rd; r incl breakfast from $50;) For budget chains, try this Super 8: no fuss, clean rooms, decent breakfast.

MIDRANGE & TOP END

El Rey Inn (☎ 505-982-1931, 800-521-1349; www.elreyinnsantafe.com; 1862 Cerrillos Rd; r incl breakfast $99-190, ste $150-230;) A highly recommended classic courtyard hotel, with super rooms, a great pool and hot tub, and even a kids' playground scattered around 5 acres of greenery. The inn recycles and takes a lot of green-friendly steps to conserve resources. Most rooms have air con.

Santa Fe Sage Inn (☎ 505-982-5952; www.santafesageinn.com; 725 Cerrillos Rd; r incl breakfast $135-160;) Bold colors, wrought-iron lamps and crisply patterned Navajo pillows and rugs enliven midsize rooms at this motel-style inn. Shuttle to downtown and an on-site Laundromat are nice perks.

Santa Fe Motel & Inn (☎ 505-982-1039, 800-930-5002; www.santafemotel.com; 510 Cerrillos Rd; r $139-149, casitas $154;) It's the aesthetic and technological attention to detail that make this downtown-adjacent motel a great pick. Bright tiles, clay sunbursts, LCD TVs and a welcoming chili pepper carefully placed atop your towels are just a few memorable pluses. Savor hot breakfasts on the kiva-anchored patio.

Eating

BUDGET

Five and Dime General Store (58 E San Francisco St) For a memorable local dish, sidle up to the counter at this sundries shop and order a Frito pie ($4.35). They say this delicacy – a bag of Fritos topped with meat, beans and onions – has been served here since 1962.

our pick **Santa Fe Farmers Market** (www.santafefarmersmarket; 1607 Paseo de Peralta; 7am-noon Sat mid-Apr–Oct, 9am-1pm Sat Nov–mid-Apr, 7am-noon Tue mid-May–Oct) If fresh produce is more your style, don't miss this market at the redeveloped rail yard (Amtrak doesn't come through here but a few cargo trains do). Free samples and a festive mood make for a very pleasant morning.

Santa Fe Baking Company & Café (☎ 505-988-4292; 504 W Cordova Rd; mains $5-10; 6am-8pm Mon-Sat, 6am-6pm Sun) An upbeat café serving burgers, sandwiches and hearty breakfasts all day. Place your order at the counter then savor Southwestern-style specialties drenched in red, green or 'Christmas' (a combination of both) chili sauce.

Tia Sophia's (☎ 505-983-9880; 210 W San Francisco St; mains $7-10; 7am-2pm Mon-Sat) The plaza workforce joins knowledgeable collectors for this top spot's fabulous lunch specials and other great New Mexican offerings.

MIDRANGE

Chocolate Maven Bakery & Cafe (☎ 505-984-1980; 821 W San Mateo Rd; pastries under $5, mains $9-14; 7am-3pm regular menu & 3-5:30pm high-tea menu Mon-Fri, 9am-3pm Sat, 9am-4pm Sun) Foodies arrive early for decadent breakfasts – strawberries-and-cream waffles, cheesy eggsadillas – and up-close views of the bakers prepping food behind a large glass wall. Part of the fun is finding the place; it's hidden in a nondescript warehouse. As for the chocolate – from chocolate almond crepes to Mayan Chile hot chocolate – there's a sinful array of choices. Bakery items and drinks available to go.

Shed (☎ 505-982-9030; 113½ E Palace Ave; lunch mains $6-10, dinner mains $6-32; 11am-2:30pm & 5:30-9pm Mon-Sat) It's touristy, but the location is great, the patio is made for sipping margaritas, and the chicken enchiladas with red chili sauce will send you home satisfied. For fun, award-winning New Mexican fare, stop here.

Cowgirl Hall of Fame (☎ 505-982-2565; 319 S Guadalupe St; mains $8-15; 11am-midnight Mon-Fri, 10am-midnight Sat, 10am-11pm Sun, bar open later) Two-step up to the cobblestoned courtyard and try the salmon tacos, butternut-squash casserole or the BBQ platter – all served with Western-style feminist flair. Youngsters are welcome, with buckets of coloring crayons to draw on the lengthy kids' menu. It also has a perennially popular bar with live music – some say it's the only meat market in town (youngsters perhaps not as welcome).

Mu Du Noodles (☎ 505-983-1411; 1494 Cerrillos Rd; mains $16-22; 🕑 5:30-9pm Tue-Sat, 11am-2pm Sun) Pan-Asian organic dishes, like lamb dumplings, Vietnamese spring rolls and tofu laksa, inspire lines out the door of this cozy contemporary spot; the noodles and specials are recommended, and almost everything has a vegan version.

TOP END

Geronimo (☎ 505-982-1500; 724 Canyon Rd; dishes $28-44; 🕑 5:45-10pm Mon-Thu, 5:45-11pm Fri & Sat) Housed in a 1756 adobe, Geronimo is among the finest and most romantic restaurants in town. Gourmands will be happy to hear that Chef Eric DiStefano has recently returned. The short but diverse menu currently includes fiery sweet chili and honey-grilled prawns and peppery elk tenderloin with applewood-smoked bacon.

Drinking & Entertainment

For a rooftop view with your margarita, try the convivial **Rooftop Cantina** (☎ 505-983-1616; 132 W Water St) perched atop Coyote Café, or ascend five floors to the **Bell Tower Bar** (☎ 505-982-5511; 100 E San Francisco St) at La Fonda, where you can watch one of those patented New Mexico sunsets. Both spots are open seasonally, as long as the cold's not nipping at your toes.

For microbrews and friendly conversation, settle in at the **Sleeping Dog Tavern** (☎ 505-982-4335; 114 W San Francisco St), a low-key gastropub just off the plaza. For a grungier, grumpier crowd, head over to the basement-y confines of divey **Matador** (Galisteo St). Descend the steps near the corner of W San Francisco St, slap on your best frown and open the door.

There's foot-stompin' live music nightly at **Evangelo's** (☎ 505-982-9014; 200 W San Francisco St) and the sounds of rock, blues, jazz and Latin combos spill into the street. You'll also find live music and good drinking most nights at the Cowgirl Hall of Fame (opposite).

For live performances and movies, see what's doing at the **Lensic Performing Arts Theater** (☎ 505-988-1234; www.lensic.org; 211 W San Francisco St). This beautifully renovated 1930s movie house is the city's premier venue for performing arts. Continuing its film history, it also holds $5 classic-movie screenings.

At the **Santa Fe Opera** (☎ 505-986-5900, 800-280-4654; www.santafeopera.org; tickets $26-188; 🕑 Jul & Aug) you can be a decked-out socialite or show up in cowboy boots and jeans; it doesn't matter. Opera fans (and those who've never attended an opera in their lives) come to Santa Fe for this alone: an architectural marvel, with views of wind-carved sandstone wilderness crowned with sunsets and moonrises, and at center stage internationally renowned vocal talent performing masterworks of aria and romance. The opera is 7 miles north of Santa Fe. Follow I-285 north to exit 168. Turn left off the ramp then right onto Opera Dr and continue 1.4 miles.

Shopping

Offering carved howling coyotes, turquoise jewelry and fine art, Santa Fe attracts shoppers of all budgets.

Plaza Mercado (112 W San Francisco St) A swish spot packed with art galleries, antique stores and Santa Fe–style clothing.

Pueblo of Tesuque Flea Market (Hwy 84/285; 🕑 8am-4pm Fri-Sun Mar-Nov) This outdoor market a few minutes' drive north of Santa Fe at Tesuque Pueblo offers deals on high-quality rugs, jewelry, art and clothing.

Getting There & Around

At press time, **Santa Fe Municipal Airport** (SAF; ☎ 505-955-2900; wwwsantafenm.gov; 121 Aviation Dr) was offering one daily flight to/from Dallas–Fort Worth (DFW) via **American Eagle** (☎ 800-433-7300; www.aa.com). By 2010, there should be two daily American Eagle flights to/from DFW, plus one daily flight to/from Los Angeles (LAX).

Greyhound (☎ 505-471-0008; www.greyhound.com; 858 St Michael's Dr) has two daily buses to Albuquerque ($20, 80 minutes) and one daily bus to Taos ($27 to $30, 95 minutes). **Twin Hearts Shuttle** (☎ 800-654-9456) runs between Santa Fe and the Albuquerque Sunport ($25) and Taos ($40); make reservations in advance.

Amtrak (☎ 800-872-7245; www.amtrak.com) stops at Lamy; buses continue 17 miles to Santa Fe.

Santa Fe Trails Downtown Transit Center (☎ 505-955-2001; www.santafenm.gov; 🕑 6am-10:45pm Mon-Fri,

8am-7:40pm Sat, 9:30am-6:15pm Sun, times may vary slightly) provides local bus service (adult/senior and child $1/50¢ per ride; day pass $2/1).

AROUND SANTA FE

Don't get too comfy in Santa Fe, because there's lots to see nearby.

Pueblos

North of Santa Fe is the heart of Puebloan lands. The **Eight Northern Pueblos** (ENIPC; ☎ 505-747-1593) publish the excellent and free *Eight Northern Indian Pueblos Visitors Guide*, available at area visitor centers.

Eight miles west of Pojoaque along Hwy 502, the ancient **San Ildefonso Pueblo** (☎ 505-455-3549; per vehicle $7, camera/sketching/video permits $10/25/20; 8am-5pm daily, visitor center closed Sat & Sun in winter) was the home of Maria Martinez, who in 1919 revived a distinctive traditional black-on-black pottery style. Several exceptional potters (including Maria's direct descendants) work in the pueblo; stop at the **Maria Poveka Martinez Museum** (admission free; 8am-4pm Mon-Fri), which sells the pueblo's pottery.

Las Vegas

Not to be confused with the glittery city to the west in Nevada, this Vegas is one of the loveliest towns in New Mexico and one of the largest and oldest towns east of the Sangre de Cristo Mountains. Its eminently strollable downtown has a pretty Old Town Plaza and some 900 historic buildings listed in the National Register of Historic Places. Its architecture is a mix of Southwestern and Victorian. Ask for a walking-tour brochure from the **chamber of commerce** (☎ 505-425-8631, 800-832-5947; www.lasvegasnewmexico.com; 701 Grand Ave; 9am-5pm Mon-Fri).

Built in 1882 and carefully remodeled a century later, the recently expanded **Plaza Hotel** (☎ 505-425-3591, 800-328-1882; www.plazahotel-nm.com; 230 Plaza; r/ste incl breakfast from $89/159;) is Las Vegas' most celebrated and historic lodging. The elegant building now offers 72 comfortable accommodations. Choose between Victorian-style, antique-filled rooms in the original building or bright, monochromatic rooms in the new adjoining wing.

Indulge in a good New Mexican meal at **Estella's Café** (☎ 505-454-0048; 148 Bridge St; mains lunch under $10, dinner $10-12; 11am-3pm Mon-Wed, 11am-8pm Thu & Fri, 7am-2pm Sat). Estella's devoted patrons treasure their homemade red chili, *menudo* (tripe and grits) and scrumptious enchiladas.

From the plaza, Hot Springs Blvd leads 5 miles north to Gallinas Canyon and the massive **Montezuma Castle**, an eye-popping structure on the flanks of the Sangre de Cristo Mountains; once a hotel, it's now the United World College of the West. Along the road there, you can soak in a series of natural **hot spring pools**.

Los Alamos

The top-secret Manhattan Project sprang to life in Los Alamos in 1943, turning a sleepy mesa-top village into a busy, community-wide laboratory. Here, in the 'town that didn't exist,' the nation's leading scientists developed the first atomic bomb in almost total secrecy. Today you'll encounter a fascinating dynamic in which souvenir T-shirts emblazoned with atomic explosions and 'La Bomba' wine are sold next to books on pueblo history and wilderness hiking.

You can't actually visit the **Los Alamos National Laboratory**, where the first atomic bomb was conceived, but you can visit the well-designed, interactive **Bradbury Science Museum** (☎ 505-667-4444; www.lanl.gov/museum; cnr Central Ave & 15th; admission free; 10am-5pm Tue-Sat, 1-5pm Sun & Mon;), which covers atomic history. A short film traces the community's wartime history and reveals a few fascinating secrets. Don't miss the small **Los Alamos Historical Museum** (☎ 505-662-6272; www.losalamoshistory.org; 1921 Juniper St; admission free; 10am-4pm Mon-Sat, 1-4pm Sun winter, 9:30am-4:30pm Mon-Sat, 11am-5pm Sun summer) on the nearby grounds of the former Los Alamos Ranch School – an outdoorsy school for boys that closed when the scientists arrived. Displays highlight the school's history (surprisingly interesting), atomic culture artifacts and the social history of life 'on the hill' during the secret project. Pick up one of its great downtown walking-tour pamphlets or download it from the website.

Bandelier National Monument

Because of its convenient location and spectacular landscape, **Bandelier** (☎ 505-672-3861; www.nps.gov/band; per vehicle $12; 8am-6pm summer, 9am-5:30pm spring/fall, 9am-4:30pm winter) is an excellent choice for folks interested in ancient pueblos. The adventurous can climb four ladders to reach an ancient cave dwelling inhabited by Ancestral Puebloans, who lived here until the mid-1500s. Although none of the sites are restored, there are almost 50 sq miles of protected canyons offering backpacking trails and camping at **Juniper Campground** (campsites $12), set among the pines near the monument entrance. It has about 100 campsites and is first-come, first-served, though rarely full.

Abiquiu

The tiny community of Abiquiu (sounds like 'barbecue'), on Hwy 84 about 45 minutes' drive northwest of Santa Fe, is famous because the renowned artist Georgia O'Keeffe lived and painted here permanently from 1949 until her death in 1986. With the Chama River flowing through farmland and spectacular rock landscape, the ethereal setting continues to attract artists, and many live and work in Abiquiu. O'Keeffe's adobe house is open for limited visits, and the Georgia O'Keeffe Museum (p893) offers one-hour **tours** (☎ 505-685-4539; www.okeeffemuseum.org) on Tuesday, Thursday and Friday from March to November ($30), and also on Saturdays from June to October ($40), often booked months in advance.

A retreat center on 21,000 acres at the foot of the Sangre de Cristo Mountains (and a shooting location for the movie *City Slickers*), **Ghost Ranch** (☎ 505-685-4333, 877-804-4678; www.ghostranch.org; campsites $19, RV sites $22-28, dm incl breakfast $50, r with private/shared bath incl breakfast from $80/50) is a spectacular spot with basic lodging and cafeteria-style meals. No phones or TVs in the rooms.

The lovely **Abiquiú Inn** (☎ 505-685-4378, 888-735-2902; www.abiquiuinn.com; Hwy 84; RV sites $18, r $140-200, ste $170, 4-person casitas $190; ⊠ ❄) is a sprawling collection of shaded adobes; spacious casitas have kitchenettes. Wi-fi is available in the lobby and the on-site restaurant, **Cafe Abiquiú** (breakfast mains under $10, lunch & dinner mains $10-20; 7am-9pm). The lunch and dinner menu includes numerous fish dishes, from chipotle honey-glazed salmon to trout tacos.

Ojo Caliente

At 140 years old, **Ojo Caliente Mineral Springs Resort & Spa** (☎ 505-583-2233, 800-222-9162; www.ojospa.com; 50 Los Baños Rd; r $139, cottages $199-239, ste $269-329; ⊠) is one of the country's oldest health resorts. Located 50 miles north of Santa Fe on Hwy 285, the newly renovated resort offers 10 soaking pools with several combinations of minerals. If you're feeling out-of-sorts, try a cup of the Lithia water, rumored to help relieve the blues. In addition to the pleasant, if nothing special, historic hotel rooms, the resort has added 12 plush, boldly colored suites with kiva fireplaces and private soaking tubs, and 11 New Mexican–style cottages. Wi-fi is available in the lobby. The on-site **Artesian Restaurant** (breakfast mains $5-10, lunch mains $9-10, dinner mains $11-26; 7:30am-10:30am, 11:30am-2:30pm & 5-9pm Sun-Thu, 5-9:30pm Fri & Sat) prepares organic and local ingredients with aplomb.

Cuba

Set in 360 beautiful acres in the Nacimiento Mountains, the friendly **Circle A Ranch Hostel** (☎ 505-289-3350; www.circlearanchhostel.com; dm $25, r $40-55, ste $65, yurt bed/whole yurt $30/75; May–mid-Oct;), just off Hwy 550, is a gem. The lovely old adobe lodge, with exposed beams, grassy grounds, hiking trails and a classic kitchen, is a peaceful place to hang out. Choose between private bedrooms (some with quilts and iron bedsteads), shared bunkrooms and a yurt. It also offers work exchanges.

TAOS

Nestled in the snow-peaked Sangre de Cristo Mountains, this small town has a big reputation. Isolated Taos boasts – with a pleasant but ever-so-disinterested tone – a long history of luring artists with its fabled clear light, a stunning multistory adobe pueblo and a magnificent mountain setting.

It's an eccentric place, full of bohemians and mainstream dropouts, alternative-energy aficionados, fine chefs, acculturated B&B owners and old-time Hispanic families who still farm hay fields. It's rural and worldly, a place where grazing horses and a disproportionate number of artists hold equal sway.

Information

Taos Vacation Guide (www.taosvacationguide.org) Great resource with lots of easy-to-navigate links.

Visitor center (☎ 575-758-3873, 800-732-8267; www.destinationtaos.com; 1139 Paseo del Pueblo Sur; 9am-5pm;)

Wired? (☎ 575-751-9473; 705 Felicidad Lane; 8am-6pm Mon-Fri, 8:30am-6pm Sat & Sun) Coffee shop with internet access ($7 per hour). Free wi-fi for customers.

Sights

Four miles south of Taos in Ranchos de Taos, the oft-photographed **San Francisco de Asís Church** (☎ 575-758-2754; St Francis Plaza; 9am-4pm Mon-Fri) was built in the mid-18th century but didn't open until 1815. It's been memorialized in Georgia O'Keeffe paintings and Edward Weston photographs.

At 650ft above the Rio Grande, the steel **Rio Grande Gorge Bridge** is the second-highest suspension bridge in the US; the view down is eye-popping. For the best pictures of the bridge itself, park at the rest area on the western end of the span. Just 1.5 miles west of the bridge is the fascinating community of **Earthships** (☎ 575-751-0462; www.earthship.net; Hwy 64; adult/child under 12 $5/free; 🕑 10am-4pm), with self-sustaining, environmentally savvy houses built with recycled materials that are completely off the grid. You can also stay overnight in one (see right).

Taos Historic Museums (☎ 575-758-0505; www.taoshistoricmuseums.com; adult/child individual museums $8/4, both museums $12; 🕑 10am-5pm Mon-Sat, noon-5pm Sun) runs two great houses: the **Blumenschein Home** (222 Ledoux St), with spectacular art, and the **Martínez Hacienda** (708 Lower Ranchitos Rd), a 21-room colonial trader's former home dating from 1804.

The **Millicent Rogers Museum** (☎ 575-758-2462; www.millicentrogers.org; 1504 Millicent Rogers Museum Rd; adult/child $10/6; 🕑 10am-5pm, closed Mon Nov-Mar), is filled with pottery, jewelry, baskets and textiles, and has one of the best collections of Native American and Spanish-Colonial art in the US.

Housed in a historic mid-19th-century adobe compound, the **Harwood Museum of Art** (☎ 575-758-9826; www.harwoodmuseum.org; 238 Ledoux St; adult/senior & student $8/7; 🕑 10am-5pm Tue-Sat, noon-5pm Sun) features paintings, drawings, prints, sculpture and photography by northern New Mexico artists, both historical and contemporary.

Although the collection of artifacts at the **Kit Carson Home & Museum** (☎ 575-758-4613; www.kitcarsonhome.com; 113 Kit Carson Rd; admission $5; 🕑 9am-5pm) is pretty light, you can watch an interesting 20-minute History Channel video about the famed frontiersman's life and explore his one-story home. For a more interesting – if haphazard – collection of period artifacts, walk across the street to the tiny museum inside El Rincón Trading Post (opposite).

Activities

During the summer, **white-water rafting** is popular in the Taos Box, the steep-sided cliffs that frame the Rio Grande. Day-long trips begin at around $100 per person; contact the visitor center for local outfitters. **Hiking** options are plentiful; trailheads line the road to the ski valley.

With a peak elevation of 11,819ft and a 2612ft vertical drop, **Taos Ski Valley** (☎ 866-968-7386; www.skitaos.org; lift ticket adult/teen 13-17 & senior/child $65/55/38) offers some of the most challenging skiing in the US and yet remains low-key and relaxed. Once exclusive to skiers, the resort now allows snowboarders on its slopes.

Sleeping

Abominable Snowmansion (☎ 575-776-8298; www.abominablesnowmansion.com; 476 State Hwy 150, Arroyo Seco; campsites $12, dm $22, tipis $34, cabins $37, r with shared/private bath $52/57; P ⊠ 💻 wi-fi) About 9 miles northeast of Taos, this well-worn and welcoming hostel is a cozy mountainside alternative to central Taos. A big, round fireplace warms guests in wintertime, and kitschy tipis are available in summer. There's a $3 discount on dorms and private rooms for HI members.

Sun God Lodge (☎ 575-758-3162, 800-821-2437; www.sungodlodge.com; 919 Paseo del Pueblo Sur; r $69-102, ste $145; P ✤ wi-fi) The hospitable folks at this well-run two-story motel can fill you in on local history as well as the craziest bar in town. Rooms are clean – if a bit dark – and decorated with low-key Southwestern flair. The highlight is the lush-green courtyard dappled with twinkling lights, a scenic spot for a picnic or enjoying the sunset. Wi-fi works best in the courtyard. Located 1.5 miles south of the plaza, the Sun God is a great budget choice.

Historic Taos Inn (☎ 575-758-2233, 888-518-8267; www.taosinn.com; 125 Paseo del Pueblo Norte; r $75-275; P ⊠ wi-fi) Even though it's not the plushest place in town and the front desk was a tad flakey when we visited, it's still fabulous, with a cozy lobby, a garden for the restaurant, heavy wooden furniture, a sunken fireplace and lots of live local music at its famed Adobe Bar. Parts of this landmark date to the 1800s. Wi-fi available in the lobby and some rooms.

Earthship Rentals (☎ 575-751-0462; www.earthship.net; Hwy 64; r $110-190) Experience an off-grid overnight in a boutique-chic, solar-powered dwelling. A cross between organic Gaudí architecture and space-age fantasy, these sustainable dwellings are put together using recycled tires, aluminum cans and sand, with rain catchment and gray-water systems to minimize their footprint. Half-buried in a valley surrounded by mountains, they *could* be hastily camouflaged alien vessels – you never know.

Eating

Taos Pizza Out Back (☎ 575-758-3112; 712 Paseo del Pueblo Norte; slices $3.50-7, whole pies $13-27; 🕑 11am-10pm daily May-Sep, 11am-9pm Sun-Thu, 11am-10pm Fri & Sat Oct-Apr) Warning: these pizza pies may be cruelly habit-forming. Located behind another business (no, it's not Australian), it uses organic ingredients and serves epicurean combos like a Portabella Pie with sun-dried tomatoes and camembert. Slices are the size of a small country.

our pick **Taos Diner** (☎ 575-758-2374; 908 Paseo del Pueblo Norte; mains $4-12; 🕑 7am-2:30pm) It's with some reluctance that we share the existence of this marvelous place, a mountain-town diner with wood-paneled walls, tattooed waitresses, fresh-baked biscuits and coffee cups that are never less than half-full. This is diner grub at its finest, prepared with a Southwestern, organic spin. Mountain men, scruffy jocks, solo diners and happy tourists – everyone's welcome here. We like the Copper John's eggs with a side of green chili sauce.

Orlando's (☎ 575-751-1450; 1114 Don Juan Valdez Lane; mains $8-11; 🕑 10:30am-3pm & 5-9pm) After a morning at the Gorge, stop here on your return for Taos' best New Mexican food, period. Those chicken enchiladas and huge burritos are all dressed to perfection and served up in the beautiful dining room.

Joseph's Table (☎ 575-751-4512; 108A S Taos Plaza; mains $26-38; 🕑 11:30am-2:30pm Fri-Mon Jun-Sep, 5:30-10pm daily) Inside the Hotel La Fonda, Chef Joseph Wrede doles out unique and creative Southwestern dishes with an emphasis on ingredients from local farms. The dining room sprouts pussywillow chandeliers and a lush flowery mural painted by his wife and his mother. Couples should go for a 'loveshack,' one of the cozy, romantic window booths.

Also good, if a bit touristy, is perennial breakfast fave **Michael's Kitchen** (☎ 575-758-4178; 304 Paseo del Pueblo Norte; mains $7-16; 🕑 7am-2:30pm).

Drinking

Adobe Bar (☎ 575-758-2233; Historic Taos Inn, 125 Paseo del Pueblo Norte) Everybody's welcome in 'the living room of Taos.' And there's something about it: the chairs, the Taos Inn's history, the casualness, the tequila. The packed streetside patio has some of the state's finest margaritas, along with an eclectic lineup of great live music and never a cover.

Alley Cantina (☎ 575-758-2121; 121 Teresina Lane) It's a bit-cooler-than-thou, but maybe 'tude happens when you inhabit the oldest building in town. Catch live rock, blues, hip-hop or jazz almost nightly.

Eske's Brew Pub & Eatery (☎ 575-758-1517; 106 Des Georges Lane) For a communal vibe grab an outdoor table at easygoing Eske's and order up a house specialty microbrew. Maybe an Artist Ale? Or a Taos Green Chile Beer? This crowded hangout spotlights local bands, from acoustic guitar to jazz.

DON'T MISS: TAOS PUEBLO

Built around AD 1450 and continuously inhabited ever since, the streamside **Taos Pueblo** (☎ 575-758-1028; www.taospueblo.com; Taos Pueblo Rd; adult/child $10/5, photography or video permit $5; 🕑 8am-4pm Nov-Feb, 8am-4:30pm Mar-Oct, closed for 6 weeks around Feb & Mar) is the largest existing multistoried pueblo structure in the US and one of the best surviving examples of traditional adobe construction.

Shopping

Taos has historically been a mecca for artists, demonstrated by the huge number of galleries and studios in and around town. Indie stores and galleries line the **John Dunn Shops'** (www.johndunnshops.com) pedestrian walkway linking Bent St to Taos Plaza. Here you'll find the well-stocked **Moby Dickens Bookshop**, the welcoming **Steppin' Out** boutique, and the tiny but intriguing **G Robinson Old Prints & Maps** – a treat for cartography geeks.

Even if you're not looking to buy anything, stop by **El Rincón Trading Post** (☎ 575-758-9188; 114 Kit Carson Rd) to browse through the dusty museum of artifacts, an engaging jumble of Native American crafts, jewelry and Old West memorabilia. There's even a detailed discourse on the role of the peyote plant.

Getting There & Away

From Santa Fe, take either the scenic 'high road' along Hwys 76 and 518, with galleries, villages and sites worth exploring, or follow the lovely unfolding Rio Grande landscape on Hwy 68.

Greyhound (☎ 575-758-1144, 800-231-2222; www.greyhound.com; 710h Paseo del Pueblo Sur) has a daily bus service to Albuquerque ($43, three hours) and Santa Fe ($27, 1½ hours).

NORTHWESTERN NEW MEXICO

Dubbed 'Indian Country' for good reason – huge swaths of land fall under the aegis of the Navajo, Pueblo, Zuni, Apache and Laguna tribes – this quadrant of New Mexico showcases remarkable ancient Indian sites alongside modern, solitary Native American settlements.

Farmington & Around

The largest town in New Mexico's northwestern region, Farmington makes a good base from which to explore the Four Corners area. The **visitors bureau** (☎ 505-326-7602, 800-448-1240; www.farmingtonnm.org; Gateway Park, 3041 E Main St; 8am-5pm Mon-Sat) has more information.

Shiprock, a 1700ft-high volcanic plug that rises eerily over the landscape to the west, was a landmark for the Anglo pioneers and is a sacred site to the Navajo.

An ancient pueblo, **Salmon Ruin & Heritage Park** (☎ 505-632-2013; adult/senior/child $3/2/1; 8am-5pm Mon-Fri, 9am-5pm Sat & Sun) features a large village built by the Chaco people in the early 1100s. Abandoned, resettled by people from Mesa Verde and again abandoned before 1300, the site also includes the remains of a homestead, petroglyphs, a Navajo hogan and a wickiup (a rough brushwood shelter). Take Hwy 64 east 11 miles toward Bloomfield.

Fourteen miles northeast of Farmington, the 27-acre **Aztec Ruins National Monument** (☎ 505-334-6174; www.nps.gov/azru; adult/child under 16 $5/free; 8am-5pm Sep-May, 8am-6pm Jun-Aug) features the largest reconstructed kiva in the country, with an internal diameter of almost 50ft. A few steps away, let your imagination wander as you stoop through low doorways and dark rooms inside the West Ruin. In summer, rangers give early-afternoon talks at the c 1100 site about ancient architecture, trade routes and astronomy.

About 35 miles south of Farmington along Hwy 371, the undeveloped **Bisti Badlands & De-Na-Zin Wilderness** is a trippy, surreal landscape of strange, colorful rock formations; desert enthusiasts shouldn't miss it. The Farmington **BLM office** (☎ 505-599-8900; www.nm.blm.gov; 1235 La Plata Hwy; 7:45am-4:30pm Mon-Fri) dispenses information.

The lovely, three-room **Silver River Adobe Inn B&B** (☎ 505-325-8219, 800-382-9251; www.silveradobe.com; 3151 W Main St; r incl breakfast $105-175) offers a peaceful respite among the trees along the San Juan River.

Managing to be both trendy *and* kid-friendly, the hippish **Three Rivers Eatery & Brewhouse** (☎ 505-324-2187; 101 E Main St; mains $8-26; 11am-10pm) has good steaks and pub grub and its own microbrews.

Chama

Nine miles south of the Colorado border, Chama's **Cumbres & Toltec Scenic Railway** (☎ 575-756-2151, 888-286-2737; www.cumbrestoltec.com; late May–mid-Oct) is both the longest (64 miles) and highest (over the 10,015ft-high Cumbres Pass) authentic narrow-gauge steam railroad in the US. It's a beautiful trip, particularly in September and October during the fall foliage, through mountains, canyons and high desert.

Chaco Culture National Historic Park

Featuring massive Ancestral Puebloan buildings set in an isolated high-desert environment, intriguing **Chaco** (per vehicle $8; sunrise-sunset) contains evidence of 5000 years of human occupation. In its prime, the community at Chaco Canyon was a major trading and ceremonial hub for the region – and the city the Puebloan people created here was masterly in its layout and design. Pueblo Bonito is four stories tall and may have had 600 to 800 rooms and kivas. As well as taking the self-guided loop tour, you can hike various **backcountry trails**. For stargazers, there's the **Night Skies** program offered Tuesday, Friday and Saturday evenings April through October. After a ranger-led talk, visitors view starry skies through park telescopes.

The **visitor center** (☎ 505-786-7014; www.nps.gov/chcu; 8am-5pm) is in a remote area approximately 80 miles south of Farmington. **Gallo Campground** (campsites $10) is 1 mile east of the visitor center; no RV sites. Campsites are first-come, first-served.

NORTHEASTERN NEW MEXICO

East of Santa Fe, the lush Sangre de Cristo Mountains give way to high and vast rolling plains. Dusty grasslands stretch to infinity and further – to Texas. Cattle and dinosaur prints dot the landscape, a land of extremes with formerly fiery volcanoes in Capulin and hot springs in Montezuma. Ranching is an economic mainstay, and on many stretches of the road you'll see more cattle than cars.

The Santa Fe Trail, along which pioneer settlers rolled in wagon trains, ran from New Mexico to Missouri. You can still see the wagon ruts in some places off I-25 between Santa Fe and Raton. For a bit of the Old West without a patina of consumer hype, this is the place.

Cimarron

Cimarron once ranked among the rowdiest of Wild West towns; it's name even means 'wild' in Spanish. According to local lore, murder was such an everyday occurrence in the 1870s that peace-and-quiet was newsworthy, one paper going so far as to report: 'Everything is quiet in Cimarron. Nobody has been killed in three days.'

Today, the town is indeed quiet, luring nature-minded travelers who want to enjoy the great outdoors. Driving here to or from Taos, you'll pass through gorgeous **Cimarron Canyon State Park**, a steep-walled canyon with several hiking trails, excellent trout fishing and camping.

Each of the 15 spotless motel rooms at the **Cimarron Inn & RV Park** (☎ 505-376-2268, 800-546-2244; www.cimarroninn.com; Hwy 64; campsites $10, RV sites $30, r $45-110, 6-/12-person cabins $135/240) comes with a Cimarron-related theme, from fishing and hunting to Native American and Will James, a cowboy writer and illustrator. There's a fun rock shower in the ski room. Units range from small singles to cabins that can bunk the extended family. Some have kitchenettes. It's a good budget choice before reaching the more expensive mountain resorts.

Capulin Volcano National Monument

Rising 1300ft above the surrounding plains, **Capulin** (☎ 575-278-2201; www.nps.gov/cavo; per vehicle $5; 🕒 8am-4pm Sep-May, 7:30am-6:30pm Jun-Aug) is the most accessible of several volcanoes in the area. From the visitor center, a 2-mile road spirals up the mountain to a parking lot at the crater rim (8182ft), where trails lead around and into the crater. The entrance is 3 miles north of Capulin village, which itself is 30 miles east of Raton on Hwy 87.

SOUTHWESTERN NEW MEXICO

The Rio Grande Valley unfurls from Albuquerque down to the bubbling hot springs of funky Truth or Consequences. Crops, while plentiful, often grow on a wing and a prayer. Residents are few and far between, except in lively Las Cruces, the state's second-largest city.

I-10 cuts through the Chihuahua Desert, dominated by yucca and agave. This is ranching country, though the cattle are sparse. North of the desert and west of I-25, the rugged Gila National Forest is wild with backpacking and fishing adventures.

Truth or Consequences & Around

An offbeat joie de vivre permeates this funky little town, which was built on the sight of natural hot springs in the 1880s. A bit of the quirkiness stems from the fact that the town changed its name from Hot Springs to Truth or Consequences (or 'T or C') in 1950, after a popular radio program of the same name. Publicity these days comes courtesy of Virgin Galactic CEO Richard Branson, Governor Bill Richardson and other space-travel visionaries driving the development of nearby Spaceport America, scheduled to launch tourists into the great beyond by the end of 2010.

Wander around the hole-in-the-wall cafés, pop into a gallery, check out the engaging mishmash of exhibits at the **Geronimo Springs Museum** (☎ 575-894-6600; www.geronimosprings museum.com; 211 Main St; adult/child $5/2.50; 🕒 9am-5pm Mon-Sat, noon-5pm Sun) and definitely enjoy a soak in a hot-spring spa. The **visitor center** (☎ 575-894-1968, 800-831-9487; www.truthorconsequencesnm.net; 211 Main St; 🕒 9am-4:30pm Mon-Fri, 9am-5pm Sat, noon-5pm Sun) has local listings.

About 60 miles north of town, sandhill cranes and Arctic geese winter in the 90 sq miles of fields and marshes at **Bosque del Apache National Wildlife Refuge** (☎ 575-835-1828; per vehicle $5; State Hwy 1; 🕒 refuge sunrise-sunset, visitor center 7:30am-4pm Mon-Fri, 8am-4:30pm Sat & Sun). There's a visitor center and driving tour.

Many local motels double as spas. Former hostel **Riverbend Hot Springs** (☎ 575-894-7625; www.riverbendhotsprings.com; 100 Austin St; r with shared/private bath $55/75, ste $88, cottages $110; ⊠ ✣ ☰) now offers more traditional motel-style accommodations – no more tipis – from its fantastic perch beside the Rio Grande. Rooms exude a bright, quirky charm, and several units work well for groups. Private hot-spring tubs are available by the hour (guest/nonguest $15/10 for the first hour then $10/5 additional hours), as is a public hot spring pool (guest/nonguest free all day/$10 for the first hour then $5 per hour or $20 per day).

our pick **Blackstone Hotsprings** (☎ 575-894-0894; www.blackstonehotsprings.com; 410 Austin St; r $75-125;), new on the scene, embraces the T or C spirit with an upscale wink, decorating each of its seven rooms in the style of a classic TV show. From the *Jetsons* to the *Golden Girls* to *I Love Lucy*, the decor is simultaneously sassy, chic and comfortable, not to mention right on theme. Best part? Each room comes with its own hot-spring tub so you can fill 'er up then soak to your muscles' content. Built as a U-shaped motor-court motel in the 1930s, the property today uses its central courtyard as a flower-dappled patio. Great digs, and a primo spot for a post-hike soak.

When it comes to food, the upbeat **Happy Belly Deli** (☎ 575-894-3354; 313 N Broadway; mains under $10; 7am-3pm Mon-Fri, 8am-3pm Sat, 8am-noon Sun) draws the morning crowd with fresh breakfast burritos, while the new **Café BellaLuca** (☎ 575-894-9866; 303 Jones St; lunch mains $6-10, dinner mains $10-23; 11am-9pm Mon, Wed & Thu, 11am-10pm Fri & Sat, 10am-8pm Sun) earns raves for its Italian specialties.

Las Cruces & Around

The second-largest city in New Mexico is home to New Mexico State University (NMSU), which keeps things somewhat lively with about 17,000 students. The **visitors bureau** (☎ 575-541-2444, 800-343-7827; www.lascrucescvb.org; 211 N Water St; 8am-5pm Mon-Fri) has information.

For many, a visit to neighboring **Mesilla** is the highlight of their time in Las Cruces. Wander a few blocks off the plaza to gather the essence of a mid-19th-century Southwestern town of Hispanic heritage.

our pick **El Comedor** (☎ 575-524-7002; 2190 Ave de Mesilla; mains under $10; 9am-9pm Mon-Fri, 9am-3pm Sat & Sun), off the plaza in Mesilla, is highly recommended. Trust us, the hearty chili-and-cheese smothered New Mexican dishes at this bustling adobe are worth the extra two blocks of walking. Every dish looks good as it passes, but the chicken enchiladas with green chili sauce are so darn cheesy and good that if you don't lick your plate and yell hallelujah, you probably never will.

White Sands Missile Test Center Museum (☎ 575-678-8824; www.wsmr-history.org; admission free; 8am-4pm Mon-Fri, 10am-3pm Sat & Sun), about 25 miles east of Las Cruces along Hwy 70 (look for the White Sands Missile Range Headquarters sign), has been a major military testing site since 1945, and it still serves as an alternative landing site for the space shuttle. Look for the crazy outdoor missile park. Since it's on an army base, everyone entering over the age of 18 must show ID, and the driver must present car registration and proof of insurance.

In Las Cruces, **Lundeen Inn of the Arts** (☎ 575-526-3326, 888-526-3326; www.innofthearts.com; 618 S Alameda Blvd; incl breakfast r $79-125, ste $99-155;), a large turn-of-the-19th-century Mexican territorial-style inn, has seven guest rooms (all wildly different), an airy living room with soaring ceilings (made of pressed tin) and a 300-piece fine-art gallery.

Join the student crowd at **Spirit Winds Coffee Bar** (☎ 575-521-1222; 2260 S Locust St; mains under $10; 7am-7pm Mon-Fri, 7:30am-7pm Sat, 8am-6pm Sun) for excellent cappuccino, good sandwiches, salads, soups and pastries. The adjoining gift store has Bettie Page lunch boxes, decorative Buddhas and hilarious cards. **Nellie's Cafe** (☎ 575-524-9982; 1226 W Hadley Ave; 8am-2pm) is a favored local Mexican restaurant. Cash only.

Greyhound (☎ 575-524-8518; www.greyhound.com; 390 S Valley Dr) has buses traversing the two interstate corridors (I-10 and I-25), as well as daily trips to Albuquerque ($30 to $39, 3¾ hours), Roswell ($37 to $54, 3¾ hours) and El Paso ($11.50, one hour).

> **EATING SOUTHWEST: GREEN CHILI CHEESEBURGER**
>
> If you're anywhere close at mealtime, pull into the **Owl Bar & Cafe** (☎ 575-835-9946; 215 San Antonio St; 8am-8:30pm Mon-Sat) for a green chili cheeseburger. Many New Mexican restaurants claim to serve the state's best, but the Owl Bar's pancake-flat beef patty piled high with mayo, cheese, pickles, tomato, onion and green chili has got 'em all beat. It's a spicy hot mess on a toasted bun. And oh so good. It's in San Antonio, 90 miles south of Albuquerque.

Silver City & Around

One word of caution when strolling through downtown Silver City – look carefully before you step off the sidewalk. Because of monsoonal summer rains, curbs are higher than average, built to keep the Victorian and the

IF YOU HAVE A FEW MORE DAYS

For those heading west into Arizona from Socorro, Hwy 60 makes a remote, scenic alternative to I-40. Past the town of Magdalena is the **Very Large Array** (VLA; www.vla.nrao.edu; admission free; 8:30am-dusk) radio telescope facility, a complex of 27 huge antenna dishes sprouting like giant mushrooms in the high plains. At the visitor center, watch a short film about the facility and take a self-guided walking tour with a window peek into the control building. Drive 4 miles south of Hwy 60 off Hwy 52 near mile-marker 93.

brick and cast-iron buildings safe from quick rising waters. The spirit of the Wild West still hangs in the air here, as if Billy the Kid himself – a former resident – might amble past at any moment.

Silver City is also the gateway to outdoor activities in the Gila National Forest, which is rugged country suitable for remote cross-country skiing, backpacking, camping, fishing and other activities.

The **visitor center** (575-538-3785, 800-548-9378; www.silvercity.org; 201 N Hudson St; 9am-5pm Mon-Fri, 10am-2pm Sat if volunteer available) and the **Gila National Forest Ranger Station** (575-388-8201; www.fs.fed.us/r3/gila; 3005 E Camino Del Bosque; 8am-4:30pm Mon-Fri) have area information. To learn about the town's contentious mining history, watch the blacklisted 1954 movie *Salt of the Earth*.

Two hours north of Silver City, up a winding 42-mile road, is **Gila Cliff Dwellings National Monument** (575-536-9461; admission $3; 8am-6pm Jun-Aug, 9am-4pm Sep-May), occupied in the 13th century by Mogollons. Mysterious and relatively isolated, these remarkable cliff dwellings are easily accessed from a 1-mile loop trail and look very much as they would have at the turn of the first millennium. For **pictographs**, stop by the Lower Scorpion Campground and walk a short distance along the marked trail.

Rounded volcanic towers make the **City of Rocks State Park** (575-536-2800; www.emnrd.state.nm.us/prd/cityrocks.htm; Hwy 61; day use $5, campsites $8-10) an intriguing playground. You can also camp among the towers in secluded campsites with tables and fire pits. Campsites are a mix of first-come, first served and reservable. For a rock-lined gem of a spot, check out campsite 43, the Lynx. Head 24 miles northwest of Deming along Hwy 180, then 3 miles northeast on Hwy 61. For more creature comforts, continue north on Hwy 180 to the **Silver City KOA** (575-388-3351, 800-562-7623; www.silvercitykoa.com; 11824 Hwy 180E; campsites $24-31, RV sites $28-46, cabins $50-63;), where you'll find 'kamping kabins' and a laundry.

For a smattering of Silver City's architectural history, overnight in the 22-room **Palace Hotel** (575-388-1811; www.zianet.com/palacehotel; 106 W Broadway; incl breakfast d $52-65, ste $79;). Exuding a low-key, turn-of-the-19th-century charm (no air con, older fixtures), the Palace is a great choice for those tired of cookie-cutter chains. On the corner, the lofty **Javalina** (575-388-1350; 201 N Bullard St; pastries $2-4; 6am-9pm Mon-Thu, to 10pm Fri & Sat, to 7pm Sun) offers coffee, snacks and wi-fi in a comfy, come-as-you-are space.

You have the choice of three sizes – tapa, mezze, entrée – for meals at **Shevek & Co Restaurant** (575-534-9168; 602 N Bullard St; tapa under $10, mezze $8-18, entrée $20-30; 5-8:30pm Sun-Tue & Thu, 5-9pm Fri & Sat, slightly longer hours in summer), an upscale bistro where locally grown Slow Food specialties are prepared with Mediterranean flair.

SOUTHEASTERN NEW MEXICO

With the exception of the forests surrounding the resort towns of Cloudcroft and Ruidoso, southeastern New Mexico is marked by seemingly endless horizons and grassy plains. It's also marked by awesome White Sands National Monument and magnificent Carlsbad Caverns National Park. Spend dusk at both places if you can. It's all here: alien sightings in Roswell, Billy the Kid in Lincoln, and Smokey Bear just west in Capitan.

White Sands National Monument

Slide, roll and slither through brilliant, towering sand hills. Sixteen miles southwest of Alamogordo (15 miles southwest of Hwy 82/70), gypsum covers 275 sq miles to create a dazzling white landscape at this crisp, stark **monument** (575-679-2599; www.nps.gov/whsa; adult/child under 16 $3/free; 7am-9pm Jun-Aug, 7am-sunset Sep-May). These captivating windswept dunes are a highlight of any trip to New Mexico.

Spring for a $15 plastic saucer at the visitor center gift store then sled one of the back dunes. It's fun, and you can sell the disc back for $5 at day's end (no rentals to avoid liability). Check the park calendar for sunset strolls and occasional moonlight bicycle rides (adult/child under 16 $5/2.50), the latter best reserved far in advance. Backcountry campsites, with no water or toilet facilities, are a mile from the scenic drive. Pick up one of the limited permits ($3, issued first-come, first-served) in person at the visitor center at least one hour before sunset.

Alamogordo & Around

Alamogordo is the center of one of the most historically important space- and atomic-research programs in the country. The four-story **New Mexico Museum of Space History** (☎ 505-437-2840, 877-333-6589; www.nmspacemuseum.org; Hwy 2001; adult/senior/child 4-12yr $6/5/4; 9am-5pm) has excellent exhibits on space research and flight. Its **Tombaugh IMAX Theater & Planetarium** (adult/senior/child $6/5.50/4.50) shows outstanding films on a huge wraparound screen on anything from sharks to space exploration.

Numerous motels stretch along White Sands Blvd, including **Best Western Desert Aire Motor Inn** (☎ 575-437-2110; www.bestwestern.com; 1021 S White Sands Blvd; r $74-120; P), with standard-issue rooms and suites (some with kitchenettes), along with a sauna. Before heading to White Sands, try a homespun American or Mexican dish at the kid-friendly **Our Country Kitchen** (☎ 575-434-3431; cnr 12th & New York Aves; mains $6-9; 6am-2:30pm;), or save up for a post-hike feast at **Wok Inn** (☎ 575-434-4388; 1010 S White Sands Blvd; mains & buffet under $10; 11am-10pm), where the seven enormous buffet counters could qualify as the next wonder of the world. Even if you're not eating here, check 'em out.

Cloudcroft

Pleasant Cloudcroft, with turn-of-the-19th-century buildings, offers lots of outdoor recreation, a good base for exploration and a low-key feel. Situated high in the mountains, it provides welcome relief from the lowlands heat to the east. The **chamber of commerce** (☎ 575-682-2733, 866-874-4447; www.cloudcroft.net; 1001 James Canyon Hwy; 10am-5pm Mon-Sat) is inside a log cabin on Hwy 82.

The **Lodge Resort & Spa** (☎ 575-682-2566, 800-395-6343; www.thelodgeresort.com; 1 Corona Pl; r from $125, ste $185-315;) is one of the Southwest's best historic hotels. Rooms in the main Bavarian-style hotel are furnished with period and Victorian pieces. Within the lodge, **Rebecca's** (☎ 575-682-3131; breakfast & lunch mains $8-15, dinner mains $28-36; 7-10:30am Mon-Sat, 7-10am Sun, 11:30am-2pm & 5:30-9pm, slightly longer hours summer), named after the resident ghost, offers by far the best food in town.

Ruidoso

Downright bustling in the summer and big with racetrack bettors, resorty Ruidoso (it means 'noisy' in Spanish) has an utterly pleasant climate thanks to its lofty and forested perch near Sierra Blanca (12,000ft). It's spread out along Hwy 48 (known as Mechem Dr or Sudderth Dr), the main drag. The **chamber of commerce** (☎ 575-257-7395, 877-784-3676; www.ruidosonow.com; 720 Sudderth Dr; 8am-4:30pm Mon-Fri, 9am-3pm Sat) has visitor information.

SIGHTS & ACTIVITIES

Serious horse racing happens at the **Ruidoso Downs Racetrack** (☎ 575-378-4431; www.ruidownsracing.com; Hwy 70; grandstand seats free, boxes $35-45; races Thu-Sun late May–early Sep, casino 11am-11pm year-round). The fine **Hubbard Museum of the American West** (☎ 575-378-4142; www.hubbardmuseum.org; 841 Hwy 70 W; adult/senior/child $6/5/2; 9am-5pm;) displays Western-related items, with an emphasis on Old West stagecoaches, Native American artifacts and, well, all things horse.

The best ski area south of Albuquerque is **Ski Apache** (☎ 575-464-3600, snow conditions 575-257-9001; www.skiapache.com; all-day lift ticket adult/child $39/25; 9am-4pm), 18 miles northwest of Ruidoso on the slopes of beautiful Sierra Blanca Peak (about 12,000ft). To get there, take exit 532 off Hwy 48.

Circle the wagons and ride over to **Flying J Ranch** (☎ 575-336-4330; www.flyingjranch.com; Hwy 48 N; adult/child $24/14; from 5:30pm Mon-Sat late May–early Sep, plus Sat during Sep & first two Sat of Oct;), about 1.5 miles north of Alto, for a meal. This 'Western village' stages gunfights and offers pony rides with its cowboy-style chuckwagon.

To stretch your legs, try the easily accessible **forest trails** on Cedar Creek Rd just west of Smokey Bear Ranger Station. Choose from the USFS Fitness Trail or the meandering paths at the Cedar Creek Picnic Area.

SLEEPING & EATING

Numerous motels, hotels and cute little cabin complexes line the streets.

Sitzmark Chalet (☎ 575-257-4140, 800-658-9694; www.sitzmark-chalet.com; 627 Sudderth Dr; r $75-89, ste $99;) This ski-themed chalet offers 17 simple but nice rooms. Picnic tables, grills and an eight-person hot tub are welcome perks.

Ruidoso Lodge Cabins (☎ 575-257-2510, 800-950-2510; www.ruidosolodge.com; 300 Main Rd; cabins $109-209;) Attractively set along the river, these cabins have full kitchens and wood-burning fireplaces.

Cornerstone Bakery (☎ 575-257-1842; 359 Sudderth Dr; mains under $10; 7:30am-2pm Mon-Sat, 7:30am-1pm Sun) Stay around long enough and this eatery may become your touchstone. Everything on the menu, from the omelets to croissant sandwiches, is worthy, and the pinyon-flavored coffee is wonderful.

Café Rio (☎ 575-257-7746; 2547 Sudderth Dr; mains $5-25; 11am-9pm) Friendly service isn't the first description that leaps to mind at this scruffy pizza joint, but oh…take one bite of a pillowy slice and all will be forgiven.

Casa Blanca (☎ 575-257-2495; 501 Mechem Dr; lunch mains $6-8, dinner mains $10-20; 11am-9pm) Dine on Southwestern cuisine in a renovated Spanish-style house. The *chilis rellenos* are to die for.

Lincoln & Capitan

Fans of Western history won't want to miss little Lincoln. Twelve miles east of Capitan along the **Billy the Kid National Scenic Byway** (www.billybyway.com), this is where the gun battle that turned Billy the Kid into a legend took place. The whole town is beautifully preserved in close to original form and the main street has been designated the **Lincoln Town Monument**; modern influences (such as neon-lit motel signs, souvenir stands, fast-food joints) are not allowed.

Buy tickets to the most historic buildings at the **Anderson Freeman Visitors Center & Museum** (☎ 575-653-4025; Hwy 380; admission to 5 sites adult/child $5/free; 8:30am-4:30pm), where you'll also find exhibits on Buffalo soldiers, Apaches and the Lincoln County War. Make the fascinating **Courthouse Museum** your last stop; this is the well-marked site of Billy's most daring – and violent – escape. There's a plaque where one of his bullets slammed into the wall.

For overnighters, the **Ellis Store Country Inn** (☎ 575-653-4609, 800-653-6460; www.ellisstore.com; Mile 98, Hwy 380; r incl breakfast $89-119;) offers three antique-filled rooms (complete with wood stove) in the main house; five additional rooms are located in a historic mill on the property. From Wednesday to Saturday the host offers a six-course dinner ($75 per person), served in the lovely dining room. Perfect for special occasions; reservations recommended.

Like Lincoln, cozy Capitan is surrounded by the beautiful mountains of **Lincoln National Forest**. The main reason to come is so the kids can visit **Smokey Bear Historical State Park** (☎ 575-354-2748; www.smokeybearpark.com; adult/child 7-12yr $2/1; 9am-5pm;), where Smokey (yes, there actually was a real Smokey Bear) is buried.

Roswell

If you believe The Truth is Out There, then the Roswell Incident is already filed away in your memory banks. In 1947 a mysterious object crashed at a nearby ranch. No one would have skipped any sleep over it, but the military made a big to-do of hushing it up, and for a lot of folks, that sealed it: the aliens had landed! International curiosity and local ingenuity have transformed the city into a quirky extraterrestrial-wannabe zone. Bulbous white heads glow atop the downtown streetlamps and busloads of tourists come to find good souvenirs.

Pick up local information and have your picture snapped with an alien at the **visitors bureau** (☎ 575-624-0889, 888-767-9355; www.roswellmysteries.com; 912 N Main St; 8:30am-5:30pm Mon-Fri, 10am-3pm Sat & Sun;).

Believers and kitsch-seekers must check out the **International UFO Museum & Research Center** (☎ 575-625-9495; www.roswellufomuseum.com; 114 N Main St; adult/child $5/2; 9am-5pm), displaying documents supporting the cover-up as well as lots of far-out art and exhibitions. The annual **Roswell UFO Festival** (www.roswellufofestival.com) beams down over the July 4 weekend, with an otherworldly costume parade, guest speakers, workshops and concerts.

Ho-hum chain motels line N Main St. About 36 miles south of Roswell, the **Heritage Inn** (☎ 575-748-2552, 866-207-0222; www.artesiaheritageinn.com; 209 W Main St; r incl breakfast $94;) in Artesia offers 11 Old West–style rooms and is the nicest lodging in the area.

Take a break from the downtown heat with a glass of wine and a cheese plate inside the cool confines of **Pecos Flavors Winery** (☎ 575-627-6265; 305 N Main St; 10am-7pm Mon-Thu, 10am-8pm Fri & Sat). Beer-drinkers can swig an Alien Amber Ale. Superhero-themed **Farley's** (☎ 575-627-1100; 1315 N Main St; mains $7-13; 11am-11pm Sun-Thu, to 1am Fri & Sat) has 29 beers on tap as well as pub food and pizza in a huge industrial space. For simple, dependable Mexican fare downtown, try **Martin's Capitol Café** (110 W 4th St; mains $6-10; 6am-8:30pm Mon-Sat).

The **Greyhound Bus Depot** (☎ 575-622-2510; www.greyhound.com; 1100 N Virginia Ave) has buses to Carlsbad ($29 to $32, 1½ hours) and El Paso, TX, via Las Cruces ($55 to $60, 5½ hours).

Carlsbad

Travelers use Carlsbad as a base for visits to nearby Carlsbad Caverns National Park (right) and the Guadalupe Mountains. The **chamber of commerce** (☎ 575-887-6516, 866-822-9226; www.carlsbadchamber.com; 302 S Canal St; 9am-5pm Mon, 8am-5pm Tue-Fri year-round, 9am-3pm Sat May-Sep) has information on both.

On the northwestern outskirts of town, off Hwy 285, **Living Desert State Park** (☎ 575-887-5516; 1504 Miehls Dr; adult/child 7-12yr $5/3; 8am-8pm late Jun–Aug, 9am-5pm Sep-May;) is a great place to see and learn about cacti, coyotes and wildlife. The park has a good 1.3-mile trail that showcases different habitats of the Chihuahua Desert.

Most Carlsbad lodging consists of chain motels on S Canal St or National Parks Hwy. The no-frills **Motel 6** (☎ 575-885-0001; www.motel6.coms; 3824 National Parks Hwy; s/d $50/54;) is clean, cheap and on the way to the park. For more personal service, spend a night or two at the red-tiled, Mediterranean-style **Sousorrone Viento** (☎ 575-628-0446; www.sousorronev.com; 20 Vincent Rd; r $125;) north of town. The lovely owners of this welcoming B&B offer three tidy, well-appointed rooms and serve full, made-to-order breakfasts. Hikers are welcome, and they'll even pack you a trail lunch. Just north of the B&B is the highly recommended **Carlsbad KOA** (☎ 575-457-2000; www.carlsbadrv.com; 2 Mantei Rd; tent sites $27-30, RV sites $39-44, cabins $53-95;), the cleanest campground you'll ever visit. The campground is located between mileposts 51 and 52 off Hwy 285.

The perky **Blue House Bakery & Cafe** (☎ 575-628-0555; 609 N Canyon St; mains under $10; breakfast 6am-noon Mon & Sat, breakfast & lunch 6am-2pm Tue-Fri) brews the best coffee in this quadrant of New Mexico. Get there before 10am for the full selection of pastries. There's drive-through 'cue at **Danny's Place** (☎ 575-885-8739; 902 S Canal St; mains $5-11; 11am-9pm), as well indoor seating. The sandwiches here, served in a basket, are hearty, messy and a little bit spicy. For convivial beer-swigging, locals and visitors crowd **Lucy's** (☎ 575-887-7714; 701 S Canal St; mains $7-16; 11am-9pm Mon-Thu, 11am-9:30pm Fri & Sat), where you can also scarf down cheap New Mexican meals.

Greyhound (☎ 575-628-0768; www.greyhound.com; 3102 National Parks Hwy) buses depart from the Shamrock gas station inside Food Jet South. Destinations include El Paso, TX ($50 to $54, three hours), and Lubbock, TX ($50 to $54, 4¾ hours).

Carlsbad Caverns National Park

Scores of wondrous caves hide under the hills at this unique **national park** (☎ 575-785-2232, bat info 505-785-3012; www.nps.gov/cave; 3225 National Parks Hwy; adult/child $6/free; caves 8:30am-3:30pm late May–early Sep, 8:30am-2pm early Sep–late May), which covers 73 sq miles. The cavern formations are an ethereal wonderland of stalactites and fantastical geological features. You can ride an elevator from the visitor center or take a 2-mile subterranean walk from the cave mouth to the Big Room, an underground chamber 1800ft long, 255ft high and over 800ft below the surface. For claustrophobics and those prone to panic attacks, the chamber and the elevator ride down to it (which descends the length of the Empire State Building in under a minute) may be a less than enjoyable experience.

Guided tours of additional caves are available (adult $7 to $20, child $3.50 to $10), and should be reserved well in advance (call ☎ 877-444-6777 or visit www.recreation.gov). Bring long sleeves and closed shoes; it gets chilly.

The cave's other claim to fame is the 300,000-plus Mexican free-tailed bat colony that roosts here from mid-May to mid-October. Be here by sunset, when they cyclone out for an all-evening insect feast.

California

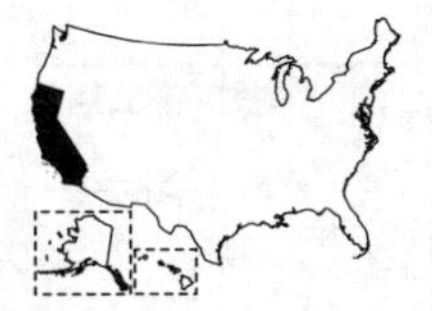

More than anything else, California is iconic. It was here that naturalist John Muir rhapsodized about the Sierra Nevada's 'range of light,' and Jack Kerouac and the Beat Generation defined what it meant to hit the road. Today, winemakers craft world-beating vintages in their biodynamic vineyards, while a new generation of civil-rights activists, progressive social thinkers and environmentalists leave their mark on not just the state, but also the nation.

Think of California as the USA's most futuristic social laboratory. If humans develop an appetite, it will be fed here. If technology identifies a new useful gadget, Silicon Valley will build it at light speed. If postmodern Southern California celebrities, bizarrely famous merely for the fact of being famous, make a fashion statement, its ripples will be felt across the country. The California 'nation state' is worlds apart from most of the rest of America. But perhaps no other pop culture has as big of an effect on how the rest of us work, play, eat, love, consume and, yes, recycle.

Ever since the hurly-burly mid-19th-century gold-rush era, brave women and men filled with ambition and desire from across America and around the world have been streaming into California. It's here that, for millions of recent immigrants, the American dream still beckons like a golden sun hanging above the shimmering surf and windblown palm trees at the end of Route 66 in Los Angeles. And that's not a bad place for you, too, to start.

HIGHLIGHTS

- Chasing waterfalls and climbing granite domes in **Yosemite National Park** (p1006)
- Surfing the waves off **San Diego** (p939) and **Orange County** (p938) beach towns
- Experiencing multicultural neighborhoods and glam nightlife in **Los Angeles** (p914)
- Trekking to sand dunes and Old West ghost towns around **Death Valley** (p954)
- Cruising Hwy 1 past redwood forests on the rocky coast of **Big Sur** (p960)
- Devouring Mission-style burritos and fresh, farmers-market fare in **San Francisco** (p982)
- Wallowing in a mud bath near the vineyards in **Calistoga** (p992)
- Looking up at the world's tallest trees in **Redwood National Park** (p998)

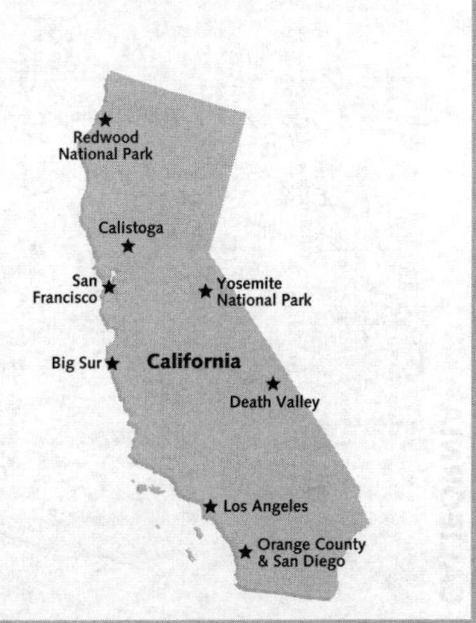

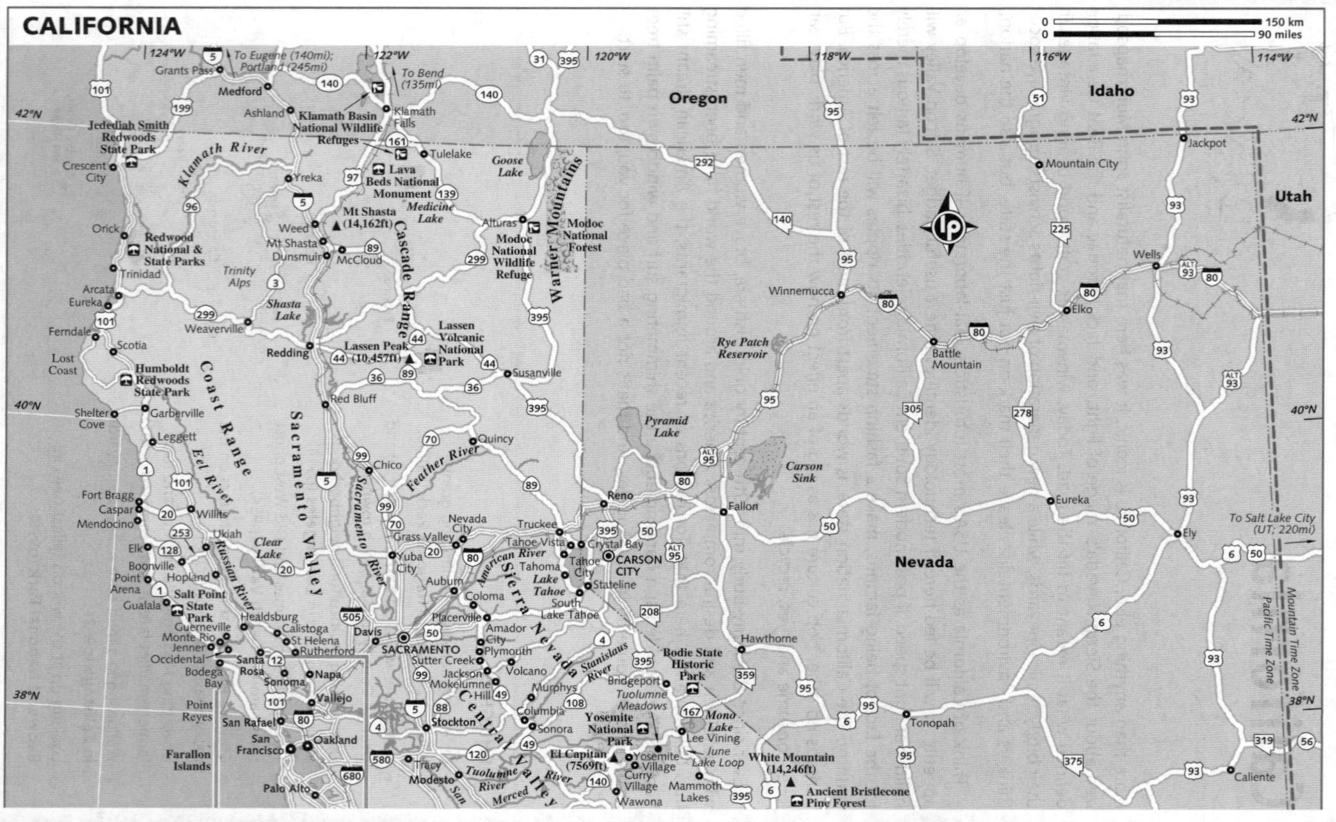
CALIFORNIA
0 150 km
0 90 miles
Oregon
Idaho
Utah
Nevada
Mountain Time Zone
Pacific Time Zone
To Salt Lake City (UT; 220mi)
To Eugene (140mi); Portland (245mi)
To Bend (135mi)
Jackpot
Mountain City
Wells
Elko
Eureka
Ely
Battle Mountain
Winnemucca
Tonopah
Caliente
Rye Patch Reservoir
Carson Sink
Pyramid Lake
Fallon
Hawthorne
Reno
CARSON CITY
Stateline
Crystal Bay
White Mountain (14,246ft)
Ancient Bristlecone Pine Forest
Bodie State Historic Park
Mono Lake
Lee Vining
June Lake Loop
Mammoth Lakes
Bridgeport
Tuolumne Meadows
Yosemite National Park
Yosemite Village
Curry Village
Wawona
El Capitan (7569ft)
Warner Mountains
Modoc National Forest
Modoc National Wildlife Refuge
Goose Lake
Alturas
Susanville
Lassen Volcanic National Park
Lassen Peak (10,457ft)
Cascade Range
Tulelake
Lava Beds National Monument
Medicine Lake
Klamath Falls
Klamath Basin National Wildlife Refuges
Mt Shasta (14,162ft)
McCloud
Weed
Mt Shasta
Dunsmuir
Yreka
Ashland
Medford
Grants Pass
Klamath River
Jedediah Smith Redwoods State Park
Crescent City
Redwood National & State Parks
Orick
Trinidad
Arcata
Eureka
Ferndale
Scotia
Lost Coast
Humboldt Redwoods State Park
Garberville
Shelter Cove
Trinity Alps
Shasta Lake
Redding
Weaverville
Red Bluff
Chico
Quincy
Feather River
Sacramento River
Sacramento Valley
Coast Range
Eel River
Leggett
Willits
Ukiah
Fort Bragg
Caspar
Mendocino
Elk
Boonville
Hopland
Point Arena
Gualala
Salt Point State Park
Russian River
Clear Lake
Healdsburg
Guerneville
Monte Rio
Jenner
Occidental
Bodega Bay
Santa Rosa
Sonoma
Calistoga
St Helena
Rutherford
Napa
Vallejo
Point Reyes
San Rafael
San Francisco
Oakland
Palo Alto
Farallon Islands
Davis
SACRAMENTO
Yuba City
Grass Valley
Nevada City
Auburn
Coloma
Placerville
American River
Truckee
Tahoe Vista
Tahoe City
Tahoma
Lake Tahoe
South Lake Tahoe
Sierra Nevada
Amador City
Plymouth
Sutter Creek
Jackson
Mokelumne Hill
Volcano
Murphys
Columbia
Sonora
Stanislaus River
Stockton
Central Valley
Tracy
Modesto
Tuolumne River
Merced River
San
42°N
40°N
38°N
124°W
122°W
120°W
118°W
116°W
114°W

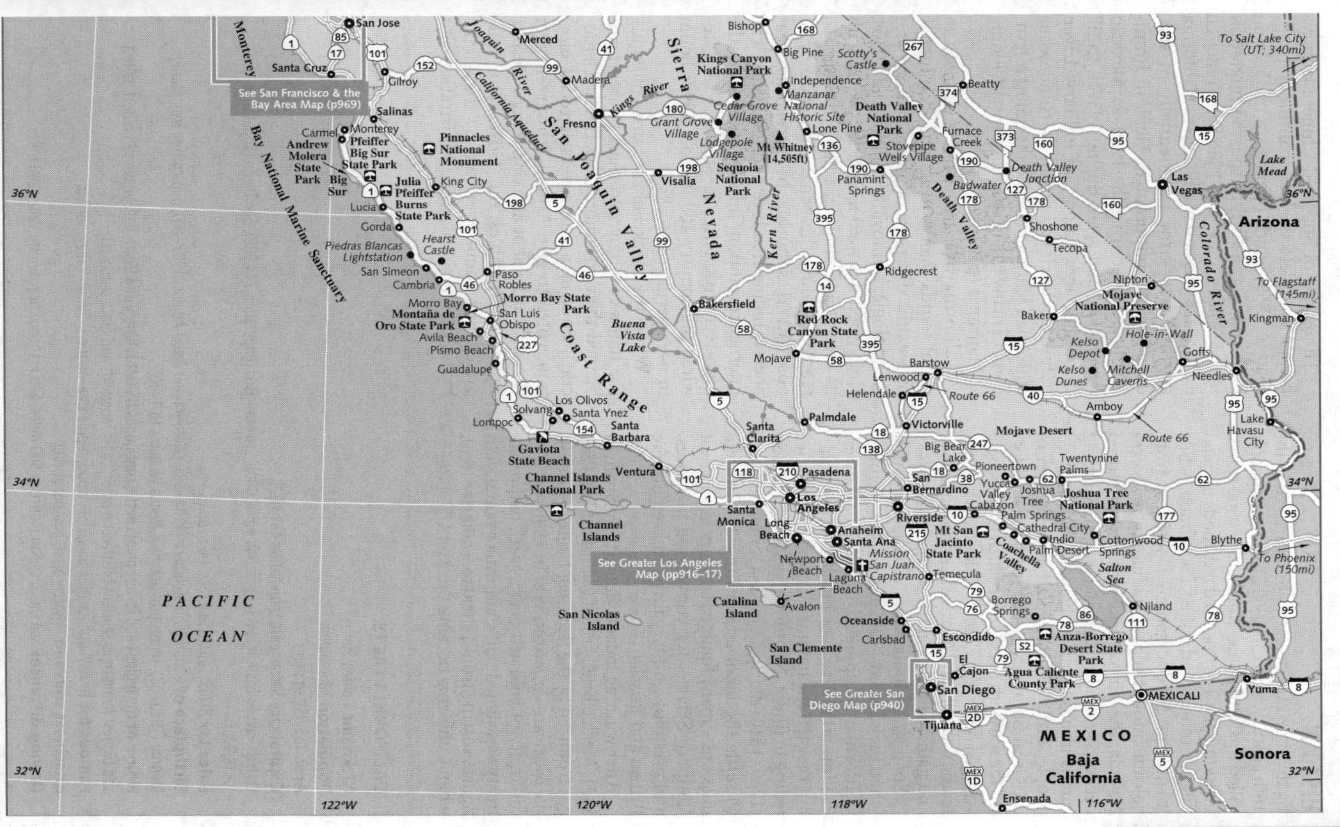
To Salt Lake City (UT; 340mi)
Lake Mead
Arizona
To Flagstaff (145mi)
Kingman
Colorado River
Las Vegas
Lake Havasu City
Needles
Goffs
Nipton
Mojave National Preserve
Hole-in-Wall
Mitchell Caverns
Kelso Depot
Kelso Dunes
Route 66
Amboy
To Phoenix (150mi)
Blythe
Twentynine Palms
Joshua Tree National Park
Cottonwood Springs
Salton Sea
Niland
Yuma
Sonora
MEXICALI
MEXICO
Baja California
Anza-Borrego Desert State Park
Agua Caliente County Park
Ensenada
Tijuana
San Diego
El Cajon
Escondido
Borrego Springs
Coachella Valley
Indio
Palm Desert
Cathedral City
Palm Springs
Cabazon
Mt San Jacinto State Park
Temecula
Yucca Valley
Joshua Tree
Pioneertown
Big Bear Lake
San Bernardino
Riverside
Mojave Desert
Baker
Shoshone
Tecopa
Death Valley Junction
Badwater
Death Valley
Furnace Creek
Beatty
Stovepipe Wells Village
Death Valley National Park
Scotty's Castle
Panamint Springs
Ridgecrest
Barstow
Lenwood
Helendale
Victorville
Red Rock Canyon State Park
Palmdale
Mojave
Bishop
Big Pine
Independence
Manzanar National Historic Site
Lone Pine
Mt Whitney (14,505ft)
Kern River
Kings Canyon National Park
Cedar Grove Village
Grant Grove Village
Lodgepole Village
Sequoia National Park
Sierra Nevada
Kings River
Visalia
Bakersfield
Santa Clarita
Pasadena
Los Angeles
Santa Monica
Long Beach
Newport Beach
Anaheim
Santa Ana
Mission San Juan Capistrano
Laguna Beach
Oceanside
Carlsbad
Avalon
Catalina Island
San Clemente Island
San Nicolas Island
Channel Islands
Channel Islands National Park
See Greater Los Angeles Map (pp916–17)
See Greater San Diego Map (p940)
Ventura
Santa Barbara
Buena Vista Lake
Coast Range
Santa Ynez
Los Olivos
Solvang
Lompoc
Gaviota State Beach
San Joaquin Valley
Fresno
Madera
Merced
Joaquin River
California Aqueduct
Morro Bay State Park
San Luis Obispo
Paso Robles
Guadalupe
Pismo Beach
Avila Beach
Montaña de Oro State Park
Morro Bay
Cambria
San Simeon
Hearst Castle
Piedras Blancas Lightstation
Gorda
Lucia
Julia Pfeiffer Burns State Park
Big Sur
Pfeiffer Big Sur State Park
Andrew Molera State Park
Carmel
Monterey
Salinas
King City
Pinnacles National Monument
Gilroy
San Jose
Santa Cruz
Monterey Bay National Marine Sanctuary
See San Francisco & the Bay Area Map (p969)
PACIFIC OCEAN
36°N
34°N
32°N
116°W
118°W
120°W
122°W

HISTORY

By the time European explorers arrived in the 16th century, up to 300,000 indigenous people called this land home. Northern coastal tribes, including the Tolowa, used redwoods to build dugout canoes and fished for salmon, while inland the Modoc gathered obsidian from volcanic mountains for trading. In the Sierra Nevada, the Miwok and other tribes moved between foothill villages and seasonal hunting camps in mountain highlands. Paiute tribespeople subsisted further east at the border of the Great Basin desert. Chumash villages dotted the southern coast, from which tribespeople voyaged out to the Channel Islands, while nomadic Cahuilla and Mojave bands found oases and gathered plants in the southern deserts.

Spanish conquistadors combed through what they called 'Alta California' (Upper California, as opposed to Baja, or Lower, California) in search of a fabled 'city of gold,' but they left the territory virtually alone after failing to find it. Not until the Mission Period (1769–1810) did Spain make a serious attempt to settle the land, establishing 21 Catholic missions – many founded by Franciscan priest Junípero Serra – for conversion purposes, and presidios (military forts) to keep out the British and Russians.

After winning independence from Spain in 1821, Mexico briefly ruled California, but then got trounced by the fledgling United States in the Mexican–American War in 1846–48. The discovery of gold just over a week before the treaty was signed sent California's population figures soaring from 14,000 to 92,000 by 1850, when California became the 31st US state.

Thousands of imported Chinese laborers helped complete the transcontinental railroad in 1869, which opened up markets on both coasts and further spurred migration to the Golden State. The 1906 San Francisco earthquake was barely a hiccup as California continued to grow exponentially in size, diversity and importance. Mexican immigrants arrived during the 1910–21 Mexican Revolution, and again during WWII, to fill labor shortages. Important military-driven industries developed during wartime, while anti-Asian sentiments led to the unjust internment of many Japanese Americans, including at Manzanar (p1013).

California has long been a pioneer in social trends thanks to its size; confluence of wealth, diversity of immigration; and technological innovation. Since the 1930s, Hollywood has mesmerized the world with its dreams and fashions, while San Francisco reacted against the banal complacency of post-WWII suburbia by spreading beat poetry, hippie free love and gay pride. The internet revolution, initially spurred by the high-tech visionaries in Silicon Valley, rewired the country and led to a 1990s boom in overspeculated stocks.

When the stock bubble burst, plunging the state's economy into chaos, Californians blamed their governor, Gray Davis (Democrat), and, in a controversial recall election, voted to give Arnold Schwarzenegger (Republican) a shot at fixing things. Despite some early fumbles, the 'Governator' surprised just about everyone by distancing himself from the Bush administration and

CALIFORNIA FACTS

Nickname Golden State
Population 38.3 million
Area 155,959 sq miles
Capital city Sacramento (population 481,000)
Other cities Los Angeles (population 4,003,000), San Francisco (population 744,000), San Diego (population 1,336,900)
Sales tax 8.25%, additional local taxes up to 1%
Birthplace of author John Steinbeck (1902–68), photographer Ansel Adams (1902–84), pop-culture icon Marilyn Monroe (1926–62), tennis pros Serena & Venus Williams (b 1980)
Home of the highest and lowest points in the contiguous US (Mt Whitney and Death Valley); world's oldest, tallest and biggest living trees (ancient bristlecone pines, coast redwoods and giant sequoias)
Famous for Disneyland, earthquakes, Hollywood, hippie tree-huggers, Silicon Valley, surfing
Kitschiest souvenir 'Mystery Spot' bumper sticker
Driving distances San Diego to San Francisco 500 miles, San Francisco to Yosemite Valley 200 miles

CALIFORNIA...

In One Week

California in a nutshell: Start in **Los Angeles** (p914), maybe detouring to **Disneyland** (p938), and then head up the breathtaking Central Coast, stopping in **Santa Barbara** (p956) and **Big Sur** (p960), before soaking up a dose of city culture in **San Francisco** (p966). Head inland to **Yosemite** (p1006) before returning to LA.

In Two Weeks

Follow the one-week itinerary at a saner pace. Add a jaunt to NorCal's **Wine Country** (p991), **Lake Tahoe** (p1004) or **Death Valley** (p954).

With Kids

Rug rats will be head over heels after seeing all the treasures waiting in the Golden State. Few can resist the magic of **Disneyland** (p938), but speed-crazed teens might prefer the roller-coaster thrills at nearby **Knott's Berry Farm** (p938) or **Six Flags Magic Mountain** (p937). Movie magic awaits at **Universal Studios** (p924) in LA, while San Diego is all about animal magnetism with its famous **zoo** (p943), **wild animal park** (p948) and **SeaWorld** (p944). In Northern California, don't miss the **Monterey Bay Aquarium** (p962) and **Santa Cruz Boardwalk** (p964).

putting environmental issues and controversial stem-cell research at the top of his agenda.

Then, in 2009, budget shortfalls caused another staggering financial crisis that lawmakers had yet to resolve at press time. Meanwhile, California's all-important high-tech sector struggles to regain its momentum, the need for public education reform builds, overcrowded prisons keep filling, state parks are chronically underfunded and the conundrum of illegal immigration from Mexico, which fills a critical cheap labor shortage (especially in agriculture), continue to bedevil the state.

LOCAL CULTURE

Currently the world's 12th-largest economy, California is a state of extremes, where grinding poverty shares urban corridors with fabulous wealth. Waves of immigrants keep arriving, and their neighborhoods are often miniversions of their homelands. Extreme tolerance for others is the norm in California, and so is intolerance, which you'll encounter on freeways or if you smoke. Untraditional and unconventional attitudes have made California a trendsetter by nature. After all, this state invented the internet and the iPod, power yoga and reality TV. Image is important, appearances are stridently youthful and outdoorsy, and an automobile often defines who you are and how important you consider yourself, especially in Southern California (SoCal).

LAND & CLIMATE

Deserts, forests, high alpine zones, river deltas, coastal wetlands, valleys – you want 'em, California's got 'em. The highest mountain in the contiguous USA (Mt Whitney, 14,505ft) is here and so is the lowest point in the nation (Badwater in Death Valley, 282ft below sea level). And those earthquakes? There isn't a day without one, but don't worry as most are so small that you won't even notice.

California's northern and eastern mountain regions get inundated with winter snow, while in summer the mercury can soar as high as 120°F (49°C) in the Central Valley and deserts. At the same time, inland heat pulls chilly blankets of fog over the coast from Big Sur northward, so don't forget a fleece jacket. Fog briefly hovers over SoCal in late spring, but by July the coast is usually clear, so to speak.

PARKS & WILDLIFE

Yosemite (p1006) and Sequoia (p1010) became California's first national parks in 1890, and today there are six more: Kings Canyon (p1010) Death Valley (p954), Joshua Tree (p951), Channel Islands (p956), Redwood (p998) and Lassen Volcanic (p1004). The **National Park Service** (NPS; www.nps.gov) also manages over two dozen other historic sites, monuments, nature preserves and recreational areas statewide. For camping on federal lands, see p1132.

California's over 270 **state parks** (☎ 916-653-6995, 800-777-0369; www.parks.ca.gov) are a diverse bunch, including everything from underwater marine preserves to redwood forests; they protect nearly a third of the coastline and 3000 miles of hiking, biking and equestrian trails. At press time, over 100 state parks were temporarily closed to California's budget crisis. Check the website to see which ones have reopened by the time you read this. Day-use parking fees range from $4 to $15; campsites cost $10 to $65 per night. **ReserveAmerica** (☎ 800-444-7275; www.reserveamerica.com) handles camping reservations.

When it comes to animals in California, think big. Gray whales, which migrate from Alaska to northern Mexico and back between December and April, are as large as a school bus. Year-round pods of bottle-nosed dolphins and porpoises frolic just offshore, while barking seals and sea lions laze under piers and on beaches. The California grizzly survives only on the state flag, but black bears are common, especially in the Sierra Nevada range.

Almost half of the bird species found in North America use coastal and inland refuges along the Pacific Flyway for rest and refueling. Look for bald eagles, which soared off the endangered species list in 2007. Ambitious captive-breeding programs have reintroduced California condors into the wild, although they're still exceedingly rare. Many migratory and native birds also flock to desert watering holes in native fan-palm oases, as bighorn sheep do. Also keep an eye out for the slow-moving, endangered Mojave desert tortoise.

INFORMATION

California Division of Tourism (www.visitcalifornia.com)

California Highway Conditions (☎ 800-427-7623; www2.dot.ca.gov/hq/roadinfo)

Department of Forestry & Fire Protection (www.fire.ca.gov) For wildfire updates.

USGS Earthquake Hazards Information (http://quake.usgs.gov/recenteqs/latest.htm) Maps of current seismic activity.

GETTING THERE & AROUND

Los Angeles (LAX) and San Francisco (SFO) are major international airports. Smaller airports such as Sacramento, Oakland, San Jose, Orange County and San Diego handle primarily domestic travel.

Four main Amtrak (p1166) routes connect California with the rest of the USA: *California Zephyr* (Chicago–San Francisco/Emeryville), *Coast Starlight* (Seattle–Los Angeles), *Southwest Chief* (Chicago–LA) and *Sunset Limited* (New Orleans–LA). Useful intrastate routes include the *Pacific Surfliner* (San Diego to San Luis Obispo via LA), *Capitol Corridor* (San Jose to Auburn via Oakland and Sacramento) and *San Joaquin* (Sacramento and San Francisco Bay Area to Bakersfield, with a bus link to Yosemite from Merced).

Greyhound (p1160) reaches into many corners of the state. But to really get out and explore, especially away from the coast, you'll need a car. National car-rental agency (p1164) offices are ubiquitous, with rates generally lowest in LA, San Diego and San Francisco.

LOS ANGELES

While 'All-American' isn't the first thought that comes to mind when thinking of Los Angeles, no other city is more American. Virtually every facet of this nation is represented here in its extremes. Its people are among the nation's richest and poorest, most established and newest arrivals, most refined and roughest, most beautiful and most plain, most erudite and most airheaded.

What Angelenos share is that they are seekers – or descendants of seekers – drawn by a dream, be it fame on the silver screen or money to send back to the family. In America's largest county (it would be the eighth largest state in population all by itself, with 10.2 million residents), success can be spectacular and failure equally so. If that's not America, we don't know what is.

If you think you've already got LA figured out – smog, traffic, celebrity murders, Botox babes and wannabes – think again. Although it's the world's undisputed entertainment capital, the city's truths aren't delivered in gossip rags or on movie screens. Rather, they are doled out in small portions of everyday experiences. Chances are, the more you explore, the more you'll enjoy.

Now is an exciting time to visit LA. Hollywood and Downtown are undergoing

LOS ANGELES...

Distances are ginormous in LA, so allow for traffic and don't try to pack too much into a day. These itineraries are already ambitious enough.

In One Day

Fuel up for the day at **Waffle** (p932) and then go star-searching on the **Walk of Fame** (p922) along revitalized Hollywood Blvd. Up your chances of spotting actual celebs by hitting the f|ashion-forward boutiques on paparazzi-infested **Robertson Blvd** (p936) and having lunch at the **Ivy** (p932). Then drive to the lofty **Getty Center** (p926), before heading west to the **Venice Boardwalk** (p927) to see the seaside sideshow. Watch the sunset over the ocean in **Santa Monica** (p933) and have dinner here.

In Two Days

Keep up with rapidly evolving Downtown LA. Start with its roots at **El Pueblo de Los Angeles** (p918), and catapult to the future at the dramatic **Walt Disney Concert Hall** (p920) and **Cathedral of our Lady of the Angels** (p920). Dim sum brunch in **Chinatown** (p932) is best walked off with a stroll among the nearby art galleries (p918). The new LA Live entertainment center is home to the **Grammy Museum** (p920), and if you're lucky you can join Leo, Jack and other celebs watching the Lakers next door at **Staples Center** (p921). Top it off with cocktails at the rooftop bar of the **Standard Downtown LA** (p930).

In More Days

Now that you've begun to get the hang of the city, it's time to branch out. Take the following suggestions at your own pace; each has its own brand of fabulousness: **Beverly Hills** (p924), **Los Angeles County Museum of Art** (p924), **Hollywood Bowl** (p935), **Huntington Library** (p928), **Surfrider Beach** (p926), **Abbot Kinney Blvd** (p927), **Fashion District** (p920), and **Spaceland** (p935).

an urban renaissance; a climate of openness and experimentation energizes the art, music and fashion scenes; and innovative chefs have kicked local cuisine into high gear.

ORIENTATION

LA County's landmass is vast (88 cities in over 4,000 square miles), but the areas of visitor interest are fairly well defined. About 12 miles inland, Downtown combines history, highbrow culture and global-village pizzazz. Hip-again Hollywood is to the northwest, and urban designer chic and lesbi-gays rule West Hollywood. South of here, Museum Row is Mid-City's main draw, while further west are ritzy Beverly Hills, Westwood (home to UCLA) and Brentwood, with the hilltop Getty Center. Santa Monica is the most tourist-friendly beach town; others include swish but low-key Malibu, boho Venice and hopping Long Beach. Stately Pasadena lies northeast of Downtown.

Getting around is easiest by car, although public transport is usually adequate to most of these neighborhoods.

INFORMATION

Bookstores

Book Soup (Map p925; ☎ 310-659-3110; www.booksoup.com; 8818 W Sunset Blvd, West Hollywood) Frequent celeb sightings.

Distant Lands (Map pp916-17; www.distantlands.com; ☎ 626-449-3220; 56 S Raymond Ave, Pasadena) Treasure chest of travel books, guides and gadgets.

Emergency & Medical Services

Cedars-Sinai Medical Center (Map p925; ☎ 310-423-3277; 8700 Beverly Blvd, West Hollywood; 24hr emergency)

National Sexual Assault Hotline (☎ 800-656-4673; 24hr)

Rite-Aid pharmacies (☎ 800-748-3243; some 24hr) Call for the nearest branch.

Internet Access

Libraries offer free access. Below are the main branches; phone or visit their websites for branch locations.

Los Angeles Public Library (Map p919; ☎ 213-228-7000; www.lapl.org; 630 W 5th St, Downtown;)

Santa Monica Public Library (Map p927; ☎ 310-458-8600; www.smpl.org; 601 Santa Monica Blvd;)

GREATER LOS ANGELES

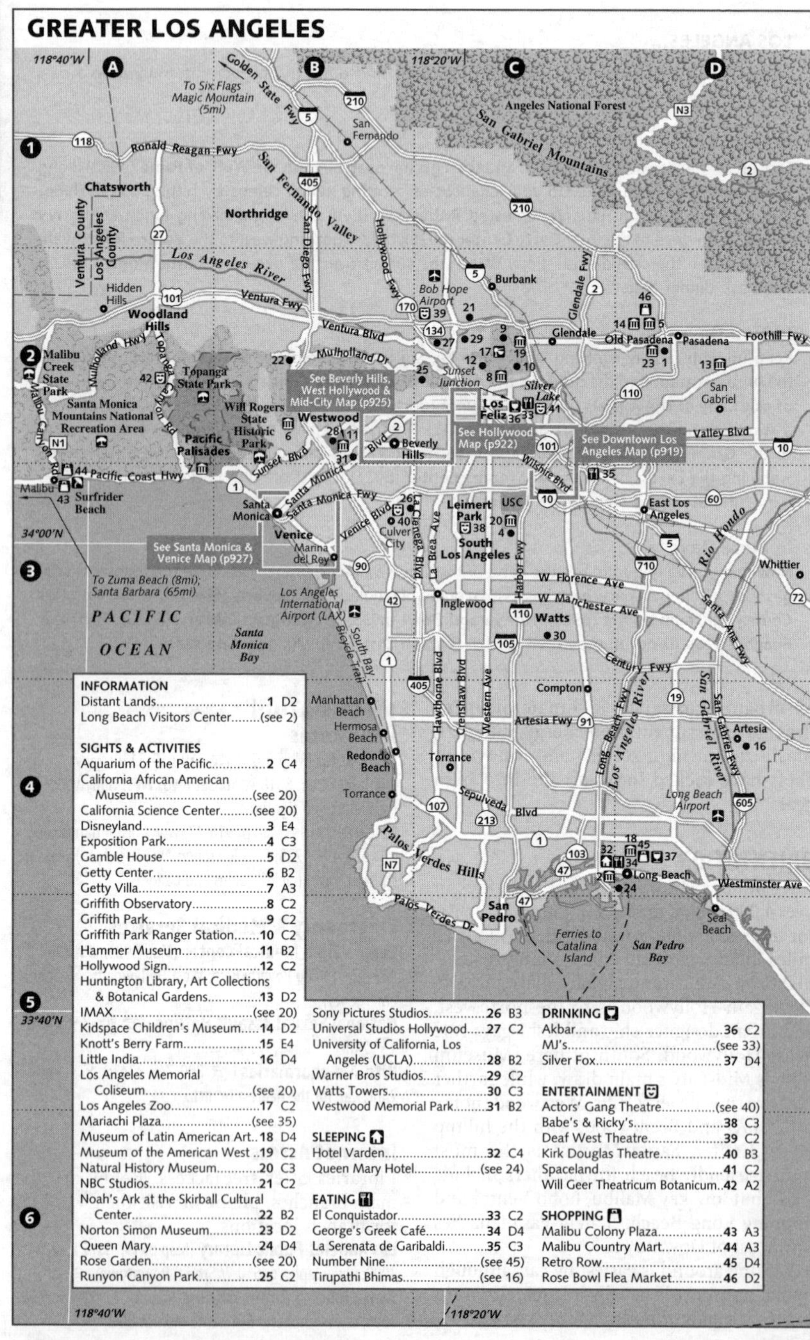

INFORMATION
Distant Lands....1 D2
Long Beach Visitors Center....(see 2)

SIGHTS & ACTIVITIES
Aquarium of the Pacific....2 C4
California African American Museum....(see 20)
California Science Center....(see 20)
Disneyland....3 E4
Exposition Park....4 C3
Gamble House....5 D2
Getty Center....6 B2
Getty Villa....7 A3
Griffith Observatory....8 C2
Griffith Park....9 C2
Griffith Park Ranger Station....10 C2
Hammer Museum....11 B2
Hollywood Sign....12 C2
Huntington Library, Art Collections & Botanical Gardens....13 D2
IMAX....(see 20)
Kidspace Children's Museum....14 D2
Knott's Berry Farm....15 E4
Little India....16 D4
Los Angeles Memorial Coliseum....(see 20)
Los Angeles Zoo....17 C2
Mariachi Plaza....(see 35)
Museum of Latin American Art....18 D4
Museum of the American West....19 C2
Natural History Museum....20 C3
NBC Studios....21 C2
Noah's Ark at the Skirball Cultural Center....22 B2
Norton Simon Museum....23 D2
Queen Mary....24 D4
Rose Garden....(see 20)
Runyon Canyon Park....25 C2
Sony Pictures Studios....26 B3
Universal Studios Hollywood....27 C2
University of California, Los Angeles (UCLA)....28 B2
Warner Bros Studios....29 C2
Watts Towers....30 C3
Westwood Memorial Park....31 B2

SLEEPING
Hotel Varden....32 C4
Queen Mary Hotel....(see 24)

EATING
El Conquistador....33 C2
George's Greek Café....34 D4
La Serenata de Garibaldi....35 C3
Number Nine....(see 45)
Tirupathi Bhimas....(see 16)

DRINKING
Akbar....36 C2
MJ's....(see 33)
Silver Fox....37 D4

ENTERTAINMENT
Actors' Gang Theatre....(see 40)
Babe's & Ricky's....38 C3
Deaf West Theatre....39 C2
Kirk Douglas Theatre....40 B3
Spaceland....41 C2
Will Geer Theatricum Botanicum....42 A2

SHOPPING
Malibu Colony Plaza....43 A3
Malibu Country Mart....44 A3
Retro Row....45 D4
Rose Bowl Flea Market....46 D2

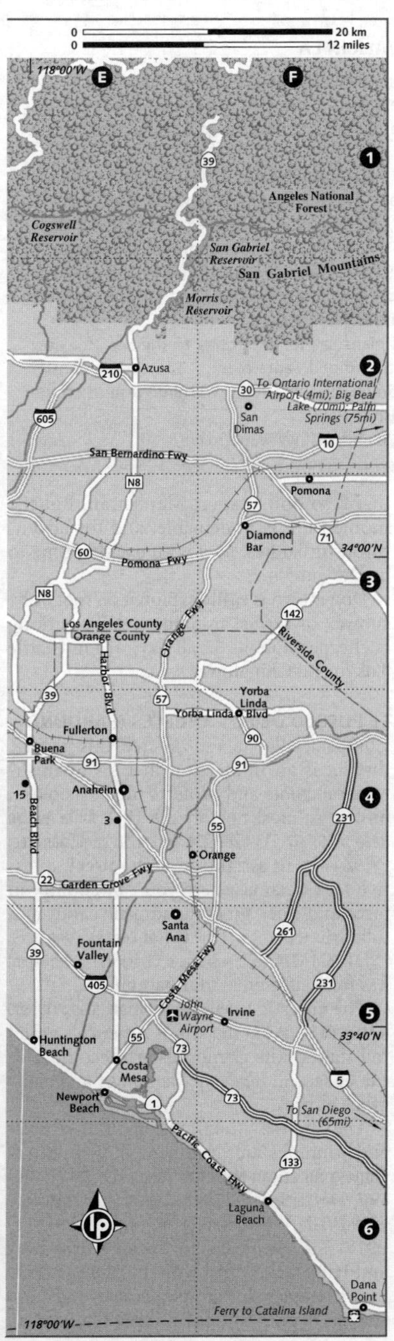

Internet Resources

Daily Candy LA (www.dailycandy.com) Little bites of LA style.

Discover Los Angeles (http://discoverlosangeles.com) Official tourist office site.

Flavorpill (http://flavorpill.com/losangeles) Hip city culture guide.

Gridskipper LA (www.gridskipper.com/travel/los-angeles) Urban travel guide to the offbeat.

LA Observed (www.laobserved.com) News blog that rounds up – and often scoops – other media.

LA.com (www.la.com) Clued-in guide to shopping, dining, nightlife and events.

Media

KCRW 89.9 FM (www.kcrw.org) A Santa Monica–based National Public Radio (NPR) station that plays cutting-edge music and airs well-chosen public affairs programming.

KPCC 89.3 FM (www.kpcc.org) Pasadena-based NPR station with NPR and BBC programming and intelligent local talk shows.

LA Weekly (www.laweekly.com) Free alternative news and listings magazine.

Los Angeles Magazine (www.losangelesmagazine.com) Glossy lifestyle monthly with a useful restaurant guide.

Los Angeles Times (www.latimes.com) The West's leading daily and winner of dozens of Pulitzer Prizes. Embattled but still useful.

Money

American Express (Map p925; ☎ 310-659-1682; Beverly Connection; 8493 W 3rd St, Mid-City; 🕑 9am-6pm Mon-Fri, 10am-3pm Sat)

Travelex (Map p925; ☎ 310-659-6093; US Bank, 8901 Santa Monica Blvd; 🕑 9am-2pm & 3pm-6pm Mon-Fri, 9am-1pm Sat)

Post

Call ☎ 800-275-8777 or visit www.usps.com for the nearest branch.

Telephone

LA County is covered by nearly a dozen area codes, some shared with neighboring counties. Dial 1 + area code before all numbers.

Tourist Information

Beverly Hills (Map p925; ☎ 310-248-1015, 800-345-2210; www.lovebeverlyhills.org; 239 S Beverly Dr, Beverly Hills; 🕑 8:30am-5pm Mon-Fri)

Downtown LA (Map p919; ☎ 213-689-8822; http://discoverlosangeles.com; 685 S Figueroa St; 🕑 8:30am-5pm Mon-Fri)

HOT TOPIC: ACTUALLY, SOME PEOPLE *DO* WALK IN LA

'No one walks in LA,' the '80s band Missing Persons famously sang. That was then. Fed up with traffic, smog and high gas prices, the city that defined car culture is developing a foot culture. Angelenos are moving into more densely populated neighborhoods and walking, cycling and taking public transit.

The turning point was the extension of Metro Red Line subway in 2003, connecting Union Station in Downtown LA to the San Fernando Valley via Koreatown, Hollywood and Universal Studios. Base yourself near one of the arty stations, and you may not need a car at all. Particularly convenient stations include Pershing Sq and 7th St/Metro Center in Downtown, and Hollywood/Highland in Hollywood. Unlimited-ride tickets at $5 a day are a downright bargain; plus, given LA's legendary traffic, it's often faster to travel below ground than above. Light-rail lines connect Downtown with Long Beach, Pasadena, East LA and Culver City.

The catch: going further afield. While eventual plans call for a 'Subway to the Sea', for now you'll be busing it to Mid-City, Beverly Hills, Westwood and Santa Monica. The easiest transfer is to the Rapid 720 bus (at Wilshire/Vermont station on the Red Line or Wilshire/Western on the Purple Line), which makes limited stops along Wilshire Blvd.

For more information see Getting Around (p936) and visit www.metro.net.

Hollywood (Map p922; ☎ 323-467-6412; Hollywood & Highland complex, 6801 Hollywood Blvd; ⏰ 10am-10pm Mon-Sat, 10am-7pm Sun)

Long Beach (Map pp916-17; ☎ 562-628-8850; www.visitlongbeach.com; ⏰ 11am-7pm daily Jun-Sep, 11am-5pm Sat & Sun Oct-May) Outside Aquarium of the Pacific.

Santa Monica (☎ 310-393-7593, 800-544-5319; www.santamonica.com) Visitor Center (Map p927; 1920 Main St; ⏰ 9am-6pm); Information Kiosk (Map p927; ☎ 1400 Ocean Ave; ⏰ 9am-5pm Jun-Aug, 10am-4pm Sep-May)

SIGHTS

Each LA neighborhood has its unique appeal. For great museums and architecture, head to Downtown, Mid-City or Pasadena. West Hollywood has the legendary Sunset Strip and trendy shopping, and the beach towns are great for soaking up the laid-back SoCal vibe.

Downtown

For decades, Downtown was LA's historic core and main business and government district – and empty nights and weekends. That's changing, as evidenced by the crowds at LA Live entertainment district and Walt Disney Concert Hall, cheering the Lakers at Staples Center arena and strolling the Grand Ave cultural corridor.

The real changes are more subtle. Thousands of young professionals, college kids and artists have moved into newly created lofts. Bars, restaurants and movie theaters have followed, and there's a growing gallery district. Of course, things don't change overnight, so don't expect Manhattan. But the momentum is undeniable, and for adventurous urbanites, now is an exciting time to be Downtown.

Downtown is easily explored on foot or by subway or DASH minibus (p937). Parking is cheapest (about $6 all day) around Little Tokyo and Chinatown.

EL PUEBLO DE LOS ANGELES & AROUND

Compact, colorful and car-free, this historic district is an immersion in LA's Spanish-Mexican roots and protects the city's oldest buildings, most notably the 1818 **Avila Adobe** (Map p919; ☎ 213-628-1274, Olvera St; admission free; ⏰ 9am-4pm). It's right on **Olvera Street**, a festive tack-o-rama where you can chomp on tacos and stock up on handmade candy and folkloric trinkets. The **visitor center** (Map p919; ☎ 213-628-1274; Sepulveda House, Olvera St; ⏰ 9am-4pm) has free self-guided tour pamphlets.

The majestic 1939 **Union Station** (Map p919; 800 N Alameda St; 🅿) is the last of America's grand rail stations; its glamorous art-deco interior can be seen in *Blade Runner*, *Bugsy* and many other movies.

The Chinese-American community's trials and triumphs are documented in the small **Chinese American Museum** (Map p919; ☎ 213-485-8567; www.camla.org; 425 N Los Angeles St; adult/student/senior $3/2/2; ⏰ 10am-3pm Tue-Sun); **Chinatown** (Map p919) is a few blocks north along Broadway and Hill St, crammed with dim sum parlors, exotic temples, herbal apothecaries and curio shops. On once run-down **Chung King Road**, an

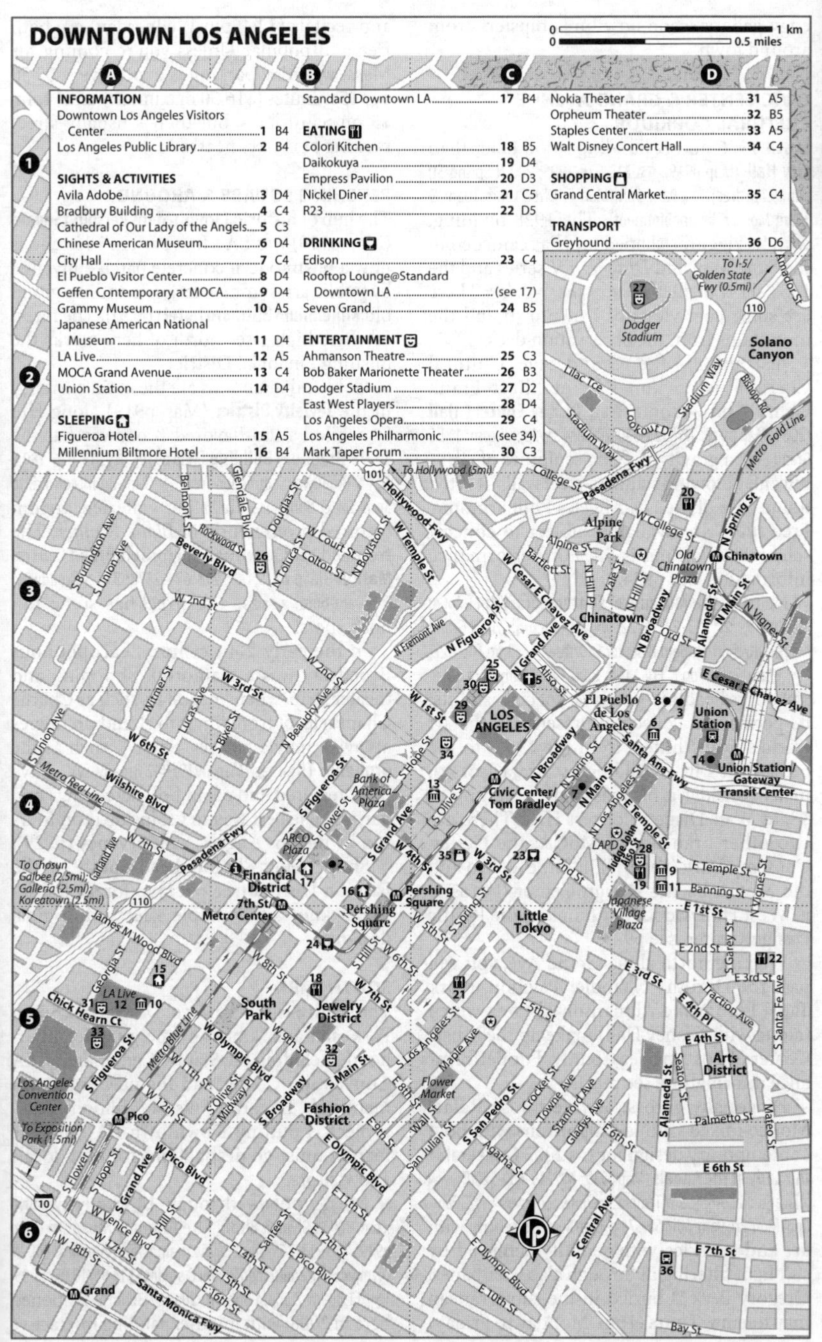
DOWNTOWN LOS ANGELES
0 1 km
0 0.5 miles
A
B
C
D
1
2
3
4
5
6
INFORMATION
Downtown Los Angeles Visitors Center 1 B4
Los Angeles Public Library 2 B4
SIGHTS & ACTIVITIES
Avila Adobe 3 D4
Bradbury Building 4 C4
Cathedral of Our Lady of the Angels 5 C3
Chinese American Museum 6 D4
City Hall 7 C4
El Pueblo Visitor Center 8 D4
Geffen Contemporary at MOCA 9 D4
Grammy Museum 10 A5
Japanese American National Museum 11 D4
LA Live 12 A5
MOCA Grand Avenue 13 C4
Union Station 14 D4
SLEEPING
Figueroa Hotel 15 A5
Millennium Biltmore Hotel 16 B4
Standard Downtown LA 17 B4
EATING
Colori Kitchen 18 B5
Daikokuya 19 D4
Empress Pavilion 20 D3
Nickel Diner 21 C5
R23 22 D5
DRINKING
Edison 23 C4
Rooftop Lounge@Standard Downtown LA (see 17)
Seven Grand 24 B5
ENTERTAINMENT
Ahmanson Theatre 25 C3
Bob Baker Marionette Theater 26 B3
Dodger Stadium 27 D2
East West Players 28 D4
Los Angeles Opera 29 C4
Los Angeles Philharmonic (see 34)
Mark Taper Forum 30 C3
Nokia Theater 31 A5
Orpheum Theater 32 B5
Staples Center 33 A5
Walt Disney Concert Hall 34 C4
SHOPPING
Grand Central Market 35 C4
TRANSPORT
Greyhound 36 D6
To I-5/ Golden State Fwy (0.5mi)
Amador St
110
Dodger Stadium
Solano Canyon
Lilac Tce
Stadium Way
Bishops Rd
Lookout Dr
Metro Gold Line
101
To Hollywood (5mi)
College St
Pasadena Fwy
Hollywood Fwy
Alpine Park
W College St
N Spring St
Chinatown
Old Chinatown Plaza
Alpine St
Bartlett St
N Hill Pl
Yale St
N Hill St
N Broadway
N Alameda St
N Main St
N Vignes St
Ord St
Chinatown
W Cesar E Chavez Ave
N Grand Ave
Aliso St
E Cesar E Chavez Ave
El Pueblo de Los Angeles
Union Station
Santa Ana Fwy
Union Station/ Gateway Transit Center
Belmont St
Glendale Blvd
Douglas St
Rockwood St
Beverly Blvd
W Court St
Colton St
N Toluca St
N Boylston St
W Temple St
S Burlington Ave
S Union Ave
W 2nd St
N Fremont Ave
N Figueroa St
W 2nd St
W 3rd St
Witmer St
Lucas Ave
S Bixel St
N Beaudry Ave
W 1st St
LOS ANGELES
W 6th St
S Union Ave
Metro Red Line
Wilshire Blvd
S Figueroa St
Bank of America Plaza
S Hope St
S Olive St
Civic Center/ Tom Bradley
N Broadway
N Spring St
N Main St
N Los Angeles St
E Temple St
LAPD
Judge John Aiso St
E Temple St
Banning St
E 1st St
N Vignes St
Garland Ave
W 7th St
Pasadena Fwy
ARCO Plaza
S Flower St
S Grand Ave
W 4th St
W 3rd St
E 2nd St
Japanese Village Plaza
To Chosun Galbee (2.5mi); Galleria (2.5mi); Koreatown (2.5mi)
Financial District
7th St/ Metro Center
Pershing Square
Pershing Square
Little Tokyo
W 5th St
S Spring St
E 2nd St
S Garey St
E 3rd St
James M Wood Blvd
W 8th St
S Hill St
W 6th St
E 3rd St
Traction Ave
E 4th Pl
Georgia St
LA Live
Chick Hearn Ct
South Park
Jewelry District
W 7th St
E 5th St
E 4th St
Arts District
S Santa Fe Ave
Metro Blue Line
W Olympic Blvd
W 9th St
S Main St
S Los Angeles St
Maple Ave
S Figueroa St
W 11th St
S Olive St
Midway Pl
S Broadway
Fashion District
Flower Market
E 8th St
Crocker St
Towne Ave
Stanford Ave
Gladys Ave
S Alameda St
Seaton St
Mateo St
Los Angeles Convention Center
W 12th St
Pico
To Exposition Park (1.5mi)
E 9th St
Wall St
S San Pedro St
Palmetto St
E 6th St
E Olympic Blvd
San Julian St
Agatha St
E 6th St
S Flower St
S Hope St
S Grand Ave
W Pico Blvd
10
S Hill St
W Venice Blvd
W 17th St
W 18th St
Santee St
E 11th St
E 12th St
E Pico Blvd
E 14th St
E 15th St
E 16th St
S Central Ave
E Olympic Blvd
E 10th St
E 7th St
Grand
Santa Monica Fwy
Bay St

edgy gallery scene now lures hipsters from around town.

CIVIC CENTER & GRAND AVENUE CULTURAL CORRIDOR

Until 1966 no LA building stood taller than **City Hall** (Map p919; ☎ 213-978-1995; 200 N Spring St; admission free; 🕓 9am-5pm Mon-Fri, free tours 10am & 11am Mon-Fri by appointment). The 1928 building, with its ziggurat-shaped top, has cameoed in the *Superman* and *Dragnet* TV series and the 1953 sci-fi thriller *War of the Worlds*. There are some cool views of Downtown and the mountains from the observation deck.

Just uphill, the Grand Ave Cultural Corridor is anchored by architect Frank Gehry's now-iconic **Walt Disney Concert Hall** (2003; Map p919; ☎ 323-850-2000; www.laphil.com; 111 S Grand Ave), a gravity-defying sculpture of curving and billowing stainless-steel walls; it is the home base of the Los Angeles Philharmonic. Free tours are available subject to concert schedules. Parking is $8. For performance information, see p934.

Nearby, the **Museum of Contemporary Art** (MoCA; Map p919; ☎ 213-626-6222; www.moca.org; 250 S Grand Ave; adult/child/student & senior $10/free/5, 5-8pm Thu free; 🕓 11am-5pm Mon & Fri, 11am-8pm Thu, 11am-6pm Sat & Sun) offers headline-grabbing special exhibits; its permanent collection presents all the art world's heavy hitters from the 1940s to the present. It's in a building by Arata Isozaki; many consider it his masterpiece. Parking is $8, at Walt Disney Concert Hall. There are two other branches of MoCA: the Geffen Contemporary (Map p919) in Little Tokyo and the MoCA Pacific Design Center (Map p925) in West Hollywood. For more on the Pacific Design Center, see p923.

Walking north along Grand Ave, you will pass the Dorothy Chandler Pavilion, Mark Taper Forum and Ahmanson Theater, which (along with Disney Hall) make up the Music Center of Los Angeles County. For performance information, see p934.

Diagonally across, architect José Rafael Moneo mixed Gothic proportions with bold contemporary design for his 2002 **Cathedral of Our Lady of the Angels** (Map p919; ☎ 213-680-5200; www.olacathedral.org; 555 W Temple St; admission free; 🕓 6:30am-6pm Mon-Fri, 9am-6pm Sat, 7am-6pm Sun). It teems with art and sparkles with serenity achieved by soft light filtering in through alabaster panes; Gregory Peck is buried in the subterranean mausoleum. Tours (1pm, Monday to Friday) and recitals (12:45pm Wednesday) are both free and popular Unless you're coming for Mass, weekday parking is expensive – $3.50 per 15 minutes ($16.50 maximum) until 4pm, $5 on Saturday – but there's usually street parking at meters nearby.

PERSHING SQUARE & AROUND

The hub of historic Downtown, **Pershing Square** (Map p919) was LA's first park in 1866 and is now a postmodern concrete patch enlivened by public art, summer concerts and the grand old **Millennium Biltmore Hotel** (p930). The forest of office high-rises north of here marks the bustling Financial District.

Gold and diamonds are the main currency in the **Jewelry District** (Map p919) along Hill St, while Latino-flavored Broadway has the 1893 **Bradbury Building** (Map p919; ☎ 213-626-1893; 304 S Broadway; admission free; 🕓 9am-6pm Mon-Fri, to 5pm Sat & Sun); its dazzling galleried atrium featured prominently in *Blade Runner*. The frenzied and sawdust-sprinkled **Grand Central Market** (Map p919; ☎ 213-624-2378; 317 S Broadway; 🕓 9am-6pm) across the street has some fun nosh spots.

In the early 20th century, cacophonous Broadway was a glamorous shopping and theater strip, where megastars such as Charlie Chaplin leapt from limos to attend premieres at lavish movie palaces. Some – such as the **Orpheum Theater** (Map p919; 842 Broadway) – have been restored and again host screenings and parties. The best way to get inside is on tours run by the Los Angeles Conservancy (p929).

Shopaholics should head south to the Fashion District (see p921) to forage for designer knockoffs, sample sales and original designs.

SOUTH PARK

The southwestern corner of Downtown, South Park isn't a park but an emerging neighborhood, including the Staples Center arena, LA Convention Center and the new entertainment hub, LA Live. This $1.7 billion megaproject is putting Downtown LA onto the map of must-go destinations for both locals and visitors.

Music pulses through **LA Live** (www.lalive.com, 800 W Olympic Blvd). The **Grammy Museum** (Map p919; ☎ 213-765-6800; www.grammymuseum.org; 800 W Olympic Blvd; adult/child/senior & student $14.95/10.95/11.95; 🕓 11:30am-7:30pm Sun-Fri, 10am-7:30pm Sat) opened here in 2008, with mind-expanding interactive displays of the history of American music and plenty of listening opportunities. Nearby is the 7100-seat **Nokia Theatre** (Map p919; 213-763-6030, www.nokiatheatrelive.com, 777 Chick Hearn Ct), which hosts the MTV Music Awards and *American Idol* finals. LA Live also includes live-music clubs, a megaplex movie theater, a dozen restaurants and a 54-story hotel tower shared by Marriott and Ritz-Carlton.

The flying-saucer-shaped **Staples Center** (Map p919; ☎ 213-742-7340; www.staplescenter.com; 1111 S Figueroa St) is a sports and entertainment arena with all the high-tech trappings. It's home to the Lakers, Clippers and Sparks basketball teams, as well as the Kings ice hockey team. Major headliners – Barbra Streisand to Justin Timberlake – also perform here.

Heading east on Olympic Blvd takes you into the heart of the **Fashion District** (Map p919; ☎ 213-488-1153; www.fashiondistrict.org), a 90-block nirvana for bargain hunters, even if shopping around here is more Middle Eastern bazaar than Rodeo Dr, and haggling is ubiquitous. There's a head-spinning selection of samples, knockoffs and original designs at cut-rate prices.

Nearby, LA's **flower market** (Map p919; ☎ 213-627-3696; Wall St; Mon-Fri $2, Sat $1; 8am-noon Mon, Wed & Fri, 6am-noon Tue, Thu & Sat), between 7th and 8th Sts, is the largest in the country and dates back to 1913.

Parking at South Park is in private lots ($8 to $20). South Park is near the Blue Line light-rail.

LITTLE TOKYO

Little Tokyo swirls with shopping malls, Buddhist temples, public art, traditional gardens, and authentic sushi bars and *izakaya* (pubs). The **Japanese American National Museum** (Map p919; ☎ 213-625-0414; www.janm.org; 369 E 1st St; adult/child/student & senior $9/free/5, 5-8pm Thu free; 11am-5pm Tue, Wed & Fri-Sun, noon-8pm Thu) offers an in-depth look at the Japanese immigrant experience, including the painful chapter of the WWII internment camps.

Arty types can pop next door to gawk at the cutting-edge and often provocative exhibits at the **Geffen Contemporary at MOCA** (Map p919; ☎ 213-626-6222; www.moca.org; 152 N Central Ave).

Exposition Park & Around

Just south of Downtown LA, **Exposition Park** (Map pp916-17; 24hr) has enough kid-friendly museums, historic sports facilities and green spaces to keep you busy for a day. Parking is $8.

Dinos to diamonds, bears to beetles, hissing roaches to an ultra-rare megamouth shark – the old-school **Natural History Museum** (Map pp916-17; ☎ 213-763-3466; www.nhm.org; 900 Exposition Blvd; adult/child/senior & student $9/2/6.50; 9:30am-5pm;) will take you around the world and back millions of years in time. Kids love digging for fossils in the Discovery Center and making friends with creepy crawlies in the Insect Zoo.

A simulated earthquake, hatching baby chicks and a giant techno-doll named Tess bring out the kid in all of us at the **California Science Center** (Map pp916-17; ☎ 323-724-3623; www.californiasciencecenter.org; 700 State Dr; admission free; 10am-5pm;), a great hands-on science museum. The **IMAX** (Map pp916-17; ☎ 213-744-7400; adult/child/senior & student $8/4.75/5.75;) next door is ideal for capping off an action-filled day.

More grown-up attractions are the **California African American Museum** (Map pp916-17; ☎ 213-744-7432; www.caamuseum.org; 600 State Dr; admission free; 10am-5pm Tue-Sat, 11am-5pm Sun), a handsome showcase of African American art, culture and history; the romantic **Rose Garden** (Map pp916-17; admission free; 9am-dusk mid-Mar–Dec); and the 1923 **Los Angeles Memorial Coliseum** (Map pp916–17), site of the 1932 and 1984 Summer Olympic Games.

The area south of Exposition Park, known as South Los Angeles, is no stranger to poverty and crime. But one good reason to venture here is the world-famous **Watts Towers** (Map pp916-17; ☎ 213-847-4646; 1727 E 107th St; tours adult/child/senior & teen $7/free/3; 10am-4pm Tue-Sat, noon-4pm Sun, tours 10:30am-3pm Thu-Sat, 12:30-3pm Sun; P), a huge and fantastical free-form sculpture cobbled together from found objects – from green 7-Up bottles to seashells and pottery shards – by artist Simon Rodía.

Hollywood

Aging movie stars know that a facelift can pump up a drooping career. The legendary **Hollywood Boulevard** has received similar preening and sprucing in recent years. While it still hasn't recaptured its Golden Age glamour (1920s–40s), much of its late-20th-century seediness is gone.

Even the most jaded visitor may thrill in the famous forecourt of **Grauman's Chinese Theatre** (1927; Map p922; ☎ 323-464-6266; 6925 Hollywood Blvd;), where generations of screen legends have left their imprints in cement: feet, hands, dreadlocks (Whoopi Goldberg), and even magic wands (the young stars of the *Harry Potter* films). Actors dressed as Superman, Marilyn Monroe and the like are usually on hand to pose for photos (for tips), and it's a good bet you'll be offered free tickets to TV shows (those in season). It's on the **Hollywood Walk of Fame** (Map p922), which honors more than 2000 celebrities with stars embedded in the sidewalk.

Real-life celebs sashay along the red carpet for the Academy Awards next door at the **Kodak Theatre** (Map p922; ☎ 323-308-6363; www.kodaktheatre.com; adult/child & senior $15/10; 🕑 10:30am-4pm Jun-Aug, 10:30am-2:30pm Sep-May; closed irregularly). Pricey 30-minute tours take you inside the auditorium, the VIP room and past an actual Oscar statuette.

The spark plug for the neighborhood's rebirth was **Hollywood & Highland** (Map p922; ☎ 323-467-6412; www.hollywoodandhighland.com; 6801 Hollywood Blvd; admission free; 🕑 24hr), a multistory mall marrying kitsch and commerce. The main plaza is designed to frame views of LA's most recognizable landmark, the **Hollywood Sign** (Map pp916–17), which was erected in the Hollywood Hills in 1923 as an advertising gimmick for a real-estate development called Hollywoodland.

Across Hollywood Blvd is the flamboyant 1926 **El Capitan Theatre** (Map p922; ☎ 323-467-7674; 6838 Hollywood Blvd), which shows Disney blockbusters. Down the street, the exotic

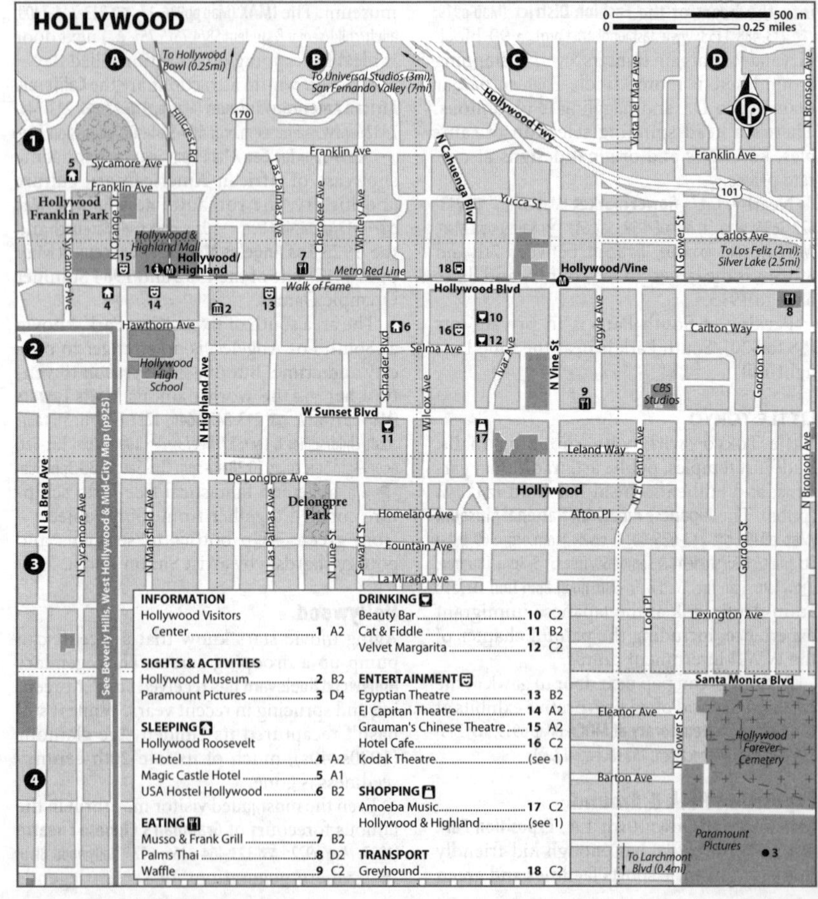

TOURING THE STUDIOS

Half the fun of visiting Hollywood is hoping you'll see stars. Up the odds by being part of the studio audience of a sitcom or game show, which usually tape between August and March. For free tickets, contact **Audiences Unlimited** (☎ 818-260-0041; www.tvtickets.com) or stop by its booth inside Universal Studios Hollywood (p924).

For an authentic behind-the-scenes look, take a small-group tour by open-sided shuttle at **Paramount Pictures** (Map p922; ☎ 323-956-1777; 5555 Melrose Ave, Hollywood; tours $35, minimum age 12yr; Mon-Fri), **Warner Bros Studios** (Map pp916-17; ☎ 818-972-8687; www2.warnerbros.com/vipstudiotour; 3400 Riverside Dr, Burbank, San Fernando Valley; tours $45, minimum age 8yr; 8:30am-4pm Mon-Fri, longer in spring & summer) or walking tours of **Sony Pictures Studios** (Map pp916-17; ☎ 323-520-8687; 10202 W Washington Blvd, Culver City; tours $25; 9:30am, 10:30am, 12:30pm, 1:30pm & 2:30pm Mon-Fri; P). All of these show you around sound stages and backlots (outdoor sets), and into such departments as wardrobe and make-up. Reservations are required; bring photo ID.

1922 **Egyptian Theatre** (Map p922; ☎ 323-466-3456; www.americancinematheque.com; 6712 Hollywood Blvd) is home to the American Cinematheque, which presents arty retrospectives and Q&As with directors, writers and actors.

The slightly musty **Hollywood Museum** (Map p922; ☎ 323-464-7776; www.thehollywoodmuseum.com; 1660 N Highland Ave; adult/student/senior $15/12/12; 10am-5pm Wed-Sun) is a 35,000-sq-ft shrine to the stars, crammed with kitsch, knickknacks and props out of shows starring celebrities from Charlie Chaplin to Zac Efron.

The Metro Red Line (see p918) stops beneath Hollywood & Highland Mall. Validated parking here costs $2 for four hours.

Griffith Park, Silver Lake & Los Feliz

America's largest urban park, **Griffith Park** (Map pp916-17; ☎ 323-913-4688; admission free; 6am-10pm, trails close at dusk; P) is a playground for all age levels and interests. Five times the size of New York's Central Park, it embraces an outdoor theater, zoo, observatory, museum, antique trains, golf, tennis, playgrounds, bridle paths, 53 miles of hiking trails, Batman's caves and even the Hollywood Sign. The **Ranger Station** (4730 Crystal Springs Dr) has maps.

For family fun, make friends with 1200 finned, feathered and furry creatures at the **Los Angeles Zoo** (Map pp916-17; ☎ 323-644-4200; www.lazoo.org; 5333 Zoo Dr; adult/child/senior $12/7/9; 10am-5pm; P). Then hop over to the **Museum of the American West** (Map pp916-17; ☎ 323-667-2000; www.autrynationalcenter.org; 4700 Western Heritage Way; adult/child/student/senior $9/3/5/5, free 2nd Tue each month; 10am-5pm Tue-Sun, to 8pm Thu Jun-Aug; P), where exhibits on the good, the bad and the ugly of America's westward expansion rope in even the most reluctant of cowpokes. Star exhibits include an original stagecoach, a large Colt firearms collection and a nymph-festooned saloon.

Above Los Feliz loom the iconic triple domes of the 1935 **Griffith Observatory** (Map pp916-17; ☎ 213-473-0800; www.griffithobservatory.org; 2800 Observatory Rd; admission free, planetarium shows adult/child/senior $7/3/5; noon-10pm Tue-Fri, 10am-10pm Sat & Sun; P). A recent makeover brought a super-techie star projector to its planetarium and doubled the exhibit space, including films in the Leonard Nimoy Event Horizon Theater. During clear night-time skies, you can often peer through the telescopes at heavenly bodies.

West Hollywood

Rainbow flags fly proudly over Santa Monica Blvd. Celebs keep the gossip rags happy by misbehaving at the clubs on the fabled Sunset Strip. Boutiques on Robertson Blvd and Melrose Ave are ground zero for sassy and chic. Welcome to the city of West Hollywood (WeHo), 1.9 sq miles of pure personality.

WeHo's also a hotbed of cutting-edge design for furniture and furnishings, particularly along the **Avenues of Art and Design** around Beverly Blvd and Melrose Ave. Some 130 galleries fill the monolithic 'blue whale' and 'green whale' of the **Pacific Design Center** (PDC; Map p925; ☎ 310-657-0800; www.pacificdesigncenter.com; 8687 Melrose Ave; 9am-5pm Mon-Fri), designed by Cesar Pelli (of Malaysia's Petronas Towers fame), though most sales are to the trade only; a 'red whale' was under construction at the time of writing this book. There's also a small offshoot of the **Museum of Contemporary Art** (MoCA, p920, Map p925, admission free) behind PDC's main buildings. Parking is $4.50 per hour.

WORTH A TRIP: UNIVERSAL STUDIOS HOLLYWOOD

Universal Studios (Map pp916-17; ☎ 818-622-3801; www.universalstudioshollywood.com; 100 Universal City Plaza; admission over/under 48in $67/57; open daily, hours vary;) first opened to the public in 1915, when studio head Carl Laemmle invited visitors at a quaint 25¢ each (including a boxed lunch) to watch silent films being made. Nearly a century later, Universal remains one of the world's largest movie studios, even if today's visitors are directed to movie-based theme parks at which their chances of seeing an actual movie shoot are approximately nil.

Nonetheless, generations of visitors have had a ball here. Start with the 45-minute narrated **Studio Tour** aboard a giant, multicar tram that takes you past working soundstages and outdoor sets like *Desperate Housewives* (when there's no filming). Also prepare to survive a shark attack à la *Jaws* and an 8.3-magnitude earthquake. It's hokey but fun.

Of Universal's thrill rides, top billing goes to the **Simpsons Ride**, a motion-simulated romp 'designed' by Krusty the Klown. **Special Effects Stages** give you the park's best glimpse into the craft of movie-making (green-screening, sound, etc). **Water World** may have bombed as a movie, but the live action show based on it is a runaway hit, with stunts including giant fireballs and a crash-landing seaplane.

Parking is $12, or arrive via Metro Red Line.

A point of pilgrimage is the **Schindler House** (Map p925; ☎ 323-651-1510; www.makcenter.org; 835 N Kings Rd; adult/senior & student $7/6, 4-6pm Fri free; 11am-6pm Wed-Sun), which pioneering modernist architect Rudolph Schindler (1887–1953) made his home. It now houses changing exhibits and lectures.

Mid-City

Among LA's dozens of great museums, some of the best line Museum Row, a short stretch of Wilshire Blvd just east of Fairfax Ave.

Los Angeles County Museum of Art (LACMA; Map p925; ☎ 323-857-6000; www.lacma.org; 5905 Wilshire Blvd; adult/child under 17yr/student & senior $12/free/8, 'pay what you wish' after 5pm, free on 2nd Tue of each month; noon-8pm Mon, Tue & Thu, noon-9pm Fri, 11am-8pm Sat & Sun) is one of the country's top art museums and the largest in the western USA. A major 2008 revamp masterminded by Renzo Piano brought to LACMA the three-story **Broad Contemporary Art Museum** (B-CAM); the collection includes seminal pieces by Jeff Koons, Roy Lichtenstein and Andy Warhol, and two gigantic works in rusted steel by Richard Serra.

The rest of LACMA brims with thousands of paintings, sculpture and decorative arts: Rembrandt, Cézanne and Magritte; ancient pottery from China, Turkey and Iran; photographs by Ansel Adams or Henri Cartier-Bresson; and a jewelbox of a Japanese pavilion. There are often headline-grabbing touring exhibits. Parking is $7.

A four-story ode to the auto, the **Petersen Automotive Museum** (Map p925; ☎ 323-930-2277; www.petersen.org; 6060 Wilshire Blvd; adult/child/senior & student $10/3/5; 10am-6pm Tue-Sun;) exhibits shiny vintage cars galore, plus a fun LA streetscape showing how the city's growth has been shaped by the automobile. Parking is $8.

Between 10,000 and 40,000 years ago, tarlike bubbling crude oil trapped saber-toothed cats, mammoths and other extinct ice age critters, which are still being excavated at the **La Brea Tar Pits**. Check out their fossilized remains at the **Page Museum** (Map p925; ☎ 323-934-7243; www.tarpits.org; 5801 Wilshire Blvd; adult/child/senior/student $7/2/4.50/4.50; 9:30am-5pm;). New fossils are being discovered all the time, and an active staff of archaeologists works behind glass. Parking is $6.

Museum Row is easily combined with a romp around the **Original Farmers Market** (6333 W 3rd St; P), with plenty of food stalls for a fill-up before you hit the adjacent **Grove**, an open-air shopping mall with a musical fountain.

Beverly Hills

The mere mention of Beverly Hills conjures images of Maseratis, manicured mansions and mega-rich moguls. Stylish and sophisticated, this is indeed a haven for the well-heeled and famous. Stargazers could take a guided bus tour (p929), snag a map and scout for the stars' homes – or maybe just book a table at Spago (p933), the flagship restaurant of celebrity chef Wolfgang Puck.

It's pricey and pretentious, but no trip to LA would be complete without a saunter along **Rodeo Drive** (Map p925), the famous

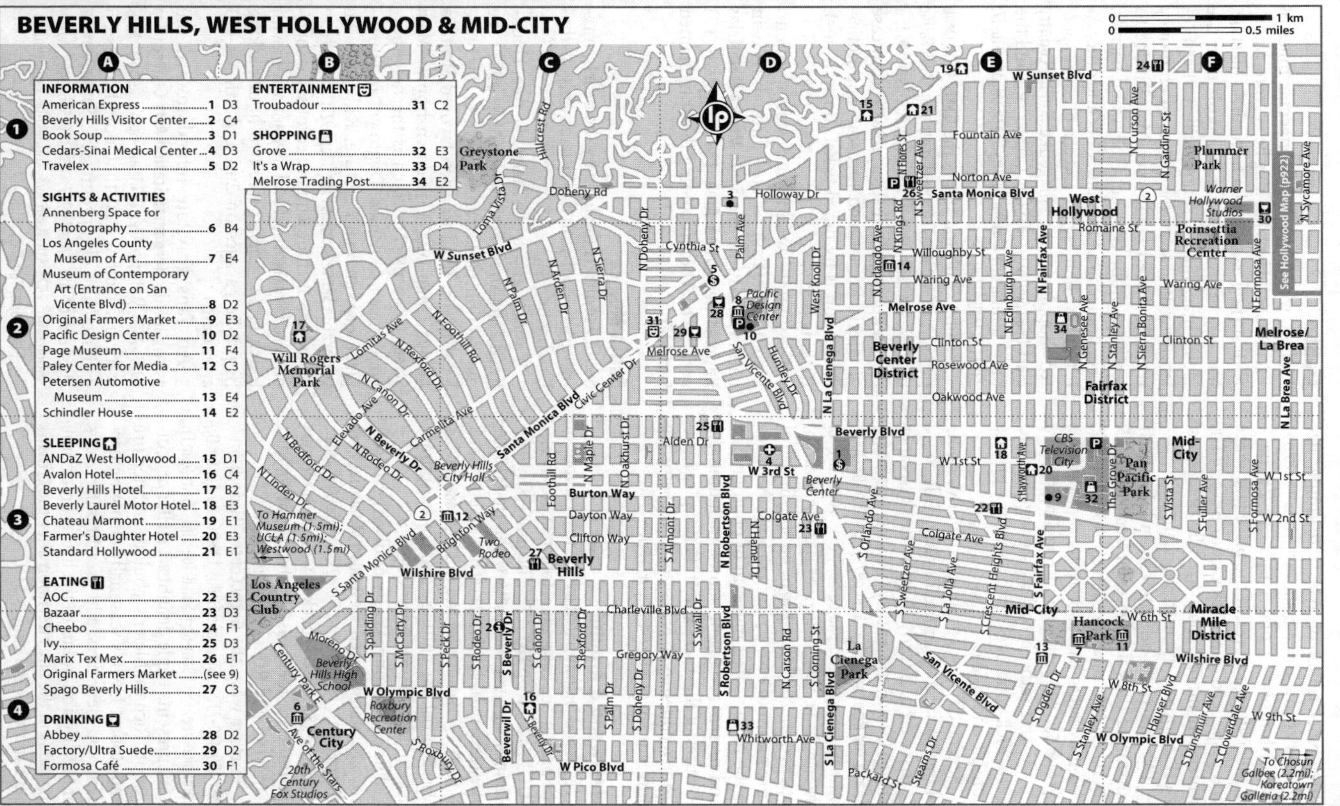
BEVERLY HILLS, WEST HOLLYWOOD & MID-CITY
0 1 km
0 0.5 miles
INFORMATION
American Express 1 D3
Beverly Hills Visitor Center 2 C4
Book Soup 3 D1
Cedars-Sinai Medical Center 4 D3
Travelex 5 D2
SIGHTS & ACTIVITIES
Annenberg Space for Photography 6 B4
Los Angeles County Museum of Art 7 E4
Museum of Contemporary Art (Entrance on San Vicente Blvd) 8 D2
Original Farmers Market 9 E3
Pacific Design Center 10 D2
Page Museum 11 F4
Paley Center for Media 12 C3
Petersen Automotive Museum 13 E4
Schindler House 14 E2
SLEEPING
ANDaZ West Hollywood 15 D1
Avalon Hotel 16 C4
Beverly Hills Hotel 17 B2
Beverly Laurel Motor Hotel 18 E3
Chateau Marmont 19 E1
Farmer's Daughter Hotel 20 E3
Standard Hollywood 21 E1
EATING
AOC 22 E3
Bazaar 23 D3
Cheebo 24 F1
Ivy 25 D3
Marix Tex Mex 26 E1
Original Farmers Market (see 9)
Spago Beverly Hills 27 C3
DRINKING
Abbey 28 D2
Factory/Ultra Suede 29 D2
Formosa Café 30 F1
ENTERTAINMENT
Troubadour 31 C2
SHOPPING
Grove 32 E3
It's a Wrap 33 D4
Melrose Trading Post 34 E2
See Hollywood Map (p922)
Greystone Park
Will Rogers Memorial Park
West Hollywood
Plummer Park
Warner Hollywood Studios
Poinsettia Recreation Center
Pacific Design Center
Beverly Center District
Fairfax District
Melrose/La Brea
CBS Television City
Pan Pacific Park
Mid-City
Beverly Hills City Hall
Beverly Center
Two Rodeo
Beverly Hills
Los Angeles Country Club
Beverly Hills High School
Roxbury Recreation Center
Century City
20th Century Fox Studios
La Cienega Park
Hancock Park
Miracle Mile District
To Hammer Museum (1.5mi); UCLA (1.5mi); Westwood (1.5mi)
To Chosun Galbee (2.2mi); Koreatown Galleria (2.2mi)
W Sunset Blvd
Santa Monica Blvd
Melrose Ave
Beverly Blvd
W 3rd St
Burton Way
Wilshire Blvd
W Olympic Blvd
W Pico Blvd
San Vicente Blvd
N La Cienega Blvd
S La Cienega Blvd
N Robertson Blvd
S Robertson Blvd
N Fairfax Ave
S Fairfax Ave
N La Brea Ave
N Beverly Dr
S Beverly Dr
Fountain Ave
Holloway Dr
Doheny Rd
Hillcrest Rd
Loma Vista Dr
Cynthia St
Palm Ave
Civic Center Dr
Charleville Blvd
Gregory Way
Whitworth Ave
Packard St
Stearns Dr
Colgate Ave
Dayton Way
Clifton Way
Alden Dr
Willoughby St
Waring Ave
Romaine St
Norton Ave
Clinton St
Rosewood Ave
Oakwood Ave
W 1st St
W 2nd St
W 6th St
W 8th St
W 9th St
Century Park E
Ave of the Stars
Moreno Dr
Brighton Way
S Santa Monica Blvd

three-block ribbon of style. Here sample-size fembots browse for fashions from international houses – from Armani to Zegna – in killer-design stores. If the price tags make you gasp, head one block east to Beverly Dr, which has more budget-friendly boutiques, local shops and mainstream chains.

TV and radio addicts can indulge their passion at the **Paley Center for Media** (Map p925; ☎ 310-786-1000; www.paleycenter.org; 465 N Beverly Dr; suggested donation adult/child/senior/student $10/5/8/8; 🕑 noon-5pm Wed-Sun), a mind-boggling archive of TV and radio broadcasts going back to 1918. Pick your faves, grab a seat at a private console and enjoy.

Several city-owned garages offer two hours of free parking in central Beverly Hills.

Just west of Beverly Hills, in the skyscraper village known as Century City, the **Annenberg Space for Photography** (Map p925; ☎ 213-403-3000; www.annenbergspaceforphotography.org; 2000 Ave of the Stars, No 10; admission free; 🕑 11am-6pm Wed-Sun) opened in 2009. Built around a cylindrical core meant to evoke a camera lens, the space is the region's first museum of photography and presents changing shows, including the Pictures of the Year exhibit. Parking is $3.50 from Wednesday to Friday, or $1 on Saturday and Sunday or after 4:30pm daily.

Westwood & Around

Westwood is dominated by the vast campus of the prestigious **University of California, Los Angeles** (UCLA; Map pp916–17). The university-run **Hammer Museum** (Map pp916-17; ☎ 310-443-7000; www.hammer.ucla.edu; 10899 Wilshire Blvd; adult/child/senior $7/free/5; 🕑 11am-7pm Tue, Wed, Fri & Sat, 11am-9pm Thu, 11am-5pm Sun) has cutting-edge contemporary art exhibits. Hammer parking is $3.

Tucked among Westwood's high-rises, postage stamp-sized **Westwood Memorial Park** (Map pp916-17; ☎ 310-474-1570; 1218 Glendon Ave; admission free; 🕑 8am-dusk) is packed with such famous 6ft-under residents as Marilyn Monroe, Burt Lancaster and Rodney Dangerfield.

Further west, the **Getty Center** (Map pp916-17; ☎ 310-440-7300; www.getty.edu; 1200 Getty Center Dr; admission free; 🕑 10am-6pm Sun & Tue-Thu, 10am-9pm Fri & Sat) presents triple delights: a stellar art collection, Richard Meier's fabulous architecture and Robert Irwin's seasonally changing gardens. On clear days, add breathtaking views of the city and ocean to the list. A great time to visit is in the late afternoon after the crowds have thinned. Parking is $10.

Malibu

Malibu, which hugs 27 spectacular miles of Pacific Coast Hwy, has long been synonymous with surfing, stars and a hedonistic lifestyle, but it actually looks far less posh than the glossy mags make it sound. Still, it's been celebrity central since the 1930s, when money troubles forced landowner May Rindge to lease out property to her Hollywood friends. Leo, Brangelina, Streisand, Cher and other A-listers have homes here and can often be spotted shopping at the villagelike **Malibu Country Mart** (Map pp916-17; 3835 Cross Creek Rd; P) and the more utilitarian **Malibu Colony Plaza** (Map pp916-17; 23841 W Malibu Rd; P).

Malibu's cultural star is the **Getty Villa** (Map pp916-17; ☎ 310-440-7300; www.getty.edu; 17985 Pacific Coast Hwy; admission free; 🕑 10am-5pm Thu-Mon; P), a replica Roman villa that's a fantastic showcase of Greek, Roman and Etruscan antiquities. Admission is by timed ticket (no walk-ins). Parking is $10.

Despite its wealth and star quotient, Malibu is best appreciated through its twin natural treasures: the **Santa Monica Mountains National Recreation Area** (Map pp916–17) and the beaches, including the aptly named **Surfrider**.

Santa Monica

Santa Monica is the belle by the beach, mixing urban cool with a laid-back only-at-the-beach vibe.

Tourists and teens make car-free, chain-lined **Third Street Promenade** (Map p927) the most action-packed zone; however, for more local flavor, head to celeb-favored **Montana Avenue** (Map p927) or down-homey **Main Street** (Map p927), which is the neighborhood once nicknamed 'Dogtown' and birthplace of skateboard culture. Kids love the venerable **Santa Monica Pier** (Map p927; 👶), where diversions include a quaint carousel, a solar-powered Ferris wheel and tiny aquarium with touch tanks. There's free two-hour parking in public garages on 2nd and 4th Sts ($3 after 6pm).

Art fans gravitate inland toward the avant-garde **Bergamot Station Arts Center** (Map p927; 2525 Michigan Ave; 🕑 10am-6pm Tue-Sat; P), a former trolley stop that now houses 35 galleries and the progressive **Santa Monica Museum of Art** (Map p927; ☎ 310-586-6488; www.smmoa.org; 2525 Michigan Ave; suggestion donation $5; 🕑 11am-6pm Tue-Sat).

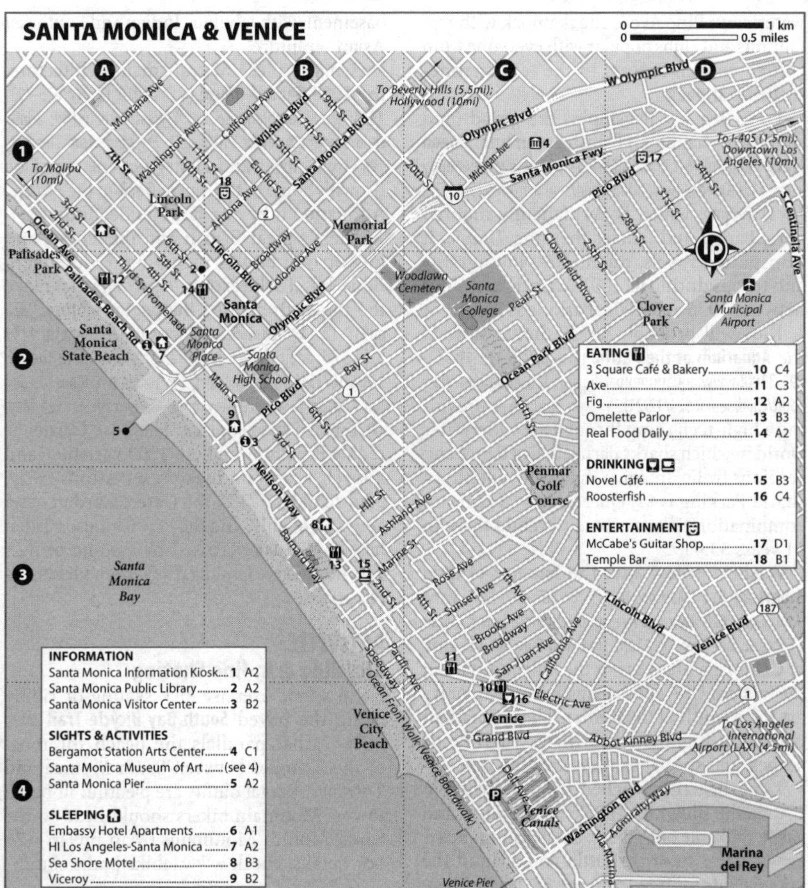

Venice

It's a freak show, a human zoo and a wacky carnival, but as far as LA experiences go, the **Venice Boardwalk** (Ocean Front Walk; Map p927) is truly essential. This cauldron of counter-culture is the place to get your hair braided, your karma corrected or a *qi gong* back massage. Encounters with wannabe Schwarzeneggers, hoop dreamers, a Speedo-clad snake charmer or a roller-skating Sikh minstrel are pretty much guaranteed, especially on hot summer days. Alas, the vibe gets a bit creepy after dark.

To escape the hubbub, meander inland to the **Venice Canals** (Map p927), a vestige of Venice's early days when gondoliers poled visitors along quiet man-made waterways. Today, ducks preen and locals lollygag in row boats in this serene, flower-festooned neighborhood.

The hippest Westside strip is funky, sophisticated **Abbot Kinney Boulevard** (Map p927), a palm-lined mile of restaurants, yoga studios, art galleries and eclectic shops selling mid-century furniture and handmade perfumes.

There's street parking around Abbot Kinney, and parking lots ($6 to $15) on the beach.

Long Beach

LA County's southernmost seaside town hosts the world's third-busiest container port, after Singapore and Hong Kong. But Long Beach's industrial edge has worn smooth in its humming downtown and along the restyled waterfront. Pine Ave is chockablock with restaurants and clubs popular with everyone from coiffed conventioneers to the testosterone-fuelled frat pack.

Long Beach's 'flagship' is the grand (and supposedly haunted!) British ocean liner **Queen Mary** (Map pp916-17; ☎ 562-435-3511; www.queenmary.com; 1126 Queens Hwy; adult/child/senior from $25/13/22; 🕑 10am-6pm), which is permanently moored here. Larger and fancier than the *Titanic*, it transported royals, dignitaries, immigrants and troops during its 1001 Atlantic crossings between 1936 and 1964. Parking is $12.

Kids will probably have a better time at the **Aquarium of the Pacific** (Map pp916-17; ☎ 562-590-3100; www.aquariumofpacific.org; 100 Aquarium Way; adult/child/senior $24/12/21; 🕑 9am-6pm; 👶), providing a high-tech romp through an underwater world in which sharks dart, jellyfish dance and sea lions frolic. Imagine the thrill of petting a shark! Parking is $7. *Queen Mary*/Aquarium combination tickets cost adult/child three to 11 years $35/19.

A short ride away, the **Museum of Latin American Art** (Map pp916-17; ☎ 562-437-1689; www.molaa.org; 628 Alamitos Ave; adult/child/student & senior $9/free/6, Sun free; 🕑 11am-5pm Wed-Sun; P) is one of California's best as it is the only museum in the western USA specializing in contemporary art from south of the border. The permanent collection highlights spirituality and landscapes, and special exhibits are first-rate.

Long Beach is reached from Downtown LA via the Blue Line (p937, 55 minutes) and easily walkable once there. Passport minibuses (www.lbtransit.org) shuttle you around the above sights for free – you pay $1.25 elsewhere in town.

Pasadena

Resting below the lofty San Gabriel Mountains, Pasadena drips wealth and gentility and feels like a world apart from urban LA. It's famous for art museums, grand estates, fine craftsman architecture and the Rose Parade on New Year's Day (opposite).

The main fun zone is **Old Town Pasadena** (Map pp916–17), along Colorado Blvd and between Pasadena Ave and Arroyo Pkwy. Stroll west and you'll see Rodin's *The Thinker*, a mere overture to the full symphony of European art at the **Norton Simon Museum** (Map pp916-17; ☎ 626-449-6840; www.nortonsimon.org; 411 W Colorado Blvd; adult/child & student/senior $8/free/4; 🕑 noon-6pm Wed-Thu & Sat-Mon, noon-9pm Fri; P). Don't skip the basement, with fabulous Indian and Southeast Asian sculpture.

A masterpiece of craftsman architecture, the 1908 **Gamble House** (Map pp916-17; ☎ 626-793-3334; www.gamblehouse.org; 4 Westmoreland Pl; adult/child/student & senior $10/free/7; 🕑 noon-3pm Thu-Sun; P) by Charles and Henry Greene was Doc Brown's home in the movie *Back to the Future*. Admission is by one-hour guided tour.

There's great British and French art and lots of rare books, including a Gutenberg Bible, but it's the exquisite gardens that make the modestly named **Huntington Library** (Map pp916-17; ☎ 626-405-2100; www.huntington.org; 1151 Oxford Rd; adult/child/student/senior $15/6/10/12 Tue-Fri, $20/6/10/15 Sat, Sun & holidays; 🕑 10:30am-4:30pm Tue-Sun Jun-Aug, Sat & Sun Sep-May, noon-4:30pm Tue-Fri Sep-May; P) such a special place. The Rose Garden is redolent with more than 1200 varieties (and a lovely tearoom; make reservations early, adult/child $25/13), the Desert Garden has a Seussian quality, and the new Chinese garden has a small lake crossed by a stone bridge. The interactive Children's Garden yields lots of surprises.

ACTIVITIES

Bicycling & In-line Skating

Get a scenic exercise kick skating or riding along the paved **South Bay Bicycle Trail** (Map pp916-17) that parallels the beach for most of the 22 miles between Santa Monica and Torrance. Rental outfits are plentiful in beach towns. Mountain bikers should head to the Santa Monica Mountains (Map pp916–17). For details, check www.labike paths.com.

Hiking

Turn on your celeb radar while strutting it with the hot bods along **Runyon Canyon Park** (Map pp916–17) above Hollywood. **Griffith Park** (Map pp916–17) is also laced with trails. For longer rambles, head to the Santa Monica Mountains, where **Will Rogers State Historic Park**, **Topanga State Park** and **Malibu Creek State Park** (all Map pp916–17) are all excellent gateways to beautiful terrain. Parking costs $10 to $12.

Swimming & Surfing

Top beaches for swimming are Malibu's **Zuma** (off Map pp916–17), **Santa Monica State Beach** (Map p927) and **Hermosa Beach** (Map pp916–17). **Surfrider Beach** (Map pp916–17) in Malibu is a legendary surfing spot.

'Endless Summer' is, sorry to report, a myth, so much of the year you'll want to wear a wet suit in the Pacific. Water temperatures become tolerable by June and peak at about 70°F (21°C) in August and September. Water quality varies. For updated conditions check the 'Beach Report Card' at www.healthebay.org.

LOS ANGELES FOR CHILDREN

Keeping the rug rats happy is child's play in LA. Many museums and attractions have kid-oriented exhibits, activities and workshops, but the excellent **Kidspace Children's Museum** (Map pp916-17; ☎ 626-449-9144; www.kidspacemuseum.org; 480 N Arroyo Blvd, Pasadena; admission $8, 🕑 9:30am-5pm Mon-Fri, 10am-5pm Sat & Sun; Ⓟ 👶) specifically lures the single-digit set with hands-on exhibits, outdoor learning areas and gardens. It's best after 1pm, when the field-trip crowd has left.

Kids love animals, making the sprawling Los Angeles Zoo (p923) in family-friendly Griffith Park a sure bet.

our pick **Noah's Ark at the Skirball Cultural Center** (Map pp916-17 ☎ 310-440-4500, tickets 877-722-4849; www.skirball.org; 2701 N Sepulveda Blvd; adult/child 2-12yr/student & senior $10/5/7, free on Thu; 🕑 noon-5pm Tue-Thu, 10am-5pm Sat & Sun, closed major Jewish holidays; 👶), great for those rare days when the weather does not cooperate, is an indoor playground of imaginative creatures made from car mats, couch springs, metal strainers and other recycled items.

Dino-fans gravitate to the Page Museum at the La Brea Tar Pits (p924) and Natural History Museum (p921), while budding scientists love the California Science Center (p921) next door.

For live sea creatures, head to the Aquarium of the Pacific (opposite) in Long Beach; teens might get a kick out of the ghost tours of the *Queen Mary* (opposite).

The adorable singing and dancing marionettes at **Bob Baker Marionette Theater** (Map p919; ☎ 213-250-9995; www.bobbakermarionettes.com; 1345 W 1st St, near Downtown; admission $12, reservations required; 🕑 10:30am Tue-Fri, 2:30pm Sat & Sun; Ⓟ 👶) have enthralled generations of wee Angelenos.

Among SoCal's amusement parks, Santa Monica Pier (p926), Disneyland (p938) and Knott's Berry Farm (p938) are meant for kids of all ages. Activities for younger children are more limited at Universal Studios Hollywood (p924) and Six Flags Magic Mountain (p937).

TOURS

Esotouric (☎ 323-223-2767; www.esotouric.com; bus tours $58) Hip, offbeat, insightful and entertaining walking and bus tours themed around famous crime sites (Black Dahlia, anyone?), literary lions (Chandler to Bukowski) and historical neighborhoods.

Los Angeles Conservancy (☎ 213-623-2489; www.laconservancy.org; tours $10) Thematic walking tours, mostly of Downtown LA, with an architectural focus.

Red Line Tours (☎ 323-402-1074; www.redlinetours.com; tours $25) 'Edutaining' walking tours of Hollywood and Downtown using headsets that cut out traffic noise.

Starline Tours (☎ 323-463-333, 800-959-3131; www.starlinetours.com; tours from $39) Narrated bus tours of the city, stars' homes and theme parks.

FESTIVALS & EVENTS

Rose Parade (☎ 626-449-4100; www.tournamentofroses.com) New Year's Day cavalcade of flower-festooned floats along Pasadena's Colorado Blvd, followed by the Rose Bowl football game.

Toyota Grand Prix of Long Beach (☎ 888-827-7333; www.longbeachgp.com) Week-long auto-racing spectacle in mid-April drawing world-class drivers.

Fiesta Broadway (☎ 310-914-0015; www.fiestabroadway.la) Huge street fair along historic Broadway in Downtown, on the last Sunday in April, with performances by Latino stars.

Sunset Junction Street Fair (☎ 323-661-7771; www.sunsetjunction.org) Silver Lake weekend street party with grub, libations and edgy bands in late August.

West Hollywood Halloween Carnival (☎ 323-848-6400; www.visitwesthollywood.com) Free rambunctious street fair with eccentric, and often NC17-rated, costumes on Santa Monica Blvd in WeHo on October 31.

SLEEPING

Your choice of lodging location may determine the LA you experience. For beach life, base yourself in Santa Monica or Long Beach. Cool-hunters and party people will be happiest in Hollywood or WeHo; culture-vultures, in Downtown; and the posh lot, in Beverly Hills. Rates are pretty steep and further swelled by a lodging tax of 12% to 14%; always ask whether discounts are available.

Downtown

Figueroa Hotel (Map p919; ☎ 213-627-8971, 800-421-9092; www.figueroahotel.com; 939 S Figueroa St; r $134-164, ste $225-265; ❄ 💻 📶 🏊) A rambling 1920s oasis across from LA Live, the Fig welcomes guests with a richly tiled Spanish-style lobby that segues to a sparkling pool and buzzy outdoor bar. Rooms are furnished in a world-beat mash-up of styles (Morocco, Mexico, Japan…), comfy but varying in size and configuration. Parking is $12.

Millennium Biltmore Hotel (Map p919; ☎ 213-624-1011, 800-245-8673; www.thebiltmore.com; 506 S Grand Ave; r $119-399, ste $460-3000;) Drenched in tradition and gold leaf, this palatial hotel has bedded stars, presidents and royalty since 1923, although some rooms lack elbow space. The gorgeous art-deco health club takes the work out of workout. Parking is $40.

our pick **Standard Downtown LA** (Map p919; ☎ 213-892-8080; www.standardhotel.com; 550 S Flower St; r from $165;) This 207-room design-savvy hotel in a former office building goes for a young, hip and shag-happy crowd – the rooftop bar fairly pulses – so don't come here with kids or to get a solid night's sleep. Mod, minimalist rooms have platform beds and peek-through showers. Parking is $31.

Hollywood

USA Hostel Hollywood (Map p922; ☎ 323-462-3777, 800-524-6783; www.usahostels.com; 1624 Schrader Blvd; incl breakfast & tax dm from $30-37, r from $70-85;) Not for introverts, this energetic hostel puts you within steps of Hollywood's party circuit. Make new friends during staff-organized BBQs, comedy nights and tours, or during free pancake breakfast in the guest kitchen.

Magic Castle Hotel (Map p922; ☎ 323-851-0800, 800-741-4915; www.magiccastlehotel.com; 7025 Franklin Ave; r from $164;) Walls are thin, but this renovated former apartment building around a courtyard boasts contemporary furniture, attractive art, comfy bathrobes and fancy bath amenities. Most rooms have a separate living room. For breakfast: freshly baked goods and gourmet coffee on your balcony or poolside. Ask about access to the namesake private club for magicians. Parking is $10.

Hollywood Roosevelt Hotel (Map p922; ☎ 323-466-7000, 800-950-7667; www.hollywoodroosevelt.com; 7000 Hollywood Blvd; r from $399;) This venerable hotel has hosted elite players since the first Academy Awards were held here in 1929. It pairs a palatial Spanish lobby with sleek Asian contemporary rooms, a busy pool scene and rockin' restos. Marilyn Monroe shot her first commercial by the pool. Parking is $30.

West Hollywood & Mid-City

Beverly Laurel Motor Hotel (Map p925; ☎ 323-651-2441, 800-962-3824; 8018 W Beverly Blvd; r $109-155;) Ride the retro wave on the cheap at this slicked up 52-room 1950s motel near the Original Farmers Market and Grove. Rooms are just above basic and the pool tiny, but the attached Swingers diner (mains $5 to $11) makes colossal burgers and wicked Bloody Marys.

Standard Hollywood (Map p925; ☎ 323-650-9090; www.standardhotel.com; 8300 W Sunset Blvd; r $160-225, ste from $350;) This white-on-white property on the Sunset Strip is a scene with a model in a glass case behind the front desk, Astroturf-fringed pool with a view across LA, and rooms with condoms in the minibars and temperature controls that read 'blow, blow harder, stop.' Parking is $29.

our pick **Farmer's Daughter Hotel** (Map p925; ☎ 323-937-3930, 800-334-1658; www.farmersdaughterhotel.com; 115 S Fairfax Ave; r $179-209;) Opposite the Original Farmers Market, Grove and CBS Studios, this perennial pleaser gets high marks for its sleek 'urban cowboy' look. Adventurous lovebirds should ask about the No Tell Room… Parking is $17.

ANDaZ West Hollywood (Map p925; ☎ 323-656-1234; www.andaz.com; 8401 W Sunset Blvd; r from $245;) Like many a rockstar who used to stay here, the former 'rock 'n' roll Hyatt' has been transformed by a new name and face-lift. Rooms face Sunset Blvd (larger but noisier) or the Hollywood Hills, and boast clean lines, sleek oak furniture and bamboo-fiber robes. The rooftop pool deck has sweeping views, and the lobby lounge offers morning coffee, pastries and all-day snacks. Parking is $25.

Chateau Marmont (Map p925; ☎ 323-656-1010, 800-242-8328; www.chateaumarmont.com; 8221 W Sunset Blvd; r $345-785;) Its French-flavored indulgence may look dated, but this faux-chateau has long attracted A-listers – Greta Garbo to Bono – with its legendary discretion. The garden cottages are the most romantic, but not everyone is treated like a star. Parking is $28.

Beverly Hills

Avalon Hotel (Map p925; ☎ 310-277-5221, 800-535-4715; www.avalonbeverlyhills.com; 9400 W Olympic Blvd; r from $289;) Mid-century modern gets a 21st-century twist at this high-octane hot spot where the moneyed and metrosexual vamp it up by the hourglass-shaped pool and at the groovy Blue on Blue restaurant–bar. Parking is $30.

our pick **Beverly Hills Hotel** (Map p925; ☎ 310-276-2251, 800-283-8885; www.beverlyhillshotel.com; 9641 Sunset

Blvd; r from $450;) The legendary Pink Palace from 1912 oozes opulence. The pool deck is classic, the grounds are lush, and the Polo Lounge remains a clubby lunch spot for the well-heeled and well-dressed. Rooms are comparably old-world, with gold accents and marble tile. Parking is $33.

Santa Monica & Venice

HI Los Angeles-Santa Monica (Map p927; ☎ 310-393-9913, 800-909-4776, ext 137; www.lahostels.org; 1436 2nd St; dm members/nonmembers $28/31, r with shared bath from $104;) This 260-bed hostel is in an architecturally interesting building, but it's the killer location – between the beach and Third Street Promenade – that really makes it. Rates include linen and continental breakfast.

Sea Shore Motel (Map p927; ☎ 310-392-2787; www.seashoremotel.com; 2637 Main St; r from $110, ste from $180;) These clean, friendly, family-owned lodgings are steps from the beach and right on happening Main St (read: some street noise). Spanish-tiled rooms are basic but attractive enough, and lofty kitchen suites are ideal for families.

Embassy Hotel Apartments (Map p927; ☎ 310-394-1279; www.embassyhotelapts.com; 1001 3rd St; r $175-390;) This hushed 1927 Spanish-colonial hideaway delivers charm by the bucket. A rickety elevator takes you to units oozing old-world flair but equipped with internet. Kitchens make many rooms well suited to do-it-yourselfers.

our pick **Viceroy** (Map p927; ☎ 310-260-7500, 800-622-8711; www.viceroysantamonica.com; 1819 Ocean Ave; r from $390;) Ignore the high-rise eyesore exterior and plunge headlong into *Top Design*'s Kelly Wearstler's campy 'Hollywood Regency' decor and color palette from dolphin gray to mamba green. Look for poolside cabanas, Italian designer linens, and chic bar and restaurant. Parking is $28.

Long Beach

Hotel Varden (Map pp916-17; ☎ 562-432-8950, 877-382-7336; www.thevardenhotel.com; 335 Pacific Ave; r from $109;) The designers clearly had a field day with their modernist renovation of the diminutive rooms in this 1929 hotel: tiny desks, tiny sinks, lots of right angles, cushy beds, white, white and more white. Rates include simple continental breakfast and wine hour. It's a block from Pine Avenue's restaurants and night spots. Parking is $10.

Queen Mary Hotel (Map pp916-17; ☎ 562-435-3511; www.queenmary.com; 1126 Queens Hwy, Long Beach; r $159-259;) Take a trip without leaving the dock aboard this grand ocean liner (p928). Staterooms brim with original art-deco details – avoid the cheapest ones that are on the inside. Rates include admission to guided tours. Parking is $15.

EATING

LA's culinary scene is one of the world's most vibrant and eclectic. Celebrity chefs whip up the latest in farmers-market-fab, alongside authentic international cooking in ethnic neighborhoods. For Angelenos, whether it's burritos or *bulgogi* (marinated, grilled Korean beef), dim sum, sushi or tapas, it's all just good food.

Downtown

Colori Kitchen (Map p919; ☎ 213-622-5950; 429 W 8th St; mains lunch $8-14, dinner $12-18; 11am-3pm Mon-Fri, 6-9pm Wed-Sat) Everybody feels like family in this colorful, cozy dining room with exposed brick walls, where owner–chef Luigi kicks Italian comfort food into high gear. BYOB.

Nickel Diner (Map p919; ☎ 213-623-8301; 524 S Main St; mains $8-14; 8am-3:30pm Tue-Sun, 6pm-11pm Tue-Sat) In Downtown's boho historic district, this place feels like a throwback to the 1920s, though decidedly non-'20s ingredients appear here: quinoa, arugula, chimichurri, etc. 'Smac and cheese' is a classic, and desserts are bountiful.

R23 (Map p919; ☎ 213-687-7178; 923 E 2nd St; mains lunch $9-13, dinner $12-30; 11:30am-2pm Mon-Fri, 5:30-10pm Mon-Sat) Not even the bold art and Frank Gehry–designed cardboard chairs can distract sushi lovers from the exquisite treats in this industrial-flavored hideaway.

Also, browse **LA Live** (Map p919) for about a dozen restaurants from chichi Japanese (Katsuya by Starck) to rockin' fish (Rock n Fish), Tiki tributes (Trader Vic's) and all-American beer hall (Yard House).

Hollywood

Musso & Frank Grill (Map p922; ☎ 323-467-7788; 6667 Hollywood Blvd; mains $12-35; 11am-11pm Tue-Sat) Hollywood history hangs thickly in the air at the boulevard's oldest eatery. Waiters balance platters of steaks, chops, grilled liver and other dishes harking back to the days when cholesterol wasn't part of our vocabulary. Service is smooth, so are the martinis.

EATING LA: ESSENTIAL ETHNIC NEIGHBORHOODS

Taking nothing away from LA's top-end eateries, no less than Ruth Reichel – editor of *Gourmet* and former *LA Times* restaurant critic – has said that LA's real food treasures are its ethnic restaurants. With some 140 nationalities in LA, we can just scratch the surface, but here are some of the most prominent neighborhoods for authentic cuisine.

Little Tokyo– Downtown LA; Essential dish: steaming bowl of ramen at **Daikokuya** (Map p919; ☎ 213-626-1680; 327 East 1st St; 🕑 11am-2.30pm & 5pm-midnight Mon-Sat) While there, visit the Japanese American National Museum (p921)

Chinatown – Downtown LA; Essential dish: dim sum at **Empress Pavilion** (Map p919; ☎ 213-617-9898; 2nd fl, 988 N Hill St; dim sum per plate $2-6, most mains $10-25; 🕑 10am-2:30pm & 5:30-9pm, to 10pm Sat & Sun)While there, view contemporary art in galleries along Chung King Rd

Boyle Heights (Mexican) – East LA; Essential dish: gourmet tortilla soup at **La Serenata de Garibaldi** (Map pp916-17; ☎ 323-265-2887; 1842 E 1st St; mains $10-25; 🕑 11:30am-10:30pm Mon-Fri, 9am-10:30pm Sat & Sun) While there, listen to mariachis at Mariachi Plaza

Koreatown – West of Downtown LA; Essential dish: barbecue cooked at your table with lots of *banchan* (side dishes) at **Chosun Galbee** (off Map pp916-17; ☎ 323-734-3330; 3300 Olympic Blvd; mains $12-24; 🕑 11am-11pm) While there, browse the giant Koreatown Galleria mall (Olympic Blvd and Western Ave) for housewares and more food

Thai Town – East Hollywood; Essential dish: curries with accompaniment by an Elvis impersonator at **Palms Thai** (Map p922; ☎ 323-462-5073; 5900 Hollywood Blvd; mains $6-19; 🕑 11am-midnight Sun-Thu, 11am-2am Fri & Sat) While there, pick up a flower garland at Thailand Plaza shopping center (5321 Hollywood Blvd)

Little India – Pioneer Blvd, Artesia; Essential dish: vegetarian *thali* (set meal) at **Tirupathi Bhimas** (Map pp916-17; ☎ 562-809-3806; www.tirupathibhimas.com; Little India Village, 18792 Pioneer Blvd; mains $5-10; 🕑 11:30am-2:30pm Tue-Fri, 6pm-9:30pm Tue-Thu, 6pm-10pm Fri) While there, shop for a sari down the street

Waffle (Map p922; ☎ 323-465-6901; 6255 W Sunset Blvd; most mains $9-12; 🕑 6:30am-2:30am Sun-Thu, 6:30am-4:30am Fri & Sat) After a night out clubbing, do you really feel like filling yourself with garbage? Us, too. But the Waffle's 21st-century diner food – cornmeal-jalapeño waffles with grilled chicken, carrot cake waffles, mac 'n' cheese, samiches, heaping salads – is organic and locally sourced, so it's (almost) good for you. Bonus: short but well-chosen wine list.

El Conquistador (Map pp916-17; ☎ 323-666-5136; 3701 W Sunset Blvd, Silver Lake; mains $10-17; 🕑 11am-10pm Sun-Thu, 11am-11pm Fri & Sat) Halloween meets Margaritaville at this campy cantina, which is a perfect launchpad for a night on the razzle. One cocktail may suffice to drown your sorrows, so be sure to fill up on yummy nachos, quesadillas, enchiladas and other above-average classics.

West Hollywood, Mid-City & Beverly Hills

Cheebo (Map p925; ☎ 323-850-7070; 7533 W Sunset Blvd; mains $9-14, dinner $10-25; 🕑 8am-11pm) Cheap and cheerful, this joint makes heaping salads, bulging sandwiches and fabulous organic pizzas sold by the foot. (Inner) kids love the free paper and crayons.

Marix Tex Mex (Map p925; ☎ 323-656-8800; 1108 N Flores St; mains $9-19; 🕑 11:30am-11pm) Many an evening in Boystown has begun flirting on Marix's patios over kick-ass margaritas, followed by fish tacos, fajitas, chipotle chicken sandwiches, and all-you-can-eat on Taco Tuesdays.

our pick **Bazaar** (Map p925; ☎ 310-246-5555; 465 S La Cienega Blvd; dishes $8-18; 🕑 brunch 11am-3pm Sat & Sun, 6pm-11pm daily) In the SLS Hotel, the Bazaar dazzles with over-the-top design by Philippe Starck and futuristic tapas by José Andrés. Caprese salad pairs cherry tomatoes with mozzarella balls that explode in your mouth, or try cotton-candy foie gras or a Philly cheesesteak on 'air bread.' Cocktails and patisserie are similarly *outré*. Caution: those small plates add up.

Ivy (Map p925; ☎ 310-274-8303; 113 N Robertson Blvd; mains $20-38; 🕑 11:30am-11pm Mon-Fri, 11am-11pm Sat, 10am-11pm Sun) In the heart of Robertson's fashion frenzy, the Ivy's picket-fenced porch and rustic cottage are *the* power lunch spot in town. Chances of catching A-lister babes nibbling on a carrot stick or studio execs discussing sequels over the lobster omelet are excellent – if you're willing to put up with self-conscious servers and steep prices.

Spago Beverly Hills (Map p925; ☎ 310-385-0880; 176 N Cañon Dr; mains lunch $19-48, dinner $32-66; noon-2:30pm Mon-Thu & Sat, 11:30am-2:30pm Fri, 6-10pm Sun-Fri, 5:30-11pm Sat) Wolfgang Puck's flagship emporium is still tops for celebrity-spotting and fancy eating. Book early if you want to scan the power crowd for famous faces while nibbling on expertly crafted global fusion fare.

Original Farmers Market (Map p925; cnr 3rd St & Fairfax Ave;) The market hosts a dozen worthy, budget-priced eateries, most *al fresco*. Try the classic diner Du-par's, Cajun-style cooking at the Gumbo Pot, ¡Loteria! Mexican grill or Singapore's Banana Leaf.

Santa Monica & Venice

Omelette Parlor (Map p927; ☎ 310-399-7892; 2732 Main St; mains $6-12; 6am-2:30pm Mon-Fri, 6am-4pm Sat & Sun;) An institution since the time Main St was known as Dogtown, festooned with black-and-whites of old Santa Monica, a soundtrack of oldies and a leafy courtyard out back. Big-as-your-head omelets and famous waffles for breakfast may last you to dinner.

Real Food Daily (Map p927; ☎ 310-451-7544; 514 Santa Monica Blvd; mains $8-17; 11:30am-10pm; V) If you're tempted by tempeh or seduced by *seitan*, or even if you're not, RFD is worth checking out – a vegan place minus the hippie commune trappings, plus food courtesy of celeb chef Ann Gentry.

3 Square Café & Bakery (Map p927; ☎ 310-399-6504; 1121 Abbot Kinney Blvd; mains $8-20; café 8am-10pm Mon-Thu, to 11pm Fri, 9am-11pm Sat, to 10pm Sun, bakery 7am-7pm) Tiny café at which you can devour Hans Röckenwagner's German-inspired pretzel burgers, gourmet sandwiches and apple pancakes. Bakery shelves are piled high with rustic breads and fluffy croissants.

Axe (Map p927; ☎ 310-664-9787; 1009 Abbot Kinney Blvd; mains lunch $6-12, dinner $18-26; 11:30am-3pm Wed-Fri, 9am-3pm Sat & Sun, 6-10pm Wed & Thu, 6-10:30pm Fri & Sat, 5:30-9:30pm Sun) It's good vibes all around at this industrial-chic space (pronounced ah-*shay*) on Abbot Kinney's restaurant row, where artsy bohos tuck into sharp-flavored dishes woven together from whatever is local, organic and in season.

Fig (Map p927; ☎ 310-319-3111; Fairmont Miramar Hotel, 101 Wilshire Blvd; mains lunch $9-24; dinner $19-34; 7am-2pm daily, 5-10pm Tue-Sat) It's all about the ingredients at this unpretentious newcomer with a really refined palate. They're sourced locally, and the menu kindly notes what's in season, for the freshest market salads or sides to steak and seafood, plus housemade charcuterie and lovely *fromages*. For dessert, fig bars (*duh!*).

Long Beach

Number Nine (Map pp916-17; ☎ 562-434-2009; 2118 E 4th St; mains $7-9; noon-midnight) An enthusiastic, artsy couple of owners serves Vietnamese noodles in maximalist portions in minimalist surrounds on Retro Row (p936). Try the five-spice chicken with egg roll.

George's Greek Café (Map pp916-17; ☎ 562-437-1184; 135 Pine Ave; mains $7-19; 11am-10:30pm Sun-Thu, 11am-11:30pm Fri & Sat) George's is the heart of the Pine Ave restaurant row, both geographically and spiritually. George himself may greet you at the entrance on the generous patio, and locals cry *'Opa!'* for the *saganaki* (flaming cheese) and lamb chops.

DRINKING

ourpick Edison (Map p919; ☎ 213-613-0000; 108 W 2nd St, off Harlem Alley; Wed-Sat) *Metropolis* meets *Blade Runner* at this industrial-chic basement boîte, where you'll be sipping mojitos surrounded by turbines and other machinery back from its days as a boiler room. Don't worry: it's all tarted up nicely with cocoa leather couches, three cavernous bars and a dress code.

Seven Grand (Map p919; ☎ 213-614-0737; 515 W 7th St) It's as if hipsters invaded mummy and daddy's hunt club, amid the tartan-patterned carpeting and deer heads mounted on the wall. Whisky is the drink of choice: choose from over 100 from Scotland, Ireland and even Japan.

Formosa Café (Map p925; ☎ 323-850-9050; 7156 Santa Monica Blvd) Bogart and Gable used to knock 'em back at this bat cave of a watering hole that's so authentically noir that scenes from *LA Confidential* were filmed here.

Dresden (Off Map p922; ☎ 323-665-4294; 1760 N Vermont Ave, Los Feliz) Dresden's answer to Bogey is the campy songster duo Marty & Elayne. They're an institution: you saw them crooning 'Stayin' Alive' in *Swingers*.

Cat & Fiddle (Map p922; ☎ 323-468-3800; 6530 W Sunset Blvd) Morrissey to Frodo, you never know who might be popping by for a Boddingtons on the fountain courtyard. Fortunately, this Brit-pub staple is more about friends and conversation than faux-hawks and working the deal.

Velvet Margarita (Map p922; ☎ 323-469-2000; 1612 N Cahuenga Blvd) Sombreros, velvet Elvises,

LA: SO GAY

Simply put, LA is one of America's gayest cities. The *Advocate* magazine, PFLAG (Parents and Friends of Lesbians and Gays), and America's first gay church and synagogue all started here. Gays and lesbians are woven into every segment of society: entertainment, politics, business and actors/waiters/models.

'Boystown', Santa Monica Blvd in West Hollywood (WeHo), is ground zero for LA's gay community. Dozens of high-energy bars, cafés, restaurants, gyms and clubs here are especially busy from Thursday to Sunday; most cater to gay men. Elsewhere, the gay scenes are considerably more laid-back. Silver Lake, LA's original gay enclave, has evolved from largely leather and Levi's to encompass cute multiethnic hipsters. Long Beach also has a significant gay community.

LA's Gay Pride celebration (mid-June, www.lapride.org) attracts hundreds of thousands for nonstop partying and a parade down Santa Monica Blvd. Here are some party places to get you started the rest of the year. Freebie listings magazines and the websites www.westhollywood.com and www.gaycities.com have comprehensive listings.

WeHo

Abbey (Map p925; ☎ 310-289-8410; www.abbeyfoodandbar.com; 692 N Robertson Blvd; mains $9-13; 🕑 8am-2am) From its beginnings as a humble coffeehouse, the Abbey has grown into WeHo's funnest, coolest and most varied bar and restaurant, with dozens of flavored martinis and upscale pub grub. Take your pick of spaces from leafy patio to Goth-mod lounge.

Factory/Ultra Suede (Map p925; ☎ 310-659-4551; www.factorynightclub.com; 652 La Peer Dr) This giant double dance club has an edgy New York feel and sports different stripes nightly – from fashion-forward femmes to male hot bods.

Silver Lake

Akbar (Map pp916-17; ☎ 323-665-6810; www.akbarsilverlake.com; 4356 W Sunset Blvd) Best jukebox in town, Casbah atmosphere, and a crowd that's been known to change from hour to hour – gay, straight or just hip, but not too-hip-for-you. Some nights, the back room's a dance floor; other nights, it might feature comedy or crafts.

MJ's (Map pp916-17; ☎ 323-660-1503; www.mjsbar.com; 2810 Hyperion Ave) Popular contempo hangout for dance nights, 'porn star of the week' and cruising. It attracts a younger but diverse crowd.

Beach Cities

Roosterfish (Map p927; ☎ 310-392-2123; www.roosterfishbar.com; 1302 Abbot Kinney Blvd) The Fish has been serving the men of Venice for over three decades, but still feels current and chill, with a pool table and back patio. Friday nights are busiest.

Silver Fox (Map pp916-17; ☎ 562-439-6343; www.silverfoxlongbeach.com; 411 Redondo Ave) Despite its name, all ages frequent this mainstay of gay Long Beach, especially on karaoke nights. It is a short drive from shopping on Retro Row.

cheesy Mexican cult movie projections and margarita-swilling scenesters – it's Cabo San Lucas meets Graceland at this dark palace of kitsch on the Cahuenga Corridor party drag.

Also recommended:

Beauty Bar (Map p922; ☎ 323-464-7676; 1638 N Cahuenga Blvd) Beautilicious martinis and manicures.

Novel Café (Map p927; ☎ 310-396-8566; 212 Pier Ave) Low-key indie java shop favored by writers, beach bums and Main St shoppers.

ENTERTAINMENT

LA Weekly (www.laweekly.com) and the *Los Angeles Times* (http://theguide.latimes.com) have extensive entertainment listings. Snag tickets online, at the box office or through **Ticketmaster** (☎ 213-480-3232; www.ticketmaster.com). Get half-price tickets to selected stage shows through **Goldstar** (www.goldstar.com); for theater, use **LAStageTIX** (www.theatrela.org) and **Plays 411** (www.plays411.com); or go in person to the visitor centers in Hollywood and Downtown LA (p917).

Live Music & Nightclubs

Troubadour (Map p925; ☎ 310-276-6168; www.troubadour.com; 9081 Santa Monica Blvd, West Hollywood; ⏲ Mon-Sat) This legendary rock hall helped catapult the Eagles and Tom Waits to stardom and is still great for catching tomorrow's headliners. A beer-drinking crowd serious about its music keeps attitude to a minimum.

our pick Spaceland (Map pp916-17; ☎ 323-661-4380; www.clubspaceland.com; 1717 Silver Lake Blvd, Silver Lake) Beck played some early gigs at what is still LA's best place for indie and alterna-sounds. When the ad says 'special guest,' you never know what level of star might show up for quick and dirty impromptu sessions.

Hotel Cafe (Map p922; ☎ 323-461-2040; www.hotelcafe.com; 1623.5 N Cahuenga Blvd, Hollywood) The 'it' place for handmade music sometimes features big-timers such as Suzanne Vega, but it's really more of a stepping stone for message-minded newbie balladeers. Get there early and enter from the alley.

McCabe's Guitar Shop (Map p927; ☎ 310-828-4403; www.mccabes.com; 3101 Pico Blvd, Santa Monica) This mecca of musicianship sells guitars and other instruments, and the likes of Jackson Browne, Liz Phair and Michelle Shocked perform live in the postage-stamp-sized back room.

Babe's & Ricky's (Map pp916-17; ☎ 323-295-9112; www.bluesbar.com; 4339 Leimert Blvd, Leimert Park; ⏲ Mon & Thu-Sat) This legendary blues joint is great any time, but Mondays are cult: $8 buys Mama Laura's late-night soul food buffet.

The Sunset Strip is lined with legendary music halls from Whisky A-Go-Go to House of Blues.

Classical Music & Opera

Los Angeles Philharmonic (Map p919; ☎ 323-850-2000; www.laphil.org; 111 S Grand Ave, Downtown) The world-class LA Phil performs classics and cutting-edge works at the Walt Disney Concert Hall. In 2009, the Phil welcomed Venezuelan wunderkind Gustavo Dudamel as its music director.

our pick Hollywood Bowl (off Map p922; ☎ 323-850-2000; www.hollywoodbowl.com; 2301 N Highland Ave, Hollywood; ⏲ late Jun-Sep) This historic natural amphitheater is the LA Phil's summer home and also a stellar place to catch big-name rock, jazz, blues and pop acts. Come early for a preshow picnic (alcohol is allowed).

Los Angeles Opera (Map p919; ☎ 213-972-8001; www.laopera.com; Dorothy Chandler Pavilion; 135 N Grand Ave, Downtown) Helmed by Plácido Domingo, this renowned opera ensemble plays it pretty safe with crowd-pleasers.

Theater

Centre Theatre Group (☎ 213-628-2772; www.centretheatregroup.org) New and classic plays and musicals, including some Broadway touring companies, are presented in – count em – three venues: Ahmanson Theatre (Map p919) and Mark Taper Forum (Map p919) in Downtown LA and Kirk Douglas Theatre (Map pp916–17) in Culver City. Phone for $20 'Hot Tix' to shows (when available).

Actors' Gang Theatre (Map pp916-17; ☎ 310-838-4264; www.theactorsgang.com; 9070 Venice Blvd, Culver City) Cofounded by Tim Robbins, this socially mindful troupe has won many awards for its bold and offbeat interpretations of classics and new works pulled from ensemble workshops.

Deaf West Theatre (Map pp916-17; ☎ 818-762-2773; www.deafwest.org; 5112 Lankershim Blvd, North Hollywood, San Fernando Valley; tickets vary) Hearing-impaired actors perform classic and contemporary plays in sign language with voice interpretation and/or supertitles; its 'Big River' soared on Broadway.

Other thespian venues:

East West Players (Map p919; ☎ 213-625-7000; www.eastwestplayers.org; 120 N Judge John Aiso St, Downtown) Pioneering Asian American ensemble.

Will Geer Theatricum Botanicum (Map pp916-17; ☎ 310-455-3723; www.theatricum.com; 1419 N Topanga Canyon Blvd, north of Santa Monica) Enchanting summer repertory in the woods.

Spectator Sports

Dodger Stadium (Map p919; ☎ 866-363-4377; www.dodgers.com; 1000 Elysian Park Dr, Downtown) LA's Major League Baseball team plays from April to October in this legendary stadium.

Staples Center (Map p919; ☎ 213-742-7340; www.staplescenter.com; 1111 S Figueroa St, Downtown) This state-of-the-art venue is home base for all three of LA's professional basketball teams – the LA Lakers, LA Sparks and LA Clippers – as well as the LA Kings NHL ice-hockey team.

SHOPPING

Beverly Hills's **Rodeo Drive** (Map p925; btwn Wilshire & Santa Monica Blvds) may be the world's most famous shopping street, but LA drips with other options for retail therapy. Fashionistas, and their paparazzi piranhas, flock to **Robertson**

IT'S A WRAP

Dress like a movie star – in their actual clothes! Packed-to-the-rafters **It's a Wrap** (Map p925; ☎ 310-246-9727; 1164 S Robertson Blvd, Mid-City, 11am-8pm Mon-Fri, 11am-6pm Sat & Sun) sells wardrobe castoffs – tank tops to tuxedos – worn by actors and extras working on TV or movie shoots. Tags are coded (there's a list at the check-out counter), so you'll know whose clothing you can brag about wearing.

Boulevard (Map p925; btwn Beverly Blvd & 3rd St), **Melrose Avenue** (Map p925; btwn San Vicente Blvd & La Brea Ave) in Hollywood and West Hollywood, and **Montana Avenue** (Map p927; btwn Lincoln Blvd & 20th St) in Santa Monica.

Hollywood is ground zero for groovy tunes at **Amoeba Music** (Map p922; ☎ 323-245-6400; 6400 W Sunset Blvd). East of here, Silver Lake has cool kitsch, collectibles and emerging LA designers, especially around **Sunset Junction** (Map p922; cnr Hollywood & Sunset Blvds). Other 'chain-gang-free' strips are Main St in Santa Monica (Map p927), Abbot Kinney Blvd in Venice (p927) and Larchmont Blvd in Hollywood (Map p922).

Bargain hunters haunt Downtown's Fashion District (p920), Jewelry District (p920) and Flower Market (p921), while Long Beach's **Retro Row** (Map pp916-17; E 4th St btwn Junipero & Cherry Aves) brims with shops selling vintage clothing and mid-century furniture at prices from 'how much?' to '*how* much?'

Good flea markets include the weekly **Melrose Trading Post** (Map p925; Fairfax High School, 7850 Melrose Ave, West Hollywood; admission $2; 9am-5pm Sun), which brings out hipsters in search of retro treasure, and the monthly **Rose Bowl Flea Market** (Map pp916-17; ☎ 323-560-7469; www.rgcshows.com; Rose Bowl, 1001 Rose Bowl Dr, Pasadena; admission $8-20; 5am-4:30pm 2nd Sun of the month), the 'mother' of all flea markets with more than 2200 vendors.

GETTING THERE & AWAY

Air

LA's main gateway is **Los Angeles International Airport** (LAX; Map pp916-17; ☎ 310-646-5252; www.lawa.org/lax), one of the world's five busiest. The nine terminals are linked by the free Shuttle Bus A, on the lower (arrival) level. Hotel and car-rental shuttles stop here as well.

Long Beach Airport (LGB; Map pp916-17) and Burbank's **Bob Hope Airport** (BUR; Map pp916-17) handle mostly domestic flights.

Bus

The main **Greyhound bus terminal** (Map p919; ☎ 213-629-8401, 800-231-2222; 1716 E 7th St) is in an unsavory part of Downtown, so avoid arriving after dark. Some buses go directly to the **Hollywood terminal** (Map p922; ☎ 323-466-6381; 1715 N Cahuenga Blvd).

Car

The usual international car-rental agencies have branches throughout Los Angeles (see p1164 for central reservation numbers and websites). At LAX, if you don't have a prior booking, use courtesy phones in the arrival areas and catch free shuttles to the agencies' off-airport locations.

Train

Amtrak trains roll into Downtown's historic **Union Station** (Map p919; ☎ 800-872-7245; 800 N Alameda St). The *Pacific Surfliner* travels daily to San Diego ($34, 2¾ hours), Santa Barbara ($25, 2½ hours) and San Luis Obispo ($36, 5½ hours).

GETTING AROUND

To/From the Airport

At LAX, door-to-door shuttles operated by **Prime Time** (☎ 800-473-3743; www.primetimeshuttle.com) and **Super Shuttle** (☎ 310-782-6600; www.supershuttle.com) leave from the lower level of all terminals. Typical fares to Santa Monica, Hollywood or Downtown are $21, $26 and $16, respectively. **Disneyland Express** (☎ 714-978-8855; www.grayline.com) travels at least hourly between LAX and Disneyland-area hotels for one way/round-trip $22/$32.

Curbside dispatchers will summon a taxi for you. There's a flat fare of $46.50 to Downtown LA, and metered fares average $30 to Santa Monica, $42 to Hollywood, and up to $90 to Disneyland. There is a $2.50 surcharge for taxis departing LAX. See opposite for further information.

LAX Flyaway Buses (☎ 866-435-9529; www.lawa.org/flyaway) depart LAX terminals every 30 minutes, from about 5am to midnight, nonstop to both Westwood ($5, 30 min) and Union Station ($7, 45 min) in Downtown LA.

Other **public transportation** is slower and less convenient but cheaper. From the lower level outside any terminal, catch a free shuttle bus to parking lot C, from where it is a walk of under a minute to the LAX Transit Center, the hub for buses serving all of LA. You can also take shuttle bus G to Aviation Station and the Metro Green Line light rail, from where you can connect to the Blue Line and Downtown LA or Long Beach (40 minutes). See Public Transportation (below) for further information.

Car & Motorcycle

Unless time is no factor or money is extremely tight, you'll probably find yourself behind the wheel, although this means contending with some of the worst traffic in the country. Avoid rush hour (roughly 7:30am to 9am and 4pm to 6:30pm).

Parking at motels and cheaper hotels is usually free, while fancier ones charge from $8 to $36. Valet parking at nicer restaurants, hotels and nightspots is commonplace, with rates ranging from $2.50 to $10.

For local parking recommendations, see each of the neighborhoods in the Sights section (p918).

Public Transportation

LA's **Metro**(☎ 800-266-6883; www.metro.net) operates about 200 bus lines and six subway and light-rail lines:

Blue Line Downtown (7th St/Metro Center) to Long Beach
Expo Line Downtown (7th St/Metro Center) to Culver City, via Exposition Park
Gold Line Union Station to Pasadena and East LA
Green Line Norwalk to Redondo Beach
Purple Line Downtown to Koreatown
Red Line Union Station to North Hollywood, via Downtown, Hollywood and Universal Studios

Tickets cost $1.25 per boarding (get a transfer when boarding if needed). There are no free transfers between trains and buses, but 'TAP card' unlimited ride passes cost day/week $5/17. Bus drivers sell regular fares and same-day passes (exact fare required). Purchase train tickets at vending machines in stations. Trip-planning help is available at ☎ 800-266-6883 or online at www.metro.net.

Local **DASH minibuses** (☎ your area code + 808-2273; www.ladottransit.com; 25¢) serve Downtown and Hollywood. Santa Monica–based **Big Blue Bus** (☎ 310-451-5444; www.bigbluebus.com, 75¢) serves much of the western LA area and LAX. Its Line 10 Freeway Express connects Santa Monica with Downtown LA ($1.75, one hour).

See also p918 for further information.

Taxi

Except for taxis lined up outside airports, train stations, bus stations and major hotels, it's best to phone for a cab. Fares are metered, $2.85 at flag fall plus $2.70 per mile. Taxis serving the airport accept credit cards, though sometimes grudgingly. Some recommended companies:

Checker (☎ 800-300-5007)
Independent (☎ 800-521-8294)
Yellow Cab (☎ 800-200-1085)

AROUND LOS ANGELES

CATALINA ISLAND

Mediterranean-flavored **Catalina Island** (www.visitcatalina.org, www.catalinachamber.com) is a popular getaway for harried Angelenos, but seems to sink under the weight of day-trippers in summer. Commercial activity concentrates in the pint-sized port town of **Avalon** where the tourist office on the Green Pier has maps and information on sights and activities.

Catalina isn't famous for its beaches, but it does have some excellent snorkeling at Descanso Beach, Lovers' Cove and Casino Point Marine Park, a marine reserve that is also the best shore dive. Gear rentals cluster on the Green Pier. Other ways to escape the throngs are by kayaking the quiet coves of Catalina's rocky coastline or by visiting the nature-protected backcountry. On the Inside Adventure by **Catalina Adventure Tours** (☎ 877-510-2888; www.catalinaadventuretours.com; $35), you'll enjoy memorable views of the rugged coast and sandy coves and may even run into a herd of bison. The only other way to access the inland areas is by foot, boat or mountain bike (free pass required; call ☎ 310-510-1421).

Catalina Express (☎ 310-519-1212, 800-481-3470; www.catalinaexpress.com; round-trip $66.50) operates ferries to Avalon from San Pedro, Long Beach and Dana Point (in Orange County). Reservations are recommended in summer.

SIX FLAGS MAGIC MOUNTAIN

Velocity is king at **Six Flags** (off Map pp916-17; ☎ 661-255-4111; www.sixflags.com/parks/magicmountain; 26101 Magic Mountain Pkwy, Valencia; adult/child under 4ft $54/30; 🕑 from 10:30am daily late Mar-early Sep, open Sat, Sun, holidays & some Fridays rest of year, closing times vary 6pm-midnight;), the ultimate roller-coaster park, where you can go up, down and inside-out faster and in more baffling ways than anywhere aside from a space shuttle. Check the website for discounts. It's about 30 miles north of central LA off the I-5 (Golden State Fwy). Parking is $15.

SOUTHERN CALIFORNIA COAST

ORANGE COUNTY

Oh sure, you've seen *the OC*, then *Real Housewives*, and you *think* you know what to expect from this giant quilt of suburbia connecting LA and San Diego: affluence, aspiration and anxiety. Indeed, there is much living large in Orange County: shopping is a major passion, and tony resorts and restaurants serve its affluent residents. But it's also home to a burgeoning arts community, 42 miles of glorious beaches and – don't forget – the 'Happiest Place on Earth,' aka Disneyland.

Disneyland Resort

The mother of all theme parks, **Disneyland** (Map pp916-17; ☎ 714-781-4000 or 714-781-7290; www.disneyland.com; 1313 Harbor Blvd, Anaheim; 1-day pass either park adult/child 3-9yr $69/59, both parks $94/84;) lures you into a parallel world that's as enchanting as it is freaky and frenzied. The most popular rides and attractions include the wildly creative Indiana Jones Adventure, the white-knuckle Space Mountain and the Pirate's Lair where Jack Sparrow welcomes wannabe swashbucklers. The Finding Nemo Submarine Voyage is a gentle adventure for little ones.

Bigger and less crowded, **Disney's California Adventure** celebrates the natural and cultural glories of the Golden State but lacks the density of attractions and depth of imagination. The best rides are Soarin' over California, a virtual hang-glide, the Twilight Zone Tower of Terror that drops you 183ft down an elevator chute, and the new 3-D Toy Story Mania.

Nearby, **Downtown Disney** offers plenty of opportunities to drop even more cash in its stores, restaurants and entertainment venues.

You can see either park in a day, but going on all the rides requires at least two days (three if visiting both parks), as waits for top attractions can be an hour or more. To minimize wait times, especially in summer, arrive midweek before the gates open and use the Fastpass system, which assigns boarding times for selected attractions. A variety of multiday passes are available. Check the website for discounts and seasonal park hours. Parking is $12.

Chain hotels are a dime a dozen in the surrounding city of Anaheim, but a recommended indie is flowery, family-friendly **Candy Cane Inn** (☎ 714-774-5284, 800-345-7057; www.candycaneinn.net; 1747 S Harbor Blvd; r $99-189;), where rates include a fitness center and poolside continental breakfast.

Knott's Berry Farm

Smaller and less commercially frenzied than Disney, Old West–themed **Knott's Berry Farm** (Map pp916-17; ☎ 714-220-5200; www.knotts.com; 8039 Beach Blvd, Buena Park; adult/child 3-11yr & senior $52/23; from 10am;) often teems with packs of speed-crazed adolescents testing their mettle on an intense line-up of thrill rides. Gut-wrenchers include the wooden Ghost Rider and the '50s-themed Xcelerator, while the single-digit-aged find tamer action at Camp Snoopy. If your stomach's up for it, wrap up with a visit with Mrs Knott's classic fried-chicken dinner (mains $10 to $16). Save time and money by printing tickets online. Parking costs $10 (free for restaurant patrons). Closing times vary from 6pm to 1pm; check website.

Orange County Beaches

Hummer-driving hunks and Botoxed beauties mix it up with surfers and artists to give Orange County's beach towns their distinct vibe. Just across the LA–OC county-line, **Seal**

WHAT THE...?

Hey, did that painting just move? Welcome to the **Pageant of the Masters** (☎ 949-497-6582, 800-487-3378; www.pageanttickets.com; admission $20-100; 8:30pm Jul & Aug), in which elaborately costumed humans step into painstaking recreations of famous paintings on an outdoor stage. The pageant began in 1933 as a sideshow to Laguna Beach's **Festival of the Arts** (www.LagunaFestivalofArts.org) and has been a prime attraction ever since. Our favorite part: watching the paintings deconstruct.

Beach is refreshingly noncommercial with its pleasantly walkable downtown, while gentrified **Huntington Beach** (aka Surf City, USA) epitomizes the California surfing lifestyle. Next up is the ritziest of the OC's beach communities: **Newport Beach**, portrayed in *The OC* and nirvana for luxe shoppers. Families should steer toward Balboa Peninsula for its beaches, vintage wooden pier and quaint amusement center.

Laguna Beach is the OC's most cultured and charming seaside town, where secluded beaches, glassy waves and eucalyptus-covered hillsides create a Riviera-like feel. Art galleries dot Coast Hwy here, and Laguna's summer art festivals are institutions.

Mission San Juan Capistrano (☎ 949-234-1300; cnr Ortega Hwy & Camino Capistrano; incl audio tour adult/child/senior $9/5/8; 🕒 8:30am-5pm), about 10 miles south and inland from Laguna, is one of California's most beautiful missions, featuring lush gardens and the charming Serra Chapel.

SAN DIEGO

San Diegans shamelessly yet endearingly promote their hometown as 'America's Finest City.' Smug? Maybe, but it's easy to see why. The weather is practically perfect, with coastal high temperatures hovering around 72°F (22°C) all year. Beaches or forests are rarely more than 10 minutes drive away. Its population (about 1.26 million) makes it America's eighth-largest city (or about 1.5 times the size of San Francisco), yet we're hard-pressed to think of a more laid-back big city anywhere.

San Diego languished as a relative backwater until WWII, when the Japanese attack on Pearl Harbor prompted the US Navy to relocate the US Pacific Fleet from Hawaii to San Diego's natural harbor. Growth has been phenomenal ever since in military, tourism, education and research (especially medicine and oceanography), alongside high-tech companies in the inland valleys and businesses involved in cross-border trade. It all makes San Diego seem more all-American than its California *compadres,* despite its borderland location.

For visitors, San Diego bursts with world-famous attractions: including the San Diego Zoo (p943), SeaWorld (p944), and Legoland (p948). The ritzy, picturesque enclave of La Jolla (p945) has pride of place on San Diego's coast. Conventions are big business too, and next to the convention center is the always buzzing Gaslamp Quarter (p941). San Diego's beach cities make for 'hanging 10' or dipping in the world's largest pool (aka the Pacific).

Orientation

San Diego's compact downtown revolves around the historic Gaslamp Quarter, a beehive of restaurants, bars and boutiques with the convention center just to its south. Southwest of here, Coronado is reached via a stunning bridge, while Little Italy and museum-rich Balboa Park (home of the San Diego Zoo) are to the north. The park segues into Hillcrest, the city's lesbi-gay hub. West of here are tourist-oriented Old Town, and the water playground around Mission Bay.

Heading north along the coast, Ocean Beach, Mission Beach and Pacific Beach epitomize the laid-back SoCal lifestyle, while La Jolla sits pretty and privileged. The I-5 Fwy cuts through the region north–south, while the I-8 Fwy is the main east–west artery. The CA163 Fwy heads north from downtown through Balboa Park.

Information

BOOKSTORE

Le Travel Store (Map p942; ☎ 619-544-0005; 745 4th Ave, Downtown)

INTERNET ACCESS

For wi-fi hot-spot locations, check www.jiwire.com.

San Diego Public Library (Map p942; ☎ 619-236-5800; www.sandiego.gov/public-library; 820 E St, Downtown; 📶) Call or check the website for branch locations.

INTERNET RESOURCES

Accessible San Diego (www.asd.travel) Excellent resource for barrier-free travel around San Diego.

Gaslamp.org (www.gaslamp.org) Everything you need to know about the bustling Gaslamp Quarter, including parking secrets.

VISITING TIJUANA

Tijuana, Mexico, has long been a popular side trip; however, at the time of writing, safety conditions were such that it's not recommended. A triple-whammy of drug-related violence, the global economic downturn and the 2009 H1N1 swine flu virus has turned once-bustling tourist areas into ghost towns.

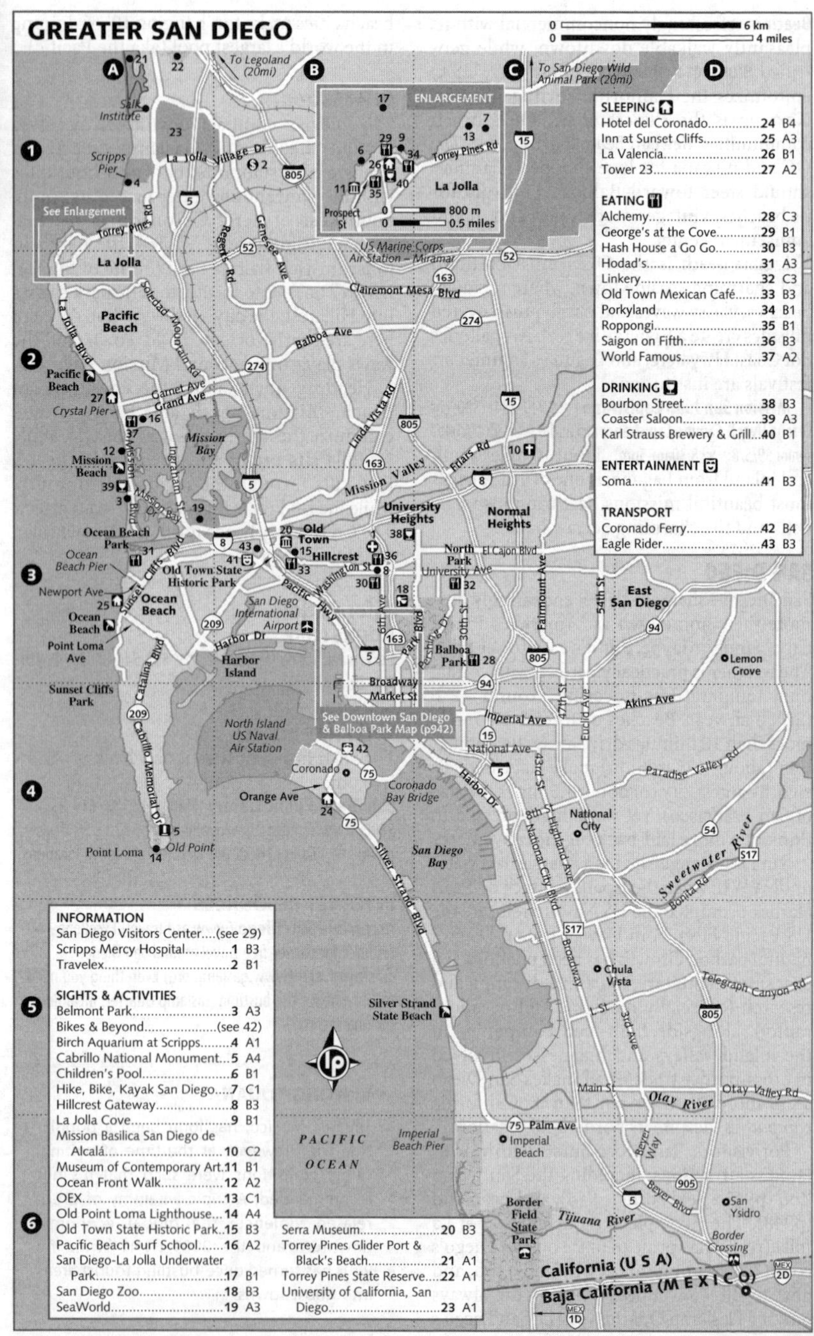
GREATER SAN DIEGO
0 6 km
0 4 miles
To Legoland (20mi)
To San Diego Wild Animal Park (20mi)
ENLARGEMENT
See Enlargement
See Downtown San Diego & Balboa Park Map (p942)
PACIFIC OCEAN
California (U S A)
Baja California (M E X I C O)
SLEEPING
Hotel del Coronado....24 B4
Inn at Sunset Cliffs....25 A3
La Valencia....26 B1
Tower 23....27 A2
EATING
Alchemy....28 C3
George's at the Cove....29 B1
Hash House a Go Go....30 B3
Hodad's....31 A3
Linkery....32 C3
Old Town Mexican Café....33 B3
Porkyland....34 B1
Roppongi....35 B1
Saigon on Fifth....36 B3
World Famous....37 A2
DRINKING
Bourbon Street....38 B3
Coaster Saloon....39 A3
Karl Strauss Brewery & Grill....40 B1
ENTERTAINMENT
Soma....41 B3
TRANSPORT
Coronado Ferry....42 B4
Eagle Rider....43 B3
INFORMATION
San Diego Visitors Center....(see 29)
Scripps Mercy Hospital....1 B3
Travelex....2 B1
SIGHTS & ACTIVITIES
Belmont Park....3 A3
Bikes & Beyond....(see 42)
Birch Aquarium at Scripps....4 A1
Cabrillo National Monument....5 A4
Children's Pool....6 B1
Hike, Bike, Kayak San Diego....7 C1
Hillcrest Gateway....8 B3
La Jolla Cove....9 B1
Mission Basilica San Diego de Alcalá....10 C2
Museum of Contemporary Art....11 B1
Ocean Front Walk....12 A2
OEX....13 C1
Old Point Loma Lighthouse....14 A4
Old Town State Historic Park....15 B3
Pacific Beach Surf School....16 A2
San Diego-La Jolla Underwater Park....17 B1
San Diego Zoo....18 B3
SeaWorld....19 A3
Serra Museum....20 B3
Torrey Pines Glider Port & Black's Beach....21 A1
Torrey Pines State Reserve....22 A1
University of California, San Diego....23 A1

San Diego Convention & Visitors Bureau (www.sandiego.org) Search hotels, sights, dining, rental cars and more, and make reservations.
San Diego.com (www.sandiego.com) Comprehensive ad-based portal to all things San Diegan, from fun stuff to serious business.

MEDIA

Gay & Lesbian Times (www.gaylesbiantimes.com) Free weekly.
KPBS 89.5 FM (www.kpbs.org) National public radio.
San Diego Magazine (www.sandiegomagazine.com) Glossy monthly.
San Diego Reader (www.sdreader.com) Free tabloid-sized listings magazine.
San Diego Union-Tribune (www.signonsandiego.com) The city's major daily.

MEDICAL SERVICES

Rite-Aid pharmacies (☎ 800-748-3243) Call for the nearest branch.
Scripps Mercy Hospital (Map p940; ☎ 619-294-8111; 4077 5th Ave, Hillcrest; 24hr emergency room)

MONEY

Travelex (10:30am-7pm Mon-Fri, 10am-6pm Sat, 11am-4pm Sun); Airport (Map p940; ☎ 619-295-2501; 8am-5pm); Downtown (Map p942; ☎ 619-235-0901; Horton Plaza;); La Jolla (Map p940; ☎ 858-457-2412; University Towne Centre mall, 4417 La Jolla Village Dr); Foreign currency exchange services.

POST

Call ☎ 800-275-8777 or log on to www.usps.com for the nearest branch.

TOURIST INFORMATION

Balboa Park Visitors Center (Map p942; ☎ 619-239-0512; www.balboapark.org; 1549 El Prado; 9:30am-4:30pm) In the House of Hospitality. Sells park maps and the Passport to Balboa Park (adult/child $39/21, with zoo admission $65/39), which allows one-time entry to 13 of the park's museums within seven days.
San Diego Visitors Centers (☎ 619-236-1212, 800-350-6205; www.sandiego.org) Downtown (Map p942; cnr W Broadway & Harbor Dr; 9am-5pm Jun-Sep, 9am-4pm Oct-May); La Jolla (Map p940; 7966 Herschel Ave; 11am-4pm, possible longer hours Jun-Sep & Sat & Sun)

Sights

DOWNTOWN

In 1867, creative real-estate wrangling by developer Alonzo Horton created the so-called 'New Town' that is today's downtown San Diego. Downtown's main street, 5th Ave, was once a notorious strip of saloons, gambling joints and bordellos known as Stingaree.

These days, Stingaree has been beautifully restored as the thumping heart of downtown San Diego and rechristened the **Gaslamp Quarter** (Map p942), a playground of restaurants, bars, clubs, shops and galleries. For the full historical picture, peruse the exhibits inside the 1850 **William Heath Davis House** (Map p942; ☎ 619-233-4692; www.gaslampquarter.org; 410 Island Ave; adult/child/senior $5/free/4; 10am-6pm Tue-Sat, 11am-3pm Sun), which also offers guided walking tours (adult/senior and student $10/8; tours 11am Saturday) of the quarter.

Just a quick stroll southeast of the Gaslamp is Downtown's newest landmark, **Petco Park** (Map p942; ☎ 619-795-5011; www.padres.com; 100 Park Blvd; tours adult/child/senior $9/5/6; tours 10:30am, 12:30pm & 2:30pm Tue-Sun May-Aug, 10:30am & 12:30pm Apr & Sep, subject to game schedule), home of the San Diego Padres baseball team. Take an 80-minute behind-the-scenes tour.

Downtown's commercial focal point is the colorful, mazelike shopping mall **Westfield Horton Plaza** (Map p942; Broadway & 4th St; P). West of here, the **Museum of Contemporary Art** (Map p942; ☎ 858-454-3541; www.mcasd.org; 1001 & 1100 Kettner Blvd; adult/student/senior $10/free/5; 11am-5pm Thu-Tue, to 7pm third Thu each month, with free admission 5pm-7pm) emphasizes minimalist and pop art, as well as conceptual works and cross-border art. The 1100 Kettner Bldg is at the historic Santa Fe Depot. Another branch is in La Jolla (p945; one ticket admits you to all venues).

The museum is little more than a Frisbee toss away from the Embarcadero waterfront, where you can catch a harbor cruise or the Coronado Ferry (p943). The main attraction, though, is the **USS Midway Museum** (Map p942; ☎ 619-544-9600; www.midway.org; Navy Pier; adult/child/senior & student $17/9/13; 10am-5pm;), which is aboard the Navy's longest-serving aircraft carrier (1945–91). A self-guided audio tour takes in berthing spaces, galley, sick bay and, of course, the flight deck with its restored aircraft, including an F-14 Tomcat. Allow at least two hours. Parking costs from $5.

Other salty Embarcadero sights include the historic sailing vessels of the **Maritime Museum** (Map p942; ☎ 619-234-9153; www.sdmaritime.com; 1492 N Harbor Dr; adult/child/senior $14/8/11; 9am-8pm, to 9am late May-early Sep), most notably the 1863 *Star of India*.

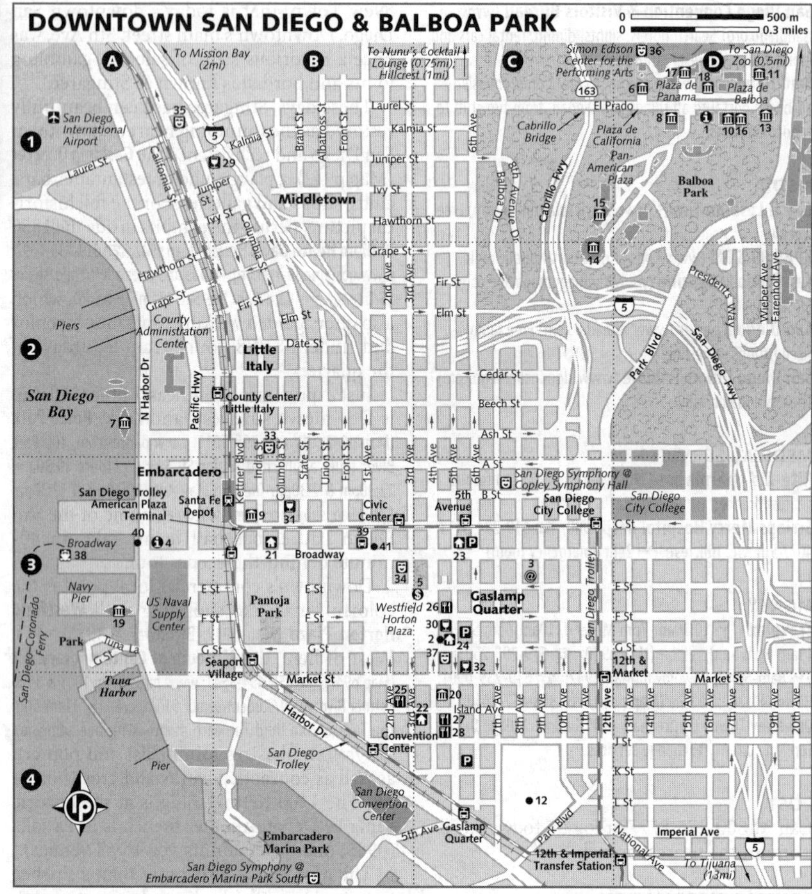

INFORMATION

Balboa Park Visitors Center......1 D1
Le Travel Store......2 C3
San Diego Public Library......3 C3
San Diego Visitors Center......4 A3
Travelex......5 C3

SIGHTS & ACTIVITIES

California Building......6 D1
Maritime Museum......7 A2
Mingei International Museum......8 D1
Museum of Contemporary Art......9 B3
Museum of Man......(see 6)
Museum of Photographic Arts......10 D1
Natural History Museum......11 D1
Old Globe Theaters......(see 36)
Petco Park......12 C4
Reuben H Fleet Science Center......13 D1
San Diego Air & Space Museum......14 C2
San Diego Automotive Museum......15 C1
San Diego Model Railroad Museum......16 D1
San Diego Museum of Art......17 D1
Timken Museum of Art......18 D1
USS Midway Museum......19 A3
William Heath Davis House......20 C4

SLEEPING

500 West Hotel......21 B3
Horton Grand Hotel......22 C4
Se San Diego......23 C3
USA Hostel San Diego......24 C3

EATING

Café 222......25 B4
Croce's Restaurant & Jazz Bar......26 C3
Gaslamp Strip Club......27 C4
Oceanaire......28 C4

DRINKING

Airport Lounge......29 B1
Bitter End......30 C3
Karl Strauss Brewery & Grill......31 B3
Side Bar......32 C3

ENTERTAINMENT

Anthology......33 B2
Arts Tix......34 B3
Casbah......35 A1
Imax Theater......(see 13)
Old Globe Theaters......36 D1
Shout House......37 C3

TRANSPORT

Coronado Ferry......38 A3
Greyhound......39 B3
San Diego Harbor Excursion......40 A3
Transit Store......41 B3

In northern downtown, **Little Italy** (Map p942; www.littleitalysd.com) has evolved into one of the city's hippest places to live, eat and shop. India St is the main drag.

CORONADO

Technically a peninsula, Coronado Island (Map p940) is joined to the mainland by a soaring, boomerang-shaped bridge. The main draw here is the **Hotel del Coronado** (p946), famous for its buoyant Victorian architecture and illustrious guest book, which includes Thomas Edison, Brad Pitt and Marilyn Monroe (its exterior stood in for a Miami hotel in the classic film *Some Like it Hot*). The hourly **Coronado Ferry** (Map p942; ☎ 619-234-4111; www.sdhe.com; one way/round-trip $3.25/6.50; 🕑 9am-10pm) shuttles between the Broadway Pier on the Embarcadero (Map p942) to the ferry landing at the foot of Orange Ave (Map p940), where **Bikes & Beyond** (Map p940; ☎ 619-435-7180; rental per hr/day from $7/30; 🕑 9am-8pm, call for seasonal hours) rents bicycles.

SAN DIEGO ZOO

If it slithers, crawls, stomps, swims, leaps or flies, chances are you'll find it in this world-famous **zoo** (Map p940; ☎ 619-231-1515; www.sandiegozoo.org; 2920 Zoo Dr; adult/child $28.50/18.50, with guided bus tour & aerial tram ride $35/26; 🕑 opens 9am, closing times vary; 👪) in northern Balboa Park. It's home to 3000-plus animals representing 800-plus species in a beautifully landscaped setting, including the new 7.5-acre Elephant Odyssey. Arrive early, when the animals are most active. Attractions include animal shows and an aerial tram. See also the affiliated **San Diego Wild Animal Park** (off Map p940); combination tickets are available.

BALBOA PARK & AROUND

Balboa Park is an urban oasis brimming with more than a dozen museums, gorgeous gardens and architecture, performance spaces and the famous zoo. Early 20th-century beaux arts and Spanish-colonial buildings (the legacy of world's fairs) are grouped around plazas along the east–west El Prado promenade. Balboa Park (parking free) is easily reached from downtown on bus 7. A free tram shuttles visitors around.

The Balboa Park Visitors Center sells park maps and the Passport to Balboa Park; see p941 for details. Some museums occasionally have free admission on Tuesday – check with the visitors center.

The scenic park approach from the west across Cabrillo Bridge drops you at Plaza de California, dominated by the flamboyant **California Building** (Map p942). Inside, the **Museum of Man** (Map p942; ☎ 619-239-2001; www.museumofman.org; Plaza de California; adult/child 6-12yr/child 13-17yr & senior $10/5/7.50; 🕑 10am-4:30pm) exhibits world-class pottery, jewelry, baskets and other artifacts. Behind the museum are the **Old Globe Theaters**.

Further east, a trio of museums rings Plaza de Panama, including the **San Diego Museum of Art** (Map p942; ☎ 619-232-7931; www.sdmart.org; Plaza de Panama; adult/child/student/senior $10/4/7/8; 🕑 10am-5pm Tue-Sat, noon-5pm Sun, to 9pm Thu), which gets accolades for its European old masters and good collections of American and Asian art. The **Mingei International Museum** (Map p942; ☎ 619-239-0003; www.mingei.org; 1439 El Prado, Plaza de Panama; adult/child/senior $7/4/5; 🕑 10am-4pm Tue-Sun) exhibits folk art from around the globe, while the small but exquisite **Timken Museum of Art** (Map p942; ☎ 619-239-5548; www.timkenmuseum.org; 1500 El Prado; admission free; 🕑 10am-4:30pm Tue-Sat, from 1:30pm Sun) showcases European and American heavyweights, from Rembrandt to Cézanne and John Singleton Copley.

East along El Prado, the **Museum of Photographic Arts** (Map p942; ☎ 619-238-7559; www.mopa.org; adult/child/student & senior $6/free/4; 🕑 10am-5pm) exhibits fine-art photography and hosts an ongoing film series. The **San Diego Model Railroad Museum** (Map p942; ☎ 619-696-0199; www.sdmrm.org; adult/senior/student $6/3/5; 🕑 11am-4pm Tue-Fri, 11am-5pm Sat & Sun; 👪) is one of the largest of its kind with brilliantly 'landscaped' train sets.

Next up is Plaza de Balboa, flanked by the **Reuben H Fleet Science Center** (Map p942; ☎ 619-238-1233; www.rhfleet.org; 1875 El Prado; adult/child & senior $10/8.75; 🕑 9:30am-varies; 👪), which is a family-oriented hands-on museum-cum-**Imax theater** (adult/child $14:50/11.75 incl Science Center admission, additional films $5). Opposite is the **Natural History Museum** (Map p942; ☎ 619-232-3821; www.sdnhm.org; 1788 El Prado; adult/child/student/senior $13/7/8/11; 🕑 10am-5pm; 👪), with dinosaur skeletons, an impressive rattlesnake collection, an earthquake exhibit and nature-themed movies in a giant-screen cinema.

Buildings around Pan-American Plaza in the park's southern section date from the 1935 Pacific–California Exposition. It's all about polished chrome and cool tailfins at the **San Diego Automotive Museum** (Map p942; ☎ 619-231-2886;

www.sdautomuseum.org; 2080 Pan-American Plaza; adult/child/senior $8/5/6; 10am-5pm). The **San Diego Air & Space Museum** (Map p942; 619-234-8291; www.aerospacemuseum.org; adult/child/student & senior $15/6/12; 10am-5:30pm Jun-Aug, to 4:30pm Sep-May) offers a fun-filled look at the history and mystique of flight. Highlights include an original Blackbird SR-71 spy plane and a replica of Charles Lindbergh's *Spirit of St Louis*, as well as simulators that require an extra charge.

North of Balboa Park, **Hillcrest** (off Map p942) is the hub of San Diego's gay community, but everyone's welcome in its buzzing restaurants, boutiques, bookstores, bars and cafés. Start your stroll at the **Hillcrest Gateway** (Map p940), a neon arch near 5th St and University Ave. **North Park** (Map p940) is a budding neighborhood with a youngish, urban vibe and a growing restaurant and nightlife scene around 30th St and University Ave.

OLD TOWN & MISSION VALLEY

In 1769, a band of missionaries led by the Franciscan friar Junípero Serra founded the first of the 21 California missions on San Diego's Presidio Hill; a small village (pueblo) grew around it. The spot turned out to be less than ideal for a mission, however, and in 1774 the mission was moved about 7 miles upriver, closer to a steady water supply and fertile land.

Today the **Mission Basilica San Diego de Alcalá** (Map p940; 619-281-8449; www.missionsandiego.com; 10818 San Diego Mission Rd at Friars Rd; adult/child/student & senior $3/1/2; 9am-4:45pm) is secluded in a corner of what's now called Mission Valley. It's a modest rectangle embracing a tranquil garden. Unfortunately, reaching it requires passing through the valley itself, via an unlovely freeway flanked by three massive shopping malls.

The original pueblo is now called **Old Town**. On the site of the original mission stands the handsome **Serra Museum** (Map p940; 619-297-3258; 2727 Presidio Dr; adult/child/student & senior $5/2/4; 10am-4:30pm), which highlights life during the city's rough-and-tumble early period.

Downhill, **Old Town State Historic Park** (Map p940; 619-220-5422; San Diego Ave at Twiggs St; visitor center 10am-5pm; P) preserves five original adobe buildings and several re-created structures from the first pueblo, including a schoolhouse and a newspaper office. Most now contain museums, shops or restaurants, and there are more restaurants along San Diego Ave. The visitor center operates free tours.

POINT LOMA

This peninsula wraps around the entrance to crescent-shaped San Diego Bay like an arm around a shoulder. Enjoy stunning bay panoramas from the **Cabrillo National Monument** (Map p940; 619-557-5450; www.nps.gov/cabr; per car $5 or per person $3; 9am-5pm; P), which honors the leader of the first Spanish exploration of the West Coast. In winter enjoy whale-watching and tide-pooling. The nearby 1854 **Old Point Loma Lighthouse** helped guide ships until 1891 and is now a museum.

MISSION BAY & BEACHES

After WWII, coastal engineering turned the mouth of the swampy San Diego River into a 7-sq-mile playground of parks, beaches and bays. Amoeba-shaped Mission Bay sits just inland. Surfing is popular in Ocean Beach and Mission Beach, and all the beaches are naturals for swimming, kiteflying and cycling along miles of paved bike paths.

Mission Bay's four-star attraction is **SeaWorld** (Map p940; 800-257-4268, 619-226-3901; www.seaworld.com/seaworld/ca; 500 SeaWorld Dr; adult/child 3-9yr $65/55; 9am-11pm Jul–mid-Aug, shorter hours rest of year;). It's easy to spend a day here, shuttling among shows, rides and exhibits. The biggest draws are live animal shows, particularly *Believe*, featuring Shamu, the world's most famous killer whale, and his killer whale amigos leaping, diving and gliding. Some may find the presentation a little, well, awww, but the animals induce *awe*. Dolphin shows are also popular. Avoid marked 'soak zones' near the tanks or you will get wet. There are also zoolike animal exhibits and a few amusement-park-style rides, such as the Journey to Atlantis flume. Lines can be long in summer and around holidays. Parking is $12.

San Diego's three major beaches are ribbons of hedonism where armies of tanned, taut bodies frolic in the sand and surf. South of Mission Bay, hippie-flavored **Ocean Beach** (OB; Map p940) has a fishing pier, beach volleyball, sunset BBQs and good surf. Newport Ave is chockablock with bohemian bars, eateries and shops selling beachwear, surf gear and antiques.

West of Mission Bay, **Mission Beach** (MB; Map p940) and its northern neighbor, **Pacific Beach** (PB; Map p940), are connected by the car-free **Ocean Front Walk** (Map p940), which swarms with skaters, joggers and cyclists year-round. The small **Belmont Park** amusement park in MB beckons with a historic wooden roller coaster and large indoor pool. PB has the better-quality restaurants and nightlife.

LA JOLLA

Snuggling against one of Southern California's loveliest sweeps of coast, La Jolla (Spanish for 'the jewel;' say la-*hoy*-ah, if you please) is a ritzy suburb with shimmering beaches and a tight, upscale downtown. Noteworthy sights include the **Children's Pool** (Map p940; no longer a kids' swim area but now home to sea lions), kayaking at **La Jolla Cove** (Map p940), exploring **sea caves** and snorkeling the **San Diego-La Jolla Underwater Park** (Map p940). The **Museum of Contemporary Art** (Map p940; ☎ 858-454-3541; www.mcasd.org; 700 Prospect St; adult/student/senior $10/free/5; ⏰ 11am-5pm Thu-Tue, to 7pm third Thu each month, with free admission 5pm-7pm) is the sister venue of the Downtown branch (above; same ticket for both locations).

Outside La Jolla's central village is the **University of California, San Diego** (UCSD) (Map p940), with its renowned research facilities. The **Birch Aquarium at Scripps** (Map p940); ☎ 858-534-3474; http://aquarium.ucsd.edu; 2300 Exhibition Way; adult/child/student/senior $11/7.50/8/9; ⏰ 9am-5pm; P ♿) has a spectacular oceanfront setting. Up the coast, the **Torrey Pines State Reserve** (Map p940; ☎ 858-755-2063; www.torreypine.org; 12600 N Torrey Pines Rd; car $10; ⏰ 8am-dusk) protects the endangered Torrey pine and is perfect for leisurely ocean-view strolls on 2000 acres. Parking here costs $8. Hang-gliding at Torrey Pines State Beach takes you by **Black's Beach** (Map p940), which is legendary among naturists.

Activities

Surfing and windsurfing (for surf reports, call ☎ 619-221-8824) are both excellent, although in some areas territorial locals are a major irritation. Learn to hang 10 at the **Pacific Beach Surf School** (Map p940; ☎ 858-373-1138; www.pacificbeachsurfschool.com; 4150 Mission Blvd; private lessons per person $75-85). Snorkeling and scuba diving in the **San Diego-La Jolla Underwater Park** (Map p940), you'll encounter glowing orange garibaldi flitting around giant kelp forests. For gear or instruction, try **OEX** (Map p940; ☎ 858-454-6195; www.oeexpress.com; 2158 Avenida de la Playa) in La Jolla.

Tours

Hike, Bike, Kayak San Diego (Map p940; ☎ 858-551-9510, 866-425-2925; www.hikebikekayak.com; 2246 Avenida de la Playa, La Jolla) Just what it says.

Old Town Trolley Tours (☎ 619-298-8687; www.trolleytours.com; adult/child $32/16) Hop-on, hop-off loop tour to the main attractions.

San Diego Harbor Excursion (Map p942; ☎ 619-234-4111; www.sdhe.com; 1050 N Harbor Dr; adult/child from $20/10) A variety of bay and harbor cruises.

Sleeping

Rates quoted here are 'rack' rates, and can skyrocket downtown during big conventions and the summer peak and plummet at other times. The San Diego Conventions & Visitor Bureau runs a **room reservation line** (☎ 800-350-6205; www.sandi ego.org).

DOWNTOWN

USA Hostel San Diego (Map p942; ☎ 619-232-3100, 800-438-8622; www.usahostels.com; 726 5th Ave; dm/d incl breakfast from $26/65; 💻 📶) In a former Victorian-era hotel, this convivial Gaslamp hostel has cheerful rooms, a full kitchen and a lounge for chilling. Rates include linen, lockers and a pancake breakfast.

500 West Hotel (Map p942; ☎ 619-234-5252, 866-315-4251; www.500westhotel.com; 500 W Broadway; s/d/tw with shared bath $59/69/79; ⊠ 💻 📶) Rooms are shoebox-sized and baths are down the hallway in this renovated 1920s YMCA, but hipsters on a budget love the bright decor, flat-screen TVs, communal kitchen (and diner-style restaurant, 7am to 1pm) and fitness studio.

Horton Grand Hotel (Map p942; ☎ 619-544-1886, 800-542-1886; www.hortongrand.com; 311 Island Ave; r from $199; ⊠ 📶) This brick hotel in the Gaslamp dates from 1886. All rooms are individually decorated with Victoriana and gas fireplaces, and some have street-facing wrought-iron balconies. Rooms facing the inner courtyard are quieter. Parking is $25.

Se San Diego (Map p942; ☎ 619-515-3000; www.sesandiego.com; 1047 5th Ave; r from $249; ⊠ 💻 📶 🐾) This new hotel brings Hollywood glam to San Diego. The 9,000lb bronze front door pivots open on to Nepalese carpets and walls covered in silver leaf, and the texture fest continues with crystal beads, stingray skin and woven leather. There's doting service, a chic restaurant, lovely spa and, should you need it, a music studio. Parking is $36.

BEACHES

Inn at Sunset Cliffs (Map p940; ☎ 619-222-7901, 866-786-2543; www.innatsunsetcliffs.com; 1370 Sunset Cliffs Blvd, Ocean

Beach; r from $175;) Hear the surf crashing onto the rocky shore at this 24-room charmer wrapped around a flower-bedecked courtyard. Breezy rooms are on the small side (and may have the occasional cracked tile), but it's still tops in Ocean Beach. Some suites have full kitchens.

Tower 23 (Map p940; 866-869-3723; www.t23hotel.com; 723 Felspar St, Pacific Beach; r from $199;) A mod and modernist showplace for a contempo-cool beach stay, with lots of teals and mint blues and a sense of humor. There's no pool – but dude, you're right on the *beach*. Parking is $20.

La Valencia (Map p940; 858-454-0771, 800-451-0772; www.lavalencia.com; 1132 Prospect St, La Jolla; r from $295;) Publicity stills of Lon Cheney, Lillian Gish and Greta Garbo line the hallways of this 1926 landmark: pink-walled, Mediterranean-style and designed by William Templeton Johnson. Its 116 rooms are rather compact (befitting the era), but it wins for Old Hollywood romance. Parking is $25.

Hotel del Coronado (Map p940; 619-435-6611, 800-468-3533; www.hoteldel.com; 1500 Orange Ave, Coronado; r from $380;) San Diego's iconic hotel, the Del provides more than a century of history, tennis courts, spa, shops, splashy restaurants, manicured grounds and a white-sand beach. Some rooms are in a 1970s seven-story building; book the original building. Parking is $25.

Eating

With more than 6000 restaurants, San Diego's dynamic dining scene will please everyone from fast-food junkies to serious gourmets. Reservations are advised at dinnertime, especially on weekends.

DOWNTOWN

Café 222 (Map p942; 619-236-9902; 222 Island Ave; mains $6-11; 7am-1:45pm) Downtown's favorite breakfast place for pumpkin waffles; buttermilk, orange-pecan or granola pancakes; and eggs in scrambles or benedicts. There are lunchtime sandwiches and salads, but we can't get enough of breakfast (available until closing).

Croce's Restaurant & Jazz Bar (Map p942; 619-233-4355; 802 5th Ave; mains breakfast & lunch $7-19, dinner $23-35; 5:30pm-midnight Mon-Fri, 10am-midnight Sat & Sun) Empty tables are a rare sight at this sizzling restaurant – a pioneer of the Gaslamp and Ingrid Croce's tribute to her late husband, singer Jim Croce. The contemporary American menu has few false notes, nor have the musicians who perform nightly at the jazz bar.

Gaslamp Strip Club (Map p942; 619-231-3140; 340 5th Ave; mains $14-24; kitchen 5-10pm Sun-Thu, 5pm-midnight Fri & Sat, bar open later) Pull a bottle from the wine vault and then char your own favorite cut of steak, chicken or fish on the open grills in this retro-Vegas dining room. Fab, creative martinis, 'pin-up' art by Alberto Vargas and reasonable prices. No one under 21 allowed.

our pick **Oceanaire** (Map p942; 619-858-2277; 400 J St; mains $20-35; 5-10pm Sun-Thu, 5-11pm Fri & Sat) The look is art-deco ocean liner and the service is just as refined, with an oyster bar (get them for a buck during happy hour, 5pm to 6pm Monday to Friday) and inventive creations, including Maryland blue crab cakes and horseradish-crusted Alaskan halibut.

OLD TOWN, HILLCREST & NORTH PARK

our pick **Old Town Mexican Café** (Map p940; 619-297-4330; 2489 San Diego Ave, Old Town; dishes $3-14; 7am-midnight;) Watch the staff turn out fresh tortillas in the window while waiting for a table. Besides breakfast (great *chilaquiles* – soft tortilla chips covered with mole), there's a big bar (try the Old Town ultimate margarita) and rambling dining room serving famous *machacas* (shredded pork with onions and peppers).

Hash House a Go Go (Map p940; 619-298-4646; 3628 5th Ave, Hillcrest; breakfast mains $8-16; 7.30am-2pm Tue-Fri, 7.30am-2.30pm Sat-Mon, 5:30-9pm Sun & Tue-Thu, 5:30-10pm Fri & Sat) This buzzing bungalow makes biscuits and gravy straight outta Carolina, towering benedicts, large-as-your-head pancakes and, of course, hash seven different ways. Come hungry.

Saigon on Fifth (Map p940; 619-220-8828; 3900 5th Ave, Hillcrest; mains $7-16; 11am-midnight;) This Vietnamese place tries hard and succeeds, with dishes such as fresh spring rolls, fish of Hue (with garlic, ginger and lemongrass) and rockin' 'spicy noodles.' Elegant but not overbearing.

Alchemy (Map p940; 619-255-0616; 1503 30th St, North Park; mains $11-20; 4pm-midnight Sun-Thu, 4pm-1am Fri & Sat, 11am-2pm Sat & Sun) It's a spin-the-globe menu of local ingredients from small plates (including charcuterie or Parmesan frites with garlic aioli), and Jidori chicken with bok choy and shiitake dumplings, in an art-filled blondwood room.

Linkery (Map p940; ☎ 619-255-8778; 3794 30th St, North Park; mains $9-20; ⏲ 5.30-11:30pm Mon-Thu, noon-11:30pm Fri-Sun) A daily changing menu of housemade sausages and hand-cured meats from sustainably raised animals is the thing here – on a roll, in tacos, on a board with cheese or in *choucroute* (French stew). Vegetarians: don't worry; you're covered too.

BEACHES

Porkyland (Map p940; ☎ 858-459-1708; 1030 Torrey Pines Rd, La Jolla; dishes $3-7; ⏲ 9am-7pm) *Ay, caramba!* This mini-mall Mexican joint just outside La Jolla village has no atmosphere, but the burritos and fish tacos have a devoted following. The *habanero* burrito ($4.50) will make your taste buds roar and still leave you beer money.

Hodad's (Map p940; ☎ 619-224-4623; 5010 Newport Ave, Ocean Beach; burgers $4-9; ⏲ 11am-9pm Sun-Thu, 11am-10pm Fri & Sat) OB's legendary burger joint serves great shakes, massive baskets of onion rings and succulent hamburgers wrapped in paper. The walls are covered in license plates, grunge/surf-rock plays (loud!) and your bearded, tattooed server might sidle in to your booth to take your order.

World Famous (Map p940; ☎ 858-272-3100; 711 Pacific Beach Dr, Pacific Beach; mains breakfast & lunch $8-15, dinner $10-24; ⏲ 7am-11pm) Watch the surf while enjoying 'California coastal cuisine,' an ever-changing menu of inventive dishes from the sea (think banana rum mahi and bacon-and-spinach-wrapped scallops), plus steaks, salads, lunchtime sandwiches and burgers and breakfasts, like the Newport omelet with crab, shrimp and spicy sauce.

Roppongi (Map p940; ☎ 858-551-5252; 875 Prospect St, La Jolla; most dishes $10-25; ⏲ 11:30am-9:30pm Sun-Thu, 11:30am-10:30pm Fri & Sat) Tapas-style Asian fusion shines at this gorgeous eatery with clever lighting that makes everyone look good. The Polynesian crab stack, piled high and tossed at table, is a killer choice, and the ahi tuna with watermelon is a surprising flavor bomb.

George's at the Cove (Map p940; ☎ 858-454-4244; www.georgesatthecove.com; 1250 Prospect St, La Jolla; mains $11-48; ⏲ 11am-11pm) If you've got the urge to splurge, the Euro-Cal cooking is as dramatic as the oceanfront location thanks to the bottomless imagination of chef Trey Foshee. George's has graced just about every list of top restaurants in California, and indeed the USA. Three venues allow you to enjoy it at different price points: Ocean Terrace, George's Bar and George's California Modern.

Drinking

Bitter End (Map p942; ☎ 619-338-9300; 770 5th Ave, Downtown) The crowd wears khakis and drinks martinis at this former Gaslamp brothel that has been turned into an atmospheric watering hole. There's an extensive selection of beers on tap. Dancing is downstairs.

Side Bar (Map p942; ☎ 619-696-0946; www.sidebarsd.com; 536 Market St, Downtown) Good vibrations accompany good libations – watermelon mojito, martini with blue cheese-stuffed olives – at this Gaslamp lounge, while you lounge on a long banquette beneath 'oh my'-enducing art.

Karl Strauss Brewery & Grill Downtown (Map p942; ☎ 619-234-2739; 1157 Columbia St; ⏲ hrs vary); La Jolla (Map p940; ☎ 858-551-2739; cnr Wall St & Herschel Ave; ⏲ hrs vary) Local microbrewery serving surprisingly decent pub grub (most mains $10 to $19). Pints cost $3.50 and pitchers are $12.95 during happy hour (4pm to 6:30pm Monday to Friday).

Airport Lounge (Map p942; ☎ 619-685-3881; 2400 India St, Little Italy) The clientele is Euro-cool, the DJs hot, the design mod, the drinks strong and the servers dressed like flight attendants at this buzzy watering hole in the flight path of San Diego Airport.

Nunu's Cocktail Lounge (off Map p942; ☎ 619-295-2878; 3537 5th Ave, Hillcrest) Dark and divey, this hipster haven started pouring when JFK was president and still looks the part with its curvy booths, big bar and lovably kitsch decor. Smoking is permitted on the patio.

Bourbon Street (Map p940; ☎ 619-291-4043; www.bourbonstreetsd.com; 4612 Park Blvd, North Park) This gay spot's warren of bars, courtyards and dancefloor makes for easy mingling. Look for bingo nights, guest DJs and wickedly cheap martini happy hours.

Coaster Saloon (Map p940; ☎ 858-488-4438; 744 Ventura Pl, Mission Beach) This old-fashioned neighborhood bar has front-row views of the Belmont Park roller coaster, and draws an unpretentious crowd with its beer selection and good margaritas.

Entertainment

Check the *San Diego Reader* or the Thursday edition of the *San Diego Union-Tribune* for the latest happenings around town (see p941). **Arts Tix** (p942; www.sdartstix.com; 3rd Ave &

Broadway, Downtown; 11am-6pm Tue-Thu, 10am-6pm Fri & Sat, 10am-5pm Sun), in a kiosk on Broadway outside Horton Plaza, has half-price tickets for same-day evening or next-day matinee performances and discounted tickets to all types of other events. **Ticketmaster** (☎ 619-220-8497; www.ticketmaster.com) and **House of Blues** (www.hob.com) sell other tickets.

LIVE MUSIC & NIGHTCLUBS

Anthology (Map p942; ☎ 619-595-0300; www.anthologysd.com; 1337 India St, Downtown; cover free-$60) Near Little Italy, Anthology presents live jazz in a swank supper-club setting, from both up-and-comers and big-name performers.

Casbah (Map p942; ☎ 619-232-4355; 2501 Kettner Blvd; cover free-$15) Liz Phair, Alanis Morissette and the Smashing Pumpkins all rocked this funky Casbah on their way up the charts, and it's still a good place to catch local acts and tomorrow's headliners.

Shout House (Map p942; ☎ 619-231-6700; 655 4th Ave, Downtown; cover free $10) Dueling pianos entertain at this rowdy but innocent Gaslamp bar. Pianists have an amazing repertoire: standards, rock and more; we once heard the cult comedy number 'D*ck in a Box.'

Soma (Map p940; ☎ 619-226-7662; www.somasd.com; 3350 Sports Arena Blvd, near Old Town; cover $8-23) This all-ages venue (no booze) spotlights up-and-coming local bands of the alterna-rock and punk persuasion. Electric and edgy, with fiercely loyal crowds.

Getting There & Away

San Diego International Airport (Lindbergh Field; Map p940; ☎ 619-400-2400; www.san.org) sits about 3 miles west of Downtown; plane-spotters will thrill watching jets come in for a landing over Balboa Park.

Greyhound (Map p942; ☎ 619-515-1100; 120 W Broadway, Downtown) has hourly direct buses to Los Angeles (one way/round-trip $17/30, two to three hours).

Amtrak (☎ 800-872-7245; www.amtrak.com) runs the *Pacific Surfliner* several times daily to Los Angeles ($34, three hours) and Santa Barbara ($37, 6½ hours) from the **Santa Fe Depot** (Map p942; 1055 Kettner Blvd, Downtown).

All major car-rental companies have desks at the airport, or call the national toll-free numbers (p1164). **Eagle Rider** (Map p940; ☎ 619-222-8822, 877-437-4337; 3655 Camino del Rio W, Old Town; 9am-5pm) rents motorcycles from $89 per day.

Getting Around

Bus 992 ('the Flyer,' $2.25) operates at 10- to 15-minute intervals between the airport and Downtown, with stops along Broadway. Airport shuttles such as **Super Shuttle** (☎ 800-974-8885; www.supershuttle.com) charge about $13 to Downtown. A taxi fare to Downtown from the airport is $10 to $15.

Local buses and the San Diego Trolley, which travels south to the Mexican border, are operated by **Metropolitan Transit System** (MTS; www.sdcommute.com). The **Transit Store** (Map p942; ☎ 619-234-1060; Broadway & 1st Ave; 9am-5pm Mon-Fri) has route maps, tickets and Day Tripper passes for $5/9/12/15 for one/two/three/four days. Single-day passes are available for purchase on board buses. The taxi flag fall is $2.40, plus $2.60 for each additional mile.

AROUND SAN DIEGO

San Diego Zoo's Wild Animal Park

Take a walk on the 'wild' side at this 1800-acre **open-range zoo** (off Map p942; ☎ 760-747-8702; www.sandiegozoo.org; 15500 San Pasqual Valley Rd, Escondido; general admission adult/child $28.50/18.50, incl tram adult/child $35/26; opens 9am, closing times vary;). Giraffes graze, lions lounge and rhinos romp more or less freely on the valley floor. For that instant safari feel, board the Journey to Africa tram ride, which tours you around the second-largest continent in under half an hour. Combination tickets with the San Diego Zoo are $60/43.

The park is in Escondido, about 35 miles north of downtown San Diego. Take I-15 Fwy to the Via Rancho Pkwy exit and then follow the signs. Parking is $9.

Legoland

This enchanting **fantasy park** (off Map p940; ☎ 760-918-5346; www.legoland.com/california; 1 Legoland Dr, Carlsbad; adult/child $63/53; opens 10am, closing hours vary, closed most Tue & Wed Sep-May;) of rides, shows and attractions is mostly suited to the elementary-school set. Tots can dig for dinosaur bones, pilot helicopters and earn their driver's license. Mom and dad will probably get a kick out of Miniland, recreating such American landmarks as the White House, the Golden Gate Bridge and Las Vegas entirely of Lego blocks. From Downtown San Diego (about 32 miles), take the I-5 Fwy north to the Cannon Rd E exit. Parking is $12.

CALIFORNIA DESERTS

From swanky Palm Springs to desolate Death Valley, this remote desert region – swallowing 25% of California – is a land of contradictions: vast yet intimate; searing yet healing. Over time, you may find that what first seemed harrowingly barren will transform in your mind's eye to perfect beauty: weathered volcanic peaks, sensuous sand dunes, purple-tinged mountains, cactus gardens, tiny wildflowers pushing up from hard-baked soil in spring, lizards scurrying beneath colossal boulders, and uncountable stars. California's deserts are serenely spiritual, surprisingly chic and ultimately irresistible, whether you're a boho artist, movie star, rock climber or 4WD adventurer.

PALM SPRINGS

The Rat Pack is back, baby – or, at least, its hangout is. In the 1950s and '60s, Palm Springs (population 47,900), some 100 miles east of LA, was the swinging getaway of Sinatra, Elvis and other big stars. Once the Rat Pack packed it in, however, the Coachella Valley swarmed with retirees in golf clothing. In the 1990s, a new generation latched onto PS' retro-chic charms: kidney-shaped pools, midcentury modernist steel-and-glass bungalows, boutique hotels with vintage decor and piano bars serving perfect martinis. Today, retirees mix with hipsters and there's a significant gay and lesbian community.

Orientation

Palm Springs is the principal city of the Coachella Valley, south of the I-10 Fwy. In its compact downtown, Palm Canyon Dr (Hwy 111) runs one-way south, while Indian Canyon Dr runs northbound. East–west Tahquitz Canyon Way runs toward the airport. Southeast of PS, Hwy 111 crawls from commercial Cathedral City to Indio, passing tony 'Down Valley' towns with world-class golf resorts and ritzy shopping.

DON'T MISS

- **Tahquitz Canyon** (p950) – hike Native American stream-fed lands
- **Pioneertown** (p952) – Hollywood's timeless Western movie set
- **Salvation Mountain** (p953) – folk art near the Salton Sea
- **Route 66** (p954) – cruise along America's 'Mother Road'
- **Rhyolite** (p955) – well-preserved, atmospheric mining ghost town

Information

High season is October to April, but PS stays busy in summer, when temperatures spike above 100°F (38°C), hotel rates drop and many businesses keep shorter hours.

Desert Regional Medical Center (☎ 760-323-6511; 1150 N Indian Canyon Dr; 24hr) Emergency room.

Palm Springs Koffi Downtown (☎ 760-416-2244; 515 N Palm Canyon Dr; 5:30am-8pm; wi-fi); South (☎ 760-322-7776; 1700 S El Camino Real at E Palm Canyon Dr; 5:30am-8pm; wi-fi) Hand-brewed java and free wi-fi.

Palm Springs Official Visitors Center (☎ 760-778-8418, 800-347-7746; www.palm-springs.org; 2901 N Palm Canyon Dr; 9am-5pm) North of downtown at the tramway turnoff, offers specialty tourism guides (mobility-impaired, GLBT etc) and sells touring maps inside a 1965 Albert Frey–designed gas station.

Post office (☎ 760-322-4111; 333 E Amado Rd; 8am-5pm Mon-Fri, 9am-3pm Sat)

Public library (☎ 760-322-7323; 300 S Sunrise Way; 9am-8pm Tue-Wed, 9am-6pm Thu-Sat; internet; wi-fi) Free internet access.

Sights & Activities

our pick **Palm Springs Aerial Tramway** (☎ 760-325-1449, 888-515-8726; www.pstramway.com; 1 Tramway Rd; adult/child $23/16; 10am-8pm Mon-Fri, 8am-8pm Sat & Sun, last tram down 9:45pm; family-friendly) offers dizzying views as you're whisked 2.5 miles from sunbaked desert to pine-scented alpine wonderland. Temperatures can be 30°F to 40°F (17°C to 22°C) cooler up top at the mountain station (8516ft). Outside, hiking trails lead through the wilderness of **Mt San Jacinto State Park** (car $8), including a 5.5-mile nontechnical summit trek. In winter, rent snowshoes and cross-country skis at the **Adventure Center** (10am-4pm Thu-Mon, last rental 2:30pm), which is just outside the station.

In the cooler months, especially when spring wildflowers bloom, ramble around the lands owned by Cahuilla tribespeople. **Indian Canyons** (☎ 760-323-6018; www.indian-canyons.com; off S Palm Canyon Dr; adult/child $8/4, 90-min guided hike $3/2; 8am-5pm

WHAT THE...?

West of Palm Springs, you may do a double-take when you glimpse the **World's Biggest Dinosaurs** (☎ 951-922-0076; www.cabazondinosaurs.com; 50770 Seminole Dr, off I-10 exit Main St, Cabazon; 10am-6pm Mon-Thu, 10am-7pm Fri-Sun). Claude K Bell, a sculptor for Knott's Berry Farm (p938), spent over a decade crafting these concrete behemoths, now owned by Christian creationists promoting 'intelligent design.' In the gift shop, alongside the sort of dino-swag you might find at science museums, you can read about hoaxes and fallacies of evolution and Darwinism, and 'evidence' that dinosaurs and humans existed simultaneously.

Oct-Jul, Fri-Sun only Jul-Sep) is rare veins of green; picnic by a palm-shaded stream or beneath towering rock formations. **Tahquitz Canyon** (☎ 760-416-7044; www.tahquitzcanyon.com; 500 W Mesquite Ave; adult/child $12.50/6; 7:30am-5pm Oct-Jul, Fri-Sun only Jul-Sep, last entry 3:30pm) is famous for its seasonal waterfall and ancient rock art; tribal ranger-guided hikes leave from the visitor center, which has natural and cultural history exhibits.

The **Palm Springs Art Museum** (☎ 760-322-4800; www.psmuseum.org; 101 Museum Dr; adult/child/student $12.50/free/5, free 4-8pm Thu; 10am-5pm Tue-Wed & Fri-Sun, noon-8pm Thu) features contemporary painting, photography and sculpture, as well as pre-Columbian antiquities and Native American art.

On hot days, kids go nuts at **Knott's Soak City** (☎ 760-327-0499; www.knotts.com/soakcity/ps; 1500 S Gene Autry Trail; adult/child $30/20, after 3pm $20/20; mid-Mar–Sep, hr vary) water park, boasting an 800,000-gallon wave pool, towering water slides and tube rides. Parking is $9.

Worth the 30-minute drive down-valley, **Living Desert Zoo & Gardens** (☎ 760-346-5694; www.livingdesert.org; 47900 Portola Ave, off Hwy 111, Palm Desert; adult/child $12/7.50; 9am-5pm Sep–mid-Jun, 8am-1:30pm mid-Jun–Aug) harbors a walk-through wildlife hospital, native plants and animals, desert geology exhibits and hiking trails.

Sleeping

High-season winter rates are quoted below; ask about summer discounts. Motels cluster south of downtown PS and along the I-10 Fwy heading east to Indio. For gay-friendly lodgings, browse www.purpleroofs.com.

Caliente Tropics (☎ 760-327-1391, 800-658-6034; www.calientetropics.com; 411 E Palm Canyon Dr; d $66-111) This Polynesian-style motor lodge, where Elvis once splashed poolside, has blazing tiki torches poolside and spacious rooms with surprisingly comfy beds. It can get raucous, but it's near downtown.

Alpine Gardens Hotel (☎ 760-323-2231, 888-299-7455; www.alpinegardens.com; 1586 E Palm Canyon Dr; r $70-155) If PS' yeah-baby groove leaves you cold, all 10 rooms at this impeccably kept 1950s motel have redwood-beamed ceilings, fridges and slightly kitsch furnishings; suites have kitchens.

our pick **Del Marcos Hotel** (☎ 760-325-6902, 800-676-1214; www.delmarcoshotel.com; 225 W Baristo Rd; r $99-289) Newly remodeled, this 1947 gem finally looks like it should. Groovy tunes in the lobby usher you toward a saltwater pool and ineffably chic rooms named for architectural luminaries.

Chase Hotel (☎ 760-320-8866, 877-532-4273; www.chasehotelpalmsprings.com; 200 W Arenas Rd; r $119-159) On a side street downtown, this classic midcentury, modern motel has immaculately kept, oversized rooms with contemporary cool furnishings and some kitchenettes.

Orbit In (☎ 760-323-3585, 877-996-7248; www.orbitin.com; 562 W Arenas Rd; r $149-259) Swing back to the '50s during the 'Orbitini' happy hour, and then enjoy the high-end, original midcentury furniture (Eames, Noguchi *et al.*) and retro record players juxtaposed with flat-screen TVs. Free loaner bikes are available.

Viceroy (☎ 760-320-4117, 800-670-6184; www.viceroypalmsprings.com; 415 S Belardo Rd; r $170-290) Wear a Pucci dress to blend in at this 1960s-chic miniresort done up in black, white and lemon-yellow (think Austin Powers meets Givenchy). Full-service spa, fitness center and cruiser bikes are available to borrow.

Also recommended:

Century (☎ 760-323-9966, 800-475-5188; www.centurypalmsprings.com; 598 Grenfall Rd; r $179-299) To stay gay with that midcentury modern aesthetic.

Hope Springs (☎ 760-329-4003; www.hopespringsresort.com; 68075 Club Circle Dr, Desert Hot Springs; d from $195) Modernist 10-room mecca with hot-springs pools, north of I-10.

Eating

PS is famous for fabulous cocktails, not dining.

Sherman's (☎ 760-325-1199; 401 E Tahquitz Canyon Way; mains $5-15; 🕒 7am-9pm; 👶) With a breezy sidewalk patio, this 1950s Jewish deli serves lox-and-bagel breakfasts and early-bird dinners. It's festooned with headshots of aficionados no less than Don Rickles.

Cheeky's (☎ 760-327-7595; 622 N Palm Canyon Dr; mains $7-14; 🕒 8am-2pm) Never mind the subpar service and tiny portions – you can't beat the fresh, often organic menu for witty inventiveness: oatmeal brûlée with mascarpone cheese, custardy scrambled eggs and bacon bar 'flights.' Be prepared to wait.

Matchbox (☎ 760-778-6000; 2nd level, Mercado Plaza, 155 S Palm Canyon Dr; pizzas $11-21; 🕒 5-11pm Sun-Thu, to 1am Fri & Sat) A winner for its gourmet wood-oven-fired pizzas, killer California wine list and happy-hour cocktails and noshes. Nab a terrace table for prime people-watching.

Copley's on Palm Canyon (☎ 760-327-9555; 621 N Palm Canyon Dr; mains $29-37; 🕒 6pm-late Tue-Sun, from 5:30pm Jan-Apr) On the former Cary Grant estate, chef Andrew Manion Copley gets seriously inventive: think lavender-crusted rack of lamb and 'Oh my lobster pie.' Bring your sweetie and credit card.

Also recommended:

Cactusberry (☎ 760-325-3228; 116 La Plaza; dishes $3-6; 🕒 noon-10pm) Super-cool frozen yogurt with fresh-fruit toppings in biodegradable bowls.

Hadley Fruit Orchards (☎ 888-854-5655; 48980 Seminole Dr, Cabazon; date shake $5; 🕒 9am-7pm Mon-Thu, 8am-8pm Fri-Sun) Allegedly invented trail mix, it's near the outlet malls.

Native Foods (☎ 760-416-0070; Smoke Tree Village, 1775 E Palm Canyon Dr; mains $8-15; 🕒 11:30am-9:30pm Mon-Sat; 👶 V) Fresh, organic, vegan-friendly fare in an airy strip mall.

Drinking & Entertainment

Arenas Rd, east of Indian Canyon Dr, is lesbigay nightlife central.

Wang's in the Desert (☎ 760-325-9264; 424 S Indian Canyon Dr) With a so-so Chinese menu, indoor koi pond and giant cocktails, this resto-bar's a perennial gay darling. Kiss, kiss.

Melvyn's (☎ 760-325-2323; Ingleside Inn, 200 W Ramon Rd) Loll with a stiff martini with retired celebrities while torch singers backed by live combos croon at this old-guard standby, which was once a haunt of Sinatra. Shine your shoes.

Camelot Theatres (☎ 760-325-6565; www.camelottheatres.com; 2300 Baristo Rd) With a full bar and café, the desert's premier art-house cinema screens foreign and indie flicks. Film festivals happen in January and June.

> **A BLAST FROM THE PAST**
>
> Downtown's 1936 Plaza Theater hosts the **Palm Springs Follies** (☎ 760-327-0225; www.psfollies.com; 128 S Palm Canyon Dr; tickets $50-92; 🕒 Nov-May), a three-hour Ziegfeld Follies–style revue of music, dancing, showgirls and off-color comedy. The twist? Many of the performers are as old as the theater – all are over 50, and some are octogenarians. But this is no amateur hour: in their heyday, these old-timers hoofed it alongside Hollywood and Broadway's biggest, who occasionally guest-star.

Shopping

Go art-gallery hopping downtown along North Palm Canyon Dr.

Trina Turk (☎ 760-416-2856; 891 N Palm Canyon Dr) Find shagadelic resort-chic drag at PS' unique clothing boutique, inside a 1960s Albert Frey–designed storefront.

Angel View (☎ 760-320-1733; 454 N Indian Canyon Dr) At this charitable thrift-store chain, today's hipsters can buy clothes as cool as when they were first worn a generation ago.

Getting There & Around

Ten minutes' drive from downtown, **Palm Springs International Airport** (PSP; ☎ 760-318-3800; www.palmspringsairport.com; 3400 E Tahquitz Canyon Way) is served by several domestic and Canadian airlines; major car-rental agencies (p1164) are on-site.

Thrice-weekly Amtrak trains to/from LA ($35, 2¾ hours) stop at the unstaffed, kinda-creepy North Palm Springs Station, 5 miles north of downtown, as do several daily Greyhound buses to/from LA ($37, 2¾ hours). **SunLine** (☎ 760-343-3451, 800-347-8628; www.sunline.org; single ride/day pass $1/3) runs slow-moving local buses throughout the valley.

JOSHUA TREE NATIONAL PARK

Straddling the transition zone between the Colorado and Mojave deserts, this park is popular with rock climbers and hikers, especially when spring wildflowers bloom and Joshua trees (actually, tree-sized yucca plants) dramatically send out cream-colored

WHAT THE...?

Just north of Yucca Valley, **Pioneertown** (www.pioneertown.com; admission free) was built as a Hollywood Western movie set in 1946, and it hasn't changed much since. On Mane St, witness mock gunfights at 2:30pm on Saturdays and Sundays from April to October. Enjoy BBQ, cheap beer and live music at honky-tonk **Pappy & Harriet's Pioneertown Palace** (760-365-5956; www.pappyandharriets.com; 53688 Pioneertown Rd; mains $8-27; 11am-1am Thu-Sun, 5pm-midnight Mon). Then bed down where yesteryear silver-screen stars slept at **Pioneertown Lodge** (760-365-4879; www.pioneertownmotel.com; 5040 Curtis Rd; r $78-99;), whose quaint memorabilia-filled rooms have kitchenettes and satellite TV (no phones).

flowers. The mystical quality of this stark, wondrously boulder-strewn landscape has inspired many artists, most famously the band U2. The trees themselves were named by Mormon settlers, who envisioned their twisted branches stretching up toward God like a biblical prophet's arms.

Twentynine Palms Hwy (Hwy 62) parallels the north side of the park, where most of the attractions are (including all of the Joshua trees), while I-10 borders the remote south side. Entry permits ($15 per vehicle) are valid for seven days; ask for a free map and newspaper guide. There are no tourist services or facilities besides restrooms, so gas up and bring food and plenty of water. Get information at the main **visitor centers** (760-367-5500; www.nps.gov/jotr; Oasis Utah Trail & National Park Dr, Twentynine Palms; 8am-5pm; Joshua Tree Park Blvd, off Hwy 62; 8am-5pm; Cottonwood north of I-10, Cottonwood Springs; 9am-3pm).

The epic **Wonderland of Rocks**, a mecca for climbers, dominates the park's north side. Sunset-worthy **Keys View** overlooks the San Andreas Fault and as far as Mexico. For Western pioneer history, visit **Keys Ranch** (reservations 760-367-5555; 90-min walking tour adult/child $5/2.50; 10am & 1pm Sat & Sun Oct-May, weekday hours vary). Hikers can search out native desert fan-palm oases like **49 Palms Oasis** (3-mile round-trip) or **Lost Palms Oasis** (7.2-mile round-trip). Kid-friendly nature trails include **Barker Dam** (1.3-mile loop), which passes Native American petroglyphs; **Skull Rock** (1.7-mile loop); and **Cholla Cactus Garden** (0.25-mile loop). For a scenic 4WD route, tackle the bumpy 18-mile **Geology Tour Road**, also open to hardy mountain-bikers.

Sleeping & Eating

Of the park's eight **campgrounds** (campsites $10-15), only Black Rock Canyon and Cottonwood accept **reservations** (877-444-6777; www.recreation.gov) and have potable water, flush toilets and dump stations. Backcountry camping (no campfires) is allowed 1 mile off-road and 500ft from any trail; free self-registration is required at backcountry boards scattered throughout the park.

Otherwise, base yourself in Twentynine Palms (home of the world's largest US marine base), arty Joshua Tree or suburban Yucca Valley, all north of the park. Standouts from the run-of-the-mill Hwy 62 motels include the **Pioneertown Lodge** (see boxed text, above) and **Spin & Margie's Desert Hide-a-Way** (760-366-9124; www.deserthideaway.com; off Sunkist Rd, Joshua Tree; ste $125-160;), a hacienda-style inn with striking design motifs using corrugated tin, old license plates and cartoon art. The **Best Western Yucca Valley Hotel & Suites** (760-365-3555, 800-780-7234; www.bestwestern.com; 56525 Hwy 62, Yucca Valley; d incl breakfast $88-126;) has business-class comforts.

For inventive sustenance, drop by ubercool **Crossroads Café** (760-366-5414; 61715 Hwy 62, Joshua Tree; mains $4-11; 6:30am-8pm Sun-Tue & Thu, 6:30am-9pm Fri & Sat), with its tree-hugger-friendly menu, from dragged-through-the-garden salads to fresh smoothies. There's a cute bakery across the street. **Sam's Pizza & Subs** (760-366-9511; 61380 Twentynine Palms Hwy, Joshua Tree; mains $8-11; 11am-8pm Mon-Thu, 11am-7pm Fri & Sat, 3-8pm Sun) doubles as a vegetarian-friendly Indian restaurant. Atmosphere: nil. Solution: takeout.

ANZA-BORREGO DESERT STATE PARK

Extending south almost to Mexico, this 640,000-sq-mile untamed desert beast is the USA's largest state park outside Alaska. It claims spectacular scenery (especially when spring wildflowers bloom – call 760-767-4684 for updates) and rare wildlife such as endangered bighorn sheep, plus untrammeled backcountry byways and Native American, Spanish conquistador and Old West historical sites to explore. It's all within reach of the retro resort town of Borrego Springs (population 2800). In summer, Hades-like heat makes daytime exploring dangerous.

In Borrego Springs, you'll find ATMs, gas stations, a post office, supermarket and public library offering free internet-access terminals and wi-fi. The park's comprehensive **visitor center** (☎ 760-767-4205; www.california-desert.org; 200 Palm Canyon Dr; admission free; 9am-5pm Oct-May, Sat & Sun only Jun-Sep) is 2 miles west. You'll need your own wheels to explore the park (car $8); 4WD vehicles can tackle over 500 miles of backcountry dirt roads. If you hike the park's nature trails or go mountain biking along dirt roads, pack extra water and don't go at midday.

Park highlights include: **Fonts Point** desert lookout; **Clark Dry Lake** for birding; the **Elephant Tree Discovery Trail**; Split Mountain's **wind caves**; and **Blair Valley**, with its Native American pictographs and *morteros* (seed-grinding stones). Further south, **Agua Caliente County Park** (☎ 760-765-1188; 39555 Rte S2; entry $5; 9:30am-5pm Sep-May) has indoor and outdoor hot-springs pools.

Besides the state park's two **developed campgrounds** (☎ 800-444-7275; www.reserveamerica.com; campsites/RV sites $25/35) – Tamarisk Grove is shady and Borrego Palm Canyon has hookups – and several primitive campgrounds (no water), you can camp for free anywhere that's off-road and at least 100ft from water. Open ground fires and gathering vegetation (dead or alive) are prohibited.

In Borrego Springs, adobe-style **Borrego Valley Inn** (☎ 760-767-0311, 800-333-5810; www.borregovalleyinn.com; 405 Palm Canyon Dr; r incl breakfast $185-265;) has 15 lovely rooms with Southwestern decor, plus a clothing-optional pool and hot tub. **Stanlunds Inn & Suites** (☎ 760-767-5501; www.standlunds.com; 2771 Borrego Springs Rd; r $65-150;) is an ultra-basic, cinder-block motel with some kitchenettes, but no phones.

Inside a refurbished Quonset hut (the sign just says 'Eat'), **Red Ocotillo** (☎ 760-767-7400; 818 Palm Canyon Dr; mains $6-15; 7am-8:30pm;) diner serves all-day skillet breakfasts, giant sandwiches and cold beer. More run-of-the-mill eateries line up west of Christmas Circle.

For country-style B&Bs and famous apple pie, the gold-mining town of **Julian** (☎ 760-765-1857; www.julian.ca) is a 45-minute drive southwest of Borrego Springs.

MOJAVE NATIONAL PRESERVE

If you're on a quest for the 'middle of nowhere,' you'll find it in the wilderness of the **Mojave National Preserve** (☎ 760-252-6100; www.nps.gov/moja; admission free), a 1.6-million-acre jumble of sand dunes, Joshua trees, volcanic cinder cones and habitat for desert tortoises, jackrabbits and coyotes. No gas is available here.

Southeast of Baker and the I-15 Fwy, Kelbaker Rd crosses a ghostly landscape of cinder cones before arriving at **Kelso Depot**, a handsome 1920s Spanish mission revival-style railroad station, which houses an art gallery, an old-fashioned **lunch counter** (dishes $2-8; 9am-5pm Fri-Tue) and a **visitor center** (☎ 760-252-6108; 9am-5pm) with excellent natural and cultural history exhibits. It's another 11 miles southwest to 'singing' **Kelso Dunes**. When conditions are right, they emanate low, booming sounds that are caused by shifting sands – try running downhill to jump-start the effect.

From Kelso Depot, Kelso–Cima Rd takes off northeast. After 19 miles, Cima Rd heads back toward I-15, which takes you around almost perfectly symmetrical **Cima Dome**, a 75-sq-mile, 1500ft hunk of granite with crusty lava outcroppings. Its slopes are smothered in the world's largest **Joshua tree forest**. For a close-up look, summit Teutonia Peak (4 miles round-trip); the trailhead is 6 miles northwest of Cima.

WHAT THE...?

It's an unexpected sight: California's largest lake in the middle of its biggest desert. After the Colorado River flooded in 1905, it took 1500 workers and half a million tons of rock to put the river back on course. With no natural outlet, the artificial **Salton Sea** (www.saltonsea.ca.gov) is here to stay: its surface is 220ft below sea level and its waters 30% saltier than the Pacific – it's an environmental nightmare that's yet to be cleaned up.

An even stranger sight near the lake's eastern shore is **Salvation Mountain** (www.salvationmountain.us), a 100ft-high hill of concrete and hand-mixed adobe, covered with acrylic paint. With the motto 'God Never Fails,' it's the vision of folk artist Leonard Knight. Turn off Hwy 111 at Niland, drive east on Beal Rd and you can't miss it.

ROUTE 66: GET YOUR KICKS IN CALIFORNIA

Through California's deserts, Route 66 mostly follows the National Old Trails Hwy, which is prone to potholes and heart-stopping vistas. After crossing into California near Needles and running a gauntlet of Mojave ghost towns, you'll motor through the railroad towns of Barstow and Victorville – each with its own Route 66 museum – and then ride I-15 over Cajon Summit into San Bernardino. On Foothill Blvd, keep cruising west all the way to Pasadena (p928). Swing by old-fashioned **Fair Oaks Pharmacy & Soda Fountain** (☎ 626-799-1414; 1526 Mission St, Pasadena; 9am-9pm Mon-Sat, 10am-7pm Sun;) before braving traffic on the final stretch through LA, where crashing ocean waves await at the end of Route 66 near Santa Monica Pier (p926), over 300 miles from the Arizona–California border. Surf to www.cart66pf.org for directions, photos, news and events. Feeling ambitious? To drive the entire 2400mi route, see p44.

East of Kelso–Cima Rd, Mojave Rd is the backdoor route to two first-come, first-served **campgrounds** (campsites $12) with potable water at Mid Hills (no RVs) and Hole-in-the-Wall. They bookend a rugged 10-mile scenic drive along **Wild Horse Canyon Rd**. Ask at Hole-in-the-Wall's **visitor center** (☎ 760-252-6104; 9am-4pm Wed-Sun Oct-Apr, Fri-Sun only May-Sep) about the slot-canyon **Rings Trail**. Roads in this area are mostly unpaved but well maintained.

Southwest of Hole-in-the-Wall, **Mitchell Caverns** (☎ 760-928-2586; adult/child $6/3; tours 1:30pm daily year-round, also 10am & 3pm Sat & Sun early Sep-late May) unlock a world of quirky limestone formations; make reservations. The caverns are inside Providence Mountains State Recreation Area, where no-reservation **primitive campsites** ($25) perch dizzyingly high above the desert floor.

Free backcountry and roadside **camping** is permitted throughout the Mojave National Preserve in areas already used for this purpose. For a roof over your head, there are a few cheap, bare-bones motels in Baker.

Off the beaten path, B&B-style **Hotel Nipton** (☎ 760-856-2335; www.nipton.com; 107355 Nipton Rd, Nipton; d $65-99; reception 8am-6pm;) inhabits a century-old adobe villa with tent cabins in a lonely railway outpost northeast of the preserve. Check-in is at the well-stocked trading post, which is next to the bar and café (mains $6 to $25).

DEATH VALLEY NATIONAL PARK

The name itself evokes all that is harsh and hellish – a punishing, barren and lifeless place of Old Testament severity. Yet closer inspection reveals that nature is putting on a spectacular show with water-sculpted canyons, singing sand dunes, palm-shaded oases, eroded mountains and plenty of endemic wildlife. It's a land of superlatives, holding the US records for hottest temperature (134°F, or 57°C), lowest point (Badwater, 282ft below sea level) and largest national park outside Alaska (over 5000 sq miles). Peak tourist season is when spring wildflowers bloom.

Entry permits ($20 per vehicle) are valid for seven days. Purchase them at self-service pay stations throughout the park. For a free map and newspaper, show your receipt at the **visitor center** (☎ 760-786-3200; www.nps.gov/deva; 8am-5pm) in Furnace Creek, which also has a general store, gas station, post office, ATM, lodging and restaurants. Stovepipe Wells, a 30-minute drive northwest, has a general store, gas station, ATM, motel and café. Panamint Springs, on the park's western edge, has gas and snacks.

Sights & Activities

Drive up to **Zabriskie Point** at sunrise or sunset for spectacular valley views across golden badlands eroded into waves, pleats and gullies. Less than 20 miles further south, at **Dante's View**, you can simultaneously see the highest (Mt Whitney, 14,505ft) and lowest (Badwater) points in the contiguous USA. En route, detour along the bone-rattling scenic one-way loop through **Twenty Mule Team Canyon**.

Badwater itself, an eternal landscape of crinkly salt flats, is a 17-mile drive south of Furnace Creek. Along the way, narrow **Golden Canyon** and **Natural Bridge** are both easily explored on short hikes. On the **Devils Golf Course**, crystallized salt has piled up into saw-tooth mini mountains. A 9-mile detour along **Artists Drive** is best in late afternoon when eroded hillsides erupt in fireworks of color.

Near Stovepipe Wells, you can scramble along the smooth marble walls of **Mosaic Canyon** or roll down the Saharan-esque **Mesquite Flat sand dunes** – magical during a full moon. Another 36 miles north is whimsical **Scotty's Castle** (☎ 760-786-2392; adult/child $11/6; tours 9am-5pm Nov-Apr, 9am-4:30pm May-Oct), where costumed interpreters bring to life the strange tale of con-man Death Valley Scotty. Eight miles west, giant **Ubehebe Crater** is evidence of a massive volcanic eruption.

In summer, stick to paved roads (dirt roads can quickly overheat vehicles), limit your exertions (eg no hiking midday) and visit higher-elevation areas. For example, the scenic drive up **Emigrant Canyon Road**, starting west of Stovepipe Wells, ends 21 miles later at the historic beehive-shaped **Charcoal Kilns**, near the trailhead for the exhilarating 8.4-mile round-trip hike up telescopic **Wildrose Peak** (9064ft). At the park's western edge, utterly remote **Panamint Springs** offers volcanic vistas, Joshua tree forests and a pint-sized springtime waterfall.

Back at Furnace Creek Ranch, the **stables** (☎ 760-786-3339; 1hr/2hr ride $45/65) offer guided horseback rides daily, except during summer. For novelty's sake, play a round at the **golf course** (☎ 760-786-2301; greens fees $25-55; mid-Oct–early May), which has the world's lowest-elevation greens.

Sleeping & Eating

During spring, accommodations are often booked solid and campgrounds fill by mid-morning, especially on weekends. All of the following in-park lodgings are run by **Xanterra** (☎ reservations 303-297-2757, 888-786-2387).

Stovepipe Wells Village (☎ 760-786-2387; www.stovepipewells.com; Hwy 190; RV sites $23, r $81-121;) The freshly renovated roadside motel rooms are quiet and spacious (no phones or TVs), so it's definitely the most bang for your buck in the valley. The small pool is cool. The cowboy-style restaurant (mains $5 to $25) delivers three square meals a day.

Furnace Creek Ranch (☎ 760-786-2345; www.furnacecreekresort.com; cabins $126-162, r $157-213;) Tailor-made for families, this rambling resort has cramped cabins and slightly larger motel rooms that are dated but comfortable. There's a children's playground, spring-fed swimming pool and tennis courts. Skip the breakfast and lunch buffets at the steakhouse (dinner mains $19-29). Next door, the café (mains $6 to $19) cooks up American standards all day long.

> **WHAT THE...?**
>
> Four miles west of Beatty, NV, **Rhyolite** (☎ 775-553-2967; www.rhyolitesite.com; Hwy 374; admission free; sunrise-sunset) ghost town recounts the hurly-burly, boom-and-bust story of so many Western gold-rush mining towns. Don't overlook the 1906 'bottle house' or the skeletal remains of a three-story bank. Next door is the bizarre **Goldwell Open Air Museum** (☎ 702-870-9946; www.goldwellmuseum.org; admission free; 24hr) of trippy installation art started by Belgian artist Albert Szukalski in 1984.

Furnace Creek Inn (☎ 760-786-2345; www.furnacecreekresort.com; r $320-435; mid-Oct–mid-May;) At this elegant, mission-style hotel you can count the colors of the desert while unwinding by the spring-fed pool, which has sweeping vistas across the valley. The restaurant (mains $12 to $38) isn't quite as gourmet as advertised. Nice Sunday brunch, though.

Northeast of the park, the casino pit-stop of Beatty, NV, is your best bet for motels. Southbound toward I-15, Shoshone has a gas station, general store and the charming solar-powered 'flexitarian' **Cafe Çest Si Bon** (☎ 760-852-4307; 118 Hwy 127; dishes $3-8; 8am-4pm Wed-Sun;) for espresso, crepes and free wi-fi. Nearby Tecopa has hot-springs pools, a date farm, RV parks and the quirky, low-tech **Ranch House Inn and Hostel** (☎ 760-852-4580; www.ranchhouseinn.com; 2001 Old Spanish Trail Hwy; dm $22-25, d $75-118, tipis $148, all with shared bath).

CAMPING

Of the park's nine **campgrounds** (campsites free-$18), only Furnace Creek accepts **reservations** (☎ 877-444-6777; www.recreation.gov) from mid-April to mid-October. In summer, Furnace Creek is first-come, first-served, and the only other campgrounds open are Mesquite Spring, near Scotty's Castle, and those along Emigrant Canyon Rd. West of Stovepipe Wells, tent-only Emigrant campground is open year-round. Other valley-floor campgrounds – like roadside Stovepipe Wells, Sunset and shadier Texas Springs – are mostly for RVs; they're open October to April.

Backcountry camping (no campfires) is allowed 2 miles off paved roads and away from developed and day-use areas, and

IF YOU HAVE A FEW MORE DAYS

Rugged **Channel Islands National Park** (www.nps.gov/chis; admission free) earns the nickname 'California's Galápagos' for its unique wildlife. The islands are now preserved as wilderness, offering superb snorkeling, scuba diving, sea kayaking and wildlife watching. Spring is a gorgeous time to visit; summer and fall can be bone-dry, and winter stormy.

Anacapa, which is closest to the mainland, is the best island for day-tripping, with easy hiking trails and unforgettable views. Santa Cruz, the largest island, is convenient for overnight trips, offering a campground, sea kayaking and rugged hiking trails. Other islands require longer channel crossings and multiday trips: San Miguel is often shrouded in fog; Santa Barbara supports seabird and elephant-seal colonies, as does Santa Rosa, which also has Chumash archaeological sites.

Boat trips leave from Ventura Harbor, off Hwy 101, where an **NPS visitor center** (☎ 805-658-5730; 1901 Spinnaker Dr; ⏰ 8:30am-5pm) has information and maps. The main tour-boat operator is **Island Packers** (☎ 805-642-1393; www.islandpackers.com; 1691 Spinnaker Dr). Rates start at $45/28 per adult/child for day trips; $30/21 for whale-watching cruises. Primitive **campgrounds** (☎ 877-444-6777; www.recreation.gov; tent sites $15) require reservations; bring food and water.

100yd from any water source; pick up free permits at the visitor center.

Furnace Creek Ranch and Stovepipe Wells Village offer public showers ($5, including swimming-pool access).

CENTRAL COAST

No trip to California is worth its salt without a jaunt along the surreally scenic Central Coast. Hwy 1, one of the most iconic roads in the US (see p45), skirts past posh Santa Barbara, retro Pismo Beach, collegiate San Luis Obispo, fantastical Hearst Castle, soul-stirring Big Sur, down-to-earth Monterey Bay and hippie-haunt Santa Cruz. Slow down – this idyllic coast deserves to be savored, not gulped. (That same advice goes for the incredible locally grown wines, too.)

SANTA BARBARA

Life is certainly sweet in Santa Barbara, a coastal Shangri-La where the air is redolent with citrus and jasmine, flowery bougainvillea drapes whitewashed buildings with red-tiled roofs, and it's all cradled by seemingly endless pearly beaches. You won't regret slowing down for the Mediterranean architecture, California cuisine or local wines. Just ignore those pesky oil derricks out to sea.

State St is the main drag with bars, cafés, theaters and boutique shops. Near the waterfront, the **visitor center** (☎ 805-965-3021; www.santabarbaraca.com; 1 Garden St; ⏰ 9am-5pm Mon-Sat, 10am-5pm Sun) has maps and self-guided tour brochures. Helpful websites http://greensantabarbara.com and www.santabarbaracarfree.org offer ecotravel tips and valuable discounts.

Sights & Activities

The Spanish-Moorish revival style **county courthouse** (☎ 805-962-6464; 1100 Anacapa St; admission free; ⏰ 8am-5pm Mon-Fri, 10am-4:30pm Sat & Sun) is an absurdly beautiful place to be on trial (or get married). Marvel at the hand-painted ceilings and intricate murals, and then climb the *Vertigo*-esque clocktower for panoramic views.

The 1786 **Mission Santa Barbara** (☎ 805-682-4713; www.sbmission.org; 2201 Laguna St; adult/child $5/1; ⏰ 9am-4:30pm), nicknamed California's 'Queen of the Missions,' was the only one to escape secularization under Mexican rule. Look for Chumash artwork inside the vaulted church and a moody cemetery out back.

Uphill from the mission, **Santa Barbara Botanic Garden** (☎ 805-682-4726; www.sbbg.org; 1212 Mission Canyon Rd; adult/child $8/4; ⏰ 9am-6pm Mar-Oct, to 5pm Nov-Feb; 👪) is devoted to native flora. For a quirkier garden experience, book ahead for **Lotusland** (☎ 805-969-9990; www.lotusland.org; adult/child $35/10; ⏰ tours 10am & 1:30pm Wed-Sat mid-Feb–mid-Nov), the legacy of eccentric Madame Ganna Walska; two-hour walking tours take in rare botanical species.

Downtown, the **Santa Barbara Museum of Art** (☎ 805-963-4364; www.sbma.net; 1130 State St; adult/child $9/6, Sun free; ⏰ 11am-5pm Tue-Sun) has a well-edited collection of contemporary California artists, modern masters, like Matisse and Chagall, and Asian art. It also puts on sophisticated special exhibits.

Along the waterfront, 1872 **Stearns Wharf** is the West's oldest continuously operating wooden pier, now strung with restaurants and shops. A paved multi-use recreational trail skirts miles of beautiful beaches. **Wheel Fun** (805-966-2282; 23 E Cabrillo Blvd; 8am-8pm) rents bicycles (from $8 per hour).

Farther east at the harbor, **Santa Barbara Maritime Museum** (805-962-8404; www.sbmm.org; 113 Harbor Way; adult/child $7/4, free 3rd Thu of the month; 10am-5pm Thu-Tue, to 6pm in summer;) celebrates the town's briny history with memorabilia, hands-on and virtual-reality exhibits, and a movie theater. Nearby, **Paddle Sports** (805-899-4925; www.kayaksb.com; 117b Harbor Way; hr vary) rents kayaks (singles two hour/four hour $20/30) and teaches stand-up paddle surfing (two-hour lesson $65).

For traditional board-surfing lessons (from $99) and guided kayaking tours (from $85), talk to **Santa Barbara Adventure Co** (805-452-0671; www.sbadventureco.com). Year-round, **Condor Express** (805-882-0088; www.condorcruises.com; 301 W Cabrillo Blvd; adult/child from $48/28) runs narrated whale-watching tours.

Outside Santa Barbara, along Hwy 101, you'll find gorgeous, palm-fringed **state beaches** (per car $10), including Carpinteria State Beach, 10 miles south, and El Capitan and Refugio, just over 20 miles north.

Sleeping

Prepare for sticker shock: even basic rooms command over $200 in summer. Bargains may be found on motel row along upper State St, a few miles north of downtown. For state beaches' developed campgrounds along Hwy 101, make **reservations** (800-444-7275; www.reserveamerica.com; campsites $35-65).

Marina Beach Motel (805-963-9311, 877-627-4621; www.marinabeachmotel.com; 21 Bath St; r incl breakfast $119-284;) Old-fashioned one-story motor lodge right near the ocean has been done up inside. Some of the comfy rooms have kitchenettes. Free bikes are available to borrow.

Presidio Motel (805-963-1355; www.thepresidiomotel.com; 1620 State St; r incl breakfast $120-150;) Like the H&M of motels, this affordable gem has panache and personality thanks to buzzy art, dreamy bedding, and hip and helpful owners. Noise can be an issue, but loaner bikes are free.

Brisas del Mar (805-966-2219, 800-468-1988; www.sbhotels.com; 223 Castillo St; r incl breakfast $145-235;) Big kudos for the freebies (DVDs, wine and cheese, milk and cookies) and new Mediterranean-style front section, although the motel wing is unlovely. The hotel's respectable sister properties are lower-priced.

El Capitan Canyon (805-685-3887, 866-352-2729; www.elcapitancanyon.com; 11560 Calle Real, off Hwy 101; safari tents $155, cabins $225-350;) Go glamping in this car-free zone near El Capitán State Beach, a 30-minute drive up Hwy 101 northbound. Creekside cedar cabins come with heavenly mattresses, kitchenettes, outdoor firepits and, if you're lucky, therapeutically deep soaking tubs.

Eating

To fill picnic baskets for the beach, stop at **C'est Cheese** (805-965-0318; 825 Santa Barbara St; 10am-6pm Mon-Fri, 8am-6pm Sat) and **Our Daily Bread** (805-966-3894; 831 Santa Barbara St; 6am-5:30pm Mon-Fri, 7am-4pm Sat).

our pick **Santa Barbara Shellfish Company** (805-966-6676; 230 Stearns Wharf; dishes $5-16; 11am-9pm) 'From sea to skillet to plate' best describes this end-of-the-wharf crab shack that's more of a counter joint. Great lobster bisque, ocean views and the same owners for 25 years.

Brophy Brothers (805-966-4418; mains $9-20; 11am-10pm Sun-Thu, to 11pm Fri & Sat) The raw-bar seafood at this raucous harbor hangout is so fresh that you half expect it to leap straight up out of the Pacific. Social upstairs deck for sunset drinks.

Tupelo Junction (805-899-3100; 1218 State St; mains $12-18; 8am-2pm) Southern-style comfort food is the specialty at this busy downtown storefront café, showing off fresh takes on good ol' standards like cinnamon-apple beignets, vanilla-dipped French toast and gouda mac 'n' cheese.

Square One (805-965-4565; 14 E Cota St; mains $14-25; 5:30-10pm Tue-Sun) Postmodern Californian cuisine reaches stratospheric heights of inventiveness, piquing even jaded palates with the likes of grapefruit gelée and avocado mousse laid atop seafood. Sculpted desserts are challenging. Svelte wine bar.

Drinking & Entertainment

Nightlife revolves around lower State St. Pick up free alt-weekly *Santa Barbara Independent* (www.independent.com) for a current calendar and venue listings.

Soho (☎ 805-962-7776; www.sohosb.com; 1221 State St; cover $12-30) This unpretentious brick room located upstairs behind a McDonald's has live bands nightly, from indie rock, funk and folk to jazz and blues.

Santa Barbara Brewing Co (☎ 805-730-1040; 501 State St) They've got microbrews on tap, including a killer Rincon Red ale made with Oregon hops. Pool tables are in the tatty lounge out back.

Getting There & Around

Greyhound (☎ 805-965-7551; 34 W Carrillo St) has several daily buses to LA ($18, three hours) and San Francisco ($60, nine hours) via San Luis Obispo ($27, two hours). **Amtrak** (209 State St) runs directly to LA ($25, three hours) and San Luis Obispo ($30, three hours).

Metropolitan Transit District (☎ 805-963-3366; www.sbmtd.gov; 1020 Chapla St; single-ride $1.75) buses travel across the city. MTD's **Downtown-Waterfront shuttle** (25¢; 9am-6pm daily year-round, to 10pm Fri & Sat Jun-Aug) hums down State St to Stearns Wharf and along Cabrillo Blvd by the beach.

SANTA BARBARA TO SAN LUIS OBISPO

You can speed up to San Luis Obispo in just two hours along Hwy 101, or take all day detouring to wineries, historical missions and hidden beaches.

A scenic backcountry drive north from Santa Barbara follows Hwy 154, where you can go for the grape in the **Santa Barbara County wine country** (www.sbcountywines.com). For all-day winery tours with an eco-angle, check out **Sustainable Vine** (☎ 805-698-3911; www.sustainablevine.com; tour $125). Otherwise, start exploring at **Los Olivos Tasting Room** (☎ 805-688-7406; 2905 Grand Ave, Los Olivos; tasting fee $7; 11am-5:30pm), which stocks rare vintages inside a 19th-century general store, and then follow the **Foxen Canyon Wine Trail** (www.foxencanyonwinetrail.com) north past cult winemakers' vineyards.

Further south, the Danish-immigrant village of **Solvang** (http://solvangusa.com) is a kitsch lovers' dream with its decorative windmills and fairytale-esque bakeries. If you need an espresso, picnic lunch or BBQ take-out, stop by **El Rancho Marketplace** (☎ 805-688-4300; 2886 Mission Dr (Hwy 246), Solvang; 6am-10pm). Farther west near Hwy 101, **Hitching Post II** (☎ 805-688-0676; 406 E Hwy 246, Buellton; mains $21-48; 5-9:30pm) is an old-guard steakhouse that makes its own pinot noir (which is damn good, by the way); reservations are essential.

DON'T MISS

- **Lotusland** (p956) – tour an eclectic botanical legacy
- **Piedras Blancas elephant-seal colony** (p960) – giant marine mammals in action
- **Andrew Molera State Park** (p961) – solitude, beachcombing and California condors
- **Tor House** (p962) – a poet's eccentric coastal hideaway
- **Kuumbwa Jazz Center** (p965) – live shows by musical masters

Follow Hwy 246 about 15 miles west of Hwy 101 to **La Purísima Mission State Historic Park** (☎ 805-733-3713; www.lapurisimamission.org; 2295 Purisima Rd, Lompoc; per car $6; 9am-5pm). Completely restored, it's one of California's most evocative Spanish-colonial missions, with flowering gardens, livestock pens and adobe buildings. South of Lompoc, Jalama Rd travels 14 twisting miles to utterly isolated **Jalama Beach County Park** (☎ 805-736-3504; www.jalamabeach.com; per car $8). Its crazy-popular **campground** (campsites/RV sites $20/30) doesn't take reservations – look for the 'campground full' sign a half-mile south of Hwy 1, to save yourself a wasted trip

Heading north on Hwy 1, rough-and-tumble **Guadalupe** is the gateway to North America's largest coastal dunes. The **Dunes Center** (☎ 805-343-2455; www.dunescenter.org; 1055 Guadalupe St; 10am-4pm Wed-Sun) has simple displays on the mystical Dunites of the 1930s and the 'Lost City of DeMille' (www.lostcitydemille.com), the entire movie set of the 1923 version of *The Ten Commandments* that lies buried beneath the sands. More recently, scenes from *Pirates of the Caribbean: At World's End* were filmed here. The best dune access is west of town via Hwy 166. Back downtown, dig into juicy steaks at genuine Old West–flavored **Far Western Tavern** (☎ 805-343-2211; 899 Guadalupe St; dinner mains $20-32; 11am-9pm Tue-Thu, 11am-10pm Fri & Sat, 9am-9pm Sun).

Where Hwy 1 rejoins Hwy 101, **Pismo Beach** has a nice long stretch of sand and a **monarch butterfly grove**, where migratory monarchs perch in eucalyptus trees from late October to February. The grove is just south of **Pismo State Beach campground** (☎ reservations 800-444-7275; www.reserveamerica.com; Hwy 1; campsites $35), which offers beach access and hot showers. Pismo Beach has dozens of motels, but rooms fill up quickly and prices skyrocket in summer. Grab breakfast at **Old West Cinnamon Rolls** (☎ 805-773-1428; 861 Dolliver St; dishes $3-5; 🕒 6:30am-5:30pm) bakery. By the pier, lines go out the door at hole-in-the-wall **Splash Cafe** (☎ 805-773-4653; 197 Pomeroy Ave; dishes $3-10; 🕒 8am-9pm; 👶), which is known for its clam chowder served in sourdough-bread bowls. When the fresh bucket o' seafood gets dumped on your butcher paper-covered table at the **Cracked Crab** (☎ 805-773-2722; 751 Price St; mains $9-48; 🕒 11am-9pm Sun-Thu, to 10pm Fri & Sat), make sure you're wearing a plastic bib.

SAN LUIS OBISPO

Halfway between LA and San Francisco, San Luis Obispo (SLO) is a lively yet low-key place. University students inject a healthy dose of hubbub into the streets, pubs and cafés, especially during the Thursday-night **farmers market** (🕒 6-9pm), which turns downtown's Higuera St into a festive street party with live music and sidewalk BBQs. SLO's **visitor center** (☎ 805-781-2777; www.visitslo.com; 1039 Chorro St; 🕒 10am-5pm Sun-Wed, 10am-7pm Thu-Sat) is off Higuera St. Like so many other California towns, SLO grew up around a **mission** (☎ 805-543-6850; www.missionsanluisobispo.org; 751 Palm St; admission $2; 🕒 9am-4pm), founded in 1772 by peripatetic Junípero Serra. These days, SLO is just a grape's throw from thriving **Edna Valley wineries** (www.slowine.com), known for chardonnays and syrahs.

Sleeping & Eating

San Luis Obispo's motel row is north of downtown along Monterey St, with cheaper chains along Hwy 101. Downtown Higuera St has cafés, restaurants, wine-tasting rooms and brewpubs.

HI Hostel Obispo (☎ 805-544-4678; www.hostelobispo.com; 1617 Santa Rosa St; dm $24-27, r from $45; 🕒 check-in 8-10am & 4:30-10pm; 💻 📶) This solar-powered ecohostel inhabits a converted Victorian one block from the train station. Amenities include a kitchen and bike rentals ($10/day). No credit cards are accepted.

Peach Tree Inn (☎ 805-543-3170, 800-227-6396; www.peachtreeinn.com; 2001 Monterey St; r incl breakfast $79-200; ❄ 💻 📶) The folksy motel rooms are relaxing, especially those creekside or with rocking chairs overlooking rose gardens and lawns. Hearty breakfasts include homemade breads.

Big Sky Café (☎ 805-545-5401; www.bigskycafe.com; 1121 Broad St; mains $8-20; 🕒 7am-9pm Mon, 7am-10pm Tue-Fri, 8am-10pm Sat, 8am-9pm Sun) With the tagline 'analog food for a digital world,' this ecoconscious café gets top marks for imaginative market-fresh breakfasts, but big-plate dinners can be bland.

Novo (☎ 805-543-3986; 726 Higuera St; small plates $6-22, dinner mains $16-32; 🕒 11am-10pm Mon-Thu, 11am-midnight Fri & Sat, 10am-10pm Sun) Novo spins out hit-or-miss Mediterranean, Brazilian and Asian-inspired tapas, with an eye towards freshness and presentation. Pick from dozens of international beers, wines or sakes, and savor the view from creekside decks.

> **WHAT THE...?**
>
> The fantastically campy **Madonna Inn** (☎ 805-543-3000, 800-543-9666; www.madonnainn.com; 100 Madonna Rd; r $179-449; ❄ 🏊) is a garish confection visible from Hwy 101. Japanese tourists, vacationing Midwesterners and irony-loving hipsters adore the 110 themed rooms – including Yosemite Rock, Caveman and hot-pink Floral Fantasy (check out photos online). The urinal in the men's room is a bizarre waterfall. But the best reason to stop here? Old-fashioned cookies from the storybook bakery.

Getting There & Around

A half-mile walk east of downtown, **Amtrak** (1011 Railroad Ave) runs the daily Seattle–LA *Coast Starlight* and twice-daily *Pacific Surfliner*, stopping at Santa Barbara ($30, 2¾ hours), LA ($37, 5¾ hours) and San Diego ($55, 8¾ hours). **Greyhound** (1023 Railroad Ave) has daily buses to Santa Barbara ($27, 2¼ hours), LA ($38, 5¼ hours) and San Francisco ($48, seven hours).

SLO's **Regional Transit Authority** (RTA; ☎ 805-541-2228; www.slorta.org; one-way fares $1.25 to $2.75, day pass $4.50) operates daily buses with limited weekend services, converging on downtown's **transfer center** (cnr Palm & Osos Sts).

MORRO BAY TO HEARST CASTLE

About 15 miles north of SLO via Hwy 1, **Morro Bay** is home to a commercial fishing fleet; however, its claim to fame is **Morro Rock**, a volcanic peak jutting up from the ocean floor, giving your first hint of the coast's upcoming drama. (Too bad about those power plant smokestacks obscuring the views though.) Boat tours and kayak rentals are available along the Embarcadero, where **Giovanni's Fish**

Market & Galley (☎ 805-772-2123; 1001 Front St; mains $6-10; 9am-6pm;), a classic California seafood shack, has killer garlic fries and fish-and-chips. Midrange motels cluster uphill between Harbor and Main Sts.

Nearby are fantastic state parks for coastal hiking and **camping** (☎ reservations 800-444-7275; www.reserveamerica.com). South of town, **Morro Bay State Park** (☎ 805-772-2694; campsites/RV sites $35/50) has a natural-history museum and heron rookery. The park's **Inn at Morro Bay** (☎ 805-772-5651, 800-321-9566; www.innatmorrobay.com; 60 State Park Rd; d $109-279;) is a tranquil, two-story waterfront lodge, where most rooms have feather beds and gas fireplaces to ward off coastal fog. Further south in Los Osos, west of Hwy 1, wilder **Montaña de Oro State Park** (☎ 805-772-7434; campsites $5-25) features coastal bluffs, tidepools, sand dunes, peak-climbing and mountain biking trails, and primitive camping. Its Spanish name ('mountain of gold') comes from native poppies that blanket the hillsides in spring.

North along Hwy 1, surfers love the Cal-Mexican **Taco Temple** (☎ 805-772-4965; 2680 Main St, Morro Bay; mains $6-12; 11am-8:30pm Sun, 11am-9pm Mon & Wed-Sat), a cash-only joint, and **Ruddell's Smokehouse** (☎ 805-995-5028; 101 D St, Cayucos; mains $4-10; 11am-6pm), which serves smoked-fish tacos by the oceanfront pier in small-town Cayucos. Vintage beach motels line Cayucos' Ocean Ave, including family-run **Seaside Motel** (☎ 805-995-3809, 800-549-0900; www.seasidemotel.com; 42 S Ocean Ave, Cayucos; r $75-140; W), which has kitchenettes.

Twenty miles north of Morro Bay, quaint **Cambria** village has deluxe lodgings along unearthly beautiful Moonstone Beach Dr, including the charming, Tudor-style **Fogcatcher Inn** (☎ 805-927-1400, 800-425-4121; www.fogcatcherinn.com; 6400 Moonstone Beach Dr; d incl breakfast $145-399;), harboring modern rooms with romantic fireplaces. Inland, **HI Cambria Bridge Street Inn** (☎ 805-927-7653; www.bridgestreetinncambria.com; 4314 Bridge St; dm $22-25, r $40-75, all with shared bath; reception 5-9pm;) sleeps like a hostel but feels like a grandmotherly B&B. The artisan cheese and wine shop **Indigo Moon** (☎ 805-927-2911; 1980 Main St; lunch mains $5-10; 10am-4pm daily, 5-9pm Wed-Sun) has breezy bistro tables, market-fresh salads and gourmet sandwiches. With a sunny patio and take-out counter, **Linn's Easy as Pie Cafe** (☎ 805-924-3050; 4251 Bridge St; dishes $4-10; 11am-7pm;) is famous for its olallieberry pie and preserves.

Ten miles north of Cambria, hilltop **Hearst Castle** (☎ 805-927-2020, 800-444-4445; www.hearstcastle.org; tours adult/child from $24/12; 8:20am-3:20pm, later in summer) is California's most famous monument to wealth and ambition. William Randolph Hearst, the newspaper magnate, entertained Hollywood stars and royalty at this fantasy estate dripping with European antiques, accented by shimmering pools and surrounded by flowering gardens. Tours last 1¾ hours, including the round-trip bus ride. Make reservations, especially for evening living-history and Christmas holiday tours. Five miles south, **San Simeon State Park** (☎ reservations 800-444-7275; www.reserveamerica.com; campsites $20-35) has creekside campgrounds.

Heading north, Point Piedras Blancas is home to an enormous **elephant-seal colony** that breeds, molts, sleeps, frolics and, occasionally, goes aggro on the beach. Keep your distance from these wild animals as they can move faster on the sand than you can. The main viewpoint, 4.8 miles north of Hearst Castle, has interpretive panels. Seals are here year-round, but the exciting birthing and mating season is from January to March, peaking on Valentine's Day. Nearby, the 1875 **Piedras Blancas Lightstation** (☎ 805-927-7361; www.piedrasblancas.org; adult/child $10/5; 9:45am Tue, Thu & Sat) is an outstandingly scenic spot; tours meet at the old motel, 1.5 miles north of the lighthouse off Hwy 1.

BIG SUR

Much ink has been spilled extolling the raw beauty and energy of this 100-mile stretch of craggy coastline shoehorned south of the Monterey Peninsula. More a state of mind than a place you can pinpoint on a map, Big Sur has no traffic lights, banks or strip malls. When the sun goes down, the moon and stars provide the only illumination – if summer fog hasn't extinguished them. Lodging, food and gas are scarce and pricey. Demand is high year-round, so book ahead. The free, information-packed newspaper *Big Sur Guide* (www.bigsurcalifornia.org) is available everywhere along the way. Note the $10 parking fee at state parks is valid for same-day access to all.

It's about 25 miles from Hearst Castle to blink-and-you-miss-it Gorda, home of **Treebones Resort** (☎ 877-424-4787; www.treebonesresort.com; 71895 Hwy 1; d with shared bath incl breakfast $155-290;), which offers back-to-nature clifftop yurts, some with oceanview decks. Don't expect much privacy though.

About 10 miles north of Lucia is the new-agey **Esalen Institute** (☎ 831-667-3047; www.esalen.org; 55000 Hwy 1), famous for its esoteric workshops and ocean-view hot-springs baths. With a reservation you too can frolic nekkid in the latter – but only from 1am to 3am ($20, credit cards only). It's surreal.

Three miles north, **Julia Pfeiffer Burns State Park** (car $10) harbors California's only coastal waterfall, 80ft-high McWay Falls, which is reached via a quarter-mile stroll. Perched on a cliff are two **walk-in campsites** (☎ 800-444-7275; www.reserveamerica.com; tent sites $30). Two more miles north, a steep dirt trail descends from a hairpin turn on Hwy 1 to **Partington Cove**, a raw and breathtaking spot where crashing surf salts your skin – truly scenic, but swimming isn't safe.

Seven miles further is **Deetjen's Big Sur Inn** (☎ 831-667-2377; www.deetjens.com; 48865 Hwy 1; d $130-200, with shared bath $80-185), where quirky, rustic rooms and cottages nestle among redwoods and wisteria. Its quaint **restaurant** (dinner mains $12-32; 🕑 8-11:30am & 6-9pm) serves country comfort-style fare.

Just north, the funky **Henry Miller Memorial Library** (☎ 831-667-2574; www.henrymiller.org; Hwy 1; 🕑 11am-6pm Wed-Mon; 💻 📶) is the art and soul of Big Sur bohemia, with a jam-packed bookstore, live-music concerts, open-mic nights and an outdoor film series. Nearly opposite, food takes a backseat to dramatic ocean views at clifftop **Nepenthe** (☎ 831-667-2345; 48510 Hwy 1; mains $14-37; 🕑 11:30am-10pm), meaning 'island of no sorrow.' The Ambrosia burger is famous.

Heading north, the **USFS Big Sur Ranger Station** (☎ 831-667-2315; 🕑 8am-4:30pm) will clue you in about hiking and camping options and issue overnight parking ($4) and campfire permits (free) for backpacking trips into the Ventana Wilderness, including the popular 10-mile trek to Sykes Hot Springs.

Across the highway, detour onto the obscurely marked Sycamore Canyon Rd, which drops for two narrow, twisting miles to crescent-shaped **Pfeiffer Beach** (per vehicle $5; 🕑 6am-sunset), with its towering offshore sea arch and strong currents that make it too dangerous for swimming. Dig down into the sand – it's purple!

Next up, **Pfeiffer Big Sur State Park** is crisscrossed by sun-dappled trails through redwood forests, including a lazy 1.4-mile round-trip to Pfeiffer Falls, which usually runs from October to May. Make campground **reservations** (☎ 800-444-7275; www.reserveamerica.com; campsites $35-50) or stay in the rambling, 1930s **Big Sur Lodge** (☎ 831-667-3100, 800-424-4787; www.bigsurlodge.com; 47225 Hwy 1; r $209-369; 🏊), which has renovated, single-story attached cottages, a well-stocked general store and simple **restaurant** (mains $8-25; 🕑 7:30am-9pm).

Most of Big Sur's commercial activity is concentrated along the next 6 miles, including a post office, shops, gas stations, private campgrounds, motels and restaurants. Chic, ecoconscious **Glen Oaks Motel** (☎ 831-667-2105; www.glenoaksbigsur.com; Hwy 1; d $195-300; 📶) is a redesigned 1950s redwood-and-adobe motor lodge, where snug rooms and cabins have gas fireplaces. A California-style **burrito bar** (mains $5-8) hides inside the Big Sur River Inn's **general store** (☎ 831-667-2700; 46840 Hwy 1; 🕑 11am-7pm). Nearby, **Maiden Publick House** (☎ 831-667-2355) has an encyclopedic beer menu, decent pub grub and live-music jams.

Heading north, visitors often overlook **Andrew Molera State Park** (vehicles $10), but locals love this trail-laced pastiche of grassy meadows, waterfalls, ocean bluffs, rugged beaches and wildlife watching, including California condors. From the parking lot, a half-mile trail leads to a first-come, first-served **campground** (tent sites $25).

Six miles before the famous Bixby Bridge, take a tour of 1889 **Point Sur Lightstation** (☎ 831-625-4419; www.pointsur.org; tours from adult/child $10/5; 🕑 schedules vary). Meet your guide at the locked gate; arrive early as space is limited (no reservations).

CARMEL

Once a bohemian artists' seaside resort, too-quaint Carmel-by-the-Sea now has the well-manicured feel of a country club. Simply plop down in any café (Ocean Ave is the main drag) and watch the parade of behatted ladies toting fancy-label shopping bags, dapper gents driving top-down convertibles and frazzled nannies wheeling their pampered charges.

A mile south of downtown, gorgeous **San Carlos Borroméo de Carmelo Mission** (☎ 831-624-1271; www.carmelmission.org; 3080 Rio Rd; adult/child under 17/senior $6.50/2/4; 🕑 9:30am-5pm Mon-Sat, 10:30am-5pm Sun) is an oasis of calm and solemnity, ensconced in flowering gardens. Its stone basilica is filled with original art, while a separate chapel holds the memorial tomb of founder Junípero Serra.

They bark, they bray, they bathe and they're fun to watch – sea lions are the stars of **Point Lobos State Reserve** (☎ 831-624-4909; http://pt-lobos.parks.states.ca.us; per car $10; 8am-30min after sunset), 4 miles south of Carmel. Its dramatically rocky coastline offers excellent tidepooling. The full perimeter hike is 6 miles, but even short walks take in Bird Island and Whalers Cove. Arrive early on weekends; parking is limited.

Even if you've never heard of 20th-century poet Robinson Jeffers, a pilgrimage to **Tor House** (☎ 831-624-1813; www.torhouse.org; 26304 Ocean View Ave; tours $7; 10am-3pm Fri & Sat), which was built with his own hands, offers fascinating insights into bohemian Old Carmel. A porthole in the Celtic-inspired Hawk Tower reputedly came from the wrecked ship that carried Napoleon from Elba. Make reservations for tours (no children under 12).

Downtown, **Bruno's Market & Deli** (☎ 831-624-3821; cnr 6th & Junípero Aves; sandwiches $5-8; 7am-8pm) makes a mean tri-trip beef sandwich and has all the accoutrements for a picnic. Southeast of the mission, **Rio Grill** (☎ 831-625-5436; 101 Crossroads Blvd, off Hwy 1 exit Rio Rd; mains $9-26; 11:30am-9pm Sun-Thu, to 10pm Fri & Sat) is a jazzy bistro, where local ingredients find their destiny in wickedly flavored Southwestern dishes.

MONTEREY

Working-class Monterey is all about the sea. Today, it lures visitors with a top-notch aquarium that's a veritable temple to Monterey Bay's underwater universe. A National Marine Sanctuary since 1992, the bay begs for exploration by kayak, boat, scuba or snorkel. Meanwhile, downtown's historic quarter preserves California's Spanish and Mexican roots with restored period buildings. Don't waste time on the tourist ghettos of Fisherman's Wharf and Cannery Row; the latter was immortalized by novelist John Steinbeck back when it was the hectic, smelly epicenter of the sardine-canning industry, Monterey's lifeblood till the 1950s.

The **visitor center** (☎ 831-657-6400, 877-668-3739; www.montereyinfo.org; 401 Camino El Estero; 9am-6pm Mon-Sat, to 5pm Sun, closing 1hr earlier Nov-Mar) has free phones for checking lodgings availability. There's a smaller **branch** (5 Custom House Plaza; 9am-5pm) inside the Maritime Museum. Ask for the free *Monterey County Film & Literary Map*.

Sights

MONTEREY BAY AQUARIUM

our pick **Monterey Bay Aquarium** (☎ 831-648-4800, tickets 866-963-9645; www.montereybayaquarium.org; 886 Cannery Row; adult/child $30/18; 9:30am-6pm Mon-Fri, to 8pm Sat & Sun Jun-Aug, 10am-6pm daily Sep-May) – we dare you not to be mesmerized and enriched by this ecoconscious aquarium. Give yourself at least half a day to watch sharks and sardines play hide-and-seek in fast-growing kelp forests, observe the antics of frisky otters, meditate upon ethereal jellyfish and get touchy-feely with sea cucumbers, bat rays and other tide-pool creatures. Feeding times are best, especially for watching the penguins. To avoid the worst crowds, get tickets in advance, be there when doors open and stick around during lunchtime.

MONTEREY STATE HISTORIC PARK

Old Monterey is a cluster of lovingly restored 19th-century brick-and-adobe buildings, including stately Casa Soberanes; novelist Robert Louis Stevenson's one-time boardinghouse residence; and the Cooper–Molera adobe, built by a sea captain. All these and more are covered on a 2-mile self-guided walking tour called the **Path of History**. Admission to the buildings is free, but opening hours and guided tour times vary. At press time, all of the park's historic buildings were temporarily closed to the public, due to the state's budget crisis. Pick up maps and find out what's open inside the **Pacific House Museum** (☎ 831-649-7118; 20 Custom House Plaza), which has in-depth period exhibits on California's multinational history.

Opposite, the **Maritime Museum** (☎ 831-372-2608; 5 Custom House Plaza; admission free; 10am-5pm Tue-Sun) illuminates Monterey's salty past, including the roller-coaster-like rise and fall of the local sardine business. Gems include a ship-in-a-bottle collection and the historic Fresnel lens from Point Sur Lightstation.

Activities

A favorite activity is walking or bicycling the paved 18-mile **Monterey Peninsula Recreation Trail**, which edges the coast through Monterey and ends at Lovers Point in Pacific Grove. The much-vaunted **17-Mile Drive** connects Monterey and Pacific Grove with Carmel-by-the-Sea. For maps and rentals, drop by **Bay Bikes** (☎ 831-655-2453; www.baybikes.com; 585 Cannery Row; per hr/day from $8/32).

WORTH THE TRIP: NATIONAL STEINBECK CENTER

A 30-minute drive east of Monterey, Salinas is the birthplace of John Steinbeck (1902–68), a Stanford University dropout who went on to win a Nobel Prize for Literature. Tough, funny and brash, he sensitively portrayed the troubled spirit of rural, working-class Americans in such novels as *The Grapes of Wrath, Cannery Row* and *East of Eden*.

Smack in the middle of the fertile Salinas Valley, the **National Steinbeck Center** (☎ 831-775-4721; www.steinbeck.org; 1 Main St; adult/child $11/6; 🕑 10am-5pm) brings his novels to life with interactive, kid-accessible exhibits and short movie clips. One cherished possession is Rocinante, the camper Steinbeck drove across America while writing *Travels with Charley*. A surprisingly interesting agricultural museum also inhabits the center.

In August, the **Steinbeck Festival** (www.steinbeck.org) is four days of films, lectures, music, tours and storytelling. Just south of the museum, Salinas' Main St is chockablock with eateries and bars, including First Awakenings diner, Habanero Cucina Mexicana and Monterey Coast Brewing Co.

Kayaking is especially magical at sunset; rent from the friendly folks at **Monterey Bay Kayaks** (☎ 800-649-5357; www.montereybaykayaks.com; 693 Del Monte Ave; per day $30-35). Lessons and guided tours of Monterey Bay or nearby Elkhorn Slough start at $50.

Diving and snorkeling reign supreme, although the water is rather frigid. Rent a full get-up, including wetsuit, at **Monterey Bay Dive Company** (☎ 831-656-0454; www.montereyscubadiving.com; 225 Cannery Row; snorkel/scuba rental per day $39/80), which runs guided boat dives (from $60).

Year-round, Fisherman's Wharf is the launch pad for whale-watching trips. But it's worth the 20-minute drive north to Moss Landing, where **Sanctuary Cruises** (☎ 530-778-3344; www.sanctuarycruises.com; adult/child under 3yr/child 3-12yr $45/10/35) operates highly recommended whale-watching and dolphin-spotting cruises led by marine biologists; reservations are essential.

Festivals & Events

Castroville Artichoke Festival (☎ 831-633-2465; www.artichoke-festival.org) 'Agro-art' sculptures, cooking demos and field tours in mid-May.

Monterey County Fair (☎ 831-372-5863; www.montereycountyfair.com) Old-fashioned carnival, wine-tasting competitions and live music in mid-August.

Monterey Jazz Festival (☎ 831-275-9255; www.montereyjazzfestival.org) One of the USA's longest-running jazz festivals in mid-September.

Sleeping

Peak summer rates are quoted below. Skip the frills and save a bunch at chain and indie motels along Munras Ave, south of downtown, and N Fremont St, east of Hwy 1.

Veterans Memorial Park Campground (☎ 831-646-3865; walk-in/drive-in campsites $5/25) Tucked into the forest, this municipal campground has 40 well-kept, grassy nonreservable sites with hot showers, drinking water and firepits.

HI Monterey Hostel (☎ 831-649-0375; www.montereyhostel.org; 778 Hawthorne St, Monterey; dm $25-28, r $59-91, all with shared bath; 🕑 reception 8am-10pm; 💻) Four blocks from Cannery Row, this simple, clean hostel is just the ticket for backpackers; reservations are strongly recommended. Take MST bus 1 from downtown's Transit Plaza.

Asilomar Conference Grounds (☎ 831-372-8016, 866-654-2878; www.visitasilomar.com; 800 Asilomar Ave, Pacific Grove; r incl breakfast $115-185; 📶 🏊 👪) At the peninsula's western edge, this state-park lodge has buildings designed by architect Julia Morgan, of Hearst Castle fame (see p960). Historic rooms are small and thin-walled, but charming nonetheless. The lodge's rec room has fireside reading nooks, ping-pong and pool tables, and bicycle rentals (per day $10).

Monterey Hotel (☎ 831-375-3184, 800-966-6490; www.montereyhotel.com; 406 Alvarado St, Monterey; r $159-319; 📶) Right downtown, this 1904 grand edifice harbors small, somewhat noisy, but freshly renovated rooms sporting reproduction Victorian furniture; there is no elevator. Book online for discounts. Parking costs $17.

Sanctuary Beach Resort (☎ 831-883-9478, 877-944-3863; www.thesanctuarybeachresort.com; 3295 Dunes Dr, Marina; r $189-369; 📶 🏊 👪) Be lulled to sleep by the surf at this low-lying retreat, hidden in the dunes north of Monterey. Petite town house rooms have gas fireplaces, kitchenettes and binoculars for whale-watching. The beach is off-limits, as it's a nature preserve, though there are other beaches and hiking trails nearby.

Eating & Entertainment

More eateries, bars, live music and cinemas line Alvarado St downtown and Cannery Row.

First Awakenings (☎ 831-372-1125; American Tin Cannery, 125 Oceanview Blvd, Pacific Grove; 🕑 7am-2pm Mon-Fri, to 2:30pm Sat & Sun; mains $5-11; 👶) Sweet and savory, creative breakfasts and lunches, plus bottomless pitchers of coffee, make this hideaway café near the aquarium worth seeking out.

our pick **Passionfish** (☎ 831-655-3311; 701 Lighthouse Ave, Pacific Grove; mains $17-24; 🕑 5-9:30pm Sun-Thu, to 10:30pm Fri & Sat) Here it is. You found it. A perfect, chef-owned seafood restaurant where the sustainable fish is dock-fresh, every preparation divine and the wine list more than affordable. Reservations are recommended.

Montrio Bistro (☎ 831-648-8880; 414 Calle Principal. Monterey; dishes $5-10, mains $14-38; 🕑 4:30pm-10pm Sun-Thu, to 11pm Fri & Sat; 👶) In a 1910 firehouse, the tables of this sophisticated-looking restaurant are covered in butcher paper with crayons for kids. The New American cooking often features local, organic ingredients. Tapas-sized tasting dishes and local wine list show flair.

Also recommended:

Wild Plum Cafe & Bakery (☎ 831-646-3109; 731 Munras Ave, Monterey; mains $6-11; 🕑 7am-6:30pm Tue-Fri, to 5pm Mon & Sat; 👶) Sidewalk café serving organic egg breakfasts, housemade soups and sandwiches.

East Village Coffee Lounge (☎ 831-373-5601; 498 Washington St, Monterey; dishes $2-6; 🕑 6am-late Mon-Fri, 7am-late Sat & Sun) Sleek coffeehouse with a liquor license and live-music, film and DJ nights.

Getting Around

Local buses run by **Monterey-Salinas Transit** (☎ 831-899-2555, 888-678-2871; www.mst.org; single-ride/day pass from $2.50/6) converge at the **Transit Plaza** (cnr Pearl & Alvarado Sts), including routes to Salinas, Carmel and, in summer, Big Sur. Also in summer, free daytime trolleys loop around downtown, Fisherman's Wharf and Cannery Row.

SANTA CRUZ

SoCal beach culture meets North California (NorCal) counterculture in Santa Cruz. The University of California (UCSC) student population makes this old-school radical town way more youthful, hip and lefty-political than Silicon Valley over the redwood-forested mountains farther north. Some worry that Santa Cruz's weirdness quotient is dropping, but you'll disagree when you witness the freak show (and we say that with love) along Pacific Ave, downtown's main drag. For the beach and boardwalk, head south. The **visitor center** (☎ 831-425-1234, 800-833-3494; www.santacruzca.org; 1211 Ocean St; 🕑 9am-5pm Mon-Fri, 10am-4pm Sat, 11am-3pm Sun) can help find accommodations. KPIG (107.5 FM) plays the classic Santa Cruz soundtrack – think Bob Marley, Janis Joplin and Willie Nelson.

Sights & Activities

There's free admission to the vintage 1907 **boardwalk** (☎ 831-423-5590; www.beachboardwalk.com; 400 Beach St; rides $2.25-4.50, all-day pass $30; 🕑 daily Memorial Day–Labor Day, off-season hr vary), which boasts the West Coast's oldest beachfront amusement park, with the 1924 Giant Dipper coaster and a 1911 Looff carousel.

About 1.5 miles west along the coast road, the tiny **Surfing Museum** (☎ 831-420-6289; www.santacruzsurfingmuseum.org; 701 W Cliff Dr; admission by donation; 🕑 noon-4pm Thu-Mon Sep-Jun, 10am-5pm Wed-Mon Jul & Aug), which is inside the old lighthouse, is packed with memorabilia, including vintage redwood boards. The museum overlooks experts-only **Steamers Lane** and beginners' **Cowells**, both popular surf breaks.

Further west, **Natural Bridges State Beach** (☎ 831-423-4609; per car $10; 🕑 8am-sunset; 👶) bookends the scenic drive, about 3.5 miles from the wharf. There are tide pools for exploring and leafy trees in which monarch butterflies hibernate from mid-October to late February. Nearby, UCSC's **Seymour Center at Long Marine Lab** (☎ 831-459-3800; www2.ucsc.edu/seymourcenter; off Delaware Ave; adult/student $6/4; 🕑 10am-5pm Tue-Sat, noon-5pm Sun; 👶) has cool interactive exhibits for kids.

They don't call Santa Cruz 'Surf City' for nothing. **Richard Schmidt Surf School** (☎ 831-423-0928; www.richardschmidt.com; per 2hr lesson $80) can get you out there, all equipment included. For surfing tips from in-the-know staff, head east to Capitola for women-owned **Paradise Surf Shop** (☎ 831-462-3880; www.paradisesurf.com; 3961 Portola Dr; wetsuit/surfboard rental $10/20, 2hr lesson $100; 🕑 10am-6pm Mon-Fri, 9am-6pm Sat & Sun) and internationally renowned **O'Neill Surf Shop** (☎ 831-475-4151; www.oneill.com; 1115 41st Ave; wetsuit/surfboard rental $10/20; 🕑 9am-8pm Mon-Fri, 8am-8pm Sat & Sun). Or experience the craggy coastline with **Venture Quest** (☎ 831-427-2267; www.kayaksantacruz.com; 2 Santa Cruz Wharf; kayak rentals/tours/lessons from $30/55/70; 🕑 10am-7pm Mon-Fri, 9am-7pm Jun-Sep, off-season hr vary; 👶), which guides sea-cave and

WHAT THE...?

A kitschy, old-fashioned tourist trap, the **Mystery Spot** (☎ 831-423-8897; www.mysteryspot.com; off Branciforte Dr; admission $5; 🕒 10am-5pm Sep-May, 10am-6pm Mon-Fri, 9am-7pm Sat & Sun Jun-Aug) has scarcely changed since 1940. On a steeply sloping hillside, compasses seem to point crazily, mysterious forces push you around and buildings lean at silly angles. Make reservations, or risk getting stuck waiting. It's 3 miles north of town. Parking costs $5. Don't forget your bumper sticker!

whale-watching kayak tours, including to Elkhorn Slough and Point Lobos (p962).

A 45-minute drive north of Santa Cruz into the mountains via Hwys 9 and 236, **Big Basin Redwoods State Park** (☎ 831-338-8860; www.bigbasin.org; per car $10; 🕒 6am-10pm) protects 20,000 acres of redwood forest and 80 miles of trails, one of which drops to the Pacific. Closer to town, **Henry Cowell Redwoods State Park** (☎ 831-438-2396; per car $10; 🕒 sunrise-sunset) has riverside trails through old-growth redwood forests. It's near Felton, the terminus of **Roaring Camp Railroads** (☎ 831-335-4484; www.roaringcamp.com; adult/child from $20/14; 🕒 schedules vary), which operates narrow-gauge steam trains up into the redwoods and a standard-gauge train from Santa Cruz's boardwalk; parking costs $7.

Sleeping

Hotel prices soar in summer. For motels, try Ocean St near downtown and Mission St near the UCSC campus. Make **reservations** (☎ 800-444-7275; www.reserveamerica.com) for state-park **campgrounds** (campsites $35-65, RV sites $65) at beaches south of town off Hwy 1 or up in the redwood forests (above).

HI Santa Cruz Hostel (☎ 831-423-8304; www.hi-santacruz.org; 321 Main St; dm $25-28, r $60-100, all with shared bath; 🕒 reception 8-11am & 5-10pm; 💻) Budget overnighters dig this cute hostel at the Carmelita Cottages in a flowery garden setting, just two blocks from the beach. One bummer: the 11pm curfew. Make reservations.

Redwood Croft (☎ 831-458-1939; www.redwoodcroft.com; 275 Northwest Dr, Bonny Doon; r incl breakfast $145-230; 👶) A 25-minute drive into the mountains, this country B&B with old-fashioned charm is a rejuvenating, back-to-nature retreat, with hammocks, fireplaces, hot tubs and a trampoline for the kiddos.

Adobe on Green B&B (☎ 831-469-9866; www.adobeongreen.com; 103 Green St; r incl breakfast $149-199; 📶) Peace and quiet are the mantras here. The hosts are practically invisible, but their thoughtful touches are everywhere: from boutique-hotel-style amenities inside spacious, stylish and solar-powered rooms to breakfast spreads from their organic gardens.

Pleasure Point Inn (☎ 831-475-4657; www.pleasurepointinn.com; 23665 E Cliff Dr; r incl breakfast $250-295; 📶) Live out your fantasy of California beachfront living here. Clean-lined, contemporary rooms have hardwood floors, Jacuzzi tubs, kitchenettes and private patios. Step onto the rooftop deck for drop-dead views.

Eating & Drinking

Downtown, especially Pacific Ave, is chockablock with mostly mediocre cafés. Mission St, near the UCSC campus, offers cheap take-out and multi-ethnic joints.

Tacos Moreno (☎ 831-429-6095; 1053 Water St; dishes $2-6; 🕒 11am-8pm) Who cares how long the line is, especially at lunchtime? You're guaranteed to find taqueria heaven here – from pork, chicken and beef soft tacos to supremely stuffed burritos.

Emily's (☎ 831-429-9866; 1129 Mission St; items $2-7; 🕒 5:30am-6pm Mon-Fri, 6:30am-6pm Sat & Sun) Their motto is simply 'good things to eat.' Stop by for hot, cheddar-cheese scones or the daily soup-and-salad combo, and nosh on the shady creekside porch.

Engfer Pizza Works (☎ 831-429-1856; 537 Seabright Ave; pizzas $8-23; 🕒 4-9:30pm Tue-Sun; 👶) Detour to find this old factory, where wood-fired oven pizzas are made from scratch with love – the no-name specialty is almost like a giant salad on roasted bread. Play ping-pong and sip draft microbrews while you wait.

Drinking & Entertainment

Pacific Ave downtown has prolific bars, live-music lounges, cinemas and coffeehouses. Check the free newspaper *Santa Cruz Weekly* for listings.

Kuumbwa Jazz Center (☎ 831-427-2227; www.kuumbwajazz.org; 320 Cedar St; 🕒 hr vary) books big-name jazz sounds. **Moe's Alley** (☎ 831-479-1854; www.moesalley.com; 1535 Commercial Way; 🕒 4pm-2am Tue-Sun) is a warm, intimate venue for jazz, blues and world beats. With its leafy sidewalk verandah, arty **Caffe Pergolesi** (☎ 831-426-1775; 418 Cedar St; 🕒 7am-11pm; 📶) is the place to discuss conspiracy theories over strong coffee, organic juices or beer.

Getting There & Away

Local buses run by **Santa Cruz Metro** (☎ 831-425-8600; www.scmtd.com; single-ride/day pass $1.50/4.50) cover the region, converging on **Metro Center** (920 Pacific Ave). Nearby, **Greyhound** (☎ 831-423-1800; 425 Front St) runs frequent buses to San Francisco ($21, three hours) and Los Angeles ($55, nine hours).

SANTA CRUZ TO SAN FRANCISCO

Far more scenic than any freeway, this curvaceous, 70-mile stretch of coastal Hwy 1 is bordered by wild beaches, organic farmstands and sea-salted villages, all scattered like so many loose diamonds in the rough.

Twenty miles north of Santa Cruz, **Año Nuevo State Natural Reserve** (☎ 650-879-0227; per car $10; 8:30am-3:30pm Apr-Nov, by reservation only mid-Dec–mid-Mar) is home base for the world's largest colony of northern elephant seals. Call ahead to reserve space on a 2½-hour, 3-mile guided **walking tour** (☎ 916-638-5883, 800-444-4445; per person $7) during the cacophonous winter birthing and mating season. On a quiet windswept coastal perch further north, green business certified **HI Pigeon Point Lighthouse Hostel** (☎ 650-879-0633; dm $23-28, r $53-118; check-in 3:30-10:30pm;) inhabits the historic lightkeepers' quarters. It's popular, so book ahead.

Five miles north, **Pescadero State Beach & Marsh Natural Preserve** (☎ 650-879-2170; per car $10; 8am-sunset) attract beachcombers and birders. Just inland, Pescadero village is home to famed **Duarte's Tavern** (☎ 650-879-0464; 202 Stage Rd; dinner mains $25-40; 7am-9pm), where creamy artichoke soup and olallieberry pie are crowd-pleasers. For a beach picnic, visit the bakery-deli at **Arcangeli Grocery Co** (☎ 650-879-0147; 287 Stage Rd; 10am-6pm) and family-owned **Harley Farms Cheese Shop** (☎ 650-879-0480; 250 North St; 11am-5pm). Camp inside a redwood canyon at **Butano State Park** (☎ reservations 800-444-7275; www.reserveamerica.com; campsites $35), which is 5 miles southeast via Cloverdale Rd.

Less than 20 miles farther north, busy Half Moon Bay is defined by seductive, 4-mile-long **Half Moon Bay State Beach** (☎ 650-726-8819; per car $10, campsites $35-50), offering Spartan campsites. For oceanfront luxury, the **Inn at Mavericks** (☎ 650-728-1572; www.innatmavericks.com; 364 Princeton Ave; r $185-245;) offers spacious, romantic roosts, most with deep-soaking tubs. It overlooks Pillar Point Harbor, which has a decent brewpub with a sunset-view patio. Better cafés, restaurants and eclectic shops line Half Moon Bay's quaint, five-block-long Main St, inland from Hwy 1.

Five miles farther north, follow the signs to **Moss Beach Distillery** (☎ 650-728-5595; 140 Beach Way; appetizers $11-16; noon-8:30pm Mon-Thu, noon-9pm Fri & Sat, 11am-8:30pm Sun), a historic spot with good fish-and-chips and an ocean-view deck for sunset drinks. Two more miles along, **HI Point Montara Lighthouse Hostel** (☎ 650-728-7177; Hwy 1 & 16th St; dm $23-28, r $63-114; check-in 3:30-10:30pm;) is an airy, ecofriendly hostel with a private beach; reservations are essential. From here, it's just 25 miles to San Francisco via Devil's Slide.

SAN FRANCISCO & THE BAY AREA

SAN FRANCISCO

Somewhere between waking and sleeping, there's a costumed pug parade already in progress past candy-colored Victorian houses, a street-corner prophet reciting Beat poetry through a megaphone, and skateboarders grinding to an awed halt to see an orange bridge poking through a blanket of fog. This dreamscape is an actual city called San Francisco, where East meets West, and fact meets fiction.

If you've ever wondered where the envelope goes when it's pushed, here's your answer. Psychedelic drugs, newfangled technology, gay liberation, green ventures, free speech and culinary experimentation all became mainstream long ago in San Francisco. Not afraid to go for broke, the city has lost fortunes – but never its spirit – in gold-rush panics and dot-com crashes, not to mention earthquakes and fires. Losing your shirt is now a favorite local pastime with the clothing-optional Bay to Breakers race, Pride Parade and hot Sundays on the nude north end of Baker Beach. This is no place to be shy: out here among eccentrics of every stripe, no one's going to notice a few tan lines. So long, inhibitions; hello, San Francisco.

History

Oysters and acorns would have been your main dinner options in the Mexico-run

Ohlone settlement of San Francisco circa 1847; however, a year and some gold nuggets later, beer and steak were the order of the day. By 1849, gold found in the nearby Sierra Nevada foothills had turned a waterfront village of 800 into a port city of 100,000 prospectors, card sharks, con men, prostitutes and honest folk trying to make an honest living – good luck telling which was which. That friendly bartender might drug your drink, and you'd wake up a mile from shore, shanghaied into service on some ship bound for Argentina. (No wonder San Franciscans still prefer their bartenders surly.)

By 1850, California had been nabbed from Mexico and fast-tracked for US statehood, presenting San Francisco with the problem of introducing public order to 200 saloons and an untold number of brothels and gambling dens. Panic struck when Australia glutted the market with gold in 1854, and ire turned irrationally on the city's Chinese community, who from 1877 to 1945 were restricted to living and working in Chinatown by anti-Chinese laws and periodic race riots. The main way out of debt was dangerous work building railroads for the city's robber barons, who dynamited, mined and clear-cut their way across the Golden West, and built grand Nob Hill mansions towering above Chinatown.

The city's lofty ambitions and 20-plus theaters came crashing down in 1906, when earthquake and fire left 3000 dead, 100,000 homeless and much of the city reduced to rubble – including almost every mansion on Nob Hill. Theater troupes and opera divas performed for free amid smoldering ruins downtown, reviving a performing arts tradition that continues to this day.

Ambitious public works projects continued through the 1930s, when Diego Rivera, Frida Kahlo and federally funded muralists began the tradition of leftist politics in paint visible in 250-plus Mission murals.

WWII brought seismic shifts to San Francisco's community as women and African Americans working in San Francisco shipyards created a new economic boom, and President Franklin Delano Roosevelt's Executive Order 9066 mandated the internment of the city's historic Japanese American community. A 40-year court battle ensued, ending in an unprecedented apology from the US government. San Francisco became a testing ground for civil rights and free speech, with Beat poet Lawrence Ferlinghetti and City Lights Bookstore winning a landmark 1957 ruling against book banning, with the publication of Allen Ginsberg's splendid, incendiary *Howl*.

The Central Intelligence Agency (CIA) hoped an experimental drug called LSD might turn San Francisco test subject Ken Kesey into the ultimate fighting machine, but instead the author of *One Flew Over the Cuckoo's Nest* served it up in Kool-Aid and kicked off the psychedelic '60s. The Summer of Love brought free food, love and music to the Haight – an out and proud gay community to the Castro – and back-to-nature California cuisine to natural food co-ops and restaurants nationwide.

The 1980s meant bloated stock market gains and devastating losses from AIDS, but the city rallied from recession in the early '90s to become a model for disease treatment and prevention. When other California cities systematically shut out homeless people by closing clinics and forbidding sitting on sidewalks, San Francisco absorbed homeless Vietnam veterans, runaways and addicts, and continues the work of repairing shattered lives today.

The city's arty cyberpunk crowd introduced wild ideas to Silicon Valley in the 1990s, spawning a dot-com boom that abruptly changed San Francisco's public image from grungy downtown bike messengers to slick South of Market venture capitalists. Then just as suddenly, the bubble popped in 2000. But rents and hopes were never entirely deflated, and San Francisco's quintessential bohemians are clutching their rent-controlled leases for dear life as the recession hits, social media takes off and a biotech boom begins. This is where you come in, just in time for San Francisco's next wild ride.

Orientation

The tongue of land that sticks out into the Pacific mocking the rest of the continental US is San Francisco. The 7 x 7-mile city is laid out on a staid grid, but its main street downtown is a diagonal contrarian streak called Market St. South of Market (SoMa) are the warehouses, galleries and rampant hedonism, while north of Market you'll find pinstriped Financial District (FiDi) with the wild parrots of North Beach on its shoulders.

From here to the waterfront, the scenery gets weirder and wilder. Decor choices shift from the Tuscan faux-finish of North Beach to pagoda-topped Chinatown Deco along Columbus St, which points north toward the sea lions belly flopped on Fisherman's Wharf. To the West it's a steep slide from swanky Nob Hill and Russian Hill through the shopping and entertainment gauntlet that is Union Square, all the way downhill to seedy Tenderloin back alleys.

Alongside the squalor of the 'Loin are the grandiose ambitions of Civic Center and the east–west dividing line of Van Ness Ave. Follow Van Ness south until you see taco trucks and graffiti art, and you'll know you've arrived in the Mission. Further west is witty, pretty and gay Castro, and north of the Castro, freak flags fly high above rainbow Victorians in the historic hippie Haight. Keep heading north and you'll rub shoulders with old money in Pacific Heights and wonder how everyone suddenly got so blonde in the Marina. Westward, ho: the Richmond and Sunset districts flank Golden Gate Park, where the city gets back to nature.

Keep your city smarts and wits about you, especially at night in the Tenderloin, SoMa and the Mission. Expect to be asked for spare change often, but don't feel obliged – to address the causes of homelessness instead of the symptoms, consider making a donation to nonprofit Haight Ashbury Food Program (p977).

From San Francisco International Airport, take Hwy 101 north. See p987.

Information

BOOKSTORES

A Different Light Bookstore (Map pp972-3; ☎ 415-431-0891; www.adlbooks.com; 489 Castro St; ⏲ 10am-10pm Mon-Sat, 11am-9pm Sun) The USA's largest gay bookseller: raucous readings; gay, lesbian, bisexual and transgender (GLBT) resources; and literary cruising.

Adobe Books (Map pp972-3; ☎ 415-864-3936; http://adobebooksbackroomgallery.blogspot.com; 3166 16th St; ⏲ 11am-midnight) Every book you never knew you needed used and cheap, if you can find it in the obstacle course of sofas, cats, art installations and German philosophy.

Bound Together Anarchist Book Collective (Map pp972-3; ☎ 415-431-8355; www.boundtogetherbooks.com; 1369 Haight St; ⏲ 11:30am-7:30pm) All-volunteer nonprofit bookstore stocked with conspiracy theory comics, alternative histories, organic farming manuals and other radical notions.

City Lights Bookstore (Map pp972-3; ☎ 415-362-8193; www.citylights.com; 261 Columbus Ave; ⏲ 10am-midnight) Landmark bookseller, publisher and free-speech champion; trust excellent staff picks, browse Muckraking and Stolen Continents downstairs and find Nirvana upstairs in Poetry.

Green Apple (Map pp972-3; ☎ 415-387-2272; www.greenapplebooks.com; 506 Clement St; ⏲ 10am-10:30pm Sun-Thu, 10am-11:30pm Fri & Sat) Three-story mother lode of new releases, remaindered titles and used books; mags, music and used novels two doors down.

Kayo Books (Map pp972-3; ☎ 415-749-0554; www.kayobooks.com; 814 Post St; ⏲ 11am-6pm Thu-Sat) Pulp fiction, and proud of it: vintage noir novels, trashy romances, wild Westerns and an entire Bizarre Nonfiction section.

EMERGENCY & MEDICAL SERVICES

American College of Traditional Chinese Medicine (Map pp972-3; ☎ 415-282-9603; www.actcm.edu; 450 Connecticut St; ⏲ 8:30am-9pm Mon-Thu, 9am-5:30pm Fri & Sat) Acupuncture, herbal remedies and other traditional Chinese medical treatments.

Pharmaca (Map pp972-3; ☎ 415-661-1216; www.pharmaca.com; 925 Cole St; ⏲ 8am-8pm Mon-Fri, 9am-8pm Sat & Sun) Pharmacy plus naturopathic remedies and weekend chair massage.

Police, fire & ambulance (☎ 311)

San Francisco General Hospital (Map pp972-3; ☎ emergency room 415-206-8111, main 415-206-8000; www.sfdph.org; 1001 Potrero Ave)

Trauma Recovery & Rape Treatment Center (☎ 415-437-3000; http://traumarecoverycenter.org)

Walgreens (Map pp972-3; ☎ 415-861-6276; www.walgreens.com; 498 Castro at 18th; ⏲ 24hr) Pharmacy and over-the-counter meds; dozens of locations citywide.

INTERNET ACCESS

There are more than 370 free wi-fi hot spots citywide. Connect for free in Union Sq, BrainWash (p970), and most cafés and hotel lobbies. Walgreens (above) can burn digital photos on to a CD for $2.99.

Apple Store (Map pp972-3; ☎ 415-392-0202; www.apple.com/retail/sanfrancisco; 1 Stockton St; ⏲ 10am-9pm Mon-Sat, 11am-6pm Sun; wi-fi) Free wi-fi access and internet terminal usage.

San Francisco Main Library (Map pp972-3; ☎ 415-557-4400; http://sfpl.lib.ca.us; cnr 100 Larkin St, at Grove St; ⏲ 10am-6pm Mon & Sat, 9am-8pm Tue-Thu, noon-6pm Fri & Sun; wi-fi) The main library provides free internet terminal usage and free (although spotty) wi-fi access.

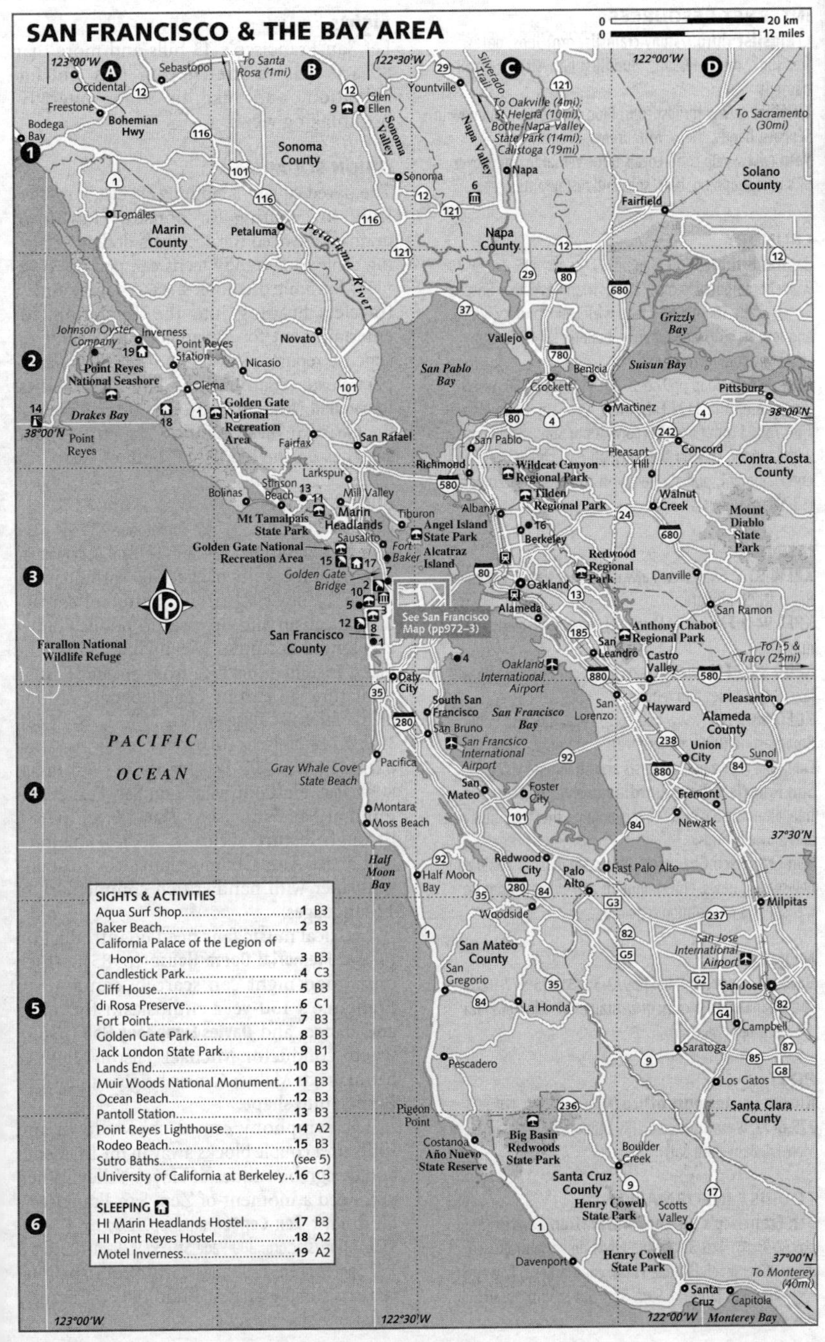
SAN FRANCISCO & THE BAY AREA
0 20 km
0 12 miles
123°00'W
122°30'W
122°00'W
38°00'N
37°30'N
37°00'N
To Santa Rosa (1mi)
To Oakville (4mi); St Helena (10mi); Bothe-Napa Valley State Park (14mi); Calistoga (19mi)
To Sacramento (30mi)
To I-5 & Tracy (25mi)
To Monterey (40mi)
Sonoma County
Marin County
Napa County
Solano County
Contra Costa County
Alameda County
San Mateo County
Santa Clara County
Santa Cruz County
San Francisco County
PACIFIC OCEAN
San Pablo Bay
Suisun Bay
Grizzly Bay
San Francisco Bay
Drakes Bay
Monterey Bay
Farallon National Wildlife Refuge
See San Francisco Map (pp972–3)
SIGHTS & ACTIVITIES
Aqua Surf Shop 1 B3
Baker Beach 2 B3
California Palace of the Legion of Honor 3 B3
Candlestick Park 4 C3
Cliff House 5 B3
di Rosa Preserve 6 C1
Fort Point 7 B3
Golden Gate Park 8 B3
Jack London State Park 9 B1
Lands End 10 B3
Muir Woods National Monument 11 B3
Ocean Beach 12 B3
Pantoll Station 13 B3
Point Reyes Lighthouse 14 A2
Rodeo Beach 15 B3
Sutro Baths (see 5)
University of California at Berkeley 16 C3
SLEEPING
HI Marin Headlands Hostel 17 B3
HI Point Reyes Hostel 18 A2
Motel Inverness 19 A2

INTERNET RESOURCES

Craigslist (http://sfbay.craigslist.org) Jobs, dates, free junk, tango lessons, Buddhist babysitters – you name it.
Thrillist (www.thrillist.com) Blog on the new and now in SF: bars, bands, shops, restaurants, events.
Yelp (www.yelp.com) Locals trade verbal fisticuffs over SF's best shopping, bars, spas and restaurants.

LAUNDRY

Bernal Bubbles (off Map pp972-3; ☎ 415-821-9530; www.bernalbubbles.com; 397 Cortland Ave near Bocana St; 7am-10pm;) Free wi-fi, coin laundry, wash and fold service, video games, bulletin board for stray socks and free lecture series.
BrainWash (Map pp972-3; ☎ 415-255-4866; www.brainwash.com; 1122 Folsom St; 7am-10pm Mon-Thu, 7am-11pm Fri & Sat, 8am-10pm Sun;) Come with laundry, stay for breakfast all day, cheap beer, live entertainment, pinball, free wi-fi and internet terminals ($3 per 20 minutes).

MEDIA

KALW 91.7 FM (www.kalw.org) Local National Public Radio (NPR) affiliate.
KPFA 94.1 FM (www.kpfa.org) Alternative news and music.
KPOO 89.5 FM (www.kpoo.com) Community radio with jazz, R & B, blues and reggae.
KQED 88.5 FM (www.kqed.org) Local NPR and Public Broadcasting (PBS) affiliate featuring original shows, California reportage, podcasts and streaming video.
San Francisco Bay Guardian (www.sfbg.com) SF's free, alternative weekly covers politics, theater, music, art and movie listings.
San Francisco Chronicle (www.sfgate.com) Main daily newspaper; news, entertainment and event listings on website (no registration required).

MONEY

Bank of America (Map pp972-3; ☎ 415-977-0278; www.bankamerica.com; downstairs, One Market Plaza; 9am-6pm Mon-Fri)

POST

Rincon Center post office (Map pp972-3; ☎ 800-275-8777; www.usps.com; 180 Steuart St; 8am-6pm Mon-Fri, 8am-2pm Sat)

TOURIST INFORMATION

San Francisco's Visitor Information Center (Map pp972-3; ☎ 415-391-2000; www.onlyinsanfrancisco.com; lower level, Hallidie Plaza, cnr Market & Powell Sts; 9am-5pm Mon-Fri, 9am-3pm Sat & Sun, closed Sun Nov-Apr)

Sights

Let San Francisco's 43 hills and more than 80 arts venues stretch your legs and imagination, and take in some (literally) breathtaking views.

UNION SQUARE

The paved square is nothing special, but offers front-row seating for nonstop downtown drama: bejeweled theater-goers dodging clanging cable cars, trendy teens camped out overnight for limited-edition sneakers and business travelers heading into the Tenderloin for entertainment too scandalous to include on expense reports. The action begins with shoppers clustered around the Powell St **cable-car turnaround** (Mapp972–3), gets dramatic along the Geary St **Theater District** (Mapp972–3) and switches on the red lights south of Geary.

CIVIC CENTER

City Hall (Map pp972-3); ☎ docent tours 415-554-6139; www.sfgov.org; 400 Van Ness Ave; 8am-8pm Mon-Fri) rose from the ashes of the 1906 earthquake to house the city's signature mixture of corruption, idealism and opposition politics under a splendid rotunda. Meanwhile across the plaza, imaginations race from ancient Persian miniatures to cutting-edge Japanese fashion at the **Asian Art Museum** (Map pp972-3; ☎ 415-581-3500; www.asianart.org; 200 Larkin St; adult/senior/student & child 13-17yr $12/8/7; 10am-5pm Tue, Wed, Fri-Sun, to 9pm Thu). Find out what's on San Francisco's mind at San Francisco's **Main Library** (p968), through lecture series, historical exhibits, and artist Ann Chamberlain's card-catalog wallpaper with handwritten commentary in 12 languages.

Classical music fans need no introduction to **War Memorial Opera House** (p985), which on a good night can scarcely contain San Francisco's 150-year enthusiasm for opera and dance, and **Davies Symphony Hall** (p985), where conductor Michael Tilson Thomas' baton prods Mahler to new heights and whips Berlioz into shape.

The symphony crowd chows down and spiffs up a couple blocks away in the brasseries and design boutiques of Hayes Valley. When you need a moment of Zen, San Francisco's landmark **Zen Center** (Map pp972-3; ☎ 415-863-3136; http://sfzc.org; 300 Page St; 9:30am-12:30pm & 1:30-5pm Mon-Fri, 8:30am-noon Sat) offers spiritual retreats for the largest Buddhist community outside Asia.

SAN FRANCISCO IN…

Stretch your dollars and ditch the car: bus fare and calf muscles let you see SF at its best.

One Day

Since the gold rush, great San Francisco adventures have started in **Chinatown** (p975), where you can still wander back alleys in search of hidden fortunes – in cookies, that is. Beat it to **City Lights Bookstore** (p968) to revel in Beat poetry and free speech, and then walk downhill past the **Transamerica Pyramid** (p975) to **City View** (p982) for scrumptious dumplings. Hit the **San Francisco Museum of Modern Art** (below) and the downtown **gallery scene** (p975), and then head over to the **Asian Art Museum** (opposite), where art transports you across centuries and oceans within an hour. Two blocks away, conductor Michael Tilson Thomas brings down the house with Beethoven at **Davies Symphony Hall** (p985). Toast hearts lost and inspiration found in SF with passion-fruit cocktails and Nuevo Latino cuisine at **Destino** (p984). End the night with film festival premieres at the **Castro Theatre** (p986), or swaying to glam-rock anthems in a converted speakeasy at **Café du Nord** (p985).

Two Days

Start your day amid the unlikely splendors of mural-covered **Balmy Alley** (p976), and then window-shop up to **826 Valencia** (p976) to load up on pirate supplies and literary mags and to watch ichthyoid antics in the Fish Theater. By the time you walk to 16th and Valencia, you should be hungry enough to eat a horse – maybe even a burrito (p983). Hoof it up to the Haight for flashbacks at vintage clothing boutiques and follow starry-eyed hippies to the Summer of Love site: **Golden Gate Park** (p977). Head to the **MH de Young Fine Arts Museum** (p978) for far-out tower views and farther-out art, take a walk on the wild side in the rainforest dome of the **California Academy of Sciences** (p977), and then dig into organic Cal-Moroccan feasts at **Aziza** (p984).

For Foodies

Graze your way across San Francisco, starting with the farmers' market at the **Ferry Building** (p982) or the gamut of local temptations indoors: sourdough baguettes, artisanal chocolate, sustainably farmed caviar and organic goat blue cheese. Your crash course in dim sum awaits along Chinatown's **Stockton Street** (p975), where florescent-lit mom-and-pop shops dole out shrimp and chive dumplings, crowd-pleasing barbecue pork buns and sweet lotus-root mooncakes. From here it's a BART ride to 24th Street and Mission, where bodegas revive tired palates with fragrant corn tortillas and habañero-spiked salsa; **La Taquería** (p983) sets the standard for Cal-Mex burritos. Cross town to shop Clement Street's restaurant supply stores for fearsome cleavers and dainty *amuse-bouche* plates, and scour **Green Apple** (p968) for remaindered cookbooks. Your grand finale awaits at **Jardinière** (p982), with a mood-enhancing meal by James Beard award-winning chef Traci des Jardins.

SOMA

Don't let the high-rises and warehouses fool you: SoMa is packed with outrageous art venues, adventurous dining and anything-goes after-hours clubs. At **San Francisco Museum of Modern Art** (SFMOMA; Map pp972-3; ☎ 415-357-4000; www.sfmoma.org; 151 3rd St; adult/senior/student/child under 12 $12.50/8/7/free; ⏰ 11am-5:45pm Fri-Tue, to 8:45pm Thu), Mario Botta's glowing lightwell illuminates massive mural installations, outstanding photography from Dorothea Lange's Depression documentaries to Daido Moriyama's dreamscapes, a rooftop sculpture garden featuring Louise Bourgeois' eerie super-spider, and new media mavericks, such as Matthew Barney, who debuted his dazzling Vaseline-smeared videos at SFMoMa.

Comics earn serious consideration at the **Cartoon Art Museum** (Map pp972-3; ☎ 415-227-8666; www.cartoonart.org; 655 Mission St; adult/child 6-12yr $6/2; ⏰ 11am-5pm Tue-Sun) with shows of original *Watchmen* covers, too-hot-to-print political cartoons and hands-on workshops with comics legends. On this same block is the always moving **Museum of African Diaspora** (Map pp972-3; ☎ 415-358-7200; www.moadsf.org; 685 Mission; ⏰ 11am-6pm Wed-Sat), tracing connections among African communities through

SAN FRANCISCO

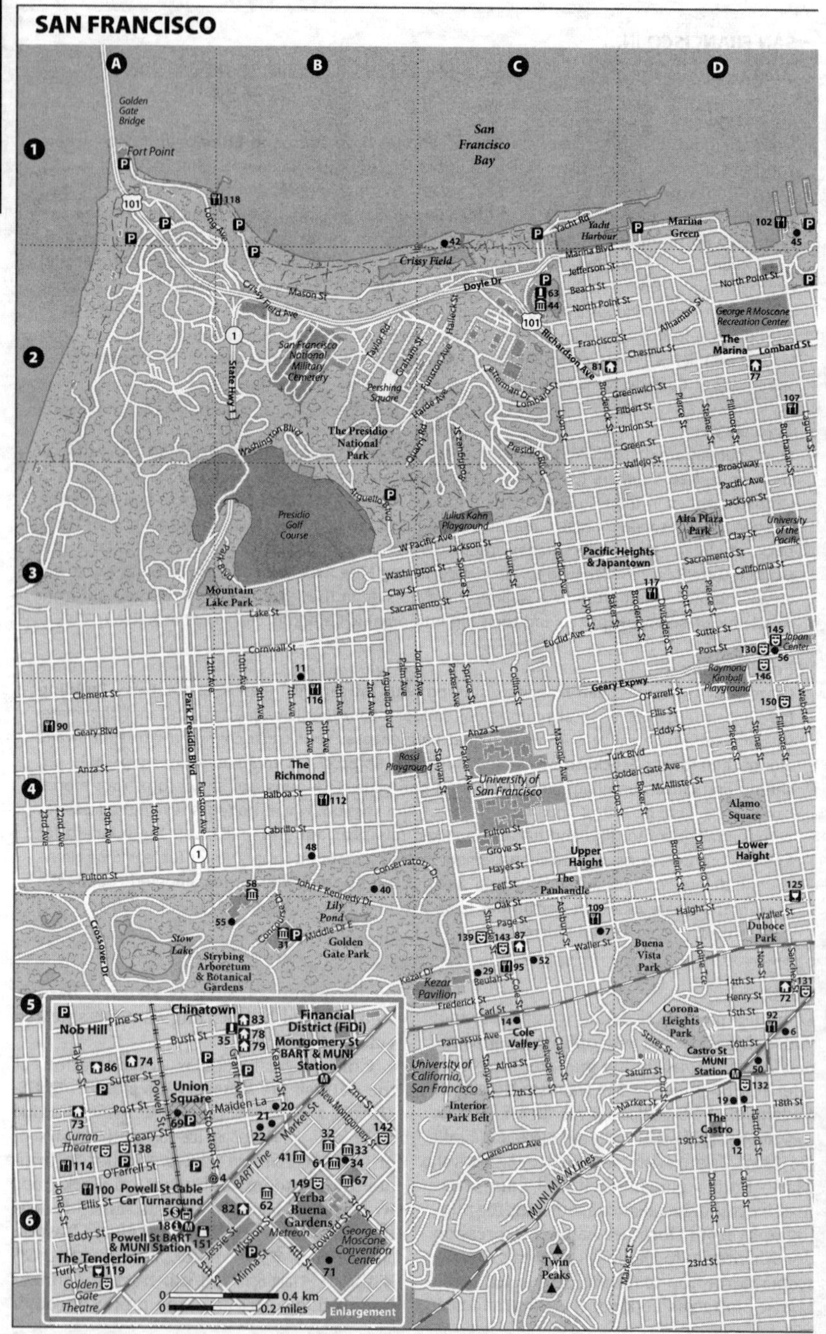

INFORMATION

A Different Light Bookstore 1 D5
Adobe Books 2 E5
American College of Traditional Chinese Medicine 3 G5
Apple Store 4 B6
Bank of America 5 A6
Books Inc 6 D5
Bound Together Anarchist Book Collective 7 C5
BrainWash 8 F4
California Welcome Center 9 F1
City Lights Bookstore 10 F2
Green Apple 11 B3
Human Rights Campaign 12 D6
Kayo Books 13 F3
Pharmaca 14 C5
Rincon Center Post Office 15 G3
San Francisco General Hospital 16 F6
San Francisco Main Library 17 F4
San Francisco's Visitor Information Center 18 A6
Walgreens 19 D5

SIGHTS & ACTIVITIES

14 Geary 20 B5
49 Geary 21 B6
77 Geary 22 B6
826 Valencia 23 E6
Adventure Cat 24 F1
Alcatraz Cruises 25 F1
Aquarium of the Bay 26 F1
Art Institute 27 E2
Asian Art Museum 28 F4
Avenue Cyclery 29 C5
Beat Museum 30 F2
Blazing Saddles (see 101)
California Academy of Sciences 31 B5
California Historical Society 32 B6
Cartoon Art Museum 33 B6
Catharine Clark Gallery 34 B6
Chinatown Gate 35 B5
Chinese Historical Society of America Muesum 36 F3
City Hall 37 E4
City Kayak 38 H4
Coit Tower 39 F2
Conservatory of Flowers 40 B4
Contemporary Jewish Museum 41 B6
Crissy Field 42 C1
Davies Symphony Hall (see 136)
Dolores Park 43 E6
Exploratorium 44 C2
Ferry Building (see 99)
Fort Mason 45 D1
Galería de la Raza 46 F6
George Sterling Park 47 E2
Golden Gate Bike & Skate 48 B4
Gold's Gym 49 F5
Gold's Gym 50 D5
Grace Cathedral 51 F3
Haight Ashbury Food Program 52 C5
Hyde Street Pier 53 E1
Jack Hanley Gallery 54 E5
Japanese Tea Garden 55 B5
Kabuki Hot Springs 56 D3
Meeting Point for Fire Engine Tours 57 E1
MH de Young Fine Arts Museum 58 B4
Mission Dolores 59 E5
Musée Mécanique 60 E1
Museum of African Diaspora 61 B6
Museum of Craft & Folk Arts 62 B6
Oceanic Society Expeditions (see 45)
Palace of Fine Arts 63 C2
Precita Eyes Mural Arts Center 64 F6
San Francisco Lesbian, Gay, Bisexual, Transgender Community Center 65 E4
San Francisco Maritime National Historical Park 66 E1
San Francisco Museum of Modern Art (SFMOMA) 67 B6
Transamerica Pyramid 68 F2
Union Square 69 A6
War Memorial Opera House (see 148)
Yerba Buena Centre for the Arts (see 149)
Zen Center 70 E4
Zeum Art & Technology Center 71 B6

SLEEPING

24 Henry 72 D5
Dakota Hotel 73 A6
Golden Gate Hotel 74 A5
HI San Francisco Fisherman's Wharf 75 E1
Hotel Bohème 76 F2
Hotel Del Sol 77 D2
Hotel des Arts 78 B5
Hotel Triton 79 B5
Hotel Vitale 80 G3
Marina Motel 81 C2
Mosser 82 B6
Orchard Garden Hotel 83 B5
Pacific Tradewinds 84 F3
Parker Guest House 85 E5
Petite Auberge 86 A5
Red Victorian 87 C5
San Francisco Elements 88 E6
San Remo Hotel 89 F2

EATING

Aziza 90 A4
Bocadillos 91 F2
Cafe Flore 92 D5
Cinecittá 93 F2
City View 94 F2
Cole Valley Cafe 95 C5
Crown & Crumpet 96 E1
Delfina 97 E5
Destino 98 E5
Ferry Building 99 G2
Fish & Farm 100 A6
Gary Danko 101 E1
Greens 102 D1
Home 103 E5
House of Nanking 104 F2
Ideale 105 F2
Jardinière 106 E4
La Boulange 107 D2
La Taquería 108 E6
Magnolia Brewpub 109 C5
Mission Beach Café 110 E5
Molinari 111 F2
Namu 112 B4
Rosamunde Sausage Grill (see 125)
Saigon Sandwich Shop 113 E3
Shalimar 114 A6
Suppenküche 115 E4
Taiwan 116 B4
Tataki 117 D3
Warming Hut 118 B1

DRINKING

Aunt Charlie's 119 A6
Eagle Tavern 120 F5
Hôtel Biron 121 E4
Koko Cocktails 122 E3
Lexington Club 123 E6
Powerhouse 124 F4
Toronado 125 D4
Tosca Cafe 126 F2
Zeitgeist 127 E5

ENTERTAINMENT

Annie's Social Club 128 F4
AT&T Park 129 G4
Boom Boom Room 130 D3
Café du Nord 131 D5
Castro Theater 132 D5
Cat Club 133 F4
Climate Theater 134 F4
Club Fugazi 135 F2
Davies Symphony Hall 136 E4
DNA Lounge 137 F5
Geary Theater 138 A6
Honey Soundsystem (see 141)
Magic Theater (see 45)
Milk 139 C5
New Conservatory Theater 140 E4
Paradise Loft 141 F4
Qoöl 142 B6
Red Vic 143 C5
Roxie Cinema 144 E5
Sundance Kabuki Cinema 145 D3
The Fillmore 146 D3
Theater Rhinoceros 147 E5
TIX Bay Area (see 69)
War Memorial Opera House 148 E4
Yerba Buena Center for the Arts 149 B6
Yoshi's 150 D4

SHOPPING

Westfield San Francisco Shopping Center 151 A6

TRANSPORT

Blue & Gold Ferries 152 G2
Blue & Gold Ferries 153 F1
City Rent-a-Car 154 E3
Transbay Terminal 155 G3

SAN FRANCISCO ART ATTACK

Think you can keep up with SF's creative leaps? Once your imagination limbers up at **SFMoMa** (p971), catch art while it's hot and controversial at the **Catharine Clark Gallery** (Map pp972-3; ☎ 415-399-1439; www.cclarkgallery.com; 150 Minna St; ⏲ noon-6pm Tue-Thu). Next, follow the steady stream of hipsters across 3rd St into **Yerba Buena Center for the Arts** (Map pp972-3; ☎ 415-978-2787; www.ybca.org; 701 Mission St; gallery admission adult/senior/student & teacher $7/5/5; ⏲ noon-5pm Tue-Sun, to 8pm Thu) for avant-garde shows and openings that draw art freaks by the thousands.

Duck into Yerba Buena Lane to celebrate creative breakthroughs in skilled hands at the **Museum of Craft & Folk Arts** (Map pp972-3; ☎ 415-227-4888; www.mocfa.org; 51 Yerba Buena Lane; adult/senior/child under 18yr $5/4/free; ⏲ 11am-5pm Tue-Sun), and then hit the galleries at **14, 49 and 71 Geary** (below) to see SF's latest high-concept photography and installation art. Afterwards, crash inside a hotel room designed to look like a conspiracy theorist's lair at **Hotel des Arts** (p981).

art, storytelling and technology. Across the street, architect Daniel Liebskind reshaped San Francisco's 1881 brick power plant with a blue steel extension to form the Hebrew word *l'chaim* ('to life'). Welcome to the **Contemporary Jewish Museum** (Map pp972-3; ☎ 415-655-7800; www.jmsf.org; 736 Mission St at 3rd; adult/child/senior & student $10/free/8; ⏲ 11am-5:30pm Fri-Tue, 1-8:30pm Thu), where recent shows explore Chagall's theatre backdrops and the life of Gertrude Stein. To keep the artistic inspiration coming, see above.

THE FINANCIAL DISTRICT

Back in its Barbary Coast heyday, loose change would buy you time with loose women in this neighborhood – now you'd be lucky to see a loose tie during happy hour. But the area still has redeeming quirks: a redwood grove has taken root in the remains of old whaling ships below the rocket-shaped **Transamerica Pyramid** (Map pp972-3; www.thepyramidcenter.com; 600 Montgomery St; ⏲ not open to the public), and eccentric art collectors descend from hilltop mansions for First Thursday gallery openings at **14, 49 and 77 Geary** (Map pp972-3; www.sfada.com; San Francisco Art Dealers Association; ⏲ most galleries 10:30am-5:30pm Tue-Fri, 11am-5pm Sat). Hedonism is alive and well at the **Ferry Building** (Map pp972-3; ☎ 415-983-8000, www.ferrybuildingmarketplace.com; ⏲ 10am-6pm Mon-Fri, 9am-6pm Sat, 11am-5pm Sun), where foodies happily miss their ferries slurping local oysters and bubbly.

CHINATOWN

More than pagoda phone booths and dragon-draped streetlights, it's astounding resilience that defines these 22 blocks and 40 alleyways. Since the 1840s, this community has survived riots, discrimination, fires, bootlegging gangsters and politicians' attempts to relocate it down the coast – the amazing-but-true story unfolds before your eyes at the landmark **Chinese Historical Society of America Museum** (Map pp972-3; ☎ 415-391-1188; www.chsa.org; 965 Clay St; adult/child 6-17yr $3/1; ⏲ noon-5pm Tue-Fri).

In the 1930s, Chinatown merchants rallied to oust back-alley brothels and opium dens, and gave **Grant Avenue** its signature Chinatown deco look. One block uphill, **Stockton Street** is lined with dim sum dives, vegetable sellers and apothecaries with walls of wooden drawers. But since you'll never really know Chinatown until you roam its alleys, take our Walking Tour (p978) or reserve ahead for **Chinatown Alleyway Tours** (p980).

NORTH BEACH

Parrots and poetry make the air of North Beach seem rarified – or maybe that's just the heady aroma of espresso brewing and pizza baking. Beat writers Jack Kerouac, Allen Ginsberg and Lawrence Ferlinghetti made this Italian neighborhood the proving ground for free spirits and free speech in the 1950s, as chronicled in the **Beat Museum** (Map pp972-3; ☎ 800-537-6822; www.thebeatmuseum.org; 540 Broadway; admission $5; ⏲ noon-10pm Tue-Thu, 10am-10pm Fri-Sun), and the escaped parrots who flock here make it an actual urban jungle. Some things stay the same: in cafés and pizzerias lining **Columbus** and upper **Grant Street**, you'll still hear Italian spoken. Up the **Filbert Street steps** at **Coit Tower** (Map pp972-3; ☎ 415-362-0808; admission free, elevator rides $5; ⏲ 10am-6pm), you'll find 360-degree views of downtown and wrap-around 1930s murals glorifying SF workers – once denounced as Communist, but now a landmark.

RUSSIAN HILL & NOB HILL

Gardeners, fitness freaks and suckers for sunsets all brave dizzying climbs west of North

Beach up Russian and Nob Hills. Drivers test their mettle on the crooked 1000 block of **Lombard Street** (Map pp972–3), but many obliviously roll past one of the city's best sunset vista points over the Golden Gate bridge at **George Sterling Park** (Map pp972–3) and a splendid Diego Rivera mural at the nearby **Art Institute** (Map pp972-3; ☎ 415-771-7020; www.sfai.edu; 800 Chestnut St; ⏰ 8am-9pm).

Stairways lead urban hikers past hidden cottages and scrap-sculpture gardens, but there's a shortcut to heaven in SF: hop the cable car uphill to **Grace Cathedral** (Map pp972-3; ☎ 415-749-6300; www.gracecathedral.com; 1100 California St; ⏰ 7am-6pm Mon-Fri, 8am-6pm Sat, 8am-7pm Sun, services with choir at 11am & 3pm Sun). This progressive Episcopal church keeps pace with its parishioners: the AIDS Interfaith Memorial Chapel features a bronze Keith Haring altarpiece; stained-glass windows illuminate Human Endeavors, including Albert Einstein in a swirl of nuclear particles; and pavement labyrinths guide restless souls through the spiritual stages of releasing, receiving and returning.

FISHERMAN'S WHARF

With the notable exception of sea lions gleefully belching after fish dinners at **Pier 39** (Map pp972-3; ☎ 415-981-7437; www.pier39.com), most piers are packed with landlubbers attempting to digest sourdough-bread bowls of gloppy clam chowder (don't bother: it can't be done). For a real taste of the city's seafaring past, head to the **San Francisco Maritime National Historical Park** (Map pp972-3; ☎ 415-561-7100; www.nps.gov/safr; 499 Jefferson at Hyde; ⏰ 9:30am-7pm Jun-Sep, 9:30am-5pm Oct-May) to tour 19th-century ships moored at **Hyde Street Pier** (Map pp972-3; ☎ 415-447-5000; 2905 Hyde at Jefferson Sts; boarding pass $5, national park passes accepted), including triple-masted 1886 *Balclutha*. At Pier 45 you can guillotine a man for a quarter at the **Musée Mécanique** (Map pp972-3; ☎ 415-346-2000; www.museemecaniquesf.com; admission free; ⏰ 10am-7pm Mon-Fri, 10am-8pm Sat & Sun), where 19th-century arcade games like the macabre French Execution compete for your spare change with Ms Pac-Man.

THE MARINA & PRESIDIO

Army sergeants would surely be scandalized by the frolicking in former army bases in the Marina and Presidio, including comedy improv and kiddie art classes at **Fort Mason** (Map pp972-3; ☎ 415-345-7500; www.fortmason.org). Geeks and freaks flock to the **Exploratorium** (Map pp972-3; ☎ 415-561-0360; www.exploratorium.edu; 3601 Lyon St; adult/child 4-12yr $14/9, Tactile Dome $17; ⏰ 10am-5pm Tue-Sun) to learn the scientific secrets to cuteness and grope through the Tactile Dome. Outside, ducklings march through the 1915 **Palace of Fine Arts** (Map pp972–3), Bernard Maybeck's faux-Roman rotunda depicting Art under attack by Materialists, with Idealists leaping to her rescue.

The Presidio's coastal airstrip has been stripped of asphalt and reinvented as **Crissy Field** (Map pp972-3; ☎ 415-561-7690; www.crissyfield.org), a haven for coastal birds, kitefliers and urban beachgoers. Take a hike for spectacular views of Golden Gate Bridge: see it from below like Alfred Hitchcock for a thrilling case of *Vertigo* at **Fort Point** (Map p969; ☎ 415-561-4395; www.nps.gov/fopo), or see it *au naturel* on the Presidio's west side at clothing-optional **Baker Beach** (Map p969; ⏰ sunrise-sunset). When the fog rolls in, the **Warming Hut** (Map pp972-3; ⏰ 9am-5pm) serves Fair Trade coffee and organic pastries within walls insulated with old denim.

THE MISSION

The Mission would have you believe every underground art movement started here – that's not entirely untrue. Ever since the local Ohlone painted pulsating hearts behind the altar at **Mission Dolores** (Map pp972-3; ☎ 415-621-8203; www.missiondolores.org; cnr Dolores & 16th Sts; adult/senior & child $5/3; ⏰ 9am-4pm Nov-Apr, 9am-4:30pm, May-Oct) around 1795, the Mission has kept art close to its heart.

Before SF skate-graffiti art became an international hit through such galleries as **Jack Hanley** (Map pp972-3; ☎ 415-522-1623; www.jackhanley.com; 395 Valencia St; ⏰ 11am-6pm Tue-Sat), there were 1970s political murals lining Mission side streets and the **Balmy Alley** (off Map pp972-3; off 24th St near Folsom). For tours, see Precita Eyes Mission Mural Tours (p980). Politics come with the territory: protests are held almost every weekend at **Dolores Park** (Map pp972–3), and Latino artists take on politics and pop culture at **Galería de la Raza** (Map pp972-3; ☎ 415-826-8009; www.galeriadelaraza.org; 2857 24th St; ⏰ noon-6pm Wed-Sat, 1-7pm Tue).

Given a Mission diet of burritos, margaritas and coffee, creative types seem to thrive – hence the local design boutiques, 'zine bookstores and nonprofit arts venues clustered around Valencia and Mission Sts. When a Pirate Supply Store landed at **826 Valencia** (Map pp972-3; ☎ 415-642-5905; www.826valencia.org;

826 Valencia St; noon-6pm), selling eye patches and McSweeney's publications to fund youth writing workshops, the Mission found its dream mission.

THE CASTRO

San Francisco's other neighborhoods have their share of gays; however, in the landmark Castro district, the GLBT community is extra-strength, like superheroes or condoms. Here they don't just get mad about half-ass drag and laws prohibiting same-sex marriage, they get organized: hence the historic **Human Rights Campaign** (Map pp972-3; ☎ 415-431-2200; www.hrc.org; 600 Castro St) and half-million-strong **Pride parade** (see p980), trailing boas and bridal veils by the mile.

You'll know you're entering the Castro from downtown when you see that glorious aqua Victorian with a glass front, so anyone inside the **San Francisco Lesbian, Gay, Bisexual, Transgender Community Center** (Map pp972-3; ☎ 415-865-5555; www.sfcenter.org; 1800 Market St) can still be out and proud. Stop by for art shows by transgendered artists, GLBT parenting groups, Friday crafts extravaganzas for under-26 arty types, and the annual Queer Prom. But you've officially arrived when you see the marquee of the **Castro Theatre** (p986), where every film begins with the rise of a mighty organ…no, really. When the vintage Wurlitzer rises from the orchestra pit and the crowd sings the theme song from *San Francisco* ('San Francisco, open your Golden Gate…'), the moment is pure movie magic.

THE HAIGHT

Better known as the hazy hot spot of the Summer of Love, the Haight still has its swinging '60s tendencies. Only a very mysterious, very local illness could explain the number of neighborhood medical marijuana clubs, and tie-dyes and ideals have never entirely gone out of fashion here – hence the **Bound Together Anarchist Book Collective** (p968), the cooperative indie **Red Vic Movie House** (p986) and the **Haight Ashbury Food Program** (Map pp972-3; ☎ 415-566-0366; www.thefoodprogram.org; 1525 Waller St), serving anyone in need with hot meals and job training.

North of Divisadero St, the **Upper Haight** features head shops, cafés, boutiques, vintage clothes and used CDs. Across Divisadero, **Lower Haight** is big on hairdressers, bars, skater gear and, um, gardening supply shops, all clustered around the picture-perfect Victorians lining hilltop **Alamo Square Park**. Anywhere you go on Haight, punks, artistes, aesthetes, oddballs and misfits all blend into the scenery.

JAPANTOWN & PACIFIC HEIGHTS

Atop every noodle house counter and karaoke bar in Japantown perches a *maneki neko*, the porcelain cat with one paw raised in permanent welcome. This neighborhood works hard to put you completely at ease, including shiatsu massages at **Kabuki Hot Springs** (p978), eco-entertainment and non-GMO popcorn at Robert Redford's **Sundance Kabuki Cinema** (p986), and **Yoshi's** (p985), featuring such world-class talents as New Orleans' Preservation Hall Jazz Band and SF's own funk-fusion Broun Fellinis. Across the street is the **Fillmore** (p985), the legendary birthplace of 1960s psychedelic rock, with the Day-Glo poster gallery to prove it.

GOLDEN GATE PARK & AROUND

San Francisco was way ahead of its time in 1866, when the city decided to turn 1017 acres of sand dunes into the world's largest city park. This ambitious green scheme scared off Frederick Law Olmstead, the celebrated architect of New York's Central Park, and thwarted real estate speculators' plans to turn Golden Gate Park into a theme-park resort. The park does have its outlandish attractions, including carnivorous plants and outer-space orchids in the 1879 **Conservatory of Flowers** (Map pp972-3; ☎ 415-666-7001; www.conservatoryofflowers.org; adult/senior & youth age 12-17/age 5-11/under 5 $5/3/1.50/free; 9am-4:30pm Tue-Sun). But instead of hotels and casinos, park architect William Hammond Hall insisted on botanical gardens, the **Japanese Tea Garden** (Map pp972-3; ☎ 415-752-4227; www.parks.sfgov.org; Hagiwara Tea Garden Dr; adult/senior & age 12-17/age 5-11/under 5 $5/3/$1.50/free, free 9-10am Mon, Wed & Fri; 9am-6pm Mar-Oct, 9am-5pm Nov-Feb) and boating on scenic **Stow Lake** (Map pp972-3; ☎ 415-752-0357; per hr paddleboats/canoes/rowboats $24/20/19, surreys/tandem bikes/bikes $20-35/12/6-8; rentals 10am-4pm).

Though even in Hammond's wildest dreams, he might not have imagined the Park's newest attractions. Architect Renzo Piano's 2008 landmark LEED-certified **California Academy of Sciences** (Map pp972-3; ☎ 415-379-8000; www.calacademy.org; 55 Concourse Dr; weekday adult/age 11-17/age 7-11/under 7 $24.95/19.95/14.95/free, third Wednesdays free, Thursdays 6-10pm $10 (age 21+ only); 9:30am-5pm Mon-Sat, 11am-5pm Sun) houses Pierre the Penguin and

38,000 other weird and wonderful animals under a 'living roof' of California wildflowers. Across the music concourse is another showstopper: Herzog & de Meuron's sleek, copper-clad **MH de Young Fine Arts Museum** (Map pp972-3; ☎ 415-750-3600; www.famsf.org/deyoung; adult/senior/student over 13 $10/7/6, $2 discount with Muni ticket, first Tue of month free; 9:30am-5:15pm Tue-Sun, to 8:45pm Fri Jan-Nov) is oxidizing green to blend into the park. But don't be fooled by the de Young's camouflaged exterior: inside are standout shows that celebrate inspired handiwork, from Andy Warhol's silkscreened pop-star portraits to Oceanic ceremonial masks.

Toward the Pacific, the Park scenery turns quixotic, with bison stampeding in their paddock toward dilapidated windmills. The park ends in blustery **Ocean Beach** (Map p969; ☎ 415-556-8371; sunrise-sunset), too chilly for bikini-clad clambakes but ideal for wet-suited pro surfers braving rip tides (casual swimmers beware). At the north end of Ocean Beach, the recently rebuilt and sadly soulless **Cliff House** (Map p969; ☎ 415-386-3330; www.cliffhouse.com; 1090 Point Lobos) overlooks the splendid ruin of **Sutro Baths** (Map p969), where Victorian dandies once converged for bracing baths and workouts.

Follow the trail above Sutro Baths around **Lands End** (Map p969) for postcard-worthy views of Marin Headlands and the Golden Gate Bridge. The trail leads to the **California Palace of the Legion of Honor** (Map p969; ☎ 415-750-3600; www.famsf.org/legion; 34th Ave at Clement Street; adult/senior/student over 13 $10/7/6, $2 discount with Muni ticket, first Tue of month free; 9:30am-5pm Tue-Sun), which mixes blockbuster exhibits of Fabergé eggs with Max Klinger's obscure, macabre 19th-century *Waking Dream* etchings.

SAN FRANCISCO BAY

Imagine a squat concrete bridge striped black and caution yellow spanning the San Francisco Bay – that's what the US Navy initially had in mind. Luckily, engineer Joseph B Strauss and architects Gertrude and Irving Murrow insisted on a soaring art-deco design and International Orange paint that harmonized with the natural environment. The result is the 1937 **Golden Gate Bridge** (Map pp972-3; ☎ 415-921-5858; www.goldengatebridge.org). Cars pay a $6 toll to cross from Marin to San Francisco; pedestrians and cyclists stroll the east sidewalk for free.

There is one impressive hunk of concrete in the Bay: the notorious island prison Al Capone called home, better known as **Alcatraz** (Map p969). Prison authorities boasted it was inescapable; however, since importing guards and all other necessities cost the state more than putting up prisoners at the Ritz, it was closed in 1963. Native American leaders took over the island from 1969–71 to protest US occupation of Native lands, and their standoff with the FBI is commemorated in a small museum and 'Red Power' signs near the ferry dock. Ferry tickets must be reserved in advance from **Alcatraz Cruises** (Map pp972-3; ☎ 415-981-7625; www.alcatrazcruises.com; adult/child 5-11yr day $26.00/16.00, night $32.00/19.50; reservations 9am-6:45pm; tours depart from Pier 33 about every half-hr 9am-4pm, plus 6:10pm & 6:45pm), which covers a captivating audio tour with prisoners and guards recalling life on the Rock.

Activities

Rent wheels at **Avenue Cyclery** (Map pp972-3; ☎ 415-387-3155; www.avenuecyclery.com; 756 Stanyan St;) at Golden Gate Park, or **Blazing Saddles** (Map pp972-3; ☎ 415-202-8888; www.blazingsaddles.com; 2715 Hyde St; per hr/day $7/28;), at Fisherman's Wharf. Cross the Golden Gate Bridge, and take the Sausalito ferry back to SF. On Sundays, Golden Gate Park's JFK Drive closes to vehicular traffic.

For a cool view of SF, paddle the bay with **City Kayak** (Map pp972-3; ☎ 415-357-1010; www.citykayak.com; Pier 38, cnr Embarcadero & Townsend Sts; per hr $15-25), or take a 1½-hour catamaran cruise with **Adventure Cat** (Map pp972-3; ☎ 415-777-1630; www.adventurecat.com; Pier 39; adult from $30).

Surfers head to **Ocean Beach** (Map p969), where wintertime swells rise 12ft or higher. **Aqua Surf Shop** (Map p969; ☎ 415-242-9283; http://aquasurfshop.com; 2830 Sloat Blvd; 10am-5:30pm Sun-Tue, 10am-7pm Wed-Sat) rents boards and wetsuits. Check the surf report (☎ 415-273-1618).

For stellar whale-watching trips, contact **Oceanic Society Expeditions** (Map pp972-3; ☎ 800-326-7491; www.oceanic-society.org; Fort Mason, bldg E; adult $100).

our pick **Kabuki Hot Springs** (Map pp972-3; ☎ 415-922-6000; www.kabukisprings.com; 1750 Geary Blvd; admission $22-25; 10am-9:45pm) is the place for soaking in Japanese baths; men and women use the baths on alternate days; bathing suits are required on coed Tuesdays.

Walking Tour

Limber up and look sharp: on this walk, you'll discover revolutionary plots, find hidden fortunes, meet birds that swear like sailors, shimmy up a giant fire hose and go gourmet with Gandhi.

Starting at **Chinatown's Dragon Gate** (**1**; Grant Ave at Bush St), head north one block past the gilded dragon lamps and trinket shops of Grant St and hang a right on Pine St. On your left, **Old St Mary's Park (2)** marks the spot of a notorious brothel leveled in the 1906 fire, but now the only tricks here are performed by renegade skateboarders under the watchful eye of Beniamino Bufano's 1929 statue of revolutionary leader Sun Yat-Sen. Backtrack and walk one block past Old St Mary's Church, turning left on Sacramento and taking the next right to spot flag-festooned temple balconies along **Waverly Place (3)**. Pay your respects at **Tien Hou Temple** (**4**; 125 Waverly Place, 4th fl; free, but offerings appreciated; hours vary), or hang your next left onto Clay St. One block up is the **Chinese Historical Society of America Museum** (**5**; p975), in the majestic Chinatown YWCA built by Julia Morgan, California's first female architect and the only person William Randolph Hearst trusted to build his castle (p960).

Walk back down Clay past Stockton, and the first lane on your left is **Spofford Alley (6)**, where you'll hear the click of mah-jongg tiles, a Chinese orchestra warming up and beauticians gossiping indiscreetly over blow-dryers. Once you might have overheard the whispers of Sun Yat-Sen and his conspirators at no 36 plotting the 1911 overthrow of China's last dynasty, or gunfire blasts during the 1920s bootlegger turf wars. At Washington St, jog right and left to enter **Ross Alley (7)**, once packed with brothels and more recently pimped as the picturesque setting for forgettable sequels such as *Karate Kid II* and *Indian Jones and the Temple of Doom.* Get your fortune while it's hot here, folded into warm cookies on vintage machines at **Golden Gate Fortune Cookie Factory** (**8**; 56 Ross Alley).

Head right back to Grant, and turn left; up a block and a half on your right is **Jack Kerouac Alley (9)**. The alleyway where Kerouac once passed out is now marked with poetry on the sidewalk and murals on the walls. At the end is **City Lights Bookstore** (**10**; p968), home of Beat poetry and champion of free speech. Get some lit to read a block and a half away at **Caffe Trieste** (**11**; ☎ 415-982-2605; www.caffetrieste.com; 601 Vallejo St; 6:30am-11pm daily, to midnight Fri & Sat), beloved since the '50s for its opera jukebox, accordion jams and offbeat regulars. Cross Columbus on Vallejo to the **Good Luck Parking Garage** (**12**; 735 Vallejo), where every parking spot

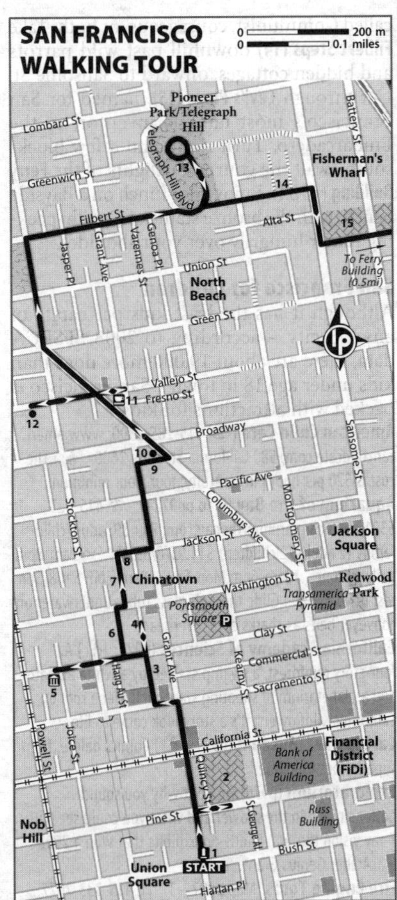

WALK FACTS

Start Chinatown's Dragon Gate
Finish Ferry Building
Distance 1.8 miles
Duration 1/2 day

comes with stenciled fortunes by artist Harrell Fletcher, such as 'You are not a has-been.'

Back on Columbus, head north, turn right at Stockton and again at Filbert St, and then pace yourself for the climb to **Coit Tower** (**13**; p975). The tower was built by eccentric millionaire Lillie Hitchcock Coit to honor firefighters and resemble a giant hose, which controversial WPA murals critics have called Communist, courageous, or both. Take **Filbert Steps (14)** downhill past wild parrots and hidden cottages, onward to Sansome St. Cut through **Levi's Plaza (15)**, named for San Francisco's most famous inventor, to the Embarcadero. Turn right, and a few blocks south await the gourmet delights of the **Ferry Building** (p982). Enjoy your lunch on a Bayside bench, with the bronze statue of Gandhi peeking rather hungrily over your shoulder.

San Francisco for Children

Although it has the least kids per capita of any US city – according to 2008 SFSPCA data, there are about 19,000 more dogs than kids under age 18 in town – San Francisco is packed with attractions for kids.

American Child Care (☎ 415-285-2300; www.americanchildcare.com; 580 California St, Suite 1600;) The cost is $20 per hour plus gratuity; four-hour minimum.

Aquarium of the Bay (Map pp972-3; ☎ 415-623-5301; www.aquariumofthebay.com; Pier 39; adult/child/family (2 adults, 2 children) $15.95/8/39.95; 9am-8pm daily summer, 10am-6pm Mon-Fri & 10am-7pm Sat & Sun rest of year;) Glide through glass tubes underwater on conveyer belts as sharks circle overhead.

California Academy of Sciences (p977;) A four-story rainforest, a swamp stalked by a white alligator, and a planetarium of shooting stars, all under a roof of California wildflowers: it's a storybook come to life.

Cartoon Art Museum (p971;) Comics galore, from superheroes to anime.

Exploratorium (p976) Find out why you sound better singing in the shower and what you could see with X-ray vision through hands-on exhibits that won a 2008 MacArthur Genius Grant.

Fire Engine Tours (Map pp972-3; ☎ 415-333-7077; www.fireenginetours.com; Beach St at the Cannery; adult/child under 12/teen $50/30/40; tours depart 1pm Wed-Mon;) Hot stuff: a 75-minute, open-air vintage fire engine ride over Golden Gate Bridge.

Golden Gate Park (p977;) Kid heaven: buffalo, a carousel, playgrounds, miniature trees and paddle boats.

Zeum Art & Technology Center (Map pp972–3; ☎ 415-822-3320; www.zeum.org; 221 4th St; adult/child 4-18yr $7/5; 11am-5pm Tue-Sun Jun-Aug, 1pm-5pm Wed-Fri & 11am-5pm Sat-Sun Sep-May;) Technology that's too cool for school: robots, live-action video games, DIY music videos, and animation workshops with Silicon Valley innovators.

Tours

California Historical Society (Map pp972-3; ☎ 415-357-1848; www.californiahistoricalsociety.org; 678 Mission St) When eccentric urban planner Gary Holloway isn't dressing in monk's robes, he leads Historical Walkabouts to little-known sights hidden in San Francisco neighborhoods.

Chinatown Alleyway Tours (☎ 415-984-1478; www.chinatownalleywaytours.org; adult/student 10-17yr/age 6-9/under 6 $18/12/5/free) Teens who grew up in the neighborhood lead two-hour tours for an up-close-and-personal peek into Chinatown's past. Tours depart 11am Saturday or by appointment.

Precita Eyes Mission Mural Tours (☎ 415-285-2287; www.precitaeyes.org; for public tour, adult/senior & under 17/under 12 $10-12/5/2) Run by the Precita Eyes Mural Arts Center, local artists lead two-hour tours on foot or bike covering 60-70 murals in a 6-10 block radius of mural-bedecked Balmy Alley. Tours depart 11am weekdays & 1:30pm weekends.

Public Library City Guides (☎ 415-557-4266; www.sfcityguides.org; public tours free) Local historians lead tours by neighborhood and theme: Art Deco Marina, Gold Rush Downtown, Pacific Heights Mansions and more. See website for meeting times and locations.

Festivals & Events

Chinese New Year Parade (☎ 415-986-1370; www.chineseparade.com) Chase the 200ft dragon, and see lion dancers and toddler kung-fu classes through Chinatown in late January/early February.

SF International Film Festival (☎ 415-561-5000; www.sffs.org) Sunglasses and paparazzi are must-have accessories at the nation's oldest film festival in late April.

Bay to Breakers (☎ 415-359-2800; www.baytobreakers.com; race registration $44-48) Many run costumed, others naked, some scared – from Embarcadero to Ocean Beach the third Sunday in May.

Carnaval (☎ 415-826-1401; www.carnavalsf.com) Brazilian, or just faking it with a wax and a tan? Come shake your tail feathers in the Mission the last weekend of May.

SF Gay Pride Month (☎ 415-864-0831; www.sfpride.org) A day isn't enough to do SF proud: June begins with the Gay & Lesbian Film Festival, and goes out in style the last weekend with the Dyke March (☎ 415-241-8882; www.dykemarch.org) and the frisky, fun, half-million-strong Lesbian, Gay, Bisexual and Transgender Pride Parade.

Folsom Street Fair (☎ 415-777-3247; www.folsomstreetfair.com) Work that leather look and enjoy public spankings for local charities the last weekend of July.

LitQuake (415-750-1497 www.litquake.org) Authors spill true stories and trade secrets over drinks at the legendary Lit Crawl, held the second weekend in October.

SF Jazz Festival (☎ 415-398-5655; www.sfjazz.org) Old-school greats and breakthrough talents blow horns and minds in late October.

Diá de los Muertos (☎ 415-821-1155; www.dayofthedeadsf.org) Party to wake the dead with a spooky costume parade, sugar skulls and fabulous altars in the Mission on November 2.

Sleeping

San Francisco is the birthplace of the boutique hotel; they're all over town – for a price: in SF, $100 to $200 rooms are midrange. The San Francisco's Visitor Information Center (p970) runs a multilingual **reservation line** (☎ 888-782-9673; www.onlyinsanfrancisco.com). **Bed & Breakfast SF** (☎ 415-899-0060; www.bbsf.com) is a B&B–apartment service. Lombard St (Hwy 101) is packed with motels. San Francisco hotel tax is 14% (hostels are exempt).

UNION SQUARE & CIVIC CENTER

Dakota Hotel (Map pp972-3; ☎ 415-931-7475; 606 Post St at Taylor St; r $98-110; ⊠ 💻 📶) Vintage 1920s hotel with clean, basic rooms and clawfoot bathtubs; the elevator is temperamental. Parking costs $16.

our pick Hotel des Arts (Map pp972-3; ☎ 415-956-3232; www.sfhoteldesarts.com; 447 Bush St; r without bath $99-149, with bath $139-199; ⊠ 📶) A budget hotel for art freaks, with specialty rooms painted by underground artists – it's like sleeping inside a painting. Standard rooms are less exciting, but are clean and good value. Parking costs $24.

Golden Gate Hotel (Map pp972-3; ☎ 415-392-3702, 800-835-1118; www.goldengatehotel.com; 775 Bush St; r without/with bath $105/165; ⊠ 💻 📶) Like an old-fashioned pensione, the Golden Gate has kindly owners and simple rooms inside a 1913 Edwardian hotel, safely uphill from the Tenderloin. Parking is $25.

Mosser (Map pp972-3; ☎ 415-986-4400, 800-227-3804; www.themosser.com; 54 4th St; r without bath $75-109, with bath $149-179; ⊠ 💻 📶) This tourist-class hotel has some stylish details in its tiny rooms and tinier baths. Parking costs $29.

Petite Auberge (Map pp972-3; ☎ 415-928-6000, 800-365-3004; 863 Bush St; r $169-219; ⊠ 💻 📶) Like a country inn – a French-provincial charmer with cheerful rooms, some with gas fireplaces. Parking is $32.

Hotel Triton (Map pp972-3; ☎ 415-394-0500, 800-800-1299; www.hoteltriton.com; 342 Grant Ave; r $149-239; ⊠ ❄ 💻 📶) The lobby thumps with high-energy music at this snappy boutique hotel. Least-expensive rooms are tiny; great beds though. Parking costs $38.

Orchard Garden Hotel (Map pp972-3; ☎ 415-399-9807; www.theorchardgardenhotel.com; 466 Bush St; r $179-249; ⊠ ❄ 💻 📶) SF's first all-green-practices hotel has soothingly quiet rooms with luxe touches, like Egyptian-cotton sheets. Parking costs $40.

THE FINANCIAL DISTRICT & NORTH BEACH

Pacific Tradewinds (Map pp972-3; ☎ 415-433-7970, 888-734-6783; www.sanfranciscohostel.org; 680 Sacramento St; dm $24-26; ⊠ 💻 📶) SF's smartest-looking all-dorm hostel has a blue-and-white nautical theme, full kitchen and spotless showers. There's no elevator, but three flights of stairs.

San Remo Hotel (Map pp972-3; ☎ 415-776-8688, 800-352-7366; www.sanremohotel.com; 2237 Mason St; r $55-85; 💻 📶) The 1906 San Remo is long on old-fashioned charm, with simple rooms and mismatched turn-of-the-century furnishings; all share bathrooms. Note: the cheapest rooms face the hallway; for air and light, request one with a window.

Hotel Bohème (Map pp972-3; ☎ 415-433-9111; www.hotelboheme.com; 444 Columbus Ave; r $174-194; ⊠ 📶) Our favorite boutique hotel is like a love letter to the Jazz era, with rooms in burnt-orange, black and sage-green, and ceiling lights are covered with Chinese umbrellas.

Hotel Vitale (Map pp972-3; ☎ 415-278-3700, 888-890-8688; www.jdvhotels.com; 8 Mission St; r $279-319; ❄ 💻 📶) The shagadelic-chic Vitale is SF's sexiest splurge, with a soothing spa theme and sumptuous beds. Parking costs $51.

FISHERMAN'S WHARF & THE MARINA

HI San Francisco Fisherman's Wharf (Map pp972-3; ☎ 415-771-7277; www.norcalhostels.org; Fort Mason, Bldg 240; dm/r $23-30/60-100; Ⓟ ⊠ 💻 📶) Superbig dorms and communal showers, but the in-park setting is unparalleled. There's no curfew.

Marina Motel (Map pp972-3; ☎ 415-921-9406, 800-346-6118; www.marinamotel.com; 2576 Lombard St; r $75-129; Ⓟ ⊠ 📶) This vintage 1930s motor court is perfect for backpackers and families. The rooms are homey; some have kitchens. The quietest are in the back.

Hotel Del Sol (Map pp972-3; ☎ 415-921-5520, 877-433-5765; www.thehoteldelsol.com; 3100 Webster St; r $169-199; Ⓟ ⊠ ❄ 📶 🏊 👶) A revamped 1950s motor lodge, the Del Sol is a riot of color. Kids love the heated outdoor pool. It also has family suites.

THE MISSION

San Francisco Elements (Map pp972-3; ☎ 415-647-4100; www.elementssf.com; 2524 Mission St; dm/d $28/79; ⊠ 💻 📶) The good-looking (if institutional) coed and segregated dorms all have in-room baths. The rooftop bar is fantastic. You'll find yourself at the center of Mission nightlife.

THE CASTRO

24 Henry (Map pp972-3; ☎ 415-864-5686, 800-900-5686; www.24henry.com; 24 Henry St; r without/with bath $105-110/$149; ⊠ 💻 📶) A converted Victorian on a quiet street, 24 Henry is decorated with cast-off antiques and utilitarian furniture. It is great for no-fuss gay travelers.

Parker Guest House (Map pp972-3; ☎ 415-621-3222, 888-520-7275; www.parkerguesthouse.com; 520 Church at 17th St; r without bath from $119, with bath $150-199; ⊠ 💻 📶) SF's best gay B&B has cushy rooms in adjoining Edwardian mansions. Parking ($15) is limited, so reserve ahead.

THE HAIGHT

Red Victorian (Map pp972-3; ☎ 415-864-1978; www.redvic.com; 1665 Haight St; r $86-200; ⊠ 📶) The year 1968 lives at the tripped-out Red Vic. Individually decorated rooms pay tribute to peace, ecology and friendship. Only four have baths; all include breakfast in the organic café. Wi-fi is available in the lobby.

Eating

Hope you're hungry – there are 10 times more restaurants per capita in San Francisco than in any other US city, and every red-blooded resident has an opinion on which one you absolutely, positively, cannot miss. The city even has a monument to gourmet glory: the **Ferry Building** (Map pp972-3; ☎ 415-983-8000; www.ferrybuildingmarketplace.com); see the boxed text, opposite. On **Chowhound** (www.chowhound.com/boards/1), informed foodies explain exactly where to eat what.

UNION SQUARE & CIVIC CENTER

Saigon Sandwich Shop (Map pp972-3; ☎ 415-474-5698; 560 Larkin St; sandwiches $3-3.50; 🕑 6:30am-5pm Mon-Sat, 7am-4:30pm Sun) Join the line for Vietnamese *banh mi*, baguettes piled with roast meat, pâté, meatballs and/or tofu with pickled carrots, jalapeno, onion, and cilantro. Order two now, and spare yourself a return trip.

Suppenküche (Map pp972-3; ☎ 415-252-9289; www.suppenkuche.com; 525 Laguna; mains $8-18.50; 🕑 5-10pm daily, 10am-2:30pm Sun) Feast on Bratwurst sausages and spaetzle oozing with cheese, and toast your new friends at the unvarnished communal table with a 2L glass boot of draft beer – then cure Sunday hangovers with 'Emperor's Pancakes' studded with brandied raisins.

Shalimar (Map pp972-3; ☎ 415-928-0333; www.shalimarsf.com 532 Jones St; mains under $10; 🕑 noon-3pm & 5-11:30pm) Follow your nose to tandoori chicken straight off the skewer and naan bread still bubbling from the oven. Vegetables are leaden, so don't hold back on the roasted meats.

Fish & Farm (Map pp972-3; ☎ 415-474-3474; www.fishandfarmsf.com; 339 Taylor St; dinner mains $17-28; 🕑 5-10pm) Ecocomfort food showcases organic produce, sustainable seafood and humanely raised meats, all sourced within 100 miles – plus cocktails blended with seasonal, organic fruit.

Jardinière (Map pp972-3; ☎ 415-861-5555; www.jardiniere.com; 300 Grove St; mains $23-40; 🕑 5-10:30pm Sun-Wed, 5-11:30pm Thu-Sat) Iron Chef champ Traci Des Jardins has a way with organic vegetables, free-range meats and sustainable seafood that's slightly naughty, topping succulent octopus with crispy pork belly, and drizzling Sonoma lavender honey over squash blossoms bursting with molten sheep's cheese. Don't miss Mondays, when $45 scores three decadent courses with wine pairings.

FINANCIAL DISTRICT, CHINATOWN & NORTH BEACH

City View (Map pp972-3; ☎ 415-398-2838; 662 Commercial St; small plates $3-5; 🕑 11am-2:30pm Mon-Fri, 10am-2:30pm Sat & Sun) Dim sum aficionados used to cramped quarters and surly service are wowed by impeccable shrimp and leek dumplings, tender asparagus and crisp Peking duck, all served with a flourish in a spacious, sunny room.

Bocadillos (Map pp972-3; ☎ 415-982-2622; www.bocasf.com; 710 Montgomery St; small plates lunch $4.50-7, dinner $5-15; 🕑 7am-10pm Mon-Wed, 7am-10:30pm Thu-Fri, 5-10:30pm Sat) Lunchtime fine dining that won't break the bank or pop buttons, with just-right Basque bites of lamb burger, snapper ceviche with Asian pears, Catalan sausages and wines by the glass.

Molinari (Map pp972-3; ☎ 415-421-2337; 373 Columbus Ave; sandwiches $5-8; 🕑 9am-5pm Mon-Fri, 7:30am-5:30pm Sat) Grab an Italian roll and get it stuffed with translucent sheets of Parma prosciutto, milky buffalo mozzarella, marinated artichokes and legendary house-cured salami.

House of Nanking (Map pp972-3; ☎ 415-421-1429; 919 Kearny St; mains $7-14; 🕑 11am-10pm Mon-Fri, from noon Sat, noon-9pm Sun) Meekly suggest seafood, nothing deep-fried, perhaps some poultry – and your server nods, snatches the menu, and returns within minutes with meltaway scallops, minced squab lettuce cups and a tea ball that blossoms in water. Come prepared to wait, and bearing cash.

FIVE TASTY REASONS TO MISS THAT FERRY

When it comes to fine dining, you'll be missing the boat unless you stop and taste the treats on offer at the Ferry Building:

- Today's catch at **Hog Island Oyster Company** (☎ 415-391-7117; www.hogislandoysters.com; half-dozen $15-17; ⌚ 11:30am-8pm Mon-Fri, 11am-6pm Sat & Sun, happy hour 5-7pm Mon & Thu), including $1 oysters at happy hour.
- Free-range beef burgers and sweet-potato fries at **Taylor's Automatic Refresher** (☎ 415-318-3423; www.taylorsrefresher.com; burgers $7-10; ⌚ 10:30am-10pm)
- Chef Traci des Jardins' *nuevo* Mexican street eats at **Mijita** (☎ 399-0814; www.mijitasf.com; menu items under $10; ⌚ 10am-7pm Mon-Thu, 10am-8pm Fri, 9am-8pm Sat, 10am-4pm Sun).
- Cal-Vietnamese Dungeness crab over cellophane noodles at Charles Phan's family-run **Slanted Door** (☎ 415-861-8032; http://slanteddoor.com; mains $11-26; ⌚ 11am-10pm).
- The Ferry Building weekend **farmers' market** (☎ 415-291-3276; www.cuesa.org; ⌚ 10am-2pm Tue, 8am-2pm Sat year-round, also 4-8pm Thu & 10am-2pm Sun in summer).

Cinecittà (Map pp972-3; ☎ 415-291-8830; 663 Union St; pizzas $9-14; ⌚ noon-10pm Sun-Thu, noon-11pm Fri & Sat) That aroma you followed into this 18-seat eatery is thin-crust Roman pizza, probably the crowd-pleasing Capricciosa: artichoke hearts, olives, fresh mozzarella, prosciutto and egg. Save room for housemade tiramisu – hands down the best in North Beach.

Ideale (Map pp972-3; ☎ 415-391-4129; www.idealerestaurant.com; 1315 Grant Ave; mains $13-26; ⌚ 5:30-10:30pm Tue-Thu, 5:30-11pm Fri & Sat, 5-10pm Sun) Expat Italian regulars are stunned that a restaurant this authentic borders the Pacific, with proper *bucatini ammatriciana* (Roman tube pasta with tomato-pancetta-pecorino sauce), seafood risotto made with superior Canaroli rice, a well-priced selection of Italian wines, and wisecracking Tuscan waitstaff.

FISHERMAN'S WHARF

Crown & Crumpet (Map pp972-3; ☎ 415-771-4252 www.crownandcrumpet.com; 207 Ghirardelli Square; tea & cake $8-12, 5-course tea service $32; ⌚ 10am-6pm Mon-Thu, 9am-10pm Fri, 9am-9pm Sat, 9am-6pm Sun) Designer style and rosy cheer usher teatime into the 21st century: girlfriends rehash hot dates over scones with strawberries and Champagne, and dads and daughters clink porcelain teacups with crooked pinkies and 38 kinds of tea. Reservations are recommended on weekends.

Gary Danko (Map pp972-3; ☎ 415-749-2060; www.garydanko.com; 800 North Point St; 2/3/4/5 courses prix-fixe $44/66/83/98; ⌚ 5:30-10pm) Smoked-glass windows prevent passersby from tripping over their tongues at the sight of roasted lobster with trumpet mushrooms, blushing duck breast with rhubarb compote, trios of crème brûlée and the lavish cheese cart. Ladies receive tiny cakes as parting gifts.

THE MARINA

La Boulange (Map pp972-3; ☎ 415-440-4450; www.baybread.com; 1909 Union St; lunch under $10; ⌚ 7am-6pm) The best buy amid Union boutiques is here: 10 bucks gets you half a tartine (open-faced sandwich) with soup or salad, a fresh-baked macaroon, and all the cornichons and Nutella you can grab from the condiment bar.

Greens (Map pp972-3; ☎ 415-771-6222; www.greensrestaurant.com; Fort Mason Center, bldg A; mains $7-20; ⌚ noon-2:30pm Tue-Sat, 5:30-9pm Mon-Sat, 10:30am-2pm Sun; Ⓥ) Career carnivores won't realize there's no meat in roasted eggplant panini or hearty black bean chili with *crème fraiche* and pickled jalapeños. On weekends, enjoy take-out at redwood-stump café tables or on sunny docks outside.

THE MISSION

La Taquería (Map pp972-3; ☎ 415-285-7117; 2889 Mission St at 25th; burritos $5-6.50; ⌚ 11am-9pm Mon-Sat, 11am-8pm Sun) No debatable tofu, saffron rice, spinach tortilla or mango salsa here: just classic tomatillo or mesquite salsa, marinated, grilled meats and flavorful beans inside a flour tortilla – optional housemade spicy pickles and sour cream are highly recommended.

Mission Beach Café (Map pp972-3; ☎ 415-861-0198; www.missionbeachcafesf.com; 198 Guerrero St; brunch $9-14; ⌚ 7am-10pm Tue-Thu, 7am-11pm Fri, 9am-11pm Sat, 9am-10pm Sun) Brunch gets upgraded to first class with soufflé pancakes, organic huevos rancheros with sustainably raised pulled pork, and farm eggs with caramelized onions and English muffins made by the in-house pastry chef.

Delfina (Map pp972-3; ☎ 415-552-4055; www.delfinasf.com; 3621 18th St; mains $18-26; 5:30-10pm Mon-Thu, 5:30-11pm Fri & Sat, 5-10pm Sun) Simple, sensational, seasonal California fare: Sonoma duck with Barolo-roasted cherries, wild nettle tagliatelle pasta, profiteroles with coffee gelato and candied almonds. Reserve ahead, or settle for Delfina Pizza next door.

THE CASTRO

Cafe Flore (Map pp972-3; ☎ 415-621-8579; http://cafeflore.com; 2298 Market St; mains $8-11; 7am-2am;) Mind your pasta-slurping and racy IM-ing with free wi-fi: this all-glass corner venue maximizes opportunities to see and be seen.

Home (Map pp972-3; ☎ 415-503-0333; www.home-sf.com; 2100 Market St; mains $12-18; 11am-midnight Mon-Fri, 10am-midnight Sat & Sun) There's no place like it, especially if you enjoy comfort food – mac 'n' cheese, roast chicken, pot roast – served fireside, with a gaggle of gym-fresh men and $4 Homegirls (aka Cosmo plus Champagne) during the 4pm to 7pm happy hour.

Destino (Map pp972-3; ☎ 415-552-4451; www.destinosf.com; 1815 Market St; small plates $10-13.30, 3-course prix-fixe $32; 5-10pm Mon-Thu, 5-11pm Fri & Sat, 11am-2pm & 5-10pm Sun) Your taste buds will think tectonic plates have shifted at this Peru-meets-California bistro, starring ahi ceviche with organic mango and achiote oil, duck breast with bacon-plantain cakes and passion-fruit Pisco sour cocktails.

THE HAIGHT

Rosamunde Sausage Grill (Map pp972-3; ☎ 415-437-6851; 545 Haight St; sausages $4-5.50; 11:30am-10pm) Impress a dinner date for $10: load up classic Brats or fig-duck links with complimentary roasted peppers, grilled onions, wholegrain mustard and mango chutney, washed down with one of 50-plus microbrews at Toronado (opposite).

Cole Valley Cafe (Map pp972-3; ☎ 415-668-5282; www.colevalleycafe.com; 701 Cole St; sandwiches $5.75; 7am-8pm;) Powerful coffee, free wi-fi and hot gourmet sandwiches that are a bargain at any price, let alone $6 for lip-smacking thyme-marinated chicken with lemony avocado spread.

Magnolia Brewpub (Map pp972-3; ☎ 415-864-7468; www.magnoliapub.com; 1398 Haight St; mains $8-19; noon-midnight Mon-Thu, noon-1am Fri, 10am-1am Sat, 10am-midnight Sun) Organic pub grub and home-brew samplers keep conversation flowing at communal tables, while grass-fed Prather Ranch burgers satisfy stoner appetites in the side booths – it's like the Summer of Love is back, only with better food.

JAPANTOWN & PACIFIC HEIGHTS

our pick **Tataki** (Map pp972-3 ☎ 415-931-1182; www.tatakisushibar.com; 2815 California St; small plates $4-13; 11:30am-2pm & 5:30-10:30pm Mon-Thu, 11:30am-2pm & 5:30-11:30pm Fri, 5-11:30pm Sat, 5-9:30pm Sun) Rescue dinner dates and the oceans with sensational, sustainable sushi: silky arctic char drizzled with yuzu-citrus and capers replaces at-risk wild salmon, and the Golden State Roll is a local hero with spicy dive-caught scallop, Pacific tuna, organic apple slivers and edible gold.

THE RICHMOND

Taiwan (Map pp972-3; ☎ 415-387-1789; 445 Clement St; meals $10; 11am-10pm Sun-Thu, 11am-midnight Fri, 10am-midnight Sat) Feast for days on heaping, housemade sesame hot-sauce noodles, dumplings made fresh to order, smoky dry braised green beans and feisty black bean chicken.

Namu (Map pp972-3; ☎ 415-386-8332; www.namusf.com; 439 Balboa St; small plates $9-15; 5-10:30pm Mon-Fri, 10am-3pm & 5:30-10:30pm Sat & Sun) SF's unfair culinary advantages – top-notch organic ingredients, Silicon Valley inventiveness and Pacific Rim flair – are showcased in Korean-inspired small plates of buttery kampachi with chili oil and fleur de sel, bacon-wrapped enoki mushrooms, and Niman Ranch Kobe beef with organic vegetables in a sizzling stone pot.

Aziza (Map pp972-3; ☎ 415-752-2222; www.azizasf.com; 5800 Geary Blvd; mains $18-26; 5:30-10:30pm Wed-Mon) Mourad Lahlou's inspiration is Moroccan and his produce organic Californian, but his flavors are out of this world: quail dazzles with huckleberries and cumin-orange glaze, and the prawn *tagine* (stew) with Meyer lemons is pizzazz in a pot.

Drinking

Crawl the Mission, Haight, North Beach, and Polk St (north of Geary St) for bars.

Hôtel Biron (Map pp972-3; ☎ 415-703-0403; 45 Rose St) Our favorite for an intimate weeknight tête-à-tête and bottle of wine. (Weekends are too crowded.)

Koko Cocktails (Map pp972-3; ☎ 415-885-4788; 1060 Geary St) This retro-cool cocktail lounge spins reggae, soul and sometimes hip-hop – a snappy place to start a pub crawl.

Toronado (Map pp972-3; ☎ 415-863-2276; www.toronado.com; 547 Haight St) Beer mavens dig the 50-plus microbrews, with hundreds more in bottles. Stumble next door to Rosamunde (opposite) for sausages.

Tosca Cafe (Map pp972-3; ☎ 415-391-1244; 242 Columbus Ave) With red-vinyl booths and a jukebox of opera and Sinatra, Tosca is quintessential old-guard North Beach.

Zeitgeist (Map pp972-3; ☎ 415-255-7505; 199 Valencia St) On warm evenings, bikers and hipsters head for Zeitgeist's huge outdoor beer garden – an underground SF institution.

Entertainment

Pick up the *SF Weekly* for listings; look online at Nitevibe (www.nitevibe.com), SF Station (www.sfstation.com) and SF Gate (www.sfgate.com); and – most importantly – strike up conversations with locals to gather tips. **TIX Bay Area** (Map pp972-3; ☎ 415-433-7827; www.theatrebayarea.org; Tue-Sun), at Union Sq, has half-price theater tickets.

NIGHTCLUBS & LIVE MUSIC

Annie's Social Club (Map pp972-3; ☎ 415-974-1585; www.anniessocialclub.com; 917 Folsom St) Annie's stages kick-ass new music, burlesque, punk-rock-and-schlock karaoke, and open-mic comedy; check the website.

Boom Boom Room (Map pp972-3; ☎ 415-673-8000; www.boomboomblues.com; 1601 Fillmore St; Tue-Sun) John Lee Hooker owns this vintage '30s blues and jazz club, which hops six nights a week. Advance tickets are necessary for major acts, but not usually.

Café du Nord (Map pp972-3; ☎ 415-861-5016; www.cafedunord.com; 2170 Market St) The former speakeasy in the basement of the Swedish-American Hall rocks revelers with a cool, ever-changing lineup; check their calendar.

El Rio (off Map pp972-3; ☎ 415-282-3325; www.elriosf.com; 3158 Mission St at Cesar Chavez) 'Salsa Sundays' are legendary: arrive at 3pm for lessons; dress sexy. Other nights: awesome specials, eclectic music, pan-sexual crowd.

Fillmore (Map pp972-3; ☎ 415-346-6000; www.thefillmore.com; 1805 Geary Blvd) Hendrix, Zeppelin, the Who – they all played the Fillmore. Its 1250 capacity means you're close to the stage. Dig the priceless collection in the upstairs poster-art gallery.

Yoshi's (☎ 415-655-5600; www.yoshis.com; 1300 Fillmore St; 8pm & (sometimes) 10pm shows nightly) San Francisco's definitive jazz club draws the world's top talent, and adjoins a pretty-good sushi restaurant.

DANCE CLUBS

Cat Club (Map pp972-3; ☎ 415-703-8965; www.catclubsf.com; 1190 Folsom St) Thursday's '1984' lures '80s pop lovers; other nights vary, but are usually way cool. Check the website.

DNA Lounge (Map pp972-3; ☎ 415-626-1409; www.dnalounge.com; 375 11th St) One of SF's last mega clubs hosts live bands and big-name DJs. The second and fourth Saturdays are Bootie, the kick-ass original mashup party (now franchised worldwide); Monday's 18-and-over night is Goth. Check the website.

Milk (Map pp972-3; ☎ 415-387-6455, www.milksf.com; 1840 Haight St) Get down to hip-hop at this tufted-white-vinyl Upper Haight club. There is no cover before 9pm.

our pick **Qoöl at 111 Minna** (Map pp972-3; ☎ 415-974-1719; www.qoolsf.com; 111 Minna St; 5-10pm Wed) SF's coolest weekly dance party is a Wednesday-evening techno happy hour in an art gallery. Afterward, follow the crowd to Satellite, at Anu (43 6th St), for techno-dance till 2am.

CLASSICAL MUSIC & OPERA

Yerba Buena Center for the Arts (Map pp972-3; ☎ 415-978-2787; www.ybca.org; 701 Mission St) The center hosts top-notch modern music, dance and theater.

Davies Symphony Hall (Map pp972-3; ☎ 415-864-6000; www.sfsymphony.org; 201 Van Ness Ave) Home of the world-renown SF Symphony. Season runs September to July.

The glorious 1932 **War Memorial Opera House** (Map pp972-3; 301 Van Ness Ave) is home to the **San Francisco Opera** (☎ 415-864-3330; www.sfopera.com; season Jun-Dec) and the **San Francisco Ballet** (☎ 415-861-5600; www.sfballet.org; season Jan-May).

THEATER

SF is home to the professional group and actor-training program **American Conservatory Theater** (ACT; ☎ 415-749-2228; www.act-sf.org), which performs at the **Geary Theater** (Map pp972-3; 415 Geary St). **SHN** (☎ 415-512-7770; www.shnsf.com) hosts touring Broadway shows.

GAY/LES/BI/TRANS SAN FRANCISCO

San Francisco is America's pinkest city. New York Marys may label SF the retirement home of the young – the sidewalks roll up early – but for sexual outlaws and underground weirdness, SF kicks New York's ass. The intersection of 18th and Castro Streets is the heart of the gay scene, with bars a go-go. Dancing queens and slutty boys head South of Market (SoMa) for thump-thump clubs and sex venues. Cruise Castro by day, SoMa by night. On sunny days, Speedo-clad gay boys and grrrls colonize the hill at 20th and Church Streets, in Mission Dolores Park. (Be prepared for pot smoke: SF is stoner central.) The sexy bitches also connect on Valencia St, south of 16th St, in happening cafés, thrift stores and bookstores. Check Get Your Girl On (http://gogetyourgirlon.com) for concerts and parties; or plug into the A-gay scene on Betty's List (www.bettyslist.com). The *San Francisco Bay Times* (www.sfbaytimes.com) has good resources for transsexuals; the *Bay Area Reporter* (aka BAR; www.ebar.com) has news and listings.

Some gay faves:

Aunt Charlie's (Map pp972-3; ☎ 415-441-2922; www.auntcharlieslounge.com; 133 Turk St; 9am-2am) Total dive. The city's best classic drag happens Fridays and Saturdays at 10pm. Thursday nights, art-school boys pack in for bathhouse disco at Tubesteak ($5).

Cafe Flore (Map pp972-3; p984) Coffee, wi-fi and hot dishes.

Eagle Tavern (Map pp972-3; ☎ 415-626-0880; www.sfeagle.com; 398 12th St; noon-2am) *The* place on Sunday afternoons; wear leather and blend right in. All-you-can-drink beer from 3pm to 6pm ($10).

Gold's Gym (Map pp972-3; ☎ 415-626-4488; www.goldsgym.com; 2301 Market St; ☎ 415-552-4653; 1001 Brannan St; admission $15) Circuit queens and Castro boys go to Market St; testosterone-y daddies go to Brannan.

Honey Soundsystem (Map pp972-3; ☎ 415-252-5018; www.honeysoundsystem.com; at Paradise Loft, 1501 Folsom St; 9pm-2am Sun) Kick-ass dance party – from obscure disco b-sides to German techno.

Lexington Club (Map pp972-3; ☎ 415-863-2052; 3464 19th St; 3pm-2am) SF's bitchinest lesbian bar.

Powerhouse (Map pp972-3; ☎ 415-552-8689; www.powerhouse-sf.com; 1347 Folsom St) Thursdays to Sundays are best at this sometimes-hot, sometimes-not, slutty-men's cruise bar. Weird smokers' patio.

Sisters of Perpetual Indulgence (☎ 415-820-9697; www.thesisters.org) For guerrilla antics, follow the 'leading-edge order of queer nuns.' Our fave event: Easter's 'Hunky Jesus Contest' in Dolores Park – legendary.

Club Fugazi (Map pp972-3; ☎ 415-421-4222; www.beachblanketbabylon.com; 678 Green St; seats $25-78) Home of ribald, hilarious *Beach Blanket Babylon* – an only-in-SF must-see.

For cool new plays and experimental shows, check the following (also see p990):

Climate Theater (Map pp972-3; ☎ 415-263-0830; www.climatetheater.com; 285 9th St)

Magic Theater (Map pp972-3; ☎ 415-441-8822; www.magictheatre.org; Fort Mason, Bldg D)

New Conservatory Theater (Map pp972-3; ☎ 415-861-8972; www.nctcsf.org; 25 Van Ness Ave)

Theater Rhinoceros (Map pp972-3; ☎ 415-861-5079; www.therhino.org; 2926 16th St)

CINEMA

our pick Castro Theatre (Map pp972-3; ☎ 415-621-6120; www.thecastrotheatre.com; 429 Castro St) The city's grandest movie place screens vintage, foreign, documentary and new films.

Sundance Kabuki Cinema (☎ 415-929-4650; www.sundancecinemas.com/kabuki.html; 1881 Post St; admission adult/child & senior $9/6.25 plus $1-3 amenities fee; call/website) The silver screen gone green, from recycled-fiber reserved seating to local Hangar vodka cocktails served in the Auditorium 1 Balcony Bar.

Also recommended for indie celluloid:

Red Vic Movie House (Map pp972-3; ☎ 415-668-3994; www.redvicmoviehouse.com; 1727 Haight St)

Roxie Cinema (Map pp972-3; ☎ 415-863-1087; www.roxie.com; 3117 16th St)

SPORTS

San Francisco 49ers (☎ 415-656-4900; www.sf49ers.com) For garlic-fries, beer and NFL football, head to Candlestick Park (Map p969).

San Francisco Giants (☎ 415-478-2277; http://sanfrancisco.giants.mlb.com) The major-league Giants plays AT&T Park (Map pp972–3).

Shopping

So much for traveling light: SF souvenirs start out packable in Chinatown with silk slippers; however, on Grant Ave between Bush and Filbert Sts, you'll discover custom zoot suits, local designer dresses and rare vinyl. Anyone tempted by locally designed earrings, handmade felt rugs and mod candelabras should beware Union St from Steiner to Van Ness Sts, as well as Hayes St between Franklin and Laguna Sts. Foot fetishists, CD hoarders and vintage clotheshounds can't resist the siren call of the Upper Haight, while used books and thrift-store scores await along Valencia and Mission Sts between 16th and 24th Sts. Mall rats may never escape the 400 stores of **Westfield San Francisco Shopping Center** (Map pp972-3 ☎ 415-512-6776; http://westfield.com/sanfrancisco; 865 Market St; ⏰ most shops 9:30am-9pm Mon-Sat, 10am-7pm Sun), and with designer finds dotting Fillmore between Bush and Clay, you might need another suitcase…

Getting There & Away

AIR

San Francisco International Airport (SFO; Map p969; ☎ 650-821-8211, 800-435-9736; www.flysfo.com) is 14 miles south of downtown off Hwy 101. SFO's AirTrain connects terminals with parking garages, rental-car centers and Bay Area Rapid Transit (BART; right).

BUS

At intercity transit hub **Transbay Terminal** (Map pp972-3; 425 Mission St), catch **AC Transit** (☎ 511; www.actransit.org) buses to the East Bay, **Golden Gate Transit** (☎ 415-455-2000; http://goldengatetransit.org) buses north to Marin and Sonoma Counties, and **SamTrans** (☎ 800-660-4287; www.samtrans.com) buses south to Palo Alto and the Pacific coast.

Greyhound (☎ 415-495-1569, 800-231-2222; www.greyhound.com) buses leave daily for Los Angeles ($39 and up, from eight hours), Truckee near Lake Tahoe ($66 round-trip, 5½ hours), and other destinations.

TRAIN

Amtrak (☎ 800-872-7245; www.amtrakcalifornia.com) offers low-emissions, leisurely travel to and from San Francisco. The *Coast Starlight*'s spectacular 35-hour run from Los Angeles to Seattle stops across the Bay in Oakland, and the *California Zephyr* takes its sweet time (51 hours) traveling from Chicago through the ruggedly handsome Rockies en route to Emeryville (near Oakland). Both have sleeping cars and dining/lounge cars with panoramic windows. Amtrak runs free shuttle buses to San Francisco's Ferry Building and CalTrain station, with connecting buses to Martinez and onward to Napa, Santa Rosa and Healdsburg.

CalTrain (☎ 800-660-4287; www.caltrain.com; cnr 4th & King Sts) connects San Francisco with towns along the Peninsula, including Millbrae (connecting to BART and SFO, 30 minutes).

Getting Around

For Bay Area transit options with departure and arrival times, check www.511.org or call ☎ 511.

TO/FROM THE SAN FRANCISCO AIRPORT

BART (Bay Area Rapid Transit; ☎ 415-989-2278; www.bart.gov; one way $5.35) offers a cheap, fast, direct ride to downtown San Francisco.

SamTrans (☎ 800-660-4287; www.samtrans.com; one way $4.50) express bus KX gets you to Transbay Terminal in about 30 minutes.

SuperShuttle (☎ 415-558-8500, 800-258-3826; www.supershuttle.com; one way $17) door-to-door vans depart from baggage-claim areas, taking 45 minutes to most locations within San Francisco.

Taxis to downtown San Francisco cost $35 to $50, plus tip.

TO/FROM THE OAKLAND INTERNATIONAL AIRPORT

SuperShuttle (above) offers shared van rides to downtown SF for an average fare of $25. **Airport Express** (☎ 800-327-2024; www.airportexpressinc.com) runs a scheduled shuttle every two hours (from 6am to midnight) between Oakland Airport and Sonoma ($32) and Marin ($24) counties.

Taxi fares from Oakland Airport average $25 to Oakland and $50 to $60 to SF, plus tip. To avoid higher fares during rush hours, ask for a flat rate to/from the airport.

BART is the cheapest way to get to San Francisco from the Oakland Airport. AirBART shuttle ($3) runs every 10 minutes to the Coliseum station to catch BART to downtown SF ($3.55 to Powell St, 25 minutes).

BOAT

Blue & Gold Ferries (Map pp972-3; ☎ 415-705-8200; www.blueandgoldfleet.com) runs the Alameda–Oakland ferry from Pier 41 and the Ferry Building. **Golden Gate Ferry** (☎ 415-455-2000; www.goldengate.org) runs from the Ferry Building to Sausalito and Larkspur in Marin County.

CAR

If you can, avoid driving in San Francisco: street parking is harder to find than true love, and meter readers are ruthless. Convenient downtown parking lots are at the Embarcadero Center, at 5th and Mission Sts, under Union Sq, and at Sutter and Stockton Sts.

National car-rental agencies have 24-hour offices at the airport and downtown; see p1164 for toll-free contact information. **City Rent-a-Car** (Map pp972-3; ☎ 415-359-1331; www.cityrentacar.com; 1433 Bush St) is a competitively priced independent agency.

PUBLIC TRANSPORTATION

San Francisco **MUNI** (Municipal Transit Agency; ☎ 415-701-2311 & 311 inside San Francisco; www.sfmuni.com) operates bus and streetcar lines and three cable-car lines; two cable-car lines leave from Powell and Market Sts, and one leaves from California and Markets Sts. A detailed *MUNI Street & Transit Map* ($3) is available at newsstands and the Powell St MUNI kiosk. Standard fare for buses or streetcars is $1.50; cable-car fare is $5. A MUNI Passport (one-/three-/seven-days $11/18/24) allows unlimited travel on all MUNI transport, including cable cars; it's sold at San Francisco's Visitor Information Center (p970) and at the TIX Bay Area kiosk at Union Sq. A seven-day City Pass ($59) includes transit and admission to six attractions.

BART (p987) links San Francisco with the East Bay and runs beneath Market St, down Mission St and south to SFO and Millbrae, where it connects with CalTrain.

TAXI

Fares run about $2.25 per mile; meters start at $3.50. Major cab companies include the following:

DeSoto Cab (☎ 415-970-1300)
Green Cab (☎ 415-626-4733; www.sfgreencab.com) Fuel-efficient hybrids; worker-owned collective.
Veteran's Taxicab (☎ 415-648-1313)
Yellow Cab (☎ 415-626-2345)

MARIN COUNTY

Majestic redwoods cling to coastal hills just across the Golden Gate Bridge in woodsy, wealthy, laid-back **Marin** (www.visitmarin.org). **Sausalito**, the southernmost town, is a cute, touristy bayside destination for bike trips over the bridge (take the ferry back). At the harbor, the **San Francisco Bay-Delta Model** (☎ 415-332-3871; www.spn.usace.army.mil/bmvc; 2100 Bridgeway Blvd; admission free; ⏲ summer 9am-4pm Tue-Fri, 10am-5pm Sat & Sun, closed Sun-Mon winter) is a way-cool 1.5-acre hydraulic re-creation of the entire bay and delta.

Marin Headlands

The windswept, rugged Headlands are laced with hiking trails, providing stunning views of SF and the Golden Gate. To reach the **visitor center** (☎ 415-331-1540; ⏲ 9:30am-4:30pm), take the Alexander Ave exit from the Golden Gate Bridge, turn left under the freeway, and then turn right on Conzelman Rd and follow signs. Attractions include the **Point Bonita Lighthouse** (⏲ 12:30-3:30pm Sat-Mon; ♿), climbable Cold War–era bunkers and **Rodeo Beach** (Map p969) – and there's free walk-in camping (reserve with the visitors center). At Fort Baker, **Bay Area Discovery Museum** (☎ 415-339-3900; www.baykidsmuseum.org; 557 McReynolds Rd, Sausalito; adult/child 1-17yr $8.50/7.50; ⏲ 9am-4pm Tue-Fri, 10am-5pm Sat & Sun; ♿) is a cool destination for kids.

Near the visitor center, the **HI Marin Headlands Hostel** (Map p969; ☎ 415-331-2777, 800-909-4776; dm from $20, r from $60; P ⊠ 💻) occupies two historic 1907 buildings on a forested hill. Private rooms in the former officer's house are sweet.

Mt Tamalpais State Park

Majestic 2571ft 'Mt Tam' is fantastic for mountain biking and hiking. **Mt Tamalpais State Park** (Map p969; ☎ 415-388-2070; www.mttam.net; per car $8) encompasses 6300 acres of parklands, plus over 200 miles of trails; get a map and don't miss East Peak. Panoramic Hwy climbs from Hwy 1 through the park to Stinson Beach, a mellow seaside town with a great beach. **Park headquarters** are at **Pantoll Station** (801 Panoramic Hwy; campsites $25), the nexus of many trails and location of a wooded first-come, first-served campground. Or make reservations and hike in food, linen and towels to the rustic, electricity-free **West Point Inn** (☎ 415-646-0702; www.westpointinn.com; 1000 Panoramic Hwy, Mill Valley; r per adult/child $50/25; reservations essential).

Near park headquarters, **Mountain Home Inn** (☎ 415-381-9000; www.mtnhomeinn.com; 810 Panoramic Hwy; dinner/brunch $38/10-20; ⏲ Wed-Sun ⊠ 💻 📶) sits atop a wooded ridge. Its romantic, woodsy rooms ($195 to $345) have gorgeous views; the restaurant serves good brunches and prix-fixe dinners.

IF YOU HAVE A FEW MORE DAYS

Right across the bay, gritty-urban Oakland's got attitude, the A's and deep African American roots that shine through in world-celebrated music, lit and art. It kicks SF's fog with daily sunshine, and has a lovely historic downtown, saltwater lake fun for joggers and kids, and some happening clubs and restaurants.

Oakland Museum of California (☎ 510-238-2200; www.museumca.org; cnr 10th & Oak Sts; adult/child $8/5; 🕑 10am-5pm Wed-Sat, noon-5pm Sun) is a must-see. Relevant, fascinating exhibits have included knockout Yosemite photography and interactive Great Quake rooms. (It may close temporarily in 2012 for renovations.)

Heinhold's First & Last Chance Saloon (☎ 510-839-6761; 48 Webster), in Jack London Sq, is a lopsided quake survivor and National Literary Landmark; open daily for inspirational drinking. Yes, your beer *is* sliding off the counter.

Yoshi's (☎ 510-238-9200; www.yoshis.com; 510 Embarcadero West; mains $15-20; 🕑 5:30-10pm Mon-Thu, to 10:30pm Fri & Sat, 5-9pm Sun) is one of the country's major jazz clubs; pretty-good sushi too.

Muir Woods National Monument

Wander among an ancient stand of the world's tallest trees in 550-acre **Muir Woods** (☎ 415-388-2595; www.nps.gov/muwo; adults/under 16 $5/free), 12 miles north of the Golden Gate. The easy 1-mile Main Trail Loop leads past thousand-year-old redwoods at Cathedral Grove and returns via Bohemian Grove. Come midweek to avoid crowds; otherwise arrive early morning or late afternoon. Take Hwy 101 to the Hwy 1 exit, and follow the signs. No camping or picnicking is permitted.

The **Muir Woods shuttle** (Bus No 66; ☎ 415-923-2000; www.goldengatetransit.org; adult/senior & child 6-18yr $3/1) operates weekends and holidays, May to September, and runs about every 30 minutes from Marin City and Mill Valley, with limited service to the Sausalito ferry terminal.

Point Reyes National Seashore

The windswept peninsula of **Point Reyes National Seashore** (Map p969) juts 10 miles out to sea on an entirely different tectonic plate, and covers 110 sq miles of beaches, lagoons and forested hills.

our pick **Point Reyes Lighthouse** (🕑 Thu-Mon), crowns the peninsula's westernmost point and is ideal for whale-watching. Our favorite hike: the bluff-top trail on the peninsula's north tip, Tomales Point, through herds of Tule elk. Take Pierce Point Rd. The **Bear Valley Visitors Center** (☎ 415-464-5100; www.nps.gov/pore) is just past Olema and has trail maps and cool displays. Point Reyes has four hike-in **campsites** (☎ reservations 415-663-8054; campsites $15), two near the beach.

The **West Marin Chamber of Commerce** (☎ 415-663-9232; www.pointreyes.org) can point out loads of cozy inns and cottages. The upmarket **Motel Inverness** (Map p969); ☎ 415-669-1081; www.motelinverness.com; 12718 Sir Francis Drake Blvd; r $100-200; ⊠ 📶) has comfy rooms and a common area with roaring fireplace. Budgeteers bunk at the only in-park lodging, **HI Point Reyes Hostel** (Map p969; ☎ 415-663-8811; dm from $22), off Limantour Rd, 8 miles from the visitors center. Wintertime bird-watching is incredible – especially Tomales Bay from a kayak. Contact **Blue Waters Kayaking** (☎ 415-669-2600; www.bwkayak.com; guided trips $68-98, rentals $40-120), which has two locations: one in Inverness, and one in Marshall.

our pick **Drake's Bay Oyster Farm** (☎ 415-669-1149; 1 dozen oysters $10-14; 🕑 8am-4:30pm), off Sir Francis Drake Blvd in the park, is the place for oyster-lovers. Make reservations to picnic. Nearby, cute little Point Reyes Station has restaurants and supplies.

BERKELEY

Not much has changed since the 1960s heyday of anti-Vietnam War protests – except the bumper stickers: 'No Blood For Oil' has supplanted 'Make Love Not War.' Birkenstocks and pony tails remain perennially in fashion. You can't walk around nude anymore, but 'Berserkeley' remains the Bay Area's radical hub, crawling with university students, scoffing skateboarders and aging hippies. Stroll its wooded university grounds and surrounding streets to soak up the vibe.

Sights & Activities

The **University of California at Berkeley** (Map p969) – 'Cal' – is one of the country's top universities and home to 33,000 diverse, politically conscious students. The university's

Visitor Services center (☎ 510-642-5215; http://visitors.berkeley.edu; 101 University Hall, 2200 University Ave at Oxford St; 🕓 8:30am-4:30pm Mon-Fri, tours 10am Mon-Sat, 1pm Sun) has info and leads free campus tours. Cal's landmark is the 1914 Sather Tower (also called the 'Campanile'), with elevator rides ($2) to the top. The Bancroft Library displays the small gold nugget that started the California gold rush in 1848.

Other campus highlights include the **Berkeley Art Museum** (☎ 510-642-0808; www.bampfa.berkeley.edu; 2626 Bancroft Way; adult/child under 13yr/senior & child 13-17yr $8/free/5; 🕓 11am-5pm Wed-Sun), whose 11 galleries showcase a wide range of works, from ancient Chinese to cutting-edge contemporary; and the world-renowned **Pacific Film Archive** (☎ 510-642-1124), which screens little-known independent and avant-garde films.

Leading to the campus's south gate, **Telegraph Avenue** is as far-out and gritty as San Francisco's Haight St, and packed with cafés, cheap-eats, record stores and bookstores – including beatnik-era **Moe's** (☎ 510-849-2087; www.moesbooks.com; 2476 Telegraph Ave; 🕓 10am-10pm).

Kick back in **Tilden Regional Park** (☎ 510-562-7275; www.ebparks.org; 🚸), in the Berkeley hills, which has hiking, picnicking, swimming at Lake Anza, and fun stuff for kids, including a merry-go-round and steam train.

Sleeping

Basic and midrange motels are clustered west of campus along University Ave.

Bancroft Hotel (☎ 510-549-1000, 800-549-1002; www.bancrofthotel.com; 2680 Bancroft Way; r from $149; ⊠ 📶) Simple and homey are the 22 rooms at this 1928 historic-landmark Craftsman hotel that's threadbare like grandma's house, sans doilies. There's no elevator. Parking costs $15.

Hotel Durant (☎ 510-845-8981, 800-238-7268; www.hoteldurant.com; 2600 Durant Ave; r $135-180; ⊠ 💻 📶) The 140-room Durant is Berkeley's spiffiest – and green-certified – but some rooms are tiny (request a big one); the beds are sumptuous. Parking is $16.

Eating & Drinking

our pick **Chez Panisse** (☎ 510-548-5049; www.chezpanisse.com; 1517 Shattuck Ave; set-price menu $65-95, café mains $18-25; 🕓 café lunch & dinner Mon-Sat; restaurant dinner Mon-Sat) Genuflect at the temple of Alice Waters: the birthplace of California cuisine remains at the pinnacle of Bay Area dining. Book one month ahead for its legendary prix-fixe meals (no substitutions); or book upstairs at the less-expensive, a-la-carte café.

Also in the Gourmet Ghetto, along Shattuck Ave north of University Ave, are the fabulous **Cheese Board Pizza** (☎ 510-549-3055; http://cheeseboardcollective.coop; 1512 Shattuck Ave; about $20/pie or $2.50/slice; 🕓 11:30am-3pm & 4:30-8pm Tue-Sat) for knockout artisanal pizzas; and the adjacent **Cheese Board Collective** (☎ 510-549-3183; 1504 Shattuck Ave; 🕓 10am-6pm Tue-Fri, to 5pm Sat) for gooey cheeses.

Vik's Chaat Corner (☎ 510-644-4412; 2390 4th St; items $3.50-6; 🕓 11am-6pm Tue-Fri, to 8pm Sat & Sun) This is our favorite Berkeley cheap-eats, with all-fresh-made Indian classics (no tikka masala here) ordered at the counter.

Caffe Strada (☎ 510-843-5282; 2300 College Ave; 🕓 7am-midnight) University students get wired on caffeine on the giant outdoor patio and study, ardently talk philosophy or make eyes at each other. Good pastries.

For the best social introduction to Berkeley's bar scene, head to the back patio at **Jupiter** (☎ 510-843-8277; 2181 Shattuck Ave).

Entertainment

Berkeley Repertory Theatre (☎ 510-845-4700; www.berkeleyrep.org; 2025 Addison St) This is the Bay Area's top professional theater company.

Shotgun Players (☎ 510-841-6500; www.shotgunplayers.org; 1901 Ashby Ave) America's first solar-powered theater, it showcases classic works and innovative new plays.

Getting There & Around

AC Transit (☎ 510-817-1717; www.actransit.org) runs local buses in Berkeley, as well as between Berkeley and Oakland ($2) and Berkeley and San Francisco ($4). **BART** (www.bart.gov) trains run from SF to Downtown Berkeley ($3.40), which is four blocks from the main campus gate.

NORTHERN CALIFORNIA

The Golden State goes wild in Northern California, with giant redwoods emerging from coastal mists, wallows formed in volcanic mud amid Wine Country vineyards, and the majestic Sierra Nevadas framing Yosemite and Lake Tahoe. Northern California's backwoods are surprisingly forward-thinking, with organic diners, ecoresorts, and the nation's earliest national and state parks. Pack your trash and be mindful of private property since local goatherds and medical marijuana growers can get touchy about trespassers. Come for the scenery, but stay for superb wine and cheese, the obligatory hot tub, and conversations that begin with 'Hey dude!' and end hours later.

WINE COUNTRY

The West has gone wild for spas, gourmet grub and the almighty grape for 150 years in the patchwork of vineyards stretching from sunny Napa to coastal Sonoma. Napa has art-filled tasting rooms by big-name architects with prices to match; in down-to-earth Sonoma, you'll drink in sheds and probably meet the vintner's dog.

DON'T MISS...

- Taste Napa's newest craze: **farm-to-table dining,** fresh and affordable at **Ubuntu** (p992) and **Ad Hoc** (p992)
- Bike Sonoma's sun-dappled Dry Creek Valley, braking for Zin in a cave at **Bella Vineyards** (p994) and Pinot in a toolshed at **Porter Creek Vineyards** (p994)
- Breathe rarified air amid 1000-year-old redwoods at **Armstrong Redwoods State Reserve** (p993)
- Find inspiration among the vineyards, peacocks and surreal sculpture at Napa's **di Rosa Art + Nature Preserve** (left)
- Race otters and turtles down the lazy **Russian River** in a canoe (p994)
- Wallow in **Calistoga's volcanic mud baths** at Indian Springs (p992)

Napa Valley

Some 230 wineries crowd 30-mile-long Napa Valley along three routes:

Hwy 121 Off Carneros Hwy (Hwy 121) towards Sonoma, landmark wineries specialize in cool-climate sparkling wines.

Hwy 29 Napa's blockbuster wines are poured in splashy tasting rooms along this highway.

Silverado Trail The trail is lined with boutique wineries, featuring bizarre architecture and cult-hit Cabs.

SIGHTS & ACTIVITIES

When you notice scrap-metal sheep-grazing Carneros vineyards, you've spotted **di Rosa Art + Nature Preserve** (☎ 707-226-5991; www.dirosapreserve.org; 5200 Carneros Hwy 121; ⌚ gallery 9:30am-3pm Wed-Fri, tours depart 10am, 11am & 1pm Wed-Fri, 10am, 11am, noon Sat). Reserve ahead for tours of the main house filled with contemporary art, from Tony Oursler's grimacing video projections in the wine cellar to million-dollar Robert Bechtel paintings hung on the living-room ceiling.

A few miles northeast is **Downtown Napa**, a Victorian boomtown with trend-setting restaurants, tasting rooms and mansions reinvented as B&Bs. Picky picnickers head to Napa's **Oxbow Public Market** (p992) for artisanal eats, while bargain-hunters hit **Napa Valley Visitors Bureau** (☎ 707-226-7459; www.napavalley.com; 1310 Napa Town Center; ⌚ 9am-5pm) for spa deals, wine-tasting passes and the free *Preiser Key to Napa Valley,* which has comprehensive winery maps. You can check your email before wine-tasting at **Napa Library** (☎ 707-253-4241; www.co.napa.ca.us/library; 580 Coombs St; ⌚ 10am-9pm Mon-Thu, 10am-5pm Fri & Sat, 2-9pm Sun).

Downtown at the **Vintners' Collective** (☎ 707-255-7150; www.vintnerscollective.com; 1245 Main St; tasting $25; ⌚ 11am-6pm Wed-Mon), sample six wines from 20 wineries in a former 19th-century brothel. Then discover affordable Pinot blends in the mural-lined tasting room of **Ceja** (☎ 707-226-6445; www.cejavineyards.com; 1248 First St, Napa; tasting $10; ⌚ noon-6pm Sun-Thu, noon-10pm Fri & Sat), which was founded by former vineyard workers. Northwest of town, the **Hess Collection** (☎ 707-255-1144; www.hesscollection.com; 4411 Redwood Rd; tasting per person $10; ⌚ 10am-4pm) pairs monster Cabs with art by mega modernists like Francis Bacon and Robert Motherwell.

Head northeast from Napa to boutique wineries along the **Silverado Trail**, starting with super-Tuscan-style Sangiovese at **Luna Vineyards** (☎ 707-255-5862; www.lunavineyards.com; 2921 Silverado Trail; ⌚ 10:30am-4pm). Stone bulls glower atop pillars lining the driveway of **Darioush** (☎ 707-257-2345; www.darioush.com; 4240 Silverado Trail; tasting $25; ⌚ 10:30am-5pm), a Persian-temple winery with monumental Merlots. Veer off to **Frog's Leap** (☎ 707-963-4704; www.frogsleap.com; 8815 Conn Creek Rd, Rutherford; tours with tasting $25; ⌚ by appointment, 10am-4pm Mon-Thu) for organically grown Cabs generously poured on irreverent tours of the LEED-certified winery.

Off Hwy 29, **Yountville** was once a stagecoach stop; now this two-horse town is home to **French Laundry** (right) and the most Michelin-starred eateries per capita in the US. Up Hwy 29, **St Helena** has historic charm and impeccable taste, with boutiques, bistros, and an 1889 stone chateau housing the **Culinary Institute of America** (☎ 707-967-2320; 2555 Main St; mains $21-34, cooking demonstration $15; restaurant 11:30am-9pm, cooking demonstrations 1:30pm & 3:30pm Mon & Fri, 10:30am & 1:30pm Sat & Sun).

Calistoga is Napa's down-to-earth north end, where **Indian Springs** (☎ 707-942-4913; www.indianspringscalistoga.com; 1712 Lincoln Ave; 10am-7:30pm) offers volcanic mud baths with access to its hot-springs pool ($85). **Dr. Wilkinson's Hot Springs** (☎ 707-942-4102; www.drwilkinson.com; 1507 Lincoln Ave; 8:30am-5:30pm) features wallows in volcanic mud and peat moss, mineral whirlpools, steam rooms, and blanket wraps ($89).

SLEEPING

Napa's best values are midweek and off-season in Calistoga and downtown Napa motels and B&Bs – see www.lonelyplanet.com and www.legendarynapavalley.com for more options.

Bothe-Napa Valley State Park (☎ 707-942-4575, reservations 800-444-7275; www.parks.ca.gov; campsites $35;) Hillside campsites with gorgeous hiking beneath redwoods to the historic Bale Grist Mill.

Calistoga Inn (☎ 707-942-4101; www.calistogainn.com; 1250 Lincoln Ave, Calistoga; r with shared bath midweek/weekend $89/139) Snug rooms lack phones and TVs, but there's a lively brewery-restaurant downstairs and spas within walking distance.

Hotel St Helena (☎ 707-963-4388; www.hotelsthelena.net; 1309 Main St, St Helena; r with shared bath $95;) Period-furnished rooms in the heart of historic St Helena.

Golden Haven (☎ 707-942-8000; www.goldenhaven.com; 1713 Lake St, Calistoga; r midweek/weekend from $115/149) Bland motel rooms at bargain rates – ask about package deals with mud bath treatments.

EATING

Oxbow Public Market (☎ 707-226-6529; www.oxbowpublicmarket.com; 610 & 644 First St; 9am-7pm Mon-Sat, 10am-5pm Sun) is a gourmet food court, featuring Hog Island's sustainably harvested oysters (six for $15), Pica Pica's Venezuelan cornbread sandwiches ($7), and Three Twins certified organic ice cream ($4 fo a single waffle cone).

Oakville Grocery (☎ 707-944-8802; www.oakvillegrocery.com; 7856 St Helena Hwy at Oakville Crossroad; 8am-6pm) Gourmet meals on the go: serious espresso, crusty bread, Sonoma cheese, cured meat and more.

JoLé (☎ 707-942-5938; www.jolerestaurant.com; 1457 Lincoln Ave, Calistoga; mains $7-22; 5pm-10pm Sun & Tue-Thu, to 11pm Fri & Sat) Small plates, modest prices and outsize flavor, from the local catch of the day to organic roast veggies and seasonal desserts from the in-house pastry chef.

our pick **Ad Hoc** (☎ 707-944-2487; www.adhocrestaurant.com; 6476 Washington St; h5pm-9pm Mon, Wed, Thu-Sun dinner, 10:30am-2pm Sun brunch) Don't bother asking for a menu at Thomas Keller's most innovative restaurant since French Laundry: chef Dave Cruz dreams up his four-course, $48 market menu daily. No substitutions are offered unless you mention dietary restrictions when making reservations, but none are needed – every dish is comforting, fresh and fabulous.

Ubuntu (☎ 707-251-5656; www.ubuntunapa.com; 1140 Main St; 5:30pm-9pm Mon-Thu, 11:30am-2:30pm & 5:30pm-10pm Fri & Sat, 11:30am-2:30pm & 5:30pm-9pm Sun; V) The seasonal, vegetarian menu features natural wonders from the biodynamic kitchen garden, satisfying hearty eaters with four to five inspired small plates and ecosavvy drinkers with 100-plus sustainably produced wines.

French Laundry (☎ 707-944-2380; www.frenchlaundry.com; 6640 Washington St, Yountville; fixed-price menu $240; 5:30-9:30pm daily, 11am-1pm Fri-Sun) The definition of California fine dining: inspired and seasonal, setting international trends with ingredients plucked from the organic garden out the back. A culinary experience worthy of lifetime achievements – a 40th birthday, say, or a Nobel Prize? Book one to six months ahead; call at 10am sharp.

Sonoma Valley

More casual and less commercial than Napa, Sonoma Valley has 70 wineries clustered around Hwy 12 – and unlike Napa, most welcome picnicking.

SIGHTS & ACTIVITIES

Downtown Sonoma was once the capital of a rogue nation, and though Sonoma Plaza looks stately with its chic boutiques and stone **visitor center** (☎ 707-996-1090, 800-576-6662; www.sonomavalley.com; 453 1st St E; 9am-5pm), the plaza gets plenty lively on summer nights and **farmers' market** (9am-noon Fri & 5:30-8pm Tue Apr-Oct) days.

Down a country road from downtown, **Gundlach-Bundschu** (☎ 707-938-5277; www.gunbun.com; 2000 Denmark St) is a solar-powered castle perched above a reclaimed water lake producing legendary Tempranillo. GunBun also runs nearby **Bartholomew Park Winery** (☎ 707-939-3026; www.bartpark.com; 1000 Vineyard Ln; tasting $5-10, museum & park entry free; tasting room & museum 11am-4:30pm daily), which is a 400-acre preserve with vineyards originally cultivated in 1857 and now certified organic, yielding citrus-sunshine Sauvignon Blanc and smoky-midnight Merlot.

Obey the call of the wild up Hwy 12 at **Jack London Historic State Park** (☎ 707-938-5216; www.jacklondonpark.com; 2400 London Ranch Rd; car $8; 10am-5pm Oct-Apr, 9:30am-7pm May-Sep), where adventure-novelist Jack London brought Sonoma's slash-and-burned hillsides back to life. Hike to the lake to overlook London's pristine 129-acre farmstead, ride through fragrant redwood groves with **Triple Creek Horse Outfit** (☎ 707-887-8700; www.triplecreekhorseoutfit.com; 2400 London Ranch Rd; group rides 1/2/3 hr with lunch $60/90/250; by reservation), or visit the House of Happy Walls to peruse London's life story, sustainable farming methods, best-selling books and 600 rejection letters.

Turn off Hwy 12 near Kenwood to **Kaz Winery** (☎ 707-833-2536; www.kazwinery.com; 233 Adobe Canyon Rd, Kenwood; tasting $5-10 (applicable to purchase); 11am-5pm Fri-Mon) for offbeat, organically grown Nebbiolo Blush Port and Cabernet Franc poured in the barn.

SLEEPING

At the northern end of Sonoma Valley, **Santa Rosa** offers affordable chain motels along Cleveland Ave, west of Hwy 101.

Sugarloaf Ridge State Park (☎ 707-833-5712, reservations 800-444-7275; www.parks.ca.gov; Adobe Canyon Rd; campsites $30) North of Kenwood wineries, 50 sites without hookups are nestled in two mellow meadows.

Hillside Inn (☎ 707-546-9353; www.hillside-inn.com; 2901 Fourth St, Sonoma; s/d Nov-Mar $70/78, Apr-Oct $74/82; P) Downtown Sonoma's best-kept motel is close to wine-tasting action; add $4 for kitchens.

Sonoma Hotel (☎ 707-996-2996, 800-468-6016; www.sonomahotel.com; 110 W Spain St, Sonoma; r incl breakfast midweek/weekend $140/170 Nov-Mar, $170/198 Apr-Oct;) Stylish 1880 landmark hotel on happening Sonoma Plaza, with larger/smaller rooms for $30 more/less; there is a two-night minimum on weekends.

our pick **Beltane Ranch** (☎ 707-996-6501; www.beltaneranch.com; 11775 Hwy 12; r incl breakfast $150-220; P) In the 1890s this ranch belonged to Mary Ellen Pleasant, daughter of slaves and former brothel owner turned abolitionist leader and California pioneer. Her graceful yellow homestead offers bucolic splendor amid olive orchards, without phones or TVs. Guests enjoy ranch-raised meals, hike trails, play tennis and watch horses graze from porch swings.

EATING

Sonoma Market (☎ 707-996-3411; 500 W Napa St, Sonoma; 6am-9pm) Superior deli with hot-pressed panini created by the in-house chef.

Red Grape (☎ 707-996-4103; www.theredgrape.com; 529 First St West; pizzas $10-16; 11:30am-10pm;) Thin-crust pizza with local cheeses and cured meats, plus small-production Sonoma wines by the half-bottle.

Fig Cafe (☎ 707-938-2130; www.thefigcafe.com; 13690 Arnold Dr, Glen Ellen; mains $15-20; 5:30-9pm daily, brunch 10am-2:30pm Sat & Sun) Sonoma's take on comfort food: organic salads, Sonoma duck cassoulet and free corkage on Sonoma wines, served in a converted living room.

Cafe la Haye (☎ 707-935-5994; www.cafelahaye.com; 140 E Napa St, Sonoma; mains $17-25; from 5:30pm Tue-Sat) In an open kitchen, this tiny bistro whips up big-city cuisine with ingredients grown within a 60-mile radius.

Russian River Valley

The West preserves its wild ways in Russian River, two hours north of San Francisco (via Hwys 101 and 116) in western Sonoma County. Here ancient redwoods tower over independent wineries and the 10-mile, aptly named **Bohemian Highway** is lined with resorts for rebels, hippie craft galleries, and gay-friendly honky-tonks. **Guerneville visitor center** (☎ 707-869-9000; www.russianriver.com; 16209 1st St; 10am-5pm) offers maps and last-minute lodging info.

Old-growth redwoods at 805-acre **Armstrong Redwoods State Reserve** (☎ 707-869-2015; www.parks.ca.gov; 17000 Armstrong Woods Rd; entry per car $8, campsites $20; 8am-sunset) were saved by lumber baron Colonel James Boydston Armstrong, who bought these woods in 1874 and saved them from the axe, including the 308ft, 1400-year-old Colonel Armstrong Tree.

Paddle downriver past herons and otters in **Burke's Canoe Trips** (☎ 707-887-1222; www.burkescanoetrips.com; 8600 River Rd; canoes $59), or enjoy nature while sipping bubbly served to US presidents at the outdoor hilltop tasting bar at **Iron Horse Vineyards** (☎ 707-887-1507; www.ironhorsevineyards.com; 9786 Ross Station Rd; $10-15 tasting; 🕑 10am-3:30pm), 15 minutes south of Guerneville. Dinner and a movie awaits at **Rio Theater** (☎ 707-865-0913; www.riotheater.com; 20396 Bohemian Hwy, Monte Rio; adult/senior, child & matinees $8/6; 🕑 Wed-Sun), a converted 1940s Army shed featuring Oscar contenders and gourmet hot dogs ($7).

Occidental is the heart of the Boho Hwy, with its organic **farmers market** (☎ 707-793-2159; www.occidentalfarmersmarket.com, 🕑 4pm-dusk Fri, Jun-Oct), clever crafts from reclaimed materials at **Renga Arts** (☎ 707-874-9407; www.rengaarts.com; 3605 Main St; 🕑 11am-5pm Fri-Mon), and outlandish April 1 Fool's Day Parade.

For European classics with California creativity – and bargain three-course weeknight menus – head to **Bistro des Copains** (☎ 707-874-2436; www.bistrodescopains.com; 3782 Bohemian Hwy; 🕑 5-9pm Sun-Thu, 5-10pm Fri & Sat).

Healdsburg to Boonville

More than 90 wineries dot the Russian River, Dry Creek and Alexander Valleys within a 30-mile radius of **Healdsburg**, where upscale eateries, wine-tasting rooms and stylish inns surround the Spanish-style Plaza. For tasting passes and Wine Country maps, hit the **Healdsburg Visitors Center** (☎ 707-433-6935, 800-648-9922; www.healdsburg.org; 217 Healdsburg Ave; 🕑 9am-5pm Mon-Fri, 9am-3pm Sat, 10am-2pm Sun).

Picture-perfect farmstead wineries await discovery in Dry Creek Valley, across Hwy 101 from downtown Healdsburg. Rent a bike from **Spoke Folk Cyclery** (opposite), and peddle from Zin-tasting in the caves at **Bella Vineyards** (☎ 707-473-9171, 866-572-3552; www.bellawinery.com; 9711 W Dry Creek Rd; tastings $5-10; 🕑 11am-4:30pm) to organic, certified biodynamic **Porter Creek Vineyards** (☎ 707-433-6321; www.portercreekvineyards.com; 8735 Westside Rd; tastings free; 🕑 10:30am-4:30pm) for woodsy Pinot Noir served on a bar made from a bowling alley lane.

North of Healdsburg, take Hwy 128 to **Anderson Valley** for organic eats and award-winning beer amid vineyards and apple orchards. In **Boonville**, brake for disc golf, beer-tasting and tours of the solar-powered facilities at **Anderson Valley Brewing Company** (☎ 707-895-2337; www.avbc.com; 17700 Hwy 253; tastings $5 (applicable to purchase); 🕑 11am-6pm Thu-Mon; tours 11:30am & 3pm daily).

SLEEPING & EATING

Healdsburg's budget options include Vegas-kitschy **L&M Motel** (☎ 707-433-6528; www.landmmotel.com; 70 Healdsburg Ave; r $75-99) and spiffy **Best Western Dry Creek** (☎ 707-433-0300, 800-222-5784; www.drycreekinn.com; 198 Dry Creek Rd; r $115-135)

Bovolo (☎ 707-431-2962; www.bovolorestaurant.com; 106 Matheson St; lunch mains $8-14; 🕑 9am-6pm Thu-Tue, to 9pm Sat & Sun) puts a Slow Food spin on fast food, making salads, panini and pizza with meats cured in-house. Critics rave about **Cyrus** (☎ 707-433-3311; www.cyrusrestaurant.com; 29 North St; fixed-price menus $102-130; 🕑 6-11pm Wed-Mon), but the local secret is the bar, where truffle-laced dishes are served à la carte with mad-scientist cocktails. **Boonville General Store** (☎ 707-895-9477; 14077 #A Hwy 128, Boonville; 🕑 9:30am-3pm) serves house-baked pastries and pizza, plus locally grown organic salads.

Getting There & Around

Wine Country is about 90 minutes north of San Francisco via Hwy 101 or I-80. For transit information, dial ☎ 511.

PUBLIC TRANSPORTATION

Take the scenic route to Napa from SF on the **Vallejo Ferry** (415-877-643-3779; www.baylinkferry.com; adults/seniors & youth/under 6 $13/6.50/free), departing from the Ferry Building about every hour from 6:30am to 7pm on weekdays, and every two hours from 11am to 7:30pm on weekends. Otherwise, take **BART** (p987) to El Cerrito and transfer to **Vallejo Transit** (☎ 707-648-4666; www.vallejotransit.com) to Vallejo. **Napa Valley Vine** (☎ 707-251-2800, 800-696-6443; www.napavalleyvine.net) buses connect Vallejo to Napa and Calistoga.

For Sonoma, **Greyhound buses** (☎ 800-231-2222; www.greyhound.com) run from San Francisco to Santa Rosa ($21). **Golden Gate Transit** (☎ 415-923-2000; www.goldengate.org) links San Francisco to Petaluma ($7.60) and Santa Rosa ($8.40), where you connect with **Sonoma County Transit** (☎ 707-576-7433; www.sctra nsit.com).

Napa Valley Vine provides public transit within Napa Valley; Golden Gate Transit, and Sonoma Valley Transit provide transit around Sonoma.

BICYCLE

The best way to explore Wine Country's scenic backroads is by bicycle. Rent yours for about $30 to $45 per day at **Calistoga Bike Shop** (☎ 707-942-9687, 866-942-2453; www.calistogabikeshop.com; 1318 Lincoln Ave), **Sonoma Valley Cyclery** (☎ 707-935-3377; 20093 Broadway), and Healdsburg's **Spoke Folk Cyclery** (☎ 707-433-7171; www.spokefolk.com; 201 Center St).

Napa Valley Adventure Tours (☎ 707-259-1833, 877-548-6877; www.napavalleyadventuretours.com; Oxbow Public Market, 610 1st St, Napa) offers bicycle rentals and Silverado Trail rides introducing cyclists to winemakers, artisans and organic farmers ($139/6.5 hours). **Getaway Adventures** (☎ 707-568-3040, 800-499-2453; www.getawayadventures.com) offers easy Sip-n-Cycle tours around Calistoga or Dry Creek ($149/6 hours).

TRAIN

Napa Valley Wine Train (☎ 707-253-2111, 800-427-4124; www.winetrain.com; adult/child under 12 $49.50/25, plus lunch $44.50/25, dinner $49.50/30) offers cushy, touristy three-hour trips with an optional winery stop ($25 extra) and a bar car ($10/4 tastings).

AUTO-RICKSHAW

Napa Valley Hoppers (☎ 707-224-4677; www.nvhoppers.com) offer motorized rickshaw excursions, making three to four winery stops from 10am to 2pm ($89 per person/5 hours); reservations are required.

NORTH COAST

Valleys of redwoods amble into the moody crash of the Pacific along the North Coast, home to hippies, hoppy microbrews and flora that famously includes some of the tallest trees and most potent marijuana in the world. This is the part of California to slow down and get lost under the giant trees as you soak up the scenic route through massive forests and foggy, two-stoplight towns.

Bodega Bay to Fort Bragg

The coast between Bodega Bay and Fort Bragg is on the gorgeous, jagged edge of the continent, where cows graze on cliffs above the frothing, frigid roar of the Pacific. The metropolitan charms of San Francisco, only a few hours south, feel eons away. Compared to Hwy 1 along the Big Sur coast, the snaking route through the North Coast is more challenging, more remote and more *real*: white-knuckled drivers pass farms, fishing towns and hidden beaches, pausing on roadside pullouts where gusty cliffs overlook migrating whales. The drive takes four hours of daylight driving without stops. At night in the fog, it takes steely nerves and much, much longer.

Bodega Bay is the first pearl in a string of sleepy fishing towns, and the setting of Hitchcock's terrifying 1963 avian horror flick *The Birds*. The skies are free from bloodthirsty gulls today (though you'd best keep an eye on the picnic); it's Bay Area weekenders who descend en masse on B&Bs and extraordinary state beaches between here and Jenner, 10 miles north. **Bodega Bay Sportfishing** (☎ 707-875-3344; 1410 Bay Flat Rd) runs whale-watching trips ($35 per person, 3½-to-four-hours) and **Bodega Bay Surf Shack** (☎ 707-875-3944; www.bodegabaysurf.com; 1400 N Hwy 1; surfboards per day $13, kayaks per 4hr single/double $45/65) rents surfboards and kayaks.

There isn't much to **Jenner**, just a cluster of shops and restaurants dotting the coastal hills where the Russian River meets the Pacific. The main attraction is the resident harbor seal colony. Look for them from Hwy 1 turnouts north of town. Volunteers protect the seals and educate tourists at **Goat Rock State Beach** (☎ 707-875-3483; Mile 19.15) during pupping season, between March and August.

The centerpiece of **Fort Ross State Historic Park** (☎ 707-847-3286, 707-847-3708; www.fortrossstatepark.org; 19005 Hwy 1; per car $8, campsites $25), 12 miles north of Jenner, is an 1812 trading post and salt-weathered Russian Orthodox church, once the southernmost reach of Tsarist Russia's North American trading expeditions. The small, wood-scented museum offers historical exhibits and respite from wind-swept cliffs. There's drive-in, first-come, first-served camping 2 miles south of the fort. It's open from April to November.

Salt Point State Park (☎ 707-847-3221, reservations 800-444-7275; www.reserveamerica.com; Mile 39; per car $8, campsites $35) has hiking trails, tide pools and two campgrounds where pink blooms spot the green, misty woods in springtime. Cows graze the surrounding rock-strewn fields on the bluffs, which are home to organic dairy cooperatives.

Continuing north is **Gualala** (pronounced wah-*la*-la), an 1850s milltown that enjoys a breathtaking coastal location. Staying in town is pricy, but a mile south, **Gualala Point Regional Park** (☎ 707-785-2377, reservations 707-565-2267; www.sonoma-county.org/parks; 42401 S Highway 1; per car $6, campsites $22) has campsites under the redwoods, a windswept beach and trails to the shore.

Just north, **Point Arena**, has a cute downtown and a stilting pier. A little further north are rapturous views atop the 1908 **Point Arena Lighthouse** (☎ 707-882-2777; www.pointarenalighthouse.com; 45500 Lighthouse Rd; 🕑 10am-3:30pm; admission $7.50), one of the tallest on the West Coast.

Eight miles north of Elk, **Van Damme State Park** (☎ 707-937-5804, reservations 800-444-7275; www.reserveamerica.com; per car $8, campsites $35) has the popular **Fern Canyon Trail**, which passes through a pygmy forest and a fern- and elderberry-lined canyon. The car-accessible camping is pleasant, but an easy 2 mile hike-in offers a secluded option.

The most popular village on this stretch, **Mendocino**, is the North Coast's salt-washed gem, with New England saltbox B&Bs and a gorgeous headland. Walk the headland among berry bramble and wildflowers, where cypress trees stand guard over dizzying cliffs. Nature's power is evident everywhere: from driftwood littered fields and cave tunnels to the raging surf. The town itself is full of cute shops – no chains – and has earned the nickname 'Spendocino' for its upscale goods. Quasi-bohemian bourgeoisie with fat wallets love wandering the streets; most are up from San Francisco for the weekend. The **visitor center** (☎ 707-937-5397; www.gomendo.com; 735 Main St; 🕑 11am-4pm) is in the Ford House and is the place to start.

Medocino's scrappy sister city, **Fort Bragg**, is trying to lure some of the moneyed travelers a bit further north, but it still has a way to go. You'll find cheap gas, large motels and a mess of fast food, but it's not without its charm. The thick, hoppy brews at **North Coast Brewing Co** (☎ 707-964-2739; www.northcoastbrewing.com; 455 N Main St; pint $4, 10-beer sampler $12) are reason enough to pull over. Fort Bragg also boasts the 1885 **Skunk Train** (☎ 800-866-1690; www.skunktrain.com; adult/child 3-11yr $47/22), whose diesel and steam engines make half-day trips through the woods to Ukiah.

SLEEPING & EATING

The following options are listed from south to north.

The **Bodega Harbor Inn** (☎ 707-875-3594; www.bodegaharborinn.com; 1345 Bodega Ave; r $80-155; ⊠), in Bodega Bay, has affordable cottage-style rooms. Golden-battered baskets of local rock cod are the highlight of the **Boat House** (☎ 707-875-3495; 1445 N Hwy 1; mains $11-15; 🕑 noon-8pm), a buoy-strung shack with a sloping floor.

Jenner's **River's End Cabins** (☎ 707-865-2484; www.ilovesunsets.com; 11048 Hwy 1; cabins $120-220) are peaceful and rustic (no TV or phone), with a connected restaurant offering carefully prepared, elegant dishes and captivating views.

In Gualala, the first stop for lunch is the best: **Bones Roadhouse** (☎ 707-884-1188; 39350 S Hwy 1; mains $10-20; 🕑 11:30am-9pm Sun-Thu, 11:30am-10pm Fri & Sat). On weekends, they may even have a codgerly blues outfit growling 'Mustang Sally.' The gorgeous, quirky **St Orres** (☎ 707-884-3303; www.saintorres.com; 36601 Hwy 1; r with shared bath incl breakfast from $95, cottages incl breakfast $140-445) has a hand-hewn Russian-style redwood hotel, secluded cottages and dramatic California cuisine (dinner mains $40).

our pick **Mar Vista Cottages** (☎ 707-884-3522, 877-855-3522; www.marvistamendocino.com; 35101 S Hwy 1; cottages from $155; ⊠ 📶) is a cluster of a dozen elegantly remodeled fishing cottages that's idyllic: chickens cluck around the grounds laying the morning's eats; guests swing on the tire swing and pick from the organic garden. The cabins have wi-fi and require a two-night minimum stay.

Lovely Mendocino has lots of upscale sleeping and dining options, but the coziest of these, **Brewery Gulch Inn** (☎ 800-578-4454; www.brewerygulchinn.com; 9401 N Hwy 1; r $210-450; 💻), wins with fireplace rooms and hosts who pour heavily at the complimentary wine hour and leave sweets out for midnight snacking. It's just south of town, on a hill overlooking the ocean. If it's late, you'll thank heavens for **Patterson's Pub** (☎ 707-937-4782; www.pattersonspub.com; 10485 Lansing St; mains $10-15), which serves big entree salads and first-class pub fare.

Jughandle Creek Farm (☎ 707-964-4630; www.jughandlecreekfarm.org; 15501 N Hwy 1; r & cabins adult/child/student $40/$13/$33, campsites $12/5/10) is an educational center in Caspar, opposite Jug Handle State Reserve. Rooms and cabins are set up like a hostel (bring a sleeping bag) with communal baths and kitchens. An hour's worth of work earns a small discount.

Fort Bragg has many dreary midrange motels, though an unbelievable bargain is available at the cute **Colombi Motel** (☎ 707-964-5773; www.colombimotel.com; 647 Oak St; r with kitchenette $45-70).

Free local folk and jazz performances set up nightly at the **Headlands Coffeehouse** (☎ 707-964-1987; www.headlandscoffeehouse.com; 120 E Laurel St; panini sandwiches $7-8; 7am-10pm Sun-Thu, to 11pm Fri & Sat), a coffee shop and café that's a godsend for idle Fort Bragg teens.

GETTING THERE & AWAY

A car is nearly a necessity along Hwy 1, though the **Mendocino Transit Authority** (MTA; 800-696-4682; www.4mta.org) operates a daily bus from Fort Bragg south to Santa Rosa via Willits and Ukiah ($20, 3 hours); at Santa Rosa, catch San Francisco–bound bus 80 ($8.80), operated by **Golden Gate Transit** (415-923-2000; www.goldengate.org). Neither Greyhound (p1160) nor Amtrak (p1166) serves towns along Hwy 1.

Ukiah to Scotia

Ukiah is mostly a place to gas up or get some food along the ride north. The best thing going in the area is **Vichy Springs Resort** (right).

North of tiny **Leggett** on Hwy 101, lose yourself under giant redwoods at **Standish-Hickey State Recreation Area** (707-925-6482, 69350 Hwy 101; per car $8). It has river swimming and fishing, as well as 9 miles of hiking trails in virgin and second-growth redwoods (look for the 225ft-tall Miles Standish tree). Fourteen miles further north is **Richardson Grove State Park** (per car $8), for 1400 acres of more virgin redwoods and camping (campsites $35).

Garberville became famous in the 1970s for the sinsemilla (potent, seedless marijuana) grown in the surrounding hills. Today Garberville is a quiet, one-street town with cheap motels and diners, and a curious culture clash of burly loggers and burned-out hippies. (You'll be able to tell them apart pretty easily.)

The **Lost Coast** tops a serious hiker's itinerary, offering the best coastal camping in California. It became 'lost' when the state's highway system bypassed the rugged mountains of the King Range, which rise 4000ft within several miles of the ocean, leaving the region largely undeveloped. The scenery is stunning. From Garberville it's 23 miles along a rough road to Shelter Cove, a seaside subdivision with a deli, restaurant and motels. Talk to locals before venturing along back roads or wandering off trail, lest you encounter farmers who are extremely protective of the county's illicit cash crop.

Along Hwy 101, 80-sq-mile **Humboldt Redwoods State Park** (707-946-2409, reservations 800-444-7275; www.reserveamerica.com; campsites $35-45) protects some of the world's oldest redwoods and has three-quarters of the world's tallest 100 trees. Even if you don't have time to hike in, drive (vehicle entry $8) the park's awe-inspiring **Avenue of the Giants**, a 32-mile, two-lane road parallel to Hwy 101. Book ahead for magnificent campsites near the informative **visitor center** (707-946-2409; 9am-5pm).

SLEEPING & EATING

The camping options are plentiful and extremely high quality, though every one-horse town guarantees at least a deli or *taqueria*. The following listings run south to north.

In Ukiah, chain motels line S State St, though the best value is the independent **Sunrise Inn** (707-462-6601; www.sunriseinn.net; 650 S State St; r $48-68;). Seven-hundred-acre **Vichy Springs Resort** (707-462-9515; www.vichysprings.com; 2605 Vichy Springs Rd, Ukiah; RV sites $20, lodge s/d $135/195, creekside r $195/245, cottages from $280;) has the only warm-water, naturally carbonated mineral baths in North America. Two-hour day-use costs $30; all-day use runs to $50. Unlike other nearby hot springs, it also requires swimwear – you'll be thankful.

The most fun dining in town is at the **Ukiah Brewing Company** (707-468-5898; www.ukiahbrewingco.com; 102 S State St; dinner mains $15-25; 5:30-9pm Tue-Sat, 11:30am-2pm Thu & Fri), where the brews are better than the food, but the dancefloor rocks to live music on the weekend.

The historic Tudor-style **Benbow Inn** (707-923-2124, 800-355-3301; www.benbowinn.com; 445 Lake Benbow Dr, Garberville, r $130-200;), just south of Garberville off Hwy 101, indulges guests with complimentary decanted sherry in each lovely room; consider splurging for riverside rooms. The white-tablecloth restaurant and wood-paneled bar are particularly inviting on foggy evenings.

Along the Avenue of the Giants is *excellent* camping – the best of which is in Humboldt Redwoods State Park (left) – and scads of musty midcentury motels, to be approached with caution.

GETTING THERE & AROUND

Greyhound (800-231-2222; www.greyhound.com) operates from San Francisco to Ukiah ($29.20). The **Redwood Transit System** (707-443-0826; www.hta.org) operates buses Monday through Saturday between Scotia and Trinidad ($1.95, 2½ hours).

Eureka to Crescent City

Passing the strip malls that sprawl from the edges, **Eureka** is unlikely to have you shouting the town's name from the hills; however, it does have an Old Town with fine Victorians, inviting shops and restaurants. The **Eureka visitor center** (☎ 707-442-3738, 800-356-6381; www.eurekachamber.com; 2112 Broadway; 🕑 8:30am-5pm Mon-Fri, 10am-4pm Sat) has maps and information. In Old Town, **Going Places** (☎ 707-443-4145; 328 2nd St; 🕑 10:30am-5:30pm Mon-Sat, 11am-5pm Sun) is a fabulous travel bookstore.

The best thing going in Eureka is **Blue Ox Millworks** (☎ 707-444-3437; www.blueoxmill.com; adult/child 6-12yr $7.50/3.50; 🕑 9am-4pm Mon-Sat), one of a small handful of mills in the nation that hand-tools Victorian detailing using traditional carpentry and 19th-century equipment. Fascinating self-guided tours let you watch the craftsmen work.

Cruising the harbor aboard the blue-and-white 1910 **Madaket** (☎ 707-445-1910; www.humboldtbaymaritimemuseum.com; adult/child 5-12yr/senior & teen $15/7.50/13; 🕑 May-Oct) is also fun. It departs from the foot of F St and the $10 sunset cocktail cruise serves from the smallest licensed bar in the state.

Nine miles north of Eureka, **Arcata** is a patchouli-dipped bastion of radical politics set around a quaint square, where trucks run on biodiesel and recycling gets picked up by tandem bicycle. On the northeast side of town lies the pretty campus of **Humboldt State University** (☎ 707-826-3011; www.humboldt.edu). At the junction of Hwys 299 and 101 is a **California Welcome Center** (☎ 707-822-3619; www.arcatachamber.com; 🕑 9am-5pm), with area info.

Trinidad, a working fishing town 16 miles north of Arcata, sits on a bluff overlooking a glittering harbor. There are lovely sand beaches and short hikes on Trinidad Head. Nearby Luffenholtz Beach is popular (but unpatrolled) for surfing; and north of town, Patrick's Point Rd is dotted with lodging and forested campgrounds. **Patrick's Point State Park** (☎ 707-677-3570; reservations 800-444-7275; www.reserveamerica.com; day-use $8, campsites $35-45) has stunning rocky headlands, tide pools and camping.

On Hwy 101, a mile south of tiny **Orick**, is **Redwood National & State Parks Visitor Center** (☎ 707-464-6101, ext 5265; www.nps.gov/redw; 🕑 9am-5pm). Together, Redwood National Park and Prairie Creek, Del Norte and Jedediah Smith State Parks are a designated World Heritage Site containing almost half the remaining old-growth redwood forests in California. The national park is free; the state parks have a $8 day-use fee in some areas and the only developed campsites ($35). Peering out of the tent at the surreal size of the trunks makes this excellent camping. The visitor center has info about the parks and free permits for backcountry camping.

The jaw-dropping highlights at **Redwood National Park** are **Lady Bird Johnson Grove** and **Tall Trees Grove**, home to several of the world's tallest trees and roaming elk herds.

But for the giant cast-metal golden bears at the bridge, you could drive right past **Klamath** and never know it existed. Isolated amid trees and water, it's a well-placed launching pad for outdoor adventures. Several miles north, **Del Norte Coast Redwoods State Park** (☎ 707-464-6101, ext 5120) contains redwood groves and 8 miles of unspoiled coastline.

Sprawling over with a crescent-shaped bay, **Crescent City** is the only sizable coastal town north of Arcata. More than half the town was destroyed by a tidal wave in 1964 and then rebuilt with drab utilitarian architecture. When the tide's out, you can check out the 1865 **Battery Point Lighthouse** (☎ 707-464-3089; admission $3; 🕑 10am-4pm Wed-Sun Apr-Oct) at the south end of A St.

Jedediah Smith Redwoods State Park (☎ 707-464-6101, ext 5112), 5 miles northeast of Crescent City, is less crowded than the other parks but no less beautiful. The redwood stands are so dense that there are few trails, but the outstanding 11-mile **Howland Hill Scenic Drive** is the best way to see the forest if you can't hike.

SLEEPING & EATING

The following options are listed south to north. A mixed bag of midcentury motels are scattered throughout every town along Hwy 101.

In Eureka, the cheapest options are south of downtown, but the family-run **Bayview Motel** (☎ 707-442-1673, 866-725-6813; www.bayviewmotel.com; 2844 Fairfield St; r $90-95; ⊠ 📶) is a bright, clean midrange choice (some rooms *do* have a bay view). **Carter House Inns** (☎ 707-444-8062, 800-404-1390; www.carterhouse.com; 301 L St; r incl breakfast $185-213; ⊠ 📶) is the cush option near Old Town, a complex of several lovingly tended Victorian properties. The French fusion at Restaurant 301 is the most haute dining around.

The **Lost Coast Brewery** (☎ 707-445-4480; 617 4th St; pints $3.50, 10-beer sampler $10, mains $6-13; 📶) is another excellent North Coast brewery. The Downtown Brown and Great White are both delicious, the kitchen turns out great wings, fries, and good burgers from 11am until midnight and – bonus – there's wi-fi.

On the nearby Samoa Peninsula, the popular **Samoa Cookhouse** (☎ 707-442-1659; www.samoacookhouse.net; all-you-can-eat meals $12-15; 7am-9pm) is the dining hall of an 1893 lumber camp. Hikers, hippies and lumberjacks get stuffed while sharing long red-checked oilcloth-covered tables.

On the Arcata town square, the stately 1915 **Hotel Arcata** (☎ 707-826-0217, 800-344-1221; www.hotelarcata.com; 708 9th St; r $96-156;) is a bit stuffy but right in the center of the town.

In Klamath, the 1914 **Requa Inn** (☎ 707-482-1425, 866-800-8777; www.requainn.com; 451 Requa Rd; r $85-155;) caters to hikers, with country-style rooms overlooking the river.

GETTING THERE & AROUND

Greyhound (☎ 800-231-2222; www.greyhound.com) serves Arcata; from San Francisco budget $38 and seven hours. **Redwood Transit buses** (☎ 707-443-0826; www.hta.org) serve Arcata and Eureka on the Trinidad–Scotia routes ($1.95, 2½ hours), which don't run on Sunday.

SACRAMENTO

Even though Sacramento was the first (non-mission) European settlement in California, the state's capital is an anomalous place: the first city to shoot up from gold discovery is flat and fairly bland with shady trees, withering summer heat and jammed highways.

In 1839, eccentric Swiss immigrant John Sutter built a fort and after gold was discovered nearby in 1848, the town's population exploded. In 1854, after several years of legislative waffling, it became California's capital. Old Sacramento remains the visitor's magnet – an authentic riverside settlement with raised wooden sidewalks that can feel like ye olde tourist trap – but better food and culture lie hidden among the grid of streets in midtown, where a fledgling arts scene is quietly defying the city's reputation as a cow town.

The **visitor center** (☎ 916-442-7644; www.discovergold.org; 1004 2nd St; 10am-5pm) in Old Sacramento can recommend hotels.

Sights

The 19th-century **state capitol** at 10th St is the white jewel rising from the immaculately manicured Capitol Mall; inside, it's stunning. The **Capitol Museum** (☎ 916-324-0333; www.statecapitolmuseum.com; admission free; 9am-5pm), gives tours through period-furnished chambers. The Assembly and Senate rooms are open to the public.

A few blocks away is the attractive, modern **California Museum** (☎ 916-653-7524; www.californiamuseum.org; 1020 O St; adult/child 6-13yr $8.50/7; 10am-5pm Mon-Sat, noon-5pm Sun;), home to the California Hall Of Fame – perhaps the only place to simultaneously encounter Cesar Chavez, Dr Seuss and Amelia Earhart.

It's a little stagey, and the candy-scented streets rumble with baby boomers on Harleys, but **Old Sacramento** (www.oldsacramento.com) offers a stroll past California's largest concentration of historic buildings and three great museums. The **California State Railroad Museum** (☎ 916-323-9280, 916-445-6645; www.californiastaterailroadmuseum.org; 125 I St; adult/child 6-17yr $9/4; 10am-5pm) is a train lover's dream. You can board dozens of meticulously restored beasts of steam and diesel; ride a steam train ($8) at summer weekends. Next door, the **Sacramento History Museum** (☎ 916-264-7059; www.sachistorymuseum.org; 101 I St; adult/child 13-17yr/child 4-12yr $5/4/3; 10am-5pm, closed Mon in winter) focuses on the gold rush. The city's small but handsome house of fine art, the **Crocker Art Museum** (☎ 916-264-5423; www.crockerartmuseum.org; 3rd & O Sts; adult/child 7-17yr $6/3, free 10am-1pm Sun; 10am-5pm Tue-Sun, to 9pm Thu) is in the former residence of 19th-century California Supreme Court Judge Edwin B Crocker. It contains his visionary collection of California art.

Restored to its 1850s appearance, **Sutter's Fort** (☎ 916-445-4422; cnr 27th & L Sts; adult/child under 5yr/child 6-16yr $5/free/3; 10am-5pm;) has historical actors in summer and some Saturdays throughout the year. Adjacent to the fort, the well-done **California State Indian Museum** (☎ 916-324-0971; adult/child under 5yr/child 6-17yr $3/free/2; 10am-5pm) is tiny but informative and has Ishi artifacts.

Sleeping & Eating

Downtown has a glut of midrange chain hotels. For restaurants, make for J St between 16th and 25th Sts.

our pick HI Sacramento Hostel (☎ 916-443-1691; 925 H St; dm $25, r $55.75;) This is a *hostel*? Sweet! The public areas in this restored Victorian mansion are B&B quality, the spacious dorms are clean and the staff is kind.

The cozy **Mulvaney's B & L** (☎ 916-441-6022; www.culinaryspecialists.com; 1215 19th St; mains $20-40;

(11:30am-2:30pm, 5-10pm Tue-Fri, 5-10pm Sat) is the class place in town; an expert French-touched menu changes every day.

The best vegetarian fare in all of California might be at **Andy Nguyen's** (916-736-1157; 2007 Broadway; meals $8-16; 11:30am-9pm Mon-Sat; V), a tranquil Buddhist Thai diner. Try the steaming curries and artful fake meat dishes (the 'chicken' leg has a little wooden bone).

For award-winning IPAs and decent pub grub, hit **Rubicon** (916-448-7032; www.rubiconbrewing.com; 2004 Capitol Ave; sandwiches $6-9; 11am-11:30pm Mon-Thu, to 12:30am Fri & Sat, to 10pm Sun).

Getting There & Around

Sacramento is 91 miles east of San Francisco via I-80, and 386 miles north of LA via I-5. **Sacramento International Airport** (916-929-5411; www.sacairports.org), is a great small airport to access Lake Tahoe, 15 miles north of downtown off I-5.

Greyhound (800-231-2222; 7th & L Sts) serves San Francisco ($22, two hours), Los Angeles ($66, nine hours), Seattle ($150, 19 hours) and other major towns.

Sacramento's **Amtrak** (800-872-7245; cnr 5th & I Sts) is the best way to travel to the Bay Area, with frequent trains. The depot is near downtown. Trains leave daily for Oakland ($24, two hours) and Los Angeles ($56, 14 hours).

Sacramento Regional Transit (916-321-2877; www.sacrt.com) runs a bus and light rail system (fare $2.25).

GOLD COUNTRY

This is where California was born with a sparkle: a curiously shiny rock caught the eye of James Marshall in 1848, the sighting of which started a chaotic stampede of some 300,000 Forty Niners whose lust for gold had little time for the rules of civilized society or the environment. You'd never know to visit the region today: the scars of mining have healed, leaving hills dotted with pine and oak, and once lawless towns are either restored to the showy Victorian elegance or slouching under the blistering summer heat. Historical markers tell tales of bloodlust and banditry, but a traveler's more tactile pleasures on offer include an icy plunge into one of the area's swimming holes or a molar-rattling mountain bike descent.

Many small cities exude historical quaintness, but all have similar features: antiques, ice-cream parlors and musty gold-rush museums. Situated along Hwy 49, the area warrants a two-day detour. For something adventurous, try a white-water trip down the American River; its three forks are inviting for beginners and experts alike.

In the summer when temperatures soar, rafting trips explore the icy currents of the American, Tuolumne, Kings and Stanislaus Rivers. **All-Outdoors California Whitewater Rafting** (800-247-2387; www.aorafting.com) is the favorite; the family-run outfitter does single- and two-day wilderness adventures. **Wolf Creek Wilderness** (530-477-2722; www.wolfcreekwilderness.com; 595 E Main St, Grass Valley; kayaks per day from $40) has kayak rentals and lessons ($40 to $150).

Outside of Auburn off I-80, at exit 121, the **California Welcome Center** (530-887-2111; www.visitplacer.com; 13411 Lincoln Way; 9:30am-4:30pm Mon-Fri, 9am-3pm Sat, 11am-3pm Sun) has statewide information. The **Gold Country Visitors Association** (800-225-3764; www.calgold.org) has detailed local information.

Northern Mines

Highway 50 divides the Southern and Northern Mines; the latter stretch south from Nevada City to Placerville. Winding Hwy 49, which connects it all, has plenty of pull-outs and vistas of the surrounding hills. If it's sweltering and you see a line of cars parked roadside, it's likely a swimming hole. Don't ask questions; just park, strip and jump. One of the best is where North and South Forks of the American River join up, 3 miles south of Auburn on Hwy 49.

Nevada City was known as the 'Queen City of the Northern Mines' and her streets still gleam with lovingly restored buildings, an arty folk scene, organic cafés and boutiques. The **chamber of commerce** (530-265-2692, 800-655-6569; www.nevadacitychamber.com; 132 Main St; 9am-5pm Mon-Fri, 11am-4pm Sat, 11am-3pm most Sundays) has self-guided walking tours and tons of information. The **Tahoe National Forest Headquarters** (530-265-4531; 8am-4:30pm Mon-Fri, plus Sat in summer), on Hwy 49 at the north end of Coyote St, has hiking and backcountry info, including details about area mountain biking trails.

About 5 miles southwest, **Grass Valley** is Nevada City's functional sister, where artists, hippies and ranchers get their oil changed. Two miles east of town, the landscaped **Empire Mine State Historic Park** (530-273-8522; www.empiremine.org; adult/child 6-16yr $5/3; 9am-6pm summer, 10am-5pm winter) marks the site of one of the richest mines in the state; from 1850 to 1956 it produced 5.8 million ounces of gold – about $5 billion in today's market. In summer, living-history weekends are popular; an underground tour is due to open in 2010.

Coloma is where the gold rush started, and the **Marshall Gold Discovery State Historic Park** (☎ 530-622-3470; per car $8; 🕑 8am-dusk) makes an eerily quiet tribute to the riotous discovery, with a replica of Sutter's Mill, restored buildings and short hikes. There's a statue of Sutter himself, who, in one of the many ironic twists of the gold rush, died a ward of the state.

SLEEPING & EATING

The following sleeping and eating options are listed north to south. Cafés, ice-cream parlors and upscale eateries are in nearly every sizable town along Hwy 49.

In Nevada City, there's an abundance of budget sleeping options, but the best is just outside of town. **Northern Queen Inn** (☎ 530-265-5824; www.northernqueeninn.com; 400 Railroad Ave; r $99-154;) is an 86-room motel with separate cottages with kitchens. The most fun is **Outside Inn** (☎ 530-265-2233; www.outsideinn.com; 575 E Broad St; r $75-150;), which has themed rooms and is run by exceedingly friendly outdoor enthusiasts.

More upscale than the many cute cafés at which folkies gather is **New Moon Café** (☎ 530-265-6399; www.thenewmooncafe.com; 230 York St; mains $13-28; 🕑 11am-9pm Tue-Sun). It has a regularly changing, French-Asian menu with an organic, local bent.

In Grass Valley, the register of the 1852 **Holbrooke Hotel** (☎ 530-273-1252, 800-933-7077; www.holbrooke.com; 212 W Main St; r midweek/weekend from $90/105;) boast Ulysses Grant and Mark Twain. Elegant Victorian rooms have claw-foot tubs. A recommended restaurant is on-site.

If you're cruising this part of the state without time to explore, the best pit stop is off I-80 at exit 121. There, **Ikedas** (☎ 530-885-4243; www.ikedas.com; 13500 Lincoln Way; 🕑 8am-7pm, to 8pm weekends) feeds Tahoe-bound travelers amazing burgers, homemade pies and snacks, including a deliriously good, seasonal fresh peach shake.

Southern Mines

The towns of the Southern Mines – from Placerville to Sonora – receive less traffic and the dusty streets still have a whiff of Wild West, which is evident in the motley assortment of Harley cruisers, weed farmers, vineyard owners and gold prospectors (still!) who populate them. Some, like **Plymouth** (Ole Pokerville) and **Mokelumne Hill** (Moke Hill), are virtual ghost towns, slowly crumbling into photogenic oblivion. Others, like **Jackson**, **Murphys** and **Sutter Creek**, are frilly slices of historical Americana. Get off the beaten path for family-run vineyards (especially around Plymouth in Amador County, a region that invented Zinfandel) and underground caverns, where geological wonders reward those willing to navigate the touristy gift shops above.

To get perspective on the region's history, take Hwy 88 north toward Pine Grove to the **Indian Grinding Rock State Historic Park** (☎ 206-296-7488; 14881 Pine Grove-Volcano Rd, per car $8, campsites $25; 🕑 sunrise-susnet), which is sacred ground for the local Miwok Indians. The magnificent 'grinding rock' is covered with ancient petroglyphs and mortar holes called *chaw'Ses*. Camping in reconstructed bark houses, called *U'macha'tam'ma*', provides a more tactile Miwok experience than any museum could.

Columbia (☎ 209-536-1672; www.columbiacalifornia.com;) is one of Gold Country's best historic sites, with four square blocks of authentic 1850s buildings and concessionaires in period costumes right in the middle of town. It's crazy with kids panning for gold. The park itself doesn't close, but most businesses are open from 10am to 5pm.

SLEEPING & EATING

Sleeping and eating listings that follow are ordered north to south. This area's best value is in the national forests, where camping is free. Lacy B&Bs are in nearly every town and usually priced over $100 per night.

our pick **Taste** (☎ 209-245-3463; www.restauranttaste.com; 9402 Main St, Plymouth; mains $31-50; 🕑 5pm-10pm Thu-Mon) is where the region's best food is at, with artfully constructed fresh, seasonal dishes that are well paired with bold Zinfandels from the surrounding hills of Amador County. It was recently named among the top 50 restaurants in the nation.

our pick **St George Hotel** (☎ 209-296-4458; www.stgeorgehotel.com; 16104 Main St, Volcano; r incl breakfast $98-127;) was built in 1862. The attractive rooms in the grand main hotel share baths, while six bungalows have private baths. In the adjoining bar, brave travelers brace themselves before sipping the historic local tipple, 'Moosemilk.'

Murphys Historic Hotel & Lodge (☎ 209-728-3444, 800-532-7684; www.murphyshotel.com; 457 Main St, Murphys; r midweek $89-109, add $20 weekends;) is a trip back in time with shared baths, no phones or TVs, and a creaky saloon. Can't live without TV? Book the adjacent motel.

In Columbia, the co-run **City Hotel & Fallon Hotel** (☎ 209-532-1479, 800-532-1479; www.cityhotel.com; Fallon Hotel r incl breakfast from $80-145, City Hotel r incl breakfast $115-145) have 24 stunning, museum-worthy rooms. The City Hotel has an acclaimed **restaurant** (meals $14-30; 5-9:30pm Tue-Sun, plus 9am-2pm Sun), and Fallon Hotel hosts a repertory theater. Ask about packages.

Busy Sonora is a bit drab, but it's just over an hour from Yosemite National Park (see p1006) and has serviceable midrange hotels. The best is just off Main St: **Gunn House Hotel** (☎ 209-532-3421; www.gunnhousehotel.com; 286 S Washington St; r $69-109; P) has historic rooms that are a work of love. The poolside breakfast room is the place to fuel up before the drive to Yosemite.

GETTING THERE & AROUND

About 26 miles northeast of Sacramento, Hwy 49 intersects I-80 in the town of Auburn. Local bus systems include **Gold Country Stage** (☎ 530-477-0103), which links Nevada City, Grass Valley and Auburn (fare $1.50 to $3), and **Placer County Transit** (☎ 530-885-2877). No public transit serves the Southern Mines on Hwy 49.

NORTHERN MOUNTAINS

Remote and eerily beautiful, the Northern Mountains are some of California's least-visited turf; it's an endless show of geological wonders, alpine lakes, rivers and desert. The major peaks – Lassen, Shasta, Lava Beds National Monument and the Trinity Alps – have little geological features in common, but all offer isolated backcountry camping under sparkling night skies. The towns dotted along the region's routes aren't attractions, but they make good places to gas up for the launch into the wild.

Redding to Yreka

Much of the drive north of Redding is dominated by **Mt Shasta**, a 14,162ft snow-capped monster that rises out of the Central Valley as dramatically as the anticipation felt by outdoor enthusiasts who seek adventure along its slopes. An extremely helpful pit stop just off I-5 is the **Shasta-Cascade Wonderland Association** (☎ 530-365-1180, 800-474-2782; www.shastacascade.com; 9am-10pm Mon-Fri, 9am-4pm Sat & Sun). It's 10 miles south of Redding in the Shasta Factory Outlets Mall.

Despite what their brochures may say, **Redding** itself is a snooze. The best reason to stop is the **Sundial Bridge**, a glass-deck pedestrian marvel designed by world-class architect Santiago Calatrava. It leads over the Sacramento River and to the **Turtle Bay Exploration Park** (☎ 800-887-8532; www.turtlebay.org; 840 Auditorium Dr; adult/child 4-12yr $13/9; 9am-5pm; closed Tue in winter;), a kid-friendly science center.

Eight miles west of Redding on Hwy 299 (the Trinity Scenic Byway) is the **Whiskeytown National Recreation Area**, home of **Whiskeytown Lake**, a vast reservoir with hiking, camping and several sandy beaches. The **visitor center** (☎ 530-246-1225; 9am-6pm summer, 10am-4:30pm winter) has maps, permits and information. **Weaverville**, another 35 miles west, is the launching point for mountains, and a lovely detour from Redding. The **Weaverville Ranger Station** (☎ 530-623-2121; 210 N Main St; 8am-5pm Mon-Fri, to 4:30pm Sat) issues backcountry permits to surrounding **Trinity Alps**, some of the most pristine wilderness in California.

North of Redding, I-5 crosses deep-blue **Shasta Lake**, California's biggest reservoir, which is surrounded by hiking trails and paved RV parks. High in the limestone megaliths at the north end of the lake are the prehistoric caves of **Lake Shasta Caverns** (☎ 530-238-2341, 800-795-2283; www.lakeshastacaverns.com; adult/child 3-11yr $22/12; tours 9am-3pm). Tours come with a pontoon ride.

Teensy **Dunsmuir**, a historic railroad town, is rustic like its neighbors, but distinguishes itself with a healthy scene for culture and cuisine. If for no other reason, stop to fill your water bottle from the public fountains; Dunsmuir claims it's got the best H_20 on earth.

Gorgeous **Mt Shasta town** lures climbers, burnouts and back-to-nature types, all of whom revere the majestic mountain that looms overhead with varying degrees of mystical and physical engagement. **Mt Shasta visitor center** (☎ 530-926-4865, 800-926-4865; www.mtshastachamber.com; 300 Pine St; 9am-5:30pm Mon-Thu, to 6pm Fri & Sat, to 4pm Sun) is a useful info hub.

Everitt Memorial Hwy climbs the mountain to 7900ft; to access it, simply head east from town on Lake St and keep going. Ask the rangers' advice to find a hiking trail that's a good match for the season and your ability. Ten-thousand-foot-plus climbs require a $20 Summit Pass from the **Mt Shasta Ranger Station** (☎ 530-926-4511; 204 W Alma St; 8am-4:30pm Mon-Sat).

Campers note: even in summer, temperatures on the mountain drop below freezing. Ski or board its south slope, off Hwy 89, at **Mt Shasta Board & Ski Park** (☎ 530-926-8610, 800-754-7427; www.skipark.com); take a mountain bike or chairlift ride in summer.

SLEEPING & EATING

Sleeping and eating listings are ordered south to north. The best option in this part of the state is to camp. Midcentury motels are abundant in all but the remote northeast.

Clustered near major thoroughfares, lodgings in Redding can be noisy. Situated north of downtown on N Main are a few clean, quiet motels; chain options lie along the freeway.

To get out in the wilderness, rent gear in Redding at **Hermit's Hut** (☎ 888-507-4455; www.hermitshut.com; 3184 Bechelli Ln; 2-person tents $20, backpacks per day $9).

The most memorable indoor stay is in a wood-paneled caboose at the **Railroad Park Resort** (☎ 530-235-4440, 800-974-7245; www.rrpark.com; d from $115;), off I-5 just south of Dunsmuir.

Among Dunsmuir's gourmet eateries is Thai restaurant **Sengthongs** (☎ 530-235-4770; www.sengthongs.com; 5855 Dunsmuir Ave; mains $15-22; 5-9pm Thu-Mon). It also hosts live music in an adjoining room.

Even though it's tiny, McCloud has loads of B&Bs, most of which are charming. The intensely scenic three-hour **Shasta Sunset Dinner Train** (☎ 800-733-2141; www.shastasunset.com; set-price menu $89, tax & drinks extra; 6pm) departs on weekends.

If you want to carb-up before heading up Shasta or stuff your face after a week of granola, head for **Mike and Tony's** (☎ 530-926-4792; www.mikeandtonys.net; 501 S Mount Shasta Blvd; dinner mains $16-24; 5pm-9pm Thu-Mon, to 10pm Fri & Sat) in Mount Shasta town.

Comfy motels line Yreka's Main St, including the **Klamath Motor Lodge** (☎ 530-842-2751, 800-551-7255; 1111 S Main St; d $64;). Ask for the crunchy crust at popular **Brickhouse Bakery & Pizzeria** (☎ 530-841-0553; 313 W Miner St; dinner mains from $8; 6:30am-9pm).

GETTING THERE & AROUND

Amtrak trains (☎ 800-872-7245; www.amtrak.com) service Redding and Dunsmuir; **Greyhound buses** (☎ 800-231-2222; www.greyhound.com) serve Redding and Yreka. **Stage buses** (☎ 530-842-8295, 800-2478243) cover Siskiyou County from Dunsmuir to Yreka, weekdays only. By car, San Francisco to Redding is 215 miles (four hours). For updated road conditions call **Siskiyou County** (☎ 530-842-4438).

Northeast Corner

Site of one of the last major Indian wars and a half-million years of volcanic destruction, **Lava Beds National Monument** is a quiet monument to centuries of turmoil. This park's got it all: lava flows, craters, cinder and spatter cones, and more than 500 lava tubes. It was the site of the Modoc War, and Native Americans maintain a strong presence here today – their ancestors' petroglyphs adorn some cave walls. Info, maps and flashlights (for cave exploring) are available at the **visitor center** (☎ 530-667-8113; www.nps.gov/labe; 1 Indian Well; 8am-6pm May-Oct, to 5pm Nov-Sep). Coming from the north on Hwy 161, turn south on Hill Rd to the park's north entrance. Nearby is the park's only **campground** (campsite $10). The simple sites (no showers) are suitable for tents and small RVs. Free wilderness camping is available; ask at the visitor center.

Winged migrants find safe haven just north at **Klamath Basin National Wildlife Refuges**, a reserve consisting of six separate refuges. This is a prime stopover on the Pacific Flyway and an important wintering site for bald eagles. The **visitor center** (☎ 530-667-2231; http://klamathbasinrefuges.fws.gov; 4009 Hill Rd; 8am-4:30pm Mon-Fri, 10am-4pm Sat & Sun) is along the road to Lava Beds Monument on Hwy 161. Self-guided 10-mile auto tours (free) of the Lower Klamath and Tule Lake reserves provide excellent viewing.

Overall, this area has very few commercial services, though the friendly, tidy **Ellis Motel** (☎ 530-667-5242; r $50-55, with kitchen extra $5) is 1 mile north of Tulelake on Hwy 139. One of the most popular (and only) restaurants around is **Captain Jack's Stronghold** (☎ 530-664-5566; mains $8-14; 8am-8pm Tue-Sun), which is located 5 miles south of Tulelake on Hwy 139 and named for the nearby lava-rock fortress where the Modoc took their final stand.

Modoc National Forest blankets over 3000 sq miles of California's northeast corner. Camping here is free and no reservations are accepted, though you need a permit for a campfire. **Medicine Lake**, 14 miles south of Lava Beds Monument on Hwy 49, is a pristine, blue, gleaming crater lake surrounded by pine forest, hulking volcanic formations and cool, secluded campgrounds (also free).

Alturas, at the junction of Hwys 299 and 395, is the Modoc County seat, and mostly for local ranchers. The Modoc National

Forest **Supervisor's Headquarters** (☎ 530-233-5811; www.fs.fed.us/r5/modoc; 800 W 12th St; 8am-4:30pm Mon-Fri) provides hiking info and maps. The **Modoc National Wildlife Refuge** (☎ 530-233-3572; http://modoc.fws.gov; 7:30am-4pm Mon-Fri) is 3 miles southeast of Alturas. Just 24 miles east of Alturas, on the California–Nevada border, is the high desert of **Surprise Valley**, which is the gateway to the wild **Warner Mountains**.

The region's impressive **Lassen Volcanic National Park** (per car $10, campsites $16-18) is further south. Steaming hydrothermal sulfur pools and cauldrons, with names like 'Devil's Kitchen,' can be visited at some distance. At 10,457ft Lassen Peak is the world's largest plug-dome volcano. The park has two entrances with visitor centers: the smaller on Hwy 44 at Manzanita Lake, and a newly remodeled one off Hwy 89, where **park headquarters** (☎ 530-595-4444; www.nps.gov/lavo; 8am-4:30pm daily Jul-Sep, Mon-Fri Oct-Jun) is located. Hwy 89 through the park is open to cars from June to October (and to cross-country skiers in winter). All camping is first-come, first-served. Outside the park, lodges and cabins line Hwy 89 between Hat Creek and Old Station.

SIERRA NEVADA

The mighty Sierra Nevada – baptized the 'Range of Light' by naturalist John Muir – is California's backbone. This 400-mile phalanx of craggy peaks, chiseled and gouged by glaciers and erosion, both welcomes and challenges outdoors enthusiasts. Cradling three highland national parks (Yosemite, Sequoia and Kings Canyon), the Sierra is a magical wonderland of superlatives, embracing the contiguous USA's highest peak (Mt Whitney), North America's tallest waterfall and the world's biggest trees.

LAKE TAHOE

Shimmering in myriad blues and greens, Lake Tahoe is the nation's second-deepest lake. It straddles the California–Nevada state line. Driving around its spellbinding 72-mile scenic shoreline gives you quite a workout behind the wheel. The north shore is quiet and upscale; the west shore, rugged and old-timey; the east shore, undeveloped; and the south shore, busy and tacky with aging motels and flashy casinos. The horned peaks surrounding the lake are four-seasons playgrounds.

Tahoe gets packed in summer, on winter weekends and around holidays, when reservations are essential. The **Lake Tahoe Visitors Authority** (☎ 800-288-2463; www.bluelaketahoe.com) and **North Lake Tahoe Visitors Bureaus** (☎ 888-434-1262; www.gotahoenorth.com) can help with accommodations and vacation packages. Room rates tend to be lowest in South Lake Tahoe. There's camping in state parks and on USFS lands.

South Lake Tahoe & West Shore

With retro motels and eateries lining busy Hwy 50, South Lake Tahoe feels oddly suburban. Gambling at Stateline's casino hotels, just across the Nevada border, attracts thousands, as does the world-class ski resort of **Heavenly** (☎ 775-586-7000; www.skiheavenly.com; cnr Wildwood Ave & Saddle Rd;). In summer, a trip up the gondola (adult/child $30/20) guarantees fabulous views of the lake and **Desolation Wilderness** (www.fs.fed.us/r5/ltbmu/recreation/wilderness/desowild). This stark and beautiful landscape of raw granite peaks, glacier-carved valleys and alpine lakes is a favorite of hikers. Get maps, information and overnight wilderness permits at the **USFS Taylor Creek Visitor Center** (☎ 530-543-2674; Hwy 89; 8am-5:30pm late May-Sep, to 4:30pm Oct). It's 3 miles north of the 'Y' intersection of Hwys 50 and 89, at **Tallac Historic Site** (☎ 530-541-5227; admission by donation; 10am-4:30pm mid-Jun–mid-Sep, Fri & Sat only mid-May–mid-Jun), which preserves early 20th-century vacation estates. **Lake Tahoe Cruises** (☎ 530-543-6191; www.zephyrcove.com; 2hr narrated tour adult/child $39/15) ply the 'Big Blue' year-round. Back on shore, vegetarian-friendly **Sprouts** (☎ 530-541-6969; 3123 Harrison Ave/US 50; mains $6-9; 8am-9pm) is a delish natural-foods café.

Hwy 89 threads northwest along the thickly forested west shore to **Emerald Bay State Park** (☎ 530-541-6498; entry per car $8, campsites $35; late May-Sep), where granite cliffs and pine trees frame a fjordlike inlet, truly sparkling green. A steep 1-mile trail leads down to **Vikingsholm Castle** (tours adult/child $5/3; 10am-4pm). From this 1920s Scandinavian-style mansion, the 4.5-mile **Rubicon Trail** ribbons north along the lakeshore past an old lighthouse and small coves to **DL Bliss State Park** (☎ 530-525-7277; entry per car $8, walk-in tent sites $7, campsites $35-50), with its sandy beaches. North of Meeks Bay, **Tahoma Meadows B&B Cottages** (☎ 530-525-1553, 866-525-1533; www.tahomameadows.com; 6821 W Lake Blvd, Tahoma; d incl breakfast $125-199) rents darling country cabins.

North & East Shores

The north shore's commercial hub, **Tahoe City** is great for grabbing supplies and renting outdoor gear. It's also close to **Squaw Valley USA** (☎ 530-583-6985; www.squaw.com; off Hwy 89;), a megasized ski resort that hosted the 1960 Winter Olympics. Après-ski crowds gather for beer 'n' burgers at woodsy **Bridgetender** (☎ 530-583-3342; 65 W Lake Blvd; dishes $6-12; 11am-11pm, to midnight Thu-Sat) restaurant. Fuel up on French toast and eggs Benedict at down-home **Fire Sign Cafe** (☎ 530-583-0871; 1785 W Lake Blvd; dishes $6-12; 7am-3pm).

Little towns farther east are more fetching. In summer, swim or kayak at **Tahoe Vista** or **Kings Beach**. For a taste of old Tahoe, spend a night at **Rustic Cottages** (☎ 530-546-3523, 888-778-7842; www.rusticcottages.com; 7449 N Lake Blvd, Tahoe Vista; cabins incl breakfast $89-230;), whose 1940s-era cabins come with full kitchens and modern amenities. Kings Beach has filling eats, including old-world pastas at **Lanza's** (☎ 530-546-2434; 7739 N Lake Blvd; mains $12-25; 5-10pm).

Hwy 28 barrels east into Nevada at Crystal Bay. Try your luck at the casinos, including landmark **Cal Neva Resort** (☎ 775-832-4000; www.calnevaresort.com; 2 Stateline Rd), whose one-time owner Frank Sinatra entertained JFK, Marilyn Monroe and mobsters here in the early 1960s. Or catch a live-music show at **Crystal Bay Club Casino** (☎ 775-831-0512; 14 Hwy 28; tickets $10-50; schedule varies).

With pristine beaches, lakes and miles of multiuse trails, **Lake Tahoe-Nevada State Park** (☎ 775-831-0494; http://parks.nv.gov/lt.htm; entry per bicycle/car $2/8) is the east shore's biggest draw. Summer crowds splash in the turquoise waters of **Sand Harbor**. The 15-mile **Flume Trail**, a mountain biker's holy grail, starts further south at **Spooner Lake**. Conveniently, you can rent bikes ($45) and arrange shuttles ($13) at the trailhead.

Truckee & Donner Lake

North of the lake off I-80, Truckee is not in fact a truck stop but a thriving mountain town, with organic-coffee shops, trendy boutiques and dining in its historical downtown district. Inside the train depot, the **visitor center** (☎ 530-587-8808; www.truckee.com; 10065 Donner Pass Rd; 9am-6pm;) offers free wi-fi and pay-as-you-go internet terminals (per hour $12).

Ski bunnies have several resorts, including glam **Northstar-at-Tahoe** (☎ 530-562-1010; www.northstarattahoe.com; off Hwy 267, 6mi south of I-80;); **Sugar Bowl** (☎ 530-426-9000; www.sugarbowl.com; Hwy 40, off I-80 exit 174;), cofounded by Walt Disney; and **Royal Gorge** (☎ 800-666-3871; www.royalgorge.com; 9411 Hillside Dr, off I-80 exit 174;) cross-country ski resort.

Nearby Donner Summit (7239ft) is where the infamous Donner Party became trapped during the fierce winter of 1846–47. Led astray by an erroneous guidebook, less than half survived – by cannibalizing their dead friends. The grisly tale is chronicled at the **Emigrant Trail Museum** (adult/child $5/3; 9am-4pm) inside **Donner Memorial State Park** (☎ 530-582-7892; Donner Pass Rd, off I-80 exit 184; entry per car $8, walk-in tent sites $7, campsites $35; campground mid-May–mid-Sep), where **Donner Lake** is popular for swimming and windsurfing.

our pick Cedar House Sport Hotel (☎ 530-582-5655, 866-852-5655; www.cedarhousesporthotel.com; 10918 Brockway Rd; r incl breakfast $170-200;) is ecoconscious and green building-certified, and has stylishly modern boutique rooms as well as an outdoor hot tub. For DJs, live jazz and a killer wine list, sophisticated bistro-lounge **Moody's** (☎ 530-587-8688; 10007 Bridge St; dinner mains $20-38; 11:30am-9:30pm Sun-Thu, to 10pm Fri & Sat) sources locally ranched meats and seasonal produce. Down pints of 'Donner Party Porter' at **Fifty Fifty Brewing Co** (☎ 530-587-2337; 11197 Brockway Rd) across the tracks.

Getting There & Around

Major airlines serve **Reno-Tahoe International Airport** (p835). **South Tahoe Express** (☎ 866-898-2463; www.southtahoeexpress.com) runs frequent airport shuttles to Stateline ($26, two hours). **North Lake Tahoe Express** (☎ 866-216-5222; www.northlaketahoeexpress.com) connects the airport with Truckee, Squaw Valley and north-shore towns ($40).

From Truckee's **Amtrak depot** (10065 Donner Pass Rd), which has daily trains to Sacramento ($39, 4½ hours) and Reno ($17, 1½ hours), Greyhound has twice-daily buses to Reno ($20, one hour), Sacramento ($42, 2½ hours) and San Francisco ($46, six hours). Amtrak's Thruway buses connect Sacramento with South Lake Tahoe ($34, 2½ hours).

Tahoe Area Rapid Transit (TART; ☎ 530-581-3922; www.laketahoetransit.com; single-ride/day pass $1.75/3.50) runs local buses to Truckee and around the north and west shores. South Lake Tahoe is served by **BlueGO** (☎ 530-541-7149; www.bluego.org; single-ride/day pass $2/6), which operates a summer-only trolley up the west shore to Tahoma, connecting with TART.

Hwy 89 (Emerald Bay Rd) may partly close in winter, when tire chains are often required on I-80 and US 50.

YOSEMITE NATIONAL PARK

There's a reason why everybody's heard of it: the granite-peak heights are dizzying, the mist from thunderous waterfalls drenching, the Technicolor wildflower meadows amazing, and the majestic, hulking silhouettes of El Capitan and Half Dome almost shocking against a crisp blue sky. It's a landscape of dreams, relentlessly surrounding us oh-so-small people on all sides. Then, alas, the hiss and belch of another tour bus, disgorging dozens, rudely breaks the spell. While staggering crowds can't be ignored, these rules will shake most of 'em:

- Avoid summer. Spring's best, especially when waterfalls gush in May. Autumn is blissfully peaceful, and snowy winter days can be magical too.
- Park your car and leave it – simply by hiking a short distance up almost any trail, you'll lose the car-dependent majority of visitors.
- To hell with jet lag. Get up early, or go for moonlit hikes and do unforgettable stargazing.

SCENIC DRIVES IN THE SIERRA NEVADA

- Lake Tahoe Eastshore Dr (Hwy 28 & US 50; p1005) – coast beside the 'Big Blue'
- Tioga Rd (Hwy 120; p1008) – Yosemite's rooftop of the world
- Generals Hwy (Hwy 198; p1010) – historic byway past giant sequoias
- Kings Canyon Scenic Byway (Hwy 180; p1010) – dive into North America's deepest canyon
- Eastern Sierra Scenic Byway (US 395; p1012) – where snowy mountains overshadow the desert

Orientation & Information

Yosemite's entrance fee ($20 per car, $10 on bicycle, motorcycle or foot) is valid for seven days and includes a free map and helpful newspaper guide. The primary entrances are: Arch Rock (Hwy 140), South Entrance (Hwy 41), Big Oak Flat (Hwy 120 west) and Tioga Pass (Hwy 120 east). Open seasonally, Hwy 120 traverses the park as Tioga Rd (see boxed text, p1011), connecting Yosemite Valley with Hwy 395 in the Eastern Sierra Nevada (p1012).

Overrun, traffic-choked Yosemite Village is home to the park's main visitor center, museum, general store and many other services. Curry Village is another Yosemite Valley hub, offering showers, self-service laundry and outdoor equipment rental and sales, including for camping. Along scenic Tioga Rd, Tuolumne (pronounced *twol*-uh-mee) Meadows draws hikers, backpackers and climbers to the park's northern region. Wawona, near the southern entrance, has a pioneer-history village, golf course and giant sequoias.

Yosemite Village, Curry Village and Wawona stores all have ATMs. Fill up the tank before entering the park, or buy high-priced gas at Wawona or Crane Flat year-round or at Tuolumne Meadows in summer.

Peak summer hours are listed below for the following:

Post office (☎ 209-372-4475; 9017 Village Dr, Yosemite Village; 🕑 8:30-5pm Mon-Fri, 10am-noon Sat)

Public library (☎ 209-372-4552; www.mariposalibrary.org; Girls Club Bldg, 58 Cedar Ct, Yosemite Valley; 🕑 8:30am-11:30am Mon, 10am-2pm Tue, 8:30am-12:30pm Wed, 4-7pm Thu; 💻) Two free internet terminals.

Yosemite Lodge at the Falls (☎ 209-372-1274; Northside Dr, Yosemite Valley; per 10min $1; 💻) Self-service internet kiosks.

Yosemite Medical Clinic (☎ 209-372-4637; Ahwahnee Dr, Yosemite Valley; 🕑 8am-7pm, emergencies 24hr) Also runs a dental clinic.

Yosemite Valley Visitor Center (☎ 209-372-0200; www.nps.gov/yose; Yosemite Village; 🕑 9am-7:30pm) Smaller visitor centers at Wawona, Tuolumne Meadows and Big Oak Flat are open seasonally.

Valley Wilderness Center (☎ 209-372-0740; Yosemite Village; 🕑 7:30am-5pm) Backcountry permits and bear-canister rentals also available seasonally at Wawona, Tuolumne Meadows and Big Oak Flat.

Sights

YOSEMITE VALLEY

From the ground up, this dramatic valley cut by the meandering Merced River is song-inspiring: rippling green meadow-grass; stately pines; cool, impassive pools reflecting looming granite monoliths and cascading, glacier-cold whitewater ribbons.

You can't ignore monumental **El Capitan** (7569ft), an El Dorado for rock climbers, while toothed **Half Dome** (8842ft) is Yosemite's spiritual centerpiece. The classic photo-op is up Hwy 41 at **Tunnel View**. Sweat it out and you'll get better views – sans crowds – from the **Inspiration Point Trail** (2.6 miles round-trip), starting near the tunnel. Early or late in the day, head up the 2-mile round-trip trail to **Mirror Lake** to catch the ever-shifting reflection of Half Dome in the still waters, full only in spring and early summer.

Spring snowmelt turns the valley's famous waterfalls into thunderous cataracts; most are reduced to a mere trickle by late summer. **Yosemite Falls** is North America's tallest, dropping 2425ft in three tiers. A wheelchair-accessible trail leads to the bottom of this cascade or, for solitude and different perspectives, you can trek the grueling trail to the top (7.2 miles round-trip). No less impressive are nearby **Bridalveil Fall** and other waterfalls scattered throughout the valley. A strenuous staircase climb (see p1008) beside **Vernal Fall** leads you, gasping, right to the top edge of the falls for a vertical view – look for rainbows in the clouds of mist.

GLACIER POINT & WAWONA

Rising 3200ft above the valley floor, dramatic **Glacier Point** (7214ft) practically puts you at eye level with Half Dome. It's about an hour's drive from Yosemite Valley up Glacier Point Rd (usually open late May to mid-November) off Hwy 41, or a strenuous hike along the **Four-Mile Trail** (actually, 4.8 miles one way) or the less-crowded, waterfall-strewn **Panorama Trail** (8.5 miles one way). To avoid backtracking, reserve a seat on the hikers' shuttle bus (p1009).

At Wawona, a 45-minute drive south of Yosemite Valley, drop by the **Pioneer Yosemite**

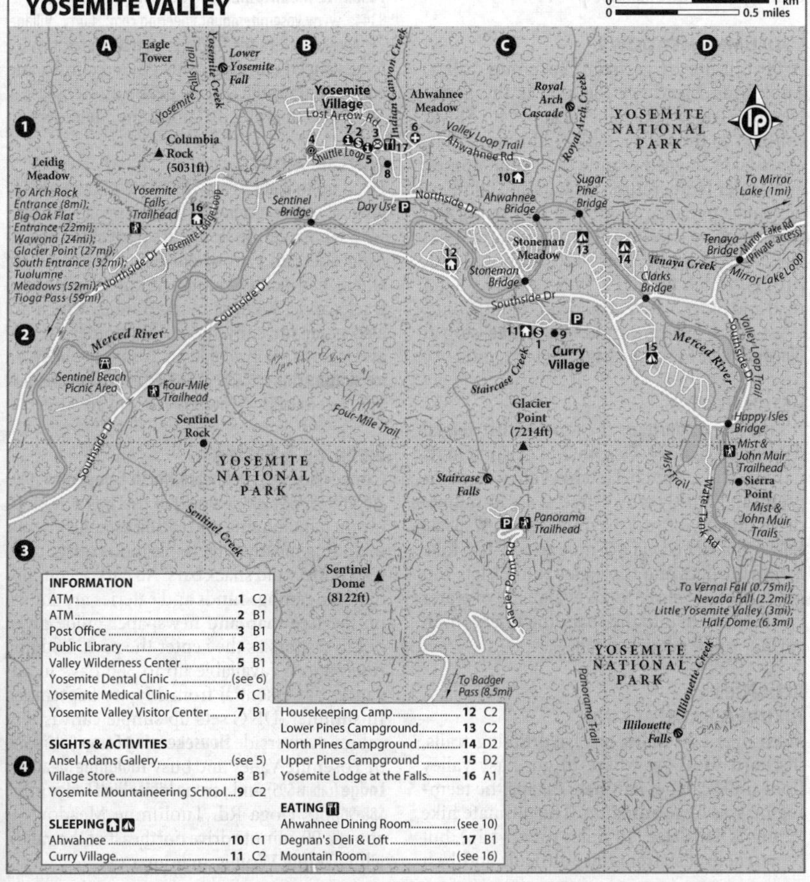

DARKROOM SHOW

Few know about it, but *original* Ansel Adams photographic prints are shown at Yosemite Valley's **Ansel Adams Gallery** (☎ 209-372-4413; www.anseladams.com; Yosemite Village; ⏲ 9am-5pm, later in summer). The curator-led 'Fine Print' tour is limited to five people; call in advance to reserve a spot. For budding photographers, free guided 'Camera Walks' are offered at 8:30am thrice weekly in summer; space is limited to 15 people.

History Center, with its covered bridge, pioneer cabins and historic Wells Fargo office. Farther south, wander giddily in the **Mariposa Grove**, home of the 1800-year-old Grizzly Giant and other giant sequoias (see p1012).

TUOLUMNE MEADOWS

A 90-minute drive from Yosemite Valley, Tuolumne Meadows (8600ft) is the Sierra Nevada's largest subalpine meadow. It's a vivid contrast to the valley, with wildflower fields, azure lakes, ragged granite peaks and domes, and cooler temperatures. Hikers and climbers will find a paradise of options; swimming and picnicking by lakes are also popular. Access is via scenic Tioga Rd (Hwy 120; see boxed text, p1011), which follows a 19th-century wagon road and older Native American trading route. West of the meadows and **Tenaya Lake**, stop at **Olmsted Point** for epic vistas of Half Dome.

HETCH HETCHY

It's the site of perhaps the most controversial dam in US history. Despite not existing in its natural state, Hetch Hetchy Valley remains pretty and mostly crowd-free. It's a 40-minute drive northwest of Yosemite Valley. **Wapama Falls**, approached via a 5-mile round-trip hike across the dam and through a tunnel, lets you get thrillingly close to an avalanche of water crashing down into the sparkling reservoir. In spring, you'll get drenched.

Activities

HIKING & BACKPACKING

With over 800 miles of varied hiking trails, it's hard to know where to go. Easy valley floor trails can get jammed; escape the teeming masses by heading up. The ultimate hike summits **Half Dome** (14 miles round-trip), but be warned: it's strenuous, difficult and best tackled in two days. It's rewarding to hike just as far as the top of **Vernal Fall** (3 miles round-trip) or **Nevada Fall** (5.8 miles round-trip) via the **Mist Trail**. A longer, alternate route to Half Dome follows a more gently graded section of the long-distance **John Muir Trail**.

Wilderness permits are required year-round for overnight trips. A quota system limits the number of people leaving from each trailhead. Make **reservations** (☎ 209-372-0740; www.nps.gov/yose/planyourvisit/wildpermits.htm; permit fee $5, plus $5 per person) up to 24 weeks before your trip, or try your luck grabbing a permit at a wilderness center on the day before or morning of your hike.

ROCK CLIMBING

With sheer spires, polished domes and soaring monoliths, Yosemite is rock-climbing nirvana. **Yosemite Mountaineering School** (YMS; ☎ 209-372-8344; www.yosemitemountaineering.com; Curry Village; ⏲ Apr-Oct) offers topflight instruction for novice to advanced climbers, plus guided climbs and equipment rental. During peak summer season, YMS also operates at Tuolumne Meadows.

WINTER SPORTS

Head up to **Badger Pass** (☎ 209-372-8430; www.badgerpass.com; ⏲ 9am-4pm mid-Dec–late Mar, weather permitting; 🚼), whose gentle slopes are perfect for beginning skiers and snowboarders. Cross-country skiers can schuss along 40km of groomed tracks and 150km of marked trails, which are also great for snowshoers. Equipment rental and lessons are available. In Yosemite Valley, an **ice-skating rink** (☎ 209-372-8319; Curry Village; adult/child $8/6, skate rental $3; ⏲ hours vary) opens in winter.

Sleeping & Eating

Concessionaire **Delaware North Companies** (DNC; ☎ 801-559-4884; www.yosemitepark.com) has a monopoly on park lodging and eating establishments, including mostly forgettable food courts, cafeteria buffets and snack bars. All park accommodations, campgrounds and eateries are shown on the free map and newspaper guide given out to visitors as they enter the park. Lodging reservations (available up to 366 days in advance) are essential from May to September. In summer, DNC sets up simple canvas-tent cabins at riverside **Housekeeping Camp** (cabins $73) in Yosemite Valley and busy **Tuolumne Meadows Lodge** (cabins $95) and serene **White Wolf Lodge** (cabins $88-96) off Tioga Rd. Tuolumne Meadows is about a 90-minute drive northeast of the valley, while White Wolf is an hour away.

Curry Village (Yosemite Valley; tent cabins $95-97, cabins without/with bath $102/140, cottage r $179; Apr–mid-Oct;) With a nostalgic summer-camp atmosphere, Curry Village has hundreds of helter-skelter units scattered beneath towering evergreens. Tent cabins resemble Civil War army barracks with scratchy wool blankets; wooden cabins are smaller but cozy.

Yosemite Lodge at the Falls (Northside Rd, Yosemite Valley; r $179-207;) Spacious motel-style rooms have patios or balconies overlooking Yosemite Falls, meadows or the parking lot. Fork into grass-fed steaks, river trout and organic veggies at the lodge's Mountain Room (dinner mains $16 to $30), open nightly (no reservations). The casual lounge offers the same menu and has a convivial open-pit fireplace.

Wawona Hotel (Wawona Rd, Wawona; r without/with bath incl breakfast buffet $145/217;) Filled with ghosts and character, this Victorian-era throwback has wide porches, manicured lawns and a golf course. Half the thin-walled rooms share baths and need some paint and attention. The romantic dining room with vintage details serves three gourmet Western meals a day (dinner mains $17 to $33). Wawona is about a 45-minute drive south of the valley.

Ahwahnee (Ahwahnee Dr, Yosemite Valley; r from $488;) Sleep where Charlie Chaplin, Eleanor Roosevelt and JFK bedded down at this national historic landmark, built in 1927. Browse the artisan gift shop, and then sit a spell by the roaring fireplace beneath soaring sugar-pine timbers. Skip the formal dining room, serving only mediocre Californian fare (dinner mains $30 to $50), for the lobby bar with its signature inspired cocktails.

Degnan's Deli & Loft (Yosemite Village; mains $6-21; deli 7am-5pm year-round, restaurant 4-9pm Mon-Fri, noon-9pm Sat & Sun Apr-Oct;) Grab a custom-made deli sandwich and bag of chips downstairs before hitting the trail. After dark, head upstairs for pool tables, cold brewskies and crispy pizzas.

CAMPING

All campgrounds have bearproof lockers and campfire rings; most have potable water.

In summer, most campgrounds are noisy and booked to bulging, especially **North Pines** (campsites $20; mid-Mar–Nov), **Lower Pines** (campsites $20; Mar-Oct) and **Upper Pines** (campsites $20; year-round) in Yosemite Valley and **Tuolumne Meadows** (campsites $20; Jul-late Sep) off Tioga Rd, a 90-minute drive northeast of the valley. In summer, some campgrounds require **reservations** (518-885-3639, 877-444-6777; www.recreation.gov), which are available up to five months in advance.

Camp 4 (shared tent sites per person $5; year-round), a rock climber's hangout in the valley, and **Bridalveil Creek** (campsites $14; Jul-early Sep), a 45-minute drive south of the valley off Glacier Point Rd, are first-come, first-served and often full by noon, especially on weekends. Looking for a quieter, more rugged experience? Try smaller spots like **Tamarack Flat** (campsites $10; late Jun-Sep), **Yosemite Creek** (tent sites $10; Jul-early Sep) and **Porcupine Flat** (campsites $10; Jul–mid-Oct) off Tioga Rd, 45 minutes to 1¼ hours' drive northeast of the valley.

OUTSIDE YOSEMITE NATIONAL PARK

Gateway towns with sometimes better-value lodgings include Fish Camp, Oakhurst, El Portal, Midpines, Mariposa, Groveland and Lee Vining.

Yosemite Bug (209-966-6666, 866-826-7108; www.yosemitebug.com; 6979 Hwy 140, Midpines; dm $22-25, tent cabins $35-55, r $75-155, cabins with shared bath $65-85;) Tucked into a forest about 25 miles west of Yosemite Valley, this rustic mountain hostelry hosts globetrotters who dig the clean rooms, yoga studio and spa, swimming hole, shared kitchen access and laundry. The café's fresh, organic and vegetarian-friendly meals (mains $5 to $15) get raves.

our pick **Evergreen Lodge** (209-379-2606, 800-935-6343; www.evergreenlodge.com; 33160 Evergreen Rd, Groveland; tents $50-90, cabins $145-299;) Near the entrance to Hetch Hetchy, this welcoming resort lets roughing-it guests cheat with comfy, prefurnished tents and deluxe mountain cabins. Outdoor recreational activities abound, with equipment rentals available. There's a tavern, general store, bar with pool tables and restaurant (dinner mains $18 to $30) serving three hearty meals every day.

Narrow Gauge Inn (559-683-7720, 888-644-9050; www.narrowgaugeinn.com; 48571 Hwy 41, Fish Camp; r incl breakfast $120-195; restaurant 5:30-9pm Wed-Sun mid-Apr–mid-Oct;) Swiss chalet–esque, this small inn has 26 comfy rooms, each with balcony or patio, and the Yosemite Mountain Sugar Pine steam railway next door. The 'buffalo bar' is authentic, and elk, venison and rib-eye appear on the Euro-Cal menu. It's 4 miles south of the park.

Getting There & Around

The nearest Greyhound and Amtrak stations are in Merced. **Yarts** (209-388-9589, 877-989-2787;

www.yarts.com) buses travel from Merced to the park along Hwy 140, stopping at towns along the way. In summer, Yarts buses run from Mammoth Lakes (p1012) along Hwy 120 via Tioga Pass. One-way tickets including the park-entry fee cost $25 from Merced, $30 from Mammoth Lakes.

Free shuttle buses loop around Yosemite Valley and, in summer, the Tuolumne Meadows and Wawona areas. DNC runs hikers' buses from the valley to Tuolumne Meadows ($14.50/$23) or Glacier Point (one way/round-trip $25/41). Bike rentals (per hour/day $9.50/25.50) are available at Yosemite Lodge and Curry Village, both in the valley. In winter, valley roads are plowed and the highways to the parks are kept open (except Tioga Rd/Hwy 120) – although snow chains may be required – and a free twice-daily shuttle bus connects Yosemite Valley with Badger Pass.

SEQUOIA & KINGS CANYON NATIONAL PARKS

In these neighboring parks, the famous rust-red giant sequoia trees are bigger – up to 30 stories high! – and more numerous than anywhere else in the Sierra Nevada. Tough and fire-charred, they'd easily swallow two freeway lanes each. Giant, too, are the mountains – including Mt Whitney (14,505ft), the tallest peak in the lower 48 states. Finally, there is the giant Kings Canyon, carved out of granite by ancient glaciers and a powerful river. These are what lure the vast majority of 1.5 million annual visitors here; however, for quiet, solitude and close-up sightings of wildlife, including black bears, hit the trail to quickly lose yourself in the epic wilderness.

Orientation & Information

Sequoia was designated a national park in 1890; Kings Canyon, in 1940. Though distinct, the two parks operate as one unit with a single admission fee (valid for seven days) of $20 per car, $10 on motorcycle, bicycle or foot. For updates and general info, call ☎ 559-565-3341 or check the park website (www.nps.g ov/seki).

From the south, Hwy 198 enters Sequoia National Park beyond the town of Three Rivers at Ash Mountain, from where it ascends the zigzagging Generals Hwy. From the west, Hwy 180 leads to the Big Stump entrance near Grant Grove before plunging into Kings Canyon.

Lodgepole Village (☎ 559-565-4436), in Sequoia, and **Grant Grove Village** (☎ 559-565-4307), in Kings Canyon, are the main hubs. Both have year-round visitor centers, post offices, markets, ATMs and public showers (summer only). **Foothills Visitor Center** (☎ 559-565-3135) at Ash Mountain is open year-round. **Cedar Grove Visitor Center** (☎ 559-565-3793) and the **Mineral King Ranger Station** (☎ 559-565-3768) are open during summer. Check the free park newspaper for opening hours of visitor centers and other services.

Expensive gas is available at Hume Lake (year-round) and Stony Creek (summer only) outside park boundaries on national forest land.

Sights

SEQUOIA NATIONAL PARK

We dare you to try hugging the trees in **Giant Forest**, a 3-sq-mile grove protecting the park's most gargantuan specimens; the world's biggest is the **General Sherman Tree**. With sore arms and sticky sap fingers, lose the crowds by venturing onto any of the many forested trails (bring a map).

Two miles south is the kid-friendly **Giant Forest Museum** (☎ 559-565-4480; 9am-4:30pm, to 7pm in summer;). More hiking trails start there, including a wheelchair-accessible route. For 360-degree views of the Great Western Divide, climb the steep quarter-mile staircase up **Moro Rock**.

Discovered in 1918, **Crystal Cave** (☎ 559-565-3759; www.sequoiahistory.org; adult/child $11/6; open early May-late Oct, tour hours vary;) has marble formations estimated to be 10,000 years old. Tickets for the 45-minute basic tour are available at the Lodgepole and Foothills visitor centers, *not* at the cave. Bring a jacket as it's chilly.

Worth a detour is **Mineral King**, a late-19th-century mining and logging camp ringed by craggy peaks and alpine lakes. The 25-mile one-way scenic drive – navigating over 700 hair-raising hairpin turns – is usually open from late May to late October.

KINGS CANYON NATIONAL PARK

North of Grant Grove Village, **General Grant Grove** brims with majestic giants. Beyond here, Hwy 180 begins its 35-mile descent into **Kings Canyon**, serpentining past chiseled rock walls laced with spring waterfalls. Near **Boyden Cavern** (☎ 559-338-0959; 45min tour adult/child $13/6.50; May–mid-Nov;) the road meets the Kings River, its roar ricocheting off granite cliffs soaring over 4000ft high, making this one of North America's deepest canyons.

Cedar Grove Village is the last outpost of civilization before the rugged grandeur of the Sierra Nevada backcountry. A popular day hike climbs 4 miles one way to roaring **Mist Falls** from Roads End; continue alongside the river 2.5 more miles to **Paradise Valley**. A favorite of birders, an easy 1.5-mile nature trail loops around **Zumwalt Meadow**, just west of Roads End. Watch for rattlesnakes, black bear and mule deer.

Activities

Hiking is why people come here – with over 800 miles of marked trails to prove it. Cedar Grove and Mineral King offer the best backcountry access. Trails usually begin to open by mid-May, though there's hiking year-round in the Foothills area. Overnight backcountry trips require wilderness permits ($15), subject to a quota system in summer; for details, see www.nps.gov/seki/planyourvisit/wilderness.htm.

You can take a naturalist-led field trip with the **Sequoia Natural History Association** (SNHA; ☎ 559-565-3759; www.sequoiahistory.org). Horseback riding is offered at **Grant Grove Village** (☎ 559-335-9292) and the **Cedar Grove Pack Station** (☎ 559-565-3464). In summer, cool off by swimming at Hume Lake, on national forest land off Hwy 180, and at riverside swimming holes in both parks. In winter, you can cross-country ski or snowshoe among the snow-draped giant sequoias. Equipment rental is available at Grant Grove Village and Wuksachi Lodge; for the best cross-country skiing and other winter sports, visit old-fashioned Montecito Sequoia Lodge (right) off the Generals Hwy between the two parks.

Sleeping & Eating

Outside Sequoia's southern entrance, several independent and chain motels line Hwy 198 through unexciting Three Rivers town.

John Muir Lodge & Grant Grove Cabins (☎ 559-335-5500, 866-522-6966; www.sequoia-kingscanyon.com; Hwy 180, Grant Grove Village; d $62-188; wi-fi) Woodsy lodge has good-sized, if generic, rooms and a cozy lobby with a stone fireplace and board games. Oddly assorted cabin types range from thin-walled canvas tents to nicely furnished historical cottages with private bathrooms.

Cedar Grove Lodge (☎ 559-335-5500, 866-522-6966; www.sequoia-kingscanyon.com; Hwy 180, Cedar Grove Village; r $119-135; mid-May–mid-Oct; wi-fi) The 21 motel-style rooms with common porches overlooking Kings River are simple and well worn, but they're still your best option down the canyon.

Montecito Sequoia Lodge (☎ 559-565-3388, 800-227-9900; www.mslodge.com; 63410 Generals Hwy, btwn Sequoia & Kings Canyon National Parks; d incl meals $119-169; family-friendly) Basic, recently renovated rooms include all meals. Family-fun camps keep things raucous all summer long; in winter there's cross-country skiing lessons and 50 miles of groomed trails.

Wuksachi Lodge (☎ 559-565-4070, 866-807-3598; www.visitsequoia.com; 64670 Wuksachi Way, 4 miles north of Lodgepole Village; r $181-241; wi-fi) Don't be misled by the grand lobby – because oversized motel-style rooms are nothing to brag about. For an unforgettable wilderness adventure, the lodge's Bearpaw High Sierra Camp (tent cabin per person, including meals, $175) is open from mid-June to mid-September.

Camping **reservations** (☎ 518-885-3639, 877-444-6777; www.recreation.gov) are accepted only at Lodgepole and Dorst in Sequoia National Park. The parks' dozen other campgrounds are first-come, first-served. Most have flush toilets; sites cost $12 to $20. Lodgepole, Azalea, Potwisha and South Fork are open year-round. Overflow camping is available in the surrounding Sequoia National Forest.

The markets in Grant Grove, Lodgepole and Cedar Grove have limited, pricey groceries; the latter two have snack bars serving

IMPASSABLE TIOGA PASS

Hwy 120 is the only road connecting Yosemite National Park with the Eastern Sierra, climbing through Tioga Pass (9945ft). Most California maps mark this road 'closed in winter,' which, while literally true, is also misleading. Tioga Rd is usually closed from the first heavy snowfall in October or November until May or June. If you are planning a trip through Tioga Pass in spring, you'll likely be out of luck. The earliest date that the road through the pass is plowed is April 15, yet it has only opened in April once since 1980. In 1998, it didn't open until July 1! Call ☎ 209-372-0200 or check the website (www.nps.gov/yose/planyourvisit/conditions.htm) for current road and weather conditions.

burgers and basic meals for under $10. The Wuksachi Lodge's upscale **restaurant** (☎ 559-565-4070; dinner mains $18-33; 🕑 7-10am, 11am-2:30pm & 5-9:45pm) is hit-or-miss.

Getting There & Around

In summer, free shuttle buses cover the Giant Forest and Lodgepole Village areas of Sequoia National Park, while the **Sequoia Shuttle** (☎ 877-287-4453; www.sequoiashuttle.com) connects the park with Three Rivers and Visalia (round-trip fare $10 to $15), with onward connections to Amtrak (p1166); reservations are required. Currently, there is no public transportation into Kings Canyon National Park.

EASTERN SIERRA

Vast, empty and majestic, here jagged peaks plummet down into the Great Basin desert, a dramatic juxtaposition that creates a potent scenery cocktail. Hwy 395 runs the entire length of the Sierra Nevada range, with turnoffs leading to pine forests, wildflower-strewn meadows, placid lakes, simmering hot springs and glacier-gouged canyons. Hikers, backpackers, mountain bikers, fishers and skiers love to escape here. The main visitor hubs are Mammoth Lakes and Bishop.

At **Bodie State Historic Park** (☎ 760-647-6445; adult/child $5/3; 🕑 8am-6pm Jun-Aug, 8am-4pm Sep-May), a gold-rush ghost town is preserved in a state of 'arrested decay.' Weathered buildings sit frozen in time on a dusty, windswept plain. To get there, head east for 13 miles (the last three unpaved) on Hwy 270, about 7 miles south of Bridgeport. The access road is often closed in winter.

Further south, **Mono Lake** (www.monolake.org) is famous for its unearthly tufa towers, which rise from the alkaline water like drip sand castles. The best photo ops are from the south shore's **Mono Lake Tufa State Natural Reserve** (admission $3). Off Hwy 395, **Mono Basin Scenic Area Visitor Center** (☎ 760-647-3044; 🕑 8am-5pm Mon-Fri, 8am-7pm Sat & Sun Jun-Aug, shorter hours Sep-May) has excellent exhibits and schedules of guided walks and talks. From the nearby town of Lee Vining, Hwy 120 heads west into Yosemite National Park via the Tioga Pass (see boxed text, p1011).

Continuing south on Hwy 395, detour along the scenic 16-mile **June Lake Loop** or push on to **Mammoth Lakes**, a fast-growing four-seasons resort guarded by 11,053ft **Mammoth Mountain** (☎ 760-934-2571, 800-626-6684; www.mammothmountain.com; 1 Minaret Rd; ski-lift tickets adult/child $69/34; 🚸), a top-notch skiing area. The slopes morph into a mountain-bike park in summer, when there's also camping, fishing and day hiking in the Mammoth Lakes Basin and Reds Meadow areas. Nearby are the near-vertical, 60ft-high basalt columns of **Devil's Postpile National Monument**, formed by volcanic activity. Hot-springs fans can soak in the boiling-hot pools of the **Hot Creek Geological Site** (admission free; 🕑 sunrise-sunset), 3 miles south of town. The **Mammoth Lakes Welcome Center & Ranger Station** (☎ 760-924-5500, 888-466-2666; www.visitmammoth.com; Hwy 203; 🕑 8am-5pm Mon-Fri) has maps and information about all of these places.

Farther south, Hwy 395 descends into the Owens Valley, soon arriving in frontier-flavored **Bishop**, whose minor attractions include art galleries and an interesting railroad museum. Bishop provides access to the best fishing and rock climbing in the entire Eastern Sierra, and it's the main gateway for packhorse trips. Covered sidewalks and vintage neon signs line Bishop's busy main street.

To check out some of the earth's oldest living things, budget a half-day for the thrilling trip up to the **Ancient Bristlecone Pine Forest** (☎ 760-873-2500). These gnarled, otherworldly looking trees are found above 10,000ft on the slopes of the parched White Mountains, where you'd think nothing could grow. The oldest tree – called Methuselah – is estimated to be over 4700 years old. The road (usually open May to October) is paved to the top, where there are hikes of varying length, primitive camping and a visitor

SUPERSIZED FORESTS

In California you can stand under the world's oldest trees (ancient bristlecone pines, see right) and its tallest (coast redwoods, see p998), but the record for biggest in terms of volume belongs to the giant sequoias *(Sequoiadendron giganteum)*. They grow only on the western slope of the Sierra Nevada range and are most abundant in Sequoia, Kings Canyon and Yosemite National Parks. John Muir called them 'Nature's forest masterpiece,' and anyone who's ever craned their neck to take in their soaring vastness has probably done so with the same awe. These trees can grow 300ft tall and nearly 40ft in diameter with bark up to 2ft thick. The **Giant Forest Museum** (p1010) in Sequoia National Park has exhibits about the trees' unusual ecology.

DON'T MISS

- **Bodie State Historic Park** (opposite) – a real gold-rush ghost town
- **Mono Lake** (opposite) – unearthly, mysterious-looking mineral formations
- **Whoa Nellie Deli** (right) – creative comfort food, like buffalo meatloaf
- **Ancient Bristlecone Pine Forest** (opposite) – the world's oldest living trees
- **Manzanar National Historic Site** (below) – uncensored history of WWII-era internment camps

center. From Hwy 395, take Hwy 168 east for 12 miles and then head uphill another 10 miles from the marked turnoff.

Hwy 395 barrels on south to Independence and **Manzanar National Historic Site** (☎ 760-878-2194; www.nps.gov/manz; 5001 Hwy 395; admission free; sunrise-sunset, visitor center 9am-4:30pm, to 5:30pm Apr-Oct), which memorializes the war relocation camp where some 10,000 Japanese Americans were unjustly interned during WWII following the attack on Pearl Harbor. Interpretive exhibits and a short film vividly chronicle life at the camp.

South of here, in Lone Pine, you finally catch a glimpse of **Mt Whitney** (14,505ft), the highest mountain in the lower 48 states. The heart-stopping, 11-mile scenic drive up **Whitney Portal Road** (closed in winter) is spectacular. Climbing the peak is hugely popular, but requires a permit issued on a lottery basis. For details, consult www.fs.fed.us/r5/inyo or stop by the **Eastern Sierra InterAgency Visitor Center** (☎ 760-876-6222; 8am-5pm) at the Hwy 395/136 junction. West of Lone Pine, the bizarrely shaped boulders of the **Alabama Hills** have enchanted filmmakers of such Hollywood Western classics as *How the West Was Won* (1962). Peruse vintage memorabilia and movie posters at the **Museum of Lone Pine Film History** (☎ 760-876-9909; www.lonepinefilmhistorymuseum.org; 701 S Main St; admission $5; 10am-6pm Mon-Wed, 10am-7pm Thu-Sat, 10am-4pm Sun).

Sleeping

The Eastern Sierra is freckled with campgrounds. Backcountry camping requires fire permits (including for campstoves), available free at any ranger station. Bishop, Lone Pine and Bridgeport have the most motels. Mammoth Lakes has countless inns, B&Bs and condo and vacation rentals

Dow Hotel & Dow Villa Motel (☎ 760-876-5521, 800-824-9317; www.dowvillamotel.com; 310 S Main St; r $50-135;) John Wayne and Errol Flynn are among the movie stars who have stayed at this venerable hotel. Built in 1922, it has been restored with rustic charm, though modern motel rooms are generic.

Redwood Motel (☎ 760-932-7060, 888-932-3292; www.redwoodmotel.net; 425 Main St, Bridgeport; d $70-110; mid-Mar–early Dec;) A cow in a Hawaiian shirt and other wacky farm animal sculptures give a cheerful welcome to this spotless motel. Your host will shower you with travel tips. There is limited free wi-fi.

Winnedumah Hotel (☎ 760-878-2040; www.winnedumah.com; 211 N Edwards St, Independence; r incl breakfast $85-130) Off the beaten path, this 1927 country-style inn with welcoming owners was once a popular movie-star hangout when the cameras were rolling in the nearby Alabama Hills.

Tamarack Lodge & Resort (☎ 760-934-2442, 800-626-6684; www.tamaracklodge.com; off Lake Mary Rd, Mammoth Lakes; r $109-169, cabins $169-469;) In business since 1924, this ecosavvy lodge offers cabins with kitchens, ranging from very simple to simply deluxe, and some even have wood-burning stoves.

Eating & Drinking

Erick Schat's Bakkery (☎ 760-873-7156; 763 N Main St, Bishop; sandwiches $5-8; 6am-6pm) Touristy, oh yes. But it's still the best place on Hwy 395 to satisfy cravings for fresh-baked breads (try the jalapeño-cheese), apple fritters and pecan-kiss cookies.

Good Life Café (☎ 760-934-1734; 126 Old Mammoth Rd, Mammoth Lakes; mains $8-12; 6:30am-3pm) Stomach-stuffing Mexican breakfasts, healthy veggie wraps, brawny burgers and big salad bowls make this place perennially popular. Expect a wait, but it's worth it.

Whoa Nellie Deli (☎ 760-647-1088; Hwys 120 & 395, Lee Vining; mains $8-20; 7am-9pm mid-May–Oct) Great food in a gas station? Really, you gotta try this amazing kitchen, where chef Matt 'Tioga' Toomey serves up delicious fish tacos, wild buffalo meatloaf and other tasty morsels.

For strong brews, visit **Looney Bean Roasting Co** (☎ 760-872-2326; 399 N Main St, Bishop; 6am-8pm Sun-Thu, to 10pm Fri & Sat;). Before you hit the trail, stop by **Mahogany Smoked Meats** (☎ 888-624-6426; 2345 N Sierra Hwy, Bishop; 9am-6pm) for elk, buffalo and turkey jerky.

Pacific Northwest

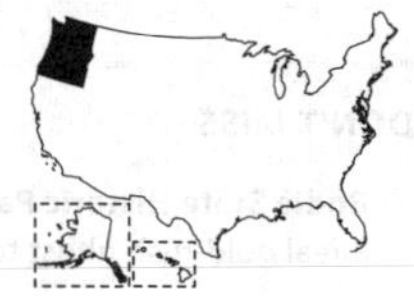

Test Carl Jung's theory of word association out on the Pacific Northwest and you'll get a variety of different answers: evergreen, rain, volcanoes, fleece-wear, coffee, Starbucks, beer, Boeing, Nirvana, Nike, grunge, Gates. These are the well-known symbols, the nationally and internationally recognizable cultural icons. But what of the other stuff? Who knew about llama trekking in the North Cascade Mountains, the authentic Bavarian 'village' of Leavenworth, the fruity Cab Savs of up-and-coming Walla Walla or the eclectic food carts of downtown Portland?

So pack up your lightweight rucksack/suitcase and leave all your rainy/grungy/caffeine-concocted preconceptions at home. This ripe outdoor Eden wedged between Northern California and the Canadian border is not just about philanthropic dot-com millionaires and tall dark-roast skinny lattes (although the coffee ain't half bad). Much of it isn't even that green, comprised instead of high plateaus, scrubby steppe, grand coulees and dusty desert – yes, desert!

If the USA's East Coast is prone to overwork, the West undoubtedly suffers from the opposite affliction. Spend time in the overcast Pacific Rim cities and you'll quickly understand the Northwest's conundrum. It's hard to resist the lure of the great outdoors when resplendent volcanoes like Rainier, Hood and Baker take their cloudy hats off and allow a little sun to shine through. Seattleites and Portlanders don't merely live to work; they work to live – hiking around Rainier's Wonderland Trail, kayaking the San Juan Islands, sipping homemade beer in homegrown microbreweries and discussing the protest potential of 'tree-sitting' with reformed anarchists from Eugene. Take a leaf out of their tree and come join them.

HIGHLIGHTS

- Climbing up or hiking around **Mt Rainier** (p1043) on a guided five-day ascent or the circuitous 10-day Wonderland Trail
- Quaffing local wine and watching cowpokes at the Northwest's biggest rodeo in **Ellensburg** (p1044)
- Sharing a tall dark skinny latte with wannabe rock stars, dot-com millionaires and aging fetish freaks in caffeine-fueled **Seattle** (p1021)
- Taking a bike ride around clean, green, serene **Portland** (p1046) energized by beer, coffee and food-cart pizza
- Watching West Coast thespians get their tongues around Elizabethan English in Ashland at the world-renowned **Oregon Shakespeare Festival** (p1065)

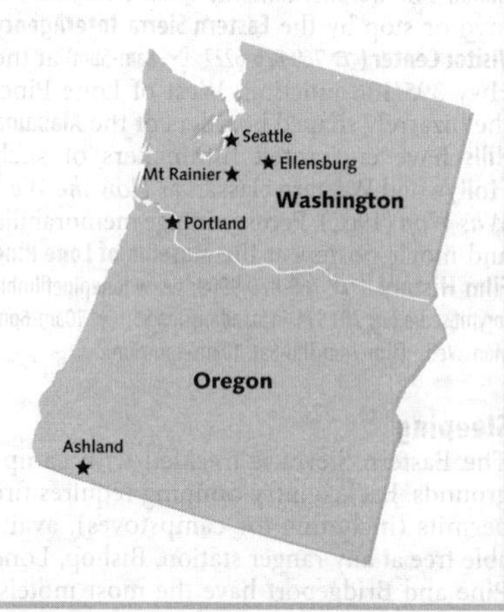

HISTORY

Native American societies including the Chinook and the Salish had long-established coastal communities by the time Europeans arrived in the Pacific Northwest in the 18th century. Inland, on the arid plateaus between the Cascades and the Rocky Mountains, the Spokane, Nez Percé and other tribes thrived on seasonal migration between river valleys and temperate uplands.

Three hundred years after Columbus landed in the New World, Spanish and British explorers began probing the northern Pacific coast, seeking the fabled Northwest Passage. In 1792, Capt George Vancouver was the first explorer to sail the waters of Puget Sound, claiming British sovereignty over the entire region. At the same time, an American, Capt Robert Gray, found the mouth of the Columbia River. In 1805 the explorers Lewis and Clark crossed the Rockies and made their way down the Columbia to the Pacific Ocean, extending the US claim on the territory.

In 1824 the British Hudson's Bay Company established Fort Vancouver in Washington as headquarters for the Columbia region. This opened the door to waves of settlers but had a devastating impact on the indigenous cultures, assailed as they were by the double threat of European diseases and alcohol.

In 1843 settlers at Champoeg, on the Willamette River south of Portland, voted to organize a provisional government independent of the Hudson's Bay Company, thereby casting their lot with the USA, which formally acquired the territory from the British by treaty in 1846. Over the next decade, some 53,000 settlers came to the Northwest via the 2000-mile-long Oregon Trail.

Arrival of the railroads set the region's future. Agriculture and lumber became the pillars of the economy until 1914, when the opening of the Panama Canal and WWI brought increased trade to Pacific ports. Shipyards opened along Puget Sound, and the Boeing aircraft company set up shop near Seattle.

Big dam projects in the 1930s and '40s provided cheap hydroelectricity and irrigation. WWII offered another boost for aircraft manufacturing and shipbuilding, and agriculture continued to thrive. In the postwar period Washington's population, especially around Puget Sound, grew to twice that of Oregon. But hydroelectricity production and the massive irrigation projects along the Columbia have nearly destroyed the river's ecosystem. Logging has also left its scars, especially in Oregon. The environment remains a contentious issue in the Northwest; flash points are the logging of old-growth forests and the destruction of salmon runs in streams and rivers.

In the 1980s and '90s, the economic emphasis shifted again with the rise of the high-tech industry, embodied by Microsoft in Seattle and Intel in Portland. The region has also reinvigorated its eco-credentials and stands at the forefront of US efforts to offset climate change.

LOCAL CULTURE

The stereotypical image of a Pacific Northwesterner is of a casually dressed, latte-supping urbanite who drives a Prius, votes Democrat and walks around with an unwavering diet of Nirvana-derived indie rock programmed into their iPod. But, as with most fleeting regional generalizations, the reality is far more complex.

Noted for their sophisticated café culture and copious microbrew pubs, the urban hubs of Seattle and Portland are the Northwest's most emblematic cities. But head east into the region's drier and less verdant interior and the cultural affiliations become increasingly more traditional. Here, strung out along the Columbia River Valley or nestled amid the arid steppes of southeastern Washington, small towns host raucous rodeos, tourist centers promote cowboy culture, and a cup of coffee is served 'straight up' with none of the fancily fashioned chai lattes and icy frappés that are par for the course in Seattle.

In contrast to the USA's hardworking eastern seaboard, life out West is more casual and less frenetic than in New York or Boston. Idealistically, Westerners would rather work to play than live to work. Indeed, with so much winter rain, the citizens of Olympia or Bellingham will dredge up any excuse to shun the nine-to-five treadmill and hit the great outdoors a couple of hours (or even days) early. Witness the scene in late May and early June when the first bright days of summer prompt a mass exodus of hikers and cyclists making enthusiastically for the national parks and wilderness areas for which the region is justly famous.

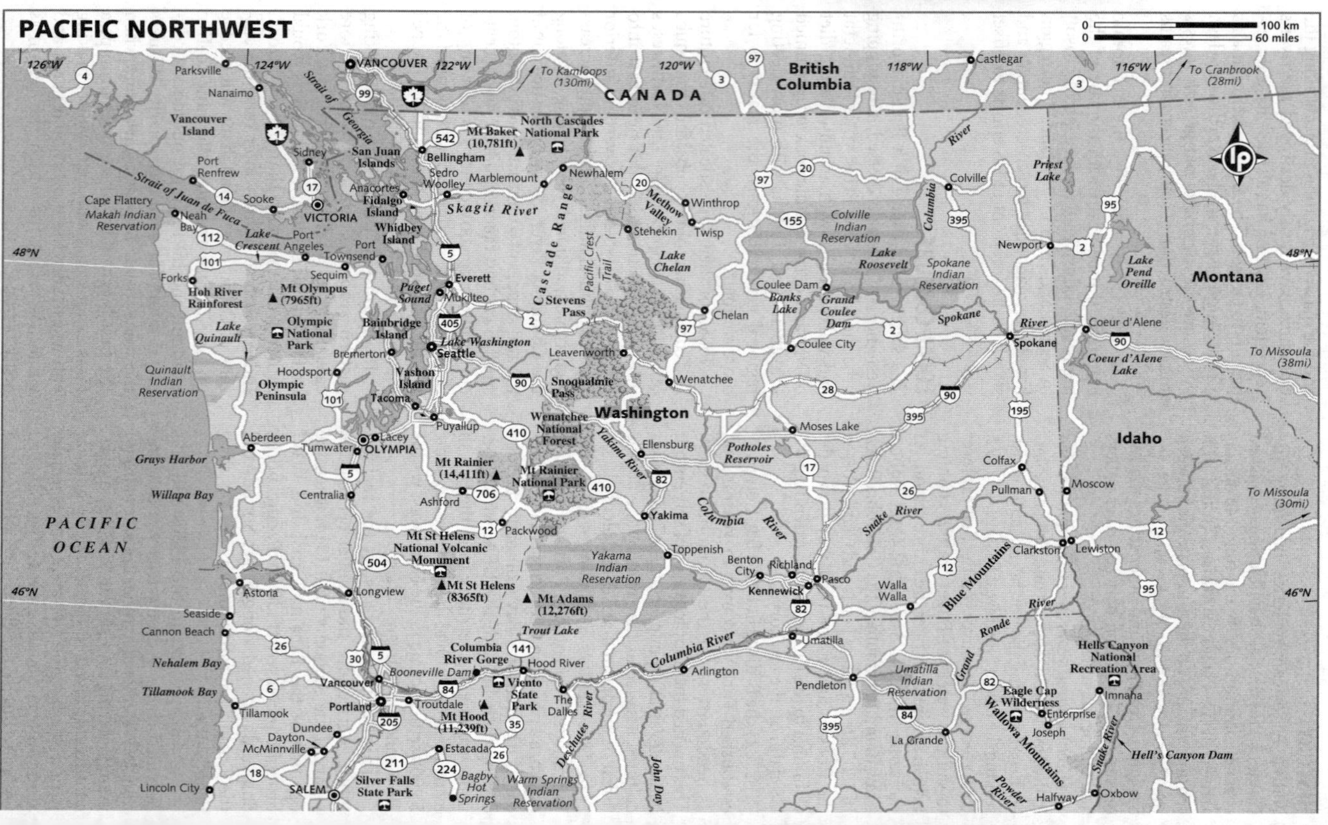
PACIFIC NORTHWEST
0 100 km
0 60 miles
To Cranbrook (28mi)
To Missoula (38mi)
To Missoula (30mi)
To Kamloops (130mi)
CANADA
British Columbia
Montana
Idaho
Washington
PACIFIC OCEAN
Vancouver Island
VANCOUVER
VICTORIA
OLYMPIA
SALEM
Parksville
Nanaimo
Port Renfrew
Sooke
Sidney
Cape Flattery
Makah Indian Reservation
Neah Bay
Strait of Juan de Fuca
Strait of Georgia
San Juan Islands
Anacortes
Fidalgo Island
Whidbey Island
Port Townsend
Port Angeles
Lake Crescent
Sequim
Forks
Hoh River Rainforest
Lake Quinault
Quinault Indian Reservation
Mt Olympus (7965ft)
Olympic National Park
Olympic Peninsula
Hoodsport
Bremerton
Bainbridge Island
Vashon Island
Tacoma
Lacey
Tumwater
Aberdeen
Grays Harbor
Willapa Bay
Centralia
Longview
Astoria
Seaside
Cannon Beach
Nehalem Bay
Tillamook Bay
Tillamook
Lincoln City
McMinnville
Dayton
Dundee
Portland
Vancouver
Troutdale
Estacada
Bagby Hot Springs
Silver Falls State Park
Bellingham
Sedro Woolley
Skagit River
Marblemount
Newhalem
Mt Baker (10,781ft)
North Cascades National Park
Cascade Range
Everett
Mukilteo
Puget Sound
Lake Washington
Seattle
Puyallup
Mt Rainier (14,411ft)
Mt Rainier National Park
Ashford
Packwood
Mt St Helens National Volcanic Monument
Mt St Helens (8365ft)
Mt Adams (12,276ft)
Trout Lake
Columbia River Gorge
Booneville Dam
Viento State Park
Hood River
The Dalles
Mt Hood (11,239ft)
Warm Springs Indian Reservation
Deschutes River
John Day
Stevens Pass
Snoqualmie Pass
Leavenworth
Wenatchee National Forest
Pacific Crest Trail
Stehekin
Lake Chelan
Methow Valley
Winthrop
Twisp
Chelan
Wenatchee
Ellensburg
Yakima River
Yakima
Yakama Indian Reservation
Toppenish
Benton City
Richland
Kennewick
Pasco
Columbia River
Arlington
Umatilla
Pendleton
Umatilla Indian Reservation
La Grande
Grand Ronde River
Blue Mountains
Wallowa Mountains
Eagle Cap Wilderness
Joseph
Enterprise
Imnaha
Hells Canyon National Recreation Area
Hell's Canyon Dam
Snake River
Oxbow
Halfway
Powder River
Walla Walla
Potholes Reservoir
Moses Lake
Coulee City
Coulee Dam
Banks Lake
Grand Coulee Dam
Colville Indian Reservation
Lake Roosevelt
Spokane Indian Reservation
Spokane River
Spokane
Colville
Castlegar
Newport
Priest Lake
Lake Pend Oreille
Coeur d'Alene
Coeur d'Alene Lake
Colfax
Pullman
Moscow
Clarkston
Lewiston
126°W
124°W
122°W
120°W
118°W
116°W
48°N
46°N

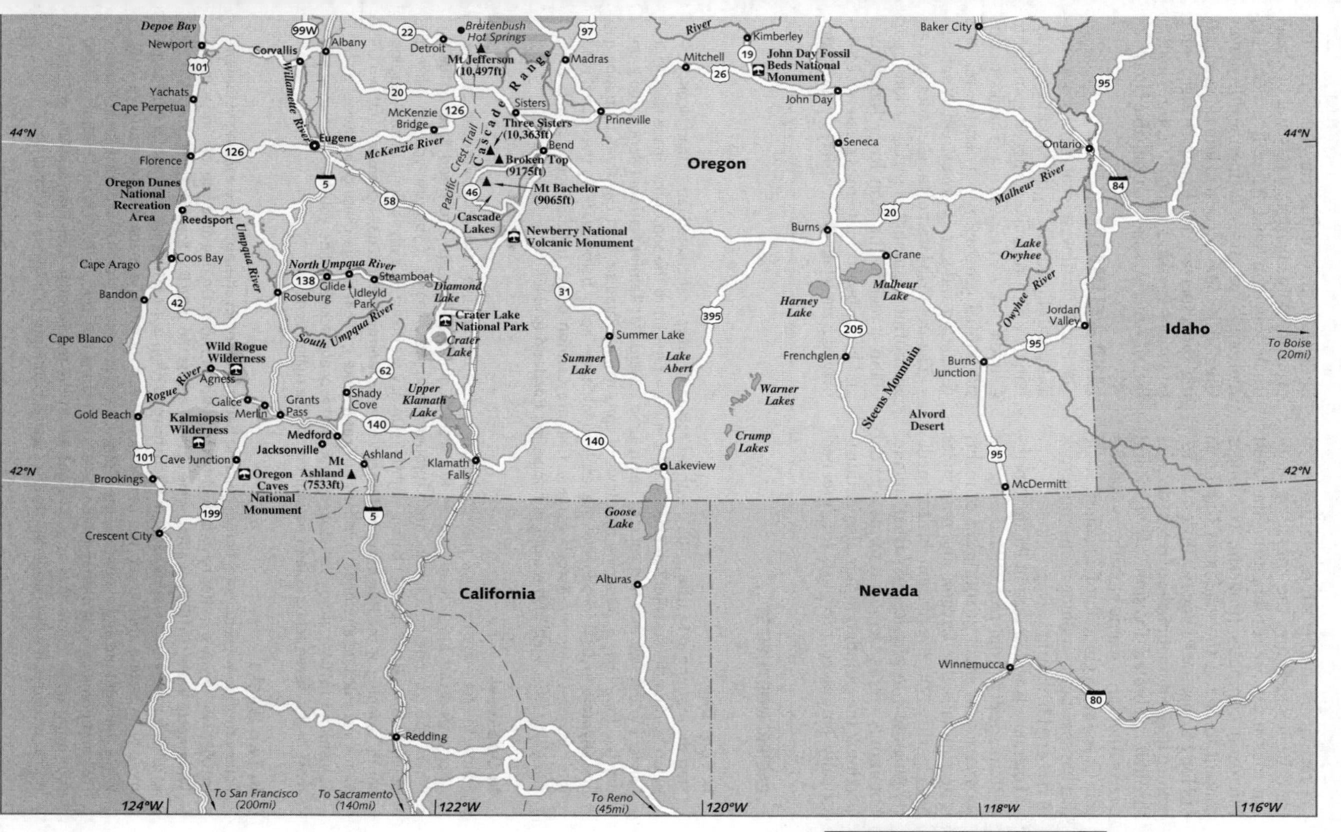

Depoe Bay
Newport
Corvallis
Albany
Detroit
Breitenbush Hot Springs
Mt Jefferson (10,497ft)
Madras
River
Kimberley
Baker City
Mitchell
John Day Fossil Beds National Monument
Yachats
Cape Perpetua
Willamette River
McKenzie Bridge
Cascade Range
Sisters
Three Sisters (10,363ft)
Prineville
John Day
44°N
Eugene
McKenzie River
Pacific Crest Trail
Bend
Broken Top (9175ft)
Seneca
Oregon
Ontario
Florence
Mt Bachelor (9065ft)
Malheur River
Oregon Dunes National Recreation Area
Reedsport
Cascade Lakes
Newberry National Volcanic Monument
Burns
Umpqua River
Crane
Lake Owyhee
Cape Arago
Coos Bay
North Umpqua River
Glide
Idleyld Park
Steamboat
Diamond Lake
Bandon
Roseburg
Malheur Lake
Owyhee River
Harney Lake
Jordan Valley
Crater Lake National Park
Crater Lake
South Umpqua River
Summer Lake
Idaho
To Boise (20mi)
Cape Blanco
Wild Rogue Wilderness
Lake Abert
Frenchglen
Burns Junction
Steens Mountain
Agness
Rogue River
Warner Lakes
Galice
Merlin
Grants Pass
Shady Cove
Upper Klamath Lake
Alvord Desert
Gold Beach
Kalmiopsis Wilderness
Medford
Jacksonville
Crump Lakes
Cave Junction
Ashland
Mt Ashland (7533ft)
Klamath Falls
Lakeview
42°N
Brookings
Oregon Caves National Monument
McDermitt
Goose Lake
Crescent City
Alturas
California
Nevada
Winnemucca
Redding
To San Francisco (200mi)
To Sacramento (140mi)
To Reno (45mi)
124°W
122°W
120°W
118°W
116°W

Creativity is another strong Northwestern trait, be it redefining the course of modern rock music or reconfiguring the latest Microsoft computer program. No longer content to live in the shadow of California or Hong Kong, the Pacific Northwest has redefined itself internationally in recent decades through celebrated TV shows (*Frasier* and *Grey's Anatomy*), iconic global personalities (Bill Gates) and a groundbreaking music scene that has spawned everything from grunge rock to riot grrrl feminism.

Tolerance is widespread in Pacific Northwestern society, from recreational drug use (possession of small quantities of cannabis is decriminalised in Oregon, and both states have legalised the use of cannabis for medical purposes) to physician-assisted suicide. Commonly voting Democrat in presidential elections, the population has also enthusiastically embraced the push for 'greener' lifestyles in the form of car clubs, recycling programs, organic restaurants and biodiesel whale-watching tours. An early exponent of ecofriendly practices, former Seattle mayor Greg Nickels has advocated himself as a leading spokesperson on climate change, while salubrious Portland regularly features high in lists of America's most sustainable cities.

LAND & CLIMATE

The Pacific Northwest is cut in half both physically and climatically by the looming Cascade Range, which runs like a rugged spine from Canada down to California. Thanks to this substantial geographic barrier, the region's vegetation and terrain are extremely varied.

The area to the west of the Cascades receives an enormous amount of precipitation (up to 200in a year in the Hoh River Rainforest) and hence boasts numerous glaciers, record-breaking snowfalls and a lush temperate rain-

PACIFIC NORTHWEST...

In Four Days

Start the morning in **Seattle** (p1021) with brunch and a brew – caffeinated rather than alcoholic – before surfing the stalls in Pike Place Market and taking a lift to the top of the Space Needle. If Rainier's visible you may find yourself being lured towards **Mt Rainier National Park** (p1043) on day two for a hike in the alpine meadows of aptly named Paradise. Start day three by popping into **Olympia** (p1034) for a look at the resplendent State Capitol before tracking the coastal road into Oregon via historic **Astoria** (p1068). Call into **Cannon Beach** (p1068) before it gets dark, and enjoy what's left of the night in happening **Portland** (p1046).

In One Week

Follow the four-day itinerary, spending a bit of time on day five to discover Portland by bike. After a food-cart lunch head east on the scenic Columbia River drive to **Hood River** (p1060) where you can ride on a historic train through the apple orchards. If you rush you can make it down as far as **Bend** (p1063) before nightfall. On day six breakfast early in Bend before heading south, stopping at the **Newberry National Volcanic Monument** (p1063). Continue south on US 97 for a scenic late-afternoon epiphany at **Crater Lake** (p1064) before chasing the sunset as far as **Ashland** (p1064). If you've booked your Shakespeare tickets online you'll be able to spend most of day seven relaxing (and eating) before the main event.

In Two Weeks

Follow the one-week itinerary before heading back north for an afternoon and evening in **Eugene** (p1059) where you'd better have brought your running shoes. On day nine you can linger in the **Willamette Valley** (p1058) quaffing wine or head across the state line towards the **Yakima Valley** (p1044) for more of the same. Gentile **Ellensburg** (p1044) is a worthwhile overnighter with some more wine tasting after which you can book a quaint room in Germanic **Leavenworth** (p1040). While there get out and experience the Alpine Lakes Wilderness. From Leavenworth cross Stevens Pass and home in on **Whidbey Island** (p1037) for some true bucolic relaxation. Finish the grand tour using up as many days as you've got left in the recuperative **San Juan Islands** (p1038) – no car required, it's the Pacific Northwest's perfect antidote to a two-week road trip.

forest that shelters some of the world's oldest and largest trees. Traveling inland, the lofty mountains – which culminate in 14,411ft Mt Rainier – suck up much of this moisture from the atmosphere, leaving the areas to the east of the range languishing in arid steppe and semidesert (Pasco in southeast Washington gets less than 6in of rain a year).

Cocooned on a massive ice-age floodplain, the eastern parts of Oregon and Washington lie on the dry Columbia River plateau, a region characterized by its many coulees, canyons and gorges. Indeed, the spectacular Columbia River is the fourth-largest river by volume in the US (after the Mississippi) and drains the whole region through a magnificent river gorge that provides the only natural break in the Cascade Mountains south of the Canadian border. The Columbia is also renowned for its numerous dams that provide vital hydroelectric power and have transformed a once barren desert into a veritable Garden of Eden that produces fine wines, classic vegetables and more than half of the US apple crop.

PARKS & WILDLIFE

Oregon has one national park, Crater Lake (p1064); Washington has three: Olympic (p1034), North Cascades (p1041) and Mt Rainier (p1043). Maps and passes are available at various ranger stations or through **Nature of the Northwest** (www.naturenw.org).

There are 240 state parks in Oregon (p1046) and 215 in Washington (p1020). Other areas noted for their natural beauty include the Oregon Coast (p1068), the Columbia River Gorge (p1060) and Hells Canyon (p1067), which borders with Idaho. Mt St Helens (p1044) offers visitors a unique look at America's most well known National Volcanic Monument.

The Northwest's parks contain numerous fauna including black bear, rare Roosevelt elk (in Olympic National Park), mule deer, bighorn sheep, coyote, raccoons and pronghorn antelope. Meanwhile the seas boast plentiful whales and sea lions. Resident birds include herons, kingfishers, loons, ospreys, meadowlarks and bald eagles.

INFORMATION

Oregon and western Washington have a 10-digit dialing system for local calls. To make a local call within the ☎ 206, ☎ 253, ☎ 425, ☎ 360 and ☎ 564 area codes in Washington, and throughout Oregon, dial the area code first (without a preceding 1).

GETTING THERE & AROUND

Seattle-Tacoma International Airport (p1032), aka 'Sea-Tac,' is the main international airport in the Northwest, with daily service to Europe, Asia and points throughout the US and Canada. Portland International Airport (p1057) serves the US and Canada and has nonstop flights to Frankfurt (Germany) and Guadalajara (Mexico).

Both passenger-only and car ferries operate around Puget Sound and across to Vancouver Island, BC (Canada). **Washington State Ferries** (WSF; ☎ 206-464-6400, in Washington 888-808-7977; www.wsdot.wa.gov/ferries) links Seattle with Bainbridge and Vashon Islands. Other WSF routes cross from Whidbey Island to Port Townsend on the Olympic Peninsula, and from Anacortes through the San Juan Islands to Sidney, BC. Victoria Clipper (p1032) operates services from Seattle to Victoria, BC. Ferries to Victoria also operate from Port Angeles (p1036). Alaska Marine Highway (p1077) ferries go from Bellingham, WA, to Alaska.

Greyhound (p1160) provides service along the I-5 corridor from Bellingham in northern Washington down to Medford in southern Oregon, with connecting services across the US and Canada. East–west routes fan out toward Spokane, Yakima, the Tri-Cities (Kennewick, Pasco and Richland), Walla Walla and Pullman in Washington, and Pendleton, Bend, Hood River and Newport in Oregon with numerous stops in between.

Driving your own vehicle is a convenient way of touring the Pacific Northwest. Major rental agencies can be found throughout the region. I-5 is the major north–south road artery. In Washington I-90 heads east from Seattle to Spokane and into Idaho. In Oregon I-84 branches east from Portland along the Columbia River Gorge via Pendleton to link up with Boise in Idaho.

Amtrak (p1166) runs an excellent train service north (to Vancouver, Canada) and south (to California) linking Seattle, Portland and other major urban centers with the *Cascades* and *Coast Starlight* routes. The famous *Empire Builder* heads east to Chicago from Seattle and Portland (joining up in Spokane, WA).

WASHINGTON

Divided in two by the spinal Cascade Mountains, Washington isn't so much a land of contrasts as a land of polar opposites. Centered on Seattle, the western coastal zone is wet, urban, liberal and famous for its fecund evergreen forests; splayed to the east between the less celebrated cities of Spokane and Yakima, the inland plains are arid, rural, conservative and covered by mile after mile of scrublike steppe.

Of the two halves it's the west that harbors most of the quintessential Washington sights, while the more remote east is less heralded, understated and full of surprises.

History

The first US settlement in Washington was at Tumwater, on the southern edge of Puget Sound, in 1845. Both Seattle and Port Townsend were established in 1851 and quickly became logging centers. Lumber was shipped at great profit to San Francisco, the boomtown of the California gold rush.

In 1853, Washington separated from the Oregon territory. Congress reduced the amount of land open to native hunting and fishing, and opened up the eastern part of the state to settlement. The arrival of rail links in the last decades of the century created a readily accessible market for the products of the Pacific Northwest and brought in floods of settlers.

Washington was admitted to the union in 1889, and Seattle began to flourish in 1897, when it became the principal port en route to the Alaska and Yukon goldfields. The construction of the Bonneville Dam (1937) and Grand Coulee Dam (1947) accelerated the region's industrial and agricultural development by providing cheap hydroelectric power and irrigation.

The rapid postwar urbanization of the Puget Sound region created an enormous metropolitan area linked by perpetually jammed freeways that mar some of the waterfront vistas. Industry switched from lumber to computer technologies as Seattle rode the dot-com boom, suffered a small recession and emerged to fight another day. Placed firmly on the world map through the work of homegrown global giants such as Starbucks and Microsoft, Washington is looking to the future with a greener face. Former Seattle mayor Greg Nickels has been instrumental in rallying more than 400 American cities to reduce carbon emissions in line with the Kyoto Protocol and the knock-on effect in other towns is palpable.

Information

Washington road conditions (☎ Seattle 206-368-4499, elsewhere in the state 800-695-7623)

Washington State Parks & Recreation Commission (☎ 360-902-8844, 800-233-0321; www.parks.wa.gov; PO Box 42650, Olympia, WA 98504) You can reserve up to nine months in advance at 50 of Washington's 90 state park campgrounds. There's a $6.50 online booking fee. Prices are approximately$19 for a standard campsite, $26 for a hook-up.

Washington State Tourism Office (☎ 360-725-5052; www.tourism.wa.gov; 🕒 7am-7pm) Useful website; 'travel counselors' offer travel-related advice over the phone.

WASHINGTON FACTS

Nickname Evergreen State
Population 6.5 million
Area 71,342 sq miles
Capital city Olympia (population 44,645)
Other cities Seattle (population 582,454), Spokane (population 198,081), Yakima (population 82,805), Bellingham (population 75,150), Walla Walla (population 30,945), Ellensburg (population 15,414)
Sales tax 6.5%
Birthplace of singer and actor Bing Crosby (1903–77), guitarist Jimi Hendrix (1942–70), computer geek Bill Gates (b 1955), Denver Broncos quarterback John Elway (b 1960), saxophonist Kenny G (b 1956), musical icon Kurt Cobain (1967–94)
Home of Mt St Helens, Microsoft, Starbucks, Nordstrom, Evergreen State College
Famous for grunge rock, coffee, *Grey's Anatomy*, *Twin Peaks*, volcanoes, apples, wine, precipitation
State vegetable Walla Walla sweet onion
Driving distances Seattle to Portland 174 miles, Spokane to Port Angeles 365 miles

SEATTLE

Built on seven hills like a modern Rome, Seattle is an entrepreneurial Pacific Rim city whose groundbreaking homegrown inventions have a habit of becoming international brands. Think anarchistic grunge music and cool coffee bars, zillionaire computer geeks and Boeing planes. But, in the fast-moving economy of the Pacific Northwest, Seattle doesn't rest on its laurels. In a city still less than 160 years old, what happened last month, let alone last year, is quickly confined to ancient history. Tucked beneath the shadow of the Cascade Mountains, the splayed metropolis has grown up and moved on since the nihilistic '90s. Belltown, grunge music's former spiritual home, is now a nexus for wine-quaffing condo dwellers; the global conglomerate known as Starbucks is locally challenged by more low-key indie roasters; and the traffic jams on I-5, while still legendary, have been countered by the green sprouts of a concerted environmental revolution led by proactive former city mayor, Greg Nickels. The moral of the story is: when in Seattle never stand still. This is a city at the vanguard with a boom-bust cycle that has been replaying itself ever since the 1890s when the Klondike gold rush created the 19th-century equivalent of the dot-com millionaire.

History

Seattle was named for Chief Sealth, leader of the Duwamish tribe that inhabited the Lake Washington area when David Denny led the first group of white settlers here in 1851. The railway came through in 1893, linking Seattle with the rest of the country. For a decade, prospectors headed for the Yukon gold territory would stop in Seattle to stock up on provisions.

The boom continued through WWI, when Northwest lumber was in great demand and the Puget Sound area prospered as a shipbuilding center. In 1916 William Boeing founded the aircraft manufacturing business that would become one of the largest employers in Seattle, attracting tens of thousands of newcomers to the region during WWII.

In November 1999, the city drew attention as protesters and police clashed violently outside a World Trade Organization (WTO) summit. Two of the city's biggest business successes, Starbucks and Microsoft, are loved and loathed almost equally. Boeing has relocated its headquarters to Chicago, though it's still a major presence in Seattle.

Orientation

Seattle's Sea-Tac Airport is 13 miles south of the city. Amtrak trains use the King Street Station, north of the new Seahawks Stadium, just south of Pioneer Square. Greyhound's bus terminal is on the corner of 8th Ave and Stewart St, on the north edge of downtown.

Seattle is neighborhood-oriented: Capitol Hill and the U District are east of I-5, while downtown, Seattle Center, Fremont and Ballard lie to the west. To reach Fremont from downtown, take 4th Ave to the Fremont Bridge; from here, hang a left on NW 36th Ave (which becomes Leary) to reach Ballard. Eastlake Ave goes from downtown to the U District.

Information

BOOKSTORES

Bulldog News & Espresso (☎ 206-632-6397; www.bulldognews.com; 4208 University Way NE) A very thorough newsstand in the U District.

Elliott Bay Book Company (☎ 206-624-6600; www.elliottbaybook.com; 101 S Main St) Labyrinthine store in historic Pioneer Square has readings almost nightly.

Metsker Maps (☎ 206-623-8747; www.metskers.com; 1511 1st Ave) Great selection of maps and travel guides.

EMERGENCY & MEDICAL SERVICES

45th St Community Clinic (☎ 206-633-3350; 1629 N 45th St, Wallingford) Medical and dental services.

Harborview Medical Center (☎ 206-731-3000; 325 9th Ave) Full medical care, with emergency room.

Seattle Police (☎ 206-625-5011)

Seattle Rape Relief (☎ 206-632-7273)

Washington State Patrol (☎ 425-649-4370)

INTERNET ACCESS

Seattle is a computer geek's heaven and practically every bar and coffee shop has free wi-fi, as do most hotels. For laptop-free travelers, internet cafés include the following:

Cyber-Dogs (☎ 206-405-3647; 909 Pike St; 1st 20min free, then per hr $6; 🕑 10am-midnight) A veggie hot dog stand (dogs $2 to $5), espresso bar, internet café and youngster hangout/pick-up joint.

Online Coffee Company (www.onlinecoffeeco.com; per min 14¢; 🕑 7:30am-midnight); Olive Way (☎ 206-328-3731; 1720 E Olive Way); Pine St (☎ 206-323-7798; 1404 E Pine St) The Olive Way location is in a cozy former residence, while the Pine St shop is more utilitarian-chic. The first hour is free for students.

PACIFIC NORTHWEST

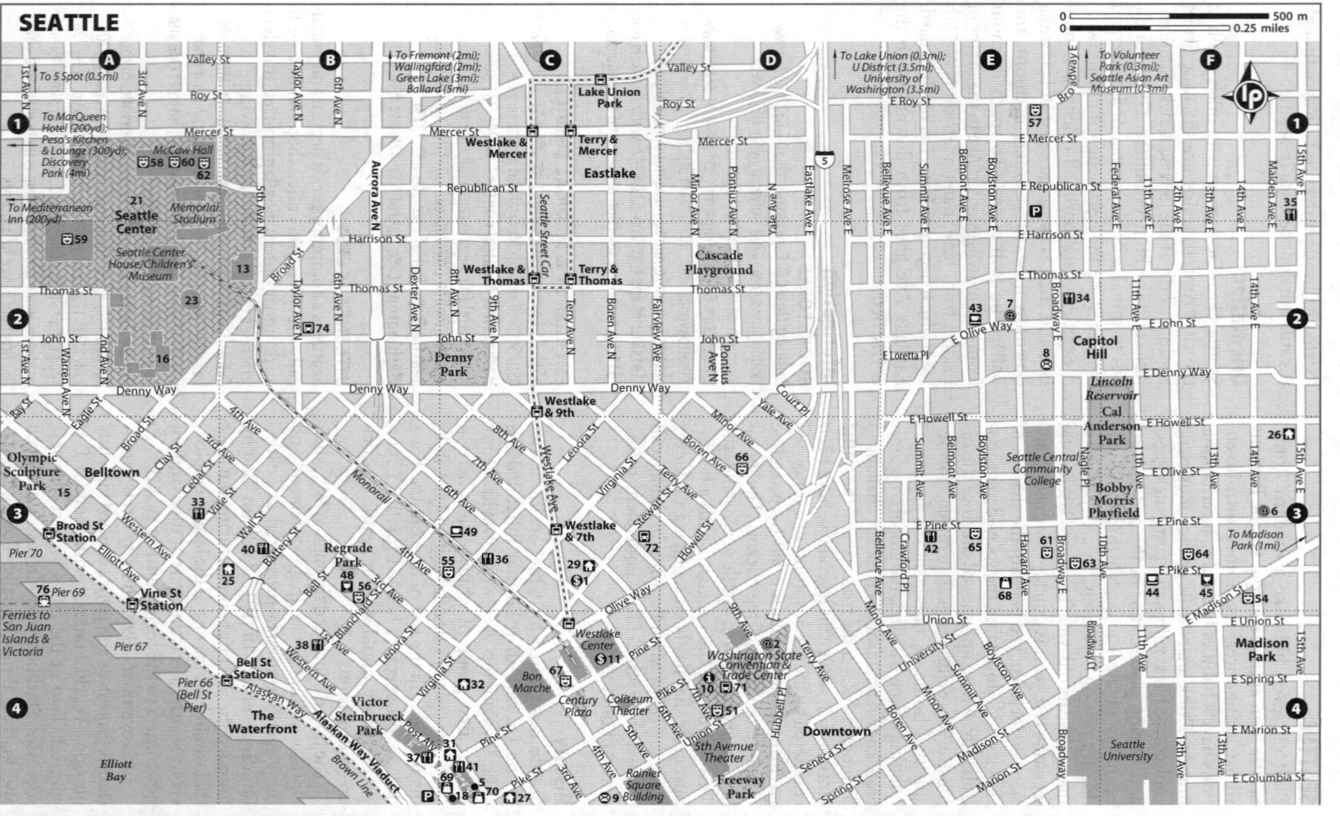

SEATTLE
0 500 m
0 0.25 miles
To 5 Spot (0.5mi)
To MarQueen Hotel (200yd); Peso's Kitchen & Lounge (300yd); Discovery Park (4mi)
To Mediterranean Inn (200yd)
To Fremont (2mi); Wallingford (2mi); Green Lake (3mi); Ballard (5mi)
To Lake Union (0.3mi); U District (3.5mi); University of Washington (3.5mi)
To Volunteer Park (0.3mi); Seattle Asian Art Museum (0.3mi)
To Madison Park (1mi)
Seattle Center
McCaw Hall
Memorial Stadium
Seattle Center House/Children's Museum
Lake Union Park
Westlake & Mercer
Terry & Mercer
Eastlake
Westlake & Thomas
Terry & Thomas
Cascade Playground
Seattle Street Car
Denny Park
Westlake & 9th
Westlake & 7th
Capitol Hill
Lincoln Reservoir
Cal Anderson Park
Bobby Morris Playfield
Seattle Central Community College
Madison Park
Seattle University
Olympic Sculpture Park
Belltown
Broad St Station
Vine St Station
Bell St Station
Regrade Park
Monorail
Victor Steinbrueck Park
The Waterfront
Alaskan Way Viaduct
Alaskan Way
Brown Line
Westlake Center
Bon Marche
Century Plaza
Coliseum Theater
Washington State Convention & Trade Center
5th Avenue Theater
Rainier Square Building
Freeway Park
Downtown
Pier 70
Pier 69
Pier 67
Pier 66 (Bell St Pier)
Ferries to San Juan Islands & Victoria
Elliott Bay
Denny Way
Aurora Ave N
Westlake Ave
Mercer St
E Pine St
E Pike St
E Madison St
E Union St
Post Alley

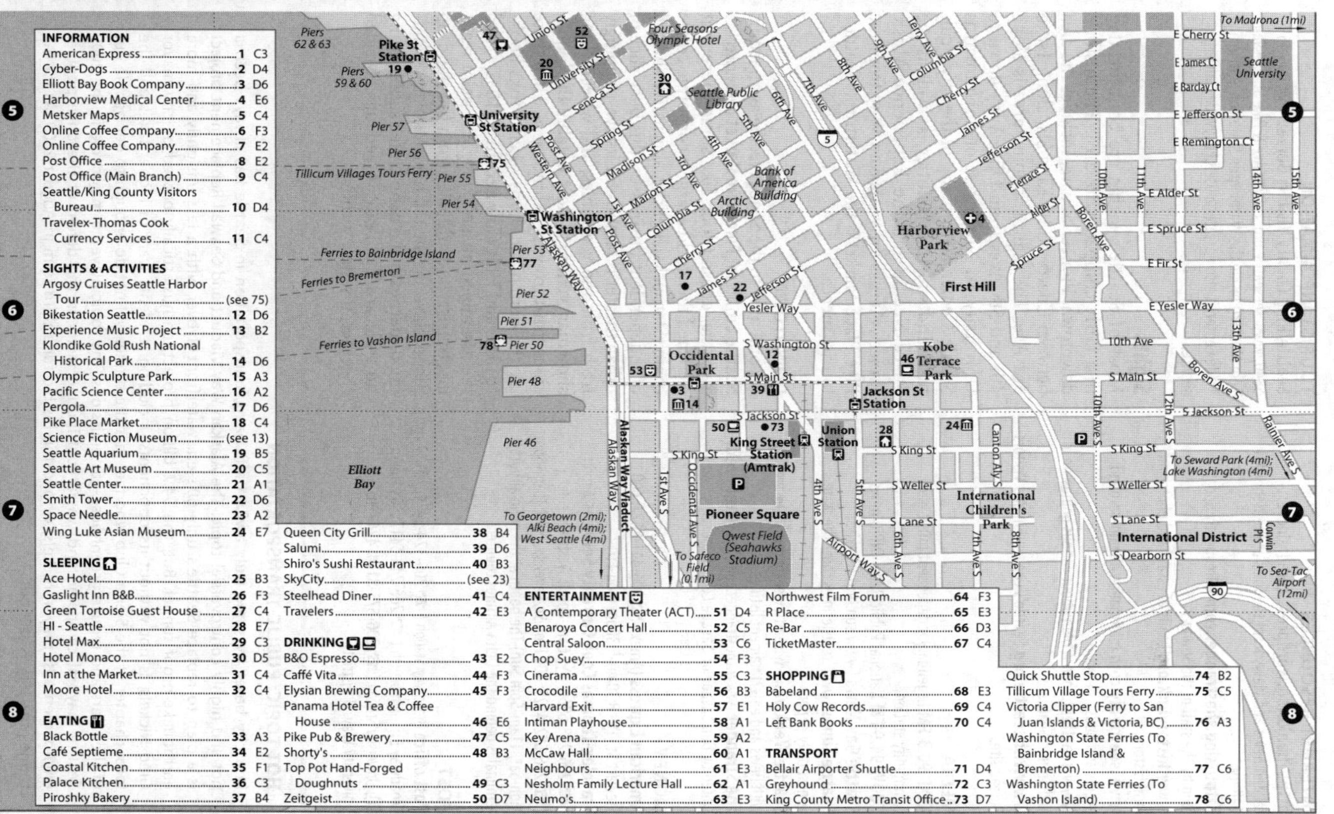
INFORMATION
American Express 1 C3
Cyber-Dogs 2 D4
Elliott Bay Book Company 3 D6
Harborview Medical Center 4 E6
Metsker Maps 5 C4
Online Coffee Company 6 F3
Online Coffee Company 7 E2
Post Office 8 E2
Post Office (Main Branch) 9 C4
Seattle/King County Visitors Bureau 10 D4
Travelex-Thomas Cook Currency Services 11 C4
SIGHTS & ACTIVITIES
Argosy Cruises Seattle Harbor Tour (see 75)
Bikestation Seattle 12 D6
Experience Music Project 13 B2
Klondike Gold Rush National Historical Park 14 D6
Olympic Sculpture Park 15 A3
Pacific Science Center 16 A2
Pergola 17 D6
Pike Place Market 18 C4
Science Fiction Museum (see 13)
Seattle Aquarium 19 B5
Seattle Art Museum 20 C5
Seattle Center 21 A1
Smith Tower 22 D6
Space Needle 23 A2
Wing Luke Asian Museum 24 E7
SLEEPING
Ace Hotel 25 B3
Gaslight Inn B&B 26 F3
Green Tortoise Guest House 27 C4
HI - Seattle 28 E7
Hotel Max 29 C3
Hotel Monaco 30 D5
Inn at the Market 31 C4
Moore Hotel 32 C4
EATING
Black Bottle 33 A3
Café Septieme 34 E2
Coastal Kitchen 35 F1
Palace Kitchen 36 C3
Piroshky Bakery 37 B4
Queen City Grill 38 B4
Salumi 39 D6
Shiro's Sushi Restaurant 40 B3
SkyCity (see 23)
Steelhead Diner 41 C4
Travelers 42 E3
DRINKING
B&O Espresso 43 E2
Caffé Vita 44 F3
Elysian Brewing Company 45 F3
Panama Hotel Tea & Coffee House 46 E6
Pike Pub & Brewery 47 C5
Shorty's 48 B3
Top Pot Hand-Forged Doughnuts 49 C3
Zeitgeist 50 D7
ENTERTAINMENT
A Contemporary Theater (ACT) 51 D4
Benaroya Concert Hall 52 C5
Central Saloon 53 C6
Chop Suey 54 F3
Cinerama 55 C3
Crocodile 56 B3
Harvard Exit 57 E1
Intiman Playhouse 58 A1
Key Arena 59 A2
McCaw Hall 60 A1
Neighbours 61 E3
Nesholm Family Lecture Hall 62 A1
Neumo's 63 E3
Northwest Film Forum 64 F3
R Place 65 E3
Re-Bar 66 D3
TicketMaster 67 C4
SHOPPING
Babeland 68 E3
Holy Cow Records 69 C4
Left Bank Books 70 C4
TRANSPORT
Bellair Airporter Shuttle 71 D4
Greyhound 72 C3
King County Metro Transit Office 73 D7
Quick Shuttle Stop 74 B2
Tillicum Village Tours Ferry 75 C5
Victoria Clipper (Ferry to San Juan Islands & Victoria, BC) 76 A3
Washington State Ferries (To Bainbridge Island & Bremerton) 77 C6
Washington State Ferries (To Vashon Island) 78 C6
Piers 62 & 63
Piers 59 & 60
Pike St Station
University St Station
Washington St Station
Pier 57
Pier 56
Pier 55
Pier 54
Pier 53
Pier 52
Pier 51
Pier 50
Pier 48
Pier 46
Tillicum Villages Tours Ferry
Ferries to Bainbridge Island
Ferries to Bremerton
Ferries to Vashon Island
Elliott Bay
Alaskan Way
Alaskan Way Viaduct
Alaskan Way S
To Georgetown (2mi); Alki Beach (4mi); West Seattle (4mi)
To Safeco Field (0.1mi)
Four Seasons Olympic Hotel
Seattle Public Library
Bank of America Building
Arctic Building
Union St
University St
Seneca St
Spring St
Madison St
Marion St
Columbia St
Cherry St
James St
Jefferson St
Yesler Way
Western Ave
Post Ave
1st Ave
2nd Ave
3rd Ave
4th Ave
5th Ave
6th Ave
7th Ave
8th Ave
9th Ave
Terry Ave
E Terrace St
Alder St
Spruce St
Boren Ave
Harborview Park
First Hill
Occidental Park
Kobe Terrace Park
Jackson St Station
Union Station
King Street Station (Amtrak)
Pioneer Square
Qwest Field (Seahawks Stadium)
S Washington St
S Main St
S Jackson St
S King St
S Weller St
S Lane St
S Dearborn St
1st Ave S
Occidental Ave S
4th Ave S
5th Ave S
6th Ave S
7th Ave S
8th Ave S
Canton Aly S
Airport Way S
International Children's Park
International District
10th Ave S
12th Ave S
Rainier Ave S
Boren Ave S
Corwin Pl S
To Seward Park (4mi); Lake Washington (4mi)
To Sea-Tac Airport (12mi)
To Madrona (1mi)
E Cherry St
E James Ct
E Barclay Ct
E Jefferson St
E Remington Ct
E Alder St
E Spruce St
E Fir St
E Yesler Way
10th Ave
11th Ave
13th Ave
14th Ave
15th Ave
Seattle University

INTERNET RESOURCES

http://hankblog.wordpress.com Insider art-related news and views from the folks at the Henry Art Gallery.
http://slog.thestranger.com A frequently updated blog by the staff of the *Stranger*.
www.historylink.org Loads of essays and photos on local history.
www.seattlediy.com Information on underground events and house shows.
www.seattlest.com A blog about various goings-on in and around Seattle.
www.visitseattle.org Seattle's Convention and Visitors Bureau site.

MEDIA

KEXP 90.3 FM Legendary independent music and community station.
KUOW 94.9 FM National Public Radio (NPR) news.
Seattle Gay News (www.sgn.org) Weekly.
Seattle Times (www.seattletimes.com) The state's largest daily paper.
Seattle Weekly (www.seattleweekly.com) Free weekly with news and entertainment listings.
The Stranger (www.thestranger.com) Irreverent weekly edited by Dan Savage of 'Savage Love' fame.

MONEY

American Express (Amex; ☎ 206-441-8622; 600 Stewart St; 🕑 8:30am-5:30pm Mon-Fri)
Travelex-Thomas Cook Currency Services Airport (☎ 206-248-6960; 🕑 6am-8pm); Westlake Center (☎ 206-682-4525; 400 Pine St, Level 3; 🕑 9:30am-6pm Mon-Sat, 11am-5pm Sun) The booth at the main airport terminal is behind the Delta Airlines counter.

POST

Post office Broadway Station (☎ 206-324-5474; 101 Broadway E); main branch (☎ 206-748-5417; 301 Union St); University Station (☎ 206-675-8114; 4244 NE University Way, U District)

TOURIST INFORMATION

Seattle/King County Visitors Bureau (☎ 206-461-5840; www.seeseattle.org; cnr 7th Ave & Pike St; 🕑 9am-5pm Mon-Fri) Inside the Washington State Convention and Trade Center; it also operates a useful citywide concierge service.

Sights

Most of Seattle's sights are concentrated in a fairly compact core area. The historic downtown, Pioneer Square, includes the area between Cherry and S King Sts, along 1st to 3rd Ave. The main shopping area is along 4th and 5th Aves from Olive Way down to University St. Northwest of downtown is Seattle Center, with many of the city's cultural and sporting facilities, as well as the Space Needle and the Experience Music Project. Across busy Alaskan Way from the Pike Place Market is the Waterfront, Seattle's tourist mecca.

DOWNTOWN

Second only to the Space Needle as an iconic Seattle emblem, **Pike Place Market** (www.pikeplacemarket.org) doesn't look like somewhere that spawned the world's largest corporate coffee chain (Starbucks). Quirky, alternative and full of independent businesses, this busy slice of urban theater is famous for its eye-poppingly fresh fruit and vegetables, and wisecracking showman vendors, most notably the loquacious fish-throwing fishmongers. Then there are the anarchistic shops – Left Banks Books (p1032) and Holy Cow Records (p1032) – and the assembled buskers, jugglers, palm readers, tourists and oddballs, from the stand-up piano player in the tall hat to the guy standing underneath the neon coffee sign holding up a placard that reads 'Free Hugs'. Melded together, it's quite a show.

HOT TOPIC: PUBLIC TRANSPORTATION

In a city beset by some truly awful traffic jams, transportation in Seattle has always been a hot and highly controversial topic. The Alaskan Way Viaduct and Seawall Replacement project is a plan to replace Seattle's ugly 60's-era waterfront flyover with a less unsightly and more earthquake-proof tunnel. But, the $4.2 billion project, enthusiastically backed by city mayor Greg Nickels, is not without its opponents, including residents wary of higher taxes and the local chapter of the Sierra Club who feel that the tunnel will not do enough to get people out of their cars and reduce greenhouse-gas emissions. The topic played a major role in the 2009 Seattle mayoral campaign and was a contributing factor in the defeat of the once popular environmentalist mayor, Nickels, who lost in his bid for a third term in August 2009. As for the tunnel, the jury is still out.

DON'T MISS

- **Pike Place Market** (opposite) – street theater in Seattle's urban hub
- **Seattle Art Museum** (below) – up-to-the-minute international art skillfully laid out in a classic downtown gallery
- **Capitol Hill** (p1026) – where the counterculture meets modern yuppie-dom in a funky hilltop domain
- **Brouwer's** (p1030) – an enormous beer hall with an epic bar and cool industrial decor

Extensively renovated and expanded in 2007, the **Seattle Art Museum** (☎ 206-654-3100; www.seattleartmuseum.org; 1300 1st Ave; adult/child/student/senior $13/free/7/10, 1st Thu of month free; 🕑 10am-5pm Tue-Sun, to 9pm Thu & Fri) now has 118,000 extra square feet. Some have criticized the new section for having a clinical feel, but it's difficult not to be struck by a sense of excitement upon entering. Above the ticket counter hangs Cai Guo-Qiang's *Inopportune: Stage One*, a series of white cars exploding with neon. Between the two museum entrances (one in the old building and one in the new) is the 'art ladder,' a free space with installations cascading down a wide stepped hallway. And the galleries themselves are much improved. The museum's John H Hauberg Collection is an excellent display of masks, canoes, totems and other pieces from Northwest coastal tribes.

Northwest of Pike Place Market is **Belltown**, a one-time haven of grunge that is anything but grungy these days. Aside from sharing lattes with the now upscale condo crowd you can mosey on over to the experimental new **Olympic Sculpture Park** (☎ 206-654-3100; 2901 Western Ave; admission free; 🕑 sunrise-sunset), an outpost of the Seattle Art Museum overlooking Elliott Bay.

PIONEER SQUARE

A riot of Richardson Romanesque (the red-bricked revivalist architectural style that embellished Seattle after the 1889 fire (a devastating inferno that destroyed 25 city blocks including the entire central business district), Pioneer Square is Seattle's oldest quarter. In the early years its boom-bust fortunes turned its arterial road, Yesler Way, into the original 'skid row' – an allusion to the skidding logs that were pulled downhill to Henry Yesler's pier-side mill. When the timber industry fell on hard times, the road became a haven for the homeless and its name subsequently became a byword for poverty-stricken urban enclaves countrywide.

Pioneer Square's most iconic building is the 42-story **Smith Tower** completed in 1914 and, until 1931, the tallest building west of the Mississippi. Thanks to a concerted public effort, the neighborhood avoided being laid to waste by the demolition squads in the 1960s and is now protected in the Pioneer Square–Skid Rd Historic District.

The quarter today mixes historic with seedy and harbors art galleries, cafés and nightlife. Highlights include the 1909 **Pergola**, a decorative iron shelter reminiscent of a Parisian Metro station; **Occidental Park**, containing totem poles carved by Chinookan artist Duane Pasco; and the Central Saloon (p1031), a bar that has been in operation since 1892.

The **Klondike Gold Rush National Historical Park** (☎ 206-553-7220; www.nps.gov/klse; 117 S Main St; admission free; 🕑 9am-5pm) is a shockingly good museum with exhibits, photos and news clippings about Seattle during the boom years of the 1897 Klondike gold rush that sent prospectors to the Yukon Territory in Canada.

INTERNATIONAL DISTRICT

East of Pioneer Square (take S Jackson St), Asian shops and restaurants line the streets. The **Wing Luke Asian Museum** (☎ 206-623-5124; www.wingluke.org; 407 7th Ave S; adult/child/student $4/2/3; 🕑 11am-4:30pm Tue-Fri, noon-4pm Sat & Sun) documents the city's wealth of Asian cultures and their often fraught meeting with the West through artwork, special exhibits, historic photographs, a replica of a WWII Japanese American internment camp and recorded interviews with people who were forced into the camps.

SEATTLE CENTER

The remnants of the futuristic 1962 World's Fair hosted by Seattle and subtitled Century 21 Exposition are still visible nearly 50 years later at the **Seattle Center** (☎ 206-684-8582; www.seattlecenter.com; 400 Broad St). The fair was a major success, attracting 10 million visitors, running a profit (rare for the time) and inspiring a skin-crawlingly kitschy Elvis movie, *It Happened at the World's Fair* (1963).

Visible all over the city, the instantly recognizable **Space Needle** (☎ 206-905-2100; www.spaceneedle.com; adult/child/senior $16/8/14; 9am-midnight) is a 605ft-high observation station with a revolving restaurant. The **monorail** (☎ 206-905-2600; www.seattlemonorail.com; adult/child/senior $4/1.50/2; 9am-11pm), a 1.5-mile experiment in mass transit that many American cities have yet to cotton on to, runs every 10 minutes daily from downtown's Westlake Center to a station next to the Experience Music Project.

Microsoft cofounder Paul Allen's **Experience Music Project** (EMP; ☎ 206-367-5483; www.emplive.com; 325 5th Ave N; adult/child/student & senior $19.95/14.95/15.95; 9am-6pm Sun-Thu, 9am-9pm Fri & Sat May-Sept, 10am-5pm Sun-Thu, 10am-9pm Fri & Sat Nov-Apr) is worth a look for the architecture alone. Whether it's worth the admission price depends on how old and music-obsessed you are. The Frank Gehry building houses 80,000 music artifacts, including handwritten lyrics by Nirvana's Kurt Cobain and a Fender Stratocaster demolished by Jimi Hendrix. Attached to the EMP is the **Science Fiction Museum** (☎ 206-724-3428; www.sfhomeworld.org; 325 5th Ave N; adult/child $15/12; 10am-8pm May-Sept, 10am-5pm Wed-Mon Nov-Apr), a nerd paradise of costumes, props and models from sci-fi movies and TV shows. Admission is free between 5pm and 8pm on the first Thursday of the month.

CAPITOL HILL

Seattle's counterculture is never far from the surface in irreverent Capitol Hill, a well-heeled but liberal neighborhood rightly renowned for its fringe theater, alternative music scene, indie coffee bars, and vital gay and lesbian culture. You can take your dog for a herbal bath here, go shopping for ethnic crafts on Broadway, or blend in (or not) with the young punks and the old hippies on the eclectic Pike-Pine Corridor. The junction of Broadway and E John St is the nexus from which to navigate the quarter's various restaurants, brewpubs, boutiques and dingy but not dirty dive bars. Further north, in stately **Volunteer Park**, the **Seattle Asian Art Museum** (☎ 206-654-3100; www.seattleartmuseum.org; 1400 E Prospect St; adult/child/student & senior $5/free/3, 1st Thu & Sat of month free; 10am-5pm Tue-Sun, to 9pm Thu; P) houses the extensive art collection of Dr Richard Fuller, who donated this severe art-moderne-style gallery to the city in 1932. Also in Volunteer Park is the glass-sided Victorian **conservatory** (admission free), filled with palms, cacti and tropical plants.

WHAT THE...?

The **Fremont Troll** lurks beneath the north end of the Aurora Bridge at N 36th St. The troll's creators – artists Steve Badanes, Will Martin, Donna Walter and Ross Whitehead – won a competition sponsored by the Fremont Arts Council in 1990. The 18ft-high cement figure snacking on a Volkswagen Beetle is now a favorite place for late-night beer drinking.

FREMONT

Fremont, about 2 miles north of Seattle Center, is known for its lefty vibe, farmers market and wacky public sculpture, including a rocket sticking out of a building and a statue of Lenin shipped over from Slovakia. People come from all over town for the **Fremont Sunday Market** (☎ 206-781-6776; www.fremontmarket.com/fremont; Stone Way & N 34th St; 10am-5pm Sun May-Sept, 10am-4pm Sun Nov-Apr). The market features fresh fruits and vegetables, arts and crafts, and all kinds of people getting rid of junk.

Another piece of public art, **Waiting for the Interurban** (cnr N 34th St & Fremont Ave N) is a cast-aluminum statue of people awaiting a train that never comes: the Interurban linking Seattle and Everett stopped running in the 1930s (it started up again in 2001 but the line no longer passes this way). Check out the human face on the dog; it's Armen Stepanian, once Fremont's honorary mayor, who made the mistake of objecting to the sculpture.

THE U DISTRICT

The 700-acre **University of Washington** (www.washington.edu) campus sits at the edge of Lake Union in a commercial area about 3 miles northeast of downtown. The main streets are University Way, known as 'the Ave,' and NE 45th St, both lined with coffee shops, restaurants and bars, cinemas and bookstores. The core of the campus is **Central Plaza**, known as Red Sq because of its brick base. Get information and a campus map at the **visitor center** (☎ 206-543-9198; 4014 University Way; 8am-5pm Mon-Fri).

Near the junction of NE 45th St and 16th Ave is the **Burke Museum** (☎ 206-543-5590; adult/student/senior $8/5/6.50, 1st Thu of month free; 10am-5pm, 1st Thu of month 10am-8pm), with an excellent collection of Northwest-coast Native American artifacts. At the corner of NE 41st St and 15th Ave is the **Henry Art Gallery**

(☎ 206-543-2280; adult/student/senior $10/free/6, Thu free; 11am-5pm Tue-Sun, to 8pm Thu), a sophisticated space centered on a remarkable permanent exhibit by light-manipulating sculptor James Turrell, and featuring various temporary and touring collections.

BALLARD

Six miles northwest of Downtown, Ballard, despite its recent veneer of hipness, still has the feel of an old Scandinavian fishing village – especially around the locks, the marina and the Nordic Heritage Museum. The old town has become a nightlife hot spot, but even in the daytime its historic buildings and cobblestoned streets make it a pleasure to wander through.

Here, the waters of Lake Washington and Lake Union flow through the 8-mile-long Lake Washington Ship Canal and into Puget Sound. Construction of the canal began in 1911; today 100,000 boats a year pass through the **Hiram M Chittenden Locks** (☎ visitors center 206-783-7059; 3015 NW 54th St; 24hr), about a half-mile west of Ballard off NW Market St. Take bus 17 from downtown at 4th Ave and Union St. On the southern side of the locks you can watch from underwater glass tanks or from above as salmon navigate a **fish ladder** on their way to spawning grounds in the Cascade headwaters of the Sammamish River, which feeds Lake Washington.

Activities

HIKING

There are great hiking trails through old-growth forest at Seward Park, which dominates the Bailey Peninsula that juts into Lake Washington, and longer but flatter hikes in 534-acre Discovery Park northwest of Seattle. The **Sierra Club** (☎ 206-523-2019; www.sierraclub.org) leads day-hiking and car-camping trips on weekends; most day trips are free.

CYCLING

A cycling favorite, the 16.5-mile **Burke-Gilman Trail** winds from Ballard to Log Boom Park in Kenmore on Seattle's Eastside. There, it connects with the 11-mile **Sammamish River Trail**, which winds past the Chateau Ste Michelle winery in Woodinville before terminating at Redmond's Marymoor Park.

More cyclists pedal the oft-congested loop around **Green Lake**, situated just north of Fremont and 5 miles north of the downtown core. Closer in, the 2.5-mile **Elliott Bay Trail** runs along the Waterfront.

Get a copy of the *Seattle Bicycling Guide Map*, published by the City of Seattle's **Transportation Bicycle & Pedestrian Program** (☎ 206-684-7583; www.cityofseattle.net/transportation/bikemaps.htm) online or at bike shops.

The following are recommended for bicycle rentals and repairs:

Bicycle Center (☎ 206-523 8300; 4529 Sand Point Way; rentals per 1-/24hr $3/15) A longstanding bike shop that does rentals and repairs; it's right off the Burke-Gilman Trail.

Bikestation Seattle (☎ 206-224-9252; 309A 3rd Ave S; 9am-5pm Mon-Fri) Affiliated to the Bicycle Alliance of Washington, this place offers secure 24/7 bike parking, on-site repair and rental facilities in the adjacent JRA shop.

Gregg's Cycles (☎ 206-523-1822; 7007 Woodlawn Ave NE; 10am-8pm Mon-Fri, 10am-6pm Sat & Sun) Here since 1932, Gregg's is a higher-end shop with two new storefronts in Bellevue and Alderwood; rentals are still out of the Green Lake shop. Fancy road bikes rent for $30 to $56 per hour, or you can get a more standard model for $18 per hour or $135 per week.

WATER SPORTS

On Lake Union, **Northwest Outdoor Center Inc** (☎ 206-281-9694, 800-683-0637; www.nwoc.com; 2100 Westlake Ave N; kayaks per hr $13-20) rents kayaks and offers tours and instruction in sea and white-water kayaking.

The **UW Waterfront Activities Center** (☎ 206-543-9433; canoes & rowboats per hr $7.50; usually 10am-7pm Feb-Oct), at the southeast corner of the Husky Stadium parking lot off Montlake Blvd NE, rents canoes and rowboats. Bring ID or a passport.

The **Agua Verde Paddle Club** (☎ 206-545-8570; 1303 NE Boat St; per 1/2hr single kayak $15/25, double kayak $18/30; 10am-dusk Mon-Sat, 10am-6pm Sun Mar-Oct), near the university on Portage Bay, rents kayaks.

Seattle for Children

The whole of Seattle Center will fascinate youngsters, but they'll get the most out of the **Pacific Science Center** (☎ 206-443-2001; www.pacsci.org; 200 2nd Ave N; adult/child 3-5yr/child 6-12yr $11/6/8, IMAX Theater & Laserium with general admission extra $3, without general admission $8/6/7; 10am-6pm;). It entertains and educates with virtual-reality exhibits, laser shows, holograms, an IMAX theater and a planetarium – parents won't be bored either. Parking costs between $5 and $10.

Downtown on Pier 59 is the fascinating **Seattle Aquarium** (☎ 206-386-4300; www.seattleaquarium.org; 1483 Alaskan Way at Pier 59; adult/child $16/10.50; 9:30am-5pm;), another fun way to learn all about the natural world of the Pacific

Northwest. 'Window on Washington Waters' is a look at the seafloor of the Neah Bay area, where rockfish, salmon, sea anemones and more than 100 other fish and invertebrate species live. The centerpiece of the aquarium is a glass-domed room where sharks, octopuses and other deepwater denizens lurk in the shadowy depths.

Tours

Argosy Cruises Seattle Harbor Tour (206-623-1445, 800-642-7816; www.argosycruises.com; adult/child $18.61/7.81) Argosy's popular Seattle Harbor Tour is a one-hour narrated tour of Elliott Bay, the Waterfront and the Port of Seattle. It departs from Pier 55.

Coffee Crawl (800-838-3006; www.seattlebyfoot.com; tours $20; 10am selective days) Touring Seattle's coffee bars is a local experience akin to exploring Rome's ruins. This two-hour caffeine-fuelled romp starts at Pike Place Market under the famous coffee sign and continues along Post Alley with explanations on the city's coffee history and culture.

Seattle Food Tours (425-725-4483; www.seattlefoodtours.com; tours $39) A culinary hike in and around Pike Place Market, this 2½-hour excursion takes in a bakery, chowder house, Vietnamese restaurant and Mexican kitchen. You'll also get some historical and artistic background.

Festivals & Events

Northwest Folklife Festival (206-684-7300; www.nwfolklife.org) Memorial Day weekend in May. International music, dance, crafts, food and family activities at Seattle Center.

Seafair (206-728-0123; www.seafair.com) Late July and August. Huge crowds attend this festival on the water, with hydroplane races, a torchlight parade, an air show, music and a carnival.

Bumbershoot (206-281-8111; www.bumbershoot.com) Labor Day weekend in September. A major arts and cultural event at Seattle Center, with live music, author readings and lots of unclassifiable fun.

Sleeping

From mid-November through to the end of March, most downtown hotels offer Seattle Super Saver Packages – generally 50% off rack rates, with a coupon book for savings on dining, shopping and attractions. Call the **Seattle Hotel Hotline** (800-535-7071). You can make reservations on its website at www.seattlesupersaver.com.

BUDGET

Green Tortoise Guest House (206-340-1222; www.greentortoise.net; 105 Pike St; dm $24-29, r $77-80, incl breakfast;) The only hostel in the city center now that HI (Hostelling International) Seattle has closed, this once-super-grungy place has moved around the corner from its old home and is right across the street from Pike Place Market. There are 30 bunk rooms and 16 European-style rooms (with shared bath and shower).

Moore Hotel (206-448-4851, 800-421-5508; www.moorehotel.com; 1926 2nd Ave; s/d with shared bath $59/71, private bath $74/86;) Old-world and a little moth-eaten, the Moore nonetheless has a friendly front desk and a prime location. If that doesn't swing you, the price should.

College Inn (206-633-4441; www.collegeinnseattle.com; 4000 University Way NE; s/d incl breakfast from $60/70;) This pretty, half-timbered building in the U District, left over from the 1909 Alaska-Yukon-Pacific Exposition, has 25 European-style guest rooms with sinks and shared baths. Note there are four flights of stairs and no elevator. Pub in the basement!

MIDRANGE

Gaslight Inn B&B (206-325-3654; www.gaslight-inn.com; 1727 15th Ave E; r $88-158;) The Gaslight Inn has 15 rooms available (12 with private baths) in two neighboring homes. In summer, it's refreshing to dive into the outdoor pool or just hang out on the sun deck.

Ace Hotel (206-448-4721; www.acehotel.com; 2423 1st Ave; r with shared/private bath $99/190;) Emulating (almost) its hip Portland cousin, the Ace sports minimal, futuristic decor (everything's white or stainless steel, even the TV), antique French army blankets, condoms instead of pillow mints and a Kama Sutra in place of the Bible. Parking costs $15.

our pick **Mediterranean Inn** (206-428-4700; www.mediterranean-inn.com; 425 Queen Anne Ave N; r from $119;) There's something about the surprisingly un-Mediterranean Med Inn that just clicks. Maybe it's the handy cusp-of-downtown location, or the genuinely friendly staff, or the kitchenettes in every room, or the small downstairs gym, or the surgical cleanliness in every room. Don't try to define it – just go there and soak it up.

Hotel Max (206-441-4200, 800-426-0670; www.hotelmaxseattle.com; 620 Stewart St; s/d from $179/199;) Original artworks hang in the (small but cool) guest rooms, and it's tough to get any hipper than the Max's super-saturated color scheme – not to mention package deals such as the Grunge Special or the Gaycation. Rooms feature menus for your choice of pillows and spirituality services. Parking costs $15.

TOP END

Inn at the Market (☎ 206-443-3600, 800-446-4484; www.innatthemarket.com; 86 Pine St; r $175-300, with water views $230-400; P ⊠ ✲ ☰) The elegant Inn at the Market is the only lodging in the venerable Pike Place Market. This 70-room boutique hotel has large rooms, many of which enjoy grand views onto market activity and Puget Sound. Parking costs $20.

MarQueen Hotel (☎ 206-286-7407; www.marqueen.com; 600 Queen Anne Ave N; r from $225; P ☰) In some old (by Seattle standards) apartment buildings spruced up and turned into a hotel, the MarQueen's rooms come with their original kitchenettes and retain enough early 20th-century elegance to keep them feeling authentic. While falling a little shy of the full-on luxury bracket, the hotel's location adjacent to the Seattle Center and next to a fine strip of restaurants is a big advantage.

Hotel Monaco (☎ 206-621-1770; www.monaco-seattle.com; 1101 4th Ave; d/ste from $260/309; P ⊠ ☐ ☰) Whimsical with dashes of European elegance, the downtown Monaco is worthy of all four of its illustrious stars. Injecting a bit of down-to-earth ambience into the brew, the assistant manager runs (quite literally) early-morning jogging sessions along the Waterfront with guests.

Eating

BUDGET

The best budget meals are to be found in Pike Place Market. Take your pick and make your own from fresh produce, baked goods, deli items and take-out ethnic foods.

our pick Piroshky Bakery (☎ 206-441-6068; 1908 Pike Pl; snacks $2-7; 🕒 8am-6:30pm Oct-Apr, 7:30am-6:30pm May-Sep) Proof that not all insanely popular Pike Place holes-in-the-wall go global (à la Starbucks), Piroshky's is still knocking out its delectable mix of sweet and savory Russian pies and pastries in a space barely big enough to swing a small kitten. Join the melee and order one 'to go.'

Travelers (☎ 206-329-6260; 501 E Pine St; snacks $5-10; 🕒 10am-7pm Mon-Thu, 10am-8pm Fri & Sat, noon-8pm Sun) This Capitol Hill Indian store-cum-café sells everything from tiffin boxes to Kama Sutra postcards, but comes into its own for its slow-brewed masala chai tea, a sweet, spicy and powder-free taste of the real Asian subcontinent. If you're feeling peckish the subtly nuanced *thali* tray is highly recommended.

Peso's Kitchen & Lounge (☎ 206-283-9353; 605 Queen Anne Ave N; breakfast $6-9, dinner $9-13; 🕒 9am-2am) A place that wears many hats – or should that be sombreros. Fine Mexican food is served here in the evenings amid a cool trendy 'scene' that is anything but Mexican. But the trump card comes the next morning, after the beautiful people have gone home, with an acclaimed egg-biased breakfast.

Salumi (☎ 206-621-8772; 309 3rd Ave S; sandwiches $7-10, plates $11-14; 🕒 11am-4pm Tue-Fri) The line waiting at Mario Batali's dad's place is like its own little community. People chat, compare notes, talk about sandwiches they've had and loved…it's nice. Sandwiches come with any of a dozen types of cured meat and fresh cheese. There aren't many seats, so plan to picnic.

MIDRANGE

Shiro's Sushi Restaurant (☎ 206-443-9844; 2401 2nd Ave; sushi $2-9, specials $9-13, mains $20-21; 🕒 5:30-9:45pm) There's barely room for all the awards and kudos that cram the window in this sleek Japanese joint. Grab a pew behind the glass food case and watch the experts concoct delicate and delicious Seattle sushi.

Café Septieme (☎ 206-860-8858; 214 Broadway E; starters $5-9, breakfast & lunch $7-9, dinner $15-18; 🕒 9am-midnight) A pretty, Euro-style restaurant-bar with red walls and white-clothed tables, Septieme serves filling but sophisticated burgers, salads, pastas and fish dishes; the bacon-provolone cheeseburger is great.

Palace Kitchen (☎ 206-448-2001; 2030 5th Ave; salads $7-9, mains $12-25; 🕒 5pm-1am) Owned by celebrity chef Tom Douglas, Palace Kitchen is a late-night hot spot that fills up when the cocktail crowd gets peckish. Its bar snacks are anything but ordinary; try the king-crab omelet.

5 Spot (☎ 206-285-7768; 1502 Queen Anne Ave N; brunch $8-10, dinner $13-17 🕒 8:30am-midnight) Top of the hill, top of the morning and top of the pops; the queues outside 5 Spot at 10am on a Sunday testify to a formidable brunch. The crowds mean a great atmosphere and the hearty menu, which has perfected French toast, huevos rancheros and plenty more American standards, will shift even the most stubborn of hangovers.

Black Bottle (☎ 206-441-1500; 2600 1st Ave; plates $8-12; 🕒 4:30pm-2am) This trendy minimalist bar-restaurant showcases the new Belltown of smart condo dwellers and avid wine quaffers. The food is mainly appetizers, but with menu items such as grilled lamb and sumac hummus, and braised artichoke heart and greens, even the nostalgic grunge groupies of yore will find it hard to resist the lure.

Coastal Kitchen (☎ 206-322-1145; 429 15th Ave E; lunch $8-12, dinner $14-20; 🕑 8am-11pm) This longtime favorite turns out some of the best food in the neighborhood – it has an eclectic mix of Cajun, Mayan and Mexican inspirations, and an Italian-language instruction tape running in the restroom, if that gives a clue toward influences.

TOP END

Queen City Grill (☎ 206-443-0975; 2201 1st Ave; mains $12-33; 🕑 5pm-2am) This longtime Belltown favorite serves daily seafood specials and menus that change to reflect the use of seasonal ingredients. The room is warmly lit and cozy, yet sophisticated, and service is all class.

Steelhead Diner (☎ 206-625-0129; www.steelheaddiner.com; 95 Pine St; sandwiches $9-13, mains $15-33; 🕑 11am-10pm Tue-Sat, 10am-3pm Sun) Homey favorites such as fish and chips, grilled salmon or braised short ribs and grits become fine cuisine when they're made with the best of what Pike Place Market has to offer.

SkyCity (☎ 206-905-2100; 219 4th Ave N; mains $34-54; 🕑 11:30am-2pm & 5-8:45pm Mon-Fri, 10am-2:45pm & 5-9:45pm Sat & Sun) Balanced on top of the Space Needle (p1026), this revolving restaurant makes a full turn every 47 minutes. The steep prices reflect both the setting (all tables have a full city view) and the fine dining incorporating fresh ecofriendly ingredients.

Drinking

You'll find cocktail bars, dance clubs and live music on Capitol Hill. The main drag in Ballard has brick taverns old and new, filled with the hard-drinking older set in daylight hours and indie rockers at night. Belltown has gone from grungy to shabby chic, but has the advantage of many drinking holes neatly lined up in rows. Industrial Georgetown is an up-and-coming barfly's paradise, still rough around the edges. And, this being Seattle, you can't walk two blocks without hitting a coffee shop.

Coffeehouses get brewing between 6am and 7am and keep going until 7pm. Some of the hip places hold out until 11pm or even midnight. Bars usually open from 5pm to 2am, unless there's a restaurant attached in which case they'll often open for lunch.

COFFEEHOUSES

Starbucks is the tip of the iceberg. Seattle has spawned plenty of smaller indie chains, many with their own roasting rooms.

B&O Espresso (☎ 206-322-5028; 204 Belmont Ave E; 🕑 7am-late Mon-Thu, 8am-late Fri-Sun) Full of understated swank, this is the place to go for Turkish coffee – if you can get past the pastry case up front.

Caffé Vita (☎ 206-709-4440; 1005 E Pike St; 🕑 6am-11pm) The laptop fiend, the date, the radical student, the homeless hobo, the philosopher, the business guy on his way to work; watch the whole neighborhood pass through this Capitol Hill institution (one of four in Seattle) with its own on-site roasting room visible through a glass partition.

Top Pot Hand-Forged Doughnuts (☎ 206-728-1966; 2124 5th Ave; 🕑 6am-7pm) Another nascent Seattle chain, Top Pot still only has a manageable four branches. This trendy Belltown location is perhaps the quirkiest with its floor-to-ceiling library shelves, art-deco signage, and legendary coffee and doughnuts.

Panama Hotel Tea & Coffee House (☎ 206-515-4000; 607 S Main St; 🕑 8am-7pm Mon-Sat, 9am-7pm Sun) The Panama, a historic 1910 building that contains the only remaining Japanese bathhouse in the US, doubles as a memorial to the neighborhood's Japanese residents forced into internment camps during WWII.

Zeitgeist (☎ 206-583-0497; 171 S Jackson St; 🕑 6am-7pm Mon-Fri, 8am-7pm Sat & Sun; 📶) Plug into the spirit of the times with the rest of the laptop crew at this lofty, brick-walled café near the train station.

BARS

Brouwer's (☎ 206-267-2437; 400 N 35th St; 🕑 11am-2am) This dark cathedral of beer in Fremont has rough-hewn rock walls and a black metal grate in the ceiling. Behind an epic bar are tantalizing glimpses into a massive beer fridge. A replica *Mannequin Pis* statue at the door and the Belgian crest everywhere clue you in to the specialty.

Shorty's (☎ 206-441-5449; 2222 2nd Ave) An unpretentious oasis in a block of *très chic* lounges, Shorty's has cheap beer and hot dogs, alcohol slushies and a back room of pinball heaven.

Blue Moon (☎ 206-633-626; 712 NE 45th St) Legendary former haunt of Dylan Thomas and Allen Ginsberg, the Blue Moon is exactly a mile from the university campus, thanks to an early zoning law. Be prepared for impromptu poetry recitations, jaw-harp performances and inspired rants.

Copper Gate (☎ 206-706-3292; 6301 24th Ave NW) Formerly one of Seattle's worst dives, the Copper Gate in Ballard is now an upscale bar-restaurant focused on meatballs and naked ladies. A Viking longship forms the bar, with a peepshow pastiche for a sail and a cargo of helmets and gramophones.

Nine Pound Hammer (☎ 206-762-3373; 6009 Airport Way S) This darkened beer hall in Georgetown is generous with the pours and the peanuts, and the mixed crowd of workers, hipsters, punks and bikers vacillates between energetic and rowdy.

BREWPUBS

Jolly Roger Taproom (☎ 206-782-6181; 1514 Leary Way NW; Mon-Sat) Less scurvy-barnacle than placid-yachtsman, Maritime Pacific Brewing's Jolly Roger Taproom in Ballard is a tiny, pirate-themed bar with a nautical chart painted onto the floor, good seafood and about 15 taps.

Hale's Ales Brewery (☎ 206-706-1544; 4301 Leary Way NW) Hale's makes fantastic beer, notably its ambrosial Cream Ale. Its flagship brewpub in Fremont feels like a business-hotel lobby, but it's worth a stop. There is a self-guided tour near the entrance.

Pike Pub & Brewery (☎ 206-622-6044; 1415 1st Ave) This pub in Pike Place Market serves great burgers and brews in a funky neoindustrial multilevel space.

Elysian Brewing Company (☎ 206-860-1920; 1221 E Pike St) On Capitol Hill, the Elysian's huge windows are great for people-watching – or being watched, if your pool game's good enough.

Entertainment

Consult the *Stranger*, *Seattle Weekly* or the daily papers for listings. Tickets for big events are available at **TicketMaster** (☎ 206-628-0888), which operates a **discount ticket booth** (☎ 206-233-1111) at Westlake Center.

LIVE MUSIC

Crocodile (☎ 206-441-5611; www.thecrocodile.com; 2200 2nd Ave) Reopened in March 2009 after a year in the doldrums, the sole survivor of Belltown's once influential grunge scene (formerly known as the Crocodile Café) will have to work hard to reclaim an audience who grew up listening to Nirvana, Pearl Jam and REM at this formerly hallowed music venue.

Neumo's (☎ 206-709-9467; www.neumos.com; 925 E Pike St) A punk/hip-hop/alternative music venue that counts Radiohead and Bill Clinton (not together) among its former guests, Neumo's (formerly known as Moe's) fills the big shoes of its original namesake. You can mark the passage of time at 'Sad Bastards Mondays' which offer 'tunes to cry into your beer to.'

Chop Suey (☎ 206-324-8000; www.chopsuey.com; 1325 E Madison St) Chop Suey is a dark, high-ceilinged space with a ramshackle faux-Chinese motif and eclectic bookings.

Central Saloon (☎ 206-622-0209; 207 1st Ave) The launching pad for many a musical career, Pioneer Square's 'Central' has been in operation since 1892 and has seen it all from the Klondike gold rush to a Mudhoney sound rush.

CINEMAS

The biggest event of the year for Seattle cinephiles is the **Seattle International Film Festival** (SIFF; ☎ 206-464-5830; www.siff.net; tickets $5-11, 6-/20-pack pass $57/180). The festival uses a half-dozen cinemas but also has its own dedicated cinema, in McCaw Hall's **Nesholm Family Lecture Hall** (321 Mercer St, Seattle Center), and typically starts in mid-May.

The **Seattle Lesbian & Gay Film Festival** (☎ 206-323-4274; www.threedollarbillcinema.org; tickets $6-8), a popular festival in October, shows new gay-themed films from directors worldwide.

Cool cinemas include the following:

Cinerama (☎ 206-441-3653; www.cinerama.com; 2100 4th Ave) One of the very few Cineramas left in the world, it has a fun, sci-fi feel.

Harvard Exit (☎ 206-781-5755; www.landmarktheatres.com; cnr E Roy St & Harvard Ave) Built in 1925, Seattle's first independent theater.

Northwest Film Forum (☎ 206-329-2629; www.nwfilmforum.org; 1515 12th Ave) Impeccable programming, from restored classics to cutting-edge independent and international films.

THEATER & CULTURE

Check local newspapers for reviews and schedules.

One of the three big companies in the city, **A Contemporary Theatre** (ACT; ☎ 206-292-7676; www.acttheatre.org; 700 Union St) fills its $30-million home at Kreielsheimer Place with performances by Seattle's best thespians and occasional big-name actors. The Intiman Theatre Company, Seattle's oldest, takes the stage at **Intiman Playhouse** (☎ 206-269-1900; www.intiman.org; 201 Mercer St).

The **Pacific Northwest Ballet** (☎ 206-441-9411; www.pnb.org) is the foremost dance company in the Northwest and does more than a hundred performances a season from September through June at Seattle Center's McCaw Hall. **Seattle Opera** (☎ 206-389-7676; www.seattleopera.org), also at McCaw Hall, features a program of four or five full-scale operas every season, including a summer Wagner's *Ring* cycle that draws sellout crowds.

The **Seattle Symphony** (☎ 206-215-4747; www.seattlesymphony.org) is a major regional ensemble. It plays at the Benaroya Concert Hall, which you'll find downtown at 2nd Ave and University St.

SPORTS

The beloved **Seattle Mariners** (☎ 206-628-3555; www.mariners.org; tickets $7-60) baseball team plays in Safeco Field just south of downtown, while the **Seattle Seahawks** (☎ 425-827-9777; www.seahawks.com; tickets $42-95), the Northwest's only National Football League (NFL) franchise plays in the 72,000-seat Seahawks Stadium.

GAY & LESBIAN VENUES

Storied dance club **Re-Bar** (☎ 206-233-9873; 1114 Howell St), where many of Seattle's defining cultural events happened (such as Nirvana album releases etc), welcomes gay, straight, bi or undecided revelers to its lively dance floor.

Check out the always-packed dance factory **Neighbours** (☎ 206-324-5358; 1509 Broadway Ave E) for the gay club scene and its attendant glittery straight girls.

R Place (☎ 206-322-8828; 619 E Pine St) offers three floors of dancing to hip-hop/R & B DJs and plenty of sweaty body contact make this club a blast for pretty much everyone who isn't terribly uptight.

Shopping

The main big-name shopping area is downtown between 3rd and 6th Aves and University and Stewart Sts. Pike Place Market (p1024) is a maze of arts-and-crafts stalls, galleries and small shops. Pioneer Square and Capitol Hill have locally owned gift and thrift shops.

Some only-in-Seattle shops to seek out:

Babeland (☎ 206-328-2914; 707 E Pike St; 🕒 11am-10pm Mon-Sat, noon-7pm Sun) The answer to the question 'Where can I buy pink furry handcuffs and a glass dildo?'

Holy Cow Records (☎ 206-405-4200; 1501 Pike Pl, Suite 325; 🕒 10am-10pm Mon-Sat, 10am-7pm Sun) Proceed to Pike Place Market and let your fingers flick through the ageing vinyl at this shrine to music geekdom; you might just stumble upon that rare Psychedelic Furs 12-inch that has been eluding you since 1984.

Left Bank Books (☎ 206-622-0195; 92 Pike St; 🕒 10am-7pm Mon-Sat, 11am-6pm Sun) This 35-year-old collective displays zines in *español,* revolutionary pamphlets, a 'fuck authority' notice board and plenty of Chomsky. You're in Seattle, just in case you forgot.

Getting There & Away

AIR

Aka 'Sea-Tac,' **Seattle-Tacoma International Airport** (SEA; ☎ 206-433-5388; www.portseattle.org/seatac), 13 miles south of Seattle on I-5, has daily service to Europe, Asia, Mexico and points throughout the USA and Canada, with frequent flights to and from Portland, OR, and Vancouver, BC.

BOAT

Victoria Clipper (☎ 206-443-2560, 800-888-2535; www.victoriaclipper.com) operates several high-speed passenger ferries to Victoria, BC, and to the San Juan Islands. It also organizes package tours which can be booked in advance through the website. Victoria Clipper runs from Seattle to Victoria up to six times daily; round-trips cost from $77.

The **Washington State Ferries** (☎ 206-464-6400, in Washington 888-808-7977; www.wsdot.wa.gov/ferries) website has maps, prices, schedules, trip planners and weather updates, plus estimated waiting time for popular routes. Fares depend on the route, vehicle size and trip duration, and are collected either for round-trip or one-way travel depending on the departure terminal.

BUS

The **Bellair Airporter Shuttle** (☎ 1-866-235-5247; www.airporter.com) buses passengers as far afield as Ellensburg, Yakima, Anacortes and Bellingham.

Greyhound (☎ 206-628-5561, 800-231-2222; www.greyhound.com; 811 Stewart St; 🕒 6am-midnight) connects Seattle with cites all over the country, including Chicago, IL ($195 one way, two days, three daily), Spokane, WA ($38, five to seven hours, three daily), San Francisco, CA ($95, 20 hours, four daily), and Vancouver, BC ($25, three to four hours, six daily).

More comfortable and offering free on-board wi-fi is the super-efficient **Quick Shuttle** (☎ 800-665-2122; www.quickcoach.com) that runs five times daily along I-5 between Sea-Tac Airport and central Vancouver (BC) stopping in downtown Seattle (at the Best Western Executive Inn, 200 Taylor Ave N), Tulalip, Bellingham airport, South Surrey (Canada), Vancouver airport and downtown Vancouver.

TRAIN

Amtrak (☎ 800-872-7245; www.amtrak.com) serves Seattle's **King Street Station** (303 S Jackson St; 🕑 6am-10:30pm, ticket counter 6:15am-8pm). Three main routes run through town: the *Amtrak Cascades* (connecting Vancouver, Seattle, Portland and Eugene), the very scenic *Coast Starlight* (connecting Seattle, Oakland and Los Angeles) and the *Empire Builder* (a cross-continental roller-coaster to Chicago).

Some examples of one-way ticket prices from Seattle:

Chicago, IL From $334, 46 hours, daily
Oakland, CA $92, 23 hours, daily
Portland, OR $28, three to four hours, five daily
Vancouver, BC $35, three to four hours, five daily

Getting Around

TO/FROM THE AIRPORT

There are a number of options for making the 13-mile trek from the airport to downtown Seattle.

Gray Line's **Airport Express** (☎ 206-626-6088; www.graylineseattle.com; one way adult/child $11/8.25) fetches passengers in the parking lot outside door 00 at the south end of the baggage-claim level. It will drop you at a choice of eight different downtown hotels (handy if you want to get downtown).

Taxis and limousines (about $35 and $40, respectively) are available at the parking garage on the 3rd floor. Rental-car counters are located in the baggage-claim area.

Catch **Metro** (☎ schedule info 206-553-3000; www.transit.metrokc.gov) buses outside door 6 by baggage carousel 5 on the baggage-claim level. Buses 194 Express and 174 go downtown ($1.75 to $2). From there, the free 99 bus goes to the Waterfront, Pioneer Square and the International District. Use the online trip planner for more information.

CAR & MOTORCYCLE

Trapped in a narrow corridor between mountains and sea, Seattle is a horrendous traffic bottleneck and its nightmarish jams are famous. I-5 has a High-Occupancy Vehicle lane for vehicles carrying two or more people. Otherwise try to work around the elongated rush 'hours'.

PUBLIC TRANSPORTATION

Buses are operated by **Metro Transit** (☎ schedule info 206-553-3000, customer service 206-553-3060; www.transit.metrokc.gov), part of the King County Department of Transportation. Fares cost $1.75 to $2.

The new **Seattle Street Car** (☎ 206-553-3000; www.seattlestreetcar.org) runs from the Westlake Center to Lake Union along a 2.6-mile route. There are 11 stops allowing interconnections with numerous bus routes.

TAXI

All Seattle taxi cabs operate at the same rate, set by King County; at the time of research the rate was $2.50 at meter drop, then $2.50 per mile.

Any of the following offer reliable taxi service:

Orange Cab Co (☎ 206-444-0409; www.orangecab.net)
Yellow Cab (☎ 206-622-6500; www.yellowtaxi.net)

AROUND SEATTLE

Puget Sound

Bainbridge Island is a popular destination with locals and visitors alike; the ferry ride provides stunning views of Seattle and the Sound, and it's the quickest and easiest way to get out on the water from Seattle. Prepare to stroll around lazily, tour some waterfront cafés, taste unique wines at the **Bainbridge Island Winery** (☎ 206-842-9463; www.bainbridgevineyards.com; Hwy 305; 🕑 tastings 11am-5pm Fri-Sun), 4 miles north of Winslow, and maybe rent a bike and cycle around the invitingly flat countryside.

Another easy way to get onto the Sound from Seattle is with **Tillicum Village Tours** (☎ 206-933-8600, 800-426-1205; www.tillicumvillage.com; adult/child/senior $79/30/72), which operates from March and December, departing from Pier 55. The four-hour trip to Blake Island – the birthplace of Seattle's namesake, Chief Sealth – includes a salmon bake, a native dance and a movie at an old Duwamish Native American village.

Washington State Ferries (☎ 206-464-6400, in Washington 888-808-7977; www.wsdot.wa.gov/ferries) runs many times daily from Seattle to Bainbridge (adult/child/car and driver $6.70/5.40/14.45, bicycle surcharge $1).

Olympia

In many ways a microcosm of Seattle, Olympia is an edgy, culturally vivacious city that also doubles up as the state capital. Long hailed as a nexus for the fine arts, it's noted for its progressive university (Evergreen) and white-hot music scene, a force that served as an important catalyst for grunge and fermented its own angry post-punk genre: riot grrrl, a radical '90s incarnation of proactive third-wave feminism. While the nightlife has lost a little of its luster since Kurt Cobain roamed the bars of 4th Ave, Olympia can still put on a show and its gritty underground music scene is complemented by some decent brewpubs and a growing cluster of nonfranchise coffee bars. Beyond the grunge, the city's position at the tip of Puget Sound sandwiched between two national parks (Olympic and Mt Rainier) makes it a viable base for the wilderness-bound. The **State Capitol Visitor Center** (☎ 360-586-3460; cnr 14th Ave & Capitol Way) offers information on the capitol campus, the Olympia area and Washington state.

Be sure to look inside the vast, marble-clad **Legislative Building** (1927) in the Washington State Capitol. Free tours are offered hourly between 8am and 4:30pm every day except Christmas and Thanksgiving. Visitors can also tour the **campus** (admission free; 8am-4pm Mon-Fri) and see the Temple of Justice and the Capitol Conservatory, which houses a large collection of tropical plants.

The **State Capital Museum** (☎ 360-753-2580; 211 W 21st Ave; admission $2; 10am-4pm Tue-Fri, noon-4pm Sat) has exhibits on the Nisqually Native Americans. The **Olympia Farmers Market** (☎ 360-352-9096; 10am-3pm Thu-Sun Apr-Oct, 10am-3pm Sat & Sun Nov-Dec), at the north end of Capitol Way, is one of the state's best with fresh local produce, crafts and live music.

For cheap digs, try the **Olympia Inn** (☎ 360-352-8533; 909 Capitol Way S; s/d $50/57; P), a central downtown motel with no frills but clean rooms. A little more upmarket is the slick and efficient **Phoenix Inn Suites** (☎ 360-570-0555; 415 Capitol Way N; s/d $99/109;), well tuned in dealing with demanding state government officials.

Batdorf & Bronson (☎ 360-786-6717; 513 Capitol Way S; 6am-7pm Mon-Fri, 7am-6pm Sat & Sun) is a local roaster offering ethical coffee. Aside from this downtown café, you can buy or try the latest blends at its popular **Tasting Room** (☎ 360-753-4057; 200 Market St NE; 9am-4pm Wed-Sun). The equally famous Olympia oysters can be sampled at the **Budd Bay Café** (☎ 360-357-6963; 525 Columbia St NW; seafood dinners $17-24; 6:30am-11pm). The **Spar Bar** (☎ 360-357-6444; 114 4th Ave E; breakfast $4-5, lunch $5-8; 7am-9pm) is a cozy old café-cum-bar-cum-cigar store with good brews, classic comfort food and supersonic service.

The city's never-static music scene still makes waves on 4th Ave at the retrofitted **4th Avenue Tavern** (☎ 360-786-1444; 210 4th Ave E) or the graffiti-decorated **Le Voyeur** (☎ 360-943-5710; 404 4th Ave E), an anarchistic, vegan-friendly dive bar with a busker often guarding the door.

OLYMPIC PENINSULA

Surrounded on three sides by sea and exhibiting many of the insular characteristics of a full-blown island, the remote Olympic Peninsula is about as 'wild' and 'west' as America gets. What it lacks in cowboys it makes up for in rare, endangered wildlife and dense primeval forest. The peninsula's road-less interior is largely given over to the notoriously wet Olympic National Park while the margins are the preserve of loggers, Native American reservations and a smattering of small but interesting settlements, most notably Port Townsend. Equally untamed is the western coastline, America's isolated end point, where the tempestuous ocean and misty old-growth Pacific rainforest meet in aqueous harmony.

Olympic National Park

Declared a national monument in 1909 and a national park in 1938, the 1406-sq-mile **Olympic National Park** (www.nps.gov/olym) shelters one of the world's only temperate rainforests and a 57-mile strip of Pacific coastal wilderness that was added in 1953 – it exists as one of North America's last great wilderness areas. Opportunities for independent exploration abound, with visitors enjoying such diverse activities as hiking, fishing, kayaking and skiing.

INFORMATION

The park entry fee is $5/15 per person/vehicle, valid for one week, payable at park entrances. Many park visitor centers double as United

WHAT THE....?

With their sharp, crenellated ridges and brooding, snowcapped volcanoes, Washington's peaks share much in common with the Andes in South America – including llamas.

Deli Llama Adventures (☎ 360-757-4212; www.delillama.com; 17045 Llama Lame, Bow, WA 98232) is a small, well-established local outfit that offers llama/hiking excursions in both the North Cascades and Olympic National Parks for groups of up to 10 people from May through September. Prices start at $140 per person per day (depending on group size) and include tents, cooking gear, all meals and – of course – the llamas themselves who, with their sure-footed dignity and instinctive climbing skills, can penetrate the rugged backcountry like a fleet of environmentally friendly SUVs.

States Forestry Service (USFS) ranger stations, where you can pick up permits for wilderness camping ($5 per group, valid up to 14 days, plus $2 per person per night).

Forks Visitor Information Center (☎ 360-374-2531, 800-443-6757; 1411 S Forks Ave, Forks; 🕓 10am-4pm) Suggested itineraries and seasonal information.

Olympic National Park Visitor Center (☎ 360-565-3130; 3002 Mt Angeles Rd, Port Angeles; 🕓 9am-5pm) The best overall center is situated at the Hurricane Ridge gateway, a mile off Hwy 101 in Port Angeles.

Wilderness Information Center (☎ 360-565-3100; 3002 Mt Angeles Rd, Port Angeles; 🕓 7:30am-6pm Sun-Thu, 7:30am-8pm Fri & Sat May-Sept, 8am-4:30pm daily Nov-Apr) Directly behind the visitor center, you'll find maps, permits and trail information.

EASTERN ENTRANCES

The graveled Dosewallips River Rd follows the river from US 101 (turn off approximately 1km north of Dosewallips State Park) for 15 miles to **Dosewallips Ranger Station**, where the trails begin; call ☎ 360-565-3130 for road conditions. Even hiking smaller portions of the two long-distance paths – with increasingly impressive views of heavily glaciated **Mt Anderson** – is reason enough to visit the valley. Another eastern entry for hikers is the **Staircase Ranger Station** (☎ 360-877-5569; 🕓 May-Sept only), just inside the national park boundary, 15 miles from Hoodsport on US 101. Two state parks along the eastern edge of the national park are popular with campers: **Dosewallips State Park** (☎ 888-226-7688; campsites/RV sites $19/24 and **Lake Cushman State Park** (☎ 888-226-7688; campsites/RV sites $20/26). Both have running water, flush toilets and some RV hookups. Reservations are accepted.

NORTHERN ENTRANCES

The park's easiest – and hence most popular – entry point is at **Hurricane Ridge**, 18 miles south of Port Angeles. At the road's end, an interpretive center overlooks a stupendous view of Mt Olympus (7965ft) and dozens of other peaks. The 5200ft altitude can mean inclement weather and the winds here (as the name suggests) can be ferocious. Aside from various summer trekking opportunities, the area boasts one of only two US national-park-based ski runs operated by the small, family-friendly **Hurricane Ridge Winter Sports Club** (☎ 360-417-1542; www.hurricaneridge.net).

Popular for boating and fishing is **Lake Crescent**, the site of the park's oldest and most reasonably priced **lodge** (☎ 360-928-3211; www.lakecrescentlodge.com; 416 Lake Crescent Rd; lodge r with shared bath $68-85, cottages $132-211; 🕓 May-Oct; P ⊠ ✳ wi-fi). Sumptuous and sustainable food is served in the lodge's ecofriendly restaurant. From **Storm King Information Station** (☎ 360-928-3380; 🕓 May-Sept only) on the lake's south shore, a 1-mile hike climbs through old-growth forest to Marymere Falls. Along the Sol Duc River, the **Sol Duc Hot Springs Resort** (☎ 360-327-3583; www.northolympic.com/solduc; 12076 Sol Duc Hot Springs Rd, Port Angeles; r $115-169, RV sites $23; 🕓 late Mar–Oct; ✳ ♿) has lodging, dining, massage and, of course, hot-spring pools (adult/child $10/7.50), as well as great day hikes.

WESTERN ENTRANCES

Isolated by distance and one of the US' rainiest microclimates, the Pacific side of the Olympics remains its wildest. Only US 101 offers access to its noted temperate rainforests and untamed coastline. The **Hoh River Rainforest**, at the end of the 19-mile Hoh River Rd, is a Tolkienesque maze of dripping ferns and moss-draped trees. You can get better acquainted with the area's complex yet delicate natural ecosystems at the **Hoh visitor center and campground** (☎ 360-374-6925; campsites $12; 🕓 9am-6pm Jul & Aug, 9am-4:30pm Sep-Jun), which has information on guided walks and longer backcountry hikes. No hook-ups or showers; first-come first-served.

A little to the south lies **Lake Quinault**, a beautiful glacial lake surrounded by forested peaks. It's popular for fishing, boating and swimming and is punctuated by some of the nation's oldest trees.

our pick **Lake Quinault Lodge** (☎ 360-288-2900; www.visitlakequinault.com; 345 S Shore Rd; lodge r $134-167, cabins $125-243;), a luxury classic of 1920s 'parkitecture', boasts a heated pool and sauna, a crackling fireplace and a memorable dining room noted for its sweet-potato breakfast pancakes. For a cheaper sleep nearby try the ultrafriendly **Quinault River Inn** (☎ 360-288-2237; 8 River Dr; r $69; P) in Amanda Park, a favorite with anglers.

A number of short hikes begin just outside the Lake Quinault Lodge or you can try the longer **Enchanted Valley Trail**, a medium-grade 13-miler that begins from the Graves Creek Ranger station at the end of South Shore Rd and climbs up to a large meadow resplendent with wildflowers and copses of alder trees.

Port Townsend

Historical relics are rare in the Pacific Northwest which makes time-warped Port Townsend all the more fascinating. Small, nostalgic and culturally vibrant, this showcase of 1890s Victorian architecture is the 'New York of the West that never was,' a one-time boomtown that went bust at the turn of the twentieth century only to be rescued 70 years later by a group of far-sighted locals. Port Townsend today is a buoyant blend of inventive eateries, elegant fin de siècle hotels and quirky annual festivals. To get the lowdown on the city's rollercoaster boom-bust history call in at the **visitor center** (☎ 360-385-2722; www.ptchamber.org; 2437 E Sims Way; 9am-5pm Mon-Fri, 9am-4pm Sat & Sun). Further enlightenment can be gleaned at the **Jefferson County Historical Society Museum** (☎ 360-385-1003; 540 Water St; adult/child 12yr & under $4/1; 11am-4pm Mon-Sat & 1-4pm Sun Mar-Dec).

Blustery **Fort Worden State Park** (☎ 360-344-4400; 200 Battery Way; 6:30am-dusk Apr-Oct, 8am-dusk Nov-Mar), located 2 miles north of the ferry landing (take Cherry St from uptown), was featured in the film *An Officer and a Gentleman*. Within the complex are the **Commanding Officer's Quarters** (☎ 360-385-4730; admission $2; 10am-5pm daily Jun-Aug, 1-4pm Sat & Sun Mar-May & Sep-Oct), a restored Victorian-era home, the **Coast Artillery Museum** (☎ 360-385-0373; admission $2; 11am-4pm daily Jun-Aug, 11am-4pm Sat & Sun Mar-May & Sep-Oct) and plenty of opportunities to fly kites and view nature.

Within Fort Worden State Park, the **HI Olympic Hostel** (☎ 360-385-0655; www.hihostels.com; 272 Battery Way; dm $17-20, r from $50) has impeccable if spartan quarters in a former barracks; it's up the hill behind the park office. Downtown is bedecked with numerous red-bricked Victorian hotels, including the **Waterstreet Hotel** (☎ 360-385-5467; www.waterstreethotelporttownsend.com; 635 Water St; r $50-160;), with a selection of period rooms set above a pub (read: noise), some with ocean views. The turreted, Prussian-style **Manresa Castle** (☎ 360-385-5750, 800-732-1281; www.manresacastle.com; cnr 7th & Sheridan Sts; r from $109; P) is a quieter (though purportedly haunted) 40-room mansion built in 1892 that is light on cheap gimmicks but heavy on period authenticity.

Port Townsend has a whole range of unfancy but funky places to eat, drink and be merry. The **Salal Café** (☎ 360-385-6532; 634 Water St; breakfast $7-8, lunch $8-9; 7am-2pm) is an insanely popular brunch spot famous for its egg burritos. Arrive early to nab a table.

our pick **Waterfront Pizza** (☎ 360-385-6629; 951 Water St; pizzas from $10 11am-10pm) is a hole-in-the-wall drawing people regularly across Puget Sound from Seattle for legendary hand-tossed sourdough pizza crust topped with a delicious range of fresh ingredients. Eat it upstairs or/and order a slice to go. The **Silverwater Cafe** (☎ 360-385-6448; 237 Taylor St; lunch $6-10, dinner $10-17; 11:30am-10pm Sun-Thu, 11:30am-11pm Fri & Sat) provides a romantic atmosphere for a creatively prepared dinner.

Port Townsend can be reached from Seattle in a ferry/bus connection via Bainbridge Island and Poulsbo (bus 90 followed by bus 7). **Washington State Ferries** (☎ 206-464-6400, in Washington 888-808-7977; www.wsdot.wa.gov/ferries) goes to and from Keystone on Whidbey Island (car and driver/passenger $8.90/2.60, 35 minutes).

Port Angeles

Despite the name, there's nothing Spanish or particularly angelic about Port Angeles. Propped up by the lumber industry and backed by the steep-sided Olympic Mountains, people come here to catch a ferry for Victoria, BC, or plot an outdoor excursion into the nearby Olympic National Park rather than for the town per se. The **visitor center**

(☎ 360-452-2363; 121 E Railroad Ave; ⏲ 8am-8pm May-Oct, 10am-4pm Nov-Apr) is adjacent to the ferry terminal. For information on the national park there's another center just outside town (see p1035). You can get kitted out for impending outdoor adventures at **Olympic Mountaineering** (☎ 360-452-0240; 140 W Front St).

Port Angeles' cheapest central budget accommodation can be found at the comfortable **Downtown Hotel** (☎ 360-565-1125; www.portangelesdowntownhotel.com; 101 E Front St; r with shared/private bath $55/75;) adjacent to the ferry dock. Downstairs, the cheerful **Corner House Restaurant** (☎ 360-452-9692; 101 E Front St; mains $6-8; ⏲ 6am-9pm) does a bustling trade and its no-nonsense table/booths are nearly always full.

Bella Italia (☎ 360-457-5442; 118 E 1st St; mains $11-19; ⏲ from 4pm) boasts a comprehensive wine list and offers last-gasp carb-loading for hikers heading for the Olympic wilderness.

Two ferries run from Port Angeles to Victoria, BC: the **Coho Vehicle Ferry** (☎ 360-457-4491; passenger/car $13.50/50), taking 1½ hours, and the passenger-only **Victoria Express** (☎ 360-452-8088; adult/child $12.50/7; ⏲ May-Sep), which takes one hour.

Olympic Bus Lines (☎ 360-417-0700) runs twice daily to Seattle ($39) from the public transit center at the corner of Oak and Front Sts. **Clallam Transit** (☎ 360-452-4511) buses go to Forks and Sequim where they link up with other transit buses, enabling you to circumnavigate the whole peninsula.

Northwest Peninsula

Several Native American reservations cling to the extreme northwest corner of the continent and welcome interested visitors. Hit hard by the decline in the salmon-fishing industry, the small settlement of Neah Bay on Hwy 112 is characterized by its weather-beaten boats and craning totem poles. This is home to the **Makah Indian Reservation** (www.makah.com), whose **Makah Museum** (☎ 360-645-2711; 1880 Bayview Ave; admission $5; ⏲ 10am-5pm daily Apr-Aug, 10am-5pm Wed-Sun Sep-May) displays artifacts from one of North America's most significant archaeological finds. Exposed by tidal erosion in 1970, the 500-year-old Makah village of Ozette quickly proved to be a treasure trove of native history, unearthing a huge range of materials including whaling weapons, canoes, spears and combs. Seven miles beyond the museum, a short boardwalk trail leads to **Cape Flattery**, a 300ft promontory that marks the most northwesterly point in the lower 48 states.

Convenient to the Hoh River Rainforest and the Olympic coastline is **Forks**, a one-horse lumber town 57 miles from Neah Bay. Get cozy in the amiable **Forks Motel** (☎ 360-374-6243; www.forksmotel.com; 432 S Forks Ave; s/d $65/70;) and sample home-style cooking at the **In Place** (☎ 360-372-6258; 320 S Forks Ave; mains $9-17; ⏲ 7am-10pm) nearby.

NORTHWEST WASHINGTON

Wedged between Seattle, the Cascades and Canada, northwest Washington draws influences from three sides. Its urban hub is laidback Bellingham with its collegiate coffee bars and organic ethnic restaurants, while its outdoor highlight is the pastoral San Juan Islands, an extensive archipelago accessible by ferry that glimmers like a sepia-toned snapshot from another era. Equally verdant, and simpler to reach, Whidbey Island contains beautiful Deception Pass State Park and the quaint oyster-fishing village of Coupeville. Situated on Fidalgo Island and attached to the mainland via a bridge, the settlement of Anacortes is the main hub for ferries to the San Juan Islands and Victoria, BC. If your boat's delayed you can pass time in expansive Washington Park or sample the local halibut and chips in a couple of classic downtown restaurants.

Whidbey Island

Measuring 41 miles north to south, Whidbey Island is one of the largest contiguous islands in the United States. It is also quite possibly one of the greenest. Endowed with six state parks, a unique National Historical Reserve, a budding artists and writers community, plus a free – yes, free – island-wide public bus service, there's more to this lush oasis than meets the eye.

Deception Pass State Park (☎ 360-675-2417; 41229 N State Hwy 20) straddles the eponymous steep-sided water chasm that flows between Whidbey and Fidalgo Islands, and incorporates lakes, islands, campsites and 27 miles of hiking trails.

Ebey's Landing National Historical Reserve (☎ 360-678-3310; www.nps.gov/ebla; admission free; ⏲ 8am-5pm mid-Oct–Mar, 6:30am-10pm Apr–mid-Oct) comprises 17,400 acres encompassing working farms, sheltered beaches, two state parks and the town of **Coupeville**. This small settlement is one of

PACIFIC NORTHWEST

Washington's oldest towns and boasts an attractive seafront, antique stores and a number of old inns. Call at the **visitor center** (☎ 360-678-5434; www.centralwhidbeychamber.com; 107 S Main St; 10am-5pm) for more details. Whidbey has multiple inns and B&Bs and even the motels are markedly different. Head for the **Coupville Inn** (☎ 800-247-6162; www.thecoupevilleinn.com; 200 Coveland St; r without/with balcony $105/140; P), which bills itself as a French-style motel (if that's not an oxymoron) with fancy furnishings and a tasty breakfast. For fresh local clams and hand-crafted microbrews look no further than **Toby's Tavern** (☎ 360-678-4222; 8 Front St; 11am-9pm Sun-Thu, 11am-10pm Fri & Sat).

Washington State Ferries (☎ 206-464-6400, in Washington 888-808-7977; www.wsdot.wa.gov/ferries) link Clinton to Mukilteo (car and driver/passenger $6.85/3.95, 20 minutes, every 30 minutes) and Keystone to Port Townsend (car and driver/passenger $8.90/2.60, 30 minutes, every 45 minutes). Free **Island Transit buses** (☎ 360-678-7771) run the length of Whidbey every hour daily except Sunday, from the Clinton ferry dock.

Bellingham

Bellingham exudes green; not just in its trees (of which there are plenty), but in its whole progressive approach to life. You can walk or cycle along well-maintained intra-urban trails here, sort your waste into six different recycling bins, and go shopping in pioneering community food co-ops. But, rather than being a commune of tree-hugging granola-munchers, Washington's 10th-largest population center is widely touted as being one of the USA's most livable communities. There's precious history to be found here, showcased in the gentile quarter of Old Fairhaven, erudite intellectualism available in an assortment of secondhand bookstores, and, just outside the city limits, the magical outdoors – from the rugged tip of Mt Baker down to the kayak-friendly inlets of the San Juan Islands. The best downtown tourist information can be procured at the **Visitor Info Station** (☎ 360-527-8710; www.downtownbellingham.com; 1304 Cornwall St; 9am-6pm).

Victoria/San Juan Cruises (☎ 360-738-8099, 800-443-4552) has whale-watching trips to Victoria, BC, via the San Juan Islands. Boats leave from the Bellingham Cruise Terminal in Fairhaven.

The secret of a good 'chain' hotel is that it doesn't seem like a chain at all. To put this theory into practice, check out the clean, personable **Guesthouse Inn** (☎ 360-671-9600; www.bellinghamvaluinn.com; 805 Lakeway Dr; s/d $79/89; P) just off I-5. Handily, the Vancouver-Seattle Airporter Shuttle also stops here. The **Fairhaven Village Inn** (☎ 360-733-1311; www.fairhavenvillageinn.com; 1200 10th St; r with bay/park view $169/189; P) blends in with the vintage tones of Old Fairhaven without losing its modern sheen. Service is slick but subtle.

Bellingham has so many good independent cheap eats, it's a dice roll where to go first. Try the **Bagelry** (☎ 360-676-5288; 1319 Railroad Ave; bagels $4-7; 6:30am-5pm Mon-Fri, 8am-4pm Sat & Sun) where preservative-free New York–style bagels are baked on the premises and served with a good-morning grin. The **Swan Cafe** (☎ 360-734-0542; 1220 N Forest St; dishes $5-7; 8am-9pm; V) is a Community Food Co-op with an on-site café-deli that offers an insight into Bellingham's organic, fair-trade, community-based mentality. You can walk the 2.5-mile South Bay Trail down to Fairhaven where book-browsing in **Village Books** (☎ 360-671-2626; www.villagebooks.com; 1200 11th St) can be combined with a visit to the adjacent **Colophon Café** (☎ 360-647-0092; 1208 11th St; mains $7-10; 9am-10pm), famous for its African peanut soup and chocolate brandy cream pies. The emblematic **Mt Baker Theatre** (☎ 360-734-6080; 106 N Commercial St) punches way above its weight and regularly draws top-name acts for music and plays.

San Juan Islands Shuttle Express (☎ 360-734-3431) offers daily summer service to Orcas and San Juan Islands ($20). Alaska Marine Highway ferries (p1077) go to Juneau (60 hours) and other southeast Alaskan ports (from $353 without car). The **Bellair Airporter Shuttle** (☎ 360-380-8800; www.airporter.com) runs to Sea-Tac airport ($34) with connections en route to Anacortes and Whidbey Island.

SAN JUAN ISLANDS

Take the ferry west out of Anacortes and you'll feel like you've dropped off the edge of the continent. A thousand metaphoric miles from the urban inquietude of Puget Sound, the nebulous San Juan archipelago conjures up Proustian flashbacks from another era and often feels about as American as – er – Canada (which surrounds it on two sides). Street crime here barely registers, fast-food franchises are a nasty mainland apparition, and cars – those most essential of US travel accessories – are best left at home.

There are over 450 landfalls in this expansive archipelago but unless you're rich enough to charter your own yacht or seaplane you'll be restricted to seeing the big four – San Juan, Orcas, Shaw and Lopez Islands – all served daily by Washington State Ferries. Communally, the islands are famous for their tranquillity, whale-watching opportunities, sheltered sea kayaking and seditious nonconformity.

For good general information about the San Juans, contact the **San Juan Islands Visitor Information Center** (☎ 360-468-3663; www.guidetosanjuans.com; 10am-2pm Mon-Fri).

The best way to explore the San Juans is by sea kayak or bicycle. Kayaks are available for rent on Lopez, Orcas and San Juan Island. Expect a guided half-day trip to cost $30 to $45. Note that most beach access is barred by private property, except at state or county parks. Cycling-wise, Lopez is flat and pastoral and San Juan is worthy of an easy day loop, while Orcas offers the challenge of undulating terrain and the steep 5-mile ride to the top of Mt Constitution.

Airlines serving the San Juan Islands include **Harbor Air Lines** (☎ 800-359-3220; www.harborair.com), **Kenmore Air** (☎ 800-543-9595; www.kenmoreair.com) and **West Isle Air** (☎ 800-874-4434; www.westisleair.com). Public transportation is pretty much nonexistent, but most motels will pick up guests at the ferry landing with advance notice.

Washington State Ferries (☎ 206-464-6400, in Washington 888-808-7977; www.wsdot.wa.gov/ferries) leaves Anacortes for the San Juans; some continue to Sidney, BC, near Victoria. Ferries run to Lopez Island (45 minutes), Orcas Landing (60 minutes) and Friday Harbor on San Juan Island (75 minutes). Fares vary by season; the cost of the entire round-trip is collected on westbound journeys only (except those returning from Sidney, BC). To visit all the islands, it's cheapest to go to Friday Harbor first and work your way back through the other islands.

Lopez Island

If you're going to Lopez – or 'Slow-pez,' as locals prefer to call it – take a bike. With its undulating terrain and salutation-offering locals (who are famous for their three-fingered 'Lopezian wave') this is the ideal cycling isle. A leisurely pastoral spin can be tackled in a day with good overnight digs available next to the marina in the **Lopez Islander Resort** (☎ 360-468-2233; www.lopezislander.com; 2864 Fisherman Bay Rd; d from $120;), which has a restaurant, gym and pool and offers free parking in Anacortes (another incentive to dump the car). If you arrive bike-less, call up **Lopez Bicycle Works** (☎ 360-468-2847; 2847 Fisherman Bay Rd; 10am-6pm May-Sep) who can deliver a bicycle to the ferry terminal for you.

San Juan Island

San Juan Island is the archipelago's unofficial capital, a verdant mix of low forested hills and small rural farms that resonate with a dramatic and unusual 19th-century history. The main settlement is Friday Harbor, where the **chamber of commerce** (☎ 360-378-5240; www.sanjuanisland.org; 135 Spring St; 10am-5pm Mon-Fri, 10am-4pm Sat & Sun) is situated inside a small arcade off the main street.

San Juan Island National Historical Park (☎ 360-378-2240; www.nps.gov/sajh; 8:30am-4pm), commemorating a mid-19th-century British-US territorial conflict, consists of two former military camps on opposite ends of the island. Both of these day-use sites contain remnants of the old officers' quarters; the American Camp, on the island's southeast end, features a splendid hike up Mt Finlayson, from which three mountain ranges can be glimpsed on a clear day. On the western shore, **Lime Kiln Point State Park** (8am-5pm mid-Oct–Mar, 6:30am-10pm Apr–mid-Oct) is devoted to whale-watching.

Wayfarer's Rest (☎ 360-378-6428; www.rockisland.com/~wayfarersrest; 35 Malcolm St; dm/cabins $30/70) in Friday Harbor is a backpackers hostel. **Roche Harbor Resort** (☎ 800-451-8910; www.rocheharbor.com; Roche Harbor; r $79-99, 2-bedroom town houses from $299, condos from $149; P) is a splendid seaside village on the island's northwest corner. Friday Harbor has several great places to eat near the ferry landing.

Orcas Island

Precipitous, unspoiled and ruggedly beautiful, Orcas Island is the San Juan's emerald jewel. The ferry terminal is at Orcas Landing, 13.5 miles south of the main population center, Eastsound. On the island's eastern lobe is **Moran State Park** (☎ 360-376-2326; 6:30am-dusk Apr-Sep, 8am-dusk Oct-Mar), dominated by Mt Constitution (2409ft), with 40 miles of trails and an awe-inspiring 360-degree mountaintop view. Reservations are accepted.

Orcas Island has some stellar accommodation options, from cheap cottages to luxury resorts.

IF YOU HAVE A FEW MORE DAYS

Washington's Cascades are full of latent surprises – both natural and constructed. If you're keen to get off the main tourist routes and fly by the seat of your pants, try taking in some of the following treats.

- **Ross Lake Resort** is a cluster of floating cabins on the west side of Ross Lake just north of the Ross Dam. There's no road in, so guests either hike the 2-mile trail from Hwy 20 or take the resort's tugboat-taxi-and-truck shuttle from the parking area near Diablo Dam.
- Hike the trail up to **Desolation Peak** (6102ft) overlooking Ross Lake and ponder the hut where Beatnik novelist Jack Kerouac once spent two months alone as a fire lookout in 1956. The hike is 6.8 miles one-way and pretty strenuous, although you'll be richly rewarded with the same stunning vistas that inspired Kerouac. The trailhead is best accessed via water taxi from the Ross Lake Resort.

our pick **Rosario Resort & Spa** (☎ 360-376-2222; www.rosario-resort.com; 1400 Rosario Rd, Eastsound; r $188-400; P ⊠ ⊠ ⊠ ⊠), at the top end of the market, is a magnificent seafront mansion built by former shipbuilding magnate Robert Moran in 1904 and now converted into an exquisite, upscale resort and spa. A cheaper but no less historic option is **Outlook Inn** (☎ 360-376-2200; www.outlookinn.com; 171 Main St, Eastsound; r with shared/private bath $84/140; P ⊠ ⊠), a vintage 1888 structure that has kept up with the times by adding motel-style rooms and fancy suites. The on-site **New Leaf Café** (☎ 360-376-2200; mains $17-25; ⏲ 5:30-11pm Thu-Mon) is one of the island's classiest eating spots. Campers will find solace at **Moran State Park** (☎ 360-376-2326; standard sites $13, hiker & cyclist sites $6), which has more than 150 campsites (no hookups).

Cafe Olga (☎ 360-376-5098; 11 Point Lawrence Rd, Olga; mains $9-11; ⏲ 9am-6pm Mon-Fri, 9am-8pm Sat & Sun, closed Wed Mar-Apr) is tucked inside a barn alongside a crafts gallery 6 miles southeast of Eastsound. It specializes in homemade pies and provides a sweet treat for cyclists and hikers who just conquered lofty Mt Constitution. For *fuerte* Mexican flavors look no further than **Bilbo's Festivo** (☎ 360-376-4728; 310 A St, Eastsound; dinner mains from $14; ⏲ 4-9pm).

NORTH CASCADES

Geologically different from their southern counterparts, the North Cascade Mountains are peppered with sharp, jagged peaks, copious glaciers and a preponderance of complex metamorphic rock. Thanks to their virtual impregnability, the North Cascades were an unsolved mystery to humans until relatively recently. The first road was built across the region in 1972 and, even today, it remains one of the Northwest's most isolated outposts.

Mt Baker

Rising like a ghostly sentinel above the sparkling waters of upper Puget Sound, Mt Baker has been mesmerizing visitors to the northwest for centuries. A dormant volcano that last belched smoke in the 1850s, this haunting 10,781ft peak shelters 12 glaciers and in 1999 registered a record-breaking 95ft of snow in one season.

Well-paved Hwy 542 – known as the Mt Baker Scenic Byway – climbs 5100ft to **Artist Point**, 56 miles from Bellingham. Near here you'll find the **Heather Meadows Visitor Center** (Mile 56 Mt Baker Hwy; ⏲ 8am-4:30pm May-Sep) and a plethora of varied hikes.

Boasting the greatest annual snowfall of any ski area in North America, Mt Baker is a skier's paradise and the **Mt Baker Ski Area** (☎ 360-734-6771; www.mtbakerskiarea.com) has 38 runs, eight lifts and a vertical rise of 1500ft. Due to its rustic facilities, ungroomed terrain and limited après ski options, the resort has gained something of a cult status among snowboarders, who flock here for the Legendary Baker Banked Slalom, held every January.

On the 100 or so days a year when Baker breaks through the clouds, the views from the deck at the **Inn at Mount Baker** (☎ 360-599-1359; www.theinnatmtbaker.com; 8174 Mt Baker Hwy; r from $149; P ⊠ ⊠) can divert your attention away from the rather scrumptious breakfast. Situated 7 miles east of Maple Falls this six room B&B is welcoming, private and mindful of its pristine setting.

Leavenworth

Blink hard and rub your eyes. This isn't some strange Germanic hallucination. This rather is Leavenworth, a former lumber town that underwent a Bavarian makeover back in the 1960s after the rerouting of the cross-continental railway threatened to put it permanently out of business. Swapping wood for tourists, Leavenworth today has successfully reinvented itself as a traditional Romantische Strasse village, right down to the beer and sausages and the lederhosen-loving locals (25% of whom are German). The classic *Sound of Music* mountain setting helps, as does the fact that Leavenworth serves as the main activity center for sorties into the nearby Alpine Lakes Wilderness. The **Leavenworth Ranger Station** (☎ 509-548-6977; 600 Sherbourne St; 7:30am-4:30pm daily mid-Jun–mid-Oct, 7:45am-4:30pm Mon-Fri mid-Oct–mid-Jun) can advise on the local outdoor scene, while **Der Sportsmann** (☎ 509-548-5623; 837 Front St) will happily kit you out for anything from skiing and climbing to biking and snowshoeing.

Far too cozy to be classified as a standard motel, the **Linderhof Inn** (☎ 509-548-5283; www.linderhof.com; 690 Hwy 2; r $99-149) is an authentic take on a Bavarian B&B with king-sized beds, flat-screen TVs, a decent buffet breakfast and super-friendly staff. Taking the German theme up a notch is the quirky **Enzian Inn** (☎ 509-548-5269; www.enzianinn.com; 590 Hwy 2; d $120-150) with an 18-hole putting green, a racquetball court, a sunny breakfast room and a lederhosen-clad owner who entertains guests with an early-morning blast on the alphorn.

For Wiener Schnitzel served with classic Bavarian sauce, red cabbage and spaetzle, head to **Andreas Keller** (☎ 509-548-6000; 829 Front St, Lower Level; lunch $7-9, dinner $14-18; 11am-10pm), where traditional accordionists serenade diners every night from 6pm. The alfresco **München Haus** (☎ 509-548-1158; 709 Front St; sausages & snacks from $6; 11am-11pm daily May-Oct, 11am-11pm Fri-Sun Nov-Apr) serves the best charbroiled Bavarian sausage this side of Bavaria.

Lake Chelan

Long, slender Lake Chelan is central Washington's playground. **Lake Chelan State Park** (☎ 509-687-3710), on South Shore Rd, has 144 campsites ($19 to $24; reservations accepted); a number of lakeshore campgrounds are accessible only by boat. The town of **Chelan**, at the lake's southeastern tip, is the primary base for accommodations and services, and it has a **USFS ranger station** (☎ 509-682-2549; 428 Woodin Ave). **Link Transit** (☎ 509-662-1155; www.linktransit.com) buses connect Chelan with Wenatchee and Leavenworth ($1).

Beautiful **Stehekin**, on the northern tip of Lake Chelan, is accessible only by **boat** (☎ 509-682-4584; www.ladyofthelake.com; round-trip from Chelan $39), **seaplane** (☎ 509-682-5555; round-trip from Chelan $159) or a long hike across Cascade Pass, 28 miles from the lake. Most facilities are open mid-June to mid-September.

Methow Valley

The Methow's combination of powdery winter snow and abundant summer sunshine has transformed the valley into one of Washington's primary recreation areas. Bike, hike and fish in the summer; cross-country ski on the second-biggest snow trail network in the US in the winter.

The USFS maintains the **Methow Valley Visitor Center** (☎ 509-996-4000; 24 West Chewuch Rd; 8am-5pm May-Oct) on Hwy 20 at the west end of Winthrop. For classic accommodations and easy access to cross-country skiing, hiking and biking trails, decamp at the exquisite **Sun Mountain Lodge** (☎ 509-996-2211; www.sunmountainlodge.com; Box 1000, Winthrop, WA 98862; lodge r $160-620, cabins $160-345), 10 miles west of the town of Winthrop.

North Cascades National Park

The wildest of all Pacific Northwest wildernesses, the lightly trodden **North Cascades National Park** (www.nps.gov/noca) has no settlements, no overnight accommodations and only one unpaved road. The names of the dramatic mountains pretty much set the tone: Desolation Peak, Jagged Ridge, Mt Despair and Mt Terror. Not surprisingly, the region offers some of the best backcountry adventures outside of Alaska.

The **North Cascades Visitor Center** (☎ 206-386-4495; 502 Newhalem St; 9am-4:30pm daily mid-Apr–Oct, 9am-4:30pm Sat & Sun Nov-Mar, extended hours mid-Jun–Labor Day), in the small settlement of Newhalem on Hwy 20, is the best orientation point for visitors and is staffed by expert rangers who can enlighten you on the park's highlights.

NORTHEASTERN WASHINGTON

Bordered by Canada to the north and Idaho to the east, northeastern Washington is dominated by the understated yet populous city of Spokane and is internationally famous for producing one of the 20th century's greatest engineering marvels, the gargantuan Grand Coulee Dam.

WORTH THE TRIP: WINTHROP

Welcome to the not so Wild West. Winthrop (population 349) is – along with Bavarian Leavenworth (p1040) – one of two themed towns on the popular Cascade Loop. But rather than extolling the virtues of lederhosen, Winthrop has been made over to resemble a scene from swaggering 1950s cowboy flick *High Noon*.

The area was first settled in 1891 by Harvard-educated Guy Waring, who built a trading post at the confluence of the Chewuch (*chee*-wok) and Methow Rivers. When the mining business dried up after 1915, Winthrop teetered catastrophically on the brink of extinction, until an enterprising local couple drafted in Robert Jorgenson, the architect who had redesigned Leavenworth, to rebuild the town with false-fronted shops and assorted cowboy memorabilia in the hope of attracting tourists.

It did. Today, Winthrop is a perennially popular pit stop on the Cascade Loop rightly lauded for its fishing, cross-country skiing and mountain-biking opportunities. In keeping with its esoteric image Winthrop is often seen as the birthplace of modern smokejumping and you can learn all about it by visiting the **North Cascade Smokejumper Base** (☎ 509-997-2031; 23 Intercity Airport Rd; admission free; usually 8am-5pm Jun-Oct) halfway between Winthrop and Twisp. Cheap lodging and great food can be found in town at the **Duck Brand Hotel** (☎ 509-996-2192; www.methownet.com/duck; 248 Riverside Ave; s/d $69/79;), a classic Wild West–style cantina.

PACIFIC NORTHWEST

Grand Coulee Dam

The colossal Grand Coulee Dam is the country's largest hydroelectric project and one of the great engineering marvels of the modern world. While many people visit the area to admire the dam itself, an equal number are drawn by the fishing, hunting and swimming opportunities that the structure and the adjoining 150-mile-long Lake Roosevelt have inadvertently created.

Visitors can orientate themselves at the **Grand Coulee Visitor Arrival Center** (☎ 509-633-9265; 9am-5pm), an interactive exhibit center that details the history of the dam, offers free guided tours and showcases a spectacular nightly laser show.

Spokane

Bucking cultural trends in eastern Washington, Spokane is a city that exhibits style and panache. As well as hosting the 1974 World's Fair, this understated metropolis has spawned history's most popular recording artist (Bing Crosby), its largest organized running race (Bloomsday), one of the nation's most successful college basketball teams (Gonzaga Bulldogs) and a stunning Gilded Age hotel (the Davenport). Shoehorned among the highlights you'll find restored steam mills, classic art-deco skyscrapers, an inviting river trail and the Browne's Addition historic district – a treasure trove of Queen Anne architecture. Stop by the **Spokane Area Visitor Information Center** (☎ 509-747-3230; www.visitspokane.com; 201 W Main Ave at Browne St; 8:30am-5pm Mon-Fri, 9am-6pm Sat & Sun) for a raft of information.

On the former site of Spokane's 1974 World's Fair, the **Riverfront Park** (☎ 509-456-4386; www.spokaneriverfrontpark.com) provides a welcome slice of urban greenery in the middle of downtown. It has been redeveloped in recent years with a 17-point **sculpture walk**, along with plenty of bridges and trails to satisfy the city's plethora of amateur runners. The park's centerpiece is **Spokane Falls**, a gushing combination of scenic waterfalls and foaming rapids. There are various viewing points over the river, including a short **gondola ride** (admission $7; 11am-6pm daily, to 9pm Fri, Sat & holidays), which takes you directly above the falls. Walkers and joggers crowd the interurban **Spokane River Centennial Trail** (☎ 509-624-7188), which extends for 37 miles to the Idaho border and beyond.

Encased in a striking state-of-the-art building in the posh Browne's Addition neighborhood, the **Northwest Museum of Arts & Culture** (☎ 509-456-3931; www.northwestmuseum.org; 2316 W 1st Ave; adult/child/senior & student $7/free/5; 11am-5pm Tue-Sun, to 8pm Wed & Fri) has – arguably – one of the finest collections of indigenous artifacts in the Northwest.

The **Davenport Hotel** (☎ 509-455-8888; www.thedavenporthotel.com; 10 S Post St; r standard/deluxe $219/239;) is a historic Spokane landmark (opened in 1914) that is considered one of best hotels in the US. If you can't afford a room, linger in the exquisite lobby. Equally charming is the smaller but similarly polished **Montvale**

Hotel (☎ 509-747-1919; www.montvalehotel.com; 1005 W 1st Ave; r queen/king $89/159; ⊠ ❄ 📶). The third in the boutique triumvirate is the **Hotel Lusso** (☎ 509-747-9750; www.hotellusso.com; North One Post; s/d $155/295; ⊠ ❄ 📶), with sparkling marble bathrooms and expensive wood furnishings.

Rock City Grill (☎ 509-455-4400; 505 W Riverside Ave; lunch $6-10; 🕑 11am-11pm Sun-Thu, to midnight Fri & Sat), is an atmospherically lit, youthful bar-restaurant with an expansive menu of old staples prepared in imaginative ways. The **Steam Plant Grill** (☎ 509-777-3900;159 S Lincoln; wraps $7-9, mains $15-23; 🕑 11:30am-9:30pm Mon-Thu & Sun, 11:30am-11pm Fri & Sat) serves everything from Thai wraps to New Zealand lamb chops in a converted neo-industrial steam plant.

With a vibrant student population based at Gonzaga University, Spokane has a happening nighttime scene. You can sample the local handcrafted ales at the **Northern Lights Brewing Company** (☎ 509-242-2739; 1003 E Trent Ave), an enticing microbrewery near the university campus. For an alternative gay-friendly nighttime establishment try **Dempsey's Brass Rail** (☎ 509-747-5362; 909 W 1st). For concerts, plays, film festivals and the Spokane Opera check out the **Metropolitan Performing Arts Center** (☎ 509-455-6500; www.metmtg.com/themet; 901 W Sprague Ave).

Buses and trains depart from the **Spokane Intermodal Transportation Station** (221 W 1st Ave). **Amtrak** (☎ 509-624-5144) has a daily service on the esteemed *Empire Builder* to Seattle ($56, 7½ hours), Portland ($56, 9½ hours) and Chicago ($237, 14½ hours).

SOUTH CASCADES

The South Cascades are taller but less clustered than their northern counterparts extending from Snoqualmie Pass east of Seattle down to the mighty Columbia River on the border with Oregon. The highpoint in more ways than one is 14,411ft Mt Rainier. Equally compelling for different reasons is Mt St Helens (8365ft), still recovering from a devastating 1980 volcanic eruption. Lesser known Mt Adams (12,276ft) is renowned for the huckleberries and wildflowers that fill its grassy alpine meadows during the short but intense summer season.

Mt Rainier National Park

Majestic Mt Rainier, the USA's fourth-highest peak (outside Alaska), is also one of its most beguiling. Encased in a 368-sq-mile national park (the world's fifth national park when it was inaugurated in 1899), the mountain's snowcapped summit and forest-covered foothills harbor numerous hiking trails, huge swaths of flower-carpeted meadows and an alluring conical peak that presents a formidable challenge for aspiring climbers. The park has four entrances. Nisqually, on Hwy 706 via Ashford, near the park's southwest corner, is the busiest and most convenient gate, being close to the park's main nexus points and open year-round. The other entrances are Ohanapecosh, via Hwy 123; White River, off Hwy 410; and Carbon River, the most remote entryway, at the northwest corner. Call ☎ 800-695-7623 for road conditions.

For information on the park check out the National Park Service (NPS) website at www.nps.gov/mora, which includes downloadable maps and descriptions of 50 park trails.

Park entry is $15 per car or $5 per pedestrian. For overnight trips, get a wilderness camping permit (free) from ranger stations or visitor centers. The six campgrounds in the park have running water and toilets, but no RV hookups. **Reservations** (☎ 800-365-2267; www.mount.rainier.national-park.com/camping.htm; reserved campsites May-Sept/Oct-Apr $15/12, unreserved campsites $10) are strongly advised during summer months and can be made up to two months in advance by phone or online.

The park's two main nexus points are Longmire and Paradise. Longmire, 7 miles inside the Nisqually entrance, has a **Museum/Information Center** (☎ 360-569-2211, ext 3314; admission free; 🕑 9am-6pm Jun-Sep, 9am-5pm Oct-May), a number of important trailheads and the rustic **National Park Inn** (☎ 360-569-2275; www.guestservices.com/rainier; r with shared/private bath $104/139, 2-room units $191; P ❄) complete with an excellent restaurant. More hikes and interpretive walks can be found 12 miles further east at loftier Paradise, which is served by the flying-saucer-shaped **Henry M Jackson Visitor Center** (☎ 360-569-2211, ext 2328; 🕑 9am-7pm daily May-Sep, 10am-5pm Sat & Sun Oct & Apr) and the vintage **Paradise Inn** (☎ 360-569-2275; r with shared/private bath $105/154; 🕑 May-Oct; P ⊠ ❄). Climbs to the top of Rainier leave from here and can be organized through the **American Alpine Institute** (☎ 360-671-1505; www.aai.cc; 1515 12th St, Bellingham, WA 98225), which offers guided five-day climbs from $1540.

The **Wonderland Trail** is a 93-mile path that completely circumnavigates Mt Rainier via a well-maintained unbroken route. The hike is normally tackled over 10 to 12 days with walkers staying at one of 18 registered campsites along the way. Before embarking you'll need to organize a free backcountry permit from the **Wilderness Information Center** (☎ 877-617-9950; www.nps.gov/mora; 55210 238th Ave E, Ashford, WA 98304-9751); forms are available online.

The remote Carbon River entrance gives access to the park's inland rainforest. The **ranger station** (☎ 360-829-9639), just inside the entrance, is open daily in summer.

Gray Line (☎ 206-624-5077; www.graylineseattle.com) runs tours from Seattle from May to September (one/two days $62/145).

Mt St Helens National Volcanic Monument

Thanks to a 1980 eruption that set off an explosion bigger than the combined power of 21,000 atomic bombs, Washington's 87th-tallest mountain needs little introduction. What it lacks in height Mt St Helens makes up for in fiery infamy; 57 people perished on the mountain on that fateful day in May 1980 when an earthquake of 5.1 on the Richter scale sparked the biggest landslide in human history and buried 230 sq miles of forest under millions of tons of volcanic rock and ash.

For the car-less, Mt St Helens can be seen in a day trip by bus from Portland with **Eco Tours of Oregon** (☎ 503-245-1428; www.ecotours-of-oregon.com) for $59.50. If traveling independently, your first port of call should be the **Mt St Helens Visitor Center** (☎ 360-274-2100; 3029 Spirit Lake Hwy; admission $3; ⏰ 9am-5pm), 5 miles east of Castle Rock on Hwy 504, which showcases films, exhibits and free information on the mountain.

For a closer view of the destructive power of nature, venture to the **Coldwater Ridge Visitor Center** (☎ 360-274-2131; ⏰ 10am-6pm May-Oct, 9am-5pm Nov-Apr) with vistas toward Mt St Helens' gaping northern crater.

An off-beat ambience is provided at the **Eco Park Resort** (☎ 360-274-7007; www.ecoparkresort.com; 14000 Spirit Lake Hwy; tent sites/yurts/cabins $17.50/75/100).

Mt Adams

Further from Seattle than Mts Rainier and St Helens, and covered on its eastern flanks by the Yakama Indian Reservation, Mt Adams receives nowhere near as many visitors as its more famous neighbors. Yet it is enchantingly beautiful. Protected in the 66-sq-mile **Mt Adams Wilderness**, Adams sports plenty of picturesque hikes including the much-loved **Bird Creek Meadow Trail**, a 3-mile loop that showcases the best of the mountain's meadows, wildflowers and waterfalls. Another unique activity in the area is blue-huckleberry picking in the high meadows around the Indian Heaven Wilderness. For huckleberry permits and information on hiking and climbing, consult the **Mt Adams Ranger District USFS office** (☎ 509-395-3400; 2455 Hwy 141; ⏰ 8am-4:30pm Mon-Sat, plus Sun May-Sept) in Trout Lake.

The most enticing local accommodation option can be found at **Serenity's** (☎ 509-395-2500; www.serenitys.com; 2291 Hwy 141; cabins $89-129; P ☎), a mile south of Trout Lake on Hwy 141, which offers four beautifully presented cabins in the woods in the shadow of Mt Adams.

CENTRAL & SOUTHEASTERN WASHINGTON

While they're rarely the first places visitors to Washington head for, the central and southeastern parts of the state harbor one secret weapon: wine. A Johnny-come-lately to the viticultural world, the fertile land that borders the Nile-like Yakima and Columbia River valleys is awash with enterprising new wineries producing quality grapes which now vie with California for national recognition. Yakima and its smaller and more attractive cousin Ellensburg have traditionally held the edge, but look out too for emerging Walla Walla, where talented restaurateurs and a proactive local council have begun to craft a wine destination par excellence.

Yakima & Ellensburg

Situated in its eponymous river valley, the city of Yakima is a rather bleak trading center that doesn't really live up to its 'Palm Springs of Washington' tourist label. The main reason to stop here is to visit one of the numerous wineries that lie between Yakima and Benton City; pick up a map at the **Yakima Valley Visitors & Convention Bureau** (☎ 509-575-3010; www.visityakima.com; 10 N 8th St; ⏰ 9am-5pm Mon-Sat, 10am-4pm Sun).

A better layover is Ellensburg, a diminutive settlement 36 miles to the northwest that juxtaposes the state's largest rodeo (each Labor Day) with a town center that has more coffee bars per head than anywhere else in the world (allegedly). Grab your latte at local roaster **D&M Coffee** (☎ 509-925-5313; 301 N Pine St), browse the history section in the **Kittitas County Museum**

(☎ 509-925-3778; donations accepted; ⌚ 10am-4pm Mon-Sat Jun-Sep, noon-4pm Tue-Sat Oct-May) opposite, and seriously consider staying over in **Guesthouse Ellensburg** (☎ 509-962-3706; www.guesthouseellensburg.com; 606 Main St; r $135), a small two-bedroom B&B set above Ellensburg Wineworks, a retail shop and wine-tasting room where guests can quaff the local flavors free of charge.

Walla Walla

Over the last decade, Walla Walla has converted itself from an obscure agricultural backwater, famous for its sweet onions and large state penitentiary, into the hottest wine-growing region outside of California's Napa Valley. While venerable Marcus Whitman College is the town's most obvious cultural attribute, you'll also find zany coffee bars here, along with cool wine-tasting rooms, fine Queen Anne architecture and one of the state's freshest and most vibrant farmers markets.

A good starting point for aspiring wine quaffers is **Walla Walla Wineworks** (☎ 509-522-1261; 31 E Main St; ⌚ 11am-6pm Mon-Thu, 11am-9pm Fri & Sat) in the town center, a tasting room affiliated to the local Waterbrook winery that offers local wines, cheese, cured meats along with live music at weekends.

For information on wine tasting and maps of four fascinating urban walking tours call in at the **chamber of commerce** (☎ 509-525-0850; www.wallawalla.org; 29 E Sumach St; ⌚ 8:30am-5pm Mon-Fri, 9am-4pm Sat & Sun May-Sept).

The remains of the 1836 **Whitman Mission** are 7 miles west of Walla Walla off US 12. Marcus Whitman and 14 other missionaries died in 1847 when, after a measles epidemic killed half their tribe, a band of Cayuse Native Americans attacked the 11-year-old mission. When news of the uprising reached Washington, DC, Congress established the Oregon Territories, the first formal government west of the Rockies. The **visitor center** (☎ 509-522-6357; adult/family $3/5; ⌚ 8am-4:30pm) has exhibits and maps.

Walla Walla's best-known landmark and most salubrious hotel is the independently run **Marcus Whitman Hotel** (☎ 509-525-2200; www.marcuswhitmanhotel.com; 6 W Rose St; r from $99; ❄ 📶). To immerse yourself in the real flavor of the area you can stay in a cottage at the pricey but lovely **Inn at Abeja** (☎ 509-529-2660; www.abeja.net; 2014 Mill Creek Rd; cottages from $215-285; ⊠ ❄), a working winery 4 miles east of town in the foothills of the Blue Mountains.

The wine boom has lured a number of notable restaurateurs to the area. One of the best fine-dining experiences can be found at **Saffron Mediterranean Kitchen** (☎ 509-525-2112; 125 W Alder St; mains $15-27; ⌚ 2-10pm Tue-Thu & Sun, 2-11pm Fri & Sat), which takes fresh local ingredients and turns them into Mediterranean-tinged wonders. Local wines are sold and hearty brunches concocted at **Merchants Delicatessen** (☎ 509-525-0900; 21 E Main St; breakfast $5-8; ⌚ 5:30am-5pm Mon-Sat), a hybrid café, deli, wine store and bakery bang in the town center.

OREGON

Spatially larger than Washington but with only half the population, Oregon is the Pacific Northwest's warm, mild-mannered elder cousin (it joined the union 30 years earlier than Washington). Physically, the state shares many characteristics with its northern neighbor including a rain-lashed coast, a spectacular spinal mountain range and a drier, more conservative interior plateau. But, with better urban planning laws and less sprawl, Oregon retains a more laid-back and tranquil feel.

History

Oregon started as an ad hoc collection of New England missionaries and French and British trappers, officially becoming a US territory in 1848 and a state in 1859. Settlers populated most of the coastal and central region by the 1860s, many having made the arduous six-month journey across the continent on the Oregon Trail.

The new Oregonians proceeded to appropriate the homelands of the various Native American groups. In what came to be called the Rogue River Wars, one such group – the Takelma, dubbed *coquins* (rogues) by French beaver trappers early in the 19th century – attacked immigrant parties and refused to negotiate with the army to allow passage through their land. Consequently, tensions mounted, and butchery escalated on both sides. Eventually the Takelma retreated into the canyons of the western Rogue Valley, but they surrendered after several winter months of skirmishing with little food or shelter. They were sent north to the Grand Ronde Reservation on the Yamhill River, and they weren't alone. By the late 1850s,

OREGON FACTS

Nickname Beaver State
Population 3.8 million
Area 95,997 sq miles
Capital city Salem (population 152,000)
Other cities Portland (population 537,081), Eugene (population 146,356), Bend (population 71,892)
Sales tax Oregon has no sales tax
Birthplace of former US president Herbert Hoover (1874–1964); writer and Merry Prankster Ken Kesey (1935–2001); actress and dancer Ginger Rogers (1911–1995); *The Simpsons* creator Matt Groening (b 1954); filmmaker Gus Van Sant (b 1952)
Home of Oregon Shakespeare Festival, tree-sitting, Nike, McMenamins
Famous for the Oregon Trail, forests, rain, beer, not being able to pump your own gas
State beverage milk (dairy's big here)
Driving distances Portland to Eugene 110 miles, Pendleton to Astoria 295 miles

PACIFIC NORTHWEST

most of the Native Americans in the region had been confined to reservations.

The railroad reached Portland in 1883, and by 1890 the city was one of the world's largest wheat-shipment points. The two world wars brought further economic expansion, much of it from logging. In the postwar era, idealistic baby boomers flooded into Oregon from California and the eastern states, seeking alternative lifestyles and natural surroundings. These arrivals brought pace-setting policies on many environmental and social issues.

Since the 1960s, Portland and western Oregon have been particularly influenced by the new, politically progressive settlers, while small towns and rural areas have remained mostly conservative. Its ballot-initiative system gives Oregonians the opportunity to advance citizen-proposed laws to the ballot box, and Oregon has become a stage for political dramas on divisive issues – such as physician-assisted suicide and gay marriage – in which the whole country has an interest.

Information

Nature of the Northwest (☎ 503-872-2750, 800-270-7504; www.naturenw.org/forest-directory.htm; 800 NE Oregon St, Suite 177, Portland, OR 97232; 🕑 9am-5pm Mon-Fri) Recreational information on national forests and state parks of the region; sells the Northwest Forest Pass ($5/30 per day/year), required at many parks, trailheads, visitor centers and boat launches.
Oregon road conditions (☎ 503-588-2941, in Oregon 800-977-6368)
Oregon State Parks & Recreation Dept (☎ 503-378-6305, 800-551-6949; www.oregonstateparks.org; 1115 Commercial St NE, Salem, OR 97310) Roughly half of Oregon's state park campgrounds accept reservations (up to 9 months in advance), the rest are first-come first-served. You can book online. Tent sites run from $14 to $18, electric hook-ups $16 to $22.
Oregon Tourism Commission (☎ 503-986-0000, 800-547-7842; www.traveloregon.com; 775 Summer St NE, Salem, OR 97301; 🕑 8am-5pm Mon-Fri) Sends out information and brochures on accommodations, camping, state parks and recreation outfitters.

PORTLAND

If there's a blueprint for a successful 21st-century city, Portland must surely be it. While New York continuously reinvents itself and San Francisco has priced its Haight hippies out of the property market, this zany but precocious mini-metropolis stands at the cutting edge of all that's cool, hip and forward-thinking about modern America.

Irony is one of Portland's biggest hallmarks. Known as 'Stumptown' by early pioneers for the proliferation of tree stumps that littered downtown, the city's erstwhile tree-fellers have turned into modern tree-huggers and the urban area now exhibits more parks than any other city in the US. Portland green credentials also extend to its environmentalism. You can ride a bike here and still live to tell the tale, breeze around downtown on a free European-style tram, or sup organic coffee with a zine-reading lesbian beside a Bosnian food cart.

And if that's not enough, consider that Portland has more strip clubs per head than either Vegas or New York. Intrigued? You will be.

History

The Portland area was first settled in 1844 when two New Englanders bought a claim on the Willamette's west bank. They tossed a coin to decide the new settlement's name – 'Portland' won over 'Boston.'

Portland's location near the confluence of the Columbia and Willamette Rivers helped drive the young city's growth. The California gold rush clamored for Oregon lumber, while the growing population of settlers in the Willamette Valley demanded supplies. The Northern Pacific Railroad (which arrived in 1883) and the WWII shipbuilding boom didn't hurt the local economy either.

Today more than half a million people live in the greater Portland area. Shipping operations have since moved north of downtown, the Old Town's been revitalized and the once-industrial Pearl District now brims with expensive lofts and boutiques. Outdoor-clothing manufacturers Nike, Adidas and Columbia Sportswear help drive the economy, along with high-tech companies such as Intel and Tektronix.

Orientation

Portland lies just south of the Washington border and about an hour's drive from the Pacific Coast. The Willamette River flows through the center of town, dividing the city into east and west. Burnside St divides north from south, organizing the city into four quadrants: Northwest, Southwest, Northeast and Southeast. Make sure you understand this, as the same address could exist on both NE Davis St and NW Davis St, which are on opposite sides of the river!

Downtown is in Southwest Portland. The historic Old Town, rough-and-tumble Chinatown, trendy 23rd Ave, chic Pearl District and exclusive West Hills are in Northwest Portland. Close to the center but across the river is the Lloyd District, an extension of downtown.

Northeast and Southeast Portland are mostly tree-lined, late 19th-century residential neighborhoods, each with its own trendy cluster of shops and restaurants. Popular commercial streets include N Mississippi Ave, NE Alberta St, SE Hawthorne Blvd and SE Division St. Sellwood is furthest south and a pretty neighborhood with antique stores and yuppies.

Information

BOOKSTORES

CounterMedia (☎ 503-226-8141; 927 SW Oak St) Portland personified. Liberally minded books on fringe culture and vintage erotica.

In Other Words (☎ 503-232-6003; www.inotherwords.org; 8 NE Killingsworth St) Feminist bookstore and resource center, just north of the Lloyd District.

Powell's City of Books (☎ 503-228-4651; www.powells.com; 1005 W Burnside St) The largest independent bookstore in the US, this place is dangerously addictive. Bank on your quick one-hour 'browse' turning into three. Fantastic travel section.

Reading Frenzy (☎ 503-274-1449; www.readingfrenzy.com; 921 SW Oak St) Flick through *Yeti, Rolling Thunder, Bitch, Craphound, Giant Robot* and other such indie zine classics.

EMERGENCY & MEDICAL SERVICES

Legacy Good Samaritan Hospital & Medical Center (☎ 503-413-7711; 1015 NW 22nd Ave)

Portland Police (☎ 503-823-0000)

Walgreens (☎ 503-238-6053; 940 SE 39th Ave) Has a 24-hour pharmacy; to the city's east.

INTERNET ACCESS

Backspace (☎ 503-248-2900; www.backspace.bz; 115 NW 5th Ave; 🕑 7am-11pm Mon-Wed, to midnight Thu & Fri, 10am-midnight Sat, to 11pm Sun) Youth-oriented hangout with arcade games, coffee and long hours.

Urban Grind Coffeehouse (www.urbangrindcoffee.com); NE Oregon St (☎ 503-546-0649;2214 NE Oregon St); NW 14th Ave (☎ 503-546-5919; 911 NW 14th Ave; 🕑 6am-10:30pm) Slick café with computers and free wi-fi.

INTERNET RESOURCES

City of Portland (www.portlandonline.com) Stumptown's official website.

Gay Oregon (www.gaypdx.com) A resource for Portland's gay and lesbian communities.

PDX Guide (www.pdxguide.com) Fun and spot-on food and drink reviews by a guy who knows, plus other happenings around town.

Portland Independent Media Center (www.portland.indymedia.org) Community news and lefty activism.

MEDIA

Just Out (www.justout.com) Free biweekly serving Portland's gay community.

KBOO 90.7 FM Progressive local station run by volunteers; alternative news and views.

Portland Mercury (www.portlandmercury.com) The local sibling of Seattle's *Stranger*, this free weekly is published on Thursdays.

Portland Monthly (www.portlandmonthlymag.com) Excellent subscription magazine focusing on the city's happenings.

Willamette Week (www.wweek.com) Free alt-weekly covering local news and culture, published on Wednesdays.

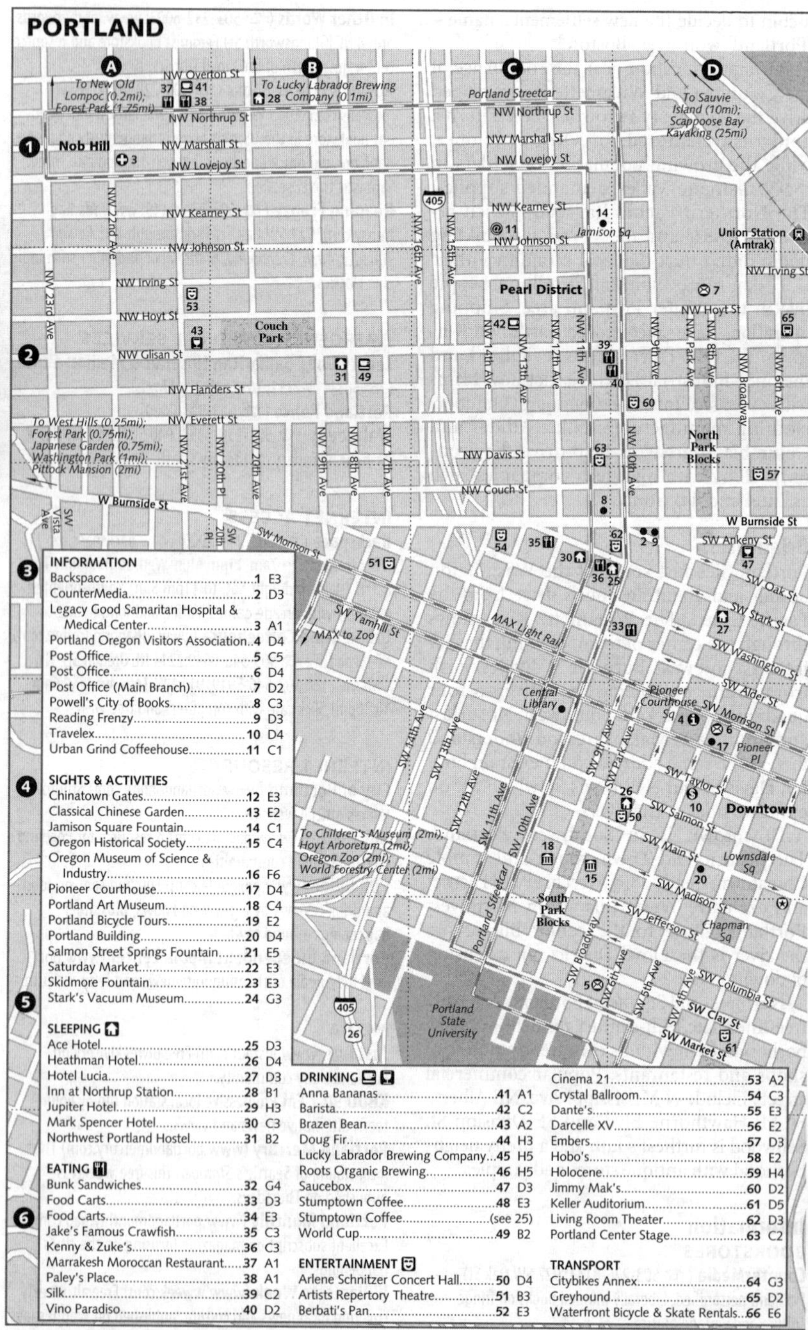
PORTLAND
To New Old Lompoc (0.2mi); Forest Park (1.75mi)
To Lucky Labrador Brewing Company (0.1mi)
To Sauvie Island (10mi); Scappoose Bay Kayaking (25mi)
To West Hills (0.25mi); Forest Park (0.75mi); Japanese Garden (0.75mi); Washington Park (1mi); Pittock Mansion (2mi)
To Children's Museum (2mi); Hoyt Arboretum (2mi); Oregon Zoo (2mi); World Forestry Center (2mi)
MAX to Zoo
Nob Hill
Pearl District
Couch Park
Jamison Sq
Union Station (Amtrak)
North Park Blocks
South Park Blocks
Central Library
Pioneer Courthouse Sq
Pioneer Pl
Downtown
Lownsdale Sq
Chapman Sq
Portland State University
Portland Streetcar
MAX Light Rail
NW Overton St
NW Northrup St
NW Marshall St
NW Lovejoy St
NW Kearney St
NW Johnson St
NW Irving St
NW Hoyt St
NW Glisan St
NW Flanders St
NW Everett St
NW Davis St
NW Couch St
W Burnside St
SW Morrison St
SW Yamhill St
SW Ankeny St
SW Oak St
SW Stark St
SW Washington St
SW Alder St
SW Taylor St
SW Salmon St
SW Main St
SW Madison St
SW Jefferson St
SW Columbia St
SW Clay St
SW Market St
NW 23rd Ave
NW 22nd Ave
NW 21st Ave
NW 20th Pl
NW 20th Ave
NW 19th Ave
NW 18th Ave
NW 17th Ave
NW 16th Ave
NW 15th Ave
NW 14th Ave
NW 13th Ave
NW 12th Ave
NW 11th Ave
NW 10th Ave
NW 9th Ave
NW Park Ave
NW 8th Ave
NW Broadway
NW 6th Ave
SW Vista Ave
SW 20th Pl
SW 14th Ave
SW 13th Ave
SW 12th Ave
SW 11th Ave
SW 10th Ave
SW 9th Ave
SW Park Ave
SW Broadway
SW 6th Ave
SW 5th Ave
SW 4th Ave
405
26

INFORMATION
Backspace 1 E3
CounterMedia 2 D3
Legacy Good Samaritan Hospital & Medical Center 3 A1
Portland Oregon Visitors Association 4 D4
Post Office 5 C5
Post Office 6 D4
Post Office (Main Branch) 7 D2
Powell's City of Books 8 C3
Reading Frenzy 9 D3
Travelex 10 D4
Urban Grind Coffeehouse 11 C1

SIGHTS & ACTIVITIES
Chinatown Gates 12 E3
Classical Chinese Garden 13 E2
Jamison Square Fountain 14 C1
Oregon Historical Society 15 C4
Oregon Museum of Science & Industry 16 F6
Pioneer Courthouse 17 D4
Portland Art Museum 18 C4
Portland Bicycle Tours 19 E2
Portland Building 20 D4
Salmon Street Springs Fountain 21 E5
Saturday Market 22 E3
Skidmore Fountain 23 E3
Stark's Vacuum Museum 24 G3

SLEEPING
Ace Hotel 25 D3
Heathman Hotel 26 D4
Hotel Lucia 27 D3
Inn at Northrup Station 28 B1
Jupiter Hotel 29 H3
Mark Spencer Hotel 30 C3
Northwest Portland Hostel 31 B2

EATING
Bunk Sandwiches 32 G4
Food Carts 33 D3
Food Carts 34 E3
Jake's Famous Crawfish 35 C3
Kenny & Zuke's 36 C3
Marrakesh Moroccan Restaurant 37 A1
Paley's Place 38 A1
Silk 39 C2
Vino Paradiso 40 D2

DRINKING
Anna Bananas 41 A1
Barista 42 C2
Brazen Bean 43 A2
Doug Fir 44 H3
Lucky Labrador Brewing Company 45 H5
Roots Organic Brewing 46 H5
Saucebox 47 D3
Stumptown Coffee 48 E3
Stumptown Coffee (see 25)
World Cup 49 B2

ENTERTAINMENT
Arlene Schnitzer Concert Hall 50 D4
Artists Repertory Theatre 51 B3
Berbati's Pan 52 E3
Cinema 21 53 A2
Crystal Ballroom 54 C3
Dante's 55 E3
Darcelle XV 56 E2
Embers 57 D3
Hobo's 58 E2
Holocene 59 H4
Jimmy Mak's 60 D2
Keller Auditorium 61 D5
Living Room Theater 62 D3
Portland Center Stage 63 C2

TRANSPORT
Citybikes Annex 64 G3
Greyhound 65 D2
Waterfront Bicycle & Skate Rentals 66 E6

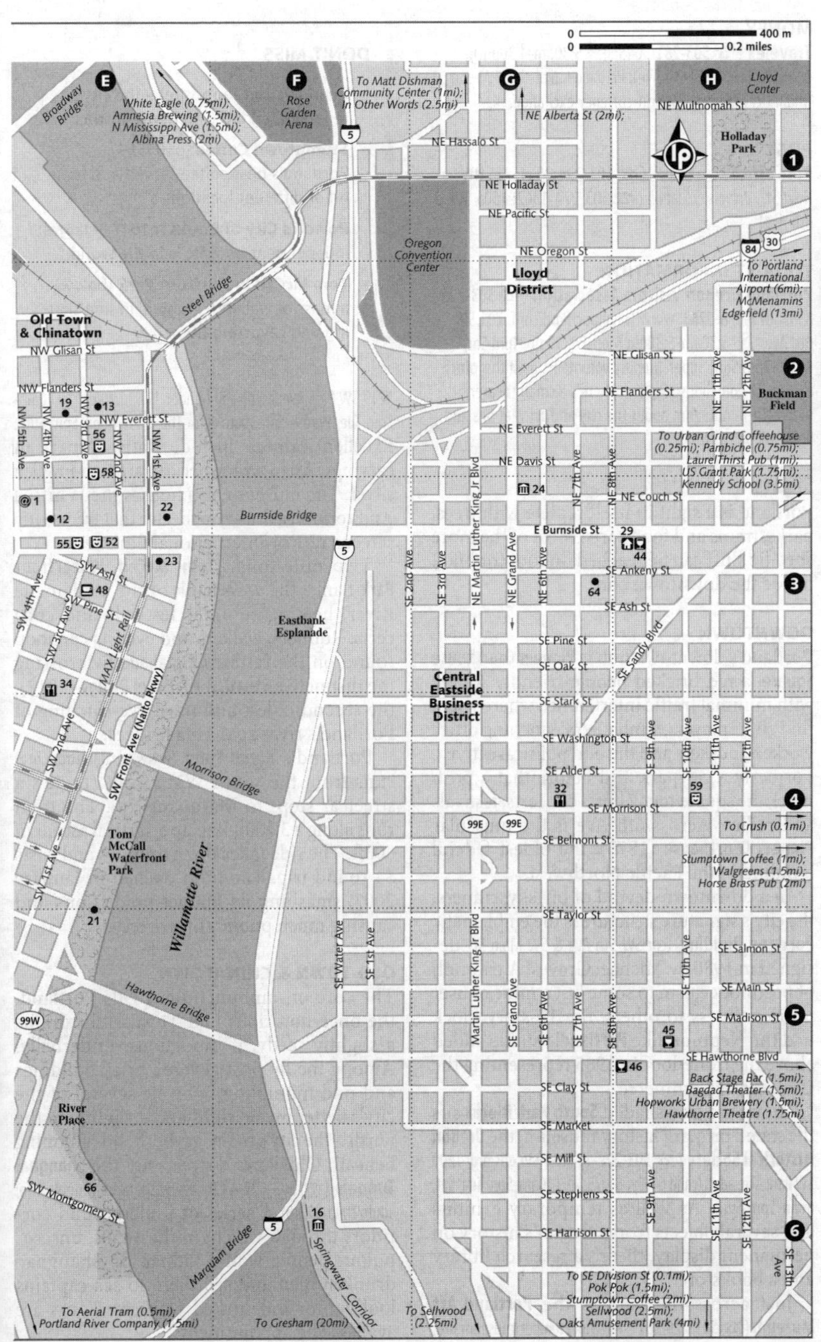

0 400 m
0 0.2 miles
To Matt Dishman Community Center (1mi); In Other Words (2.5mi)
White Eagle (0.75mi); Amnesia Brewing (1.5mi); N Mississippi Ave (1.5mi); Albina Press (2mi)
NE Alberta St (2mi);
Broadway Bridge
Rose Garden Arena
Lloyd Center
NE Multnomah St
Holladay Park
NE Hassalo St
NE Holladay St
NE Pacific St
Oregon Convention Center
NE Oregon St
Lloyd District
To Portland International Airport (6mi); McMenamins Edgefield (13mi)
Steel Bridge
Old Town & Chinatown
NW Glisan St
NE Glisan St
NW Flanders St
NE Flanders St
Buckman Field
NW Everett St
NE Everett St
NE Davis St
NE Couch St
To Urban Grind Coffeehouse (0.25mi); Pambiche (0.75mi); LaurelThirst Pub (1mi); US Grant Park (1.75mi); Kennedy School (3.5mi)
NW 5th Ave
NW 4th Ave
NW 3rd Ave
NW 2nd Ave
NW 1st Ave
Burnside Bridge
E Burnside St
SE Ankeny St
SE Ash St
SW Ash St
SW Pine St
SE Pine St
SE Oak St
SE Stark St
SE Sandy Blvd
SW 4th Ave
SW 3rd Ave
SW 2nd Ave
SW 1st Ave
MAX Light Rail
SW Front Ave (Naito Pkwy)
Eastbank Esplanade
Central Eastside Business District
SE Washington St
SE Alder St
SE Morrison St
Morrison Bridge
To Crush (0.1mi)
SE Belmont St
Stumptown Coffee (1mi); Walgreens (1.5mi); Horse Brass Pub (2mi)
Tom McCall Waterfront Park
Willamette River
SE Taylor St
SE Salmon St
SE Main St
SE Madison St
SE Hawthorne Blvd
Hawthorne Bridge
Back Stage Bar (1.5mi); Bagdad Theater (1.5mi); Hopworks Urban Brewery (1.5mi); Hawthorne Theatre (1.75mi)
SE Clay St
SE Market
SE Mill St
SE Stephens St
SE Harrison St
River Place
SW Montgomery St
Marquam Bridge
Springwater Corridor
SE 2nd Ave
SE 3rd Ave
NE Martin Luther King Jr Blvd
Martin Luther King Jr Blvd
NE Grand Ave
SE Grand Ave
NE 6th Ave
SE 6th Ave
NE 7th Ave
SE 7th Ave
NE 8th Ave
SE 8th Ave
SE 9th Ave
SE 10th Ave
SE 11th Ave
SE 12th Ave
SE 13th Ave
NE 11th Ave
NE 12th Ave
SE Water Ave
SE 1st Ave
To SE Division St (0.1mi); Pok Pok (1.5mi); Stumptown Coffee (2mi); Sellwood (2.5mi); Oaks Amusement Park (4mi)
To Aerial Tram (0.5mi); Portland River Company (1.5mi)
To Gresham (20mi)
To Sellwood (2.25mi)
PACIFIC NORTHWEST

MONEY

Travelex (☎ 503-281-3045; 🕑 5:30am-4:30pm); downtown (900 SW 6th Ave); Portland International Airport (main ticket lobby) Foreign-currency exchange.

POST

Post office Main branch (☎ 503-294-2564; 715 NW Hoyt St); University Station (☎ 503-274-1362; 1505 SW 6th Ave)

TOURIST INFORMATION

Portland Oregon Visitors Association (☎ 503-275-8355, 877-678-5263; www.travelportland.com; 701 SW 6th Ave; 🕑 8:30am-5:30pm Mon-Fri, 10am-4pm Sat, 10am-2pm Sun) Super-friendly volunteers man this office in Pioneer Courthouse Square. There's a small theater with a 12-minute film about the city and Tri-Met bus and light-rail offices inside.

Sights

Portland is a sight in itself replete with trees, parks, trams and food carts. Most of the more specific stuff can be reached on foot (or bike) inside the downtown core.

DOWNTOWN

Portland's downtown hub is **Pioneer Courthouse Square**, a red-bricked people-friendly square with minimal traffic interference where you'll find chess players, sunbathers, lunching office workers, buskers and the odd political activist. Formerly a car park and before that a posh hotel, the square today hosts concerts, festivals and rallies. Across 6th Ave is the muscular **Pioneer Courthouse** (1875), the oldest federal building in the Pacific Northwest.

In a downtown devoid of big skyscrapers, the city's signature structure is the emblematic **Portland Building** (cnr SW 5th Ave & SW Main St) designed in 1980 by Michael Graves. A triumph of postmodernism to some but a mine of user unfriendliness to others, the 15-story block had the Neptune-like **Portlandia** statue added above the front door in 1985 representing the Goddess of Commerce.

Along the tree-shaded **South Park Blocks** sits the state's primary history museum, the **Oregon Historical Society** (☎ 503-222-1741; www.ohs.org; 1200 SW Park Ave; adult/child 6-18yr $11/5; 🕑 10am-5pm Tue-Sat, noon-5pm Sun). As well as temporary exhibits and several objects from Oregon's history on permanent display, there's a research library and a bookstore.

Just across the park is the **Portland Art Museum** (☎ 503-226-2811; www.portlandartmuseum.org; 1219 SW Park Ave; adult/child under 17 $10/free; 🕑 10am-5pm Tue, Wed & Sat, 10am-8pm Thu & Fri, noon-5pm Sun). Excellent exhibits include Native American carvings, Asian and American art, and English silver. The museum also houses the Whitsell Auditorium, a first-rate theater that frequently screens rare or international films.

Two-mile-long **Tom McCall Waterfront Park** flanks the west bank of the Willamette River, hosting summer festivals and concerts. Runners, walkers and cyclists can loop round on the **Eastbank Esplanade** by crossing the distinctive vertical lift **Steel Bridge** (1912), the second-oldest and most eye-catching of Portland's river-spanning bridges.

Portland's **Aerial Tram** (www.portlandtram.org) runs from the south Waterfront (there's a streetcar stop) to Marquam Hill. The tram runs along a 3,300ft line up a vertical ascent of 500ft. The ride takes three minutes and costs $4 round-trip. The tram opened in January 2007, smashing its budget predictions and causing much public controversy.

OLD TOWN & CHINATOWN

The core of rambunctious 1890s Portland, the once-notorious Old Town still exhibits a slightly seedy, if innocuous, underbelly. Among the fly-post covered brick buildings and odd mumbling hobo lie several of the city's better music clubs and – slightly to the north – the city's main 'gayborhood.' Running beneath Old Town's streets are the **Shanghai Tunnels** (☎ 503-622-4798; www.shanghaitunnels.info; adult/child $12/8), a series of underground corridors through which, in the 1850s, unscrupulous people would kidnap or 'shanghai' drunken men and sell them to sea captains looking for indentured workers. Tours are available by appointment.

DON'T MISS

- **Pearl District** (opposite) – the city's rehabilitated old warehouse district
- **Stumptown Coffee** (p1055) – Portland's best coffee served at a handful of different locations
- **Powell's City of Books** (p1047) – largest independent bookstore in the world
- **Tom McCall Waterfront Park** (below) – a mass of walking, jogging, in-line skating and cavorting humanity

The impressive pagoda-style **Chinatown Gates** (cnr W Burnside St & NW 4th Ave) belie a rather lackluster Chinese quarter where you'll struggle to find a palatable dim sum restaurant. Aside from some token chow mein takeouts, the main attraction here is the **Classical Chinese Garden** (☎ 503-228-8131; www.portlandchinesegarden.org; cnr NW 3rd Ave & NW Everett St; adult/child under 5/senior $7/free/6; 10am-5pm). It's a one-block haven of tranquillity, reflecting ponds and manicured greenery. Free tours are available with admission.

Victorian-era architecture and the attractive **Skidmore Fountain** give the area beneath the Burnside Bridge some nostalgic flair. The best time to hit the river walk is on a weekend to catch the famous **Saturday Market** (☎ 503-222-6072; www.portlandsaturdaymarket.com; 10am-5pm Sat & 11am-4:30pm Sun Mar-Dec), which showcases handicrafts, street entertainers and food carts.

NORTHWEST & PEARL DISTRICT

Nob Hill – or 'Snob Hill' to its detractors – has its hub on NW 23rd Ave, a trendy neighborhood thoroughfare that brims with clothing boutiques, home decor shops and cafés. Restaurants – including some of Portland's finest – lie mostly along NW 21st Ave. This is a great neighborhood for strolling, window-shopping and people-watching.

Just east and closer to downtown, the Pearl District is an old industrial quarter that has transformed its once grotty warehouses into expensive lofts, upscale boutiques and trendy restaurants. On the first Thursday of every month, art galleries extend their evening hours and the area turns into a fancy street party of sorts. The Pearl is bordered by NW 9th Ave, NW 14th Ave, W Burnside St and NW Lovejoy St.

WEST HILLS & WASHINGTON PARK

Behind downtown Portland is the West Hills area, known for its exclusive homes, windy streets and huge **Forest Park** – America's largest green urban space.

The grand **Pittock Mansion** (☎ 503-823-3623; www.pittockmansion.com; 3229 NW Pittock Dr; adult/child 6-18yr/senior $7/4/6; 11am-4pm; P) was built in 1914 by Henry Pittock, who revitalized the Portland-based *Oregonian* newspaper. It's worth visiting the (free) grounds just to check out the spectacular views – bring a picnic.

Massive Washington Park contains a day's worth of attraction in its own right. See Portland's famous blooms on show at the **International Rose Test Gardens** (☎ 503-823-7529; www.rosegardenstore.org; admission free; sunrise-sunset; P) with 400 types of roses and good views. Further uphill is the tranquil **Japanese Garden** (☎ 503-223-1321; www.japanesegarden.com; 611 SW Kingston Ave; adult/child 6-17yr $8/5.25; noon-7pm Mon, 10am-7pm Tue-Sun; P). Prettiest in the fall, **Hoyt Arboretum** (☎ 503-865-8733; www.hoytarboretum.org; 4000 Fairview Blvd; admission free; trails 6am-10pm, visitor center 9am-4pm Mon-Fri, 9am-3pm Sat; P) is home to more than 1000 species of native and exotic trees and has 12 miles of walking trails. There's also a popular zoo (p1052).

NORTHEAST & SOUTHEAST

Across the Willamette River from downtown is the **Lloyd Center** shopping mall (1960), the usual florescent amalgamation of fast-food franchises and chain stores, of interest only because it was – apparently – the first of its kind in the US. A few blocks to the southwest is the slightly more attractive glass-towered **Oregon Convention Center** and the **Rose Garden Arena**, home of local basketball heroes, the Trailblazers.

Further up the Willamette, **N Mississippi Avenue** used to be full of run-down buildings but they've been transformed into trendy shops and restaurants. Northeast is artsy **NE Alberta Street**, a ribbon of art galleries, boutiques and cafés. Don't miss the summertime street party that takes place every last Thursday of the month – it's a hoot. For a dose of hippie-hipster culture, visit **SE Hawthorne Boulevard** (near SE 39th Ave), a bohemian string of bookstores, colorful shops and cafés. A mile to the south the connecting thoroughfare of **SE Division Street** has in recent years become a kind of SE Delicious Street with an ample quota of excellent new restaurants bars and pubs.

Activities

HIKING, MOUNTAIN BIKING & CYCLING

Hiking and mountain biking are to Portland what driving is to LA – a cultural rite of passage. You may need a few weeks of training in order to keep up with the svelte-looking locals.

Hikers and joggers will find an unbelievable 70 miles of trails in **Forest Park**, all within the city limits. The **Wildwood Trail** starts at the Hoyt Arboretum and winds through

WHAT THE...?

Only in America (or should that be 'only in Portland'): **Stark's Vacuum Museum** (☎ 503-232-4101; www.starks.com; 107 NE Grand Ave; admission free; 🕑 8am-7pm Mon-Fri, 9am-5pm Sat, 11am-4pm Sun) is an anally retentive collection of 300 or more Hoovers, Busy Bees, Electroluxes and Pneumatics that document the esoteric history of floor-cleaning from 1950s housewife classics to 21st-century lightweights. The museum is located – surprise, surprise – in Stark's vacuum cleaner store and, after sifting through the throwaway collection of modern models, you'll undoubtedly end up pining for one of the museum's space-dog machines of yore.

30 miles of forest, with many spur trails allowing for loop hikes. Other trailheads into Forest Park are at the western ends of NW Thurman and NW Upshur Sts.

Cyclists have the riverside **Springwater Corridor**, which starts near the Oregon Museum of Science & Industry (as an extension of the Eastbank Esplanade) and goes all the way to the suburb of Gresham – over 21 miles long. For mountain biking try **Leif Erikson Drive**, a great old logging road leading 11 miles into Forest Park and offering occasional peeks over the city. Avoid riding on hiking paths here, as you'd be poaching the trails.

For scenic farm country, head to **Sauvie Island**, 10 miles northwest of downtown Portland. This island is prime cycling land – it's flat, has relatively little traffic and much of it is wildlife refuge. For bike rentals, see p1058.

WATER SPORTS

Summer in Portland means finding cool things to do on hot days, and fortunately there's a few.

For simple pleasures, visit the **Salmon Street Springs Fountain** in the Tom McCall Waterfront Park or the **Jamison Square Fountain** (cnr NW Johnson St & NW 10th Ave), both of which attract splashing kids.

Swim indoors at **Matt Dishman Community Center** (☎ 503-823-3673; 77 NE Knott St; admission $2-3.25), north of the Lloyd District. For an outdoor experience, try the pool at **US Grant Park** (☎ 503-823-3674; cnr NE 33rd Ave & NE US Grant Pl; admission $2-3.25), northeast of the Lloyd District. Hours at both pools vary for different activities, so call beforehand.

Kayakers have **Portland River Company** (☎ 503-459-4050; www.portlandrivercompany.com; 6320 SW Macadam Ave) or **Scappoose Bay Kayaking** (☎ 503-397-2161, 877-272-3353; www.scappoosebaykayaking.com; 57420 Old Portland Rd), both with tours and rentals.

Portland for Children

Fear not, overworked parent. Kids love Portland especially the **Oregon Museum of Science & Industry** (OMSI; ☎ 503-797-6674; www.omsi.edu; 1945 SE Water Ave; adult/senior & child 3-13yr $11/9; 🕑 9:30am-5:30pm; 👶), which offers hands-on science exhibits for the whole age range. There's also an Omnimax theater, planetarium shows and a submarine tour (all separate charge).

In summer, the Zoo Train connects the Washington Park rose garden with the **Oregon Zoo** (☎ 503-226-1561; www.oregonzoo.org; 4001 SW Canyon Rd; adult/child $9.75/6.75; 🕑 8am-6pm Apr-Sep; 👶). Don't miss 'zoolights' during the holiday season, when the zoo becomes a winter wonderland filled with lit-up trees and animal figures. In summer there are concerts on the zoo's lawns. Parking costs $1.

Parents can also seek solace at the nearby **Children's Museum** (☎ 503-223-6500; www.portlandcm.org; 4015 SW Canyon Rd; admission $8; 🕑 9am-5pm Mon-Sat, 11am-5pm Sun; 👶), a great place to keep kids busy with interesting learning activities and exhibits. Next door, the **World Forestry Center** (☎ 503-228-1367; www.worldforestry.org; 4033 SW Canyon Rd; adult/child 3-18yr/senior $8/7/5; 🕑 10am-5pm; 👶) offers similar experiences but with a woodsy twist.

For rides and go-karts, head south to **Oaks Amusement Park** (☎ 503-233-5777; www.oakspark.com; 7805 SE Oaks Park Way; admission free, ride bracelets $11.75-14.40; 👶). Hours vary widely, so call ahead.

Tours

For kayak tours, see above.

Eco Tours of Oregon (☎ 503-245-1428, 888-868-7733; www.ecotours-of-oregon.com) Naturalist tours of northwest Oregon and Washington, including the Columbia River Gorge, Mt St Helens and the wine country.

Portland Bicycle Tours (☎ 503-360-6815; www.intrepidexperience.com; 345 NW Everett St) Bike the 'City of Roses' on a parks, bridges or market tour energized with plenty of Stumptown coffee. Two-hour tours with own/rented bike cost $30/40.

Portland Walking Tours (☎ 503-774-4522; www.portlandwalkingtours.com) Art, food, neighborhood, history, underground and even ghost-oriented tours.

Festivals & Events

Portland International Film Festival (☎ 503-221-1156; www.nwfilm.org) Oregon's biggest film event highlights nearly 100 films from over 30 countries. Held mid to late February.

Portland Rose Festival (☎ 503-227-2681; www.rosefestival.org) Rose-covered floats, dragon-boat races, fireworks, roaming packs of sailors and the crowning of a Rose Queen all make this Portland's biggest celebration. Held late May to early June.

Queer Pride Celebration (☎ 503-295-9788; www.pridenw.org) Keep Portland queer in mid-June: enjoy a kick-off party, take a cruise or join the parade.

Oregon Brewers Festival (☎ 503-778-5917; www.oregonbrewfest.com) Quaff microbrews during the summer (late July) in Tom McCall Waterfront Park and during the winter (early December) at Pioneer Courthouse Square.

Sleeping

Reserve ahead in summer.

BUDGET

Northwest Portland Hostel (☎ 503-241-2783; www.nwportlandhostel.com; 425 NW 18th Ave; dm $20-25, d $42-74;) Perfectly located between the Pearl District and NW 21st and 24th Aves, this friendly hostel is spread across a couple of quintessential Northwest District houses and features plenty of common areas (including a small deck), good rooms and bike rentals. Non-HI members pay $3 extra.

our pick **McMenamins Edgefield** (☎ 503-669-8610; www.mcmenamins.com; 2126 SW Halsey St, Troutdale; dm $30, d with shared bath $60-80, with private bath $110-145;) This former county poor farm, restored by the McMenamin brothers, is now a one-of-a-kind, 38-acre hotel complex with a dizzying variety of services. Taste wine and homemade beer, play golf, watch movies, shop at the gift store, listen to live music, walk the extensive gardens and eat at one of its restaurants. It's about a 20-minute drive east from downtown.

White Eagle (☎ 503-335-8900, 866-271-3377; www.mcmenamins.com; 836 N Russell St; dm $40, d $45-60;) A rock-and-roll crash pad (ZZ Top used to play here), the White Eagle is a McMenamins-run bar and live-music saloon which keeps 11 upstairs basic rooms (all with shared baths) for night owls, incurable music fans and very heavy sleepers. The hotel was opened in 1905 and, while the upstairs brothel and opium den may been sidelined, the home-brewed beer still hits the mark. It's north of the Lloyd District on the MAX light-rail line.

MIDRANGE

Jupiter Hotel (☎ 503-230-9200; www.jupiterhotel.com; 800 E BurnsideSt; d Sun-Thu $100-145, Fri & Sat $128-178;) Take a dull concept – in this case a motel – give it a sleek makeover and behold! The Jupiter has hijacked America's most ubiquitous cheap-sleep idea and personalized it with retro furnishings, chalkboard doors (on which you can write instructions to the room maid) and splashes of vivid color. No two rooms are alike (ironic given the motel shell) and the adjacent Doug Fir (p1055) is one of the city's coolest live-music venues. Hit the bar with the band roadies and check in after midnight for a discount.

our pick **Ace Hotel** (☎ 503-228-2277; www.acehotel.com; 1022 SW Stark St; d with shared/private bath from $107/147;) A microcosm of the Portland scene, Ace is frequented by some of the city's brightest sparks who recline on the ample lobby sofas supping on Stumptown coffee and conversing on everything from Brangelina to Derrida. If you make it upstairs, you'll find attractive retro-industrial rooms glittering with chic minimalist appeal. Parking costs $20.

Kennedy School (☎ 503-249-3983, 888-249-3983; www.mcmenamins.com; 5736 NE 33rd Ave; d $109-130;) At this Portland institution, a former elementary school, you can relive those halcyon days when you used to fall asleep in biology classes. A few miles from the city center, the school is now home to a hotel (yes, the bedrooms are converted classrooms), a restaurant, several bars, a microbrewery and a movie theater. There's a soaking pool, and the whole school is decorated with mosaics, fantasy paintings and historical photographs.

Mark Spencer Hotel (☎ 503-224-3293, 800-548-3934; www.markspencer.com; 409 SW 11th Ave; d incl breakfast from $125;) If the Ace is too trendy for your taste head next door to this more refined and down-to-earth (some would say 'boring') choice where spacious, unmemorable rooms (all with kitchens) are economically priced for such a well-placed, comfortable city center option. There's complimentary tea with cookies in the afternoon. Parking costs $16.

Hotel Lucia (☎ 503-225-1717; www.hotellucia.com; 400 SW Broadway; d from $127;) A boutique hotel with sleek black and white furnishings topped with arty displays of polished (but still edible) apples. Rooms are design-show funky and geek-friendly gadgets include wi-fi, flat-screen TVs and i-Pod docking

EATING PORTLAND: FOOD CARTS

Perhaps one of the best (and cheapest) ways to uncover Portland's cultural pastiche is to explore its delicious food carts. Largely a product of the last decade, these semipermanent kitchens-on-wheels inhabit parking lots around town and are usually clustered together in rough groups or 'pods'. As most of the owners are recent immigrants (who can't afford a hefty restaurant start-up), the carts are akin to an international potluck with colorful kitchen hatches offering soul food from everywhere from Bosnia and Czechoslovakia to Vietnam and Mexico. While prices are low ($5 to $6 for a filling and tasty lunch), standards of hygiene – thanks to tight city regulations – are kept high and the banter between customer-proprietor is a kind of geography lesson meets recipe exchange.

Food-cart locations vary, but you'll find two significant clusters at the corners of SW Alder St and SW 9th Ave, and SW Washington St and SW 3rd Ave.

stations. The downtown location is handy for everywhere.

Inn at Northrup Station (☎ 503-224-0543, 800-224-1180; www.northrupstation.com; 2025 NW Northrup St; d incl breakfast from $156; P ⊠ ✱ 🖳 ᯤ) Almost over the top with its bright color scheme and funky decor, this super-trendy hotel boasts huge artsy suites, many with a patio or balcony. There's a cool rooftop patio with plants.

TOP END

Heathman Hotel (☎ 503-241-4100, 800-551-0011; www.heathmanhotel.com; 1001 SW Broadway; d from $200; ✱ 🖳 ᯤ) Portland's token 'posh' hotel has a doorman dressed as a London beefeater (without the accent) and one of the best restaurants in the city. It also boasts high tea in the afternoons, jazz in the evenings and a library stocked with signed books by authors who have stayed here. Rooms are elegant, stylish and luxurious. Parking costs $30.

Eating

Portland's rapidly evolving food scene has won plenty of plaudits, especially in recent years, with its globally-influenced dishes. Vegetarians are well catered for while budget travelers can enjoy the city's quirky international food carts with cultural roots in Bosnia, Egypt and everywhere in between.

Bunk Sandwiches (☎ 503-477-9515; 621 SE Morrison St; light meals $5-7; ⌚ 8am-3pm) This unfussy hole-in-the-wall brunch/lunch spot is well worth crossing the river for. Choose from a blackboard of po'boys, tuna melts and meatball parmigianas and you'll be licking your lips all day long.

Silk (☎ 503-248-2172; 1012 NW Glisan St, Pearl District; mains $7-10; ⌚ 11am-3pm & 5-10pm Mon-Sat) Vietnamese-food lovers will adore this gorgeous restaurant. Everything is delicious, from the banana-blossom salad and lemongrass shrimp to the pho (noodle soups). The original restaurant (called Pho Van) can be found on SE 82nd Ave.

Pok Pok (☎ 503-232-1387; 3226 SE Division St; mains $8-11; ⌚ 11.30am-10pm Mon-Fri, 5-10pm Sat) Popular Thai hole-in-the-wall with some of Portland's best Thai food.

Kenny & Zuke's (☎ 503-222-3354; 1038 SW Stark St; sandwiches $9-13; ⌚ 7am-8pm Sun-Thu, 7am-9pm Fri & Sat) Portland takes on New York in this new traditional Jewish-style deli next to the Ace Hotel where the pièce de résistance is – surprise, surprise – the hand-sliced pastrami (cured for five days, smoked for10 and steamed for three). Once you've demolished the classic pastrami on rye leave room for a blintz, latke or formidable desert.

Vino Paradiso (☎ 503-295-9536; 417 NW 10th Ave; mains $11-16; ⌚ 4-11pm Tue-Sat, 3-9pm Sun) A cool Pearl District wine bar-cum-bistro with small, tasty portions of mainly Italian fare skillfully paired with some amazing vinos. Try the risotto and watch the beautiful people come and go.

Pambiche (☎ 503-233-0511; 2811 NE Glisan St; mains $11-17; ⌚ 11am-10pm Sun-Thu, 11am-midnight Fri & Sat) Americans might not be able to legally visit Cuba, but they can get the next best thing at this multicolored Cuban restaurant in the Northeast district. Open all day, *la hora del amigo* (Cuban happy hour) is the best time to chow (2pm to 6pm Monday to Friday, 10pm to midnight Friday and Saturday). The menu? No Castro speeches, but plenty of *ropa vieja* (shredded beef), snapper in coconut sauce and that rich Cuban coffee. Warning – the place is insanely popular, but tiny. Arrive early!

our pick Jake's Famous Crawfish (☎ 503-226-1419; 401 SW 12th Ave; mains $17-32; 11am-11pm Mon-Thu, 11am-midnight Fri, noon-midnight Sat, 3-11pm Sun) Portland's best seafood lies within this elegant old-time venue. The oysters are divine, the crab cakes a revelation and the horseradish salmon your ticket into heaven. Come at 3pm and praise the lord for (cheap) happy hour.

Marrakesh Moroccan Restaurant (☎ 503-248-9442; 1201 NW 21st Ave; mains $20-30; 5pm-midnight Mon-Sat) You'll be hitting Powell's bookstore to buy Lonely Planet's *Morocco* guide after a visit to this Nob Hill classic which serves up authentic tagine that you eat with your hands while sitting on puffy cushions.

Paley's Place (☎ 503-243-2403; 1204 NW 21st Ave; mains $20-32; 5:30-10pm Mon-Thu, 5:30-11pm Fri & Sat, 5-10pm Sun) Vitaly and Kimberly Paley have established one of Portland's premier restaurants, offering a creative blend of French and Pacific Northwest cuisines. Whether it's the duck confit, Kobe burger or veal sweetbreads, you can count on fresh ingredients, excellent service and a memorable experience.

Drinking

Check www.barflymag.com for eclectic, spot-on reviews. As of 2009, Oregon bars and pubs are nonsmoking.

COFFEEHOUSES

To Seattleites it's anathema to suggest that Portland brews equitable coffee, but word on the street says it's a close run thing.

our pick Stumptown Coffee (☎ 503-230-7797; Ace Hotel 1022 SW Stark St; Belmont 3356 SE Belmont St; Division 3377 SE Division St; Downtown 128 SW 3rd Ave;) The hottest, the coolest, the greatest and the most ubiquitous.

Barista (☎ 503-274-1211; 539 NW 13th Ave) Forget the beans, it's all about the confection. Star barista Billy Wilson concocts caffeine-infused miracles out of an eclectic selection of different coffees in this made-over Pearl District warehouse.

Albina Press (☎ 503-282-5214; 4637 N Albina Ave;) Pure nirvana for its delicious cups of coffee artistically constructed by competition-winning baristas. The cafe is situated just off I5 two miles north of the Lloyd District.

World Cup (☎ 503-228-4152; 1740 NW Glisan St;) Not a soccer tournament but a world-class coffee bar with its own on-site roasting room. It also rejuvenates the marathon book-browsers in Powell's bookstore.

Anna Bannanas (☎ 503-274-2559; 1214 NW 21st Ave;) Funky hangout in an old renovated house with a comfortable feel, gourmet food and a good crowd.

BARS

Brazen Bean (☎ 503-234-0636; 2075 NW Glisan St) Located in a antique Victorian house, this very popular bar is known for its martinis – more than 25 different kinds. During happy hour (5pm to 8pm weekdays) the prize drinks are $4 and service slows to molasses.

Saucebox (☎ 503-241-3393; 214 SW Broadway) Metro-sleek restaurant with pretty bar staff serving upscale Asian-fusion cuisine, but also very popular for its wide selection of drinks, including creative cocktails. DJs fire up at 10pm.

Horse Brass Pub (☎ 503-232-2202; 4534 SE Belmont St) Portland's most authentic English pub, cherished for its dark-wood atmosphere, excellent fish and chips, and 50 beers on tap. Play some darts, watch soccer on TV or just take it all in.

Doug Fir (☎ 503-231-9663; 830 E Burnside St) Paul Bunyan meets the *Jetsons* at this ultratrendy venue with edgy, hard-to-get talent, drawing crowds from tattooed youth to suburban yuppies. Sample its restaurant (open 21 hours), then stumble next door to the rock-star quality Jupiter Hotel.

Crush (☎ 503-235-8150; 1400 SE Morrison St) Slip into this sexy lounge with all the pretty people and order one of the exotic cocktails. The menu's gourmet (try brunch) and there's a 'vice' room just for smokers. Great for a girls' night out, straight or lesbian.

LaurelThirst Pub (☎ 503-232-1504; 2958 NE Glisan St) Crowds sometimes spill onto the sidewalk at this dark, funky neighborhood joint. Regular live music is free in the early evening, but incurs a cover charge after 9pm. Good beer and wine selection (but no liquor), along with fine breakfasts.

Back Stage Bar (☎ 503-236-9234; 3702 SE Hawthorne Blvd) Hidden gem behind the Bagdad Theater with a seven-story-high space, pool tables galore and tons of personality.

BREWPUBS

It's enough to make a native Brit jealous. Portland has about 30 brewpubs within its borders – more than any other city on earth. Here's a starting list.

Amnesia Brewing (☎ 503-281-7708; 832 N Beech St) Hip N Mississippi Ave's main brewery, with a casual feel and picnic tables out front. Excellent beer – try the Desolation IPA or Wonka Porter. Outdoor grill offers burgers and sausages.

Hopworks Urban Brewery (☎ 503-232-4677; 2944 SE Powell Blvd) The newest kid on the block opened in March 2008 and furnished Portland with its first 100% ecobrewery – all organic ales, local ingredients, composting and even a 'bicycle bar.'

Lucky Labrador Brewing Company (Hawthorne ☎ 503-236-3555; 915 SE Hawthorne Blvd; Pearl District ☎ 503-517-4352; 1945 NW Quimby St) Large, no-nonsense beer hall with a wide selection of brews and, at the Hawthorne branch, a dog-friendly back patio, where movies are shown in summer.

New Old Lompoc (☎ 503-225-1855; 1616 NW 23rd Ave) Eclectic pub offering more than a dozen taps with treats such as Condor Pale Ale, Sockeye Cream Stout and Bald Guy Brown. The leafy back patio is a must on warm days.

Roots Organic Brewing (☎ 503-235-7668; 1520 SE 7th Ave) Relative newcomer on the scene focusing on fully organic brews.

Entertainment

Check the *Mercury* or *Willamette Week* for schedules and cover charges.

LIVE MUSIC

See also Doug Fir (p1055), LaurelThirst Pub (p1055) and Holocene (right).

Dante's (☎ 503-226-6630; www.danteslive.com; 1 SW 3rd Ave) This steamy red bar books vaudeville shows along with national acts including the Dandy Warhols and Concrete Blonde. Drop in on Monday night for the ever-popular 'Karaoke from Hell.'

Berbati's Pan (☎ 503-248-4579; www.berbati.com; 10 SW 3rd Ave) This established rock club nabs some of the more interesting acts in town. Expect big band, swing, acid rock and R & B music. Outdoor seating and pool tables a plus.

Crystal Ballroom (☎ 503-225-0047; www.mcmenamins.com; 1332 W Burnside St) Major bands play at this historic ballroom, from the Grateful Dead to Steve Earl. The 'floating' dance floor bounces at the slightest provocation.

Jimmy Mak's (☎ 503-295-6542; www.jimmymaks.com; 221 NW 10th Ave) Stumptown's premier jazz venue, serving excellent Mediterranean food; casual smoking bar-lounge in the basement. Music starts at 8pm.

Hawthorne Theatre (☎ 503-233-7100; www.hawthornetheatre.com; 1507 SE 39th Ave) All-ages music venue good for live rock, reggae, punk, pop, metal and country music. Intimate stage, high balcony and 21-and-over section for legal boozehounds.

GAY & LESBIAN VENUES

For current listings see *Just Out*, Portland's free gay biweekly. Or grab a *Gay and Lesbian Community Yellow Pages* (www.pdxgayyellowpages.com) for other services. For an upscale, mixed-crowd bar, see Crush (p1055). A selection:

Darcelle XV (☎ 503-222-5338; 208 NW 3rd Ave) Portland's premier drag show, featuring queens in big wigs, fake jewelry and over-stuffed bras. Male strippers perform at midnight on weekends.

Holocene (☎ 503-239-7639; 1001 SE Morrison St) Best for lesbians on 'Tart Night,' which takes place every second

MIKE MCMENAMIN

A Portland native, Mike is one of two McMenamin brothers who started the quirky Pacific Northwest McMenamins empire that includes more than 50 brewpubs, hotels, restaurants, music venues and movie theaters – most located in historic buildings and decorated in highly eclectic style. They're all very fun places to visit, stay at and have a drink at (or three). See www.mcmenamins.com for a taste.

What are the best things about Portland? I think the neighborhoods here are fabulous. There are dozens of them that feel good and have their own life. Portland is charming: rolling hills, proximity to a lot of stuff. It's a good spot, small-town feel…but it's getting faster, or I'm getting slower.

How did you go about finding buildings to restore? In the early days, we used to have to drive around and snoop stuff out. But now we get piles of suggestions, photos, brochures and calls from people who like that we preserve things. It's rewarding that they think of us like that, but it's also kind of unfortunate because we can't do everything.

What role did you play in starting Portland's microbrew movement? There was a group of people – Portland Brewing, Widmer, us and Bridgeport – that were instrumental in getting that whole thing going. In 1985 [pubs could legally brew their own beer] and it's been a great thing. You tend to think of a brewery as a vast thing, but it can be in the corner of the kitchen.

Sunday of the month. Otherwise it's your typical hipster crowd dance scene in a modern industrial space.

Embers (☎ 503-222-3082; 110 NW Broadway) Regulars come to meet up for the music (from '80s tunes to techno and pop), amateur drag shows, a fun dance floor and friendly camaraderie. Mixed crowd.

Hobo's (☎ 503-224-3285; 120 NW 3rd Ave) Past the old historic storefront is a classy restaurant–piano bar popular with older gay men. It's a quiet, relaxed place for a romantic dinner or drink.

CINEMAS

Another Portland quirk is the cinemas where you can sit down for a movie and be served wine, beer, food and snacks without taking your eyes off the screen.

Kennedy School (☎ 503-249-3983; www.mcmenamins.com; 5736 NE 33rd Ave) is the McMenamin brothers' premier Portland venue. Watch movies in the old school gym. **Bagdad Theater** (☎ 503-236-9234; www.mcmenamins.com; 3702 SE Hawthorne Blvd), another awesome McMenamin venue, has bargain flicks. **Cinema 21** (☎ 503-223-4515; www.cinema21.com; 616 NW 21st Ave) is Portland's premier art- and foreign-film theater. **Living Room Theater** (☎ 971-222-2005; www.livingroomtheaters.com; 341 SW 10th Ave) has six theaters with cutting-edge digital technology screen art-house, foreign and retro movies while the cool staff serves you drinks and tapas in front of the big screen. There's an adjacent bar with wine, wi-fi, coffee and comfy sofas. Sublime.

THEATER & CULTURE

The Oregon Symphony performs in **Arlene Schnitzer Concert Hall** (☎ 503-228-1353, 800-228-7343; www.pcpa.com/events/asch.php; 1037 SW Broadway), a beautiful, if not acoustically brilliant, downtown venue. You can catch some of Portland's best plays, including regional premieres, in the intimate space at the **Artists Repertory Theatre** (☎ 503-241-1278; www.artistsrep.org; 1516 SW Alder St). The Portland Opera, Oregon Ballet Theatre and Oregon Children's Theatre all stage performances at **Keller Auditorium** (☎ 503-248-4335; www.pcpa.com/events/keller.php; 222 SW Clay St), while **Portland Center Stage** (☎ 503-445-3700; www.pcs.org; 128 NW 11th Ave), the city's main theater company, now performs in the Portland Armory – a newly renovated Pearl District landmark that boasts state-of-the-art features.

SPORTS

Portland's only major-league sports team is the **Trail Blazers** (www.nba.com/blazers), who play basketball at Rose Garden Arena. The **Winter Hawks** (www.winterhawks.com), Portland's minor-league hockey team, and the **LumberJax** (www.portlandjax.com), the city's lacrosse team, both play here too.

PGE Park hosts the Portland's minor-league baseball team, the **Portland Beavers** (www.portlandbeavers.com), along with the A-League soccer team, the **Portland Timbers** (☎ 503-553-5555).

Shopping

Portland's downtown shopping district extends in a two-block radius from Pioneer Courthouse Square and displays all of the usual suspects. Pioneer Place, an upscale mall, is between SW Morrison and SW Yamhill Sts, east of the square. The Pearl District is dotted with high-end galleries, boutiques and home-decor shops – don't miss Powell's City of Books (p1047). On the first Thursday of each month galleries stay open longer and people fill some of the Pearl's streets amid a party atmosphere. And on weekends, visit the quintessentially Portland Saturday Market (p1051).

Eastside has lots of trendy shopping streets that also host a few restaurants and cafés. SE Hawthorne Blvd is the biggest, N Mississippi Ave is the most recent and NE Alberta St is the most artsy and funky. Down south, Sellwood is known for its antique shops.

Getting There & Away

Portland International Airport (PDX; ☎ 877-739-4636; www.flypdx.com) has daily flights all over the US, as well as to seven international destinations. It's situated just east of I-5 on the banks of the Columbia River (20 minutes' drive from downtown) Amenities include money changers, restaurants, bookstores (including three Powell's branches) and business services like free wi-fi.

Greyhound (☎ 503-243-2357; www.greyhound.com; 550 NW 6th Ave) connects Portland with cities along I-5 and I-84. Destinations include Chicago, IL (50 hours, $170), Boise, WA (9½ hours, $60), Denver, CO (28 hours, $120), San Francisco, CA (17½ hours, $76), Seattle, WA (four hours, $36) and Vancouver, BC (8½ hours, $48).

Amtrak (☎ 503-241-4290; www.amtrak.com; cnr NW 6th Ave & NW Irving St) serves Chicago, IL ($237, two days, two daily), Oakland, CA ($69, 18 hours, one daily), Seattle, WA ($28, 3½ hours, four daily) and Vancouver, BC ($42, four hours, two daily).

Getting Around

Tri-Met's MAX light-rail train runs between the airport and downtown ($2, 45 minutes). If you prefer a bus, **Blue Star** (☎ 503-249-1837; www.bluestarbus.com) offers a shuttle service between PDX and several downtown stops ($14, 30 minutes). Taxis from the airport cost about $30.

Portland is regularly touted as the most bike-friendly city in the US and there are miles of dedicated paths. Rent bikes from **Citybikes Annex** (☎ 503-239-6951; www.citybikes.coop; 734 SE Ankeny St) or **Waterfront Bicycle & Skate Rentals** (☎ 503-227-1719; 315 SW Montgomery St). A ballpark price for day rental is $35. Some hotels (eg Ace Hotel) offer bikes free of charge.

Another Portland tour de force is its comprehensive public transportation network. The city runs standard local buses, a MAX light-rail system – run by Tri-Met with an **information center** (☎ 503-238-7433; www.trimet.org; 8:30am-5:30pm Mon-Fri) at Pioneer Courthouse Square – and a streetcar (tram) introduced in 2001 which runs from Portland State University, south of downtown, through the Pearl District to NW 23rd Ave. Within the downtown core, public transportation is free; outside downtown, fares run $1.70 to $2. Services run until 1:30am.

Major car-rental agencies have outlets at Portland International Airport and around town. Oregon law prohibits you from pumping your own gas. Most of downtown is metered parking; a free option is to park along an inner-Southeast street and walk across a bridge to the city center.

Cabs are available 24 hours by phone. Downtown, you can often just flag them down. Try **Broadway Cab** (☎ 503-227-1234) or **Radio Cab** (☎ 503-227-1212)

AROUND PORTLAND

A short and scenic drive from Portland are some of the best wineries in the state, mostly scattered around the towns of Dundee and McMinnville along Hwy 99W. To get started, contact **Willamette Valley Wineries Association** (☎ 503-646-2985; www.willamettewines.com).

There are many wineries in the area but, for a decent overview visit **Ponzi Vineyards** (☎ 503-628-1227; 14665 SW Winery Lane, Beaverton; 10am-5pm), 30 minutes southwest of downtown Portland, where you taste current releases and visit the historic cellars and vineyards.

Meandering through plush green hills on winding country roads from one wine-tasting room to another is a delightful way to spend an afternoon (just make sure you designate a driver). Alternatively, Portland-based **Pedal Bike Tours** (☎ 503-916-9704; pedalbiketours.com) run five-hour spins from the town of Dundee on Hwy 99W for $79. If you only have time for a quick sampling, head for the **Oregon Wine Tasting Room** (☎ 503-843-3787; 11am-6pm), 9 miles south of McMinnville on Hwy 18, where you'll find around 70 of the area's wineries represented. **Grape Escape** (☎ 503-282-4262; www.grapeescapetours.com) specializes in wine-country tours.

For something different, head to McMinnville's **Evergreen Aviation Museum** (☎ 503-434-4180; www.sprucegoose.org; 500 NE Captain Michael King Smith Way; adult/child 3-17yr/senior $14/12/13; 9am-5pm) and check out Howard Hughes' **Spruce Goose**, the world's largest wood-framed airplane. There's also a replica of the Wright brothers' Flyer, along with an IMAX theater (movie admission separate).

There are several fine restaurants in the area, but for something spectacular consider the **Joel Palmer House** (☎ 503-864-2995; www.joelpalmerhouse.com; 600 Ferry St, Dayton; mains $20-37; 5-9pm Tue-Sat); its dishes are peppered with wild mushrooms collected by hand from the surrounding woods. And if you need an interesting place to stay, consider **McMenamins Hotel Oregon** (☎ 503-472-8427; www.mcmenamins.com; 310 NE Evans St, McMinnville; d $60-130;), an older building renovated into a charming hotel. It boasts a pub with an awesome rooftop bar.

WILLAMETTE VALLEY

The Willamette Valley, a fertile 60-mile-wide agricultural basin, was the holy grail for Oregon Trail pioneers who headed west more than 150 years ago. Today it's the state's breadbasket, producing more than 100 kinds of crops – including renowned Pinot Noir grapes. Salem, Oregon's capital, is about an hour's drive from Portland at the northern end of the Willamette Valley, and most of the other attractions in the area make easy day trips as well. Toward the south is Eugene, a dynamic college town worth a few days of exploration.

Salem

Another leafy Oregon city, state capital Salem is renowned for its cherry trees, capitol building and Willamette University. Find information at the **visitor center** (☎ 503-581-4325; 1313 Mill St SE; 8:30am-5pm Mon-Fri, 10am-5pm Sat).

Following an Oregon trend, Salem's best museum is housed in the local university. Willamette University's **Hallie Ford Museum of Art** (☎ 503-370-6300; 900 State St; adult/senior $3/2; 10am-5pm Tue-Sat, 1-5pm Sun) boasts the state's best collection of Pacific Northwest art, including an impressive Native American gallery.

The 1938 **Oregon State Capitol** (☎ 503-986-1388; 900 Court St NE) looks like a sci-fi film director's vision of an Orwellian White House. Free tours run hourly between 9am and 4pm in summer. Rambling 19th-century **Bush House** (☎ 503-363-4714; 600 Mission St SE; adult/child 6-12yr/senior $4/2/3; noon-5pm Tue-Sun) is an Italianate mansion now preserved as a museum with historic accents, including original wallpapers and marble fireplaces.

Silver Falls State Park (☎ 503-873-8681; car per day $3) is 26 miles east of Salem on Hwy 214 (via Hwy 22). South Falls, a 177ft waterfall, is just a few feet from the main parking lot. For something longer, hike a 7-mile loop trail that covers 10 waterfalls – including a few you can walk behind. There's also camping, swimming and a 4-mile paved bike path.

A couple of hours drive east of Salem are **Bagby Hot Springs**, a revitalizing free hot-tub in a rustic forest bathhouse 1.5 miles down a hiking trail. From Estacada head 26 miles south on Hwy 224 (which becomes Forest Rd 46). Turn right onto Forest Rd 63 and go three miles to USFS Rd 70. Turn right and go 6 miles to the parking area ($5 Northwest Forest Pass required). If the communal bathing doesn't cut it, enjoy more salubrious climes at **Breitenbush Hot Springs** (☎ 503-854-3320; www.breitenbush.com), a fancier spa with massages, yoga and the like. Day-use prices are $12 to $25. Breitenbush is east of Salem on Hwy 46 just past the settlement of Detroit.

Eugene

If Eugene was a person, it would be a countercultural Merry Prankster dressed in recycled running shoes with a penchant for anarchistic politics. Located in a central location close to coast, mountains, rivers and plains, this is the city that launched Nike, food co-ops, tree-sitting and Ken Kesey, the zany author of *One Flew Over the Cuckoo's Nest*.

Arcane antics aside, Eugene is an interesting mid-state stopover with plenty of outdoor recreation possibilities and several world-class wineries. It also has – not surprisingly – more dedicated running paths than anywhere else in the US. For more information visit the **Convention & Visitors Association of Lane County** (☎ 541-484-5307, 800-547-5445; www.visitlanecounty.com; 754 Olive St; 8am-5pm Mon-Fri, 10am-4pm Sat & Sun).

SIGHTS & ACTIVITIES

The **5th St Public Market** (www.5stmarket.com; cnr E 5th Ave & Pearl St) is an old mill that now anchors several dozen restaurants, cafés and boutiques around a pretty courtyard. Performers occasionally entertain here.

Housed in a replica of a Native American longhouse, the **University of Oregon Museum of Natural History** (☎ 541-346-3024; http://natural-history.uoregon.edu; 1680 E 15th Ave; adult/senior & child 3-18yr $3/2; 11am-5pm Wed-Sun) contains the state's best display of fossils, Native American artifacts and geologic curiosities.

The renowned **Jordan Schnitzer Museum of Art** (☎ 541-346-3027; http://jsma.uoregon.edu; 1430 Johnson Lane; adult/senior $5/3; 11am-8pm Wed, 11am-5pm Tue & Thu-Sun) offers a rotating permanent collection of world-class art, from Korean scrolls to Rembrandt paintings.

Eugene has some of the best running facilities in the nation. Many trails hug the Willamette River including **Pre's Trail** (named for Eugene running icon Steve Prefontaine) in Alton Barker Park. The **Adidas Oregon Trail** (cnr 24th & Amazon Pkwy) is a one-mile loop popular with interval runners (it's floodlit at night). **Spencer Butte Park** south of town offers more challenging, hillier terrain.

SLEEPING

Prices can rise sharply during key football games and graduation.

Eugene Kamping World (☎ 541-343-4832, 800-343-3008; www.eugenekampingworld.com; 90932 S Stuart Way; campsites/RV sites $18/30) Large, tidy campground 6 miles north of Eugene (I-5 exit 199). Reservations are accepted.

Campus Inn (☎ 541-343-3376, 800-888-6313; www.campus-inn.com; 390 E Broadway; d from $66;) An independent family-run motel (recently remodeled) perched between the university and downtown with friendly helpful staff, a Jacuzzi and a small gym. Prices depend on the season but are negotiable.

River Walk Inn (☎ 541-344-6506, 800-621-2904; www.ariverwalkinn.com; 250 N Adams St; d $100-120; P) Dutch colonial B&B with four simple, pretty rooms (two with private bath) and a casual, homey atmosphere. Close to the river.

Campbell House (☎ 541-343-1119, 800-264-2519; www.campbellhouse.com; 252 Pearl St; d incl breakfast from $129;) Large 1892 inn with 19 rooms, suites and a cottage; lovely common spaces and garden too.

EATING & DRINKING

Papa's Soul Food Kitchen (☎ 541-342-7500; 400 Blair Blvd; mains $6-9; noon-2pm & 5-9pm Tue-Fri, 2-9pm Sat) Line up with the locals at this outrageously popular Southern-food spot, which grills up awesome fried catfish and seafood gumbo. The best part is the live blues music, which keeps the joint open late on weekends.

McMenamins (11am-11pm Sun-Thu, 11am-midnight Fri & Sat) E 19th St (☎ 541-342-4025; 1485 E 19th St) High St (☎ 541-345-4905; 1243 High St); North Bank (☎ 541-343-5622; 22 Club Rd) Gloriously located on the banks of the mighty Willamette, the North Bank pub–restaurant boasts riverside patio tables. The other two locations lack water views but offer similar fare ('classic pub food with a Northwest kick' – pasta, salads, burgers and steaks).

Morning Glory Café (☎ 541-687-0709; 450 Willamette St; 7:30am-3:30pm; V) Eugene in a nutshell, or should that be a nut-roast. This sustainable place is good for breakfast, lunch and brunch and rarely will vegans have a better choice – everything on the menu is either vegan or can be made vegan. Try the biscuits, tofu sandwiches or cookies, and as the in-shop sign says 'make tea not war.'

Ambrosia (☎ 541-342-4141; 174 E Broadway; mains $14-22; 11:30am-9:30pm Mon-Thu, 11:30am-11:30pm Fri, 4:30-11pm Sat, 4:30-9pm Sun) Long bar, cozy interior, fine wine and great Italian food from the standard (spaghetti bolognese) to the more adventurous (curried pasta salad). There's weekly wine-tasting and small plate specials Monday to Friday 2:30pm to 5:30pm.

GETTING THERE & AROUND

Eugene is serviced by the **Eugene Airport** (EUG; ☎ 541-682-5430; www.eugeneairport.com), **Amtrak** (☎ 541-687-1383; www.amtrak.com; cnr E 4th Ave & Willamette St) and **Greyhound** (☎ 541-344-6265; www.greyhound.com; 987 Pearl St).

Local bus service is provided by **Lane Transit District** (LTD; ☎ 541-687-5555; www.ltd.org). For bike rentals there's **Paul's** (☎ 541-344-4150; 152 W 5th St; 9am-7pm Mon-Fri, 10am-5pm Sat & Sun).

COLUMBIA RIVER GORGE

The fourth-largest river in the US by volume, the mighty Columbia runs 1243 miles from Alberta, Canada, into the Pacific Ocean just west of Astoria. For the final 309 miles of its course the heavily dammed waterway delineates the border between Washington and Oregon and cuts though the Cascade Mountains via the spectacular Columbia River Gorge. Showcasing numerous ecosystems, waterfalls and magnificent vistas the land bordering the river is protected as a National Scenic Area and is a popular sporting nexus for windsurfers, cyclists, anglers and hikers.

Hood River & Around

Surrounded by apple orchards and wineries, the small town of Hood River, 63 miles east of Portland on I-84, is famous for its windsurfing (on the Columbia River) and mountain biking south of town off Hwy 35 and Forest Rd 44. A sporting triumvirate is completed by year-round skiing facilities on nearby Mt Hood. For more outdoor information call in at the **chamber of commerce** (☎ 541-386-2000; www.hoodriver.org; 405 Portway Ave; 9am-5pm Mon-Fri, 10am-5pm Sat & Sun), across I-84 from the city center.

In operation since 1906, the 22-mile **Mount Hood Railroad** (☎ 541-386-3556; 110 Railroad Ave; www.mthoodrr.com; adult/child $30/18;) was built to carry lumber to the Columbia River. Today it serves mainly as a tourist train. Spectacular two-hour trips run Wednesdays to Sundays from April through December starting from the historic rail depot in Hood River on the corner of 1st St and Cascade Ave.

The **Columbia River Gorge Hostel** (☎ 509-493-3363; www.bingenschool.com; cnr Cedar & Humbolt Sts; dm/r from $19/49), across the Columbia in Bingen, WA, has simple and affordable lodging in an old schoolhouse. The **Inn at the Gorge** (☎ 541-386-4429; www.innatthegorge.com; 1113 Eugene St; d $119-159;) is an attractive Queen Anne–style B&B with five rooms (some with kitchenette) and wide porches.

Full Sail Brewery (☎ 541-386-2247; 506 Columbia St; mains $9-23; 11:30am-8pm) has a cozy tasting-room bar with a small pub menu. Free 20-minute brewery tours end up here. **Sage's Café** (☎ 541-386-9404; 202 Cascade Ave; sandwiches $4-7; 7:30am-4pm Mon-Fri, 8am-4pm Sat & Sun), situated in a little mall, offers great pancakes, oatmeal and brunch along with 25 different sandwich concoctions in a warm and unpretentious coffee bar-cum-restaurant.

SCENIC DRIVE: HISTORIC COLUMBIA RIVER HIGHWAY

Finished in 1915, this gorgeous winding highway between Troutdale and the Dalles was the first paved road in the Northwest. It was also part of the Oregon Trail and the last leg of Lewis and Clark's expedition. There are gushing waterfalls in spring, wildflower displays in summer and awe-inspiring views all year round. Hikers have plenty of trailheads to choose from, and cyclists can cruise two stretches of the old highway renovated for nonvehicle use (cars 'detour' onto I-84).

Be sure to stop at the interpretive center **Vista House** (☎ 503-695-2230; 🕑 9am-6pm), boasting an amazing view. It's atop Crown Point on the E Historic Columbia River Hwy, 3 miles east of the town of Corbett and 45 miles west of Hood River. Must-see **Multnomah Falls** is a 642ft waterfall – Oregon's tallest – with a one-hour hike to the top. There's a **visitor center** (☎ 503-695-2372; 🕑 9am-5pm) here with plenty of area information. Finally, hikers will appreciate the **Eagle Creek Trail**, the gorge's premier trail.

To reach the historic 74-mile highway, take exit 17 or 35 off I-84.

OREGON CASCADES

An extension of their Washington cousins, the Oregon Cascades offer plenty of dramatic stand-alone volcanoes that dominate the skyline for miles around. Mt Hood overlooking the Columbia River Gorge is the state's highest and offers year-round skiing plus a relatively straightforward summit ascent. Tracking south you pass Mt Jefferson and the Three Sisters before reaching Crater Lake, the ghost of erstwhile Mt Mazama that collapsed in on itself after blowing its top approximately 7000 years ago. More volcanic tourism is available in the Newberry National Volcanic Monument, or you can enjoy flatter, less fiery adventures in the nearby town of Bend.

Mt Hood

Mt Hood (11,239ft), or Wy'east as it was known to the Native Americans, is Oregon's highest peak and the fourth-highest in the Cascades. First climbed in 1857, the summit ascent is relatively easy compared to other mountains but still requires technical climbing know-how. Hood has six ski areas, including Timberline, which lies above the eponymous lodge and offers the only year-round skiing in the US. In summer, hiking reigns supreme with the Timberline Trail, a 40.7-mile circumnavigation of the mountain, attracting the most ambitious walkers.

The prettiest approach to Hood by car is from Hood River (44 miles) on Hwy 35. Alternatively you can take Hwy 26 directly from Portland (56 miles). The historic Timberline Lodge offers the mountain's loftiest and most scenic accommodation and dining. Otherwise you're better off in Government Camp, 6 miles away.

If you're approaching from Hood River visit the **Hood River Ranger Station** (☎ 541-352-6002; 6780 Hwy 35, Parkdale; 🕑 8am-4:30pm Mon-Sat). The **ZigZag Ranger Station** (☎ 503-622-3191; 70220 E Hwy 26, Zigzag; 🕑 7:45am-4:30pm Mon-Sat) is more handy for Portland arrivals. There's another helpful office in Government Camp. The weather changes quickly here; carry chains in winter. For road conditions, dial ☎ 800-977-6368.

ACTIVITIES

Hiking

A Northwest Forest Pass ($5) is required at most trailheads.

Loop 7 miles to beautiful **Ramona Falls**, which tumbles down mossy columnar basalt. Or head 1.5 miles up from US 26 to **Mirror Lake**; continue a half-mile around the lake, then 2 miles beyond to a ridge.

The 40.7-mile **Timberline Trail** circumnavigates Mt Hood along a scenic wilderness. Noteworthy portions of it include the hike to McNeil Point and the short climb to Bald Mountain. From Timberline Lodge, Zigzag Canyon Overlook is a 4.5-mile round-trip.

Climbing Mt Hood should be taken seriously – deaths do occur. Contact a ranger station for details.

Skiing

Timberline Lodge (☎ 503-622-0717; www.timberlinelodge.com; lift tickets adult/child 7-14yr/child 15-17yr $52/30/40) is the USA's only year-round skiing option. **Mt Hood SkiBowl** (☎ 503-272-3206; www.skibowl.com; lift tickets adult/child 7-12 $38/20) meanwhile, is the nation's largest night-ski area and the closest skiing to Portland. The largest ski area on Hood is **Mt Hood Meadows** (☎ 503-337-2222; www.skihood.com; lift tickets adult/child 7-14 $52/30).

CLIMBING OREGON'S PEAKS

Unless you're a mountaineering expert (or a Sherpa) don't even think about trying to ascend one of Oregon's volcanoes without a guide. Good all-round programs are offered by **Timberline Mountain Guides Inc** (☎ 541-312-9242; www.timberlinemtguides.com).

- **Mt Hood** (11,239ft) Each year 10,000 people scale Hood via its textbook southern route (crossing the Palmer and Coalman glaciers), making it the second most climbed mountain in the world over 10,000ft (after Mt Fuji in Japan). Though it's a relatively straightforward ascent, don't underestimate the latent dangers – Hood has claimed 130 lives in the last 100 years.
- **Mt Jefferson** (10,497ft) A breathtaking wilderness mountain, Jefferson's remote summit makes for a difficult but rewarding ascent. Expert rock- and ice-climbing skills are necessary.
- **North Sister** (10,085ft) The oldest of Oregon's three sisters, the north peak is also the trio's most rugged and offers what is potentially its most dangerous climb with high levels of erosion…possible rock-falls.
- **Middle Sister** (10,047ft) The difficult middle child is also the Sisters' most mysterious summit, although climbing here is less complicated than the north peak with no previous mountaineering experience required.
- **Broken Top** (9,175ft) An often overlooked extinct volcano that offers a wide variety of ascents and experiences from rugged rock climbing to adrenalin-charged ice-axe adventures.

For backcountry skiing, ski mountaineering and other adventures contact **Timberline Mountain Guides Inc** (☎ 541-312-9242; www.timberlinemtguides.com).

SLEEPING & EATING

Mazama Lodge (☎ 503-272-9214; www.mazamas.org; 30500 E West Leg Rd; dm members/nonmembers $15/20, d $45-60) Run by mountaineering group Mazamas, this lodge just outside Government Camp has mostly dorms (bring bedding), decks with mountain views, and a restaurant. Open weekends mostly. In winter, trek 10 minutes from the parking lot; in summer, park at the lodge.

Huckleberry Inn (☎ 503-272-3325; www.huckleberry-inn.com; 88611 E Government Camp Loop, Government Camp; d $85-135, 2 bedrooms with kitchen $155; ⊠ 💻 ᯤ) A family-run rustic inn and restaurant with dorm and private rooms, along with a 24-hour restaurant serving up formidable milk shakes and – as the name suggests – pie! Handily located in Government Camp village.

our pick **Timberline Lodge** (☎ 800-547-1406; www.timberlinelodge.com; d $115-270; ⊠ 💻 ᯤ 🏊) Stanley Kubrick fans will have no trouble recognizing this historic 1937 lodge as the fictional Outlook Hotel from the film *The Shining* (exterior shots only). 'All work and no play make Jack a dull boy,' typed Jack Nicholson repeatedly in the movie. If only he'd known about the year-round skiing, the hikes, the cozy fires and the hearty restaurant.

Backyard Bistro (☎ 503-622-6302; 67898 E US 26, Welches; mains $6-9; 🕒 11am-8pm Tue-Sat, 10am-4pm Sun) This tiny but elegant bistro serves up rather delicious soups, salads and sandwiches; there's a great patio for warm days.

Rendezvous Grill & Tap Room (☎ 503-622-6837; 67149 E US 26, Welches; mains $20-30; 🕒 11:30am-9pm) Outstanding dishes such as porterhouse steak and Dungeness crab linguine are served here. Great desserts and wine list also.

Reserve **campsites** (☎ 877-444-6777; www.reserveusa.com; campsites $12-14) in summer. On US 26 are streamside campgrounds Tollgate and Camp Creek. Large and popular Trillium Lake has great views of Mt Hood.

Sisters

Named for the trio of eponymous 10,000ft-plus peaks that dominate the skyline, congenial Sisters straddles the Cascades and high desert that demarcate western and eastern Oregon. Once a stagecoach stop for loggers and ranchers, the town is now a hot spot full of boutiques and art galleries. Throw in some splendid mountain scenery, spectacular hiking and a sunny climate and the brew is hard to resist. For local orientation, see the **chamber of commerce** (☎ 541-549-0251; www.sisterschamber.com; 291 Main St; 🕒 9am-5pm) or the **ranger station** (☎ 541-549-7700; www.fs.fed.us/r6/centraloregon; 207 N Pine St; 🕒 8am-4pm).

At the southern end of Sisters, the city park has **campsites** (per site $10); no showers.

For more comfort there's the **Sisters Inn** (☎ 541-549-7829; www.sistersinnandrvpark.com; 540 US 20 W; RV sites $35-38, d $87-109;) with great rooms and an indoor pool. Or try the central but quiet **Blue Spruce B&B** (☎ 541-549-9644; www.blue-spruce.biz; 444 Spruce St; d $169-189;), offering four woody rooms with fireplaces and bike rental.

Bend

Salubrious, livable and embellished with attractive riverside parks, Bend is Oregon personified. Though ostensibly prosperous, the area got hit badly by the 2008–09 economic downturn with unemployment hitting over 12%. Yet, despite the recession, this 52,000-strong city of sporty fresh-air fiends has held onto its green sheen.

Information is available at the **visitor and convention bureau** (☎ 541-382-8048; www.visitbend.com; 917 NW Harriman St; 9am-5pm Mon-Fri, 10am-4pm Sat) and the **Bend-Fort Rock Ranger District** (☎ 541-383-5300; www.fs.fed/us/r6/centraloregon; 1230 NE 3rd St; 7:45am-4:30pm Mon-Fri).

SIGHTS & ACTIVITIES

The extraordinary **High Desert Museum** (☎ 541-382-4754; www.highdesertmuseum.org; 59800 S US 97; adult/child 5-12yr/senior $15/9/12; 9am-5pm), 6 miles south of Bend, is undoubtedly one of the best in the state. It charts the settlement of the West, along with the region's natural history. The sea-otter exhibit and trout pool are highlights.

As improbable as it may seem on a hot spring day, Bend boasts Oregon's best skiing 22 miles southwest of the town at glorious Mt Bachelor (9065ft). With 370in of snow a year, the season at **Mt Bachelor Ski Resort** (☎ 541-382-7888; www.mtbachelor.com; lift tickets adult/child 6-12yr/senior $58/35/50) begins in November and can last until May. Cross-country skiing is also possible.

SLEEPING & EATING

Look out for a new downtown boutique hotel still being built at the time of writing and due to open in late 2009.

Tumalo State Park (☎ 541-388-6055, 800-551-6949; www.oregonstateparks.org; 64120 OB Riley Rd; campsites/RV sites/yurts $17/22/29) Located 5 miles northwest of Bend off US 20. Reservations are accepted.

Bend Riverside Motel (☎ 541-389-2363, 800-284-2363; 1565 Hill St; d from $60;) Away from the main motel strip, the Riverside sits on the cusp of the downtown core and enjoys an attractive watery setting. For a slightly higher fee you can bag a room with a river-facing view. There's a small covered swimming pool and a pleasant park next door.

our pick **McMenamins Old St Francis School** (☎ 541-382-5174; www.mcmenamins.com; 700 NW Bond St; d $145-175, cottages $190-330;) Another highly original McMenamins invention; this time an old schoolhouse remodeled into a classy 19-room hotel complete with saltwater Turkish bath (nonguests pay $5), restaurant-pub, three bars, pool tables and a movie theater. You'll struggle to tear yourself away to delve into the town itself.

Victorian Café (☎ 541-382-6411; 1404 NW Galveston Ave; mains $7-12; 7am-2pm) A Bend classic and a must-see for anyone with a hearty morning appetite, the Victorian is a formidable American brunch stop housed in an inviting red chalet in the city's leafy western suburbs. Brave the weekend queues to get in – you won't regret it.

Deschutes Brewery & Public House (☎ 541-382-9242; 1044 NW Bond St; 11am-11pm Mon-Thu, 11am-midnight Fri & Sat, 11am-10pm Sun) Bend's first microbrewery, gregariously serving up plenty of food and handcrafted beers.

Newberry National Volcanic Monument

This volcanic region (day use $5) showcases 500,000 years of volcanic activity. Start your visit at the recently refurbished **Lava Lands Visitor Center** (☎ 541-593-2421; 9am-5pm Jul-Sep, limited hours May, Jun, Sep & Oct, closed Nov-Apr), 13 miles south of Bend. Nearby attractions include **Lava Butte**, a perfect cone rising 500ft, and **Lava River Cave**, a lava tube. Four miles west of the visitor center is **Benham Falls**, a good picnic spot on the Deschutes River.

Newberry Crater was once one of the most active volcanoes in North America, but after a large eruption a caldera was born. Close by are **Paulina Lake** and **East Lake**, deep lakes rich with trout, while looming above is 7985ft **Paulina Peak**.

Cascade Lakes

Hwy 46, also called the Cascade Lakes Hwy, loops roughly 100 miles between high mountain peaks, linking together lovely alpine lakes. There are several trailheads in the area, along with campgrounds at most lakes. Beyond Mt Bachelor the road is closed from November to May.

Many lakes have cabins ranging from rustic to upscale. These include **Twin Lakes Resort** (☎ 541-382-6432; www.twinlakesresortoregon.com), **Elk Lake Resort** (☎ 541-480-7378; www.elklakeresort.net) and **Crane Prairie Resort** (☎ 541-383-3939; www.crane-prairie-resort-guides.com). Reserve ahead.

Crater Lake National Park

Get ready for a sharp intake of breath. It may be a cliché but it certainly isn't an exaggeration: the still, deep, blue waters of Crater Lake reflect the surrounding cliffs like a giant mirror. The secret lies in the water's purity. No rivers or streams feed the lake meaning its H_2O content is made up entirely of rain and melted snow. It is also exceptionally deep – indeed at 1949ft (maximum) it's the deepest lake in the US. The classic tour is the 33-mile self-guided rim drive (open approximately June to mid-October), but there are also exceptional hiking and cross-country skiing opportunities. As Oregon's sole national park, there's a $10 vehicle fee to enter the Crater Lake area. It receives some of the highest snowfalls in North America and the rim drive and north entrance are sometimes closed up until early July. Check ahead. For more park information head to **Steel Visitor Center** (☎ 541-594-3100; 9am-5pm May-Sept, 10am-4pm Nov-Apr).

You can stay overnight from early June to early October at the **Cabins at Mazama Village** (☎ 541-830-8700, 888-774-2728; www.craterlakelodges.com; d $126;) or the majestic old **Crater Lake Lodge** (☎ 541-594-2255, 888-774-2728; www.craterlakelodges.com; d $151-282;), opened in 1915 as a classic example of rustic 'parkitecture.' The updated facilities still retain their rustic elegance. Nearby campgrounds include the large **Mazama Campground** (campsites/RV sites $21/25), managed by Crater Lake Lodge.

SOUTHERN OREGON

With a warm and sunny climate that belongs in nearby California, southern Oregon is the state's banana belt. Rugged landscapes, scenic rivers and a couple of attractive towns top the highlights list, while breathtaking Crater Lake (above) isn't too far away. Centrally located between Seattle and San Francisco, southern Oregon is certainly worth more than a short gas break as you cruise I-5.

Ashland

The pretty settlement of Ashland is as synonymous with William Shakespeare as the great Bard's hometown, Stratford-upon-Avon, in England. People come from all over the world to see its famous Shakespeare festival (see opposite) which has been held here under various guises since the 1930s. The word 'festival' is a little misleading; the shows are a permanent fixture occupying nine months of the annual town calendar and attracting up to 400,000 theater-goers per season. An attractive town in its own right, Ashland is propped up by a plethora of wineries, upscale B&Bs and fine restaurants. Adjacent to the three splendid theaters (one of which is outdoor) is lovely, 93-acre Lithia Park, which winds along Ashland Creek above the center of town and is embellished with fountains and flowers. For detailed information visit the **chamber of commerce** (☎ 541-482-3486; www.ashlandchamber.com; 110 E Main St; 9am-5pm Mon-Fri, 11am-3pm Sat, noon-3pm Sun).

ACTIVITIES

Powdery snow is surprisingly abundant at **Mt Ashland Ski Resort** (☎ 541-482-2897; www.mtashland.com; lift pass adult/child $36/29), 18 miles southwest on 7533ft Mt Ashland. Pedal-pushers can rent a bike at **Siskiyou Cyclery** (☎ 541-482-1997; 1729 Siskiyou Blvd; per day $35; 10am-5:30pm Tue-Sat) and explore the countryside on Bear Creek Greenway.

Noah's River Adventures (☎ 541-488-2811; www.noahsrafting.com; 53 N Main St) offers white-water rafting and fishing trips on the Rogue and Upper Klamath Rivers. For a more refined water-based excursion ask about the wine floats and wine/culinary trips.

For a good soak check out **Jackson Wellsprings** (☎ 541-482-3776; www.jacksonwellsprings.com; 2253 Hwy 99), a casual New Age–style place which boasts an 85°F (29°C) mineral-fed swimming pool ($6) and 103°F (39°C) private Jacuzzi tubs ($20 to $30 for 75 minutes). It's 2 miles north of town.

SLEEPING

Reserve in summer when the thespians descend in their droves.

Glenyan Campground (☎ 541-488-1785, 877-453-6929; www.glenyanrvpark.com; 5310 Hwy 66; campsites/RV sites $22/28;) Pleasant campground 4 miles southeast of Ashland; go for a creekside spot. Reservations are accepted.

Manor Motel (☎ 541-482-2246; www.manormotel.net; 476 N Main St; d from $59;) Handily located independent hotel on the threshold

OREGON SHAKESPEARE FESTIVAL

Highly respected and wildly popular, the OSF repertoire is rooted in Shakespearean and Elizabethan drama but also features revivals and contemporary theater from around the world. Eleven productions run February through October in three theaters near Main and Pioneer Sts: the outdoor **Elizabethan Theatre**, the **Angus Bowmer Theatre** and the intimate **New Theatre**.

Performances sell out quickly; obtain tickets in advance at www.osfashland.org. You can also try the **box office** (☎ 541-482-4331; 15 S Pioneer St; tickets $20-80). Backstage tours (adult/youth $12/6) also need to be booked well in advance.

Check the OSF Welcome Center (on the north side of the complex facing Main St) for other events, which may include scholarly lectures, play readings, concerts and preshow talks.

of the central area with 11 rooms, friendly service and plenty of greenery.

our pick **Columbia Hotel** (☎ 541-482-3726, 800-718-2530; www.columbiahotel.com; 262 1/2 E Main St; d $78-136;) Get in a Shakespearean mood at this quaint European-style hotel with period rooms (some with shared baths), comfy sitting area, complimentary morning coffee and ideal theater-side location.

Ashland Springs Hotel (☎ 541-488-1700, 888-795-4545; www.ashlandspringshotel.com; 212 E Main St; d $139-249;) An Ashland institution and National Historic Landmark that was painstakingly restored in 2000, the Springs glistens with plenty of Shakespearean splendor, although it actually dates from 1925. Elegant rooms are bedizened with pastel colors and common areas include a grand ballroom, a conservatory, an English garden and Larks Restaurant.

Cowslip's Belle B&B (☎ 541-488-2901, 800-888-6819; www.cowslip.com; 159 N Main St; d $145-165;) A top-rated B&B with four luxurious rooms in a 1913 bungalow along with a couple of suites ($215 to $245) in a separate town house. There's a beautiful garden and classic touches such as love seats, rockers, private decks and Jacuzzi tubs (in the suites).

EATING

Sesame Asian Kitchen (☎ 541-482-0119; 21 Winburn Way; mains $11-16; 11:30am-9pm) The newest place in town is a chic but relatively cheap Asian-fusion restaurant where quick service and hearty but healthy portions make for an ideal pre-performance dinner. Try the tangerine chicken or the Mongolian beef short ribs as you discuss the merits of Hamlet over Macbeth.

New Sammy's Cowboy Bistro (☎ 541-535-2779; 2210 S Pacific Hwy; mains $23-36; 5-8:30pm Thu-Sun) Some consider this funky spot, run by an eclectic couple, Oregon's best restaurant. Located in Talent, about 3 miles north of Ashland. Reserve weeks in advance; limited winter hours.

Chateaulin (☎ 503-482-2264; 50 E Main St; mains $24-36; 5-9pm Wed-Sun) More European fantasies are stirred at this fine-dining French bistro right next to the theaters. The decor and menu are *très* Parisian (dishes include duck, vol-au-vent and filet mignon) but the wine list stays patriotically local with some hard-to-find Oregonian vintages. There's a wine shop next door.

Jacksonville

This small but endearing ex-gold-prospecting town is the oldest settlement in southern Oregon and a National Historic Landmark. The main drag is lined with well-preserved buildings dating from the 1880s, now converted into boutiques and galleries. Music-lovers can't miss the **Britt Festival** (☎ 541-773-6077; www.brittfest.org; September), a world-class musical experience with top-name performers. Seek more enlightenment at the **chamber of commerce** (☎ 541-899-8118; www.jacksonvilleoregon.org; 185 N Oregon St; 10am-5pm Mon-Fri, 11am-4pm Sat & Sun).

Jacksonville is full of fancy B&Bs; for budget motels head 6 miles east to Medford.

Jacksonville Stage Lodge (☎ 541-899-3953, 800-253-8254; www.stagelodge.com; 830 N 5th St; d $98-112;) is a modern hotel with 27 spacious and fine contemporary rooms.

Wild Rogue Wilderness

Situated between the town of Grants Pass on I-5 and Gold Beach on the Oregon coast, the Wild Rogue Wilderness lives up to its name, with the turbulent Rogue River cutting through 40 miles of untamed, roadless canyon. The area is known for challenging white-water rafting (classes III and IV) and long-distance hikes.

Grants Pass is the gateway to adventure along the Rogue. The **chamber of commerce** (☎ 541-476-7717, 800-547-5927; www.visitgrantspass.org; 1995 NW Vine St; 8am-5pm Mon-Fri) is right off I-5 exit 58. For raft permits and backpacking advice, contact the Bureau of Land Management's (BLM) **Smullin Visitors Center** (☎ 541-479-3735; www.blm.gov/or/resources/recreation/rogue/index.php; 14335 Galice Rd; 7am-3pm) in Galice.

Rafting the Rogue is not for the faint of heart; a typical trip takes three days and costs upward of $650. Outfitters include **Raft the Rogue** (☎ 800-797-7238; www.raftthe rogue.com; 21171 Hwy 62), **Rogue Wilderness Adventures** (☎ 800-336-1647; www.wildrogue.com). The latter is based in the small town of Shady Cove, 20 miles north of Medford.

A highlight of the region is the 40-mile **Rogue River Trail**, once a supply route from Gold Beach. The full trek takes four to five days; day hikers might aim for Whiskey Creek Cabin, a 6-mile round-trip from the Grave Creek trailhead. The trail is dotted with rustic lodges ($110 to $140 per person with meals; reservations required) – try **Black Bar** (☎ 541-479-6507; www.blackbarlodge.net). There are also primitive campgrounds along the way.

North Umpqua River

This 'Wild and Scenic' river boasts world-class fly-fishing, fine hiking and serene camping. The 79-mile **North Umpqua Trail** begins near Idleyld Park and passes through Steamboat en route to the Pacific Crest Trail. A popular sideline is pretty **Umpqua Hot Springs**, east of Steamboat near Toketee Lake. Not far away, stunning, two-tiered **Toketee Falls** (113ft) flows over columnar basalt, while **Watson Falls** (272ft) is one of the highest waterfalls in Oregon. For information stop by Glide's **Colliding Rivers Information Center** (☎ 541-496-0157; 18782 N Umpqua Hwy; 9am-5pm May-Oct). Adjacent is the **North Umpqua Ranger District** (☎ 541-496-3532; 8am-4:30pm Mon-Fri).

Between Idleyld Park and Diamond Lake are dozens of riverside campgrounds; these include lovely **Susan Creek** and primitive **Boulder Flat** (no water). A few area accommodations fill up quickly in summer; try the log-cabin-like rooms at **Dogwood Motel** (☎ 541-496-3403; www.dogwoodmotel.com; 28866 N Umpqua Hwy; d $65-70;).

Oregon Caves National Monument

This very popular cave (there's only one) lies 19 miles east of Cave Junction on Hwy 46. Three miles of passages are explored via 90-minute **walking tours** (☎ 541-592-2100; www.nps.gov/orca; adult/child 16yr & under $8.50/6; 10am-4pm Apr-May & Oct-Nov, 9am-5pm Jun-Sep, closed Dec-Mar) that include 520 rocky steps and dripping chambers running along the River Styx. Dress warmly, wear shoes with good traction and be prepared to get dripped on.

Cave Junction, 28 miles south of Grants Pass on US 199 (Redwood Hwy), provides the region's services. Here you'll find the decent **Junction Inn** (☎ 541-592-3106; 406 Redwood Hwy; d from $65;), along with a few restaurants. For fancy lodgings right at the cave there's the impressive **Oregon Caves Chateau** (☎ 541-592-3400, 877-245-9022; www.oregoncaveschateau.com; d from $90-137; May-Oct); grab a milk shake at the old-fashioned soda fountain here. Campers should head to **Cave Creek Campground** (☎ 541-592-2166; campsites $10), 14 miles up Hwy 46, about 4 miles from the cave.

EASTERN OREGON

Mirroring Washington, Oregon east of the Cascades bears little resemblance to its wetter western cohort. Despite a tiny population – the biggest town Pendleton numbers only 20,000 – the region hoards some of the state's most diverse and unusual sights. Picture high plateaus, painted hills, alkali lakebeds and the country's deepest river gorge. Many of the smaller towns will whisk you back in time with still-palpable spaghetti-Western touches.

John Day Fossil Beds National Monument

Within the soft rocks and crumbly soils of John Day country lies one of the world's greatest fossil collections, laid down between six and 50 million years ago. Roaming the forests at the time were saber-toothed nimravids, pint-sized horses, bear-dogs and other early mammals.

The national monument includes 22 sq miles at three different units: Sheep Rock Unit, Painted Hills Unit and Clarno Unit. Each has hiking trails and interpretive displays. To visit all of the units in one day requires quite a bit of driving, as more than 100 miles separate the fossil beds.

Visit the excellent **Thomas Condon Paleontology Center** (☎ 541-987-2333; www.nps.gov/joda; 32651 Hwy

19, Kimberly; 9am-5:30pm May-Sep, to 4pm Nov-Apr) 2 miles north of US 26 at the Sheep Rock Unit. Displays include a three-toed horse and petrified dung-beetle balls, along with many other fossils and geologic history exhibits. If you feel like walking, take the short hike up the **Blue Basin Trail**, which will make you feel like you've just landed on the sunny side of the moon.

The Painted Hills Unit, near the town of Mitchell, consists of low-slung, colorfully banded hills formed about 30 million years ago. Ten million years older is the Clarno Unit, which exposes mud flows that washed over an Eocene-era forest and eroded into distinctive, sheer-white cliffs topped with spires and turrets of stone.

Rafting is popular on the John Day River, the longest free-flowing river in the state. **Oregon River Experiences** (800-827-1358; www.oregonriver.com) offer trips of up to five days. There's also good fishing for smallmouth bass and rainbow trout. Enquire at the **Oregon Department of Fish & Wildlife** (541-575-1167; www.dfw.state.or.us).

Every little town in the area has at least one hotel; these include the charming **Historic Hotel Oregon** (541-462-3027; www.theoregonhotel.net; 104 E Main St; dm $15, d $29-79;) in Mitchell and the friendly **Sonshine B&B** (541-575-1827; www.sonshinebedandbreakfast.com; 210 NW Canton St; d $75-105;), in John Day itself, which has four rooms, formidable breakfasts and a warm welcome. There are several campgrounds in the area including Lone Pine and Big Bend (sites $8) on Hwy 402.

Wallowa Mountains

The Wallowa Mountains, with their glacier-hewn peaks and crystalline lakes, are among the most beautiful natural areas in Oregon. The only drawback is the large number of visitors who flock here in summer, especially to the pretty **Wallowa Lake** area. Escape them all on one of several long hikes into the nearby **Eagle Cap Wilderness** area, such as the 6-mile one-way jaunt to **Aneroid Lake** or the 9-mile trek on the **West Fork Trail**. From the upper Lostine Valley, or from the Sheep Creek Summit of USFS Rd 39, there is easier day-hike access to the Eagle Cap's high country.

Just north of the mountains, in the Wallowa Valley, **Enterprise** is a homely backcountry town with several motels such as the **Ponderosa** (541-426-3186; 102 E Greenwood St; d $67-74;). If you like beer, don't miss the town's microbrewery, Terminal Gravity. Just 6 miles south is Enterprise's fancy cousin, the upscale town of **Joseph**. Expensive bronze galleries and artsy boutiques line the main strip, and accommodations comprise mostly B&Bs.

Hells Canyon

North America's deepest river gorge (yes – even deeper than the Grand Canyon) provides Oregon with its northeastern border (with Idaho) and visitors with one of the state's wildest and jaw-dropping vistas. The mighty Snake River (a 1000-mile-long tributary of the even mightier Columbia) has taken 13 million years to carve its path through the high plateaus of eastern Oregon to its present depth of 8000ft. The canyon itself is a true wilderness bereft of roads but replete with plenty of outdoor adventures.

For perspective, drive 30 miles from Joseph to Imnaha, where a 24-mile slow gravel road leads up to the excellent lookout at **Hat Point** (USFS Rd 4240). From here you can see the Wallowa Mountains, Idaho's Seven Devils, the Imnaha River and the wilds of Hells Canyon. This road is open from late May until snowfall; give yourself two hours each way for the drive. In Enterprise, the **Wallowa Mountains Visitor Center** (541-426-5546; www.fs.fed.us/r6/w-w; 88401 Hwy 82; 8am-6pm Mon-Sat) has a wealth of information on road conditions and area details.

For white-water action and spectacular scenery, head down to **Hells Canyon Dam**, 25 miles north of the small community of Oxbow. **Hells Canyon Adventures** (541-785-3352, 800-422-3568; www.hellscanyonadventures.com; 4200 Hells Canyon Dam Rd) runs raft trips and noisy **jet-boat tours** from May through September (reservations required). Just past the dam the road ends at the **Hells Canyon Visitor Center** (541-785-3395; 8am-4pm May-Sept), which has good advice on the area's campgrounds and hiking trails.

The area has many campgrounds. Just outside Imnaha is the huntsman-style **Imnaha River Inn** (541-577-6002, 866-601-9214; www.imnahariverinn.com; d $120), a B&B replete with Hemingway-esque animal trophies, while Oxbow has the good-value **Hells Canyon B&B** (541-785-3373; www.hellscanyonb-b.com; 49922 Homestead Rd; d $70). For more services head to the towns of Enterprise, Joseph and Halfway.

Steens Mountain & Alvord Desert

Steens Mountain, the highest peak (9670ft) in southeastern Oregon, is part of a massive,

30-mile fault-block range. On the west slope of the range, ice-age glaciers bulldozed massive U-shaped valleys into the flanks of the mountain. To the east, delicate alpine meadows and lakes flank the Steens, dropping off dizzyingly into the Alvord Desert 5000ft below.

Beginning in Frenchglen, the 66-mile gravel **Steens Mountain Loop Road** offers access to Steens Mountain Recreation Area; it's open from late June to October (depending on the weather) and requires a high-clearance vehicle in parts. Call the **Bureau of Land Management** (BLM; ☎ 541-573-4400; www.blm.gov; 7:45am-4:30pm Mon-Fri) for information. If you happen to be in the area outside these months or have a low-clearance vehicle, consider seeing the Steens via the flat eastern gravel road through the scenic Alvord Desert. Take a full gas tank and prepare for weather changes year-round.

There are campgrounds on the Steens Mountain Loop, such as the BLM's pretty Page Springs and fine South Steens Campgrounds (campsites $6 to $8, water available). Free 'dispersed' camping is allowed in the Steens and Alvord Desert (bring water). The historic **Frenchglen Hotel** (☎ 541-493-2825; fghotel@yahoo.com; 39184 Hwy 205, Frenchglen; d $67-100; mid-Mar–Oct;) has small, cute rooms with shared bath, plus five modern rooms with private bathroom. Dinners are available (reserve ahead).

OREGON COAST

While Washington's mountains might pack more punch than Oregon's less well known peaks, Oregon wins hands down when it comes to beaches. Oregon's 362 miles of gorgeous coastline is paralleled by spectacular US 101, a scenic highway that winds its way through towns, resorts, state parks (over 70 of them) and wilderness areas.

Astoria

The oldest Caucasian-founded settlement west of the Rockies, the port town of Astoria was founded by John Jacob Astor – a millionaire fur trader and the Bill Gates of his day – in 1811. Sitting at the wide mouth of the Columbia River, the town retains some typical Victorian heritage houses, a handful of good seafood restaurants and plenty of poignant Lewis and Clark memorabilia; the two great American explorers concluded their epic cross-continental journey at Fort Clatsop, just south of here, in 1805. The impossible-to-miss 4.1-mile-long **Astoria-Megler Bridge** (1966) takes US 101 into Washington state and is the world's longest continuous truss bridge. Find information at the **visitor center** (☎ 503-325-6311; www.oldoregon.com; 111 W Marine Dr; 9am-5pm).

Astoria's 150-year-old seafaring heritage is well interpreted at the fine **Columbia River Maritime Museum** (☎ 503-325-2323; www.crmm.org; 1792 Marine Dr; adult/child 6-17yr/senior $10/5/8; 9:30am-5pm). The less flashy **Heritage Museum** (☎ 503-338-4849; www.cumtux.org; 1618 Exchange St; adult/child 6-17yr/senior $4/2/3; 10am-5pm) has historical exhibits which include Ku Klux Klan (KKK) paraphernalia.

The extravagant **Flavel House** (☎ 503-325-2203; www.cumtux.org; 441 8th St; adult/child 6-17yr/senior $5/2/4; 10am-5pm) is a Queen Anne Victorian built by Capt George Flavel, one of Astoria's leading citizens during the 1880s. For a good view, head uphill to the **Astoria Column**, a 125ft tower painted with scenes from the westward sweep of US exploration and settlement.

Five miles south of Astoria, the **Lewis & Clark National Historical Park** (☎ 503-861-2471; www.nps.gov/lewi; adult/child under 16 $3/free; 9am-6pm Jun-Aug, 9am-5pm Sep-May) offers a reconstructed fort similar to one the Corps of Discovery occupied during their miserable winter of 1805–06. And 10 miles west of Astoria off US 101 is **Fort Stevens State Park** (☎ 503-861-1671; campsites/RV sites/yurts $18/22/30), which commemorates the historic military reservation that guarded the mouth of the Columbia River. There's beach access, camping and bike trails. Reservations are accepted.

The oldest hotel in the West Coast's oldest town, the **Hideaway Inn & Hostel** (☎ 503-325-6989; www.hideawayinnandhostel.com; 443 14th St; dm $20, r $33-88;) has cheap bunks and private rooms. The **Commodore Hotel** (☎ 503-325-4747; www.commodoreastoria.com; 258 14th St; d with shared/private bath from $69/129;) is an early 20th-century hotel that recently reopened after 45 years as a pigeon coop. The birds and moths have been replaced by a stylish set of European-style rooms and suites.

TPaul's Urban Café (☎ 503-338-5133; 1119 Commercial St; mains $9-16; 9am-9pm Mon-Thu, 9am-10pm Fri & Sat, 11am-4pm Sun) cooks up memorable lunchtime quesadillas served with nachos and a homemade salsa dip. **Baked Alaska** (☎ 503-325-7414; 1 12th St; mains $18-24; 11am-10pm) is one of Astoria's finer restaurants, with great water views.

Cannon Beach

The low-key antidote to gaudy Seaside 9 miles to the north, Cannon Beach is a sensitively laid-out small resort where upmarket serenity is juxtaposed against the thunderous Pacific breakers and fickle weather. Immense basalt promontories and a sweeping sandy beach have given the town its tourist-brochure wrapping paper, but Cannon Beach is uniquely beautiful and far from spoiled. Photogenic **Haystack Rock** (a 295ft sea stack) is the most spectacular landmark just offshore, while stunning views grace the Oregon Coast Trail over Tillamook Head in nearby Ecola State Park. The town itself is replete with small art galleries and esoteric shops. For the full rundown ask at the **chamber of commerce** (☎ 503-436-2623; www.cannonbeach.org; 207 N Spruce St; 10am-5pm Mon-Sat, 11am-4pm Sun).

our pick **Cannon Beach Hotel** (☎ 503-436-1392, 800-238-4107; www.cannonbeachhotel.com; 1116 S Hemlock St; d from $132-242) dates from 1914 and has small but tasteful rooms and a café. For budget lodgings head north a few blocks to the **Blue Gull Inn Motel** (☎ 800-507-2714; www.haystacklodgings.com; 487 S Hemlock St; d/cottages from $69/125), a modest but pleasant arc of rooms clustered around an outdoor fountain. Campers have **Sea Ranch RV Park** (☎ 503-436-2815; www.cannon-beach.net/searanch; 415 Fir St; campsites/RV sites/cabins $26/30/80).

There are plenty of eateries in town; try the clams, snapper or halibut at the oceanfront **Wayfarer Restaurant** (☎ 503-436-1108; 1190 Pacific Drive; mains $19-28; 9am-3pm & 5-10pm) or the burgers and pizza at **Lumberyard** (☎ 503-436-0285; 264 3rd St; mains $9-23; 11am-10pm).

There's a daily **Amtrak Bus** (☎ 800-872-7245) to Portland ($17), via Astoria, leaving from outside the Beach Store at 1108 S Hemlock St.

Newport

Oregon's second-largest commercial port, Newport is a lively tourist city with several fine beaches and a world-class aquarium. Good restaurants – along with some tacky attractions, gift shops and barking sea lions – abound in the historic Bayfront area, while bohemian Nye Beach offers art galleries and a friendly village atmosphere. The **Newport Seafood & Wine Festival** in late February draws the West's top chefs and literally dozens of wineries from California up to Washington. Get information at the **visitor center** (☎ 541-265-8801, 800-262-7844; www.newportchamber.org; 555 SW Coast Hwy; 8am-5pm Mon-Fri, 10am-3pm Sat).

The top-notch **Oregon Coast Aquarium** (☎ 541-867-3474; www.aquarium.org; 2820 SE Ferry Slip Rd; adult/child 3-13yr/senior $13.25/7.75/11.25; 9am-6pm) is well known on the scenic coast, featuring a sea otter pool, surreal jellyfish tanks and Plexiglas tunnels through a shark tank. An alternative is the **Oregon Coast History Center** (☎ 541-265-7509; www.oregoncoast.history.museum; 545 SW 9th St; suggested donation $2; 10am-5pm Tue-Sun) housed in the turreted Burrows House and adjacent Log Cabin. There's more history at the breezy **Yaquina Head Outstanding Area** (☎ 541-574-3100; 750 Lighthouse Dr; admission $7; sunrise-sunset), site of the coast's tallest lighthouse and an interesting interpretive center.

Campers can head to **South Beach State Park** (☎ 541-867-4715, 800-452-5687; www.oregonstateparks.org; campsites/RV sites/yurts $22/22/29), 2 miles south on US 101, which has 227 reservable campsites and 27 yurts. Book-lovers shouldn't miss the **Sylvia Beach Hotel** (☎ 541-265-5428; www.sylviabeachhotel.com; 267 NW Cliff St; d incl breakfast $105-208), with simple but comfy rooms, each named after a famous author; reservations are mandatory. For a fancy meal, try **Saffron Salmon** (☎ 541-265-8921; 859 SW Bay Blvd; mains $22-30; 11:30am-2:30pm & 5-8:30pm Thu-Tue). Once you get past the stellar wall-to-wall view, dig into grilled Chinook salmon or herb-crusted rack of lamb. Reserve for dinner.

Yachats

One of the Oregon coast's best-kept secrets, this neat and friendly little town lies at the base of beautiful **Cape Perpetua**. Volcanic intrusions to the south form a beautifully rugged shoreline, with dramatic features such as the Devil's Churn and the Spouting Horn. Ten miles south is the much-photographed **Heceta Head Lighthouse**, built in 1894 and perched above the churning ocean. Five miles further south on US 101 is the almost tourist trap but fun **Sea Lion Caves** (☎ 541-547-3111; www.sealioncaves.com; adult/child 6-12yr/senior $11/7/10; 8am-6pm Jul & Aug, 9am-5:30pm Sep-Jun), a noisy grotto filled with groaning sea lions accessed via an elevator. Get more tips at the **visitor center** (☎ 800-929-0477; www.yachats.org; cnr US 101 & 3rd St; 10am-5pm).

Camp at **Beachside State Park** (☎ 541-563-3220, 800-452-5687; www.oregonstateparks.org.com; campsites/RV sites/yurts $17/21/29), 5 miles north on US 101 (reservations accepted). A mile further on is the quirky Lesbian-owned **See Vue Motel** (☎ 541-547-3227, 866-547-323787; www.seevue.com; 95590 Hwy 101 S; d $80-120), whose 11 individually crafted rooms are perched high above the Pacific breakers. In town you can bed down at the welcoming **Ya'Tel Motel** (☎ 541-547-3225; www.yatelmotel.com; cnr US 101 & 6th St; d $55-90; ⊠ 💻 📶) where eight specially named rooms come with the usual motel amenities plus popcorn, board games and – priceless one this – genuine hospitality.

Oregon Dunes National Recreation Area

Stretching for 50 miles between Florence and Coos Bay, the Oregon Dunes form the largest expanse of coastal dunes in the USA. The dunes tower up to 500ft and undulate inland as far as 3 miles to meet coastal forests, harboring curious ecosystems that sustain an abundance of wildlife. Hiking trails, bridle paths, and boating and swimming areas are available, but avoid the stretch south of Reedsport as noisy dune buggies dominate this area. Inform yourself at the Oregon Dunes National Recreation Area's **headquarters** (☎ 541-271-3495; www.fs.fed/us/r6/sius law; 855 Highway Ave; 🕑 8am-4:30pm Mon-Fri, 8am-4pm Sat & Sun) in Reedsport.

State parks include popular **Jessie M Honeyman** (☎ 541-997-3641; US 101; campsites/RV sites/yurts $17/22/29), 3 miles south of Florence, and pleasant **Umpqua Lighthouse** (☎ 541-271-4118; US 101; campsites/RV sites/yurts/cabins $16/20/27/35), 6 miles south of Reedsport. USFS campgrounds include **Eel Creek** (☎ 877-444-6777; US 101; campsites $17), 10 miles south of Reedsport.

Bandon

Optimistically touted as Bandon-by-the-Sea, this little town happily sits at the bay of the Coquille River. Its harbor has gentrified into a picturesque shopping district, while south of town are vacation resorts and occasional beach access points. The **Bandon Historical Society Museum** (☎ 541-347-2164; 270 Fillmore Ave; admission $2; 🕑 10am-4pm Mon-Sat) has interesting displays on shipwrecks, the Coquille Native Americans and the town's fiery past (two fires devastated the town in 1914 and 1936). For more details harass the **chamber of commerce** (☎ 541-347-9616; www.bandon.com; cnr 2nd St & Chicago Ave; 🕑 10am-5:30pm).

You can book a campsite at **Bullards Beach State Park** (☎ 541-347-2209, 800-452-5687; US 101; campsites/yurts $20/27), 2 miles to the north. At the harbor is **Sea Star Guesthouse** (☎ 541-347-9632; www.seastarbandon.com; 370 1st St; d $80-115; ⊠), offering pleasant homey rooms, some with loft and kitchenette. Just outside town is **Lighthouse B&B** (☎ 541-347-9316; www.lighthouselodging.com; 650 SW Jetty Rd; d $150-263; ⊠ 💻 📶), boasting fine river views and excellent rooms.

For fancy food head to **Wild Rose Bistro** (☎ 541-347-4428; 130 Chicago St; mains $18-24; 🕑 5-10pm Wed-Mon), which uses fresh ingredients to whip up some of the coast's best dishes.

Gold Beach

Situated at the mouth of the fabulous Rogue River, Gold Beach attracts anglers and folks looking to zip upstream via jet boat into the Wild Rogue Wilderness area. Hikers can appreciate the area's spectacular coastline; visit **Cape Sebastian State Park**, a rocky headland 7 miles south, for a panorama stretching from California to Cape Blanco. Get details at the **chamber of commerce** (☎ 541-247-7526, 800-525-2334; www.goldbeachchamber.com; 29279 S Ellensburg Ave; 🕑 9:30-5:30pm Tue-Sun).

For rustic, modern or beach cabins (along with RV sites) head to **Ireland's Rustic Lodges** (☎ 541-247-7718; www.irelandsrusticlodges.com; 29346 Ellensburg Ave; d $58-149; 💻 📶). There's a glorious garden area in front and beach views in back. Awesome cheeses, meats, soup and sandwiches can be had at **Patti's Rollin 'n Dough Bistro** (☎ 541-247-4438; 94257 N Bank Rogue Rd; mains $7-14; 🕑 10:30am-3pm Tue-Sat), one of the coast's best cheap eats, though it only serves lunch (reserve ahead).

Brookings

Just 6 miles from the California border is this balmy and bustling commercial town. Other than great fishing and the scenic coastline, visitors come to visit the remote and unique vegetation of the **Kalmiopsis Wilderness** area. North of town is **Samuel H Boardman State Park**, with 11 miles of Oregon's most beautiful coastline. Oregon's only redwood forests, along with old-growth myrtle, are found in **Alfred A Loeb State Park** (☎ 541-469-2021, 800-452-5687; www.oregonstateparks.org; N Bank Chetco River Rd; tents/cabins $16/35), 10 miles east. The **chamber of commerce** (☎ 541-469-3181; www.brookingsor.com; 16330 Lower Harbor Rd; 🕑 9am-5pm Mon-Fri) is at the harbor.

Alaska

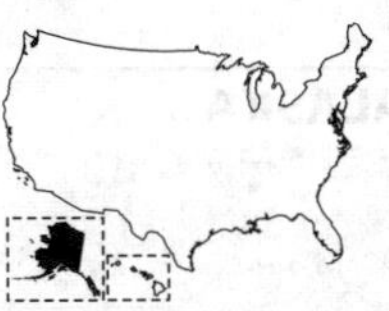

Big, beautiful and wildly bountiful. Far away, rurally isolated and very expensive. Alaska is a traveler's dilemma.

There are few places in the world with the grandeur and breathtaking beauty of Alaska. Not only is Mt McKinley the highest peak in North America, it's also a stunning sight when you catch its alpenglow in Wonder Lake. Forty bald eagles perched on a single tree is something seen in Haines, not in Iowa. A 5-mile-wide glacier shedding chunks of ice the size of small cars is not something you'll see anywhere else in the USA.

Alaska is a remote and costly destination for anybody tripping through the rest of the country. To reach the 49th state takes a week on the road, two to three days on a ferry or, from any region outside the Northwest, a $600-to-$800 airline ticket. And once there you'll find accommodations expensive, bus and train options meager and much of the state roadless and inaccessible.

But for those who have a strong sense of adventure, a little extra time and a love for life on the grand scale, whether it's watching a 40-ton humpback whale breaching or witnessing the northern lights snake mysteriously across the sky, Alaska is a hard place to pass up. And once there, even on a short side-trip, you'll marvel at this amazing land and begin plotting your return.

HIGHLIGHTS

- Zip-lining down to a stream full of bears feasting on salmon in **Ketchikan** (p1078)
- Kayaking among icebergs and seals at **Glacier Bay National Park & Preserve** (p1083)
- Following the Klondike gold rush into the mountains with a ride on the historic **White Pass & Yukon Route Railroad** (p1085)
- Exploring Alaska's history and culture at the newly renovated **Anchorage Museum of History & Art** (p1087)
- Watching **Childs Glacier** (p1097) crackle and send giant icebergs into the Copper River from only 300 yards away.
- Exploring the copper-mining town of **Kennecott** (p1097) and spending the night in the funky town of **McCarthy** (p1097)
- Looking for brown bears and Mt McKinley from the shuttle bus in **Denali National Park** (p1100)
- Enjoying a strenuous mountain hike and then a soothing soak at **Chena Hot Springs** (p1101)
- Following the **Dalton Highway** to the Arctic Ocean and the top of the world…or close to it (p1103)

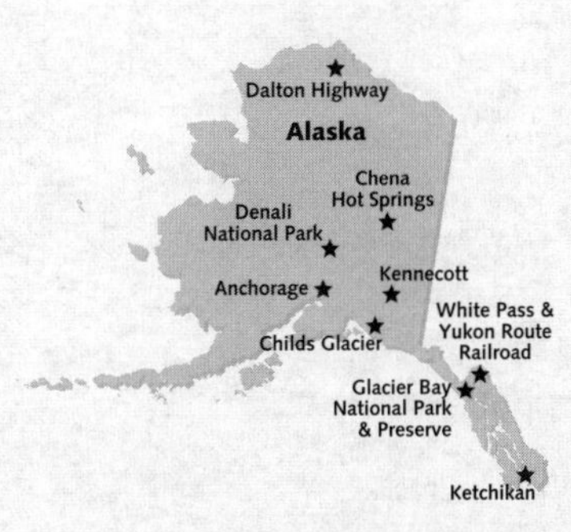

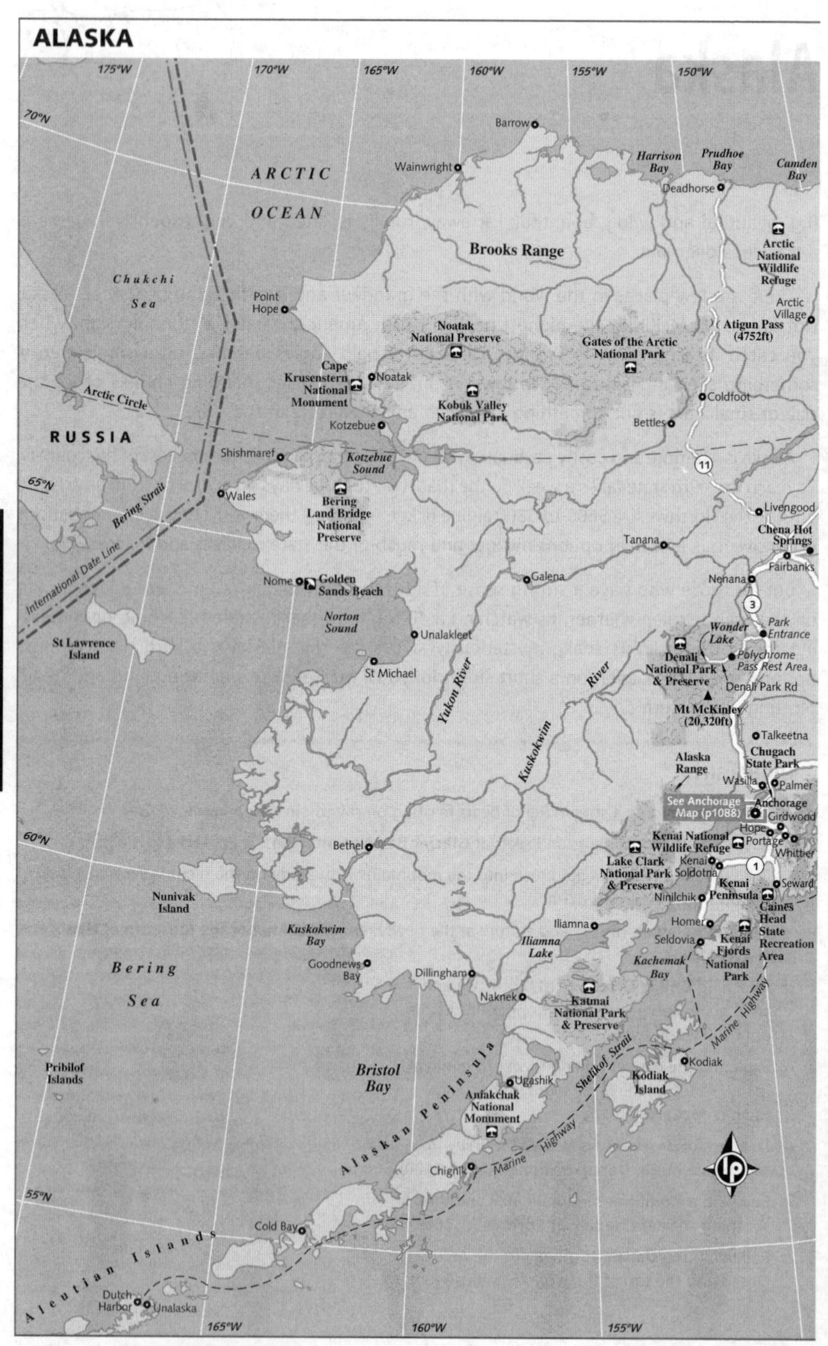
ALASKA
175°W
170°W
165°W
160°W
155°W
150°W
70°N
65°N
60°N
55°N
ARCTIC OCEAN
Chukchi Sea
RUSSIA
Bering Strait
International Date Line
Arctic Circle
Barrow
Wainwright
Harrison Bay
Prudhoe Bay
Camden Bay
Deadhorse
Brooks Range
Arctic National Wildlife Refuge
Arctic Village
Point Hope
Noatak National Preserve
Atigun Pass (4752ft)
Gates of the Arctic National Park
Cape Krusenstern National Monument
Noatak
Kobuk Valley National Park
Coldfoot
Kotzebue
Bettles
Shishmaref
Kotzebue Sound
Wales
Bering Land Bridge National Preserve
Livengood
Chena Hot Springs
Tanana
Fairbanks
Nome
Golden Sands Beach
Galena
Nenana
Norton Sound
Park Entrance
Unalakleet
Wonder Lake
St Lawrence Island
Denali National Park & Preserve
Polychrome Pass Rest Area
St Michael
Denali Park Rd
Yukon River
Kuskokwim River
Mt McKinley (20,320ft)
Talkeetna
Chugach State Park
Alaska Range
Wasilla
Palmer
See Anchorage Map (p1088)
Anchorage
Girdwood
Hope
Kenai National Wildlife Refuge
Portage
Whittier
Bethel
Kenai
Soldotna
Lake Clark National Park & Preserve
Seward
Kenai Peninsula
Ninilchik
Nunivak Island
Caines Head State Recreation Area
Homer
Iliamna
Kenai Fjords National Park
Seldovia
Kuskokwim Bay
Iliamna Lake
Kachemak Bay
Goodnews Bay
Bering Sea
Dillingham
Naknek
Katmai National Park & Preserve
Marine Highway
Kodiak
Shelikof Strait
Kodiak Island
Pribilof Islands
Bristol Bay
Alaskan Peninsula
Ugashik
Aniakchak National Monument
Chignik
Cold Bay
Aleutian Islands
Dutch Harbor
Unalaska
165°W
160°W
155°W
11
3
1

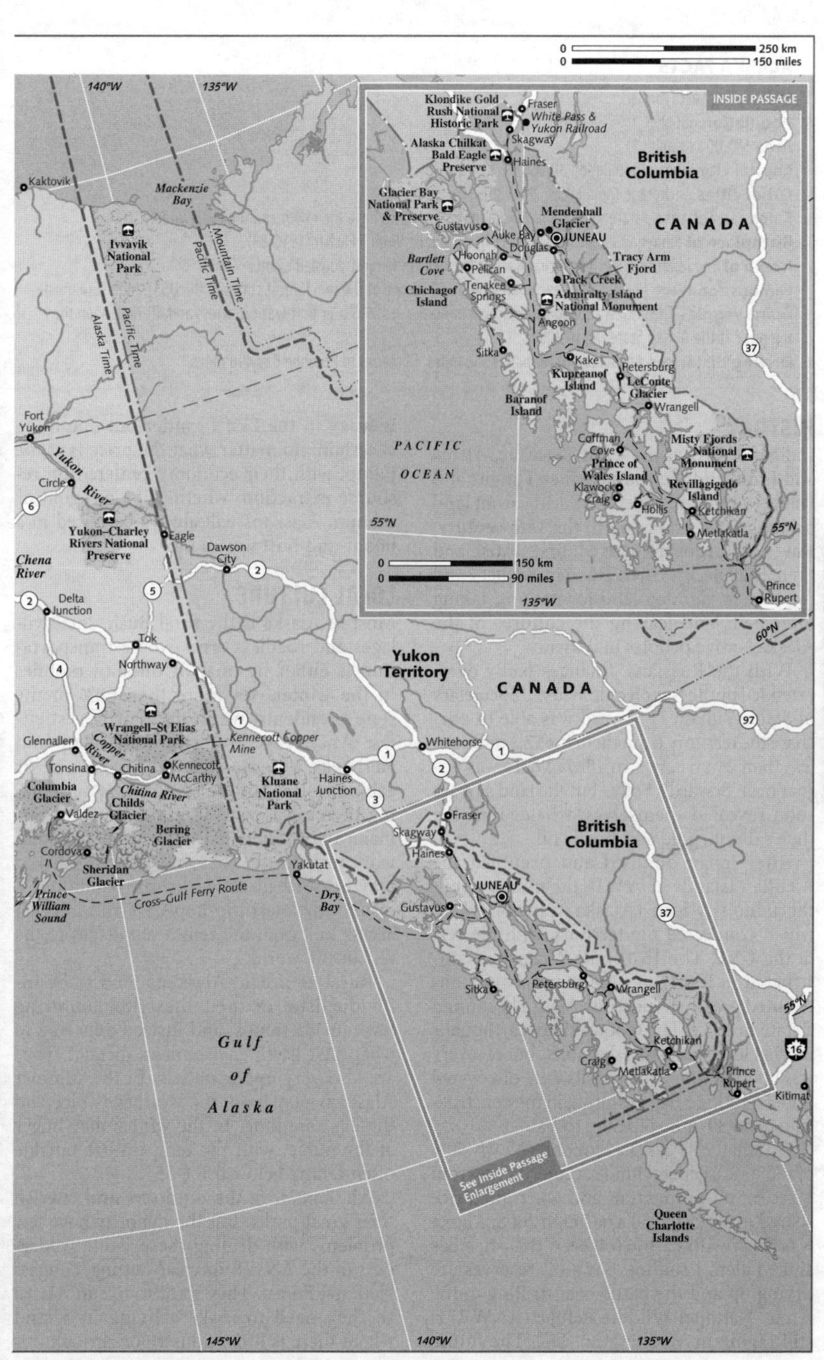
INSIDE PASSAGE
Klondike Gold Rush National Historic Park
Fraser
White Pass & Yukon Railroad
Skagway
Alaska Chilkat Bald Eagle Preserve
Haines
British Columbia
Glacier Bay National Park & Preserve
Mendenhall Glacier
Gustavus
Auke Bay
JUNEAU
Douglas
CANADA
Bartlett Cove
Hoonah
Pelican
Tracy Arm Fjord
Pack Creek
Chichagof Island
Tenakee Springs
Admiralty Island National Monument
Angoon
Sitka
Kake
Petersburg
Kupreanof Island
LeConte Glacier
Baranof Island
Wrangell
PACIFIC OCEAN
Coffman Cove
Misty Fjords National Monument
Prince of Wales Island
Klawock
Craig
Revillagigedo Island
Hollis
Ketchikan
Metlakatla
Prince Rupert
150 km
90 miles
250 km
150 miles
Kaktovik
Mackenzie Bay
Ivvavik National Park
Mountain Time
Pacific Time
Alaska Time
Fort Yukon
Yukon River
Circle
Yukon–Charley Rivers National Preserve
Eagle
Dawson City
Chena River
Delta Junction
Tok
Northway
Yukon Territory
Wrangell-St Elias National Park
Kennecott Copper Mine
Glennallen
Copper River
Tonsina
Chitina
Kennecott
McCarthy
Chitina River
Columbia Glacier
Valdez
Childs Glacier
Bering Glacier
Kluane National Park
Haines Junction
Whitehorse
Cordova
Sheridan Glacier
Yakutat
Dry Bay
Prince William Sound
Cross-Gulf Ferry Route
Gulf of Alaska
See Inside Passage Enlargement
Queen Charlotte Islands
Kitimat
140°W
135°W
145°W
55°N
60°N

ALASKA FACTS

Nickname Last Frontier.
Population 686,293
Area 591,004 sq miles
Capital city Juneau (population 30,966).
Other cities Anchorage (population 283,938).
Sales tax There is no state sales tax in Alaska, but many cities have their own and they vary widely.
Birthplace of Singer and poet Jewel (b 1974), cartoonist Virgil F Partch (1916-84).
Home of The Iditarod – the 'Last Great Race' is the world's longest dogsled event.
Famous for Its size (even if split, each half would still be one of the two largest states in the USA); Inuit (Eskimos).
Giant veggies The largest cabbage ever grown in Alaska, a 105.6lb-er that was 6ft across and 4ft high, won the top prize at the Alaska State Fair in 2000.
Driving distances Anchorage to Fairbanks 358 miles, Fairbanks to Prudhoe Bay 498 miles

HISTORY

Indigenous Alaskans – Athabascans, Aleuts and Inuit, and the coastal tribes Tlingits and Haidas – migrated over the Bering Strait land bridge 20,000 years ago. In the 18th century, waves of Europeans arrived: first British and French explorers, then Russian whalers and fur traders, naming land formations, taking otter pelts and leaving the cultures of the Alaska Native peoples in disarray.

With the Russians' finances badly overextended by the Napoleonic Wars, US Secretary of State William H Seward was able to purchase the territory from them for $7.2 million – less than 2¢ an acre – in 1867. There was uproar over 'Seward's Folly,' but the land's riches soon revealed themselves: whales initially, then salmon, gold and finally oil.

After Japan bombed and occupied the Aleutian Islands in WWII, the military built the famous Alcan (Alaska–Canada) Hwy, which connected the territory with the rest of the USA. The 1520-mile Alcan was constructed in less than nine months and contributed greatly to postwar Alaska becoming a state in 1959. The Good Friday earthquake in 1964 left Alaska in a shambles, but recovery was boosted when oil deposits were discovered under Prudhoe Bay, resulting in the construction of a 789-mile pipeline to Valdez.

Oil still fuels Alaska's economy. Nearly 90% of the state's general fund revenue comes from taxes on oil production and when the price soared to almost $150 a barrel in 2008, Alaska was flush with cash. However, the price has since fallen, Prudhoe Bay's oil reserves are drying up and the battle over drilling in the Arctic National Wildlife Refuge (ANWR) is still raging in Washington, DC. The future is fuzzy in the Last Frontier but one thing is certain, no matter what the price is at the pump: with their economy centered on resource extraction, whether it's oil, gold or salmon, Alaskans will always be mired in a boom-and-bust way of life.

LOCAL CULTURE

Most of Alaska is the rural Bush, small villages and roadless areas where transportation is either by boat or on snowmobiles in the winter. Yet more than 60% of the state's residents live in the four largest cities: Anchorage, Juneau, Ketchikan and Fairbanks. You can still find Alaskans in log cabins in the middle of nowhere supporting themselves with traplines, but the vast majority of residents live in neighborhoods, work nine-to-five jobs and look forward to playing softball at weekends. Satellite TV dishes, the latest hip-hop CDs and internet access link even the remotest villages to the rest of the world.

Rural or urban, Alaskans tend to be individualistic in their lifestyles, following few outside trends, and instead adhering to what their harsh environment dictates. They are also very opportunistic. In the summer Alaskans play hard: the weather is nice and the days are long. In the winter they linger at the office, with the temperature outside often falling below 0°F (-15°C).

Alaskans love the outdoors and cherish their great parks. But the majority have few problems with drilling the pristine wilderness of the ANWR or clear-cutting Tongass National Forest. They want to live in Alaska so they need to make a living in a land where there is little industry or agriculture.

LAND & CLIMATE

Simply put, Alaska is huge. Or, as residents love to point out: if Alaska was divided in half each half would rank as the top two largest states in the country, dropping Texas to third. At latitudes spanning the Arctic Circle, the main body of Alaska is about 800 sq miles, with the arc of the Aleutian Islands chain stretching some 1600 miles south and west, and a 'panhandle' strip running 600 miles southeast down the North American coast.

The coastal regions, such as Southeast and Prince William Sound, have lush coniferous forests, while the Interior is dominated by boreal forest of white spruce, cottonwood and birch. Further north is a taiga zone – a moist, subarctic forest characterized by muskeg, willow thickets and stunted spruce – then the treeless Arctic tundra, with grass, mosses and a variety of tiny flowers thriving briefly in summer.

Alaska's size is the reason for its extremely variable climate. The Interior can top 90°F (32°C) during the summer, while the Southeast and Southcentral maritime regions will average 55°F (13°C) to 70°F (21°C). In the Southeast it rains almost daily from late September through October, while even a week of good weather in the summer will include a day or two when you need to pull out your rain gear. In winter, residents experience long nights (in Juneau it gets dark between 4 and 5pm, in Barrow the sun never comes up so it's always dark), -50°F (-55°C) temperatures and the mesmerizing northern lights.

HOT TOPIC: THE METEORIC RISE OF SARAH PALIN

From mayor of a small Alaskan town to being considered as a presidential contender in the 2012 election, it's been a wild ride for Sarah Palin. Few politicians from any state have risen in the national spotlight as fast as Alaska's former governor.

Palin was only three when her father, a science teacher, moved his family from Idaho to Skagway, AK, in 1964 to accept a teaching position. Eventually they relocated to Wasilla, where senior point-guard Palin led her high-school girls' basketball team to the Alaska state championship. Over the next few years, Palin finished third in the 1984 Miss Alaska pageant, worked as a sports reporter for an Anchorage TV station and married her high school sweetheart.

Then in 1992, the self-described 'hockey mom' won a seat on the Wasilla City Council; four years later, at 32, she was Wasilla's mayor. But the turning point for Palin was in 2004 when she resigned as the head of the Alaska Oil and Gas Conservation Commission over ethical violations by another commissioner. Two years later when Palin ran for governor, promising 'transparency and trust' in Alaska politics, she struck a chord with many residents disillusioned with the career politicians, corruption and cronyism. The results were stunning. In the Republican primary she crushed incumbent Gov Frank Murkowski by more than 30 percentage points. In the general election, she handily beat former Democratic Gov Tony Knowles to not only become Alaska's first female governor but also, at age 42, its youngest.

Two years later Republican presidential candidate John McCain chose Palin as his running mate, making her the first Alaskan and only the second woman to run on a major US party ticket. The highlight of the campaign came early when she delivered a spirited, 40-minute acceptance speech at the Republican National Convention that was praised by conservatives and watched by more than 40 million people on TV.

The national campaign was rough for Palin: there was a wardrobe controversy, the announcement of her unwed teenage daughter's pregnancy, and an interview with CBS News anchor Katie Couric in which she stumbled badly over foreign policy questions. But Palin's views on abortion (pro-life, not pro-choice), gun ownership and conservative fiscal policy excited the right wing of the Republican party while her trademark 'you betcha' phrase became a rallying cry for the so-called Joe Six-Packs of America. McCain had no more lost the 2008 presidential campaign when a Draft Palin movement was organized to position the Alaska governor for the Republican nomination in 2012.

With eighteen months remaining in her term as governor, Palin shocked the political world in 2009 by announcing her resignation, fueling even more speculation that she was eyeing a run for president.

The peak tourist season runs from early July to mid-August, when the best-known parks are packed and it's essential to make reservations for ferries and accommodations. In May and September you'll still find mild weather, but fewer crowds and lower prices.

PARKS & WILDLIFE

Alaska has land to roam and plenty of parks to do it in. Within the state the National Park Service (NPS) administers 54 million acres as national parks, preserves and monuments. The most popular national parks are Klondike Gold Rush National Historical Park in Skagway (p1085), Denali National Park in the Interior (p1099) and Kenai Fjords National Park near Seward (p1094).

Various agencies administer Alaska's parks, refuges and forests. The US Forest Service (USFS) administers **Tongass National Forest** (☎ 907-586-8800; www.fs.fed.us/r10/tongass); US Fish & Wildlife Service (USFWS) manages **Kenai National Wildlife Refuge** (☎ 907-262-7021; http://kenai.fws.gov); while the Bureau of Land Management (BLM) is responsible for **White Mountains National Recreation Area** (☎ 907-474-2200; www.blm.gov/ak/st/en/prog/sa/white_mtns.html). **Alaska State Parks** (☎ 907-269-8400; dnr.alaska.gov/parks) account for another 3 million acres, and most parks offer **camping** (campsites per night $10-20; reservations generally not accepted), hiking and paddling. At 773 sq miles, Chugach State Park (on the edge of Anchorage) is the country's third-largest state park.

All the above agencies have wilderness cabins you can rent (see Information, below) and plenty of places to watch wildlife. On land, Alaska's most popular species to view are moose, bears and bald eagles. Harder to spot are caribou, which inhabit the Interior in large herds; mountain goats and Dall sheep, which also live in remote areas; and wolves, which are reclusive by nature. Marine life includes seals, porpoises, whales, sea otters and walruses. During summer, millions of spawning salmon fill the rivers and streams.

INFORMATION

The **Alaska Travel Industry Association** (www.travelalaska.com) is the official tourism marketing arm for the state and publishes a vacation planner with listings of B&Bs, motels, tours and more. An excellent source for tour companies and outfitters committed to responsible tourism and minimizing visitor impact is **Alaska Wilderness Recreation and Tourism Association** (☎ 907-258-3171; www.awrta.org).

The best place for information on national parks, state parks and all public land agencies along with their cabin rental programs is one of the four Alaska Public Lands Information Centers (APLICs) scattered around the state. Anchorage has the largest **APLIC** (☎ 907-271-2737; www.alaskacenters.gov) and is the best one to contact in advance of your trip.

ACTIVITIES

Alaska is many things, but first and foremost it is the great outdoors. Travelers come here for the mountains, the trails, the wildlife, the camping – the adventure. Hiking trails are boundless and are the best way to escape the summer crowds in places like Juneau and the Kenai Peninsula. Mountain biking is allowed on many trails, and bikes can be rented throughout the state. You can also rent kayaks in coastal towns such as Ketchikan, Sitka, Juneau, Seward and Valdez, where paddlers enjoy sea kayaking in protective fjords, often within view of glaciers. Other popular outdoor activities are white-water rafting, wildlife-watching, canoeing, fishing, ziplining and just pulling over on the road and admiring the scenery.

GETTING THERE & AROUND

Air

The vast majority of visitors to Alaska, and almost all international flights, fly into **Ted Stevens Anchorage International Airport** (ANC; ☎ 907-266-2526; www.dot.state.ak.us/anc).

Alaska Airlines (☎ 800-426-0333; www.alaskaair.com) has direct flights to Anchorage from Seattle, Chicago and many West Coast cities. It also flies between many towns within Alaska, including daily northbound and southbound flights year-round through Southeast Alaska, with stops at all main towns. Round-trip advance-purchase routes include Seattle–Ketchikan, Anchorage–Juneau and Ketchikan–Juneau.

Since absorbing Northwest, **Delta** (☎ 800-221-1212; www.delta.com) offers direct flights from Minneapolis, Detroit, Atlanta and New York, while **American Airlines** (☎ 800-443-7300; www.aa.com) flies in from St Louis and Dallas.

'Bush planes' can be chartered to the most remote areas of the state. Smaller airlines serving the Southeast Alaska region include **Taquan Air** (☎ 907-225-8800, 800-770-8800;

ALASKA...

In One Week

From Washington state, hop on one of the Alaska Marine Highway ferries for a cruise through **Southeast Alaska** (p1078). Spend a day in **Ketchikan** (p1078) zip-lining and watching bears feast on salmon, then three days in **Juneau** (p1081) to check out its great hiking and glaciers. Jump back on the Alaska Marine Highway to Skagway and relive the **Klondike gold rush** (p1085).

In Two Weeks

Fly to **Anchorage** (p1086), rent a car and beat it out of town. Head south, following the beautiful Seward Hwy to **Seward** (p1093) and go kayaking in Resurrection Bay. Continue the road trip by driving to artsy **Homer** (p1094). Begin the second week in Anchorage exploring Alaska's biggest city, then jump on the Alaska Railroad for charming **Talkeetna** (p1100). Continue north on the train to spend three days in **Denali National Park** (p1099), viewing wildlife and hopefully Mt McKinley.

In Wilderness Cabins

Explore the Southeast wilderness by reserving rustic **National Forest cabins** (☎ 877-444-6777; www.recreation.gov.com). The Anan Bay Cabin near Wrangell includes an observatory where you can watch bears feed on salmon. A short flight from Juneau delivers you to West Turner Lake Cabin, a classic log structure overlooking the lake. At the White Sulphur Springs Cabin near Sitka, you can spend the evenings sipping wine and soaking in hot springs.

www.taquanair.com) and **Wings of Alaska** (☎ 907-789-0790; www.wingsofalaska.com).

Boat

The **Alaska Marine Highway** (☎ 800-642-0066; www.ferryalaska.com) connects Bellingham, WA, with 14 towns in Southeast Alaska (p1078) and is a very popular way to travel to this roadless region, with calls on the main towns almost daily in summer. The complete trip (Bellingham–Haines; $353, 3½ days) stops at ports along the way and should be scheduled in advance. Trips within the Inside Passage include Ketchikan-Petersburg ($60, 11 hours), Sitka-Juneau ($45, five hours) and Juneau-Haines ($37, two hours). Alaska Marine Highway ferries are equipped to handle cars (Bellingham–Haines $462), but space must be reserved months ahead. The ferries also service five towns in Southcentral Alaska, and make five runs a year from Kodiak to Unalaska in the Aleutian Islands (p1102) and 11 between Whittier and Juneau.

You can also pick up the **state ferries** (☎ 800-642-0066; www.ferryalaska.com) from Prince Rupert, British Columbia, to Ketchikan ($54), or twice a month join the special runs across the Gulf of Alaska from Juneau to Whittier ($221).

Bus

Bus services link all the main towns in Alaska, with connections to the lower 48. Traveling by bus is not that much cheaper than flying, but you do get to experience the Alcan Hwy. From Seattle, WA, **Greyhound** (☎ 206-628-5526; 800-231-2222; www.greyhound.com; cnr 8th Ave & Stewart St) can get you to Whitehorse, Canada, via Vancouver ($181, 52 hours); see p1157 for further information. From Whitehorse, **Alaska Direct** (☎ 800-770-6652; www.alaskadirectbusline.com; 509 Main St) leaves three days a week for Anchorage ($220, 16 hours).

Car

Be sure to allow at least a week to drive from northern USA through Canada to Fairbanks on the mostly paved Alcan Hwy. It's not worth the time it takes unless you can make some stops along the way and spend a few weeks in Alaska. Local rental cars are handy to get around the countryside; they start at $45 a day, with 100 miles free.

Train

The **Alaska Railroad** (☎ 907-265-2494, 800-544-0552; www.akrr.com) offers a service between Seward and Anchorage and from Anchorage to Denali, before ending in Fairbanks. Book seats in advance on this popular train.

The narrow-gauge 1890s **White Pass & Yukon Route Railroad** (☎ 800-343-7373; www.wpyr.com) links Skagway and Fraser, British Columbia, with a bus connection to Whitehorse, Yukon, which is situated on the Alcan Hwy ($116, 10 hours). It also offers short excursions from Skagway (p1085).

SOUTHEAST ALASKA

The Southeast is as close as Alaska comes to continental USA, but most of it is inaccessible by road. It's possible to fly to the panhandle for a quick visit, but a better option if you can spare a week or two is to cruise the Inside Passage, a waterway made up of thousands of islands, glacier-filled fjords and a mountainous coastline. You can jump on a state ferry and stop at a handful of ports for hiking, kayaking and whale-watching.

KETCHIKAN

Ketchikan, the first stop of the Alaska Marine Highway, is a thin town: several miles long, never more than 10 blocks wide and crammed with Alaskan character, adventure and the scenery you came looking for.

Information

Crow's Nest (☎ 907-225-6119; 308 Grant St; per 30min/hr $2.50/5; 6am-6pm) Cheapest internet in town plus a huge espresso machine.

Ketchikan Visitors Bureau (☎ 907-225-6166, 800-770-3300; www.visit-ketchikan.com; 131 Front St; 7am-5pm) Helpful staff will book tours and accommodations.

Southeast Alaska Discovery Center (☎ 907-228-6220; 50 Main St; adult/child $5/free; 8am-5pm) Houses an impressive exhibit hall; provides details of outdoor activities.

Sights & Activities

Fly through the trees! **Alaska Canopy Adventures** (☎ 907-225-5503; www.alaskacanopy.com; 116 Wood Rd; $179 per person), uses eight zip lines, three suspension bridges and 4WD vehicles so you can zip 4600ft down a mountain. Afterwards you can watch bears feast on a salmon run.

The star of Ketchikan's former red-light district, Creek St, is **Dolly's House** (☎ 907-225-6329; 24 Creek St; adult/child $5/free; 8am-5pm), the parlor of Ketchikan's most famous madam, Dolly Arthur. The **Totem Heritage Center** (☎ 907-225-5900; 601 Deermont St; adult/child $5/free; 8am-5pm) features a collection of 19th-century totems in a spiritual setting.

The 3-mile **Deer Mountain Trail** begins near the city center and provides access to the alpine world above the timberline and wonderful views of the town. There are more trails in the **Ward Lake Recreation Area**. **Southeast Sea Kayaks** (☎ 907-225-1258, 800-287-1607; www.kayakketchikan.com; 1621 Tongass Ave; single/double kayak per day $50/60, day trip $219) offers rentals and guided trips.

Sleeping

Ketchikan Hostel (☎ 907-225-3319; ktnyh@eagle.ptialaska.net; 400 Main St; dm $15; ⊠) A friendly, clean hostel located in a Methodist church downtown and open from June through August.

Gilmore Hotel (☎ 907-225-9423, 800-275-9423; www.gilmorehotel.com; 326 Front St; d $115-155; ⊠ 💻 📶) Built in 1927, the Gilmore has 38 'historically proportioned' (ie small) rooms that include cable TV, coffeemakers and hair dryers.

our pick **New York Hotel** (☎ 907-225-0246, 866-225-0246; www.thenewyorkhotel.com; 207 Stedman St; r $129-144, ste $189-209; ⊠ 💻 📶) A historic boutique hotel in the heart of town with antique-filled rooms and unique suites overlooking Creek Street.

Black Bear Inn (☎ 907-225-4343; www.stayinalaska.com; 5528 N Tongass Hwy; r $160-230; ⊠ 💻 📶) This incredible B&B, 2.5 miles north of the downtown madness, offers both rooms and small apartments. Among the many amenities is a covered outdoor hot tub where you can soak while watching eagles soaring overhead.

Eating & Drinking

Burger Queen (☎ 907-225-6060; 518 Tongass Ave; burgers $5-8; 11am-3pm Mon, 11am-7pm Tue-Sat) Ketchikan's favorite shake-and-burger joint. They'll deliver your hamburger to the Arctic Bar across the street where you can be sipping a beer.

Sushi Harbor (☎ 907-225-1233; 629 Mission St; lunch specials $9-11, rolls $7-13; 10am-10pm). This Japanese restaurant bustles with locals, tourists and cruise-ship workers. Just a bowl of their udon noodles will fuel you all afternoon.

Bar Harbor Restaurant (☎ 907-225-2813; 2813 Tongass Ave; lunch mains $9-12, dinner mains $15-30; 11am-9pm Mon-Fri, 5-9pm Sat & Sun; ⊠) A cozy place with a covered outdoor deck, between downtown and the ferry terminal. Yea, they serve seafood here – who doesn't in Southeast? – but their signature dish is Ketchikan's best prime rib.

IF YOU HAVE A FEW MORE DAYS

Real Alaska is only a three-hour ferry ride away from the cruise-ship madness of Ketchikan. Prince of Wales Island, the third-largest island in the USA, features Alaska Native villages, the Southeast's most extensive road network and a lot of clear-cuts, but no cruise ships. For information, **Prince of Wales Chamber of Commerce** (☎ 907-755-2626; www.princeofwalescoc.org; Klawock Bell Tower Mall, Craig-Klawock Hwy; 🕑 10am-3pm Mon-Fri) is in Klawock and a **USFS office** (☎ 907-826-3271; 900 9th St; 🕑 8am-5pm Mon-Fri) is in Craig.

Bring a mountain bike and you can spend a week exploring the 300 miles of paved and graded gravel roads or the 1800 miles of shot-rock logging roads. Bring a kayak and you can do the same along 990 miles of contorted coastline. You can also rent bikes and kayaks from **A5 Outdoor Recreation** (☎ 907-329-2399; www.a5outdoorrec.com; 103a Sea Otter Dr, Coffman Cove; bike per day $25, single/double kayak $50/60).

In Craig, stay at **Ruth Ann's Hotel** (☎ 907-826-3378; cnr Main & Water Sts; r $110-135; ☒) or the delightful **Inn of the Blue Heron** (☎ 907-826-3608; www.littleblueheroninn.com; 406 9th St; s $79-99, d $99-115; ☒ 💻).

The **M/V Stikine** (☎ 866-308-4848; www.interislandferry.com; adult/child $37/18) makes a daily Hollis–Ketchikan run. The main communities of Klawock and Craig are 25 miles and 31 miles southwest of Hollis respectively.

First City Saloon (☎ 907-225-1494; 830 Water St; 📶) A sprawling club that rocks with live music during the summer, often impromptu when cruise-ship bands are looking to let loose.

Getting There & Around

Alaska Airlines and Alaska Marine Highway ferries service Ketchikan (see p1076). For wheels, try **Alaska Car Rental** (☎ 907-225-5123, 800-662-0007; 2828 Tongass Ave; compacts $55).

AROUND KETCHIKAN

Ten miles north of Ketchikan, **Totem Bight State Historical Park** (☎ 907-247-8574; admission free; 🕑 6am-10pm) contains 14 restored totem poles, a colorful community house and viewing deck overlooking Tongass Narrows.

Misty Fjords National Monument begins 22 miles east of Ketchikan, offering wildlife-watching and spectacular views of 3000ft sheer granite walls that rise from the ocean. **Allen Marine Tours** (☎ 907-225-8100, 877-686-8100; www.allenmarinetours.com; adult/child $168/115) runs a four-hour trip around the monument. **Family Air Tours** (☎ 907-247-1305 800-380-1305; www.familyairtours.com; adult/child $229/179) offers a two-hour tour of flightseeing and hiking in the monument's old-growth forests.

WRANGELL

Strategically located near the mouth of the Stikine River, Wrangell is the only town to have existed under three flags and be ruled by four nations – Tlingit, Russia, Britain and the USA. Today Wrangell is one the few ports where the state ferries dock downtown, so at the very least jump off the boat for a quick look around town.

At the Nolan Center is the **visitor center** (☎ 907-874-3901, 800-367-9745; www.wrangell.com; 296 Outer Dr; 🕑 10am-5pm Mon-Sat; 💻) and the impressive **Wrangell Museum** (☎ 907-874-3770; 296 Outer Dr; adult/child/family $5/3/12; 🕑 10am-5pm Mon-Sat), where you can learn about gold-rush Wrangell or why Wyatt Earp filled in as the town's deputy marshal for 10 days.

For its size, Wrangell has an impressive collection of totems. Pick up the free *Wrangell Guide* at the visitor center and spend an afternoon locating them all. Make sure you stop at **Chief Shakes Island**, near the boat harbor downtown.

Sleeping & Eating

Alaskan Sourdough Lodge (☎ 907-874-3613, 800-874-3613; www.akgetaway.com; 1104 Peninsula St; s/d $104/114; ☒ 💻) This family-owned lodge offers 16 rooms, a sauna, steam bath and a front deck full of wicker furniture with a view of the harbor.

Stikine Inn (☎ 907-874-3388, 888-874-3388; www.stikineinn.com; 107 Stikine Ave; s $115-143, d 134-151; 📶) Wrangell's largest motel is on the waterfront near the ferry dock and underwent a major renovation in 2008 that included its bar, restaurant and many of the 33 rooms.

Diamond C Café (☎ 907-874-3322; 223 Front St; breakfast dishes $6-12, lunch mains $8-14; 🕑 6am-3pm; ☒) Eat

ALASKA

what the locals eat (eggs, biscuits and deep-fried fish-and-chips) while listening to the conservative pulse of this community.

The **City Park Campground** (Zimovia Hwy; campsites free), 1.75 miles south of the ferry terminal, is a delightful place to pitch a tent, while **Wrangell Hostel** (☎ 907-874-3534; 220 Church St; dm $18; ⊠) is in the Presbyterian church.

PETERSBURG

At the north end of the spectacular Wrangell Narrows lies the picturesque community of Petersburg, a town known for its Norwegian roots and home to Alaska's largest halibut fleet.

The **Petersburg Chamber of Commerce** (☎ 907-772-4636; www.petersburg.org; cnr Fram & 1st Sts; 9am-5pm Mon-Sat, noon-4pm Sun) has B&B and USFS information. You can also visit the **USFS office** (☎ 907-772-3871; Federal Bldg, 12 N Nordic Dr; 8am-5pm Mon-Fri).

Sights & Activities

The center of old Petersburg was **Sing Lee Alley**, which winds past weathered homes and boathouses perched on pilings above the water. The **Clausen Memorial Museum** (☎ 907-772-3598; 203 Fram St; adult/child $3/free; 10am-5pm Mon-Sat) features local artifacts and fishing relics, and a small but excellent museum store.

Tongass Kayak Adventures (☎ 907-772-4600; www.tongasskayak.com; single/double kayak $55/65) offers rentals and drop-off transportation, as well as several guided paddles, including a day-long paddle at **LeConte Glacier** ($225), North America's southernmost tidewater glacier and often the site of spectacular falling ice and breaching whales.

Sleeping, Eating & Drinking

Alaska Island Hostel (☎ 907-772-3632, 877-772-3632; www.alaskaislandhostel.com; 805 Gjoa St; dm $25; ⊠ 💻) This is Petersburg's excellent and only budget-lodging alternative. The nine-bunk hostel, a short walk from downtown, is clean, comfortable, casual and fun.

Nordic House (☎ 907-772-3620; www.nordichouse.net; 806 S Nordic Dr; s/d $82/92; ⊠ 💻) Within an easy walk of the ferry terminal, this place offers five large rooms and a common area overlooking the boat harbor.

Scandia House (☎ 907-772-4281, 800-722-5006; www.scandiahousehotel.com; 110 Nordic Dr; s/d $110/130; 📶) The most impressive place in town, this hotel has 33 modern rooms (some with kitchenettes), a courtesy shuttle service, and a main-street location.

Coastal Cold Storage (☎ 907-772-4177, 306 Nordic Dr; breakfast dishes $4-6, lunch mains $9-12; 7am-3pm) The local specialty is halibut beer bits and this place serves the best ones in this seafood town.

Kito's Kave (☎ 907-772-3207; 11 Sing Lee Alley; dinner mains $8-12) Serves up Petersburg's best Mexican, with live music and dancing at night.

our pick **Beachcomber Inn** (☎ 907-772-3888; 384 Mitkof Hwy; dinner mains $15-30; 5:30-9pm) This wonderful restaurant is built on pilings over the sea so every table has a fabulous maritime-and-mountain view.

SITKA

Russians established Southeast Alaska's first nonindigenous settlement here in 1799, and the town flourished on fur. Today Sitka sees itself as both the cultural center of the Southeast and, because it's the only one facing the Pacific Ocean, the region's most beautiful city.

The **Sitka Convention & Visitors Bureau** (☎ 907-747-5940; www.sitka.org; 330 Harbor Dr; 8am-5pm Mon-Fri) is located across the street from St Michael's Cathedral, and also staffs a desk in the Centennial Building. The **USFS office** (☎ 907-747-6671; 204 Siginaka Way; 8am-4:30pm Mon-Fri) can provide hiking and kayaking information for the area.

Sights & Activities

Sitka National Historical Park has an intriguing trail that winds past 15 totem poles, while its **visitor center** (☎ 907-747-0110; Lincoln St; adult/child $4/free; 8am-5pm) features Russian and indigenous artifacts and traditional carving demonstrations. For an eye-to-eye encounter with a bald eagle, head to the nearby **Alaska Raptor Center** (☎ 907-747-8662, 800-643-9425; www.alaskaraptor.org; 101 Sawmill Creek Rd; adult/child $12/6; 8am-4pm; 👪) where injured birds relearn to fly in its flight training center.

St Michael's Cathedral (☎ 907-747-8120; 240 Lincoln St; admission $2; 9am-4pm Mon-Fri) is a replica of the original 1840s Russian Orthodox cathedral destroyed by fire in 1966; priceless treasures were salvaged by residents. Castle Hill is the site of **Baranof's Castle**, where Alaska was officially transferred from Russia to the USA. Built in 1842, the **Russian Bishop's House** (☎ 907-747-6281; Lincoln St; adult/child $4/free; 9am-5pm) is Sitka's oldest intact Russian building. **Sheldon Jackson Museum** (☎ 907-747-8981; 104 College

Dr; adult/child $4/free; 9am-5pm) houses an excellent indigenous culture collection.

Sitka has superb hiking, and the **Gaven Hill Trail** into the mountains is accessible from the downtown area. There are also many kayaking trips around Baranof and Chichagof Islands. **Sitka Sound Ocean Adventures** (907-747-6375; www.ssoceanadventures.com; single/double kayak $55/65) rents kayaks and runs guided day trips; its office is a blue bus at the Centennial Building. Thanks to Sitka's ocean location, marine-wildlife boat tours have mushroomed in the town. **Allen Marine Tours** (907-747-8100, 888-747-8101; www.allenmarinetours.com; adult/child $79/49; 8:30-11:30am Sat & Sun) offers three-hour tours that often include spotting otters and whales. **Sea Life Discovery Tours** (907-966-2301, 877-966-2301; www.sealifediscoverytours.com; adult/child $86/63;) operates two-hour tours from a glass-bottomed boat that provides underwater views of the area's marine life.

Sleeping

Sitka International Youth Hostel (907-747-8661; 109 Jeff Davis St) Sitka's new – and only – hostel is downtown less than a block from Crescent Harbor and is expected to be open by 2010.

Ann's Gavan Hill B&B (907-747-8023; www.annsgavanhill.com; 415 Arrowhead St; s/d $75/95;) An easy walk from downtown, this lovely Alaskan home has three guestrooms and a wrap-around deck with two hot tubs. Ahhh!

Sitka Hotel (907-747-3288; www.sitkahotel.net; 118 Lincoln St; s/d Oct 1–Apr 30 $85/90, May 1–Sep 30 $99/105;) This venerable hotel is right downtown and its new back rooms are large, comfortable and feature views of Sitka Sound.

Shee Atika Totem Square Inn (907-747-3693; www.totemsquareinn.com; 201 Katlian St; r $144-189;) Extensively renovated, this is Sitka's finest hotel, with 68 large, comfortable rooms perched above a harbor that bustles with boats bringing in the day's catch.

Eating & Drinking

Highliner Coffee (907-747-4924; 327 Seward St, Seward Sq Mall; light fare under $5; 5:30am-5pm Mon-Sat, 8am-4pm Sun;) At the Highliner they like their coffee black and their salmon wild. Come here to catch the buzz from a latte and the local issues.

Victoria's (907-747-9301; 118 Lincoln St; breakfast $8-13, lunch mains $9-14, dinner mains $15-24; 4:30am-10pm;) Sitka's early-morning breakfast joint also serves a good selection of seafood in the evening.

Little Tokyo (907-747-5699 315; Lincoln St; lunch $8-10, fish & tempura rolls $6-12; 11am-9pm;) Even crew members from the commercial fleet, who know a thing or two about raw fish, say Sitka's only sushi bar is a good catch.

our pick **Ludvig's Bistro** (907-966-3663; 256 Katlian St; dinner mains $20-33; 2-10pm;) Sitka's boldest restaurant is steadily becoming known as the Southeast's best. The menu is described as 'rustic Mediterranean fare' and almost everything is local, even the sea salt.

Fly-in Fish Inn Bar (907-747-7910; 485 Katlian St) A delightfully little six-stool bar on the back side of a inn. On the covered deck outside you can watch deckhands unload the day's catch.

Getting There & Away

Sitka Airport (SIT; 907-966-2960), on Japonski Island, is served by **Alaska Airlines** (800-426-0333; www.alaskaair.com). **Northstar Rental** (907-966-2552, 800-722-6927; Sitka Airport) has compacts from $55 per day. **Alaska Marine Highway** (907-747-8737, 800-642-0066; www.ferryalaska.com) ferries stop almost daily at the terminal, which is 7 miles north of town. **Ferry Transit Bus** (907-747-8443; one way/round-trip $8/10) will take you into town.

JUNEAU

The first town to be founded after Alaska's purchase from the Russians, Juneau became the territorial capital in 1906 and today is the most scenic capital in the country. Its historic downtown clings between snow-capped mountains and a bustling waterfront. The rest of the city spreads north into the Mendenhall Valley. Juneau is also Alaska's cruise-ship capital and the gateway to many attractions, including Glacier Bay National Park (p1083) and Admiralty Island National Monument (p1083).

Information

Juneau Convention & Visitors Bureau (907-586-2201, 800-587-2201; www.traveljuneau.com; 101 Egan Dr; 9am-5pm) In Centennial Hall.

Juneau Library (907-586-5249; 292 Marine Way; 11am-9pm Mon-Thu, noon-5pm Fri-Sun;) Provides free internet access.

Juneau Ranger Station (907-586-8800; 8510 Mendenhall Loop Rd; 8am-5pm Mon-Fri) This new office is in Mendenhall Valley and has information on cabins, trails and kayaking.

Sights & Activities

The **Alaska State Museum** (☎ 907-465-2901; 395 Whittier St; adult/child $5/free; 8:30am-5:30pm) has artifacts from Alaska's six major indigenous groups, plus a full-size eagles' nest atop a two-story tree.

The **Juneau-Douglas City Museum** (☎ 907-586-3572; 114 W 4th St; adult/child $4/free; 9am-5pm Mon-Fri, 10am-5pm Sat & Sun) highlights the area's gold-mining history. The **Last Chance Mining Museum** (☎ 907-586-5338; 1001 Basin Rd; adult/child $4/free; 9:30am-12:30pm & 3:30-6:30pm) is an impressive complex of railroad lines, ore cars and repair sheds. A short hike will take you to the very interesting **Treadwell Mine ruins**, just south of Douglas.

About 3 miles northwest of downtown, the **Macaulay Salmon Hatchery Visitor Center** (☎ 907-463-4810; 2697 Channel Dr; adult/child $3.25/1.75; 10am-6pm Mon-Fri, 10am-5pm Sat & Sun) has huge seawater aquariums and underwater viewing windows so you can watch thousands of salmon fighting their way upstream to spawn.

The area's numerous glaciers include **Mendenhall Glacier**, the famous 'drive-in' glacier; the informative **USFS Visitor Center** (☎ 907-789-0097; Glacier Spur Rd; adult/child $3/free; 8am-7:30pm) is 13 miles from the city. **Mendenhall Glacier Transport** (☎ 907-789-5460; round-trip $14) runs a bus from downtown to the visitor center.

Hiking is the most popular activity in the area, and some trails access USFS cabins. **Juneau Parks & Recreation** (☎ 907-586-0428; www.juneau.org/parksrec) organizes free hikes. **West Glacier Trail**, which sidles along Mendenhall Glacier, has the most stunning scenery. The **Mt Roberts Trail** is the most popular hike to the alpine country above Juneau.

Or skip the hike – the **Mt Roberts Tram** (☎ 907-463-3412, 888-461-8726; 490 S Franklin St; adult/child $27/13.50; 9am-9pm) takes passengers from the dock to the timberline, where there is a nature center and a restaurant.

The Juneau area is wonderful for kayaking and whale-watching. **Alaska Boat & Kayak** (☎ 907-364-2333; www.juneaukayak.com; 11521 Glacier Hwy; single/double kayak $50/70; 9am-6pm) rents boats and offers a self-guided Mendenhall Lake paddle. **Orca Enterprises** (☎ 907-789-6801, 888-733-6722; www.alaskawhalewatching.com; adult/child $120/88) uses a 42ft jet boat for whale-watching tours.

our pick **Adventure Bound Alaska** (☎ 907-463-2509, 800-228-3875; www.adventureboundalaska.com; adult/child $150/95) offers a wonderful day-trip to steep-sided Tracy Arm fjord, 50 miles southeast of Juneau, to see seals, glaciers and icebergs.

Sleeping

Downtown accommodations are heavily booked during summer, but Juneau has more than 50 B&Bs; stop at the visitor center to find one.

Juneau International Hostel (☎ 907-586-9559; www.juneauhostel.org; 614 Harris St; dm adult/child $10/5) Alaska's best hostel is a five-minute walk from the state capitol.

Driftwood Lodge (☎ 907-586-2280, 800-544-2239; www.driftwoodalaska.com; 435 Willoughby Ave; r $94-110) The rooms are no-frills but clean, and many have kitchenettes. There's a courtesy airport and ferry van, a coin laundry and bike rental.

Juneau Hotel (☎ 907-586-5666; www.juneauhotels.net; 1200 W 9th St; ste $169) New, freshly painted and located within easy walking distance of the downtown attractions, this all-suites hotel is Juneau's best deal in accommodations.

Silverbow Inn (☎ 907-586-4146, 800-586-4146; www.silverbowinn.com; 120 2nd St; r $169-209) A wonderful boutique inn on top of a downtown bagel shop. Along with 11 rooms, there's an outdoor hot tub with a view of the mountains.

WORTH THE TRIP: SMALL PORTS IN SOUTHEAST ALASKA

The **LeConte ferry** (☎ 800-642-0066; www.ferryalaska.com) services a handful of small ports between Sitka and Juneau, offering the chance to experience a Southeast Alaska not overrun by cruise-ship passengers. Stay for a day or two and then hop on a **Wings of Alaska** (☎ 907-789-0790; www.wingsofalaska.com) plane.

On Chichagof Island, **Hoonah** boasts the world's longest zip line at 5330ft and great whale-watching while roadless **Tenakee Springs** is known for its relaxed pace, alternative lifestyle and public bathhouse, built around a 108°F (42°C) hot spring. Twice monthly, the *LeConte* travels to the lively fishing town of **Pelican**, a unique day trip from Juneau ($100). Built on pilings over tidelands, Pelican's main street is a mile-long wooden boardwalk.

EATING ALASKA: SALMON BAKES

One popular eating event during summer in much of the state, but especially in the Southeast, is the salmon bake. It's an outdoor affair, with grilled locally caught salmon smothered with somebody's homemade barbecue sauce and served all-you-can-eat style. A dinner costs $20 to $27 and it's strictly something tourists do, but is often the dining highlight of many trips to Alaska. Two of the state's best bakes are at **Thane Ore House** (below) in Juneau and the **Alaska Salmon Bake** (☎ 907-452-7274; www.akvisit.com) at Fairbank's Pioneer Park (p1101).

Eating & Drinking

Seong's Sushi Bar & Chinese Takeout (☎ 907-586-4778; 740 W 9th St; sushi $4-6, Chinese lunch $7-9, dinner $11-13; 10am-8:30pm Mon-Thu, to 9pm Fri, 4-9pm Sat; ☒) Across from the Federal Building, the menu at this sushi bar is extensive and loved by locals.

Rainbow Foods (☎ 907-586-6476; 224 4th St; food bar per lb $7.50; 9am-7pm Mon-Sat, 10am-6pm Sun; ☒) A cool natural-foods store with a deli that makes for a happening lunch spot.

Hot Bite (☎ 907-790-2483; 11465 Auke Bay Harbor Dr; hamburgers $8-13; 11am-7pm; ☒) You have to drive out to the Auke Bay Harbor for the best milk shakes and burgers in Juneau. The small café also has seating outside where you can watch the state ferry sail out of Auke Bay.

Island Pub (☎ 907-364-1595; 1102 2nd St; large pizza $13-16; 11:30am-10pm) Across the channel in Douglas is the capital city's best pizzeria, serving firebrick-oven focaccias and gourmet pizza to a mountainous view.

Twisted Fish (☎ 907-463-5033; 550 S Franklin St; dinner mains $15-22; 11am-10pm; ☒) Beef be gone! Located between Taku Smokeries and a wharf where commercial fishermen unload their catch, this restaurant is about local seafood.

Thane Ore House (☎ 907-586-3442; 4400 Thane Rd; dinner adult/child $24/12; 11am-9pm; ☒) Juneau's best salmon bake, 4 miles south of town, is an all-you-can-eat affair of grilled salmon, halibut and ribs…plus sides. There's courtesy-van transportation.

S Franklin St is Juneau's drinking sector. The (in)famous **Red Dog Saloon** (☎ 907-463-3658; 278 S Franklin St) has a sawdust floor and relic-covered walls. Hidden in the **Alaskan Hotel** (☎ 907-586-1000; 167 S Franklin St) is a unique bar with historic ambience and occasional live music.

Getting There & Around

The main airline serving Juneau is **Alaska Air** (☎ 800-426-0333; www.alaskaair.com). Smaller companies such as **Wings of Alaska** (☎ 907-789-0790; www.wingsofalaska.com) provide services to isolated communities.

The terminal for the **Alaska Marine Highway** (☎ 800-642-0066; www.ferryalaska.com) is 14 miles from downtown; M/V *LeConte* runs to Angoon ($37, nine hours) and Tenakee Springs ($35, eight hours), while the high-speed M/V *Fairweather* connects to Petersburg ($66, four hours) and Sitka ($45, 4½ hours).

Juneau's public bus system, **Capital Transit** (☎ 907-789-6901; adult/child $1.50/1), can take you from the airport to the city center, but not the ferry terminal. Numerous car-rental places offer pick up/drop off and unlimited mileage. Compacts at **Rent-A-Wreck** (☎ 907-789-4111, 888-843-4111; 2450 C Industrial Blvd) are $45, while **Evergreen Ford** (☎ 907-789-9386; 8895 Mallard St) rents them for $54.

ADMIRALTY ISLAND NATIONAL MONUMENT

Fifteen miles southeast of Juneau, this island has 1406 sq miles of designated wilderness, featuring brown bears, eagles, whales, harbor seals and sea lions. Stock up on supplies in Juneau and contact the **Juneau Ranger District office** (☎ 907-586-8800; www.fs.fed.us/r10/tongass/districts/admiralty) for information.

The single settlement on Admiralty Island, **Angoon**, is a dry community with only one café. **Favorite Bay Inn** (☎ 907-788-3234; www.favoritebayinn.com; s/d with shared bath $119/139; ☒) will pick you up from the ferry terminal and rent you a canoe to paddle into the heart of Admiralty Island.

The best bear-viewing in Southeast Alaska is at **Pack Creek**, on the eastern side of Admiralty Island. The bears are most abundant in July and August, when the salmon are running, and visitors can watch them feed from an observation tower. The tower is reached by a mile-long trail, usually as part of a guided tour. **Alaska Discovery/Mt Sobek** (☎ 800-586-1911; www.mtsobek.com) offers a three-day tour from Juneau ($1295 per person) that includes kayaking and camping and **Alaska Fly 'N' Fish** (☎ 907-790-2120; www.alaskabyair.com) has a five-hour, fly-in tour ($600).

GLACIER BAY NATIONAL PARK & PRESERVE

Eleven tidewater glaciers spill from the mountains and fill the sea with icebergs around the icy wilderness of **Glacier Bay National Park**

& Preserve. To see the glaciers, most visitors board the *Fairweather Express* operated by **Glacier Bay Lodge & Tours** (☎ 907-264-4600, 888-229-8687; www.visitglacierbay.com; adult/child $190/95) for an eight-hour cruise up the West Arm of Glacier Bay.

The only developed hiking trails are in Bartlett Cove, but there is excellent kayaking; rent equipment from **Glacier Bay Sea Kayaks** (☎ 907-697-2257; www.glacierbayseakayaks.com; single/double kayak per day $45/50). **Spirit Walker Expeditions** (☎ 907-697-2266, 800-529-2537; www.seakayakalaska.com) offers day paddles for $160 to $435.

The **park headquarters** (☎ 907-697-2230; www.nps.gov/glba; 1 Park Rd; 8am-4:30pm Mon-Fri) in Bartlett Cove maintains a free campground and a **visitor center** (☎ 907-697-2627; 6am-10:30pm) at the dock, which provides backcountry permits and maps. The park is served by the settlement of **Gustavus** (www.gustavusak.com), which has lodging, restaurants and supplies.

Glacier Bay Lodge (☎ 888-229-8687; www.visitglacierbay.com; 199 Bartlett Cove Rd; r $171-196; ☒) is the only hotel and restaurant at Bartlett Cove.

In Gustavus, **Good River B&B** (☎ 907-697-2241; www.glacier-bay.us; Good River Rd; s/d/cabin $120/140/130; ☒) is a three-story log home with three guestrooms and a Honeymoon Cabin (no running water) tucked in the woods. The much larger **Annie Mae Lodge** (☎ 907-697-2346; 800-478-2346; www.anniemae.com; Grandpa's Farm Rd; s $120-150, d $170-200; ☒) has 11 rooms, most with private entrances and bathrooms.

On the way to the dock, **Beartrack Mercantile** (☎ 907-697-2358; Dock Rd; 9am-7pm Mon-Sat, 10:30am-6pm Sun) has limited groceries and surprisingly good deli sandwiches.

Unfortunately, the Alaska state ferry doesn't stop at Gustavus. **Alaska Airlines** (☎ 800-426-0333; www.alaskaair.com) has daily flights between Gustavus and Juneau. The Glacier Bay Lodge bus meets flights for $12.

HAINES

Haines is Southeast Alaska's most scenic departure point and a crucial link to the Alcan Hwy for thousands of RVers every summer on their way to Interior Alaska. The Northwest Trading Company arrived here in 1878, followed by gold prospectors and the US Army, which built its first permanent post in Alaska, Fort Seward, in 1903. The perceived threat of a Japanese invasion in WWII resulted in the construction of the Haines and Alcan Hwys, connecting Haines to the rest of the USA. If mammoth cruise ships depress you, Haines is a much better destination choice than Skagway.

Collect information from the **Haines Convention & Visitors Bureau** (☎ 907-766-2234, 800-458-3579; www.haines.ak.us; 122 2nd Ave; 9am-5pm).

Sights & Activities

Haines has the most affordable museums in Alaska. The **Sheldon Museum** (☎ 907-766-2366; 11 Main St; adult/child $3/free; 10am-5pm Mon-Fri, 1-4pm Sat & Sun) features indigenous artifacts upstairs, and gold-rush relics downstairs. The **American Bald Eagle Foundation** (☎ 907-766-3094; 113 Haines Hwy; adult/child $3/1; 10am-5pm Mon-Fri, 1-5pm Sat & Sun;) displays more than 100 species of animals, including almost two dozen eagles, in their natural habitat. For something quirky, hit the **Hammer Museum** (☎ 907-776-2374; 108 Main St; adult/child $3/free; 10am-5pm Mon-Fri), a 1200-hammer monument to owner Dave Pahl's obsession with the tool.

Haines offers two major hiking-trail systems – Mt Riley and Mt Ripinsky – as well as afternoon walking tours of **Fort Seward** (the visitor center has details). **Chilkat Guides** (☎ 907-766-2491, 888-292-7789; www.raftalaska.com; adult/child $89/62) runs a four-hour Chilkat River raft float and **Sockeye Cycle** (☎ 907-766-2869, 877-292-4154; www.cyclealaska.com; rental 4-/8hr $25/35) will rent you a mountain bike and suggest rides.

Sleeping

Bear Creek Cabins & Hostel (☎ 907-766-2259; www.bearcreekcabinsalaska.com; Small Tract Rd; dm/cabins $20/48; ☒) To escape the metropolis of Haines, head a mile out of town to this pleasant hostel on the edge of the woods.

Fort Seward Lodge (☎ 907-766-2009, 877-617-3418; 39 Mud Bay Rd; s/d $95/110, r without bath $75; ☒) The former Post Exchange of Fort Seward offers Haines' best value in accommodations, with updated rooms and a friendly bar.

Lynn View Lodge (☎ 907-766-3713; www.lynnviewlodge.com; Mile 6.5 Lutak Rd; r $95-135, cabins $95; ☒) This B&B near the ferry terminal offers rooms, suites, cabins and a great view of Lynn Canal.

Captain's Choice Motel (☎ 907-766-3111, 800-478-2345; www.capchoice.com; 108 2nd Ave; s/d $113/123; ☒) The nicest motel in town, with a huge sun deck that overlooks the bay.

Eating & Drinking

Mountain Market & Spirits (☎ 907-766-3340; 151 3rd Ave S; sandwiches $6-8; 7am-7pm Mon-Fri, 8am-7pm Sat,

8am-6pm Sun; ⊠) Great coffee, innovative wraps, cool atmosphere.

Chilkat Restaurant & Bakery (☎ 907-766-3653; Dalton St at 5th Ave; breakfast dishes $6-8, lunch mains $7-8; 🕑 7am-3pm Mon-Sat; ⊠) Locals have been gathering here for a slice of rhubarb-strawberry pie for 25 years.

Fireweed Restaurant (☎ 907-766-3838; 37 Blacksmith St; pasta $11-15, pizza $11-21; 🕑 4:30-9pm Tue, 11:30am-3pm & 4:30-9pm Wed-Sat; ⊠) This bright and laid-back bistro looks like it belongs in California rather than Haines. Vegetarians actually have a choice here (try the veggie baked ziti).

Mosey's Cantina (☎ 907-766-2320; 31 Tower Rd; lunch $8-15, dinner $14-18; 🕑 11:30am-2:30pm & 5:30-8:30pm Mon-Sat; ⊠) A cute and cozy Mexican restaurant serving halibut-stuffed burritos and the local beer.

It's well worth the walk to the **Haines Brewing Company** (☎ 907-766-3823; Dalton City; 🕑 1-7pm Mon-Sat), the town's delightful one-room brewery.

Getting There & Away

Several air-charter companies service Haines, the cheapest being **Wings of Alaska** (☎ 907-789-0790; www.wingsofalaska.com).

Haines-Skagway Fast Ferry (☎ 907-766-2100, 888-766-2103; www.hainesskagwayfastferry.com; one way adult/child $35/18) will get you to and from Skagway.

Eagle Nest Car Rentals (☎ 907-766-2891, 800-354-6009; 1183 Haines Hwy), in the Eagle Nest Motel, has cars available for $50 per day with 100 miles included.

AROUND HAINES

The 75-sq-mile **Alaska Chilkat Bald Eagle Preserve**, along the Chilkat River, protects the world's largest-known gathering of bald eagles. The greatest numbers of birds are spotted in December and January, but you can see eagles here any time during summer. Lookouts on the Haines Hwy between Miles 18 and 22 allow motorists to glimpse the birds. **Alaska Nature Tours** (☎ 907-766-2876; www.alaskanaturetours.net; adult/child $65/50; 👶) offers a three-hour tour of the preserve.

SKAGWAY

The northern terminus of the Alaska Marine Highway, Skagway was a gold-rush town infamous for its lawlessness. In 1887 the population was two; 10 years later it was Alaska's largest city, with 20,000 residents. Today, Skagway survives entirely on tourism and gets packed when a handful of cruise ships pull in and thousands of passengers converge on the town as if the Klondike gold rush was still on.

Information

Klondike Gold Rush National Historical Park Visitors Center (☎ 907-983-9223; www.nps.gov/klgo; 154 Broadway St; 🕑 8am-6pm) For everything outdoors; local trails, public campgrounds and National Park Service (NPS) programs.

Skagway Convention & Visitors Bureau (☎ 907-983-2854; www.skagway.com; cnr Broadway St & 2nd Ave; 🕑 8am-6pm Mon-Fri, 9am-6pm Sat & Sun) In the can't-miss Arctic Brotherhood Hall (think driftwood).

Sights & Activities

The **Klondike Gold Rush National Historical Park** is a seven-block corridor along Broadway St that features 15 restored buildings, false fronts and wooden sidewalks from Skagway's golden era as a boom town. Thanks to the cruise ships, it's the most popular national park in Alaska. To best appreciate this amazing moment in Skagway's history, join a free, ranger-led walking tour, offered five times a day from the NPS Center.

The **Skagway Museum** (☎ 907-983-2420; Skagway City Hall, cnr 7th Ave & Spring St; adult/child $2/1; 🕑 9am-5pm Mon-Fri, 10am-5pm Sat, 10am-4pm Sun) is one of the best in Southeast, and its gold-rush relics are some of the most interesting exhibits in a town filled with museums. **Moore's Cabin** (cnr 5th Ave & Spring St; admission free; 🕑 10am-5pm) is the town's oldest building, while **Mascot Saloon** (290 Broadway St; admission free; 🕑 8am-6pm) is a museum devoted to Skagway's heyday as the 'roughest place in the world.'

White Pass & Yukon Route Railroad (☎ 907-983-2217, 800-343-7373; www.wpyr.com; 231 2nd Ave; adult/child $103/52) offers the best tour: the three-hour Summit Excursion climbs the high White Pass in a historic narrow-gauge train.

Sleeping

Skagway Home Hostel (☎ 907-983-2131; www.skagwayhostel.com; 456 3rd Ave; dm $15-20; ⊠ 💻) A half-mile from the ferry terminal, this is a relaxed hostel with a kitchen, laundry facilities and daily chores.

Cindy's Place (☎ 907-983-2674, 800-831-8095; www.alaska.net/~croland; Mile 1 Dyea Rd; cabins s $50-140, d $65-150) Two miles from town are Cindy's cabins: two large log units with private baths and a smaller, cozy one without a shower. In

ALASKA

the morning freshly baked goods magically appear on your doorstep.

Sgt Preston's Lodge (☎ 907-983-2521, 866-983-2521; www.sgt-prestonslodgeskagway.com; 370 6th Ave; s $80-115, d $90-130; ☒ 🖳) Recently updated, this motel is the best bargain in Skagway and just far enough from Broadway St to escape most of the cruise-ship crush.

Mile Zero B&B (☎ 907-983-3045; www.mile-zero.com; 901 Main St; r $135; ☒ 🖳) This B&B is like a motel with the comforts of home as the six large rooms have their own bath and a private entrance on the wraparound porch.

Eating & Drinking

North Eden (☎ 907-983-2784; 21st Ave at State St; breakfast dishes $4-6, lunch mains $5-6; 🕑 6:30am-2pm; ☒) Skagway's most affordable espresso bar, with cheap breakfasts and lunch bowls heaped with spicy red beans, lentils or rice for $5 or less.

Starfire (☎ 907-983-3663; 4th Ave at Spring St; lunch mains $12-15, dinner mains $14-19; 🕑 11am-10pm Mon-Fri, 4-10pm Sat & Sun; ☒) Order pad Thai or spicy drunken noodle here and then enjoy it with a beer on the outdoor patio.

Stowaway Café (☎ 907-983-3463; 205 Congress Way; dinner mains $18-27; 🕑 4-10pm; ☒) Near the Harbor Master's office, this funky and fantastic café serves excellent fish and Cajun-style steak dinners. Try the wasabi salmon.

Skagway Fish Company (☎ 907-983-3474; Congress Way; lunch mains $10-14, dinner mains $17-35; 🕑 11am-10pm) Despite a menu loaded with seafood, what locals rave about at this restaurant located next to Stowaway Café are its ribs – great barbecue even if you weren't in Alaska.

Red Onion Saloon (☎ 907-983-2222; 205 Broadway St) This former brothel is now Skagway's liveliest bar. Naturally.

Getting There & Away

Regularly scheduled flights from Skagway to Juneau, Haines and Glacier Bay are available from **Wings of Alaska** (☎ 907-983-2442; www.wingsofalaska.com).

Alaska Marine Highway (☎ 800-642-0066; www.ferryalaska.com) has ferries departing every day in summer, and **Haines-Skagway Fast Ferry** (☎ 907-766-2100, 888-766-2103; www.hainesskagwayfastferry.com; one way adult/child $35/18) runs daily to Haines.

Sourdough Car Rentals (☎ 907-983-2523; 6th Ave at Broadway St; 🕑 8am-5pm) has compacts for $69 a day with unlimited miles.

Yukon-Alaska Tourist Tours (☎ 866-626-7383, in Whitehorse 867-668-5944; www.yukonalaskatouristtours.com) offers a minibus service three times a week to Whitehouse (one way $60).

White Pass & Yukon Route Railroad (☎ 800-343-7373; www.whitepassrailroad.com; 231 2nd Ave) goes to Fraser, British Columbia, where there's a bus connection to Whitehorse (adult/ child $116/58).

SOUTHCENTRAL ALASKA

Southcentral Alaska is where Alaskans and travelers alike come to play, with its mountains, glaciers, good fishing, great hiking and kayaking and lots of campgrounds to stay at. Even better, there are roads between towns and other regions of the state, making Southcentral Alaska one of the most accessible places to visit.

ANCHORAGE

Anchorage offers the comforts of a large US city but is only a 30-minute drive from the Alaskan wilderness. Founded in 1914 as a work camp for the Alaska Railroad, the city was devastated by the 1964 Good Friday earthquake but quickly rebounded as the industry headquarters for the Prudhoe Bay oil boom. Today almost half the state's residents live in or around the city, as Anchorage (population 283,938) serves as the economic and political heart of Alaska. Sorry, Juneau.

Orientation

A surveyor was obviously in charge of laying out Anchorage. Its downtown is pedestrian-friendly, with numbered avenues running east–west and lettered streets north–south. East of A St, street names continue alphabetically, beginning with Barrow.

Midtown Anchorage is generally considered to span the area between Fireweed Ave south to 36th Ave and Minnesota Avenue east to Old Seward Hwy. Anything south of 36th Ave is clumped together as South Anchorage.

MAPS

The best free city map is the *Alaska Activities Map*, distributed all over town. For more detail there's Rand McNally's *Anchorage* ($4). The best selection of maps is at Title Wave Books (opposite) or the Alaska Public Lands Information Center (opposite)

DON'T MISS

The **Chilkoot** is the most famous trail in Alaska and often the most popular. It was the route used by the Klondike gold miners in the 1898 gold rush, and walking it is not so much a wilderness adventure as a history lesson. The 34-mile trek takes three to four days and includes the Chilkoot Pass – a steep climb up to 3525ft that has most hikers scrambling on all fours. The highlight of the hike for many is riding the historic White Pass & Yukon Route Railroad (WP&YR; p1085) from Lake Bennett back to Skagway. There are cheaper ways to return, but don't pass up the train. Experiencing the Chilkoot and returning on the WP&YR is probably the ultimate Alaska trek, combining great scenery, a historical site and an incredible sense of adventure.

Interested? Stop at the **Trail Center** (☎ 907-983-9234; Broadway St at 2nd Ave, Skagway; 🕑 8am-5pm) to obtain backpacking permits and set up the hike. Then cross the street to WP&YR depot to book a seat on the train.

Information

BOOKSTORES

Title Wave Books (☎ 888-598-9283; 📶) Northern Lights Center (1360 W Northern Lights Blvd); W 5th Ave (415 W 5th Ave) The best bookstore in Anchorage with two branches, both equipped with internet cafés.

INTERNET ACCESS

Cyber City (☎ 907-277-7601; 1441 W Northern Lights Blvd; per hr $4; 🕑 11am-midnight Mon-Sat, from noon Sun) Midtown location for late-night gamers.

ZJ Loussac Public Library (☎ 907-343-2975; 3600 Denali St; 🕑 10am-9pm Mon-Thu, to 6pm Fri-Sat, 1-5pm Sun) Free internet access.

MEDIA

Tourist freebies are available everywhere, including the *Official Anchorage Visitors Guide.*

Anchorage Daily News (www.adn.com) This top-rate paper has the largest daily circulation in the state.

Anchorage Press (www.anchoragepress.com) A fabulous free weekly with events listings and social commentary.

MEDICAL SERVICES

Alaska Regional Hospital (☎ 907-276-1131; 2801 DeBarr Rd; 🕑 24hr) For emergency care.

First Care Medical Center (☎ 907-248-1122; 3710 Woodland Dr, Suite 1100; 🕑 7am-midnight) Walk-in clinic in midtown.

Providence Alaska Medical Center (☎ 907-562-2211; 3200 Providence Dr)

MONEY

Key Bank (☎ 257-5500, 800-539-2968; 601 W 5th Ave) Downtown.

Wells Fargo (☎ 800-869-3557; 301 W Northern Lights Blvd) The main bank is in midtown.

POST

Post office (344 W 3rd Ave) Downtown in the Village at Ship Creek Center.

TOURIST INFORMATION

Alaska Public Lands Information Center (☎ 907-271-2737; www.alaskacenters.gov; 605 W 4th Ave, Suite 105; 🕑 9am-5pm) Has park, trail and cabin information as well as excellent displays.

Log Cabin Visitor Center (☎ recorded event information 907-274-3531, 907-276-3200; www.anchorage.net; 524 W 4th Ave; 🕑 7:30am-7pm Jun-Aug, 8am-6pm May & Sep) Has pamphlets, maps, bus schedules and city guides in several languages.

Sights & Activities

Experiencing Alaska Native culture firsthand in the Bush is expensive. Instead, come to the **Alaska Native Heritage Center** (☎ 800-315-6608; www.alaskanative.net; 8800 Heritage Center Dr; adult/child $25/17; 🕑 9am-5pm) and see how humans survived – even thrived – before central heating. Spread over 26 acres are studios with artists carving baleen or sewing skin-boats, a small lake and five replica villages.

our pick **Anchorage Museum of History & Art** (☎ 907-343-4326; 121 W 7th Ave; adult/child $8/2; 🕑 9am-6pm; 👶) is Alaska's crowning cultural experience. A $75 million renovation that doubled its size was completed in 2009. If you don't have an entire afternoon for this jewel then visit the much smaller **Heritage Library Museum** (☎ 907-265-2834; 301 W Northern Lights Blvd; admission free; 🕑 noon-5pm Mon-Fri) for its displays of Alaska Native costumes, weapons and artwork.

For something wild head to the **Ship Creek Viewing Platform** (Whitney Rd at Ship Creek Bridge) when from mid- to late summer king, coho and pink salmon spawn up Ship Creek and the banks are lined with locals and visitors alike trying to catch dinner. On the other side of the creek, beginning at the west end of 2nd Ave, is the 11-mile **Tony Knowles Coastal Trail**, the most scenic of the city's 122

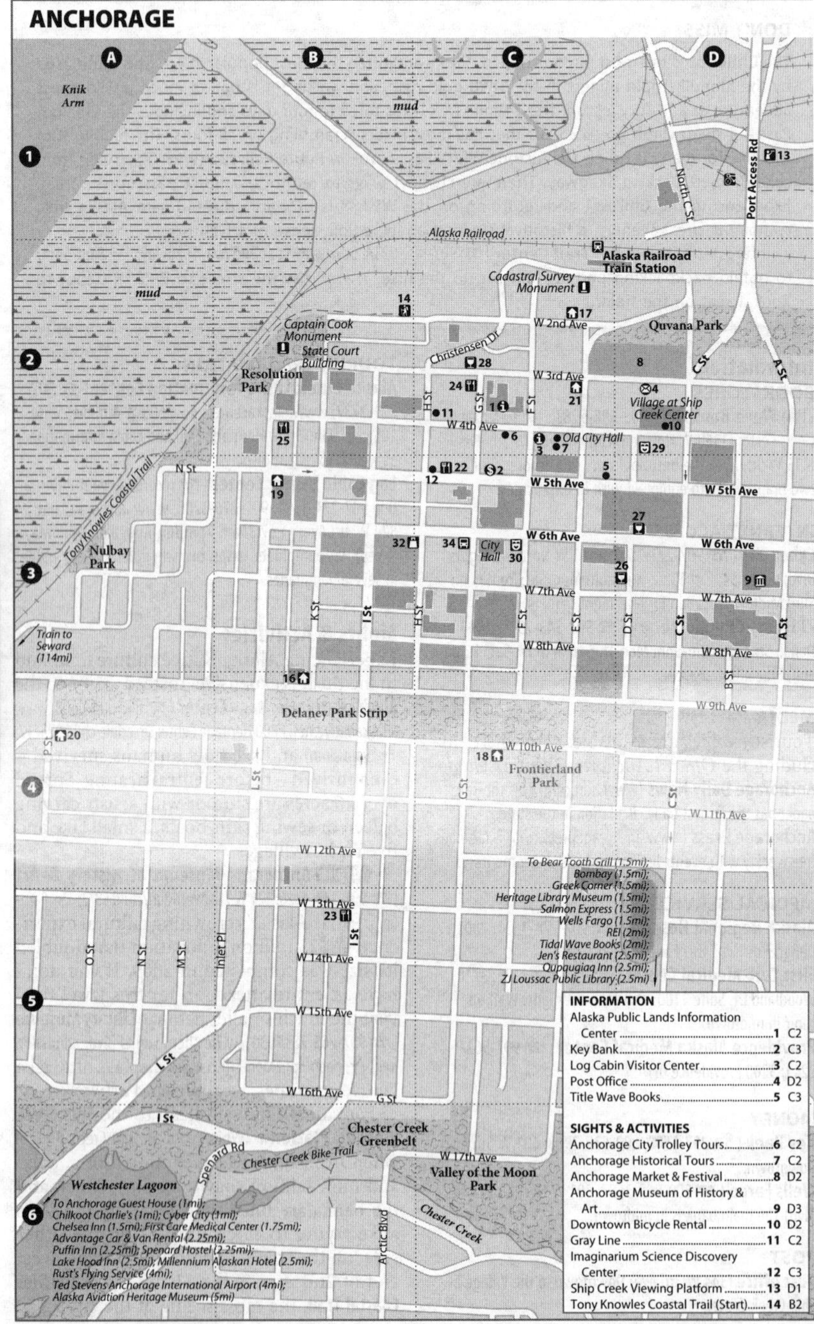
ANCHORAGE
A
B
C
D
1
2
3
4
5
6
Knik Arm
mud
mud
Alaska Railroad
Alaska Railroad Train Station
Cadastral Survey Monument
Port Access Rd
North C St
13
14
17
W 2nd Ave
Quvana Park
Captain Cook Monument
State Court Building
Christensen Dr
28
Resolution Park
W 3rd Ave
8
C St
A St
24
1
21
4
Village at Ship Creek Center
10
H St
G St
F St
11
W 4th Ave
6
3
7
Old City Hall
29
25
Tony Knowles Coastal Trail
N St
22
12
2
5
W 5th Ave
W 5th Ave
19
27
W 6th Ave
W 6th Ave
32
34
City Hall
30
Nulbay Park
26
9
W 7th Ave
W 7th Ave
K St
I St
H St
F St
E St
D St
C St
A St
Train to Seward (114mi)
W 8th Ave
W 8th Ave
16
B St
Delaney Park Strip
W 9th Ave
20
P St
W 10th Ave
18
Frontierland Park
L St
G St
C St
W 11th Ave
W 12th Ave
To Bear Tooth Grill (1.5mi);
Bombay (1.5mi);
Greek Corner (1.5mi);
Heritage Library Museum (1.5mi);
Salmon Express (1.5mi);
Wells Fargo (1.5mi);
REI (2mi);
Tidal Wave Books (2mi);
Jen's Restaurant (2.5mi);
Qupqugiaq Inn (2.5mi);
ZJ Loussac Public Library (2.5mi)
W 13th Ave
23
I St
O St
N St
M St
Inlet Pl
W 14th Ave
W 15th Ave
L St
W 16th Ave
G St
I St
Chester Creek Greenbelt
Spenard Rd
Chester Creek Bike Trail
W 17th Ave
Valley of the Moon Park
Westchester Lagoon
To Anchorage Guest House (1mi);
Chilkoot Charlie's (1mi); Cyber City (1mi);
Chelsea Inn (1.5mi); First Care Medical Center (1.75mi);
Advantage Car & Van Rental (2.25mi);
Puffin Inn (2.25mi); Spenard Hostel (2.25mi);
Lake Hood Inn (2.5mi); Millennium Alaskan Hotel (2.5mi);
Rust's Flying Service (4mi);
Ted Stevens Anchorage International Airport (4mi);
Alaska Aviation Heritage Museum (5mi)
Arctic Blvd
Chester Creek
INFORMATION
Alaska Public Lands Information Center 1 C2
Key Bank 2 C3
Log Cabin Visitor Center 3 C2
Post Office 4 D2
Title Wave Books 5 C3
SIGHTS & ACTIVITIES
Anchorage City Trolley Tours 6 C2
Anchorage Historical Tours 7 C2
Anchorage Market & Festival 8 D2
Anchorage Museum of History & Art 9 D3
Downtown Bicycle Rental 10 D2
Gray Line 11 C2
Imaginarium Science Discovery Center 12 C3
Ship Creek Viewing Platform 13 D1
Tony Knowles Coastal Trail (Start) 14 B2

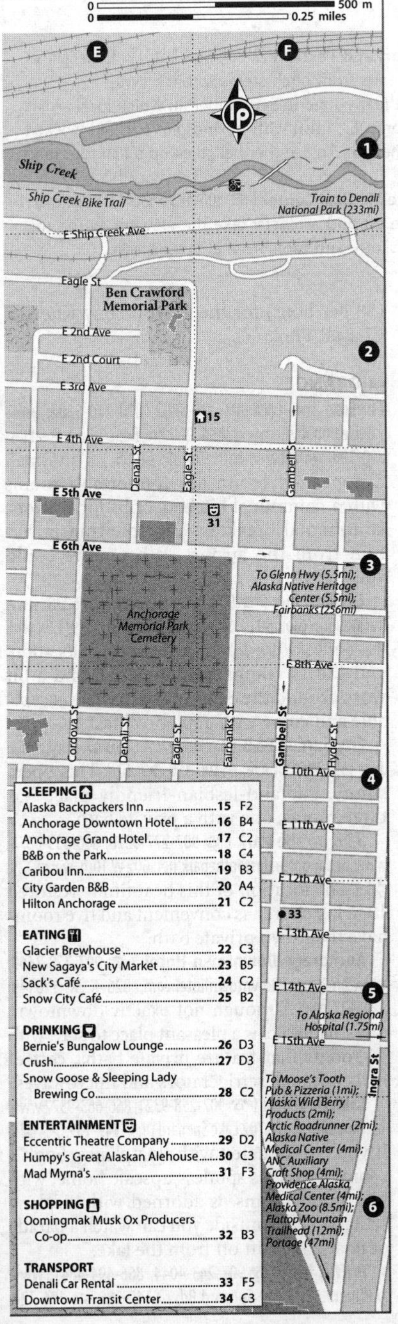

miles of paved path. Rent bikes at **Downtown Bicycle Rental** (☎ 907-279-5293; 333 W 4th Ave; 3/24hr rental $16/32).

Ideally located on the south shore of Lake Hood, the world's busiest floatplane lake, is the **Alaska Aviation Heritage Museum** (☎ 907-248-5325; 4721 Aircraft Dr; adult/child $10/6; 9am-5pm), a tribute to Alaska's colorful bush pilots and their faithful planes. Housed inside are 25 planes along with historic photos and displays of pilots' achievements, from the first flight to Fairbanks (1913) to the early history of Alaska Airlines.

Flattop Mountain is Alaska's most-climbed peak; a three- to five-hour, 3.4-mile round-trip starts from a trailhead on the outskirts of Anchorage. Maps are available at the Alaska Public Lands Information Center (p1087) and the **Flattop Mountain Shuttle** (☎ 907-279-3334; round-trip adult/child $22/15) will run you to the trailhead.

Anchorage Historical Tours (☎ 907-274-3600; Old City Hall, 524 W 4th Ave; adult/child $5/1; 1pm Mon-Fri) takes visitors on hour-long downtown walking tours. **Anchorage City Trolley Tours** (☎ 907-775-5603; 612 W 4th Ave; per person $15; tours on the hour 9am-5pm) One-hour rides in a bright red trolley past Lake Hood, Earthquake Park and Cook Inlet, among other sights.

'Flightseeing' – touring in a small plane – is popular in Anchorage. Tours are short and expensive, but if time is limited they offer a glimpse into Alaska's grandeur not otherwise possible. More than a dozen charter companies peddle flightseeing: **Rust's Flying Service** (☎ 907-243-1595, 800-544-2299; www.flyrusts.com; 4525 Enstrom Circle) has 30-minute tours ($100), a three-hour flight to view Mt McKinley in Denali National Park ($365) and a full day of guided fly-in fishing ($485).

Anchorage for Children

Anchorage is exceptionally kid-friendly – more than 40 city parks boast playscapes. Close to downtown, **Frontierland Park** (corner of 10th Ave & E St) is a local favorite. **Valley of the Moon Park** (cnr Arctic Blvd & W 17th Ave) makes a delightful picnic spot. If the Flattop Mountain hike (above) is overly ambitious for your kids, head to **Alaska Wild Berry Products** (☎ 907-562-8858; 5525 Juneau St; admission free; 10am-11pm). Inside the sprawling gift shop is a chocolate waterfall and the Wild Berry Theater; outside there's a short nature trail that leads to a handful of caribou that kids can feed and pet.

DON'T MISS

On the weekend head over to the **Anchorage Market & Festival** (W 3rd Ave & E St; 10am-6pm Sat & Sun) for live music, cheap food and great souvenirs from birch steins to birch syrup.

The **Wild Salmon On Parade**, an annual event (early June to September) in which local artists turn fiberglass fish downtown into a 'Marilyn MonROE,' a fish with boxing gloves titled 'Socked Eye Salmon,' and 'Fish & Chips', a poker-playing halibut. To see them all, pick up a fish tour map at the Log Cabin Visitor Center (p1087).

Even if you're not sick, stop at the **Alaska Native Medical Center** (800-478-1636; 4315 Diplomacy Dr) to see its fantastic collection of Alaska Native art and artifacts: take the elevator to the top floor and wind down the staircase past dolls, basketry and tools from all over Alaska.

The unique wildlife of the Arctic is on display at the **Alaska Zoo** (907-346-3242; 4731 O'Malley Rd; adult/child $12/6; 9am-6pm Sat-Mon, Wed & Thu, 9am-9pm Tue & Fri), the only zoo in North America that specializes in northern animals, including three species of Alaskan bear and other Alaska native species, from wolverines and moose to caribou and Dall sheep.

To add some science to Alaska's nature, check out the **Imaginarium Science Discovery Center** (907-276-3179; 737 W 5th Ave; adult/child $5.50/5; 10am-6pm Mon-Sat, noon-5pm Sun). This award-winning center features creative, hands-on exhibits that explain the northern lights, earthquakes, oil exploration and other Alaskan topics.

Sleeping

BUDGET

Spenard Hostel (907-248-5036; www.alaskahostel.org; 2845 W 42nd Pl; dm $25) This friendly, independent hostel is near the airport and has 24-hour check-in – great for red-eye arrivals in Alaska. There's free coffee in the morning and bike rentals ($3 per hour) are available.

Alaska Backpackers Inn (907-277-2770; www.alaskabackpackers.com; 327 Eagle St; dm/s/d $25/50/60) Anchorage's newest hostel is roomy, comfortable and professional. A bit east of central downtown, it's still within walking distance to restaurants and bars.

our pick **Qupqugiaq Inn** (907-563-5633; www.qupq.com; 640 W 36th Ave; dm $24, s/d $87/104, with shared bath $69/90) This colorful establishment has a continental breakfast that includes French-pressed coffee and roll-your-own oats. The large dorms sleep eight, and the private rooms are bright and clean.

Anchorage Guest House (907-274-0408; www.akhouse.com; 2001 Hillcrest Dr; dm/r $39/92) This beautiful place feels more like a B&B than a hostel, and the prices reflect that. Rent a bike ($8 per hour) for the nearby Tony Knowles Coastal Trail.

MIDRANGE

Chelsea Inn (907-276-5002, 800-770-5002; www.chelseainnalaska.com; 3836 Spenard Rd; s/d incl breakfast $90/100, with shared bath $79/89) This small European-style inn has comfortable rooms with a communal kitchen, cribs for the tots, continental breakfast and free transportation from the airport. What more could you want?

Caribou Inn (907-272-0444, 800-272-5878; www.cariboubnb.com; 501 L St; s/d incl breakfast $119/129, with shared bath $99/109) Ideal downtown location, and the 14 rooms, though small and a bit worn around the edges, are definitely acceptable and come with a full breakfast.

City Garden B&B (907-276-8686; www.citygarden.biz; 1352 W 10th Ave; r $100-150) This open, sunny, gay-and-lesbian-friendly place has three rooms, one with a private bath.

B&B on the Park (907-277-0878, 800-353-0878; www.bedandbreakfastonthepark.net; 602 W 10th Ave; r $125) The location of this beautifully restored 1946 log church is convenient and five rooms have their own private bath.

Anchorage Downtown Hotel (907-258-7669; www.anchoragedowntownhotel.com; 826 K St; r $149) Although not exactly downtown, this small hotel is a pleasant place to stay, with 16 rooms that feature private baths, coffeemakers, small refrigerators and microwaves.

Lake Hood Inn (907-258-9321; 866-663-9322 www.lakehoodinn.com; 4702 Lake Spenard Dr; r $149-169) If you're infatuated with floatplanes, book a room here. This spotless upscale home, with four guest rooms, is adorned with airplane artifacts while outside you can watch a parade of floatplanes lift off from the lake.

Puffin Inn (907-243-4044, 866-494-4841; www.puffininn.net; 4400 Spenard Rd; r $149-185, ste 194-221;

) The Puffin Inn has three tiers of fine rooms, from 26 sardine-can economy rooms to full suites. Accessible via a free 24-hour airport shuttle.

TOP END

Anchorage Grand Hotel (907-929-8888, 888-800-0640; www.anchoragegrand.com; 505 W 2nd Ave; r $205;) This small but luxurious hotel features 30 spacious suites that include full kitchens and separate living and bedroom areas. Many rooms overlook Ship Creek and Cook Inlet, and the hotel's downtown location is convenient to everything.

Millennium Alaskan Hotel (907-243-2300, 800-544-0553; www.milleniumhotels.com; 4800 Spenard Rd; r $219-349;) A large, 248-room resort with a woodsy lodge feel overlooking Lake Spenard four miles from downtown. Kids love the mounted animals and fish.

Hilton Anchorage (907-272-7411, 800-245-2527; www.hiltonanchorage.com; 500 W 3rd Ave; r $290;) The Hilton has the best location of any of the luxury hotels, right in the heart of downtown. If you're going to pay this much, ask for a room with a view of Cook Inlet.

Eating

In Anchorage you'll enjoy great menus, from Polynesian and Mexican to good old burgers, and clean air. All restaurants and bars went smoke-free in 2007.

BUDGET

New Sagaya's City Market (907-274-6173; W 13th Ave; 6am-10pm Mon-Sat, 8am-9pm Sun) Eclectic and upscale, this grocery store has a great deli specializing in Asian fare and has seating indoors and outdoors.

Arctic Roadrunner (907-561-1245; 5300 Old Seward Hwy; burgers $5-6; 10:30am-9pm Mon-Sat) Since 1964 this place has been turning out beefy burgers that can be enjoyed outdoors while watching salmon spawn up Campbell Creek.

Salmon Express (606 W Northern Lights Blvd; fast food $5-9; 10:30am-6pm Mon-Fri) It serves salmon chowder, salmon kabobs and the recommended salmon quesadillas from the most ramshackle little drive-through stand imaginable.

our pick **Snow City Café** (907-272-2489; 1034 W 4th Ave; breakfast dishes $7-13; lunch mains $9-11; 7am-4pm Sat) This busy café serves healthy grub to a mix of clientele that ranges from the tattooed to the up-and-coming. For breakfast skip the usual eggs and toast and try a bowl of Snow City granola with dried fruit, honey and nuts instead.

Bear Tooth Grill (907-276-4200; 1230 W 27th St; burgers $8-12, dinner mains $10-20; 11am-11:30pm) A popular hangout with an adjacent movie theatre, the Bear Tooth Grill serves excellent burgers and seafood as well as Mexican and Asian fusion dishes.

MIDRANGE

Greek Corner (907-276-2820; 302 W Fireweed Ln; lunch mains $7-12, dinner mains $12-20; 11am-10pm Mon-Fri, noon-10pm Sat, 4pm-10pm Sun) Best moussaka and stuffed grape leaves in Alaska.

Sack's Café (907-274-4022; 328 G St; lunch mains $9-13, dinner mains $18-34; 11am-2:30pm & 5-9pm Mon-Thu, 11am-2:30pm & 5-10:30pm Fri & Sat, 10am-2:30pm & 5-9pm Sun) A bright, colorful restaurant serving Asian-Mediterranean fusion fare that is consistently creative (reservations recommended).

Bombay (907-277-1200; 555 W Northern Lights Blvd; mains $15-20; 11am-2pm & 5-9pm) Skip the mediocre lunch buffet and order straight off the menu. Don't forget to try the samosas.

Moose's Tooth Pub & Pizzeria (907-258-2537; 3300 Old Seward Hwy; medium pizza $16-22; 10:30am-11:30pm Mon-Thu, to 12:30am Fri & Sat, 11am-11:30pm Sun) An Anchorage institution serving 18 custom-brewed beers including monthly specials, and 50 gourmet pizzas.

TOP END

Glacier Brewhouse (907-274-2739; 737 W 5th Ave; lunch mains $11-17, dinner mains $18-37; 11am-10pm Sun-Thu, 11am-11pm Fri & Sat) Grab a table overlooking the three giant copper brewing tanks and enjoy Alaskan seafood and rotisserie-grilled ribs and chops with a pint of oatmeal stout.

Jen's Restaurant (907-561-5367; 701 W 36th Ave; lunch mains $10-22; dinner mains $18-36; 11am-2pm Mon-Fri, 6-10pm Tue-Sat) Innovative, Scandinavian-accented cuisine emphasizing fresh ingredients and elaborate presentation. There's also a wine bar with music and a menu of tapas.

Drinking

Crush (907-865-9198; 343 W 6th Ave) This swanky wine bar serves 'bistro bites' – a menu of appetizers and salads. It a great place for a nibble and a glass wine.

Snow Goose & Sleeping Lady Brewing Co (907-277-7727; 717 W 3rd Ave) If the sun is setting over Cook Inlet and the Alaska Range, head to the rooftop deck of this brewpub. Only the beer is better than the view.

Bernie's Bungalow Lounge (☎ 907-276-8808; 626 D St) Pretty people, pretty drinks: this is the place to see and be seen. On Thursdays bands play on the tiki torch-lit patio, on the weekends it's DJs.

Entertainment

Check the *Anchorage Press* and Friday's *Anchorage Daily News* for the latest entertainment listings.

Mad Myrna's (☎ 907-276-9762; 530 E 5th Ave; cover Sat & Sun $5-10) A fun, cruisy bar with line-dancing on Thursday, drag shows on Friday and dance music most other nights after 9pm.

our pick **Chilkoot Charlie's** (☎ 907-272-1010; 2435 Spenard Rd) 'Coots,' as locals call this beloved landmark, is big and brash, with 10 bars, four dance floors and sawdust everywhere. Some amazing bands have played here: Doobie Brothers, Blue Oyster Cult and Green Day, among others.

Humpy's Great Alaskan Alehouse (☎ 907-276-2337; 610 W 6th Ave) Live music nightly from around 9pm, running the gamut from acoustic folk and ska to disco retrospective. All of it can be enjoyed with more than 40 drafts on tap, the most of any bar in Anchorage.

Eccentric Theatre Company (☎ 907-274-2599; 413 D St) This may be the best live theater in town, staging everything from Hamlet to a Mel Brooks' jazz musical based on the poetry of Don Marquis. Only in Anchorage…

ALASKA

Shopping

Oomingmak Musk Ox Producers Co-op (☎ 907-272-9225; www.qiviut.com; 604 H St; 10am-6pm) Handles a variety of very soft, very warm and very expensive garments made of arctic musk-ox wool, hand-knitted in isolated Inupiaq villages.

REI (☎ 907-272-4565; 1200 W Northern Lights Blvd; 10am-8pm Mon-Fri, 10am-7pm Sat, 10am-6pm Sun) The newly expanded REI has the city's finest selection of backpacking, kayaking and camping gear.

ANC Auxiliary Craft Shop (☎ 907-729-1122; 4315 Diplomacy Dr; 10am-2pm Mon-Fri, 11am-2pm 1st & 3rd Sat of month) On the 1st floor of the Alaska Native Medical Center; has some of the finest Alaska Native arts and crafts available to the public.

Getting There & Around

Ted Stevens Anchorage International Airport (ANC; ☎ 907-266-2525; www.dot.state.ak.us/anc/index.shtml) has frequent inter- and intrastate flights. Terminals are off International Airport Rd. **Alaska Airlines** (☎ 800-426-0333; www.alaskaair.com) flies to 19 Alaskan towns, including Fairbanks, Juneau, Nome and Barrow. **Era Aviation** (☎ 800-866-8394; www.flyera.com) flies to Cordova, Valdez, Kodiak and Homer. **Pen Air** (☎ 800-448-4226; www.penair.com) serves southwest Alaska.

Alaska Shuttle (☎ 907-338-8888, 907-694-8888; www.alaskashuttle.net) offers door-to-door transportation between the airport and downtown and South Anchorage (one to three people $30) and Eagle River ($45). The city's bus service (People Mover) picks up from both terminals (bus 7) on a route that heads back downtown.

Advantage Car & Van Rental (☎ 907-243-8806, 888-877-3585; 4211 Spenard Rd) rents compacts for daily/weekly $70/42, as does **Denali Car Rental** (☎ 907-276-1230, 800-757-1230; 1209 Gambell St) for daily/weekly $65/390. Avoid picking up a car at the airport as you will be hit with a 32% rental tax, as opposed to 18% in the city.

Alaska Direct Bus Line (☎ 800-770-6652; www.alaskadirectbusline.com) has regular services to Glennallen ($75, three hours), and Tok ($105, eight hours). **Alaska/Yukon Trails** (☎ 800-770-7275; www.alaskashuttle.com) goes to Denali ($75, five hours) and Fairbanks ($99, nine hours). **Seward Bus Lines** (☎ 907-563-0800; www.sewardbuslines.net) goes to Seward ($50, 2½ hours), while **Homer Stage Lines** (☎ 907-868-3914; www.homerstageline.com) will take you to Homer ($78, five hours).

Alaska Railroad (☎ 907-265-2494, 800-544-0552; www.akrr.com) goes south to Whittier (adult/child $65/33, 2½ hours) and Seward (adult/child $75/38, four hours), and north to Denali (adult/child $146/73, eight hours) and Fairbanks (adult/child $210/105, 12 hours).

People Mover (☎ 907-343-6543; www.peoplemover.org; adult/child $1.75/1) is the local bus service; its main terminal is at the **Downtown Transit Center** (cnr W 6th Ave & G St).

AROUND ANCHORAGE

Seward Hwy runs south of Anchorage, squeezed between the mountains and Turnagain Arm, where motorists often pull over to watch beluga whales. At Portage, a short railroad and toll road runs to Whittier for the ferry to Valdez. Portage Glacier Access Rd leads to the **Begich-Boggs Visitors Center** (☎ 907-783-2326; 9am-6pm), 5 miles south of Portage, and **Portage Glacier**. **Gray Line** (☎ 907-277-5581; www.graylinealaska.com; 6441 Interstate Circle) offers hour-long cruises (adult/child $29/14.50),

WORTH THE TRIP: GIRDWOOD

Enfolded into mighty peaks famed for skiing, and overlooking the beauty of Turnagain Arm, Girdwood is a magnet for epicurean urbanites, artists and hippies successful in spite of themselves. With fine restaurants, great hiking, a colorful town center and not one but two trams, it's a must.

At **Hotel Alyeska** (☎ 907-754-2111; www.alyeskaresort.com; 1000 Arlberg Ave; d $199-239, ste $440-2200;) in Girdwood, you can ride a tram to explore the alpine area, and then enjoy its mountaintop restaurant, **Seven Glaciers** (☎ 907-754-2237; dinner mains $28-52; 5:30-9:30pm), before heading back down.

The Crow Pass Trail, 5.8 miles north of Alyeska Hwy on Crow Creek Rd, is a short but beautiful alpine hike that features gold-mining relics and an alpine lake, and Dall sheep are usually on the slopes above. It's 4 miles to Raven Glacier, the traditional turnaround point of the trail. Refuel after the hike at **Maxine's Glacier City Bristol** (☎ 907-783-1234; Crow Creek Rd; dinner mains $15-22; 5pm-midnight; Wed-Mon), a Mediterranean bistro with a Girdwood feel (friendly dogs congregate outside while their owners eat). Your lamb shawarma is accompanied by live music on Friday and Saturday nights.

the only way to see the entire glacier. There are two USFS campgrounds along Portage Glacier Access Rd: **Black Bear Campground** (campsites $14) and **Williwaw Campground** ($28).

Northeast of Anchorage, Glenn Hwy runs 13 miles to Eagle River Rd – a beautiful mountainside trip. The **Eagle River Nature Center** (☎ 907-694-2108; 32750 Eagle River Rd; 10am-5pm; admission per vehicle $5) offers wildlife displays and scenic hiking. Near Palmer, 42 miles north of Anchorage, **Hatcher Pass** is an alpine paradise, with hiking, parasailing, gold-rush artifacts and panoramas of the Talkeetna Mountains.

our pick Hatcher Pass Lodge (☎ 907-745-5897; www.hatcherpasslodge.com; Mile 17.5 Hatcher Pass Rd; r/cabin $95/165;) puts you above the treeline for spectacular views of the mountains surrounding Independence Mine State Historic Park and offers cabins and a restaurant. Or you can stay at **Hatcher Pass B&B** (☎ 907-745-6788, 877-745-6788; www.hatcherpassbb.com; Mile 6.6 Palmer-Fishhook Rd; cabin s/d $109/124;).

KENAI PENINSULA

This wonderful region, broken up by mountains, fjords and glaciers and laced with hiking trails and salmon-filled rivers, is a popular playground for both tourists and locals. More than half the population of the state lives within a two-hour drive of Kenai Peninsula. Even if you despise crowds, there are easy escapes into the wilderness.

Seward

Seward is an unpolished gem, rewarding visitors with small-town charm and phenomenal access to the mountains and sea. Founded in 1903 as an ice-free port at the southern end of the Alaska Railroad, Seward prospered in the gold rush as it was located at the beginning of the Iditarod Trail. It also survived the devastating 1964 Good Friday earthquake.

The **Chamber of Commerce** (☎ 907-224-8051; www.sewardak.org; 2001 Seward Hwy/3rd Ave; 8am-6pm Mon-Thu, to 8pm Fri, 9am-5pm Sat, 10am-3pm Sun) serves as the visitor center. There's also a **USFS office** (☎ 907-224-3374; 334 4th Ave; 8am-5pm Mon-Fri) and the **Kenai Fjords National Park Visitor Center** (☎ 907-224-3175; www.nps.gov/kefj; 1212 4th Ave; 8am-6pm) for hiking and paddling information. **Grant Electronics** (☎ 907-224-7015; 222 4th Ave; per hr $8; 9am-6pm) has internet access.

SIGHTS & ACTIVITIES

our pick Alaska SeaLife Center (☎ 800-224-2525; www.alaskasealife.org; 301 Railway Ave; adult/child $20/10; 8am-7pm;) is the only cold-water marine-science facility in the western hemisphere. It's home to a thousand fish, nearly all from Alaskan waters, and is the top attraction on the Kenai Peninsula. Plan to spend an afternoon here watching puffins, otters and 2000lb Steller sea lions glide past the two-storey viewing windows.

Six miles south of town is **Caines Head State Recreation Area** (per person $5), which was fortified during WWII to guard the entrance of Resurrection Bay after the Japanese bombed the island of Unalaska. Exploring the bunkers, gun emplacements and surrounding alpine country makes for an intriguing way to spend a day. You can access the area on foot at low tide along the Coastal Trail, or paddle to it with

Kayak Adventures Worldwide (☎ 907-224-3960; www.kayakak.com; 328 3rd Ave; day trip $125). **Miller's Landing Campground** (☎ 907-224-5739, 866-541-5739; www.millerslandingak.com; Lowell Point Rd; one way/round-trip $38/48) also runs a water taxi to the state park.

Seward's other great hike is the **Mt Marathon Trail**, a 3-mile (round-trip) walk to spectacular views on the mountain overlooking Seward.

SLEEPING

Snow River Hostel (☎ 907-440-1907; www.snowriverhostel.org; Mile 16 Seward Hwy; dm/d $20/50; ☒) Out of town, but highly recommended for its wooded tranquility.

Ballaine House B&B (☎ 907-224-2362; www.superpage.com/ballaine; 437 3rd Ave; r $50-82; ☒) This B&B is in one of the original Seward homes and does cook-to-order breakfasts.

Van Gilder Hotel (☎ 800-204-6835; www.vangilderhotel.com; 308 Adams St; d with/without bath $139-219/109; ☒) Seward's oldest hotel, which means two things: Victorian charm and brass beds. The European pensions with shared baths are a bargain.

Seward Windsong Lodge (☎ 907-224-7116; www.sewardwindsong.com; Mile 0.5 Exit Glacier Rd; r $179-309; ☒) This Alaska Native–corporation-owned place is immaculate, modern and snazzy, but devoid of good views and soul. There's free shuttle transportation to downtown.

EATING & DRINKING

Smoke Shack (☎ 907-224-7427; 411 Port Ave; breakfast & lunch dishes $6-11; 6am-8pm) Housed in a rail car, this tiny joint has the best breakfast in town, with biscuits and gravy made from scratch.

Yoly's Bistro (☎ 907-224-3295; 220 4th Ave; lunch mains $7-14, dinner mains $12-25; 11am-10pm) The menu has a delicious blend of curries, seafood, and burgers, with a decent wine and beer selection. Listen to live music on weekends.

Ray's Waterfront (☎ 907-224-5606; breakfast & lunch dishes $10-16, dinner mains $19-31; 11am-10pm) Hands down, this is Seward's culinary high point, with attentive service, picture-postcard views and the finest seafood above water.

Yukon Bar (☎ 907-224-3063; cnr 4th Ave & Washington St) has live music and can get festive at night. Head to **Resurrect Art Gallery Coffee House** (☎ 907-224-7161; 320 3rd Ave; 7am-7pm; ☒) for a latte and a quieter atmosphere.

GETTING THERE & AWAY

Seward Bus Lines (☎ 907-224-3608; www.sewardbuslines.net) runs daily to Anchorage ($50, 2½ hours). **Alaska Railroad** (☎ 800-544-0552; www.akrr.com) takes a spectacular daily route to Anchorage (adult/child $75/38, four hours).

Kenai Fjords National Park

South of Seward is Kenai Fjords National Park. The park's main features are the 917-sq-mile **Harding Icefield** and the tidewater glaciers that calve into the sea. Even though it's making a fast retreat, **Exit Glacier**, at the end of Exit Glacier Rd, is still the most popular attraction. There's a visitor center and a paved 0.25-mile trail to a glacier overlook. Hikers can climb a difficult 5 miles to the edge of the ice field – worth it for the spectacular views. The park visitor center is in Seward (p1093).

The best marine-wildlife cruises in the state are the tour boats that run into Kenai Fjords. **Major Marine Tours** (☎ 907-224-8030, 800-764-7300; www.majormarine.com) offers a half-day Resurrection Bay tour (adult/child $69/34) and a full-day tour viewing Holgate Arm ($136/68). The latter tour is a local favorite for its wildlife and prime rib and salmon buffet feast (adult/child $19/9).

Sterling Hwy

Paved Sterling Hwy arcs around the Kenai Peninsula, passing **Kenai National Wildlife Refuge**, where you might see moose, bears, eagles, salmon and anglers. Head to **Kenai**, which has good views and some Russian history, and then to Captain Cook Strait Recreation Area, which is off the fishing circuit. South of Soldotna, the scenic highway hugs the coastline, passing through small villages with campgrounds and great clamming beaches. Picturesque **Ninilchik** has a Russian accent, and **Eagle Watch Hostel** (☎ 907-567-3905; home.gci.net/~theeaglewatch; Mile 3 Oil Well Rd; dm/r $15/40; ☒) is 3 miles east of the Sterling Hwy in a gorgeous rural setting where you can see eagles.

Homer

Colorful and hip Homer sits on beautiful Kachemak Bay at the end of Sterling Hwy, facing awe-inspiring mountains and glaciers. The town began attracting alternative types in the 1960s, and is now home to artists and aging hippies. **Homer Visitor Center** (☎ 907-235-7740; www.homeralaska.org; 201 Sterling Hwy; 9am-7pm Mon-Fri, 10am-6pm Sat & Sun) has courtesy phones to book rooms or tours. The **Homer Library** (☎ 907-235-3180; 500 Hazel Ave; 10am-6pm Mon, Wed, Fri & Sat, 10am-8pm Tue & Thu) is impressive and has free internet access.

SIGHTS & ACTIVITIES

The recently renovated **Pratt Museum** (☎ 907-235-8635; 3779 Bartlett St; adult/child $6/3; ⌚ 10am-6pm) is the best on the peninsula, with exhibits on the *Exxon Valdez* oil spill and the dangers fisherman face on Kachemak Bay. Intriguing wildlife exhibits are found at the free **Alaska Islands & Ocean Visitor Center** (☎ 907-235-6961; www.islandsandocean.org; 95 Sterling Hwy; ⌚ 9am-6pm).

Homer Spit is a 4.5-mile sand bar that hums with tourists clamming, camping on the beach and exploring the harbor by boat. The best hiking is along the beaches, particularly Bishop's Beach Trail at Homer's Bishop Park, and at Kachemak Bay State Park, located across Kachemak Bay.

SLEEPING

Karen Hornaday Memorial Campground (tent/RV sites $8/15) Below the bluffs just north of downtown, this campground is less busy than those on the Spit.

Homer Hostel (☎ 907-235-1463; www.homerhostel.com; 304 W Pioneer Ave; dm $25, s/d $52/65) A bit cluttered, this hostel is perfectly located right downtown with no lockout.

Driftwood Inn (☎ 907-235-8019, 800-478-8019; www.thedriftwoodinn.com; cnr Main St & Bunnell Ave; d $85-170; wi-fi) Quiet yet centrally located, this inn has rooms ranging from tiny 'ship quarters' to large rooms with oceanfront views. Fall asleep to the sound of the waves.

Old Town B&B (☎ 907-235-7558; www.oldtownbedandbreakfast.com; 106 W Bunnell Ave; d $95-115) Three beautiful rooms with great views and lots of antiques; rates include a gourmet breakfast at Panarelli's Café next door.

Ocean Shores Motel (☎ 907-235-7775, 800-770-7775; www.akoceanshores.com; 451 Sterling Hwy; d $129-199; wi-fi) A downtown motel with clean and spacious rooms, most with pleasant decks. Operated by a serious kayak buff.

Bear Creek Lodging (☎ 907-235-8484; Bear Creek Dr; www.bearcreekwineryalaska.com; ste $225; ☒) Situated on a stunning hillside at the Bear Creek Winery, this place has two posh suites and a hot tub overlooking the vineyard. This is Alaska?

EATING & DRINKING

Two Sisters Bakery (☎ 907-235-2280; 233 W Bunnell Ave; light meals $3-9; ⌚ 7am-8pm Mon-Sat, 9am-4pm Sun) A beloved Homer institution with espresso and tables on a porch overlooking the bay.

Fresh Sourdough Express (☎ 907-235-7571; 1316 Ocean Dr; breakfast dishes $6-10, lunch & dinner mains $6-11; ⌚ 7am-9pm; ♿) Alaska's first green restaurant where everything is organic and as much as possible locally grown.

Café Cups (☎ 907-235-8330; 162 W Pioneer Ave; dinner mains $11-30; ⌚ 4:30-9:30pm Tue-Sat) Has a wacky exterior (think Antoni Gaudí) and an equally fun, eclectic-yet-refined menu that includes excellent curries and hand-cut rib-eyes.

our pick **Fat Olives** (☎ 907-235-8488; 276 Ohlson Ln; dinner mains $16-29; ⌚ 11am-9:30pm) In this chic and hyper-popular pizza joint/wine bar, you could gorge affordably on appetizers such as prosciutto-wrapped Alaska scallops, delicious mains like wood oven-roasted rack of lamb or a huge slice of pizza to go ($4).

Salty Dawg Saloon (Homer Spit Rd) Maybe the most-colorful bar on the Kenai Peninsula, the Salty Dawg is one of those places that's famous for being famous.

GETTING THERE & AWAY

Era Aviation (☎ 800-866-8394; www.flyera.com) flies frequently from Anchorage. The **Alaska Marine Highway** (☎ 907-235-8449; www.ferryalaska.com) sails three times a week to Seldovia ($33) and four to five times weekly to Kodiak ($74). **Polar Car Rental** (☎ 800-876-6417; Homer airport terminal; ⌚ 24hr) rents subcompacts for $65 a day. **Homer Stage Line** (☎ 907-235-2252; www.homerstageline.com) provides a bus service to Anchorage ($78, five hours).

PRINCE WILLIAM SOUND

Enclosed in a jagged-edged circle and infused with fjords and glaciers, Prince William Sound is a stunner. With only three cities, the 15,000-sq-mile region is mostly wilderness packed with quiet coves, rainy islands and abundant wildlife. Don't pass through without splurging on a marine-wildlife boat tour or a kayak adventure.

Whittier

At the western end of Prince William Sound, this strange little town was built by the military as a WWII warm-water port. A tunnel was drilled through solid rock to connect it with the main line of the Alaska Railroad. In 2000, the tunnel was converted to handle vehicles and Whittier's first luxury hotel opened up shortly after that.

Prince William Sound Kayak Center (☎ 907-472-2452, 877-472-2452; www.pwskayakcenter.com; Eastern

ALASKA

Ave) offers rentals (single/double $50/80) and guided tours, including day-long excursions to Blackstone Bay (for two people $425).

If you're looking for a place to stay, **June's B&B** (☎ 907-472-2396, 888-472-2396; www.breadnbuttercharters.com; Lot 7, Harbor View Rd; condos $155-275; ☒) offers insight into the local lifestyle by putting you up in comfortable suites atop Begich Towers. At the **Inn at Whittier** (☎ 907-472-7000; www.innatwhittier.com; 1 Harbor Loop Rd; r $219-399; ☐ ☒) the rooms are bland but the view isn't – make sure you spend the $20 extra for a seaside room.

A train leaves Whittier daily for Anchorage (adult/child $65/33, 2½ hours). The Alaska Marine Highway sails three times per week direct to Valdez ($89) and Cordova ($89).

Valdez

Just 25 miles east of Columbia Glacier, the ice-free port of Valdez is the southern terminus of the Trans-Alaska Pipeline. Valdez first boomed when 4000 gold seekers passed through, heading for the Klondike. After the 1964 earthquake, the city was rebuilt 4 miles further east.

ALASKA

The **Valdez Visitor Information Center** (☎ 907-835-4636; www.valdezalaska.org; 200 Fairbanks Dr; ⏲ 8am-7pm Mon-Sat, noon-7pm Sun) has information about the area and courtesy phones to book accommodations. **Valdez Consortium Library** (☎ 907-835-4632; 212 Fairbanks St; ⏲ 10am-6pm Mon & Fri, 10am-8pm Tue-Thu, to 6pm Sat) has free internet access.

SIGHTS & ACTIVITIES

The **Valdez Museum** (☎ 907-835-2764; 217 Egan Dr; adult/child $6/free; ⏲ 9am-5pm) is packed with displays, including the first barrel of oil to flow from the Trans-Alaska Pipeline and photos of Valdez being shaken by the 1964 Good Friday earthquake. The **Maxine & Jesse Whitney Museum** (☎ 907-834-1690; 303 Lowe St; adult/child $5/3; ⏲ 9am-7pm; ♿) is devoted to Alaska Native culture and Alaskan wildlife, and features ivory and baleen artwork and natural-history displays.

The magnificent **Columbia Glacier** is retreating, but its 3-mile-wide face can still be seen from Alaska Marine Highway ferries going to or from Whittier. For a longer and much closer look, **Stan Stephens Glacier & Wildlife Cruises** (☎ 907-835-4731, 866-867-1297; www.stanstephenscruises.com; 112 N Harbor Dr) runs seven-hour boat tours to Columbia Glacier (adult/child $112/56) and a nine-hour tour that also includes Meares Glacier (adult/child $147/73).

Although not blessed with the hiking options that Anchorage and Juneau possess, Valdez still offers a number of scenic trails. The 12.8-mile **Shoup Bay Trail**, which leads to its namesake bay, includes walk-in campsites halfway through the hike. For white-water enthusiasts, **Keystone Raft & Kayak Adventures** (☎ 907-835-2606, 800-328-8460; www.alaskawhitewater.com; ½-day $105) runs raft trips on the Class IV Tsaina River. **Anadyr Adventures** (☎ 907-835-2814, 800-865-2925; www.anadyradventures.com; 225 Harbor Dr) offers kayak rentals (single/double per day $45/65), water-taxi service and guided day trips.

SLEEPING

Bear Paw RV Campground (☎ 907-835-2530; 101 N Harbor Dr; tent/RV sites $20/30) Conveniently located right downtown; has showers and laundry – and a great little wooded glade just for tents!

L&L's B&B (☎ 907-835-4447; www.lnlalaska.com; 533 W Hanagita St; r with/without bath $85/75; ☒ ☐) Five rooms in a big, airy suburban home with two bicycles at your disposal.

Downtown B&B Inn (☎ 907-835-2791; 800-478-2791; www.alaskan.com/downtowninn; 113 Galena Dr; r incl breakfast $110, with shared bath $95; ⊜) More hotel than B&B, though you do get breakfast with your clean, basic room.

Lakehouse B&B (☎ 907-835-4752; www.cvinternet.net/~devens; Mile 6 Richardson Hwy; r $130-145; ☒ ☐) This ambling, sunny place has six rooms, all spacious and each with its own deck overlooking the pretty Robe Lake. If you've got your own wheels, this is a good option.

EATING

Alaska Halibut House (☎ 907-835-2788; 208 Meals Ave; fish $4-10; ⏲ 11am-8pm Mon-Sat) Frying up delicious local fish, this place is what every fast-food joint should be.

Ernesto's Taqueria (☎ 907-835-2519; 328 Egan Dr; fast food $7-9; ⏲ 5:30am-9:30pm) Locally loved, this place serves large portions of serviceable Mexican food with a selection of Mexican beer.

Fu Kung (☎ 907-835-5255; 207 Kobuk Dr; lunch mains $7-10, dinner mains $12-17; ⏲ 11am-11pm Mon-Sat, 4pm-11pm Sun) In a structure that wonderfully fuses Asian and Alaskan themes, this restaurant has fantastic Chinese food and lunch specials including egg roll and quality wonton soup.

GETTING THERE & AWAY

Era Aviation (☎ 800-866-8394; www.flyera.com) makes the 40-minute flight daily to Anchorage. **Alaska**

Marine Highway (☎ 800-642-0066; www.ferryalaska.com) ferries sail regularly to Whittier ($89) and Cordova ($50).

Cordova

At the eastern end of the sound, this beautiful little town's population of 2600 doubles in summer with fishery and cannery workers. First settled by the nomadic Eyak, who lived on the enormous salmon runs, Cordova became a fish-packing center in 1889.

The **Cordova Library** (☎ 907-424-6667; 622 1st Ave; 10am-8pm Tue-Fri, 1-5pm Sat & Sun) has visitor information, including B&B listings, and internet access. The **USFS office** (☎ 907-424-7661; 612 2nd St; 8am-5pm Mon-Fri) has free maps of hiking trails accessible from the road.

SIGHTS & ACTIVITIES

The **Cordova Museum** (☎ 907-424-6665; 622 1st Ave; admission $1; 10am-6pm Mon-Fri; 10am-5pm Sat, 2-4pm Sun) has a small but intriguing collection that ranges from when the Russians arrived in the area to a heart-wrenching display on the *Exxon Valdez* oil spill. It will also store your pack during the day. The **Ilanka Cultural Center** (☎ 907-424-7903; 110 Nicholoff Way; admission free; 10am-5pm Mon-Fri) has a small but high-quality collection of Alaska Native art.

our pick Childs Glacier calving into the Copper River is a magnificent sight – it's part of the stunning scenery to be found along the 50-mile Copper River Hwy. **Alaska River Expeditions** (☎ 907-424-7238, 800-776-1864; www.alaskarafters.com; Mile 13 Copper River Hwy) offers a full-day bus tour to Childs Glacier ($85) or a half-day raft and hike adventure to **Sheridan Glacier** ($95).

SLEEPING & EATING

Northern Nights Inn (☎ 907-424-5356; www.northernnightsinn.com; cnr 3rd St & Council Ave; r from $85;) Rooms in this century-old house range from basic to suites with kitchenettes. Some have peek-a-boo views of the bay.

Reluctant Fisherman Inn (☎ 907-424-3272, 800-770-3272; www.reluctantfisherman.com; cnr Railroad & Council Aves; r $130-155;) Overhanging Orca Inlet, this place is as close to luxurious as Cordova gets.

Baja Taco Wagon (☎ 907-424-5599; Harbor Loop; fast food $7-12; 8am-9pm) Graft a bus onto a cabin, add flowers and nautical implements, and what do you have? The best fish-taco stand north of San Diego.

Killer Whale Café (☎ 907-424-7733; 1st St; breakfast $5-10, sandwiches & burgers $8-10; 6:30am-3pm Mon-Sat, to 1pm Sun) Serves hearty breakfasts and fresh soups, wraps and sandwiches.

Powder House Bar (☎ 907-424-3529; Mile 1.5 Copper River Hwy; dinner mains $9-11; 10am-late Mon-Sat, noon-late Sun) Features folk and country music along with its grub and drinks.

GETTING THERE & AWAY

Alaska Airlines (☎ 907-424-7151, 800-252-7522; www.alaskaair.com) flies daily from Anchorage and Juneau. **Alaska Marine Highway** (☎ 800-642-0066; www.ferryalaska.com) ferries run daily to Valdez ($50, 4 hours) or Whittier ($89, 6½ hours). Rent a car at **Chinook Auto Rentals** (☎ 907-424-5279, 877-424-5279; www.chinookautorentals.com; Mile 13 Copper River Hwy) for $55 per day.

Wrangell–St Elias National Park

Part of a 31,250-sq-mile wilderness area, this park is a crossroad of mountain ranges: Wrangell, Chugach and St Elias. Extensive ice fields and 100 major glaciers spill from the peaks, including one bigger than the state of Rhode Island. It's more difficult to visit than Denali National Park but no less impressive with mountainous scenery and numerous opportunities for wilderness adventure whether on foot or in a raft.

From Valdez, the Richardson Hwy is a jaw-dropping scenic route to Glennallen, past canyons, mountain passes and glaciers. The **Wrangell–St Elias National Park Visitor Center** (☎ 907-822-5234; www.nps.gov/wrst; Mile 106.8 Richardson Hwy; 9am-7pm) is in Copper Center.

A side road at Tonsina goes southeast to Chitina, which has the last place to fill up your tank. From there, the rugged Mt McCarthy Rd follows former railroad tracks 60 miles east through the stunning Chugach Mountains and across the mighty Copper River to the Kennicott River, where the road dead-ends. Here a footbridge is used to cross the river and access historic McCarthy and the abandoned copper-mining town of Kennecott.

McCarthy & Kennecott

Scenic and funky little McCarthy was the Wild West counterpart of the Kennecott company town and, to a degree, still is today. The historic buildings in McCarthy are inns, restaurants and bars that serve visitors arriving from the other side of the Kennicott River. The company town of Kennecott is the remains of what was one of the greatest and richest copper mines in the USA.

In 1900 miners discovered the rich Kennecott copper deposit, and a syndicate built 196 miles of railroad through the wilderness to take the ore to Cordova. For 30 years Kennecott worked around the clock, but in 1938 management closed the mine, giving workers two hours to catch the last train out. Despite some pilferage, Kennecott remains a remarkably preserved piece of US mining history. The **Kennecott Visitor Center** (☎ 907-554-1105; Kennicott Railroad Depot; 9am-5:30pm) is staffed by the NPS during the summer (June to August), and has displays and maps of the company town.

There's some good hiking around the glaciers, peaks and mines, as well as rafting on the Kennicott River. **St Elias Alpine Guides** (☎ 907-544-4445, 888-933-5427; www.steliasguides.com) offers historical walking tours of Kennecott ($25) and a half-day hike on Root Glacier ($65). **Copper Oar** (☎ 907-554-4453, 800-523-4453; www.copperoar.com) has a full-day whitewater raft trip that ends with a bush plane flight ($275).

our pick **Kennicott River Lodge & Hostel** (☎ 907-554-4441; www.kennicottriverlodge.com; dm/cabin/ste $28/100/150;) is a beautiful log lodge on the west side of the river with a 12-person sauna. A bit run-down but offering the lowest rates in McCarthy is **Lancaster's Backpacker Hotel** (☎ 907-554-4402; www.mccarthylodge.com; s/d $48/68). Near the ruins, **Kennicott Glacier Lodge** (☎ 907-258-2350, 800-582-5128; www.kennicottlodge.com; s/d from $169/259;) is a sprawling lodge and restaurant overlooking its namesake glacier.

Backcountry Connection (☎ 907-822-5292, in Alaska 866-582-5292; www.kennicottshuttle.com) buses leave Glennallen daily for McCarthy via Chitina ($79). In McCarthy there's a five-hour layover to visit Kennecott; this long day trip costs $99. **Ellis Air** (☎ 907-822-3368; www.ellisair.com) flies from Anchorage to McCarthy via Gulkana twice weekly (one way/round-trip $300/600).

KODIAK ISLAND

Southwest of Kenai Peninsula, Kodiak Island is most famous for Kodiak brown bears, which grow huge from gorging on salmon. Accommodations and transportation are expensive, but the town is a refreshing change after visiting areas overrun by cruise ships and RVers.

The **Kodiak Island Visitors Center** (☎ 907-486-4782, 800-789-4782; www.kodiak.org; 100 Marine Way; 8am-7pm Mon-Tue, 9am-5pm Wed-Thu, 8am-7pm Fri, 10am-2pm & 5-9pm Sat, noon-5pm Sun) has lists of accommodations (including 20 B&Bs). The **Homes Johnson Library** (☎ 907-486-8686; 319 Lower Mill Rd; 10am-9pm Mon-Fri, 10am-5pm Sat, 1-5pm Sun) has free internet access.

Bear-watching is best from July to September, but usually involves a charter flight to a remote salmon stream through a company like **Sea Hawk Air** (☎ 907-486-8282, 800-770-4295; www.seahawkair.com; adult/child $475/350). **Orcas Unlimited** (☎ 907-539-1979; www.orcasunlimited.com) has guided full-day kayak outings ($160 to $200).

Bev's Bed & Make Your Own Darn Breakfast (☎ 907-486-8217; www.bevsbedandbreakfast.com; 1510 Mission Rd; r $90-120;) You can't beat the price for what you get at Bev's; comfortable queen-size beds, a fully-stocked kitchen and 15-minute walk to downtown.

Salmon Run Guesthouse (☎ 907-486-0091; www.salmonrunguesthouse.com; 410 Hillside Dr; r $120-160;) It's a climb to this downtown B&B but the three guestrooms are like small apartments with fully-equipped kitchens and private entrances.

Both **Alaska Airlines** (☎ 800-252-7522; www.alaskaair.com) and carrier **Era** (☎ 800-866-8394; www.flyera.com) fly to Kodiak from Anchorage daily. **Alaska Marine Highway** (☎ 907-486-3800; www.ferryalaska.com) ferries connect Kodiak with Homer ($74) several times a week.

DENALI & THE INTERIOR

Mt McKinley, known to the native Athabascans as Denali, presides regally over Alaska's vast and diverse Interior, a region that stretches from lowland forests to the towering peaks and glaciers of the Alaska, Talkeetna and Wrangell ranges. This is Alaska's heartland: dogsleds and gold pans, roadhouses and fish wheels, moose on the side of the road and a seemingly endless stretch of pavement disappearing into the mountains.

The main route into this region is George Parks Hwy (Hwy 3), which winds 358 miles from Anchorage to Fairbanks, passing Denali National Park. The Richardson Hwy (Hwy 4) extends 366 miles south from Fairbanks to Valdez while the Glenn Hwy (Hwy 1) completes this Interior triangle by extending 189 miles from Anchorage to Glennallen. All the Interior roads are lined with turnoffs, campgrounds and hiking trails and are serviced by small towns with limited facilities and high prices.

DENALI NATIONAL PARK

This breathtaking wilderness area, which includes North America's highest mountain, attracts 400,000 visitors a year. A single road curves 91 miles through the heart of the park, leading to off-trail hiking opportunities, wildlife and stunning panoramas. The Denali Park Rd can be used only by official shuttle buses, which have limited seating. Numbers of overnight backpackers in the wilderness zones are also strictly limited. This means Disneyland-level crowds at the entrance but relative solitude once you're inside.

Wildlife, including mammals from marmots to moose, is easy to spot. Caribou, wolves and brown bears are crowd favorites. However, the main attraction is magnificent Mt McKinley, a high pyramid of rock, snow and glaciers rising from the valley floor. Clouds will obscure McKinley more often than not, so be prepared to wait for the big picture.

Information

The park entrance is at Mile 237.3 George Parks Hwy. The highway north and south of the park entrance is 'Glitter Gulch,' a touristy strip of private campgrounds, lodges, restaurants and facilities.

Begin your trip to Denali at the **Wilderness Access Center** (WAC; ☎ 907-683-9274; Mile 1 Denali Park Rd; 5am-8pm) to obtain shuttle-bus tickets, campsites and pay entrance fees (per person/family $10/20). Then head across the parking lot to the **Backcountry Information Center** (BIC; ☎ 907-683-9510; 9am-6pm) for a free backcountry permit if you want to overnight in Denali's backcountry. Finally stop at the new **Denali Visitor Center** (☎ 907-683-2294; www.nps.gov/dena; 8am-6pm;) to learn what makes this park so special. If possible, plan the exact days you will be at Denali and reserve bus seats and campsites through **Denali National Park Reservations** (☎ 907-272-7275, 800-622-7275; www.reservedenali.com).

Shuttle buses provide access for day hiking and sightseeing, and can be reserved from late February for the following summer. In the backcountry you can get on or off buses along their routes. Buses leave the WAC regularly (5:30am to 4pm) for various stops, including Eielson Visitor Center (adult/child $31/free, four hours) and Wonder Lake ($43/free, 6½ hours). Special camper shuttle buses, with space for backpacks and mountain bikes, cost $30 per adult (children are free) to any point on the road.

Activities

For day hiking, get off the shuttle bus at any valley, riverbed or ridge that takes your fancy (no permit needed). For a guided walk, book at the WAC one or two days ahead.

For backcountry camping, you must get a backcountry permit from the BIC one day in advance. The park is divided into 43 zones, each with a regulated number of visitors. Some are more popular than others. Watch the Backcountry Simulator Program video at the BIC – it covers bears, river and backcountry safety – and check the quota board for an area you can access. You then go to the counter to book a camper shuttle bus and buy your maps.

Most cyclists book campsites at the WAC and then carry their bikes on the camper shuttle. Cycling is only permitted on roads. Rent bikes from **Denali Outdoor Center** (☎ 907-683-1925, 888-303-1925; www.denalioutdoorcenter.com; Mile 240.5 & Mile 247 Parks Hwy; per hr/day $7/40).

Several rafting companies run daily floats on the Nenana River. **Denali Raft Adventures** (☎ 907-683-2234, 888-683-2234; www.denaliraft.com; Mile 238 Parks Hwy) offers a wild canyon run through the gorge, as well as a milder Mt McKinley float ($84 per person).

Sleeping & Eating

Campsites inside the park cost between $9 and $20, and most can be reserved for a $4 fee. That includes Riley Creek, just inside the park entrance, which is usually overrun by RVers. Other campgrounds are spaced along the park road, the most popular being Wonder Lake (Mile 85 Park Rd; campsites $16), overlooking Mt McKinley, while Sanctuary River (Mile 23 Park Rd; campsites $9) makes a great base for day hikes.

Denali Mountain Morning Hostel (☎ 907-683-7503; www.hostelalaska.com; Mile 224 Parks Hwy; dm/d $32/80-95;) A great place to get a bunk, stash your gear (or rent some) and catch a free shuttle to the park. Make reservations!

Denali Grizzly Bear Resort (☎ 907-683-2696, 866-583-2696; www.denaligrizzlybear.com; Mile 231.1 George Parks Hwy; campsites $24, r $192, tent cabin from $30-35, cabin $65-260) This place offers wooded campsites, platform tent cabins, rooms and 23 cabins, some featuring tons of Alaskan character.

Carlo Creek Lodge (☎ 907-683-2576; www.ccldenaliparkalaska.com; Mile 224 George Parks Hwy; cabins with/without bath $145/85; 💻 📶) About 13 miles south of the park entrance, this lodge offers a variety of creek-side accommodations.

Earthsong Lodge (☎ 907-683-2863; www.earthsonglodge.com; Mile 4 Stampede Rd, off Mile 251 Parks Hwy; cabins $155-195) North of Healy; rents out 12 private-bathroom cabins above the timberline at 1900ft – just a short climb away from stunning views of Mt McKinley.

Overlook Bar & Grill (☎ 907-683-2641; Mile 238.5 Parks Hwy; sandwiches & burgers $11-15; 🕑 11am-11pm) Way up on the hill over Glitter Gulch, the 'Big O' gets raves for its view, beer list and as the best bar at the entrance.

229 Parks (☎ 907-683-2567; Mile 229 Parks Hwy; dinner $24-34; 🕑 8-11am, 5-10pm Tue-Sun) South of McKinley Village, this excellent restaurant manages to be both epicurean and ardently environmental at the same time, emphasizing organic and locally grown foods.

Getting There & away

From the WAC inside the park, the **Alaska/Yukon Trails** (☎ 800-770-7275; www.alaskashuttle.com) bus departs for Anchorage ($75, six hours) and Fairbanks ($55, three hours).

The **Alaska Railroad** (☎ 907-265-2494, 800-544-0552; www.akrr.com) train departs from a depot near Riley Creek campground; it's expensive (adult/child Anchorage $146/73, Fairbanks $64/32) but very scenic.

GEORGE PARKS HWY

North of Anchorage, just past the Glenn Hwy (Hwy 1) turnoff, George Parks Hwy passes through Wasilla – the now famous home of ex-Gov Sarah Palin. A dramatic detour, the Fishook-Willow Rd between Palmer and Willow goes through **Hatcher Pass** (p1093), an alpine paradise with foot trails, gold-mining artifacts and panoramas of the Talkeetna Mountains.

Talkeetna

At Mile 98.7, a side road heads north to this interesting town. It was a miners supply center in 1901, and later a riverboat station and a railroad-construction headquarters. Since the 1950s, Mt McKinley mountaineers have made Talkeetna their staging post, and today the town is the most interesting along the George Parks Hwy. Just be aware that loads of cruise ship visitors invade this town throughout the summer. The **Talkeetna/Denali Visitors Center** (☎ 907-733-2688; www.talkeetnadenali.com; George Parks Hwy; 🕑 10am-6pm) has information about the area.

The **Mountaineering Ranger Station** (☎ 907-733-2231; cnr 1st & B Sts; 🕑 8am-6pm) handles expeditions to Mt McKinley and has displays that will interest even those who have no desire to stand on North America's highest peak. The four restored buildings of the **Talkeetna Historical Society Museum** (☎ 907-733-2487; adult/child $3/free; 🕑 10am-6pm) are a block south of Main St and houses exhibits on bush pilots and McKinley climbs.

For scenic flights to view Mt McKinley ($190 to $330), check out **Hudson Air Service** (☎ 907-733-2321, 800-478-2321; www.hudsonair.com) or **K2 Aviation** (☎ 907-733-2291, 800-764-2291; www.flyk2.com). If the day is clear, be prepared for a long wait, made worthwhile by an unforgettable flight.

SLEEPING & EATING

Talkeetna Hostel International (☎ 907-733-4678; www.talkeetnahostel.com; I St; dm/s/d $22/50/65; ⊠ 💻) This well-loved hostel has coed dorm rooms, private rooms, a shared kitchen and even a converted VW van you can sleep in ($35). How cool is that?

Latitude 62 Lodge/Motel (☎ 907-733-2262; Mile 13.5 Talkeetna Spur Rd; s/d $68/79) If downtown Talkeetna is just too hippie-dippy for you, there's always this place, with hunting-lodge decor.

Talkeetna Alaskan Lodge (☎ 907-733-9500, 888-959-9590; www.talkeetnalodge.com; Mile 12.5 Talkeetna Spur Rd; r $309-409, ste 479-569; 💻 📶) This luxurious Alaska Native–corporation-owned place has 153 rooms and suites, a restaurant, a lounge and high prices. The hillside setting offers great views of Mt McKinley.

Mountain High Pizza Pie (☎ 907-733-1234; Main St; pizza slice $4, sandwiches $6-12; 🕑 11:30am-11pm) This arty, airy restaurant makes fabulous pizza that is served with a mug of one of Alaska's favorite microbrews.

Wildflower Café (☎ 907-733-2694; Main St; sandwiches $14, mains $22-32; 🕑 11am-9pm) This new entrant to the Talkeetna culinary scene is doing well with yummy burgers and large wholesome mains served on a large deck that's a perfect perch for people-watching.

Café Michele (☎ 907-733-5300; Talkeetna Spur Rd & 2nd St; lunch mains $13-17, dinner mains $18-35; 🕑 11am-10pm; ⊠) Talkeetna's fanciest restaurant with international cuisine that takes off in Asia

SCENIC DRIVE: CHENA HOT SPRINGS

Start the morning hiking in Chena River State Recreational Area, which has a variety of walks, including the impressive Granite Tors Trail, a 15-mile loop. Then end the day at **Chena Hot Springs Resort** (☎ 907-451-8104; www.chenahotsprings.com; Mile 56.5 Chena Hot Springs Rd; campsites/yurts $20/65, r $189-249), where you can soak away those sore feet or have a cold one in its Aurora Ice Museum, the world's only year-round ice palace. The resort also offers economical yurts, a good restaurant and a bar where you can belly up and drink as if you were a local.

with dishes like coconut-curry rice, then suddenly jets down to the US South for a romping jambalaya.

GETTING THERE & AWAY

The **Alaska Railroad** (☎ 800-544-0552; www.akrr.com) from Anchorage stops at Talkeetna daily in summer (adult/child $89/45, 3½ hours) and heads north to Denali National Park (adult/child $89/45, four hours) and Fairbanks (adult/child $124/62, 8½ hours). **Denali Overland Transportation** (☎ 907-733-2384, 800-651-5221; www.denalioverland.com) runs shuttles between Anchorage and Talkeetna ($75, three hours).

FAIRBANKS

A spread-out, low-rise city, Fairbanks (population 96,888) features extremes of climate, colorful residents and gold fever. In a city that can hit -60°F (-70°C) in the winter, summer days average 70°F (21°C) and occasionally top 90°F (32°C). Downtown is roughly centered on Golden Heart Park, and Cushman St is more or less the main street.

Fairbanks was founded in 1901, when a trader could not get his riverboat any further up the Chena River. A gold strike made Fairbanks a boom town, with 18,000 residents settling there by 1908, but by 1920 the population had slumped to 1000. WWII, the Alcan Hwy and military bases produced minor booms, but the town took off as a construction base for the Trans-Alaska Pipeline in 1973 and still serves as a gateway to the North Slope. Just north of the city is Fort Knox, Alaska's largest gold mine.

Information

The new **Morris Thomson Cultural & Visitor Center** (☎ 907-456-5774, 800-327-5774; www.explorefairbanks.com; 101 Dunkel St; 🕑 8am-7pm), combines the maps and exhibits of the former Alaska Public Lands Information Center with the travel brochures and helpful staff of the Fairbanks Convention and Visitors Center.

Sights & Activities

Pioneer Park (☎ 907-459-1087; cnr Airport Way & Peger Rd; admission free; 🕑 stores noon-8pm, park 24hr; 👪) is a 44-acre park and the city's biggest attraction. The historical displays are impressive and include an old stern-wheeler, the railroad car that carried President Warren Harding, and giant gold dredgers.

Museum of the North (☎ 907-474-7505; 907 Yukon Dr; adult/child $10/free; 🕑 9am-9pm;) at the University of Alaska rivals the Anchorage Museum of History & Art as the state's most impressive cultural center. A $42 million expansion added a Alaska Native art gallery and a sound-and-light theatre that features the northern lights. But the most popular exhibit is still Blue Babe, a 36,000-year-old bison found preserved in the permafrost.

Canoeing options range from afternoon paddles to overnight trips; ask at **7 Bridges Boats & Bikes** (☎ 907-479-0751; www.7gablesinn.com/7bbb; 4312 Birch Lane; canoe per day $35), at 7 Gables Inn. Alternatively, cruise the calm Chena River with a 3½-hour tour on the historic stern-wheeler **Riverboat Discovery** (☎ 907-479-6673, 866-479-6673; www.riverboatdiscovery.com; 1975 Discovery Dr; adult/child $55/38; 🕑 8:45am & 2pm; 👪).

Sleeping

Go North Hostel (☎ 907-479-7272; 866-236-7272; 3500 Davis Rd; tent cabins $25, campsites $12; 💻 📶) Fairbanks' best hostel houses backpackers in comfortable tent cabins, offers communal cooking in a bright kitchen cabin and boasts a dazzling array of services, including canoe-trip shuttles and guided backcountry expeditions.

Ah, Rose Marie (☎ 907-456-2040; www.akpub.com/akbbrv/ahrose.html; 302 Cowles St; s/d incl breakfast $65/90; ⊠ 💻) This highly recommended downtown B&B has cozy rooms at an amazingly affordable rate and great breakfasts.

Golden North Motel (☎ 907-479-6201, 800-447-1910; www.goldennorthmotel.com; 4888 Old Airport Rd; s/d $79/89-106; 💻 📶) A friendly, family-owned place that is the cheapest respectable motel in town.

ALASKA

WORTH THE TRIP: CRUISING THE ALEUTIANS

The easiest way to see 'Bush Alaska' without flying is to hop onto the **Alaska Marine Highway** (☎ 800-642-0066; www.ferryalaska.com) when it makes its special runs to the eastern end of the Aleutian Islands. The MV *Tustumena*, a 290ft vessel that holds 220 passengers, is one of only two ferries in the Alaska Marine Highway fleet rated as an oceangoing ship; hence its nickname, the 'Trusty Tusty.' It is also one of the oldest vessels in the fleet, thus its other nickname: the 'Rusty Tusty.'

Once a month from May through September, the *Tustumena* leaves Kodiak on a Wednesday, and continues west to Chignik, Sand Point, King Cove, Cold Bay and False Pass, docking at each village for two hours, which is plenty of time to get off for a quick look around. It reaches Unalaska/Dutch Harbor by Saturday morning and stays put for five hours before backtracking.

A Kodiak–Unalaska ticket is adult/child $293/146, making the cruise one of the best bargains in public transportation. The scenery and wildlife are spectacular. You'll pass the perfect cones of several volcanoes, the treeless but lush green mountains of the Aleutians and distinctive rock formations and cliffs. Whales, sea lions, otters and porpoises are commonly sighted, and birdlife abounds. Occasionally a brown bear is seen rambling along the beach. More than 250 species of birds migrate through the Aleutians and if you don't know a puffin from a kittiwake, you can attend daily presentations by naturalists from the US Fish & Wildlife Service.

Viewing wildlife and scenery depends, however, on the weather. It can be an extremely rough trip at times, deserving its title 'the cruise through the cradle of the storms.' The smoothest runs are from June to August, while in the fall 40ft waves and 80-knot winds are the norm. That's the reason for barf bags near the cabins and Dramamine in the vending machines, right above the Reese Peanut Butter Cups. Its tiny bar – three stools, two tables – is called The Pitch And Roll Cocktail Lounge.

Keep in mind that the Tusty's solarium isn't as comfortable as most of the Southeast ferries for cabinless sleeping. Bring a good sleeping pad and loads of Cup-of-Noodles, instant oatmeal and tea (there's free hot water) if you want to avoid the restaurant onboard. Also bring a good book. On days when the fog surrounds the boat, there is little to look at but the waves lapping along the side.

ALASKA

Rooms tend to be on the small side but come with coffee and muffins in the morning.

7 Gables Inn (☎ 907-479-0751; www.7gablesinn.com; 4312 Birch Lane; r $90-130, apt $130-200; 💻) This B&B, just off the Chena River, is entered via a hothouse garden and offers plush rooms, some with Jacuzzis, as well as private apartments.

Pike's Waterfront Lodge (☎ 907-456-4500, 877-774-2400; www.pikeslodge.com; 1850 Hoselton Rd; r from $235; 💻 📶) An upscale place on the banks of the Chena River, amenities at this lodge include a steam room, sauna and a deck on the river.

Eating & Drinking

College Coffeehouse (☎ 907-374-0468; 3677 College Rd; 🕑 7am-midnight Mon-Fri, 8am-midnight Sat & Sun; 💻 📶) In Campus Corner Mall, this is one of the best spots in Fairbanks to pick up on the city's offbeat vibe. They often have live music.

Sam & Sharon's Sourdough Cafe (☎ 907-479-0523; University Ave at Cameron St; breakfast, burgers & sandwiches $7-11; 🕑 6am-10pm) Considered by many to be the town's best diner, this place, just down University Ave from campus, serves up sourdough pancakes all day long.

Lemongrass (☎ 907-456-2200; 388 Old Chena Pump Rd; mains $9-11; 🕑 11am-4pm & 5pm-10pm) Ignore the out-of-the-way, strip-mall setting – Fairbanks' best Thai food and most gracious service is found here.

Gambardella's Pasta Bella (☎ 907-457-4992; 706 2nd Ave; lunches $9-12, dinners $12-28; 🕑 11am-9pm Mon-Thu, to 10pm Fri & Sat, 4-9pm Sun) *The* place for Italian food in Fairbanks, with luscious pasta dishes, pizza and homemade bread. There's an outdoor café that's a delight during Fairbanks' long summer days.

Big Daddy's Barbecue (☎ 907-452-2501; 107 Wickersham St; sandwich $9-12, dinner $13-30; 🕑 11am-10pm Mon-Thu, to 11pm Fri & Sat) Claiming to be the 'northernmost southern barbecue,' Big Daddy's has great beef brisket, ribs, and pulled pork with all the down-home fixin's. There's live music Thursday through Saturday.

Palace Theatre & Saloon (☎ 907-456-5960; www.akvisit.com; adult/child $18/9) At Pioneer Park, this saloon comes alive at night with honky-tonk piano, can-can dancers and other acts in the *Golden Heart Revue.*

Getting There & Around

Alaska Airlines (☎ 800-252-7522; www.alaskaair.com) has seven flights daily to Anchorage with occasional bargains. **Frontier Alaska** (☎ 907-450-7200, 800-478-6779; www.frontierflying.com) also flies to Anchorage as well as throughout Arctic Alaska.

Arctic Rent-A-Car (☎ 907-479-8044; www.arcticrentacar.com; 4500 Dale Rd), near the airport, rents out compacts for around $50 a day with 200 free miles.

Alaska Direct Bus Lines (☎ 800-770-6652; www.alaskadirectbusline.com) makes a Fairbanks–Whitehorse run ($200, 15 hours) stopping at Tok ($80, five hours) along the way. **Alaska/Yukon Trails** (☎ 800-770-7275; www.alaskashuttle.com) offers daily connections to Denali National Park ($55, 2½ hours) and Anchorage ($99, eight hours). It also services Dawson City ($169, 10 hours).

The **Alaska Railroad** (☎ 800-544-0552; www.akrr.com) departs at 8:15am daily for Denali National Park (adult/child $64/32, three hours) and Anchorage (adult/child $210/105, 12 hours).

The **Metropolitan Area Commuter Service** (☎ 907-459-1011; www.co.fairbanks.ak.us/transportation) provides a local bus service (single ride/daily pass $1.50/3).

THE BUSH

The Bush is the vast area of Alaska that is not readily accessible by road or ferry. It includes Arctic Alaska, the Brooks Range, the Alaska Peninsula–Aleutian Islands chain and the Bering Sea coast. Traveling to the Bush usually involves small, expensive chartered aircraft. Facilities for travelers are pricey and very limited.

To visit **Arctic Alaska**, take the Dalton Hwy, a rough gravel road that goes 490 miles north from Fairbanks to Deadhorse, near Prudhoe Bay. You can tour the oil complex at Prudhoe, but you can't camp on the shores of the Arctic Ocean. The highlight of the long drive is the **Arctic Circle** and **Atigun Pass** (4752ft) in the Brooks Range, 300 miles from Fairbanks, for the views of the North Slope. **Dalton Hwy Express** (☎ 907-474-3555; www.daltonhighwayexpress.com) makes the run to Prudhoe Bay twice a week. It's $168 round-trip from Fairbanks to the Arctic Circle (six hours one way), and $442 to Prudhoe Bay (16 hours one way). **Arctic Outfitters** (☎ 907-474-3530; www.arctic-outfitters.com) offers a self-drive package to Prudhoe Bay for $1,313, which includes a car and three nights' lodging for two people.

WHAT THE ...

Muktuk is an Inupiat delicacy that is made up of the outer skin of a whale and the attached pink blubber. It can be eaten pickled, boiled or even fresh with hot mustard, and is said to have the consistency of stale Jell-O. Needless to say, muktuk is an acquired taste. Fly to Barrow in late June for the town's Nalukataq Festival to acquire it.

The Dalton Hwy passes the remote **Gates of the Arctic National Park**, which has great hiking and paddling, but the park is best accessed from the town of **Bettles**, which can be reached only by air. For information, contact the **NPS Ranger Station** (☎ 907-692-5494; www.nps.gov/gaar). For guided and unguided trips into the park as well as accommodations in Bettles, contact **Bettles Lodge** (☎ 800-770-5111, 907-692-5111; www.bettleslodge.com).

On the Bering Sea coast, the legendary gold-rush town of **Nome** is friendly and an intriguing place to visit, whether you want to explore the still-visible links to its golden past or have a go panning for nuggets yourself. The **visitor center** (☎ 907-443-6624; www.nomealaska.org; 9am-9pm) has information about accommodations and trips in the surrounding area. You can camp for free on **Golden Sands Beach**, where gold is still being sought by a small band of miners who set up their sluice boxes and other equipment every summer. You can talk to them, see the nuggets they find and then give panning a whirl for yourself. **Swanberg's Gold Dredge** is on display nearby. **Alaska Airlines** (☎ 800-252-7522; www.alaskaair.com) offers nonstop flights from Anchorage.

Hawaii

So many states claim uniqueness, and Hawaii does too. It now even boasts that it's the birthplace of the USA's 44th president, Barack Obama. But this string of emerald islands in the cobalt-blue Pacific Ocean, over 2000 miles from any continent, takes a little work to get to. So you may wonder: will that be time and money well spent?

We're so glad you asked: cue the galloping *Hawaii Five-0* theme music and watch surfers carve a thunderous ocean, Elvis croon and lei-draped beauties dance hula 'neath wind-rustled palms.

Hawaii, as tourist bureaus and Hollywood constantly remind us, is 'paradise.' Push past the hype and what do you find? Darned if they're not right. Hawaii is hiking sculpted cliffs or diving coral-reef cities in the morning and drinking mai tais to slack-key guitar at sunset. It's slurping chin-dripping papayas with hibiscus flowers in your hair; it's Pacific Rim cuisine, fiery volcanoes and cavorting whales. By serendipity and design, Hawaii is an almost flawless destination. It's an enchanting multicultural society with roots in Polynesia, Asia, North America and Europe, and it's an expression of nature at its most luscious and divine.

About seven million visitors come to experience paradise annually, but the islands are not as crushed with sun-baked tourists and cooing honeymooners as that sounds. If you want a cushy resort vacation, head for Oahu's Waikiki or West Maui. For something cheaper or more adventurous, aim for the Big Island or Kaua'i. If time is short, stick to one island and make the most of it. Honolulu is a teeming cultural and economic powerhouse, but in under an hour you can be alone in the rainforest or snoozing on white sand.

Locals know that Hawaii isn't really paradise, but on any given day it can sure feel like it.

HIGHLIGHTS

- Exploring multicultural Honolulu, particularly the herbalists and eats of **Chinatown** (p1111)
- Snorkeling with tropical fish in O'ahu's **Hanauma Bay** (p1117)
- Hiking the smoldering crust of a living volcano at **Hawai'i Volcanoes National Park** (p1122)
- Catching sunset in the 'house of the rising sun,' Maui's **Haleakalā** (p1127)
- Kayaking or hiking Kaua'i's wrinkly **Na Pali Coast** (p1128)

HISTORY

Little is known about Hawaii's first settlers, who arrived around AD 500. Tahitians arrived around AD 1000, and for the next 200 years navigated thousands of miles back and forth across the ocean in double-hulled canoes. Ruled by chiefs, ancient Hawaiian society was matriarchal, and its religion followed strict laws known as *kapu*.

In 1778, famed British explorer Captain James Cook stumbled upon the islands, and he returned in 1779. The first white Westerner to arrive, Cook was initially feted like a high chief (perhaps even a deity) as Hawaiians plied him with food and goodwill. However, on the second visit, tensions escalated over a series of small thefts and insults. During a confrontation on the beach, Cook lost his temper and shot a Hawaiian, sparking a violent melee during which Cook himself was killed.

Beginning in the 1790s, King Kamehameha, chief of the Big Island, conquered and united all the Hawaiian islands. He is credited with bringing peace and stability to a society that was often in flux due to wars and the power struggles of the ruling class. However, after his death in 1819 his son Liholiho inherited the throne, while Kamehameha's favorite wife, Queen Ka'ahumanu, became regent. In a stunning repudiation of traditional Hawaiian religion, Liholiho and Ka'ahumanu deliberately violated the *kapu* and destroyed many temples.

As fate would have it, Christian missionaries arrived not long after, and in the midst of Hawaii's social and spiritual chaos they found it relatively easy to 'save souls.' New England whalers also arrived, seeking different quarry, and by the 1840s Lahaina and Honolulu were the busiest whaling towns in the Pacific. Meanwhile, foreigners made a grab for Hawaii's fertile land, turning vast tracts into sugarcane plantations; needing workers in cane fields, they encouraged a flood of immigrants from China, Japan, Portugal and the Philippines. This gave rise to Hawaii's multiethnic culture, but it also displaced Native Hawaiians, most of whom became landless.

In 1893 a group of American businessmen overthrew the Hawaiian monarchy. The US government was initially reluctant to support the coup, but it soon rationalized its colonialism by citing the islands' strategic importance and annexed Hawaii in 1898. Hawaii played an infamous role in US history when a surprise attack on Pearl Harbor vaulted America into WWII. Hawaii became the 50th US state in 1959.

LOCAL CULTURE

Compared to 'the mainland' – the blanket term for the rest of the USA – Hawaii may as well be another country. In fact, some Native Hawaiians would like to restore Hawaii's status as an independent nation. It makes sense. Geologically, historically and culturally, Hawaii developed in isolation, and, like its flora and fauna, its society is unique, endemic and even fragile. Locals treasure their customs and sensibilities and constantly guard them against the diluting influence of *haole* (white or mainland) ways – which arrive like so many invasive species.

In Hawaii, no ethnicity claims a majority, but this diversity is also distinct from typical American multiculturalism. Hawaii has large Asian populations and very small African American and Mexican Hispanic communities, with about 20% of residents identifying themselves as full or part Native Hawaiian.

As befits a tropical paradise, Hawaii has a decidedly casual personality. Except in cosmopolitan Honolulu, aloha shirts and sandals ('rubbah slippahs') are acceptable attire for any occasion, socializing revolves around food and family, and fun means sports and the outdoors. In local and Hawaiian sensibilities, caring for the land and caring for the community are integral and intertwined.

Then there is aloha – or alooooooоHA, as they say at the luau. It is of course a greeting, but, more than that, it describes a gentle,

HAWAII FACTS

Nickname Aloha State
Population 1.3 million
Area 6423 sq miles
Capital city Honolulu (population 375,570)
Sales tax 4.16% (plus 8.25% room tax, due to increase to 9.25% in 2010)
Birthplace of entertainer Don Ho (1930–2007), President Barack Obama (b 1961), actor Nicole Kidman (b 1967), pro golfer Michelle Wie (b 1989)
Home of ukuleles, America's only royal palace
Famous for surfing, hula, mai tais, the world's most active volcano
Most famous state fish humuhumunukunukuapua'a (or, 'fish with a nose like a pig')

HAWAII

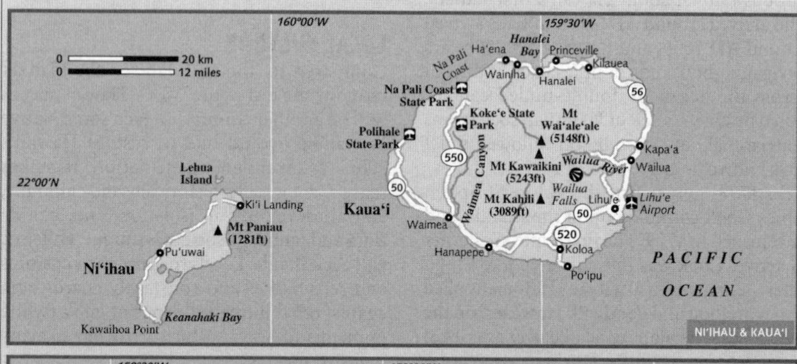
160°00'W
159°30'W
22°00'N
0 20 km
0 12 miles
Na Pali Coast
Ha'ena
Hanalei Bay
Princeville
Kilauea
Wainiha
Hanalei
Na Pali Coast State Park
Koke'e State Park
Mt Wai'ale'ale (5148ft)
Polihale State Park
Waimea Canyon
Mt Kawaikini (5243ft)
Wailua River
Kapa'a
Wailua
Lehua Island
Wailua Falls
Mt Kahili (3089ft)
Lihu'e
Lihu'e Airport
Ki'i Landing
Kaua'i
Mt Paniau (1281ft)
Waimea
Pu'uwai
Hanapepe
Koloa
Po'ipu
Ni'ihau
Keanahaki Bay
Kawaihoa Point
PACIFIC OCEAN
NI'IHAU & KAUA'I

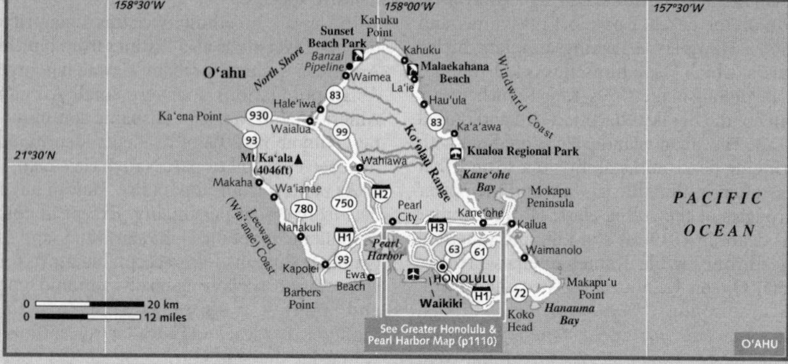
158°30'W
158°00'W
157°30'W
21°30'N
Kahuku Point
Sunset Beach Park
Banzai Pipeline
Kahuku
Malaekahana Beach
O'ahu
North Shore
Waimea
La'ie
Windward Coast
Hale'iwa
Hau'ula
Ka'ena Point
Waialua
Ka'a'awa
Ko'olau Range
Kualoa Regional Park
Mt Ka'ala (4046ft)
Wahiawa
Kane'ohe Bay
Makaha
Wa'ianae
Mokapu Peninsula
Pearl City
Kane'ohe
Kailua
Leeward (Wai'anae) Coast
Nanakuli
Pearl Harbor
Waimanolo
Kapolei
HONOLULU
Ewa Beach
Makapu'u Point
Barbers Point
Waikiki
Koko Head
Hanauma Bay
PACIFIC OCEAN
0 20 km
0 12 miles
See Greater Honolulu & Pearl Harbor Map (p1110)
O'AHU

157°00'W
156°30'W
156°00'W
21°00'N
20°30'N
'Ilio Point
Mo'omomi Beach
Kalaupapa Peninsula
Moloka'i
Papohaku Beach Park
Kalaupapa
Molokai Airport
Kalawao
Halawa Bay
Kualapu'u
Maunaloa
Kamakou Preserve
Kamakou Peak (4970ft)
Halawa Valley
Waialua
Kaunakakai
Puko'o
Kamalo
PACIFIC OCEAN
Honolua Bay
West Maui Airport
Kahakuloa
Kapalua
Kahana
Ferry
Pu'u Kukui (5788ft)
Kahului Bay
Ho'okipa Beach
Kahului Airport
Maui
Ka'anapali
Waihe'e
Lana'i
Kahokunui
Wailuku
Kahului
Pa'ia
Haiku
Huelo
Hana Hwy
Keomuku
Lahaina
'Iao Valley State Park
Ke'anae
Lana'i City
Munro Trail
Kahe'a
Olowalu
Ma'alaea
Hana Airport
Kaumalapau
Lana'ihale (3370ft)
Kihei
Wai'anapanapa State Park
Hana
Papawai Point
Ma'alaea Bay
Lana'i Airport
Hulopo'e Beach Park
Manele Bay
Keokea
Haleakalā National Park
Wailea
Makena
Pu'u 'Ula'ula (10,023ft)
'Ohe'o Gulch
Kipahulu
Molokini Crater
'Ahihi-Kina'u Natural Area Reserve
Kaupo
Lua Makika (1477ft)
La Pérouse Bay
Kaho'olawe
0 20 km
0 12 miles
LANA'I, MOLOKA'I, KAHO'OLAWE & MAUI

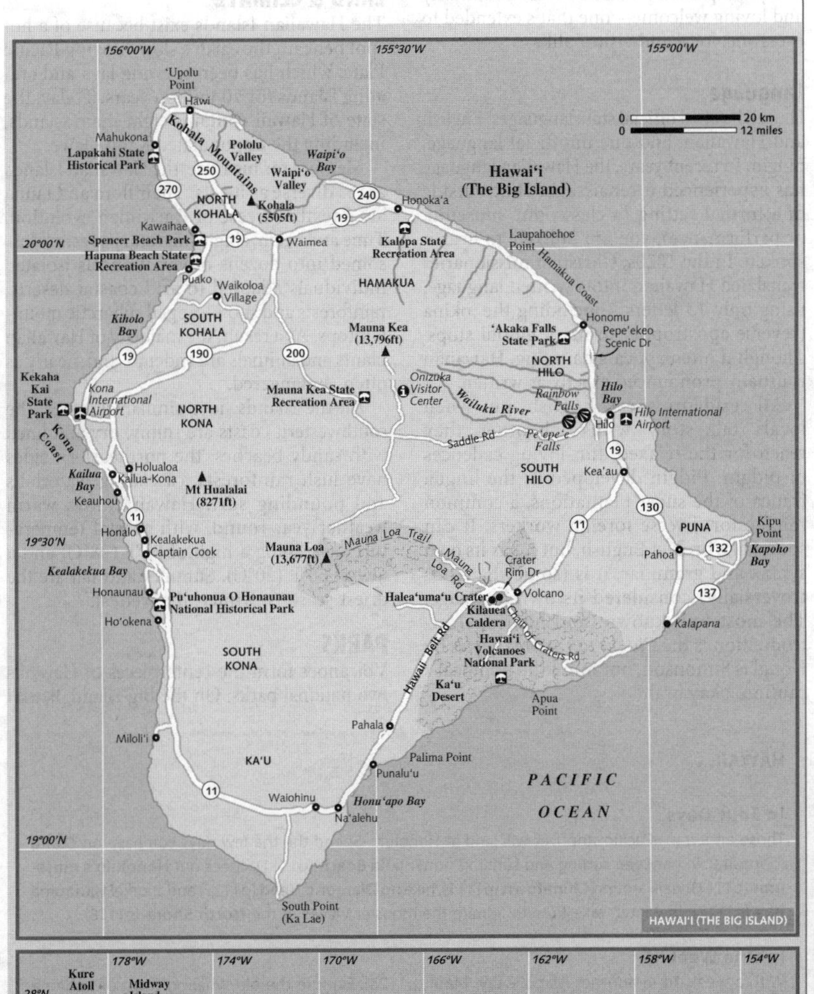
HAWAI'I (THE BIG ISLAND)
Hawai'i
(The Big Island)
156°00'W
155°30'W
155°00'W
20°00'N
19°30'N
19°00'N
0 20 km
0 12 miles
'Upolu Point
Hawi
Mahukona
Lapakahi State Historical Park
Kohala Mountains
Pololu Valley
Waipi'o Bay
Waipi'o Valley
NORTH KOHALA
Kohala (5505ft)
Honoka'a
Kawaihae
Spencer Beach Park
Waimea
Kalopa State Recreation Area
Hapuna Beach State Recreation Area
Laupahoehoe Point
Hamakua Coast
Puako
HAMAKUA
Waikoloa Village
Kiholo Bay
SOUTH KOHALA
Mauna Kea (13,796ft)
Honomu
'Akaka Falls State Park
Pepe'ekeo Scenic Dr
NORTH HILO
Kekaha Kai State Park
Kona International Airport
NORTH KONA
Mauna Kea State Recreation Area
Onizuka Visitor Center
Wailuku River
Rainbow Falls
Hilo Bay
Hilo International Airport
Hilo
Kona Coast
Saddle Rd
Pe'epe'e Falls
Kailua Bay
Holualoa
Kailua-Kona
Keauhou
Mt Hualalai (8271ft)
SOUTH HILO
Kea'au
Honalo
Kealakekua
Captain Cook
PUNA
Kipu Point
Mauna Loa Trail
Mauna Loa (13,677ft)
Mauna Loa Rd
Crater Rim Dr
Pahoa
Kapoho Bay
Kealakekua Bay
Honaunau
Pu'uhonua O Honaunau National Historical Park
Halea'uma'u Crater
Volcano
Kilauea Caldera
Ho'okena
Chain of Craters Rd
Kalapana
Hawai'i Volcanoes National Park
SOUTH KONA
Hawaii Belt Rd
Ka'u Desert
Apua Point
Pahala
Miloli'i
Palima Point
KA'U
Punalu'u
PACIFIC OCEAN
Waiohinu
Honu'apo Bay
Na'alehu
South Point (Ka Lae)
178°W
174°W
170°W
166°W
162°W
158°W
154°W
28°N
24°N
20°N
Kure Atoll
Midway Island
Pearl and Hermes Atoll
Lisianski Island
Maro Reef
Laysan Island
Gardner Pinnacles
Tern Island
Necker Island
French Frigate Shoals
Tropic of Cancer
Nihoa Island
Main Hawaiian Islands
Kaua'i
Ni'ihau
O'ahu
Moloka'i
Lana'i
Maui
Kaho'olawe
Hawai'i (The Big Island)
0 400 km
0 250 miles

everyday practice of openness, hospitality and loving welcome – one that's extended to everyone, local and visitor alike.

Language

Hawaii has two official state languages, English and Hawaiian, and one unofficial language, pidgin. In recent years, the Hawaiian language has experienced a renaissance, but outside of a formal setting (a classroom, museum, or performance), you are unlikely to hear it spoken. In the 1820s, Christian missionaries translated Hawaiian into a written language, using only 13 letters – including the ʻokina (reverse apostrophe) to mark glottal stops. Though it often appears daunting, Hawaiian is usually pronounced exactly as written.

All residents speak English, but when locals 'talk story' with each other, they reach for the relaxed, fun-loving cadences of pidgin. Pidgin developed as the lingua franca of the sugar plantations, a common tongue for diverse foreign workers. It can sound like broken English, but it has its own syntax and grammar; it is (somewhat controversially) considered its own language. The most well-known (and hilarious) introduction is the *Pidgin to Da Max* series by Douglas Simonson, but mind the nonlocal's caution, okay brah?

LAND & CLIMATE

The Hawaiian Islands exist because of a hot spot beneath the earth's slow-moving Pacific Plate, which has been spewing lava and creating islands for 70 million years. Today, the state of Hawaii contains eight main islands, including the unpopulated Kahoʻolawe.

Measure for measure, the Hawaiian Islands are as diverse as it gets. Their flora and fauna are a textbook case of Darwinian evolution. Time and again, single migratory species blossomed into dozens of variations as isolated individuals adapted to arid coastal deserts, rainforests and snow-capped subarctic mountaintops. As a result, the majority of Hawaiian plants and animals are endemic and, nearly as often, endangered.

All the islands have similar climates: the southwestern coasts are sunny, dry and lined with sandy beaches; the northeastern sides have lush rainforests, cascading waterfalls and pounding surf. Hawaii enjoys warm weather year-round, with coastal temperatures averaging a high of 83°F (28°C) and a low of 68°F (20°C). Summer and fall are the driest seasons; winter, the wettest.

PARKS

Volcanoes form the centerpieces of Hawaii's two national parks. On the Big Island, **Hawaiʻi**

HAWAII…

In Four Days

Those on a trans-Pacific stopover will land at Honolulu. Spend the the few days you have on **O'ahu** (opposite). In between surfing and sunning on **Waikiki Beach** (p1111), check out **Honolulu's museums** (p1111), walk around **Chinatown** (p1111), hike up **Diamond Head** (p1117) and snorkel **Hanauma Bay** (p1117). In winter, take time to admire the monster waves of the **North Shore** (p1118).

In One Week

With a week, fit in another island – say, **Maui** (p1123). Explore the old whaling town of **Lahaina** (p1123), head to **Haleakalā National Park** (p1127) to see the sunrise above the crater, take a **whale-watching cruise** (see boxed text, p1125), snorkel **Molokini Crater** (p1125) and drive the **Road to Hana** (see boxed text, p1126).

In Two Weeks

With two weeks, be more leisurely and visit two or three islands. If you choose the **Big Island** (p1118), visit the ancient Hawaiian **Pu'uhonua O Honaunau National Historical Park** (p1119), lounge on **Gold Coast beaches** (see boxed text, p1121), catch the farmers market and museums in **Hilo** (p1121), and say aloha to Pele at **Hawai'i Volcanoes National Park** (p1122). If you choose to visit **Kaua'i** (p1127), kayak the **Wailua River** (p1127), hike **Waimea Canyon** and **Koke'e State Park** (p1129), surf **Hanalei Bay** (p1128), snorkel **Ke'e Beach** (p1128) and don't miss hiking the **Kalalau Trail** on the Na Pali Coast (p1128).

Volcanoes National Park (p1122) contains two active volcanoes and a wondrous collection of landscapes, from lava deserts to rainforests to freezing mountaintops. Maui's **Haleakalā National Park** (p1127) focuses on Haleakalā Crater, which so resembles the lunar surface that astronauts have trained there.

Hawaii's many state parks range from beachfront sites with full facilities to undeveloped wilderness. For more information and to make camping reservations, contact the **Division of State Parks** (Map p1112; ☎ 808-587-0300; www.hawaiistateparks.org; 1151 Punchbowl St, Honolulu). The state-sponsored **Na Ala Hele** (Map p1110; ☎ 808-587-0300; www.hawaiitrails.org) has hiking-trail information.

INFORMATION

For in-depth coverage of the islands, see Lonely Planet's *Hawaii* guide.

Hawaii Ecotourism Association (www.hawaiieco tourism.org) This nonprofit certifies and lists businesses committed to ecotourism.

Hawaii Visitors & Convention Bureau (www.go hawaii.com) The state's official tourism site.

GETTING THERE & AROUND

Honolulu International Airport (HNL; Map p1110; ☎ 808-836-6413; www.honoluluairport.com) is a major Pacific air hub and an intermediate stop on many flights between the US mainland and Asia, Australia and the South Pacific. From Europe, ask about an add-on fare from the US West Coast or perhaps a round-the-world ticket (p1155). From the US mainland, the cheapest fares often start at around $700 from the east coast and $400 from California. Most major US airlines fly to Honolulu, Maui and the Big Island.

Hawaiian Airlines (☎ 800-367-5320; www.hawaii anair.com) and **go!** (☎ 888-435-9462; www.iflygo.com) are the main carriers flying between the Hawaiian Islands. Service is frequent and flight times are short. One-way fares to/from Honolulu can be as low as $40, but other interisland flights typically run $70 to $90.

Standard ferry services connect Maui to Lana'i and Moloka'i. The high-speed Hawaii Superferry, connecting Honolulu and Maui, shut down in 2009 (due to legal troubles).

O'ahu is the only island that can be explored extensively by public bus. Maui, the Big Island and Kaua'i have infrequent bus services between major towns and very limited service to sightseeing destinations.

Rental cars are widely available on all the main islands, and typically begin around $30 to $40 a day and $130 to $170 a week. It's wise to book a car before arrival.

Specialized tours include whale-watching cruises, bicycle tours, snorkeling trips, overnight tours and helicopter tours. All can be booked after arrival in Hawaii. On the larger islands, half- and full-day sightseeing bus tours are available for $60 to $100; the largest companies are **Discover Hawaii Tours** (☎ 800-946-4432; www.discoverhawaiitours.com), **Roberts Hawaii** (☎ 866-898-2519; www.robertshawaii .com), and **Polynesian Adventure Tours** (☎ 800-622-3011; www.polyad.com).

O'AHU

O'ahu is preeminent among Hawaii's islands – so much so that the others are referred to as 'Neighbor Islands.' O'ahu is the center of Hawaii's government, commerce and culture. It's home to three-quarters of state residents, and it's the destination of two-thirds of all visitors. Honolulu is one of the nation's major cities, and its nearby Waikiki beaches gave birth to the whole tiki-craze Hawaii fantasia. If you want to take the measure of diverse Hawaii, O'ahu offers the full buffet in one tidy package: in the blink of an eye you can go from crowded metropolis to remote turquoise bays teeming with sea life. Known as 'the gathering place,' O'ahu is the USA's best combination of urban living, natural beauty and rural community.

Getting There & Around

O'ahu's extensive public bus system, **TheBus** (☎ 808-848-5555; www.thebus.org; Kalihi Transit Center, 811 Middle St), has some 80 routes that collectively cover most of O'ahu; all fares are $2. From Honolulu International Airport to Waikiki, take bus 19 or 20. Buses 2, 19 and 20 connect Waikiki with downtown Honolulu and Chinatown. Another option for getting between Honolulu and Waikiki is the **Waikiki Trolley** (☎ 808-593-2822; www.waikikitrolley.com; all-day pass adult/child $30/14). See also left.

HONOLULU & WAIKIKI

Among its many museums and cultural offerings, Honolulu has the only royal palace in the USA, and it is a foodie heaven of cheap noodle joints and fancy Pacific Rim cuisine.

Saunter over to gorgeous Waikiki to lounge on the sand, play in the water and listen to splendid Hawaii music in the evening.

Orientation & Information

Honolulu International Airport (Map p1110) is on the outskirts of Honolulu; airport buses pass through Honolulu's city center on their way to Waikiki. Diamond Head, the extinct volcano looming above the eastern side of Waikiki, is such a major landmark that islanders typically say 'go Diamond Head' when they give directions.

BOOKSTORES

Bestsellers (Map p1113; ☎ 808-953-2378; Hilton Hawaiian Village, 2005 Kalia Rd, Waikiki; 🕑 8am-10pm)

Native Books/Nā Mea Hawai'i (Map p1110; ☎ 597-8967; www.nativebookshawaii.com; Ward Warehouse, 1050 Ala Moana Blvd, Honolulu; 🕑 10am-9pm Mon-Sat, 10am-7pm Sun) Specializes in Hawaiiana books and hosts cultural performances and classes.

INTERNET ACCESS

Kuhio Ave has internet shops; average surfing costs $6 to $12 an hour.

Hawaii State Library (Map p1112; ☎ 586-3500; www.librarieshawaii.org; 478 S King St; 🕑 10am-5pm Mon & Wed, 9am-5pm Tue, Fri & Sat, 9am-8pm Thu) A temporary visitor card ($10) allows free internet access at any branch.

MEDIA

Honolulu Advertiser (www.honoluluadvertiser.com) Hawaii's largest daily newspaper.

Honolulu Star-Bulletin (www.starbulletin.com) Honolulu's other daily newspaper.

KINE (105.1 FM) Hawaiian music.

MEDICAL SERVICES

Longs Drugs (Map p1110; ☎ 808-949-4781, pharmacy 808-947-2651; www.longs.com; 2220 S King St, Honolulu; 🕑 24hr) Honolulu has numerous Longs with varying hours.

Queen's Medical Center (Map p1110; ☎ 808-538-9011; www.queensmedicalcenter.net; 1301 Punchbowl St, Honolulu; 🕑 24hr) A major full-service hospital.

MONEY

These banks have island-wide branches.

Bank of Hawaii (Map p1113; ☎ 808-543-6900, 888-643-3888; www.boh.com; 2155 Kalakaua Ave, Waikiki)

First Hawaiian Bank (Map p1112; ☎ 808-525-6888; www.fhb.com; 2 N King St, Honolulu)

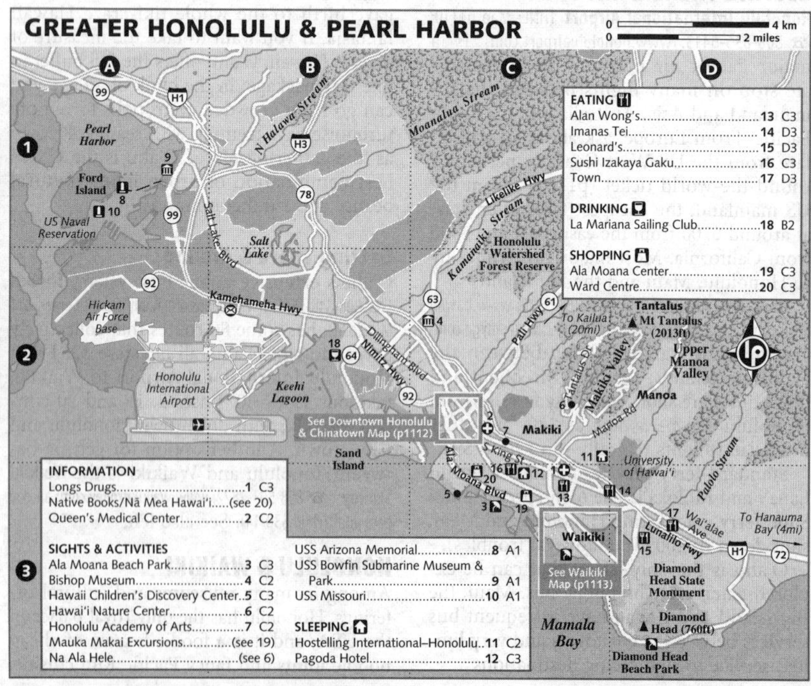

POST

Post office Downtown (Map p1112; ☎ 800-275-8777; 335 Merchant St); Waikiki (Map p1113; ☎ 800-275-8777; 330 Saratoga Rd)

TOURIST INFORMATION

Hawaii Visitors & Convention Bureau (Map p1113; ☎ 808-923-1811, 800-464-2924; www.gohawaii.com; Waikiki Shopping Plaza, 2270 Kalakaua Ave, Suite 801)
O'ahu Visitors Bureau (☎ 877-525-6248; www.visit-oahu.com) Stock up on brochures at the airport counter.

Sights & Activities

DOWNTOWN HONOLULU

At the heart of downtown Honolulu, the 19th-century **'Iolani Palace** (Map p1112; ☎ 808-522-0832; www.iolanipalace.org; cnr S King & Richards Sts; tours/gallery only $20/6; 9am-5pm Tue-Sat, guided tour 9-11:15am, self-guided audio tour 11:45am-3:30pm) offers a unique glimpse of Hawaii's intriguing history. At the adjacent, postmodern **State Capitol** (Map p1112), visitors can wander through the rotunda without charge. Built of coral slabs, the nearby 1842 **Kawaiaha'o Church** (Map p1112; ☎ 808-522-1333; 957 Punchbowl St; admission free; 8am-4pm Mon-Fri) is O'ahu's oldest church.

A central piece of the island art scene, the **Hawai'i State Art Museum** (Map p1112; ☎ 808-586-0900; www.hawaii.gov/sfca; 250 S Hotel St; admission free; 10am-4pm Tue-Sat) showcases the work of Hawaiian artists.

CHINATOWN

Immediately north of downtown Honolulu, Chinatown is an intriguing quarter that lends itself to exploring. Bring an appetite since grazing the superb Asian food is a prime activity as you wander among the herbalists, temples and tattoo parlors. Get started at the colorful **O'ahu Market** (Map p1112; cnr Kekaulike & N King Sts) – the bustling heart of Chinatown for more than a century. For a bizarro-tropical escape, visit Chinatown's overwhelming **Foster Botanical Garden** (Map p1112; ☎ 522-7066; www.co.honolulu.hi.us/parks/hbg/fbg.htm; 180 N Vineyard Blvd; adult/child 6-12yr $5/1; 9am-4pm, guided tour usually 1pm Mon-Sat).

BE YOUR OWN TOUR GUIDE

No car? No worries, brah! Make a fun, easy day excursion circling the island by public bus. Routes 52 and 55 combine, taking you in four nonstop hours from Honolulu's Ala Moana Center, up H1 to Haleiwa, past the North Shore, down the Windward Coast, and back to Honolulu via the Pali Hwy. Stop as many times as you like and simply catch the next bus; they run every 30 to 60 minutes daily. Each ride costs $2, or buy a four-day visitor pass ($20) and have unlimited usage for a multiday trip. What a deal!

WAIKIKI

Waikiki is all about that loooong beach. Catamarans and outriggers pull up onto the sand offering rides, and concession stands rent surfboards, boogie boards, kayaks and windsurfing gear at reasonable prices. If you need just a *little* help perfecting your technique, lessons are readily available.

GREATER HONOLULU

Bishop Museum (Map p1110; ☎ 808-847-3511; www.bishopmuseum.org; 1525 Bernice St; adult/child $16/13; 9am-5pm Wed-Sun) is considered the finest Polynesian anthropological museum in the world. Impressive cultural displays include the newly refurbished, epic Hawaiian Hall, while the Science Adventure Center puts you inside an erupting volcano.

The exceptional **Honolulu Academy of Arts** (Map p1110; ☎ 808-532-8700; www.honoluluacademy.org; 900 S Beretania St; adult/child $10/free; 10am-4:30pm Tue-Sat, 1-5pm Sun) has must-see collections of Asian, European and Pacific art.

Several hiking trails offer sweeping city views in the Tantalus area, the lush Upper Manoa and Makiki Valleys, and the hills above the University of Hawai'i. Some trailheads are accessible by bus. Run by the state Division of Forestry & Wildlife, **Na Ala Hele** (Map p1110; ☎ 808-973-9782; www.hawaiitrails.org; 2135 Makiki Heights Dr; 7:45am-4:30pm Mon-Fri) distributes free trail maps.

For a great place to swim without the tourist crowds, head to **Ala Moana Beach Park** (Map p1110; 1201 Ala Moana Blvd), between downtown and Waikiki.

Honolulu & Waikiki for Children

O'ahu spills over with activities for *keiki* (children). While the above-average **Honolulu Zoo** (Map p1113; ☎ 808-971-7171; www.honoluluzoo.org; 151 Kapahulu Ave; adult/child $8/1; 9am-4:30pm) is worth a look, the nearby **Waikiki Aquarium** (☎ 808-923-9741; www.waquarium.org; 2777 Kalakaua Ave; adult/child $9/2; 9am-4:30pm) will knock your

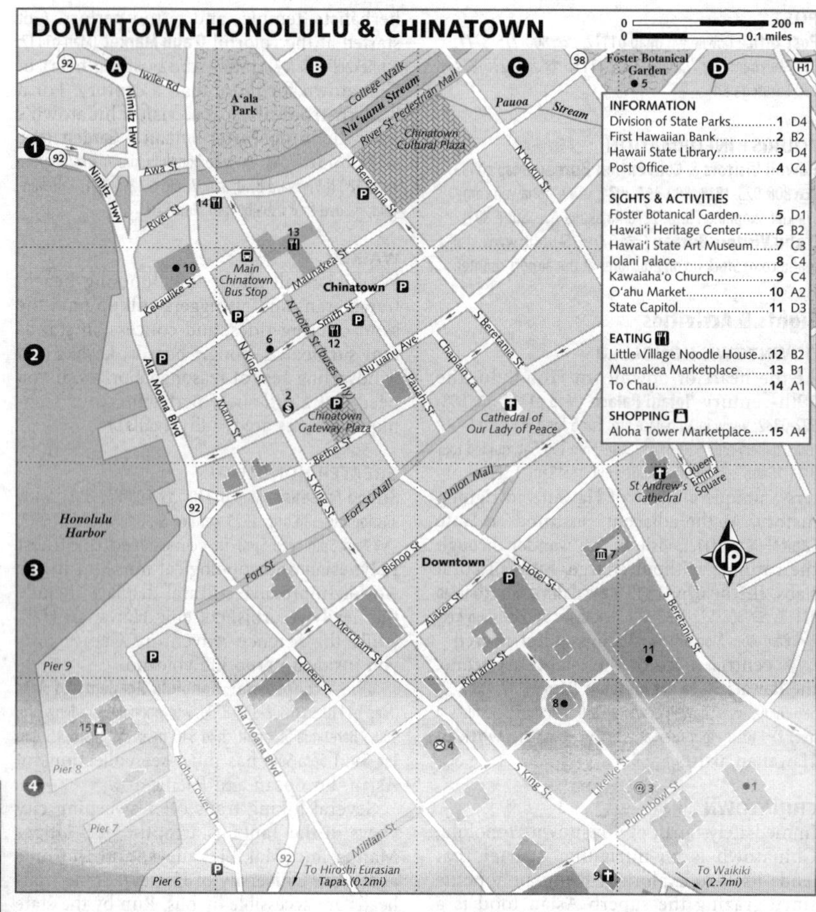

socks off, with fantastic exhibits and hands-on touch tanks.

The kid-centered **Hawai'i Nature Center** (Map p1110; ☎ 808-955-0100; www.hawaiinaturecenter.org; 2131 Makiki Heights Dr;) conducts family programs and hikes on most weekends; see the website for a schedule.

Of course, what kid doesn't love Waikiki Beach? When the sun fails to shine, the hands-on **Hawaii Children's Discovery Center** (Map p1110; ☎ 808-524-5437; www.discoverycenterhawaii.org; 111 'Ohe St; admission $10; 9am-1pm Tue-Fri, 10am-3pm Sat & Sun;) is a perfect let-'em-loose kind of place.

Tours

For something more interesting than the typical bus tour, try the following.

Hawaii Food Tours (☎ 808-926-3663; www.hawaiifoodtours.com; tours $100-200) From holes-in-the-wall to gourmet temples.

Hawai'i Heritage Center (Map p1112; ☎ 808-521-2749; 1117 Smith St; tours $10; 9:30-11:30am Wed & Fri) Chinatown walking tours.

Mauka Makai Excursions (☎ 866-896-0596; www.hawaiianecotours.net; 350 Ward Ave, Ste 106; tours $52-85) Hawaiian-run cultural ecotours; some hiking.

Festivals & Events

In April, the only-in-Hawaii **Waikiki Spam Jam** (www.spamjamhawaii.com) is a rhapsodic celebration of canned meat. **King Kamehameha Celebration** (☎ 808-586-0333), a state holiday in early June, includes festivities at 'Iolani Palace. Across the state from September into

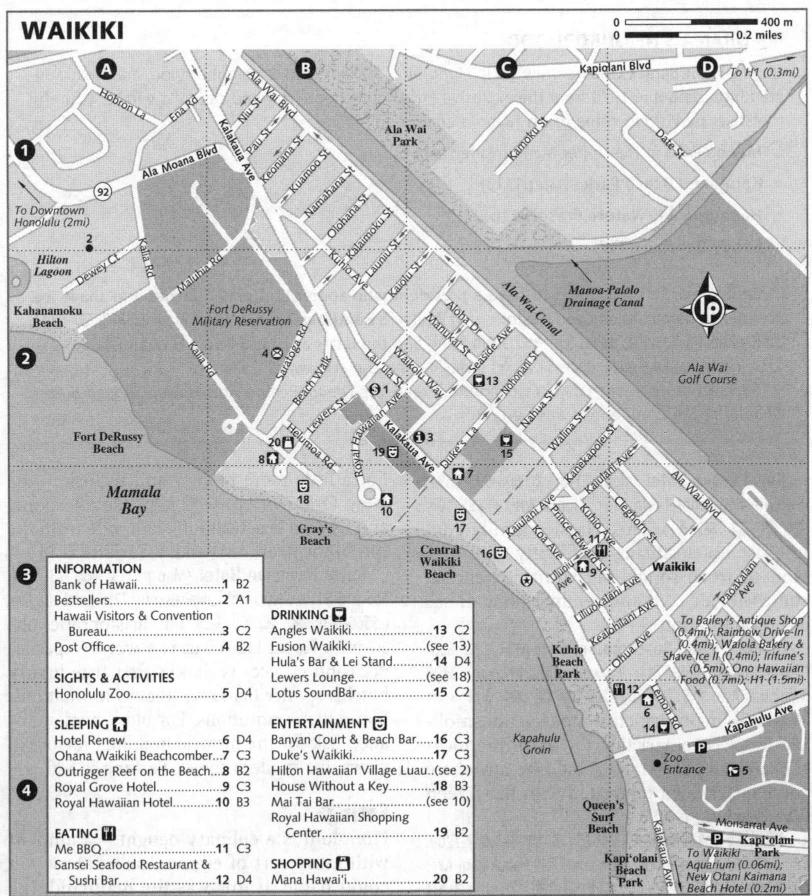

October, **Aloha Festivals** (http://alohafestivals.com) inspires two months of cultural performances and celebrations. The North Shore comes alive for the **Triple Crown of Surfing** (http://triplecrownofsuring.com) from November to December. For much more, see www.gohawaii.com.

Sleeping

As a rule, the best selection of hotels is in Waikiki, while Honolulu has far better eats.

HONOLULU

Hostelling International–Honolulu (Map p1110; ☎ 946-0591; www.hostelsaloha.com; 2323-A Seaview Ave; dm $20-23, r $50-56; reception 8am-noon & 4pm-midnight; P) This small, tidy hostel is in a residential neighborhood near the university, a short bus ride from Waikiki. There are sex-segregated dorms, plus kitchen, laundry and lockers.

Pagoda Hotel (Map p1110; ☎ 808-923-4511, 800-472-4632; www.pagodahotel.com; 1525 Rycroft St; r from $125, 1br from $155; P) Adorably kitschy or just outdated? Either way, it's a popular, good-value alternative to hectic Waikiki, with 12 floors of comfortable, no-frills rooms. Parking is $5.

WAIKIKI

Waikiki is the center of the action, and Kalakaua Ave, the main beachfront strip, is lined with swanky high-rise hotels. That idyllic location comes at a price; for better value, look off the beach and along Kuhio Ave.

MR OBAMA'S NEIGHBORHOOD

US President Barack Obama grew up in Honolulu's Makiki Heights neighborhood, and he graduated high school in 1979 from the exclusive Punahou School. Now you can follow in his youthful footsteps by visiting some of his favorite childhood places:

- **Manoa Falls** in the Upper Manoa Valley (p1111)
- **Kapi'olani Beach Park** (Map p1113)
- **Hanauma Bay Nature Preserve** (p1117)
- **Sandy Beach** (p1117)

If nothing else, it's refreshing to have a president who appreciates plate lunches and shave ice. President Obama has enjoyed the former at Waikiki's **Rainbow Drive-In** (off Map p1113; 808-737-0177; cnr Kapahulu & Kanaina; dishes $5; 7:30am-9pm), and the latter at **Island Snow Hawaii** (808-263-6339; 130 Kailua Rd, Kailua; items $4-7; 10am-7pm) on the Windward Coast.

To learn more about Obama's childhood, read *The Dream Begins: How Hawaii Shaped Barack Obama* by Stu Glauberman and Jerry Burris.

Royal Grove Hotel (Map p1113; 808-923-7691; www.royalgrovehotel.com; 161 Uluniu Ave; r $55-100;) This classic, family-run, low-rise hotel satisfies the thrifty with spacious if worn rooms (all with kitchenette, some with air-con) and genuine aloha. It has a central location.

Ohana Waikiki Beachcomber (Map p1113; 808-922-4646, 866-968-8744; www.ohanahotels.com; 2300 Kalakaua Ave; r $120-230;) On Waikiki's main strip, this modern nonsmoking hotel is remarkable for its prime location and subprime rates. Could-be-anywhere rooms have been renovated with flat-screen TVs. Parking is $18.

our pick **Hotel Renew** (Map p1113; 808-687-7700, 888-485-7639; www.hotelrenew.com; 129 Paoakalani Ave; r incl breakfast $160-225;) Just a half block from the beach, this ecoconscious, gay-friendly boutique hotel satisfies sophisticated urbanites nursing romantic island dreams. There are only 72 stylish, design-savvy rooms, attentive staff and lots of little niceties. Parking is $22.

Outrigger Reef on the Beach (Map p1113; 923-3111, 866-956-4262; www.outriggerreef.com; 2169 Kalia Rd; r $160-375, 1br from $270;) Looking sharp after a recent remodel, this Outrigger eschews the hoity-toity attitudes of its higher-priced beachfront neighbors. Enjoy atmospheric Hawaiiana – from the handmade outrigger canoe to free hula classes – and modern, functional rooms. Parking is $25.

New Otani Kaimana Beach Hotel (off Map p1113; 808-923-1555, 800-356-8264; www.kaimana.com; 2863 Kalakaua Ave; r $190-440, ste $340-920;) For a little more privacy and seclusion, the New Otani offers well-kept, small rooms and its own beach about a half mile from the throbbing heart of Waikiki. Parking is $18.

Royal Hawaiian Hotel (Map p1113; 923-7311, 866-716-8110; www.royal-hawaiian.com; 2259 Kalakaua Ave; r $560-920;) The aristocratic, oh-so-pink Royal Hawaiian is a worthy special-occasion choice. Waikiki's first true luxury hotel is spiffier than ever, thanks to multimillion-dollar renovations. For old-school ambiance, ask for the historic building; for ocean views, the modern tower. Parking is $20.

Eating

Honolulu is a culinary delight – abundant with every sort of ethnic Asian eatery you could name. If this was the mainland, the scene would get much more press.

HONOLULU

Maunakea Marketplace (Map p1112; 1120 Maunakea St; meals $5; 7am-3:30pm) This Chinatown food court serves the ultimate local grinds, with mom-and-pop vendors whipping up home-style Chinese, Filipino and Thai fare.

To Chau (Map p1112; 808-533-4549; 1007 River St; soups $5-8; 8:30am-2:30pm) This Chinatown staple makes Honolulu's best *pho*, a delicious, steamy Vietnamese soup spiced with heaps of fresh basil and tasty extras.

Little Village Noodle House (Map p1112; 808-545-3008; 1113 Smith St; mains $7-15; 10:30am-10:30pm Sun-Thu, to midnight Fri & Sat) A quiet, air-conditioned restaurant in Chinatown? That's only the beginning. The kitchen sets a gold stand-

HAWAII

ard, particularly for black-bean sauce and noodles.

Imanas Tei (Map p1110; ☎ 808-941-2626; 2626 S King St; plates $5-30; ⏰ 5-11:30pm Mon-Sat) At this top-rated *izakaya* (a Japanese pub serving food), enjoy world-class sake while grazing on delectable sushi and crowd-pleasing *nabemono* (do-it-yourself meat and vegetable soups).

Sushi Izakaya Gaku (Map p1110; ☎ 589-1329; 1329 S King St; plates $8-25; ⏰ 5-11pm Mon-Sat) Another wildly popular *izakaya*, near the university, Gaku plates traditional, supremely fresh sushi and hard-to-find specialties like *chazuke* (tea-soaked rice porridge) and *natto* (fermented soybeans). Reservations are recommended.

Hiroshi Eurasian Tapas (off Map p1112; ☎ 808-533-4476; www.hiroshihawaii.com; 500 Ala Moana Blvd; plates $15-25; ⏰ 5:30-9:30pm) The Honolulu culinary scene is all about East–West fusions, and chef Hiroshi Fukui adds his own personal stamp with his subtle, unlikely, unforgettable creations.

Town (Map p1110; ☎ 735-5900; www.townkaimuki.com; 3435 Wai'alae Ave at 9th Ave; mains lunch $6-15, dinner $15-22; ⏰ 6:30-9:30pm Mon-Thu, 6:30am-10pm Fri & Sat) Laid-back locavores love the Mediterranean-inspired cuisine at Town. Leave your attitude at the door, be patient (it helps), and enjoy coffee-shop gourmet with the occasional *Lost* cast member.

our pick **Alan Wong's** (Map p1110; ☎ 949-2526; www.alanwongs.com; 1857 S King St; mains $27-52; ⏰ 5-10pm) Celebrity chef Alan Wong continues to redefine classic Pacific Rim and Hawaii Regional cuisine with flare, whimsy and farm-to-table freshness. You can't miss with signature dishes like ginger-crusted snapper and twice-cooked *kalbi* short ribs. Reservations are essential.

WAIKIKI

Leonard's (Map p1110; ☎ 808-737-5591; 933 Kapahulu Ave; pastries 75¢-$2; ⏰ 6am-9pm Mon-Thu, 6am-10pm Fri & Sat) This classic Portuguese bakery is famous for *malasadas*, an addictive, spongy, often-cream-filled donut. Try coconut cream; you'll be hooked.

Waiola Bakery & Shave Ice II (☎ 808-735-8886; 525 Kapahulu Ave; snacks $2-4; ⏰ 7:30am-6pm) For a lesson in shave ice, Waiola is the place. The superfine ice and the add-ons set it apart: try azuki beans, condensed milk, *mochi* (sticky-sweet Japanese-pounded rice cakes) and island-style *li hing mui* crack seed.

Me BBQ (Map p1113; ☎ 808-926-9717; 151 Uluniu Ave; plate meals $4-12; ⏰ 7am-9pm Mon-Sat) This hole-in-the-wall Korean takeout counter delivers the goods fast and plentiful. Order a plate lunch, grab some napkins and take it to the beach.

Ono Hawaiian Food (☎ 808-737-2275; 726 Kapahulu Ave; meals $12-16; ⏰ 11am-8pm Mon-Sat) A legendary destination for traditional Hawaiian dishes and local grinds – get a combo plate, but don't miss the *kalua* pig.

Sansei Seafood Restaurant & Sushi Bar (Map p1113; ☎ 808-931-6286; http://sanseihawaii.com; 3rd fl, Marriott Resort, 2552 Kalakaua Ave; mains $16-35; ⏰ 5:30-10pm Sun-Thu, 5:30pm-1am Fri & Sat) Chef DK Kodama's 'new wave sushi' is a certified hit, playfully dribbling truffled sauces, deep-frying panko-crusted rolls and adding Dungeness crab to simmering ramen. The torch-lit veranda enjoys prime sunset views.

EATING HAWAII: LOCAL GRINDS & HAWAII REGIONAL CUISINE

Hawaii is a feast for the senses, and that includes your palate. For two decades, 'Hawaii Regional Cuisine' has referred to Hawaii's robust, distinctive gourmet fusion of Pacific Rim flavors. Once this meant seared *'ahi* and macadamia-crusted mahimahi, a dash of *shōyu* and a *liliko'i* glaze. Today, it means menus built almost exclusively around the bounty of organic, locally grown produce, sustainably harvested seafood and island ranches. It's a 21st-century amalgam of locavore politics and international inspirations that can reach far beyond the Pacific Rim. Mix Spanish tapas and sushi? Burritos, backyard mangoes, and *kalua* pork? *Por que no?*

In everyday life, though, Hawaii lives on 'local grinds,' a catch-all pigdin term for the satisfying comfort foods of the state's polyglot cultures. Local grinds include Native Hawaiian favorites such as *kalua* pork (roasted pig in an underground oven), *laulau* (savory meats wrapped in steamed taro leaves), and poi (mashed taro). It includes endless varieties of *poke*, or seasoned, raw fish. It's a morning *loco moco* (rice, two fried eggs, hamburger patty, and gravy) followed by an afternoon plate lunch (fried or grilled meat, 'two-scoops rice,' and potato-macaroni salad). It's Japanese *saimin* (egg noodles in broth), Chinese crack seed (preserved fruit), and a classic, rainbow-hued, melon-sized, postswim shave ice.

Drinking & Entertainment

BARS & NIGHTCLUBS

The free *Honolulu Weekly* (www.honolulu-weekly.com) has full details on bars, clubs and entertainment. The hippest nightlife scene is around N Hotel St and Nu'uanu Ave in Chinatown, which was once a notorious red-light district.

Lewers Lounge (Map p1113; ☎ 808-923-2311; Halekulani Hotel, 2199 Kalia Rd; music 7:30pm-1am) This sophisticated lounge is old-school Waikiki, with top-shelf, fresh-juice cocktails and smooth live jazz music.

La Mariana Sailing Club (Map p1110; ☎ 808-848-2800; 50 Sand Island Access Rd; 11am-10pm Sun-Thu, 11am-midnight Fri & Sat) They don't make kitschy 1950s tiki bars like this anymore – and who knows how long this one will last? Grab a waterfront table, order a mai tai with tiki-head swizzle stick, and dream.

Lotus SoundBar (Map p1113; ☎ 808-924-1688; Waikiki Town Center, 2301 Kuhio Ave; cover $10-20; 9pm-2am Sun-Wed, 9pm-4am Thu-Sat) This nightclub has cutting-edge DJs spinning soulful hip-hop and chill-out grooves.

HAWAIIAN MUSIC & HULA

Waikiki has plenty of Hawaiian-style entertainment on offer.

our pick **Kuhio Beach Torch Lighting & Hula Show** (☎ 808-843-8002; www.honolulu.gov/moca; admission free; 6:30-7:30pm Tue, Thu & Sat;) Bask in the warm aloha with performances by local hula troupes at this city-sponsored show at Kuhio Beach Park (Map p1113).

Royal Hawaiian Shopping Center (Map p1113; ☎ 808-922-2299; 2201 Kalakaua Ave; 6pm Mon-Fri) Oddly enough, this shopping center hosts interesting Hawaiian music and hula performances on the 2nd floor and provides free weekday classes.

Hilton Hawaiian Village Luau (Map p1113; ☎ 808-941-5828; www.hiltonhawaiianvillage.com/luau; 2005 Kalia Rd; adult/child 4-11yr $95/48; 5:30-8:30pm Sun-Thu;) This beachside luau is a kitschy classic, with a huge buffet, mid-20th-century *hapa haole* hula, and high-energy fire twirlers.

Many beachfront hotels offer evening Hawaiian music and hula at their outdoor bars and restaurants. Head for these at sunset:

Banyan Court & Beach Bar (Map p1113; ☎ 808-921-4600; www.moana-surfrider.com; Moana Surfrider, 2365 Kalakaua Ave; 10:30am-midnight, live music 6-9pm) The famous *Hawaii Calls* radio show once broadcast under the banyan tree here; name musicians arrive on weekends.

Duke's Waikiki (Map p1113; ☎ 808-922-2268; www.dukeswaikiki.com; Outrigger Waikiki, 2335 Kalakaua Ave; 4pm-midnight, live music 4-6pm Fri-Sun) Duke's hosts a raucous, surf-themed party most nights, with the crowds for weekend concerts spilling onto the sand.

House Without a Key (Map p1113; ☎ 808-923-2311; www.halekulani.com; Halekulani Hotel, 2199 Kalia Rd; 7am-9pm, live music 5:30-8:30pm) At this classy open-air bar, catch live music and solo hula by two former Miss Hawaii pageant winners.

Mai Tai Bar (Map p1113; ☎ 808-923-7311; www.royal-hawaiian.com; Royal Hawaiian Hotel, 2259 Kalakaua Ave; 10:30am-12:30am, live music 6-10pm) The Royal Hawaiian's low-key bar includes a view to Diamond Head. Their signature mai tai packs a punch.

Shopping

our pick **Bailey's Antique Shop** (☎ 808-734-7628; 517 Kapahulu Ave; 10am-6pm) This famous mecca for vintage and used aloha shirts promises over 15,000 choices. You're guaranteed to find something memorable.

Mana Hawai'i (Map p1113; ☎ 808-923-2220; 2nd fl, Waikiki Beach Walk; 9am-10pm) This airy space offers authentic Hawaii-made products (eg woodcarving and bowls) as well as photos and books on Hawaii, and hosts classes in Hawaiian language, hula, lauhala weaving etc.

Honolulu's main shopping centers also have Hawaiian crafts, food and clothing:

GAY & LESBIAN WAIKIKI

Waikiki is the heart of Honolulu's well-developed gay scene. The free monthly magazine **Odyssey** (www.odysseyhawaii.com) has full details; visit also **Gay Hawaii** (www.gayhawaii.com). Queen's Surf Beach (Map p1113) is the destination for the sun-worshipping gay crowd.

Waikiki's top gay venue, **Hula's Bar & Lei Stand** (Map p1113; ☎ 808-923-0669; www.hulas.com; Waikiki Grand Hotel, 134 Kapahulu Ave; 10am-2am), is a cheery open-air bar with views of Diamond Head. Other good spots include **Angles Waikiki** (Map p1113; ☎ 808-926-9766; www.angleswaikiki.com; 2256 Kuhio Ave; 10am-2am), a bar by day and a nightclub after dark; and **Fusion Waikiki** (Map p1113; ☎ 808-924-2422; 2260 Kuhio Ave; 10pm-4am Sun-Thu, 8pm-4am Fri & Sat), which features karaoke and drag shows.

Ala Moana Center (Map p1110; ☎ 808-955-9517; www.alamoanacenter.com; 1450 Ala Moana Blvd; 9:30am-9pm Mon-Sat, 10am-7pm Sun)
Aloha Tower Marketplace (Map p1112; ☎ 808-528-5700; www.alohatower.com; 1 Aloha Tower Dr; 9am-9pm Mon-Sat, to 6pm Sun)
Ward Centre (Map p1110; ☎ 808-591-8411; www.wardcenters.com; Ward Ave; 10am-9pm Mon-Sat, to 6pm Sun) Adjacent to Ward Warehouse.

PEARL HARBOR

On December 7, 1941, a Japanese attack on Pearl Harbor took 2500 lives, sank 21 ships and fatefully catapulted the US into WWII. Today more than 1.5 million people a year 'remember Pearl Harbor' by visiting the **USS Arizona Memorial** (Map p1110).

The memorial sits directly over the sunken *Arizona;* visitors look down at the shallow wreck, still a tomb for 1177 sailors. The **visitors center** (☎ 808-422-0561; www.nps.gov/usar; Arizona Memorial Dr; admission & tour free; 7am-5pm) runs 1¼-hour tours that include a documentary film and a boat ride to the memorial. Tours run on a first-come, first-served basis; arrive early to beat the long queues. No purses, fanny packs or camera bags are allowed; the parking lot has storage ($3).

If you have to wait, walk to the adjacent **USS Bowfin Submarine Museum & Park** (Map p1110; ☎ 808-836-0317; www.bowfin.org; Arizona Memorial Dr; museum $5, submarine tours $10; 8am-5pm), poke around the WWII relics and clamber down into a retired submarine. Got more time? From the Bowfin, shuttles go to the **USS Missouri** (Map p1110; ☎ 877-644-4896; www.ussmissouri.org; tours $16; 9am-5pm) and the hangar-sized **Pacific Aviation Museum** (☎ 808-441-1000; www.pacificaviationmuseum.org; adult/child 4-12yr $14/7; 9am-5pm) on Ford Island (Map p1110). The Mighty Mo's deck hosted the Japanese surrender that ended WWII, while authentically restored planes including a Japanese Zero are on display at the museum.

From Waikiki, bus 42 goes to Pearl Harbor ($2) or take the **VIP Trans** (☎ 808-836-0317; http://viptrans.com; round-trip $11), which picks up from Waikiki hotels.

SOUTHEAST O'AHU

The southeast coast abounds in dramatic scenery and offers plenty of activities. For a sweeping view of the area, make the 1.5-mile climb up **Diamond Head** (Map p1110; Diamond Head Rd; per person/car $1/5; 6am-6pm), the 760ft extinct volcano that forms the famous backdrop to Waikiki.

The best place on O'ahu to go eyeball to eyeball with tropical fish is at **Hanauma Bay Nature Preserve** (☎ 808-396-4229; www.honolulu.gov/parks/facility/hanaumabay; Hwy 72; adult/child $5/free; 6am-7pm Wed-Mon Apr-Oct, to 6pm rest of yr), a gorgeous turquoise bathtub set in a rugged volcanic ring. For the best conditions, head to the outer reef; you can rent snorkel gear on-site. Parking costs $1.

Long and lovely **Sandy Beach**, along Hwy 72 about a mile north of Hanauma, offers very challenging bodysurfing with punishing shorebreaks, making it a favorite of pros – and exhilarating to watch!

From Waikiki, bus 22 ($2) stops at most southeast-area beaches.

WHAT THE...?

Craving a little Istanbul in the islands? Hawaii might be the last place you'd expect a show-stopping paean to Islamic art and architecture, but the stunning, graceful mansion of heiress Doris Duke is just that. Named **Shangri La** (☎ 866-385-3849; www.shangrilahawaii.org; 2½hr tour $25; usually 8:30am, 11am & 1:30pm Wed-Sat, closed Sep), it's open only for guided tours, which depart from the Honolulu Academy of Arts (p1111).

WINDWARD COAST

The deeply scalloped Ko'olau mountains form a scenic backdrop for the entire windward coast, where near-constant trade winds create ideal conditions for windsurfing.

The reef-protected **Waimanalo Bay** contains O'ahu's longest beach (5.5 miles of gleaming white sand), and it's great for swimming. From Hwy 72, make a detour south on Hwy 61 to reach the stunning panorama at **Nu'uanu Pali Lookout** (1200ft).

Beneath the windswept *pali* (cliffs) sits beautiful **Kailua Beach**, the island's top **windsurfing** spot. Just beyond the beach, the bird sanctuary of **Popoi'a Island** is a popular destination for kayakers. Gear rental and windsurfing lessons are available weekdays. **Kailua** has plenty of sleeping and eating options, and makes a good place to stay. For area B&Bs and condos, check with **Affordable Paradise** (☎ 808-261-1693; www.affordable-paradise.com).

Other notable beaches are the scenic **Kualoa Regional Park** and, further on, **Malaekahana Beach**, a marvelous spot for swimming, windsurfing and snorkeling, particularly at Goat Island, a near-shore bird sanctuary.

Run by the Mormon Church, the **Polynesian Cultural Center** (☎ 808-293-3333, 800-367-7060; www.polynesia.com; Hwy 83, La'ie; admission $60; ⏰ noon-9pm Mon-Sat) is a Polynesian theme park (and all that implies) with villages, performances and luau buffets. Only Pearl Harbor draws more visitors.

NORTH SHORE

O'ahu's North Shore is legendary for the massive 30ft winter swells that thunder against its beaches. In the 1960s, surfers first learned to ride these deadly waves, and today the North Shore hosts the world's most awesome surf competitions, particularly December's famed Triple Crown.

The gateway to the North Shore, **Hale'iwa** is the region's only real town – along its main road you'll find a funky surf museum, shops selling surfing paraphernalia, and rusty pickup trucks with surfboards tied to the roof. When the surf's up, folks really do drop everything to hit the waves. They don't have to go far: **Hale'iwa Ali'i Beach Park**, right in town, gets towering swells.

The North Shore's most popular beach, **Waimea Bay Beach Park**, in the town of Waimea, flaunts a dual personality. In summer the water can be as calm as a lake and ideal for swimming and snorkeling; in winter it rips with the island's highest waves.

Just north, the **Banzai Pipeline** breaks over a shallow reef, creating a death-defying ride for pros only. Next up is **Sunset Beach Park**, O'ahu's classic winter surf spot, famous for its incredible surf and tricky breaks; sunbathers favor the fit and fashionable.

Hale'iwa Joe's (☎ 808-637-8005; www.haleiwajoes.com; 66-011 Kamehameha Ave, Hale'iwa; lunch mains $9-18, dinner mains $15-30; ⏰ 11:30am-9:30pm), a North Shore institution, serves up hearty seafood-inspired meals. Emma's Poke (marinated raw *'ahi*) and coconut shrimp are favorites.

WAI'ANAE COAST

For a day-trip escape from Honolulu, explore the rural, underpopulated and sometimes impoverished Wai'anae Coast. **Makaha** has a fantastic beach with excellent surfing, and inland in the Makaha Valley is the beautifully restored **Kane'aki Heiau** (☎ 808-695-8174; admission free; ⏰ 10am-2pm Tue-Sun). At jagged **Ka'ena Point**, lovely windswept trails and a pretty beach offer a perfect perch for sunset.

HAWAI'I THE BIG ISLAND

Diverse in every way, and twice the size of the other Hawaiian Islands combined, the Big Island contains a whole continent's worth of adventures. Even more thrillingly, it's still growing. Of Hawai'i's two active volcanoes, Kilauea (p1122) has been erupting almost nonstop for the last 25 years. Along with red-hot lava, the Big Island offers stargazing from subarctic mountaintops, ancient Hawaiian places of refuge, an artistic working-class city, well-preserved plantation towns, horseback riding in cowboy country, rugged hikes and a full range of soporific beaches, from bone-white strands to green to tan to black and cratered with lava-rock tide pools.

Getting There & Around

Mainland flights arrive at both Kona and Hilo International **airports** (www6.hawaii.gov/dot/airports/hawaii); both have taxi stands and car-rental booths. The public bus system, **Hele-On** (☎ 808-961-8744; www.heleonbus.org), is free and circles the island, but has limited Monday-to-Saturday commuter-focused routes.

KAILUA-KONA

Kailua-Kona is the sort of overbright tourist town where you sit in open-air cafés and count sunburnt vacationers for amusement. But with sun-drenched beaches north and south and stacks of ocean-centric activities at hand, this condo-rich area makes a great base for wider explorations.

Sights & Activities

The grounds of King Kamehameha's Kona Beach Hotel at **Kamakahonu Beach** were once the site of Kamehameha the Great's royal residence. They include the restored **Ahu'ena Heiau**, a temple at which Kamehameha died in 1819.

Meander south on Ali'i Dr and visit the lava-rock **Moku'aikaua Church** (☎ 808-329-0655; www.mokuaikaua.org; Ali'i Dr; admission free; 8am-5pm), built in 1836 by Hawaii's first Christian missionaries. Across the street, and currently closed for renovations, **Hulihe'e Palace** (☎ 808-329-1877; www.daughtersofhawaii.org; 75-5718 Ali'i Dr; call for hr & admission) was a vacation spot for Hawaiian royalty and is packed with amazing Hawaiian artifacts. Several miles south of Kailua on Ali'i Dr, get sunning and bodysurfing at sparkling **White Sands Beach**. In Keauhou, **Kahalu'u Beach** offers fab snorkeling with sea turtles; gear rental is available.

Sleeping

For condos, check with **ATR Properties** (☎ 808-329-6020, 888-311-6020; www.konacondo.com) or **Kona Hawaii Vacation Rentals** (☎ 808-329-3333, 800-244-4752; www.konahawaii.com).

Koa Wood Hale Inn/Patey's Place (☎ 808-329-9663; www.alternative-hawaii.com/affordable/kona.htm; 75-184 Ala Ona Ona St; dm/s/d from $25/55/65; P) This well-managed, well-located hostel is Kona's best deal, with plain, quiet and clean dorms and private rooms.

Kona Tiki Hotel (☎ 808-329-1425; www.konatiki.com; 75-5968 Ali'i Dr; r $72-96;) It's all about the price, the location and the surf outside your window; rooms are straightforward but atmospheric to the max. Some have kitchenettes.

Royal Kona Resort (☎ 329-3111, reservations 800-222-5642; www.royalkona.com; 75-5852 Ali'i Dr; r $185-285, ste $300-430; P) Sporting '70s-era Polynesian kitsch, the Royal Kona is a Brady Bunch–style good time; the full-amenity hotel has attractive rooms, killer views and a classic tiki bar.

Eating

Island Lava Java (☎ 808-327-2161; 75-5799 Ali'i Dr; mains $8-20; 6am-10pm;) This local gathering spot provides that irresistible combo of good coffee, ocean breezes and internet access ($4 per 20 minutes).

Kanaka Kava (☎ 808-883-6260; www.kanakakava.com; Coconut Grove Marketplace, 75-5803 Ali'i Dr; kava $4, plates $13-16; 10am-10pm Sun-Wed, to 11pm Thu-Sat) Join locals for some mildly intoxicating kava (juice of the *'awa* plant) at this hidden counter; the well-made Hawaiian fare is fresh and tasty.

Big Island Grill (☎ 808-326-1153; 75-5702 Kuakini Hwy; plate lunches $10, mains $10-19; 6am-9pm Mon-Sat) Hawaiian-style home cooking draws everyone and their auntie to this beloved institution; look no farther than the plate lunches and loco mocos.

Kona Brewing Company (☎ 808-334-2739; www.konabrewingco.com; 75-5629 Kuakini Hwy; mains & pizza $11-26; 11am-9pm Sun-Thu, to 10pm Fri & Sat) The Big Island's first microbrewery makes top-notch ales with a Hawaiian touch. They also make great pizza, and their torchlit patio packs 'em in nightly; reserve ahead.

SOUTH KONA COAST

Linger along the verdant, romantic South Kona Coast for its fragrant coffee farms (see boxed text, p1120), ancient Hawaiian sites, colorful small towns and exquisite snorkeling.

A side road off Hwy 11 leads to the sparkling waters of mile-wide **Kealakekua Bay**. At the bay's northern end is Ka'awaloa Cove, where Captain Cook was killed and now the Big Island's premier **snorkeling** destination. You can hike to it, but it's far more fun to kayak (sometimes with dolphins). For kayak rentals and tours, try the Hawaiian-owned **Aloha Kayak Company** (☎ 808-322-2868, 877-322-1444; www.alohakayak.com; Hwy 11, Honalo; kayak rentals $35-60, half-day tours $65-160). For snorkel and dive cruises – and an epic, unforgettable nighttime manta-ray trip – try **Sea Paradise** (☎ 808-322-2500, 800-322-5662; www.seaparadise.com; adult/child snorkel cruise $99/59, manta snorkel $89/59).

South of Kealakekua Bay, the awesome **Pu'uhonua O Honaunau National Historical Park** (☎ 808-328-2288; www.nps.gov/puho; per car $5; 7am-8pm) is an ancient place of refuge – or *pu'uhonua*, a sanctuary where *kapu*-breakers could have their lives spared. The evocative grounds and temples are right next to a terrific snorkeling spot called 'Two-Step,' north of the park.

In Captain Cook, the 1917 **Manago Hotel** (☎ 808-323-2642; www.managohotel.com; 82-6155 Hwy 11; r without/with bath $36/64) is a classic experience: stay in the simple, well-kept roadhouse rooms and order the restaurant's signature pork chops.

our pick **Ka'awa Loa Plantation** (☎ 323-2686; www.kaawaloaplantation.com; 82-5990 Napo'opo'o Rd; r incl breakfast $125-145, ste $195, cottage $150;), a stylish, jungly estate with four-poster beds, outdoor shower and a view-licious lanai, is perfect for those wishing to indulge in romance.

Another window on local life is **Teshima Restaurant** (☎ 808-322-9140; Hwy 11; mains $13-23;

6:30am-1:45pm & 5-9pm), in Honalo. Families and immigrant coffee pickers have been ordering delicious Japanese comfort food here since the 1940s.

NORTH KONA & KOHALA COASTS

North of Kailua-Kona, the lava-blackened coast from North Kona to North Kohala is strung with secluded, palm-lined beaches, ancient Hawaiian sites and posh resorts. For beaches, see the Gold Coast Beaches boxed text (opposite).

our pick **Kona Village Resort** (808-325-5555, 800-367-5290; www.konavillage.com; 1 Kahuwai Bay Dr; 1-r hale $660-$1200, 2-r hale $975-1475;) offers low-key but luxurious seclusion and the warmest aloha of any Big Island resort. Rates include all meals. Plus, they host the island's best **luau** (adult/child 6-12yr $98/67; 6pm Wed & Fri), with great food and authentic hula.

The Waikaloa resort area is home to a huge ancient petroglyph field and two shopping malls with tons of free entertainment. Blurring the line between resort and theme park is the **Hilton Waikoloa Village** (808-886-1234, 800-445-8667; www.hiltonwaikoloavillage.com; 69-425 Waikoloa Beach Dr, Waikoloa; r $230-650;), with pools, lagoons and activities to please all ages.

The Mauna Lani resort area also has ancient Hawaiian sites, a shopping mall, and the notably ecoconscious **Mauna Lani Bay Hotel** (808-885-6622, 800-367-2323; www.maunalani.com; 68-1400 Mauna Lani Dr; r $445-965, ste from $995;).

For live jazz and dancing under the stars, head to Kawaihae and **Blue Dragon Musiquarium** (808-882-7771; www.bluedragonhawaii.com; 61-3616 Kawaihae Rd; mains $15-30; 5-10pm Wed-Sun, bar to 11pm), whose eclectic, above-average menu matches its engaging roster of performers.

WAIMEA

Waimea is the epicenter of the USA's largest cattle ranch, and you can learn all about Hawai'i's unusual cowboy history at **Parker Ranch Historic Homes** (808-885-5433, 877-885-7999; www.parkerranch.com; 67-1435 Mamalahoa Hwy; adult $10; 10am-5pm Tue-Sat); Parker Ranch also books horse rides. More museum than gallery, the **Isaacs Art Center** (808-885-5884; http://isaacsartcenter.hpa.edu; 65-1268 Kawaihae Rd; admission free; 10am-5pm Tue-Sat) has a stunning collection of Hawaii painters, including Madge Tennent and Herb Kawainui Kane.

It's easy to live well in Waimea. First, book a cozy, memorable room at **Aaah, the Views B&B** (808-885-3455; www.aaahtheviews.com; 66-1773 Alaneo St; d incl breakfast $150-195;). Then take your pick among the town's gourmet restaurants. A romantic choice is **Merriman's** (808-885-6822; www.merrimanshawaii.com; Opelo Plaza, 65-1227 Opelo Rd; dinner mains $30-45; 11:30am-1:30pm & 5:30-9pm Mon-Fri, 5:30-9pm Sat & Sun). An early innovator of Hawaii Regional Cuisine, the service is perfect and the cuisine always farm fresh.

MAUNA KEA

Measured from its base beneath the sea, this sacred **mountain** (13,796ft) is the tallest on earth, and its summit, nearly touching the sky, is clustered with world-class astronomical observatories. Partway up the mountain, the **Onizuka Center for International Astronomy** (808-961-2180; www.ifa.hawaii.edu/info/vis; admission free; 9am-10pm) offers displays, free astronomy presentations, awesome stargazing and summit tours (BYO 4WD). Continuing to the summit for sunset is unforgettable, but it requires a 4WD, a grueling 6-mile, high-altitude hike (10 hours round-trip), or a guided tour. One of the best is run by **Hawaii Forest & Trail**

WORTH THE TRIP: KONA COFFEE FARMS

Lots of good coffee is grown in Hawaii, but none has the gourmet cachet of 100% Kona coffee, which is grown on about 700 small family-run farms in the Kona Coffee Belt – a narrow strip of land just 2 miles wide and 22 miles long. With harvesting still done by hand, the region has a lost-in-time feel, seemingly unchanged from when Japanese and other immigrants first established themselves in the 19th century.

An easy way to experience this is to drive south from Holualoa, on Hwy 180, through the South Kona towns along Hwy 11. In Kealekekua on Hwy 11, get a free tour at the historic **Greenwell Farms** (808-323-2295; www.greenwellfarms.com; 8am-5pm Mon-Sat, tours to 4pm). Then, just south, check out the **Kona Coffee Living History Farm** (808-323-2006; www.konahistorical.org; adult $20; tours on the hour 9am-1pm Mon-Thu), which recreates rural Japanese-immigrant life in the early 20th century. In November, catch the 10-day **Kona Coffee Cultural Festival** (www.konacoffeefest.com).

DON'T MISS

All these Gold Coast beaches and parks are free and signed from Hwy 19.

Kekaha Kai State Park (closed Wed) Four dreamy sugar-sand beaches; all but Manini'owali Beach require hot hiking or 4WD to reach.

Kiholo Bay Less-crowded, easy-access black sand beach.

Puako Off Hwy 19, turn left for tide pools, turn right for kid-friendly Beach 69.

Hapuna Beach State Recreation Area World-renowned swoon-worthy Hapuna also has recommended camping cabins (808-974-6200; www.hawaiistateparks.org; cabins $20).

Mau'umae Beach Mauna Kea Resort's beach is every bit Hapuna's equal.

Spencer Beach Park The waters are silty, but it has the region's best camping (808-961-8311; www.hawaii-county.com/parks/parks.htm; campsites $5).

(808-331-8505, 800-464-1993; www.hawaii-forest.com; tours $185).

To reach the Onizuka Center, you must drive the 50-mile Saddle Rd (Hwy 200); though ridiculously scenic, it's historically accident prone and some car-rental companies prohibit travel on it; ask when renting.

HAMAKUA COAST

The Hamakua Coast offers some of the Big Island's most spectacular scenery – it's a *Lost*-worthy show of deep ravines, lush jungle valleys and cascading waterfalls.

Most scenic of all is **Waipi'o Valley**, the largest of seven magnificent amphitheater valleys on the windward coast. Hwy 240 dead-ends at a dramatic overlook; the road down is so steep that only 4WDs can make it. It's worth the 20-minute hike down – or really, the grueling return – to meditate on the thunderous black-sand beach, surrounded by ribbony waterfalls feeding ancient taro patches.

Another moody stop is beautiful **Laupahoehoe Point**, where in 1946 Hawaii's worst tsunami swept away half the town, as well as dozens of children. **'Akaka Falls State Park** (Hwy 220) contains two stunning waterfalls that are easily accessed along a short rainforest loop trail. **Pepe'ekeo Scenic Dr** makes for a delightful 4-mile detour, cutting through a thick forest of flowering tulip trees on the way south to Hilo.

HILO

The island capital, Hilo has been dubbed the 'rainiest city in the US,' and that soggy reputation tends to keep tourists away. It's their loss because Hilo – ethnically diverse, largely working class, with a walkable, historic downtown – provides visitors with an evocative slice of real Hawaii. Browse its vibrant farmers market and its first-rate museums and galleries, and you find a proud community undampened by mass tourism.

Sights & Activities

With its waterfront of century-old buildings, downtown Hilo brims with weather-beaten charm. Pick up a walking-tour map at the **Big Island Visitors Bureau** (808-961-5797; www.bigisland.org; 250 Keawe St; 8am-4:30pm Mon-Fri).

One of Hawaii's most fascinating museums, **'Imiloa Astronomy Center of Hawai'i** (808-969-9700; www.imiloahawaii.org; 600 'Imiloa Pl; adult/child $17.50/9.50; 9am-4pm Tue-Sun) explores Native Hawaiian culture, Hawaiian ecology and environment, and astronomical discoveries about our universe – all filtered through the lens of Mauna Kea. It's an eye-popping, thought-provoking journey.

The **Lyman Museum** (808-935-5021; www.lymanmuseum.org; 276 Haili St; adult/child $10/3; 10am-4:30pm Mon-Sat) provides an excellent overview of Hawaii's natural and cultural history. Hilo has survived several major tsunamis, and the dramatic **Pacific Tsunami Museum** (808-935-0926; www.tsunami.org; 130 Kamehameha Ave; adult/child $7/5; 9am-4pm Mon-Sat) brings these chilling events to life.

If possible, time your visit for Hilo's twice-weekly **farmers market** (www.hilofarmersmarket.com; cnr Mamo St & Kamehameha Ave; 6am-3pm Wed & Sat), an islandwide event that's equal parts gossip and shopping, both for fresh produce and Hawaiian crafts and clothing.

Sleeping

Hilo Bay Hostel (808-933-2771; www.hawaiihostel.net; 101 Waianuenue Ave; dm $25, r with/without bathroom $75/65;) Put simply, this hostel is great. Perfectly situated downtown, it's well maintained and welcoming; private rooms are a great deal.

HAWAII

Dolphin Bay Hotel (☎ 808-935-1466, 877-935-1466; www.dolphinbayhilo.com; 333 Iliahi St; r $100-160;) This is a perennial favorite with volcanoes-bound travelers who like to settle in. Rooms aren't snazzy, but they're comfortably clean and have kitchens.

our pick **Hilo Honu Inn** (☎ 808-935-4325; www.hilo honu.com; 465 Haili St; r incl breakfast $140-250;) This friendly B&B with hilltop views has three great rooms, but the top-floor Samurai Suite is a memorable treat, boasting authentic Japanese furnishings and an awesome *ofuro* (soaking tub).

Shipman House B&B (☎ 808-934-8002, 800-627-8447; www.hilo-hawaii.com; 131 Ka'iulani St; r incl breakfast $210-250;) Hilo's most gracious and historic B&B occupies a Victorian mansion packed with museum-quality Hawaiiana. Queen Lili'uokalani once entertained on the grand piano.

Eating

Nori's Saimin & Snacks (☎ 808-935-9133; Suite 124, 688 Kino'ole St, in Kukuau Plaza; noodle soups $5.50-9; 10:30am-11pm Tue-Sat, 10:30am-10pm Sun) *Saimin* is Japanese soup for the soul, and this no-frills Hilo institution serves it in rich steaming bowls packed with goodies.

Café Pesto (☎ 808-969-6640; www.cafepesto.com; 308 Kamehameha Ave; pizzas $12-19, dinner mains $17-30; 11am-9pm Sun-Thu, to 10pm Fri & Sat) A buzzing, friendly downtown choice with a varied menu; pizzas and seafood are noteworthy.

our pick **Hilo Bay Café** (☎ 808-935-4939; Waiakea Center, 315 Maka'ala St; mains $16-30; 11am-9pm Mon-Sat, 5-9pm Sun) The Hilo-style, unpretentious-yet-sophisticated gourmet dishes whipped up here will keep your palate happy and your honey's heart warm even when the rain is pounding.

HAWAI'I VOLCANOES NATIONAL PARK

Even among Hawaii's many wonders, this **national park** (☎ 808-985-6000; www.nps.gov/havo; 7-day pass per car $10) stands out: its two active volcanoes testify to the ongoing birth of the islands. Majestic Mauna Loa (13,677ft) looms like a sleeping giant, while young Kilauea – the world's most active volcano – has been erupting almost continually since 1983. With luck, you'll witness the primal event of molten lava tumbling into the sea. But the park contains much more – overwhelming lava deserts, steaming craters, lava tubes and ancient rainforests. For hikers, it's heaven.

Near the park entrance, **Kilauea Visitor Center** (☎ 808-985-6017; 7:45am-5pm) makes a great introduction, and rangers provide updates on trail conditions, volcanic activity and guided walks. The **Volcano Art Center** (☎ 808-967-7565, 866-967-7565; www.volcanoartcenter.org; 9am-5pm) coordinates special events.

Sights & Activities

The 11-mile **Crater Rim Drive** circles Kilauea Caldera, offering almost nonstop views of the goddess Pele's scorched, smoldering home. If time is short, drive this, making sure to peek into **Halema'uma'u Crater** (where eruption activity resumed in 2008); hike **Thurston Lava Tube**, an enormous cave left by flowing lava; and visit **Jaggar Museum** (☎ 808-985-6049; admission free; 8:30am-8pm), with working seismographs, lava displays and a stupendous vista. Note that shifting eruptions can cause unexpected road and trail closures.

The best two-hour hike is the 4-mile **Kilauea Iki Trail**, which crosses the top of steaming Kilauea Iki Crater; this hike can be easily extended by joining up with the **Halema'uma'u Trail**, a 7-mile loop. For an all-day or overnight adventure, **Napau Crater Trail** (a 14-mile round-trip) leads to tremendous views of the smoke-belching Pu'u O'o vent.

The park's equally scenic 18-mile **Chain of Craters Road** leads down to the coast, ending abruptly where recent lava flows have buried it. Rangers can advise you on how, or if it's possible, to hike to the active flow from here; a tell-tale steam plume marks the spot where lava enters the water. Stay for sunset as darkness brings out the fiery glow.

For **lava updates**, check with the **USGS** (☎ 808-967-8862; http://hvo.wr.usgs.gov) and **Hawai'i County** (☎ 808-961-8093; www.lavainfo.us), which, at the time of writing, was maintaining a lava-viewing site outside the park at Kalapana, in the Puna district.

Sleeping & Eating

All but the campgrounds listed below are in the nearby village of Volcano, which has many nice B&Bs and vacation homes. **Volcano Gallery** (☎ 800-967-8617; www.volcanogallery.com) is a locally managed rental agency.

The national park maintains two excellent, free, first-come, first-served campgrounds: **Namakanipaio**, off Hwy 11 outside the park entrance, and **Kulanaokuaiki**, along Hilina Pali Rd inside the park. Backcountry camping is limited; register at the visitor center no more than one day ahead. Also, Namakanipaio has 10 simple, A-frame **cabins** (☎ 808-967-7321; cabins $55).

Holo Holo In (☎ 808-967-7950; www.enable.org/holoholo; 19-4036 Kalani Honua Rd; dm $19, r $50-65; 💻) This friendly hostel is a great budget choice.

My Island B&B (☎ 808-967-7216; www.myislandinnhawaii.com; 19-3896 Old Volcano Rd; d incl breakfast $85-120, house $165) Occupying an historic 1886 house, this European-style B&B is delightful; it is run by gracious, gregarious hosts who make you feel like family.

Kilauea Lodge (☎ 808-967-7366; www.kilauealodge.com; 19-3948 Old Volcano Rd; r incl breakfast $175-225; ⊠ 📶) With a variety of well-appointed, country-cozy rooms, this rambling lodge is a nicely romantic choice. Plus, it runs the area's best restaurant (mains $25 to $35; open 5:30pm to 9pm), serving hearty steaks and German comfort food (*hassenpfeffer*, anyone?).

ourpick Thai Thai Restaurant (☎ 808-967-7969; 19-4084 Old Volcano Rd; mains $15-23; 🕑 4-9pm) Inspired by Pele, perhaps, the superior Thai cuisine here is satisfyingly hot and authentic; leftovers make the perfect trail lunch.

MAUI

According to some, you can't have it all. Perhaps those folks haven't been to Maui, which consistently lands atop travel-magazine reader polls as one of the world's most romantic islands. And why not? With its wealth of glorious beaches, luxe resorts, friendly B&Bs, gourmet cuisine, fantastic luau and world-class windsurfing, whale-watching, snorkeling, diving and hiking, what's missing? More adventure? Drive the jungly road to Hana (p1126) or traverse the moonlike volcanic crater of Haleakalā (p1127). More privacy? Maui is the gateway to secluded Moloka'i (p1129) and Lana'i (p1129). But is Maui *really* all that? Well, it does weave a gauzy spell that leaves most visitors more in love than when they arrived, so you'll just have to excuse those who, when the magazines call, wax a little enthusiastic.

Getting There & Around

Most travelers to Maui arrive at **Kahului International Airport** (OGG; ☎ 808-872-3803; http://hawaii.gov/ogg), the busiest airport in Hawaii outside Honolulu. From the airport, shuttle buses service the main tourist destinations. Using biodiesel vehicles, **Speedi Shuttle** (☎ 808-871-7474, 877-242-5777; www.speedishuttle.com) is the green-friendly airport shuttle service; it's $35 to Kihei, and $50 to Lahaina.

The island's public bus system, **Maui Bus** (☎ 808-871-4838; www.mauicounty.gov/bus), operates several daily routes (fares $1) that service the main towns, including Kahului, Lahaina, Wailuku, Kihei and Wailea. To rent your own wheels, consider the ecofriendly, biodiesel-fueled cars at **Bio-Beetle** (☎ 808-873-6121, 877-873-6121; www.bio-beetle.com), which start at $50/250 a day/week.

LAHAINA & KA'ANAPALI

For cook-it-yourself condo life, head to Kihei (p1124). For the megahotel and resort experience, bunk down in Ka'anapali, which also has prime beaches. And for atmosphere, entertainment and fine dining, make time for Lahaina, a 19th-century whaling town rich with well-preserved period architecture. Maui's best festivals occur in Lahaina and, for romantics, it's tough to beat the town's combination of history, gourmet restaurants and dazzling Pacific Ocean sunsets.

Sights & Activities

The focal point of Lahaina is its bustling small-boat harbor, backed by the historic **Pioneer Inn** and Banyan Tree Sq – the latter is home to the largest **banyan tree** in the US. The main drag and tourist strip is Front St, which runs along the ocean and is lined with shops, galleries and restaurants.

Lahaina's main sightseeing attractions are within walking distance of the waterfront. They include a host of fine small museums, missionary homes, prisons built for rowdy sailors and the remains of a royal palace. For a free walking-tour map, visit the **Lahaina Visitor Center** (☎ 808-667-9175, 888-310-1117; www.visitlahaina.com; 648 Wharf St; 🕑 9am-5pm), inside the old courthouse.

As for those world-famous beaches? Head north and keep going: between Ka'anapali and Kapalua, one impossible perfect strand follows another. All water sports are possible, and eager outfitters abound. Three top-ranked gems are **Kahekili Beach Park, Honolua Bay** and **DT Fleming Beach Park.**

In Ka'anapali, visit the evocative **Whalers Village Museum** (☎ 808-661-5992; www.whalersvillage.com; 2435 Ka'anapali Parkway; admission free; 🕑 9am-10pm) in the Whalers Village mall.

HAWAII

In May, don't miss Maui's signature cultural event, the two-week **International Festival of Canoes** (www.mauifestivalofcanoes.com), held in Lahaina.

Sleeping

House of Fountains (808-667-2121, 800-789-6865; www.alohahouse.com; 1579 Lokia St; r incl breakfast $150-170;) In addition to museum-quality Hawaiiana, this friendly B&B has well-equipped, modern rooms and a great breakfast. It's near Wahikuli Beach Park, between Lahaina and Ka'anapali.

our pick **Lahaina Inn** (808-661-0577, 800-669-3444; www.lahainainn.com; 127 Lahainaluna Rd; r $150-170, ste $205;) Forget cookie-cutter resorts – if you want an authentic taste of Lahaina, book a room at this painstakingly resorted boutique hotel, furnished with Hawaiian quilts and antiques. Your TV is a rocking chair on the lanai above town.

Ka'anapali Beach Hotel (808-661-0011, 800-262-8450; www.kbhmaui.com; 2525 Ka'anapali Parkway; r incl breakfast $235-355;) While not the fanciest, newest or biggest, this low-key Ka'anapali resort hotel has an enviable beach location and, most of all, genuine Hawaiian aloha. There are free guest lessons in ukulele, hula and lei-making.

Eating & Drinking

Pioneer Inn (808-661-3636; 658 Wharf St; 11am-10pm) With its whaling-era atmosphere and harborside veranda, this is unquestionably the most popular place for a drink in Lahaina.

Bakery (808-667-9062; 991 Limahana Pl; snacks $1.50-6; 5:30am-12:30pm Mon-Fri, to noon Sat) Lahaina's finest bakery, in a nondescript industrial park, offers sinfully sweet pastries, crispy croissants and generously heaped sandwiches.

Aloha Mixed Plate (808-661-3322; www.alohamixedplate.com; 1285 Front St; plates $6-14; 10:30am-10pm) This fun Lahaina beach shack is the best place to go local with a Hawaiian plate lunch or to catch sunset with a tropical drink, a few *pupu* and Hawaiian music.

Sansei Seafood Restaurant (808-669-6286; www.sanseihawaii.com; 600 Office Rd; sushi $4-15, mains $17-40; 5:30-10pm Sat-Wed, to 1am Thu & Fri) In Kapalua, trendy Sansei is always packed, serving out-of-this-world sushi and intriguing Japanese–Hawaiian fare; Thursday and Friday have half-price food after 10pm.

Hula Grill & Barefoot Bar (808-667-6636; www.hulagrill.com; Whalers Village; grill menu $9-18, dinner mains $19-34; 11am-10pm) Watch the swimsuit parade in Ka'anapali as you dine under coconut-frond umbrellas on creative *pupu* and robust dinner mains, like kiawe wood-grilled steaks.

I'O (808-661-8422; www.iomaui.com; 505 Front St; mains $28-38; 5:30-10pm) For Lahaina's best waterfront fine dining, stop searching. I'O features nouveau Hawaii cuisine using organic, farm-fresh ingredients and a bounty of just-caught seafood.

Entertainment

our pick **Old Lahaina Lu'au** (808-667-1998, 800-248-5828; www.oldlahainaluau.com; 1251 Front St; adult/child $92/62; 5:15-8:15pm) For a night to remember, this beachside luau is unsurpassed for its authenticity and all-around aloha – the hula troupe is first rate and the feast superb. Book far ahead.

Feast at Lele (808-667-5353, 866-244-5353; www.feastatlele.com; 505 Front St; adult/child $110/80; 6-9pm) No half-hearted buffet, this gourmet luau is a delicious culinary tour of Pacific cultures, accompanied by an excellent music-and-dance performance.

MA'ALAEA BAY

Ma'alaea Bay runs along the low isthmus separating the mountain masses of western and eastern Maui. Prevailing winds from the north funnel between the mountains, creating strong midday gusts and some of the best **windsurfing** conditions on Maui.

The superb **Maui Ocean Center** (808-270-7000; www.mauioceancenter.com; 192 Ma'alaea Rd, Ma'alaea; adult/child $25/18; 9am-6pm Jul & Aug, to 5pm rest of yr;), the largest tropical aquarium in the USA, is a dazzling feast for the eyes. The aquarium, dedicated to Hawaii marine life, is as close as you can get to being underwater without donning dive gear!

With a breezy harbor view, the **Waterfront** (808-244-9028; 50 Hauoli St, Ma'alaea; mains $26-35; 5-9pm) serves Central Maui's best seafood.

KIHEI

Sun-kissed, gleaming beaches run for miles and miles south of Kihei, which is less ritzy than West Maui. Vacationers flock to this coast for the excellent swimming, snorkeling, windsurfing and kayaking, and abundant condos keep prices reasonable.

For kayak rentals and adventurous tours, try **South Pacific Kayaks** (808-875-4848, 800-776-2326; www.southpacifickayaks.com; 95 Hale Kuai St;

WHALES IN LOVE

Every winter from November through May, some 10,000 humpback whales crowd the shallow waters along the western coast of Maui for breeding, calving and nursing. These awesome creatures are easy to spot from shore, particularly when they perform their acrobatic breaches. It's one of nature's grandest spectacles.

To get an even closer look, take a whale-watching cruise with the nonprofit **Pacific Whale Foundation** (☎ 808-249-8811, 800-942-5311; www.pacificwhale.org; adult/child $32/17; Dec-Apr;), which sails out of both Lahaina and Ma'alaea harbors. Another place to get acquainted with these creatures is in Kihei at the **Hawaiian Islands Humpback Whale National Marine Sanctuary Headquarters** (☎ 808-879-2818, 800-831-4888; www.hawaiihumpbackwhale.noaa.gov; 726 S Kihei Rd; 10am-3pm Mon-Fri). You can volunteer for one of the sanctuary's ocean counts.

Think the whales aren't happy to be in Maui? Listen to them singing at www.whalesong.net.

single/double kayaks per day $40/60, tours $65-100). South Pacific's paddle to **Molokini Crater** (per person $140) is a workout that leads to Maui's best snorkeling and diving spot. Or opt for a two-hour Molokini Express boat trip with **Blue Water Rafting** (☎ 808-879-7238; www.bluewaterrafting.com; Kihei Boat Ramp; tours $50-120).

Sleeping

To begin sorting through Kihei's condo possibilities, check out **Bello Realty** (☎ 808-879-3328, 800-541-3060; www.bellomaui.com) or **Kihei Maui Vacations** (☎ 808-879-7581, 888-568-6284; www.kmvmaui.com).

Two Mermaids on Maui B&B (☎ 808-874-8687, 800-598-9550; www.twomermaids.com; 2840 Umalu Pl; studio/1-br incl breakfast $115/140;) For a more personal touch, try the two kitchenette units at this friendly, cheerful B&B.

Kihei Kai Nani (☎ 808-879-9088, 800-473-1493; www.kiheikainani.com; 2495 S Kihei Rd; 1-br units $148-168;) This inviting low-rise complex has roomy, well-equipped one-bedroom units. It has good off-season discounts.

Punahoa (☎ 808-879-2720, 800-564-4380; www.punahoabeach.com; 2142 Ili'ili Rd; studio/1br/2br $156/240/270;) This tasteful boutique condo, hidden on a side street, fronts a quiet beach frequented by sea turtles. Who needs a pool?

Eating

Eskimo Candy (☎ 808-879-5686; www.eskimocandy.com; 2665 Wai Wai Place; meals $8-17; 10:30am-7pm Mon-Fri) If you've never tried *poke* (cubed, marinated raw fish), this local fish market is a required stop. If you *have* tried *poke,* same thing. Delicious ahi wraps and fish tacos round out the takeout menu.

Da Kitchen Express (☎ 808-875-7782; www.da-kitchen.com; Rainbow Mall, 2439 S Kihei Rd; meals $9-12; 9am-9pm) This quintessential Hawaiian diner serves tasty, sizeable plate lunches. Try *laulau, loco moco* and other local grinds, but don't miss the *kalua* pork.

Café O'Lei (☎ 808-891-1368; http://cafeoleirestaurants.com; Rainbow Mall, 2439 S Kihei Rd; lunch $8-13, dinner $18-30; 10:30am-3:30pm & 5-9pm Tue-Sun) For superb Hawaii Regional cuisine at honest prices, no other Kihei dining spot comes close. It has fierce martinis too.

WAILEA & MAKENA

As Maui's most upscale seaside community, Wailea boasts million-dollar homes and extravagant resorts with prices to match – all because this stretch of coastline cradles tawny beaches of dreamy perfection. The mile-long **Wailea Beach Walk** is a superb place to enjoy shoreline whale-watching in winter.

South of Wailea, Makena has several knockout undeveloped beaches – particularly **Big Beach** and secluded **Little Beach** – as well as the **'Ahihi-Kina'u Natural Area Reserve**, which encompasses trails, historic ruins and hidden coves ideal for snorkeling.

A class act, **Pineapple Inn Maui** (☎ 808-298-4403, 877-212-6284; www.pineappleinnmaui.com; 3170 Akala Dr; r/cottage $150/215;) is a boutique inn where all the attractive rooms have kitchenettes – the only thing lacking is a high price.

KAHULUI & WAILUKU

Kahului and Wailuku, Maui's two largest communities, flow together in one urban sprawl. Kahului hosts Maui's windsurfing shops, whose employees give lessons at perpetually breezy **Kanaha Beach**. The **Maui Arts & Cultural Center** (☎ 808-242-7469; www.mauiarts.org; 1 Cameron Way) is Maui's premier concert venue, which also runs an excellent

SCENIC DRIVE: ROAD TO HANA

The most spectacular coastal drive in all Hawaii, the Hana Hwy (Hwy 360) winds its way deep into jungle valleys and back out above a rugged coastline. The road is a real cliff-hugger with 54 one-lane bridges, roadside waterfalls and head-spinning views. Gas up and buy lunch in Pa'ia before starting.

Swimming holes, heart-stopping vistas and awesome hikes call out almost nonstop. Definitely explore the lava tubes and black-sand beach at **Wai'anapanapa State Park**, with inviting camping ($5) and cabins ($45). For permits, contact the **Division of State Parks** (☎ 808-984-8109; www.hawaiistateparks.org/camping).

To really get away? In Huelo, book the **Tea House** (☎ 572-5610, 800-215-6130; www.mauiteahouse.com; Ho'olawa Rd, Huelo; 1br cottage $150), a meditative, off-the-grid cottage made from a former Zen temple, with open-air shower, kitchen and soulful views.

art gallery (☎ 808-242-2787; admission free; 11am-5pm Tue-Sun).

On the outskirts of Wailuku, **'Iao Valley State Park** ('Iao Valley Rd; admission free; 7am-7pm) centers on the picturesque 'Iao Needle rock pinnacle, which rises 1200ft from the valley floor.

Information

Maui Memorial Medical Center (☎ 808-244-9056; 221 Mahalani St, Wailuku; 24hr) The island's main hospital.

Maui Visitors Bureau (☎ 808-872-3893, 808-244-3530; www.visitmaui.com; Kahului Airport; 7:45am-9:45pm) Operates a staffed booth in the airport's arrivals area.

Sleeping & Eating

Old Wailuku Inn (☎ 808-244-5897, 800-305-4899; www.mauiinn.com; 2199 Kaho'okele St, Wailuku; r $165-195;) Step back into the 1920s in this elegant period home, built by a wealthy banker and authentically restored by the friendly innkeepers. Rooms are large and comfy, with traditional Hawaiian quilts.

Thailand Cuisine (☎ 808-873-0225; Maui Mall, 70 E Ka'ahumanu Ave, Kahului; mains $10-15; 10:30am-3pm & 5-9:30pm) Stop here for superior Thai cuisine, and a menu with dozens of tasty vegetarian options. It's a perennial award winner.

Drinking

Wow-Wee Maui's Kava Bar & Grill (☎ 808-871-1414; 333 Dairy Rd, Kahului; 10am-9pm Sun-Thu, to 11pm Fri & Sat) This hip café is the place to try the mildly relaxing drink kava. If it tastes too much like dirt, try it mixed with chocolate.

PA'IA

But for the incessant winds, Pa'ia would be a forgotten former sugar town. Instead, it's become the Windsurfing Capital of the World and draws an eclectic, international crowd and a burgeoning selection of superb restaurants. To admire the windsurfing and kitesurfing action, head to **Ho'okipa Beach.**

our pick **Mama's Fish House** (☎ 808-579-8488; www.mamasfishhouse.com; 799 Poho Pl; mains $36-50; 11am-2:30pm & 5-9:30pm) is Maui's most celebrated seafood restaurant, which pairs beachside romance with impeccably prepared fish. Reservations are essential. **Pa'ia Fish Market Restaurant** (☎ 808-579-8030; 100 Hana Hwy; meals $9-15; 11am-9:30pm) is the place to go for fresh fish sandwiches.

HANA & AROUND

The mainland influences so evident everywhere else on Maui are missing in Hana, where many residents are Native Hawaiian, and they treasure the town's relaxed pace and quiet isolation. Surfers head to **Waikoloa Beach**, while sunbathers favor **Kaihalulu (Red Sand) Beach**, which is reached by a trail at the end of Uakea Rd.

The road south from Hana is incredibly beautiful. 'Ohe'o Stream cuts its way through **'Ohe'o Gulch** as a gorgeous series of wide pools and waterfalls, each tumbling into the one below. Just past the gulch is the sleepy village of **Kipahulu**, the burial site of aviator Charles Lindbergh.

Maintenance at this Hana condo complex can be uneven, but **Hana Kai Maui** (☎ 808-248-8426, 800-346-2772; www.hanakaimaui.com; 1533 Uakea Rd; studio/1-br from $185/210;) has an ideal oceanfront spot and great views from upper-floor rooms.

Hana isn't known for great eats, but it has one gourmet destination: **Ka'uiki** (☎ 808-248-8211, 800-321-4262; Hotel Hana-Maui,

5031 Hana Hwy; full dinner $50-65; ⌚ 11:30am-2:30pm & 6-9pm). Dinner is a locavore's treat with Hana-caught fish, Nahiku greens and other homegrown delights.

HALEAKALĀ NATIONAL PARK

No trip to Maui is complete without visiting this **national park** (www.nps.gov/hale; 3-day entry pass per car $10), containing the mighty volcano that gave rise to East Maui. The volcano's floor measures a whopping 7.5 miles wide, 2.5 miles long and 3000ft deep – more than enough to swallow Manhattan. From its towering rim there are dramatic views of its lunarlike surface. But the adventure needn't stop at the viewpoints: with a good pair of hiking boots, you can walk down into the crater on trails that meander around eerie cinder cones and peer up at towering walls.

For an unforgettable experience, arrive in time to see the sunrise – an event that Mark Twain called the 'sublimest spectacle' he'd ever seen. Check on weather conditions and sunrise times (☎ 866-944-5025) before driving up. **Park headquarters** (☎ 808-572-4400; ⌚ 6:30am-4pm) can give you details on free guided hikes and nature talks.

Free drive-up **camping** (first-come, first-served) is allowed at Hosmer Grove, near the main entrance. Another amazing option is primitive **cabins** on the crater floor; demand is so high that you must book online (https://fhnp.org/wcr) exactly 90 days in advance. Camping and cabins have a three-night maximum.

KAUA'I

Lush, rural Kaua'i is the Pacific Ocean's magnificent jade temple. On Hawaii's oldest major island, nature's fingers have had time to dig deep – carving the unbelievable fluted cliffs of the Na Pali Coast (p1128) and the tremendous ragged gash of Waimea Canyon (p1129). A mecca for hikers and kayakers, Kaua'i is beloved by outdoor enthusiasts of all stripes, and it has been the darling of honeymooners ever since Elvis tied the knot here in *Blue Hawaii*. Forget coddling resorts, decadent shopping or bustling nightlife. Come to Kaua'i for its heavenly art gallery – the one you find outdoors. The price for these works? Just a pair of boots and a little sweat.

Getting There & Around

All commercial flights land at **Lihu'e Airport** (LIH; ☎ 808-246-1448; www6.hawaii.gov/dot/airports/kauai/lih). Taxis and the major car-rental companies are available here. Kaua'i has a limited public **bus service** (☎ 808-241-6410; www.kauai.gov; ⌚ Mon-Sat), which serves most towns but not tourist destinations like Kilauea Point and Koke'e State Park. Fares are $1.50.

LIHU'E

This former plantation town is Kaua'i's capital and commercial center. Seek information at the **Kaua'i Visitors Bureau** (☎ 808-245-3971, 800-262-1400; www.kauaidiscovery.com; 4334 Rice St; ⌚ 8am-4:30pm Mon-Fri). The insightful **Kaua'i Museum** (☎ 808-245-6931; www.kauaimuseum.org; 4428 Rice St; admission $10; ⌚ 9am-4pm Mon-Fri, 10am-4pm Sat) traces the island's intriguing history.

Garden Island Inn (☎ 808-245-7227, 800-648-0154; www.gardenislandinn.com; 3445 Wilcox Rd; r $100-150, ste $145-180; ⊠ ⁂ ☰) offers modest but cheerful rooms just minutes from the beach. Fish lovers may find themselves coming to **Fish Express** (☎ 808-245-9918; 3343 Kuhio Hwy; lunch $6-7.50; ⌚ 10am-6pm Mon-Sat, to 5pm Sun, lunch served to 3pm daily) every day for its heavenly gourmet takeout.

Luau Kalamaku (☎ 877-622-1780; www.luaukalamaku.com; Kilohana Plantation; adult/child 3-11yr/child 12-18yr $95/45/65; ⌚ 5pm Tue & Fri) offers a theatrical, Cirque du Soleil–style Polynesian show with its above-average luau buffet.

WAILUA & AROUND

You wouldn't know it from the shopping strip-lined Kuhio Hwy, but the Wailua area contains great outdoor opportunities. Families should head to **Lydgate Beach Park** (www.kamalani.org), with the best kids' playground in Hawaii and safe swimming at a well-protected beach. The mountains above Wailua hold some recommended **hikes**, such as the Kuilau Ridge Trail, the Moalepe Trail and the Nounou Mountain Trails.

However, most come to kayak the **Wailua River**. The easy, bucolic 5-mile kayak – including swimming holes and hikes to waterfalls – is so popular that it's restricted almost completely to guided tours. Book a day ahead with **Kayak Kaua'i** (☎ 808-826-9844, 800-437-3507; www.kayakkauai.com; double kayaks per person $27, tours adult/child $85/60) and **Outfitters Kaua'i** (☎ 808-742-9667, 888-742-9887; www.outfitterskauai.com; kayaks per person per day $40, tours adult/child $98/78); both also offer other kayak and guided trips. Or try **Kayak Wailua** (☎ 808-822-3388; www.kayakwailua.com; Kuhio Hwy, Wailua; tour per person $40), a small, family-owned outfit specializing in Wailua River tours.

NA PALI COAST & NORTH SHORE

Unspoiled and unhurried, Kaua'i's mountainous north shore features otherworldly scenery and enough outdoor adventures for a lifetime. Be sure to stop at **Kilauea Point National Wildlife Refuge** (☎ 808-828-1413; www.fws.gov/kilaueapoint; Kilauea Rd, Kilauea; admission $5; 10am-4pm) to enjoy its historic lighthouse and thriving seabird sanctuary.

Gentle **'Anini Beach Park** is spacious, with calm water perfect for kids, lazy kayaking, easy snorkeling and the best beginner windsurfing on the island. Camping is recommended (and quieter midweek); get permits from the **Division of Parks & Recreation** (☎ 808-241-4463; www.kauai.gov; campsites per person $3).

The Princeville area makes for glamorous living and provides glorious sunset perches, such as at the tiny but magnificent **Pali Ke Kua Beach** (accessible through the Princeville Resort). A satisfying, and more affordable, lodging choice is **Westin Princeville Ocean Resort Villas** (☎ 808-827-8700; www.westinprinceville.com; 3838 Wyllie Rd; studio/1 br from $250/375;); the condo-like 'villas' boast full kitchens, flat-screen TVs and washer/dryer. The Westin also contains **Nanea** (☎ 808-827-8700; breakfast $8-22, dinner mains $31-38; 6:30-10:30am & 5:30-9:30pm), an inventive restaurant featuring elegant locally grown Hawaii fusion cuisine.

In **Hanalei**, the hippie-surfer vibe is palpable and, indeed, in magnificent **Hanalei Bay** the surfing is spectacular; it really swells in winter. Also popular are quiet, easy kayak trips up the **Hanalei River**; for rentals, try **Pedal & Paddle** (☎ 808-826-9069; www.pedalnpaddle.com; Ching Young Village; single/double kayaks per day $20/40).

An attractively well-kept place to stay is **Hanalei Inn** (☎ 808-826-9333; www.hanaleiinn.com; 5-5468 Kuhio Hwy; r $150; W). Its four studios have kitchens and a killer locale.

Hanalei makes a good meal stop. Doubters become converts at **Hanalei Taro & Juice Company** (☎ 826-1059; 5-5070-B Kuhio Hwy; smoothies $3-4.50, sandwiches $6.50; 11am-4pm Mon-Fri), where the taro-based smoothies are exquisite; the other Hawaiian fare is great too. For a gourmet plate lunch (on paper plates), head for **Polynesia Café** (☎ 808-826-1999; www.polynesiacafe.com; Ching Young Village; mains $11-17; 8am-9pm). For firmer tableware and a stylishly rustic atmosphere, **Postcards Café** (☎ 808-826-1191; www.postcardscafe.com; 5-5075 Kuhio Hwy; mains $18-27; 6-9pm) creates gourmet, vegetarian-friendly organic cuisine.

Marking the western end of Hwy 56, at the little village of **Ha'ena**, are **Tunnels Beach** and lovely **Kee Beach**, both of which have excellent snorkeling. Camping is allowed (with a permit) at **Ha'ena Beach Park** (☎ 808-241-4463; www.kauai.gov; campsites per person $3), close to the Kalalau trailhead.

In Ha'ena, **Hanalei Colony Resort** (☎ 808-826-6235, 800-628-3004; www.hcr.com; 5-7130 Kuhio Hwy; 2-br from $250;) has a tad dated '70s-era décor, but the condos are kept well and in a nicely secluded waterfront location.

Hikers shouldn't miss the challenging but oh-so-rewarding 11-mile **Kalalau Trail**, which runs along the folded Na Pali cliffs and winds through a series of breathtakingly lush valleys in **Na Pali Coast State Park**. To hike past the first valley or for backcountry camping ($10 per person per night), you need a **permit** (☎ 808-274-3444; www.hawaiistateparks.org). Allow three days for the whole shebang.

Hard-core paddlers can admire the same scenery from the sea along the strenuous 17-mile Na Pali Coast kayak. It takes all day (and feels longer) and is only possible from May to September. Two good outfitters are **Kayak Kaua'i** (☎ 808-826-9844, 800-437-3507; www.kayakkauai.com; Na Pali tours $205) and **Na Pali Kayak** (☎ 808-826-6900, 866-977-6900; www.napalikayak.com; Na Pali tours $200).

SOUTH SHORE

Sunny, family-friendly **Po'ipu**, Kaua'i's main resort area, fronts a fabulous run of sandy beaches. It's good for swimming and snorkeling year-round and for surfing in summer. Tour the stunning gardens at the **National Tropical Botanical Garden** (NTBG; ☎ 808-742-2623; www.ntbg.org; 4425 Lawa'i Rd; tours $20-85; 8:30am-5pm) and admire the windswept limestone cliffs of the Maha'ulepu Coast along the 2-mile **Maha'ulepu Heritage Trail** (www.hikemahaulepu.org).

Po'ipu is awash in condos and vacation rentals for all budgets; check the listings of **Po'ipu Beach Resort Association** (☎ 808-742-7444; www.poipubeach.org) and **Parrish Collection Kaua'i** ((☎ 808-742-2000, 800-742-1412; www.parrishkauai.com).

In Koloa, the magnificent valley views from **Marjorie's Kaua'i Inn** (☎ 808-332-8838, 800-717-8838; www.marjorieskauaiinn.com; Hailima St, Lawa'i; r incl breakfast $130-175;) could be a trip highlight. Rooms are nicely appointed with kitchenettes.

our pick **Casa di Amici** (☎ 808-742-1555; www.casadiamici.com; 2301 Nalo Rd; mains $23-29; ⏰ from 6pm) is the place to head to at dinnertime. This overlooked, unpretentious gem serves Italian-influenced island cuisine.

WEST SIDE

The top destinations here are **Waimea Canyon** – the 'Grand Canyon of the Pacific' with cascading waterfalls and spectacular gorges – and the adjacent **Koke'e State Park**. Both feature breathtaking views and a vast network of hiking trails; some, like Koke'e's Awa'awapuhi and Nu'alolo Trails, stroll the knife edge of precipitously eroded cliffs. Waimea Canyon Dr (Hwy 550) starts in the town of Waimea and is peppered with scenic lookouts. Pick up trail information at the park's **Koke'e Museum** (☎ 808-335-9975; www.kokee.org; 3600 Koke'e Rd; donation $1; ⏰ 10am-4pm).

Those with tents should aim for the comfortable Koke'e State Park campground; for permits, contact the **Division of State Parks** (☎ 808-274-3446; www.hawaiistateparks.org; campsites $5). The town of **Waimea** makes a good base for park explorations; in town, **Inn Waimea** (☎ 808-338-0031; www.innwaimea.com; 4469 Halepule Rd, Waimea; ste from $110, cottage $150; ⊠ 💻 📶) is a lovely old missionary home with four guest rooms and two-bedroom cottages.

Also worth exploring is **Hanapepe**, a quaint, historic town with false-fronted Old West buildings housing fun galleries and shops. Friday night is **Hanapepe Art Walk** (⏰ 6-9pm Fri), when galleries stay open late and the town comes alive. Near town, **Salt Pond Beach Park** is perfect for swimming and ideal for families. The best West-side meal is at the artfully quaint **Hanapepe Café** (☎ 808-335-5011; 3830 Hanapepe Rd; lunch $6-10, dinner $18-25; ⏰ 7:30am-3pm Mon-Thu, 5-9pm Fri); the menu focuses on seafood and vegetarian mains, and dinner Friday night includes live music (reservations are required).

MOLOKA'I

Sparsely populated by mostly Native Hawaiians and largely undeveloped for tourism, rural Moloka'i is ideal for those seeking the 'other' Hawaii: unpackaged, traditional, still wild and exuding genuine aloha. It is for travelers who willingly trade comfort for a taste of an untamed landscape – this one recalling Hawaii's awe-inspiring natural glory as it was half a century or more ago.

The quintessential Moloka'i experience is riding a mule (or hiking) down the steep, towering cliff face of the Kalaupapa Peninsula. Designated as the **Kalaupapa National Historical Park** (www.nps.gov/kala; ⏰ Mon-Sat), the beautiful peninsula was once a settlement for people with leprosy (now called Hansen's disease); from 1873 to 1889, they were served by Catholic priest Father Damien, who achieved sainthood in 2009. Guided tours of the settlement are included in the cost of the **Moloka'i Mule Ride** (☎ 808-567-6088, 800-567-7550; www.muleride.com; tours $175).

From Moloka'i's main town, **Kaunakakai** (with simple lodgings and eateries), a gorgeous 27-mile drive leads along the south coast past small towns and fishponds to the lush **Halawa Valley**, which shelters ancient heiau and waterfalls. Raw, nearly prehistoric forests are found in the **Moloka'i Forest Reserve** and the adjacent **Kamakou Preserve**, in central Moloka'i. Access is difficult (almost exclusively by 4WD and/or long hike), so it's worth joining the excellent monthly hike with the **Nature Conservancy** (☎ 808-553-5236; www.nature.org/hawaii; suggested donation $25), which provides transportation.

For cottages, houses and condos **Molokai Vacation Properties** (☎ 808-553-8334, 800-367-2984; www.molokai-vacation-rental.com) and **Moloka'i Resorts Vacation Rental Center** (☎ 808-553-3666, 800-600-4158; www.molokairesorts.com) have choices in all price ranges.

To reach Moloka'i, **Island Air** (☎ 808-484-2222, 800-652-6541; www.islandair.com) and **Mokulele Airlines** (☎ 808-426-7070, 866-260-7070; www.mokuleleairlines.com) both have daily flights from Honolulu and Kahului, Maui. Or take a 90-minute passenger ferry from Lahaina, Maui, on the **Molokai Princess** (☎ 808-662-3355, 866-307-6524; www.molokaiferry.com; adult/child $40/20), which runs two round-trips Monday to Saturday and one on Sunday. It will also arrange ferry-car packages.

LANA'I

Once home to the world's largest pineapple plantation, Lana'i has been refashioned into a plaything for the wealthy. Home to a pair of Hawaii's most elite resorts, between them boasting more stars than the night sky, and two world-class golf courses, Lana'i can nevertheless make a satisfying visit or day trip for mere-mortal travelers.

At its center is **Lana'i City**, a charming, well-preserved historic plantation town where the pace evokes a gentler, slower era. Swim, snorkel and dive in the dolphin-rich waters off beautiful **Hulopo'e Beach**, and enjoy unparalleled views hiking along the ridgetop **Munro Trail**.

You can also **golf**, and sample the good life, at the resorts, which are run by **Four Seasons Resort Lana'i** (☎ 800-321-4666; www.fourseasons.com/lanai). Get your gourmet restaurants, spas and first-class lodgings at either **Manele Bay** (☎ 808-565-2000; r from $415;) or **Lodge at Koele** (☎ 808-565-4000; r from $345;). To spend the night without breaking the bank, the 1923 **Hotel Lanai** (☎ 808-565-7211, 877-665-2624; www.hotellanai.com; 828 Lana'i Ave; r $160-180;) is a 10-room former plantation guesthouse that is a delightful throwback.

The recommended way to reach Lana'i is by ferry from Lahaina, Maui, since you often see whales and spinner dolphins en route. **Expeditions** (☎ 808-661-3756, 800-695-2624; www.go-lanai.com; adult/child $30/20) runs a round-trip passenger ferry five times daily. Also, **Island Air** (☎ 808-484-2222, 800-652-6541; www.islandair.com) and **Mokulele Airlines** (☎ 808-426-7070, 866-260-7070; www.mokuleleairlines.com) both have daily flights from Honolulu.

OTHER ISLANDS

KAHO'OLAWE

This uninhabited island, 7 miles southwest of Maui, was used exclusively by the US military as a bombing target from WWII until 1990. Despite a $400-million, 10-year cleanup by the military, the island remains littered with unexploded ordnance and is thus off-limits to tourists.

Considered sacred by Native Hawaiians, Kaho'olawe is currently managed by the **Kaho'olawe Island Reserve Commission** (www.kahoolawe.hawaii.gov). With the help of **Protect Kaho'olawe 'Ohana** (www.kahoolawe.org), it is rehabilitating the island's ecosystems and restoring cultural sites in the hopes of making the island livable once again. To learn more or to volunteer to help during monthly visits, see the websites.

NI'IHAU

The smallest of the inhabited Hawaiian Islands and a Native Hawaiian preserve, Ni'ihau has long been closed to outsiders, earning it the nickname 'The Forbidden Island.' No other place in Hawaii has more successfully turned its back on change. The island's 160 residents still speak Hawaiian as a first language, and Ni'ihau has no paved roads, no airport, no islandwide electricity and no telephones.

The only way to visit the island is through **Ni'ihau Helicopters** (☎ 877-441-3500; www.niihau.us; per person $365/half day); arrange helicopter tours well in advance.

PAPAHANAUMOKUAKEA MARINE NATIONAL MONUMENT

On June 15, 2006, President Bush declared the Northwestern Hawaiian Islands the USA's first Marine National Monument. Encompassing around 140,000 sq miles and containing 33 islands and atolls, it is now the largest protected marine area in the world and is scattered across 1200 miles of ocean northwest of Kaua'i.

The islands are home to the USA's largest and healthiest coral reef, and they support 7000 marine species and around 14 million seabirds. Governed by some form of protection since 1909, **Papahanaumokuakea Marine National Monument** (www.hawaiireef.noaa.gov) has only one island that can be visited by tourists, Midway Island, which was the site of a pivotal WWII battle between Japanese and American naval forces. Renewed in 2007 by the **US Fish & Wildlife Service** (www.fws.gov/midway), Midway visits are limited, costly ($5000 per week) and only allowed from November to July – to coincide with Midway's spectacular albatross nesting season.

Directory

CONTENTS

ACCOMMODATIONS

This guide includes recommendations for all budgets, but it emphasizes midrange accommodations. Unless otherwise noted, 'budget' is considered under $80 per room per night, 'midrange' $80 to $200 and 'top end' over $200. Accommodation rates are based on standard double-occupancy in high season (usually during summer from late May to early September). These rates are a general guide only. Special events, busy weekends, conventions and holidays can drive prices higher; in some places, low-season rates can be significantly lower. Note: *prices do not include hotel tax,* which can add 10% to 15%, or more. When booking, always ask for the rate including taxes.

Since nearly every US hotel has nonsmoking rooms, the nonsmoking icon ( ) is used only when a property bans smoking entirely. Accommodations that cater to families are marked with the child-friendly icon ( ). The wi-fi icon ( ) is used when wireless internet access is available, whether free or paid. The internet icon ( ) denotes an online computer terminal is available for guests' use. To find ecofriendly accommodations, consult the GreenDex (p1212).

For all but the cheapest places and the slowest seasons, reservations are advised. In high-season tourist hot spots, hotels can book up months ahead. Walking in off the street without a reservation gets you a good deal only when things are really dead. In general, many hotels offer specials on their websites, but low-end chains sometimes give a slightly better rate over the phone. Chain hotels also increasingly offer frequent-flyer mileage deals and other rewards programs; ask when booking. Online travel booking, bidding and comparison websites (see p1154) are another good way to find discounted hotel rates; also check out **Hotels.com** (www.hotels.com) and **Hotwire** (www.hotwire.com).

B&Bs

In the USA, many B&Bs are high-end romantic retreats in restored historic homes that are run by personable, independent innkeepers who serve gourmet breakfasts. These B&Bs often take pains to evoke a theme – Victorian, rustic, Cape Cod and so on – and amenities range from merely comfortable to hopelessly indulgent. Rates normally top $100, and the best run $200 to $300+. Many B&Bs have minimum-stay requirements, and some exclude young children.

BOOK YOUR STAY ONLINE

For more accommodation reviews and recommendations by Lonely Planet authors, check out the online booking service at www.lonelyplanet.com/hotels. You'll find the true, insider low-down on the best places to stay. Reviews are thorough and independent. Best of all, you can book online.

PRACTICALITIES

Electricity

- AC 110V is standard; buy adapters to run most non-US electronics

Newspapers & Magazines

- National newspapers: *New York Times, Wall Street Journal, USA Today*
- Mainstream news magazines: *Time, Newsweek, US News & World Report*

Radio & TV

- Radio news: National Public Radio (NPR), lower end of FM dial
- Broadcast TV: ABC, CBS, NBC, FOX, PBS (public broadcasting)
- Major cable channels: CNN (news), ESPN (sports), HBO (movies), Weather Channel

Video Systems

- NTSC standard (incompatible with PAL or SECAM)
- DVDs coded for Region 1 (US and Canada only)

Weights & Measures

- Weight: ounces (oz), pounds (lb), tons
- Liquid: oz, pints, quarts, gallons (gal)
- Distance: feet (ft), yards (yd), miles (mi)

To convert weights, liquid measures and distances to the metric system, see the inside front cover.

Still, European-style B&Bs exist: these may be rooms in someone's home, with plainer furnishings, simpler breakfasts, shared baths and cheaper rates. These often welcome families.

B&Bs can close out of season and reservations are essential, especially for top-end places. To avoid surprises, always ask about bathrooms (whether shared or private). B&B agencies are sprinkled throughout this guide. Also check listings online:

Bed & Breakfast Inns Online (www.bbonline.com)
BedandBreakfast.com (www.bedandbreakfast.com)
BnB Finder (www.bnbfinder.com)
Pamela Lanier's Bed & Breakfast Inns (www.lanierbb.com)
Select Registry (www.selectregistry.com)

Camping

Most federally managed public lands (see p1134) and many state parks offer camping. First-come, first-served 'primitive' campsites offer no facilities; overnight fees range from free to under $10. 'Basic' sites usually provide toilets (flush or pit), drinking water, fire pits and picnic tables; they cost $5 to $15 a night, and some or all may be reserved in advance. 'Developed' campsites, usually in national or state parks, have nicer facilities and more amenities: showers, barbecue grills, RV sites with hookups etc. These run $12 to $35 a night, and many can be reserved in advance.

Camping on most federal lands – including national parks (p114), national forests, Bureau of Land Management land and so on – can be reserved through **Recreation.gov** (☎ 518-885-3639, 877-444-6777; www.recreation.gov). Camping is usually limited to 14 days and can be reserved up to six months in advance. For some state park campgrounds, you can make bookings through **ReserveAmerica** (www.reserveamerica.com). Both websites let you search for campground locations and amenities, check availability and reserve a site, view maps and get driving directions online.

Private campgrounds tend to cater to RVs and families (tent sites may be few and lack atmosphere). Facilities may include playgrounds, convenience stores, wi-fi networks, swimming pools and other activities. Some rent camping cabins, ranging from canvas-sided wooden platforms to log-frame structures with real beds, heating and private baths. **Kampgrounds of America** (KOA; http://koa.com) is a national network of private campgrounds with a full range of facilities. You can order KOA's free annual directory (shipping fees apply) or browse its comprehensive campground listings and make bookings online.

Hostels

Hostels are clustered mainly in the northeast, the Pacific Northwest, California and the Southwest. Cities stock a handful, but across swathes of the Great Plains, the Midwest and the South, it's hard to find even one.

Hostelling International USA (HI-USA; ☎ 301-495-1240; www.hiusa.org; annual membership adult/child under 18/senior $28/free/$18) runs over 40 hostels in the US. Most have gender-segregated dorms, a few private rooms, shared baths and a communal kitchen. They usually provide linen (free or for a small fee; sleeping bags not allowed), prohibit alcohol and smoking, and organize social activities. In cities, hostels may stay open 24 hours, have wheelchair-accessible accommodations and amenities such as swimming pools, while others may close in the afternoon (usually between 10am and 5pm). Overnight fees for dorm beds range from $20 to $35. HI-USA members are entitled to small discounts and a free hostel handbook upon request. Reservations are accepted and advised during high season, when there may be a three-night maximum stay. Book online or through HI-USA's central **booking service** (☎ 888-464-4872).

The USA has many independent hostels not affiliated with HI-USA. For online listings, check the following:

Hostel Handbook (www.hostelhandbook.com)
Hostels.com (www.hostels.com)
Hostelworld.com (www.hostelworld.com).
Hostelz.com (www.hostelz.com)

Hotels

These days, every town's 'hotel corridor' seems to be an interchangeable row of bland, chain-owned choices. There's no escaping this, though what you lose in personality you gain in dependability. With chains, you have the (sometimes stifling) comfort of knowing what you'll get by looking at the sign. Sigh.

In this guide, we aim to highlight independently owned, family-run, quirky and otherwise stand-out establishments – places designed to be remembered, not instantly forgotten. When these are too few to sustain the traveler, we also include the best choices among the chains. Some chains, as well, have made not-unwelcome stabs at individualism; it sounds oxymoronic, but they occasionally offer unique stays.

Hotels in all categories typically include in-room phones, cable TV, alarm clocks, private baths and a simple continental breakfast. Many midrange properties provide minibars, microwaves, hairdryers, internet access, air-conditioning and/or heating, swimming pools and writing desks, while top-end hotels add concierge services, fitness and business centers, spas, restaurants, bars and much more.

The downside to an independent hotel is that decor and cleanliness can vary greatly, even from room to room. Don't like surprises? Ask to see your room before paying, particularly at cheaper places. In general, rooms will have one king-size bed or two double or queen-size beds, and rates will cover two adults, with small surcharges for a third or fourth person. Even if hotels advertise that children 'sleep free,' cots or rollaway beds may cost extra. Always ask about the hotel's policy for telephone calls; all charge an exorbitant amount for long-distance and international calls, but some also charge for dialing local and toll-free numbers.

CHAIN HOTELS

Budget

Choice Hotels (☎ 877-424-6423; www.choicehotels.com)
Days Inn (☎ 800-329-7466; www.daysinn.com)
Motel 6 (☎ 800-466-8356; www.motel6.com)
Red Roof Inn (☎ 800-733-7663; www.redroof.com)
Super 8 (☎ 800-800-8000; www.super8.com)
Travelodge (☎ 800-578-7878; www.travelodge.com)

Midrange

Best Western (☎ 800-780-7234; www.bestwestern.com)
Choice Hotels (☎ 877-424-6423; www.choicehotels.com)
Hampton Inn (☎ 800-426-7866; www.hamptoninn.com)
Holiday Inn (☎ 888-465-4329; www.holidayinn.com)
Howard Johnson (☎ 800-446-4656; www.hojo.com)
La Quinta (☎ 800-753-3757; www.lq.com)
Marriott (☎ 888-236-2427; www.marriott.com)
Radisson (☎ 800-395-7046; www.radisson.com)
Ramada (☎ 800-272-6232; www.ramada.com)

Top End

Four Seasons (☎ 800-819-5053; www.fourseasons.com)
Hilton (☎ 800-445-8667; www.hilton.com)
Hyatt (☎ 888-591-1234; www.hyatt.com)
Ritz-Carlton (☎ 800-542-8680; www.ritzcarlton.com)
Sheraton (☎ 800-325-3535; www.sheraton.com)
W Hotels (☎ 877-946-8357; www.whotels.com)
Westin (☎ 800-937-8461; www.westin.com)

Motels

Motels were originally 'drive-up rooms' along the highway, where you parked your car outside your door. Today, many motels are equivalent to hotels, with one leftover distinguishing characteristic: motels usually have exterior room doors opening onto a parking lot, while most hotel rooms open into secured interior hallways.

Motels tend to cluster around interstate exits and along main routes into towns. Some remain smaller, less-expensive 'mom-and-pop' operations; breakfast is rarely included (unless you count burnt coffee and donuts); and amenities might top out at a phone and a TV (maybe with cable). However, motels often have a few rooms with simple kitchenettes.

Don't judge a motel solely on looks. Facades may be faded and tired, but the proprietor may keep rooms spotlessly clean. Of course, the situation could be decidedly reversed. Try to ask to see your room before you commit.

ACTIVITIES

For inspiration, see the Outdoors chapter (p131) and the special section on national parks (p105). Here, we've provided some practical details and contact information for national outdoors organizations. See the regional chapters for more destinations, outdoor outfitters and local organizations.

The **Great Outdoor Recreation Pages** (GORP; http://gorp.away.com) are an all-round online resource. A general-interest magazine for outdoor enthusiasts is **Outside** (http://outside.away.com). If you just need gear, national retailers include co-op–owned **REI** (☎ 253-891-2500, 800-426-4840; www.rei.com) and the corporate **Sports Authority** (☎ 888-801-9164; www.sportsauthority.com).

For comprehensive instruction in a range of outdoor skills, contact the **National Outdoor Leadership School** (☎ 800-710-6657; www.nols.edu). REI offers outdoor activity and skills classes, weekend getaways and longer multisport adventure tours. **Outward Bound** (☎ 866-467-7651; www.outwardbound.org) is known for its challenging courses emphasizing wilderness skills and personal growth. For more regional outdoor activity schools, see p132.

The USA has a wealth of public lands. **Wilderness.net** (www.wilderness.net) provides descriptions, maps, contact information and links for every national wilderness area. **Recreation.gov** (www.recreation.gov) has a searchable database of recreational opportunities on public lands managed by federal agencies:

Bureau of Land Management (BLM; www.blm.gov)
National Park Service (NPS; www.nps.gov)
US Fish & Wildlife Service (USFWS; www.fws.gov)
US Forest Service (USFS; www.fs.fed.us)

For advice on low-impact camping and 'Leave No Trace' wilderness etiquette, see p126.

Canoeing, Kayaking, Rafting & Sailing

If a river, lake or reservoir is big enough to support watercraft, an outfitter or rental operation will usually be found nearby. In national parks, rafting, kayaking and canoeing usually require a permit, and in some cases – such as white-water rafting on the Colorado River – waitlists for individual permits can be years long. In these cases, book in advance with an organized tour.

Helpful resources for paddlers:

American Canoe Association (www.americancanoe.org) Canoeing and kayaking organization publishes *Paddler* magazine (www.paddlermagazine.com), has a water trails database and offers courses.

American Whitewater (www.americanwhitewater.org) Advocacy group for responsible recreation works to preserve America's wild rivers.

Canoe & Kayak (www.canoekayak.com) Special-interest magazine for paddlers.

Kayak Online (www.kayakonline.com) Advice for buying gear and helpful links to kayaking outfitters, schools and associations.

Cycling & Mountain Biking

Bike rental outfits are common across the whole country; see the regional chapters for recommendations. Turn to p1159 for advice on bicycle touring; buying, renting and reselling bicycles; and transporting your own bicycle to, from and around the USA. If you bring your own bike, bring a heavy-duty lock too – bicycle theft is big business here.

Some national and state parks have multi-use or recreational cycling trails, but bikes are almost always banned from dedicated hiking trails. Bikes are typically allowed on the parks' paved or dirt roads, but ask the rangers about local regulations first. Trail etiquette requires that cyclists yield to other users on trails. Elsewhere, bicycles are subject to the same rules of the road as automobiles. Check out www.mtbr.com or www.dirtworld.com for free online reviews of hundreds of mountain-biking trails.

Helpful resources for cyclists:

Adventure Cycling Association (www.adventurecycling.org) Organizes tours, sells bike routes and maps, maintains a cyclists' yellow pages and publishes *Adventure Cyclist* magazine.

Backroads (www.backroads.com) Offers a variety of cycling and multisport tours nationwide, from cushy to strenuous.

Bicycling (www.bicycling.com) Primarily for road cyclists, *Bicycling* magazine highlights cycling routes across the country and advises on gear and fitness training.

Bike (www.bikemag.com) *Bike* magazine publishes news and features online, with links to a database of national mountain-biking trail reviews.

Cycle America (www.cycleamerica.com) Specializes in supported cross-country rides and national park cycling tours.

League of American Bicyclists (www.bikeleague.org) National advocacy group publishes *American Bicyclist* magazine; its informative website has links, touring advice and a database of local bike clubs and repair shops.

Hiking & Backpacking

With few exceptions, most of America's wilderness areas are open to hikers. The best-maintained trails are usually in national and state parks; these range from easy, paved, wheelchair-accessible nature paths to overnight and multiday backcountry adventures.

At national and state parks, free trail maps are usually adequate for day hikes. For backpacking and day hiking on other public lands, topographic maps (p1143) may be useful and even necessary. Before hiking, always ask at a ranger station or visitor center about current weather and trail conditions. It's usually required that you get a permit or at least register with park rangers or at a sign-in board before departing on overnight trips. Whether free or costing a few dollars, backcountry permits are sometimes limited; in popular national parks they can book up months ahead. In environmentally sensitive areas areas, backcountry use may have many restrictions.

Be prepared for a wilderness journey and know what to do if things go wrong. **Survive Outdoors** (www.surviveoutdoors.com) dispenses tons of safety and first-aid tips, plus helpful photos of dangerous critters. *How to Stay Alive in the Woods: A Complete Guide to Food, Shelter, and Self-Preservation that Makes Starvation in the Wilderness Next to Impossible,* by Bradford Angier, covers almost every contingency.

Helpful resources for hikers and backpackers:

American Hiking Society (www.americanhiking.org) Links to local hiking clubs and 'volunteer vacations' building trails.

Backpacker (www.backpacker.com) Premier national magazine for backpackers, from novices to experts.

Rails-to-Trails Conservancy (www.railstotrails.org) Converts abandoned railroad corridors into hiking and biking trails; publishes free trail reviews at www.traillink.com.

Trails.com (www.trails.com) Searchable database of over 45,000 trails from coast to coast, plus printable topo maps and hike guides; membership fee required.

The continental USA's three mountain systems are traversed by legendary, epic trails, which can be broken up into smaller segments. For more information:

Appalachian Trail Appalachian Trail Conservancy (www.appalachiantrail.org)

Continental Divide Trail Continental Divide Trail Alliance (www.cdtrail.org); Continental Divide Trail Society (www.cdtsociety.org)

Pacific Crest Trail Pacific Crest Trail Association (www.pcta.org)

Rock Climbing & Canyoneering

Listed here are some helpful resources for climbers and canyoneers:

American Canyoneering Association (www.canyoneering.net) An online canyons database and links to courses, local climbing groups and more.

Climbing (www.climbing.com) Killer magazine for cutting-edge rock-climbing news and information since 1970.

SuperTopo (www.supertopo.com) One-stop shop for rock-climbing guidebooks, free topo maps and route descriptions.

Skiing & Snowboarding

Most of the USA's ski resorts are all-inclusive experiences: they typically offer equipment rental, lessons, kids' programs, restaurants and lodging. The ski season typically runs from mid-December to April, though some resorts have longer seasons. In summer, many resorts are great places to go mountain biking and hiking courtesy of chair lifts. Ski packages (including airfare, hotel and lift tickets) are easy to find through resorts, travel agencies and online travel booking sites; these packages can be a good deal if your main goal is to ski.

Charles Leocha's *Ski Snowboard America* has up-to-date overviews of North America's major resorts. Virtually every ski resort has its own website. Most downhill ski resorts also have snowboarding areas and some have cross-country (Nordic) ski trails. In winter, popular areas of national parks, national forests and city parks often have cross-country ski and snowshoe trails and ice-skating rinks.

These are some helpful resources for skiers and snowboarders:

Cross-Country Ski Areas Association (www.xcski.org) Comprehensive information and gear guides for skiing and snowshoeing across North America.

Cross Country Skier (www.crosscountryskier.com) Magazine with Nordic skiing news articles, online trail reports, and race and events information.

Powder (www.powdermag.com) Online version of *Powder* magazine for skiers.

SkiNet (www.skinet.com) Online versions of *Ski, Skiing* and *Snow* magazines.

Ski Resorts Guide (www.skiresortsguide.com) Comprehensive guide to resorts, with downloadable trail maps, lodging info and more.

SnoCountry Mountain Reports (www.snocountry.com) Snow reports for North America, plus events, news and resort links.

Snowboard.com (http://snowboard.colonies.com) A community website for snowboarders; lots of unvarnished advice.

Surfing, Kitesurfing & Windsurfing

Pick up **Surfer** (www.surfermag.com) magazine for news, features and an events calendar, along with travel reports that cover just about every break in the USA, plus online discussion boards. For a comprehensive surfing atlas, buy the *Stormrider Guide: North America*. The **US Kitesurfing Association** (www.uskite.org) has links to kitesurfing schools nationwide. For online articles and kitesurfing news, check out www.ikiteboarding.com. Windsurfers should contact the **US Windsurfing Association** (www.uswindsurfing.org). For water babies of all kinds, the **Surfrider Foundation** (www.surfrider.org), a grassroots nonprofit organization, strives to protect coastal biodiversity and ecological integrity worldwide.

BUSINESS HOURS

Unless otherwise noted, standard business hours in this guide are as follows. Businesses are open 9am to 5pm Monday to Friday. Banks are open 8:30am to 4:30pm Monday to Thursday, until 5:30pm Friday. Some post offices and banks are also open 9am to noon or 1pm on Saturday.

Stores are usually open 10am to 6pm Monday to Saturday, noon to 5pm Sunday. In malls and downtown shopping areas, hours may be extended to 8pm or 9pm. Supermarkets are generally open 8am to 8pm, and most cities have 24-hour supermarkets. In some parts of the country, all businesses except a few restaurants may close on Sunday.

Restaurant hours can fluctuate with seasonal demand and the owners' whim. We provide peak-season restaurant hours for every listing, but if it's winter, and your heart's set and/or you're making a special trip, call ahead to confirm. Generally, breakfast is served from 7am to 10:30am Monday to Friday, with weekend brunch 9am to 2pm Saturday and Sunday; lunch runs from 11:30am to 2:30pm Monday to Friday; and dinner is served between 5pm to 9:30pm, often later on Friday and Saturday.

Bars and pubs are usually open 5pm to midnight, extended to 2am on Friday and Saturday. Nightclubs and dance clubs tend to open after 9pm and close around 2am Wednesday to Saturday; hours may be longer in major cities.

CHILDREN

Traveling with children is often like possessing a secret key that unlocks locals, who brighten and coo and embrace your family like long-lost cousins. From the city to the country, most facilities are ready to accommodate a child's needs, and there are boundless options for entertaining restless young minds.

Practicalities

Restaurants of all stripes have high chairs, and if a restaurant doesn't have a specific children's menu, it can usually make a kid-tailored meal. Many diners and family restaurants break out paper placemats and crayons for drawing. Many public toilets have a baby changing table (sometimes in men's toilets too), and gender-neutral 'family' facilities appear in airports.

Motels and hotels typically have rooms with two beds, which are ideal for families. They also have roll-away beds or cots that can be brought into the room for an extra charge. Some have 'kids stay free' programs, for children up to 12 or sometimes 18 years old. Some B&Bs, to preserve a romantic atmosphere, don't allow children; ask when reserving.

Every car rental agency should be able to provide an appropriate child seat or restraint, since these are required in every state, but you need to request it when booking and expect to pay around $10 more per day. Airlines sometimes offer 'kids fly free' promotions, and they usually offer steep discounts for traveling infants.

Resort hotels may have on-call babysitting services; otherwise, ask the front-desk staff or concierge to help you make arrangements. Always ask if babysitters are licensed and bonded, what they charge per hour per child, whether there's a minimum fee, and if they charge extra for transportation or meals. Most tourist bureaus list local resources for childcare and recreation facilities, medical services and so on.

To find family-oriented sights and activities, accommodations, restaurants and entertainment throughout this guide, just look for the child-friendly icon ( ).

Sights & Activities

In this guide, many big cities include a 'for children' section that highlights the area's best kids' activities and resources. The USA is full to bursting with hands-on science museums, playgrounds, theme parks and family fun centers, too. Most national and state parks gear at least some exhibits, trails and programs (eg junior ranger activities) towards families with kids.

For more outdoor advice, read *Kids in the Wild: A Family Guide to Outdoor Recreation* by Cindy Ross and Todd Gladfelter, and Alice Cary's *Parents' Guide to Hiking & Camping*. For all-around information and advice, check out Lonely Planet's *Travel with Children*.

Helpful resources for families:

Family Travel Files (www.thefamilytravelfiles.com) Ready-made vacation ideas, destination profiles and travel tips.

Go City Kids (www.gocitykids.com) Excellent coverage of kid-centric activities and entertainment in over 50 US cities.

Kids.gov (www.kids.gov) Eclectic, enormous national resource; download songs and activities, or even link to the CIA Kids' Page.

CLIMATE CHARTS

For general advice on seasonal travel in the USA, see p25. Every regional chapter provides specific destination information. The **National Weather Service** (www.nws.noaa.gov) has an array of radar and satellite maps. Our climate charts (p1138) provide a snapshot of the USA's weather patterns.

CUSTOMS

For a complete list of US customs regulations, visit the official portal for **US Customs and Border Protection** (www.cbp.gov); the downloadable 'Know Before You Go' brochure covers the basics.

US Customs allows each person to bring 1L of liquor (provided you are at least 21 years old) and 100 cigars and 200 cigarettes (if you are at least 18) duty-free into the USA. US citizens are allowed to import, duty-free, $800 worth of gifts and purchases from abroad, while non-US citizens are allowed to bring in $100 worth.

US law permits you to bring in, or take out, as much as $10,000 in US or foreign currency, traveler's checks or money orders without formality. There's no maximum limit, but larger amounts of money must be declared to customs.

There are heavy penalties for attempting to import illegal drugs. It's also forbidden to bring in to the US drug paraphernalia, lottery tickets, items with fake brand names, and most goods made in Cuba, Iran, North Korea, Myanmar (Burma), Angola and Sudan. Any fruit, vegetables, or other food or plant material must be declared or left in the bins in the arrival area. Most food items are prohibited to prevent the introduction of pests or diseases.

The USA, like over 170 other countries, is a signatory to the Convention on International Trade in Endangered Species of Wild Flora and Fauna (CITES). As such, it prohibits the import and export of products made from species that may be endangered in any part of the world, including ivory, tortoiseshell, coral and many fur, skin and feather products. If you bring or buy a fur coat, bone carving or alligator-skin boots, you may have to show a certificate when you enter and/or leave the USA that states your goods were not made from endangered species. For more information, contact the **US Fish and Wildlife Service** (☎ 800-358-2104; www.fws.gov).

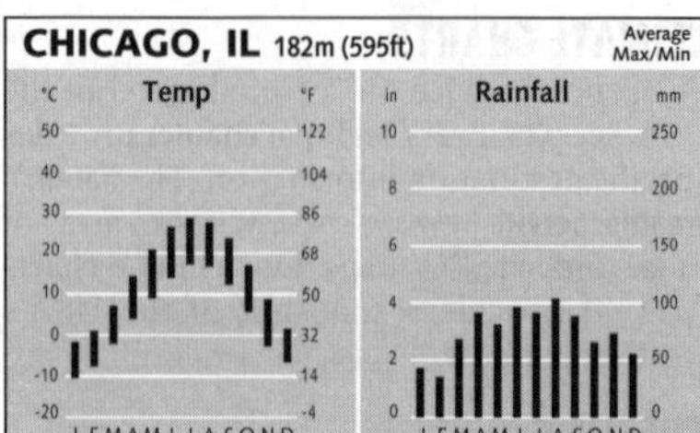
CHICAGO, IL 182m (595ft)
Average Max/Min
°C Temp °F
50 40 30 20 10 0 -10 -20
122 104 86 68 50 32 14 -4
in Rainfall mm
10 8 6 4 2 0
250 200 150 100 50 0
J F M A M J J A S O N D

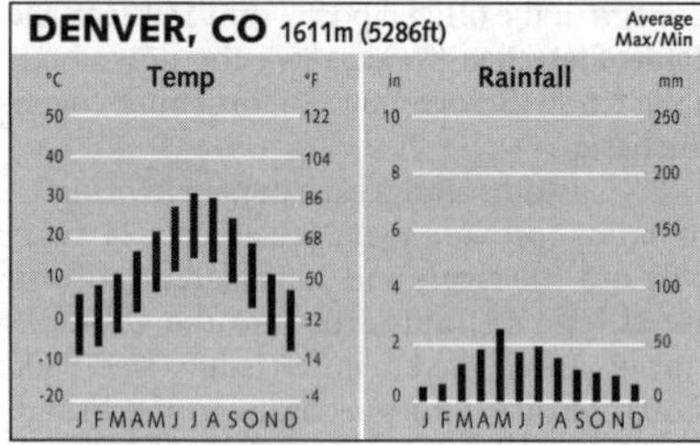
DENVER, CO 1611m (5286ft)
Average Max/Min
°C Temp °F
50 40 30 20 10 0 -10 -20
122 104 86 68 50 32 14 -4
in Rainfall mm
10 8 6 4 2 0
250 200 150 100 50 0
J F M A M J J A S O N D

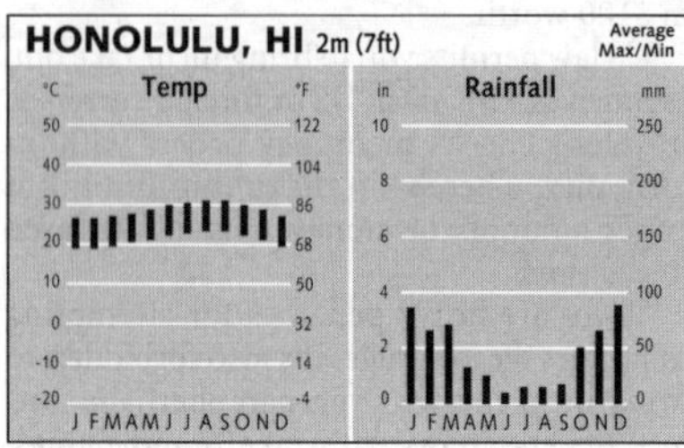
HONOLULU, HI 2m (7ft)
Average Max/Min
°C Temp °F
50 40 30 20 10 0 -10 -20
122 104 86 68 50 32 14 -4
in Rainfall mm
10 8 6 4 2 0
250 200 150 100 50 0
J F M A M J J A S O N D

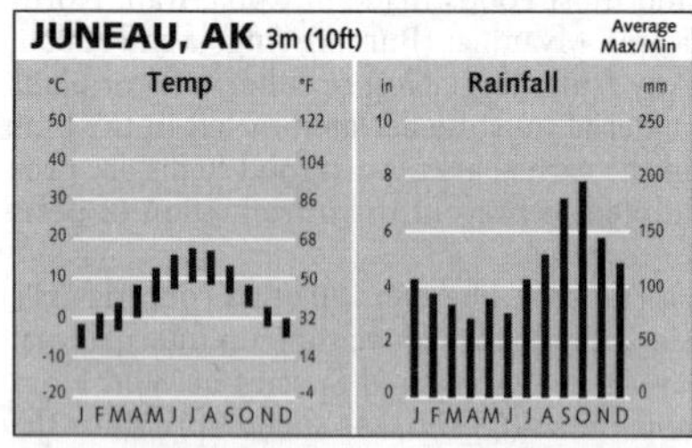
JUNEAU, AK 3m (10ft)
Average Max/Min
°C Temp °F
50 40 30 20 10 0 -10 -20
122 104 86 68 50 32 14 -4
in Rainfall mm
10 8 6 4 2 0
250 200 150 100 50 0
J F M A M J J A S O N D

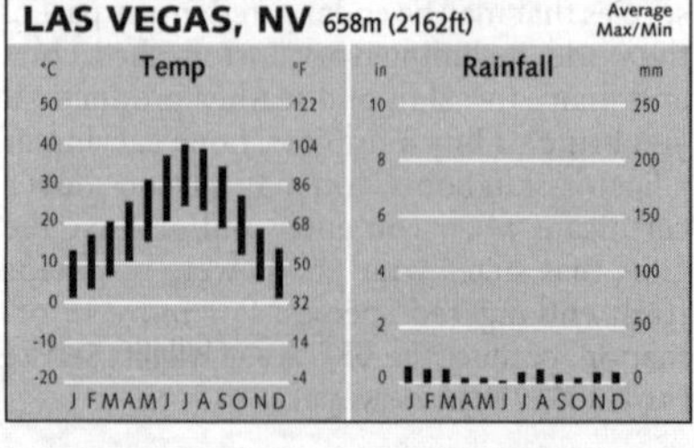
LAS VEGAS, NV 658m (2162ft)
Average Max/Min
°C Temp °F
50 40 30 20 10 0 -10 -20
122 104 86 68 50 32 14 -4
in Rainfall mm
10 8 6 4 2 0
250 200 150 100 50 0
J F M A M J J A S O N D

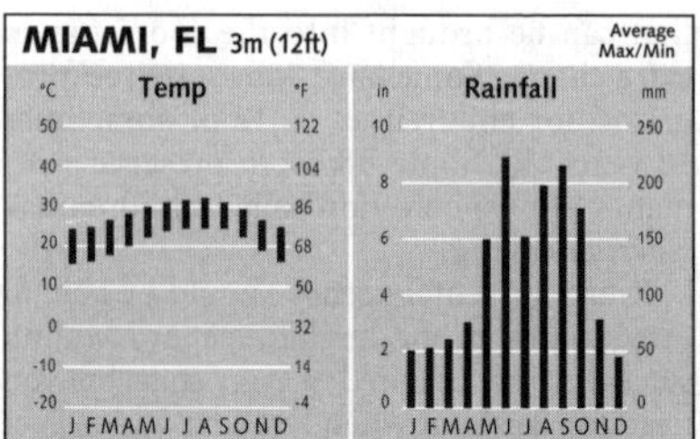
MIAMI, FL 3m (12ft)
Average Max/Min
°C Temp °F
50 40 30 20 10 0 -10 -20
122 104 86 68 50 32 14 -4
in Rainfall mm
10 8 6 4 2 0
250 200 150 100 50 0
J F M A M J J A S O N D

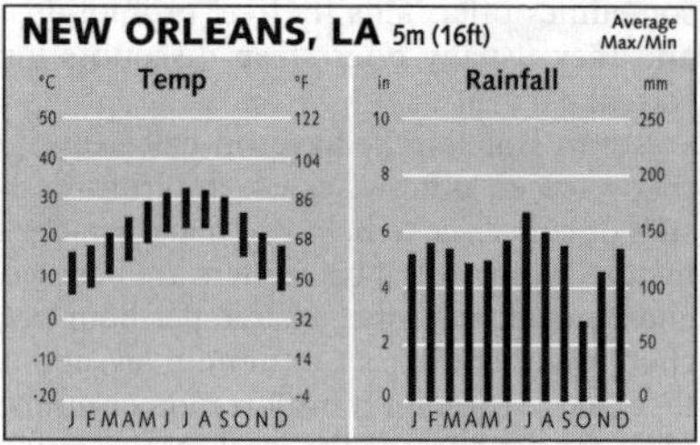
NEW ORLEANS, LA 5m (16ft)
Average Max/Min
°C Temp °F
50 40 30 20 10 0 -10 -20
122 104 86 68 50 32 14 -4
in Rainfall mm
10 8 6 4 2 0
250 200 150 100 50 0
J F M A M J J A S O N D

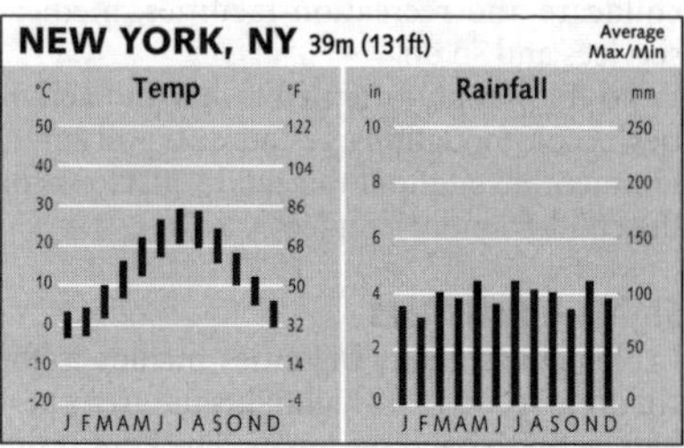
NEW YORK, NY 39m (131ft)
Average Max/Min
°C Temp °F
50 40 30 20 10 0 -10 -20
122 104 86 68 50 32 14 -4
in Rainfall mm
10 8 6 4 2 0
250 200 150 100 50 0
J F M A M J J A S O N D

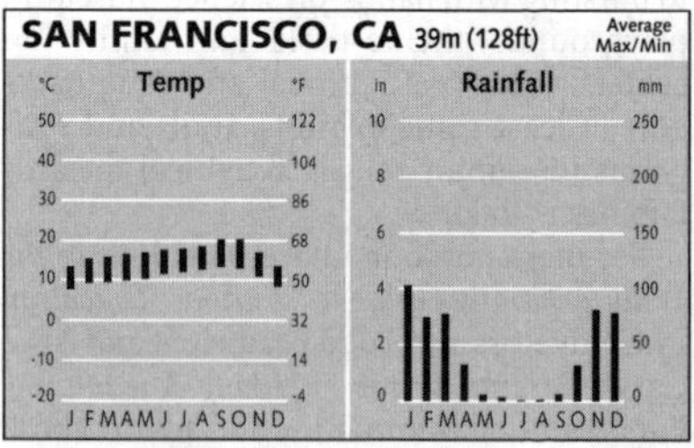
SAN FRANCISCO, CA 39m (128ft)
Average Max/Min
°C Temp °F
50 40 30 20 10 0 -10 -20
122 104 86 68 50 32 14 -4
in Rainfall mm
10 8 6 4 2 0
250 200 150 100 50 0
J F M A M J J A S O N D

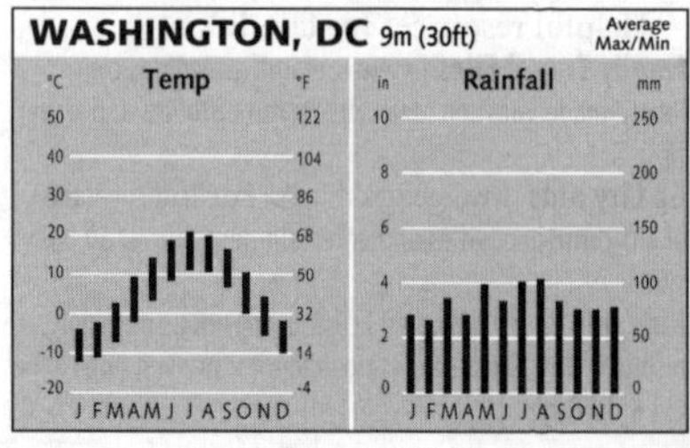
WASHINGTON, DC 9m (30ft)
Average Max/Min
°C Temp °F
50 40 30 20 10 0 -10 -20
122 104 86 68 50 32 14 -4
in Rainfall mm
10 8 6 4 2 0
250 200 150 100 50 0
J F M A M J J A S O N D

DANGERS & ANNOYANCES

Despite its seemingly Babylonian list of dangers – guns, violent crime, riots, earthquakes, tornadoes – the USA is actually a pretty safe country to visit. The greatest danger for travelers is posed by car accidents (buckle up – it's the law). The greatest annoyances are urban traffic and crowds at popular tourist attractions. Otherwise, there are few traveler troubles unique to the USA.

Crime

For the traveler, petty theft is the biggest concern, not violent crime. When possible, withdraw money from ATMs during the day, or at night in well-lit, busy areas. When driving, don't pick up hitchhikers, and lock valuables in the trunk of your car before arriving at your destination. In hotels, you can secure valuables in room or hotel safes.

Guns, so prominent in the news, would seem to be everywhere, but unless it's hunting season, you'll rarely see them (except perhaps in Alaska and Texas). Then again, if it *is* hunting season, wear bright colors when hiking in the woods.

Scams

Pack your street smarts. In big cities, you know that three-card-monte card games are always rigged, and that expensive electronics, watches and designer items sold on the cheap from sidewalk tables are either fakes or stolen? You realize there is no such thing as 'bargain-priced authentic handicrafts?' Good. Those truly fascinated by all the myriad ways small-time American hucksters make a living today (usually with credit card, real estate and investment frauds), browse the 'Consumer Guides' on the government's website, www.usa.gov.

Natural Disasters

Most areas with predictable natural disturbances – tornadoes in the Midwest, tsunamis in Hawaii, hurricanes in the South, earthquakes in California – have an emergency siren system to alert communities to imminent danger. These sirens are tested periodically at noon, but if you hear one and suspect trouble, turn on a local TV or radio station, which will be broadcasting safety warnings and advice.

The **US Department of Health & Human Services** (www.dhhs.gov/disasters) has preparedness advice, news and information on all the ways your vacation could go horribly, horribly wrong. But relax: it probably won't.

DISCOUNTS

Travelers will find a plethora of ways to shave costs off hotel rooms, meals, rental cars, museum admissions and just about anything else that can be had for a price. Persistence and ingenuity go a long way when it comes to finding deals in the USA.

Students and seniors over age 62 (sometimes 55 or 60) are not issued separate discount cards, but they benefit from savings of all kinds. As a matter of policy, ask about a discount every time you book a room, reserve a car or pay an entrance fee. Most of the time this saves 10% or so, but sometimes as much as 50%. Simply carry proof of age or student status.

International students should consider getting an **International Student Identity Card** (ISIC; www.isiccard.com), which provides its own discounts and should convince any dubious merchants of your student status. For international nonstudents under 26, the International Youth Travel Card (IYTC) offers some of the same savings. International and US students can buy the **Student Advantage Card** (www.studentadvantage.com) and get 15% off Amtrak train and Greyhound bus tickets, plus discounts of up to 40% at some hotels, shops and cinemas.

US seniors should consider getting an 'America the Beautiful' Senior Pass (p114), which grants free access to all federal recreational lands (eg national parks) and 50% off use fees such as camping. For US citizens aged 50 years and older, the nonprofit **American Association of Retired Persons** (AARP; www.aarp.org) is another source of travel discounts, typically 10% to 25% off hotels, car rentals, entertainment etc.

Card-carrying members of automobile associations (p1161) are entitled to similar travel discounts; AAA has reciprocal agreements with several international auto associations, so bring your membership card from home. Other people whose status might lead to discounts are: US military personnel and veterans, travelers with disabilities, children, business travelers and foreign visitors. These discounts may not always be advertised – it pays to ask.

Discount coupons can be found at every tourist locale. They always have restrictions

GOVERNMENT TRAVEL ADVICE

- Australia (www.smartraveler.gov.au)
- Canada (www.voyage.gc.ca)
- New Zealand (www.safetravel.govt.nz)
- UK (www.fco.gov.uk)
- USA (www.travel.state.gov)

and conditions, so read the fine print. Some are hardly worth the effort, but scour tourist information offices and highway welcome centers for brochures and flyers, and you'll find a few gems. For online hotel coupons, browse **Roomsaver.com** (www.roomsaver.com).

EMBASSIES & CONSULATES

International travelers who want to contact their home country's embassy while in the United States should visit www.embassy.org, which lists contact information for all foreign embassies in Washington, DC. Most countries have an embassy for the UN in New York City. Some countries also have consulates in other large cities; look under 'Consulates' in the yellow pages, or call local directory assistance.

FESTIVALS & EVENTS

Festivals and events listed here are celebrated nationally, though with much more fanfare in some places. For more festival highlights nationwide, see 'Parties & Parades' (p28) and the 'Festivals & Events' sections of the regional chapters. Contact individual tourist information offices for more details. See also Holidays (opposite).

JANUARY

Chinese New Year Late January or early February. Celebrated with parades, fireworks and lots of food; San Francisco's Chinatown is a fantastic place to be.

FEBRUARY

Black History Month African American heritage is celebrated nationwide.

Valentine's Day The 14th. For some reason, St Valentine is associated with romance; shops sell out of boxes of chocolate candy, flowers and cards.

Mardi Gras In late February or early March, the day before Ash Wednesday. Parades, revelry and abandonment accompany the finale of Carnival; New Orleans's celebrations are legendary.

MARCH

St Patrick's Day The 17th. The patron saint of Ireland is honored; huge celebrations occur in New York, Boston and Chicago. Wear green – if you don't, you could get pinched.

Easter In late March or April, on the Sunday following Good Friday (which is not a public holiday); after morning church services, kids hunt for eggs hidden by the Easter bunny.

MAY

Cinco de Mayo The 5th. The day the Mexicans won the Battle of Puebla against the French in 1862; especially in the South and West, communities celebrate their Mexican heritage with parades.

Mother's Day The second Sunday. Children send cards and call their mothers (or feel guilty for a whole year).

JUNE

Father's Day The third Sunday. Same idea as Mother's Day, different parent, less guilt.

Gay Pride Month (www.interpride.org) In some cities, gay pride celebrations last a week, but in San Francisco, it's a month-long party, where the last weekend in June sees giant parades.

JULY

Independence Day The 4th. The historic anniversary of the US becoming independent inspires parades and fireworks; Chicago pulls out all the stops with fireworks on the 3rd.

OCTOBER

Halloween The 31st. Kids dress in costumes and go door-to-door trick-or-treating for candy; adults dress in costumes and act out alter egos at parties – New York and San Francisco are the wildest.

NOVEMBER

Day of the Dead The 2nd. Areas with Mexican communities honor deceased relatives with candlelit memorials; candy skulls and skeletons are popular.

Thanksgiving The fourth Thursday. A latter-day harvest festival: family and friends gather for daylong feasts, traditionally involving roast turkey. New York City hosts a huge parade.

DECEMBER

Chanukkah Date determined by the Hebrew calendar, but usually begins before Christmas. This eight-day Jewish holiday is also called the Festival of Lights.

Christmas The 25th. Christ's birth inspires midnight church services, tree-lighting ceremonies, caroling in the streets and of course, a visit from Santa.

Kwanzaa (www.officialkwanzaawebsite.org) From December 26th to January 1st. This African American celebration is a time to give thanks and honor the seven principles.

New Year's Eve The 31st. Out with the old, in with the new: millions get drunk, resolve to do better, and the next day nurse hangovers while watching college football.

FOOD

In this book, restaurant prices typically refer to an average main dish at dinner; the same dish at lunch will usually be significantly cheaper, perhaps half-price. Quoted prices do not usually include drinks, appetizers, desserts, taxes or tips, unless otherwise stated. When price categories are used in the regional chapters, 'budget' means a meal under $12, 'midrange' means most dinner meals or mains $12 to $25, and 'top end' means most dinner meals or mains over $25.

Note many US restaurants ban or restrict smoking. For the lowdown on cuisine, customs and table manners, see the Food & Drink chapter, p101.

GAY & LESBIAN TRAVELERS

Most major US cities have a visible and open GLBT community that is easy to connect with. In this guide, many cities include a boxed text or section that describes the city's best GLBT offerings. For highlights, see the 'We're Here, We're Queer' itinerary (p43).

The level of acceptance varies nationwide. In some places, there is absolutely no tolerance whatsoever, and in others acceptance is predicated on GLBT people not 'flaunting' their sexual preference or identity. Make no mistake: bigotry still exists. When in doubt, assume locals follow a 'don't ask, don't tell' policy. Same-sex marriage, a hotly debated topic, is now legal in a handful of states.

Damron (www.damron.com) publishes the classic gay travel guides, but they're advertiser-driven and sometimes outdated. **OutTraveler** (www.outtraveler.com), **Out & About** (www.gay.com/travel) and **PlanetOut** (www.planetout.com/travel) publish downloadable gay travel guides and articles. **Purple Roofs** (www.purpleroofs.com) lists gay-owned and gay-friendly B&Bs and hotels nationwide.

The Queerest Places: A Guide to Gay and Lesbian Historic Sites by Paula Martinac is full of juicy details and history, and covers the country.

Other helpful resources:

Advocate (www.advocate.com) Gay-oriented news website reports on business, politics, arts, entertainment and travel.

Gay & Lesbian National Help Center (☎ 888-843-4564; 🕑 1-9pm PST Mon-Fri, 4pm-midnight PST Sat) A national hotline for counseling, information and referrals.

Gay Yellow Network (www.gayyellow.com) Yellow-page listings for over 30 US cities.

National Gay and Lesbian Task Force (www.thetaskforce.org) National activist group's website covers news, politics and current issues.

HOLIDAYS

On the following national public holidays, banks, schools and government offices (including post offices) are closed, and transportation, museums and other services operate on a Sunday schedule. Holidays falling on a weekend are usually observed the following Monday.

New Year's Day January 1
Martin Luther King Jr Day Third Monday in January
Presidents' Day Third Monday in February
Memorial Day Last Monday in May
Independence Day July 4
Labor Day First Monday in September
Columbus Day Second Monday in October
Veterans' Day November 11
Thanksgiving Fourth Thursday in November
Christmas Day December 25

During spring break, college students get a week off from school so they can overrun beach towns and resorts with wild shenanigans. Colleges don't all choose the same week, so spring breaks occur throughout March and April. For students of all ages, summer vacation runs from June to August.

INSURANCE

No matter how long or short your trip, make sure you have adequate travel insurance, purchased before departure. At a minimum, you need coverage for medical emergencies and treatment, including hospital stays and an emergency flight home if necessary. Medical treatment in the USA is of the highest caliber, but the expense could kill you. See p1168 for more information.

You should also consider getting coverage for luggage theft or loss and trip cancellation. If you already have a home-owner's or renter's policy, see what it will cover and consider getting supplemental insurance to cover the rest. If you have prepaid a large portion of your trip, cancellation insurance is a worthwhile expense. A comprehensive travel insurance policy that covers all these things can cost up to 10% of the total cost of your trip.

THE LEGAL AGE FOR...

- Drinking: 21
- Driving: 16
- Heterosexual consensual sex: 16-18 (varies by state)
- Homosexual consensual sex: where legal, 16-18 (varies by state)
- Voting: 18

Travelers should note that they can be prosecuted under the laws of their home country regarding age of consent for sexual activity, even while traveling abroad.

If you will be driving, it's essential that you have liability insurance. Car rental agencies offer insurance that covers damage to the rental vehicle and separate liability insurance, which covers damage to people and other vehicles. See p1163 for details.

Worldwide travel insurance is available at www.lonelyplanet.com/travel_services. You can buy, extend and claim online anytime – even if you're already on the road.

INTERNET ACCESS

Travelers will have few problems staying connected in the tech-savvy USA.

This guides uses an internet icon (💻) when a place has an internet terminal for public use and the wi-fi icon (📶) when it offers wireless internet access, whether free or fee-based. These days, most hotels and some motels have either a public computer terminal or wi-fi (sometimes free, sometimes for a surcharge of $10 or more per day); ask when reserving. For more on wi-fi hotspots, see the boxed text, below.

Most towns have at least one internet café or copy center (rates average $3 to $12 per hour) and cities have dozens; in this guide, city 'Internet Access' sections list convenient options. In addition to providing internet access, full-service internet cafés may let you hook up your own peripherals to upload photos and/or burn them onto CDs (see also p1144).

For quick internet surfing and email, other dependable bets are public libraries, which offer public terminals (though they have time limits) and sometimes wi-fi. Occasionally out-of-state residents are charged a small fee.

If you're not from the US, remember that you will need an AC adapter for your laptop, plus a plug adapter for US sockets; both are available at larger electronics shops, such as **Best Buy** (☎ 888-237-8289; www.bestbuy.com).

See p32 for some useful websites for trip planning and traveling in the USA.

LEGAL MATTERS

In everyday matters, if you are stopped by the police, bear in mind that there is no system of paying traffic or other fines on the spot. Attempting to pay a fine to an officer is frowned upon at best and may result in a charge of bribery. For traffic offenses, the police officer or highway patroller will explain the options to you. There is usually a 30-day period to pay a fine. Most matters can be handled by mail.

If you are arrested, you have a legal right to an attorney, and you are allowed to remain

LOOK MA, NO WIRES

Wi-fi hotspots don't entirely cover the USA yet, but wireless internet access is common. Most cities and college towns have neighborhood hotspots, and even the smallest towns usually have at least one coffee shop, internet café or hotel with wi-fi. You can even connect in the woods: private campgrounds (like KOA) increasingly offer it, and so do some state parks (for example, in California, Michigan, Kentucky and Texas).

The following websites provide lists of free and fee-based wi-fi hotspots nationwide, as well as lots of helpful advice and links to gear:

- www.hotspot-locations.com
- www.jiwire.com
- www.wi-fi.com (run by the nonprofit Wi-Fi Alliance).
- www.wififreespot.com
- www.wi-fihotspotlist.com

silent. There is no legal reason to speak to a police officer if you don't wish, but never walk away from an officer until given permission to do so. Anyone who is arrested is legally allowed to make one phone call. If you can't afford a lawyer, a public defender will be appointed to you free of charge. Foreign visitors who don't have a lawyer, friend or family member to help should call their embassy; the police will provide the number upon request.

As a matter of principle, the US legal system presumes a person innocent until proven guilty. Each state has its own civil and criminal laws, and what is legal in one state may be illegal in others. Federal laws are applicable to the postal service, US government property and many interstate activities.

One wrinkle for international visitors is the USA Patriot Act, passed after September 11. Among other things, it expanded the federal government's ability to detain foreign visitors and immigrants they believe are linked to terrorism or terrorist organizations for an extended period of time without submitting charges or bringing them to trial. While this should be taken seriously, it is extremely unlikely to affect you. For more information and legal-defense referrals, contact the **American Civil Liberties Union** (ACLU; www.aclu.org/safeandfree).

Drinking

Bars and stores often ask for photo ID to prove you are of legal drinking age (ie 21 or over). Being 'carded' is standard practice; don't take it personally. The sale of liquor is subject to local government regulations; some counties prohibit liquor sales on Sunday, after midnight or before breakfast. In 'dry' counties, liquor sales are banned altogether.

Driving

In all states, driving under the influence of alcohol or drugs is a serious offense, subject to stiff fines and even imprisonment. For more information on driving in the USA and road rules, see p1165.

Drugs

Recreational drugs are prohibited by federal and state laws. Some states, such as California and Alaska, treat possession of small quantities of marijuana as a misdemeanor, though it is still punishable with fines and/or imprisonment.

Possession of any illicit drug, including cocaine, ecstasy, LSD, heroin, hashish or more than an ounce of pot, is a felony potentially punishable by lengthy jail sentences. For foreigners, conviction of any drug offense is grounds for deportation.

MAPS

For a good road atlas or driving maps, try **Rand McNally** (www.randmcnally.com) and its Thomas Brothers city guides; both are stocked at many bookstores and some gas stations. If you are a member of an automobile association (p1161), you can get free high-quality maps from regional offices; AAA has reciprocal agreements with some international auto clubs. For online driving directions and free downloadable maps, visit **Google Maps** (http://maps.google.com).

If you're heading into the wilderness backcountry, don't venture out on the trail without a good topographic map, often sold at park visitor centers, outdoor outfitters and supply stores. The most detailed topo maps are published by the **US Geological Survey** (USGS; ☎ 877-275-8747; http://store.usgs.gov), which offers online downloads and orders; the website has a comprehensive list of retailers. You can pay to create custom, downloadable topo maps at **Trails.com** (www.trails.com) or buy personalized topo-map creation software from **National Geographic** (www.nationalgeographic.com), whose online store has all the mapping products you'd ever want.

For on- and off-road driving and outdoor adventures on foot and bicycle, GPS gear and mapping software are available from **Garmin** (www.garmin.com) and **Magellan** (www.magellangps.com). Of course, GPS units can sometimes fail and may not work in all areas of the country, such as in thick forests or deep canyons.

MONEY

The US dollar ($) is the only currency generally accepted in the country, though a few places near the Canadian border also accept Canadian dollars.

The US dollar is divided into 100 cents (¢). Coins come in denominations of 1¢ (penny), 5¢ (nickel), 10¢ (dime), 25¢ (quarter), the seldom-seen 50¢ (half-dollar) piece and $1 coin. Quarters are most commonly used in vending machines and parking meters. Bills come in $1, $2 (rare), $5, $10, $20, $50 and $100 denominations.

Most locals do not carry large amounts of cash for everyday use, relying instead on credit cards, ATMs and debit cards. Smaller businesses may refuse to accept bills over $20. Prices quoted in this book are in US dollars and exclude taxes, unless otherwise noted. For a list of currency-exchange rates at press time, see the inside front cover. For typical US travel costs, see p25.

ATMs

ATMs are available 24/7 at most banks, and in shopping centers, airports, grocery stores and convenience shops. Most ATMs charge a service fee of $2 or more per transaction and your home bank may impose additional charges. Withdrawing cash from an ATM using a credit card usually incurs a hefty fee; check with your credit-card company first.

For foreign visitors, ask your bank or credit card company for exact information about using its cards in stateside ATMs. If you will be relying on ATMs (not a bad strategy), bring more than one card and carry them separately. The exchange rate on ATM transactions is usually as good as you'll get anywhere. Before leaving home, notify your bank and credit-card providers of your upcoming travel plans. Otherwise, you may trigger fraud alerts with atypical spending patterns, which may result in your accounts being temporarily frozen.

Credit Cards

Major credit cards are almost universally accepted. In fact, it's almost impossible to rent a car or make phone reservations without one (though some airlines require your credit card billing address to be in the USA – a hassle if you're booking domestic flights once there). It's highly recommended that you carry at least one credit card, if only for emergencies. Visa and MasterCard are the most widely accepted.

Before leaving home, notify your bank/credit-card providers of your upcoming travel plans. Carry copies of your credit card numbers separately. If your credit cards are lost or stolen, contact the issuing company immediately:

American Express (☎ 800-528-4800; www.americanexpress.com)
Diners Club (☎ 800-234-6377; www.dinersclub.com)
Discover (☎ 800-347-2683; www.discovercard.com)
MasterCard (☎ 800-622-7747; www.mastercard.com)
Visa (☎ 800-847-2911; www.visa.com)

Currency Exchange

Banks are usually the best places to exchange foreign currencies. Most large city banks offer currency exchange, but banks in rural areas may not. Currency-exchange counters at the airport and in tourist centers typically have the worst rates; ask about fees and surcharges first. **Travelex** (☎ 888-457-4602; www.travelex.com) is a major currency-exchange company, but **American Express** (☎ 800-297-2977; www.americanexpress.com) travel offices may offer better rates.

Taxes

Sales tax varies by state and county; see each state's 'Facts' boxed text in the regional chapters for specifics. Hotel taxes vary by city, and these are listed under cities' Sleeping sections.

Tipping

Tipping is *not* optional; only withhold tips in cases of outrageously bad service.

Airport & hotel porters $2 per bag, minimum per cart $5
Bartenders 10-15% per round, minimum per drink $1
Hotel maids $2-4 per night, left under the card provided
Restaurant servers 15-20%, unless a gratuity is already charged on the bill
Taxi drivers 10-15%, rounded up to the next dollar
Valet parking attendants At least $2 when handed back the keys

Traveler's Checks

Since the advent of ATMs, traveler's checks are becoming obsolete, except as a trustworthy backup. If you carry them, buy them in US dollars; local businesses may not cash them in a foreign currency. Keep a separate record of their numbers in case they are lost or stolen. American Express and Visa traveler's checks are the most widely accepted.

PHOTOGRAPHY & VIDEO

Print film can be found in drugstores and at specialty camera shops. Digital camera memory cards are widely available at chain retailers such as Best Buy and Target.

Drugstores and supermarkets will process print film cheaply – about $7 for a roll of 24 exposures. One-hour processing services are more expensive, usually around $12. FedEx Office is a major chain of copy shops with one-stop digital-photo printing and CD-burning stations. Many internet cafés (p1142) offer digital photo uploading and CD-burning services.

Some Native American tribal lands prohibit photography and video completely; when it's allowed, you may be required to purchase a permit. Always ask permission if you want to photograph someone close up; anyone who then agrees to be photographed may expect a small tip.

For more advice on picture-taking, consult Lonely Planet's *Travel Photography* book.

POST

For 24-hour postal information, including post office locations and hours, contact the **US Postal Service** (USPS; ☎ 800-275-8777; www.usps.com), which is reliable and inexpensive. You'll find branch post offices and post office centers in some drugstores and supermarkets.

For sending urgent or important letters and packages either domestically or overseas, **Federal Express** (FedEx; ☎ 800-463-3339; www.fedex.com) and **United Parcel Service** (UPS; ☎ 800-742-5877; www.ups.com) offer more-expensive door-to-door delivery services.

Postal Rates

At press time, the postal rates for 1st-class mail within the USA were 44¢ for letters weighing up to 1oz (17¢ for each additional ounce) and 28¢ for postcards. First-class mail goes up to 13oz, and then priority-mail rates apply.

International airmail rates (except to Canada and Mexico) are 98¢ for a 1oz letter or a postcard; to Canada it's 75¢, and to Mexico it's 79¢.

Sending & Receiving Mail

If you have the correct postage, you can drop mail weighing less than 13oz into any blue mailbox. To send a package weighing 13oz or more, go to a post office.

Poste-restante mail can usually be sent to you c/o General Delivery at any post office that has its own zip code. Domestic mail is usually held for 10 days and international mail for 30 days before it's returned to the sender; you might ask the sender to write 'Hold for Arrival' on the envelope. You'll need photo ID to collect mail. In some big cities, general-delivery mail is not held at the main post office but at a postal facility away from downtown.

SHOPPING

Most visitors won't want to leave before procuring a little American kitsch, and you'll find it's merely abundant even when it isn't truly bizarre. Some tacky roadside souvenirs achieve the status of folk art, and if nothing else, they prove that Americans really do have a sense of humor.

Many regions are known for excellent local handicrafts or Native artwork and goods. Traditional quilts, Pueblo jewelry, Navajo blankets, traditional and contemporary pottery, Gullah sweetgrass baskets and tooled leather cowboy boots are just a few of the things to look for. Good pieces will be expensive; if they are cheap, they are probably not authentic.

Another popular purchase is antiques. As with handicrafts, bargains are rare and sometimes suspect. The most popular antiques – anything colonial, Victorian, Amish, Shaker, art-deco or 1950s mid-century-modern – will likely have a hefty price tag.

For hip, unusual souvenirs, browse museum stores, which specialize in items that play off the museum's collections. They also often sell high-quality original designs by local artists and artisans.

Bargain hunters should track down factory outlet malls. These are usually near a freeway exit on the outskirts of cities or towns. There, brand-name stores sell their damaged, leftover or out-of-season stock at discounts ranging from modest to practically giveaway. Service will be minimal and choices limited, but the chance of half-price Levi's jeans, Nike shoes or a Coach handbag can be a sirens' song.

SOLO TRAVELERS

There are no particular problems traveling alone in the USA.

Hotels often offer lower rates for a single person, but single rooms tend to be small and badly located; for more comfort, reserve a double. To meet people, eat at the restaurant bar.

Hitchhiking is always risky and not recommended, *especially* hitchhiking alone. Definitely don't pick up hitchhikers when driving alone.

When first meeting someone, don't advertise where you are staying, or even that you are traveling alone. Americans can be eager to help and even take in solo travelers. However, don't take all offers of help at face value. If someone who seems trustworthy invites you to his or her home, let someone (eg hostel or hotel manager) know where you're going. This advice also applies if you go for a hike by yourself. If something happens and you don't return as expected, you want to know that someone will notice and know where to begin looking for you.

More advice for women travelers can be found on p1151.

TELEPHONE

The US phone system comprises regional service providers, competing long-distance carriers and several mobile-phone and payphone companies. Overall, the system is very efficient, but it can be expensive. Avoid making long-distance calls on a hotel phone or on a pay phone. It's usually cheaper to use a regular landline or cell phone.

Telephone books can be fantastic resources: in addition to complete calling information, they list community services, public transportation and things to see and do. Online phone directories include www.411.com and www.yellowpages.com.

Cell Phones

In the USA cell phones use GSM 1900 or CDMA 800, operating on different frequencies from other systems around the world. The only foreign phones that will work in the USA are GSM tri- or quad-band models. If you have one of these phones, check with your service provider about using it in the USA. Ask if roaming charges apply, as these will turn even local US calls into pricey international calls.

You can rent a mobile phone from one of several major US airports or have it delivered anywhere in the USA by **TripTel** (☎ 877-874-7835; www.triptel.com); pricing plans vary, but typically are expensive. **T-Mobile** (www.t-mobile.com) is another company that rents cell phones with a set amount of prepaid call time.

It might be cheaper to buy a compatible prepaid SIM card for the USA, like those sold by AT&T or Cingular, which you can insert into your international mobile phone to get a local phone number and voicemail. **Planet Omni** (☎ 925-686-9945; www.planetomni.com) and **Telestial** (☎ 213-337-5560, 800-707-0031; www.telestial.com) offer these services, as well as cell phone rentals.

You may also be able to take the SIM card from your home phone, install it in a rented mobile phone that's compatible with the US systems, and use the rental phone as if it were your own phone – same number, same billing basis. Ask your mobile phone company about this before departure.

Huge swathes of rural America, including many national parks and recreation areas, don't pick up a signal. Check your provider's coverage map.

Dialing Codes

If you're calling from abroad, the international country code for the USA is ☎ 1 (the same as Canada, but international rates apply between the two countries). To make an international call from the USA, dial ☎ 011, then the country code, followed by the area code (usually without the initial '0') and the phone number. For assistance making international calls, dial ☎ 00.

All phone numbers within the USA consist of a three-digit area code followed by a seven-digit local number. Typically, if you are calling a number within the same area code, you only have to dial the seven-digit number; however, some places now require you to dial the entire 10-digit number even for a local call. If dialing the seven-digit number doesn't work, try all 10.

If you are calling long distance, dial ☎ 1 plus the area code plus the phone number. If you're not sure whether the number is local or long distance (new area codes are added all the time, confusing even residents), try one way, and if it's wrong, usually a recorded voice will correct you.

For local directory assistance, dial ☎ 411. For directory assistance outside your area code, you can dial ☎ 1 plus the three-digit area code of the place you want to call plus 555-1212, but this will be charged as a long-distance call. For free nationwide directory assistance, dial ☎ 800-466-4411.

Toll-free numbers begin with ☎ 800, ☎ 888, ☎ 877 and ☎ 866 and when dialing, must be preceded by ☎ 1. Most can only be used within the USA, some only within the state, and some only from outside the state. You won't know until you try dialing. For directory assistance for toll-free numbers, call ☎ 800-555-1212.

The 900-series of area codes and a few other prefixes are for calls charged at a premium per-minute rate – phone sex, horoscopes, jokes etc.

Pay Phones

Local calls at pay phones cost 35¢ to 50¢ for the first few minutes; talking longer costs more.

Only put in the exact amount because pay phones don't give change. Some pay phones (eg in national parks) only accept credit cards or prepaid phone cards. Local calls from pay phones get expensive quickly, while long-distance calls can be prohibitive, especially if you use the operator (☎ 0) to facilitate long-distance or collect (reverse-charge) calls. It's usually cheaper to use a prepaid phone card (see the next section) or the access line of a major carrier like **AT&T** (☎ 800-321-0288).

Phone Cards

A prepaid phone card is a good solution for travelers on a budget. Phone cards are easy to find in larger towns and cities, where they are sold at newsstands, convenience stores, supermarkets and major retailers. Be sure to read the fine print, as many cards contain hidden charges such as 'activation fees' or per-call 'connection fees' in addition to the rates. AT&T sells a reliable phone card that is widely available in the USA.

TIME

The USA uses Daylight Saving Time (DST). On the second Sunday in March, clocks are set one hour ahead ('spring ahead'). Then, on the first Sunday of November, clocks are turned back one hour ('fall back'). Just to keep you on your toes, Arizona (except the Navajo Nation), Hawaii and much of Indiana don't follow DST.

The US date system is written as month/day/year. Thus, 8 June 2008 becomes 6/8/08.

TOURIST INFORMATION

There is no national office promoting US tourism. However, visit the federal government's official web portal (www.usa.gov), go to the 'Travel and Recreation' page, and you'll find links to every US state and territory tourism office and website, plus more links to indoor and outdoor recreation, from museums and historical landmarks to scenic byways, beaches and parks.

In this book, state tourism offices are listed in the Information section at the start of each regional chapter, while city and county visitor information centers are listed throughout the regional chapters.

Any tourist office worth contacting has a website, where you can download free travel e-guides, and will send out a clutch of free promotional material (though typically only to US addresses). They also field phone calls; some local offices maintain daily lists of hotel room availability, but few offer reservation services. All tourist offices have self-service racks of brochures and discount coupons; some also sell maps and books.

State-run 'welcome centers,' usually placed along interstate highways, tend to have materials that cover wider territories, and offices are usually open longer hours, including weekends and holidays.

Many cities have an official convention and visitors bureau (CVB); these sometimes double as tourist bureaus, but since their main focus is drawing the business trade, CVBs can be less useful for independent travelers.

Keep in mind that, in smaller towns, when the local chamber of commerce runs the tourist bureau, their lists of hotels, restaurants and services usually mention only chamber members; the town's cheapest options may be missing.

Similarly, in prime tourist destinations, some private 'tourist bureaus' are really agents who book hotel rooms and tours on commission. They may offer excellent service and deals, but you'll get what they're selling and nothing else.

TRAVELERS WITH DISABILITIES

If you have a physical disability, the USA can be an accommodating place. The Americans with Disabilities Act (ADA) requires that all public buildings, private buildings built after 1993 (including hotels, restaurants, theaters and museums) and public transit be wheelchair accessible. However, call ahead to confirm what is available. Some local tourist offices publish detailed accessibility guides.

Telephone companies offer relay operators, available via teletypewriter (TTY) numbers, for the hearing impaired. Most banks provide ATM instructions in Braille and via earphone jacks for hearing-impaired customers. All major airlines, Greyhound buses and Amtrak trains will assist travelers with disabilities; just describe your needs when making reservations at least 48 hours in advance. Service animals (guide dogs) are allowed to accompany passengers, but bring documentation.

Some car rental agencies – such as Budget and Hertz – offer hand-controlled vehicles and vans with wheelchair lifts at no extra charge, but you must reserve them well in advance. **Wheelchair Getaways** (☎ 800-642-2042;

www.wheelchairgetaways.com) rents accessible vans throughout the USA. In many cities and towns, public buses are accessible to wheelchair riders and will 'kneel' if you are unable to use the steps; just let the driver know that you need the lift or ramp.

Many national and some state parks and recreation areas have wheelchair-accessible paved, graded dirt or boardwalk trails. US citizens and permanent residents with permanent disabilities are entitled to a free 'America the Beautiful' Access Pass (p114), which gives free entry to all federal recreation lands (eg national parks).

Some helpful resources for travelers with disabilities:

Access-Able Travel Source (☎ 303-232-2979; www.access-able.com) General travel website with useful tips and links, including the Travelin' Talk Network.

Disabled Sports USA (☎ 301-217-0960; www.dsusa.org) Offers sports and recreation programs for those with disabilities and publishes *Challenge* magazine.

Flying Wheels Travel (☎ 507-451-5005, 877-451-5006; www.flyingwheelstravel.com) A full-service travel agency.

Mobility International USA (☎ 541-343-1284; www.miusa.org) Advises disabled travelers on mobility issues and runs educational international-exchange programs.

Moss Rehabilitation Hospital (☎ 800-225-5667; www.mossresourcenet.org/travel.htm) Extensive links and tips for accessible travel.

Society for Accessible Travel & Hospitality (☎ 212-447-7284; www.sath.org) Advocacy group provides general information for travelers with disabilities.

VISAS

Warning: all of the following information is highly subject to change. US entry requirements keep evolving as national security regulations change. All travelers should double-check current visa and passport regulations *before* coming to the USA.

Although you can also access visa information through www.usa.gov, the **US State Department** (www.travel.state.gov/visa) maintains the most comprehensive visa information, providing downloadable forms, lists of US consulates abroad and even visa wait times calculated by country. **US Citizenship and Immigration Services** (USCIS; www.uscis.gov) mainly serves immigrants, not temporary visitors.

Visa Applications

Apart from most Canadian citizens and those entering under the Visa Waiver Program (see opposite), all foreign visitors will need to obtain a visa from a US consulate or embassy abroad. Most applicants must schedule a personal interview, to which you must bring all your documentation and proof of fee payment. Wait times for interviews vary, but afterward, barring problems, visa issuance takes from a few days to a few weeks.

Your passport must be valid for at least six months after the end of your intended stay in the USA. You'll need a recent photo (2in by 2in), and you must pay a $131 processing fee, plus in a few cases an additional visa issuance reciprocity fee. In addition to the main nonimmigrant visa application form (DS-156), all men aged 16 to 45 must complete an additional form (DS-157) that details their travel plans.

Visa applicants are required to show documents of financial stability (or evidence that a US resident will provide financial support), a round-trip or onward ticket and 'binding obligations' that will ensure their return home, such as family ties, a home or a job. Because of these requirements, those planning to travel through other countries before arriving in the USA are generally better off applying for a US visa while they are still in their home country, rather than while on the road.

The most common visa is a nonimmigrant visitor's visa, type B-1 for business purposes, B-2 for tourism or visiting friends and relatives. A visitor's visa is good for multiple entries over one or five years, and specifically prohibits the visitor from taking paid employment in the USA. The validity period depends on what country you are from. The actual length of time you'll be allowed to stay in the USA is determined by US immigration at the port of entry.

If you're coming to the USA to work or study, you will need a different type of visa, and the company or institution to which you are going should make the arrangements. Other categories of nonimmigrant visas include an F-1 visa for students attending a course at a recognized institution; an H-1, H-2 or H-3 visa for temporary employment; and a J-1 visa for exchange visitors in approved programs. See p1151 for more information about working in the USA.

VISA WAIVER PROGRAM

Currently under the Visa Waiver Program (VWP), citizens of the following countries may enter the USA without a visa for stays of 90 days or fewer: Andorra, Australia, Austria, Belgium, Brunei, Czech Republic, Denmark, Estonia, Finland, France, Germany, Hungary, Iceland, Ireland, Italy, Japan, Latvia, Liechtenstein, Lithuania, Luxembourg, Malta, Monaco, the Netherlands, New Zealand, Norway, Portugal, San Marino, Singapore, Slovakia, Slovenia, South Korea, Spain, Sweden, Switzerland and the UK.

If you are a citizen of a VWP country, you do not need a visa *only if* you have a passport that meets current US standards (see p1152) *and* you have gotten approval from the Electronic System for Travel Authorization (ESTA) in advance. Register online with the Department of Homeland Security at https://esta.cbp.dhs.gov at least 72 hours before arrival; once travel authorization is approved, your registration is valid for two years.

Visitors from VWP countries must still produce at the port of entry all the same evidence as for a nonimmigrant visa application. They must demonstrate that their trip is for 90 days or less, and that they have a round-trip or onward ticket, adequate funds to cover the trip and binding obligations abroad.

In addition, the same 'grounds for exclusion and deportation' apply (see the next section), except that you will have no opportunity to appeal the grounds or apply for an exemption. If you are denied under the Visa Waiver Program at a US point of entry, you will have to use your onward or return ticket on the next available flight.

GROUNDS FOR EXCLUSION & DEPORTATION

If on your visa application form you admit to being a subversive, smuggler, prostitute, drug addict, terrorist or an ex-Nazi, you may be excluded. You can also be refused a visa or entry to the USA if you have a 'communicable disease of public health significance' or a criminal record, or if you've ever made a false statement in connection with a US visa application. However, if these last three apply, you are still able to request an exemption; many people are granted them and then given visas.

The US immigration department has a very broad definition of a criminal record. If you've ever been arrested or charged with an offense, that's a criminal record, even if you were acquitted or discharged without conviction. Don't attempt to enter through the VWP if you have a criminal record of any kind; assume US authorities will find out about it.

Communicable diseases include tuberculosis, the Ebola virus, SARS and most particularly HIV. US immigration doesn't test people for disease, but officials at the point of entry may question anyone about his or her health. They can exclude anyone whom they believe has a communicable disease, perhaps because they are carrying medical documents, prescriptions or AIDS/HIV medicine. Being gay is not grounds for exclusion; being an IV drug user is. Visitors may be deported if US immigration finds out they have HIV but did not declare it. Being HIV-positive is not grounds for deportation, but failing to provide accurate information on the visa application is.

Often USCIS will grant an exemption (a 'waiver of ineligibility') to a person who would normally be subject to exclusion, but this requires referral to a regional immigration office and can take some time (allow at least two months). If you're tempted to conceal something, remember that US immigration is strictest of all about false statements. It will often view favorably an applicant who admits to an old criminal charge or a communicable disease, but it is extremely harsh on anyone who has ever attempted to mislead it, even on minor points. After you're admitted to the USA, any evidence of a false statement to US immigration is grounds for deportation.

Prospective visitors to whom grounds of exclusion may apply should consider their options *before* applying for a visa.

Entering the USA

If you have a non-US passport, you must complete an arrival/departure record (form I-94) before you reach the immigration desk. It's usually handed out on the plane along with the customs declaration. For the question, 'Address While In the United States,' give the address where you will spend the first night (a hotel address is fine).

No matter what your visa says, US immigration officers have an absolute authority to refuse admission to the USA or to impose conditions on admission. They will ask about your plans and whether you have sufficient funds; it's a good idea to list an itinerary, produce an onward or round-trip ticket and have at least one major credit card. Showing that you have over $400 per week of your stay should be enough. Don't make too much of having friends, relatives or business contacts in the USA; the immigration official may decide that this will make you more likely to overstay. It also helps to be neatly dressed and polite.

The Department of Homeland Security's registration program, called **US-VISIT** (www.dhs.gov/us-visit), includes every port of entry and nearly every foreign visitor to the USA. For most visitors (excluding, for now, most Canadian and some Mexican citizens), registration consists of having a digital photo and electronic (inkless) fingerprints taken; the process takes less than a minute.

The National Security Entry/Exit Registration System (NSEERS) applies to certain citizens of countries that have been deemed particular risks; however, US officials can require this registration of any traveler. Currently, the countries included are Iran, Iraq, Libya, Sudan and Syria, but be sure to visit www.ice.gov for updates. Registration in these cases also includes a short interview in a separate room and computer verification of all personal information supplied on travel documents.

Visa Extensions

To stay in the USA longer than the date stamped on your passport, go to a local **USCIS** (☎ 800-375-5283; www.uscis.gov) office to apply for an extension well *before* the stamped date. If the date has passed, your best chance will be to bring a US citizen with you to vouch for your character, and to produce lots of other verification that you are not trying to work illegally and have enough money to support yourself. However, if you've overstayed, the most likely scenario is that you will be deported. Travelers who enter the USA under the VWP are ineligible for visa extensions.

Short-Term Departures & Reentry

It's temptingly easy to make trips across the border to Canada or Mexico, but upon return to the USA, non-Americans will be subject to the full immigration procedure. Always take your passport when you cross the border. If your immigration card still has plenty of time on it, you will probably be able to reenter using the same one, but if it has nearly expired, you will have to apply for a new card, and border control may want to see your onward air ticket, sufficient funds and so on.

Traditionally, a quick trip across the border has been a way to extend your stay in the USA without applying for an extension at a USCIS office. Don't assume this still works. First, make sure you hand in your old immigration card to the immigration authorities when you leave the USA, and when you return make sure you have all the necessary application documentation from when you first entered the country. US immigration will be very suspicious of anyone who leaves for a few days and returns immediately hoping for a new six-month stay; expect to be questioned closely.

Citizens of most Western countries will not need a visa to visit Canada, so it's really not a problem at all to cross to the Canadian side of Niagara Falls, detour up to Québec or pass through on the way to Alaska. Travelers entering the USA by bus from Canada may be closely scrutinized. A round-trip ticket that takes you back to Canada will most likely make US immigration feel less suspicious. Mexico has a visa-free zone along most of its border with the USA, including the Baja Peninsula and most of the border towns, such as Tijuana and Ciudad Juárez. You'll need a Mexican visa or tourist card if you want to go beyond the border zone. See Border Crossings, p1157.

VOLUNTEERING

Volunteer opportunities abound in the USA, and they can be a great way to break up a long trip. They can also provide truly memorable experiences: you'll get to interact with people, society and the land in ways you never would by just passing through.

Casual, drop-in volunteer opportunities are plentiful in big cities, where you can socialize with locals while helping out nonprofit organizations. Check weekly alternative newspapers for calendar listings, or browse the free classified ads online at **Craigslist** (www.craigslist.org). The public website **Serve.gov** (www.serve.gov) and private websites **Idealist.org** (www.idealist.org) and **VolunteerMatch** (www.volunteermatch.org) offer free searchable databases of short- and long-term volunteer opportunities nationwide.

More formal volunteer programs, especially those designed for international travelers, typically charge a hefty fee of $250 to $1000, depending on the length of the program and what amenities are included (eg housing, meals). None cover travel to the USA.

Recommended volunteer organizations:

Green Project (☎ 504-344-4884; www.thegreenproject.org) Working to rebuild New Orleans post-Katrina in sustainable, green ways.

Habitat for Humanity (☎ 800-422-4828; www.habitat.org) Focuses on building affordable housing for those in need.
Sierra Club (☎ 415-977-5522; www.sierraclub.org) 'Volunteer vacations' restore wilderness areas and maintain trails, including in national parks and nature preserves.
Volunteers for Peace (☎ 802-259-2759; www.vfp.org) Grassroots, multiweek volunteer projects emphasize manual labor and international exchange.
Wilderness Volunteers (☎ 928-556-0038; www.wildernessvolunteers.org) Weeklong trips helping maintain national parklands and outdoor recreation areas.
World Wide Opportunities on Organic Farms–USA (www.wwoofusa.org) Represents more than 1000 organic farms that host volunteer workers in exchange for meals and accommodation, with opportunities for both short- and long-term stays.

WOMEN TRAVELERS

Women traveling alone or in groups should not expect to encounter any particular problems in the USA. The community website www.journeywoman.com facilitates women exchanging travel tips, and has links to other helpful resources. The booklet 'Her Own Way,' published by the Canadian government, is filled with general travel advice, useful for any woman; click to www.voyage.gc.ca/publications/menu-eng.asp to download the PDF or read it online.

These two national advocacy groups might also be helpful:
National Organization for Women (NOW; ☎ 202-628-8669; www.now.org)
Planned Parenthood (☎ 800-230-7526; www.plannedparenthood.org) Offers referrals to women's health clinics throughout the country.

In terms of safety issues, single women just need to practice the same street smarts as any solo traveler (p1145), but they are sometimes more often the target of unwanted attention or harassment. Some women carry a whistle, mace or cayenne-pepper spray in case of assault. If you purchase a spray, contact a police station to find out about local regulations. Laws regarding sprays vary from state to state; federal law prohibits them being carried on planes.

If you are assaulted, consider calling a rape-crisis hotline before calling the police, unless you are in immediate danger, in which case you should call ☎ 911. But be aware that not all police have as much sensitivity training or experience assisting sexual assault survivors, whereas rape-crisis-center staff will tirelessly advocate on your behalf and act as a link to other community services, including hospitals and the police. Telephone books have listings of local rape-crisis centers, or contact the 24-hour **National Sexual Assault Hotline** (☎ 800-656-4673; www.rainn.org). Alternatively, go straight to a hospital emergency room.

WORK

If you are a foreigner in the USA with a standard nonimmigrant visitor's visa, you are expressly forbidden to partake in paid work in the USA and will be deported if you're caught working illegally. Employers are required to establish the bona fides of their employees or face fines, making it much tougher for a foreigner to get work than it once was.

To work legally, foreigners need to apply for a work visa before leaving home. A J-1 visa, for exchange visitors, is issued to young people (age limits vary) for study, student vacation employment, work in summer camps, and short-term traineeships with a specific employer. Organizations that can help arrange international student exchanges, work placements and J-1 visas:
American Institute for Foreign Study (☎ 866-906-2437; www.aifs.com)
Au Pair in America (☎ 800-928-7247; www.aupairinamerica.com)
BUNAC UK (☎ 020-7251-3472; www.bunac.org)
Camp America UK (☎ 020-7581-7373; www.campamerica.co.uk)
Council on International Educational Exchange (☎ 207-553-4000; www.ciee.org)
InterExchange (☎ 212-924-0446; www.interexchange.org)
International Exchange Programs (IEP) Australia (☎ 1300-300-912; www.iep.org.au); New Zealand (☎ 0800-443-769; www.iep.co.nz)

For nonstudent jobs, temporary or permanent, you need to be sponsored by a US employer who will have to arrange an H-category visa. These are not easy to obtain, since the employer has to prove that no US citizen or permanent resident is available to do the job. Seasonal work is possible in national parks and at tourist attractions and ski resorts. Contact park concessionaire businesses, local chambers of commerce and ski-resort management. Lonely Planet's *Gap Year Book* has more ideas on how to combine work and travel.

Transportation

CONTENTS

GETTING THERE & AWAY

Flights and tours can be booked online at www.lonelyplanet.com/travel_services.

ENTERING THE USA

The USA is working hard to counter any lingering 'Fortress America' imagery that came about post–September 11, and in fact, despite new security procedures, it's not really any more time-consuming to enter the country now than pre–September 11. That said, US officials are strict and vigilant: have all your papers in order; neatness and politeness count.

If you are flying to America, the first airport that you land in is where you must go through immigration and customs, even if you are continuing on the flight to another destination. Upon arrival, all international visitors must register with the US-VISIT program, which entails having your fingerprints scanned and a digital photo taken. For more information on visa requirements for visiting the USA, including the Electronic System for Travel Authorization (ESTA) now required before arrival for citizens of Visa Waiver Program (VWP) countries, see p1148.

Once you go through immigration, you collect your baggage and pass through customs (p1137). If you have nothing to declare, you'll probably clear customs without a baggage search, but don't assume this. If you are continuing on the same plane or connecting to another one, it is your responsibility to get your bags to the right place. There are usually airline representatives just outside the customs area who can help you.

If you are a single parent, grandparent or guardian traveling with anyone under 18, carry proof of legal custody or a notarized letter from the nonaccompanying parent(s) authorizing the trip. This isn't required, but the USA is concerned with thwarting child abduction, and not having authorizing papers could cause delays or even result in being denied admittance to the country.

Passports

Adult US citizens returning from any foreign country, including Canada, Mexico, the Caribbean and Bermuda, must present a passport, passport card, enhanced driver's license or trusted traveler program card to re-enter the USA. Children under 16 who are US citizens are currently exempt from this rule; they need only show a birth certificate, naturalization certificate or citizenship card. For more on the mercurial re-entry requirements for US citizens, click to the US Department of State's website, www.getyouhome.gov.

Every foreign visitor entering the USA from abroad needs a passport. Your passport must be valid for at least six months longer than your intended stay in the USA. Also, if your passport does not meet current US standards,

THINGS CHANGE...

The information in this chapter is particularly vulnerable to change. Check directly with the airline or a travel agent to make sure you understand how a fare (and ticket you may buy) works and be aware of the security requirements for international travel. Shop carefully. The details given in this chapter should be regarded as pointers and are not a substitute for your own careful, up-to-date research.

CLIMATE CHANGE & TRAVEL

Climate change is a serious threat to the ecosystems that humans rely upon, and air travel is the fastest-growing contributor to the problem. Lonely Planet regards travel, overall, as a global benefit, but believes we all have a responsibility to limit our personal impact on global warming.

Flying & Climate Change

Pretty much every form of motor travel generates CO_2 (the main cause of human-induced climate change) but planes are far and away the worst offenders, not just because of the sheer distances they allow us to travel, but because they release greenhouse gases high into the atmosphere. The statistics are frightening: two people taking a return flight between Europe and the US will contribute as much to climate change as an average household's gas and electricity consumption over a whole year.

Carbon Offset Schemes

Climatecare.org and other websites use 'carbon calculators' that allow jetsetters to offset the greenhouse gases they are responsible for with contributions to energy-saving projects and other climate-friendly initiatives in the developing world – including projects in India, Honduras, Kazakhstan and Uganda.

Lonely Planet, together with Rough Guides and other concerned partners in the travel industry, supports the carbon offset scheme run by climatecare.org. Lonely Planet offsets all of its staff and author travel.

For more information check out our website: lonelyplanet.com.

you'll be turned back at the border. If your passport was issued before October 26, 2005, it must be 'machine readable' (with two lines of letters, numbers and <<< at the bottom); if it was issued between October 26, 2005, and October 25, 2006, it must be machine readable and include a digital photo; and if it was issued on or after October 26, 2006, it must be an e-Passport with a digital photo and an integrated RFID chip containing biometric data.

AIR

Airports & Airlines

The USA has over 375 domestic airports, but only a baker's dozen are the main international gateways. Many other airports are called 'international' but may have only a few flights from other countries – typically Mexico or Canada. Even travel to an international gateway sometimes requires a connection in another gateway city (eg London–Los Angeles flights may involve transferring planes in Houston).

International gateway airports in the USA:

Atlanta Hartsfield-Jackson International (ATL; ☎ 404-530-7300; www.atlanta-airport.com)
Boston Logan International (BOS; ☎ 800-235-6426; www.massport.com/logan)
Chicago O'Hare International (ORD; ☎ 800-832-6352; www.flychicago.com)
Dallas-Fort Worth (DFW; ☎ 972-574-8888; www.dfwairport.com)
Honolulu (HNL; ☎ 808-836-6413; www.honoluluairport.com)
Houston George Bush Intercontinental (IAH; ☎ 281-230-3000; www.fly2houston.com)
Los Angeles (LAX; ☎ 310-646-5252; www.lawa.org/lax)
Miami (MIA; ☎ 305-876-7000; www.miami-airport.com)
New York John F Kennedy (JFK; ☎ 718-244-4444; www.panynj.gov)
Newark Liberty International (EWR; ☎ 973-961-6000; www.panynj.gov)
San Francisco (SFO; ☎ 800-435-9736; www.flysfo.com)
Seattle Seattle-Tacoma International (SEA; ☎ 206-433-5388; www.portseattle.org/seatac)
Washington, DC Dulles International (IAD; ☎ 703-572-2700; www.metwashairports.com/dulles)

AIRLINES FLYING TO/FROM THE USA

The national airlines of most countries have flights to the USA, and the USA has several airlines serving the world. Online, www.seatguru.com and http://seatexpert.com have extensive airline info, including seat-by-seat reviews for each aircraft.

Aer Lingus (EI; ☎ 800-474-7424; www.aerlingus.com)
Aerolíneas Argentinas (AR; ☎ 800-333-0276; www.aerolineas.com.ar)
Aeroméxico (AM; ☎ 800-237-6639; www.aeromexico.com)
Air Canada (AC; ☎ 888-247-2262; www.aircanada.com)
Air China (CA; ☎ 866-270-5897; http://us.fly-airchina.com)
Air France (AF; ☎ 800-237-2747; www.airfrance.com)

YOU MAY NOW BOARD YOUR FLIGHT

By now, most everyone knows that airport security measures restrict many common household items from being carried on planes. These regulations change often, so get up-to-date information on current restrictions from the **Transportation Security Administration** (TSA; ☎ 866-289-9673; www.tsa.gov), which also provides average security wait times by airport (30 minutes is standard).

To get through airport security checkpoints, you need a boarding pass and photo ID. If you beep going through the metal detector, or x-rays of your carry-on bags look suspicious, you will undergo a second screening, involving hand-wand and pat-down checks and opening your bags. You can request a private room.

If you suspect you were stopped because your name appears on the TSA Watch List, afterwards file a complaint with the DHS Traveler Redress Inquiry Program (DHS TRIP; www.dhs.gov); this doesn't remove your name from the list, but it establishes that you are not the 'Jane Doe' they want, expediting screening next time.

All checked luggage is screened for explosives; TSA may open your suitcase for visual confirmation, breaking the lock if necessary. Either leave your bags unlocked or use a TSA-approved lock such as **Travel Sentry** (www.travelsentry.org). Also, screening machines damage undeveloped film, so carry this on the plane and request a hand inspection.

As for gels and liquids, you *can* bring them: just put each of 'em in a 3oz container and gather them all together into a single quart-size zip-top bag. That's TSA's 3-1-1 rule. For more information, see its website.

Air India (AI; ☎ 800-223-7776; http://home.airindia.in)
Air New Zealand (NZ; ☎ 800-262-1234; www.airnewzealand.com)
Alitalia (AZ; ☎ 800-223-5730; www.alitalia.com)
All Nippon Airways (NH; ☎ 800-235-9262; www.fly-ana.com)
American Airlines (AA; ☎ 800-433-7300; www.aa.com)
Asiana Airlines (OZ; ☎ 888-437-7718; http://us.flyasiana.com)
British Airways (BA; ☎ 800-247-9297; www.britishairways.com)
British Midland Airways (BD; ☎ 800-788-0555; www.flybmi.com)
Cathay Pacific Airways (CX; ☎ 800-233-2742; www.cathaypacific.com)
Continental Airlines (CO; ☎ 800-523-3273; www.continental.com)
Delta Air Lines (DL; ☎ 800-221-1212; www.delta.com)
El Al Airlines (LY; ☎ 800-223-6700; www.elal.com)
Iberia Airlines (IB; ☎ 800-772-4642; www.iberia.com)
Icelandair (FI; ☎ 800-223-5500; www.icelandair.com)
Japan Airlines (JL; ☎ 800-525-3663; www.jal.com)
KLM Royal Dutch Airlines (KL; ☎ 800-225-2525; www.klm.com)
Korean Air (KE; ☎ 800-438-5000; www.koreanair.com)
LAN Airlines (LA; ☎ 866-435-9526; www.lan.com)
Lufthansa (LH; ☎ 800-399-5838; www.lufthansa.com)
Mexicana Airlines (MX; ☎ 800-531-7921; www.mexicana.com)
Northwest Airlines (NW; ☎ 800-225-2525; www.nwa.com)
Philippine Airlines (PR; ☎ 800-435-9725; www.philippineairlines.com)
Qantas Airways (QF; ☎ 800-227-4500; www.qantas.com.au)
Scandinavian Airlines (SK; ☎ 800-221-2350; www.flysas.com)
Singapore Airlines (SQ; ☎ 800-742-3333; www.singaporeair.com)
South African Airways (SA; ☎ 800-722-9675; www.flysaa.com)
Spanair (JK; ☎ 888-545-5757; www.spanair.com)
Swiss (LX; ☎ 877-359-7947; www.swiss.com)
Thai Airways (TG; ☎ 800-426-5204; www.thaiair.com)
United Airlines (UA; ☎ 800-864-8331; www.united.com)
US Airways (US; ☎ 800-622-1015; www.usairways.com)
V Australia (VA; ☎ 800-444-0260; www.vaustralia.com)
Virgin Atlantic (VS; ☎ 800-821-5438; www.virgin-atlantic.com)
WestJet Airlines (WS; ☎ 888-937-8538; www.westjet.com)

Tickets

Getting a cheap airline ticket is a matter of research, reserving early – at least three to four weeks in advance – and timing. Flying midweek and in the off-season (normally, fall to spring, excluding holidays) is always less expensive, but fare wars can start anytime. To ensure you've found the cheapest possible ticket for the flight you want, check every angle: compare several online travel booking sites with the airline's own website. Engage a living, breathing travel agent if your itinerary is complex.

Keep in mind your entire itinerary. Some deals for travel within the USA can only be purchased overseas in conjunction with an international air ticket, or you may get discounts for booking air and car rental together. Or, you may find domestic flights within the USA are less expensive when added on to your international airfare.

For a good overview of online ticket agencies, visit **Airinfo** (http://airinfo.aero), which also lists travel agents worldwide. The big three US travel-booking websites are **Travelocity** (www.travelocity.com), **Orbitz** (www.orbitz.com) and **Expedia** (www.expedia.com). Similar to these and worth trying are **Cheap Tickets** (www.cheaptickets.com) and **Lowest Fare** (www.lowestfare.com). Typically, these sites don't include budget airlines such as Southwest.

Meta sites are good for price comparisons, as they gather from many sources (but don't provide direct booking). Try **Farecast** (www.farecast.com), **Kayak** (www.kayak.com), **Mobissimo** (www.mobissimo.com), **Qixo** (www.qixo.com) and **Sidestep** (www.sidestep.com).

Bidding for travel can be very successful, but read the fine print carefully before bidding. Try **Hotwire** (www.hotwire.com), **Skyauction** (www.skyauction.com) and **Priceline** (www.priceline.com). See www.biddingfortravel.com for advice about Priceline, which can be great for car rentals.

INTERCONTINENTAL (RTW) TICKETS

Round-the-world (RTW) tickets can be great if you want to visit other regions besides the USA; otherwise, a simple round-trip ticket is usually cheaper. RTW tickets are of most value for trips that combine the USA with Europe, Asia and/or Australasia.

RTW tickets typically let you fly in only one direction on the combined routes of an airline alliance, such as **Star Alliance** (www.staralliance.com) and **One World** (www.oneworld.com). They are valid for a fixed period, usually a year; some are segment-based, while others are tiered by total mileage. Most RTW fares restrict the number of stops within the USA and Canada. The cheapest fares permit only one stop; others allow multiple stops. Some airlines 'black out' heavily traveled routes (eg Honolulu–Tokyo). In most cases a 14-day advance purchase is required. After the ticket is purchased, dates can usually be changed without penalty, and tickets can be rewritten to add or delete stops, for an extra charge.

For RTW tickets, try:

Air Brokers (www.airbrokers.com)
Air Treks (www.airtreks.com)
Circle the Planet (www.circletheplanet.com)
Just Fares (www.justfares.com)

Africa

Only a few cities in West and North Africa have direct flights to the USA, including Abidjan (Côte d'Ivoire), Accra (Ghana), Cairo (Egypt), Casablanca (Morocco), Dakar (Senegal) and Lagos (Nigeria). Delta Air Lines and South African Airways fly direct between Johannesburg and New York. Otherwise, most flights from Africa to the USA go via a European hub, commonly London.

Agents serving South Africa:

Flight Centre (☎ 0860-400-727; www.flightcentre.co.za)
STA Travel (☎ 0861-781-781; www.statravel.co.za)

Asia

Bangkok, Singapore, Kuala Lumpur, Hong Kong, Seoul and Tokyo all have good connections to the US West Coast. Many flights to the USA go via Honolulu, but stopovers may cost extra. Bangkok is the discounted-fare capital of the region, though its cheapest agents can be unreliable.

Agents serving Asia:

Concorde Travel Hong Kong (☎ 852-2526-3391; www.concorde-travel.com)
No 1 Travel Tokyo (☎ 03-3205-6073; www.no1-travel.com)
STA Travel Bangkok (☎ 662-236-0262; www.statravel.co.th); Singapore (☎ 65-6737-7188; www.statravel.com.sg); Tokyo (☎ 03-5391-2922; www.statravel.co.jp)
Traveller Services Hong Kong (☎ 852-2375-2222; www.taketraveller.com)
Zuji (www. zuji.com)

Australia

Some flights go from Sydney and Melbourne direct to Los Angeles and San Francisco. Flights to other US cities usually involve a stop in Los Angeles, or possibly San Francisco or Honolulu. Qantas, V Australia, Air New Zealand, United, American and US Airways are the main airlines on the route. Fares from Melbourne, Sydney, Brisbane and sometimes Cairns are 'common rated' (the same for all cities). For other cities such as Hobart and Perth, there'll usually be an add-on fare.

Agents serving Australia:

Flight Centre (☎ 1300-133-133; www.flightcentre.com.au)
STA Travel (☎ 1300-134-782; www.statravel.com.au)
Travel.com (☎ 1300-130-482; www.travel.com.au)
Zuji (☎ 1300-888-180; www.zuji.com.au)

Canada

Daily flights go from Toronto, Montreal, Vancouver and many smaller cities to all US gateways. Commuter flights to cities such as New York and Chicago can be expensive. Some of the best deals are charter and package fares to sunny destinations like Florida, California, Las Vegas and Hawaii, with higher prices during winter.

It may be much cheaper to travel by land to the nearest US city, then take a discounted domestic flight. For example, round-trip fares to New York are often much cheaper from Seattle, WA, than from Vancouver, British Columbia, which is only 140 miles north across the US–Canadian border.

Agents serving Canada:

Expedia (☎ 888-397-3342; www.expedia.ca)
Travel Cuts (☎ 866-246-9762; www.travelcuts.ca)
Travelocity (☎ 800-457-8010; www.travelocity.ca)

Continental Europe

There are nonstop flights to many US cities, but the discounted fares often involve indirect routes and changing planes. The main airlines between Europe and the USA include Air France, Alitalia, American Airlines, British Airways, Continental Airlines, Delta Air Lines, Icelandair, KLM, Lufthansa, Scandinavian Airlines, Spanair and United Airlines. Sometimes an Asian or Middle Eastern carrier will have cheap deals on flights in transit to the USA, but these seats can be difficult to book.

BELGIUM

Airstop (☎ 070-233-188; www.airstop.be)

FRANCE

Anyway (☎ 0892-302-301; www.anyway.fr)
Easyvols (☎ 0899-700-207; www.easyvols.fr)
Nouvelles Frontières (☎ 01-4920-6587; www.nouvelles-frontieres.fr)
Voyages Wasteels (☎ 0892-051-155; www.wasteels.fr)

GERMANY

Expedia (☎ 01805-900-560; www.expedia.de)
Opodo (☎ 01805-676-361; www.opodo.de)
Reisebörse (☎ 030-2800-2800; www.reiseboerse.com)
STA Travel (☎ 069-743-032-92; www.statravel.de)

ITALY

CTS (☎ 06-441-111; www.cts.it)
Opodo (☎ 199-404-044; www.opodo.it)

NETHERLANDS

Airfair (☎ 0900-7-717-717; www.airfair.nl)

SCANDINAVIA

Kilroy Travels (www.kilroytravels.com) Denmark (☎ 7015-4015); Finland (☎ 0203-545-769); Norway (☎ 2149-2633); Sweden (☎ 0771-545-769)

SPAIN

Barceló Viajes (☎ 902-200-400; www.barceloviajes.com)

Latin America

The main US gateway from Central and South America is Miami, FL, but there are also direct flights to Los Angeles, CA, and Houston, TX. Check the national airlines of the countries you want to connect to, as well as major US carriers such as American, Continental, Delta and United.

At times, it can be much cheaper to fly to a Mexican border town than to the adjacent town on the US side. A flight from Mexico City to Tijuana, right by the border, can cost quite a bit less than a flight to San Diego, which is just a few miles north of the US–Mexico border. Check safety conditions for US–Mexico overland border crossings first (see opposite).

Agents serving Latin America:

Despegar Mexico (☎ 55-1084-0450; www.despegar.com.mx)
Mundo Joven Mexico (☎ 01800-000-0789; www.mundojoven.com)
OTEC Viajes (www.otecviajes.com) Costa Rica (☎ 506-2523-0500); El Salvador (☎ 503-2264-0200); Honduras (☎ 504-220-6165); Nicaragua (☎ 505-278-3788); Panama (☎ 507-264-2842)
Star Travel Argentina (☎ 11-5199-4445; www.startravel.com.ar)
Student Travel Bureau Brazil (☎ 11-3038-1555; www.stb.com.br)
Viajo.com (www.viajo.com) Argentina (☎ 0810-888-8425; www.viajo.com.ar); Mexico (☎ 55-5004-4120; www.viajo.com.mx)

New Zealand

Air New Zealand has direct flights from Auckland to Los Angeles. Flights from Christchurch and Wellington require changing planes in Auckland or one of the Pacific Islands.

Agents serving New Zealand:

Flight Centre (☎ 0800-243-544; www.flightcentre.co.nz)
STA Travel (☎ 0800-474-400; www.statravel.co.nz)
Travelocity (☎ 0800-451-297; www.travelocity.co.nz)

UK & Ireland

One of the busiest and most competitive air sectors in the world is between the UK and the USA, with hundreds of scheduled flights between London and major US gateways offered by American, British Airways, BMI, Continental, Delta, Northwest/KLM, United, US Airways and Virgin Atlantic. From UK regional airports, discounted flights may be routed via London, Paris or Amsterdam, and will probably not fly direct to smaller US cities such as Las Vegas or Denver.

Agents serving the UK and Ireland:

Ebookers.com (☎ 0871-223-5000; www.ebookers.com)
Flight Centre (☎ 0870-499-0040; www.flightcentre.co.uk)
North-South Travel (☎ 01245-608-291; www.northsouthtravel.co.uk) Donates part of its profits to projects in the developing world.
Opodo (☎ 0871-472-5112; www.opodo.co.uk)
Quest Travel (☎ 0845-263-6963; www.questtravel.com)
STA Travel (☎ 0871-230-0040; www.statravel.co.uk)
Trailfinders (☎ 0845-058-5858; www.trailfinders.com)
Travel Bag (☎ 0871-703-4700; www.travelbag.co.uk)
Travelocity (☎ 0870-472-5116; www.travelocity.co.uk)

LAND

Border Crossings

The USA shares long land borders with Canada in the north and Mexico in the south. It is relatively easy crossing from the USA into either country; it's crossing *into* the USA that can pose problems if you haven't brought all your documents (see p1148). **US Customs & Border Protection** (http://apps.cbp.gov/bwt/) tracks current wait times at every border crossing. Some borders are open 24 hours, but most are not.

The USA has more than 20 official border crossings with Canada. Busy entry points include those at Detroit (MI)/Windsor, Buffalo (NY)/Niagara Falls and Blaine (WA)/British Columbia. The downside to choosing a quiet border crossing is that officers have plenty of time to take apart your luggage. For border wait times returning to Canada, visit www.cbsa-asfc.gc.ca/general/times/menu-e.html.

The USA has almost 40 official entry points with Mexico. The main ones are San Diego (CA)/Tijuana, Nogales West (AZ)/Nogales East, El Paso (TX)/Ciudad Juárez and Brownsville (TX)/Matamoros. As always, have your papers in order, act polite and don't make jokes or casual conversation with US border officials.

In 2009 the **US State Department** (http://travel.state.gov) issued a travel alert about a dangerous increase in Mexican drug cartel violence and crime along the US–Mexico border. Foreign visitors should exercise extreme caution, avoid large-scale gatherings and demonstrations, and not drive after dark, especially in a car with US license plates. For more specific travel warnings, see p752 for Ciudad Juárez and p939 for Tijuana.

Canada

BUS

Greyhound has direct connections between main cities in Canada and the northern USA, but you may have to transfer to a different bus at the border. Book through **Greyhound USA** (☎ 800-231-2222, international customer service 214-849-8100; www.greyhound.com) or **Greyhound Canada** (☎ in Canada 800-661-8747; www.greyhound.ca). Greyhound's Discovery Pass (p1160) allows unlimited travel in both the USA and Canada.

CAR & MOTORCYCLE

If you're driving into the USA from Canada, bring the vehicle's registration papers, proof of liability insurance and your home driver's license. Canadian auto insurance is typically valid in the USA, and vice-versa. Canadian driver's licenses are also valid, but an International Driving Permit (IDP) is a good supplement (p1163).

If your papers are in order, taking your own car across the US–Canadian border is usually fast and easy, but occasionally the authorities of either country decide to search a car *thoroughly*. On weekends and holidays, especially in summer, traffic at the main border crossings can be heavy and waits long.

TRAIN

Amtrak (☎ 800-872-7245; www.amtrak.com) and **VIA Rail Canada** (☎ 888-842-7245; www.viarail.ca) run daily services between Montreal and New York, Toronto and New York via Niagara Falls, Toronto and Chicago via Detroit, and Vancouver and Seattle. Customs inspections happen at the border, not upon boarding.

Mexico

BUS

Greyhound US (☎ 800-231-2222, international customer service 214-849-8100; www.greyhound.com) and **Greyhound México** (☎ in Mexico 800-710-8819; www.greyhound.com.mx) operate direct bus routes between main towns in Mexico and the USA. Northbound buses can take time to cross the border, as sometimes US immigration insists on checking every person on board.

For connections to smaller destinations south of the border, there are numerous domestic Mexican bus companies; **Ticketbus** (☎ in Mexico 5133-2424, 800-702-8000; www.ticketbus.com.mx) is an alliance of several.

CAR & MOTORCYCLE

If you're driving into the USA from Mexico, bring the vehicle's registration papers, proof of liability insurance and your driver's license from your home country. Mexican driver's licenses are valid, but an IDP (p1163) is a good supplement.

Very few car-rental companies will let you take a car from the US into Mexico. US auto insurance is not valid in Mexico, so even a short trip into Mexico's border region requires you to buy Mexican car insurance, available for $25 per day at most border crossings, as well as from **AAA** (☎ 800-874-7532; www.aaa.com). At some border towns, including Tijuana or Ciudad Juárez, there can be long lines of vehicles waiting to re-enter the USA. For a short visit, it's often more convenient to leave your car in a private parking lot on the US side and walk or take a bus across the border.

For a longer driving trip into Mexico beyond the border zone or Baja California, you'll need a Mexican *permiso de importación temporal de vehículos* (temporary vehicle import permit). See Lonely Planet's *Mexico* guide for details, or call Mexico's tourist information number in the USA (☎ 800-446-3942).

TRAIN

Amtrak gets close to the Mexican border at San Diego (CA), Yuma (AZ) and El Paso and Del Rio (TX), but there are currently no cross-border services. There are no Mexican train services to US border towns.

SEA

If you're interested in taking a cruise ship to America – as well as to other interesting ports o' call – a good specialized travel agency is **Cruise Web** (☎ 800-377-9383; www.cruiseweb.com).

You can also travel to and from the USA on a freighter, though it will be much slower and less cushy than a cruise. Nevertheless, freighters aren't spartan (some advertise cruise-ship-level amenities), and they are much cheaper (sometimes by half). Trips range from a week to two months; stops at interim ports are usually quick.

For more information:

Cruise & Freighter Travel Association (☎ 800-872-8584; www.travltips.com)

Freighter World Cruises (☎ 800-531-7774; www.freighterworld.com).

TOURS

Group travel can be an enjoyable way to get to and tour the USA. For tours once you're in the country, see p1166.

Reputable tour companies:

American Holidays (☎ 01-673-3840; www.americanholidays.com) Ireland-based company specializes in tours to North America.

Contiki (☎ 866-266-8454; http://contiki.com) Party-hardy sightseeing tour-bus vacations for 18- to 35-year-olds.

North America Travel Service (☎ 020-7569-6710; www.northamericatravelservice.co.uk) UK-based tour operator arranges luxury US trips.

Trek America (☎ in North America 800-221-0596, in UK 0845-313-2614; www.trekamerica.com) For active outdoor adventures; group sizes are kept small.

GETTING AROUND

AIR

When time is tight, book a flight. The domestic air system is extensive and reliable, with dozens of competing airlines, hundreds of airports and thousands of flights daily. Flying is usually more expensive than traveling by bus, train or car, but it's the way to go when you're in a hurry. Advice for buying international plane tickets (p1154) also applies to domestic flights.

Main 'hub' airports in the USA include all international gateways (p1153) plus many other large cities. Most cities and towns have a local or county airport, but you usually have to travel via a hub airport to reach them.

The website www.parkingaccess.com offers information, reservations and discounts on parking at most major airports.

Airlines in the USA

Several domestic airlines have entered and emerged from bankruptcy recently, but are still flying. Mergers and downsizing have had an impact on traveler experiences. Free meal service has often been replaced with for-purchase sandwiches, and thinly spread staff mean that any disruptions (say, from a winter snowstorm) can strand flights for hours or even days.

Overall, air travel in the USA is very safe (much safer than driving out on the nation's highways); for comprehensive details by carrier, check out **Airsafe.com** (www.airsafe.com), which has good advice on current airport security procedures (see the boxed text, p1154).

The main domestic carriers:

AirTran Airways (☎ 800-247-8726; www.airtran.com) Atlanta-based airline; primarily serves the South, Midwest and eastern US.

Alaska Airlines/Horizon Air (☎ 800-252-7522/547-9308; www.alaskaair.com) Serves Alaska and the western US, with flights to the East Coast and Hawaii.

American Airlines (☎ 800-433-7300; www.aa.com) Nationwide service.

Continental Airlines (☎ 800-523-3273; www.continental.com) Nationwide service.

Delta Air Lines (☎ 800-221-1212; www.delta.com) Nationwide service.

Frontier Airlines (☎ 800-432-1359; www.frontierairlines.com) Denver-based airline with nationwide service, including to Alaska.

Hawaiian Airlines (☎ 800-367-5320; www.hawaiianair.com) Serves the Hawaiian Islands and West Coast, plus Las Vegas and Phoenix.

JetBlue Airways(☎ 800-538-2583; www.jetblue.com) Nonstop connections between eastern and western US cities, plus Florida, New Orleans and Texas.

Midwest Airlines (☎ 800-452-2022; www.midwestairlines.com) Milwaukee-based carrier serves many US gateway cities.

Northwest Airlines (☎ 800-225-2525; www.nwa.com) Nationwide service.

Southwest Airlines (☎ 800-435-9792; www.southwest.com) Service across the continental USA.

Spirit Airlines (☎ 800-772-7117; www.spiritair.com) Florida-based airline; serves many US gateway cities.

United Airlines (☎ 800-864-8331; www.united.com) Nationwide service.

US Airways (☎ 800-428-4322; www.usairways.com) Nationwide service.

Virgin America (☎ 877-359-8474; www.virginamerica.com) Flights between East and West Coast cities and Las Vegas.

Air Passes

International travelers who plan on doing a lot of flying might consider buying a North American air pass. Passes are normally available only to non–North American citizens, and they must be purchased in conjunction with an international ticket. Conditions and cost structures can be complicated, but all passes include a certain number of domestic flights (from two to 10) that typically must be used within a 60-day period. Often you must plan your itinerary in advance, but sometimes dates (and even destinations) can be left open. Talk with a travel agent to determine if an air pass will save you money. Two of the biggest airline networks offering air passes are **Star Alliance** (www.staralliance.com) and **One World** (www.oneworld.com).

BICYCLE

Regional bicycle touring is popular. It means coasting winding backroads (because bicycles are often not permitted on freeways), and calculating progress in miles per day, not miles per hour. Cyclists must follow the same rules of the road as automobiles, but don't expect drivers to respect your right of way. **Better World Club** (p1161) offers a bicycle roadside assistance program.

For bicycling associations, tour groups and magazines, see p1134. For highlights of the USA's cycling and mountain-biking trails, turn to p132. For epic cross-country journeys, get the support of a tour operator; it's about two months of dedicated pedaling coast to coast.

For advice, and lists of local bike clubs and repair shops, browse the **League of American Bicyclists website** (www.bikeleague.org). If you're bringing your own bike to the USA, visit the **International Bicycle Fund website** (www.ibike.org), which lists bike regulations by airline and has lots of advice. In the past, most international and domestic airlines have carried bikes as checked baggage without charge when they're in a box; recently, many have changed their regulations and imposed or increased fees (averaging $50 to $100, but sometimes higher). Amtrak trains and Greyhound buses will transport bikes within the USA, sometimes charging extra.

It's not hard to buy a bike once you're here and resell it before you leave. Every city and town has bike shops; if you prefer a cheaper, used bicycle, try garage sales, bulletin boards at hostels and colleges, or the free classified ads at **Craigslist** (www.craigslist.org). These are also the best places to sell your bike, though stores selling used bikes may also buy from you.

Long-term bike rentals are also easy to find; recommended rental places are listed throughout this guide. Rates run from $100 per week and up, and a credit card authorization for several hundred dollars is usually necessary as a security deposit.

BOAT

There is no river or canal public transportation system in the USA, but there are many smaller, often state-run, coastal ferry services, which provide efficient, scenic links to the many islands off both coasts. Most larger ferries will transport private cars, motorcycles and bicycles. For details, see the regional chapters.

The most spectacular coastal ferry runs are on the southeastern coast of Alaska and along the Inside Passage (p1077). The Great Lakes have several islands that can be visited only by boat, such as Mackinac Island, MI (p624); the Apostle Islands, off Wisconsin (p635); and remote Isle Royale National Park (p625), MN. Off the coast of Washington, ferries reach the scenic San Juan Islands (p1039). Several of California's Channel Islands (p956) are accessible by boat, including Catalina Island (p937), offshore from Los Angeles.

BUS

To save money, travel by bus, particularly between major towns and cities. Gotta-go middle-class Americans prefer to fly or drive, but buses let you see the countryside and meet folks along the way. As a rule, buses are reliable, cleanish and comfortable, with air-conditioning, barely reclining seats, onboard lavatories and no smoking on board.

Greyhound (☎ 800-231-2222; www.greyhound.com) is the major long-distance bus company, with routes throughout the USA and Canada. To improve efficiency and profitability, Greyhound has recently stopped service to many small towns; routes generally trace major highways and stop at larger population centers. To reach country towns on rural roads, you may need to transfer to local or county bus systems; Greyhound can usually provide their contact information.

Competing with Greyhound are the 75-plus franchises of **Trailways** (☎ 703-691-3052; www.trailways.com). Trailways may not be as useful as Greyhound for long trips, but fares can be competitive. Upstart long-distance bus lines that may offer cheaper fares include **Megabus** (☎ 877-462-6342; www.megabus.com), primarily operating routes in the Northeast and Midwest.

Most baggage has to be checked in; label it loudly and clearly to avoid it getting lost. Larger items, including skis, surfboards and bicycles, can be transported, but there may be an extra charge. Call to check.

The frequency of bus services varies widely, depending on the route. Despite the elimination of many tiny destinations, nonexpress Greyhound buses still stop every 50 to 100 miles to pick up passengers, and long-distance buses stop for meal breaks and driver changes.

Many bus stations are clean and safe, but some are in dodgy areas; if you arrive in the evening, it's worth spending the money on a taxi. Some towns have just a flag stop. If you are boarding at one of these, pay the driver with exact change.

Bus Passes

Greyhound's **Discovery Pass** (☎ 888-454-7277; www.discoverypass.com), which is available to both domestic and international travelers, allows unlimited, unrestricted travel for periods of seven ($199), 15 ($299), 30 ($399) or 60 ($499) consecutive days in both the USA and Canada. Besides the length of the pass, the only real decision to make is which country you want to start your travels in. This pass is also accepted by a few dozen regional bus companies; check with Greyhound for a list.

You can buy passes at select Greyhound terminals up to two hours before departure, or purchase them online at least 14 days in advance, then pick them up using the same credit card, with photo ID, at least an hour before boarding.

Costs

For lower fares on Greyhound, purchase tickets at least seven days in advance. Round trips are also cheaper. Special promotional fares are regularly offered on Greyhound's website, especially for online bookings. If you're traveling with family or friends, Greyhound's companion fares let up to three additional travelers get 50% off with a minimum three-day advance purchase.

As for other Greyhound discounts: tickets for children aged two to 11 get 40% off; seniors over 62 get 5% off; and students get 15% off if they have purchased the Student Advantage Discount Card ($20), or 10% off with any valid student ID.

Here are some sample standard one-way adult fares and trip times on the 'Hound:

Service	Price ($)	Duration
Boston–Philadelphia	65	8hr
Chicago–New Orleans	130	22hr
Los Angeles–San Francisco	45	8hr
New York–Chicago	110	18hr
New York–San Francisco	245	2-3 days
Washington, DC–Miami	149	27hr

Reservations

Tickets for some Trailways and other buses can only be purchased immediately prior to departure. Greyhound bus tickets can be bought over the phone or online. If you make your purchase 10 days in advance with a major US credit card, tickets will be mailed to you. International credit cards are accepted when buying in person at the terminal, by calling ☎ 214-849-8100 or by booking online in advance for 'Will Call' tickets, which you can pick up at the terminal (bring photo ID). Greyhound terminals also accept traveler's checks and cash.

On Greyhound, a prepurchased ticket does not reserve or guarantee a seat on a bus. Seating is normally first-come, first-served. Greyhound recommends arriving an hour before departure to get a seat; allow extra time on weekends and holidays. In select gateway cities, priority seating costs $5 extra, but guarantees you a seat and lets you board ahead of other passengers.

CAR & MOTORCYCLE

The American love of the auto runs so deep it often verges on the pathological. And it will abide for at least one practical reason: the continent is too damn big. Public transportation can't cover it. For maximum flexibility and convenience, and to explore rural America and its wide-open spaces, you have to have a car. Independence costs, though, as rental rates and gas prices can eat a good chunk of your travel budget. Only for stays in major metro areas can you easily dispense with an auto.

For recommended driving routes, turn to the special Road Trips chapter (p44) and Scenic Drive boxed texts throughout the regional chapters.

Automobile Associations

The **American Automobile Association** (AAA; ☎ 800-874-7532; www.aaa.com) has reciprocal membership agreements with several international auto clubs (check with AAA and bring your membership card from home). For its members, AAA offers travel insurance, tour books, diagnostic centers for used-car buyers and a wide-ranging network of regional offices. AAA advocates politically for the auto industry.

A more ecofriendly alternative, the **Better World Club** (☎ 866-238-1137; www.betterworldclub.com) donates 1% of revenue to assist environmental cleanup, offers ecologically sensitive choices for every service it provides and advocates politically for environmental causes.

In either organization, the primary member benefit is 24-hour emergency roadside assistance anywhere in the USA. Both also offer trip planning, free travel maps, travel agency services, car insurance and a range of travel discounts (eg on hotels, car rentals, attractions).

Bring Your Own Vehicle

For details on driving your own car over the border from Canada, see p1157, and from Mexico, see p1158. Unless you're moving to the USA, don't even think about freighting your car.

Drive-Away Cars

'Drive-away cars' refers to the business of driving cars across the country for people who are moving or otherwise can't transport their cars themselves. For flexible travelers, they can be a dream come true: you can cover the long distances between A and B for the price of gas. Timing and availability are key.

To be a driver you must be at least 23 years old with a valid driver's license (non-US citizens should have an International Driving Permit); you'll also need to provide a $300 to $400 cash deposit (which is refunded upon safe delivery of the car), a printout of your 'clean' driving record from home, a major credit card and/or three forms of identification (or a passport).

The drive-away company provides insurance; you pay for gas. The stipulation is that you must deliver the car to its destination within a specified time and mileage, which usually requires that you drive no more

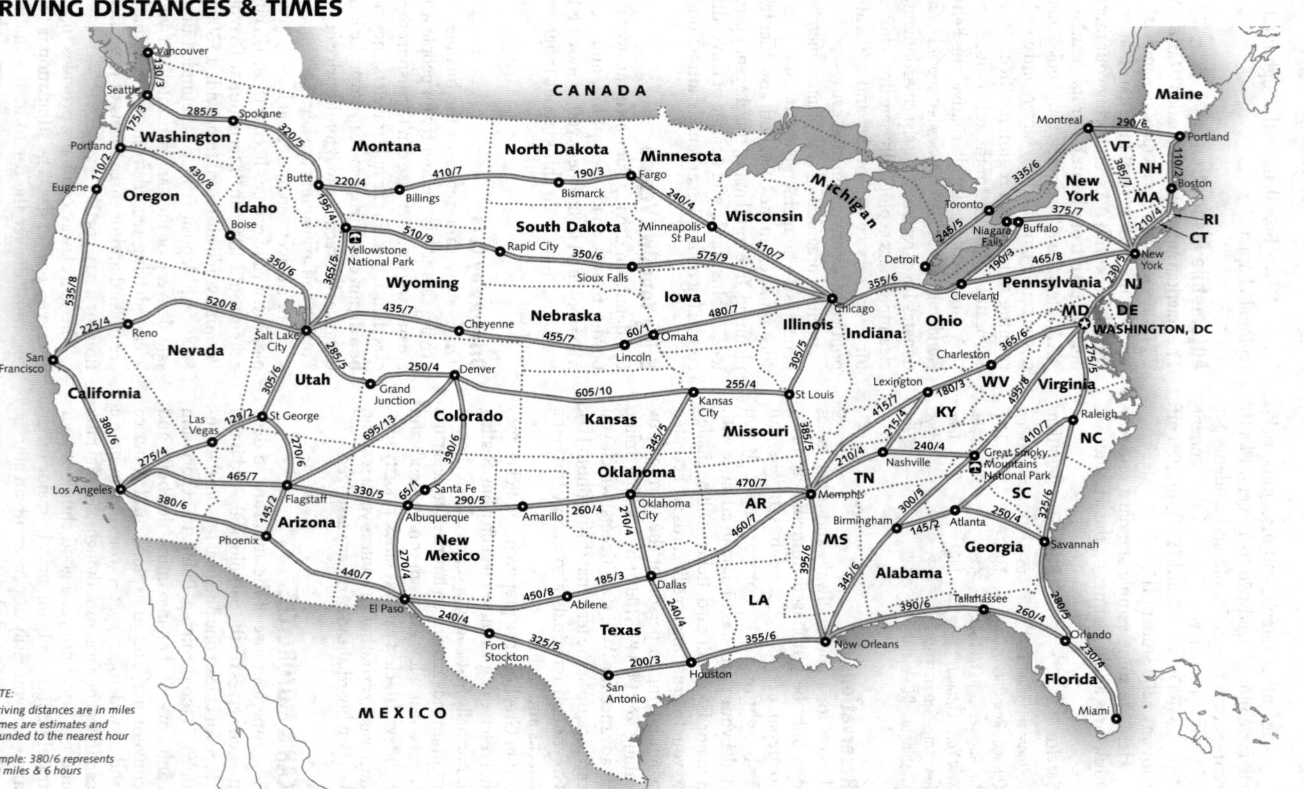
DRIVING DISTANCES & TIMES
CANADA
MEXICO
Washington
Oregon
California
Nevada
Idaho
Montana
Wyoming
Utah
Arizona
Colorado
New Mexico
North Dakota
South Dakota
Nebraska
Kansas
Oklahoma
Texas
Minnesota
Iowa
Missouri
AR
LA
Wisconsin
Illinois
Michigan
Indiana
Ohio
KY
TN
MS
Alabama
Georgia
Florida
SC
NC
Virginia
WV
Pennsylvania
New York
VT
NH
MA
Maine
RI
CT
NJ
DE
MD
WASHINGTON, DC
Vancouver
Seattle
Portland
Eugene
San Francisco
Los Angeles
Las Vegas
Reno
Boise
Spokane
Butte
Billings
Yellowstone National Park
Salt Lake City
St George
Phoenix
Flagstaff
Grand Junction
Denver
Cheyenne
Rapid City
Bismarck
Fargo
Minneapolis-St Paul
Sioux Falls
Omaha
Lincoln
Kansas City
St Louis
Chicago
Santa Fe
Albuquerque
Amarillo
Oklahoma City
El Paso
Fort Stockton
Abilene
Dallas
San Antonio
Houston
Memphis
Nashville
Lexington
Charleston
Great Smoky Mountains National Park
Birmingham
Atlanta
New Orleans
Tallahassee
Savannah
Raleigh
Orlando
Miami
Detroit
Cleveland
Toronto
Niagara Falls
Buffalo
Montreal
Portland
Boston
New York
130/3
175/3
110/2
535/8
225/4
285/5
320/5
430/8
350/6
220/4
195/4
410/7
190/3
240/4
410/7
510/9
365/5
350/6
575/9
520/8
435/7
455/7
60/1
480/7
380/6
275/4
125/2
305/6
285/5
250/4
605/10
255/4
305/5
465/7
270/6
695/13
390/6
145/2
330/5
65/1
290/5
260/4
210/4
345/5
470/7
385/5
440/7
270/4
450/8
185/3
240/4
240/4
325/5
200/3
355/6
460/7
395/6
210/4
415/7
215/4
180/3
365/6
495/8
240/4
410/7
275/5
300/5
145/2
250/4
325/6
345/6
390/6
260/4
280/5
230/4
355/6
245/5
190/3
335/6
375/7
465/8
230/5
385/7
290/6
110/2
210/4
NOTE:
- Driving distances are in miles
- Times are estimates and rounded to the nearest hour
Example: 380/6 represents 380 miles & 6 hours

than eight hours and about 400 miles a day along the shortest route (ie no sightseeing). Availability depends on demand.

One major company is **Auto Driveaway** (☎ 800-346-2277; www.autodriveaway.com), which has more than 40 offices nationwide.

Driver's License

Foreign visitors can legally drive a car in the USA for up to 12 months using their home driver's license. However, an IDP will have more credibility with US traffic police, especially if your home license doesn't have a photo or isn't in English. Your automobile association at home can issue an IDP, valid for one year, for a small fee. Always carry your home license together with the IDP.

To drive a motorcycle in the USA, you will need either a valid US state motorcycle license or an IDP specially endorsed for motorcycles.

Insurance

Don't put the key into the ignition if you don't have insurance, which is legally required, else you risk financial ruin and legal consequences if there's an accident. If you already have auto insurance, or if you buy travel insurance that covers car rentals, make sure your policy has adequate liability coverage for where you will be driving; it probably does, but beware that states specify different minimum levels of coverage.

Rental-car companies will provide liability insurance, but most charge extra. Rental companies almost never include collision-damage insurance for the vehicle. Instead, they offer an optional Collision Damage Waiver (CDW) or Loss Damage Waiver (LDW), usually with an initial deductible cost of $100 to $500. For an extra premium, you can usually get this deductible covered as well. Paying extra for some or all of this insurance increases the cost of a rental car by as much as $30 a day.

Many credit cards offer free collision damage coverage for rental cars if you rent for 15 days or less and charge the total rental to your card. This is a good way to avoid paying extra fees to the rental company, but note that if there's an accident, sometimes you must pay the rental car company first and then seek reimbursement from the credit-card company. There may be exceptions that are not covered, too, such as 'exotic' rentals (eg 4WD Jeeps, convertibles). Check your credit-card policy.

Purchase

Buying a car is usually much more hassle than it's worth, particularly for foreign visitors and trips under four months. Foreigners will have the easiest time arranging this if they have stateside friends or relatives who can provide a fixed address for registration, licensing and insurance, or by working with one of the companies below.

To find a new or used auto, check newspapers and websites and visit dealers. To evaluate used-car prices, check the **Kelley Blue Book** (www.kbb.com). It's smart to pay an independent auto mechanic to inspect any used car before you buy it. Once purchased, the car's transfer of ownership papers must be registered with the state's Department of Motor Vehicles (DMV) within 10 days; you'll need the bill of sale, the title (or 'pink slip') and proof of insurance. Some states also require a 'smog certificate.' This is the seller's responsibility, so don't buy a car without a current certificate. A dealer will submit all necessary paperwork to the DMV for you.

For foreigners, independent liability insurance is difficult to virtually impossible to arrange without a US driver's license. A car dealer or AAA may be able to suggest an insurer who will do this. Even with a local license, insurance can be expensive and difficult to obtain if you don't have evidence of a good driving record. Bring copies of your home auto-insurance policy if it helps establish that you are a good risk. All drivers under 25 will have problems getting insurance.

Finally, selling a car can become desperate business. Selling to dealers gets you the worst price but involves a minimum of paperwork. Otherwise, fellow travelers and college students are the best bets – but be sure the DMV is properly notified about the sale, or you may be on the hook for someone else's traffic tickets later on.

Based in Seattle, WA, **Auto Tour USA** (☎ 206-999-4686; www.autotourusa.com) specializes in helping foreign visitors purchase, license and insure cars. For US citizens, **Adventures on Wheels** (☎ 800-943-3579; www.adventuresonwheels.com) offers a six-month buy-back program: you buy one of their cars, they register and insure it, and when your trip's done, they buy it back for a pre-established price.

TRANSPORTATION

Rental

CAR

Car rental is a competitive business in the USA. Most rental companies require that you have a major credit card, be at least 25 years old and have a valid driver's license (p1163). Some major national companies may rent to drivers between the ages of 21 and 24 for an additional charge of around $25 per day. Those under 21 are usually not permitted to rent at all.

Good independent agencies are listed in this guide. Online, **Car Rental Express** (www.carrentalexpress.com) rates and compares independent agencies in US cities; it's particularly useful for searching out cheaper long-term rentals.

Major national car-rental companies:

Alamo (☎ 877-222-9075; www.alamo.com)
Avis (☎ 800-331-1212; www.avis.com)
Budget (☎ 800-527-0700; www.budget.com)
Dollar (☎ 800-800-3665; www.dollar.com)
Enterprise (☎ 800-261-7331; www.enterprise.com)
Hertz (☎ 800-654-3131; www.hertz.com)
National (☎ 877-222-9058; www.nationalcar.com)
Rent-a-Wreck (☎ 877-877-0877; www.rentawreck.com)
Thrifty (☎ 800-847-4389; www.thrifty.com)

Car-rental prices vary wildly. As when buying plane tickets, shop around, checking every angle and several websites. Airport locations may have cheaper rates but higher fees; city-center offices may do pick-ups and drop-offs. Adjusting the days of your rental even slightly can completely change the rate; weekend and weekly rates are usually cheaper. The average daily rate for a small car ranges from around $30 to $75, or $200 to $500 per week. If you belong to an auto club or frequent-flier program, you may get a discount (or earn rewards points or miles). Check out arranging a cheaper fly–drive package, too. No matter what, advance reservations are recommended.

Some other things to keep in mind: most national agencies make 'unlimited mileage' standard on all cars, but independents might charge extra for this; limited mileage plans rarely work out unless you aren't going far. Some rental companies let you pay for your last tank of gas upfront; this is almost never a good deal. Tax on car rentals varies by state and agency location; always ask for the total cost *including* all taxes and fees. Most agencies charge more if you pick the car up in one place and drop it off in another; usually only national agencies even offer this option. Be careful about adding extra days or turning in a car early; extra days may be charged at a premium rate, or an early return may jeopardize any weekly or monthly discounts you originally arranged.

Some major national companies, including Avis, Budget and Hertz, offer 'green' fleets of hybrid rental cars (eg Toyota Priuses, Honda Civics), although you'll usually have to pay a lot extra to rent a more fuel-efficient car. Some independent local agencies, especially on the West Coast, also offer hybrid-vehicle rentals. Try Southern California's **Simply Hybrid** (www.simplyhybrid.com) and Hawaii's **Bio-Beetle** (p1123).

For car-sharing rentals in cities and towns in 25 states, **Zipcar** (☎ 866-494-7227; www.zipcar.com) charges hourly/daily rental fees with free gas, insurance and limited mileage included; prepayment is required. Check the website for locations and to apply (some foreign drivers OK). No one-way rentals allowed.

MOTORCYCLE & RECREATIONAL VEHICLE (RV)

If you dream of cruising across America on a Harley, **EagleRider** (☎ 888-900-9901; www.eaglerider.com) has offices in major cities nationwide and rents other kinds of adventure vehicles, too. Beware that motorcycle rental and insurance are expensive.

Companies specializing in RV and camper rentals:

Adventures on Wheels (☎ 800-943-3579; www.wheels9.com)
Cruise America (☎ 800-671-8042; www.cruiseamerica.com)
Happy Travel Camper Rental & Sales (☎ 800-370-1262; www.camperusa.com)

Road Conditions & Hazards

America's highways are legendary ribbons of unblemished asphalt, but not always. Road hazards include potholes, city commuter traffic, wandering wildlife and, of course, cell-phone-wielding, kid-distracted and enraged drivers. Caution, foresight, courtesy and luck usually gets you past them. For nationwide traffic and road-closure information, click to www.fhwa.dot.gov/trafficinfo/index.htm.

In places where winter driving is an issue, many cars are fitted with steel-studded snow tires; snow chains can sometimes be required in mountain areas. Driving off-road, or on dirt roads, is often forbidden by rental-car companies, and it can be very dangerous in wet weather.

In deserts and range country, livestock sometimes graze next to unfenced roads. These areas are signed as 'Open Range' or with the silhouette of a steer. Where deer and other wild animals frequently appear roadside, you'll see signs with the silhouette of a leaping deer. Take these signs seriously, particularly at night.

Road Rules

In the USA, cars drive on the right-hand side of the road. The use of seat belts and child safety seats is required in every state. Most car rental agencies rent child safety seats for around $10 per day, but you must reserve them when booking. In some states, motorcyclists are required to wear helmets.

On interstate highways, the speed limit is sometimes raised to 75mph. Unless otherwise posted, the speed limit is generally 55mph or 65mph on highways, 25mph to 35mph in cities and towns and as low as 15mph in school zones (strictly enforced during school hours). It's forbidden to pass a school bus when its lights are flashing.

Unless signs prohibit it, you may turn right at a red light after first coming to a full stop, so long as you don't impede intersecting traffic, which has the right of way. At four-way stop signs, cars should proceed in order of arrival; when two cars arrive simultaneously, the one on the right has the right of way. When in doubt, just politely wave the other driver ahead. When emergency vehicles (ie police, fire or ambulance) approach from either direction, pull over safely and get out of the way.

Most states have laws against (and hefty fines for) littering along the highway. Sure, few people ever get caught, but don't do it anyway. In an increasing number of states, it is illegal to talk on a handheld cell (mobile) phone while driving; use a hands-free device (eg Bluetooth headset) instead.

The maximum legal blood-alcohol concentration for drivers is 0.08%. Penalties are very severe for 'DUI' – driving under the influence of alcohol and/or drugs. Police can give roadside sobriety checks to assess if you've been drinking or using drugs. If you fail, they'll require you take a breath test, urine test or blood test to determine the level of alcohol or drugs in your body. Refusing to be tested is treated the same as if you'd taken the test and failed.

In some states it is illegal to carry 'open containers' of alcohol in a vehicle, even if they are empty. Containers that are full and sealed may be carried, but if they have ever been opened, you must transport them in the trunk.

HITCHHIKING

Hitchhiking in the USA is potentially dangerous and definitely not recommended. Indeed, drivers have heard so many lurid reports they tend to be just as afraid of those with their thumbs out. Hitchhiking on freeways is prohibited. You'll see more people hitchhiking in rural areas and in Alaska and Hawaii, but these places aren't safer than anywhere else, and with sparse traffic, you may well get stranded. In and around national parks, hitching to and from trailheads is common, but a safer bet is to check ride-share boards at hostels, park visitor centers and wilderness information stations.

LOCAL TRANSPORTATION

Except in large US cities, public transportation is rarely the most convenient option for travelers, and coverage can be sparse to outlying towns and suburbs. However, it is usually cheap, safe and reliable. For details, see the Getting Around sections for the main cities and towns covered in the regional chapters. In addition, more than half the states in the nation have adopted ☎ 511 as an all-purpose local-transportation help line.

Airport Shuttles

Shuttle buses provide inexpensive and convenient transport to/from airports in most cities. Most are 12-seat vans; some have regular routes and stops (which include the main hotels) and some pick up and deliver passengers 'door to door' in their service area. Costs average $15 to $30 per person.

Bicycle

Some cities are more amenable to bicycles than others, but most have at least a few dedicated bike lanes and paths, and bikes can usually be carried on public transportation. See p1159 for more on bicycling in the USA, including rentals.

Bus

Most cities and larger towns have dependable local bus systems, though they are often designed for commuters and provide limited service in the evening and on weekends. Costs range from free to between $1 and $3 per ride.

Subway & Train

Some cities have underground subways or elevated metropolitan rail systems, which often provide the fastest local transport. The largest systems are in New York, Chicago, Boston, Philadelphia, Washington, DC, Chicago, Los Angeles and the San Francisco Bay Area. Other cities may have small, one- or two-line rail systems that mainly serve downtown.

Taxi

Taxis are metered, with flagfall charges of around $2.50 to start, plus $1.50 to $2 per mile. They charge extra for waiting and handling baggage, and drivers expect a 10% to 15% tip. Taxis cruise the busiest areas in large cities; otherwise, it's easiest to phone and order one.

TOURS

Hundreds of companies offer all kinds of organized tours of the USA; most focus on either cities or regions. See Tours in the city sections throughout this book for more recommendations, and above for sightseeing tours that take you to and around the USA.

Popular tour companies:

Backroads (☎ 510-527-1555, 800-462-2848; www.backroads.com) Designs a range of active, multisport and outdoor-oriented trips for all abilities and budgets.

Elderhostel (☎ 978-323-4141, 800-454-5768; www.elderhostel.org) For those aged 55 and older, this venerable nonprofit offers 'learning adventures' in all 50 states.

Gray Line (www.grayline.com) For those short on time, Gray Line offers a comprehensive range of standard sightseeing tours across the country.

Green Tortoise (☎ 415-956-7500, 800-867-8647; www.greentortoise.com) Offering budget adventures for independent travelers, Green Tortoise is famous for its sleeping-bunk buses. Most trips leave from San Francisco, traipsing through the West and nationwide.

TRAIN

Amtrak (☎ 800-872-7245; www.amtrak.com) has an extensive rail system throughout the USA, with Amtrak's Thruway buses providing connections to and from the rail network to some smaller centers and national parks. Compared with other modes of travel, trains are rarely the quickest, cheapest, timeliest or most convenient option, but they turn the journey into a relaxing, social and scenic all-American experience.

Amtrak has several long-distance lines traversing the nation east to west, and even more running north to south. These connect all of America's biggest cities and many of its smaller ones. Long-distance services (on named trains) mostly operate daily on these routes, but some run only three to five days per week. See Amtrak's website for detailed route maps, as well as the Getting There & Around sections in this guide's regional chapters.

Commuter trains provide faster, more frequent services on shorter routes, especially the northeast corridor from Boston, MA, to Washington, DC. Amtrak's high-speed Acela Express trains are the most expensive, and rail passes (opposite) are not valid on these trains. Other commuter rail lines include those serving the Lake Michigan shoreline near Chicago, IL, major cities on the West Coast and the Miami, FL, area.

Classes & Costs

Amtrak fares vary according to the type of train and seating; on long-distance lines, you can travel in coach seats (reserved or unreserved), business class, or 1st class, which includes all sleeping compartments. Sleeping cars include simple bunks (called 'roomettes'), bedrooms with en-suite facilities and suites sleeping four with two bathrooms. Sleeping-car rates include meals in the dining car, which offers everyone sit-down meal service (pricey if not included). Food service on commuter lines, when it exists, consists of sandwich and snack bars. Bringing your own food and drink is recommended on all trains.

Various one-way, round-trip and touring fares are available from Amtrak, with discounts of 15% for seniors aged 62 and over and for students with a 'Student Advantage' card ($20) or an International Student Identity Card (ISIC), and 50% discounts for children aged two to 15 when accompanied by a paying adult. AAA members get 10% off. Web-only 'Weekly Specials' offer deep discounts on certain undersold routes.

Generally, the earlier you book, the lower the price. To get many of the standard discounts, you need to reserve at least three

ALL ABOARD!

Who doesn't enjoy the steamy puff and whistle of a mighty locomotive as glorious scenery streams by? Dozens of historic narrow-gauge railroads still operate today as attractions, rather than as transportation. Most trains only run in the warmer months, and they can be extremely popular – so book ahead.

Here are some of the best:

Cass Scenic Railroad Nestled in the Appalachian Mountains in West Virginia (p382).

Cumbres & Toltec Scenic Railroad Living, moving museum from Chama, NM, into Colorado's Rocky Mountains (p902).

Durango & Silverton Narrow Gauge Railroad Ends at historic mining town Silverton in Colorado's Rocky Mountains (p784).

Great Smoky Mountain Railroad Rides from Bryson City, NC, through the Great Smoky Mountains (p403).

Mount Hood Railroad Winds through the scenic Columbia River Gorge outside Portland, OR (p1060).

Roaring Camp Railroads Rises through coast redwood forests in the mountains above Santa Cruz, CA (p965).

Skunk Train Runs between Fort Bragg, CA, on the coast and Willits farther inland, passing through redwoods (p996).

White Pass & Yukon Route Railroad Klondike Gold Rush–era railroad has departures from Skagway, AK (p1085), and Fraser (British Columbia) and Carcross and Whitehorse (Yukon) in Canada.

Also worth riding are the vintage steam and diesel locomotives of Arizona's **Grand Canyon Railway** (p849), New York State's **Delaware & Ulster Line** (p198), and Colorado's **Pikes Peak Cog Railway** (p767).

days in advance. If you want to take an Acela Express or Metroliner train, avoid peak commute times and aim for weekends.

Amtrak Vacations (☎ 800-268-7252; www.amtrakvacations.com) offers vacation packages that include rental cars, hotels, tours and attractions. Air-Rail packages let you travel by train in one direction, then return by plane the other way.

Sample standard, one-way, adult coach-class fares and trip times on Amtrak's long-distance routes:

Service	Price ($)	Duration (hr)
Chicago–New Orleans	$110	20
Los Angeles–San Antonio	$135	30
New York–Chicago	$85	19
New York–Los Angeles	$195	61
Seattle–Oakland	$95	23
Washington, DC–Miami	$120	24

Reservations

Reservations can be made any time from 11 months in advance up to the day of departure. Space on most trains is limited, and certain routes can be crowded, especially during summer and holiday periods, so it's a good idea to book as far in advance as you can; this also gives you the best chance of fare discounts.

Train Passes

Amtrak's USA Rail Pass offers coach-class travel for 15 ($389), 30 ($579) or 45 ($749) days, with travel limited to 8, 12 or 18 one-way 'segments,' respectively. A segment is *not* the same as a one-way trip. If reaching your destination requires riding more than one train (for example, getting from New York to Miami with a transfer in Washington, DC) that one-way trip will actually use two segments of your pass.

Present your pass at an Amtrak office to pick up your ticket(s) for each trip. Reservations should be made by phone (call ☎ 800-872-7245, or ☎ 215-856-7953 from outside the USA) as far in advance as possible. Each segment of the journey must be booked. At some rural stations, trains will only stop if there's a reservation. Tickets are not for specific seats, but a conductor on board may allocate you a seat. Business-class, 1st-class and sleeper accommodations cost extra and must be reserved separately.

All travel must be completed within 180 days of purchasing your pass. Passes are not valid on the Acela Express, Auto Train, Thruway motorcoach connections or the Canadian portion of Amtrak routes operated jointly with Via Rail Canada.

Health

Dr David Goldberg

CONTENTS

The North American continent encompasses an extraordinary range of climates and terrains, from the freezing heights of the Rockies to tropical areas in southern Florida. Because of the high level of hygiene, infectious diseases will not be a significant concern for most travelers, who will experience nothing worse than a little diarrhea or a mild respiratory infection.

BEFORE YOU GO

INSURANCE

The USA offers possibly the finest health care in the world. The problem is that, unless you have good insurance, it can be prohibitively expensive. It's essential to purchase travel health insurance if your regular policy doesn't cover you when you're abroad.

Bring any medications you may need in their original containers, clearly labeled. A signed, dated letter from your physician that describes all medical conditions and medications, including generic names, is also a good idea.

If your health insurance does not cover you for medical expenses abroad, consider supplemental insurance. Check the Travel Services section of the **Lonely Planet website** (www.lonelyplanet.com) for more information. Find out in advance if your insurance plan will make payments directly to providers or reimburse you later for overseas health expenditures. For more information on insurance, see p1141.

RECOMMENDED VACCINATIONS

No special vaccines are required or recommended for travel to the USA. All travelers should be up-to-date on routine immunizations. See the following table.

Vaccine	Recommended for	Dosage	Side effects
chicken pox	travelers who've never had chicken pox	two doses a month apart	fever; mild case of chicken pox
influenza	all travelers during flu season (Nov-Mar)	one dose	soreness at injection site; fever
measles	travelers born after 1956 who've had only one measles vaccination	one dose	fever; rash; joint pains; allergic reactions
tetanus-diphtheria	all travelers who haven't had a booster within 10 years	one dose lasts 10 years	soreness at injection site

MEDICAL CHECKLIST

Recommended items for a medical kit:

- acetaminophen (Tylenol) or aspirin
- adhesive or paper tape
- antibacterial ointment (eg Bactroban) for cuts and abrasions
- antihistamines (for hay fever and allergic reactions)
- anti-inflammatory drugs (eg ibuprofen)
- bandages, gauze, gauze rolls
- DEET-containing insect repellent for the skin
- permethrin-containing insect spray for clothing, tents and bed nets
- pocket knife
- scissors, safety pins, tweezers
- steroid cream or cortisone (for poison ivy and other allergic rashes)
- sunblock
- thermometer

INTERNET RESOURCES

There is a wealth of travel health advice available on the internet. The World Health Organization publishes a superb book, called *International Travel and Health,* which is revised annually and is available online at no cost at www.who.int/ith/en. Another website of general interest is **MD Travel Health** (www.mdtravelhealth.com), which provides complete travel health recommendations for every country, updated daily, also at no cost.

It's usually a good idea to consult your government's travel health website before departure, if one is available:

Australia (www.smarttraveller.gov.au)
Canada (www.hc-sc.gc.ca/index-eng.php)
UK (www.dh.gov.uk/travellers)
USA (wwwn.cdc.gov/travel)

IN THE USA

AVAILABILITY & COST OF HEALTH CARE

In general, if you have a medical emergency, the best bet is for you to find the nearest hospital and go to its emergency room. If the problem isn't urgent, you can call a nearby hospital and ask for a referral to a local physician, which is usually cheaper than a trip to the emergency room. Stand-alone, for-profit urgent-care centers can be convenient, but may perform large numbers of expensive tests, even for minor illnesses.

Pharmacies are abundantly supplied, but you may find that some medications that are available over-the-counter in your home country require a prescription in the USA and, as always, if you don't have insurance to cover the cost of prescriptions, they can be shockingly expensive.

INFECTIOUS DISEASES

In addition to more common ailments, there are several infectious diseases that are unknown or uncommon outside North America. Most are acquired by mosquito or tick bites.

Giardiasis

This parasitic infection of the small intestine occurs throughout the world. Symptoms may include nausea, bloating, cramps and diarrhea, and may last for weeks. To protect yourself from Giardia, avoid drinking directly from lakes, ponds, streams and rivers, which may be contaminated by animal or human feces. The infection can also be transmitted from person to person if proper hand washing is not performed. Giardiasis is easily diagnosed by a stool test and readily treated with antibiotics.

HIV/AIDS

As with most parts of the world, HIV infection occurs throughout the USA. You should never assume, on the basis of someone's background or appearance, that they're free of this or any other sexually transmitted disease. Be sure to use a condom or other prophylactic device for all sexual encounters.

Lyme Disease

This disease has been reported from many states, but most documented cases occur in the northeastern part of the country, especially New York, New Jersey, Connecticut and Massachusetts. A smaller number of cases occur in the northern Midwest and in the northern Pacific coastal regions, including northern California. Lyme disease is transmitted by deer ticks, which are only 1mm to 2mm long. Most cases occur in the late spring and summer. The **Center for Disease Control** (CDC; www.cdc.gov/ncidod/dvbid/lyme) has an informative, if slightly scary, web page on Lyme disease.

The first symptom is usually an expanding red rash that is often pale in the center, known as a bull's-eye rash. However, in many cases, no rash is observed. Flu-like symptoms are common, including fever, headache, joint pains, body aches and malaise. When the infection is treated promptly with an appropriate antibiotic, usually doxycycline or amoxicillin, the cure rate is high. Luckily, since the tick must be attached for 36 hours or more to transmit Lyme disease, most cases can be prevented by performing a thorough tick check after you've been outdoors. For information, see Tick Bites (p1171).

Rabies

Rabies is a viral infection of the brain and spinal cord that is almost always fatal. The rabies virus is carried in the saliva of infected animals and is typically transmitted through an animal bite, though contamination of any break in the skin with infected saliva may result in rabies. In the USA, most cases of human rabies are related to exposure to bats. Rabies may also be contracted from raccoons, skunks, foxes, and unvaccinated cats and dogs.

If there is any possibility, however small, that you have been exposed to rabies, you should seek preventative treatment, which consists of rabies immune globulin and rabies vaccine, and is quite safe. In particular, any contact with a bat should be discussed with health authorities, because bats have small teeth and may not leave obvious bite marks. If you wake up to find a bat in your room, or discover a bat in a room with small children, rabies prophylaxis may be necessary.

West Nile Virus

These infections were unknown in the USA until a few years ago, but have now been reported in almost all 50 states. The virus is transmitted by culex mosquitoes, which are active in late summer and early fall, and generally bite after dusk. Most infections are mild or asymptomatic, but the virus may infect the central nervous system, leading to fever, headache, confusion, lethargy, coma and sometimes death. There is no treatment for West Nile virus. For the latest update on the areas affected by West Nile, go to the **US Geological Survey website** (http://diseasemaps.usgs.gov).

ENVIRONMENTAL HAZARDS

Bites & Stings

Common sense approaches to these concerns are the most effective: wear boots when hiking to protect from snakes, wear long sleeves and pants to protect from ticks and mosquitoes. If you're bitten, don't overreact. Stay calm and follow the recommended treatment.

ANIMAL BITES

Do not attempt to pet, handle or feed any animal, with the exception of domestic animals known to be free of any infectious disease. Most animal injuries are directly related to a person's attempt to touch or feed the animal.

Any bite or scratch by a mammal, including bats, should be promptly and thoroughly cleansed with large amounts of soap and water, followed by application of an antiseptic, such as iodine or alcohol. The local health authorities should be contacted immediately for possible post-exposure rabies treatment, whether or not you've been immunized against rabies. It may also be advisable to start an antibiotic, since wounds caused by animal bites and scratches frequently become infected.

MOSQUITO BITES

When traveling in areas where West Nile or other mosquito-borne illnesses have been reported, keep yourself covered (wear long sleeves, long pants, hats and shoes rather than sandals) and apply a good insect repellent, preferably one containing DEET, to exposed skin and clothing. In general, adults and children over 12 should use preparations containing 25% to 35% DEET, which usually lasts about six hours. Children between two and 12 years of age should use preparations containing no more than 10% DEET, applied sparingly, which will usually last about three hours. Neurologic toxicity has been reported from DEET, especially in children, but appears to be extremely uncommon and generally related to overuse. DEET-containing compounds should not be used on children under age two.

Insect repellents containing certain botanical products, including oil of eucalyptus and soybean oil, are effective but last only 1½ to two hours. Products based on citronella are not very effective.

Visit the **Center for Disease Control's website** (CDC; www.cdc.gov/ncidod/dvbid/westnile/prevention_info.htm) for prevention information.

SNAKE BITES

There are several varieties of venomous snakes in the USA, but unlike those in other countries they do not cause instantaneous death, and antivenins are available. First aid is to place a light constricting bandage over the bite, keep the wounded part below the level of the heart and move it as little as possible. Stay calm and get to a medical facility as soon as possible. Bring the dead snake for identification if you can, but don't risk being bitten again. Do not use the mythic 'cut an X and suck out the venom' trick; this causes more damage to snakebite victims than the bites themselves.

SPIDER & SCORPION BITES

Although there are many species of spider in the USA, the only ones that cause significant human illness are the black widow, brown recluse and hobo spiders. The black widow is black or brown in color, measuring about 15mm in body length, with a shiny top, fat body, and distinctive red or orange hourglass figure on its underside. It's found throughout the USA, usually in barns, woodpiles, sheds, harvested crops and bowls of outdoor toilets. The brown recluse spider is brown in color, usually 10mm in body length, with a dark violin-shaped mark on the top of the upper section of the body. It's usually found in the South and southern Midwest, but has spread to other parts of the country in recent years. The brown recluse is active mostly at night, lives in dark sheltered areas, such as under porches and in woodpiles, and typically bites when trapped. Hobo spiders are found chiefly in the northwestern USA and western Canada.

If bitten by a black widow, you should clean the wound with an antiseptic such as iodine or alcohol and apply ice or cold packs, then go immediately to the nearest emergency room. Complications of a black-widow bite may include muscle spasms, breathing difficulties and high blood pressure. The bite of a brown recluse or hobo-spider typically causes a large, inflamed wound, sometimes associated with fever and chills. The symptoms of a hobo spider bite are similar to those of a brown recluse, but milder. If bitten, apply ice and see a physician.

The only dangerous species of scorpion in the USA is the bark scorpion, which is found in the southwestern part of the country, chiefly Arizona. If stung, you should immediately apply ice or cold packs, immobilize the affected body part and go to the nearest emergency room. To prevent scorpion stings, be sure to inspect and shake out clothing, shoes and sleeping bags before use, and wear gloves and protective clothing when working around piles of wood or leaves.

TICK BITES

Ticks are parasitic arachnids that may be present in brush, forest and grasslands, where hikers often get them on their legs or in their boots. Adult ticks suck blood from hosts by burrowing into the skin and can carry infections such as Lyme disease.

Always check your body for ticks after walking through high grass or thickly forested area. If ticks are found unattached, they can simply be brushed off. If a tick is found attached, press gently down around the tick's head with tweezers, grab the head and pull steadily upwards – do not twist or force it. (If no tweezers are available, use your fingers, but protect them from contamination with a piece of tissue or paper.) Do not rub oil, alcohol or petroleum jelly on it. If you get sick in the next couple of weeks, consult a doctor.

Glossary

The best primer for what has happened to the English language since it landed on the continent is Bill Bryson's *Made in America* (1994), which tackles American slang and expressions (along with good dollops of history) from the arrival of the *Mayflower* onwards.

4WD – four-wheel-drive vehicle
9/11 – September 11, 2001; the date of the Al-Qaeda terrorist attacks, in which hijacked airplanes hit the Pentagon and destroyed NYC's World Trade Center
24/7 – 24 hours a day, seven days a week

AAA – the American Automobile Association, also called 'Triple A'
Acela – high-speed trains operating in the northeast
adobe – a traditional Spanish-Mexican building material of sun-baked bricks made with mud and straw; a structure built with this type of brick
aka – also known as
alien – official government term for a non-US citizen, visiting or resident in the USA (as in 'resident alien,' 'illegal alien' etc); impolite generally
Amtrak – national government-supported passenger railroad company
Angeleno/Angelena – a resident of Los Angeles
antebellum – of the period before the Civil War; pre-1861
ANWR – Arctic National Wildlife Refuge; contains a 1.5-million-acre wilderness area that's the subject of controversial oil and gas drilling proposals
Arts and Crafts – an architecture and design movement popular at the turn of the 20th century; also called (American) Craftsman
ATF – Bureau of Alcohol, Tobacco & Firearms, a federal law enforcement agency
ATM – automated teller machine
ATV – all-terrain vehicle, used for off-road transportation and recreation; see also *OHV*

back east – a West Coast reference to the East Coast
backpacker – one who hikes or camps out overnight; less commonly, a young, low-budget traveler
bling – hip-hop term for expensive jewelry and goods, the status symbols of success
BLM – Bureau of Land Management, an agency of the federal Department of the Interior that manages certain public lands for resources and recreation
blog – short for web log; a personal journal available online
blue book – the *Kelley Blue Book,* a used-car pricing guide
bluegrass – a form of Appalachian folk music that evolved in the bluegrass country of Kentucky and Tennessee
bodega – especially in NYC, a small local store selling liquor, food and other basics
boomtown – as during the gold rush, a town that experiences rapid economic and population growth
booster – an avid promoter of a town or university; sometimes has parochial connotations
brick-and-mortar – a business' actual premises, as opposed to its internet presence
buffalo soldier – an African American soldier serving in the West after the Civil War
burro – a small donkey used as a pack animal
Bush, the – the greater part of Alaska, inaccessible by road or sea; to get there, charter a 'bush plane'
BYOB – bring your own booze; a staple of party invitations

Cajun – corruption of 'Acadia'; refers to Louisiana people who descended from 18th-century French-speaking Acadian exiles from eastern Canada
camper – pickup truck with a detachable roof or shell fitted out for camping
carded – asked to show your ID to buy liquor or cigarettes, or to enter a bar
carpetbaggers – political Northerners who migrated to the South following the Civil War
CCC – Civilian Conservation Corps, a Depression-era federal program established in 1933 to employ young, single men
CDW – collision damage waiver; optional insurance against damaging a rental car
cell – cellular (or mobile) phone
chamber of commerce – an association of local businesses that often provides tourist information
Chicano/Chicana – a Mexican American man/woman
clambake – seashore cookout featuring clams, fish and other fresh seafood
CNN – Cable News Network, a 24-hour cable TV news station
coach class – an economical class of travel on airplanes, trains, etc
coed – coeducational, open to both males and females; often used in noneducational contexts (eg hostel dorms)
conch (pronounced conk) – pink mollusk eaten as seafood; also a nickname for long-term Key West residents (new Key Westers are freshwater conchs)
Conestoga wagon – a big covered wagon drawn by horses or oxen, the vehicle of 18th- and 19th-century westward migration; also called a 'prairie schooner'
Confederacy – the 11 Southern states that seceded from the USA in 1860–61
contiguous states – all states except Alaska and Hawaii; also called the 'lower 48'

cot – camp bed (babies sleep in cribs)
country and western – an amalgam of folk music of the South and the West
coyote – a small wild dog; also a person who assists illegal immigrants to cross the Mexican border into the USA
cracker – in the South, a derogatory term for a poor white person
CVB – convention and visitors bureau, a city-run organization promoting tourism and assisting visitors

DEA – Drug Enforcement Agency, the federal body responsible for enforcing US drug laws
Deep South – in this book, the states of Louisiana, Mississippi and Alabama
Dixie – the South; the states south of the *Mason-Dixon Line*
DIY – do it yourself
DMV – Department of Motor Vehicles, the state agency that administers the registration of vehicles and the licensing of drivers
docent – a guide or attendant at a museum
downtown – the center of a city, central business district (CBD); in the direction of downtown (eg a downtown bus)
DUI – driving under the influence of alcohol or drugs or both; sometimes called DWI (driving while intoxicated)

East – generally, the states east of the Mississippi River
efficiency – a small furnished apartment with a kitchen, often for short-term rental
Emancipation – refers to Abraham Lincoln's 1863 Emancipation Proclamation, which freed all slaves in the Confederate-controlled states (made official with the US Constitution's 13th Amendment)
entrée – the main course of a meal
express bus/train – stops only at selected stations, not at 'local' stations
express stop/station – served by express buses/trains as well as local ones

fanzine – an amateur DIY magazine, often written by obsessive fans
flag stop – a place where a bus stops only if you flag it down
foldaway – portable folding bed in a hotel
forty-niners – immigrants to California during the 1849 gold rush; also, San Francisco's pro-football team (49ers)
funnel cake – a specialty of the Pennsylvania Dutch, these deep-fried, spiral-shaped pastries are served dusted with powdered sugar, usually at outdoor fairs and carnivals
gallery – a commercial establishment selling artwork; institutions that exhibit art collections are usually called museums
gated community – walled upscale residential area accessible only through security gates
general delivery – poste restante
Generation X – 1980s disaffected youth, replace by Generation Y
gimme cap – promotional baseball cap with company logo; often used pejoratively to refer to rural or lower-class white culture
GLBT – gay, lesbian, bisexual, transgender (ie inclusive of all nonheterosexuals); *aka* LGBT
GOP – Grand Old Party, nickname for the Republican Party
graduate school – advanced-degree study, after completion of a bachelor's degree
green card – technically, an Alien Registration Receipt Card, issued to holders of immigrant visas that allows them to live and work legally in the USA; being issued in various colors, it's actually not green
Gullah – African American culture from the Georgia and South Carolina coast

hale – Hawaii thatched-roof bungalow
hip-hop – rap music; also African American urban youth culture generally
Hispanic – of Latin American descent or culture (often used interchangeably with *Latino/Latina*)
HI-USA – Hostelling International USA; refers to US hostels affiliated with Hostelling International, a global federation
hogan – a traditional Navajo one-room structure used for religious practices
honky-tonk – country music club
hookup – at campgrounds, refers to *RV* connections for electricity, water and sewage; in social situations, refers to a casual sexual encounter
'Hound, to ride the – to travel by Greyhound bus

Imax – specialized, giant-screen movie theaters
INS – Immigration & Naturalization Service; as of 2002 replaced by the *USCIS* and no longer operating
interstate – an interstate highway, part of the national, federally funded highway system
IRS – Internal Revenue Service, the branch of the US Treasury Department that oversees tax collection

Jim Crow laws – in the post–Civil War South, laws intended to limit the civil or voting rights of blacks; Jim Crow is an old pejorative term for a black person
Joshua tree – a tall, treelike type of yucca plant, common in the arid Southwest
juke joints – roadside dance halls with live music

kachina – Hopi sacred spirits; also refers to kachina dolls (traditional Hopi carvings)
kiva – a round underground chamber built by indigenous Southwestern cultures for ceremonial and everyday purposes
KOA – Kampgrounds of America, a private chain of campgrounds throughout the USA

lagniappe – (lan-yap) a little something extra, often refers to a free gift, bonus or perk
Latino/Latina – a man/woman of Latin American descent (often used interchangeably with *Hispanic*)
LDS – from the Church of Jesus Christ of Latter-Day Saints, the formal name of the Mormon church
live oak – a hardwood, evergreen oak, native to the South; dead live oaks make excellent boat-building timber
local – a bus or train that stops at every bus stop or station; see also *express bus/train*
lower 48 – the 48 *contiguous states* of the continental USA; all states except Alaska and Hawaii

Mason-Dixon Line – the 1767 delineation between Pennsylvania and Maryland that was later regarded as the boundary between free and slave states in the period before the Civil War
MLB – Major League Baseball
MLS – Major League Soccer
mojito – sweet rum drink laden with mint
moonshine – illegal liquor, usually corn whiskey, associated with backwoods stills in the Appalachian Mountains
morteros – hollows in rocks used by Native Americans for grinding seeds and nuts; also called mortar holes or grinding stones
Mother Road – nickname for Route 66, once the main route from Chicago to Los Angeles

NAACP – National Association for the Advancement of Colored People
National Guard – each state's federally supported military reserves, used most often in civil emergencies
National Recreation Area – National Park Service areas of scenic or ecological importance that are also reserved for recreation; they often incorporate public works, such as dams
National Register of Historic Places – the National Park Service list of historic sites; designation restricts modifications to help preserve the integrity of original buildings
NBA – National Basketball Association
NCAA – National Collegiate Athletic Association, the body that regulates intercollegiate sports
New Deal – wide-ranging domestic program of public works and regulations introduced by President Franklin D Roosevelt to counteract the effects of the Depression
NFL – National Football League
NHL – National Hockey League
NHS – National Historic Site
NM – National Monument
NOW – National Organization for Women, a political organization dedicated to promoting women's rights and equality
NPR – National Public Radio, a noncommercial, listener-supported national network of radio stations; notable for news and cultural programming
NPS – National Park Service, the division of the Department of the Interior that administers US national parks, monuments, historic sites, preserves and more
NRA – National Recreation Area; also National Rifle Association, an influential pro-gun lobby
NWR – National Wildlife Refuge

OHV – off-highway vehicle
OMG – oh my God
ORV – off-road vehicle
out west – the opposite of *back east;* any place west of the Mississippi River
outfitter – business providing supplies, equipment, transport, guides etc for fishing, canoeing, rafting and hiking trips

panhandle – a narrow piece of land projecting from the main body of a state (eg the Florida panhandle); also, to beg from passersby
parking lot/garage – paved area/building for parking cars (the phrase 'car park' is not used)
PBS – Public Broadcasting System, a noncommercial TV network; the TV equivalent of *NPR*
PC – politically correct; also personal computer
petroglyph – a work of rock art in which the design is pecked, chipped, incised or abraded into the surface of the rock
PGA – Professional Golfers' Association
pickup – small truck with an open bed
pictograph – indigenous work of art in which the design is painted, often on a rock surface
po'boy – a Louisiana-style submarine sandwich on a thick bread roll
powwow – a social and ceremonial gathering of Native American people
pueblo – Native American village in the Southwest, with adjoining dwellings of *adobe* or stone

ranchero – a Mexican rancher; also a Mexican American musical style blending German and Spanish influences, often featuring accordions
rancho – a small ranch (Mexican Spanish)
raw bar – a restaurant counter that serves raw shellfish
Reconstruction – a period after the Civil War, when secessionist states were placed under federal control before they were readmitted to the Union
redneck – derogatory term for a politically conservative, working-class rural person
ristra – dried, usually red chili peppers tied on a string and hung vertically, often seen in New Mexico
RV – recreational vehicle, also known as a motor home

scalawags – Southern whites with Northern sympathies who profited under *Reconstruction* after the Civil War
schlep – carry awkwardly or with difficulty (Yiddish)

schlock – cheap, trashy products (Yiddish)
shotgun shack – a small timber house with rooms in a line (as if you could fire a shotgun straight through from front to back); once-common dwellings for poor whites and blacks in the South
sierra – mountain range (Spanish)
snail mail – stamped letters and packages, as opposed to email
snowbirds – term for retirees who travel to sunny vacation spots during winter, often around the Southwest, California, Texas, Florida and Hawaii
SoCal – Southern California
soul food – a traditional Southern cuisine (such as chitterlings, ham hocks and collard greens) of African Americans
sourdough – a 19th-century California miner; also old-time Alaskans who, it is said, are 'sour on the country but without enough dough to get out'; also, a yeast mixture used to make bread or pancakes
SSN – social security number, a nine-digit ID code required for employment
stick, stick shift – manually operated gearshift; a car with manual transmission ('Can you drive a stick?')
strip mall – any collection of businesses and stores arranged around a parking lot
SUV – sports utility vehicle
swag – free promotional items given away to function as advertisements

terroir – a French term used in wine countries referring to the unique characteristics of a particular place where grapes are grown
Trail of Tears – in the 1830s, the forced relocation of some Native American tribes to the western US; hardships along the route resulted in starvation, exposure, disease and death
trailer – transportable dwelling; a trailer park is a residential collection that doesn't move and provides low-cost housing
TTY/TDD – telecommunications devices for those who are deaf
two-by-four – standard-size timber, 2in thick and 4in wide

Underground Railroad – series of safe havens for runaway slaves heading North
Union, the – the United States; in a Civil War context, the Union refers to the northern states at war with southern Confederate states
USAF – United States Air Force
USCIS – US Citizenship & Immigration Services, the agency within the Department of Homeland Security that oversees immigration, naturalization and visa processing
USFS – United States Forest Service, the division of the Department of Agriculture that manages federal forests for resources and recreation
USGS – United States Geological Survey, an agency of the Department of the Interior responsible for, among other things, creating detailed topographic maps of the country
USMC – United States Marine Corps
USN – United States Navy

wash – a watercourse in the desert, usually dry but subject to flash flooding
Wasp – White, Anglo-Saxon Protestant; often used to refer to affluent white upper-class values
well drinks – bar drinks with less-expensive, generic-brand hard liquor, as opposed to name-brand 'top-shelf' drinks
wickiup – a portable shelter of grasses, reeds or brushwood made by Native Americans
WNBA – Women's National Basketball Association
wonk – a person overly obsessed with minute details, usually pejorative; equivalent to geek
WPA – Works Progress (later, Works Projects) Administration; a Depression-era, New Deal program to increase employment by funding public works projects

zip code – a five- or nine-digit postal code
zydeco – music style of southern Louisiana combining influence from French, Caribbean and blues cultures

The Authors

SARA BENSON

Coordinating Author, California

Midwestern by birth and Californian by choice, Sara has traveled extensively to all states except Alaska – though she dreams of heading to that wild north land as soon as possible. Already the author of more than 30 travel and nonfiction books, Sara has contributed to many Lonely Planet travel guides, including *California, Las Vegas Encounter, Southwest USA* and *Hawaii*. Her travel writing features on websites and in magazines and newspapers from coast to coast, including *National Geographic Traveler*. She has also worked as a national-park ranger. Follow her adventures at www.indietraveler.net.

AMY C BALFOUR

Southwest

Amy has hiked, biked, skied and gambled her way across the Southwest, finding herself returning with particular fondness to Moab, Zion, Park City and Taos. On this trip she discovered a few new favorites – Albuquerque, Silver City, Monument Valley – and she's already plotting her return. When she's not daydreaming about red rocks and green chili stew, Amy's writing about travel, food and the outdoors.

ANDREW BENDER

California

Yet another Lonely Planet author with an MBA, this native New Englander first came to LA after B-school to work in film production, but he ended up leaving the industry to do what every MBA (and production dude) secretly dreams of: traveling and writing about it. Since then, his writing and photography have appeared in the *Los Angeles Times, Forbes, Hemispheres* (United Airlines' in-flight magazine), *SilverKris* (Singapore Airlines' in-flight magazine), some two dozen Lonely Planet titles including *Los Angeles & Southern California*, and his blog, www.wheres-andy-now.com. When not on the road, he can be seen biking the beach in Santa Monica or discovering LA's next great ethnic joint.

LONELY PLANET AUTHORS

Why is our travel information the best in the world? It's simple: our authors are passionate, dedicated travelers. They don't take freebies in exchange for positive coverage so you can be sure the advice you're given is impartial. They travel widely to all the popular spots, and off the beaten track. They don't research using just the internet or phone. They discover new places not included in any other guidebook. They personally visit thousands of hotels, restaurants, palaces, trails, galleries, temples and more. They speak with dozens of locals every day to make sure you get the kind of insider knowledge only a local could tell you. They take pride in getting all the details right, and in telling it how it is. Think you can do it? Find out how at **lonelyplanet.com**.

ALISON BING

California

Over 15 years in San Francisco, Alison has done everything you're supposed to do in the city and many things you're not, including falling in love on the 7 Haight bus and gorging on Mission burritos before Berlioz symphonies. Alison holds degrees in art history and international diplomacy – respectable diplomatic credentials she regularly undermines with opinionated culture commentary for radio, newspapers, foodie magazines, and books, including Lonely Planet's *San Francisco Encounter, San Francisco City Guide* and *California Trips*.

BECCA BLOND

Rocky Mountains

The author of more than 30 Lonely Planet guides, including *Thailand, Australia, South Africa, Tahiti & French Polynesia* and *Madagascar & Comoros,* Becca's adventures in travel writing have taken her across five continents in six years. But she's never happier than when she's assigned to write about her home turf, the Rocky Mountains. A Colorado resident for half her life, Becca has worked on the last two editions of this guide, and was the coordinating author of *Southwest USA* and *Arizona, New Mexico & the Grand Canyon Trips*. When not on the road, she lives in Boulder with her husband Aaron and their bulldog Duke.

JEFF CAMPBELL

Hawaii

Jeff first made it to the Big Island in 1993, and he's been finding excuses to get back to Hawaii ever since (his honeymoon, for one – just like Elvis!). For Lonely Planet, he's been the coordinating author of the last two editions of *Hawaii* and the previous three editions of *USA*, plus other US titles. He lives with his wife and two kids in New Jersey.

NATE CAVALIERI

California

A native of Michigan, Nate Cavalieri first dipped a toe in the Pacific while playing piano in a touring rock-and-roll outfit. He got hooked and moved West a few years later. He's lived in Northern California for six years, working as a journalist, travel writer and music critic. He's the author of seven Lonely Planet titles, including guides to California, Chicago, Puerto Rico and *Volunteer: A Traveller's Guide*.

JIM DUFRESNE **Alaska**

Jim has lived, worked and wandered across Alaska and even cashed a Permanent Fund Dividend check. As the sports and outdoors editor of the *Juneau Empire*, he was the first Alaskan sportswriter to win a national award from the Associated Press. As a guide for Alaska Discovery he has witnessed Hubbard Glacier shed icebergs the size of pickup trucks off its 8-mile-wide face. Jim now lives in Michigan but is constantly returning to the far north to write books on Alaska, including Lonely Planet's *Alaska* and *Hiking in Alaska*.

LISA DUNFORD **Texas**

As she moved there 15 years ago, and married a native, Lisa might be considered a naturalized Texan. She's driven the length and breadth of her very large adopted state, always on the lookout for good BBQ or a dance hall she hasn't seen. Before writing freelance, Lisa was an editor and restaurant reviewer at the *Corpus Christi Caller-Times*. Now, no matter where this wanderer roams, she always returns to the patch of east Texas riverfront that she, her husband and their dogs call home.

NED FRIARY & GLENDA BENDURE **New England**

Ned grew up in Massachusetts, Glenda in California, and together they've spent years traveling throughout Europe, Asia and the USA. They've set foot on 49 states – well, make it 50 if you count that two-hour stopover in Anchorage. When it finally came time to plant a garden, they zeroed in on Cape Cod, which remains their home base. Road trips and ocean swims are favorite pastimes. They've written extensively on the region and are coauthors of Lonely Planet's *New England* guide.

MICHAEL GROSBERG **New York, New Jersey & Pennsylvania**

Growing up in the Washington, DC, area, Michael spent holidays with his large New York City family and grew to know their neighborhoods as if they were his own. After several long overseas trips and many careers, including journalism and NGO work in South Africa, Michael returned to New York City for graduate school in comparative literature and taught literature and writing in several NYC colleges. He's lived in Manhattan, Queens and Brooklyn (and taught in the Bronx), and claims to know much of the city like the back of his hand. Of course, every chance he gets, he ditches Brooklyn and heads upstate or to Pennsylvania for the outdoors, or to the Jersey shore.

ADAM KARLIN **Washington, DC & the Capital Region; The South**

Adam's Lonely Planet career has taken him from the Andaman Islands to the Zimbabwean border, but his first gig for the company was writing on his backyard: good ol' America, still one of his favorite places in the world to travel. For this *USA* guide, Adam, who can't figure out where or what to call home, got to write on the two cities in America that could most closely fit the definition for him. New Orleans vs Washington, DC – crawfish vs crabs – is a debate Adam happily engages in.

MARIELLA KRAUSE **Florida**

As a fan of amusement parks, kitschy tourist attractions and states with panhandles, Mariella was thrilled to take to the highways of Florida to uncover its every eccentricity. Having spent her formative years in the middle states, she's delighted to now call San Francisco home. She started her career as an advertising copywriter and now writes a little bit of everything, from books to newspaper articles to glossy brochures, all from her Victorian flat in Noe Valley, often with a cat in her lap. Mariella can tell you the difference between an alligator and a crocodile, if you'd like.

JOSH KRIST **Southwest**

An Arizona State University alum, Josh has traveled all over Arizona and Nevada for business, pleasure and adventure. For Lonely Planet he's written about Vietnam, the Caribbean, Mexico and Thailand, and is a freelance alcohol and travel writer living in San Francisco. He won the 'Little Mr Phoenix' personality contest in 1976.

EMILY MATCHAR **The South**

Emily was raised in the Tar Heel State and can still sometimes be found around Chapel Hill (though lately she's been bopping between New Mexico, Singapore and Sydney, Australia). Though she doesn't have an accent, her Southern nature manifests in an unlimited tolerance for pork and biscuits. She writes about travel, food and culture for a number of magazines, and has contributed to several other Lonely Planet guides, including the previous edition of *USA* and *The Carolinas, Georgia & the South Trips*.

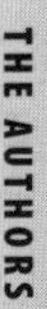

BRENDAN SAINSBURY
Pacific Northwest

An expat Brit, Brendan's first exposure to Pacific Northwest culture came via a well-used copy of *Nevermind* by Washington grunge merchants Nirvana in 1992. Moving to BC, Canada, in 2004, he made his first sorties across the border to the Evergreen State in search of snow-capped volcanoes, enlightening music and a half-decent cup of coffee. Somewhere between Mt Baker and Seattle he found all three. Brendan has also coauthored Lonely Planet's *Washington, Oregon & the Pacific Northwest* guide.

CÉSAR SORIANO
Washington, DC & the Capital Region

Born in Washington, DC, and raised in Virginia on countless bushels of Chesapeake Bay blue crabs, César is one of the few folks who can actually call themselves a native Washingtonian. After graduating from George Mason University, César served in the US Army and worked as a celebrity reporter and war correspondent for *USA Today*. He's traveled to 55 countries but frequently returns home to some of his favorite DC-area attractions, including the National Mall, Shenandoah, Arlington, Rehoboth Beach and Washington Capitals hockey games. He lives in London with his equally wanderlusting wife and Baltimore native 'hon,' Marsha.

ELLEE THALHEIMER
The South

Ellee Thalheimer was born and raised in Little Rock, AR, under her mother's credo that you can't get any better than GRITS – Girls Raised in the South. Though she has left the Bible Belt to be a wilderness guide, yoga instructor, massage therapist and freelance writer based in Portland, OR, she's still able to appreciate the rich culture and unsung beauty of the South. Ellee has contributed to guidebooks to Mexico, the Caribbean and the Pacific Northwest for Lonely Planet, and has authored Lonely Planet's *Cycling Italy*.

RYAN VER BERKMOES
Great Plains

Ryan Ver Berkmoes first drove across the Great Plains with his family in the 1960s. Among the treasured memories are a pair of Wild West six-shooters he got at Wall Drug in South Dakota and which he still has (in a box someplace, not under his pillow). Through the years he has never passed up a chance to wander the back roads of America's heartland, listening to podcasts aplenty, finding beauty and intrigue where it's least expected and debating whether heaven would be a perpetual tank of gas or a bottomless plate of Kansas City burnt ends. Find more of his dreams at www.ryanverberkmoes.com.

JOHN A VLAHIDES

California

John A Vlahides lives in San Francisco. He cohosts the television series *Lonely Planet: Roads Less Travelled*, on the National Geographic channel, and is also cofounder of the California travel site 71miles.com. John studied cooking in Paris with the same chefs who trained Julia Child, and is a former luxury-hotel concierge and member of the prestigious Les Clefs d'Or, the international union of the world's elite concierges. John spends free time singing with the San Francisco Symphony, sunning on the nude beach beneath the Golden Gate Bridge, skiing the Sierra Nevada, and touring California on his motorcycle.

KARLA ZIMMERMAN

Great Lakes

As a lifelong Midwesterner, Karla is well versed in the region's beaches, ballparks, breweries and pie shops. When she's not home in Chicago watching the Cubs…er, writing for newspapers, books and magazines, she's out exploring. For this gig, she polka danced in Wisconsin, picked blueberries in Michigan, faced Vikings in Minnesota and drank an embarrassing number of milk shakes in Ohio. Karla has traveled to more than 55 countries, and written for several Lonely Planet guidebooks covering the USA, Canada, Caribbean and Europe.

CONTRIBUTORS

Karen Levine earned a master's degree in art history at San Francisco State University and currently serves as managing editor, publications, at the San Francisco Museum of Modern Art. She has contributed essays, interviews and reviews to a number of art publications, including *Tema Celeste* and *Artweek*.

John Mariani is the author of *The Encyclopedia of American Food & Drink, America Eats Out: An Illustrated History of Restaurants, Taverns, Coffee Shops, Speakeasies, and Other Establishments That Have Fed Us for 350 Years* and, with his wife, Galina, *The Italian-American Cookbook*. He is also a food and travel correspondent for *Esquire* magazine and a wine columnist for Bloomberg news, radio and TV. He publishes and writes the weekly *Mariani's Virtual Gourmet Newsletter* (www.johnmariani.com).

Amy Marr has explored every US national park, hoofed and pedaled all over the world, and led more than 40 biking and hiking trips. Now a cookbook publisher and travel writer, she's rooted in Marin County, where she bikes and hikes on Mt Tam and cooks up Italian feasts.

Regis St Louis is now a resident of NYC but is a Hoosier by birth, and grew up dreaming of big journeys across America and beyond. He's crossed the US by bus, train and automobile, and has traveled in dozens of countries across six continents. He has written for numerous Lonely Planet guides, including *New England, New York City* and *USA*, and his articles have appeared in the *Chicago Tribune* and the *Los Angeles Times*, among other publications.

TophOne is a DJ, graffiti artist and music writer from San Francisco. He grew up skating and going to punk-rock shows, but now rides his bike between bars and gigs across the West. A senior writer for *XLR8R* magazine, he pens the popular 'Lucky 13' column, is founder of the RedWine DJs and loves baseball.

Behind the Scenes

THIS BOOK

For this 6th edition of USA, Sara Benson coordinated a stellar author team (see the Authors, p1176). Jeff Campbell coordinated or contributed to the 5th and previous editions. This guidebook was commissioned in Lonely Planet's Oakland, California, office and produced by the following:

Commissioning Editors Suki Gear, Emily K Wolman
Coordinating Editor Averil Robertson
Coordinating Cartographer Brendan Streager
Coordinating Layout Designer Margaret Jung
Managing Editors Imogen Bannister, Laura Stansfeld
Managing Cartographer Alison Lyall
Managing Layout Designer Laura Jane
Assisting Editors Susie Ashworth, Lindsay Brown, Monique Choy, Jocelyn Hargrave, Victoria Harrison, Kim Hutchins, Sally O'Brien, Dianne Schallmeiner, Gabrielle Stefanos, Angela Tinson
Assisting Cartographers Ross Butler, Dennis Capparelli, Eve Kelly, Mick Garrett, Birgit Jordan, Joelene Kowalski, Ross Macaw
Cover Research Naomi Parker, lonelyplanetimages.com
Project Managers Chris Girdler, Craig Kilburn

Thanks to Lucy Birchley, Sally Darmody, Indra Kilfoyle, Wayne Murphy, Raphael Richards

THANKS

SARA BENSON

Thanks to Suki Gear, Craig Kilburn and everyone in-house for such a sweet gig. Kudos to Jeff Campbell for shepherding *USA* through many previous incarnations. Without such helpful coauthors, I never could have pieced together this behemoth – thanks, everybody! PS Ranger Mike: life's always better with you.

AMY C BALFOUR

Many thanks to Mari Hoidal and Gib Berry for sharing the best – and strangest – of Salt Lake City and Park City. It was fun! Big props to Marcus Garcia and Susan Cooper for helping me with all things Albuquerque and New Mexico. The patient rangers, docents and volunteers who answered all my crazy questions across two big states also get my warmest regards. Thank you Suki for entrusting me with two wonderful states, and kudos to Sam for bringing it all together with patience and good cheer.

ANDREW BENDER

Carol Martinez, Robin McClain, Megan Rodriguez, Madison Fisher, Joe Timko, Kate Buska and Erik Dahlerbruch and, in-house, Suki Gear and Sam Benson for the opportunity and their good cheer and advice.

THE LONELY PLANET STORY

Fresh from an epic journey across Europe, Asia and Australia in 1972, Tony and Maureen Wheeler sat at their kitchen table stapling together notes. The first Lonely Planet guidebook, *Across Asia on the Cheap,* was born.

Travelers snapped up the guides. Inspired by their success, the Wheelers began publishing books to Southeast Asia, India and beyond. Demand was prodigious, and the Wheelers expanded the business rapidly to keep up. Over the years, Lonely Planet extended its coverage to every country and into the virtual world via lonelyplanet.com and the Thorn Tree message board.

As Lonely Planet became a globally loved brand, Tony and Maureen received several offers for the company. But it wasn't until 2007 that they found a partner whom they trusted to remain true to the company's principles of traveling widely, treading lightly and giving sustainably. In October of that year, BBC Worldwide acquired a 75% share in the company, pledging to uphold Lonely Planet's commitment to independent travel, trustworthy advice and editorial independence.

Today, Lonely Planet has offices in Melbourne, London and Oakland, with over 500 staff members and 300 authors. Tony and Maureen are still actively involved with Lonely Planet. They're traveling more often than ever, and they're devoting their spare time to charitable projects. And the company is still driven by the philosophy of *Across Asia on the Cheap*: 'All you've got to do is decide to go and the hardest part is over. So go!'

ALISON BING

Many thanks and shameless California bear hugs to editorial superhero Suki Gear; California coauthors John Vlahides and Sam Benson, fellow travelers and inspired raconteurs; fearless leaders Brice Gosnell and Heather Dickson at Lonely Planet; the Sanchez Writers' Grotto for steady inspiration; and above all to Marco Flavio Marinucci, whose powerful kindness and bracing espresso makes everything possible.

BECCA BLOND

This book is dedicated to two very special boys, Austin Van de Weghe Pugh (born March 8, 2009) and Cooper Maxwell Marshall (born June 18, 2009), the first-born sons of two of my best friends, Natalie and Danielle. Thanks also to my in-house editors, Averil Robertson and Susie Ashworth.

JEFF CAMPBELL

Jeff owes thanks to many people, but none more than Sara Benson – a consummate pro who has so gracefully taken the *USA* baton. Here's to slack key in Waimea again! I am also indebted to the work of Luci Yamamoto, Ned Friary and Glenda Bendure, and I owe a huge *mahalo nui loa* to Bobby Camara, as always.

NATE CAVALIERI

Nate Cavalieri would like to thank Florence Chien, Suki Gear and Sam Benson for their support on this project.

LISA DUNFORD

I'm much obliged to friends and family across Texas, including Anna and Seth Sosolik, Tara and Doug Hrbacek, Lindsay and Jack Day, Daryn and Mark Polanco, Nancy Shropshire, Joe Kulbeth, Terri Haas, Catherine Navarro and the kula. Much love to Helen Dickman and my mom and dad. Thanks, too, to Sam Benson and Suki Gear for all their organizing efforts. And Billy – what can I say? icau.

NED FRIARY & GLENDA BENDURE

We'd like to thank everyone who pointed us in the right direction, from the farmer in Quechee who told us to drive 6 miles down that rutted dirt road (oops…wrong turn) to Bob Prescott, Patti Bangert, Julie Lipkin, Susan Milton and Bryan Lantz for sharing the insider scoop on their favorite haunts. And a toast to our commissioning editor, Suki Gear, and coordinating author, Sam Benson, for making everything flow so smoothly.

MICHAEL GROSBERG

This book and everything I do is dedicated to the memory of Rebecca Tessler, my love and life. You are always with me forever. I love you.

A huge thanks to the following for all of their support, knowledge and recommendations: Ahna and Emma Tessler, Ryan and Hayley Geftman, Katie Sanders, Carolyn and Rebecca Yaffe, Brooke Farrell, Matt Silverman, Betsy Freeman, Claire Shubik, Seth Richards, Nirav Mehta, Deb Roth, Jonathan Rosen, Sharon and Mike Nisengard, Daryl Hirsch, Karen Greenstein, Andrew Krouk, Tara Cooney, Marisa Crandall, Adam Feinberg, Jeffrey Dashevsky, Allan Cohen, Camille McNutt, Kevin Kauffunger and Eric Eto.

ADAM KARLIN

My people, as always: my family and my friends in two of America's greatest cities, who make it nigh on impossible for me to pick one to live in. There's not enough space to list all your names, but I am ever indebted to all of you for your hospitality and love.

MARIELLA KRAUSE

Thanks to Annette Simon for kicking the trip off right with her wonderful hospitality and tour of Jax Beach. Hats off to the fabulous Lonely Planet crew – in particular, Suki Gear and Sam Benson – for your guidance and support. Thanks to my husband, Tim Bauer, for keeping me company, even during some of the less-glamorous parts of the trip. And thanks to Brady Lea's husband, David, who should always be thanked in acknowledgments.

JOSH KRIST

Thanks to my wife, Hélène Goupil, who dealt with wedding arrangements while I wrote this book. Quadruple thanks to Didier Bruneel. Jesse Krist, 'kingbilly.' Kerri, Miriam and William Krist, Jacob and Rosemary Whitt, and Joelle, Elodie, and Regis Goupil. Lonely Planet shout outs: Suki Gear, Sam Benson, Jay Cooke. My AZ and NV friends, old and new.

EMILY MATCHAR

Thanks to Suki Gear, Sam Benson, and everyone else at Lonely Planet. Thanks to Jamin, for those late-night directions over the phone when I was lost in South Carolina and all the other innumerable ways you support your peripatetic girlfriend. Thanks to my parents for letting me write most of my chapter from their living room. Thanks to Beth Hatcher for helping me get my boot-stompin' groove on in Nashville and to Claire Napier Galofaro for being my guide to Louisville. And thanks to everyone on Twitter who gave me awesome suggestions, even though we might not know each other.

BRENDAN SAINSBURY

Many thanks to all the untold park rangers, bus drivers, tourist-info volunteers, restaurateurs and innocent bystanders who helped me during my research. Thanks particularly to Suki Gear for offering me the gig in the first place and to Sam Benson for being such a supportive coordinating author. Special thanks, as always, to my wife Liz and three-year-old son Kieran for their company in various remote parts of Washington and Oregon.

CÉSAR SORIANO

Thanks to Capitol Region USA; Wink, Kris, KC and Aly for your hospitality, love and crabs; Ron, Franco, Mark, Craig for your friendship over many pints of Amber Waves; to my wanderlust wife Marsha, whose love always guides me home – here's to the next phase of our global adventure.

ELLEE THALHEIMER

Lots of thanks are due but I particularly want to thank Joe Partridge, Mammaw, my people in Arkansas, Mammaw, Kristin, Tom, and Lily Hayes, Daniel Woodrow, Jesse Sibly, Allan and Ann Perry, Lynda Churchfield and Dennis, Aly Heard, Andrea Habern, Tom Scarborough, McCoy Buford, and Dad, for making my Atlanta trip.

RYAN VER BERKMOES

Serious thanks to my parents, who believed in the value of road trips. And special thanks to my sister Cynthia, who always sided with me regarding the importance of the motel pool having a slide. In Iowa I was reunited with my senior prom date Kathy Berge (how'd we get from Santa Cruz to Des Moines?), while a great journalist, Dan Piller, showed me the ins and outs (a lot of those…) of pigs. At Lonely Planet, wide open thanks to Suki and Sam for their hard work. And more special thanks go to the person who invented the recipe for garlic salad at Doc's in Wichita. Can I have some more?

JOHN A VLAHIDES

John is grateful to his coauthors Sam Benson and Alison Bing, as well as commissioning editor Suki Gear, for their unending support. Many thanks to those who helped during research: Christine Murray, Marc Kate, Monique Jenkinson, Warren Longmire, Paul Marchegiani, Marianne Wong, DJ Gray and Sam Khedr. But I'm most grateful to you, dear reader. Have a blast on the road!

KARLA ZIMMERMAN

Many thanks to Sam Benson, Carrie Biolo, Nancy Castagnet, Ruggero Fatica, Suki Gear, Rhoda Henderson, Val and Jeff Johnson, Julie Lange, Sarah Leugers, Kari Lydersen, Elizabeth Miller, Amanda Powell, Susan H Stephan, Don and Karen Zimmerman, Sara Zimmerman, and the Cleveland, Chicago and Detroit CVBs. Thanks most to Eric Markowitz, the world's best partner-for-life.

OUR READERS

Many thanks to the travelers who used the last edition and wrote to us with helpful hints, useful advice and interesting anecdotes:

Juan Albier, Paul Maximilian Alex, Jennifer Anderson, Matt Battaglia, Anne Katrine Bjerregaard, Mirjam Buitelaar, Cessie Cerrato, Marissa Comstock, Dara Conlan, Wendy Costa, Dale Desena, Marcellina Garcia, Neil Govan, Monica Griffin, Elizabeth Gunther, Price Gutshall, Blake Harrison, Tricia Hayes, Jason Hutchison, Mark Jitlal, Marlise Kast, Alice Leeder, Brian & Lorna Lewis, Queen Becky M, Ashish Maharjan, Ty Markham, Steve Marsh, Hilary Maslon, Nima Matias Jokilaakso, Perry Michelle, Janet Mitchelson, Harald Mueller, Jean Munsee, Melanie Nisbet, Alex Omand, Xavier Ottolini, Oliver Pearman, Emma Rabbitts, Nathan Reynolds, Joan Roco, A Ross, Rob Sandie, Markus Schorn,

SEND US YOUR FEEDBACK

We love to hear from travelers – your comments keep us on our toes and help make our books better. Our well-traveled team reads every word on what you loved or loathed about this book. Although we cannot reply individually to postal submissions, we always guarantee that your feedback goes straight to the appropriate authors, in time for the next edition. Each person who sends us information is thanked in the next edition and the most useful submissions are rewarded with a free book.

To send us your updates – and find out about Lonely Planet events, newsletters and travel news – visit our award-winning website: **lonelyplanet.com/contact**.

Note: we may edit, reproduce and incorporate your comments in Lonely Planet products such as guidebooks, websites and digital products, so let us know if you don't want your comments reproduced or your name acknowledged. For a copy of our privacy policy visit lonelyplanet.com/privacy.

Skyler Schrempp, Mara Senra, Robin Shannon, Jon Sigurjonsson, Sebastian Steinfeld, John Stolzenbach, Joost Taverne, Elizabeth Tobey, Carton Tsutomu, Herjan Velding, James Vol Hartwell, Jessica Vowels, Sue Wallis, Alasdair Warwood, Steven Weiss, Kathryn Williams, Dale Woitas, Andrew Young, Francois Zermeno, Nan Zosel

ACKNOWLEDGMENTS

Many thanks to the following for the use of their content:

Globe on title page ©Mountain High Maps 1993 Digital Wisdom, Inc.

Internal photographs: p15 (#8) Franck Fotos/ Alamy; p13 (#5) Ron Niebrugge/Alamy; All other photographs by Lonely Planet Images: p12 (#7) Ann Cecil; p9 (#6), p11 (#2), p15 (#5) Richard Cummins; p8 (#1) John Elk III; p13 (#3) Lee Foster; p11 (#8) Dennis Johnson; p11 (#5), p14 (#1) Ray Laskowitz; p7, p10 (#1 & #3) Mark Newman; p16 (#bottom) Emily Riddell; p8 (#8) Stephen Saks; p15 (#2), p16 (#1) Douglas Steakley; p14 (#3) Oliver Strew, p9 (#2) Jon Stromme; p13 (#1) David Tomlinson.

Index

ABBREVIATIONS

AK	Alaska	KY	Kentucky	NY	New York
AL	Alabama	LA	Louisiana	OH	Ohio
AR	Arkansas	MA	Massachusetts	OK	Oklahoma
AZ	Arizona	MD	Maryland	OR	Oregon
CA	California	ME	Maine	PA	Pennsylvania
CO	Colorado	MI	Michigan	RI	Rhode Island
CT	Connecticut	MN	Minnesota	SC	South Carolina
DC	District of Columbia	MO	Missouri	SD	South Dakota
DE	Delaware	MS	Mississippi	TN	Tennessee
FL	Florida	MT	Montana	TX	Texas
GA	Georgia	NC	North Carolina	UT	Utah
HI	Hawaii	ND	North Dakota	VA	Virginia
IA	Iowa	NE	Nebraska	VT	Vermont
ID	Idaho	NH	New Hampshire	WA	Washington
IL	Illinois	NJ	New Jersey	WI	Wisconsin
IN	Indiana	NM	New Mexico	WV	West Virginia
KS	Kansas	NV	Nevada	WY	Wyoming

INDEX

C

000 Map pages
000 Photograph pages

INDEX

000 Map pages
000 Photograph pages

INDEX

000 Map pages
000 Photograph pages

INDEX

000 Map pages
000 Photograph pages

000 Map pages
000 Photograph pages

N

000 Map pages
000 Photograph pages

INDEX

INDEX

INDEX

INDEX

Y

GreenDex

It seems like almost everyone is going 'green' in the USA these days. But how can you really know which businesses are ecofriendly and which are simply jumping on the bandwagon?

The following sights and attractions, activities, tour operators, outdoor outfitters, nonprofit and educational organizations, festivals, restaurants, coffeehouses, shops, accommodations, transportation methods and more have been handpicked by our authors because they are in harmony with sustainable-tourism goals. Some of those picked are involved in environmental conservation and cleanup. Others may be locally owned and operated, helping to preserve regional identity, arts and culture, especially that of Native Americans (including Alaskans and Hawaiians).

We want to keep developing our sustainable-tourism content. If you think we've omitted somewhere that should be listed here, or if you disagree with our choices, email us at talk2us@lonelyplanet.com.au and set us straight for next time. For more information about sustainable tourism and Lonely Planet, see lonelyplanet.com/about/responsible-travel.

TEXAS

USA-WIDE

WASHINGTON, DC & THE CAPITAL REGION

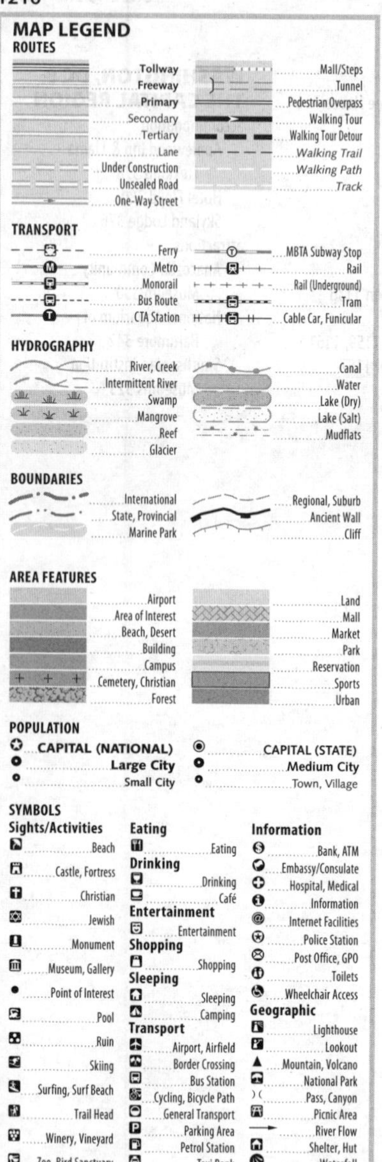

LONELY PLANET OFFICES

Australia (Head Office)
Locked Bag 1, Footscray, Victoria 3011
☎ 03 8379 8000, fax 03 8379 8111
talk2us@lonelyplanet.com.au

USA
150 Linden St, Oakland, CA 94607
☎ 510 250 6400, toll free 800 275 8555
fax 510 893 8572
info@lonelyplanet.com

UK
2nd fl, 186 City Rd,
London EC1V 2NT
☎ 020 7106 2100, fax 020 7106 2101
go@lonelyplanet.co.uk

Published by Lonely Planet Publications Pty Ltd
ABN 36 005 607 983

Cover photograph: Mt Rushmore with full moon, Randy Wells/Getty. Many of the images in this guide are available for licensing from Lonely Planet Images: lonelyplanetimages.com.

Printed by Toppan Security Printing Pte. Ltd.
Printed in Singapore